Macroeconomic Factors in the Commodity Market Outlook 7

Managing Interest-Rate Risk on Both Sides of the Balance Sheet 11

Market for Cocoa 34

Market for Coffee 35

Market for Sugar 38

Mathematical Aids 17

Measuring Commodity Trading Performance 22

Mechanics of Futures Trading 2

Money Management Concepts 21

Oats 28

Orange Juice 36

Platinum and Palladium 46

Pork Complex 32

Potato Market 37

Preference Space Evaluation of Trading System Performance 23

Primary Factors Constituting a Dynamic Cattle Industry 31

Quantitative Trading Methods 15

Refined Sugar Cash and Futures Markets 39

Regulation of the Futures Industry 5

Selecting a Trading System 16

Silver Market 44

Soybean Complex Cash and Futures Markets 30

Stock Index Futures 49

Taxation of Commodity Transactions 6

U.S.D.A. Crop and Livestock Information System 8

Wheat 26

Winnipeg Grain Markets 29

*Understanding, Selecting and Using Computers.

HANDBOOK OF FUTURES MARKETS

HANDBOOK OF FUTURES MARKETS

Commodity, Financial, Stock Index, and Options

PERRY J. KAUFMAN

A Wiley-Interscience Publication

JOHN WILEY & SONS New York • Chichester • Brisbane • Toronto • Singapore

This publication is designed to provide accurate and authoritative information in regard to the subject matter covered. It is sold with the understanding that the publisher is not engaged in rendering legal, accounting, or other professional service. If legal advice or other expert assistance is required, the services of a competent professional person should be sought. *From a Declaration of Principles jointly adopted by a Committee of the American Bar Association and a Committee of Publishers.*

Library of Congress in Publication Data
Main entry under title:

Handbook of futures markets.

"A Wiley-Interscience publication."
Bibliography: p.
Includes index.
1. Commodity exchanges—Handbooks, manuals, etc.
I. Kaufman, Perry J.
HG6046.h36 1984 332.63'28 84-3504
ISBN 0-471-08714-9

Printed in the United States of America

10 9 8 7 6 5 4 3 2

For Jason and Aaron,

may you grow up with the free markets that we know

FOREWORD

This book is about commodity futures, a market which provides both industry and investors a forum for the economics of supply and demand. It offers opportunity for reducing the risks involved in the purchase or sale of raw materials, interest rates or currency fluctuations and even the stock market. For the investor it has many vehicles for participating in a market which permits you to earn above average returns.

The goal of this book is to provide a complete, accurate, and straightforward reference for futures markets. To the sophisticated business person as well as the generally interested reader, there is still much mystery about futures markets. This book eliminates that mystery. Chapter by chapter questions are answered creating a total comprehension of the inter-workings of commodity trading.

This book contains the tools and the methods of analysis needed to operate in the commodity futures markets. It is designed as a learning manual and a reference guide. Extensive examples and graphics make it possible to visualize problems and their solutions. The book concentrates on techniques, analysis, calculation and explanation. The result is an accurate, yet easily understood presentation of the subject matter of an advanced investment course.

Many people have contributed to the growth, interest, and development of this book. Each chapter is a self-contained unit, but each fits into an integrated whole. Step by step, you will be given the fundamentals of market analysis as these fundamentals apply to the world of commodities. I really believe that a thorough reading of this book will make it possible for readers to use the market confidently, for either avoiding or taking risks and to make investment decisions confidently, knowing that they have satisfied the basic rule of successful trading: knowledge.

This book will save you time. It is easy to understand and enables you to have answers to complex questions in one volume. Hedging strategies and tax questions that seemed complicated before are answered in language that is easy to understand.

This book provides a crystal clear explanation of techniques that most practitioners need to give their clients valuable advice even if their specialty is some other area of commodities. Quite often a professional who is not familiar with a particular area of commodities may tend to avoid that area. This book provides its readers with a practical knowledge of the problems and benefits relating to commodities and enables them to feel comfortable when advising their clients to take a course of action in that area.

The outlook for commodity futures is bright. The futures markets will continue to play a dramatic and significant role in the decade ahead. Continued price volatility will keep the futures industry squarely in the world economic spotlight for the next ten years. Futures markets will continue to be the measures of panic, risk spreaders for the world's holders and users of resources, and an economic shock absorber—a stabilizing force in destabilized times. As long as markets perform that function, we will survive the next ten years.

There will no doubt be unforeseen developments that will affect the economic system during the next ten years. However, it is unlikely that they will be greater than those witnessed during the 1970s, such as the oil embargo, the move of the USSR and China into the mainstream of world trade, the record high inflation and interest rates that revolutionized investment thinking.

Developing Third World nations may continue to come to the brink of collapse as they are forced to roll over huge debts continuously, but bankers and governments will cooperate more closely to avoid a chain of economic crashes. World leaders will be more pragmatic and realistic in dealing with economic and political problems. Despite protectionist attitudes of some leaders, the trend seems to be toward a more free market rather than a Keynesian approach.

In today's world, nations are beoming more economically inter-related in what will become a one-economy world more and more in the next ten years. The United States and the dollar will remain leaders in this trend. The microcomputer will have macro implications in these trends. The world's financial center will continue to concentrate in the United States, and futures markets will boom, possibly even at its current explosive rate. Two new markets, stock index futures and commodity options, will become big new investment markets in the decade ahead. Exchanges will link together more. Moves will be made toward central clearing and probably computerized exchange trading in some areas during the decade. New, expanded futures centers will emerge in London and the Far East (Hong Kong, Singapore or Tokyo), but U.S. exchanges will remain dominant in financial and agricultural commodities.

The markets of the 1980s will be more sophisticated as microcomputers become even more pervasive and new risk management tools are developed. More institutions and investors of all types will look to the futures markets to manage risk. Against this type of background the continued boom in the futures industry seems assured.

If this book increases your own knowledge and confidence as you make key investment decisions, then it will have been worth the money, time and effort spent in mastering these principles.

FREDERICK F. HORN

Senior Vice President & Director
Prudential-Bache Securities Inc.
Commodity Division

PREFACE

The scope of this book is broad. It is intended to reach all sectors of the industry and provide an organized, helpful, and comprehensive reference. In doing that it is necessary to start at the beginning—the history and operation of the futures markets—before advancing to the more subtle areas which are usually of more interest to the professionals. Rather than treat the basic introductory material in a "ho-hum" manner, the origins of the market have been recalled with photographs and some memorabilia. Those traders and commercial users of the commodities markets who have participated for the past few decades may find a picture of the old buildings or exchange floors a pleasant reminder of the way things were. They have been captured here with the hope that the past will not be lost. I expect that subsequent editions of The *Handbook of Futures Markets* will gather more of market history and tradition.

The participants in the futures markets and the tools for watching and analyzing price data are in transition. Microcomputers and integrated circuit boards are revolutionizing communications in the industry. Instantaneous real-time displays and the possibility of computerized exchanges such as INTEX are on the threshhold of change which may eliminate "open outcry" and the way we have always envisioned order execution. It may not be long before the roar of the opening and closing seconds are only a memory—replaced by twenty-four hour computerized trading, with dozens of display screens prompting traders to place orders. Even more, computers may automatically place orders instantaneously when their analysis indicates that an arbitrage, spread, or other opportunity exists. No more tossing of filled tickets onto the Board of Trade floor, no more "runners," no more hoarse throats. Many sections of the book have tried to account for changes in the markets. David Handmaker's "The Computer in a Commodity Futures Environment" is a comprehensive discussion of the state-of-the-art, however, by the time this volume is in print, the advancements may be far greater.

"Hedging," by David Rinehimer, discusses another topic that has not been covered in depth before. The commercial use of the markets, with special emphasis on *basis risk,* is an area which has always been assumed as understood by those who would need such information. But the markets have expanded to products and concepts beyond the traditional agricultural groups. Financial, stock index, energy, and inflation related items now comprise well over half of the total trading in futures markets. Many of the sections on specific commodities and commodity groups illustrate hedging applications unique to that product.

Anyone familiar with the mix of business will know that *managed accounts* now represent a significant part of the open interest. While it is not the purpose of this book to evaluate the effects of such large blocks of money on price movements, the area of *money management* has been covered in detail, from the managers themselves to performance evaluation and the risk preference of the investors. Since many commodity market participants are not trading by their own decisions, this section gives them tools to understand and assess performance.

All the sections are comprehensive and represent a special effort by the contributing authors. I would like to express my gratitude to each one of them. They represent the highest level of professionalism in the futures industry and I am proud to have worked with them.

I would like to thank the commodity exchanges for their full support. The Chicago Board of Trade, the Chicago Mercantile Exchange, Commodity Exchange, Inc., the Coffee, Sugar and Cocoa Exchange, the MidAmerica Exchange, the New York Mercantile Exchange and the Kansas City Board of Trade have all provided the unlimited use of their publications. Many of the contributing authors represent the high level of expertise existing in their economic and research departments. Bill Jiler of Commodity Research Bureau has been extremely generous in providing many of the excellent charts and tables used in this volume.

Although the articles were intended to be general in nature, some of them, by necessity, are timely—"Regulation of the Futures Industry" required a separate foreword to explain recent changes and interpretations. Many other chapters, including "Taxation of Commodity Transactions" by Frank A. Ernst and Joseph P. Tyrrell, "Commodity Money Management" by Leon Rose, and parts of each of the commodity sections, especially "Energy Futures" by David Hirschfeld. The time it takes to coordinate an effort of this size has made it impossible to effect last minute changes to all these sections to provide the most timely data. The quality of these sections loses nothing by this.

My appreciation also goes to Jeff LaPlante, who helped to organize and schedule the *Handbook* in addition to writing a fine introductory piece. Special thanks to my good friend and editor, Stephen Kippur, who worked closely with me during the past three years.

PERRY J. KAUFMAN

Chatham, New Jersey
January 1984

CONTENTS

PART I THE MARKETS AND THEIR OPERATION

1 **Growth and Organization of Commodity Markets**
J. DUNCAN LAPLANTE

2 **The Mechanics of Futures Trading**
RICHARD J. TEWELES

3 **The Clearinghouse**
THEODORE R. HARTLEY

4 **Comparing the U.S. and U.K. Futures Markets**
MICHAEL RIESS

5 **Regulation of the Futures Industry**
MARK H. MITCHELL, CARL N. DUNCAN, DAVID M. KOZAK, STANLEY M. KLEM

6 **Taxation of Commodity Transactions**
FRANK A. ERNST, JOSEPH P. TYRRELL

PART II MARKET INFLUENCES

7 **Macroeconomic Factors in the Commodity Market Outlook**
GREGORY M. KIPNIS

8 **The USDA Crop and Livestock Information System**
WALTER SPILKA, JR.

PART III USE OF THE MARKETS

9 **Hedging**
DAVID RINEHIMER

10 **The Development of the Financial Futures Markets**
DR. FRANK J. JONES

11 **Managing Interest-Rate Risk on Both Sides of the Balance Sheet: Use of Futures by Financial Institutions**
JAMES KURT DEW

12 **Commodity Spreads**
COURTNEY SMITH

13 **Commodity Options**
JOHN W. LABUSZEWSKI, JEANNE CAIRNS SINQUEFIELD, LAWRENCE I. SHULMAN

PART IV FORECASTING METHODS AND TOOLS

14 **Bar Charting**
JOHN J. MURPHY

15 **Quantitative Trading Methods**
PERRY J. KAUFMAN

16 **Selecting a Trading System**
W. FREDERICK HITSCHLER

17 **Mathematical Aids**
PERRY J. KAUFMAN

18 **The Computer in a Commodity Futures Environment: Understanding, Selecting, and Using Computers**
DAVID HANDMAKER

PART V RISK AND MONEY MANAGEMENT

19 **Commodity Money Management**
LEON ROSE

20 **Effects of Capitalization on Money Management**
EDWARD CORBALLIS

21 **Money Management Concepts**
MARY CATHERINE SHOUSE

22 **Measuring Commodity Trading Performance**
JACK SCHWAGER

23 **Preference Space Evaluation of Trading System Performance**
NORMAN D. STRAHM

24 **Evaluating a Managed Account**
FRANK S. PUSATERI

PART VI THE COMMODITIES

Grains and Soybean Complex

25 **Agriculture**
PERRY J. KAUFMAN

26 **Wheat**
DONNA NEILSEN MURPHY

27 **Corn**
DONNA NEILSEN MURPHY

28 **Oats**
KING S. KEARNS, II

29 **Winnipeg Grain Markets**
KING S. KEARNS, II.

30 **The Soybean Complex Cash and Futures Markets**
FRANK S. ROSE, RANDALL E. SHELDON

Livestock

31 **Primary Factors Constituting a Dynamic Cattle Industry**
BRUCE A. GINN

32 **The Pork Complex**
PATRICK J. LUBY

33 **Broilers**
STAN OSTROWSKI

Foods

34 **The Market For Cocoa**
TODD E. PETZEL

35 **The Market For Coffee**
TODD E. PETZEL

36 **Orange Juice**
CHARLES M. BARLEY

37 **The Potato Market**
PERRY J. KAUFMAN

38 The Market For Sugar
Todd E. Petzel, Kevin P. Klarnet

39 Refined Sugar Cash and Futures Markets
Donna Neilsen Murphy

40 The Cotton Market
Herman S. Kohlmeyer, Jr.

41 An Introduction to the Lumber and Plywood Markets
Michael Gorham

Energy

42 Energy Futures
David J. Hirschfeld

Metals

43 The Gold Market
Robert C. Teetsell

44 The Silver Market
Avner S. Wolf

45 The Copper Market
Robert J. Anthes

46 Platinum and Palladium
Karen Marie Forstik

47 Foreign Exchange Futures
Allen M. Loosigian, James E. Higgens

48 Interest-Rate Futures
Paul T. Wilkinson, Steven G. Saltzgaber

49 Stock Index Futures The Kansas City Board of Trade Value Line Average (VLA) Contract
Neil S. Weiner

Appendix A: Chicago Board of Trade Membership Transactions
Jeff Requarth

Appendix B: Low-Frequency Filters for Seasonal Analysis
David Handmaker

Appendix B: Low-Frequency Filters for Seasonal Analysis
DAVID HANDMAKER

GLOSSARY

BIBLIOGRAPHY

INDEX

CONTRIBUTORS

ROBERT J. ANTHES is the Coordinator of Market Surveillance at Commodity Exchange Inc. where he is involved in the monitoring and analysis of all COMEX markets. He also serves as a liaison to two committees of the COMEX Board of Governors, the Margin Committee and the Control Committee. In addition to his knowledge of the COMEX futures markets, Mr. Anthes is a student of both domestic and international commodities markets for copper, gold, silver, aluminum and other metals. Mr. Anthes holds a B.S. in Economics from Rutgers University.

CHARLES M. BARLEY is a hedging specialist in orange juice along with other agricultural and livestock markets in the southeastern United States. He has been a contributor to *Commodities Magazine* and the Florida Cattleman's Association publications. Mr. Barley helped establish the futures market in Frozen Concentrated Orange Juice and worked with the Chicago Mercantile Exchange in establishing a southeastern delivery point for feeder cattle. He is Vice-President of Commodities with Shearson/American Express in Winter Park, Florida.

EDWARD CORBALLIS is Vice-President of Thomson McKinnon Securities, Inc., where he is national commodity sales manager and responsible for commodity managed accounts. Mr. Corballis has served as a member of the New York Coffee and Sugar Exchange and the New York Mercantile Exchange and has been a frequent speaker on managed accounts. Previously, Mr. Corballis was an independent commodity trading advisor and Manager of the Guided Accounts Program for Merrill Lynch. He graduated from Rollins College in 1964 and attended the New York University Graduate School of Business.

JAMES KURT DEW is President of Manufacturers Hanover Futures, Inc. Previously, Dr. Dew served as a consultant to Manufacturers Hanover and other financial institutions using futures. Dr. Dew writes extensively on risk management and has developed the Synthetic Fixed Rate Loan and the concept of the Effective Gap. Dr. Dew was Manager of Financial Research and Senior Financial Economist for the International Monetary Market, where he helped to develop futures contracts in the Standard and Poor's 500 Stock Index, domestic negotiable CDs, and the IMM's original contract in Eurodollar deposits. Previously, Dr. Dew served as monetary economist for the Federal Reserve Bank of San Francisco. He received his Ph.D. in economics from Texas A&M and has degrees in mathematics from Xavier University and the College of Wooster.

CARL N. DUNCAN is a partner of Abramson & Fox, a Chicago law firm specializing in securities and commodities law and representing a commodity exchange, commodity trading advisors and pool operators, brokerage firms, banks, and all aspects of the commodities industry. Previously, Mr. Duncan was Senior Attorney in the Office of Tender Offers and Acquisition at the Securities and Exchange Commission and a member of the Corporate Counsel Department of Continental Illinois National Bank and Trust Company of Chicago, specializing in securities and bank holding company law. A 1970 graduate of New York University School of Law, Mr. Duncan has an M.B.A. in finance from American University.

FRANK A. ERNST is a frequent speaker and author of several articles for various business and tax publications, including a significant article on taxation of inventories which appeared in the January, 1983 issue of *Taxation For Accountants*. In addition to his extensive involvement with the commodities industry through Coopers & Lybrand's Commodities and Securities Industry Team, Mr. Ernst specializes in the tax issues relating to the inventory and bankruptcy tax law. Frank Ernst is a Tax Manager with Coopers & Lybrand's Chicago office. He previously served with the Internal Revenue Service in auditing, management and teaching positions. Mr. Ernst is a C.P.A. and a graduate of Loras College.

KAREN MARIE FORSTIK is a 1980 graduate of Cook College, Rutgers University, where she received her B.S. in animal science and was awarded membership in Alpha Zeta, an honorary service organization for outstanding academic performance. Ms. Forstik is Marketing Assistant for the New York Mercantile Exchange, where she held a previous position as Research Analyst.

BRUCE A. GINN is an agricultural consultant, economist, and Director of Research for the Livestock Business Advisory Service. He specializes in research, analysis, and price forecasting for the livestock and meat industry, including econometric models and hedging strategies. Mr. Ginn was Project Leader for the Western Livestock Marketing Information Program and served as a livestock economist for Clayton Brokerage Company. He holds both B.S. and M.S. degrees in agricultural economics from Texas Tech University.

MICHAEL GORHAM is Vice-President of Commodity Research for the Chicago Mercantile Exchange. Prior to his move to the Exchange in 1979, Mr. Gorham was an economist with the Federal Reserve Bank of San Francisco. He has written about a number of business and financial issues for the Christian Science Monitor as well as popular and scholarly articles on such topics as: the effect of ocean mining on mineral exporting countries, the effect of U.S.D.A. announcements on grain prices, lower cost alternatives to Japan's current food policy, the coffee price rise of 1976/77, and the effect of drought on food prices. Mr. Gorham holds a Ph.D. in agricultural economics from the University of Wisconsin.

DAVID HANDMAKER is a consultant specializing in computer hardware and software for market analysis and commodity trading. *Commodities Magazine, The Journal of Futures Markets,* and various computer industry periodicals have published Mr. Handmaker's contributions to this growing field. Mr. Handmaker studied economics at Brandeis University, the University of Vienna, and the London School of Economics. He built and managed the Commodities Service Division of Data Resources, Inc. and was Manager of financial applications at Software Resources, Inc. before forming his own firm in Massachusetts.

THEODORE R. HARTLEY has managed large blocks of investment capital in the futures markets since 1972. He has been a member of all the principal commodities and futures exchanges and a lecturer at the Harvard Business School on the use of the futures markets as a part of corporate strategy. Mr. Hartley served as a principal consultant to organizations, advising on the feasability of proposed and existing futures markets. Ted Hartley has written extensively while living in Aspen, Colorado, where he is an avid outdoorsman, and in Los Angeles, where he also pursues his interests in old motion pictures. He graduated from the United States Naval Acadamy at Annapolis and holds graduate degrees from Pepperdyne University and Harvard Business School.

JAMES E. HIGGINS is a strategy consultant residing in Boston. He specializes in the theory of financial markets. A graduate of Harvard University and a former writer for *International Moneyline,* Mr. Higgins also served as researcher for Allan Loosigian's *Stock Index Futures*.

W. FREDERICK HITSCHLER is President of Comtectra Systems, Inc. He has been managing money and researching and developing computerized trading methods for the commodity markets since 1972, and he is a senior research computer-commodity consultant to Remote Computing Corporation. He has created the computer programs used since 1978 by Merrill Lynch Pierce Fenner and Smith as the basis of their commodity research and weekly market signals; these programs have been used by other major brokerage firms as well. He is also coauthor of *Stock Market Trading Systems* (Dow Jones-Irwin, 1980). Mr. Hitschler holds a degree in economics from the Wharton School and a Master's in communications.

DAVID J. HIRSCHFELD is the Chief Architect of the Chicago Board of Trade's Crude Petroleum contract. He received his undergraduate education from Duke University and his graduate education from the University of Chicago. He is a broker in the "energy pits" of the CBT. In addition to trading, he runs a small consulting firm that specializes in energy futures and serves the Chicago Board of Trade, the Mid-America Commodity Exchange, and Argonne National Laboratory.

FRANK J. JONES is Executive Vice President and Chief Operating Officer of the New York Futures Exchange and Chairman of the Board of the New York Futures Clearing Corporation. Previously he was Vice President of Research for the Chicago Mercantile Exchange. He holds a Ph.D. in economics from Stanford University, an M.B.A. from the University of Pittsburgh, and an M.S. in nuclear engineering from Cornell. Dr. Jones has authored several books, including *Macro Finance—The Financial System and the Economy,* as well as articles and chapters in books on financial futures markets, the financial system, and related topics.

He is a frequent speaker on financial futures, the financial markets, and futures exchanges.

PERRY J. KAUFMAN, editor, has specialized in technical and econometric analysis for both commercial and speculative users of the commodities markets since 1970. He has developed significant theories of price forecasting and risk aversion, and he has consulted for many brokerage houses and commodity users. He is a frequent lecturer at universities and professional seminars worldwide. Mr. Kaufman is the author of *Technical Analysis in Commodities* (John Wiley & Sons, 1980), *Commodity Trading Systems and Methods* (John Wiley & Sons, 1978), and *Commodity Point and Figure Trading Techniques* (Investor Publications, 1975) He is the founder of *The Journal of Futures Markets* and is President of Comrand Corporation in Chatham, New Jersey.

KING S. KEARNS, II is Executive Assistant to the President of the Winnipeg Commodity Exchange. Since joining the Winnipeg Exchange in 1975 he has written articles on Canadian commodity trading for numerous publications in Canada, the United States, and Europe. Mr. Kearns is a journalism graduate from Central Michigan University and has done post graduate work at Central Michigan University and the University of Manitoba. Prior to joining the exchange, he was editor of business publications in western Canada. He is member of the Canadian Public Relations Society and the Canadian Farm Writers and Broadcasters Association.

GREGORY M. KIPNIS is Vice-President in charge of equity futures trading at Donaldson, Lufkin and Jenrette. Previously he was Chief Economist and Commodity Research Director at ACLI International Commodity Services, a subsidiary of DLJ. He has also been an economist at both DLJ and IBM. Mr. Kipnis coedited *Using Stock Index Futures* (Dow Jones) to be published in early 1984. He holds a B.S. and an M.B.A. from New York University.

KEVIN P. KLARNET is a staff economist at the Coffee, Sugar & Cocoa Exchange, Inc. Before joining the Exchange in 1980 he was involved in alternative energy research for the Alcohol Fuels Commission. Mr. Klarnet received an A.B. in economics from Colgate University and an M.S. in natural resource economics from the University of Rhode Island.

STANLEY M. KLEM is Corporate Counsel of Managcare, Inc. in Chicago. From 1981 to 1983 Mr. Klem was associated with Abramson & Fox, a Chicago law firm which specializes in securities and commodity law. A member of the Chicago Bar Association, Mr. Klem received his B.A. from Augustana College (Illinois) in 1978, graduating magna cum laude, and his J.D. from the University of Michigan in 1981, where he was associate editor of the University of Michigan *Journal of Law Reform*. Mr. Klem is the author of "Qualification Requirements for Foreign Corporations: The Need for a New Defintion of 'Doing Business' Based on In-State Sales Volume" (14 *U. Mich. J. L. Ref.* 86, 1980).

HERMAN S. KOHLMEYER, JR. is a first vice-president and cotton specialist at Thomson McKinnon Securities, Inc. After graduation from Yale university and having served in the United States Navy, Mr. Kohlmeyer worked continuously at Kohlmeyer and Company until its merger in 1973. He is the third generation of his family to work in the cotton futures industry.

DAVID M. KOZAK is an attorney with the Chicago law firm of Chapman & Cutler. He specializes in the areas of commodity futures law and securities law. He is an honors graduate of Lake Forest College (B.A.), holds an M.A. from the University of Chicago in political science, and is a cum laude graduate of Loyola University (Chicago) Law School.

JOHN W. LABUSZEWSKI is Director of Economic Research at MidAmerica Commodity Exchange, where he is responsible for the development of new commodity futures and option contracts. Mr. Labuszewski came to MidAmerica from the Chicago Board of Trade where he served as a staff economist. He holds an M.B.A. from the University of Illinois.

J. DUNCAN LAPLANTE, Assistant Editor for The *Handbook of Futures Markets,* is a writer and editor living in Princeton, New Jersey. His work is usually concerned with subjects of an historical nature. He holds degrees in English and history from the American University in Washington, D.C. Past works include an historical perspective of madness from the sixteenth century to present day and various articles on the Vietnam war. He has recently completed a book based on the experience of a Soviet defector.

ALLAN M. LOOSIGIAN is President of A. M. Loosigian & Co. in Stamford Connecticut, an investment firm which specializes in financial futures. He is the author of *Foreign Exchange Futures* (Dow Jones-Irwin, 1981) and *Interest Rate Futures* (Dow Jones-Irwin, 1979). Mr. Loosigian was a magna cum laude graduate of Princeton University's School of Public and International Affairs, and a Fulbright Scholar in economics at the University of Munster in West Germany. He did graduate studies at Stanford University and at Columbia University's Graduate School of Business, and has taught finance and investments at Fairfield University in Connecticut.

PATRICK J. LUBY has been Vice-President and Corporate Economist of Oscar Meyer Foods Corp. since 1974, following 25 years of experience with the company. Mr. Luby has written numerous articles for industry trade publications and the *Journal of Agricultural Economics.* He is a member of the Chicago Mercantile Exchange, American Agricultural Economic Association, Wisconsin Business Economists Association, and the Food and Agricultural Committee, U.S. Chamber of Commerce. He is a former chairman of the American Meat Institute and was on the Board of Directors at the National Livestock and Meat Board from 1970–1982. Mr. Luby holds a B.A. from the University of Dayton, an M.S. and Ph.D. from Purdue University, and received the Gamma Sigma Delta Award from the University of Wisconsin School of Agriculture and Life Sciences, 1979.

MARK H. MITCHELL is a partner with the Chicago law firm of Chapman & Cutler, where he specializes in commodity futures and securities law. Mr. Mitchell represents the National Association of Futures Trading Advisors, a number of brokerage firms, banks, and a wide range of financial institutions engaged in futures trading. He formerly served in the Office of Chief Counsel, Division of Trading and Markets, Commodity Futures Trading Commission. He is an honors graduate of Dartmouth College and the University of California Law School.

DONNA NIELSEN MURPHY is a soybean complex and livestock analyst at the Quaker Oats Company in Chicago. Ms. Murphy has published "How to Hedge Interest Rate Risk with Financial Futures" in *The Southern Banker*. Before joining Quaker Oats she served as an economist at the MidAmerica Commodity Exchange where she researched contract feasibility and wrote the gold coins futures contract submission as well as the Exchange's *Application for Designation as a Contract Market in Refined Sugar*. Ms. Murphy received a B.S. in International Relations from Georgetown University and an M.A. in Agricultural Economics from the University of Wisconsin.

JOHN J. MURPHY is a charting specialist and head of JJM Technical Advisors in New York. He teaches courses on commodity technical analysis for the New York Institute of Finance and is a contributing editor to Commodity Research Bureau's "Commodity Chart Service." Mr. Murphy holds a B.A. in economics and an M.B.A. from Fordham University. He was Manager of the Commodity Technical Analysis Department and Senior Manager Account Trading Advisor for Merrill Lynch Pierce Fenner Smith, Inc., and Director of Commodity Research for Brascan International. He publishes a technical letter on financial, metals, and energy futures and is preparing a book on Commodity Technical Analysis.

STAN OSTROWSKI is Senior Agricultural Economist for the Chicago Mercantile Exchange. He specializes in the lumber, plywood, pork bellies, broilers, and eggs markets. Mr. Ostrowski previously served with the Commodity Futures Trading Commission as Assistant Regional Director, Division of Economics and Education. He holds a B.S. in economics from the University of Illinois and attended the University of Chicago Graduate School on the U.S.D.A. competitive grant program.

TODD E. PETZEL is Chief Economist at the Coffee, Sugar & Cocoa Exchange. Prior to joining the Exchange in 1982, he taught at the Food Research Institute of Stanford University and Macalester College, St. Paul, Minnesota. He received his A.B., A.M., and Ph.D. degrees in economics from the University of Chicago, and his research interests include the political economy of agriculture and the time series behavior of commodity prices.

FRANK S. PUSATERI is a financial analyst with a broad analytical background in the preparation and interpretation of financial data, using both manual and computer-based techniques. Before forming his own company, Mr. Pusateri was Director of Managed Commodity Accounts for E.F. Hutton & Company. He was responsible for the evaluation and selection of the commodity trading advisors used in E.F. Hutton's Managed Accounts Program, developing the statistical and analytic techniques employed in the selection process. Mr. Pusateri gained his training with W. T. Grant and Exxon Chemical Co. He holds an M.B.A. in accounting and finance from the Amos Tuck School of Business Administration, Dartmouth College, and a B.A. in mathematics from Colgate University.

JEFF REQUARTH is a commodity trading advisor and pool operator working on the floor of the Chicago Board of Trade. He is President of Requarth Trading in Chicago.

MICHAEL RIESS is a management consultant who has been extensively involved in many phases of the commodity business. He is a member of the Advisory Board of the Center for the Study of Futures Markets and teaches "Metals and Metal Trading" at the Columbia University Graduate School of Business. He has published several articles on commodity trading. For the past fifteen years he has traded physical metals as well as metal futures in both London and New York. He has managed futures trading, brokerage, and research operations. Mr. Riess holds graduate degrees from Columbia University's Graduate Schools of Business Adminstration and International Affairs. He is President of Michael Riess & Co. in Greenwich, Connecticut.

DAVID RINEHIMER is Vice-President and Director of Commodity Research for Thomson McKinnon Securities. He is a specialist in agricultural commodities and coauthored "U.S. Cotton Export Prospects Brighten in Southern Europe," published in *Foreign Agriculture*. Prior to his position at Thomson McKinnon, Mr. Rinehimer was a commodity analyst for other leading brokerage firms and an agricultural economist for the Foreign Agricultural Service of the U.S.D.A. He received his M.S. in agricultural economics from Rutgers University.

FRANK S. ROSE is an advisory economist with the Department of Economic Analysis and Planning, Chicago Board of Trade. Mr. Rose holds degrees in agricultural economics from Cornell and Michigan State Universities. Previously, he has held research positions with the U.S. Department of Agriculture and the Organization for Economic Cooperation and Development.

LEON ROSE is Publisher of *Managed Account Reports* and *Futures Industry* newsletters, publications of LJR Communications, Inc. in Columbia, Maryland. He is also President of MAR/Consultants, Inc. in Columbia, Maryland. Mr. Rose has been involved with the futures markets since 1971, when he co-founded *Commodities Magazine,* following nearly twenty years of experience as a newspaper reporter, radio news editor, and advertising copywriter. The highly regarded newsletters were established following the sale of the magazine in 1976. Mr. Rose is often quoted in the nation's press, is a frequent speaker at conferences, and has written numerous articles on the subject of commodity money management.

STEPHAN G. SALTZGABER has been a government bond trader in New York since leaving the Chicago Board of Trade, where he worked for the Financial Instruments Group of the Economic Analysis Department. Mr. Saltzgaber gained his experience researching and designing new interest rate contracts for the Board of Trade after joining the industry in 1980. He holds a B.A. from Wesleyan University and an M.B.A. in Finance from the University of Chicago.

LAWRENCE I. SCHULMAN is Director of Financial Futures at Singer/Wanger Trading Company, where he is responsible for developing interest rate futures and option trade. He comes to this position from the Chicago Board of Trade where he was a staff economist, and he holds an M.B.A. from the University of Chicago.

JACK SCHWAGER combines experience in both fundamental and technical analysis of commodities markets. He has written numerous articles on market analysis for *Commodities Magazine,* authored an article in the 1981 Commodity Yearbook (Commodity Research Bureau) and is coauthoring *A Complete Guide To The Futures Markets* (John Wiley & Sons), which will be released in 1984. He is a frequent speaker at industry seminars. Mr. Schwager was Senior Vice-President of Commodities Corporation and Director of Research at both Smith Barney, Harris Upham and Co. and Loeb Rhoades, Hornblower. He holds a B.A. in economics from Brooklyn College and an M.A. in economics from Brown University.

RANDALL E. SHELDON is Manager of the Agricultural Group of the Department of Economic Analysis and Planning, Chicago Board of Trade. He has degrees in Agricultural Economics from Kansas State University. He previously held a research position with Kansas State University.

MARY CATHERINE SHOUSE is Senior Vice-President of Mellon Capital Management Corporation, a subsidiary of Mellon National Corporation, and she is a well-known speaker at both the professional and university levels. Ms. Shouse is best known for her research and development of new products. She helped bring Core Portfolios, representing the entire U.S. Equity Market, to the institutional equity marketplace, in addition to a Stock Index Futures Service which complements the S&P 500 Index Funds. She resides in Los Altos Hills, California.

JEANNE CAIRNS SINQUEFIELD is Manager of Financial Instruments at the Chicago Board of Trade where she has developed a number of interest rate futures and option contracts. She holds an M.B.A. and Ph.D. from the University of Chicago.

COURTNEY SMITH is Director of Commodity Futures Research for Paine, Webber, Jackson and Curtis. He is the author of *Commodity Spreads* (John Wiley & Sons, 1982) and coauthor of *Profits Through Seasonal Trading* (John Wiley & Sons, 1980), as well as numerous articles and pamphlets. Mr. Smith is the Editor of the research publications issued by the Futures Department of Paine, Webber, Jackson and Curtis. He was educated in Canada where he was president of one of the first futures money management firms in Canada. His specialties include commodity spreads and stock index futures.

WALTER SPILKA, JR. is a grain analyst with Smith Barney, Harris Upham and Co. in New York, following his position as a feed grain analyst with the U.S. Department of Agriculture. He received his doctorate in Agricultural Economics from the Virginia Polytechnic Institute and State University. The views expressed in his chapter, "The U.S.D.A. Crop and Livestock Information System" are solely those of the author.

NORMAN D. STRAHM received a Ph.D. in Electrical Engineering from the Massachusetts Institute of Technology, then taught and researched physics at the University of Illinois in Chicago for four years before entering the commodity futures industry. He has served as Research Analyst with Hornblower & Weeks-Hemphill, Noyes, Inc. and with Loeb Rhoades Hornblower and Co.; as Senior Grain Analyst with Smith Barney Harris Upham and Co.; and as Vice-President with Commodities Corporation. He is currently Vice-President of James Orcutt and Co., a commodity trading advisor in Chicago.

ROBERT C. TEETSELL is Director of Commodity Options at Commodity Exchange, Inc. (COMEX), where he has been extensively involved in the development of the Exchange's option on the gold futures contract. He serves as a technical advisor to the Options Committee of the COMEX Board of Governors, the Board of Governors of the COMEX Clearing Association, and the Option Settlement Price Committee. Mr. Teetsell teaches courses on COMEX gold futures options at the New School for Social Research in New York City. Before joining COMEX, Mr. Teetsell was an economist for the Irving Trust Company. He has a B.S. from Penn State University and an M.B.A. from New York University.

RICHARD J. TEWELES is chairman of the Department of Finance, Real Estate and Law at the California State University, Long Beach. He is the author of *The Stock Market* (John Wiley & Sons, 1983), *The Commodity Futures Game: Who Wins? Who Loses? Why?* (McGraw-Hill, 1974), *The Commodity Futures Trading Guide* (McGraw-Hill, 1969), and over fifty articles on finance, law, marketing, and education. Dr. Teweles has been a consultant to brokerage firms, exchanges, law firms and government agencies in the areas of commodities and securities and has held memberships on the major futures exchanges.

JOSEPH P. TYRRELL is a C.P.A. and tax manager at the Chicago office of Coopers & Lybrand. He is a member of the Coopers & Lybrand Chicago Commodities and Securities Group and the Coopers and Lybrand National Insurance Tax Group. He received his B.B.A. in accounting from the University of Notre Dame and his Masters of Science in taxation from DePaul University.

NEIL S. WEINER, as consulting economist to the Kansas City Board of Trade, wrote the economic justification studies leading to CFTC approval for the initial trading of stock index futures contracts. He is the author of *Stock Index Futures: A Guide for Traders, Investors, and Analysts* (John Wiley & Sons, 1983), as well as a contributor to *The Journal of Futures Markets, Commodities Magazine, Quarterly Journal of Economics,* and *The American Statistician.* Prior to specializing in futures trading and capital markets, Dr. Weiner held senior economic and statistical positions at the Institute for Defense Analyses in Arlington, Virginia, and at the Executive Office of the President (OMB), in Washington, D.C. He holds B.S. and M.B.A. degrees in finance from U.C.L.A. and a Ph.D. in economics from Harvard University.

PAUL T. WILKINSON is an Assistant Vice-President with the Prudential-Bache Institutional Financial Futures Department, where he is involved in the development of risk management programs for institutional clients. Prior to joining

Prudential-Bache, Mr. Wilkinson was a financial futures specialist with A.G. Becker's Hedge Department and was involved in the management of internal hedge applications. He also served as Economist in the Financial Instruments Group, Department of Economic Analysis and Planning at the Chicago Board of Trade. There he was involved in new financial futures contract development and financial futures research. Mr. Wilkinson holds a B.A. in economics and an M.M. in finance and economics from Northwestern University.

AVNER S. WOLF is an Assistant Professor in the Department of Economics and Finance at Baruch College. Mr. Wolf has served as a consultant to Commodity Exchange, Inc. as well as taught at Columbia University's Graduate School of Business in business economics and finance. Mr. Wolf holds a B.A. from the Hebrew University and an M.A. and Ph.D. from Columbia University.

PART I

THE MARKETS AND THEIR OPERATION

CHAPTER 1

GROWTH AND ORGANIZATION OF COMMODITY MARKETS

CONTENTS

EARLY EVOLUTION 3
EARLY JAPANESE MARKET 5
THE MEIJI REGIME 8
DEVELOPMENT OF MARKETS IN THE WESTERN WORLD 9
Early Markets in America—
New York (1725–1862) 9
Chicago (1835–1875) 10
New York (1870–1947) 11
SELF-REGULATION 17
STANDARDIZATION OF CONTRACTS 18
EVOLUTION OF FUTURES TRADING—1850s–1870s 18
FORMS OF MARKET TRANSACTIONS 19
SPECULATION 20
Role of the Speculator 20
Hedger 21
FUTURES TRADING AND TELECOMMUNICATIONS 21
RELATIONSHIP OF DOMESTIC EXCHANGES 22
ORGANIZATION OF THE EXCHANGES 23
COMMITTEES 23
ARBITRATION COMMITTEES 24
GENERAL MEMBERSHIP 25
THE MARKETS TODAY 25
OPEN INTEREST 27
THE FINANCIALS 29
NEW AND PENDING CONTRACTS 30
The Exchanges and Commodities Traded 32
FOREIGN EXCHANGES 41
BERMUDA 41
Intex—International Futures Exchange Ltd. 41
FRANCE 41
Bourse De Commerce 41
ENGLAND 43
NETHERLANDS 45
HONG KONG 53

CHAPTER 1

GROWTH AND ORGANIZATION OF COMMODITY MARKETS

J. Duncan LaPlante

EARLY EVOLUTION

Any examination of the history of commodity trading must go back to the origins of man and his exchange, through barter, of articles for food and other goods. Though primitive, it is this same premise that is the backbone of modern open trade. If we concern ourselves only with the markets of today, and their foundations, we need not look earlier than medieval Europe to see a structure that still remains in the commodity exchanges.

The signing of the Magna Carta by King John on June 15, 1215 confirmed the right of merchants to freely enter and leave England in possession of goods. This act in itself opened the doors for many merchants to expand their markets into England. In that era the most extensive trading was done in cloth and wool, but trading also occurred in domestic livestock and foodstuffs.

A *bill of exchange* which was similar to a *warrant* was conceived by medieval traders in the 13th century. It was known as the "Fair letter." This form of payment evolved primarily out of necessity because carrying gold and silver was not only cumbersome, but the trade routes in medieval times were too dangerous. The Fair letter represented the goods traded, and would be settled at a later date upon delivery in the city where the seller lived.

Merchant associations formed as tradespeople saw the strength in acting as one unit in their common interest. The function of these associations was to arrange the dates of fairs where they would display and sell their goods. The associations also coordinated their efforts with the local authorities to ensure smooth operations. This could be construed as similar to the relationship between the Futures Industry Association (FIA) and the Commodity Futures Trading Commission (CFTC).

Attending these fairs were merchants from Holland, France, Italy, Spain, and England. Certain fairs were stronger in one nationality than others. For instance, the Winchester Fair catered mostly to Italian and French merchants, whereas the Stourbridge Fair was dominated by Flemish merchants.

As the towns and villages strengthened economically and grew in population, they formed their own markets. These were usually organized in some central location, such as the village square. Many of the articles traded in the European marketplace were brought from the East through Constantinople and the Medi-

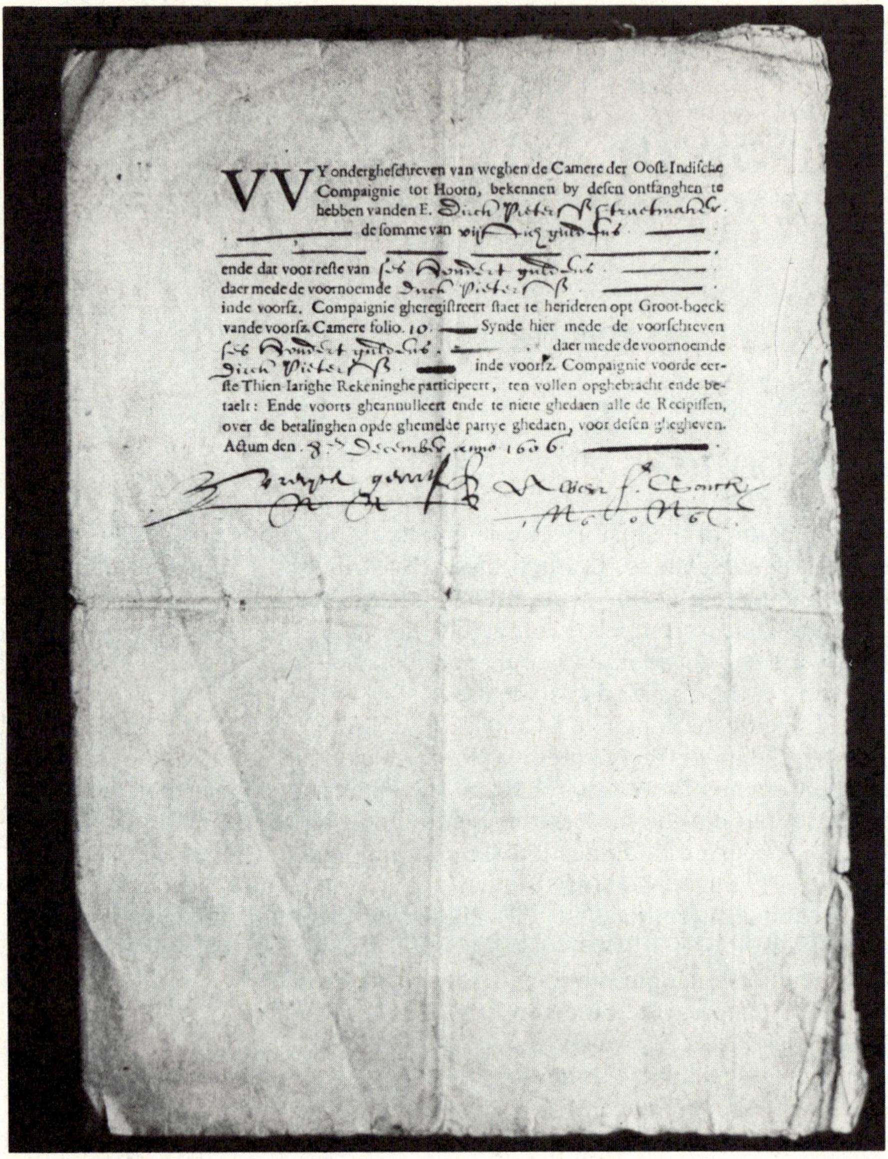

VVY ondergheſchreven van weghen de Camere der Ooſt-Indiſche Compaignie tot Hoorn, bekennen by deſen ontfanghen te hebben vanden E. [illegible] de ſomme van [illegible] ende dat voor reſte van [illegible] daer mede de voornoemde [illegible] inde voorſz. Compaignie ghereginſtreert ſtaet te herideren opt Groot-boeck vande voorſz. Camere folio. 10. Synde hier mede de voorſchreven [illegible] daer mede de voornoemde [illegible] inde voorſz. Compaignie voorde eerſte Thien-Iarighe Rekeninghe participeert, ten vollen opghebracht ende betaelt: Ende voorts gheannulleert ende te niete ghedaen alle de Recipiſſen, over de betalinghen opde ghemelde partye ghedaen, voor deſen ghegheven. Actum den [illegible] anno 1606.

[illegible]

FIGURE 1. Certificate of Trade from the Dutch East India Company.

terranean. These were items such as colored silk and spices such as ginger, pepper, and cinnamon.

Doubtless there were *rules of trade* that were established by the 17th century. In Holland in the early 1600s there were markets that dealt in the products of whole fisheries. The well-known speculation in Dutch tulips that occurred between 1634 and 1637 is still frequently referred to by critics to illustrate the negative aspects of unlimited speculation.[1] The exchanges, or bourses, as they were known

[1]The most popular version of the Tulipomania and other phenomena of speculation can be found in MacKay, *Extraordinary Popular Delusions and The Madness of Crowds*, Page, London, 1932.

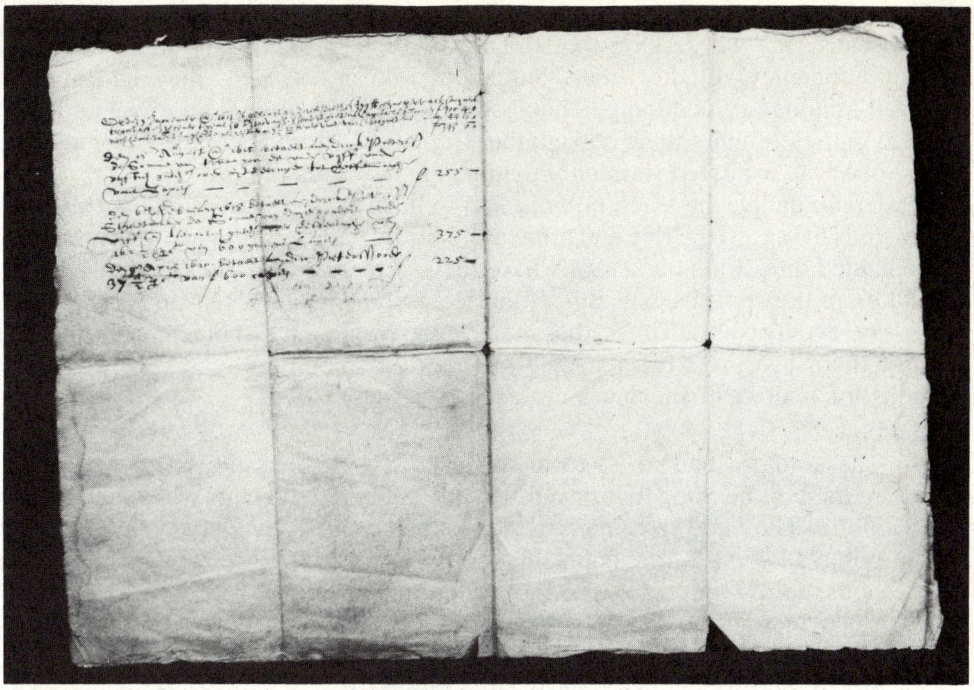

FIGURE 1. Continued.

in most European countries, evolved out of the marketplace. The name bourse (boerse, beurs, bolsa) comes from an 18th-century innkeeper named Van der Beurs, which would explain the adoption of the name into the many languages that used it. The inn was located in Bruges, Belgium, became a gathering place for merchants, and eventually became the center for local commerce. These bourses continued to serve essentially the same function as the fair, but on a more permanent basis.

Europe was not the only part of the world developing its trading markets. There were others, too numerous to mention here, that were either short-lived or absorbed into larger organizations. One market that does merit attention is the rice market in Japan. This was a highly organized commodity market that eventually established the use of forward contracts.

EARLY JAPANESE MARKET

According to Henry Bakken, credit must go to the feudal landowners of Japan for being the innovators of a futures market. During the Tokugawa era (1603–1868, eight generations), the feudal lords were required to spend at least half a year in Edo (Tokyo) where the central government (Tokugawa Shogunate) was located. This was by decree of the Shogunate, who wanted his lords to remain where he could keep an eye on them, as a measure of precaution. He did not want them to create a rebellion in some remote part of the empire, form an army, and separate him from his position.

The rents these absentee landlords collected were paid in kind, (in this case, rice) because the workers on the land were in feudal tenure and in an economy of self-sufficiency. In the urban centers of Edo and Osaka, they had already evolved a monetary economy. The absentee landlords were living well and they needed money to meet their obligations. In that era, if one belonged to the upper class, one was expected to maintain appearances.

Understandably, the titled nobility had to have cash to participate in this form of gracious living, so the rice and other agricultural products grown on their manors were hauled into Edo and Osaka where they were sold for cash. This, of course, would be in the spot market. Since the rice crop in Japan is seasonal, shipments were not evenly spread over the year. Moreover, some of the nobles did not confine themselves to a budget; they ran out of cash before the next harvest. The reasons for their cash shortages are examined below.

1. The landlord had to go to his estate to check operations and collect his rents, but the Shogunate would not permit him to take his wife and children along. They had to remain in Edo as hostages. They were a pledge of the noble's loyalty to the court. Thus, the nobles were forced to maintain two households—one in the country and one in the city.
2. When the nobles ventured out they had to travel in style to impress the country people. This called for an elaborate entourage, much formality, and dignified ritualism. This was not a matter of individual choice. The Shogunate prescribed what had to be done, since the noble was in a sense his traveling ambassador. A large number of samurai were present on the trip.
3. The Shogunate frequently required his nobles to contribute liberally to public works such as building and repairing castles, constructing roads, reclaiming land, and providing for the maintenance of armed forces.

It is easy to see how the nobles could find themselves short of cash. Often they had to raise cash quickly to meet some emergency; so at first they issued tickets (warehouse receipts) against supplies they had stored in the country or in rented warehouses in the city. Wholesale and retail merchants bought these tickets against anticipated needs. This was similar to what is today known as hedging. Eventually these rice tickets were made negotiable and became a form of currency to facilitate the transaction of business. The warehouse receipts were avidly bought up by the mercantile class. They were first administered by public officials of the Shogunate, but later the whole matter of the issue and supervision of the receipts was taken over by the merchants.

In time, the merchants began extending credit to the nobles in advance of the sale of the tickets, naturally at a high interest rate. Soon some of the merchants manipulated the market and became very wealthy. When they became affluent, they expanded their business operations and grew even weathier—richer by a good deal than some of the nobles. All they lacked was a title.

One particularly wealthy merchant named Yodoya in Osaka dominated the rice trade in that city; his house became the center where many of the merchants met to exchange information and negotiate transactions with one another. "The price at Yodoya's" was regarded as the prevailing price in the city of Osaka. This actually became the first commodity exchange formed in Japan in 1650. Later, in 1697, Yodoya was moved to another location, the Dojima district of Osaka, and thereafter the rice exchange became known as the *Dojima rice market*.

The striking feature about this market was that only trading in futures was permitted. A rule was formulated which stipulated that all transactions were limited to "cho-ai-mai-kaisho" which means "the market place." In 1730 the Tokugawa Shogunate officially recognized this commodity exchange which had been voluntarily developed by private traders. This institution and the system evolved for consumating transactions were declared legally permissible and protected by the highest authority of the realm.

Traders on the Oriental commodity exchange were orderly and well-disciplined. Their rules, according to Bakken, were as follows:

1. The contract term was limited to 4 months.
2. The year was divided into three 4-month periods.
3. At the end of each contract period the market was closed for a few days.
4. Trading was done in rice only.
5. All contracts in any 4-month period were standardized.
6. The basic grade for any contract period was chosen by the traders by majority vote. There were four grades available.
7. No physical delivery of grain against outstanding contracts was allowed.
8. All differences in value had to be settled in cash.
9. All contracts had to be settled and accounts cleared on or before the last day of the trading period.
10. No contracts could be carried over into the new contract period.
11. All trades had to be cleared through a clearinghouse.
12. Any default in payments was borne by the clearinghouse.
13. Traders were required to establish a line of credit with the clearinghouse of their choice.
14. The clearinghouses were nonprofit operations, but a commission was charged for services rendered.
15. No new contracts could be made during the last 3 days of any trading period. Bakken interprets this rule to mean that these days were reserved for the business of clearing trades by matching long against short, and so forth.
16. An arbitration committee was evidently in existence, and it was empowered to adjudicate disputes and judiciously settle issues concerning values and prices. The cho-ai-mai ("rice trade on book") futures market preceded our first futures market in the Western hemisphere by 129 years, that is, England in 1826, or the earliest futures transactions in this country by 170 years.

Toward the end of the Tokugawa era, the economic situation became erratic and prices fluctuated wildly, so much so, that the prices in the spot market had little relationship to the prices made in the futures market. In 1863 the length of the contract was shortened to 2 months, and it was shortened to 1 month in 1869.

THE MEIJI REGIME

The Meiji regime came to power succeeding the Tokugawa dynasty. It was called the Meiji restoration. At the time it assumed leadership in 1869 several rice exchanges had been established other than the one at Osaka. The new regime proved antagonistic to futures trading because it regarded all futures markets as a form of gambling and ordered them closed before the end of the first year in office. Only 2 years passed, however, before the government was forced to reopen the exchanges to circumvent complete chaos in the grain markets. This same phenomenon occurred in Germany in 1896. On the restoration of futures markets, physical deliveries were authorized in lieu of a cash settlement, which effectively tied the cash market to the futures market for the first time in Japanese trading. Commodity exchanges were in operation in Tokyo (Edo), Nagoya, and Osaka. Even though physical deliveries were permissible as a means of settling futures commitments at that time, it should be noted that very few contracts were offset by actual delivery of grain.

In 1876 the Meiji government passed laws designed to eliminate abuses and more firmly establish the honorable, time-tested customs handed down from past generations of futures traders. At this time, the government insisted that ownership and management of the building and facilities provided to expedite futures trading be owned by an independent company instead of a nonprofit association of traders. Soon after the passage of this act, rice exchanges developed in more than 10 cities in Japan. The addition of all these facilities attracted more traders to the exchanges. The more traders there were, the greater became the speculative excesses. The more money that was made or lost in speculation, the more attention the futures markets received from the public. Moreover, producers, consumers, politicians, lawyers, and academicians became increasingly critical of the futures market transactions.

The end product of this turbulence was the passage of the Commodity Exchange Act of 1893. After extensive studies were made of exchanges in other countries, this act made it permissible to form commodity exchanges either as joint-stock companies for profit or as nonprofit membership associations. Nearly all the exchanges formed in the 1890s were profit-seeking joint-stock companies, and by 1898 in the course of 5 years Japan was well-supplied with 128 commodity exchanges. While most of these were specialized in dealing in rice, a number of the exchanges offered contracts in other products such as salt, sea products, tea, silk, textiles, and sugar. The government, fearing promiscuous gambling, aggressively moved to reduce the number of exchanges, and apparently it was successful since only a few exchanges were recorded actively in business in the first decade of this century.

In 1914 the Commodity Exchange Act was revised, making it illegal for officers and employees to engage in trading through the exchange which they served. In 1922 the Exchange Act was revised as well as the law relating to the taxation of the exchanges. A number of the exchanges thereafter hastily reorganized as nonprofit membership associations. The records show eight such associations in 1927.

Following the occupation of Japan in 1949, there has been a resurgence of futures trading. A new Commodity Exchange Act was passed in 1950. The first exchange to be established under this act was the *Osaka Chemical Fibre Exchange*. By 1960 there were 20 new commodity exchanges in operation; five were dealing in fibers and textiles, two in silk, two in dried cocoons, two in rubber, two in sugar, six in grain, and one in sea products.

DEVELOPMENT OF MARKETS IN THE WESTERN WORLD

In 1733, in England, the use of warrants was initiated in the business of the East India Company. Warrants and their relationship to grading will be discussed in more detail later. For the moment it is important to realize that the use of warrants was an advancement to the industry in that it enabled one to transfer ownership without the actual transfer of any goods. This would clearly expedite the trading process for all parties concerned. By about 1734, England had a fixed system for grading metals, especially iron. This meant that once graded, a specific lot of a commodity could be transferred in the form of a warrant. (*Note*: Futures contracts were traded in Holland and France before 1832. Futures trading was reported in Berlin around the same year. In all three cases the contracts themselves were different in nature and specifications from the futures contracts in use today.)

EARLY MARKETS IN AMERICA—NEW YORK (1725–1862). In the early stages of America's economic development, several small markets existed in New York that had originally been formed without a permanent location from which to conduct business. There was one market in about 1725 that was actually located for a time at the east end of Wall Street. The commodities that were traded included domestic wheat and tobacco, and, as was common in that period, slaves.

As early as 1752 an exchange was formed in New York at the foot of Broad Street. It was primarily a spot market whose membership traded in domestic produce such as eggs and butter. A major problem with the early markets was that they lacked organization. Their membership was unstable and they often were without a stable base of operations. They did, however, lay the groundwork for the commodity exchanges of today and provided a place to trade for shipowners, brokers, financiers, producers, and speculators with risk capital.

The first forward contract on record is dated March 13, 1851. The transaction involved 3,000 bushels of corn for delivery in June at $0.01 below the March price. Forward trading has essentially the same contractual commitments as spot trading, the difference being that in a forward transaction the buyer and seller agree to defer delivery until some point in the future. In negotiating a contract of this nature the buyer may require a guarantee of a specific quality from the seller. Usually both parties will agree to the price adjustments that will be made, depending on if the quality, or grade, is inferior or superior to the predetermined standard of the commodity.

Forward contracts were originally made between country merchants and terminal receivers with both parties intending to make and take delivery. By the mid-1850s contracts frequently changed hands several times before being purchased by someone who was interested in taking delivery. In time, other businesspeople began trading, with no intention of taking delivery.

In 1850 the *Commercial Exchange* was founded in New York. It was incorporated as the *New York Produce Exchange* in 1862 and operated primarily as a spot market for several years. Though this exchange is no longer in operation, it, and others like it, through the use of forward contracts, provided the foundation for the emergence of futures markets.

CHICAGO (1835–1875). New York in the early 1830s was a thriving urban environment, the center of business for most of the nation. Chicago on the other hand was in the midst of rapid growth. It was incorporated as a village in 1833 and did not become a city until 1837. At that point the population was a mere 4,107. Despite its modest size, Chicago had all the requisites for becoming a large and successful city.

As early as 1832 there had been export shipments of beef and pork from Chicago. The first large commodity shipment occurred in 1839 when 1,678 bushels of wheat were shipped by boat from Chicago to Black Rock, New York. Chicago's rapid development as a grain terminal was largely due to the agricultural wealth of the surrounding area. Another contributing factor was simply its ideal location with access to water transportation. Processing facilities were set up to accommodate the eastbound trade .There were three major reasons why Chicago was the center for grain:

Grain was shipped to Chicago for reshipment east.
Grain was shipped to Chicago for processing.
Grain was shipped to Chicago to support the livestock population.

Despite the use of forward contracts, the market could not always sustain the often sudden shifts in supply, demand, and, consequently, price. Just after harvest it was common for the supply to far exceed the immediate needs. As was often the case, the farmer or producer got the short end of the deal. The processors could afford to bid low due to the existing glut of commodities on the market. There were cases where even though the prices were extremely low, there were still a vast amount of goods that simply were not sold.

This situation was aggravated by the lack of suitable storage space and the primitive condition of the cold storage facilities that were available at the time. In addition to this, the means of transportation did not allow for swift passage to and from the city. Once the goods had arrived there was not only the problem of storage space with which to contend, but because of underdeveloped harbor facilities, any goods that were scheduled for shipment east were frequently delayed.

In 1848 there were two major occurrences that greatly improved the situation in Chicago. The first was the completion and opening of the Illinois–Michigan Canal, which served to expedite transportation to and from Chicago. Shortly thereafter railroads began to spread in all directions, connecting producers with the markets and enabling goods to retain their value longer due to the lessened duration of their trip.

The other important occurrence of 1848 was the founding of the *Chicago Board of Trade*. There were 82 original members of what is today the world's oldest active commodity futures exchange. Initially, the objective of the Board of Trade was to promote the commerce of Chicago itself. However, this objective became secondary to the regional development of commerce that occurred as the surrounding area prospered. The Chicago Board of Trade was incorporated in 1859, just prior to the outbreak of the Civil War.

During the Civil War (1861–1865) Chicago served as the primary concentration point for the Union army. Certain elements of futures trading began to evolve as the government purchased pork under contract for later delivery. Formalization of futures contracts was stimulated by the compounded supply-and-demand problems which were perpetrated by the war. After the war, eastbound commerce expanded as futures trading came into full force within the business communities.

The *MidAmerica Commodity Exchange* was founded in 1868 as *Pudd's Exchange*. The founders were each former members of the Chicago Board of Trade. In 1880 it was incorporated as the *Chicago Open Board of Trade*. The exchange was literally *open* in that the public could stand in trading pits and observe their orders being filled. In 1882 the exchange became the first to institute third-party clearing, a practice that was later adopted by all other commodity exchanges.

Another exchange came into being in 1874. The *Chicago Produce Exchange* was formed by a group of agricultural dealers who traded eggs, butter, poultry, and other produce. This exchange would later become the *Chicago Butter and Egg Board* and eventually the *Chicago Mercantile Exchange*.

Chicago was clearly on the road to diversified expansion. Processing facilities grew and new exchanges were established. But an event took place in 1871 that caused many of the currently operating processing plants to be totally refurbished. The event was of course the Chicago Fire. It seems somehow ironic that it was started by a cow in the city of livestock. Many records were destroyed which, had they survived, may have revealed the full details of what had transpired within that period.

NEW YORK (1870–1947). In 1870 the *New York Cotton Exchange* was formed. It was incorporated in 1872 and that same year it established its rules for trading. These rules, as would be the case with most of the other exchanges, developed out of existing forward contracting practices. They also applied to brokers as they governed their trading practices. Some of the major elements involved in these regulations are

Standardized contract.
Margin deposit.
Transfer of contracts.
Described delivery grades.
Delivery procedure.

The *New York Mercantile Exchange* was founded in 1872 under the name of the *Butter and Cheese Exchange of New York*. In 1882 it was changed to the current name. That same year the *New York Coffee Exchange* was formed. The exchange

FIGURE 2. Benjamin Arnold—first president of the New York Coffee Exchange.

was originally created to trade in coffee futures only, but in 1914 sugar futures were added to replace the European raw sugar markets that were closed by World War I. Two years later the name was changed to the *New York Coffee and Sugar Exchange*. Both the New York Cotton Exchange and the New York Coffee and Sugar Exchange have similar provisions in their bylaws for arbitration. Among the early exchanges in New York speculation was a dominant force, which led to numerous disputes among the members. Thus it was appropriate and wise for such bylaws to be put into effect in order to minimize conflict and to arrive at swift settlements.

In 1925 the *New York Cocoa Exchange* was founded as the world's first exchange for trading exclusively in cocoa futures. After 1920 several new commodities were added to the general markets. The exchanges each traded their share of the new list of commodities. Some of the commodities added included cocoa, tin, soybeans, lead, black pepper, soybean meal, soybean oil, rubber, copper, silk, silver, zinc, potatoes, millfeeds, wool tops, grease wool, hides, and

FIGURE 3. Coffee Exchange—circa 1900.

FIGURE 4. Sugar ring—1933.

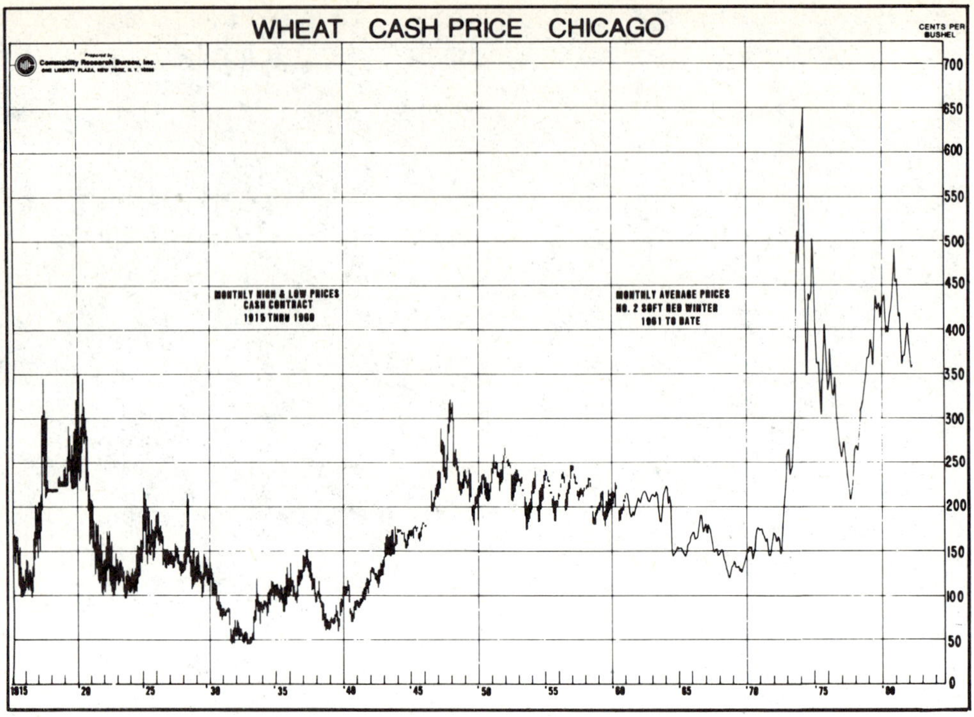

FIGURE 5. Cash wheat at Chicago.

FIGURE 6. The Chicago Mercantile Exchange—1928.

FIGURE 7. The Chicago Mercantile Exchange (building), 1928–1972.

cottonseed meal. Prior to World War II trading was suspended in tin, lead, and silk in order that supplies would be sufficient to sustain the United States through the duration of the war.

Commodity Exchange, Incorporated (COMEX) was formed on July 5, 1933 by the consolidation and merger of several smaller independent exchanges in New York. These included the *National Silk Exchange,* the *National Metal Exchange,* the *National Hide Exchange,* and the *Rubber Exchange of New York.* Each of these exchanges had previously traded futures in their respective commodities. In addition to those, COMEX eventually established futures trading in lead and zinc. Trading in silver was discontinued in 1934 when the federal government nationalized silver.

Just prior to World War II, trading in most futures markets was suspended because of the establishment of price ceilings and the initiation of allocation controls. The grain and cotton exchanges remained open, but there was little trading of any significance. By 1947 normal trading had resumed, though with minor exceptions.

FIGURE 8. The Chicago Mercantile Exchange (trading floor), 1921–1928.

FIGURE 9. COMEX (trading floor)—circa 1935.

CHICAGO (1898–1960). In 1898 the *Chicago Butter and Egg Board* (formerly the *Chicago Produce Exchange*) was organized to provide a national marketplace for trading in cash and futures contracts in various agricultural commodities. By 1915, 28 rules had been set down governing the trading of butter. After World War I industry leaders formed an organization to permit the public participation of trading under supervised commodity trading regulations.

The Chicago Egg and Butter Board was renamed the *Chicago Mercantile Exchange* late in 1919. The first day of trading was December 1, 1919 at the corner of LaSalle and Lake Streets. On and around April 25, 1928, the entire operation was moved to the North Franklin and Washington Street location due to the lack of available space at the original building.

Up until the early 1950s almost all trading had been done in eggs and butter. In the 1950s and 1960s many new contracts were developed for trading and some of the contracts already traded were discontinued. The unsuccessful contracts included onions, frozen shrimp, scrap iron, apples, hides, and frozen broilers. The surviving original contracts included frozen pork bellies, live hogs, live cattle, and Idaho potatoes.

In 1973 the *Chicago Open Board of Trade* adopted a new name—the *MidAmerica Commodity Exchange*. Along with the change of name, they moved to modern facilities and initiated trading in "minicontracts." Through the development of smaller minimum trading units, MidAmerica has made futures trading possible for a much broader segment of growers, processors, and the public investor or speculator.

SELF-REGULATION

Self-regulation in commodity futures markets began with grading specifications. The Chicago Board of Trade (CBOT) developed the first system of standards for wheat and initiated a system of inspection and weighing for the various types of grain that were (and are) traded there. In 1859 the CBOT was authorized by the state of Illinois to hire and instruct individuals to measure, gauge, weigh, and inspect grain.

It was the substitution of weight for volume that made the development of grain-handling machinery possible. By 1860 most of the grain in Chicago was inspected and graded. It should be noted that the grading system in the United States developed independently within the area of agricultural products. For instance, as wheat was presented for storage, it was inspected and classified within the established grades. Receipts, or warrants, were issued by the elevator or warehouse according to grade. The warrants then represented the commodity that was being stored.

The major problem that evolved within this system of classification was that the warrants that were issued applied to specific lots of grain. The warrants then changed hands several times which created a great deal of difficulty at delivery time. Some 10 years later in about 1870 all grain was stored according to grade. There was no longer any reference made to a specific lot of grain. A system of generalized receipts evolved, allowing delivery to take place with much less confusion.

STANDARDIZATION OF CONTRACTS

In order to maintain stability within the futures markets, it became neccessary to create a standard on which contracts could be based. This meant that there would have to be uniform contracts drawn up for the specific commodities traded. These contracts were based on previously established standards of quality (grade) and were uniform for both domestic and international trade.

This does not mean that one contract can properly represent an entire commodity. Depending on the commodity, there could be several different contracts, each valid for a specific grade. Also, depending on the commodity, there could be several grades, each uniform within the general classification of standard. Of course samples of the various grades of the commodity were made available upon request.

For each commodity there is a "basis" or "standard" grade. When compared to the basis grade, all other grades are judged as either superior or inferior in quality. The basis grade represents the largest proportion of the total quantity of a given commodity. Where prices are concerned, the price of the basis or standard grade would move above or below the current base price, depending upon the supply of the commodity and the demand.

There are several different individuals or groups that undertake the grading of samples. They are as follows:

1. A committee of the given exchange, who is authorized by them to perform the grading function.
2. Individuals not on a committee of any kind, but still licensed by the exchange.
3. Individual graders who are employed under government authority.

The end result of the self-regulatory process is that there is an expanded volume of trading and perhaps what is more important is that the expansion is not haphazard in nature; it is organized and efficient. The organization, especially in the area of grading, expedites the manufacture of products. The standardization of contracts expedites the completion of trades and instills future delivery confidence because one knows exactly what to expect.

EVOLUTION OF FUTURES TRADING—1850s–1870s

Between 1850 and 1857 there occurred a great deal of growth and industrialization accompanied by a rapid increase in production and shipment. Unfortunately, this resulted in frequent price fluctuations. There were severe market gluts and subsequent price declines. Forward contracts, as they were at the time, could not sustain the increase in technology and its resultant production levels.

Forward contracts were originally made between country merchants and terminal operators with both parties intending to make and take delivery. By the mid-to-late 1850s, contracts frequently changed hands several times before being sold to someone who had intentions of taking delivery. In time, more diverse businesspeople (speculators, business investors, and so forth) began trading without any intention of taking delivery.

There had been much trading in forward contracts outside of the board and its members. In 1858 the Chicago Board of Trade adopted a rule which restricted trade to members of the exchange. The following year the arbitration committee was established at the CBOT. On March 27, 1863 another rule was adopted to enforce compliance of contract terms. This rule stated that failure to comply with the terms would result in the suspension of membership privileges. The first rule that dealt specifically with time or forward contracts was enacted in May 1865. It required the deposit of a margin, not to exceed 10% of the value of the commodity, when demanded by either party.

The Chicago Board of Trade adopted its "general" rules and regulations on October 13, 1865. This included the margin rule that had been written in May 1865. The six basic points covered were:

1. Procedures to follow in the event that one fails to complete delivery.
2. Standardization of delivery procedure.
3. Prescribed terms of payment.
4. Contracts for other than the exchange of title.
5. Deposit of funds to guarantee performance.
6. Standardized contract terms.

Four years later, the first rules for futures trading were established by the Chicago Board of Trade. Futures trading had already been going on for several years before anyone made any attempt to specifically regulate the process. Naturally, most of the rules evolved from those that had been written for forward contracts, but some, particularly those that dealt with the delivery procedure, had to be initiated separately due to the delivery arrangements that are unique to futures trading. Evidence given to a congressional committee on agriculture in February 1892 stated that the government contracts for pork during the Civil War were the first futures transactions made.

There was no major futures trading in New York until the late 1870s. The first important futures trading in New York was done on the *New York Cotton Exchange*. The *New York Produce Exchange* became an active market for futures early in 1876. The first public call in pork and lard was on January 31, 1876, and the first public call in grain was on May 17, 1877. As early as 1885 there were futures contracts traded in Milwaukee, Toledo, and St. Louis.

FORMS OF MARKET TRANSACTIONS

Since people first realized that they were to some extent dependent on others, they have conducted some form of trade. Such interdependency resulted first in barter and eventually in more sophisticated means of trading. The descriptions below provide a brief explanation of the various forms of market transactions.

Barter. Barter is an exchange of need for need. These bilateral transactions were isolated and seldom were influenced by other trades.

Cash Markets. The cash markets originated with the medium of the exchange. Goods were exchanged simultaneously for cash.

Spot Markets. Spot markets evolved out of the cash markets. Samples of specific lots of a commodity being offered for sale were displayed at the exchange. Delivery need not occur simultaneously with the sale. The title to the goods is transferred at the time of payment which occurs following delivery. "Spot" is also used to refer to the futures contract of the current month, in which case the trading is still considered to be in futures, but delivery is possible at any time.

Forward (to arrive). A contract is purchased for specific goods or their equivalent. Delivery occurs at a predetermined point in time which has been agreed to by both parties. Payment is made upon delivery. The sale is usually made on a sample, but it may be made on a description instead.

Contract to Deliver On Sale. This was the primary bridge between forward and futures contracts. The sale was made on the basis of samples or on description. There was a time lapse prior to delivery at which point payment was made.

Futures Markets. There are several futures markets in various locations throughout the world. A *futures contract* is a standardized agreement whereby a purchase is made of a specific commodity of a specific quality or grade. There are designated months for delivery for each commodity and standardized procedures for making and taking delivery. The first known futures transaction took place in Japan around 1697, in England around 1826, and in the United States around 1868. Sale or purchase of a contract is not dependent on samples, but on the description referencing standardized grades. The exchanges maintain uniformity in contracts, trade terms, trade customs, and practices in order to effect standards of classification and to arbitrate disputes.

SPECULATION

An individual who enters the futures market for a purpose other than hedging is a speculator. Although spreading is a sophisticated form of speculation in that more than one commodity or contract of futures are involved in trading, more commonly a speculator is simply a commodity trader who is outright long or short in futures attempting to forecast price movement for profit.

ROLE OF THE SPECULATOR. The speculator fulfills several vital economic functions that facilitate the production, processing, and marketing of basic commodities. The speculator provides the risk-shifting opportunity for the hedger and the liquidity that allows the hedger to buy and sell in large volume.

The speculator examines the likely price movement and risks venture capital for the sake of profiting on an accurate forecast of that price movement. Active speculation tends to lessen the extremes of price movement that would otherwise occur. Analysis of the composition of commodity futures trading prepared monthly by the CFTC indicates that in periods of less speculative activity, price volatility will tend to be more extreme than in periods when there is relatively more speculative activity.

A futures position, whether long or short, carries with it both the positive and negative aspects of price movement that exist in owning the actual commodity, but without the problems of storage and handling. The speculator will buy or sell, depending on whether a forecast calls for an increase or decrease in price. The offsetting sale or purchase will result in a profit if the market has moved true to the forecast. The profit potential remains the same in assuming either a long or short position and the profit potential is of course proportional to the speculator's forecasting acumen.

There are those who equate speculation with gambling and there are those who make a distinction between the two and base the difference on the nature of risk itself and its relation to the social good. Gambling involves the creation of risk for the sole purpose of assuming that risk. Any form of gambling, whether it is a poker game, roulette wheel, or horse race, creates a risk that would not otherwise exist.

Speculation, however, involves risks that are necessarily present in the process of marketing goods in a free capitalistic system. These risks of investment exist and if the speculator did not assume them the open market system would soon fail. The clearest distinction is that the gambler creates a game to satisfy a desire to partake in a risk situation, while the speculator is not creating the game, but merely assuming a risk that is already present by the nature of the economic system.

If hedgers (see the chapter on hedging for more detail) operated solely to reduce their risks, and this were only made possible by the involvement of the speculator, then it would seem clear that the speculator provided a service of substantial social value. However, hedgers operate in the futures markets not just to reduce their risk, but also as speculators, to realize profit. In some cases they might find it in their interest to carry their entire risk unhedged, thus maximizing their profits should the market move to their advantage.

HEDGER. A hedger is an individual or organization which assumes a position in a futures market that is intended as a temporary substitute for the sale or purchase of the actual commodity. A hedge is the sale of futures contracts in anticipation of future sales of cash commodities as a protection against possible price declines, or it is the purchase of futures contracts in anticipation of future purchases of cash commodities as a protection against the possibility of increasing costs.

FUTURES TRADING AND TELECOMMUNICATIONS

Other than a person's drive for more efficient means to attain personal goals, there is another element involved in the evolution of futures trading that merits attention. The development of telecommunications has played a major role in the day-to-day business operations of the commodities industry.

It began with the telegraph, linking western states with the East coast and the producers of livestock and grains with the markets. Telegraph lines had been in use in Chicago by 1848, the same year that the Chicago Board of Trade was founded. The introduction of the telephone in 1878 connected the brokerage houses to the trading floors, thus establishing connections between investors, brokers, and the exchanges. The advent of the teletype or electric ticker provided almost immediate access to price changes through the transmission of quotations. It also established the first efficient means by which to monitor and record changes in price and subsequent price trends.

There is an entire chapter in this book devoted to the computer and information systems, so it will be sufficient to say here that without the computer, there would still be chalk written price quotations and the idea of a totally automated exchange would still remain a vision, rather than the reality it has become.

RELATIONSHIP OF DOMESTIC EXCHANGES

Futures exchanges provide an active and organized marketplace where members trade in standard or basis contracts under established regulations. The exchanges also assume responsibility for the grading of cash commodities. The exchanges themselves do not actually trade commodities, nor do they set prices for the commodities traded. The prices are decided in the open market through open outcry. This may evolve into a more advanced technological approach through the use of computer systems designed to enable one to trade without the use of the trading floor. But for the moment, the method of open outcry is the most equitable means of arriving at a fair market price.

The primary objective of a futures exchange is to provide the facilities for the trading of futures contracts. Members alone are permitted to do the actual trading, but they in turn represent various trade interests and the public. Hieronymus suggests that there are seven major functions (objectives) that are common to all futures exchanges[2]:

1. To establish equitable principles of business conduct by members.
2. To provide an organized marketplace and establish the time(s) of trading.
3. To provide uniform rules and standards for the conduct of trading.
4. To establish uniformity of contract size and trade customs regarding quality, time and place of delivery, and terms of payment.
5. To collect and disseminate price information to members of the exchange and to the public.
6. To provide machinery to guarantee the settlement of contracts and the payment of financial obligations in connection with trading among members.
7. To provide a mechanism for the adjustment of disputes among members.

The functions will vary somewhat depending upon the individual exchange. It is safe to say that the similarities in procedure and regulation are greater than the differences in management and operations.

There is another side to the relationship between the exchanges. Though they share certain structural aspects, each exchange has developed independently from

[2]T. A. Hieronymus, *The Economics of Futures Trading*, Commodity Research Bureau, NY, 1971.

the others, and as such has its own history and traditions (though they maintain some common members). There does exist some competition, but it is most evident where the same commodity is being traded by more than one exchange. Because most exchanges trade in different commodities, there is a strong basis for cooperation. Many have suggested an unspoken competition between the exchanges in New York and those in Chicago, but this is more of an industry rivalry than it is an economic competition and this book will not pursue this matter.

In addition to the trading of futures contracts, there are a number of other responsibilities in which the exchanges are involved. Perhaps the most important of these is the establishment of grades and the inspection of the commodities themselves. Exchanges also supervise the weighing of commodities moving through the terminal. The various grain exchanges operate cash markets where buyers and sellers negotiate on the exchange of title. Another nonfutures function is the establishment of commission rates (and rules) for trading in cash commodities.

ORGANIZATION OF THE EXCHANGES

All of the commodity exchanges in the United States are nonprofit membership associations and are incorporated in the states in which they are located. Most exchanges limit the number of members, but it should be noted that companies, partnerships, cooperatives, and corporations are frequently registered for certain membership privileges. As mentioned earlier, it is common for one to maintain memberships on more than one exchange simultaneously.

Each exchange is governed by a Board of Governors, Board of Directors, or Board of Managers. The board is generally elected by the members of the exchange though sometimes it is elected by board members themselves, as in the case of a retiring member whose position needs to be filled.

The administration of an exchange is comprised of executive officers and staff. The staff members are not members of the exchange. The officers of the exchange are usually made up of a chairman, one or two vice-presidents, and sometimes a treasurer and/or secretary. Staff officers include the president, one or more vice-presidents, each usually in charge of a committee or department of the exchange, the treasurer, and secretary. The specific titles of these executive and staff officers vary somewhat depending upon the exchange. The responsibilities of the staff are to carry out the decisions of the Board of Governors and to maintain the policies of the exchange.

COMMITTEES

Within every exchange there exist a number of committees that are designed to deal with the various aspects of maintaining and optimizing the exchange's operations. These committees advise the board on specific areas of operation and assist other committees and departments in matters of their unique concentration. The members of these committees are either appointed by the Board of Directors or elected by other members of the exchange. All of the committees are ultimately responsible to the Board of Directors.

Below is a list of committees that are common to most of the exchanges in the United States. A brief explanation of their purposes is provided as well. Again, the committees within each individual exchange may vary or have different names. In addition to the general committees listed, most have committees that focus on the specific commodities that are traded on that exchange as follows:

1. *Arbitration.* Arbitration committees are discussed in detail below.
2. *Business Conduct.* Supervision and investigation of the business conduct of exchange members.
3. *Finance.* Management of the finances and investments of the exchange.
4. *Floor Conduct.* Supervision of activity on the exchange trading floor.
5. *Government Relations.* Relations with state and federal governments and organizations thereof—CFTC, SEC, FTC, and so forth.
6. *Management.* Management of the physical facilities of the exchange.
7. *Nominations.* Nominations of candidates for the board, its officers, and those committees elected by the exchange membership.
8. *Public Relations.* Relations with the city, public, and investors.
9. *Quotations and Market Reports.* Supervision of the reporting of market prices, information, and statistics.
10. *Regulations.* Amendments to Rules and Regulations pertinent to the exchange and the industry in general.
11. *Warehouse and License.* Supervision of weighing, warehousing, and inspection of commodities for delivery against the futures contracts of the exchange.

ARBITRATION COMMITTEES

Organized exchanges uniformly provide for adjudication by voluntary or compulsory arbitration of all disputes between members without recourse to courts of law. All members of an exchange subject themselves to the provisions of its charter and bylaws. Controversies are usually disposed of with a minimum of expense and delay. The machinery of arbitration makes for a swift and just determination without the rigidity and legal formalities found in a court of law.

Charges of misconduct that may render an exchange member subject to disciplinary action may be preferred by

The Board of Governors.

Committees or arbitrators that have the authority to prefer such charges.

Any member of the exchange.

GENERAL MEMBERSHIP

The general membership of any exchange is comprised of individuals whose financial position and integrity are found to be consistent with the standards set by the exchange. An extensive investigation of an applicant for membership may be undertaken by the exchange to ensure that the applicant qualifies on the basis of his or her credit standing and financial responsibility. Members are often given a better rate of commission for the execution of an order if they do not choose to execute the order themselves or they pay a minimum exchange and clearing fee if they actually execute their own orders.

Other personnel that are essential to the day-to-day operation of the exchange include market reporters and runners. The market reporters stand either adjacent to the pit or ring, or else within the center on the trading floor. Their function is to record price changes as they occur. The prices which they record are displayed on the computer-operated electronic display boards which are clearly visible from any point on the trading floor. These prices eventually become the "ticker" or narrow tape which gets transmitted by the communications services.

The runners or messengers have the responsibility of getting the orders and their subsequent executions to and from the trading pit. When an order is relayed by phone to a commission house's order desk on the trading floor, the runner then delivers the order to the appropriate broker in the trading pit. Following the execution of the order, the runner delivers the order back to the commission house's quarters on the trading floor and the confirmation of the order is then documented and sent on to the customer.

THE MARKETS TODAY

There are currently 11 major commodity exchanges operating in the United States. Of these, the Chicago Board of Trade is the largest and the exchanges in Chicago are the most active.

Before 1960 nearly all of the commodities traded on futures exchanges were storable agricultural products such as cotton, grains, coffee, and so forth. During the 1960s, trading expanded to include futures contracts in livestock. This generated a substantial amount of new trading activity as contracts in hogs, cattle, and pork bellies, among others, became available.

The 1970s saw additional expansion within the futures markets as foreign currency and interest-rate futures contracts were introduced. Many attribute the growth in volume to the introduction of the financial instrument contracts. Between 1970 and 1980, volume increased 676%. The number of contracts traded went from 13.62 million in 1970, to 92.10 million in 1980.

In addition to the increased number of new contracts being listed on the futures exchanges, the growth of futures markets can be explained by the increase in international trade, the development of Third World countries, and a general expansion of world economics. The rise in interest rates caused more volatile markets, resulting in increased use of futures for risk transference.

FIGURE 10. Trading activity—New York Mercantile Exchange.

Between 1970 and 1981, the number of different futures contracts more than doubled, going from 40 in 1970 to 86 in 1981. In 1960 there were only 30 different contracts being traded, and of those only five are now inactive. Of course not all of the contracts that were added during the period from 1961 to 1981 have been successful. Contracts in leather, onions, and diamonds, to name a few, have not survived.

In 1982 many exchanges began trading stock index futures, conceptually a major step forward for the futures markets. These indices link the futures markets with the stock market to provide a vehicle for hedging large or institutional portfolios. The unique aspect of the contract is its *cash settlement*. Unlike agricultural products, there is no physical delivery of a stock portfolio which represents the index. In the case of the Value Line or the New York Stock Exchange Index that would mean a weighted index portfolio of over 1,500 stocks. Cash settlement is not a new concept. The earliest exchange in Kioto, Japan in the early 1500s met with difficulties from their government when it introduced contracts with similar cash settlement. The government claimed that such a contract violated the basic meaning of futures "exchange" which, it contended, *must* have physical delivery of the commodity. This conflict led to the closing of the Kioto exchange in 1526.

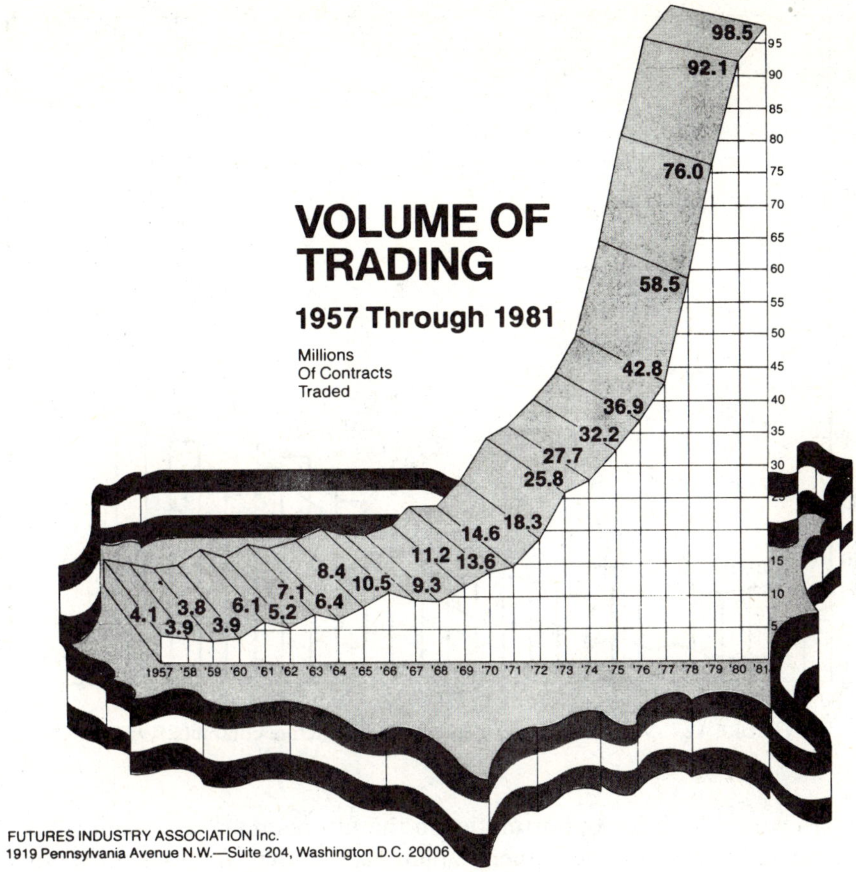

FIGURE 11. Volume of trading, 1957–1981.

OPEN INTEREST

As volume expanded, the total open interest also expanded. Open interest is the number of open positions at the close of any business day. As indicated by Table 1, open interest between the years 1960 and 1980 increased by about 14% per year. Trading volume during the same time span increased at about 17% per year. This difference has been attributed to the many speculators who entered the markets and in doing so created an exceptional increase in contract liquidity.

This expansion represents increased use of the market by both commercial and speculative interests. In the 1960s there was only slow growth in trading based on a new awareness of the futures markets and a shift of capital from the stock market to commodities. During the late 1960s and through the 1970s, it was common to associate the increases and decreases in commodity market participation to the rise and fall of the stock market. Whenever stock prices declined,

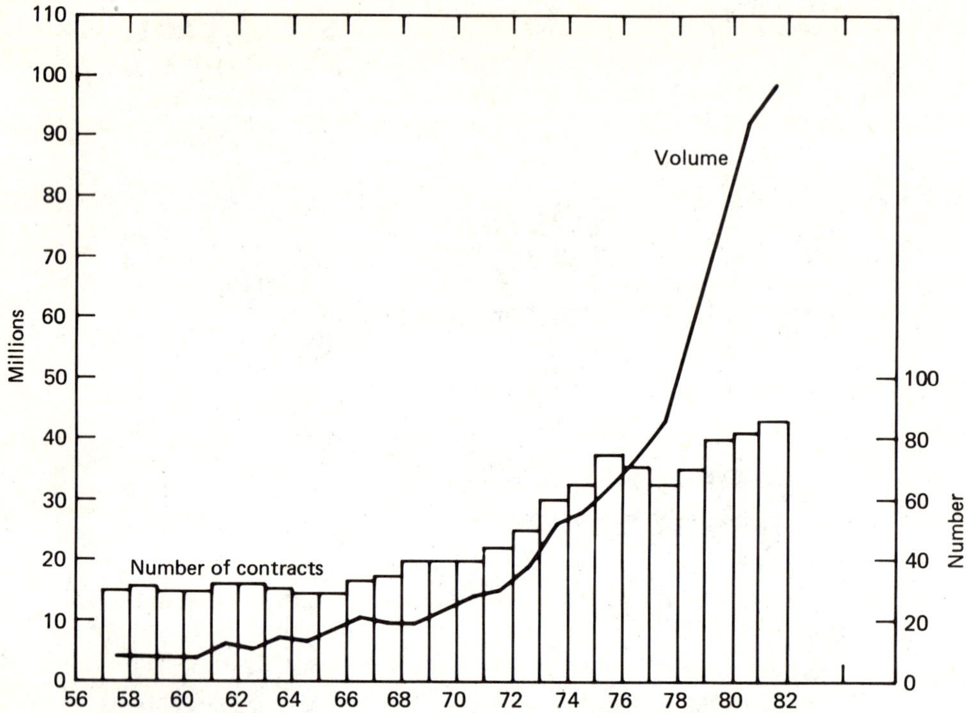

FIGURE 12. Volume of trading and number of active contracts, 1957–1981.

investors would look for opportunities in the futures markets; when stock prices began to rise they would move their capital back to their favored stock portfolios.

The events of the 1970s and the introduction of new contracts caused a more rapid and stable growth in the futures markets. Public awareness focused on the grain markets in 1974 when the Russian wheat sales left the United States with an inadequate grain reserve, and prices at twice the level of the previous year.

TABLE 1. Trading-Volume/Open-Interest (Vol/OI) Ratio by Commodity Groups, 1978–1980 Averages

Futures Group	Vol/OI Ratio	Average Value Per Contract ($1,000)
Livestocks	80.7	$ 23.84
Foreign currencies	73.4	67.99
Grains and oilseeds	61.3	22.90
Industrials	43.2	28.65
Interest rates	41.3	328.50
Tropicals	39.2	31.52
Precious metals	28.6	45.72
All groups	47.8	$ 56.83

Source: ACLI Research Department, White Plains, NY, 1981.

In 1975 the U.S. dollar began its sharpest decline. Manufacturers and producers realized that the export demand and the value of the U.S. dollar, previously ignored, were real parts of product pricing. Fluctuations in price directly related to changes in the value of the U.S. dollar were enough to cause serious financial problems in industry. It brought about an awareness of better inventory control and the need for a new and more sophisticated program of commodity purchases and sales.

As discussed in the section "New and Pending Contracts" the financial futures markets have been the greatest asset to the industry. Instability of interest rates and acute public awareness have brought both speculators and institutions en masse into the markets as active participants, which has substantially increased contract liquidity.

Along with the increase in volume and open interest there was also an increase in the dollar value. Collective trading value went from $30.8 billion in 1960 to $6.3 trillion in 1980. The value of open interest went from $0.96 to $91.5 billion over the same time span. This rate of expansion was around 30.5% per year and was caused by the rapid increase in the average dollar value of each contract. The average contract was worth $7,950 in 1960 as opposed to $9,320 in 1970. In the decade between 1970 and 1980, the average value increased more than seven times to about $68,710 per contract. With the exclusion of the financial instruments, the average dollar value per contract in 1980 would be approximately $31,000. The annual growth rate would be only 7% from 1960 to 1980, which is barely higher than the general rate of inflation. One must therefore conclude that the drastic increase in trading value between 1970 and 1980 was almost exclusively due to the introduction of the financial instrument futures.

THE FINANCIALS

Ginnie Maes (Government National Mortgage Association) began trading at the Chicago Board of Trade during October 1975. Treasury bills (90-day) followed shortly thereafter on January 6, 1976 on the Chicago Mercantile's International Monetary Market (IMM). Both contracts proved to be highly successful and during August 1977 and again in September of the same year, the CBOT added contracts in long-term Treasury bonds and short-term (90-day) commercial paper. A year later in September, 1978 the CBOT introduced a new Ginnie Mae contract and the IMM simultaneously added a contract for 1-year Treasury bills. Debt instrument futures were rapidly becoming the most popular contracts traded in the United States.

This popularity resulted in a flood of applications to the CFTC, (Commodity Futures Trading Commission) by most of the major exchanges. The CFTC, however, was reluctant because of pressure from several federal agencies such as the Treasury Department and the SEC (Securities Exchange Commission); they wished to limit the trading of such contracts because of the potential negative effects on future government borrowings in the cash markets. Another reason the CFTC was hesitant was the increase in speculation in a market that had been designed primarily for hedgers. In late 1978 the financial futures markets presented certain profits for the speculator because interest rates were on a constant upswing.

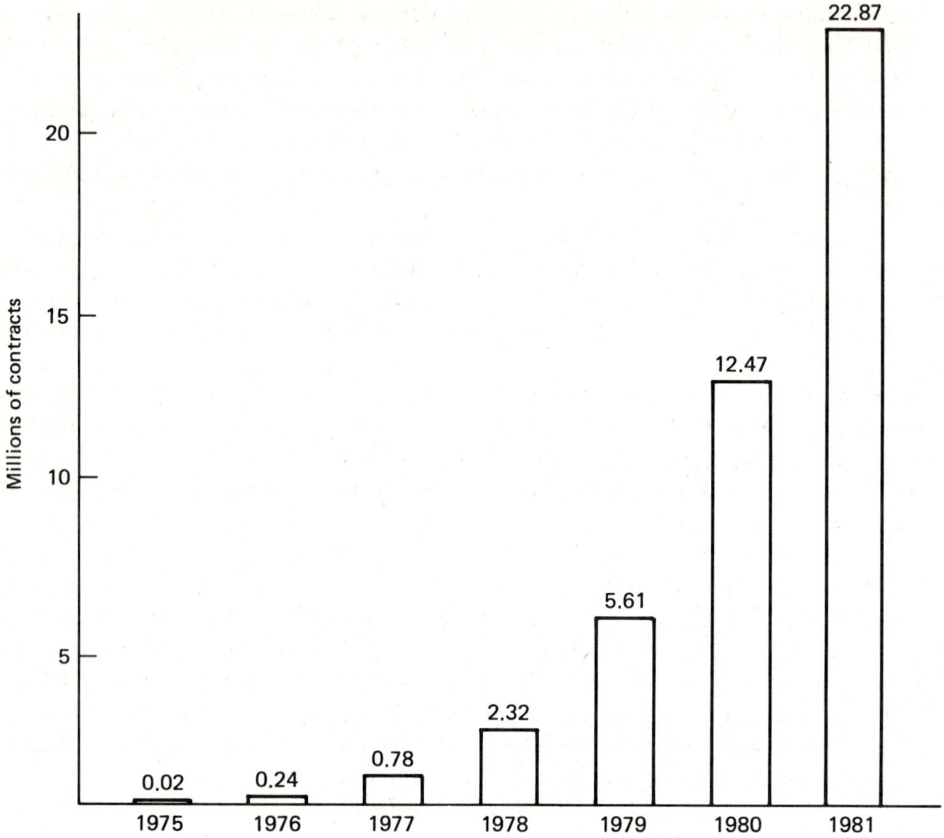

FIGURE 13. Volume chart, interest-rate futures.

Our concern here is with the growth of the industry in general. It would be difficult to elaborate on that growth without citing its main proponent—the financial instruments. This is most evident when one examines the volume that was generated over a relatively short span of time. During the first 2 years of activity, the Ginnie Mae contract on the CBOT produced a volume of 450,000 contracts. During 1978 that volume doubled to 900,000 contracts. The year 1978 was an exceptional one because of the singular direction of interest rates. On another exchange (IMM), trading in Treasury bills for the first 2 years generated 430,000 contracts and again in 1978 the volume soared to over 740,000 contracts. Normally, interest rates fluctuate seasonally due to the influences of government and corporate borrowings, but due to the economic and political climate of 1978, the direction of interest rates went in one direction—up.

NEW AND PENDING CONTRACTS

Since 1979 there have been several new contracts traded in the United States. The Chicago Mercantile Exchange added 4-year Treasury notes on July 10, 1979, domestic Certificates of Deposit on July 21, 1979, and Eurodollars on December

9, 1981. The Chicago Board of Trade has added contracts for Certificates of Deposit and 10-year Treasury notes.

Of all the new contracts, none has raised as many questions and created as much controversy as the stock index futures contract. This contract was first traded on the Kansas City Board of Trade (Value Line Index) on February 24, 1982. The Chicago Mercantile Exchange followed with the Standard & Poor's 500 Index and shortly thereafter (May 6, 1982) the New York Futures Exchange began trading the New York Stock Exchange (NYSE) Composite Index. For a more detailed discussion of the nature of the contract and its functions, a section has been provided in another part of the book.

Another area of great interest to the futures industry has been the recently developed "energy" contracts. These include futures contracts in heating oil, crude oil, industrial fuel, and liquid propane. These contracts are either already being traded, or are still pending before the CFTC.

There are indications that new contracts are being considered by several exchanges and it seems likely that the energy futures markets will continue to expand.

As of this writing, the CFTC has yet to decide on the feasibility of several proposed contracts. Table 2 shows the exchanges and the contracts they have proposed for trading.

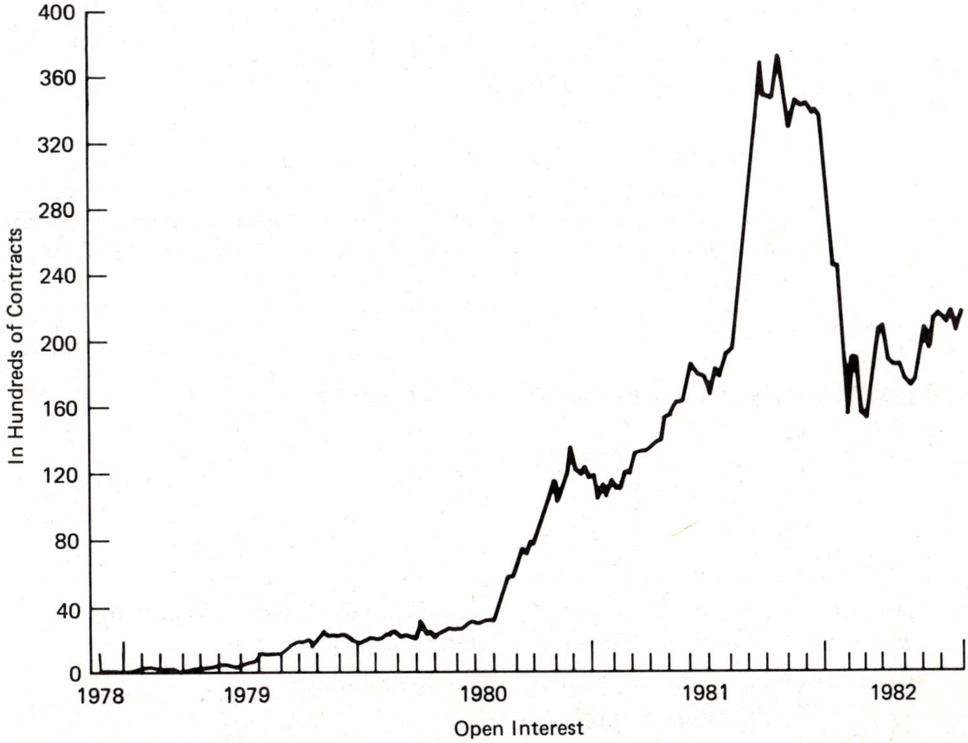

FIGURE 14. Heating and open interest charts.

TABLE 2. Pending Applications for Contract-Market Designation

Exchange	Contract	Letter Date	Received Date	Federal Register Publication Date	Federal Register Comment Period Ends
CBOT	Portfolios (13 contracts)[a]	2/20/80	2/26/80	1/22/81	3/23/81
		2/26/82	3/ 1/82	4/ 7/82	5/ 7/82
	Industry composite amended	7/28/82	7/28/82	7/29/82	
	Treasury bills (90-day)	3/31/80	4/ 1/80	4/24/81	5/26/81
	Gold coins	3/26/81	3/30/81	10/ 1/81	11/ 2/81
	Treasury notes (intermediate-term)	3/27/81	4/ 2/81	10/ 1/81	11/ 2/81
	Crude petroleum	12/ 2/81	12/ 2/81	12/22/81	2/22/82
	Options: T-bonds (designated 8/31)	12/ 9/81	12/ 9/81	12/29/81	3/ 1/82
				3/25/82	4/ 9/82
				4/30/82	5/28/82
	Prime rate	12/11/81	12/14/81	1/22/82	3/23/82
CBOE	CBOE 100 Index Value	5/19/82	5/20/82		
CME	Treasury bills (6-month)	9/ 3/80	9/ 5/80	1/27/81	3/30/81
	Gold coins	2/20/81	2/23/81	4/23/81	6/22/81
	Leaded and unleaded regular gasoline (2 contracts)	2/ 8/82	2/ 8/82	3/19/82	5/18/82
	Options: S&P 500	7/ 2/82	7/ 2/82	8/10/82	9/ 9/82

[a]Ten industry portfolios: air transport, automotive, banking, chemical, drug, information processing, photo-optic, retail, telecommunications, and industry composite portfolio; and two indices: transport, and gas and electric.

THE EXCHANGES AND COMMODITIES TRADED

A. MidAmerica Commodity Exchange.

1. Origin—founded in 1868.
   a. Incorporated as the Chicago Open Board of Trade in 1880.
   b. Name changed to MidAmerica in 1973.
2. Trading—trades transacted on MidAmerica are in smaller minimum units than on most other exchanges (''minicontracts'').
   a. Corn, wheat, and soybeans—1,000 bushel units.
   b. Oats—5,000 bushel units.
   c. Live hogs—15,000 lb.

(As of August, 1982)

Exchange	Contract	Letter Date	Received Date	Federal Register Publication Date	Federal Register Comment Period Ends
CSC	Options: sugar	12/ 8/81	12/ 9/81 9/21/81 12/ 9/81	12/29/81	3/ 1/82
COMEX	Gold coins	9/14/81		11/17/81	1/ 4/81
	Options: gold	12/ 8/81		12/29/81	3/ 1/82
Cotton	None				
KCBT	Treasury-bills (90-day)	12/ 7/81	12/ 9/81	1/15/82	3/16/82
	Options: Value Line Average	3/22/82	3/23/82	4/30/82	5/28/82
MACE	Gold coins	12/18/80	12/19/80	4/ 8/81	6/ 8/81
	Refined sugar	8/31/81	9/ 2/81	11/17/81	1/18/81
	New York silver	9/ /81	9/25/81	12/21/81	2/19/82
	Options: Gold	12/ 8/81	12/ 9/81	12/29/81	3/ 1/82
	Foreign currencies (5)[b]	7/19/82	7/23/82		
MGE	White wheat	7/14/82	7/15/82	6/28/82	8/27/82
NOCE	Corn	5/14/82	5/17/82		
NYFE	NYSE Equity	4/15/81	4/16/81	6/11/81	8/10/81
	Indexes (4)[c]	1/27/82	2/ 4/82	3/31/82	6/ 1/82
	Corporate bonds (25-year; AT&T)	4/30/81	5/ 4/81	6/11/81	8/10/81
	Options: NYSE Indexes	3/29/82	4/ 1/82	4/30/82	5/28/82
NYME	Options: N.Y. #2 Heating Oil	3/ 8/82	3/10/82	4/30/82	5/28/82
	Crude oil: sweet and sour (2 contracts)	3/ 9/82	3/11/82	4/29/82	6/28/82

[b]British pounds, Canadian dollars, Deutsche marks, Japanese yen, and Swiss francs.
[c]Financial, transportation, utility, and industrial.

d. Live cattle—20,000 lb.
e. Gold in 33.2 troy oz.
f. Silver in 1,000 troy oz.
g. Silver coins in $5,000 face value.

3. Membership—between 1971 and 1976 the total membership of Mid-America grew from 170 to its current 1,205, making it the second largest exchange in the United States.

B. Chicago Board of Trade.

1. Origin—founded in 1848, making it the oldest as well as the largest exchange in the United States.
2. Trading in—grains, soybeans, soybean products, silver, gold, iced broil-

ers, plywood, Ginnie Maes, 90- and 30-day commercial paper, long-term U.S. Treasury bonds, and 4- to 6-year Treasury notes.

3. Membership—1,402 full-time members and 100 financial instrument members.

C. Chicago Mercantile Exchange.

1. Origin—agricultural dealers formed the Chicago Produce Exchange in 1874.
2. Trading in—butter, eggs, poultry, and other perishable agricultural products.
   a. In 1898 the butter and egg dealers formed their own market—the Chicago Butter and Egg Board.
   b. Commodities were added to the list already traded and the exchange was renamed the Chicago Mercantile Exchange in 1919.
   c. Exchange moved to Franklin Street location; Will Rogers spoke at the opening ceremony.
   d. Additional commodities added and the dates of their entry to the markets:
      eggs—December 1, 1919
      potatoes—January 12, 1931
      pork bellies—September 18, 1961
      live cattle—November 30, 1964
      R/L lumber—October 1, 1969
      feeder cattle—November 10, 1971
      British pound, Canadian dollar, Deutsche mark, Japanese yen, Mexican peso, Swiss franc—May 16, 1972
      U.S. silver coins—October 1, 1973
      Dutch guilder—May 16, 1973
      French franc—September 23, 1974
      gold—December 31, 1974
      90-day bill—January 6, 1976
      stud lumber—November 28, 1977
      1-year Treasury bill—September 11, 1978
      4-year Treasury note—July 10, 1979
      broilers—November 6, 1979
3. International Monetary Market (division of CME).
   a. Established in 1972 for futures trading in foreign currencies.
   b. Futures added—gold bullion, December 31, 1974;
      3-month Treasury bills, January 1976; and
      1-year Treasury bills, September 1978.
4. Associate Mercantile Market (division of CME).
   Commodities traded—lumber, stud lumber, milo, butter, eggs, turkeys, and russet Burbank potatoes.
5. Membership—1,300 total members.
   a. Chicago Mercantile Exchange, 500.
   b. International Monetary Market, 650.
   c. Associate Mercantile Market, 150.

TABLE 3. Chicago Mercantile Exchange, Associate Mercantile Market, International Monetary Market Futures Trading Opening Dates[a]

Apples	January	1949
Boneless beef	April	1970
British pound	May 16,	1972
Broiler chickens	November 6,	1979
Butter	December 1,	1919
Canadian dollar	May 16,	1972
Canadian silver coins	October 1,	1973
Cattle (fat)	November 30,	1964
Cattle (fat western)	November	1965
Certificate of Deposit: 3 months	July 29,	1981
Cheese	October	1929
Chickens (frozen)	April	1962
Copper	July 1,	1974
Deutsche mark	May 16,	1972
Dressed beef	February	1965
Dressed poultry	June	1949
Dutch guilder	May 16,	1973
Eggs (fresh)	December 1,	1919
Feeder cattle	November 30,	1971
French franc	September 23,	1974
Gold bullion	December 31,	1974
Grain sorghum (milo)	March 2,	1971
Hogs	February 28,	1966
Iron and steel scrap	September	1954
Italian lira	May 16,	1972
Japanese yen	May 16,	1972
Lumber (random lengths)	October 1,	1969
Mexican peso	May 16,	1972
Nest run eggs	July 1,	1974
Onions	September 8,	1942
Plywood	July 28,	1982
Pork bellies	September 18,	1961
Potatoes	January 12,	1931
Shrimp	November	1963
Skinned hams	February 3,	1964
Stud lumber	November 28,	1977
Swiss franc	May 16,	1972
Treasury bills: 90-day	January 6,	1976
1-year	September 11,	1978
Treasury notes: 4-year	July 10,	1979
Turkeys	October 1,	1945
United States silver coins	October 1,	1973

Source: Prepared by Jeanne Rickey, CME Stat. Dept.
[a]CME/IMM Merger effective March 18, 1976.

D. New York Cotton Exchange.
   1. Origin—formed by 106 cotton merchants and brokers in 1870.
   2. Trading in—exclusively cotton, however separate corporations have been established to facilitate trading in other commodities.
      a. Wool Associates—founded 1931.
      b. Citrus Associates—founded 1966.
      c. Petroleum Associates—founded 1971.
   3. Membership.
      a. New York Cotton Exchange, 450.
      b. Citrus Associates of New York Cotton Exchange, 200.
      c. Petroleum Associates of New York Cotton Exchange 100.

E. Commodity Exchange, Incorporated (COMEX).
   1. Origin—formed in 1933 through merger and consolidation.
   2. Trading in—copper, gold, silver, and zinc.
      a. Rubber and hides were suspended in 1970.
      b. Mercury was suspended in 1975.
   3. Membership—386.

F. Coffee, Sugar, and Cocoa Exchange.
   1. Origin—founded as the Coffee Exchange of the City of New York. Name changed on December 1, 1916.
   2. Trading in—coffee, sugar (added in 1914), and cocoa (added in a merger on September 28, 1979). The New York Cocoa Exchange had been in existence since May 21, 1925.
   3. Membership—527.

G. AMEX Commodities Exchange (ACE).
   1. Origin—affiliate of the American Stock Exchange (AMEX).
   2. Trading in—GNMA futures, Treasury bill, Treasury bond, Treasury note, Canadian dollar, Deutsche mark, British pound, Japanese yen, and Swiss franc.

H. New York Mercantile Exchange.
   1. Origin—founded in 1872 as the American Exchange; mostly traded in eggs, butter, and so forth.
      a. April 27, 1880—name changed to the Butter, Cheese, and Egg Exchange of the City of New York.
      b. June 6, 1882—name changed to the New York Mercantile Exchange (NYME).
   2. Trading—Maine round white potatoes, imported lean beef, gold, platinum, palladium, heating oil, industrial fuel oil, and nine international currencies.
   3. Membership—408.

TABLE 4. COMEX

Commodity	Date of Inauguration	First Suspension	First Resumption	Second Suspension	Second Resumption	Third Suspension	Third Resumption	Fourth Suspension	Fourth Resumption
Burlap	9/ 9/53	11/19/59							
Copper	7/ 5/33	5/ 5/41[a]	7/15/47	1/29/51[b]	2/19/51	7/27/51[c]	6/ 1/53	8/15/71[d]	8/19/71
Crude oil	3/ 5/35								
Gasoline	3/ 5/35								
Gold	12/31/74								
Hides	7/ 5/33	6/13/41[a]	11/19/46	1/29/51[b]	3/12/51	3/22/51[c]	3/10/52	10/16/70	
Lead	7/ 2/34	6/30/41[a]	1/17/50	1/29/51[b]	2/19/51	7/27/51[c]	5/26/52	10/15/70	
Mercury	1/16/67	8/15/71[d]	8/23/71	7/10/75					
Propane gas	9/18/67	2/ 1/71							
Rubber	7/ 5/33	6/23/41[a]	5/ 1/47	3/31/51[c]	3/ 2/52	10/14/70	12/ 2/74	6/12/75	
Silk	7/ 5/33	7/26/41[a]	3/15/54	12/12/56					
Silver	7/ 5/33	8/ 9/34[e]	6/12/63	8/15/71[d]	8/19/71				
Tin	7/ 5/33	8/13/41[a]	1/ 5/50	1/29/51[b]	2/19/51	11/19/59	8/ 8/64	7/14/71	
Zinc	7/ 2/34	3/ 3/41[a]	7/22/47	1/29/51[b]	2/19/51	7/27/51[c]	6/23/52	10/15/70	2 8/78

[a]World War II.
[b]1951 price freeze.
[c]Korean conflict.
[d]1971 Wage-price freeze.
[e]Depression—executive order nationalizing silver.

FIGURE 15. Trading activity—the New York Mercantile Exchange.

I. Kansas City Board of Trade.
   1. Origin—organized in 1856, incorporated July 1, 1973.
   2. Trading in—hard red winter wheat.
   3. Membership—214.

J. Minneapolis Grain Exchange.
   1. Origin—founded in 1881. The largest cash grain market in the world.
   2. Trading in—grain; futures contracts in spring wheat.
   3. Membership—420.

K. New Orleans Commodity Exchange.
   1. Origin—founded in 1871 as the New Orleans Cotton Exchange, ceased operations in 1961; reopened on April 9, 1981 as the New Orleans Commodity Exchange.
   2. Trading—the only active exchange in the southern United States and the only exchange to offer futures in milled rice, rough rice, short staple cotton, and Gulf delivery soybeans.
   3. Membership—500.
   4. Additional Information.

      New Orleans Board of Trade—originally the New Orleans Produce Exchange (1880). Dealt in domestic produce shipped on the Mississippi River from local farms.

FIGURE 16. Trading at the New Orleans Commodity Exchange—soybean pit (''New Markets for the New South'').

FIGURE 17. Trading in the soybean pit on the New Orleans Commodity Exchange on opening day of the contract, October 29, 1981.

FIGURE 18. Trading floor—the New Orleans Commodity Exchange.

In 1883 moved to the new building and in 1889 the name was changed to the New Orleans Board of Trade (NOBT). It still traded in produce, but was linked with the Chamber of Commerce and the New Orleans Mercantile, which dealt in marine negotiations for barges and the marine exchange.

In 1938 the Product Exchange (NOBT) ceased operations due to the advent of futures contracts. The exchange had primarily been a spot market.

FOREIGN EXCHANGES

BERMUDA

INTEX— INTERNATIONAL FUTURES EXCHANGE LTD. The brainstorm of two Americans (Eugene M. Grummer and Junius W. Peake), the *International Future Exchange Ltd.* is located in Bermuda. It is the first attempt at creating a totally automated international exchange. Proposed trading will be initially conducted in gold futures and long-term U.S. Treasury bonds.

The unique aspect of INTEX is its total automation. The computer system is designed to facilitate worldwide trading without employing the traditional open outcry method of arriving at a market price. The system is capable of handling 70,000 trades an hour.

Members would conduct their trading from computer terminals that could be located anywhere in the world. One clear advantage to automated trading is that there is room for unlimited expansion of contracts. Rather than moving the entire facility to a larger trading floor, one need only add additional pages to the computer program output. If all goes well, there are plans to eventually expand the trading hours so that one could trade 24 hours a day. There are major computer centers for INTEX in New York, Chicago, and London.

FRANCE

BOURSE DE COMMERCE. The Paris International Futures Market opened in 1964, at the site of a prior futures market at the Paris Bourse, and is currently providing facilities for trading in white sugar. France is the largest producer of white sugar in the free world (about 4 million tons per year) and is an exporter of more than half of its production. The volume chart shown in Figure 20 indicates the growth of the market since 1976.

There are major sugar futures markets in both London and New York, but most others trade in raw sugar. The market in London, for instance, is primarily intended for the refiners of raw sugar and, consequently, their white sugar market does not have the volume that is generated on the Paris Bourse.

```
AUDIT
10:17:31  LIMIT   777777  BUY       50  EUR JUN82  LIMIT:   86.19  IMM/CAN? NO
          ID: 0000000000000  PRINCIPAL    MEMO: Limit Order

ACKNOWLEDGEMENT
10:17:39  LIMIT   777777  BUY       50  EUR JUN82 at   86.19
          ID: 0000000000000  Limit Order Added to Open Order File

AUDIT
10:18:41  LIMIT   777777  BUY      100  EUR JUN82  LIMIT:   86.20  IMM/CAN? NO
          ID: 0000000000000  PRINCIPAL    MEMO: Limit Order

EXECUTION CONFIRMATION
10:18:49  LIMIT   777777  BUY      100  EUR JUN82 at   86.20
          ID: 0000000000000  Limit Order Contract Confirmation
```

FIGURE 19. INTEX—sample printout.

```
XM-TSD VERSION VC06-00
*
+------------------------------------------------------------------------------+
|                                                                              |
|INTEX/05-AUG-82/12:10                    INTEX                       EUROMONEY|
|                                                                              |
+------------------------------------------------------------------------------+


                    ****************************************
                    *        BULLETIN BOARD NOTICE         *
                    ****************************************

   This is line one of the bulletin board
   This is line 2
   This is line 3

   Todays Bulletin Password is:  ABC


+------------------------------------------------------------------------------+
|                                                                              |
|INTEX/14-APR-82/10:01                    INTEX                       EUROMONEY|
|                                                                              |
+------------------------------------------------------------------------------+

AUDIT--------------------------------------------------------------------------------
10:05:43  LIMIT    NBM    BUY       50   EUR-JUN82  LIMIT:    86.19  IMM/CAN? NO
          ID: NBM -002  PRINCIPAL     M#: ORDER2  MEMO: Limit Order

ACKNOWLEDGEMENT----------------------------------------------------------------------
10:05:50  ID: NBM -002  LIMIT    BUY       50  EUR-JUN82 at    86.19
          Added to Open Order File

AUDIT--------------------------------------------------------------------------------
10:06:57  LIMIT    NBM    BUY       50   EUR-JUN82  LIMIT:    86.20  IMM/CAN? NO
          ID: NBM -002  PRINCIPAL     M#: ORDER2  MEMO: Limit Order

EXECUTION CONFIRMATION---------------------------------------------------------------
10:07:00  ID: NBM -002  LIMIT    BUY       50  EUR-JUN82 at    86.20
          Contracts Executed

AUDIT--------------------------------------------------------------------------------
10:09:30  LIMIT    NBM    BUY      100   EUR-JUN82  LIMIT:    86.20  IMM/CAN? NO
          ID: NBM -002  PRINCIPAL     M#: ORDER2  MEMO: Limit Order

EXECUTION CONFIRMATION---------------------------------------------------------------
10:09:37  ID: NBM -002  LIMIT    BUY      100  EUR-JUN82 at    86.20
          Contracts Executed

AUDIT -------------------------------------------------------------------------------
10:10:35  LIMIT    NBM    SELL      50   EUR-JUN82  LIMIT:    86.19  IMM/CAN? NO
          ID: NBM -002  PRINCIPAL     M#: ORDER2  MEMO: Limit Order

EXECUTION CONFIRMATION---------------------------------------------------------------
10:10:44  ID: NBM -002  LIMIT    SELL      50  EUR-JUN82 at    86.19
          Contracts Executed

AUDIT--------------------------------------------------------------------------------
10:11:52  LIMIT    NBM    SELL      50   EUR-JUN82  LIMIT:    86.19  IMM/CAN? NO
          ID: NBM -002  PRINCIPAL     M#: ORDER2  MEMO: Limit Order

ACKNOWLEDGEMENT----------------------------------------------------------------------
10:12:00  ID: NBM -002  LIMIT    SELL      50  EUR-JUN82 at    86.19
          Added to Open Order File
```

FIGURE 19. Continued.

The International Futures Exchange (Bermuda) Limited

One World Trade Center
Suite 2029
New York, NY 10048
212/524-0700
Telex: 226078 AEGIS

The Perry Building
40 Church Street
Hamilton 5-24, Bermuda
809/295-6400
Telex: 3278 INTEX BA

UPDATE

May 14, 1982

Attached is an example of the printed order record which INTEX will be able to generate. The format and data are adaptable to individual needs. INTEX is also able to handle STOP and SPREAD orders.

10:05:43 The first entry shows the "Audit" record of the entry of an order to buy 50 June 1982 Euromoney contracts at 86.19. Since the "IMM/CAN?" question (immediate or cancel) is answered in the negative, the central market will keep the order on file if there is no immediate execution. The "Audit" record is a positive report of the actual instruction transmitted by the local station.

10:05:50 The second entry, "Acknowledgement", shows that Bermuda has received the Limit Order and that it has been added to the central Open Order File.

10:06:57 Here is the "Audit" record of the entry of an order to buy 50 June 1982 Euromoney contracts at 86.20.

10:07:06 Here is an "Execution Confirmation" showing that the preceeding order was matched against offerings in the market and has been executed.

****

Accuracy...positive response...speed (answers in seconds) are characteristics of INTEX.

FIGURE 19. Continued.

Coffee and cocoa are also traded on the Bourse, but neither contract is very active (less than 30,000 contracts a year) when compared to other world coffee and cocoa markets.

ENGLAND

The most important exchange in England is the *London Metal Exchange* (LME). Trading is conducted in copper, silver, zinc, lead, and tin; options are traded in all metals. Options were traded regularly on the London Metal Exchange and other London markets until World War II. Following the war there was little activity until the late 1960s.

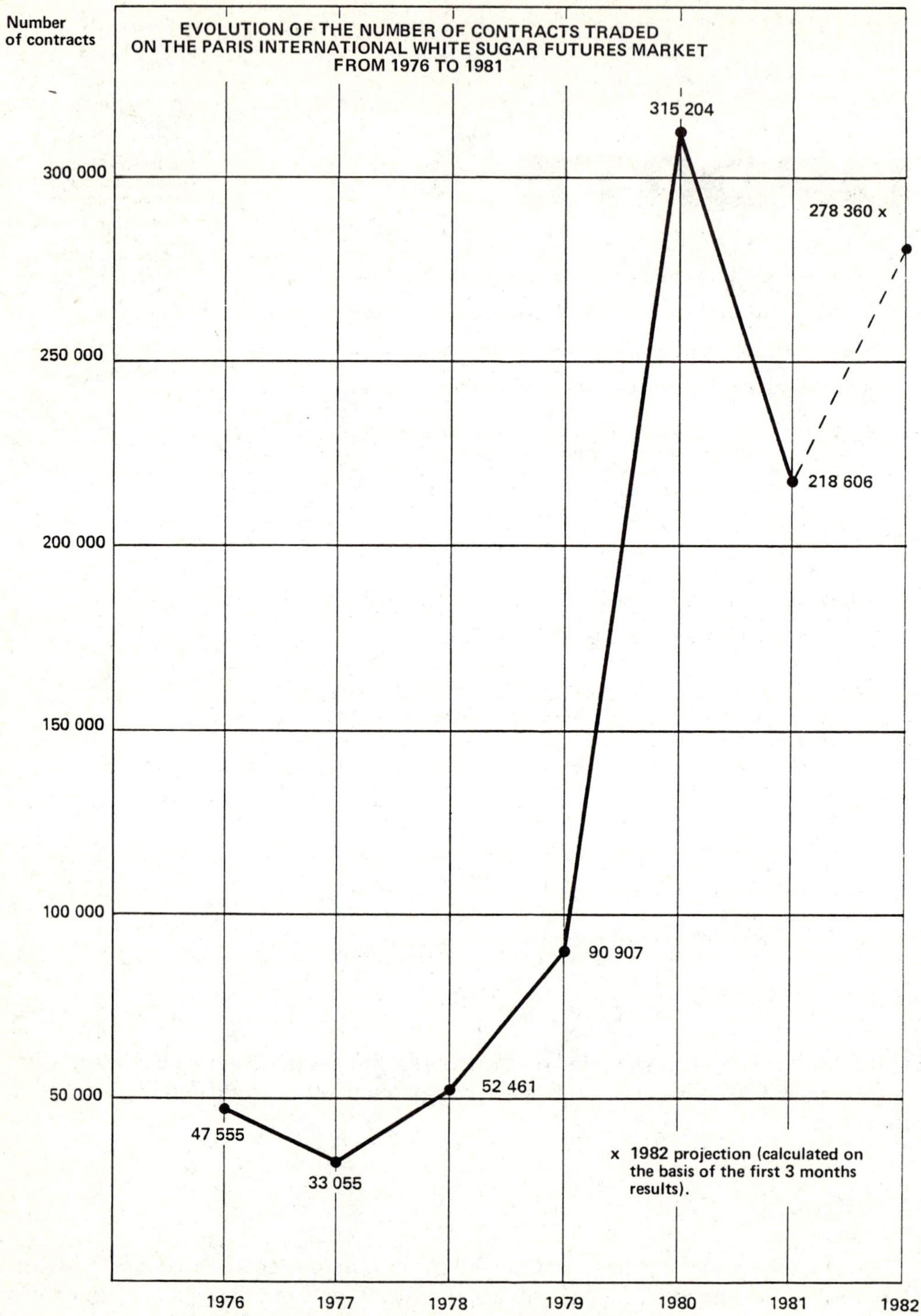

FIGURE 20. Volume chart—Paris international white sugar.

FIGURE 21. Normal trading day market scene at the London Grain Futures Market.

The *London Commodity Exchange* (LCE) was established in 1954. The following associations are members of the LCE:

the London Cocoa Terminal Market Association Ltd.
the Coffee Terminal Market Association of London Ltd.
the GAFTA Soya Bean Meal Futures Association Ltd.
the London Rubber Terminal Market Association Ltd.
the Vegetable Oil Terminal Market Association Ltd.
the London Wool Terminal Market Association Ltd.
the United Terminal Sugar Market Association Ltd.
the International Petroleum Exchange of London Ltd.

Table 5 provides specific information regarding the commodities traded in London. Included is a list of the currencies that are traded and a conversion table of weights and measures.

NETHERLANDS

The Dutch have a long tradition of international trade. In the past they have traded in coffee, sugar, cocoa, rubber, hides, and other products. Today there are only two active commodity markets in Amsterdam: the *Potato Terminal Market* and the *Pork Terminal Market*.

TABLE 5. London Commodities

Commodity	Exchange Trading Hours (Local time)	Contract Size Minimum Fluctuation	Value $0.01 Move	Daily Trading: Limit	Daily Trading: Maximum Range	Commissions: Regular	Commissions: Spread	Commissions: Day Trade
Aluminum	London Metal Exchange: 9:00 a.m.–5:30 p.m. including specific rings	25 metric tons £0.50 = £12.50	—	—	—	0.375%		
Barley—home grown	Grain and Feed Trade Association: 11:00 a.m.–12:30 p.m. and 2:45 p.m.–4:00 p.m.	100 metric tons £0.05 = £5.00	—	— —	— —	£38.50 plus £1.00	£38.50 plus £2.00	£19.80 plus £1.00
Cocoa	London Cocoa Terminal Market Association: 10:00 a.m.–1:00 p. m. and 2:30 p.m.–4:45 p.m.	10 metric tons £1.00 = £10.00	—	Market is permitted to move £40.00 either up or down and will then close for 15 min and reopen limit-free for rest of the day.		£42.60 plus £1.40	£41.20 plus £2.80	£20.60 plus £1.40
Coffee—arabica	London Coffee Terminal Market Association: 10:15 a.m.–12:15 p.m. and 2:45 p.m.–4.45 p.m. Kerb trading, 5:30 p.m.–7:45 p.m.	37,500 lb. $0.05 = $17.25	$375	—	—	$94.00 plus $1.60	$94.00 plus $1.60	$47.00 plus $0.80
Coffee—robusta	London Coffee Terminal Market Association: 10:30 a.m.–12:30 p.m. and 2:30 p.m. –4:50 p.m.	5 metric tons £1.00 = £5.00	—	—	—	£38.60 plus £1.40	£37.20 plus £2.80	£18.60 plus £1.40
Copper	London Metal Exchange: 9:00 a.m.–7:00 p.m. including specific rings	25 metric tons £0.50 = £12.50	—	—	—	0.375% minimum	—	—

Gas oil	International Petroleum Exchange: 9:30 a.m.–12:20 p.m. and 2:45 p.m.–5:20 p.m.	100 metric tons $0.25 = $25	—	—	—	$76.70 plus $3.30	$73.40 plus $6.60	$36.70 plus $3.30
Gold	London Bullion Market: 8:30 a.m.–7:30 p.m. Gold fixing, 10:30 a.m. and 3:00 p.m. Orders may be entered during the fixing.	400 fine troy oz 100 fine troy oz Tradeable but not deliverable	— —	— —	— —	0.50% value minimum	—	—
(Orders for Hong Kong basis London Bullion Market can be worked outside these hours.)								
Lead	London Metal Exchange: 9:00 a.m.–5:30 p.m. including specific rings	25 metric tons £0.25 = £6.25	—	—	—	1% minimum	—	—
Nickel	London Metal Exchange: 9:00 a.m.–5:30 p.m. including specific rings	6 metric tons £1.00 = £6.00	—	—	—	0.375% minimum	—	—
Rubber	London Rubber Terminal Market Association: 9:45 a.m.–12:45 p.m. and 2:30 p.m.–4:30 p.m. Kerb trading, 4:45 p.m.–5:30 p.m. approximately.	15 metric tons £0.10 = £15.00	—	Market is permitted to move 3 pence either up or down and will then close for 15 min and reopen limit-free for rest of day.		£16.00 £7.00	£16.00 £7.00	£8.00 £3.50
Silver	London Metal Exchange: 9:00 a.m.–7:30 p.m. including specific rings	10,000 troy oz £0.001 = £10.00	—	—	—	0.50% minimum	—	—
Silver	London Bullion Market: 9:00 a.m.–7:30 p.m. Silver fixing, 12:15 p.m. and orders must be entered by 12:05 p.m.	5,000 troy oz £0.001 = £5.00	—	—	—	0.50% minimum	—	—

TABLE 5. (*Continued*)

Commodity	Exchange Trading Hours (Local time)	Contract Size Minimum Fluctuation	Value $0.01 Move	Daily Trading		Commissions		
				Limit	Maximum Range	Regular	Spread	Day Trade
Soybean meal	Grain and Feed Trade Association: 10:30 a.m.–12:20 p.m. and 2:50 p.m.–5:00 p.m.	100 metric tons £0.10 = £10.00	—	Market is permitted to move £5 either up or down and will then close for 15 min and reopen limit-free for the rest of the day.		£40.26 plus £2.74	£37.52 plus £5.48	£18.76 plus £2.74
Sugar	London No. 4 United Terminal Sugar Market: 10:30 a.m.–12:30 p.m. and 2:30 p.m.–4:40 p.m. Kerb trading committee after 4:40 p.m., call until 7:10 p.m.	50 metric tons £0.05 = £2.50	—	£20 up or down lunchtime close to following day lunchtime close.		£38.50 plus £11.00	£38.50 plus £11.00	£19.80 plus £5.50
Tin	London Metal Exchange: 9:00 a.m.–5:30 p.m. including specific rings	5 metric tons £1.00 = £5.00	—	—	—	0.50% minimum	—	—
Wheat—home grown	Grain and Feed Trade Association: 11:00 a.m.–12:30 p.m. and 2:45 p.m.–4:00 p.m.	100 metric tons £0.05 = £5.00	—	—	—	£38.50 plus £1.00	£38.50 plus £2.00	£19.80 plus £1.00
Wool, New Zealand No. 2	London Wool Terminal Market Association: 2:45 p.m.–3:45 p.m. and after hours, 3:50 p.m.–4:45 p.m.	2,500 kilos $0.001 = $2.50	—	—	—	£35.00 plus £1.34	£35.00 plus £2.68	£18.00 plus £1.34
Zinc	London Metal Exchange: 9:00 a.m.–5:30 p.m. including specific rings	25 metric tons £0.25 = £6.25	—	—	—	0.75%	—	—

[a]Table 5 is based on data available 12/25/81.

TABLE 5 (*Continued*)

London Metal Exchange Market Calls	
First Session	
Silver	11:50 a.m.–11:55 a.m.
Aluminum	11:55 a.m.–12:00 noon
Copper	12:00 noon–12:05 p.m.
Tin	12:05 p.m.–12:10 p.m.
Lead	12:10 p.m.–12:15 p.m.
Zinc	12:15 p.m.–12:20 p.m.
Nickel	12:20 p.m.–12:25 p.m.
(Interval)	12:25 p.m.–12:30 p.m.
Copper wirebars	12:30 p.m.–12:35 p.m.
Copper cathodes and fire refined	12:35 p.m.–12:40 p.m.
Tin	12:40 p.m.–12:45 p.m.
Lead	12:45 p.m.–12:50 p.m.
Zinc	12:50 p.m.–12:55 p.m.
Aluminum	12:55 p.m.–1:00 p.m.
Nickel	1:00 p.m.–1:05 p.m.
Silver	1:05 p.m.–1:10 p.m.
Official kerb	1:10 p.m.–1:25 p.m.
Second Session	
Lead/zinc	3:30 p.m.–3:35 p.m.
Copper wirebars/cathodes	3:35 p.m.–3:40 p.m.
Tin	3:40 p.m.–3:45 p.m.
Aluminum/nickel	3:45 p.m.–3:50 p.m.
Silver	3:50 p.m.–3:55 p.m.
(Interval)	3:55 p.m.–4:00 p.m.
Lead	4:00 p.m.–4:05 p.m.
Zinc	4:05 p.m.–4:10 p.m.
Copper wirebars	4:10 p.m.–4:15 p.m.
Copper cathodes	4:15 p.m.–4:20 p.m.
Tin	4:20 p.m.–4:25 p.m.
Aluminum	4:25 p.m.–4:30 p.m.
Nickel	4:30 p.m.–4:35 p.m.
Silver	4:35 p.m.–4:40 p.m.
Kerb	4:40 p.m.–5:00 p.m.
Rooms to close at 5:10 p.m.	

On November 30, 1977, the *European Options Exchange* (EOE) was established in Amsterdam. In the developmental stages, the securities were selected from among the major stocks listed on the principal stock exchanges of the world.

Volume has increased consistently over the years since its inception. In 1981 more than one million options were traded. In addition to trading stock options, investors also took advantage of opportunities to use call options to buy shares below the stock market price, or to sell them above the stock exchange price by means of put options.

On April 2, 1981 the EOE opened markets in gold options and, on November 24, 1981, three classes of Dutch state loans (bond options). As a result of these

TABLE 5 (*Continued*)

		Interbank New York (as traded through London)			
				Commissions (typical retail commissions per min contract size)	
Contract	Trading Hours[b] (New York time)	Contract Size (minimum in dollars)	Daily Trading Limit	Regular	Spread
British pound	9 a.m.–3 p.m.	1 million	None	$ 85.00	$170.00
Canadian dollar	9 a.m.–3 p.m.	1 million	None	$110.00	$220.00
Swiss franc	9 a.m.–3 p.m.	1 million	None	$ 85.00	$170.00
German mark	9 a.m.–3 p.m.	1 million	None	$ 85.00	$170.00
French franc	9 a.m.–3 p.m.	1 million	None	$ 85.00	$170.00
Italian lira	9 a.m.–3 p.m.	1 million	None	$ 85.00	$170.00
Japanese yen	9 a.m.–3 p.m.	1 million	None	$ 85.00	$170.00

[b]Depending upon prevailing market conditions.

Weights, Measures, and Conversion Factors

Bushel weights:
- Wheat and soybeans = 60 lb
- Corn, sorghum and rye = 56 lb
- Barley (grain) = 48 lb; malt = 34 lb
- Oats = 32 lb

Bushels to metric tons:
- Wheat and soybeans = bushels × 0.027216
- Barley = bushels × 0.021722
- Corn, sorghum, and rye = bushels × 0.025400
- Oats = bushels × 0.014515

1 metric ton equals:
- 2204.622 lb
- 22.046 cwt
- 10 quintals
- 1,000 kg
- 36.7437 bushels wheat or soybeans
- 39.3679 bushels
- 45.9296 bushels barley
- 68.9844 bushels oats

Area:
- 1 acre = 0.404694 hectares
- 1 hectare = 2.4710 acres

Yields:
- Wheat = bushels per acre × 0.6725 = quintals per hectare
- Rye, and corn = bushels per acre × 0.6277 = quintals per hectare
- Barley = bushels per acre × 0.5380 = quintals per hectare
- Oats = bushels per acre × 0.3587 = quintals per hectare

Dealer Options

Dealer options are offered on:

Gold	— 100 oz
Silver	— 1,000 oz
Silver	— 5,000 oz
Copper	—25,000 lb
Platinum	— 50 oz
Krugerrand	— 50 coins
Maple leaf	— 10 coins
Silver $ bags	—$1,000 face value
Silver clad bags	—$1,000 face value

Commissions: Buy—$50.00 or 5% of premium, whichever is greater.

Commissions: Sell—$50.00 or 5% of premium, whichever is greater.

TABLE 6. Dutch Commodity Clearing House Since 1888

Commodity	Traded During the Following Years		
Coffee	1888–1916	1919–1940	1954–1962
	1965–1971		
Pepper	1892–1915	1920–1931	1936–1939
	1955–1962	1968–1971	
Tin	1891–1914		
Cloves	1898–1915		
Copra	1899		
Raw sugar	1902–1917		
White sugar	1921–1939		
Nutmeg	1914–1917		
Rubber	1919–1940	1950–1965	
Cocoa	1937–1940	1953–1976	
Hides	1957–1961		
Potatoes	1958–present		
Pulse	1960–1968		
Eggs	1976–1979		
Pork meat	1977–1980		
Slaughter porks	1980–present		

TABLE 7. European Options Exchange Volume in Contracts for 1981

		Monthly Turnover in Contracts[a]			Open Interest	
Month	Number of Trading Days	Total	Calls	Puts	Daily Average	(End of Month)
January	21	56,276	44,028	12,248	2,680	55,511
February	20	66,588	56,350	10,238	3,329	72,846
March	22	87,018	63,318	23,700	3,955	96,806
April	19	114,825	88,859	25,966	6,043	68,942
May	20	81,055	63,927	17,128	4,053	83,719
June	21	125,816	103,299	22,517	5,991	113,681
July	23	119,230	87,459	31,771	5,184	96,964
August	21	87,691	68,887	18,804	4,176	114,234
September	22	106,187	70,270	35,917	4,827	126,685
October	22	73,990	54,039	19,951	3,363	83,439
November	21	73,587	51,778	21,809	3,504	100,086
December	21	51,318	36,686	14,632	2,444	113,078
Total	253	1,043,581	788,900	254,681	4,125	

[a]The highest daily turnover in 1981 was 14,069 contracts, recorded on June 4; the highest turnover in 1980 was 9,179 contracts, on March 18.

new markets, there are 27 classes of options (23 stock, 3 bond, and 1 commodity) listed as active on the European Options Exchange.

HONG KONG

The *Hong Kong Commodity Exchange* was incorporated in December 1976. The first commodities traded were cotton on May 9, 1977 and sugar on November 15, 1977. A soybean market was added 2 years later in November 1979 which proved

TABLE 8. Contract Specifications for Hong Kong Commodity Exchange

	COTTON 原棉	SUGAR 原糖	SOYBEANS 黃豆	GOLD 黃金
Standard Grade **標準品級**	SLM 1 inch US grown white cotton 1英吋中下級 美棉，白色	Raw cane Sugar of 96° Polarization 原蔗糖 96度旋光度	Unselected China Yellow Soybeans 未經選擇 中國黃豆	Refined Gold of not less than 995 fineness 純度不低於 九九五黃金
Trading Units **交易單位**	50,000 lbs. 磅 (100 bales) (綑)	50 long tons 長噸 (112,000 lbs.) (磅)	500 bags of 袋 60 kg each 公斤	100 oz. 盎斯 fine Gold
Tenderable Grades **可交收品級**	31/32 inch staple or longer 31/32 英吋 或較長	Growth of S.E. Asian Countries 東南亞國家出產	US I.O.M. Soybeans 美國印第安那州 俄亥俄州及密芝根州	Bars of 100 oz. 50 oz. & 1kg. 100盎斯，50盎斯 及1公斤金條
Delivery Point **交收地點**	Galveston Texas U.S.A. 美國德薩斯州 加爾維斯頓市	F.O.B., S.E. Asian Countries 離岸價 東南亞國家	Tokyo or Kanagawa, Japan 日本東京或神奈川	Hong Kong 香港
Price Quotation **報價**	US Currency 美金	US Currency 美金	HK Currency 港幣	US Currency 美金
Min. Fluctuations **最低價格波幅**	1/100 cents per lb. 每磅1/100美仙	1/100 cents per lb. 每磅1/100美仙	20 cents per bag 每袋20仙	10 cents per oz. 每盎斯10美仙
Trading Months **交易合約月份**	Mar. May. July. Oct. Dec. 三月、五月、七月 十月、十二月	Jan. Mar. May. July. Sept. Oct. 一月、三月、五月 七月、九月、十月	Each consecutive month up to six months ahead. 連續六個 月份	Even months Spot month and the following two months 雙數月份，現貨月 及隨後兩個月份
Trading Hours **交易時間**	9:30 – 11:30 15:30 – 16:30 上午9:30至上午11:30 下午3:30至下午4:30	10:30 – 12:00 14:30 – 16:00 上午10:30至中午12:00 下午2:30至下午4:00	9:50 10:50 12:50 14:50 上午9:50 10:50 下午12:50 2:50	9:00 – 12:00 14:30 – 17:30 上午9:00至中午12:00 下午2:30至下午5:30
Trading Method **交易方式**	Group & Open Outcry 集體及公開叫價	Group & Open Outcry 集體及公開叫價	Group Trading 集體一價	Open Outcry 公開叫價
Original Margin **基本按金**	US$2,000 美元	US$2,500 美元	HK$2,500 港元	US$3,000 or 美元或 HK$15,000 港元
Daily Limits **每日價格變動限額**	*US 3 美仙	+*US 1 美仙	Nil 無	+*US$40 美元

* No limit is imposed on spot month.
現貨月份並無限制

\+ Market is closed for 30 minutes and reopened without limit on price movement.
市場暫停30分鐘重開，再無價格變動限制。

The information stated above is a summary of some important facts of the relative contract. It should not be regarded as comprehensive and may be subject to alternation at any time. 上述資料係有關之期貨合約之括要並會隨時修改。

to be highly successful. Further developments have included the revision of the cotton contract and the doubling of the size of the soybean contract. On August 19, 1980, the Hong Kong Commodity Exchange opened trading in gold futures contracts. Because Hong Kong is located in a time zone where its business hours are 12 hours different than those of New York, it provides an open market when all other gold markets are closed. This time difference is a perfect complement to the New York and London markets. Combined with substantial local interest in the gold contract, the Hong Kong market has become the third largest gold market in the world. (*Note*: For a more comprehensive survey of the world's commodity markets, readers should refer to the *Guide To World Commodity Markets*, published in England by Kogan Page, London, and in the United States by Nichols Publishing, New York. The *Guide to World Commodity Markets* is in its third edition.)

CHAPTER 2

THE MECHANICS OF FUTURES TRADING

CONTENTS

TRADING FACILITIES 3

ESTABLISHING A COMMODITY ACCOUNT 4

THIRD PARTY ACCOUNTS 9

MARGINS 10

COMMODITY ORDERS 12

Types of Orders 12

CONTRACT FACTS 17

LIQUIDATING TRANSACTIONS 19

PRICES 20

Time and Sales 21

PROFIT-OR-LOSS CALCULATION 22

UNUSUAL LIQUIDATION 25

CLOSING COMMODITY ACCOUNTS 26

CHAPTER 2

THE MECHANICS OF FUTURES TRADING

Richard J. Teweles

TRADING FACILITIES

Few people who decide to trade in the commodity futures markets choose to join a commodity exchange and must therefore trade through brokerage houses that are members of one or more such exchanges. Such brokerage houses vary somewhat in size, services offered, and costs. Some are full-service wire houses that deal in securities, commodities, and other financial areas such as real estate and insurance. They provide a considerable number of such customer conveniences as the ability to transfer funds as desired among various types of accounts and offices in many locations. They tend to be large and well-financed and so provide a measure of safety in financial strength and concern for their reputations.

Smaller firms, such as those that handle only commodity transactions, compensate for their inability to service all of their customers' needs by offering an ostensibly greater degree of sophistication in their limited area. They may profess to have more extensive research facilities, better local and trading floor services, lower commissions, or some combination of these.

The claims made for the value of fast executions and brokerage house research are not always accepted without reservation. A client may justifiably conclude that speed may not be worth much in that a bad trade is no less bad if traded rapidly. They may believe that any information available from a brokerage house is almost certainly widely known and to know that everyone else knows is to know nothing. Most firms claim to employ especially well-qualified floor brokers, but most floor brokers are utilized by several firms, and the differences in competence do not appear especially noteworthy. Clients who consider themselves to be self-traders may demand only satisfactory personal service, financial integrity of their brokers, and the lowest margins and commissions that are offered or that may be negotiated.

A new trader is well-advised to choose the registered representative who will service his or her account as carefully as he or she chooses the firm with which to open this account. The differences in training, experience, and integrity among representatives are quite wide and may bear little correlation with the reputations or advertised images of the firms with which they happen to be associated. There are some small firms with excellent representatives and large firms who may be afflicted with self-serving charlatans. A new customer should try to choose a representative just as wisely as he or she would choose a doctor, dentist, or lawyer and not open an account with someone who happens to be designated "broker of the day," or who chooses to offer a "seminar" at some local hotel meeting room.

ESTABLISHING A COMMODITY ACCOUNT

When the decisions have been made to trade, where to trade, and with whom to trade, opening a commodity account is not difficult. Certain papers must be signed which do not vary much from one brokerage house to another. A commodity account agreement [Figure 1(b)] is similar to a stock margin account agreement in that it indicates the responsibilities and obligations of both parties and the procedure to be followed in the event of a dispute. An account may be in the name of one or more individuals, a partnership, or a corporation. Accounts in the name of two or more individuals may be as tenants in common, or as joint tenants with rights of survivorship. The latter should not be chosen casually and may warrant advice from an accountant or attorney. Many problems caused by death, divorce, or disputes among various parties to an account can be quite time-consuming and expensive if a wrong choice of account type is made.

An authority to transfer funds may be part of the new account form or it may be a separate form [see Figure 1(c)]. This authority allows a broker to transfer funds as required from one commodity account to others owned by the same customer. Most commonly this involves transfers of funds as needed between regulated and unregulated accounts which would otherwise require individual written authorizations from the customer. Unregulated commodity accounts are utilized for trading in commodities on markets not regulated by the Commodity Futures Trading Commission (CFTC).

Brokers require commodity customers to sign so-called risk letters [see Figure 1(d)] which warn that most commodity trades are quite speculative and that the customers are responsible even for any losses that exceed funds deposited in an account. This is an attempt to protect the brokerage house against clients who might maintain that they were unaware of the risks involved in trading or that their registered representatives misrepresented the exposure. For instance, a client might conclude that spread positions virtually ensure profits while eliminating risk. The risk letter typically corrects this misconception by pointing out that spreads may be subject to variations greater than net positions and, hence, be even more risky. Parenthetically, it should be noted that a risk letter in itself does not necessarily protect a broker from claims by clients who maintain after the fact that they were misled. Customers who might reasonably be deemed unable to understand risk letters because of their lack of education or financial sophistication or their states of mind might well be able to hold successfully that they were not bound by them. They might be able in some cases to prove that they received and believed oral representations to the effect that the risks described in a letter were exaggerated or inaccurate.

Risk letters are one of the devices used by brokers obligated to know their customers to determine suitability. Suitability is widely assumed to include financial and temperament aspects. Although temperament is difficult to ascertain

R5100

STANDING INSTRUCTIONS

AUTOMATIC DIVIDEND (OPT.)
AD - Add Account on Auto Div
LEAVE BLANK - Not on Auto Div

PRIMARY TRANSFER CODES (OPT.)
TØØ - Transfer into Client Account N & A Deliver to Branch Office
T11 - Transfer into Client Account N & A Deliver to Client MAPS Address
T12 - Transfer into Client Account N & A Hold in Safekeeping

MANDATORY MONEY FUND CODES
AMM - Add MoneyMart
AGT - Add Chancellor Government Trust
AOF - Add Bache International Money Fund
ATD - Add Chancellor Tax Free Money Fund
NMF - No Money Fund

Bache NEW ACCOUNT FORM

CHECK ONE — THIS FORM MUST BE COMPLETED FOR ANY ONE OF THE FOLLOWING PURPOSES:
☐ TO OPEN A NEW ACCOUNT
☐ TO UP-DATE BACKGROUND AND FINANCIAL INFORMATION OF AN ALREADY EXISTING ACCOUNT.

OFFICE | ACCOUNT NUMBER | A E | TAX I.D. NUMBER / SOCIAL SECURITY NUMBER (F) | DATE OF BIRTH

NAME AND ADDRESS INFORMATION
1
2 DO NOT
3
4 WRITE IN
5
6 THIS SPACE

DOMESTIC TELEPHONE NUMBER: AREA CODE | PRINCIPLE TELEPHONE NUMBER
AUTOMATIC DIVIDEND | TRANSFER INSTRUCTIONS (T) | MANDATORY MONEY FUND INSTRUCTIONS

7 INTERNATIONAL TELEPHONE NUMBER
CODES ARE ON THE FORM STUB ABOVE

Duplicate Mailing Instructions (Attach Form 1481 C-2)
DUP. STATEMENTS ☐
DUP. CONFIRMATION ☐

8 **RESIDENCE** ☐ RENT ☐ OWN RESIDENCE | YEARS THERE | LEGAL RESIDENCE IF DIFFERENT THAN MAILING ADDRESS

9 **EMPLOYMENT** JOB TITLE | EMPLOYERS NAME (STATE IF SELF EMPLOYED) | YEARS THERE | IS CLIENT'S OR SPOUSE'S EMPLOYER A BROKERAGE FIRM, INSURANCE CO., OR BANK? ☐ YES ☐ NO IF 'YES', SEE NYSE RULE 407

10 BUSINESS ADDRESS | CITY | STATE | ZIP CODE | AREA CODE | BUSINESS PHONE NO.

11 **CLIENT PROFILE**

(A) MARITAL STATUS (PLEASE CIRCLE): a. Single d. Widow(er) b. Married e. Separated c. Divorced
(B) NUMBER OF DEPENDENTS

(C) OCCUPATION (PLEASE CIRCLE): a. Doctor i. Clerical b. Lawyer j. Salesperson c. Finance k. Government d. Engineer l. Educator e. Self Employed m. Retired f. Home Maker n. Other (Specify) g. Student h. Not Employed

PLEASE CIRCLE	D. STATED INCOME	E. LIQUID ASSETS	F. NET WORTH (EXC. RES.)
\$ 0 to 19,999	a.	a.	a.
\$20,000 to 24,999	b.	b.	b.
\$25,000 to 34,999	c.	c.	c.
\$35,000 to 74,999	d.	d.	d.
\$75,000 to 124,999	e.	e.	e.
\$125,000 or more	f.	f.	f.

IS CLIENT AN OFFICER, DIRECTOR OR 10% STOCKHOLDER IN ANY CORPORATION? ☐ YES ☐ NO
CITIZEN OF U.S.A. (IF OTHER PLEASE SPECIFY) ☐ YES ☐ NO
FORMER BACHE CLIENT? STATE ACCOUNT NUMBER ☐ YES ☐ NO
(G) ACCOUNT WITH OTHER FIRM ☐ YES ☐ NO NAME IF YES

12 IF MARRIED, NAME OF SPOUSE | ADDRESS (IF DIFFERENT) | CITY | STATE | ZIP CODE

13 NAME OF SPOUSE'S EMPLOYER | BUSINESS ADDRESS | CITY | STATE | ZIP CODE

14 IS CLIENT RELATED TO A BACHE EMPLOYEE? ☐ YES ☐ NO IF 'YES', NAME AND RELATIONSHIP | HOW LONG HAS A.E. KNOWN CLIENT?

INVESTMENT PROFILE

15 (H) CLIENT'S STATED INVESTMENT OBJECTIVE (CIRCLE ONE OR MORE): a. Safety of Principal d. Speculation b. Tax Sheltered Income e. Income c. Long Term Growth

(I) INVESTMENT EXPERIENCE | YEARS | INVESTMENT EXPERIENCE | YEARS: a. Options; b. Stocks & Bonds; c. Commodities; d. Other

INTRODUCTION

(J) SOURCE OF ACCT. OPENING (PLEASE CIRCLE): a. Seminars e. Local Advertising b. Walk/Phone In f. Personal Acquaintance c. National Advertising g. Referral By d. National Direct Mail h. Other

IS A.E. LICENSED IN STATE OF CLIENT'S RESIDENCE? ☐ YES ☐ NO

16 **REFERENCES** NAME OF BANK | BRANCH AND ADDRESS | ☐ SAVINGS ☐ CHECKING | BANK REFERENCE CHECK NAME OF BANK OFFICER

17 **POWER OF ATTORNEY** DOES ANYONE HAVE POWER OF ATTORNEY? IF 'YES', STATE NAME AND ATTACH A NEW ACCOUNT FORM FOR THE AGENT ☐ YES ☐ NO Name | IS POWER OF ATTORNEY A.E.? ☐ YES ☐ NO

ACCOUNT DESCRIPTION

18 (K) TYPE OF ACCOUNT (PLEASE CIRCLE): a. Cash e. Speculative Commodity b. Margin f. Hedge Commodity c. Command g. Other (Specify) d. Option

(L) ACCOUNT DESCRIPTION (PLEASE CIRCLE): a. Individual g. Estate b. Joint WROS h. Investment Club c. Joint TIC i. Trust d. Corporation j. Custodian e. Partnership k. IRA/KEOGH f. Other

IF AN INSTITUTION PLEASE DESCRIBE
IS THIS AN ASSET MANAGEMENT ACCOUNT? IF 'YES' NAME OF INVESTMENT ADVISOR: ☐ YES ☐ NO
IS ADVISOR REGISTERED? ☐ YES ☐ NO | DOES CLIENT HAVE IRA OR KEOGH PLAN? ☐ YES ☐ NO

19 **INITIAL TRANSACTION** WAS INITIAL TRANSACTION ☐ ORDER ☐ TRANSFER | DESCRIPTION OF ORDER ☐ SALE ☐ PURCHASE ☐ SHORT SALE | QUANTITY | DESCRIPTION | PRICE

20 IF AN ORDER, WAS IT SOLICITED? ☐ YES ☐ NO | IF TRANSFER - NAME OF PRIOR FIRM AND ACCOUNT NO. | DEPOSIT RECEIVED OR VALUE OF SECURITIES \$

21 **REVIEW/SIGNATURE** A.E. NAME (PRINTED) | MANAGER'S NAME (PRINTED)

22 A.E. SIGNATURE | DATE | MANAGER'S SIGNATURE | DATE

FORM 1233L-3

NEW ACCOUNT COPY

(a)

FIGURE 1. The four documents shown represent some, but not all, of the forms required for opening a commodity account. (*a*) New Account Form—filled in by the customer, this form shows the type of account and the financial suitability for trading commodities. (*b*) Customer's Agreement—standard customer agreement for an individual account. (*c*) Supplemental Commodity Customer's Agreement—provides for a transfer of funds from other accounts held at that same brokerage firm in order to reduce debit equities. (*d*) Risk Disclosure Statement—explaining the risks associated with commodity trading and high leverage as required by the CFTC.

Bache Halsey Stuart Shields Incorporated CUSTOMER'S AGREEMENT	ACCOUNT NAME (HEREIN REFERRED TO AS I)	ACCOUNT NO.	DOC ID.	DATE
			42	

1. I agree as follows with respect to all of my accounts, in which I have an interest alone or with others, which I have opened or open in the future, with you for the purchase and sale of securities and commodities:

2. I am of full age and represent that I am not an employee of any exchange or of a Member Firm of any Exchange or the NASD, or of a bank, trust company, or insurance company and that I will promptly notify you if I become so employed.

3. All transactions for my account shall be subject to the constitution, rules, regulations, customs and usages, as the same may be constituted from time to time, of the exchange or market (and its clearing house, if any) where executed.

4. Any and all credit balances, securities, commodities or contracts relating thereto, and all other property of whatsoever kind belonging to me or in which I may have an interest held by you or carried for my accounts shall be subject to a general lien for the discharge of my obligations to you (including unmatured and contingent obligations) however arising and without regard to whether or not you have made advances with respect to such property and without notice to me may be carried in your general loans and all securities may be pledged, repledged, hypothecated or re-hypothecated, separately or in common with other securities or any other property, for the sum due to you thereon or for a greater sum and without retaining in your possession and control for delivery a like amount of similar securities or other property. At any time and from time to time you may, in your discretion, without notice to me, apply and or transfer any securities, commodities, contracts relating thereto, cash or any other property therein, interchangeably between any of my accounts, whether individual or joint or from any of my accounts to any account guaranteed by me. You are specifically authorized to transfer to my cash account on the settlement day following a purchase made in that account, excess funds available in any of my other accounts, including but not limited to any free balances in any margin account or in any non-regulated commodities account, sufficient to make full payment of this cash purchase. I agree that any debit occurring in any of my accounts may be transferred by you at your option to my margin account.

5. I will maintain such margins as you may in your discretion require from time to time and will pay on demand any debit balance owing with respect to any of my accounts. Whenever in your discretion you deem it desirable for your protection, (and without the necessity of a margin call) including but not limited to an instance where a petition in bankruptcy or for the appointment of a receiver is filed by or against me, or an attachment is levied against my account, or in the event of notice of my death or incapacity, or in compliance with the orders of any Exchange, you may, without prior demand, tender, and without any notice of the time or place of sale, all of which are expressly waived, sell any or all securities, or commodities or contracts relating thereto which may be in your possession, or which you may be carrying for me, or buy any securities, or commodities or contracts relating thereto of which my account or accounts may be short, in order to close out in whole or in part any commitment in my behalf or you may place stop orders with respects to such securities or commodities and such sale or purchase may be made at your discretion on any Exchange or other market where such business is then transacted, or at public auction or private sale, with or without advertising and neither any demands, calls, tenders or notices which you may make or give in any one or more instances nor any prior course of conduct or dealings between us shall invalidate the aforesaid waivers on my part. You shall have the right to purchase for your own account any or all of the aforesaid property at any such sale, discharged of any right of redemption, which is hereby waived.

6. All orders for the purchase or sale of commodities for future delivery may be closed out by you as and when authorized or required by the Exchange where made. Against a "long" position in any commodity contract, prior to maturity thereof, and at least five business days before the first notice day of the delivery month, I will give instructions to liquidate, or place you in sufficient funds to take delivery; and in default thereof, or in the event such liquidating instructions cannot be executed under prevailing conditions, you may, without notice or demand, close out the contracts or take delivery and dispose of the commodity upon any terms and by any method which may be feasible. Against a "short" position in any commodity contract, prior to maturity thereof, and at least five business days before the last trading day of the delivery month, I will give you instructions to cover, or furnish you with all necessary delivery documents; and in default thereof, you may without demand or notice, cover the contracts, or if orders to buy in such contracts cannot be executed under prevailing conditions, you may procure the actual commodity and make delivery thereof upon any terms and by any method which may be feasible.

7. All transactions in any of my accounts are to be paid for or required margin deposited no later than 2:00 p.m. on the settlement date.

8. I agree to pay interest and service charges upon my accounts monthly at the prevailing rate as determined by you.

9. I agree that, in giving orders to sell, all "short" sale orders will be designated as "short" and all "long" sale orders will be designated as "long" and that the designation of a sell order as "long" is a representation on my part that I own the security and, if the security is not in your possession that it is not then possible to deliver the security to you forthwith and I will deliver it on or before the settlement date.

10. Reports of the execution of orders and statements of my account shall be conclusive if not objected to in writing within five days and ten days, respectively, after transmittal to me by mail or otherwise.

11. All communications including margin calls may be sent to me at my address given you, or at such other address as I may hereafter give you in writing, and all communications so sent, whether in writing or otherwise, shall be deemed given to me personally, whether actually received or not.

12. No waiver of any provision of this agreement shall be deemed a waiver of any other provision, nor a continuing waiver of the provision or provisions so waived.

13. I understand that no provision of this agreement can be amended or waived except in writing signed by an officer of your Company, and that this agreement shall continue in force until its termination by me is acknowledged in writing by an officer of your Company; or until written notice of termination by you shall have been mailed to me at my address last given you.

14. This contract shall be governed by the laws of the State of New York, and shall inure to the benefit of your successors and assigns, and shall be binding on the undersigned, his heirs, executors, administrators and assigns. Any controversy arising out of or relating to my account, to transactions with or for me or to this Agreement or the breach thereof, and whether executed or to be executed within or outside of the United States, except for any controversy arising out of or relating to transactions in commodities or contracts related thereto executed on or subject to the rules of a contract market designated as such under the Commodity Exchange Act, as amended, shall be settled by arbitration in accordance with the rules then obtaining of either the American Arbitration Association or the Board of Governors of the New York Stock Exchange as I may elect. If I do not make such election by registered mail addressed to you at your main office within five (5) days after demand by you that I make such election, then you may make such election. Notice preliminary to, in conjunction with, or incident to such arbitration proceeding, may be sent to me by mail and personal service is hereby waived. Judgment upon any award rendered by the arbitrators may be entered in any court having jurisdiction thereof, without notice to me.

15. If any provision hereof is or at any time should become inconsistent with any present or future law, rule or regulation of any securities or commodities exchange or of any sovereign government or a regulatory body thereof and if any of these bodies have jurisdiction over the subject matter of this agreement, said provision shall be deemed to be superseded or modified to conform to such law, rule or regulation, but in all other respects this agreement shall continue and remain in full force and effect.

DATE ______________ CUSTOMER'S SIGNATURE X ______________ X ______________

SIGN IN BOTH PLACES

LENDING AGREEMENT

YOU AND ANY FIRM SUCCEEDING TO YOUR FIRM ARE HEREBY AUTHORIZED FROM TIME TO TIME TO LEND SEPARATELY OR TOGETHER WITH THE PROPERTY OF OTHERS EITHER TO YOURSELVES OR TO OTHERS ANY PROPERTY WHICH YOU MAY BE CARRYING FOR ME ON MARGIN. THIS AUTHORIZATION SHALL APPLY TO ALL ACCOUNTS CARRIED BY YOU FOR ME AND SHALL REMAIN IN FULL FORCE UNTIL WRITTEN NOTICE OF REVOCATION IS RECEIVED BY YOU AT YOUR PRINCIPAL OFFICE IN NEW YORK.

DATE ______________ CUSTOMER'S SIGNATURE X ______________ X ______________

KINDLY SIGN THIS FORM IN THE TWO SIGNATURE SPACES INDICATED ABOVE. IN THE CASE OF JOINT ACCOUNTS, BOTH TENANTS SHOULD SIGN IN BOTH SIGNATURE SPACES. RETURN THIS ORIGINAL (WHITE) TO THE BACHE OFFICE WHICH SERVICES YOUR ACCOUNT. THE DUPLICATE (BUFF) SHOULD BE RETAINED FOR YOUR PERSONAL RECORDS.

PRINTED IN U.S.A.

(b)

FIGURE 1. *Continued*

SUPPLEMENTAL COMMODITY CUSTOMER'S AGREEMENT

Account Number ______________________

Branch Number ______________________

Bache

Bache Halsey Stuart Shields Incorporated
Bache Plaza, 100 Gold Street
New York, N.Y. 10038

Dear Sirs:

Until further notice in writing, you are hereby authorized, at any time and from time to time, without prior notice to the undersigned, to transfer from my/our Regulated Commodity Account to any other account, held by you in which I/we have any interest, such excess funds, equities, securities, and/or other property as in your judgment may be required for margin, or to reduce or pay in full any debit balance and/or to reduce or satisfy deficits in such other security and/or commodity accounts. By "Regulated Commodity" is meant any commodity covered by the Commodity Exchange Act at the time of such transactions. You agree, however, that within a reasonable time after making any such transfer, you will confirm the same in writing to the undersigned.

Dated ...., 19........

....
Customer's Signature

WHITE COPY MUST BE SENT TO MAIN OFFICE.
YELLOW COPY TO BE RETAINED BY CUSTOMER.
PINK COPY TO BE FILED IN BRANCH OFFICE.

Form 1888C-3

PRINTED IN USA

(c)

FIGURE 1. *Continued*

ACCOUNT NO. ______________________

ACCOUNT NAME ______________________

____

BACHE HALSEY STUART SHIELDS INCORPORATED

RISK DISCLOSURE STATEMENT

This statement is furnished to you because rule 1.55 of the Commodity Futures Trading Commission requires it.

The risk of loss in trading commodity futures contracts can be substantial. You should therefore carefully consider whether such trading is suitable for you in light of your financial condition. In considering whether to trade, you should be aware of the following:

(1)You may sustain a total loss of the initial margin funds and any additional funds that you deposit with your broker to establish or maintain a position in the commodity futures market. If the market moves against your position, you may be called upon by your broker to deposit a substantial amount of additional margin funds, on short notice, in order to maintain your position. If you do not provide the required funds within the prescribed time, your position may be liquidated at a loss, and you will be liable for any resulting deficit in your account.

(2)Under certain market conditions, you may find it difficult or impossible to liquidate a position. This can occur, for example, when the market makes a "limit move."

(3)Placing contingent orders such as "stop loss" or "stop limit" order will not necessarily limit your losses to the intended amounts, since market conditions may make it impossible to execute such orders.

(4)A "spread" position may not be less risky than a simple "long" or "short" position.

(5)The high degree of leverage that is often obtainable in futures trading because of the small margin requirements can work against you as well as for you. The use of leverage can lead to large losses as well as gains.

This brief statement cannot, of course, disclose all the risks and other significant aspects of the commodity markets. You should therefore carefully study futures trading before you trade.

IN OPENING A COMMODITY FUTURES ACCOUNT WITH BACHE HALSEY STUART SHIELDS INCORPORATED I, AS THE BENEFICIAL HOLDER OF INTEREST IN THIS ACCOUNT (OR, AS AN AUTHORIZED REPRESENTATIVE OF A BUSINESS ENTITY WHICH IS THE BENEFICIAL HOLDER OF INTEREST THEREIN), ACKNOWLEDGE THAT I HAVE RECEIVED AND UNDERSTAND THE RISK DISCLOSURE STATEMENT.

______________________ DATE

______________________ SIGNATURE OF CLIENT

Form 4594-3

(d)

FIGURE 1. *Continued*

and define precisely, most brokerage firms at least try to establish a satisfactory quantitative approach to the financial aspect of suitability. They do this by requiring a new client to indicate some combination of income, net worth, and liquid net worth (discretionary funds) to justify trading in speculative areas such as commodities or stock options. Accordingly, they may require the customer to prepare and sign a financial statement. Some registered representatives who are somewhat too eager to begin generating commissions from a new account prepare a statement for a client's account by following a few questions with a considerable amount of pure conjecture. A few are so misguided that they prepare the statement themselves with little or no basis in fact and then sign the client's name to it. Such actions as these place both a salesperson and his or her firm in a position of considerable jeopardy if the client later loses money and maintains successfully that he or she was clearly unsuitable for trading.

THIRD-PARTY ACCOUNTS

Sometimes a client chooses to allow a third party to make trades in his or her account without prior discussion of the positions to be established or liquidated. Such accounts are usually designated as discretionary, but sometimes are described as controlled or managed. The party who is delegated the right to make trades may be a registered representative or a personal friend of the customer who is believed to have some special skill in trading. The right to trade in such cases is granted by a limited power of attorney, usually called a trading authority.

Sometimes control is given to a person or company paid to trade the account. Compensation may take the form of a share of profits generated, if any, a percentage of the capital utilized, or a combination of both. Some consider the term "managed account" to apply only to those managed for compensation and reserve the term "discretionary account" for cases where trading power is given to a registered representative. Actually, any third-party account which has been established properly may correctly be designated as discretionary.

All third-party accounts are subject to special documentation by the brokerage house to make certain that the client is suitable for such an account. Some third-party accounts are subject to controls by exchanges or government agencies. A minimum deposit might be required and the amount to be maintained may be specified. The registered representative may be subject to special requirements such as minimum length of experience and careful supervision. Group accounts may be deemed subject to approval by the state.

All parties to such accounts should be especially cautious particularly if discretion is awarded to a registered representative. Registered representatives may be accused of churning accounts whether or not money is made or lost by their trading. Even if the allegation is not true, discretion supported by a limited power of attorney provides a strong legal base for proof that the registered representative controlled the account. Control of the account is material in proving a churning allegation. A customer who directs or discusses each transaction before it is made may claim that he or she was wronged in some way, but can hardly maintain that he or she lacked control of this account.

It would appear that most brokers would be wise not to allow discretionary accounts or, at least, only in unusual and carefully supervised circumstances. It would also appear that a customer should grant discretion only after considerable thought. Even those who admit that they know less than a third party about trading could at least keep informed of the status of his or her account and perhaps learn enough by observing a successful trader carefully to justify the loss of some time and flexibility.

MARGINS

Low margins provide much of the appeal of commodity trading for many people and also cause considerable trouble. It is essential that customers and their brokers understand this subject thoroughly. Some confusion is caused by the fact that many registered representatives and their customers are more familiar with the trading of securities and gained their knowledge of margins from that part of the financial world.

Margins in securities are nothing more than that industry's special word for credit. The minimum amounts required to be deposited for various security transactions are set by the Board of Governors of the Federal Reserve System and the requirements are enforced by the Securities and Exchange Commission. Margins are sometimes set at higher levels by stock exchanges or by individual brokerage houses, or by both. The customer is subject to the highest level required by any of the three. Miminum initial deposit requirements and maintenance levels are typically set by exchanges.

If margin is utilized for the purchase of securities, the broker is a creditor of the customer and is paid interest on the debt owed. The amount owed is usually referred to as the customer's debit balance. Interest is charged at a specified level above the current cost of call money. The exact rate depends upon the size of the debit balance; the larger the balance, the lower the rate.

Short sales require margin in a different sense. Such margins act as good-faith deposits to ensure the broker that he or she will suffer no loss if a customer enters a short position and is later forced to cover the position at a higher price, thereby losing money. In the case of short sales, as in the case of purchases, the minimum amount of margin is a fixed percentage, commonly 50%, of the dollar amount of the transaction.

Commodity margins do not involve the extension of credit to a customer by a brokerage house. Rather, as with security short sales, they act as good-faith deposits. Margins are deposited with a clearinghouse usually in the form of cash. Some clearinghouses permit a large part of margin required to be deposited in the form of such cash equivalents as Treasury bills or warehouse receipts, but even in such cases, some cash is required.

Commodity margins are designated as initial and maintenance or variation margins. Initial margins are specified as fixed amounts per contract and do not vary with the current value of the commodity traded. Maintenance margins ranging from 50 to 75% of initial margins are also required by the exchanges. If a customer's equity is impaired by adverse market action to the point where the customer is below the specified maintenance margin at the close of a market, the equity must be promptly restored, not just to the minimum maintenance level but up to the initial requirement. Failure to respond to a call for additional funds may result in a position being liquidated by the broker. Brokers' actions in liquidating accounts too rapidly or too slowly in response to such variation margin calls frequently result in disputes. Most such disputes revolve around the interpretation of the term "promptly," but exchanges have preferred to permit some flexibility to allow consideration of such factors as the volatility of the market, amount of the exposure, and experience with a particular customer's account. Accordingly, there are no lengthy periods for payment customarily allowed. The fact that security settlements are usually allowed 5 days and that some commodity exchanges do not demand an explanatory report for 5 days have caused some customers to think that they have 5 days to meet a call in an undermargined account. This is not the case.

Margins on spread positions may or may not total the margins required by the legs considered separately. For example, a client may buy May wheat on one exchange and sell July wheat on another. The broker must deposit funds in unrelated clearinghouses and may, therefore, require full margins on both sides of the transaction. A customer may buy sugar and sell coffee on the same exchange believing the products to be related, but find that the exchange regards these products as not sufficiently related to consider the trade as a spread and so charge full margins on each side. The purchase and sale of different but related commodities, such as corn and wheat, might require a margin equal only to the higher of the two. If wheat, for example, required a margin higher than corn, the customer who buys wheat and sells corn is required to deposit an amount equal only to the wheat margin alone. The customer who sells a contract of a commodity for delivery in one month against the purchase of the same amount of the same commodity for delivery in another month of the same crop year might find that the margin requirement for the spread position is considerably less than even that which would be required for either of the two sides taken individually. The purchase of March wheat against the sale of May wheat, for example, would be less than the margin required for either the purchase or the sale if made alone. This is true because the exchange regards the chance of equity variation on such spreads to be less than that of net positions. Traders should remain aware, however, that the latter is not always true.

Requirements on cash positions are usually much higher than those on futures. This means that a customer who deliberately or carelessly takes delivery of a futures contract may be subjected to a substantial call for additional funds. Firms able and willing to extend or arrange for credit on cash positions usually require a cash deposit of about 30% which compares with the 5–10% typically required against futures positions.

Customers are well-advised to check margin requirements with their brokers before entering positions. Registered representatives, in turn, should carefully maintain records of margin requirements. These may be changed by exchanges as markets become more or less volatile. Customers who are misinformed as to margin requirements may justifiably claim damage if they enter too much or too little of a position because they were misinformed about current margins required.

It should be noted further that margin changes may be retroactive and therefore affect previously established positions. A customer trading a maximum position with minimum capital might therefore be forced out of a position if margins were unexpectedly increased. This is only one of the several valid reasons for not trading beyond one's means.

COMMODITY ORDERS

An order is initiated when a customer decides to enter or liquidate a position in a futures market. Such decisions might be based on the advice of someone else, such as the customer's broker or an advisory service, or upon such technical devices or fundamental sources in which the customer has some confidence. The order to enter or exit a market is placed with a member broker who has contact with the trading floor upon which the commodity is traded. The customer usually contacts a broker by telephone unless the customer happens to be in the broker's office. Less often, orders may be placed by telegram or even by mail.

The broker, having received an order, contacts the trading floor by telephone, direct line, or teletype. The order may be transmitted directly from a branch office to a floor or may be transmitted to a regional office and then redirected to a floor. When the order is received on the trading floor it is taken by the runner or transmitted by hand signal to floor brokers, who attempt to execute the order. Floor brokers congregate on the trading floor in pits or rings, which are merely areas where particular commodities are traded. After a trade is made with another floor broker who takes the opposite side of the transaction for another customer or for his or her own account, confirmation is made to the originating office of the brokerage firm and thence to the customer. Confirmation is made immediately, usually by telephone, but in any case, confirmation is also made by mail as quickly as possible. Confirmations are usually mailed on the same day that the transaction is made [see Figure 5(a)]. This allows possible disputes to be resolved as quickly as possible.

TYPES OF ORDERS. There is a large number of types of orders some of which are too obscure to warrant detailed discussion here. Some types of orders are allowed by some exchanges and not by others. Some orders may be allowed at some times but not allowed at others, depending upon the degree of market activity. Brokers should know which orders are currently acceptable and by which exchanges in order to avoid delays caused by entry of improper orders. Ignorance in this area may not only cause a customer to lose confidence in a broker, but may well result in losses in an account.

The most common type of order and one which is always acceptable is the market order. This instructs a broker to buy or sell a specified number of contracts as quickly as possible at the best possible price. The advantage of this type of order is that it is always filled unless there is an error in its handling, or if the price of a commodity is already at its specified limit for the day and remains there.

Some customers utilize market orders to enter or exit a market but specify that their orders be filled only on the opening or closing of the market on that day. Given the often heavy and even frantic trading early and late in a trading session, it is sometimes difficult to understand the motivation that causes a customer to decide to trade at those times.

A second type of order commonly used is the limited or limit order. This type

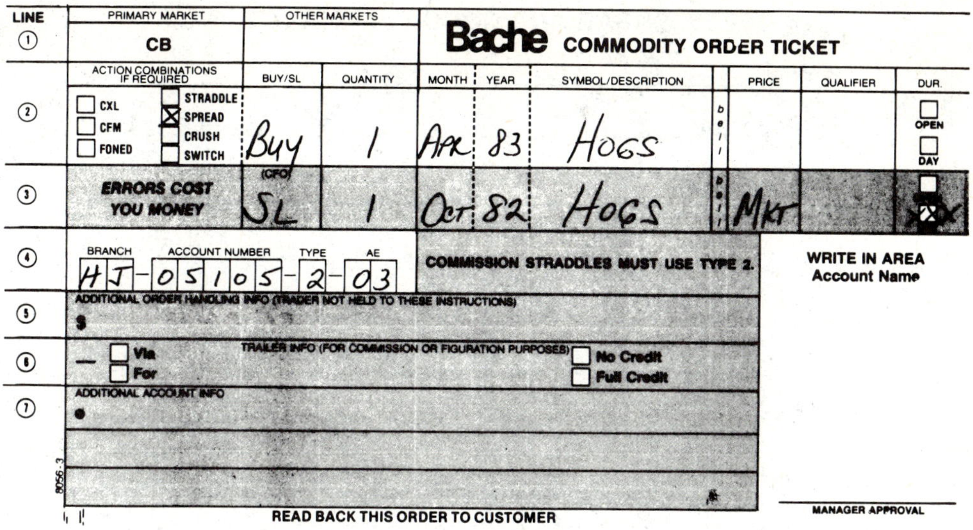
LINE
PRIMARY MARKET | OTHER MARKETS
① CB
Bache COMMODITY ORDER TICKET
ACTION COMBINATIONS IF REQUIRED | BUY/SL | QUANTITY | MONTH | YEAR | SYMBOL/DESCRIPTION | PRICE | QUALIFIER | DUR.
② CXL CFM FONED STRADDLE SPREAD CRUSH SWITCH | Buy | 1 | Apr | 83 | Hogs | | | OPEN DAY
③ ERRORS COST YOU MONEY | (CFO) SL | 1 | Oct | 82 | Hogs | Mkt
④ BRANCH ACCOUNT NUMBER TYPE AE | HJ-05105-2-03 | COMMISSION STRADDLES MUST USE TYPE 2.
WRITE IN AREA Account Name
⑤ ADDITIONAL ORDER HANDLING INFO (TRADER NOT HELD TO THESE INSTRUCTIONS)
⑥ Via For | TRAILER INFO (FOR COMMISSION OR FIGURATION PURPOSES) | No Credit | Full Credit
⑦ ADDITIONAL ACCOUNT INFO
8056-3
READ BACK THIS ORDER TO CUSTOMER
MANAGER APPROVAL

(a)

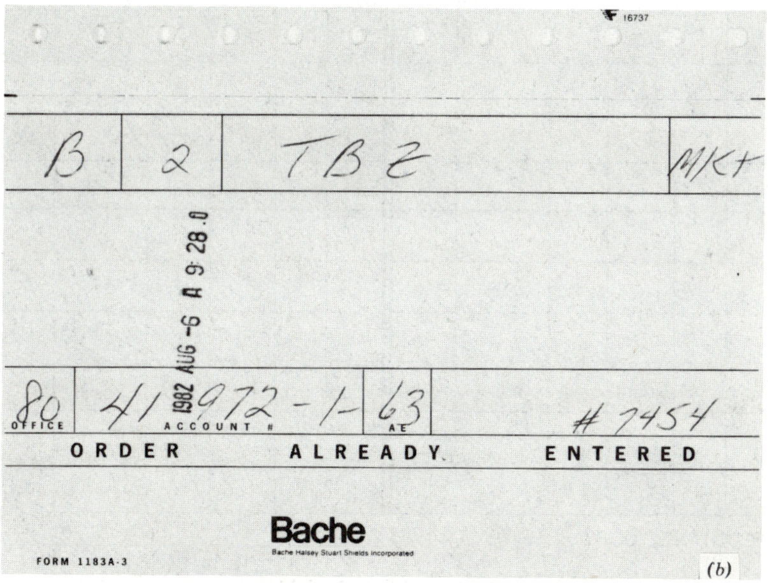
16737
B | 2 | TBZ | MKT
1982 AUG -6 A 9:28.0
80 OFFICE | 41 972 ACCOUNT # | 1 | 63 AE | #7454
ORDER ALREADY ENTERED
Bache
Bache Halsey Stuart Shields Incorporated
FORM 1183A-3

(b)

FIGURE 2. Order Tickets—both forms are used when commodity orders are given by the brokerage firm to the floor broker. The complete form (*a*) is filled out by the account executive, while the short form (*b*) is often used by the order desk which receives many telephone orders within a short time span. (*a*) Commodity Order Ticket—showing a spread order in hogs. (*b*) Short Form—showing an order to buy two contracts of December Treasury bills "at the market."

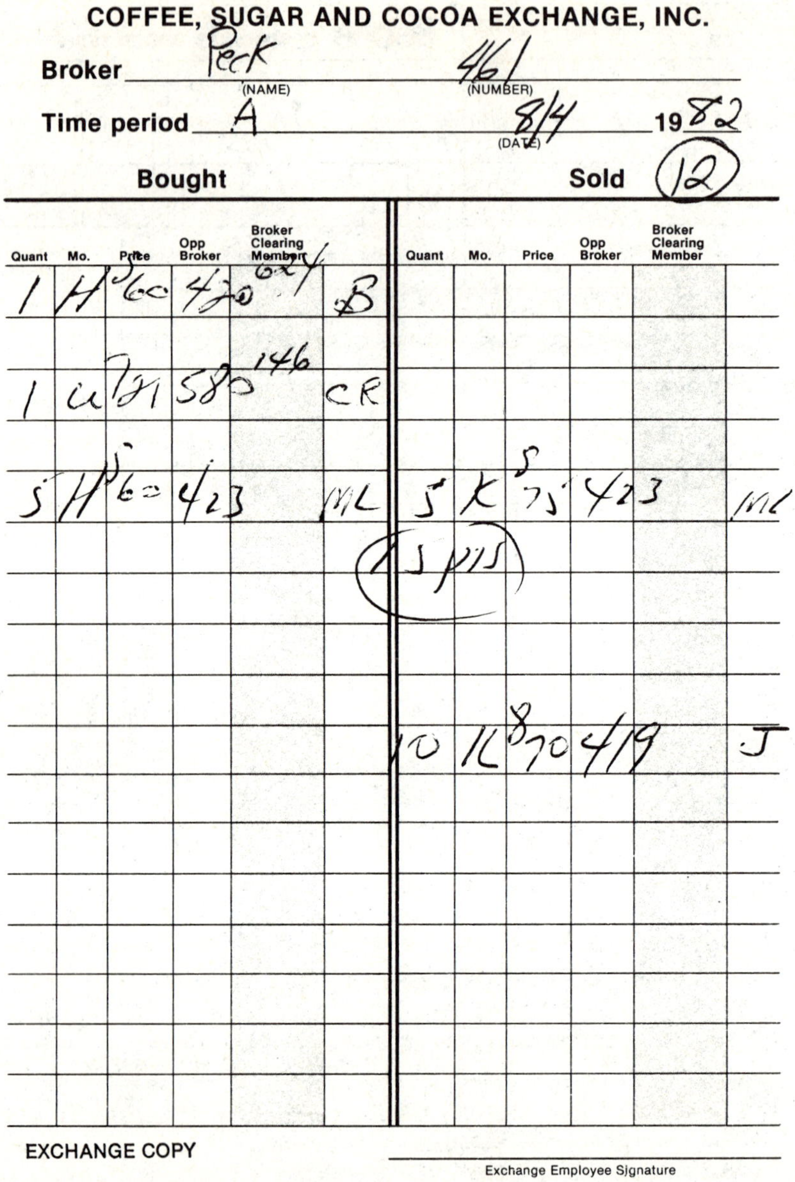

COFFEE, SUGAR AND COCOA EXCHANGE, INC.

Broker Peck (NAME) 461 (NUMBER)

Time period A 8/4 (DATE) 1982

Bought | Sold (12)

Quant	Mo.	Price	Opp Broker	Broker Clearing Member		Quant	Mo.	Price	Opp Broker	Broker Clearing Member	
1	H	860	420	624	B						
1	U	721	580	146	CR						
5	H	860	423		ML	5	K	875	423		ML
						15 pts					
						10	K	870	419		J

EXCHANGE COPY

Exchange Employee Signature

FIGURE 3. Floor Broker's Transaction Record—entered while completing orders in the trading pit, this record shows 1 March sugar bought at 8.60, a September sugar bought at 7.21, a spread of 5 March and 5 May sugar completed at a 15-point premium May over March, and 10 May sugar sold at 8.70.

of order specifies the highest price which a buyer is willing to pay or the lowest price at which a seller is willing to sell. It appears to some that such orders will save traders money because they often result in buying below or selling above the current market level. Like most tradeoffs in the financial world, however, the apparent advantage is offset by a cost. The price limits preclude some orders from being filled at all because the broker is unable to fill them at or better than their specified limits. Some traders believe that the amount saved on such orders in the long run exceeds that which is lost by missing favorable opportunities, whereas others believe the opposite.

Limit orders may be placed for a day or for a longer period including an indefinite one. The latter are usually referred to as open or good-til-canceled (GTC). They are held by the broker until they are filled or until they are canceled by the customer. Some brokers accept orders good for the remainder of the week, remainder of the month, or until a specified day or even a specified time of day. If a limit order does not specify a time at which it expires, it is presumed to be a day order. Brokers should make certain that the time intended by the customer is clearly understood. Orders allowed to lapse at the end of a day or allowed to remain for more than a day can cause problems if inconsistent with the customer's intention.

Some traders, and even some brokers, incorrectly add the words "or better" to limit orders. This not only yields no advantage, but can cause a problem by confusing the floor broker, who may return it for clarification and thereby miss a market. It is always assumed that a buyer would be happy to pay less than a specified limit and that a seller would always be glad to sell for more than a limit. The term "or better" is correctly used on a buy order only when such an order is placed at a price well above the last sale, or on a sell order well below the price of the last sale. The purpose is to indicate to the floor broker that the order is correct. Such an order is usually placed after the release of some news item that is anticipated to have a substantial effect upon the price of a commodity.

An order similar to a limit order is the market-if-touched (MIT) order. Such orders are also commonly called board orders. Like the limit order, an MIT order to sell a position is placed above the current level of the market and an MIT order to buy is placed below the present level. Unlike the limit order, however, the MIT order instructs the broker to execute it at the market when there is a transaction at the price specified on the order. A seller therefore might receive a price lower than is specified on the order and a buyer might pay more. Such orders are placed by those who believe that they can identify the precise levels to which markets might rise or fall. Such beliefs are based, in most cases, either upon a supremely inflated ego or abysmal ignorance. It is difficult to justify their use.

Stop orders may be used either to liquidate or establish positions in the market. A sell stop is placed below the current level of the market and a buy stop is placed above. Most commonly such orders are used to limit the extent of losses. For example, a person might buy a contract of silver at $7.85 per oz and instruct a broker to enter a sell stop at $7.70. This order would be elected when a transaction took place at or below $7.70. The person could get the price specified on the stop order, and on rare occasions a higher price, but most often would receive a lower price. No broker can guarantee and no customer should expect protection at the level specified in a stop order. (The CFTC risk disclosure statement, Figure 1(d), specifically addresses this point.) A customer may choose to utilize a variation of the stop order called a stop limit if permitted by the exchange upon which the trading is being done. In this case a price is specified and acts as a limit when the stop is elected. Although this prevents a fill far from the stop level, it also may serve to prevent a fill at all. In such cases losses can be virtually limitless and the stop order's purpose of exiting badly chosen trades is defeated.

A customer with a profit in a position who wishes to maintain the position in the hope of gaining additional profit may use a stop in an effort to accomplish this. For example, the buyer of the silver at \$7.85 could still be holding that position after the price has risen to, say, \$8.25. The buyer might enter a stop (or raise an existing stop) at \$8.10. If the price fell to that level the buyer would be reasonably sure of liquidating with some profit, whereas if the price rise continued without first reacting to \$8.10 the buyer could keep the position and perhaps have the opportunity to raise the stop to still higher levels.

A third use of the sell stop order is to establish a short position on market weakness. A customer might believe, for example, that if the price of silver fell to \$7.45 from its present level of \$7.85, such weakness would indicate a downtrend and the price would probably go significantly lower. The customer would instruct a broker to sell a position at \$7.45 so the market would be entered only after weakness had been clearly indicated. Obviously, if the customer was quite certain that the order would be filled, he or she would have sold at the \$7.85 level in the first place, but if the customer believed that a downtrend must first be seen to be believed, he or she might prefer to see the weakness first. The customer would therefore believe he or she was in a position to make less profit, but with a higher degree of probability of making it.

Buy stops are mirror images of the above three uses of sell stops and are used for similar purposes; that is, to limit losses on short positions that have already produced an open profit, or to enter long positions on market strength.

Stop orders, despite those who maintain the contrary, do not in themselves provide a trading strategy. If trades or entrance levels are not well-chosen, the use of stops, trailing or otherwise, might enable a trader to avoid ruin for a longer period, but the ultimate result will almost certainly be the same. It might be further noted that many important exchanges do not permit the use of stop orders in the case of spread positions.

Alternative orders are utilized by some traders who plan their exit points when a position is entered. For example, a trader might buy a contract of September corn at \$2.65 per bushel and decide when the position is established that he or she will accept a profit of \$0.20 per bushel, or liquidate with a loss of \$0.10. The trader could enter a combination order which instructs a broker to sell at \$2.85 or \$2.55 stop OCO. The \$2.85 is a limit order to sell at that price or higher. The \$2.55 is an order to sell at the market if September corn trades at \$2.55. The OCO means "one cancels the other" or "order cancels order."

Those using alternative orders are usually rather sophisticated traders. They have predetermined their objectives and maximum risk points, presumably based on some thought or experience, and have sufficient discipline to follow their plans. Some who do not use such orders prefer to "watch the market," although most would be hard put to explain just what it was they were watching. Rising markets rise and falling markets fall whether watched or not and the manner of their rising or falling does not tell much of a story. In that orders are not in the market, it is possible for prices to reach objectives or risk limits with no action being taken. Reaching an objective and then missing it or watching a loss become materially greater than was regarded as acceptable are not good for a trader's morale, to say nothing of a trader's trading capital.

Of course, some traders use technical devices which are supposed to indicate when a market should be exited although they are unable to establish specific price levels in advance. Despite the inability of such traders to use alternative orders effectively, they could at least use stop orders to eliminate unreasonable adversity.

A customer may wish to cancel an order already placed. This is done with a cancellation which itself is considered to be an order. The original order is canceled when instructions reach the floor of the exchange and not when the cancellation is placed with the registered representative. Some customers believe that they have been mistreated because an order is filled after they thought it had been canceled, but most such misunderstandings are caused by underestimating the time required to cancel the previous order.

A cancellation may also be entered as part of a replacement order. For example, a customer may offer to sell November soybeans at $7.56 per bushel. Being unsuccessful, the customer may then order a broker to attempt to sell at $7.43 at the same time canceling the $7.56. Such an order is often called a CFO (cancel former order).

Special orders based on price differences may be used for spreads. A customer may believe that the price of March pork bellies is too low relative to that of May pork bellies and therefore instruct a broker to buy March bellies and sell May bellies at a difference of 150-points premium May. Such a customer does not care what prices are actually paid or received as long as the price paid for March is at least 150 points below the price received for the May. Orders to liquidate spreads may be entered in the same way.

There is a long list of other types of orders, but most are merely variations of those already discussed and are not too frequently used. If a customer upon the advice of an astrologer insists on entering or exiting a market at 10:47 a.m. Philadelphia time, the customer can probably find an exchange and brokerage house to accept and enter such an order.

CONTRACT FACTS

Virtually all brokers can provide customers with a publication called "Contract Facts" or "Contract Terms" or some similar title. A trader should procure such a publication and make every effort to keep it current, especially for those commodities in which the trader is particularly interested. Such a document is reproduced here, but it will be out of date soon. Contract facts change frequently, and ignorance of correct facts can have serious consequences. It might be valuable, however, to indicate the kind of information that is available in such publications and why it is important.

The customer who decides to trade a particular commodity future may find that trading in that commodity may take place on several commodity exchanges.

Drexel Burnham Lambert

MARKETS IN FUTURES: SELECT CONTRACT TERMS AND OTHER INFORMATION

COMMODITY	EXCHANGE/ LOCAL TRADING HOURS	CON-TRACT UNIT	MINIMUM FLUCTUATION		DAILY PRICE LIMIT (3)	ROUND TURN COMMISSION	ORDER & REPORT SYMBOL	CONTRACT MONTHS
			A PRICE CHANGE OF	RESULTS IN A PROFIT OR LOSS OF PER CONTRACT				
ALUMINUM	London Metals Exchange 12:00 P.M.- 5:00 P.M.	25 Metric Tons	£ .50	£ 12.50	NONE	½% of Value buy and sell side	LAL	Date 3 months forward
BANK CERTIFICATE OF DEPOSIT	Chicago Board of Trade 8:00 A.M.- 2:00 P.M.	1,000,000 face value	1 basis point $.01	$25.00	60 basis points (.60) $1500/contract	$90.00	BC	First half month: March, June, September, December
BANK CERTIFICATE OF DEPOSIT	International Monetary Market 8:00 A.M.- 2:00 P.M.	1,000,000 face value	1 basis point $.01	$25.00	80 basis points (.80) $2000/contract	$90.00	DC	March, June, September, December
BANK CERTIFICATE OF DEPOSIT	New York Futures Exchange 9:00 A.M.- 3:00 P.M.	1,000,000 face value	1 basis point $.01	$25.00	100 basis points (1.00) $2500/contract	$90.00	YC	First half month: March, June, September, December, plus two nearby months, e.g. September, October, November, December, March
BRITISH POUNDS (1)	International Monetary Market of CME 7:30 A.M.- 1:24 P.M.	25,000 B.P.	$.0005	$12.50	$.05 $1250/contract	$90.00	BP	January, March, April, June, July, September, October, December and the current month
BROILERS ICED (1)	Chicago Board of Trade 9:15 A.M.- 1:20 P.M.	30,000 lbs.	$.00025/lb.	$7.50	$.02 $600/contract	$80.00	IB	January, March, May, July, September, November
CANADIAN DOLLARS (1)	International Monetary Market of CME 7:30 A.M. 1:22 P.M.	100,000 C.D.	$.0001	$10.00	$.0075 $750/contract	$90.00	CD	January, March, April, June, July, September, October, December
CATTLE FEEDER (1)	Chicago Mercantile Exchange 9:05 A.M.- 12:45 P.M.	44,000 lbs.	$.00025/lb.	$11.00	$.015 $660/contract	$80.00	FN	January, March, April, May, August, September, October, November
CATTLE LIVE (1)	Chicago Mercantile Exchange 9:05 A.M.- 12:45 P.M.	40,000 lbs.	$.00025/lb.	$10.00	$.015 $600/contract	$80.00	LC	January, February, April, June, August, October, December
COCOA	10:00 A.M.- 1:00 P.M. London Cocoa Terminal Market 2:30 A.M.- 4:45 P.M.	10 Metric Tons	£ .5	£ 5.00	Market closes after £ 20 more, then resumes on limitless trading	£ 50.00	LCC	March, May, July, September, December
COCOA (1)	N.Y. Coffee Sugar Cocoa Exchange 9:30 A.M.- 3:00 P.M.	10 Metric Tons	$1.00/ton	$10.00	$88.00 $880/contract	$90.00	CM	March, May, July, September, December

Information Bulletin I Issued: July 1982

(Prepared for our clientele by the Commodity Operations and New York Research Staff)

This chart covers the more active commodity futures and include those in which trading has recently been started or is about to start. Information is not guaranteed, but is based on sources considered reliable and is subject to change without prior notice.

FIGURE 4. Commodity Fact Sheet.

Although the brokerage house should know where the commodity trades and be able to reach the market routinely, the customer may learn that the choice of market may affect him or her in various ways. One of these is trading hours. Gold futures, for example, trade actively on several exchanges in New York and Chicago, as well as in various foreign countries. A customer who lives in Phoenix and wishes to buy gold on the opening of a market needs to know what time the market opens relative to time in Phoenix.

Contracts on different exchanges may vary in size. Some exchanges trade in full-sized contracts, whereas others trade the same commodities in smaller contract sizes, sometimes referred to as minicontracts. The size of the contract has implications for the amount of money that can be gained or lost relative to a given change in price levels. It also affects the margins required and the commissions charged. It is impossible for a customer to manage capital intelligently without knowing the size of the contracts in which he or she is dealing.

All commodity futures contracts are not traded in all future months. A commodity future traded on two exchanges might be traded in different months on each of the exchanges. For example, silver is traded for January delivery in New York on the Commodity Exchange, Incorporated, but not on the Chicago Board of Trade. This can be important to a customer who has a strong feeling about events in January or who perhaps wishes to spread a silver position against some other related commodity, such as platinum, which trades for January delivery.

A customer holding a commodity position until delivery time is vitally concerned with first notice and delivery dates, both of which are frequently listed in the contract fact publication. Other items frequently listed, such as the interpretation of price changes, limit moves, and limit ranges, are discussed below.

LIQUIDATING TRANSACTIONS

A person who buys a commodity future has contracted to perform either of two acts. First, he or she may accept delivery of the commodity according to the terms of the contract during the month specified. Delivery will be in an amount, form, and at a location specified in the contract. The form is frequently as a warehouse receipt. An alternative to delivery is an offset to the contract, which involves selling the position before delivery is made. It is rare for delivery to be accepted or even contemplated. The commodity futures markets are designed to provide a proxy for the cash markets and thereby act as a pricing mechanism and not act as part of, or as a substitute for, the cash markets.

A person who has sold a commodity contract has also agreed to perform one of two acts. He or she may meet an obligation by delivering the commodity in accordance with the terms of the contract, or may offset the contract by buying the same amount of the commodity that he or she previously sold before being obliged to take delivery. As delivery time approaches, virtually all contracts are settled by offset as those who are long sell to those who are short. This acts to reduce the open position for the maturing delivery month. The few contracts not settled by offset are eventually settled by delivery. The clearinghouse will act for any customers who fail to meet their obligation. Any cost of arranging a delivery is charged to the brokerage house which has failed to act. The brokerage house, in turn, charges the customer who created the problem by failing to offset or to arrange delivery.

Except for those with trade connections, delivery should be taken only after careful thought. There is an obligation to pay for the commodity received. Although it is possible to arrange credit for such purchases, the amount of money required is considerably more than was necessary to carry the futures position and any loans require the payment of interest. A person who is unsophisticated in cash market transactions may find liquidation of a reluctant cash position expensive, difficult, or even impossible if the quality of the commodity delivered deteriorates. The customer who takes delivery merely to avoid realizing an open loss on a futures position is often destined to lose a far greater amount on the cash position which he or she has acquired.

PRICES

Prices for a commodity futures contract are expressed in terms of the units specified in the contract in which the commodity trades. Some futures, such as grains and oilseeds, trade in bushels. Others, such as precious metals, trade by the ounce. Soybean oil, coffee, and pork bellies trade by the pound. Currencies trade by the unit and financial instruments in terms of basis points. Still other commodity futures trade by the foot, ton, kilo, or gallon. Clearly, it is necessary for a trader to know the size of the contract in which he or she is trading and how prices are expressed in order to be able to evaluate his or her position intelligently. All of these facts are clearly and simply expressed in the commodity "Contract Facts" sheets previously discussed. Because most traders are active in only a limited number of commodities, particularly at any one time, it is not difficult to learn the essential facts about what is being traded. This can best be illustrated by example.

Assume that a trader believes that the price of cattle will rise after the middle of the year in sufficient amount and with a great-enough probability to justify a long position in that market. By looking at the financial page of a newspaper or by asking a broker, the trader learns that the basic market for cattle is on the Chicago Mercantile Exchange, that the standard contract is 40,000 lb, that the price is expressed in terms of cents per pound, and that delivery is permitted in January, February, April, June, August, October, and December. The trader notes that the October delivery closed the previous day at a price of 61.50 cents per lb. A rise to 61.51 would represent an increase of $4 in the value of a contract ($0.0001 multiplied by 40,000). This would be a profit to anyone long the contract and a loss to anyone short. The amount of the change is often referred to as one point. A full cent would therefore constitute 100 points.

The trader would further note that the minimum fluctuation between sales may be one point or more depending upon exchange rules. In the contract facts, therefore, the trader should determine the minimum fluctuation. The trader would discover that the minimum fluctuation, or tick, allowed in cattle is 2½ points which represents a value of $10 per contract. The minimum uptick from the close of 61.50 would therefore increase the price to 61.52½ and the minimum downtick would lower the price to 61.47½. Most newspapers omit the ½ to save space and assume that those interested in cattle would know that the 61.47 which appears in the price column really means 61.47½.

In order to give markets time to absorb sudden startling news events, most exchanges designate the limit to which prices may move in 1 day. Such limits are generally referred to as "limit up" or "limit down." The maximum allowable range over which the price may move in any 1 day is designated as the limit range which is almost always the sum of the allowable limits up and down. The latter are invariably equal in amount. The limit in cattle is usually 1½ cents per lb or 150 points up or down from the closing settlement price of the previous market day. On one contract this represents a change of value of $600 (40,000 lb multiplied by $0.015). When markets become especially volatile, most exchanges provide for temporary increases in the limits, and this is the case in the cattle market.

Limit moves may preclude a trader from liquidating an unfavorable position when he or she wishes to do so, and thereby lead to some rather common misconceptions. Some believe that the possibility of unfavorable limit moves can make commodity markets especially dangerous because positions cannot be liquidated. Actually, a limit is established only to provide a cooling-off period. Being able to liquidate at a highly unfavorable price today rather than a price no worse and possibly better tomorrow provides small comfort. The trader who blames a misfortune on an adverse limit move is overlooking the real cause; that is, being on the wrong side of the market.

Others incorrectly believe that a market closes when a limit is reached. Actually, any number of contracts may be traded at the limit and prices may move in from the limit before the market closes for the day. A customer who wishes to exit a position with the market limit against him or her has nothing to lose by entering a market order to liquidate. If entered it may be filled. If not entered, it will certainly not be filled.

Unfilled orders to buy a limit-up market or to sell in a limit-down market are said to be in a "pool." The strength or weakness of a market in such a state can be estimated by asking the exchange floor for the size of the pool. A person short a market which is limit up with a large pool is probably destined to be forced to wait until the next day if he or she wishes to liquidate. If the loss is large and the position substantial, the person is also destined to find that the night seems somewhat longer than usual.

"TIME AND SALES." Commodity exchanges make every effort to keep accurate records of the price of all transactions made during a trading session and the exact times at which they took place. A customer who thinks that his or her trade might have been unduly delayed thereby giving an execution price less favorable than deserved is entitled to ask for a time and sales report covering the period during which his or her order was or should have been on the floor. Because each order must be time-stamped when received, again when it is transmitted to the floor, and again when any kind of report on its status is received, it is not too difficult to discover if it was delayed or otherwise mishandled. A broker who does not time-stamp and preserve his or her orders fails to do so at his or her own peril. The CFTC appears to be particularly humorless in their enforcement of these requirements. (Strangely enough, neither the exchanges nor the regulatory bodies require the sealing of the time stamps).

Unless a broker is intentionally delaying orders, cases of errors in transmission or mishandling by floor personnel are rare. Most customers who believe that they have valid complaints in these areas overestimate the speed and reliability of the quote machines or tapes that they may be watching and they do not really have the accurate grasp of exchange floor activity that they think they do.

PROFIT-OR-LOSS CALCULATION

Although commodities differ in contract sizes and other details, it should not be difficult for anyone to understand commodity bookkeeping especially with a little help from a well-trained broker. Because we have already spent a little time here with October cattle, let us continue with that example.

The customer has decided that the price of October cattle is likely to rise from its present level of 61.50 cents per lb. This decision may be based upon technical observations, fundamental conditions, or a combination of both. The sources of information may be the broker or any others utilized by the customer. The customer may subscribe to advisory services, have a friend who raises cattle, or take advice from a butcher. The customer may utilize technical devices based upon price, volume, open interest, or some combination of these, or may keep charts or try to analyze some combination of numbers. In any case, the customer reaches a conclusion in which he or she has confidence. The customer believes, say, that the price of cattle will rise to at least 70 cents per lb by the middle of September. This would represent an increase of $8\frac{1}{2}$ cents per lb from the present 61.50 level and would yield a gross profit of $3,400 on each contract purchased (850 points at $4 per point). The customer's broker tells the customer that the current margin required per contract is $2,000. The round-turn commission (covering both the entry and the exit from the trade) is $70. The client is aware, or should be, that margins and commissions may vary from one brokerage house to another and that higher numbers may not represent a higher level of service. The client further decides that he or she is willing to risk a loss of 5 cents per lb ($2,000) per contract should the client's information or interpretation of the information prove to be wrong. In that the client has liquid net worth of $20,000 available for trading, the client concludes that a position of two cattle contracts seems reasonable.

An order to buy two October cattle is given to the broker. The order may be at the market which directs that the contracts be bought as soon as possible at the lowest price available or, alternatively, the order may specify a price. Let us assume that a bid is made at the previous close of 61.50 cents and that the order is filled at that price. The customer may then enter a sell stop at 56.50 and a limit order to sell at 70.00. Some may choose to "watch the market" rather than enter either or both such orders, but failure to enter them is almost impossible to justify under the conditions outlined. The only alternative to withholding the orders is to be in constant contact with the broker when the market is in the areas of either of those price levels. At such times, an order to liquidate should be entered anyhow. If contact is missed a market may be missed. If, as a result, a loss is extended or an objective which could have been realized is missed, the client has only himself or herself to blame. A plan which is not followed is no better than no plan at all.

If the market price should rise to 70.00 before delivery becomes a threat, and if a sell order were entered and filled, the customer would now realize a profit of 850 points on each of the two contracts. The total of 1,700 points multiplied by $4 would yield a gross profit of $6,800 less a $140 commission, or $6,660. The entire commission would be charged upon liquidation rather than partly when entered and partly when liquidated as is the case in security markets.

If the market had fallen to 56.50 and if a stop order had been entered, the customer's position would be liquidated at the market. Assume the customer would get filled at 56.40. The customer's loss would be 510 points on each contract or a total of 1,020 points on both. At $4 per point the customer would lose $4,080 plus the commission of $140, or a total of $4,220. It might be noted that commissions on commodities trading are figured on the basis of the number of contracts traded and not in terms of the dollar amounts of transactions as is usually true in the cases of such securities as stocks. The commission would therefore be $140 regardless of the level at which the contracts were liquidated.

Following the liquidation, the customer would receive a confirmation of the liquidation just as he or she received a confirmation of the entry of the trade at 61.50. Such confirmations [see Figure 5(*a*)], usually mailed the day a trade is made, indicate the date and description of the transaction including the price at which it took place. The liquidating confirmation, often called a purchase-and-sale report (P&S) [see Figure 5(*b*)] also summarizes the results of the entire trade. It indicates the price of the exit, as well as that of the entry, the difference in terms of points, the commission, and resulting net profit or loss in the customer's account. This information is summarized on a monthly statement [see Figure 5(*c*)] sent to the customer. Such statements also usually indicate the cash balance in the account as well as the status of any open positions.

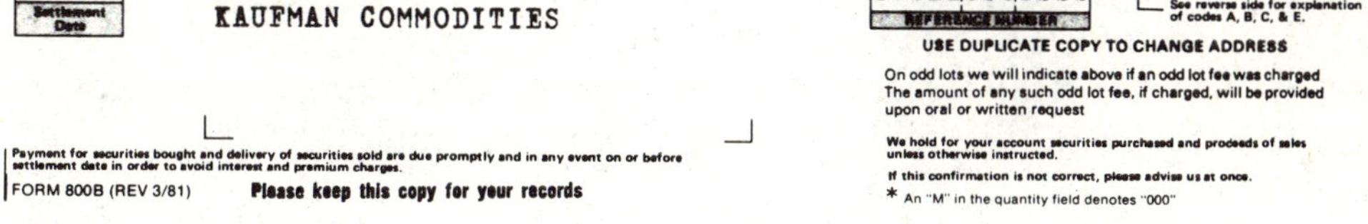

EF HUTTON & COMPANY INC. CHESTNUT HILL PL CHESTNUT HILL MA 02167

We confirm the following transaction subject to the agreement on the reverse side.

EFHutton

YOU	QUANTITY*	CUSIP NUMBER FOR EFH USE ONLY	PRICE	AMOUNT	COMMISSION OR SERVICE FEE	INTEREST OR STATE TAX	REG. AND/OR MAILING FEE	NET AMOUNT
SLD	1							
CT MAR82 COTTON			6516					

DUPLICATE

Trade Date: 011182

Settlement Date

SPECIAL ACCT 2
KAUFMAN COMMODITIES

ACCOUNT NO.	A	A.E.	B	C		E
J36212821		46	9			

8201100000000 — REFERENCE NUMBER

U - Indicates unsolicited order

See reverse side for explanation of codes A, B, C, & E.

USE DUPLICATE COPY TO CHANGE ADDRESS

On odd lots we will indicate above if an odd lot fee was charged The amount of any such odd lot fee, if charged, will be provided upon oral or written request

We hold for your account securities purchased and proceeds of sales unless otherwise instructed.

If this confirmation is not correct, please advise us at once.

* An "M" in the quantity field denotes "000"

Payment for securities bought and delivery of securities sold are due promptly and in any event on or before settlement date in order to avoid interest and premium charges.

FORM 800B (REV 3/81) **Please keep this copy for your records**

(*a*)

FIGURE 5. Customer Accounting—the three forms represent typical records of transactions provided to the customer by a major brokerage firm. (*a*) Confirmation of Transaction—this form confirms the sale on 1/11/82 of one contract of March 1982 cotton at a price of 65.16. (*b*) Purchase and Sale Statement (P&S)—this identifies that the current cotton transaction caused the liquidation of a prior purchase made on 12/28/81 at 64.62. The result of the trade is shown as a $270 profit less a $2 exchange fee and an $82 commission. (*c*) Monthly Statement—all confirmations, purchases and sales, cash transactions, and open positions are summarized on a monthly statement. The customer can verify the month-end account equity by adding the net profit or loss on open trades (a debit of $722) to the new cash balance of $63.61. Note that this account is secured by $20,000 in U.S. Government Treasury bills.

PAGE 1

BOUGHT OR RECEIVED				SOLD OR DELIVERED			
TRADE DATE MO DAY YR	QUAN.	DESCRIPTION	PRICE	TRADE DATE MO DAY YR	QUAN.	DESCRIPTION	PRICE
122881	1	CT MAR82 COTTON	6462	011182	1	CT MAR82 COTTON	6516

ACCOUNT NUMBER OFF NUMBER A.E.
J3621282146

DIFFERENCE	FEE AND / OR TAX	COMMISSION	NET DR OR CR TO YOUR ACCOUNT
27000CR	200	8200	18600C

DUPLICATE

1 - REGULATED
2 - NON-REGULATED
3 - SPOT
4 - OPTIONS

SPECIAL ACCT 2
KAUFMAN COMMODITIES

011182 P & S DATE ← S - STRADDLE 820111081 09 * B

ACCOUNT PURCHASE AND SALE OF COMMODITY CONTRACTS DESCRIBED ABOVE FOR YOUR ACCOUNT.

* SEE REVERSE SIDE FOR EXPLANATION OF "B"

ERRORS AND OMISSIONS EXCEPTED. IF NOT CORRECT, PLEASE ADVISE AT ONCE.
ALL INQUIRIES, CHECKS, INSTRUCTIONS, ETC. SHOULD BE SENT TO THE OFFICE SERVICING YOUR ACCOUNT.
PLEASE MENTION YOUR ACCOUNT NUMBER ON ALL CORRESPONDENCE.

FORM 458 (REV. 7/79)

CUSTOMER'S COPY

EF Hutton
E. F. HUTTON & COMPANY

(b)

BALANCES	OPENING CREDIT (CR) DEBIT (DR)	CLOSING CREDIT (CR) / DEBIT (DR)	OPEN POSITION GAIN (G) / LOSS (L)	EQUITY CREDIT (CR) / DEBIT (DR)	
REGULATED ACCOUNT	52200DR	6361CR	722L	OPENING	3DR
NON-REGULATED ACCOUNT				CLOSING	658DR
SPOT ACCOUNT				US TREASURIES (COMMODITY DEPOSIT)	20,000
TOTAL	52200DR	6361CR		USDOLLARS	

ACCOUNT NUMBER	OFFICE	NUMBER	A.E.
	J36		46
SOC. SEC. NO. OR TAX I.D. NO.			
STATEMENT DATE	FROM	01 01 82	
	TO	01 31 82	

PAGE 1

SPECIAL ACCT 2
KAUFMAN COMMODITIES

CL

*	DATE	BOT OR LONG	SLD OR SHORT	DESCRIPTION	PRICE	DEBIT	CREDIT
1	01 05	1		CT MAR82 CGBRPOUND	19125.0		
1	01 05		1	CT MAR82 US T BILL	8748.0		
1	01 06	1	1	CT MAR82 GINMAES	P & S	1,91950	
1	01 06		1	CT MAR82 GINMAES	5906.0		
1	01 06	5M		BU MAR82 CORN	275 1/2		
1	01 07		1	CT FEB82 CEICENGLD	39750.0		
1	01 07	1	1	CT MAR82 SWISS FR	P & S	1,12200	
1	01 07		1	CT MAR82 SWISS FR	55250.0		
1	01 07		1	CT MAR82 JA YEN	45530.0		
1	01 11	1	1	CT MAR82 COTTON	P & S		18600
1	01 11		1	CT MAR82 COTTON	6516.0		
1	01 11	1	1	CT MAR82 CGBRPOUND	P & S	69700	
1	01 11		1	CT MAR82 CGBRPOUND	18875.0		
1	01 12	1		CT MAR82 GINMAES	5821.0		
1	01 12		1	CT APR82 LIVECATTL	5810		
1	01 13	1	1	CT MAR82 GINMAES	P & S	95100	
1	01 13		1	CT MAR82 GINMAES	5725.0		
1	01 14		1	CT APR82 LIVE HOGS	4632 1/2		
1	01 18	1	1	CT APR82 LIVE HOGS	P & S		7250
1	01 18	1		CT APR82 LIVE HOGS	4585		
1	01 19			TFR FM STK ACCT			3.41400
1	01 21			147129		62496	
1	01 21			147130		6793	
1	01 21	1		CT MAR82 CGBRPOUND	18905.0		
1	01 22	1		CT APR82 LIVE HOGS	4770		
1	01 22	1	1	CT MAR82 CGBRPOUND	P & S	53450	
1	01 22		1	CT MAR82 CGBRPOUND	18720.0		
1	01 25		1	CT MAR82 CGGERMARK	42980.0		
1	01 26	1		CT MAR82 SB OIL	1990.0		
1	01 26	1	1	CT MAR82 CGGERMARK	P & S	59700	
1	01 26	1		CT MAR82 CGGERMARK	43400.0		
1	01 26	1	1	CT MAR82 JA YEN	P & S		1,40300
1	01 26	1		CT MAR82 JA YEN	44350.0		
1	01 27	1		CT MAR82 COTTON	6535.0		
1	01 27		1	CT MAR82 CGGERMARK	43200.0		
1	01 28	1	1	CT FEB82 CEICENGLD	P & S		1,25850
1	01 28	1		CT FEB82 CEICENGLD	38400.0		
1	01 28		1	CT APR82 CEICENGLD	39130.0		
1	01 28	1	1	CT MAR82 US T BILL	P & S		1,25000
1	01 28	1		CT MAR82 US T BILL	8695.0		
1	01 29	1		CT MAR82 CGBRPOUND	18860.0		
1	01 29	1	1	CT MAR82 CGGERMARK	P & S	48450	
1	01 29	1		CT MAR82 CGGERMARK	43530.0		
*	* * *	* * * *	* * * *	* O P E N T R A D E S *	* TRD PR	SETT PR	GAIN/LOSS
1	12 29	5M		BU MAR82 CORN	272	274	10000G
1	01 06	5M		BU MAR82 CORN	275 1/2	274	7500L
1	01 26	1		CT MAR82 SB OIL	1990.0	2018.0	16800G
1	01 12		1	CT APR82 LIVECATTL	5810	6170	1,44000L
1	01 22	1		CT APR82 LIVE HOGS	4770	4945	52500G
1	01 28		1	CT APR82 CEICENGLD	39130.0	39180.0	5000L
1	01 27	1		CT MAR82 COTTON	6535.0	6580.0	22500G
1	01 29	1		CT MAR82 CGBRPOUND	18860.0	18790.0	17500L

ATTENTION: NEW COMMODITY STATEMENT OF ACCOUNT
THIS NEW COMMODITY STATEMENT HAS BEEN DESIGNED FOR YOUR CONVENIENCE. A DETAILED EXPLANATION OF MONEY FIELDS AND SYMBOLS ARE DESCRIBED ON REVERSE SIDE.

*TYPE OF ACCOUNT

YOUR ACCOUNT EXECUTIVE IS

HIS/HER TELEPHONE NUMBER IS

FOR THE ACCOUNT OF:

STATEMENT OF ACCOUNT WITH

EF Hutton

MAIN OFFICE:

ONE BATTERY PARK PLAZA
NEW YORK, NY 10004

TELEPHONE: (212) 742-5000

PLEASE RETAIN THIS STATEMENT FOR INCOME TAX PURPOSES AND ALSO BECAUSE IT CONTAINS INFORMATION REQUIRED BY YOU TO VERIFY INTEREST ENTRIES APPEARING ON SUBSEQUENT STATEMENTS. IF NOT CORRECT, PLEASE RETURN IT TO US IMMEDIATELY.

CHECKS SHOULD BE SENT TO THE OFFICE SERVICING YOUR ACCOUNT. INSTRUCTIONS AND INQUIRIES SHOULD BE DIRECTED TO YOUR ACCOUNT EXECUTIVE. WHEN MAKING INQUIRIES, PLEASE MENTION YOUR ACCOUNT NUMBER. PLEASE NOTIFY US PROMPTLY OF ANY CHANGE OF ADDRESS.

NO ONE CONNECTED WITH E.F. HUTTON & COMPANY INC. IS AUTHORIZED TO RENDER TAX ADVICE OR TO INSURE THE TAX CONSEQUENCES OF ANY TRANSACTION.

ALL ACCOUNT STATEMENTS FURNISHED TO YOU SHALL BE CONSIDERED ACCURATE AND COMPLETE AND ACKNOWLEDGED BY YOU TO BE CORRECT UNLESS YOU REPORT ANY DIFFERENCES IMMEDIATELY TO THE MANAGER OF THE OFFICE SERVICING YOUR ACCOUNT.

ERRORS AND OMISSIONS EXCEPTED.

SEE REVERSE SIDE FOR EXPLANATION OF SYMBOLS USED ON THIS STATEMENT.

FORM 3305

(c)

FIGURE 5. *Continued*

Before the customer's trade is liquidated, the customer may easily determine his or her current equity in that open trade by simply learning the current price and then multiplying advances or declines from the entry price by $4 per point per contract. In addition, virtually all brokerage houses provide each registered representative with a daily running account of each customer's positions and this information is available to any customer who requests it. A customer who maintains that he or she does not know how he or she stands on an open transaction really has little basis for such an assertion. The knowledge required to enter a position in the first place is sufficient to enable anyone to calculate open profits or losses on the position after entry. Daily prices are available from any broker, daily newspapers, and, in most large cities, from television financial channels.

UNUSUAL LIQUIDATIONS

Most positions are liquidated because a customer chooses to accept a profit or loss. At least two types of liquidation are less usual. The first involves liquidation by delivery. In most cases, delivery is preceded by a notice of intention to deliver which can usually be transferred almost immediately to someone else. Sometimes the customer chooses to accept or make delivery. Customers who choose to do so may be in the trade and deal in the commodity involved. Sometimes, however, delivery involves customers too stubborn to accept a loss and who are too naive to understand the possibly expensive consequences of entering the unfamiliar cash market.

A second unusual liquidation takes place as a result of adversity. Sometimes market action causes severe impairment of a customer's trading capital. The customer may have no additional resources. Sometimes the customer may have additional resources, but does not choose to make them available for trading commodities. Such situations may arise from sheer misfortune, lack of planning, overtrading an account, or a combination of all. In such cases, the broker may liquidate all or part of the open positions in the customer's account with or without notice. Notice need not be given if the conditions are deemed serious enough, but most brokers prefer to give customers a reasonable time to meet margin calls. Margin calls must be met promptly. The definition of the word "prompt" may vary with the size of the position, capital remaining in the account, volatility of the account, and the broker's estimate of the probability of the customer sending additional funds. Certainly there is no defined number of hours or days to which a client is entitled despite some belief to the contrary. Brokers who tell their customers that they will always be given a specified length of time to meet initial or variation margin calls do so at their own peril.

If a position deteriorates so rapidly that the money utilized for margin is gone, it is possible for an account to go into a deficit (negative equity) position. Barring an error or improper procedure by the broker, the customer is liable for such deficits. If the customer refuses to meet an obligation to remit funds to make up such deficits, disputes may result leading to arbitrations or even lawsuits. Both the broker and the broker's customer should be aware of the problems that can be caused by overtrading or overstaying markets.

CLOSING COMMODITY ACCOUNTS

If a customer wishes to close a commodity account which has no currently open positions, the customer requests a check for his or her credit balance, if any, and cancels any open orders. If the account is discretionary, the customer should cancel the trading authority in writing. If there are open positions, they must be liquidated before the account is closed.

Sometimes a customer wishes to transfer an account from one brokerage house to another. In the commodities area, unlike securities, this may involve an extra commission cost. An open position transferred from one brokerage house to another is deemed by the clearinghouses to have been traded one to the other and a commission is incurred on such trades. Although the commission house receiving the new account may be willing to waive a commission in order to facilitate getting it, the house losing the account is understandably less willing to be accommodating. A customer wishing to place an account elsewhere may be well-advised to deposit funds in the new account and make any desired new entries there. At the same time, the customer can close out the old positions in due course in an earlier account and then withdraw the credit balance when all positions have been liquidated. This will avoid needless commission expense. Customers who are sufficiently angry about some aspect of the service they have received from a broker or who are concerned about the company's financial stability may prefer to transfer accounts immediately regardless of cost.

A broker who learns of the death of a customer normally will cancel all open orders and close out open positions. A security account can reasonably be held intact awaiting instructions from an executor, but this is hardly practical in a highly leveraged account.

CHAPTER 3

THE CLEARINGHOUSE

CONTENTS

EVOLUTION	4	DAILY REPORTING	8
THEORY AND PURPOSE OF THE MODERN CLEARING HOUSE	5	ORIGINAL MARGIN, VARIATION MARGIN, AND MARGIN CALLS	8
PRINCIPLE OF SUBSTITUTION	6		
FINANCIAL SAFEGUARDS	6	HANDLING OF DELIVERIES	9

CHAPTER 3

THE CLEARINGHOUSE

Theodore R. Hartley

The success of the futures market system depends upon the confidence of all parties that the contractual obligations of the *buyer* and *seller* which comprise *futures transactions* will be met with consistent dispatch. To ensure performance by both longs and shorts in keeping with the rules of the various exchanges a third participant is made party to every futures transaction. This party has the responsibility to enforce the contractual agreements, which are the essence of a transaction on a futures exchange. This participating authority *clears* the completed trades by matching up buyers and sellers and then "standing in for them," by holding good-faith deposits (margin deposits) as security, and by instituting and enforcing procedures to promote the efficiency and the integrity of the futures markets. This clearinghouse exercises its authority through its members (mostly Futures Commission Merchants and large commercial trading firms) who in turn deal directly with and are responsible for the initiating trader who is the ultimate party to the futures transaction. Thus the futures exchange clearinghouse functions in a way analogous to a bank clearinghouse, which offsets the claims and obligations of its member banks, minimizing the actual transfer of cash and notes, and reducing the need for physical delivery of legal tender (or in the case of the futures clearinghouse, the delivery of the physical commodity).

The critical assignment of *matching up* the buyer and seller in a futures transaction is not a trivial task. In the vast majority of cases, the buyer of a futures contract does not know the identity of the seller. The buyer places an order through a broker and so originates a series of operations, including transmission, execution, and reporting, which finally results, after the close of the market, in the complex activity of matching up broker–members on opposing sides of the transaction and of adjusting their margin requirements accordingly. These broker–members in their turn deal with their originating customer requiring margin adjustments and compliance with the rules governing the transaction. The clearinghouse guarantees the transaction to both parties and, with the power of its backing by its member firms, effectively reaches down through the transacting broker to the individual trader or hedger and ensures that his or her contractual rights are protected.

The rights of the holder of a futures contract are guaranteed by a hierarchy of financial resources provided by the member firms to the clearinghouse for that purpose. These resources include member good-faith deposits or margins, special guarantee funds levied from the members and the assets and reserves of the

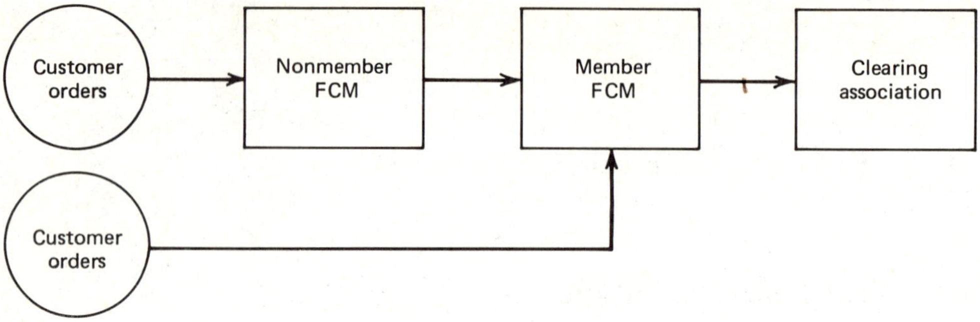

FIGURE 1. Order flow.

clearinghouse itself. The ability of the clearinghouse to guarantee the contracts it clears provides the basis of trust in the futures trading institutions and their transactions, an essential factor if they are to function successfully. The clearinghouse is an adjunct of the exchange it serves and provides housekeeping, policing, and insuring operations: it identifies and matches contracting parties and then assumes the obligations of each; it thereafter administers the procedures which assure that the contractual agreements will be kept.

The clearinghouse provides four essential services in futures trading:

1. It *regulates* the dealings between member firms in regard to futures transactions between them.
2. It *allocates* physical delivery rights and obligations at the expiration of a futures contract to qualified receivers who are long the futures contract and intend to take delivery.
3. It *facilitates trading* on the exchange by providing an efficient manner of offsetting trades thus reducing transaction costs and delays.
4. It *ensures against default* on futures contracts on a routine and continuing basis.

Modern futures trading at current levels of volume would not be possible without this highly sophisticated clearinghouse operation. However, clearing functions have not always been so organized and well-administered. The clearing function has evolved through the many levels since futures trading began.

EVOLUTION

The futures markets grew out of "cash" exchanges where buyers and sellers met to deal in physical commodities. In those early days, parties to the transactions made their own arrangements for payment and delivery. Inevitably, customs developed which led to standard practices of futures trading. This simplification created the opportunity for deferred delivery agreements which would parallel cash agreements in later times. Since meeting to exchange goods and payments at the moment of delivery was not always convenient or possible, brokers began assuming the responsibility of arranging for delivery and the acceptance of payment and were paid a fee for their services. This third-party representation allowed a new method of transacting and marketing commodities. Instead of paying *today* for the delivery of a commodity at some future specified date, the buyer and seller could contract to *complete the transaction at some future date* at a specified price. These contracts then began taking on a life of their own and soon brokers could offer producers and speculators the opportunity to offset existing contractual obligations without actually waiting for the delivery date. Thus the futures markets were born. But with the buyer and seller no longer facing each other with goods-in-hand, a new problem developed which heralds the birth of the clearinghouse, namely, how to match up offsetting contracts and thus provide a quick and simple support for market liquidity to satisfy the increasing demand for futures commitments.

Toward the end of the 19th century, the use of the futures markets grew rapidly as commercial producers and users found that they could take a short futures position to limit the risk of holding physical commodities, while speculators discovered that they could take a position in the market without the hazards and costs of actually owning the commodity. The volume in futures trading bulged to previously unseen numbers after the turn of the century. *Ad hoc* methods were developed by brokers to deal with the increasingly complex string of transactions in which a single contract might be bought and sold many times. Brokers employed clerks who threaded executed orders (for contracts with the same expiration period) on large snap rings so that the net position could be ascertained more easily. This became the *ring method* of clearing transactions.

Not all brokerage firms proved able or willing to stand behind their customers' transactions at times of large price movements and for a while customers and firms had to be sure that that broker who represented the opposite side of the transaction had the reputation and the financial means to meet a client's contractual obligations. Out of the search for assurance that contracts would be honored, grew the clearinghouse. As the clearinghouse was accepted, buyers and sellers ceased being obligated to each other, but rather created financial obligations to the clearinghouse through the brokerage firms which made up the membership of the clearinghouse association. Thus a structure evolved which suited the purposes of producers, shippers, speculators, and brokers, and ensured that contractual obligations would be met to the benefit of all contracting parties.

THEORY AND PURPOSE OF THE MODERN CLEARINGHOUSE

Today the clearinghouse acts as a principal in the commodity transaction. It sells the contract to the buyer and buys the identical contract from the seller; thus both buyer and seller need look only to the clearinghouse through their executing broker to complete the transaction. The seller and buyer no longer deal with each other, nor do they need even to know the identity of the holder of the opposite side of their contract. Should the brokerage house (FCM) fail to perform, the clearinghouse and the financial commitment of all of its members stand behind the integrity of the contract.

Since the buyer and seller do not create obligations to each other but only to the clearinghouse through the member firm, the two parties are independent of each other and thus can make market decisions independently. Each can decide to buy (or sell) their side of the contract or to take (or make) delivery without reference to the other, each knowing that the clearinghouse guarantees performance for each transaction which it clears, and guarantees payment when such is due at the time their contracts are closed out by offsetting transactions.

The clearinghouse, by clearing and guaranteeing every trade on the exchange for which it is an adjunct, permits its members to act for their customers with assurance that transactions conducted according to the rules of the exchange will be honored. Thus the clearinghouse serves the most significant market purpose—to create confidence in the integrity and security of the exchange and its transactions.

PRINCIPLE OF SUBSTITUTION

At the end of each trading day, the clearinghouse accepts all the trades from the exchange which have been matched up and properly executed; thereafter, the original parties have no further relationship to each other in regard to those trades. A member firm which executed an order thereafter deals only with the clearinghouse in the administration of that contract; the clearinghouse assumes the position of the other party to the contract.

With the clearinghouse acting as the ultimate buyer and seller (i.e., the same delivery month of the same commodity) it can easily match *buys and sells* of identical contracts. By this arrangement one contract is offset against any other of the same specifications and can therefore be freely substituted in the daily matching process. Thus a trader is not obligated to buy back the original contract sold in order to cover a position; the clearinghouse may substitute any contract of the same specifications and the trader is nevertheless relieved of a contractual obligation.

A second useful effect of substitution also stems from the role of the clearinghouse as the ultimate buyer and seller. It can offset a contract executed by a member firm without obtaining the permission of the originator of the trade. This ability to substitute the contract without recourse provides flexibility and facility to the futures markets. Trading is conducted with an ease and freedom which would not be possible if each trade were closed out only if the originating parties agreed to do so.

FINANCIAL SAFEGUARDS

The integrity of the clearing system relies heavily on the ability of the clearinghouse to perform on its guarantee that the futures contract will be honored, and that no member will bear the burden of risk of financial loss caused by a default on a contractual obligation by another party. By taking the place of every buyer and every seller and assuming their obligations, the clearinghouse guarantees performance on every contract.

To create the financial depth to assume this awesome responsibility, the clearinghouse relies not only on its own assets, but on guarantees and deposits from its member firms. To ensure that the financial liability is covered for every contract, it requires that each member firm deposit in an escrow account funds or margin for every contract cleared for that firm, but not offset by other positions which that firm may hold (net positions). Since this deposit is required each time a new trade is originated it is termed *original margin*. The escrow provides that margin funds are held for the mutual use of the firm and the clearinghouse and cannot be released except as financial liability is reduced.

In addition to cash, two types of securities may be deposited to fulfill margin requirements:

1. Equity shares in the clearinghouse, assessed at current book value, which are owned by the member firms (members are required to own stock in the clearinghouse in an amount dependent upon the size and volume of their transactions).
2. Obligations of the U.S. Government, that is, Treasury bills, bonds, or notes, the interest on which accrues to the benefit of the member firm even when deposited in escrow.

In addition to original margin deposits, firms are required to make additional deposits (variation margin) whenever a price movement of their holding creates the possibility of additional financial liability.

There is still a further safeguard: the *guarantee fund* which is held in either cash or government securities in a bank and which cannot be withdrawn except on an order signed by not less than three directors of the clearinghouse (a rule which on some exchanges has been simplified to require only one authorized signature). The guarantee fund is made up of contributions required of members as a condition of membership. These contributions not only guarantee that funds are available to absorb deficits not promptly covered by a member in his or her margin account, but may be used to absorb losses not covered by margin deposits in any member's account. Thus the guarantee fund stands to cover the naked losses of any member of the clearinghouse.

In addition to margin deposits and guarantee deposits, the net assets of the clearinghouse and in particular the *surplus* are available to the directors as a final safeguard against default on a contract obligation. The surplus, sometimes called the *surplus fund*, accumulates to the credit of the clearinghouse from the fees, billed monthly to each member, for the clearing of trades. Although the fees charged per contract are small, they are large in the annual aggregate.

The rules and bylaws of each clearinghouse dictate the specific steps which may or must be taken in the event of the failure of a member to meet margin obligations or to make good on the contractual provisions of a futures contract. The first step is either to close out all contracts held at the clearinghouse in the member's name, offsetting them by purchase or sale on the exchange floor or to transfer them to another clearinghouse member. Next, the defaulting member's account must be debited or credited with the resulting losses or gains. When the contracts have been closed out and the net profits or losses have been posted to the member's account a deficit may remain. This deficit is covered by applying in succession (to the extent necessary) funds available from the safeguards, respectively:

1. The member's margin account.
2. The member's contributions to the guarantee fund.
3. The surplus fund, as the Board of Directors may direct.
4. The contributions of all members to the guarantee fund.

Should the general guarantee fund be drawn down, a special assessment is immediately levied on all the clearing members to replenish the guarantee fund. The amounts required of each member are proportional to its share of the trading volume of the exchange.

DAILY REPORTING

The account which each member firm holds with the clearinghouse is settled daily by the clearinghouse. Through the applied principle of substitution the clearinghouse closes out any contracts which have been offset by subsequent transactions for both sides. Thus after balancing its books each day, the clearinghouse knows and reports the number of contracts not yet liquidated or fulfilled by delivery for each delivery period (contract month) for every commodity or futures contract which it clears. This is the daily *open interest.* Each contract traded on the exchange is reported to the clearinghouse which can therefore report the total number of contracts traded in each delivery month in every commodity each trading day. These important data, *volume* and *open interest* for each futures delivery month, are made available to all interested parties on a daily basis in accordance with the requirements of the *Commodity Futures Trading Commission Act of 1974.* The CFTC itself makes use of the data in its monthly *Report on Traders' Commitments* and its statistical analysis of the makeup of current open interest.

The clearinghouse may also be responsible for computing and disseminating a third type of daily numerical information, the *settlement price,* so called because it is the price used to settle and adjust the debits and credits of the member firms' margin accounts (variation margin requirements). The settlement price is determined each day by the clearinghouse personnel based on closing prices or closing ranges announced from the exchange floor, but may take into consideration prevailing price differences between succeeding contract months (spread differences).

ORIGINAL MARGIN, VARIATION MARGIN, AND MARGIN CALLS

The margin deposits which member firms are required to post (sometimes called *clearing margins*) are established by the directors of the clearinghouse and are normally the same for all members, although this may be modified where the directors feel unusual risks warrant such action. In the interest of market liquidity, margins are kept as low as the clearing organizations believe is prudent. On most American exchanges, *initial margins* or *original margins* reflect the *net* position, long or short, of a member; however, some clearinghouses dictate that both the long and the short positions be margined in each commodity. It is expected that initial margins are large enough to cover losses incurred even from maximum daily price moves (limit moves). Nevertheless, the clearinghouse may issue a *variation margin call* to a member whose position has been affected adversely during the trading day, and the member must deliver a certified check in the amount specified within 1 hour. These member margin requirements, both initial and variation, are separate and distinct from margin requirements which the brokerage firms, in their turn, impose upon their individual client accounts in accordance with exchange regulations.

After the close of the market each day, when the settlement price has been computed and posted, the clearinghouse figures the net change in value of the futures contracts held by the member firms. This variation in value creates the *variation margin* or *pay* which the member must meet before the opening of the market on the following day if the price movement has created a loss. Should the price movement and the resulting change in value be in favor of a member, a *collect* is created which is a sum the clearinghouse pays to the member. By this procedure, margin requirements are "marked to the market" daily and original margin is maintained at its initial level.

In addition to daily adjustments to margin requirements due to price variations, original margin requirements may change because of the addition or the reduction in numbers of contracts held. Most clearinghouses create individual daily margin statements for their members which show the new open position count of contracts in all delivery months, the margins required for each, and the amount of margin which the clearinghouse is holding for the member's account. Any deficit must be made up before the opening of the market the following day.

Member credit created by favorable variation margin adjustments (*pays* or *collects*) cannot be used to offset a call by the clearinghouse for original margin. Thus the integrity of the original margin is maintained as a safeguard.

HANDLING OF DELIVERIES

The option to actually make or receive delivery of the goods or commodity which is the subject of the futures contract keeps futures prices in a valid relationship with cash prices. Most buyers and sellers of futures contracts ultimately offset their original position by taking an opposite position in the futures market so that, by the principle of substitution, they terminate their contract obligations. However, some small percentage of futures contracts are settled by delivery of the physical commodity against the contract. Although the clearinghouse does not make or take delivery itself, it establishes the mechanism and sets the procedures by which deliveries are made. Through substitution, the clearinghouse matches up a short who wishes to make delivery with a long contract holder who wishes to receive delivery; on most exchanges this delivery is directed to the eligible long who has held his or her futures contract the longest. Of course, the clearinghouse deals with the ultimate receiver only through the member firm which represents him or her, and the member firm may have its own internal methods for selecting the long, from the firm's list of clients who are long, to whom they will pass delivery.

The member firm representing the delivering seller starts the delivery process by issuing a *delivery notice* to the clearinghouse during trading hours or during another time period specified by clearinghouse rules. Since the notice is delivered to the clearinghouse as a request to match up a buyer, the buyer's name will not appear on the notice; however, all other essential contract facts are included—the day on which delivery will be made, the delivery point, the grade, the price, and any other relevant details. If the delivery notice was issued during the period stipulated by the exchange for making and taking delivery against an expiring contract, then the next trading day becomes the *delivery day*. The price that the deliverer receives and that which appears on the delivery notice is the settlement price of the previous trading session.

Once the clearinghouse has received a delivery notice it passes it along to a clearing member who is shown on the books as being long and eligible for delivery. Each clearinghouse has its own rules and procedures for selecting which member firm will receive the notice if more than one is an eligible long. In most cases the first notice is given to the firm holding the oldest long position; however, some exchanges distribute delivery notices in proportion to the relative numbers of long contracts held by the various members.

When a long receives a delivery notice, the long must accept it regardless of his or her ultimate intention not to accept delivery. Thereafter, procedures vary slightly from one exchange to another and depending upon whether the exchange rules and contract specifications describe the notice as *transferable* or *nontransferable*.

The issue of transferability is important only if the party to whom the delivery notice was issued does not want to take delivery and thus wishes to transfer the delivery to another buyer. If the delivery notice is transferable as it is, for example, on the New York Cotton Exchange, the unwilling buyer needs only to resell it on the exchange floor, thus transferring obligations to another buyer. This transfer transaction must take place within one-half hour of the time the buyer receives the delivery notice or the notice will be considered accepted and that buyer must take delivery.

If the delivery notice is nontransferable, the buyer to whom the notice is delivered must keep it until the next trading day, paying all storage charges for the physical commodity which is construed to be in the buyer's possession. Then, if the notice holder does not wish to retain the physical commodity, the holder issues a new delivery notice and the delivery notice process is repeated on the next trading day. In this latter case, the unwilling receiver is said to "retender" the notice. The Chicago Board of Trade employs nontransferable delivery notices.

The obligation and participation in the delivery process by the clearinghouse ends when the ultimate buyer accepts the *delivery notice* and both buyer and seller are identified. The rest of the process of physical delivery involves the buyer and seller directly and consists of making adjustments for variations from contract

TABLE 1. Comparative Analysis of Clearing Associations

Organizational Structure and Solvency Regulations	COMEX	Chicago Mercantile	Chicago Board of Trade	Coffee, Sugar, and Cocoa	New York Mercantile	MidAmerica	International Commodity Clearing House (ICCH)
Organizational structure	Separate affiliated corporation	Clearing association is part of exchange	Separate affiliated corporation	Separate affiliated corporation	Clearing association is part of exchange	Clearing association is part of exchange	Separate corporation owned by six banks
Minimum capital requirements for membership	$1 million net capital	CFTC minimum, but Clearing House Committee may set higher requirements	$200,000 stated capital; or $50,000 adjusted net capital; or 4% of funds required to be segregated, whichever is larger	$1 million working capital	$500,000 net capital	$100,000 net capital	£100,000 to £1 million, depending on the commodity
Financing reporting requirements	In compliance with CFTC	In compliance with CFTC	In compliance with CFTC	In compliance with CFTC	In compliance with CFTC	In compliance with CFTC	Annual Reports, quarterly net worth
Guaranty fund requirements	$200,000 to $2 million based upon net worth	$50,000	None	$100,000 to $500,000 based on net capital	$50,000	None	None
Primary assets used by members to fulfill contribution to guaranty fund	U.S. Government securities and bank letters of credit	U.S. Government securities and negotiable Certificates of Deposit of accepted banks	n.a.[a]	U.S. Government securities, cash or bank letters of credit	U.S. Government securities	n.a.[a]	n.a.[a]

TABLE 1. (*Continued*)

Organizational Structure and Solvency Regulations	COMEX	Chicago Mercantile	Chicago Board of Trade	Coffee, Sugar, and Cocoa	New York Mercantile	MidAmerica	International Commodity Clearing House (ICCH)
Margin requirements calculation	Net	Gross	Net	Combination of net and gross[b]	Gross	Net	Net on larger side of a position
Original margin	Increases with position size	Constant for all position sizes	Constant for all position sizes	Increases with position size	Increases with position size	Constant for all position sizes	May change with position size, at discretion of ICCH
Payment form	Cash, U.S. Government securities, and letters of credit	Cash only on CME; also letters of credit on IMM and OIM	Cash, U.S. Government securities, and letters of credit	Cash, U.S. Government securities, and letters of credit	Cash and U.S. Government securities[c]	Cash, U.S. Government securities, and letters of credit, bullion	Cash, foreign currency, U.K. Treasury bills, and letters of credit
Investment of margin funds	Interest accrues to clearing association	Interest accrues to clearing members[d]	Interest accrues to members	Interest acrrues to clearing association	Interest accrues to clearing members	Interest accrues to clearing members	Interest accrues to ICCH
Variation margin payment form	Cash only	Cash only	Cash only	Cash only	Cash only	Cash only	Same assets acceptable for initial margin
Position limits	Tied to net capital	No fixed position limits, but Clearing-house Committee may require more capital the larger the position, at its discretion[e]	No fixed position limits, but clearing association may impose them on individual members, at its discretion	Tied to net capital	Tied to net capital	No fixed position limits	No fixed position limits, but at the discretion of the ICCH

Daily price limits[f]	Yes	Yes	Yes	Yes	Yes	Yes	Depends on specific exchange[g]
Procedure in event of default: attachable assets and assessment procedure	CM assets Association's guaranty fund Association's surplus funds Pro-rata assessment on CM's cleared trades Limited to lower of 25% of CM's net capital or $10 million Not more than one assessment every 10 days[h]	CM assets Exchange's trust fund Guaranty fund Exchange's surplus funds Unlimited *pro-rata* on net capital, cleared trades, and open interest	CM assets Association's surplus funds No assessment of members permitted	CM assets Association's guaranty fund Association's surplus funds *Pro-rata* assessment on CM's cleared trades and open interest Limited to lower of 25% of net capital or $10 million	CM assets Association's guaranty fund Exchange's surplus funds Unlimited, shared equally by all members of exchange	CM assets Exchange's surplus funds Unlimited, shared equally by all exchange members	CM assets ICCH's capital

TABLE 1. *(Continued)*

Organizational Structure and Solvency Regulations	COMEX	Chicago Mercantile	Chicago Board of Trade	Coffee, Sugar, and Cocoa	New York Mercantile	MidAmerica	International Commodity Clearing House (ICCH)
Number of members	76	100	155	68	85	35	450
Size of guaranty fund in July 1982	$75 million	$29 million[i]	n.a.[a]	$24 million	$2.5 million[j]	n.a.[a]	n.a.[a]
Size of surplus funds in July 1982 (either CA or exchange where relevant)	$2.5 million	$30 million	$14 million	$7 million	$6 million	$6 million	£16–£20 million
Annual contract volume in 1981	13,293,049	24,527,020	49,085,763	3,562,613	1,781,407	2,588,540	4,883,398[k]
Percentage of total U.S. futures trading in 1981	13.49	24.89	49.82	3.62	1.81	2.63	

Source: From Edwards, Franklin R., "The Clearing Association in Futures Markets: Guarantee and Regulator," presented at the Conference on the *Industrial Organization of Futures Markets: Structure and Conduct,* Center for the Study of Futures Markets, Columbia University, New York, November 4 and 5, 1982.

[a]n.a. means "not applicable"; CM refers to clearing member.

[b]Net on FCM proprietary accounts; on FCM customer accounts it is net plus the smaller side of gross.

[c]Varies with commodity: for potatoes, only cash is acceptable; for petroleum products, letters of credit are also acceptable.

[d]Except for investment of discount on U.S. Treasury bills, interest on which accrues to clearing association.

[e]There are fixed position limits only for agricultural commodities.

[f]Limits are set by respective exchanges; are different for different commodities; and are usually not imposed in delivery month.

[g]Most exchanges have intraday limits: when they are hit the market closes for 30 min, after which trading is resumed.

[h]A clearing member has the option of resigning from the clearing association in periods between assessments.

[i]Includes a $24 million trust fund and a $5 million guarantee fund.

[j]When new rules are instituted, fund will rise to about $5 million.

[k]Does not include options.

specifications and exchanging a certified check for payment of the physical commodity for a warehouse receipt representing the commodity in approved storage or safekeeping.

By taking the place of both buyer and seller in the futures contract transaction the clearinghouse guarantees the integrity of the futures contract and compliance with its obligations. In so doing it ensures order and confidence in the complex series of financial and administrative operations which make up the futures market.

CHAPTER 4

COMPARING THE U.S. AND U.K. FUTURES MARKETS

CONTENTS

THE LONDON METAL EXCHANGE 11

Principals' Market 12
Settlement 13
Delivery by Value Date 13
Official Rings and the KERB 14
Transfer of Contracts 14
Trading Limits 17
Commissions 17
Membership and Management 17

THE LONDON BULLION BROKERS 18

THE LONDON GOLD FUTURES MARKET 18

THE LONDON COMMODITY EXCHANGE GROUP OF COMMODITIES 18

THE LONDON INTERNATIONAL FINANCIAL FUTURES EXCHANGE 20

LONDON GRAIN FUTURES MARKETS 21

CLEARING ASSOCIATIONS AND SECURITY BACKSTOPS 21

Margining on the LME 22
Margining ICCH Commodities 23
Margining and Software Services 23
Interest Payment Versus Equity Disbursement 23
Underlying Support 23
Legal and Regulatory Safeguards 24

A BRIEF WORD ABOUT OPTIONS 25

SUMMARY: ARBITRAGE BETWEEN THE U.S. AND U.K. MARKETS 26

CHAPTER 4

COMPARING THE U.S. AND U.K. FUTURES MARKETS

Michael Riess

The U.S. and London exchanges are similar enough to encourage a substantial volume of arbitrage, but there are significant differences, especially in the metals markets. There are also differences in the clearing systems and in the quality of regulatory protection; and, of course, there is always the English/American language barrier!

London offers several contracts that are unique to the United Kingdom along with some that are shared with the United States. Table 1 shows the contracts traded in London along with their U.S. counterparts.

There are five groups of London exchanges, each under different supervision:

1. The London Metal Exchange (LME).
2. The London Gold Futures Market (LGFM).
3. The London Commodity Exchange Group (LCE).
4. The London International Financial Futures Exchange (LIFFE).
5. The London Grain Futures Markets supervised by the Grain and Feed Trade Association (GAFTA).

These different groups share two characteristics which contrast with U.S. practice:

1. *Few Local Traders.* Although many London exchanges trade in substantial volume (some larger than their U.S. counterparts) the trading rings themselves are small. This is because there are virtually no independent "local" traders or scalpers which in the United States can account for over half the daily volume. Most London floor traders represent large dealers or brokerage firms, and if they day trade ("jobbing" in U.K. parlance) or carry positions it is for the firm's account. Unlike the United States, England has no restrictions on brokers carrying house positions (see Figure 1).

2. *Sterling-Denominated Contracts.* Since they are traded in the United Kingdom, most of London's futures contracts are denominated in pounds sterling. The trading implications are significant since commodities are generally perceived as "hard assets" whose prices move inversely to the currency in which they are bought and sold. So prices for the same commodity can look more bullish or bearish depending on the currency in which they are traded (see Figure 2).

TABLE 1. U.K./U.S. Comparison of Trading Specifications (U.K. Contracts Italicized)

U.K. Exchange	Market	U.S. Exchange	Contract	Quote	Minimum Fluctuation	Limit
LME	*Silver*		*10,000 oz*	*pence/troy oz*	*0.10 pence*	*None*
		COMEX	5,000 oz	cents/troy oz	$0.10	$0.50
		CBOT (old)	5,000 oz	cents/troy oz	$0.10	$0.40
		(new)	1,000 oz	cents/troy oz	$0.10	$0.40
		MidAmerica	1,000 oz	cents/troy oz	0.05	$0.40
	Copper					
	Regular		*25 metric tons*	*£/metric ton*	*£0.50/metric ton*	*None*
	HiGrade		*25 metric tons*	*£/metric ton*	*£0.50/metric ton*	*None*
		COMEX	25,000 lb	cents/lb	$0.05/lb	$0.05
	Lead		*25 metric tons*	*£/metric ton*	*£50/metric ton*	*None*
	Zinc		*25 metric tons*	*£/metric ton*	*£50/metric ton*	*None*
	Tin		*5 metric tons*	*£/metric ton*	*£1/metric ton*	*None*
	Aluminum		*25 metric tons*	*£/metric ton*	*£0.50/metric ton*	*None*
	Nickel		*6 metric tons*	*£/metric ton*	*£1/metric ton*	*None*
LGFM	*Gold*		*100 oz*	*$/troy oz*	*$0.10/oz*	*$30*
		COMEX	100 oz	$/troy oz	$0.10/oz	$25
		CBOT	100 oz	$/troy oz	$0.10/oz	$25
		IMM	100 oz	$/troy oz	$0.10/oz	$50
		MidAmerica	33.2 oz	$/troy oz	$0.25/oz	$50

GAFTA	*Wheat*		*100 metric tons*	*£/metric ton*	*£0.5/metric ton*	*None*
		CBOT	5,000/bushel units	cents/bushel	$0.25/bushel	$0.20
	Barley		*100/metric tons*	*£/metric ton*	*£0.05/metric tons*	*None*
	Potatoes		*40/metric tons*	*£/metric ton*	*£10/metric tons*	*None*
	Soyabean meal		*100/metric tons*	*£/metric ton*	*£10/metric tons*	*£5 +*
		CBOT	100/metric tons	$/short ton	$0.10/ton	$10
LIFFE	*Deutsche mark* (DM)		DM*125,000*	DM/*dollars*	DM*0.001*	DM*0.05*
		IMM	DM125,000	cents/DM	0.0001/DM	0.0100
	Japanese yen (JY)		¥*12,500,000*	¥*/$*	¥*.01*	¥*5*
		IMM	¥12,500,000	cents/¥	0.000001/¥	0.0001
	Swiss franc (SF)		SF*125,000*	SF/*dollars*	SF*0.0001*	SF*0.04*
		IMM	SF125,000	cents/SF	$0.01/SF	0.015
	Sterling (£)		*£25,000*	*dollars*	*$0.01*	*$0.05*
		IMM	£25,000	cents/£	0.005/£	$0.05
	3-Month Eurodollars		*$1 million*	*100 Yield*	*0.01%*	*100 Pts.*
		IMM	$1 million	IMM Index	0.01	100 Pts.
	3-Month Sterling deposit		*£250,000*	*100 Yield*	*0.01%*	*100 Pts.*
	20-Year gilt		*£50,000*	*£/50,000*	£1/32/£100	£2/5100

TABLE 1 (*Continued*)

U.K. Exchange	Market	U.S. Exchange	Contract	Quote	Minimum Fluctuation	Limit
LCE	*Cocoa*		*10 metric tons*	*£/metric ton*	*£1/metric ton*	*£40+*
		New York Coffee, Sugar, and Cocoa Exchange	10 metric tons	$/metric ton	$1/metric ton	$88
	Coffee		*5 metric tons*	*£/metric ton*	*£1/metric ton*	*None*
		New York Coffee, Sugar, and Cocoa Exchange	37,500 lbs	cents/lb	$0.001/lb	$0.04
	Sugar		*50 metric tons*	*£/metric ton*	*0.05/metric ton*	*£20 +*
		New York Coffee, Sugar, and Cocoa Exchange	112,000 lbs	cents/lb	$0.01/lb	$0.50
	Wool		*2,500 kilos*	*NZ¢/kilo*	*1 NZ¢/kilo*	*None*
	Rubber		*15 metric tons*	*0.10/kilo*	*£0.01/kilo*	*£0.003/kilo*
	Soyabean oil		*25 metric tons*	*dollars/metric ton*	*$0.50/metric ton*	*None*
		CBOT	60,000 lbs	cents/lb	$0.01/lb	$0.01
	Gasoil		*100 metric tons*	*dollars/metric ton*	*$0.25/metric ton*	
		New York Mercantile (Heating oil)	42,000 gallons	cents/gallon	$0.01/gallon	$0.02

TABLE 1 (*Continued*)

U.K. Exchange	Market	U.S. Exchange	Delivery Months	Hours (United States)		Shared Time
LME	*Silver*		Daily up to 3 months forward	11:50–11:55 4:35–4:40	General trading	All day
		COMEX	Spot/Jan./Feb./Mar./May/July/Sept./Dec.	9:05–2:30		All day
		CBOT (old)	Spot/Feb./Apr./June/Aug./Oct./Dec.	9:05–2.45		All day
		(new)	Spot/Feb./Apr./June/Aug./Oct./Dec	9:05–2:45		All day
		MidAmerica	Spot/Feb./Apr./June/Aug./Oct./Dec.	9:05–3:00		All day
	Copper					
	Regular		Daily:Spot/1month/3months			
	HiGrade		Daily:Spot/1month/3months			
		COMEX	Spot/Jan./Feb./Mar./May/July/Sept./Dec.	9:50–2:00		All day
	Lead		Daily up to 3 months forward	12:10–12:15 3:25–3:30	General trading	
	Zinc		Daily up to 3 months forward	12:15–12:20 3:30–3:35	General trading	
	Tin		Daily up to 3 months forward	12:40–12:45 3:40–3:45	General trading	
	Aluminum		Daily up to 3 months forward	11:55–12:00 4:25–4:30	General trading	
	Nickel		Daily up to 3 months forward	1:00–1:05 4:30–4:35	General trading	
LGFM	*Gold*		Monthly:Spot + each month for 6 months	9:30–12:20 2:00–4:45		
		COMEX	Spot/Jan./Feb./Apr./June/Aug./Oct./Dec.	9:00–3:00		9:00–11:45
		CBOT	All months	9:00–3:00		9:00–11:45
		IMM	Spot/Jan./Feb./Mar./Apr./June/July/Oct./Dec.	9:05–3:00		9:05–11:45
		MidAmerica	Mar./June/Sept./Dec.	9:05–3:10		9:05–11:45

TABLE 1 (*Continued*)

U.K. Exchange	Market	U.S. Exchange	Delivery Months	Hours (United States)	Shared Time
GAFTA	*Wheat*		Spot/Jan./Mar./May/July/Sept./Nov.	11:00–12:30	
		CBOT	Spot/Mar./May/July/Sept./Dec.	10:30–2:15	10:30–11:00
	Barley		Spot/Jan./Mar./May/July/Sept./Nov.	11:00–12:30 2:45–4:00	
	Potatoes		Spot/Feb./Apr./May/Nov.	11:00–12:30 2:45–4:00	
	Soyabean meal		Spot/Feb./Apr./June/Aug./Oct./Dec.	10:30–12:45 2:50–5:10	
		CBOT	Spot/Jan./Mar./May/July/Aug./Sept./Oct./Dec.	10:30–2:15	10:30–12:10 + kerb
LIFFE	*Deutsche mark* (DM)		Mar./June/Sept./Dec. with first 5 delivery months	8:35–3:00	
		IMM	Spot/Jan./Mar./Apr./June/July/Sept./Oct./Dec.	8:30–2:20	8:30–10:00
	Japanese yen (JY)		Mar./June/Sept./Dec. with first 5 delivery months	8:45–3:00	
		IMM	Spot/Jan./Mar./Apr./June/July/Sept./Oct./Dec.	8:30–2:26	8:30–10:00
	Swiss franc (SF)		Mar./June/Sept./Dec. with first 5 delivery months	8:40–3:00	
		IMM	Spot/Jan./Mar./Apr./June/July/Sept./Oct./Dec.	8:30–2:16	8:30–10:00
	Sterling (£)		Mar./June/Sept./Dec. with first 5 delivery months	8:30–3:00	
		IMM	Spot/Jan./Mar./Apr./June/July/Sept./Oct./Dec.	8:30–2:24	8:30–10:00
	3-Month Eurodollars		Mar./June/Sept./Dec. with first 5 delivery months	8:30–3:00	
		IMM	Mar./June/Sept./Dec.	8:30–3:00	8:30–10:00
	3-Month Sterling deposit		Mar./June/Sept./Dec. with first 5 delivery months	9:00–3:00	
	20-Year Gilt		Mar./June/Sept./Dec. with first 5 delivery months	9:15–3:15	
LCE	*Cocoa*		Spot/Mar./May/July/Sept./Dec.	10:00–1:00 2:30–5:00	

TABLE 1 *(Continued)*

U.K. Exchange	Market	U.S. Exchange	Delivery Months	Hours (United States)	Shared Time
		New York Coffee, Sugar, and Cocoa Exchange	Spot/Mar./May/July/Sept./Dec.	9:30–3:00	9:30–12:00
	Coffee		Spot/Jan./Mar./May/July/Sept./Nov.	10:30–12:30 2:30–5:00	
		New York Coffee, Sugar, and Cocoa Exchange	Spot/Mar./May/July/Sept./Dec.	9:45–2:30	9:45–2:30
	Sugar		Spot/Jan./Mar./May/Aug./Oct.	10:30–12:45 2:30–5:00 + kerb	
		New York Coffee, Sugar, and Cocoa Exchange	Spot/Jan./Mar./May/July/Sept./Oct.	10:00–1:45	10:00–12:00 + kerb
	Wool		Spot/Jan./Mar./May/Aug./Oct./Dec.	2:45–3:45	
	Rubber		Quarterly and every individual month	9:45–1:00 2:30–4:45	
	Soyabean oil		Spot/Feb./Apr./June/Aug./Oct./Dec.	10:15–12:15 2:30–5:00	
		CBOT	Spot/Jan./Mar./May/July/Aug./Sept./Oct./Dec.	10:30–2:15	10:30–12:00
	Gasoil		Spot and following 9 months	9:30–12:30 2:45–5:20	
		New York Mercantile (Heating Oil)	Spot/Jan./Feb./Mar./May/July/Aug./Sept./Nov./Dec.	10:30–2:45	10:30–12:20

THE RING

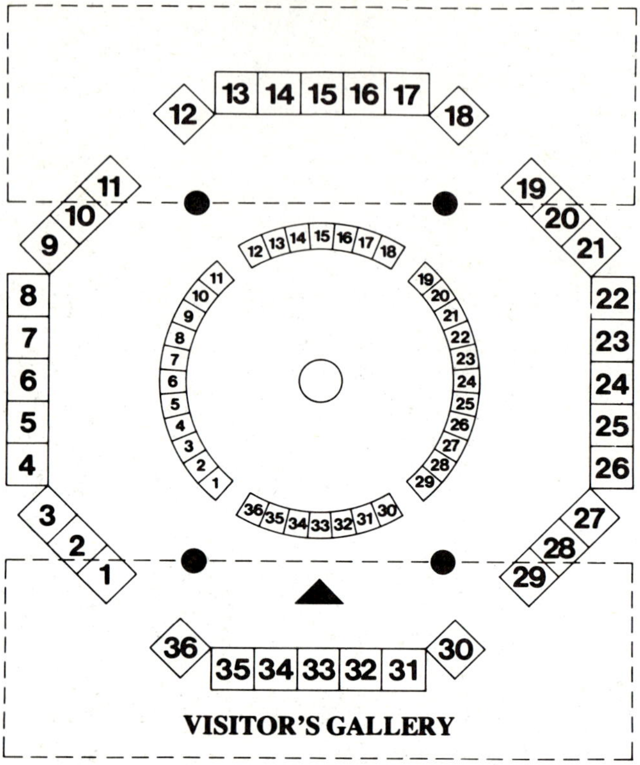

Seat No.		Seat No.	
1.	Empty — None	19	Amalgamated Metal Trading Ltd.
2.	Tennant Trading (Metals) Ltd.	20.	Holco Trading Co. Ltd.
3.	Philipp & Lion	21.	Cominco (U.K.) Ltd.
4.	Lonconex Ltd.	22.	Continental Ore Europe Ltd.
5.	The Commercial Metal Co. Ltd.	23.	Gerald Metals Ltd.
6.	Empty — None	24.	L.M.E. Executive
7.	Cerro Metals (U.K.) Ltd.	25.	Henry Bath & Son Ltd.
8.	J. H. Rayner (Mincing Lane) Ltd.	26.	Anglo Chemical Metals Ltd.
9.	Ametalco Trading Ltd.	27.	Johnson Matthey Commodities Ltd.
10.	Billiton-Enthoven Metals Ltd.	28.	Leopold Lazarus Ltd.
11.	Empty — None	29.	Rudolf Wolff & Co. Ltd.
12.	Brandeis Instel (Brokers) Ltd.	30.	Gill & Duffus Ltd.
13.	Metdist Ltd.	31.	Metallgesellschaft Ltd.
14.	Triland Metals Ltd.	32.	Boustead Davis (Metal Brokers) Ltd.
15.	Sogemin (Metals) Ltd.	33.	Wilson, Smithett & Cope Ltd.
16.	Empty — None	34.	Sharps, Pixley Ltd.
17.	Maclaine, Watson & Co. Ltd.	35.	Entores (Metal Brokers) Ltd.
18.	Empty — None	36.	Empty — None

FIGURE 1. The London Metals Exchange. (*a*) The ring. (*b*) The exchange during trading.

(b)

THE LONDON METAL EXCHANGE

The LME is the oldest metals exchange in the world. Metals traded are

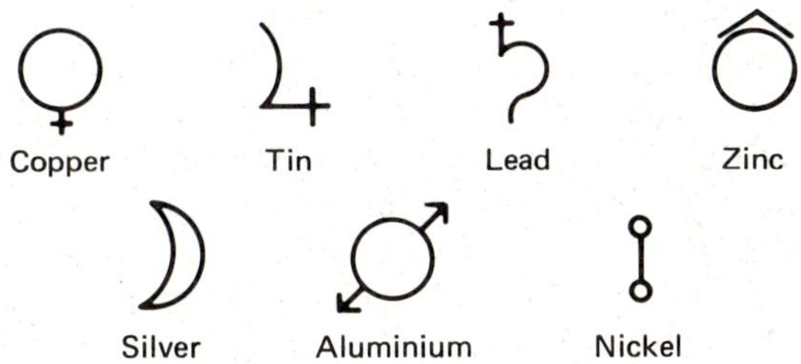

(The LME uses the alchemical symbols to indicate the metal being traded.)

The LME, which began as a group of merchants that gathered at the Jerusalem Coffee House to conduct physical metals business (or, in England, "actuals" metals business), still retains many characteristics of a physical forward market. Metal actually delivered accounts for more than 15% of volume; in the United States, the figure is usually under 5%. At the same time, the LME operates enough like a futures market for a London trader to participate comfortably on a U.S. exchange, and vice versa. As on a U.S. exchange, official trading on the LME is

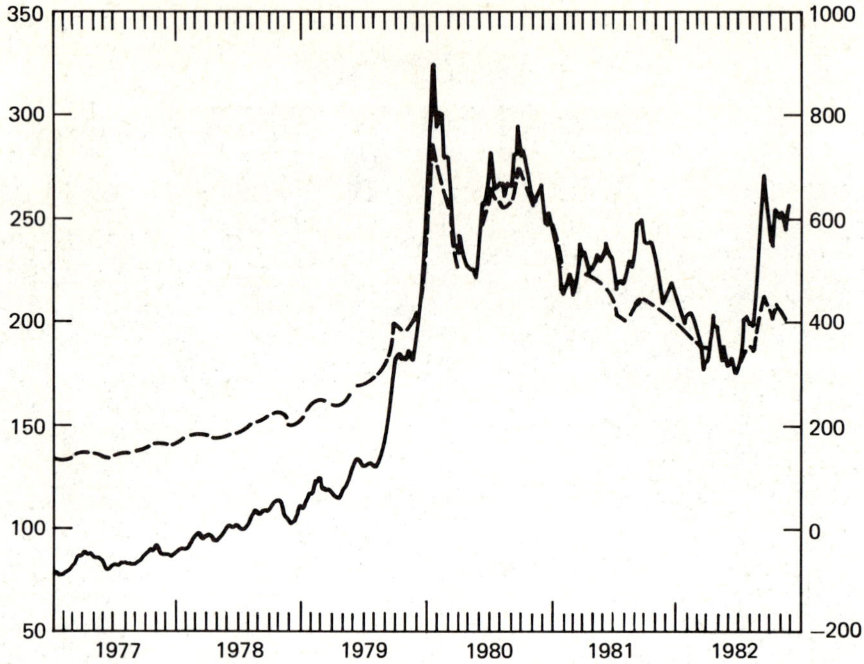

FIGURE 2. Handy & Harman gold prices.

by open outcry in a trading ring. Contracts are standardized and can be liquidated either by delivery or by offset. That is where the similarities end.

PRINCIPALS' MARKET. The LME is a principals' market, just as it was a century ago. Contracts are between single members and opposite contract parties, principal-to-principal. There is no anonymous clearinghouse interposed between buyer and seller, so each contract is with an identifiable company. LME business is thus more personal than U.S. exchange dealings. Rules, regulations, and standards of behavior do exist and are administered by a board, an elected committee of subscribers, and various subcommittees; but, the real standards of behavior lie in the strong tradition of what is acceptable and what is not. Comparing the slim book of LME rules to the 10-lb tome of COMEX bylaws and regulations makes the force of tradition quite clear. In fact, most of the rules used appear—and fit!—on every LME contract. With the advent of computerized back offices, conventional contracts are being replaced by computerized confirmation slips, but the traditional contract is worth perusing as a distillation of LME rules and standards. Although physical forward contracts are traditionally individualized, the grades of materials traded and the contract terms used on the LME are standardized. Still, LME contracts retain their character as agreements between principals for forward delivery of physical goods. On U.S. exchanges, business is done through a broker who acts as agent, not principal. Brokers are authorized to execute trades on behalf of clients and guarantee their clients' credit, but the client is the beneficial owner of the contract and has the ultimate responsibility of performance.

FIGURE 3. "Near hysteria rages at the London Metals Exchange."

SETTLEMENT. Like any physical forward contract between principals, LME profits or losses on contracts liquidated by offset are not paid until the contract matures. (A contract for delivery 3 months forward that is liquidated after a month is not settled for another 2 months, when the contract matures.) On the LME, a contract that has been offset by an opposite trade for the same maturity date no longer bears a price risk; however, there is a credit risk that persists until the maturity date. A nonmember would have to collect profits from the receiver if the member went bankrupt. This would be the case with unrealized profits and also on profits that have been locked in by offsetting trades, but that have not yet matured. United States contracts are paid upon liquidation, and liquidation terminates the contract in every respect.

DELIVERY BY VALUE DATE. LME deliveries are specific "value dates." Formal deliveries are dated *spot, 1 month,* and *3 months forward* from the date of the transaction, although the LME can be used to contract for any forward date. Contracts for longer than 3 months are on "white" forms, on terms which are negotiated for each transaction. In contrast, U.S. deliveries are by month, extend over a year forward, and give the seller the option to deliver on any day during the delivery month.

The LME's 3-month delivery period originally reflected the time for a vessel to bring copper from Chile to England. Today, the 3-month delivery period is appropriate for a different reason: recent studies indicate that the useful price-determination ability of futures markets extends about 3 months forward. Anticipation of future developments that might affect price are discounted independently by forward deliveries up to about 3 months ahead. Beyond 3 months, the market's ability to discount supply-and-demand shifts diminishes.

Price differences beyond 3 months are determined mainly by the interest rate yield curve. It is interesting to note that the LME 3-month silver contract enjoys a good level of activity but a 7-month contract was tried and eventually dropped. Prior to 1981, U.S. tax laws made it advantageous to use distant contracts here; however, since this advantage disappeared with the Tax Reform Act of 1981 it is interesting to note that volume in the distant deliveries has fallen off considerably, particularly in the nonagricultural commodities.

OFFICIAL RINGS AND THE KERB. A fundamental rule of U.S. futures trading is that all futures contracts must be executed on the floor through competitive bidding. This is not true of the LME. Each metal is traded by open outcry in an official ring twice a day in the morning and twice in the afternoon for a few minutes. The main purpose of the morning rings is not so much to conduct the day's business, which can be done outside the ring, but primarily to establish an official price. The LME official prices then serve to fix the price of most of the world's variable price contracts on exchange-traded metals. The afternoon rings are held to reflect prices traded on the U.S. markets and to take into account the events that affect prices after the morning market closes.

General trading takes place on the exchange floor between the ring sessions and on the telephone all day long. Most trading is by phone and never reaches the exchange floor. In addition, the LME allows trading on the "kerb." After each session, dealers gather in the exchange to trade in the various metals.

An official price based on a few minutes of ring trading can seem unrealistic when most of the volume is done off the exchange. From time to time, exchange officials have tried in vain to limit nonring activity and channel more trading into the official rings to keep the official prices credible, but the attempts have generally been fruitless. In fact, kerb trading found its name when exchange officials closed the exchange to prevent unofficial trading after the rings were over. Trading simply moved outside to the kerb. Rather than resist the inevitable, the exchange sanctioned and institutionalized the practice. The alternative would be to extend the brief rings and allow official trading throughout the day.

LME settlement prices are also used for margining (see "Margining on the LME") and to expedite physical delivery of a contract through a series of members. Allocation of material between longs and shorts is handled by the "clearing" staff of the exchange. As on U. S. exchanges, transfer is made at the settlement price at the time when material is due for delivery. On the LME, differences between the settlement and contract prices are settled directly between buyer and seller. On U.S. exchanges, such differences are settled through the clearinghouse. On the LME, trades liquidated by offset are invoiced in much the same way as in the United States. The main differences are semantic, that is, a *confirmation* is called a *contract,* and a *P&S* is called a *difference* or *settlement account*.

TRANSFER OF CONTRACTS. On the LME, it is normal practice to buy from one member and sell the contract to another. Trades with the same maturity date but executed with different LME members are liquidated through the exchange

CONTRACT RULES

Rule A. Members of the London Metal Exchange, in their dealings with other Members, shall be responsible to and entitled to claim against one another, and one ‚er only, for the fulfilment of every Contract for Metals.

Rule B. In these Rules the expression "Members of the London Metal Exchange" includes Firms and Companies who, although not themselves Subscribers to the ange, are represented and deal thereon by and through "Representative Subscribers" to the Exchange acting as the representatives or Agents of such Firms or Companies.

Rule C. If any Member of the Metal Exchange fails to meet his engagements to another Member, whether by failing to provide on the due date documents (*i.e.* Bills of ıg, Warrants or Delivery Orders according to the metals dealt in) to meet sales made or money to pay for metals bought, or by making default in fulfilling any other ation arising out of dealings made subject to the Rules and Regulations of the London Metal Exchange, notice of the default shall be given at once in writing to the mittee of the Exchange and the Committee shall immediately fix and publish a settlement price or prices as at the date of such communication to them for all contracts n the defaulter may have open under these Rules, whether with Members or with parties who are not Members. All such contracts shall forthwith be closed and balanced, lling to or buying from the defaulting Member such metals as he may have contracted to deliver or take, at the settlement prices fixed for this purpose by the Committee, ıny difference arising whether from or to the party in default shall become payable forthwith notwithstanding that the prompt day or other day originally stipulated for the ment of the transaction may not have arrived. In fixing settlement prices under this Rule the Committee may in their discretion take into consideration the extent and ·e of the transactions which the defaulting Member has open and any other circumstance which they may consider should affect their decision. In any case where the mittee shall be of opinion that the default is not due to the insolvency of the defaulter the Committee shall by resolution negative the application of this rule. Any claim ıg out of a default not due to insolvency shall be settled by arbitration in the usual manner. This rule shall apply to cases in which at or after the decease of a Member the gements entered into by him are not duly met.

Rule D. In any Contract made subject to the Rules and Regulations of the London Metal Exchange between a Member and a non-Member in the event of the non-ber failing to meet his engagement arising out of any such contract whether by failing to provide on the due date documents to meet sales or money to take up documents e case may be) or otherwise howsoever or of his failing to supply or maintain such margin (if any) for which the Member is entitled to call and has called, or in the event of on-Member's suspending payment or becoming bankrupt or committing any act of bankruptcy or (being a Company) in the event of its going into liquidation whether ıtary or otherwise, the Member shall have the right to close all or any such Contracts outstanding between them by selling out or buying in against the non-Member (as the nay be) and any differences arising therefrom shall be payable forthwith notwithstanding that the prompt day or other day originally stipulated for settlement may not have ·d.

Rule E. Payments for Warrants or other documents (when deliverable under the Contracts), unless otherwise stipulated on the contract, shall be made by cash in on, or by cheque on a London *clearing* bank, either mode in Seller's option. The documents shall be tendered in London against the cash or cheque, as the case may be, ıot later than 2.30 p.m. on the prompt or settling day.

Rule F. Contracts wherein Buyer or Seller (as the case may be) has the option to uplift or to deliver, prior to the prompt or settlement date by giving previous notice of tention, shall have the notice reckoned by market days; such notices, unless otherwise stipulated at time of purchase or sale, shall be as follows: On a Contract with the n to uplift or to deliver during one calendar month or less, one day's notice shall be given; on a Contract with the option beyond one and up to two calendar months two notice shall be given; and on a Contract with the option beyond two and up to three calendar months three days' notice shall be given previous to the date on which ·ry is required, or will be made. Notice shall be given for the whole quantity stated in the contract and shall be tendered in writing and delivered at the office of the seller of ption not later than 11.30 a.m. on the day of notice. Rent shall only be allowed to Buyer to actual day of settlement; and there shall not be any allowance of interest for a ent made prior to the prompt date.

Rule G. Prompt or settlement dates falling on Saturday, Sunday, or a Bank Holiday which days are not market days, shall be settled as follows. Prompts falling on day shall be settled on the Friday previous; but should the preceding Friday be a Bank Holiday the prompt shall be extended to the Monday following; should both the y preceding and the Monday following be Bank Holidays, the prompt shall be settled on the Thursday previous. Prompts falling on Sunday should be extended to the ay following, but should that Monday be a Bank Holiday the prompt shall be extended to the Tuesday following; should both the following Monday and Tuesday be Bank lays, the prompt shall then be extended to the Wednesday following. Prompts falling on a Bank Holiday shall be extended to the day following; and if the Bank Holiday fall iday the prompts shall be extended to the Monday following; but should the Friday be Good Friday, prompts falling on that day shall be settled on the Thursday previous. ristmas Day falls on Monday, prompts falling on that day shall be extended to the Wednesday following, but if Christmas Day falls on Tuesday, Wednesday, Thursday, or y, prompts falling on that day shall be settled on the day previous.

Rule H. The establishment, or attempted establishment of a "corner", or participation directly or indirectly in either, being detrimental to the interest of the Exchange, Committee shall, if in their opinion a "corner" has been or is in the course of being established, have power to investigate the matter and to take whatever action it ders proper to restore equilibrium between supply and demand. Any member or members may be required to give such information as is in his or their possession relative matter under investigation.

Rule J. (Options). On the day on which notice is due, the holder of the option shall, except in cases to which Rule C applies, declare in writing before 11.30 a.m. ner he exercises or abandons the option, and if he fails to make such declaration the option shall be considered as abandoned. Options (subject to Rule F above) may be red for less than the total optional quantity in quantities of 25 tonnes for Copper (Higher Grade, Standard Cathodes or Fire Refined), 5 tonnes for Standard Tin and High e Tin, 25 tonnes for Standard Lead, 25 tonnes for Standard Zinc, 25 tonnes for Aluminium, 6 tonnes for Primary Nickel and 10,000 troy ounces for Silver, or multiples of, only one declaration against each contract being allowed. In cases to which Rule C applies the price fixed by the Committee, at which outstanding contracts are to be d, shall equally apply to all option contracts; and all options shall be automatically determined, and be deemed to have been either exercised or abandoned, according as rices may be in favour of or against the defaulter and whether the defaulter be the seller or the buyer of an option, and the option money shall be brought into account. In acts with optional prompts, the price which shall be taken as the basis of settlement shall be the settlement price fixed by the Committee under Rule C for the prompt most rable to the holder of the option.

Rule K. (Clearing). All contracts made between Members of the London Metal Exchange who are entitled to deal in the Ring, either for Copper (Higher Grade, ard Cathodes or Fire Refined), Tin (Standard or High Grade), Standard Lead, Standard Zinc, Aluminium, Primary Nickel or Silver, shall be settled through the ing, except when a Member insists on his right to receive cash instead of a cheque from the Member to whom he has sold, in which case the Seller shall give notice to his r before 11.30 a.m. on the market day preceding the settling day, and such transactions shall then be exempted from settlement through the Clearing. The Rules governing earing of all contracts shall be those in existence at the time fixed for the fulfilment of the contract. Copies of such rules may be obtained from the Secretary of the ange.

Rule L. In case of strikes, lock-outs or other unforeseen contingencies in London or other authorised port or point of delivery, which prevent or delay the discharge r warehousing of Copper (Higher Grade, Standard Cathodes or Fire Refined), Tin (Standard or High Grade), Standard Lead, Standard Zinc, Aluminium, Primary el and/or Silver, the Seller may be allowed to postpone delivery if he can prove to the satisfaction of the Committee (of which proof the Committee shall be the sole judge) e does not hold available metal in warehouse or vault with which to fulfil his contracts and that he has metal of the requisite quality which has arrived in London or any authorised port or point of delivery at least ten days prior to the earliest prompt for which relief is asked, or has metal of the requisite quality in his works, but the delivery, arge and/or warehousing of which is prevented or delayed as aforesaid. He must also deposit with the Secretary of the Exchange such sums as the Committee may require ot exceeding £5 per tonne in the case of Copper, Lead, Zinc and Aluminium, £10 per tonne in the case of Tin and Primary Nickel and £5 per thousand troy ounces in the of Silver. No interest will be allowed on deposits, which will be returned after delivery of Warrants. Should his application be passed by the Committee, he shall deposit nents or other proof to the satisfaction of the Committee with the Secretary of the Exchange, who shall issue Certificates for Copper, Lead, Zinc and Aluminium in tities of 25 tonnes, Certificates for Tin in quantities of 5 tonnes, Certificates for Nickel in quantities of 6 tonnes and Certificates for Silver in quantities of 10,000 troy s. The Seller shall deliver these Certificates to his Buyer. The Certificates will then constitute a good delivery on the Clearing within the period stated thereon and ences must be settled on the prompt day. The holder of a Certificate must present it to the firm named thereon not later than 2.30 p.m. on the day following that on which eives notice in writing from his Seller that the Warrant for the actual Copper, Tin, Lead, Zinc, Aluminium, Nickel or Silver is ready. He must take up the Warrant against ent at the settlement price fixed on the preceding market day, receiving or paying any difference between this and the price mentioned on the Certificate. In the event of ice on the Certificate being above or below the settlement price operative on the day of delivery the receiver shall pay or be paid the amount of any difference. No other ents shall pass except against delivery of the actual Warrant. In case of any dispute, the Committee's ruling to be final. A fee of £5 to be paid by the Applicants for each ficate issued.

FIGURE 4. Sample LME contract rules.

ARBITRATION

Rule 1. **All disputes arising out of or in relation to contracts subject to the Rules and Regulations of the London Metal Exchange shall be referred to arbitration as herei provided. The Executive Secretary of the Committee of the London Metal Exchange (hereinafter referred to as "the Secretary") shall be notified of such disputes in writing ar party first notifying the difference shall at the time of such notification deposit with the Metal Market & Exchange Co. Ltd., the sum of £100. All such disputes shall be refer two arbitrators, one to be appointed by each party to the difference from the Arbitration Panel of the London Metal Exchange, such arbitrators having power to appoint a arbitrator from the Panel and having all the powers conferred on arbitrators by the Arbitration Act 1950 or any statutory modifications thereof for the time being in force Secretary shall be notified in writing by each party of the appointment of the arbitrators. The arbitration and any Appeal made pursuant to Rule 8 of these Rules from the A of the Arbitrators to the Committee shall take place at the London Metal Exchange (unless mutually agreed by the Arbitrators and the parties to the dispute that the venue s be elsewhere in England or Wales) and English procedure and law shall be applied thereto.**

Rule 2. Persons eligible for appointment to the Arbitration Panel shall be members of the Exchange, their partners or co-directors (as the case may be) or members o staff. Appointment to and removal from the Panel shall be made, at their sole discretion, by the Committee of the London Metal Exchange who will also be responsib maintaining a panel of sufficient size.

Rule 3. In the event of either party to the difference (*a*) failing to appoint an arbitrator, or (*b*) failing to give notice in writing or by cable of such appointment to rea other party within 14 days after receiving written or cabled notice from such other party of the appointment of an arbitrator (any notice by either party being given to the either by cable or by registered post addressed to the usual place of business of such other party), or (*c*) in the case of death, refusal to act, or incapacity of an arbitrator, upon written or cabled request of either party an arbitrator shall be appointed from the said Arbitration Panel by the Committee of the London Metal Exchange.

Rule 4. In case the two arbitrators appointed as aforesaid, whether originally or by way of substitution, shall not within three calendar months after the appointment arbitrator last appointed deliver their Award in writing, or choose a third arbitrator, then the said Committee on the written request of either party shall appoint a arbitrator selected from the said Arbitration Panel to act with the two aforesaid arbitrators.

Rule 5. The Award in writing of the arbitrators or any two of them shall be made and delivered in triplicate to the Secretary within a period of three calendar months the date of the acceptance of the appointment by the arbitrator last appointed.

Rule 6. Every Award made pursuant to any provision of this Rule shall be conclusive and binding on the parties to the arbitration, subject to appeal as herei mentioned.

Rule 7. The procedure upon an arbitration shall be as follows:

(*a*) Within a period of 21 days after the appointment of the second of the two arbitrators so appointed, each party shall deliver to the arbitrators and to other a statement of case in writing with the originals, or copies, of any documents referred to therein. All such documents to be in the English langu accompanied by certified translations into English.

(*b*) If either party shall make default in delivering such statements and documents (due consideration being given to time occupied by mails) the arbit shall proceed with the case on the statement before them, provided always that, in the sole discretion of the arbitrators, an extension of time m allowed for the delivery of such statements and documents.

(*c*) The arbitrators shall appoint a day for a hearing within 28 days, or such further time as the arbitrators shall in their sole discretion allow after the exp the 21 days in accordance with Rule 7(*a*), and shall give due notice in writing thereof to the parties, who may, and if required by the arbitrators shall, a and shall submit to examination by the arbitrators and produce such books and documents as the arbitrators may require. Each party shall be entit produce verbal evidence before the arbitrators.

(*d*) Neither Counsel nor Solicitor shall be briefed to appear for either party without the consent of the arbitrators.

(*e*) The arbitrators may engage legal or other assistance.

(*f*) The arbitrators may adjourn the hearing from time to time, giving due notice in writing to the parties of the resumed hearing, and the arbitrators m they think fit, proceed with such a resumed hearing in the absence of either party or of both parties.

(*g*) Where any change takes place in the constitution of the tribunal of arbitrators, either by substitution or otherwise, the new tribunal shall appoint a d the hearing which shall be not later than 28 days, nor earlier than 7 days, after the change. Each party, if desiring to do so, may submit an Am Statement of Case, with a copy to the other party, which must reach the new tribunal within seven days of its appointment.

(*h*) In the event of a third arbitrator being appointed, the provisions contained in Section 9 Sub-Section 1 of the Arbitration Act 1950 shall not apply reference.

(*i*) The cost of the arbitration shall be at the sole discretion of the arbitrators. The arbitrators shall fix the amount of their remuneration. The Award shall separately the amount of such costs and remuneration and by whom they shall be paid and whether the whole or any part of the deposit referred to in 1 of these Rules shall be returned to the party lodging the same or be forfeited. In the event of either or both parties having been granted permission t arbitrators to be legally represented at the hearing the arbitrators may take into consideration any legal costs which have been incurred.

(*j*) The Award shall be deposited with the Secretary who shall forthwith give notice of receipt thereof in writing to both parties, and a copy of such Award be delivered to both parties on payment by either party of the costs specified in the Award, which payment shall not affect any provision of the A

(*k*) In the event that after the deposit referred to in Rule 1 of these Rules has been made the parties to the arbitration shall (i) settle their differences, (ii) proceed as directed by the arbitrators under sub-clause (*c*) of this Rule, (iii) fail to take up the Award within 28 clear days of notification being given sub-clause (*j*) of this Rule, such deposit shall be forfeited.

(*l*) At the time of issuing their Award, all statements and all documents lodged with the arbitrators shall be delivered by them to the Secretary, by whom shall be retained until the expiration of the time for giving notice of appeal, as hereafter mentioned, after which the Secretary shall, unless there sh such appeal, return them to the parties concerned.

Rule 8. Either party shall have the right to appeal against the Award to the Committee of the London Metal Exchange.

Rule 9. The method of appeal against the Award shall be as follows:

(*a*) The party making the appeal shall (i) within 21 days of the date of the Award give notice in writing of such appeal to the Secretary, and to the other and shall at the same time state the grounds for appeal, (ii) deposit with the Secretary the sum of £200, and in addition the sum, if any, which sh payable under the Award by the Appellant.

(*b*) Upon the receipt of such Notice of Appeal the Committee shall within 4 weeks nominate not less than five members, (hereinafter called "the A Committee") to hear the Appeal. Members of the Appeal Committee shall be members of the Committee of the London Metal Exchange and/or me of the Board of the Metal Market & Exchange Co. Ltd.

(*c*) The procedure on appeal shall as far as possible be similar to that above provided for the original hearing, except that all statements and docu delivered to the Secretary under Rule 7(*l*) shall be laid before the Appeal Committee, who may, however, require such further statement or stateme other information or documents from either or both of the parties as the Appeal Committee may think necessary. The provisions of Rule 7(*k*) shall ap like manner to the deposit referred to in sub-paragraph (*a*) (ii) of this Rule as the deposit in connection with the original hearing.

(*d*) The decision in writing of the majority of the Appeal Committee (which latter shall not at any time number less than five) shall be final and binding parties, and the Appeal Committee shall also decide whether the whole or any part of the said deposit of £200 shall be returned to the Appellant forfeited.

(*e*) The Appeal Committee shall have the same discretion regarding costs as is given to the arbitrators under Rule 7(*i*) and shall fix the amount of remuneration and direct by whom it shall be paid.

(*f*) All statements and all documents lodged with the Appeal Committee shall together with the Award be deposited by them with the Secretary by whom shall be retained until the costs and fees specified in the Award have been paid by either party. On payment, which shall not affect any provision Award, a copy of the Award shall be delivered to both parties and all documents returned to the parties concerned.

FIGURE 4. Continued.

when they mature. This leaves customers free to open trades with one member and liquidate them with another. Such a facility is important in a principals' market where all the business is not done by open outcry and a member offering an attractive sales price might not be a competitive buyer when the customer wants to liquidate.

TRADING LIMITS. Unlike the U.S. exchanges, the LME has no daily price limits. In the United States, where a significant part of the volume is from the speculative public, price limits provide a cooling-off period and allow brokers to update margin deposits. But margins on the LME have never been a preeminent consideration because on the LME there is a strong merchant orientation, and merchants tend to benefit from price dislocations; and the LME is a principals' market, where traditionally members have dealt with each other on an ongoing basis.

The existence of this completely "free" market has been a comfort to American brokers and traders, who know that there is a market on which they can lay off risk when the U.S. markets are locked at the limit.

COMMISSIONS. Commissions on the LME are not handled as they are on U.S. exchanges or on other U.K. markets. Rather than charging "round-turn" commissions, LME commissions are typically charged "one way" when a trade is opened and again when it is closed. Commissions are stated as a part of a percentage of the face value of the contract price (e.g., $\frac{1}{16}$, $\frac{1}{8}$, $\frac{1}{2}$, etc.) rather than as a fixed amount per lot, so transaction costs increase and decrease with commodity prices. These differences can be significant. Being a principals' market, LME commissions have always been negotiable, both in size and method of payment.

MEMBERSHIP AND MANAGEMENT. There are two classes of LME trading membership: *ring dealing* and *nonring dealing*. Ring-dealing members are entitled to trade on the exchange floor; nonring-dealing members are not. Nonring-dealing members can issue LME contracts, but do not enjoy the financial guarantees or have the credit requirements of ring-dealing members.

Unlike the U.S. exchanges, which are governed by a Board of Directors, the LME is run by its *directors* and by a *committee of subscribers*. The committee was formed early in 1880 as a result of a dispute between the directors and the subscribers. At that time the directors decided to abolish the formal rings and have only an informal kerb. The general membership, through the newly formed committee, objected and the rings continued. The committee has kept its important role as a counterweight to the directors in the management of the exchanges.

Joint action between the directors and the committee is required in many important areas, specifically, the election of new members and agreement to new rules or amendments. The *directors* are responsible for assuring the financial capability of each of the members and, through the Metal Market Exchange Company Ltd., to provide the services to run the markets. The *committee of subscribers* can be likened to a strong and independent executive committee of a corporation's Board of Directors. It is responsible for the day-to-day running of the exchange.

THE LONDON BULLION BROKERS

Although the daily meeting of London's leading bullion dealers[1] does not constitute a futures market, it is an important part of the process of setting the world's precious metal prices. Twice a day the brokers closet themselves in a closed meeting at N. M. Rothschild's and produce two daily "fixings" for gold. Silver is fixed only once. The price is a consensus of the five brokers and is the level at which most of their bids and offers would be cleared at that moment. The fixing price influences all the other precious metal markets and, in turn, reacts to them. Nowadays the second gold fixing, which takes place when the U.S. markets are open, is becoming more important, reflecting the fact that the New York and Chicago markets have become the leading price benchmarks.

THE LONDON GOLD FUTURES MARKET

After what must be the longest, most difficult gestation period of any new futures contract, gold futures trading opened on the London Gold Futures Market in April 1982. This exchange is a joint effort of the LME and the Bullion Brokers, each of whom have three members on the Board of Directors. The Gold Exchange trades on its own floor and clears its trades through the International Commodities Clearing House, which works very much like a U.S. clearing association, as will be discussed in detail later.

The gold exchange contract was initially denominated in sterling, but after a disappointing start, was changed to dollars. It is now similar to the U.S. and Hong Kong contracts, which means that there is now a dollar-denominated gold contract trading somewhere in the world at virtually every hour of the day (see Table 2).

The London markets are open for about 5 hours before New York or Chicago. During this time, London dealers will make a dollar-denominated *forward physical market* in gold and other commodities. When the U.S. market opens, it is possible to exchange this physical forward contract for a U.S. futures contract at the same price. This is done through the *Exchange for Physical (EFP)* mechanism. The trade is then margined and ultimately liquidated in the United States, like any other trade.

THE LONDON COMMODITY EXCHANGE GROUP OF COMMODITIES

The LCE structure is much like New York's Commodity Exchange Center. It is a confederation of exchanges, including the following:

the London Cocoa Terminal Market Association Ltd.
the Coffee Terminal Market Association of London Ltd.

1. N.M. Rothschild & Sons Ltd., Johnson Matthey (Bankers) Ltd., Sharps Pixley Ltd., Mocatta & Goldschmidt Ltd., Samual Montagu & Co. Ltd.

TABLE 2. International Gold Exchanges[a]

Country	Exchange	Quotations	Trading Hours
Canada	Winnipeg Commodity Exchange	U.S. dollars	0925–1430
United States	Chicago Board of Trade	U.S. dollars	0900–1430
	Chicago Mercantile Exchange IMM	U.S. dollars	0905–1430
	Commodity Exchange of New York	U.S. dollars	0900–1430
	MidAmerica Exchange	U.S. dollars	0905–1440
United Kingdom	London Gold Futures Market	U.S. dollars	0430–0720
Singapore	Singapore Gold Exchange	U.S. dollars	2200–0130 0330–0530
Hong Kong	Hong Kong Commodity Exchange	U.S. dollars	2100–2400 0230–0530
Japan	Tokyo	Japanese yen	2300–0600 (six fixings)
Australia	Sydney Futures Exchange	Australian dollars	0130–0330 0500–0700

[a]Additional forward markets exist in Zurich, Luxemburg and The Netherlands.

the United Terminal Sugar Market Association Ltd.
the London Rubber Terminal Market Association Ltd.
the London Wool Terminal Market Association Ltd.
the GAFTA Soya Bean Meal Futures Association Ltd.
the International Petroleum Exchange of London Ltd.
the London Vegetable Oil Terminal Market Association Ltd.

Each exchange has its own board and the chairman of each exchange is invited to serve on the LCE Board. While each exchange is fairly independent, with its own rules and regulations, general policy matters are referred to the LCE Board.

There are two categories of membership in the LCE markets:

1. *Floor Members* (of each exchange), who have full voting rights, are limited to EEC companies, and are permitted to trade on the exchange floor.
2. *Associate Members*, who have restricted voting rights and who must trade through floor members, but who may issue exchange contracts in their own name.

The LCE markets are similar to the U.S. exchanges rather than to the LME. All LCE contracts are cleared by the International Commodities Clearing House; all LCE trades must be cleared. The LCE have delivery months rather than value dates, continuous trading (except for a lunch break), liquidation upon offset rather than upon contract maturation, and published price and volume information. Material tendered for physical delivery averages less than 1% of volume traded.

One noteworthy difference from the U.S. exchanges is the handling of daily price limits. Daily limits are points at which the market is temporarily closed for a brief "cooling-off period." When prices reach a limit up or down, trading stops so brokers have a chance to straighten their books, issue margin calls, and reconcile errors and discrepancies. The limit closings are typically for half an hour, but the time can be extended at the discretion of the *Call Chairman*, part of whose job is to assure an orderly market. Trading then resumes with *no limit*.

On all London exchanges, except the LME, commissions are stated as a flat sterling amount rather than as a percentage of the contract value. On the LME, commissions are negotiable. On the other exchanges, there are official published rates; however, discounting has been a general practice for some years. Commissions will be officially negotiable now that discussions on this matter with the EEC have been concluded.

The sugar market differs from the other LCE markets in allowing after-hours or kerb trading to permit arbitrage between London and New York until the New York market closes. Rubber also has kerb trading. Trades done on the kerb are cleared in the next day's transactions. So although London sugar and rubber futures contracts can be traded off the exchange for part of the day, all contracts must be registered with the exchange and entered with the clearinghouse. In this respect, the LCE contracts follow the practice of the U.S. exchanges.

The London rubber contract has a unique delivery: the contract is either for 15 metric tons, deliverable in any calendar quarter, or in three 5-ton contracts for single nearby months. In the quarterly contract, delivery is for 5 tons in each month of the quarter. For example, the January–March delivery is really three lots of 5 tons deliverable in each of the months January, February, and March.

The gas/oil contract on the International Petroleum Exchange and the #2 heating oil contract on the New York Mercantile Exchange have virtually identical delivery terms and specifications. To facilitate trading between the markets, the two are linked by wire and share an on-line video price display.

THE LONDON INTERNATIONAL FINANCIAL FUTURES EXCHANGE

London's traditional place as a world financial center coupled with the great success of the U.S. financial futures markets encouraged London to establish its own financial futures exchange in 1982. The LIFFE, its contracts, and trading hours are designed to encourage arbitrage with other financial markets. Like the U.S. exchanges, LIFFE has futures contracts being traded, or soon to begin, in both interest rates and currencies. These include

Interest rates:

- 3-month Eurodollar deposits

3-month sterling deposits
20-year gilt (based on 20-year U.K. Government stock)
Currencies (against the dollar):
Sterling
Swiss franc
Deutsche mark
Yen

LIFFE clears its trades through the ICCH.

Unlike the U.S. exchanges, LIFFE chose to establish its operations independently of the commodity futures markets. The rationale was that the instruments and market participants differ from those in the commodity industry, therefore a new exchange, separate from the existing markets, was required. This judgment seems to have been accurate, for the initial memberships represented a spectrum of banks, merchant banks, commodity and stock brokers, and commodity and security dealers. In the United States it took several years for the markets to develop such broadly based participation.

LONDON GRAIN FUTURES MARKETS

There are a few U.K. exchanges, now under the supervision of the Grain and Feed Trade Association (GAFTA) that were established to serve the needs of the U.K. farmer, whose contracts have been adapted to fit European Economic Community (EEC) needs. These include

the London Grain Futures Market (wheat & barley)
the Soya Bean Meal Futures Association Ltd.
the London Potato Futures Association Ltd.

Clearing on the wheat and barley exchanges is through the GAFTA Clearing House. However, recent GAFTA markets such as potatoes and soya bean meal use the ICCH facilities. Operating methods are similar to the U.S. markets. Delivery terms adhere to EEC commercial practice. As markets with primarily a domestic following, they have not enjoyed significant volume or open interest.

Until now, Europe has focused on the Chicago Board of Trade for its futures needs relating to grains, and of course the Board of Trade's volume, open interest, and liquidity tend to self-perpetuate it as the market of choice. However, the EEC, in aggregate, is a major grain producer and it is conceivable that its business could shift to the United Kingdom, where the futures markets reflect the internal economics of the EEC more closely.

CLEARING ASSOCIATIONS AND SECURITY BACKSTOPS

All the U.K. exchanges now have some form of daily margining mechanism. The LME is policed by the London Metal Exchange Monitoring Operation (MEMO) and trades done on the LCE, LIFFE, and LGFM are cleared and margined by the International Commodities Clearing House (ICCH). These give direct protection to member firms (as do their U.S. counterparts). By assuring financial performance among the members, they also help insulate nonmembers from a member's failure. Direct protection to nonmembers is very different in the United States and the United Kingdom.

MARGINING ON THE LME. The LME is the only major futures exchange in the world with no associated clearinghouse. As a principals' market, trades are backed only by the capital and credit of ring dealers who make the contract. If they fail, contract parties have no recourse except to the receiver and to a share of the funds available from the Members' Compensation Fund. In addition, in the wake of a member's default, the committee is empowered to make a call on the membership to make the affected members whole.

In point of fact, there have been very few failures among ring-dealing members. Beyond their capital, members are backed by parent companies and bank guarantees. To become a member, a firm must be well-known and must have a strong reputation, in addition to meeting the financial requirements. A major bankruptcy did take place in the early 1970s and highlighted the members' interdependence and vulnerability to a chain reaction of failures. In response, the LME revamped its security mechanisms.

It used to be that if the market moved adversely between the contract and maturation dates, no margin was called for—cash changed hands only on the value date, as was (and still is) the norm in principal-to-principal forward contracts. As a price move progressed, it left the exchange and increasingly vulnerable to default by a weak member on the wrong side of the market. Margining assures that each member pays as he or she goes, but may introduce cash demands not normally associated with a principal's market.

The MEMO system was established as a compromise solution. Based on the member's net worth, each member is assigned a credit line. Within the bounds of this line, the member can deal free of margins. However, if the loss in the member's position (the sum of its own positions along with those of its brokerage customers) exceeds the member's credit line, the member will be called for additional funds or security to make up the difference.

The margin calculations are performed by the computer bureau of the ICCH. Members submit their trades daily to the ICCH for evaluation. If a member exceeds its credit line the *Monitoring Committee* is notified. At the discretion of the LME Monitoring Committee, the additional security required may be more than the deficit. If the member does not replace the security, that member is declared in default. While the possibility of a chain reaction of deficits remains, MEMO substantially buffers its potential impact. Hence, members can deal free of margins within predetermined parameters, so the cash flow implications of a full margining system are minimized. At the same time, the membership is spared catastrophic surprises.

All told, the financial integrity of the LME is greater today than it was a decade ago. LME members now face the possibility of a margin call resulting from clients' positions, so they are more conservative in offering credit lines. Like U.S. brokerage firms, LME members often require original margin deposits and variation margin payments.

Whereas there used to be a great difference between United States and LME margining practice, they are now becoming more similar. In both cases, with the U.S. shift from "good to the last drop" to limited liability clearing, members' liability to other members is limited, and exposure is minimized by variation margin payments, backstopped by large but limited bank lines.

There are still important differences: the U.S. clearing mechanisms have the security of original margin deposits, which are not mandatory on the LME, and MEMO allows credit lines, whereas U.S. systems do not. Even so, the trend toward increased security in London and easing of security in the United States is bringing the systems closer.

MARGINING ICCH COMMODITIES. While U.S. clearing associations clear the trades of one exchange, the ICCH covers all the U.K. exchanges except the LME (and several overseas exchanges as well). It functions very much like a U.S. clearinghouse—it interposes itself between all buyers and sellers, and it collects original margin deposits on net positions and settles variation margin daily (or more often if markets are volatile). However, there are a few key differences.

1. *Clearing for Profit.* United States clearing bodies are not-for-profit corporations whose shares are held by the clearing members. In contrast, the ICCH is owned by a group of major banks and has a profitable operating history. Being a money-making venture, the ICCH is aggressive in seeking new clearing business. In addition to the London exchanges, it clears for the Kuala Lumpur Exchange and the Hong Kong Gold Exchange, and participates in the clearing of the Sydney and Paris Exchanges.

2. *Bank Guarantees.* In contrast to the U.S. clearing associations, the ICCH permits the use of bank guarantees and letters of credit to cover variation margin calls and original margin deposits.

MARGINING AND SOFTWARE SERVICES. Like any modern clearinghouse, the ICCH has a substantial computer capability. Unlike the others, it uses this capability to sell members on-line margin reports for themselves and for their individual clients, and will prepare confirmations, P&S accounts, and other statements.

INTEREST PAYMENT VERSUS EQUITY DISBURSEMENT. In addition to clearing fees and income from software services, the ICCH earns interest revenue. The ICCH gives credit and pays interest on equity in open positions, but it does not disburse unrealized profits. Interest on equity balances is at a competitive rate, with the ICCH earning a small spread between what it pays members and the prevailing interbank rates.

UNDERLYING SUPPORT. ICCH members are liable only for their own obligations. Should a member default, the deficit is assumed by the clearinghouse. The ICCH, in turn, is owned by a syndicate of the U.K. clearing banks. Like the U.S. clearinghouses, in the late 1970s the ICCH's backing came under question. It was then owned by the United Dominions Trust (UDT). UDT's capital had been gradually eroding at a time when futures volume and price volatility were soaring. As a result in 1981 the Bank of England arranged new backing by organizing the bank consortium that now owns the ICCH.

The trend in the United States and the United Kingdom is clearly toward increased reliance on the major banks to underwrite the clearinghouse. In the case of the ICCH, the dependence is direct; in the case of the LME and those U.S. exchanges where members can use letters of credit or guarantees to support their commitments, reliance is indirect but, nonetheless, critically important.

LEGAL AND REGULATORY SAFEGUARDS. The security of nonmember clients is improved by clearing and margining mechanisms, but only indirectly, to the extent that members' liabilities are kept current.

In the United States customers are protected directly in several ways. If a customer feels aggrieved, the customer can petition for arbitration under the aegis of the exchange or can take his or her case to the courts. These protections are also available to the client doing business on a U.K. exchange.

1. *CFTC* vs. *the Bank of England.* While the U.S. futures markets are regulated by the Commodity Futures Trading Commission there is no U.K equivalent. The CFTC conducts customer reparations procedures, polices broker registration and minimum capital requirements, and enforces the consumer protection laws promulgated by Congress. It audits commission merchants, trading advisors, and pool operators. If it senses a violation, it can issue cease-and-desist orders. It can take its case to court and frequently acts as *amicus curiae*.

The closest U.K. equivalents are the Bank of England and the Department of Trade. The Bank and the Department of Trade are politically independent and their specialists are career officers with extensive experience and in-depth knowledge of the industry. The Bank focuses on matters that affect foreign exchange, whereas the Department of Trade is more concerned with internal regulation. Both have accrued considerable informal administrative power, and the industry depends on their knowledgeability in overseeing the futures business.

The U.S. and the U.K. bodies have fundamentally different styles of governing. Whereas the CFTC's mandate is defined and circumscribed by the letter of its regulations and by specified bureaucratic processes, the Bank of England and the Department of Trade have broad discretionary powers.

2. *Differences in the Law.* In the United States, customers' funds must be kept segregated from the broker's capital in a special account. Segregation is policed by the CFTC and violation of customer fund segregation is fraud. If a broker should default, the receiver can pay out segregated funds immediately and in full because they are not part of the broker's assets.

In the United Kingdom, the law discourages rather than requires segregation. A broker can separate customers' funds from his or her own capital if the broker chooses. Up to now, if a broker went bankrupt, the receiver would pierce the separation and treat the customers' funds as part of the broker's capital. Customers became general creditors. However, new regulations that would allow effective segregation are being formulated. Once effective, segregation will be similar in the United States and the United Kingdom.

3. *Regulatory Powers of the Exchanges.* United States and U.K. futures markets share vulnerability to manipulation. Material available for delivery is small relative to total volume and open interest, so the markets are susceptible to squeezes and corners. The U.K. exchanges have powers similar to the U.S.

markets in preventing manipulation and, like the U.S. exchanges, have forced liquidations and increased original margins when necessary. Like the CFTC, the Bank of England takes an active interest in such exchange action (as it does in any situation that could disrupt the normal flow of commerce and finance in the United Kingdom).

A BRIEF WORD ABOUT OPTIONS

For decades, exchange-traded options on futures contracts have been an important part of the London markets. For the last 10 years, the U.S. exchanges have tried to follow suit; they have now established a pilot program in options on a few commodity and financial futures contracts. The LME and LCE have option contracts associated with all of their commodities, while LIFFE and the gold exchange have no option contracts yet. The other differences between U.S. and London options are:

1. *London Options not Transferable.* The major difference between London and the new U.S. options is that in England, options cannot be transferred—a put or call cannot be resold to a third party. It can be hedged (or blocked) by an offsetting futures trade, but must be held until exercised. Grantors of options can buy options to hedge their sales, but the purchase and sale will not liquidate. Options will offset but will be liquidated only upon maturation. Because London options are not transferable, the trading of in-the-money and out-of-the-money options is not possible. The exception to this rule is the United Terminal Sugar Market Association. The rules for London sugar have been changed. As of March 1, 1983 the options will be transferable and traded in much the same way as U.S. exchange-traded options. The main differences will be

a. The deliveries traded—in London, options can be traded only in December, March, and August months.

b. Margining—in London, the option buyer (taker) pays his or her premium when the buyer exercises (declares) or abandons the option.

On the U.S. exchanges, the buyer pays his premium immediately. The premium passes through the clearinghouse and is credited to the grantor's account, but is offset by an original margin requirement equal to the premium (plus a further original margin deposit, the size of which depends on whether the granted position is naked).

In both cases, the grantor does not receive the option until it is exercised or until it expires. However, in the United States, the exchanges permit original margin deposits to be held in Treasury bills, so the grantor has the benefit of earning interest. For purposes of valuation, London options should trade at a discount reflecting present value.

If the new sugar option contract is successful, the other markets will probably shift to transferable contracts.

2. *Hedging Versus Exercising an Option.* In London, option buyers can exercise their options at any time during the holding period but generally hold the options until they mature to benefit from the full-time value. Profits can be locked in just as effectively by selling futures against a *call* or buying against a

put as by reselling the option. In effect, *buying against a put* converts it to a *call* and *selling against a call* converts it to a *put:*

call: downside exposure limited to premium, unlimited upside potential

put: upside exposure limited to premium, unlimited downside potential

call plus futures short: no upside potential because call hedged by short. Unlimited downside potential on short position limited only by cost of premium on call.

put plus futures long: no downside potential because put hedged by long. Unlimited upside potential on long position limited only by cost of premium on put.

Since puts can be readily converted to calls and vice versa, puts and calls generally trade at roughly equal premiums. The difference is generally no more than the cost of a commission. *Double options* can be created by hedging half of a call or put position. Only one side of a double option can be exercised.

Trades against London options require no margins, so hedging an option entails no more risk than selling it, and trading against an option has the advantage of maintaining the profit potential until the option expires. Each trade against an option entails some commission, but details vary among brokers and exchanges. The disadvantage of trading against (or hedging) an option rather than selling it is that selling an unexpired option allows the seller to recapture some of the premium, but trading against it does not.

Since profitable options must be exercised, taking profits requires, first, exercising the option to receive the futures contract and then liquidating the futures contract.

SUMMARY: ARBITRAGE BETWEEN THE U.S. AND U.K. MARKETS

The London/U.S. arbitrage is conceptually the same as a domestic intermarket spread, that is, equal and opposite positions, established simultaneously on different exchanges, but in similar price-related contracts, tend to move in parallel. Several factors cause differences in arbitrage spreads:

1. *Market Orientation.* For instance, the U.S. coffee and cocoa businesses focus on Central and Latin American sources. London looks primarily to African growths. A strike in Ghana or port congestion in Kenya will enhance London prices relative to New York. Poor Brazilian crops will strengthen U.S. prices.

2. *Spread Discrepancies.* Shifting differentials between time periods create opportunities for "straddle arbitrage" or offsetting positions in different deliveries.

3. *Changes in Convenience Costs.* Shifts in freight, storage, and other costs and changes in duties and tariffs move the arbitrage.

4. *Foreign Exchange Fluctuations.* Currency fluctuations between the dollar and sterling can cause major arbitrage shifts.

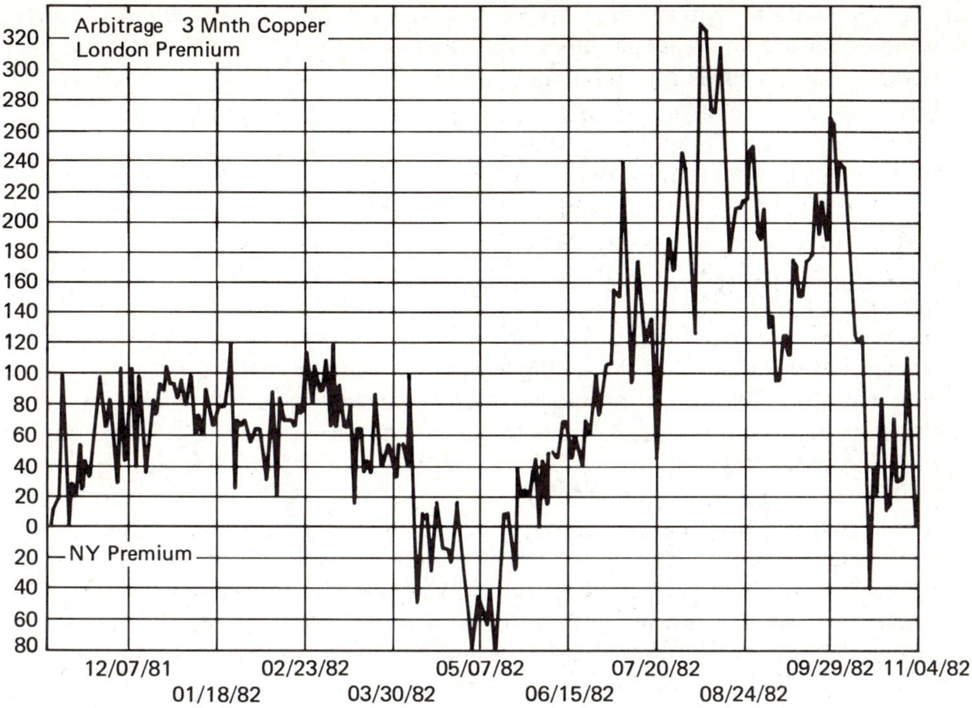

FIGURE 5. Arbitrage—3-month copper.

Arbitrage can be done to take advantage of immediate market aberrations or in anticipation of longer-term differential movements.

Straddle arbitrage is a further refinement. When spread differences in London diverge from the United States, it can be profitable to establish the arbitrage in different deliveries. If the markets are in a normal carrying charge mode (known in England as a *contango*) and the spread is wider in London, selling a distant London delivery and buying a nearby U.S. delivery might make sense. Inverted markets (or *backwardations*) are more difficult to analyze but the same principles generally apply. Other considerations in United States-London arbitrage are:

1. *Contract Disparities.* The sizes of contracts in London and the United States are sometimes different, so positions have to be adjusted. For example, London silver contracts are 10,000 troy oz, whereas U.S. contracts are for 5,000 and 1,000 troy oz; depending on a U.S. contract, 2 or 10 U.S. lots would have to be executed to offset each London lot.

Similarly, many U.K. commodities are quoted in *pounds sterling per ton,* whereas their U.S. equivalents are in *cents per lb.* These disparities have to be brought to a common denominator to calculate the arbitrage.

In the case of the LME, deliveries are by value date whereas the U.S. exchanges trade by month. In other cases, the delivery month might be different. The differences in time must be corrected to make the values of the positions equivalent.

Finally, to make the positions comparable, currency has to be converted. For a commodity arbitrage 3 months forward, the 3-month currency rate is used to make the positions equivalent. Exchange rate fluctuations between the sterling and the dollar are so great that unless the currency risk is hedged, the commodity arbitrage position turns into a currency play.

2. *Cash Flow Considerations.* Because margining practices in the United States and United Kingdom are different, cash flow considerations can be important. On the LME, unrealized equity in a position is not paid out until maturation. In the ICCH commodities, variation margin credits earn interest, but can be collected only when the position is liquidated. (It is possible to draw down ICCH balances by liquidating and reestablishing a position, but this adds to transaction costs.)

Since they are on different exchanges, the legs of an arbitrage position are margined independently. If the losing leg of an arbitrage position is in the United States it requires variation margin payments, but equity in the winning London leg cannot be drawn down to cover the U.S. call. As a result, arbitrage can be margin-intensive if the adverse position is in the United States, so it is generally done by well-financed professionals.

There is a way that hedger and speculator alike can participate effectively in the arbitrage: at any one time, in price-related markets, there is only one best purchase or one best sale. When London seems to be at a high premium, it is possible to earn the arbitrage differential by selling in the United Kingdom rather than the U.S. market (or buying a London market instead of a U.S. market when London seems comparatively cheap). The flexibility of having an alternative market gives all market participants the opportunity to attain the best price available.

CHAPTER 5

REGULATION OF THE FUTURES INDUSTRY

CONTENTS

FOREWORD 3

Commodity Options 3
Leverage Transactions 3
Private Right of Action 4
CFTC Emergency Powers 4
New Registration Categories 4
Commodity Trading Advisors and Commodity Pool Operation 5
State Enforcement Powers 5
Enhanced Authority of National Futures Association (NFA) 5
SEC/CFTC Jurisdictional Agreement 5

CURRENT FRAMEWORK OF COMMODITY REGULATION 6

The Creation of the Modern Commodity Exchange Act 6
The Commmodity Futures Trading Commission 8
Regulation of Contract Markets 12
Regulation of Trading Professionals 17
Regulation of Trading 24
Remedying Violations of the CEA 29

CURRENT REGULATORY ISSUES 33

The Role of the National Futures Association 33
Commodity Options: CFTC Pilot Program 35
CFTC Jurisdictional Issues 37
Conclusion: Regulation and Beyond 41

NOTES 42

APPENDIX 48

CHAPTER 5

REGULATION OF THE FUTURES INDUSTRY

Mark H. Mitchell
Carl N. Duncan
David M. Kozak
Stanley M. Klem

FOREWORD

The chapter entitled "Regulation of the Futures Industry" was drafted in early 1982. In January 1983 President Reagan signed into law the Futures Trading Act of 1982 (1982 Act), which expanded the authority of the Commodity Futures Trading Commission (CFTC) and made important changes to the regulatory framework for futures trading. However, publication schedules did not permit substantial revisions of the chapter to permit it to conform to the state of the law at the time of this writing. Therefore, this Foreword has been prepared to describe briefly some of the major recent developments in the regulation of the industry. In addition, the text of the chapter has been annotated where appropriate to indicate that changes have occurred in the law as described.

COMMODITY OPTIONS. In October, 1982, the CFTC's options pilot program began. Exchanges were initially permitted to offer a limited number of options on nonagricultural futures contracts, and options on nonagricultural physical commodities were then authorized as additions to the pilot program. The 1982 Act removed a prior prohibition on the trading of options on agricultural futures contracts and authorized the CFTC to establish a pilot program involving agricultural option contracts.[a] The CFTC has recently established an advisory committee to consider such a pilot program.

LEVERAGE TRANSACTIONS. As mandated by the 1982 Act, the CFTC has proposed regulations governing leverage transactions. The proposed regulations continue the moratorium on new entry into this field, propose definitions of leverage transactions, and establish a larger role for the CFTC in establishing customer

[a]CEA, §§ 4c(b) and 4c(c).

protections procedures relating to registration and capital requirements, review of sales materials, and specification of leverage contract terms.[b]

PRIVATE RIGHT OF ACTION. The 1982 Act created an express private right of action against commodity professionals whose actions injure a customer. Exclusive jurisdiction over such actions was conferred on the federal courts, and recovery of actual financial damages was specified as the exclusive remedy in such actions.[c] Arbitration and reparations remain as alternative means of resolving customer disputes.

CFTC EMERGENCY POWERS. The authority of the CFTC to act in market emergencies was expanded under the 1982 Act to permit retroactive imposition of speculative position limits.[d]

NEW REGISTRATION CATEGORIES. The 1982 Act expanded the number of registration categories in the futures industry to include introducing brokers and associated persons of introducing brokers, commodity pool operators, and commodity trading advisors. The status of introducing broker was defined in the 1982 Act in terms of soliciting or accepting orders for futures trades without accepting money, securities, or other property or extending credit in regulation to those trades.[e] Many persons who formerly acted as "agents" of FCMs are now required to register as introducing brokers.

Introducing brokers and their associated persons will be registered and regulated by the National Futures Association.[f] Registration requires completion of an application, including evidence that minimum financial requirements have been satisfied. Two alternatives are provided for meeting the minimum financial requirements: (1) maintenance of minimum net capital of at least $20,000 or (2) execution of a guarantee agreement, in a form established by the CFTC, with an FCM that agrees to be responsible for the liabilities of the introducing broker.[g]

The 1982 Act extended the status of "associated person" to include persons who: (1) solicit or accept orders for introducing brokers; (2) solicit or accept discretionary accounts for commodity trading advisors; and (3) solicit or accept subscriptions to commodity pools for commodity pool operators.[h] The registration procedure for these new categories is virtually identical to that for associated persons of FCMs—the sponsoring entity with which the applicant seeks an association must certify the applicant's fitness, generally after a review of his or her background.[i] The sponsor is required to assume responsibility for the acts of its associated persons. An associated person may be associated with more than

[b]CEA, § 19; the proposed regulations may be found at 48 Fed. Reg. 122 (June 23, 1983), CCH ¶ 21,742.
[c]CEA, § 22(a)(1), (b)(1), and (c).
[d]CEA, § 8a(9).
[e]CEA, § 2(a)(1)(A); CFTC Reg. § 3.15.
[f]CEA, § 4(d) and 4(f); CFTC Reg. § 3.2; 48 Fed. Reg. 35159 (August 3, 1983), CCH ¶ 21,791; 48 Fed. Reg. 35248, 35259 (August 3, 1983), CCH ¶ 21,792.
[g]CFTC Reg. § 1.17 (a)(1)(ii); 48 Fed. Reg. 35248, 35261 (August 3, 1983), CCH ¶ 21,792.
[h]CEA, § 4k; CFTC Reg. §§ 3.12 and 3.16.
[i]CFTC Reg. § 3.16; 48 Fed. Reg. 35248, 35253 (August 3, 1983), CCH ¶ 21,792.

one trading advisor and/or pool operator but may be associated with only one FCM or one introducing broker at a given time.[j]

COMMODITY TRADING ADVISORS AND COMMODITY POOL OPERATORS. The 1982 Act modified the statutory definition of "commodity trading advisor" to exclude under many circumstances (1) persons rendering advice solely in connection with cash commodities, (2) employees of banks and trust companies, (3) fiduciaries of defined benefit plans regulated under the Employee Retirement Income Security Act of 1974, and (4) representatives of the electronic media.[k]

STATE ENFORCEMENT POWERS. State enforcement authority under the 1982 Act is clearly confined to enforcement of the antifraud provisions of the Commodity Exchange Act. The states are required to provide the CFTC with written notice prior to commencement of such actions, and a copy of the complaint must be provided to the CFTC after it has been filed. Moreover, the CFTC may intervene in these proceedings or appeal a decision in such proceedings, and either the CFTC or the defendant may remove such actions from state court to federal district court.[l] State actions against persons registered with the CFTC on the basis of state law are curtailed. However, all federal and state laws have been declared applicable to off-exchange transactions and to persons required to be registered with the CFTC but who are not.[m]

The scope of the authority of the states to impose substantive restrictions on the terms of commodity pool offerings was addressed in the legislative history of the 1982 Act but not in the Act itself. In September 1983, the North American Securities Administrators Association adopted guidelines for commodity pool programs which take effect on January 1, 1984. The limits of state authority in this area are still a subject of controversy at this writing.

ENHANCED AUTHORITY OF NATIONAL FUTURES ASSOCIATION (NFA). The 1982 Act directs the NFA to establish training and proficiency standards for persons affiliated with NFA members who solicit commodity transactions. Audit and enforcement programs are also required, as are standards relating to sales practices of members and their associated persons.[n]

SEC/CFTC JURISDICTIONAL AGREEMENT. The 1982 Act largely adopted legislative proposals prepared by the CFTC and the Securities and Exchange Commission (SEC) with respect to their particular jurisdictions. The CFTC retained primary responsibility for all futures trading and for all options trading on futures, including stock index futures contracts. However, the latter are required to meet requirements enunciated in the statute. Consultation with the SEC on such contracts is required, and a procedure for judicial review is now in place to resolve disagreements between the SEC and CFTC.[o]

[j] CFTC Reg. § 3.16; 48 Fed. Reg. 35248, 35255 (August 3, 1983), CCH ¶ 21,792.
[k] CEA, § 2(a)(2).
[l] CEA, § 6d.
[m] CEA, § 12(e).
[n] CEA, § 17(p).
[o] CEA, § 2(a)(1)(B).

The SEC retains regulatory responsibility for options on individual stocks and on stock indices, options on exempted securities, and options on certificates of deposit. Options on foreign currencies are to be jointly regulated; the SEC will regulate foreign currency options traded on a stock exchange, and the CFTC will regulate other options on foreign currencies. Finally, the 1982 Act confirmed that the federal securities laws apply to offers and sales of commodity pool interests.[p]

MARK H. MITCHELL
DAVID M. KOZAK

November 1983

This chapter is intended as a brief overview of the regulatory environment of the commodities industry. It is divided into two parts: (1) a discussion of the framework of commodity regulation, and (2) a review of the major issues which will affect the shape of this framework in the future. In addition, the historical development of the present legal environment is discussed in the Appendix.

This chapter is of necessity only a summary of the law affecting the industry. It would be impractical to mention every aspect of state and federal law which has an impact on the various industry participants. It should also be noted that the rules of the various commodity exchanges, other than certain major rules required by law, are not discussed. Furthermore, the topics which are treated in this chapter are discussed in general terms which do not always reflect the intricacies and technicalities which are often important in deciding how the law should be applied to a particular person or situation.

This chapter reflects the state of the law only at the time of its writing. It is important to note that commodity regulation is a rapidly changing area of the law,[1] and it is likely that substantial changes in the legal provisions discussed in this chapter will take place in the near future. In particular, the 1982 congressional reauthorization hearings for the Commodity Futures Trading Commission will likely lead to significant changes (see "Conclusion: Reauthorization and Beyond" under "Current Regulatory Issues"). Legal decisions should be made only after consulting with competent counsel, and should not be made solely on the basis of statements made in this chapter.

THE CURRENT FRAMEWORK OF COMMODITY REGULATION

THE CREATION OF THE MODERN COMMODITY EXCHANGE ACT. The legislation which underlies the scheme of commodity regulation in the United States is the Commodity Exchange Act (CEA).[2] It was enacted in 1936 (see the Appendix), but was dramatically changed by legislation known as the Commodity Futures Trading Commission Act of 1974.[3] These amendments created the Commodity Futures Trading Commission and established the current framework for federal regulation of the commodities industry. Numerous factors brought about

[p] CEA, § 4m(2).

the passage of these amendments, which completely overhauled the then-existing regulatory structure.

Hedgers' Concerns. The legislation was, in part, a response to certain concerns of persons using the commodity futures markets for hedging purposes. In the period just before 1974, the federal government had significantly reduced its practice of purchasing and stockpiling certain agricultural commodities to stabilize prices. The resulting higher degree of price risk led to greater use of the commodity markets for hedging purposes. In addition, the markets had experienced a general increase in interest in hedging as the result of the introduction of a number of new contracts. This increased use of the markets by hedgers led Congress to perceive a need for greater supervision.[4]

Concerns were also voiced over the definition of "hedging" for purposes of applying speculative limits: regulators expressed the fear that the definition was being misused by speculators, while some hedgers felt that the definition was too mechanical and did not include certain types of hedging transactions. Finally, Congress became aware of concerns expressed by hedgers over the increased cost of hedging resulting from the breakdown in some markets of the traditional relationship between cash and futures prices.[5]

Speculators' Concerns. Congress was also influenced by certain factors relating to the use of the commodity markets by speculators. The early 1970s saw many investors in the securities markets develop a new interest in speculation in commodities. In addition, a substantial amount of new speculative activity had developed in unregulated commodities and options.[6] Congressional attention focused on the potential for abuses in connection with this new surge of trading activity. Congress was also influenced by perceptions that unsophisticated investors were being lured into speculation in commodity markets. This was brought about in part by certain widely publicized instances of outright fraud in connection with sales of unregulated commodity options.[7]

Concerns Over Self-Regulation. Another factor which led to the major changes effected in the CEA was congressional concern over the adequacy of the self-regulatory programs of the exchanges. This concern resulted in part from the perception that many new market participants did not view membership in an exchange as important or even desirable. Such persons included those dealing in unregulated commodities.[8] The increasing number of lawsuits against exchanges for failure to enforce their own rules also raised doubts about the effectiveness of self-regulation.[9] In addition, the continued ability of exchanges to control their members was brought into question by a federal antitrust action against the Chicago Board of Trade.[10] This action ended the fee-setting practices of that exchange, and raised the possibility that other self-regulatory measures would be attacked as unlawful restraints on trade.

Concerns Over Existing Regulation. Congress was also aware of justifiable concerns as to whether the existing government regulatory structure was adequate to carry out its functions. The insufficient staffing of the Department of Agriculture's Commodity Exchange Authority (the agency administering the CEA) had been brought to the attention of Congress. In addition, Congress was concerned about the Commodity Exchange Authority's ability to regulate adequately the large number of new contracts. Regulatory initiatives by the states were also a cause of concern: the proliferation of actual and proposed state laws governing areas not regulated by federal law created the spectre of the lack of uniform regulation. Finally, the growing confusion concerning the distinction between securities and commodities induced Congress to take legislative action with the purpose of clarifying the issue.[11] An example of this confusion was the treatment of discretionary commodity trading accounts by some states as securities. Congress sought to resolve these problems by creating a single expert regulator for the commodities industry.

THE COMMODITY FUTURES TRADING COMMISSION. The 1974 amendments to the CEA gave the Commodity Futures Trading Commission (hereinafter referred to as "CFTC" or "Commission") the authority to administer the CEA's new regulatory scheme. Under the former regulatory structure, this administrative function had been assigned to the Department and Secretary of Agriculture and to the Commodity Exchange Authority.[12] The 1974 amendments transferred this function to the CFTC and gave it additional powers. The CFTC is an independent regulatory commission with five members. One of its five members is the chairman, who has specific powers. All of the members of the Commission are appointed by the President, and are subject to confirmation by the Senate.[13]

Jurisdiction

Generally. The 1974 amendments dramatically increased the number of commodity transactions subject to regulation. With regard to commodity futures contracts, the approach of the former legislation had been that only those commodities specifically enumerated in the CEA were covered. This necessitated periodic amendment to the CEA as new types of contracts gained popularity. However, certain widely traded commodity futures contracts were never covered by the old CEA (see the Appendix).

Commodity Futures Contracts. The amended CEA adopted an approach which gave the CFTC exclusive jurisdiction over

> accounts, agreements . . . and transactions involving contracts of sale of a commodity for future delivery, traded or executed on a contract market designated pursuant to section 5 of this Act or any other board of trade, exchange or market.[14]

The CEA definition of "commodity" is broad, and includes all goods and articles (except onions), and all services, rights, and interests "in which contracts for future delivery are presently or in the future dealt in,"[15] that is, nearly anything which is the subject of a futures contract. Thus, a "commodity" under the CEA can be a tangible or intangible item (corn or Treasury bills), but is not subject to CFTC jurisdiction unless it becomes the subject of futures trading.

The requirement that a contract be one "for future delivery" means that the CFTC has jurisdiction over futures contracts, but not over contracts for the "sale of any cash commodity for deferred shipment or delivery"[16] ("forward" contracts) or cash transactions. For example, neither forward contracts for foreign currencies traded in the interbank market nor cash sales of agricultural commodities by farmers are subject to the CFTC's jurisdiction. However, certain antifraud and antimanipulation provisions of the amended CEA *do* apply to cash and forward transactions[17] (see "Regulation of Trading Professionals" and "Regulation of Trading"). The CEA also states that none of its provisions apply to

> transactions in foreign currency, security warrants, security rights, resales of installment loan contracts, repurchase options, government securities, or mortgages or mortgage purchase commitments, unless such transactions involve the sale thereof for future delivery conducted on a board of trade.[18]

This provision principally affects the large institutions which enter into forward and cash contracts for these items outside of the futures markets.

Commodity Options. The CFTC also has jurisdiction over commodity option transactions. The approach under the old legislation was that option contracts in the agricultural commodities enumerated in the CEA were illegal. This ban remains in force.[19] However, the CEA now gives the CFTC jurisdiction over

> any transaction which is of the character of, or is commonly known to the trade as, an "option," "privilege," "indemnity," "bid," "offer," "put," "call," "advance guaranty," or "decline guaranty."[20]

For these transactions, the amended CEA permits trading in commodities not listed in the old CEA if, or under such terms as, the CFTC decides.[21] A framework for an options pilot program was established by the CFTC in November 1981 (see "Commodity Options: CFTC Pilot Program" under "Current Regulatory Issues"). [Substantial changes not reflected here have recently occurred in this area of the law. See Foreword.]

Leverage Transactions. The CFTC also has jurisdiction over "leverage" transactions. A "leverage" transaction is defined as any transaction for the delivery of a commodity

> under a standardized contract commonly known to the trade as a margin account, margin contract, leverage account, or leverage contract, or under any contract, account, arrangement, scheme, or device that the Commission determines serves the same function or functions as such a standardized contract, or is marketed or managed in substantially the same manner as such a standardized contract.[22]

The CEA groups the treatment of leverage transactions into three categories[23]: (1) leverage transactions in the agricultural commodities enumerated in the old CEA are prohibited; (2) leverage transactions in silver or gold bullion and bulk coins may be regulated by CFTC rules "designed to ensure the financial solvency of the transaction or prevent manipulation or fraud"; and (3) leverage transactions in other commodities may be regulated or prohibited by the CFTC. The CFTC also has the power to treat leverage transactions in commodities not listed in the old CEA as futures transactions.

The CFTC placed a moratorium on new entries in the gold and silver leverage transaction business in 1978,[24] and extended it to all other commodities in 1979[25]. In 1979, the CFTC decided to treat gold and silver leverage transactions as futures transactions,[26] but has deferred the effective date of its regulations until after the 1982 reauthorization process[27] in order to give Congress an opportunity to deal with the issue. As noted above, the CFTC has the authority to regulate, but not ban, gold and silver leverage transactions. However, the treatment of these transactions as futures transactions would probably lead to the demise of that industry because, as the industry presently exists, leverage contracts in gold and silver cannot meet the requirement that they be traded only on a designated contract market (see "Regulation of Contract Markets"). [Substantial changes not reflected here have recently occurred in this area of the law. See Foreword.]

Duties

Generally. The CEA gives the CFTC numerous duties. The manner in which many of the duties described below are carried out is described in greater detail later in this chapter.

Regulation of Contract Markets. One of the duties of the CFTC is the regulation of commodity exchanges. The CFTC has the power to designate contract markets, pursuant to which it determines the exchanges on which various commodity futures contracts are traded. The Commission also has authority to establish commodity grades, change delivery points, affirmatively approve exchange rules, and alter or supplement those rules. It can exercise certain other powers in an "emergency" (see full discussion of "Regulation of Contract Markets").

Regulation of Trading Professionals. The 1974 amendments gave the CFTC authority to regulate certain commodity trading professionals. It was given the power over the registration process for futures commission merchants and floor brokers. In addition, it acquired newly created authority to implement new registration requirements for commodity trading advisors, commodity pool operators, and associated persons of futures commission merchants. The CFTC was authorized to set fitness standards for floor brokers, futures commission merchants, and associated persons (see detailed discussion of "Regulation of Trading Professionals"). The 1974 amendments also established the framework for the formation of self-regulatory associations for the commodities industry by giving the CFTC the authority to approve and register such associations (see "Futures Associations"). The 1978 amendments to the CEA also gave the CFTC the power to issue rules governing commodity broker bankruptcies.[28] [Substantial changes not reflected here have recently occurred in this area of the law. See Foreword.]

Regulation of Trading. The CFTC also has broad authority to regulate commodity trading. First, it is responsible for the enforcement of the CEA's various antifraud provisions. CEA prohibitions on specific types of trading activity and practices and market manipulation are also enforced by the CFTC. The CFTC also has the power to set speculative limits, which affect large traders, and to enforce reporting requirements for traders whose market positions exceed levels established by the CFTC (see full discussion of "Regulation of Trading").

Remedying Violations of the CEA. The CFTC has substantial powers to enforce the CEA and remedy violations thereof. The CFTC operates an administrative reparations procedure for adjudicating private claims against persons registered under the CEA. The CFTC also has a role in the disciplinary procedures of the exchanges: the Commission may discipline exchange members for rule violations if exchanges fail to do so, and has the power to review exchange disciplinary proceedings. The Commission has retained the authority to suspend or revoke the contract market designation of an exchange as a penalty for a violation of the CEA. In addition, it has the power to bring administrative enforcement actions and to issue cease-and-desist orders against all violators except contract markets. The CFTC may also bring an action in federal district court in order to obtain an injunction against violations of the CEA. Finally, the CFTC has the authority to investigate anyone subject to the CEA (see later discussion of "Remedying Violations of the CEA"). [Substantial changes not reflected here have recently occurred in this area of the law. See Foreword.]

Informational Activities. The CFTC also serves the function of assuring dissemination of various types of public information. Contract markets are required by the CFTC to make public before the beginning of trading each day the volume of trading for each contract for the previous day and other information.[29] The Commission is also authorized to investigate commodity futures markets and publish regular market reports.[30]

The CEA requires the CFTC to cooperate with other federal agencies in order to avoid unnecessary duplication of information-gathering activities. Other agencies are required to furnish market information to the CFTC, but the CFTC must abide by rules of confidentiality which apply to such information.[31] In addition, certain rules of confidentiality apply to information gathered in the course of investigations of persons subject to the CEA and to investigations conducted in order to furnish market reports.[32] The CFTC is prohibited from disclosing information which would separately disclose the business transactions, trade secrets, or names of customers of any person. However, such information may be disclosed in the course of a congressional investigation or CFTC administrative proceeding.

Organization and Coordination of Activities. The daily operations of the five-man CFTC are carried on through its three principal divisions and its other sections and offices. The Division of Trading and Markets is responsible for carrying out the CFTC's programs for the regulation of contract markets and trading professionals (see "Regulation of Contract Markets" and "Regulation of Trading Professionals"). The CFTC's Division of Enforcement is in charge of enforcing the provisions of the CEA by bringing various administrative actions and conducting investigations (see "Remedying Violations of the CEA"). The Division of Economics and Education engages in economic research in various areas and conducts public educational programs. The CFTC's other administrative divisions include a Complaints Section and a Hearings Section, which together are responsible for conducting the reparations proceedings which may be brought against persons registered under the CEA (see "Remedying Violations of the CEA" and "Reparations Proceedings").

The CEA requires the CFTC generally to cooperate with other agencies of federal, state, and local government.[33] The CFTC is also specifically required to maintain ties with the Department of Agriculture, the Department of the Treasury, the Federal Reserve System, the Securities and Exchange Commission, the Department of Justice, and the Comptroller General.[34] The CEA requires the CFTC to carry out its duties by the "least anticompetitive means" and by endeavoring to take into consideration "the public interest to be protected by the antitrust laws."[35]

REGULATION OF CONTRACT MARKETS

Contract Market Designation

Generally. The process of "designation" of contract markets is an essential element of the scheme of market regulation under the CEA. Under this system, first introduced in 1922 (see the Appendix), certain transactions may be effected only by or through a member of a contract market. A commodity exchange must receive a separate designation for each type of contract traded.

Significance of Contract Market Membership. The scheme of contract market regulation rests on the special status given to contract markets and their members. The CEA defines "member of a contract market" as any individual or entity owning, holding membership, or having membership representation on, or given a member's trading privileges on, a contract market.[36] This special status is given by the section of the CEA which makes it unlawful for any person

> to deliver for transmission through the mails or in interstate commerce . . . any offer to make or execute, or any confirmation of the execution of, or any quotation or report of the price of, any contract for the sale of any commodity for future delivery on or subject to the rules of any board of trade in the United States, or for any person to make or execute such contract of sale . . . except . . . where such contract is made by or through a member of a board of trade which has been designated by the Commission as a "contract market."[37]

A similar but somewhat differently worded provision of the CEA makes it unlawful for any person

> to conduct any office or place of business anywhere in the United States or its territories for the purpose of soliciting or accepting any orders for the purchase or sale of any commodity for future delivery, or for making or offering to make any contracts for the purchase or sale of any commodity for future delivery, or for conducting any dealings in commodities for future delivery . . . if such orders, contracts, or dealings are executed or consummated otherwise than by or through a member of a contract market.[38]

The former provision applies only to transactions on or subject to the rules of a board of trade. The latter provision applies only to the conduct of an office or business, but is not limited to transactions subject to such rules. Since most persons involved in such transactions are likely to have an "office," the second provision is generally broader in scope.

The importance of these provisions is reflected by the CEA's treatment of misrepresentations concerning contract market membership. The CEA makes it illegal to make certain false representations concerning a person's membership in a contract market in connection with the solicitation or handling of an order or contract for the purchase or sale of any commodity in interstate commerce or for future delivery.[39] [Substantial changes not reflected here have recently occurred in this area of the law.]

Location. Designated contract markets must meet requirements as to their location.[40] These requirements can be met in two ways. First, a contract market may be designated if it is located at a terminal market where the cash commodity underlying the contract is sold in such a manner as to reflect its general value and where inspection services approved by the Secretary of Agriculture are available for that commodity. As an alternative, the contract market may be designated if the CFTC approves the market location and the terms of delivery for that contract.

Exchange Operations. As a condition of designation, the governing board of the exchange must adhere to numerous requirements relating to the conduct of business on the exchange.[41] The governing board must itself file, and must require members to file, reports required by the CFTC, including those showing the details and terms of all transactions by the exchange and its members. The exchange must establish procedures aimed at prohibiting the dissemination of false information which would tend to affect commodity prices. It must also establish procedures designed to prohibit price manipulation and the cornering of any commodity market and make provision for implementing all decisions made by the exchange or the CFTC in accordance with the Commodity Exchange Act.

Agricultural Cooperatives. Another condition of designation of a contract market is that the governing board of the exchange may not exclude from exchange membership

> any duly authorized representative of any lawfully formed and conducted cooperative association of producers having adequate financial responsibility which is engaged in any cash commodity business, if such association has complied, and agrees to comply, with such terms and conditions as are or may be imposed lawfully on other members of such exchange.[42]

To ensure that a "cooperative association of producers" is truly "agricultural," it must be "in good faith owned or controlled, directly or indirectly" by agricultural producers.[43]

"Public Interest" Requirement. The 1974 amendments to the CEA added an important new requirement for contract market designation. This condition requires

the governing board of the exchange to show that futures transactions in the commodity, which is the subject of the contract, will not be contrary to the "public interest." The CFTC is empowered to make the determination as to whether this test is met.[44] The legislative history of the CEA indicates that Congress intended this test to include an "economic purpose" test, which would require an exchange to show something more than the expectation of the occasional use of the contract for price basing or hedging.[45] [Substantial changes not reflected here have recently occurred in this area of the law.]

CFTC Guidelines. The CFTC has issued additional guidelines for designation.[46] The guidelines formally establish and elaborate the "economic purpose" test. In addition, they require that any lack of conformity of the terms of the proposed contract to normal commercial practices must be shown to be necessary or desirable for hedging purposes. The guidelines also require that the exchange demonstrate that the contract will result in the delivery of supplies which will not be conducive to price manipulation or distortion, and which can reasonably be expected to be available. [Substantial changes not reflected here have recently occurred in this area of the law.]

Proposed CFTC Rules. The CFTC has proposed replacing its present guidelines with new rules.[47] The proposed rules would require that (1) the exchange furnish a profile of the cash markets underlying the proposed contract; (2) the contract terms can be expected to promote hedging or price discovery (i.e., establishing a price for the underlying cash commodity), while minimizing the potential of manipulation or other market distortions; (3) the "economic purpose" test be satisfied; and (4) the exchange furnish certain additional information bearing on other public interest considerations such as rule enforcement, the price and quantity of deliverable supplies, and the monitoring of the positions of large traders. The proposed rules also contain special requirements which would govern the designation of markets for contracts based upon an aggregation of securities or securities indexes, and for contracts based on securities issued or guaranteed by the federal government or a federal agency (with respect to futures contracts involving securities and securities indexes, see "CFTC Jurisdictional Issues" and "CFTC–SEC Jurisdictional Boundaries" under "Current Regulatory Issues". [Substantial changes not reflected here have recently occurred in this area of the law.]

Denial, Suspension, or Revocation of Designation. The CFTC can refuse to designate a contract market if an application does not show satisfaction of the applicable conditions or does not give sufficient assurance of future compliance.[48] If the CFTC's Division of Trading and Markets refuses to designate an exchange to trade a proposed contract, the exchange has a right to a hearing before the full Commission. An adverse decision of the CFTC may be appealed to the U.S. Court of Appeals. The designation of a contract market may be suspended for up to 6 months, or may be revoked, only after the CFTC gives notice and holds a hearing.[49] Such action may be taken only if the exchange (or any of its directors, officers, agents, or employees) has violated the CEA or CFTC regulations, or if the exchange has failed to enforce rules made by it as a condition of designation. A decision by the CFTC to suspend or revoke a designation may also be appealed to the U.S. Court of Appeals. [Substantial changes not reflected here have recently occurred in this area of the law.]

Duties of Contract Markets

Generally. Another element of the scheme of contract market regulation is the large number of continuing duties imposed on designated contract markets.[50] As noted above, the failure to carry out these duties can result in suspension and revocation of designation. Contract markets are required to furnish the CFTC with copies of all of their rules and bylaws, and all of the changes made therein. They must keep records for at least 3 years with respect to all matters discussed and actions taken by the contract market's governing board (including committees), and any of their subsidiaries or affiliates. The CFTC has also imposed certain reporting requirements on contract markets.[51]

Delivery Terms. A number of duties relate to the terms of delivery. Each contract market is required to comply with CFTC orders to allow delivery of the actual commodity 3 to 10 days after a delivery month if the CFTC determines that such action is needed in order to prevent "squeezes" and market congestion endangering price stability.[52] The contract market must establish a delivery notice requirement of at least 1 business day prior to delivery, and must comply with CFTC orders for up to 10-days notice, where the CFTC finds it necessary to prevent or diminish unfair trading practices.[53] These CFTC actions may be carried out only after notice and an opportunity for a hearing, and such orders cannot be applied to existing contracts.

In addition, contract markets must require that all commodities to be delivered conform to U.S. standards if such standards have been officially promulgated and adopted by the CFTC.[54] The delivery of a commodity must be permitted at points, in grades, and in locational price differentials which tend to prevent or diminish price manipulation, market congestion, or the "abnormal movement of such commodity in interstate commerce."[55] If the CFTC determines that the rules of a contract market do not accomplish these purposes, it may require the appropriate changes; if these changes are not made within 75 days after the contract market receives notice, the CFTC can effect the changes itself (except with respect to existing contracts).

Warehouses. Other duties relate to the warehouses at which delivery is to be made. Each contract market must provide that warehouse receipts issued under the U.S. Warehouse Act are acceptable in satisfaction of the contract if the commodity is delivered from a warehouse subject to that act. Warehouse receipts must also be of contract specifications with respect to kind, quality, and quantity, and the warehouse must meet reasonable requirements with respect to location, accessibility, and suitability for the purpose.[56] The operators of warehouses used for delivery of the commodity traded are also subject to certain recordkeeping and inspection requirements.[57]

Enforcement Programs. The CEA requires contract markets to enforce all rules approved by the CFTC and to revoke those which are disapproved.[58] The CFTC has issued guidelines that require a contract market to establish an enforcement program which includes: (1) surveillance of market activity and trading practices; (2) examination of members' records; (3) investigation of customer complaints and alleged or apparent violations; and (4) maintenance of prompt, effective procedures for disciplinary and/or corrective action.[59] Contract markets are also required to enforce their own rules relating to CFTC-approved minimum financial standards and related reporting requirements for futures commission merchants who are market members.[60]

Arbitration Procedures. Contract markets are required to establish procedures for the arbitration of the claims of customers (other than floor brokers and futures commission merchants) against contract market members and their employees.[61] These procedures must be voluntary, may not be applied to claims exceeding $15,000, and may not provide for compulsory payment unless the parties so agree. The CFTC has issued detailed regulations governing these arbitration procedures.[62] Although not required by the CEA, exchanges have established procedures which also provide for the settlement of disputes between different contract market members.[63] [Substantial changes not reflected here have recently occurred in this area of the law.]

Contract Market Rules

Rule Approval Process. The 1974 amendments changed the procedure by which the rules of contract markets are reviewed by the CFTC. Under the former law, the Department of Agriculture was given the power to disapprove rules which were in violation of the CEA or CFTC regulations. The 1974 amendments changed this approach to a process of affirmative approval.[64] Under this new approach, all bylaws, rules, regulations, and resolutions relating to the terms and conditions of contracts, or any trading requirements, must receive the prior approval of the CFTC.[65] In addition, the CFTC must provide the opportunity for interested persons to participate in the approval process of any rule which the CFTC determines to be "of major economic significance." Approval is not required for rules setting levels for margin, rules adopted in emergency situations, and administrative rules which the CFTC chooses to exempt.

The CFTC, by regulation, has adopted the position that it will disapprove not only those rules which are directly contrary to a specific requirement of the CEA, but also those which conflict or are inconsistent with any of the policies, purposes, and public interest considerations embodied in the CEA or CFTC regulations.[66] The CFTC is required to reach a decision within 30 days unless it gives notice that a longer time is required; otherwise, disapproval requires notice and an opportunity for a hearing.[67] [Substantial changes not reflected here have recently occurred in this area of the law.]

Altering or Supplementing Rules. The CFTC has the power under certain circumstances to alter or supplement the rules of a contract market.[68] This power allows the CFTC to make changes only in those rules dealing with (1) contract terms and conditions; (2) the form or manner of purchases or sales; (3) other trading requirements (except margin requirements); (4) financial responsibility requirements; and (5) recordkeeping and accounting requirements for customer transactions. Rules may be altered or supplemented only if the CFTC makes a determination that the changes are necessary or appropriate for the protection of persons dealing in commodities traded on a contract market.

CFTC "Emergency" Powers. A final power given the CFTC in 1974 with respect to contract market rules allows it to act in an emergency situation by directing a contract market to take any action necessary to maintain or restore orderly trading.[69] An "emergency" is defined by the CEA as a threatened or actual market manipulation or corner, any act of the United States or a foreign government affecting a commodity, or any major market disturbance preventing the market from accurately reflecting the forces of supply and demand. [Substantial changes not reflected here have recently occurred in this area of the law. See Foreword.]

Recordkeeping and Reporting Requirements for Members. A contract market member must comply with reporting and recordkeeping requirements imposed by the market as a condition of designation. In addition, the CEA requires contract market members to keep records of all of their commodity transactions.[70] The CFTC has issued rules detailing the types of records required and the period for which they must be retained,[71] and has imposed certain reporting requirements.[72]

REGULATION OF TRADING PROFESSIONALS

Floor Brokers and Futures Commission Merchants

Definitions. The regulatory system administered by the CFTC includes not only the markets, but also the various individuals and other entities involved in the commodity futures industry. Two of these groups of persons, floor brokers and futures commission merchants, have been subject to federal regulation since the enactment of the CEA in 1936. The CEA defines a floor broker as

> any person who, in or surrounding any "pit," "ring," or "post," or other place provided by a contract market for the meeting of persons similarly engaged, shall purchase or sell for any other person any commodity for future delivery on or subject to the rules of any contract market.[73]

A futures commission merchant (FCM) is defined as including

> individuals, associations, partnerships, corporations, and trusts engaged in soliciting or in accepting orders for the purchase or sale of any commodity for future delivery on or subject to the rules of any contract market and that, in or in connection with such solicitation or acceptance of orders, accepts any money, securities, or property (or extends credit in lieu thereof) to margin, guarantee, or secure any trades or contracts that result or may result therefrom.[74]

Registration. All floor brokers and FCMs are required to register with the CFTC.[75] All registrations expire on December 31 of each year, and are renewed upon application unless the registration has been suspended or revoked. Beginning in July 1982, fingerprinting is required for all floor brokers and FCMs registering for the first time.[76] [Substantial changes not reflected here have recently occurred in this area of the law.]

Regulation of Business Practices. The business operations of floor brokers and FCMs are subject to various forms of control. The CFTC has issued regulations prohibiting and restricting the various types of trading activities of both floor brokers and FCMs (see "Regulation of Trading" and "Trading Practices of Floor Brokers and FCMs"). The CFTC has the authority to establish standards for floor brokers and FCMs with respect to training, experience, and other qualifications, and can require written proficiency examinations.[77] Although the CFTC has not exercised its authority to establish such requirements, the National Futures Association may soon set such standards (see "The Role of the National Futures Association" under "Current Regulatory Issues"). The CFTC also has authority to require floor brokers and FCMs to report and keep records of their own transactions and positions, and those of their customers,[78] and has issued regulations specifying certain types of records to be kept and transactions to be reported by FCMs.[79]

Dual Trading. The CFTC was given the power by the 1974 amendments to deal with "dual trading" by floor brokers and FCMs. Specifically, the CFTC was given the power to determine (1) whether floor brokers could trade for their own account (or for an account over which they have discretionary authority) and also execute a customer order, and (2) whether FCMs could trade for their own account of for any proprietary account.[80] The CFTC has agreed to allow these practices subject to regulations which allow the reconstruction of sequence of trading, and has promulgated regulations requiring each contract market to bracket each trading day into half-hour periods.[81]

FCM Net-Capital Requirements. Ensuring the financial stability of FCMs is another goal of the CEA's regulatory scheme. The CFTC has the power to set minimum financial requirements for FCMs. These requirements will be met if the FCM is a member of a contract market and conforms to its financial standards and related reporting requirements.[82] The CFTC has issued regulations which require registered FCMs to maintain an adjusted net capital equal to or greater than the greatest of (1) $100,000 ($50,000 for members of a contract market or a registered futures association); (2) 4% of the funds required to be segregated by the CEA and CFTC regulations; or (3) for securities brokers and dealers, 4% of aggregate debit items computed in accordance with the formula for determination of reserve requirements.[83] The CFTC has proposed to change this formula so that the $100,000 and $50,000 figures would be raised to $250,000 and $100,000, respectively,[84] and this proposal may be adopted shortly. Special regulations deal with the definition of adjusted net capital.[85] [Substantial changes not reflected here have recently occurred in this area of the law.]

FCM Handling of Customer Funds. The CEA also regulates the handling of customer funds by FCMs.[86] The act requires that customer funds be accounted for separately and prohibits the commingling of such funds. However, "commingling" does not include the depositing of funds in the account of a clearinghouse organization for normal clearinghouse purposes.

The CFTC has also issued regulations which specify the manner of segregation and accounting for customer funds.[87] Customer monies used as margin must be dealt with as belonging to the customer upon their receipt by the FCM from the customer. In addition, the margin money of one customer may not be used by any FCM to margin the trades of another customer. The investment of customer funds is restricted to government or government-guaranteed securities (such as Treasury bills or GNMA certificates), and all FCMs are required to keep certain records of customer funds which are invested. Investments made with customer funds may not be appraised at greater than current market value. However, FCMs are specifically permitted to retain any interest earned on such investments. Loans made by any FCM to a customer must be treated as belonging to such customer.

Associated Persons

Generally. The 1974 amendments to the CEA initiated registration and other requirements for "associated persons." Specifically, this category of persons includes

> any person . . . associated with any futures commission merchant or with any agent of a futures commission merchant, as a partner, officer, or employee (or any person occupying a similar status or performing similar functions), in any capacity which involves (i) the solicitation or acceptance of customers' orders (other than in a clerical capacity), or (ii) the supervision of any person or persons so engaged.[88]

Registration. Associated persons, other than individuals who are registered as floor brokers or FCMs, must register with the CFTC.[89] The registration of an associated person expires 2 years after its effective date, and may be renewed upon application unless revoked or suspended. The CEA makes it unlawful for any FCM or its agent to permit a person to become associated with it in the capacity of an associated person if the FCM or agent knew or should have known that the person was not registered (or that the registration had been revoked, had expired, or was currently under suspension). [Substantial changes not reflected here have recently occurred in this area of the law. See Foreword.]

New Requirements. The CFTC will initiate additional registration requirements for associated persons in July 1982.[90] These new regulations will require that a person applying for associated person status must be fingerprinted. In addition, the prospective associated person must obtain from the FCM with whom he or she is to be associated the following written certifications: (1) that the FCM or its agent intends to hire the applicant, and that the applicant will not be permitted to engage in the activities of an associated person until registration is completed; (2) that the FCM has verified the information supplied by the applicant to the CFTC relating to his or her education and employment history during the preceding 5 years; (3) that to the best of the FCM's knowledge, all of the publicly available information supplied by the applicant to the CFTC is accurate and complete; and (4) that the FCM has taken, and will take, measures to prevent the unwarranted dissemination of the information contained in the application or in the records obtained in support of the certifications made by the FCM.

It will be unlawful for the FCM to certify as to the accuracy and completeness of the information in the application of a prospective associated person if the

FCM knew or should have known that any of the information was not accurate and complete. These required certifications will have the effect of requiring an FCM to assume a large degree of responsibility for the fitness of associated persons employed by it or any of its agents. An FCM must retain the records which are necessary to support its certifications. These new regulations will also mandate that an individual may only be associated with one FCM or one agent of an FCM at a time. [Substantial changes not reflected here have recently occurred in this area of the law. See Foreword.]

Customer Protection Rules. The CFTC requires both FCMs and associated persons to conform to certain rules designed to protect their customers. CFTC regulations prohibit any FCM or associated person from directly or indirectly effecting a transaction for a customer unless either specific authorization is given or written authority is given to effect transactions without specific authorization.[91] A transaction is "specifically authorized" if the customer (or person designated by the customer to control his or her account) specifies the precise commodity interest and the exact amount to be purchased or sold.

The CFTC has also sought to protect customers by imposing certain supervisory duties on FCMs, associated persons (except those with no supervisory duties) and all other CFTC registrants.[92] These persons must "diligently supervise" the handling of all commodity interest accounts carried, operated, or advised by them, as well as all other activities of their partners, officers, employees, and agents (or persons occupying a similar status or performing a similar function) relating to their business as a registrant.

Commodity Trading Advisors and Commodity Pool Operators

Definitions. The 1974 amendments to the CEA authorized the establishment of a comprehensive scheme for the regulation of commodity trading advisors and commodity pool operators. Congressional awareness of the importance of their activities is reflected in a recitation in the CEA that such activities are "affected with a national public interest."[93]

A commodity trading advisor (CTA) is described by the CEA as

> any person who, for compensation or profit, engages in the business of advising others, either directly or through publications or writings, as to the value of commodities or as to the advisability of trading in any commodity for future delivery on or subject to the rules of any contract market, or who for compensation or profit, and as part of a regular business, issues or promulgates analyses or reports concerning commodities.[94]

By itself, this description includes many types of persons principally engaged in other professions or businesses. The definition in the CEA therefore excludes the following categories of persons who engage in the activities described above solely as an incident to the conduct of their business or profession: banks and trust companies; newspaper reporters, columnists, and editors; lawyers; accountants; teachers; floor brokers; FCMs; publishers of *bona fide* newspapers, news magazines, or business or financial publications of general or regular circulation (including their employees); and contract markets. These persons, so long as their commodity advisory activities are solely incidental to their principal business or profession, are not subject to any of the provisions of the CEA affecting CTAs.[95] In addition, the CFTC has issued a number of interpretative letters applying this definition to more specific situations.[96] [Substantial changes not reflected here have recently occurred in this area of the law. See Foreword.]

A commodity pool operator (CPO) is defined by the CEA as

> any person engaged in a business which is of the nature of an investment trust, syndicate, or similar form of enterprise, and who, in connection therewith, solicits, accepts or receives from others, funds, securities, or property, either directly or through capital contributions, the sale of stock or other forms of securities, or otherwise, for the purpose of trading in any commodity for future delivery on or subject to the rules of any contract market, but does not include such persons not within the intent of this definition as the Commission may specify by rule or regulation or by order.[97]

The CFTC has issued a number of interpretative letters clarifying this definition.[98]

Registration. Both CTAs and CPOs are required to register with the CFTC. Registrations expire annually on June 30. The CFTC has been given authority under the CEA to exempt certain CTAs and CPOs from registration requirements.[99] Beginning in July 1982, fingerprinting is required for all CTAs and CPOs registering for the first time.[100]

Various classes of persons have been exempted from registration as a CTA (to be distinguished from those persons specifically excluded from the definition of "commodity trading advisor"). First, certain CTAs furnishing a very limited amount of services need not register.[101] This class includes those CTAs who, during the preceding 12 months, did not furnish commodity trading advice to more than 15 persons, and do not hold themselves out generally to the public as CTAs. In addition, CFTC regulations exempt from registration certain CTAs for whom registration is not necessary for the protection of the public.[102] These persons include dealers, processors, brokers, and sellers in cash market transactions of any commodity; nonprofit, voluntary membership trade associations or farm organizations; registered associated persons; registered CPOs; and persons exempt from registration as a CPO who give trading advice solely for the use of the pool for which they are exempt. [Substantial changes not reflected here have recently occurred in this area of the law. See Foreword.]

The CFTC has also proposed regulations which would require registration as a CTA for any person who either solicits customers on behalf of a CTA or CPO, or supervises any person engaging in such solicitation. However, this registration requirement would not apply to individuals registered with the CFTC in some other capacity. These proposed regulations would also make it unlawful for a CTA or CPO to allow any individual to solicit customers on its behalf if the CTA or CPO knows or should know that the individual is not registered as a CTA. The usual disclosure and recordkeeping requirements for CTAs (discussed below) would not apply to persons registering under these proposed regulations.[103] [Substantial changes not reflected here have recently occurred in this area of the law. See Foreword.]

The CFTC has also exempted two classes of commodity pool operators from registration requirements. First, registration is not required for a CPO who (1) receives no compensation for operating the pool (except reimbursement for ordinary administrative expenses), (2) operates only one pool at a time, (3) is not otherwise required to register and is not a business affiliate of any person required to register with the CFTC, and (4) operates a pool for which no person does any advertising.[104] Second, CPOs operating a small pool or a number of small pools are not required to register.[105] This class includes CPOs operating pools where the gross capital contributions for all of the pools do not exceed $200,000, and where none of the pools have more than 15 participants at any time (not counting certain affiliated persons).

The regulatory scheme covering CTAs and CPOs includes specific provisions in the CEA governing the procedure which must be followed in order to deny, suspend, or revoke a person's registration as a CTA or CPO.[106] The CFTC is required to provide a hearing before such action is taken, except if the applicant is subject to an outstanding CFTC order denying the applicant contract market trading privileges, suspending or expelling the applicant from contract market membership, or suspending or revoking the applicant's CEA registration. In order to deny, suspend, or revoke registration, the CFTC must determine, after holding such hearing, that (1) the denial, suspension, or revocation is in the public interest; (2) the operations of the person tend to disrupt orderly marketing conditions or tend to cause unreasonable price fluctuations in commodities; and (3) either (a) the applicant has been convicted of a securities or commodity law violation, (b) the person is subject to a certain type of injunction, or (c) a controlling person has been subjected to a certain type of CFTC order.[107] [Substantial changes not reflected here have recently occurred in this area of the law. See Foreword.]

Disclosure Documents. The scheme of regulation for CTAs and CPOs requires that they make certain disclosures to the recipients of their services in the form of a "Disclosure Document." The regulations governing Disclosure Documents were recently revised, and became effective in August 1981.[108] A CTA must deliver a Disclosure Document to each prospective client for each trading program it employs before the CTA solicits or enters into an agreement to direct the client's account, or to guide a client's trading, by means of a systematic approach that recommends specific transactions.[109] A CPO must deliver a Disclosure Document to any prospective pool participant before it solicits, accepts, or receives funds, securities, or property from that participant.[110]

CFTC regulations require that Disclosure Documents contain certain information for prospective clients (CTAs) or pool participants (CPOs). A CTA's Disclosure Document must contain the names of FCMs with whom clients will be required to maintain their accounts, a description of the CTA's trading program, business background, performance record, fees, conflicts of interest, whether such CTA will trade for its own account, and material litigation. The Disclosure Document must include certain specifically worded disclaimers, including a "Risk Disclosure Statement." The Disclosure Document must also contain any other information which would be "material" to the prospective client's decision whether to utilize the CTA's trading program.[111]

Disclosure Documents for CPOs must contain the same categories of information with respect to the pool as CTA Disclosure Documents. In addition, the performance record of both the pool and the pool's CTA must be disclosed. Any ownership interest in the pool held by the CPO or pool's CTA must also be disclosed, as must all types of pool expenses. Other requirements mandate the disclosure of the amount of funds necessary for the commencement of trading; the manner in which margin requirements will be fulfilled; the form in which pool funds not deposited as margin will be held after the commencement of trading; any restrictions on the transferability of a participant's interest in the pool; the manner in which a participant may redeem his or her interest in the pool; the extent to which a participant may be liable for the obligations of the pool in excess of the amount of the participant's contribution; pool policies with respect to distributions of profits or capital and the federal-income-tax effects of such payments for a participant (including a discussion of tax consequences of the form or organization of the pool and such payments therefrom); and any commissions or fees paid in connection with the solicitation of pool contributions. In addition, the Disclosure Document must contain any other information which would be "material" to the prospective participant's decision whether or not to participate in the pool.[112] Simulated or hypothetical performance records may be presented by CTAs or CPOs only when accompanied by a specific disclaimer.[113]

The CFTC has established recordkeeping requirements for both the CTAs and CPOs.[114] CPOs must also make available to pool participants certain records.[115] In addition, because interests in commodity pools are generally considered "securities," their offering must comply with applicable state and federal securities laws (see "CFTC Jurisdictional Issues" under "Current Regulatory Issues").[116]

Handling of Funds. CTAs and CPOs are subject to restrictions on the handling of client and participant funds. A CTA may not solicit, accept, or receive client funds in the CTA's own name unless the CTA is also registered as an FCM, or is a leverage transaction merchant registered as a CTA.[117] A CPO must operate the pool as a separate legal entity, although he or she may be exempted from this requirement under certain circumstances.[118] A CPO must also receive funds of pool participants for interests in the pool only in the pool's name, and may not commingle the property of the pool with any other property.[119]

CPO Reporting Requirements. CFTC regulations require CPOs to furnish pool participants with periodic statements relating to the pool's performance.[120] CFTC regulations require that participants be furnished with an "Account Statement" which consists of a Statement of Income (or Loss) and a Statement of Changes in Net Asset Value. The Account Statement must be furnished monthly if the net assets of the pool exceed $500,000; for other pools, the statement must be furnished quarterly. The Statement of Income (or Loss) must contain: (1) realized net trading gain or loss; (2) unrealized net trading gain or loss; (3) other income; (4) management, advisory, and other fees; (5) brokerage commissions; and (6) other expenses incurred or accrued by the pool for the period. The Statement of Changes in Net Asset Value must show the effect of additions to and withdrawals from the pool (including redemptions), and must include the total net income or loss and the net asset value of each outstanding participation unit in the pool at the end of the period.

In addition, pool participants must be furnished with an Annual Report within 90 days of the close of the pool's fiscal year.[121] It must include: (1) the net asset value of the pool, the participation units therein, and the participant's units; (2) a Statement of Financial Condition; (3) a Statement of Income or Loss; (4) a Statement of Changes in Financial Position; and (5) a Statement of Changes in Ownership Equity. This information must relate not only to the fiscal year just concluded, but also to certain preceding fiscal years.

Antifraud Rules. Certain conduct by CTAs and CPOs is prohibited by the CEA (see also "Regulation of Trading"). CTAs and CPOs are forbidden by the CEA from representing or implying that they have been sponsored, recommended, or approved, or have had their abilities or qualifications passed on by any U.S. Government agency or official.[122] In addition, the CEA contains a general prohibition against fraudulent conduct by CTAs and CPOs making it unlawful for them

> by the use of the mails or any means or instrumentality of interstate commerce, directly or indirectly—
>
> (A) to employ any device, scheme, or artifice to defraud any present or prospective client or participant; or
>
> (B) to engage in any transaction, practice, or course of business which operates as a fraud or deceit upon on any present or prospective client or participant.[123] In addition, CFTC regulations contain a similar antifraud provision which applies to advertising practices of CTAs and CPOs.[124]

REGULATION OF TRADING

Trading, Antifraud Rules. Another aspect of the regulatory scheme established by the CEA is the regulation of various types of trading activity. This includes the prohibition of certain types of fraudulent conduct. In addition to the previously mentioned antifraud provision governing CTAs and CPOs (see "Regulation of Trading Professionals" "Commodity Trading Advisors and Commodity Pool Operators," and "Antifraud Rules"), the CEA forbids certain types of fraudulent conduct (1) by contract market members and their correspondents, agents, and employees in interstate commerce or other persons with respect to futures contracts, acting for or on behalf of any other person, or (2) by any person in or in connection with any order to make, or the making of any contract of sale of any commodity made, or to be made, on or subject to the rules of any contract market. Within these parameters, section 4b of the CEA makes it unlawful

> (A) to cheat or defraud or attempt to cheat or defraud such other person;
>
> (B) willfully to make or cause to be made to such other person any false report or statement thereof, or willfully to enter or cause to be entered for such person any false record thereof;
>
> (C) willfully to deceive or attempt to deceive such other person by any means whatsoever in regard to any such order or contract or the disposition or execution

of any such order or contract, or in regard to any act of agency performed with respect to such order or contract for such person; or

(D) to bucket such order, or to fill such order by offset against the order or orders of any other person, or willfully and knowingly and without the prior consent of such person to become the buyer in respect to any selling order to such person, or become the seller in respect to any buying order of such person.[125]

Antifraud rules have also been established by CFTC regulation for other types of transactions. The CFTC has promulgated antifraud rules modeled after section 4b for commodity option transactions[126] and futures contracts traded on foreign exchanges.[127] The CFTC has also issued a rule prohibiting fraudulent conduct with respect to leverage transactions in silver or gold bullion or bulk coins.[128] This rule is a general prohibition employing language similar to that of Rule 10b-5 under the Securities Exchange Act of 1934. It makes it unlawful, in connection with such transactions, to employ any device, scheme, or artifice to defraud, to make an untrue statement or omission of a material fact, or to engage in any act, practice, or course of business which operates or would operate as a fraud or deceit upon any person. The wording of this provision is similar to the previously discussed antifraud provision governing conduct by CTAs and CPOs. [Substantial changes not reflected here have recently occurred in this area of the law.]

Other General Trading Prohibitions. In addition to the antifraud rules, the CEA makes it unlawful for any person to offer to enter into, enter into, or confirm the execution of certain specific types of transactions. These transactions include "wash sales," that is, transactions involving no change in ownership; "cross trades," that is, noncompetitive matching of orders of different customers of a floor broker or FCM; "accommodation trades," that is, trades made by a floor broker unlawfully assisting another floor broker; other types of fictitious sales; and any transaction used to cause the reporting of a price which is not "true and *bona fide*." In addition, option transactions in those commodities covered by the CEA prior to 1974 are still prohibited.[129] However, certain other option transactions will be allowed under the CFTC's recently proposed pilot program (see "Commodity Options: CFTC Pilot Program" under "Current Regulatory Issues").

Trading Practices of Floor Brokers and FCMs. As a part of its regulatory program for floor brokers and FCMs, the CFTC has issued rules designed to ensure that these persons refrain from certain trading practices. These rules require each contract market to establish certain rules regulating the trading practices of floor brokers.[130] Such rules must include prohibitions on a floor broker (1) trading for his or her own account (or an account he or she controls), while holding the order of another for the same commodity or commodity option which is executable at the market price, or the price at which the broker's own trade can be made; (2) executing any transaction for any account of another person for which orders can be placed or originated, or for which transactions can be executed, without the prior specific consent of the account holder, regardless of any general authorization pursuant to a written agreement (however, such orders may be placed with another member for execution); (3) disclosing the orders held by the broker for another person, or divulging an order revealed to the broker by another by reason of their relationship, except where the broker has discretionary trading authority, or at the request of the CFTC or the contract market; (4) taking, directly or indirectly, the other side of any order of another person revealed to the broker by reason of their relationship, except with such person's consent and in conformity with contract market rules; (5) making a purchase or sale which has been directly or indirectly prearranged; (6) allocating trades among accounts other than in accordance with contract market rules; and (7) withholding or withdrawing from the market any order or part of an order of another person for another broker's convenience. In addition, these rules require that every execution of a transaction on the floor by a broker be confirmed promptly by the opposite floor broker or floor trader. However, under certain circumstances and upon petition, the CFTC may exempt contract markets from this confirmation requirement.[131] This confirmation must identify the price, quantity, future, and respective clearing members. However, the contract market may be exempted from requiring identification of clearing members if it can be shown that the requirement would seriously disrupt the functions of the marketplace and that every trade can effectively be matched.

The CFTC also requires all FCMs to establish and enforce certain internal controls to ensure that to the extent possible every customer order executable at or near the market price is transmitted to the floor before any order in the same commodity or commodity option for a proprietary account (or any account in which an affiliated person has an interest or controls) is transmitted to the floor by an affiliated person gaining knowledge of such customer's order prior to its transmission.[132] The internal controls must be designed to avoid circumvention of this prohibition.

FCMs and their affiliated persons are prohibited by CFTC rule from disclosing that an order of another person is being held by the FCM or any of its affiliated persons, unless necessary to the effective execution of the order, or unless requested by the CFTC, the contract market, or a registered futures association.[133] In addition, FCMs and their affiliated persons may not knowingly take, directly or indirectly, the other side of any order of another person revealed to them or any of their affiliated persons by reason of the relationship to such other person, except with the other person's prior consent and in conformity with contract-market rules.

CFTC regulations prohibit any FCM from knowingly handling the account of an affiliated person of another FCM unless it receives certain written authorization from the other FCM, identifies the orders in the account in a specified manner, and regularly transmits to the other FCM certain documents relating to the account.[134] In addition, affiliated persons of an FCM are permitted to have an account, directly or indirectly, with another FCM only if they receive certain written authorization from the FCM with which they are affiliated, and copies of certain documents relating to the account are regularly transmitted to the affiliated FCM.[135]

Speculative Limits

Generally. The CEA authorizes the CFTC to establish limits on either the amount of trading that may be done, or the positions that may be held, by any person in futures contracts on or subject to the rules of a contract market.[136] The CFTC is empowered to set different limits for different commodities, delivery months, markets, and for buying versus selling transactions. A general justification for these limits is contained in the text of the CEA which states:

> Excessive speculation in any commodity under contracts of sale of such commodity for future delivery on or subject to the rules of contract markets causing sudden or unreasonable fluctuations or unwarranted changes in the price of such commodity, is an undue and unnecessary burden on interstate commerce in such commodity.[137]

An additional rationale for speculative limits is that these limits reduce the impact on commodity markets of individual speculators, and thereby reduce opportunities for market manipulation. [Substantial changes not reflected here have recently occurred in this area of the law.]

Position Limits. At one time the CFTC established and enforced daily limits on the volume of speculative trading. However, these daily limits were repealed in 1979.[138] The reasons given by the CFTC for this repeal were that such limits were not necessary to limit or prevent excessive speculation, and that such limits at times could limit market liquidity. The CFTC therefore presently exercises its authority over speculative trading only to establish aggregate position limits. Speculative position limits have been established by the CFTC for positions in futures contracts for oats, barley, flaxseed, cotton, rye, soybeans, eggs, potatoes, corn, and wheat.[139] In addition, since February 1982 the CFTC has required designated contract markets establish their own position limits for all commodities except those for which no months are listed for trading.[140] [Substantial changes not reflected here have recently occurred in this area of the law.]

Hedging Exemption. Position limits are subject to a number of special rules. The most important of these is that position limits do not apply to *bona fide* hedging transactions or positions. The dangers popularly associated with large positions are deemed not likely to arise if the person holding the position is a hedger. The CFTC definition for "*bona fide* hedging transactions and positions" includes transactions and positions which (1) normally represent a substitute for transactions to be made or positions to be taken at later time in a physical marketing channel; (2) are economically appropriate to the reduction of risk in the conduct and management of a commercial enterprise; and (3) arise from potential changes in the value of assets, liabilities, or services.[141] These transactions and positions must also have the purpose of offsetting price risks incidental to commercial cash or spot operations, and must be established and liquidated in an orderly manner in accordance with sound commercial practices. The regulations also provide a nonexclusive list of hedging transactions.[142] A trader must file certain statements with the CFTC if the trader wishes to have the CFTC classify a nonenumerated transaction as a hedging transaction.[143]

Other Exemptions. In addition, speculative position limits do not apply to transactions made by, for, or at the direction of the U.S. Government or one of its agencies. FCMs and floor brokers do not have to take into account transactions which are not made by them on their own behalf or for their own account (e.g., transactions in nonproprietary customer accounts) in determining whether they have exceeded these limits.[144] The CFTC has the power to exempt certain other transactions (spreads, straddles, and international arbitrage) from these limits,[145] but has not done so.

Aggregation of Positions. In applying speculative position limits, the CEA requires that the CFTC take into account trading by controlled persons, or trading by several persons pursuant to an express or implied agreement, or understanding.[146] The positions of such individuals are aggregated and treated as the position of one person. The CFTC has adopted a statement of policy on the issue of "aggregation."[147] The statement generally treats any person as "owning" an account if the person has an interest in the account of 10% or more. In addition, positions of discretionary accounts and customer trading programs of FCMs (and their officers, partners, and employees) are considered to be controlled by the FCM except where (1) the trading in the account is directed by someone other than the FCM; (2) the FCM maintains only the amount of control over the account required to fulfill its duty to supervise diligently the trading; and (3) the trading decisions are determined independently of trading decisions in other accounts of the FCM.

Prohibition of Manipulation. Another aspect of the regulation of trading under the CEA is the prohibition of price manipulation. Certain provisions of the CEA prohibit the manipulation or attempted manipulation of the market price of a commodity.[148] This prohibition applies to conduct in either cash or futures markets. The CEA does not define "manipulation"; instead, the CFTC (and its administrative law judges) and various courts have struggled to establish a definition. However, it has generally been held that manipulation includes not only activity which causes the raising or lowering of prices, but also that which prevents the rise or fall of prices which would otherwise be caused by the forces of supply and demand.[149] Both the CFTC and certain courts have held that manipulation requires an intent to manipulate;[150] although this intent may be proven by circumstantial evidence.[151] In proving that manipulation occurred, the CFTC and certain courts have also held it is irrelevant whether the alleged manipulator made a profit.[152]

Reporting Requirements. An additional element of the regulation of trading under the CEA is the large trader reporting requirements.[153] The purpose of these requirements is to enable the CFTC to engage in market surveillance by monitoring traders holding large positions. Traders holding, controlling, or having a financial interest in an open futures position equaling or exceeding the applicable reporting level are required to file reports with the CFTC so long as their position equals or exceeds the limit. The three categories of traders for reporting purposes are (1) FCMs and foreign brokers (who file '01 reports); (2) persons holding *bona fide* hedging positions and merchants, processors, and dealers in cotton (who file '04 reports); and (3) all other traders (who file '03 reports). Reporting levels are different for different categories of traders.[154] [Substantial changes not reflected here have recently occurred in this area of the law.]

The CFTC requires '01 reports to be filed daily and '04 reports to be filed weekly.[155] The CFTC formerly required '03 reports to be filed daily; however, CFTC regulations were recently changed, and these reports now must be filed only on special call from the CFTC.[156] Traders who file '04 reports are not required to report positions in certain commodities which persons filing '01 reports must report.[157] In addition, traders who may be required to file '03 reports are required to maintain certain books and records.[158]

REMEDYING VIOLATIONS OF THE CEA. One of the significant changes in the CEA as a result of the 1974 amendments was the addition of a number of new provisions for dealing with violations of the act. The CEA now includes procedures by which persons harmed by violators of the CEA may seek redress, as well as means by which the CFTC and other government authorities can punish violations.

Private Claims

Reparations Proceedings. The 1974 amendments to the CEA added a new administrative remedy for persons harmed by violations of the CEA or CFTC regulations. This remedy involves "reparations" proceedings, which may be brought against any person required to register as a floor broker, FCM, associated person, CTA, or CPO.[159] A complaint must be filed by the aggrieved party with the Complaints Section of the CFTC within 2 years of the occurrence of the alleged violation. The alleged violator is required to answer the complaint if the Complaints Section feels that the facts stated in the complaint warrant an answer. The CFTC may also conduct an investigation into the alleged violation. After the Complaints Section reviews the complaint, it may decide to forward the matter to the Hearings Section for the institution of a formal adjudicatory proceeding. This proceeding will include a hearing before an administrative law judge (ALJ) if the damages exceed $5,000; otherwise, the Hearings Sections may choose to allow only affidavits in support of the complaint and answer. Although the CFTC may review the decision made by the ALJ if such review is "necessary or appropriate to resolve an important issue of law of public policy,"[160] there is no right to such review. However, the CFTC has proposed new regulations which would establish such a right.[161] [Substantial changes not reflected here have recently occurred in this area of the law. See Foreword.]

The CEA contains specific provisions for judicial review and enforcement of reparations awards.[162] Such awards are enforceable for 3 years through a federal district court. Costs and attorney's fees can be awarded by the court. The awards are reviewable in the U.S. Court of Appeals, but the findings of fact made in the reparations proceeding are conclusive if supported by the weight of the evidence. If an award is made, either it must be paid or the decision must be appealed within 15 days of the period allowed for compliance. A failure to do either will result in the party being prohibited from trading on contract markets and having his/her registration automatically suspended.

Arbitration. An alternative to a reparations proceeding in some circumstances is arbitration. CFTC regulations require all contract markets to provide for fair and equitable procedures, through arbitration or otherwise, for the settlement of customers' claims and grievances against members (or their employees) which do not exceed $15,000.[163] These procedures must meet certain minimum requirements to ensure that they are fair and equitable. The procedures are also required to be voluntary.[164] Because of the enormous backlog of reparations cases, the CFTC recently proposed to amend its regulations in order to encourage the choice of arbitration over reparations proceedings.[165]

Private Lawsuits Under the CEA. A possible third alternative for a person seeking compensation for losses arising from a violation of the CEA is a suit for damages in federal court. The federal courts are divided on the question of whether a person can bring a suit for damages for violations for certain provisions of the CEA.[166] Although the CEA does not specifically authorize such suits, a number of courts have allowed such actions under the theory that such a private right of action can be "implied" from the act and its legislative history. This theory has been employed to find private judicial remedies for violations of the federal securities laws.[167] The U.S. Supreme Court will soon decide whether such a right exists under the CEA, and if so, under which provisions.[168] [Substantial changes not reflected here have recently occurred in this area of the law. See Foreword.]

Governmental Enforcement Actions

CFTC Power Over Exchanges. The CEA now contains numerous ways for the CFTC and other government authorities to bring enforcement actions against violators of the act. One way in which this may be accomplished is by CFTC action to discipline members of exchanges for the violation of exchange rules. The CFTC may take such action whenever the exchange fails to discipline a member for such a violation.[169] In addition, the CFTC has discretionary authority to review all exchange disciplinary actions. The CFTC may affirm, set aside, or remand the decision for further proceedings, or it may modify the decision.[170] The CEA requires an exchange to make public its findings and reasons for disciplinary action, including the action taken or penalty imposed. However, the evidence gathered may be disclosed only to the persons subjected to the proceeding and to the CFTC.[171]

CFTC Administrative Actions. The CFTC has the power to initiate administrative actions against violators of the CEA.[172] Such a proceeding may be initiated if the CFTC has reason to believe that a person (other than a contract market)[173] either (1) is manipulating commodity prices or attempting to do so; (2) has willfully made a material false statement or omission in a registration application or report; or (3) has violated any provision of the CEA, CFTC regulations, or a CFTC order. An action may also be initiated against any person who has induced, or aided and abetted in, such a violation.[174]

The person against whom an administrative action is initiated has the right to notice of the charges and a hearing.[175] Upon a finding of a violation, the CFTC has authority to prohibit the party from trading on contract markets, suspend for up to 6 months or revoke his or her registration, or assess a civil penalty of up to $100,000 for each violation. However, the CFTC is required to consider certain factors before it assesses any money penalty.[176] If the violator's primary business involves the use of commodity futures markets, the size of its business and the extent of its ability to continue in business must be considered. For other violators, the CFTC must consider their net worth. The penalty assessed can be recovered by court action if it is not paid. Any order issued may be appealed to the U.S. Court of Appeals.

CFTC Cease-and-Desist Orders. The CFTC also has the authority to issue cease-and-desist orders against certain violations of the CEA.[177] An order to cease and desist from such violations may be issued against any person (other than a contract market)[178] if that person is manipulating or attempting to manipulate the market price of a commodity, or is violating or has violated any provision of the CEA or a CFTC regulation. Before an order is issued, the alleged violator must receive notice of the charges against him or her and be given a hearing. A cease-and-desist order is also subject to judicial review. The significance of a cease-and-desist order is that the failure to comply with such an order is a crime. Ordinarily, it is a misdemeanor, although it is a felony if the violation involved embezzlement of customer funds, or the manipulation, cornering, or transmitting of false market information (see "Criminal Conduct").

CFTC Injunctions and Compliance Orders. The CFTC has the authority, as another enforcement alternative, to bring actions in court to obtain injunctions and compliance orders.[179] It may bring an action in federal district court to enjoin any person (including a contract market) or to enforce compliance with the CEA or CFTC regulations if that person (1) has engaged, is engaging, or is about to engage in a violation of the CEA or (2) is restraining trading in any commodity futures contract.

CFTC Denial of Registration. Another sanction available to enforce the CEA and its policies is the denial of registration. CFTC regulations govern the manner in which registration in any capacity under the CEA may be denied.[180] In some instances, the applicant has the right to notice and a hearing regarding the grounds for denial of registration. Those grounds include: (1) a conviction of a felony, debarment from contracting with the United States, willfully making a material statement which is false or misleading, or willfully omitting a material fact in the application; (2) a conviction of a misdemeanor involving certain commodity or securities transactions; (3) a prohibition by court injunction, or by agreement or settlement with the CFTC or SEC, from engaging in certain commodity or securities activities; or (4) a finding within the past 10 years by a court, the CFTC, or the SEC, that the applicant violated certain federal commodity and securities laws, or aided or abetted a violation, or failed reasonably to supervise with a view toward preventing such violations; or (5) an outstanding CFTC order denying the applicant trading privileges on any contract market, suspending or revoking the registration of the applicant in some capacity, or suspending the applicant from membership on any contract market. No hearing is required if the applicant's registration has been revoked or is currently under suspension. [Substantial changes not reflected here have recently occurred in this area of the law.]

CFTC Investigative Powers. Finally, the CFTC has certain investigative powers.[181] It may make such investigations as it deems necessary to ascertain the facts regarding the operations of exchanges and other persons subject to the CEA. It may publish the results of these investigations, although it may not publish data and information that would separately disclose the business transactions or market positions of any person and trade secrets or names of customers.

State Enforcement Powers. The 1978 amendments to the CEA also gave state officials certain powers to enforce the CEA.[182] State attorneys general and securities commissioners are authorized to bring civil actions in federal district court on behalf of their citizens seeking injunctions or damages, or both, for violations of the CEA. However, these actions may not be brought against contract markets or floor brokers. [Substantial changes not reflected here have recently occurred in this area of the law. See Foreword.]

Criminal Conduct

Generally. Violations of certain provisions of the CEA are criminal offenses.[183] As such, these violations may be prosecuted by U.S. District Attorneys. The maximum fines for felonies which can be imposed on individuals and the maximum fines for misdemeanors were raised in 1974 from $10,000 to $100,000.

Felonies. The following acts are felonies punishable by a fine of up to $500,000 ($100,000 for individuals), imprisonment of up 5 years, and costs of prosecution: (1) embezzlement by an FCM (or any of its employees or agents) of customer funds exceeding $100; (2) manipulating or attempting to manipulate the price of a commodity; (3) cornering or attempting to corner a commodity; (4) knowingly delivering false information tending to affect the price of a commodity; (5) failing to comply with a CFTC cease-and-desist order relating to the aforementioned offenses; (6) acquiring, using, trading on the basis of, or imparting of nonpublic ("inside") information by persons associated with the CFTC; (7) violating the antifraud rules; (8) engaging in a business which must be carried on through or by a member of a contract market by a nonmember; (9) misrepresenting one's membership in a contract market; and (10) engaging in options transactions in commodities regulated prior to 1974.[184]

Misdemeanors. The following acts are misdemeanors punishable by a fine of up to $100,000, imprisonment of up to 1 year, and costs of prosecution: (1) failure to register with the CFTC; (2) failure to file trader reports; (3) exceeding speculative limits; (4) engaging in wash sales, cross trades, accommodation trades, fictitious sales, or transactions resulting in the reporting of a false price (5) violation of a cease-and-desist order relating to certain offenses; and (6) violation of a CFTC order prohibiting a person from trading.[185]

FUTURES ASSOCIATIONS. The 1974 amendments to the CEA gave the CFTC the power to register self-regulatory associations of registrants. The purpose of such associations is to assume a large portion of the present regulatory responsibilities of the CFTC. The CEA establishes certain requirements for such associations. A registered futures association must be designed to promote just and equitable principles of trade, and must provide for discipline of members who violate its rules.[186] In addition, it must make provision for the election by customers of arbitration of claims of $15,000 or less.[187] [Substantial changes not reflected here have recently occurred in this area of the law. See Foreword.]

The CFTC has the authority to impose sanctions on any registered association and its members. It can also review disciplinary proceedings of the association and, in some cases, abrogate association rules. The CFTC may require persons who are not members of an association to pay fees to defray regulatory costs and subject them to such regulation as it finds necessary.[188] The 1978 amendments to the CEA also gave the CFTC the authority to approve association rules requiring membership in at least one such association.[189] The National Futures Association recently became the first organization to be registered as a self-regulatory association (see "The Role of the National Futures Association" under "Current Regulatory Issues").

CURRENT REGULATORY ISSUES

The regulatory framework under which the development of the commodities industry will take place was established by the 1974 amendments to the CEA. Several changes to this framework were made in 1978. Nevertheless, a number of unresolved regulatory issues remain, the most important of which warrant some discussion.

THE ROLE OF THE NATIONAL FUTURES ASSOCIATION

Approval. As mentioned above, the CFTC recently approved the registration of the first registered futures association. The official recognition of the National Futures Association (NFA) followed 5 years of discussion between the industry and the CFTC. While most of the comments regarding the application of the association were favorable, concerns about the anticompetitive aspects of the NFA were voiced by the Antitrust Division of the Department of Justice.[190] However, as previously noted, Congress amended the CEA in 1978 to permit mandatory membership in such associations (see "Futures Associations" under "The Current Framework of Commodity Regulation").

Objective. The objective of the NFA is to implement a comprehensive regulatory program for the commodities industry, with special attention devoted to the uniform regulation of the retail activities of its members.[191] The NFA plans to devote its first year of operations to the hiring of a professional staff, and to the gradual commencement of its programs for FCMs, which will include the registration of associated persons. Its second year will be devoted to phasing-in its program for CTAs and CPOs. The NFA plans to be fully operational by the fall of 1983. [Substantial changes not reflected here have recently occurred in this area of the law. See Foreword.]

Board of Directors. The NFA will be headed by a Board of Directors composed of 38 members.[192] Each contract market will have either one or two seats, depending upon its size. Fourteen of the members will represent FCMs. CTAs and commercial users of the markets will each have three seats, while CPOs and commercial bankers will each have two seats. Three seats are reserved for "public" directors, that is, individuals with no direct affiliation with the industry. With the exception of contract markets, not more than one-half of the directors in any of these categories may be from the same geographic region; the three regions are the eastern, central, and western.

The duties of the day-to-day supervision of the NFA management will be performed by an Executive Committee of the Board, which will have nine members.[193] One member will be the President of the Board. Two members will be directors representing contract markets, three will be FCM directors, two will be directors representing other industry participants (except commercial banks), and one will be a "public" director. Membership on the executive committee is also subject to geographic diversity requirements.

Mandatory Membership. The Articles of Incorporation of the NFA are designed to take advantage of the provision of the CEA which permits a registered futures association to require membership in one such association.[194] The articles prohibit a member of the NFA from accepting futures orders from another person (except a direct customer) unless the other person belongs to either the NFA or another registered futures association. The mandatory membership requirement will therefore result in an interruption in the flow of customer orders when an ineligible person becomes involved. This rule makes an exception for floor brokers, who are not required to join the NFA in order to accept orders for execution. The rationale for the exception is that floor brokers are already regulated by the contract market where they conduct business.

FCM Financial Requirements. The NFA intends to devote considerable attention to establishing and enforcing minimum financial requirements for its FCM members.[195] However, it does not intend to establish such requirements for other members, such as agents of FCMs, CPOs, or CTAs. With regard to this aspect of its operations, the NFA intends to relieve the contract markets of some of their present regulatory duties.

Ethical Standards. The NFA will also adopt ethical standards to apply to its members.[196] These will include prohibitions against fraud, manipulative or deceptive acts and practices, and unjust or inequitable dealings. Bucketing will be prohibited, and members will be required to establish procedures for supervising employees and handling discretionary accounts.

Admission. Membership in the NFA is open to practically any industry participant: any CFTC registrant, any contract market, any agent of an FCM, and any other person engaged in the commodity futures business, unless the person is subject to certain specified membership disqualifications (which include revocation of CFTC registration).[197] Other persons may become members if the CFTC designates them by rule as being eligible. In addition, each employee of an FCM member must register with the NFA as an "associate." Applicants will be screened initially by the NFA staff. If there is reason to believe that the applicant is not qualified, or if the applicant wishes to appeal a preliminary determination to that effect, the Membership Committee of the NFA Board will decide the matter. An applicant may be disqualified on the basis of certain grounds enumerated in the CEA, and must also meet the fitness standards used by the CFTC to screen applicants for registration. The CFTC has the power to order a person admitted to the NFA.

Discipline. The disciplinary function of the NFA will be carried out through its Office of Compliance.[198] The office will engage in financial auditing and ethical surveillance. Infractions will be reported to a nine-member Business Conduct Committee, which may conduct disciplinary proceedings. The committee will make the decision whether or not to serve a formal complaint on the accused. If a complaint is issued, the accused must answer, and is entitled to a hearing before the committee. Adverse decisions may be appealed to the Appeals Committee of the NFA Board. This disciplinary authority may be exercised over any member or associate required to register with the CFTC, except for floor brokers (who are subject to exchange regulation). In addition, summary action (including actions without a prior hearing) may be taken by the President of the Board, with the concurrence of the Executive Committee, in certain emergency situations. [Substantial changes not reflected here have recently occurred in this area of the law. See Foreword.]

Arbitration. The establishment of a system of arbitration is another important objective of the NFA.[199] Its goal is to replace the arbitration procedures of the various exchanges with one centralized system. The NFA arbitration system will hear complaints by customers against members who are FCMs, CTAs, and CPOs (or their employees), and complaints against associates. The system will not deal with claims over $15,000, although the NFA has the discretionary authority to hear other claims or claims for larger amounts. There is no right of appeal and awards may be enforced by court proceedings.

Funding. The NFA by-laws have established a funding plan to be phased-in by the board.[200] Annual assessments for contract markets are based upon the number of futures transactions, with minimum and maximum assessments. Assessments for FCMs are based upon a flat fee plus an amount related to the number of transactions. Fees for other members have been set in flat amounts, and some may be waived or reduced by the board.

COMMODITY OPTIONS: CFTC PILOT PROGRAM

Scope of the Pilot Program. Another current regulatory issue relates to the establishment by the CFTC of a scheme of regulation for commodity options. As mentioned above, the 1974 amendments to the CEA gave the CFTC the authority either to ban or to regulate options transactions in all commodities other than those regulated prior to that date (see "The Commodity Futures Trading Commission" and "Jurisdiction" under "The Current Framework of Commodity Regulation"). The CFTC established the framework for an options pilot program in November 1981.[201] The program is scheduled to last for 3 years, during which time the CFTC will gather information in order to decide whether, or in what manner, it should continue to permit options trading. The original pilot program involves only options on futures contracts traded on domestic exchanges. However, the CFTC proposed at the time of initiation of the program that it be expanded to include dealer options, that is, options on physical commodities.[202]

Under the pilot program, each domestic exchange may apply for designation to trade options on one futures contract for which it is already designated as a contract market.[203] The program limits participation to those FCMs who are members of either the contract market on which the option is traded or a registered futures association which has undertaken to regulate its members in a manner equivalent to a contract market.[204] [Substantial changes not reflected here have recently occurred in this area of the law. See Foreword.]

Designation Requirements

The Contract. An exchange desiring designation as a contract market for the trading of a commodity-option contract must demonstrate that the contract meets certain standards.[205] Specifically, it must show that it is likely to serve a legitimate economic purpose; (2) that commercial interests have participated in formulating the option contract and have expressed an interest in using it; and (3) that there is sufficient liquidity in the cash and futures markets for the commodity underlying the option to prevent market disruption. (This requirement is automatically satisfied if the volume of trading in all contract months for the underlying futures contract has averaged at least 1,000 contracts per week for the preceding 12 months.)

Exchange Rules. Any exchange seeking designation is also required to adopt certain rules governing options trading.[206] These rules pertain to strike prices, deep-out-of-pocket options, and notification of option grantors of the exercise of the options. In addition, exchanges must require member FCMs (1) to establish specific procedures for making and retaining records of customer complaints; (2) to establish procedures for supervising customer accounts; (3) to disclose any disciplinary action taken against them or their associated persons; (4) to submit to the exchange all promotional material to determine that it is not fraudulent; (5) to establish certain procedures governing discretionary accounts; and (6) to refrain from fraudulent or high-pressure tactics. Exchanges must also establish procedures for, and conduct sales practice audits of, member FCMs.

Exchange Procedures. Various other procedures must be adopted by exchanges seeking designation.[207] These procedures include (1) a system for the general dissemination and quotation of volume and last-sale-price information for the option; (2) a system of clearance and processing of option transactions which will not adversely affect the corresponding system for futures transactions; and (3) a comprehensive listing of occupational or business categories of commercial users of the physical commodity. [Substantial changes not reflected here have recently occurred in this area of the law. See Foreword.]

Other Features. Much of the remainder of the pilot program consists of the same types of rules governing futures trading. For example, segregation of customer funds by FCMs is required,[208] and similar recordkeeping[209] and reporting[210] requirements apply. In addition, the pilot program allows individual exchanges to determine the appropriate levels of margin to be required of option grantors. The CFTC has taken this approach because it feels that the risk of the grantor of an uncovered option is sufficiently similar to that of a futures customer to allow the same deference to the expertise of the exchanges.[211]

However, other aspects of the program differ from the regulatory scheme for futures trading, reflecting the differences in the two types of transactions. For example, options traded under the pilot program may be exercised only by the "book-entry" method; that is, by the establishment by book entry in the clearing organization of positions in the underlying futures contracts.[212] The alternative method, which was rejected, would have required an option grantor to establish a position in the appropriate futures contract and to provide instructions to the clearing organization to transfer that position to the person exercising the option. The reason for its rejection by the CFTC was to avoid possible congestion or disorder in the underlying futures contract and the resultant distortion in futures prices.[213]

In addition, the pilot-program regulations require that option premiums be paid in full to the FCM carrying the option customer's account at the time the option is purchased.[214] Clearing members must receive the full amount of the premium from their customers, and clearing organizations are required to receive this premium from their members. The reasons given by the CFTC for not allowing the margining of option premiums were (1) to avoid customer confusion concerning the extent of their obligation and (2) to ensure the financial stability of FCMs, clearing members, and clearing organizations.[215]

The pilot-program regulations also contain special rules governing disclosures to option customers. No FCM may open a commodity option account for a customer unless the FCM furnishes the customer with a written disclosure statement whose content is specifically set forth in the regulations.[216] The FCM must also receive an acknowledgment from the customer that he or she has read and understands the statement. In addition, exchanges are required as a condition of designation to adopt rules requiring member FCMs to comply with these disclosure requirements.[217]

CFTC JURISDICTIONAL ISSUES

Background. A current area of controversy which has stimulated much debate involves the question of the CFTC's "exclusive jurisdiction" in the area of commodity trading. As previously noted (see "The Commodity Futures Trading Commission" and "Jurisdiction" under "The Current Framework of Commodity Regulation"), the 1974 amendments to the CEA gave the CFTC

> exclusive jurisdiction with respect to accounts, agreements (including any transaction which is of the character of, or is commonly known to the trade as, an "option" . . .) and transactions involving contracts for sale of a commodity for future delivery, traded or executed on a contract market designated pursuant to section 5 of this Act or any other board of trade, exchange, or market.[218]

The legislative history of both the 1974 and 1978 amendments to the CEA reflects a congressional intent to vest the CFTC with exclusive jurisdiction in the area of commodity futures trading. For example, the Conference Report on the 1974 amendments states:

> Under the exclusive grant of jurisdiction to the Commission, the authority in the Commodity Exchange Act (and the regulations issued by the Commission) would preempt the field insofar as futures regulation is concerned. Therefore, if any substantive state law regulating futures trading was contrary or inconsistent with federal law, federal law would govern. In view of the broad grant of authority to the Commission to regulate the futures industry, the conferees do not contemplate that there will be a need for any supplementary regulation by the states.[219]

Thus the Senate Committee Chairman Talmadge remarked during floor debates on the 1974 amendments: "In establishing this Commission, it is the Committee's intent to give it exclusive jurisdiction over those areas delineated in the Act."[220] Moreover, the Senate Committee emphasized in its report on the 1974 amendments that "The Committee wished to make clear that where the jurisdiction of the Commodity Futures Trading Commission is applicable, it supercedes State as well as Federal agencies."[221] Congress repeated its support for this policy when it amended the CEA again in 1978, and spoke of the necessity for a "single, unified system" and a "coherent and consistent. . .national policy" for futures trading.[222]

However, this congressional grant of "exclusive jurisdiction" to the CFTC has raised a number of questions. In reality, the CFTC has exclusive jurisdiction only in certain areas. In other areas it either shares jurisdiction with other regulators, or has no jurisdiction at all. Some of those areas are discussed below. [Substantial changes not reflected here have recently occurred in this area of the law. See Foreword.]

CFTC–SEC Jurisdictional Boundaries

Background. One of the principal areas of jurisdictional controversy involves the respective regulatory domains of the CFTC and the Securities and Exchange Commission (SEC). Of importance in this regard is the proviso which accompanies the "exclusive jurisdiction" provision of the CEA. It states

> except as herinabove provided, nothing contained in this section shall (i) supercede or limit the jurisdiction at any time conferred on the Securities and Exchange Commission or other regulatory authorities under the laws of the United States or of any State, or (ii) restrict the Securities and Exchange Commission and such other authorities from carrying out their duties and responsibilities in accordance with such laws.[223]

The phrase "except as hereinabove provided" in the above proviso indicates that it does not apply to the objects of the CFTC "exclusive jurisdiction" mentioned earlier in the same section of the CEA. However, the SEC took a contrary position soon after the adoption of the 1974 amendments. The SEC contended that it retained jurisdiction over any futures contract on a financial instrument defined as a "security" under the federal securities laws. This dispute arose in connection with the approval by the CFTC of a futures contract on GNMA certificates, which began trading on the Chicago Board of Trade in 1975. However, the SEC took no formal action in the matter.[224] During the 1978 reauthorization of the CFTC, the SEC attempted unsuccessfully to amend the CEA in order to acquire from the CFTC its regulatory jurisdiction over futures transactions involving securities.[225]

December 1981 Jurisdictional Agreement. In December 1981, following discussions between CFTC Chairman Philip McB. Johnson and SEC Chairman John S. R. Shad, the two agencies reached agreement on a number of issues relating to jurisdiction over financial instruments and other matters. The two agencies subsequently prepared legislative proposals to codify the agreement.[226] This draft legislation will be considered during the 1982 reauthorization process for the CFTC (see "Conclusion: Reauthorization and Beyond").

A principal part of the agreement deals with the division of authority with respect to options and futures contracts involving securities. Under the agreement, the SEC would assume regulatory responsibility for options on securities and Certificates of Deposit, and on all groups or indexes of securities or Certificates of Deposit. This provision would allow the SEC to continue its efforts to regulate the options on "physical" securities which are presently traded on national securities exchanges and to assume jurisdiction over any options on aggregates of securities which may be traded in the future.

The agreement would give the CFTC jurisdiction over both futures contracts, and options on those futures contracts, on securities exempted from SEC regulation (other than municipal securities), and on certain broad-based groups or indexes of securities. However, the CFTC's authority over futures contracts (and options thereon) on stock indexes would be subject to a number of limitations. First, futures contracts on such indexes or groups would have to provide for settlement either in cash or by delivery of a security for which the CFTC would have authority to approve a futures contract (e.g., a U.S. Government security). Second, futures or options contracts in securities indexes or groups would be required to be such that trading in the contract would not be likely to produce manipulation in the corresponding futures or other related markets. Third, the securities group or index underlying any such contract would be required to be predominantly composed of the securities of unaffiliated issuers. Fourth, this group or index would be required to be a widely published measure of, and to reflect, the market for all publicly traded equity or debt securities or a substantial segment of such market, or be comparable to such a measure.

The CFTC–SEC agreement recognizes the SEC's strongly expressed concern that it be given a role in the designation by the CFTC of contract markets for futures contracts (or options thereon) on securities groups or indexes. The agreement therefore would require the CFTC to consult with the SEC in connection with such designations. The CFTC would be required to establish a public-comment period and to hear SEC objections with respect to whether the minimum requirements for designation have been met. The CFTC would also be required to provide the SEC with an oral hearing, and would be required to give appropriate weight to any SEC objections. Finally, if the CFTC designated such a contract market, the SEC would have the right to seek judicial review of the order.

The remaining category of securities addressed by the CFTC–SEC agreement is that of individual nonexempt corporate or municipal securities. Under the agreement, the trading of futures contracts (and options thereon) on such securities (or contracts or options based on the value thereof) would be banned. However, the agreement expresses the intention of the two agencies to study the issues raised by the trading of these futures and options with a view toward eventually recommending the repeal of this prohibition.

The CFTC–SEC agreement also allocates regulatory responsibility with respect to options contracts on foreign currencies. This responsibility would be shared by giving the SEC jurisdiction over such options traded on national securities exchanges, and by giving the CFTC authority to regulate these options when they are traded on the commodities markets.

One last aspect of the CFTC–SEC agreement attempts to clarify the shared regulatory responsibilities of the two agencies with respect to commodity pools. The agreement recognizes that the CFTC will continue its comprehensive regulation of commodity pool operators, and that the CEA grants the CFTC exclusive jurisdiction with respect to state regulation. The agreement would reserve to the SEC its authority related to the registration of interests in commodity pools. Specifically, it recognizes the applicability to commodity pools of the Securities Act of 1933 and the Securities Exchange Act of 1934 with respect to the securities issued by the pools and transactions therein. The agreement also recognizes the applicability to commodity pools and commodity pool operators, in certain circumstances, of the Investment Advisers Act of 1940 and the Investment Company Act of 1940. [Substantial changes not reflected here have recently occurred in this area of the law. See Foreword.]

CFTC–State Jurisdictional Boundaries. Another current jurisdictional issue relates to the respective domains of the CFTC and the states in the regulation of commodity futures trading. In addition to the legislative history already discussed, it is noteworthy that when Congress amended the CEA in 1974, it repealed a section of the act which had provided that "nothing in this section or section 4b shall be construed to impair any state law applicable to any transaction enumerated or described in such section."[227] This had been the only language in the CEA specifically reserving regulatory authority to the states.

In 1978, Congress added to the CEA Section 6d, which gave state attorneys general and securities administrators authority to bring civil actions in federal court on behalf of the state's citizens for violations of the CEA.[228] In enacting this section, Congress noted that in these suits the states would not be enforcing "their local laws," but rather CFTC policies, and that the provision was "(c)onsistent with the Commission's exclusive jurisdiction and preemption of state regulatory activity enacted in 1974. . ."[229] To assure a "national policy established by the Commission,"[230] Congress specified in Section 6d that state regulators must immediately notify the CFTC of any actions brought by them under the section, and that the CFTC may intervene in any such action.

The area in which the respective jurisdictional realms of the CFTC and the states have been subject to the greatest dispute is the area of the regulation of commodity pools. As previously discussed (see "Regulation of Trading Professionals" and "Commodity Trading Advisors and Commodity Pool Operators" under "The Current Framework of Commodity Regulation"), an extensive system of regulation of commodity pool operators has been established by the CFTC. However, the interests in commodity pools organized as corporations or limited partnerships are considered "securities," and are therefore also within the scope of state securities laws. The controversy with respect to commodity pools stems from the attempts by a number of states to regulate the operational aspects of commodity pools by conditioning the right to make a public offering of commodity pool interests in those states on compliance with certain operational standards.

Representative "guidelines" for public commodity pools utilized by state securities administrators were adopted in April 1978 by the Central Securities Administrators Council (CSAC), a group of seven midwestern state securities administrators.[231] The guidelines established standards relating to the qualifications of the sponsor of the pool; the suitability of investors for participation in the pool; the amount and types of fees, compensation, and expenses charged to the pool; the rights and obligations of participants; and the manner of marketing the interests in the pool (including certain disclosure requirements). In September 1980 the North American Securities Administrators Association (NASAA) proposed certain commodity pool guidelines modeled after the CSAC guidelines.[232] The proposed NASAA guidelines contain very strict limitations on the types and amounts of fees and compensation which can be charged to a pool.

The proposed NASAA guidelines have been widely criticized by the industry. The guidelines conflict with the CFTC treatment of commodity pools inasmuch as they impose numerous additional restrictions, many of which were specifically considered and rejected by the CFTC. In addition, many of the proposed guidelines are based upon inappropriate analogies to other guidelines for oil and gas and real-estate ventures, and to investment advisor and investment company laws. A strong argument can be made that such guidelines, if implemented, would be preempted by the CFTC'S "exclusive jurisdiction" over commodity trading. The future of the commodity pool industry is dependent upon how closely the guidelines finally adopted by NASAA, if any, resemble the guidelines which have been proposed. At the date of this writing, there are no existing public commodity pools which could meet the proposed NASAA guidelines. [Substantial changes not reflected here have recently occurred in this area of the law. See Foreword.]

CONCLUSION: REAUTHORIZATION AND BEYOND. At the time of this writing, the 1982 "reauthorization" process for the CFTC has begun. The 1978 amendments to the CEA required Congress to decide whether to reauthorize appropriations for the CFTC by providing for the expiration of such appropriations in September 1982.[233] Reauthorization hearings commenced in February 1982.

The reauthorization process will provide Congress with the opportunity to address numerous issues effecting the system of federal commodities regulation. Of course, the first issue Congress must face is whether to continue the CFTC's existence. It is anticipated that Congress will opt for its continued existence. In addition, a number of other issues are likely to be dealt with. In particular, the jurisdictional matters discussed above are very likely to receive consideration. These hotly contested matters are likely to be at the center of Congress' attention. Congress is also likely to consider proposals

1. to decide the status of leverage contracts (since the CFTC has deferred its ruling on these transactions until after reauthorization);
2. to establish criteria and standards for the setting of speculative position limits;

3. to expand the scope of information protected from CFTC disclosure;
4. to improve the procedures for contract market designation and approval of contract market rules;
5. to establish judicial review of CFTC "emergency" actions;
6. to establish conflict-of-interest rules for exchange governing boards;
7. to protect persons accused of violating the CEA, CFTC regulations, or exchange rules from exposure to multiple proceedings;
8. to establish automatic renewal of registration;
9. to revise or even eliminate the reparations procedure;
10. to establish "user fees" on futures transactions as a source of CFTC funding;
11. to establish a new registration category for persons soliciting either clients for CTAs or pool participants for CPOs;
12. to expand the CFTC's authority to establish testing and qualification requirements for registrants;
13. to clarify or alter the authority of the states to bring enforcement actions aimed at off-exchange fraud;
14. to alter the manner in which levels of margin are set; and
15. to clarify the CEA with a view toward eliminating ambiguities and inconsistencies in the act.

NOTES

1. An excellent research tool in the area of commodity law, which is updated to reflect new developments, is the *Commodity Futures Law Reporter*, published by the Commerce Clearing House, Inc. (For purposes of citation, this source shall hereinafter be referred to as "CCH" with citation to the pertinent paragraph number.)
2. 7 U. S. C. §§1–24 (1976); CCH ¶¶1001–1471. (For purposes of citation, the Commodity Exchange Act shall hereinafter be referred to as "CEA," and all citations shall be the CEA rather than to the corresponding section of the U.S. Code.)
3. Pub. L. 93–463, 88 Stat. 1389, CCH¶¶ 1501–1548. (For purposes of citation, the Commodity Futures Trading Commission Act of 1974 shall hereinafter be referred to as "CFTC Act," and all citations shall be to the CFTC Act rather than to the corresponding section of statutory compilations.)
4. S. Rep. No. 93–1131, 93rd Congress, 2nd Session 18 (1974).
5. H. R. Rep. No. 93–1131, 93rd Congress, 2nd Session 48 (1974).
6. See J. Rainbolt, "Regulating the Grain Gambler and His Successors," 6 *Hofstra L. Rev* **1**, 13–15 (1977) (hereinafter referred to as "Rainbolt").
7. Customer losses in one scheme were estimated at over $71 million. See H. R. No. 93–975, 93rd Congress, 2nd Session 48 (1974).
8. See Ref. 6, pp. 13–15.
9. H. R. Rep. No. 93–975, 93rd Congress, 2nd Session 48 (1974).
10. See *United States* v. *Board of Trade, Inc.*, CCH ¶ 20,011 (N.D. I11. 1974).
11. H. R. Rep. No. 93–975, 93rd Congress 2nd Session 48 (1974).
12. The authority of the Department of Agriculture and Secretary of Agriculture under the CEA was delegated to the Commodity Exchange Authority, an agency within the department.
13. CEA §2(a) (2).

14. CEA §2(a)(1).
15. *Ibid.*
16. *Ibid.*
17. CEA §§ 40 (antifraud); §§ 6(b) and 9(b) (antimanipulation).
18. CEA § 2(a) (1).
19. CEA § 4c(c).
20. CEA § 4c(b).
21. CEA § 4c.
22. CEA §§ 2(a)(1) and 19(a).
23. CEA §§ 19(a), 19(b), and 19(c).
24. 17 C.F.R. § 31.1, *as promulgated* 43 Fed. Reg. 56885 (December 5, 1978), CCH ¶ 20,704. (Regulations promulgated by the Commodity Futures Trading Commission under the Commodity Exchange Act, found in Part 17 of the Code of Federal Regulations, shall hereinafter be referred to for citation purposes as "Reg." They may be found in CCH ¶¶ 2001–3326.)
25. Reg. § 31.2, *as promulgated* 44 Fed. Reg. 55820 (September 28, 1979), CCH ¶ 20,898.
26. 44 Fed. Reg. 44177 (July 27, 1979), CCH ¶ 20,863.
27. 44 Fed. Reg. 69304 (December 3, 1979), CCH ¶ 20,929.
28. Pub. L. 95–405, 92 Stat. 865, CCH ¶¶ 1601–1627, *codified at* CEA § 19. (For purposes of citation, the 1978 amendments to the CEA, which are known as the Futures Trading Act of 1978, shall hereinafter be referred to as the Futures Trading Act, and all citations shall be to the Futures Trading Act rather than to the corresponding section of statutory compilations.) Certain rules have been proposed for commodity broker bankruptcies; see 46 Fed. Reg. 57535 (November 24, 1981), CCH ¶ 21,282.
29. Reg. §§ 16.01–16.02.
30. CEA § 16(a).
31. CEA § 16(c).
32. CEA §§ 8 and 16(d).
33. CEA § 12(a).
34. CEA § § 2(a)(8)(A) (Department of Agriculture), 2(a)(8)(B)(i) (Department of the Treasury, Federal Reserve Board, Securities and Exchange Commission), 4g(1), 4n(3), 5a(2) (Department of Justice), and 9(g) (Comptroller General).
35. CEA § 15.
36. CEA § 2(a)(1).
37. CEA § 4.
38. CEA § 4h(1).
39. CEA § 4h(2).
40. CEA § 5(a).
41. CEA §§ 5(b), 5(c), 5(d), and 5(f).
42. CEA § 5(e).
43. CEA § 2(a)(1).
44. CEA § 5(g).
45. H. R. Rep. No. 93–975, 93rd Congress, 2nd Session 29 (1974); S. Rep. No. 93–1131, 93rd Congress, 2nd Session 6 and 7 (1974).
46. *Guidelines on Economic and Public Interest Requirements for Contract Market Designation*, CCH ¶ 6145.
47. 45 Fed. Reg. 73504 (November 5, 1980), CCH ¶ 21,104.
48. CEA § 6.
49. CEA § 6(a).
50. CEA §§ 5a(1) and 5a(2).
51. Reg. §§ 16.00–16.06.

52. CEA § 5a(4).
53. CEA § 5a(5).
54. CEA § 5a(6).
55. CEA § 5a(10).
56. CEA § 5a(7).
57. CEA § 5a(3).
58. CEA § 5a(8).
59. Contract Market Rule Enforcement Program, Guideline No. 2, CCH ¶ 6430.
60. CEA § 5a(9).
61. CEA § 5a(11).
62. Reg. §§ 180.1–180.6.
63. See, for example, Rule 610.00 of the Chicago Board of Trade.
64. CFTC Act § 210.
65. CEA § 5a(12).
66. Standard to be Applied by the CFTC in Disapproving Contract Market Rules, CCH ¶ 6526.
67. CEA § 5a(12).
68. CEA § 8a(7).
69. CEA § 8a(9).
70. CEA § 5(b).
71. Reg. §§ 1.31, 1.35, and 1.37.
72. Reg. §§ 17.00–17.04.
73. CEA § 2(a)(1).
74. CEA § 2(a)(1).
75. CEA § 4f(1).
76. 45 Fed. Reg. 80485 (December 5, 1980), CCH ¶ 21,114, *effective date deferred* 46 Fed. Reg. 24940 (May 4, 1981), CCH ¶ 21,179.
77. CEA § 4p.
78. CEA § 4g.
79. Reg. §§ 1.33, 1.35–1.37 and 17.00–17.04.
80. CEA § 4j.
81. Reg. § 1.35
82. CEA § 4f(2).
83. Reg. § 1.17(a)(1).
84. 45 Fed. Reg. 79498 (December 1, 1980), CCH ¶ 21,111.
85. Reg. § 1.17(c)(1).
86. CEA § 4d(2).
87. Reg. §§ 1.20–1.30.
88. CEA § 4k (1).
89. CEA §§ 4k(1) and 4k(2).
90. 45 Fed. Reg. 80485 (December 5, 1980), CCH ¶ 21,114, *effective date deferred* 46 Fed. Reg. 24940 (May 4, 1981), CCH ¶ 21,179.
91. Reg. § 166.2.
92. Reg. § 166.3.
93. CEA § 41.
94. CEA § 2(a)(1).
95. *Ibid.*
96. See CCH ¶ 4375.

97. CEA § 2(a)(1).
98. See CCH ¶ 4400.
99. CEA § 4m.
100. 45 Fed. Reg. 80485 (December 5, 1980), CCH ¶ 21,114 *effective date deferred* 46 Fed. Reg. 24940 (May 4, 1981), CCH ¶ 21,179.
101. *Ibid.*
102. Reg. § 4.14.
103. 47 Fed. Reg. 2325 (January 15, 1982), CCH ¶ 21,310.
104. Reg. § 4.13(a)(1).
105. Reg. § 4.13(a)(2).
106. CEA 4n(5).
107. CEA 4n(6). The CFTC has promulgated regulations governing the procedure and grounds for the denial of registration in any capacity under the CEA (see note 162 and accompanying text, *infra*).
108. 46 Fed. Reg. 26004 (May 8, 1981), CCH ¶ 21,188, *effective date deferred* 46 Fed. Reg. 34799 (July 6, 1981).
109. Reg. § 4.31(a).
110. Reg. § 4.21(a).
111. Reg. § 4.31.
112. Reg. § 4.21.
113. Reg. § 4.41(b).
114. Reg. §§ 4.32 (CTAs) and 4.23 (CPOs). The records which CTAs are required to maintain include certain information and documents relating CTAs and their clients, certain confirmations and purchase-and-sale statements, literature distributed and records of oral presentations by the CTA, and books and records of the CTA's other commodity business dealings. The records which a CPO is required to maintain include certain accounting records and documents relating to the CPO and the operation of the pool, certain confirmations and purchase-and-sale statements, literature distributed and records of oral presentations by the CPO, certain financial statements relating to the pool, and books and records of all other activities in which the CPO engages.
115. Reg. § 4.23. The CPO must make available to pool participants all those records it is required to maintain, with the exception of certain information on other pool participants and certain information concerning the CPO.
116. Moreover, a person engaged in the business of selling interests in commodity pools may be required to register as a broker–dealer (see Section 15 of the Securities Exchange Act of 1934, 15 U. S. C. § 780 (1976)].
117. Reg. § 4.30.
118. Reg. § 4.20(a).
119. Reg. §§ 4.20(b) and 4.20(c).
120. Reg. §§ 4.22(a), 4.22(b) and 4.22(h).
121. Reg. §§ 4.22(c)–4.22(f) and 4.22(h).
122. CEA § 40(2).
123. CEA § 40(1).
124. Reg. § 4.41(a).
125. CEA § 4b(1).
126. Reg. § 32.9.
127. Reg. § 30.02.
128. Reg. § 31.03.
129. CEA § 4c(a).

130. Reg. §§ 155.2(a)–155.2(h).
131. Reg. § 155.2(i).
132. Reg. § 155.1 and Reg. § 155.3(a). These regulations define an "affiliated person" of a futures commission merchant for purposes of these regulations as any general partner, officer, director, owner of more than 10% of the equity interest, correspondent, agent or person associated therewith, associated person or employee of the futures commission merchant, and any relative or spouse of any of the foregoing persons, or any relative of such spouse, who shares the same home as any of the foregoing persons.
133. Reg. § 155.3(b).
134. Reg. § 155.3(c).
135. Reg. § 155.3(d).
136. CEA § 4a(1).
137. *Ibid.*
138. 44 Fed. Reg. 7124 (February 6, 1979), CCH ¶ 20,756.
139. Reg. §§ 150.1–150.12.
140. Reg. § 1.61.
141. Reg. § 1.3(z)(1).
142. Reg. § 1.3(z)(2).
143. Reg. §§ 1.3(z)(3) and 1.47.
144. CEA § 4a(4).
145. CEA § 4a(1).
146. *Ibid.*
147. *Statement of Aggregation Policy and Adoption of Related Reporting Rules*, 44 Fed. Reg. 33839 (June 13, 1979), CCH ¶ 20,837.
148. See, for example, CEA §§ 6(b), 6(c), and 9(b).
149. *Cargill, Inc.* v. *Hardin*, 452 F.2d 1154 and 1163 (8th Cir. 1971); Hohenberg Bros. Co., CCH ¶ 20,271 (CFTC 1977), p. 21,477.
150. *Ibid.*
151. *G. H. Miller & Co.* v. *United States*, 201 F.2d 476 and 479–484 (7th Cir. 1953).
152. *Cargill, Inc.* v. *Hardin*, 452 F.2d 1154 and 1163 (8th Cir. 1971); Hohenberg Bros. Co., CCH ¶ 20,271 (CFTC 1977), p. 21,478.
153. Reg. § 15.01(c).
154. Reg. § 15.03. For example, the reporting level for wheat is 3 million bushels for traders filing '04 reports, 1 million bushels for traders filing '03 reports, and 500,000 bushels for traders filing '01 reports.
155. Reg. §§ 17.00–17.04 and 19.00–19.10.
156. Reg. §§ 18.00–18.07, *as amended* 46 Fed. Reg. 59960 (December 8, 1981), CCH ¶ 21,285.
157. Reg. § 15.02
158. Reg. § 18.05.
159. CFTC Act § 106, *codified at* CEA § 14.
160. Reg. § 12.101.
161. 46 Fed. Reg. 9958 (January 30, 1981), CCH ¶ 21,148.
162. CEA §§ 14(f), 14(g), and 14(h).
163. CEA § 5a(11).
164. Reg. §§ 180.1–180.6.
165. 46 Fed. Reg. 60834 (December 14, 1981), CCH ¶ 21,286.
166. Compare *Curran* v. *Merrill Lynch, Pierce, Fenner and Smith, Inc.*, 622 F.2d 216 (8th Cir. 1980), *cert. granted* 68 L. Ed. 2d 293 (1981)(private right exists) with *Rivers* v. *Rosenthal & Company*, 634 F.2d 774 (5th Cir. 1980), *petition for cert. filed* 49 U.S.L.W. 3712 (United States, March 10, 1981) (No. 80–1542) (private right does not exist).

168. See, for example, *Kardon* v. *National Gypsum & Co.*, 69 F. Supp. 512 (E.D. Pa. 1946).
168. See 67 L.Ed. 2d 332 (1981) and 68 L. Ed. 2d 293 (1981) (granting *writ of certiorari* in four cases).
169. CEA § 8c(1)(A); Reg. §§ 8.01–8.28.
170. CEA § 8c(2), 8c(3); Reg. §§ 9.1–9.50.
171. CEA § 8c(1)(B).
172. CEA § 6(b).
173. Although not subject to administrative enforcement actions, contract markets may be subject to proceedings to suspend or revoke their designation should they engage in certain prohibited conduct (see note 46 and accompanying text, *supra*). They are also subject to CFTC injunctive actions (see note 161 and accompanying text, *infra*).
174. CEA § 13.
175. CEA § 6(b).
176. CEA § 6(d).
177. CEA § 6(c).
178. See note 157a, *supra*.
179. CEA § 6(c).
180. Reg. § 1.10e.
181. CEA § 8(a); Reg. §§ 11.1–11.8.
182. Futures Trading Act § 15, *codified at* CEA § 6(d).
183. CFTC Act § 212(d).
184. CEA §§ 9(a), 9(b), 9(d), and 9(e).
185. CEA § 9(c).
186. CEA §§ 17(b)(1)–17(b)(9).
187. CEA § 17(b)(10).
188. CEA §§ 17(c)–17(1).
189. CEA § 17(m).
190. Remarks of John H. Stassen, Fourth Annual Commodities Law Institute, Chicago, Ill. (September 24, 1981).
191. *Ibid.*
192. National Futures Association, "Registration Statement Under Section 17 of the Commodity Exchange Act for Approval As a Registered Futures Association" (March 16, 1981), pp. 3–7.
193. *Ibid*, pp. 4 and 5.
194. *Ibid*, pp. 7 and 8.
195. *Ibid*, pp. 8 and 9.
196. *Ibid.*, p. 9.
197. *Ibid.*, p. 10.
198. *Ibid.*, pp. 11 and 12.
199. *Ibid.*, pp. 12 and 13.
200. *Ibid.*, pp. 13 and 14.
201. 46 Fed. Reg. 54500 (November 3, 1981), CCH ¶ 21,263.
202. 46 Fed. Reg. 54570 (November 3, 1981), CCH ¶ 21,264.
203. Reg. §§ 33.4 (a)(3).
204. Reg. §§ 33.3 (b)(1).
205. Reg. § 33.4(a)(5).
206. Reg. §§ 33.4(b) and 33.4(c).
207. Reg. §§ 33.4(e), 33.4(f), and 33.4(g).
208. Reg. §§ 1.20–1.30.
209. Reg. §§ 1.32–1.39.
210. Reg. §§ 15.00–15.05, 16.00–16.05, 17.00–17.04, 18.00–18.07, and 21.00–21.02.

211. CCH ¶ 21,263, p. 25,291.
212. Reg. § 33.4 (a)(1)(ii).
213. CCH ¶ 21,263, p. 25,290.
214. Reg. § 33.4(a)(2).
215. CCH ¶ 21,263, p. 25,290.
216. Reg. § 33.7.
217. Reg. § 33.4(b)(7).
218. CEA § 2(a)(1).
219. S. Rep. No. 1194, 93rd Congress, 2nd Session 35 (1974) (Conference Report).
220. 120 Cong. Rec. 30459 (September 9, 1974).
221. S. Rep. No. 93–1131, 93rd Congress, 2nd Session 23 (1974).
222. S. Rep. No. 95–850, 95th Congress 2nd Session 75 (1978).
223. CEA § 2(a)(1).
224. See CCH ¶ 20,177 (correspondence between SEC and CFTC).
225. See S. Rep. No. 95–850, 95th Congress, 2nd Session 20–22 (1978).
226. CFTC–SEC Joint Release, CFTC No. 883–82, SEC No. 82-9 (February 2, 1982).
227. CFTC Act § 402.
228. CEA § 6(d), *as amended by*, Section 15 of the Futures Trading Act of 1978, Pub. L. No. 95–405, 92 Stat. 865, 872, and 873 (1978).
229. S. Rep. No. 95–850, 95th Congress, 2nd Session 25 and 26 (1978).
230. *Ibid.*, p. 26.
231. Central Securities Administrators Council, "Guidelines for the Registration of Commodity Pool Programs," *1 Blue Sky L. Rep.* ¶ 5441 (January 24, 1978).
232. North American Securities Administrators Association, Guidelines for the Registration of Commodity Pool Programs (September 17, 1980).
233. CEA § 12(d).

APPENDIX

Regulation Prior to 1974: A Brief History

The scheme of commodities regulation in the United States today reflects American historical experiences. However, it does not represent the first attempt by a national government to control commodities markets and trading.

Foreign experiences include the regulation of the Japanese *cho-ai-mai* rice-ticket market, which was the world's first organized futures market. This market was organized in the 1600s, and was officially recognized by the Japanese Imperial government in 1730. The *cho-ai-mai* market was a futures market with a peculiar rule which prohibited the delivery of cash commodities. This led to large differences between cash and futures prices, and caused the Imperial government to ban trading on the exchange in 1869. However, even more severe fluctuations in the cash market for rice subsequently occurred, and trading was allowed to reopen 2 years later with provision for physical delivery. [See R. Teweles, C. Harlow, and H. Stone, *The Commodity Futures Game*, New York: McGraw-Hill, 1974. pp. 8–9 (hereinafter referred to as Teweles, Harlow, and Stone).]

A contrasting foreign experience is that of the English commodity exchanges, which have existed since the 1500s. For example, the London Commodity Exchange is a group of exchanges evolving from the Royal Exchange, which was opened in London in 1570. The London commodity markets historically have operated with a minimal amount of governmental regulation. [See J. Rainbolt, "Regulating the Grain Gambler and His Successors," 6 Hofstra L. Rev. 1, 4 and 5 (1977) (hereinafter referred to as Rainbolt).]

The first organized commodity markets in the United States were established in the middle of the 19th century. One difference which developed between the London and Chicago markets was that on American exchanges the risk-assuming role of the London dealer was assumed by the speculator. This difference was the result of the much larger volume of trading on American markets and the corresponding greater amount of risk which needed to be assumed.

The early history of exchange regulation in the United States is a history of self-regulation. The Chicago Board of Trade, organized in 1848, established numerous rules to facilitate trading by its members. Early in its life, the board established systems of weighing and inspection of commodities. It also established a set of trading rules which eventually included the following: (1) commodities selected for trading were to be susceptible to easy grading; (2) commodities were to be subject to regular government inspection in order to maintain proper standards of grading; (3) payment was to be in cash at the time of delivery; (4) prices were to be publicly reported and available to all traders; (5) traders were required to establish financial responsibility; and (6) markets were required to have enough buyers and sellers to provide a continuous opportunity to trade.

American commodity exchanges completed their evolution into true "futures" markets about the time of the Civil War. However, after the war there arose political forces which were opposed to the existence of commodity futures exchanges as strictly self-regulated entities. These forces were a part of the Populist movement, and during the latter part of the 19th century their political attacks on futures trading gained in intensity.

The object of the reformers' attacks was the speculator. Because these reformers and their supporters failed to acknowledge the value to the markets of speculators, speculation commonly was equated with gambling. An inclination to blame market losses on factors other than their own shortcomings, as well as a tendency to resent the accumulation of profits from activities which seemed "unproductive," undoubtedly played a large part in the support of this movement by agricultural producers. As a political force, defenders of the futures markets were outnumbered in the state legislatures and Congress by this "farm block." Several state legislatures, mainly in the South, passed laws in the 1880s treating futures contracts as gambling contracts and making them unlawful. The Illinois legislature enacted such a piece of legislation in 1867, although it repealed the law the following year. During that period seven members of the Chicago Board of Trade were arrested for violations.

In Congress the first bill to ban futures trading was introduced in 1844. By the 1890s congressional sentiment in opposition to futures trading reached a peak. In 1893 a bill imposing a prohibitive tax on all futures trading in farm products passed both houses in different forms, and only narrowly failed to become law. A number of years later, in 1916, Congress successfully enacted the Cotton Futures Act, which regulated certain aspects of cotton futures trading (see Teweles, Harlow, and Stone, pp. 10–12).

After the conclusion of World War I, the price of agricultural commodities declined sharply. Much of the blame was placed on speculators, and in particular on the practice of short-selling. The result of the rekindled hostility toward speculators was the passage by Congress in 1922 of the Futures Trading Act. This act included a tax of $0.20 per bushel on transactions conducted from a government-designated exchange. However, the act was declared unconstitutional by the Supreme Court the same year as being beyond the congressional taxing power.

Later the same year Congress rewrote the Futures Trading Act, and removed the tax provision. The new act, entitled the Grain Futures Act, was based on the congressional power to regulate interstate commerce. This new law was upheld by the Supreme Court. The Grain Futures Act regulated futures trading only in grain, and only on certain exchanges. The Department of Agriculture was given authority to administer the act. The act was designed principally to regulate the exchanges rather than individual traders, its most important provision being a procedure for the "designation" of exchanges. Under this provision, futures trading could lawfully be conducted only as a "designated contract market." One important condition of designation was that the exchange take steps to ensure that its members would not engage in price manipulation. If the exchanges failed to fulfill their obligations to comply with the conditions of designation, the suspension or revocation of the designation was the only available penalty. Apart from this draconian measure (which seldom could be expected to be imposed) little could be done to enforce this law. The act also contained some provisions for enforcement of the prohibition against price manipulation by governmental legal action.

The Grain Futures Act was an ineffective tool for carrying out the objectives of its supporters. It contained no prohibition on many types of fraud, required no registration or reporting by market participants, set no financial requirements for futures commission merchants, and did not allow the imposition of effective sanctions. However, the Department of Agriculture was authorized by the act to engage in fact-finding and investigative activities. As a result, Secretaries of Agriculture began recommending as early as 1925 that their regulatory powers be expanded (see Rainbolt, pp. 6–8).

The Stock Market Crash of 1929 resulted in demands for investor protection, including new legislation to regulate commodity exchanges. Although there was never an analogous "crash" on the commodity exchanges, this distinction was not articulated by the advocates of greater regulation. Soon after the passage of the Securities Act of 1933 and the Securities Exchange Act of 1934, Congress held extensive hearings to review the regulatory experience of the Grain Futures Act. These hearings culminated in the passage in 1936 of the Commodity Exchange Act (CEA). The legislative history of the CEA reflects a mixture of the traditional animosity toward "speculators," and Congress's recently acquired concern for the protection of "investors." Of course, the investors in commodity markets *are* speculators. [See P. Johnson, "The Commodity Futures Trading Commission Act: Selected Challenges to Agriculture," *1976 Illinois Law Forum*, pp. 509 and 512–14 (1976).] In an address to Congress in 1934, President Roosevelt called for more regulation of the securities and commodities industries, and proposed the elimination of "unnecessary, unwise, and destructive speculation," with the object being to "restrict, as far as possible, the use of these exchanges for purely speculative purposes." [see 78 Cong. Rec. 2264 (1934)] However, certain views expressed by Congress reflected somewhat less hostility toward speculators. A House committee described them as "that class of citizens who have a fondness, and perhaps some aptitute, for speculative investment in commodities and who like to test their judgement concerning values and price trends by occasional and moderate speculation therein." [see H. R. Rep. No. 421, 74th Congress, 1st Session 3 (1935)]

The Commodity Exchange Act represented a significant expansion of regulatory structure established by the Grain Futures Act and the Cotton Futures Act. The coverage of the CEA was extended to agricultural commodities other than cotton and grains. The CEA continued the system of contract-market designation. In addition, many new regulatory devices and other requirements were introduced. Exchanges, floor brokers, and futures commission merchants were now required to register with the Secretary of Agriculture. The manipulation of both futures markets and the underlying cash commodities was made a criminal offense. Futures commission merchants were required for the first time to segregate the funds of their customers. The CEA contained a general provision making it unlawful to cheat, defraud, or deceive customers, or to bucket their orders.

The CEA also made it unlawful to engage in "wash sales" and option transactions. The enforcement powers of the Department of Agriculture were increased: the department was given the power to investigate reported violations of the act, to obtain cease-and-desist orders against violators, and to deny trading privileges. The suspension or withdrawal of exchange designation was retained as another available sanction.

In addition, the CEA authorized the Department of Agriculture to establish limits on the amount of trading done and the size of positions held by speculators. Those persons using the markets for hedging purposes could not be subjected to these limits. However, this distinction between speculators and hedgers represented something more than the traditional prejudice against the former group. Although this provision restricted speculation, it did not amount to a ban and thereby acknowledged the legitimacy of the role of the speculator within the market mechanism (see Rainbolt, pp. 9 and 10).

The CEA also introduced several new provisions affecting contract markets. The CEA relaxed the requirement that a designated contract market be located at the site of a terminal market for the cash commodity. It also permitted designation if the exchange provided for delivery of commodities at a location and on terms acceptable to the Secretary of Agriculture. The CEA required that books and records be kept for all transactions and proceedings on the contract market, and that the markets permit inspections. Contract markets were also required to file their rules with the Department of Agriculture. Finally, standards were set for contracts and the warehouses at which delivery was to be made.

The CEA applied only to those commodities specifically mentioned in its provisions. As a result, many commodities and entire organized exchanges (e.g., the New York Cocoa Exchange) were left unregulated. The CEA resulted in a division of regulatory responsibilities between the federal government and the exchanges, with the self-regulatory aspect assuming greater importance. For a number of reasons, the CEA also remained largely agricultural in nature. It applied only to the agricultural commodities, which were of greatest concern to farmers. The act was administered by the Secretary of Agriculture. In addition, agricultural interests were given special status under the CEA: speculative limits did not apply to agricultural hedgers, and the CEA continued the right of agricultural cooperatives to membership in exchanges under certain conditions, while providing a procedure for review of the decision of an exchange to deny such a membership. However, other aspects of the CEA reflected its more limited function as a device for the protection of investors, including speculators. This group of market users benefited from the new provisions governing brokers, as well as the new antifraud provision (see Johnson, p. 514).

For the next 30 years few changes were made in the CEA. Various agricultural commodities were added to the list of those regulated by the CEA, including wool, wool tops, soybeans, oils and fats, cottonseed, and the byproducts of some of these commodities. Following allegations of manipulation, and after several years of debate, Congress banned all futures trading in onions in 1958. Demands were also made for restrictive legislation governing potato futures, but such legislation was never enacted (see Teweles, Harlow, and Stone, pp. 12–13).

Significant amendments were made to the CEA in 1968. New commodities, including livestock, livestock products, and frozen concentrated orange juice were brought under regulation. In addition, numerous amendments were made in order to better protect investors in the commodity futures markets. A new class of floor brokers was subjected to registration requirements and supervision, and the antifraud provisions were amended to apply to a broader class of persons. New protections also were established for the handling of investors' funds: limitations on the investment of customer funds by brokers were established, and banks and clearing organizations were brought within the requirements for the segregation of those funds.

Another significant group of 1968 amendments changed the way in which the CEA dealt with the establishment and enforcement of exchange rules. The Secretary of Agriculture was authorized for the first time to disapprove any exchange rule which violated the CEA. The amendment also authorized the Secretary of Agriculture to take action against exchanges which failed to enforce their own rules relating to contract terms and trading. As a result, some courts held that persons had a right to bring a suit in federal court under the latter provision against exchanges for failing to enforce their rules (see Johnson, p. 515).

CHAPTER 6

TAXATION OF COMMODITY TRANSACTIONS

CONTENTS

AUTHORS NOTE 3

PRIOR TAX TREATMENT OF COMMODITY TRANSACTIONS 4

Types of Commodity Futures Transactions 4
Tax Consequences of Nonhedge Transactions 4
Straddles 6
Cash-and-Carry Transactions 9

THE ECONOMIC RECOVERY TAX ACT OF 1981 10

Regulated Futures Contracts and the Mark-to-Market Concept 11
Carry-Back Provisions 13
Transitional Rules 15
Loss Deferral Rule 16
Identified Straddle Election 18
Wash-Sale Rules 19
Taxes, Short-Sale Rule 20
Taxes, Constructive Ownership Rules 20
Taxes, Mixed Straddles and Mixed Straddle Election 21
Taxes, Cash-and-Carry Transactions 22
Reporting Considerations 22
Identification Requirements for Dealers in Securities 23

TREASURY-BILL FUTURES 24

HEDGING 25

TAXATION OF STOCK INDEX FUTURES AND OPTIONS ON FUTURES 26

Options on Futures

TAXATION OF COMMODITY TRADERS 26

Treatment of Trading Gains and Losses 27
Tax-Deductible or Tax-Deferred Retirement Plans 27

TAXATION OF DOMESTIC COMMODITY FUNDS 27

TAXATION OF OFFSHORE COMMODITY FUNDS 28

STOCK OPTIONS 29

Tax Effect on the Investor Purchasing an Option 30
Tax Effect on the Investor Granting and Option 30
Tax Effect on the Investor Writing a Straddle 30
Tax Effect on the Market Maker 31

IRS ACTIVITY IN THE COMMODITIES AREA 31

BIBLIOGRAPHY 32

CHAPTER 6

TAXATION OF COMMODITY TRANSACTIONS

Frank A. Ernst, C.P.A.
Joseph P. Tyrrell, C.P.A.

AUTHORS' NOTE

The taxation of transactions in commodity futures contracts has changed significantly with the enactment of the Economic Recovery Tax Act of 1981 (ERTA). The new provisions were designed to eliminate what Congress perceived as abusive tax sheltering arrangements. To fully understand the operation of the new provisions, one must review the Congressional intent behind its enactment. To facilitate this understanding, we have included discussions from the Congressional Committee Reports analyzing the prior tax treatment of commodity transactions and the changes to such treatment.

At the time of this writing, the Internal Revenue Service (IRS) had not yet published the Income Tax Regulations interpreting the commodity futures provisions as enacted by Congress. The purpose of the regulations is to expand the discussion and application of the new statutory provisions. Throughout this chapter, references have been made to such unissued regulations and every attempt has been made to provide discussions and examples as to the most commonly accepted interpretation of the new commodity tax laws.

It is our understanding that the regulations will be issued in three stages.

1. Regulations dealing exclusively with the transitional year elections available in 1981.
2. Regulations dealing with the identification of commodity straddle transactions.
3. General regulations.

The provisions of ERTA were aimed at eliminating a variety of techniques which had been used to defer income, convert ordinary income into capital gain, or convert short-term capital gain into long-term capital gain. Prior to the enactment of ERTA, there were relatively few provisions in the Internal Revenue Code dealing specifically with the intricacies of commodity futures transactions. Certain wash-sale and short-sale rules applicable to stocks and securities which effectively (1) disallowed losses where taxpayers did not terminate their interest and (2) disallowed the conversion of short-term gains into long-term gains, did not apply to commodity futures transactions. The IRS attempted to provide authority in this area by issuing Revenue Rulings in 1977 and 1978 on silver straddles and transactions in Treasury-bill futures. The courts had not issued any decisions on the deductibility of commodity straddle losses. Finally, in 1981, Congress added specific statutory rules to the Internal Revenue Code to govern the taxation of commodity futures transactions and commodity straddle transactions.

PRIOR TAX TREATMENT OF COMMODITY TRANSACTIONS

Prior to the enactment of the ERTA, a variety of techniques utilizing commodity futures transactions were utilized to defer income, convert ordinary income into capital gain, or convert short-term capital gain into long-term capital gain. The following discussion analyzes such tax-saving techniques and focuses on the tax treatment of commodity futures transactions prior to the enactment of the new commodity tax laws.

TYPES OF COMMODITY FUTURES TRANSACTIONS. Generally, transactions in commodity futures fall into four categories:

1. *Hedge Transactions.* Used to protect against losses caused by fluctuations in the price of a commodity which is included in inventory to be used or sold in the normal course of business. Gains and losses from such transactions will receive ordinary income or loss treatment. ERTA did not alter such ordinary income or loss treatment for hedge transactions. Hedge transactions will be discussed in greater detail in a later section.
2. *Nonhedge Transactions.* Entered into for speculation or investment purposes with a view towards making a profit. Generally, these transactions generate capital gain or loss.
3. *Straddle Transaction.* A simultaneous purchase and sale of commodity futures contracts requiring delivery in different months, with the expectation of realizing gain by the variation in the prices of the futures contracts as a result of market conditions. Such transactions generally result in capital gain or loss.
4. *Cash-and-Carry Transaction.* A simultaneous purchase of a ''spot'' commodity or a futures contract requiring present delivery of the commodity (or purchase of the nearest-month futures contract with expectation of taking delivery of the contract) and a sale of a futures contract with the expectation of realizing an overall gain due to a change in interest rates and other economic factors on the subsequent delivery of the commodity upon the closing of the futures contract. Prior to the enactment of ERTA, the expenses incurred (e.g., insurance, interest, storage) to store the commodity were treated as ordinary deductions, and any gain or loss realized upon the closing of the futures contract and the sale of the commodity was treated as capital gain or loss.

TAX CONSEQUENCES OF NONHEDGE TRANSACTIONS. In general, commodity futures contracts, which are not hedges, are treated as capital assets, and gain or loss from the sale or exchange of such contracts will receive capital gain or loss treatment. The holding period of the capital asset generally determines whether the gain or loss upon disposition will be treated as long-term or short-term. Prior to the enactment of ERTA, the sale or exchange of a "long" commodity futures contract, held for more than 6 months, would generate a long-term capital gain or loss. The sale or exchange of a "long" commodity futures contract, held for less than 6 months, or the sale or exchange of any "short" commodity futures contract would result in short-term capital gain or loss. In determining the holding period of a physical commodity received in satisfaction of the commodity futures contract, the holding period of the commodity futures contract was tacked onto the holding period of the physical commodity. The physical commodity must have been held for 1 year to receive long-term capital gain treatment.

Generally, a futures contract would be considered sold or exchanged as of the moment an offsetting trade is made. The offsetting trade must be for the same commodity, in the same market, for the delivery in the same contract period as the original futures contract. The offsetting trade "covers" the original trade and is considered a sale or exchange which may generate capital gain or loss.

The definition of capital gains and losses in Internal Revenue Code Section (IRC) 1222 requires that there be a "sale or exchange" of a capital asset. Court decisions prior to ERTA interpreted this requirement to mean that when a disposition is not a sale or exchange, for example, a lapse, cancellation, or abandonment, such disposition produces ordinary income or loss. This interpretation applied even to dispositions which were economically equivalent to a sale or exchange of a capital asset.

Some taxpayers and tax-shelter promoters attempted to exploit these court decisions, holding that ordinary income or loss results from certain dispositions of property whose sale or exchange would produce capital gain or loss. As a result of these interpretations, losses from the termination, cancellation, lapse, abandonment, and other dispositions of property, which were not considered sales or exchanges of the property, were reported as fully deductible ordinary losses instead of as capital losses, the deductibility of which was restricted. However, if such property increased in value and the holding-period requirements were met, the taxpayer sold or exchanged such property so that the gains were reported as long-term capital gains, taxed at preferential rates.

Some of the more common of these tax-oriented ordinary loss and capital gain transactions involved cancellations of forward contracts for foreign currency or securities. For example, a taxpayer might have simultaneously entered into a contract to buy German marks for future delivery and a contract to sell German marks for future delivery. If the price of German marks thereafter declined, the taxpayer sold his or her contract to sell marks to a bank or other institution for a gain equivalent to the excess of the contract price over the lower market price and canceled an obligation to buy marks by payment of an amount in settlement of an obligation to the other party to the contract. The taxpayer treated the sale proceeds as capital gain, but treated the amount paid to terminate the obligation to buy as an ordinary loss. Such treatment is no longer possible under ERTA.

However, such ordinary loss treatment for years prior to ERTA may be subject to IRS attack due to a recent Tax Court decision. In *Vickers v. Comr.*, 80 T.C. 2/14/83, the Tax Court addressed the question of whether the closing of a commodity future position through an exchange clearinghouse met the definition of a sale or exchange.

The taxpayer in the case argued that the closing of his long and short commodity positions through the exchange's clearing function did not meet the definition of a sale or exchange, but were simply a release or discharge of his contracted obligation under each open position. Accordingly, he argued that the losses resulted from the discharge of a contracted obligation and were therefore ordinary in nature.

The court concluded that the mechanical details of how commodity exchanges and their clearing houses handle their records and record transactions cannot serve to change the substance of the transaction. This conclusion was based upon the reasoning that the offsetting transactions recorded to clear the trades effectively transfer the right to receive or the obligation to deliver and that money was received or paid as a consideration for the transfer, thereby triggering a sale or exchange.

Although this decision dealt with what is now defined as a regulated futures contract (RFC), the IRS may apply it to the cancellation of forward contracts.

STRADDLES. Simple commodity tax straddles had been used to defer tax on short-term capital gain from one tax year to the next tax year and to convert short-term capital gain into preferentially taxed long-term capital gain in a later year. In addition, it was possible to use straddles to defer tax on ordinary income and convert that income into long-term capital gain. A simple commodity straddle is constructed by taking equal long and short positions in futures contracts in the same commodity with different delivery dates. The two positions, called "legs," are expected to move in opposite directions but with approximately equal absolute changes. Thus, for example, if one leg of a straddle in futures contracts increases $500 in value, the other leg can be expected to decrease in value by about the same amount. By maintaining balanced positions, the economic risks of the transaction are reduced. Due to the reduced risk, the IRS had ruled (Rev. Rul. 77-185, 1977-1 C.B. 48) that the loss from certain silver futures contracts, constituting part of a straddle, was not deductible, as the taxpayer "had no reasonable expectation of deriving an economic profit from the transaction." The ruling also stated that the loss claimed on the disposition of one leg of the straddle was not a loss from a closed and completed transaction. This ruling has been the subject of controversy and the IRS has litigated the deductibility of certain losses claimed in commodity straddle transactions.

Prior to ERTA, the Internal Revenue Code did not contain specific rules dealing with straddles in commodities and commodity futures contracts. Neither the wash-sale rules nor the short-sales rules applicable to stocks and securities applied to the typical straddle in commodities (i.e., the acquisition of a contract to buy a commodity in one month and the acquisition of a contract to sell the same commodity in a different month).

The wash-sale rules provide for nonrecognition of certain losses from the sale or exchange of stock and securities if the taxpayer has not terminated his or her investment in the loss property. The wash-sale rules disallow any loss from the disposition or stock or securities where substantially identical stock or securities (or an option or contract to acquire such stock or securities) are acquired by the taxpayer during the period beginning 30 days before the date of sale and ending

30 days after such date. This provision prevents a taxpayer from selling stock which has declined in value to establish a loss for tax purposes, but then immediately reacquiring substantially identical stock. Since the sale and reacquisition together do not significantly alter the taxpayer's position in that stock, the wash-sale rule precludes the "loss" deduction. Such a strategy is analogous to closing the loss "leg" of a commodity futures straddle to report a tax loss and immediately thereafter acquiring a similar position in a contract of a different month.

However, the wash-sale rules apply only with respect to the disposition of stock or securities. The Internal Revenue Service, in a wash-sale ruling, has ruled (Rev. Rul. 71-568, 1971-2 C.B. 312) that commodity futures contracts are not treated as stock or securities.

In the case of a "short sale" (i.e., where the taxpayer sells borrowed property and later closes the sale by repaying the lender with identical property), any gain or loss on the closing transaction is ordinarily considered short-term capital gain or loss if the property used to close the short sale is a capital asset in the hands of the taxpayer. Entering into a contract to sell (i.e., a short position) is treated as a short sale for purposes of these rules.

The Internal Revenue Code contains several rules which were intended to eliminate specific devices in which short sales could be used to transform short-term gains into long-term gains. Under these rules, if a taxpayer holds property (i.e., long position) for less than the long-term holding period and sells short substantially identical property, the holding period of the "long" position is suspended and is generally considered to run again on the date of the closing of the short sale. These rules preclude the taxpayer from "aging" his or her holding period so as to convert short-term capital gain into long-term capital gains, where the taxpayer is free of any significant risk of loss. Also, if a taxpayer holds property for more than 1 year and then sells substantially identical property short, any loss on the closing of the short sale is considered long-term capital loss. This rule prevents the conversion of long-term capital loss into short-term capital loss. For purposes of these rules, property includes stock, securities, and commodity futures. However, commodity futures are not considered substantially identical property if they call for delivery of the commodity in a different calendar month.

The following examples illustrate the workings of a commodity futures straddle.

Example 1. This example details a transaction which would have generated long-term gain and short-term loss and could have been used to convert short-term capital gain to long-term capital gain.

On June 1, 1977, T enters into a contract to buy 5,000 oz of March 1978 silver and at the same time enters into a contract to sell 5,000 oz of May 1978 silver. On December 2, 1977, more than 6 months later, assume both futures have risen in value by $0.50 per oz (normally the price movement of each part of the straddle changes separately causing significant economic potential, i.e., profit or loss). T, by closing out each contract separately, will realize a long-term capital gain of $2,500 on the long position of March 1978 silver and a $2,500 short-term capital loss on the short sale of May 1978 silver. (Gain or loss recognized on the closing of a short position in commodity futures will always be short-term.) Should the taxpayer have short-term capital gain from other commodity transactions of $2,500, the short loss on May 1978 silver will offset such other commodity gain. The taxpayer will report a long-term capital gain on March 1978 silver, effectively converting other commodity short-term capital gain into long-term capital gain.

If both futures had declined in value, T should close out the long position before his holding period was more than 6 months in order to prevent the loss from becoming long-term. The closing of both contracts prior to such a 6-month holding period, except for differences in fluctuations of price, will result in a wash of gain and loss, both being short-term.

Example 2. This example details a transaction whereby capital gains and losses are generated in different years. This example is very similar to the IRS silver straddle ruling discussed earlier.

Assume T has short-term gains in the amount of $2,500 realized in the current taxable year. The use of commodity futures will enable him to recognize a $2,500 offsetting loss in such year, with comparable gain in the next year, while subjected to little market risk.

In November 1977, T could enter into the transaction described in Example 1. Assuming that the market value of silver rises in value by $0.50 per oz, T would close out his short position in May 1978 silver by December 31, 1977, recognizing a short-term loss of $2,500.

He immediately would sell short July 1978 silver in order to be protected against a price decline. In the subsequent year, both the March 1978 long position and July 1978 short position would be sold with a resulting net short-term gain approximately equivalent to the $2,500 short-term loss recognized in December 1977. Similar action on the part of T in case of market decline will accomplish the same results.

It was possible under the transactions described in Examples 1 and 2 to defer paying tax on the short-term gains realized in the earlier year and also convert the short-term gains into long-term gains in the succeeding year, provided there was a rise in the market value of the future and there was sufficient time left before the maturity dates of the contracts to accomplish the latter objective.

The possibility that certain transactions called spreads or straddles might afford taxpayers an opportunity to defer income and convert ordinary income and short-term capital gain into long-term capital gain had been recognized by the investment industry for decades. In the last 10–15 years, the use of commodity futures tax shelters had extended beyond investment professionals to significant numbers of taxpayers, individual and corporate, throughout the economy. The tax advantages of spread transactions, especially those structured in commodity futures contracts, were touted in commodity manuals. Domestic and offshore syndicates advertised tax spreads or straddles to their clients. Such blatant advertising of tax losses was accompanied by IRS attack.

Although the IRS issued Revenue Rulings in 1977 and 1978 disallowing certain tax straddle losses, they did not win a court decision until their apparent victory in 1982. A court decision addressing the deductibility of commodity tax straddle losses was decided by the Tax Court in March 1982. In *Harry Lee Smith and Patricia Ann Smith* v. *Commissioner, Herbert J. Jacobson and Ruth D. Jacobson* v. *Commissioner,* the taxpayers sold their interest in a partnership they had formed to develop and sell apartments. Both realized substantial short-term capital gains on the sale. A stockbroker who was acquainted with one of the taxpayers contacted them about participating in a commodity tax straddle to convert their short-term capital gains into long-term capital gains. After some discussion of the tax advantages to be gained, the taxpayers agreed to participate in the stock brokerage firm's tax straddle program. To that end, they each deposited funds with the brokerage firm and instructed the firm to acquire commodity tax straddles for them.

The IRS made the following arguments in support of the disallowance of the tax straddle losses:

1. There were no genuine losses realized;
2. The alleged losses were but one step in a series of transactions which must be integrated and recognized only upon conclusion of the scheme;
3. The transactions lacked economic substance; and
4. The losses, if real, were not deductible under IRC 165(c)(2) because they were not incurred in a transaction entered into for profit.

To these arguments the taxpayers and amicus responded:

1. Straddles are not shams, but rather, are economically useful investments with significant nontax consequences;
2. Prior case law has treated futures contracts with different months as independent transactions;
3. Congressional activity and inactivity indicate that losses arising out of a commodity tax straddle should be recognized;
4. Respondent's step-transaction argument would effectively write a wash sale provision into the Internal Revenue Code for commodity futures trading where, as respondent concedes in Rev. Rul. 71-568, 1971-2 C.B. 312, none now exists; and
5. Straddling presents real possibilities for gain and loss; and petitioners possessed adequate nontax profit objectives to avoid disallowance of their straddle losses on the basis of section 165(c)(2).

Based on these facts, the Tax Court held that the losses incurred by the taxpayers in silver futures were not deductible because they were not sustained in transactions entered into for profit, that is, the taxpayers did not have a nontax motive for engaging in the straddle transaction. It is important to note that the court rejected the IRS technical arguments (i.e., points one to three above) and supported the taxpayer's position (i.e., points one to four above). Therefore, there is currently no basis in tax law for the disallowance of commodity straddle losses incurred by a commodity trader in transactions entered into for profit.

CASH-AND-CARRY TRANSACTIONS. A cash-and-carry transaction is similar to a commodities straddle except that the investor purchases a "spot" commodity contract in lieu of a futures contract and takes delivery of the commodity, ordinarily through a warehouse receipt. (The investor could also purchase the nearest-month futures contract and take delivery of the commodity.) The investor simultaneously sells a commodity future requiring delivery preferably more than 1 year out. The investor hopes to make money in this transaction due to expectations of changes in interest rates and other costs of carrying the spot commodity, when compared to the "locked-in" spread between the cost of the spot and the selling amount of the futures contract. Silver, gold, and other metals lend themselves to cash-and-carry transactions.

Prior to ERTA, the expenses for storage, insurance, and interest on indebtedness incurred or continued to purchase or carry a commodity held for investment, were deductible as an ordinary expense (the interest deduction was subject to the investment interest limitation) paid or incurred for the management, conservation, or maintenance of property held for the production of income, notwithstanding the fact that the taxpayer held an offsetting position to minimize his or her risk. The sale of the commodity held in storage would result in long-term capital gain or loss if held for more than 1 year. (The 6-month holding-period rule applies only to commodity futures.) Short-term gain or loss would result from the closing of the short position by buying a "long" position with the same delivery date.

Because the price differential between the current (or spot) price of the physical commodity and the price of the futures contract for a distant month is largely a function of interest and other carrying charges, the futures contract has a contract price approximately equal to the total payment for the physical commodity plus interest and carrying costs.

Therefore, a taxpayer executing a cash-and-carry transaction would acquire the silver and the offsetting contract in one year and hold them into the next year. When the 12-month holding period qualifying the physical commodity for long-term treatment had elapsed, and assume the price of silver had declined, the silver could be delivered to satisfy the taxpayer's obligation under the short futures contract, thereby realizing a gain on the silver. If the price of silver had increased, the taxpayer could sell the silver, producing long-term capital gain, while closing out the short futures position, creating a short-term capital loss. In either event, the net long-term capital gain on the two positions was about equal to the interest and carrying charges paid and deducted during the period the commodity was held. Thus, in years prior to 1982, investment income taxable at rates as high as 70%, might have been deferred for a year and converted into long-term capital gains taxable at rates no higher than 28%.

THE ECONOMIC RECOVERY TAX ACT OF 1981

The Economic Recovery Tax Act of 1981 (ERTA) added express statutory rules dealing specifically with commodity futures contracts and commodity straddle transactions. These statutory provisions relate to the following:

1. Regulated futures contracts (IRC 1256).
2. Treatment of gain or loss from certain terminations (IRC 1234A).
3. Carry-back of RFC capital losses [IRC 1212(c)].
4. Straddles (IRC 1092).
5. Interest and carrying charges in cash-and-carry transactions [IRC 263(g)].

6. Certain governmental obligations issued at a discount [IRC 1232(a)(4)].
7. Identification of securities by dealers in securities [IRC 1236(a)].

REGULATED FUTURES CONTRACTS AND THE MARK-TO-MARKET CONCEPT. Due to the rapid and significant growth in the use of commodity tax straddles, Congress believed it necessary to enact specific and simple statutory rules to prohibit any further attempts to use straddles for tax avoidance.

Congress believed that laws based on the actual operations of futures trading would establish an accurate method of determining a taxpayer's future income or loss, and end the use of commodity futures for tax-sheltering purposes.

The U.S. commodity futures exchanges employ a unique system of accounting for every futures contract's gain or loss on a daily basis. Even though a futures trader does not close out an open position, the trader may receive any gain on the position in cash as a matter of right each trading day.

If a trader's position has increased in value during the day, the net increase in the position is computed and transferred to the trader's account before the beginning of trading the next day. The trader has the right to withdraw the full amount of such gains immediately every trading day. However, if a trader's position decreases in value, the trader will have to meet a margin call, that is, deposit additional funds, before the next business day. Money paid on position losses is paid into the exchange clearing association which transfers such amounts to accounts which gained during the trading day. This daily accounting which includes the determination of contract settlement prices and margin adjustments to reflect gains and losses is called "marking-to-market."

Marking-to-market requires daily cash adjustments through the exchange clearing association to reconcile exchange members' net gains and losses on their positions. At the close of trading each day, every member must mark all customer accounts to the settlement prices (current market value) for the day. Gains and losses are immediately deposited into or withdrawn from the customer accounts. Customers in turn are entitled to withdraw their gains, or are required to deposit any margin required because of losses in their accounts, at the close of every day under this mark-to-market system.

ERTA has adopted a mark-to-market system for the taxation of regulated commodity futures contracts (RFCs). This rule corresponds to the daily cash settlement mark-to-market system employed by U.S. commodity futures exchanges for determining margin requirements, and applies the doctrine of constructive receipt to gains in a futures trading account at year-end. The application of the constructive receipt rule elsewhere in the tax law generally means, for example, that taxpayers must include in their income any interest which has accrued in their savings account during the year, even though they may not have withdrawn the interest. Because a taxpayer who trades futures contracts receives profits as a matter of right or must pay losses in cash daily, Congress believed it appropriate to measure the taxpayer's futures income on the same basis for tax purposes.

Unless specifically excepted, all RFCs are subject to the mark-to-market rules. The specific exceptions relate to RFCs identified in hedge, identified straddle, and mixed straddle transactions.

A regulated futures contract (RFC) is defined as a contract (1) which requires delivery of personal property or an interest in personal property; (2) which is marked-to-market under a system of the type used by U.S. commodity futures exchanges to determine the amount which must be deposited, in case of losses, or the amount which may be withdrawn, in the case of gains, as a result of price changes with respect to the contract during the day; and (3) which is traded on or subject to the rules of a domestic board of trade designated as a contract market by the Commodity Futures Trading Commission, or of any board of trade or exchange which the Treasury Department determines operates under rules adequate to carry out the purposes of the mark-to-market provisions. The Technical Corrections Act of 1982 expanded the definition of RFCs to include cash settlement contracts and foreign currency contracts. Cash settlement contracts (e.g. stock index futures) do not require the delivery of personal property and would therefore not qualify as an RFC as defined by ERTA. The Technical Corrections Act deleted the ERTA delivery of personal property requirement.

Trading in foreign currency for future delivery is conducted through RFCs and is also conducted through contracts negotiated with any one of a number of commercial banks which comprise an informal market for such trading (bank foward contracts). Bank forward contracts differ from RFCs in that they are private contracts in which the parties remain entitled to performance from each other. Furthermore, bank forward contracts do not call for daily reservation margin to reflect market changes, and the interbank market has no mechanism for settlement terminating a taxpayer's position prior to the delivery date.

The Technical Corrections Act provides that certain foreign currency contracts, generally those that are also traded through RFCs, are subject to the same tax treatment as RFCs. Generally, the change in the treatment of foreign currency contracts applies to contracts entered into after May 11, 1982. However, special transitional rules allowed a taxpayer who held a foreign currency contract during 1981 to treat such contract as an RFC in 1981. Such retroactive election must have been made by April 11, 1983.

Each RFC held by a taxpayer is treated as if it were sold or otherwise liquidated for fair market value on the last business day of the tax year. Ordinarily, the settlement prices determined by an exchange for its futures contracts on the year's last business day are to be considered the contract's fair market value. Any gain or loss on the contract is taken into account for the taxable year, together with the gain or loss on other futures contracts which were held during the year but closed out before the last business day.

If a taxpayer holds RFCs at the beginning of a taxable year, any gain or loss subsequently realized on these contracts must be adjusted to reflect any mark-to-market gain or loss taken into account with respect to these contracts in a prior year.

Any RFC capital gain or loss which is recognized due to the closing of a position or recognized due to marking-to-market is treated as if 40% of the gain or loss is short-term capital gain or loss, and 60% of the gain or loss is long-term capital gain or loss. For 1982 and later years, this allocation of capital gain between short-term and long-term results in a maximum effective tax rate of 32% on such gains. RFCs continue to constitute capital assets in all cases in which they would have constituted capital assets under prior law. Treatment of gains and losses as partially short-term and partially long-term is not intended to affect the character of such contracts as capital assets nor to eliminate the holding-period requirements applicable to assets which are not RFCs. Thus, for example, a physical commodity must still be held for 1 year to qualify for long-term capital gain treatment, and any gain or loss on an RFC identified as part of a hedging transaction will constitute ordinary income or loss and is not subject to the 60/40 rule. Likewise, gains and losses from RFCs which are part of a mixed straddle will not be subject to the mark-to-market rules, if so elected.

Adaptation of the mark-to-market system in the determination of taxable gain or loss from RFCs requires that every position held at any time during the taxable year be determined by marking-to-market, using the settlement price on each relevant date as necessary to include in taxable income all RFC gains and losses from such positions. Accordingly, the mark-to-market rules, including the allocation between long-term and short-term capital gain or loss, apply to any termination of a taxpayer's obligation with respect to an RFC whether the termination is executed by offsetting, by taking or making delivery, by transfer of the taxpayer's interest in the contract, or in some other manner. These mark-to-market rules apply to a transfer notwithstanding that nonrecognition of gain or loss would result from the application of any other provision of the Internal Revenue Code. Gain or loss upon termination is determined on the basis of the contract's fair market value at the time of termination, ordinarily the actual price received or paid if the termination is a closing transaction.

The following example illustrates the application of the mark-to-market rules:

Example. During 1982 an individual trader had the following RFC net gains and losses:

	Prior-Law Classification		ERTA
	Long-Term	Short-Term	Total
Realized on closed trades	$18,000	$(5,000)	$13,000
Marked-to-market on year-end open positions	3,000	(4,000)	(1,000)
Gain from RFC	$21,000	$(9,000)	$12,000

The RFC net $12,000 gain is reported as $7,200 (60%) long-term and $4,800 (40%) short-term capital gain and is then combined with other non-RFC capital gain and loss transactions to determine the overall net capital gain or loss for the taxable year.

Note that the holding period has no effect on the ERTA 60/40 classification. Therefore, the typical commodity trader realizing all short-term capital gains and losses will have 60% of such gains and losses classified as long-term.

CARRY-BACK PROVISIONS. ERTA permits an election under which "net commodity futures capital losses" may be carried back 3 years and applied against "net commodities futures capital gains." The carry-back is available only if, after netting RFCs subject to the mark-to-market rule with capital gains and losses from other sources, there is a net capital loss for the taxable year. The lesser of such net capital loss or the net loss resulting from RFC transactions constitutes the "net commodity futures loss" which may be carried back.

The amount carried back may be applied only against net commodity futures gains resulting from application of the mark-to-market rule in the carry-back year. Net commodities futures gains are defined as the lesser of the net RFC gains or net capital gain from all sources.

Amounts carried back under the election are to be treated as if 40% are short-term capital losses and 60% are long-term capital losses. Such losses must be absorbed in the earliest year to which they may be carried back and any remaining amount is then carried forward to the next year in the same proportions of 40 and 60%. Losses are not allowable to the extent they would create or increase a net operating loss in the carry-back year.

Amounts against which losses may be applied in the carry-back year (i.e., "net commodities futures gain"), are determined without regard to "net commodity futures loss" for the loss year or any year thereafter. Because the mark-to-market system begins in 1981 and no taxpayer has net RFC gains under ERTA provisions, 1981 is the earliest year to which net commodity futures capital losses can be carried back. If RFC capital losses are carried forward, they continue to be treated as RFC losses in the year to which they are carried.

The capital loss carry-back election for RFCs may be illustrated by the following example.

Example. Assume the taxpayer had the following 1985 capital gains and losses:

1985	Short-Term	Long-Term	Total
RFC mark-to-market net losses	$(40,000)	$(60,000)	$(100,000)
Other short-term capital loss	(3,000)		(3,000)
Other long-term capital gain		50,000	50,000
Subtotal	$(43,000)	$(10,000)	$ (53,000)
Capital loss applied against ordinary income (limited to $3,000)	3,000		3,000
Net capital loss	$(40,000)	$(10,000)	$ (50,000)
Net commodity futures loss (Lesser of RFC loss of $100,000 or net capital loss of $50,000)			$ (50,000)
RFC carry-back amount classification	$(20,000)	$(30,000)	$ (50,000)

Should the taxpayer make the RFC capital loss carry-back election, net RFC losses from 1985 (i.e., $50,000) are carried back 3 years to 1982. The amount carried back is treated in the carry-back year as 40% short-term and 60% long-term. Therefore the $50,000 carry-back will be treated as $20,000 short-term loss and $30,000 long-term loss. The amount carried back may be applied only against gains from RFCs in the carry-back year and only to the extent that the taxpayer had a net capital gain in such year.

Assume the taxpayer had the following 1982 capital gains and losses:

1982	Short-Term	Long-Term	Total
RFC mark-to-market net gain	$ 20,000	$ 30,000	$ 50,000
Other long-term capital loss	———	(30,000)	(30,000)
Net capital gain in 1982	20,000	0	20,000
RFC loss carry-back from 1985 utilized in 1982	(20,000)	———	(20,000)
Net 1982 capital gain (loss) after RFC carry-back	None	None	None

Note that only $20,000 of the 1985 RFC loss carry-back is utilized in 1982. If the taxpayer had no net RFC gain in 1983 or 1984, the $30,000 of unused RFC losses would be carried forward to 1986 and would be treated as losses from RFCs in that year. Therefore the $30,000 RFC carry-forward will be treated as $12,000 short-term capital loss and $18,000 long-term capital loss in 1986.

TRANSITIONAL RULES. The mark-to-market rules created significant tax burdens for some taxpayers who had large RFC unrealized net gain positions at the end of the tax year immediately preceding the first year to which the new rules applied (i.e., as of December 31, 1980 for calendar-year taxpayers). Therefore, Congress provided some transitional relief provisions. Consequently, the taxpayer had three different options in determining when the mark-to-market rules would be effective and what income-tax rates would be utilized in determining the tax liability on RFC gains. With respect to RFCs owned by commodity partnerships, the election is made at the partnership level. The options or elections, which pertain only to 1981, are as follows:

1. Full-year election.
2. June 23, 1981 election.
3. No election.

Full-Year Election. The taxpayer could elect to apply the new mark-to-market rules to all RFCs held at any time during 1981. Under this election, the 1982 income-tax rates would be applied to any gains or losses recognized. This resulted in a maximum blended effective tax rate of 32% for the RFC gains of a taxpayer making a full-year election. The full-year election also allows a taxpayer to pay the tax on commodity gains rolled into 1981 in up to five annual installments subject to certain limitations. Interest is imposed on the deferred installments.

June 23, 1981 Election. The taxpayer could elect to apply the new mark-to-market rules to RFCs held on or after June 23, 1981. The 1981 income-tax rates were utilized under this election. The taxpayer used the tax rules in effect prior to ERTA to determine the character of the gains or losses on RFCs closed-out prior to June 23, 1981.

The June 23 election would have been advantageous when RFC long-term capital gains were recognized on dispositions prior to June 24, 1981 and RFC short-term capital gains were recognized on dispositions on or after June 23, 1981.

No Election. The third taxpayer option was to make no election. This resulted in the application of the mark-to-market rules to RFCs acquired after June 23, 1981. All RFCs marked-to-market in 1981 were subject to 1981 rates. The taxpayer utilized the pre-ERTA tax rules to determine the gain-or-loss character of RFCs acquired prior to June 24, 1981.

Temporary Regulations. The IRS issued Temporary Regulations in August, 1982 explaining the mechanics of the above elections. The Temporary Regulations also provide that an election may be revoked with the consent of the Commissioner of the Internal Revenue Service.

LOSS DEFERRAL RULE. The mark-to-market provisions discussed above apply only to positions held in RFCs. However, commodity tax straddles were also constructed using non-RFC property. Therefore ERTA also modified the short-sale and wash-sale rules already contained in the Internal Revenue Code and provided a loss deferral rule to cover positions and straddles in non-RFC property. In addition, ERTA set forth constructive ownership rules and provided an identified straddle election. Congress also directed the Treasury Department to issue regulations to carry out these various ERTA commodity provisions. These regulations should help to clarify many of the unanswered questions left by the new tax legislation.

The new IRC 1092 provides for a loss deferral rule and is designed to eliminate straddle transactions in non-RFC property. Essentially, IRC 1092 provides that in the year a loss is realized from the sale of a position in a straddle, such loss will be deductible only to the extent that it exceeds the gain from the offsetting position in the straddle. The term unrealized gain is the amount of gain that would have been recognized had the offsetting position been sold on the last day of the tax year.

Losses which are deferred under IRC 1092 are carried forward to the succeeding year and will be subject to the application of the loss deferral rule in that succeeding year. Such losses may not be carried back to a prior taxable year as are net RFC losses. Rather the deferred losses are recognized in the first taxable year in which there is not unrealized appreciation in offsetting positions acquired before the disposition of the loss position.

A straddle for the purposes of the loss deferral rule is defined as offsetting positions with respect to personal property where there is a substantial reduction in the taxpayer's risk of loss from holding any position in personal property because of one or more other positions held with respect to personal property. Positions in personal property may be treated as offsetting whether or not the underlying property is the same kind. For example, a long futures contract for soybean meal and a short futures contract for soybean oil can be considered offsetting positions. In addition, a straddle may consist of two positions which are not the same type of interest in property. This would be the case where the taxpayer holds a cash position in silver and a futures contract to sell the same amount of silver.

ERTA defines "personal property" as any personal property, other than stock, of a type which is actively traded. A "position" is an interest in personal property, including a futures contract, a forward contract, or an option. In addition to corporate stock, the ERTA rules do not apply to real property or to property which is not actively traded. United States currency does not constitute personal property as defined since only property or interests in property that may result in gain or loss on their disposition are subject to the straddle limitations.

The term "position" includes options to buy or sell stock if such stock is actively traded, provided either that the period during which the option may be exercised exceeds the period required for long-term capital gain treatment or that the options are not traded on a domestic or designated foreign exchange. Thus the loss deferral rules apply to offsetting positions in stock options which can be held for more than 12 months. The definition of position excludes, and thus the major rules are inapplicable to, stock options traded on U.S. exchanges or similar foreign exchanges designated by the Secretary of the Treasury, if the options have an exercise period less than the minimum time required to hold a capital asset to produce long-term capital gain or loss, that is, more than 12 months.

IRC 1092 provides a rebuttable presumption as to when positions will be considered offsetting and therefore part of a straddle. If any of the following factors are present, the positions will be presumed to constitute a straddle and it will be necessary for the taxpayer to demonstrate that his or her intent was otherwise:

1. Positions held in the same personal property where the values of the positions vary inversely, regardless of whether the physical commodity itself or a contract for the commodity is held.
2. Positions held in the same personal property where their values ordinarily vary inversely with respect to each other even though the property may be in a substantially altered form.
3. Positions held in debt instruments of similar maturities where their values ordinarily vary inversely in relation to each other.
4. Positions which are sold or marketed as offsetting positions or straddles.
5. Positions on which the aggregate margin requirement is lower than the sum of the margin requirements for each of the positions, if held separately.

The following examples illustrate the application of the loss deferral rule:

Example 1. In 1982 the taxpayer holds long and short forward contracts which constitute a straddle. The gain and loss on such contracts are as follows:

The long forward position has a gain of $5,000.
The short forward position has a loss of $10,000.

Upon the disposition of the short contract the taxpayer realizes a loss of $10,000. If the long contract is retained at year-end, the taxpayer would be limited to a $5,000 tax loss on the forward position closed during the year—the $10,000 realized loss less the $5,000 unrealized gain in the long forward position.

Example 2. A taxpayer holds three forward contracts with the following gain and losses:

Position #1 $ 5,000 gain.
Position #2 $ (7,000) loss.
Position #3 $(10,000) loss.

At year-end Position #3 is closed, thereby incurring a $10,000 loss. Positions #1 and #2 have not been designated as part of an identified straddle. If Position #1 can be paired with Position #3 under the loss deferral rule, the realized loss of $10,000 will be limited to $5,000 due to the $5,000 unrealized gain in an offsetting position.

Had Positions #1 and #2 been acquired on the same day and designated as an identified straddle, they could not be paired with any other positions and the taxpayer would be able to report the entire Position #3 $(10,000) loss.

Example 3. Assume the taxpayer has a $5,000 deferred loss carry-forward from 1982 and the deferred loss offsetting position has an unrealized gain of $7,000. During 1983 the taxpayer disposes of the offsetting position (and thus had no unrealized gain in an offsetting position at year-end) and realizes a gain of $7,000. The deferred loss carry-forward of $5,000 would then be fully deductible against the $7,000 realized gain. If the taxpayer were to hold the long forward contract during all of 1983, the $5,000 deferred loss would continue to be deferred. The taxpayer would be allowed to recognize additional loss only to the extent that the unrecognized gain of his or her offsetting position declined from its $7,000 unrealized gain amount. Should the unrealized gain in the offsetting position on December 31, 1983 be $4,500, the $500 excess deferred loss ($5,000 loss carry-forward less $4,500 unrealized gain) would be deductible in 1983.

IDENTIFIED STRADDLE ELECTION. IRC 1092 also provides taxpayers with an election to identify certain non-RFC positions as "identified straddles." Positions which are part of an identified straddle do not offset any positions not included in the identified straddle, nor will an identified straddle position defer losses or require capitalization of carrying costs as to any position not included in the identified straddle. Losses on positions which make up an identified straddle are treated as sustained not earlier than the day on which the taxpayer disposes of all positions comprising such a straddle.

To qualify as such, an "identified straddle" must be:

1. Identified on the taxpayer books on the close of the day in which the offsetting positions are acquired.
2. All the original positions must be acquired on the same day.
3. The original positions must be disposed of on the same day of the tax year they were acquired or held together throughout such tax year.
4. The straddle cannot be part of a larger straddle (i.e., part of a butterfly straddle).

The following example illustrates the application of the identified straddle rules:

Example 1. Assume the taxpayer acquires Position #1 and closes such position at a $5,000 loss. Within the specified period of time designated under the wash-sale regulations (discussed later) the taxpayer establishes Positions #2 and 3. If Position #3 is similar to Position #1 it will be considered an offsetting position with respect to Position #1, and the loss realized on closing Position #1 would be deferred under the wash-sale provisions.

This deferral could have been avoided by identifying Positions #2 and 3 as an "identified straddle" whereby they could not be paired with other positions held by the taxpayer.

Example 2. Assume a taxpayer holds a physical position in a certain commodity and is incurring interest and storage charges to carry the position. The position is not intended to be part of a cash-and-carry spread transaction. Should the taxpayer hold an offsetting position that could be matched with such physical commodity, the IRC 1092 loss deferral rule and the IRC 263(g) interest and carrying charges capitalization rule would apply. However, if such offsetting position had been previously identified as part of an "identified straddle" it could not be matched with any other position held. Therefore the interest and carrying charges would be fully deductible as would any loss on the disposition of the physical position (subject to the general capital loss limitations).

As a practical matter, the requirement that the positions of an identified straddle be designated as such on the day they are established could prove burdensome to a trader holding many positions and incurring gains and losses on possibly hundreds of trades during a taxable period. These bookkeeping aspects should be clarified somewhat in the forthcoming regulations; however, it can be assumed that the IRS will not provide traders much relief from problems of this nature.

WASH-SALE RULES. Congress directed the IRS to issue regulations under IRC 1092 similar to the stocks and securities wash-sale provisions already contained in IRC 1091. The IRC 1091 wash-sale rule defers the loss on the disposition of stock or securities if, within 30 days before or after such disposition, the taxpayer acquires substantially identical property.

The new commodity wash-sale regulations to be issued under IRC 1092 will substitute the concept of "offsetting positions" for the concept of "substantially identical" property. These regulations will defer losses sustained on the sale of a position in a straddle if, within a yet-to-be-determined designated period, the taxpayer replaces that position with another offsetting position. The Senate Finance Committee Report indicates that the wash-sale rules will be applied prior to the loss deferral rules, both of which are contained in the new IRC 1092.

Assuming that the commodity wash-sale regulations to be issued closely parallel the existing regulations relating to stocks and securities, the following example demonstrates its anticipated application and interaction with the loss deferral rule.

Example. A taxpayer acquires and maintains long and short forward contracts. The long position has a gain of $5,000 and the short position a $6,000 loss. The short position is closed and a $6,000 loss is realized. Another short position is immediately established and offsets the long contract. No other movement in the price of the contracts takes place before year-end.

Under the loss deferral rule, $5,000 (the amount of the unrealized gain in an offsetting position) of the realized $6,000 loss would be deferred. However, under the wash-sale provisions, the entire $6,000 loss would be deferred due to the fact that a new offsetting position was established within the designated wash-sale period.

SHORT-SALE RULES. Congress also directed the IRS to issue regulations applying rules to positions in straddles similar to the stock-and-securities short-sale provisions contained in IRC 1233. The short-sale regulations will provide rules to determine the holding period of positions in a straddle and will be aimed at limiting the taxpayers' ability to convert short-term gain into long-term gain and long-term loss into short-term loss.

Under the pre-ERTA short-sale rules, the acquisition of a futures contract to sell property was treated as a short sale. However, because a long contract for delivery of the same property in a different month was not "substantially similar" property, the pre-ERTA short-sale rules did not apply to futures contracts. The regulations should direct that offsetting positions of a straddle will now constitute substantially similar property for purposes of the short-sale rules. Therefore the holding period of offsetting positions in a straddle will stop running while such position is part of a straddle.

In applying the short-sale rules to loss straddle positions, any loss incurred when closing a short position will be treated as a long-term capital loss if the taxpayer holds an offsetting position for 6 months prior to the time the short contract was acquired.

The short-sale rules should only affect the holding period of non-RFCs. Under the RFC mark-to-market provisions, the actual holding period is irrelevant in determining the character of an RFC gain or loss. All gains and losses on RFCs are treated as 60% long-term and 40% short-term regardless of actual holding period. (An exception to this rule is explained under the "mixed straddle" election.)

CONSTRUCTIVE OWNERSHIP RULES. For purposes of the loss deferral, wash-sale, and short-sale rules, a taxpayer will be deemed to hold a position held by a partnership, trust, or Subchapter S corporation. These entities are considered "flow-through" entities as they are not generally taxed directly; rather, the partners, beneficiaries, or shareholders are taxed on the income or loss passed through from such entities. It is unclear at this time whether a taxpayer will be deemed to hold the entire position held by the flow-through entity or only his or her proportional share. This point along with the carryover of holding period on flow-through-entity positions should be addressed in the forthcoming regulations.

The constructive ownership rules could provide numerous practical problems for taxpayers holding interests in partnerships, trusts, and Subchapter S corporations which hold and trade positions, and, where the taxpayer trades in his or her own account. It would seem that the individual would have to be aware of all transactions and positions held by the flow-through entity in order to correctly determine the treatment of individual transactions.

The regulations should reduce the adverse effect and practical problems that the constructive ownership rules seem to present. It seems likely that the regulations will exempt passive investments in widely held entities or in situations where the individual involved has no say in the management of the flow-through entity. It would also seem that without some limiting provisions in the regulations, IRS agents would have unlimited discretion to match up positions between individuals and related entities where there was no intent to enter into an abusive tax straddle transaction.

MIXED STRADDLES AND MIXED STRADDLE ELECTION. ERTA provides special rules for the taxation of straddles composed of at least one position in RFCs and one or more positions in interests in property which are not RFCs. For example, a taxpayer may hold a forward contract for delivery of wheat and an offsetting wheat futures contract, or a Treasury bill and a Treasury bill futures contract.

In situations involving these "mixed straddles" the following rules will apply:

1. The gain or loss attributable to the RFC position will be treated under the mark-to-market provisions, that is, 60% long-term and 40% short-term.
2. The loss realized on the disposition of the non-RFC or the RFC will be subject to the loss deferral rule of IRC 1092.
3. All positions of the mixed straddle are also subject to the wash-sale and short-sale rules of IRC 1092 and the capitalization of interest and carrying charge rules of IRC 263(g).

The application of these rules is illustrated by the following example.

Example. A taxpayer established a long forward contract (non-RFC) and a short position in an RFC. At year-end the long forward position has an unrealized gain of $2,500 and the short RFC has an unrealized loss of $2,000.

Under the mark-to-market provisions, the unrealized loss would be recognized in the current year and treated as 60% long-term and 40% short-term. However, the loss deferral rule will defer the loss until a later year when the unrealized gain in the offsetting non-RFC long position is realized or the unrealized gain declines to less than $2,000.

Under the short-sale rule, the holding period of the long contract is suspended while it is part of the mixed straddle. To be treated as long term, it must be held without any offsetting positions, for the required long-term holding period.

A taxpayer may make a one-time affirmative election out of the mark-to-market provisions with respect to RFCs that are part of a "mixed straddle." Once the mixed straddle election is made, it applies to all mixed straddles identified by the taxpayer in the year of the election and thereafter. This election does not mean, however, that any straddle consisting of an RFC and a non-RFC is automatically a mixed straddle. In order to be a mixed straddle, it must be identified as such on the taxpayer's records. The taxpayer may revoke the mixed straddle election only with the consent of the IRS.

The "mixed straddle" election and the "identified straddle" rule are mutually exclusive in that the "mixed straddle" election does not also make the straddle an "identified straddle." A taxpayer may at his or her option designate a "mixed straddle" as an "identified straddle" or designate an "identified straddle" without also classifying it as a "mixed straddle." The forthcoming regulations should clarify the interactions of these two provisions.

A mixed straddle election will change the character of the gain or loss realized on the disposition of an RFC. For example, if there is a realized gain on the RFC leg of a mixed straddle, the mixed straddle election will convert such RFC gain, normally treated as 60% long-term and 40% short-term, to all short-term under the short-sale rules. Another disadvantage of the mixed straddle election is the loss of the new RFC carry-back provisions.

CASH-AND-CARRY TRANSACTIONS. Under prior law, carrying charges incurred or continued to purchase or carry a commodity held for investment, were deductible as an ordinary expense paid or incurred for the management, conservation, or maintenance of property held for the production of income, notwithstanding that the taxpayer held an offsetting position to minimize risk and may have claimed long-term capital gain on the sale of the commodity.

Under ERTA, taxpayers are now required to capitalize certain otherwise deductible expenditures for personal property if the property is held as part or all of an offsetting position belonging to a straddle. Such expenditures must be charged to the capital account of the property for which the expenditures are made. Thus these expenditures will reduce the capital gain or increase the capital loss recognized upon the disposition of the property.

Expenditures subject to this capitalization requirement are interest on indebtedness incurred or continued to purchase or carry the property, as well as amounts paid or incurred for insuring, storing, or transporting the property. The amount of these expenditures, called carrying charges, to be capitalized is reduced by any interest income from the property (including original issue discount) which is included in gross income for the taxable year, and any amount of ordinary income acquisition discount (discussed with Treasury-bill futures) included in gross income for the taxable year.

Because Congress recognized that certain legitimate business transactions, such as hedging, which result only in ordinary income or loss, lack significant tax avoidance potential, it exempted such activities from the new rules on cash-and-carry transactions. Therefore the capitalization requirements do not apply to any identified hedging transactions or to any position which is not part of a straddle. Thus, for example, a farmer can still deduct currently the costs of financing crops. Similarly, securities dealers' expenses for financing their inventory and trading accounts which generate ordinary income or loss remain deductible currently.

REPORTING CONSIDERATIONS. ERTA outlines specific tax-return reporting requirements relating to commodity trading activities. The Treasury Department issued Form 6781, Gains and Losses from Commodity Futures Contracts and Straddle Positions, to accommodate this reporting. Form 6781 is to be attached to all individual, corporate, and partnership tax returns that include commodity-related transactions, unrealized gains from open year-end positions, and gains and losses from straddle positions.

Form 6781 is divided into four parts. Part I is used to report gains or losses on RFCs either closed during the year or marked-to-market at year-end. The resulting net gain or loss is then divided into the 60% long-term and 40% short-term portions and carried to Schedule D—Capital Gains and Losses to be included with other capital gain and loss transactions.

Part II is for reporting gains and losses from non-RFC straddle positions and mixed straddles for which the mixed straddle election has been made. The straddle gains and losses from Part II are classified as long-term or short-term based upon the actual holding period. Such amounts are also carried to Schedule D to be included with other capital gains and losses.

Part III is used to report the unrealized gains from positions held on the last day of the tax year. These transactions are only for identification purposes and the resulting gain amount is not carried to any other tax return schedule. The purpose of Part III is to alert the IRS to open position gains that should be considered under the loss deferral rule.

ERTA also authorizes penalties for failure to provide the required information in Part III for any year in which a loss was sustained on any position. The additional tax will be treated as a negligence penalty. The penalty will be 5% of the tax underpayment.

Part IV is used to compute the tax due as a result of the ERTA full-year election available during the 1981 transition year. This part is also used to compute the amount of the deferred tax under the 5-year installment method of paying unrealized gains rolled into 1981.

IDENTIFICATION REQUIREMENTS FOR DEALERS IN SECURITIES. The income tax regulations define a dealer in securities as an individual, partnership, or corporation regularly engaged in the purchase of securities and their resale to customers. The brokers' gains and losses from these securities held primarily for sale to customers in the ordinary course of business are taxed as ordinary gains or losses. However, brokers' gains and losses from securities held for investment, and not for resale to customers, are taxed as capital gains and losses.

Prior to ERTA, the tax law contained a provision which allowed a securities dealer to identify and segregate certain of its assets as held for investment. A security that was "clearly identified" on the dealer's records as held for investment, within 30 days following the date of acquisition, would receive capital gains treatment. Congress felt that the law allowing 30 days for a dealer to identify securities held for investment was subject to abuse. Because of the opportunity for designating appreciated securities as held for investment, to treat gains as capital gains, and securities which had declined in value as held primarily for sale to customers, to treat such losses as ordinary losses, broker–dealer partnerships were formed which exploited these opportunities. Hundreds of investors were sold interests in these partnerships which allowed them to receive ordinary losses with which to offset other taxable income.

ERTA now requires a dealer in securities to identify a security as held for investment not later than the close of business on the date of the security's acquisition. No security which is part of an offsetting position may be treated as clearly identified in the dealer's records as a security held for investment unless all securities belonging to the offsetting position are properly identified in a timely manner.

ERTA contains a separate provision for floor specialists. A floor specialist is a person who is a member of a national securities exchange, is registered as a specialist with the exchange, and meets the requirements for specialists established by the Securities and Exchange Commission. A floor specialist is allowed seven business days after the acquisition of stock, in which the specialist is registered with the exchange, to identify such stock as held for investment.

TREASURY BILL FUTURES

Prior to ERTA, certain governmental obligations (e.g., Treasury bills) issued on a discount basis and payable without interest at a fixed maturity not exceeding 1 year from the date of issue were treated as ordinary income property rather than capital assets. This provision was originally added to the Internal Revenue Code in 1941 to relieve taxpayers of the requirement of separating the interest element from the short-term capital gain or loss element when an obligation is sold before maturity. Thus all gains and losses from transactions in such obligations were treated as ordinary income or ordinary loss at the time the obligation was paid at maturity, sold, or otherwise disposed of.

A Treasury bill future, like a commodity future, is a contract to purchase or sell a fixed amount of Treasury bills, at a future date, for a fixed amount. The Internal Revenue Service had ruled (Rev. Rul. 78-414, 1978-2 C.B. 213) that a future contract to purchase Treasury bills is a capital asset if held for investment. Because of the ordinary income character of Treasury bills, these obligations had been used together with capital assets in the design of tax shelters to convert ordinary income to capital gains. In combination with other bonds, all of which were capital assets, and with futures contracts for Treasury bills, straddles had been structured which were intended to result in significant tax savings.

Straddles in Treasury bill futures generally were structured in the same way as other futures straddles. The execution of these "Treasury bill" shelters involved one difference. In the case of a loss on a long leg, when the delivery month arrived, the taxpayer took delivery of the bills and then disposed of the bills themselves, creating an ordinary loss; in the case of a loss on a short leg, the taxpayer purchased the bills at the market price and delivered the bills themselves at the contract's lower price, creating an ordinary loss. Ordinary losses are fully deductible against any type of ordinary income. The gain leg of the straddle would be terminated by disposing of the futures contract through a transaction on the exchange and the taxpayer would claim capital treatment, usually short-term. If necessary to achieve the desired tax saving, the taxpayer could then enter into a new straddle, not involving Treasury bills, to generate a year-end capital loss to preclude current taxation of the gain from the Treasury bill future, and hopefully convert it into long-term gain in the following year by having gain occur on the long position of the taxpayer's new straddle.

Congress was concerned about the adverse impact of Treasury bill straddles on government tax revenues. Moreover, the number of contract holders demanding performance on Treasury bill futures contracts at the end of some years had threatened to exceed the supply of deliverable bills. This delivery problem could disrupt Treasury bill markets and damage government financing generally. Therefore Congress believed that government revenue and finance considerations required that these shelter activities be discouraged and that Treasury bills be characterized as capital assets. This change, coupled with a rule to facilitate that determination of discount income, would protect both government revenues and debt management.

Thus ERTA now provides that obligations of the United States, of its possessions, of a state or political subdivision of a state or the District of Columbia, issued on a discount basis and payable without interest in less than 1 year, be treated as capital assets in determining gain or loss. However, state and municipal obligations, the interest on which is tax exempt per IRC 103, are excepted from this rule.

In order to facilitate the determination of discount applicable to any holder, the gain from the disposition of such short-term government obligations is treated as ordinary income to the extent of the ratable share of "acquisition discount" received by the taxpayer. The ratable share is that portion equal to the ratio of the number of days the obligation is held by the taxpayer to the number of days between the date of acquisition by the taxpayer and the date of maturity. Acquisition discount is the excess of the stated redemption price at maturity over the taxpayer's basis for the obligation. For purposes of this provision, stated redemption price at maturity includes any interest payable at maturity.

This formulation will enable each holder to determine the portion of any proceeds from disposition of such an obligation to be treated as ordinary discount income without reference to original issue discount or the treatment applicable to any other holder. Any gain exceeding the taxpayer's ratable share of acquisition discount is short-term capital gain and any loss on disposition of an obligation is short-term capital loss.

Because securities dealer's inventories are ordinary income or loss accounts, this change does not affect their operations. The computation of discount income should entail only a minor increase in the taxpayers' paperwork. Thus Congress adopted the new rule as the simplest and most reasonable method of measuring income on such governmental obligations issued at a discount.

HEDGING

Transactions qualifying as hedges will not receive capital gain or loss treatment, and are exempted from the mark-to-market, straddle loss deferral, wash-sale, short-sale, and cash-and-carry capitalization rules of ERTA.

Gains and losses on these hedging transactions will be treated under general tax rules and precedents established in pre-ERTA years using the Corn Products Doctrine. The Corn Products Doctrine deems a hedge to exist where the transactions constitute an integral part of the taxpayer's trade or business. Thus a hedging transaction for these purposes is an identified transaction executed by the taxpayer in the normal course of his or her trade or business primarily to reduce certain risks.

Such transactions are executed to reduce the risk of price or currency fluctuations with respect to property which is held or to be held by the taxpayer, and which if disposed of, produces ordinary income or loss. In addition, hedging transactions are executed to reduce the risk of price or interest rate changes, or currency fluctuations, with respect to borrowings made or to be made or obligations incurred or to be incurred by the taxpayer. The income on such borrowings or obligations, of course, must be ordinary. Transactions resulting in capital gain or loss do not qualify for this hedging exemption. Therefore should a taxpayer enter into an offsetting position to protect a capital asset from price fluctuations (e.g., a Treasury bond held for investment), such offsetting position's gain or loss is not subject to the hedging exception.

Hedging transactions must be clearly identified in the taxpayer's records as being such before the close of the day on which the transaction was entered into. In situations where hedging transactions are numerous and complex, and opportunities for manipulation of transactions to obtain deferral or conversion of income are minimal, it is generally unnecessary to require taxpayers to identify and match hedging activities with hedged properties in their records. In such cases, it may be sufficient to mark an entire account as a hedged account for this identification requirement. However, in cases where taxpayers do not maintain and manage their ordinary income transactions separately from their capital transactions, and, where other factors indicate a danger of manipulation, more detailed identification records may be required.

Should a taxpayer fail to identify a true hedge as such on his or her books and records, the transactions will still generate ordinary income treatment; however, it appears the mark-to-market rules will apply to the RFC making up such a hedge. Regulations to be issued should address this issue of recordkeeping and clarify many unanswered questions in this area.

TAXATION OF OPTIONS ON FUTURES

In the fall of 1981, the Commodity Futures Trading Commission established a pilot program for exchange-traded futures options. Generally, exchange-traded futures options are options to buy or sell RFCs. The Federal income tax consequences of speculative trading in futures options is unclear at this time. The provisions of ERTA did not specifically address the taxation of futures options nor has the IRS issued regulations or rulings on this matter. The Commodity Exchange, Incorporated (COMEX) and the Coffee, Sugar, and Cocoa Exchange had requested the IRS rule on the proper tax treatment of such options on futures contracts. The ruling requested that buyers and sellers of exchange-traded options receive the 60% long-term and 40% short-term capital gain treatment applicable to RFC gains and losses. However, the ruling requested that holders of long options would not be subject to the mark-to-market RFC provisions. (The mark-to-market RFC provisions require that the RFC be treated as sold on the last business day of the taxable year.)

Therefore, holders of long options would be taxed at the time the contract is exercised, closed-out, or permitted to lapse. This difference in the mark-to-market treatment was requested because holders of long options do not receive the benefit of margin payments based on daily marking-to-market at the settlement prices as do holders of RFCs.

TAXATION OF COMMODITY TRADERS

Commodities traders generally fall into relatively distinct categories, the broadest distinction being between specialists and nonspecialists. The former are full-time professionals who have no other active sources of income; they are almost always exchange members. Nonspecialists invest in commodities speculatively to supplement income from other sources.

TREATMENT OF TRADING GAINS AND LOSSES. Gains and losses from both the specialist and nonspecialist commodity trader's transactions in futures contracts receive capital gain and loss treatment. Clearly, the speculator or investor should receive capital gain treatment; however, there was once a question as to whether the professional commodity trader, whose primary source of income is from the active trading of commodity futures, on a daily basis, should receive capital gain treatment. This question was answered in 1956, when the Seventh Circuit Court of Appeals held in *Faroll* v. *Jarecki,* [231 F2d 281 (7th Cir. 1956) Sup. Ct.—cert. denied, 352 U.S. 830], that losses realized by a professional trader from commodity futures transactions entered into on the trader's own behalf were capital losses. Accordingly, gains realized by a trader, on transactions entered into on the trader's own behalf, are treated as capital gains. This case was actually an IRS victory. Faroll, the taxpayer, was a general partner in a brokerage firm and also a member of the Chicago Board of Trade, where he bought and sold commodity futures for his own account. He attempted to deduct his commodity futures losses as ordinary losses. The IRS contested such treatment and the issue was litigated. The court agreed with the IRS and characterized Faroll's futures losses as capital losses, subjecting such losses to the general limitation on the deductibility of capital losses.

Generally, the new mark-to-market provisions have been beneficial for the commodity trader. Commodity traders' RFC gains and losses are now marked-to-market and treated as 60% long-term and 40% short-term. Typically, the commodity trader would not hold a futures position for the 6-month long-term holding period. Therefore, under prior law, all such gains would have been treated as short-term capital gains taxed as high as 70%. However, due to ERTA, those same gains are now split and therefore subject to a maximum blended tax rate of 32%.

TAX-DEDUCTIBLE OR TAX-DEFERRED RETIREMENT PLANS. The commodity trader whose sole source of income is from gains on futures contracts and other passive income (i.e., stock gains, interest, and dividends) will be unable to establish a tax-deductible or tax-deferred retirement plan. To establish such a plan, the taxpayer must first have earnings from self-employment. Generally, self-employment income is salary, wages, or income from personal services. Capital gains and other passive income are not considered self-employment income and thus the commodity trader does not meet the self-employment income prerequisite and may not establish a tax-deductible or tax-deferred retirement plan.

It should be noted that brokerage commissions are considered self-employment income and thus eligible for a tax-deductible or tax-deferred retirement plan.

TAXATION OF DOMESTIC COMMODITY FUNDS

Generally, a commodity fund represents a pooling of investors' assets which are managed by the commodity pool trading advisors and commodity pool operators.

A commodity fund, organized as a partnership for federal income tax purposes, will not be subject to federal income tax. Rather, each partner is allocated his or her distributive share of partnership income, gain, loss, deductions, credits, and tax preferences and, must take these items into account in computing his or her own federal-income-tax liability. Because the commodity fund purchases commodity futures contracts for investment, only for its own account and not for the account of others, the gains and losses generated by the fund will be treated as capital gains and losses. Such gains and losses are subject to the ERTA commodity provisions (i.e., 60/40 long-term/short-term classification).

A partner who is an individual, Subchapter S corporation, or closely held corporation can only deduct its share of the commodity fund's loss (including capital loss) to the extent to which the partner is "at risk." Generally, the amount at risk is equal to the partner's initial cost increased by additional contributions and the partner's share of income, and decreased by the partner's share of losses and distributions. In addition, the amount considered at risk includes the partner's proportionate share of liabilities for which there is a personal liability. Generally, a limited partner will not be personally liable for any portion of the partnership's liabilities. If a partner has a loss for which it is not at risk, that loss is carried over and may be deducted by the partner in a later year in which there is an at-risk amount.

Generally, the limited partner's tax basis of his partnership interest will be the same as his at-risk amount. Any cash distribution in excess of a partner's tax basis will be treated as a capital gain from the sale or exchange of his partnership interest. A capital loss will be recognized to the extent there is any tax basis remaining in the partnership interest, in which case he will recognize loss to the extent of that basis.

TAXATION OF OFFSHORE COMMODITY FUNDS

Offshore commodity funds are generally organized in "tax-haven" countries for the purpose of trading in commodity and currency futures contracts on U.S. and foreign exchanges. A tax-haven country, such as the Cayman Islands, Bermuda, the Bahamas, and Panama, will generally not impose an income tax on the gains and losses of the commodity fund.

An offshore commodity fund may be organized as a partnership or a corporation. An offshore commodity fund partnership should not be subject to U.S. income tax; however, the U.S. partner will be required to report his or her distributive share of partnership income and loss just as a U.S. partner in a domestic commodity fund.

Similarly, an offshore commodity fund corporation, that does not engage in business in the United States, will not be subject to U.S. income tax. An offshore commodity fund corporation will not be considered to be engaged in a U.S. trade or business if it does not maintain an office or other fixed place of business in the United States through which or by the direction of which the transactions in commodities are effected. Therefore, to be exempt from U.S. income tax, the offshore corporation must conduct its commodity trading through a resident broker, commission agent, or other independent agent. Commodity trading decisions must be made by either third-party trading managers located in the United States or fund personnel located outside the United States.

Generally, the U.S. investor in the offshore commodity fund corporation will be taxed upon dividend distributions from the fund or at the time the investor's shares in the fund are sold or exchanged. This differs from the treatment of the U.S. investor in an offshore commodity fund partnership who is taxed currently on his or her distributive share of fund income and losses.

An exception to the above-mentioned general rule applies to "controlled foreign corporations" (CFC). A CFC is defined as any foreign corporation which is owned more than 50% by U.S. shareholders. A U.S. shareholder is defined as any U.S. citizen, resident, domestic partnership, domestic corporation, certain estates, or trusts which own 10% or more of the voting power of the offshore corporation.

A U.S. shareholder in a CFC is generally subject to current taxation, at ordinary income tax rates, on his or her proportionate share of the CFC's earnings. Note that a U.S. partner in an offshore commodity fund partnership is also taxed currently, however, the partner's distributive share of trading gains and losses will be treated as capital gains and losses. Such gains are taxed at ordinary rates to the CFC sharehoders.

STOCK OPTIONS

Stock options are options to buy or sell securities and are utilized to reduce risk from stock holdings through a hedging-type arrangement or to maximize potential gain from expected price fluctuations. Stock options are generally referred to as either "puts" or "calls." A "put" option is an option to sell 100 shares of a particular stock at a specified price within a defined period of time. A "call" is an option to buy 100 shares of a particular stock at a specified price within a defined period of time. Listed option trading began in 1973 on the Chicago Board Options Exchange and subsequently commenced on major exchanges throughout the nation.

Currently, listed options do not have expiration dates beyond 1 year, and, therefore, may not generate long-term capital gain or loss upon disposition. The terms of a listed option are fixed, with the only variable being the premium to be paid or received. Ordinary dividends will not affect the striking price of a listed option.

Unlisted options are those options which are not traded on an exchange and may have expiration dates more than 1 year following the day they are granted. The terms of an unlisted option are not fixed and are determined by negotiation between the buyer and seller. In addition, the rights and obligations are between the buyer and seller and not between the party and the Options Clearing Corporation as with listed options. Furthermore, ordinary dividends will affect the striking price of the unlisted option.

The tax ramifications of a transaction in options depend upon whether the party involved is an investor purchasing an option, an investor writing an option, or a "market maker," that is, a person who writes options in the ordinary course of his or her trade or business.

TAX EFFECT ON THE INVESTOR PURCHASING AN OPTION. Options purchased by an investor are considered to be capital assets and the tax treatment depends upon whether the option is sold, allowed to lapse, or exercised.

If the option is sold, the difference between the cost of the option and the proceeds from the sale is treated as a capital gain or loss. The period for which the investor has held the option determines whether the capital gain or loss is short-term or long-term. The contract must be held for 1 year to generate long-term capital gain or loss.

Should an option lapse, it will be treated as a capital gain or loss.

Should a put or call be exercised, the investor will treat the cost thereof as follows: The amount paid for the call will increase the cost of the stock acquired, while the amount paid for the put will decrease the proceeds of the stock sold. Upon the exercise of a call, the holding period of the stock so acquired does not include the holding period of the call, but starts the day after the call is exercised.

Stock options traded on an exchange, with expiration dates of less than 1 year, are not subject to the mark-to-market and straddle provisions of the ERTA. Therefore, under current law, losses generated from stock option straddles are not subject to the ERTA loss deferral provisions.

TAX EFFECT ON THE INVESTOR GRANTING AN OPTION. Generally, income is not recognized on the receipt of the premium for writing an option, nor will any gain or loss be recognized until the option is exercised, expires, or is terminated by the grantor. Such gain or loss will be short-term capital gain or loss. Should the grantor be required to purchase stock due to the exercise of a "put," the stock basis in the hands of the grantor will be the price paid less the premium received on the writing of the "put." The holding period for the stock acquired begins on the date after the exercise of the option. Should the grantor be required to sell stock due to the exercise of a "call", gain or loss will be determined by increasing the proceeds realized upon sale of the stock by the call premium received upon granting the call option. If the stock was held by the investor for more than 1 year, any gain or loss, including that portion attributable to the call premium, shall be treated as long-term capital gain or loss.

TAX EFFECT ON THE INVESTOR WRITING A STRADDLE. If the writer of a Chicago Board Options Exchange (CBOE) straddle sells the put and call components for separate, identifiable premiums, the writer must utilize the separate premiums received for the put and the call in determining the respective gains and losses. However, where the writer of a CBOE straddle sells the put and call components for a single premium so that the amount attributable to the put and call components cannot be determined, the writer must either allocate the premium between the component options according to the relative market value of each component option or in accordance with Revenue Procedure 65-29, allocate 55% of the premium received with respect to straddle contracts involving corporate stock to the call option and 45% of the premium to the put option. That portion of the premium allocated to the exercised call must be added to the amount realized on the sale of the stock by the taxpayer. That portion of the premium allocated to the exercised put decreases the writer's basis in the stock purchased pursuant to the put. That portion of the premium allocated to the lapsed put or call must be reported by the taxpayer as a short-term capital gain.

Gain or loss from any closing transaction with respect to, and gain on the lapse of, an option written as part of a CBOE straddle is a short-term capital gain or loss, regardless of whether the writer's obligation pursuant to the other option comprising the straddle is terminated by reason of the passage of time, by exercise, or by cancellation in a closing transaction.

TAX EFFECT ON THE MARKET MAKER. Market makers are writers of options in the ordinary course of their trade or business. They, in essence, make a market with respect to a particular option. As market makers, gains and losses generated from the disposition of stock options will be treated as ordinary gains and losses.

The straddle provisions of ERTA do not apply to market-maker gains and losses. Therefore, under current law, losses from market-maker stock option straddles are not subject to ERTA loss deferral rules. The IRS has taken exception to this treatment and will probably litigate this issue.

IRS ACTIVITY IN THE COMMODITIES AREA

The *Internal Revenue Manual* (IRM) contains guidelines and audit techniques to agents for dealing with returns reporting commodity trading activity. These provisions are contained under the *Specialized Industries Audit Guidelines and Examination of Tax Shelters Handbook*. These IRM sections have not been updated since the enactment of ERTA.

With the enactment of ERTA and the 1981 Tax Court decision in the Smith–Jacobson case, it would seem that the IRS would not pursue pre-ERTA commodity issues, at least on the returns of individuals actively engaged in commodity trading activities.

Senators Dole, Percy, Dixon, and Moynihan have written to the Commissioner of Internal Revenue, Roscoe Egger, to clarify congressional intent with respect to sections of ERTA commodity provisions. Senator Dole states in a letter dated June 23, 1982, that "We did, however, act on the assumption that there were straddles that appeared to have been legitimate for tax purposes, that the transition provisions would apply to them and that the IRS would seek to formulate its position with respect to straddles rolled into 1981 in such a way that the transition provisions would provide meaningful relief to persons engaged in such legitimate transactions."

Senators Percy and Dixon, in a coauthored letter dated March 15, 1982 state, "We believe that commodity traders should have the benefit of the statutory transition relief that was designed for the specific purpose of alleviating the financial calamity that would result in many instances . . . The intent of the law was to stop the roll-over of gains as of 1981, not to punish traders who had rolled gains forward in the past." The Senators go on to state ". . . We are requesting that in formulating the regulations to implement the 1981 Act you make clear that the statutory transition relief is applied as intended and that in the meantime, you review auditing practices to insure that Congressional intent in this area is honored."

These statements clearly indicate that Congress did not anticipate that the IRS would pursue straddle trading issues on returns of legitimate commodity traders after the enactment of ERTA. This reasoning is also in line with the *Smith–Jacobson* decision.

BIBLIOGRAPHY

Bernstein, Joseph E. "Trading in Commodity Futures Contracts Through Tax Haven Corporations." *The Tax Advisor,* September 1981.

Bowers, William P. "New Law Eliminates Most Tax Straddle Benefits: An Analysis of the Drastic Changes." *Journal of Taxation,* December 1981, pp. 338–346.

Crestol, Jack and Schneider, Herman M. *Tax Planning for Investors.* Princeton, NJ: Dow Jones Books, Coopers & Lybrand, 1978.

Economic Recovery Tax Act of 1981 (H.R. 4242, P.L. 97-34, 97th Congress). General explanation prepared by the staff of the Joint Committee on Taxation, U.S. Government Printing Office, Washington, D.C. 1981.

Futures Industry Association, Inc. Transcript of the Proceedings of the Tax Seminar on the "Coverage and Application of Title V ("Tax Straddles") of the Economic Recovery Tax Act of 1981—Public Law 97-34." Washington, D.C., September 9, 1981.

Grody, Allan D. *Commodities, The Economics and Mechanisms of the Markets.* Princeton, NJ: Coopers & Lybrand, 1978.

Harry Lee Smith and Patricia Ann Smith v. *Commissioner,* and *Herbert J. Jacobson and Ruth D. Jacobson* v. *Commissioner,* 78 T.C. No. 26 (March 5, 1982).

Internal Revenue Code and *Income Tax Regulations* issued thereunder.

Shapiro, Donald. "Commodities, Forwards, Puts, and Calls—Things Equal to the Same Things are Sometimes Not Equal to Each Other." *The Tax Lawyer,* **34**(3), 581–604.

"Stock Index Futures—Plunging into an Untapped Market." *Commodities, The Magazine of the Futures Industry,* May 1982.

"Stock Index Futures—22 Variations on a Theme." *Commodities, The Magazine of the Futures Industry,* May 1982.

Strategies: Tax and Financial Planning. Princeton, NJ: Coopers & Lybrand, 1981.

Strauss, Stuart. "An Analysis of the Tax Straddle Provisions of the Economic Recovery Tax Act of 1981." *Taxes, The Tax Magazine,* March 1982, pp. 163–182.

Commodity Code Sections Enacted by Economic Recovery Tax Act of 1981

IRC §263(g)—Certain Interest and Carrying Costs.

IRC §1092—Straddles.

IRC §1212(c)—Carry-back of Losses from Regulated Futures Contracts to Offset Prior Gains From Such Contracts.

IRC §1232(a)(4)—Certain Short-Term Government Obligations.

IRC §1234A—Gains or Losses from Certain Terminations.

IRC §1236—Dealers in Securities.

IRC §1256—Regulated Futures Contracts Marked-to-Market.

PART II

MARKET INFLUENCES

CHAPTER 7

MACROECONOMIC FACTORS IN THE COMMODITY MARKET OUTLOOK

CONTENTS

COMMODITIES ARE A CRITICAL FACTOR OF PRODUCTION 3

ROLE OF COMMODITIES IN WORLD TRADE 4

LINKAGE OF COMMODITY PRODUCTION AND TRADE TO THE FUTURES MARKETS 6

THE GROWTH OF THE U.S. FUTURES MARKETS 7

THE 1979–1982 CRUCIBLE 14

SPIKES AND CRATERS 14

THE IRON GRIP OF HIGH, REAL INTEREST RATES: A 70 YEAR PERSPECTIVE 16

THE OIL CONNECTION 19

THE DEMAND SIDE—WORLD TRADE 22

EXCHANGE RATE EFFECTS 25

INVENTORIES—A MEASURE OF IMBALANCE 27

CHAPTER 7

MACROECONOMIC FACTORS IN THE COMMODITY MARKET OUTLOOK

Gregory M. Kipnis

A balanced and thorough analysis of the outlook for commodity prices should include a consideration of the technical condition of the market, microlevel supply and demand fundamentals, and the international macroeconomic backdrop. Perhaps one of the greatest mistakes made in attempting to gauge the outlook for individual commodity prices would be to overlook the broad economic context within which each commodity is competing for scarce economic resources and markets. Factors such as the business cycle, in the United States and abroad, shifts in the growth of world trade, swings in the dollar exchange rate, the price and availability of credit, changes in oil prices, the financial fortunes of the OPEC countries, and the balance of political forces, are all examples of issues and events which can radically alter the behavior of some or all commodity prices.

In this chapter we will establish the worldwide economic significance of commodities and the futures markets, and a number of quantitative relationships which should be monitored and analyzed by the analyst, hedger, investor, or speculator. The conclusions gleaned from such an analyses should prove essential in the development of longer-term trading strategies and the assessment of the risk/reward characteristics of that strategy.

COMMODITIES ARE A CRITICAL FACTOR OF PRODUCTION

The goods and services output of a society are derived from three factors of production: *land, labor,* and *capital.* These three fundamental factors combine in varying proportions to produce everything consumed. The prices these factors command in a competitive marketplace, which economists refer to as rents, wages, interest, and profits, are largely determined by the revenue contribution each factor makes in the production process.

Most economic textbooks pay great attention to the labor and capital inputs. They are the more interesting because they are the most politically visible and the most variable factors. Land, by comparison, does not vote and is a relatively fixed factor. The moral and ethical concerns of society regarding its efficiency and equity in the distribution of income revolve around the use and compensation of labor and capital. It should not be overlooked that in the political process, labor and the owners of capital represent the two largest voting and lobbying forces.

Land is a gift of nature. In one sense it is finite, yet nature's resources are so vast that, except for considerations of cost of use and extraction, we tend to consider land as limitless.

Land and its byproducts have been virtually overlooked in most academic research on the production capabilities of the United States, that is, until recently. Typically, the production function used to characterize the actual and potential output of the U.S. economy has required careful measurements of such variables as labor inputs, capital inputs, and allowances for improvements in the productivity of labor and capital.

Land, though critical, has been an omitted factor of production in most of the equations describing the economy. This shortcoming, however, came crashing into the consciousness of government and private-sector economists in the aftermath of the oil embargo of 1973 and the ensuing fourfold price increase in 1974 imposed by OPEC on Western economies. This brings us to commodities, for oil and all other raw materials are the manifestations of land. The uncertainty of supply and the huge distortion in relative prices radically altered the economics of production throughout the world. As a result, the semipermanent change in the relative price of the commodity oil brought about the obsolescence of much plant and equipment.

Strictly speaking, *commodities are one step removed from land.* They are byproducts of the land. Oil can be extracted only after extensive expenditures for exploration and drilling. Copper has to be mined and refined; wood has to be harvested, hauled, and milled; agricultural products must be cultivated. Commodities, as we commonly know them, are the useful forms of land which can be easily traded, shipped, and transformed into finished goods.

Sudden changes in the availability and price of critical commodities can have an enormous impact on the direction and outlook for most economies. In the near term, few commodities can be easily substituted in the production process. This is true because of rigidities in tastes and values, and the technology employed. One need only look at the effects of the 1973–1974 and subsequent OPEC oil price shocks on Western economic growth; the cumulative effects on the Soviet Union of grain crop failures; or the shift in the Humbolt currents and the disappearance of anchovies off the coast of Peru and their effects on the worldwide price of soybeans and fertilizers.

ROLE OF COMMODITIES IN WORLD TRADE

In 1980 world trade reached the staggering figure of nearly $2 trillion. This contrasts with the size of U.S. Gross National Product of $2.6 trillion in the same year. A little over half of world trade was accounted for by raw materials, that is, commodities. A careful examination of Table 1 reveals some rather remarkable details about the structure of world commodity trade. First, however, let us explain the data.

The export figures by product are collected in great detail by the United Nations. The data only encompass the market economies, however; thus they exclude the

TABLE 1. Value of Top 15 and Selected Other World Traded Commodities (billions of dollars, F.O.B. basis)

Rank	Top 15 Commodities	Annual Average 1977–1979
1	Crude petroleum[a]	$159.50
2	Iron and steel	52.17
3	Lumber[a]	13.53
4	Diamonds	13.11
5	Coffee[a]	12.89
6	Natural gas	11.43
7	Wheat and flour[a]	10.66
8	Soybean complex[a]	10.07
9	Copper[a]	8.80
10	Coal	8.57
11	Aluminum	8.03
12	Cattle and beef[a]	7.93
13	Fish	7.84
14	Corn[a]	7.81
15	Sugar[a]	7.00
Total		$339.34
	Selected Other Commodities	
	Cocoa[a]	$4.93
	Cotton[a]	4.84
	Rubber, natural	4.22
	Plywood and veneer[a]	3.60
	Wool	3.07
	Rice[a]	2.76
	Hogs and pork[a]	2.67
	Butter	2.26
	Silver[a]	1.98
	Cowhide	1.76
	Poultry and eggs[a]	1.70
	Oranges[a]	1.45
	Zinc	1.30
	Platinum[a]	0.91
	Potatoes[a]	0.71
Total: All Commodities		$704.31
Total: World Trade		$1,350.60
Commodities as percent of world trade		52%

Sources: U.N. International Trade Statistics; ACLI/DLJ.
[a]Commodities which are actively traded on U.S. futures exchanges.

USSR, China, Cuba, and the other COMECON countries. Furthermore, they are expressed on a F.O.B. basis, that is, the value of export *free on board* the means of transportation. To smooth out year-to-year swings in the rankings, we calculated a 3-year average for the 1977–1979 period.

If asked, many might correctly guess that *crude petroleum* would be at the top of the world export list, at $159.50 billion. Few, however, might suspect that *diamonds* ranked number 4 at $13.11 billion, or *coffee* ranked fifth at $12.89 billion. In total we identify 30 commodity items in Table 1; the first 15 are ranked according to dollar importance. The second group of 15 are shown because they are commodities which are traded in the U.S. futures markets or the terminal markets in London. Although they appear to be in rank order, many commodities were deleted.

Commodity trade is a gigantic business. The total of all raw and semifinished materials (e.g., copper, iron, and steel) weighed in at an average of $704.31 billion per annum in the 1977–1979 period. That accounted for 52% of world trade.

These figures clearly dramatize the enormity of the role played by commodities in world economic affairs. The fluctuations in supply and demand are inextricably linked to world political and economic forces. In turn, swings in the world economic and financial conditions have a huge impact on the political and economic outlook for commodity-producing nations.

LINKAGE OF COMMODITY PRODUCTION AND TRADE TO THE FUTURES MARKETS

It is in the nature of competitive markets, which have large numbers of buyers and sellers, and especially commodity markets, that the brokers and traders in the pits of the New York and Chicago futures exchanges know little, nor care much, about the size of their markets in relation to world commodity trade. It would probably come as somewhat of a surprise to many that, though the commodity futures markets are limited, their trading volume is double the size of world trade for all commodities. This would be especially surprising considering that not all world-traded commodities have a counterpart contract on the futures exchanges. If one looked at individual commodities it can be found that futures trading in many cases is many times greater than foreign trade.

In 1981 nearly 90 different futures contracts were traded on 12 U.S. futures exchanges, threefold the number traded in 1960. This impressive list included some of the most actively traded commodities worldwide, such as petroleum products, lumber, coffee, wheat, soybeans, copper, and sugar. Futures contracts also exist for some of the lesser world-traded commodities such as potatoes, feeder cattle, and pork bellies.

The fact that a commodity is not of major importance in world trade, in no way indicates that it is unimportant in an absolute sense. For example, there are a number of commodities which have huge U.S. or world-production figures, yet only a small fraction of the product finds its way into the export market. Most notably, *cattle* is probably one of the three largest world-produced commodities at about $273 billion in the 1978–1980 period, yet only about 3% of output found its way into the export market; the rest was consumed domestically. Other examples include world hog production, at over $50 billion, with barely 5% exported. Potatoes are produced throughout the world as well, at an estimated value of $31 billion, yet a mere 2% finds its way into world commerce (see Table 2).

Commodities play an enormous role in the growth and devopment of the wealth of nations. As economies grow and the extent of world integration expands, world trade grows proportionately more rapidly. In the 10-year period 1970–1980 world trade grew at an annual compound rate of 20.5%, which is about double the rate of world GNP growth during the same period. However, this rapid growth increased risks to producers, users, and financiers of commodities. Small shifts in world prosperity can have magnified effects on commodity-producing countries. The greater extent of economic integration also means that volatile exchange rates, interest rates, and prices become a worldwide shared problem.

THE GROWTH OF THE U.S. FUTURES MARKETS

It was mentioned above that currently there were nearly 90 actively traded futures contracts in the United States. However, for many years prior to 1960 only 20 contracts were actively traded, including the most nonperishable agricultural crops such as grain, cotton, soybeans, sugar, cocoa, and coffee. In the 1960s trading expanded to include livestock; in the 1970s the futures markets expanded into metals and opened up windows on other capital markets with the introduction of foreign currency and interest-rate futures. In 1982, yet another capital market window was opened, this time on the stock market, with the advent of the stock

TABLE 2. Approximate Export Fractions of Major World-Traded Commodities

Commodity	Export Percents[a]
Lumber	28%
Coffee	69
Wheat	16
Soy complex	24
Copper	60
Cattle	3
Corn	17
Sugar	16
Cocoa	97
Cotton	21
Plywood	14
Hogs and pork	5
Silver	52
Oranges	29
Gold	80
Platinum	32
Potatoes	2

Sources: Various; ACLI/DLJ.

[a]Exports as a percent of world production of each commodity.

index futures. What did this expansion in numbers of commodites covered do to the volume of trading?

It was not until 1973, or more than 100 years after the start of trading of the traditional commodity futures in 1848, that trading volume reached 25 million contracts per year. It took only 8 years, however, for the financial futures trading to top this figure. As shown in Figure 1, which depicts both total trading volume and number of different contracts, trading volume expanded more than fourfold from 3.9 million contracts in 1960 to 13.6 million in 1970, and almost sevenfold in the next 10 years to 92.1 million in 1980. In 1981 volume reached 98.5 million contracts and was divided at 69.5 million contracts for commodities futures and 29.0 million for financial futures instruments.

There are several reasons for the dramatic growth in trading experienced in the 1970s:

1. A greatly increased economic base for most of the commodities as economies grew and world markets became more integrated.
2. A large increase in the number of net new contracts approved for trading.
3. A broadening in the understanding, acceptance, and utilization of the economic functions of futures markets.
4. The increased level and volatility of inflation and interest rates, which

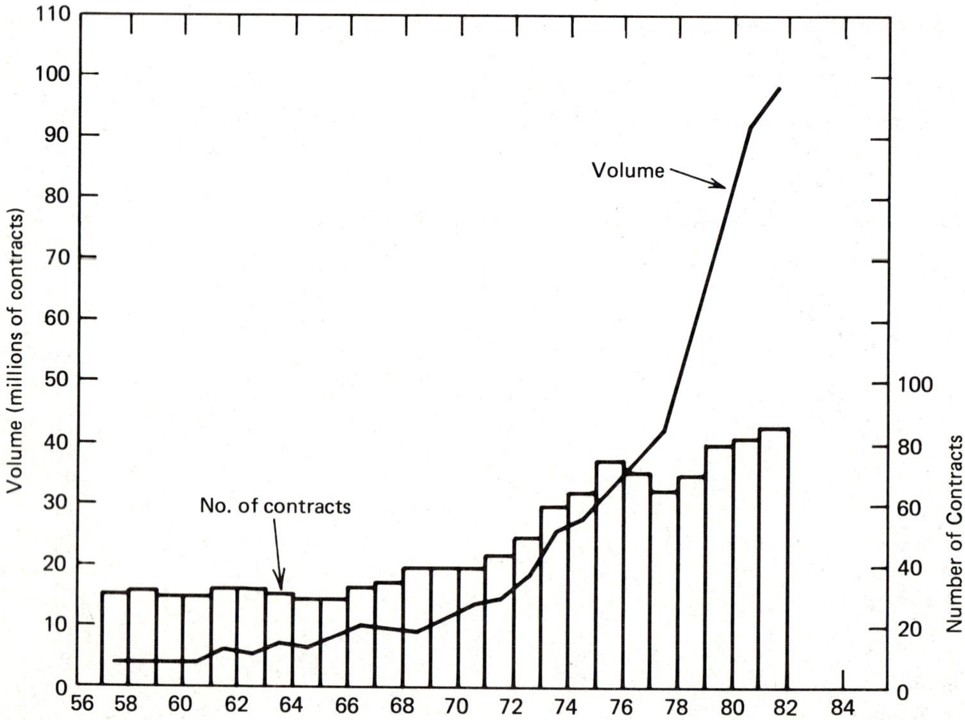

FIGURE 1. Volume of trading and number of active contracts, 1957–1981. *Sources*: Various exchanges; ACLI/DLJ.

convinced many commercial firms of the need to hedge and thus transfer price risks.

Not all futures contracts have succeeded. The markets' imagination has often outdistanced the markets' needs. As a result, the maternity ward and the mortuary for commodity justification studies have been quite active. For example, of the 30 contracts traded in 1960, only five are still traded today. Furthermore, the contracts which have been added since 1961 account for 55% of the total trading volume today. Without these new additions, current trading volume would be significantly reduced. Many of the newer contracts have not been a success. For example, contracts were born and later buried for tomato paste, onions, diamonds, leather, and lard—just to mention a few.

As shown in Table 3, the growth of the futures markets has accelerated in the 1970–1980 decade, in comparison with 1960–1970. The number of different commodity contracts more than doubled in the second decade, versus a one-third growth in the 1960–1970 period. Trading volume growth also accelerated from an annual average increase of 13.4% in the first decade to 21.1% in the second decade. It is interesting to note that this later figure matches closely the 20.5% growth rate cited earlier for world trade for the same period.

Perhaps the most astounding aspect of the futures markets has been the magnitude and growth in the underlying dollar value of trading. In 1980 the face value of trading in all futures contracts reached $6.3 trillion! That is 50-fold the value of trading 10 years earlier (see Table 3). The compound annual growth rate was 47.8% from 1970 to 1980. Even between 1960 and 1970 growth was rapid at 15.2%, but not nearly as breathtaking.

This extraordinary rate of growth came from rapid gains in the average value per contract traded. In 1960, the average contract value was $7,950; in 1970, $9,320; and in 1980, $68,710. Part of the increase in average contract value, in fact about half of the increase, was the result of price inflation without any changes in per contract units. The other part of the increase lies in the introduction of financial futures contracts which had an average face value of about $328,500 in the 1978–1980 period.

In order to get more perspective on the dollar magnitude of futures trading, we have calculated the volume and value data on a 3-year average basis for the

TABLE 3. Growth of Futures Markets, 1960–1980

				Annual Growth Rate	
	1960	1970	1980	1960–1970	1970–1980
Number of contracts	30	40	82	33.3%	105.0%
Volume (millions of contracts)	3.9	13.6	92.1	13.4%	21.1%
Value of trading (billions of dollars)	$30.1	$126.9	$6,328.5	15.2%	47.8%

period 1978–1980 (see Table 4), to make them more comparable to the trade data shown in Table 1.

The 3-year trading volume averaged 75.5 million contracts, with seven-eighths coming from commodity futures. The value of trading was $4.5 trillion, with commodities accounting for only 42%, at $1.9 billion; whereas interest-rate futures accounted for 54% of the total.

In contrast with the stock market, commodity futures trading was nearly seven times the value of trading on the New York Stock Exchange. If all futures are taken together, the ratio would be 16 times.

However, the amount of equity capital actually deployed in the futures markets is substantially less than suggested by these figures. Margins on outright positions are usually in the 5–10% range, and in the case of spreads, the margins are even smaller. We estimate that in the 1978–1980 period, original margin (deployed equity) was about $6 billion.

Relative to value of production, commodity futures trading is at least two times greater, and relative to just U.S. supply of each of the traded commodities, eight times greater.

To complete the picture of the linkage between the futures markets and the physical world of trade and production, we will examine futures trading by commodity in relation to the world and U.S. supply for each of the individual commodities. It is worth noting that more than one-third of the nearly 90 contracts are not actively traded. Furthermore, 31 of the most actively traded contracts accounted for more than 96% of total trading in the 1978–1980 period. Within the commodity futures group, 23 futures contracts accounted for 95.8% of all volume.

In Table 5 we present detailed information for 23 commodities including trading volume and value, open interest, world production, and U.S. supply. The commodities are ranked by the volume of trading. These data provide insight into the extent to which the futures markets are integrated into the physical markets.

Since one of the primary functions of the futures markets is to provide an efficient means to transfer price risks, an examination of futures markets activity in relation to the physical market provides a rough indicator of the extent of mutual interrelation, and the liquidity and depth of the futures market.

For example, looking at the first line in Table 5, one sees that soybean trading volume averaged 9.786 million contracts during the 3-year period 1978–1980. This trading volume was the equivalent of 1,332 million metric tons with a market value of $352.2 billion. The number of open positions in the futures market av-

TABLE 4. Volume and Value of U.S. Futures Trading, by Category (1978–1980 Averages)

	Volume (Thousands)	Value (Billions of Dollars)
Commodity futures	66,040	$1,875
Interest-rate futures	6,801	2,396
Foreign currency futures	2,669	185
	75,510	$4,456

Sources: Various exchanges; ACLI/DLJ.

TABLE 5. Average Commodity Futures Trading Volume, Open Interest, World Production, and U.S. Available Supply for Selected Major Commodities for 1978–1980

Name	Units[b]	Average Exchange Trading Volume			Daily Exchange Open Interest			World Production		U.S. Available Supply[a]	
		Contracts (1,000)	Unit Amounts	Value (Billions of Dollars)	Contracts (1,000)	Unit Amounts	Value (Millions of Dollars)	Unit Amounts	Value (Billions of Dollars)	Unit Amounts	Value (Billions of Dollars)
Soybeans	million metric tons	9,786	1,332	$ 352.2	123.0	16.74	$ 4,417	84.0	$ 22.21	60.30	$ 15.94
Gold	million ounces	9,067	907	376.6	202.6	20.26	8,744	38.8	16.12	16.44	6.83
Corn	million metric tons	8,915	1,132	131.0	169.6	21.54	2,473	400.0	46.29	219.17	25.36
Cattle	million heads	6,268	232	168.7	71.4	2.71	1,878	238.5	169.05	39.33	27.88
Wheat	million metric tons	5,199	707	107.2	77.3	10.52	1,560	435.8	66.08	84.27	12.78
Silver	million ounces	4,894	24,470	271.7	293.8	1,469.00	15,285	343.1	3.81	532.70	5.91
Soy oil	million metric tons	3,053	83	46.6	58.2	1.58	887	12.5	7.02	5.67	3.18
Soy meal	million metric tons	2,811	255	54.7	52.7	4.78	1,025	55.7	11.95	23.40	5.02
Sugar	million metric tons	2,129	108	53.2	53.8	2.73	1,229	87.2	42.95	13.03	6.42
Hogs	million heads	1,908	260	25.4	25.0	3.26	331	499.4	50.94	82.33	8.40
Copper	million metric tons	1,853	21	40.7	50.7	0.57	1,076	7.6	14.73	4.04	7.83
Cotton	million bales	1,778	185	67.7	38.8	4.04	1,444	63.3	23.16	16.33	5.98
Pork bellies	million metric tons	1,735	30	33.7	18.7	0.32	351	2.1	2.40	0.73	0.83
Feeders	million heads	808	57	27.7	17.8	1.07	594	214.0	104.00	35.80	17.40
Lumber	billion board feet	683	89	17.0	9.6	1.25	237	250.0	47.75	51.67	9.87
Coffee	million bags	507	144	32.8	9.3	2.64	606	81.6	18.59	23.30	5.31
Platinum	million ounces	457	23	10.9	8.6	0.43	205	6.6	3.13	2.01	0.95
Potatoes	million cwt	344	172	1.3	8.9	4.45	33	5,296.4	30.79	336.67	2.54
Cocoa	thousand metric tons	281	2,810	9.0	8.0	80.00	267	1,601.0	5.13	181.20	0.58
Oats	million metric tons	251	18	2.1	5.8	0.42	48	46.9	5.47	11.60	1.35
Orange juice	thousand metric tons	211	1,436	3.6	8.6	58.51	146	1,975.1	4.95	481.95	1.21
Plywood	billion square feet	193	15	3.0	4.9	0.37	75	126.0	25.20	18.80	3.76
Heating oil	million barrels	136	136	4.6	3.4	3.40	118	4,868.0	164.65	1,387.60	46.93
Subtotal		63,267	—	$1,841.4	1,320.5	—	$43,029	—	$886.07	—	$222.26
All others		2,773	—	33.6	59.5	—	791	—			
Total commodities		66,040		$1,875.0	1,380.0		$43,820				

Sources: Various; ACLI/DLJ.

[a]Available supply equals production, plus imports, plus inventories.

[b]Units apply to unit-amount column.

eraged 123,000 contracts, equal to 16.74 million metric tons with a face value of $4.4 billion.

World production of soybeans averaged 84 million metric tons, valued at $22.25 billion; and the U.S. supply (defined in Table 5 as production plus imports, plus inventories) was 60.3 million metric tons, about three-quarters of world production, and valued at $15.94 billion.

The raw information in Table 5 enables one to derive two important analytical ratios about the U.S. futures markets. For example, trading volume should be taken as an indication of market liquidity rather than the size of a market. Large trading volumes may imply fast order execution and narrower bid/asked spreads. However, size is relative to the amount of business to be done. A speculator may find the volume large, but a major producer may find the volume small. Thus to measure market *liquidity* we have calculated the ratio of trading volume, recalculated to physical units, to world production and U.S. supply. These ratios are shown in the first two columns of Table 6. The resulting ratios are a relative measure of liquidity.

The second two columns provide a measure of *market penetration,* that is, the percentage of total market which is hedged on average. We calculate this ratio from the open interest (OI) data, that is, the number of open contracts, and world production and U.S. available supply.

Looking at the data we see, for example, that soybean trading during the 1978–1980 period was 15.9 times (15.9 ×) world production and 22.1 times (22.1 ×) U.S. supply. Relatively speaking gold, silver, the soybean complex, and pork bellies are very liquid markets with double-digit multiples relative to world production. Despite a relatively small trading volume, platinum is also a very liquid market in relation to its market size. On the other hand, heating oil, potatoes, and plywood markets are less liquid, which may imply difficulty in accommodating large hedging volumes. However, this also implies potential for enormous growth.

Inferences from direct comparison of the market liquidity ratios (MLR) should be made with care. For example, the MLR was 6.2 × for coffee in the U.S. market as compared with only 5.2 × for corn. It would be inappropriate to assume that the coffee futures market is more liquid than corn because the corn market has a much larger trading base. Also, coffee is a much more world-trade-oriented commodity, with exports normally accounting for about 80% of the world production as compared with only 20% for corn.

Based upon total trading value, total U.S. commodity futures trading was about 2.1 × larger than the value of world production of those commodities and 8.3 × the size of U.S. supply in the 1978–1980 period.

The depth of market penetration ratios shown in the last two columns of Table 6 are presented in percentage terms rather than multiples because the figures are smaller.

Obviously, there are some overcounting and undercounting problems in using such ratios as a market penetration measure. Although most of the contracts traded on futures exchanges cover a period about 1 year forward, such as grains and meats, there are some contracts which cover much longer forward periods, including gold, silver, and copper. But even in the case of grains and tropicals, where only up to 1 year forward is possible, it is often the case that two crop years are active at the same time. Thus the market risks represented by futures' OIs lack a basic uniformity. On the other hand, some commodities are not produced

TABLE 6. Market Liquidity and Penetration Ratios for Selected Major Commodities, 1978–1980

	Market Liquidity Ratio (×)[a]		Market Penetration Ratio (%)[b]	
Name	World Production	U.S. Supply	World Production	U.S. Supply
Soybeans	15.9 ×	22.1 ×	19.93%	27.76%
Gold	23.4	55.1	52.22	123.24
Corn	2.8	5.2	5.39	9.83
Cattle	1.0	5.9	1.14	6.89
Wheat	1.6	8.4	2.41	12.48
Silver	71.3	45.9	428.15	275.76
Soy oil	6.6	14.6	12.64	27.87
Soy meal	4.6	10.9	8.58	20.43
Sugar	1.2	8.3	3.13	20.95
Hogs	0.5	3.2	0.65	3.96
Copper	2.8	5.2	7.50	14.11
Cotton	2.9	11.3	6.38	24.74
Pork bellies	14.3	41.1	15.24	43.84
Feeders	0.3	1.6	0.50	2.99
Lumber	0.4	1.7	0.50	2.42
Coffee	1.8	6.2	3.24	11.33
Platinum	3.5	11.4	6.52	21.39
Potatoes	—	0.5	0.08	1.32
Cocoa	1.8	15.5	5.00	44.15
Oats	0.4	1.6	0.90	3.62
Orange juice	0.7	3.0	2.96	12.14
Plywood	0.1	0.8	0.30	1.97
Heating oil	—	0.1	0.07	0.25
Total	2.1	8.3	4.85%	19.36%

Sources: Table 5; ACLI/DLJ.
[a]Market liquidity is production (or supply) divided by volume.
[b]Market penetration is production (or supply) divided by open interest.

entirely for direct commercial uses. For example, a farmer produces corn for his or her own hog feeds; thus the risk exposure, as measured by either production or total supply, would be overstated.

Despite the risk measurement problems, the market penetration ratios (MPR) reveal some interesting results. As shown in Table 6, the total OI for silver accounted for more than 428% of the annual average world production in the period 1978–1980. For gold, the average OI on the same two exchanges was more than the total available supply in the United States. The OI for notoriously speculative soybean markets, on the other hand, represented only 27.8% on the U.S. supply and ranked sixth among the 23 commodities. The cocoa futures also had a high MPR of 44.2% and ranked third in the U.S. market, but only 5% in terms of world production and thus ranked 11th.

The average MPR for the 23 commodities covered was about 19.4% in terms of the U.S. available supply or about 4.9% in terms of total world production. Both are surprisingly high numbers. However, excluding gold and silver, the MPR would drop to only about 9.1% for the U.S. market and about 2.2% for the world. Since the MPRs for most of the commodities are relatively low in relation to total market risk exposures, it appears that the current utilizations of futures market for risk transference are low and the prospect for futures trading growth seems promising if economic uncertainties and volatility remain a permanent feature of the landscape.

THE 1979–1982 CRUCIBLE

Commodity market events of the past few years have probably been the most tumultuous and yet instructive since the Great Depression of the 1930s. The confluence of flexible exchange rate regimes, synchronized international shocks and economic distress, and the high degree of international integration revealed relationships and introduced new considerations for the commodity markets. Analysts and traders, trained and experienced during calmer, earlier decades, were easily overtaken and mesmerized by overpowering events and seemingly unstructured and unfamiliar variables.

What makes this period so interesting is that during the 4-year interval, 1979–1982, we witnessed a major blowoff and subsequent collapse in commodity prices in the midst of massive and protracted declines of worldwide economic activity. In late 1979–early 1980 prices generally, and real estate, collectibles, and commodities specifically, were bounding upward at the tail end of the longest economic expansion which was not the product of a major war. For example, the U.S. economic expansion, 1961–1969, was quickened and extended by the Vietnam War, whereas the expansion from early 1975 to late 1979 was militarily tranquil for the United States.

In 1978 and early 1979 OPEC was spending nearly every dollar it was taking in, following larger surpluses in the previous 2 years. This reversal helped stimulate economic activity on a worldwide basis. World trade was booming, and monetary policies were generally highly expansionary throughout the world. As a result few nations were feeling any economic pain from the cumulative oil price hikes of the previous several years, 1973–1979.

By early 1980 economic growth came to a screeching halt. Many economies plunged into recessions under the weight of the ravages of high double-digit inflation rates and abrupt shifts by monetary authorities to more stringent policies, causing high real interest-rate environments throughout the world. Furthermore, the arithmetic of towering debt levels and declining world trade produced onerous debt service burdens for the less developed countries. This precipitated efforts to "beggar-thy-neighbor" through competitive devaluations and protectionist trade measures. With this background, commodity prices collapsed by astonishing proportions, plunging downward by 80% in a number of cases.

SPIKES AND CRATERS

In Table 7 we show the extraordinary commodity price swings experienced over the period 1976–1982. The upswings from the lows to the highs were breathtaking. Few commodity prices failed to double in price. The typical gain was 311%. For example, silver prices zoomed by more than *11-fold,* from nearly $4 per oz in

TABLE 7. Spikes and Craters in Commodity Prices 1976–1982[a]

	SPIKES Percent Rise from Low to High	CRATERS Percent Collapse from High to Low
Gold	770%	−66%
Silver	150	−90
Copper	181	−64
Heating oil	160	−31
Lumber	159	−58
Cotton	85	−38
Wheat	157	−44
Corn	114	−47
Soybeans	90	−45
Potatoes	305	−67
Sugar	650	−88
Coffee	313	−73
Cocoa	320	−75
Live cattle	126	−30
Live hogs	87	−52
(Simple average)	(+31%)	(−58%)
CRB Index	76	−32

Sources: Commodity Research Bureau, Incorporated; ACLI International Commodity Services.

[a]Data calculated from specific highs and lows for each commodity's futures prices. In the case of soybeans, 1976 to early 1977 data were ignored.

1976 to $50 per oz in early 1980. Thereafter, silver prices rapidly slumped by *90%*, reaching $5 per oz in mid-1982. Only cotton (up 85%), soybeans (90%), and live hogs (87%) failed to double in price.

Not all of the price surges were related to the general inflationary environment. Real fundamentals such as supply shortages caused by production failures or consumption simply outstripping available supply, were frequently a contributory factor.

In contrast to the remarkable prices gains of the individual commodities, the overall index of commodity prices, published and calculated by the Commodity Research Bureau, Incorporated (CRB), increased by 76%—less than any of the individual commodities. Such a figure represents a large percentage gain and should not be underrated. However, the difference between the aggregate index and the individual details does require explanation.

The reason for the disparity is the difference in the way the statistics are calculated. First, the CRB index is a geometric mean of 27 commodities, *not* an arithmetic or weighted average. It is the nature of the mathematics of a geometric mean that it produces a lower rate of gain than simple averages (a point that will not be proved here). Second, the reference dates used to calculate the trough-to-peak and peak-to-trough percent changes were different for each commodity. For example, the CRB index reached its all-time high in October 1980, yet many individual commodities, such as the metals, attained their peaks earlier in the year. At those dates the CRB index was at considerably lower levels. Agricultural prices, however, tended to peak late in 1980.

The declines in prices were equally as breathtaking. The typical plunge from peak to the 1982 lows was 58%. Sugar and silver led the way free-falling by 88% and 90%, respectively. By contrast, the decline in the index was only 32%. Once again, not all of the price declines were associated with the general deflationary forces caused by slumping demand. Many commodities were caught up in a series of bumper crop years.

In the remaining sections we will examine the broad macroeconomic factors which we consider largely responsible for the long-term swings in commodity prices. No one factor alone was totally responsible for the swings in prices. We do, however, beg the reader's forgiveness for having limited ourselves to so few factors. But, we did so for a reason. The variables we focused on had the virtue that they are generally accurate measurements, which are readily available on a timely basis and are of themselves the object of much analysis and forecasting.

THE IRON GRIP OF HIGH, REAL INTEREST RATES: A 70-YEAR PERSPECTIVE

Interest rates have been one of the most powerful monetary forces acting on commodity inflation rates. Interest rates affect commodity prices in a number of ways, for example, they are a significant cost of the production and distribution of raw materials. Every step of the way requires financing. As rates rise, producers at first attempt to adjust prices upward to pass along the higher cost as they try to maintain profit margins. As prices rise, demand gradually begins to soften, eventually exerting downward pressure on prices.

Another factor is that as interest rates rise more rapidly than prices generally, everyone in the distribution chain attempts to reduce inventory holdings. This has the effect of putting more supply pressure on the market until the liquidation phase is over.

As interest rates reach levels considerably above the expected inflation rate for the commodity, speculators and investors begin to look to other arenas to deploy capital, usually short-term debt instruments. This further reduces the demand for commodities.

Another consideration is the effect high international, and especially dollar, interest rates have on commodity-producing countries. High U.S. interest rates usually cause foreign exchange pressures on developing countries, as capital flows to the higher-yielding market. As the producing country's exchange rates fall, so do their commodity export prices in dollar terms. Even if they try to maintain a steady dollar price, this will usually backfire because the prices paid by other industrial countries will rise in their currency terms, thus reducing demand. Keep in mind that most producing countries price and take payment in dollars since most of their debts are dollar denominated.

Figures 2 through 4 show the history of *real interest rates* over the 70-year period 1913–1982, in relation to U.S. commodity prices. Real interest rates are calculated by taking the difference between the prime rate and the general con-

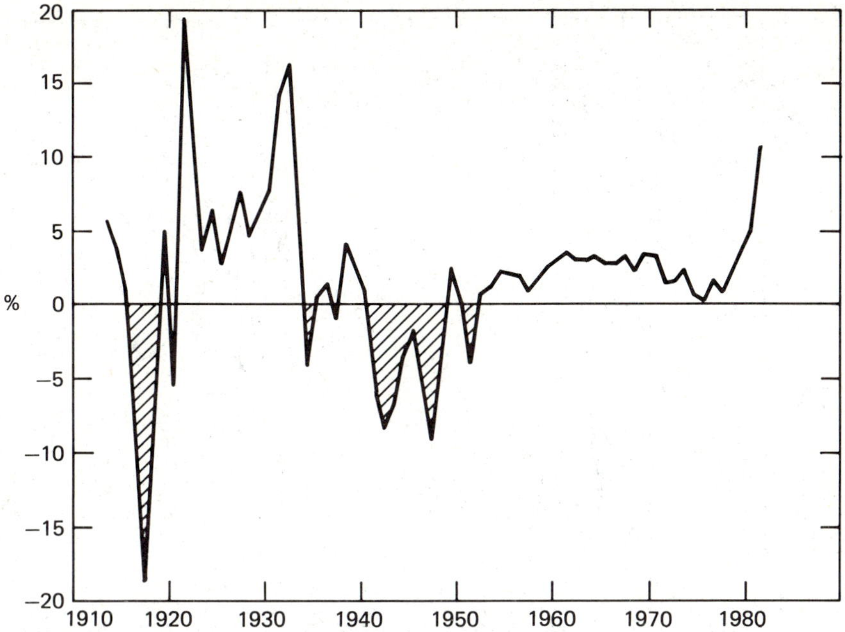

FIGURE 2. Real interest rates (prime less PCE deflator), annual data, 1913–1981. *Sources*: FRB; U.S. Department of Commerce; ACLI/DJL.

sumer inflation rate. The general consumer inflation rate used was the GNP deflator for personal consumption expenditures. This measure is used, rather than the more familiar consumer price index (CPI) because it suffers less from the measurement distortions caused by pricing a fixed market basket over long periods of time. Also, the item coverage is much broader than for the CPI.

Commodity price inflation is represented by the wholesale price index (also called the producer price index today) for raw materials.

It is quite clear from Figure 2 that there have been many periods when there have been very high and very low real interest rates. For example, we frequently regard 1981 as a watershed for high real rates; the prime rate averaged 18.9% and the consumer inflation rate (hereafter *PCE* deflator) averaged 8.3%. This put real interest rates at a premium over the inflation rate by 10.6%. However, real rates have been higher. In 1921 the real rate was 19.3%, and in 1930 and 1931, 14.3% and 16.1%, respectively.

At the other extreme, interest rates have sometimes fallen to large discounts to the inflation rate. For example, as shown in Figure 2, this was true for the 1916–1918 period and the 1940–1950 period. In 1974 the real rate was almost zero.

In Figures 3 and 4 the graphic correlations between real interest rates and commodity prices for the period 1913–1954 are shown two ways. In Figure 3 the two series are plotted over time and in Figure 4 they are plotted as a scatter diagram, with the real interest rates measured along the vertical axis and the commodity inflation rate along the horizontal axis. Both figures show a strong tendency for the two series to be *negatively correlated* on an annual basis. In the scatter diagram the two extremes points in the upper left-hand corner and lower

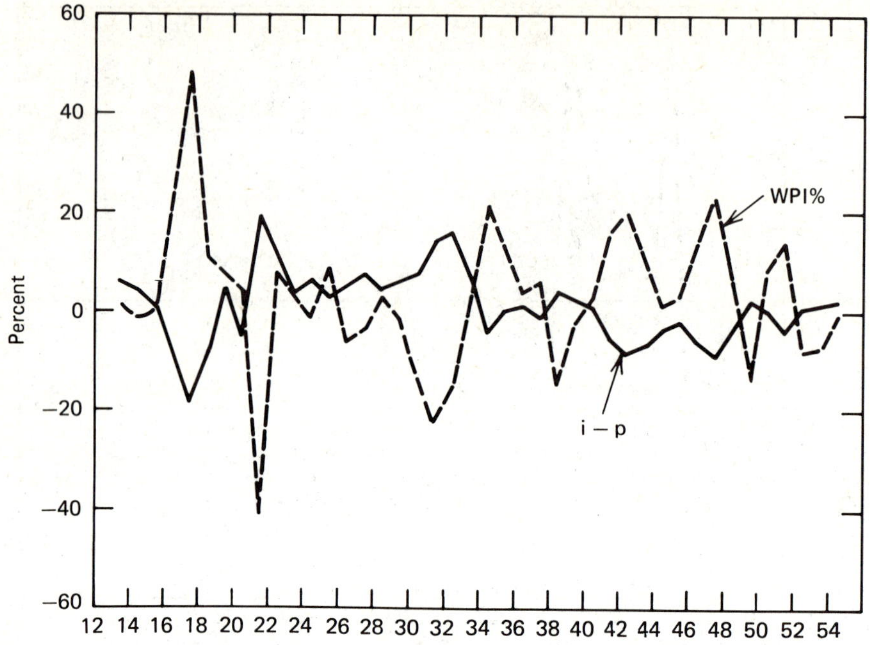

FIGURE 3. Real interest rates (i-p) versus WPI–commodities (percent change), annual data, 1913–1954. *Sources*: FRB; BLS; ACLI/DLJ.

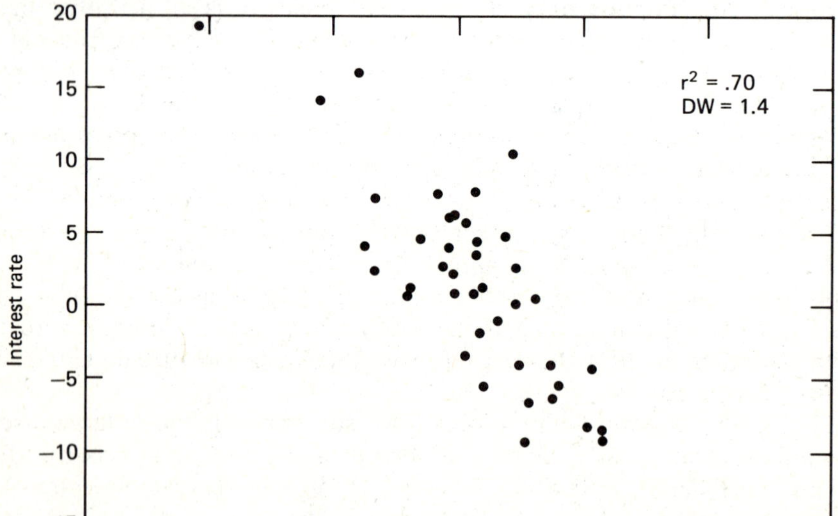

FIGURE 4. Scatter diagram: mean interest rates versus WPI–commoditites (percent change), annual data, 1913–1954. *Sources*: FRB; BLS; ACLI/DLJ.

right-hand corner anchor the regression line, which shows significant negative correlation with a correlation coefficient of 70%. The observation in the upper left-hand corner occurred in 1921 when the real interest rate was 19.3% and commodity prices tumbled by 41.5%. The observation in the lower right-hand corner occurred in 1917 when the real interest rate was −18.7% and commodity prices surged by 48.5%.

Turning to more recent times, Figures 5 through 7 depict the experience from 1978 through the third quarter of 1982, on a quarterly basis. During this period the relationship is also seen to be negative, though less strongly so. The correlation coefficient is 46%. This weaker correlation may be due to the fact that the data for the first half of 1981 for the commodity inflation rate are somewhat aberrant. Since the commodity inflation rate is calculated on a year-over-year basis, early 1981 is distorted by the high volatility in commodity prices experienced in the first half of 1980, the base period for the calculation.

The omitted period, 1955–1977, is not shown because little was happening to real interest rates and commodity prices until the tail end of the period. As a result there was an insignificant statistical relationship.

THE OIL CONNECTION

Upon reflection it may not seem surprising that crude oil and commodity prices have traced similar paths over the past quarter of a century. However, the closeness of those paths is quite remarkable, as can be seen in Figure 8. In round numbers every 10 percentage point change in international crude oil prices has been associated with about a 1.4 percentage point change in the same direction

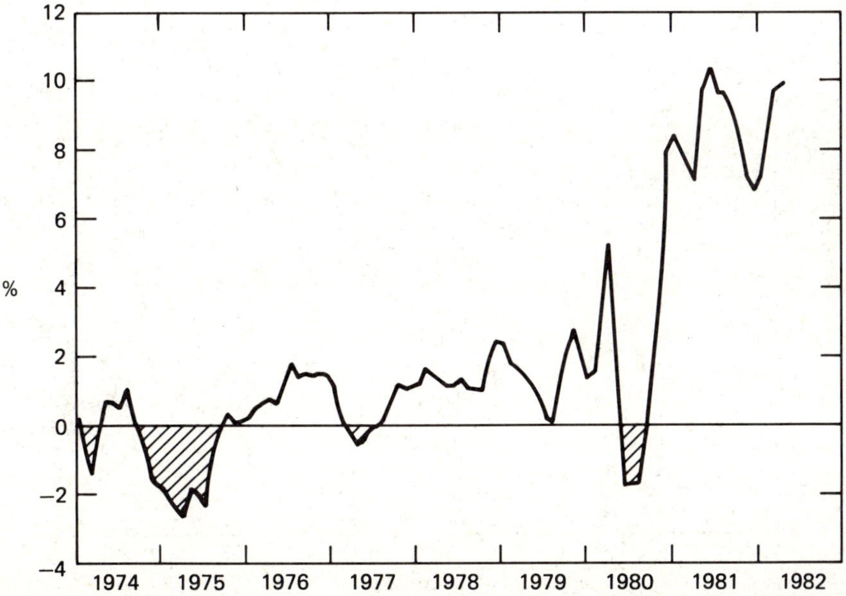

FIGURE 5. Real interest rate (prime rate less percent change from prior year in the CPI), quarterly data, 1974–1982, first quarter. *Sources*: FRB; U.S. Department of Commerce; ACLI/DLJ.

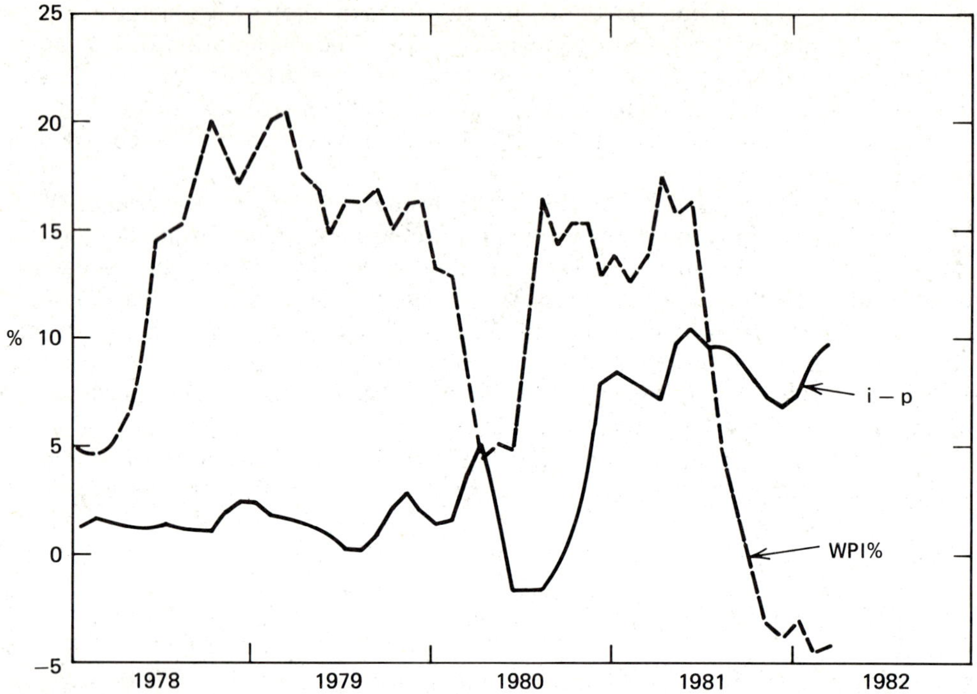

FIGURE 6. Real interest rate (i-p) versus WPI–commodities (percent change), quarterly data, 1978–1982, first quarter. *Sources*: FRB; U.S. Department of Commerce; ACLI/DLJ.

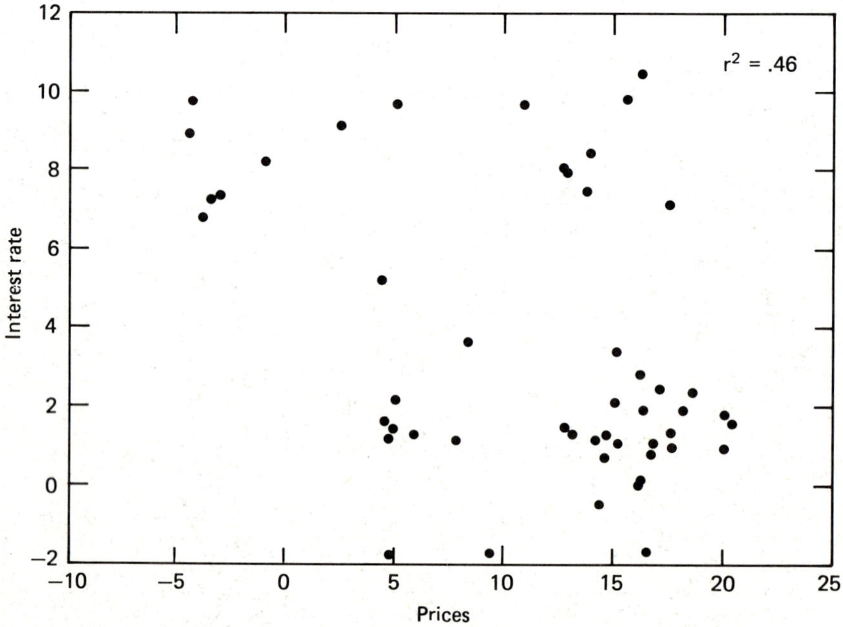

FIGURE 7. Scatter diagram: real interest rate versus WPI–commodities (percent change), quarterly data, 1978–1982, first quarter. *Sources*: FRB; U.S. Department of Commerce; ACLI/DLJ.

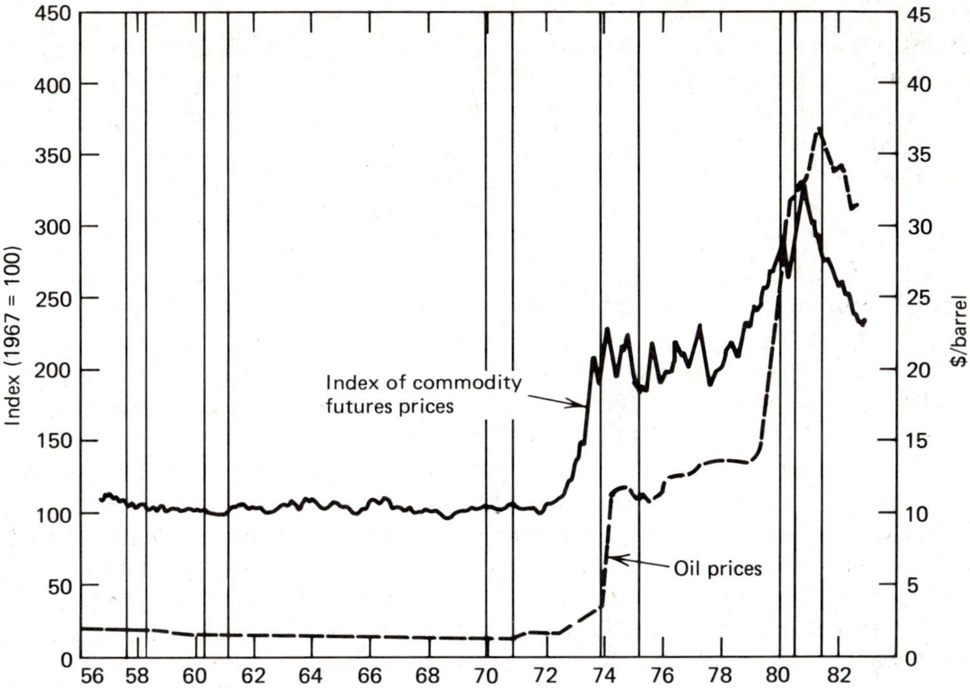

FIGURE 8. Index of commodity futures prices versus price of imported oil (vertical lines designate economic turning points). *Sources*: Commodity Research Bureau, Inc.; U.S. Department of Commerce; ACLI/DLJ.

in the CRB index of commodity prices. These percentages are a rough indicator of the extent of the relationship and should not be used for predicative purposes. In fact during the short time span of the past 2 years, the commodity price index has fallen by about twice as much as crude oil prices (as can be seen in the figure).

The logic chain which connects these two prices' phenomena, and the high degree of correlation, is complex and may not prove stable in the years to come. Furthermore, it is not clear which way causality runs. Nonetheless, one should have a firm idea where oil prices are headed as part of a general commodity price outlook study.

There are four reasons why crude oil and commodity prices may be related:

1. *Cost Push*. As we learned in an earlier section, commodities, whether in raw form or in the form of finished products, are at the base of almost all economic activity. Energy costs are a critical cost in the cultivation, harvesting and distribution, or extraction, refinement, fabrication and distribution of most commodities. Thus, as energy prices rise so should commodity prices in order that producers can recoup their higher expenses. Directly and indirectly, energy costs may account for one-tenth of the finished cost of raw materials.

2. *Terms of Trade Indexing*. In the face of rising energy prices, many commodity-producing nations, which are heavily dependent on imported oil and trade generally, will attempt to balance their terms of trade by raising export prices. For example, if nations were able to buy 10 barrels of oil for 1 ton of commodity

export, and oil prices doubled, they would certainly attempt to double their export prices. Otherwise, they would have to double their export quantity to 2 tons to pay for the same quantity of imported oil.

3. *Implied OPEC Pricing Formula.* A reason why oil prices may follow commodity prices comes from a careful monitoring of the OPEC meetings. As recently as 1981 OPEC was considering tying the price of oil by formula to the value of the dollar, to the growth rate of industrial economies, and to the rate of inflation of imported commodities. Furthermore, at many meetings there were discussions about the responsibility of OPEC to aid the oil-importing developing world (the countries devastated by high oil prices) by supporting higher commodity prices. Of course, these two ideas are in fundamental conflict, but they do point out that OPEC was cognizant of commodity prices as a variable in pricing oil. (In 1983, it was hoped that they would consider lowering oil prices, inasmuch as commodity prices had fallen so precipitously.)

4. *Monetary Accommodations.* Finally there is the issue of monetary and fiscal accommodation. When the first OPEC price shock hit the industrial world in early 1974 there was great fear among government leaders and bankers that the high oil prices would in effect impoverish their economies and that the non-oil-exporting developing countries would be unable to finance their prospective huge current account deficits. The implicit conclusion reached by many government leaders, though not all, was to engage in stimulatory policies to offset the oil price shock through deficit spending and rapid expansion of the domestic and international money supply (Eurodollar market). Those who understood the inflationary implications of these collective policies in many cases looked the other way believing that maybe the West could get away with paying for oil with depreciating dollars. Thus, the other major industrial countries adopted less stimulatory policies than the United States, thereby ensuring a collapse of the dollar.

In this way the United States, in effect, allowed the inflation in one commodity's price (oil) to spread and become a generalized inflation phenomenon for all other commodities, finished goods, and services.

THE DEMAND SIDE—WORLD TRADE

So far we have reviewed two important variables, real interest rates and the price of crude oil, which have both micro and macro impacts on the cost structure of commodities and the inflation process generally. In this section we focus on the *demand side* as an equally important determinant of commodity prices. Unfortunately, it is virtually impossible to obtain timely, frequent, and accurate data for total domestic and foreign consumption of all commodities. However, reasonably timely data are available for that part of commodity output which enters into foreign trade. In fact, for many commodities, more than half of production is exported. Furthermore, more than half of world trade, 52% to be exact, is made up of raw materials and semifinished goods which collectively are referred to as commodities. Industrial nations as a group are the major importers of commodities.

World trade can be defined in terms of *total exports* or *total imports*. In our analysis we prefer to use the International Monetary Fund (IMF) data on world imports. We do so for two major reasons. Commodity imports tend to be more sensitive to the business cycle in the industrial world and reported imports of industrial nations tend to be more accurate and timely than export data from developing countries.

During the 29-year period 1951–1980, world trade has expanded by more than 23-fold, rising from $83.1 billion in 1951 to $1.92 trillion in 1980. The most rapid growth has taken place in the last 10 years of this interval, when imports expanded at a compound annual rate of 20.5%. Much of the recent growth was spurred by the sharp increases in oil prices rather than unit growth. For example, in 1974 and 1980, years when oil prices advanced rapidly, world imports grew by 46.2% and 22.9%, respectively.

In the period 1980–1982, however, world trade suffered a number of serious reversals. Not since 1958 have world imports registered a decline in nominal terms and not since 1952 and 1953 has this occurred for two consecutive years. Both of these periods were associated with major recessions in both the United States and in the major industrial countries. These were also periods of sharply declining prices of world-traded items (see Figure 9 and Table 8).

During the most recent period of trade weakness the world was once again in the grips of protracted recessions, compounded by dramatically reduced oil consumption (and more recently lower oil prices as well), low auto sales, growing barriers to trade (particularly in autos, steel, fibers, high technology, and agriculture), and generally restrictive monetary and fiscal policies in the United States, United Kingdom, West Germany, and Japan.

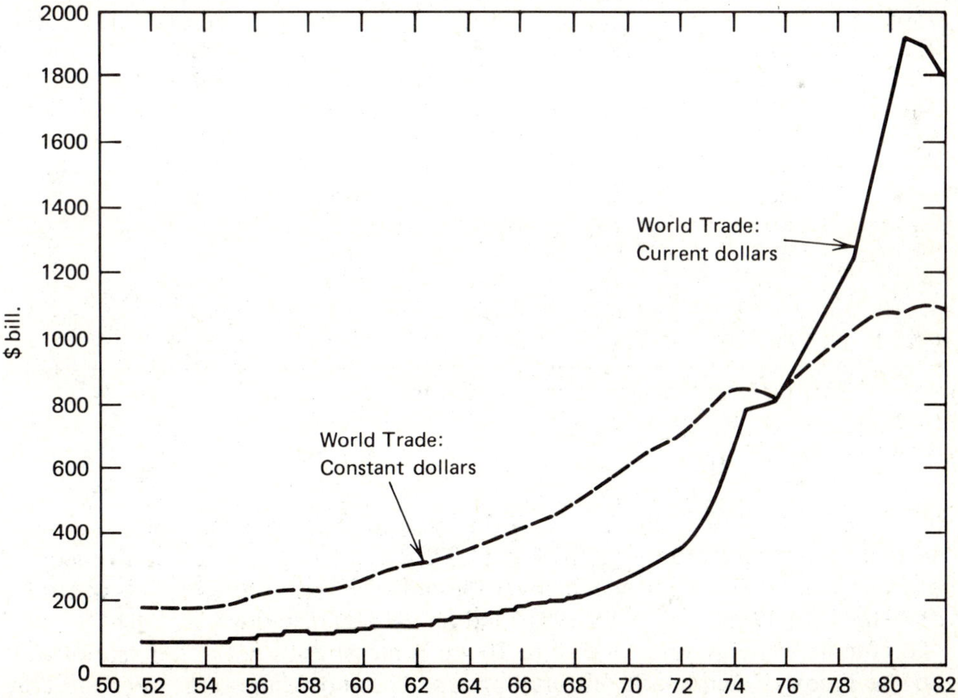

FIGURE 9. World trade, measured by imports, in current and constant dollars. *Sources*: International Monetary Fund; ACLI/DLJ.

TABLE 8. World Trade—Current and Constant Dollars

	Total World Imports (Billions)	Percent Change	Unit Import Prices (1975 = 100)	Percent Change	Unit World Imports (Billions of 1975 Dollars)	Percent Change
1951	83.1	n.a.[a]	48.1	n.a.	172.6	n.a.
1952	82.1	−1.2	46.7	−3.0	175.8	1.9
1953	78.0	−4.9	43.4	−7.1	179.9	2.3
1954	81.1	3.9	42.9	−1.2	189.1	5.1
1955	91.0	12.2	43.3	0.9	210.2	11.1
1956	100.1	10.0	44.4	2.5	225.5	7.3
1957	110.1	9.9	45.8	3.1	240.5	6.6
1958	102.7	−6.7	42.7	−6.7	240.3	−0.1
1959	108.9	6.1	41.6	−2.7	262.1	9.1
1960	122.0	12.0	42.0	1.0	290.8	11.0
1961	127.7	4.7	41.7	−0.7	306.7	5.5
1962	134.8	5.6	41.1	−1.3	327.8	6.9
1963	146.8	8.9	41.6	1.2	352.6	7.5
1964	163.2	11.2	42.5	2.1	384.0	8.9
1965	177.2	8.6	43.0	1.3	411.9	7.3
1966	194.9	10.0	43.6	1.4	446.9	8.5
1967	204.3	4.8	43.2	−0.9	472.7	5.8
1968	227.5	11.3	43.0	−0.5	528.7	11.8
1969	259.3	14.0	44.1	2.4	588.2	11.3
1970	298.4	15.1	46.3	4.9	645.1	9.7
1971	333.6	11.8	48.9	5.7	682.4	5.8
1972	391.3	17.3	52.8	7.9	741.8	8.7
1973	539.3	37.8	64.8	22.8	832.3	12.2
1974	788.6	46.2	91.9	41.9	857.7	3.1
1975	817.3	3.6	100.0	8.8	817.3	−4.7
1976	926.4	13.4	101.2	1.2	915.3	12.0
1977	1,067.6	15.2	110.1	8.8	969.3	5.9
1978	1,240.6	16.2	121.2	10.1	1,023.5	5.6
1979	1,560.8	25.8	144.2	19.0	1,080.1	5.9
1980	1,920.4	23.0	178.6	23.9	1,075.8	−0.4
1981	1,899.8	−1.1	174.4	−2.3	1,089.5	+1.3
1982[b]	1,774.7[b]	−6.6	163.6	−6.5	1,084.8	−.4

Sources: International Monetary Fund; ACLI/DLJ.
[a]n.a. = not applicable.
[b]ACLI estimate.

The recent spell of weakness in world trade in real (constant dollar) terms is also quite impressive. Only in 1958 and 1975 were there similar occurrences; in those years unit volume of trade fell by 0.1% and 4.7%, respectively. This contrasts with −0.4% in 1980, +1.3% in 1981, and an estimated −0.4% in 1982.

To complete the picture, in Figure 10 we contrast constant dollar world trade with the index of commodity futures prices. The most important message conveyed by this relationship is that commodity prices have declined during periods when world trade has weakened. This is particularly noticeable in the 1974–1975

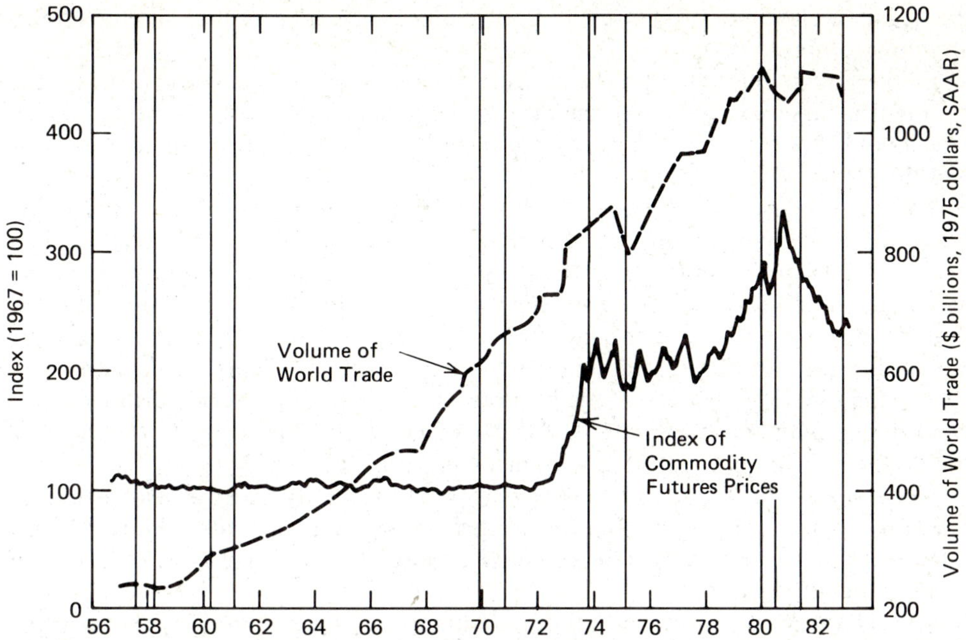

FIGURE 10. Index of commodity futures prices versus volume of world trade (vertical lines designate economic turning points). *Sources*: Commodity Research Bureau, Inc.; IMF; ACLI/DLJ.

and 1980–1982 periods. Thus another variable the commodity price forecaster should take into account is the outlook for world trade.

It would be totally foolhardy to entertain bullish views on commodity prices without a strong prospect of world trade growth in both nominal and real terms.

EXCHANGE RATE EFFECTS

A myopia shared by many commodity price analysts is to look at commodity prices only in terms of U.S. dollars. However, since changes in the value of the dollar affect the prices paid by non-U.S. consumers in their own domestic currency, swings in the value of the dollar will impact foreign demand. Furthermore, since roughly 70–80% of world commodity consumption takes place outside of the United States, changes in the value of the dollar can have an inverse effect on the U.S. dollar price.

For example, assume that producers of commodity X price and receive payment in dollars, and initially price the commodity at $10 per lb. Furthermore, assume that the United States consumes 20% of world production and demand is negatively sensitive to price changes on a one-to-one basis. Thus should the dollar rise in value, say by 10%, against a basket of foreign currencies, then the rest-of-the-world price would rise by 10%, even though the U.S. price initially remained unchanged. As foreign prices rose, consumption would fall by a similar percentage, that is, by 10%. As demand falls in 80% of the world market, in effect there would be an increase in the available supply to the U.S. market. This in turn would put downward pressure on U.S. prices. A good example of a well-known commodity which is priced and paid for (for the most part) in dollars is crude oil. However, the negative elasticity of demand to price changes is less than one, and the effects are slow to unfold.

Even though this example is an oversimplification of the world pricing and payment arrangements for commodity trade, it does make the simple point that one should expect a negative relationship between the dollar price of commodities and the value of the dollar.

There are many reasons why this inverse relationship will not work perfectly. First, there are many producing countries which do not price and take payment in dollars. For example, the Ivory Coast and Cameroon, major producers of cocoa, are on a French franc pegged system. Other countries will price their output in pounds sterling or Deutsche marks. Second, not all commodities have a large negative price elasticity of demand in the short term. Finally, in a number of cases, combinations of buffer stock, quota, or other supply-altering arrangements can operate sufficiently rapidly that the demand effects of swings in the value of the dollar can be partly offset by changes in supply.

Nonetheless, as Figure 11 makes reasonably clear, there is a strong inverse relationship between commodity futures prices and exchange rates. The exchange rate series is based on a trade weighted average of the dollar against 10 major industrial countries.

The relationship is not exact; there are numerous significant divergences (e.g., 1974). Furthermore, there are a number of cases where it appears that currency rates have turned in advance of changes in commodity prices (1973 and 1980). This characteristic, however, is highly desirable from a forecasting viewpoint.

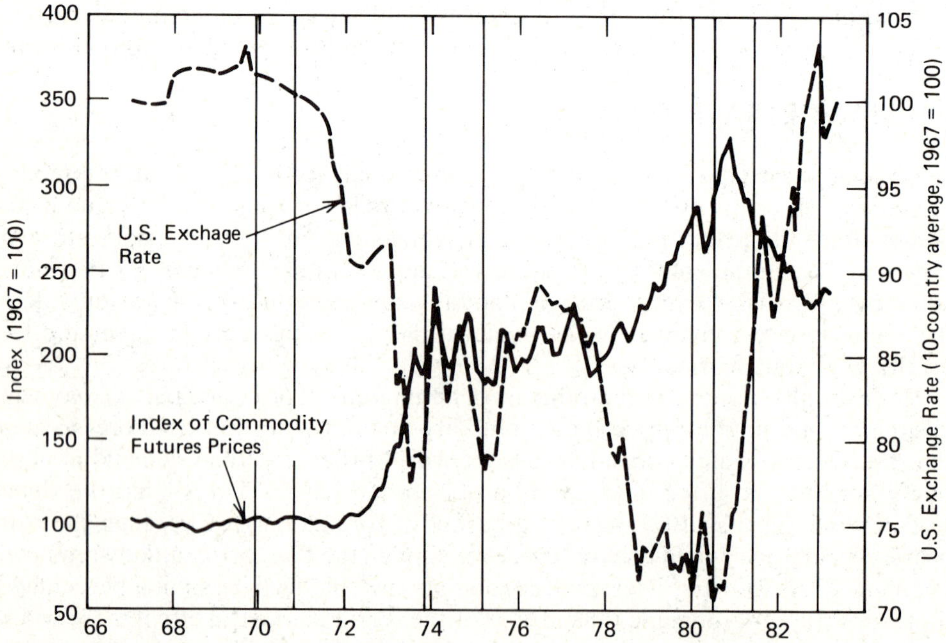

FIGURE 11. Index of commodity futures prices versus weighted exchange rate of the U.S. dollar (vertical lines designate economic turning points). *Sources*: Commodity Research Bureau, Inc.; FRB; ACLI/DLJ.

It is clear from Figure 11 that there are major inverse trend moves: 1970–1973 when commodity prices rose and the dollar weakened; 1973–1977 when both series on balance moved sideways; 1977–1980 when the dollar once again weakened and commodity prices soared; and finally, the remarkable period 1980–1982 when the dollar rebounded so sharply that all the losses of the previous decade were reversed, while at the same time commodity prices collapsed nearly back to their 1977 levels.

No commodity price forecast should be made without careful analysis of the exchange rate outlook.

INVENTORIES—A MEASURE OF IMBALANCE

Commodity price behavior and inventory cycles are broadly related to each other. This is true because changes in inventory levels reflect shifts in the consumption/production balance. Whenever consumption falls substantially below production, or production surges ahead of consumption, inventories mount rapidly. If inventory levels are expected to rise above a threshold level, and aggressive quota restrictions or buffer stock building programs are not implemented, prices tend to crumble sharply, and fall to the marginal unit cost of the most efficient producers. Conversely, when consumption outstrips production, and inventories are expected to fall below a critical level, prices tend to explode. The upside to

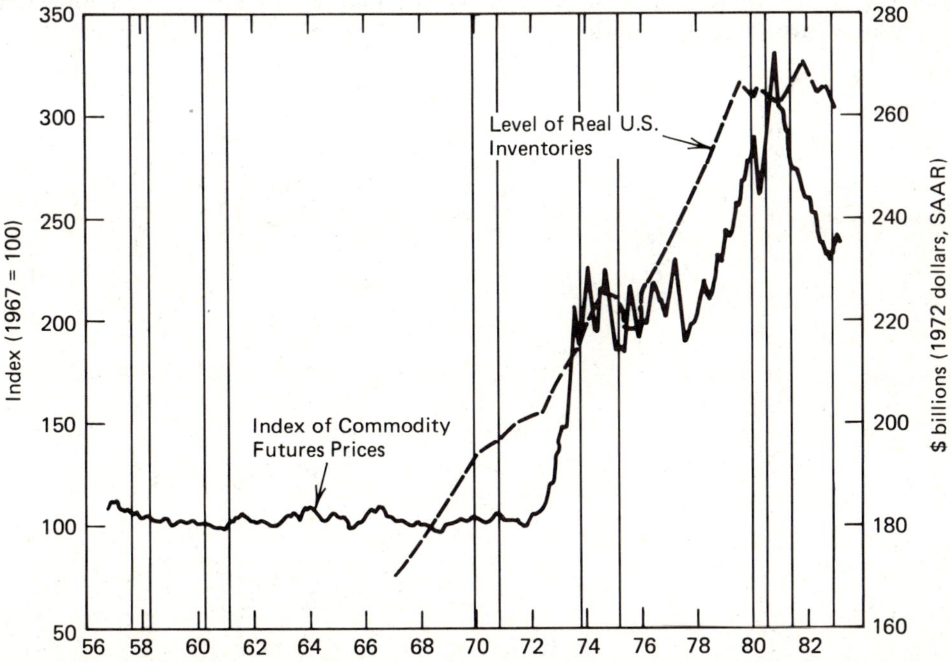

FIGURE 12. Index of commodity futures prices versus level of real U.S. inventories (vertical lines designate economic turning points). *Sources*: Commodity Research Bureau, Inc.; U.S. Department of Commerce; ACLI/DLJ.

prices is not neatly bounded and depends very much on the short-run elasticity of demand with respect to price.

This type of inventory price relationship holds for most commodities at the micro level. For example, the prospect of a sugar shortage in 1980 pushed prices to high levels, only to be reversed when the feared shortage never materialized. Weak demand resulted in high inventories of copper and lumber in the 1981–1982 period, depressing their prices throughout this period.

At the aggregate level the inventory commodity price relationship is more elusive, partly because of deficiencies in the accuracy and timeliness of worldwide inventory data, and partly because of aggregation problems for both the price and inventory data. Inventories might be heavily influenced by one or two commodities, whereas the price index may be unaffected because of the peculiar weighting scheme employed.

Despite many shortcomings, and acceding to the inescapability of some data compromises, reasonably persuasive graphical evidence on an aggregate inventory price relationship can be gleaned from Figure 12. In this figure commodity futures prices are contrasted with total U.S. constant dollar (in 1972 dollars) inventory levels since 1967. During the two periods of significant weakness in commodity futures prices (1975–1976 and 1980–1982) a substantial degree of inventory liquidation was also witnessed.

Of course, inventories are not the only factor influencing commodity futures prices, but they are a very useful summary measure of aggregate imbalances in the supply-and-demand situation. It would be highly unlikely to see a significant bull market in commodity futures develop when inventory levels are excessive and are being liquidated. Conversely, a bear market would be unlikely when inventories are lean and building.

CHAPTER **8**

THE USDA CROP AND LIVESTOCK INFORMATION SYSTEM

CONTENTS

DECISION-MAKING FACTORS 10
SOYBEAN COMPLEX 12
COTTON 15
WHEAT 18

CHAPTER **8**

THE USDA CROP AND LIVESTOCK INFORMATION SYSTEM

Walter Spilka, Jr.

Participants in the commodity futures markets rely on a continuous flow of information by which to evalute their current or prospective positions in the market. One such source of information is the Department of Agriculture (USDA), which provides a large amount of basic data and analyses for public use. A major segment of the USDA's information deals with the traditional agricultural commodities, that is, grains, oilseeds, and livestock. The long and successful history of trading in these commodities is due not only to their widespread use as a hedging vehicle, but also to the amount of public-sector information available concerning supplies, demand, and prices of these commodities.

As the size and importance of the agricultural sector has grown in relation to the rest of the economy, so has the amount of information provided by the USDA. Part of the reason for the increase in information stems from the growth in agricultural exports, particularly grains, which has injected a measure of uncertainty into farm prices. One need only examine a continuation chart of wheat futures prices over the period of 1960–1980 (see Figure 1) to observe the increase in volatility that occurred in 1972 and 1973. A look at the supply-and-demand data during this period would show it characterized by a surge in exports.[1] Prices prior to this time were generally steady and closely related to the loan rate. The increase in exports, particularly to countries with changing demands and political decisions to meet crop shortfalls through imports led to more variation in supply-and-demand balances and prices.

The response by the USDA to the increased importance of international trade in the grain market was twofold. First, agricultural policy and farm programs became oriented more toward trying to prevent the sharp price fluctuations by establishing trade agreements and grain reserves that would accumulate grain at low prices and release stored grain when prices reach higher price levels. Thus, farmers could be insulated from very low prices in times of overproduction, while consumers were protected from high prices in times of excessive demand. Trade agreements were negotiated with larger customers to assure some continuity and consistency in purchases. The second response was to increase the quantity of data and analysis flowing both into and out of the USDA, in order to provide

[1]Wheat exports between 1971/72 and 1972/73 rose 86%.

FIGURE 1. Monthly Chicago Wheat Prices.

USDA policymakers with more information with which to shape policy in the increasingly complex agricultural sector. Additionally, the widening scope of the farm programs and their potential expense required more data for USDA budget analysis. Finally, the public benefited by receiving more information about agriculture at a time when it was becoming more internationally oriented.

To accomplish the goal of providing the public with timely and accurate information, the USDA issues a wide variety of publications on all segments of agriculture. For the purposes of commodity futures market participants, the most important reports are those concerning livestock, grains, soybeans, and cotton. The USDA publishes two major report series on the livestock sector, the *Hogs and Pigs* reports and the *Cattle on Feed* reports. These publications provide the public with an estimate of the potential livestock slaughter by detailing current inventories by number and weight breakdown. As a result, the reports can have a strong impact on cash and futures prices. These reports are issued after the close of the commodity markets. The *Hogs and Pigs* reports are issued quarterly, with the March, September, and June reports showing data from the 10 major hog-producing states, while the December issue contains data for all states. The report provides details of inventories, number of sows farrowing and to farrow, litter size, and the pig crop. The monthly *Cattle on Feed* report indicates number of cattle on feed, placements on feed, and marketings in the seven major producing states. The reports for January, April, July, and October show the same data for the 13 largest producing states. The publication *Cattle* details the inventory in January and July for 50 states. Examples of the reports are shown in Tables 1 and 2.

These reports are assembled and issued by the USDA's Crop Reporting Board (CRB). As is the procedure with all CRB reports, the data is collected at the state level, at statistical offices, and then sent to the CRB in Washington. All data analysis is done under secure conditions to prevent premature leakage of information. At the CRB, the data is aggregated to regional and national levels and cross-checked with other data, such as commercial slaughter, before it is released to the public. The gathering of the basic data is accomplished using statistical survey techniques. The survey procedure categorizes producers by size of operation. A sample of producers in each category are then interviewed using mailed questionnaires, telephone interviews, and personal interviews. The structure of the sample is such that larger producers are sampled more frequently. The samples then are expanded to represent all producers.

Detailed economic analysis of the implications of the livestock reports is contained in the publication *Livestock and Meat Situation and Outlook,* which is issued approximately six times a year. These reports note the implications of inventories for future supplies of animals and meat. The analysis examines grain prices, forage supplies, and price trends, and forecasts livestock prices. Since expansion of livestock herds is dependent on profitability, analysis of costs of production and returns is included. Current and projected supply-and-demand balances and price forecasts are contained also in the *World Agricultural Supply and Demand Estimates*.

For the grains, soybeans, and cotton, USDA's Crop Reporting Board issues a number of reports which estimate the sizes of crops, as well as current stock levels. The most important series of reports are *Prospective Plantings, Acreage, Crop Production,* and *Grain Stocks. Prospective Plantings* publishes results of a survey that asks producers to indicate their planting intentions for the coming season. The report is issued during February and provides some early indications of the amount of corn, soybeans, spring wheat, and cotton to be grown; as it precedes actual planting by a few months, its indications are subject to frequent change.[2] The *Acreage* report is issued in late June and is based on a survey conducted around June 1. It indicates plantings and expected harvested acreage in all states for corn, all wheat, soybeans, and cotton as well as smaller crops such as sorghum, oats, barley, and sunflowers. Since this report occurs at the beginning of the planting season, it provides a much clearer idea of the potential size of the crop. The monthly *Crop Production* reports are probably the most widely anticipated releases. These reports are issued at midmonth and are based on surveys taken at the beginning of the month. They indicate, by state, harvested acreage, yield, and production of the crop. Yields are determined by actual surveying and observation of crop areas. As the *Crop Production* report provides a good estimate of the size of the crop, it can have an impact on futures prices.

[2]Some years *Prospective Plantings* has been issued in January and March.

TABLE 1. Hogs and Pigs: Inventory Number, June 1 and December 1, Sows Farrowing and Pig Crop, 1980–1982, United States

Item	1980	1981	1982	1982 as % of 1980	1982 as % of 1981
		1000 Head		Percent	
Inventory Number—June 1					
All hogs and pigs	65255	59740	51990	80	87
kept for breeding	9481	8358	7389	78	88
market	55774	51382	44601	80	87
Market hogs and pigs by weight groups:					
under 60 lb	25002	23069	18941	76	82
60–119 lb	13550	12204	10954	81	90
120–179 lb	9781	9041	8200	84	91
180 lb and over	7441	7068	6506	87	92
Inventory number—December 1					
All hogs and pigs	64512	58691			
kept for breeding	9148	7844			
market	55364	50847			
Market hogs and pigs by weight groups:					
under 60 lb	22139	19465			
60–119 lb	13982	12924			
120–179 lb	11000	10453			
180 lb and over	8243	8005			
Sows farrowing:					
December[a]–February	3317	2914	2587	78	89
March–May	3913	3526	2991	76	85
December[a]–May	7229	6440	5578	77	87
June–August	3399	3196			
September–November	3430	3062			
June–November	6829	6258	[b]5637	83	90
Pig crop:					
December[a]–February	23682	21046	18436	78	88
March–May	28604	26554	22520	79	85
December[a]–May	52286	47600	40956	78	86
June–August	24341	23540			
September–November	24915	22636			
June–November	49256	46176	[c]40900	83	89
year	101542	93776	[c]81856	81	87
		Number			
Pigs per litter:					
December[a]–February	7.14	7.22	7.13	100	99
March–May	7.31	7.53	7.53	103	100
December[a]–May	7.23	7.39	7.34	102	99
June–August	7.16	7.37			
September–November	7.26	7.39			
June–November	7.21	7.38	[c]7.26	101	98

Source: Hogs and Pigs, June 1982, Crop Reporting Board, SRS, USDA.

[a]December preceding year.

[b]Intentions.

[c]Average number of pigs per litter with allowance for trend used to compute indicated June–November pig crop.

The *Crop Production* forecasts are generally regarded as accurate; because they are based on conditions only up to a given point in time, however, they are subject to revision as weather conditions change. As more becomes known about the crop over the season, the reports become more accurate forecasts of the final crop size. The *Grain Stocks* report is issued at the beginning of each crop quarter.[3] This release gives the results of a survey of farmers and elevator operators, and provides an indication of the amount of grain on farms and in off-farm storage. The difference between the current quarter's stocks and the previous quarter's stocks is usage, which provides the market with a barometer of demand. A monthly schedule of these reports can be found in Table 8 at the end of this chapter.

At the same time that the CRB releases crop-production data for the United States, the USDA also issues the *World Crop Production* report. This release provides country data on foreign production of coarse grains, soybeans, and cotton. The release of these reports is the first step in a two-step process of economic analysis. These reports provide vital input for the next day's analysis of the U.S. supply-and-demand situation titled *World Agricultural Supply and Demand Estimates*.

The responsibility for making the analysis and estimates contained in this report falls on what are termed Interagency Committees (IAC). Since 1977, the USDA has employed a more centralized approach to the dissemination of economic information by the IAC. The World Agricultural Outlook Board (WAOB) was formed to provide a focal point, which would coordinate the analysis and release of the IAC deliberations. The WAOB does this by providing a chairperson for each committee. The IAC meet following the release of all major CRB reports. The meetings are held under secure conditions, and the results are released after the closing of the commodity markets. The IAC analysis is contained in *World Agricultural Supply and Demand Estimates*.

The IAC are made up of representatives of the various USDA agencies that collect data and conduct economic analyses. The specific agencies represented are: the Economic Research Service (ERS), the Foreign Agricultural Service (FAS), the Agricultural Stabilization and Conservation Service (ASCS), and the Agricultural Marketing Service (AMS)—in addition to the WAOB. The ERS provides the committee with economic analysis of the impact of changes in domestic supply and disappearance on price. Analysis of foreign countries also is provided, particularly with regard to economic issues such as exchange rates, tariffs, and trade agreements. The FAS provides the committee with detailed data and analyses of foreign production, usage, trade, and prices for each commodity. The FAS, in particular, relies on its network of agricultural attachés, representatives who are stationed in embassies around the world. A continuous flow of information from the attachés on crop conditions provides the FAS with a primary source of country-by-country data. Additionally, the Export Sales Reporting Division of the FAS provides the latest data on exports. The ASCS provides the committee with data and analyses of the commodity programs. This would include the amounts of grain under price-support loan, in reserves, and under government ownership. The ASCS, which administers the farm programs, receives its data from a network

[3]For corn and wheat, the crop quarters begin in January, April, June, and October, while for soybeans they are January, April, June, and September.

TABLE 2. Cattle and Calves: Number on Feed, Placements, Marketed, and Other Disappearance, Seven States, April 1–May 1 and February 1–May 1[a]

Item	April 1–May 1				
				1982 as percent of	
	1980	1981	1982	1980	1981
		1,000 Head		Percent	
On feed April 1[b]	7,156	6,837	7,024	98	103
Placed on feed during April	1,237	1,721	1,565	127	91
Fed cattle marketed during April	1,435	1,386	1,414	99	102
Other disappearance during April[c]	130	142	109	84	77
On feed May 1[b]	6,828	7,030	7,066	103	101

State	February 1–May 1											
	Number on feed			Placed			Marketed			Other Disappearance		
	1981	1982	1982 and 1981	1981	1982	1982 and 1981	1981	1982	1982 and 1981	1981	1982	1982 and 1981
	1,000 Head		Percent	1,000 Head		Percent	1,000 Head		Percent	1,000 Head		Percent
	February 1			During February			During February			During February		
Arizona	400	325	81	40	38	95	32	33	103	26	8	31
California	625	540	86	57	78	137	83	100	120	20	11	55
Colorado	820	730	89	118	179	152	185	180	97	28	14	50
Iowa	1,310	1,140	87	180	170	94	190	150	79	10	15	150
Kansas	1,080	1,060	98	200	235	118	230	250	109	10	5	50
Nebraska	1,550	1,600	103	350	380	109	380	380	100	20	30	150
Texas	1,720	1,660	97	245	240	98	340	320	94	15	10	67
Totals	7,505	7,055	94	1,190	1,320	111	1,440	1,413	98	129	93	72
	March 1			During March			During March			During March		
Arizona	382	322	84	32	35	109	52	37	71	16	12	75
California	579	507	88	63	72	114	100	104	104	16	9	56
Colorado	725	715	99	181	255	141	210	185	88	31	15	48

Iowa	1,290	1,145	89	175	190	109	225	175	78	10	10	100
Kansas	1,040	1,040	100	312	341	109	246	241	98	6	10	167
Nebraska	1,500	1,570	105	320	420	131	350	400	114	20	20	100
Texas	1,610	1,570	98	300	480	160	370	400	108	20	20	100
Totals	7,126	6,869	96	1,383	1,793	130	1,553	1,542	99	119	96	81
	April 1			During April			During April			During April		
Arizona	346	308	89	46	40	87	46	50	109	13	9	69
California	526	466	89	57	82	144	83	91	110	13	15	115
Colorado	665	770	116	205	206	100	140	155	111	30	11	37
Iowa	1,230	1,150	93	205	190	93	170	183	108	15	12	80
Kansas	1,100	1,130	103	368	327	89	217	215	99	11	12	109
Nebraska	1,450	1,570	108	470	400	85	360	380	106	40	30	75
Texas	1,520	1,630	107	370	320	86	370	340	92	20	20	100
Totals	6,837	7,024	103	1,721	1,565	91	1,386	1,414	102	142	109	77
	May 1											
Arizona	333	289	87									
California	487	442	91									
Colorado	700	810	116									
Iowa	1,250	1,145	92									
Kansas	1,240	1,230	99									
Nebraska	1,520	1,560	103									
Texas	1,500	1,590	106									
Totals	7,030	7,066	101									

Source: Cattle on Feed, May 1982, Crop Reporting Board, SRS, USDA.

[a]Estimates in this *Cattle on Feed* report are based on data provided voluntarily by cattle feeders. The state statistical offices maintain an up-to-date list of cattle feeders stratified by feedlot capacity. Data are collected by mail and by personal and telephone interviews on or about the first day of each survey period. Survey procedures are designed to obtain reports from all feeders in the larger-size strata, and feeders in the smaller-size strata are sampled. Of the total inventory of cattle on feed estimated on this report 69% were actually reported in the survey.

[b]Cattle and calves on feed are animals for slaughter market being fed a full ration of grain or other concentrates and are expected to produce a carcass that will grade good or better.

[c]Includes death losses, movement from feedlots to pastures, and shipments to other feedlots for further feeding.

of county and regional offices. The AMS provides the committee with information on cash markets. The committee also makes use of current weather information, based on cooperation of the USDA meteorologists with the National Oceanographic and Atmospheric Administration. When a special situation requires it, the interagency committee is briefed by a USDA meteorologist.

DECISION-MAKING FACTORS

This section provides a description of some of the factors considered by the interagency committees when making supply, demand, and price estimates for the feed grains, soybeans, wheat, and cotton. Often, the same factors are considered for each commodity, although their relative importance may vary from commodity to commodity. The IAC meets on a continuing basis, constantly updating its estimates as new information becomes available. The estimates are made within a range of predictable error, even though the midpoint of the range often is cited as the official USDA estimate. As the season progresses and more information becomes available—leaving less uncertainty—the range of the estimate becomes progressively smaller.

For corn, which is analyzed with oats, barley, and sorghum, the first information about the new crop is found in the Prospective Plantings report, which indicates producers' planting intentions for the crop. In May, the IAC issues its first estimates of supply and demand for the new crop, based primarily on trends and analysts' judgments. The June Acreage report provides a more accurate plantings forecast, while the monthly Crop Production reports give updated estimates of the size of the crop. The quarterly Grain Stocks report indicates usage of the crop: one function of the committee is to determine respective usage by category. Domestic disappearance falls into two categories: feed and food, seed and industrial. In estimating feed usage, the committee considers availabilities and price relationships among various substitute feeds. With relation to corn—by far the largest in feed usage—an important consideration is the price of soybean meal, since high meal prices imply higher rates of corn usage. Sorghum availability and price is important, also, as sorghum is a direct substitute for corn, particularly in feedlots in the Southwest. Barley and oats, too, act as substitutes for corn, although to a lesser degree. A recent trend has been toward feeding livestock soft wheat, mostly in the Southeast. Low wheat prices relative to corn during the June–August period can imply lower corn feed usage. Another consideration is the amount of hay available and the quality of pastures. When pastures are rated good, there will be more grazing and less use of feedlots.

The second factor affecting feed use is the size of the animal population. The ERS provides the committee with livestock and poultry data, in terms of standardized units of grain-consuming animal units and protein-consuming animal units. By employing standardized units, it is easier to determine the amount of grain to be consumed. Also considered are projected prices for livestock and poultry. Measures of the price of livestock to feed prices, for example, the hog/corn ratio, are useful in estimating feed usage.

The other category of domestic feed-grain disappearance is for food, seed, and industrial purposes. Usage in this category has grown, recently, because of the expansion of corn sweetener and fuel-alcohol production. Estimates of food, seed, and industrial feed-grain usage are made by ERS analysts based on surveys of the wet and dry milling industries, breakfast cereal and pet-food industries, malt and distilled liquor industry, and fuel-alcohol producers. Seed use is, of course, directly related to planted acreage. Most of the basic data come from the Census Bureau's survey of manufacturing industries, which is issued every 5 years. This data are then extrapolated to account for population growth and the emergence of new products such as gasohol. While, over the last few years, increases in food, seed, and industrial uses have been somewhat predictable, the rapid growth of fructose production and changes in federal support for fuel-alcohol production have made projections in the category subject to greater variation.

Export estimates are made on the basis of analysis conducted by the Foreign Agriculture Service and the ERS International Economics Division. A primary source of information for this analysis is information gathered by agricultural attachés who are stationed at embassies in various countries. These attachés are responsible for monitoring the countries' production prospects and exports and their import needs, as well as policies which might affect trade. The attachés file reports on a regular basis with the FAS containing estimates and any new information that would be useful to the export analysis. Information on export sales and shipments also is provided by the FAS Export Sales Division. In addition, analysts examine trends in foreign production and trade by looking at population and income growth, weather, acreage changes, exchange rates, tariffs, subsidies, and procurement rates of food-purchasing agencies. Of particular importance to U.S. exports have been the export policies followed by marketing boards in Australia, Canada, Argentina and South Africa. All of these countries have been making concerted efforts to expand exports. Separate analysis of the situation in the Soviet Union is done by a group of specialists called the USSR Task Force. The end result of all analysis is the seasons' export projection.

There are three data sources which monitor the export situation and help the committee determine if the export estimate is still on track. The first is the weekly export inspection data provided by the Federal Grain Inspection Service. This report indicates the amount of feed grains, wheat, and soybeans shipped out of export locations during the previous week. The second is the Census Bureau, which issues a monthly export report that indicates not only grain exports, but also product exports including soybean meal and oil, and wheat flour. At the end of the season, the Census Bureau export data become the official USDA export estimate. A final gauge of the export situation is provided by the FAS *Export Sales* report, which indicates amounts that have been exported, as well as outstanding sales which have been contracted for, but not delivered. The report provides some indication of the pending export rate. A big increase in outstanding sales would indicate that exports are likely to increase, while a decline would signal the opposite. As new data and information become available to the committee, the export estimates are reexamined and, if necessary, revised.

The difference between total supplies of grain (beginning stocks plus production and any imports) and total disappearance (domestic plus exports) is termed ending stocks. A certain amount of stocks at the end of the marketing year are necessary to provide a continuous flow of grain to processors and exporters before the new crop is harvested. These stocks are referred to as pipeline supplies: for corn, they are usually placed at 400–500 million bushels. Ending stocks projected below this level could mean spot shortages may appear. While ending stocks are the arithmetic difference between supplies and use, they provide the quickest comparison of the grain balance from one crop year to the next.

With the development of the farmer-owned grain reserve (FOR), the disposition of ending stocks has become important in determining how much grain will be free stocks or in marketable channels and how much will remain under government contract or ownership. Because the FOR is designed to accumulate grain when market prices are low and release stocks when prices reach higher levels, it is necessary for the committee to project the inventory, since this will impact prices. It is necessary, also, to estimate Commodity Credit Corporation (CCC) inventories, since these represent grain not in marketable channels. The CCC stocks are accumulated through direct purchasing programs and through defaults on price-support loans. The ASCS is the agency that administers the programs and is responsible for projecting participation in them. Through its network of county offices, the ASCS monitors the flow of grain into and out of different programs. Perhaps the most important program is the price support or nonrecourse loan program in which producers take out short-term loans using their grain as collateral. Widespread use of the program would imply higher prices early in the season. Because the producer has the option of either defaulting on the loan and turning the grain over to the CCC or moving it into the longer-term FOR program, it becomes important to watch loan activity and its relation to market prices. The committee must also monitor prices as they increase, since FOR and CCC stocks can be released once prices reach designated levels.

The link between supply and usage is price. The IAC is responsible for forecasting season-average farm prices based on the projected supply-and-demand balance and the current economic outlook. The projected farm prices are used by the USDA to estimate farm income, an important measure of agriculture's economic well-being. One economic relationship that is closely watched is the strong correlation between the ratio of ending stocks to use and price. Increases in the ratio are highly related to lower prices. The price forecast is confirmed in the monthly USDA publication *Agricultural Prices,* which indicates the average price received by producers for their products. The committee takes the monthly price and weights it by marketings of the product in a given month to determine the average weighted price. The heaviest marketings for corn are normally in October and November. As the season progresses, the monthly weighted prices become part of the season's price history, and the projected price will vary less and less. An example of the results of the IAC for feed-grains analysis is shown in Table 3. Detailed economic analysis of the corn and feed-grain market is found in the ERS publication *Feed Outlook and Situation,* which is issued four times a year. This report also contains a large amount of data, including quarterly breakouts of the supply-and-demand estimates and various price series for grains and substitute products.

SOYBEAN COMPLEX

The analysis and estimating procedure for soybeans, soymeal, and soyoil is similar to that for the feed grains, except that somewhat different economic relationships are examined. Soybeans derive their value from the products that are obtained in the crushing process—meal and oil. Meal is used as a high-protein livestock

TABLE 3. United States Feed Grains and Corn[a]

Commodity	1980/1981	1981/1982 Estimated	1982/1983 Projections May	1982/1983 Projections Probable Variation[b]
Feed grains:				
Area		Million acres		
Planted	121.3	123.5		
Harvested	101.5	106.9		
		Metric tons		
Yield per harvested acre	1.95	2.32		
		Million metric tons		
Beginning stocks	52.4	34.6	62.5	
Production	198.0	248.4	231.5	+21/−21
Imports	.3	.3	.3	
Supply, total	250.7	283.3	294.3	+21/−21
Feed and residual	123.0	130.3	131.8	+10/−10
Food, seed, and industrial	23.8	25.1	25.9	+1/ −1
Domestic, total	146.8	155.4	157.7	+10/−10
Exports	69.3	65.4	67.2	+6/ −6
Use, total	216.1	220.8	224.9	+14/−14
Ending stocks, total	34.6	62.5	69.4	+11/−11
Farmer-owned reserve	4.9	38.0	42.2	
CCC inventory	7.1	9.1	10.9	
Free stocks	22.6	15.4	16.3	
Corn:				
Area		Million acres		
Planted	84.0	84.2		
Harvested	73.0	74.6		
		Bushels		
Yield per harvested acre	91.0	109.9		
		Million bushels		
Beginning stocks	1,617	1,034	1,976	
Production	6,645	8,201	7,685	+770/−770
Imports	1	1	1	
Supply, total	8,263	9,236	9,662	+770/−770
Feed and residual	4,139	4,300	4,350	+350/−350
Food, seed, and industrial	735	785	815	+25/ −25
Domestic, total	4,874	5,085	5,165	+365/−365
Exports	2,355	2,175	2,300	+200/−200
Use, total	7,229	7,260	7,465	+500/−500
Ending stocks, total	1,034	1,976	2,197	+400/−400
Farmer-owned reserve	185	1,250	1,400	
CCC inventory	238	315	375	
Free stocks	611	411	422	
Average farm price[d]	3.11	2.50	2.50–2.90	

[a]Marketing year beginning October 1 for corn and sorghum; June 1 for barley and oats.
[b]The "probable variation" reflects the root-mean-square error and/or standard error of estimate from trend and judgement. Chances are about 2 out of 3 that the outcome will fall within the implied ranges.
[c]Reserve loans that were called in January 1981, and extended indefinitely in April.
[d]Season-average farm price, dollars per bushel.

and poultry-feed ingredient in mixed rations, while oil is used mainly for food and industrial purposes. Disappearance of soybeans falls into three categories: exports, crushing, and a residual group that includes the small amounts used for feed and seed.

Export demand for soybeans is the sum of the crushing demand by importing countries. A given country's decision to import soybeans instead of products is a function of available crush capacity, demand for both products instead of an individual one, and the availability and price of substitute oilseeds and products. Because both the variety and quantity of internationally traded oilseeds have increased, price has played an important role in exports. Since a majority of U.S. soybeans go to Western Europe and Japan, the strength of the dollar against the currencies of these countries is a major consideration in the import decision. Because crushing plants store soybeans to ensure continuous operations, and then store products until sold, interest rates become a factor also. High interest rates discourage inventory buildup and thus reduce demand.

Crushing demand represents the largest category of usage. A gauge of the crush is provided in the weekly National Soybean Processor's Association crush report and the monthly Census Bureau crush report. Since the crushing process yields more than four times as much meal as oil, it follows that demand for soybeans to crush is derived primarily from demand for soymeal. The difference between the prices that the crusher receives for the respective products and the price of the soybeans is termed the crushing margin. Most soybean crushers use the futures market to determine when it is profitable to crush beans. When the difference between the value of the products and the soybeans is large enough, the crusher will lock in a profit in the futures market by buying soybean futures and selling product futures. A margin of $0.30/bushel–$0.40/bushel usually is needed to ensure a profitable crush. Projected prices of soybeans and products which yield lower margins are usually indicative of reduced crushing activity.

Demand for meal is a function of both numbers of livestock and poultry, and rates of use. Projections of animal numbers are made at the ERS and are usually put on a standardized basis of protein-consuming animal units. Relative rates of use are a function of prices and availabilities of competing feeds and protein meals. How much soymeal will be used can be determined, in part, from a historical comparison of product and input prices. Such price ratios as the pork/meal and broiler/meal are often employed to determine rate of use. Meal use is somewhat more responsive to increases in livestock prices than to lower meal prices, but both will increase usage. Meal, also, is exported, and demand in an importing country is affected by the same factors as in the United States. The export market has grown, in part, because of changing consumer tastes, and the upgrading of diets to include more meat. At the same time, increased world demand has encouraged other countries to develop crushing capacity as well as trade policies which protect the industry. Most notable has been Brazil, which now has a large crushing industry and provides the United States with its most significant export competition. Brazilian trade policy favors exporting products instead of soybeans. The situation in Brazil, therefore, becomes an important consideration for the IAC when projecting meal export estimates.

Demand for soyoil is highly related to population changes and real income growth. As economic activity expands and consumer incomes rise, more money is spent on meals away from home. Fast-food outlets and restaurants are large users of soyoil, making it necessary that the committee consider the outlook for economic growth and consumer income when making soyoil projections. In the export market, soyoil is subject to competition not only from other-origin soyoil, but also from other edible cooking oils such as palm oil, coconut oil, and rapeseed oil. Very often, the major considerations in projecting soyoil exports are the availability and prices of different oils. Consumer tastes, also, have played a part in exports as some oils are preferred to others. Another consideration in the export outlook is the existence of credit programs such as PL480. These programs enable poor countries to purchase larger amounts of oil on more favorable terms. An example of estimates made for the soybean complex are shown in Table 4. Analysis of the current situation in the soybean complex is found in the ERS report: *Fats and Oils Outlook and Situation*. Issued four times a year, this publication provides detailed economic and statistical analysis not only of the soybean complex, but also of competing oilseeds.

COTTON

The analysis and estimate procedures used by the interagency committee for cotton are the same as for the grains, with the exception that by law cotton price forecasts are not published. There are two categories of cotton disappearance: mill use and exports. Projections of mill use are made after consideration of several factors. The first is the level of domestic economic activity and interest rates. Since cotton mills normally carry large inventories, high interest rates increase the cost of holding raw- and processed-cotton inventories. High interest rates discourage inventory accumulation and reduce mill rates. High interest rates are associated, also, with slow economic growth and higher unemployment. This results in reduced consumer income and fewer expenditures on durable textile products. The reduction in textile demand tends to lag recessions by three to nine months.

Cotton's major substitutes are polyester fibers, which find extensive use in clothing, housing, and automobiles. Recessions, therefore, can have a greater impact on their demand. Since cotton and polyester fiber are close substitutes, relative fiber prices can affect the mill's use of cotton. In general, however, the mill does not have wide leeway in substitution, particularly in products such as clothing, where both fibers are blended to produce desirable characteristics. Another factor affecting the level of mill use is the balance of textile trade. Imports of finished textile products have increased in recent years and thus has reduced the demand for domestically produced textile products. The nature of textile trade agreements, particularly with the People's Republic of China, is an important consideration for the committee when projecting mill use.

Exports of cotton fiber are related to the balance between foreign cotton supplies and foreign mill use. The major foreign producers are the Soviet Union, China, Pakistan, and India. The FAS analysis of production trends in these countries is important to the committee's export projection. While foreign mill use is affected by basically the same factors as U.S. mills, the extent of competition in the export market dictates that importers consider such factors as exchange rates and relative prices. An example of supply–demand estimates for cotton is shown in Table 5. The economic situation in cotton is described in the ERS publication

TABLE 4. United States Soybeans and Products (Domestic Measure)[a]

Commodity	1980/1981	1981/1982 Estimated	1982/1983 Projections May	1982/1983 Projections Probable Variation[b]
Soybeans:				
Area		Million acres		
Planted	70.0	68.1		
Harvested	67.9	66.7		
		Bushels/acre		
Yield per harvested unit	26.4	30.4		
		Million bushels		
Beginning stocks	359	318	315	
Production	1,792	2,030	2,100	+170/ −170
Supply, total	2,151	2,348	2,415	+170/ −170
Crushings	1,020	1,055	1,080	+65/ −65
Exports	724	890	915	+60/ −60
Seed and feed	66	68	70	
Residual	23	20	20	
Use, total	1,833	2,033	2,085	+100/ −100
Ending stocks	318	315	330	+100/ −100
Average farm price (dollars/bushel)	7.57	6.05	5.85–7.50	
Soybean oil:		Million pounds		
Beginning stocks	1,210	1,736	1,525	
Production	11,270	11,289	11,775	+700/ −700
Supply, total	12,480	13,025	13,300	+700/ −700
Domestic	9,115	9,550	9,850	+300/ −300
Exports	1,629	1,950	2,250	+400/ −400
Use, total	10,744	11,500	12,100	+350/ −350
Ending stocks	1,736	1,525	1,200	+350/ −350
Average price[c]	22.7	19.0	20.0–26.0	
Soybean meal:		Thousand short tons		
Beginning stocks	226	163	230	
Production	25,312	25,267	25,760	+1550/−1550
Supply, total	24,538	25,430	25,900	+1550/−1550
Domestic	17,597	18,000	18,400	+1000/−1000
Exports	6,778	7,200	7,350	+600/ −600
Use, total	24,375	25,200	25,750	+1000/−1000
Ending stocks	163	230	240	+50/ −50
Average price[d]	218.20	185	175–210	

[a]Marketing year beginning September 1 for soybeans; October 1 for soybean oil and meal.
[b]The "probable variation" reflects the root-mean-square error and/or standard error of estimate from trend and judgement. Chances are about 2 out of 3 that the outcome will fall within the implied ranges.
[c]Simple average of crude soybean oil, Decatur, cents per lb.
[d]Simple average of 44% protein, Decatur, dollars per short ton.

TABLE 5. United States Cotton: Upland and Extra Long Staple[a]

Commodity	1980/1981	1981/1982 Estimated	1982/1983 Projections May	1982/1983 Projections Probable Variation[b]
		Domestic Measure		
Area		Million acres		
Planted	14.5	14.3		
Harvested	13.2	13.8		
		Pounds		
Yield per harvested acre	404	543		
		Million 480-lb bales		
Beginning stocks[c]	3.0	2.7	6.4	+0.4/ −0.4
Production	11.1	15.6	12.5	+1.5/ −1.5
Supply, total[d]	14.1	18.3	18.9	+1.7/ −1.7
Mill use	5.9	5.3	5.8	+0.7/ −0.7
Exports	5.9	6.8	7.5	+1.5/ −1.5
Use, total	11.9	12.1	13.3	+1.8/ −1.8
Difference unaccounted[e]	0.3	0.2	0.2	
Ending stocks	2.7	6.4	5.8	+2.0/ −2.0
Average farm price[f]	74.7	54.7[g]	[h]	
		Metric Measure		
Area		Million hectares		
Planted	5.88	5.79		
Harvested	5.35	5.59		
Yield per harvested		Metric tons		
hectare	0.45	0.61		
		Million metric tons		
Beginning stocks[c]	0.65	0.59	1.39	+0.09/−0.09
Production	2.42	3.40	2.72	+0.33/−0.33
Supply, total[d]	3.07	3.99	4.12	+0.37/−0.37
Mill use	1.28	1.15	1.26	+0.15/−0.15
Exports	1.28	1.48	1.63	+0.33/−0.33
Use, total	2.59	2.63	2.90	+0.39/−0.39
Difference unaccounted[e]	0.07	0.04	0.04	
Ending stocks	0.59	1.39	1.26	+0.44/−0.44
Average farm price[f]	1.65	1.21[g]	[h]	

[a]Marketing year beginning August 1.
[b]The "probable variation" reflects the root-mean-square error and/or standard error of estimate from trend and judgment. Chances are about 2 out of 3 that the outcome will fall within the implied ranges.
[c]Based on Bureau of the Census data.
[d]Includes imports.
[e]Difference between ending stocks based on Bureau of Census data and preceding season's supply less distribution.
[f]Season-average farm price, domestic measure, cents per lb; metric measure, dollars per kg.
[g]Weighted average for the first 8 months of the marketing season; not a projection for 1981 and 1982.
[h]USDA is prohibited from publishing cotton-price projections.
Note: Totals may not add due to rounding.

Cotton and Wool Outlook and Situation, which is issued four times a year. The analysis includes manmade fibers as well.

WHEAT

The analysis of the wheat market differs somewhat from that of the feed-grains market in that wheat is harvested at two separate times each crop year. Winter wheat, which includes hard red and soft red winter and white wheat is seeded in the fall and harvested in early summer. About 75% of the total crop is winter wheat. The first indications of the size of the winter wheat crop are contained in the December CRB publication, *Small Grains*. This report shows planted acreage while the May *Crop Production* report contains the first production estimate. Spring wheat is planted in the spring and harvested in late summer. Acreage is estimated in the June *Acreage* report while the first production estimate is contained in the August *Crop Production* report. The interagency wheat committee not only provides supply and demand estimates of all wheat, but also makes periodic estimates of each class of wheat (see Table 6). The outlook for the different classes is significant for analysis of intermarket spreads. Soft-red-wheat prices are represented on the Chicago Board of Trade, while hard red wheat is traded at the Kansas City Board of Trade and spring wheat is priced on the Minneapolis Grain Exchange.

Disappearance of all wheat falls into three categories: food, feed, and exports. Food use of wheat represents consumption by mills in the production of flour. The amount of wheat milled each year generally increases with the population, although some variation can occur due to flour export demand. Feed use of wheat has varied widely from season to season. There has been a trend toward increased feeding of soft red wheat in Southeast poultry producing areas. These regions are deficit in corn, which must be barged in or moved by train, so that low wheat prices relative to corn can make feeding profitable. In addition, wheat is double-cropped with soybeans in the South where poultry feeding provides a ready outlet for the crop particularly during the June–September quarter.

Export estimates of wheat are based on analysis done by the FAS and the ERS International Economics Division. The major wheat importers are the Soviet Union and China. The Soviet Union's import needs stem largely from production shortfalls and consist mostly of hard red wheat. The Chinese import demand has increased because of increased consumption of bakery products in that country. The majority of imports are of soft red wheat. The major wheat exporters are Canada, Australia, the European Community, and Argentina. Aggressive export policies adopted by the marketing boards in these countries have enabled them to increase production, as well as exports. The analysis of production trends, as well as of export policies, is important in the determination of U.S. exports. In determining the disposition of ending stocks, the committee employs the same methods of analysis used for the feed grains. Stocks of wheat may be under government contract, owned by the CCC, or free. Again, there is a close relationship between wheat prices and the ratio of ending stocks to use. Important

TABLE 6. United States Wheat by Classes: Supply and Disappearance[a]

Year Beginning June 1	Hard Winter	Hard Spring	Soft Red	White	Durum	Total
			Million bushels			
1979/1980						
Beginning stocks	423	320	27	68	86	924
Production	1,089	363	317	259	106	2,134
Supply, total[b]	1,512	684	344	327	193	3,060
Domestic use	347	182	150	55	49	783
Exports	725	217	154	196	83	1,375
Use, total	1,072	399	304	251	132	2,158
Ending stocks	440	285	40	76	61	902
1980/1981 Estimated						
Beginning stocks	440	285	40	76	61	902
Production	1,181	312	435	338	108	2,374
Supply, total[b]	1,621	598	475	414	171	3,279
Domestic use	383	153	138	54	52	780
Exports	697	188	299	267	59	1,510
Use, total	1,080	341	437	321	111	2,290
Ending stocks	541	257	38	93	60	989
1981/1982 Projected						
Beginning stocks	541	257	38	93	60	989
Production	1,115	468	673	351	186	2,793
Supply, total[b]	1,656	726	711	444	247	3,784
Domestic use	364	174	219	59	51	867
Exports	780	210	450	275	85	1,800
Use, total	1,144	384	669	334	136	2,667
Ending stocks						
April projection	507	337	62	105	106	1,117
May projection	512	342	42	110	111	1,117

[a]Includes flour and products in wheat equivalent.
[b]Total supply includes imports.

in the analysis of ending stocks is the breakdown between classes of wheat, which, again, has implications for intermarket spreads. Price projections are made in a manner similar to the other commodities with the one difference being that projected wheat prices represent a weighted average of the price of each class of wheat. A shortage of one type of wheat, therefore, might not translate into higher prices. An example of the supply-and-demand estimates for wheat is shown in Table 7. An economic analysis of the current situation in the wheat market is found in the ERS report *Wheat Outlook and Situation*. This publication is issued four times a year and includes analysis and statistical data on each class of wheat.

TABLE 7. United States Wheat and Rice[a]

Commodity	1980/81	1981/82 Estimated	1982/83 Projections May	1982/83 Projections Probable Variation[b]
Wheat:				
Area		Million acres		
Planted	80.6	88.9		
Harvested	71.0	80.9		
		Bushels		
Yield per harvested acre	33.4	34.5		
		Million bushels		
Beginning stocks	902	989	1,117	
Production	2,374	2,793	2,648	+215/−215
Imports	3	2	2	
Supply, total	3,279	3,784	3,767	+215/−215
Food	614	620	625	+5/ −5
Seed	114	112	110	+5/ −5
Feed and residual	52	135	125	+50/ −50
Domestic, total	780	867	860	+55/ −55
Exports	1,510	1,800	1,700	+150/−150
Use, total	2,290	2,667	2,560	+175/−175
Ending stocks, total	989	1,117	1,207	+175/−175
Farmer-owned reserves	360	560	650	
CCC inventory	196	185	195	
Free stocks	433	372	362	
Average farm price[c]	3.91	3.70	3.60–4.00	
Rice (rough equivalent):				
Area		Million acres		
Allotment	1.80	1.80		
Planted	3.38	3.84		
Harvested	3.31	3.80		
		Pounds		
Yield per harvested acre	4,413	4,873		
		Million cwt		
Beginning stocks	25.7	16.5	54.0	
Production	146.2	185.4	163.0	+9/ −9
Imports	0.2	0.1	0.1	
Supply, total	172.1	202.0	217.1	+9/ −9
Domestic	54.5	56.5	59.0	+2/ −2
Exports	91.4	86.5	86.5	+7/ −7
Use, total	145.9	143.0	145.5	+8/ −8
Ending stocks	16.5	54.0	66.6	+8/ −8
Differences unaccounted	+9.7	+5.0[d]	+5.0[d]	
Average farm price[c]	12.80	9.25	8.50–10.00	

[a]Marketing year beginning June 1 for wheat and August 1 for rice.
[b]The "probable variation" reflects the root-mean-square error and/or standard error of estimate from trend and judgement. Chances are about 2 out of 3 that the outcome will fall within the implied ranges.
[c]Season-average farm price; dollars per bushel for wheat and dollars per cwt for rice.
[d]Projected, based on historical relationships.

TABLE 8. Monthly Issue Schedule of USDA Reports

Month	Titles of Major Reports
January	*Cattle on Feed* (13-state), *Crop Production* (cotton, annual summary), *Grain Stocks* (corn, soybeans, all wheat) and *Cattle* (50-state inventory)
February	*Cattle on Feed* (seven-state) and *Prospective Plantings* (corn, soybeans, cotton, and spring wheat)
March	*Cattle on Feed* (seven-state) and *Hogs and Pigs* (10-state)
April	*Cattle on Feed* (13-state) and *Grain Stocks* (corn, soybeans, all wheat)
May	*Cattle on Feed* (seven-state) and *Crop Production* (winter wheat)
June	*Cattle on Feed* (seven-state), *Hogs and Pigs* (10-state), *Acreage* (corn, soybeans, cotton, all wheat), *Grain Stocks* (corn, soybeans, all wheat), and *Crop Production* (winter wheat)
July	*Cattle on Feed* (13-state), *Crop Production* (winter wheat), and *Cattle* (50-state inventory)
August	*Cattle on Feed* (seven-state) and *Crop Production* (corn, soybeans, cotton, all wheat)
September	*Cattle on Feed* (seven-state), *Hogs and Pigs* (10-state), *Crop Production* (corn, soybeans, cotton, all wheat), and *Grain Stocks* (soybeans)
October	*Cattle on Feed* (13-state), *Crop Production* (corn, soybeans, cotton), and *Grain Stocks* (corn, all wheat)
November	*Cattle on Feed* (seven-state) and *Crop Production* (corn, soybeans, cotton)
December	*Cattle on Feed* (seven-state), *Hogs and Pigs* (50-state), *Crop Production* (cotton), and *Small Grains* (winter wheat plantings)

PART III

USE OF THE MARKETS

CHAPTER 9

HEDGING

CONTENTS

Hedging Price Risk 3
Price Risk 7
Objectives of Hedging 8
Types of Hedges 9

BASIS 11

Cost of Carry 12
Convergence 14
Seasonality of Basis 14
Distortions in Carrying Charges 16
Inverted Markets 17
Basis Risk and Profit Maximization 17
Seasonality 19
Hedging the Basis 19
Hedging Applications 21

HEDGING IN AN INVERTED MARKET 31

BENEFITS OF HEDGING 36

Taking Advantage of Price Distortions 37
Reduced Costs 39
Financing 39

QUESTIONS TO ANSWER BEFORE HEDGING 39

Evaluating a Hedge 40
Evaluation of Hedging Costs 40
Indirect Hedging Relationships 41
Hedging Quantity and Method 41

INTEGRATED HEDGES 42

Case 1: Feedlot Hedge 42
Case 2: Soybean Processing Hedge 45

THE COMPLETE HEDGE 48

SUMMARY 50

CHAPTER 9

HEDGING

David Rinehimer

Over time prices for agricultural commodities have been characterized by their volatile and many times unpredictable nature. Unexpected occurrences often called "shocks" which affect future supplies and/or demand are quickly reflected in prices. Since the early 1970s commodity price fluctuations have been even more excessive for not only agricultural commodities, but also industrial raw material prices. From 1972 through late 1980 the Commodity Research Bureau index of 27 futures prices more than tripled, rising to a record high of 337.6; however, by the end of 1982, that index, an indicator of the general trend in futures, lost close to one-half of that gain, falling to the 230.0 level. In comparison, the CRB index had moved within a narrow range of only 90.0–120.0 (see Figure 1) prior to 1970.

Over an even shorter time span, from 1979 to 1982, commodity price movements were extremely erratic. For example, the nearest cotton futures price rose from $0.60 per lb to over $0.90 per lb, then declined steadily back to about $0.60. Corn futures in Chicago jumped from $2.60 per bushel to nearly $4 per bushel, then, just as quickly, slumped back to under $2.20. The price of copper skyrocketed to well over $1.40 per lb in 1980, but in just 10 months prices were under the $0.80–$0.84 per lb cost of production level, and eventually declined another $0.30 per lb. Gold prices soared from $250 per oz to an all-time high of $875 per oz in early 1980. By mid-1982, gold had fallen back to the $300 per oz area (see Figure 2). In addition to agricultural and industrial raw commodities, interest-rate sensitive markets such as government and corporate bonds, commercial paper as well as foreign currencies have also displayed volatile price patterns.

Figure 3 displays a weekly high-, low-, and closing-price bar chart of nearest contract Swiss franc and Treasury-bond futures from mid-1979, showing the recent extreme price movements.

HEDGING PRICE RISK. More frequent imbalances between the supply and demand for essential agricultural, industrial, and financial commodities have produced the volatile price swings of the past 20 years. Natural and manmade occurrences such as rapidly changing weather patterns, a burgeoning demand for a better standard of living, hyperinflation, increased government involvement in world trade, a greater need for capitalization, currency devaluations, and expanding world markets have all enlarged the importance of risk management.

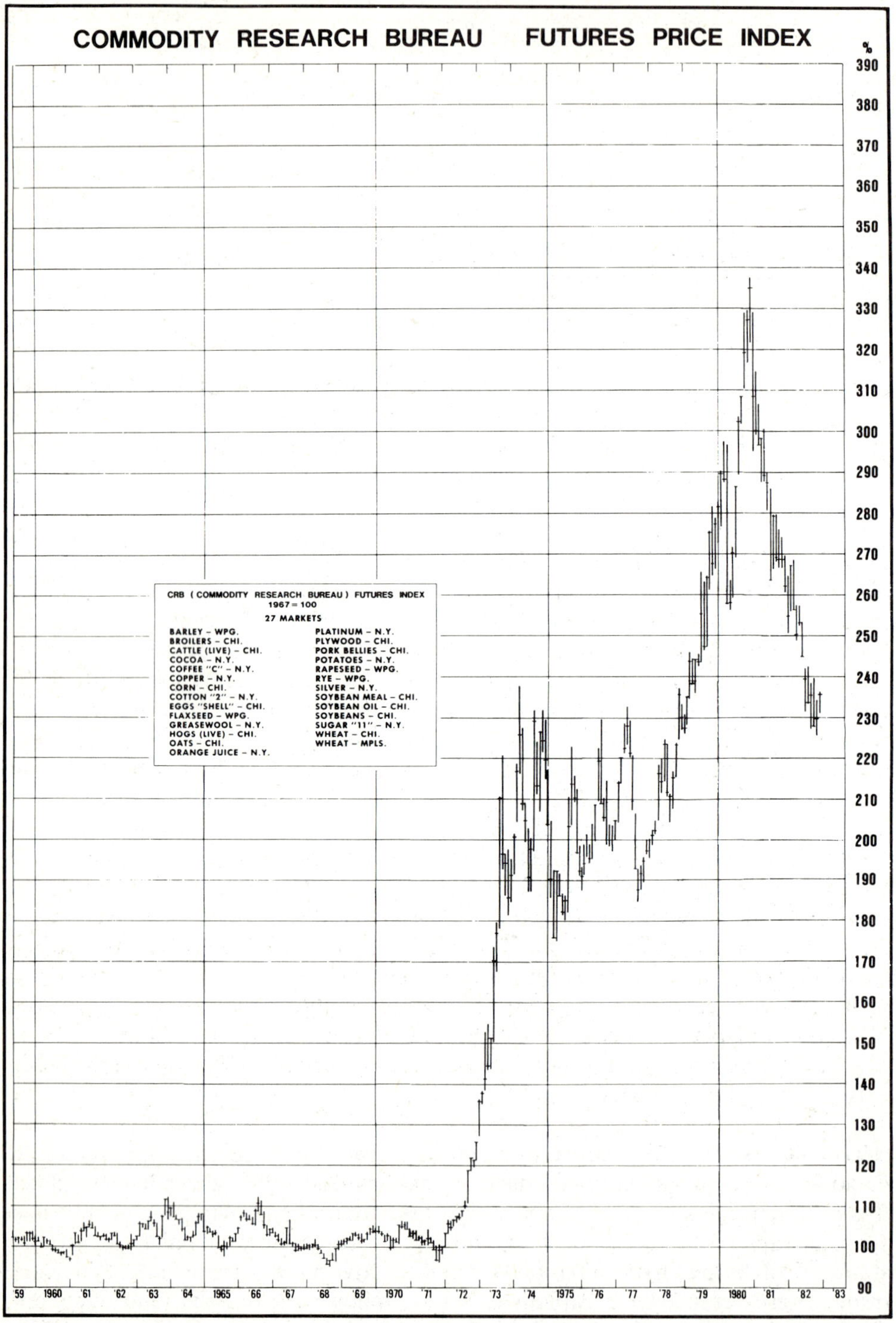

FIGURE 1. Commodity Research Bureau futures price index from 1959–1982 (monthly high–low–close bar chart).

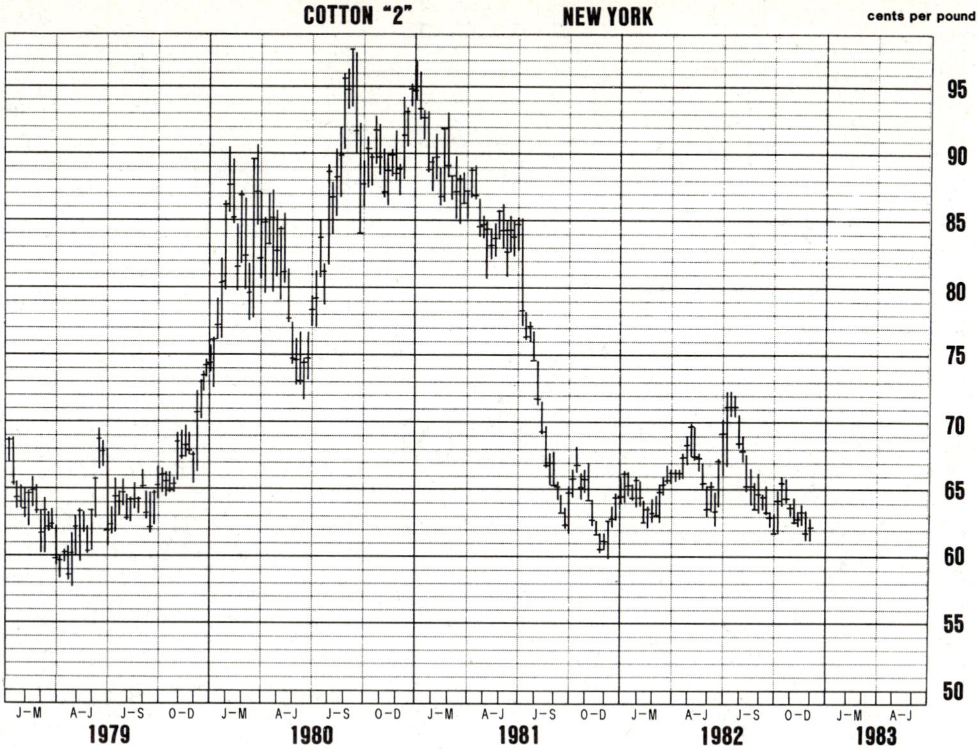

FIGURE 2. Price trends for cotton, corn, copper and gold from 1979–1982 (weekly high–low–close bar chart of the nearest futures).

JULY 15, 1983

FIGURE 2. *(Continued)*

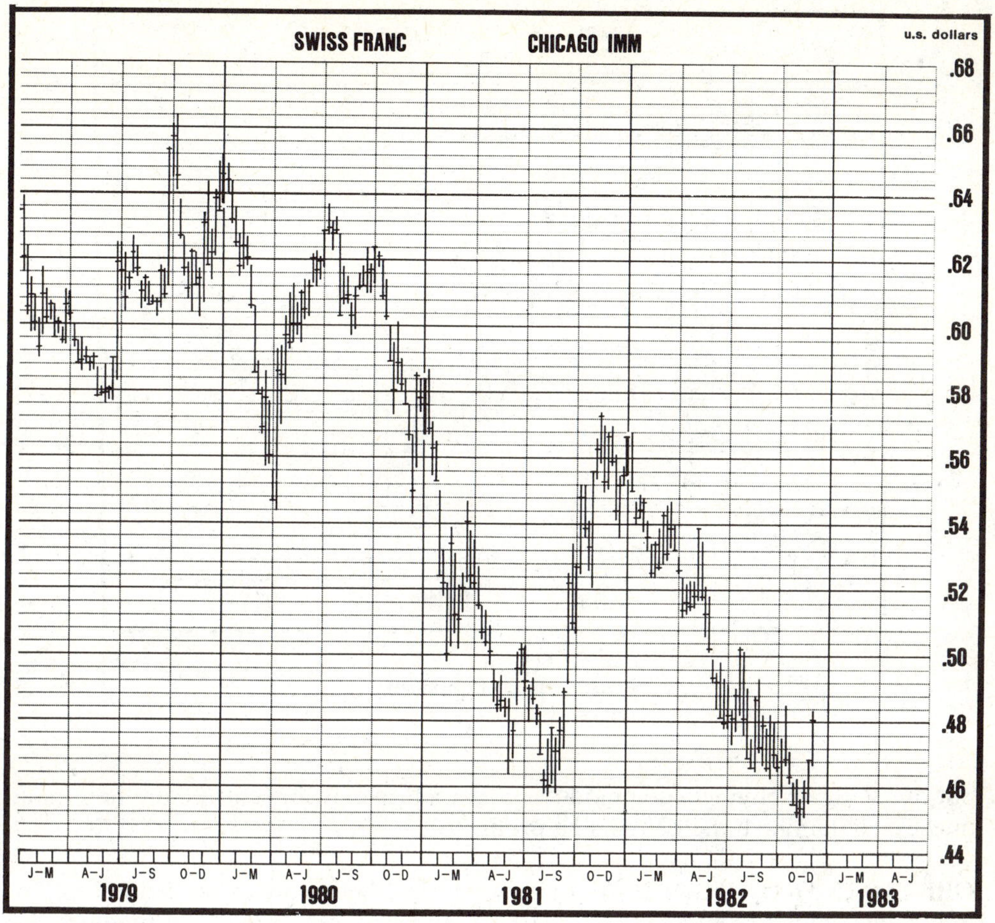

(*a*)

FIGURE 3. Price trends for the Swiss franc and U.S. Treasury bonds from 1979–1982 (weekly high–low–close bar chart of nearest futures).

PRICE RISK. The financial risk associated with commodity price change is assumed by the producer, warehouser, merchant, dealer, processor, exporter, and manufacturer as the product moves through the distribution process.

The use of *hedging* through *futures* is one technique which has grown in importance as a business management tool to minimize risk and increase profit opportunities. The futures contract, in fact, evolved to minimize the price risk in the lag between production and consumption as far back as 1877. A firm that does not hedge is speculating on cash prices and must assume the financial risks associated with an unfavorable price change and subsequent effects on profits. The greater the percentage that the unhedged raw material accounts for the total product cost, the greater the risk and effect on the firm's earnings. In particular, an industry which is characterized by high volume and narrow profit margins, such as the grain industry, can be devastated if cash positions are unhedged during either a rise or fall in price. A good hedging program can take enough of the risk

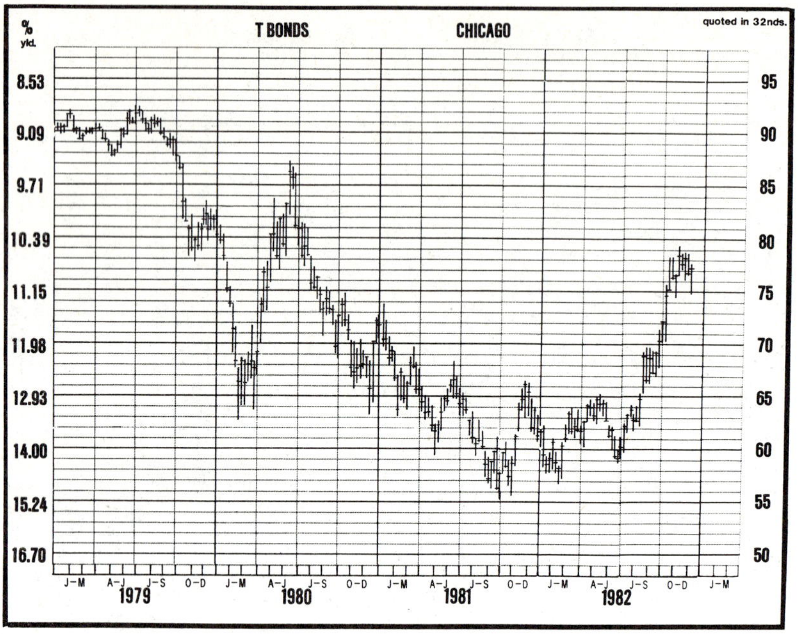

(b)

FIGURE 3. Continued.

out of selling or buying a commodity so that a firm can concentrate on their main interest: obtaining a merchandising profit.

OBJECTIVES OF HEDGING. For our purposes, hedging can be defined as *establishing a position in a futures contract approximately equal, but opposite to, an already existing or anticipated net cash position* to protect profit margins against an adverse change in price. Essentially, a hedge is a *temporary substitute for a cash position to be taken at a later date.* Through the hedge, absolute price risk is transferred to a speculator who seeks to profit from a favorable change in price, usually over a different time period. The speculator provides the market with liquidity and continuity, which is necessary for the hedging process to work efficiently.

In October 1977 the Commodity Futures Trading Commission (CFTC) developed a broader definition of hedging for the purpose of explaining the use of futures by the business community. The CFTC defined "a *bona fide* hedging transaction" as

> positions in a contract for future delivery on any contract market, where such positions normally represent a substitute for transactions to be made or positions to be taken at a later time in a physical marketing channel, and where they are economically appropriate to the reduction of risks in the conduct and management of a commercial enterprise, and where they arise from:
>
> **1.** The potential change in the value of assets which a person owns, produces,

manufactures, processes, or anticipates owning, producing, manufacturing, processing, or merchandising.

2. The potential change in the value of liabilities which a person owes or anticipates incurring.
3. The potential change in the value of services which a person provides, purchases or anticipates providing or purchasing.

Positions shall not be classified as *bona fide* hedging transactions unless their purpose is to offset price risks incidental to commercial cash or spot operations and such positions are established and liquidated in an orderly manner in accordance with sound commercial practices.

The definition of "*bona fide* hedging transaction" includes, but is not limited to the following specific transactions:

1. Sales of any commodity for future delivery on a contract market which do not exceed in quantity:
   a. Ownership or fixed-price purchases of the same cash commodity by the same person.
   b. Twelve months unsold anticipated production of the same commodity by the same person provided that no such position is maintained in any future during the five last trading days of that future.
2. Purchase of any commodity for future delivery on a contract market which do not exceed in quantity:
   a. The fixed-price sale of the same cash commodity by the same person.
   b. The quantity equivalent of fixed-price sales of the cash products and by-products of such commodity by the same person.
   c. Twelve months unfilled anticipated requirements of the same cash commodity for processing, manufacturing, or feeding by the same person, provided that such transactions and positions in the five last trading days of any one future do not exceed the person's unfilled anticipated requirements by the same cash commodity for that month and for the next succeeding month.
3. Sales and purchases for future delivery described in paragraphs above of this section may also be offset other than by the same quantity of the same cash commodity, provided that the fluctuations in value of the position for future delivery are substantially related to the fluctuations in value of the actual or anticipated cash position, and provided that the positions in any one future shall not be maintained during the last five trading days of that future.

TYPES OF HEDGES. There are two basic types of hedge transactions, the selling hedge and the buying hedge. The selling hedge or "short hedge" involves ownership or purchases of a cash commodity and subsequent or simultaneous sale of an equivalent quantity of futures. The objective of a selling hedge is to protect the value of existing inventory or prospective production against a decline in price, and whenever possible, to earn a return on storage. When a short futures position is established against a cash commodity and prices decline, the decrease in value of the cash product is partially offset by profits on the short futures position. In a selling hedge the owner of the cash product forgoes the opportunity to profit if the price increases.

For example, a farmer expecting to harvest 10,000 bushels of wheat wants to receive a price which covers the costs and returns a reasonable profit. If a futures contract with a delivery time approximately equivalent to when the farmer would harvest the crop was trading at a price which was attractive to the grower, then a short futures position should be considered. By selling futures short as a hedge the farmer would reduce the potential for loss if prices declined, as well as establish an expected future profit margin. If, when the farmer is ready to sell wheat, the local cash market had dropped by $0.20 per bushel, the farmer would receive $2,000 less than the farmer's initial objective. If hedged, since both cash and futures are influenced by the same general factors, part of the farmer's loss would be offset by profits from the futures transaction.

In another case, a company receiving future payments due in foreign currencies could use futures to protect against a depreciation in the value of that currency through a selling hedge. If a firm was due payment in Swiss francs 3 months forward, a short futures position would significantly offset losses that would result if the value of the franc dropped by the time payment was received. The primary objective of the selling hedge is to insulate the cash product against a decline in value. Reducing carrying charges pertains to basis trading of storable commodities which will be discussed later.

In contrast to the selling hedge, the buy hedge involves the purchase of futures to protect against a possible price increase of the actual commodity prior to its physical purchase. Buy hedges, also termed "long hedges," are usually used as a way to fix the cost of a raw material or establish a price against a forward commitment. Operators of grain elevators, processors, cattle ranchers, feedlot operators, manufacturers, and exporters all have a need to use futures to establish a buy hedge.

For example, a soybean oil exporter receives an order in April for 180,000 lb of crude soybean oil to be shipped in 3 months at a predetermined price. The exporter sets the price for this order on the basis of the cash price of soybean oil on the day the deal was made, but will not purchase the oil until shortly before making delivery. If the exporter wished to protect against the risk of an upward price movement resulting in a reduced profit margin, the exporter would purchase three July contracts of soybean oil futures, equivalent to 180,000 lb of oil. Let us further assume that 3 months later (or when the exporter must buy the cash oil to fulfill the contract) the cash price has risen $10 per cwt and July futures moved up $8 per cwt. The increase of $10 in the exporter's cost is partially offset by the $8 gross profit on the futures position. Through the use of the buy hedge the cost of soybean oil was only $2 higher than the exporter had planned to pay, rather than $10 more if the exporter was unhedged.

If the raw material was purchased and held until the date of delivery, then considerable capital would also have been tied up for storage and insurance with an added loss of interest. The buy hedge allowed the exporter to fix the raw material cost without using a large amount of capital. If both cash and futures had dropped by $10 per cwt then the opportunity for reduced costs and larger profits would have been negated by the loss in the futures transaction.

In another case, a feedlot operator can fix the cost of corn used in the feeding operation through a long hedge. If in February the operator determines a reasonable profit margin can be locked-in at current futures prices, the operator would establish long futures positions to fix the feeding cost. If cash prices rose by the time the operator required the corn, the operator's increased costs would be offset by the gain on the futures position.

For both a sell and buy hedge the main objective is to protect a margin of profit against an unfavorable change in price. However, if prices move in a hedger's favor then the gain realized from the cash position will be considerably offset by the loss from the futures positions which is opposite to that of cash.

BASIS

The most important concept in understanding the application of futures to hedging price risk is basis. *Basis* is the difference between a particular cash price and a futures price (*cash–futures*), where the cash item is of a definite quality at a specific location. The cash price can be for the par deliverable quality at the designated futures delivery point(s) or for a comparable quality at other locations. A basis relationship can be derived wherever a commodity similar in quality to futures is traded.

The relationship between cash and futures prices is usually quoted by the cash price as a premium or discount to futures rather than as an absolute price level, that is, *cash is $0.10 over (or under) futures*. If, for example, on February 10th the Chicago F.O.B. cash price for No. 2 yellow soybeans was at $6.20 per bushel and the May futures closed at $6.50 per bushel, then the Chicago soybean basis per the May futures would be $6.20 less $6.50 or −$0.30. This case is called "30 under," meaning the cash price is $0.30 under the May futures.

As the location, cost of carry, and quality of the cash product being quoted change, so will the basis. For example, on the same day cash C.I.F. (cost, insurance, and freight) soybeans of a better quality, say No. 1 yellow soybeans at New Orleans, could be trading at 7 over the May futures for an equivalent cash price of $6.57 per bushel. Figure 4 illustrates how the cash–futures relationship can differ depending upon location and quality. At one location futures are at a premium to cash, whereas at the other location the opposite relationship holds (i.e., futures are at a discount to cash).

Basis differences due to location reflect the costs of moving the cash commodity from one local market to the designated delivery points, and the difference in supply-and-demand factors between the local market and the delivery points for the futures contract. Availability of transportation facilities, unfavorable weather which affects product movement, and unexpected labor disruptions can influence the transportation component of the basis calculation. Each local market has a specific set of supply-and-demand fundamentals which differentiates it from other areas. As these fundamentals change relative to the situation at the futures terminals the basis will adjust accordingly. Futures prices reflect the outlook for the par deliverable quality at the designated delivery points for specific delivery periods. If imbalances between supply and demand develop in one area and not at the futures delivery locations then a change in basis must occur as cash and futures prices diverge.

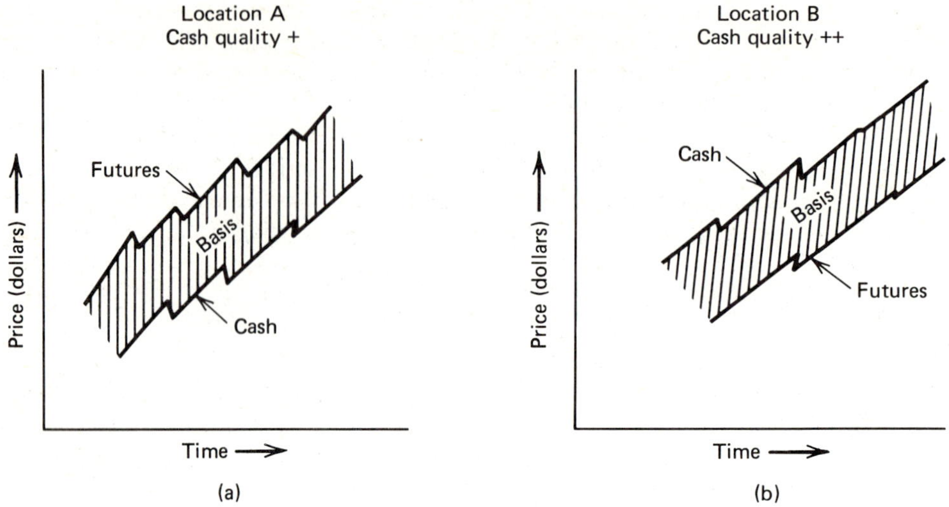

FIGURE 4. Cash–futures relationship at different locations.

For example, growing conditions may cause an adverse supply shortage in one particular region while supplies at other locations are ample to meet demand. This could result in the local cash price moving to an abnormal relationship to futures because of the local imbalance between supply and demand. Differences in basis can also reflect differences in the type of cash market price being quoted. For example, for the same location a C.I.F. will carry a premium to an F.O.B. (free on board) price because it reflects additional costs. The two prices, although representing the same quality and location, will have a different basis.

COST OF CARRY. A futures price, in addition to reflecting the cash market price and expectations of market conditions at a future point in time, includes the cost of carrying inventory for delivery against futures. If the commodity is storable, carrying charges primarily include storage (at rental rates), insurance, interest, and handling. Other costs which vary in importance are capital and quality depreciation along with the cost of maintaining the condition of storage facilities.

Under normal conditions cash prices at the delivery points will remain under futures prices reflecting the cost of carrying the commodity until it can be delivered against futures. When the nearest futures is above the cash price and subsequent futures within the crop year are successively selling for a higher premium because of the additional cost of carry to that point in time, the market is referred to as a *normal* or *carrying charge* market. A normal cash–futures relationship is usually associated with adequate deliverable supplies relative to current and prospective demand.

As time passes and the delivery period for the futures contract approaches, the costs of carrying inventory becomes less of a factor. Consequently, the difference between cash and the nearest futures becomes smaller reflecting the reduced cost of carry. For this difference to narrow, either cash prices rise to meet futures and/or futures decline to meet cash.

For example, on February 11, 1982 the following cash and closing futures prices were taken from the *Wall Street Journal* for No. 2 yellow corn at Chicago:

Contract	Dollars per Bushel	Basis (Cents/Bushel)
Cash	2.63¼	
Futures		
March 1982	2.71¼	8
May 1982	2.82¾	19½
July 1982	2.92	28¾
September 1982	2.96	32¾

Figure 5 illustrates how the basis (cash–futures) is largest for the more distant contracts in the same crop year because the longer holding period requires greater carrying charges. Each futures contract price reflects some percentage of the total cost of carrying the cash product up until it can be delivered. The basis will vary with the changes in the cost of the components which make up the carrying charge: interest rates, storage and handling, and insurance, as well as the value of the commodity itself. Using a 15% interest rate and a monthly storage and insurance charge of $210 per contract, the cost of carrying 5,000 bushels of corn priced at $2.63 per bushel for 30 days would be $0.07 per bushel. If the corn was bought on February 11 and held until July 1, the first delivery day for the July contract, the cost of carrying the cash product until it would be delivered against futures would be $0.34 per bushel or $1,700 per contract. The difference between the cash price and the July futures on February 11 was $0.28¾ per bushel, less than the full cost of carry. Assuming carrying charges remained constant, the spread

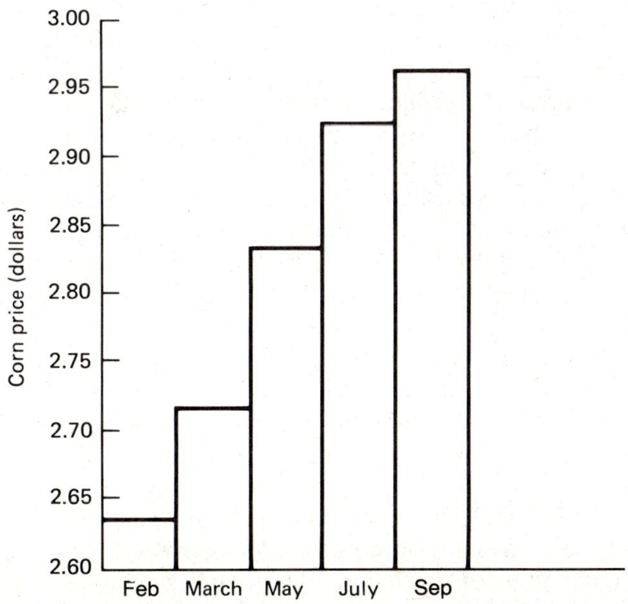

FIGURE 5. Cash–futures price relationship in a "carrying charge" market.

between the cash price and the July futures would be expected to narrow because carrying charges become less of a consideration during the shorter time period required to carry the product for delivery in July. In fact, with the expiration of the July contract the price of cash corn at the designated delivery points and the nearest futures should converge because the cost of carry is approaching zero.

CONVERGENCE. Although cash and futures tend to converge, very seldom do they meet. Technical differences between merchandising the cash commodity relative to futures and the inconvenience of delivery against the futures contract are the main reasons the two prices are not identical at the time of expiration. Many times cash prices will move to a premium against the expiring futures because the cash product has greater value since the exact quality, time, and place of delivery can be determined in a cash transaction. When taking delivery of futures the buyer does not know the specific time (most futures deliveries are made at the seller's option) or the location of where the delivery can be received. More importantly, the buyer is uncertain of the exact quality delivered. Although there is only one par deliverable quality, other varieties can be delivered against futures at either a premium or discount to the par grade. This may result in the buyer receiving a grade that is unacceptable for the buyer's needs.

There may also be added cost associated with taking a futures delivery, including surcharges or levies in moving the futures product. Consequently, commercial firms will not be inclined to take delivery of futures unless the basis relationships offer an attractive profit opportunity. Basis can also change instantly as the value of the factors that create the carrying charge structure change. For example, if the cost of money increases from 10 to 15% it becomes more expensive to hold the cash commodity. This increased cost will be reflected in a greater difference between cash and the futures contract, as well as between futures within the same crop year.

Hedging price risk through futures is possible because of the similarity and eventual convergence of cash and futures prices (see Figure 6). Since both markets are influenced by changes in the same general market factors, prices tend to change in the same direction, but not necessarily by the same magnitude. The extent of price risk exposure which can be minimized is related to the degree of correlation between the change in cash prices and the change in futures prices. This in turn reflects how closely the underlying characteristics of the cash product are represented by the standard futures contract, especially in regard to quality, location, and time. Price changes between futures and cash prices are not usually identical because each price represents a somewhat different set of factors that determine price.

Basis tends to measure the relative price change between a specific local delivery (regional price) and a standard market price that represents fundamental developments at the primary marketing center for that commodity.

SEASONALITY OF BASIS. The basis between the cash price and the nearest futures for storable, seasonally produced commodities follows a pattern determined by the availability of par deliverable supplies relative to prospective demand. In a normal market when harvest supply pressure is at its peak and storage

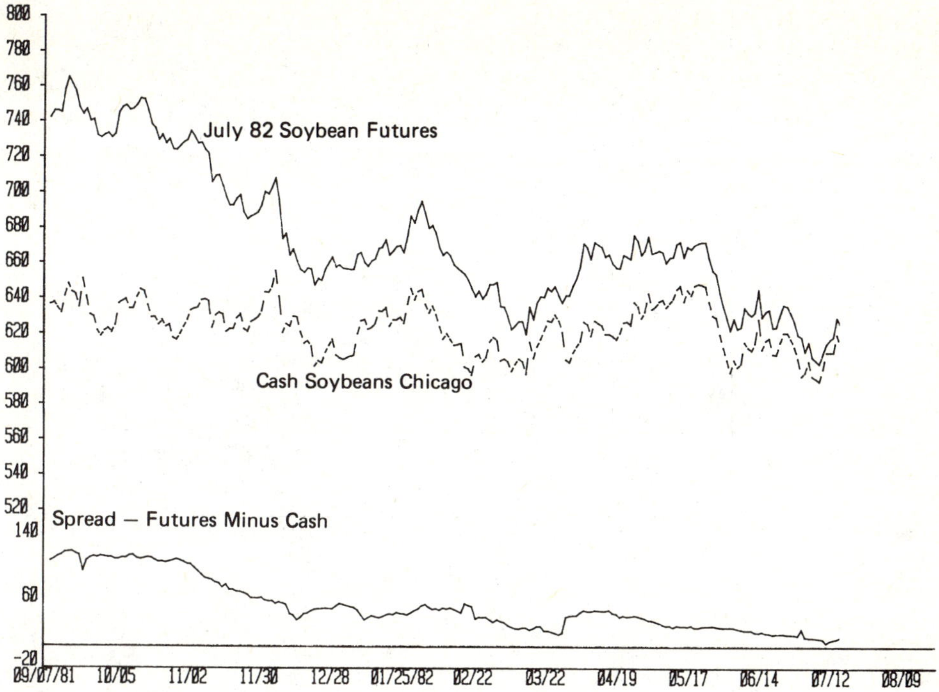

FIGURE 6. Soybeans, no. 1 yellow Chicago versus July 1982 soybean futures. Spread–futures minus cash.

space is in demand, cash prices are usually below futures by the greatest amount for the season. This relatively wide basis is called "weak." During this period the growing demand for storage space increases storage cost and the total cost of carry. Cash prices, reflecting surplus supplies and limited storage space, will maintain a wide basis to futures, until supply and demand move more toward equilibrium.

For example, harvesting of soybeans in the United States from October through December significantly increases available supplies relative to domestic and export demand. As the season progresses, supplies are consumed and, with the demand for storage space lessening, the soybean basis will tend to narrow. At this time the cash prices also reflect the added costs of storing and maintaining the cash product. There are no added costs to futures since carrying charges have already been included in its price when the basis was weak.

When supplies tighten relative to the rate of usage, the cash–futures difference declines and the basis is said to be "strengthening." Figure 7 illustrates the seasonal basis tendency from a period of surplus to supply tightness.

Variations in basis can (1) follow a seasonal pattern reflecting the changing relationship between supply and demand during the course of the growing season, (2) reflect changes in market factors that influence futures price variables at the par delivery points or at a particular location, or (3) reflect changes in the variables that comprise the cost of carry, that is, interest rates, storage charges, insurance, handling, and conditioning.

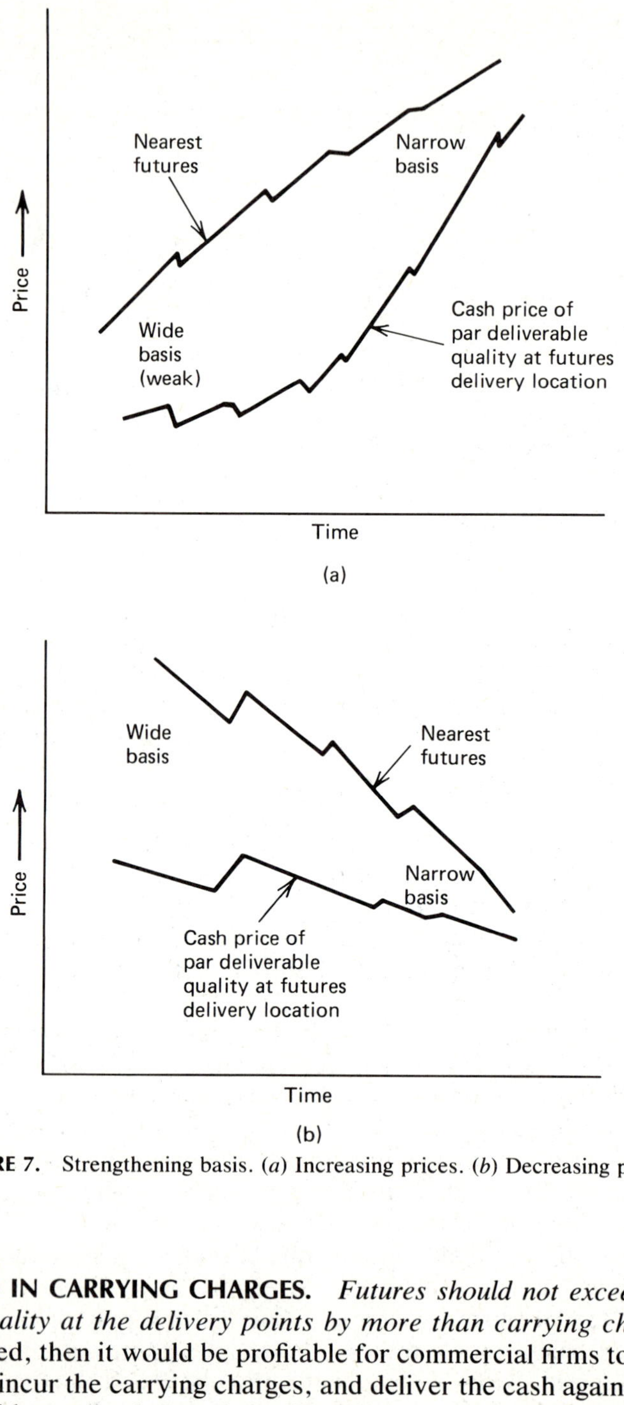

FIGURE 7. Strengthening basis. (*a*) Increasing prices. (*b*) Decreasing prices.

DISTORTIONS IN CARRYING CHARGES. *Futures should not exceed cash prices for the par quality at the delivery points by more than carrying charges.* If that situation existed, then it would be profitable for commercial firms to purchase the cash product, incur the carrying charges, and deliver the cash against the futures. A profit would be realized on at least the difference between the basis when the cash was purchased and the maximum cost of carry. As this profit potential becomes more obvious, increased selling of futures and buying of the cash product would narrow the cash–futures relationship and reduce the difference in prices until a profit could not be realized, that is, futures must fall to full carry or less.

Selling of futures would also come from commercial firms who hold long futures positions, because it would be more economical to purchase the lower-priced cash and pay the carrying charges than hold futures which are selling beyond the cost of carry. Conversely, if the basis narrows to a point where it proved economical to take delivery of futures rather than hold the more expensive cash product, the stronger demand for futures relative to cash would tend to widen the basis. It could then prove more economical to sell cash rather than hold short futures positions. More aggressive selling of cash compared with futures would also widen the basis relationship. As the expiration of the nearest futures approaches, supplies available for delivery against futures relative to immediate demand will determine the basis relationship between cash prices and the nearest futures.

Futures for *nonstorable commodities,* produced on a continual basis, such as live cattle and live hogs, have no cost of carry. A basis relationship is only relevant between the spot delivery month during expiration and the cash price for deliverable supplies. Cash and the nearest futures for nonstorable commodities also tend to converge during futures expiration. For example, if on March 1 cash prices were $5 per cwt under the March futures, then merchants would buy the cash commodity and deliver the product against futures. If this profit opportunity persisted, then futures during expiration would reflect the values that exist in the cash market.

INVERTED MARKETS. When supplies become tight and/or demand for immediate delivery becomes excessive cash prices may move to a premium over futures, while the nearest futures moves to a premium over the deferred months. This type of market is referred to as an *inverted market* (see Figure 8). Expectations of an increase in future supplies and softer demand will cause the back months to rise less than the nearby futures, since the nearby deliveries are more representative of conditions in the cash market. In a normal market, cash prices should not fall under the nearest futures by more than the cost of carry. But in an inverted market, there is no way to determine the premium which the cash price will maintain over futures and the difference between nearby and forward contracts. Prices eventually distribute the supplies among buyers who are willing to pay a premium for immediate delivery.

As the cash price moves to a larger premium relative to futures, the basis level will increase in value. If the cash price declines at a faster rate than futures or if futures start to catch up to cash, the basis would tend to decline in value in an inverted market structure. An inverted market is much more common for futures that have no cost of carry associated with it. The bar graph shown in Figure 9 illustrates the cash–futures relationship for an inverted market.

BASIS RISK AND PROFIT MAXIMIZATION. At the time a hedge is closed out, if the basis is identical to the entry basis level, the hedge transaction is said to be *perfect.* The gain or loss in the cash transaction is totally offset by the gain or loss in futures. Perfect hedges are extremely unlikely since cash and futures prices do not usually change by the same amount on a consistent basis. In the same way

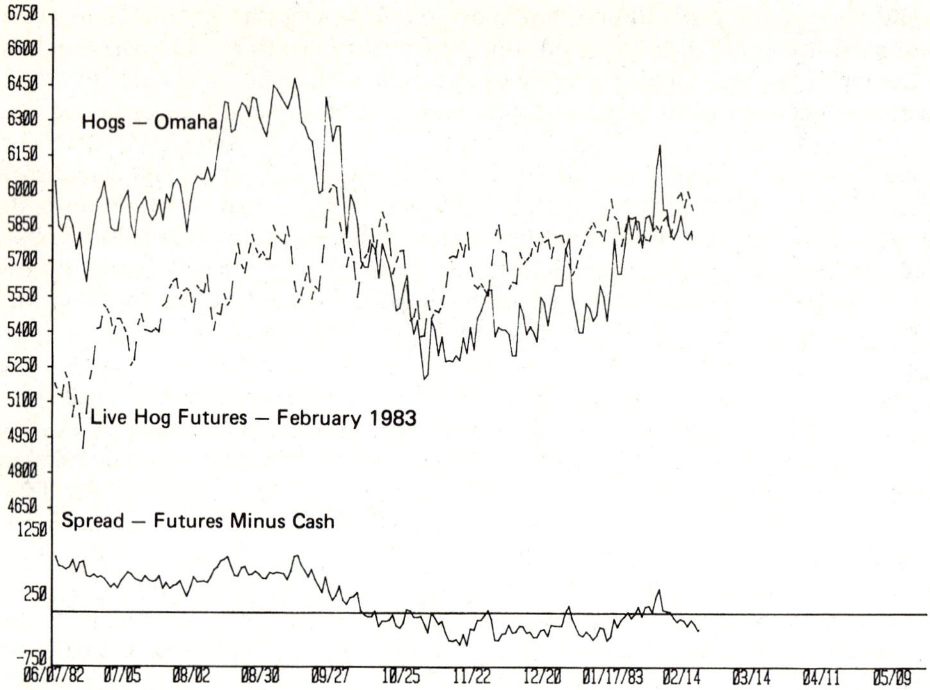

FIGURE 8. Hogs, Omaha versus February 1983 live hog futures. Spread–futures minus cash.

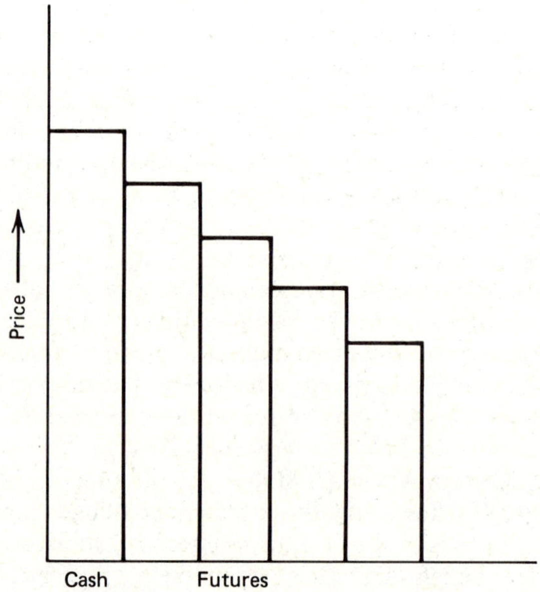

FIGURE 9. Inverted market structure.

as absolute prices, basis can move in one's favor causing a gain, or trend opposite to expectations and result in a loss.

Basis change is a risk that is not always minimized. Its management, however, is less risky than that of absolute prices because basis variation is less volatile and more predictable than either cash or futures prices.[1] A hedger should be more willing to assume the risk of an unfavorable move in the basis rather than the risk of an unhedged position. A hedger substitutes the major risk of the commodity's value for the smaller risk of basis variation. If the change in basis can be accurately forecast, then not only can the hedge minimize price risk, but it may realize a profit as well.

SEASONALITY. A thorough knowledge of the seasonal tendencies for a particular market should be acquired by a prospective hedger to provide insight into the most advantageous time to "lock-in" a favorable basis. Each local market may follow a different seasonal basis pattern since local cash prices are affected by unique marketing factors intrinsic to that region. To estimate the expected basis patterns, a hedger should compare the historical price pattern of the local cash price with the futures delivery month in which the hedge is being placed. Comparing the historical relationships between the two prices during the course of many seasons familiarizes a hedger with the usual cash–futures relationship. This aids in determining a favorable entry or exit level, especially if the basis greatly deviates from the norm. Techniques for calculating the seasonal basis factor are the same as those used to calculate normal price seasonality.

Hedgers should also be aware of differences between the *current basis* and *calculated* or *ideal basis*. Carrying charges can be calculated by taking all the costs (i.e., transportation, interest, storage, and certification) in moving the cash product from the local market to a location eligible for futures delivery. By incorporating these costs with quality premiums and discounts, a theoretical basis can be computed and a forward cash price estimated from futures. Comparing the hedger's expected costs with the corresponding anticipated price at the local market for some future delivery will help the hedger decide whether the hedge should be placed. If a basis relationship deviates considerably from the calculated value, a hedger may decide to lock-in the basis and make or accept delivery of futures in anticipation of cash and futures converging at the contract expiration.

A hedge is usually liquidated when the cash transaction is fulfilled and before the futures contract expires. Fewer than 3% of futures transactions are settled by actual delivery. Because of the potential for a profitable basis change, a hedger should consider delivery against futures as an available option; however, the delivery procedure and specific costs associated with delivery must be evaluated before that decision can be made. Uncertainties with regard to quality and location many times deter commercial firms from using futures as a delivery mechanism, especially if local cash market supplies are readily available.

HEDGING THE BASIS. In addition to reducing absolute price risk, hedging can generate trading profits if the change in basis can be successfully forecasted.

[1]R. J. Teweles, C. V. Harlow, and H. L. Stone, *Commodity Futures Game: Who Wins? Who Losses? Why?* McGraw-Hill, N.Y., 1974, p. 35.

Whether profits are realized by a narrowing or widening of the cash–futures relationship will depend upon both the type of hedge (either a *buy* or *sell* hedge) and whether the market structure is *normal* or *inverted*. A holder of a sell hedge (long cash, short futures) is said to be *long the basis*; that is, if the basis in a normal market increases in value by narrowing, an unrealized profit results. For example, if a sell hedge is established at 200 points under futures, for a profit to be realized the sell hedge must be closed-out at a basis greater in value than −200 points, less brokerage commissions.

A buy hedge (short cash, long futures), referred to as *short the basis*, generates profits in a normal market when the basis value declines or widens. Using the previous example, the close-out basis would have to be less than −200 points net brokerage for a buy hedge to be profitable.

For the basis to widen in a normal market when the price trend is down, the cash prices must decline at a faster rate than futures. If both cash and futures were in downtrends but futures were declining faster than cash, then the basis would narrow, resulting in gains for hedgers who are long the basis and losses for those who are short the basis. When the price trend is up and cash prices are gaining on futures the basis will narrow. A widening of the basis will result if futures gain relative to cash. Regardless of the direction of the general price trend, in a normal market structure a narrowing of the basis benefits the sell hedge (long the basis), while profits on the buy hedge (short the basis) occur when the basis widens (see Figure 10).

The opposite relationships apply when the market structure is *inverted* and

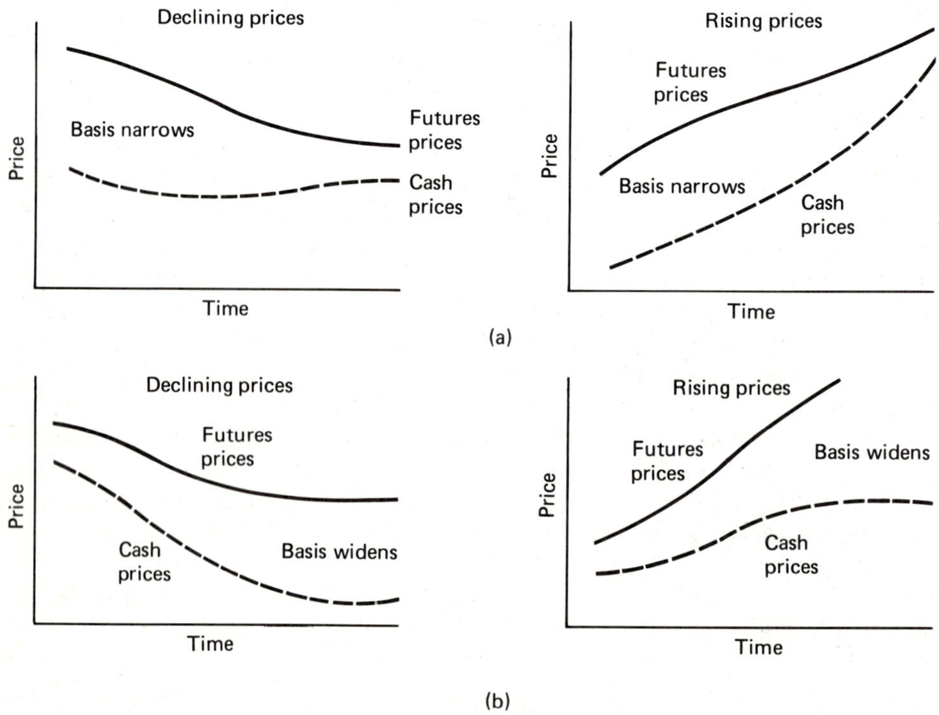

FIGURE 10. Basis relationships in a normal market.

cash prices are at a premium to futures. For the cash–futures difference to increase in value, the basis must widen and when the basis narrows the cash–futures value must decline. To realize a hedging profit when you are long the basis, short futures, and the market is inverted requires a widening of the basis compared to a narrowing of the basis in a normal market. In this situation, a hedger who is short the basis is attempting to profit by a narrowing of the basis either by cash prices declining faster than futures or futures outdistancing cash (see Figure 11). Unlike a normal carrying charge market, an inverted market has no limit to the premium which cash or the more nearby months can hold over the more distant contracts. A firm attempting to hedge price risk must be aware of the consequences of basis variation in both a normal carrying charge and an inverted market.

HEDGING APPLICATIONS. Profits realized from a hedge result from successfully speculating on basis change. Although an unfavorable change in basis may reduce the effectiveness of the hedge, the risk associated with basis variation is usually far less than the risk of an unhedged position. The following examples illustrate different applications for sell and buy hedges under different market situations. These examples will better clarify how a hedge can result in minimizing absolute price risk and, at times, produce profits.

Case 1: A Sell Hedge in a Normal Carrying Charge Market Where the Hedger is Attempting to Protect the Value of Inventory and Cover Part or All of the Cost of Carry Until the Inventory Can Be Sold. Since this is a short hedge in a normal

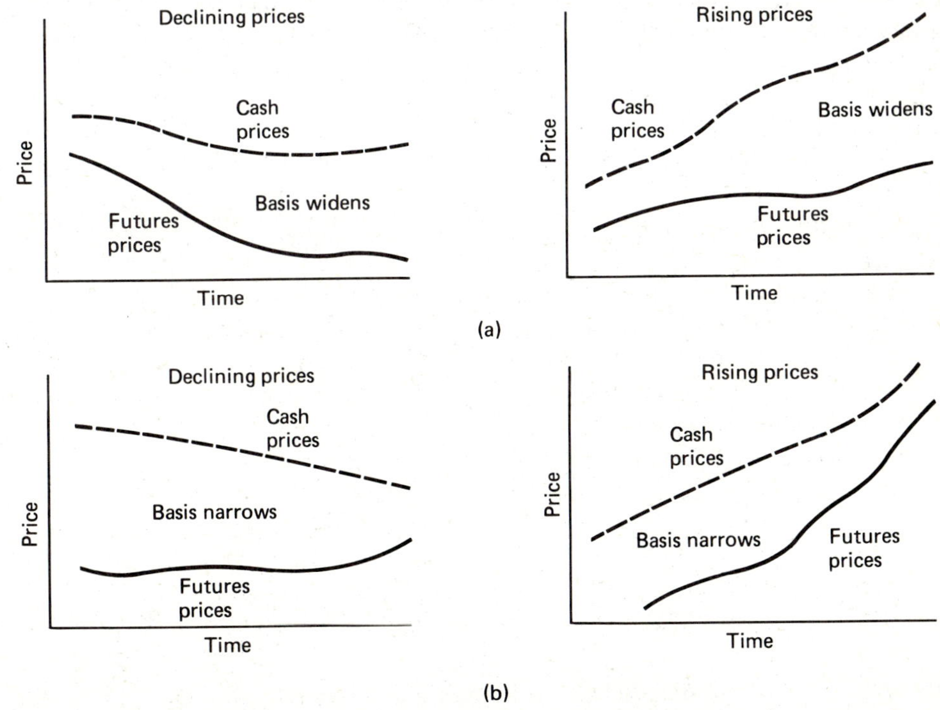

FIGURE 11. Basis relationships in an inverted market.

market, the objective would be to sell futures at a basis as close to the full cost of carry as possible. It was earlier explained that a basis cannot be maintained beyond the full cost of carry because it would be attractive for commercial firms to buy the cash commodity, sell futures, incur the carrying charges, and deliver against the futures contract. The cash–futures relationship will tend to converge causing the basis to narrow as a result of the decreasing total cost of carry as time for delivery against futures nears. The profits realized from the sell hedge due to the narrowing of the basis offset part of the total cost of carrying the cash product until it can be sold. The risk of the basis widening declines over time since the maximum cost of carry decreases, assuming the components that make up these carrying charges do not change in value.

We should not forget that a primary motive for hedging is that the farmer may have already constructed and/or paid for "on-farm" storage. Once this storage is available, the producer must sell as far into the future as possible and recapture the cost of building the storage facilities. In doing this the producer has the latitude to find the situation or situations in which the carrying charges and/or the absolute prices are to the producer's greatest advantage. The following examples show how this sell hedge would work.

Assume on July 1st a Chicago elevator operator purchased 15,000 bushels of No. 2 soft red winter wheat at $3.50 per bushel in the local market. The operator will hold the inventory until a buyer can be found and calculates that it will cost $0.085 per bushel per month to carry the inventory. The December contract is trading on July 1 at $3.75 per bushel and the hedger feels a $0.25 per bushel basis offers an attractive opportunity to cover part of the carrying charges when compared to the maximum cost of carry of $0.42½ per bushel. A short December futures position is taken at $3.75 per bushel. By October 1st the elevator operator has found a buyer for the wheat; however, the local cash price has declined to $3.35 per bushel. The basis narrowed to $0.17 per bushel, reflecting the shorter time period and lower cost of carrying inventory from October to December compared with July to December. The results of the cash and futures transactions are presented below:

	Cash Market	Futures Market[a]	Basis
July 1st	Purchases 15,000 bushels of No. 2 soft red winter wheat at $3.50 per bushel. Total value is $52,500.	Sells 15,000 bushels of December Chicago wheat futures at $3.75 per bushel.	$−0.25
October 1st	Sells 15,000 bushels of No. 2 soft red winter wheat at $3.35 per bushel. Total value is $50,250.	Buys back 15,000 bushels of December Chicago futures at $3.52 per bushel.	$−0.17
Result	Loss of $2,250	Gain of $3,450	Basis change: $0.08
Net result	Gain of $1,200 less brokerage commissions.		

[a]A change of $0.01 per bushel is equivalent to $50 per contract in the futures market where each contract is 5,000 bushels.

By hedging, the elevator operator was able to insulate the value of the cash inventory from a price decline and to cover part of the cost of carrying the cash wheat from July 1st to October 1st. If the hedge was not established, then a loss of $2,250 would have occurred. The net result was a gain of $1,200 less the commission charges for the futures transaction.

Now let us look at the same example but assume that prices rise from July 1st to October 1st and the operator sells the cash wheat at $3.65 and covers the December futures at $3.85 per bushel. The results of the cash/futures transactions would be as follows:

	Cash Market	Futures Market	Basis
July 1st	Purchases 15,000 bushels of No. 2 soft red winter wheat at $3.50 per bushel. Total value is $52,500.	Sells 15,000 bushels of December Chicago wheat futures at $3.75 per bushel.	$−0.25
October 1st	Sells 15,000 bushels of No. 2 soft red winter wheat at $3.65 per bushel. Total value is $54,750.	Buys back 15,000 bushels of December Chicago wheat futures at $3.85 per bushel.	$−0.20
Result	Gain of $2,250	Loss of $1,500	Basis change: $0.05
Net result	Gain of $750 less brokerage commissions.		

In this situation the gain realized in the cash transaction is partially offset by the loss from the short futures position. The hedger would have realized a greater gain if the hedge was not established; however, the risk of lower prices would have been assumed. Once again the basis narrowed because of the reduced cost of carry and improved the effectiveness of the hedge.

If the basis is unusually narrow and the monthly storage cost represented by the futures is less than the hedger's own carrying charge, then it may prove profitable to sell cash and buy futures thereby realizing a lower cost of carry. A significant amount of cash would be freed since only about 10% of the value received from the cash transaction would be required to meet the futures initial margin. This option will be more attractive when storage costs are more variable compared to a situation where a large amount of capital has been fixed to storage facilities.

Case 2: A Sell Hedge in a Normal Market Where a Farmer Attempts to Establish a Profitable Sales Price for a Commodity Not Ready for Market. Assume that in early July a soybean farmer expects to produce 10,000 bushels of soybeans and have it harvested and ready for sale by the end of October. The November soybean contract closed at $6.50 per bushel on July 1st. By November the local cash price is, on average, about $0.20 per bushel under the November futures. After factoring-in the farmer's cost of production, the soybean farmer calculates that a profit can be realized on anticipated production if the farmer can receive $6.30 per bushel as a local price. To try to lock-in this attractive price, the farmer sells 10,000 bushels of November soybean futures at $6.50 per bushel on July 2nd. By October, when the crop is harvested and ready for sale, cash prices are much lower due to larger-than-expected yields and weaker-than-expected export and domestic feed demand. The local cash market price is now equivalent to $5.75 per bushel, $0.55 or 9% under the July price objective. Futures also responded to the bearish developments and by late October the November contract was trading at $6 per bushel. On October 28th the farmer sold 10,000 bushels of soybeans to a local elevator operator at $0.25 under the November contract which by then was at $6 per bushel. By having a hedge the farmer received only $0.05 per bushel less than the farmer's price objective because the $0.55 per bushel decline in the cash market was mostly offset by the $0.50 per bushel profit, less commissions, from the futures transaction. The following illustrates the cash and futures transactions:

	Cash Market	Futures Market	Basis
July 2nd	Farmer seeks $6.30 per bushel when 10,000 bushels of new crop soybeans are ready for sale in local market. Total expected value is $63,000.	Sells 10,000 bushels of November soybean futures at $6.50 per bushel.	$−0.20
October 28th	Sells 10,000 bushels in local cash market at $5.75 per bushel. Total value is $57,500.	Covers 10,000 bushels of short November soybean futures at $6.00 per bushel.	$−0.25
Result	Loss of $5,500	Gain of $5,000	Basis change: $−0.05
Net result	Loss of $500 plus brokerage commissions.		

The farmer received $5.75 per bushel for the new crop plus $0.50 per bushel on the short futures position to realize a total return of $6.25 per bushel. The farmer did not realize the $6.30 per bushel price objective because the basis was wider than the expected basis of *$0.20 under,* but by hedging the farmer only missed the cash objective by less than 10% of the loss that would have subsequently occurred if the hedge had not been taken.

Case 3: A Sell Hedge Used to Forward Price a Nonstorable Commodity. Basis variation for nonstorable commodities can be excessive at times since expectations of future supply and demand for each contract individually are the dominant determinants of basis rather than carrying charges for storable commodities. Futures can move from premiums to discounts relative to the cash market price depending upon changing expectations. Knowledge of basis trends is essential for a hedge to be effective. In this example we will examine how a livestock producer combines costs, the desired profit margin, and expected basis to determine the target price the producer wishes to receive.

In December a feedlot operator purchases 200 feeder cattle averaging 750 lb each. The operator expects to feed the cattle to an average weight of 1,100 lb for marketing in May. To cover the costs of feeder cattle and feed the operator must receive an average price of at least $55 per cwt. Once the break-even price is determined, the expected basis and margin of profit are added on to determine the target price for the sell hedge. Analyzing local cash and futures price trends for the past 10 years indicates that, on average, the local cash price for steers is $1.25 per cwt under the June futures during May. Adding an expected profit of $3 per cwt to the break-even price and anticipated basis gives the operator a target price $59.25 per cwt for the sell hedge. The 200 live cattle at an average finished weight of 1,100 lb would be equivalent to five and one-half contracts. Since a futures contract cannot be purchased or sold for less than the standard contract unit, in this case 40,000 lb, the operator must decide whether to sell five or six contracts. Analysis of future supply-and-demand considerations, along with recent technical price behavior, suggest that cash prices could be considerably lower than either the expected basis or June futures would suggest. To protect the value of the operator's entire anticipated production, the operator decides to use six contracts for the hedge. The operator realizes that there is an equivalent increase in risk should prices and/or basis move against the operator.

On December 15th the June live cattle contract is trading between $59 and $59.50 per cwt. The operator instructs the broker to enter a limit order to sell six June *live cattle* contracts at $59.25. The sell hedge is established at an average price of $59.35. On May 15th, following a steep price decline, the operator is ready to market the cattle. A packer purchases the 200 head for $53.50 per cwt, $1.50 under the break-even price. In addition, the average weight per steer of 1,080 lb is 20 lb under the expected market weight. The short June futures position is covered the same day as the cash sale at $54.70, realizing a basis of 120 points. The results of the sell hedge are presented below:

	Cash Market	Futures Market[a]	Basis
December 15th	An operator expects to have 200 cattle weighing an average of 1,100 lb ready for market by May. A price of $58 per cwt would cover costs and assure a reasonable profit. Expected revenues = $127,600.	Sells six June live cattle contracts at an average price of $59.35 per cwt.	− 135 points

[a]A change of $0.01 (100 points) per lb is equivalent to $400 in the futures market where each contract is 40,000 lb.

May 15th	Sells 200 finished cattle weighing an average of 1,080 lb per head at $53.50 per cwt. Total revenue = $115,560.	Buys back six June live cattle futures at $54.70 per cwt.	− 120 points
Result	Loss of $12,040.	Gain of $11,160.	Basis change: + 15 points
Net result	Loss of $880 plus brokerage commissions.		

The decline in the cash price and lower-than-expected average market weight resulted in realized revenue falling $12,040 under expectations. However, profits of $11,160 from the short futures position offset all but $880 of the lower return. The loss could have been greater if the basis had not moved in the hedger's favor by narrowing, and if the operator had selected five rather than six contracts. When deciding upon the number of contracts to use for a hedge, consideration should be given to the probability of an unfavorable move in price. If the probability of an unfavorable price move is small, then the hedger may desire to hedge only a portion of the hedger's anticipated sale or purchase. If the hedger is quite confident that prices in the cash market could move against him or her by the time the cash position is transacted, then a full hedge would be recommended.

Case 4: A Buy Hedge in a Normal Market to Protect the Margin of Profit for an Uncovered Forward Sale. Many times selling prices are quoted months ahead of the purchase of (1) the product to be delivered, or (2) the raw materials needed for the production process. The offering price is based upon expected costs and a desired margin of profit. If, by the time the cash purchase is made, prices have declined below expectations, then additional profits can be realized. But if costs increase beyond expectations, then profits can erode and losses may even result. The seller has many options, each with a different level of risk. The option of greatest risk would be to speculate that prices will not rise above their expected values. The second option would be to purchase the commodity and hold it until delivery. The main disadvantages of the second option are the large capitalization needed to complete the transaction and the associated lost opportunity cost of taking capital away from alternative productive resources. In addition, costs must be incurred in storing, insuring, and maintaining the cash commodity until it is needed.

A *buy hedge* can minimize the disadvantages of the other two alternatives. A long futures position is taken to protect against an absolute increase in price, with the hedger assuming the risk of an unfavorable change in basis. A profit can be realized from a buy hedge in a normal market when the closed-out basis is wider than the expected basis. If the forward sale is based upon the current cash price, then a basis loss will ultimately result because cash and the nearest futures will tend to converge over the life of the futures contract. In a normal market structure this will result in a narrowing of the basis either by cash prices rising faster than futures or futures declining faster than cash. The basis loss incurred over the longer term will be directly offset by the savings in cost realized by not having to carry the physical inventory until some future date. Over a shorter time period profits are more likely to occur from a buy hedge when the basis relationship widens by either cash declining more than futures or futures increasing faster than cash. The following example illustrates how a buy hedge can be used as a temporary substitute for a future cash transaction and how results can differ depending upon whether the basis widens or narrows over the life of the hedge.

An exporter of corn in December agrees to sell 10,000 bushels of No. 2 yellow corn (par deliverable grade for Chicago futures) for February delivery at $0.20 per bushel over the March futures. On December 10th the sale price of $3.10 per bushel is set when the March futures is at $2.90 per bushel. In determining the offering quote, the exporter must take into consideration the expected cost of corn when it is purchased in the local cash market and the anticipated margin of profit. Historical price relationships between the local cash corn price and March futures indicate that, on average, the March futures price is usually $0.07 per bushel over the local cash market during February. Based upon the current March futures price of $2.90 per bushel the exporter decides to lock-in the cost of the corn when purchased in February at $2.83 per bushel, plus basis variation. To protect against increased cost and a reduced margin of profit the exporter establishes a *long March futures position* in corn of 10,000 bushels at $2.90 on December 10th.

At the time the hedge is established the local cash market price for corn is $2.70 per bushel. From December to February corn prices move higher reflecting larger-than-expected purchases from the Soviet Union and reduced-crop prospects in some of the major corn-producing countries. On February 10th the exporter purchases corn from a local elevator operator for $0.05 per bushel under the March futures which is then at $3 per bushel. The buy hedge is closed out at a basis of $0.05 under, $0.02 narrower than the expected closed-out basis. The $0.02 per bushel basis loss was a small premium to pay when compared to the $0.12 per bushel rise in the local cash price. The gain from the long futures position offset more than 80% of the increase in cost. The corresponding cash and futures transactions for the hedge are presented below:

	Cash Market	Futures Market[a]	Basis
December 10th	Sells 10,000 bushels of No. 2 yellow corn for shipment in February at $3.10 per bushel based upon an expected corn cost of $2.83 per bushel. Expected cost = $28,300.	Buys 10,000 bushels of March corn futures at $2.90 per bushel.	$−0.07

[a]A change of $0.01 per bushel is equivalent to $50 per contract in the futures market where each contract is 5,000 bushels.

February 10th	Purchases 10,000 bushels of No. 2 yellow corn from local elevator operator at $2.95 per bushel. Cost = $29,500.	Sells 10,000 bushels of March corn futures at $3 per bushel.	$−0.05
Result	Loss of $1,200	Gain of $1,000	Basis change: $0.02
Net result	Loss of $200 plus brokerage commissions.		

In addition to offsetting the higher-than-expected cost of corn, the buy hedge allowed the exporter to fix the price of the corn while committing capital equivalent to less than 10% of the value of the contract, assuming no additional margin had to be posted.

What would be the results of the buy hedge if prices had declined by February and the basis narrowed by $0.02 more than anticipated? Let us assume that the cash corn was purchased on February 10th at *$0.05 under,* when the March futures was at $2.75 per bushel. The results of the hedge would be as follows:

	Cash Market	Futures Market	Basis
December 10th	Sells 10,000 bushels of No. 2 yellow corn for shipment in February at $3.10 per bushel based upon expected corn cost of $2.83 per bushel. Expected cost = $28,300.	Buys 10,000 bushels of March corn futures at $2.90 per bushel.	$−0.07
February 10th	Purchases 10,000 bushels of No. 2 yellow corn from local elevator operator at $2.70 per bushel. Cost = $27,000.	Sells 10,000 bushels of March corn futures at $2.75 per bushel.	$−0.05
Result	Reduction in cost of $1,300	Loss of $1,500	Basis change: $0.02
Net result	Loss of $200 plus brokerage commissions.		

The greater profit that would be realized by purchasing the cash corn at a lower cost than was anticipated is totally offset by the loss suffered from the long futures position. In addition, a loss of $200 resulted because the closed-out basis was narrower than was anticipated. The reason the exporter decided to hedge was to lock-in an attractive profit from the sale of corn based upon a cost of $2.83 per bushel. The exporter was willing to forgo the additional profit that could have been earned if prices moved lower in order to prevent an erosion of the exporter's anticipated profit from prices moving substantially higher. This is similar to the case of the hedger buying the basis who cannot fully benefit from a rise in price because a short futures position is being held. In both instances the margin of profit will decline or increase depending upon the movement of the basis.

Case 5: A Buy Hedge Not Only Offsets an Increase in Cost But Also Results in a Profitable Basis Trade. A manufacturer of electrical components receives an order in March for September delivery. To manufacture the components, 50,000 lb of copper will be needed, but the actual cash purchase will not be necessary until July. The cost of copper accounts for the largest percentage of the total cost of production; therefore paying a higher-than-expected cost for the copper would certainly cut the anticipated profit level of the cash transaction. Since the cash copper purchase will take place after the July futures contract expires, the manufacturer establishes the *buy hedge* in the September contract.

Assuming a normal basis of 70 points between the September futures and the local cash price during July, the manufacturer estimates the purchase price to be 84.30¢ per lb when the September futures is at 85.00 per lb. Two long September futures, totaling 50,000 lb, are purchased at 85.00¢ per lb on March 20th. When the buy hedge is established, the local cash market price is 81.25¢ per lb, 3.75¢ per lb (375 points) under the September contract. The manufacturer was considering buying the lower priced cash and storing it until it would be needed in July. However, when carrying charges for the months April–July were added to the spot price it was found that the September futures price of 85.00¢ was below the total cost associated with buying spot copper and carrying it until July.

By July 25th when the manufacturer purchases the copper, both the cash and futures are above their March levels. The 50,000 lbs of copper are bought at $0.01 (100 points) under the September futures when it was at 88.00¢ per lb. Profits from the long futures position not only offset the entire cost increase for copper, but also produced a gross profit of 0.30¢ per lb per contract. The cash and futures transactions are as follows:

	Cash Market	Futures Market	Basis
March 20th	Expects to purchase 50,000 lb of copper during July at an estimated cost of 84.30¢ per lb. Expected cost = $42,150.	Buys two September copper futures at 85.00¢ per lb.	−70 points

July 25th	Buys 50,000 lb of copper in the cash market at a price of 87.00¢ per lb. Total cost = $43,500.	Sells two September copper futures at 88.00¢ per lb.	−100 points
Result	Increased cost of $1,350	Gain of $1,500	Basis change: −30 points
Net result	Gain of $150 less brokerage commissions.		

As the previous example shows, the buy hedge was liquidated at a wider-than-anticipated basis. Not only was the higher cost offset, but a gross profit of $150 was realized. Inclusion of brokerage charges will reduce the actual futures profit.

We will now examine the same case but, in this illustration, the price will move lower from March to July with the hedge still being covered at a wider basis than was originally anticipated. Let us assume that cash copper is purchased at $0.01 (100 points) under the September futures on July 25th when the September contract is at 80.00¢ per lb. The cash and futures transaction would be as follows:

	Cash Market	Futures Market	Basis
March 20th	Expects to purchase 50,000 lb of copper during July at an estimated cost of 84.30¢ per lb. Expected cost = $42,150.	Buys two September copper futures at 85.00¢ per lb.	−70 points
July 25th	Buys 50,000 lb of copper in the cash market at a price of 79.00¢ per lb. Total cost = $39,500.	Sells two September copper futures at 80.00¢ per lb.	−100 points
Result	Decrease in cost of $2,650	Loss of $2,500	Basis change: −30 points
Net result	Gain of $150 less brokerage commissions.		

In this case the lower-than-anticipated cost is offset by the loss on the futures trade. Because of the gain from the favorable move in basis, the net cost of the copper is 84.00¢ per lb, 30 points under expectations.

HEDGING IN AN INVERTED MARKET

When the market structure is inverted, that is, cash prices at a premium to futures, the principles of hedging are completely the opposite of those which were applied in a normal carrying charge market. A hedger who is long the basis with the long cash position at a premium to the short futures will realize basis trading profits only when the cash–futures price relationship widens beyond expectations. In a normal market a narrowing of the basis is needed to generate trading profits. A *buy hedge in an inverted market requires a narrowing of the basis for a profitable basis trade*. In contrast, a widening of the basis is needed for profits in a normal market.

The concept of convergence of cash and the nearest futures during futures expiration applies regardless of whether the market structure is inverted or normal. When the price trend is down and the cash price is at a premium to futures, the decline in cash must be greater than that of futures for the two prices to converge. If the trend is up then futures prices must outpace the gain in cash. If a hedge is held until expiration and the market is inverted, the basis will tend to narrow just as in a normal market. This narrowing of basis over time will benefit the uncovered buy hedger who has sold forward at a fixed price and prove costly for the sell hedger. However, since there is no limit to the premium cash can move over futures, there is also no constraint on how wide the basis can get and the amount of profits that can be realized from a sell hedge. In contrast, the risk associated with an unfavorable basis move is unlimited for a hedger who is short cash and long futures unless the hedge is held until the futures contract is near expiration. Remember, in a normal market the cash price can be discounted to futures at most by the maximum cost of carry. We will now examine some examples which will illustrate hypothetical results for both sell and buy hedges in an inverted market.

CASE 1. In November a distributor of petroleum products purchases 200,000 gal of No. 2 heating oil for delivery in mid-February to fulfill supply contracts to an apartment complex. The price the distributor receives will be fixed at time of delivery. The purchase price of the oil is 100 points over the December futures contract, which at the time of sale was trading at 90.00¢ per gal. Cash prices are at a premium to futures because of strong demand reflecting an extremely cold winter and the potential for tight supplies because of political tensions in the Mideast.

To protect against a decline in the value of the distributor's inventory by February, a short futures position is established. On November 10th the distributor instructs the broker to sell five March No. 2 heating oil contracts. The five contracts, equivalent to 210,000 gal of No. 2 heating oil New York harbor delivery, are sold at 87.00¢ per gal, for a long basis position of *400 points cash premium to futures*. On February 15th the distributor sells 200,000 gal of heating oil to the apartment complex at 87.00¢ per gal and then covers the five short March contracts at 86.00¢ per gal. The long basis position is closed out 300 points narrower than when it was established because the cash price declined at a greater rate than futures. The results of the cash and futures transactions are as follows:

	Cash Market	Futures Market	Basis
November 10th	Purchases 200,000 gal of No. 2 heating oil at 91.00¢ per gal. Total value = $182,000.	Sells five March heating oil futures (42,000 gal per contract) at 87.00¢ per gal.	400 points
February 15th	Sells 200,000 gal to an apartment complex at 87.00¢ per gal. Total value = $174,000.	Covers five short March heating oil futures at 86.00¢ per gal.	100 points
Result	Loss of $8,000	Gain of $2,100	Basis change: −300 points
Net result	Loss of $5,900 plus brokerage commissions.		

In this particular case the sell hedge was only effective in offsetting 26% of the loss realized from the decline of the cash market price. The narrowing of the basis by 300 points resulted in a basis trading loss of $5,900 compared with a loss of $8,000 if a hedge had not been established.

CASE 2. Let us examine the same example assuming that both cash and futures prices moved higher by February 15th. Regardless of whether the trend is up or down, cash and futures will tend to converge as futures near expiration. Last trading day for the March futures is the last business day in February. We will assume that the cash product is sold at 93.00¢ per gal and the short futures position is covered at 92.00¢ per gal. The basis once again narrowed resulting in a basis trading loss as futures rose at a faster rate than cash. The results of the hedge are presented below:

	Cash Market	Futures Market	Basis
November 10th	Purchases 200,000 gal of No. 2 heating oil at 91.00¢ per gal. Total value = $182,000.	Sells five March heating oil futures (42,000 gal per contract) at 87.00¢ per gal.	400 points
February 15th	Sells 200,000 gal to an apartment complex at 93.00¢ per gal. Total value = $186,000.	Covers five short March heating oil futures at 92.00¢ per gal.	100 points

Result	Gain of $4,000	Loss of $10,500	Basis change: −300 points
Net result	Loss of $6,500 plus brokerage commissions.		

The loss from the futures side of the hedge completely offset the gain realized from the cash transaction and resulted in an additional loss of $6,500 by having the cash position hedged. When a long basis position is established in an inverted market and the basis narrows, basis trading losses can be anticipated.

CASE 3. We will now reexamine the case of the heating oil distributor and illustrate what the results would have been if the hedge was liquidated at a wider basis than it was established. After the sell hedge is entered the cash and futures prices continue to move higher. By December 20th the local cash price had risen by 5.00¢ per gal over its November 10th level, while the March futures had experienced a gain of 300 points per contract to 90.00¢ per gal. The distributor decided to sell the inventory in the attractively priced cash market and also realized a basis trading profit by covering the long basis position at a wider point than initially established. The 200,000 gal of heating oil are sold in the local cash market for 96.00¢ per gal and the five short March futures are covered at an average price of 90.00¢ per gal. The results of the cash and futures transactions are as follows:

	Cash Market	Futures Market	Basis
November 10th	Purchases 200,000 gal of No. 2 heating oil at 91.00¢ per gal. Total value = $182,000.	Sells five March heating oil futures (42,000 gal per contract) at 87.00¢ per gal.	400 points
December 20th	Sells 200,000 gal of No. 2 heating oil at 96.00¢ per gal in the local cash market. Total value = $192,000.	Covers five short March heating oil futures at 90.00¢ per gal.	600 points
Result	Gain of $10,000	Loss of $6,300	Basis change: 200 points
Net result	Gain of $3,700 less brokerage commissions.		

Since the cash price increased at a faster rate than the March futures, a widening of the basis occurred. Not only did the hedge serve to minimize the risk of a decline in price but, in addition, a trading profit was realized. The gain of $10,000 from the cash sale more than offset the futures loss of $6,300 on the five contracts and left a trading profit of $3,700. Basis trading profits would have been realized in a declining market by futures falling at a faster pace than the cash price which would again result in a widening of basis.

The next few examples will illustrate how a commercial firm may use a buy hedge when the market is inverted and how results can differ depending upon the extent of widening or narrowing from the initial basis.

CASE 4. Let us assume that in January a hog producer estimates that by April 10,000 bushels of No. 2 yellow corn will be required for a feeding operation. Because of very urgent export demand due to poor crop prospects in the United States and South America, local cash prices are at a premium to the more distant futures. On January 20th the local cash market for corn is $0.25 per bushel over the May futures. The cost of corn accounts for a significant percentage of the producer's total feeding cost so any unexpected increase in its price could considerably reduce the anticipated margin of profit. If the current price for the May futures of $2.75 per bushel can be fixed then the producer feels a reasonable profit margin can be earned. Establishing a buy hedge seems very attractive when compared to the alternative options of buying higher-priced cash corn and incurring the additional cost of carry or speculating that feed costs will be under the May futures by April.

Estimating an expected closed-out basis and corresponding cash price is very difficult since there is no limit to the premium the cash market can maintain over futures up until futures expiration. The producer expects a narrowing of the basis from its current level of $0.25 per bushel (cash premium over futures) as the May contract becomes the nearest futures. Based upon historical basis patterns during periods when market fundamentals were similar to current market conditions, a closed-out basis of $0.10 per bushel cash over the May futures is estimated by the producer. The hedger is looking to lock-in an estimated cash price equivalent to $2.85 per bushel. A buy hedge is established on January 21st at $2.75 per bushel in the May futures. By April 15th when the hog producer is ready to purchase feed, the local price for corn is $3.10 per bushel, $0.10 per bushel higher than the local price when the hedge was taken. The May futures also moved sharply higher since it reflected more of the cash market conditions than it did 3 months earlier. The long May futures is liquidated at $3.05 per bushel when the 10,000 bushels of corn are purchased at $3.10. The closed-out basis is $0.05 compared with the expected basis of $0.10. The following illustrates the results of the hog-producer's hedge:

	Cash Market	Futures Market	Basis
January 21st	Hog producer expects to purchase 10,000 bushels of No. 2 yellow corn in April at $2.85 per bushel. Total cost = $28,500.	Buys 10,000 bushels of May corn futures at $2.75 per bushel.	$0.10

April 15th	Purchases 10,000 bushels of No. 2 yellow corn in local market at $3.10 per bushel. Total cost = $31,000.	Sells 10,000 bushels of May corn futures at $3.05 per bushel.	$0.05
Result	Loss of $2,500	Gain of $3,000	Basis change: $-0.05
Net result	Gain of $500 less brokerage commissions.		

The above illustration shows how the long futures position was effective in offsetting the higher-than-expected cost for corn and the additional $0.05 per bushel or $500 (less commission) gain realized by the basis narrowing beyond expectations. The same net result would have occurred if prices moved lower from January to April as long as the closed-out basis was $0.05 per bushel compared with an expected basis of $0.10. For example, assume the local purchase price on April 15th was $2.70 and the long May futures is liquidated at $2.65. The loss of $1,000 (less commission charges) sustained from the futures position is offset by a savings on the cost for cash corn of $1,500 for a net gain of $500. This is the same net result as in the first case.

When maintaining buy hedges in an inverted market the hedger assumes unlimited risk since there is no constraint on the premium of cash prices to futures. Although a hedger may assume cash and futures will converge, there is no guarantee this will occur by the time the cash commodity is purchased. The long futures position will serve to offset a part of the increased costs associated with higher prices; however, the difference between the actual and expected closed-out basis will determine the hedge's effectiveness. We will now examine results of the hog-producer's buy hedge when the cash and futures position are closed-out at a wider basis than was initially anticipated.

CASE 5. Let us assume that on April 15th the hog producer purchases 10,000 bushels of cash corn for $3.20 per bushel and simultaneously liquidates the long May futures at $3.00 per bushel. The closed-out basis of $0.20 is $0.10 greater than the producer had forecast. The gain from the long May futures only offset $2,500 of the higher-than-expected cost of $3,500. Here are the results of the hedge:

	Cash Market	Futures Market	Basis
January 21st	Hog producer expects to purchase 10,000 bushels of No. 2 yellow corn in April at $2.85 per bushel.	Buys 10,000 bushels of May corn futures at $2.75 per bushel.	$0.10

	Total cost = $28,500.		
April 15th	Purchases 10,000 bushels of No. 2 yellow corn in local market at $3.20 per bushel. Total cost = $32.000.	Sells 10,000 bushels of May futures at $3 per bushel.	$0.20
Result	Loss of $3,500	Gain of $2,500	Basis change: $0.10
Net result	Loss of $1,000 plus brokerage commissions.		

The net result of the hedge in the above example is that the producer paid $2.95 per bushel or $29,500 for the feed. If the producer decided not to hedge and waited until April, the increased cost would be $3.20 or $32,000, $2,500 more than the cost with the hedge. Buying the corn at $3.00 per bushel and carrying it until April 15th would have resulted in a total cost of $3.14 per bushel, assuming a monthly cost of carry of $0.05 per bushel. The total cost for corn would have been $1,900 more when compared to the net cost, using a hedge. Even though the buy hedge only partially covered the increased cost, it still proved more cost effective than the other available options.

The examples presented in this section were intended to illustrate how hedging results can be affected by basis changes. Before undertaking a hedging program, commercial firms must have a thorough understanding of the historical and expected basis patterns of each cash market they trade. Table 1 summarizes how the movement in basis relative to the market structure influences the results for a firm seeking to profit from a favorable basis change.

TABLE 1. Basis Trading Results for Buy and Sell Hedges in Normal and Inverted Markets As Basis Widens and Narrows

Basis		Sell Hedge	Buy Hedge
Narrows	Normal market	Profit	Loss
	(Inverted market)	(Loss)	(Profit)
Widens	Normal market	Loss	Profit
	(Inverted market)	(Profit)	(Loss)

BENEFITS OF HEDGING

The function of a hedging program is to *minimize the financial liability* associated with an unfavorable change in price. This absolute price risk is transferred to a speculator which allows the hedger to assume the less volatile risk associated with basis variation. As operational risks are reduced, a firm can more effectively direct its resources toward maximizing profits and corporate growth. Maintaining both cash and futures positions allows a firm the opportunity to realize additional revenues by accurately anticipating basis change. Numerous other benefits resulting in cost minimization or profit maximization can also be derived from hedging. Foremost among these is the increased flexibility provided a firm in the production, warehousing, distribution, and marketing of its product. Producers, merchandisers, and end users have the opportunity to take advantage of attractively priced futures and readily adjust strategies as market conditions change.

Since futures partially offset cash losses, greater leverage can be applied in the timing of cash transactions. A buyer or seller in the cash market who is not satisfied with current prices can delay transactions in anticipation of more favorable price levels. In contrast, the firm that speculates on the movement of cash prices by being unhedged does not have this flexibility and may be forced into poor marketing decisions if potential profit margins are diminished by an unfavorable price move. The availability of continuous trading of futures during the times that the exchanges are open allows for ease in entering and exiting positions. The contract size and choice of delivery months for the futures side of the hedge can be quickly adjusted as cash market conditions change.

For some commodities, futures are the only available markets where forward prices can be set. Cash market participants have the option of hedging costs or product value as far forward as 9–24 months. Although there are cash forward markets for some commodities they tend to offer less flexibility since cash commitments cannot be as easily offset as futures positions. For example, a cotton producer, prior to harvest, may enter into a forward contract to deliver a specific quantity of cotton meeting certain quality standards at a set price for delivery 3 months forward. The grower runs the risk of not being able to fulfill the conditions of the contract if the harvest does not meet expectations. If that did occur the grower could be forced to purchase cotton on the cash market, most likely resulting in higher costs and reduced profit margins. In contrast, the quantity of futures used in a sell hedge could be quickly increased or decreased depending upon the expected size of the crop.

An additional consideration when comparing cash and futures contracts is the *chance of default*. The performance of the futures contract is guaranteed by the clearing member firms of the exchange which, as a group, provide a solid financial backing. The possibility of a default in a cash transaction will depend solely upon the financial strength of the parties involved.

TAKING ADVANTAGE OF PRICE DISTORTIONS. Hedgers not only have the opportunity for profit from a favorable change in basis, but can also take advantage of short-term disparities between futures prices. Price distortions can occur between (1) different delivery months in the same commodity on the same exchange (December copper versus July copper), (2) the same or different delivery months in the same commodity traded on different exchanges (Chicago September wheat versus Kansas City September wheat), (3) the same or different delivery months of different but related commodities on the same or different exchanges (Chicago December corn versus Chicago December oats), and (4) processed products and the raw materials used for their production (Chicago March soybeans versus Chicago March soybean meal and March soybean oil).

The simultaneous purchase of an underpriced commodity against the sale of an overpriced one to profit from price disparity is called an *arbitrage*. Excessive distortions between the value of different futures contracts can result from changes in the fundamental factors responsible for the normal price differential or from short-term volatility concentrated in one delivery month. For example, temporary price distortions can occur when a large number of buy or sell orders are triggered at a particular price. These technical variations are usually short-lived unless there is a change in the fundamental factors responsible for the price difference.

Consider the situation where coffee, cocoa, and sugar are traded on futures exchanges in both New York and London. Differences in price between the same commodity and delivery month reflects differences in the quality delivered against each contract, local supply-and-demand conditions for the deliverable qualities, variation in the pound sterling, delivery procedures on the two exchanges, and the costs associated with moving the commodity from one market to the other. Prices must be adjusted for the above fundamental differences if they are to be equated. The arbitrageur looks to establish a position at a price differential which exceeds the fundamental difference in price in order to profit when that spread adjusts to reflect current and anticipated fundamentals.

Differences in price between delivery months for the same futures such as Chicago September wheat and Chicago March wheat will reflect the cost of carry from one month to the other and the expected future supply and demand during those particular delivery periods. If carrying charges increase and the fundamental outlook remains unchanged, then the premiums of the distant futures in a normal market should increase. However, if current available supplies are low and demand is strong relative to expected fundamentals for the more distant futures, then that premium may narrow even if carrying charges rise. When the demand for one or more delivery months completely offsets the cost of carry the market structure becomes *inverted*.

Price differences between interrelated commodities and commodities traded on different exchanges will generally reflect fundamental differences in the supply of, or demand for, that the particular quality of commodity and the transportation cost of moving the product from one market to another. Firms may decide to adjust a hedge if price distortions are excessive and the potential gain from switching the position from one delivery month or exchange to another offsets the cost.

For example, heavy selling or buying of one delivery month relative to the rest of the board may prompt the moving of a hedge to a different month because a more attractive basis can be established. A hedger attempting to cover part of the carrying charges may decide to roll a short March position into May if volume buying of May pushes its premium temporarily beyond the total costs of carrying the cash commodity until May. A chocolate manufacturer looking to hedge against an increase in raw material costs will compare the differential between prices of New York and London futures to see if any disparities exist before placing the hedge. The historical deviation between prices and seasonal tendencies will be evaluated before a decision is made. As with the study of basis, a hedger must be completely familiar with the factors that cause price differences between exchanges or between different delivery months for the same futures when deciding where to hedge. In the final decision, the anticipated benefit of using one contract over another must outweigh the cost of switching into another option.

REDUCED COSTS. Both variable and fixed costs associated with a firm's daily operations can be reduced if a hedging program is followed. Earlier we illustrated how a sell hedge can result in reducing some of the costs of carrying inventory if the hedge is placed at a wide enough basis in a normal market. A buy hedge can improve profit margins by reducing capital requirements and freeing more excess funds to be allocated to alternative productive resources. By using futures to hedge forward requirements, a firm forgoes the large capital outlay to build storage facilities and the costs of maintenance associated with holding the cash product until it is needed in the future. Since futures are bought and sold on margin, a hedger needs only 10% of the contract value to establish a position; however, additional funds would be required for maintenance margin calls. Consequently, capital is free to be allocated to more productive resources and total interest costs are reduced.

FINANCING. Maintaining a hedged position can improve the likelihood of receiving favorable financing terms. Because of the seasonal and cyclic patterns of production and consumption within many industries, the demand for working capital can vary greatly from one period to the next. Since hedging reduces to some extent a firm's operating risks, loans are more secure and banks are willing to lend more capital at favorable borrowing rates. For example, an elevator operator using inventory as collateral may be able to borrow up to 90% of the inventory's value if a short hedge was maintained. In contrast, only 70–80% may be borrowed if the cash position was unhedged. The increased working capital will allow the operator to handle more volume and turnover, resulting in expanded profits.

Receiving additional working capital enables a firm to maintain its operational schedule even during periods of seasonally slow cash flow. In some cases an agreement can be made with a bank to finance any additional margin calls required to maintain the hedge. Finally, hedging can help in planning future decisions more efficiently. Both costs and prices received can be better estimated. Since hedging reduced the variability of prospective profit margins, a firm is more certain of future cash flow and can better plan where the resources will be allocated and improve operational efficiency.

QUESTIONS TO ANSWER BEFORE HEDGING

Hedging involves a series of equally important decisions which must be carefully evaluated in order to effectively reduce risk exposure and offer profitable basis trading opportunities. The initial consideration is deciding "*is the risk worth hedging?*" The degree of risk associated with an unhedged position can be quantified using the expected price change and the probability of that change occurring compared with the cost of hedging and the firm's tolerance for risk. Hedging costs include commissions charged for the transaction, opportunity costs associated with interest not realized in the margin deposit, financial loss that could result from an unfavorable basis change, and the expected difference between the desired entry price on the futures trade and actual execution price (also referred to as slippage). Let us now review an example to show how the calculations would be made in this cost analysis.

EVALUATING A HEDGE. In October a firm in the United States has ordered electronic equipment from a Japanese company for delivery and payment by February 1st. The cost of the equipment is 25 million Japanese yen, equivalent to two IMM futures contracts. The comptroller of the firm is considering hedging using futures since the comptroller feels there is a high probability that the yen will increase in value by the time payment is due. The comptroller feels there is a 70% chance that the spot yen will rise 5% from its current value to 0.4200¢ per yen by February. The expected loss from not hedging would be calculated by multiplying the current spot rate of 0.4000¢ per yen by the anticipated rate change of 5% and then multiplying the estimated 70% probability of that price change occurring:

$$0.4000¢ \text{ per yen} \times 0.05 \times 0.70 = 0.0140¢ \text{ per yen}$$

Thus the risk exposure of an increase of 0.0140¢ on 25 million yen is equivalent to $3,500.

EVALUATION OF HEDGING COSTS. The next step is to evaluate the different costs associated with the hedge and compare them to the calculated risk exposure. The most significant cost among these is the risk of an unfavorable change in basis. As was mentioned earlier, accurate forecasting of a basis change will likely determine the effectiveness of the hedge. Knowledge of the historical and seasonal relationships between cash and futures prices combined with a thorough understanding of the current fundamental situations are needed. The more the underlying characteristics of the cash product deviate from the standardized futures contract, the greater the basis volatility should be.

Calculation of the *correlation statistics* between cash and futures and between their respective rate of change is a good indicator of the type of basis variation to expect. The more positive the correlation between prices, the greater the chance of a stable basis. When a raw material goes through various stages of processing, the correlation between futures price and the price of the processed product declines because the value of the raw commodity accounts for less of the product's final value. For example, the change in the price of cotton can have a significant impact on a cotton exporter's earnings; however, since that fiber is first processed into yarn, then fabric, and eventually into a finished product, the risk associated with the price of cotton becomes less of a consideration since the other costs of labor, transportation, equipment, and marketing significantly affect the product's final value. Consequently, the risk exposure and correlation between the price of cotton and that of the finished product does not justify the hedge.

In our currency example the comptroller expects to close-out the futures hedge at a 30-point differential, futures premium to cash. If the hedge is liquidated at a wider futures premium, additional revenue will be realized. The comptroller figures the probability of an unfavorable basis move of 20 points per contract is 30% for an expected cost of $150 (20 points × $12.50 × two contracts × 0.30). Adding commission costs of $120 to estimates for opportunity costs and slippage of $100 and $125, respectively, brings the total expected cost of the hedge to $495. In this example, because the risk of being unhedged far exceeds its expected cost, hedging the firm's currency exposure should be considered.

INDIRECT HEDGING RELATIONSHIPS. When the cash commodity is distinctly different but related in an indirect way to the underlying futures, the hedge is referred to as a "cross hedge." This type of hedge is particularly common in financial futures because of the large variety of cash debt instruments which have significant differences from the specifications of the limited available futures. Hedging corporate bonds using Treasury-bond futures or banker's acceptances with Treasury bills or CD futures are possible cross hedges. Even if the correlations between cash and futures are not high, a firm may decide to hedge and assume the high basis risk because the absolute price risk is considerable. Evaluation of a cross hedge requires a thorough understanding of the expected basis. Regression analysis can be used to estimate the change in the value of futures when cash changes by a set percent. This will help determine the number of contracts used for the hedge.

HEDGING QUANTITY AND METHOD. Once it is determined that a hedge is economical, the next questions are "how much of the risk should be hedged?" and "what trading approach should be used?" A hedging program should be coordinated with the firm's overall corporate objectives and industry pricing structure. If the risk is considered small relative to a firm's net worth, working capital and liquidity, then the cash position may be left unhedged or only a small portion of the risk will be hedged. Hedging should be considered in context with maintaining or increasing profit margins of finished products, stockpiling, or forward pricing in the cash market. The larger the percent of a firm's assets represented by a commodity value, the greater the exposure associated with an unfavorable price change.

A hedger's tolerance for risk will determine the hedger's strategy for trading. A pure hedge attempts to manage as much risk as possible until the future cash transactions are completed. The futures contract and delivery month used by a pure hedger should match the quality and time period for the cash transaction as closely as possible. A hedger who has a greater tolerance for risk may choose to hedge based upon what the hedger feels is the probability of an unfavorable price change. The selective hedge is established and maintained based upon expectations of trends for cash and futures. Firms may decide to adjust a hedge if price distortions are excessive and the potential gain from switching the position from one delivery month or exchange to another offsets the cost. For example, heavy selling or buying of one delivery month relative to the rest of the board may prompt the moving of a hedge to a different month because a more attractive basis can be established. A hedger attempting to cover part of the carrying charges may decide to roll a short March position into May if volume buying of May pushes its premium temporarily beyond the total cost of carrying the cash commodity until May.

A chocolate manufacturer looking to hedge against an increase in raw material costs will compare the differential between prices of New York and London futures to see if any disparities exist before placing the hedge. The historical deviation between prices and seasonal tendencies will be evaluated before a decision is made. The size of the hedge can be adjusted depending upon changes in the outlook for production and price. A general rule to which some farmers adhere is to hedge one-third of future production before planting, one-third when the crop first emerges, and leave one-third unhedged until the new crop outlook can be accurately estimated. A selective hedge should have the financial leverage necessary to assume the expected loss of an unhedged position. A farmer heavily in debt is less likely to assume risk compared to one with a significantly larger amount of working capital.

Regardless of whether the hedge is pure or selective the following factors should be considered before establishing a futures hedge:

Compare risk exposure against cost of hedge.
Decide how much risk to hedge.
Decide which exchange and delivery month to use.
Decide when the hedge should be lifted and if it should be reestablished.

INTEGRATED HEDGES

Because of the wide array of actively traded futures, many different risks associated with a business operation can be hedged simultaneously. Future profit margins can be locked-in when both the future selling price and costs of production are established. The opportunity to reduce price risks has increased significantly over the past 10 years due to the introduction of imaginative new futures contracts and options on futures contracts.

A merchant dealer can now hedge against a decline in the value of a firm's inventory or increase in production costs, as well as minimize the risks associated with fluctuations in the U. S. dollar, short- or long-term interest rates, and even equity values if circumstances warrant. The following examples will illustrate how future profit margins can be set when both sell and buy hedges are incorporated. In these examples we will assume that hedging has been determined to be an appropriate strategy for the operation and that a fully hedged position will be maintained at all times.

CASE 1: FEEDLOT HEDGE. A cattle feedlot operator purchases feeder cattle weighing anywhere from 650 to 800 lb per head and raises them to an average market weight of about 950 to 1,200 lb or more. Future profit margins will be determined mostly by the costs of feeders and feed versus the selling price of the fat cattle when they are ready for market. By hedging all three price risks, future profit margins can also be estimated.

To calculate the expected local cash price the hedger must have a knowledge of local basis trends for feeder cattle, feed, and live cattle. A daily log can be kept to compare expected costs to the expected selling price based upon futures prices and the local basis at the time the cash transaction is completed. The operator will hedge these risks once the estimated margin of profit is at a level which assures the operator a reasonable return.

Let us assume that in July the livestock operator plans to purchase 170 head of feeders by September and market the finished steers in March. The operator figures, on average, the feeders will weight 700 lb per head and the market weight will be around 1,050 lb per head. Approximately 5,000 bushels of No. 2 yellow corn will be needed to raise the feeders to market weight. The operator feels a profit of about $30 per head can be gained based upon current futures prices (October CME feeder cattle, December CBT corn, April CME live cattle and their expected close-out basis) when the future cash transactions are complete. The *integrated hedge* will be established by:

1. Buying October feeder cattle futures.
2. Buying December corn futures.
3. Selling April live cattle futures.

On July 20th the October feeder futures and December corn futures are selling at $53.50 per cwt and $3 per bushel, respectively. Seasonal basis patterns and the operator's analysis of future market factors suggests that by September the local cash price for feeders will be $1.50 per cwt over October futures and that No. 2 yellow corn will be selling at $0.12 per bushel under the December delivery. Consequently, by establishing long hedges the operator has set future costs for feeders and corn at the local cash market at $55 per cwt and $2.88 per bushel, respectively. To break even on the feeding operation the producer must receive a price of $58.50 per cwt on a 1,050-lb choice steer.

On July 20th the April live cattle futures is trading at $62 per cwt. By selling the April "fat" cattle contract at $62 per cwt the operator figures a local cash price of $61.30 per cwt can be locked-in since the local basis is on average $0.70 per cwt under April futures during March. If the basis estimates are accurate then a profit of about $29 per head can be realized. To hedge the cost of 170 feeders weighing, on average, 700 lb each would require three futures contracts (700 lb × 170 feeders per 42,000-lb contract = 2.8 contracts). The operator assumes a 1% death loss; consequently, the operator decides to hedge the value of 168 steers weighing an average of 1,050 lb by using a combination of four April CME live cattle contracts and one of the smaller April MidAmerican cattle contracts (where one contract is 20,000 lb.).

On September 10th the long side of the hedge is liquidated when (1) the cash feeders are purchased at $58 per cwt and (2) the cash corn is bought at $2.70 per bushel and futures are liquidated at $2.80 per bushel. The results of the long hedges are as follows:

	Cash Market	Futures Market	Basis
July 20th	A livestock producer expects to purchase 170 feeder cattle weighing an average of 700 lb per head for $55 per cwt. Expected cost = $65,450.	Buys three October feeder cattle futures at $53.50 per cwt.	$1.50 per cwt
September 10th	Purchases 170 feeder cattle, average weight 700 lb per head at $58 per cwt. Total cost = $69,020.	Sells three October feeder cattle futures at $56.90 per cwt.	$1.10 per cwt
Result	Increase cost of $3,570	Gain of $4,488	Basis change: −$0.40 per cwt.
Net result	Gain of $918 less brokerage commissions.		

July 20th	A livestock producer expects to purchase 5,000 bushels of No. 2 yellow corn for $2.88 per bushel. Expected cost = $14,400.	Buys 5,000 bushels of December corn futures at $3 per bushel.	$−0.12 per bushel
September 10th	Purchases 5,000 bushels of No. 2 yellow corn at $2.70 per bushel. Total cost = $13,500.	Sells 5,000 bushels of December corn futures at $2.80 per bushel.	$−0.10 per bushel
Result	Reduction in cost of $900	Loss of $1,000	Basis change: $0.02 per bushel.
Net result	Loss of $100 plus brokerage commissions.		

By hedging future feeder cattle and corn requirements the livestock operator not only averted a higher-than-expected net cost, but also realized additional income because of a favorable basis change in the feeder cattle long hedge. These examples again illustrate how the outcome of a hedge in both an inverted (feeder cattle case) and a normal (corn situation) market is influenced by the change in basis.

The profit in the long feeder cattle hedge not only reflected favorable basis change, but also the additional profit from having more than the total risk value of the expected cash transaction covered by the value of the three futures.

If prices had declined from July to September, then the operator's decision to use three contracts would have caused a net loss from the hedge transaction even if the basis did not change. When the cattle are ready for market in March the local cash market price is at $59 per cwt. The fat cattle are sold and the short hedges on the CME and MidAmerica Exchange are covered at $60.20 per cwt on March 15th. The results of the short hedge are as follows:

	Cash Market	Futures Market	Basis
July 20th	A livestock producer expects to sell 168 head (assuming 1% death loss) weighing, one average, 1,050 lb in March in the local market at $61.30 per cwt. Expected revenue = $108,133.	Sells four CME live cattle contracts (equivalent to 152 head) and one MidAmerican live cattle contract (equal to 19 head) at $62 per cwt.	−$0.70 per cwt
March 15th	Sells 168 head of live cattle, weighing, on average, 1,050 lb at $57 per cwt. Total revenue = $100,548.	Buys four contracts of live cattle and one MidAmerican live cattle futures at $58 per cwt	−$1 per cwt
Result	Decrease in income of $7,585	Gain of $7,200	Basis change: −$0.30 per cwt.
Net result	Loss of $385 plus brokerage commissions.		

The net result of the sell hedge was that the operator was under the expected revenue by $385. If no hedge had been established the March revenue would have been only 93% of the expectations in July. The combination of both sell and buy hedges allowed the feedlot operator to achieve an attractive profit even though the cost of feeders increased and the selling price of the fat cattle declined below earlier expectations.

CASE 2: SOYBEAN PROCESSING HEDGE. To realize a gross profit margin from processing soybeans the combined value of the products produced—soybean meal and soybean oil—must exceed the cost of the soybeans. The availability of futures allows the soybean processor to fix a gross profit margin while minimizing the risk of an unfavorable price change for soybeans, soybean oil, and soybean meal. The processing of 1 bushel of soybeans, equivalent to 60 lb, yields an average of 11 lb of soybean oil and 47 lb of soybean meal. From 1 to 2 lb are lost in the manufacturing (crushing) process. The crushing margin is calculated by comparing the cost of soybeans to the combined value of the processed products. Since soybean meal is quoted in terms of dollars per short ton, its price must be divided by 0.0235 (which equals 47 lb/2,000 lb = 1 short ton) to derive the corresponding value of meal per bushel of soybeans. If soybeans cost $6 per bushel and oil and meal can be sold for $0.18 per lb and $182 per ton, respectively, then the gross crushing margin would be calculated as follows:

Cost of soybeans = $6 per bushel	
Value of soybean oil = $0.18 per pound × 11 lb/bushel	= $1.98 per bushel
Value of soybean meal = $182 per ton × 0.0235 tons/bushel	= $4.28 per bushel
Total product value	= $6.26 per bushel
Gross crushing margin (combined product value minus soybean cost) = $6.26 per bushel − $6 per bushel	= $0.26 per bushel

In a manner similar to the feedlot operator, the soybean crusher can calculate daily potential future profit margins by comparing CBT soybean futures against the combined value of soybean oil and soybean meal futures. The three-way hedge which requires the buying of soybean futures and the selling of oil and meal futures is referred to as "putting on the crush."

There are three basis risks related to this hedge since three cash–futures combinations are involved. For example, a processor in August knows that 50,000 bushels of soybeans will be required for September in order to satisfy October oil and meal commitments. The processor feels an attractive gross profit can be locked-in based upon current prices for November soybeans, December soybean oil, December soybean meal, and the expected basis when the crush transactions are completed. The hedge is implemented on August 5th by (1) buying 50,000 bushels of November soybeans at $5.75 per bushel, (2) selling nine contracts of December soybean oil at $0.17 per bushel, and (3) selling 12 December contracts of soybean meal at $179 per ton. The nine contracts of oil and 12 contracts of meal approximate the total quantity of products produced from crushing 50,000 bushels of soybeans. The gross processing margin is equal to $6.08 per bushel less $5.75 per bushel, or $0.33 per bushel, where

Value of soybean oil = $0.17 per lb × 11 lb	= $1.87 per bushel
Value of soybean meal = $179 per ton × 0.0235 tons/bushel	= $4.21 per bushel
Total product value	= $6.08 per bushel

The crusher expects to purchase cash soybeans in the local market at $0.20 per bushel under November futures and sell oil and meal at $0.01 per lb and $4 per ton under the respective December futures deliveries. If these basis expectations are realized, then a gross margin of $0.32 per bushel will be realized from hedging.

On September 8th the processor purchases 50,000 bushels of soybeans in the local cash market at $5.85 per bushel and sells the same quantity of November futures at $6 per bushel. The results of the long side of the crush spread are presented below:

	Cash Market	Futures Market	Basis
August 5th	A processor expects to purchase 50,000 bushels of soybeans in the local market at $5.55 per bushel. Expected cost = $277,500.	Buys 50,000 bushels of November soybean futures at $5.75 per bushel.	−$0.20 per bushel
September 8th	Purchases 50,000 bushels of soybeans in the local market at $5.85 per bushel Total cost = $292,500.	Sells 50,000 bushels of November soybean futures at $6.00 per bushel.	−$0.15 per bushel
Result	Increase cost of $15,000	Gain of $12,500	Basis change: $0.05 per bushel
Net result	Loss of $2,500 plus brokerage commissions.		

The net result of the long hedge was that the processor paid $0.05 per bushel more for the soybeans than was expected in September. This was a relatively small premium considering the local price was $0.30 per bushel higher than was anticipated. On October 15th the soybean oil and soybean meal are sold at $0.185 per lb and $190 per ton, respectively. The short December futures are covered at $0.195 per lb for the oil and at $192 per ton for the meal. The results of the short side of the crush spread are as follows:

	Cash Market	Futures Market	Basis
August 5th	A processor expects to sell 550,000 lb of soybean oil in October at $0.16 per lb. Expected revenue = $88,000.	Sells nine contracts of December soybean oil futures at $0.17 per lb.	$0.01 per lb
October 15th	Sells 550,000 lb of soybean oil in the local market at $0.185 per lb. Total revenue = $101,750.	Buys nine contracts of December soybean oil futures at $0.195 per lb.	$0.01 per lb
Result	Gain of $13,750	Loss of $13,500	Basis change: $0
Net result	Gain of $250 less brokerage commissions.		
August 5th	A processor expects to sell 1,175 tons of	Sells 12 contracts of December soybean	−$4 per ton

	soybean meal in October at $175 per ton. Expected revenue = $205,625.	meal futures at $179 per ton.	
October 15th	Sells 1,175 tons of soybean meal in the local market at $190 per ton. Total revenue = $223,250.	Buys 12 contracts of December soybean meal futures at $192 per ton.	−$2 per ton
Result	Gain of $17,625.	Loss of $15,600	Basis change: $2 per ton.
Net result	Gain of $2,025 less brokerage commissions.		

With the hedge the soybean processor realized a gross profit margin of $0.31 per bushel instead of the target of $0.32 per bushel. The net result was nearly perfect but, as we mentioned earlier, perfect hedges are seldom achieved. The crush example did illustrate the three different consequences of basis movement:

1. Profitability, as in the soybean meal selling hedge, because the basis narrowed more than expected due to cash increasing faster than futures.
2. Unprofitability, when the same basis pattern occurred in the soybean hedge, but since a buy hedge had been established the narrowing resulted in a higher net cost.
3. Unchanged, as in the case of the soybean oil selling hedge, since the change in the final price of cash was equal to that of the December futures.

In this example a greater return would have been earned if the crush was not established; however, the corresponding financial risk would have been much greater. Of course, the "selective hedger" may have placed hedges in only one or two futures and/or adjusted the quantity of contracts employed. The strategy of the selective hedger would reflect appraisal of price and basis trends.

There are many variations of an integrated hedge that can be established depending upon the market outlook of each futures. For example, when the cost of soybeans is greater than the combined product value of oil and meal it becomes unprofitable to crush beans. Rather than stop processing, the manufacturer can put on what is referred to as a "reverse crush" spread, selling soybean futures and buying oil and meal futures. If this position is taken by a large number of processors the action would weaken soybean prices and provide strength to oil and meal futures allowing for a readjustment in the raw material cost relative to the value of the processed products.

THE COMPLETE HEDGE

To a hedger, the greatest concern is an unfavorable basis change. Once a hedge has been established the basis trend takes priority over the movement of the local market price. Within some industries, such as grains, cotton, sugar, coffee, and cocoa, the basis risk can be offset by setting the basis at which the hedge will be closed-out. The actual price of the cash transaction will be determined from the price at which the futures position is offset plus the predetermined basis level. For example, assume a grain exporter who is short the corn basis at $0.10 per bushel under March futures agrees to buy the needed quantity of corn from an elevator operator at $0.12 per bushel under March futures. The actual price the exporter pays will be determined by the value of the March futures minus $0.12 per bushel.

Regardless of the subsequent cash price, the exporter gained $0.02 per bushel from the profitable basis trade. Establishing the transaction price from a predetermined basis is known by different terms depending upon the commodity. It is termed "on-call" for cotton, "ex-pit" for grains, "against actuals" for sugar and coffee, and "exchange for physicals" in the cocoa and metals industries. In all of the above, basis risk is offset once the forward basis has been set thereby canceling the only other price risk for the hedger.

For an "on-call" trade the timing of when to offset the futures position will be determined by either the buyer (*buying "on-call"*) or seller (*selling "on-call"*). For example, assume a cotton merchant in March wishes to purchase 1,000 bales of strict low middling cotton for April delivery. To protect against a price advance the merchant is long 10 May futures from 70.00 per lb with the expectation of purchasing the cotton at 50 points off May futures. The merchant contracts with a grower to purchase 1,000 bales of the required quality at 75 points off the May "seller's call" price fixed later. The seller can then fix the transaction price on any day up until April 15th. The time limit is mutually agreed upon between buyer and seller.

From March through early April the price of cotton rises and on April 10 the grower decides to fix the cash price. This is done by instructing the cotton merchant's futures broker to buy 10 contracts of May cotton futures for the *cotton merchant's account*. The 10 May futures were sold at 73.00¢ per lb resulting in a cash price of $0.7225 per lb. The futures transactions also affect the merchant's long hedge. In this case the grower had the option of waiting until the price level became more attractive to sell the crop. The merchant benefited from being completely insulated from increased costs in addition to earning 0.25¢ per lb on the basis trade.

In a "buyer's call" transaction the buyer has the option of deciding within a certain time limit when the cash price is established. Assume a cotton merchant owns 5,000 bales and is *long the local basis* at 100 points off the December futures. A cotton mill, in need of cotton 2 months forward, agrees to purchase the 5,000 bales at 70 points off the December futures, *"buyer's call" price fixed later*. The mill has 45 days from the day of the sale to establish the transaction price. If prices move lower, the cost of cotton to the mill will decline while just the opposite will occur on a price advance. For the merchant, a basis trading profit is guaranteed in addition to full price protection from a price decline. Two weeks later the mill fixes the cash price by instructing the merchant's broker to buy 50 contracts of December futures for the merchant's account. As with the previous case the futures transaction established the cash price and offset the merchant's hedge.

At any one time a merchant can simultaneously be involved in a seller's and buyer's call transaction. The only concern of the merchant is selling at a more favorable basis than the commodity was purchased. The results will not vary regardless of whether the merchant's buying or selling price is set first because the initial and closed-out basis are already determined.

"Ex-pit," "against actuals," "exchange for physicals" are offset differently from "on-call" transactions. For these, the futures trade is completed outside the trading ring between the buyer's broker and the seller's broker. This is the one exception to the rule that all trades must be completed by open outcry. Once the respective brokers meet outside the trading ring, they close-out each side of the buyer's and seller's hedge at either the market price or at a previously agreed-upon price. In doing so they also establish the cash price of the transaction.

For example, assume a corn elevator operator is long the basis at \$0.20 per bushel under December for 10,000 bushels of corn and the operator agrees to sell this quantity to an exporter who is short the basis from \$0.10 per bushel under December futures. They agree to sell the corn at \$0.15 per bushel under December. The elevator operator is short 10,000 bushels of December corn and the exporter is long 10,000 bushels of December corn. To complete the ex-pit transaction the brokers for the elevator operator and exporter meet outside the ring and establish the price. This is the price that will offset the respective hedges and establish the cash price. If completed inside the ring then there is no guarantee that the two brokers would be able to complete the entire transaction without another broker taking the other side of the trade. Therefore, the transaction would not result in offsetting both sides of the hedge. Ex-pit transactions must only involve brokers representing participants of the cash transaction.

SUMMARY

Examples used throughout this chapter have been intended to illustrate how hedging can be implemented, in different market situations, to reduce absolute price risk and be a tool to produce trading profits. The degree of correlation between cash and futures along with the accuracy of basis forecasts will determine the success of the hedge in reaching these objectives.

Near perfect conditions between cash and futures rarely occur since there are usually differences between the two market prices in quality, quantity, delivery points, and delivery procedures. For example, the cash quality being hedged may be of a better or substandard grade when compared with the futures basis grade. Since the size of the futures contract is fixed, the cash quantity being hedged may not match the standardized futures or multiples of that contract. Differences between supply availability at the local market and that at the futures delivery locations will also cause prices to differ. Each local market price will reflect the current situation and outlook at that location, which at most times will be somewhat different than that reflected by futures prices.

Cash/futures correlations can also vary depending upon which delivery month is used, since each option does not change by the same magnitude. Accurate basis forecasts will depend upon the hedger's knowledge of seasonal and cyclic patterns of the different cash–futures relationships, knowledge of the situation, and outlook for both cash and futures and an understanding of the factors that influence the cost of carry.

Many times it is difficult to forecast the close-out basis because the cash–futures positions are not liquidated simultaneously. If a cash transaction is made after futures are closed-out, then the seller and/or buyer must wait until the following day to hedge. By then futures could be sharply higher or lower than the preceding day and result in the hedge establishing a less attractive forward price.

Hedging cannot guarantee profits by correcting for poor management, unprofitable price levels, or a noncompetitive industrial price structure. It can, however, be extremely effective in reducing price risk and allowing a firm to expect a reasonable return with a high degree of certainty. Hedging applications should continue to expand as long as price volatility and uncertainty characterize the trading environment of cash commodities.

CHAPTER 10

THE DEVELOPMENT OF THE FINANCIAL FUTURES MARKETS

CONTENTS

THE CHRONOLOGICAL DEVELOPMENT OF THE FINANCIAL FUTURES MARKET **3**

The Advent of Financial Futures **5**
The Development of the Financial Futures Markets **7**
A Series of Failures **10**
The Second Wave of Successful Contract **13**
The Uses and Users of the Interest-Rate Futures Contracts **15**
The Structure of the Interest-Rate Futures Markets **17**
The Regulatory Posture **18**
Equity Index Futures Contracts **20**
A Quantitative View of the Growth of the Interest-Rate Futures Markets **23**

THE DEVELOPMENT OF THE INTERACTIONS BETWEEN THE CASH AND FINANCIAL FUTURES MARKETS **23**

Alternative Investments (Over Holding Period Beginning at Present) **30**
Integration of the Cash and the Futures Markets Interest Rates **33**
Arbitrage Strategies Revisited **43**
Overview of the Interactions **49**

CHAPTER 10

THE DEVELOPMENT OF THE FINANCIAL FUTURES MARKETS

Dr. Frank J. Jones

The financial futures markets have been a recent addition to the very sophisticated financial system of the United States. During their short existence, they have become an essential part of this financial system.

The section "The Chronological Development of the Financial Futures Markets" summarizes the development of these markets with respect to the new financial futures contracts listed, the growth in the trading volume of these contracts, and the uses of each type of contract. The section "The Development of the Interactions Between the Cash and Futures Financial Markets" discusses, in a somewhat more technical manner, the development of the interactions between the cash and futures financial markets. The section "Overview" provides a summary and conclusions.

THE CHRONOLOGICAL DEVELOPMENT OF THE FINANCIAL FUTURES MARKETS[1]

Commodity markets, or futures markets as they have recently come to be called, were developed for agricultural products over 100 years ago in the United States. While these markets are widely recognized for their speculative uses (although it is difficult to define speculation, it can be considered a high-risk, often short holding period investment), they became essential tools of risk management for institutions in the cash markets for agricultural products, that is, for institutions "hedging" their exposure due to the price risk of their agricultural products.

Specifically, producers of agricultural products have exposure to decreasing or uncertain prices before they can market their product. Similarly, purchasers of agricultural products are exposed to increasing or uncertain prices of the agricultural products before they actually buy the products. Agricultural futures markets have been used to hedge these price exposures. Producers can sell futures

[1]I would like to acknowledge Mr. Stephen Storch of the New York Stock Exchange for his helpful comments on this section.

contracts to hedge against price decreases ("short hedges"), while purchasers can buy futures contracts to hedge against price increases ("long hedges").

Futures markets are necessary and successful only when prices are volatile. With stable prices, speculators would find no profit potential in futures markets and hedgers would have no need for hedging to obtain price protection. Given that volatile prices are considered undesirable, futures markets would be expected to be, parasitically, successful only in undesirable times. Thus futures markets present the obverse case to Shakespeare's farmer who hanged himself in fear of plenty. They flourish only in adverse times.

Agricultural futures markets have become successful because they have achieved a high degree of "liquidity." The liquidity of a market means that the "spread" between the price at which a customer in the market can buy (the dealer's offer price in the market) or sell (the bid price), essentially called the transaction cost, is small. In a liquid market larger quantities of contracts can be bought or sold with only small changes in the offer or bid prices.

One reason for this liquidity is that the futures markets are highly leveraged. This leverage in the futures markets relates to a large extent to the margining practices in the futures markets. In the "cash" or "spot" markets, which require immediate delivery, the title or ownership is transferred from the seller to the buyer immediately. At the same time payment must be made in full from the buyer to the seller, or a substantial down payment must be made (the "margin") and the remainder borrowed with an interest paid on the borrowed amount by the buyer.

However, in futures markets, title or ownership is not transferred when futures contracts are bought or sold. Futures contracts are commitments to future spot transactions at a specific time in the future at a specific price, not to an immediate transaction. Buyers of futures contracts (longs) commit to paying the full value of the futures contract in cash and accepting delivery of the specified commodity. Sellers of futures contracts (shorts) commit to delivering the specified commodity and receiving the full value of the futures contract, both at the specified time in the future.

Thus, the "margin" on futures contracts represents only earnest money or collateral, guaranteeing that the spot transaction will be made at the specified time in the future, if the futures position is still held at that time. Consequently, the difference between the value of the futures contract and the margin need not be borrowed by the borrower and no interest is paid on the difference since there is no loan at the time the futures position is entered into.

Margins on futures contracts are low, typically 5% of the contract value or less. This alone would seem to indicate that the futures contract between the buyer and seller would not be very secure; that is, either the buyer or seller could default on a losing position. However, another margin practice provides security to the futures contract. If the price of the futures contract increases, buyers (longs) profit from the increase and sellers (shorts) lose. While in the spot markets, these profits and losses are not realized until an asset is sold or a liability redeemed, in the futures markets losers must immediately make good for their losses in cash, and these payments are transferred to those who profit on a daily basis. This practice is called "marking to the market."

In the futures markets it is easy for either longs or shorts to liquidate or reverse their positions (i.e., longs sell a futures contract or shorts buy a futures contract) before the settlement or maturity date of the futures contract. If a futures contract is liquidated prior to its settlement date, the position no longer exists. Thus, if liquidated, the long need never put up in cash the full value of the futures contract and accept delivery of the specified commodity, and the short need never make delivery of the specified commodity and accept in cash the value of the futures contract. Additionally, most futures contracts are liquidated or reversed prior to their settlement dates. Thus, the original margins and the payment due to losses or the receipts due to gains are the only transactions in which most buyers and sellers of futures contracts participate.

Due largely to the low margins and the easy reversibility of futures contracts, it is much easier to make transactions in the futures markets than in the spot markets. For this reason and, as a result, due to the diverse participants in the futures markets (hedgers, speculators, and arbitrageurs, as discussed below), the agricultural futures markets have become much more liquid than the spot markets. This has not only made the markets easier for hedgers and speculators to use, and, thus, more liquid, but has also caused the futures markets to be used for *pricing* spot-market transactions in many agricultural commodities.

If the futures markets are more liquid than the spot markets, it seems reasonable to price spot-market transactions off futures prices. Such pricing means that the spot price of future spot-market transactions are set relative to a specific futures price on that date. For example, the price of a corn transaction to be consummated on December 13, 1983 may be set at $0.10 over the price of the December 1983 Chicago Board of Trade corn futures contract on that date.

Prior to the development of financial futures markets, agricultural futures had become an integral part of the spot markets for those same agricultural commodities due to their hedging and pricing functions and not due to their speculative uses. The commercial need for these futures markets is greater when the prices of the agricultural commodities are more volatile.

THE ADVENT OF FINANCIAL FUTURES.[2] For a variety of reasons, interest rates, and hence the prices of debt securities, were relatively stable from the end of World War II until the beginning of the 1960s. The first highly volatile postwar interest-rate episode occurred during the "credit crunch" of 1966. Subsequently, there were periods of much greater interest-rate volatility during 1969, 1973, and 1974.

It seems no accident that soon after the volatile interest-rate periods of 1973 and 1974 the first interest-rate futures contract was initiated in 1975. The GNMA (Government National Mortgage Association) futures contract was offered by the Chicago Board of Trade (CBT) on October 20, 1975. Soon after that, the International Monetary Market (IMM) of the Chicago Mercantile Exchange (CME) initiated a futures contract based on a 90-day U.S. Treasury bill on January 6, 1976. Approximately 1½ years later, on August 22, 1977, the CBT initiated a futures contract on 20-year U.S. Treasury bonds.

[2]While the first financial futures contracts were the foreign currency futures contracts initiated by the International Monetary Market of the Chicago Mercantile Exchange in 1972, this chapter considers only futures contracts based on debt and, more recently, equity indexes.

A chronology of the dates of the Commodity Futures Trading Commission (CFTC) approval and initial trading by an exchange is provided in Tables 1–3 for interest-rate futures contracts, foreign currency futures contracts, and stock index futures contracts, respectively.

While these futures contracts were initially greeted with skepticism by participants in the fixed income markets, they soon became integral parts of their related fixed income cash markets, just as agricultural futures markets had become integral parts of the agricultural cash markets.

These interest-rate futures markets were initially described as revolutionary and innovative. On the contrary, the advent of interest-rate futures markets was long overdue. It always seemed surprising that the world's most sophisticated financial system lacked a market for the deferred delivery of debt and equity securities, even though this country's agricultural markets had long had such deferred delivery markets.

TABLE 1. Interest-Rate Futures Contracts Designated by the CFTC as of September 1982

Instrument	Exchange	Date of Designation	Date First Traded
GNMA (CDR)	CBOT	9/11/75	10/20/75
Treasury bills (90-day)	CME	11/26/75	1/06/76
Commercial paper (90-day)	CBOT	7/12/77	9/26/77
Treasury bonds (15-year)	CBOT	8/02/77	8/22/77
GNMA (CD)[a]	ACE	8/22/78	9/12/78
Treasury bills (1-year)	CME	8/25/78	9/11/78
Commercial paper (30-day)	CBOT	9/11/78	5/14/79
GNMA (CD)	CBOT	9/11/78	9/12/78
Treasury bills (90-day)[a]	ACE	6/19/79	6/26/79
Treasury bills (90-day)	COMEX	6/19/79	10/20/79
Treasury notes (4–6 year)	CBOT	6/19/79	6/25/79
Treasury notes (3½–4½ year)	CME	6/19/79	7/10/79
GNMA (CD)	COMEX	10/16/79	11/13/79
Treasury bonds (20-year)[a]	ACE	10/16/79	11/14/79
Treasury bills (90-day)	NYFE	7/15/80	8/14/80
Treasury bonds (20-year)	NYFE	7/15/80	8/07/80
Treasury notes (2-year)	COMEX	9/30/80	12/02/80
Domestic CD	NYFE	6/30/81	7/09/81
Domestic CD	CBOT	7/21/81	7/22/81
Domestic CD	CME	7/28/81	7/29/81
Treasury bonds (15-year)	MACE	9/09/81	9/18/81
Treasury notes (long-term)	CBOT	9/23/81	5/03/82
GNMA (CD)	NYFE	9/23/81	—
Treasury notes (short-term)	CBOT	9/30/81	—
Eurodollars	CME	12/08/81	12/09/81
Eurodollars	CBOT	12/15/81	—
Eurodollars	NYFE	12/15/81	—
Treasury bills (90-day)	MACE	3/29/82	4/02/82
Treasury bills (6-month)	CME	9/21/82	—

[a]These contracts ceased trading when ACE terminated operations.

TABLE 2. Foreign Currency Futures Designated by the CFTC as of September 1982

Instrument	Exchange	Date of Designation	Date First Traded
Belgian franc	NYME	7/18/75	9/12/74
British pound	CME	7/18/75	5/16/72
	NYME	7/18/75	9/12/74
	NYFE	5/28/80	8/07/80
Canadian dollar	CME	7/18/75	5/16/72
	NYME	7/18/75	9/12/74
	NYFE	5/28/80	8/07/80
Deutsche mark	CME	7/18/75	5/16/72
	NYME	7/18/75	9/12/74
	NYFE	5/28/80	8/07/80
Dutch guilder	CME	7/18/75	5/16/73
	NYME	7/18/75	9/12/74
French franc	CME	7/18/75	9/23/74
Italian lira	NYME	7/18/75	9/12/74
	CME	9/30/81	—
Japanese yen	CME	7/18/75	5/16/72
	NYME	7/18/75	9/12/74
	NYFE	5/28/80	8/07/80
Mexican peso	CME	7/18/75	5/16/72
	NYME	7/18/75	9/12/74
Swiss franc	CME	7/18/75	5/16/72
	NYME	7/18/75	9/12/74
	NYFE	5/28/80	8/07/80

The earliest significant users of the interest-rate futures markets were the U.S. Treasury security dealers, the most sophisticated participants in the cash markets. The participation of these individuals in the futures markets greatly benefited the development of these futures markets.

THE DEVELOPMENT OF THE FINANCIAL FUTURES MARKETS. The development of the debt and equity futures markets can be considered relative to the structure of the cash markets for debt and equity securities. As shown in Table 4 the cash markets can be divided into the debt and equity markets. The debt markets can then be divided according to two variables—the maturity and the degree of credit risk of the issuer. The maturity can then be subdivided into short term, intermediate term, and long term. The most important distinction with respect to the credit risk of the issues is whether it is public credit, that is, U.S. Government credit or private credit which in most cases is corporate credit. Of course, while public credit is homogeneous—U.S. Government securities are all considered as virtually "riskless"—there are many gradations of private credit

TABLE 3. Stock Index Futures Contracts Designated by the CFTC as of September 1982

Instrument	Exchange	Date of Designation	Date First Traded
Value Line Average Stock Index	KCBT	2/16/82	2/24/82
Standard & Poors 500 Stock Index	CME	4/20/82	4/21/82
COMEX 500 Stock Index	COMEX	4/28/82	—
NYSE Composite Index	NYFE	5/04/82	5/06/82
CBT Stock Market Index	CBT	5/13/82	—
NYSE Financial Sector Stock Index	NYFE	9/21/82	—
NYSE Utility Sector Stock Index	NYFE	9/21/82	—
NYSE Industrial Sector Stock Index	NYFE	9/21/82	—

risk. For example, for long-term corporate debt, private credit risk varies from AAA to C as rated by Standard & Poors.

The chronological development of the debt and equity futures markets can be considered with respect to the structure in Table 4, as shown in Table 5. The first interest-rate futures contract was developed at the CBT in 1975, and listed for trading on October 20, 1975. This contract was based on an intermediate-term public security, the GNMA.

In many ways, the GNMA was not an obvious choice as the basis for the first interest-rate futures contract. The GNMA was a relatively new instrument (the GNMA security was initiated by the U.S. Government National Mortgage Association during 1972) and a relatively complicated instrument. However, there was a considerable interest-rate risk exposure borne by the originators of mortgages that could be hedged by such a futures contract. The developer of this futures contract received a research grant from the Federal Home Loan Bank of San Francisco during his doctoral studies to examine the feasibility of a GNMA futures contract to hedge such mortgage-originator exposure.

TABLE 4. Structure of Cash Debt and Equity Markets

Debt	Public Issuer (government)	Private Issuer
Short term		
Intermediate term		
Long term		
Equity		

TABLE 5. Development of Financial Futures Contracts[a]

	Public	Private
Short-term debt	(2) 90-day Treasury bill (IMM: 1/76)	(4) 90-day bank CD (IMM: 8/81) (5) 90-day Eurodollar[b] (IMM: 12/81)
Intermediate-term debt	(1) GNMA (CDR) (CBT: 9/75) (6) 10-year Treasury note (CBT: 5/82)	
Long-term debt	(3) 20-year Treasury bond (CBT: 8/77)	
Equity	Not applicable	(7)–(9) Stock indexes (KCBT: 2/82, IMM: 4/82, NYFE: 5/82)

[a]Foreign currency futures were initiated by the IMM in 1972. Exchanges other than the four indicated here listed contracts on these same products which failed (see Table 8). These and other exchanges not indicated here listed contracts on other products which failed. Among them are: C.P. (30- and 90-day), 1-year Treasury bill; 4-year Treasury note; 2-year Treasury note, and GNMA (CD) (see Table 8).
[b]First futures contract based on cash settlement.

The GNMA futures contract was also a relatively complicated futures contract. It, in many ways, was a hybrid of the CBT's futures contracts on grains and on plywood, developed in this way to facilitate the understanding of the new futures contract by government regulators and by the CBT floor traders.[3]

Three months after the initiation of the GNMA futures contract, the IMM initiated a futures contract based on 90-day Treasury bills on January 6, 1976. In many ways, this seemed a more obvious choice for an interest-rate futures contract. Ninety-day Treasury bills had been regularly issued, widely held, and actively traded for a considerable time. On the other hand, the "originator" or issuer of Treasury bills, the U.S. Treasury, was not a likely hedger. The design of the Treasury bill futures contract was tailored quite closely to the practices in the primary and secondary markets for Treasury bills and was, indeed, relatively simple.

The fact that the CBT initiated a GNMA futures contract and that the CME developed a 90-day Treasury bill contract was consistent with their heritage of a high degree of specialization according to whether the underlying products were "storable" or "perishable."

Storable products can be delivered on any of several consecutively maturing futures contracts because they can be stored and retain the characteristics nec-

[3]R. L. Sandor and H. Sosin, "Inventive Activity in Futures Markets: A Case Study of the Development of the First Interest Rate Futures Market," July 1980 (unpublished paper).

essary to be deliverable on these consecutive futures contracts. Grain is an example of a storable product. For example, soybeans received from January 83 delivery could be stored and redelivered on the following March, May, July, or much later futures contracts. Delivery of any storable product can be taken on a nearby long futures position and the product can then be redelivered on a deferred short futures position.

Perishable products however, cannot be delivered on any of several consecutively maturing futures contracts because they do not retain the deliverable characteristics, that is, they perish in the interim. For example, cattle can be delivered on one, and only one, futures contract because they meet the quality standards of the contract for only a short time during their life. Similarly, perishable products cannot be taken on delivery using nearby long position and redelivered against a deferred short position because, again, they perish in the interim.

Most of the successful futures contracts of the CBT were based on storable products, such as the grains, before the initiation of interest-rate futures contracts. The CME, on the other hand, had achieved success mainly in nonstorable products, such as cattle, before the initiation of their first interest-rate futures contract. Thus, the fact was not accidental that the first CBT interest-rate contract was based on the GNMA, which is "storable," and even more so that the GNMA contract was written in a manner similar to their grain and lumber contracts. Neither was it accidental that the CME's first interest-rate futures contract, the Treasury bill contract, was based on the "perishable" Treasury bill.

Approximately 19 months after the IMM listed the Treasury-bill futures contract, on August 22, 1977, the CBT listed a futures contract based on long-term U.S. Treasury bonds. This contract grew very quickly from its initiation and is currently the largest futures contract both in terms of open interest and trading volume.

Thus the first three interest-rate futures contracts introduced became successful. In addition, they represented three different maturity ranges, the intermediate term, short term, and long term, chronologically. All three were based on public debt; that is, none of the first three interest-rate futures contracts was based on private debt.

A SERIES OF FAILURES. After the first three interest-rate futures contracts listed succeeded, a high degree of euphoria existed concerning new interest-rate futures contracts. However, after the onset of the Treasury-bond futures contract, 4 years passed before the initiation of another successful interest-rate futures contract. During this time, there were several failures—failures of new types of contracts and failures of other exchanges imitating the existing successful contracts.

Soon after the initiation of the CBT's Treasury-bond futures contract, the CBT listed a 90-day commercial paper contract, on September 26, 1977, and the IMM listed a 1-year Treasury-bill futures contract on September 11, 1978. Neither achieved success. The reasons for their failures are, most likely, quite different.

The 1-year Treasury-bill futures contract was based on another public security, the 1-year U.S. Treasury bill. However, the trading activity in the cash market for 1-year Treasury bills was substantially less than the 90-day U.S. Treasury bills. In addition, a 1-year Treasury-bill futures contract could be synthesized by "stripping" four consecutive 90-day Treasury-bill futures contracts. For example, during April 1982, a March 1983 1-year Treasury-bill futures contract is equivalent to a June 1982 cash Treasury bill and a sequence of June, September, and December, 1982 90-day U.S. Treasury-bill futures contracts. Thus, in some ways, the 1-year U.S. Treasury-bill futures contract provided no new hedging or trading opportunities.

The analysis of the failure of the 90-day commercial paper contract is more interesting. Among the reasons for the failure were (1) There is no secondary market for commercial paper (this is particularly important since the major early users of the GNMA, Treasury bill and Treasury bond futures contracts were the secondary dealers in those instruments). (2) Most commercial paper is issued with a 30-day maturity rather than with a 90-day maturity. (3) There was already a 90-day instrument hedging vehicle with the 90-day Treasury-bill futures contract. (4) This was the first interest-rate futures contract based on private credit.

Consider in more detail the fourth reason, which was considered by many to be the determining reason for the failure. Public securities, that is U.S. Treasury securities, have virtually no credit risk. On the other hand, private securities have varying degrees of credit risk depending on the identity of the issuer. In order to have an adequate deliverable supply on a futures contract based on private securities, the securities of several different issuers have to be specified as deliverable. Thus securities of necessarily different credit risks are deliverable.

Obviously, the greater the credit risk of a security the higher the interest rate. Since all futures contracts are based on seller's, or short's, option, the seller will choose to deliver the cheapest deliverable security, that is, the security with the highest interest rate or the highest credit risk. Thus the futures contract will trade-off (or price-off) the deliverable security with the highest credit risk.

Many analysts, due to the failure of the CBT's 90-day commercial paper futures contract, concluded that a futures contract based on private securities could not succeed because of the heterogeneity of credit risks of deliverable securities and the uncertainty of the long regarding the credit risk of the deliverable securities. Related to this, the CBT declared two new issuers of commercial paper deliverable which had a higher credit risk than any of the previously deliverable issuers of commercial paper after the contract had begun trading. These newly added issues thus became the cheapest deliverable issues on the futures contract and reduced the futures contract price because it increased the degree of credit risk of the deliverable securities. This addition of new issuers undoubtedly affected the confidence of some users of the contract in the contract's performance.

Thus, it remained to be seen whether this 90-day commercial paper futures contract failed due to the heterogeneity of credit risk on the deliverable securities and, if so, whether this meant that no contract based on private credit could succeed, as many asserted. Of course, the alternative hypothesis, that one or more of the first three potential reasons for failure were the actual reason(s), might also have been true.

It is likely however, that the CBT commercial paper contract failed due to the absence of a secondary market for commercial paper and, thus, the absence of any dealers to use the futures contract. The way that the list of the deliverable commercial paper was chosen in the futures contract and subsequently changed may also have contributed to its problems.

During June and July 1979 two 4-year Treasury-note futures contracts were initiated by the IMM and the CBT (actually the IMM contract was based on Treasury notes with 4½–5½ years to maturity and the CBT contract had 4–6 years to maturity). Both failed. The next era of interest-rate futures contracts was by additional existing exchanges or *de nov* futures exchanges entering the interest-rate futures area.

New exchanges attempted to get into the interest-rate futures market. First, on September 12, 1978, the American Commodities Exchange (ACE), a wholly owned subsidiary of the American Stock Exchange, began trading contracts on the GNMA-CD (Certificate of Delivery), a new type of GNMA contract based on delivery of an actual GNMA certificate rather than a depository receipt, as was the CBT GNMA-CDR contract. This was thought to be a significant improvement in contract design over the GNMA-CDR. In fact, this perception was so common that the CBT also filed a contract on a GNMA-CD which was approved by the CFTC at essentially the same time as the ACE's contract and began trading on the same day. Although both contracts started trading at essentially the same time and each achieved some early trading volume, neither became successful. The question resulting from this experience was "Can a newly listed contract, even one with superior technical design, supplant a previously listed contract of the same general type which already has a high degree of liquidity?"

The ACE also listed the Treasury-bill and Treasury-bond futures contract during 1979, but neither could compete successfully with their Chicago counterparts. Subsequently, the ACE terminated operations during 1980 and the ACE members were given the opportunity to become members of the New York Futures Exchange, mentioned below.

COMEX, the preeminent metals trading exchange also attempted to enter the interest-rate futures markets during 1979. On October 20, 1979, COMEX listed a 90-day Treasury-bill contract and on November 13, 1979 a GNMA-CD contract. Finally, on December 2, 1980 COMEX listed a 2-year Treasury-note contract. None of these contracts succeeded.

Finally, the New York Futures Exchange, a wholly owned subsidiary of the New York Stock Exchange entered the interest-rate futures markets and foreign currency futures markets during 1980. Amid much publicity, the New York Futures Exchange listed futures contracts based on the same five foreign currencies traded successfully by the IMM, a 90-day Treasury bill, and a 20-year Treasury bond during August, 1980. Despite initial success, particularly in the Treasury-bond futures contract, none is currently active.

By mid-1981 many observers, having witnessed the failure of several interest-rate futures contracts listed during the 4-year period from mid-1977 to mid-1981, began to believe that there would be no new successful interest-rate futures contracts. And, in particular, the skepticism regarding the prospects for interest-rate futures contracts based on private securities increased.

In fact, rationale were developed that no new interest-rate futures contracts were needed. There are two essential ingredients of an interest-rate futures contract for hedging use. The first is liquidity, and the second is low basis risk. Additional futures contracts based on new types of underlying securities would decrease the degree of basis risk for a particular hedge, thus improving the hedging performance of a futures contract.

However, by fragmenting hedge and speculative users of futures contracts among more and more futures contracts, it would be harder for new futures contracts to achieve liquidity and each of many futures contracts may be less liquid than each of fewer futures contracts. Given that analysis can be done to minimize the degree of basis risk, but that there is no cure for illiquidity, it can be argued that it is better to have a few liquid contracts than a myriad of moderately liquid or illiquid contracts. Thus, it could be argued, the onus is on the hedge users of the existing financial futures contracts to better understand cash–cash and cash–futures interest-rate relationships, thus being better able to hedge the interest-rate exposure of several different securities with the few existing interest-rate futures contracts.

During early 1981, after the consecutive failures of so many financial futures contracts, the market began to accept the fact that there may be no more successful interest-rate futures contracts. In particular, the skepticism increased regarding the prospects for interest-rate futures contracts based on private debt.

THE SECOND WAVE OF SUCCESSFUL CONTRACTS. However, beginning in August 1981 a series of successful interest-rate futures contracts were introduced.

Bank CD Futures Contracts. An important development was the introduction of futures contracts based on 90-day commercial bank Certificates of Deposit (CDs), which are private securities. Such contracts were listed by the NYFE, the IMM, and the CBT on July 9, 22, and 29, 1981 respectively. The competition among these three exchanges for this new product was closely monitored by the press and the public. Although the NYFE contract was listed first, was initially quite successful, and had an early lead in commercial participation, the IMM contract soon thereafter became the dominant contract in this market. Today, only the IMM contract is trading and, indeed, quite successfully.

The reasons commonly ascribed to the success of the IMM contract were the superior floor resources of the IMM and the ability of the IMM floor traders to spread the CD against the Treasury bill to hedge their CD risk. In addition, as mentioned above, the IMM floor was well-experienced in trading perishable instruments, which the bank CD is.

Since it was thought, particularly in view of the CBT commercial paper experience, that a futures contract based on private credit could not succeed, it is interesting to consider how private credit was handled in the CD contracts, the first successful contract based on private credit. The banks whose CDs were deliverable on the NYFE and IMM contracts were determined by a mechanism whereby the exchange itself did not specify the lists of deliverable banks, but used a practice among the dealers in bank CDs to determine the deliverable lists. Secondary market CD dealers have a practice to facilitate the liquidity of their CD secondary market whereby the "top-tier" or "on-the-run" CDs, the most credit-worthy banks, are all traded at the same rate, and, in fact, the CD of any one of these on-the-run banks is accepted for a bid for any on the list. This list of banks is called the "no-name" list. Thus the bids and offers among dealers for no-name banks apply to any bank on the list and delivery on these bids would be accepted of any bank on this list. Banks with more credit risk than the on-the-run banks would be traded on the "named" basis only; that is, bids and offers would apply only to the specified bank.

The NYFE and IMM contracts specified that the CDs deliverable on a contract would be the dealers' no-name list. Periodically, a survey of the dealers would be taken by the exchange to determine the list of CDs deliverable on the contract. In this way, the market itself, specifically the dealers, rather than the exchange, would determine the deliverable list. This mechanism proved successful when initiating the futures contract based on private debt. Finally, a futures contract based on private debt had succeeded, and the contract design was a significant aspect of this success.

Eurodollar Futures Contract. Another interesting development in interest-rate futures occurred later in 1981. Eurodollar futures contracts had been widely discussed for several years. One aspect of the consideration of the Eurodollar futures contract was that during 1981 the CFTC was in receipt of Eurodollar futures contracts from the CBT, the IMM, and NYFE of quite different contract designs. The CBT contract was based on the delivery of "Eurodollar CDs," which were Eurodollar securities very much like U.S. bank CDs and traded on a secondary market. On the other hand, the IMM contract was based on the delivery of Eurodollar time deposits of banks which were not transferable and which were not traded on a secondary market. The NYFE contract was based on cash settlement, a new concept in interest-rate futures (although equity futures contracts, discussed below, had previously been submitted to the CFTC based on cash settlement).

The potential disadvantage of the Eurodollar CD futures contract was the small size of the market and the concern over the adequacy of deliverable supply. The potential limitation of the Eurodollar TD futures contract was the nontransferability of the underlying security.

The disadvantage of the cash settlement futures contract was that no such contract had previously been approved by the CFTC. The cash settlement procedure, as specified by the NYFE contract, was based on taking the average of the offer rates for 90-day deposits from the principal London offices of several major banks in the Eurodollar TD market. Before these quotes were averaged, the high and the low quotes would be eliminated.

An advantage of this cash settlement procedure for futures contracts based on private credit is that while futures contracts normally trade at the cheapest or the lowest common denominator, a contract based on such a cash settlement specification trades to the average bank rates. Thus there would be less basis risk if one bank was particularly weak relative to the others. Before the approval of their contracts, both the IMM and the CBT changed their Eurodollar submissions to cash settlement.[4]

While all three contracts were approved during a short-time period during December 1981, only the IMM listed their Eurodollar futures contract, on December 9, 1981. While this contract has, perhaps, not traded to the level expected, the trading volume has been consistent at a reasonable level and the open interest continues to be significant.

[4]For a more detailed discussion of cash settlement, see F. J. Jones, "The Economics of Futures and Options Contracts Based on Cash Settlement," *Journal of Futures Markets* (Volume 2).

10-Year Treasury Note. Next, on May 3, 1982 the CBT successfully launched a new intermediate-term Treasury-note futures contract, based specifically on the Treasury notes with 7–10 years maturity. This contract had a record first-day trading volume—31,872—with a large initial open interest—and continues to trade quite well. It appears to have filled the need for an instrument in the intermediate maturity range.

Overview of Successful Contracts Based on Debt. With respect to Table 5, there are currently successful futures contracts based on short-, long-, and intermediate-public debt and two successful futures contracts based on short-term private debt. What are the prospects for futures contracts based on intermediate-term and long-term private debt? Probably not very good. Although futures contracts have been discussed on intermediate-term and long-term private debt (in fact a contract based on long-term private debt, specifically AAA AT&T majority-owned debentures, was submitted by NYFE to the CFTC), due to the heterogeneity of intermediate-term and long-term corporate bonds and notes, it is difficult to design futures contracts based on such instruments. It seems that the intermediate- and long-term public-debt futures contracts will continue to be used to hedge corporate counterparts.

THE USES AND USERS OF THE INTEREST-RATE FUTURES CONTRACTS. The initial users of each futures contract were the secondary market dealers in the specific underlying securities, initially, U.S. Government securities, and later bank CD dealers and Eurodollar dealers. These dealers certainly used financial futures contracts to trade for a profit, as they used the cash market securities.

The dealers also used the interest-rate futures contracts to hedge their portfolios. Dealers buy for and sell from their portfolios. Thus, in order to make markets, that is, to be able to sell securities, they must maintain an inventory.

Dealers have three sources of profits. The difference between the bid/ask quotation, the spread, is their "bread-and-butter" source of profits. They may also profit from the "carry" on their portfolio. If the cost of financing their portfolio (usually the repo rate) is less than the interest-rate return on the securities in their portfolio, they profit on the financing from carrying the securities. This is the case if the yield curve is upward sloping, that is, long-term interest rates are greater than short-term rates. In the opposite case, with a downward-sloping yield curve, the result is "carry loss" rather than carry profit.

The third source of profit or loss for these dealers is the capital gains or capital losses from changes in the value of the securities in their portfolio. Specifically, when interest rates go up, prices on their securities in their portfolio go down, and the dealers experience a loss. In particularly volatile times, the losses on the portfolio position may exceed the profits from the bid/ask spread and the carry.

So dealers, to a significant extent, have locked in the profits from the bid/ask spread and carry by hedging the inventory values of their portfolios by using the interest-rate futures markets. As a specific example, U.S. Government securities dealers have said that, due to hedging, they are able to bid more aggressively at U.S. Treasury auctions for U.S. Treasury securities to keep in their portfolios until they are able to distribute them. They are able to hedge their "takedown" at the auction from the time they are awarded securities by the U.S. Treasury until they are able to actually distribute the securities to the customers. Nondealer hedgers have also become active in the interest-rate futures markets, as indicated below.

In addition, the speculative use of interest-rate futures markets has increased significantly, by introducing a whole new class of speculators into the overall futures markets. Prior to 1975, only those familiar with the agricultural and metal markets (and after 1972 the foreign currency markets) speculated in the financial futures markets. However, after 1975 anyone, particularly those in the business community, who had a view on interest rates could speculate on the basis of this view in the financial futures markets. Thus the advent of interest-rate futures substantially expanded the potential speculative use of the financial futures markets. (Some data on the increase in the trading volume in the interest-rate futures markets since their inception are considered below.)

In many ways, the interest-rate futures markets developed in the same way as the agricultural futures markets. The interest-rate futures markets quickly became very liquid as a result of broad participation by dealers, other hedgers, speculators, and arbitrageurs. Approximately 2 years ago, a U.S. Treasury security dealer said that the futures markets on Treasury bonds and Treasury bills were more liquid than the corresponding cash markets for Treasury bonds and Treasury bills. His statement was viewed with skepticism. Now this observation is accepted as a truism.

The trading volume in the interest-rate futures markets is greater than the corresponding trading volume in the cash markets. Specifically, the average daily trading volume of Treasury-bill and Treasury-bond futures has been approximately $30 billion and $5 billion, respectively, while the average daily trading volume of Treasury bills and bonds in the cash markets has been $5 billion and $10 billion, respectively. In addition, it is easier to make sizable transactions in the futures markets than in the corresponding cash markets without "moving the market." The interest-rate futures markets for Treasury bonds and bills are undoubtedly more liquid than the cash markets for Treasury bonds and bills.

This liquidity also provides another important function for the interest-rate futures market—they are widely used for "pricing." Government securities dealers have said that when making markets (bids and offers) for normal sizes in the Treasury-bond and Treasury-bill cash markets, they may or may not pay attention to the corresponding futures markets, depending on their view of the market. However, they say, when making bids or offers for larger than normal sizes, they always look at the interest-rate futures markets at least to observe where the futures price is. They do so because the interest-rate futures markets are more liquid than the cash market and they also want to base the quote (bid or offer) for the less-liquid cash market relative to where the more-liquid futures price is. In addition, they may also use the market to hedge this transaction. But, they say, they always use the futures market as a basis for pricing.

Another important class of market users, mentioned above, is the "arbitrageur." There is a definite conceptual relationship between the futures price and the cash price of the underlying securities, as discussed below. Arbitrageurs evaluate the relationships between futures market prices and cash market prices and engage in transactions to profit from discrepancies between the two prices. For example, if the futures price is "cheaper" than it should be relative to the cash market price, the arbitraguer will buy the cheaper futures contract and sell the cash-market security until the relative prices "come into line" and, thereby, profit. Arbitrageurs conduct the opposite transactions in the opposite case.

In general, arbitrageurs provide an important function in the futures market, that is, correct pricing. In order for futures markets to be useful for hedgers, both long and short hedgers, the prices have to be "right" relative to cash-market prices. Futures prices which are too high may be good for short hedgers, but they would not be good for long hedgers; similarly if futures prices are too low they would be good for long hedgers, but not for short hedgers. Arbitrageurs tend to make futures prices "right" relative to the cash market prices, so that the futures prices are useful to both long hedgers and short hedgers.

THE STRUCTURE OF THE INTEREST-RATE FUTURES MARKETS. The structure of the interest-rate futures markets can be thought of as a tripod, as shown in Table 6. At the top of the tripod is the main intended user of the interest-rate futures markets, the commercial hedgers, which may be dealers, banks, or other hedgers. The intended purpose of any futures contract is hedging. Table 7 provides some categories of actual hedge users of the interest-rate futures markets.

The next two parts of the tripod are speculators. There are two important types of speculators. The on-floor speculators are the market makers whose sole occupation is making markets on the floor of the exchange that trades the futures contract. The on-floor speculator, or market maker, is essential in providing liquidity to futures markets.

Another very different type of speculator is the off-floor speculator. These are

TABLE 6. Structure of Financial Futures Markets

Commercial Users

Hedgers (Used for risk aversion)
- Banks
  - —Trading department
  - —Liability
  - —Portfolio
  - —Trust
- S & Ls
- Dealers
- Pensions
- Corporations

Arbitrageurs
- —Access to both cash and futures

"On-floor"	"Off-floor"
Scalpers or market makers	Retail speculators
—Provide liquidity	—Risk takers
—Take short-term positions	—Take longer-term positions
	—Proverbial "Doctor from Dubuque"

TABLE 7. Examples of Actual Uses and Users of Financial Futures

1. Treasury security and CD dealers, including commercial banks hedging their portfolios of Treasury bills, Treasury notes, Treasury bonds, GNMAs, and CDs.
2. Treasury security dealers for *pricing* their purchases and sales.
3. Investment banks hedging underwriting of *corporate* bonds.
4. Corporations hedging future issues of C.P.
5. Banks hedging future issues of CDs.
6. Banks funding a term loan (e.g., 1-year) by selling a strip of CD (or Treasury bill) futures to hedge future issues of 90-day CDs or rollovers of 90-day CDs to fund the term loan.
7. Bond portfolio managers hedging against increasing interest rates.
8. Municipal-bond underwriters hedging underwritings.
9. Dealers for arbitrage and trading.
10. Banks for asset/liability mismatch.

the typical retail speculators who attempt to profit by taking a view on the market. A very important distinction between the on-floor and the off-floor speculators, is that the on-floor speculators are market makers, whereas the off-floor speculators are market takers.

As discussed above, another important user of the interest-rate futures markets, which can be thought of at the center of the tripod, is the arbitrageur. The function of the arbitrageur is to profit by providing price corrections to the futures markets. By participating in the futures markets, they also provide liquidity—often a very important source of liquidity.

Overall, the on-floor market makers and arbitrageurs participate in the futures market to provide important functions—liquidity and correct pricing, respectively—and continue to participate in the market only if they profit. Thus, these two types of participants can be thought of as, in aggregate, taking a profit out of the futures markets, although obviously some on-floor speculators and some arbitrageurs lose money and go out of business. Obviously, the other two types of participants, the hedger and the off-floor speculator, pay a premium, in the aggregate, for participating in the futures markets which are transferred through the markets to the on-floor speculator and the hedger.

THE REGULATORY POSTURE. The futures markets have been under the purview of the Commodity Futures Trading Commission (CFTC), an independent regulatory body, since 1975. The initial interest-rate futures contracts, the GNMA, and the Treasury-bill and Treasury-bond futures contracts, were approved by the CFTC after considerable analysis. Little attention was paid by other regulatory bodies such as the Federal Reserve System (the Board of Governors of which is called "the Fed"), the U.S. Department of the Treasury (the "Treasury"), and the Securities Exchange Commission (SEC), to these approvals.

However, as these markets grew, the Fed, the Treasury, and the SEC became very interested and concerned about the initiation of these new markets. Thus, before the next round of interest-rate futures markets were approved, the 1-year U.S. Treasury bill and the intermediate-term U.S. Treasury note, the Fed and the Treasury demonstrated interest and had considerable input.

The Fed and the Treasury were concerned about several aspects of the interest-rate futures markets. First, they were concerned that the markets would be used only by speculators and would thereby potentially increase the volatility of the cash markets. They were also concerned that this aspect and other aspects of the interest-rate futures markets, such as the Treasury's having to issue certain types of debt to provide deliverable supply on futures contracts, would interfere with the process of the Treasury's funding of its debt and, thus, in the overall government financing process. Finally, they were concerned that the use of the interest-rate futures markets would divert funds away from the cash markets, thereby harming not only the government-funding process, but also the private-capital formation process in the country. The SEC had these and also other concerns, as discussed below, with respect to the equity index futures contract.

During the 1978 reauthorization of the CFTC by Congress, there were some attempts to put the regulation of the interest-rate futures contracts under the jurisdiction of the SEC as well as, or in lieu of, the CFTC. While this did not occur, the CFTC was obliged to provide an opportunity for the SEC, the Fed, and the Treasury to comment to the CFTC on any of the financial futures contracts it was considering before the contracts were approved or disapproved. This process has been followed since 1978.

In addition, during 1979 a temporary *de facto* moratorium was imposed on the approval of new interest-rate futures contract by the CFTC, while the Federal Reserve System and the Treasury completed a Fed/Treasury study on the effects of the interest-rate futures markets on the financial system and the economy. When this study began, it appeared to most observers that the views of the Fed and the Treasury toward the interest-rate futures markets would be very negative. In conducting the study, the authors interviewed many actual users of the interest-rate futures market. In particular, they interviewed many U.S. Government securities dealers who used the markets. These dealers informed the Fed/Treasury study authors of the values of the interest-rate futures markets for their market making in U.S. Treasury securities, as described above, and also indicated that the interest-rate futures market made it easier rather than more difficult and costly for the Treasury to finance its debt. Such interviews considerably affected the outcome of the study.

Thus, the Fed/Treasury study turned out to be neutral overall and because it was less negative toward the markets than many expected, it was commonly interpreted as the Fed and Treasury granting approbation of these markets. The following is a quote from the study[5].

> . . . to the extent that financial futures markets encourage more speculation by lowering the cost of doing so, they also lead to the production of a greater amount

[5] *Treasury/Federal Reserve Study of Treasury Futures Markets*, a study by the staffs of the U.S. Treasury and the Federal Reserve System, May 1979, Vol. 1, p. 9.

> of information than would otherwise be available. In other words, while the spot market yield curve may incorporate all available information, that yield curve may itself be altered by the existence of financial futures.

It would be incorrect, however, to state that the study was without severe reservations about the financial futures markets, particularly the proliferation of identical contracts on different exchanges. The concern over deliverable supply was a theme of the study.

After the completion of the Fed/Treasury study, neither the Fed nor the Treasury was concerned about the new interest-rate futures contract for some time. The Fed and Treasury continued to comment, however, on particular contracts, as provided in the 1978 reauthorization. Mostly, however, the comments have concerned the specifications of the contracts, and their more general concerns have been less serious. Recently, the Fed has not recommended against the approval of futures contracts based on securities of direct interest to banks, specifically bank CDs and Eurodollars, by the CFTC.

The U.S. Department of the Treasury became even less concerned during the Reagan administration than it had been during previous administrations about the approval of new interest-rate futures contracts.

The current position was articulated by Deputy Assistant Secretary of the Treasury, Mark E. Stalnecker, before the Subcommittee on Conservation, Credit, and Rural Development of the House Committee on Agriculture, who said

> In summary, we believe that the futures markets, including financial futures, provide important services to the Nation's economy and that the existing regulatory structure should be able to deal with any potential problems. For our part, we will not act to impede the growth and evolution of futures markets, though we will of course continue to monitor developments in these markets and their implications for the Nation's financial markets.

This change in the regulatory posture in Washington set the stage for consideration of equity index futures contracts, which are discussed next.

EQUITY INDEX FUTURES CONTRACTS. The change in regulatory posture described above paved the way for the consideration and approval of the equity index futures contracts. Even though the interest-rate futures contracts had initially been called revolutionary and these contracts had subsequently become an integral part of the financial system, the concept of equity index futures contracts was now considered to be revolutionary.

There were several concerns about equity index futures contracts. The first was the regulatory jurisdiction. According to the 1978 reauthorization of the CFTC, the CFTC had complete jurisdiction over these futures contracts although they were bound to consult with other regulatory agencies before approving new financial contracts. However, some in the SEC, Congress, and elsewhere thought that the SEC should have jurisdiction over futures contract related to stocks or stock indexes. Thus it was not clear whether the CFTC could or would approve stock index futures contracts until this contention was resolved. In fact, a senior staff member of the SEC, informed about the nature of the stock index futures contracts in 1979 said that the futures exchanges "would trade these contracts over my dead body."

The second issue concerned margins. The CFTC has never had authorization to set margins on futures contracts—margins were set solely by the exchanges. Many, however, including some in Congress, thought that the Federal Reserve System and/or the CFTC should set margins on equity index futures contracts.

The third concern related to the cash settlement specified as the means of settling equity index futures contracts. Prior to December 1981, no futures contracts based on cash settlement had been approved by the CFTC.

Many of the states' gaming laws distinguish futures markets from gambling by the requirement of delivery of an actual commodity on futures contracts; consequently, any futures contract based on cash settlement would according to these laws be considered gambling and would thus be illegal. Other observers, however, asserted that the Commodities Exchange Act provides the CFTC with the preemption of all state laws, specifically preempting the state gaming laws which thus have no standing with respect to futures contracts based on cash settlement.

This legal issue, however, was resolved before stock index futures contracts were seriously considered by the CFTC. During December 1981 the CFTC approved three Eurodollar futures contracts based on cash settlement, as discussed above. The CFTC thus ruled that CFTC preemption of state gaming laws applied. There have been no legal repercussions of this decision to date. Some observers continue to assert, however, that the cash settlement aspect of equity index futures contracts relegate these contracts to vehicles for gambling.

Finally, there again arose the concern, in this case more serious, that the advent of stock index futures contracts would affect national capital formation by decreasing the level of investment in the stock market and diverting funds into the stock index futures markets. This, indeed, was a subjective issue.

All of these issues were resolved fairly quickly, if not easily. Two appointees of President Reagan whose policies were consistent with his more laissez-faire approach to government were instrumental in the resolution of these issues. They are CFTC Chairman Philip Johnson and SEC Chairman John Shad. Upon assuming their respective duties, these two men negotiated a pact between the SEC and the CFTC that has come to be called the "Shad/Johnson Agreement" which resolves the jurisdictional issue, the first issue. Among the elements of this agreement were

The SEC would have jurisdiction over options on all securities.

The CFTC would have jurisdiction over all futures contracts based on broadly based and widely accepted stock indexes which were settled in cash.

Neither agency would have jurisdiction over futures contracts based on narrow stock indexes, or on futures contracts on stocks or stock groups which were settled by the actual delivery of stock.

The CFTC would have jurisdiction over options on all futures contracts, and options on physical commodities which were not securities.

This agreement, although it has not yet been completely codified by Congress, satisfied the jurisdictional issue, at least between the SEC and the CFTC.

As indicated above, the cash settlement issue was resolved with the approval of the Eurodollar futures contracts during December 1981.

With respect to the margin issue, Chairman Philip Johnson negotiated with the Board of Governors of the Federal Reserve System, and the Chairman of the Board, Paul Volker. These two men mutually agreed that while the Fed could officially exert jurisdiction over setting margins on equity index futures contracts, that the Fed would not exert such jurisdiction if the exchanges being approved for such contracts would agree to set their initial speculative margins at levels equal to at least 10% of the value of the contracts. As indicated below, all the relevant exchanges have heretofore complied with this requirement and the Fed has withheld the exercise of margin-setting jurisdiction. It should be noted that the margin issue is far from being settled. Chairman Dingell of the House Energy and Commerce Committee, which has jurisdiction over the SEC, noted on April 23, 1982, that "the setting of margin is not something to be negotiated between the Federal government and the sponsoring market . . ." In addition, the Fed is currently engaged in a special study of margin regulation.

The capital formation issue was not dealt with definitively as were the other three concerns, but this did not deter the CFTC's approval (although it may have affected the negative vote in the CFTC's 4-1 vote on these contracts).

The first submission on the stock index futures contracts to the CFTC was by the Kansas City Board of Trade (KCBOT) during 1978 for a futures contract based on the Dow Jones Industrial Average. Since the KCBOT did not have authorization by Dow Jones, Incorporated to use their average, and Dow Jones, Incorporated threatened suit, the KCBOT changed from the Dow Jones Industrial Average. In fact, more than one change was made and the KCBOT contract finally approved by the CFTC was based on the Value Line Composite Index.

The CBT on December 3, 1980 submitted futures contracts based on 10 different industry groups, each of which was composed of five stocks, and an 11th futures contract based on the composite of these 10 industry groups, that is a 50-stock index. The CBT developed the composition of the 10 industry groups and the overall group. Soon thereafter, on January 3, 1981, the IMM of the CME submitted a futures contract based on the S&P 500 Index. Finally, on June 8, 1981, the New York Futures Exchange submitted a futures contract based on the New York Stock Exchange Composite Index and the New York Stock Exchange's four subindexes—the financial, utility, transportation, and industrial subindexes.[6]

With Chairman Philip Johnson having dealt with the jurisdictional and margin issues, the CFTC expeditiously approved the contracts of the KCBOT, the IMM, and the NYFE between February and May 1982. The KCBOT Value Line contract began trading on February 24, 1982, the IMM S&P 500 contract on April 24, 1982, and the NYFE New York Stock Exchange Composite Index on May 6, 1982.

However, the CBT's 11 contracts were not approved by the CFTC because they were not based on broad stock indexes which were widely available, as required by the Shad/Johnson Agreement. Although the CBT changed their futures contract to be based on the Dow Jones Industrial Average, Dow Jones has through

[6]Subsequently, on September 10, 1981, the COMEX submitted a futures contract based on the S&P 500 Index. However, while the IMM had S&P's approval to use their index, the COMEX did not and the IMM, through the courts, has prevented COMEX from using the index.

the courts heretofore prevented the CBT from trading this contract even though it was approved by the CFTC.

Although these equity index futures contracts were approved by the CFTC prior to most observers' expectations, the reader will be pleased to know that the senior SEC staffer referred to previously remains in good health. The change in the regulatory posture and the effectiveness of Chairman Philip Johnson and Chairman John Shad in dealing with these issues was instrumental in the advent of these equity index contracts.

Many potential users of these equity index futures contracts, prior to their approval, thought that the stock index futures market would be even larger than the Treasury-bond futures contracts, then the largest futures contract. It was thought that these contracts would have great interest both for speculative uses and for commercial hedging by professionals. Indeed, the trading volume and open interest on these contracts developed quickly, even more quickly than the Treasury-bond futures contract initially developed. These contracts had significant participation both for speculators and for professional hedgers.

A QUANTITATIVE VIEW OF THE GROWTH OF THE INTEREST-RATE FUTURES MARKETS. The previous sections discuss, in general, the development and growth of the interest-rate and stock index futures markets. As indicated qualitatively, this growth has been significant.

However, it is also interesting to quantify this growth by considering the data on trading volume of these contracts relative to the trading volume of traditional futures contracts over the period since 1977. Such data are provided in Table 8, which includes data on not only the successful contracts, but those which have not been successful.

As indicated in the summary of Table 8, not only has the absolute trading volume of all interest-rate, equity index, and foreign currency futures contracts increased substantially, but the market share, based on the number of contracts traded, of the entire financial futures markets has increased considerably from 3.2% in 1977 to 6.6% in 1978, 10.3% in 1979, 18.1% in 1980, 29.4% in 1981, and up to 36.9% during the first eight months of 1982. In some specific months this market share has been 50%.

These financial futures contracts have obviously made significant penetration into the total futures markets, and more importantly have significantly expanded the futures markets both for speculative and hedging purposes. Most observers expect the share of the total futures markets represented by financial futures to continue to increase. In addition, most observers expect the financial futures to continue to have an integral and beneficial effect on their related cash markets. The relationship between the interest-rate futures markets and their related cash markets is the topic of the next section.

THE DEVELOPMENT OF THE INTERACTIONS BETWEEN THE CASH AND FINANCIAL FUTURES MARKETS

The nature of the interaction between the cash market for a product and its related futures market has been a topic of interest for many people over the past years.

TABLE 8. Financial Futures Contracts Traded January 1977–August 1982

Successful Interest Rate and Equity		1977	1978	1979	1980	1981	January/August 1982
GNMA (CDR):	CBT	422,421	953,161	1,371,078	2,325,892	2,292,882	1,389,214
Treasury bills:	IMM	321,703	768,980	1,930,482	3,338,773	5,631,290	4,631,719
Treasury bonds:	CBT	32,101	555,350	2,059,594	6,489,555	13,907,988	10,723,694
CDs:	IMM	—	—	—	—	423,718	1,170,337
Eurodollar:	IMM	—	—	—	—	15,171	159,462
Treasury note:	CBT	—	—	—	—	—	557,004
Value Line Composite Index:	KCBT	—	—	—	—	—	290,053
S & P 500 Index:	IMM	—	—	—	—	—	1,022,394
NYSE Composite Index:	NYFE	—	—	—	—	—	541,691
Total		776,225	2,277,491	5,361,154	12,154,220	22,271,049	20,485,568

Unsuccessful Interest Rate		1977	1978	1979	1980	1981	January/August 1982
Commercial paper (30-day):	CBT	—	—	1,292	67	—	—
Treasury note (4–6 year):	CBT	—	—	11,599	450	2,721	—
Commercial paper (90-day):	CBT	3,553	18,767	39,702	15,996	49	—
GNMA (CD):	CBT	—	6,527	77,365	12,619	175	—
Bank CD (90-day):	CBT	—	—	—	—	158,920	144,495
Treasury bill (1-year):	IMM	—	5,564	11,769	604	—	—
Treasury note (4-year):	IMM	—	—	11,072	338	—	—
Treasury bill (90-day):	COMEX	—	—	27,860	76,081	1,052	—
Treasury note (2-year):	COMEX	—	—	—	17,653	30,188	—
GNMA (CD):	COMEX	—	—	873	7,403	—	—
GNMA (CD):	ACE	—	16,671	52,493	4,530	—	—
Treasury bill (90-day):	ACE	—	—	4,334	5	—	—
Treasury bond:	ACE	—	—	7,492	8,050	—	—
Treasury bill (90-day):	NYFE	—	—	—	32,452	9,766	—
Treasury bond:	NYFE	—	—	—	139,410	162,942	4,364
Bank CD (90-day):	NYFE	—	—	—	—	117,807	132
Total		3,553	47,529	245,851	315,658	483,620	148,991

Other Interest Rate		1977	1978	1979	1980	1981	January/August 1982
Treasury bond:	MidAmerica	—	—	—	—	109,944	270,498
Treasury bill (90-day):	MidAmerica	—	—	—	—	—	55,492
Total		—	—	—	—	109,944	325,990
Total of all interest-rate and equity contracts		779,778	2,325,020	5,607,005	12,469,878	22,864,613	20,960,549

TABLE 8 (*Continued*)

Successful Foreign Currency		1977	1978	1979	1980	1981	January/August 1982
British pound:	IMM	78,701	240,099	513,682	1,263,750	1,491,102	913,883
Canadian dollar:	IMM	161,139	207,654	399,885	601,925	475,585	728,150
Deutsche mark:	IMM	134,368	400,569	450,856	922,608	1,654,891	1,185,215
Japanese yen:	IMM	82,261	361,731	329,645	575,073	960,598	1,119,640
Swiss franc:	IMM	106,968	321,451	493,944	827,884	1,518,767	1,716,322
Mexican peso:	IMM	17,029	17,844	29,982	19,301	18,905	50,338
French franc:	IMM	3,150	4,449	406	144	2,080	4,814
Total		583,616	1,553,797	2,218,400	4,210,685	6,121,928	5,718,362

Unsuccessful Foreign Currency		1977	1978	1979	1980	1981	January/August 1982
Dutch guilder:	IMM	2,812	3,585	22	4	4	—
British pound:	NYME	—	500	420	—	—	—
Canadian dollar:	NYME	—	181	3,866	—	—	—
Deutsche mark:	NYME	—	1,844	182	—	—	—
Japanese yen:	NYME	—	441	43	—	—	—
Swiss franc:	NYME	—	401	45	—	—	—
British pound:	NYFE	—	—	—	7,352	37	—
Canadian dollar:	NYFE	—	—	—	692	4	—
Deutsche mark:	NYFE	—	—	—	258	3	—
Japanese yen:	NYFE	—	—	—	199	13	—
Swiss franc:	NYFE	—	—	—	3,630	13	—
Total		2,812	6,952	4,578	12,135	74	—
Total of all foreign currency contracts		586,428	1,560,749	2,222,978	4,222,820	6,122,002	5,718,362

Summary	1977	1978	1979	1980	1981	January/August 1982
Total of all interest-rate and equity contracts	779,778	2,325,020	5,607,005	12,469,878	22,864,613	20,960,549
Total of all foreign currency contracts	586,428	1,560,749	2,222,978	4,222,820	6,122,002	5,718,362
Total of all financial contracts (Interest-rate, equity, and foreign currency)	1,366,206	3,885,769	7,829,983	16,692,698	28,986,615	26,678,911
Total of all futures contracts	42,847,064	58,462,172	75,966,471	92,096,109	98,522,371	72,386,784
Percentage of interest-rate and equity contracts to all futures contracts	1.8%	4.0%	7.4%	13.5%	23.2%	29.0%
Percentage of all financial contracts to all futures contracts	3.2%	6.6%	10.3%	18.1%	29.4%	36.9%

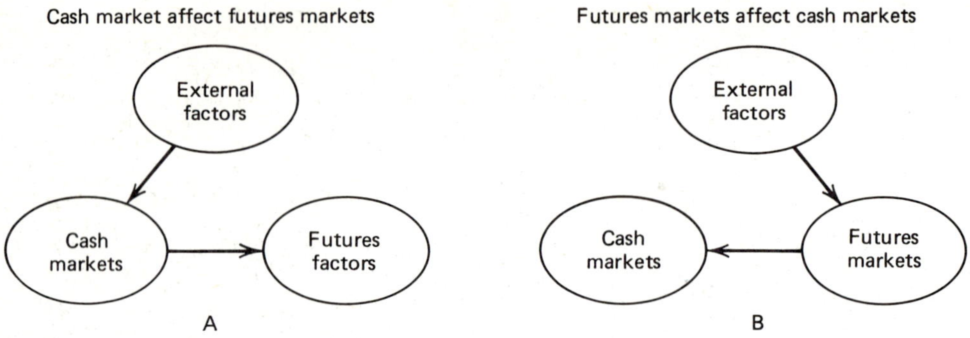

FIGURE 1. Potential relations between cash and futures markets.

Often the related question is phrased as: "Does the cash market affect the futures market?" or "Does the futures market affect the cash market?"

Assuming that there are some external factors that affect one or the other (or both) of these markets, these two views of causality could be depicted as shown in Figure 1, parts A and B respectively.

Consider Figure 1 with respect to the interest-rate futures markets. In this context, the external factors can be considered to be changes in the money supply and other Fed-policy variables, the strength of the economy, the demand and supply of funds in the financial markets, inflationary expectations, and several other factors.

The question concerns the nature of the causality of these external factors on the cash and futures markets for debt or interest-rate instruments. Asserting that cash market affects the futures markets, as shown in Figure 1, part A, assumes that the external factors affect the cash markets, which then affect the futures markets. This relationship assumes that the participants in the cash market are well-informed of the external factors mentioned above and responded quickly to changes in these external factors, thereby affecting the cash market interest rates. It also assumes that the participants in the futures markets observe and respond to the cash market interest rates, but not to the external factors, and on this basis make decisions that affect futures markets interest rates.

On the other hand, asserting that the futures markets affect the cash markets, as shown in Figure 1, part B, assumes that the participants in the futures markets are well-informed of, and respond quickly to, the external factors, causing the futures markets interest rates to change quickly in response to the external factors. It also assumes that participants in the cash markets, while not in contact with the external factors, are aware of changes in the futures markets and respond in ways that cause changes in cash market interest rates.

Early in the development of the interest-rate futures markets, the situation described in Figure 1, part A, may have been the actual situation. However, as indicated above, government securities dealers were early participants and remain important participants in both the cash and the futures markets for government debt instruments. And the government securities dealers are familir are familiar with and respond quickly to the external factors mentioned above. Thus it would

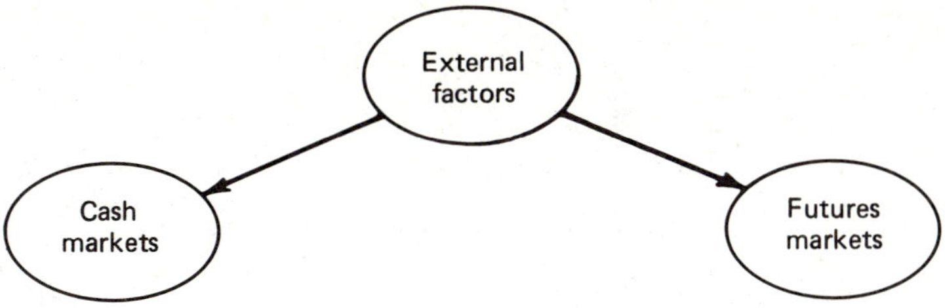

FIGURE 2. External factors affect both cash and futures markets.

seem that neither part A nor part B of Figure 1 accurately describe the relationship between the cash and futures markets.

Rather, it seems that causality shown in Figure 2, that is, the same external factors affect both the cash and the futures markets, is accurate. Certainly government securities dealers and many other participants both in the cash and futures markets for government securities are in close contact with, and respond quickly to, the external factors which affect interest rates. Thus, the external factors directly affect both the cash market and the futures markets, essentially simultaneously.

In this case, is there any direct relationship between the cash and the futures markets? This question is the subject of this section, "The Development of the Interaction Between the Cash and Futures Financial Markets." Do the external factors affect the cash and the futures markets for government securities at the same time and in the same direction without, on the other hand, having any specific direct relationship between the cash and futures market? The answer to this question is "no." While due to the fact that many of the same users are in both the cash and futures markets and thus the same external factors affect both markets, in addition, as now discussed, there are also direct specific relationships between the cash and futures markets. These relationships are the result of arbitrage between the cash and futures markets.

Arbitrage is the consummation of two similar but offsetting transactions which have no or little risk but yet, due to price discrepancies between the two transactions, have profit potential. In this context, arbitrageurs conduct two offsetting transactions between the cash and the futures markets based on the relationships that should prevail between these two markets, thereby profiting from discrepancies between these markets and causing the relationships that should prevail to actually prevail. As shown below, transactions can be made between the cash and futures markets which are essentially identical, or at least very similar; that is, futures markets transactions can synthesize or generate synthetic cash market transactions. Such synthetic transactions, and the actions of arbitrageurs to conduct such types of transactions in an offsetting way, causes an integration of the cash and the futures markets for debt and equity securities, that is, a direct relationship between these two markets, as shown in Figure 3.

Overall, external factors affect both the cash and futures markets and, arbitrage between the cash and futures markets keeps a direct relationship between the two markets, as shown in Figure 3.

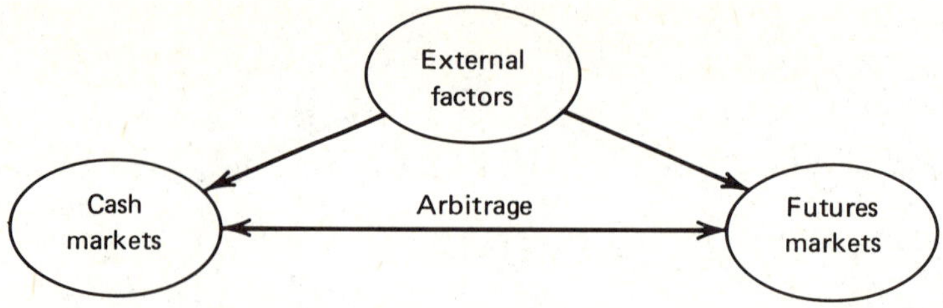

FIGURE 3. Complete relationships between cash and futures markets.

ALTERNATIVE INVESTMENTS (OVER HOLDING PERIOD BEGINNING AT PRESENT).[7] This section discusses mechanisms for achieving riskless returns over a holding period[8] at present. The only mechanism for achieving a riskless investment over a holding period beginning at present by using only the cash markets is to purchase a cash security with a maturity exactly at the end of the intended holding period. Of course, if the investors were willing to accept some risk over their specific holding periods, two other alternatives are available.

First, the investors could purchase a cash security with a maturity longer than the intended holding period and sell the security on the secondary market at the end of the holding period. This technique is called "riding the yield curve." Of course, there is some risk in this strategy because if interest rates increase during the holding period, there will be a capital loss on the security held. This type of risk is the *risk of principal*.

The second cash market mechanism for achieving an investment, with some risk, over a specific holding period, is to buy a cash market security with a maturity shorter than the intended holding period and use the receipts from the maturity value of this security to purchase another cash market security which then matures at or before the end of the intended holding period. If necessary, a sequence of short-maturity cash securities may have to be purchased to complete the holding period. However, if interest rates decline before the maturity of the first security, the interest return on the second security purchased will be less than that on the first; and subsequent securities sequentially purchased during the holding period could experience even lower returns. This type of risk is the *risk of income*.

Thus, by using only the cash markets, a riskless return over a holding period beginning at present can be achieved only by purchasing a cash market security with a maturity exactly at the end of the holding period. However, by using the futures markets, either in conjunction with the cash markets or alone, there are other alternatives for achieving a riskless return over a holding period beginning now. An overview of the types of these alternatives is provided in Table 9.

The first type of alternative is to construct a "synthetic" security of the intended

[7]The sections "Alternative Investments (Over Holding Period Beginning at Present)," "Integration of Cash and the Futures Markets Interest Rates," and "Arbitrage Strategies Revisited" appeared originally in F. J. Jones, "The Integration of the Cash and Futures Markets for Treasury Securities," *The Journal of Futures Markets,* **1**(1), 33–57.

[8]A "holding period" is the period of time between when an investment is made and when the investor plans to terminate or liquidate the investment.

TABLE 9. Various Holding-Period Returns: Holding Period Beginning at Present

Cash Market Only	Joint Use of Cash and Futures Markets
No risk: Buy cash security with maturity exactly at the end of the holding period. With risk: 1. Buy a cash security with maturity longer than the end of the intended holding period and sell the security at end of holding period—this is called "riding the yield curve." However, if interest rates rise during the holding period, there will be a capital loss. This type of risk is a *risk of principal*. 2. Buy a cash security with a maturity shorter than the end of the intended holding period and use the receipts from the maturity value of the security to purchase another cash market security that matures at or before the end of the intended holding period. However, if interest rates decline while the first security purchased is being held, the return on the second security purchased will be lower. This element of risk is a *risk of income*.	1. Construct a "synthetic security" of the desired holding period by purchasing a cash security with a maturity less than the end of the intended holding period and a series of one or more futures contracts, the securities which would be delivered thereon would complete the holding period. This is called a "strip of futures." [See (2) under Alternative Investments in Table 10 for an example.] 2. Construct a "synthetic security" of the desired holding period by purchasing a cash security with a maturity greater than the end of the holding period and selling a futures contract with a maturity at the end of the holding period on which the security held can be delivered. This is called a "hedged yield curve ride." [See (3) and (4) under Alternate Investments in Table 10 for examples.]

holding period by purchasing a cash market security with a maturity less than the end of the holding period and a series of one or more futures contracts, the holdings of the securities which would be delivered thereon and would complete the intended holding period. This technique is called a "strip of futures."

For example, as illustrated in (2) under Alternative Investments Table 10, an investor with an intended holding period on July 20, 1980 from the present to December 20, 1980 could purchase a 2-month cash Treasury bill, which matures on September 20, 1980, and purchase a September 1980 90-day Treasury-bill futures contract. The investor would hold the Treasury bill delivered on the futures contract from September 20 until December 20, 1980, thus completing the 5-month holding period. Longer holding periods provide a larger number of alternative strips of futures.

The first mechanism for achieving a riskless return over a holding period beginning at present, the strip of futures, involves the purchase of a cash security with a maturity shorter than the intended holding period, and taking long positions in one or more futures contracts to extend the holding period to the intended holding period. The second mechanism uses the cash and futures markets in the opposite way. It involves the purchase of a cash security with a maturity longer than the intended holding period and taking a short position in the futures market with a maturity at the end of the intended holding period to shorten the holding period of the cash security to the intended holding period. The second mechanism

TABLE 10. Various Holding-Period Returns: Holding Period Beginning at Present (July 20, 1980)

	Holding Period					
Alternative Investments	July 20, 1980	September 20, 1980	December 20, 1980	March 20, 1981	December 20, 1981	December 1984
Example: Desire a riskless 5-month holding-period investment beginning on July 20, 1980–December 20, 1980.						
1. Pure cash market investment: purchase 5-month December 20, 1980 Treasury bill	5-month cash security—long (July 20, 1980 to December 20, 1980)					
2. "Strip of futures": purchase 2-month September 20, 1980 Treasury bill and a December 1980 3-month Treasury-bill futures contract.	2-month cash security—long (July 20, 1980 to September 20, 1980)	December 1980 3-month Treasury-bill futures contract—long (September 20, 1980 to December 20, 1980)				
3. Hedged yield curve ride with 3-month Treasury-bill futures contract: purchase an 8-month, March 1981 cash Treasury bill and sell a December 1980 3-month Treasury-bill futures contract. (Deliver the cash security, which will have a maturity of 3 months on December 20, 1980.)	8-month cash security—long (July 20, 1980 to March 20, 1981)		December 1980 3-month Treasury-bill futures contract—short			
4. Hedged yield curve ride with Treasury-bond futures contract: purchase a cash 20-year Treasury bond and sell a December 1980 Treasury-bond futures contract. (Deliver the cash security on December 1980 Treasury-bond futures contract.)	July 20, 1980 December 20, 1980 July 20, 2000 20-year cash security—long			December 1980 Treasury-bond futures contract—short		

is a hedge variation of riding the yield curve, and can be considered a "hedged yield-curve ride."

In a yield curve ride, the investor purchases a security with a maturity longer than the intended holding period and sells the security on the secondary market at the end of the intended holding period. The sales price of the security depends on cash market conditions at the time of the sale and this strategy is, therefore, subject to risk. However, by selling a futures contract whose maturity is the same as the end of the intended holding period and which permits the delivery of the cash market security at the maturity of the futures contract, the sales price of the cash market security can be locked-in at the time it is purchased. By selling a futures contract upon which the cash market security can be delivered at the maturity of the futures contract, which is also the end of the holding period, the investor has essentially locked-in the sale price of the cash security, thereby making the yield curve ride riskless, thus a "hedged yield curve ride."

A hedged yield curve ride, thus, is buying a cash security, holding or "carrying" it, and delivering it on a short futures position. This mechanism is utilized by the grain and metals markets and is called a "cash and carry." Basically, this mechanism represents an intertemporal arbitrage. Thus a hedged yield curve ride is equivalent to a cash and carry.[9]

Under (3) and (4) in Alternative Investments in Table 10 is illustrated hedged yield curve rides over the holding period from July 20, 1980 through December 20, 1980 by using 90-day Treasury-bill and 20-year Treasury-bond futures contracts, respectively.

Overall, an investor desiring to make a riskless investment over the holding period from July 20, 1980 through December 20, 1980 can choose among alternatives (1)–(4) in Table 10. Alternative (1) is a pure cash market investment; alternative (2) is a strip of futures; and alternatives (3) and (4) are hedged yield curves rides. An investor with this holding period would calculate the return on each of these alternative investments and select the alternative with the highest return, since all the alternatives are riskless. The choice among these various alternatives results in the purchase or sale of different cash market securities, different futures contracts, and different contract months of the same futures contracts and, thus, the cash and futures market prices are influenced and the markets are integrated.

An analytical framework for considering the returns on the alternative investments is considered next.

INTEGRATION OF THE CASH AND THE FUTURES MARKETS INTEREST RATES. The previous section concludes with the observation that investors with holding periods beginning at present can choose between a pure cash market investment and a combination of cash and futures markets' investments based on potentially different but riskless rates of return over the holding period. Thus, investors purchase or sell different cash market securities, different futures contracts, and different contract months of the same futures contracts. In this way, the futures market and cash market prices for the appropriate securities are related. This section describes the nature of the integration of the cash and futures market prices due to such relationships.

In an ideal market, with complete integration of the cash and futures markets, the effective holding-period returns for all riskless investments over all specific holding periods will be equal. Under these circumstances, there would be no opportunity for yield improvement among alternative riskless investments over the same holding period. However, at present there are opportunities for yield improvement on equivalent riskless investments over an identical holding period by selecting among alternative investments.

And, even in the long run, some discrepancies between cash and futures mar-

[9]This mechanism is feasible only for contracts on which deliverables can be carried, that is, for which the intercontract deliveries are possible. For example, this can be done for all Treasury-bond futures contract months, but not all Treasury-bill futures contract months.

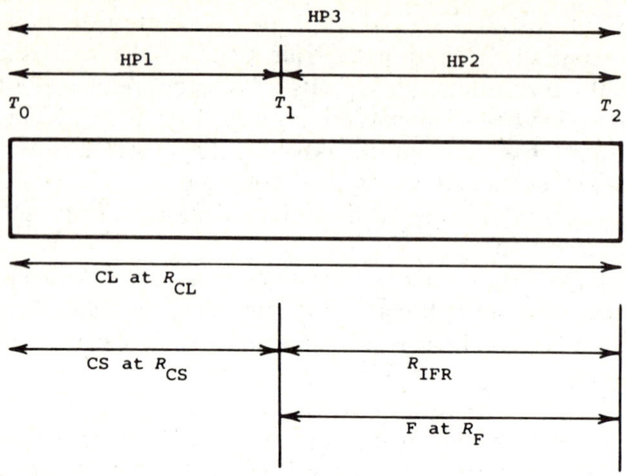

FIGURE 4. Schematic of assumptions for discussion of the section "The Chronological Development of the Financial Futures Markets"

kets interest rates may remain due to differences in tax and accounting treatments, the perceived credit risk of futures markets, differences in margins, margin practices, and commissions, or regulatory policies. In addition, different investors and borrowers may have access to different effective investment and borrowing rates of return. At present, however, there are greater differences among alternative riskless holding-period returns than would be due only to these effects.

Before discussing the nature of the integration between the cash and futures markets, some background is provided. Consider an important cash market concept called "the implicit forward rate" (denoted herein by R_{IFR}), or simply the forward rate. To address this concept, consider a 2-year holding period HP3, from time T_0 to T_2, which is divided into two sequential 1-year holding periods HP1, from T_0 and T_1, and HP2, from T_1 to T_2, as shown in Figure 4. Cash market interest rates can be observed for the 1-year holding period HP1 and the 2-year holding period HP3, both beginning at T_0. Denote these rates R_{CS} and R_{CL}, respectively. From R_{CL} and R_{CS}, the long- and short-term cash market interest rates, an effective implied interest rate over the holding period HP2, which can be called the implicit forward rate, R_{IFR}, can be calculated by[10]

[10]The derivation of the relationship between R_{IFR} and R_{CS} and R_{CL} for the two annual subperiods HP1 and HP2 within the overall 2-year period HP3 is as follows:

$$(1 + R_{CS})(1 + R_{IFR}) = (1 + R_{CL})^2$$

and

$$1 + R_{CS} + R_{IFR} + R_{CS}R_{IFR} = 1 + 2\,R_{CL} + R_{CL}^2$$

Assume $R_{CS}R_{IFR} = 0$ and $R_{CL}^2 = 0$, and the following approximation obtains

$$R_{CS} + R_{IFR} = 2R_{CL}$$

or

$$R_{IFR} = 2R_{CL} - R_{CS}$$

The last equation, used herein, is typically used to calculate the implicit forward rate.

$$R_{IFR} = 2R_{CL} - R_{CS}$$

The implicit forward rate, R_{IFR}, represents the return over the holding period HP2 represented in the 2-year investment over HP3 at R_{CL}, given the current 1-year rate over HP1 of R_{CS}. In other words, R_{IFR} represents what investors would have earned over HP2 by holding CL at R_{CL} over HP3 over and above what they would have earned over HP1 at the rate R_{CS}. Thus R_{IFR} can be thought of as the interest rate over the forward holding period HP2 implicit in the explicit interest rates R_{CS} over HP1 and R_{CL} over HP3.

Conceptually, this return could be realized in the cash market by purchasing the HP3 holding-period investment at R_{CL} and shorting (i.e., borrowing and selling) the HP1 holding-period investment at R_{CS}, or borrowing over the HP1 investment at R_{CS}. Practically, however, it is difficult to short securities and the private borrowing rate may be much higher than the short-term interest rate, R_{CS}, on the security. Although, conceptually, implicit forward rates represent the return over a future holding period implicit in the current cash market structure of long- and short-term interest rates, it is difficult to achieve this rate using only the cash markets.[11]

It can be shown that there is a relationship between R_{IFR} and the interest rate that is expected, at time T_0, to prevail over HP2 at time T_1—that is, the rate that at time T_0 is expected to prevail over HP2. Denote this expected rate by R_{EXP}. There will be pressures to make the implicit forward rate, R_{IFR}, equal to this expected rate, R_{EXP}, as now shown. Note that both R_{IFR} and R_{EXP} apply to the holding period HP2 as of T_0.

Investors can achieve a return over holding period HP3 by either buying a security CL with a holding period HP3 and a return R_{CL}; or alternatively, by buying a security CS with holding period HP1 and a return R_{CS}, and subsequently, at the maturity of CS at time T_1, purchasing a security with holding period HP2 at the prevailing interest rate over HP2 at that time. Of course, the first alternative provides a certain return over HP3, the return on the second alternative is not certain. Presently, the interest rate expected to prevail over HP2 is R_{EXP}. If R_{CL} is greater than the joint return from R_{CS} over HP1 and R_{EXP}, the rate currently expected over HP2, investors would prefer a long-term investment at R_{CL}, and borrowers would prefer the short-term market, borrowing at R_{CS}. Such preferences would cause the long-term rate R_{CL} to decrease and the short-term rate R_{CS} to increase. And such changes would continue until the return R_{CL} over holding period HP3 was equal to the expected joint return from R_{CS} over HP1 and R_{EXP} over HP2. The equality of these two returns would occur only if the implicit forward rate, R_{IFR}, derived from R_{CS} and R_{CL}, were equal to the expected

[11]Alternatively, the implicit forward rate also represents what an investor would earn over holding period HP1 by buying CL at R_{CL}, holding it over period HP1, and selling it at the end of HP1 if the initial maturity structure of interest rates remains the same at the end of HP1; that is, R_{CS} and R_{CL} remain the long- and short-term interest rates over subsequent holding periods of length HP1 and HP3, respectively, at the end of HP1. An alternative way to state this is that the yield curve at the end of HP1, at T_1, is the same as it was at the beginning of HP1, at T_0. According to this interpretation, R_{IFR} is the return over HP1 to buying CL at R_{CL}, holding it until the end of HP1, and selling it on the cash market, that is, riding the yield curve, if the yield curve remains constant. Obviously, the yield curve may shift between T_0 and T_1, so this rate over HP1 is not assured.

rate over HP2, R_{EXP}. The reason is that, by calculation, R_{IFR} is the rate that makes the return from R_{CL} over HP3 equal to the joint return from R_{CL} over HP1 and R_{IFR} over HP2.

The conclusion of this discussion is that choices by investors and borrowers among pure cash market investments tend to make the implicit forward rate, R_{IFR}, equal to the short-term rate currently expected to prevail in the future, R_{EXP}, and thus the "average" of R_{EXP} and R_{CS} equal to R_{CL}. Pressures toward such equality exist. It is such pressures that make the cash market yield curve slope upward during times when interest rates are expected to increase and slope downward at times when interest rates are expected to decline, as illustrated in Table 11.

R_{EXP} will not necessarily, however, be systematically such that the average of R_{CS} and R_{EXP} will equal R_{CL}, that is, R_{EXP} equals R_{IFR}. The major reason for the

TABLE 11. Relation Between Slope of Yield Curve and Interest-Rate Expectations

Cash Market Security		Implicit Forward Rate		
Maturity (years)	Yield	Period	Rate	(Proof)
		Upward-Sloping Yield Curve		
1	6%	0 to 1	6%	
2	7%	1 to 2	8%	$\left(\frac{8+6}{2} = 7\%\right)$
3	8%	2 to 3	10%	$\left(\frac{2 \times 7 + 10}{3} = 8\%\right)$
4	9%	3 to 4	12%	$\left(\frac{3 \times 8 + 12}{4} = 9\%\right)$
5	10%	4 to 5	14%	$\left(\frac{4 \times 9 + 14}{5} = 10\%\right)$
Conclusion: Upward-sloping yield curve implies expectations of increasing interest rates.				
		Downward-Sloping Yield Curve		
1	10%	0 to 1	10%	
2	9%	1 to 2	8%	$\left(\frac{10+8}{2} = 9\%\right)$
3	8%	2 to 3	6%	$\left(\frac{2 \times 9 + 6}{3} = 8\%\right)$
4	7%	3 to 4	4%	$\left(\frac{3 \times 8 + 4}{4} = 7\%\right)$
5	6%	4 to 5	2%	$\left(\frac{4 \times 7 + 2}{5} = 6\%\right)$
Conclusion: Downward-sloping yield curve implies expectations of decreasing interest rates.				

difference, as indicated above, is that long-term investments are subject to a greater degree of market risk than short-term investments. Specifically, in the case being considered, investors experience greater price volatility from a long-term investment, CL, than short-term investment, CS. And investors typically require a risk premium for investing long term, such that R_{CL} is greater than the average of R_{CS} and R_{EXP}. Nevertheless, if the risk premium is relatively constant, the relationship between the R_{CS}, R_{CL}, and R_{EXP} will be stable.[12]

An important aspect of the implicit forward rate is that it applies to a holding period that begins in the future. Specifically, it applies to HP2. This holding period begins at T_1, at the end of HP1, and extends to T_2 through holding period HP2. Futures market rates also apply to holding periods that begin in the future. By analogy, then, since implicit forward rates reflect investors' expectations about interest rates over future holding periods, futures interest rates should similarly reflect such expectations; and since both implicit forward rates and futures rates apply to identical holding periods, these two rates are theoretically equal over the same holding period.

But, of course, futures rates may not require the same type of risk premium adjustments that implicit forward rates do, if calculated from contemporaneous R_{CS} and R_{CL}. As discussed above, implicit forward rates include a risk premium adjustment due to market risk. However, futures rates may include adjustments for factors such as for credit risk involved in futures market transactions and institutional factors such as taxation and accounting treatment and margin levels and practices. Implicit forward rates and futures rates, thus, over the same holding period, should differ only due to their relative risk premiums and these institutional and margining factors. Nevertheless, since these differences should be stable, there should be a stable relationship between implicit forward rates and futures rates over identical holding periods.[13]

Thus three interest-rate constructs apply to holding period HP2. They are R_{IFR}, which is not observable but is calculated from R_{CS} and R_{CL}; R_{EXP}, which is neither

[12]The conceptual and empirical relationships among short-term and long-term interest rates and the related risk premium are discussed by R. B. Worley and S. Diller in "Interpreting the Yield Curve," *Financial Analyst Journal* **32**(68), November/December, 1967, pp. 37–45. The relationship among R_{CS}, R_{CL}, and R_{EXP} is as follows:

$$(1 + R_{CS})(1 + R_{EXP}) = (1 + R_{CL})^2$$

where R_{CL} would be expected to contain a risk premium RP which could be measured by

$$RP = (1 + R_{CL})^2 - (1 + R_{CS})(1 + R_{EXP}),$$

where R_{EXP} could be measured empirically by the actual interest rate over HP2 at time T_1. Measuring R_{IFR} from R_{CS}, R_{CL}, and the equation

$$(1 + R_{CS})(1 + R_{IFR}) = (1 + R_{CL})^2$$

would provide an upward bias in R_{IFR} by the amount of the risk premium. A conclusion of this article is as follows: "Historical yield spreads suggest that, other things equal, market participants require additional yield to extend the maturity of their holdings; three-month forward rates have, on average, exceeded subsequent spot rates by 58 basis points."

[13]See papers by D. Breeden and B. Cornell, E. Kane, J. Pomrenze, and S. Jonas presented at "The Pricing of Futures and Forward Contracts," a Research Colloquium sponsored by the Center for the Study of Futures Markets, Columbia Business School, NY, May 19, 1980.

observable nor calculable; and R_F, a futures market rate over HP2, which is observable. Theoretically, in equilibrium all should be equal. However, in practice, there will be differences among all three because of the risk premium for market risk in the cash market which affects R_{CL} and hence the calculation of R_{IFR} and potentially perceived credit risk and institutional and margining factors in the futures markets which may affect R_F.

The remainder of this section deals with the fundamental relationship between the cash market implicit forward rates and the futures market rates over the same holding period and this relationship relative to the integration of the cash and futures markets. The integration of the cash and futures markets is discussed with reference to Figure 4. As indicated, holding period HP1 extends from the present time T_0 to until time T_1. Holding period HP2 extends from time T_1 in the future until time T_2. The holding period HP3 extends from T_0 to T_2. A long-term cash investment CL at the interest rate R_{CL} applies to the holding period HP3. A short-term cash investment CS at the interest rate R_{CS} applies to holding period HP1. Both R_{CL} and R_{CS} are observable interest rates on actual outstanding cash market securities. The implicit forward rate derived from R_{CS} and R_{CL} over HP2, R_{IFR}, is not an observable quantity—it is calculated from R_{CS} and R_{CL}.

Assume there is also a futures market with a futures contract, F, which has a maturity T_1, and a security deliverable on this contract with a maturity at time T_2, that is, the security has a term to maturity on the delivery day, T_1, of HP2. Assume that the current interest rate on this contract is R_F. This futures rate R_F is also observable.

Thus there are observable interest rates R_{CS} over HP1, R_{CL} over HP3, and R_F over HP2. And an implicit forward rate, R_{IFR}, can be calculated from the short and long cash market interest rates R_{CL} and R_{CS}.Note that both the implicit forward rate, R_{IFR}, and the futures rate, R_F, apply to the same holding period HP2.

The remainder of this section discusses, with respect to Figure 4, alternate investment strategies involving both the cash and futures markets over the holding periods HP1 and HP3 and also arbitrage strategies between the cash and futures markets over these holding periods. The approach is to determine whether the optimal investments over these holding periods are pure cash market investments or investments involving a combination of the cash and futures markets, and to determine the conditions for the optimality of various strategies. Optimal arbitrage strategies and the related conditions are also considered.

Investment Over HP1. With respect to investment alternatives over the holding period HP1, investors can either buy the short-term security CS at R_{CS}, the first alternative shown in Table 12, or buy the long-term security CL at R_{CL} and sell a futures contract at R_F to hedge the sale of CL, the end of holding period HP1, the second alternative in Table 12. The second alternative is, of course, a hedged yield curve ride, which, as discussed above, can also be considered a "cash and carry." Since both of these investments are riskless over HP1, investors will select the alternative which has the higher return over the holding period HP1. On the basis of the previous discussion, it is obvious that whichever of these two alternatives has the higher return depends on the relationship between R_{IFR} and R_F over HP2. Investors choosing the first alternative earn an explicit R_{CS} over

TABLE 12. Investment Alternatives Over HP1

Alternatives:
Alternative (1): buy CS at R_{CS}
Alternative (2): buy CL at R_{CL} and sell F at R_F

Descriptions:
Alternative (1): a pure cash market transaction
Alternative (2): a hedged yield curve ride, which can also be considered a "cash and carry"

Decision rules:
Select alternative (1) if $R_{IFR} < R_F$
Select alternative (2) if $R_{IFR} > R_F$

HP1. Investors choosing the second alternative buy CL at R_{CL} and sell F at R_F. By buying CL at R_{CL}, they are implicitly taking a long position over HP2 at R_{IFR}. By selling F at R_F, they are explicitly taking a short position over HP2 at R_F.

As discussed above, R_{IFR} is calculated from R_{CS} and R_{CL} and is the return over HP2 in excess of the return R_{CS} over HP1. Thus since the second alternative consists of taking a long position over HP2 at R_{IFR} and a short position over HP2 at R_F, the second alternative will be superior to the first alternative only if R_{IFR} exceeds R_F.

Thus, as indicated in Table 12, if $R_{IFR} > R_F$, the second alternative, the hedged yield curve ride, has a higher return. On the other hand, if $R_{IFR} < R_F$, the first alternative, the pure cash market investment, is superior. The decision rule for determining the alternative which provides the higher return, is based on the relationship between R_{IFR}, the return over HP2 implicit in R_{CL} and R_{CS}, and R_F, the return over HP2 on F.

Arbitrage Over HP1. The investments over HP1 described in Table 12 require a net commitment of funds and provide a return on the invested funds. An investor could also profit from the discrepancies between the potentially different returns on the alternate investments over identical holding periods with no net commitment of funds by arbitraging the difference in the returns on the alternative investments. In an arbitrage, the investor would take advantage of the discrepancy in equivalent returns by taking a "long position" in the investment alternative with the higher return and a "short position" in the investment alternative with the lower return. Arbitrage requires no net commitment of funds, as does simply investing in and committing funds to the superior investment alternative, as considered above. In this context, "taking a long position" means to conduct the transaction in the way it is presented in Table 12, while "taking a short position" means to conduct the transaction in the opposite of the way it is presented in Table 12, that is, "selling" instead of "buying" and "buying" instead of "selling."

Thus, if $R_{IFR} > R_F$, arbitrageurs would conduct the second alternative described in Table 12, the superior alternative, and the opposite of the first alternative, the inferior alternative. So, under this condition arbitrageurs would buy CL at R_{CL} and sell F at R_F, the second alternative, and "sell CS" at R_{CS}, the opposite of the first alternative. Practically, "selling" the cash market security CS at R_{CS}

TABLE 13. Arbitrage Over HP1

Investment over HP1, as summarized in Table 12, involves a net commitment of funds. However, an arbitrageur could take advantage of differences in the returns on two investment alternatives in Table 12 with no commitment of funds by arbitraging between the two investments over HP1.

Decision rules:

1. If $R_{IFR} > R_F$, conduct alternative (2) and the opposite of alternative (1), that is,

buy CL at R_{CL}, sell F at R_F, and "sell CS" at R_{CS}.

"Selling CS" at R_{CS} means shorting CS or borrowing short-term funds at the short-term rate, R_{CS}.

In effect, then, arbitrageurs obtain short-term funds at R_{CS} (by shorting a security CS, or borrowing by issuing CS at R_{CS}), use these funds to buy a long-term security CL at R_{CL}, and sell the futures contract F at R_F to lock-in the sale value of CL, which will be sold at the maturity of the short-term loan CS. This transaction represents a hedged yield curve ride where the long-term cash security purchased and held is financed, hence called a "financed hedged yield curve ride."[a] Alternatively, it is a cash and carry that is financed by short-term borrowing. Thus this form of arbitrage can also be called a "financed cash and carry."

2. If $R_{IFR} < R_F$, conduct alternative (1) and the opposite of alternative (2), that is,

buy CS at R_{CS}, "sell CL" at R_{CL}, and buy F at R_F.

"Selling CL" at R_{CL} means shorting CL or borrowing long-term funds at the long-term rate R_{CL}.

In effect, then, arbitrageurs borrow long-term funds at R_{CL} and use these funds to buy a short-term cash security CS at R_{CS}. They also buy a futures contract on which they take delivery of a security immediately after the short-term cash security CS matures. They use the maturity value of CS to make payment for taking delivery on the futures contract. They hold the security taken on delivery on the futures contract until its maturity and use the payment received for its maturity value to repay the long-term cash loan (or when taken on delivery redeliver it on their short position in CL).

The combination of buying CS at R_{CS} and buying F at R_F and taking delivery represents a strip of futures over HP3. The remaining transaction, "selling CL at R_{CL}," represents a borrowing of funds to finance the strip of futures. Overall, then, this transaction can be called a "financed strip of futures."

---

[a]An alternative method of describing the same situation is as follows. By buying CL at R_{CL} and selling F at R_F, arbitrageurs lock-in a return over holding period HP1. This short-term rate has been called an "implied repo rate,"—denoted as R_{IRR}. The implied repo rate, R_{IRR}, can be compared with the actual short-term interest rate, or "repo rate," R_{CS}, to determine the optimality of alternative investments over HP1 or arbitrages. Thus

1. If $R_{IRR} > R_{CS}$
   a. For investment over HP1, buy CL and sell F (hedged yield-curve ride).
   b. For arbitrage, buy CL and sell F and borrow at R_{CS} (sell CS at R_{CS}) (financed hedged yield curve ride).
2. If $R_{IRR} < R_{CS}$
   a. For investment over HP1, buy CS (cash market investment).
   b. For arbitrage, buy CS and borrow CL at R_{CL} (or sell CL at R_{CL}) and buy F (financed strip of futures).

TABLE 13. (*Continued*)

These decision rules based on R_{IRR} and R_{CS} provide equivalent results to the decision rule based on R_{IFR} aı**. R_F, discussed above as shown below:**

Observed:

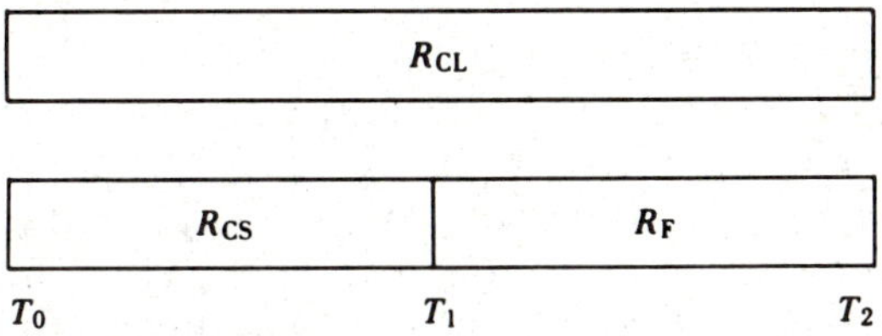

(a) *Decision Rule Based on Comparison of* R_{IFR} *and* R_F*:*

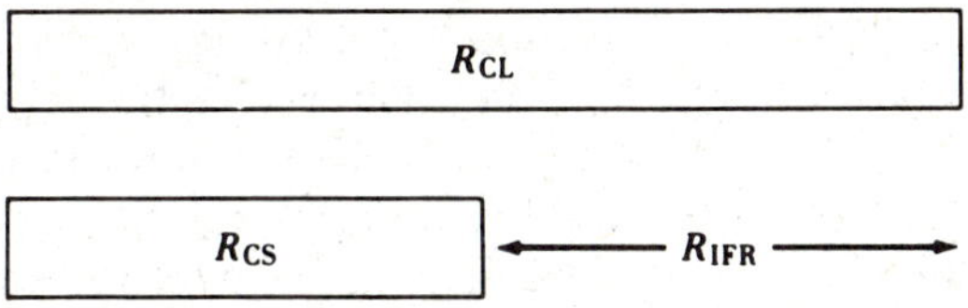

(1) Calculate R_{IFR} from R_{CS} and R_{CL}.
(2) The decision rule is based on a comparison of R_{IFR} and R_F.

(b) *Decision Rule Based on Comparison of* R_{IRR} *and* R_{CS}*:*

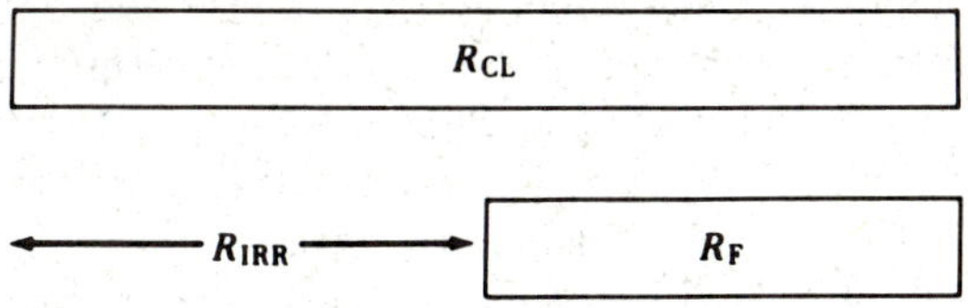

(1) Calculate R_{IRR} from R_{CL} and R_F.
(2) The decicion rule is based on a comparison of R_{IRR} and R_{CS}.

Resolution of Two Decision Rules:

It is clear that $R_{IFR} > R_F$ is equivalent to $R_{IRR} > R_{CS}$
and that $R_{IFR} < R_F$ is equivalent to $R_{IRR} < R_{CS}$.

Thus, the outcomes based on these two decision rules are identical. Similar relationships could be developed for invectments and arbitrage over holding period HP3.

means either shorting CS, that is, borrowing it and selling it, or borrowing short-term funds at the short-term rate R_{CS}. Overall, then, under this condition, arbitrageurs borrow short-term funds at R_{CS}, and sell futures contracts F at R_F to lock-in the sale value of CL, which will be sold before its maturity at the maturity of the short-term loan CS which is also the maturity of the futures contract F. Since the funds used to finance the investment in CL are obtained via the issue of CS at R_{CL} (either selling the borrowed security CS or borrowing at R_{CL}),[14]

[14]This distinction is discussed in more detail in "The Integration of the Cash and the Futures Market Interest Rates."

there is no net commitment of funds. Hence, the hedged yield curve ride, buying CL and selling F, is financed by borrowing short-term funds. This overall transaction can thus be called a "financed hedged yield curve ride" and is described in Table 13. Since, as discussed above, hedged yield curve rides are essentially cash and carrys, this financial transaction can also be considered a "financed cash and carry."

Second, as indicated in Table 13, if $R_{IFR} < R_F$, arbitrageurs would select the first alternative and the opposite of the second alternative in Table 12. That is, arbitrageurs would buy CS at R_{CS}, "sell CL" at R_{CL}, and buy F at R_F. "Selling CL" at R_{CL} means either shorting CL, that is, borrowing CL and selling it, or borrowing long-term funds at the long-term rate R_{CL}. In effect, then, the arbitrageurs borrow long-term funds at R_{CL} and use these funds to buy a short-term cash security CS at R_{CS}. The arbitrageurs also buy futures contracts, on which they would take delivery of a short-term security immediately after the maturity of the short-term cash security CS. At this time, the arbitrageurs would use the maturity value of CS to make payment for taking delivery of the short-term security on the futures contracts. The investor, then, holds the short-term security taken on delivery on the futures contract until its maturity, and uses its maturity value payment to repay the long-term cash loan. The combination of buying CS and subsequently taking delivery on the futures contract, F, represents a strip of futures over the holding period HP3. The transaction, "selling CL" at R_{CL}, represents a borrowing of funds to finance the strip of futures. Consequently, the overall transaction can be called a "financed strip of futures."

Summarily, then, if $R_{IFR} > R_F$, the optimal arbitrage is a "financed hedged yield curve ride." On the other hand, if $R_{IFR} < R_F$, the optimal arbitrage is a "financed strip of futures." Both of these strategies are financed, that is, require no net commitment of funds. Both are thus arbitrages rather than investments.

The footnote to Table 13 discusses an alternative way of considering the decisions presented in Tables 12 and 13. The footnote shows that rather than comparing R_{IFR}, the implicit forward rate in the cash market over HP2, with R_F, the futures rate over HP2, instead R_{IRR}, the rate implicit in R_{CL}, can be compared with R_F, the short-term cash rate R_{CS}, over HP1 as the decision rule. The rate R_{IRR} is often called the "implied repo rate." The conclusions based on the comparison of R_{IRR} and R_{CS} are identical to those by comparing R_{IFR} and R_F, as demonstrated in the footnote to Table 13. These types of arbitrage are discussed in greater detail in the section "Arbitrage Strategies Revisited."

Investment Over HP3. The two previous sections have considered alternate investment and arbitrage strategies over holding period HP1. The next two parts discuss investment and arbitrage strategies, respectively, over the longer holding period HP3. As indicated in Table 14, to achieve a riskless return over the holding period HP3, investors can buy CL at R_{CL}, a pure cash market transaction. Alternatively, investors can buy both CS at R_{CS} and F at R_F, a strip of futures. Which of these alternatives provides a higher return depends on whether R_{IFR} or R_F is greater over the holding period HP3. Obviously, if $R_{IFR} > R_F$, the first alternative, the pure cash market transaction, provides a higher return because the return implicit in the cash market, R_{IFR}, is greater over HP3 than the futures rate, R_F. On the other hand, if $R_F > R_{IFR}$, the strip of futures provides a higher

TABLE 14. Investment Alternatives Over HP3

Alternatives:
  Alternative (1): buy CL at R_{CL}
  Alternative (2): buy CS at R_{CS} and buy F at R_F

Description:
  Alternative (1): a pure cash market transaction
  Alternative (2): a strip of futures

Decision rules:
  Select alternative (1) if $R_{IFR} > R_F$
  Select alternative (2) if $R_{IFR} < R_F$

return because the return in the futures markets, R_F, is greater over HP3 than the return implicit in the cash market, R_{IFR}.

Arbitrage Over HP3. As indicated in Table 13, differences in the returns on equivalent riskless investments over HP1 can be arbitraged with no net commitment of funds. Equivalently, Table 15 considers arbitrage based on differences in alternative riskless investments over the holding period HP3.

If $R_{IFR} > R_F$, the first alternative in Table 14 is preferable to the second alternative. In these circumstances, arbitrageurs would buy CL at R_{CL}, the first alternative, and do the opposite of the second alternative, that is "sell CS" at R_{CS} and sell F at R_F. This arbitrage strategy is the same as the first arbitrage alternative in Table 13, which is a financed hedged yield curve ride.

On the other hand, if $R_{IFR} < R_F$, an arbitrageur would buy CS at R_{CS} and buy F at R_F, the second alternative in Table 14, and do the opposite of the first alternative, that is, "sell CL" at R_{CL}. Note this is the same as the second alternative in Table 13, which is a financed strip of futures. Thus the potential arbitrages and the corresponding decision rules over HP3 in Table 15 are identical with those over HP1 in Table 13, and need be considered no further.

As indicated, these types of arbitrage strategies are discussed in greater detail in the section "The Development of the Interactions Between the Cash and Futures Financial Markets."

ARBITRAGE STRATEGIES REVISITED. "Arbitrage Over HP1" and "Arbitrage Over HP3" provide a discussion of arbitrage strategies over holding periods HP1 and HP3, respectively, and relate these arbitrage strategies to the investment alternatives over these same holding periods. This section extends and completes the discussion of arbitrage strategies. Short arbitrages and long arbitrages are discussed in the sections "Short (Futures) Arbitrage (Financed Hedged Yield Curve Ride)" and "Long (Futures) Arbitrage (Financed Strip of Futures)," respectively.

Short (Futures) Arbitrage (Financed Hedged Yield Curve Ride). Table 16 summarizes the transactions that take place over holding period HP1, between T_0 and T_1, which are discussed in the section "Arbitrage Over HP1." For ease of reference, the transactions undertaken at time T_0 are denoted as follows: buying a

TABLE 15. Arbitrage Over HP3

Investment over HP3, as summarized in Table 14, involves a net commitment of funds. However, an arbitrageur could take advantage of differences in the returns on the two investment alternatives in Table 14 with no commitments of funds by arbitraging between the two investments over HP3.

Decision rules:

1. If $R_{IFR} > R_F$, conduct alternative (1) and opposite of alternative (2) in Table 14, that is,

buy CL at R_{CL}, sell CS at R_{CS}, and sell F at R_F.

Note that this is the same as alternative (1) in Table 13, which is a financed hedged yield curve ride.

2. If $R_{IFR} < R_F$, conduct alternative (2) and the opposite of alternative (1) in Table 14, that is,

buy CS at R_{CS}, buy F at R_F, and "sell CL" at R_{CL}.

Note that this is the same as alternative (2) in Table 13 which is a financed strip of futures.

long-term cash security is denoted by (1); borrowing short-term funds to finance the purchase of the long-term cash is denoted by (2); and the sale of the futures contract is denoted by (3).

As discussed in the section "Arbitrage Over HP1," conducting all three transactions at time T_0 is an arbitrage, since there is no net commitment of funds, that can be considered a financed hedged yield curve ride. This type of arbitrage can

TABLE 16. Short (Futures) Arbitrage: Financed Hedged Yield Curve Ride (Over HP1)

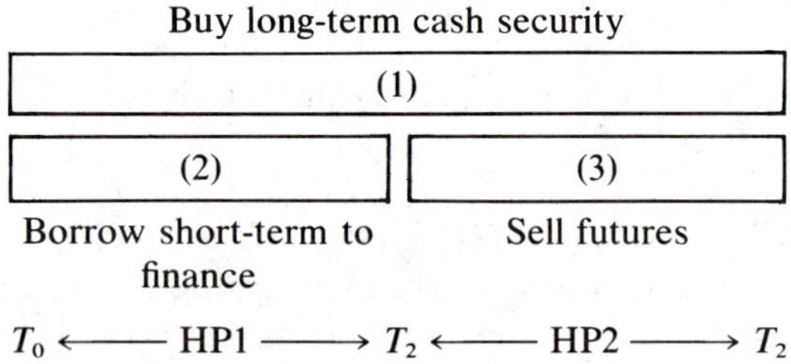

Transactions at times T_0 and T_1:

T_0—

1. Buy long-term cash.
2. Borrow short-term funds to finance purchase of long-term cash.
3. Sell futures.

T_1—

1. Deliver long-term cash on futures and collect receipts.
2. Use receipts to pay off short-term borrowing.

also be called a "short arbitrage" because it involves a short position in the futures contract.

However, in addition to all three transactions being done at T_0, various combinations of these transactions can be done at T_0 as well. Various combinations of these transactions, and their nature, are summarized in Table 17.

Transaction (1) alone is a yield curve ride of an asset over HP1. Specifically, the investor buys the long-term cash security at T_0 and sells it at T_1, thereby recognizing a holding-period return over HP1. As discussed above, this investment is not riskless. To conduct this type of transaction, the investor must expect that either interest rates will remain constant or decrease during the holding period; that is, the price of the security purchased will either remain constant or increase.

The combination of transactions (1) and (3), that is, adding transaction (3) to transaction (1), is a hedged yield curve ride. Selling a futures contract at T_0 which matures at T_1, in addition to buying the long-term cash security, hedges the holding of the long-term cash security, thereby making the investment riskless over HP1.

The combination of transactions (1)–(3) conducted at T_0, that is, adding transaction (2) to transactions (1) and (3), finances the hedged yield curve ride. This combined transaction is called a financed hedged yield curve ride, or alternatively, a *short futures arbitrage*.

Finally, the combination of only transactions (1) and (2), both cash market transactions, is a pure cash market arbitrage. Borrowing funds with one maturity and investing in an asset of another security is often called a "mismatched book." In this type of a mismatched book, the arbitrageur borrows short-term funds and invests long-term funds. This type of arbitrage would be conducted in an environment wherein interest rates were expected to decrease. With expectations of decreasing interest rates, the arbitrageur would invest long term, thereby locking-in a long-term investment rate, and borrow short term, planning to refinance borrowing at a later date at a lower interest rate.

Long (Futures) Arbitrage (Financed Strip of Futures). Table 18 summarizes the transactions that occur at time T_0 in a long futures arbitrage over holding period HP3, between T_0 and T_2, as discussed in the section "Arbitrage Over HP3." Again, the various specific transactions are denoted by numbers: the long-term

TABLE 17. Nature of Various Combinations of Transactions in a Short Arbitrage (Over HP1)

Transactions	Description
(1)	Yield curve ride (of an asset) (buy at T_0, sell at T_1) (expect interest rates to remain constant or decrease, that is, prices to remain constant or increase between T_0 and T_1)
(1) + (3)	Hedged yield curve ride
(1) + (2)[a]	Cash arbitrage (mismatched book) (expect interest rates to decrease)
(1) + (2) + (3)[a]	Financed hedged yield curve ride (short arbitrage)

[a]The combination of (1) + (2) may be the result of a repurchase agreement ("repo").

borrowing is denoted by (1); the short-term cash investment is denoted by (2); and the purchase of a futures contract is denoted by (3).

Raising long-term funds in a long arbitrage, transaction (1), can be accomplished in either of two ways. First, according to method (A), the arbitrageur can borrow and sell a security with a commitment to repay the security at the end of HP3 at T_2, that is, "short" the cash security. For a perfect arbitrage, as discussed below, the cash security shorted must be one that is deliverable on the futures contract and therefore the one which the arbitrageur will take delivery of on a long futures position at T_1. In this way, the arbitrageur could repay on a short cash position the security the arbitrageur receives on delivery on a long futures position at T_1.

Alternatively, according to method (B), the arbitrageur could raise long-term funds by borrowing long-term funds directly or by issuing a long-term security. In these cases the arbitrageur would not be able to repay the direct loan or retire the security issued with the security taken on delivery on the long futures position.

An important difference between a long arbitrage and a short arbitrage results from the fact that futures contracts are based on "seller's option," according to which if more than one security is eligible for delivery (as there is on the Treasury-bond futures contracts, but not on the Treasury-bill futures contracts), the short may choose which deliverable security to deliver and the long must accept which-

TABLE 18. Long (Futures) Arbitrage: Financed Strip of Futures (Over HP3)

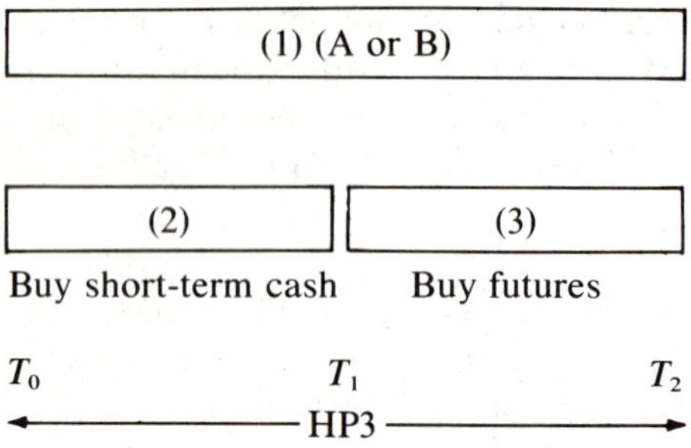

A. Short long-term cash security deliverable on futures contract (borrow long-term cash security and sell the security)[a]

or

B. Borrow long-term funds (direct loan or issue long-term security).

Transactions at times T_0 and T_1

T_0—(A)

1. Short long-term cash security, that is, borrow long-term cash security and sell the security to raise funds.
2. Buy short-term cash security—with funds raised in (1).
3. Buy futures.

T_0—(B)

1. Borrow long-term funds (direct loan or issue long-term security).
2. Buy short-term cash security—with funds raised in (1).
3. Buy futures.

T_1—(A)

1. Use maturity value of short-term cash security to take delivery on futures (or could liquidate futures position and use receipts of maturity value of maturing short-term cash security to buy security shorted on the cash market, which should be the same due to convergence).

T_1—(B)

1. Use maturity value of maturing short-term cash security to take delivery on futures position (so the arbitrageur owns the security received on the futures contract and has an outstanding long-term loan, both of which have the same maturity, and the rate on both of which was locked-in at T_0).

TABLE 18. (*Continued*).

2. Use security received on delivery on futures (or purchased on cash market) to repay short position on long-term cash. (May have to swap out of deliverable security received on delivery into deliverable security shorted if more than one security is deliverable on the futures contract, with possible basis risk).	2. Sell security received on delivery and buy back long-term security issued, if marketable, or prepay long-term loan if privately placed (if interest rates have decreased, the value of the long-term loan is higher, but profits are in the long futures position). (Could also invest receipts until maturity of long-term loan until T_2 and then pay-off long-term loan.) This arbitrage will be exact if the spread between the cash security specified in the futures contract and the cash security issued by the arbitrageur (the long-term loan) due to credit risk, that is, after adjusting for difference in maturities—the credit risk basis—remains constant. If this basis changes, the arbitrage is not exact. Thus, while case (A) is a perfect, or riskless, arbitrage, case (B) is not a riskless arbitrage.[b]

[a]Mechanism A can also be accomplished by a reverse repurchase agreement (reverse repo). Thus the combination of transactions 1-A and 2 would be accomplished by "reverse-repoing-in" a security with term to maturity HP3 (maturity at T_2) over the term of the reverse repo agreement of HP1 (maturity T_1). Of course, to effectively complete the shorting of the long-term security and to finance the reverse repo, the long-term security reverse-repoed-in would be sold on the cash market. At T_1, the arbitrageur would receive delivery on the futures contract of a security that could be used to fulfill the reverse repo agreement.

[b]Examples of riskless (perfect) arbitrages of type (B): (1) If the yield curves at T_0 and T_1 for Treasury debt and private debt differ by same amounts for all same maturities, as shown in Figure 5, then the arbitrage is perfect or riskless. (2) If the yield curves at T_0 and T_1 for Treasury debt and private debt differ by different amounts for all maturities at T_0 and T_1, as shown in Figure 6, then arbitrage is imperfect or risky.

ever eligible security the short chooses, although with typically some price adjustment. In a long futures arbitrage thus the arbitrageur will receive which of the eligible deliverables the short chooses—the long has no control in this regard.

Thus, in the Treasury-bond futures contract with several deliverable bonds, the short arbitrageur could buy a long-term bond and be assured of being able to deliver the same bond on a short futures position. Of course if the bond purchased was not the cheapest deliverable even though the bond could be delivered, it might not be economical for the arbitrageur to do so—the arbitrageur might swap a bond for the cheapest deliverable bond.

However, the long arbitrageur who shorted a deliverable bond would not be assured that he or she would receive the same bond on delivery on the long futures position that had been shorted. The arbitrageur may choose to deliver a different deliverable bond than the bond the long arbitrageur had shorted. Of course, in this case the long arbitrageur would simply have to swap out of the bond he or she received on delivery on the futures contract and into the bond that was shorted.

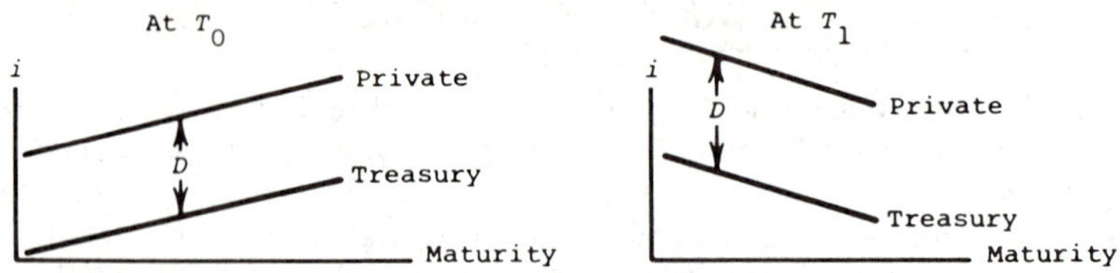

FIGURE 6. Treasury-debt and private-debt yield curves for risky arbitrage.

And the spread between the two, for example, the spread between two deliverable Treasury securities, should remain approximately the same and the effectiveness and precision of the arbitrage should, therefore, not be greatly affected. However, there is the possibility of some basis risk in such a long arbitrage transaction.

Table 18 summarizes the transactions that take place at the times T_0 and T_1 in a long arbitrage, according to the two different specific ways of raising long-term funds: (A) raising long-term funds by shorting a long-term cash security and (B) borrowing long-term funds by issuing a security or by a direct loan.

The only risk in an arbitrage financed via mechanism (A) is due to the seller's options, discussed above, according to which if there was more than one deliverable security, the arbitrageur may have to swap out of the security taken on delivery and swap into the deliverable bonds shorted. This long arbitrage can thus be called a *pure long arbitrage*.

However, according to mechanism (B) for raising long-term funds, there is no potential for using the security taken on delivery on the long futures position to retire the security issued or to repay the direct loan. In this case, the security taken on delivery on the long futures position must be sold and the funds received used to retire the loan. As indicated in Table 18, in order for this arbitrage to be exact, the spread between the cash security specified in the futures contract and the long-term cash security issued by the arbitrageur, which is most likely due primarily to credit risk but possibly also due to maturity differences, remains constant. However, if this spread or basis changes because of changing risk premiums due to either factor, the arbitrage is imperfect and is not riskless. And it is likely that there will be a smaller degree of basis change between different securities deliverable on the same futures contract, as in mechanism (A), than between a security deliverable on the futures contract and the private security issued, as in mechanism (B). Thus there is more risk in an arbitrage financed according to mechanism (B). Thus the long arbitrage financed by mechanism (B) is called a *cross long arbitrage* in contrast to the pure long arbitrage financed by mechanism (A).

As in the short arbitrage, various combinations of the transactions undertaken at time T_0 in a long arbitrage can be interpreted as summarized in Table 19.

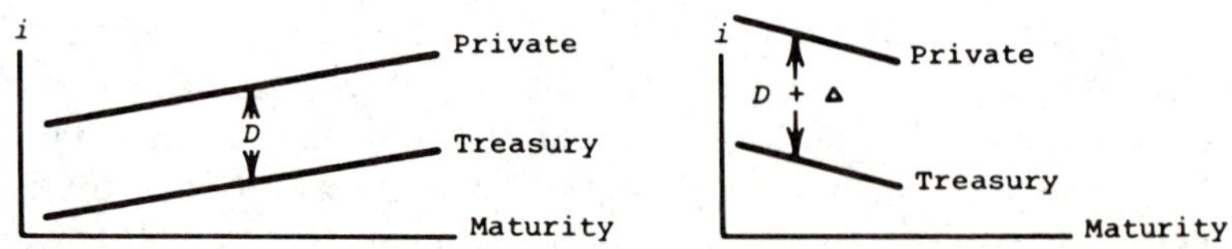

FIGURE 5. Treasury-debt and private-debt yield curves for riskless arbitrage.

TABLE 19. Nature of Various Combinations of Transactions in a Long Arbitrage (Over HP3)

Transactions	Description
(1)	Hedged yield curve ride (of a liability) (borrow funds or issue security at T_0, prepay loan or retire issue at T_1) (expect interest rates to remain constant or increase, that is, prices to remain constant or decrease between T_0 and T_1)
(2) + (3)	Strip of futures
(1) + (2)[a]	Cash arbitrage (mismatched book) (expect interest rates to increase)
(1) + (2) + (3)[a]	Financed strip of futures (long arbitrage)

[a]The combination of transactions (1) + (2) can be accomplished by a reverse repurchase agreement (''reverse repo'') and selling the security ''reverse-repoed-in'' on the cash market.

Transaction (1) alone can be considered a yield curve ride of a liability in that the arbitrageur borrows or issues a security at T_0 and plans to retire the security or prepay the loan at time T_1. A borrower would conduct this transaction if the borrower expected interest rates to remain constant or increase, thus security prices to remain constant or to decrease, so that the borrower could retire the loan or security issued at a price below its initial value. Yield curve rides are typically in terms of assets. This yield curve ride, however, is in terms of liabilities.

Transactions (1) and (2) together represent a cash arbitrage, or as discussed above, a mismatched book. This type of mismatched book is of the opposite type of that in Table 19. To conduct transactions (1) and (2) together at time T_0, the arbitrageur would expect interest rates to increase between T_0 and T_1, so that the price of the long-term security issued would decline by more than the price of the short-term asset purchased.

The combination of transactions (2) and (3) represents a strip of futures, as discussed above.

Finally, the combination of transactions (1)–(3) represents a financed strip of futures, or a long arbitrage.

OVERVIEW OF THE INTERACTIONS. The sections ''Alternative Investment (Over Holding Period Beginning at Present),'' ''Integration of Cash and the Futures Markets Interest Rates,'' and ''Arbitrage Strategies Revisited'' discuss the nature of arbitrage between the cash and futures markets on debt instruments. These arbitrage relationships provide exact relationships between the cash and futures markets. When there are discrepancies from these relationships between the cash and futures markets, arbitrageurs conduct transactions that, while generating a profit for the arbitrageurs, reestablish, with bounds, these relationships.

These arbitrage relationships, and the transactions of arbitrageurs to establish these relationships, causes the integration of the cash and futures markets for debt instruments. Thus, Figure 3 describes the actual relationship between the cash and futures markets, wherein the relevant external factors have a direct effect on both the cash and futures markets and, in addition, there is a direct relationship, due to arbitrage, between the cash and futures markets.

CHAPTER 11

MANAGING INTEREST-RATE RISK ON BOTH SIDES OF THE BALANCE SHEET: USE OF FUTURES BY FINANCIAL INSTITUTIONS

CONTENTS

FORECAST-DRIVEN BALANCE-SHEET MODELS 4

GAP-DRIVEN BANK BALANCE-SHEET PLANNING MODELS 5

SHORTCOMINGS OF GAP ANALYSIS REPAIRED: THE EFFECTIVE GAP 6

THE BEST BENCHMARK 9

INTEGRATED RISK-RETURN MANAGEMENT: QUALITATIVE ANALYSIS 11

CHAPTER 11

MANAGING INTEREST-RATE RISK ON BOTH SIDES OF THE BALANCE SHEET: USE OF FUTURES BY FINANCIAL INSTITUTIONS

James Kurt Dew

The use of financial futures by financial institutions has received enormous attention in the 1980s. Yet banks, for the most part, still do not use them. To the extent they do, most observers believe that the use of futures by banks is still primarily speculative. Why? After all, financial futures, used as vehicles to reduce the riskiness of banking, are tailor-made to address the greatest problem the financial system faces today—the problem of interest-rate risk.

The reason for the divergence between potential benefit and realized benefit of futures use is a shortfall in the technology of risk management. This chapter discusses the technology of risk management in banking today, and considers what might be done to improve this technology so that futures use will become feasible.

The technology of bank risk management will never be changed for the purpose of making futures markets useful. Futures are not, in the long run, important enough to warrant such a major adjustment. However, luckily for futures markets, the adjustment of the technology of bank risk management necessary to put banks on firm ground in their ordinary risk-management operations will also facilitate the use of futures. Thus the banking system is moving in the direction of greater use of the financial instruments available in the futures markets. This chapter addresses the changes that will occur in any event, to manage interest-rate risk properly, and how futures will fit into risk management in the end.

The chapter describes the two prevalent existing risk-management techniques, and how they fail to address the management of interest-rate risk adequately. Then a third method is developed, one that facilitates the solution of risk-management problems of banks and accommodates the prudent and effective use of futures.

FORECAST-DRIVEN BALANCE-SHEET MODELS

Most currently available models of bank balance-sheet management are not powerful enough to consider interest-rate risk in a common-sense way. Such models tend to hinder the bank interested in using futures primarily because they do not allow the bank to gain an understanding of their actual interest-rate risk in the first place.

There are three kinds of models being applied by banks to the analysis of interest-rate risk. The first of the three kinds of models is driven by the bank's interest-rate forecast. These first models have great intuitive appeal to bankers because they most closely approximate the pre-1980s-type of interest-rate risk management. Presently none of them accommodates the use of futures, and if one ever does, will nonetheless not be particularly effective for this purpose.

These interest-rate–forecast-driven models help to facilitate bank risk-management activities to some extent, by providing a rough estimate of bank future earnings, if bank interest-rate forecasts are correct. These models also give a bank a limited idea of its interest-rate risk exposure, by allowing the model user to forecast earnings under assumed interest-rate scenarios that differ from the bank's "best guess."

Any good model builds the bank from the ground up, product by product. A useful model should forecast deposit and loan volumes by type, and interest rates for the bank that does not supply its own, but will also allow a bank to base earnings on its own forecasts.

First, the model identifies a bank's planning period. Some models allow you to decide how far ahead you want to plan, but most do not. Typically, the model decides how far ahead a bank will manage its interest-rate risk. Usually the designated planning period is 1 year. For most banks, however, the flexibility to manage interest-rate risk for future periods more than 1 year hence is essential. The extent of this risk must be considered, even if it must be done by guesswork.

Using a forecast-driven model, the bank can experiment with the values of "driver" rates, volumes of assets and liabilities, and the prices of loans relative to the cost of funds. But one problem that arises with some models is a failure to indicate limitations that exist in real-life bank management. A model sometimes assumes more latitude than the bank has in practice. In using "best guess," optimistic, and pessimistic values of all three variables described above, for example, the bank would examine 27 possible outcomes—none of them necessarily feasible as a practical matter. For instance, the model is able to double the volume of loans, all granted at floating rates, three percentage points above prime, fund them with fixed-rate liabilities, and have interest rates rise 500 points. This is not possible for the bank. Furthermore, no comments about the riskiness of this strategy would be made by the model. A better model would challenge this set of assumptions and encourage the user to consider interaction between assumptions.

The second weakness of this kind of model is that it does not provide guidance in choosing among the alternative scenarios it constructs. The model reports the earnings resulting from a given management decision under prescribed management assumptions. The risk involved may only be determined indirectly by showing what happens if assumptions are changed. The model never asks how much risk is acceptable to bank management. If the model could work under the risk restraints placed upon it to produce the strategy that would maximize income under the conditions expected to prevail, much better understanding of actual options available to the bank could be achieved.

GAP-DRIVEN BANK BALANCE-SHEET PLANNING MODELS

The gap-driven models of bank balance-sheet management focus on the measurement of risk to the exclusion of the projection of earnings. Thus in their way they are as inadequate as the forecast-driven models discussed in "Forecast-Driven Balance-Sheet Models", that focus on earnings while ignoring risk. These gap models are easily adapted to the use of futures. Unfortunately, the futures market positions these models "spin off" as a by-product are rarely the right ones. The futures positions produced by gap models are rarely the ones that will lead to lower risk for the financial institution. However, where these two kinds of models are all that is available to a bank, the bank must analyze its exposure using a combination of the two, liberally seasoned with the collective judgment of bank management. Both risk and earnings are too important to focus on one while neglecting the other.

The shortcomings of the currently fashionable analysis of bank balance sheets—known as gap analysis—fall into one of two categories: reparable and irreparable. The most widely available versions of gap analysis fail to take into account a variety of factors, each of which has an important impact on the interest-rate risk exposure of banks. These errors include the following:

1. Failure to recognize the fact that the risk exposure of a bank is not the result of errors in the pricing of existing fixed-rate assets or liabilities, but, rather, the result of the possibility that subsequent assets and liabilities will be repriced at levels inconsistent with future profitability. The current earnings problems of savings institutions, for example, are not the result of underpriced mortgages. Instead, they are the result of the institutions' inability to ensure that the costs of the deposit liabilities issued following the granting of the original mortgages would not exceed the earnings on the mortgages themselves.

2. Most gap measurement packages dwell upon the risk exposure of the institution in the nearer term, ignoring exposure resulting from the inability to adequately control the risk resulting from unfunded longer-term commitments. Since this second risk is usually the more critical to the future profitability of the bank, better treatment of the longer-term risk is well-advised.

3. In measuring the risk exposure of a bank over some specified period of time, the bank should focus on the maturities of new balance-sheet items. Maturities of new liabilities determine the exposure of the institution, not maturities of roll-off liabilities. In assessing interest-rate risk, it is necessary to do more than simply determine which liability is maturing at what time. This fact does not describe the risk resulting from the repricing of a liability. If a maturing asset or liability is rolling into a 6-month maturity, for example, the risk at the time of repricing is six times the risk resulting from repricing the same current liability, at the same yield, but with a new liability having a 1-month maturity. The deciding factor is the risk created by the new liability, not the maturing one.

4. Currently available measures of the gap fail to take account of the relative volatilities of different instruments. A bank funded by liabilities at a 3-month average maturity and carrying loans that float with the prime is not as risky as a bank that funds itself in the same way, but puts its money into the fed funds market instead of prime loans. The reason is that the prime rate and the fed funds rate do not behave alike. Fed funds, a very short-term market-determined rate of interest, is a far more volatile rate than the prime, an administered rate. Thus an adjustment for the effect of the relative volatilities of various instruments will result in more accurate measures of the relative riskiness of the bank.

These four shortcomings of the gap have one common characteristic—they can be fixed. An improved version of the gap—call it the "adjusted gap"—does not suffer from the above deficiencies. In the next section, "Shortcomings of Gap Analysis Repaired: The Effective Gap" these problems, and how they may be rectified, are considered.

Unfortunately, gap analysis suffers from a more fundamental problem, one that cannot be rectified. The nature of this problem, and a new technique, maximum-earnings–minimum-risk banking, is described in "Integrated Risk-Return Management: Qualitative Analysis."

SHORTCOMINGS OF GAP ANALYSIS REPAIRED: THE EFFECTIVE GAP

There are four basic factors that ordinary gap analysis simply overlooks unnecessarily. All of them are critical issues to a bank seeking to measure and to manage its interest-rate risk. The factors are as follows:

1. Failure to recognize the fact that the risk exposure of a bank is not the result of errors in the pricing of existing fixed-rate assets or liabilities.

First, the effective gap recognizes risk more accurately by focusing on the anticipated new assets or liabilities to be added to the balance sheet, rather than existing assets and liabilities. If, for example, an MMC is going to mature 2 months hence, to be rolled-over into another MMC, the risk exposure of the bank bears no relationship to the MMC currently on the books of the bank—a 2-month exposure. Instead the risk exposure of the bank depends upon the MMC to be written in the future—a 6-month exposure, to be incurred in 2 months. Suppose these MMC's were funding an 8-month fixed-rate loan. Then the adjusted gap resulting from these combined assets and liabilities on a month-to-month basis is described in Table 1.

TABLE 1. Adjusted Gap

Month:	January	February	March	April	May	June	July	August
Gap:	0	0	Effect of MMC	0	0	0	0	0

The risk exposure of the bank in each month is zero, with the exception of the month of March. If the bank could "lock up" the cost of the March MMC, the bank would have no further risk exposure, since the bank already knows both the cost of money and earnings in January and February, and earnings through August. Knowing the cost of the MMC, then, is the only element of uncertainty and, once this uncertainty is removed, net earnings for the period as a whole are tied down.

This fact has important implications. First, interest-rate exposure is never precisely measurable. One cannot know the amount of interest-rate exposure of an institution in advance without also knowing future deposit volumes. Second, the sole significance of knowing the current balance sheet is that it provides some idea of the past performance of the bank, that will perhaps bear upon the future performance of the bank.

2. Most gap measurement packages dwell upon the risk exposure of the institution in the nearer term, ignoring exposure resulting from the inability to adequately control the risk resulting from unfunded longer-term commitments.

The risk exposure of the bank is a longer-term risk, not a shorter-term risk. Events that occur during the next month may well be the primary focus of a good bank manager. But a bank manager should not confuse the risk emanating from next-month's events with the risk that determines next-month's earnings. Only for a dealer, who marks an entire portfolio to the market on a daily basis, are these two notions one in the same.

This month's events are important because they will affect the income of the bank for years to come. When the cost of funds of savings institutions rose during the late 1960s, it was painful to the institutions, but not critical to their survival. When costs of funds for savings institutions rose above earnings in 1980, on the other hand, it was another matter entirely. The reason for this difference was that the duration of the first period of high rates was brief; of the second period, not so brief. Both events—a rapid run-up in interest rates—occurred quickly, but the importance of the run-up depended not upon the time it took for rates to rise, but rather upon the length of time over which the effects of this event persisted.

Thus, although we may be attempting to protect the bank from changes in interest rates that might occur during the next month only, protection must nonetheless be sought for every period in which the effect of the events might possibly persist. This, potentially, is as long as the maturity of the longest-dated asset or liability of significant size on the balance sheet—for most institutions up to 20 years.

3. Maturities of new liabilities determine the exposure of the institution, not maturities of roll-off liabilities.

A good example of the relative importance of existing deposit categories, compared to projected new levels of these same deposit categories, is the earlier example of the MMC maturing in 2 months, to be replaced by another MMC. The magnitude of the risk exposure of the bank depended on two factors: the time at which the reset occurred—in 2 months—and the length of time the new liability would remain on the books—6 months. If the maturing liability had been replaced by a 3-month Certificate of Deposit instead of a 6-month MMC, the exposure of the bank funding the same 8-month fixed-rate loan described in our previous example would be slightly altered to the new exposure described in Table 2.

TABLE 2. Adjusted Gap

Month:	January	February	March	April	May	June	July	August
Gap:	0	0	Effect of CD	0	0	Effect of second CD	0	0

The March exposure of this operation is less than the March exposure of the bank in Table 1. This is due to the shorter maturity of the CD compared to the MMC. On the other hand, a new source of risk enters the picture, the risk due to the June repricing of the March CD.

How would a bank examine its risk exposure in the month of June, from the perspective of the beginning of the year? To measure the bank's adjusted gap, the bank must forecast assets and liabilities that will have their rates reset during the month of June. The first step in this process is to forecast the amount of expected deposits received at federally mandated ceiling rates (e.g., MMC's) in June. This might be done, for example, by assuming that existing MMC's will roll-over in June, and that new MMC's will be booked at about the same rate that new deposits have been booked in the recent past.

Next, the bank will also need to estimate the extent of its reliance upon purchased money. An important aspect of this forecast, needless to say, will be the bank estimate of loan demand. The bank will certainly need to purchase liabilities in sufficient volume to fund projected loan demand.

4. Currently available measures of the gap fail to take account of the relative volatilities of different instruments.

Rather than look at the contractural maturities of assets and liabilities, some statistical measure of the effective gap—a statistical measure of maturities of assets and liabilities that takes into account the relative volatilities of various instruments—would be more useful. Such a measure could be constructed in a variety of ways, depending on the needs of the institution.

To do this, a benchmark financial instrument is chosen and the gaps for other instruments "normalized" relative to the benchmark. Suppose we let the benchmark instrument be one-month commercial paper, for example, measuring the effective gap on a monthly basis using month-end to month-end changes in rates. So an institution with a one-year fixed-rate asset, funded by monthly rollovers of one-month commercial paper, would have a gap that changed each month by the negative of the amount being rolled over (by assumption, since we are defining all other interest rate gaps in terms of their volatilities relative to this one).

The contribution of all other instruments to changes in the institutional gap will depend on two factors:

1. The average change from the most recent month-end to the next most recent month-end of the yield for the instrument relative to the yield on one-month commercial paper.
2. The change in earnings resulting from a given change in the yield of the instrument, relative to the change in earnings resulting from a reset of the one-month commercial paper rate. For example, the change in the effective gap for a reset of an instrument at a six-month maturity ought to be roughly twice the change in the effective gap for the same instrument at a three-month maturity, and six times its gap at a one-month maturity.

Using month-end data from January 1977 to March 1981, the contribution of various financial instruments to the effective gap, per million dollars bought, was determined using ordinary least squares regression coefficients.

TABLE 3. Effective Contribution to the Gap, on a Month-to-Month Basis, the Gap of Various Financial Instruments Against One-Month Commercial Paper

Instrument	Change in Gap (In Millions)
1 Month commercial paper	1.00
Federal funds	1.16
Floating prime-related loans	0.86
3 Month CD's	3.10
MMC's	4.54

These effective gaps differ substantially from the contractual gap. As the first example suggested, the Fed funds gap is somewhat larger than the effective gap of the prime, due to the greater volatility of Fed funds. Three-month CDs add about three times the amount to the gap that one-month commercial paper does, since CDs and commercial paper have about the same volatility but CDs have three times the maturity. Finally, although money market certificates have six-month maturities, the MMC rate is less volatile than the commercial paper rate, so that the contribution of an MMC to the effective gap is only about 4.5 times that of one-month commercial paper.

THE BEST BENCHMARK

There are several factors to consider in choosing the benchmark to use in estimating the effective contribution of other money instruments to the gaps. First, the relationship between the benchmark rate and other rates affecting the net interest margin of the institution should not vary substantially with the passage of time, since the measures of contributions of other instruments to the rate exposure of the firm have been based on the historical relationship between the benchmark rate and these other rates.

TABLE 4. Effective Gaps: 90-Day Bill Futures Benchmark

Instrument	Effective Gap
30-day commercial paper	0.335
Month-to-month changes—fed funds	0.364
90-day CDs	1.361
Month-to-month changes—prime rate	0.260
Six-month MMCs	2.181

One property that would make a desireable benchmark rate from this point of view is that the benchmark rate should have a maturity as close as possible to the average maturity of other instruments on the balance sheet, thus minimizing the impact of shifts in the slope of the yield curve on the accuracy of the estimated relationship between the benchmark rate and other rates affecting the gap.

A second factor in assuring the reliability of the estimates of the effective gap is choosing a benchmark rate that is market-determined. Administered rates may change their relationships to be predominantly market-determined rates found on the balance sheets of most financial institutions at present. Thus, it seems reasonable to avoid the prime rate, the money market CD rate, the Federal Reserve discount rate, and perhaps the Fed funds rate in choosing a benchmark.

Another desirable characteristic of the benchmark rate is that it be as useful as possible in adjusting the gap in the direction desired by the firm. Suppose, for example, that the increment to the effective gap between five and six months hence was plus $3 million, based on the one-month commercial paper benchmark used earlier. This gap could only be brought to zero, using the benchmark rate, by simultaneously entering a five-month reverse repurchase agreement and a six-month repurchase agreement, both collateralized by $3 million in commercial paper. This would be impossible since term repurchase agreements at longer maturities are basically mythical beasts.

This suggests that financial futures would make desirable benchmark rates, since this sort of fine-tuning of the gap is not only possible with futures, it is easy.

Table 4 displays the effective gap for various instruments based on the 90-day bill futures benchmark. As the table indicates, the primary difference between these effective gaps and those for 30-day commercial paper is that the different maturities of the two instruments reduce the gaps by about a factor of three.

In summary, then, the effective gap does a number of things better than the ordinary gap. First, it better identifies the source of risk—yields on assets and liabilities not yet booked. Second, it characterizes the extent of the risk more adequately by looking at risk over all relevant future periods, rather than limiting the examination to a short period in the future. Third, it captures the role of maturity of not-yet-booked liabilities more accurately. Finally, it captures the effects of the different volatilities of rates on interest-rate exposure. Unfortunately, there are some major issues that gap analysis does not, and cannot, address. In the following analysis, the crucial importance of these unaddressed issues will be described, and a means for including them in the analysis of risk developed.

INTEGRATED RISK-RETURN MANAGEMENT: QUALITATIVE ANALYSIS

From the discussions of the previous two sections on Gap-driven models and their improvements, it is possible to look through the veil of the balance-sheet models themselves and see the real predicament that leads to the difficulty in adapting models to real banks. For just as these models are not capable of dealing with the problem of maximizing return while simultaneously minimizing risk, banks themselves find it quite difficult to simultaneously manage both risk and return. Within the scope of the risk a bank finds acceptable, there are limits to the aggressiveness of its stance. The banker must seek the maximum return consistent with an acceptable level of risk.

But the technology exists to make substantial improvements in the terms of loans, that is, changes that can improve the bank loan loss performance in adverse rate environments, and can also bring new business to the bank. If this program is managed with appropriate concern for the risk involved, it can enhance the profitability of the bank in the short run, through stable income growth, and also in the long run, through expanded customer base.

Running a maximum-profit, minimum-risk bank requires, above all, the ability to juggle concerns of the short run along with concerns of the long run. If earnings must be sacrificed to protect the bank risk position, formal methods of coming to grips with the issues are recommended. The analysis of this problem is accomplished through consideration of risk and return on two levels. The first level is quantitative. Where possible, risk should be subjected to careful statistical analysis. This process yields two benefits. First, it puts a burden on the staff support of management decision making to generate and analyze all information that would bear on the judgement that must be made. Second, it divides the decision-making process into those decisions that emanate from assumed continuation of experience of the past, and those decisions that bear the stamp of new management-instigated initiatives.

Of the two types of analysis, qualitative analysis will always be the more important since qualitative analysis, by its nature, deals with intangibles and thus requires judgement, not arithmetic. On the other hand, problems that *do* lend themselves to quantitative analysis should definitely be pursued in a quantitative manner, since the bank is better served by use of arithmetic where arithmetic will suffice. That is, 2 + 2 = 4, regardless of whether or not management judges that 2 + 2 = 5.

CHAPTER **12**

COMMODITY SPREADS

CONTENTS

SPREAD AND SPREAD TERMINOLOGY	3	MORE ATTRACTIVE REWARD/RISK RATIO	17
INTERDELIVERY SPREADS	4	USEFUL TO OUTRIGHT TRADER	18
INTERCROP SPREADS	5	CARRYING CHARGES	18
INTERCOMMODITY SPREADS	8	STORAGE AND INSURANCE	20
COMMODITY VERSUS PRODUCT	8	FINANCING COSTS	20
BUTTERFLY SPREADS	9	CARRYING CHARGE MARKETS	20
INTERCOMMODITY SPREAD QUOTES	9	INVERTED MARKETS	21
TRADING TECHNIQUES	11	THE MEANING OF INVERTED OR CARRYING CHARGE MARKETS	22
MARKET, LIMIT, AND TIME ORDERS	11	SPREADS RARELY GO TO FULL CARRY	23
INTERMARKET SPREAD ORDERS	12	IMPLIED YIELDS	24
STOP ORDERS	13	BULL AND BEAR SPREADS	24
ENTERING THE ORDER	13	INTERMARKET SPREADS	26
LEGGING-IN OR LEGGING-OUT	14	INTERMARKET WHEAT SPREADS	27
LEGGING MISTAKES	15	INTERCOMMODITY SPREADS	28
BAD SPREAD INTO GOOD OUTRIGHT	15	WHEAT VERSUS CORN	29
WHY TRADE SPREADS	15	CRUSH SPREADS	30
LIMITED RISK	16	SOURCES OF INFORMATION	34
LOWER RISK	16	BIBLIOGRAPHY	34
LESS MARGIN	16		
LOCKED LIMIT DAYS	17		

CHAPTER **12**

COMMODITY SPREADS

Courtney Smith

Commodity spreads are an exciting trading vehicle. They allow for exceptional variations in risk, from the small changes of the carrying charge spread to the highly leveraged intercommodity spread. Opportunities are plentiful and the situations can be more complex and subtle than outright positions. Until recently, professional traders and hedgers have long dominated spread trading. More and more speculators, however, are learning about and trading spreads.

SPREAD AND SPREAD TERMINOLOGY

There is confusion in the nomenclature of spreads. The word "spread" is not universally accepted. In New York City, "straddle" and "switch" are often used. In this chapter we use the term "spread," but remember that other terms may be used.

A spread is the purchase of one futures contract and the simultaneous sale of another futures contract. The spread trader becomes *simultaneously* long one futures contract and short another futures contract. A spread is composed of two *legs*. The long contract is one leg and the short contract is the other leg.

The components of a spread can relate time or location or commodities or a combination of the three. An example of a time spread would be September lumber versus November lumber. One can also spread different commodities, such as wheat and corn. Different markets can be spread, such as Kansas City wheat and Chicago wheat; or a location spread could be London silver versus New York silver.

A spread between different contract months in the same commodity is called an *interdelivery* or *intracommodity spread*. A spread between different commodities is called an *intercommodity spread*. The examples of spreading commodities in different markets are *intermarket spreads*.

When one trades spreads, the spread trader is trying to profit from the change in the difference in price between the two contracts. The spread trader is concerned with the relative prices of two contracts rather than the absolute level of prices. This is not to say that the price level of a commodity does not affect the spread, but it is not a main ingredient for making money, only a secondary characteristic. Let us look at an example of a common intracommodity spread.

Let us say that on May 1, 1976, you had sold one December 1976 contract of copper at $0.73 and simultaneously bought one May 1977 contract of copper at $0.74. The difference in price was $0.01 in favor of the May contract (May premium over December). Your margin would have been $250. On August 6, 1976, the difference between December and May copper has widened to $0.03 (the December contract was selling for $0.70 and the May for $0.73). Because of carrying charges (which are explained later) you knew that the spread was not likely to widen any further. You liquidated the position by buying the December contract and selling the May contract. Your profit comes to $500 minus approximately $60 commission for a net profit of $440. Nearly 200% on your money in 3 months! Let us put this transaction into step form:

Date	December Contract	May Contract
May 1, 1976	Sell December 1976 copper at $0.73/lb	Buy May 1977 copper at $0.74/lb
August 6, 1976	Buy December 1976 copper at $0.70/lb	Sell May 1977 copper at $0.73/lb

The result is $0.03/lb gain on December 1976 contract multiplied by 25,000 lb and $0.01/lb loss on May 1977 contract multiplied by 25,000 lb. There is a $750 gain on the December 1976 contract minus $30 commission (half of the total spread commission) which equals a $720 net profit; a $250 loss on the May 1977 contract plus $30 commission which equals a $280 net loss; and a $720 profit on the December 1976 contract minus $280 loss on the May 1977 contract which equals a $440 net profit on the spread.

INTERDELIVERY SPREADS

Interdelivery spreads are subdivided into two types, the *bull spread* and the *bear spread*. A bull spread for most commodities is one in which the trader is long the nearby contract and short the deferred contract. For example, a bull spread is long July 1978 cocoa and short December 1978 cocoa. The trader who has a bull spread is looking for the nearby contract to be stronger than the deferred contract. In other words, if the absolute price levels are rising, the trader is looking for the nearby to rise more than the deferred. Conversely, if the absolute price level is declining, the trader is looking for the nearby contract to decline less than the deferred. The reason for this is that the current supply-and-demand situation and recent news will have a greater impact on the nearbys and a more diffused impact on the far contract. This is the case for the agricultural, financial, and foreign exchange markets (see Figure 1). Of course, there is always the possibility the nearby will gain in price and the deferred will decline in price when the news specifically affects the new agricultural crop or the long-term view of prices. We will discuss later several commodities that have the far contract gain more than the nearby in normal bullish conditions.

The bear spread is the reverse of the bull spread. The trader is short the nearby

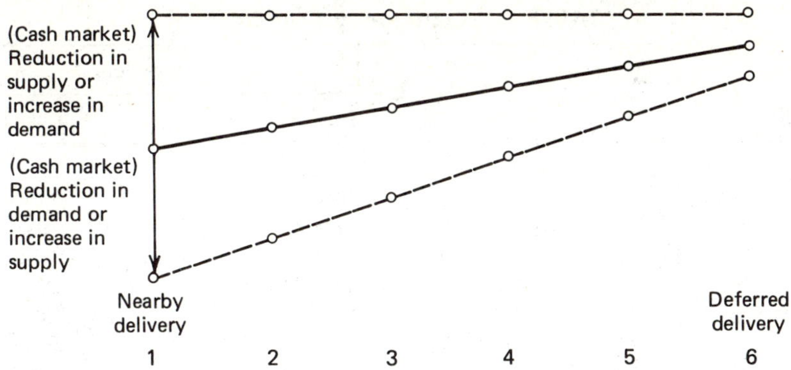

FIGURE 1. Relative price changes of deferred contracts.

month and long the deferred month and is therefore looking for the deferred month to be relatively stronger than the nearby month. Being short October 1982 hogs and long February 1983 hogs would be considered a bear spread.

INTERCROP SPREADS

Another type of intracommodity spread is the *intercrop spread*. An intercrop spread involves taking a long position in one crop year and a short position in a different crop year. For example, the crop year for Kansas City wheat begins with the July contract and ends with the following May contract (the crop is actually harvested in May and June). A trader who is long the May 1981 contract and short the July 1981 contract would have an intercrop spread. Note, however, that being long the July 1981 contract and short the May 1982 contract is not an intercrop spread because those particular two delivery months are in the same crop year.

There is a significantly greater amount of volatility in intercrop spreads than in interdelivery spreads involving the same crop year. This is because the variation in supply from one year to the next can cause major price distortions, while within one crop year price fluctuations are limited to changes in short-term demand and carrying charges. As a result, margins are often higher for intercrop spreads. A dramatic example of an intercrop spread is the August pork bellies versus the February contract of the following calendar year. The crop year in pork bellies, for futures market purposes, is from February to August. The exchange rules dictate that August pork bellies may not be redelivered against the following February pork bellies. So, although the two contracts are in the same commodity, they are governed by different supply-and-demand considerations. It is therefore quite possible for August and February bellies to move in opposite directions. Although there is significantly more volatility, there is also greater profit potential. Table 1 is a list of the various commodities and their crop years relative to futures markets contracts. The price of an intracommodity spread is the difference between the two contracts. A trader who was long December corn at $3 and short March corn at $3.10 was *bull spread* December/March corn at $0.10 *premium* the March. An alternative way to say this is to say the trader was in the spread at

TABLE 1. Commodity Crop Year

Commodity	Crop Year	
	First Future	Last Future
Wheat		
K.C., Chicago	July	May
Minneapolis	September	July
Corn	December	September
Oats	July	May
Soybeans	September	August
Soybean oil	October	September
Soybean meal	October	September
Live hogs	None	None
Frozen pork bellies	February	August
Cattle—live	None	None
Cattle—feeder	None	None
Treasury bonds	None	None
Treasury bills	None	None
GNMA	None	None
Lumber	None	None
Plywood	None	None
Foreign currencies	None	None
Cotton	October	July
Frozen concentrated orange juice	January	November
Potatoes	November	April
Cocoa	December	September
Coffee	December	September
Sugar	None	None
Platinum	None	None
Heating oil	None	None

March \$0.10 over December. Note that if December rises above March, we would quote the spread at, for example, December \$0.12 over March. Thus one has to specify the difference in value between the contracts as well as which contract is the premium month.

Figure 2 shows the price behavior of the March 1981/July 1981 corn spread. The price started at about \$0.12 premium the July and moved up to a high of about \$0.02 premium the March where it began a choppy downtrend until, at the end of the chart, it traded at about \$0.09 premium the July. (The prices on this spread chart, as well as all other spread charts in this chapter, are the differences between settlement prices.) The trader should note that the contract differences are plotted in cents per bushel. As we will see later, other types of spreads are graphed as the difference in dollar value between the two spread contracts. All intracommodity spreads are graphed and quoted as the unit difference between the contracts.

Spreads are always quoted with the *long contract first*. Thus the trader would initiate a long July wheat/short May wheat trade, but would not initiate a short May wheat/long July wheat trade. Even though the short contract may be chronologically first, the long contract is always the first quoted.

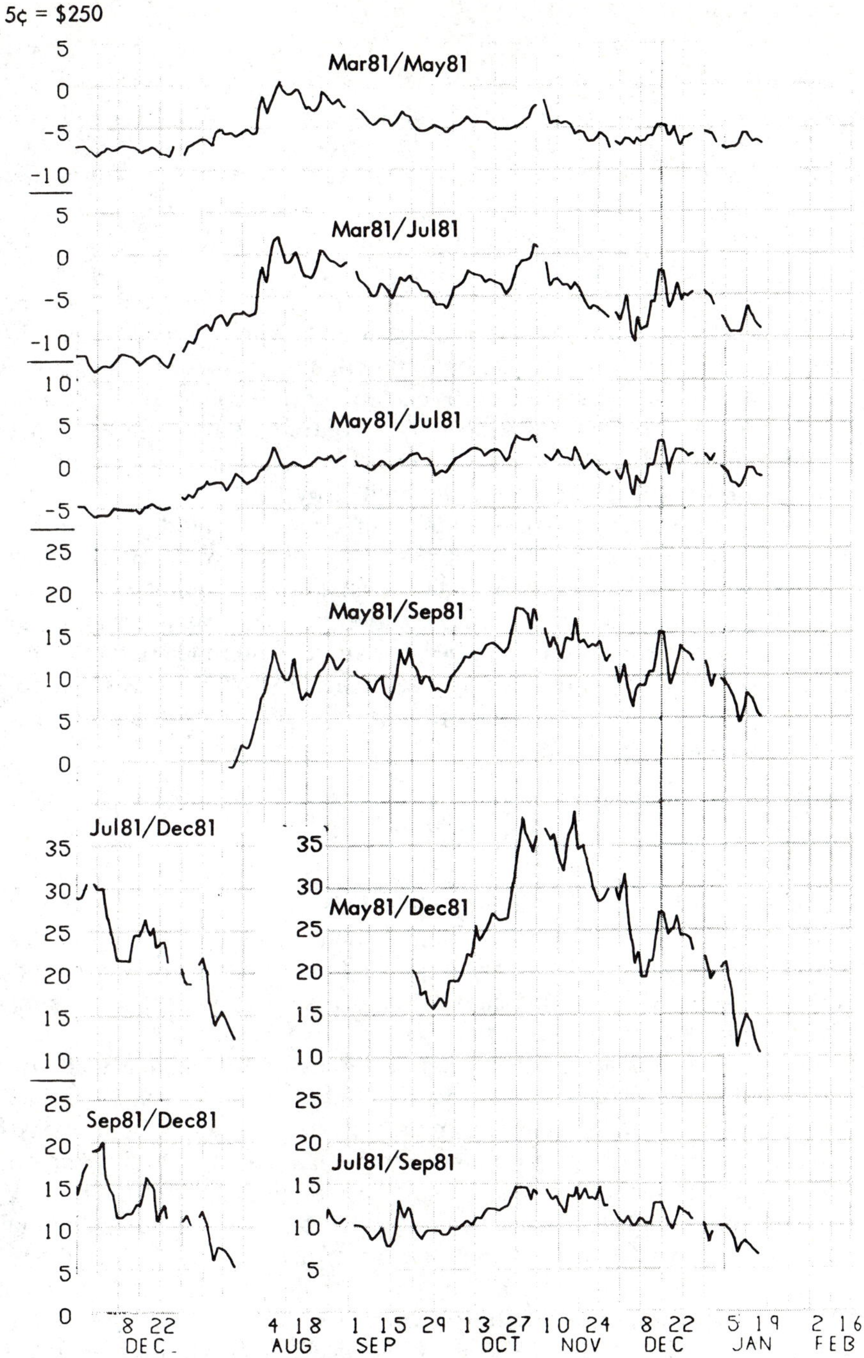

FIGURE 2. 1981 corn spreads (source: *Spread Scope*).

INTERCOMMODITY SPREADS

An *intercommodity spread* is a spread between two different commodities. Long December gold and short December silver would be such a spread. It is not necessary to spread the same months in the two different commodities. Intercommodity spreads should be thought of as spreads between two different but related commodities.

In the previous example, gold and silver are different commodities but related due to their intrinsic value as precious metals. The spreads of soybean meal versus corn, or wheat versus corn, or oats versus corn, are examples of different commodities related by their protein ratios and availability for animal feeds. Although it is not always the case, it is common to find that the contracts which are objects of a spread are possible substitutes for each other or have a product relationship. The potential substitutability gives the two contracts a relationship that can be traded by the spread trader. If wheat can be fed to animals instead of corn, the price discount of wheat to corn will be limited by the nutritional relationship of the grains. Thus a long gold/short orange juice spread would not be considered an intercommodity spread for our purposes because there is no relationship between the two commodities other than perhaps color. Obviously, it is an intercommodity spread in that it is a long position in one commodity and one short position in another commodity but, because there is no fundamental relationship between the commodities, it is considered by traders to be two outright positions rather than an intercommodity spread; the exchanges offer no margin benefit for these transactions.

COMMODITY VERSUS PRODUCT

A special type of intercommodity spread is the spread between a commodity and its products. The most common example is the spread between soybeans and its two products—soybean oil and soybean meal. This is usually considered to be the most complex of spreads because it involves analysis of three commodities rather than the usual two contracts.

Very few soybeans are used in their unprocessed form. Nearly all soybeans are crushed into two products—soybean oil and soybean meal. Each bushel of soybeans, weighing 60 lb, yields approximately 11 lb of oil, 48 lb of meal, and 1 lb of waste. The analyst must do some simple mathematics to find the value of oil and meal per bushel of soybeans. Since oil is quoted in cents per lb, we simply multiply the oil price by 11 to get the value of bean oil per bushel. To obtain the value of meal, the analyst multiplies the price of meal by 0.024 (0.024 is 48 lb divided by the 2,000 lb in a ton). This converts the price of meal in dollars per ton to the value of the meal per bushel of beans.

A soybean processor or crusher makes a profit from the difference between the cost of buying the beans and the price for selling the products. This difference is called the gross processing margin (GPM), or the coversion margin. In the futures industry the difference is commonly called the *crush margin*.

The spread created by buying soybean futures and simultaneously selling soybean oil and soybean meal futures is called the *crush spread*. When one buys the oil and meal futures and sells the bean futures, it is called the *reverse crush spread*.

This spread is most frequently quoted in cents per bushel representing product value after subtracting the cost of the beans. For instance, "the May crush is running at $0.30" means that the combined value of the May contracts for the products, expressed in cents per bushel is worth $0.30 more than the value of the May contract for beans.

BUTTERFLY SPREADS

A *butterfly spread* can be viewed as two interdelivery spreads combined. A butterfly spread is not the simultaneous purchase and sale of two different contracts but the simultaneous purchase and sale of three contracts. For example, the following combination of positions is considered a butterfly spread:

Short 1 April live cattle contract.
Long 2 June live cattle contracts.
Short 1 August live cattle contract.

One should note that the middle leg of the spread has two contracts, whereas each outside leg has only one. This is because a spread comprised of contracts of equal value usually has equal numbers of longs and shorts.

A butterfly spread is of typically lower volatility and lower risk than a simple spread. The fact that it is both a bull spread (long June/short August) and a bear spread (short April/long June) leads to low volatility, since the result is the net of two spreads rather than the net of two delivery months.

INTERCOMMODITY SPREAD QUOTES

Intercommodity spreads are quoted in several different ways. If the two commodities have a similar unit of measure, for example, wheat and corn are measured in bushels, the spread will most likely be quoted as the difference between the two commodities in relation to their common unit. For instance, Figure 3 shows May wheat with the price of May corn subtracted from it. The chart is graphed as the number of cents per bushel between the commodities.

Alternatively, but less likely, the prices can be quoted as the ratio between one commodity and a second commodity. In Figure 4 we can see a chart of the price of May 1981 wheat divided by the price of May 1981 corn. Nonetheless, when orders are placed for execution, the common way of quoting this type of spread is the difference in cents per bushel.

The third major way to quote spreads is the difference between the dollar value of the contracts. In other words, the contract size times the current price of one commodity is subtracted from the contract size times the current price of a second contract. In Figure 4 we can see that the value of September 1981 soybean oil, subtracted from the value of September 1981 soybean meal, was worth about $10,000 in October 1980. In other words, the value of the contract of soybean

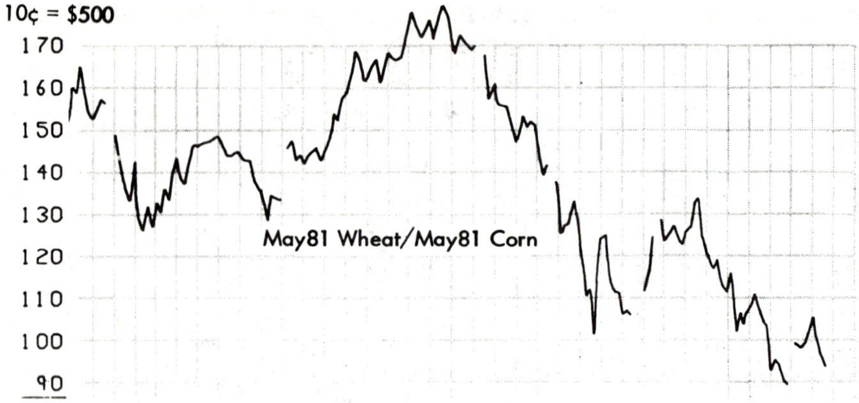

FIGURE 3. 1981 wheat corn spreads (source: *Spread Scope*).

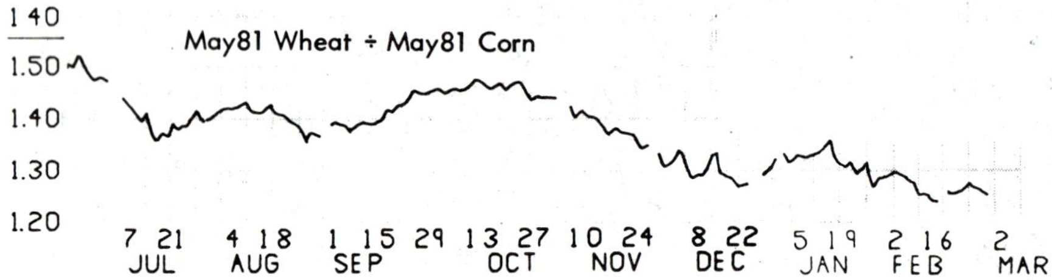

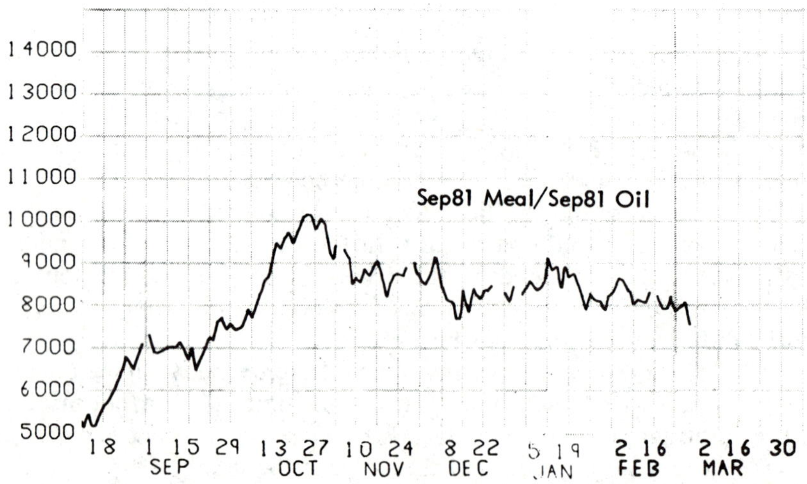

FIGURE 4. 1981 meal/oil spread (source: *Spread Scope*).

meal was worth $10,000 more than the value of the contract of soybean oil. Oil/meal is the most common spread quoted in this manner, although intercommodity currency spreads can often be found quoted this way.

TRADING TECHNIQUES

The mechanics of spread trading are relatively simple. The exchanges will accept fewer types of orders for spreads than for outright or "net" positions. The proper use of spread orders can be the difference between a profitable trade and an unprofitable trade. Because spreads require the simultaneous purchase and sale of two contracts, entry and exit are necessarily more difficult.

MARKET, LIMIT, AND TIME ORDERS

There are three types of spread orders, each with a specific use. There are times when the trader will use one type of order and not another type. The trader, however, should check to see which of the orders described below are acceptable at which exchanges. Some exchanges take orders that other exchanges will not accept.

A *market order* is perhaps the most common way to execute a spread. The trader tells the broker how many spreads he or she wishes to buy or sell, but does not specify the price at which to initiate the spreads. The order means to do the trade as quickly as possible at the current market price. The main purpose of a market order is speed, not the best possible price. The floor broker will attempt to get a good price, but the broker's goal is to make the trade quickly.

Market orders work well in a large liquid market. The floor broker can easily find other brokers willing to take the other side of the trade. The spread between the bid and ask prices is often the minimum tic for that commodity. Thus, during June, a popular spread like the July/November soybean spread can be easily filled at the market at the prevailing prices.

However, an illiquid market having low volume or open interest can be treacherous to the trader using a market order. When the floor broker receives the order to execute an illiquid spread at the market, the broker may have a hard time finding another party to take the opposite side. By offering more favorable prices to others, the broker will eventually execute the spread with varying degrees of loss to the customer.

Suppose it is June and a trader wants to initiate a long March/short May orange juice spread at about 100-points premium the May. The March/May orange juice spread and May orange juice will be illiquid in June. Even though March and May orange juice may settle 100 points apart for a month, the trader will have a difficult time obtaining that price. The floor broker, after receiving the order, will have to find someone to take the other side of the transaction. As there are few trades in March and May orange juice and even fewer in the March/May orange juice spread, the broker will have to discount the spread more and more to induce someone to take the other side. The broker may have to offer more than 50 points to find a trading partner.

The trader, looking to obtain the spread at 100-points premium the May, now becomes the unproud owner at 50-points premium in May. And yet, at the end of the day, the March and May contracts may continue to close 100 points apart.

A *limit order* can prevent the unfortunate experience of the orange juice spreader. A limit order specifies the price that the floor broker can accept for the trade. The trader instructs the broker to execute the trade at that price or better. The orange juice spreader could have entered an order to buy March and sell May orange juice at 100-points premium May. The broker is being instructed to buy the March and sell May but only if the May can be sold at least 100 points higher than the March. The broker could not put the trade on by selling May 50 points or 60 points or, for that matter, 99 points above the March. The broker is allowed to obtain a better price than specified.

The drawback to the limit order is that no one may wish to take the side of the spreader's offered trade. The orange juice spreader may offer 100-points premium May and nobody wants it; the orange juice spreader may never be able to execute the spread.

A limit order does not guarantee a fill. It is possible for the trader to see the price move through the "limit price" on the tape or quote machine and yet not execute the trade. It is possible that the trade took place on the opposite side of the pit and the floor broker did not hear it or was unable to get there in time, or there might have been inadequate volume at that price.

Further, it must be remembered that spread quotes frequently differ from the difference between the two outrights. That difference is a rough guide but may not represent the actual spread quotes. It is quite possible that one of the two contracts has not traded for some time and the other contract's price has moved away from the first one. Before choosing the spread difference for your limit order in an illiquid market, it is best to get a quote directly from the floor of the exchange.

A *time order* specifies the time of day that the trader wishes an order to be filled. It may be at any time of day but, more commonly, on the open or close. Thus the spread trader could conceivably put in an order such as "buy June, sell December silver at 11:15 a.m. central time." This would become a market order at 11:15. Most time orders are intended to initiate or exit trades at the market on the open or close. A typical order might be to "buy August, sell December live cattle, market on close."

INTERMARKET SPREAD ORDERS

Intermarket spread orders are the hardest to execute. The floor broker must buy a contract of one commodity at the market, then quickly contact a counterpart in another market's pits. The built-in delay makes it difficult for the broker to execute limit orders. Some brokers will accept intermarket spreads only on a "not held" basis. This means that they will try their best but will not be held responsible for poor executions. They do this to protect themselves from buying one market's contract, having the other market's price fall away from them, and being stuck holding the first contract because of an inability to get the required price on the other contract. Some brokers will accept intermarket limit spread orders on a "take your time" (TYT) basis. This gives the floor broker more time to use discretion in executing the order.

There is no delay in getting an intermarket spread market order filled. The broker merely executes this spread as two separate market orders.

STOP ORDERS

A stop order is an order that becomes a market order as soon as a given price level is reached. Thus the order "buy July, sell August pork bellies at 50-points premium July stop" becomes a market order if the July/August belly spread trades at 50 points or higher, premium July.

It should be noted, however, that it is extremely rare to find an exchange that accepts spread stop orders. The Chicago Board of Trade accepted them in the past but no longer does. The Chicago Mercantile Exchange accepts them, but only at the discretion of the floor broker, and it is unlikely you will find a broker willing to execute a spread stop order. For all practical purposes, traders should assume that they will not be able to use spread stop orders, and should check with their brokers to find out the latest policies.

Although spread stop orders may not exist, many spread advisors and traders act as if they did. Newsletters, advisors, and brokers often tell their clients to put on a spread with a stop at such and such a level. Some will even use the term "close-only stop."

The terms "stop" and "close-only stop" are not strictly correct but serve a useful purpose. These "stops" should be considered mental stops. The trader can enter *market* or *limit* orders when the spread appears to be trading at or near the exit point. This obviously requires more awareness on the part of the trader and the trader's broker.

"Close-only stops" are more complicated. The trader should look at the settlement or closing prices of the two legs of the spread. If the difference is not beyond the exit point, the trader does nothing. If it is past the "stop," the trader calls the broker just after the opening the following morning and asks for a quote on the spread. If the quote from the floor is also beyond the "stop," the trader should place an order to liquidate the spread *at the market*.

ENTERING THE ORDER

The trader should obtain from the broker the latest spread quotes from the floor before entering any trades. This gives the trader the best indication of the price of the spread. Alternatively, the trader should check the spread differences based on the settlement prices. Other than quotes direct from the floor, the settlement prices give the best indication of spread price levels.

Traders should use limit orders whenever possible. The spread trader is often looking for rather small changes in price differences. A market order may nullify whatever price advantage the spreader had. Market orders should be used only when speed of execution is the paramount concern. This might be a concern if news causes dramatic moves in the market, and the trader wants to quickly enter or exit a position.

LEGGING-IN OR LEGGING-OUT

Legging-in is the process of putting on a spread by buying or selling one leg of the spread followed, some time in the future, by the opposite position in the second leg. Legging-out is the same process to exit a trade. Legging-in or -out turns an outright position into a spread or vice versa. It is usually done for the wrong reasons. The technique is only useful when the trader wants to convert an outright position into a spread or a spread into an outright.

The trader holding an outright position may decide that the outright position will no longer be a wise investment. Simultaneously, the trader discovers a good spread prospect that has, as one of its legs, the outright position the trader wishes to eliminate. The trader legs into the other side of the spread. Eventually, and most probably, the spread is liquidated as a spread.

The purpose of this exercise is to save a small amount of money on commissions. The trader does not liquidate the outright position, pay full commission for it, and then initiate the spread. Legging into the spread saves the trader half of a round-turn comission. In past years, when long-term capital gains was an issue, spreading a position would allow the trader to carry the long leg for 6 months without loss of outright profits, although a price reversal would shift some profits to the short side.

Changing the outright position into a spread must be considered coincidental. That is, the two positions must have been considered as two separate trades that happened to coincide in time. This will typically happen only when a major government report is to be released. A speculator, long August cattle, deems the situation too risky to carry a long position into the July 1 *Cattle on Feed* report. The speculator believes that the report will be bullish, but does not want to take on the additional risk going into the report. Rather than liquidating the long August position, a December cattle is sold. The speculator has reduced the risk substantially by shorting the December cattle, but also substantially reduced the reward. The speculator has thus replaced a high-stake bet on the outcome of the report with a low-stake one. Again, when there was a holding period for long-term capital gains, it was common practice to spread a long position.

It should be noted that the trader may be right in the bullishness of the report and still lose money. The report might show fewer cattle on feed to be marketed in December than in August. This may force all contracts higher, but may also force the December cattle to be stronger than the August cattle. This demonstrates the need to consider the outright positions and the spread to be different trades, each initiated and liquidated for its own reasons. It is too easy for the trader to use a simplistic approach when substituting spreads for outrights. They must be considered separate trades. The legging into the spread should be considered only as a minor commission saver.

LEGGING MISTAKES

Most legging-in and -out is done for the wrong reasons. The most common mistake is to leg into a spread from an unprofitable outright position. Suppose a trader is short December copper and is losing $2,000. The trader may not want to confront the fact that the loss in equity is a failure. The trader believes that by hanging onto the trade there is a chance to make back the loss. No one can disagree that the speculator has a chance to turn the trade into a winner, but at that moment it is a failure.

It is common for traders to think that a realized loss of $2,000 is worse than an unrealized loss of $2,000. By realizing the loss, the trader feels forced to admit failure. Faced with the potential for psychological trauma and the necessity of putting up more margin, the trader decides to stall for time by shorting March copper. The trader has drastically reduced the chance of losing any more money and has reduced his or her margin needs. Temporarily, the trader has forestalled the need to admit failure and has no need to put up more margin.

Nothing has been accomplished, however, except increased commission costs. By totally eliminating the losing outright the trader would have no margin requirements and would be psychologically free to look for new profit potentials. The trader's chances of recouping his or her losses on the outright by profiting from the new spread position must be considered somewhere between slim and none. There is no point in locking-in a loss by spreading.

BAD SPREAD INTO GOOD OUTRIGHT

Much the same mistake, though less severe, is seen while legging-out of spreads. Traders will seek to convert an unprofitable spread into a profitable outright. Assume that a speculator is short December, long March copper and is currently losing $500. The speculator, seeing a downtrend developing in copper, decides to liquidate the long March copper and go net short December copper in an effort to regain the loss of $500.

This is not a bad tactic if the speculator coincidentally decides that short December copper is a good trade and that short December/long March copper is a bad trade. However, these types of coincidences are rare. The speculator must have the discipline to mentally separate the spread and the outright positions. The speculator must fight the fear of losing, a fear that might motivate the speculator to compound his or her losses by legging-out of a bad spread into a bad outright.

WHY TRADE SPREADS?

There are a number of significant reasons why the commodity futures trader should trade spreads or, at the least, watch them closely. A significant advantage is usually lower volatility, hence lower risk. The major exception to the rule of lesser volatility is intercommodity spreads. A common move in wheat is about $0.05 per day for an outright position, but the wheat spreads move only about $0.0025 per day. In other words, instead of a move worth $250, as in the case of an outright position, the spread will move only about $12.50.

Many commodities are so volatile that they require constant supervision. Spreads, on the other hand, are generally sedate enough that they can be monitored once a day or less. If an outright position account is fluctuating widely, the speculator must have more money in his or her account in order to weather the possible string of losses. Through the use of spreads, even small traders can participate in the commodity markets.

LIMITED RISK

Spreads are the only commodity investment that can have a limited risk. Storable commodities have what are called *carrying charges* (storage, insurance, and financing costs). As a result, there often occurs a situation where the price of a spread will rarely go past "full carry." This means that the trader can initiate a spread near that level and know the amount of risk involved.

LOWER RISK

Spreads usually offer a lower risk alternative to outright positions because of their hedged nature. This is an important consideration when comparing spreads versus outright positions. The spread trader should note that there are some spreads that can have higher volatility than outright positions, as in cattle versus hogs. Because one is trading two different commodities, it is possible that the prices of the two commodities go in opposite direction, resulting in losing or gaining money on both sides of the spread. This happens most frequently in intercommodity spreads and, to a lesser extent, in intermarket spreads.

LESS MARGIN

The exchanges allow the spread trader to deposit a much smaller amount of margin money because of their reduced volatility. For example, a brokerage firm may require that the trader put up $1,800 for an outright wheat position, but only $300 to initiate a wheat spread. This allows the small trader to trade commodities and allows any trader to acquire a greater degree of diversification. Also, new commodity traders have an opportunity to learn about the commodity futures market while risking smaller amounts of money.

The lower margins allow the trader to place more trades in more commodities, thus giving the trader the ability to diversify and not depend on the success of a single commodity. The result of diversification is a reduction in the volatility in the trader's equity. With a $10,000 account, the trader may safely be able to enter two to four outright positions, but can safely initiate 10 or more spread positions.

This ability to spread the account risk can have an important impact on the trader's profitability. For example, a trader who is long wheat would have lost margin money if the price of wheat dropped limit-down for two consecutive days. If the wheat trader had started an account with $2,000, the loss of the original margin money would mean the trader was no longer a wheat trader. On the other hand, it would take six consecutive losses of margin money to turn the trader from a wheat spread trader to an ex-wheat spread trader. This ability to withstand more losses can contribute greatly to the trader's staying power in the marketplace.

LOCKED-LIMIT DAYS

The hedged nature of most spreads provides a protection against locked-limit moves. Commodity prices can move dramatically because of political action, weather, government reports, and so on. This can create locked-limit days, where prices move their daily allowable limit and no trading takes place. An outright trader with the wrong position can lose thousands of dollars before being able to liquidate the position. This can cause the trader's account to go into a deficit and force the trader to add money. In the same circumstance, the spread trader is largely protected. Because the spread trader is both long and short in a commodity, locked-limit days, though possibly anxiety-producing, do not usually create deficit positions. Although the spread may move against the trader after the prices cease being locked, the loss is usually substantially less than the outright would have suffered. If both contracts of the spread closed "at the limit" there is no change in the quoted spread value and no profit or loss to the trader on those days.

It is also worth noting that, because spreads are executed simultaneously, not as two separate positions, they may be liquidated during locked-limit days, whereas no outright positions can be liquidated. Thus it is possible that a person may wish to liquidate a spread opposite to our hypothetical trader's spread and be willing to take the other side of our trader's position. Frequently, this is the only trading that takes place on locked-limit days.

MORE ATTRACTIVE REWARD/RISK RATIO

A given spread may well provide a more attractive reward/risk ratio than a given outright position. For example, the value of the May/July wheat spread is largely determined by the carryover of soft red winter wheat. In the spring, the price of May wheat frequently is dominated by prospects for the new crop. This can create a situation where the outright price has fully discounted the known fundamentals and is trading in a tight trading range, while the May contract is gaining or losing substantially to the July contract. Thus the May/July wheat spread can provide the opportunity for trading in wheat while the outright long or short has very little opportunity.

The determination of whether a trader should initiate a spread or an outright position is up to the individual. It should be noted, however, that the outright position must provide a higher profit in order to return the same percentage gain. In wheat, because the spread margin may be $300 and the outright margin $1,800, the outright position must yield a net profit six times greater than the spread profit to yield the same return on investment.

USEFUL TO OUTRIGHT TRADER

A knowledge of spreads and spread action can be a powerful tool for the outright trader, since spread movements frequently signal the direction of the next move. If the near months of corn gain relative to the far months, this generally indicates a tightening of the supply-and-demand situation and a bull move could be in the works. Conversely, if the nearby does not gain on the far contract during a bull move, this may be an indication that the run up is technical in nature rather than representing a fundamental change in the market. Thus the astute trader can be tipped off to a potential short or the use of a bear spread.

A close examination of spreads also may tell the trader which particular contract month should be traded. Suppose the trader wishes to be long cattle. By examining the spreads and buying the contract that has been the strongest, the trader may get an increased return on the invested dollar. The trader who wished to short a commodity can examine the spreads and sell the weakest option. This one simple technique should significantly improve profit performance.

CARRYING CHARGES

Carrying charges occupy an important place in spread trading. They permeate the analysis of many commodities. No matter what type of analysis is being used, the trader must be cognizant of carrying charges. Carrying charges can be used to delineate risk as well as to provide profit opportunities. Prior to 1976, carrying charges were very stable because the financing component, mainly the interest charges on the cost of inventory, was slow to change. Recent years have shown so much increase in volatility that a silver spread, which is largely an interest-rate position, is highly risky. But first let us look at the grains, a ''traditional'' carrying charge market.

Suppose a person decided, for whatever reason, to buy 5,000 bushels of corn on September 1 and carry (or hold or store) it until December 1. The traders would have to pay several costs to carry the corn—storage for the corn, insurance against loss or damage, perhaps interest on a loan if the trader borrowed the money to buy the corn. Storage, insurance, and financing make up the carrying charges. Carrying charges are the cost of carrying a commodity for a particular period of time.

Carrying charges can vary for different people for the same commodity. If a person or company owned a corn bin that was built and paid for 20 years ago, the storage costs could be considered negligible. Storing the corn at a public elevator would cost much more. Some people or companies are in a position to borrow money less expensively than others. A very large company may be able to borrow money at less than the prime rate, whereas a smaller company may have to pay something above the prime rate. Hence the interest-rate component can change. It can be seen that the cost of carry is variable; nonetheless, an industry standard exists. *Full carrying charges* are considered to be the cost of storage and insurance at a public warehouse and financing at the prime rate plus 1%.

It is important to realize that a commodity can be held for less than the commonly accepted full carry cost. A commercial cash corn firm may charge customers $0.042 per bushel per month to store the corn, but the firm's actual cost may only be $0.030 per bushel per month. The commercial firm's carrying charge can therefore be less than its clients'. This is one reason why grain spreads rarely reach the commonly accepted full carrying charges. The common carrying charges mentioned by spread market participants should therefore be considered as only a rule of thumb. Any brokerage house will be able to provide the current cost of carry.

Carrying charges affect the futures market. The carrying charges for futures are identical to those in the cash market with the minor additional cost of delivery and redelivery. Carrying charges in the futures market apply only to commodities which are storable, deliverable, and redeliverable. The trader must be able to take delivery of a commodity, store it until the next futures contract expires, and deliver it against that contract.

Commodities which are easily storable and redeliverable include

Wheat
Corn
Oats
Soybeans
Soybean oil
Cotton
Orange juice
Coffee
Copper
Silver
Gold
Platinum
Plywood

Commodities which are not storable and cannot be redelivered and hence do not have carrying charges include

Live cattle
Live hogs
Feeder cattle

There are commodities that do not quite fall into these two neat categories. They include

Pork bellies
Sugar
Lumber
Soybean meal
Potatoes
Foreign currencies
Interest rates

Let us take a look at some of these unusual commodities.

Pork bellies have carrying charges only within a single calendar year. The carrying charges in sugar are unknown because the product can be delivered anywhere in the world outside the United States; the sugar market therefore ignores the existence of carrying charges. Lumber is storable but not redeliverable. Although soybean meal is perishable, the certificate delivery system creates a market with carrying charges. Potatoes are perishable. Currencies spreads are governed by the absolute price level and the levels of interest rates in the two countries. Treasury bills and Certificates of Deposit are not redeliverable. Treasury bonds are redeliverable, but have a very tricky delivery process that can push prices away from apparent carrying charges.

STORAGE AND INSURANCE

Storage and insurance charges change occasionally, and spreaders should be alert for such changes. Traders should also note that storage charges vary from one warehouse to another. For instance, grain storage always includes a 3-month minimum commitment following harvest. The current charges can be obtained from a broker or the exchange on which the commodity is traded.

FINANCING COSTS

Financing costs make up the greatest portion of carrying charges. It is always assumed that the money necessary to buy and hold the cash commodity is borrowed. Even when the money is not borrowed, there is a cost to use it. The user loses the opportunity to use the money in other investments. Even though this opportunity cost is usually less than the cost of borrowing, the latter is considered the financing cost.

The borrowing cost used for calculating carrying charges is the prime rate plus an additional 1%. If the prime rate is 20%, the financing cost would be 21%. This simulates the cost to most businesses in the position of carrying the cash commodity.

With March copper at $0.70 and the prime rate at 18%, it would cost $0.0665 to finance the copper until September. Half the finance costs are charged because it is 6 months from March to September. The interest rate used would be 18% plus 1%, or 19%. This would be divided in half, because of the 6-month time span, and multiplied by the price of copper. Thus 9.5% times $0.70 equals $0.0665. Storage and insurance would be extra.

There is sometimes confusion as to how many months there are between futures contracts. For instance, some people contend that traders should count the first month in the spread, so that from March to September would count as 7 months. The correct way, however, is to assume 6 months from March to September. This is counting from the typical first delivery day in March, March 1, to the typical first delivery day in September, September 1.

CARRYING CHARGE MARKETS

A market where the back months are priced higher than the near months is called a *carrying charge market*. Figure 5 shows wheat contract prices in a carrying charge market. Table 2 presents full carrying charges for each possible spread at the time this chart was constructed (June 23, 1981).

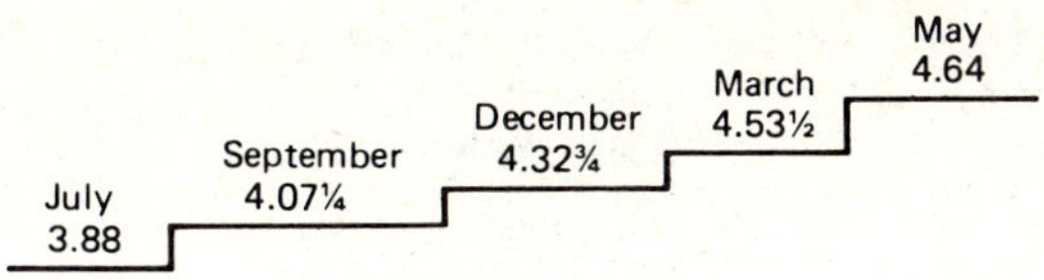

FIGURE 5. Wheat, normal carry market.

The actual spreads were therefore at the percentages of full carry given in Table 3. It is apparent that spreads within one commodity, one market, and one crop year can fall within a large range of percentage of full carry. In this example, spreads ranged from a low of 44% to a high of 81% of full carry.
The percentage of full carry the spreads represent gives the spreader a lot of useful information. If the spreader wanted to be bull spread, the spreader would have more confidence in the bull spread that was at 81% of full carry than the one at 44%, all other things being equal. Conversely, the bear spreader would be more comfortable bear spreading March/May rather than July/December.

Traders should not think that they only need to find the spread at the greatest or least percentage of full carry. There can be reasons for the divergence in percentage of full carry. The trader must examine the fundamentals to ensure that the reasons for the divergence may not work against the proposed spread. For example, the spread at 81% of full carry could be that close to full carry because the market expects low exports as a result of the winter closing of the Great Lakes. Perhaps a bullish bias is built into the back spreads because the market is less sure that the situation will be as bearish in the far future as it is in the near future.

INVERTED MARKETS

An inverted market is a market in which the near contracts sell for more than the far contracts. This occurs in storable and redeliverable commodities when there is an exceptional demand for the commodity in the face of a tightness in supply. An example of an inverted market is seen in Figure 6.

TABLE 2. Wheat Carrying Charges

Spread	Full Carrying Charges
July/September	22
July/December	55
July/March	88
July/May	110
September/December	34
September/March	68
September/May	91
December/March	35
December/May	59
March/May	24

TABLE 3. Wheat Spreads Percentage of Full Carry

Spreads	Spread Value	Percentage of Full Carry
July/September	15 ¼	69
July/December	44 ¾	81
July/March	65 ½	74
July/May	76	69
September/December	25 ½	75
September/March	46 ¼	68
September/May	56 ¾	62
December/March	20 ¾	59
December/May	31 ¼	53
March/May	10 ½	44

In a nonstorable commodity, an inverted market simply means that the market has ascertained that the supply-and-demand situation is more bullish in the near contracts than in the far.

THE MEANING OF INVERTED OR CARRYING CHARGE MARKETS

The carrying charges that exist in many markets are an inducement to carry the cash commodity into the future. The closer the spread is to full carry, the greater the inducement is to carry the cash commodity. In effect, the market is bidding a higher price for the commodity in the future than now. It may be advantageous for a cash merchant to sell corn in the March futures at $3.25 than to sell it in the cash market now, in December, at $3.00. The greater the spread between the future price and the current price, the greater the quantity of corn will be offered in the future. This carrying charge also allows farmers to recoup the cost of building their own storage facilities.

Notice that only the most bearish situation could get the spread to full carrying charges. Full carrying charges are a message from the market to the holder of the cash commodity to store the commodity as long as possible. The cash holder can sell a futures contract in the future which will fully reimburse the holder for the carrying charges. Thus the carrying charges represent what the market is willing to pay someone to store the commodity. As the price differential moves away from full carry there becomes less incentive for someone to carry the commodity and more incentive to sell it on the spot market.

When spreads invert, with the nearby contracts trading for higher prices than the far contracts, the market is giving an incentive to the cash commodity holder

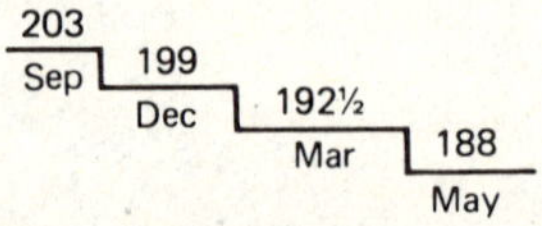

FIGURE 6. Oats, invested market.

not to store the commodity but to sell it on the spot market as soon as possible. The market may be saying, "Here, we will give you $2.03 a bushel for your oats now, but only $1.90 a bushel if you wait until March to sell them." The incentive to sell now is obvious. The cash commodity holder might not want to sell immediately, however, if it appears that the price will rise. The oats owner who was only offered $1.90 a bushel for March oats in the futures market may believe oats will actually be selling for $2.25 a bushel when March rolls around. This belief might provide enough incentive to hold the oats rather than to sell them now. Nonetheless, by not selling the oats a the current spot price of $2.03, this oats owner is not only speculating on a price rise but is also losing the opportunity to use the cash in other ways. For instance, the oats owner could sell the oats now for $2.03 and put the money in Treasury bills (if the oats owner sold enough oats). Because of this option, the oats owner must face the possibility that the oats will not rise in price enough to yield the same as an investment in Treasury bills. At yields of 12% a farmer must get an additional $0.06 per bushel plus storage for deferred delivery of 3 months at levels of $2.00 per bushel.

An inverted market thus provides a negative inducement to hold the commodity. It is sometimes called *negative carrying charges* when a market is inverted. One can consider this as a negative return for holding inventories. However negative this may appear to the cash commodity holder, it is a useful tool for speculators.

When spreads in storable commodities invert, there is usually a tightness in the supply-and-demand situation. The spread trader can capitalize on this situation by initiating bull spreads.

SPREADS RARELY GO TO FULL CARRY

Carrying charges rarely go to full carry for two reasons. First, if a spread were to trade at full carry, speculators would step in to sell the carrying charges (buy the spread) with very little risk, except for the slim possibility that the carrying charges might widen. Because the market does not consider this much of a risk, the spreads rarely get to full carry. As the spread gets closer to full carry and has less risk, more traders will buy the spread (buy the nearby contract and sell the far contract) until the spread reaches a point where buying pressure halts the spread from moving closer to full carry. This buying of the near contract and selling of the far contract exerts a pressure to move the spreads away from full carry and occurs before the spreads reach full carry.

Second, the full carrying charges represent the *theoretical* costs. A large commercial interest may not have to pay the full carrying costs. It is conceivable that a commercial interest will not borrow the money necessary to carry the inventory. Perhaps the commercial interest will simply carry the inventory rather than sell it and put the proceeds in the bank. Storage costs are usually lower for a commercial interest than for individuals. The costs outlined above were the price that the commercial interests are charging their customers. Since we can presume that they are making a profit, their own costs must be lower. It is therefore quite possible for a commercial interest to consider carrying charges to be significantly lower than the theoretical full carry. It is probable that commercial interests would be locking-in a profit if they were to sell futures contracts at theoretical full carry.

IMPLIED YIELDS

Carrying charges can also be looked at as yields on an investment. Since financing costs are the bulk of the cost of carry in some commodities, particularly the precious metals, a person could collect the financing charges instead of paying them.

Here is how it works. Gold is selling for $408 per oz and a trader has about $40,000 to invest. The investor seeks a high return with low risk (as we would). By looking in the newpaper the trader sees that a gold contract for delivery 1 year in the future is trading at $472. The investor buys 100 oz of cash gold for $408 per oz and simultaneously sells a 100-oz contract of gold for delivery 1 year in the future at $472 per oz. As far as the gold market is concerned the trader is long 100 oz of cash gold and short 100 oz of future delivery gold. But the trader has bought the gold at $408 and, in effect, presold it at $472. The difference between the buying and selling prices, $64, is the profit.

The profit of $64 is also the return on investment. It is the same as if the trader had placed $408 in a time deposit and was guaranteed by the bank that the $408 would grow to $472. In either case, the investment yields 15.7% per annum. (The $64 profit divided by the initial investment of $408 is 0.157 or 15.7%.) The investor may prefer to get long the nearby and take delivery rather than buy in the cash market. This gives the investor the option of redelivering against the short position. Unfortunately, this transaction may have complications. The trader must realize that additional margin may be required to be posted if the price of gold rallies. As the price of gold continues higher, the investor will find that the short gold position is an increasing loss. But, the net position is flat, or hedged. That is, the loss in the short futures is made up in the long cash position. Nonetheless, additional cash will have to be posted as margin for the futures position. The cash gold may not be used for margin purposes, although the value of the cash gold can be used as collateral for a bank loan. A trader expecting to use this method frequently can structure a three-way agreement with a bank to provide margin whenever necessary.

Precious metal spreads all have an implied yield feature. It is this direct correlation with short-term interest rates which allows the trader to seek profits by changes in carrying charge spreads.

BULL AND BEAR SPREADS

Bull and bear spreads are surrogate outright positions. In other words, the trader has an option of putting on an interdelivery bull or bear spread instead of an outright long or short position. Since nearby contracts generally gain on distant contracts in a bull market and lose value in a bear market, a bull spread consists of being long the nearby contract and short the deferred contract. Conversely, a bear spread is long the far contract and short the near contract. We can assume that spreads act this way because the effects of changes in supply and demand are more easily related to nearby contracts while the effects are more difficult to assess with regard to the deferred contracts.

When a trader, through various types of analyses, decides that a market will be in an upward trend, the trader may place bull spreads instead of outright long positions. The reverse is also true. A trader, looking at a market which appears to have burdensome supplies, has the option of placing bear spreads instead of shorting the market. The most common substitute for an outright position is an intercrop spread. The trader who wishes to go long could instead buy the old crop and sell the new crop if a near-term tightness in supplies is expected.

There are some commodities for which bull and bear spreads work and there are commodities where the reverse is true or where there is no such relationship. Bull and bear spreads work on commodities where, in fundamentally oriented bull markets, the nears gain on the fars. In technically oriented markets, even spreads in the commodities listed below will not necessarily follow the general pattern. Commodities in which the usual pattern applies include

Cocoa	Pork bellies
Copper	Soybean
Corn	Soybean meal
Oats	Soybean oil
Orange juice	Sugar
Plywood	Wheat

You might notice that these products are highly seasonal and therefore are subject to severe changes in nearby supply and demand. The effects of changes in the supply-and-demand situation are more significant in the near contracts than the deferred.

The commodities which work in the opposite direction include

Gold	Potatoes
Platinum	Silver

What would be called a bear spread in most commodities would be a bull spread in the later commodities. In other words, the trader would put on a short nearby/long deferred spread if the trader anticipated higher prices in the underlying commodity. This is the exact reverse of the general pattern of most commodities. These commodities tend to be in a pattern of the far contracts always being higher than the nears.

Bull markets in the precious metals, gold, silver, and platinum, occur because of a change in the market's evaluation of the commodity price level. Bull markets do not occur in precious metals because of a tightness of supplies. There are huge worldwide stocks of each of these commodities, which, though not necessarily in deliverable positions, can be quickly pulled into deliverable positions. Thus what might be a burdensome supply in other commodities keeps the value of spreads at or very near full carry. When the price of the commodity goes up, the amount of full carry widens; since the contract value increases with the price, the total interest will increase, with the most deferred contracts having greater costs (interest costs over longer time periods).

Potatoes, on the other hand, do not conform to the general pattern because they have a high degree of perishability and a seasonal production cycle. The round white potato contract, traded on the New York Mercantile Exchange, calls for delivery of potatoes grown in New York, Connecticut, and Maine and harvested in the fall. November is considered the first new crop futures contract for potatoes. The potatoes are placed in storage in November and are consumed throughout the winter, but the supplies are usually used up by June of the following year. Until recently, there had been a May contract which was considered the last futures in the crop year. Since the Commodity Futures Trading Commission banned May potato contracts, however, the April contract has now become potentially tight. Thus the April contract will always be at a premium to the November contract. If something is going to be bullish for the November contract, it is going to be even more bullish for the April contract.

The far contract also commands a premium because the market must compensate the holder of the potatoes for the loss of opportunities to use the money invested in the potatoes, lost interest on the money invested in the potatoes, and the risks due to the high perishability of the potatoes.

Nonstorable commodities (cattle, feeder cattle, and live hogs) tend to have no relationship between the outright price movement and the movement of the spreads, because it is virtually impossible to hold and redeliver such a commodity from one period to another. In other words, the trader who took delivery of live cattle in June would be extremely unlikely to redeliver them against the August contract. The cost of feed, weight, and time would make it undesirable. Each contract month is considered as a separate commodity.

INTERMARKET SPREADS

Several commodities are traded on more than one market. For example, wheat is traded on three separate markets, the Chicago Board of Trade, the Kansas City Board of Trade, and the Minneapolis Grain Exchange. Silver is traded on the Chicago Board of Trade, the Commodity Exchange in New York, and the London Metal Exchange. Coffee is traded in New York and London. Gold is traded in Chicago and New York.

Intermarket spreads entail the purchase of a contract in one market and the sale of another in the other market. For instance, a trader could buy Chicago wheat and sell Kansas City wheat. Intermarket spreads are relatively hard to initiate because they take place in different markets, cities, or even continents. Brokers accept them as basically two outright positions. An intermarket spread based on the temporary distortions in the same delivery month may also be considered an arbitrage. We will consider a spread to involve both a longer time interval and an underlying shift or change in the price relationship of the markets involved.

Intermarket spreads generally are regarded as the most complicated spreads. The necessity of analyzing two markets and the fine distinctions between contract specifications is sometimes too complicated for the novice commodity trader.

Intermarket spreads are usually left until some degree of confidence and competence has been built up by trading other types of spreads.

INTERMARKET WHEAT SPREADS

The most common type of intermarket spreads are the wheat spreads between the Chicago Board of Trade, the Kansas City Board of Trade, and the Minneapolis Grain Exchange. This happens in large volume every day as traders try to profit from the changes in the supply and demand between the three different exchanges. These changes are not obvious since each exchange trades a different type of wheat.

There are three types of wheat traded on commodity exchanges in the United States. Hard red winter wheat is traded at the Kansas City Board of Trade, northern spring wheat is traded at the Minneapolis Grain Exchange and, theoretically, hard red winter, northern spring, and soft red winter wheat can all be delivered at the Chicago Board of Trade. As a practical matter, trading focuses on the supply and demand for soft red winter wheat. This is because the three exchanges concentrate on the type of wheat grown in their immediate areas. Soft red winter wheat is the type of wheat grown nearest Chicago, but the exchange allows the delivery of the other two types of wheat against their wheat contract. The other two exchanges allow the delivery of one type of wheat only.

Traders should note that the three types of wheat tend to have different uses. The differences are often related to their protein content. The hard red wheat with a relatively high protein content is used for bread while the soft red wheat with a lower protein level is usually used for crackers. All three types of wheat are, to a limited extent, interchangeable. This means that the prices of the various types of wheat cannot be too different from one another. If the price of one variety of wheat gains too much on another variety of wheat, wheat users will change the blend of wheat in their processing to increase the use of the more inexpensive wheat.

The ability to deliver any type of wheat against the Chicago contract is a major factor in keeping the prices of the various types of wheat closely related. If the price of the futures contract in Chicago, which is mainly based on the fundamentals of soft red wheat, were to gain dramatically over Kansas City contract, wheat owners might find it to their advantage to barge hard red wheat from Kansas City to Chicago and deliver it against the contract there. The net effect of this is to limit the amount that Chicago futures can rise above Kansas City and Minneapolis futures by approximately the cost of purchasing and shipping the wheat from Kansas City or Minneapolis to Chicago. It is possible, however, for the Chicago contract to rise above these costs for a short time. If the price of the Chicago contract moves high enough to induce people to move wheat from outlying areas to Chicago, the price may stay high during the time it takes for the outlying wheat to be loaded and shipped to Chicago. Also, it will most likely take more than one bargeload of wheat to change the fundamental picture in Chicago enough to bring it in line with Kansas City and Minneapolis. The net effect is that prices will rarely go above the point that will bring wheat into Chicago from other points, but once it happens there may be a time lag before it moves back below that point. It is also possible that the ability to spread the two markets might bring prices back into line and physical delivery may prove unnecessary in most cases.

This more or less limiting factor can be compared with the concept of carrying charges. The price can move to a certain point but is unlikely to go beyond it. Both factors work consistently because the grain futures markets are inseparable from the cash markets and an integral part of the agricultural marketing program in the United States. The trader can thereby profit by putting on short Chicago and long Kansas City or Minneapolis spreads when prices reach the point where wheat will be shipped into Chicago. The trader should contact a broker to find out the costs to ship wheat from the various markets into Chicago. These costs change and the trader should be alert to its effect on trading.

It is important to note that since the Chicago market is the only market that allows the delivery of more than one variety of wheat the correction of price distortions is only one-way. This means that the Kansas City and Minneapolis contract prices can go above the Chicago price added to the costs of moving the wheat to those markets. The three wheat markets, however, rarely get to a point where barge rates come into play. Only a large relative shortage of soft red wheat could cause intermarket deliveries to become a market factor. The spreads between the three markets mainly respond to the relative supply and demand between the markets.

One major factor affecting price changes between the markets is the different growing seasons. The two winter wheats, traded in Kansas City and Chicago, are harvested in May, June, and July. The first new crop contract is the July contract and the last old crop contract is the May contract. The spring wheat, traded on the Minneapolis exchange, is harvested in late summer. The first new crop contract is the September contract and the last old crop contract is the July contract. This creates a number of seasonal trades. The July contracts in Kansas City and Chicago will tend to lose to the July Minneapolis contract because they will be burdened with large new crop supplies while the Minneapolis July contract will be scraping the bottom of the old crop barrel. The Minneapolis September contract will tend to lose to the Chicago and Kansas City September contracts for much the same reason but to a lesser degree. The Kansas City and Chicago contracts will be starting a seasonal rise in price while the Minneapolis contract will be dropping due to the increasing supplies of harvest.

Commission costs on intermarket spreads are usually double because traders must pay full commissions on both sides of the spread. There is typically a reduction in margins though. Brokerage houses will usually allow the intermarket spreader to put up the margin on the side of the spread which requires the highest margin. Thus if the Chicago wheat margin in $1,500 and Kansas City wheat margin is $1,200, the spread trader would be required to place $1,500 as a margin deposit.

INTERCOMMODITY SPREADS

Many commodities have similar uses and can be substituted for one another in certain circumstances. Spreads between these types of commodities are called intercommodity spreads. As an example, corn and oats are both used for feeding animals. The prices of these two commodities can vary over a wide range but there is a limit as to how far the price of one commodity can go over the price of the other commodity. If the price of corn were to gain too much on the price of oats, animal feeders would stop using the corn and substitute oats based on their relative protein content. This substitution would depress the price of corn while increasing the price of oats. Thus the price relationship between the two commodities would be forced back into line.

The strong relationship between commodities which are subject to spreading is most often their ability to be substituted for one another. Wheat versus corn, corn versus oats, hogs versus cattle, and Treasury bonds versus GNMAs are all examples of popular intercommodity spreads. Not quite as strong is the relationship between silver and gold (investments) and copper and lumber (housing).

Another popular intercommodity-spread relationship is that of a commodity and its products. Probably the two most popular intercommodity spreads of this type are the soybean versus soybean meal and soybean oil spread and the hog versus bellies spread. These are commodities which are related by one side of the spread being a product of the other side of the spread. Another spread of this type gaining in popularity is the cattle-feeding profit-margin spread, feeder cattle plus corn versus live cattle.

A third type of intercommodity spread is the soybean meal versus soybean oil spread. These two commodities are not related because of substitutability but because they are both products of the same commodity—soybeans. The supply and demand for one of the commodities has a strong effect on the supply and demand for the other commodity.

All other spreads between two commodities do not fall into the category we have delineated as intercommodity spreads. They may, in fact, be between "intercommodity," but unless there is some type of relationship between the two commodities we do not call them spreads.

Perhaps the largest volume of intercommodity spreads is between the various grains. Wheat, corn, and oats can all be used as feedgrains. However, the grains do not have a one-to-one relationship with each other. For instance, wheat contains roughly 15% more protein than does corn. Thus the price of wheat will typically be at least 15% more than the price of corn. Let us examine closer the wheat/corn spread as an example of an intercommodity.

WHEAT VERSUS CORN

Wheat versus corn is one of the most popular intercommodity spreads, if not the most popular. It has several interesting features of which the spread trader should be aware. The major factors to keep in mind are the supply and demand of the two commodities and the seasonality of production. If all things were equal, wheat would sell for 15% more than corn because of the extra feed value, but things are never equal. Hence wheat will trade for a greater or lesser premium than 15%. Because wheat is used mainly as a food grain rather than a feed grain, its uses tend to be different from corn. It is this extra utility as a food grain which typically allows it to trade for greater than its feed value over the price of corn. If corn was selling for $3 a bushel, one would expect wheat to trade at $3.45 a bushel based on its feed value. However, because of its use in bread, crackers, pastries, and so on, its value is usually much higher than 15% above the corn price. It is not unusual to see wheat sell for $4 a bushel when corn is selling for $3 a bushel. The 15% differential often serves to denote the narrowest point of the spread.

The major value of examining supply and demand is to try to discover the expected range of the spread. A year with a very large supply of wheat and a low supply of corn will cause wheat to sell for a much closer value to corn than if the reverse were true. In fact, in several years, where there was a large supply of wheat relative to corn, the price of wheat actually was below the price of corn. While it did not sell there for a particularly long period of time, it should alert traders of the possibility that the 15% greater feed value does not *necessarily* present a floor to the value of wheat over corn. It takes time to adjust feeding rations and the different feed properties of wheat will result in other dietary changes necessitating planning on the part of the feedlot. The major types of wheat in the United States were developed for bread and bread products, not for livestock feed. Therefore, the animal feeders, even with the price of wheat below corn, will not turn to exclusively wheat over corn. The wheat creates a meat slightly different from the corn. Feeders will introduce larger quantities of wheat to the diet, but they do not feed exclusively wheat.

One potential clue to the value of the wheat versus the corn is the ratio of their total supplies. When there is a large supply of wheat relative to corn, the demand for wheat will have to be exceptionally strong to move its price to a level much higher than the corn's price.

The other major factor to consider when trading wheat versus corn is the seasonality of production. Wheat is harvested mainly in June and July while corn is harvested in October–December. The first new crop contract of wheat is July and the first new crop contract for corn is December. Both wheat and corn reach their price lows for the year typically during the harvest period. The July contract tends to be the weakest contract for corn.

Because July is a seasonally strong month for corn due to the slowly reducing supply and yet consistent demand, the price of July corn tends to gain on the price of July wheat from the period of the preceding December through to the expiration of the July contract. From that point until the following December the situation changes. December corn typically is the weakest month for corn while December is a reasonably firm wheat contract. Thus from July through to December wheat prices are reasonably firm; from July through to December, the December contract of wheat tends to gain on December corn. Figures 7 and 8 show the seasonality of the various contracts.

The wheat/corn spread has been a favorite of seasonal traders for many years. The specific highs and lows and the exact timing are a function of the supply and demand of the two commodities for that particular year.

CRUSH SPREADS

The most complex spread is the *crush spread*. This is used extensively by soybean crushers as a hedge mechanism. It involves the purchase or sale of soybean contracts with the opposite transaction in its two products, soybean oil and soybean meal. There are two separate spreads that can be achieved with these three

DECEMBER WHEAT

11 YEARS

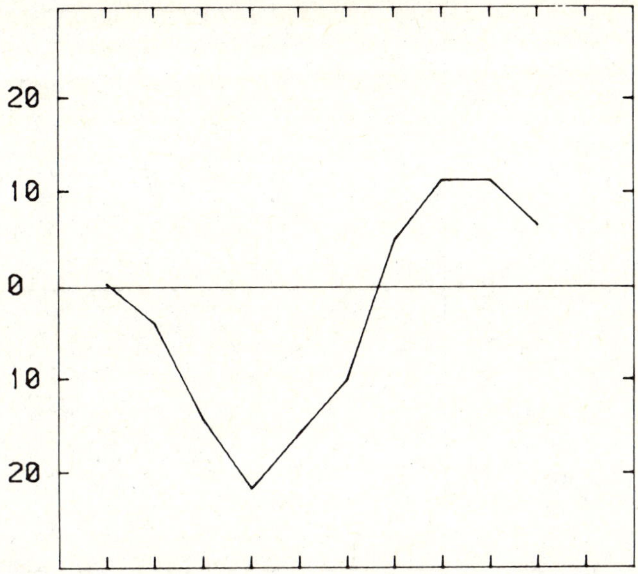

	J-F	F-M	M-A	A-M	M-J	J-J	J-A	A-S	S-O	O-N	N-D	D-J
Average Move		-4.3	-10.1	-7.5	5.9	5.8	14.8	6.3	0	-4.9		
% Reliable		63.7	81.9	81.9	45.5	45.5	36.4	54.6	72.8	45.5		
Avg. Up Move		5.6	4.9	15.3	19.4	22.5	60.3	16.5	11.6	9.2		
Avg. Down Move		9.9	13.5	12.5	5.4	8.2	11.2	5.9	30.9	21.9		
Greatest Up Move		12.1	8.1	29	46.1	41	152	43.9	63.8	17.8		
Greatest Down Move		37.7	61.8	39.3	7.9	14	40.6	20	43.4	50.8		

FIGURE 7. December wheat seasonality (11 years).

commodities. One is the *crush spread* and the other is the *reverse crush spread*. The first spread, also called "putting on the crush," is a duplication of soybean crusher transactions. The crush spread entails buying one contract of soybean futures and selling one contract each of soybean oil and soybean meal.

Soybean crushing or processing as a business requires a premium of the value of the meal and oil over the value of the soybeans. The soybean crusher receives profit largely depending on the margin between the products and the beans. This difference is called the *gross processing margin*. The soybean processor must buy soybeans, crush them into its components—meal and oil—and sell the meal and oil for a combined price higher than what the processor paid for the soybeans plus other costs and overhead. Many soybean crushers hedge their production by putting on the crush spread. They are typically trying to lock-in a profitable crush margin instead of leaving the profits to the vagaries of the marketplace.

The crush spread is particularly attractive during periods of large supply of the products and a strong demand for the soybeans. The soybean demand could

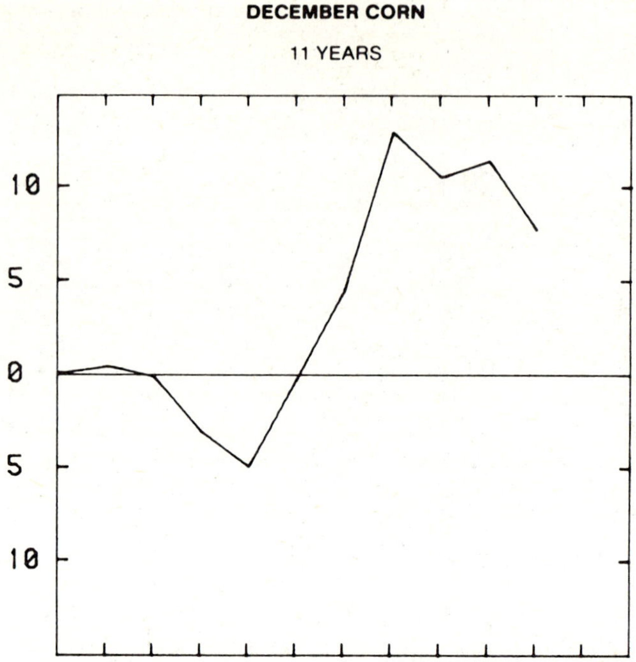

	J-F	F-M	M-A	A-M	M-J	J-J	J-A	A-S	S-O	O-N	N-D	D-J
Average Move	0.3	-0.6	-3	-1.9	4.7	4.7	8.4	-2.4	0.8	-3.7		
% Reliable	45.5	54.6	45.5	63.7	45.5	45.5	45.5	54.6	36.4	63.7		
Avg. Up Move	5.4	3.7	3.3	7.1	14.2	20.3	30.8	6.1	11.2	6.8		
Avg. Down Move	3.9	4.3	10.5	7.1	3.3	8.3	10.2	9.5	5.1	9.7		
Greatest Up Move	19.1	8.9	7.7	19.6	26	59.9	59.8	10.2	31.7	12.5		
Greatest Down Move	13.4	10.7	29	17.4	6.9	21.3	19.8	36.4	17.4	22.9		

FIGURE 8. December corn seasonality (11 years).

potentially stem from exports. Traders should watch the weekly and monthly crush figures as a clue to the actions of the soybean crushers. By watching these figures the spread trader may be able to tell whether the soybean crushers are reducing their volume of crush due to a lack of profitability. The spreader should not be confused, however, by the normal period of shutdown around Labor Day and Christmas. Crushings take a sharp drop during those two periods as soybean processors shut their plants for their staff to take holidays and for routine maintenance. Traders should also be examining the cash crush margins at all times, since they also give a clue to the current conditions in the marketplace.

There is also a seasonality to crush margins. They tend to be widest (the products are worth the most compared to the beans) just at harvest time. This makes perfect sense when you consider that harvest time is the point of the greatest supply of the soybeans and at the same time may be the period of strong demand for meal and oil.

The reverse crush spread is more common than the crush spread. It is the opposite of what a soybean crusher would be doing in the marketplace. As was mentioned previously, sometimes the gross processing margin will deteriorate to a point where there is little or no profit in crushing soybeans. This typically comes about as an overproduction of the meal and oil in the face of a relatively strong market in soybeans. It is difficult to ascertain exactly when soybean crushing becomes unprofitable. Depending on where they are and how much hedging they have done and what percentage of their capacity they are running at, the minimum crush margin necessary to profile a profit can vary from company to company and even over a wide area within a particular company.

When the gross processing margin becomes unprofitable, the soybean processor begins to think of reducing or stopping the processing of soybeans. Typically, the soybean crusher will continue to process soybeans for some time after moving into an unprofitable situation. This is not as strange as it sounds at first. The loss on the processing of soybeans is usually less than the loss that the crusher will suffer if the crusher had no revenue coming in. Even without processing any soybeans, the processor must continue to pay heat, light, financing charges on inventory, and so on. There may also be labor problems if the crusher is continually shutting down and reopening. It is often a more prudent plan to lose a small amount of money on the processing of beans rather than more money by shutting down. Also, the plant will sometimes lose less money if it processes a lot of soybeans than when it produces just a few. The higher the production is as a percentage of capacity, the more efficient the processing. Thus the per unit cost of processing is reduced.

Nonetheless, after a few months of losing money, soybean processors will begin to cut back production or shut down entirely. They will sometimes move from a two-shift schedule to a one-shift schedule or take an extra week of holidays near Labor Day or Christmas. The eventual aim of cutting back production is to decrease the apparent surplus of soybean products on the marketplace. This obviously does not happen overnight. It can take several months for an apparent surplus to be worked down to a level which increases the gross processing margins. Thus the reverse crush spreader typically does not have to rush into positions.

The crush and reverse crush spreader should be aware that the crush margins usually trade within a wide range. Crush spreads placed at the high end of this range and reverse crushings put on at the low end can be a very profitable strategy over the long run. It does, however, require nerves of steel and a large bankroll. It is not uncommon for a crush margin to go against the trader by $0.10, $0.20, or even $0.30. This is particularly true of the normal crush spread. The reverse crush spread, though theoretically of less risk, can also become unprofitable by tens of cents. It is obvious that the situation will eventually return to normal, but the spread trader must be well capitalized in order to withstand the margin calls.

The crush and reverse crush spreader must also consider the ratio of the various contracts to each other. The exchanges allow the placing of crush and reverse crush spreads in the ratio of one meal and one oil contract for every one soybean contract. Unfortunately, the number of bushels in one soybean contract does not yield the number of tons of soybean meal and the number of pounds of soybean oil in one contract each. Nonetheless, spreaders should be aware that most brokerage houses will allow the crush and reverse crush spread for the margin necessary to carry just the soybeans.

SOURCES OF INFORMATION

The following is a list of sources of information that will be of interest to spread traders. A packet of information on spreads may also be obtained by simply writing to Courtney Smith, 1614-675 West Hastings, Vancouver, B.C., V6R 4W8, Canada. It would be worth checking with major brokerage houses for information and even a newsletter specifically for spread traders.

BIBLIOGRAPHY

Commodity Spread Trader, Hadady Publications, 61 South Lake Avenue, Suite 309, Pasadena, CA 91101. This is a biweekly publication that issues specific spread suggestions. A telephone recorder message comes with the service. They have had a good track record but need more space devoted to justifying the suggested spreads.

Smith, Courtney D. *Commodity Spreads, Techniques and Methods For Trading Financial Future, Grain, Meat, and Other Spreads,* Wiley, NY, 1982. This book expands on the material presented in this chapter. In addition, most of the book deals with methods of analyzing and trading commodity spreads. Most of the trading techniques described are also useful for the trader of outright positions.

Dobson, Ed. *Commodity Spreads,* Traders Press, Box 10344, Greenville, SC, 29603; 1971. The book is composed of charts of spread price action going back to 1971. It is indispensable when using historical comparison analysis. It is also very useful for examining seasonal tendencies and obtaining prices for regression and correlation analysis. Highly recommended.

Esserman, Wayne. *Odds On Grain Spreading,* Ewe Publishing, Box 201, Delphi, IN 46923. This is an examination of the monthly seasonality of intramarket wheat, corn, and soybean spreads. The method used to determine the seasonality is the examination of historical price patterns rather than the ratio to the moving average method. Recommended for the grain spreader.

Spread Scope, Box 5841, Mission Hills, CA 93145. No spread trader can be without a subscription to *Spread Scope*. It is a weekly chart service totally devoted to spread price charts. It is timely and complete. One very useful feature is the table of carrying charges at the back of each issue. Highly recommended. The same company also publishes an advisory letter which analyzes spreads from a technical perspective.

CHAPTER 13

COMMODITY OPTIONS

CONTENTS

FUNDAMENTAL CONCEPTS 4

Pull and Call Options 4
Option Expiration 4
Strike Force 4
Option Premium 5
Option Identification 5

RISK/REWARD STRUCTURE 6

Ways to Profit from an Option 6
"In-the-Money" and "Out-of the Money" 7
Options Diagram 8

HISTORY OF OPTIONS TRADING IN THE UNITED STATES 10

The Precommodity Exchange Act Era 10
The London Markets 11
Options Banned 11
Options Pilot Program of 1981 12
Security Exchanges 12

COMMODITY OPTION MARKETS TODAY 13

Options on Futures Contracts 14
Options on Actual Securities 14
Dealer Options 17

OPTION PRICING 17

Leverage and Insurance Value 17
Relatoinship Between Market and Strike Price 21
Underlying Market Volatility 23
Short-Term Interest Rates 24
Term Until Expiration 25
Pricing Model 25

OPTION TRADING STRATEGIES 26

Option Buying 29
Naked Option Selling 30
Covered Option Writing 31
"Covered" Option Buying 33
Option Spreads 34
Option Straddles 36

COMMERCIAL APPLICATIONS OF COMMODITY OPTIONS 38

Options as an Alternative to Futures 38
Price and Quantity Risk 40
Delta Hedging 40

MARGINING 42

GLOSSARY 44

BIBLIOGRAPHY 47

CHAPTER 13

COMMODITY OPTIONS

John W. Labuszewski
Jeanne Cairns Sinquefield
Lawrence I. Schulman

Interest in commodity trading has grown tremendously during the past decade as evidenced by the almost exponential growth in commodity futures volume. Unfortunately, commodity options trading has not kept pace with the growth of commodity futures. This relative inactivity may be attributed, of course, to government regulations, which have effectively relegated commodity options to a secondary role in the commodity marketplace. Interest in commodity options has never died, however, and recent developments suggest that commodity options are likely to reemerge within the next few years as important trading and risk-management vehicles, perhaps even rivaling or surpassing futures volume.

Commodity options are nothing new—they have been offered in many different forms for commodities as diverse as wheat, gold, and even tulip bulbs. Trading of commodity options, however, has often been surrounded by controversy. The controversy was so great in the early part of the century that Congress prohibited options trading for traditional agricultural commodities such as grains and livestock. Other restrictions have been enacted in response to other controversies and by the 1970s, options were domestically available from only a handful of closely supervised gold and silver dealers.

In 1981 the Commodity Futures Trading Commission (CFTC) introduced an options pilot program which permits the nation's commodity futures exchanges to offer options on a limited number of commodities. Commodity options have also captured the imaginations of the nation's security exchanges, which have introduced options on debt securities. Introduction of commodity options by organized exchanges is an event analogous to the introduction of the Chicago Board Options Exchange (CBOE), which was organized in 1973 to trade stock options. The CBOE presented an alternative to the loosely organized over-the-counter (OTC) market for stock options which dominated prior to 1973. The OTC market now plays a relatively minor role relative to option exchanges. Similarly, one might expect that exchange-traded commodity options eventually will dominate commodity options traded off-exchange. Before we continue with our story, let us review the fundamentals of options trading.

FUNDAMENTAL CONCEPTS

Any analysis of options trading—commodity or stock options—must begin with a review of the fundamental concepts and terminology associated with the option trade. Fortunately, commodity options share much of the same fundamentals with stock options. The reader who is familiar with stock options, therefore, might wish to proceed ahead to "Risk/Reward Structure."

PUT AND CALL OPTIONS. An option is a contractual agreement contingently to purchase or sell a particular asset or financial right, such as a commodity or a commodity futures contract, for a specific price within a specific time period. There are two basic types of options, a "call" option and a "put" option. A *call* option gives the holder (or option buyer) the right, but not the obligation, to *purchase* the underlying commodity. The call writer (or option seller) is obligated to sell the particular commodity upon the holder's demand and in accordance with the previously agreed-upon conditions. Similarly, a *put* option gives the holder the right, but not the obligation, to *sell* the underlying commodity. The put writer is obligated to buy the particular commodity upon the holder's demand and in accordance with the previously agreed-upon conditions.

The easiest way to recall the distinction between a call and a put option is by associating the implications of the terms "call" and "put" with the contractual rights of the option holder. The call option holder buys the right to purchase the commodity underlying the call option. The right to purchase is implied by the term "call." On the other hand, the put option buyer buys the right to sell the commodity underlying the put option. Again, the right to sell is implied by the term "put." Often, one will hear of a call option holder "calling" the underlying commodity from the writer; or, conversely, of the put option holder "putting" the underlying commodity to the writer. This process is also referred to as *exercising* the option.

OPTION EXPIRATION. The option holder's right to exercise the option contract expires on the expiration date. There is an important distinction between the option expiration date and the exercise date. The exercise date is the date upon which the option is actually exercised while the expiration date is the last day upon which the option may be exercised. These terms are needed to differentiate between a "European" and an "American" option. A "European" option can only be exercised on the expiration date. Its expiration date is the same as the exercise date (if indeed the option is exercised by the holder). An "American" option, on the other hand, can be exercised at any time prior to the expiration date at the holder's discretion. Thus the exercise date can be different from the expiration date. We will concentrate our attentions on American options common to the domestic option markets.

STRIKE PRICE. When a holder of an option exercises the option the holder buys, in the case of a call option, or sells, in the case of a put option. This trade is transacted at a particular price agreed upon by both buyer and seller at the time the option is "written." (A writer or option seller is considered to have "written" or "granted" an option when the option is sold.) This price is known as the "strike" or "exercise" price. If two individuals enter an option contract they would negotiate the strike price as well as other contract terms. Where there are a large number of option buyers and sellers, however, it is rather inconvenient or even chaotic to negotiate the strike price of individual option contracts. Exchange-traded options, therefore, are characterized by a standardized strike price and other contract terms. Exchanges will only permit traders to negotiate the option price or "premium."

Typically, there will be more than one strike price established for each commodity option with a particular expiration date. The strike price will be set so that there are strike prices in the immediate pricing vicinity above and below the price of the underlying instrument. Normally, these strike prices will be set at regular intervals.

OPTION PREMIUM. The option "premium" is the price one pays to buy the option, or the price one receives for selling the option. The premium is negotiated between the buyer and seller at the time the option is written. Generally, a call option premium will rise as the price of the underlying instrument rises and drop as the underlying price drops. The holder of a call option, then, is hoping that the underlying price will rise. A put option premium will generally decline as the price of the underlying instrument rises and rise as the underlying price declines. In this case, the holder is hoping that the underlying price will go down while the writer is hoping that the underlying price goes up.

This type of price behavior may be explained with an example. Assume that the price of gold was $500 and the strike price on a gold call option was $400. The holder would make $100 by exercising the option. When the holder exercises the call option, the holder pays the writer $400 and receives the gold. The gold may subsequently be sold for $500 in the open market and the holder will thereby realize a $100 profit. (This profit is decreased to the extent of the premium originally paid to acquire the option.) Clearly, a call option is more valuable when the underlying price is $500 than when the underlying price equals $400 or even $300. This example is reversed for put options. If the price of gold was $300 and the put option strike price equaled $400, the holder would make $100 by exercising the put. If the underlying price was $400 or $500, the put option would be considerably less valuable.

OPTION IDENTIFICATION. An option contract for a particular commodity may be fully identified by reference to whether it is a put or a call, the expiration date, and the strike price. These contract terms are called the option "type," "class," and "series." All put options are regarded as options of the same type as are all call options. Options of the same type which share a common expiration date are said to be of the same class. Finally, all options of the same type and class which have the same strike price comprise an option series.

Exchange-traded options are standardized with respect to the option contract terms. The exchange will set particular strike prices and particular expiration dates. Only the premium will vary once the option is listed as available for trading. This standardization or "fungibility" generally differentiates exchange-traded options from dealer options which are not always so standardized. Exchange-traded options also permit traders to liquidate or offset long and short positions before expiration and without exercising the option. Thus, if one were to enter an "opening sale" or an "opening purchase" of a particular option series, the trader could subsequently cancel that short or long position by engaging in a "closing purchase" or a "closing sale," respectively.

RISK/REWARD STRUCTURE

The central and perhaps most confusing feature of an option contract is that the holder and writer assume very different risk/return postures. The holder's risk is limited to the price of the option or premium paid on purchase, whereas the writer's risk is practically unlimited. The holder's potential return is practically unlimited while the writer's potential return is limited to the premium received on purchase. Why, given this arrangement, would a trader want to sell an option? Let us examine the risk/reward structure of an option contract more closely.

WAYS TO PROFIT FROM AN OPTION. There are two ways in which a holder can profit from buying an option contract. A holder can take a profit by exercising the option or by selling the option contract before it expires. Let us assume that the holder bought a sugar call option contract for \$0.01 per lb when sugar was selling for \$0.15 per lb. The strike price is \$0.16 per lb.

If the price of sugar stayed at the \$0.15 level, the holder would not be inclined to exercise the option—if the holder did so, the holder would be buying sugar at \$0.16 when it is only worth \$0.15 in the market. But let us say that the price of sugar went up to \$0.20. At \$0.20 the holder could exercise the option at \$0.16 and sell the sugar in the cash market for \$0.20, or \$0.04 less the \$0.02 premium for a \$0.02 profit. As we learned in "Fundamental Concepts," the premium would have gone up if the price of the underlying commodity—in this case sugar—had gone up. Assume that the premium had risen to \$0.07—in this case, the holder can sell the option at the increased premium and realize a profit of \$0.05. The holder's profit equals the difference between the closing sale price of \$0.07 and the opening purchase price of \$0.02.

Similarly, there are only two ways in which an option grantor can profit from writing an option. An option writer can take a profit by "buying back" the option contract before it expires or by waiting for the option to expire. If our sugar call option buyer in the previous example had not exercised the option because sugar prices remained static or declined, the writer would receive the full premium paid to him or her when the writer sold the option contract to the holder. Let us say that the price of sugar went down to \$0.10 per lb. In this case, the call option premium would have declined—the writer could buy the same call option with the same expiration and strike price at the lower premium. In this way, the writer cancels or offsets the original option sale with an option purchase. The profit is implied in the difference between the premium at the time of the opening sale and the time of the closing purchase. Tables 1, 2, and 3 summarize the fundamental concepts of options.

TABLE 1. Identifying an Option

	Type	Class	Series
Put or call	A gold put		
Expiration		A December gold put	
Strike price			A $400 December gold put

"IN-THE-MONEY" AND "OUT-OF-THE-MONEY." An option holder would only exercise an option when profit can be realized—naturally, it would be foolish to exercise an option when one incurred a loss by so doing. An option writer is also interested in whether the holder can be expected to exercise the option because if there is no exercise, the writer keeps the premium, which could then be regarded as pure profit.

In order to identify options which represent likely candidates for exercise, one must examine the relationship between the strike price and the underlying commodity price. In the case of a call option, the holder could profitably exercise an option when the underlying commodity price is greater than the strike price. The holder would be buying at the low strike price and would be able to sell at the higher prevailing price. (The price that was originally paid for the option or premium is irrelevant in the consideration of whether or not to exercise the option because it is a "sunk" or irretrievable cost.) If the prevailing price were lower than the strike price, there would be no incentive to exercise a call option because to do so would result in a loss to the holder.

Because the question of whether an option might be exercised or not is asked so frequently, the option trade has developed expressions to distinguish options which are likely to be exercised from those which are not likely to be exercised. An "in-the-money" option is one which is likely to culminate in an exercise, whereas an "out-of-the-money" option is one which is not likely to be exercised. Specifically, an in-the-money call is one where the underlying commodity price exceeds the strike price, while an out-of-the-money call is one where the underlying commodity price is less than the strike price. The terms are simply reversed for put options—an in-the-money put is one where the underlying commodity price is less than the strike price, while an out-of-the-money put is one where the

TABLE 2. Option Premium Movement

	Underlying Price Goes Up	Underlying Price Goes Down
Call option premium	Goes up	Goes down
Put option premium	Goes down	Goes up

TABLE 3. Results of an Option Transaction

	Holder	Writer
Exercising the option	Profits by exercise by the in-the-money amount (less the premium).	Loses by exercise by the in-the-money amount (cushioned by the premium).
Option expiration	Loses the entire premium.	Profits by the entire premium.
Closing or offsetting transaction	Profits if premium increases; loses if premium decreases.	Profits if premium decreases; loses if premium increases.

underlying commodity price is greater than the strike price. If the underlying market price equals the strike price, then the option is referred to as an "at-the-money" option and it is indeterminate whether the holder would want to exercise it or not.

OPTIONS DIAGRAM. Figure 1 illustrates the potential profit or loss which may accrue to the holder or writer of a call option contract. Let us assume that the call may be exercised for a gold futures contract and that the holder will wait until the expiration date to decide whether to exercise the option or let it expire. The option premium is \$40 per oz and the striking price is \$400 per oz. The holder loses while the writer receives the entire premium if the option is permitted to expire (regardless of whether the option is in-the-money or out-of-the-money).

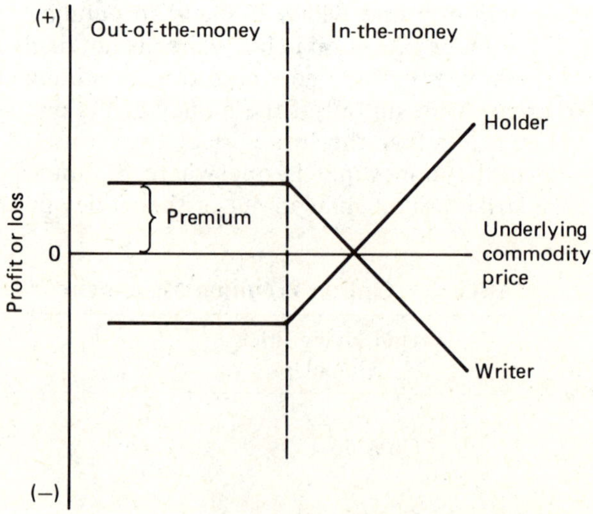

FIGURE 1. Risk/reward structure of a call option.

The holder can be expected, however, to exercise the option if it is in-the-money. The holder profits when exercising the option by the in-the-money amount less the price originally paid as premium. If, for example, the holder exercises the option when the underlying gold contract is worth $450, the holder makes $50 upon exercise less the $40 premium for a net profit of $10 per oz. If the holder exercises the option when the underlying gold contract is worth only $430, then the holder makes $30 upon exercise less the $40 premium for a net loss of $10 per oz. If the price of gold upon exercise equals $440 per oz, then the holder breaks even, that is, there are neither profits nor losses as a result of the transaction.

The writer's profit-and-loss scenario is represented as a mirror image of the buyer's profit-and-loss scenario. When the price of gold equals $450 upon exercise, the writer loses $50 upon exercise, but the writer's loss is cushioned by the $40 premium and the writer's net loss is $10. When the price of gold equals $430 upon exercise, the writer loses $30 through the exercise but retains the $40 premium for a $10 net profit.

It is interesting to note that it may be in the best interest for the holder to exercise an in-the-money option even when a net loss results. A holder always turns a profit by exercising an in-the-money option, which at the least, helps to cushion the original outlay to buy the option. If, of course, the option is out-of-the-money, the holder will almost invariably prefer to let the option expire and lose the premium to the writer.

The profit or loss associated with a put option is illustrated in Figure 2. The call option holder profits from an increase in the underlying gold price while a put option holder profits from a decline in the underlying price. The call option writer profits when the underlying price remains constant or declines, and the put option writer profits when the underlying price remains constant or increases.

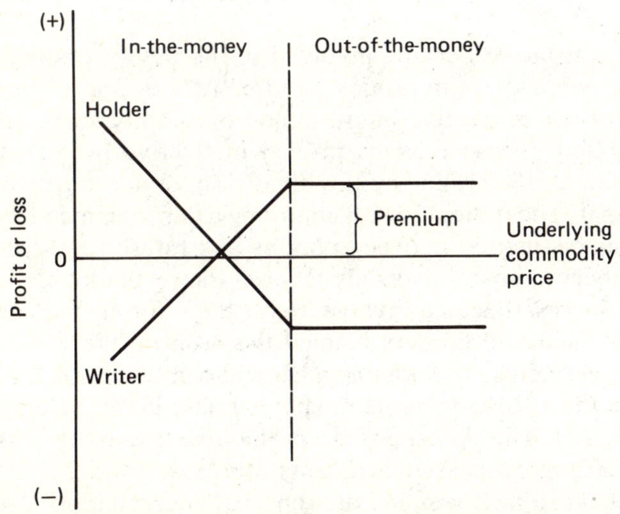

FIGURE 2. Risk/reward structure of a put option.

HISTORY OF OPTIONS TRADING IN THE UNITED STATES

The history of options trading in the United States is replete with instances of federal government intervention. This discussion, therefore, deals more with episodes of regulatory intercession than with trading experience.

THE PRECOMMODITY EXCHANGE ACT ERA. Commodity options have been known by many names including privileges, indemnities, bids, offers, advance guaranties, and decline guaranties. Commodity options first surfaced domestically somewhat over 100 years ago when privileges, a form of commodity options, appeared on the floors of the nation's grain exchanges. There were two types of privileges—bids and offers, which correspond roughly to puts and calls. The buyer of a bid had the privilege of selling grain futures to the privilege seller, while the buyer of an offer had the privilege of buying grain futures from the privilege seller. Rather than negotiate premiums, a fixed commission was charged for a bid and an offer, the strike price of which was adjusted below and above current market prices. Privileges could be obtained which expired by the end of the day, within a week or within a month, thus they were referred to as "dailies," "weeklies," and "monthlies."

Privileges proved to be very popular during the volatile up and down markets of the 1860s. They were met with considerable opposition, however, from farm groups who petitioned their state governments to prohibit option and futures trading. These farmers felt that malevolent speculators were responsible for volatile grain prices and were guilty of price manipulation. Accordingly, privileges were officially frowned upon by grain exchanges such as the Chicago Board of Trade, which adopted a rule in 1865 which denied privilege traders the protection of the exchange: "Privileges bought or sold to deliver or call for grain or other property by members of the Association shall not be recognized as a business transaction by the Directors or the Committee of Arbitration." This did not effectively discourage trading of privileges, and the rule was subsequently eliminated in 1869.

The Illinois legislature became involved in the option trading controversy in the 1870s. Lobbyists for farm groups and for traders, and businessmen pushed hard to protect their respective interests and eventually some compromised reforms were passed. These reforms proved ineffective in curbing the trade of privileges despite an 1885 ruling by the Illinois Supreme Court which found privileges to be illegal. The difficulty with enforcing a ban stemmed from the difficulty of making a fair distinction between options and futures and from the fact that exchange members almost universally ignored the regulations.

The U.S. Congress became involved with the issue in the early 1890s when grain prices declined and farmers blamed the drop on the evils of speculation. Congress came very close to adopting a general ban on options, but nevertheless failed to act. In the 1920s, the issue reemerged, and in 1921 Congress passed the Futures Trading Act. This Act imposed a prohibitive tax on earnings from privilege trading. In 1922 Congress passed the Grain Futures Act, which required exchanges and their members to maintain and file reports concerning privilege trading, and authorized the Secretary of Agriculture to conduct investigations of exchange operations. Failure to comply with the act could result in revocation of an exchange's status as a futures market. The effect of the 1921 and 1922 acts was effectively to end all commodity option trading on exchanges. A subsequent 1926 decision by the Supreme Court in *Trusler* v. *Crooks,* however, found the tax imposed by the 1921 act unconstitutional. Option trading immediately reemerged on the grain markets.

The dates of July 19 and 20, 1933 are significant in the grain trade. On those dates, wheat prices collapsed dramatically and privilege trading was labeled the culprit. As a result of political pressure from the farm lobby, Congress passed the Commodity Exchange Act of 1936, which banned all commodity option trading in certain enumerated domestic commodities including wheat, cotton, rice, corn, oats, barley, rye, flaxseed, grain sorghums, mill feeds, butter, eggs, and Irish potatoes. In 1938 the list was expanded to include wool tops; in 1940, fats, oils, cottonseed meal, cottonseed, peanuts, soybeans, and soybean meal; and in 1968, livestock, livestock products, and frozen orange juice. The result was that commodity options completely disappeared from the domestic commodity exchanges.

THE LONDON MARKETS. Meanwhile, options trading continued actively in London until the outbreak of World War II. Volumes remained minimal until the late 1960s when Americans, who were prohibited from trading options in the United States, "discovered" the London markets. Many domestic brokerage firms began to offer their services as intermediaries between American customers and members of the London exchanges. The American customer was at something of a disadvantage in this respect because the London exchanges' clearinghouse guaranties extend only to the local exchange members and not to the American customer.

Options were available in London in a number of diverse commodities including cocoa, coffee, copper, silver, sugar, lead, tin, and zinc. In contrast to so-called "American" options, London options could only be exercised on the expiration date. London options were and are available for expiration in 3-, 6-, and 9-month time. The London options are exercisable for a futures contract in the particular commodity.

The popularity of London options grew tremendously in the early 1970s. Unfortunately, the domestic option market during this period was characterized by some widely publicized scandals involving option-based get-rich-quick schemes. Some domestic retailers sold options to the public at excessive premiums and without "covering" their short option positions through ownership of the underlying commodity. The most notable case during this period was the *SEC* v. *Goldstein, Samuelson, Incorporated.* Goldstein allegedly had become the proprietor of a "Ponzi" arrangement; that is, he sold options uncovered under the assumption that if some of the options were exercised, they could be paid out of premiums received from new customers. Unfortunately, the bubble burst and the resulting scandal had far-reaching implications—reports were that investors who had become involved in this pyramid scheme lost $70 million.

OPTIONS BANNED. None of the retail sales abuses which allegedly occurred during this period was actually connected with exchange-traded options. Nevertheless, Congress decided to review federal regulation of commodity futures and option trading in order to prevent further scandals of this nature. The Commodity Futures Trading Commission Act of 1974 was the result of this review. The new law created the CFTC as an independent agency charged with the administration of the Commodity Exchange Act.

The new law continued the prohibition of exchange-traded options for the commodities enumerated prior to 1974. In addition, the CFTC was empowered to extend the prohibition to any other commodities covered under the new Act or to permit options on previously nonenumerated commodities to trade under whatever conditions it deemed appropriate.

Congress initially required the CFTC to develop regulations which would permit options to begin trading within a year. The CFTC responded by adopting regulations which would permit options to be traded off-exchange by closely supervised firms already engaged in the offer and sale of the physical commodity underlying the option. The regulations were made effective in 1977 when the CFTC licensed some 60 firms to transact business in London options and "dealer" options. The latter type of option is sold by the dealer in the physical commodity and is "covered" by the dealer's inventory of goods.

Sales abuses continued to occur, however, and in June 1978 the CFTC decided temporarily to suspend all sales of commodity options in the United States. The only exceptions to the ban included options traded between commercials and dealer options offered to the public, provided that the grantor firm was able to demonstrate financial capability. The exception to the ban was made in response to intense congressional pressure and near-certainty that Congress itself would act to permit existing dealer-option grantors to remain in business if the CFTC did not.

In 1978 Congress passed the Futures Trading Act of 1978. This law had the effect of reinforcing the CFTC's ban on options and required the CFTC to develop a plan which would adequately regulate options before the ban was lifted. It also recognized and sanctioned dealer options under specific circumstances.

OPTIONS PILOT PROGRAM OF 1981. For some time, the CFTC has discussed the possibility of permitting domestic commodity exchanges to trade options exercisable in futures contracts, much like London options. The purported purpose of the pilot program was to gather evidence to determine the economic benefits of options, to examine the effectiveness of customer protection rules, and to examine the effect that options trading would have on futures.

In September 1981 the CFTC published final rules which would govern exchange-traded options on the commodities which were not enumerated prior to 1974. In December 1981 eight domestic commodity futures exchanges submitted applications to trade options exercisable in futures contracts ranging from precious metals to imported agricultural commodities to financial instruments to stock indexes. The CFTC is also considering expansion of the pilot program to include options on physical commodities although no action has been taken as of this writing.

SECURITY EXCHANGES. While Congress and the CFTC had often taken measures which prohibited options trading on commodities, there was no similar ban on options exercisable for security instruments such as corporate stock. Consequentially, options exercisable in stock were traded actively in the over-the-counter markets under the auspices of the Put and Call Dealers Association. In

1973 the Chicago Board Options Exchange (CBOE), an offshoot of the Chicago Board of Trade, began trading stock options under strictly supervised conditions. In 1973 only 18 stocks were listed for trading, but this number grew to over 200 to date. In addition, other security exchanges such as the American Stock Exchange, the Pacific Stock Exchange, the Philadelphia Stock Exchange, and the Midwest Stock Exchange began to list stock options.

In the 1980s these security exchanges became interested in expanding the scope of their option markets to include trading of debt instruments, such as Treasury securities and GNMAs, domestic CDs, and foreign currencies. In December 1981 the Chairman of the Securities and Exchange Commission (SEC), which regulates the security exchanges and the CFTC, agreed that the SEC would have jurisdiction over options on actual security instruments such as Treasury bills and Treasury bonds, while the CFTC was to retain jurisdiction over options on futures contracts for security instruments as well as other physical commodities which are not security instruments. Although the legal status of this "Johnson–Shad" agreement is still being debated, it is likely that this regulatory framework will ultimately be endorsed by Congress.

COMMODITY OPTION MARKETS TODAY

Option contracts may be written for just about any kind of asset or financial right. Of course the regulatory framework permits only certain kinds of option contracts to be traded. Nevertheless, commodity option markets are or will soon be available for a wide range of different commodities.

The commodities which are the subject of option contracts or "underlying" commodities, may be categorized on the basis of whether they may be exercised for a "physical" or "actual" commodity, or a futures contract. For example, there are dealer options for physical gold bullion, while options for gold futures contracts are being proposed by commodity futures exchanges. There are also options for futures contracts based upon Treasury securities, and options for actual Treasury securities offered by security exchanges.

Actual commodities may be further classified on the basis of whether they generate interest income or not. For example, an actual Treasury bond will generate interest income for the holder of the security, whereas any income generated from a commodity such as gold or silver must be in the form of price appreciation. An option for an interest-bearing commodity closely resembles a stock option which generates periodic dividend income with the qualification that interest income is guaranteed while dividend income is contingent upon the corporation's success and dividend policy. A futures contract, whether it is based upon an interest-bearing commodity or not, will never generate interest income, and so options on futures are very much like options on non-interest-bearing commodities.

Option contracts written for futures contracts or actual commodities serve the same basic economic functions. Options provide insurance against adverse price movements for commercial market participants and provide speculators with a vehicle which may be used to profit from commodity price movement while limiting the risk associated with adverse fluctuations. There are, however, some important differences which arise from the use of options on different underlying commodities.

OPTIONS ON FUTURES CONTRACTS. Futures contract options are offered by the nation's commodity futures exchanges and are regulated by the Commodity Futures Trading Commission's option pilot program of 1981. The pilot program limits each commodity exchange to a single option market on those commodities for which option trading was not prohibited prior to 1974. This means that options may be traded for futures contracts on precious metals such as gold, silver, and platinum; financial instruments such as Treasury bills, Treasury bonds, GNMAs, bank Certificates of Deposit, and Eurodollars; some agricultural commodities such as sugar, cocoa, and coffee; and energy products such as heating oil and gasoline.

These new option markets offer some unique advantages over options exercisable in actual commodities. First, futures prices are widely disseminated over telecommunication devices, whereas cash market prices for many commodities which are not exchange-traded are sometimes more difficult to come by. Superior price dissemination may make it easier to trade options on futures contracts than options on actuals.

A second advantage of options on futures is that it is much easier to exercise the option contract. For example, when a put option on an actual is exercised, the buyer must have that physical commodity available. This means that the buyer would have to go into the cash market and buy that commodity for its full purchase price. In contrast, when a put option on futures is exercised, the buyer enters into a short futures position while the seller enters into a long futures position at the option strike price. Because the futures contract is highly margined, the cost associated with the exercise is minimal. Table 4 provides a description of the option contract terms proposed by domestic commodity exchanges under the CFTC's option pilot program.

OPTIONS ON ACTUAL SECURITIES. Options on interest-bearing commodities such as actual Treasury bills and Treasury bonds will be offered by the nation's security exchanges, which are regulated by the Securities and Exchange Commission. Options trading on securities exchanges first surfaced in 1973 with the formation of the Chicago Board Options Exchange. Although the CBOE only traded stock options initially, the question of whether or not there was any regulatory barrier to trading options on other securities did not appear until 1981. The success of financial futures such as Treasury bill, Treasury bond, and GMNA futures in the late 1970s and continuing into the 1980s has prompted these exchanges to explore ways to trade options on actual debt securities in addition to corporate stock. Although several commodity futures exchanges have contended that options on actual commodities traded for future delivery are most appropriately regulated by the CFTC, the Johnson–Shad agreement of 1981 has, for the most part, silenced this debate.

The primary advantage to trading options based on actual commodities is that it is somewhat simpler than trading options for futures contracts. A futures contract is a derivative instrument once removed from the actual commodity, and an option for a futures contract is a derivative to a derivative and is thus twice removed from the actual commodity.

TABLE 4. Summary of Futures Contract Options

Exchange	MidAmerica	CBT	COMEX	CME	KCBT	NYFE	CSCE	NYMEX
Underlying commodity	33.2 oz of gold	$100,000 Treasury bonds	100 oz of gold	Standard & Poor's 500 Index multiplied by $500	Value Line Index multiplied by $500	NYSE Index multiplied by $500	112,000 lb raw sugar	1,000 barrels No. 2 heating oil
Trading months	March, April, June, August, September, and December	March, June, September, and December	April, August, and December	March, June, September, and December	March, June, September, and December	Not available as of this writing	March, July, and October	March, July, September, and December
Last trading day	Second Friday of month prior to option month	First Friday at least ten business days before first notice day of futures	Second Friday of month prior to option month	Third Thursday of contract month (same as futures)	Last business day of contract month	Not available as of this writing	Second Friday of month prior to option month	Second Friday of month prior to option month
Expiration	Saturday following last trading day	Saturday following last trading day	Last trading day	Last trading day	Last trading day	Not available as of this writing	Saturday following last trading day	Last trading day
Strike price intervals	Depends on current gold price: $10 under $300; $20 between $300 and $500; $30 between $500 and $800; and $40 over $800	2 points	Depends on current gold price: $10 under $300; $20 between $300 and $500; $30 between $500 and $800; and $40 over $800	5 index points	5 index points	Not available as of this writing	Depends on current sugar price: ½¢ in 2 nearby months and 1¢ in deferred under $0.15, $.02 between $.15 and $.40 and $0.4 over $0.40	Depends on current oil price: $0.01 under $0.50, $0.02 between $0.50 and $1.10, $0.03 between $1.10 and $2, $0.04 over $2

TABLE 4. (*Continued*)

Exchange	MidAmerica	CBT	COMEX	CME	KCBT	NYFE	CSCE	NYMEX
Premium quotation	2.5¢ per oz ($0.83)	1/64 point ($15.625)	$0.10 per oz ($10)	0.05 index point ($25)	0.05 basis point ($25)	Not available as of this writing	$0.01 per lb ($11.20)	$0.01 per gal ($4)

MidAmerica — MidAmerica Commodity Exchange
CBT — Chicago Board of Trade
COMEX — Commodity Exchange, Incorporated
CME — Chicago Mercantile Exchange
KCBT — Kansas City Board of Trade
NYFE — New York Futures Exchange
CSCE — Coffee, Sugar, and Cocoa Exchange
NYMEX — New York Mercantile Exchange

An actual commodity option may be attractive to commercial market participants who are interested in taking or making delivery of the actual debt instrument and not a futures contract. Table 5 provides a description of the option contract terms proposed by the nation's security exchanges.

DEALER OPTIONS. Options on non-interest-bearing actual commodities such as gold and silver are offered over-the-counter by a handful of domestic commodity dealers and are regulated by the Commodity Futures Trading Commission. These options are available for a number of different precious metals in various forms. The options traded by commodity exchanges may be contrasted to dealer options on a number of levels. Dealer options are exercisable for the physical commodity while futures options may be exercised for a highly leveraged futures contract based on a particular commodity. Exchange-traded options can be both bought and sold whereas dealer options have usually been available only for purchase. Table 6 provides a description of some of the dealer options available today. Note that the terms of these dealer options correspond to a large extent to the terms of popular futures contracts traded on-exchange.

It is likely that in the near future, the CFTC will permit commodity exchanges to offer options on physical commodities. In addition, there has been increasing pressures on Congress to lift the ban on domestic agricultural commodities. If these two developments are realized, we can expect to see options on physical soybeans, corn, and wheat offered by exchanges.

OPTION PRICING

Successful option trading hinges on one's ability to identify the fair value of an option. If a trader consistently pays less than the fair-market value of an option or sells options at more than their fair-market value, then that trader will, over the long run, make a profit. Therefore it is important to understand the basics of option pricing.

The value of an option contract, as with all other types of investment instruments which are actively traded, depends upon the interplay of the forces of supply and demand. Options are traded competitively on the floors of the nation's exchanges and will increase in price when there are more buyers than sellers and decrease in price when there are more sellers than buyers. Buyers do not want to pay any more than necessary for an option while sellers want to get the highest possible price for writing the option. These countervailing forces will tend to cause the option premium to seek an equilibrium level. But how do buyers and sellers recognize when an option is overpriced or underpriced? Let us consider some of the basic factors which influence this assessment.

LEVERAGE AND INSURANCE VALUE. An option contract has value because of two attributes.

1. Options may provide leverage and permit the holder to enjoy the same potential return which may accrue to the outright buyer of the underlying commodity for a smaller investment.

TABLE 5. Summary of Security Exchange Options

Exchange	AMEX	AMEX	AMEX	CBOE	CBOE
Underlying commodity	Treasury bills; four contracts, $1 million with 13 weeks to maturity, $200,000 13-week, $500,000 26-week, and $100,000 26-week	Treasury notes, 5 to 7-year term, two contracts, $100,000 and $20,000	90-day domestic CDs $1 million	30-year Treasury bonds, two contracts, $100,000 and $20,000	$100,000 GNMA pass-through certificates
Trading months	March, June, September, and December	March, June, September, and December	March, June, September, and December		March, June, September, and December
Last trading day	Third Friday of expiration month	Third Friday of expiration month	Third Friday of expiration month	Third Friday of expiration month	Third Friday of expiration month
Expiration	Saturday following last trading day	Saturday following last trading day	Saturday following last trading day	Saturday following last trading day	Saturday following last trading day
Strike price intervals	100 basis points	2 points	100 basis points	2 points	2 points
Premium quotation	1 basis point ($25 and $5)	$\frac{1}{32}$ point ($31.25 and $6.25)	1 basis point ($25)	$\frac{1}{32}$ point ($31.25 and $6.25)	$\frac{1}{32}$ point ($31.25)

AMEX American Stock Exchange
CBOE Chicago Board Options Exchange
PSE Philadelphia Stock Exchange
NYSE New York Stock Exchange

TABLE 5 (*Continued*)

PSE	Exchange	NYSE	NYSE
Foreign currencies; 12,500 British pounds, 62,500 German marks, 62,500 Swiss francs, 6,250,000 Japanese yen, 50,000 Canadian dollars	Underlying commodity	Treasury bills; four contracts, $1 million with 13 weeks to maturity, $200,000 13-week, $500,000 26-week $100,000 26-week	Specific Treasury note issues, $100,000 and $20,000
March, June, September, and December	Trading months	March, June, September, and December	February, May, August, November
Second Friday of expiration month	Last trading day	Third Friday of expiration month	Day prior to expiration
Saturday following last trading day	Expiration	Saturday following last trading day	Third business day prior to 15th calendar day
$0.05 in pounds, $0.02 in marks, $0.02 in francs, $0.02 in dollars $0.0002 in yen	Strike price intervals	100 basis points	2 points
Quoted in terms of American dollars	Premium quotation	1 basis point ($25 and $5)	$\frac{1}{32}$ point ($31.25 and $6.25)

TABLE 6. Summary of Dealer Options

Firm[a]: Mocatta Metals Corporation								
Underlying commodity	100 oz of gold	50 South African kruggerands	10 Canadian maple leafs	1,000 oz silver	$1,000 face value silver half-dollars	$1,000 face value silver dollars	25,000 lb of copper	50 oz of platinum
Trading months	January, March, April, June, July, September, October, and December	January, February, April, May, July, August, October, and December	February, March, May, June, August, September, November, and December	February, March, May, June, August, September, November, and December	January, March, April, June, July, September, November, and December	January, February, April, May, July, August, October, and November	February, March, May, June, August, September, November, and December	January, February, April, May, July, August, October, and November
Expiration	First business day of month	First business day of month	First business day of month	First business day of month	First business day of month	First business day of month	First business day of month	First business day of month
Strike price intervals	$25 per oz	$25 per oz	$25 per oz	$1 per oz	$200	$1,000	$0.04 per lb	Depends on current platinum price $25 under $700, $50 over $700

[a]Although several firms other than Mocatta offer similar options, Mocatta appears to be the most popular dealer.

2. Options provide a form of insurance for the holder because losses are limited to the original premium while potential profits are not restricted.

These factors affect different types of commodity options differently. There are three types of commodities underlying option contracts—futures contracts, interest-bearing commodities, and non-interest-bearing commodities. All commodity options provide insurance from adverse price movements, no matter which category they fall into. Some commodity options, however, have negligible or even negative leverage value.

For example, when an option for a non-interest-bearing commodity is purchased instead of the underlying commodity itself, capital equal to the difference between the purchase price of the underlying commodity and the option premium is freed for alternate investment use. Thus this type of option has significant leverage value.

Contrast this to an option which may be exercised for an interest-bearing commodity. When an option on an interest-bearing commodity is purchased, capital is also freed for alternate investment purposes. However, the alternate investment may be generating less returns than the interest-bearing commodity. If, for example, one bought an option for a bank Certificate of Deposit (CD) which paid 14% annual interest and invested the difference between the purchase price of the CD and the option premium in a short-term investment earning only 12% per annum, then the leverage associated with the option would actually be negative.

A futures contract never generates interest, but while the option premium is always less than the full purchase price of the commodity which is the subject of the futures contract, the cost of acquiring the futures contract is always less than the cost of the option. A futures contract itself is a leverage instrument—the futures market participant makes an initial margin deposit and "marks-to-market" thereafter. The initial margin deposit is, however, usually put up in Treasury securities such as Treasury bills, whereas the option premium must be paid for in cash. Therefore, the option buyer forfeits the interest which might accrue on the premium and thus incurs negative leverage.

There are a number of market conditions which impact upon the option's insurance and leverage value and, therefore, impact upon the premium. These factors include the relationship between the underlying market price and the option strike price, the characteristic or expected price volatility of the underlying market, short-term interest rates, and the time period until option expiration. Because these factors are dynamic, the option premium can be expected to constantly adjust in order to strike a new equilibrium.

RELATIONSHIP BETWEEN MARKET AND STRIKE PRICE. The relationship between the underlying market price and the strike price plays a critical role in determining the option premium. An option premium may be minimally valuated at the in-the-money amount of the option. If, for example, Treasury-bond futures were trading at 62% of par and a call option was struck at 60% of par, then the call premium would equal at least 2% of par. If it did not, then arbitrageurs would seize upon the opportunity by buying as many options as they could, exercise the options by buying Treasury bond futures at 60, and immediately turn the Treasury bond futures around by selling out of the long position at 62. In this

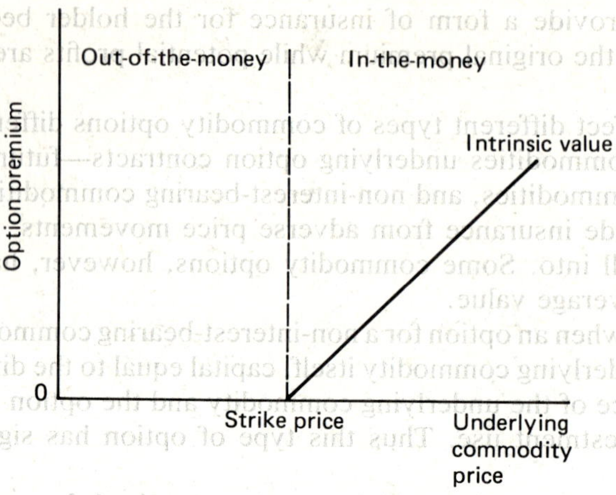

FIGURE 3. Intrinsic value of a call option.

way, they could reap the profit implied by the amount by which the premium was less than 2% of par.

A call option premium will not be less than the underlying price less the strike price, while a put option premium will not be less than the strike price less the underlying price. This, of course, is the in-the-money amount of the option and is often referred to as "intrinsic" value. When this component of the option price increases, the leverage value of the option decreases correspondingly because more premium is required to secure the option.

The intrinsic value of an option is quite easy to compute. Options will, however, usually trade at premiums well above their intrinsic value. This additional price component is referred to as the option's "extrinsic" value. Extrinsic value reflects the market's assessment of whether the option will ever be profitable, that is, whether the underlying price will rise into-the-money sufficiently to permit a profitable exercise. An option's extrinsic value is greatest when it is at-the-money or near-the-money.

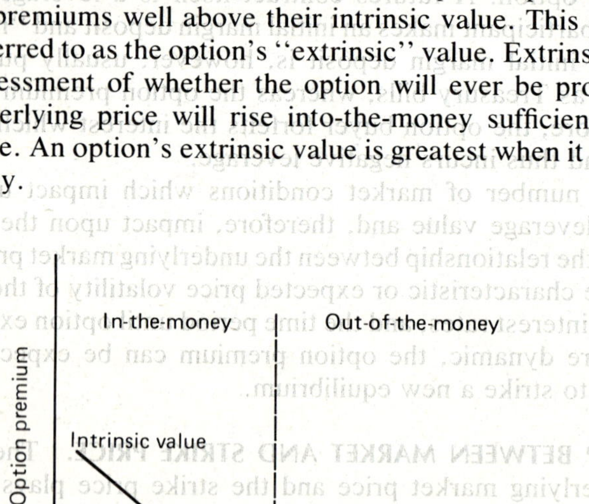

FIGURE 4. Intrinsic value of a put option.

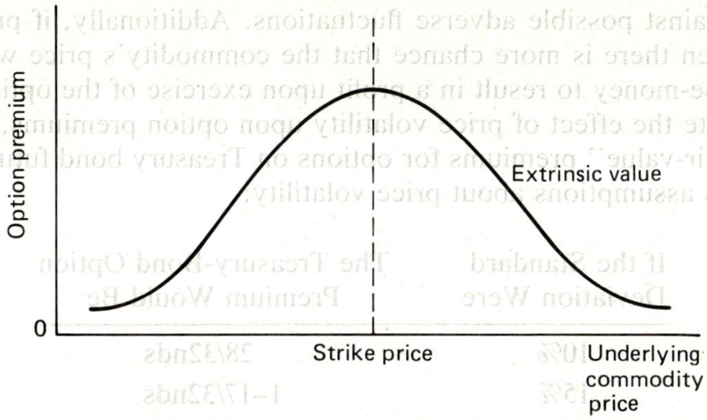

FIGURE 5. Extrinsic value of an option.

Consider the case where the option is very far out-of-the-money. In this case, there is typically a low probability that the underlying commodity price will ever approach or be in-the-money and thus permit a profitable exercise. The farther out-of-the-money, the less insurance value, and this will be reflected in the premium. To illustrate, assume that one had bought a gold call option at a $500 strike price to ensure that one would not be affected by rising gold prices, and the gold market price fell to $200. In this case, the insurance is unnecessary as it would be unlikely that gold would rise above $500 from $200.

Consider the case where the option is deep in-the-money. In this case, the intrinsic value of the option is so high as to compromise the leverage value of the option. This factor is particularly operative where the option has negative leverage value such as with an option on a futures contract. In cases like these, the holder might prefer to exercise the option promptly rather than lose the interest which might otherwise accrue. Factors which impact upon the option's extrinsic value include market volatility, the term until expiration, and short-term interest rates.

UNDERLYING MARKET VOLATILITY. The volatility of the underlying commodity refers to the price variability which is characteristic of the commodity. For example, if gold prices were expected to go up 10% over the next 6 months, but changing economic conditions suggest that they will now go up 50%, the buyers will bid up the price of call options and put option premiums will decrease accordingly. It is not always easy, however, to predict the direction in which the price will fluctuate over the next several months, let alone the next several days. If we believe that commodity markets are "efficient"—that is, that they adjust completely and immediately to reflect any new market information, then it is impossible to forecast the direction in which the market might move. Therefore, volatility is often thought of as movement in either direction—either up or down—and the magnitude rather than the direction of that movement is the relevant characteristic.

If the characteristic volatility of a commodity price increases, then the insurance value of an option increases correspondingly. Obviously, if the price were perfectly static, then there would be no need to seek price insurance. On the other hand, when prices are changing dramatically, then insurance is often necessary to protect against possible adverse fluctuations. Additionally, if price volatility increases, then there is more chance that the commodity's price will move sufficiently in-the-money to result in a profit upon exercise of the option.

To illustrate the effect of price volatility upon option premiums, consider the following "fair-value" premiums for options on Treasury bond futures contracts using various assumptions about price volatility:

If the Standard Deviation Were	The Treasury-Bond Option Premium Would Be
10%	28/32nds
15%	1–17/32nds
20%	2–15/32nds
25%	3–12/32nds
30%	4–10/32nds

(This analysis made the assumption that the Treasury-bond call option had a strike price of 64, the underlying price was 62, the short-term interest rate was 12%, and the option had 6 months to expiration.)

SHORT-TERM INTEREST RATES. When short-term interest rates increase, this implies that an investor can do more with excess capital. When the option has positive leverage value, then an increase in the prevailing rate tends to increase the option premium, whereas it tends to decrease the premium if the option has negative leverage value.

The leverage value of options on non-interest-bearing actual commodities is always positive and therefore an increase in the short-term rate will tend to increase the option premium. The leverage value of options on futures contracts, on the other hand, is always negative and therefore an increase in the alternate investment rate will decrease the option premium. The leverage value of an interest-bearing commodity depends on the interest paid on the commodity relative to the alternate investment rate. For example, an option on actual Treasury bonds would have negative leverage value if the Treasury-bond rate were to exceed the short-term rate, while the option would have positive leverage value if the Treasury-bond rate were less than the short-term rate. If one held the Treasury-bond rate constant, of course, an increase in short-term rates would result in diminished leverage value and a decreased premium.

To illustrate the effect of short-term interest rates on option premiums, consider the following "fair-value" premiums for options on gold futures:

If the Interest Rate Were	The Gold Option Premium Would Be
8%	\$18.74 per oz
10%	\$18.65 per oz
12%	\$18.55 per oz
14%	\$18.46 per oz
16%	\$18.37 per oz

(These calculations assume that the call option was struck at $400, the prevailing gold price, the option had 3 months until expiration, and the price variability was 25% per annum.)

Of course, if interest rates went up from 8 to 16%, this would no doubt have an effect upon the underlying gold futures price. This would in turn affect the relationship between the market and strike prices and thus indirectly impact upon the premium. The interplay between interest rates and premium and market price would be even more complicated and dramatic when the commodity underlying the option involved a debt instrument such as a Treasury security or a bank CD.

TERM UNTIL EXPIRATION. All commodity option premiums decrease if prices remain constant as the term until option expiration decreases. This phenomenon may be attributed to the fact that the insurance value of an option decreases as it approaches expiration. Insurance value is greater when the option term is longer because there is more possibility that adverse events will occur during a longer time period. By extending the life of the option, one extends the period over which one enjoys its insurance value.

The option premiums associated with interest-bearing commodities and futures contracts are affected less by this time factor than are premiums associated with non-interest-bearing commodities. This phenomenon may be attributed to the fact that the leverage value of the former two types of options is less than the leverage value of the latter type of option. Obviously, the longer period of time during which one may take advantage of positive leverage, the more the option is worth.

The following list illustrates the "fair-value" premiums for a call option on gold futures using different assumptions about time until expiration:

If the Time Until Expiration Were	The Gold Option Premium Would Be
1 month	$12.67 per oz
2 months	$15.60 per oz
3 months	$18.55 per oz
6 months	$27.04 per oz
9 months	$32.02 per oz

(These premiums were estimated assuming that the strike price equaled $400, the underlying market price equaled $400, short-term interest rates were at 12% and the underlying market volatility was 25%.)

The extrinsic value of an option is often referred to as its "time value." While it is true that other factors aside from the time until option expiration contribute to the extrinsic component of an option premium, it is clear that the time until option expiration has a dramatic effect on the option premium, as shown in Table 7.

PRICING MODEL. The model which was utilized to derive the "fair-value" premiums for options on futures contracts is the one developed by Fischer Black, who along with Myron Sholes developed the classic formula which is used to

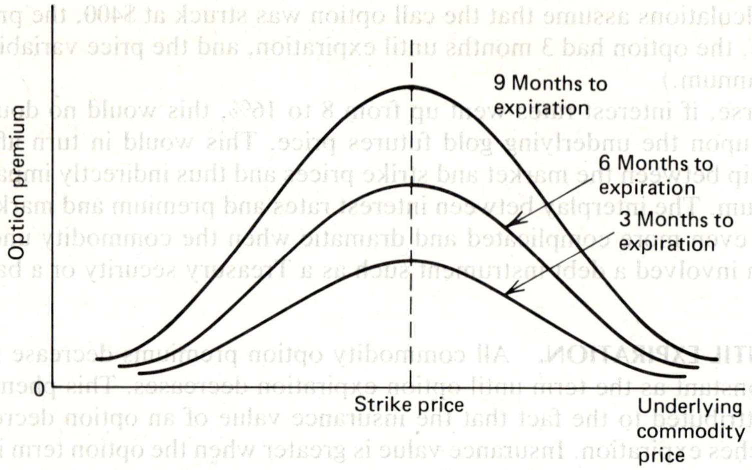

FIGURE 6. Diminishing extrinsic value as option approaches expiration.

derive the "fair-value" premiums for stock options. This model prices calls as follows:

$$(2)\ C = e^{-rt}[FN(d_1) - EN(d_2)]$$

$$d_1 = [\ln(F/E) + t\sigma^2/2]/\sigma\sqrt{t}$$

$$d_2 = d_1 - \sigma\sqrt{t}$$

where C is the call premium; r the short-term interest rates; t the term until option expiration (in years); F the underlying futures price; E the exercise price; N the cumulative normal probability distribution; and σ the annualized standard deviation of returns. Puts are priced very similarly as follows:

$$(3)\ P = -e^{-rt}\ [FN(-d_1) - EN(-d_2)]$$

where P is the put premium.

This model makes some important assumptions with which the reader should be familiar. First, the model assumes that the option will not be exercised before option expiration, that is, it is a "European" option. Second, it assumes that short-term interest rates and the option's volatility remain constant over the life of the option. Diversion from these assumptions will affect the reliability of the pricing model. Finally, this model is applicable only to options on futures; although we will not go into details, certain modifications are necessary in order to apply the model to options on physicals or securities. Table 8 gives an example of how the model is used to calculate the "fair-value" premium of an option.

OPTION TRADING STRATEGIES

There is almost an endless variety of strategies which may be developed which involve options, an option in combination with other options, and options in combination with the underlying commodities. Options provide a great deal of flexibility for the investor to utilize myriad strategies in order to protect an in-

TABLE 7. Effects of Market Conditions on the Option Premium

	Increased Short-Term Interest Rates	Increased Price Volatility	Increased Time Until Expiration
Non-interest-bearing physical commodity:			
Insurance value	0	+	+
Leverage value	+	0	+
Overall effect	+	+	+
Interest-bearing actual commodity:			
Insurance value	0	+	+
Leverage value	+	0	+ or −[a]
Overall effect	+	+	+
Futures contracts:			
Insurance value	0	+	+
Leverage value	−	0	+
Overall effect	−	+	+

[a]Leverage value can be positive or negative depending upon the relationship between the interest paid on the commodity and the alternate short-term investment rate.

vestment or to profit from options independently from other investments. While it is not possible to provide a complete description of all the different ways in which options may be used, we will attempt to summarize a few of the most basic and most popular strategies.

Option strategies may be broken down into several classes corresponding to the degree of risk associated with the transaction. For example, strategies which involve the sale of a put or a call option without an offsetting position may be considered to be very risky. Someone who, for example, sells a single put option is said to hold a "naked" position and is exposed to the full price volatility associated with the option. On the other extreme, there are strategies which

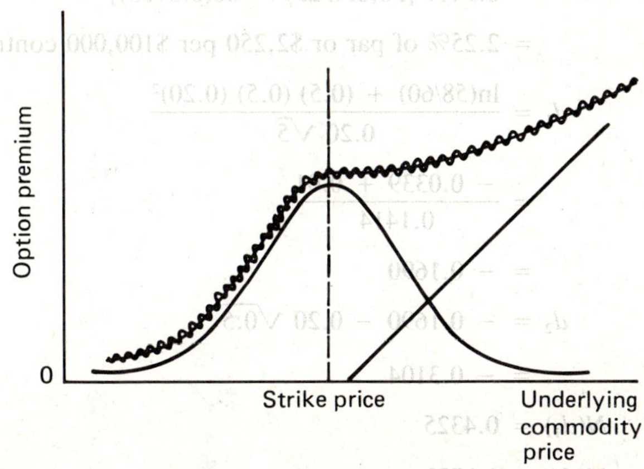

FIGURE 7. Call option premium.

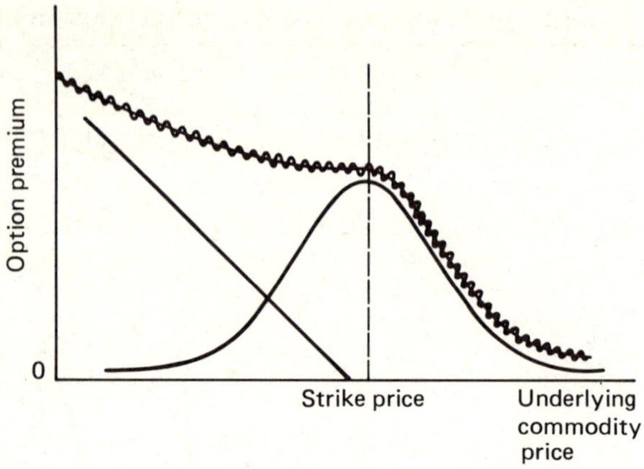

FIGURE 8. Put option premium.

involve two or more option positions which tend to fluctuate in opposite directions and so the gains in one position may offset the losses in the opposite position. Under some circumstances, for example, an investor may prefer to buy a call option and sell another call. These types of strategies are similar to spreading transactions on future markets. Somewhere in the middle are strategies which involve option contracts in combination with the underlying commodity. For example, an investor may be long platinum futures and long a put option. This is called a "covered" strategy because possible losses on the futures are "covered" by potential gains on the option.

TABLE 8. How To Calculate The "Fair-Value" Premium

Let us assume that a call option on a Treasury bond futures contract has a striking price of 60% of par and the underlying Treasury bond market is trading at 58. Short-term interest rates are at 14% and the market volatility is 20%. The option has 6 months until expiration.

$$\text{Call premium} = e^{-(0.12)(0.5)}\,[58N(d_1) - 60N(d_2)]$$

$$= 0.9417\,[58(0.4325) - 60(0.3783)]$$

$$= 2.25\% \text{ of par or } \$2{,}250 \text{ per } \$100{,}000 \text{ contract}$$

$$d_1 = \frac{\ln(58/60) + (0.5)\,(0.5)\,(0.20)^2}{0.20\sqrt{5}}$$

$$= \frac{-\,0.0339 + 0.01}{0.1414}$$

$$= -\,0.1690$$

$$d_2 = -\,0.1690 - 0.20\sqrt{0.5}$$

$$= -\,0.3104$$

$$N(d_1) = 0.4325$$

$$N(d_2) = 0.3783$$

OPTION BUYING. An investor who is bullish on a particular commodity may prefer to buy a call option rather than purchase the actual commodity. Conversely, an investor who is bearish on a commodity may find that buying a put option is a more attractive strategy than selling the commodity short. (It is usually much more difficult to sell an actual commodity short in comparison to a futures contract which may be bought or sold with equal ease.)

When an investor buys a call option, the investor profits from bull moves to the same extent as he or she would had he or she bought the underlying commodity, except that the investor initially forfeits the option premium. Likewise, a put option buyer shares in the profits resulting from price declines just like the investor who had sold short outright, except that option premium is foregone in order to buy the option. The major advantage with these strategies is that the option buyer's potential loss is limited to the price of the option.

For example, let us assume that our option enthusiast had bought an option for gold futures which was struck, or had a striking price at-the-money or equal to the prevailing market price of $380 per oz. Let us also assume that the option premium was equal to $20 per oz. Compare the results which the option buyer would have realized if the buyer had bought an option or had bought the futures contract:

Gold Price at Expiration	Returns on Long Futures	Returns on a Call Option Purchase
$300	−$80	−$20
$340	−$40	−$20
$380	0	−$20
$400	+$20	0
$420	+$40	+$20
$460	+$80	+$60

These results do not include consideration of transaction costs such as commissions. A put option buyer who had bought an at-the-money put option would also limit the maximum loss to the premium while sharing in the potential profits which would accrue to a seller of a futures contract less the premium:

Gold price at Expiration	Returns on Short Futures	Returns on a Put Option Purchase
$300	+$80	+$60
$340	+$40	+$20
$360	+$20	0
$380	0	−$20
$420	−$40	−$20
$460	−$80	−$20

This analysis assumes that the option is held until expiration or is exercised. This, of course, is not always the case as an option buyer may prefer to offset the long option by selling the option and thereby cancel the open position. Usually, however, an option premium does not move in a one-to-one ratio to the underlying commodity market. The option premium will move in a one-to-one ratio to the futures only when the option is so far in-the-money so that its extrinsic worth is practically nil and the premium represents exclusively its intrinsic in-the-money worth. On the other extreme, an option which is extremely out-of-the-money moves relatively little in comparison to the price movement of the underlying commodity. When an option is near-the-money, the premium will move by about 50% of the underlying commodity fluctuation.

Because of this phenomenon, which is discussed in a subsequent section, it may be more profitable to exercise an option which moves into-the-money rather than sell it in order to realize a profit. On the other hand, it may be more attractive to sell an option rather than holding it to expiration when it moves down if the premium has not depreciated fully in order to cut losses. Keep in mind that the option premium will naturally depreciate as it moves closer to expiration because of its diminishing time value.

An option buyer should always be cognizant of the "break-even" level. In order to profit by buying an option, the underlying price must move in-the-money. If it does not, the option will be unprofitable to exercise and, therefore, the buyer may wish to let the option expire. Sometimes the underlying commodity price will move in-the-money but not sufficiently in-the-money to permit a profitable exercise considering the premium initially paid out. This does not imply, however, that the option should not be exercised; on the contrary, the premium has already been paid and if the option is in-the-money at all, it can be exercised to cut losses. At some point, the option will be sufficiently in-the-money to permit the buyer to exercise the option and get back the initial premium. This point is the "break-even" point.

In the cases described above, the break-even point is $20 in-the-money. If the buyer exercises when the option is $20 in-the-money, the buyer makes $20 upon exercise which just covers the premium forfeited up front.

NAKED OPTION SELLING. Taking the opposite side of an option holder's position is the option seller or writer. The option writer's motive is to sell the option and retain the premium initially paid by the buyer. In order to do this, the writer must select a situation where there is little probability that the option will move sufficiently in-the-money to provide for a profitable exercise by the holder. Thus, if the commodity underlying a call option remains stagnant or moves lower, then the option will not be exercised and the writer will retain the premium. Likewise, a put writer will profit to the extent of the premium where the underlying price remains stagnant or moves up. If the price moves significantly up or down, then the call and put writers respectively will be subject to large losses.

An option writer will normally look for options which are overvalued relative to the "fair-value" premium in order to reap greater than normal returns. However, a writer cannot afford to forget that he or she holds a position which is subject to potentially unlimited loss. Let us look at the risk reward structure of a naked option seller who takes the opposite side of the transactions described in "Option Buying." The call option seller would have realized the following returns:

Gold Price at Expiration	Returns on a Put Option Purchase
$300	+$20
$340	+$20
$380	+$20
$400	0
$420	−$20
$460	−$60

As is apparent, the call option writer's returns are a mirror image of the call option holder's returns. The most the naked option writer can make in this case is $20, but can lose $60 and more if the gold price goes up by more than $80 per oz. The put option writer's returns are likewise a mirror image of the put option holder's returns:

Gold price at Expiration	Returns on a Put Options Purchase
$300	−$60
$340	−$20
$360	0
$380	+$20
$420	+$20
$460	+$20

Before anyone takes up a collection for the option writers of the world, we must point out that the option premium that writers demand will be adjusted to compensate for expected price volatility as well as the other factors described in "Option Pricing." Additionally, option writers could offset the short position with a closing purchase in order to cut short any potential losses. Remember, that if the underlying market price remains static, then the option seller will retain the full value of the premium as the option premium will naturally lose its time value as expiration draws near.

COVERED OPTION WRITING. Although naked option writing is a viable strategy for some, the majority of option writers sell the option in connection with other activities in the underlying commodity market. Specifically, an option writer may already be long in the underlying futures market and may wish to write a call on that position in order to collect the premium. Someone who is short futures may wish to sell puts and thereby collect the option premium. This type of strategy is referred to as "covered" option writing.

Covered writing strategies permit an investor to generate supplemental income while holding the commodity underlying the option. When a holder of a long futures position sells a call, the holder augments his or her income by the premium, but nonetheless risks losing an unlimited amount given a major bear move.

Let us assume that our option investor buys a Treasury-bond futures contract and sells a call option struck at-the-money or 60% of par. The premium equals 2% of par. What happens if the market moves up or down? The following table shows the possible outcome:

Treasury-bond Price at Expiration	Long Futures Value	Short Option Value	Overall Position
52	−8	+2	−6
56	−4	+2	−2
58	−2	+2	0
60	0	+2	+2
62	+2	0	+2
64	+4	−2	+2
68	+8	−6	+2

The covered writer's overall position in this case looks very much like that which is assumed by the seller of a naked put and can be regarded as a defensive position. Conversely, the covered put writer's position is very similar to that held by a naked call seller:

Treasury-bond Price at Expiration	Short Futures Value	Short Option Value	Overall Position
52	+8	−6	+2
56	+4	−2	+2
58	+2	0	+2
60	0	+2	+2
62	−2	+2	0
64	−4	+2	−2
68	−8	+2	−6

As we shall see below, most covered option writers are commercial interests who may be in the business of buying and selling the physical underlying commodity or who may produce or use the commodity. But why would a public investor want to use a covered write strategy? There are several reasons why this strategy may be attractive.

Assume that the investor is generally bullish on a particular commodity and, therefore, has acquired a long futures position. While the commodity may be going up over the medium term to long term, it may experience adverse fluctuations in the meantime. Because futures contracts are "marked-to-market" on a daily basis, the long may be subject to variation margin calls on the futures position. The sale of a call option can help an investor manage these margin calls by generating cash in the form of the premium with which to cover the temporary fluctuation. Our investor will find this covered writing strategy to be most profitable when the investor anticipates only moderate price movement (in either direction). If, for example, the market price declines to 59, the investor still pockets the 2% premium while incurring the 1% loss on the futures for a net profit of 1% of par. Of course, the investor's long-term bullish forecast may prove to be in error; the investor should then attempt to cut any losses short by selling the futures.

If the price of the futures contract starts to move up substantially, then the writer can buy back the short call option. Because the option premium does not fluctuate to the same degree as the underlying commodity, chances are that the writer's losses on the closing purchase will be less than the writer's gains on the futures. If the option is exercised before the writer can transact a closing purchase, then the writer liquidates the long futures position upon exercise, but this loss may be considered to be an opportunity loss only because, in our example, the option strike price equaled the original purchase price on the futures contract.

"COVERED" OPTION BUYING. Just as one might use a short option position to offset possible losses on an underlying commodity position, one might use a long option position to offset possible losses on the same underlying commodity position. For example, if an investor had taken a long position in gold futures, he might, under some circumstances, want to buy a put against that futures position. Similarly, a holder of a short futures position may want to buy a call against that position. A long futures position is essentially bullish while a long put is essentially bearish. Short futures and long calls also represent offsetting positions.

This type of "coverage" may be considered to be a defensive strategy from the investor's standpoint and offers only a moderate amount of risk (and potential return). Let us consider how an investor may use this strategy. Assume that our trader has already taken a long position in gold futures at a price of $400 per oz in anticipation of price appreciation. Our trader is confident that the market will be moving very quickly, and, therefore, buys a put option. Let us introduce a new twist in our analysis and assume that the put option is struck somewhat out-of-the-money at $380 per oz and sells for $10 per oz. (By buying an out-of-the-money option instead of an in-the-money or at-the-money option, our investor pays less premium. Of course, the investor has less downside protection by so doing.) Our investor's profit-and-loss scenario looks like this:

Gold Price at Expiration	Returns on Long Futures	Return on Long Put	Overall Returns
$300	−$100	+$70	−$30
$350	− $50	+$20	−$30
$400	0	−$10	−$10
$450	+ $50	−$10	+$40
$500	+$100	−$10	+$90

The investor can lose no more than the premium plus its out-of-the-money valuation, while the investor's profits remain potentially unlimited, equal as they are to the profits on the long futures contract less the $10 premium. The holder of a short futures contract can use a call option in a substantially similar way. Assume that our investor sells a gold futures contract at $400 in anticipation of substantial price decline. While the investor feels that the price will drop, the investor is concerned about dramatic price movement in either direction. For self-protection, the investor buys an out-of-the-money call struck at $420 for $10 per oz. The investor's profit-and-loss scenario is structured as follows:

Gold Price at Expiration	Returns on Short Futures	Return on Long Call	Overall Returns
$300	+$100	−$10	+$90
$350	+ $50	−$10	+$40
$400	0	−$10	−$10
$450	− $50	+$20	−$30
$500	−$100	+$70	−$30

Used in this manner, a purchased option can be considered to be a form of a stop-loss order. In the cases outlined above, our investor has effectively limited any loss to $30 per oz without substantially diminishing any profit potential. This type of strategy may be particularly effective where a trader feels strongly that there will be a major market move and is leaning in one direction, but fears that a strong move in the opposite direction is not outside of the realm of possibility.

OPTION SPREADS. An option spread involves the simultaneous purchase and sale of two options of the same type but with different strike prices, terms until expiration or both. One might construct an option spread by buying and selling calls or by buying and selling puts. An option spread is similar in concept to a futures spread in that offsetting positions are taken in the same market by buying and selling contracts with slightly different contract terms. When constructing a futures spread, the difference in the long and short legs of the spread are the contract maturities. Because option contracts can be either puts or calls, and may have different striking prices in addition to having different terms until expiration, an option spread is much more complicated than a futures spread.

A "vertical" option spread is one which involves two options of the same type and term until expiration, but have different striking prices. For example, an investor may buy a $420 call option and sell a $400 call option with the same expiration date. A "horizontal" option spread involves two options of the same type and striking price, but with different terms until expiration. For example, an option trader may buy a September $400 gold put option and sell put a December $400 gold option. This may also be referred to as "calendar" spread. A "diagonal" spread is one which involves elements of both a vertical and a horizontal spread.

For example, an option trader may buy a September $400 gold call option and sell a December $420 gold call option.

Let us illustrate how some of these spreads might work under a number of different market scenarios. Assume that our option trader is rather bullish on the price of gold, but that the trader wishes to limit any risks to a very low level. Therefore, the investor decides to use option spreads to take advantage of possible bull moves. The investor can do this by entering a vertical call spread where the short leg strike price is greater than the long leg strike price. Let us assume that gold is currently trading at $410 and our investor buys a $400 call for $20 and sells a $420 call for $10:

Gold Price at Expiration	Returns on Short Call	Return on Long Call	Overall Returns
$360	+$10	−$20	−$10
$380	+$10	−$20	−$10
$400	+$10	−$20	−$10
$410	+$10	−$10	0
$420	+$10	0	+$10
$430	0	+$10	+$10
$440	−$10	+$20	+$10
$460	−$30	+$40	+$10

In this case, if the price of gold moves up to $420, then our spreader may earn $10—the maximum profit possible on the trade, while a decline to $400 will cause the trader to lose $10—the maximum loss possible. The maximum profit or loss which may be incurred as a result of this strategy is rather low. Although this example assumed that the option positions were held until expiration, a trader might readily take advantage of bullish fluctuations by engaging in a closing purchase to cancel the outstanding short position and a closing sale to cancel the outstanding long position. Because the in-the-money call premium will respond more sharply to an increase in the underlying gold price than the out-of-the-money premium, a trader would realize a positive return by closing out the spread subsequent to a bull movement.

Let us consider a way to take advantage of a generally static price environment through the use of horizontal spread. Recall that as an option approaches expiration, its price drops dramatically to a point where the option's intrinsic value will equal its full price. In other words, its time value will diminish to zero. An option spreader can exploit this fact by selling options with a short term until expiration and buying options with a longer term until expiration. The near-term option will lose time value quicker than the long-term option.

Assume that our spreader sells a March and buys a September 60 Treasury bond call. The near-term option has 3 months until expiration, while the deferred option has 9 months until it expires. Using the model provided above, we may calculate the fair-value premiums for these options, assuming that Treasury bonds in both March and September are trading at 60 in the underlying market, that the standard deviation of returns is about 17%, and that short-term interest rates equal 14%:

If the Term Until Expiration Were	The Premium Would Equal Approximately
3 months	1-27/32nds
6 months	2-22/32nds
9 months	3-00/32nds

Assume that the underlying price remained constant and that the investor held both options for 3 months until the near-term option expired. In this case, the investor would pocket the full 1-27/32nds premium for the short option because it would become worthless when it expires. Our investor would thereupon transact a closing sale at 2-22/32nds for the long option, losing 10/32nds on the sale. The investor's net profit on the position would equal 1-17/32nds.

OPTION STRADDLES. An option straddle or "double" is the simultaneous purchase of a put and a call option, or the simultaneous sale of a put and call option. Quite appropriately, the former transaction is referred to as a "straddle purchase," while the latter transaction is a "straddle sale." A straddle transaction is distinguished from a spread in that a straddle involves two long or two short positions in the same "type" of option, that is, either put or call, while a spread involves a sale and a purchase of the same type of option.

An investor may be inclined to buy a straddle where the investor is not sure of the direction in which the underlying commodity price will move, but the investor is confident that there will be a substantial move in one direction or another. In other words, price volatility as discussed above, is very high. Conversely, an investor may be inclined to sell or write a straddle where the investor is confident that the underlying price will remain static.

The straddle buyer profits from a strong price movement in either direction while a straddle seller profits from sluggish price movement. Recall that when the underlying commodity price remains constant that an option writer generally pockets the full amount of the premium (unless the option was written somewhat in-the-money, in which case, the writer profits by the amount of the premium less the in-the-money amount). On the other hand, if the underlying price moves in-the-money by more than the option premium, then the buyer can exercise the option profitably. A straddle buyer has two possibilities of exercising the option—if the underlying price moves up significantly, the straddle buyer may exercise the call; if the underlying price declines significantly, the buyer may exercise the put. In either case, the underlying price must move up or down by the combined amounts of the put and call premiums in order to permit a profitable exercise. The writer's position is cushioned by the two premiums received initially.

Let us work through an example to illustrate the mechanics associated with a straddle strategy. Assume that gold futures are trading at $400 per oz and that there is a $400 put and $400 call option available. The premiums on the two options equal $10. Assume that our investor had sold the straddle:

Gold Price at Expiration	Returns on Call Option	Return on Put Option	Overall Returns
$360	+$10	−$30	−$20
$370	+$10	−$20	−$10
$380	+$10	−$10	0
$390	+$10	0	+$10
$400	+$10	+$10	+$20
$410	0	+$10	+$10
$420	−$10	+$10	0
$430	−$20	+$10	−$10
$440	−$30	+$10	−$20

The straddle writer's returns are maximized if the underlying gold price remains constant at the $400 original level. When the price remains static, the writer pockets the two $10 premiums for a $20 total return. If the price moves up, the call option will be exercised and if it moves down, the put will be exercised—both circumstances diminish the writer's returns. The writer's profits are cushioned to the extent of the premiums received on sale—it is only if the underlying price moves more than $20 in either direction that the writer realizes a negative return. The straddle buyer's returns are a mirror image of the straddle seller's returns:

Gold Price at Expiration	Returns on Call Option	Return on Put Option	Overall Returns
$360	−$10	+$30	+$20
$370	−$10	+$20	+$10
$380	−$10	+$10	0
$390	−$10	0	−$10
$400	−$10	−$10	−$20
$410	0	−$10	−$10
$420	+$10	−$10	0
$430	+$20	−$10	+$10
$440	+$30	−$10	+$20

Successful execution of a straddle strategy requires close observation of the volatility of the underlying commodity market. A straddle buyer would normally seek out options which are underpriced relative to their "fair value," while a straddle seller would seek out overpriced options. Implicit in the option premium is the market's general assessment of the underlying volatility of the commodity.

If an investor has observed indications that the underlying commodity is likely to become more volatile, then the investor may prefer to buy a straddle; on the other hand, if indications point to a slower-moving market, then one might prefer to sell the straddle.

COMMERICAL APPLICATIONS OF COMMODITY OPTIONS

Hedging, or the shifting of price risk from risk-averse to risk-seeking parties, is a function traditionally accomplished through the use of futures markets. Commodity option markets, as suggested above, have a similar capacity to protect against adverse price movements. Option markets, therefore, represent an alternative hedging vehicle which offers unique advantages not available to the user of futures markets.

OPTIONS AS AN ALTERNATIVE TO FUTURES. Commerical participants in the cash commodity markets, such as producers, merchants, and users of a particular commodity, are often faced with the prospect of uncertain price fluctuation. For example, a gold miner who is considering sinking a new mine shaft must consider the costs of constructing the mine as well as the expected price of gold when it will be extracted from the ground and refined into a salable product. It may be that at the current price of gold, the miner might expect to turn a profit. If, however, gold prices decline before the miner is ready to sell any gold, the miner may be faced with a large loss.

In order to "lock-in" the current price, the miner could sell gold futures or could use gold option contracts. Assume that the "break-even" price of gold equals $380 per oz and that the current market price equals $400. If our miner had gold available for sale now, the miner could make $20 per oz. The miner could also be assured of a profit of about $20 by selling gold futures now. When the gold is mined, the miner could buy back the futures contracts and sell the physical gold in the cash markets. Any decline in the price of gold in the cash markets would be compensated for by profits accruing from the short futures position.

Alternatively, our miner could either sell calls or buy puts in order to hedge price risk. If our miner sold calls, he or she would receive the premium. If gold prices declined, the premium would serve to diminish the loss. If the price of gold increases and the gold is "called" away, our miner could deliver the gold to the option holder. If the option strike price were greater than the break-even point, the miner would lock in the profit implied by the difference between the strike and break-even price and would retain the premium. Of course, the miner would forgo potential profits where the underlying market moved up in excess of the strike price plus the option premium, but these losses may be regarded as opportunity losses, not out-of-the-pocket expenses.

If our miner bought puts, any decline in the market price would encourage the miner to exercise the puts by selling the gold that was mined at the option strike price. Assuming that the strike price is greater than the break-even point, our miner turns a profit. Of course, the miner initially forgoes the option premium.

If the price of gold increases substantially, our miner would let the option expire and would count the premium as the cost of price insurance.

Let us illustrate the results of each of these transactions. Remember that the break-even point is $380 and that gold is currently selling at $400. Assume that the miner could effect a "perfect" hedge; that is, the basis, or difference between cash and futures prices remains constant throughout the life of the hedge. Our hedger can, therefore, perfectly lock-in the $20 per oz profit. Assume also that puts and calls struck at $400 are trading at $20 premiums. What would our hedger's profits or losses look like?

Gold Price at Expiration	Unhedged Position	Hedge with Futures	Hedge with Short Calls	Hedge with Long Puts
$340	−$40	+$20	−$20	0
$360	−$20	+$20	0	0
$360	0	+$20	+$20	0
$400	+$20	+$20	+$40	0
$420	+$40	+$20	+$40	+$20
$440	+$60	+$20	+$40	+$40
$460	+$80	+$20	+$40	+$60

The option strategies illustrated above are, of course, variations on the "covered" writing and "covered" buying strategies discussed previously. When a commercial market participant uses a covered buying strategy, the participant limits the downside risk to a particular level without limiting the profit potential. In our example, the gold miner would be guaranteed of at least breaking even by buying puts. If the price of gold went up, the miner would participate fully in the increase, except that the miner had initially forfeited the premium. If our miner had used a "covered" writing strategy by selling calls, then the miner would have augmented his or her income by the $20 premium provided that the price of gold did not appreciate beyond $420. Even at prices above $420, our miner would have been guaranteed of a $40 profit.

TABLE 9. Alternative Hedging Strategies

Cash Market Situation	Hedge with Futures	Hedge with Calls	Hedge with Puts
Anticipates purchase or is net short	Purchase futures	Purchase calls	Sell puts
Anticipates sale or is net long	Sell futures	Sell calls	Purchase puts

PRICE AND QUANTITY RISK. Up until now we have ignored the fact that our gold miner may not be able to forecast precisely how much gold will be produced by the new shaft. Presumably the costs of digging the mine are the same whether or not any gold is found at all. Obviously, the quantity of gold mined will have an impact on the profitability of the new mine. Even if the price of gold goes up substantially, the miner stands to lose if very little gold can be produced. On the other hand, the miner may turn a handsome profit even if gold prices declined provided that a sizable quantity of gold can be produced.

Commercials are often faced with two kinds of risks—price risk and quantity risk. Consider a construction company which has entered a bid for a parcel of real estate. The builder hopes to construct a large office building on the site and has based a bid on projected revenues and costs, the latter factor is in large part determined by financing charges. Our builder could, of course, sell futures based on debt instruments and thereby "lock-in" a particular interest rate. But what happens if the futures prices go up and the bid is rejected? In this case, our builder stands to lose a substantial amount of money. On the other hand, our builder may elect to buy a put option. If interest rates go up (and the price of debt instruments go down accordingly), *and* the bid is accepted, the builder can exercise the option and use the profits to offset the increased cost of financing. The builder may lose, of course, on the long puts if interest rates go down (and the price of debt instruments go up) and the bid is rejected. These losses, however, are limited to the premium.

DELTA HEDGING. All of our examples until now have assumed that our hedger holds an option position until expiration. This may not always be convenient, particularly when there are no options whose expiration date coincides with the anticipated termination of the cash market transaction, the risk of which is to be hedged. Recall, however, that an option trader need not hold a position until it expires. Rather, the trader can offset an outstanding option position by executing a closing sale or purchase.

Hedgers who use futures contracts typically offset outstanding futures positions to coincide with the culmination of the cash position. Likewise, one might expect that option hedgers may on occasion prefer to offset option positions prior to expiration. Just as the hedger who uses futures contracts is exposed to "basis risk," that is, the risk that the difference between the cash and futures positions will not remain constant throughout the life of the hedge, our option hedger must attempt to manage the "delta" factor.

Recall that when the underlying market price moves up or down, the option premium moves correspondingly. When the underlying price moves up, the call premium appreciates and the put premium depreciates. When the underlying price moves down, the call premium declines and the put premium increases. These premiums do not, however, fluctuate in a one-to-one ratio to the underlying market price fluctuation. Except for deep-in-the-money options, the option premium will move less than the underlying market fluctuation. The ratio of option price fluctuation to underlying market price fluctuation is termed the "delta" factor (see Figure 9).

It is possible, of course, to calculate the expected change in the option premium in response to a given change in the underlying market price. For example, an

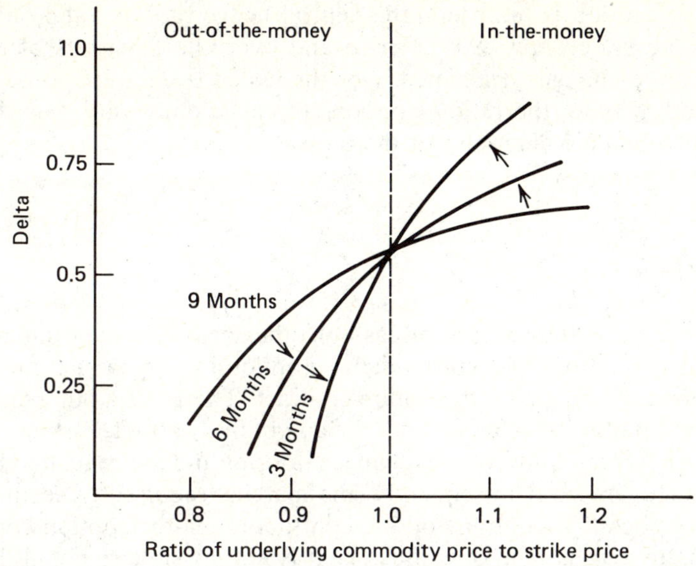

FIGURE 9. Delta factors for call options for 3-, 6-, and 9-month terms to expiration.

option which is struck at-the-money or near-the-money will typically move by 50% for a slight change in the underlying market price. This is an important concept for commercial and speculative option market participants alike. The "neutral hedge ratio" is the reciprocal of delta and tells us how many option contracts are needed to offset price risk associated with the underlying commodity. If delta approximates 50%, then our hedger may enter into two option contracts for every unit of the cash commodity which must be hedged. Thus, if the underlying price declines by $1, a put option price will increase by $0.50 or by $1 in the aggregate if two options are used. A speculator is likewise interested in this ratio because it defines the level of risk the speculator has assumed by acquiring the option contract.

Let us illustrate the procedure of delta hedging. Assume that an insurance company anticipates a cash inflow of $60,000 in a week and plans on investing the money in Treasury bonds. Bonds are selling at 60% of par currently and the insurance company fears that prices will increase as interest rates decline during the interim. In order to offset the price risk, our hedger could buy calls or sell puts. Assume that the company buys calls which expire in 3 months which are struck at-the-money, and are selling at $3,200 for every $100,000 in face value. How many calls should the firm buy?

When the strike price equals the underlying market price, delta equals 0.50 which suggests that the option price will move by 50% of the underlying market fluctuation. Taking the reciprocal of delta gives us the neutral hedge ratio of two (2). Let us say that the hedger's fears are realized and the market price of bonds moves up to 61. The fair value of the call should move up to about $3,800. Our hedger can thereupon sell the calls for a profit of $500 each or $1,000 for two calls, which exactly offsets the $1,000 higher price which must be paid for the bonds.

A word of caution is in order—the neutral hedge ratio is valid only for small changes in the underlying market price and over short periods of time. If the underlying price changes dramatically or the hedge is intended to be applied for a long period of time, the ratio of options to cash commodity must be adjusted to reflect the dynamic character of the ratio.

MARGINING

An option margin is the amount of cash or other near-cash instruments (such as Treasury bills or letters of credit) which an option investor must put up to guarantee performance or secure the option contract. There are a number of different types of commodities which may underlie an option contract; further, options are offered by a number of different exchanges or firms and are regulated by different governmental agencies. Consequently, the margins required to secure an option may vary significantly from one option contract to another option contract, possibly leading to a great deal of confusion. It is not possible to detail the specifics of every margin system which might be in use; because many option markets we have described are as of this writing pending the review of a regulatory agency, the margin systems are subject to change. We will, however, review the fundamentals of the proposed system.

A common feature of all domestically available or proposed margin systems is that they require the full payment of the option premium in cash upon option purchase. When buying an option, the buyer would pay the full premium upon purchase, and the cash is thereupon passed to the writer. Options traded on exchanges are technically contracts between the exchange clearing organization, which guarantees the financial integrity of each trade, and the individual trader. Thus the clearing organization collects the premium from the holder and passes it to the writer.

The obvious advantage associated with requiring the full payment of the option premium up front is that it eliminates the necessity for variation margin calls when the market moves adversely. The option buyer is certain of the magnitude of the maximum potential loss and is relieved of the necessity to keep a close check on his or her position. In effect, the long option position is margined in full. It may be observed, however, that futures margins are designed to cover the maximum anticipated 1-day price movement. Margins in excess of that amount are unnecessary because the futures margining system is designed to pay monies to the holders of profitable positions and collect monies from holders of unprofitable positions on a daily basis. Recall that option premiums cannot fluctuate more than the price of the underlying commodity. It stands to reason, then, that the amount required to secure an option position cannot exceed the amount required to secure a similarly sized futures contract. When an option premium is greater than the futures margin (and to the extent that a futures contract may be margined in securities), the option holder may enjoy diminished leverage relative to a futures contract.

Consider the risk associated with a naked short call position. Recall that a short option position may be liquidated in one of three ways: the option may be permitted to expire unexercised; the option may be exercised; or, the writer may buy the option back, offsetting the short position. Let us examine the risks associated with these three scenarios.

As an option moves further out-of-the-money and as expiration approaches, the probability of exercise is reflected in the diminishing value of the option premium. When the probability is negligible that the option will ever become profitable to exercise, the option premium will approach zero. It is reasonable, then, that the margin that a short is required to post should diminish in accordance with the diminished risk. Because the premium reflects the market's evaluation of risk, it is reasonable to tie the margin to the premium.

If the underlying commodity market appreciates significantly in price, the option may be driven deep into-the-money, making it economic for the holder to exercise the option. If a call is exercised, the writer will be compelled to assume a short position in the underlying commodity at a disadvantage to the market equal to the in-the-money amount. The writer may already maintain a long position in the underlying commodity and the option exercise may serve simply to offset the existing position. Or the writer may undertake to buy back the short position immediately upon exercise in order to avoid the possibility that the market will continue to rise and thereby limit the loss to the in-the-money amount. But if the writer is not able to buy back the short position immediately at the market price, the writer may be exposed to the risk of holding a short position in a rising market. Moreover, the writer may prefer to hold the short position and make no attempt to buy it back. Thus the margin must cover the in-the-money amount plus the risk of maintaining a short position.

If the underlying commodity price rises, a call premium will likewise rise, maintaining a minimum value of the in-the-money amount. If the option writer attempts to buy back the option, the writer may have to pay considerably in excess of the original premium received on purchase. Thus the margin should reflect the current value of the premium so that the writer may be able to buy the option back when desired.

Exchanges which propose to trade options exercisable in futures contracts generally require margins equal to the margin on the underlying futures contract plus the current value of the option premium. (Margin reductions are frequently permitted for out-of-the-money short positions.) By requiring the writer to post the current margin on the underlying futures contract, the exchange guarantees that sufficient funds will be available to secure a futures contract should the option be exercised. Recall that the option premium is received in cash by the writer upon purchase. Thus the writer is required to post margins initially equal to the original premium plus the futures margin. The margin requirement is thereupon "marked-to-market" or adjusted to reflect the current value of the option premium. In this manner, the exchange guarantees that sufficient funds will always be available should the writer buy the option back. And, because the premium will be at a minimum equal to the in-the-money amount, funds will be available to cover the loss of the in-the-money amount should an exercise occur.

To illustrate, assume that an option trader writes a call exercisable for one $100,000 face-value Treasury-bond futures contract. The call is currently at-the-money; the option is struck at 60% of par and the underlying market is trading at 60% of par. The margin on the underlying futures contract equals $2,000 and the call premium is at $1,000. The writer receives the $1,000 cash upon option sale, but is required to post $2,000 plus the $1,000, or $3,000, with the exchange clearing organization in order to secure the option. (Option margins generally will be accepted in noncash forms such as in Treasury securities, although the rules vary from exchange to exchange.

Treasury-bond Price	Futures Margin	Call Premium	Margin Requirement	Variation Margins
60–00	$2,000	$1,000	$3,000	—
62–00	$2,000	$2,500	$4,500	Pay $1,500
59–00	$2,000	$ 500	$2,500	Collect $2,000

Assume that the price of the Treasury-bond contract moves up to 62–00 from 60–00. The $100,000 face-value Treasury-bond contract is now $2,000 in-the-money and the premium rises to $2,500. The writer is now required to post an additional $1,500 variation margin. If the Treasury-bond price and premium drop to 59–00 and $500, respectively, the margin requirement drops to $2,500 and the writer is entitled to collect $2,000.

Margins proposed by security exchanges are similarly based upon the option premium. Instead of referencing a futures contract margin, however, a fixed amount (subject to change) will be required. For example, an option on an actual GNMA may be margined at 130% of the current value of the option premium plus the fixed sum of $1,500. This represents a notable change from the stock option margining system where the margins reference a fixed percentage of the value of the underlying security. Dealer options on physical commodities generally are margined as a fixed percentage of the value of the underlying commodity, similar in concept to stock margins.

Because the risks associated with holding a covered, spread, or straddle position generally are less than the risks associated with a naked position, the margins are decreased correspondingly. For example, the risks associated with writing a covered call, that is, selling a call option and buying the underlying commodity, are much less than the risks associated with selling the call naked or buying the commodity by itself. The prudent investor is best advised to consult an account executive or the exchange upon which the option is traded in order to understand the details of the margining system in use.

GLOSSARY

AMERICAN OPTION: An option contract which may be exercised at any time prior to expiration. This contrasts with a "European option" which may only be exercised on the expiration date.

AT-THE-MONEY: An option is at-the-money when the underlying market price equals the strike price. When an option is at-the-money, there is no obvious incentive for the option holder to exercise the option.

CALENDAR SPREAD: See "horizontal spread."

CALL OPTION: A call option gives the option buyer or holder the right, but not the obligation, to buy, and obliges the option seller or writer to sell, the underlying commodity at a specific strike price upon the holder's demand.

Class of Option: All options of the same type (see "type of options") with the same expiration date are considered to be of the same class. For example, all Treasury-bond put options which are exercisable for March Treasury-bond futures are considered to be of the same class.

Closing Purchase: A closing purchase cancels an outstanding short option position. For example, an option trader may have sold an option yesterday. By buying an option of the same series today, the trader may cancel or offset the outstanding obligation. A closing transaction results in diminished open interest.

Closing Sale: A closing sale cancels an outstanding long option position. For example, an option trader may have bought an option yesterday. By selling an option of the same series today, the trader may cancel or offset the outstanding option. A closing transaction results in diminished open interest.

Covered Writer: An option writer is "covered" when the writer holds an offsetting position in the underlying commodity market. For example, a short put option is covered by a short position in the underlying commodity. Conversely, a short call option is covered by a long position in the underlying commodity.

Delta: The amount by which an option premium will fluctuate as a percentage of the fluctuation in the underlying commodity market.

Diagonal Spread: A diagonal option spread involves the purchase and sale of two options of the same type which have different strike prices and different expiration dates.

Doubles: See "straddles."

European Option: A European option may be exercised only on its expiration date. This contrasts with "American options" which may be exercised at any time prior to the expiration date.

Exercise: When a call option holder exercises an option, the holder buys the underlying commodity from the option seller. Conversely, a put option holder who exercises an option sells the underlying commodity to the option seller.

Exercise Price: See "strike price."

Expiration Date: Every option contract becomes null and void subsequent to its expiration date. An option which is not offset by a closing transaction or exercised by the expiration date expires or lapses.

Extrinsic Value: The price of an option over and above the intrinsic value. This value is sometimes referred to as the option's "time value."

Fair Value: An option's fair value is the premium which the buyer might pay to the seller wherein both parties to the contract might expect to break even, without considering transaction costs. The actual purchase price of an option may vary from the fair value insofar as fair value is a theoretical concept.

Futures Contract: A futures contract is a contract to make or take delivery of a commodity at some future date. Some option contracts are exercisable for futures contracts rather than the actual or physical commodity.

Holder: An option holder has bought an option and therefore owns the right to exercise it. The terms option buyer and holder are synonomous.

Horizontal Spread: A horizontal or calendar spread involves the purchase and sale of two option contracts of the same type which have the same strike prices but different expiration dates.

INSURANCE VALUE: An option has insurance value insofar as an option buyer has unlimited profit potential and limited downside risk.

IN-THE-MONEY: An option is in-the-money when it may be exercised for a gross profit by the holder. A call option is in-the-money when the underlying market price exceeds the strike price. Conversely, a put option is in-the-money when the underlying market price is less than the strike price.

INTRINSIC VALUE: An option's intrinsic value is equal to its in-the-money valuation. An option premium will never be less than the option's intrinsic value. If the fair value of the option is less than its intrinsic value, the option is likely to be exercised.

LEVERAGE: Leverage refers to one's ability to participate in profits which result from favorable price fluctuations of a particular commodity without putting up the full purchase price of the commodity.

MARGIN: The monetary deposits required to secure an investment position.

MARK-TO-MARKET: This refers to the practice of assessing the requirement for more or less margin to secure a position which has lost in value or gained in value, respectively.

NAKED OPTION: An option is naked when it is bought or sold while the buyer or seller does not hold an offsetting position in the underlying commodity market.

NEUTRAL HEDGE RATIO: Option premiums normally do not fluctuate in a one-to-one ratio with fluctuations in the underlying commodity market. For example, a 10% change in the underlying market price may give rise to a 5% change in the option premium. In this case, the neutral hedge ratio equals 2. For example, one could buy two call options to offset the risk of a short position in the underlying commodity.

OPENING PURCHASE: An opening purchase establishes an open or outstanding long position in the option market.

OPENING SALE: An opening sale establishes an open or outstanding short position in the option market.

PREMIUM: The option buyer pays the option seller a premium in order to secure the rights associated with holding the option. This is the option price and is usually quoted in units of the underlying commodity rather than in the aggregate. For example, a premium for a $100,000 Treasury-bond option may equal 2% of par or $2,000 in the aggregate.

PUT OPTION: A put option gives the option buyer or holder the right, but not the obligation, to sell, and obliges the option seller or writer to buy, the underlying commodity at a specific strike price upon the holder's demand.

SERIES OF OPTIONS: All options of the same type and of the same class which are exercisable at the same strike price are considered to be of the same series.

SPREAD: An option spread involves the purchase and sale of two options of the same type which vary in terms of their strike prices or their expiration dates or both.

STRADDLE: An option straddle or double involves the purchase of two different types of options, that is, a put and a call, or the sale of two different types of options.

STRIKE PRICE: The price at which the option may be exercised. Normally, options are available at a number of different striking prices for the same underlying commodity with the same expiration date.

TIME VALUE: See "extrinsic value."

TYPE OF OPTION: Options are of two types—puts and calls.

UNDERLYING COMMODITY: The commodity for which the option may be exercised. There are generally three types of commodities underlying a commodity option contract: interest-bearing commodities, such as debt instruments, non-interest-bearing commodities, such as physical gold, and futures contracts. The former two types of commodities are also referred to as "actual" or "physical" commodities.

VERTICAL SPREAD: A purchase and sale of two options of the same type with the same expiration date and different strike prices.

BIBLIOGRAPHY

Many of these references are geared toward stock options insofar as commodity options are only now reemerging as significant trading and hedging vehicles. Literature is expected to be available shortly from the exchanges which will trade the options described above.

Black, F. "The Pricing of Commodity Contracts." *Journal of Financial Economics* (January/March 1976).

Black, F. and Scholes, M. "The Pricing of Options and Corporate Liabilities." *Journal of Political Economy* (May/June 1973.)

Bokron, N. *How to Use Put and Call Options*. Springfield, MA: John Magee, 1975.

Clasing, H. *The Dow Jones Irwin Guide to Put and Call Options*. Homewood, IL: Dow Jones Irwin, Incorporated 1978.

Cox and Ross, S.A. "The General Structure of Contingent Claim Pricing." (unpublished paper 1975).

Davis, G. and Jacobson, M. *Stock Option Strategies*. Cross Plains, WI: Badger Press, 1976.

Gastineau, G. *The Stock Options Manual*. New York, NY: McGraw-Hill, 1979.

Hoag, J. "An Introduction to the Valuation of Commodity Options." (unpublished paper, 1978).

Malkiel, B. and Quandt, R. *Strategies and Rational Decisions in the Securities Options Market*. Cambridge, MA: MIT Press, 1969.

McMillian, L. *Options as a Strategic Investment*. New York, NY: New York Institute of Finance, 1980.

Mehl, P. "Trading Privileges on the Chicago Board of Trade." U.S. Department of Agriculture Circular No. 323, 1934.

Noddings, T. *How the Experts Beat the Market*. Homewood, IL: Dow Jones Irwin, Incorporated, 1976.

Zieg, K. and Nix, W. *The Commodity Options Market*. Homewood, IL: Dow Jones Irwin, Incorporated, 1978.

PART IV

FORECASTING METHODS AND TOOLS

CHAPTER 14

BAR CHARTING

CONTENTS

DOW THEORY	5	**MAJOR REVERSAL CHART PATTERNS**	14
BAR CHARTS	6	Double Tops or Bottoms	15
Weekly and Monthly Continuation Charts	7	Triple Tops or Bottoms	16
BASIC TECHNICAL CONCEPTS	8	Head and Shoulders Top or Bottom	16
Trend	8	Spike or *V* Top or Bottom	16
Support and Resistance	9	Rounding or Saucer Top or Bottom	16
Trendlines and Channels	10	**CONTINUATION PATTERNS**	17
Percentage Retracements	12	Flags and Pennants	18
Gaps	13	Triangles	19
		SUMMARY AND CONCLUSIONS	20

CHAPTER 14

BAR CHARTING

John J. Murphy

Before discussing some of the specific techniques used by the technician or chartist, it might be useful to first discuss what chart analysis is and what it is not, to define some terms, and make a few distinctions. Probably the simplest and best definition of chart analysis is *the study of market action, through the use of price charts, for the purpose of forecasting the future direction of prices.* One slight distinction, for example, is the use of the term "market action" instead of "price action." The latter term implies just the study of price itself, while the former term includes volume and open interest, which are included by most chartists in their analysis.

The chartist uses price charts and a variety of technical tools and indicators to determine the present trend of the market first, and then, hopefully, the future trend. What the chartist is trying to do is to identify important trends in early stages of development and then to participate in those trends.

The chartist usually limits himself or herself to the study of market action, which means that the chartist is not overly concerned with the reasons why a market moves up or down. (Being a chartist means never having to ask why.) While this approach to forecasting, which tends to ignore the facts and often contradicts conventional wisdom, may seem somewhat naive and even heretical to some, there are sound and iogical philosophical premises on which the entire technical approach is based.

The first of these premises is that market action tends to discount or reflect all the factors—fundamental, psychological, and otherwise—that can possibly affect the market price. Put another way, the chartist believes that if supply exceeds demand, prices will fall. If demand exceeds supply, prices will rise. While this may sound overly simplistic, the logic is hard to disagree with. In an indirect way, the chartist is actually studying the fundamentals. Even the most "dyed in the wool" chartist would probably concede that it is the underlying forces of supply and demand that cause bull and bear markets. The charts themselves do not cause prices to go up or down, but simply reflect the fundamentals of the market, or at least the market's perception of the fundamentals.

While the fundamentalist may be concerned with the specific supply-and-demand factors, the chartist is content to look at the end result—the price. Another way of stating the basic difference between the fundamental and technical approach would be that the former approach studies the *cause* while the latter approach studies the *effect*. The chartist takes a shortcut approach. The chartist believes that if the fundamentals are bullish, prices should rise; or, put the other way, if prices rise, the fundamentals must be bullish.

The second premise actually has two parts to it, namely, that prices move in trends and that, once a trend has been established, it tends to continue in the same direction. The entire concept of trend is basic to the charting approach. If prices did not trend, charting would be fruitless. It is not within the scope of this chapter to discuss the academic question of whether or not markets do actually trend. If the reader has any serious doubts as to whether markets trend, a casual perusal of any commodity chart library covering the last 10 years should clear up that doubt.

A third premise is that history tends to repeat itself, or the key to the future lies in a study of the past. Part of the rationale behind this premise is that the study of price charts is actually a study in human psychology, which tends not to change. This particular aspect of charting—the use of the past to predict the future—has been questioned by many market observers over the years. The chartist could justifiably point out, however, that every known method of forecasting, including fundamental analysis, is based on the study of past data. So if this aspect of charting is questionable, so is every other form of forecasting that utilizes historical data.

It is unfortunate that the technical and fundamental approaches are often viewed as being in total conflict with one another when, in actuality, the practitioners of each philosophy are approaching the same problem, but from different directions. The fundamentalist believes that a study of all of the economic factors that can affect market price is necessary. The technician believes that if all of these economic factors are reflected in market price then the study of market price is all that is necessary. The correct answer may lie somewhere in between.

The technician believes that prices act as a sort of "leading indicator" of the fundamentals, that the known fundamentals are "in the market," while the market is already looking ahead to the "unknown" fundamentals. Therefore, at critical turning points in the market, there is often a time lag between what the market is actually doing and what the fundamentals say it should be doing. At some point, the fundamentals will catch up to the market action, but often too late to take action.

One final distinction should be made at this point between the terms "technical analyst" and "chartist." Up until the past decade, these terms were used interchangeably with little distinction made between the two because the terms meant the same thing. Over the past 10 years, however, with the introduction of computer technology to market analysis and the application of advanced mathematical and statistical forecasting techniques to the commodity markets, it is becoming increasingly necessary to distinguish between the "technician" and the "chartist." A technician is anyone who relies solely on the study of market action for analysis and trading. The technician may be a chartist or a mathematician. The chartist, as the name implies, relies heavily on price charts. The chartist may or may not use computers in his or her work. Several technical indicators may be used to supplement the analysis, but the chart remains the primary tool. The mathematician, on the other hand, may build statistical models based on weighted moving averages, exponential smoothing, or linear regression. The mathematician may or may not use charts, but is classified as a technician as long as the work is limited to the study of market action.

One way of making the distinction between a chartist and a technician is to say that all chartists are technicians, but not all technicians are chartists. Charting remains somewhat subjective. While it is true that the rules of chart analysis can be studied in several texts, the application of those rules is highly subjective. Chart analysis may be more art than science. Mathematical technicians seem more concerned with devising mechanical trading systems which can be programmed into a computer which then generates buy and sell signals. The intent of this approach seems to be more science than art. This particular chapter is concerned with charting. While the terms chartist and technician may be used throughout the chapter, it should be kept in mind that "charting" represents only one area of the broader topic of "technical analysis."

DOW THEORY

It would not seem appropriate to plunge into the subject of charting without paying tribute to the Dow theory, which is generally considered to be the "granddaddy" of the technical approach. First formulated by Charles H. Dow around the turn of the century, the Dow theory forms the basis for a surprising amount of what we today call the technical approach. An excellent review of the Dow theory can be found in *Technical Analysis of Stock Trends* by Robert D. Edwards and John Magee (John Magee, Springfield, MA, 1948). The work by Edwards and Magee is considered the "bible" of the charting technique and highly recommended reading for serious students of the subject.

While the original theory was meant to be applied to two stock averages, the industrials and the rails, both of which Dow created, many of the principles are widely used today, perhaps unknowingly, and form much of the basis of the "trend-following approach."

Let us mention a few of the points included. Dow first put forward the idea that the market discounted everything and that, once a trend began, it continued until it reversed. Dow broke down the concept of trend into three categories—major, secondary, and near-term. He introduced the concept of confirmation between the two averages and talked about the importance of volume in cofirming the trend. He believed that major bull and bear markets were divided into three phases, an idea that was later refined by R. N. Elliott in the Elliott Wave Theory.

The basic definition of a trend, which will be covered later, is right out of the Dow theory. While the original concept was devised for stock market averages, the followers of the Dow theory will find wide application of the principles to commodity chart analysis.

Probably the major criticism of the theory, which should sound familiar to proponents of the trend-following approach, is that the signals are "too late," that is, too much of the trend is lost while waiting for the signal. The followers of this approach, however, believe that it is fruitless to try to catch the top or bottom of market moves, and content themselves with capturing the middle portion of major moves.

Beginners in the study of commodity chart analysis could not find a better way to start their study than with a thorough review of the Dow theory. Professional chartists, who may occasionally become a bit too sophisticated looking for the perfect system or indicator, might also derive some benefit in a periodic review of the theory.

BAR CHARTS

The two most widely used types of charts in commodity chart analysis are the bar chart and the point-and-figure chart. Of these two, the bar chart is the more commonly used and is the subject of this chapter. The bar chart is sometimes referred to as the daily high, low, close chart. A quick glance at some of the accompanying charts will show what the bar chart looks like. The chart has a vertical and horizontal axis. The vertical scale is labeled with prices, while the horizontal scale represents time. Each bar on the daily chart represents 1-day's action. Each day the high, low, and closing prices are recorded on the chart. A vertical line connects the high and the low (the range), while a small horizontal bar or tick represents the closing price. The bar moves one space to the right with each passing day.

In addition to price, two other pieces of information are often recorded on the daily bar chart, namely, volume and open interest. It should be noted that official volume and open interest figures are usually reported 1 day late. Estimated volume figures, however, are made available for the latest day. These figures are recorded near the bottom of the chart under the appropriate day's price data.

There is some disagreement among chartists as to the relative importance of volume and open interest figures. Some chartists give them more importance than they probably deserve and others give them little or no credence. Most chartists, however, seem to agree that volume and open interest have some forecasting value when used in conjunction with price analysis. Of the three, price is by far the most important. Volume is probably next in line of importance, with open interest a distant third.

Volume is defined simply as the total number of contracts traded during a given time period, usually 1 day. It is marked by a vertical bar at the bottom of the chart in the appropriate day. Volume, or trading activity, measures the intensity or pressure behind the price action and helps to determine which way most of the pressure is moving. As a rule of thumb, volume tends to increase in the direction of the price trend. That is, if prices are in an uptrend, volume will tend to increase as prices advance and decrease on downside reactions. In a downtrend, the heavier volume will occur as prices move lower and decline on bounces. If the volume does behave in this fashion, then the volume is said to be ''confirming'' the price trend. If, however, volume starts to decrease as prices move up in an uptrend and increase on downside reactions, this would indicate a shift in pressure to the downside, and might be a signal of a price reversal to the downside. Volume also plays an important confirming role in the study of chart price patterns and will be discussed later.

Open interest is the number of outstanding contracts. It represents the number of outstanding longs or shorts, but not the total of both. Open interest is reported by individual delivery month and by a total number. For purposes of chart analysis, only the total number is used. Awareness of the open interest in the individual contracts can be useful, however, in helping to decide which contracts to trade, since trading is generally recommended in the more actively traded deliveries for purposes of liquidity.

The rule for interpreting open interest is similar to the rule for volume, which is that open interest should increase in the direction of the main trend. For example, in an uptrend, increasing open interest indicates new money flowing into the market and is considered bullish. Declining open interest in an uptrend indicates primarily short covering in progress, and is considered less bullish. In a downtrend, rising open interest reflects new short selling and is considered bearish. Declining open interest in a downtrend suggests primarily long liquidation in progress, and is considered less bearish.

Open interest is one area that probably requires further research by market technicians. For the past few years, the exceptions to the above-stated rule seem to be more common than the rule itself. In addition, some technicians believe that breaking down open interest figures into categories, for example, hedgers, large traders, and small traders, generally referred to as "open interest mix," has forecasting value. Finally, several chart services plot a 5-year average of open interest figures to reflect the seasonal patterns which should be taken into consideration in the forecasting process.

The above comments present the most common interpretation for volume and open interest. There are several additional refinements which are beyond the scope of this chapter.

WEEKLY AND MONTHLY CONTINUATION CHARTS. So far we have discussed only daily bar charts. However, the bar chart can be used for much longer time periods, for example, weekly or monthly. In a weekly chart, each price bar would represent 1-week's action and in a monthly chart, each bar would represent 1-month's action. The reason for using weekly and monthly charts is to compress the price action for the purpose of looking at much longer time horizons. For example, the daily bar chart might only cover the last 6–9 months. The weekly chart can go back as far as 5 years, while the monthly chart can go back as far as 20 years.

In order to do a thorough chart analysis of the trend structure of a given market, the chartist should always be aware of what the longer-range trends look like. This can only be done by using weekly and monthly charts.

This brings us to one of the basic differences between stock and commodity chart analysis, namely, the limited life span of a commodity futures contract. The average common stock chart goes back for several years. However, the average futures contract trades for about 1½ years before expiration. How then do commodity chartists perform longer-range trend analysis? The answer is the weekly and monthly continuation chart. While the method used to construct these continuation charts has some flaws, it is relatively simple and effective.

The price of the nearest expiring contract month is used. When the contract expires, the new nearest month is plotted. This technique provides continuity in the price structure and allows for longer-range trend analysis. Sometimes large gaps will appear between the expiring contract and the next contract which can, on occasion, cause near-term distortions on the chart. However, even with this criticism of the construction of the continuation chart, the chart has proven to be extremely valuable in longer-range analysis. Some analysts have tried to improve the continuity by forming a continuation chart using the second or third delivery months. While this often reduces the gaps, it may also dampen or change the pattern of the price movement. While most of the comments in this chapter will be dealing with the daily bar chart, it should be mentioned that many of the charting techniques discussed herein work quite well when applied to longer-range charts. As a matter of fact, the notion is completely erroneous that chart analysis is only useful or valid for near-term forecasting. Several texts on the subject have suggested that fundamental analysis should be used for longer-range forecasting, while chart analysis should be limited to near-term forecasting or "timing." The fact is that chart analysis can be used to great advantage over any time period, including longer-range forecasting.

BASIC TECHNICAL CONCEPTS

TREND. The interpretation of chart patterns represents the most important aspect of bar charts. However, as an introduction to that subject, there are a few basic chart concepts that should be treated first. The first of these is the *trend.*

The concept of a trend is really what charting is all about. When all of the terminology is stripped away, the chartist is simply trying to predict the trend of a market. Trend could simply be defined as the general direction of the market. Figure 1 shows a chart as it would look with all trendlines, channels, support and resistance lines (to be described later). However, several distinctions must be made as to direction and magnitude of that trend.

With regard to direction, markets can be categorized as moving in three directions—up, down, and sideways. While this statement may seem obvious, it is important to realize that at least one-third to one-half of the time markets move in a sideways direction in what is often described as a "trading range." Since most technical "systems" are trend-following in nature, they usually do not work well in sideways or "nontrending" markets. An important question is raised on how to deal with sideways markets. Traders are faced with three decisions—whether to buy, sell, or stand aside. The last of these three options, to stand aside or do nothing, is a valid decision and, for at least a third of the time, is probably the correct one.

In our earlier discussion of the Dow theory, it was mentioned that Dow broke a trend into three categories—primary or major, secondary or intermediate, and minor or near-term. In reality, there are many more classifications into which a trend could be broken down, but most chartists and texts on the subjects seem content to stick to these three. Dow classified the major trend as being in effect for more than 1 year; the secondary trend from 3 weeks to as many months; the near-term trend as less than 3 weeks. While different analysts and authors use slightly different time periods, Dow's original definition seems quite adequate.

When someone asks "What is the trend in the gold market?" it is often difficult to answer without first asking which trend is being asked about. The major trend

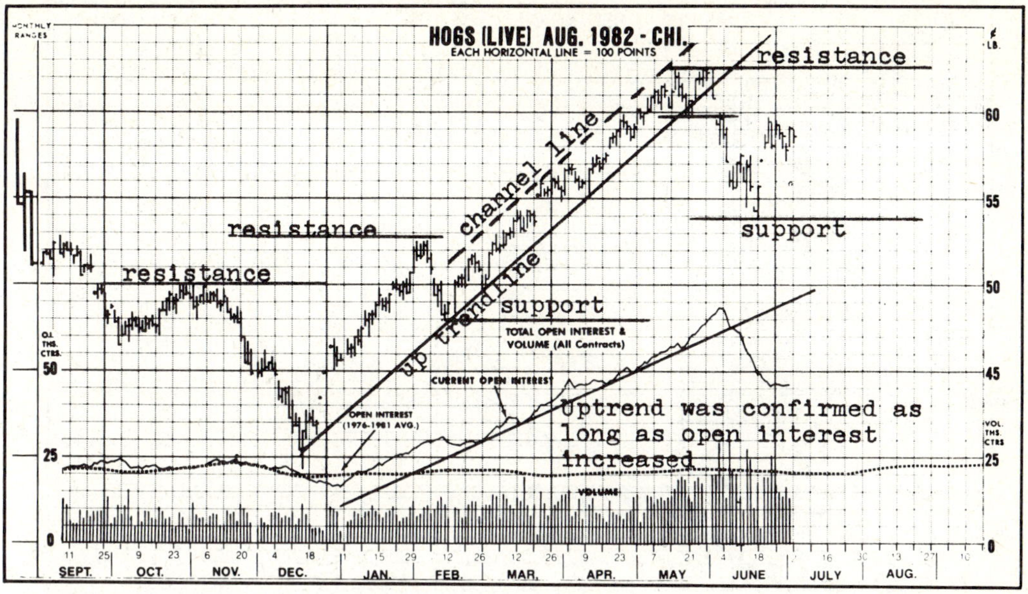

FIGURE 1. Hogs (live), August 1982, Chicago. This daily bar chart shows price, volume, and open interest and illustrates how open interest increased during the price advance. The increase in volume during the first week in June as prices fell reflected a shift in sentiment to the downside. The chart also shows support and resistance levels, the basic up trendline and channel line. (*Source:* Commodity Research Bureau.)

may be down, the intermediate sideways, and the near-term up. Distinctions must always be made. To some near-term traders, for example, a 2-day bounce in a market constitutes an uptrend. It becomes necessary when discussing the trend in a market to make sure that everyone is using the same time interval.

SUPPORT AND RESISTANCE. Markets rarely move in a straight line, but move in a wavelike motion with a series of peaks and troughs. A more precise definition of an uptrend than was given earlier would be a pattern of successively higher peaks and troughs. A downtrend would be a pattern of successively lower peaks and troughs. A sideways trend would exist where the peaks and troughs are horizontal.

In chart analysis, these peaks and troughs are referred to as *resistance* and *support*. Support is a price level under the market where prices stop going down and start moving up. Chartists say there is "support" under the market at a given level. Very often, a support level is determined by studying a price chart to see where prices met with support in the past. Previous reaction lows are referred to as support levels.

Resistance is a price level over the market where prices stop going up and start moving down. Usually, a previous rally high is referred to as a resistance level. To understand the concept of trend, one must be comfortable with support and resistance. As long as the support and resistance levels are rising, the trend is up. As long as they are declining, the trend is down. Figure 2 shows major (long-

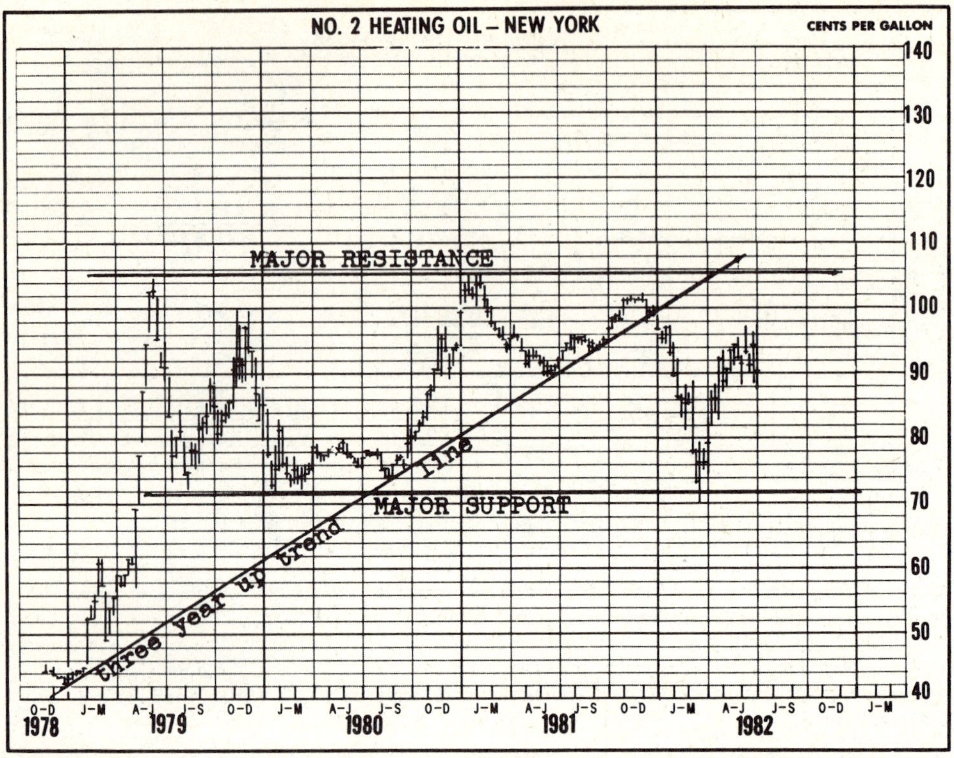

FIGURE 2. No. 2 heating oil, New York. This weekly continuation chart demonstrates how well historic support and resistance levels function even on longer-range charts. None of the above support or resistance levels was visible on the daily heating oil chart. Notice also how well the major three-year up trendline contained the major bull market until January 1982 when a bear market signal was registered. (*Source:* Commodity Research Bureau.)

term) support and resistance levels for heating oil, while Figure 3 shows a double top as major resistance.

One interesting feature of support and resistance is that, once they have been penetrated by a significant amount, they revert to the opposite function. In other words, *a support level that has been penetrated on the downside becomes a resistance level. A resistance level that has been penetrated on the upside becomes a support level.* It is a bit easier to understand why this happens when applied to support. A support level exists because there is significant buying at a certain price level. However, once that buying has been exhausted, and the support level is violated, all of those buyers now have trading losses. Because of the high leverage factor in futures trading, there is little "staying power" if one is caught on the wrong side of a market move. Therefore all or most of the previous buy orders under the market now become sell orders over the market. Support becomes resistance (see Figure 4).

TRENDLINES AND CHANNELS. The *trendline* and *channel line* are two extremely valuable technical tools used by the chartist. The trendline, which is the more important of the two, helps define the "slope" of a trend and is generally used as an early-warning signal, when violated, that a trend may be reversing.

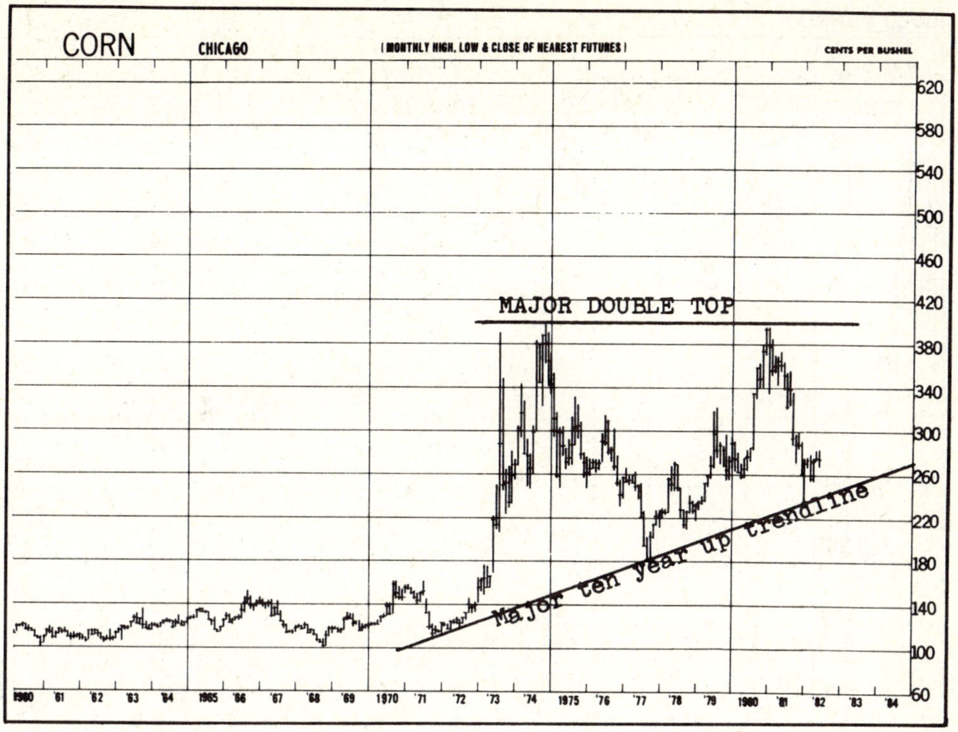

FIGURE 3. Corn, Chicago (monthly high, low, and close of nearest futures). In this monthly continuation chart of corn, showing the past twenty years of price history, notice the major resistance and double top at \$4.00, seven years apart. Also notice how the major 1981 bear market halted at the major ten-year up trendline. None of these longer-range benchmarks was visible on the daily charts of the corn market. (*Source:* Commodity Research Bureau.)

An up trendline is drawn up to the right under successively higher reaction lows. A down trendline is drawn down to the right over successively lower rally highs. The trendline should touch the extreme high or low point of each rally high or reaction low (see Figure 4).

It takes two points to draw a trendline and a third point to confirm it. In the early stages of an uptrend, for example, a tentative up trendline may be drawn under the two ascending reaction lows. If prices subsequently touch the trendline a third time and bounce off it, the trendline is "confirmed" and becomes a "valid" trendline. The correct drawing of trendlines is somewhat of an art. Several trendlines may have to be drawn in the early stages of a trend before the correct one is achieved. Sometimes even valid trendlines may have to be redrawn after a minor penetration or after the acceleration of the trend, which leaves the original trendline too far away from the market action. Most chartists will generally draw several trendlines at the same time to reflect the major, intermediate, and minor trend.

The channel line is another trendline technique which can be useful at times. Often, but not always, a price trend will assume a slope where two parallel trendlines can be drawn, over the peaks and under the troughs. For example, in a downtrend, once the valid down trendline is drawn over the rally peaks, a

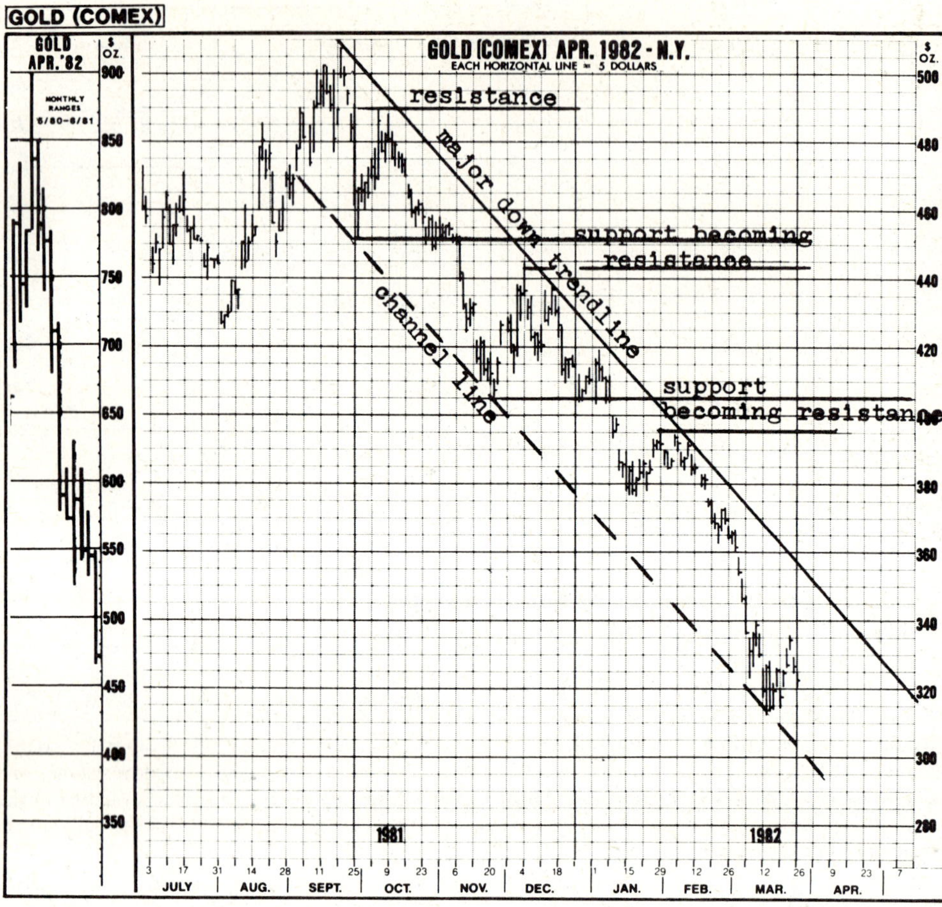

FIGURE 4. Gold (COMEX), April 1982, New York. A classic downtrend of descending peaks and troughs is shown in this daily bar chart of gold. Notice how support levels became resistance levels once violated. Also notice the major down trendline and the parallel channel line. (*Source:* Commodity Research Bureau.)

parallel channel line can be drawn down to the right under the descending reaction lows (as shown in Figure 4). In an uptrend, the channel line would be drawn parallel to the basic up trendline, but over the ascending rally peaks (see Figure 1). Sometimes prices will trend in a consistent fashion between the two parallel lines. Once a trend channel has been identified, the chart trader can use this information to great advantage by knowing in advance where the market will probably meet with support and resistance. Also, the penetration of the upper or lower boundaries tells the chartist that the trend is accelerating or decelerating.

PERCENTAGE RETRACEMENTS. One of the more intriguing and predictable aspects of market action is the *percentage retracement*. It was mentioned earlier that trends move in a wavelike motion with successive peaks and troughs. Within the framework of the overriding trend direction, prices tend to correct or "retrace" a certain percentage of the previous move before resuming the original trend. The best-known application of this tendency is the "50% retracement." For example, if a market is in a major uptrend and rallies from $3 to $4, the subsequent intermediate correction may retrace 50%, or $0.50 of the uptrend. There are also some minimum and maximum retracement parameters that chartists generally utilize. A minimum retracement is generally about one-third of the previous trend, while a maximum would be about two-thirds. This information obviously has tremendous application for the chartist. Even a strong trend will generally retrace at least one-third. If, however, the retracement exceeds the two-thirds mark, the chartist is immediately alerted to the likelihood that the retracement is more likely a trend reversal.

GAPS. The subject of "gaps" is one of those areas of which everyone seems to have a little knowledge. Unfortunately, that little bit of knowledge can often be confusing and misleading. To begin with, a *gap* is simply a space on the chart where no trading has taken place. In an extremely weak market, for example, one day's price range is significantly lower than the previous day's range, leaving a space on the chart. Sometimes these gaps are significant and sometimes they are not. They can also have a different meaning depending on where in the price structure they appear.

Gaps are generally broken down into five categories:

1. *Common Gap.* These gaps are usually spotted in trading ranges and in thinly traded markets. They have little or no forecasting value.

2. *Breakaway Gap.* These gaps usually occur at an important "breakout" point on a chart. Usually, they occur at the completion of an important topping or bottoming pattern. Sometimes they will mark the breaking of an important trendline, signaling a trend reversal. This type of gap usually signifies the beginning of an important move. They may or may not be "filled" or "closed." This last point becomes especially important in the timing of entry into a market. One of the great "clichés" of gap analysis is that they are always filled. This is simply not the case with the breakaway gap. To always wait for the closing of the gap to initiate new positions will result in several missed opportunities.

3. *Runaway or Measuring Gap.* After a trend has been underway for a while, and is moving effortlessly, very often a gap or series of gaps will appear on the price chart. This is a sign of increased momentum. They are called "measuring" gaps because they often occur at about the halfway point in the trend. Here again, these gaps are often not filled.

4. *Exhaustion Gap.* At the end of an important trend, very often prices will have one last spurt which shows up as a gap. While one is never certain which type of gap is developing, there are some guidelines that can be followed. If the trend has been in existence for some time, if the other types of gaps have already appeared, and if most chart "objectives" have been achieved, then one should be alerted to the increased possibility of "exhaustion" gaps. The final giveaway is that these gaps are always filled, usually within a few days. This is one case where the filling of a gap indicates a probable trend reversal.

5. *Island reversal.* Often near the end of a move an exhaustion gap is followed within a few days by a breakaway gap in the opposite direction. In an uptrend, for example, prices will gap higher, trade in a narrow range for a few days, and then gap lower. The result leaves a cluster of one or several days' price

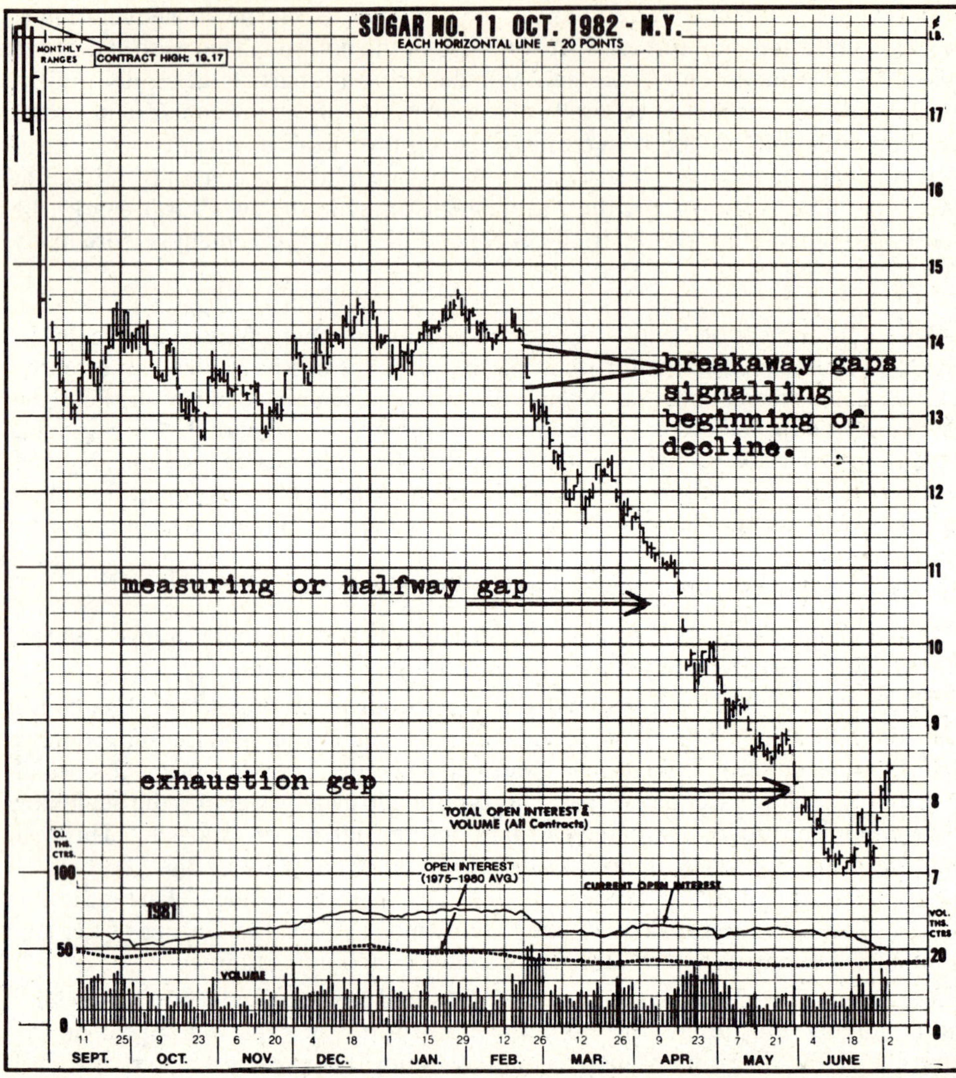

FIGURE 5. Sugar No. 11, October 1982, New York. In this chart showing the three types of gaps, notice that the breakaway and measuring gaps were not filled. Only the exhaustion gap was filled, signalling the probable end of the decline. The measuring gap occurred at about the halfway mark. (*Source:* Commodity Research Bureau.)

action standing out on the chart as an "island" with a gap on both sides. This "island reversal," as the name implies, usually indicates a trend reversal.

MAJOR REVERSAL CHART PATTERNS

Over the years, several price patterns have been identified by chartists as having predictive value. These price or chart patterns are generally divided into *reversal* and *continuation patterns*. As the name implies, reversal patterns represent im-

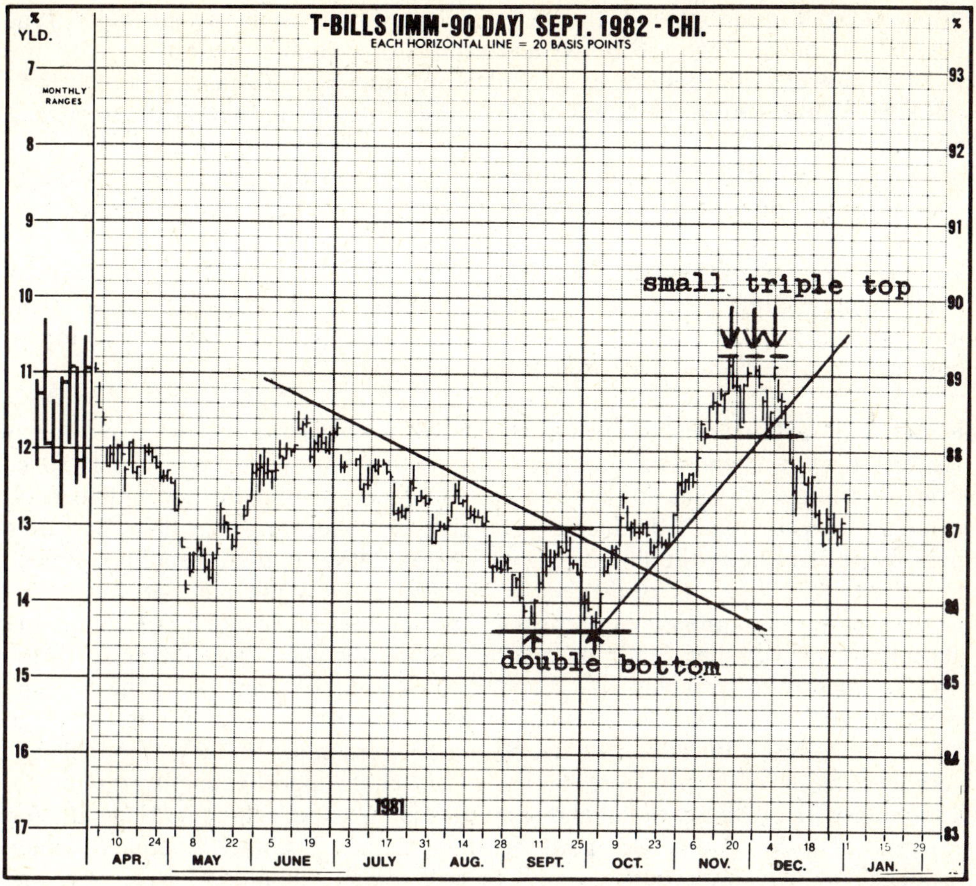

FIGURE 6. Treasury bills (IMM–90 day), September 1982, Chicago; double bottom and triple top. The chart shows a double bottom formed during September/October. Notice the inability of prices to set new lows, followed by the upside penetration of the middle peak. The triple top shows three rallies turned back at about the same level, followed by the downside violation of the intervening reaction lows. The completion of both patterns coincides with the breaking of up and down trendlines. (*Source:* Commodity Research Bureau.)

portant trend reversals in progress. A major bottoming pattern, for example, would imply that a downtrend has ended and a new uptrend is about to begin. Continuation patterns represent relatively short pauses in the existing trend after which the original trend resumes. The ability to accurately identify these patterns as early as possible obviously gives the chartist an important edge. The subject of pattern identification represents the most subjective area of chart analysis.

DOUBLE TOPS OR BOTTOMS. One of the most common of the reversal patterns is the "double top or bottom." In an uptrend, for example, prices are setting successively higher peaks and troughs, which constitutes the definition of an uptrend. The "testing" of a previous resistance peak in an uptrend or a previous support low in a downtrend is always critical because it is precisely at that point that a trend will either resume or stall. If prices are unable to move beyond a previous peak in an uptrend, this is usually the first warning signal that a trend may be in trouble. Figure 6 shows an example of a double bottom.

In an uptrend, the failure to exceed a previous peak forms a "double top" followed by a downside violation of a previous low. It is important to stress that, until the previous low is violated, the potential double top is not confirmed. In a double bottom, of course, the pattern is just the reverse. Prices are unable to penetrate previous support followed by an upside penetration of resistance.

TRIPLE TOPS OR BOTTOMS. Sometimes instead of testing an important peak twice before failing, prices will form three peaks. This is referred to as a "triple top." The triple top or bottom occurs less frequently than the double top or bottom, but usually has more significance (see Figure 6).

HEAD AND SHOULDERS TOP OR BOTTOM. A variation of the triple top is the well-known "head and shoulders" top or bottom. The only real difference from the triple top is that, in the head and shoulders, the "head," or middle peak, is higher than the two "shoulders." The head and shoulders top, then, has three peaks with the one in the middle higher than the other two. A trendline referred to as the "neckline" is drawn under the two intervening reaction lows. The reversal pattern is complete once the neckline has been penetrated. The commonly accepted "measurement" for this pattern is the distance from the head to the neckline measured vertically, and then projected from the point where the neckline is penetrated. A pullback sometimes occurs after the break of the neckline, in which prices will return near the neckline before resuming the new trend. This is another example of the principle mentioned earlier of support becoming resistance. The bottom or "inverse" head and shoulders is the exact same picture as the top except it is upside down. This pattern will sometimes become "complex" which means there may be two heads or two right or left shoulders. However, one principle which should be kept in mind is the tendency for this pattern to be symmetrical. Therefore two left shoulders would suggest the strong possibility of two right shoulders (see Figure 7).

It should be mentioned here that volume plays an important role in all of these patterns as a confirming indicator. The completion of all of these patterns, which occurs with the breaking of some important support or resistance level, or the neckline, should be accompanied by a noticeable increase in trading volume. The absence of heavy volume, especially in new uptrends, would render the chart signal suspect.

SPIKE OR *V* TOP OR BOTTOM. A fourth reversal pattern is referred to as a "spike" or "*V*" top or bottom. This pattern, which is difficult to identify in its early stages, represents an abrupt change in market direction. All of the other reversal patterns take time to develop and can be studied and evaluated. This pattern, however, occurs so quickly that one is never sure until well after the fact that it has occurred. A "V" top is shown in Figure 8.

ROUNDING OR SAUCER TOP OR BOTTOM. The last of these reversal patterns, and possibly the most rare, is the "rounding" or "saucer" top or bottom. This pattern represents a very gradual shifting of market psychology from up to

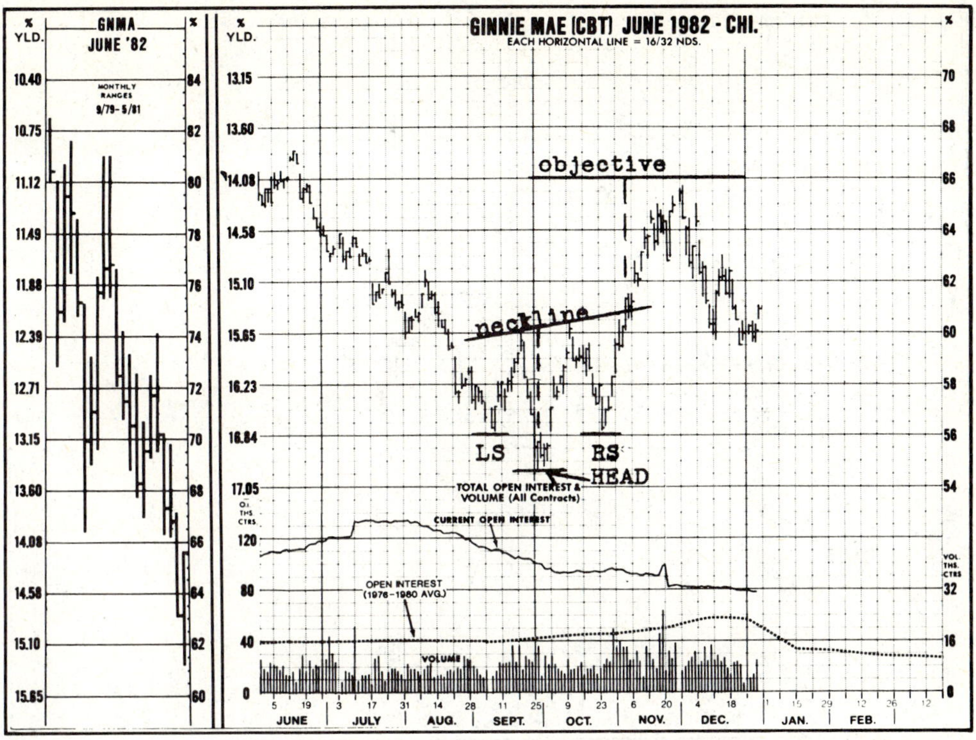

FIGURE 7. Ginnie Mae (CBT), June 1982, Chicago; head and shoulders bottom. The left shoulder (LS) and right shoulder (RS) are shown at about the same level, with the middle low (head) below the two shoulders. The measurement taken by measuring the vertical distance from the head to the neckline and then projecting from the point where the neckline is penetrated yielded a target to 66. (*Source:* Commodity Research Bureau.)

down or vice versa. As the name implies, the price pattern has a "rounding" top or bottom appearance and has been relatively rare in recent years.

A brief comment on the use of chart "terminology" or "jargon" may be in order here. In case any newcomers to the subject of chart analysis find themselves intimidated by the reliance on chart terms, it should be fairly obvious by now that most of the terms used by chartists are "self-explanatory" in nature and easily understood and mastered. These terms have been used over the years because they happen to best describe a certain chart picture. Chartists, however, should probably exercise more discretion when using these terms in the presence of the uninitiated.

CONTINUATION PATTERNS

The major reversal patterns just described usually indicate that an important reversal of trend is taking place. *Continuation patterns,* however, are usually much shorter in duration and only represent pauses in the existing trend. The most common continuation patterns are flags, pennants, wedges, rectangles, and triangles.

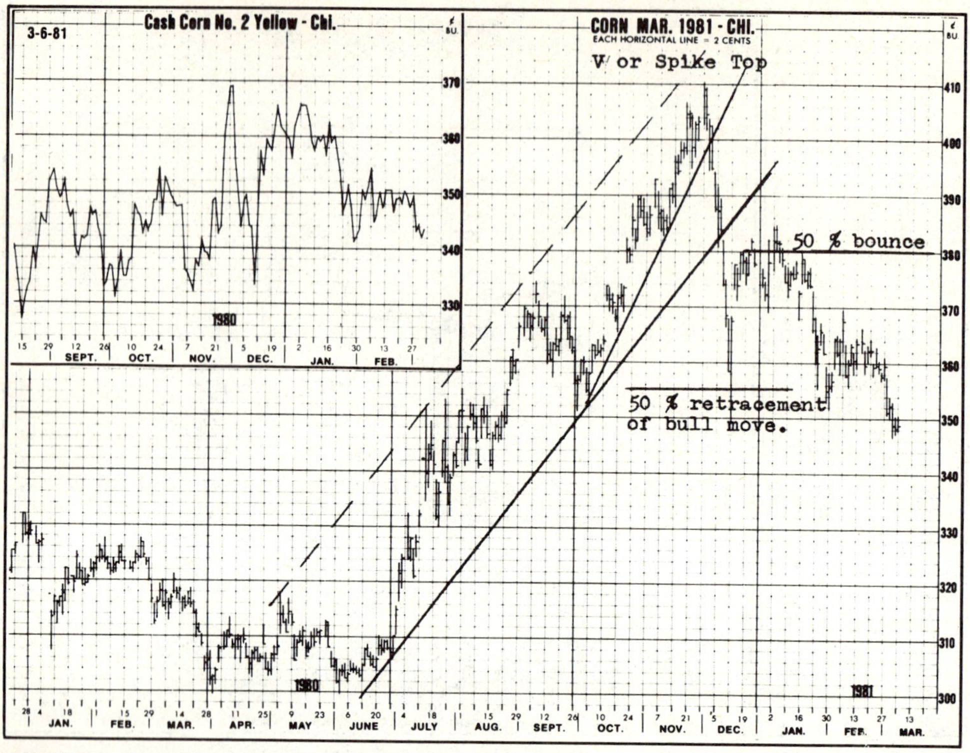

FIGURE 8. Corn, March 1981, Chicago; cash corn No. 2 yellow, Chicago. This chart shows the "V" or "spike" top that represents a sudden and dramatic reversal of trend. The pattern is especially difficult to identify until after the fact. Notice the principle of the 50% retracement. In general, prices will often retrace about 50% of the previous trend. The chart also shows the major up trendline and channel, as well as a tighter, more near-term, up trendline near the top. Chartists usually draw several trendlines. (*Source:* Commodity Research Bureau.)

FLAGS AND PENNANTS. These two patterns usually occur after a sharp price move has occurred and prices pause to consolidate or digest those sudden gains or losses. Both patterns have the same meaning, but are shaped slightly differently. The *pennant* moves sideways with the upper and lower boundaries converging. The *flag* tends to slope in a parallelogram against the prevailing trend. These patterns usually last no more than 2 or 3 weeks before the trend is resumed. Volume tends to drop off significantly during the formation and then picks up once the trend is resumed. One of the requirements of these patterns is that a "flagpole" precede their formation, or a steep price move. They are often referred to as flying at "half-mast," which means that they often occur at the halfway point of the move (see Figure 9).

The "wedge" looks something like a flag in the sense that it slopes against the trend, but its boundaries converge like a pennant. The "rectangle" represents a horizontal congestion area or "trading range" during which prices move sideways in a well-defined band.

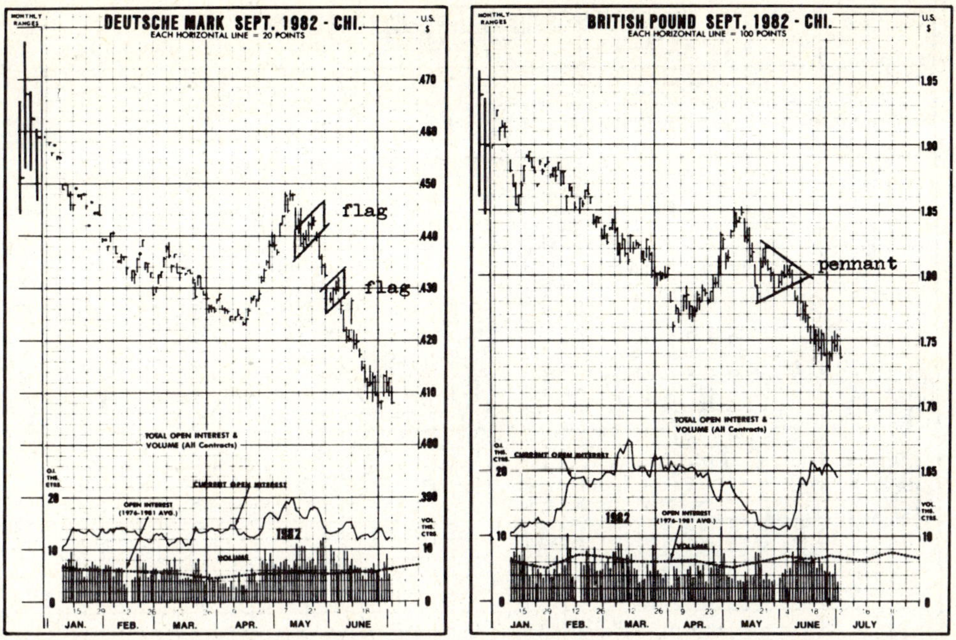

FIGURE 9. Deutsche mark, September 1982, Chicago, and British pound, September 1982, Chicago; examples of flag and pennant. The Deutsche mark chart shows two examples of bearish continuation flags that slant upward against the trend. The British pound chart shows a bearish pennant. Notice how the lines converge. The pennant in this example also resembles a symmetrical triangle. Both of these patterns, the flag and pennant, represent brief pauses in the existing trend. (*Source:* Commodity Research Bureau.)

TRIANGLES. It is difficult to classify "triangles" as either reversal or continuation patterns because they can function as either. Triangles are classified into three categories: ascending, descending, and symmetrical. All triangles have an upper and lower boundary and these are identified by a trendline.

The "ascending" triangle has a flat upper boundary and a rising lower boundary. This is a bullish pattern and indicates that buyers are more aggressive than sellers. The breakout usually occurs on the upside (see Figure 10).

The "descending" triangle is just the opposite. It has a flat lower boundary and a descending upper boundary. It indicates that sellers are more aggressive than buyers and that the breakout will probably occur on the downside.

The "symmetrical" triangle looks something like a "pennant" in the sense that both upper and lower boundaries are converging toward an "apex." The basic difference from the pennant is that the triangle can take much longer to form and usually is not preceded by a "flagpole" (see Figure 11). While it is sometimes said that the symmetrical triangle does not have any inherent forecasting value, this is only partially true. While the ascending triangle is inherently bullish, and the descending triangle inherently bearish, the symmetrical triangle is inherently neutral. But since the symmetrical triangle is a continuation pattern, it will usually break out in the direction of the prior trend. Therefore it does have forecasting value.

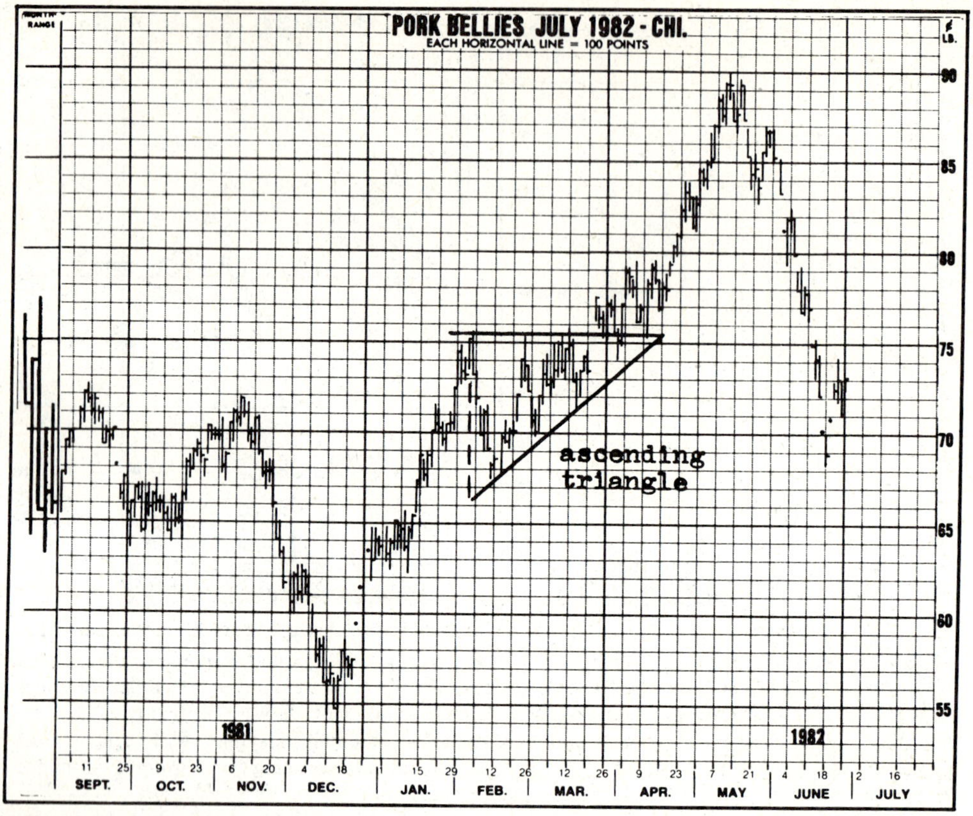

FIGURE 10. Pork bellies, July 1982, Chicago; the ascending triangle. Notice how the upper boundary is flat while the lower boundary is rising. This is a bullish pattern that means that prices will usually break out on the upside. The descending triangle has a flat lower boundary and a declining upper boundary and is usually bearish. (*Source:* Commodity Research Bureau.)

The ascending and descending triangles will sometimes function as tops or bottoms and are often referred to as "right-angle" tops or bottoms. As in other consolidation patterns, volume should show a tendency to decline during the pattern and pick up noticeably on the completion of the pattern. The most common measuring technique for triangles is the vertical height of the triangle at its left boundary measured from the "apex."

SUMMARY AND CONCLUSIONS

This discussion represents a relatively brief review of some of the more important elements of commodity bar charting. A more complete treatment of the subject would probably require several volumes. In actuality, chartists may use several other technical tools in their analysis such as momentum oscillators, moving averages, contrary opinion, weekly rules, Elliott Wave, and cycle analysis. They may also utilize point and figure charts to capture price data not apparent on bar charts.

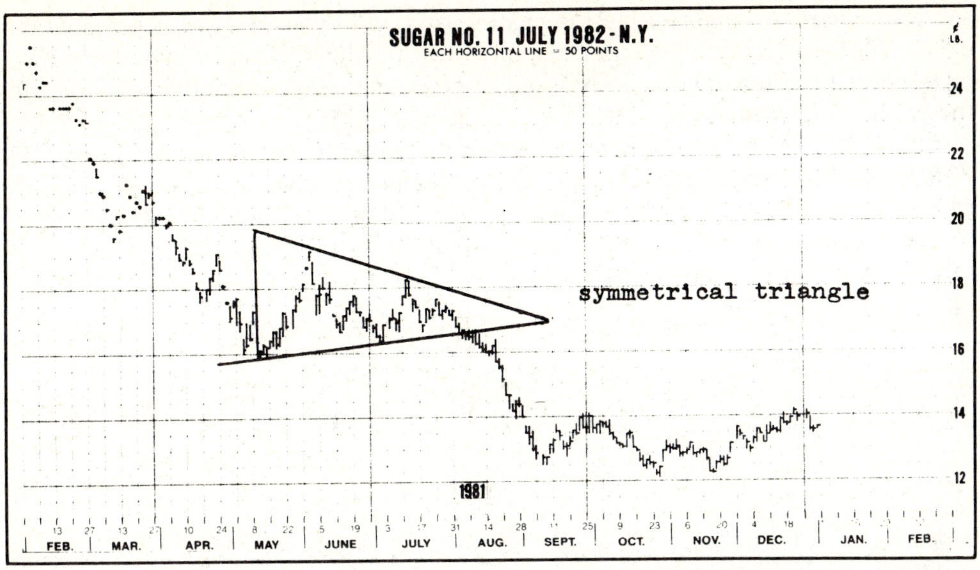

FIGURE 11. Sugar No. 11, July 1982, New York; a symmetrical triangle. The upper and lower boundaries clearly converge toward the apex. In the symmetrical triangle, the upper line is declining while the lower line is rising. This is usually a continuation pattern. In this example, since the original trend is down, the breakout will usually resume the downtrend. (*Source:* Commodity Research Bureau.)

Chartists are also well aware that individual futures markets are greatly influenced by the group to which they belong and also by the direction of commodity prices in general. Therefore chartists will supplement their chart analysis of any one market by closely monitoring various commodity group indices and one or more of the general price indices, such as the Commodity Research Bureau Futures Price Index. It is important to know, for example, whether or not the general commodity price level is in an inflationary or deflationary period. If one is watching the gold market, for example, it is also useful to know which way the metals group index is moving since related markets tend to move in the same direction.

As a corollary to the above, the principle of confirmation is important in chart analysis. A chart pattern that shows up in one contract of a commodity, for example, should be "confirmed" by a similar pattern in other contracts. A signal or pattern that is not confirmed should be suspect. Carrying that thought a bit further, bullish or bearish chart readings in one market should be "confirmed" by similar readings in related markets. The soybean complex, for example, tends to rise and fall together. Bullish readings in the soybean market would be suspect if not confirmed by similar bullish readings in at least one of the products, oil or meal. As a general guiding rule in the principle of confirmation, the more chart evidence that confirms a bullish or bearish analysis, the more confidence that analysis inspires.

In conclusion, one of the great strengths of chart or technical analysis is its flexibility and adaptability. The principles of charting can be applied to virtually any market that is traded, be it in commodities or stocks, domestic or international. The principles can be applied to broad market averages and indices as well as individual markets. They can be used in any time dimension from day trading off a "tick" chart to longer-range forecasting from a 20-year monthly continuation chart. Technical principles can be applied to "outright" long or short positions or to spread trading. They can be used to great advantage by the speculator and the commercial hedger.

Finally, chart analysis can be utilized in its purest form with no consideration of fundamental factors, or it can be utilized simply as a check or confirmation of conclusions arrived at by fundamental or economic analysis. However one chooses to use the principles of chart analysis, some knowledge of these principles of market behavior is a necessity for successful commodity analysis and trading.

CHAPTER 15

QUANTITATIVE TRADING METHODS

CONTENTS

POINT-AND-FIGURE CHARTING 3

Plotting Prices Using the Point-and-Figure Method 4
Chart Formations 5
Trendlines 6
Trading Techniques 7
Price Objectives 8
Point-and-Figure Concepts 11

SMOOTHING 11

Relating Exponential Smoothing to Standard Moving Averages 13
Trading Methods 14
Velocity and Acceleration 17

SYSTEM TRADEOFFS

Trend-Following Systems 19
Contratrend Systems 20

CYCLES 22

Seasonality 22
Other Growing Cycles 24
Major Regular Cycles 25
Phasing Using Moving Averages 27

SHORT-TERM TRADING 29

Day-Trading Techniques 29
Methods of Day Trading 30
Time of Day 30
Overnight Positions 30
Market Patterns 32
Point-and-Figure Use in Short-Term Trading 32

USE OF THE COMPUTER IN SYSTEM DEVELOPMENT 33

Computer Testing 33
Point-and-Figure 34
Real-Time Analysis 34

CHAPTER 15

QUANTITATIVE TRADING METHODS

Perry J. Kaufman

Quantitative, or numerical, methods for evaluating price movement and making trading decisions have become a dominant part of market analysis. At one time the only acceptable manner of trading was by understanding the factors which make prices move, and determining the extent or potential of future movement. The market now supports dozens of major funds and managed programs which account for a sizable part of commodity open interest and operate wholly or primarily, on decisions based upon quantitative methods. Many commercial participants in the markets, who once restricted research to supply, demand, and related factors, now include various technical methods for the purpose of "timing" or confirming price direction.

In many ways there is no conflict between traditional fundamental analysis and technical analysis. The decisions which result from economic or policy changes are far-reaching; the results of those actions may cause a long-term change in the direction of prices and may not be reflected immediately. Actions based on long-term forecasts may involve considerable risk and often can be an ineffective use of money. Integrated with a numerical method of known risk which determines price trends over shorter intervals, many commercial firms have gained practical solutions to their trading problems.

One of the earliest attempts in the development of a quantitative technical approach was to reduce the interpretive qualities of chart analysis. The trendlines drawn across the bottoms or tops of a chart formation are often imperfect; a small violation of the trendline must be ignored to maintain the integrity of the trend. If that is done, then a penetration of the line, signaling a change in the direction of the trend, becomes ambiguous. The simplest solution to this sequence of uncertainty is the *point-and-figure method* of charting.

POINT-AND-FIGURE CHARTING

Dating back to Charles Dow at the turn of the century, the point-and-figure method allows the chartist to be specific about "significant" price movements and yet retain the ability to supplement the well-defined rules with the interpretation of patterns, in a manner similar to bar charting. The earliest important work published on the subject was *The Point-and-Figure Method of Anticipating Stock Price*

Silver

854.0	X									
853.0	X	O	X							
852.0	X	O	X	O						
851.0		O	X	O	X					
850.0		O		O	X	O				
849.0				O	X	O				
848.0				O	X	O				
847.0				O						
846.0										

FIGURE 1. Point-and-figure chart.

Movements by Victor de Villiers in 1933[1]. Other studies and analyses can be found in *Profit and Profitability* by Robert Earl Davis (R.E. Davis, West Lafayette, IN, 1969) and *Point-and-Figure Commodity Trading Techniques* by K.C. Zieg and P.J. Kaufman (Investors Intelligence, Larchmont, NY, 1975). Although very popular among all levels of experience traders, very little has been written about the method in recent years. The concentration in literature seems to have shifted to more mathematical approaches to market analysis. Point-and-figure charting remains, however, an important factor in the commodities markets.

PLOTTING PRICES USING THE POINT-AND-FIGURE METHOD. To plot prices on a point-and-figure chart, we start with a piece of graph paper and mark the left scale as a conveniently small price increment. For example, each box may be set at \$1 for gold and platinum, \$0.01 for soybeans and silver, and so forth (see Figure 1). The choice of box size will make the chart more or less sensitive to changes in price direction, as will be seen in later examples. The smaller the price increment, the more changes in direction will be seen. This also corresponds to longer or shorter trends, or major and minor trends. Therefore a point-and-figure chartist looking for a long-term price movement will use a larger box size.

Although the box sizes are often related to the current volatility of the markets, Table 1 shows some possible choices for selected commodities.

Once the graph paper has been scaled, and the prices entered on the left side, the chartist can begin. The first box to be entered is that of the current closing price of the commodity. If the price of silver is 852.50 and a \$1 box is being used, then a mark is placed in the box beside the value 852. We use an X or an O to indicate that the current price trend is up or down, respectively. You may select the X or O yourself when you begin—after that it will be determined for you (see Figure 2).

The rules for plotting point-and-figure charts are easily shown as a flowchart (Figure 2). In general, preference is given to price movements which continue in the direction of the current trend. Therefore if the trend is up (represented by a

[1]Reprinted in 1966 by Traders Press, NY.

TABLE 1. Point-and-Figure Suggested Box Size

Commodity	Approximate Average Price	Box Size
Gold	$400 per oz	$2 per oz
Silver	$10 per oz	$0.03 per oz
Soybeans	$6 per bushel	$0.01 per bushel
Copper	$0.70 per lb.	$0.25 per lb
Treasury bills	90.00	5 points
Swiss francs	45.00	10 points

column of X's) the new high price is tested first; if the trend is down, the low price is of greatest importance. The opposite price is checked only if the new price fails to increase the length of the column of the current trend.

The traditional point-and-figure method calls for the use of a "three-box reversal," that is, the price must reverse direction by an amount equal to three boxes from the most extreme box of the last column (it actually must fill the forth box since the extreme box is left blank) before a new column can begin. The importance of keeping the three-box reversal has always been questional by experienced point-and-figure traders. It should be noted that the net reversal amount, the box size times the number of boxes in the reversal, is the critical value. For example, a $4 box for gold, with a three-box reversal means that gold must reverse by $12 to indicate a trend change. The opposite combination, a $3 box and a four-box reversal, would actually signal a reversal of trend at the same time. The proper selection is based on the subsequent sensitivity of the box size following the reversal. Therefore a smaller box size may interpret the smallest price movements as a continuation of the trend and ultimately capture more of the price move; it is considered the preferable alternative. The choice of box size and reversal boxes will be considered in more detail in the section on computer testing.

Additional research has questioned the preference for the trend continuation rather than plotting the trend reversal when both situations occur on a single day. Traditional point-and-figure rules ignore the reversal when there is a new high in an uptrend, or a new low in a downtrend; it may be, however, that there are more advantages to taking the reversal whenever possible. Consider the alternatives. If the reversal continues, it is better to react more quickly and be stopped-out sooner, resulting in smaller losses. If the trend reverses again, then the stop-loss point in the current trade becomes closer, which is again an advantage when the more important reversal occurs. Figure 3 shows the combination of events resulting in these patterns.

CHART FORMATIONS. The formations of a commodity point-and-figure chart are very limited compared to those expressed by a stock chart. The length of maturity of a commodity contract, the sparse number of commodities, and the high similarity between price movement of various delivery months within one commodity restricts the number of formations that a chartist might expect to find. The most comprehensive study of chart formations in both stocks and later in commodities was published by Robert E. Davis. His 1965 book *Profit and Prob-*

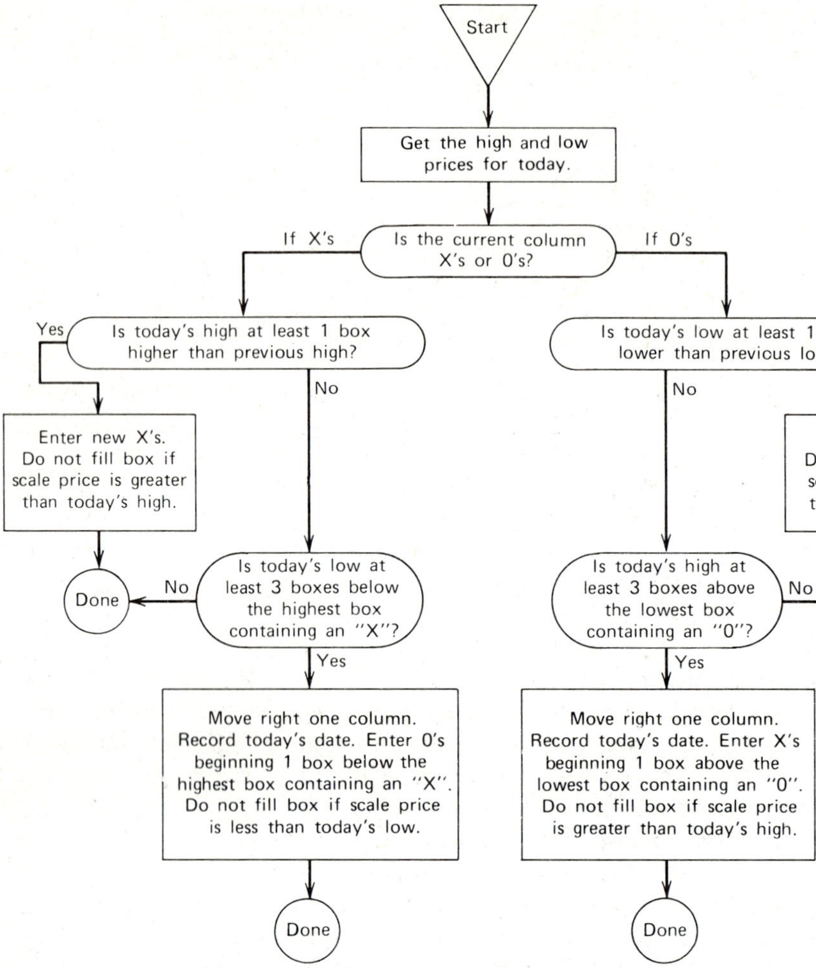

FIGURE 2. Point-and-figure daily rules.

ability and later with Charles C. Thiel, Jr., *Point-and-Figure Commodity Trading, A Computer Evaluation* (1970) analyze the success of various "buy" and "sell" formations.

The most successful of the stock market chart formations was shown by Davis to be the ascending triple top and the breakout of the triple bottom. Due to the infrequency of occurrence in commodities, only the simple buy and sell signals were tested in the later study. The results of the commodity evaluation showed that a change of box size was a critical factor in the success of the method.

TRENDLINES. The bullish and bearish trendlines important to bar charting also exist in the point-and-figure charts. The act of leaving the top or bottom box blank when reversing to the next column, often forms an ascending or decending pattern at a 45° angle (providing that the graph paper has square boxes). These 45° angles represent the major anticipated trends of the commodity. Once a top or bottom has been identified, a 45° line can be drawn down from the upper corner of the

Day	High	Low
1	802	790
2	811	795
3	813	792
4	818	796
5	825	810
6	832	808
7	840	825

a. Sample prices for plotting

Price	b			c				
840			X					X
835			X					X
830			X					X
825			X			X		X
820			X			X	O	X
815			X			X	O	X
810	X		X	X		X	O	
805	X	O	X	X	O	X		
800	X	O	X	X	O	X		
795	X	O		X	O			
790	X			X				

b. Traditional method

c. Option taken on day 6

FIGURE 3. Alternate methods of plotting point-and-figure reversals. (*a*) Sample prices for plotting. (*b*) Traditional method. (*c*) Option taken on day 6.

top box of X's toward the right or up from the bottom of the lowest box of O's toward the right (see Figure 4). These trendlines can be used to *confirm* the direction of price movement. It is common to "filter" the basic point-and-figure trading signals to conform to the longer-term concept of trends represented by the 45° lines.

TRADING TECHNIQUES. The most common point-and-figure formations are shown in Figure 5 accompanied by the 45° trendlines which apply. The simple *buy* and *sell* signals which occur when a column of X's rises above the prior column of X's or when the column of O's declines below the previous column of O's respectively, are the most commonly used. Since commodity contracts are of short duration as compared to stocks, and they are usually considered separate from other contracts, there is little opportunity to apply the more complex formations, however reliable.

A popular variation to the simple buy and sell signals is to wait for a pullback to the 45° trendline or to previous support. Rather than entering on the initial buy signal, for example, a trader will wait for the first reversal and buy as prices near

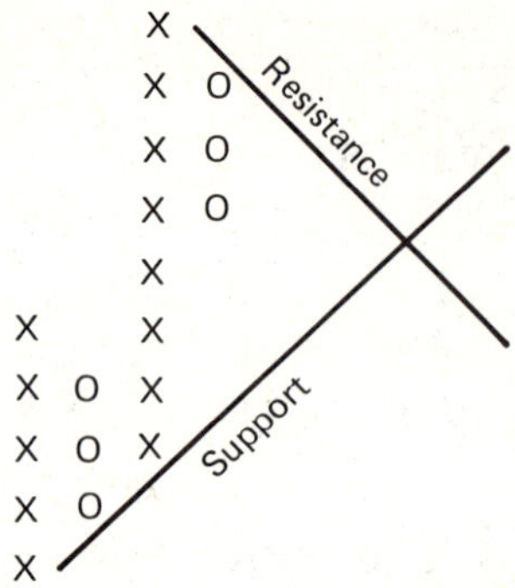

FIGURE 4. Point-and-figure trendlines.

prior lows or when they reverse again toward the upside. Figure 6(*a*) shows the reduction in risk which can be attained using this method. Figure 6(*b*) represents the new entry point following a second reversal after the initial buy signal. It can be seen that the stop is only four boxes below the entry rather than six in the initial buy signal.

A second variation is based on taking profits during sustained moves. Occasionally the market continues in one direction for an exceptional time without a setback large enough to cause a point-and-figure reversal. As a rule of thumb we will consider this any sustained move of 10 boxes or more. Rather than liquidate the trade arbitrarily to capture the profits, it is reasonable to use the first reversal (four boxes below the highest box) as your exit point. No matter how high the move, your loss on exit will remain fixed and you will have the advantage of a clear reentry point and a close stop, as shown in Figure 7. The reentry signals can also be treated as secondary entry points for adding to the original position, providing proper risk management is used.

PRICE OBJECTIVES. Point-and-figure charting has unique methods for determining price objectives. The *horizontal count* relates the time and movement spent in a consolidation area (a rectangular formation on a line chart), to the potential movement as follows:

$$\text{price objective} = \text{lowest box} + (\text{width} \times \text{reversal value})$$

The upside price objective, in box notation, is determined to be three times the width (using a three-box reversal) of the consolidation pattern, measured from the bottom upwards. For the downside horizontal objective, the *width × reversal value* is subtracted from the highest box of the distribution formation.

The *vertical count* is a measurement of volatility, and is applied to a price reversal. It is calculated as

$$\text{price objective} = \text{lowest box} + (\text{number of boxes in first reversal from a top or bottom}) \times \text{reversal value}$$

Using the standard three-box reversal, this method would set the vertical price objective as three times the size of the first reversal following the formation of a bottom (or top).

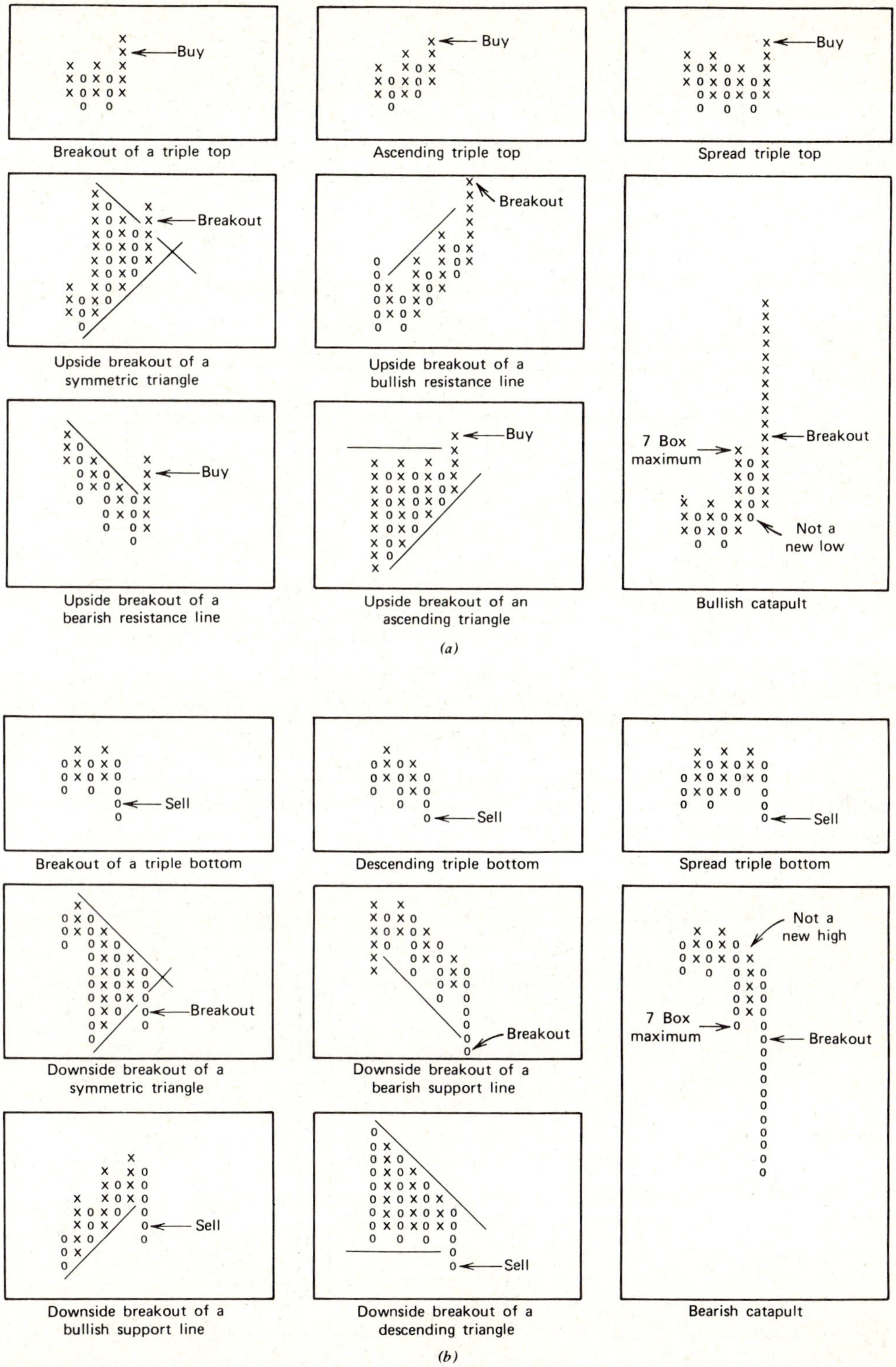

FIGURE 5. (*a*) Compound point-and-figure buy signals. (*b*) Compound point-and-figure sell signals.

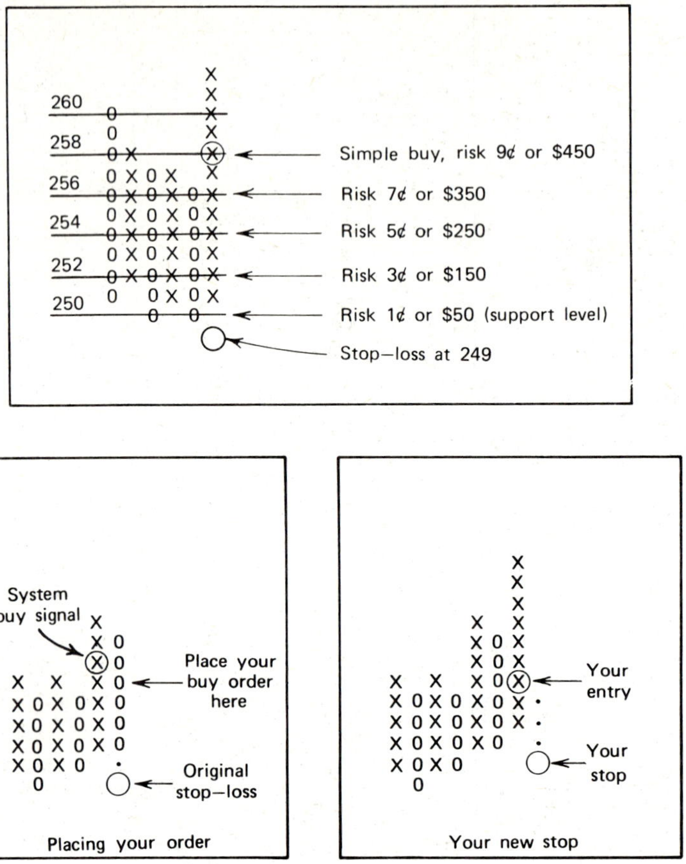

FIGURE 6. Point-and-figure entry variations applied to corn prices. (*a*) Entering on a pullback. (*b*) Entering on a confirmation of the new trend.

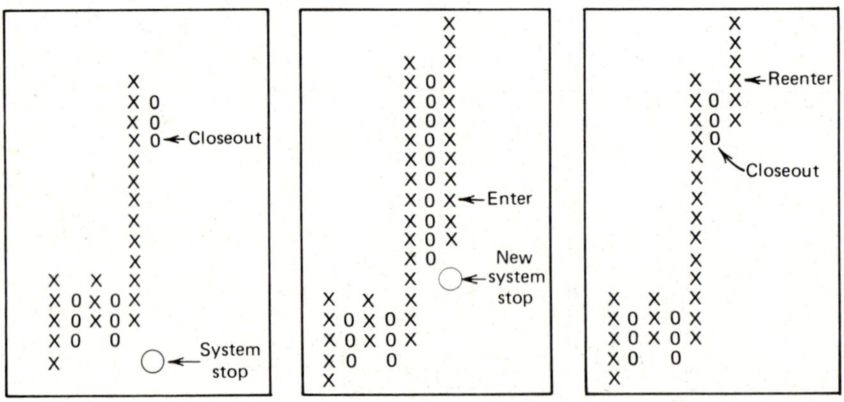

(*a*) (*b*) (*c*)

FIGURE 7. Cashing in on profits.

POINT-AND-FIGURE CONCEPTS. Point and figure is a popular and often successful trading method. It can identify trends and provide the basis for buy and sell signals as well as newer, more sophisticated methods. But this technique, as well as others, requires change. The box size used will determine the nature or speed of the trend, and the frequency of the trading signals. In addition, a box size chosen when prices are low will not usually work as prices move higher. Consider a reasonable selection of a box size for 90-day Treasury bills in 1975 as 10 points (1/10 of 1%), making a three-box reversal equal to 30 points. During 1981 a reversal of this size could easily have occurred every day, since the daily range was double the reversal value. Higher prices mean greater fluctuations, and a small box size selected at lower price levels in a less volatile period will appear more sensitive at higher prices. Similarly, a large box size selected when prices are high will be useless at lower levels, since weeks of price movement may pass before a single box could be plotted.

The methods for determining the optimum point-and-figure box size and reversal are considered along with similar analyses in the section "Computer Testing." Without such aids the trader may consider plotting each commodity using a logarithmic or other expanding scale. This serves to reduce the effects of greater volatility at higher prices which leads to more frequent reversals and signals. While this is a theoretically sound approach to charting, it entails risks which also increase logarithmically with the box size and may not be appropriate at very high price levels.

SMOOTHING

The basis for most mathematical computer-based methods is *smoothing*. In technical analysis *smoothing is the identification of a trend by the elimination of unnecessary price movement*. Although we can find a trend using a trendline in chart analysis or a vertical column of X's or O's on a point-and-figure chart, the trends found by smoothing are normally derived from a mathematical formula (or model) applied to a time series (sequential price data).

The objective of a smoothing method is to determine the current direction of price movement. The results can be simply expressed as up, down, and sideways. Smoothing techniques do not attempt to predict the extent or objective of the price movement, only the current direction. It presumes that prices will continue to move in the same general direction long enough to net a profit over some time period. The method does not refute the long-term random character of price movement, but does require that prices have sustained movement over short intervals.

The most popular smoothing technique is the *moving average*. This is simply the average of the most recent *n* days of closing (or other) prices. If 10 days are used, the result is called a *10-day moving average*. Using this method, an analyst might conclude that, if the current price was higher than the 10-day moving average, then the current trend of prices is up; if the value of the moving average was higher than the most recent price, then the price trend would be down. The number of days used in the moving average will determine the sensitivity of the price trend as well as the speed with which the analysis identifies a change of directional movement. Therefore a slow moving average will use at least 25 days and will change very little in value due to a single new price (4% of the total value), while one additional price will be 20% of the value of a 5-day moving average. Figure 8 shows the difference between trends as calculated using fast, medium, and slow moving averages.

More significance can be given to recent data by weighting the prices. It is possible to multiply the most recent day by a factor of 10, the prior day by 9, and so forth in order to give greater importance to some data. If the same weighting factor is applied to more than one consecutive price, the method is called *step-weighting*.

$$\text{Simple moving average } (n \text{ days}) = A_n = \frac{P_n + P_{n-1} + \cdots + P_1}{n} \tag{1}$$

$$\text{Weighted moving average } (n \text{ days}) = W_n = \frac{a_1 p_n + a_2 P_{n-1} + \cdots + a_n P_1}{a_1 + a_2 + \cdots + a_n} \tag{2}$$

$$\text{Step-weighted moving average } (n \text{ days}) \text{ in steps of 2} = SW_n = \frac{a(P_n + P_{n-1}) + b\,(P_{n-2} + P_{n-3}) + \cdots}{2a + 2b + \ldots} \tag{3}$$

By adjusting the weighting factors in either Eqs. (2) or (3), it is possible to put greater emphasis on the most recent price data. This technique is called *front loading*.

A popular smoothing method, which is readily automated, is *exponential smoothing*. This approach gives significance to each price by considering it as a

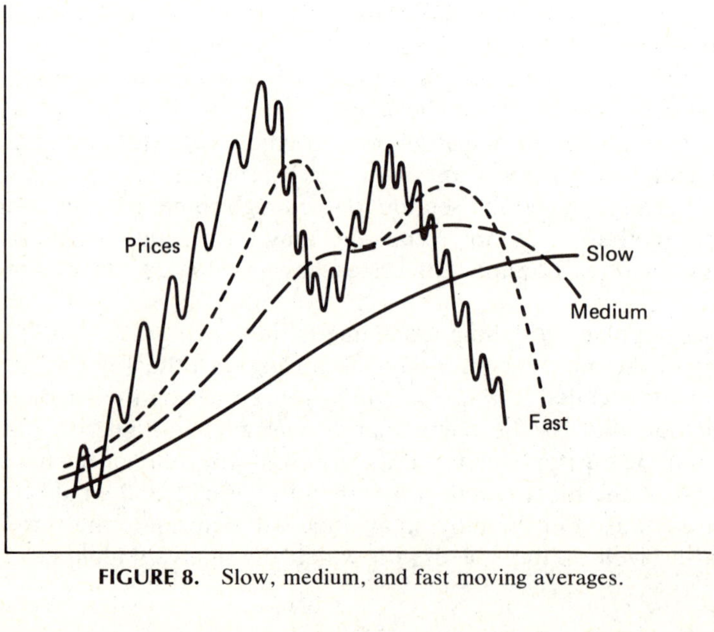

FIGURE 8. Slow, medium, and fast moving averages.

percentage of the whole. A smoothing constant c represents the part of the total value which is assigned to the new data. It is often calculated as

$$E_t = E_{t-1} + c\,(P_t - E_{t-1})$$

where E_t is today's exponential value, E_{t-1} is the previous value, P is the current price used for the calculations, and c is the smoothing constant $(0 < c < 1)$.

The nature of a smoothing method causes the trendline to lag behind the price movement. As a trend is established and prices continue to move in one direction, often at a faster rate, the trendline falls farther behind. One method of compensating for this lag is called *double exponential smoothing,* a process which applies an exponential smoothing technique to the lag itself and adds the result back into the original calculation. If we define the lag or error as

$$e_t = P_t - E_t$$

where P_t is the price on day t and E_t is the corresponding exponential smoothing value, then by smoothing these error terms e_t using smoothing constant a we get

$$\epsilon_t = \epsilon_{t-1} + a\,(e_t - \epsilon_{t-1})$$

and this accumulated smoothing value is added into the original approximation as

$$EE_t = E_t + \epsilon_t$$

The effects of the error due to lag will be corrected but not eliminated in relationship to the rate of increase or decrease in the lag.

RELATING EXPONENTIAL SMOOTHING TO STANDARD MOVING AVERAGES. Most traders understand the time relationship of a standard moving average much more readily than an exponential one. Because of the diluting effect of the exponential smoothing, a comparison with respect to days is based on both the smoothing constant and the elapsed time. Intuitively, we know that a 50% smoothing is somewhat slower than a two-day moving average, a 10% smoothing is slower than a 10-day moving average, and a 5% smoothing is slower than a 20-day moving average. The important factor is that for any specified smoothing constant the exponential moving average includes all prior data. If we were to compare a 5-day moving average with an exponential with only 5 total days included, in our relationship the two valves would be closer than if the exponential had 10 or 20 days of elapsed calculation.

One way to understand the weighting effect of the exponential smoothing method is to relate it to a corporation with 10 shareholders and 100% of the stock outstanding. The corporation chooses to add another shareholder and grant the new person 10% ownership. The original shareholders now receive a 10% reduction to 9.1% each and the new shareholder has a full 10%, totaling 100%. Afterwards the corporation again chooses to take on a new 10% shareholder and dilutes all previous holders by 10%, so that the original shareholders each have 8.19% and the first additional shareholder now has 9.1%. It can be seen that, as this procedure of diluting shares continues, the original shareholders become a very small part of the ownership although they never disappear. In the same way the prior data always remains part of each calculation using exponential smoothing.

Table 2 shows a reasonable approximation of exponential smoothing constants to standard moving averages. The proper selection of an exponential smoothing constant is essential for computer testing as one can see in part A of the table. If smoothing constants are selected at equal intervals the result would be that half of your tests will analyze time intervals of less than 3 days.

While there are many types of moving averages or trend-following systems, it is not clear that any one method is better than another. Aside from the intrinsic inaccuracy of the methods in general, it is possible to create essentially the same trendlines using two different formulas, by varying the time interval, weighting factors, or smoothing constant. The most significant part of these techniques is the time interval. An analyst who can choose the proper time span can be successful with any of the methods discussed. Computers have been used extensively to determine the number of days, or intervals, used in these calculations.

TRADING METHODS. As with other trading systems the most popular use of the various smoothing techniques is the simplest. Using a single trendline, a trader can be *long* while prices are above the trendline and *short* when prices are below. Such a simple program is subject to frequent losses or whipsaws when prices alternately close above and below the trendline without continuing in one direction for any time. By adding a *channel,* or *band,* around the moving average line, we can exchange the frequent losses for reliability, but with higher risk and fewer trades. Instead of entering a new long position when prices move up through the trendline, prices must now move through a band above the trendline. The long position is liquidated, and shorts entered, if prices move down through the lower band. The initial risk of the trade is measured by the size of the channel surrounding the trendline (see Figure 9). The band serves as a level of commitment to the trades.

Bands are often related to the volatility of the market or to the specific loss allowed by the trader. Both are effectively a measurement of risk. When the band is a function of price volatility it can be calculated as an average of the daily ranges, a percentage of the current price level, or a combination of the two. In either case, the band should widen during higher priced, more active markets and narrow at the low depressed levels. It will therefore cause a new signal based on a smaller breakout at low levels.

Two moving averages are often used together in a trading program. The slower moving average (more days or smaller exponential constant) is used to identify the trend, while the faster one serves to time the entry and exit points. The most

TABLE 2. Comparing Techniques

A. Equating Standard Moving Averages to Exponential Smoothing

Smoothing constant (%)	0.10	0.20	0.30	0.40	0.50	0.60	0.70	0.80	0.90
Standard (n-day average)	20	10	6	4	3	2.25	1.75	1.40	1.15

B. Equating Exponential Smoothing to Standard Moving Averages

Standard (n-day average)	2	4	6	8	10	12	14	16	18	20
Smoothing constant (%)	0.65	0.40	0.30	0.235	0.20	0.165	0.14	0.125	0.11	0.10

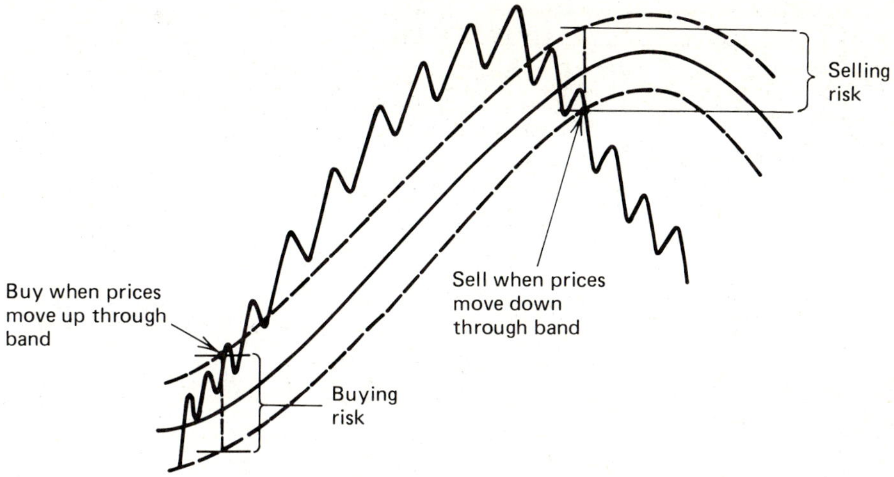

FIGURE 9. Simple trading rules for a moving average.

common rule for a double moving average system is to be long when prices are above both fast and slow moving averages and short when prices are below both. A sideways or neutral position can be assumed when prices are between the two trendlines (see Figure 10).

There are many variations on moving averages and at least as many trading rules. Some of the methods have been tested by computer and the results are available to traders; many books have been published expounding the successes of moving average systems. In the section "The Use of the Computer in System Development" the pros and cons of systems selected by computer testing are discussed.

Momentum and *oscillators* form a group of systems constructed in a manner similar to trend following, but are often used to either confirm a movement or to

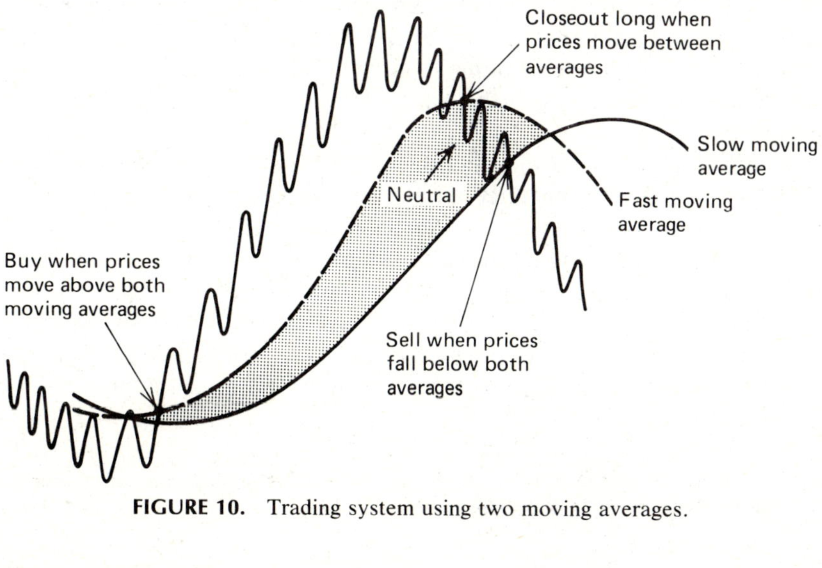

FIGURE 10. Trading system using two moving averages.

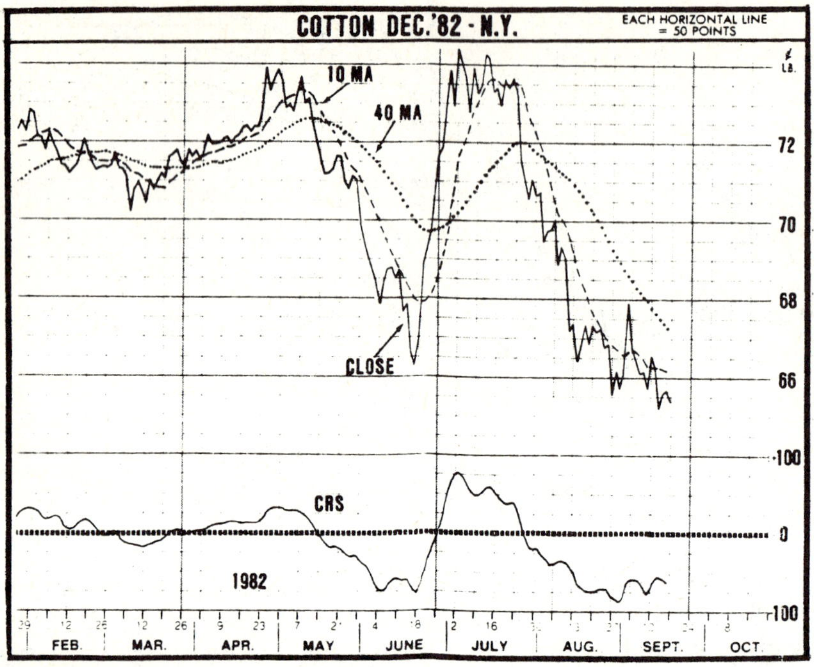

FIGURE 11. Momentum shown along the bottom of the chart: (*a*) Original price data. (*b*) Prices plotted as *n*-day momentum. (*c*) Prices plotted as oscillator. *Source:* Commodity Research Bureau.

identify price extremes. An *n*-day momentum is simply the difference between the current price P_t and the price *n* days before

$$M(n)_t = P_t - P_{t-n}$$

Although no one has shown that an $M(n)_t$ is effectively the same as an *n*-day moving average, it is difficult to distinguish any difference in the turning points identified by the two methods. Momentum can be considered a *stationary* moving average; that is, the values produced by the momentum calculation eliminate the long-term trend in a manner similar to first differences.[2] The result is that momentum values fluctuate about the value zero, shown as a horizontal line (see Figure 11).

The primary interest in a momentum value is the *rate of change* represented by high or low values. To produce an extreme value, as measured from the zero line, the difference between the 2 days observed must be large, implying that prices must have moved quickly in one direction. By noting patterns in past values, a trader can identify overbought or oversold situations and either reduce or liquidate current trades in anticipation of a reversal. High momentum is directly related to increased risk. When using moving averages or smoothing techniques the increase in momentum is reflected by an increase in the lag between current prices and the calculated trend value. However, it is difficult to compare past

[2]First differences are calculated as $D_n = P_n - P_{n-1}$, the difference between the two previous data elements. The resulting series D_i is considered *detrended*.

extremes without normalizing the values in a manner similar to the momentum calculation.

An oscillator is a refinement of the momentum concept. It is structured to allow comparisons of the extremes of past momentum values when prices move substantially higher or lower. Since the volatility tends to increase and decrease in direct relationship to the price level, we can expect higher peaks and lower valleys when prices rise; we can also expect prices to fluctuate more in the same time period. An oscillator is actually seeking a *relative* measure of extremes. We want to know what is high or low *regardless* of the price level. An oscillator may be constructed to do this by dividing the momentum value by the maximum (or near-maximum) price movement possible during this time period. For example, the divisor could be $n \times L$, where n is the number of days in the momentum and L is the limit move. Since $n \times L \leq M(n)$, the oscillator value must range between $+1$ and -1.

The use of the limit to calculate an oscillator value is not necessarily a reasonable solution since there is little continuity in the changing of limits as prices increase and decrease. A relationship based upon probable movement as a function of price level (a price-volatility relationship) would be a far better solution in identifying uniform extreme zones (see comparisons in Figure 12).

VELOCITY AND ACCELERATION. Although many of the applications of price forecasting come from techniques used in aerospace and other military areas the concepts of velocity and acceleration of price movement is a pure transfer from the science of physics. It measures the speed and the rate of change of the speed of market movement, respectively. While velocity is easily related to momentum, acceleration has no obvious counterpart in any of the mathematical approaches discussed previously. *Average velocity* $\bar{v}$ is calculated as

$$\bar{v} = \frac{D}{T}$$

where D is the total elapsed distance and T is the time interval. A plot of $\bar{v}$ over the most recent fixed time interval T would be the same as the momentum. In physics, however, it is more popular to consider *instantaneous velocity,* the velocity at a single moment in time, which causes the results to differ from momentum. Instantaneous velocity is calculated using differentiation applied to a formula representing price movement. Both formulas and techniques can be found in any text on physics but often must be modified using methods of numerical analysis.

Acceleration is calculated by applying differentiation to the equation representing velocity, with the result also called the *second derivative*. A popular way of extracting velocity and acceleration from a price series is to take the *first and second differences*. This is accomplished simply by subtracting the previous price from the current price, such that $D1_i = P_i - P_{i-1}$, where $D1_i$ is the ith first difference. We create a new price series, P', which is detrended (without velocity) by subtracting the first differences from the original series, $P'_i = P_i - D1_i$. If you perform the same operation on the series of first differences, you can find the rate of change, or second difference, $D2_i = D1_i - D1_{i-1}$. It is possible to

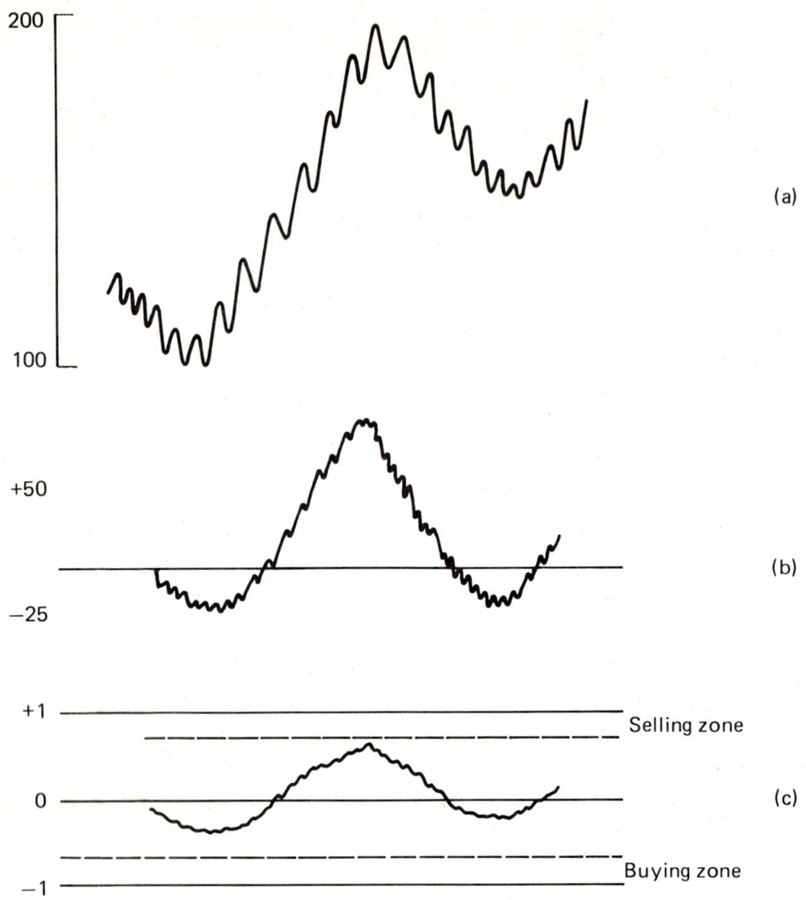

FIGURE 12. Comparative plots of price data.

TABLE 3. Interpretation of Velocity and Acceleration

Velocity	Acceleration	Price Movement
+	+	Price is moving up at an increasing rate
+	0	Price is moving up at a constant rate
+	−	Price is moving up at a decreasing rate
0	0	Price is static
−	+	Price is moving down at a decreasing rate
−	0	Price is moving down at a constant rate
−	−	Price is moving down at an increasing rate

analyze the two new series $D1$ and $D2$ to determine when there is a change or potential change in the velocity or acceleration of a price series.

The series formed by velocity and acceleration values can be used in the same way as a moving average value or as a supplemental filter. The final calculation of velocity and acceleration is remarkably similar to the concept of momentum, but with results that are more readily analyzed automatically. The combination of the two factors are summarized in Table 3 although a more precise relationship is found using actual values.

SYSTEM TRADEOFFS

While most traders are continually searching for a well-defined system which has no losses, they are realistic enough to know that most profit, loss, and risk decisions are all dependent upon one another. Just as in gambling theory, a system can be structured to have frequent small losses and occasional large profits—or frequent small profits with large losses. One cannot create a system with such small losses that these losses are essentially zero, without increasing the frequency of the losses to the point where profits rarely occur. In the commodities markets the cost of doing business prevents such an approach from being possible.

The decisions that structure a system require the trader to choose between the frequency of profits to losses, the relative size of those profits and losses, and the number of opportunities which will be available to trade. These interrelationships will be interpreted differently for different types of systems.

TREND-FOLLOWING SYSTEMS. The relative risks and rewards of a trend-following system are based on the selection of the trend speed. Using a simple moving average system (applied to closing prices) as an example we can see in Figure 13 that a faster moving average (smaller number of days) will stay closer

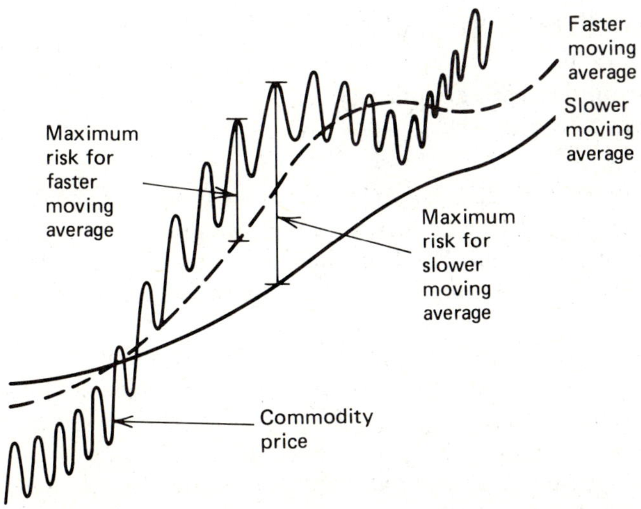

FIGURE 13. Relative risk of a moving average system.

to the current price than a moving average which uses a larger number of days. The maximum risk is equal to the largest lag as measured from the current price to the corresponding moving average value. This lag is limited by

$$M = P - (L \times N)/2$$

where P is the current closing price, L is the limit move, and N is the number of days in the moving average.

The smaller losses of the faster trend system are kept in proportion to the profits because of the same system sensitivity. The price changes of smaller magnitude which cause the moving average to change direction and hold losses to a minimum, also break the sustained trends into shorter movements. The net results are more frequent trades with relatively small losses and modest profits. Longer-term trends cause fewer trades by holding to the market direction for a longer time. This results in much larger profits and correspondingly larger losses.

The risk of a single trade being small or large is not necessarily a complete measure of trading risk. Since there are more losses than profits in normal trend-following systems, it is important to consider the sequence of losses as part of the ultimate risk of trading. It is the combination of these losses that provides a reasonable comparison in determining whether a slow or fast moving average system has the best profit-to-loss ratio.

CONTRATREND SYSTEMS. The risk and reward structure of a contratrend method is quite different from that of a trend-following approach. Since a contratrend system, such as an oscillator, contrary opinion, or any "overbought–oversold" analysis, sets restrictions on prospective profits, it should not also limit losses. As was previously mentioned, it is possible to distribute profits and losses in various ways with regard to their size and frequency. The combinations possible are:

A few large profits and frequent small losses.
Many small profits and a few large losses.
Larger profits less often.
Smaller profits more often.
More opportunities with greater risk.
Fewer opportunities with less risk.

The first two points are easily applied to trend following, while the others are most appropriate for contratrend trading. For example, consider a sideways market, or any price series that has been detrended as in Figure 14 so that it does not exhibit any overall trending bias. Assuming that there is a normal distribution of prices, we have a clustering near the center and less frequent peaks and valleys as we move farther away from the middle. We construct an overbought–oversold indicator which can be categorized as *slightly* (S), *moderately* (M), or *extremely* (E) overbought or oversold and draw lines showing their location on Figure 14.

It can be seen that there are more opportunities to buy a *slightly oversold* market and sell a *slightly overbought* market than any of the other situations since all prices must pass through the area closest to the center before attaining a more

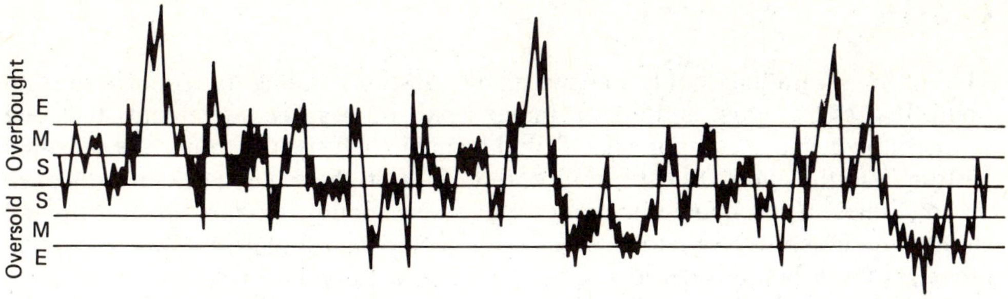

FIGURE 14. Contratrend alternatives using detrended price series.

overbought or oversold condition. Therefore the *opportunities* must increase as profit goals decrease. But what about the risk? If profits are limited, then risk must be restricted to a small part of the potential profits, or not limited by a dollar amount but by a patterned condition. For contratrend trading, an attempt to make losses small relative to a small profit objective is inconsistent. Considering the situation shown in Figure 14, the frequency of losses would increase so rapidly (as losses are kept smaller) that they would overwhelm the fixed profit potential. If losses are not restricted they will be larger when there are more opportunities with smaller price objectives. The minimum risk occurs on a single trade taken at the absolute extreme points. Figure 15 shows the relationships which exist in a standard contratrend system.

All systems have tradeoffs. If you try to reduce the losses then you must either reduce the profits or find more select opportunities for trading. If you are a trendfollower looking for the big move, you must also take a big risk. In the development of a system or trading philosophy, each person must settle on the combination of risk, reward, and opportunity that best suits him or her.

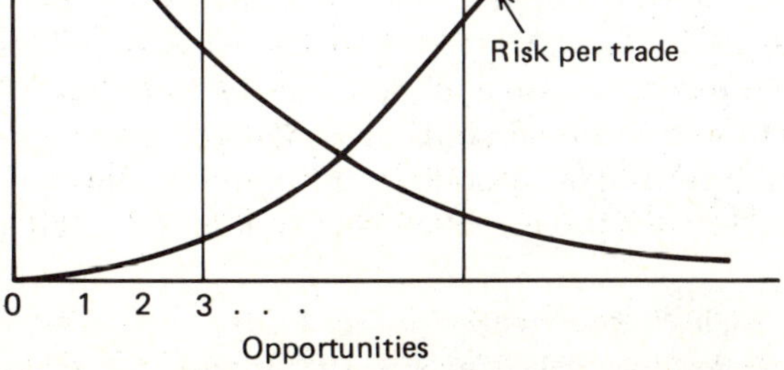

FIGURE 15. Relationship of profits to risk per trade based on opportunities.

CYCLES

The cycle as a trading tool has raised many questions among traders. There is no doubt that cycles exist and are an implicit part of all price movement. It is one of the three primary components of fundamental analysis: the trend, the seasonal pattern, and the cycle. But the ability to profit from their use has been subject to many studies. Cycles come in many forms—seasonality, production start up and shutdown, inventory or stocks, behavioral, and astronomical. Even seasonal movement can be considered a special case of a calendar cycle. Some of these cycles are *periodic,* having regular intervals between peaks and valleys, while others are more uniform in their *amplitude* or height but irregular in period. It is easiest to first examine the most definitive cycle, the seasonal price movement of agricultural crops having a 1-year growing season. In the United States this is best represented by the grains as well as by cotton, sugar beets, and potatoes. Planting of summer crops begins in about March and harvest ranges from September through November.

SEASONALITY. To find the seasonal pattern for corn, we start with average monthly prices over a substantial number of years. The simplest solution is to find the average annual price and then divide each monthly price by the respective annual average to get a ratio, or percentage variance, of the monthly prices. By averaging the ratios in the corresponding months of each year, we can find the expected variance during each month, according to past years. This simple method has a high degree of credibility, but often significant variance. There is also an inflationary bias which causes the ratios to be lowest in the early months and higher in later months.

The most effective way to determine the seasonal bias is the *moving average method.* Using a 12-point moving average applied to monthly average price data, calculate the moving average in a continuous manner from the beginning to the end of the available data. Divide the value of each data point by the corresponding moving average value at that point and then average those ratios for corresponding months. The result will be a *detrended* seasonal bias, since a 12-month moving average will trend upwards to follow the normal industrial or economic inflation patterns. By spanning an exact seasonal interval of 12 months, the moving average does not reflect any seasonal movement in its value. The use of a ratio, rather than an absolute price, provides flexibility for increased volatility, and therefore variance, as prices move to much higher or lower levels.

Figure 16 shows the results of two seasonal studies for corn. Figure 16(*a*) is a traditional monthly analysis applied to cash prices for 24-year and recent 4-year intervals ending in 1979.[3] It shows prices rising just after planting and continuing through the prime growing season and then quickly dropping as harvest proceeds. This indicates that the traditional concept of harvest lows is valid. The recent 4-year study shows the pattern of seasonality during a sustained price decline. Figure 16(*b*) is a study of weekly price movement without detrending,[4] as seen by the

[3]J. Grushcow and C. Smith, *Profits Through Seasonal Trading,* Wiley, New York, 1980.

[4]D. Handmaker, "Low Frequency Filters in Seasonal Analysis," *The Journal of Future Markets,* Vol. 1, No. 3, Wiley, New York, 1981, p. 373.

CASH CORN

24 YEARS

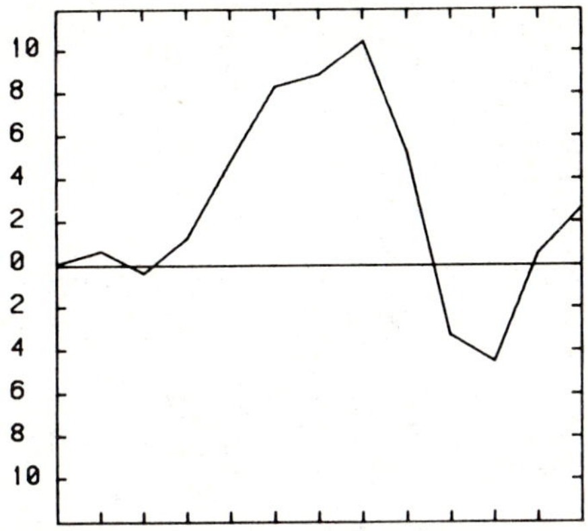

	J-F	F-M	M-A	A-M	M-J	J-J	J-A	A-S	S-O	O-N	N-D	D-J
Average Move	0.5	-1.1	1.6	3.6	3.4	0.5	1.5	-5.3	-8.5	-1.3	5	2.1
% Reliable	58.4	41.7	66.7	91.7	50	45.9	50	54.2	87.5	62.5	83.4	70.9
Avg. Up Move	3.2	2.5	5.7	5.7	10.4	6.9	11	2.2	6	9.7	7.1	6.1
Avg. Down Move	2.5	5.6	5.7	14.5	2.8	4.4	7.9	11.1	10.3	6.5	4	6.8
Greatest Up Move	18	6.1	19	38	42	20	51	6	8	30	22	25
Greatest Down Move	6.8	29	32	20	14	22	27	59	30	25	13	38

CASH CORN

4 YEARS

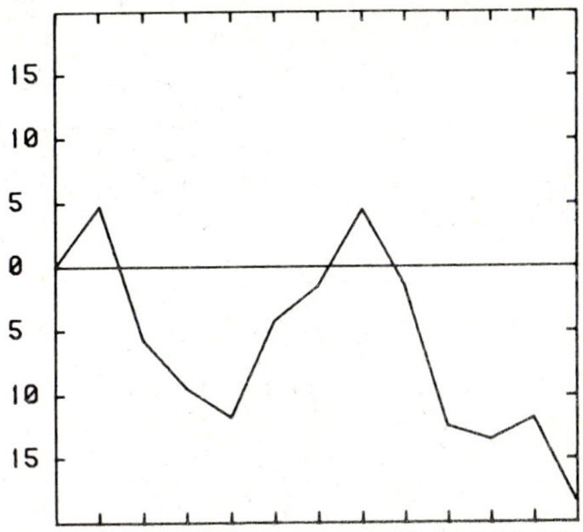

J-F	F-M	M-A	A-M	M-J	J-J	J-A	A-S	S-O	O-N	N-D	D-J
4.7	-10.5	-3.8	-2.3	7.5	2.7	6	-6	-11	-1	1.7	-6.5
75	100	50	50	75	75	50	50	50	50	75	25
7.6	0	19	10	14.6	16.5	30	2	6	18.5	6.6	6
4	10.5	17	14.5	14	22	18	13	28	20.5	13	38
18	0	19	16	23	20	51	2	8	30	11	9
4	29	32	20	14	22	27	16	28	25	13	38

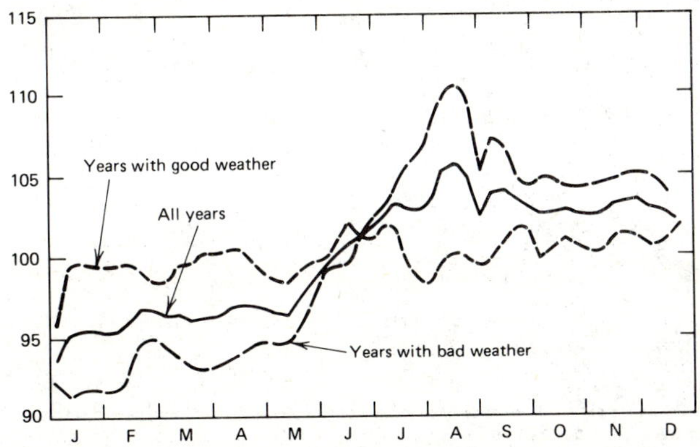

FIGURE 16. Seasonal studies. Fig 16(a) Traditional Seasonal Analysis. 16(b) Corn price seasonality during all years. (1-years with good weather . . . years with bad weather).

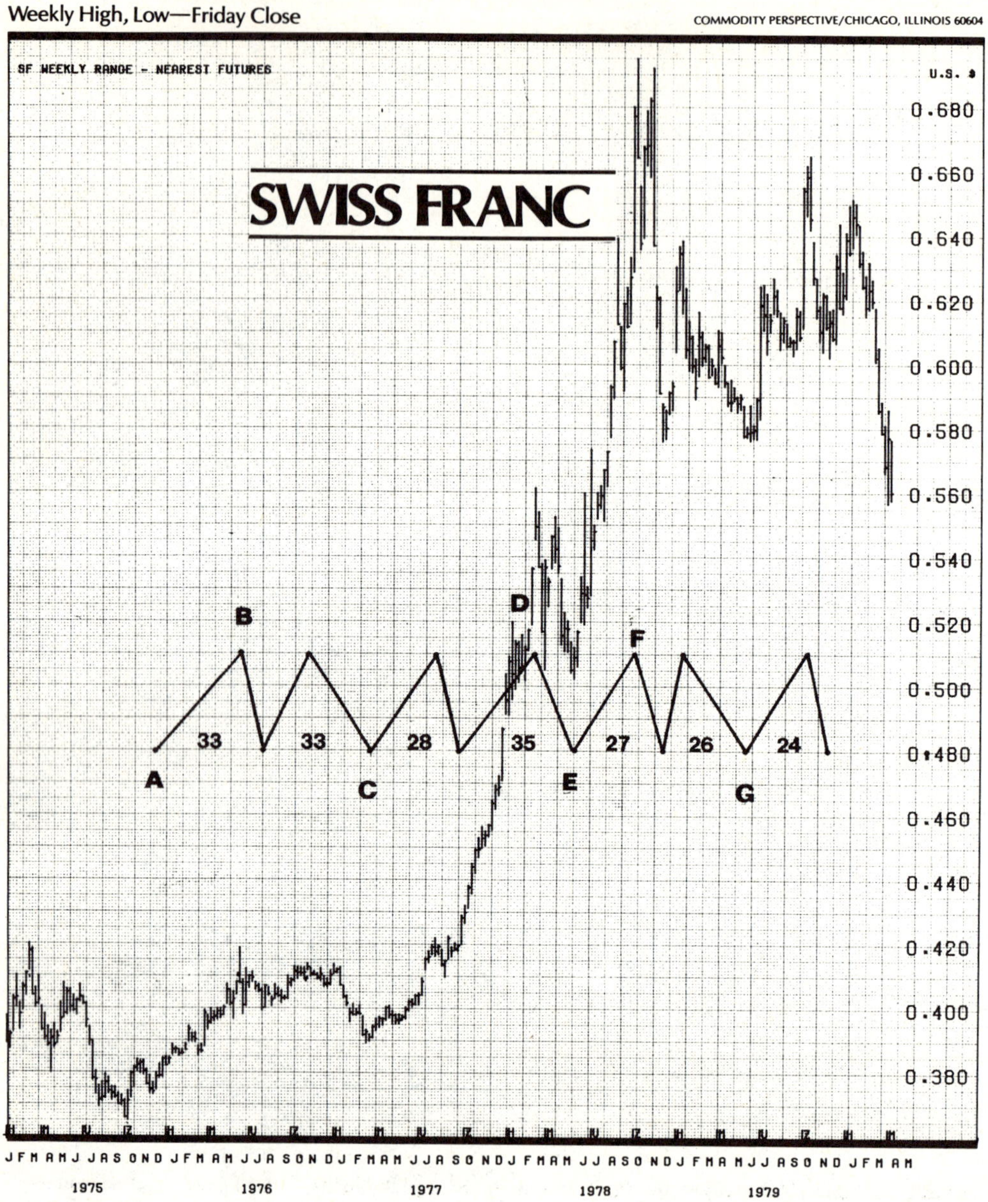

(*a*)

FIGURE 17. (*a*) Cycles in Swiss franc futures. (*b*) Cycle in cash Treasury-bill yields.

upwards bias throughout the year. This unique study also separated data which reflected good or bad weather, and shows a much more definitive seasonal pattern during years where specific growing problems existed.

OTHER GROWING CYCLES. Crops which grow in warmer climates are not necessarily confined to 12-month seasonality, although subcycles may exist. The coffee crop in Brazil is subject to yearly freezes, but recovery from a damaging frost is often a 3-year pattern. Livestock cycles have some yearly seasonality due

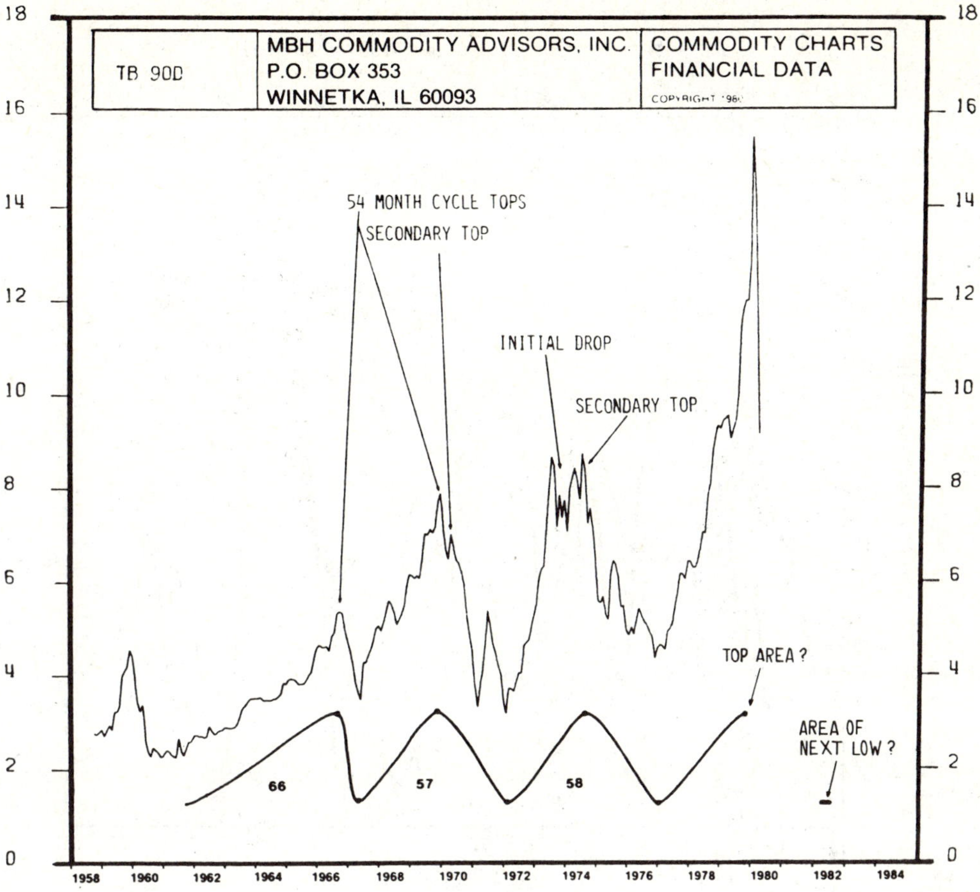

(b)

to on-farm feeding, but are dominated by breeding and feedlot patterns. Seasonality can also be reflected in a demand pattern. Potatoes reflect a market of inelastic demand with no increased selling due to harvest pressure. The demand for silver is increased sharply during the summer when most people take photographs.

MAJOR REGULAR CYCLES. The most newsworthy cycles have probably been the least practical or accurate, such as the Kondratieff wave, which shows a 54-year economic cycle. Unfortunately, a 10% shift in any one peak could cause one to buy or to sell 5 years too soon. Determining cycles of any commodity and any length have the same problems—the actual market will never correspond exactly to the predicted peaks and valleys.

Determining cycles is usually done by manually finding the tops and bottoms within fixed intervals of price movement, starting with the most obvious points. As seen in Figure 17(*a*),[5] the number of weeks in each cycle can vary 25%, making this type of cycle of little help in selecting specific buy and sell points. Figure 17(*b*) shows the longer-term cycles of Treasury bills, resulting in an interesting

[5]J. Bernstein, *The Handbook of Commodity Cycles,* Wiley, New York, NY, 1982.

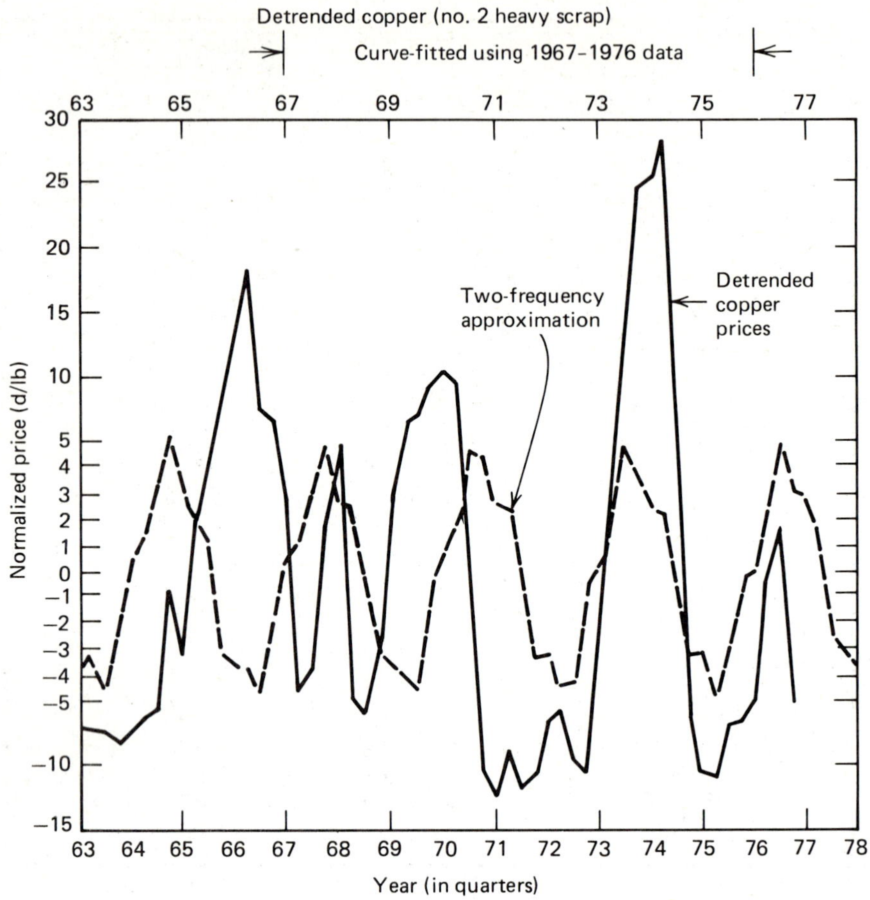

FIGURE 18. Two-frequency trigonometric approximation.

pattern, but using a small data sample. A convenient device for finding cycles of regular periods is the Ehrlich Cycle Finder,[6] an expanding tool with many points at regular intervals which can be placed on a chart to indicate where cyclic tops and bottoms should occur if patterns are consistent.

The mathematical method for finding cycles is *trigonometric curve fitting,* a form of regression analysis. It uses trigonometric functions (sine and cosine) to fit both the frequency and the amplitude of a cycle which is hidden within a price movement. Before a cycle can be found, it is necessary to detrend the data, eliminating the long-term upward or downward bias which might appear to be a leg of a cycle. Using the resulting stationary data we can apply the general formula

$$y_t = a_1 \cos \omega_1 t + b_1 \sin \omega_1 t + a_2 \cos \omega_2 t + b_2 \sin \omega_2 t$$

using a least-squares method of solution. This has been carefully explained in *Commodity Trading Systems and Methods.*[7] The results, applied to copper, are shown in Figure 18. Although the fitted cycles correspond to most major price

[6]Ehrlich Cycle Finder Company, 2220 Noyes Street, Evanston, IL 60201.

[7]P. J. Kaufman, *Commodity Trading Systems and Methods,* Wiley, New York, NY, 1978 pp. 106–117.

movements, the actual price peak occurring about 1970 is completely out-of-phase. A classic example of a regular cycle can be seen in Figure 19, which shows the 18-year pattern of construction and real-estate activity since about 1800. Although the fit was nearly perfect through the recorded data, the actual pattern in 1980–1982 must be far off from the anticipated peak. But no method should be expected to be consistently accurate. Enthusiasts of seasonal and cyclic patterns use them as a filter or bias with their trading decisions. More often they act as negative filters or as means for more heavily weighting a specific trade. They have similar risk and trading characteristics as standard fundamental analysis and are often used in the same manner.

For example, corn prices tend to be lowest in the harvest months of October and November, but often extend that trend into February. If prices are actually lowest during those months, a trader can reason that the seasonal pattern is intact and only consider long positions in the market. While there may be small opportunities for gain on the short side, the risk/reward ratio would be poor and margin money could be used better for a trade with possibilities of greater returns. Similarly, buying opportunities in February–April may be taken with greater confidence because there is substantial opportunity with little risk.

Trading the long-term cycle will tend to be easier than the shorter-term one. As in the Treasury-bill chart [Figure 17(*b*)], we can expect adjustments from peaks and valleys alternately, based on the government's ability to correct both high- and low-yield situations. Since the cycles appear to be about 60 weeks, a trader can begin to look for turning points if the current price movement is in line with the expected cycle. During the 1981–1982 interest-rate increase, a trader should be most concerned with small risk and an anticipated turn toward lower rates.

The variance of the shorter-term cycle, as seen in the Swiss franc chart [Figure 17(*a*)] is too great for accurate forecasting. From a statistical view, it may be that a signficant number of peaks and valleys occur uniformly, but the range of 24–35 weeks and the extent of movement within those intervals, seem difficult to build into a trading model. But even with these variables, cycles are an integral part of price movement not to be ignored in determining the price bias.

PHASING USING MOVING AVERAGES. Although moving averages are most commonly used as a lagged trend indicator, it is possible to use them to determine and predict cyclic movement. In the case of seasonality, the seasonal adjustment factor was determined by the difference between actual prices and a moving average value which spanned the entire season and therefore had no seasonal bias. In order to smooth the cycles and forecast their trend and turn, the moving average used must be less than the full cycle—even less than a half-cycle—otherwise the cyclic movement will be lost. In Figure 20 we see two full cycles trending upwards, each approximately 30 days in length. A selection of a 30-day moving average would result in a straight line through the center of the cycles essentially showing the current trend. For this unusually uniform pattern, the half-cycle of 15 days would show the same results. A selection of ¼ or ⅛ cycle would result in the smoothing of the cycles as shown in Figure 20; the shorter the span, the wider the gap between the straight (detrending) line and the moving average. The full cycle and ⅛ cycle averages can be used to forecast the limits of the cyclic movement and the next point of crossing, as seen in the forecasted cycle 3. A trader can use this technique to buy the low of cycle 2 and sell the high of cycle

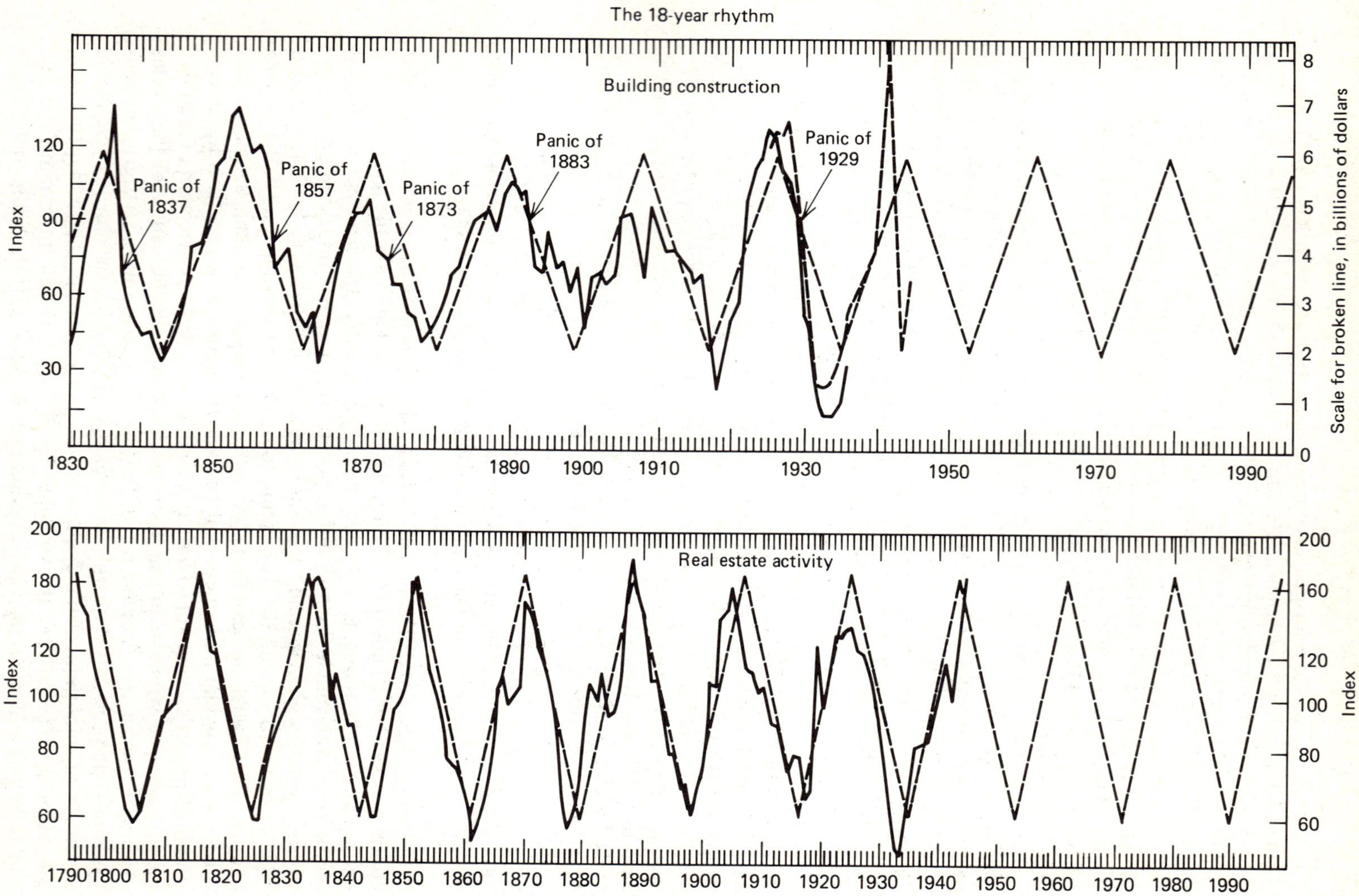

FIGURE 19. The 18-year rhythm of construction and real estate.

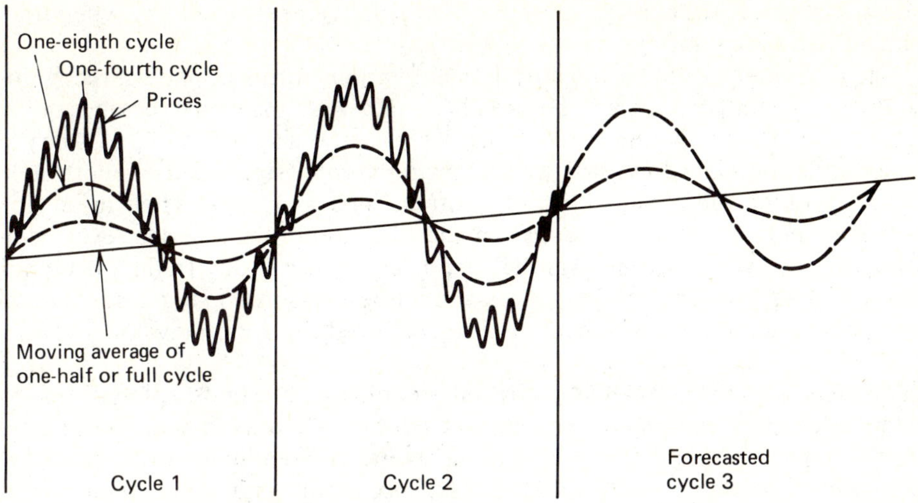

FIGURE 20. Using moving averages to predict cycles.

3, based on a turn in the moving averages at the forecasted extremes. Traded properly, by waiting for the moving average to turn, a shortened or lengthened cycle will have little effect on the method.

SHORT-TERM TRADING

Most traditional methods of technical analysis are not used for trading intervals of less than 3 days; however, short-term trading is highly technical. It is easy to see that an economic analysis of supply and demand cannot be relevant over such a short time span. Other than the immediate reactions to overnight cash market movement, anticipated daily price changes based on political events and weather have not been successfully measured. Short-term trading can be classified into day trades and overnight positions. The principles applied to short-term trading are important timing concepts, and may be used by those interested in improving their market entry and exit points.

DAY-TRADING TECHNIQUES. A day trade is a position entered and liquidated during a single trading day. The profitability of such a trade is highly dependent upon the value of the price range, the rate of commission, and the ability to follow the market movement. The first step in day trading is to select a market with ample opportunity. This means that 50% of the average daily range less commissions should provide adequate profitability. We chose 50% of the range to indicate the unlikely selection of entry and exit points corresponding to the exact extremes of the daily price range.

To improve the opportunities for day trading, it is best to find a commodity with generally high volatility and avoid those markets with isolated active days. This can be done by selecting a commodity that is at a high price level (or a financial market with high rates). Since volatility expands exponentially with the increase in price, we can expect to have large movements each day when trading a high priced commodity.

The techniques used by most traders are various forms of pattern recognition. Today's price movements are most readily compared to the most recent significant events, such as the opening price, today's high and low, yesterday's closing price, yesterday's high and low, last week's high and low, significant support and resistance points and, finally, life of contract high and low. When more points coincide, there is more confidence in the likelihood of that price level being a support or resistance point. Another important factor in day trading is liquidity. The daily range of commodity prices should be measured using a nearby active contract. Larger ranges which may exist in deferred contracts may not be realistic.

METHODS OF DAY TRADING. Recent years have brought sophisticated computerized display equipment, enabling a trader to watch an instantaneous display of price movement, enhanced by moving averages, trendlines, or presented as a point-and-figure chart, swing chart, or as an oscillator. Although moving averages and other mathematical representations of trends and price movement are popular, it is difficult to accept their significance with respect to price movement over 1- to 3-day time intervals. Based on the trader's awareness of prior highs and lows, as mentioned before, the methods discussed will exclude mathematical formulas.

The most popular trading technique for the short-term trader is to buy and sell ranges that develop during the early part of the day. Often, the highs, lows, and previous close define the most significant ranges. Combined with key times of day, it is possible to develop rules for buying and selling.

TIME OF DAY. There are natural occurrences during the trading day that make certain times more important than others. The opening gap and the continuation of that direction usually takes the first 15–20 minutes of the trading day. After that, a price reversal typically occurs and a trading range is established which lasts until the middle of the trading session. This tends to be a low volume period as well, since many of the orders originating off the floor are exhausted near the open.

Following midday, activity increases and the existing daily trading range is tested. It is common for most traders to buy the bottom of the range and sell the top. A break of either support or resistance after midday is considered a major directional change, and traders quickly shift in the direction of the breakout with the expectation of holding that position for the balance of the day. A more thorough analysis of significant times is shown in Figure 21. This table, created by Walt Bressert, uses the important highs and lows, but is very specific about relationships between the developing range, the previous days range, and the time of day.

OVERNIGHT POSITIONS. Holding a position overnight involves margin, larger commissions, and greater risk. It also greatly increases the opportunity. In modestly active markets the opening gap, the difference between the prior close and the next open, is one-half to two-thirds the size of the normal trading range. While it is nearly impossible to capture the full trading range in a day trade, it is simple

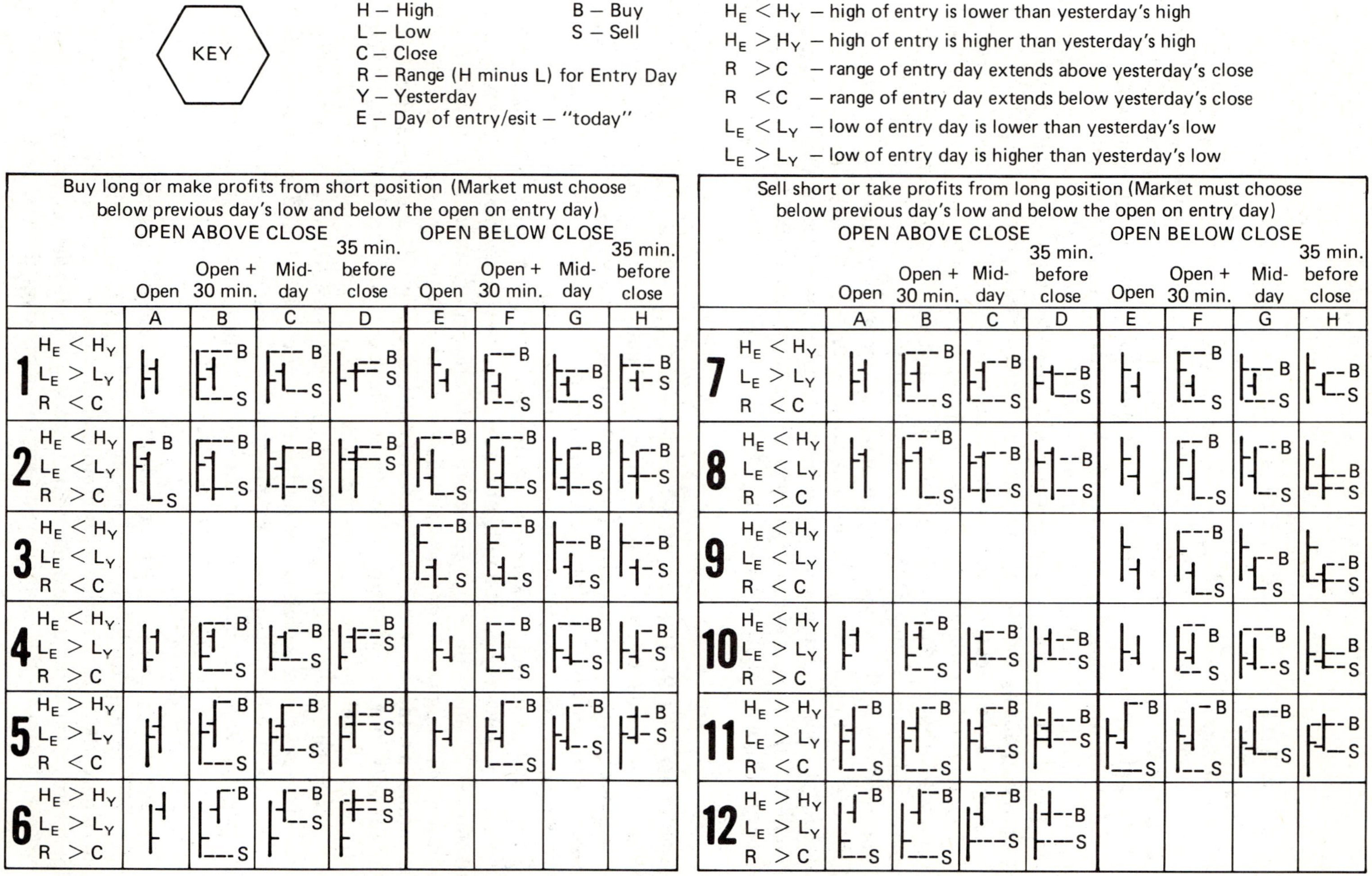

FIGURE 21. Intraday timing of market movement. *Source:* Walt Bressert.

to execute orders on the close and on the open, therefore the full overnight move can realistically be captured.

MARKET PATTERNS. A trade which lasts from 1 to 3 days can be improved if short-term patterns or cycles can be found. In a trending market, for example, there are outstanding weekly and weekend patterns. It is most common to find that the price movements from Thursday to Friday (close to close) are in the direction of the major trend, and that the movement on Monday is a continuation of that trend. By Tuesday (or sometimes Wednesday), the strength of new buyers has faded and the market sags due to lack of activity and some profit taking. It often stays in this state through Wednesday or early Thursday when it again picks up the trend. In a sideways market the Friday and Monday direction differs from the direction during the week, and often differs from each other.

During trendless markets short-term cycles may materialize. The *Taylor Trading Technique* (G. D. Taylor, Lily, 1954) is one of the few older methods of trading these cycles that has survived. Although it is in need of user interpretation, its underlying premise is that alternating 2- and 3-day cycles exist in most markets. If the trend is up, the Taylor method enters a long after the open at the bottom of the expected cycle, then carries that position up to three days as long as the subsequent opening and closing patterns conform to the expected ones. A lower open allows the long position to be held with a rally anticipated later in the day. A sharply higher open, however, is cause for liquidation due to an expected reversal.

POINT-AND-FIGURE USE IN SHORT-TERM TRADING. Point-and-figure charting has been a primary tool of the day trader for many years. Using the minimum price movement as the box size, and a three-point reversal, many analysts will keep a continuous (although lengthy) chart of price movement from day-to-day. Buy and sell signals can be taken in the standard manner, but most day traders use these charts to identify support and resistance levels in order to buy and sell, respectively. Intraday point-and-figure, as well as moving averages, often require substantial changes of direction before generating a standard new buy or sell indicator. Although new computerized displays make the plotting of these methods instantaneous, the magnitude of the price change required is usually too great to allow profits in a normal daily price range. These methods are better applied to short-term overnight positions, where the size of the move is much larger.

The standard point-and-figure method can be improved using intraday price data. Price reversals which occur during the day can be plotted using a slightly smaller box size than common for daily charting. These more frequent reversals will help define a new trend sooner, or bring the protective stop closer. In this way day traders can gain substantial information which is transparent to the interday point-and-figure users.

The use of frequent reversals provides a successful rule change for the point-and-figure method. Rather than choosing to plot the trend continuation in situations where there is a choice of a continuation or reversal, the chartist should plot the reversal. This allows the chart to reflect a reversal sooner, or bring the stop-loss closer—both possibilities an improvement over the standard rules.

USE OF THE COMPUTER IN SYSTEM DEVELOPMENT

During the previous sections the issue of *specifically* which moving average or exponential smoothing constant is best, or even which system is preferable, has been avoided. The determination of *best* is a complex decision involving individual risk preference, capitalization, and a time frame. We can, however, evaluate the performance of an individual system on an absolute profit basis. Since moving averages are foremost in trading systems, we will begin there and show the similarity in the evaluation procedure for other systems.

Implementation of a trading model on a computer involves careful planning to avoid unrealistic results. It is not unusual to find the "perfect system," one which never has a losing trade, while testing it on a computer. A closer look at the program logic would reveal, to our disappointment, that the computer was using *tomorrow's* data to determine what to do *today*.

Additional steps are necessary to make the entry and exit points of a trade assumed by the computer realistic with respect to actual market fills. In all cases, taking a more negative action—one which is less profitable—is the most conservative and acceptable approach. For example, when buying gold we can assume that a *buy stop* placed above the market at 425.00 is filled at 428.00, $3 above the desired price. The $3 *skid* was calculated as 20% of the $15 trading range on the day the order was filled. The skid should always cause a worse fill, even in the event that the resulting assumed execution price falls outside the actual trading range. The execution cost is always based on the volatility of the market, the liquidity of the specific contract, and the nature of the order. A stop order will always result in a larger cost than a limit order, since the stop order is always executed in the direction of the current price movement.

When program predetermined entry points are to be placed with the broker prior to the market open, the *opening price* should be inspected for an initial signal. For example, a buy stop placed in copper at 75.50 falls within the day's trading range of 75.00 to 76.50. However, the opening price was 75.80, triggering the order at a less favorable price. A *limit move* may also present a unique case for a computerized trading system. Some analysts assume that no trade execution would have occurred on a day where the contract price closed "at the limit." While this may be an unnecessarily severe rule, the case of a "locked-limit day" (high and low prices the same) is a clear case of a nonexecutable situation. A day with a very small range closing at the limit may be a questionable case.

Occasionally programs assume knowledge which is unavailable in the existing data. One such case would be the order of occurrence of the high and the low. It would be of great help to know that soybeans opened at 5.20, moved down to their lows, and then rallied for the remainder of the day. There is no assumption, however, that could correctly determine the order of events by only knowing the daily open, high, low, and closing prices.

COMPUTER TESTING. Consider a simple moving average system, with buy signals on upwards penetrations of the "upper" band value and sell signals on downward penetrations of the lower band value. How would one proceed in finding the proper moving average time span as well as the band width? Using a computer we can simply test every combination of moving average and band width, or a good sampling of those variables. In fact, this type of historic testing is very popular. But the mass testing or "shot-gun" testing approach, while it may identify the best combination of parameters, often has doubtful predictive qualities. Mass testing, with its known faults, is still the most direct way of arriving at an understanding of the potential for success of a trading method. If a set of trading rules can be found to be unprofitable in all cases using past data, it is not likely that a trader will want to use that method.

The organization and display of the test results are important in order to get full value from the testing. Figure 22 shows a sample test map which varies the size of the band, in percent, along the top. The map is composed of boxes, each of which contains the results of a single test run through all the data using the parameters represented by the corresponding row and column.

When displayed in the form of a map, the results of the moving average tests form an interesting pattern. The best results will cluster together with poorer returns seen as we move farther away from the area of peak success. When a long test period is used (over 5 years) the best results tend to be concentrated in the lower right-hand corner of the map, favoring the slower trends with greater risk. This can be readily understood since the one thing of which we are certain is that the trend of inflation represented a steady profitable trading pattern. An additional conclusion is that slower trends work best in low-priced, slowly moving markets. Since prices tend to remain at low levels more often than higher ones, the longer-term test will favor the longer-term trend.

As the time interval for testing decreases from over 5 years to 3 years, the average price over the period of the test has an opportunity to move above the low prices most common in long-term tests. A higher average price will usually cause the successful tests to be grouped toward the center of the map. Even shorter time intervals of less than 18 months may result in an average price which is quite high, with the stratification of success toward the very fast as well as the very slow trends. We can conclude from these results that a volatile, high-priced market can be traded quickly to profit from each price swing, or slowly to avoid the swings and remain with the long-term trend. The middle-speed trends are out of phase with either situation.

POINT-AND-FIGURE. Point-and-figure box size and reversal criteria can be tested in much the same manner. Letting the rows be the box size and the columns be the number of boxes in a reversal, we get the near-symmetric pattern shown in Figure 23(*a*). As discussed earlier, the combination of a three- and two-box size and reversal is nearly identical to a two and three combination, resulting in a mirror-image performance on the test map. If the results are plotted for all common reversal sizes (a 12-box reversal can be 1 × 12, 2 × 6, 3 × 4, 4 × 3, 6 × 2, 12 × 1) an interesting pattern may appear, as seen in Figure 23(*b*).

REAL-TIME ANALYSIS. Recent advancements in technology and communications have opened up the area of *real-time* analysis. It is possible to connect the exchange ticker lines directly to a computer so that each price movement that occurs during the trading day can be analyzed as it happens. This approach allows

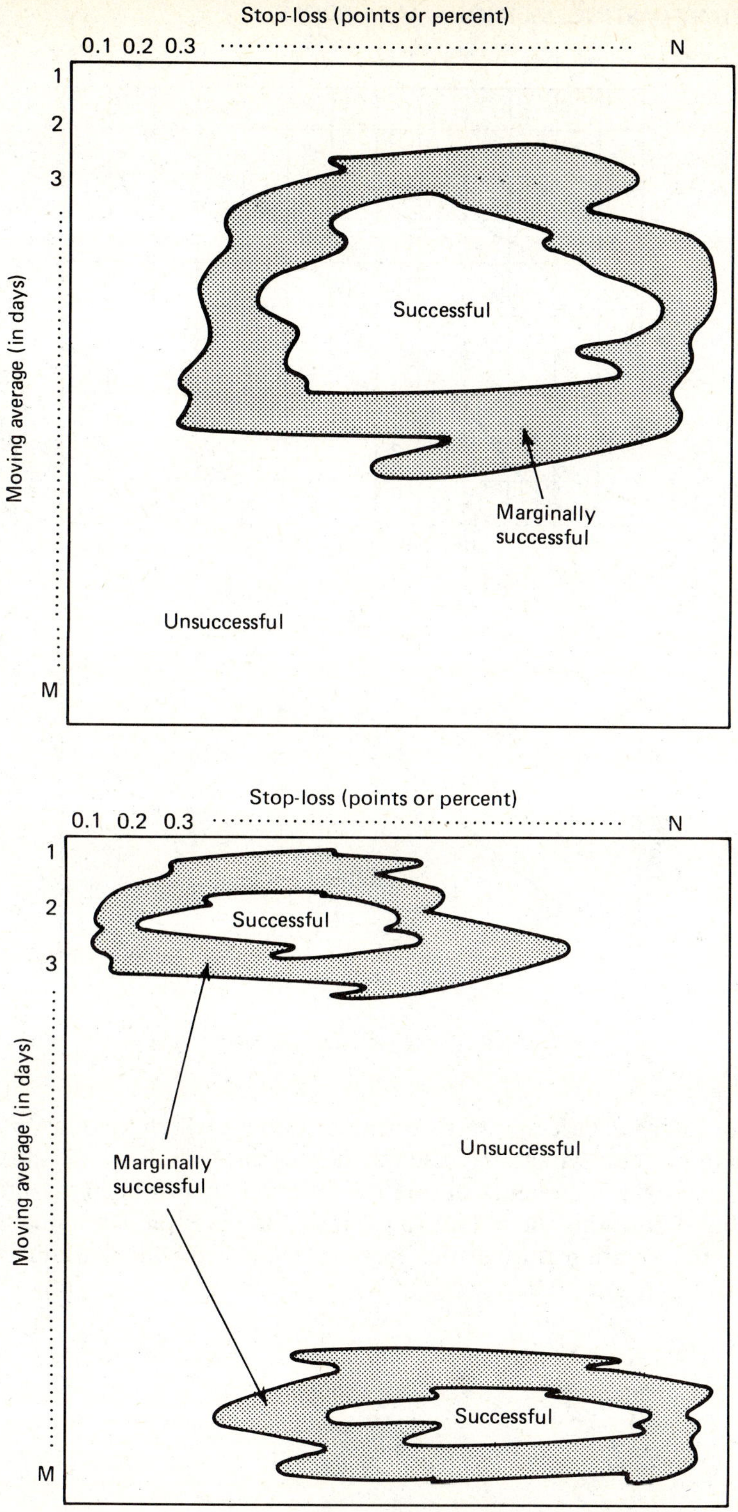

FIGURE 22. Test map patterns. (*Top*) Test map results for low prices. (*Bottom*) Test map results for high prices.

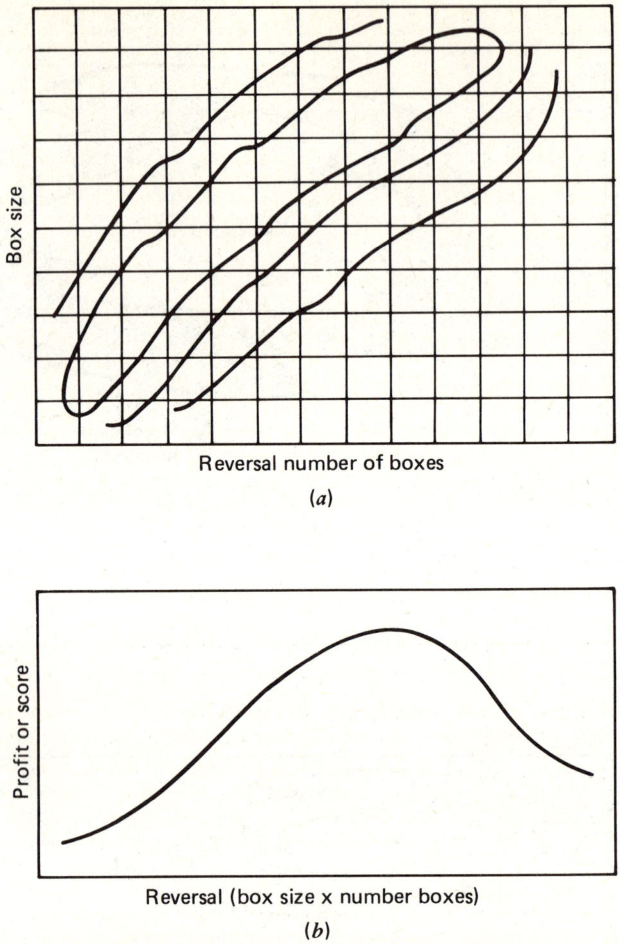

FIGURE 23. Point-and-figure mapping strategy.

the user to interpret price patterns or trend changes which are unavailable to the multitude of systems which only use the daily open, high, low, and closing prices. The sequence of price events during the day has always been a concern to the analyst, but before this the ability to retrieve and store the large quantity of data has made the solution unrealistic. Real-time analysis will continue to become more available to the trader.

CHAPTER 16

SELECTING A TRADING SYSTEM

CONTENTS

LEVERAGE RISK	4	VOLATILITY	7
TRADING APPROACHES	5	CAPITAL REQUIREMENTS	7
		RATE OF RETURN	8
COMMODITY SELECTION AND DIVERSIFICATION	6	EVALUATING RETURNS	8

CHAPTER 16

SELECTING A TRADING SYSTEM

W. Frederick Hitschler

One of the most important and immediate tasks of the commodity trader is to select a trading system which will suit the trader's personality as well as the trader's investment objectives. No matter how well a system performs in terms of return on investment, it is worthless to the trader who does not wish to follow it. Before a system can be tailored to the individual trader's profile, it is necessary to establish broad criteria for determining whether a proposed system will be of use to anyone.

It is first important to distinguish between a *trading system* and a *trading method.* A *method* will mean a single technique for determining when to buy, sell, or stand aside regarding a particular commodity. For our purposes all rules must be specific and independent of the user's judgment (capable of being automated). A method which is always in either a long or short position is called a *reversing method.* An example of a simple reversing method is the use of a single moving average of closing prices of a commodity as compared to the most recent closing price. If the most recent closing price is higher than the moving average of the closes for the past 10 days, then we assume that the price trend will continue upward, and we would *buy* (enter a long position and close out all short positions). We would recompute the moving average value daily for the most recent 10 days, then hold our long position until the most recent day's price dropped below the average. The long position would then be closed out and we would sell (enter a new short position). Of course, moving averages of longer and shorter time intervals could be used, rather than the 10-day average in the example. One of the prime functions of technical research is to determine the optimum parameter values of any method being investigated.

A *system* will be any combination of trading methods used on a portfolio of commodities, together with criteria for risk/reward and money management.

For a set of instructions to qualify as a method, it must be sufficiently specific and detailed to enable different traders to reach the same "buy" and "sell" signals unequivocally and independently. The advice to "buy low and sell high" is not a method because it does not specify how to identify when a price is either low or high. Similarly, complex models that include such expressions as "with a little practice you will be able to anticipate the low price of the day," calling as they do for the personal judgment of the trader are not methods. Also charting techniques using bar charts could not be called a method; two chartists can disagree on the forecast of timing or extent of a price movement. Therefore, to qualify as a method, a series of instructions should be programmable on a computer.

Once a method has been defined, there need to be criteria to evaluate its results. There can be no single best trading method for all investors, but there are many good ones depending on the objectives and personalities of the traders. One universal objective of trading is to make profits; however, a method that is most profitable over a period of time may not be the best, nor does the quality of profits alone make a method acceptable. For example, there are methods that lost money year after year in silver but made so much money in the violent 1979 to 1980 markets that their total profits in silver netted a greater amount than other methods which had less profit but performed with greater consistency.

LEVERAGE RISK

In the search for profits, we must always be alert to the risks. It is possible to trade commodity contracts by depositing with your broker the minimum initial speculative margin as set by the exchanges. If you are successful from your first trade, your return will be maximized by this approach; however, if your first trade is a loss you may not be able to continue trading without adding more funds for margin. Therefore, while it is possible to trade with only the minimum margin as your total capital, it is not prudent to do so. This continues to be the case later on as well, after the account has grown.

Many investors begin trading with reasonable caution, but as profits swell in their accounts, they begin taking greater and greater risks by holding more positions than their account can safely handle, effectively increasing their leverage. Virtually all who do this quickly lose their entire profits and often more because losses occur on a larger invested amount. Prudent money management demands that only a portion of the total account value be used to cover the margin requirements of the positions held in the account, while a greater portion is kept in reserve to provide for continued trading after a series of losses. Only the use of a sound method over a reasonable period of time can be expected to deliver profits. Later we will discuss how to determine the amount needed for an account to limit the risks to an acceptable range for each individual trader.

To approach trading by examining the risks and probabilities of success, may sound as if commodity trading is no more than common gambling. While it is true that the same mathematical techniques can be used to analyze both, gambling is an artificial creation of risk using dice, cards, or other means. The economic risks to the farmer, feedlot, metal fabricator or refiner, and those engaged in commerce of all types both foreign and domestic, would exist even if there were no commodity markets where their risks might be reduced by the process of hedging. Speculators provide the added liquidity by assuming the risk of both producers and processors and make the futures markets an efficient price-determining mechanism. In the search for personal gain, the speculators consequently help to reduce the overall cost of our nation's finished products, and provide price stability for those whose livelihood depends on these products.

TRADING APPROACHES

There are two distinct approaches to trading, which are known as *fundamental* and *technical*. They are distinguished by the kinds of data which are examined in arriving at a market decision. The fundamentalist uses historical economic information to establish a supply-and-demand price curve. He or she then relates estimates of this years's supply-and-demand balance to the historical price to decide if the current price is too high, too low, or just right. To arrive at an estimate of this year's supply, the fundamentalist will examine reports of the number of acres planted of a particular crop. The fundamentalist will also look at the sales of fertilizer and the sales and cost of diesel fuel for farm equipment, in addition to past weather data and predicted weather patterns for both the near- and longer-term periods of the crop's growing season. Information must be taken into account about the productivity of new seeds or strains developed for the crop being considered or for competing crops. The fundamentalist must be aware of the government stockpiles as well as those stockpiled on-farm (visible supply). Government price-support levels and the strength of the dollar will be considered, as it affects exports. The analyst will weigh the cost of interest paid on borrowed money, the impact of competition from substitutes or new products, and will be alert to changes in eating patterns and per capita income affecting demand. This list would have to be extended significantly to include all the primary determinants of price, and yet the accuracy of the current price evaluation depends upon the accuracy of the estimates and the weighting of factors. Do not be convinced that because of the complexity of the infomation involved, no fundamental method, as we have defined it, can be possible. There are econometric formulas which can reduce this mass of data to specific values, using computers, with respect to the current price and provide adequate information for trading purposes.

The difficulty with the fundamental approach for most speculators is that vast amounts of time and money can be consumed to obtain the past and present data and to work it into reliable formulations. To continue to update this data each day would then be the task of a full-time staff. (Time-sharing computer services which provide this information are equally expensive.) The individual trader who wishes to use the fundamental approach is in direct competition with the largest producers and processors in the world, with their relatively unlimited resources of information and analysis. In such a competition, the outcome is not often a surprise.

The technician may make the same assumptions about the true economic value of a commodity, but uses a different technique to take advantage of price movements. The technician makes certain assumptions about the nature of the price movements, using the format of Isaac Newton's second law of motion—*A price in motion is likely to continue in motion in the same direction,* or simply put, *prices move in trends.*

If this assumption of price continuity is correct, then it is theoritically possible to discard all facts about a commodity except its price history. Many technicians will also consider the volume of trading and changes in the open interest relative to the direction of the price.

The technician reasons that prices move in trends because the large firms which are trading in great volume over a period of time evaluate new items of fundamental importance and their resulting market actions, as a whole, move the price to effect a new balance of value. Thus the technician, instead of competing with the large companies on fundamental analysis, uses the actions of the large companies as they affect market prices by buying as the price rises and selling as the price drops. Therefore the technician should not weigh any fundamental information in market decisions since the fundamentals are assumed to be fully present in the price action itself. Fortunately, both fundamentalists and technicians can be correct about the direction of prices at the same time.

The cost of evaluating a technical method and optimizing its parameters can be significant in terms of computer simulation costs, since adequate analysis with reasonable speed is beyond the capabilities of an Apple II, for example, or other home computers. The daily updates, however, are usually simple since they involve only readily available prices or other market data. The daily update can be performed by a single individual within a reasonable amount of time, depending upon the computational tools available.

COMMODITY SELECTION AND DIVERSIFICATION

Whatever trading approach is used, the number and nature of the commodities to be traded must be carefully selected. If we could be certain which commodity was about to change in price by the greatest amount relative to its margin requirements, we could put all our funds into that one position. This would give us the possibility of the greatest returns. Since most traders use methods which are based upon probabilities rather than certainties, they try to achieve the best combination of profits and safety through the use of diversification.

Investing in a number of different commodities usually results in smaller changes in total account equity due to either profits or losses over a period of time. It practically assures the trader of being in at least one trending market most of the time, but with equal assurance of having some positions in dormant or contrary markets as well. Diversification assumes that not all markets are going to move in the same direction at the same time with the same momentum, nor will they all change direction simultaneously. That means that while we may be taking losses in some commodities, we will have profits in others to cushion their impact; and, if our system is a reasonably good one, we will survive the short-term difficulties and still be trading when there are net profits to be made.

There are some minor benefits of diversification which might be gained by trading different contract months of the same commodity or trading the same commodity on different exchanges, but they are small compared to the initial benefits of trading different commodities. Even with simple diversification there are some precautions to observe. The trading of live cattle, feeder cattle, live hogs, and pork bellies give some variety. Similarly, the trading of corn, wheat, oats, and soybeans or copper, gold, silver, and platinum offer variety. But the degree of diversification achieved by trading all meats, or all metals, or all grains, or similarly well-correlated groups is not nearly as great as trading a small number of commodities from each of the areas.

VOLATILITY

Another important criterion in the selection of what to trade is the individual *volatility pattern* of the commodity. Volatility is the *quality* of price movement measured over time. The greater the price variation, the greater the volatility. For example, suppose cattle and hogs each have a daily price range of 100 points, and cattle started the day at the day's low and rose steadily to the high where it closed. The hogs, after opening at the low, rose to the high, dropped back to the low, and rose again to the high where they closed. The hogs in this case would have been the more volatile for the day. Unfortunately, historical data, comprised only of the open, high, low, and close which is most often used for analysis, do not allow the user to determine the true daily volatility in this way. The average daily range is the most reliable indication available. An ideal measurement would be the average of the sum of the absolute intraday price movements.

Volatility can be measured for longer periods as well. One method would be to examine the weekly range of prices; another method would be to use the total of the absolute daily price changes from one close to the next for the same period; and a third would be to consider the average daily range for the week. A commodity with a large weekly or monthly range and a small total of absolute daily changes will be a better prospect for trend-following methods. This would indicate a solid trend with a minimum of price variation. When the contracts enter a trendless or consolidation period, *the weekly range normally decreases relative to the totals of absolute change*. Thus it is possible to identify the periods when most trend methods may loose money during high volatility but sideways markets. This concept could even be developed into a trading method. We would expect that a method which can adjust for degrees or patterns of volatility to be far better than one that always trades without any volatility consideration.

CAPITAL REQUIREMENTS

We must now determine the amount of capital required to trade a single commodity or a portfolio by a particular method or system. The profitability or rate of return is directly dependent on the total capital required. The less deposited into the account to trade a specific method, the greater the percentage return. Therefore we must determine the minimum of capital needed to trade as safely as our risk preference determines.

One approach to finding the best investment amount is to calculate the trades which were specified or "signaled" by the method and find the largest "continual" drop in equity. A largest loss string (LLS) or "continual" drop in equity results from a single losing trade, a continuous series or losses, or a mixture of losing and profitable trades occurring such that the difference between a previous unexceeded equity high and a subsequent equity low is greatest. It is the largest loss that would occur for an account which started at the worst possible time.

We could then take the value of the LLS, increase it to account for the rate of inflation and increased volatility since its occurrence, add the maximum exchange margin and an error factor relative to the number of trades or time period tested, and use this figure as a reasonably safe starting point. This adjusted LLS, plus the needed margin to trade the diversified program should be a good representation of the capital required to trade the system and survive the largest equity drop. Of course, we can never be completely certain of safety in the market, but for the sake of comparison among methods, the investment amount specified by the adjusted LLS can be used with a reasonable degree of confidence, even though some traders might feel comfortable only when they have twice this amount in reserve to handle losing periods.

RATE OF RETURN

We can now compute the average annual noncompounded rate of return based on a well-defined initial investment easily calculated and generally applicable. Using this technique to evaluate various methods gives us an objective criterion for stating returns and eliminates any basis for possibly distorted claims. Such distortions could occur by assuming the account started at the best possible time or adjusting the capital deposited to the minimum possible (often the minimum margin requirements). Additionally, capital could be added from outside funds and profits removed quickly; returns based on the average size of the equity would then be unreasonably large.

EVALUATING RETURNS

Using the amount of funds needed to make the chance of success highly probable, it may be that the return on investment as shown by many methods will be discouragingly low. But some traders may be willing to take greater risks for the chance of higher returns. We can judge the extent of the risks involved by manipulating the determining factors. The percentage decline in account equity is computed by dividing each of the series of losing strings by the amount of account equity at the time just before the losing string occurs or by the initial account equity if no compounding is used. Similarly, the average annual return of an account is computed by dividing the total net change in equity of the account first by the number of years involved in the performance record and then dividing that figure by the initial investment. This is, of course, a simple noncompounded annualized return. From the nature of these computations, one can see that the lower the initial investment, the greater may be both the percentage return and the potential equity decline.

Expanding on this means of evaluation, we can examine the trades of any method for any number of years and assume any initial investment value for an account. The account should be permitted to grow over the time period, but trading remains a function of the initial number of contracts (based on the initial investment) at all levels of equity. For evaluation purposes, each new trade in the trading record will assume the initiation of an additional account. For example, the first account will start with the oldest historic trade and include cumulative results from all subsequent trades; the tenth account will start with the tenth trade and include the results from the tenth trade forward. In this manner there will be as many simulated accounts as there are trades in the record.

Based upon this structure, some important questions can be asked. First, *"What percentage of the total number of the accounts would have increased by 100% without experiencing a loss string of 50%?"* By varying the percentages of profitable and losing strings, we can set up a risk/reward matrix. An examination of such a matrix would enable an analyst or trader with a conservative goal to determine the percentage of accounts that would have risen by 50% without experiencing an LLS of 20%. For the more aggressive speculator the percentage of accounts that would have risen by 200% with no LLS greater than 50% can be found.

Looking at the problem from the opposite side, we can ask *"What initial investment would have been necessary to obtain a 100% rise without a 50% LLS in at least 90% of the accounts?"* From the matrix, the trader can select any combination of risk to reward that meets the trader's financial goals without violating a sense of prudent risk; thus the variables can be matched to the specific risk preference of the individual. The well-defined method of evaluation which has been suggested here should enable the trader to compare various methods and systems on a consistent and rational basis. Once a method for trading has been selected, its trading record can be examined further by inspecting its profile for minor tactical rule changes, such as starting a new account only after a single or a series of losing trades. These decisions should be compared against alternate rules, such as waiting for at least one losing trade in a commodity before reentering a position in that commodity.

One additional refinement may be desirable. It may appear that many methods that worked well over the past few years did not work well in earlier years. There may be an inherent distortion in this comparison by reason of inflation. If the profits and losses of earlier years were multiplied by a percentage factor (inflated) which would show them in terms of constant dollars based on the present value of the U.S. dollar, they would in most instances show a much more consistent degree of profitability.

In conclusion, a rational approach to selecting and evaluating trading methods should begin with the identification of a well-defined model. More attention should be given to methods which have been optimized for the individual commodity with respect to the parameters used. Look for methods that make some provision for the inclusion of volatility factors. We should then favor those systems which are properly diversified. After obtaining a trading performance record for the method, we can create a matrix of risk and reward as discussed, and compare the profile of this system to others. By combining the best methods, we can devise a system to suit our own objectives and personality to give us our best possible individual approach to trading.

CHAPTER 17

MATHEMATICAL AIDS

CONTENTS

DISTRIBUTION 3

DISPERSION AND SKEWNESS 6

Transformations 7

REGRESSION ANALYSIS 7

Linear Regression 8
Correlation When Using a Time Series 8

NONLINEAR REGRESSION 9

MULTIVARIATE ANALYSIS 9

LEAST-SQUARES SINUSOIDAL 10

TRIGONOMETRIC CURVE FITTING 10

COMPLEX TRIGONOMETRIC CURVE FITTING 14

THE MOVING AVERAGE 15

DOUBLE EXPONENTIAL SMOOTHING 17

RISK PREFERENCE 17

PROBABILITY OF SUCCESS AND RUIN 18

Wins not Equal to Losses 18

ACTUAL VERSUS EXPECTED 20

SUPPLY AND DEMAND 21

Demand 21
Elasticity of Demand 21
Changes in Short-Run Demand Elasticity 21
Supply 22
Elasticity of Supply 23
Equilibrium 23
Building a Model 24

CHAPTER 17

MATHEMATICAL AIDS

Perry J. Kaufman

Analysis of commodity price movement and trading risk involves the specialized tools of probability and time-series analysis. All of the techniques are more or less significant based on the amount and selection of data used; smaller amounts of data lead to inconclusive results. This relationship is usually expressed as

$$\text{error} = \frac{1}{\sqrt{\text{number of data items}}} = \frac{1}{\sqrt{n}}$$

Therefore, if two items are used, the error associated with the results will be 50%, for 100 items the error is 10%. This same error factor must be applied to selection of trading methods, econometric price forecasts, and risk analysis.

The time interval used for analysis is a primary factor in determining its accuracy. For example, an econometric forecast of wheat demand uses monthly data going back 3 years. The final forecast will be accurate to $\pm\ 1/\sqrt{36}$, or $\pm$ 16.7%, a large error. An analysis of risk/reward due to trading a slow trend-following system has six losses and three profits over a 3-year interval. The error on the collective data is ⅓ and the small sampling of profitable of losing trades shows that no reasonable conclusions could be drawn.

DISTRIBUTION

The *frequency distribution* can give a good picture of the characteristics of the data. If we want to know how often sugar prices were at different price levels we can divide prices into $0.01 increments (e.g., 5.01 to 6.00, 6.01 to 7.00, etc.) and count the number of times that prices fall into each interval. The result will be a distribution of prices as shown in Figure 1. It should be expected that the distribution of prices for a commodity will be *skewed* towards the left-hand side (lower prices), and have a long *tail* towards higher prices on the right-hand side. This is because prices remain at higher levels for only a short time relative to their long-term characteristics. Commodity prices tend to be bounded on the lower end, limited in their downside movement, by production costs and resistance of the suppliers to sell at prices which represent a loss. On the higher end there is not such a clear point of limitation, therefore prices move much further up during periods of extreme shortage relative to demand.

In order to quantify the tendencies and extremes of price movement or other

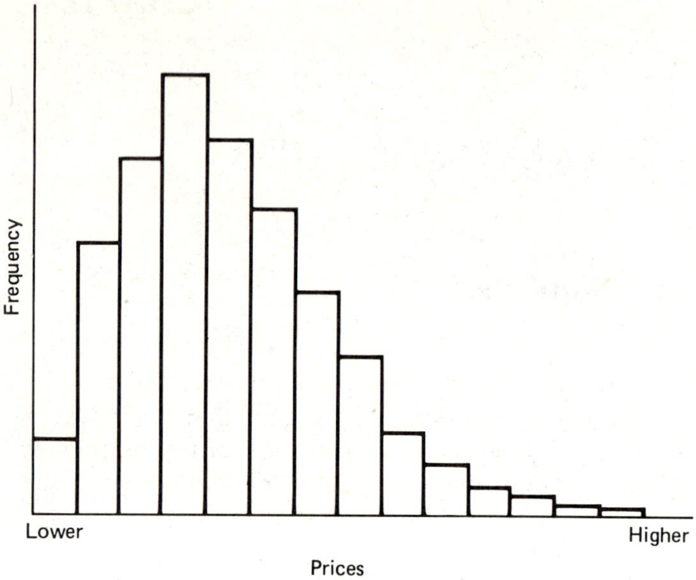

FIGURE 1. Hypothetical price distribution.

supply, demand, economic factors, or price characteristics it is necessary to start with *measures of central location,* or averages. The most important ones are:

The Arithmetic Mean,

$$\bar{a} = \frac{\sum^{N} a_i}{N} = \frac{a_1 + a_2 + \ldots + a_N}{N}$$

the sum of a series of numbers, divided by the number of items in the series.

The Median, the value of the middle item in a series. If there are an even number of items, the median is the arithmetic mean of the two central items.

The Mode, the most frequent value which occurs in the series of data. Its uniqueness often depends on the use of a large number of data points; a smaller series will usually cause it to coincide with the midpoint.

In a skewed distribution, characteristics of price data, the mean, median and mode are related as shown in Figure 2. The mode may be approximated by

$$\text{mode} = \text{mean} - 3(\text{mean} - \text{median})$$

Other measurements of central tendencies effectively *weight* or *transform* the values to reduce the effect of extreme high values. These methods are typically:

The Geometric Mean.

$$G = \sqrt[N]{a_1 \times a_2 \times \ldots \times a_N}$$

The solution to the geometric mean can be either of the two forms:

$$\ln G = \frac{\ln a_1 + \ln a_2 + \ldots + \ln a_N}{N}$$

or

$$\ln G = \frac{\ln(a_1 \times a_2 \times \ldots \times a_N)}{N}$$

The geometric mean is particularly useful in the calculation of index numbers.

The Quadratic Mean.

$$Q = \sqrt{\frac{\sum (a^2)}{N}}$$

The square root of the mean of the square of the items ("root-mean-square") is most well-known in its use in calculation of the standard deviation.

The Harmonic Mean.

$$\frac{1}{H} = \frac{\frac{1}{a_1} + \frac{1}{a_2} + \ldots + \frac{1}{a_N}}{N}$$

or

$$H = N/\sum^{N} \left(\frac{1}{a_i}\right)$$

This is often used for averaging rates, and tends to reduce the effects of extremes even more than the geometric mean.

The general relationship between the results when using the three principal means is

arithmetic mean > geometric mean > harmonic mean

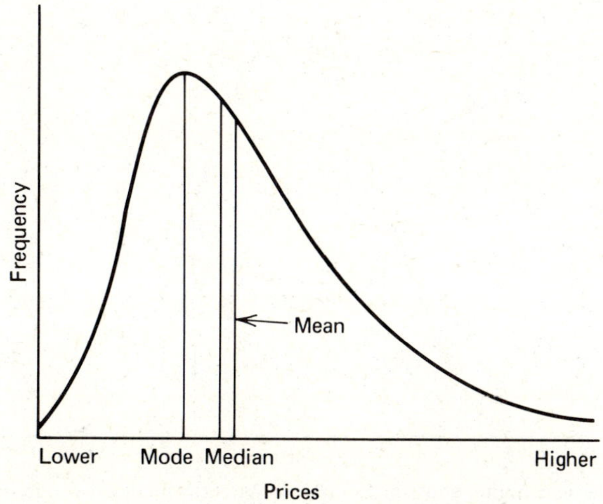

FIGURE 2. Hypothetical price distribution skewed to the right showing the relationship of the mode, median, and mean.

DISPERSION AND SKEWNESS

The center or central tendency of a data series is not a sufficient description for price analysis. The manner in which it is scattered about a given point, its *dispersion* and *skewness,* are necessary to describe the data. The *mean deviation* is a basic method for measuring distribution and may be calculated about any measure of central location, for example, the arithmetic mean. It is found by computing

$$\text{MD} = \frac{\sum |x|}{N}$$

where MD is the mean deviation and $\Sigma\,|\,x\,|$ is a sum of deviations of each value from the arithmetic mean or other measure of central location such as the median with *signs ignored.*

The *standard deviation* is a special form of measuring average deviation from the mean, which uses the root-mean-square

$$\sigma = \sqrt{\frac{\sum (x^2)}{N}}$$

where σ is the standard deviation, x is the deviation from the mean $(x_i - \bar{x})$, and N is the number of items in the data series.

The standard deviation is the most popular way of measuring the degree of dispersion of the data. The value of one standard deviation about the mean represents a clustering of about 68% of the data; two standard deviations from the mean include 95.5% of all data; and three standard deviations encompass 99.7%—nearly all the data. These values represent the groupings of a perfectly *normal* set of data, shown in Figure 3.

Most commodity data, however, is not normally distributed and must be measured and corrected for *skewness*—the degree of distortion from the normal sym-

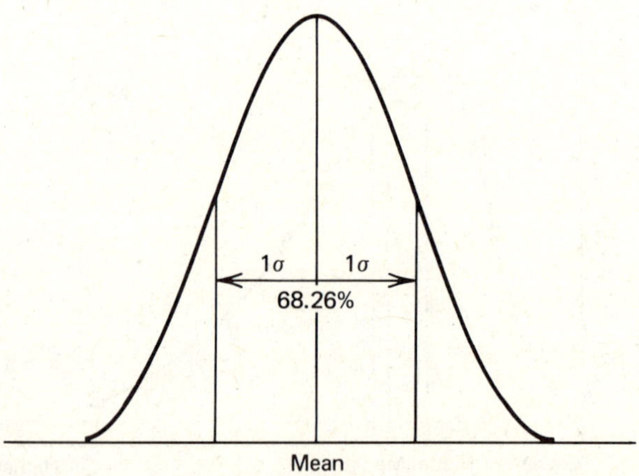

FIGURE 3. *Normal* distribution showing the percentage area included within one standard deviation about the arithmetic mean.

metry. In a perfectly normal distribution the median and mode coincide. As the data become more extreme, which might mean a very high commodity price, the *mean* will show the greatest change while the *mode* will show the least. The difference between the mean and the mode, adjusted for dispersion will give a good measure of skewness

$$K = \frac{\text{mean} - \text{mode}}{\sigma}$$

This can also be expressed using the median as

$$K = \frac{3(\text{mean} - \text{median})}{\sigma}$$

TRANSFORMATIONS. The skewness of a data series can sometimes be corrected using a *transformation* on the data. Price data may be skewed in a specific pattern. For example, if there are ¼ of the occurrences at twice the price, and 1/9 of the occurrences at three times the price, we can transform the original data into a normal distribution by taking the square root of each data item and analyzing the new data series. The characteristics of price data often show a logarithmic, power, or square-root relationship.

REGRESSION ANALYSIS

Correlation and regression analysis is a way of measuring the relationship between two sets or series of data. In economics we may want to know the relationship between gold prices and inflation, between the supply of wheat and wheat prices, or between the two related products, soybean oil and palm oil. Figure 4 shows the possible relationship between the oils as a *scatter diagram*.

There are quite a few statistical measurements which can be performed on this data. The first and most important is a *regression analysis* and *correlation coefficient*.

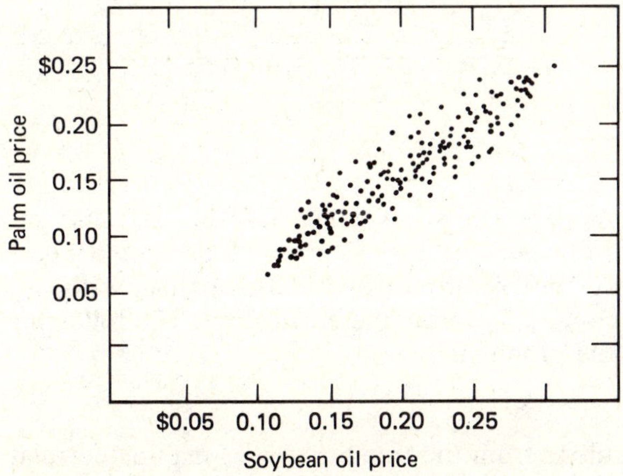

FIGURE 4. Scatter diagram of palm oil vs. soybean oil.

LINEAR REGRESSION. To find the straight line relationship between palm oil and soybean oil we solve the equation

$$Y = a + bX$$

for values a and b. The *normal equations* for the least-squares procedure allows these constants to be found by solving the formulas

$$b = \frac{N \sum xy - \sum x \sum y}{N \sum x^2 - (\sum x)^2}$$

and

$$a = \frac{1}{N}(\sum y - b \sum x)$$

where N is the number of data items in each series and x and y are the corresponding entries x_i and y_i.

The *standard error* of the calculation is a measurement of the accuracy of the line drawn through the actual data points. It is found by

$$\text{standard error} = X_y = \sqrt{\frac{\sum (y' - y)^2}{N}}$$

where y′ is the theoretical value of y_i at x_i and y is the corresponding data point y_i. The *standard error* is used in the same way as the *standard deviation* where one standard error of the estimate includes about 68% of the data points.

The *coefficient of correlation* is a percentage measurement of the correlation of the estimated and actual results. It is formed by dividing the standard error S by the standard deviation σ and adjusting such that a resulting value of 1 means a perfect relationship and a value of 0 means no relationship:

$$r = \sqrt{1 - \frac{S^2{}_y}{\sigma^2{}_y}}$$

which is also written

$$r = \frac{N \sum xy - \sum x \sum y}{\sqrt{[N \sum x^2 - (\sum x)^2]\,[N \sum y^2 - (\sum y)^2]}}$$

CORRELATION WHEN USING A TIME SERIES. Because most price analysis involves the use of two time series, precautions should be taken. A long-term similar upward (or downwards) trend will overshadow the smaller movements around the trend and exaggerate the correlation. The following methods may be used to correct the problem:

1. The deviations from the trend $(y'_i - y_i)$ may be correlated.
2. The first differences $[(y'_i - y'_{i-1}), (y_i - y_{i-1})]$ may be correlated.
3. The two series may be adjusted for trend.

NONLINEAR REGRESSION

Relationships between data series which are not linear may be represented by a curve of various forms. The most common of these curve forms are curvilinear, exponential, and power. The *curvilinear* or *first-order* case

$$y = a + bx + cx^2$$

must be solved as a series of three simultaneous equations:

$$Na + b\sum x + c\sum x^2 = \sum y$$
$$a\sum x + b\sum x^2 + c\sum x^3 = \sum xy$$
$$a\sum x^2 + b\sum x^3 + c\sum x^4 = \sum x^2y$$

The *exponential curve* has the form

$$y = ab^x$$

which can be expressed as a logarithm,

$$\ln y = a + b\ln x$$

The *power curve*

$$y = ax^b$$

can also be transformed into

$$\ln y = \ln a + b\ln x$$

and then solved using the normal equations of the linear-regression method.

MULTIVARIATE ANALYSIS

The previous regression methods were used to find the relationship between *two* data series. In econometric analysis it is often necessary to express price as dependent upon various other factors, for example, inflation, new crop supply, and carryover stocks for the case of agricultural products. This is expressed as a *multivariate* equation

$$y/\text{PPI} = a + bx_1 + cx_2$$

where y/PPI is the anticipated price adjusted by the Producer Price Index (each price used in the analysis is adjusted by the respective inflator or deflator value); x_1 is the anticipated total new crop supply; x_2 is the carryover supply from the prior year; and $a, b,$ and c are constants to be calculated in the regression analysis.

Three least-squares equations can be used to solve the multivariate problem for two independent variables x_1 and x_2 using the matrix reduction method for simultaneous linear equations:

$$an + b\sum x_1 + c\sum x_2 = \sum y$$
$$a\sum x_1 + b\sum x_1^2 + c\sum x_1x_2 = \sum x_1y$$
$$a\sum x_2 + b\sum x_1x_2 + c\sum x^2_2 = \sum x_2y$$

where every use of Σ implies $\Sigma_{i=1}^{n}$.

In general, we can express the relationship between n independent variables as

$$y = a_0 + a_1x_1 + a_2x_2 + \cdots + a_nx_n$$

The solution to this set of equations is an extension of the problems in two variables just presented, resulting in the set of simultaneous linear equations:

$$\begin{aligned}
a_0n \quad &+ a_1 \sum x_1 &&+ a_2 \sum x_2 &&+ \cdots + a_n \sum x_n &&= \sum y \\
a_0 \sum x_1 &+ a_1 \sum x_1^2 &&+ a_2 \sum x_1x_2 &&+ \cdots + a_n \sum x_1x_n &&= \sum x_1y \\
a_0 \sum x_2 &+ a_1 \sum x_1x_2 &&+ a_2 \sum x_2^2 &&+ \cdots + a_n \sum x_2x_n &&= \sum x_2y \\
& && && &&\vdots \\
a_0 \sum x_n &+ a_1 \sum x_1x_n &&+ a_2 \sum x_2x_n &&+ \cdots + a_n \sum x_n^2 &&= \sum x_ny
\end{aligned}$$

Once the system of equations has exceeded two variables it is best solved using standard programs on most computers.

LEAST-SQUARES SINUSOIDAL

A special case of the multiple linear predictor occurs when periodic peaks can be observed in the data taken at specific time intervals (time series). These peaks and valleys suggest that the time series may have a cyclic pattern. The equation for the approximation of the period movement is

$$y_t = a_0 + a_1t + a_2 \cos \frac{2\pi t}{P} + a_3 \sin \frac{2\pi t}{P} + a_4t \cos \frac{2\pi t}{P} + a_5t \sin \frac{2\pi t}{P}$$

which is a special case of the generalized multivariate approximation

$$y = a_0 + a_1x_1 + a_2x_2 + a_3x_3 + a_4x_4 + a_5x_5$$

where P is the number of data points in each cycle; $x_1 = t$, the incremental time element; $x_2 = \cos(2\pi t/P)$, a cyclic element; $x_3 = \sin(2\pi t/P)$, a cyclic element; $x_4 = t\cos(2\pi t/P)$, an amplitude-variation element; and $x_5 = t\sin(2\pi t/P)$, an amplitude-variation element.

The term a_1t will allow for the linear tendencies of the sequence. You will notice that the term 2π refers to an entire cycle and $2\pi t/P$ designates a section $(1/P)$ of a specific cycle t; this in turn adds weight to either the sine or cosine functions at different points within a cycle.

The solution is calculated in the tabular manner of the other methods, using simultaneous linear equations derived in the same way as the generalized multivariate equation.

TRIGONOMETRIC CURVE FITTING

The regression techniques using the general polynomial equation

$$y = a + bx + cx^2 + \cdots$$

as well as systems of simultaneous linear equations for solving the multivariate problem may represent a curve of a nonrepeating form. It is often convenient to study uniform waves to represent cycles of motion. Most of these cycles can be fitted using the sine and cosine trigonometric functions. These functions are also called *periodic waves* because they nominally repeat every 360° or 2π radians (where $\pi = 3.141592$). Since we can convert all notation from degrees to radians using the relationship

$$1° = \frac{2\pi}{360}$$

all work will be performed in degrees. Some other terms that must be understood when discussing wave motion are:

1. Amplitude(a)—the height of the wave from the center (x axis) at any point.
2. Frequency(ω)—the number of wavelengths that repeat every 360°, calculated as $\omega = 1/T$.
3. Period (T)—the number of time units necessary to complete one wavelength (or cycle).

A simple sine wave fluctuates from 0 to +1, then back to 0, −1, and 0 again for each cycle (one wavelength) as the degrees increase from 0° to 360°. To relate the wavelength to a specific distance in boxes (on graph paper) simply divide 360° by the number of boxes in a full wavelength and you have the increments, in degrees, represented by each box. For example, a 100-box cycle would give a value of 3.6° to each box. To change the wavelength to other than 360° we introduce a constant ω, which is a multiplier of the angle of a standard sine wave and is written

$$\sin \omega\phi$$

If $\omega > 1$ the wavelength is less than 360°; if $\omega < 1$ it will be greater than 360°. Actually, since ω is the frequency, it gives the number of wavelengths in each 360° cycle. To change the *phase* of the wave we add the value b to the angle and write the new term

$$\sin(\omega\phi + b)$$

If b is 180° the sine wave will start in the second half of the cycle; b serves to shift the wave to the left. The last variation changes the *amplitude* by multiplying the resulting value by the constant a. Since the sine will range from + 1 to − 1 the new range will be $+ a$ to $- a$. Figure 5 shows a generalized sinusoidal wave.

Since there are few examples of commodity price movement that can be represented by such a uniform wave, the concept of adding waves must be introduced. Two generalized sine waves can be added together to form a very different *compound wave:*

$$y = a_1 \sin(\omega_1\phi + b_1) + a_2 \sin(\omega_2\phi + b_2)$$

Each set of characteristic variables a_1, ω_1, b_1 and a_2, ω_2, b_2 can be different, but both waves are measured at the same point ϕ, at the same time. Consider an example that lets the phase constants b_1 and b_2 be zero:

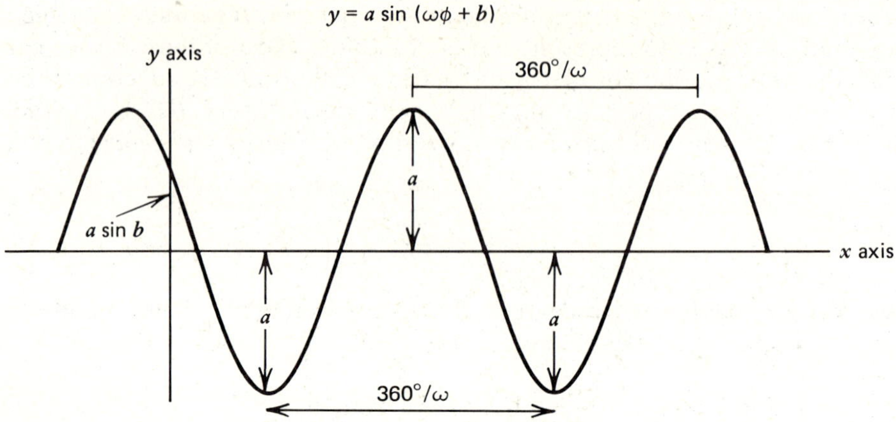

FIGURE 5. Sinusoidal wave.

$$y_1 = 3 \sin 4\phi$$

$$y_2 = 5 \sin 6\phi$$

$$y = y_1 + y_2$$

Figure 6 shows the individual regular waves y_1 and y_2 and the degenerating wave y over the interval 0° to 180°. Note that both y_1 and y_2 began the normal upward cycle at 0°; but by 180° they are perfectly out of phase. During the next 180° the two waves come back into phase. When combining periodic waves, it is useful to know the maximum and minimum amplitude of the resulting wave. Since the peaks of the two elementary waves do not necessarily fall at the same point, the sum of $a_1 + a_2$ represents only the greatest value that may be reached.

A mathematical technique, called *differentiation,* allows you to find these values directly. The first derivative, with respect to angle ϕ, is written $dy/d\phi$ or y', where y is the formula to be differentiated. The simple rules to follow are:

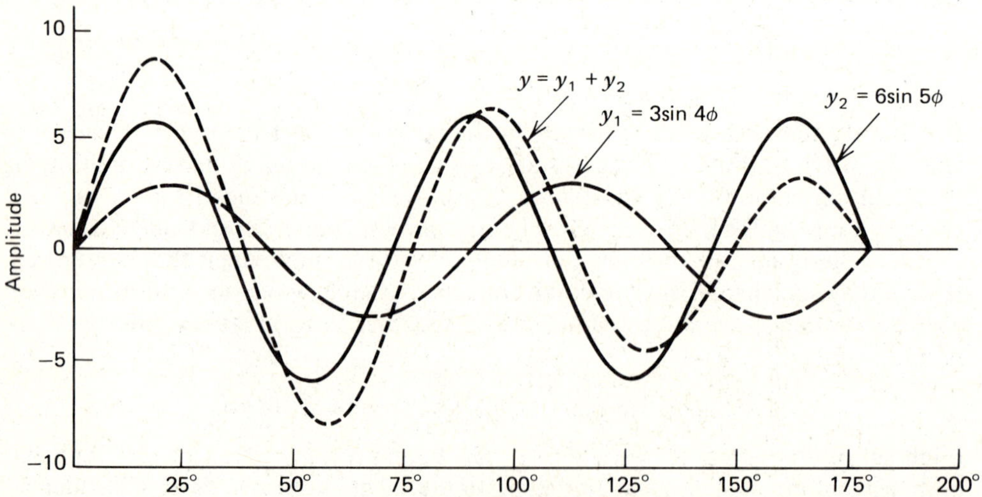

FIGURE 6. Compounded sine wave.

$$\frac{d}{d\phi}(\sin \phi) = \cos \phi; \qquad \frac{d}{d\phi}(\cos \phi) = -\sin \phi$$

$$\frac{d}{d\phi}(\sin \omega\phi) = \omega \cos \omega\phi$$

$$\frac{d}{d\phi}[\sin(\omega\phi + b)] = \omega \cos (\omega\phi + b)$$

$$\frac{d}{d\phi}[a_1 \sin(\omega_1 \phi + b_1) + a_2 \sin(\omega_2 \phi + b_2)]$$
$$= a_1 \omega_1 \cos (\omega_1\phi + b_1) + a_2 \omega_2 \cos (\omega_2\phi + b_2)$$

Applying this method to our previous example, we have

$$y = 3 \sin 4\phi + 6 \sin 5\phi$$

$$\frac{dy}{d\phi} = y' = 12 \cos 4\phi + 30 \cos 5\phi$$

The points of maximum and/or minimum value occur when $y' = 0$. Taken separately, with $y'_1 = 12 \cos 4\phi$ and $y'_2 = 30 \cos 5\phi$, we can see that $y'_1 = 0$ when $4\phi = 90°$ and $270°$, or when $\phi = 22\frac{1}{2}°$ or $67\frac{1}{2}°$, as seen in Figure 6. For y'_2 the maximum and minimum values occur when $y'_2 = 0$ or $5\phi = 90°$ and $270°$, at $\phi = 18°$ and $54°$ respectively. While we are on the simpler component equations it should be noted that the first derivative tells where the extreme high and low points are, but does not tell which one is the maximum and which is the minimum. The second derivation, y'', calculated by taking the derivative of y', is used for this distinction as follows:

if $y'(x) = 0$ and $y''(x) > 0$, then $y(x)$ is a minimum

if $y'(x) = 0$ and $y''(x) < 0$, then $y(x)$ is a maximum

From this we can determine that $y_1 = 22\frac{1}{2}°$ an $y_2 = 18°$ are maxima and $y_1 = 67\frac{1}{2}°$ and $y_2 = 54°$ are minima.

Anyone interested in pursuing the analysis of maxima and minima (extrema) will find more complete discussions in a text on calculus.

The solution to the general trigonometric single-frequency curve

$$y_t = a \cos t + b \sin \omega t$$

can more easily be found by replacing ϕ by t and considering the angle in units of 1, 2, 3, . . . rather than in degrees. This will be more convenient to visualize as well as chart. In order to find the frequency it will be necessary to first solve the equation

$$\cos \omega - \tfrac{1}{2} \alpha = 0$$

This can be done by solving the system of equations

$$\alpha y_2 = y_1 + y_3$$

$$\alpha y_3 = y_2 + y_4$$

$$\alpha y_{n-1} = y_{n-2} + y_n$$

using a least-squares method. This can be accomplished by finding the value for c and d in the equation

$$\alpha \sum c^2 = \sum cd$$

where $c = y_n$ and $d = y_{n-1} + y_{n+1}$. We can now substitute the value for α into the intermediate equation and solve for the frequency ω.

The last step in solving the equation for a single frequency is to write the *normal equations*

$$a \sum \cos^2 \omega t + b \sum \cos \omega t \sin \omega t = \sum y_t \cos \omega t$$

$$a \sum \sin \omega t \cos \omega t + b \sum \sin^2 \omega t = \sum y_t \sin \omega t$$

and solve for a and b, where $t = 1, \ldots, n$ and where ω was just found. As in the other solutions, it will be necessary to find the sums of the various terms of the equation, that is,

$$\begin{array}{ll} \sum \cos^2 \omega t & \sum \sin \omega t \cos \omega t \\ \sum \cos \omega t \sin \omega t & \sum \sin^2 \omega t \\ \sum y_t \cos \omega t & \sum y_t \sin \omega t \end{array}$$

Then the normal equations can be solved for a and b. This process is best done using a programmable calculator or computer.[1]

COMPLEX TRIGONOMETRIC CURVE FITTING

The regular cyclic component of price movement is not likely to be accurately represented by a single-frequency trigonometric curve. A combination of more than one set of sine and cosine waves of varying amplitudes and frequencies is more likely to represent the patterns. The equation for the two-frequency curve is written

$$y_t = a_1 \cos \omega_1 t + b_1 \sin \omega_1 t + a_2 \cos \omega_2 t + b_2 \sin \omega_2 t \tag{1}$$

To find the results of this complex wave it is necessary to apply the same techniques used in the single-frequency approach. The algebra for solving this problem is an expanded form of the previous solution and the use of a programmable calculator is almost a requirement. The frequencies ω_1 and ω_2 are found by solving the quadratic equation $2x^2 - \alpha_1 x - (1 + \alpha_2/2) = 0$, where $x = \cos \omega$, using the standard formula

$$x = \frac{\alpha_1 \pm \sqrt{\alpha_1^2 + 8(1 + \alpha_2/2)}}{4} \tag{2}$$

The least-squares method can be used as before derived from the general form

$$\alpha_1(y_n + y_{n+2}) + \alpha_2 y_{n+1} = y_{n-1} + y_{n+3} \tag{3}$$

[1]Sample solutions can be found in P. J. Kaufman, *Commodity Trading Systems and Methods*, Wiley, NY, 1978, pp. 112–115.

The least-squares equations for finding α_1 and α_2 are

$$\alpha_1 \sum c^2 + \alpha_2 \sum cd = \sum cp \tag{4}$$

and

$$\alpha_1 \sum cd + \alpha_2 \sum d^2 = \sum dp \tag{5}$$

where $c = y_n + y_{n+2}$, $d = y_{n+1}$, and $p = y_{n-1} + y_{n+3}$. Once α_1 and α_2 are found, ω_1 and ω_2 are calculated from the two solutions of the quadratic equation (2). The next step is to solve the normal equations to get the amplitudes, a_1, b_1, a_2, and b_2:

$$a_1 \sum \cos^2 \omega_1 t + b_1 \sum \cos \omega_1 t \sin \omega_1 t + a_2 \sum \cos \omega_1 t \cos \omega_2 t + b_2 \sum \cos \omega_1 t \sin \omega_2 t = \sum y_t \cos \omega_1 t \tag{6}$$

$$a_1 \sum \sin \omega_1 t \cos \omega_1 t + b_1 \sum \sin^2 \omega_1 t + a_2 \sum \sin \omega_1 t \cos \omega_2 t + b_2 \sum \sin \omega_1 t \sin \omega_2 t = \sum y_1 \sin \omega_1 t \tag{7}$$

$$a_1 \sum \cos \omega_2 t \cos \omega_1 t + b_1 \sum \cos \omega_2 t \sin \omega_1 t + a_2 \sum \cos \omega_2 t + b_2 \sum \cos \omega_2 t \sin \omega_2 t = \sum y_t \cos \omega_2 t \tag{8}$$

$$a_1 \sum \sin \omega_2 t \cos \omega_1 t + b_1 \sum \sin \omega_2 t \sin \omega_1 t + a_2 \sum \sin \omega_2 t \cos \omega_2 t + b_2 \sum \sin^2 \omega_2 t = \sum y_t \sin \omega_2 t \tag{9}$$

The final step is to create a 4×5 matrix to solve the four normal equations (6)–(9) for the coefficients a_1, b_1, a_2, and b_2.

THE MOVING AVERAGE

The simplest and most well-known of all *smoothing* techniques is called the *moving average*. It is the basis for most computerized trend-following methods. Using the technique for a *moving average,* the number of elements (usually closing prices) to be averaged remains the same, but the time interval advances. For the various examples of smoothing, a generalized series of closing prices $P_1, P_2, \ldots, P_t$ will be used. A *simple* moving average measured over n of these points at time t would be

$$M_t = \frac{P_t + P_{t-1} + \cdots + P_{t-n+1}}{n} = \frac{\sum_{i=1}^{n} P_{t-i+1}}{n}, \; n \leq t$$

The *weighted moving average* opens up a large area of study. Using *weighting* it is possible to assign a level of significance to each past price; in doing this the possibility of an incorrect bias is introduced. A weighted moving average is expressed in its general form as

$$W_t = \frac{w_1 P_t + w_2 P_{t-1} + \cdots + w_n P_{t-n+1}}{w_1 + w_2 + \cdots + w_n} = \frac{\sum_{i=1}^{n} w_i P_{t-i+1}}{\sum_{i=1}^{n} w_i}$$

This gives the weighted moving average at time t as the average of the previous n prices, each one weighted by w_i according to its position relative to t. A weighted moving average is called "front-loaded" if

$$w_1 \geq w_2 \geq \cdots \geq w_n$$

A popular modification to the weighting of individual prices is the weighting of a group of prices. If every two consecutive data elements had the same weighting factor, we would get

$$W_t = \frac{w_1 P_t + w_1 P_{t-1} + w_2 P_{t-2} + w_2 P_{t-3} + \cdots + w_{n/2} P_{t-n+1}}{w_1 + w_2 + \cdots + w_n}$$

or, grouped with n even,

$$W_t = \frac{w_1(P_t + P_{t-1}) + w_2(P_{t-2} + P_{t-3}) + \cdots + w_{n/2}(P_{t-n+2} + P_{t-n+1})}{w_1 + w_2 + \ldots + w_n}$$

Any number of consecutive data elements can be grouped and still satisfy the criteria for a *step-weighted* moving average.

The *geometric mean* previously shown can also be used in the same manner as a moving average, where

$$\ln G_t = \frac{\ln P_t + \ln P_{t-1} + \ldots + \ln P_{t-n+1}}{n}$$

$$= \frac{1}{n}\left(\sum_{i=1}^{n} \ln P_{t-i+1}\right)$$

A *weighted* geometric moving average would have the form

$$\ln G_t = \frac{w_1 \ln P_t + w_2 \ln P_{t-1} + \ldots + w_n \ln P_{t-n+1}}{w_1 + w_2 + \ldots + w_n}$$

$$= \frac{\sum_{i=1}^{n} w_i \ln P_{t-i+1}}{\sum_{i=1}^{n} w_i}$$

Exponential smoothing is another form of a weighted moving average. It has the advantage of being simple to calculate, using only the last exponentially smoothed value E_{t-1} and a smoothing constant a to compute the new value. Formally, the exponential smoothing method is derived from a geometric progression applied to a weighted moving average, giving

$$E_t = (1 - a)P_t + aE_{t-1}$$

It is more popularly used as

$$E_t = E_{t-1} + a(P_t - E_{t-1})$$

An important feature of the exponentially smoothed moving average is that all data previously used are always part of the new result, although with diminishing significance.

DOUBLE EXPONENTIAL SMOOTHING

As a trend continues in its direction, the exponentially smoothed moving average will lag farther behind. By selecting a smoothing constant nearer to one the magnitude of this lag will be lessened, but it will still increase. If we consider the lag as the predictive error in our calculation, then

$$\epsilon_t = P_t - E_t \qquad \text{(error)}$$

where E_t is the exponential smoothing approximation of the price P_t. By applying the same exponential smoothing technique to the pattern of increasing or decreasing error we get

$$\Sigma_t = \Sigma_{t-1} + a(\epsilon_t = \Sigma_{t-1})$$

and then adding the difference between the original smoothing value and the double (second-order) smoothing back into the approximation:

$$EE_t = E_t + \Sigma_t$$

The effect of error due to lag will be corrected so that instead of the lag increasing it will decrease. This method can be extended to "third-order" smoothing as necessary.

RISK PREFERENCE

The *risk preference* or utility of an investor for a specific venture (a trade or general speculation) can be found by adding the expected value of the investor's utilities or preferences for the various outcomes of that event,

$$P = w_1p_1 + w_2p_2 + \ . \ . \ . \ + w_np_n, \ \sum w_i = 1$$

where there are n possible outcomes. The weighting factors may be the results of personal bias or may be the calculated probabilities of each outcome. For example, a gold trade has a likely potential profit of \$4,000 with a risk of \$1,500. We can adjust the reward values by dividing by 1,000. If the probability of success is 60%, then the total utility of the trade is

$$P(\text{trade}) = 0.60 \times 4 + 0.40 \times (-1.5) = 1.8$$

If the probability of success were increased the utility P would increase in a linear fashion. But investors do not feel the same about different rewards. Given a scale of 0–100 (negative to positive reaction), an investor may rank the example (a 60% chance of a \$4,000 profit with a 40% chance of a \$1,500 loss) as a 65. If we increase only the reward to \$8,000 the investor might raise the preference of the trade to 80 altbough the utility would be 4.2, more than twice as great.

The various patterns of a curve drawn through the computed utilities can show the risk preference of the individual. Figure 7 shows the curve formations which represent a progression from extreme risk aversion to extreme risk seeking. As the risk increases in (1) in the figure the trader is less likely to participate in the trade; in (3) there is equal chance of taking the trade at all risk levels; and, in (5) the trader is more likely to enter a trade that has higher risk.

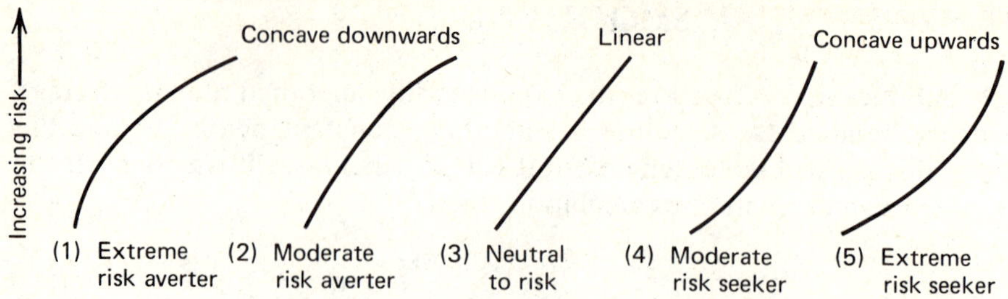

FIGURE 7. Investor utility curves. (*Source:* Teweles R. J. Teweles, C. V. Harlow, and H. L. Stone, *The Commodity Futures Game, Who Wins, Who Loses, Why?* McGraw-Hill, NY 1974. p. 133).

PROBABILITY OF SUCCESS AND RUIN

Probability theory is essential in analyzing the risk of trading. The probability or *risk of ruin* is normally expressed as

$$R = \left(\frac{1 - A}{1 + A}\right)^c$$

where $0 \leq R \leq 1$ and 0 indicates no risk and one certain ruin; $A = P - (1 - P)$; P is the proportion of winning trades, also considered the "trader's advantage"; and c is the beginning units of trading capital.

A system of trading which has 60% profitable trades and trading capital in \$10,000 units will have a risk of ruin calculated as follows:

$$A = 0.60 - (1 - 0.60) = 0.20$$

$$R = \left(\frac{1 - 0.20}{1 + 0.20}\right)^c = \left(\frac{0.80}{1.20}\right)^c = \left(\frac{1}{3}\right)^c$$

When $c = 1$ (\$10,000), R = 0.33 and when $c = 2$ (\$20,000), R = 0.11. Therefore the greater the "trader's advantage" or the greater the capital, the smaller the risk of ruin.

When dealing with profit goals, we may want to know the chance of ruin *before* achieving the goal. We can expect the results to show less chance of ruin than the unlimited case above and even smaller chances as the goal becomes smaller. The relationship can be expressed as

$$R = \frac{[(1 + A) / (1 - A)]^G - 1}{[(1 + A) / (1 - A)]^{c+G} - 1}, \quad 0 \leq R \leq 1$$

where all terms are the same as above and G is the goal units of trading capital.

WINS NOT EQUAL TO LOSSES. The basic equations just presented are generally applied to gambling situations, where the size of profits and losses are the same. This requires that the percentage of winning events to exceed the losing events in order to avoid ruin. Commodity trading, however, often results in more losing trades than profitable ones and must therefore return much *larger* profits

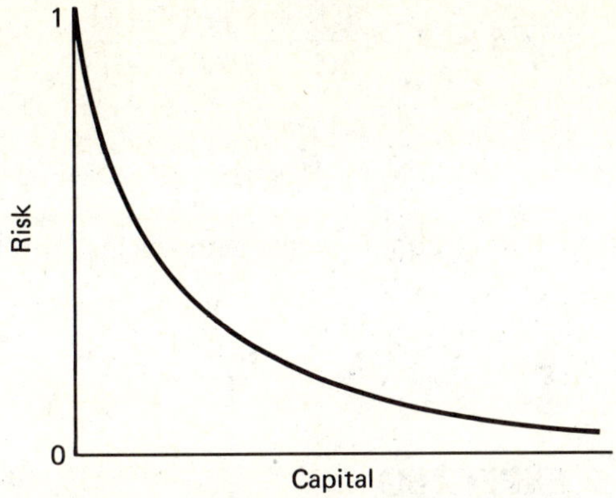

FIGURE 8. Risk of ruin based on capital.

than losses. This structure is common to all conservation of capital, or trend-following, systems. This situation can be applied to the more complex form[2]:

C_T = total capital available for trading (can be expressed in units)
C_R = cutoff point, where level of ruin is reached ($C_R < C_T$)
C_A = $C_T - C_R$, capital available to be risked
E = expected mean return per trade, the probability-weighted sum of values that a trade might take,

$$E \sum_{i}^{N} [(PL_i)\, p_i]$$

where PL_i is the possible profit or loss value and p_i is the probability of PL_i occurring ($0 < p_i < 1$)

E_2 = expected squared mean return per trade, the probability-weighted sum of all the squared values of a trade,

$$E_2 = \sum_{i}^{N} [(PL_i^2)\, p_i]$$

where PL_i and p_i are defined above,

$$D = C_A/\sqrt{E_2}$$

$$P = 0.5 + E/(2\sqrt{E_2})$$

and the *risk of ruin* is

$$R = \left(\frac{1 - P}{P}\right)^D$$

If we introduce an objective, a desired level of capital L, the *risk of ruin* R becomes

[2]F. Gehm, *Commodity Market Money Management, Wiley, New York, NY, 1983, pp. 142–143.*

$$R = 1 - \frac{[(1 - P)/P)^D - 1]}{[(1 - P)/P]^G - 1}$$

where

$$G = 1/\sqrt{E_2}$$

As in the first situation, using equal profits and losses, the risk increases as the objective L increases.

ACTUAL VERSUS EXPECTED

It is important to be able to evaluate the actual performance of a trading program against the simulated or expected performance. Remembering first that the more transactions the smaller the error and the more likely your performance analysis will be correct. The *chi-square* test is the basic method for comparing two sets of data,

$$\chi^2 = \sum_i^N \left(\frac{(O_i - E_i)^2}{E_i}\right)$$

where O_1 is the observed or actual results and E_i is the expected, simulated, or theoretic results corresponding to O_i, and there are N observations. Then χ^2 is the sum of the comparisons. The significance of the results χ^2 can be found in Table 1 since it is related to the number of observations. If χ^2 is equal or less than 5% it is considered *probably significant,* less than or equal to 1% is *significant,* and less than or equal to 1/10 of 1% is *highly significant*. The more *significant* the results, the less likely they occurred by chance.

TABLE 1. Distribution of χ^2

Cases	Probability of Occurring by Chance								
Less 1	0.70	0.50	0.30	0.20	0.10	0.05	0.02	0.01	0.001
1	0.15	0.46	1.07	1.64	2.71	3.84	5.41	6.64	10.83
2	0.71	1.39	2.41	3.22	4.61	5.99	7.82	9.21	13.82
3	1.42	2.37	3.67	4.64	6.25	7.82	9.84	11.34	16.27
4	2.20	3.36	4.88	5.99	7.78	9.49	11.67	13.28	18.47
5	3.00	4.35	6.06	7.29	9.24	11.07	13.39	15.09	20.52
6	3.83	5.35	7.23	8.56	10.65	12.59	15.03	16.81	22.46
7	4.67	6.35	8.38	9.80	12.02	14.07	16.62	18.48	24.32
8	5.53	7.34	9.52	11.03	13.36	15.51	18.17	20.09	26.13
9	6.39	8.34	10.66	12.24	14.68	16.92	19.68	21.67	27.88
10	7.27	9.34	11.78	13.44	15.99	18.31	21.16	23.21	29.59

SUPPLY AND DEMAND

Price is the balancing point of supply and demand. In order to estimate the future price of any product, or explain its historical patterns, it will be necessary to relate the factors of supply and demand and then adjust them using inflation indicators, technological improvement, and other elements common to econometric analysis. The following section briefly describes these factors.

DEMAND. The demand for a product declines as prices increase. The rate of decline is always dependent upon the need for the product and its available substitutes at different price levels. In general, as demand increases, prices increase as shown in Figure 9(*a*). D represents normal demand for a product over some fixed period. As prices rise, that demand declines fairly rapidly. D' shows greater demand, resulting in overall higher prices at all levels.

Figure 9(*b*) shows the demand relationship for potatoes for the years 1929–1939. In reality, the demand relationship is not a straight line shown in Figure 9, since production costs and demand limits prevent the curve from going to zero. On the other end of the scale, there is a lag in responding to higher prices and a consumer reluctance to reduce purchasing even at higher prices. Figure 10 shows a more representative demand curve, including extremes, where 100 represents the cost including the profit margin. The demand curve, therefore, shows the rate at which a change in quantity demanded brings about a change in price.

ELASTICITY OF DEMAND. Elasticity is an important concept in economics. It is the key factor in expressing the relationship between price and demand, a measurement of the relative change in demand as price changes,

$$E_D = \frac{\text{relative change (\%) in demand}}{\text{relative change (\%) in price}}$$

A market which always consumes the same amount of a product, regardless of price, will be called *inelastic;* as prices rise the demand remains the same and E_D is negatively very small. An *elastic* market is just the opposite. As demand increases, prices remain the same and E_D is negatively very large. Figure 11 shows the demand curve for various demand elasticities.

CHANGES IN SHORT-RUN DEMAND ELASTICITY. Demand changes gradually in response to a lasting change in price. Figure 12 shows an incremental process where the demand moves from highly inelastic (line A) to more elastic (line B). At price P_1 we find that line A represents an historic inelastic demand for a product that has always been in short supply. A permanent price change occurs due to a long-term increase in supply and prices decline to P_2 along line A to spur consumption. The points t_1, t_2, . . . represent the increased use of the product over time. As consumption adjusts to the new long-term demand line B it approaches at an increasingly slower rate.

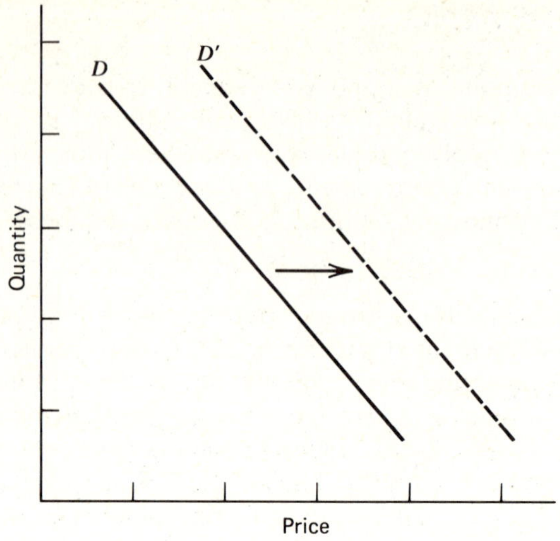

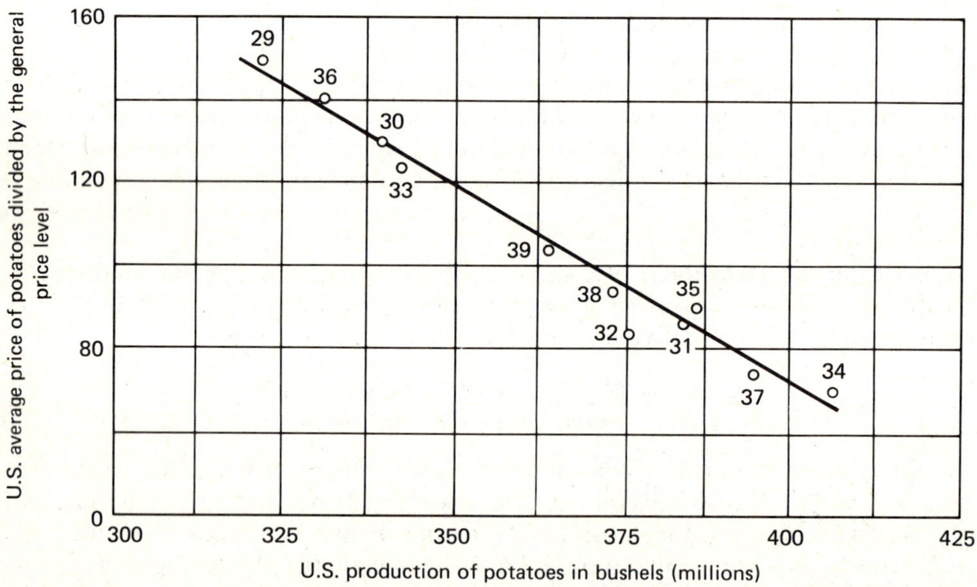

FIGURE 9. (*a*) Shift in demand. (*b*) Potatoes: U.S. average farm price on December 15th vs total production, 1929–1939. (*Source:* Geoffrey S. Shepherd, and G. A. Futrell, *Agricultural Price Analysis*, Iowa State Univ., Awes, IA, 1969. p. 53.)

SUPPLY. The supply side of the economic equation is the normal counterpart of demand. Figure 13(*a*) shows the relationship between price and quantity from the producer point of view.

As prices increase, the supplier will respond by offering significantly greater amounts of the product. Figure 13(*b*) shows the supply at price extremes. At low levels, below production costs, there is nominal supply by those producers who must maintain operations due to high fixed costs and difficulty restarting after a shutdown. At high-price levels supply is erratic. There may be insufficient supply

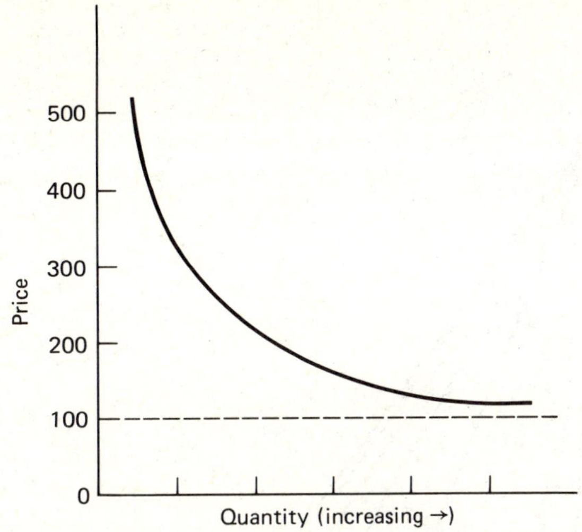

FIGURE 10. Demand curve, including extremes.

in the short term as shown in the figure, followed by the appearance of new supplies or substitutes. In most cases, however, it is demand that brings prices down.

ELASTICITY OF SUPPLY. The elasticity of supply E_S is the relationship between the change in supply and the change in price,

$$E_S = \frac{\text{relative change (\%) in supply}}{\text{relative change (\%) in price}}$$

It is the counterpart of *demand elasticity*. The elasticity of supply is a positive number since price and quantity should move in the same direction at the same time.

EQUILIBRIUM. The demand for a product and the supply of that product meet at a point of *equilibrium*. The current price of any commodity represents the point of equilibrium for that product at that moment in time. Figure 14 shows a constant demand line D and a shifting supply, increasing to the right from S to S′.

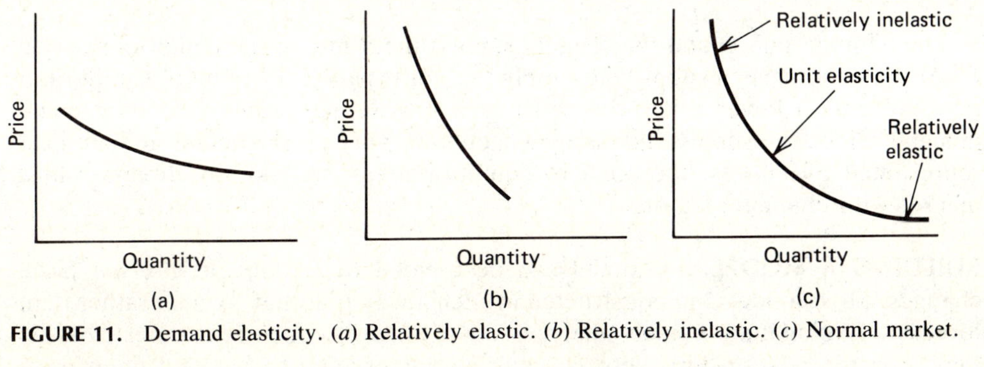

FIGURE 11. Demand elasticity. (*a*) Relatively elastic. (*b*) Relatively inelastic. (*c*) Normal market.

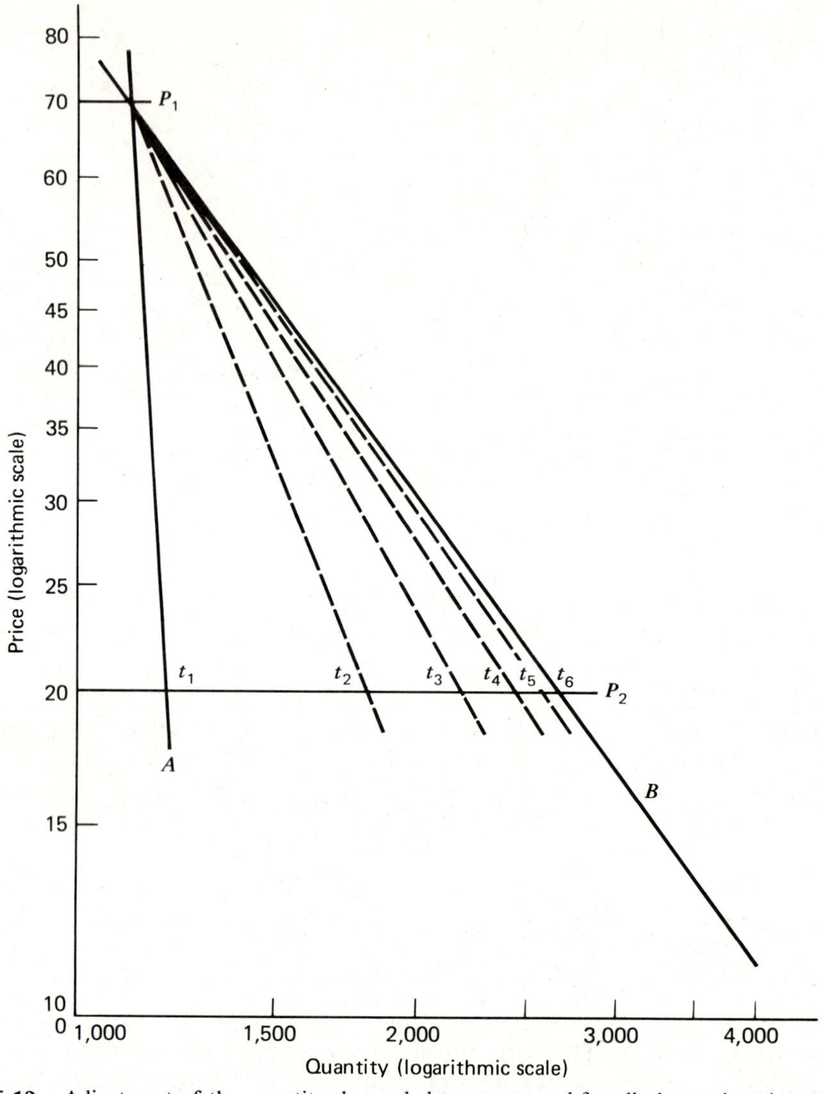

FIGURE 12. Adjustment of the quantity demanded to a once-and-for-all change in price. (*Source:* Shepherd, p. 72.)

The demand line D and the original supply line S met at the equilibrium price P; after the increase in supply the supply line shifts to S'. The point of equilibrium P' represents a lower price, the consequence of larger supply with unchanged demand. Since the supply and demand each have varying elasticities and are best represented by curves, the point of equilibrium can shift in any direction in a market with changing factors.

BUILDING A MODEL. A model can be created to *explain* or *forecast* price changes. Most models are constructed in such a way that they *explain* rather than forecast. Explanatory models analyze sets of data at concurrent times, that is, they look for relationships between multiple factors and their effect upon price

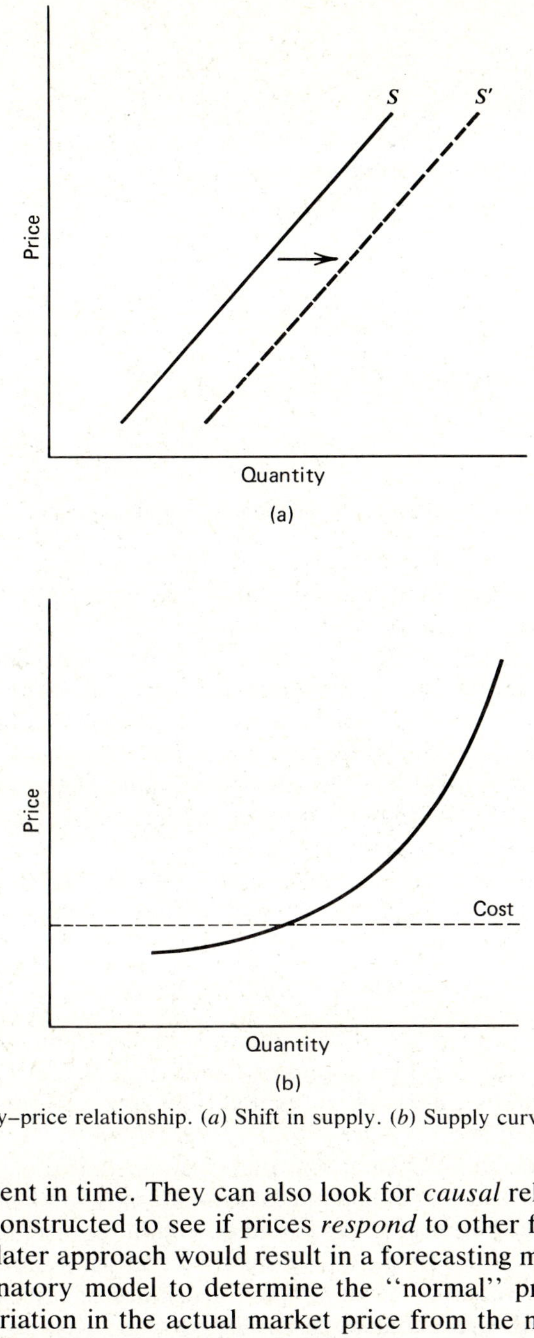

FIGURE 13. Supply–price relationship. (*a*) Shift in supply. (*b*) Supply curve, including extremes.

at the same moment in time. They can also look for *causal* relationships, that is, a model can be constructed to see if prices *respond* to other factors after one or more days. This later approach would result in a forecasting model. Is it possible to use the explanatory model to determine the "normal" price at a particular moment. Any variation in the actual market price from the normal or expected price could present trading opportunities, although not considered "forecasting."

The method of arriving at the best forecasting model can destroy its credibility. An *analytic* approach selects the factors and specifies the relationships in advance. Tests are then performed on the data to verify that the premise was correct. Many models, however, are refined by "fitting" the data using regression analysis or by "shotgun" testing, which applies a broad selection of weighting to the variables to find the best combination. These models are not necessarily "forecasting," but

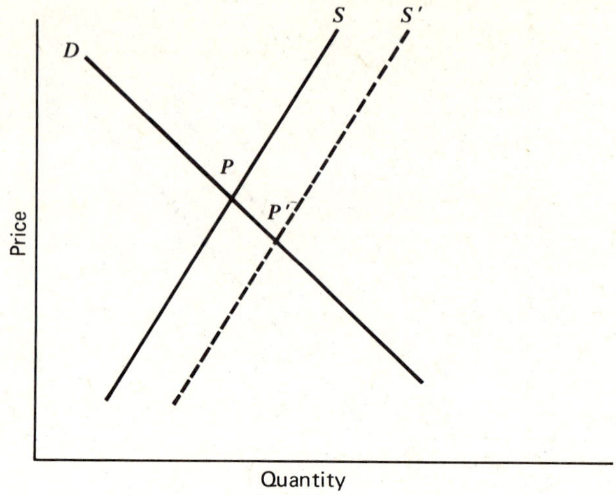

FIGURE 14. Equilibrium with shifting supply.

are definitely optimizing hindsight. Even an analytic approach that is subsequently "fine-tuned" could be in jeopardy of losing its forecasting qualities.

The factors which comprise a model can be both numerous and difficult to obtain. Figure 15 shows the interrelationship between factors in the cocoa industry. Although this chart is comprehensive in its intramarket relationships, it does not emphasize the global influences which have become a major part of price movement since the mid-1970s. The change in value of the U.S. dollar and the rapid rise of interest rates resulted in price changes that far outstripped normal "fundamental" factors for many commodities.

Models that explain price movements must be built from the primary factors of supply and demand. A simple example for estimating the price of fall potatoes[3] is

$$\mathrm{P/PPI} = a + bS + cD$$

where P is the average price of fall potatoes received by farmers; PPI is the Producer Price Index; S is the apparent domestic free supply (production less exports and diversions); D is the estimated deliverable supply; and a, b, and c are constants determined by regression analysis.

We can conclude that consumption must be constant (i.e., inelastic demand) for this model to work, since demand factors are only implicitly included in the estimated deliverable supply. Exports and diversion represent a small part of the total production. The use of the PPI gives the results in *relative* terms based on whether the index was used as an *inflator* or *deflator* of prices.

A general model, presented by Weymar[4] may be written as three behavior equations and one identity:

[3]J. D. Schwager, "A Trader's Guide to Analyzing the Potato Futures Market," *1981 Commodity Yearbook*, Commodity Research Bureau, Incorporated, New York, NY.

[4]F. H. Weymar, *The Dynamics of the World Cocoa Market*, MIT Press, Cambridge, MA, 1968.

1. Consumption: $C_t = f_c(P_t, P^L{}_t) + e_{C_t}$
2. Production: $H_t = f_H(P_t, P^L{}_t) + e_{H_t}$
3. Inventory: $I_t = I_{t-1} + H_t - C_t$
4. "Supply of storage": $P'_t - P_t = f_P(I_t) + e_P$

where C is the consumption, P is the price, P^L is the lagged price, H is the

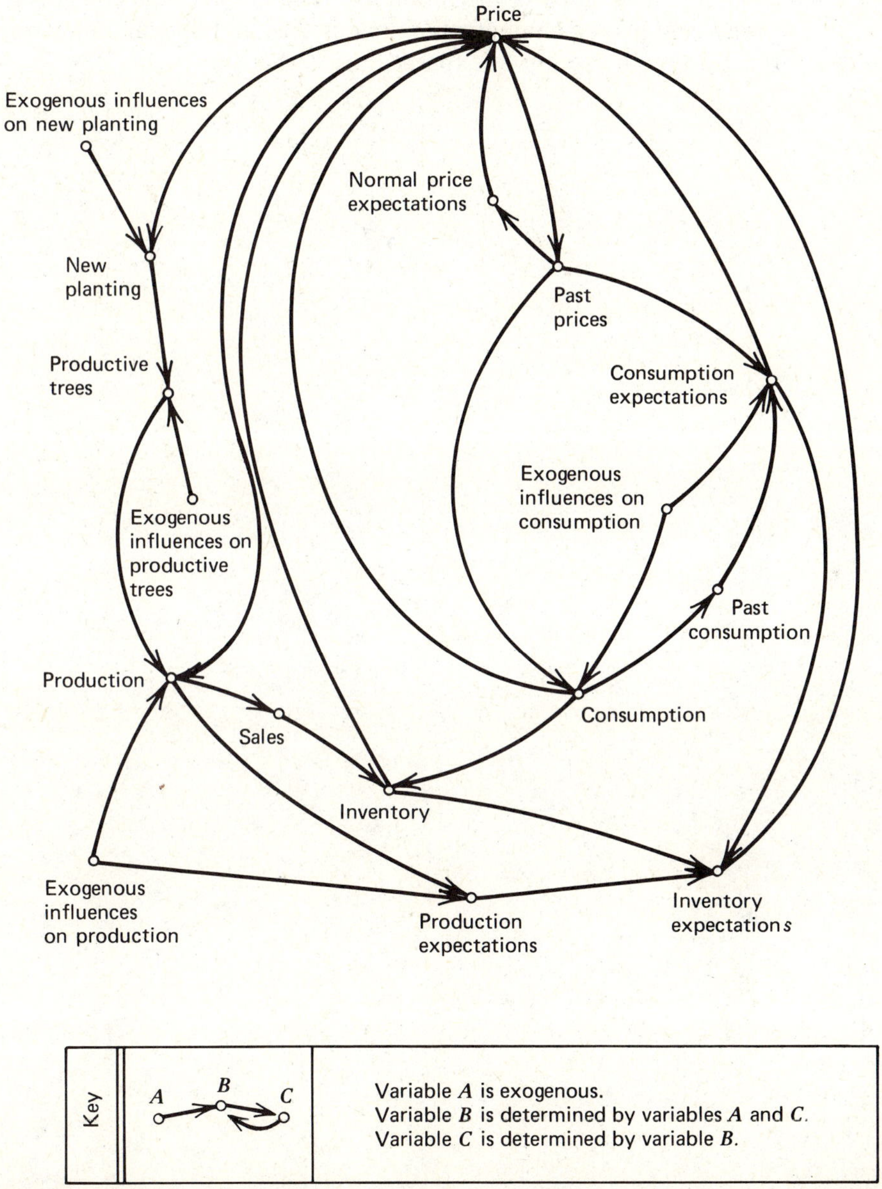

FIGURE 15. Cocoa factors. (*Source:* F. N. Waymar, *The Dynamics of the World Cocoa Market*, MIT Press, Cambridge, MA, 1968. p. 2.)

production (harvest), I is the inventory, P' is the expected price at some point in the future, and e is the corresponding error factors.

The first two equations show that both demand and supply depend on current and/or lagged price, the traditional microeconomic theory; this means that production and consumption are dependent on past prices. The third equation, inventory level, is simply the total of previous inventories plus new production less current consumption. The last equation represents the "supply of storage." This means that people are willing to carry larger inventories if they expect prices to increase substantially. The inventory function itself, equation (3), is composed of two separate relationships—manufacturer's inventories and speculator's inventories; each react quite differently to expected price change.

CHAPTER **18**

THE COMPUTER IN A COMMODITY FUTURES ENVIRONMENT: UNDERSTANDING, SELECTING, AND USING COMPUTERS

CONTENTS

DEVELOPMENT OF THE COMPUTER INDUSTRY 5

Computer Hardware 5
Computer Software 9
Development Costs 10
Futures Market Development 11
Our Dependence on Computers 13

HARDWARE CONSIDERATIONS 13

Time Sharing 14
Minicomputers 16
Microcomputers 19
Making the Hardware Decision 22

DATABASES AND SERVICES 26

Fundamental Data 27
Technical Data 28
Comparing Data Vendors 30
Database Management 32
Fulfilling Data Needs 35

COMPUTER APPLICATIONS IN THE FUTURES MARKETS 36

COMMUNICATIONS APPLICATIONS 37

Trading Applications 40
Analytical Applications 43
Accounting Applications 49
Making the Computer Work for You 51

IMPACT ON TRADING 53

APPENDIX: CATALOG OF COMMERCIAL SERVICES 56

Part 1: Category Listing 56
Part 2: Alphatbetical Listing 60

CHAPTER 18

THE COMPUTER IN A COMMODITY FUTURES ENVIRONMENT: UNDERSTANDING, SELECTING, AND USING COMPUTERS

David Handmaker

The capabilities of computer technology have broadened at exponential rates over the past three decades. What was nearly unimaginable in the 1940s and 1950s is now commonplace. In the 20th century we have watched regular data processing equipment progress from cumbersome mechanical adding machines to single-function processors the size of a city block to programmable calculators that fit in a shirt pocket and microcomputers that sit on a typewriter table. Even still we will continue to see rapid expansion in computer sciences—so rapid, that keeping aware of current developments would be a full-time occupation.

In this chapter we will look at how the developments in computing technology have been relevant to the commodity futures industry. We will discuss the differences in *hardware* and *software* capabilities and how their relationships have changed. After providing a layperson's comprehensive view in these areas, we will deal with the available applications of computers in the futures industry for trading, accounting, and analysis. The reader will then be equipped to make rational decisions as to how to use *computers* effectively in specific daily business operations.

Two distinct areas of computer usage are *information processing* and *information transmission*. Because the main reason for computers is in dealing with information, it is necessary to be concerned not only with handling data, but also with moving information or transmitting information from computer to computer. The evolution of the computer age, or information age, is a function of man's need to know, know now, and know all. Once having supplied a computer with information that can be transmitted and stored, analysis can be performed through information processing. Almost any rigorous decision-making process can be facilitated by quantitative, systematic computer analysis.

Today the uses of computers are so diverse that they show up in many areas. From information transmission and analysis to simulation and robotics, the wide-ranging effects of the computer age have changed the nature of our lives. Although it may be hard to say which came first, the massive quantities of information needing to be processed or the capability to do the processing, our governmental, industrial, and financial structures are all now based at least in some way on a foundation of computer technology.

As the capabilities in the field of computer science have grown over time, the main obstacle to their even greater penetration of our lives has been our widespread difficulty in accepting them. Despite this barrier, however, the popularity of computers has increased so that many homes now have computers used frequently by each family member. In the past the use of computers was confined to academicians and pure scientists, who conceptualized and engineered computers for computers' sake. Now, with all the different types of computer systems, we all have at least some ways we could benefit from electronic processing at work and at home. The growth in the applications of computers has made further growth faster, broader, and increasingly useful.

In the 1950s and 1960s computers were limited in capacity, usually allowing only a one-on-one computer-to-user relationship. Use of the computer was limited to the programmers and the operators. As applications became more complex, and computer languages were developed in the mid-1960s, it became possible to have many different users of one machine with a computer operator between the end users and the computer. In the 1970s *time sharing* was popularized, allowing multiple, interactive simultaneous users. Since the late 1970s the trend has been reversed towards *distributed processing* with fewer and fewer users to each computer. In fact, current microprocessor technology has taken us full circle back to a one-on-one relationship with the now well-known personal computer.

Most of us became familiar with computers and their applications through the time-sharing era. In time sharing, each user of the computer pays for however much capacity he or she needs on a large computer system which supports hundreds of simultaneous applications. Time sharing, provided by *computer service bureaus,* allows even the smallest-scale user to take advantage of significant economies of scale. The first popular computers were so massive and required such tremendous maintenance expenses that very few individuals could afford their own. Further, the vast majority of the original computer users had no need for all of the processing power available on a single machine. As computers have become smaller and less expensive, the concept of distributed or even independent processing has become a reality, replacing time sharing for many uses. There are now microcomputers and minicomputers in wide use in most large corporations, allowing accounting and research staffs to each have the same computing power previously available only through time sharing. Interfacing the small computers with a larger central machine, *distributed processing* technology signifies the acceptance of a true computer network for decision support and information handling. The current technology wave of independent processing on microcomputers has brought us power similar to that of the original behemoth computers, but requiring no more space or maintenance expenses than an electric typewriter.

Obviously, as all of the growth in computer technology has led to increased breadth of applicability, many of the changes have altered the environment of the commodity futures markets. The markets are now larger and more popular, requiring sophisticated means of information transmission, management and processing. Through this chapter we will cover computer industry developments, hardware considerations, and specific applications relevant to the commodity futures industry. We will discuss how to use computers in the markets, how to choose a computer or application, and what has been and will be the impact of this rapidly growing, high value-added scientific industry. To aid readers in making intelligent choices between all the various hardware and software, appendixes will catalog and detail many of the currently available commercial computer services and their applications in the futures markets. Throughout the chapter the effort will be made to use concepts and terminology which are easy to understand. The intent will be to equip the noncomputer professional with sufficient, not exhaustive, information about the industry. While the speed of technological advancements necessitates that any such chapter may be out of date by the time of printing, this chapter will be general enough to remain true and relevant, yet specific enough to provide valuable fundamental information.

DEVELOPMENT OF THE COMPUTER INDUSTRY

Commercial computers have changed our lives dramatically in the past 30 years. Today at least some aspects of the daily lives of each of us are affected by computers directly or indirectly. In the current age of rapid transmission and processing of voluminous data, we are all dependent on the maintenance and continued growth of computer technology. The introduction of E-COM (Electronic Computer Originated Mail) by the U.S. Postal Service in January 1982, although by no means innovative, is a cornerstone marking the legitimacy of a new age.

Although we are all familiar with computer-dependent services such as the news wires, it is not always immediately apparent that the commodity futures markets would come to a complete halt without computers. One of the main functions served by the futures markets, that of price discovery, would be almost meaningless in today's markets without rapid information transmission capabilities. The Chicago Board of Trade's *Computer Price Reporting System (CPRS),* for example, accepts floor transactions at the rate of 160 per minute, then processes and transmits the information to wallboards, tickers, and video displays within seconds. Before transmission, all transaction information is checked for validity and adherence to regulations, then recorded for future inquiry. Through news and wire services receiving this information, millions more receive a retransmission so that seconds after any given trade, individuals at all points of the country are aware of trading activity in the exchange pits. All of today's commodity futures exchanges utilize systems similar to the CBT's CPRS for price reporting, and everyone who is active in the markets is somewhat dependent on these networks.

Advances in computing technology for the futures markets range in applicability from reporting and accounting to analysis and forecasting. Each of these developments is an outgrowth of the separate innovations in hardware and software. In this section we will touch on the technological histories of both of these areas.

COMPUTER HARDWARE. *Hardware* is the physical machinery used for handling information, that is, the computer. This is distinguished from *software*—the commands which instruct the computer to perform functions. There are different types of hardware for storing, processing, and transmitting or receiving data. Over the years, advances in computer hardware technology have brought efficiencies not only in purchase price, but also in the costs of maintenance and usage. The achievement of these economies resulted from one revolutionary development after another in hardware design and microscopic circuitry. One of the first commercial computers, a UNIVAC I, was installed in 1951 at the Bureau of Census. It was the size of a large building because the thousands of internal circuits were made up of electronic tubes. These tubes generated such heat when being used that a complex cooling system was necessary throughout the machine's structure. Through the inventions in microscopic circuit technology, computers have been designed so that the same memory capacity and processing power are possible with much smaller machines. Although some of the popular microcomputers of today are nearly as powerful as their earliest ancestors, like the UNIVAC I, they occupy less than 0.001 of the space, cost less by a similar factor, and require minimal maintenance.

It used to be that housing a computer required an entire building, constructed with careful attention to design for temperature and humidity control, security, and sophisticated wiring, emergency electricity, and cooling networks. Shipping or delivering a computer was a major undertaking due to the machine's shear size and extreme fragility. It took months to assemble a computer and bring it to full functionality and then took continuing costly efforts to maintain smooth running procedures. The power requirements of the old computers were significant as were the costs of the personnel to program and maintain them. Although the salaries of programming and operating personnel have increased, thereby adding to the costs of software development, almost all of the costs associated with physical hardware have dropped drastically as smaller and smaller computers have been made a reality. The most popular computers of today are the *personal computers*. There are now millions of these computers in use in the United States and the number is climbing daily. Small computers priced below $2,000, although barely imagined before 1975, have created a new market which has grown from $65 million in 1977 to over $1 billion in 1982. In the same time the percentage of computers in use represented by personal computers has gone from under 1% to nearly 50%. These personal computers are small enough to sit on a desktop, require no more sophisticated maintenance or power supply than a typewriter, and acquiring one is as simple as the purchase of a stereo system.

Because the computers of the 1960s and early 1970s were so large and expensive, time sharing was the only popular means of obtaining computing resources. Before there was *time sharing,* the most common use of computers was through *batch processing,* a technique through which computer users specified their applications on paper, clerks keypunched the information on machine-readable cards to be input to the computer, and the user's output was available the next day at the earliest. Through time sharing, interactive computer use was realized. Any time-sharing user could sit at a terminal similar to a typewriter keyboard, enter applications directly, and get almost immediate results. The most significant impact of time sharing was that it made computers more useful by drastically lowering turnaround time and thereby greatly broadening the range of applications.

The *minicomputer,* first introduced by Digital Equipment Corporation in the early 1960s, revolutionized the hardware industry by fitting the space, budgets, and operating procedures of small businesses. Through minicomputer technology the same in-house processing capacities which had required multimillion-dollar investments before became available for only tens of thousands of dollars. These

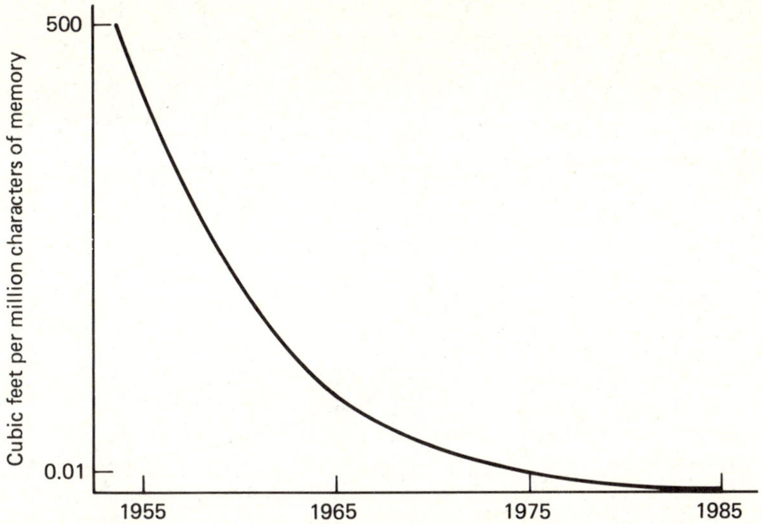

FIGURE 1. The amount of physical space required for computer memory circuits has continuously decreased with advancing technology. With the promising development of biosynthesized circuitry, this trend will continue. 1953 = 500; 1955 = 400; 1965 = 100; 1971 = 8; 1973 = 0.5; 1978 = 0.3; 1979 = 0.1; 1985 = 0.05. (*Source:* "The Waves of Change," Charles Lecht and author's estimates.)

minicomputers allow multiple, interactive usage and can match the power of much larger computers in executing computations, so that most of the advantages of time sharing on a mainframe computer can be obtained with much more manageable cost structures. As minicomputers increased in popularity through the 1970s, the concept of distributed data processing became a reality. Distributed data processing, the result of further developments in communications software and hardware, permits each department in one firm to have its own microcomputer or minicomputer designed and programmed for its individual needs, while each of these independent computer users can communicate with other departments through a central machine, or use a larger central computer for more complicated tasks.

The developments in microcircuitry have made use of computers not only affordable, but a requirement of any size commercial operation. For less than the cost of a new car, any business entity can now utilize the powers of computers without worrying about the variable costs of time sharing. Through the advent of increasingly smaller, more personal computing facilities, the reliability of computers also has been significantly increased. It used to be necessary to bring the large time-sharing computers out of service regularly in order to execute tests, perform maintenance, and make repairs. During these times the computers could not support user applications. Now the popular microcomputers stand ready for the user almost all of the time. Even those computers which support multiple, interactive users are far more reliable than their predecessors. Some of the current minicomputers, such as the DEC VAX Systems and the Tandem Non-Stop Systems are built based on multiprocessor technology with backup facilities enabling user support with almost no interruptions. Increases in dependability have been so great that many manufacturers have eliminated periodic scheduled preventative maintenance.

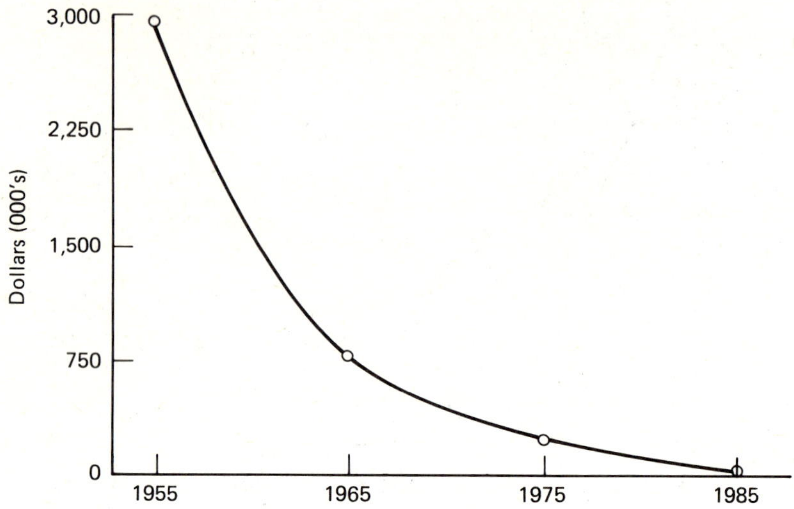

(*a*) Average computer price

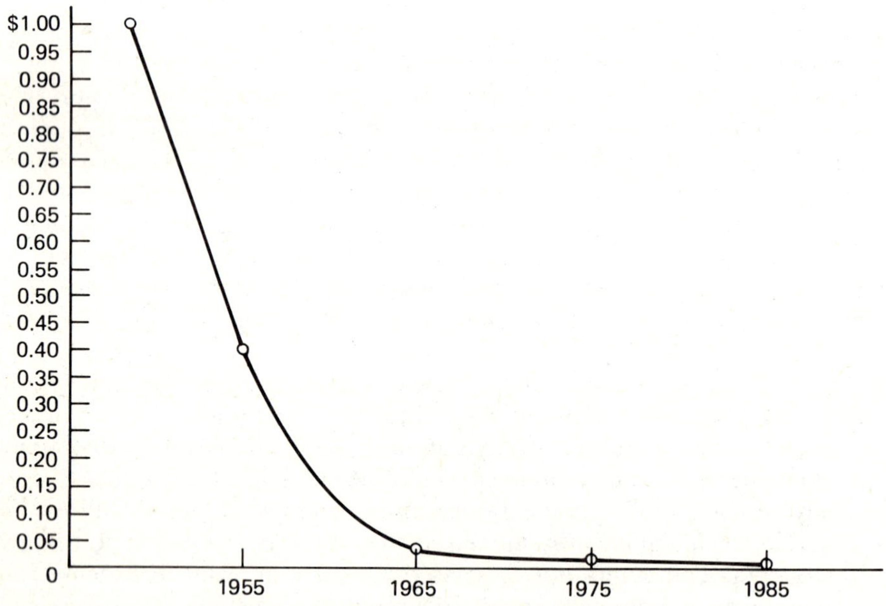

(*b*) Processor cost per 100,000 computations

FIGURE 2. Due to falling prices and greater performance capabilities, the costs of processor capacity have dropped dramatically. (*a*) 1953 = 3,000,000; 1955 = 2,900,000; 1960 = 1,200,000; 1965 = 800,000; 1970 = 500,000; 1975 = 1977 = 100,000; 1979 = 50,000; 1981 = 10,000; 1985 = 2,000. (*b*) 1953 = 0.90; 1955 = 0.40; 1960 = 0.10; 1965 = 0.03; 1970 = 0.01; 1975 = 0.004; 1980 = 0.002; 1985 = 0.001. (*c*) 1955 = 20; 1960 = 40; 1965 = 100; 1970 = 500; 1975 = 2,000; 1980 = 5,000; 1985 = 10,000. (*Source:* "The Waves of Change," Charles Lecht and author's estimates.)

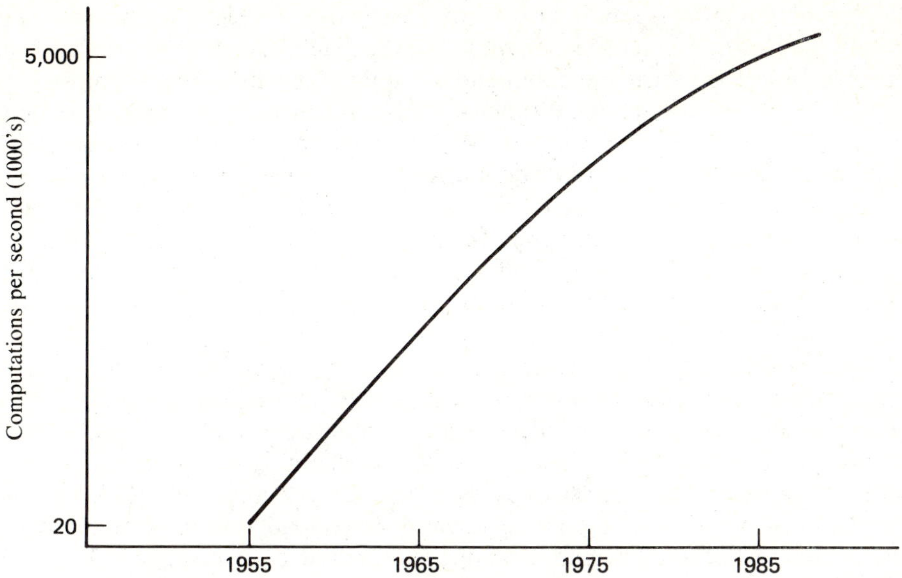

(*c*) Processor performance in 1000's of computations per second

FIGURE 2. Continued.

COMPUTER SOFTWARE. The computer hardware, comprising only an ordered collection of metal, wires, silicon, and other physical materials, is of course useless without *computer software*—the programs that make the machine run. Using software the computer can be instructed to perform operations by turning on and off thousands of internal switches. Having described generally the developments in hardware, we will now look at the evolution of software, and how the combined advances have made the commodity futures markets of today possible.

There was no software as we know it today on the UNIVAC I installed at the Bureau of Census in 1951. Programming was at a primitive stage in the early 1950s. The only way of providing a computer with instructions was through "machine language," a tedious ordering of numbers and letters identifying each datum and instruction within the computer. The impetus to the development of software was the need for regularly recurring and common calculations, but the investment incentive for software development did not yet exist. Creating software required the resources of training not only in the uses of computers, but also in their engineering design. As computers became more popular, the need for standard, comprehensive software was even greater. At this early stage, however, it was mostly scientists using computers who shared an interest in software development to avoid frequent duplication of efforts. The business applications, and therefore demand, for computers were too limited to encourage commercial investment in programming. It was only through societies of scientific computer users that standard, general programming conventions and techniques were eventually developed. Two distinct areas of software development are computer languages and operating systems.

The two main types of computer languages are *assemblers* and *compilers*. The earliest computer languages, the assemblers, convert symbolic instructions (alphabetic and numeric symbols and words, each one representing a prescribed sequence of machine language commands) into machine language. Because assemblers generally require one command per unique machine operation, they are peculiar to a specific machine. While assemblers can be complex and tedious, they allow the most effective use of their respective machines and the fastest execution of computations. Until the mid-1950s there had to be different assemblers for every type of computer and usually slightly altered versions for each installation. Assemblers are known as *lower level languages* in that they are very close to the machine. Each step higher in language levels decreases the number of commands for a given computation, but removes the user one step further from the processing hardware.

Compilers were developed to translate questions to machine code. Because there are many instructions common to almost all applications, there has always been an interest in language compilers. The first notable compiler was FORTRAN (FORmula TRANslator), developed to facilitate algebraic formula translation in the late 1950s. Over time, increasingly sophisticated versions of FORTRAN were released and other language compilers were developed through the 1950s and 1960s, such as COBOL (COmmon Business Oriented Language), ALGOL (ALGOrithmic Language), PL/1 (Programming Language 1), BASIC (Beginner's All-purpose Symbolic Instruction Code), APL (A Programming Language), and LISP (LISt Processing Language). As suggested by some of their names, each of these high-level languages was developed with particular applications in mind. They differ not only in terms of their best uses, but also in terms of their verbosity, or how many commands the user must type to executive a given computation.

Operating systems are to a computer what the human brain is to the body. Data handling, storage and retrieval, input and output, and allocation of the computer's internal resources are handled by operating systems. Operating systems were designed to reduce turnaround time by automating procedures previously performed by computer operators. They effectively teach the computer to manage its own resources and operating functions.

In the same way that the higher-level languages compile particular, frequent commands and translate them into machine language, there are software applications packages that are one step further removed from the computer, but through their design for very specific uses, require fewer commands per distinct instruction. *Applications packages* are collections of preprogrammed commands using easy-to-understand concepts designed for a particular purpose. Some of these packages facilitate processes in data file maintenance, storage and retrieval, technical analysis and graphics, screening and sorting data, or accounting and back-office settling, for example. Because most packages are designed for particular applications, they can be very easy to use. The more general the package's capabilities, the more complex it is to use as there are more commands with which the user must become familiar. The various levels of computer languages can be represented in the spectrum format in Figure 3. The ultimate sophistication in computer languages is represented in Figure 3 by the concept DWIW, a single command standing for "do what I want."

DEVELOPMENT COSTS. Expansion in the field of computer science was hindered by a "Catch-22" for years. Because there used to be very few people or companies with perceived needs for computers, little incentive existed to invest

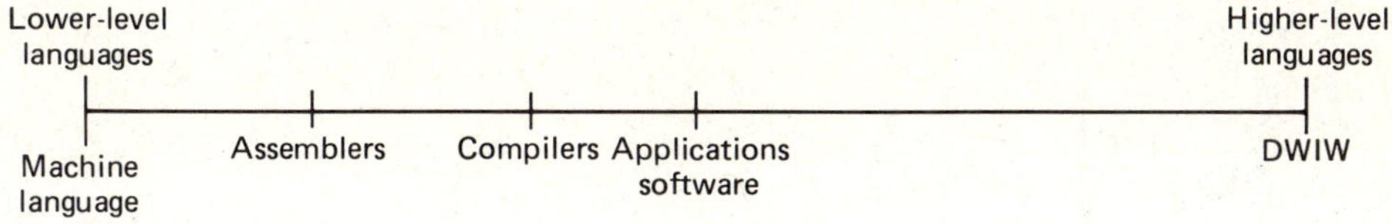

FIGURE 3. Computer language spectrum.

in the development of commonly applicable computer software. As hardware costs came down, and software developments began to grow, the feasible applications of computers came to cover a wider range and became useful in more and more industry sectors. In fact, since the early 1950s, the decreasing hardware costs and wider availability of applicable software have brought the cost of a constant computation down by magnitudes exceeding thousands. This has occurred despite the fact that software development costs, comprised mainly of the salaries of programmers, have increased dramatically. The market for program design professionals still remains one of short supply. As more and more programmers are trained, and more of the population becomes familiar with computers, we may see a decrease in the percentage of computer usage costs made up by software. Even now there are schools and universities which require courses in programming the same way that courses are required in expository writing skills. The day is approaching when almost all of us will be able to program a computer, either through a deeper understanding of computers or through easier-to-use software, and that day will bring even lower average costs for a given application.

FUTURES MARKET DEVELOPMENT. The historical changes in the cost structure of computer usage have made computers much more useful for industries such as the rapidly paced futures markets. Through the advent of broadly applicable programming languages, and especially interactive usage, there have been opportunities for programmers and users to specialize in particular applications areas. Previously only computer engineers programmed, but now since programmers need not intimately know hardware design and architecture it is feasible for someone trained in futures markets to program a computer for specific purposes. For this reason, and because there is now a market for computing resources broad enough to provide profit incentives for software development, there are now commercially available applications packages for any kind of market analysis or industry-specific use. There are time-sharing services designed for fundamental and technical analyses, commercial data bases of commonly needed information, and particular services offering preprogrammed applications available for use on microcomputers.

Companies have grown and become specialists in the use of computers in the futures industry, so that in addition to service bureaus and software shops, there are also programming and systems consultants that specialize in complete systems for particular applications in the futures markets. Most larger brokerage offices now use distributed processing systems for all of their back-office operations, such as breaking down block trades, crediting and debiting client accounts, computing commissions, and other tedious chores which must be performed in a timely fashion. In using these systems, not only can the firms eliminate the need for clerks, typists, and machine operators, but accounting errors can be detected as

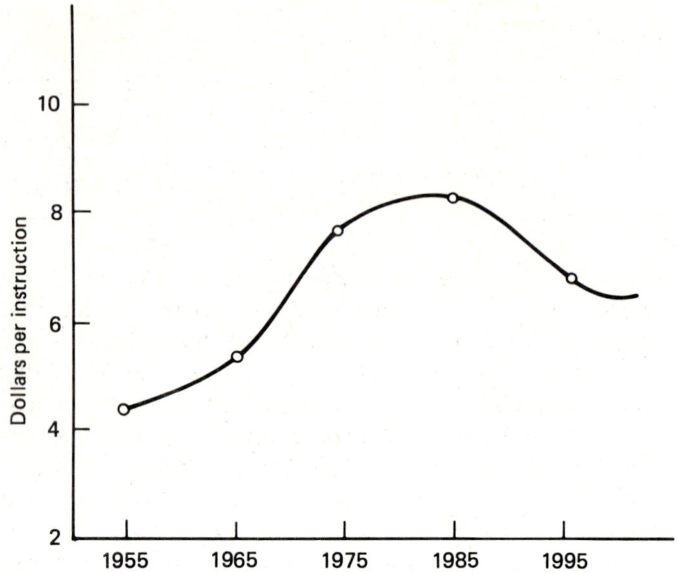

FIGURE 4. As the complexity of software has increased, so has the development cost. Increasingly sophisticated software, which will allow any computer user to write programs, along with a greater and more widely spread knowledge of computers, will reverse this trend in the future. (*Source:* "The Waves of Change," Charles Lecht and author's estimates.)

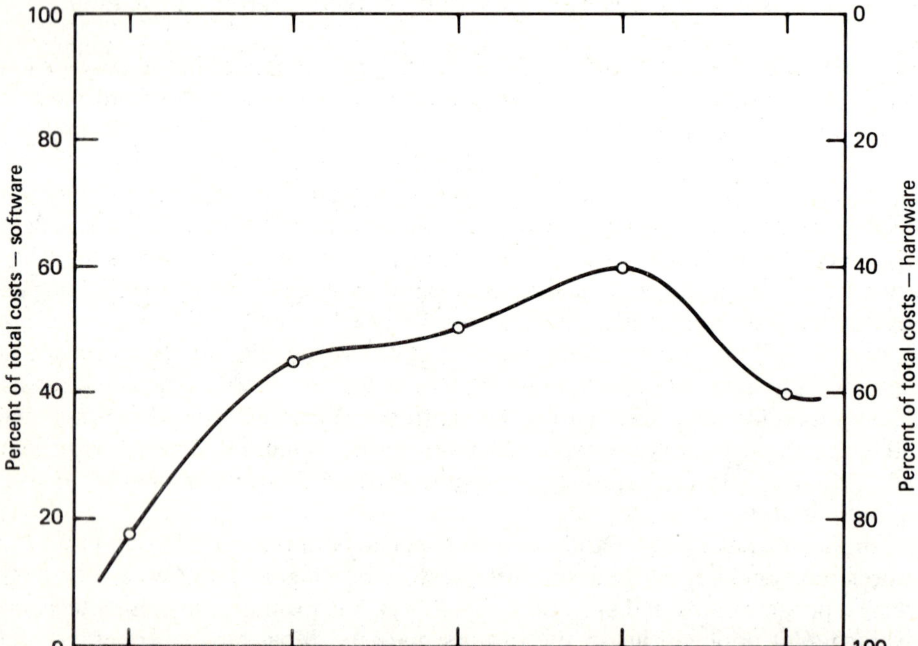

FIGURE 5. More complicated software and less expensive hardware have brought the percent of total costs made up by software higher and higher. This trend will reverse as the market for computer systems becomes more and more of a consumer-oriented market, wherein software development expenses are spread over hundreds and thousands of users' systems. (*Source:* "The Waves of Change," Charles Lecht and author's estimates.)

transactions are entered. Since brokers can sometimes directly input the information to the computer, the time gap between trade occurrence and accounting can also be narrowed and almost closed. Other computer systems have been in use for the price reporting functions performed by the exchanges, such as the Chicago Board of Trade's CPRS (Computer Price Reporting System) mentioned earlier. Systems providing trading support for futures professionals have also been designed, allowing for computer testing and implementation of buy/sell algorithms, portfolio management, accounting and reporting, margin requirement fulfillments, and other information processing needs which have to receive immediate and constant attention.

OUR DEPENDENCE ON COMPUTERS. The futures industry would have never been able to support the current volumes of trading without the computer systems that we have discussed. Not only would the absence of computers prevent the performance of functions by futures exchanges and brokerage houses, but such an absence would seriously diminish the means for analyzing and forecasting market activity, thereby discouraging some individuals from any participation in the futures markets.

We will continue to see a deeper penetration of the futures markets by computer technology. Soon there will be no need for brokers to leave their homes. To save on office space, brokerage firms will supply their account executives with home facilities for keeping apprised of market activity, computer systems for analyzing prices, and complete communications capabilities for transacting trades and generating the appropriate reports at the central office. There is already an attempt to eliminate the trading pit with the development of *INTEX*, a wholly computer-run futures exchange. When traders purchase a seat on the INTEX exchange, they receive a computer terminal and are assigned an account on a time-sharing system, so that instead of trading with hand signals and open outcry, transactions are completed with keystrokes and bid/ask entries to the computer network.

For many the computerization of the commodity futures industry is an unsettling development. Much of the personal quality of the markets will unquestionably be lost as the trading moves from an exchange floor to a central processing unit. As well, when the prevalence of computer-generated trading signals becomes overwhelming, there will no longer be the well-known seat-of-the-pants, intuitive, hunch-trading hero of the past. The widespread use of computers in trading analysis will result in much faster trading in which all of us will need the aid of a computer merely to keep pace in the markets. Therefore, in time, a general knowledge of applications of computer technology in the futures markets becomes increasingly important to all participants.

HARDWARE CONSIDERATIONS

Broad ranges of options and costs are associated with the current computer technology. Recent developments have made electronic data processing, especially the computer hardware, affordable to all. From 8-bit microcomputers to 32-bit mainframes, there are now so many different machines that choosing the foundation of a shop for computer analysis and accounting can be a difficult task. It used to be that for a given application there were only a few computers to choose from based on the software each supported. Today nearly any processing procedure can be carried out on a number of machines and the first choice becomes one of the computer hardware's size, cost, and speed. Depending on how many uses and users you have for a computer, the magnitude of processing you will be needing, and what responsibilities and costs you are prepared to bear, it may be appropriate to buy or lease a mainframe (a large-scale machine) or minicomputer, to time share on someone else's system, or to buy one or more personal computers. The choice between different hardware suppliers is one that must be made with an allowance for change. Because expansions in hardware capability are so rapid and because an individual's or a company's needs can change, any decision to purchase hardware must be made with attention to flexibility for growing and taking advantage of new technological innovations. We will look at the pros and cons of different hardware options in this section and make the necessary distinctions between size and power capacities in order to lay the foundation for rationally and confidently deciding on the most appropriate choice of hardware for particular operations.

TIME SHARING. During the 1960s and 1970s when commercial data processing became widespread, the only feasible venue for satisfying medium-scale processing needs was through *time sharing*. Because of the computers' sheer size and maintenance requirements, it was necessary to have computer service bureaus which would effectively rent time on the computer to many different users, charging them varying amounts depending on their usage. Although the time-sharing vendors often had specific, internal processing needs, they could not afford to maintain the computers on their own nor had they any need for all of one machine's computing powers. Time sharing is still a common practice today due to the user's scale economies attainable through being one of a community, instead of an individual. While today's company of almost any size can afford at least a small computer, time sharing affords the user resources otherwise unreachable due to the cost or complexity of large individual systems.

Time-sharing Costs. To use the time-sharing services of almost any vendor involves two types of costs excluding those associated with the personnel who will be employed to use the computer service. One of these costs is equivalent to a subscription fee, usually charged annually, payable in installments. Payment of this fee buys the subscriber an account on the computer and is required before taking advantage of any of the vendor's offerings. Once having established an account, the user will incur variable costs by using the computer facilities. Different vendors charge in different ways for variable factors, such as the amount of time the user is logged on to the computer, the computer resources used, use of peripherals such as graphic plotters or high-speed printers, and other components of the bureau's service.

Data Storage on Time-sharing Systems. For storing data or programs, the vendors will rent space on their tapes and disks. This allows users to have their own data within reach of the time-sharing system. Although time-sharing users customarily store all privately gathered data and written programs on the vendor's media along with many other users, the risk of these files getting into the wrong hands can be kept to a minimum. Almost all time-sharing vendors have installed operating systems which ensure that user accounts can be accessed only through the correctly input sequence of an account identifier, a secret password, and a project identifier. The only individuals who could access the user's account without this ordered procedure are the vendor's computer operators and some of the programmers, who hardly have time to search and search through accounts of files looking for valuable information. Users can exercise extra caution by naming secret files with titles that are not obvious. For instance, a program which contains your proprietary, optimal trading rule should not be titled as "BIGMONEYMAKER," but "FILE99" or something equally obscure. Most vendors also offer a program which will encipher a file so that it cannot be read or translated without the use of a secret password. The probability of having your private data and programs maliciously damaged or stolen on a time-sharing system is slim, and through proper caution can be reduced to almost none. Except for internal corporate disloyalty in your own shop or an intricate ring of sophisticated computer criminals, your worst enemy in protecting private computer files is carelessness. On most operating systems, files can be locked or mistakenly left unlocked, you or your own employees can be strict or lax on password secrecy, and other private information can be treated cautiously or recklessly.

As for accidental damage to files stored on the time-sharing vendor's media, there is also little danger. Most vendors create periodic tape backups of all information stored by users on disks so that the most work that can be lost is work completed since the last backup was made. These tapes are normally made at weekly or higher frequencies and stored in safe conditions. Often the vendor maintains an additional backup in a completely different location so that neither disk failure, electrical blackout, fire, nor flood can hopelessly destroy the valuable information users have stored on the vendor's computer media.

The Benefits of Time Sharing. The individual user's cost savings through time sharing are what made the practice popular and have kept it in the realm of options including affordable minicomputers and even smaller, less expensive personal computers. At the beginning, time sharing allows a low-risk entry into data processing, by offering a means of analyzing processing needs before purchasing a computer. Even in the long run, there are benefits to time-sharing arrangements for the large or intermediate computer resource needs. Because the time-sharing vendor is selling a service in an increasingly competitive marketplace, the user can safely leave the vendor with the responsibility for maintaining the service and expanding and improving it as new technology becomes available. As well, the more popular time-sharing vendors provide their users not only with the hardware for data processing and storage, but also programs and software packages for data maintenance, manipulation, analysis, and reporting. These packages are described in more detail in other sections, but suffice it to say for now that a time-sharing arrangement can save the user millions of dollars in software development.

As opposed to purchasing a computer, using a computer through time sharing allows some flexibility in data processing costs. In addition to the ongoing software development costs mentioned above, the independent computer user has the capital cost of the machinery or the lease to bear. Except for a comparably negligible fixed annual subscription fee, the time-sharing user has only the variable monthly usage costs which can rise and fall with data processing needs and budget allowances. This flexibility is significant throughout the year and complete from year to year. Associated with this appealing cost structure, the time-sharing computer is in most cases far more powerful than the computer one would purchase as a cost-effective alternative. Time-sharing vendors, although often selling time on minicomputers, almost always implement operating systems which allow the best possible use of a given machine's resources. On the larger machinery or with more sophisticated operating systems, much more complex tasks can be executed in less time and with less effort. In addition to a more powerful computer system, the time-sharing vendors usually provide peripheral hardware such as high-speed printers, media transfer devices, and graphic plotters.

Negative Aspects of Time Sharing. In many respects, then, using a time-sharing service seems like a least-cost alternative for unlimited data processing resources without the worry. Depending on an individual user's needs and situation, this may be true; however, sometimes a wide selection of data, software, and peripherals may be unnecessary or, the user, by leaving the vendor responsible, may be uncomfortably dependent. In such cases, the negative aspects of a time-sharing arrangement can be costly. Indirectly, the time-sharing user does pay for the available flexibility, whether or not it is necessary or sufficient.

Although time-sharing services can normally serve individual users with more speed and power than their substitutes, it is seldom a case that an individual user has the computer's full resources. Because any communal machine will be taxed at certain times, as many different users make simultaneous demands, certain applications can end up taking a long time to execute while they are held in the computer's queue. The fact that time-sharing computers are so powerful and complex also necessitates that they regularly be taken out of service temporarily for maintenance and repairs. Although the vendor will normally warn users of these maintenance periods, they can often be frustrating and debilitating if they come up at the wrong time.

When relying on a time-sharing vendor for service, the user can seldom implement major changes or expansions in hardware or software. Although the user can suggest new software or hardware investments, often even petition them through the vendor's user newsletter, or change service bureaus altogether, time sharing can be limiting in this respect. To change time-sharing vendors can be very costly, as your data processing shop will have to come to a halt, then start a learning process over with the new vendor's software and hardware conventions. This dependence on the time-sharing vendor can be a benefit when the user is satisfied with the vendor's service or when transferring responsibility for system maintenance is worth the indirect cost; however, for very large or very small needs, time sharing can be undesirable as the major means for obtaining data processing resources.

MINICOMPUTERS. A common trend for many time-sharing customers with multiple users and applications is to purchase or lease a *minicomputer*. Minicomputers, previously distinguished from mainframes by their lesser size and power, are becoming more powerful while maintaining a lower price. The popular minicomputer manufacturers—Digital Equipment Corporation (DEC), Data General,

Hewlett Packard, and IBM—all offer computers which are feasible substitutes to time-sharing services for all processing needs, especially those requiring multiple users and applications. These computers are not only smaller in terms of their physical size, but usually in terms of their "byte" size also. The computer *byte* is the internal logical and physical processing unit within the machine, and because most minicomputers have a smaller byte (16-bit) than the mainframes (32-bit), they have lower processing speeds. Because of their lower capacity, minicomputers can execute procedures as complex as any mainframe, but they process less data in a given time resulting in lower throughput. When minicomputers first made their debut in the early 1960s (DEC is credited with having offered the first commercial, mass-produced minicomputer—the PDP 8—in 1962), they were intended for use in *distributed processing*. That is, a company large enough to own a mainframe and use it in many different capacities and departments, could buy a minicomputer for each of the processing-intensive departments. Each of the minicomputers could be used for recurring, special processing within its respective department or communicate with the central computer for more complex procedures or for data access. In some cases, the central machine could be a more powerful mainframe, but in other cases, the central computer would also be a minicomputer serving as a traffic regulator and common file maintenance machine within the distributed processing network.

Leasing or Buying a Minicomputer. As minicomputer technology has progressed, the smaller, less-expensive machines have increased in power to rival the mainframes. Now minicomputers offer a sometimes fixed-cost alternative to the multiple-application time-sharing user. Depending on the user's preference, minicomputers can be bought from manufacturers or OEMs (original equipment manufacturers) who sell the same computers with different system software, or they can be leased from third parties. Leasing can allow the user a more manageable cost structure in some cases, as not only the machine but its maintenance can be purchased on a set monthly contract basis. Further, although terminating a lease may be expensive in terms of cost investment, leasing does allow the user a way out. Purchasing a minicomputer can be a preferable alternative, however, because if the right machine is chosen, then the user can maintain flexibility for growth. As minicomputers were popularized through the concept of distributed processing, most systems on the market include the option for communication between machines towards building a family of processors, all serving different necessary functions.

Minicomputer Security. With an in-house computer, for example, a minicomputer, the burden for security is only on the user. In fact, the risk of malicious damage or theft of electronically stored data is even less on an in-house computer than in a time-sharing environment. All of the common precautions to be exercised as a time-sharing user can also be implemented on a minicomputer. Further, and even more important, because the minicomputer and all associated storage devices can be kept locked in a single room, all data can be kept secure merely by acting sensibly as regards the keys to the computer room. To have complete security, against accidents as well as malice, minicomputer owners must protect all proprietary programs or data which are difficult to replace by exercising the same backup precautions as a responsible time-sharing vendor would. These include duplicate copies on tape or disk of all important files. For storage of these extra copies, most banks offer secure facilities. It is recommended that the computer owner not only use these storage facilities, but update the backup media at regular intervals to include all recently completed data collection and program development.

The Power and Independence of a Minicomputer. There are many benefits to using a minicomputer over other alternatives for satisfying hardware needs. The obvious advantages stem from having the computer within your organization. For a given application, once it has been programmed, this independence translates to very low, almost negligible variable costs. Once the computer is in-house, through either purchase or third-party lease, the user has no extra hardware usage cost for additional processing. No matter how much computer work needs to be done, the user knows ahead of time what the data processing costs will be. This independence also allows the user tremendous flexibility over an outside time-sharing vendor. If system software or applications packages are not quite as the user wants them, then for the cost of a programmer's time, the computer owner is completely free to make changes. This flexibility allows the computer to be used for any process, not only those deemed as desirable by a time-sharing vendor. Because of this, the user can buy or lease programs for research, analysis, accounting, word processing, or any other uses, all of which have made the minicomputer the backbone of the automated office of the future. The costs of using software for the more common applications is usually small when compared either to the expense for the computer or the comparable fees for time sharing. For those applications which require that the user write his or her own programs, if the user can do the programming or use a full-time programmer employed by the company then the minicomputer can be preferable to a time-sharing arrangement in which the outside vendor's personnel must be used for such proprietary programming. This is an advantage not only because it allows the user to keep secrets secret, but also because it can expedite applications programming. When the user must be concerned with computer resource usage costs, as in the case of time sharing, program efficiency is very important; however, if the computer is in-house, then the efficiency of the programs is less of an issue in the short run. Therefore new ideas or applications can be programmed accurately and quickly with no immediate need for attention to processing efficiency.

The main advantage of owning or leasing a minicomputer is that the user can have a data processing facility comparable to a time-sharing environment for lower costs with a more favorable structure. Hardware peripherals such as high-speed printers, graphic plotters, and storage media and devices can be purchased or leased when the user is ready for them. Almost any processing application feasible through a time-sharing service can be made available on an in-house computer as the user sees fit. In total, the minicomputer allows the user a comprehensive environment for computer analysis, research, and accounting at a cost that declines with increasing processing needs.

The Burdens of a Minicomputer. There are negative factors to owning or leasing a computer which do not exist when using a time-sharing service. These must also be considered before bringing computer resources in-house. The burdens of owning and maintaining a computer can be more than expected. In fact, having your own computer can be very costly when you find that the total independence can translate into being left alone out in the cold. Unless you have a complete knowledge of how to operate the minicomputer, especially in the case where there will be multiple users and applications, it will be necessary to hire a full-time operations staff or to lease a comparable service from the hardware manufacturer or another independent firm. When using these contract services, you subject yourself to the same risks present in a time-sharing situation wherein the computer and all associated work are available to outsiders. These personnel, depending on their availability, can be very costly due to the technical training necessary in electronics, engineering, and systems programming.

The prospective independent minicomputer user must also consider the costs of physical space. Although a minicomputer is usually much smaller than a mainframe, it does almost need a room of its own. Comparing in-house computer resources to a time-sharing service, physical space issues are important. The time-sharing customer must only accommodate a computer terminal for each user, but with an in-house computer there must also be a room for all the equipment, designed with attention to humidity, temperature, and working space. The independent minicomputer user must also protect his or her own important computer files with appropriate backup media, which introduce costs not always associated with use of a time-sharing service.

Still another cost to be remembered when considering in-house computer resources is the cost of upgrading hardware as technology becomes more sophisticated. Due to the fast growth in the industry the user can be left with no way of using or selling an obsolete machine. Often the old computer can be used in another department, or upgraded, starting a family of processors, but the possible options are limited. If the user finds his or her computer malfunctioning, the consequences can be worse in terms of the cost of lost computing time during repairs, which can take anywhere from a matter of hours to weeks. All of these negative factors must be considered when deciding to lease or purchase minicomputers to replace a time-sharing service or to build a distributed processing network. Through proper use of minicomputers, processing needs of any size or nature can be satisfied, but the associated costs of hardware maintenance, software development, physical space, security, and downtime represent a formidable burden to be considered.

MICROCOMPUTERS. The new wave in data processing is the *microcomputer,* or *personal computer.* Current technology enables the construction of tiny microprocessor chips which, in less room than is taken by a fingerprint, contain processing circuitry which used to be as large as a city block. Continuing technological growth has made the distinction between minicomputers and microcomputers increasingly hazy. Although minicomputers and microcomputers used to be distinguished based on whether they used a 16-bit or 8-bit processor, now there are even well-established, low-cost 16-bit microcomputers. For the sake of this chapter, however, we will make a clear and simple distinction—when we refer to microcomputers we will be talking about computers small enough to sit on a desktop and powerful enough to support only one user at a time. Although even the most popular microcomputers, such as those by Apple, IBM, and Tandy/Radio

Shack, are far less powerful than most any minicomputer or time-sharing service, they are especially useful in any of the processing tasks requiring small amounts of data and logically simple procedures. Although there were no real commercially available microcomputers before 1975, they are now very widespread, making a market of at least $1 billion. Previously confined to hobbyists and computer experts, the microcomputer market is now open to all of us with even little or no experience with computers, and must therefore be considered as far more than just a viable alternative to other computing resources.

Buying a Microcomputer. The most obvious advantage of microcomputers to the computer user is their low cost. For far less than the price of a new car, individuals can purchase microcomputers complete with storage media and devices, printers, plotters, and so on. Further, as these computers have increased in popularity, a wide range of commercial applications packages has been developed. Microcomputers, as opposed to either minicomputers or time-sharing services, are more consumer-oriented. Purchasing a microcomputer does not involve a major investment decision. Nowadays, most any major city in the country has at least one store which sells computers, associated software, and peripherals in a shopping center or mall. Merely by writing a check or using a charge card, any creditworthy customer can go to the computer store and come home with a complete microcomputer system capable of performing nearly any job possible on the larger, more expensive processing machinery.

Microcomputer Security. With a microcomputer the considerations for security are similar to those associated with minicomputers, but on a much smaller scale. The microcomputer does not need its own room with climate control, so isolation of the machine and associated hardware behind locked doors may be undesirable; however, there are ways to lock up only the microcomputer itself. As long as the owner exercises caution regarding the access to his or her computer and related storage, there is little if any risk of damage or theft of proprietary information. As in the case of a minicomputer owner, the owner of a microcomputer should maintain a complete, current library of backup information on tapes or disks for all valuable data and programs or other microcomputer files. This affords the owner security from accidental damage to or loss of any computer files which cannot be easily and inexpensively replaced. Microcomputer owners must pay special attention to this issue because in most cases the personal computer is not given any special room or environment and the whole system is more vulnerable to the dangers of carelessness, often getting less maintenance attention than it needs.

The Personal Quality of Microcomputers. Microcomputers are still far from comparable in power to the large mainframes or the other computers with sophisticated operating systems allowing time-sharing use. They are also less powerful than most any minicomputer; however, they have become amazingly popular for their low costs and many uses suitable to small-scale computer users. Personal computers, in addition to being inexpensive to purchase, are nearly free of maintenance costs. Normally, the entire system can fit on top of an ordinary table in a room without any special climate controls, and since these small computers are designed to support only one user, there is no need for technical operations personnel, sophisticated electrical wiring, or emergency power sources. Despite the fact that all associated costs are low, the majority of the popular personal computers can perform any processing that the larger machines can but with lower throughput. While the speed and ease of use associated with microcomputers may be well below that of other, larger machines, through sectorization of procedures and other ways of simplifying large jobs, the personal computers can be used for a variety of processing functions. Additionally, there is no longer a great deal of difficulty finding software packages, database access services, or hardware peripherals to use with microcomputers, so that almost all the capabilities within reach of any computer user are also available to the microcomputer owner. Other than the costs for extra effort and time due to slower processing, the purchase costs, and the time spent becoming familiar with microcomputers, there are virtually no variable costs at all in using a personal computer. Because no matter how much processing you do the cost is fixed, unless the speed and power of a larger machine are necessary, there is no reason not to use microcomputers to satisfy your processing needs. Further, although obsolescence is guaranteed as technology improves, the costs are so low that the prospective microcomputer owner need not be concerned with whether his or her computer will be the best choice available 2 years from now. In fact, we can be sure that microcomputer technology will soon render obsolete all the machines available today, but the owner's loss is minimal even if the owner ends up simply throwing away an outdated machine.

The Limitations of Microcomputers. The microcomputer is, in the truest sense of the phrase, a personal computer. Its purchase and maintenance costs are so low that given the continued proliferation of commercially available software, data, and peripherals, this will remain true. However, the personal quality of these machines can result in limitations. Although any microcomputer can serve the user well for drawing graphics, performing simple arithmetic or small file management and accounting, significant processing procedures like building large-scale econometric models, testing technical trading systems over long periods, or settling hundreds of accounts are very difficult, sometimes impossible, on a microcomputer due to its memory limits. This problem is even greater when the user does not have a deep understanding of how to program the microcomputer, because most of the commercially packaged software available can be very restrictive. Since these software packages are designed to facilitate very specific procedures, there are some types of analysis and accounting which are simply impossible to implement unless the user can do the programming. Many of the commercially available packages as well as their limitations are discussed at greater length later in this chapter.

While microcomputers afford processing power at a low cost, they are not one-to-one substitutes for their larger predecessors. Their lower power and speed can be burdensome to the large-scale computer user. Even more important, the microcomputer user has to worry about downtime just like anyone else. In the same sense that these machines can be bought much like stereo components, microcomputers have to be repaired in a similar fashion. In most cases, if your microcomputer fails to function properly, you will have to pack it up, take it to your store or service center, and leave it there until it can be repaired. Depending on the scale of your operation, setbacks could be undesirable or even intolerable.

MAKING THE HARDWARE DECISION. Twenty, even ten, years ago, choosing computer hardware was much easier than it is today. Only large corporations, government agencies, universities, and military establishments bought computers. Any of the others had no other choice but to use time-sharing services or service bureaus. Choosing one service over another was a matter of convenience, cost, reliability, and reputation. In today's market, there is a far wider range of services and products to choose from based on the same criteria. Concepts such as applicability, flexibility, and popularity come into play, making the hardware decision one that is much more complicated and one that can determine the variety of decisions that you will be able to make in the other areas.

Narrowing Down the Question of Size. The first question to ask in making your hardware decision deals with the magnitude of your processing needs. Large-scale users, such as the research departments in brokerage houses or financial and commercial firms, have to make choices between using time-sharing services and buying or leasing minicomputers. In these situations, it is always best to use a time-sharing arrangement for at least long enough to evaluate your needs. This will help not only by giving you an idea of how much computing time and power you need, but also by allowing you to gain an understanding of the issues. Very-large-scale users, such as major corporations with a variety of processing needs, make a choice on a different level. With a broad range of applications in many different departments, computer users can take advantage of the scale economies to be achieved through purchasing or leasing mainframes and operations staff or hiring systems consultants to build a distributed processing network of minicomputers and/or microcomputers. The majority of us are small-scale users and our hardware choice will almost necessarily be one of which microcomputer to buy.

Choosing a Time-sharing Vendor. In choosing a time-sharing vendor for hardware support, it is important to find a strong, well-established firm with a reputation for reliability, service, and attention to technological expansion and refinement as per the state of the art. As discussed later, it is also important to attend to the issues of applications and data when choosing a time-sharing service. Unless you have plans to do a significant amount of your own programming, you need not concern yourself with which make of machine the time-sharing vendor has, except as regards the particular hardware manufacturer's reputation for reliability and serviceability.

Choosing a Minicomputer. In purchasing or leasing a minicomputer, the main consideration is one of flexibility. It is paramount to ensure that you will be able to expand as far as you can foresee your needs may grow and then a few steps further. If a distributed processing network may be a possibility in the future, then it is essential to choose hardware designed with attention to data communications. Depending on how you obtain a minicomputer, you must keep an eye to your vendor's, original equipment manufacturer's (OEM's), or manufacturer's reputation for service, support, and accessibility. As well as in the case of choosing a time-sharing vendor, when settling on a certain minicomputer, you must investigate the types of software available for the machine, whether provided by the manufacturer, the OEM, or another firm. With in-house processing, it also becomes important to think about operations personnel to run and maintain your computer. As in any case where your business becomes dependent on the computer, but especially here, you also have to make sure that you are not dependent on one particular person or you run the risk of finding yourself left with a costly investment in a useless facility temporarily or even permanently.

Choosing a Microcomputer. The small-scale user, in choosing a microcomputer, may have the toughest decision of all to make, because he or she must acquire at least a consumer's knowledge of the hardware and its internal functions. While personal computers may serve only one master, they can offer substantial benefits at low costs to all of us, even those of us working in large firms with minicomputers, mainframes, or time-sharing arrangements. The readiness, ease of use, and freedom that come with a microcomputer can be valuable to any of us who need an easy way to deal with large quantities of information. As discussed in later sections, there are some applications, in fact most, which can be done as easily on a microcomputer as on any other equipment. Since all of us will own or at least use a microcomputer in the near future, a knowledge of the technology is important. These computers are sold in a more consumer-oriented market, so to avoid making the wrong decision, we should equip ourselves with an understanding of some basic measures for comparison. Defining some key words will be helpful in this regard.

CPU (Central Processing Unit). The main area of technological growth has been in increasingly smaller, less expensive CPUs which once were the size of a city block and now fit in the palm of your hand. The CPU is the central brain of the computer system. Different manufacturers once used any of three predominating CPUs: Intel 8088 (IBM Personal Computer); Z-80 (Tandy/Radio Shack and Xerox); MOS Technology 6502 (Apple, Atari, and Commodore). Today's processing units, while not significantly smaller than the first ones, are much more powerful (e.g., the Motorola 68000 and the Intel 8086). It is important to recognize that software written for one particular CPU will not be compatible with other CPUs.

ROM (Read-Only Memory). This is the magnetic memory internal to the computer which contains all of the operating instructions for the CPU. ROM is measured in bytes, but ROM size is not something with which to be greatly concerned as its functions are ones you cannot affect.

RAM (Random Access Memory). RAM is the internal memory that holds current programs and data while the computer is in use. Also measured in bytes, or kilobytes (1 kilobyte is equivalent to 1,024 bytes), a machine with greater RAM size can handle larger processing tasks requiring either more data, more complex programs, or both. The popular machines' RAM sizes range from 32 to 128 kilobytes, usually in multiples of 16 (32k, 48k, 64k, etc.). With most computers, it is possible to expand the RAM by purchasing extra internal storage capacity.

Floppy Disks or Diskettes. Floppy disks have replaced audio cassette tapes as the most popular choice for magnetic storage of programs and data. They have the appearance of small (5¼- or 8-inch diameter) phonograph records in protective sleeves; however, the medium for storing information on them is magnetic. In order to read information from floppy disks or write on them, you need a disk drive, comparable to a phonograph, serving to transfer data and programs to and from the disk from and to the RAM. Although floppy disks are by far the most popular storage medium for microcomputer users, the new wave in storage technology is toward hard disks which hold far more information than floppies in the same space. These hard disks are more expensive than floppies, but access to them is much faster and there is less danger of damage, because the disks and drives are all housed in one unit which the user never needs to open.

Monitor (Cathode-Ray Tube). The monitor, like a television screen in appearance, is the display unit for menus, user input, graphic or tabular results, and so on. In most cases, the computer can be used with a regular television and an rf (radio-frequency) modulator instead of a monitor, but this is not recommended. Using a television as a monitor will yield poor results for clarity and resolution and will permanently damage the television-picture quality. This should not be a significant issue, however, as the monitor is usually the least expensive of the computer system's components. Monitors usually have a black and white or black and green display. Depending on your preference, one or the other should be chosen based on comfort for your eyes. There are color monitors, which are significantly more expensive but can be especially useful in graphic applications, assuming the software you use can take advantage of the extra feature.

MODEM (Modulator/Demodulator). The MODEM is the device which connects your microcomputer to communications networks for accessing remote databases or time-sharing services via either a telephone or a direct connection to the telephone line. Due to limitations in communications technology, most MODEMs for microcomputers transmit and receive data at no more than 30 characters per second. While there are MODEMs that communicate as much as four times faster, using these MODEMs is not yet beneficial because most of those now available require that the MODEM at the other end of the transmission be an identical piece of equipment.

Printer. The printer connects to your computer to enable "hardcopy" output in addition to screen display. Access to a printer is essential to a complete system, otherwise processing results can be viewed only on the monitor. Because printers are primarily mechanical, as opposed to electronic, there are not many ways for advances in printer technology to result in lower costs. Ranging in price from around $400 to $4,000, printers for microcomputers can be compared based on whether they print letter-quality output or print with dot matrix technology. The latter, while less suitable for professional document printing, is usually a better choice for graphical output.

These are the main components of a complete microcomputer system, but some users will choose to make use of graphic plotters, different storage media, or more

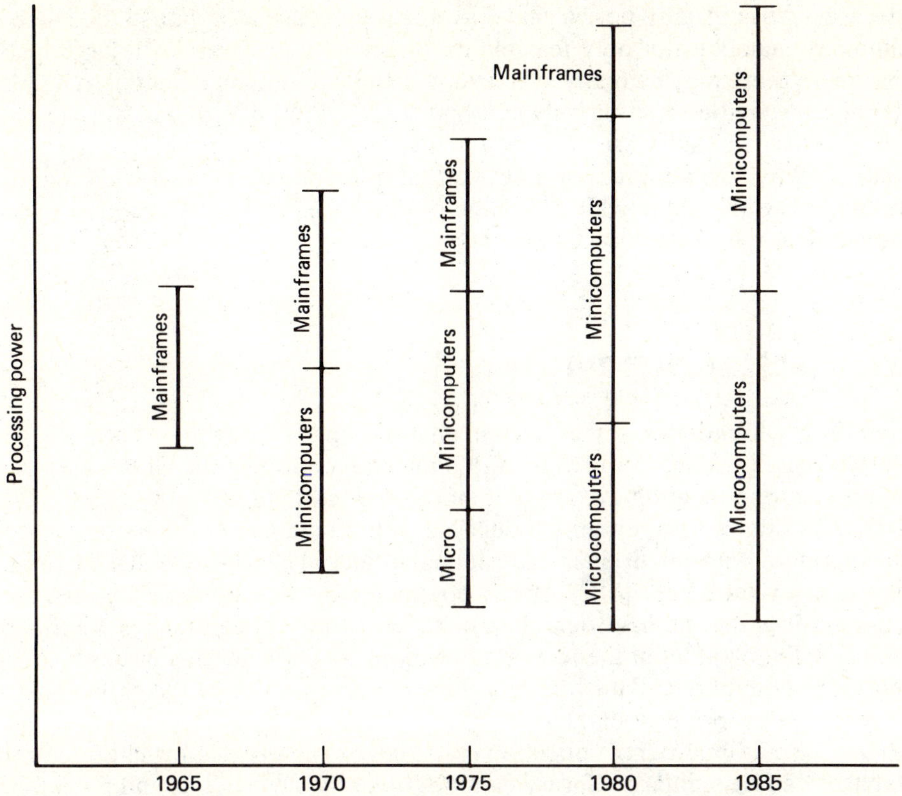

FIGURE 6. Although the distinction between minicomputers and microcomputers grows increasingly hazy, the physical machinery size for a given level of processing power has gone down, so that as the trend continues, by 1985 there will be almost no applications requiring the behemoth computers.

complicated communications technology. The overriding factor in choosing the hardware for your computer system should not be the sophistication level of the technology, but the popularity of a particular machine. A spiral ensues such that the most popular machine is the one for which the most software is developed; the more software is available, the more popular the machine becomes. Unless you plan to do most of your own programming, therefore, it is advisable to choose hardware based on the available software.

Whether the size of your processing needs directs you towards minicomputers, mainframes, time sharing, or microcomputers, the times have changed such that nowadays most all of us must deal with some type of hardware-use decision. While it is important to make a hardware choice with careful attention to future possible needs, especially in the case of a significant capital investment, keep in mind that by the time your needs have grown, there may be newer, less expensive ways to satisfy these needs. The power of popular computers and its ratio to their physical size and total cost will continue to skyrocket with the advent of increasingly complicated circuitry technology.

You may become comfortable thinking of computers as you do cars. For now, you can lease or buy what the industry offers to suit your needs and in a few years you may choose a complementary or substitute product. For small- to large-scale users, it is usually best to have as much as possible in-house, because the technology makes it not only feasible but financially preferable. In large institutions where there may be many systems, it is and will remain essential to maintain internal coordination and pay close attention to adherence to widespread, legitimate standards in software and communications. In order to make the best use of one of 50 microcomputers or a network of minicomputers, you will have to be able to choose from the available range of databases and software packages, so the best idea is to follow the pack.

DATABASES AND SERVICES

In building a foundation for computer analysis and accounting, there are many different issues to consider towards fulfilling data requirements. Given the current communications technology, any computer user can employ a MODEM (MOdulator/DEModulator) to either connect his or her machine to others or work in a time-sharing environment over the telephone lines. Using the MODEM to allow computers or terminals to interface, commercially available databases can be accessed for gathering historical data or current time-series updates. In this section, we will look at all of the relevant questions to ask regarding issues from how to choose a commercial data vendor to how to accurately and efficiently construct and maintain proprietary databases.

A *database* is an ordered collection of textual or numerical information. Textual databases can be similar to library catalogs indexing news items and publications which can be retrieved through subscription arrangements with the database vendor. There are commercial textual databases such as the Dialog Information Retrieval Service and New York Times Information Service which allow time-sharing users to screen and search millions of articles and periodical publications by author, title, or topic to facilitate the collection of written information on topics ranging from economics and government policy to engineering and aeronautics. These types of databases are convenient for certain types of historical research or primary data collection. Those databases most suited to analysis and accounting in the futures markets are more frequently numerical databases, collections of prices and volume measures, production factors, and other economic variables.

Some important concepts in numerical data collection, storage, and retrieval are those of time series, intervals, and frequencies. A *time series* is an ordered collection of numbers representing one specific variable through time. The *interval* of a time series is the period of time which it covers, and the *frequency* of a time series tells how often the variable is measured. For example, we could have a time series representing the annual levels of the Gross National Product (GNP) from 1961 to 1980. The GNP time series would have 20 values. The first value would represent the GNP of 1961, the tenth value would correspond to 1970, and so on. More or less coverage (a larger or smaller interval), or a higher (daily) or lower (annual) frequency may be best depending on the intended use of the data.

There are different ways of storing numerical data depending on how they are defined and what variables they represent. The storage technique will determine whether some types of data retrieval will be easy or difficult. Imagine a large file cabinet as being analogous to the database. In the file cabinet, there are five file drawers which we will use to store historical daily prices and volume for the Chicago Board of Trade wheat futures. We have opening, high, low, and closing prices, open interest, and volume for March, May, July, September, and December futures contracts trading in the years 1976–1980. There are different schemes we could use for storing these prices in an ordered fashion. We could put each delivery year's contract data all in one file drawer; within each drawer there would be five files, one for each delivery month. In each file, there would be six sheets of paper—one for the volume, one for the opening price, one for the closing price, and so on. If the data were filed this way and we wanted to see the closing prices for May 1976 wheat futures, from the contract's beginning to end, we could go to the 1976 drawer, open the May file, and pull out the piece of paper with closing prices. On the other hand, we could separate the drawers by calendar year, and within each drawer have chronologically ordered single sheets, each sheet having all of one particular day's price and volume data for each of the then-active contracts. Under this type of filing method, we would be easily able to access the trading activity for a specific day in the past, but it would be a tedious task to compile the historical closing prices of the May 1976 wheat futures contract, because it would be necessary to gather all of the sheets for each day that contract traded. If the data were to be stored on a computer, we would have to make the same types of decisions as to how to dimension, or structure, the electronic files, thereby determining which type of access would be easiest. Because there are many different uses of data, from accounting to analysis, we will look at how each different type of database compares to others in terms of its suitability for particular purposes. Depending on the user's data processing needs, choices must be made not only as to data storage conventions, but also as to the interval and frequency of time-series data, and the concepts that the variables represent.

FUNDAMENTAL DATA. One major area of computer-aided research is in *fundamental analysis,* the study of historical market relationships between different measures and components of supply and demand. Fundamental research, estimating the interdependencies between prices and macroeconomic and microeconomic variables, benefits most from a time-series database. Fundamental analysis is usually applied to data of weekly, monthly, quarterly, and annual frequencies. Due to some of the assumptions of fundamental analysis (e.g., perfect distribution of information) and the current speed of news travel, frequencies higher than monthly are seldom used in these studies. To draw reliable conclusions from fundamental analysis, substantial history is necessary so that despite the low frequency there is a significant number of observations.

There are many time-sharing firms that provide databases of low-frequency time series for econometric and other fundamental research. Well known for its leadership in commercially accessible databases, *Data Resources, Incorporated* (DRI), a Massachusetts economic consulting and time-sharing firm, houses millions of time series of varying frequencies for subscribers' use in research and planning. *Chase Econometrics/Interactive Data Corporation* (Chase/IDC) supplies similar databases and other services. Both firms offer subscriptions to their libraries of time series based on particular industries or economic sectors. There are macroeconomic databases containing time series of industrial and financial variables, employment figures, and demographic measures. Then there are many databases for the different microeconomies, from agriculture or energy to transportation or chemicals. An agricultural database, for example, would contain time series data for acreage planted, yield, and prices of corn, wheat, and soybeans; cattle placed on feedlots, steers slaughtered, and pork bellies in cold storage; and measures of farm machinery costs, farm profitability, and government support programs. Given the appropriate software, time-sharing subscribers to these databases can search and display data, as well as use fundamental analysis to estimate market relationships.

Microeconomic and macroeconomic data for U.S. markets are surely the most necessary for research dealing with American prices, but international data are also important. Time series of imports and exports, direction of trade, other nations' macroeconomic data, and foreign prices are also valuable to comprehensive fundamental research. These data are collected by international organizations such as the International Monetary Fund, the Organization for Economic Cooperation and Development, the European Economic Community, and others. Both DRI and Chase/IDC offer international databases in their respective arrays of time-sharing information products, as do some of the smaller firms.

Given an historical database, updates to keep the data current are an altogether different issue. Most fundamental data can be purchased for update purposes on tape, such as figures compiled by the government. Often the data can be purchased at regular intervals for the mere cost of the tape. With the increased sophistication and standarization of communications technology over recent years, however, tapes can be very burdensome and costly for updating any database, when compared to data transmission directly from one computer to another.

All of the fundamental databases are useful in estimating relationships and are therefore valuable in building econometric forecasting models. In fact, both Chase/IDC and DRI built their databases for the purpose of economic modeling and the firms offer databases not only of historical time series, but also of forecast variables that their econometric models have predicted for future market activity. Depending on the proven reliability of the specific model, these forecast data can be more or less useful in making long-term trading decisions.

TECHNICAL DATA. The type of data useful in *technical analysis* is usually of a different nature than low-frequency time-series data. Although it is important to have price data in either fundamental or technical analysis, the data needed in the latter are of a higher frequency. Databases for technical analysis in commodity futures have opening, high, low, and closing prices, volume, and open interest for all of many futures contracts at daily or even hourly frequencies. These are the data used in predicting market behavior based on trend-following models, market strength indices, or chart formations. There are many different data vendors selling data for technical analysis, but due to the high frequency and volume of the data, the choice between services should be more dependent on the vendor's facilities for updates than in the case of fundamental data.

In data for technical analysis, "history" can refer to 20 years ago, or early this morning. Services such as Comtrend, provided by *Automatic Data Processing* (ADP), distribute real-time trading information from the exchange pits to users' terminals throughout the country. ADP/Comtrend users subscribe to the Videcom Quotation Service, the original service of its kind for commodity futures markets. Through interactive CRT (cathode-ray tube) terminals, subscribers can print out settling prices, previous trades, changes in prices, bids and asks—all at the touch of particular preprogrammed function keys. Different pages, distinguished by the markets they cover, can be printed on the screen, and all data are updated automatically from the host computer.

These real-time services necessitate at least an indirect and constant link to the futures exchanges and obviously require sophisticated communications hardware and software to enable such rapid information transmission. When accessing data that are updated daily, the procedure can be identical to that for quarterly data—the procedure is just more frequently executed. However, with hourly, or real-time, continuous data access, the services are much more dependent on reliable communications facilities and time-sharing networks. Because of this, they are more accurately described as trading applications services as opposed to database vendors. Commodity Communications Corporation, Market Data Systems, and Radio Data Systems are a few of the firms that provide continuously updated data services for use in day-trading and technical analysis. Most of these services, like ADP/Comtrend, offer the data through software packages that allow data display, some manipulation of data, and often very sophisticated *graphics packages*. These services that allow intraday analysis are covered in more detail in the section "Trading Applications."

While the real-time data transmission services are very useful for the day trader, they can be very expensive for someone who wants to position trade, even though both traders may use technical analysis. For simple daily data, the real-time services are unnecessary. Although DRI and Chase/IDC are not suppliers of real-time data, their long historical databases, as well as a similar one provided by Remote Computing Corporation, are very useful in all types of technical analysis and historical performance evaluations of trading systems. These types of *data services* are designed for time-sharing users or those who maintain their own database and need daily updates. If the data are to be used in the time-sharing environment, then the vendor will most likely provide software for access and manipulation. If the user intends to load the data onto in-house storage media, such as floppy disks for a personal computer, it can be difficult to retrieve the data in a convenient form. For instance, some software enables microcomputer users to read the time-sharing database, but leaves the data in an unmanageable form on the user's computer. However, there are other applications packages, discussed later, like CompuTrac's, which transfers data from a Commodity Systems, Incorporated (CSI) computer to Apple microcomputers and includes software for simple analysis; or Software Resources, Incorporated (SRI) SMART, which not only transfers data from a time-sharing vendor in a form which can be charted and analyzed, but also restructures data files for use in various other commercial applications packages.

With data of the higher frequencies, the issues of timeliness and reliability are more important than with quarterly or annual fundamental data. When the data distribution service collects and transmits low-frequency data, there is little chance that the communications or time-sharing hardware will fail to function for an entire observation period. With high-frequency data, there is the chance that single observations or whole intervals will not be transmitted or will be sent incorrectly due to some sort of system failure. Further, when collecting high-frequency data for constant or daily transmission the vendor's margin for error is greater, as there is less time to make data integrity checks. Many of the data services that transmit in real time have programs which check for the accuracy of transmitted data so that at least if the data are wrong they will not be displayed. Some of the daily *data update services* use similar transmission software, so that if a day's data are inaccurately received, the user can reaccess the database. Commodity Systems, Incorporated (CSI) employs a "check-sum," a procedure whereby all the transmitted data are summed up and before the transmission ends, the CSI computer checks to see that the sum is the same at each end. If the sum at the transmitting computer differs from the sum at the receiving end, then the data are sent again.

COMPARING DATA VENDORS. Having determined what type of data is needed for a particular operation or area of research and analysis, there are other matters which must be considered in choosing between comparable data vendors. One issue in choosing a commercial database, in addition to coverage, interval, frequency, and reliability of data, is cost. Different data vendors have various means for pricing data, usually depending on the uniqueness of the data, their quantity, and whether history or regular updates are desired. The medium on which the data are purchased can also be important when buying historical data, be it through machine-readable tapes, printed sheets, floppy disks, or a computer-to-computer communication. Most of the data vendors will sell historical data on a variety of media so that customers can build their own databases. In most cases, such data sales are priced based on the number of time series and on how many observations are desired. The choice between services can often be made based on the pricing structure, depending on whether a long history of a few concepts is desired, or only a short history of many concepts. In the former, the optimum structure is one in which prices for a particular time series vary little depending on the interval length. In the latter case, a better pricing structure would be one in which the length of history varies prices more than the number of time series.

When the purpose of the database is for ongoing research instead of sporadic or one-time studies, the best way to purchase data is through a major commercial vendor, regardless of whether the data are to be used on a separate computer or in the vendor's time-sharing environment. A time-sharing vendor that sells data is usually large enough to achieve the scale economies that no individual user could. Some of the larger on-line data vendors spend millions of dollars annually, maintaining and updating their databases. Depending usually on whether or not particular data are public, there will be companies that offer time-sharing accounts whereby users can access the vendor's database at will. The user can then either work with the data in the time-sharing environment or store them on his or her own computer media. The major data vendors, DRI and Chase/IDC, both offer services like these, allowing customers to choose from a supermarket of databases covering a variety of subjects and time frames. The data chosen can then be effectively taken home to use at your leisure. If there are many different types of fundamental and technical data needed in your operation, an arrangement like this would be preferable to maintaining and updating your own comprehensive database.

Even for those needing only limited technical data, there are data vendors who can offer inexpensive services. MJK Associates, Commodity Systems, Incor-

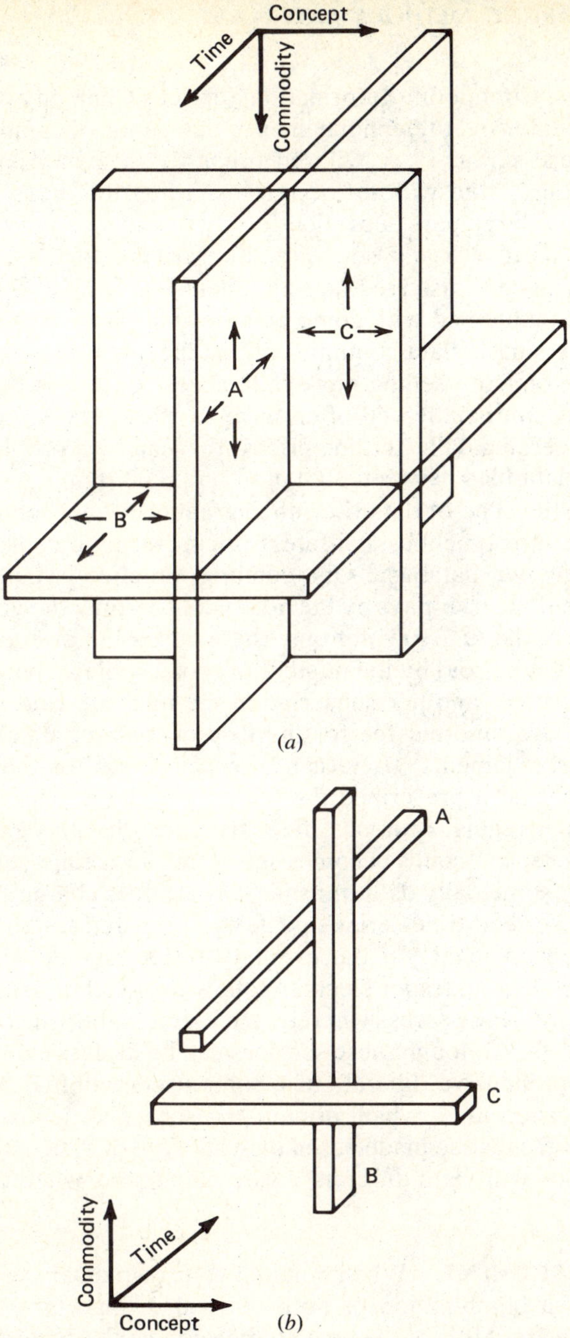

FIGURE 7. In pricing databases and in file structure, think of a three-dimensional matrix where: (1) the ''height'' of the file will be greater the more commodities included; (2) the ''width'' of the file will depend on the concepts covered (different delivery months with opening, high, low, and closing prices, volume, and open interest for each); and (3) the ''depth'' of the file will be a function of the interval. Under some pricing schemes [(as in (*a*)], database accesses can be by some sort of slice of the matrix—users pay based on how many slices they get. Other pricing structures are based on how many strips [as in (*b*)] are accessed. In either case, you should choose a database structured and priced similarly to the most frequent type of slice or strip you would be accessing. There are database vendors who sell their data by the matrix cell, so that no matter what your most common access structure is, these can be all-around favorites.

porated (CSI), and Commodity Information Services Company (CISCO) sell their daily data and updates over telephone lines to thousands of computer users across the country. These services are tailored primarily to owners of minicomputers and microcomputers, who will not be retransmitting the data. The reliability of these services is in large part dependent on the sophistication of the company's communications hardware and software. Subscribers to these services should ensure that data, once transferred, are in a manageable form. Further, when the data vendor is not equipped with complex time-sharing machinery and operating systems, but only simple data communications facilities, there are other precautions to take. A company selling more data access accounts than their communications systems can handle will often have to queue users for long times. Especially when accessing daily settling prices, this can be a problem as every user tries to retrieve data files between 3:00 p.m. and 6:00 p.m.

Depending on the type of data (i.e., their frequency, availability, or commonality, and the need for timeliness) different pricing structures may be appropriate for updating your own database. One common practice is that after paying an annual account fee, the user pays by the hour when reading the vendor's database. Often, the user may have to pay not only these costs, but also a per-unit fee. For example, data might be sold by the number of broad subjects needed; after paying an annual account fee, another subscription fee must be paid for access to the agricultural database, another fee for the macroeconomic database, and so on. Through other arrangements, users can often pay only for the number of time series needed, that is, a prescribed flat fee covers the access of any 20, 50, or 1,000 time series at regular intervals. Fee structures like this can be crippling at times when the user suddenly becomes interested in a time series not yet paid for. For example, some daily data transmission services charge a regular monthly fee to have a prescribed time-series update file prepared for their individual account to access each night. In the event that the user decides to trade new commodities (e.g., a grain trader elects to follow financial futures), it is necessary to go through an ordering process whereby the user's nightly file can be augmented for the new requests. Although these services can be far less expensive than some of the more comprehensive, liberal ones, some users will find them problematic at times. The decision as to which pricing and access structures are best for an individual customer must be made based on what type of data updates are needed. Different situations will yield different cost comparisons when considering all of these factors.

DATABASE MANAGEMENT. When building your own database of public or proprietary data, or a combination of both, it is also important to consider data management software. Most of the time-sharing companies have data management software for use on their systems. Software packages with names like AID and FILETRAN (Data Resources, Incorporated) or INSYTE (Remote Computing Corporation) can be used to manipulate and transfer data on tapes and disks, merge data files, and create new ones. These packages can be especially useful in applications requiring the use of both public and proprietary data. For example, in corporate planning decisions or even daily account settlement, some of each type of data will be needed. For use on almost any microcomputer, there are similar software programs that can be purchased on floppy disks from companies such as Peachtree Software and *VisiCorp*. Given the right data management software, all corporate or personal numerical or textual data can be stored, manipulated, and screened; reports can be generated, accounts can be settled, and databases can be updated. For more specific, complex tasks, there are many software packages for use on computers of all different types and sizes; these packages will be discussed in detail in the section "Computer Applications in the Futures Markets."

Database Accuracy. Maintenance of data integrity, or accuracy, is of paramount concern either when purchasing history or updates, or when collecting data yourself. It is important to be sure that the data are accurate in order to draw any valid conclusions from research or accounting applications. There are, therefore, many necessary precautions to be taken by you or your data vendor. Depending on your aversion to the risks of erroneous data and your confidence in the data source, some or all of these precautions should be executed using either *data management software* or simple time-series processors.

When building a database, it is important to obtain printed historical sheets, books, or other publications which can be used to verify data accuracy. With fundamental data, normally of a lower frequency than technical data, it is fairly easy to obtain historical numbers in print as well as on electronic media. There are few enough data that checking them once by eye can be sufficient. For fundamental data, it is also easy to keep the printed library current by putting your name on any of a number of appropriate government office mailing lists. Through receipt of the periodical government reports, the database can be easily updated and revised as figures are changed or found to be incorrect. When using higher-frequency technical data, checking a large historical database can be tedious and time consuming as can watching each day's updates for accuracy. It is easy enough to get a printed history of daily settling prices and volume measures from the particular futures exchange, from the *Commodity Research Bureau*, or from newspapers. Accuracy checks can be made by eye for history or updates, but using the computer to find suspect data can be much easier.

The two main types of *data errors* that the computer can be used to purge are inconsistencies and logical errors. A logical error is a data error which can be detected based on the meanings of the time series in the database. For instance, in most cases of daily settling prices for futures trading, a particular day's opening and closing prices should not be greater than the high price or less than the low price; in the same vein, there should never be a volume figure greater than the corresponding figure for the day's change in open interest. Based on the definition of these time series, data can be checked by the computer, error messages can be typed out, and then data can be checked and verified or corrected through use of the printed history.

Like checks for logical errors, checks for data consistency can be performed by the computer. An inconsistency in the data is an error which suggests unlikely market behavior. For instance, when any of a certain day's futures prices for a particular commodity contract are different from the previous day's closing price by more than the daily price limit, an error message should be printed by the checking program. An inconsistency particularly easy to find with a computer program is one called a spike, so named for how it would make a graph of the time series appear. An example of a spike would be the fourth value in a time series which had the following observations: 1.10; 1.09; 1.08; 110.; 1.09; 1.11. Because many data series would seldom contain such a spike, these inconsistencies should be programmatically purged from the database. As before, write the program to search for suspect observations, check the data through verification with reliable printed material, and then correct the error. Define a spike with the following rule: If the data observation for day t represents a change from day $t - 1$ of an amount more than two standard deviations away from the mean daily change, and the observation on day $t + 1$ represents a reversal of the change, then check the observation as a possible spike.

If the program is used to check for spikes in single data series, all major inconsistencies of this kind can be found. More concise checking can involve searching for spikes in time series representing spreads between adjacent contracts or in butterfly spreads. Through complete and comprehensive searching for inconsistencies and logical errors, and verification of all data series, a reliable and accurate database can be built.

For further insurance, the database can be copied in its accurate form, and kept in two different locations or on duplicate media, thereby lessening the chance that the whole "data cleaning" procedure will have to be repeated.

Accuracy is as important in updating the database as it is in building the original historical library, so the same checks for errors should be completed either with each regular addition to the database or at appropriate intervals throughout the year. This task can be difficult and costly with high-frequency data, so some of the data vendors such as Commodity Systems, Incorporated employ the use of check-sums. The only type of errors that these check-sums will discover, however, occur when the data are misinterpreted through the transmission process. With extremely high-frequency data, such as those provided by the real-time data services, there is little time for data errors to be detected; however, the error may remain for only a short time as the information is constantly updated. In cases like these, if the data's accuracy is essential, users can subscribe to two such services and have terminals display reported data only when the sources agree. This, of course, would involve the use of very sophisticated hardware and costly programming and is therefore not recommended.

Data Storage Media. One more area of concern in building or maintaining a database is in terms of the physical storage media. On any size machine today, the two main choices are magnetic tapes or disks. The tapes used are just like normal magnetic tapes in their purpose and appearance. In fact, the tapes that are used with most microcomputers are plain audio cassettes. *Disks* are similar in appearance to phonograph records. They are different, however, in that they employ magnetic recording techniques. Although data used to be stored on machine-readable cards, the current storage technologies make the use of cards obsolete and burdensome. The different tapes or disks used for computers from microcomputers to mainframes compare similarly for the particular machine. Tapes, due to their physical structure and the equipment for handling them, are inherently slow compared to disks. Data are written on and read from tapes sequentially. Data can be more easily accessed at random on disks. While tapes may be less expensive and more easily stored when used for recording data and putting them away for later use or database backup, disks are much more cost effective for storing frequently accessed data. Disks not only allow the user a much larger library of data ready for analysis, but require much less physical space for storage of a given amount of data, and are easier to keep clean and safe from corruption by dust or dirt. For microcomputers, there are two types of disks available—floppy disks, which require the use of a disk drive, and hard disks, which are enclosed in a single unit also containing the disk drive. The comparisons between hard and floppy disks are similar to those between floppy disks and tapes: hard disks are more expensive than floppy disks, which cost more to use than tapes; the hard disks hold more data (in a given physical space) and are much faster to access than floppies, which hold more than tapes, the slowest medium of all; and hard disks are more secure from damage than floppies, which are safer than tapes. With the promised continuation of increasing sophistication in storage technology, it will soon be as inappropriate to use tapes on any computer as it already is to use cards on large computers.

FULFILLING DATA NEEDS. Making decisions as to how to gather and store all the right data you need covers many areas. No matter what the interval or frequency of the data you will collect occasionally or regularly, there are some issues which must always be considered. The most obvious of these is the data vendor's reliability. In that some computer applications, in fact most, require not just complete accuracy, but timely accessibility, shortcomings in the data vendor's reliability in either of these qualities can cripple that part of your business dependent on data processing. The data vendor's size and popularity are also important concerns. The more customers use a particular data vendor's service, the more significant the scale economies in maintenance and coverage expansion of which you can take advantage. Of course, the vendor's popularity can be a negative factor as well, unless the equipment to serve users is sufficient to avoid bottlenecks or extended downtime. These are some of the basic considerations which you must keep in mind as you work through making other decisions regarding database pricing and content.

The first and most obvious choice in shopping for data deals with the content of the database. The type of application you have in mind will determine your needs regarding the data's interval, frequency, and coverage. Whether you need a long or short interval and a high or low frequency of data will depend on the processing application intended. It is important to keep an eye to the vendors' various levels of flexibility concerning breadth and depth of database coverage. For instance, if you want a database for technical analysis, even though you may currently need data only for futures market prices, it would be advisable to choose a vendor with a comprehensive financial database so that if you intend to follow stocks, bonds, or options, you can do so without having to initiate an arrangement with another, different vendor.

It is also important to have an understanding of a data vendor's pricing and access structure before making any decisions which could tie you into an unfavorable situation. On the issue of pricing, the best procedure is to determine what your most common types of data purchase would be and compare prices from one vendor to another based thereon. Different data vendors utilize a wide range of pricing structures and, depending on your needs, one or the other might result in the lowest costs. The means for accessing the database, whether via telephone, tape, or time sharing, can also either keep your options open or completely limit your flexibility. For instance, in some cases, access to current data has to be a separate procedure from collection of historical data, and this can result in cumbersome, regular routines to maintain the smooth flow of your processing applications.

If you attend to all of your own specific needs in each of the areas determining your choice of a data vendor, you provide yourself with a foundation for a wide range of computer applications. It is best, as always, to keep an eye to your reason for acquiring data and ensure that they will serve your purposes as easily, as reliably, and in as cost effective a manner as possible. Choose the data vendor that most closely meets your criteria for current potential needs and ensure that your environment for systematic computer usage will be based on a suitable foundation.

COMPUTER APPLICATIONS IN THE FUTURES MARKETS

As the popularity of computers and the number of users in commercial use have grown, there have been greater incentives to develop systems designed for users. As more commercially appealing systems have been developed, there has also been an increase in the number of computer users. There is now a multitude of choices allowing most any business or individual to consider some type of hardware facility in various price ranges. There are now many commercially accessible electronic databases, so that no matter what type of analysis you have in mind, there is almost always a choice of vendors for the data you need. The developments in hardware technology and database compilation have broadened the scope of commercial computer use, but it is really the development of *software* sciences that has made this breadth accessible to all of us. Developments in software, or *computer languages,* have greatly facilitated computer use to the point where most any specific industry has at least hundreds of computer users. This has provided incentives to software houses and time-sharing vendors to develop focused *applications packages*. An applications package is a collection of software programs, each written to fulfill specific needs and packaged together to provide a comprehensive computer environment for a particular type of analysis or accounting. Many of the applications packages, because they are designed to facilitate common procedures, employ a menu concept. Menu-driven packages ask the user questions, and accept a number of choices, chosen by one keystroke. Most applications packages allow the user to type some key, such as "?" or "H" (for "Help"), and the program will explain the different choices for a response. It is the applications packages that make it possible for all of us to use computers without having to understand programs.

Applications packages, otherwise known as "canned software," are available for a multitude of functions on time-sharing systems, minicomputers, and microcomputers. In this section, we will look at some of the commercially distributed packages designed for future traders and analysts. For our purposes, we will group the range of packages under four main headings: Communications, Trading, Analysis, and Accounting.

COMMUNICATIONS APPLICATIONS

Communications applications are those programs that make it possible to transfer information between two or more computers. This area of applications also includes the software which enables time sharing on terminals remote to the central computer. Had there been no communications software for time sharing on remote terminals, widespread computer usage would not have been possible before the advent of newer, less expensive, smaller hardware. Even given minicomputer and microcomputer technology, without sophisticated, somewhat standardized communications software, certain high-volume processing procedures, such as daily account settling, would be difficult because there would be no means for computer-to-computer transmission of necessary data.

Microcomputers and Time-Sharing Systems. All of the time-sharing vendors offer *communications software* to enable remote database access for on-line processing, but there are some companies that have made better use of current technology to transmit data from their big machine to your smaller unit. Through these services you can use the time-sharing service or database access service to take advantage of the scale economies in building and maintaining a database, while executing all processing procedures on your independent minicomputer or microcomputer, thereby not having to pay time-sharing fees except when necessary. These services can also be beneficial in situations where the aim is either to transmit data from your computer to theirs or access their database, use the greater sophistication of their larger, faster machine to perform complex data manipulations, and transmit the processed data back to your computer for storage or further processing. Services such as these give the user the best of both worlds: the customary power, speed, and comprehensive public databases of time sharing, and the low cost of independent or distributed processing on smaller computers. DRI offers services of this type to owners of ONYX, Apple, or IBM microcomputers. With the properly configured hardware, DRI's subscribers have the benefits of a distributed processing network. The microcomputer can be used for routine tasks such as drawing graphs, writing reports, or simple arithmetic manipulations. A wide range of fundamental data can be transmitted with DRI's database to your independent storage media; complex tasks such as econometric model construction can be executed in the time-sharing environment; and model results or forecasts can be saved for later analysis or display on microcomputers.

CISCO (Commodity Information Services Company) and MJK Associates also can support *microcomputers* as either remote time-sharing terminals or independent processors for *database access* and data transmission functions. CISCO, although supporting only a Cromemco computer, makes its complete database available for a broad collection of technical analysis applications in time-sharing mode, or data can be transmitted to the microcomputer for displaying data graphically or in tables. MJK supports the Apple, the TRS-80, and Comm-Basic hardware, so that the time-sharing computer can be used for testing trading systems, account settling, or other large jobs, and the microcomputer can be used for display and simple analysis. All of these services afford the user tremendous cost savings because with the proper database maintenance software and sufficient storage, all data can be saved for later processing with little additional expense. For owners of popular personal computers, such as Apple or Radio Shack TRS-80's, there are also commercial software packages such as VisiTerm (marketed by *VisiCorp*) which allow the microcomputer to emulate a time-sharing terminal, but not to transmit raw or processed data. VisiTerm connects Apple microcomputers to nearly any time-sharing network for database access and complex processing tasks, or to news wires and electronic mail networks for text and data transmission. Matching personal computers with VisiTerm can also communicate for transfer of programs or data. The only limit to VisiTerm and some of these other packages is that some transmissions can result in a cumbersome file structure which prohibits any use of the data other than for display. For further processing, the user has to manually enter the data in a different format. As a group, these services are best for the small- to medium-scale computer users, most of whose processing needs can be accommodated with a minicomputer or microcomputer, who occasionally need the greater power and speed of the time-sharing vendor's larger machine and more sophisticated software.

Data Transmission. There are other companies which offer sufficient communications packages to transmit data from large commercial databases, but not to allow time-sharing use of the computers. Some of the data vendors sell historical data through these transmission facilities so that users can build their own database for off-line analysis. The better ones, in fact most, also make it easy for users to update their databases at regular intervals. Software Resources, Incorporated (SRI) offers a collection of communications and database maintenance packages which enable data transmission from time-sharing networks to microcomputers such as the Apple or IBM. Without having to dial the phone or log on to the time-sharing computer, the user runs a program to build new data files or automatically update older ones with current information. One of the special benefits of this package is that it allows tremendous flexibility in database access. Users retrieve whatever data they want, given the data are in the vendor's library. Whether it is history or updates, flat or time-series structure, already in your database or not, you can retrieve what you want with the access control at your end of the transmission. CompuTrac offers a similar package which interfaces the microcomputer for vendor controlled access to the Commodity Systems, Incorporated and Interactive Data Corporation databases, each for different types of data. While any of these communications applications packages transfers data only in the format required by the same vendor's analytical applications, SRI's package includes a unique facility for reformatting data files for processing in any of a number of other analytical packages such as the *VisiCorp* software.

Day Trading and News Wires. Another interesting application of the current communications technology has been pursued actively by Quotrader Corporation and the CompuTrac Technical Analysis Group. Quotrader's software turns the Apple microcomputer into a quote machine with the capability for intraday data display, bar charts, and trading signal generation in real time. The CompuTrac group has interfaced the Apple with Commodity Communications Corporation's quote machine for the same types of applications.

Other vendors such as Dow Jones News Retrieval Service, Reuters, or Commodity News Service, offer only limited historical databases, but comprehensive

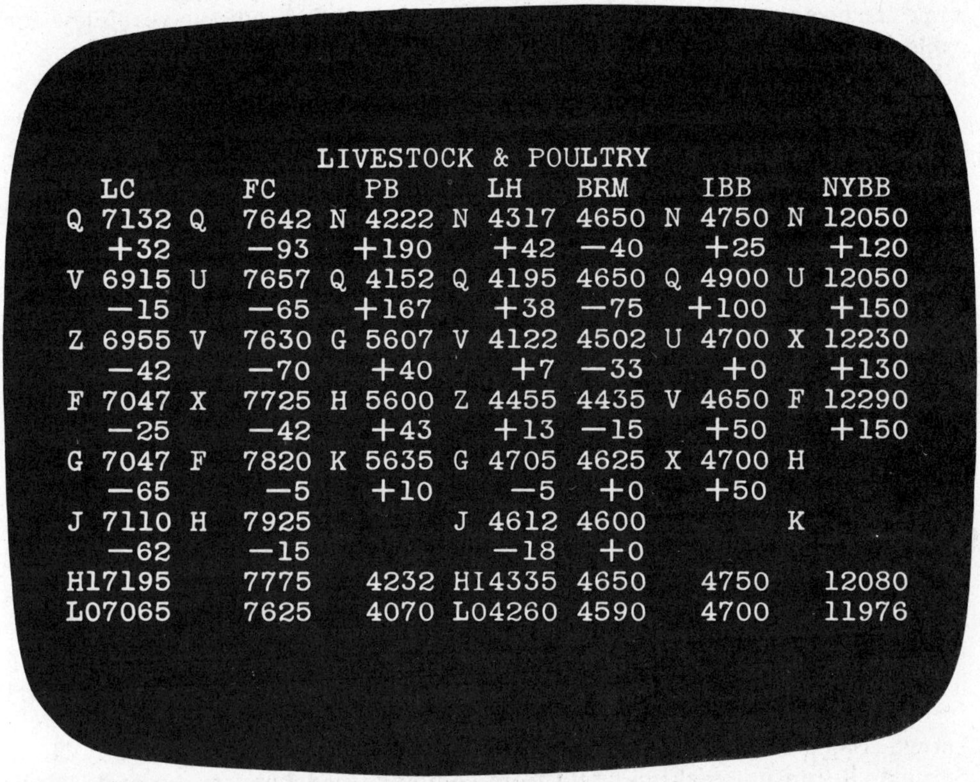

FIGURE 8. An example of one of the preselected, programmable pages as displayed on the Commodity Communications Corporation on-line quote machine.

coverage of most current market data for updating independent databases on your own computers. With these services, the main drawback is that, because the vendors offer almost no analytical applications, the user is left with a data file that cannot serve any purpose other than for display unless the information is entered manually in a suitable format. For the most part, these vendors disseminate information in formats not suitable for analysis—they are news services, not data vendors.

The main types of data for which the vending services are most valuable are the higher-frequency technical data. Not only for building historical databases, but especially for regular, timely updates, the higher the data frequency, and the more data needed, the more important these communications applications become. For database updating services, it is important to consider the format in which the data will be received. As discussed in the section on databases, the file structure of your data will determine the relative ease with which different tasks can be executed and the different pricing techniques will determine which service is most suitable for you. In communications applications for distributed processing or simple *data transmission,* however, there are other issues of concern such as the communications medium. Especially with high-frequency data, the means through which data are transmitted can determine the completeness of your database. The telephone network is the most common way, but some of the companies transmit structured data files over news wires, FM radio waves, television cable networks, or even radio signals received by a satellite disk. Depending on how high the data transmission frequency and how pressing the nature of the processing intended, in some cases more importance should be attached to the reliability of particular communications media than the costs associated with the data transmission. Because many of the communications media used are new and relatively untested, the best way to make a reliability comparison is by talking to subscribers of each of the different vendors.

Communications applications have made it possible to disseminate information, distribute data, and build whole processing networks. At frequencies as low as quarterly or as high as daily, the current technologies in communications hardware and software have made manual database updates of any size library a thing of the past. Through all of the data distribution services, the futures markets' function of price discovery can be even more broadly performed. To perform this function with even greater efficiency, the most sophisticated communications technology is used in connecting computers and terminals to each other in nationwide networks for trading applications.

TRADING APPLICATIONS. The highest-frequency data transmission is known as real time. In *real-time data* transmission, price information is relayed to users within seconds of its availability on the trading floor. Real-time data are only infrequently transmitted from computer to computer for remote storage. In most cases, real-time data are distributed over a single computer's network. The well-known companies such as Quotron, Reuters, Dow Jones, and Commodity News Service all transmit real-time data from commodity exchanges to remote, dedicated receiving terminals. The subscribers to these services can choose from a library of news or data pages to be displayed on their CRT terminal or typed out on a small printer. This type of news and data transmission service, including ones by Telerate, Technical Data, GTE, and others is suitable for data display and truly has changed the nature of the futures markets by bringing more people closer to the activity. There are a few companies, however, that have combined the current capabilities in communications and microprocessor technologies to create computer environments for real-time data transmission, display, and analysis. These services, due to the high frequency of their data, are necessarily time-sharing services. Because users' computers or terminals must be connected to the central machine throughout the trading day, real-time analysis services can be expensive, but they are the backbone of many trading operations today. These services have opened up the door to computer applications in trading that have allowed the futures markets to attract liquidity from all sections of the country and all areas of the investment world.

Dedicated Terminal Services. One of the longest established trading applications products is the Videcom Quotation Service, provided by *ADP/Comtrend*. Through Videcom terminals, subscribers can display preselected pages with 20 commodity contracts each, showing opening, high, low, and last-trade prices, as with the news and data services. These data are also updated automatically in real time, but the user can do more than just print the information. Videcom terminals are equipped to draw graphs of spreads, ratios, and moving averages, bar charts, point-and-figure charts, and trendlines. Preprogrammed graphic displays can be automatically updated and some of them can be stored for later display. Videcom also includes software for calculating profit-and-loss positions by account throughout the day. The Videcom service, although probably the best known, is no longer the only one of its kind. Market Data Systems also distributes minute-by-minute price information and exchange activity to a variety of video monitors including their Graphics One. The Graphics One draws tick-by-tick bar charts, spreads, moving averages, and point-and-figure diagrams. Both Videcom and Graphics One can be used in real-time transmission mode on daily or intraday data, so that charts can be drawn for current trading activity or for a life of contract summary. Market Data Systems keeps the intraday data on-line for the past month, and the historical daily data are accessible back to 20 years, providing the user with a comprehensive environment for making intraday trading decisions based on a wide range of information.

These trading applications services take advantage of *intelligent terminals*. The term "intelligent" is used to refer to the terminals' hardware sophistication. Unlike the terminals used by the simple news and data services which are equipped only for display, the intelligent terminals, after having received data files from the host computer, have the hardware and software to execute computations, draw graphs, and maintain small on-line databases. The more sophisticated the terminal—the higher its intelligence—the more complex the tasks it can be programmed to perform. Tradecenter takes advantage of the highly sophisticated Hewlett-Packard graphics terminals. The Tradecenter service includes instant data display and complete analysis via a connection to the master computer. Some of the more interesting features of Tradecenter, aside from the common graphics capabilities, include the ability to simultaneously view up to four separate charts or zoom in on one chart or a section of a chart. Because of the high resolution of the HP terminals, the Tradecenter graphs, even when only as large as a quarter of a page, are clear and legible.

Microcomputer Services. Radio Data Systems, transmitting data in real-time frequency through telephone, FM radio, or satellite signals, uses color graphics for its Market Monitor Service and ComChart computers. The same instant display and graphic analysis can be performed as with the other services, but the ComChart computer enhances graphics resolution by using eight different colors. Radio Data Systems subscribers can also use Apple or TRS-80 computers to receive data and news. Both of these computers and the ComChart machine allow users to save data from the day for later analysis. Using actual *microcomputers* for intraday trading applications can give the day trader a single unit for a quote machine, a graphics terminal, and an independent computer for analysis when the market is closed. The Quotrader Corporation provides a service like this on the Apple personal computer. Quotrader's system is useful for on-line, real-time systems trading, continuous price quotes, graphic displays, and instant accounting. A similar service, the Intra-Day Analyst, developed by the CompuTrac Technical Analysis Group in conjunction with Commodity Communications Corporation, combines the news and quote services of the VQP 3000 terminal with the graphic and computational facilities of the Apple personal computer, which can be used for later analysis.

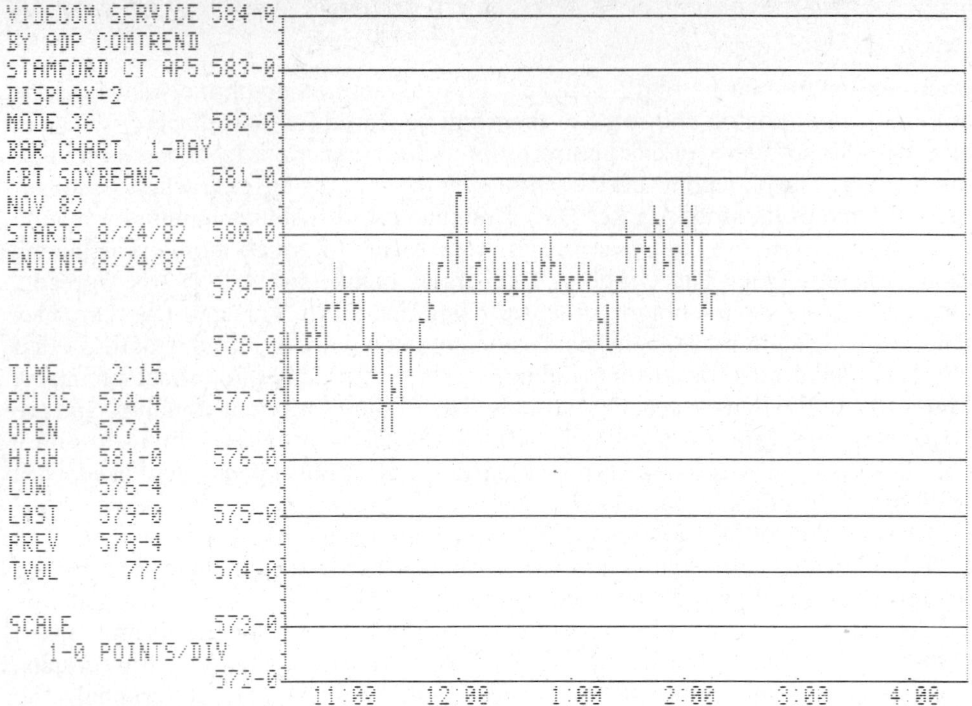

(*a*)

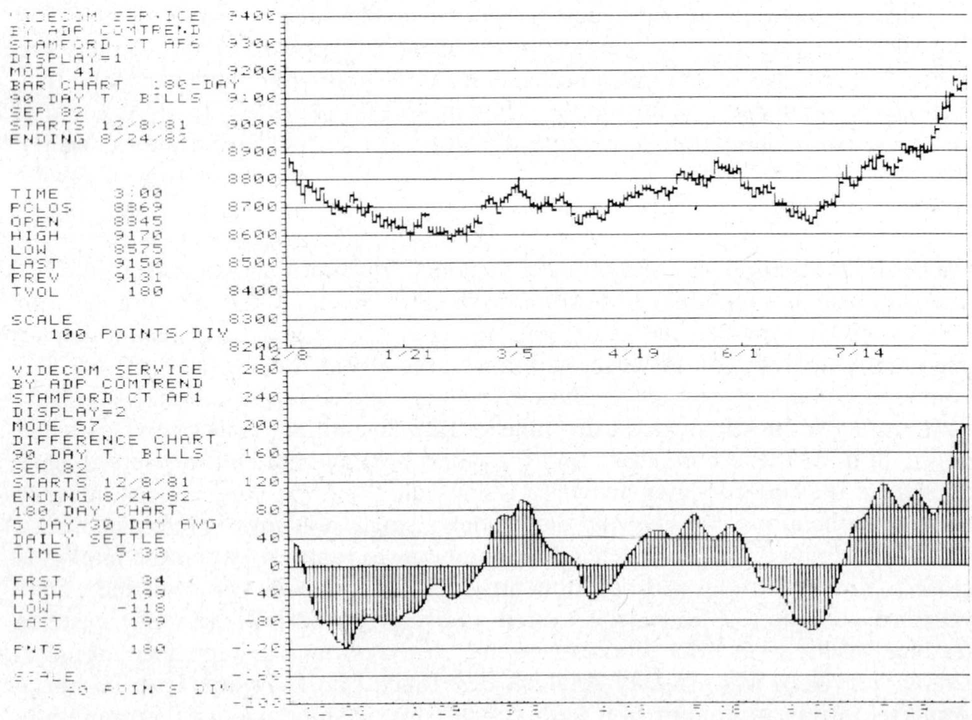

(*b*)

FIGURE 9. The Videcom Service, by ADP/Comtrend, is one of the oldest graphics and quote systems for real-time market analysis. These are just some examples of the displays which, in addition to numerical tables, Videcom users can draw up on their terminals.

There is an altogether different group of vendors supplying not only real-time data and analysis capabilities, but also trading signals generated by proprietary technical systems. Quotrader provides buy/sell recommendations from a number of *trading systems,* along with other features. Monchik–Weber Corporation's Financial Futures Service, distributed through Telerate, also includes trading recommendations, analysis, and capabilities for screening different futures contracts to make trade selections based on certain criteria specified by the user. Some companies transmit trading signals from their technical systems over time-sharing networks. In most cases, the firms selling trading signals from systems they have developed will show their prospective users track records of the trading system's performance. Evaluation of technical trading systems is covered elsewhere in this book—suffice it here to say that careful decisions must be made in guided systems trading. In some cases, historically proven technical systems can serve at least as a foundation or complement to your own daily trading analysis. In other cases, they can be your complete indisputable guide, but they must be evaluated as recommendations—not as a computer environment for your own applications.

While developments in communications applications have enabled the rapid transmission of data from trading floors to remote terminals and computers around the country, trading applications such as the graphics and real-time analysis software packages discussed have broadened the appeal of futures markets even further. By providing capabilities for almost anyone anywhere to analyze market activity as it occurs and develop structured, timely trading decisions, the combination of communication and trading applications makes it possible for a trader in Florida to react to developments at a Chicago exchange, sometimes more quickly and with more information than the traders who are there on the floor. After the markets close, however, there is a totally different area of applications in historical analysis available in time-sharing, distributed, or independent processing environments.

ANALYTICAL APPLICATIONS. The analytical applications packages, although they usually include graphics capabilities, are designed for building models. With some packages, technical *trading systems* can be structured based on historical research into statistical market relationships. Fundamental *forecasting models* can be built with packages for *econometric analysis*. Some of the packages for analytical applications are so comprehensive that they are like programming languages, while others are so specific that one only needs to type single-key responses to computer prompts. The larger, more complex packages have so many preprogrammed commands and functions included in them that it requires a large computer to run them. Because the main benefit of these complex packages is that they can be used to build large, complicated models which need massive databases, it is appropriate that they run only on the machines with greater internal memory. Some applications in historical analysis which require significant amounts of data are better performed in time-sharing environments for the machines' speed and ease of use, but for most any of the regular, day-to-day market studies there are sufficiently powerful packages for technical and fundamental analysis on *microcomputers*.

Technical Analysis Packages. There is a variety of *technical analysis* applications packages. Some of them are used on time-sharing systems and some are available for purchase or lease on independent computers. These packages include not only the trading applications mentioned earlier, but similar and even more complicated ones for analyzing historical market behavior. Most of the concepts of technical analysis are mathematically simple so that even the personal computers can handle comprehensive applications packages of this nature. The only limit of microcomputers in technical analysis is that, because of their usually more restrictive memories, they cannot handle as much data at one time as a larger computer, so certain analyses may sometimes take longer or have to be confined to small historical intervals. Beyond these limits, however, today there is very little of technical analysis which cannot be accommodated by personal computers, given the applications packages available.

The main vendors of *time-sharing* packages for technical analysis are CISCO, MJK, and Remote Computing Corporation (RCC). CISCO's time-sharing service involves a library of programs which guide the user through particular applications with computer-generated prompts for information and user-supplied responses to implement trading, hedging, and calculation applications. The programs are all very simple to run, as the user only has to answer menu questions, but by the same measure they can be limiting to the sophisticated technical trader. MJK's time-sharing service is comparable to CISCO's in that each of the technical analysis packages is similar to the trading applications packages mentioned already, but can be used on historical databases. While the applications in both of their technical analysis packages allow users to calculate spreads, butterflies, price ranges, and moving averages, and to draw bar graphs, point-and-figure charts, oscillators, and relative strength indexes, they are truly canned programs. These packages, as well as RCC's MERLIN, can be used to run historical profit-and-loss performance evaluations of common trading systems and generate up-to-the-day trading signals from the systems which are chosen. The user's flexibility is limited to the length of moving average or strength index, the commodity being traded, or the time interval, for example. While these packages are valuable for the programming time and expense that they can save for those who want to work with well-known trading systems, the computations they perform can usually be accommodated by much smaller computers with more favorable cost structures than those associated with time sharing. Remote Computing Corporation has introduced Pear Technical Analysis, a microcomputer package which draws on the database resource of the mainframe and allows for complex, user-defined model building, analysis of trading rules, and graphics. Calculations are performed using a *time series processor* on the microcomputer, a method normally available in econometric environments, such as DRI and Chase/IDC.

The EZ Model Builder System, written by MoniResearch Corporation (MRC) is a menu-driven package for technical analysis on minicomputers and is available in some time-sharing environments. Designed for evaluating technical trading systems on historical data, the EZ system prompts the user for the specifications of a trading rule, generates buy/sell, short, and cover signals, and evaluates the profitability of using the particular trading rule. MoniResearch originally programmed the EZ Model Builder System for use on Data General computers, and the system is designed primarily for these machines. For the user who needs a

The SELECTCURVE Program serves as a useful tool to test the predictive qualities of various yield curve types. Segments of the yield curve can be studied to determine whether specific shapes or levels have recurred over time. This program provides valuable information to help investors maximize returns.

```
? DO SELECTCURVE

For instructions, type 'EXPLAIN' in response to command request...

Universe consists of 1 yield curves from Thu 1/1/81 to Thu 1/1/81.

ENTER COMMAND:
```

Yield curves within the interval 5 Nov 79 to 31 Dec 81 have been requested.

```
 INTERVAL 5 NOV 79 TO 31 DEC 81
Retrieving data...please wait
Universe consists of 564 yield curves from Mon 11/5/79 to Thu 12/31/81.

ENTER COMMAND:
```

All output will print 72 characters across the page.

```
 SET WIDTH:72
Option reset...

ENTER COMMAND:
```

There will be 64 lines per page.

```
 SET LPP:64
Option reset...

ENTER COMMAND:
```

Screen for all dates after 1/1/80

```
 SCREEN ALLDATES GTR 1 JAN 80
522 curves selected from a subset of 564 curves...

ENTER COMMAND:
```

Screen for all dates where the 30 year T-Bond was greater than 10.8% and less than 11.2%. This becomes the current date subset.

```
 SCREEN CN30YY GTR 10.8 AND CN30YY LSS 11.2
37 curves selected from a subset of 522 curves...

ENTER COMMAND:
```

Screen for all dates in the current date subset where the 3-month T-Bill was greater than 14.0%. This now becomes the current date subset.

```
 SCREEN BL3Y GTR 14
2 curves selected from a subset of 37 curves...

ENTER COMMAND:
 REVIEW


Current interval is Mon 11/5/79 to Thu 12/31/81.

                Number
     Subset   Dates In
     Number   Subset              Screen Criteria
       -        ---         ------------------------------------
       *        564         Screening Universe
       1        522         ALLDATES GTR 1 JAN 80
       2         37         CN30YY GTR 10.8 AND CN30YY LSS 11.2
       3          2         BL3Y GTR 14
```

Original date subset.
Previous date subset.
Current date subset.

```
ENTER COMMAND:
 RESET 2
Current subset is subset 2 which contains 37 dates...

ENTER COMMAND:
```

The variable CN7TO20YY is defined as CN7YY/CN20YY.

```
 LET CN7TO20YY=CN7YY/CN20YY
CN7TO20YY Created

ENTER COMMAND:
```

The command, SCREEN CN7YY/CN20YY GTR 1 could have also been used here.

```
 SCREEN CN7TO20YY GTR 1
27 curves selected from a subset of 37 curves...

ENTER COMMAND:
 SCREEN BL3Y LEQ 10
2 curves selected from a subset of 27 curves...

ENTER COMMAND:
```

Lists the dates which meet all previous screening criteria.

```
 LIST

   2 curves in subset 4...

1          Wed 8/20/80
2          Fri 8/22/80
```

FIGURE 10. An example of a menu-driven program. This particular program, one of those in DRI's financial applications library, tests the predictive qualities of various types of yield curves.

large enough system to be able to take advantage of minicomputers, the EZ system can be used in-house. With this package, after the user tests and fine tunes a technical trading model, the same programs can be used to generate trading signals from the model. The buy/sell signals can be specified in logically complex or simple terms and they can be proprietary signals generated by your own trading system.

Even with applications such as MRC's EZ Model Builder System, most all of technical analyses can be handled by personal computers. Some of the more serious vendors of microcomputer software are developing applications packages designed for functions similar to the EZ system. As microcomputer technology expands, these packages will become comprehensive enough to take full advantage of the current hardware, so that soon the only need for the time-sharing services will be for database access and transmission. In the area of microcomputer applications packages for technical analysis, there are already hordes of vendors supplying programs. Many of the applications programs are provided by organizations or clubs that grew out of a group of commodity traders all interested in using microcomputers for futures market analysis, and many vendors are independent investors who are willing to sell the programs they have written for themselves. When microcomputers first became popular, there were a few commodity futures traders who saw early on that there was an opportunity for using these miniature marvels for all sorts of tedious technical analysis computations and charting applications. At that time, the choices were to do the work manually, purchase a minicomputer and write software, or to engage in a costly, ongoing time-sharing arrangement. In this environment, a limited software package for a microcomputer hit the stage as an appealing alternative, and applications programs started cropping up everywhere. The status of microcomputer software as a cottage industry is changing as some of the smaller software vendors are becoming larger and the larger ones are growing. As with any industry where customer service (though important) can be so costly, the vendors which can maintain (even strengthen) their popularity are the ones with the largest client base. The cost structure of software production and support ensures that this trend will continue, so that only the strong software vendors will be able to be competitive in the market. Even now, the more common applications packages sold for use on microcomputers are inexpensive enough that an individual trader can afford an entire hardware and software system without having to think of it as a major expenditure. Some of the vendors' packages are designed for specific hardware, and unless there are other software packages for that hardware, then choosing such services can limit the potential uses of your computer system.

One of the original cooperative organizations of microcomputer-oriented commodity traders is the CompuTrac Technical Analysis Group. In addition to having developed communications and trading applications for the Apple computer, they have written many menu-driven programs making up a complete library of technical analysis applications. For calculating or graphing spreads, averages, or oscillators there are different programs that club members can use. There are also programs for testing or using many of the well-known technical trading systems such as Wilder's techniques, momentum and oscillators, demand and strength indexes, and other calculations. The CompuTrac programs are menu driven and therefore very easy to use. The software directs the user through a sequence of choices, so that the user can run one or another program and draw a variety of different charts. The premise on which CompuTrac was built, that of a cooperative, encourages users to develop their own programs and submit them to the organization. This has led to a comprehensive library of trading systems in the different menus. Orion Enterprises, another firm supplying programs for the Apple II computer, has similar software for drawing graphs and creating spreads, averages, oscillators, and signals from a number of popular trading systems. Using the same data file structure as CompuTac, Orion's users can retrieve data from a few different vendors and be able to use the data in either Orion's or CompuTrac's programs. Orion Enterprises and the CompuTrac group must be credited with having started the proliferation of microcomputer applications packages for use in the futures markets. When personal computers first became popular, there were no software packages available for technical analysis and little apparent incentive for commercial investment in their development. It took clubs like CompuTrac and computer-oriented traders like those at Orion to develop the first generation of software designed for technical analysis on microcomputers.

Software Resources, Incorporated (SRI) has a library of applications packages which are well-suited to most any type of technical analysis on the Apple and IBM personal computers. One of the applications packages SRI leases, known as the SMART (Securities Market Analysis, Reporting, and Transaction) system is a library of menu-driven programs for computational and graphical analyses of stock or commodity futures markets. SMART, a comprehensive package with flexibility, can be used to implement any popular trading systems or even proprietary ones, because SRI designed some interesting features into SMART which make the package unique in its field. SMART is not just a library of programs, but an environment for computer analysis. Programs guide the user through all of the different menus, which include programs for computation of common or nonstandard formulas. SMART has a feature which allows the user to enter his or her own formula and the software package will write the program to generate trading signals from a proprietary system. This formula feature creates an almost limitless system, even for users who have no knowledge of programming, and can be used to evaluate the profitability of various trading systems of almost any design. To make consistent systems trading easy, the formula can be saved so that future use of the same formula requires only the push of a button or two. Although SMART does work with data files constructed in its own specific format, it has a capability for reformatting files made in the SMART environment, so that any of the information used in SRI's applications package can be considered "portable" to other software, such as the popular VisiCorp programs and others. The reverse can also be done so that data files with unsuitable structures for analysis can be reformatted.

Applications packages for technical analysis, including the high-frequency trading applications packages, are usually built on simple computation foundations. As can be surmised from the above discussions, most of the software packages designed for technical analysis are similar to one another, because the fundamental concepts are straightforward and the functions which have to be included are commonly accepted. In choosing a software package for technical analysis, the most important distinguishing factors should be the degree of flexibility and the cost. For reasons discussed elsewhere, it would be preferable to choose an applications package for a microcomputer over a time-sharing arrangement for technical analysis. The package chosen can be one which provides the user with a complete environment for executing market studies to make the best use of the microcomputer, but there are other choices for less expensive packages which are no more than libraries of programs for specific calculations. The different packages have distinct merits which must be weighed individually in each situation.

Fundamental Analysis Packages. In comparison to technical analysis, *fundamental analysis* requires a much different type of computer program. The main body of an applications package for technical analysis is made up of graphics programs and simple time-series processors. On the other hand, fundamental analysis software needs capabilities for statistics, correlation analysis, and econometrics—much more mathematically complex concepts. Using econometrics and statistics packages, historical market relationships can be tested and estimated towards constructing forecasting models. In most cases, because of the assumptions of econometrics, the fundamental analysis packages are designed for lower-frequency data, that is, monthly, quarterly, or annual time series. Given an understanding of econometrics, these packages can be used to build models for forecasting monthly or quarterly price levels, production figures, or demand measures. They can also be valuable in estimating relationships such as weather's impact on crop production, or the effect of interest rates on consumer demand.

Because the value of complete econometric and fundamental analysis applications is in using them to apply complex mathematical formulas to real data in attempts to develop forecasting models, the comprehensive packages that are easy to understand include hundreds of programs. This results in most of the packages being too large for a microcomputer to support. Because fundamental analysis covers such a broad range of mathematical concepts, the complete applications packages are usually more like complete programming languages. Users have a library of operations and functions that can be used individually or connected together to create tailored problem-solving packages.

Some of the database and analysis time-sharing vendors have proprietary applications packages such as DRI's EPS and Chase's X-Sim. DRI's package, EPS, is one of the most comprehensive, easy-to-use packages for fundamental analysis, with simple English-language commands for performing *regression analysis, autoregressive integrated moving average (ARIMA)* studies, simultaneous econometric model development and solution, as well as report writing, graphics, and programmable functions. Packages like EPS and X-Sim, both programming languages in and of themselves, exemplify the type of applications which a microcomputer simply cannot support, because they require such great amounts of internal memory to run. The users of these packages, however, pay a high price for the great flexibility they offer. Comprehensive *econometrics packages* can save tremendous amounts of expensive time and effort for the user who wants to develop highly sophisticated forecasting models, but they require the power and capacity of a large computer.

For microcomputer owners, there are plenty of slower, more cumbersome packages for limited fundamental analysis, such as *VisiCorp*'s VisiCalc and Peachtree Software's MagiCalc. These applications packages are called *electronic worksheets,* as they program the computer to replace a pencil, a pad of paper, and a calculator. The electronic worksheets are available for many microcomputers and they have become very popular because they have so many different uses in budget analysis and "what if" studies. Users type in labels, values, or formulas that correspond to specific locations on the worksheet and the program completes all the calculations. Any time a number on the worksheet is changed, all of those variables that are affected by the changed number will be automatically recalculated. The electronic worksheets, because they can be used to manipulate large data files, can be used to execute some types of fundamental analysis. There are, however, applications packages that are specifically designed for econometric and statistical analysis on microcomputers. These packages are not as sophisticated as the time-sharing ones mentioned previously, but for some types of less complicated fundamental analysis they can be suitable. SRI's SMART package has a collection of fundamental analysis menus containing programs for regression analysis and computation of correlation statistics, variance–covariance matrices, and descriptive statistics such as mean, standard deviation, and extremes. While this applications package is nowhere near as powerful as DRI's EPS, for example, it makes especially good use of the Apple hardware to perform rigorous statistical studies. Except in the case of multiple equation econometric models, the applications packages for microcomputers are adequate for most of fundamental analysis.

In the cases of DRI and Chase/IDC both time-sharing vendors originally developed their econometrics packages for their own use in building forecasting models. Although subscribers to both DRI's and Chase's services can use these packages to develop their own fundamental models, both vendors also offer access to the econometric models built by their staff economists and consultants. These commercial econometric models are updated constantly to more accurately represent the current economic situation. They are maintained and revised by specialists in the economics of certain industry sectors. For example, DRI has different models developed by specialists in agriculture, energy, manufacturing inputs, U.S. macroeconomy, European economies, and so on. These models are extremely complex, requiring the power and capacity of a time-sharing computer, so they are available only through subscription fees and usage payments. Their main value is in making alternative forecasts and "what if" analyses, using a model that represents current market relationships. For large corporate planning applications and long-term econometric forecasts, these models are very useful, but their value in day-to-day market studies or simple fundamental analysis is questionable.

The broad range of analytical applications packages for the futures markets makes it possible for almost any type of research study to be executed easily with no knowledge of computers. Packages on time-sharing systems or for use on minicomputers or microcomputers have brought the power of computer applications in technical and fundamental analysis into the reach of all of us. While none of us would deny that any successful trader has to have a good knowledge of the markets, computer analysis has become much more prevalent in futures trading and the percentage of market participants who make decisions based on seat-of-the-pants notions and hunches is constantly decreasing.

ACCOUNTING APPLICATIONS. Another area of applications important to the futures markets is in *accounting* and *back-office operations*. There are commercial packages of varying levels of sophistication available for time-sharing use, lease on minicomputers, and purchase on microcomputers that fulfill the accounting and regulatory processing needs for traders, brokers and advisors. There are two service bureaus which have specialized in providing processing applications to the brokerage industry, Commodity Accounting Systems (CAS) and Computer Information Service (CIS). CIS has programs which, after the user has provided the necessary price, purchase-and-sale data, compute margin requirements, calculate and charge commissions based on different structures, generate position reports, and CFTC reports, and even transmit information to appropriate branch offices. Subscribers to CIS send the needed input data to the host computer each night via remote terminals and processed information is received the next morning on the same terminal. CAS has a similar service in their applications package, CFATS (Commodity Fund Accounting through Time Sharing), which was written for computing performance reports, status of accounts, tax liabilities, and purchase-and-sale summaries for commodity pool operators and trading advisors. Like CIS's service, CAS's CFATS receives user data over the telephone from a remote terminal each night, processes the data overnight, and sends all output back to the user the next day. While both of these services allow data input in interactive, or time-sharing, mode they are batch processing services.

For accounting applications that necessitate interactive processing, both ADP/Comtrend and FOXSI have time-sharing packages. ADP's Commodities Processing Service is like the services mentioned previously—after submitting data by phone, the package computes, sorts, and aggregates margin, profit and loss, and commission figures for customer and house accounts; maintains CFTC records; and prints the necessary reports. Along with the Commodities Processing Service, however, ADP offers an applications package called AccountWatch. This package, which runs on the Videcom time-sharing terminals, provides instant retrieval of programmed accounts, with up-to-the-second position reports for profit-and-loss accounting, margin and equity balances, and summaries by account or broker. FOXSI also offers a batch processing service for back-office and regulatory accounting in conjunction with an interactive time-sharing applications package for listing the day's trading and open position information aggregated or sorted by customer, account, exchange, commodity, and contract. CIS's service includes the option for a distributed processing system, whereby the interactive, intraday accounting applications, such as trade entry, position reporting, or portfolio monitoring can be performed on an isolated IBM minicomputer. At the end of the day, all of the necessary data can be collected and transmitted to the central computer automatically for batch processing of accounts and settling information overnight.

For larger operations that can benefit from buying their own minicomputer, there are software firms such as Monchik–Weber and Brokerage Systems, Incorporated which lease applications packages or build custom processing programs. Monchik–Weber, using Data General and Hewlett Packard computers, has designed information systems for back-office accounting and other trading operations such as portfolio management accounting and reporting, price monitoring and position accounting, and profit-and-loss computation by account, broker, or strategy. They have also worked as systems consultants to brokerage firms setting up distributed data processing networks with central processors and desktop information terminals, Brokerage Systems, Incorporated (BSI) offers custom-designed and prepackaged software, primarily the Tracs/34 package, for accounting applications on the IBM System/34. In addition to functioning normally in any other jobs, the IBM can be used as a turnkey accounting system with BSI's applications package for trade accounting and reporting, limited research and analysis, and printing customer reports. For large brokerage houses, these companies can bring specialized programming experience and expertise to bear on the otherwise long and complex task of setting up a complete processing network for accounting applications in-house. For the smaller firms of traders and brokers, services like the batch processing and time-sharing ones are useful in the same way—they save the user the trouble of having to not only start the applications development from scratch, but also from having to cover the total cost independently.

For the independent trader or broker, there are applications packages designed for limited data processing and accounting on personal computers. SRI's SMART package has an account monitoring section which computes account appraisal reports with long and short positions, profit-and-loss statements, and trade entry figures by account, by contract, or by block trade. Complete processing sequences can be programmed with SMART's macro facility so that at the touch of only a few buttons, all necessary accounting reports can be generated. CompuTrac has a bookkeeping applications package also, the Equity Subsystem, for reviewing, selecting, posting, or listing information on trades, accounts, profit and loss, position entry and exit points, or commission charges by account or total. *The Organizer*, another package designed for future money managers, is one of the most complete packages for back-office accounting applications on a microcomputer. Designed to run on Apple, IBM, DEC, and Tandy/Radio Shack computers, it generates all of the necessary periodical reports for position and client management and CFTC compliance.

MAKING THE COMPUTER WORK FOR YOU. In choosing computer software, you determine whether all the time, effort, and expense you have put into completing your system was worthwhile. The decisions about hardware, data, and software must all be made together; however, the latter decision can usually determine the choices available for the other two decisions and will always delimit your range of applications for them. If long after choosing a particular software package you find the need to change your vendor, the results can be costly in almost every case. If you are a time-sharing user and you chose a particular vendor based on the applications software, a change of vendors will leave your processing operations at the bottom of a brand new learning curve, slowing down that part of your business dependent on using the computer. All of your proprietary work may have to be redeveloped as well, usually at tremendous expense. The same problems can arise for a minicomputer user in a similar situation. Inadequate choices for software for in-house processing, however, can result in much greater expenses for program redevelopment and possibly in hardware replacement as well. For most microcomputer users, especially those who bought a particular computer because of the software provided for it, a decision to change software can result not only in the need to restart a long learning process, but also in being forced to purchase new, different equipment. Especially with microcomputers, but also in the case of more complex hardware and even time-sharing arrangements, the purchase, lease, or investment choice concerning applications must therefore be made with very careful attention.

The first decision to make in choosing applications packages is closely related to the type of hardware you will use, because your range of choices will depend thereon. Most any commercial software firm specializes in applications programming for only one type of machine and sometimes only one make of machine. The widest range of prepackaged software is available for microcomputer owners, followed by time-sharing users, and then those with minicomputers. While there are a few vendors offering minicomputer software for accounting applications, and even fewer for analytical applications, for the most part those who opt for an in-house, multiple-user system will have to hire or contract for their own programming and operating staff or make use of professional systems consultants. Developing software in-house, while normally very costly, can result in perfectly tailored applications packages and will therefore be desirable to some. Those who do become involved in long-term, in-house software development, however, should be careful to do so only with a well-thought plan and with close attention to organization and coordination to avoid effort duplication and unnecessary future bottlenecks in expansion.

The majority of us will be choosing software packages for use on microcomputers and will be faced with as baffling a range of options as there is in brands of bread in a supermarket. The warning to microcomputer owners is to learn to distinguish between comprehensive, flexible software on the one hand and limiting, unmanageable software on the other. An applications package of the latter type will result in an inefficient use of the microcomputer and as you begin to reach the software's limits, you will find you will have to start over with a new package or learn to program on your own. By making careful decisions, you can ensure that the package you start with will be adequate for years and that as your familiarity with the computer and your ability to use it in rigorous analysis both grow, you will not find yourself backed into a corner doing only what some programmer wanted to do and not what you really had in mind. There are a few microcomputer packages well established in the market which can take simple, formulated expressions as input and actually write new programs for you. Choosing these is advisable because they allow your analysis to be as flexible as your thinking without your having to learn how to program.

If the magnitude and nature of your processing needs lead you toward a time-sharing arrangement, your object will be to choose a vendor offering not only applications packages for all of your specific needs, but the necessary data services as well. In some cases, although it may be appropriate to use different vendors for each area of applications, having the necessary data readily accessible on the computer with which they will be processed is essential. Due to this requirement, choosing a time-sharing applications package must be done with attention to the quality of the vendor's data service regarding accuracy, timeliness, and coverage.

All of the above concerns, though more important in some cases than others, should be considered whether you choose a time-sharing service, a minicomputer, or a personal computer. There are some issues, however, which are equally important no matter what the circumstances. It is always best to choose a strong, well-established software vendor to ensure that the applications package you learn to use will continue to be supported. A strong vendor is one that is not only well-established generally, but specifically suited to fulfill the needs of those in your situation. In choosing a software vendor, be aware of all the details such as service, support, and degree of specialization. It is important that the firm's programmers be well-equipped with a knowledge of the applications field as well as computer programming. For example, between two equally competent programmers, one whose specialty is chemical engineering, the other whose expertise is in technical analysis, the latter would be far better prepared to write software for futures traders.

One sign of a software vendor's strength is the degree to which a users' community has been established. If the vendor has periodical newsletters and user seminars, then these will allow a forum for discussion and future expansion requests to flourish. Occasional meetings and correspondence with your software vendor's other customers will result in your own better understanding of the package and how best to use it. In sum, you should choose a software vendor, not just an applications package. Make a distinction between the way you buy a book and the way you obtain software. An author of a book will almost never contact those who have read the book and ask whether they understood certain chapters, whether the book could be improved for the next printing, and whether the readers would like to get together to discuss such issues. A supportive, service-minded software vendor should attend to all of these types of follow-up and cooperation.

All of us will have to begin becoming familiar with computers and their applications soon. Each of us will have many complicated decisions to make and we all will have to attend to issues of our own internal coordination, whether within a firm of many computer users or only within the confines of a personal computer system. The key concepts in making a lasting choice in an applications package are organization and flexibility, and the vendor's service, strength, and specific knowledge. While the cost of the software and the ease with which it can be learned are also important, if you attend to the other issues first, these will be the easier ones to manage.

IMPACT ON TRADING

As electronic information transmission and processing technologies have grown over the years, the range of computer services for futures market professionals has blossomed into a variety of choices in hardware, data, and software affording various cost-effective means of using computers. This proliferation of computer products has obviously changed the futures markets and as it continues will do so further. In that the futures markets are ones of high speed and rapid decisions, compared to the real-estate markets for example, much of trading activity as we know it today would never have been possible without the development of affordable computer hardware, innovations in data collection and transmission, and the growth of software technology to encompass the relevant applications areas. The increasing applicability of computers has led to their greater popularity, and vice versa, in what promises to be an endless spiral.

As computers become even more deeply engrained in the daily operation of the futures markets, standards for data communications will be established to enable more widely spread penetration. As such standards are developed, it will be possible for traders to communicate with each other and with the exchanges from remote locations around the globe. Any home-computer owner will be able to access current and historical data from commercial and public news and information bases. With more and more entities having to rely on electronically transmitted data, commercial vendors will be required to adhere to regulated levels of accuracy, much as grain suppliers are now required to meet certain criteria as to their product's content. As these standards become an accepted part of the data transmission and processing industry, software products will be developed with much broader appeal. If internal hardware configuration standards also are implemented or result by default, then the day can be imagined when, in a given application, almost any program will run on any computer with any data. Although this level of standardization may be a dream, it is realistic to conceive of the day when a worldwide network of computer users in the futures markets can share software and data and mail correspondence to one another at the speed of light through electronic communications media. In this sense, the impacts of computer technology on the futures markets have hardly begun.

As a consequence of the greater use of computers in studying and trading the futures markets, many of the currently successful trading systems will become weaker, outmoded, and too slow to catch price moves. With more rapid trading, systems will have to be more finely tuned and more specifically related to individual markets. Trading systems will also have shorter profitability lifespans as redevelopment and respecification of trading models become more important, regular tasks of higher frequency. These side effects of computer analysis and trading are in some sense inevitable—if each of us has a comparably powerful computer with software designed for picking the unquestionably optimal trading system, then presumably we will all be getting similar or equivalent trading signals at the same time. The main differences in trading success would then be in execution time. Market moves would be much faster and their magnitudes would be greater. When communications capabilities and computer-user acceptance grow to the point where trades on all exchanges will be electronically executed, the impact of these factors will be even greater. To keep from getting behind in such a spiral where every trader has to constantly revise and fine tune his or her system, we will all have to become more open to new ideas and more flexible in our daily operating methods, but more disciplined in our trading decisions.

One of the obvious consequences of the new communications capabilities, which is slowly starting to take root, is a network of computer accessible exchanges far reaching enough to facilitate 24-hour trading in markets around the globe. This type of trading will open up all sorts of opportunities for arbitraging which were never even dreamed of in the past. As 24-hour trading becomes a reality, however, watching all of the markets around the clock may become the only way for a trader to maintain a competitive edge. For the large trading firms and brokerage houses, keeping a vigil on all the markets will be a costly responsibility, and for the individual trader, some opportunities will have to be forgone for purposes of sleep. To enable 24-hour trading, the futures exchanges will have to become a different type of operation from what they are now. In order to attract and support the levels of liquidity which will be available, the futures exchanges will have to become increasingly dependent on computers and communications networks for rapid and accurate data distribution to, and receival from, thousands of locations at the speed of light.

The development of INTEX the international futures exchange which has a computer-based trading environment, is a milestone in the technological progress of the futures markets. A great deal about the feasibility of a computer clearinghouse will be learned during the first few years of INTEX. In order for INTEX to succeed and therefore for other similar entities to arise, there will have to be further enhancements to current data transmission, processing, storage, and retrieval technologies, but we can be nearly certain that these will come. The most formidable obstacle to such progress will not be in the technology, but in our emotional willingness to change with the times. The floor traders, around whom the markets function, are accustomed to transacting with persons, that is, individuals, who can be seen, waved to, and signaled. It will be difficult to change from making trades by open outcry, to completing the process by numerical keyboard entry of bids and offers to a computer network through a CRT display terminal. Even though the adjustment process to the computers' penetration of the futures markets may be long and slow, it is almost a certain bet that the trader of tomorrow will be dramatically different from the trader of today. Tomorrow's trader will speak a language not of hand signals, but of computer-recognizable mnemonics and symbols. Trading will not be built around any type of social interaction or understanding of individuals' techniques or methods. To the contrary, futures trading will involve almost no human mixing, because the "trading floor" will be a central processing unit and "exchange seats" will be computer terminals in the members' homes. We can imagine, somewhat reluctantly, a generation of automaton traders who take recommendations only from computers and communicate with other traders, brokers, clients, and their offices all without ever leaving home.

As the spiral of market growth and technological progress continues upward, increasingly wider trading opportunities will arise not only in the form of more comprehensive market access, but also in terms of new futures contracts and higher levels of liquidity. With more and more interest in financial instrument futures, foreign exchange futures and equity futures, as well as options on commodities and futures, and with the increasing importance of international trade and finance in our world economy, the number of firms and individuals involved in the futures markets will continue to increase. As the comprehensive coverage of the markets, their broad accessibility, and their volume levels all grow, the futures markets will fulfill their functions much more efficiently. As the market networks become broad enough that anybody can participate effectively, limited only by their ability to afford the necessary computer services, there will be a much more fluid environment for price discovery. Information will not only flow more rapidly, but it will go from and to many more people, so that anyone who wants will be able to access all and any public information regarding each market of interest. This more rapid and comprehensive information flow will result in more efficient risk transfer through the futures markets by facilitating a greater number of transactions. Inasmuch as the markets function to transfer risk from the shoulder of the commercial hedger to that of the profit-motivated speculator, higher liquidity and more rapid information transmission and trade execution will allow the markets to serve their purpose more easily and more fully.

APPENDIX: CATALOG OF COMMERCIAL SERVICES

This chapter has centered around a discussion of the various uses of computers and related products and services which supply the futures trading industry. This appendix summarizes the specific offerings of companies that responded to our requests for information. The list of companies and the descriptions of their products and services are not exhaustive; rather, they are digests of the information received. This section should serve as a useful and easy reference for commodities professionals seeking information about hardware, software, and database products and services. Companies are cross-referenced by type of offering and then listed alphabetically. As an example, companies that offer both Technical Analysis Data (under Database Services) and software for Technical Analysis (under Software Applications), would be listed under each of those headings and separately under the alphabetical listing for a summary of the information concerning the specific company. Should a company's summary under the alphabetical listing interest you, contact them at the given address for more comprehensive information.

PART 1: CATEGORY LISTING

Computer Hardware

Time-Sharing Computer Services

Automatic Data Processing
Chase Econometrics/Interactive Data Corporation
Commodity Information Services Company
Computer Information Service
Computerized Research International
Data Resources, Incorporated
Earth Satellite Corporation
Interactive Data Services, Incorporated
MJK Associates
The Monchik–Weber Corporation
Remote Computing Corporation
I. P. Sharp Associates, Limited

Minicomputers

Digital Equipment Corporation
Hewlett Packard
International Business Machines Corporation
The Monchik–Weber Corporation
Tandem Computers, Incorporated

Microcomputers

Apple Computer, Incorporated

Comm-Basic Associates, Incorporated
Digital Equipment Corporation
Hewlett Packard
International Business Machines Corporation
Software Resources, Incorporated
Tandy Corporation/Radio Shack

Database Services

Textual Information

Commodity News Services, Incorporated
Commodity World News
CompuServe
Dialog Information Services, Incorporated
Dow Jones and Company, Incorporated
GTE, Financial Services Division
Instant Update
Logica
The New York Times Information Service, Incorporated
Quotron Systems, Incorporated
Reuters Limited
Technical Data
Telerate Systems, Incorporated

News and Quotes

Automatic Data Processing
Commodity Communications Corporation
Commodity News Services, Incorporated
Commodity World News
Dow Jones and Company, Incorporated
GTE, Financial Services Division
Instant Update
Interactive Software Research Incorporated
Kidder Reports Incorporated
Market Data Systems, Incorporated
Market Information, Incorporated
The Monchik–Weber Corporation
Quotron Systems, Incorporated
Radio Data Systems, Incorporated
Reuters Limited
Technical Data
Telerate Systems, Incorporated
Trans-Lux Corporation

Technical Analysis Data

Automatic Data Processing
Chase Econometrics/Interactive Data Corporation
Commodity Systems, Incorporated
CompuServe
Data Resources, Incorporated
Dow Jones and Company, Incorporated
Dunn and Hargitt
Market Data Systems, Incorporated
MJK Associates
The Monchik–Weber Corporation
Remote Computing Corporation
I. P. Sharp Associates, Limited
Source Telecomputing Corporation
Technical Data

Fundamental Analysis Data

Business International Corporation
Chase Econometrics/Interactive Data Corporation
CompuServe
Data Resources, Incorporated
Earth Satellite Corporation
Interactive Data Services, Incorporated
Predicasts, Incorporated
I. P. Sharp Associates, Limited
Source Telecomputing Corporation
Weather Services International

Software Applications

IntraDay Analysis

Automatic Data Processing
Commodity Communications Corporation
Commodity QuoteGraphics
CompuTrac, Incorporated
GTE, Financial Services Division
Interactive Software Research Incorporated
Market Data Systems, Incorporated
Market Information, Incorporated
Marketview Microsystems

Marketvision
The Monchik–Weber Corporation
PWA Commodity Research
Quotrader Corporation
Radio Data Systems, Incorporated
Technical Data
Tradecenter Incorporated
U.S. Futures Corporation

Technical Analysis

Anidata
Automatic Data Processing
CFM Corporation
Comm-Basic Associates, Incorporated
Commodity Concepts
Commodity Information Services Company
Computerized Research International
CompuTrac, Incorporated
Data Resources, Incorporated
Dow Jones and Company, Incorporated
H & H Trading Company
Investor's Micro Messenger
Kate's Komputers Distributing Corporation
Management Services
Marketvision
Memory Systems Incorporated
Microcomputing Research
Micro Futures
MJK Associates
MoniResearch Corporation
OCO Commodities, Incorporated
Omega Microware
Orion Management, Incorporated
Professional Farm Software
Raden Research
R & B Futures Software
Remote Computing Corporation
Software Options, Incorporated
Software Resources, Incorporated
Technical Data
Troy–Folan Productions, Incorporated

Urban Aggregates, Incorporated
Wall Street Software

Fundamental Analysis

Blue Lakes Software
Chase Econometrics/Interactive Data Corporation
Data Resources, Incorporated
Earth Satellite Corporation
MoniResearch Corporation
Peachtree Software, Incorporated
Software Resources, Incorporated
VisiCorp
The Winchendon Group

Accounting and Management

Anidata
Automatic Data Processing
Brokerage Systems, Incorporated
Commodity Accounting Systems
Computer Information Service
CompuTrac, Incorporated
Futures Order Execution Systems, Incorporated
Interactive Data Services, Incorporated
Investor's Software
Kate's Komputers Distributing Corporation
Management Services
Microcomputing Research
Olamic Systems Corporation
Organizer Systems Incorporated
Peachtree Software, Incorporated
I. P. Sharp Associates, Limited
Software Resources, Incorporated
Urban Aggregates, Incorporated
VisiCorp
The Yardley Group, Incorporated

PART 2: ALPHABETICAL LISTING

Anidata
613 Jaegar Court
Sicklerville, NJ 08081

Market Analyst—three menu-driven investment analysis and management software packages for Apple computers; Technical Analyst tracks and analyzes commodities, stocks, and bonds; Portfolio Manager automates recordkeeping and reporting for realized and unrealized gains on shorts, options, bonds, and cash purchases and sales; *News Views* and *Quotes* links Apple to *Dow Jones*, *CompuServe*, and the *Source*.

Apple Computer, Incorporated
10260 Bandley Drive
Cupertino CA 95014

Apple microcomputers—the most popular and the first commercial personal computers; distributed through retail dealers nationwide; software, peripherals, and service available at retail stores; applications packages with various functions sold by software vendors.

Automatic Data Processing (ADP/Comtrend)
25 Third Street
Stamford, CT 06905

Commodities Processing Service—services customer accounts; maintains FCM records; handles margin calculation, rate optimization, and call maintenance.

VIDECOM Quotation Service—tabular and graphic display of current day prices; *Boardwatch* with programmable pages of automatically updated price information; graphics applies tick, bar, trendline, point-and-figure, and spread charts to current data; database of price and moving average figures over life of contract for all current contracts; *Intelligent Comtrend System* interfaces ADP terminal with your in-house computer or ADP's time-sharing machine for data access and transmission.

AccountWatch—tabular display provides instant retrieval of customer accounts and updates profit and loss by position; automatically updates equity and margin balances for each account or summarizes by various categories.

Blue Lakes Software
3240 University Avenue
Madison, WI 53705

Statistical software for Apple computers—library of software packages for analysis and database management; *QUESTMOD* for questionnaire analysis, *STATMOD* for statistical analysis, *PLOTMOD* for graphic plotting, *MAILMOD* for mailing list management, and other utility programs.

Brokerage Systems, Incorporated
2 North Riverside Plaza, Suite 1135
Chicago, IL 60606

Tracs/34 Trade Accounting System—accounting software for clearing firms and futures commission merchants using in-house IBM System/34; *CPARS* bookkeeping software for standard monthly reports in pool management; manual, interactive data entry for open position reports, purchase-and-sale statements, and margin and commission maintenance and calculation; exchange, government, and month-end reporting; remote office report transmission.

Business International Corporation
One Dag Hammarskjold Plaza
New York, NY 10017

BI/DATA—judgmental forecasting service and historical data base of international statistics relevant to industry and product analysis; available through time-sharing networks, such as I.P. Sharp Associates, DIALOG Information Services, and General Electric Information Services Company.

CFM Corporation
P.O. Box 1302
Arvada, CO 80001

Software for TRS-80 microcomputers; computer-tested trading system and historical data files; emphasis on option writing strategies.

Chase Econometrics/Interactive Data Corporation
150 Monument Road
Bala Cynwyd, PA 19004

Chase/IDC—provides economic forecasting services, consulting, databases, and large-scale information management and econometric modeling systems to corporations and government; area-specific forecasting services in U.S. Economics, Food and Agriculture, International, Energy, Regional, Transportation, Industrial, and Metals and Minerals; topical databases covering U.S. Economy, Regional, PPI, CPI, Energy, Agriculture, Passenger Car, International, Financial, Flow of Funds, OECD, Insurance, and Metals; software for data management, data analysis, econometric analysis, simulation and modeling, reports, graphs, and customized applications.

Comm-Basic Associates, Incorporated
7920 Chambersburg Road
Dayton, OH 45424

Commodity System Programs—technical analysis and graphics software; programs for generation of trading signals from Welles Wilder systems, demand indices, and other popular systems; moving averages, oscillators, and spread calculation; point-and-figure charting; programs for keeping financial statements and records of small portfolios; communications software for accessing remote databases; database management software; general business accounting and word-processing packages; *Tele-Trader* programs for automatic daily database updates.

Trader Computers—Vector Graphics microcomputers for operating the Comm-Basic software and other packages; set up by Comm-Basic with Execuplan (an electronic spreadsheet), *Memorite III* (word-processing system), and *CCA Data Management System*.

COMMODEX
114 Liberty Street
New York, NY 10006

The COMMODEX System—the signals from a proprietary technical trading system are updated either daily via printed material or twice daily through the COMMODEX on-line computer network, which is accessible at any time of the day or night.

Commodity Accounting Systems
777 North First Street, #205
San Jose, CA 95112

Commodity Fund Accounting through Time Sharing (CFATS) System—accounting service for commodity trading advisors and commodity pool operators, delivered through service bureau or time sharing; preparation of personalized monthly statements for each pool participant; reports generated for performance measurement, daily status, taxes, and purchase-and-sale summaries.

Commodity Communications Corporation
420 Eisenhower Lane North
Lombard, IL 60148

VQP 2000, 3000, and 5000—on-line quotation systems for instant delivery of price and news information; graphics include bar charts, spreads, and point-and-figure charts; programmable news and quote pages; quote service can be accessed with Apple or Tandy/Radio Shack microcomputers and can be interfaced with the Technical Analysis Group's *Intra-Day Analyst*.

Commodity Concepts
P.O. Box 35324
Phoenix, AZ 85069

Commodity Programs—software for TRS-80 microcomputers; programs compute moving averages, maintain point-and-figure charts, calculate some popular indicators, and manage price-history files.

Commodity Information Services Company
327 South LaSalle
Chicago, IL 60604

CISCO Service—lists and graphs price data, moving averages, spreads, ratios, and oscillators; draws point-and-figure charts and generates cyclical and statistical analyses; trading programs for forecasting price directions and levels, such as the COMMODEX, Keltner, Donchian, and Elliott methods; all programs and 8- to 10-year historical database available in time-sharing mode; data transmission programs and simple analytical applications available for Cromemco microcomputer.

Commodity News Services, Incorporated
2100 West 89th Street
Leawood, KS 66206

Data Quote II, Data Quote IV, and American Quotation Systems—on-line quotation services for current day prices and news transmission; separate news wires for Active Commodity Trading, Baking Ingredients, Cotton Trade News, Financial Instruments, Farm Radio, Grain Instant News, Global Weather, Livestock, Feed, and Meat, Metals, Maritime Trade, Oils and Fats, Private Agricultural Markets, Poultry and Egg, Soft Commodities, Transportation News.

Uniquote—provided through Unicom News, transmits exchange prices and news to Great Britain and Western Europe; displays quotes and text on active commodities, spot, and forward foreign exchange rates; covers all futures exchanges, uses intelligent microcomputer for display terminal.

Commodity QuoteGraphics
P.O. Box 758
Glenwood Springs, CO 81602

Trader System—turns Tandy/Radio Shack microcomputer into quotation machine; programmable pages for last, open, high, low, previous close, tick volume, opening range, and volume and open interest; quote board format with multiple commodities represented on a page; price alert function to flash lights when specified criteria are met. Commodity *QuoteGraphics* collects and checks data before sending to users by wire or satellite.

Analyst System—in combination with Trader System, gives intraday graphics with frequencies from 5 to 60 minutes and intervals from 2 to 40 days; computes and displays moving averages, relative strength indices, spreads, and oscillators.

Commodity Systems, Incorporated
200 West Palmetto Road
Suite 200
Boca Raton, FL 33432

Quicktrieve—data transmission program for interfacing microcomputers with comprehensive technical database; database covers all American, Canadian, and British futures markets with data going back as far as available; complete database available only through microcomputer interfaces supplied by CSI and third-party software houses; subsets of CSI database available on some time-sharing systems; *Quick products software* for data access, analysis, and graphics on Apples, IBMs, and TRS-80s; data format compatible with Dow Jones *Market Analyzer*, *VisiCalc*, and many other software packages.

Commodity Systems Reports
335 Bryant Street, Suite 300
Palo Alto, CA 94301

Commodity Systems Reports—a quarterly, semiannual, or annual subscription service providing computer optimized, proprietary technical trading systems; the systems are described in written materials and programs are provided to run the systems on microcomputers.

Commodity World News
219 Parkade
Cedar Falls, IA 50613

Hardcopy news and quote display for intraday data; news covers major government reports and issues in daily trading.

CompuServe
5000 Arlington Centre Boulevard
Columbus, OH 43220

Database Services—*Quick Quote* service for daily technical price and volume information; Standard and Poor's General Information File; Value Line Database; MicroQuote for database access and retrieval; Commodity News Service; Archer Commodities for specialized commodity reports; Raylux Reports on economic activity; newspaper financial pages.

FEDWATCH—produced by Money Market Services, Incorporated, is a weekly newsletter covering forecasts of interest-rate trends and their effects on stock, bond, and commodity markets; includes technical comments on cash and futures markets.

Computer Information Service
300 West Adams Street
Chicago, IL 60606

Commodity Accounting System—brokerage service bureau accessible through remote terminals; variable commission and margin calculations; tracks daily charges to capital, prescribed customer limits; generates automatic exchange reports and information necessary for CFTC; monthly account management reports; daily transmission of all relevant reports to main branch offices.

Computerized Research International
720 Spadina Avenue, Suite 1308
Toronto, Ontario, Canada M5S 2T9

Technical Analysis System—time-sharing service for technical analysis of stocks, bonds, commodities, and currencies; line charts for prices, indices, and moving averages (arithmetic and exponential); variable graphics formatting and display; bar charts, point-and-figure diagrams, rate-of-change momentum programs, and primary trend and volume analysis; technical screening system for sorting and screening through databases to isolate time series that have performed up to certain criteria; databases include Federal Reserve System, Statistics Canada, the Conference Board, National Association of Home Builders, all Chase Econometrics databases, international databases, and investment databases covering stocks, bonds, commodities (American, Canadian, and London exchanges), options, and money markets.

CompuTrac, Incorporated
P.O. Box 15951
New Orleans, LA 70175

The CompuTrac Program—menu-driven microcomputer software (Apples and IBMs) with separate programs for generating charts and analyses; based on a members' cooperative, programs are added to the list. Welles Wilder studies, demand indices, HAL cyclical studies, moving averages, spreads, and ratios all can be displayed on screen or paper; other programs for regression analysis and Fourier analysis; automatic data-vendor communications programs for stock and futures prices.

Sophisticated Programming Subsystem (a program generator) allows users to input formulas for their own trading systems. *Profit Matrix* program evaluates historical profitability of simulated system trading using over 20 comparative measures. Procedure mode enables all programs to be run automatically.

Intra-Day Analyst—through a real-time connection to a *VQP3000+* Quote Machine (Commodity Communications Corporation), provides continuous graphic display of bar charts, averages, and prescribed studies; sounds alarm on specified stops; tracks contracts you specify; reviews trading action after the market.

Data Resources, Incorporated
29 Hartwell Avenue
Lexington, MA 02173

Information Plus—world's largest commercially accessible historical economic database; concepts covered include National Accounts—gross products, government receipts and expenditures, personal income and outlay, and savings and investment; Finance and Investment—balance of payments, banking, consumer credit, capital expenditures, exchange rates, interest and finance rates, and money supply; Production and Consumption—capacity and utilization, construction, consumption, employment, trade, industrial production, inventories, output, productivity, and resources; Demographics—population characteristics and vital statistics; Prices—consumer, retail, stocks, bonds, futures, and wholesale; concepts are topically arranged into models and services dealing with different areas: National—U.S. Central, U.S. County, U.S. Model, U.S. Prices, and U.S. Regional; International—Canada, Europe, Japan, IBRD, IMF, and OECD; Industrial—agriculture, automotive, chemical, consumer, defense, construction, forest products, insurance, steel, and transportation; Energy—U.S. International, Canadian Coal, Oil, and Gas; Financial—banking, commodities, COMPUSTAT, financial and credit statistics, securities, Standard & Poor's, and Value Line.

EPS Plus—time-sharing software for economic data management, manipulation, and analysis; company data, company assumptions, historical data from DRI's Information Plus, econometric forecast data, programmed report formats and graphs can be used as inputs; applications such as "what if" analyses, risks and return on investment, and regression and statistical analyses; periodic presentation-quality reports, graphs, analyses, and forecasts.

Econometric Models—forecasting models developed and maintained by DRI staff economists in specific industry areas: transportation, European energy, international automotive, European automotive, consumer research, forest products, steel, coal, chemicals, oil and drilling, energy, utilities, interindustry, East Asia, Japan, Canada, banking, U.S. economic, insurance, defense, Latin America, and agriculture and commodities.

Dialog Information Services Incorporated
3460 Hillview Avenue
Palo Alto, CA 94304

Dialog Databases—library of information covering a wide range of topics from technology and engineering to law and humanities to business and economics, of specific interest are the *AGRICOLA* (U.S. National Agricultural Library), Commonwealth Agricultural Bureaux Abstracts, The Predicasts Group (International and U.S. time series and forecasts), and U.S. exports databases.

Digital Equipment Corporation
Maynard, MA 01754

Minicomputers and microcomputers, mainframes, systems consulting and design; distributed processing design and implementation; longest established minicomputer manufacturer; products sold through original equipment manufacturers or directly.

Dow Jones & Company, Incorporated
22 Cortlandt Street
New York, NY 10007

The Dow Jones News Services—known as "the Broadtape," the oldest established news wire now available through paper or electronic media; coverage of all news areas from international politics and economics to agriculture, defense, finance, and federal government.

The Capital Markets Connection—news summaries, precious metals, foreign exchange, Euromoney, federal reserve market transactions, market sector reports, private placements, yields and prices, and commentaries.

Dow Jones News and Quote Reporter—limited news service available through telephone interface to Apple computers; news library, price quotes at 15-min delay; scanning and searching of recent, current, or coming news articles.

Market Analyzer and Portfolio Evaluator—trading analysis and money management software for Apple computers; Market Analyzer links Apple to Dow Jones News Service for access of daily database, and draws bar charts, moving averages, trend lines, and comparison charts; Portfolio Evaluator stores, modifies, updates, and reports on user-specified portfolios.

Dunn & Hargitt
P.O. Box 1100
Lafayette, IN 47902

Commodity Data Bank—futures prices and volume from mid-1959 to current quarter available through various media: floppy or minifloppy disk, tape, printout, and cards or paper tape; historical charts and programs for calculating spreads and moving averages.

Earth Satellite Corporation
7222 47th Street
Washington, D.C. 20015

CROPCAST—crop forecasting system available through time-sharing system in the United States and abroad; uses meteorological satellites, international weather services, and biological simulation models to assess crops and their environments towards forecasts of local and regional crop yields and production levels; forecasts are available daily or weekly.

Futures Order Execution Systems, Incorporated
175 West Jackson Boulevard, Suite 1259
Chicago, IL 60604

FOXSI—software services to clearing members of futures exchanges; software can be leased or purchased on turnkey basis with continuous support; on-line and batch processing for cash balance, margin requirements, open positions, purchase-and-sale statements, and CFTC reports.

GTE, Financial Services Division
100 Wall Street
New York, NY 10005

News and Quote Wire—Market Retrieval Services (securities, commodities, bonds and options price displays); Market Monitoring Service (*Marketminder*, *Limitminder*, and *Marketmonitor*); Market Broadcast Service (scrolling news, tickers, block trades, and selected trades); Newsbeat; Standard & Poor's; Commlink communications systems.

H & H Trading Company
P.O. Box 549
Clayton, CA 94517

Market Tracker—software for TRS-80 or Apple microcomputers; programs retrieve data from *Dow Jones Reporter*; computes technical market indicators such as 5-day moving average of new highs and lows, 10-day advance/decline line, 30-day oscillator, and Granville stock market techniques.

Hewlett-Packard
1820 Embarcadero Road
Palo Alto, CA 94303

Minicomputers and microcomputers, graphics terminals and plotters, and systems consulting; personal computers, peripherals, and graphics terminals distributed nationwide.

Instant Update
219 Parkade
Cedar Falls, IA 50613

Daily updates of commodity prices, news affecting markets, and Pro Farmer recommendations; accessible through television screen, computer terminal, or microcomputer.

Interactive Data Services, Incorporated
22 Cortlandt Street
New York, NY 10007

Historical Price and Notification Services—corporate pricing, municipal pricing, international securities, GNMA, and conversions.

XPRESS—portfolio review and evaluation; portfolio appraisal; time-sharing software and portfolio equity updating data.

Interactive Software Research Incorporated
P.O. Box 271, NDG, Montreal
Quebec H4A 3PS, Canada

ISR Tickwatcher—Apple II software for emulating real-time quote machine; analytical programs for drawing price charts, moving averages, and spreads; preset alarms; 144 pages of programmable display of tick-by-tick data.

International Business Machines Corporation
2 Penn Plaza
New York, NY 10021

Mainframes, minicomputers, and microcomputers—hardware and systems consulting; personal computers and peripherals distributed through retail computer stores and Sears.

Investor's Micro Software
Box 319
Harvard, MA 01451

Apple II, IBM, and TRS-80 floppy disks—programmed disks for calling buy/sells, commissions, skids, margins, profit, and loss; library of separate programs for running published trading systems includes dual moving average, breakout, exponential smoothing, trendlines, oscillators, and so forth; constantly expanding collection of individual trading systems supplied through subscription arrangement.

Investor's Software
P.O. Box 2605
San Francisco, CA 94126

Portfolio Master—software for Apple microcomputers; retrieves daily prices and updates; records and generates reports on gain, loss, current value, and percent weight calculations.

Karob Software
5808 Country View Terrace
Cincinnati, OH 45238

Commodity Package—Apple microcomputer software package for data file maintenance and technical analysis: programs for drawing bar charts, calculating moving averages, and generating hardcopy output from a printer or plotter; routines for converting CompuTrac data files to Karob format.

Kate's Komputers Distributing Corporation
P.O. Box 1675
Sausalito, CA 94965

The Analyst—software for CP/M based microcomputers, Apples, and Northstars; graphics package for line plots, bar charts, point-and-figure diagrams, relative strength ratios, moving averages, oscillators, and trendlines; data update and retrieval from Dow Jones, the Source, or CompuServe; Advisor software for account monitoring, commission recording, tax reports, and profit profiles.

Kidder Reports Incorporated
80 Wall Street, Suite 514
New York, NY 10005

Trade Evaluator—Apple II software for simulating trades in financial futures, options, and foreign exchange; systems designed for banks, dealers, and arbitrageurs; financial markets news and analysis transmitted over wire.

Logica
666 Third Avenue
New York, NY 10017

Prestel World Service—information system and communications network combined to provide telephone-accessible videotex service; data input and retrieval by independent organizations results in over 200,000 regularly updated news pages; service available via a variety of Prestel terminals or Apple computer with Appletel Software; Gateway service for interfacing Prestel with external computers for data capture.

Commodities News—European farm and trade news; EEC Green rates; Amsterdam financial information; key economic indicators for EEC countries; Dow Jones news; commodity price indices; metals prices; soft commodities; foreign exchange rates; New York, London, and Chicago futures market prices and volume; European prices and support prices; trading recommendations (chart analysis, Prescot Commodities, and COMMODEX System).

Management Services
2901 Clenenden Lane
Longview, TX 75601

Market Analyst Software—software for TRS-80 microcomputers; Datamax and Comdata data file management programs for creating and maintaining data files;

MJK package for database access to and retrieval from MJK Commodities Data Base; The Analyst II programs for testing profitability and generating trading signals from Welles Wilder technical systems; The Driver program for automating sequential runs of some trading systems; Statpac for statistical analysis, correlation, regression, variance, and frequency distribution analyses.

Market Data Systems, Incorporated
3835 Lamar Avenue
Memphis, TN 38118

Market Quotation System—news wire and intraday prices on CRT terminal; standard and programmable quote pages, crush margin calculations, most recent trades, and spreads.

Quote-Watch—electronic price board for large display area quotation system; 2-inch-tall liquid-crystal display figures.

Data Zap—transmits real-time market prices to external computers; all intraday price changes; interfaces with most computers through popular R.S. 232 protocol.

Graphics One—daily tick charts, point-and-figure charts, spread charts, intraday or daily historical bar charts, and moving averages on remote graphics terminals.

Market Information, Incorporated
Suite 360
11414 West Center Road
Omaha, NE 68144

Mitronix Commodity Quotation Services—Commodity Monitor for display of intraday data through FM radio or satellite transmission covering New York, Chicago, New Orleans, and London markets; Private New Systems for transmitting news electronically over Commodity monitor network; software for use with Apple or TRS-80 microcomputers for emulating Commodity Monitor terminal; ComChart hardware and software for intraday graphics and analysis, eight-color charting, and data retrieval and storage.

MiTicTrac—Apple microcomputer software for intraday graphic analysis including oscillators, spreads, ratios, momentum, moving averages, point-and-figure charts, and popular trading systems.

Marketview—an intraday analysis system using the IBM Personal Computer; high-resolution graphics for tick-by-tick bar charts, moving averages, relative-strength indexes, point-and-figure charting; programmable quote pages; split-screen capability and storage of up to 20 pages for quick reference.

Marketview Microsystems
133 Park Street, Suite 1201
Brookline, MA 02146

Software for Apple, North Star, and S-100 systems; retrieval, storage, and analysis of intraday futures prices data.

Marketvision
140 Cedar Street
New York, NY 10006

System 1000—intraday graphics and analysis system with quote wire. Charting programs include bar charts, point-and-figure charts, tick charts, spreads, ratios, and overlays; statistical studies include oscillators, momentum indexes, power index, daily-run figure, relative-close index, relative-strength index, and stochastic study; tabular displays include Boardvision, Quickvision, time and sales, account management, moving averages, and quotes. System 1000 tables and charts are in color, and split-screen capability allows simultaneous display of up to nine pages.

Memory Systems, Incorporated
5212 Hoffman
Skokie, IL 60077

Technical Trader—Apple microcomputer software for daily technical analysis and automatic database updates via telephone connection to Remote Computing Corporation, Commodity Systems, Incorporated, or MJK Associates; analytical programs include moving averages, historical and present position analysis, on-balance volume, Welles Wilder systems, oscillators, and proprietary systems; graphics programs for bar and line charts, histograms, and point-and-figure charts; data maintenance and report writing programs.

Microcomputing Research
29-A Estancia Drive
Marana, AZ 85238

The Computing Investor—software series for Apple microcomputers; Quoteprocessor for manual data entry; Quotecharter for generating bar charts and trendlines; Fotofolio for graphic and tabular display of portfolio management summaries; Strategy-M program gives buy/sell signals based on momentum values; Transactor recordkeeping programs for purchase-and-sale orders and executions; Vector-S generates weekly trading signals from proprietary, technical method.

Micro Futures
P.O. Box 2765
Livonia, MI 48154

Software for TRS-80 microcomputers—separate programs for popular and published trading systems computations; "Commodity System Reports" with trading signals and optimized system parameters; momentum, spreads, averages, oscillators, channels, and other technical tools.

Data Management Software—MJK access program for retrieval of current and historical data from MJK Commodities Data Base; COMDATA program for manual data entry and editing; data from MJK also available on TRS-80 disks.

MJK Associates
122 Saratoga Avenue, Suite 11
Santa Clara, CA 95050

Commodities Data Base—complete historical and current coverage of major American futures exchanges; accessible through on-line data service (MJK terminal, Apple, and TRS-80) or on magnetic tape; microcomputer software for data retrieval and storage (Apple II and TRS-80); CompuTrac or Comm-Basic compatible data file structure.

Program Library—bar charts, moving averages, daily quote pages, point-and-figure charts, price volatility, current and historical spreads, and oscillators, all in time-sharing mode with MJK database.

The Monchik-Weber Corporation
11 Broadway
New York, NY 10004

Systems Consulting—real-time systems supporting daily trading functions on desktop terminals (profit-and-loss calculations, trades entered, prices, and historical data); interactive cashiering support for brokerage operations; portfolio management and accounting programs.

Option Monitor Service—real-time access to trade and analysis data on all listed options and underlying securities; strategy planning for spreads, straddles, covered writing, and hedging.

Financial Futures Service—real-time price and volume data and analysis results and recommendations for cash and futures money market instruments.

MoniResearch Corporation
P.O. Box 19146
Portland, OR 97219

EZ Model Builder System—menu-driven software for Data General minicomputers builds, simulates, and evaluates technical trading models; *EZTREND* receives input from user to specify technical trading rule and prints out evaluation reports of different formats, varying in level of detail; *EZREVUE* accesses and prints information on prespecified trading rules; *EZFILE* data management program; *EZPLOT* graphics and package for charts and graphic display on terminal or plotter; *EZREG* for regression analysis and econometric modeling and forecasting.

The New York Times Information Service, Incorporated
Mt. Pleasant Office Park
1719A Route 10
Parsippany, NJ 07054

The Information Bank—complete electronic library of current and historical news items from hundreds of news, research, and analysis publications; software for access, searching, and displaying.

OCO Commodities, Incorporated
1001-J Bridgeway, Suite 128
Sausalito, CA 94965

CommVue—software for all major microcomputers; trendline and bar charts; manual entry of daily price data; trading signal calculation and position recommendation from single proprietary trading system.

Olamic Systems Corporation
141 West Jackson
Chicago, IL 60604

Commodity Broker's Computerized Accounting System (COCOAS)—software for back-office applications, commodity pool accounting, and brokerage management; processing through software leasing for in-house computers or through time sharing.

Omega Microware, Incorporated
222 South Riverside Plaza
Chicago, IL 60606

The Investor's Toolkit—Apple program packages including the *Chart Trader*, the *Market Analyst*, the *Financial Trader*, and the *Professional Trader*; all are different combinations of programs covering applications for data manipulation, technical analysis (graphic charting, Gann charting, and Fibonacci projection), trading systems (Welles Wilder systems, Engineer's system, Trend-master, and various other systems), and trading systems with optimization (moving average crossover, parabolic system, swing index, and relative strength index). (See Orion.)

Organizer Systems, Incorporated
2 Overlook Road
Chatham, NJ 07928

The Organizer—software for CTA and CPO back-office accounting and performance management on minicomputers and microcomputers; comprehensive reports include daily spread sheets, equity runs, monthly statements, and billing; accessible in time-sharing mode on some systems.

Orion Management, Incorporated
323 S. Franklin, Suite 804
Chicago, IL 60606

Technical Analysis Software for the Apple II—Professional Trader package (Engineer's system, moving average crossover, Welles Wilder six systems, relative strength index, directional movement, and system parameter optimization); graphic charting; data file management; Gann's Square of Nine; Fibonacci projection; spheres charting; all separate programs are compatible with CSI/Quicktrieve data file structure; distributed by Omega.

Peachtree Software, Incorporated
3 Corporate Square, Suite 700
Atlanta, GA 30329

General Purpose *Microcomputer Software*—Magic Wand Word Processing; MagiCalc data analysis; Magic Spell; Sales tracking; General Ledger; Accounts Receivable and Payable; Payroll, Inventory management.

Predicasts, Incorporated
11001 Cedar Avenue
Cleveland, OH 44106

Predicasts Terminal System—newsletters, indexes, statistical publications, and business digests; industry studies, analyses, and forecasts.

Professional Farm Software
219 Parkade
Cedar Falls, IA 50613

Software for Apple, and TRS-80 microcomputers—programs for technical analysis include bar charts, point-and-figure diagrams, moving averages, and spreads; data update service updates futures and cash prices daily through telephone connection.

PWA Commodity Research
2607 Partridge Avenue
Arlington, TX 76017

Apple Quotes—Apple software ties microcomputer to exchange lines for automatic price quotes, tick-by-tick bar charts and spreads, and daily bar and spread charts with moving averages and relative strength index.

Quotrader Corporation
257 North Greene Street
Greensboro, NC 27401

Investment Center—Apple II software for continuous price quotes, tick-by-tick bar charts; technical trading systems and recommendations; instantaneous accounting.

Quotron Systems, Incorporated
5454 Beethoven Street
Los Angeles, CA 90066

VuSet—miniature (8 lines by 16 characters) quote screen servicing commodities, options, bonds, stock markets data retrieval; market indicators; selective monitoring.

Quotron News Service—complete Dow Jones News Retrieval Service; multiple display formats; story recall; all information can be distributed to stand-alone satellite office terminals.

Financial Information Service—current prices and statistics displayed on remote terminals; programmable pages and selective monitoring; commodity trading monitor; graphics service; terminal emulation (use Quotron hardware to access inhouse system); Billboard Information Dispatch Service for electronic news network; Options Trading Information Service; Customer Account Retrieval Service.

Raden Research Group, Incorporated
120 Broadway, Suite 2114
New York, NY 10010

PRISM System—proprietary software uses Pattern Recognition Information Synthesis Modeling, an heuristic approach to discovering underlying repetitive patterns in price data; software determines whether systematic patterns exist in a particular data series and defines those patterns apparent so that predictive models can be used to signal turning points and trends.

Radio Data Systems, Incorporated
669 North 10th West
Centerville, UT 84014

Market Monitor—instantaneous price quotes from major American futures exchanges; data transmitted over FM radio or via satellite; programmable quote pages.

Private News Service—transforms internal network of Market Monitor terminals to electronic mail system.

Market Monitor Emulation—interfaces minicomputer or microcomputer with Market Monitor communications link.

ComChart System—hardware and software for use as Market Monitor during the market and historical analysis after the close; microcomputer stores daily data transmissions for bar charts (weekly or daily); spreads, moving averages volume and open interest, and point-and-figure charts.

R & B Futures Software
170 Broadway, Suite 201
New York, NY 10038

Software for technical research—different packages designed to run on Apple microcomputers, minicomputer systems, and in time-sharing mode; automatic database updates for futures prices and volume; software includes programs for technical analysis and some graphics.

Remote Computing Corporation
1044 Northern Boulevard
Roslyn, NY 11576

MERLIN—time-sharing database for securities, options, and futures prices and volume. Complete software for technical analysis and graphics includes bar/charts, volume, open interest, and uptick volume; moving averages, relative strength, and spreads; commodity trading systems, trading simulation, and system implementation and monitoring.

Dial/Data—software for interfacing Apple II with *MERLIN* database. Complete database available for transmission in CompuTrac compatible file structures; database also available in appropriate structure for *SRI/SMART* system.

Pear Technical Analysis—menu-driven microcomputer software for IBMs, generates charts and analysis of trading models. Time-series processor allows creation of more complex models without programming experience. Automatically retrieves daily and historical prices using *Dial/Data* access.

The Organizer—complete back-office accounting for CTAs, CPOs, and brokerage. For microcomputers, minicomputers, and time sharing. (See Organizer Systems, Incorporated.)

Portfolio Plus—time-sharing software for accounting, pricing, and management; handles all types of investments and financial instruments; cross-referencing, current value reporting, and auditing; automatic accuracy checking; interfaces with *MERLIN* database.

INSYTE—data management software for Burroughs mainframe computers; reporting, sorting, and updating programs; general data reporting for business functions.

Reuters Limited
2 Wall Street
New York, NY 10005

The Monitor—quote wire service distributed through CRT terminal, displaying U.S. and London commodity prices, Reuters news stories, contributed prices (from markets without central trading floors), and North American securities quotations.

The Quotation Service covers all American and Canadian commodity, financial, and currency futures, and the London Commodity Exchanges; prices can be displayed individually or on formatted pages with a selection of contracts' last trade, change, high and low, two previous trades, and time of last trade; pages can be chosen with three latest news headlines on bottom.

Marketwatch/Limitwatch displays user-specified programmed pages with prescribed limits at which *MarketAlert* will go into effect; Arbitrage allows various markets for a given commodity to be simultaneously displayed. The News Retrieval Service provides access to market reports, open interest statistics, weather reports, cash market data—all as they change; market commentaries for Grains/Oilseeds, Livestock, Metals, Financials, and so on; news headlines pages, out of which whole articles can be called up and displayed.

The Contributed Price Data Service covers markets with no central trading floor: U.S. Government securities, Fed funds, and short-term money instruments; metals—precious and nonferrous; gold coins and bullion; commodity options.

I. P. Sharp Associates Limited
Corporate Headquarters
145 King Street West
Toronto, Ontario M5H 1J8, Canada

Sharp APL—literally, "A Programming Language," APL is designed for efficient manipulation of arrays using many built-in functions. The language is the root of I. P. Sharp's time-sharing system for business-oriented applications packages and databases.

Databases—extensive socioeconomic database, including CANSIM, NBER, USCPI, and USPPI; banking database with weekly Canadian financial statistics and quarterly and annual chartered banks information; securities database covers

American and Canadian stocks and options and American, London, and Canadian commodity prices.

Applications Packages—MAGIC (retrieves, manipulates, and displays time series data); AIDS (development of planning, forecasting, and control models); Portfolio Management; Statistical Analysis; Graphics.

Software Options, Incorporated
19 Rector Street
New York, NY 10006

COTS—the Commodity Options Trading System; software for options valuation using modified Black–Scholes model runs on IBM personal computers; color graphics and tabular displays for testing options trading strategies under various scenarios.

Software Resources, Incorporated
186 Alewife Brook Parkway, Suite 310
Cambridge, MA 02138

The SMART System—menu-driven microcomputer software for technical and fundamental market analysis and graphics; technical analysis (weighted, normal, or exponential moving averages; momentum indicators; data transformations; popular, published trading systems), fundamental analysis (descriptive statistics, correlation matrices, variance, and regression analyses), graphics (bar charts, histograms, trendlines, line charts, point charts), account monitoring (profit and loss, position recording, portfolio management, and reporting), and communications (automatic database or portfolio equity updating through various sources covering all futures, listed stocks and options, bonds, and economic indices; *FORMULA* function for interpreting user input and automatically writing proprietary user programs to calculate any algebraic, logical formula; profitability evaluation of trading systems; automatic run mode and MACRO programmability.

Micro Master Portfolio System—menu-driven software for complete portfolio and investment management on personal computers; realized and unrealized gains and losses; current positions reports; account management; sorting, screening, and cross-referencing; report formatting, automating, and printing.

OASYS—the Options Analysis System for Apple microcomputers; tabular and graphic representation of results from different trading strategies and market situations; allows for flexibility in valuation technique and volatility assumptions; database updated at daily or lower frequencies.

Source Telecomputing Corporation
1616 Anderson Road
McLean, VA 22102

The Source—database services: *UPI Unistox* reports daily on all stock, commodity, bond, metals, and money market information; Raylux Financial Services Reports prepared weekly by economists, investment advisors, and financial experts; electronic mail service allowing users to send and receive messages.

Tandem Computers, Incorporated
19333 Vallco Parkway
Cupertino, CA 95014

Tandem Non-Stop Computers—multiprocessor minicomputers with software for systems operation, networking, communications, and data management; systems consulting and hardware design oriented toward uninterrupted, on-line transactions processing.

Tandy Corporation/Radio Shack
Fort Worth, TX 76102

TRS-80 microcomputers—variety of differently configured personal computers distributed through retail outlets nationwide; peripherals, software, and service available through retail stores; software available from third-party vendors.

Technical Data
One Federal Street
Boston, MA 02110

Centralized Bond Market Information Service—available in real time through Telerate Systems; 40 pages of graphic and technical information on fixed income cash and futures markets; technical commentary with short-term momentum, overbought–oversold indicators, trends, and support and resistance; closing price charts and point-and-figure diagrams; historical spreads; and arbitrage tables.

Telerate Systems, Incorporated
One World Trade Center
New York, NY 10048

Telerate News Wire and Quote Service—Dow Jones Capital Markets Report, Commodity News Service, Technical Data; commodities service (soft commodities, metal, financial, and currency futures) with current and last three trades, high, low, and open; London commodities; Monchik–Weber's financial futures service, an interactive real-time analysis and trading system.

Tradecenter Incorporated
25 Hudson Street, 12th Floor
New York, NY 10013

Tradecenter—intraday trading and analytical applications on intelligent terminals; tabular and high-resolution graphic display of long-term or tick-by-tick data; up to four charts at once can be displayed, or single sections can be enlarged to fill the screen; price charts, bar charts, spreads averages, oscillators, point-and-figure, and ratios are some of the types of charts.

Trans-Lux Corporation
110 Richards Avenue
Norwalk, CT 06854

Select 100 and *Personal Ticker*—hardcopy, real-time data transmission from exchange floors; exchange messages; key programmability for specified items.

VidiQuote—closed circuit video system with ticker display; large characters flowing from right to left; two exchange lines displayed simultaneously.

Trident Systems Publications
Box 3067
Thousand Oaks, CA 91359

MORTS—Menu-oriented Retrostatic Trading System is a package for the Apple and TRS-80 microcomputers; a user-determined risk/reward ratio and a range forecasting technique are combined to generate proprietary trading signals and track positions and equity.

Troy–Folan Productions, Incorporated
29 Miller Road
Wayne, NJ 07470

Software for Apple microcomputers—stock momentum studies and graphics for stock and commodity prices and indices; spreads and moving averages (arithmetic and exponential); database update programs for interfacing with Dow Jones, Bridge Data, and Monchik–Weber.

Urban Aggregates, Incorporated
6431 Brass Knob
Columbia, MD 21044

Investment Software Library—microcomputer software and historical data; Investment Data System for manually recording and maintaining price and volume data or reading graphical displays with digitizer; Stock Forecasting System programs for technical systems signals generated from moving average, momentum, rank, and relative strength studies; Market Trend predicts intermediate trend based on Moving Balance System's four daily indicators; graphic display of prices or computed data from Stock Forecasting System.

U.S. Futures Corporation
2214 West 18th Street, Suite 21
Houston, TX 7008

Software for Apple or IBM microcomputers—intraday price monitoring; trading signals based on proprietary trading system; color graphics and programs for technical analysis computations.

VisiCorp
1330 Bordeaux Drive
Sunnyvale, CA 94086

Software for Personal Computers—*VisiCalc*, the first electronic spreadsheet for displaying numerical data, setting up financial or business analyses, "What if" studies, simple time-series analysis; *Desktop/Plan II* organizes financial analysis, budgeting, planning, and common business calculations for modeling and reporting; *VisiPlot* is a comprehensive graphics package for formatting, labeling, and drawing line charts, histograms, scatter plots, pie charts, and other display techniques; *VisiTrend* for trend forecasting and statistical analysis, regression analysis, descriptive statistics, data transformations, and smoothing techniques; *VisiDex* is a free-format, flexible content filing system for cross-referencing, sorting, screening, and report generation; *CCA Data Management System* for mailing lists, customer files, inventory, billing, reports, and mailing labels; *VisiTerm* for using personal computer as remote time-sharing terminal, communicating between personal computers for disk file transfers, or access to large computers for data retrieval.

Wall Street Software
71 Murray Street
New York, NY 10007

Retail software for microcomputers—store sales and mail order for software packages from various manufacturers.

Weather Services International Corporation
131 The Great Road, P.O. Box B
Bedford, MA 01730

Time-sharing weather information—real-time information on worldwide weather conditions for agricultural regions; weather database for historical information, current data, and forecasts; can be accessed with microcomputer using terminal program.

The Winchendon Group
3907 Lakota Road
P.O. Box 10114
Alexandria, VA 22310

EASI/ARIMA—menu-driven software for econometric and statistical analysis on Apple microcomputers; Autoregressive Integrated Moving Average Analysis; Box–Jenkins time-series analysis; data transformations; forecasting, estimation, and diagnosis; model development and trend prediction; all programs run on CompuTrac compatible data file structures.

The Yardley Group, Incorporated
20 Exchange Place
New York, NY 10005

The Futures System—accounting and back-office settling software for in-house minicomputers or for use in time-sharing mode; daily and month-end reports for broker management, customer accounting, and CFTC reporting and clearing reports; records and manages trades, positions, commissions, and margins; proprietary database for updating account equity.

Systems Consulting—software and hardware design for customized operations in-house; custom programming for time-sharing applications using daily database.

PART V

RISK AND MONEY MANAGEMENT

CHAPTER 19

COMMODITY MONEY MANAGEMENT

CONTENTS

THE INTRODUCTION OF MANAGED ACCOUNTS 3

GROWTH OF MONEY MANAGEMENT 5

DISTRIBUTION OF SUCCESS AND FAILURE 8

SELECTING A MANAGED ACCOUNT PROGRAM 11

PERFORMANCE DISCLOSURE 12

EVALUATING A COMMODITY TRADING ADVISOR 13

COMMISSION COSTS 14

DISCLOSURE INFORMATION 15

INFORMATION SOURCES 17

CHAPTER 19

COMMODITY MONEY MANAGEMENT

Leon Rose

Speculative investment in commodities not only serves a useful economic function, but offers the possibility of large profits to the speculator. If there were no risk-taking speculators, commercial traders wishing to avert risk through hedging would have difficulty in using futures markets for that purpose. The potential for handsome profit to individuals derives primarily from the fact that commodities investments are highly leveraged.

For the very same reason, commodities investment entails an unusually high risk of loss. While that has always been the case, riskiness has increased markedly in recent years, because (among other things) interest rates and futures prices have become ever more volatile, futures contracts have proliferated in number and kind, and the amount of initial equity required for participation in the markets has steadily risen. Individuals trading for their own accounts are especially vulnerable to heavy losses in these complex, swiftly changing circumstances.

No one knows for sure how many individuals who trade commodities for their own accounts wind up net losers. The skimpy evidence from careful research, most of it of ancient vintage, suggests that the fraction is in the range 65–75%—and that excludes professional traders who, despite spending most of each working day on the floors of exchanges, take heavy losses from time to time. Among the practitioners of the commodities trade the general belief is that the fraction of losers is even higher, running between 80 and 95% of individual speculators trading on their own.

THE INTRODUCTION OF MANAGED ACCOUNTS

Managed commodity accounts are a fairly recent response to these dismal facts of life. Commodity money management's basic and declared premise is that trading in modern commodity futures markets is a vocation, a line of work best performed not by well-intentioned amateurs, but by full-time professionals armed with trading systems designed to yield a stream of profits over time, constrained by some predetermined degree of downside risk. Most such systems are technical rather than fundamental in character. This is to say that they project price movements in light of historical experience, as against forecasting by reference to the underlying conditions of supply and demand for each commodity. Furthermore the great majority of commodity money managers use computer programs to generate the trading signals on which are based the orders to buy or sell. These signals are rarely or never second-guessed by the trading advisor. True, there are a few chartists and fundamentalists who continue to manage other people's money in the futures markets, but the technical approach promises by its past performance to be the dominant technique for the foreseeable future.

The development of computerized futures trading has its roots in work done by Richard D. Donchian, a Senior Vice-President of Shearson/American Express and an active trader in futures for more than half a century. Donchian is best known for devising and, in 1957, introducing a trend-following system of trading based on moving averages, swings, and relative-strength studies of futures prices. This innovation was followed in 1960 by his "weekly rule," described and discussed in an article titled "High Finance in Copper," published in the *Commercial and Financial Chronicle* (December 1960). And in January 1961, while with Hayden, Stone (now merged into Shearson) Donchian introduced his "5-and 20-day moving average method."

As Donchian himself explained during a speech delivered at the First Annual *Managed Account Reports* Conference on Commodity Money Management in January 1980, "In some respects the 5-and 20-day moving average method is like the Model-T Ford, the forerunner of several more sophisticated methods which my associates and I are using. Also, this method and my extremely simple 'weekly rule' method have been written up as the grandfathers of most of the computerized trend-following methods in use today."

What is less well-known is that Donchian must also be credited with the idea of the publicly offered commodity fund, a notion hatched during the time he worked for Shearson, Hammill & Company immediately after World War II. His fund was patterned after the limited-partnership structure of mutual funds. Again quoting from his *Managed Account Reports* conference speech in 1980: "Carried away by the euphoria of my early easy profits in commodities, I made the unhappy decision to start the first commodity fund, Futures, Inc., in 1949. Without having experienced any of the loss pitfalls in handling commodity futures, I wasn't ready to live up to the responsibility of turning in a good performance. Also, the Street wasn't ready. The financial community considered commodities outright gambling and definitely not worthy of inclusion in a 'prudent man' investment program. Futures Inc. made a little money at first and then lost rather steadily. Public offering of the shares was discontinued in 1960. . . ."

Donchian cannot accurately be called the "father" of money management because the concept of "managing" a customer's commodities account had been an aspect of the brokerage business for some time. Individual brokers handled investors' funds on a "discretionary" basis, which meant that the broker decided what trades should be made and when, and then executed those orders either with the customer's prior agreement or at the broker's sole discretion. What Donchian did was to originate the "pure" or literally managed account and later to introduce a way by which a professional manager could employ tested criteria to identify and measure trends in commodity prices, track the acceleration or deceleration of ongoing trends, and take action in the direction of change at designated entry and exit points. By these means Donchian took most human judgment out of futures trading and replaced it with an unemotional, disciplined, technical approach.

It took more than a decade for Donchian's contributions to the "state of the art" to become fully apparent, although it is now known that a growing number of commodities traders quickly grasped the significance of his work and set about developing their own versions of the trend-following system. One by one during the 1960s and early 1970s these imaginative adaptors introduced their systems into the futures markets.

GROWTH OF MONEY MANAGEMENT

The brokerage industry gave commodity money management its biggest boost about 1974, when it resurrected Donchian's idea of the publicly offered commodity fund. A pooling of the capital of a number of investors, a fund permits persons with limited risk capital to participate in futures trading and to enjoy the fruits of risk-reducing portfolio diversification which none of the investors could undertake on his or her own. The same advantages may be had through the medium of the private pool, which in all but legal standing is identical to a public fund (funds but not private pools are considered to be securities and must be registered with the Securities and Exchange Commission). As a result, many of the individuals who before 1974 had been busily developing their own technical trading systems began to vie for designation as trading advisors for funds and pools. Concurrently, they promoted their services as advisors to individual investors with significant sums of money and a preference for maintaining a privately managed account. As the money managers prospered in these ventures, they were joined in rapidly growing number by other would-be professionals; the number of persons registered with the Commodity Futures Trading Commission (CFTC) as trading advisors and pool operators rose from just a few hundred in 1975 (when the CFTC commenced its regulatory activities) to approximately 3,000 only 6 years later.

During 1974–1978, a total of 41 publicly offered commodity funds were determined to be officially registered with the SEC. Their combined initial value, assuming all units offered were actually sold, was about $120 million. In 1979, 12 of those 41 funds were listed in the *Managed Account Reports* tables as active funds. At the end of 1981 only six of the original 12 were still on the list; four had ceased trading and two were reclassified as private pools. As the commodity markets entered a bullish phase in the early months of 1979, a number of brokerage firms moved to exploit the revealed benefits of public-fund offerings. By the end of 1979, four more public funds had begun trading; during 1980 another 11 funds entered the markets and during the following year 16 more joined the list. By the end of 1981 the monthly performance table had grown to 37 funds, the combined assets of which approximated $325 million. By the fall of 1983, the number of funds actively trading had grown to 70, and assets were nearly $500 million (see Table 1). The figure constitutes about one-third of the total estimated size of the money-management segment of the commodity futures industry, as of December 31, 1981, according to information gathered and analyzed by *Managed Account Reports*.

TABLE 1. Performance of Publicly Offered Commodity Funds[a]

Fund Name	General Partner	Sponsoring Firm	Start Date	Start NAV/ Unit ($)	NAV/ Unit ($) 1/1/82	NAV/ Unit ($) 11/30/82	NAV/ Unit ($) 12/31/82	Pct Chng 1 Mo	Pct Chng 12 Mo	Cash Distr ($)	Mar/PI 1/1/82 =100
Admiral Fund	Contifund Management	Conticommodiy Srvcs., Inc.	12/81	1,000	955	1,163	956	−17.8%	3.9[b]	200	121.0[b]
Aries Commodity Fund	The Ceres Investment Co.	A.G. Edwards & Sons	2/80	1,000	920	1,325	1,104	−16.7%	−16.3%		120.0
Boston Futures Fund I	Boston Futures Management	Thomson McKinnon Sec., Inc.	1/80	957	1,063[b]	562	547	−2.7%	−59.2[b]	86	59.5[b]
Boston Futures Fund II	Boston Futures Management	Thomson McKinnon Sec., Inc.	8/80	957	1,015[b]	516	504	−2.3%	−60.8[b]	70	56.6[b]
Boston Futures Fund III	Boston Futures Management	Eastern Capital Corporation	6/82	930	—	715	610	−14.7%	−40.4%		—
Boston Futures Fund IV	Boston Futures Management	Eastern Capital Corporation	11/82	851	—	747	583	−22.0%	—		—
Chancellor Fin Fut Fund I	Pruden'L-Bache Cmdty Mgmt Co.	Pruden'L-Bache Sec.. Inc.	3/81	1,000	952[b]	499	492	−1.4%	−60.1%	200	72.7
Chancellor Fin Fut Fund II	Pruden'L-Bache Cmdty Mgmt Co.	Pruden'L-Bache Sec.. Inc.	10/81	946	894	898	795	−11.5%	−16.1%		88.9
Chancellor Fin Fut Fund III	Pruden'L-Bache Cmdty Mgmt Co.	Pruden'L-Bache Sec.. Inc.	2/82	1,000	—	429	423	−1.4%	−58.4%		—
Chancellor Futures Fund	Pruden'L-Bache Cmdty Mgmt Co.	Pruden'L-Bache Sec.. Inc.	2/80	942	1,277	992	960	−3.2%	−31.1%	100	83.0[b]
Chancellor Futures Fund II	Pruden'L-Bache Cmdty Mgmt. Co.	Pruden'L-Bache Sec.. Inc.	4/83	1,000	—	1,167	980	−16.0%	—		—
Clark Street Futures Fund	Lasalle St. Cmdty Mgmt Corp.	A.G. Becker—Paribus	11/82	871	—	755	745	−0.5%	—	10	—
Commodity Strategy Partners	Hayden Commodities Corp.	Shearson/American Exp., Inc.	8/82	952	—	730	649	−11.1%	—		—
Commodity Trend Timing Fund	Hayden Commodities Corp.	Shearson/American Exp., Inc.	1/80	963	1,618[b]	1,515	1,343	−11.4%	−22.8%	150	92.3[b]
Commodity Trend Timing II	Hayden Commodities Corp.	Shearson/American Exp., Inc.	12/82	955	—	1,000	888	−11.2%	—		—
Commoditiy Venture Fund	Hayden Commodities Corp.	Shearson/American Exp., Inc.	11/80	950	1,525[b]	1,572	1,486	−5.5[a]	− 2.0[b]	300	117.1[b]
Commonwealth Fin Fut Fund	Virginia Futures Mgmt Corp.	Bateman Eichler.Hill Richards	4/83	893	—	903	917	1.6%	—		—
Dean Witter Cmdty Partners	Demeter Management	Dean Witter Reynolds, Inc.	3/81	1,000	968	884[r]	809[p]	−8.5%	−36.3%		83.6
Enterprise Fund	Filler, Weiner, Zaner & Assoc.	Merril Lynch Futures, Inc.	11/81	1,000	997	1,075	933	−13.2%	1.9%[b]	25	96.1
Financial Futures Fund	Dunn & Hargitt Inv Mgmt, Inc.[b]	Dunn & Hargitt, Inc.	7/81	8.08	6.71	830	7.95	−4.2%	−2.6%		118.5
Future Fund I	Heinold Commodities, Inc.	Heinold, Blyth Eastman	7/79	1,000	3,128	4,239	3,944	−7.0%	− 5.5%		126.1
Future Fund II	Heinold Commodities, Inc.	Heinold, Paine Webber	4/82	986	—	1,037	961	−7.3%	− 9.0%		—
Galileo Futures Fund	Counsellors Corp.	Clayton Brokerage	3/79	1,000	1,041[b]	1,042	941	−9.7%	−7.1%[b]	300	119.2[b]
Gemini Commodity Fund	The Ceres Investment Co.	A.G. Edwards & Sons	3/83	1,000	—	1,060	910	−14.2%	—		—
Global Fund	Heinold Commodities, Inc.	Heinold Commodities, Inc.	9/81	994	1,033	914	672	−26.5%	−37.4%		65.1
Harvest Futures Fund I	Heinold Commodities, Inc.	Heinold Commodities, Inc.	6/78	1,000	3,237[b]	2,347	2,681	14.2%	0.5[b]	650	102.9[b]
Harvest Futures Fund II	Heinold Commodities, Inc.	Heinold Commodities, Inc.	2/80	970	492	428	489	14.3%	−3.9%		99.4
Horizon Futures Fund	Heinold Commodities, Inc.	Heinold & Smith Barney Upham	10/80		1,000	1,575	1,459	7.4%	6.7%		133.2
Hutton Cmdty Partners I	Hutton Cmdty Mgmt. Inc.	EF Hutton & Company	2/80	1,000	1,058	1,124	991	−11.8%	−12.4%[b]	100	103.1[b]
Hutton Cmdty Partners II	Hutton Cmdty Mgmt. Inc.	EF Hutton & Company	12/80	1,000	1,207[b]	940	901	−4.1%	−33.9[b]	200	91.2[b]
Hutton Reserve Fund, Ltd.	[d]	EF Hutton & Company	10/82	987	—	926	905	−2.3%			—
Illinois Commodity Fund	Heinold Commodities, Inc.	Heinold Commodities, Inc.	1/78	975	2,853	2,314	2,110	−8.8%	−31.1%		74.0
Lake Forest Fund	Filler, Weiner, Zaner & Assoc.	Filler, Weiner, Zaner & Assoc.	1/81	1,000	599	605	536	−11.4%	−23.8%		89.5
Lasalle St. Futures Fund	Lasalle St. Cmdty Mgmt Corp.	A.G. Becker—Paribus	9/81	937	975	1,099	1,034	−4.6%[b]	9.7[b]	68	113.0[b]
McCormick Fund I	McCormick Futures Mgmt.	McCormick Commodities, Inc.	1/82	92	—	111	104	−6.3%	− 8.8%		—

McCormick Fund II	McCormick Futures Mgmt.	McCormick Commodities, Inc.	10/82	92	—	79	73	−7.6%	—		—
Major Trend Futures, Ltd.	Joseph D. Mills	Mills Financial Services, Inc.	10/78	500	1,020[b]	571	420	−26.4%	−42.1[b]	599	99.9[b]
Matterhorn Cmdty Partners	Hayden Commodities Corp.	Shearson/American Exp., Inc.	6/81	950	955	1,007	897	−10.9%	− 6.1[b]	100	104.4[b]
Midwest Commodity Fund I	Filler, Weiner, Zaner & Assoc.	Filler, Wiener, Zaner & Assoc.	6/81	1,000	866	859	737	−14.2%	−34.6%		85.1
Mint. Ltd.	[d]	Anderson Man Limited	1/83	10.00	—	10.97	10.03[p]	−8.6%	—		—
Monetary Futures Fund	Paine Webber Fut. Mgmt Corp.	Paine Webber Jackson Curtis	10/82	977	—	634	626	−1.3%	—		—
Palo Alto Futures Fund	Paine Webber Fut. Mgmt Corp.	Paine Webber Jackson Curtis	3/83	975	—	940	881	−6.3%	—		—
Peavey Futures Fund I	Peavey Futures Mgmt. Inc.	Peavey Company	10/80	876	1060[b]	448	412	−8.0%	−64.3%	165	54.4%[b]
Peavey Futures Fund II	Peavey Futures Mgmt. Inc.	Peavey Company	4/81	847	1,062[b]	455	420	−7.7%	−63.0%	170	55.60[b]
Peavey Futures Fund III	Peavey Futures Mgmt. Inc.	Peavey Company	8/82	919[r]	—	804	602	−25.1%	—		—
Princeton Futures Fund I	Paine Webber Fut. Mgmt. Corp.	Paine Webber Jackson Curtis	3/81	989	1,069	619	538	−13.1%	−44.2%		50.3
Princeton Futures Fund II	Paine Webber Fut. Mgmt. Corp.	Paine Webber Jackson Curtis	11/81	986	973	723	691[p]	−4.4%	−24.6%		71.0
Recovery Fund I	Heinold Commodities, Inc.	Heinold Commodities, Inc.	3/78	465	771	617	567	−8.1%	−31.4%		73.5
Recovery Fund II	Heinold Commodities, Inc.	Henold Commodities, Inc.	3/78	189	270	196	177	−9.7%	−27.2%		65.6
The Resource Fund	Heinold Commodities, Inc.	Heinold Commodities, Inc.	8/78	1,000	3,412	4,529	4,123	−9.0%	− 7.7%		120.8
Saturn Commodity Fund	The Ceres Investment Co.	A.G. Edwards & Sons	2/81	1,000	781	982	867	−11.7%	− 8.6%		111.0
Sceptre Futures Fund	Winn Management Co., Inc.	Winn Securities, Inc.	2/81	90	65	81	75	−7.4%	− 8.5%		115.4
Sek Commodity	Filler, Weiner, Zaner & Assoc.	Filler, Weiner, Zaner & Assoc.	7/82	1,000	—	672	580	−13.7%	—		—
Sunshine Futures Fund	Don Charles	Don Charles Investment Group	3/83	900	—	943	887	−5.9%	—		—
Sycamore Futures Fund	Heinold Commodities, Inc.	Smith, Barney/Tucker, Anthony	10/82	1,000	—	705	646	−8.4%	—		—
Tactical Commodity Fund	Speculation Ltd.	Speculation Ltd.	7/81	1,000	1,165	1,783	1,451	−18.6%	−3.6%		124.5
Thomson Commodity Partners	Thom. McKinnon Futures Inc.	Thomson McKinnon Sec., Inc.	8/81	1,000	1,124	884	790	−10.6%	−33.9%		70.3
Thomson Commodity Ptrs II	Thom. McKinnon Futures, Inc.	Thomson McKinnon Sec., Inc.	12/82	940	—	923	728	−21.1%	—		—
Thomson Fin Futures Ptrs I	Thom. McKinnon Futures Inc.	Thomson McKinnon Sec., Inc.	3/82	994	—	846	778	−8.0%	−25.7%		—
Thomson Futures Fund	Thom. McKinnon Futures, Inc.	Thomson McKinnon Sec., Inc.	11/78	942	1,936[b]	1,503	1,331	−11.4%	−28.2%	250	81.7[b]
Trendview Commodity Fund IV	Robert B. Conner	Rockwell Investments, Inc.	2/81	1,000	879	1,335	1,238	−7.3%	− 8.2%		140.8
Vista Futures Fund	Hayden Commodities Corp.	Shearson/American Exp., Inc.	4/81	934	1,034	1,013	786	−22.4%	−22.3%		76.0
Western Capital Fund I	Western Capital Corp.	Eastern Capital Corp.	11/81	1,000	923	402	355	−11.7%	−66.7%		38.5
Winchester Internat'l Ltd.	Drexel Burnham Lambert[c]	Drexel Burnham Lambert	11/80	9.92	8.90	10.54	8.44	−19.9%	−31.6%		94.8
Average Performance this month and last 12 months:								−9.5%	−24.5%		
Mar/Leading funds index: (1/1/82 = 100)											94.4

Notes: In some cases, starting NAV per unit does not reflect deductions for sales or organizational charges taken prior to the start of trading or during the trading period.

[a]The following information is taken from public records and reports and is believed to be reliable. However, *Managed Account Reports* cannot guarantee the accuracy of data.

[b]Includes cash payouts during period.

[c]Distributor of open-ended fund.

[d]Fund organized as corporation rather than limited partnership.

[p]Preliminary.

[r]Revised.

DISTRIBUTION OF SUCCESS AND FAILURE

An additional discovery from the *Managed Account Reports* research is that the average number of shareholders per fund at the end of 1981 was 893, which places the average limited partner's equity at roughly $4,900. On the basis of these data, the total number of limited partners in public funds at the end of 1981 was estimated at about 32,000. Although that figure represents a 270% increase in fund assets over a 30-month period, and a similar gain in the number of limited partners, it is but a tiny fraction of the assets and population of investors in securities funds.

Another important question was also investigated. Is there any evidence confirming the contention that the ratio of net losers to total investors in managed accounts is significantly lower than the reported 65–75% range for self-trading speculators? On this issue, too, the data are less than adequate but, subject to that qualification, they indicate that the probability of an investment fatality of a managed account—and a public fund, in particular—is no worse than 55% and, in years when one or more futures prices makes a sustained move, the percentage of losing accounts falls to as low as 12–15%. Furthermore, the evidence argues that the risk of complete loss diminishes dramatically for accounts kept open for 1 year or more. For an investor who kept an account open over the 30-month period from March 31, 1979 to December 31, 1981, the probability for profit was found to be 95% (see Table 2). This fortifies the axiom that rewards accrue primarily to managed-account owners who have the cash reserves and the patience to ride out the recurring draw downs that are experienced by even the most skilled commodity money managers.

As can be seen from the foregoing data, participation in commodity money management programs has its rewards—in overall gains if not in unusually high profits. This is to say that utilizers of trend-following, computer-based systems will catch trending markets often enough over time to make many accounts profitable on an annualized basis, although the size of those profits is dependent on exactly how much of each trend the money manager happens to catch; how many losses the money manager may have experienced before, during, and after each profitable move; the extent to which such losses may erode the profits the money manager has amassed; and the costs of commissions and fees applied against the account.

A look at performance over the past few years reveals that the trend in profits heavily favors the "bull" side of the market; that is, most technical systems make money, in varying degree, during upward price movements in the futures markets. Some also do well in "bear" market periods, although to a much less extent, and the evidence indicates that those who do succeed in down markets are usually trading heavily with larger amounts of account equity. The past performance of public funds shows that during the upward-trending 18 months covering 1979 and the first half of 1980, the returns to investors were, on average, quite acceptable. But during the last few months of 1980 and throughout 1981, 1982, and the first half of 1983, prices went into a steady decline and the fortunes of commodity trading advisors declined along with them, evidently because they were unable to cope with increased volatility and the choppiness generally associated with downsliding prices (see Table 3).

TABLE 2. Percentage Changes in NAV Per Unit

	3/31/79–9/30/79	9/30/79–3/31/80	3/31/79–3/31/80	3/31/80–9/30/80	9/30/80–3/31/81	3/31/80–3/31/81	3/31/81–9/30/81	3/31/79–9/30/81	3/31/80–9/30/81
Public funds:									
The Resource Fund	+ 38.4	+ 51.5	+109.7	+ 2.7	+37.1	+40.8	+29.3	+281.7	+82.1
The Future Fund (6/79)	+ 15.1	+ 57.4	+ 81.2	+ 4.6	+36.4	+42.7	+33.1	+244.2	+90.0
Illinois Commod. Fund	+ 29.5	+ 26.1	+ 58.1	− 1.7	+22.5	+20.4	+38.9	+172.9	+67.2
Recovery Fund I	+ 32.0	+ 43.0	+ 88.7	+38.2	−32.3	− 6.4	−13.7	+ 52.4	−19.2
Recovery Fund II	+ 19.7	+ 65.5	+ 98.1	+34.0	−34.9	−12.8	−22.5	+ 33.9	−32.5
Galileo Futures Fund	+ 12.4	+ 1.4	+ 13.9	+ 9.0	− 2.8	+ 6.0	−15.2	+ 2.8	−23.2
TMSI Futures Fund	+ 8.3	+45.0	+ 57.1	−11.0	+12.7	+ 0.3	+18.3	+ 86.4	+46.5
Aries Commod. Fund (2/80)	—	—	—	+ 5.3	− 1.7	+ 3.5	−15.3	—	−10.0
Commod. Tr. Timing (1/80)	—	—	—	− 0.1	−14.5	−14.6	+19.4	—	+ 1.9
Harvest Fund I	+128.4	− 7.8	+110.6	+63.4	−43.4	− 7.3	+ 3.3	+101.5	− 4.3
Harvest Fund II (1/80)	—	—	—	+36.9	−43.0	−21.9	+ 3.8	—	−18.9
Chancellor Fut. Fd. (1/80)	—	—	—	− 9.8	− 5.0	−40.0	—	+ 20.0	
Boston Fut. Fd. I (1/80)	—	—	—	+ 1.0	− 4.8	− 3.9	+45.0	—	+39.4
Hutton Commod. Ptrs. (2/80)	—	—	—	+10.8	− 9.7	0.0	− 2.5	—	− 2.5
Private pools:									
The Bay Pool	+ 1.0	+139.9	+142.3	− 8.8	+ 7.7	− 0.4	+10.2	+166.0	n.a.[a]
Commod. Trend Fund	+ 17.1	+ 25.7	+ 47.3	+14.8	+ 0.5	+15.4	−13.6	+ 46.4	− 0.5
Capital Commod. Traders	+ 45.6	+ 25.6	+ 82.8	+53.9	−30.9	+ 6.4	−15.1	+ 65.0	− 9.8
Fund "A"	+ 11.6	+ 30.6	+ 45.8	+21.5	−13.1	+ 5.6	+38.0	+112.4	+45.7
January Associates	+121.3	+ 97.9	+338.0	+ 0.5	+ 7.2	+ 7.7	+38.6	+555.4	+49.3
Rolling Eleven Com. Fd.	+ 1.3	+ 76.8	+ 79.1	+31.8	− 4.1	+26.3	+17.7	+166.2	+48.7[b]
PitCom #1 (excl. dist.)	− 13.5	+ 13.7	− 1.6	+ 9.6	+16.5	+27.6	+ 5.2	+ 32.1	+34.3[c]
Controlled Commod. Assoc.	—	+ 33.7	—	+21.1	+ 7.1	+29.6	+39.5	—	+80.9
Rainbow Fund (excl. dist.)	+ 2.6	+ 53.2	+ 57.2	+16.9	+18.3	+38.3	−12.5	+ 90.1	− 5.4[d]

TABLE 2. Continued

	3/31/79–9/30/79	9/30/79–3/31/80	3/31/79–3/31/80	3/31/80–9/30/80	9/30/80–3/31/81	3/31/80–3/31/81	3/31/81–9/30/81	3/31/79–9/30/81	3/31/80–9/30/81
Individual accounts:									
Commodity Monitors	+ 34.6	+ 47.2	+ 98.2	−29.0	− 9.5	−35.7	+44.2	+ 83.7	+ 6.4
Summit Trading Co. (5/80)	+ 18.6	+ 20.6	+ 43.0	+49.5	−16.3	+25.1	+ 1.0	+ 77.1	+24.0
Futures Equity Mgt.	+102.6	− 9.5	+ 83.4	+ 6.5	−16.7	−11.2	n.a.	n.a.	n.a.
Commodynamics Mgt. Gp.	+ 30.9	− 2.8	+ 27.3	0.0	− 8.1	− 8.1	− 9.8	+ 5.5	−17.0
Futures Mgt. (5/80)	+ 60.1	+106.0	+229.8	+35.6	−11.6	+19.9	+50.5	+495.0	+80.4
Kohl Lane Seibens	+ 5.1	− 12.1	− 7.6	+39.4	−19.0	+12.9	−40.1	− 38.5	−36.4
Phoenix Capital Mgt.	+110.6	+ 77.1	+272.9	+25.5	+25.6	+57.5	n.a.	n.a.	n.a.
AVM Associates	+ 18.9	+ 28.3	+ 52.6	+ 1.8	+ 5.5	+ 7.4	n.a.	n.a.	n.a.
TLA Ltd. Fincl. Cnslrs.	+ 8.3	+ 55.5	+ 68.4	+10.6	− 9.9	− 0.3	n.a.	n.a.	n.a.
Arithmetic mean	+ 34.4	+ 41.9	+ 91.1	+15.1	− 4.2	+ 8.7	+11.3	+134.9	+19.9
Percentage with profits	100.0	84.6	96.0	78.1	37.5	59.4	64.3	95.2	55.6

[a]n.a.: not applicable.
[b]Change of +84.5%, if amount owed by bankrupt exbroker is excluded from equity.
[c]Change of +59.6%, if cash distribution to investors during 1981 are included.
[d]Change of +48.7%, if cash distributions to investors during 1981 are included.

TABLE 3. Performance of Public Funds—1979, 1980, 1981, 1982 and 1983 (6 months)

	Average Percent Returns		Percentage of Profitable Funds	
	6 Months	12 Months	6 Months	12 Months
1979[a]	23.2%	44.6%	100.0%	76.9%
1980	18.9%	24.6%	70.6%	76.5%
1981	14.0%	3.2%	65.5%	48.6%
1982	17.2%	2.8%	82.5%	65.0%
1983	−10.1%			

[a]Since performance records were not tracked before March 1979, calculations do not include first 2 months of that year.

As can be inferred from these data, commodity funds are no different from other types of investments in their susceptibility to economic conditions. Certainly, the higher leverage in commodity investments can lead to higher rewards, and in bull market periods there is no question that such rewards have been delivered. Conversely, when recessionary periods occur, the futures markets are one of the very first barometers of declining prices, and those who had been riding bull market moves often suffer severe losses before market positions can be turned around. This was the case in the latter part of 1980, and again at different times during 1981, resulting in much lower net returns to investors than what investors had enjoyed in 1979 and in earlier years of rising prices. This is not to say investors cannot realize better returns in a commodity managed account than they might obtain in other forms of investment. The degree of return is totally dependent on the trading signal sensitivity of the system and the trading practices of the advisor with whom investors' money is entrusted.

SELECTING A MANAGED ACCOUNT PROGRAM

As with any investment, three key decisions have to be made: (1) What type of commodity money-management program do you want? (2) Can you commit the minimal required capital for the type of program you decide is best for you? (3) Which of all those offered will be your choice?

Essentially, there are three types of programs from which to choose: publicly offered commodity funds, private commodity pools, and individual accounts. In the case of public funds or private pools, an individual's exposure is nearly always limited to the amount of the initial investment, and there are funds and pools available where the investment can be as low as $2,000. Individual accounts, on the other hand, usually demand an initial investment of $20,000 or more and most have a cutoff point set at one-third to one-half the original investment. Trading for your account will be stopped by the trading advisor if equity declines to that point and your account will be liquidated unless you bring the equity up to the minimal requirement to trade the program. On liquidation, you would get back any capital remaining in the account, or you may be obligated to make up any deficit. The advisor's cutoff procedure should be clearly understood before any capital is committed.

What makes a fund or a private pool less risky than an individual account is the structure. Funds and pools are generally set up as "limited partnerships" with the investments of numerous people pooled and traded as a single account. The total combined amount is almost always very significant, permitting broad diversification in the markets, which limits risk to well below what it might be if the advisor were trading a much smaller sum of money in fewer markets. Funds also spread the costs of operation among all limited partners, according to the percentages of the total equity held by each.

The rights and obligations of limited partners in a commodity fund are very similar to those of limited partners in mutual funds. They fall under the offering registration requirements of the Securities and Exchange Commission (SEC) and therefore, the general partner must prepare a complete disclosure document in the form of a prospectus and file it for registration with the SEC. Once registered, a fund may be publicly offered to the investment community. The common practice is to break down the full amount the general partner seeks to raise into "units," which are offered in a particular amount. In most cases the price of a unit is set at $1,000 plus an additional amount to cover sales costs. In other cases, sales costs per unit are deducted from the face value of each unit. Since sales charges are not recoverable on redemption of your units, the amount has to be considered a minus figure when computing the true value of your investment.

Once SEC registration has been granted and the fund raises enough capital to become effective as a trading entity, the operation of the fund falls under the regulatory jurisdiction and reporting requirements of the Commodity Futures Trading Commission. Disclosure documents, recordkeeping, and reporting procedures to limited partners and regulatory bodies must conform with that commission's rules and regulations. The fund's prospectus always carries information about the past performance of the trading advisor (or advisors) selected by the general partner to do the trading. These data should be scrutinized with care before deciding to invest. This is not an easy job. Most major brokerage firms have been analyzing trading-advisor performance for some time, and very few advisors have been selected to be confidently recommended to customers. One major brokerage firm, which has maintained a staff of analysts for just this purpose, evaluated over 700 trading advisors during a 4-year period, but chose only 20 for inclusion on its approved list. As can be appreciated, the selection of a trading advisor for a public fund is a very critical decision, one that should command the attention of every investor.

PERFORMANCE DISCLOSURE

Until August 1981 there was no required or accepted uniform way by which trading advisors presented their performance records, so it was extremely difficult to compare one manager's performance with another's. At that time, new CFTC regulations became effective which have gone far toward establishing standardized formats for the presentation of track records. But the variations among advisors in fees and commissions, in number of commodities traded, in minimal cash requirements, and in length of time each has been actively trading and maintaining records of performance serve to complicate the evaluation process, in addition to other factors.

There are certain things to look for before making a final decision about a trading manager, things that apply to any money manager regardless of the type of program—individual account, public fund, or private pooled account. The first and most important is the largest erosion of capital to which the advisor subjected clients during the advisor's history of trading. This is vital, for you must always keep in mind that your account is being opened *after* all the performance information you have is history. That is, the advisor's track record reflects his or her *past* performance. The advisor's current level of assets under management has been achieved over time, but you are entering his or her program in the *present*, in anticipation of making gains in the *future*. If, by chance, you happen to open your account on what could be the advisor's worst possible day (when profits in the advisor's existing accounts were at a peak), you want to know how much of a loss in equity you can expect before your account turns around and starts moving in a profitable direction. The only way to estimate this is to find the largest dip in the advisor's past performance and apply that amount as a percentage of what you are contemplating as your investment. That gives you a clue as to how much you stand to lose under the worst of circumstances experienced by others investing with that advisor in the past. If the estimated percentage loss in your equity is more than you think you can live with, you should be considering other advisors who may be more conservative in their trading and have lower downside-risk potential, based on past performance.

It is always a good idea to set, however arbitrarily, your own personal risk/reward parameters before investing. Everybody dreams of doubling his or her money overnight, but the facts of life do not support such dreams. It is more logical to establish as an objective a particular percentage gain per year, and at the same time determine just how much risk you are willing to run to achieve that gain. If, for example, you feel you would be content with 30% profit per year and are willing to take a 35% of invested capital risk along the way, you have set parameters for yourself which will help immeasurably in narrowing your search for trading advisors to those with performance records that satisfy your criteria. This is not to say that future performance will equal or exceed past performance, but only that past performance is the only measuring device you have to go by. An advisor's risk/reward ratio, if favorable, at least gives you some assurance that you may not be forced out before the profits you seek begin to materialize.

EVALUATING A COMMODITY TRADING ADVISOR

Commodity industry professionals who are observers of, and participants in, the managed account segment of futures trading generally agree that careful analysis of a trading advisor should always precede an investment decision. This would require asking numerous questions of a trading advisor or pool operator which go well beyond the disclosure information currently required by the Commodity Futures Trading Commission. Revised federal regulations no longer require advisors to compute an annual rate of return, permit "compositizing" of accounts (the lumping together of all accounts in the computation of performance records, rather than revealing the performance of several individual accounts started at different times), and specify that only quarterly, not monthly, figures need be disclosed. These rules, whatever their *ratio rate* and beneficial effects, severely limit the ability of the uninitiated investor to analyze the true fortunes of separate accounts, such as he or she might open, although they do provide a broad picture of profit-and-loss potential.

To put the above in perspective, a private investor (now a consultant in money management), recently spent more than 2 years doing his own evaluations of advisors before making personal choices, using as his philosophical rule-of-thumb the analogy of "going into business with a partner." Anyone contemplating that kind of business arrangement, he pointed out, would certainly want to know everything about his partner before committing thousands of dollars to a joint venture. In a real sense, your trading advisor is your "partner," who is in the business of putting your money to work for your benefit, as well as his or her own.

Just how much the trading advisor benefits is critical to your own success. If the trading advisor generates profits for you, the advisor generates income for himself or herself, through the receipt of incentive fees. Most advisors also assess a management fee to cover recurring expenses made in the investors' behalf, and the brokerage firm receives commissions on each trade the advisor transacts. These overall costs of trading can vary significantly from one managed program to another, and can make a major difference in your realized profit picture.

It is wise to take a hard look at commissions and fees charged by each advisor, and attempt to compute them as a percent of your initial equity. Most advisors exact a management fee in the range of 4–8% of each account's average yearly equity, either computed monthly or quarterly. The incentive fee for realizing profits in your behalf generally runs in the range of 12–20%, with most advisors taking 15% of the net profits (after commissions and management fees) above the highest level of profits previously earned. In other words, if fees were charged against profits last quarter, and more profits were realized this quarter, the difference between the two profit levels would represent new assets against which an incentive fee would be taken. If there had been a loss in equity last quarter, no incentive fee should be taken until profits exceed the last amount at which the trading advisor had been compensated. Incentive fees should not be added in as a cost of trading, since they are imposed on the residual (if any) of earnings less cost of making the earnings. Management fees, on the other hand, are a direct cost.

COMMISSION COSTS

The largest expense levied upon an account is for brokerage commissions, imposed upon each trade. Commission rates vary widely from broker to broker. Some advisors permit you to place your account with a broker of your own choosing and to negotiate your own commission rates. Others insist that you trade through a designated brokerage house or one of several designees. This kind of arrangement may not be to your financial advantage. In the case of a public fund or a private pool, the brokerage arrangements are always preestablished, and the investor has no choice but to accept them. The only choice he or she has is to invest in that pool or fund, some other one, or to invest in some other kind of managed commodity account.

The best way to judge the fairness and ultimate cost of commission charges is to assume that the average of all commissions per completed trade made falls at about $80. This figure applied to trading during the year 1983, and could vary up or down from time to time, so you may find it advisable to average all commissions charged by a brokerage firm for each of the contracts traded by the advisor you are evaluating, at the time of that evaluation. The commission charged to trade a silver contract will not be the same as the commission charged to trade Treasury bills, or wheat, or gold. You want to get the entire "laundry list" of commissions and average them. Then, knowing the average number of trades made by the advisor during any given period of time, you can easily figure what percentage of your equity would be consumed by commissions. Adding in the percentage of equity taken in management fees gives you a good idea of the total costs to be applied against your account. If it runs over 30% of your initial equity, it is probably too high. The average seems to fall at about 21–24% for individual accounts as well as for funds and pools.

DISCLOSURE INFORMATION

The information an investor should accumulate about an advisor before making a final choice can be divided into four major categories: (1) information of a personal and business background nature; (2) the money manager's customer requirements; (3) the fees and commissions charged; and (4) the performance history. Below is a list of questions to which any prospective investor should have answers. Without exception, a commodity money manager should not hesitate to provide such answers. The list is not intended to be exhaustive, but is simply a guide to assist in making a determination to invest with one money manager or another.

1. The Money Manager.
    a. Name, address, telephone numbers, and full names of principals of the firm?
    b. Personal information about the principals: education, work experience, how long in futures markets and in what capacities?
    c. History of the firm: when started, types of accounts (pools, public funds, individual accounts), number of accounts at the present time, amount of money under management for past 3 years?
2. Customer Requirements.
    a. Minimal investment required for an individual account? Private pool?
    b. Amount of initial equity and/or account assets committed to margin?

   c. Amount of equity (percentage) placed in income-producing investments such as Treasury bills, money market funds, Certificates of Deposit, and so forth?
   d. Amount of investment income earned accruing to accounts?
   e. Cutoff point used by the advisor on loss of equity?

3. Fees and Commissions.

   a. Per-trade commission charged?
   b. Is there a choice of brokers, may you use your own broker, or must one use a designated broker?
   c. What percentage of equity did commissions represent in the past 12 months?
   d. What is the management or administrative fee and how is it assessed?
   e. If there is an incentive fee, what is the period of assessment (monthly, quarterly, etc.), are losses carried forward, and is it computed and charged against closed trades only, or both closed and open positions?
   f. Does the manager charge any front-end "load" or sales fee?
   g. Is there any penalty for early withdrawal of funds and, if so, how much and what time period is specified?

4. Performance History.

   a. Type of system employed: technical trend following, fundamental factors, combination of both, or other?
   b. Are results presented actual in-market trading or a simulated record?
   c. Is the track record based on cumulative results of all accounts, a unit value of all accounts, or actual individual account records? In any case, determine how many accounts are included and the starting dates of as many accounts as possible, so they can be related to economic and market conditions.
   d. How many commodities are included in the manager's trading portfolio and which commodities? (This helps you determine the past and potential volatility of the trading system, and also helps determine the amount of trading activity you can expect.)
   e. Are performance results presented to you documented by CPA audit and/or by presentation of broker firm purchase-and-sale statements?
   f. What is the ratio of profitable to unprofitable trades? Some managers can be profitable with only one-third of trades being winners, others may be less profitable with one-half or more of the trades profitable.
   g. In conjunction with (e) above, what are the average dollar gain and the average dollar loss per trade?
   h. How does the manager put an account into the market? Is the account phased-in as new signals are generated, or put into all existing positions right away?
   i. How many accounts have been closed out since the manager has been in business, and how many of these were profitable?
   j. What was the average dollar gain and average dollar loss of closed accounts, and the average number of months such accounts were active?

k. How many profitable months and unprofitable months are in the record supplied?
l. What was the greatest loss (drawdown) in the record supplied, and over what time period did it occur?
m. What was the manager's "recovery strength" after major loss periods? How much and how quickly did accounts recover?
n. What were annual net returns for a number of the manager's customers and were such returns acceptable over an extended period? Assuming your account would remain open for 3 years, would it have been worthwhile compared to other forms of investment?
o. If the manager does not supply a chart of performance, have you constructed one of your own? A picture is always worth a thousand words!
p. Have you insisted upon as current a record as possible? You are investing *now*, and today's economic and market conditions prevail. The performance record you receive should be current to at least the prior month.

Most of the above questions will be found in disclosure information the advisor sends you. Check off as you go through the document and be sure to ask the questions that are not answered in the material you have received.

INFORMATION SOURCES

One should not restrict the determination of the value of a commodity money manager's program to the material that the manager sends. Rather, find out all you can from other sources as well. This includes references to other customers of the manager and other forms of reports. Unfortunately, such sources are somewhat limited. Certainly, a prospective investor should routinely check with the Commodity Futures Trading Commission [2033 K Street, N.W., Washington, D.C. 20581, telephone: (202) 254-8630] to determine if any violations are pending against the manager, or if any administrative or criminal law decisions exist. The CFTC also requires all money managers to register as commodity trading advisors or commodity pool operators and to file disclosure documents quarterly as well as an annual report.

Another worthwhile indicator of the advisor's intention to adhere to proper business ethics is if the advisor is a member of the National Association of Futures Trading Advisors (NAFTA) [111 East Wacker Drive, Chicago, IL 60601; telephone: (312) 644-6610]. NAFTA can provide some guidance, as well, if you need answers to particular questions. The professional organization was formed in 1980 and had grown to more than 100 members by the end of 1981. Most of them are active commodity trading advisors and pool operators concerned with maintaining standards of practice and increasing the credibility of their profession.

A third source of information is *Managed Account Reports,* [5513 Twin Knolls, Columbia, MD 21045; telephone (301) 730-5365], which publishes in-depth, objective analyses of trading advisors, as well as tables of performances of private pools and public funds, in a monthly newsletter, and serves as the major clearinghouse of information for the field. The publisher has also edited an annual *Yearbook* (printed and distributed by John Wiley & Sons).

In addition, an increasing number of periodicals are publishing special articles about commodity money management. The one devoting the most space to money management is *Futures Magazine* [219 Parkade, Cedar Falls, IA 50613; telephone: (319) 277-6341].

CHAPTER **20**

EFFECTS OF CAPITALIZATION ON MONEY MANAGEMENT

CONTENTS

ALLOCATION OF CAPITAL 3

TREATMENT OF NEW ACCOUNTS 4

REDISTRIBUTION OF CAPITAL 4

BALANCING RISKS 5

TRADING PERFORMANCE AND CAPITAL CONTRIBUTION 6

DETERMINING A RISK CONTROL STRUCTURE 8

CHAPTER **20**

EFFECTS OF CAPITALIZATION ON MONEY MANAGEMENT

Edward Corballis

Money management involves the allocation of capital to balance and reduce the risks of commodity positions. The risk control measures evolving from a money management program can also lead to a more efficient use off capital. While trading approaches are directed at making profits, money management programs aim at preserving capital through loss-limiting procedures. The need for a money management program is derived from the varying degrees of risk and leverage that are associated with commodity markets and from illiquid market conditions that exist from time to time. The level of capital used and the trading system involved will exist as boundaries to the money management program.

ALLOCATION OF CAPITAL

When deploying the resources of an account, consideration must be given to the establishment of a *reserve*. A fully positioned account, one in which the full resources are committed to margin, is exposed to forced liquidations to cover margin calls when and if its equity has eroded, since exchanges require full *initial margin* to be restored when the account equity falls below 75% of the original margin. If initial margin is not met, positions must be liquidated so that initial margin is less than equity.

Liquidations, whether self-imposed or forced, should probably be arbitrarily chosen. At best they would force the trader or money manager to select which trades are expected to perform better or worse than others. The performance results could be hampered by the lost opportunity cost of a forced liquidation of a position that could eventually have proved profitable. It would also be expected that performance patterns and risk control due to diversification would become difficult to control under these circumstances. Sufficient capital is necessary to establish a reserve to prevent margin call liquidation from interfering with the trading decisions, diversification, or the overall management plan of the program.

It should be noted that reserves have an inverse effect on both leverage and risk. As larger reserves are established, less capital can be allocated to margin thereby reducing leverage. Lower leverage means lower risk and the account has considerably more "staying power" during periods of loss. No matter what approach is used, careful consideration must be given to maintaining proper diversification in order to keep the risk reduced.

TREATMENT OF NEW ACCOUNTS

A dilemma exists when trading is initiated in a new account. Does an account enter into established trading signals or wait for new signals? Risks may be increased by entering trades that already show large open profits. The effects of an adverse market reaction may reduce the profitability of an open position in an existing account while a new account may sustain a sizable loss. On the other hand, those profitable positions may only reflect the beginning of a sustained trend that may accentuate profitability. A money management program can perform a role in resolving these divergent effects on performance. When allocating the capital to different positions for a new account, the total amount allocated can be reduced and a larger reserve established. Another option is found by committing the normal amount of capital to each position and limiting the risk by setting closer stops based upon a certain predetermined percentage loss.

The alternative to diminishing normal position sizes for new accounts is a money management procedure that may be implemented whether or not trading begins with new signals, or follows established trades. A heavily positioned account with a limited reserve faces the prospect of reducing positions when the equity has been severely depleted. For example, a 50% initial equity decline requires a 100% return to restore an account to even.

If the lower level of capital or equity which is fully committed requires fewer or smaller positions, the recovery time would be considerably extended and the remaining capital would be expected to perform more productively during the rebuilding stage. An example of this situation is illustrated below:

Losing Period		Recovery Period	
Three contracts (margin $1,000)	$3,000	One contract (margin $1,000)	$1,000
50% loss	$1,500	150% profit	$1,500

A return that represents three times the original loss will merely produce an offset. Assuming that the time to achieve the gain would be longer than the holding period for the loss, rate of return calculations would also be adversely affected.

REDISTRIBUTION OF CAPITAL

The higher or lower amount of trading capital that will require position changes should be integrated into the money management plan. If the equity increases and gains are not distributed, capital allocated to positions and reserves should be adjusted for greater efficiency. The redistribution of capital should not be considered independently of the trading method. Some trading plans incorporate a system of adding to profitable positions while other programs are reducing their commitments to profitable trades.

Whatever method is employed, the allocation of capital should happen after most of the profits have been realized. Since open positions are subject to wide equity fluctuations, capital redistribution at any other time would seem premature.

The money management plans that allow for a larger reserve when an account initiates trading must also consider what increased amount of capital will dictate a reduced reserve. A money management plan is not static and should adjust to changes in trading approach, market conditions, and equity.

BALANCING RISKS

Establishing a reserve does not address the capital deployment problem of balancing the risks of various commodities, which can determine how efficiently capital is utilized. A plan to limit all position sizes to one contract does not allow for the different degrees of leverage and volatility that exist between the commodities traded. For example, an account may profitably trade one contract of a trending and reasonably stable commodity, while losing on one contract of a more leveraged, volatile commodity which is characterrized by prices bouncing up and down. The results of this imbalance are exemplified in the following situation:

Less Volatile		More Volatile	
One contract	margin $1,500	One contract	margin $5,000
$0.30 price move	profit $1,500	Six losses at 5%	loss $1,500
Return on investment	100%	Loss on investment	30%

A 100% return on margin is needed in the less volatile trade to compensate for a 30% loss on margin in the more volatile one. If the circumstances were reversed, the profit would have been $10,000 versus a $450 loss. How would the situation look if three contracts of the less volatile commodity were traded?

Less Volatile		More Volatile	
Three contracts	margin $4,500	One contract	margin $5,000
$0.30 price move	profit $4,500	Six losses at 5%	loss $1,500
Return on investment	100%		30%

A $4,500 gain was generated in the less volatile trade against a $1,500 loss for a net profit of $3,000. By transposing the situation, a $10,000 profit with a $1,125 loss would have resulted. When isolating the profitable trade from the more stable, less-volatile commodity, the 100% return seems meaningful. However, as part of a commodity portfolio the impact of the profit from one contract was diluted considerably. This inefficient use of capital drags down the results unlike the second case of the three-contract trade that contributed to profitability.

In the example, the more volatile commodity holds the greatest profit potential.

If the stable commodity has entered into the initial stages of a long-term trend, its volatility will likely increase. Any change in volatility may cause an adjustment in the allocation of capital in order to equalize the risks, otherwise a shift in volatility over time may cause the risk of the two trades to be reversed. A money management program may require that markets be continually monitored for changes in volatility.

The leverage and volatility of a commodity were not considered in the example although an element of volatility was reflected in the margin requirements. Both the leverage of a contract and the price fluctuations contribute to the degree of volatility. The different rates of leverage for various commodities is evident when comparing the initial margin requirements with the contract value. A 10% price change in a contract with 10% leverage is a 100% gain or loss as compared to a 200% gain or loss on 5% leverage. If the price changes are less for the contract with greater leverage, the difference in volatility between the two contracts is narrowed. Recent price ranges and the leverage of a commodity can be used to more accurately measure risks, rather than merely comparing margin requirements. If the risk of different positions in a commodity portfolio is balanced, the overall risk exposure should be reduced and the capital more efficiently utilized.

The risk associated with market illiquidity must also be considered when allocating capital to various positions. A commodity contract can be illiquid if an inactive deferred delivery is chosen or when events cause fast movement and limited trading at daily price limits. This market condition can profoundly affect trading systems that add contracts to profitable positions by providing poor executions, that is, entry or exit prices far different than the desired prices.

Market illiquidity is more likely to occur when a commodity is volatile and near a top. Other commodities are susceptible seasonally when, overnight, the fundamentals can be shattered by a freeze or some other devastating natural event. If positions have been added so that the average price approaches the market price, a few adverse limit moves can convert open profits into significant losses. Preferably a money management program would allow an account to endure these occasional conditions.

Planning a money management program entails leveraging a commodity portfolio by allocating capital to reserves and to particular markets. The available leverage does not have to be utilized when deploying the capital. In other words, the minimum margin requirement for a specific commodity may have been set at $2,000 but for purposes of allocating capital, the position may be margined at $5,000. By establishing these criteria, the risks related to fully leveraged and imbalanced positions are being reduced. However, limiting the risks effectively is constrained by the trading system and the amount of capital in an account.

TRADING PERFORMANCE AND CAPITAL CONTRIBUTION

The understanding of how trading systems and limited capital contributions constrain money management programs is clarified by dissecting the results of a trading system. The availability of simulated or actual results will allow for the calculation of the ratio of losing trades to profitable trades, the average size of profits and losses, and the average number of consecutive losses. These statistics can assist in matching a management program to a trading system.

A trading system that produces a 35% profit ratio, average losses of $3,000 compared to average profits of $10,000, and an average of five consecutive losses with no offsetting open positions, can potentially erode the capital of a $25,000 account to $10,000. In another trading system with a 50% profit ratio, average losses of $2,000 and average profits of $2,500, and where the average number of consecutive losing trades is three against no profitable open positions, the capital of $25,000 could depreciate to $19,000. Other trading systems have been known to generate average losses of $6,000 and profits of $3,000 while the ratio of profitable trades was 70%. If the consecutive losses average three trades, an equity decline to $7,000 would not be an unreasonable possibility. All three trading systems will require different initial capital requirements and reserves to provide them with staying power so that the trading systems are not compromised.

The calculations from the results of the three trading systems reflect one contract trade. If an account following any of the three trading systems was adequately capitalized, performance could be improved by balancing the risks and position sizes. The profitability ratio and the average number of consecutive losses will not be affected by the money management program; however, the average size of profits may be improved at a greater rate than the average size of losses. Performance is enhanced by a more efficient use of capital without altering the trading system.

The capital requirements for some trading systems are already significant without regard to an additional money management program. These systems are characterized as trend following, diversified, and always in the market. Diversification may have a greater impact on results than a money management program of balancing risks and positions. The profits from a sustained trend will often compensate for any inefficient use of capital. Test results from some of these trading systems show that profits are only achieved in trending markets. Since the system does not predict the probability or direction of a trend, it requires a continuous participation in the largest number of liquid commodity markets to improve the possibility of capturing substantial profits from an extended trend.

If the futures markets experience one year with a minimum number of trending markets, the lost opportunity cost from missing any of those trends could seriously debilitate an account. The profits from sustained trends are expected to cover the losses generated from the nontrending markets and leave enough excess for an acceptable rate of return. Calculating the profitability ratio, average gains and losses, and average number of consecutive losses will assist in determining the capital and reserve requirements of the fully diversified trading system. A preferable money management program for this trading system may need such a significant initial capital commitment that too many potential investors would be excluded from participation.

Some trend-following systems do not automatically reverse their positions. Instead they trade when various market indicators and trading signals are congruent. These systems derive their diversification by following as many markets as the trend reversal systems trade. If the calculations of the results of the two systems correspond, the initial capital requirements and reserves would be different. This would allow for the incorporation of a money management program for the nonreversal system that allocates the capital so that the risk of each market position is evenly distributed. The money management program would be compromised if many markets generated trading signals concurrently.

DETERMINING A RISK CONTROL STRUCTURE

Empirical results or simulations are often unavailable for trading systems that rely somewhat on subjective decisions, judgment, fundamentals, and a combination of technical indicators. These situations often need a money management program that controls risks and limits losses through some predetermined guidelines which may require that losses per trade be contained to 5% of the equity. Such a guideline can be damaging if the normal price fluctuations fall within the 5%. To avoid the problem of liquidating positions before they are allowed sufficient time to work, the entry points may have to be adjusted. Reentering positions that have been frequently liquidated because of the 5% requirement will not limit losses.

What is the difference between six losses, each 5% of equity, and one 30% loss over the same time frame? For those trading systems that cannot be analyzed, it would seem prudent to also set aside a large reserve until a trading pattern can be identified. The volatility of the commodity markets traded must be monitored so that the position sizes and the market risks fit into the structure of the money management program, which will contribute a disciplined approach to a subjective trading system.

Trading systems can be built to correspond to a previously defined money management structure or they can be developed solely to maximize profits without regard to any risk control. In the latter situation the system can be tested to determine the equity fluctuations of differently capitalized accounts. A profitable trading system will not necessarily succeed for all sizes of accounts. For example, a trading system may realize a net $50,000 profit after a 12-month test period. If during the course of trading the net losses totaled $20,000, a $25,000 account would have been precluded from following any new trades and probably forced to prematurely liquidate open positions. The performance of a $40,000 account would have corresponded to the test results if it was trading simultaneously. A money management program can be implemented to support a trading system so that it has an opportunity to succeed over a reasonable period of time.

A balancing process between the benefits of a money management program and the trading system is almost unavoidable unless an account is properly capitalized. It cannot be reasonably assumed that market conditions will consistently remain favorable for any trading system. Therefore preservation of capital through loss-limiting procedures must be the objective of a money management program to ensure the continued viability of a commodity account.

CHAPTER 21

MONEY MANAGEMENT CONCEPTS

CONTENTS

RISK CONTROL	3
Effects of Varying Reserve	4
Diversification of Systems and Portfolios	5
Conservation of Capital	7
PORTFOLIO SELECTION	8
Effects of Diversification Correlation	13
Efficient Frontier	15
EVALUATING RETURNS	16
CONCLUSION	17

CHAPTER 21

MONEY MANAGEMENT CONCEPTS

Mary Catherine Shouse

Money management concepts are often as important for investment survival as a trading model is for individual commodity contracts. This is especially true when the trading model is in the hands of an aggressive advisor.

Broadly speaking, money management is the art of limiting the risk of a portfolio of assets while maximizing its return. For most investment media, including commodity futures, there are many portfolios which have lower risk than any one asset alone. Note that the money management process starts after a profitable trading model has been developed for each of the commodities or assets. The idea is to build a few protective guidelines assuming you already have some valuable, though risky, trading strategies.

RISK CONTROL

There are many ways to control risk. Plain old human intuition (which needs no computer) tells you that trading several diversifying assets helps, that trading the individual contracts with the lowest risk helps, and that investing a small amount of your total investable portfolio will limit the potential losses.

Risk can be measured by the variability or standard deviation of periodic returns (see Figure 1), by the largest downside drop in account equity, or by the frequency of losses times the size of the average loss (see Figure 2). More sophisticated philosophies even consider the investors' utility or attitude towards downside drop.

Looking at the risk and return of an individual trade does contribute to the money management process, but still does not capture the interrelationships between the different commodities. It might be that a system of trading one contract each of corn, cattle, and silver would have lower risk than trading the cattle contract alone, even if cattle alone had the lowest risk of the three. Or perhaps two contracts of cattle and silver for every contract of corn would have lower risk still. A conceptual framework called *modern portfolio theory* to be described has been well-developed and tested. In many fields of investment management, it mathematically takes care of minimizing the risk of the total portfolio, for a given return level.

Meanwhile, let us turn to several "traditional" methods commonly used for risk control.

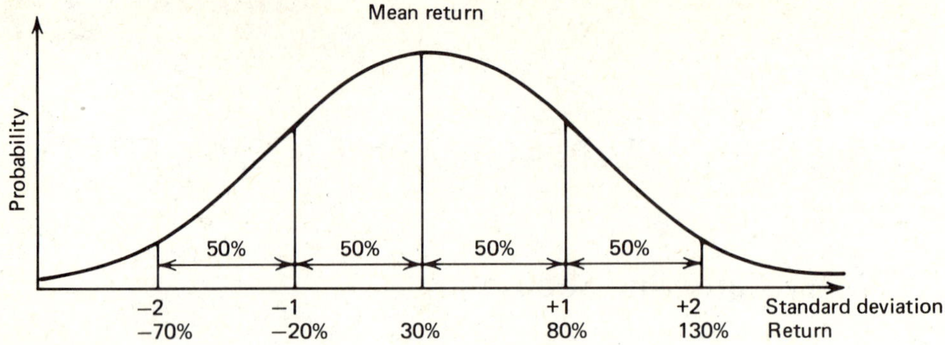

FIGURE 1. Standard deviation of returns.

EFFECTS OF VARYING RESERVE. A buy-and-hold portfolio of 10–22 commodities has not had any more risk over the past 30 years than a buy-and-hold portfolio of 10–20 stocks. Because the margin requirements of the typical commodity are usually between 5 and 15% of the value of the contract, high leverage is possible. Most commodity investment advisors and investors put up more in cash or Treasury bill reserves than the minimum required amount. In fact, most commodity advisors manage their accounts so that 30% of the value of the underlying contracts is available in the form of reserves (which thereby cover the minimum margin three times). This makes good sense if the advisor does not want to ask a client to put up new funds any time the account falls below 25%, or whatever amount is represented by the maintenance margin required.

In a leveraged account the brokerage firm requires that the investor put up an ''initial'' margin (a good-faith deposit) until the account falls below the designated ''maintenance'' margin amount. At that time the investor has 1 day to deposit new funds or else the broker may close out any open positions. If the investor initially deposited several times the initial margin required in an account, the investor would have much less risk of facing a margin call. Advisors typically manage reserves so as to keep the probability of a margin call at a low level.

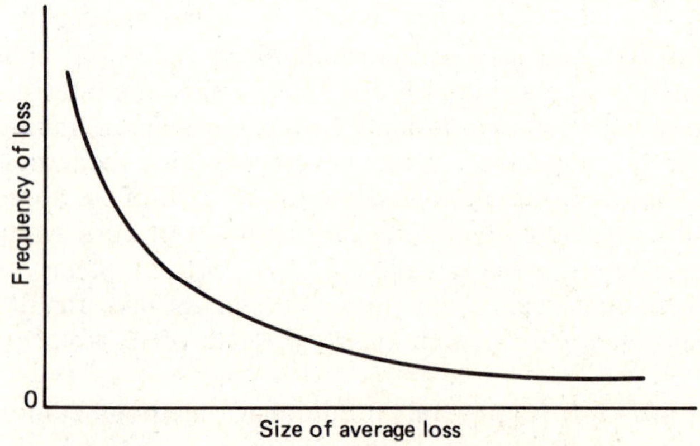

FIGURE 2. Profile of commodity or system losses.

The effect of *varying reserves* is one way of altering the risk and return of the portfolio. If one halves the reserves, the return and risk (as a proportion of the dollars invested) are both twice as great as before. If one doubles the reserves, the return and risk are both one-half as great as before.

For example, consider an account designed for a $50,000 investment with a maximum expected downside drop of 80% in a given year or variability of 80%, as measured in annual standard deviations. Let us say that the account returned 50%. If the investor or advisor was uncomfortable with the amount of risk taken on during that year, the same trading strategy and the same number of contracts might be designated as appropriate for a $100,000 account the following year. If the performance of the trading system was the same as in the previous year, the return would be 25% on the $100,000 account (as opposed to 50% on the $50,000 account) (see Figure 3).

DIVERSIFICATION OF SYSTEMS AND PORTFOLIOS. Diversification of future contracts can certainly reduce risk. The degree of risk reduction depends upon (1) how many different commodities are held, (2) whether or not they are in different classes (e.g., metals versus meats versus grains), (3) whether or not they are in long or short positions, and (4) how many of each are used. Quantification of this diversification is discussed later in "*Portfolio Selection*." Meanwhile, consider which commodities have historically shown a strong or weak diversification impact on each other. A well-diversified portfolio of commodities could well have 30% less risk than any one commodity alone.

Figure 4 shows the way in which diversification among increasing numbers of assets may help to reduce risk. Note that adding another asset of reasonably low risk (and low correlation or co-movement with the other assets) does reduce the risk of the total portfolio. However, this risk reduction occurs at a decreasing rate as more and more assets are added.

System Diversification for Investors. Some investors diversify between trading systems rather than maintain their entire account with one trading method or

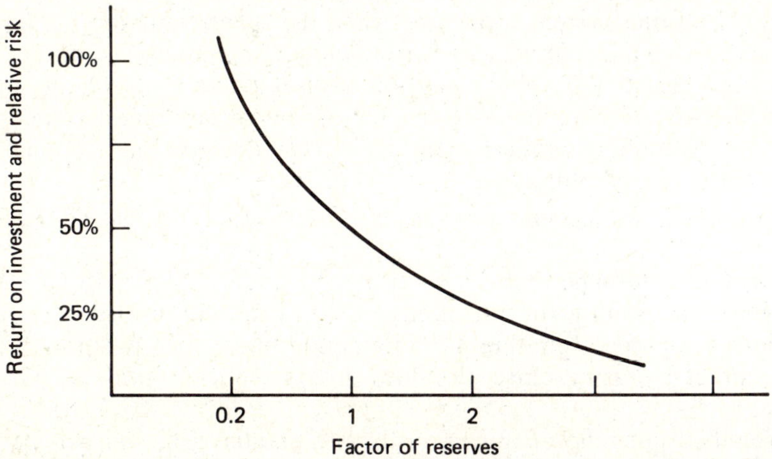

FIGURE 3. Varying reserves, assuming a 50% return on $50,000 with standard reserves (= 1).

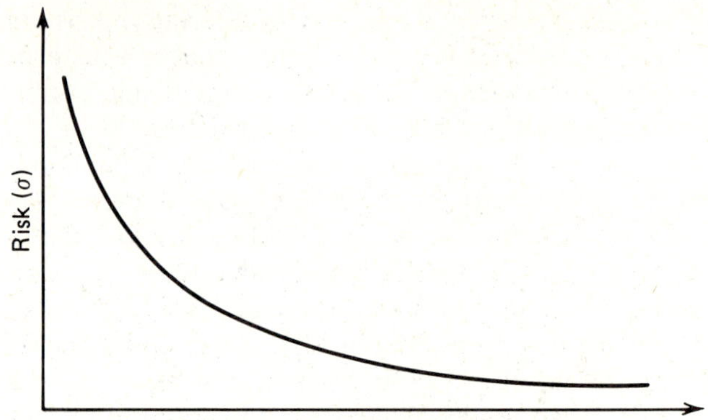

FIGURE 4. Effect of diversification on risk.

advisor. There is some benefit in diversifying between trading methods but it is limited by:

1. *The Similarity of Two Trading Methods.* If one trading system is identical to another over the same set of commodities, there is no benefit to adding the second system, in the same manner that a second contract of pork bellies does not add diversification to a first contract of pork bellies using the same system.

2. *The Size of the Incentive Within the Fee Structure.* The size of the incentive fee (if the investor is diversifying between two managed accounts) can seriously affect returns. Incentive fees are beneficial for motivation of the advisor, but decrease the total return of the investor when applied to smaller and smaller portions of the investor's portfolio. For example, the investor would like his or her account managers to be paid when the investor's total portfolio appreciates. However, if one-half appreciates by the same amount that the other half depreciates, then the net total portfolio return is zero. However, the investor still owes an incentive fee on one-half of his or her account. In the extreme, the investor would be at great disadvantage if an incentive fee were paid for each separate commodity and one system went long when the other went short. The investor would have to pay incentive fees on individual commodity contract offsetting results every period, as well as pay double brokerage firm commissions. It is better to choose a few trading methods (across numerous commodities) in which you are highly confident rather than to diversify among many trading methods when incentive fees are involved.

3. *Individual Trades and Sequences of Trades.* The risk of trading must begin with the *individual trade*. Each system creates a risk pattern by taking a longer- or shorter-term perspective for a specific trade, a commodity, or all trades. Longer-term trades allow for both greater risk and greater reward since the return fluctuations are larger. Limiting the time period of an open position in the commodity market by using close stop-loss orders reduces both the risk and the returns.

A diversified portfolio of trades, each with greater risk, will usually result in a net system risk which is still greater than a system where individual trade risks are smaller. This can be more readily determined by considering the *sequence of trades*.

Most risk-limiting trading methods will have more than one trading loss in sequence. A more accurate way of assessing the system risk is to consider sequences of profits as a single profitable trade and sequences of losses as a single losing trade. This approach will correct any problems arising from a system which has very small losses on individual trades, but has long runs of losses.

4. *Time*. Time essentially acts as a diversifying dimension. An investor can have many positive and negative returns over a larger number (e.g., 20) of commodity trades once over a 1-month period. The same effect is obtained by trading one of each of the commodities each month for 20 months. The time series method of "diversification" requires about 1/20 as much money, but takes 20 months to demonstrate the set of trades; the other method takes about 20 times as much money, but takes only 1 month to demonstrate the set of trades.

5. *Short Term Versus Long Term*. Systems that tend to trade frequently tend to generate higher commissions than those which trade infrequently in efforts to catch a long-term move. A typical managed commodity account has open positions for 1 to 2 months at a time and often produces gross commissions to the broker of 30% per year.

Frequent trades in a trend-following approach will result in a great number of losing trades relative to total trades (low *reliability*). Close stop-loss orders will result in frequent closeouts on small market reactions. Frequent trading in contratrend or arbitrage programs will result in many small profits with a few large losses.

CONSERVATION OF CAPITAL. One of the objectives in any rational investor's mind is the conservation of capital. By limiting losses on individual trades, an investor can reduce the speed at which a loss on the total portfolio takes place (as compared to holding a losing open position past normal stops). Of course, closing individual losing trades not only eliminates the potential of increased losses if the commodity were to continue to trend against the investors, but also limits the potential of increased gains, if the commodity were to turn around and trend in the investors' favor. A high profit-to-loss ratio indicates that the average profit is several times the size of the average loss. A system with high reliability—a high ratio of the number of profits to the number of losses—would also be reliable.

TABLE 1. The Investor Starts with Adverse Odds

Annual investment expenses often amount to:

Commission to the broker	=	20% of equity
Fee to the commodity advisor	=	10% of equity
Total	=	30% of equity

For every long position there is a short position, for every profit there is a loss.

Through successful trading, the typical investment manager must make 30% to break even on your investment.

TABLE 2. Performance Measuring Ratios

$$\text{The Sharpe Ratio} = \frac{\text{Reward to}}{\text{Variability}}$$

$$= \frac{\text{Mean return}}{\text{Standard deviation (risk)}}$$

$$\text{Extreme risk ratio} = \frac{\text{Average profit}}{\text{Largest downside drop in equity}}$$

For simulated performance—

$$\text{Probable risk} = \frac{\text{Distribution of returns}}{\text{Probability of particular downside drops}}$$

All of these ratios are useful in indicating the profitability of a system's past performance. Many managers use these techniques to measure and select trading systems over the past. Unfortunately, the future has never behaved quite like the past, so that creativity in money management has continued to retain its place.

PORTFOLIO SELECTION

Modern portfolio theory offers a mathematical structure for the decisions of how much of what to finally hold or trade in one's portfolio.

In the different securities markets, people have developed different ways of coming to grips with the question of portfolio selection. In the stock market a portfolio manager traditionally listens to the advice of his or her firm's security or research analysts and judges the risk of the set of stocks he or she holds in order to intuitively make the portfolio selection decisions. In the bond market a portfolio manager's holdings depend primarily upon his or her interest-rate forecast. This makes sense because bonds are primarily affected by what happens to interest rates, as opposed to what happens to corporations versus the government or other individual influences. Most bonds go up together or go down together.

Commodities futures markets tend to behave more like the stock market than the bond market when comparing one commodity to another. However, different futures contracts (maturing at different times) behave a bit like the bond market as the "hedges" within the same commodity are influenced by interest ratio to a great degree. A commodity's price variability is most determined by the specific influences of its demand and supply (or news of that demand or supply).

Let us examine this diversification benefit in more detail. This is of particular benefit to investors or money managers who have developed a trading system (even a "buy and hold until contract expiration" system) for each individual commodity he or she is interested in trading, and is at the point of considering how many contracts of what commodity to trade. They may consider the results (profits or losses) of their trading system as the assets in portfolio selection.

SELECTING PORTFOLIO ELEMENTS. Just how do you decide how many corn contracts to trade for each pork belly contract? How many copper contracts to trade for each gold contract? And how many of each contract should you trade for what size account?

The answer to these questions lies in two areas:

1. The characteristics of the trading system as it worked on the futures contracts; namely, the expected return, risk, and correlation[1] of the commodities under the trading system.
2. The risk attitude of the client.

Let us tackle these two areas one at a time.

The Characteristics of the Trading System. The goal of portfolio selection is to put together the portfolio or the set of portfolios which have the highest return possible and the lowest risk possible—two conflicting objectives. To do this, you want to choose select assets which have high returns, low individual variability, and low correlation with each. For this exercise, let us assume that the assets mentioned are not necessarily (though they may be) the buy-and-hold returns on each commodity. Instead they are the returns on the trading system as it operates in the markets.

Returns. Most commodity managers ''optimize'' their trading systems so that they would have had successful trading performance in the past. It seems to be human nature to do this, as one might wonder about a system's performance in the future if it did not at least work in the past. There is evidence to believe that the past has very little reflection on future performance. Be that as it may, most advisors still have developed a system in which they have some past performance confidence.

Discussion of how one might estimate the degree to which past returns reflect future returns was presented in a *Managed Account Reports* Conference in Los Angeles, July 1981, by the author.

It is difficult to find a trading system that works consistently over long periods of time. If the markets were ''inefficient'' and exhibited some form of predictability for a select, clever subset of superior investors to recognize, then they would tend to become more ''efficient'' as the amounts of investors' money trading this system grew and prices were coaxed back into equilibrium.

Figure 5 shows the performance of 10 public commodity funds over several periods of time. You can see that the professionally managed commodity funds that perform well in one period may or may not have performed up to ''expectations'' in the following period. With somewhat casual inspection it appears that the funds with the highest returns may also have the highest risks. One of the commodity funds had returns of over 100% during two quarters only to suffer a return of − 100% in the third quarter shown, losing not only the investors' original capital but all of the profits as well (see Figure 6).

[1]The original groundwork for this analysis was developed by Harry M. Markowitz (*Portfolio Selection*, Yale University Press, New Haven 1959). It was further developed by William F. Sharpe and explained in his book *Portfolio Theory and Capital Markets*.

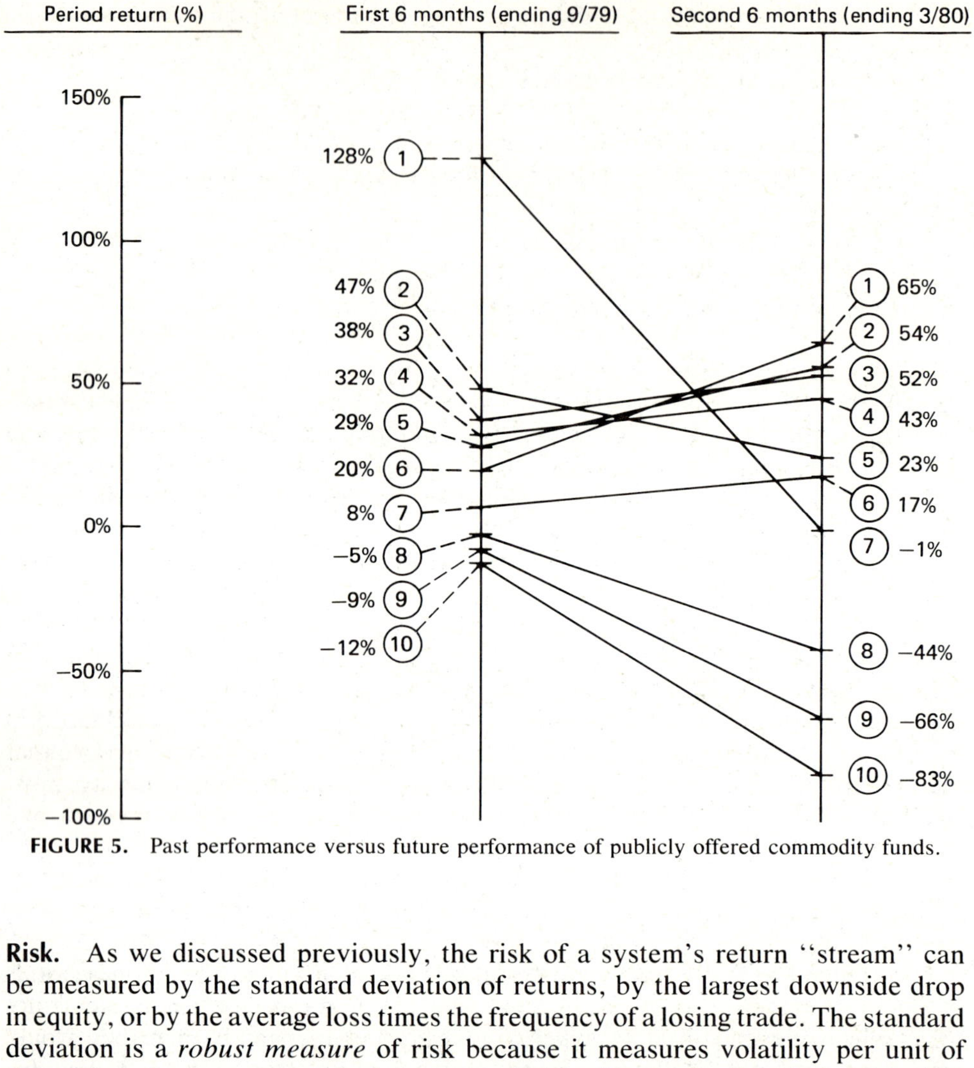

FIGURE 5. Past performance versus future performance of publicly offered commodity funds.

Risk. As we discussed previously, the risk of a system's return "stream" can be measured by the standard deviation of returns, by the largest downside drop in equity, or by the average loss times the frequency of a losing trade. The standard deviation is a *robust measure* of risk because it measures volatility per unit of time. Many investors commit their money for the "long term" meaning that they will not be distressed by short-term ups and downs in performance of the system or investment plan. Figure 7 shows an example of two assets (or systems trading the assets) with the same return, but different risk. Most healthy, risk-averse investors would prefer system A over system B. The high points would be desirable, but the low points would be distressing. All in all, the average investors would find that the lows offer more dissatisfaction, however, than the highs offer satisfaction.

This concept of *utility* (a measure of satisfaction) can be graphically shown in Figure 8. The horizontal axis is return. The vertical axis is a measure of "utility" or satisfaction. The higher the return realized, the greater the standard deviation as a measure of volatility. It may be calculated according to the equation

$$\sigma = (R_i - R^2)/(n - 1)$$

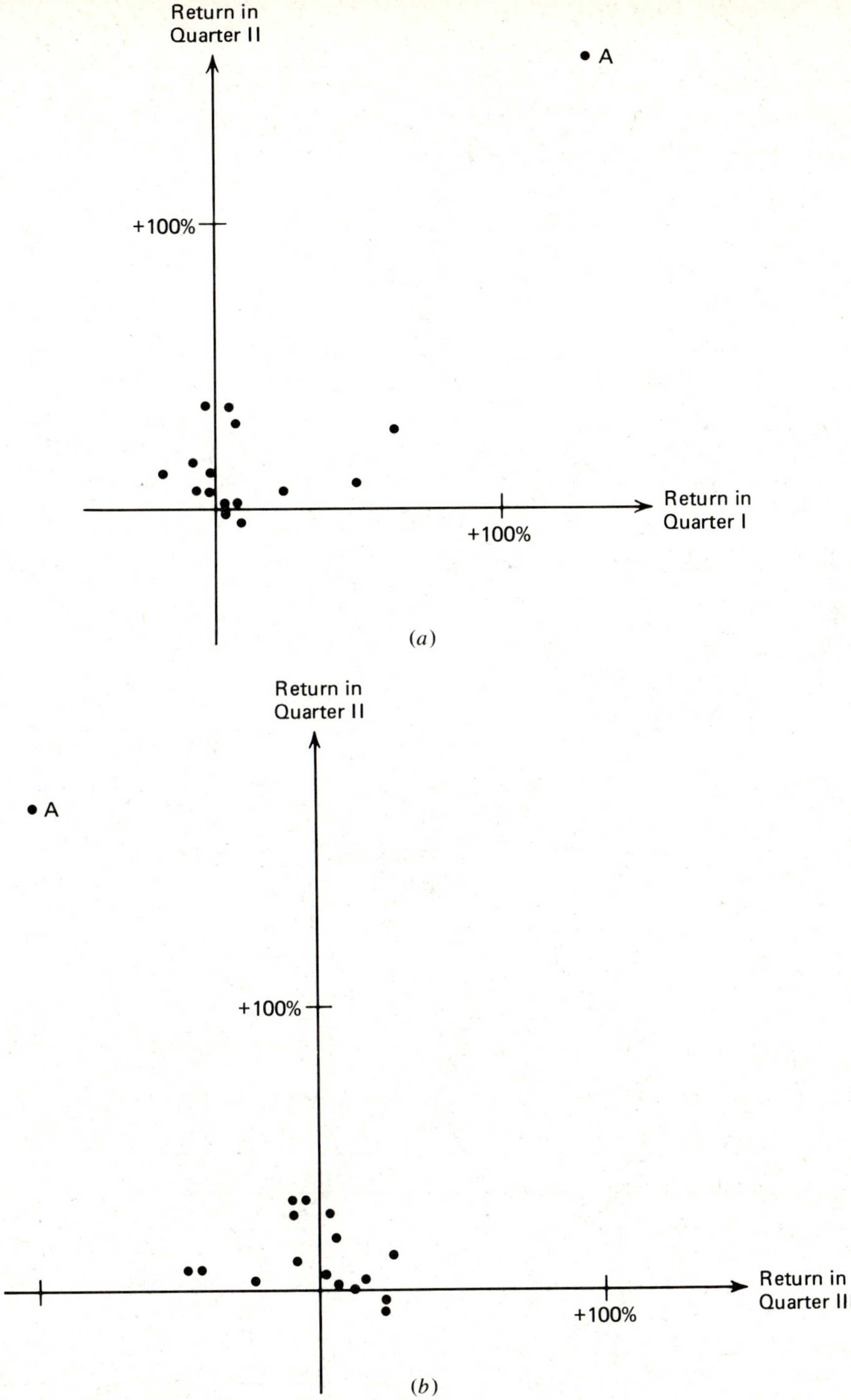

FIGURE 6. Does past performance indicate future performance? (*a*) Quarters I and II. For quarters ending 6/30/80 and 9/30/80: correlation = 0.81 and excluding A = 0.10. (*b*) Quarters II and III. For quarters ending 9/30/80 and 12/30/80: correlation = −0.79 and excluding A = −0.25. (*c*) Quarters III and IV. For quarters ending 3/31/81 and 6/30/81: correlation = 0.14.
(A = Returns achieved by Manager A).

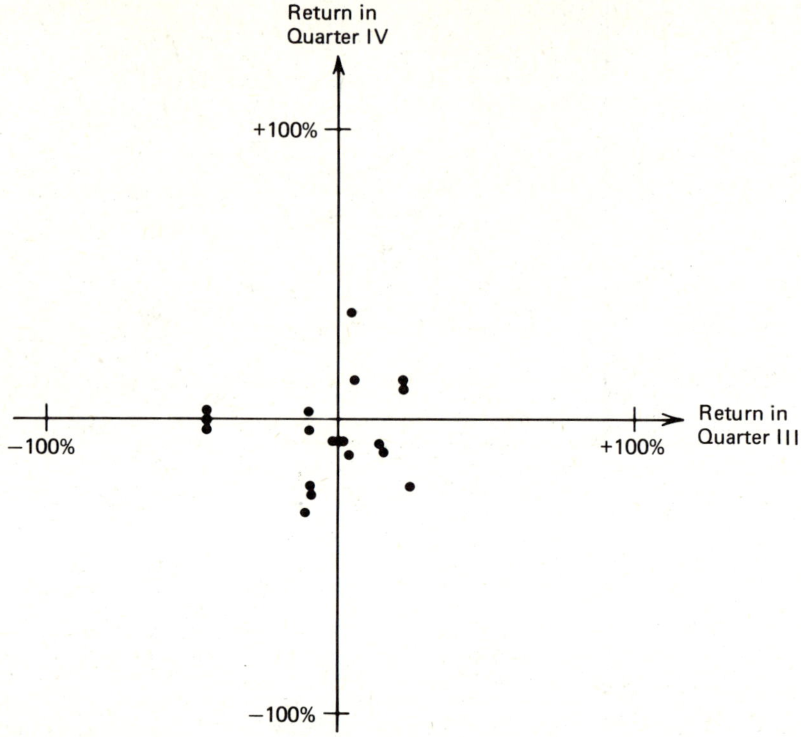

(*c*)

FIGURE 6. Continued.

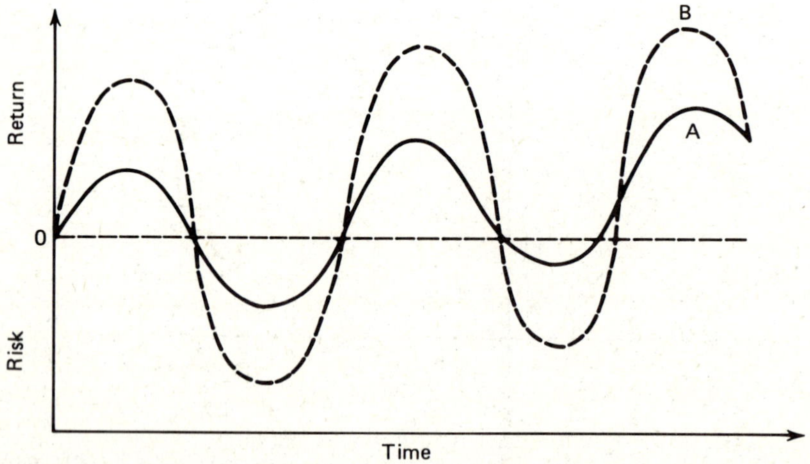

FIGURE 7. Two trading systems with identical returns, but different risk. Advisor A: standard deviation, 20%; maximum drop, 45%; return, 40%. Advisor B: standard deviation, 40%; maximum drop, 90%; return, 40%.

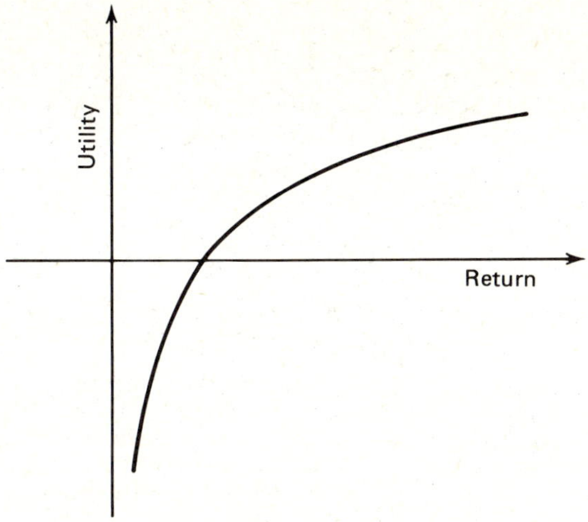

FIGURE 8. Utility.

where R_i is the return on commodity i, R is the average return across all commodities, n is the number of commodities, and σ is the utility to the client. However, this utility increases at a decreasing rate. This indicates that *more* is *better*, but after a point, not that much better. Looking at the left-hand side of the curve, we see that *less is bad,* and as the returns become more and more grimly negative, the utility to the investor becomes even worse. Losing everything is twice as bad as losing just half of the amount invested. This tends to characterize most investors' feelings.

EFFECTS OF DIVERSIFICATION CORRELATION. Assets, whether commodities or commodity trading systems, are assumed to have some imperfect correlation diversification effect with each other. This means that when one asset goes down, the other asset does not necessarily go down as well. If each of the commodities or assets had perfect correlation with each other, they would all rise and fall at exactly the same time and by exactly the same amount. There would be no such thing as "diversification." But they do not move in "lockstep" with each other.

The measurement of this diversification effect is embodied or measured by a *correlation coefficient*. The three graphs in Figure 9 demonstrate high correlation, no correlation, and negative correlation between the returns of two assets or trading systems.

Perfect correlation is 1.0, indicating that when one asset goes up, the other always goes up as well, not necessarily by the same amount, but always by the same multiple of the first asset's move. (The formula for calculating the correlation coefficient is available in any statistics book.) *No correlation* returns a value of 0 and a *high negative correlation* is represented by -1.0, showing that as one asset goes up, the other goes down.

The importance of correlation is evidenced by the relationship between the commodities in the same group versus different groups. For example, during most periods the metals all tend to move together, the meats tend to move in the same direction, and likewise for the grains. The effect is especially strong for interest-

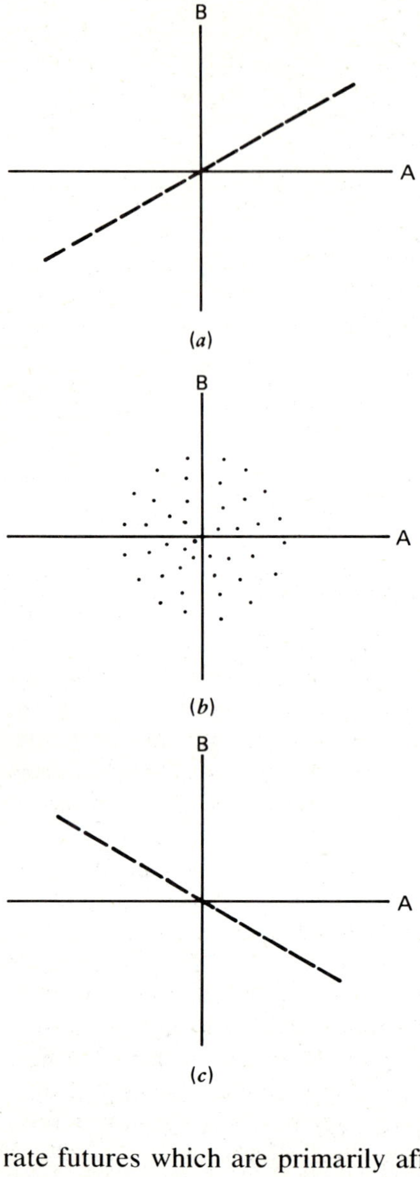

FIGURE 9. Correlation between assets (or systems) A and B. (*a*) High positive correlation. (*b*) No correlation. (*c*) High negative correlation.

rate futures which are primarily affected by government financial policy, rather than crop yields, consumption or storage costs.

In contrast, commodity futures in different groups tend to move more independently of each other. Silver tends to move independently from soybeans. Cattle tends to move independently from copper. The correlations between these commodities tend to be slightly positive, but very low.

One good way of obtaining a negative correlation between two return streams (sets of data) is to go long one commodity and short another within the same group. We call the negative correlation resulting from such a move *spreading* or *hedging*. The gains in one contract tend to offset the losses in another contract. This could be demonstrated by a long position in gold and a short position in silver over most years.

EFFICIENT FRONTIER. It is necessary to be able to select a portfolio or a set of portfolios which have the highest expected return possible for a given amount of risk. Many investment advisors find it difficult to quantify their expectations for the return of their trading system. They know that the return will not be *exactly* as they forecast, but rather a return within some range around that forecast; and, they have some associated measure, great or small, of their confidence in this forecast and the extent of its range.

We can all agree that the most attractive portfolio would be one with a high return and low risk, as opposed to a low return and high risk. Investment A would be preferred to investment B in Figure 10(*a*), which shows returns over time.

Figure 10(*b*) shows these same two investments drawn as probability distributions. You may consider the returns shown as annual returns and the height of the graph as the probability of such a return. Unfortunately, most of our choices are not so clear.

An *efficient frontier* is the set of portfolios with the highest expected return possible per unit risk. If the set of possible portfolios are shown by the circles in Figure 11, then an investor would want to choose the subset which was highest on the graph (had the highest returns) and furthest to the left (had the lowest risk). The exact proportions of the futures contracts which should be contained in each portfolio may be calculated using a "quadratic program."

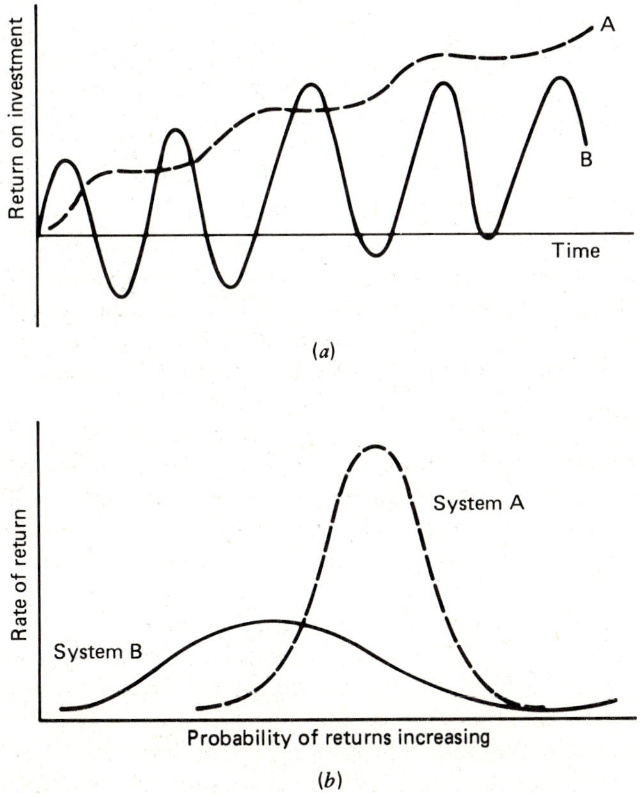

FIGURE 10. Comparative returns and risks of two systems.

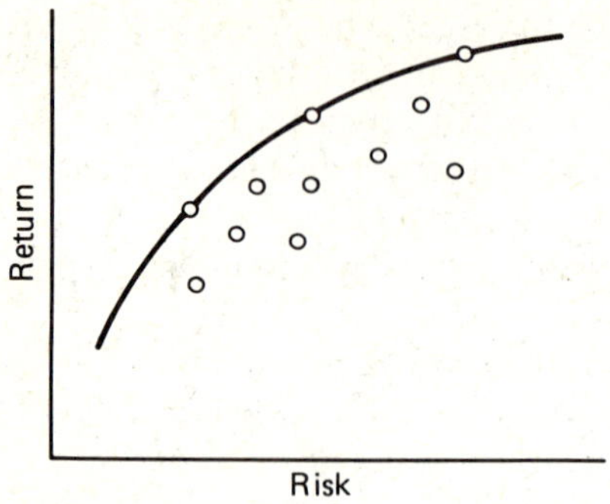

FIGURE 11. Efficient frontier.

The *objective function* of a quadratic program is to get the

$$\text{maximized return} - \text{risk}$$

Because some investors have different attitudes toward risk, we need to add a multiplier to the risk side of this equations to indicate this individual's sensitivity to risk relative to returns. Thus we get the

$$\text{Efficient frontier} = \text{maximized return} - \text{risk aversion factor} \times \text{risk}$$

EVALUATING RETURNS

Having selected a portfolio based on risk and return of individual commodity trading performance, it will be necessary to evaluate the overall returns, relative to risk, of future performance. Since there are other chapters in this book covering this topic, only the major points will be summarized.

The method selected to evaluate performance will tend to emphasize certain qualities. An *arithmetic* or *geometric* method could be used to combine returns of each month, quarter, or designated period. The arithmetic approach simply adds the returns while the geometric method multiplies them, giving a compounded return. During periods of good performance the geometric measurement will return higher results.

Performance can also be *time weighted* or *dollar weighted*. Using the time-weighted method the returns during equal periods are treated equally, regardless of the amount of money being traded. The dollar-weighted approach considers the amount of money at the beginning of each period as a factor in calculating the returns of that period. Either method could be used fairly if the method of calculation is explained with the results.

The *Sharpe ratio* is a popular way of ranking the risk and return of many systems. It is effectively a measure of the volatility or variability of the investment relative to its returns. That is, one investment with the same return as another will have a lower Sharpe ratio if the change in asset value is greater (more variable) than the other. The higher the Sharpe ratio, the better the investment relative to others. Figure 12 shows the ranking of some common investments evaluated over the period 1950–1976.

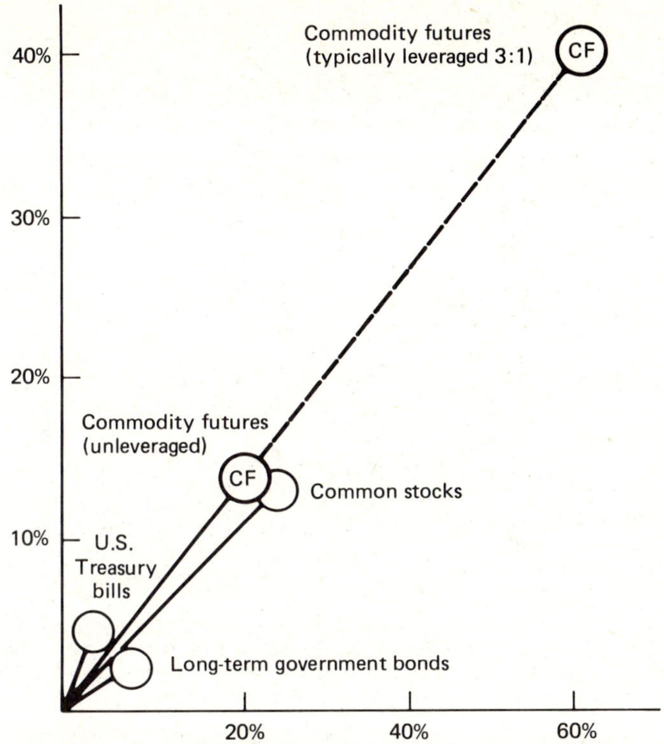

FIGURE 12. Risk/reward (Sharpe) ratios. U.S. Treasury bills, 1.9; Commodities (unleveraged), 0.7; Commodities (leveraged), 0.7; Common stocks, 0.6; Long-term government bonds, 0.4.

CONCLUSION

This chapter has looked at the various factors which are essential to money management. Most important has been an underlying theme of risk. Risk control can be achieved primarily by increasing investment reserves (using less margin for each investment) and by diversification.

Proper diversification can be the result of combining commodities which have low relative correlations. Although a well-defined mathematical approach was presented, a trader need only select from the different classes of metals, grains, livestock, and so forth to reduce risk substantially from an undiversified, or concentrated, portfolio.

Once portfolios have been structured, the best may be selected by finding the *efficient frontier*, the combination of the highest returns and the lowest risk for individual investor risk preference. Once a portfolio has been selected using this procedure, the investors or trading advisors can have a high degree of confidence that they have done their best.

CHAPTER **22**

MEASURING COMMODITY TRADING PERFORMANCE

CONTENTS

THE NEED TO NORMALIZE GAIN 3

THE SHARPE RATIO 5

FOUR PROBLEMS WITH THE SHARPE RATIO 8

ALTERNATIVE PERFORMANCE MEASURES 14

Average Maximum Retracement (AMR) as a Risk Measure 14
Margin Adjusted AMR (MAAMR) 15
Maximum Loss (ML) as a Risk Measure 16

USING THE AMR, MAAMR, AND ML TO CONSTRUCT PERFORMANCE MEASURES 16

Supplemental Performance Measures 17
Which Performance Measure is Best 18

EVALUATING PERFORMANCE FOR A MULTIMARKET SYSTEM 18

PRACTICAL CONSIDERATIONS 21

EVALUATING THE PERFORMANCE OF A MONEY MANAGER 21

Return/Risk Measure for the Money Manager 21
The Inadequacy of a Return/Risk Ratio for Evaluating Money Manager Trading Performance 22

CONCLUSIONS 25

CHAPTER 22

MEASURING COMMODITY TRADING PERFORMANCE[1]

Jack Schwager

THE NEED TO NORMALIZE GAIN

By itself, dollar gain is a meaningless statistic for judging the relative merit of a trading system. For example, given only the information that, during the same period, System A gained an average of $8,000 per year and System B $6,000 per year, there would be no way of determining which was the better system. The veracity of this statement cam be intuitively demonstrated by providing some examples.

Consider the following two cases in which additional information is provided about System A and System B:

Case 1. Both systems trade the same single market. System B initiates a one-contract position each time a signal is received. System A, on the other hand, includes rules which permit the variation of the position size from one to five contracts, depending upon the relative strength of the relevant indicators. During the period in question, the average position size in System A was three contracts.

Case 2. Both systems initiate single unit positions upon receiving signals, but System A trades coffee while System B trades corn. The significance is that contract value fluctuations in coffee far exceed those of corn.

Given the above information, insofar as any judgment is possible, in both cases, System B appears to be the better system since System A will *probably* require a substantially greater amount of funds for trading. Actually, as we will soon see, there is still not sufficient information available to compare the relative merits of System A and System B. However, the primary intention of the above examples is to highlight the total inadequacy of dollar gain as a measure of merit.

The meaningful basic measure of return is not dollar gain, but rather dollar gain *relative* to the funds required for trading, that is, a percent return figure.

[1]This chapter is adapted from *A Complete Guide to the Futures Markets* by Jack Schwager, which is scheduled for publication by John Wiley & Sons in 1984. The material is based on the results of a joint research project undertaken by the author and Norman D. Strahm. The author also wishes to acknowledge and thank Dr. Strahm for his insightful comments and suggestions.

Such a calculation is relatively straightforward if one is attempting to evaluate the performance of a money manager for a given account. In that instance, the dollar gain per year is simply divided by the total amount of funds provided to the money manager. In the case of evaluating the performance of a commodity system, however, there is no *a priori* way of determining the amount of money needed to trade the system.

Some analysts have suggested that exchange-established margins should be employed as a proxy for fund requirements in evaluating trading systems. Thus they use the dollar gain per year divided by margin as a figure of merit. At first glance, such a measure would appear to eradicate the contradictions suggested in Cases 1 and 2 which arise if gain alone is used to measure performance. In Case 1 the margin requirement would be three times as high for System A, which trades an average of three contracts, while in Case 2 the margin per contract would be much higher for coffee than corn. In both cases, the introduction of margin would tend to adjust the performance of System A downwards as appears to be intuitively desirable.

Unfortunately, a gain/margin ratio still contains a serious flaw: margin (or even a multiple of margin) is a poor proxy for the funds required to trade a system. Assume we are provided with a third case:

Case 3. Both Systems A and B trade the same market and are always in the market with a constant position size of one contract.

In case 3, a gain/margin (or a gain/multiple of margin) ratio would *always* rate System A better than System B. Now let's assume that we are dealing with a Case 3 type situation, margin equals $2,000 per contract, and the total equity streams of the two systems are reflected by the graphs in Figure 1. Although the dollar gain is greater in System A, and both systems require the same margin, it is obvious that a much greater amount of funds would be required to trade System A. Note in Figure 1 that the maximum retracement is $8,600 in System A and only $800 in System B. Furthermore, System A witnesses many more instances of substantial losses. Finally, note that these losses are far greater than the initial margin requirement. In the real world, a trader using System A would have to provide substantial additional funds beyond the initial margin to avoid being eliminated from the game. Although a trader using System B might also need to provide additional funds, the incremental amount would be substantially smaller.

Clearly, as the above example illustrates, margin can easily be a very poor relative measure of the amount of funds necessary to trade a system. It would appear that any reasonable estimate of the funds required to trade a commodity system would have to be related in some way to a risk measurement. For example, we might assume that the fund requirements are equal to the maximum retracement plus margin, or two times this figure or some other risk-based measure.

It should be noted that for the purposes of evaluating and comparing systems, it is not necessary that a risk measure directly provide an accurate estimate of the funds required to trade a system. All that is necessary is that the risk measure provide an accurate relative gauge for comparisons; that is, systems with higher risk measures should have correspondingly greater fund requirements. In any

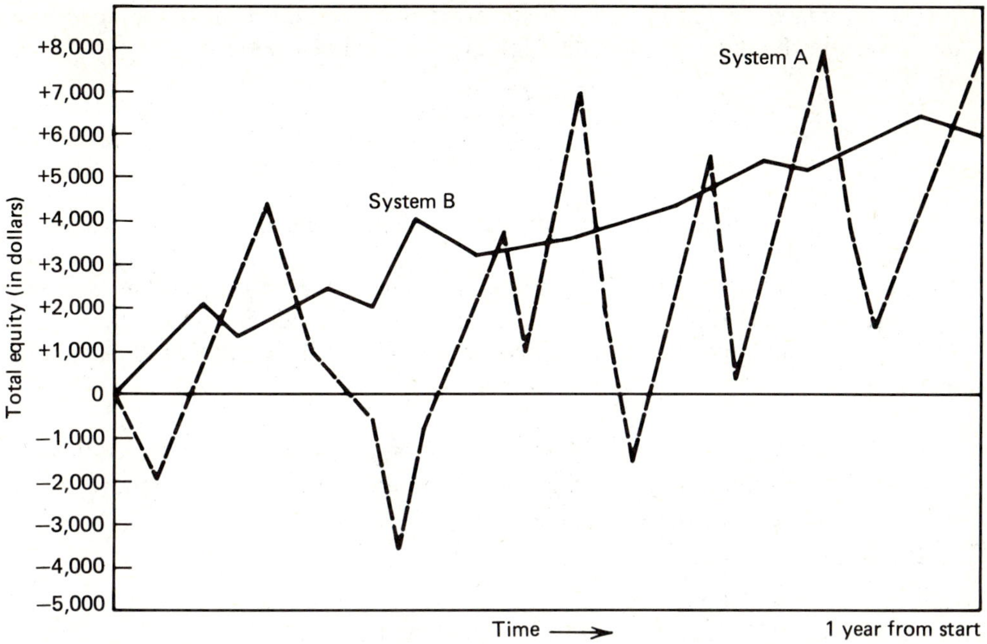

FIGURE 1. Case 3—Representation of highly volatile System A and Less volatile System B.

case, the key point is that the appropriate figure of merit for evaluating commodity trading system performance would be a gain/risk measure.

THE SHARPE RATIO

The need to incorporate risk in evaluating performance has long been recognized. The classic return/risk measure is the Sharpe ratio (SR) which can be expressed as follows:

$$\text{SR} = \frac{E - I}{\sigma}$$

where E is the expected return, I is the risk-free interest rate, and σ is the standard deviation of returns.

E is typically stated in terms of percent return. Normally, the expected return is said to equal the average past return. In view of this fact, although E always refers to the expected return (i.e., applies to a future period), we will use it synonymously with the average past return.

The incorporation of I in the Sharpe ratio recognizes that an investor could always earn a certain return "risk free," for example, by investing in Treasury bills.[2] Thus the return in excess of this *risk-free return* is more meaningful than the absolute level of the return.

[2]Of course there is some element of risk even in Treasury bills, but it is small enough to be ignored.

The *standard deviation* is a statistic which is intended to measure degree of dispersion in the data. The formula for the standard deviation is

$$\sigma = \sqrt{\frac{\sum_{i=1}^{N}(\overline{X} - X_i)^2}{N - 1}}$$

where $\overline{X}$ is the mean, X_i represents the individual data values, and N is the number of data values.

In the Sharpe ratio application, N is equal to the number of time intervals. For example, if weekly time intervals are used for a 2-year survey period, $N = 104$. The above formula indicates the following procedure for calculating the standard deviation:

1. Calculate the mean for the set of data (e.g., the average weekly return).
2. Calculate the difference between each data point and the mean.
3. Square each of these differences.
4. Sum the resulting figures.
5. Divide the sum by $N - 1$.[3]
6. Calculate the square root of the resulting figure.

In a rough sense, the standard deviation is a type of average deviation (of the individual data points from the mean) in which data points that are further from the mean have greater impact upon the calculation. (This greater weight is the result of the squaring process.)

In calculating the standard deviation it is always necessary to choose a time interval for segmenting the entire period equity data (e.g., weekly, monthly). If, for example, the percent return data for a given year were broken down into weekly figures, the standard deviation would be very high if the return of many of the individual weeks deviated sharply from the average for the period. Conversely, the standard deviation would be low if the individual weeks tended to cluster around the average. Figure 2 illustrates two sets of data with the same average weekly return but substantially different standard deviations.

The basic premise of the Sharpe ratio is that the standard deviation is a measure of risk. That is, the more widespread the individual returns from the average return, the riskier the investment. In essence, the standard deviation measures the ambiguity of the return. It should be intuitively clear that if the standard deviation is low, it is reasonable to assume that the actual return will be close to the expected return. (Assuming, of course, that the expected return is a good indicator of actual return.) On the other hand, if the standard deviation is high, it suggests that there is a good chance that the actual return may vary substantially from the expected return.

The Sharpe ratio can be calculated rather directly for a money manager because we know the amount of funds upon which percent return is based. This is not the

[3]The reason for dividing by $N - 1$ rather than N is related to a statistical concept called "degrees of freedom."

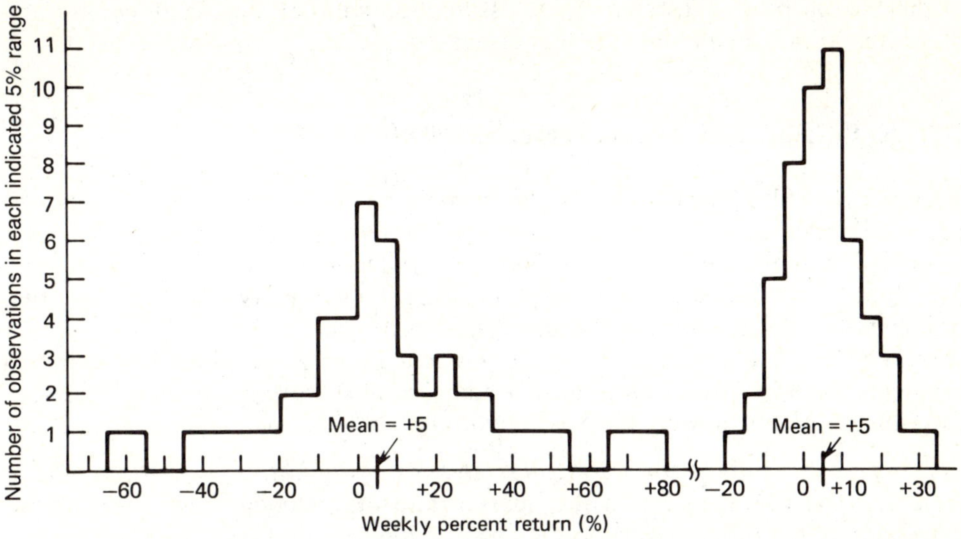

FIGURE 2. Systems with the same average weekly returns by different standard deviations.

case for a trading system. In applying the Sharpe ratio to a trading system, we have one of two options:

1. Estimate the funds required to trade the system and use this figure to calculate a percent return.
2. Simplify the Sharpe ratio by deleting the risk-free return I. Thus the Sharpe ratio would reduce to[4]:

$$\text{SR} = \frac{E}{\sigma}$$

This latter approach can be justified on the basis that, except for small accounts, the bulk of margin requirements can be met by Treasury bill deposits. Thus, in contrast to the buyer of securities, the commodity trader does not sacrifice the risk-free return in order to participate in the alternative investment.

In the form E/σ the Sharpe ratio would be the same whether E were expressed in terms of dollar gain or percent return. The reason for this is that the same unit of measurement would be used for the standard deviation. Thus, the funds requirement figure would appear in both the numerator and denominator and would cancel out.[5] In the remainder of this chapter, we will assume the reduced form

[4]As will be explained later, if this form of the Sharpe ratio is used, it is not necessary to estimate the funds required to trade the system.

[5]The implicit assumption here is that trading funds are constant (i.e., profits are withdrawn and losses replenished). In other words, there is no compounding (i.e., reinvestment of gains, reduction of investment in the event of losses). Although, generally speaking, a compounded return calculation is preferable, this consideration is more than offset by the critical advantage of not having to estimate fund requirements for a commodity system. Furthermore, in comparing two systems, the system with the higher noncompounded return will often also exhibit the higher compounded return.

of the Sharpe ratio. This simplifying assumption will not meaningfully alter any of the theoretical or practical points discussed.

FOUR PROBLEMS WITH THE SHARPE RATIO

Although the Sharpe ratio is a useful measurement, it does have a number of potential drawbacks. In this section, we use the reduced form of the Sharpe ratio discussed in the previous section (SR $= E/\sigma$). The points detailed below apply equally to the complete form of the formula. It should be noted that the first two problems cited will only be relevant if trading results in different intervals are correlated (e.g., a tendency for losses to occur in streaks), while the latter two problems would be relevant even if trading results are uncorrelated. The four potential problems in using the Sharpe ratio to measure trading performance are:

Problem 1: Failure to Distinguish Between Intermittent and Consecutive Losses. The risk measure in the Sharpe ratio—the standard deviation—is independent of the order of various data points. Figure 3 depicts the equity streams of two systems, each of which earns a total of $12,000 ($6,000 per year) for the given period. However, System A alternates $2,000 monthly gains with $1,000 monthly losses, while System B first loses $12,000 in the initial 12 months and subsequently gains $24,000 during the remainder of the period. Both systems would have identical Sharpe ratios. Despite this fact, few traders would consider the systems equivalent in risk. Virtually all traders would agree that System B is far riskier and requires a much greater sum of funds for trading. Clearly, from a trader's viewpoint, the two systems are far from identical.

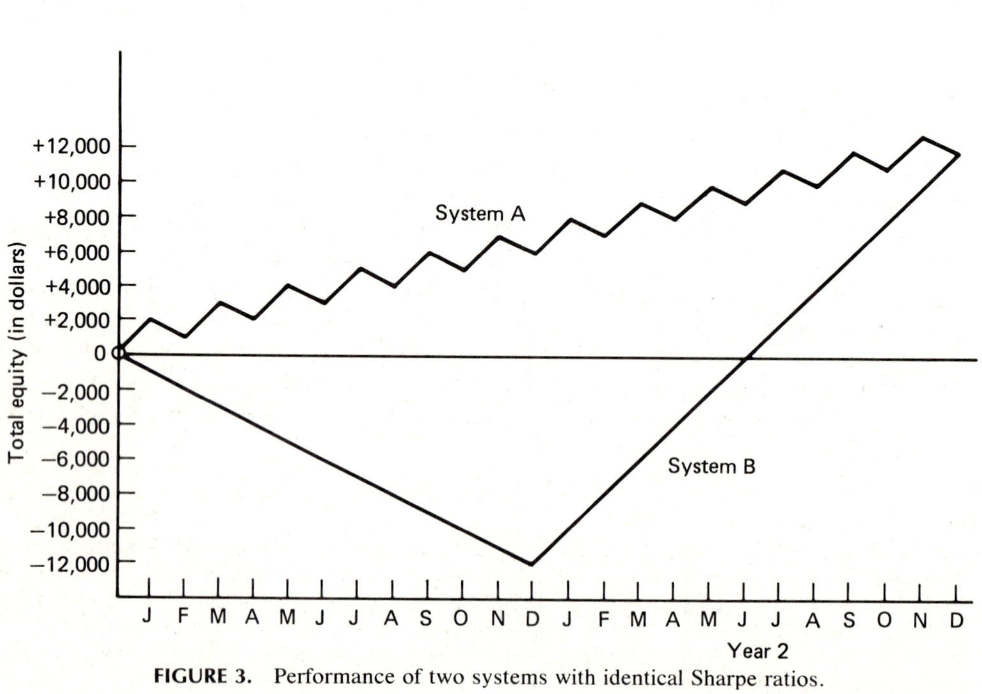

FIGURE 3. Performance of two systems with identical Sharpe ratios.

As the above illustration demonstrates, the Sharpe ratio fails to penalize systems which tend to witness consecutive losses. This can be a critical flaw if the trading results in different intervals are correlated. (If, however, interval trading results are uncorrelated, the occurrence of consecutive losses would only represent a random event and hence have no special significance. Unfortunately, although it may be possible to demonstrate that a set of results is consistent with a model based on uncorrelated results, it is impossible to prove that correlation does not exist.)

Problem 2: Dependency on Time Interval. If trading results (in different time periods) are uncorrelated, in theory, the annualized Sharpe ratio would be independent of the time interval length chosen for segmenting the data.[6] However, the assumption that trading results are uncorrelated may not always be justified. Thus, given the performance data of two systems for an extended period, we might very well consider one system better if we calculate the Sharpe ratio using weekly intervals and the other system better if we use monthly intervals. Since the choice of a time interval is arbitrary, this is an undesirable feature.

As an example, consider a system which generates the following sequence of weekly gains and losses over a 2-year period:

Week 1 +1250
Week 2 −1000
Week 3 +1150
Week 4 −1000
•
•
•
•
•
Week 101 +1250
Week 102 −1000
Week 103 +1150
Week 104 −1000

If weekly time intervals were used to calculate an annualized Sharpe ratio,[7]

$$SR = \frac{E}{\sigma} = \frac{52\left(\dfrac{(26 \times 1250) + (26 \times 1150) + [52 \times (-1000)]}{104}\right)}{\sqrt{52}\sqrt{\dfrac{26(100 - 1250)^2 + 26(100 - 1150)^2 + 52(100 + 1000)^2}{103}}}$$

$$= 0.652$$

[6]The use of different time intervals would still yield differrent Sharpe ratios, but these discrepencies would merely be a consequence of differences in sampling errors.

[7]To annualize expected return, it is necessary to multiply the expected weekly return by 52. To annualize the interval-based standard deviation, it is necessary to multiply by $\sqrt{52}$. This latter conversion is not intuitively obvious, and is due to statistical considerations which will not be discussed

If, on the other hand, we used 2-week time intervals the data sequence would be

First 2-week period	+250
Second 2-week period	+150
Third 2-week period	+250
Fourth 2-week period	+150
•	
•	
•	
•	

and the annualized Sharpe ratio would be

$$SR = \frac{26\left[\frac{26(250) + 26(150)}{52}\right]}{\sqrt{26}\sqrt{\frac{26(200-250)^2 + 26(200-150)^2}{51}}} = 20.198$$

The 0.652 Sharpe ratio calculated using 1-week intervals would seem to suggest mediocre performance, while the 20.198 Sharpe ratio calculated using 2-week intervals indicates extraordinary performance. In fact, the second Sharpe ratio figure is nearly 31 times as high as the first! Yet both these figures were derived from the same system during the same period.[8] Note that this extreme variation in the calculation results from an arbitrary factor—the length of the time interval used to segment the data.

Which of the two diverse Sharpe ratio figures is more representative of the system illustrated above? Although any answer must unavoidably be subjective, the second Sharpe ratio appears to be a better indicator of the system's behavior. Actually, the system performs extremely well: it gains a total of $52,000 per year in a steady fashion and never witnesses a loss of more than $1,000 from any start date. Even if we assume that the funds required to trade this system were equal to twice the maximum retracement, the annual percent return would still be 360%. The problem with using the 1-week intervals in this case is that the particular system witnesses wide swings over very short time periods, but behaves much more steadily over longer periods.

---

here. However, it should be emphasized that the standard deviation conversion requires that the intervals be independent—an assumption not met in this artificial example or in most actual trading cases. As a result, there is no adequate, simple way to annualize the data, or for that matter, convert it to any common period. Nevertheless, this conversion feasibility is implicitly assumed in using the Sharpe ratio, and the purpose of this example is to illustrate one of the resulting problems, that is, the dependency of the Sharpe ratio upon the choice of time interval.

[8] The huge divergence is due to the serial correlation in the data (i.e., the interdependence of time interval values) and the choice of a time interval which corresponds to a critical time scale in the serial correlation.

Problem 3: Failure to Distinguish Between Upside and Downside Fluctuations. The Sharpe ratio is a measure of volatility, not risk. The two are not necessarily synonymous. In terms of the risk calculation employed in the Sharpe ratio (i.e., the standard deviation of return), upside and downside fluctuations are considered equally bad. Thus, the Sharpe ratio would penalize a system which exhibited sporadic sharp *increases* in equity, even if equity retracements were small. To illustrate this point, Table 1 compares two systems: System A exhibits intermittent surges in equity and no equity retracements, while System B witnesses several equity retracements. Both systems gain an equal amount for the period as a whole. The equity streams for these two systems are illustrated in Figure 4. Given the data in Table 1, the *annualized* Sharpe ratios would be as follows:

$$SR_A = \frac{E}{\sigma} = \frac{\dfrac{24{,}000}{2}}{\sqrt{12}\sqrt{\dfrac{14(1000-0)^2 + 8(1000-1000)^2 + 2(1000-8000)^2}{23}}} = 1.57$$

$$SR_B = \frac{\dfrac{24{,}000}{2}}{\sqrt{12}\sqrt{\dfrac{18(1000-2000)^2 + 6(1000+2000)^2}{23}}} = 1.96$$

The expected return (E) is equal to total equity gain for the period divided by the number of years, or equivalently, the average monthly return multiplied by 12. The *annualized* standard diviation is equal to the standard deviation of the monthly returns multiplied by $\sqrt{12}$. (The rationale for multiplying by $\sqrt{12}$ here is analogous

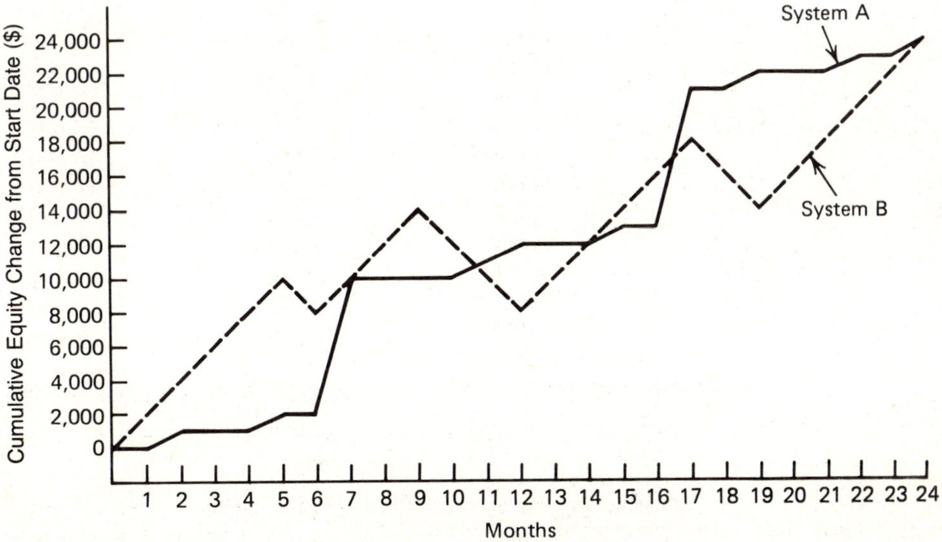

FIGURE 4. Equity streams.

to the rationale for multiplying the standard deviation of weekly data by $\sqrt{52}$—see footnote 7).

Note that although both systems gain an equal amount, and System B witnesses several retracements whereas System A does not exhibit any, the Sharpe ratio would rate System B higher. This outcome is a direct consequence of the fact that the Sharpe ratio penalizes upside volatility exactly the same as downside volatility. It should be stressed that, in contrast to the aforementioned two problems with the Sharpe ratio, this criticism applies even if the trading results in different periods are uncorrelated.

Problem 4: Failure to Distinguish Between Retracements in Unrealized Profits Versus Retracements from "Trade Entry Date" Equity.[9] Assume that after

TABLE 1. Comparison of Monthly Returns for Two Systems

	System A		System B	
Month	Equity Change	Cumulative Equity Change	Equity Change	Cumulative Equity Change
1	0	0	2,000	2,000
2	1,000	1,000	2,000	4,000
3	0	1,000	2,000	6,000
4	0	1,000	2,000	8,000
5	1,000	2,000	2,000	10,000
6	0	2,000	−2,000	8,000
7	8,000	10,000	2,000	10,000
8	0	10,000	2,000	12,000
9	0	10,000	2,000	14,000
10	0	10,000	−2,000	12,000
11	1,000	11,000	−2,000	10,000
12	1,000	12,000	−2,000	8,000
13	0	12,000	2,000	10,000
14	0	12,000	2,000	12,000
15	1,000	13,000	2,000	14,000
16	0	13,000	2,000	16,000
17	8,000	21,000	2,000	18,000
18	0	21,000	−2,000	16,000
19	1,000	22,000	−2,000	14,000
20	0	22,000	2,000	16,000
21	0	22,000	2,000	18,000
22	1,000	23,000	2,000	20,000
23	0	23,000	2,000	22,000
24	1,000	24,000	2,000	24,000
	Average Monthly Return = 1,000		Average Montly Return = 1,000	

[9] A "trade entry date" is defined as any day on which the net position shifts from neutral to long, neutral to short, long to short, or short to long. The list of all trade entry dates represents all the days on which a new trader could begin trading the system if only new signals are accepted.

many years of research John Q. Trend has found the near-perfect system. This system sets stops very close upon receiving trade signals and then continually widens the stop as the trend progresses. As a result of this structure, losses are kept low during trading range markets, while the system usually manages to hold on to a position for the duration of a major trend. The only drawback is that to achieve this latter result, the system sometimes surrenders a significant portion of unrealized profits.

Figure 5 illustrates the total equity stream of this hypothetical system (total equity includes both realized and unrealized profits). Although there are several instances of sharp retracements in total equity, note the following two key points:

1. The sharp declines represent retracements in unrealized profits.
2. The maximum loss after any possible trade entry date is very small. (It is assumed that one can only begin trading the system when a signal is received.)

Is this a risky system? From a trader's viewpoint the answer is an emphatic "no."[10] A trader using the system would never have experienced a significant decline from the trader's initial equity level regardless of when the trader started or stopped trading the system. The standard deviation measure used in the Sharpe

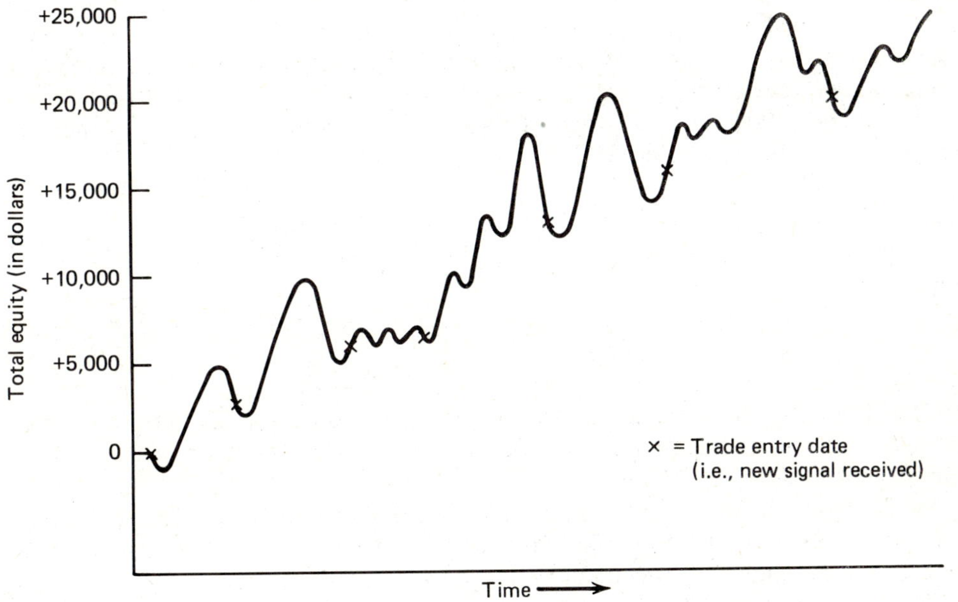

FIGURE 5. Performance of a system with initial close stops and lagging stops during major trends.

[10]It should be pointed out that this is a subjective view. Some would argue that a loss in open profits is as bad as an equivalent loss in original equity. However, the implicit philosophy in this presentation is that capital preservation is a more important criterion than minimizing retracements in open profits. Also, it should be noted that a system's predilection towards larger profit retracements will still be reflected in the gain measures. Such a system can only rate well in terms of gain if this negative quality is more than offset by other beneficial characteristics (e.g., greater immunity to whipsaw losses).

ratio, however, would rate this as a risky system. Why? Because the standard deviation is based on total equity. Therefore, sharp retracements would suggest major risk even if they always followed even larger gains subsequent to a trade entry date.

Risk measures, which are based on total equity, only make sense for very short-term trading systems (e.g., day trading), or if it is assumed that trading can begin at any time—that is, the trader does not wait for a new signal to begin trading. However, if signals are generated intermittently and one can only begin trading the system with a new signal, a risk measure based on feasible start dates appears to be preferable. This is a particularly crucial consideration for evaluating "slow" trend-following systems which generate signals infrequently (i.e., an average of 2 to 3 months or longer). Most of the risk measures discussed in the next section are based upon retracements from possible trade entry dates rather than fluctuations in total equity. If the assumption that trading can begin on any day is preferred, analogous measures can be constructed using total equity rather that trade entry date equity as the reference point.

ALTERNATIVE PERFORMANCE MEASURES

AVERAGE MAXIMUM RETRACEMENT (AMR) AS A RISK MEASURE. As previously defined, a "trade entry date" is any day on which the net position shifts from neutral to long, neutral to short, long to short, or short to long. The AMR asks the question: "For each day, what would be the retracement from initial equity if one had started trading the system on the worst possible trade entry date?"[11] The AMR is the average of these daily maximum retracement figures. The AMR can be expressed as[12]

$$\text{AMR} = \frac{1}{N} \Sigma_{i-1}^{N} \text{ POS } (\text{MCE}_i - \text{TE}_i)$$

where

$$\text{POS } (X) = \begin{bmatrix} x \text{ if } x > 0 \\ 0 \text{ if } x \leq 0 \end{bmatrix}$$

MCE is the maximum closed equity (realized profits) on any trade entry date *prior to* day i, TE_i is the total equity on day i, and N is the number of days in the survey period.

Days on which $\text{TE}_i > \text{MCE}$ imply that as of that day, those trading the system will have a net gain regardless of the trade entry date on which they began trading, that is, the maximum retracement would be zero. This is the reason for the use of the operator POS.

[11]At this point, we assume the system trades only one market and, therefore, that there are no open positions in any other market on any trade entry date.

[12]The AMR weights all daily maximum retracement figures equally. If a trader prefers a performance measure which places greater weight upon wider retracements, the following alternative form for the AMR could be considered:

$$\text{AMR} = \sqrt{\frac{\Sigma_{i=1}^{N}[\text{POS}(\text{MCE}_i - \text{TE}_i)]^2}{N}}$$

As a practical matter, the amount of computation implied by the AMR can be dramatically reduced by using only the low total equity day in each month to calculate the measure. Such an approach would provide a rough approximation of a daily-based AMR figure and would reduce the amount of computation by a factor of over 21 to 1, since N would be reduced from the number of trading days to the number of months in the survey period.

One disadvantage of the AMR is that risk measurement could be very sensitive to the time period in which losses occur. The two equity streams in Figure 6 are identical except for the time at which the large retracement materializes. Although, intuitively, both systems appear to be equivalent in terms of risk, the AMR of System B would be significantly larger.

MARGIN ADJUSTED AMR (MAAMR). It can be argued that if our primary intention is to derive a measure for the purpose of normalizing gain, a margin component term should be added to the AMR. In other words, the funds required to trade a system will be a function of margin as well as the magnitude of retracement. The MAAMR is merely the sum of the AMR and a margin estimate.

The formula for the MAAMR employs a margin estimate since it may be difficult to obtain actual margin data. The MAAMR can be expressed as follows:

$$\text{MAAMR} = \frac{1}{N}\sum_{i=1}^{N} [\text{MR}_i + (\text{MF} \times C \times V_i)]$$

where MR_i is the maximum retracement on day i and equals POS $(MCE_i - TE_i)$; MF is the margin factor, a representative constant which reflects the assumed percentage margin based on total contract value (e.g., MF = 0.08); C is the number of contracts in position; V_i is the contract value on day i, equal to the contract price times the number of units in the contract; and N is the number of trading

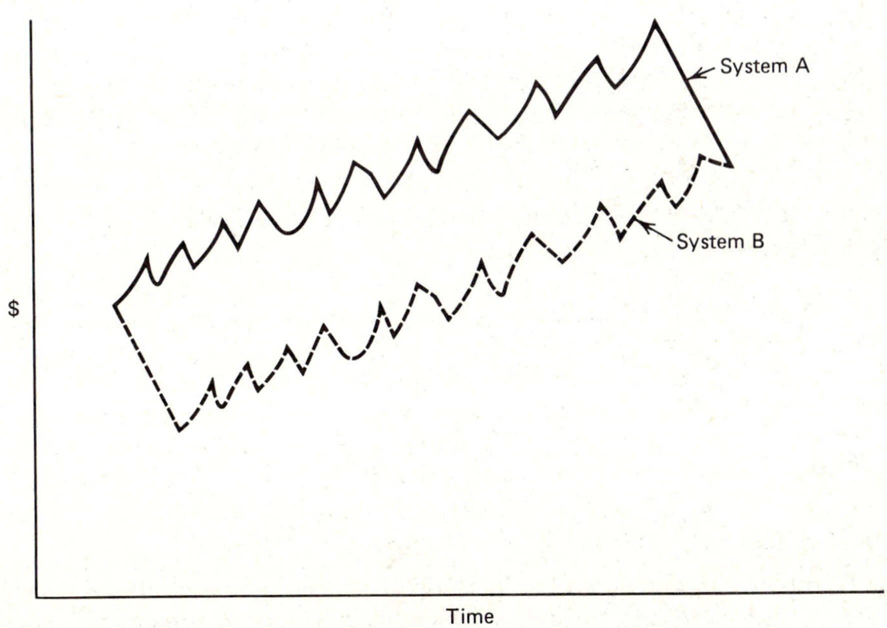

FIGURE 6. Equity streams with retracement at different times.

days in the survey period (or number of months in the survey period if only the monthly low total equity days are used in calculating the MAAMR).

The MAAMR would be subject to the same time dependency disadvantage detailed for the AMR.

MAXIMUM LOSS (ML) AS A RISK MEASURE. One number which is of particular interest is the worst case possibility in a given system. In other words, the largest retracement that would have been experienced during the entire survey period if trading was initiated on the worst possible start date. The ML is merely the largest MR_i and can be expressed as

$$ML = \text{Max}\,(MR_i)$$

The relative importance of the ML as a risk measure is somewhat dependent upon the number of markets (and/or systems) being traded. If one is trading only a single system in one market, the maximum loss becomes extremely significant in defining both the risk and the capital requirements of the system. However, if one is trading many markets (and/or systems) diversification will reduce the significance of the ML of any specific system applied to a single market.

The ML is not recommended as a sole risk measure since it depends upon only a single event and, hence, may be very unrepresentative of the overall performance of a system. Furthermore, as a result of this characteristic, the value of the ML may be highly contingent upon the choice of the survey period. However, the ML does provide important information and should be considered in conjunction with the other risk measures discussed. It is also possible to construct a margin adjusted version of the ML as we did with the AMR. However, this is probably not necessary since the ML will usually represent several multiples of the margin.

It should be emphasized that the above risk measures do not directly provide an estimate of the funds required to trade a system—they merely provide a relative measure of comparison, that is, systems with higher risk measures will have greater capital requirements. Thus, for example, although trader A may decide he needs double the MAAMR to trade a system, while trader B may triple the MAAMR to obtain his capital requirement estimate, both traders will obtain the same ordering of systems on the basis of a gain/MAAMR ratio.

USING THE AMR, MAAMR, AND ML TO CONSTRUCT PERFORMANCE MEASURES

The AMR, MAAMR, and ML are all risk measures. To obtain a performance measure, we would merely divide a gain measure (e.g., average annual gain) by one of these risk measures. Thus, the following are possible choices for performance measures:

$$G/AMR$$
$$G/MAAMR$$
$$G/ML$$

where G = average annual gain.

Each of these measures avoids the four problems discussed above regarding the Sharpe ratio. However, these measures are subject to some disadvantages which do not apply to the Sharpe ratio. Specifically, the G/ML is based on a single observation and the G/AMR and G/MAAMR are dependent on the timing of losses (see above discussion regarding the AMR and ML). Furthermore, if trading results in different intervals are uncorrelated, it can be argued that the Sharpe ratio would be a more meaningful performance measure than the alternative measures listed above. In such cases, some of the disadvantages of the Sharpe ratio (problems 1 and 2) would be dispelled, while the G/AMR, G/MAAMR, and G/ML might prove misleading since they would give greater weight to consecutive losses—a random event by definition if interval trading results are uncorrelated. Consequently, since the trader does not know whether the interval trading results for a given system are correlated or uncorrelated, it is prudent to also consider the implications of the Sharpe ratio as an additional measure even if the trader also uses one or more of the above alternative measures.

SUPPLEMENTAL PERFORMANCE MEASURES. In addition to the three performance measures suggested above the following measures may also merit supplemental attention:

1. *Expected Net Profit Per Trade.* The ENPPT can be expressed as

$$\text{ENPPT} = (\%P)\,(\text{AP}) - (\%L)\,(\text{AL})$$

where $\%P$ is the percent of total trades which are profitable, $\%L$ is the percent of total trades which result in net losses, AP is the average net profit of a profitable trade, and AL is the average net loss of a losing trade.

The usefulness of this indicator is that a low ENPPT figure will highlight systems that are vulnerable to a serious deterioration of profits given poor executions, increased commissions, or any other form of increased transaction cost. The critical disadvantage of the ENPPT is that it does not incorporate a risk measure. In addition, the ENPPT has the intrinsic drawback that it may unfairly penalize active systems. For example, a system which generated one trade for a net gain of $2,000 would rate better than a system which, during the same period, generated 100 trades with an ENPPT of $1,000 (with similar equity fluctuations).

2. *Trade-Based Profit and Loss Ratio.* The TBPLR can be expressed as follows:

$$\text{TBPLR} = \frac{(\%P)\,(\text{AP})}{(\%L)\,(\text{AL})}$$

where the components are defined as in the ENPPT. This measure indicates the ratio of dollars gained to dollars lost in all trades. The appeal of the TBPLR is that it deflates profits by a measurement of total pain suffered.

Perhaps the greatest drawback of the TBPLR is that it gives no weight to open position losses. Thus, a trade that witnesses a huge loss before it is finally closed at a slight profit would have the same effect on the TBPLR as a trade that is immediately profitable and closed at the same slight profit. The two trades, however, would hardly be equivalent in the eyes of the trader. In addition, the TBPLR does not distinguish between intermittant and consecutive losses—a potentially serious flaw if there is a tendency for losing trades to be clustered.

WHICH PERFORMANCE MEASURE IS BEST? There is no such thing as a perfect performance measure. Each measure discussed in this chapter is subject to some drawbacks. Thus, the question of which performance measure is best can only be answered subjectively. In effect, each trader must weigh the advantages and disadvantages of the various approaches. Ideally, the trader would consider several performance measures in making comparative judgments between systems. Software for calculating most of the performance measures discussed in this section is available from Commodity Information Services Company (CISCO), Chicago, Illinois.

EVALUATING PERFORMANCE FOR A MULTIMARKET SYSTEM

Thus far we have considered only the single market system. Although it is certainly possible, and even desirable, to compare the performance of different systems on a market-by-market basis, there is also a need to compare the performance of these systems for multimarket portfolios. The reason for this is that different diversification qualities can substantially alter the performance of different systems. For example, although System A outperforms System B in most markets (basis the chosen performance measures), it is entirely possible that System B might perform better for a multimarket portfolio. This could occur if the performance of different markets were less correlated using System B, thereby resulting in a more diversified portfolio and dampened retracements.

As defined for the single market case, G/AMR and G/MAAMR cannot be directly applied in evaluating the performance of a multimarket system. The problem is that there are likely to be open positions in other markets on trade entry dates (days on which a new position is entered). If a trader does not enter existing open positions when the trader starts trading the system (i.e., if the trader enters only new signal trades), the difference between the MCE_i[13] and total equity on day i (TE_i) would not be representative of the trader's retracement in equity. Why? Because $MCE_i - TE_i$ would *also* reflect the subsequent equity changes of positions which were already open on that trade entry date—positions never entered by the new trader.

It is, however, possible to express the AMR in more general form so that it encompasses the multimarket system case:

$$\text{AMR} = \frac{1}{N}\sum_{i=1}^{N} \text{POS}\,(\text{MUPE}_i - \text{TE}_i)$$

where $MUPE_i$ is the maximum unentered position equity implied by any trade entry date prior to day i, TE_i is the total equity on day i, and N is the number of trading days in the survey period (or number of months in the survey period if only the monthly low total equity days are used in calculating the AMR).

In effect, the $MUPE_i$ represents the amount of total equity as of day i which would not have been realized by a trader who started trading on the worst possible prior trade entry date. The amount by which the $MUPE_i$ exceeds total equity on

[13]As previously defined, MCE_i is the maximum closed equity (realized profit) on any trade entry date prior to day i.

day i is equal to the maximum retracement that could have been experienced as of day i if trading was started on any prior trade entry date. For example, if the $MUPE_i$ is \$100,000, it means that as of day i a trader could have missed out on \$100,000 of the prevailing total equity on day i. If TE_i is \$70,000, the implication is that the maximum retracement on day i (MR_i) is \$30,000.

How would one find the $MUPE_i$? For each trade entry date prior to day i we would sum the closed equity (CE) on that day and profit (or loss) *as of day i* on positions which were already open on that trade entry date.[14] This sum would represent the amount of total equity on day i which would not have been realized by a trader that started trading on the given prior trade entry date. The highest such sum would be the $MUPE_i$. Note that in the case of a single market system, $MUPE_i = MCE_i$ since there are no open positions (other than the newly entered trade) on trade entry dates.

It is also possible to express the MAAMR in more general form so that it is applicable to the multimarket system case:

$$\text{MAAMR} = \frac{1}{N}\sum_{i=1}^{N}\left[\text{MR}_i + \sum_{j=1}^{M} \text{MF}_j\, C_j\, V_{ij}\right]$$

where $MR_i = POS\ (MUPE_i - TE_i)$, MF_j is the margin factor (e.g., 0.08)[15], C_j is the number of contracts in market j, V_{ij} is the contract value of market j on day i, N is the number of trading days in the survey period (or number of months in the survey period if only the monthly low total equity days are used in calculating the MAAMR), and M is the number of markets.

Although the concept underlying the generalized form of the AMR and MAAMR is fairly simple, the calculation of these measures would require a great deal of computation. In essence, it would be necessary to construct a data series corresponding to each trade entry date indicating the profit (or loss) as of all subsequent trading days[16] of positions open on the given trade entry date. To reduce the magnitude of computation, the AMR and MAAMR can be roughly approximated by calculating the measures using only the first trade entry date in each month.

Note that the problem of calculating a retracement measure for the multimarket system case is greatly simplified if we assume that any time a trader begins trading the trader enters all existing open positions. In this case we can calculate a total equity average maximum retracement (TEAMR):

$$\text{TEAMR} = \frac{1}{N}\sum_{i=1}^{N}(\text{MTE}_i - \text{TE}_i)$$

where MTE_i is the maximum total equity on any trade entry date *on or prior to* day i, TE_i is the total equity on day i, and N is the number of trading days in the

[14]This profit will consist of unrealized profits for those positions still open on day i and realized profits for those positions closed prior to day i.

[15]A common MF value can be used for most markets. However, for some markets (e.g., financial futures) it will be necessary to use individualized MF values.

[16]All subsequent monthly low total equity days if only these were used to calculate the AMR or MAAMR.

survey period (or number of months in the survey period if only the monthly low total equity days are used in calculating the TEAMR).

In view of the fact that the TEAMR is so much easier to calculate than the AMR, it can also be considered as a rough proxy for the latter even when it is assumed that a trader does not enter existing open positions when he or she begins trading. However, if used in this case, retracements in total equity would not correspond to actual trading retracements and the TEAMR would be subject to Problem 3 of the Sharpe ratio.

The margin adjusted version of the TEAMR would simply be

$$\text{MATEAMR} = \frac{1}{N} \sum_{i=1}^{N} \left[\left(\text{MTE}_i - \text{TE}_i \right) + \sum_{j=1}^{M} \text{MF}_j \, C_j \, V_{ij} \right]$$

Another possible alternative to the AMR is the Closed Equity Average Maximum Retracement (CEAMR):

$$\text{CEAMR} = \frac{1}{N} \sum_{i=1}^{N} (\text{MCE}_i - \text{CE}_i)$$

where MCE_i is the maximum closed equity[17] on any trade entry date on or *prior to* day i, CE_i is the closed equity on day i, and N is the number of days in survey period (or number of months in survey period if only the monthly low closed equity days are used in calculating the CEAMR).

As indicated above, the CEAMR is a retracement measure which weighs only closed equity data. Although defining a prior equity peak (e.g., MCE_i) solely on the basis of closed equity is reasonable, if not desirable, closed equity alone is not a fully satisfactory measure of current equity. The reason is that an equity retracement that is not yet realized (i.e., an open position loss) will generate the same additional fund requirements as a retracement due to a realized loss and will cause equivalent pain; thus, it seems artificial to distinguish between the two, as is the case if closed equity is used as the measure for current equity. Nevertheless, as with the TEAMR, the argument in favor of the CEAMR is that it is far easier to calculate than the AMR. Furthermore, in combination, the TEAMR and CEAMR provide a more attractive substitute for the AMR than the TEAMR alone.

The margin adjusted version of the CEAMR is:

$$\text{MACEAMR} = \frac{1}{N} \sum_{i=1}^{N} \left[(\text{MCE}_i - \text{CE}_i) + \sum_{j=1}^{M} \text{MF}_j \, C_j \, V_{ij} \right]$$

In summary, if trades are only entered on new signals, the AMR is definitely preferable to the TEAMR or CEAMR from a theoretical standpoint.[18] However, even in this case, the latter measures are far easier to calculate and therefore may be preferred for practical reasons. Whichever of these risk measures are used, as with the single market case, a performance measure could be obtained by dividing a gain measure (e.g., G = average annual gain) by the selected risk measure.

[17]Closed equity = total equity − equity in open positions.

[18]A corresponding statement would apply to comparisons involving the MAAMR, MATEAMR, and MACEAMR.

PRACTICAL CONSIDERATIONS

The previous sections have illustrated the deficiencies of measuring performance strictly in terms of gain and have provided alternative measures which also incorporate risk. However, these theoretically preferable measures also require a great deal more computation. For this reason, it should be noted that for some applications, a simple gain measure may be adequate from a practical viewpoint. Personal experience in comparing different parameter sets for a given system in the same market suggests that there is a great deal of correlation between rankings based on gain only and rankings based on various gain/risk measures. Consequently, for a task such as optimizing a system (i.e., finding the best performing parameter set(s) in each market for a given system), in many instances very little will be lost by using a simple gain measure as opposed to the gain/risk measures discussed above. In fact, a simple gain measure may even be sufficient for comparisons of different systems, if the systems are fairly similar (e.g., if both are nonsensitive, trend-following systems).

EVALUATING THE PERFORMANCE OF A MONEY MANAGER

RETURN/RISK MEASURES FOR THE MONEY MANAGER. There are some important differences in measuring trading performance for a money manager as opposed to a system. In contrast to the trading system case, capital requirements are well-defined for the money manager. Thus, assuming no withdrawals or additions, there is no ambiguity regarding the appropriate normalizing factor for deriving a percent return figure: the average annual gain for a given account would merely be divided by the initial account size. However, note that although the money manager case is simpler than the trading system in terms of defining percent return, such a percent return measure does not reflect risk.

In evaluating performance it is essential to also incorporate risk. (This was automatically achieved in the case of a trading system since any percent-return-type measurement had to be based on risk—that is, for a trading system, fund requirements can only be defined as a function of risk.) The necessity of incorporating risk is demonstrated by Figure 7. Note that although Manager A achieves a large percent return, his performance is far more volatile. In fact, investors initiating trading in the vicinity of Manager A's peaks could have witnessed substantial losses. Given the trade record illustrated in Figure 7, most investors would readily choose Manager B over Manager A.

The above illustration highlights the importance of explicitly including risk in the performance measure. The incorporation of risk is the primary achievement of the Sharpe ratio. In this respect, the Sharpe ratio represents an important improvement over percent return alone. However, as we discussed earlier, the Sharpe ratio does have some undesirable properties, and there are other alternative return/risk measures which may be better.

The primary alternative return/risk measures discussed in this chapter employ equity retracements as a measure of risk. However, retracements cannot be directly calculated from the monthly equity figures reported by money managers because these statistics include additions and withdrawals of funds. One possible

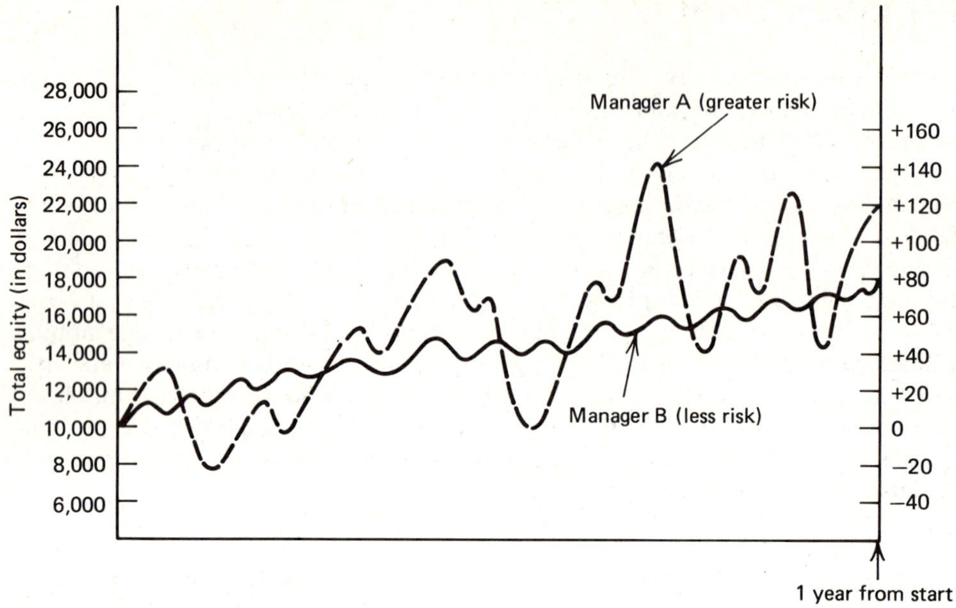

FIGURE 7. A comparison of two money managers with different risk characteristics.

way to circumvent this problem is to generate a hypothetical model account equity stream using reported monthly percent return figures. For example, if the equity at the start of the survey period is assumed to equal $100,000 (the choice of a starting equity will not affect the results) and the first month's rate of return is equal to 10%, the hypothetical model account equity at the start of the next month would be assumed to equal $110,000. Subsequent monthly beginning equity levels could be generated in similar fashion. These monthly equity figures could then be used to calculate a TEAMR. Note that in this case, the TEAMR would be based on a single observation at the end on each month, as opposed to all trading days or a single observation corresponding to the low total equity point in each month. Also note that it would not be possible to compute the AMR since the calculation of this measure would require knowledge of specific trades (e.g., prevailing open positions on trade entry dates, etc.)[19]

Although it is essential to consider risk as well as return in evaluating a money manager, in this application the combination of these two factors into a single ratio is no longer adequate. This point is fully explained in the next section.

THE INADEQUACY OF A RETURN/RISK RATIO FOR EVALUATING MONEY MANAGER TRADING PERFORMANCE. In the case of evaluating trading systems, the selected return/risk measure would yield the same ranking order of systems as the *estimated* percent return. This observation, which is a consequence

[19]Margin adjusted indicators (e.g., MATEAMR, MAAMR) also cannot be calculated for the money manager for the same reason. But this is of little consequence since these measures were specifically introduced for evaluating trading systems—a situation in which fund requirements are not known. (In many manager cases, fund requirements are precisely defined.)

of the fact that fund requirements for trading a system can only be estimated basis risk, can be proven as follows:

$$\text{Selected return/risk measure} = \frac{G}{R} \quad \text{and}$$

$$\text{Estimated percent return for a system in a given market} = \frac{G}{F}$$

where

G = average annual gain per contract
R = chosen risk measure (e.g., σ, AMR, ML, etc.)
F = total funds allocated for trading one contract of a given market in a system.

The only practical way to estimate F is as a function of risk. Most directly, F might be estimated as some multiple of a chosen risk measure. That is,

$$F = kR$$

where k = multiple of risk measure (determined subjectively).

Thus, the estimated percent return for a system could be expresses as:

$$\frac{G}{F} = \frac{G}{kR} = \frac{1}{k}\left(\frac{G}{R}\right)$$

Note that G/R is the selected return/risk measure. Thus, the percent return for a system will merely be equal to some constant times the return/risk measure. Although different traders will select different risk measures and values for k, once these items are specified, the return/risk measure and the estimated percent return would yield the same ranking order of systems. Also note that in the case of evaluating systems, the *percent risk*, which we define as the risk measure divided by fund requirements, is a constant:

$$\text{Percent risk} = \frac{R}{F} = \frac{R}{kR} = \frac{1}{k}.$$

Whereas in the case of evaluating trading systems a higher return/risk ratio *always* implies higher percent return, this is not true for the evaluation of money managers. Also, the percent risk is no longer a constant, but instead can vary from manager to manager. Thus, it is entirely possible for a money manager to have a higher return/risk ratio than another manager, but also to have a lower percent return or a higher percent risk. (The reason for this is that in the money manager case, the link between fund requirements and risk is broken—i.e., different money managers will differ in the level of risk they will assume for any given level of funds.) Consequently, a return/risk ratio is no longer a sufficient performance measure for choosing between alternative investments. We will illustrate this point by using the Sharpe ratio, but similar conclusions would apply to other return/risk measures. (In the following discussion, we assume that interest income is not included in money manager return figures, but is received by investors. Consequently, the simplified form of the Sharpe ratio, which deletes the riskless interest rate, is appropriate.)

Assume we are given the following set of *annualized* statistics for two money managers:

	Manager A	Manager B
Expected gain	$ 10,000	$ 50,000
Standard deviation of gain	$ 20,000	$ 80,000
Initial investment	$100,000	$100,000
Sharpe ratio	.50	.625

Although Manager B has the higher Sharpe ratio, not all traders would prefer Manager B since Manager B also has a higher risk measure, (i.e., higher standard deviation). Thus, a risk-averse investor might prefer Manager A, gladly willing to sacrifice the potential for greater gain in order to avoid the substantially greater risk. For example, if annual trading results are normally distributed for any given year there would be a 10% probability of the return falling more than 1.3 standard deviations below the expected rate. In such an event, an investor would lose $54,000 with Manager B [$50,000 − (1.3 × $80,000)] but only $16,000 with Manager A. For a risk-averse investor, minimizing a loss under negative assumptions may be more important than maximizing gain under favorable conditions.[20]

Next, consider the following set of statistics for two other money mangers:

	Manager C	Manager D
Expected Gain	$ 20,000	$ 5,000
Standard deviation of gain	$ 20,000	$ 4,000
Initial investment	$100,000	$100,000
Sharpe ratio	1.0	1.25

Although Manager D has a higher Sharpe ratio, Manager C has a substantially higher percent return. Investors who are not particularly risk-averse might prefer Manager C even though Manager C has a lower Sharpe ratio. The reason is that, for the major portion of probable outcomes, an investor would be better off with Manager C. Specifically in the above example, the investor will be better off as long as return does not fall more than .93 standard deviations below the expected rate—a condition which would be met 82% of the time (assuming trading results are normally distributed).[21]

Even more striking is the consideration that there are circumstances in which virtually all investors would prefer the money manager with the lower Sharpe ratio. Consider the following two money managers:

[20]An assumption is implicit in the above example: The investor cannot place a fraction of the stated initial investment with Manager B. In other words, the minimum unit size of investment is $100,000. Otherwise, it would always be possible to devise a strategy in which the investor would be better off with the manager with the higher Sharpe ratio. For example, placing $25,000 with Manager B would imply the same standard deviation as for a $100,000 investment with Manager A but a higher expected gain ($25,000).

	Manager E	Manager F
Expected gain	$ 10,000	$ 50,000
Standard deviation of gain	$ 2,000	$ 12,500
Initial investment	$100,000	$100,000
Sharpe ratio	5.0	4.0

In this example, virtually all investors (even those that are risk-averse) would prefer Manager F, despite the fact that Manager F has a lower Sharpe ratio. The reason is that the percent return is so large relative to the ambiguity of that return (standard deviation) that, even under extremely adverse circumstances, investors would almost certainly be better off with Manager F. For example, once again assuming that trading results are normally distributed, the probability of a gain more than 3 standard deviations below the expected gain is only 0.139%. Yet, even under these extreme circumstances, an investor would still be better off with Manager F: Gain = $12,500/year (12.5%) compared to $4,000/year (4%) for Manager E. This example even more dramatically illustrates the fact that, by itself, a return/risk ratio does not provide sufficient information for evaluating a money manager.[22] (This conclusion applies to all return/risk measures, not just the Sharpe ratio.)

The key point is that in evaluating money managers, it is more meaningful to consider the percent return and risk figures independently rather than as a ratio. Given both these statistics separately (as opposed to in ratio form), most investors would have sufficient information to make a reasonable choice between two managers. Since two measures are involved, an objective ordering of money managers is no longer possible. Each individual investor must determine his or her own tradeoff between percent return and risk and then order a preference of money managers based on the best combinations of these figures.

CONCLUSIONS

1. By itself, dollar gain per unit time is an insufficient measure for evaluating the performance of a trading system or a money manager.
2. In evaluating the performance of a system, a return/risk measure serves a dual role:
   a. It incorporates risk.
   b. It provides a proxy percent return measure.

[21]The following assumption is implicit in the above example: Borrowing costs for the investor are significantly greater than the interest income return realized by placing funds with a money manager. This assumption prohibits the alternative strategy of borrowing funds and placing a multiple of the initial $100,000 investment with the manager with the higher Sharpe ratio. If borrowing costs and interest income were equal (an assumption not likely to be valid in the real world), it would always be possible to devise a strategy, in which the investor would be better off with the manager with the higher Sharpe ratio. For example, the strategy of borrowing an additional $400,000 and placing $500,000 with Manager D would imply the same standard deviation as is the case for a $100,000 investment with Manager C, but a higher expected gain ($25,000).

[22]Comments analogous to footnote 21 also apply here.

3. The Sharpe ratio has several potential drawbacks as a trading performance measure:
   a. It fails to distinguish between intermittent and consecutive losses.
   b. Annualized value is dependent upon an arbitrary time interval.
   c. It fails to distinguish between upside and downside fluctuations.
   d. It fails to distinguish between retracements in unrealized profits versus retracements from trade entry date equity.
4. G ÷ MAAMR[23] is an alternative performance measure which may be preferable to the Sharpe ratio in that it appears to move closely reflect the behavioral preferences of the trader. However, the Sharpe ratio should still be considered as a supplemental measure since it is not dependent on the timing of losses. In addition, the Sharpe ratio may be the preferred performance measure if interval trading results are uncorrelated.
5. Although not suitable as a sole performance measure, G ÷ ML provides important additional information.
6. For a multimarket system, it is necessary to express the MAAMR in more general form, and the calculation of the MAAMR requires a great deal more computation.
7. For practical reasons, the MATEAMR and MACEAMR can be considered as rough proxies for the MAAMR in evaluating multimarket systems.
8. For some applications, such as optimizing a system, a simple gain measure may yield rankings which are very similar to the rankings based on the more sophisticated gain/risk measures. Practically speaking, in these situations, a simple gain measure (which requires far less computation) may be adequate.
9. Theoretically, return/risk measures applicable to the money manger would be identical to those used in evaluation a multimarket system. In practice, however, such measures usually cannot be directly calculated from available data. As a result, in order to calculate G/TEAMR it is first necessary to generate hypothetical model account data from the opposite data typically provided by money managers. (G/AMR and G/CEAMR cannot be calculated from composite data.)
10. In the case of money managers, a return/risk ratio is no longer an adequate performance measure. Rather, return and risk should be evaluated independently. The specific ordering of managers on the basis of these figures will be subjective (i.e., dependent upon the individual investor's risk/reward preferences).[24]

[23]All statements in this section regarding the MAAMR apply to the AMR as well.

[24]See N. D. Strahm, Chapter 23 of this book, for an elaboration of preference ordering in a two-dimensional space.

CHAPTER 23

PREFERENCE SPACE EVALUATION OF TRADING SYSTEM PERFORMANCE

CONTENTS

PREFERENCE ORDERING OF TRADING SYSTEMS 4

Examples of Criteria for Ordering of Trading Systems 4
Risk-Aversion Characteristics, Efficiency Criteria, and Risk-Indifference Curves 5
Quantitative Ordering 7
Normalized Versus Unnormalized Preference Spaces 10
Finding Suitable Reward and Risk Measures for a Preference Space 10

THE MEAN VARIANCE MODEL OF PREFERENCE SPACE 12

Definitions and Some Properties of (E,σ) 12
The Need for a More Restrictive Efficiency Criterion 13
The Baumol Lower Confidence Limit as a Preference Measure and The Baumol Criterion (E,L,K) as a Preference Space 16
The Sharpe Ratio: The Reward/Risk Raito in (E,σ) 17
Cautionary Warnings in the Use of Variance as a Risk 19
Measure and Discussion of Some Alternatives 19
The Kelly Measure—The Geometric Mean Rate of Return 21

SUMMARY AND CONCLUDING REMARKS 23

BIBLIOGRAPHY 25

CHAPTER 23

PREFERENCE SPACE EVALUATION OF TRADING SYSTEM PERFORMANCE

Norman D. Strahm

Commodity traders are always looking for a "better" trading system. Frequently, however, an assessment of which of two systems is better is not clear-cut. Definitions of "better" which fit a wide variety of circumstances are elusive. To some extent, judgments regarding the relative merits of different trading systems are subjective; thus, given all pertinent information, different traders will disagree on which of several systems is "best." This lack of agreement complicates the search for a standard way to report and judge the performance of a trading system or an advisor. This chapter discusses criteria which may be used to make such judgments. The presentation draws on the literature of theories of rational choice under conditions of uncertainty, much of which is based on the utility theory of preferences.

The term "trading system" can have many different connotations:

1. The performance of a trading advisor handling managed accounts, private pools, or public funds.
2. A portfolio of the performance of several advisors.
3. A set of trading rules ("technical trading system") using specific parameter[1] values applied to a single market.
4. A technical trading system simultaneously trading with several distinct sets of such parameter values.
5. A technical trading system simultaneously applied to a wide variety of markets.
6. Several technical trading systems simultaneously employed.

The possible objectives in comparing alternatives for each of the above types of trading systems would be to choose the "best":

1. Trading advisor,
2. Portfolio of trading advisors,

The author is extremely grateful to Jack Schwager for extensive comments and for editing of an early manuscript.

[1]In a trading system, a "parameter" is a quantity (e.g., the number of days in a moving average, etc.) whose value must be fixed.

3. Set of parameter values for a single system applied to a single market,
4. Portfolio of sets of parameter values for a single system applied to a single market,
5. Single system applied to a variety of markets (implicitly employing either a specific set of parameter values or a portfolio of such parameter sets for each market),
6. Portfolio of systems applied to a variety of markets.

All of the above "trading systems" can be quantitatively described by two sets of data series (1) the equity stream implied by the system and (2) a time history of the flow of funds between the trader and the "system." The effect of all fees, commissions, and other costs must be included in either the equity stream or in the flow of funds in order for fair comparisons to be made. The funds series is a record of cash flow to and from the investor; the equity stream should represent recapturable capital so that ideally the equity stream is an estimate of what would be returned to the investor if all accounts were liquidated.

In the simplest of situations an investor puts up an initial sum of money (initial equity) and makes no additions or withdrawals; all fees, commissions, and so forth are paid out of the equity of the account. At any later time an evaluation of the trading system can be made assuming the account were closed and all equity returned to the investor. Such a situation is adequately described by a single data series, the equity stream. However, situations which involve withdrawals and additions by the investor over an extended period of time cannot always be adequately described by any single series. For simplicity, the discussion in this chapter will assume that a single hypothetical equity stream is adequate.

Given the equity stream for two or more trading systems, how can the information be collapsed into a small number of performance measures which can be uniformly applied to determine which system is "best"? The answer to this question depends upon both the results of the systems and the person asking the question. We illustrate this fact with a discussion of preference ordering.

PREFERENCE ORDERING OF TRADING SYSTEMS

EXAMPLES OF CRITERIA FOR ORDERING OF TRADING SYSTEMS. Some value judgments regarding trading system performance would almost elicit universal agreement. Assuming all else equal, we can hypothesize the following statements:

Case A. Larger rates of gain are preferred to smaller rates of gain.

Case B. Small short-term fluctuations in equity are preferred to larger short-term fluctuations.

Case C. Short-term "upside" excursions in equity are preferred to "downside" excursions.

However, there would likely be disagreement in extending the list to the following:

Case D. Long-term stability is more important than short-term stability. That is, a system with a steady long-term rate of gain and greater short-term fluctuations is preferred to a system with an unstable rate of gain and smaller short-term fluctuations. Implicitly the former system would witness quick recovery from its retracements (even though they are sharper), while the latter system could witness extended periods of poor or mediocre performance.

Case E. The combination of moderate long-term gains and moderate retracements is preferred to large gains and large retracements.

In Case D, some traders would prefer to accept larger short-term retracements for the benefit of a system which recovers quickly and exhibits a steadier rate of gain over the long term. Other traders, however, might be more concerned with minimizing the size of retracements and might therefore freely choose the system which exhibits extended periods of mediocre performance. In Case E, there is a tradeoff between accepting greater short-term fluctuation in exchange for greater long-term gain. The willingness of people to accept this tradeoff varies considerably.

As the above comparisons illustrate, preferential ordering depends not only upon the characteristic behavior of the trading system, but also upon the person judging the situation. Each person's preferences can be characterized by a tradeoff pattern—how much of an increase in a desirable feature is required before that person will accept an increase in an undesirable feature. As a specific example, how much of an increase in equity retracements will a person accept for an increase of say 20% in expected percentage return. The generally desirable feature has conventionally been called "reward" (or "return") and the undesirable one "risk." That convention is adopted here even though these terms get confused with colloquial uses of the words. In particular, many traders have an *a priori* notion of what they want to call "risk"—a term usually associated with the prospect of losing money; but the measure of risk most frequently used in analysis of the financial markets emphasizes the "variability" of an outcome irrespective of whether it is a gaining or a losing situation. "Losing" is reflected in a negative value of the reward measure. It should be kept in mind that in general the terms simply denote two quantities involved in a preference tradeoff. The fact that it is desirable to *increase* one quantity and *decrease* the other is not intrinsically important; it could equally well be desirable to increase (or decrease) both quantities.

RISK-AVERSION CHARACTERISTICS, EFFICIENCY CRITERIA, AND RISK-INDIFFERENCE CURVES. A description of a person's acceptable exchange between reward and risk is referred to as his or her "risk-aversion characteristics." If for every alternative choice, reward and risk can each be adequately described by a single quantitative number then it is possible to meaningfully depict reward/risk tradeoffs. Figure 1 illustrates the risk/reward combinations implied by different systems. Each point represents the performance of a given trading system. The vertical coordinate of each point represents the reward measure, and the horizontal coordinate represents the risk measure.

Point C, at the origin, is a no-reward, no-risk choice (e.g., no trading or holding the investment in cash). Point D is a "riskless" situation which provides a positive reward. For example, this point might represent an investment in Treasury bills—

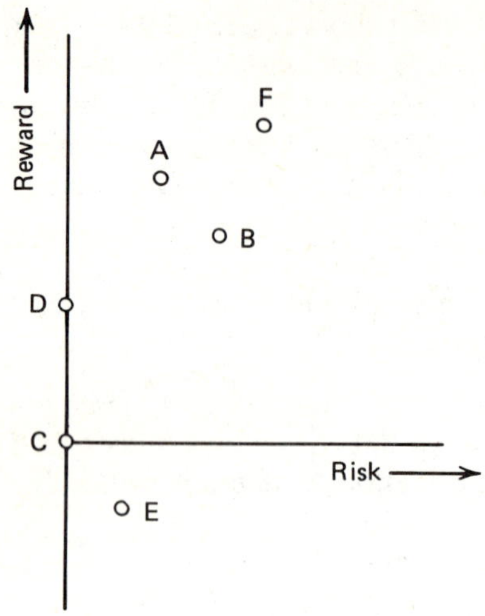

FIGURE 1. Two dimensional reward/risk diagram.

although there is a slight risk, it is negligible compared to the risk implied by any commodity trading system. Point E involves both risk and a negative reward measure. Points A, B, and F represent various combinations of risk with positive reward.

For a number of comparisons the choice between systems is clear-cut. For example, point A is preferred to point B, which has a smaller reward and a greater risk than point A. Certainly, no one who agrees that the reward and risk measures are meaningful would choose point B over point A. Some other examples of unambiguous choices include points C to E and points D to C. Any choice can be rejected if another choice has the same or higher reward and the same or lower risk (but not both the same). The rejected points would appear lower and to the right in Figure 1. The set of choices left after all such rejections is called the "efficient set" and the rule of rejection is an "efficiency criterion." The efficient set in this example consists of A, D, and F.

In general an efficiency criterion is a rejection rule which describes the choices of a broad class of individuals (e.g., all risk averters) such that the efficient set includes all choices which would be made by anyone within the class. Reward/risk space with the rejection rule described above is a special case of an efficiency criterion which can be depicted in a two-dimensional "preference space." (For an excellent general discussion of efficiency criteria see Levy and Sarnat, 1972.)

Characteristics common to the broad class of individuals are used to reject points B, C, and E from the efficient set without any further knowledge of any individual's risk-aversion characteristics. However, compare points A and F: point F implies both greater reward and greater risk. Which is better? A definite answer is not possible without considering the risk-aversion characteristic of the individual involved. The relevant question is whether the increased reward of point F over point A outweighs the increased risk of point F over point A.

Risk-aversion is described by superimposing a family of risk-indifference curves on the previous diagram (see Figure 2). By definition, any two points on a single curve have the property that systems corresponding to those two points would

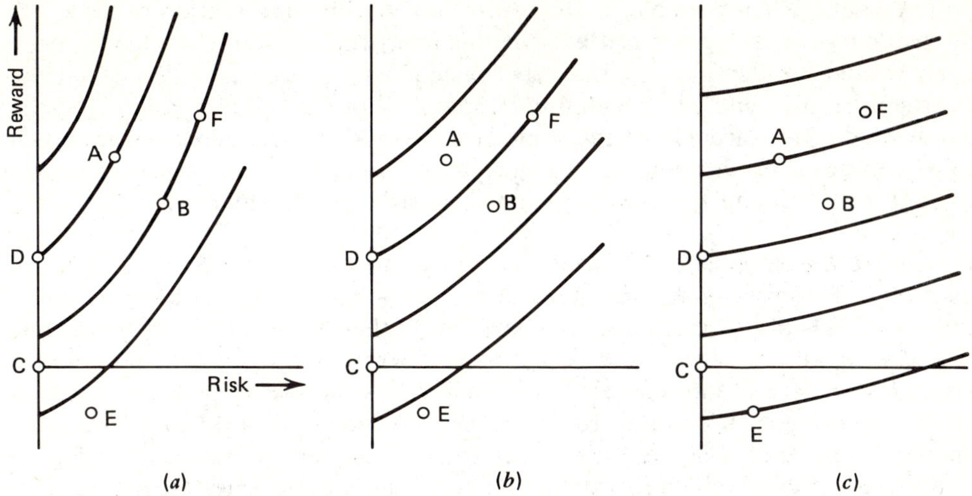

FIGURE 2. Reward/risk diagram with risk-indifference curves of three traders. (*a*) Trader X. (*b*) Trader Y. (*c*) Trader Z.

be equally desirable to the trader. More desirable systems lie on higher curves (more reward, less risk). Thus the trader's goal is to operate on the highest curve possible. However, if presented with a choice of points lying on the same curve, the trader would be completely indifferent. For example, the set of curves in Figure 2(*b*) describes the risk-aversion characteristics of one persion—Trader Y. Points D and F lie along the same curve and hence Trader Y has no preference. Point A, however, lies on a higher curve and hence would be more desirable to Trader Y than either points D or F.

Figure 2(*a*) describes the risk-aversion characteristics of Trader X, who is more risk-averse than Trader Y. The risk-indifference curves are steeper, indicating the lack of a willingness to accept as much of an increase in risk as Trader Y for a given size increase in reward. For Trader X, systems A and D are equally desirable and both are preferred to F and B. Figure 2(*c*) describes Trader Z, who is less risk averse than either Trader Y or Trader X. For Trader Z, F is the "best" system.

Including all systems, the respective preference orders are: Trader X—A and D, F and B, C, and E: Trader Y—A, D and F, B, C, and E; and Trader Z—F, A, B, D, C, and E.

Preference ordering provides a theoretical structure within which to discuss trading system performance. We have not yet been specific about how we might define "reward" or "risk."

QUANTITATIVE ORDERING

The Riskless Equivalent Reward. Reward and risk are quantitative measures (e.g., percent return, greatest percent equity drawdown, etc.). Each point in space has a pair of coordinates—a reward value and a risk value. It is also useful to attach a quantitative value to each indifference curve. A natural choice for such a quantitative value, when possible, is the reward level at the intersection of the indifference curve with the vertical axis. If this approach is used, each indifference curve would be identified by the "riskless equivalent" reward (also called the "certainty equivalent") to which it corresponds. For example, in Figure 2(*a*) the curve which runs through points D and A has a riskless equivalent reward equal to the reward level at point D. In Figure 2(*b*) the indifference curve which runs through points D and F would have the same riskless equivalent value.

Preference Measures and Performance Measures—the Reward/Risk Ratio as an Example. Preference measures, functions of reward and risk variables, are quantitative models of risk indifference. They could either be descriptive of individual behavior or be normative, that is, act as rules of thumb for action. Preference measures imply risk indifference curves which are the loci of constant value of the preference measure in reward/risk space. Reward and risk themselves are the simplest preference measures in a space. Consider the reward/risk space in Figure 2. If reward (e.g., percent return) is used as a preference measure, the indifference curves would be horizontal lines. If risk is used as a preference measure, the indifference curves would be vertical lines.

Performance measures are quantitative figures of merit describing characteristics of a trading system in a specific situation (a particular period of time, a specific market, etc.). They differ from preference measures only in a functional sense; for instance, the same mathematical formula can be used both as a performance measure (if it is used to produce quantitative measures of a trading system performance) and as a preference measure (if it is used to model preference behavior of an individual or class of individuals).

The ratio of reward to risk (e.g., percent return divided by largest percentage drawdown) is another example of a preference (or performance) measure. The indifference curves are lines emanating as spokes from the origin (see Figure 3). Each spoke has a distinct value which is equal to the ratio of the reward value to the risk value for every point on the spoke. Indifference curves which correspond to higher reward/risk ratios would be preferred to those which correspond to lower ratios. The "riskless equivalent" reward method of quantifying indifference curves does not work in this case since all curves pass through the same point of the riskless axis.

Although the reward/risk ratio is frequently used as a preference measure, it does not provide a satisfactory general behavioral model. There are three key reasons for this:

1. The area around the origin does not provide a sensible description since insignificant changes in reward or risk dramatically change the measure.
2. In certain areas of reward/risk space the reward/risk ratio model contradicts the behavioral preferences of most traders.
3. It is virtually impossible for the set of indifference curves within any broad range of the space to consistently describe the behavior of any single individual.

Although demonstration of the latter two points requires specific definitions for reward and risk, they can be made plausible by considering the implications of

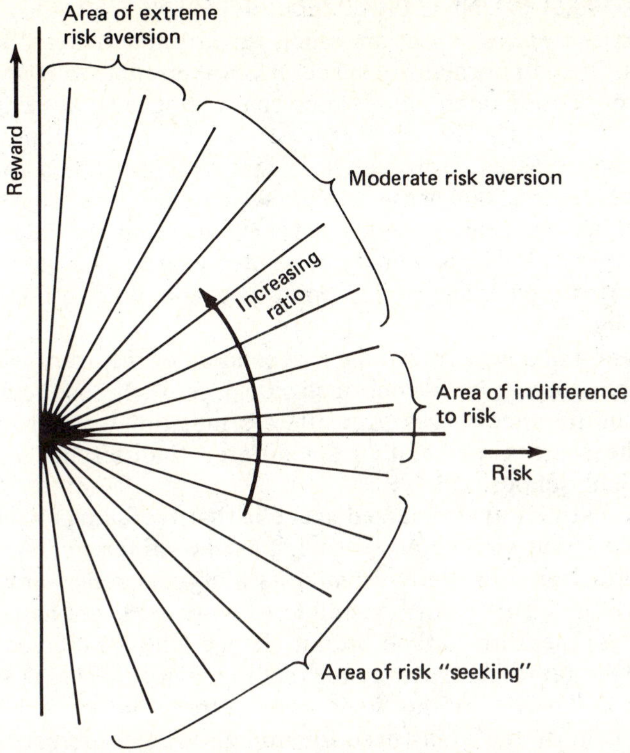

FIGURE 3. Risk-indifference curves of the reward/risk ratio preference measure.

the indifference curves represented by the reward/risk ratio model. For example, the indifference curves which correspond to high reward/risk ratios (steep, ascending lines) are those of an extremely risk-averse trader—that is, only such an individual could be indifferent between the points on one of these lines. Most traders, however, would actually prefer the higher reward points along any one of these lines since they imply a much greater return and only modestly higher risk. On the other hand, indifference curves corresponding to low positive reward/risk ratios (slowly ascending lines) are those of a near risk-indifferent trader. Most traders, however, would prefer lower reward points on these lines since they imply substantially lower risk and only modestly lower return. Furthermore, indifference curves which correspond to negative reward/risk ratios (descending lines) are those of risk seekers—that is, individuals who are willing to accept a worse return for the opportunity to take greater risk. Most traders, however, would prefer the higher reward points along these lines since they imply both a reduced risk and a less negative reward.

These illustrations just discussed highlight the severe limitations of a reward/risk ratio model. Applicability of this model would be confined to moderate positive return/risk ratios in areas away from the axes of the space. Illustrations of these points for a specific preference space are given in the section "The Sharp Ratio: The Reward/Risk Ratio in (E, σ)."

NORMALIZED VERSUS UNNORMALIZED PREFERENCE SPACES. An example of an *unnormalized space* is one in which reward and risk are represented in dollar amounts. In an unnormalized space, it is not possible to represent a system by a single point. For example, in an unnormalized space a system with a return of $10,000 per year and a risk of $5,000 per year would be represented by the corresponding coordinates. However, the same system trading two units would have the coordinates ($20,000 per year, $10,000 per year); the same system trading three units ($30,000 per year, $15,000 per year), and so forth. Each system would effectively be represented by an infinity of points (lying on a straight line emanating from the origin) with each successive point corresponding to an increase in the "size of the game."

If the evaluation of a system is to be independent of the arbitrary size in which it is traded, one is forced, in an unnormalized space, to choose reward/risk ratios as a model for indifference curves. Any other formulation would result in different multiples of the same system falling on different indifference curves. Such a restriction is highly undesirable.

The problem with an unnormalized space is that by failing to directly remove the effect of the "size of the game," it forces the preference space to contain redundant information and thereby limits its ability to reflect more meaningful tradeoffs. Therefore, it is always desirable to work with normalized return/risk measures, that is, measures which do not change with an increase in the "size of the game." One rather natural way to construct a normalized space is to divide dollar gain and dollar risk by the funds used to trade the system. For example, dividing dollar gain by the funds used for trading yields a percent return, which is a normalized preference measure. Doubling the units traded would not affect percent return. Similarly, percent retracement is also a normalized preference measure.

A preference space in which both reward and risk are normalized measures (as was implicitly the case for spaces discussed in previous sections) is called a *normalized preference space*. A trading system is characterized by a single point in a normalized preference space; thus there is no distinction between trading one unit or any multiple of units. All subsequent references to preference spaces imply normalized preference spaces.

FINDING SUITABLE REWARD AND RISK MEASURES FOR A PREFERENCE SPACE. An inherent contradiction exists in claiming the simultaneous use of

1. A two-dimensional preference space (efficiency criterion).
2. Preference measures describing arbitrarily general behavior.
3. Trading systems which have outcomes of arbitrary probability densities.[2]

Efficiency criteria for a broad class of behavior (e.g., all risk averters), justified by utility theory, and applicable to arbitrary outcome probability densities, are intrinsically infinite dimensional. A two-dimensional space will not allow com-

[2]The convention of Feller (1957) is used. Probability density is a function of unit area. The cumulative area under the density is the probability distribution, a nondecreasing function which goes from 0 to 1 in value.

pletely arbitrary specification of both preference measures and probability densities. For example, consider a space which is defined completely in terms of the first two moments of the probability densities (e.g., the mean-variance space discussed in the section "The Mean-Variance Model of Preference Space"). If any higher moment is important for preference behavior, then the preference measure could be well-defined only if probability densities were restricted in such a way that all higher moments of importance were completely determined by the first two moments.

If preference behavior is sufficiently restricted, then outcome probability densities can be general. If outcome densities are sufficiently restricted, then preference behavior can be arbitrary. In a two-dimensional space without suitable restrictions, contradictions and inconsistencies can always be found by appealing to either extreme forms of probability distributions or to extreme forms of preference behavior (Borch, 1969; Tobin, 1969; Bicksler and Samuelson, 1974). The practical necessity of using only a limited number of measures (dimensions) to evaluate trading systems implies that the range of outcome probability densities and the range of preference behavior be restricted. Such a compromise is unavoidable.

The class of individuals covered by the efficiency criterion is one example of a place for compromise. The class of all risk averters encompasses behavior which is extremely diverse. It should be possible to define a much more restrictive class of "practical traders" which would still allow reasonable range of trading system probability outcomes as well as individual preference behavior. The goal would be to find definitions of risk and reward which truly capture the elements of performance which enter into traders' preference ordering.

Also, the efficiency criterion should be such that the efficient set which results does not contain trading systems which everyone in the class would reject by preference compared to other systems in the set. That is, an efficient set should be what is left after *all possible* culling of sets without using individual preferences. Individual preferences would then be used to select from the efficient set. If it is clear that there are systems in the efficient set that everyone in the class would reject, then a more restrictive definition of reward and/or risk should be possible; that is, there should be a more restrictive efficiency criterion. If the efficient set does not contain such systems the efficiency criterion is said to be "optimal" for that class.

Are two dimensions sufficient for evaluation of trading systems? If two quantitative measures can be constructed which capture elements of reward and risk such that they allow all desired differentiation between trading systems, then a simple two-dimensional preference space is adequate. If, however, adequate information about risk, for example, cannot be compacted into a single measure, then a multidimensional risk measure would have to be adopted. How would one determine that the reward/risk measures being employed were inadequate? Such a conclusion would be indicated if, given two trading systems with identical risk and reward measures, one system is clearly preferred. In this case, there is obviously important information regarding performance of these systems which is not being captured by the reward/risk measures being used. The solution would require either the substitution of alternative risk or reward measures or the addition of other risk or reward measures (i.e., the expansion of dimensions in reward/risk space). A disagreement between traders regarding the preference ordering of two systems in the efficient set with different reward and risk measures does not suggest an inadequacy in the measures. The two traders may simply have different risk-aversion characteristics.

Some form of percent return seems to be the most natural choice for a reward measure. The practice has been to use some measure of "central tendency" of the percent return (e.g., arithmetic mean, median, mode, and so forth). The choice for a risk measure is less obvious. The most common approach has been to interpret risk as the "variability" or "fluctation" in percent return—a measure which indicates how close we can expect the actual percent return to approach the central value. Such measures include the standard deviation, mean absolute deviation, and so forth. In the following section we turn our attention to an example of a specific preference space, *mean variance,* which has been the one most extensively analyzed and widely used in the securities markets.

THE MEAN-VARIANCE MODEL OF PREFERENCE SPACE

DEFINITION AND SOME PROPERTIES OF (E,σ). In the mean variance model of reward/risk space, past history is divided into time intervals (e.g., months) and percent return is then calculated for each interval. The arithmetic mean of these returns is used as the reward measure. This average can be used as an estimate of the expected return E for a future period. The risk is defined as the standard deviation σ of the interval returns, although it could equally well be defined as *variance,* the square of standard deviation. Symbolically, we refer to this model space as (E,σ).[3]

Each system is represented by a single point in (E,σ) space. The reward coordinate equals the mean percent return of past intervals and the risk coordinate is equal to the standard deviation of percent return. As an aid to understanding some properties of (E,σ) one can picture the probability density associated with a point in the space as graphed in a third dimension such as shown in Figure 4(a). The rate of return axis is interpreted both as the independent variable for the probability densities and as the mean return E in the horizontal (E,σ) plane. The points Q, S, and T in the (E,σ) plane represent three systems, all of the same mean return, but differing in standard deviation. The standard deviation of each density enters into the picture in two ways—first, as the coordinate of the constant risk line along which the density is plotted, and second, as the "width" (degree of dispersion) of the density along that line. This interrelationship leads to some useful properties of (E,σ). Consider the densities associated with points U, V, and W along a line $E = R + k\sigma$ in Figure 4(*b*) as follows:

[3]Harry Markowitz (1952, 1959) used (E,σ) space as the base for developing his now famous portfolio theory. In that application, points in the (E,σ) space represent a *one-period* outlook into the *future*. In this chapter, points in (E,σ) space represent a multiperiod summary of the *past* statistics (i.e., sample means and variances). The two views are indistinguishable if the summary statistics of the past are used as estimates for the future as Markowitz suggested. Discussion of the concepts of portfolio theory can be found in most financial texts, for instance, Francis and Archer (1979), or Elton and Gruber (1981). The focus of this chapter is restricted to the use of (E,σ) space for evaluating performance; portfolio theory itself will not be discussed.

1. The probability that any system along this line results in a rate of return which falls below a lower line $E = R + k'\sigma$ $(k' < k)$ with representative points X, Y, and Z is the same as the probability of a rate of return falling on the low side of the mean by more than $k - k'$ standard deviations. In the special case of all probability densities having the same shape,[4] all trading opportunities along the upper line have the same probability of yielding a return less than the rate on the lower line. In other words, the lower line acts as a lower confidence limit for all systems on the upper line.
2. If all probability densities have the same shape, all trading opportunities along the line $E = R + k\sigma$ have the same probability of yielding a return less than the rate R. This follows from (1) when the lower line has constant mean return R $(k' = 0)$. The specific probability is determined by the shape of the distribution and the value of k. (For example, the probability is 2.3% for $k = 2$ and a normal distribution.)
3. Imagine lines connecting each trading system in (E,σ) space to the point $(R,0)$. That system lying on the steepest such line would have the lowest probability of yielding a return less than R (assuming probability densities of the same shape).

The desire to minimize the probability of a loss exceeding a specific level (say 30%) leads to an instructive application of property three (3). Of all the trading systems available, the one which minimizes the probability of a 30% loss is the system which has the steepest line connecting its point in (E,σ) with the point $(-0.30,0)$. This procedure, used as a criterion for choosing trading systems, has been termed the "safety-first" criterion (Roy, 1952), with the rate R (−30% in this example) known as the "disaster rate." (The criterion could be applied with any rate level, not necessarily one deserving to be called a disaster.)

THE NEED FOR A MORE RESTRICTIVE EFFICIENCY CRITERION. There are trading systems which remain in the efficient set of (E,σ) which everyone would agree should be rejected compared to other systems in the efficient set. This fact is illustrated with a simple example.

The criterion determining whether any particular trading opportunity is *not* efficient is illustrated in Figure 5(*a*). Point G is *not* efficient if there is another

[4]Probability densities which have the same "shape" differ from each other graphically by a uniform stretching or contracting along the independent and dependent axes of a graph of the density. Mathematically, a family of densities of the same shape is generated by $P_{E,\sigma}(x) = (1/\sigma)\, h(x - E)/\sigma$, where $h(x)$ is a density of zero mean and unit standard deviation. The normal distribution, the most useful one, falls into this category; some other commonly used distributions (e.g., log-normal) do not. Heuristic uses of (E,σ) would not require restriction on the shapes of probability densities, but paradoxes or inconsistencies can result (Borch, 1969; Tobin, 1969). Probability densities which are arbitrarily general (except for a restriction that there is some ceiling rate above which all densities equal zero) imply that the only permissible risk-indifference curves are families of circles, each family centered at some point on the riskless axis (above the ceiling rate). If other risk-indifference curves were used, contradictions would result. (These statements follow from utility theory. The only utility functions which are generally consistent with the mean-variance model are quadratic functions and any such function is not meaningful above some ceiling rate.)

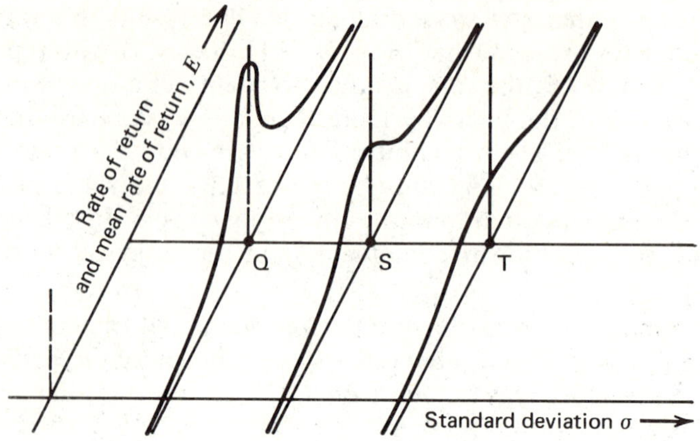

(*a*)

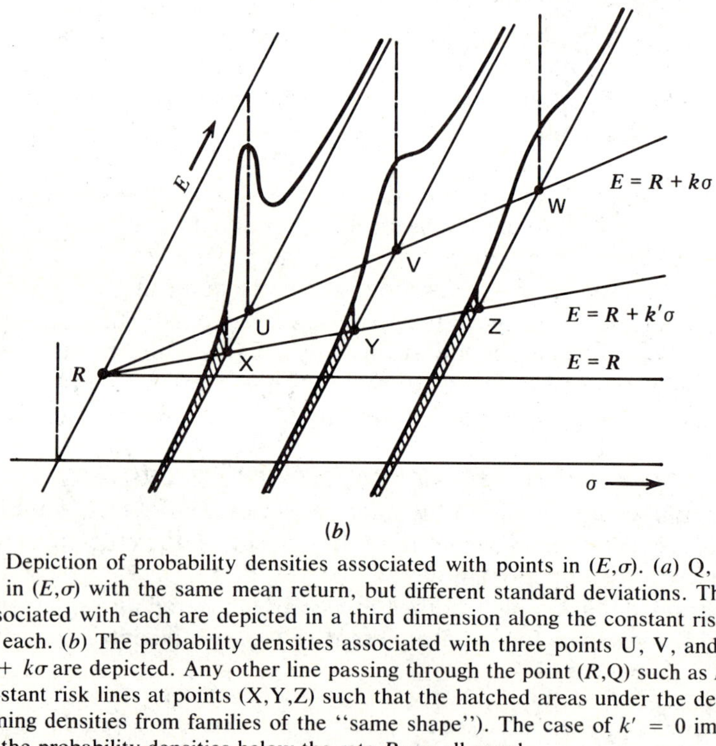

(*b*)

FIGURE 4. Depiction of probability densities associated with points in (E,σ). (*a*) Q, S, and T are three points in (E,σ) with the same mean return, but different standard deviations. The probability densities associated with each are depicted in a third dimension along the constant risk lines corresponding to each. (*b*) The probability densities associated with three points U, V, and W along the line $E = R + k\sigma$ are depicted. Any other line passing through the point (R,Q) such as $E = R + k'\sigma$ cuts the constant risk lines at points (X,Y,Z) such that the hatched areas under the densities are all equal (assuming densities from families of the "same shape"). The case of $k' = 0$ implies that the areas under the probability densities below the rate R are all equal.

choice located in the hatched area since any such point would offer both higher return and lower risk. Neither G nor H results in the other being rejected from the efficient set. However, if the probability densities of G and H do not overlap, such as in Figure 5(*b*), then the rate of return of H would always exceed the rate of return of G. In such a case, everyone would agree that G should be rejected in favor of H. In fact, agreement would result even if the probability densities overlap provided that at each level of return the probability distribution (the

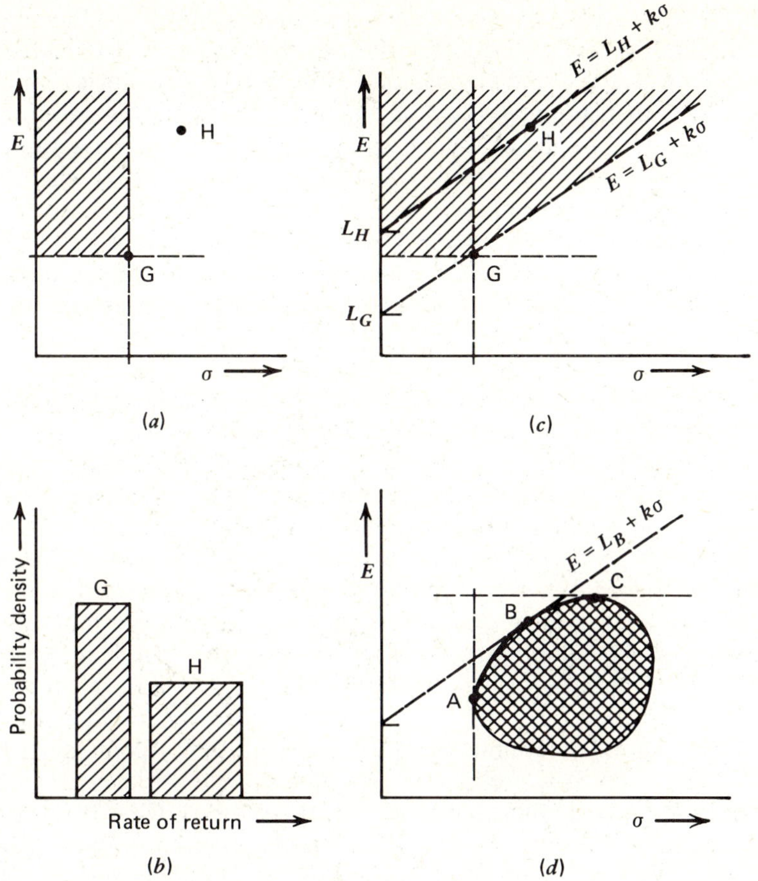

FIGURE 5. Comparison of the Baumol criterion and the mean-variance criterion. (*a*) mean-variance criterion: G is rejected from the efficient set if there is another point in the hatched area. (*b*) Non-overlapping probability densities for G and H indicate that everyone would reject G in favor of H. (*c*) The Baumol confidence limit of H, L_H, is greater than the confidence limit of G, L_G, so that the Baumol criterion rejects G in favor of H. Equivalently, any point in the hatched area results in the rejection of G. (*d*) Any point in the hatched area is assumed to be a trading opportunity. The efficient set is the line ABC according to the mean-variance criterion, but only the line BC according to the Baumol criterion.

cumulative area under the probability density) of G exceeds the distribution of H. This statement applies to risk seekers as well as risk averters. The class of risk averters would be in agreement under an even more restrictive condition—that at each level of return the *cumulative* area under the probability *distribution* of G exceeds that of H. This is the most general optimal efficiency criterion for risk averters (see Levy and Sarnat, 1972).

Regardless of the probability distributions, the probability that the rate of return from H will exceed the rate of return from G steadily increases as H moves to higher rates of return. A practical trader would agree that for sufficiently high mean rate of return the larger mean return of H would always override the effect of increased variance of H over G.

These considerations indicate the need for a more restrictive efficiency criterion than (E,σ). The general criterion for risk averters cannot be depicted in a two dimensional reward/risk space and requires far too much information (the complete probability distributions) to be of practical use. Also, this criterion does not accept the judgment of the practical trader in the previous paragraph because, for densities with tails, there is always a level of return below which it is more probable (even though an impractically small probability) for G to fall than for H. Hence there are some risk averters (although rather extreme in behavior) who will not accept H compared to G. An alternative criterion which requires no more information than that used in (E,σ) and accepts the judgment of the practical trader is suggested in the next section.

THE BAUMOL LOWER CONFIDENCE LIMIT AS A PREFERENCE MEASURE AND THE BAUMOL CRITERION *(E,L; K)* AS A PREFERENCE SPACE. William J. Baumol (1963) noted that the properties of (E,σ) space discussed in the section "Definition and Some Properties of (E,σ)" can be used to construct a more restrictive efficiency criterion which focuses on a lower confidence limit on the rate of return. The Baumol criterion states that a system with a lower mean rate of return should be rejected compared to a system with a higher mean rate of return if the higher rate system also has a higher value for its *lower confidence limit* at the *same confidence level*. By adopting a standard confidence level (e.g., two standard deviations, or about 98% for a normal distribution) one may reject any point G in favor of another point H (with higher mean) if its lower confidence limit is less than the lower confidence limit for H at the same (98%) confidence level. For example, if there is a 98% probability that G will yield a return greater than 5% and the same 98% probability that H will yield a return greater than 12%, then *G* should be rejected in favor of H (provided the mean rate of return is also higher for H). This situation is illustrated in Figure 5(*c*). Straight lines of slope k (the number of standard deviations adopted as the common confidence level—two in this example) form the risk-indifference curves of the Baumol Confidence Limit performance measure. The riskless equivalent of each line is L, the intercept of the line with the riskless axis. Any point lying within the hatched area will cause the rejection of G from the efficient set; so H will result in the rejection of G by the Baumol criterion, but not by the mean-variance criterion illustrated in Figure 5(*a*). In Figure 5(*d*) the hatched area is assumed to represent a dense selection of trading systems. The (E,σ) criterion would result in an efficient set of points along the line, ABC. The Baumol criterion would reject those points along AB, and leave the points along BC as the efficient set.

Most traders would agree with Baumol that it is more meaningful to focus on a rate of return which is a lower confidence limit than upon a rate of return which is a standard deviation. For instance, consider a trading system that has a 60% expected rate of return. The added information that there is a 98% confidence level of exceeding 14% per year is generally viewed as more instructive than the statement that there is a 23% standard deviation in return (although both these statements are equivalent, assuming a normal distribution of returns).

The confidence limit L is used to replace standard deviation in (E,σ) as the risk measure in the Baumol $(E,L;\ k)$ preference space. This efficiency criterion is a partial solution to the problems discussed in the previous section. It is not theoretically ideal; it is a practical compromise. $(E,L;\ k)$ is an optimal efficiency criterion for all risk averters if probability distributions are limited to families of the same shape, all of which have nonzero probability distribution extending down to k standard deviations below the mean, but zero distribution below that rate. For instance $(E,L;1)$ is an optimal efficiency criterion for the family of densities consisting of two equally probable outcomes (each exactly one standard deviation from the mean) and $(E,L;\sqrt{3})$ is optimal for the family consisting of uniform densities (the uniform densities extend to $\pm\sqrt{3}$ standard deviations from the mean). The criterion obtained in the limit of k going to infinity is equivalent to (E,σ) and is optimal for families with tails extending infinitely far below the mean (such as the family of normal densities). However, the "optimal" criterion is not the *practical* choice. A practical choice, for instance, would be $(E,L;2)$ used without restrictions on the probability distributions. The practical trader would accept the fact that some densities without tails are going to result in systems remaining in the efficient set which everyone would reject, and some densities with infinite tails are going to be rejected from the efficient set even though there are individual risk averters who would select these systems as "best."

THE SHARPE RATIO: THE REWARD/RISK RATIO IN (E,σ). The reward/risk ratio in (E,σ) space would be E/σ. An essentially similar preference measure has received widespread attention in the analysis of trading systems: the Sharpe ratio,[5] $(E - R)/\sigma$. R is the "riskless" market rate of return (e.g., Treasury bills). The "excess return" $E - R$ measures the amount by which the rate of return exceeds the riskless market rate. A rationale for incorporating R is that the measure should not indicate a positive reward if the system does not exceed the rate of return obtained from a riskless investment. The indifference curves implied by the Sharpe ratio are similar to those illustrated in Figure 4, with the exception that they fan out from the point $(R,0)$ instead of from the origin. Indifference curves of the Sharpe ratio and those implied by the "safety-first" criterion differ only in the interpretation and assumed value of the constant R. Similar to the "safety-first" criterion, the system with the highest Sharpe ratio is the one which has the lowest probability of yielding a return below the riskless market rate R (when only systems of the same probability shape are considered). Choosing the trading system in (E,σ) space which has the highest Sharpe ratio is equivalent to choosing the system with the steepest line between that system and the point $(R,0)$.

The section "Quantitative Ordering" under "Preference Ordering of Trading Systems" detailed some of the extreme behavioral assumptions which are implicit in the use of a reward/risk ratio model of indifference curves. Those comments would apply directly to the Sharpe ratio. As an illustration, assume that $R = 10\%$ and compare the following points:

A: Mean = 20%, standard deviation = 2%.
B: Mean = 110%, standard deviation = 20%.

Both of these points have the same Sharpe ratio (5.0) and hence should be equally

[5]The Sharpe ratio was first used by William Sharpe (1966) in a very different context—the evaluation of mutual fund performance.

preferable. However, in reality, it would be extraordinarily unlikely for System A to match or exceed the performance of System B. Assuming a normal distribution, such an event would occur less than 1 out of 250,000 times. In view of this, only a trader who is risk averse to an extreme would be indifferent between Systems A and B.

The above example considered the comparison of two points with very high Sharpe ratios. It is also instructive to compare points with very low Sharpe ratios. For simplicity, consider two points with Sharpe ratios equal to zero:

C: Mean = 10%, standard deviation = 2%.
D: Mean = 10%, standard deviation = 20%.

Note that, compared to C, D has not gained any long-term advantage in exchange for the additional risk accepted. In effect, at point D, the trader has a chance to make a greater positive return with an equal chance of making lesser (and negative) returns of comparable size. An indifference between point C and D would only make sense for a trader who is totally indifferent to risk.

The above examples illustrate that the behavior implied by high Sharpe ratio is plausible only for extremely risk-averse traders, while the behavior implied by low Sharpe ratios is plausible only for traders who are nearly totally indifferent to risk. It is highly questionable whether the indifference curves at either of these extremes are representative of many real-life traders. It is virtually impossible for the indifference curves at both extremes to accurately describe the behavior of any single individual. Even in the central part of the positive return quadrant the Sharpe ratio implies increasing risk aversion with increasing reward, a behavior which is contrary to the generally accepted sense of reward/risk tradeoffs (Pratt, 1974; Francis and Archer, 1979, pp. 267–270; Elton and Gruber, 1981, pp. 192–207).[6]

Although the Sharpe ratio is a poor model of individual behavioral indifference curves, it has a different application as a performance measure which is extremely important. If a trader can borrow (or lend) funds at an interest rate R to increase (or decrease) the leverage of a trading system at (E_0,σ_0), the net effect constitutes a trading system at (E',σ') which has both a higher (lower) expected return and a greater (lower) standard deviation. The combinations of E' and σ' which are attainable are all those which lie on the straight line, the borrowing (lending) line, running from $(R,0)$ and passing through the point (E_0,σ_0). Points located at returns above E_0 correspond to borrowing situations (increased leverage) and points below E_0 to lending situations (decreased leverage). "Lending" is equivalent to investing in a riskless system at $(R,0)$, such as Treasury bills; "borrowing" is equivalent to investing a *negative* sum in such a system. The effective point of operation, (E',σ'), lies a fraction f of the distance along the line from $(R,0)$ to (E_0,σ_0), where f is the fraction of the trader's funds in the system (E_0,σ_0) and $1-f$ is the fraction in $(R,0)$. The quantity f is greater than 1.0 for borrowing situations and less than

[6]Adherents of the utility theory of preferences would also note the Sharpe ratio is inconsistent with that theory since it cannot be derived from any utility function. However, that is true for *every* preference function in (E,σ) except for families of circles centered on the riskless axis. The more practical requirement would be that there exists some reasonable combination of a family of restricted probability densities and a utility function which together imply the indifference curves of the reward/risk ratio (excluding the area around the origin). This author's conjecture is that there is none.

1.0 for lending situations. The possibility of operating anywhere along the line implies an important use of the Sharpe ratio: Within the framework of the mean-variance model when borrowing and lending facilities are available the indifference curves of a trader will determine the degree of leveraging, but will not affect the choice of trading system; the trading system is determined solely by maximization of the Sharpe ratio. That is, all traders with the same borrowing and lending rates will choose to use the same particular system (or portfolio), but their differing risk-aversion characteristics will dictate different degrees of leveraging, that is, different operating points along the borrowing–lending line. The efficient set determined without a borrowing–lending facility is considerably altered with the use of such a facility. If the borrowing rate and the lending rates are equal, the efficient set becomes simply all the elements on the borrowing–lending line passing though the point representing that trading system with the maximum Sharpe ratio. (When arbitrary portfolios of different systems are included, the efficient set without the facility is along a boundary such as pictured in Figure 5(*d*) and the borrowing–lending line is tangent to that boundary at the point of highest Sharpe ratio just like the line tangent to the efficient set at point B in Figure 5(*d*).)

The inadequacy of the Sharpe ratio as a model of individual indifference curves can now be expressed in another way: An individual with Sharpe ratio indifference curves would be totally indifferent to the amount of leverage used in trading a system since his or her indifference curve coincides with the efficient set when a borrowing–lending facility is available. No real-life trader could be indifferent to the extent of leverage.

The Sharpe ratio is subject to several problems related to the inclusion of variance in the measure. These problems, discussed below, would apply to any use of variance in the measure of risk.

CAUTIONARY WARNINGS IN THE USE OF VARIANCE AS A RISK MEASURE AND DISCUSSION OF SOME ALTERNATIVES. The critical consideration in deciding the adequacy of variance as a risk measure is whether a variance-based ordering of trading systems is significantly different from an ordering based on some more direct measure of a trader's concept of risk (e.g., retracements). Under proper conditions, variance can be an adequate proxy for other risk measures; however, if certain assumptions are not fulfilled, variance may be a totally inadequate measure.

There are at least three important situations in which variance may yield significantly different ordering of systems than other risk measures:

1. *Strings of Losses in Excess of Those Expected From Stationary, Independent Intervals.* The presence of positive correlation between successive intervals in a system can result in significantly greater equity retracements than occur in another system with exactly the same probability distribution. This is illustrated by the equity streams depicted in Figure 6. The rates of return of System A, which are obtained from a random number generator, are normally distributed about a mean rate of 5% per month with a standard deviation of 12% per month. A noncompounded investment of $10,000 is assumed so that these rates correspond to a mean dollar gain of $500 per month and a standard deviation of $1,200. The equity stream of System B is composed of the *same* interval returns, but with

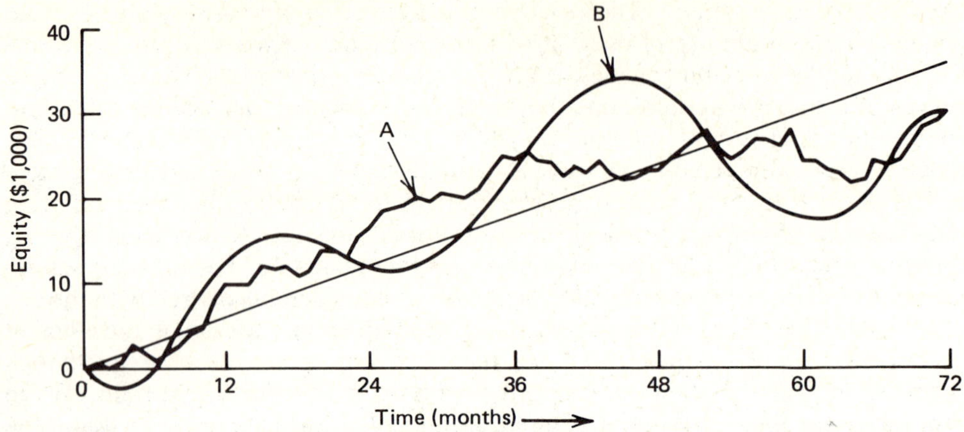

FIGURE 6. Two equity streams with the same sample mean return and the same sample variance, illustrating greater equity swings for the system with positive correlation between interval returns. The interval returns of A, selected from a normal distribution, are rearranged to show the significant gain and loss strings of B. The straight line is the long-term trend implied by the mean return of the normal distribution.

the sequence rearranged so as to reflect significant strings of losses and gains.[7] The sample mean and sample variance of these two systems are identical; yet, few traders would view the two systems producing these equity streams as equivalent.

2. *Skewness in Distributions.* Although only downside fluctuations constitute risk to a trader, variance is a measure which equally weights both downside and upside fluctuations. Thus, two systems may have the same mean and the same variance, but one may have a few large excursions to the upside with frequent but small downside fluctuations, while the second system may exhibit the reverse pattern. Most traders would consider the second more risky. Another example arises if one system, compared to the second, has the same or lower mean return and an increased variance with marked skewness to the "upside." The mean-variance criterion would reject the first system from the efficient set, but a rather normal risk averter may well prefer the first to the second. These examples illustrate the need to restrict probability distributions to those of a family of the same shape in the statement of many efficiency criteria. Markovitz (1959), however, proposed another solution to the skewness problem—a measure alternative to variance called the "semivariance" based only on downside fluctuations. Unfortunately, this measure is far less convenient to use than variance. In a different approach skewed distributions have also been treated by the introduction of a second risk measure, one which directly reflects the degree of skewness. A detailed review of both semivariance and skewness-related risk measures can be found in Francis and Archer (1979).

[7]A distinction must be made between strings of losses and gains which occur in a stochastic process with correlated intervals and strings which occur in an uncorrelated process just by chance. Any equity stream may have large strings of losses even if successive intervals are independent. The important distinction is whether or not there is an underlying mechanism which enhances excess retracements.

3. *Overstatement of Dispersion.* Sometimes variance is a poor measure of the dispersion or fluctuation in percent return because, by more strongly weighting outlying points in a distribution, it may overstate dispersion. Some distributions actually have infinite variance; in fact, arguments have been proposed (Fama, 1965) that some price series in the securities markets are best modeled with distributions which have infinite variance. If some trading systems have variances which substantially overstate dispersion while others do not, a variance-based ordering might differ substantially from an ordering based on some other measure of dispersion.

What risk measures might be used in place of variance? In addition to semivariance, Markowitz (1959) studied other possibilities including mean absolute deviation, the probability of loss, and the expected return of losing intervals. He noted that anyone behaving according to any one of these measures would "chance a substantial loss rather than select a much more conservative alternative with slightly less expected return." For instance, such an individual would be indifferent between:

A: 5% probability of an 80% loss with a 95% probability of break even.

B: A 100% probability of a 4% loss.

Such an individual would never buy insurance, and a portfolio based on these measures "can be foolishly speculative." Markovitz also rejected maximum loss as a measure of risk because it is a criterion which does not even satisfy the axioms of utility theory.

The *geometric mean rate g,* discussed in the following section, can be incorporated into risk measures by comparison to the arithmetic mean rate E. For instance, $(1 + g)/(1 + E)$ is a measure equal to 1 for a strictly uniform outcome, but decreases with increasing fluctuation.[8] (A measure of this type was suggested to the author by James Orcutt.) For probability densities of the same shape, indifference curves in (E,σ) are straight line spokes emanating from the point $(-1.00,0)$; consequently, the risk-indifference structure of this measure is identical to that of the safety-first criterion with a disaster rate of -100%.

Equity drawdown or retracement measures,[9] familiar to many commodity traders, would seem to most directly reflect most traders' sense of risk. One possible reason for avoiding retracement measures is the increased computation required; also, variance lends itself more naturally to extensions in portfolio theory.

The question of whether variance is an acceptable proxy for alternative measures must await empirical studies which compare the ordering of systems based on different risk measures.

THE KELLY MEASURE—THE GEOMETRIC MEAN RATE OF RETURN. The fluctuation of returns about an average level reduces the long-term growth rate when results are reinvested over many intervals; the greater the fluctuation, the lower the long-term rate of growth. This is a very important fact. It points out that there

[8] An alternative form, $\ln [(1 + E)/(1 + g)]$, has a numerical range similar to standard deviation; it is zero for no fluctuation and increases without bound with increasing fluctuation.

[9] See Jack Schwager, Chapter 22.

is more than a psychological reason for preferring systems of lower fluctuation. The appropriate measure of long-term growth rate is the *geometric mean rate of return, g*—that uniform rate which yields the same total return as the compounded interval rates of return. This can be expressed as

$$(1 + g)^n = (1 + r_1)(1 + r_2)(1 + r_3) \cdots (1 + r_n)$$

where

$$r_1, r_2, \ldots, r_n$$

are rates of return corresponding to each of n intervals. The name geometric mean rate arises from the fact that the geometric growth factor $(1 + g)$ is the geometric mean of the interval growth factors $\{1 + r_i\}$.

The list below compares the long-term geometric rates of return which result from fluctuations about a fixed 5% per month mean rate of return. Each month there is a 50% probability of the rate of return equaling each of the two indicated values:

Two Equally Probable Levels of Monthly Return	Long-Term Monthly Geometric Mean Rate of Return
5 , 5	5.0
0 , 10	4.9
−5 , 15	4.5
−10 , 20	3.9
−20 , 30	2.0
−30 , 40	−1.0
−40 , 50	−5.1

Note that a very profitable situation yielding 5% per month turns into a losing situation by allowing fluctuations to occur. Every month, however, there is an *expected* return of +5%, even in the losing situations.

Which of many systems has the greatest long-term return (resulting in the greatest terminal wealth) assuming reinvestment over many periods? It is *not* the system with the highest arithmetic mean return; it is the system with the highest geometric mean return. John Kelly (1956) first advocated maximization of the geometric mean rate (see Samuelson, 1971 and Thorpe, 1971 for discussion and criticism).

A point in (E,σ) may have different values of geometric mean rate for different probability shapes; that is, the geometric mean rate depends on higher moments of the density than just the first two (mean and variance). In this sense geometric mean rate is only an approximate preference measure in (E,σ).[10] If markedly different shapes of distributions were under consideration, this would have to be taken into account. When the first two moments provide an adequate approxi-

[10]Of course, geometric mean rate need not be interpreted within (E,σ); it is itself a valid reward measure and could be linked, for instance, with the risk measure $\ln [(1 + E)/(1 + g)]$ to form a preference space.

mation, the risk-indifference curves near the riskless axis are concave upward much like those in Figure 2. Each curve has a riskless equivalent rate which is just the geometric mean rate.

An alternative expression of geometric mean rate is useful: $G = \ln(1 + g)$ is the *natural exponential rate* (''natural'' rate) or *continuously compounded rate*. Use of the natural rate allows the rates of individual periods to be averaged to yield the rate of an overall period when investment is compounded. There is an overwhelming propensity for people to average interval percent returns (for instance, the monthly returns reported by commodity trading advisors on disclosure documents). This frequently gives a distorted picture of overall percent return. Using the natural rate, an individual could average the interval returns for an account over any number of intervals and have a proper percent return provided the account had no additions or withdrawals over that period. For instance, if a month's return is +20% and the next month's is −20%, the net return for two months is 0%, a conclusion which is false if the returns are simple percentage rates. (The assumption is that rate of return is based on equity at the start of the month.)

SUMMARY AND CONCLUDING REMARKS

Three decades ago formal criteria for evaluating trading systems were essentially one-dimensional. A rate of return served as the figure of merit for selection, perhaps ''adjusted'' in some way to compensate for some aspect of risk. Practitioners who did the selection, of course, incorporated considerably more information, but not with a formalized scheme. The introduction of (E,σ) in the 1950s provided a framework for formally expressing the tradeoff involved in accepting a greater equity fluctuation in order to obtain a greater return. Such a tradeoff is of prime importance in comparing performance of technical trading systems or commodity trading advisors. Preference space is a natural framework for discussing such tradeoffs, although there may be preference spaces that are more desirable than (E,σ).

The first focus of this chapter has been to present preference space concepts so that traders and researchers may use them in the analysis of commodity trading systems. In a preference space approach, an assessment of which of many alternative trading systems is ''best'' is broken into two major steps:

1. The preference behavior of a broad class of traders is considered in dividing all the alternatives available into two sets by a rejection algorithm which for each system asks whether that system is rejected in preference to another. (The rejection would have to be agreed upon by everyone in the class.) One set consists of all the rejected systems; the other set, the efficient set, then contains any system which would be selected as ''best'' by at least one member of the class. Finding the rejection algorithm, the efficiency criterion, is the task of importance. General, theoretically satisfactory efficiency criteria are not practical for use in judging trading system performance because they require more information than is reasonably well-known and need a multidimensional representation. A practical efficiency criterion is expressible in a two-dimensional reward/risk preference

space. It is particularly useful to employ scatter diagrams of system performance in such a space. The practical requirement of using a two-dimensional space limits the range of preference behavior and of probability densities of outcomes which can be treated. A wise choice of preference space would encompass only that range of preference behavior and probability densities which is met in real-life situations. The class of all risk averters seems unreasonably large for such an efficiency criterion; some more restricted class of "practical traders" would be more sensible.

2. Individual preferences within the class are expressible in the preference space by risk-indifference curves. An individual's choice of the "best" system is that member of the efficient set which lies on the most preferred indifference curve.

Once a specific set of indifference curves has been adopted it may seem unnecessary to use the intermediate step of thinking in terms of an "efficient set for a broad class of traders." Why then should one even consider such a concept? Because it effectively expresses the tradeoff choices *available* in contrast to the indifference curves expressing the tradeoff which is *acceptable*. For instance, a trading advisor will have clients who differ considerably in the risk they wish to assume. (Some advisors determine the risk characteristics of clients through questionnaires designed to probe their preference or indifference between various alternative reward/risk scenarios.) The range of alternatives which the efficient set encompasses ensures that the "best" choice of all those available from the advisor is included for any individual who fits within the broad class of traders, but possible systems or portfolio combinations which no one would choose are not included. (The efficient set concept is also useful in application of portfolio theory to formation of combinations of different trading systems. Such combinations have not been discussed in this chapter apart from a combination with a borrowing–lending facility.)

The second focus of this chapter has been the analysis of the mean-variance model of preference space in some detail. The preference measures which have been discussed within the framework of (E,σ) can, with one exception, be listed in order of increasing risk avoidance:

1. The arithmetic mean rate of return, E.
2. The Kelly measure—geometric mean rate of return, g.
3. The Sharpe ratio.
4. The safety-first criterion.
5. The ratio of geometric to arithmetic growth factors, $(1 + g)/(1 + E)$.
6. The standard deviation σ.

The other measure, the Baumol Confidence Limit $L = E - k\sigma$, would fit anywhere in this list since with adjustment of the constant k, it can range from standard deviation ($k = \infty$) to arithmetic mean rate of return ($k = 0$). The third, fourth, and fifth measures all have similar risk-indifference structures, straight lines which fan out as spokes from some point on the riskless axis. Any two measures could be candidates for reward/risk measures in a preference space. Perhaps the most instructive combination is the geometric mean rate (or alternatively, the natural rate) as a reward measure and a Baumol Confidence Limit rate of return as a (negative) risk measure. A system would be described as in the following example: A long-term compounded return of 5% per month with a 98% probability of not having a return less than a loss of 12% in any given month.

Within the context of the mean-variance model, the Sharpe ratio is of paramount importance for selection of a trading system to be used in conjunction with a borrowing–lending facility. Unrestricted use of such a facility would imply that *all* such traders would choose the *same* trading system, the one with the greatest Sharpe ratio; different traders would satisfy their differing risk indifference characteristics by using different degrees of leveraging. When borrowing and lending rates are equal, the efficient set formed with the inclusion of the facility is just the borrowing–lending line passing through the trading system with the highest Sharpe ratio.

Some criticisms of the mean-variance model emphasize that it is not formally sound as a general decision criterion, although it is considerably more practical than those efficiency criteria which are sound. In addition, certain inadequacies of variance as a risk measure may indicate that some alternative preference space or efficiency criterion will prove more useful to commodity traders in expressing the tradeoff of accepting a greater equity fluctuation to obtain a greater percent return. Also, (E,σ) is not appropriate for expressing a different kind of tradeoff, that of accepting greater short-term equity fluctuations in exchange for more stable longer-term returns. Preference measures which cannot be expressed in (E,σ) space (for instance, any measure which significantly depends on more than the first two moments of the probability densities) have not been discussed. One example is an entropy risk measure used in a mean-entropy space applied to stock portfolio formation (Philippatos and Wilson, 1972). Another example, a linear gain reward measure, was suggested by Kaufman (1981) and used by him in conjunction with a probability of loss risk measure. Equity drawdown or retracement measures are a broad class of examples of risk measures which have great appeal to many commodity traders (Schwager, Chapter 22). Studies of alternative preference spaces and comparison of preference ordering of trading systems based on (E,σ) measures with those based on alternative measures are encouraged. It is hoped that a consensus on how to best report trading system performance will emerge. The most useful form discussed in this chapter is the combination of geometric mean rate (or alternatively, the natural rate) and a Baumol Confidence Limit.

BIBLIOGRAPHY

Baumol, W.J. "An Expected Gain-Confidence Limit Criterion for Portfolio Selection." *Management Science,* **10,** October 1963, pp. 174–182.

Bicksler, J. and Samuelson, P. (Eds.). *Investment Portfolio Decision Making*. Lexington, MA: Lexington Books, 1974.

Borch, K. "A Note on Uncertainty and Indifference Curves." *Review of Economic Studies,* January 1969, pp. 1–4. (Also reprinted in Bicksler and Samuelson, 1974, pp. 29–34.)

Dickinson, J.P. (Ed.). *Portfolio Analysis, A Book of Readings*. Lexington, MA: Saxon House, London/Lexington Books, 1974.

Elton, E.J., and Gruber, M.J. *Modern Portfolio Theory and Investment Analysis*. New York, NY: Wiley, 1981.

Fama, E.F. "The Behavior of Stock Market Prices." *Journal of Business,* **38,** January 1965, pp. 34–105.

Feller, W. *An Introduction to Probability Theory and Its Applications* (2nd ed.), 1957, p. 168.

Francis, J.C., and Archer, S.H. *Portfolio Analysis* (2nd ed.). Englewood Cliffs, NJ: Prentice-Hall, 1979.

Kaufman, P.J. "Safety-Adjusted Performance Evaluation." *The Journal of Futures Markets*, **1,** 1981, pp. 17–31.

Kelly, J.L. "A New Interpretation of Information Rate." *Bell System Technical Journal,* **35,** 1956, pp. 917–926.

Levy, H., and Sarnat, M. *Investment and Portfolio Analysis*. New York, NY: Wiley, 1972.

Markowitz, H.M. "Portfolio Selection." *Journal of Finance,* March 1952, pp. 77–91.

Markowitz, H.M. *Portfolio Selection: Efficient Diversification of Investments,* Cowles Foundation Monograph #16. New York, NY: Wiley, 1959.

Philippatos, G.C., and Wilson, C.J. "Entropy, Market Risk, and the Selection of Efficient Portfolios." *Applied Economics,* **4,** 1972, pp. 209–220. (Also reprinted in Dickinson, 1974, pp. 59–73.)

Pratt, J. "Risk Aversion in the Small and in the Large." In J. Bicksler and P. Samuelson, (Eds.), *Investment Portfolio Decision Making*. Lexington, MA: Saxon House, London/Lexington Books, 1974, pp. 49–65.

Roy, A.D. "Safety First and the Holding of Assets." *Econometrica,* **20,** July 1952, pp. 431–449.

Samuelson, P.A. "The Fallacy of Maximizing the Geometric Mean in Long Sequences of Investing or Gambling." *Proceedings of the National Academy of Sciences,* **68,** October 1971, pp. 2493–2496. (Also reprinted in Bicksler and Samuelson, 1974, pp. 271–280.)

Sharpe, W.F. "Mutual Fund Performance." *Journal of Business,* **39,** January 1966, pp. 119–138.

Thorpe, E. "Portfolio Choice and the Kelly Criterion." *Business and Economic Statistics Section of Proceedings of the American Statistical Association,* 1971, pp. 215–224. (Also reprinted in Bicksler and Samuelson, 1974, pp. 253–270.)

Tobin, J. "Comment on Borch and Feldstein." *Review of Economic Studies,* January 1969, pp. 13 to 14. (Also reprinted in Bicksler and Samuelson, 1974, pp. 35–36.)

CHAPTER 24

EVALUATING A MANAGED ACCOUNT

CONTENTS

PUBLICATION OF PERFORMANCE 5

PERFORMANCE BENCH MARKS IN COMMODITIES 6

AVAILABILITY OF INFORMATION 7

PRESENTATION OF PERFORMANCE 7

PERFORMANCE CONTENT 8

SIMULATED PERFORMANCE 9

SUMMARY 9

CHAPTER 24

EVALUATING A MANAGED ACCOUNT

Frank S. Pusateri

A commodity managed account, because of its substantial leverage, will always be a high-risk/high-reward investment alternative. The most difficult mistake to avoid in the evaluation of a commodity trading advisor is one that no checklist will ever identify. There are trading approaches with actual and simulated track records that cover periods of 1, 2, or even 3 years that show substantial rewards with little or no downside risk. Sooner or later, all of these approaches demonstrate the risk level equivalent to their rewards. Even so, after many years of experience, it is hard to avoid the desire to believe that you have found a low-risk/high-reward alternative.

An investor in commodities needs to understand one of the unique rules under which commodities are traded and how it may affect his or her search. *Position limits* exist for most commodities. These limits impose a maximum number of contracts an individual or trading advisor may control in a given commodity. These limits generally have little or no relationship to market liquidity—the ability to execute a greater number of contracts at acceptable prices—but they do effectively impose a maximum on the amount of money a single commodity trader can control. As a result of position limits, most commodity traders with long records of success are not readily available to handle additional accounts. This forces the potential investor to select among commodity traders with shorter, less significant track records.

An investor seeking a professional commodity trader to manage an account is faced with the major problem of selecting one trader from among the hundreds available. The checklist that follows was designed to allow the investor who is unfamiliar with commodity managed accounts to compare managers based on background, cost, trading approach, and track records. This checklist, with some modifications, such as the omission of the questions on trading policy, can also be used to evaluate the various trading approaches which can be purchased for one's own use. Many of the questions suggested in this checklist are answered in the disclosure document required by the Commodity Futures Trading Commission of all registered commodity trading advisors and commodity pool operators. A word of caution first. It may be easier to deal with unsatisfactory answers than satisfactory ones when screening managers. It is possible for a manager to have all the right answers and yet not be a successful trader.

Evaluation Checklist

Principal and firm background.

- Name, address, and telephone number.
- Principals' background and experience.
- Firm history and starting date.
- Total number of accounts managed, number of active accounts, and number of closed accounts.
- Total money currently managed.
- Affiliations, if any, with futures commission merchants.
- Administrative, civil, or criminal proceedings.
- Other business interests.
- References, preferably well-known brokerage firms or banks.

Program background and cost.

- Types of accounts offered.
- Minimum investment.
- Commodities traded.
- Is the program highly aggressive, aggressive, or moderately aggressive?
- If losses occur, when do they recommend closing the account?
- What are their fees and how are they calculated?
- Does the client earn interest on his or her own funds?
- What percentage of equity did commissions represent last year?
- Who holds the client's money?
- At which brokerage firms are the advisors approved and what commission rate can be anticipated?
- What reports do they issue to clients?
- Are there any other charges?

Trading approach.

- What basic type of system do they use?
- Do all accounts trade the same system?
- Can the program be followed without any one principal?
- What is their maximum initial margin requirement, as a percent of equity, in total and by commodity?
- What do they estimate is the client's average and maximum exposure on any given trade?
- Do they add onto positions?
- How many contracts of a commodity do they trade and how is the portfolio balance determined?
- Do they vary the trading exposure based on current equity or use a fixed portfolio size?
- What historically has been their worst drop in equity from peak to valley?

How do they enter a new account into the market and what historically was their worst initial loss?

Are profits withdrawn or do they remain as an increase to the investment?

What ongoing research is done and when was the last time they modified their approach?

Track record.

How current is the record supplied?

Are the results shown actual or simulated?

Is the record for one account, all accounts, or some segment of the accounts?

What is the distribution of account sizes used in their record?

What commission rate and fee schedule was used for the compiled record?

Before beginning a quest to find a commodity trader, an investor should review and establish his or her overall objectives. An acceptable level of return and the comparable risk should be known in advance. The investor should decide which of the available commodity investment vehicles should be pursued based on their advantages and disadvantages and available capital. The formulation of this investment strategy in advance will result in substantial savings in time and effort by avoiding unsuitable alternatives.

PUBLICATION OF PERFORMANCE

Is a 40% annual rate of return from commodity trading good or bad? What was an acceptable rate of return in a given year from commodity trading? How do you know when your commodity managed account is performing at the average or below average? All of these questions revolve around the same issue—What benchmarks are available for evaluating commodity performance and how do you use them? Few investors, today, have the perspective to answer these questions on a year-to-year basis. This has made it difficult for them to evaluate commodities as an investment alternative.

When you discuss stock market performance, there exists a substantial number of benchmarks that can be used to determine relative performance. On an aggregate basis, you can quickly obtain the net change over practically any time period of three or four major market indicators. Each index may be representative of a different segment of the stock market, ranging from Blue Chip stocks to over-the-counter stocks, but all are fairly well understood. Any time you question an equity manager about his or her performance, the manager can usually quickly tell you how he or she did versus one or more of these indexes. In addition, there are separate statistics readily available for industry groups, such as utilities or oils, so that an investor can not only measure performance against the market as a whole but can also determine how efficient a manager trading utility stocks was when compared to the available opportunity as measured by a utility index. In commodities there exist at least two published indices. Unfortunately, they have proved to be of little or no use in measuring performance. Their value has been limited to an overall indicator of market direction. In other words, they have been used to identify major bull or bear markets.

PERFORMANCE BENCHMARKS IN COMMODITIES

A number of major problems exist in the application of commodity indices as a benchmark by which to measure performance. First, while a bias probably exists among commodity investors to prefer the long side of the market, they have the ability to trade long or short with equal costs and ease. In stocks, the typical investor trades from only the long side. A short trade in stocks, while possible, cannot be done with equal ease and cost and is therefore not done by most investors. Because the typical investor trades stocks only from the long side, the fluctuation up and down of a major index provides some measurement of opportunity. In commodities where the investor has an equal opportunity to profit from price moves which are up as well as down, the nature of the change in price is more important than the direction. For example, an overall commodity index that declined for 4 weeks and then climbed back to its initial value during the next 2 weeks, if used as most stock market indices, would indicate little or no profit opportunity. However, an investor short the commodities which comprise the index, appropriately weighted, for 4 weeks and then long for 2 weeks, could have substantially profited.

At first consideration, the measurement of potential performance in commodities, based on the investor's ability to trade both long and short, would be to calculate the sum of the net changes of the indices. This poses a second major problem. Commodity trading, because of the leverage involved, can generate substantial profits or losses in an extremely short period of time. Day traders are not rare in commodities. Traders who hold their positions 6 to 8 weeks on an average are considered to have a long-term perspective. If one is going to use net price change as the benchmark, should it be daily, weekly, or monthly change?

A second possibility in measuring change would be the calculation of the difference between the indices' peak and valley. The problem is then which peak and which valley. For example, a move in an index from 300 to 250 back up to 280 and down to 200 may yield two different answers as to the indices' net change based on what one counts as a peak and a valley. An intraday move presents a profit opportunity to some, but a *major move* which is defined in weeks and months would appear to have missed a great deal of opportunity if the intraday change were part of the measurement. Because the time frame involved in commodity trading is so short, comparatively, the use of an index as a benchmark has proved unreliable.

The last major problem in using an index as a performance benchmark involves the more basic question of whether or not a commodity index can be truly representative of commodity trading performance at all. If gold offers a substantial profit opportunity and it is only a small part of the total index composition, is a trader good or bad because he or she traded or did not trade gold? Where the trader did trade gold and profit, can the index be used to determine if the trader made the most of the opportunities offered by gold? Should we rate the trader's performance good if the trader, when measured against the index, showed substantially better performance, but when measured against the opportunity in gold, captured less than one-quarter of the possible profits? It can only be concluded that two separate and distinct benchmarks are needed: the success of the trader at selecting the markets to trade, and the trader's degree of success at taking advantage of the opportunities offered in these markets.

AVAILABILITY OF INFORMATION

The investor seeking to use the performance of similar investments as a benchmark is limited to information in stocks and bonds. The investor can get daily prices on the major mutual funds as well as individual stocks and bonds from most daily newspapers. There is an even wider variety of information from financial newspapers. In commodities little or no performance data has been published. Just recently the financial newspapers have, on occasion, published the results of the major public commodity funds. These data have also been available for about 2 years in some commodity industry trade publications. Unfortunately, these data represent only a small segment of the available commodity traders. They tend to reflect the lower-risk/lower-reward end of the spectrum of available traders.

Once or twice a year, the major business publications issue comparisons and rankings of mutual fund performance. Private newsletters and ranking services comparing not only return but risk are easy to find in stocks and bonds. Academics have been researching and publishing a broad variety of papers on investing and performance in stocks, bonds, and even real estate. To date, little data or research has ever been presented on commodities. A major problem has been the practical consideration of obtaining reliable data on a consistent basis.

The financial press reviews and prints the results of mutual funds in the stock and bond areas because of the large number of readers interested in this data. These readers may be either potential buyers or sellers of these funds. Commodities, on the other hand, are still traded by only a very limited segment of the public. The commodity fund business is in its developmental stages and to date most funds have been made available in single, short closed-ended offerings of $10–30 million to 1,000–5,000 investors. The advent of the open-ended commodity fund of a $100 million size will probably see the publishing of more frequent results and the inclusion of commodity trading results and performance comparisons and rankings. This will still leave unresolved the problem of obtaining performance data for an account of less than $1 million. A good trader will try to take advantage of the opportunities offered in trading $1 million and achieve substantially different results than the trader would have received in a $50,000 or a $100,000 account.

PRESENTATION OF PERFORMANCE

In 1981 the Commodity Futures Trading Commission adopted new rules governing the presentation of performance data by commodity trading advisors (CTAs) and commodity pool operators (CPOs). These rules were established to provide the potential investor with readily comparable performance data. Because these rules do not apply to any associated person of a futures commission merchant, a potential investor cannot, in most cases, obtain this data on *this* substantial number of available commodity traders. In addition to the required data, a CTA or CPO is allowed to present other data on performance. A substantial number of CTAs and CPOs have used this ability to present additional data to show performance in a net manner that overcomes the objections previously stated. Other CTAs and CPOs have made use of this latitude to present themselves in the most favorable light. Great care must be exercised to determine exactly how supplementary performance data was prepared.

The Commodity Futures Trading Commission requires that all CTAs and CPOs present a composite performance table of *all* accounts controlled that shows the following data on a quarterly basis for the past 3 years:

Beginning net asset value.
Additions.
Withdrawals.
Net performance.
Ending net asset value.
Rate of return.

Providing comparative data to the potential investor is an excellent idea. But the nature of the information provided has, in practice, been subject to a variety of definitions and terms for each category published. What is a *controlled account*? Must previous accounts controlled using *different systems* be included? Does net performance include or exclude *interest earnings*? Are *fees paid* treated as a withdrawal or do they decrease performance? The lack of exact definitions has created composite tables that look alike but are not comparable.

The Commodity Futures Trading Commission's new rules have also required the labeling of all simulated performance data with the following caveat:

> THE COMMODITY FUTURES TRADING COMMISSION REQUIRES A COMMODITY TRADING ADVISOR TO DISCLOSE TO PROSPECTIVE CLIENTS THAT ACTUAL PERFORMANCE RECORD OF ALL ACCOUNTS FOR WHICH THE TRADING ADVISOR AND ITS PRINCIPALS HAVE HAD THE AUTHORITY TO CAUSE TRANSACTIONS TO BE EFFECTED WITHOUT CLIENTS' SPECIFIC AUTHORIZATION. YOU SHOULD NOTE THAT THIS TRADING ADVISOR AND ITS PRINCIPALS PREVIOUSLY HAVE NOT HAD SUCH AUTHORITY.

Commodity trading advisors are allowed to present more data than the CFTC required minimums. For example, monthly data is an improvement over quarterly data for use in any type of analysis. Five years of data is better than 3 years. Obtaining enough data to draw significant conclusions has been a major problem in our young and growing industry.

PERFORMANCE CONTENT

A potential investor reviewing a trading advisor's performance record must start by defining the advisor's terms. The investor must determine what the advisor considers "equity." Does this only include cash and Treasury bills available to meet margin requirements, or does it assume assets not as readily liquid? Many advisors do their accounting based on the intended investment as shown on their customer agreement and make little or no attempt to value real assets. Their accounts are valued at the initial size plus or minus trading profits or losses. Other terminology must also be clarified:

What expenses are charged to the client within the performance data and under what headings are they included?

What commissions, on average, were charged to the accounts shown? (It is possible to have expenses in commissions 20–30% higher than those included in some performance tables.)

What account sizes predominate in the presented data? If an account is to be $50,000 and the data present the results of a $1 million account, how can that be used as any indicator of possible performance of the smaller account?

What is profit or loss? Is interest included or excluded?

What could the rate of return be if the deposits or withdrawals are applied at the beginning of the time period instead of at the end? (Most composite tables will have a substantial change in the rate of return if the order of this calculation is changed.)

Other problems in judging performance come from the fact that the disclosure gives little or no indication of how profits were made. Suppose you showed a profit of $40,000 by buying gold at $450 and selling it at $850 in a $40,000 account. Your account would have a rate of return of 80% for the time period. A potential client looking at your performance record would see impressive results but would not know that a continuation of this return would require a repetition of specific trades under unusual price moves.

SIMULATED PERFORMANCE

Simulated performance data are the subject of many potential problems. Most experienced investors, because of the problems that are potentially present in simulated data, avoid these systems. Of course, if we all avoided traders with simulated data, no new traders would succeed in proving their systems.

Simulations must first be reviewed to determine if they present a tradable system or a system that has been fitted to the underlying data. This type of review is best done with trade-by-trade data. Systems that claim to buy at bottoms and sell at tops are generally curve fitted and not tradable. Good simulation techniques require the development of the system on one time period which is then tested against another time period. While most investors cannot obtain trade-by-trade data, they can explore the simulation techniques with the trading advisor.

SUMMARY

The selection of a commodity trading advisor based on past performance assumes future markets will look like past markets. To guard against the possibility that the selected advisor has a system that cannot trade future markets, a client should establish a cutoff point prior to opening an account. Based on the advisor's historical performance, the client should pick a point that is greater than the advisor's expected downside risk parameters as the point to close the account.

PART VI

THE COMMODITIES

CHAPTER 25

AGRICULTURE

CONTENTS

PENALTIES FOR INCREASED OUTPUT 3

UNCERTAINTIES OF THE GRAIN EXPORT MARKET 3

ORGANIZING A GRAIN PRICE FORECAST 6

Determining Supply 6
Determining Demand 7
Market Price 7

MATHEMATICAL FORECASTING AND ESTIMATION 8

Price Forecasts 8
Anticipated Acreage 9
Consumption of Food 9
USDA Reports 9

CROP SPREADS 14

Diverging Prices 14
Other Spreads 15

THE LONDON GRAIN FUTURES MARKET 18

CHAPTER 25

AGRICULTURE

Perry J. Kaufman

In an era of preoccupation with money and finance the significance of agriculture in the United States becomes lost. Farming in America has been taken for granted. Each year farm output increases; in the past 5 years alone, productivity in agriculture increased five times faster than productivity in industry.

Exports of agricultural products have been a major source of revenues for the United States, totaling $41 billion in 1980. That goes a long way towards holding up the value of the dollar, considering the $80 billion paid out in the same year for imported oil.

PENALTIES FOR INCREASED OUTPUT

The increase in farm production cannot be accomplished without cost. In this case the land is paying the price. The old methods of natural fertilization, crop rotation, and contour farming have given way to faster, more economic methods of chemical fertilizers, single crops, and row planting. The cost to the soil is an annual erosion which exceeds 10 tons of topsoil per acre. This will eventually translate into dangerously lower yields. It is estimated that the topsoil in some places in Iowa has diminished from 2 to 1 ft since the land was first settled in the mid-1800s. Continuation of this rate of depletion would cause the corn yield in the Midwest to decline by as much as 30% by the year 2030.[1]

In this introduction to grain and other agricultural markets some overall concepts and analysis have been covered. Although some of these topics seem very specific, the general methods used are applicable to most crops and agricultural markets.

UNCERTAINTIES OF THE GRAIN EXPORT MARKET[2]

Although the 1980–1982 export demands did not exceed those previously anticipated, they were years of great uncertainty. The two factors which continue to

[1]R. T. Fulton, "The New Issues: Land, Water, Energy," *The Wilson Quarterly*, Summer 1981.

[2]M. Oster, "Measuring the 'China Factor' on U.S. Markets," Bache Halsey Stuart Shields, 1979; C. Leslie, "A New Look at the Soviets," Thomson McKinnon Securities, 1979.

TABLE 1. Production Growth

	1961		1980		Change	
	United States	World	United States	World	United States	World
Wheat						
Production (million metric tons)	32.4	207.3	64.5	441.7	+99%	+113%
Exports (millions of bushels)	719.4		1,525.0		+112%	
Yield per acre						
Corn						
Production (million metric tons)	94.6	196.4	185.0	402.0	+96%	+105%
Exports (millions of bushels)	435.0		2,600.0		+498%	
Yield per acre	62.4		91.0		+46%	

remain unknown are the policies of the *Soviet Union* and *China*. Each country holds such incredibly large potential as a buyer of world grain that the fundamentals of demand could be instantly changed and the balancing factor—price—could skyrocket.

The 1974–1975 USSR grain crop will be remembered as the springboard for volatile prices in the 1970s. From a total production of 223 million metric tons in 1973–1974, the Soviet production dropped to 140 (million metric tons) in 1975–1976. The small surplus gained from the larger harvest had disappeared by the next year and offered no buffer to ease the unexpected critical shortage. The export agreement signed with the United States caused all grain prices to rise, in many cases nearly double, and carried a multitude of unrelated products to exceptionally high price levels.

After 1975 the market was left with the uncertainty of future demands by the USSR. Each year farmers looked optimistically towards larger exports and higher prices. Then came Afghanistan and the U.S. embargo of grain shipments. Combined with significantly better Soviet crops, the sudden reduction in exports quickly sent prices by late 1977 to low levels never expected to be seen again.

In 1978 China purchased 3.3 million metric tons of grain from the United States out of a total imported 9.5 million metric tons. The act of purchasing was itself encouraging to the agricultural sector, since China had made its only recent purchases between 1972 and 1974. In addition, their total imports in 1978 greatly exceeded imports in 1973 and were the highest in more than 20 years. Imaginations again ran wild. A tremendous population, backward industrialization and technology, and a reentry into the U.S. market could mean unlimited demand.

What are the possibilities of unexpected demand from the Soviet Union and China? Certainly the chances of greater demand are present, although China has always been in the world market, importing primarily from Canada and Australia with smaller amounts from Argentina and France. As with the Soviets, China chose to use non-U.S. sources for their needs. The demand, however, draws down world stocks and offers only potential for U.S. grain in the event of subsequent shortages. It does not help U.S. farm prices if new supplies continue to meet demand.

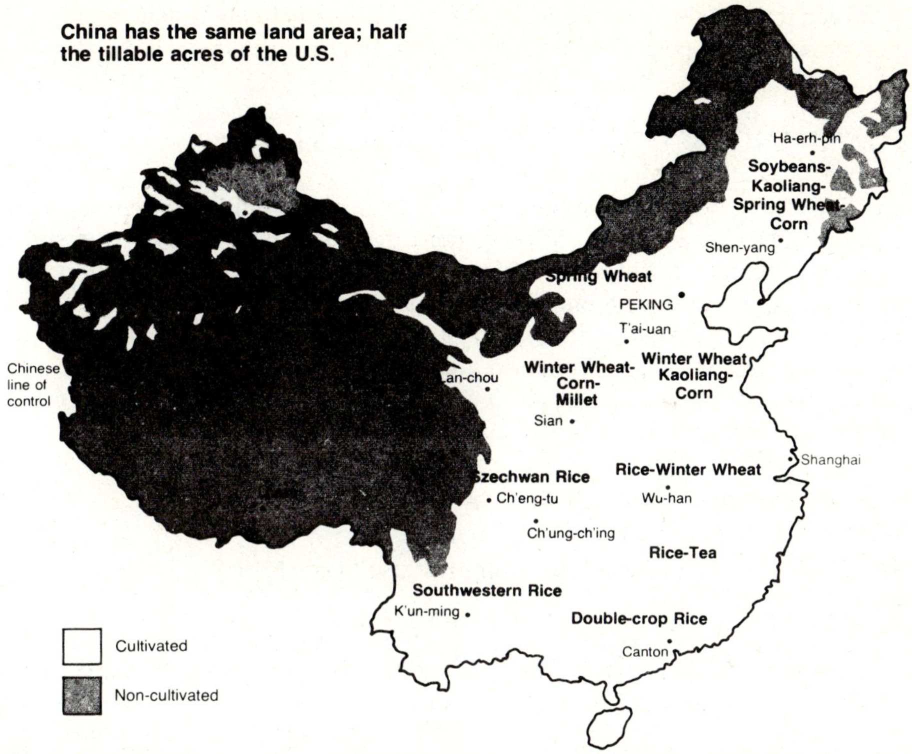

FIGURE 1. China's crop areas: China's population is crowded along her western border, forcing a population density to 3,122 people per 1,000 tillable acres, compared with 437 in the United States.

Crop surpluses in the first years of the 1980s have taken away the threat of immediate demand of U.S. grain. In the late 1970s the lingering drought in China opened possibilities of increasing demand. But there still remains some important factors. A *population* of a billion people, one-quarter of the total world population, live on the same land area as the United States, but have only one-half the tillable acreage as in the United States. If the population continues to grow (estimated at 1.5% per year) technology will have to keep a fast pace with internal consumption in order to avoid rapidly increasing imports.

The *modernization policy* of China is intended to make that country industrially competitive with other nations by the year 2000. In 1979 China planned to transfer *200 million people* from the farms to the industrial sector by 1985. In order to produce food for more people using substantially less workers China must proceed at a quick pace, and must improve output by an estimated 4.5% per year.

The Chinese government also plans *improved diets* for their people, that is, beef, pork, and poultry, as well as grains. However, feeding livestock is an inefficient way of using grain, and it will put a greater burden on production, allowing for less chance of error in the future.

If everything goes according to plan we can expect little change in the market. Occasional purchases by China and the Soviet Union will boost prices for the short term, but may be anticipated well in advance through trade agreements. However, there is certainly a chance of a "price shock." A continually increasing demand for food in the magnitudes needed by China is likely to face a crisis, and that crisis will move prices to levels far higher and faster than we have ever seen.

ORGANIZING A GRAIN PRICE FORECAST[3]

Even with the advent of computers, with access to limitless data on supply, demand, carryover, and price history, the forecasting of grain prices is still imprecise. An organized procedure, called a *balance sheet,* is a sound approach to price determination. It is intended to assess the expected price of crops for the coming season and should be applied just prior to planting of the new crop. The *balance sheet* is a simple approach to finding the supply–demand balance, which results in the net carryover for the year, and that in turn, will be the primary determinate of prices. The process asks the questions:

How much grain is stored at the beginning of the year?
What is the current production?
What is the disappearance? for domestic use? for export?
What is the resulting carryover?

DETERMINING SUPPLY. The supply of a grain depends on answering a number of questions about anticipated planting and yields:

1. Determine the total acreage to be planted.
   a. How many acres are absolutely profitable for planting of this crop?
   b. Is there going to be a shift towards or away from marginal acreage production based on forward prices?
   c. Where there is a choice of crops to plant on profitable acreage, will there be a switch from the previous year's planting?
   d. Has profitability been good in recent years for the existing crop? If so, then investment in equipment to expedite planting may cause a resistance to change.
   e. Are weather conditions such that planting is slow and a shift to a later planted crop is likely?
   f. Has recent drought required a switch to a different crop or variety?
2. What yield can be expected nationally?
   a. Weather cycles have a generally predictable impact on yields, with drought cycles likely to reduce yields by 4–6%. What are current conditions?
   b. The water table level east of the Mississippi and soil moisture reserves West relate to possible yield reduction. Is the anticipated precipitation enough to offset the moisture reserves and maintain average yields?
   c. Are proper fertilizers available for the desired crops? Were fertilizers applied earlier in the season making a change too costly?

[3]Based on G. Dike and R. Black, *Be Your Own Price Outlook Specialist . . . Some Guidelines,* Agricultural Economics Staff Paper No. 76-03, Michigan State University, 1976.

   d. Is there time to change crops without suffering reductions in yield? Keep track of planting progress in major producing states.
   e. Has marginal land been used for expanded planting? Include a reduction in yield based on land quality.

DETERMINING DEMAND. An evaluation of usage is equally important for price determination. The following questions will help find the demand figures:

1. Domestic disappearance.
   a. What are the grain levels for seed, on-farm or commercially?
   b. Trends in industrial use and food are fairly constant. What are this year's demands?
   c. Feed represents the largest consumption for most grains.
      (i) What is the status of the feeding industry? How many animal units? Unless conditions are extreme, feeders will not let facilities remain idle. Recent profitability may even result in an aggressive demand.
      (ii) What is the feeding rate? Hard winters cause higher consumption.
      (iii) Which feed was favored due to protein and price ratios?
      (iv) Is the wheat loan rate high relative to corn, causing wheat to be kept off the market?
2. Exports.
   a. What are current reserves in major importing countries? Do current weather conditions favor the crop or should additional imports be expected?
   b. Are diet patterns changing in the importing countries? Tendencies to produce more livestock will place greater demands on grain supplies and increase imports. Consider China, the Soviet Union, and developing nations.
   c. What are the existing trade agreements? Will exports be stabilized by prospective new agreements?
   d. Are any countries attempting to build reserves?
3. Stocks, reserves, and inventory.
   a. Are business "pipelines" full? Will processors be active buyers to maintain operations?
   b. Are there adequate carryover reserves in comparison with pipeline stocks?
   c. What are the government programs, loan rates, and target prices? Will they provide price support this season or prevent prices from moving higher?

MARKET PRICE. Instead of forecasting a price using complex mathematics, the information collected from answering the previous questions can be used to determine the most reasonable forecast of an average price for the current season. The answer to the following questions must assume average weather conditions in the coming crop year:

1. What is your best guess for an average price for a particular grain?

2. Based on the selected price, how will demand by the livestock sector be effected? How will that price change current feeding plans?
3. What will the level of exports be at this price?
4. Based on demand at this price what will be the resulting carryover of stocks?
5. Will the grain trade and farmers allow these carryovers at the selected price? Would they have purchased or sold more, placed more under loan or taken it out? If the balance has not been reached, pick another price that you think will clear the market and go back to (2).

In order to answer these questions, it is necessary to have reliable information. Much of this can be found in the section *Sources of Information*.

MATHEMATICAL FORECASTING AND ESTIMATION

A great amount of time and effort has been expended by the U.S. Department of Agriculture (USDA) and private industry to forecast the supply and demand and therefore the price of agricultural commodities. This work falls into two categories: forecasting crop prices and estimating current yields. While much of the USDA's work in forecasting seems to apply to potato prices and acreage, the form of the results should be applicable to most agricultural products.

PRICE FORECASTS. Forecasts of the average price take the general form[4]:

$$\text{P/PPI} = a_1 + a_2S + a_3D$$

where P is the average price received by farmers; PPI is the Producer Price Index; S is the apparent domestic free supply; D is the estimated deliverable supply; and a_1, a_2, and a_3 are the constants determined by regression analysis.

Substantial research has been performed on the potato market, resulting in the following form for forecasting average price:

$$P_f = a_1 + a_2C_f + a_3P_s + a_4D + a_5M + a_6t$$

where P_f is the average price received by farmers (adjusted by the Consumer Price Index), C_f is the apparent per capita consumption, P_s is the price of early crop of same year, D is the per capita disposable income (first quarter) adjusted by the Consumer Price Index), M is the index of the cost of marketing, t is the year (for index of technology or time-series factors), and $a_1, \ldots, a_6$ are constants determined by regression analysis.

Additional forecasts for egg prices resulted in[5]

$$P = 0.0019L + 3.52F + 0.55B \ (R^2 = 0.85)$$

where P is the monthly average price of eggs in Chicago, L is the number of layers on farms (by month), F is the monthly egg/feed ratio, and B is the average monthly retail beef price.

[4]See J. D. Schwager in the "References" section.

[5]T. Danis, *An Economic Analysis of Egg Prices in 1969*, Chicago Mercantile Exchange, Research Report No. 1, April 1970.

Other forecasts on orange juice and cocoa are available through the USDA and Weymar, respectively. General approaches to forecasting can be found in Labys, and Labys and Granger.

ANTICIPATED ACREAGE. Additional work by the USDA on anticipated acreage for the potato crop showed results of the form:

$$A_t = a_1 + a_2P_{t-1} + a_3P_{t-2} + a_4A_{t-1}$$

where A_t is the current year anticipated acreage, A_{t-1} is the previous-year planted acreage, P_{t-1} is the season-average price received by farmers in the previous year, P_{t-2} is the season-average price received by farmers 2 years prior, and a_1, . . ., a_4 are constants determined by regression analysis.

This forecast is quite simple and shows that current planting is expected to be based primarily on previous prices and recent planting decisions. In most cases the previous acreage is a strong indication of current acreage due to a natural reluctance to change.

CONSUMPTION OF FOOD[6]. The elasticity of the demand for food was estimated by E. J. Working in an article "Appraising the Demand for American Agricultural Output During Rearmament" (*Journal of Farm Economics*, Vol. 34, No. 2). The results, shown in Figure 2 indicate an elasticity of −0.251, based on the relationship

$$\log C = 1.9488 - 0.251 \log P + 0.02810 \log L$$

where C is the consumption of food, P is the price of food, and L is the income level.

This is a remarkably low elasticity of demand, indicating that demand does not decline as fast as expected. Figure 2, however, shows that demand is relatively elastic at low income levels and increasingly inelastic at higher income levels. This can be explained by the proportion of income allocated to food by each family. Increases in price cannot be absorbed at low income levels, while there is adequate excess income at higher levels to avoid changing consumer patterns as prices rise.

USDA REPORTS. The USDA has been publishing its research studies in grain yields and crop estimation for many years through the *Statistical Research Service* (SRS) and its predecessors. The following is a review of their major publications in this area.

Weather Modeling. G. A. Larsen and R. B. Peuse, *Stochastic Simulation of Daily Climate Data*, SRS, USDA 1981: This report discusses an expansion of a previous weather model designed to generate sequences of daily precipitation, maximum and minimum temperature, and solar radiation. A first order, two-state Markov chain simulates precipitation, two bivariate normal distributions simulate

[6]G. S. Shepherd, *Agricultural Price Analysis*, 5th ed., Iowa State Univ. Press, Ames, IA, 1972, p. 25.

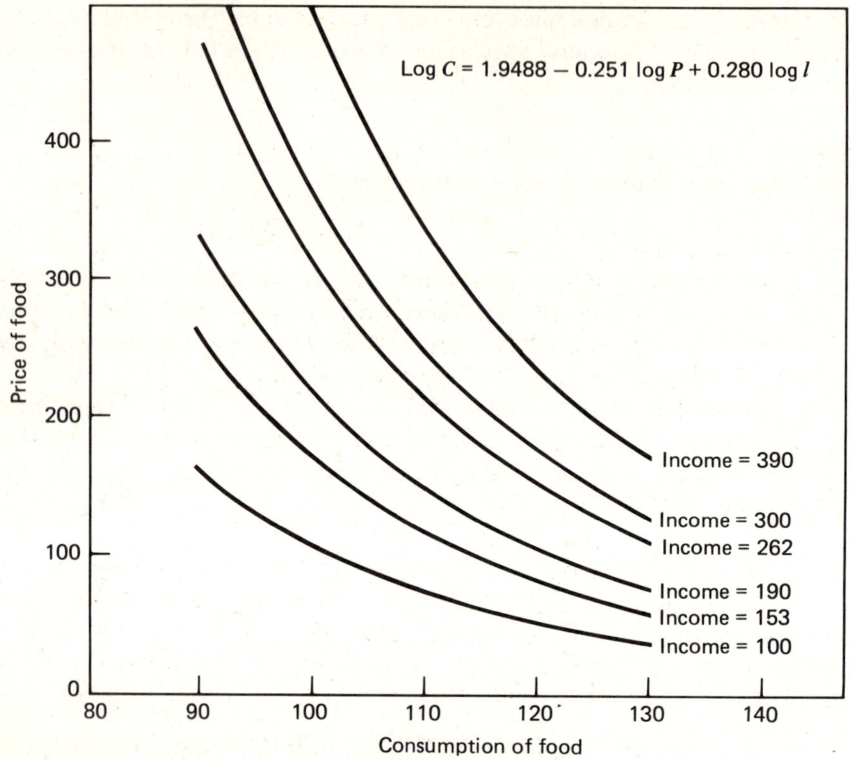

FIGURE 2. Consumption of food.

temperature, and probability distributions (gamma or beta depending on precipitation) are used for precipitation.

The purpose of simulated weather data is to fill unknown data and provide full simulation series for hydrologic models, agricultural management and risk assessment in yield determination. It is not necessary for the simulation series to follow the same patterns as actual weather at the same time as long as the long-term results are similar.

Yield Estimation for Corn and Wheat. The series of reports that follow are attempts to estimate yields using a *growth model* in different stages of refinement.

C. C. House, *A Within-Year Growth Model Approach to Forecasting Corn Yields*, SRS, USDA, September 1977: This report attempts to explain the pattern of growth of corn after it has been planted. It was expected that this study would help forecast the quality as well as the size of yields. An important consideration and motivation was speculation on climatic changes and the resulting yields in atypical growing years.

The *logistic growth and survival models* used were determined to be highly accurate representations of the growth and survival of the corn kernel formation. The model has the form

$$y_i = \frac{a}{1 + br^{t}{}_{i}} + e_i \quad (i = 1,2, \ldots, n)$$

where a, b, and r are nonnegative constants and $0<r<1$; e_i is the disturbance term (error dependent on time t); t_i is the independent time variable (time series); and y_i is the dependent variable representing growth or survival. A graphic representation of the logistic-growth-model results is shown in Figure 3.

Assuming t_0 to t_n represents the full within-year growth period, we can see that the reflection point shows a short, rapid period in which the majority of growth takes place. Major variances in yield can be associated with problems occurring in the point of the growth cycle prior to t_j.

Using a nonlinear procedure for approximation, the SRS found the constants of the growth model to be:

	a	b	r
Iowa	141.2	38.4	0.892
Texas	166.0	43.0	0.897

where a is the estimated dry kernel weight (in grams) per plant at maturity. Various adjustments were made to compensate for *heteroscedasticity*, a term referring to nonconstant variance; residuals of the regression have a significant positive correlation with time.

G. A. Larsen, *Alternate Methods of Adjusting for Heteroscedasticity in Wheat Growth Data,* Yield Research Branch, Statistical Research Division, ESCS USDA, 1978: Techniques for adjusting for heteroscedastic disturbances in growth data are discussed in this report. Logarithmic transformations and weighted least-squares methods were attempted. Both methods demonstrated the ability to adjust for a large share of the disturbances.

G. A. Larsen, *Forecasting Final Corn Grain Yield Per Plant With A Constrained Logistic Growth Model,* SRS, USDA, 1980: A study using the same model as Carol C. House applied to 1977 Illinois and Iowa corn data produced

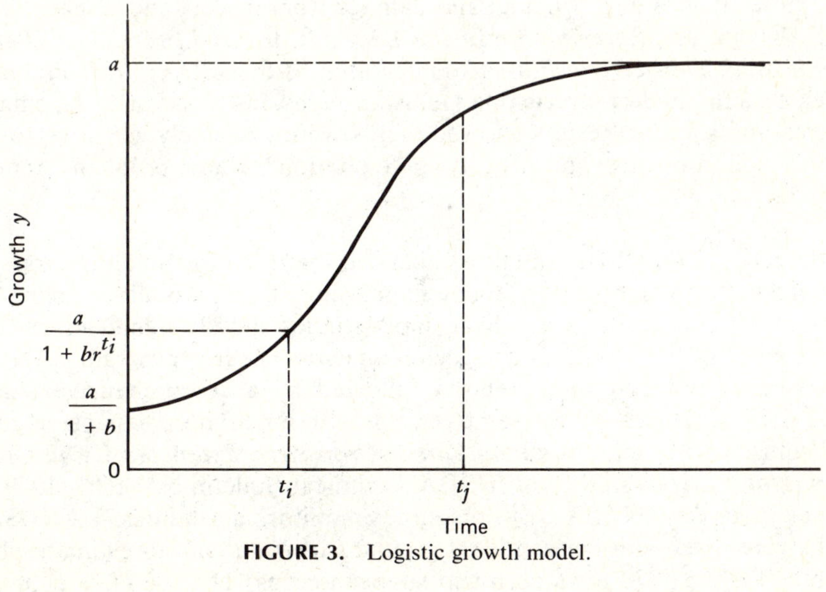

FIGURE 3. Logistic growth model.

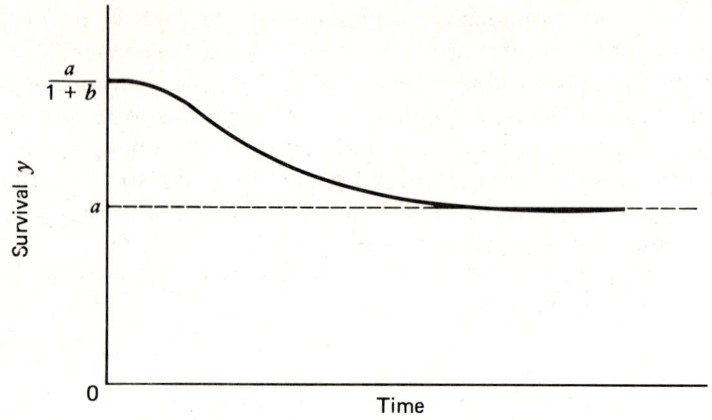

FIGURE 4. Survival growth model.

forecasts within 9% of the August 1 production and within 3% of the final production. The following assumptions were made with regard to the error term:

$$E(e_i) = 0 \text{ for all } i$$
$$\text{var } e_i = E(e^2_i) = \sigma^2 \text{ for all } i$$
$$\text{cov } e_i, e_j = E(e_i, e_j) = 0 \text{ for all } i \neq j$$

Larsen produced an adjusted growth model where the error term had a constant variance over time by dividing the basic model by $\sqrt{K_i}$, the solution to the variance-covariance equation.

G. A. Larsen, *Progress Report on the Evaluation of Plant Growth Models,* SRS, USDA, 1981: A more advanced form of yield forecasting for wheat was researched with positive, although not perfect, results. Forecasting input included soil water, temperature, solar-radiation conditions, as well as precipitation, root depth, planting (seeding) density, and factors which reduce density such as winterkill, blowout, heaving, lodging, and damage from insects and disease.

B. F. Klugh, Jr., *Examination of the Leeper Corn Yield Model, A Weather-Phenologically Timed Yield Forecasting Model,* SRS, USDA, 1979: Preliminary research on a method of forecasting yields through sensitivity analysis, small and large area application. Results showed yields were extremely sensitive to water and both soil moisture and weekly precipitation. Many problems remained unresolved.

Satellite Data. The USDA satellite-enhanced method of estimating crop yields has proved to be an extremely effective improvement over ground-sampling methods. Although concentrated in wheat, most studies show a significant reduction in the variance of the estimates using satellite data. The first program LANDSAT is reviewed in the first three reports followed by a comprehensive study of AgRISTARS, a USDA–NASA joint venture with much more expansive goals.

G. Hannschak, et al., *Obtaining Timely Crop Area Estimates Using Ground-Gathering and LANDSAT Data,* USDA Technical Bulletin No. 1609, 1979: This study describes how NASA earth resources monitoring satellites, LANDSAT II and III, were used with conventional ground-gathering data to estimate planted crop areas for the 1978 Iowa corn and soybean crops. The use of satellite information significantly improved the results of estimates made from ground data alone.

LANDSAT is an *earth resources monitoring satellite* in a sun-synchronous polar orbit at an altitude of approximately 570 miles. A multispectral scanner on board measures radiant energy reflected and emitted in four bands of the electromagnetic spectrum for each 0.45 hectare (pixel) on the earth's surface. Twelve LANDSAT scenes are required to cover most of Iowa.

Cloud cover presents a problem in obtaining good data and could make timely estimates a problem. Estimates are more precise than ground-gathering data, but are not necessarily timely primarily due to both cloud-cover problems and processing/data reduction. The satellite data-reduction method uses random sampling to solve a regression equation and determines the total area yield.

M. E. Craig, R. S. Sigman, and M. Cardenas, *Area Estimates by LANDSAT: Kansas 1976 Winter Wheat,* SRS, USDA, 1978: In this study there is an interesting and detailed description of the sampling and regression methods used to determine production. The results showed that the use of LANDSAT data reduced the final variance by an average of 64% for an 87-county area.

M. E. Craig and C. E. Miller, *Area Estimates by LANDSAT: Arizona 1979,* SRS, USDA, 1980: A study of the estimation of cotton and soghum using LANDSAT proved to be very good.

AgRISTARS (Agricultural and Resources Inventory Surveys Through Aerospace Remote Sensing) Annual Report, NASA, 1981: An extension of the LANDSAT program, this report describes the goals of AgRISTARS to determine the feasiblity of satellite sensing in accumulating crop yields (global resources). It involves the following seven information requirements:

1. Early warning of change affecting production and quality of commodities and renewable resources.
2. Commodity production forecasts.
3. Land use classification and measurement.
4. Renewable resources inventory and assessment.
5. Land productivity estimates.
6. Conservation practices assessment.
7. Pollution detection and impact evaluation.

Based on the previous information requirements, the following projects were identified:

1. Early warning/crop condition assessment.
2. Foreign commodity production forecasting.
3. Yield model development.
4. Supporting research.
5. Soil moisture.
6. Domestic crops and land cover.
7. Renewable resources inventory.
8. Conservation and pollution.

CROP SPREADS

Since wheat is traded on futures markets in Chicago at both the Board of Trade and the MidAmerica exchanges, as well as in Kansas City, Minneapolis, Winnipeg, and even London, it is not surprising that many commercial users and speculators would watch price differences for spreading or arbitrage opportunities. Even though the contract specifications show that the type of deliverable wheat may be different on each exchange, there is often a close relationship between price movements.

One of the first elements required for a viable intermarket spread is liquidity of the markets. In 1982 each of the North American markets showed the following volume[7]:

Exchange	Wheat Traded	Volume (Contracts)
Chicago Board of Trade	Most wheat	4,031,584
MidAmerica Commodity Exchange	Same as CBT	243,640
Kansas City Board of Trade	Hard red winter wheat	964,815
Minneapolis Grain Exchange	Northern spring	346,226
Winnipeg Commodity Exchange	Domestic feed wheat	178,484 (20-ton lots, about 15,000 bushels) (1981)

When you consider the conversion of the 20-ton lot of Winnipeg volume to 15,000 bushels, all wheat markets are active and able to support substantial trading. Even the MidAmerica's wheat contract, which appears to have relatively small volume, survives on arbitrage between the Board of Trade's 5,000-bushel contract and its own 1,000-bushel contract. For a small cost of doing business, the MidAmerica wheat contract can be considered as liquid as the Board of Trade's contract.

The next ingredient of a grain spread is a common basis. Since half of the wheat grown in the United States is winter wheat, harvested in May and June, it is important to be sure that the same seasonal factors move the two or more markets which are being considered for a spread. Seasonality, a major factor in long-term price movement, must be common to the commodities in order to avoid serious divergence of prices.

DIVERGING PRICES. The primary reason for diverging wheat prices is the influence of *class buyers,* those who need a specific class of wheat for baking or other food processing. A *price buyer* is one who requires the lowest price, regardless of the type of wheat. The export market is a good example of both class and price buyers. The Soviet Union has been a buyer of hard red winter wheat, while the mills in South America and the Philippines often buy spring wheat. The Far Eastern countries of India, Pakistan, and even China have been interested in the lowest available price. These export preferences, as well as U.S. processor

[7]Futures Industry Association monthly volume report.

purchasing and changing patterns make up the key demand factors which determine spread relationships.[8]

The supply of different types of wheat must impact with the demand to determine price. Because wheat production is widespread there are often substantial shifts in both *intended* production and *actual* yields. The shifts in planting can be as high as 40% of a specific crop, as in 1978 when the size of the soft red winter wheat crop declined by that amount.

There are three areas of greatest wheat production in the United States, located in substantially diverse places. While Kansas is the center of wheat production, accounting for a substantial part of the total crop, Minnesota and Washington are also large producers relative to the total. It is very likely that yields will vary considerably based on local conditions and that supplies of a particular class of wheat grown in one of those three regions will vary without a comparable change in the other areas.

Government programs are another factor which affect spreads. The spring wheat crop, located primarily in North Dakota, is marketed in Minneapolis, Duluth, and on the West Coast. Producers must incur high freight costs, which they must absorb in order to compete with local prices. The net price to the producer results in a higher percentage of spring wheat being placed under the government loan program. This in turn can lead to tight free supplies of spring wheat, causing a change in its spread relationship.

World supplies of each class of wheat is a determining factor as well in spread relationships. Since Canada is our immediate neighbor and a primary supplier of high-quality wheat to the export market, a poor Canadian crop will place sharp demand on U.S. hard red winter wheat. This will have a significant affect on the wheat price relationships.

Although the Board of Trade contract accepts a broader range of deliverable wheat than the Kansas City contract, the two most active wheat markets are most likely to be watched the closest. Since Chicago, Kansas City, and Minneapolis all satisfy the requirements for intermarket spreading, they are favorites of many speculators.

OTHER SPREADS. In addition to the intermarket spreads there are two other popular wheat (and crop) spreads. The *old–new crop spread* has always been important since the fundamentals of economics require that old and new crop prices converge at harvest of the new crop. At that time the cumulative cost of carry is lost, since the old crop must compete with the new crop. Uncertainty in the size of harvest, however, usually keeps the price of the old crop above the new until just before accurate new crop figures are released.

Other popular spreads are *feed* and *protein* relationships, which assess the best buy of all grains for the purpose of feed rations. The value of corn, wheat, oats, barley, and so forth can be related by their protein ratios.

Traders often take advantage of the fact that wheat *seasonality* is different from corn. Buying wheat during June, traditionally the harvest lows, while selling new crop corn is a common intercrop spread. The expectation is that wheat is at lows and that the lifting of hedges will cause prices to rise. Hedging for the new

[8]"Inter-Market Wheat Spreads," Minneapolis Grain Exchange, 1982.

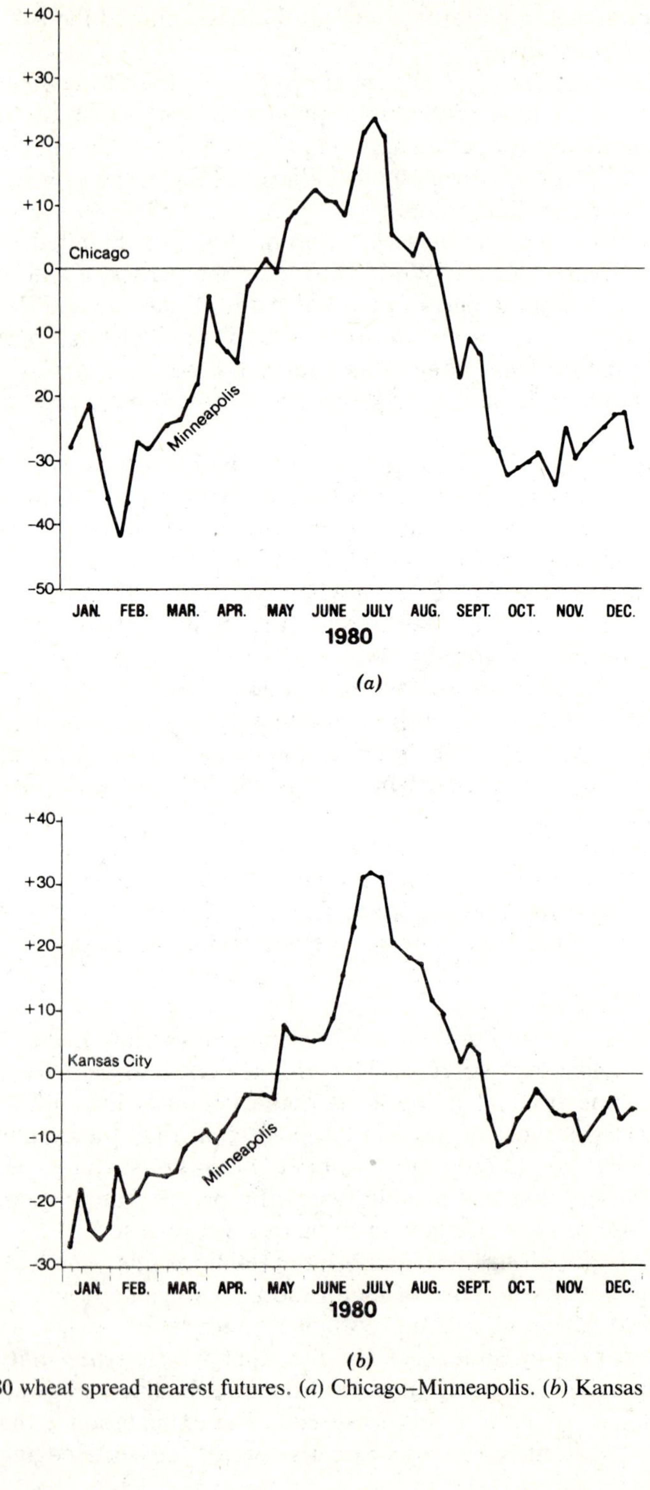

FIGURE 5. 1980 wheat spread nearest futures. (*a*) Chicago–Minneapolis. (*b*) Kansas City–Minneapolis.

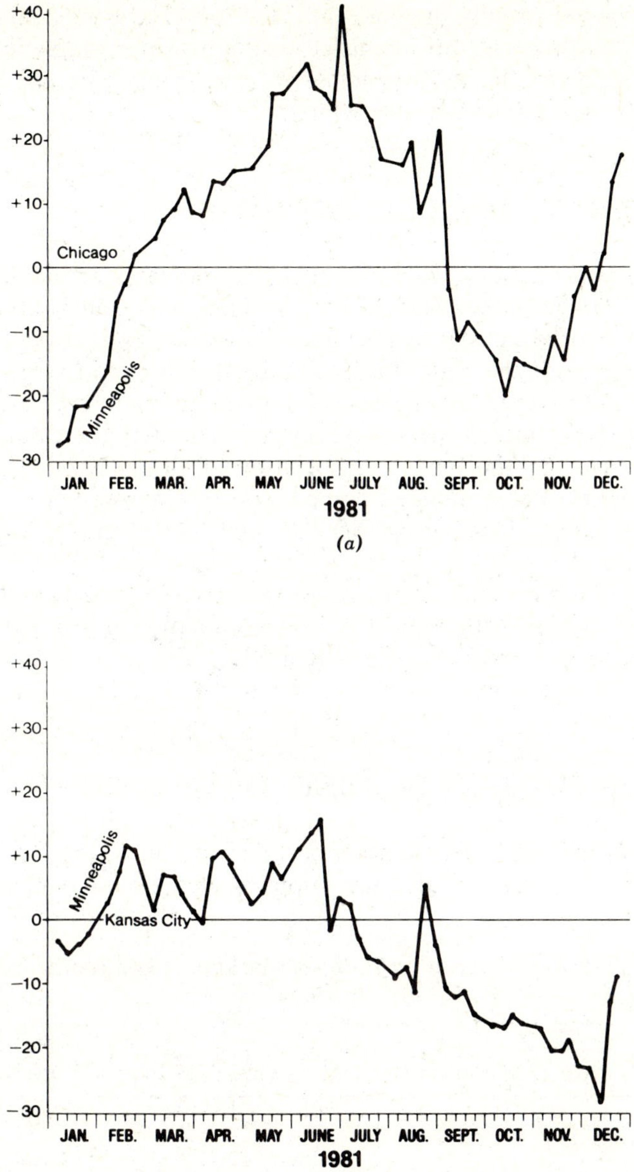

(b)

FIGURE 6. 1981 wheat spread nearest futures. (*a*) Chicago–Minneapolis. (*b*) Kansas City–Minneapolis.

wheat crop does not usually increase until the crop is put into the ground in the fall. At the same time that the wheat harvest is nearing completion, corn prices have not yet received the full impact of farm hedging. The expectation of the spread is that wheat prices will rise while corn prices will fall.

THE LONDON GRAIN FUTURES MARKET

The London grain markets are conducted in a manner similar to those in the United States. Trading takes place across a ring and all transactions are by open outcry. Official records are kept by the *Grain and Feed Trade Association* (GAFTA), which also determines the daily opening- and closing-price fixing.

The Grain Futures and Clearing House Committee is comprised of 13 members, two representing the futures market, seven nominated by the Council of GAFTA and two nominated by the British Association of Grain, Seed, Feed, and Agricultural Merchants. For a detailed comparison of clearing house functions, see M. Riess, Chapter 4, "Comparing the U.S. and U.K. Futures Markets" in this book.

The wheat and barley markets are viable within Great Britain and the European Economic Community. Although there are possibilities of arbitrage between the U.S. and U.K. wheat markets, the magnitude of business has never attracted much interest when complicated by the distance and policies of the EEC.

VOLUME OF FUTURES TRADING IN GRAINS

While grain and livestock once amounted to nearly all of the volume of trading on futures exchanges, recent burdening supplies and innovative new markets have

TABLE 2. Trading Volume on Futures Markets, 1982 (contracts of 5,000 bushels)

	CBT	MidAmerica[a]	Kansas City	London[b]	Minneapolis	New Orleans	Winnipeg[c,d]
Corn	7,948,257	274,324				971	
Flaxseed							425,865
Oats	424,595	12,981					154,209
Rapeseed							684,839
Rye							191,454
Soybean meal	2,784,423			14,099			
Wheat	4,031,584	243,640	964,815	n.a.[e]	346,226		178,484

Sources: Futures Industry Association monthly volume report, Winnipeg Commodity Exchange, International Commodity Clearing House (ICCH).

[a]1,000-bushel contract.

[b]100-ton lots, equivalent to approximately 75,000 bushels or 15 contracts.

[c]20-ton lots equivalent to approximately 15,000 bushels or three contracts.

[d]Data represents 1980–1981 crop year.

[e]n.a. = not applicable.

reduced its status among speculators. The volume of trading in all grain has declined sharply in the past few years, with corn falling another 30% from 1981 to 1982. This does not reduce the significance of futures trading in the marketing of corn as well as other grains. The futures markets are an integral part of the grain trade and will remain so as long as the United States retains its free market system (see Table 2).

SOURCES OF INFORMATION

The USDA publishes a wide variety of reports which relate to grain production and consumption. They are

Annual Summary (of crop production), third week in December.

Cattle or Feed (seven states), monthly.

Crop Production Report, monthly on the 10th of the month as of the first of the month.

Eggs, Chickens, and Turkeys Report, monthly.

Feed Situation Report, five times—February, April, May, August, and November.

Hogs and Pigs Report, March, June, September, and December.

Planting Intentions, mid-January and mid-April.

Prospective Planting Report, March 15.

Soybean Stocks, late September.

Stocks of Grains in All Positions Report, about the third week of the month as of the first of the month.

Weekly Grain Market News, including price changes, CCC sales, stocks, exports, all crop estimates, crop loan data, and domestic consumption.

Wheat Situation Report, March, May, August, and November. Current and historic analysis, narrative on fundamentals, recent developments, government programs, current outlook, future prospects, and the world situation.

Winter Wheat Seeding, late December.

The Department of Agriculture of the individual states as well provide information on the movement of crops, and in some cases, have more extensive reports. In addition, anyone can subscribe to the various reports of the *Chicago Board of Trade* which include daily prices, volume, open interest, cash prices, as well as historical supply-and-demand information. As a service to their customers, other exchanges provide daily price information upon request. Most U.S. exchanges publish an *Annual,* giving a complete recounting of prices, charts, and activity for the previous year. *Commodity Research Bureau* (Jersey City, NJ) provides a complete complement of statistics and charts for most commodities.

Information on *Canadian Grain Markets* is available as follows:

Statistics—Canadian Grain Commission, Statistics Branch, 280 Grain Exchange Building, Winnipeg, Manitoba, Canada R3B OT6.

Quarterly Summary—Winnipeg Commodity Exchange, 678 Grain Exchange Building, Winnipeg, Manitoba, Canada R3B OV7.

Annual Summary—Sanford Evans Service Limited, P.O.Box 6900, Winnipeg Manitoba, Canada R3C 3B1.

Crop Reports and Estimates—Dominion Bureau of Statistics, Ottowa, Canada.

Other reports on agriculture and food production are available from the Department of Industry, Trade and Commerce, Ottowa, Canada.

General *price information and news* on both U.S. and foreign markets are readily available in both the *Wall Street Journal* and the *Journal of Commerce*.

REFERENCES

Fulton, R. T. "The New Issues: Land, Water, Energy," *The Wilson Quarterly*, Summer 1981.

Labys, W. C. *Dynamic Commodity Models: Specification, Estimation, and Simulation*. Lexington, MA: Heath, 1973.

Labys, C., and Granger, C. W. J. *Speculation, Hedging and Commodity Price Forecasts*. Lexington, MA: Heath, 1973.

Schwager, J. D. "A Trader's Guide to Analyzing the Potato Futures Market," *1981 Commodity Yearbook*. Commodity Research Bureau, Incorporated. New York, NY:

Shepherd, G. S. *Agricultural Price Analysis*, 5th ed. Ames, IA: Iowa State Univ. Press, 1972.

Teweles, R. J., Harlow, C. V. and Stone, H. L. *The Commodity Futures Game, Who Wins? Who Loses? Why?* New York, NY: McGraw-Hill, 1974.

Weymar, F. H. *The Dynamics of the World Cocoa Market*. Cambridge, MA: MIT Press, 1968.

CHAPTER 26

WHEAT

CONTENTS

PRODUCTION	5	GOVERNMENT PROGRAMS	8
DEMAND	5	SEASONALITY	10
MARKETING	8	FUTURES MARKETS	11
PRICES	8		

CHAPTER 26

WHEAT

Donna Nielsen Murphy

Wheat is the most universal crop, grown in many countries around the world and harvested nearly every month of the year. The majority of wheat production is concentrated in the North Temperate Zone with extremely heavy concentration in Eastern Europe and adjacent parts of Russia. India and China as well are major producers. In the South Temperate Zone, Argentina and Australia are major producers.

Throughout history wheat has been one of the most valuable and widely grown cereal crops. Supposedly native to southwestern Asia, Egyptian stone carvings show farmers sowing and harvesting wheat, placing the cultivation of wheat at

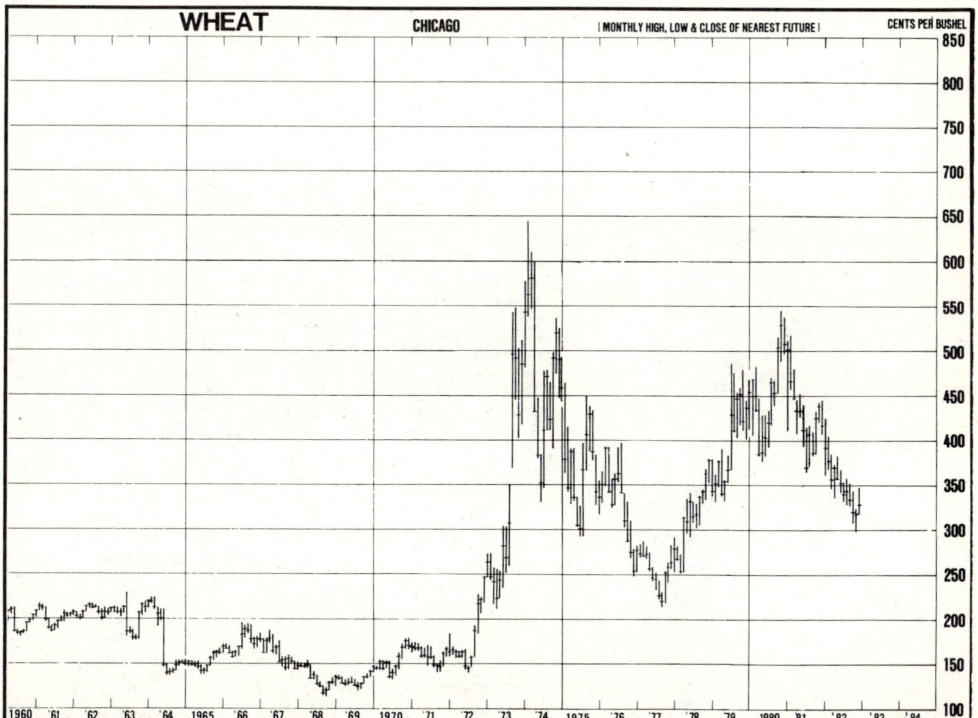

FIGURE 1. Wheat futures price—Chicago.

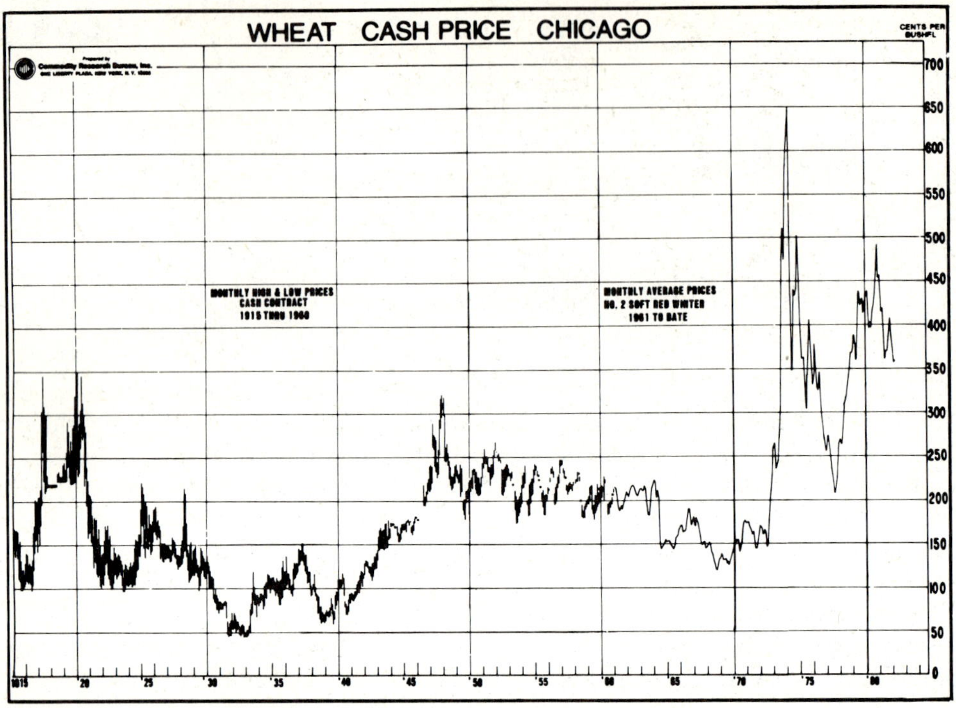

FIGURE 1. Continued. Wheat futures price—Chicago

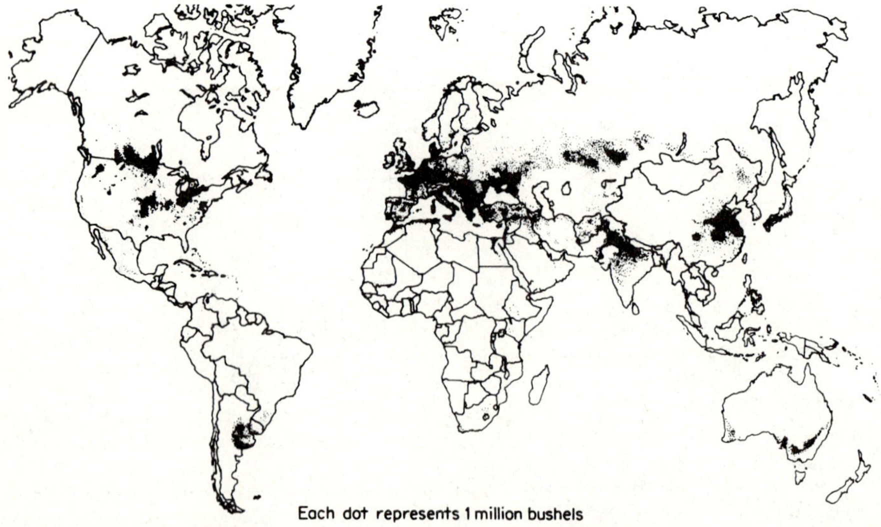

FIGURE 2. World wheat production. (*Source:* Teweles, Harlow, and Stone, *The Commodity Futures Game, Who Wins, Who Loses, Why?* McGraw-Hill, NY, 1974, p. 363.)

least 1,000 years ago. Wheat can be grown in all climates except the hottest parts of the tropical zone and the coldest areas of the frigid zones. The crop is best adapted to temperate regions, as hot, dry weather during the maturing period is important for high-quality wheat.

PRODUCTION

World production of wheat and wheat flour in 1980–1981 totaled 438.7 million metric tons—up 0.04% from the previous year. The Soviet Union is the world's largest producer of wheat, producing 98.1 million metric tons during the 1980–1981 crop year. Nevertheless, during that period the Soviet Union was a net importer of 15.5 million metric tons. The United States produced 64.5 million metric tons of wheat, 41.9 of which were exported. China produced 54.2 million metric tons of wheat; India, 31.6; Canada, 19.2; and Australia, 10.8 million metric tons during the 1980–1981 crop year.

Wheat is a member of the grass family. Its kernels grow in dense heads on top of slender, hollow stalks. The most important types of wheat grown are *common, durum,* and *club*. The kernels of common wheat may be red or white, hard or soft. The hard wheats, highest in protein, are the best bread wheats. In the United States and Canada, common wheat is also classified as winter and spring wheat. About half the wheat produced in the United States is winter wheat, so called because it is planted in the fall and lies dormant all winter long, hopefully covered by a blanket of insulating snow. Depending upon location, the crop is harvested in late May, June, or July. *Hard red winter wheat* is grown in Kansas, Nebraska, Oklahoma, and the Texas Panhandle—regions with low precipitation and cold winters. *Soft red winter wheat* is grown in the central Texas, Great Lakes, and Atlantic Coast regions—areas with higher annual precipitation rates. The North Central states usually grow varieties of hard red spring wheat because their winters are too harsh to produce winter wheat. These crops are harvested in August and September.

Durum wheat is grown in North Dakota, South Dakota, and Minnesota. Durum wheat kernels are hard, high in protein, and naturally resistant to yield-reducing rust diseases. Durum wheat is used in making pasta products. The *club* or *white wheat* crop is a relatively small proportion of all wheat produced. Both winter and spring varieties exist, and are grown in Michigan, New York, and on the Pacific Coast. Club wheat is a soft wheat used chiefly to make crackers and pastries.

North Dakota is the largest wheat-producing state, producing 332 million bushels during the 1980–1981 crop year. Kansas produced 305 million bushels; Texas, 183 million bushels; and Oklahoma and Montana each produced 173 million bushels.

DEMAND

Most of the world's wheat is milled into flour for use in bread and pastries. Wheat is also used to make pastas and breakfast foods, in brewing, in the manufacture of whiskey, and in the production of industrial alcohol. Starch from wheat is used

TABLE 1. World Production of Wheat (in Thousands of Metric Tons)[a]

Crop Year	Argentina	Australia	Canada	China	France	West Germany	India	Italy	Pakistan	Spain	Turkey	United Kingdom	USSR	United States	World Total[b]
1961–1962	190	246	283	n.a.[d]	352	148	404	305	141	126	225	196	1,900	1,232	7,880
1962–1963	190	307	566	n.a.	509	168	442	349	149	177	250	146	2,000	1,092	8,760
1963–1964	328	328	723	n.a.	377	178	398	299	155	179	290	112	1,470	1,147	8,315
1964–1965	415	369	600	n.a.	508	191	362	315	154	146	257	129	2,100	1,283	9,327
1965–1966	228	260	649	808	542	160	452	359	170	173	273	153	1,700	1,316	9,075
1966–1967	234	462	827	764	415	167	394	346	146	177	301	128	2,939	1,312	10,276
1967–1968[a]	7,320	7,547	16,137	24,500	14,287	5,644	11,393	9,596	4,393	5,650	9,000	3,902	64,200	41,030	278,516
1968–1969	5,740	14,804	17,685	22,000	14,985	6,012	16,540	9,655	6,477	5,477	8,400	3,469	76,500	42,365	307,185
1969–1970	7,020	10,546	18,623	23,000	14,459	5,820	18,652	9,585	6,711	4,624	8,300	3,364	62,300	39,263	287,739
1970–1971	4,250	7,890	9,023	24,500	12,922	5,492	20.093	9,689	7,399	4,060	8,000	4,236	82,700	36,783	291,108
1971–1972	5,680	8,651	14,412	24,000	15,360	7,142	23,832	10,070	6,476	5,457	10,700	4,815	98,760	44,029	322,562
1972–1973	6,800	6,510	14,514	26,000	18,123	6,410	26,410	9,423	6,889	4,562	9,500	4,761	85,993	42,046	331,056
1973–1974	6,560	12,094	16,459	28,000	17,792	7,134	24,735	8,900	7,800	3,915	8,000	5,003	109,784	46,407	371,600
1974–1975	5,970	11,357	13,295	37,000	19,142	7,761	22,072	9,697	7,800	4,534	8,300	6,130	83,849	48,797	356,410
1975–1976	8,570	12,024	17,078	40,000	15,013	7,014	24,104	9,610	7,673	4,302	11,500	4,488	66,224	58,078	350,057
1976–1977	11,000	11,700	23,587	50,500	16,150	6,702	28,846	9,528	8,691	4,436	13,000	4,740	96,883	58,500	421,200
1977–1978	5,700	9,400	19,900	41,000	17,046	7,126	29,082	6,650	9,100	3,988	13,500	5,267	92,200	55,700	384,200
1978–1979	8,100	18,100	21,100	54,000	21,056	8,118	31,700	9,191	8,400	4,795	13,300	6,615	120,800	48,300	446,600
1979–1980[b]	8,100	16,100	17,200	62,500	18,695	7,970	35,500	8,800	9,900	4,191	13,000	6,800	90,200	58,100	422,000
1980–1981[c]	7,800	11,000	19,100	57,000			31,600		10,800		13,800		98,100	64,500	441,700
1981–1982[c]	7,800	16,400	24,500	57,500			36,500		11,400		13,200		88,000	76,025	425,300

Source: U.S. Department of Agriculture, Foreign Agricultural Service. [a]Data prior to 1967–1968 are in millions of bushels. [b]Preliminary. [c]Estimated. [d]n.a. = not available.

TABLE 2. Stocks, Production, and Exports of Wheat, by Classes (in Millions of Bushels)

Year Beginning July	Hard Spring			Durum[b]			Hard Winter			Red Winter			White		
	July 1st Stocks	Production	Exports[a]	July 1st Stocks	Production	Exports[a]	July 1st Stocks	Production	Exports[a]	July 1st Stocks	Production	Exports[a]	July 1st Stocks	Production	Exports[a]
1961–1962	237	116	42	20	21	16	1,104	754	487	12	202	56	38	139	119
1962–1963	187	179	39	5	70	4	1,085	535	437	24	156	40	21	152	122
1963–1964	195	168	48	46	52	29	936	544	562	5	218	84	13	165	136
1964–1965	180	180	25	41	68	9	670	635	499	4	222	80	6	178	112
1965–1966	196	209	86	68	70	34	536	673	595	7	185	45	10	179	107
1966–1967	185	177	120	54	63	47	268	678	377	8	217	68	20	177	132
1967–1968	132	230	71	29	66	31	234	706	375	15	274	121	15	246	163
1968–1969	178	228	77	24	100	46	279	811	271	30	224	50	28	214	100
1969–1970	210	190	89	41	108	34	475	785	336	33	186	28	58	174	119
1970–1971	178	198	113	80	53	39	574	755	450	23	174	26	30	171	110
1971–1972	146	366	104	58	92	44	492	747	337	15	212	43	20	201	104
1972–1973	275	276	198	69	73	65	471	761	704	18	226	68	30	209	151
1973–1974	212	328	245	45	79	45	287	957	775	25	159	27	30	182	125
1974–1975	87	293	130	33	81	47	170	883	510	23	273	136	27	252	195
1975–1976	104	327	160	26	123	52	225	1,058	581	37	326	165	43	288	215
1976–1977	116	411	124	53	135	41	379	976	418	57	336	181	60	284	186
1977–1978	250	399	156	92	80	62	606	997	535	72	349	197	93	221	174
1978–1979	335	380	232	67	133	72	632	830	610	71	189	95	73	244	185
1979–1980[c]	320	363	217	86	106	83	423	1,089	725	27	317	154	68	259	196
1980–1981[d]	285	311	185	61	108	65	440	1,185	755	40	428	290	76	338	230
1981–1982[d]	244			55			470			23			117		

Source: U.S. Department of Agriculture, Economic Research Service. [a]Includes flour made from U.S. wheat and shipments to territories. [b]Includes "red durum." [c]Preliminary. [d]Estimate.

as fabric sizing. Bran, shorts, and middlings—the by-products of flour mills— are used chiefly as stock feed. Wheat straw is used as a bedding for livestock and is made into paper and cardboard.

Table 3 shows the distribution of demand for wheat. Of the total disappearance of wheat in the United States two-thirds are exports. The use of wheat for food within the United States, primarily as flour, accounts for only 25% of the total, and its use as a feed accounts for only about 6%.

MARKETING

Although intermediary steps are sometimes bypassed, wheat produced in the United States is usually sold by farmers to country elevators, which quickly turn over the grain to larger terminal elevators. Storage is generally highest at the beginning of the crop year, which runs from June to May, and lowest at the end of the crop year. Terminal elevators sell to millers, who grind the wheat into flour for use by food processors, such as bakeries and cereal manufacturers, as well as for use directly by the consumer. They also sell to elevators located at ports, from which wheat is shipped throughout the world. Of the 2,374 million bushels of wheat produced during the 1980–1981 crop year, 1,510 million bushels, or 64% were exported.

PRICES

The factor having the most immediate impact on the price of wheat is weather, as evidenced by the 1980 drought. Other longer-term factors include changes in production and consumption in countries throughout the world, size of wheat inventories, government price-support programs, and changes in foreign currency exchange rates. Political factors such as embargoes or wars involving major importing or exporting countries are also important. The grain embargo imposed against the Soviet Union from January 4, 1980 to April 24, 1981 is a case in point. The event which has had the greatest impact on wheat prices during the past 20 years was the 1973–1974 Russian grain purchase.

From 1977 to 1981 the average monthly price of Kansas City No. 1 Hard Red Winter Wheat varied from $2.31 per bushel in June and August 1977 to $4.60 per bushel in January 1981. That high is still below the average monthly price record set in February 1974, that is, $5.82 per bushel. (See Figure 1.)

GOVERNMENT PROGRAMS

The *Agriculture and Food Act of 1981* established minimum target levels for certain commodities over the next 4 years; specific support levels are determined at the discretion of the Secretary of Agriculture. The 1982 crop-year target price for wheat was $4.05 per bushel. When the 5-month weighted-average price for wheat is less than $4.05 per bushel, the government will make deficiency payments equal to the difference between the target price and the market price or the loan rate,

TABLE 3. Supply and Distribution of Wheat in the United States (in Millions of Bushels)

Year Beginning July	Supply							Domestic Disappearance							
	Stocks, July 1st										Feed				
	On Farms	Mills, Elevators[a]	Commodity Credit Corporation	Total Stocks	Production	Imports[b]	Total Supply	Food	Seed	Industry	Residuals	(On Farms Where Grown)	Total Domestic Disappearance	Exports	Total Disappearance
1961–1962	137.1	1,203.7	70.6	1,411.3	1,232.4	5.7	2,649	501.5	56.4	0.1	50.1	(22.4)	608.0	719.4	1,327
1962–1963	102.4	1,160.0	59.5	1,322.0	1,092.0	5.4	2,419	500.4	61.4	0.1	18.4	(16.1)	580.3	643.8	1,224
1963–1964	95.5	1,061.4	38.3	1,195.2	1,146.8	3.9	2,346	503.3	65.0	0.1	20.2	(15.2)	588.5	856.1	1,445
1964–1965	75.7	813.0	12.7	901.4	1,283.4	1.1	2,186	509.2	65.6	0.1	68.8	(31.4)	643.7	725.0	1,369
1965–1966	132.5	673.7	11.0	817.3	1,315.6	0.9	2,134	515.4	61.9	0.1	153.9	(41.7)	731.3	867.4	1,599
1966–1967	130.8	394.9	9.5	535.2	1,304.0	1.8	1,842	501.9	78.4	0.1	92.6	(26.1)	673.1	744.3	1,417
1967–1968	144.9	278.5	1.0	424.4	1,507.6	0.9	1,933	519.2	71.5	0.1	42.6	(42.9)	633.3	761.1	1,394
1968–1969	229.5	308.3	0.7	630.2	1,556.6	1.0	2,188	522.4	60.9	0.1	156.3	(60.8)	739.7	544.2	1,284
1969–1970	325.9	490.0	0.8	904.0	1,442.7	2.8	2,350	520.1	55.6	0.5	187.7	(61.0)	763.9	603.0	1,367
1970–1971	307.1	576.6	1.2	982.6	1,351.5	1.5	2,336	517.2	62.1	0.1	192.6	(62.0)	772.0	740.8	1,513
1971–1972	240.3	489.4	1.8	822.8	1,618.6	1.1	2,442	523.7	63.2	0.1	262.3	(71.7)	849.3	609.7	1,459
1972–1973	355.1	506.3	1.8	983.4	1,546.2	1.3	2,531	531.8	67.4	0.1	199.5	(47.0)	798.8	1,135.0	1,934
1973–1974	133.9	302.8	1.8	597.1	1,710.8	2.6	2,311	544.3	84.1	—	125.1	(31.5)	753.5	1,217.0	1,971
1974–1975	89.5	157.9	0.3	340.1	1,781.9	3.4	2,125	545.0	92.0	—	— 34.9—		671.9	1,018.5	1,690
1975–1976	132.7	194.3	—	435.0	2,126.9	2.4	2,564	588.6	99.0	0.1	— 38.1—		725.8	1,172.9	1,859
1976–1977	235.5	429.8	—	665.6	2,148.8	2.7	2,817	588.0	92.0	0.1	— 74.3—		754.4	949.5	1,704
1977–1978	426.3	685.9	—	1,113.2	2,045.5	1.9	3,161	586.5	80.0	0.1	—192.4—		859.0	1,123.9	1,983
1978–1979	492.9	683.8	—	1,176.7	1,775.5	1.9	2,955	591.8	87.0	0.1	—158.1—		837.0	1,194.1	2,031
1979–1980[c]	484.3	439.8	—	924.1	2,134.1	2.1	3,060	595.3	101.0	—	— 86.7—		783.1	1,375.2	2,158
1980–1981[d]	376.5	525.5	—	902.0	2,370.2	2.5	3,274	605.0	110.0	—	—125.0—		840.0	1,525.0	2,365
1981–1982[d]	414.3	574.5	—	988.8	2,793.4	2.0	3,784	625.0	112.0	—	—135.0—		872.0	1,850.0	2,722

Source: U.S. Department of Agriculture, Economic Research Service. [a]Also warehouses and all off-farm storage not otherwise designated, including flour mills. [b]Imports and exports are for wheat, including flour and other products in terms of wheat. [c]Preliminary. [d]Estimated.

whichever is higher. In return, the participating farmer must agree to reduce acreage planted by 15%, decreasing the total amount of wheat available to the market.

The level for regular loans for 1982 was set at $3.55 per bushel. When the price of wheat declines to this level, the participating grower may take out a 9-month loan at a subsidized interest rate. The purpose of the loan is to allow the participant to repay basic operating costs, enabling the participant to market the wheat later in the year when the markets are expected to be less congested. At the end of 9 months, the farmer may either repay the loan plus interest, surrender the crop to the Commodity Credit Corporation with the interest forgiven, or enter into the reserve loan program. In the reserve loan program, the producer signs a 3-year contract under which the producer receives a loan for $4 per bushel and agrees to store the grain for 3 years, or until the cash price reaches the trigger-level release price of $4.65 per bushel. The government pays the grower an annual storage fee of $0.265 per bushel. Interest on the loan is charged the first year, and waived during subsequent years. Should the trigger-level release price be reached, the farmer may repay the loan plus interest. If the national 5-day moving-average price continues above the trigger level after the initial release period (the remainder of the month in which the reserve is triggered plus one additional month), growers will stop earning storage payments and interest charges will resume, encouraging the farmer to repay the loan.

At the end of the 3-year period, the farmer may choose to repay the loan plus interest, to surrender the crop to the Commodity Credit Corporation, or to extend the contract for an additional 2 years.

SEASONALITY

The seasonal adjustment factor tends to follow the expected pattern of the winter crop each year, as demonstrated in the accompanying charts of the cash and nearby futures Chicago wheat markets. When the winter wheat harvest begins in June, the Great Lakes terminal elevators are anxious to buy the wheat and ship it to fulfill export commitments before the St. Lawrence Seaway is closed in December. Wheat is at a competitive advantage to other crops vis-à-vis storage space since it is the first major crop harvested. During the period when the Seaway is closed little activity occurs in the sideways trading market. In March through June the price trends downward as the Australian and Argentine export markets predominate.

Each individual futures contract also demonstrates seasonal trends. For example, both the July and December Chicago futures contracts trend downward from February through May, and upward thereafter to October. These trends may be mitigated or exaggerated by optimistic crop reports, drought, disease, and the export outlook. As is the case with all seasonal charts, these futures charts are meant to act only as guides and should not be used as definitive indicators of direction.

It is interesting to note that the futures market precedes the cash market by 1 month for lows and more than 1 month for the highs. This means that there are severe basis moves in the market. The sharpest move occurs in the futures market

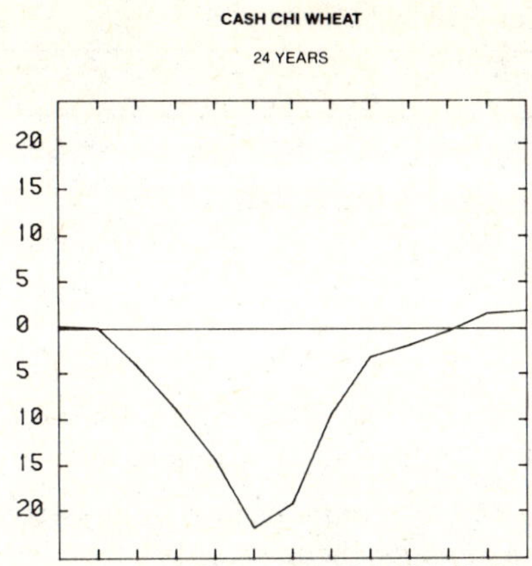

	J-F	F-M	M-A	A-M	M-J	J-J	J-A	A-S	S-O	O-N	N-D	D-J
Average Move	-0.2	-4.2	-4.7	-5.6	-7.4	2.6	9.7	6.2	1.2	1.5	1.9	0.2
% Reliable	50	50	50	62.5	70.9	50	66.7	83.4	75	83.4	62.5	62.5
Avg. Up Move	5.5	4.1	3.3	5.4	13.5	11.7	22.1	8.7	6.9	5.2	7.9	6.1
Avg. Down Move	5	11.7	12.8	11.4	16	6.4	9.6	6.3	14.7	15.5	6.4	8.2
Greatest Up Move	24	9	9	12	46	38	177	34	59	25	44	46
Greatest Down Move	22	81	94	48	62	13.3	42	20	34	38	22	51

(*a*)

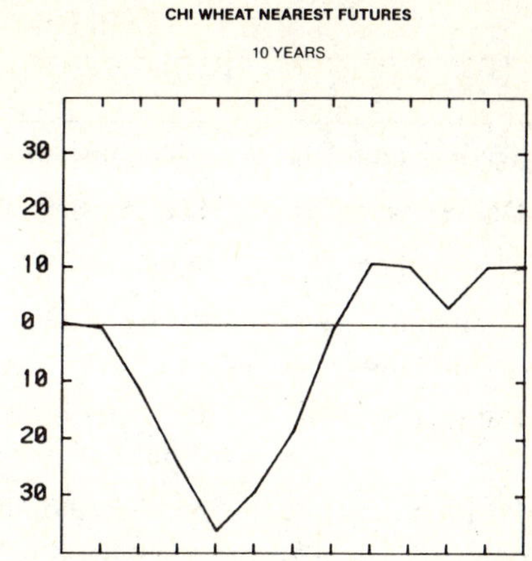

	J-F	F-M	M-A	A-M	M-J	J-J	J-A	A-S	S-O	O-N	N-D	D-J
Average Move	-0.9	-10.9	-12.8	-11.8	6.9	10.8	17.5	11.6	-0.7	-7.2	7.2	0.1
% Reliable	70	70	70	70	50	50	40	90	30	50	60	60
Avg. Up Move	14.8	5.2	4.2	7.9	19.7	25	61.7	13.6	12.3	7.5	16.4	11.4
Avg. Down Move	7.6	17.8	20.2	20.2	6	3.4	12	6.4	30.9	21.9	6.7	16.7
Greatest Up Move	21	11.8	7.3	18.4	48.1	44.4	162.9	29.5	63.8	12.1	49	51.2
Greatest Down Move	22.3	78.7	88.6	62.4	8.5	7.7	40.4	6.4	43.4	50.8	13.8	63.4

(*b*)

FIGURE 3. Wheat seasonality. (*a*) Cash Chicago wheat, 24 years. (*b*) Chicago wheat nearest futures, 10 years. (*Source:* Gruschcow and Smith, *Profits Through Seasonal Trading*, John Wiley and Sons, NY, 1980.)

where prices have large, although unreliable, movements up from July through September. At the same time the cash market has a smaller, but much more consistent, upwards move.

FUTURES MARKETS

Futures contracts in wheat are traded at the Chicago Board of Trade, the MidAmerica Commodity Exchange, the Minneapolis Grain Exchange, the Kansas City Board of Trade as well as the Winnipeg Commodity Exchange and London Grain Futures Market. Specifications are listed in Table 4.

The specifications are written to ensure that they closely mirror cash market conditions, and the months of trading are usually selected because of their significance in the crop marketing year. When a far month trades at a premium to a nearby month which exceeds the cost of carrying (storage, interest, and insurance) the physical commodity between the 2 months, the market is bullish on long-term prices. When the difference between the nearby and far months does not cover carrying charge, the market is bearish on long-term prices. An inverted market occurs when the nearby actually trades at a premium. New crop months (those months beginning with June of the subsequent year) generally trade at a premium to the prior months of old crop, although new crop may fall to a discount on reports of slackening demand or bountiful supply.

TABLE 4. Contract Specifications

	CBT
Trading unit	5,000 bushels
Delivery months	March, May, July, September, and December
Trading hours	9:30 a.m.–1:15 p.m. central time
Minimum fluctuation	¼¢ per bushel
Daily price limit	$0.20 per bushel above or below previous day's settlement price; limit expands by 50% after three successive limit days.
Position limit	Net 3 million bushels in any one future or in all futures combined. Limits do not apply to *bona fide* hedgers.
Delivery grade	No. 2 Soft Red, No. 2 Hard Red Winter, No. 2 Dark Northern Spring, and No. 1 Northern Spring is deliverable at par. No. 1 Soft Red, No. 1 Hard Red Winter, and No. 1 Dark Northern Spring is deliverable at a $0.01 per bushel premium. No. 3 Soft Red, No. 3 Hard Red Winter, No. 3 Dark Northern Spring, and No. 2 Northern Spring is deliverable at a $0.01 per bushel discount. Wheat containing moisture in excess of 13.5% is not deliverable.
Delivery	Delivery is made via a warehouse receipt issued by an exchange-approved elevator in Chicago at par, and in Toledo at a $0.02 per bushel discount.
	MidAmerica Commodity Exchange
Trading unit	1,000 bushels
Delivery months	March, May, July, September, and December
Trading hours	9:30 a.m.–1:30 p.m. central time
Minimum fluctuation	⅛¢ per bushel
Daily price limit	$0.20 per bushel above or below previous day's settlement price; limit expands by 50% after three successive limit days.
Position limit	Net 3 million bushels in any one future or in all futures combined. Limits do not apply to *bona fide* hedgers.
Delivery grade	No. 2 Soft Red, No. 2 Hard Red Winter, No. 2 Dark Northern Spring, and No. 1 Northern Spring is deliverable at par. No. 1 Soft Red, No. 1 Hard Red Winter, and No. 1 Dark Northern Spring is deliverable at a $0.01 per bushel premium. No. 3 Soft Red, No. 3 Hard Red Winter, No. 3 Dark Northern Spring, and No. 2 Northern Spring is deliverable at a $0.01 per bushel discount. Wheat containing moisture in excess of 13.5% is not deliverable.
Delivery	Delivery is made via a warehouse receipt issued by an exchange-approved elevator in Chicago at par, and in Toledo at a $0.02 per bushel discount.

TABLE 4. Continued

Minneapolis Grain Exchange	
Trading unit	5,000 bushels (1,000-bushel trading is permitted)
Delivery months	March, May, July, September, and December
Trading hours	9:30 a.m.–1:15 p.m. central time
Minimum fluctuation	¼¢ per bushel
Daily price limit	$0.20 per bushel above or below previous day's settlement price; limit expands by 50% after three successive limit days.
Position limit	Net 3 million bushels in any one future or all futures combined. Limits do not apply to *bona fide* hedgers.
Delivery grade	No. 1 Northern Spring, No. 2 Northern Spring, No. 1 Dark Northern Spring, 13.5% protein or higher at contract price; 13.0–13.4% protein at $0.03 discount. Grades with test weight of 60 lb or more per bushel are deliverable at $0.02 premium. Maximum allowable moisture is 13.5%.
Delivery	Delivery is made via a warehouse receipt issued by an exchange-approved elevator in the Minneapolis–St. Paul Switching and Barge Districts, and on the Duluth–Superior waterfront.
Kansas City Board of Trade	
Trading unit	5,000 bushels
Delivery months	March, May, July, September, and December
Trading hours	9:30 a.m.–1:15 p.m. central time
Minimum fluctuation	¼¢ per bushel
Daily price limit	$0.25 per bushel above or below previous day's settlement price
Position limit	Net 3 million bushels in any one future or in all futures combined. Limits do not apply to *bona fide* hedgers.
Delivery grade	No. 2 Hard Red Winter Wheat is deliverable at par. No. 1 Hard Red Winter is deliverable at a 1½¢ per bushel premium, and No. 3 Hard Red Winter at a 1½¢ discount.
Delivery	Delivery is made via warehouse receipt issued by an exchange-approved elevator in the Kansas City, Missouri–Kansas Switching District.
Winnipeg Commodity Exchange	
Trading unit	100-tonne board lot, 20-tonne job lot (in Canadian dollars per tonne)
Delivery months	October, December, March, May, and July
Trading hours	9:30 a.m.–1:15 p.m. central time

TABLE 4. Continued

Winnipeg Commodity Exchange	
Minimum fluctuation	\$0.10 per tonne
Daily price limit	\$5 per tonne
Position limit	None
Delivery grade	No. 3 CWRS, or No. 1 CU at \$3.50 per tonne discount, or No. 2 CU at \$5 per tonne discount, or Canada feed at \$6.50 discount.
Delivery	Thunder Bay, Ontario
London Grain Futures Market	
Trading unit	100 long tons (2,240 lb) or about 3,863 bushels
Delivery months	September, November, January, March, and May, through the 22nd of the delivery month
Trading hours	11:00 a.m.–12:30 p.m. and 2:45 p.m.–4:00 p.m.
Minimum fluctuation	£0.05 (pounds sterling) per ton
Daily price limit	None
Position limits	None
Delivery grade	Conforms to European Economic Community Standards: **1.** Wheat is to be sound and sweet and is to contain not more than 3% heat damage. **2.** Natural weight not less than 58 lb per bushel. **3.** Moisture content not to exceed 15.5%. **4.** Admixture: a. Seeds, farinaceous grains, and dirt not to exceed 2%; dirt not to exceed 1%. b. Ergot and garlic not to exceed 0.001%. **5.** Sprouted grains not to exceed 2%.
Delivery	From storage approved by the Clearing House Committee of the GAFTA and to be located within the mainland of Great Britain.

CHAPTER 27

CORN

CONTENTS

PRODUCTION	3	GOVERNMENT PROGRAMS	10
USES	6	SEASONALITY	11
MARKETING	6	FUTURES MARKETS	12
PRICES	6		

CHAPTER **27**

CORN

Donna Nielsen Murphy

There is evidence that the cultivation of maize or corn in Mexico dates as far back as 5000 B.C. making it one of the earliest of cultivated foods. Corn is unique among products grown as cereals; it is the only one originating in the Western Hemisphere. It was unknown to the rest of the world until 1492 when Columbus returned to Europe with samples of corn. After that it rapidly spread throughout Europe and within 50 years had reached as far as China.

Corn has undergone major changes in both genetics and production. *Hybridization* of various strains of corn has produced new types of seed which accentuate either endurance to extreme weather or soil conditions or bring out the specific quality of the kernel which are important for the end user. The *high-fructose* content now possible in new strains of corn has caused the rapid expansion of the corn-sweetener industry.

A *corn hybrid* is the first-generation cross between two or more inbreds. An *inbred* strain is the result of continued self-pollenation, facilitated by placing a paper bag over the ear so that no stray pollen can fall on the silks. These ears are pollenated by hand from their own tassels at the proper time. By repeating this process for a number of generations the particular traits of that corn strain are firmly fixed. Although an inbred corn tends to be small, a hybrid resulting from the cross-pollenation of two inbreds will produce a large, healthy plant. Recent research in corn hybrids has caused a dramatic increase in yields and opened new markets.

Changes in the harvesting of corn have also helped the industry. Although much of corn harvesting still leaves the corn on the ear, as it had years ago, combine harvesting of corn includes field shelling. The harvesting operation is faster with less loss from brittle field-dried ears. The higher moisture, the result of earlier harvest, however, has caused greater demands on elevator storage and drying facilities. Shelled corn cannot be placed in the traditional open cribs where it would be exposed to changes in weather, as well as to insects, birds, and rodents.

PRODUCTION

Corn has been a staple of the American diet since long before the first colonists settled in the New World. A member of the grass family, corn requires a temperate climate, fertile soil, and a good deal of moisture during the growing season. Nearly

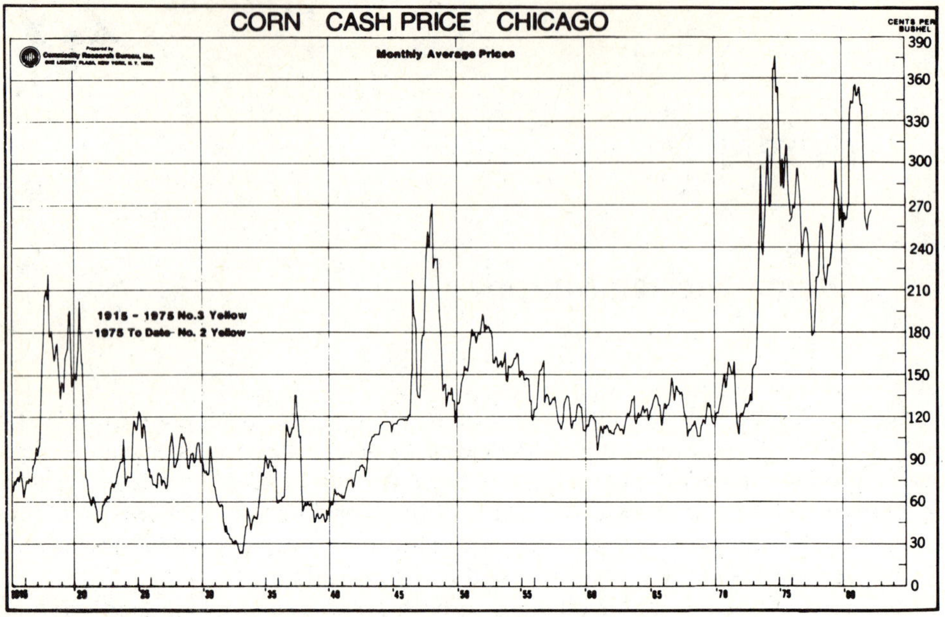

FIGURE 1. Corn cash price—Chicago.

75% of the U.S. corn crop is grown in the *Corn Belt* states, comprised of Iowa, Illinois, Indiana, Minnesota, Nebraska, Ohio, and Missouri.

Corn is classified according to the characteristics of the kernels. The most important kinds of corn are dent, flint, sweet, pop, flour, and pod corn. *Dent corn* is so named because of the the dent that appears in the crown of each kernel when the soft starch under the surface shrinks at maturity. The white or yellow kernels are wedge-shaped. Dent corn is a popular animal feed and accounts for about 90% of all corn planted. *Flint corn* is named for the flinty coat on its kernels. These kernels are smaller and rounder than dent corn kernels, and may be white, yellow, orange, brown, or purple in color. Flint corn is harder than dent corn, and is grown at the northern and southern limits of corn cultivation. *Sweet corn* contains much more sugar than other types of corn and is grown for human consumption. *Popcorn* kernels have an extremely hard coat. When the kernels are heated their hard coats resist the expansion of their soft interiors until so much pressure is built up that the kernels explode and are turned outward. Popcorn yields poorly when compared to other types of corn, but commands a higher price. *Flour corn* has soft, starchy kernels that are easy to grind with primitive means. Flour corn may be white, black, red, or purple in color and is popular with Indians in the southwestern United States. With *pod corn*, each kernel is enclosed in a separate husk. It has no commercial value.

The United States is by far the world's largest producer of corn, producing 185 million metric tons of corn during the 1980–1981 crop year, or 46% of the world total of 402 million metric tons. China was the second largest producer at 58.5 million metric tons, followed by Brazil, 20; Argentina, 11.2; and South Africa and Romania, which each produced 10.5 million metric tons.

TABLE 1. World Production of Corn or Maize (in Millions of Metric Tons)[a]

Crop Year	United States	Argentina	Brazil	Mexico	South Africa	France	China	India	Italy	Bulgaria	Hungary	Yugoslavia	Roumania	Indonesia	USSR	World Total
1961–2	3,598	210	373	219	220	1963–	1960–	168	155	45	107	179	215	91	500	7,465
1962–3	3,606	180	400	215	240		1964	180	128	61	128	208	194	126	385	7,470
1963–4	4,019	211	370	253	168	(3.6)[d]		179	136	68	140	212	237	105	335	8,060
1964–5	3,484	202	465	295	177		(425)[e]	179	156	81	138	274	263	161	360	7,835
1965–6[a]	104.2	7.0	11.4	8.0	5.1	3.4	21.4	4.8	3.3	1.2	3.6	5.9	5.9	2.4	6.4	218.9
1966–7	105.9	8.0	12.8	8.2	9.6	4.3	21.7	4.9	3.5	2.2	3.9	8.0	8.0	3.7	6.8	239.4
1967–8	123.5	6.6	12.8	8.0	5.2	4.2	25.5	6.3	3.9	2.0	3.5	7.2	6.9	2.4	8.0	253.5
1968–9	113.0	6.9	12.7	8.5	5.0	5.4	23.5	5.7	4.0	1.8	3.8	6.8	7.1	3.1	7.4	243.3
1969–0	119.1	9.4	14.2	6.5	6.2	5.7	24.3	5.7	4.5	2.4	4.8	7.8	7.7	2.3	10.1	260.0
1970–1	105.5	9.9	13.5	8.7	8.6	7.6	26.4	7.5	4.8	2.4	4.0	6.9	6.5	2.9	7.8	255.1
1971–2	143.3	5.9	12.9	9.1	9.4	8.8	25.3	5.1	4.5	2.5	4.7	7.4	7.9	2.6	8.6	292.1
1972–3	141.6	9.0	13.8	8.1	4.2	8.2	22.0	6.2	4.8	2.9	5.5	7.9	9.5	2.0	9.8	286.3
1973–4	143.4	9.9	15.0	9.0	11.1	10.7	28.0	5.8	5.1	2.6	5.9	8.3	7.4	2.9	13.2	314.7
1974–5	118.5	7.7	16.4	7.8	9.1	8.7	30.7	5.6	5.0	1.6	6.2	8.0	7.4	3.0	12.1	286.5
1975–6	147.3	5.9	17.9	9.2	7.3	8.2	32.0	7.0	5.3	3.0	7.1	9.4	9.2	2.6	7.3	321.6
1976–7	157.9	8.3	18.8	9.6	9.7	5.5	31.4	6.3	5.3	3.0	5.2	9.1	11.6	2.6	10.1	336.3
1977–8	161.8	9.7	13.9	9.7	10.2	8.6	34.4	5.9	6.4	2.6	6.0	9.9	10.1	3.0	11.0	345.6
1978–9	180.0	9.0	16.3	10.2	8.3	9.5	55.9	6.2	6.2	2.2	6.7	7.6	10.2	4.0	9.0	386.0
1979–0[b]	197.2	6.4	19.7	9.2	10.7	10.2	56.9	5.0	6.2	3.2	7.4	10.1	12.5	3.3	8.4	412.0
1980–1[c]	185.0	11.2	20.0	10.0	10.5	9.3	58.5	6.3	6.4	2.9	6.8	9.4	10.5	3.5	9.0	402.0
1981–2[2c]	208.3		23.6	11.4	9.0		59.0								8.4	436.6

[a]Data prior to 1965–1966 are in millions of bushels. [b]Preliminary. [c]Estimated. *Source*: U.S. Department of Agriculture, Foreign Agricultural Service. [d]Average 1963. [e]Average 1960–64.

On a state-by-state basis, it becomes evident how the Corn Belt region received its nickname. In 1981 Iowa produced 1,740 million bushels of corn for grain. Following Iowa were Illinois at 1,453 million bushels; Nebraska, 803 million bushels; Minnesota, 745 million bushels; and Indiana, which produced 654 million bushels.

USES

Corn is most important as a foodstuff in North and South America, in Mediterranean countries, and in eastern Europe. Corn is a less favored ingredient than wheat in making bread because it lacks the gluten that causes wheat flour to rise. Nevertheless, cornmeal is used in baking, and consumed as cornmeal mush, hasty pudding, and Johnny cake. Cornflakes, popcorn, tortillas, and whole-kernel sweet corn are popular corn products. Hominy, corn from which the hulls have been removed by a lye solution, is consumed as a vegetable mainly in the southern United States, where coarsely ground hominy, or hominy grits, is a breakfast food.

Edible cornstarch is used in foods, and industrial cornstarch in the paper and textile industries. Starch may be converted to nutritive sweeteners such as corn syrup, dextrose, and *high-fructose corn syrup* (HFCS), for use in bakery products, candies, and soft drinks. The phenomenal success of HFCS has helped boost the use of corn sweeteners such that they now account for 28% of the domestic sweetener market. Liquid dextrose may be fermented into ethyl alcohol, which is used to produce gasohol. The protein and hulls of the corn kernel produce corn gluten feed and corn gluten meal, used in livestock feed. Finally, the corn oil derived from the germ of the kernel is used to produce cooking oil, margarine, and shortening, a well as soap, glycerin, and paint.

MARKETING

At one time, most corn was fed to farm animals on the farm where it was grown. With increasing specialization of production, corn is now marketed in a variety of manners—sold to neighbors, sold to country and terminal elevators, and sold under forward contract to food processors. Storage both on and off the farm is generally highest at the beginning of the crop year, which runs from October to September, and lowest at the end of the crop year. Out of the 6,645 million bushels of corn produced during the 1980–1981 crop years, 2,355 million bushels were exported, making an important contribution to the U.S. balance of payments.

PRICES

Weather is the most important factor influencing the price of corn in the short run, as evidenced by the 1983 drought. Longer-term factors include changes in production and consumption of corn or products which utilize corn as a primary input, such as meat, gasohol, and products containing corn sweeteners. The de-

TABLE 2. Acreage And Supply Of Corn In The United States (in Millions of Bushels)

Year Beginning October	Planted	Harvested			Yield, Grain Per Harvested Acre	Carry-over, October 1st				Production For Grain	Imports[b]	Total (All Supply Grain)
		For Grain (In Millions of Acres)	For Silage	For Forage		Farm	Commodity Credit Corporation Bins	Others[a]	Total			
1961–2	65.9	57.6	6.3	1.5	62.4	588	615	813	2,016	3,598	1.4	5,615
1962–3	65.0	55.7	7.2	1.5	64.7	578	484	590	1,653	3,606	1.0	5,260
1963–4	68.8	59.2	7.7	1.4	67.9	534	396	435	1,365	4,019	1.0	5,385
1964–5	65.8	55.4	8.6	1.4	62.9	681	414	441	1,537	3,484	1.0	5,022
1965–6	65.2	55.4	8.1	1.2	74.1	581	308	258	1,147	4,103	1.0	5,251
1966–7	66.3	57.0	7.9	0.9	73.1	530	134	176	840	4,168	1.0	5,011
1967–8	71.2	60.7	8.4	1.0	80.1	569.2	97.6	156.5	823	4,860	1.0	5,687
1968–9	65.1	56.0	7.9	0.8	79.5	781.8	103.3	277.2	1,162	4,450	1.0	5,620
1969–0	64.3	54.6	7.9	0.6	85.9	728.2	143.3	241.9	1,113	4,687	1.0	5,806
1970–1	66.9	57.4	8.1	0.7	72.4	575.6	111.3	318.3	1,005	4,152	4.0	5,161
1971–2	74.2	64.1	8.8	0.7	88.1	426.7	24.5	215.5	667	5,646	1.0	6,309
1972–3	67.1	57.5	8.4	0.5	97.0	751.3	26.3	348.7	1,126	5,580	1.0	6,700
1973–4	72.3	62.1	9.0	0.6	91.3	404.6	20.3	283.7	709	5,671	1.0	6,380
1974–5	77.9	65.4	10.8	0.6	71.9	287.6	—	195.1—	483	4,701	1.8	5,187
1975–6	78.6	67.6	9.8	0.6	86.4	191.3	—	168.2—	359	5,841	1.8	6,204
1976–7	84.4	71.5	11.3	0.9	88.0	229.8	—	169.4—	399	6,289	2.5	6,691
1977–8	83.6	71.6	9.3	0.6	90.8	446.1	—	438.0—	884	6,505	2.6	7,394
1978–9	81.7	71.9	8.6	0.4	101.0	659.3	—	444.7—	1,104	7,268	1.2	8,381
1979–0	81.4	72.4	8.0	0.4	109.7	794.5	—	1,103.9—	1,304	7,939	1.1	9,244
1980–1[c]	84.1	73.1	9.3	0.6	91.0	920.9	—	696.6—	1,617	6,648	1.0	8,266
1981–2[c]	84.0	74.6	8.2	0.4	109.9	490.1	—	543.8—	1,034	8,201	1.3	9,236

[a]Interior mills and elevators and terminal markets. [b]Includes grain equivalent of cornmeal and flour. [c]Preliminary. *Source:* U.S. Department of Agriculture, Statistical Reporting Service.

TABLE 3. Distribution of Corn in the United States (in Millions of Bushels)

Year Beginning October	Breakfast Foods[a]	Food and Industrial Products[b]	Cornmeal and, so forth[c]	Wet-Process Products[d]	Alcohol and Products	Seed	Livestock Feed[e]	Exports (Including Grain Equivalent of Pdt's.)	Total Utilization	Domestic Disappearance
1961–2	17	304	102	168.7	36.4	10.9	3,212	435	3,962	3,527
1962–3	18	311	105	179.4	28.2	11.6	3,157	416	3,895	3,479
1963–4	19	352	112	195.0	25.8	11.2	3,009	500	3,848	3,348
1964–5	19	358	110	201.0	28.0	11.0	2,957	570	3,875	3,305
1965–6	20	348	111	204.0	30.0	13.0	3,361	687	4,409	3,722
1966–7	21	355	117	205.0	33.0	14.0	3,329	487	4,185	3,698
1967–8	21	365	117	213.0	34.0	12.0	3,507	633	4,518	3,885
1968–9	22	374	114	221.0	33.0	12.0	3,580	536	4,502	3,966
1969–0	22	381	116	226.0	31.0	13.0	3,795	613	4,801	4,189

	Shipments													
Year Beginning October	Wet Corn Milling (Grind)	Corn Meal[f]	Corn Flour, and so forth	Hominy Grits (Food)[g]	Breakfast Foods[g]	Distilled Liquors	Fermented Malt Liquors	Total Shipments	Seed	Livestock Feed[e]	Exports (Including Grain Equivalent of Pdt's.)	Total Utilization	Domestic Disappearance
1970–1	242	24	8	17	23	24	45	383	17	3,581	517	4,494	3,977
1971–2	246	21	10	14	24	25	45	385	15	3,997	796	5,183	4,387
1972–3	284	20	12	13	24	29	45	427	16	4,304	1,258	5,991	4,733
1973–4	295	19	14	13	25	33	47	446	18	4,205	1,243	5,896	4,653
1974–5	315	18	13	10	24	16	49	445	18	3,226	1,149	4,826	3,677
1975–6	343	18	15	11	24	21	50	482	20	3,603	1,711	5,804	4,093
1976–7	362	17	17	10	25	21	53	505	20	3,608	1,684	5,805	4,121
1977–8	405	17	18	10	25	19	52	546	20	3,783	1,948	6,282	4,334
1978–9[h]	430	18	19	9	26	18	50	570	20	4,369	2,133	7,077	4,944
1979–0[h]	455					20	31	655	20	4,544	2,433	7,626	5,194
1980–1[i]	487					20	31	715	20	4,350	2,600	7,700	5,100
1981–2[i]								765					

Sources: U. S. Department of Agriculture, Economic Research Service and Commodity Economics Division.
[a]Estimated quantities used during the calendar year following the corn harvest. [b]Total quantities processed and breakdown between domestic use and exports. [c]Estimated quantities used in producing cornmeal, flour, hominy, and grits during the calendar year following the corn harvest. [d]Starch, syrup, sugar, etc. [e]Feed and waste (residual, mostly feed). [f]Regular and degermed. [g]Assumes sizable quantities of corn flour are purchased by breakfast food manufacturers from the dry milling industry. [h]Estimate. [i]Preliminary.

velopment of substitutes, government price-support programs, and the size of corn inventories are other contributing factors. Political factors such as embargoes or wars involving major importing or exporting countries are also influential. The grain embargo imposed against the Soviet Union from January 4, 1980 to April 24, 1981 is a case in point. The event which has had the greatest impact on corn prices during the past 20 years was the 1973–1974 Russian grain purchase.

During the 1977–1981 period, the average price of No. 2 Chicago yellow corn fluctuated widely, from \$1.80 per bushel in September 1977 to \$3.56 per bushel in January 1981, although the price is still below the record average monthly price of No. 2 yellow corn, \$3.74, registered in October 1974. Recent price volatility is demonstrated in the accompanying figure.

GOVERNMENT PROGRAMS

The *Agriculture and Food Act of 1981* established minimum target levels for certain commodities over the next 4 years; specific support levels are determined at the discretion of the Secretary of Agriculture. The 1982 crop year target price for corn was \$2.70 per bushel. When the 5-month weighted average price for corn is

FIGURE 2. Corn weekly nearest futures—Chicago.

less than $2.70 per bushel, the government makes deficiency payments equal to the difference between the target price and the market price or the loan rate, whichever is higher. In return, the participating farmer must agree to reduce acreage planted by 10%, decreasing the total amount of corn available to the market.

The level for regular loans for 1982 was set at $2.55 per bushel. When the price of corn declines to this level, the participating grower may take out a 9-month loan at a subsidized interest rate. The loan is intended to allow the participant to repay basic operating costs, enabling the participant to market the corn later in the year when markets are presumably less congested. At the end of 9 months, the farmer may either repay the loan plus interest, surrender the crop to the Commodity Credit Corporation with the interest forgiven, or enter into the reserve loan program.

Under the reserve loan program, the producer signs a 3 year contract under which the producer receives a loan for $2.90 per bushel and agrees to store the grain for 3 years, or until the cash price reaches the trigger-level release price of $3.25 per bushel. The government pays the grower an annual storage fee of $0.265 per bushel. Interest on the loan is charged the first year and waived during subsequent years. Should the trigger-level release price be reached, the farmer may repay the loan plus interest. If the national 5-month moving average price continues above the trigger level after the initial release period (the remainder of the month in which the reserve is triggered plus one additional month) growers will stop earning storage payments and interest charges will resume, to encourage the farmer to repay the loan.

At the end of the 3-year period, the farmer may choose to repay the $2.90 per bushel loan plus interest, to surrender the corn to the Commodity Credit Corporation, or to extend the contract for an additional 2 years.

SEASONALITY

The price of corn tends to follow a basic pattern each year, as can be seen in the accompanying charts of the cash and nearby futures markets. During the harvest period which begins in the fall, prices plummet with an 87.5% rate of reliability. Prices are depressed when storage bins overflow and farmers are forced to bring some corn to market. At the elevators corn is at a competitive disadvantage to other earlier-harvested crops vis-à-vis storage space.

The downtrend continues through the end of harvest in November. By this time farmers have unloaded any corn they cannot store and are prepared to sit tight until prices increase, which they do in December. The increase draws some sellers and the forces of supply and demand serve to create a sideways trading market through early spring.

By May dwindling stocks lead to rising prices throughout the summer; this upward price trend may be tempered by optimistic new crop production forecasts, or exaggerated by reports of poor weather or disease. Over the past 24 years, this midsummer rally has been the least reliable portion of the pattern. Corn is not as sensitive to drought as some other crops due to the plant's extensive root structure, but late season price run-ups may be caused by an early frost.

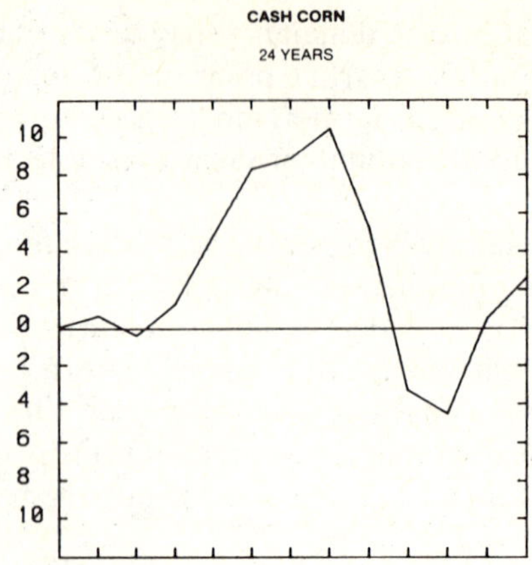

	J-F	F-M	M-A	A-M	M-J	J-J	J-A	A-S	S-O	O-N	N-D	D-J
Average Move	0.5	-1.1	1.6	3.6	3.4	0.5	1.5	-5.3	-8.5	-1.3	5	2.1
% Reliable	58.4	41.7	66.7	91.7	50	45.9	50	54.2	87.5	62.5	83.4	70.9
Avg. Up Move	3.2	2.5	5.7	5.7	10.4	6.9	11	2.2	6	9.7	7.1	6.1
Avg. Down Move	2.5	5.6	5.7	14.5	2.8	4.4	7.9	11.1	10.3	6.5	4	6.8
Greatest Up Move	18	6.1	19	38	42	20	51	6	8	30	22	25
Greatest Down Move	6.8	29	32	20	14	22	27	59	30	25	13	38

(*a*)

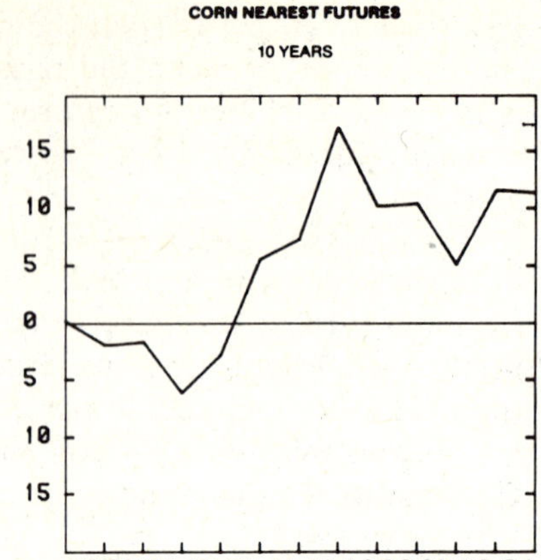

	J-F	F-M	M-A	A-M	M-J	J-J	J-A	A-S	S-O	O-N	N-D	D-J
Average Move	-2.1	0.3	-4.5	3.3	8.3	1.7	9.7	-7	0.2	-5.3	6.4	-0.3
% Reliable	70	70	60	60	60	40	50	70	30	70	90	40
Avg. Up Move	8.4	3.1	2.7	8.9	15.7	13.5	27.9	7.3	12.6	4.9	7.7	4.7
Avg. Down Move	6.6	6.4	9.3	5.1	2.7	6.1	8.6	13.1	5.1	9.7	5.4	7.7
Greatest Up Move	22.4	5	3.7	24.5	40.6	42.1	60.4	10.7	31.7	8	17.8	18.2
Greatest Down Move	32	9.5	33	16.1	4.7	11.9	18	49.8	17.4	22.9	5.4	28.5

(*b*)

FIGURE 3. Corn seeasonality. (*a*) Cash corn, 24 years. (*b*) Corn nearest futures, 10 years.

Each individual futures contract also demonstrates seasonal trends, although the reliabilities are not nearly as high as in the nearby chart. For example, both the July and December futures contracts exhibit a downtrend in prices from October to May, at which time an uptrend begins. As is the case with all seasonal charts, these futures charts are meant to act only as guides and should not be used as definitive indicators of direction.

There is bountiful information available on corn seasonality, basis, planting, maturing, and harvesting patterns as well as forecasting of both planting and yields. The University of Illinois as well as Iowa State University and other midwestern institutions are primary sources of crop pattern information. The USDA statistical services provides information of various methods of estimating production. Figure 4 shows a 9-year study by the University of Illinois on corn maturity in Illinois.

FUTURES MARKETS

Futures contracts in corn are traded at the Chicago Board of Trade and the MidAmerica Commodity Exchange. Table 4 shows the contract specifications. The specifications are written to ensure that they closely mirror cash market conditions, and the months of trading are usually selected because of their significance in the crop marketing year. When a far month trades at a premium to a nearby month which exceeds the cost of carrying (storage, interest, and insurance) the physical commodity between the 2 months, the market is bullish on

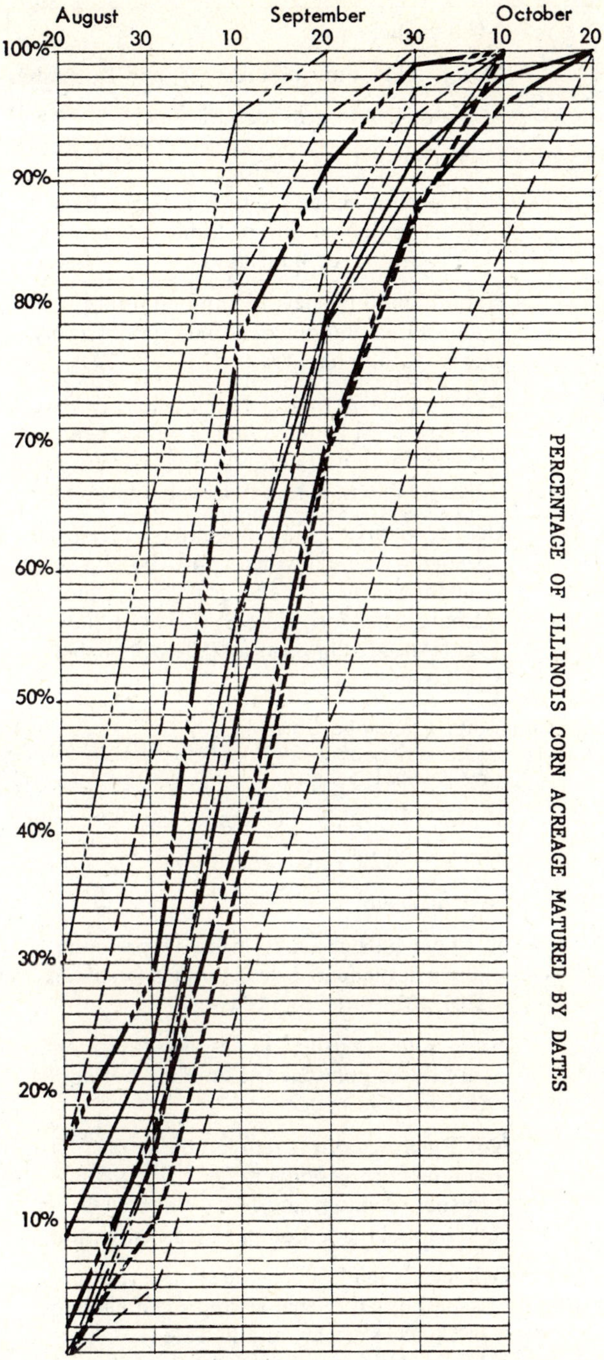

PERCENTAGE OF ILLINOIS CORN ACREAGE MATURED BY DATES

	Aug.st 20	30	September 10	20	30	October 10	20
1970	2%	17%	40%	70%	88%	96%	100%
1971	16%	29%	78%	91%	99%	100%	100%
1972	0%	10%	37%	70%	88%	100%	100%
1973	0%	15%	50%	78%	90%	100%	100%
1974	0%	5%	27%	48%	70%	85%	100%
1975	16%	45%	82%	95%	100%	100%	100%
1976	0%	15%	55%	84%	97%	100%	100%
1977	30%	65%	95%	100%	100%	100%	100%
1978	0%	18%	50%	80%	95%	100%	100%
9 Year Average	9%	24%	57%	79.5%	92%	98%	100%

FIGURE 4. Illinois corn maturing dates. (Chart by Dan Hueber.)

TABLE 4. Contract Specifications

CBT Corn	
Trading unit	5,000 bushels
Delivery months	March, May, July, September, and December
Trading hours	9:30 a.m.—1:15 p.m. central time
Minimum fluctuation	¼¢ per bushel
Daily price limit	$0.10 per bushel above or below previous day's settlement price. Limit expands by 50% after three limit days.
Position limit	Net 3 million bushels in any one future or in all futures combined. Limits do not apply to *bona fide* hedgers.
Delivery grade	No. 2 yellow corn is deliverable at par. No. 1 yellow corn is deliverable at a ½¢ per bushel premium and No. 3 yellow corn is deliverable at a 1½¢ per bushel discount.
Delivery	Delivery is made via a warehouse receipt issued by an exchange-approved elevator in Chicago at par, and in Toledo, Ohio, St. Louis, Missouri, East St. Louis, Illinois, and Alton, Illinois at a $0.04 per bushel discount.
MidAmerica Commodity Exchange Corn	
Trading unit	1,000 bushels
Delivery months	March, May, July, September, and December
Trading hours	9:30 a.m.–1:30 p.m. central time
Minimum fluctuation	⅛¢ per bushel
Daily price limit	$0.10 per bushel above or below previous day's settlement price. Limit expands by 50% after three limit days.
Position limit	Net 3 million bushels in any one future or in all futures combined. Limits do not apply to *bona fide* hedgers.
Delivery grade	No. 2 yellow corn is deliverable at par. No. 1 yellow corn is deliverable at a ½¢ per bushel premium and No. 3 yellow corn is deliverable at a 1½¢ per bushel discount.
Delivery	Delivery is made via a warehouse receipt issued by an exchange-approved elevator in Chicago at par, and in Toledo, Ohio, St. Louis, Missouri, East St. Louis, Illinois, and Alton, Illinois at a $0.04 per bushel discount.

long-term prices. When the difference between the nearby and far months does not cover the carrying charge, the market is bearish on long-term prices. An inverted market occurs when the nearby actually trades at a premium. New crop months (those months beginning with October of the subsequent year) generally trade at a premium to the prior months of old crop, although new crop may fall to a discount on reports of slackening demand or bountiful supply.

CHAPTER 28

OATS

CONTENTS

PRODUCTION 4

CONSUMPTION AND USAGE 4

SEASONAL STUDIES 5

FUTURES MARKETS 8

CHAPTER **28**

OATS

King S. Kearns, II

Like other small grains, *oats* is a cereal grass. In its wild form, oats is a persistent weed that can reduce the yields of cultivated crops.

Common oats are grown in cool, temperate regions and are second only to rye in their ability to grow in poor soils. This ability to survive conditions unsuitable for wheat and barley may have led to the cultivation of oats. Oats are thought to have spread as a weed, contaminating barley and wheat seed; they are believed to have been first cultivated in northern Europe.

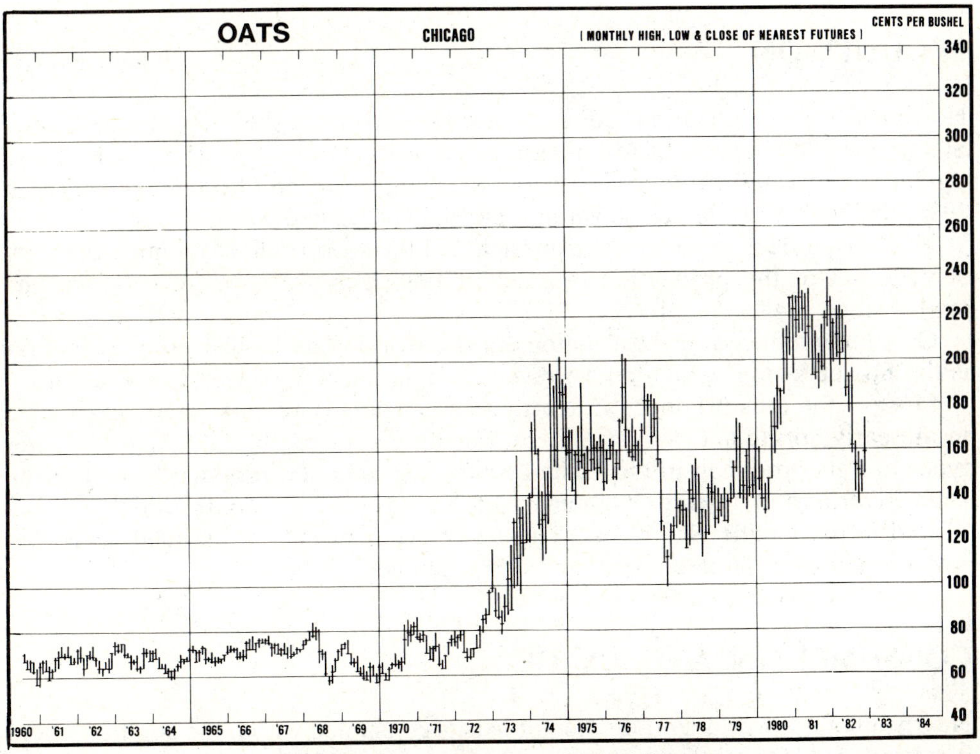

FIGURE 1. Oats cash price—United States.

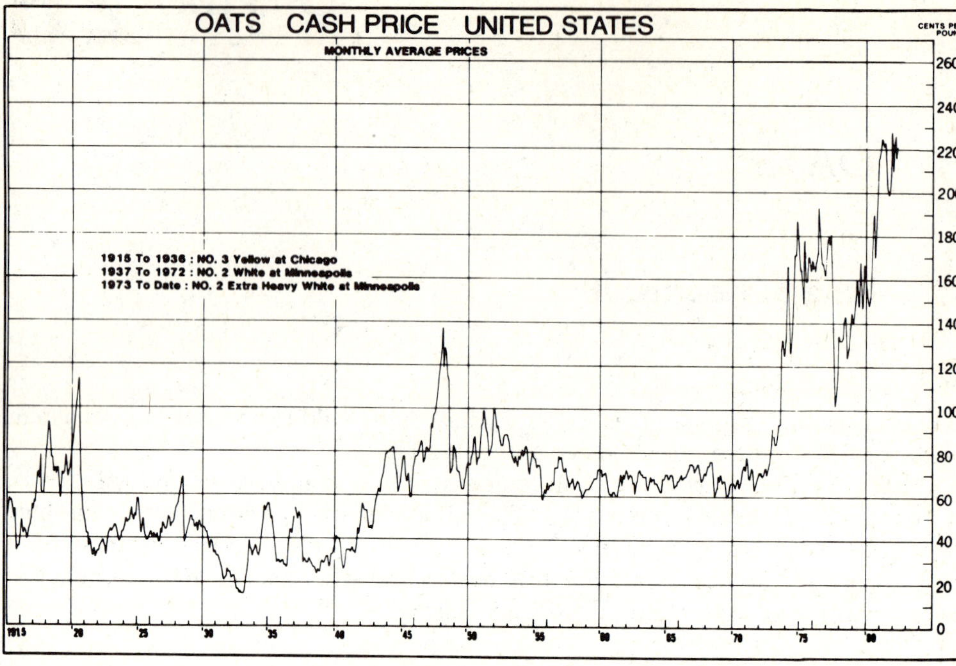

FIGURE 1. Continued.

PRODUCTION

North American and world production of oats fell through the 1970s. In the United States, the 1980 harvest of 458 million bushels was the lowest since 1881. World production also fell through the 1970s, reaching a low of 44.6 million tonnes in 1980, the lowest production level in more than 15 years.

Production declines in North America and the world reflect the movement of acreage out of the production of oats. In 1980, acreage sown to oats was the lowest since 1867.

Oats are produced in most nations in the world. The largest producer by far is the Soviet Union, which on average accounts for 40% of world production.

Most of the oats produced in North America are white oats. They are seeded in the early spring and harvesting is normally completed by late August. Other types of oats produced in the United States are red oats, produced south of the Ohio River and in Texas, Oklahoma, and Kansas, and grey oats, which are cultivated in the Pacific Northwest. These two types of oats are seeded in the fall and are harvested in late spring and early summer.

CONSUMPTION AND USAGE

Nearly all of the world's production of oats is consumed within the country where it is produced. On average, over the 10 years, only 3% of world oats production entered *export* channels.

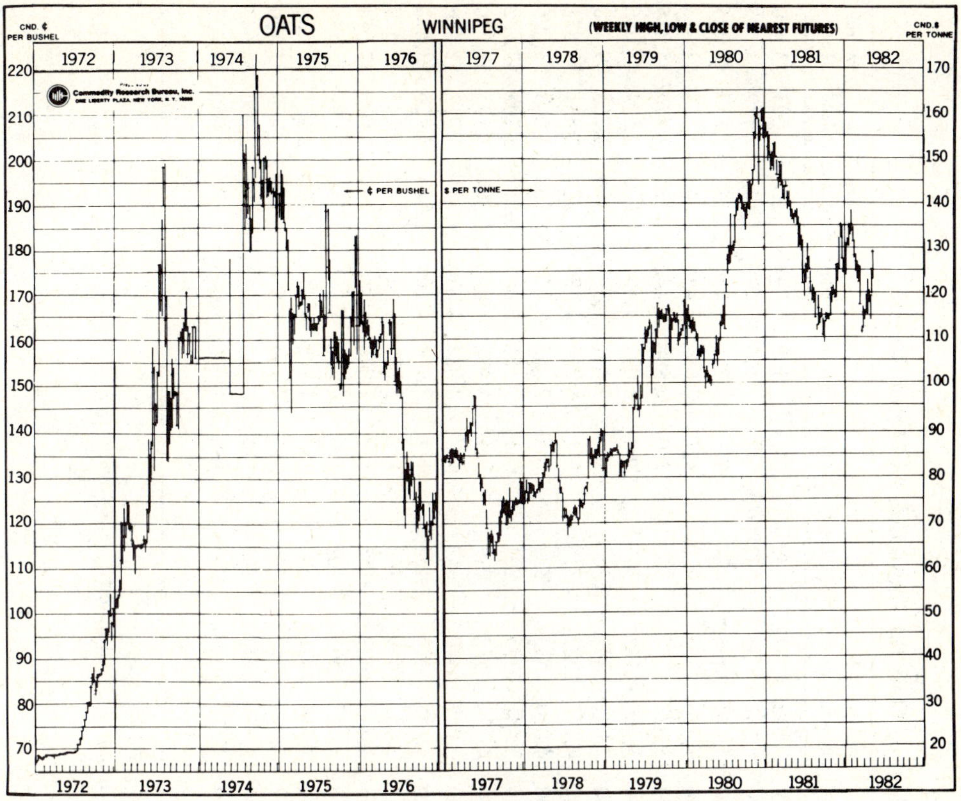

FIGURE 2. Oats weekly nearest futures—Winnipeg.

Oats are used primarily as livestock feed. They are high in carbohydrates and have the highest level of total protein among the cereal grains. They are also a source of vitamin B1 and minerals.

About 5% of the U.S. oat crop is used for edible products, including rolled oats, oatmeal, ready-to-eat cereals, and oat flour.

SEASONAL STUDIES

The cash market analysis of seasonal bias for oats appears consistent with growing patterns and shows good reliability. Lows occur in July and highs at the end of the year; the chances of a decline in January and July are greater than 70% and the chance of a rise in August and October is over 75%. Yet oats are not considered an especially good seasonal trader, since the average price move is quite small.

Figure 3 shows that the real trading opportunities are in the basis. Since the lows in the futures market precede the lows in the cash market by almost 2 months, we can translate that lag into a narrow basis (cash holding at a steady level while futures decline). A narrow basis marks the best opportunity for a producer hedge, since the basis must be widest at harvest when the cash market is under the greatest pressure.

TABLE 1. World Production of Oats (In Thousands of Metric Tons)[a]

Crop Year	United States	Canada	Argentina	Australia	Turkey	USSR	West Germany	Spain	Netherlands	Denmark	France	Sweden	United Kingdom	Poland	World Total
1961–62	1,010	284	49	69	30	600	132	34	30	47	179	93	128	203	3,410
1962–63	1,012	494	34	86	31	385	161	35	32	42	178	75	122	189	3,375
1963–64[a]	14,014	6,988	906	1,238	475	3,700	3,444	466	424	671	3,247	1,156	1,461	2,830	47,725
1964–65	12,371	5,508	805	1,271	425	3,900	3,476	390	420	821	2,680	1,448	1,346	2,218	43,278
1965–66	13,492	6,399	480	1,102	450	4,600	3,027	370	363	780	2,898	1,340	1,232	2,476	45,315
1966–67	11,660	5,778	540	1,943	450	7,500	3,366	442	357	864	3,031	1,154	1,120	2,594	47,046
1967–68	11,522	4,691	690	719	475	9,700	3,841	492	365	904	3,411	1,396	1,386	2,768	49,348
1968–69	13,799	5,591	490	1,710	450	9,700	4,135	522	318	861	3,066	1,584	1,224	2,831	52,821
1969–70	14,020	5,728	425	1,247	468	10,700	4,250	533	322	765	2,842	1,129	1,308	3,063	53,396
1970–71	13,313	5,672	360	1,613	415	11,800	3,481	395	201	631	2,556	1,685	1,217	3,209	52,882
1971–72	12,792	5,605	475	1,275	455	14,650	4,120	582	213	701	3,134	1,867	1,360	3,195	57,550
1972–73	10,044	4,630	566	740	396	14,100	3,909	440	144	637	3,084	1,630	1,255	3,212	51,286
1973–74	9,681	5,041	561	1,107	376	17,516	4,155	425	134	444	2,204	1,209	1,080	3,220	53,872
1974–75	8,912	3,929	327	874	380	15,257	3,482	559	163	472	2,081	1,686	950	3,244	49,320
1975–76	9,551	4,466	433	1,141	390	12,495	3,445	609	158	367	1,948	1,345	795	2,920	47,044
1976–77	7,930	4,831	530	1,073	400	18,113	2,497	505	103	256	1,402	1,251	764	2,695	48,744
1977–78	10,901	4,303	570	991	370	18,407	2,714	421	94	288	1,928	1,416	790	2,561	51,508
1978–79[b]	8,730	3,620	676	1,868	370	18,507	3,202	542	140	210	2,195	1,550	710	2,490	51,120
1979–80[c]	7,707	2,978	525	1,500	340	16,000	2,951	445	103	130	1,735	1,590	550	2,200	44,647
1980–81[b]	6,652	3,028	610	1,200	350	16,700	3,228	660	93	168	1,906	1,685	620	2,050	45,437
1981–82[c]	7,375														

Source: U.S. Department of Agriculture, Foreign Agricultural Service.
[a]Data prior to 1963–1964 are in millions of bushels. [b]Preliminary. [c]Estimated.

TABLE 2. Salient Statistics of Oats in the United States and Canada

	Acreage				Farm Disposition		U.S. Government Price-Support Program					
								Under Price Support				
Crop Year	Planted[a] (1,000 Acres)	Harvested[b] (1,000 Acres)	Yield Per Harvest Acre (Bushels)	Farm Value of Product (Millions of Dollars)	Feed and Seed (Millions of Bushels)	Sold (Millions of Bushels)	Owned by Commodity Credit Corporation July 1	Loans (1,000 Bushels)	Purchase Agreement	Total	Deliveries to Commodity Credit Corporation	National Average Support Rate (Dollars per Bushel)
1961–62	32,314	23,886	42.3	650	730	281	9,025	19,311	1,306	20,617	8,400	0.62
1962–63	29,500	22,377	45.2	636	720	292	16,700	29,544	2,479	32,023	19,000	0.62
1963–64	28,054	21,308	45.3	608	657	309	17,087	35,052	3,833	38,885	31,900	0.65
1964–65	25,634	19,759	43.1	541	570	282	28,254	41,200	3,700	44,900	25,100	0.65
1965–66	24,046	18,522	50.2	587	615	315	42,151	43,700	200	43,900	6,800	0.60
1966–67	23,343	17,877	44.9	540	527	277	50,573	22,700	—	22,700	6,500	0.60
1967–68	20,719	16,110	49.3	528	525	268	47,796	37,200	400	37,600	19,500	0.63
1968–69	23,342	17,708	53.7	576	592	359	45,206	89,200	5,700	89,135	35,600	0.63
1969–70	23,561	17,971	53.7	572	586	380	61,088	152,500	10,100	162,600	62,000	0.63
1970–71	24,410	18,594	49.2	582	563	355	104,254	108,900	4,800	113,700	26,600	0.54
1971–72	21,831	15,705	55.9	544	539	339	168,910			81,900	700	0.54
1972–73	19,990	13,410	51.5	507	428	262	178,128			31,800	—	0.54
1973–74	18,605	13,770	47.9	775	404	256	104,942			10,392	—	0.54
1974–75	17,013	12,608	47.6	912	389	212	24,000			3,900	—	0.54
1975–76	16,486	13,038	49.0	928	397	245	5,800			3,900	—	0.54
1976–77	16,734	11,834	45.7	845	353	193	—			4,600	—	0.72
1977–78	17,733	13,485	55.8	825	456	295	—			82,900	1,500	1.03
1978–79	16,407	11,126	52.3	706	377	219	100			25,000	500	1.03
1979–80[d]	13,957	9,679	54.4	717	348	187	2,400			12,000	—	1.08
1980–81[d]	13,360	8,640	53.0				3,000			6,000	—	1.16
1981–82[d]	13,646	9,411	54.0							9,000		1.24

Source: Department of Agriculture, Statistical Reporting Service, U.S.
[a]For all purposes. [b]For grain. [c]Including products. [d]Preliminary.

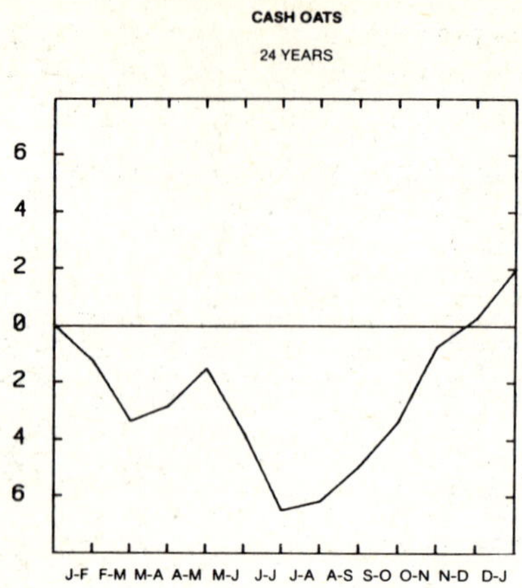

	J-F	F-M	M-A	A-M	M-J	J-J	J-A	A-S	S-O	O-N	N-D	D-J
Average Move	-1.3	-2.1	0.5	1.3	-2.3	-2.7	0.3	1.2	1.5	2.6	1	1.7
% Reliable	70.9	58.4	58.4	75	66.7	70.9	41.7	75	66.7	83.4	58.4	66.7
Avg. Up Move	2.9	1.2	3.8	2.7	5.5	5.9	6.5	2.6	3.5	3.8	3.3	4.2
Avg. Down Move	2.7	4.3	3.7	3.1	5.5	5.6	4.1	2.3	2.1	3.5	2	2.4
Greatest Up Move	11	2.6	23	9	21	20	35	9	16	17	10	23
Greatest Down Move	5.1	15	26	13	30	23	17	3.8	6	7	6	10

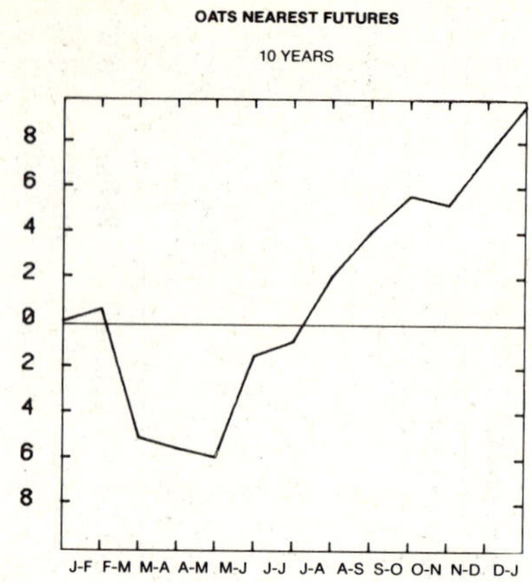

	J-F	F-M	M-A	A-M	M-J	J-J	J-A	A-S	S-O	O-N	N-D	D-J
Average Move	0.5	-5.8	-0.5	-0.4	4.5	0.6	2.8	1.9	1.5	-0.4	2.3	2
% Reliable	50	80	50	60	70	30	50	70	60	30	60	60
Avg. Up Move	3.3	1.8	4.9	4.3	7.3	11.6	10.4	4.5	5.1	2.6	5.4	7.3
Avg. Down Move	2.3	7.7	5.9	3.5	2	4.1	4.7	4.2	3.8	7.6	2.5	5.8
Greatest Up Move	8.5	2	16.4	8.2	29.4	26.8	20	7.5	18.9	4.2	9.7	22.8
Greatest Down Move	3.8	24	17.6	9.4	3.2	9.3	15.4	5.8	6.2	13.2	6.7	12.7

FIGURE 3. Oats seasonality. (*Left*) Cash Oats, 24 years. (*Right*) Oats nearest futures, 10 years.

FUTURES MARKETS

Oat futures are traded on the *Chicago Board of Trade*, the *MidAmerica Commodity Exchange*, and *The Winnipeg Commodity Exchange*. (Contract specifications appear in Table 3.)

TABLE 3. Contract Specifications

	CBT Oats
Delivery months	July, September, December, March, and May
Trading unit	5,000 bushels
Price quotations and minimum fluctuation	Quoted in dollars, cents, and quarter-cents per bushel with a minimum fluctuation of one-quarter ¢ per bushel ($12.50 per contract).
Daily price movement limits	Subject to change; consult latest official notices from the exchange.
Position limits	2 million bushels in any one future or in all futures combined; positions of 200,000 bushels or more require reports to the Commodity Futures Trading Commission.
Grades deliverable	No. 2 heavy, No. 1, and substitutions at differentials established by the exchange.

TABLE 3. Continued

	CBT Oats
Delivery	By registered warehouse receipts issued by the warehouses approved by the exchange in the Chicago Switching District or the Minneapolis or St. Paul, Minnesota, Switching Districts. Deliveries from Minneapolis or St. Paul are made at a discount of 7½¢ per bushel under contract price.
Trading hours	9:30 a.m.–1:15 p.m. central time
	MidAmerica Commodity Exchange Oats
Delivery months	March May, July, September, and December
Trading unit	5,000 bushels
Minimum fluctuation	One-eighth ¢ per bushel ($6.25 per contract)
Daily price movement limits	Subject to change; consult latest official notices from the exchange.
Position limits	2 million bushels in any one future or in all futures combined.
Grades deliverable	No. 1 oats and No. 2 heavy oats at par; other grades deliverable at differentials.
Delivery	From Chicago and Minneapolis elevators approved by the exchange.
Trading hours	9:30 a.m.–1:30 p.m. central time
	Winnipeg Commodity Exchange Domestic Feed Oats
Delivery months	October, December, March, May, and July
Trading unit	100-tonne board lot, 20-tonne job lot
Quotation	Canadian dollars per tonne
Minimum fluctuation	$1 per tonne
Daily price movement limits	$5 (Canadian) per tonne
Deliverable grade	No. 1 feed or No. 2 feed at $3.50 per tonne discount
Delivery	Thunder Bay, Ontario
Trading hours	9:30 a.m.–1:15 p.m. central time

CHAPTER **29**

WINNIPEG GRAIN MARKETS

CONTENTS

BARLEY	**3**	**RAPESEED**	**12**
Production	**3**	Production	**12**
Consumption and Usage	**3**	Consumption and Usage	**13**
Futures Markets	**4**	Futures Market	**13**
FLAXSEED	**4**	**RYE**	**13**
Production	**8**	Production	**15**
Consumption and Usage	**9**	Consumption	**15**
Futures Market	**9**	Futures Market	**20**

CHAPTER 29

WINNIPEG GRAIN MARKETS

King S. Kearns, II

BARLEY

Barley is a member of the grass family. It was domesticated in Southeast Asia and Ethiopia between 7000 and 6000 B.C. and was cultivated in Egypt as early as 5000 B.C. and in northwest Europe as early as 2500 B.C.

In Europe and the Mediterranean area, barley was used to make a flatbread, and it was the major bread plant in Europe through the 16th century.

Barley was also probably the first cereal grain used in large quantities for the production of alcoholic beverages.

PRODUCTION. Barley is second only to wheat in production in the Soviet Union, the world's largest producer with a recent average annual production of about 58 million tonnes (1 metric ton equals 45.93 bushels).

Canada and France are the next largest producers, each producing more than 10 million tonnes annually. Canada and France are also the largest exporters of barley, each with about 28% of total world trade.

Barley is the most adaptable of the cereal grains. It can be grown in subartic, temperate, and subtropic regions. It has a shorter growing season than any other cereal and is more tolerant to cold than most other cereals.

World barley yields have increased about 10% over the last decade to about 35 bushels per acre. European and North American yields are significantly higher, averaging about 45 bushels per acre. Total world production has risen about 15% in the last 10 years to 167 million tonnes.

In Canada, barley is the major cropping alternative to wheat. It is normally seeded in the prairie provinces in May and harvest may begin in early August.

CONSUMPTION AND USAGE. Barley has long held a major position as a feed in hog rations and is growing in importance in feed for cattle. More than half of world barley production is used for livestock feed. Another 10% is malted for the production of beer and other alcoholic beverages. Barley is a staple food in some countries in North Africa and Asia. As a food it is used primarily in soups and barley flour and as an extender for other vegetable proteins.

In Canada, more than half of the total production is used domestically for livestock feed. About 10% of Canadian barley production is malted and 35% moves into the export market.

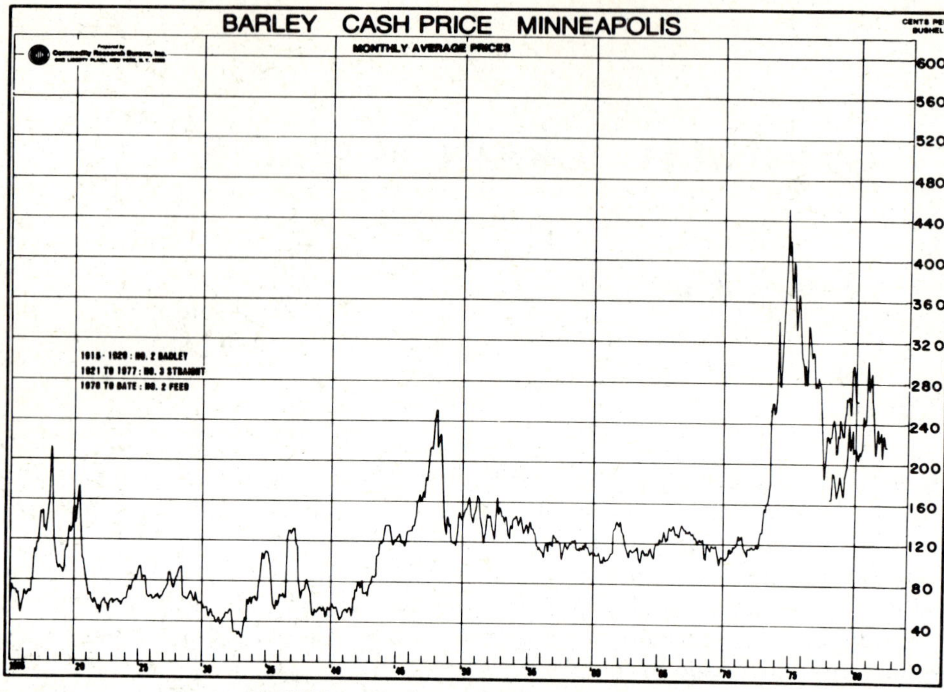

FIGURE 1. Barley cash price—Minneapolis.

The United States exports a smaller percentage of its barley production, 10–15% annually. Nearly 35% of U.S. barley production is malted to make beer and other alcoholic beverages. A small percentage of U.S. barley is used in foods.

Historically, Poland, Western Europe, and Japan have been the largest importers of barley. Since 1980, however, the Soviet Union has become the major import market for barley.

FUTURES MARKETS. Domestic feed barley futures are traded on *The Winnipeg Commodity Exchange* and on the *London Grain Futures Market*. The contract specifications are included in Table 3.

FLAXSEED

Flax has been cultivated since prehistoric times. Some types of flax are cultivated for their fiber, from which linen is made. Other types are cultivated for their seed, also known as *linseed*, which is crushed to produce *linseed oil* and *linseed meal*.

Flax is one of the oldest textile fibers known. Linen has been found in archeological sites from Egypt to northern Europe.

The flax that is grown for seed has shorter straw, more branches, and more seeds than the fiber type. The types of flax grown for seed do not produce fibers that are used to make linen.

Linseed oil was used for food by the Greeks and Romans and is still used for food in some parts of central Europe. Most of the linseed oil that is produced, however, is used as an industrial oil.

TABLE 1. World Production of Barley (in Thousands of Tonnes)[a]

Crop Years	China	United States	Argentina	Canada	Republic of Korea	Denmark	Morocco	France	India	Japan	USSR	W. Germany	Spain	Turkey	United Kingdom	World Total
1961		392	37	113		129	25	249	132	8	610	125	80	143	232	3,455
1962		428	16	166		152	55	271	145	73	720	172	99	147	269	3,910
1963		393	46	221		156	67	339	111	34	750	164	95	179	308	4,060
1964–5[a]		8,405	826	3,632	1,515	3,900	1,168	6,791	2,038	1,203	23,800	3,798	1,927	2,800	7,523	94,497
1965–6		8,558	404	4,671	1,807	4,125	1,189	7,378	2,523	1,234	19,000	3,264	1,891	3,100	8,191	93,779
1966–7		8,537	438	6,558	2,018	4,159	506	7,421	2,377	1,105	24,000	3,753	2,006	3,500	8,724	101,219
1967–8		8,137	588	5,414	1,916	4,382	1,100	9,874	2,348	1,032	20,700	4,592	2,576	3,800	9,215	103,566
1968–9		9,278	556	7,084	2,084	5,059	2,223	9,139	3,504	1,021	24,600	4,825	3,708	3,500	8,271	114,388
1969–0		9,298	570	8,238	2,066	5,255	1,310	9,452	2,424	812	26,800	4,796	3,969	3,700	8,663	117,354
1970–1		9,060	367	9,050	1,974	4,813	1,477	8,126	2,716	573	31,600	4,611	3,092	3,300	7,529	119,579
1971–2		10,094	553	13,099	1,857	5,458	1,675	8,930	2,784	503	34,564	5,601	4,783	4,170	8,558	136,475
1972–3		9,220	880	11,285	1,965	5,572	1,744	10,425	2,577	325	36,800	5,817	4,358	3,725	9,238	138,500
1973–4		9,188	732	10,224	1,778	5,507	1,255	10,844	2,379	216	55,044	6,622	4,402	2,900	9,007	157,992
1974–5		6,619	430	8,802	1,388	5,967	2,387	10,037	2,371	233	54,161	7,048	5,404	3,330	9,133	159,881
1975–6		8,361	523	9,520	1,700	5,156	1,585	9,344	3,135	221	35,808	6,971	6,728	4,500	8,513	144,467
1976–7		8,099	760	10,513	1,759	4,768	2,761	8,319	3,192	210	69,539	6,487	5,473	4,900	7,648	177,987
1977–8	6,860	9,144	353	11,799	814	6,084	1,345	10,290	2,344	206	52,687	7,483	6,693	4,750	10,520	104,546
1978–9	6,700	9,776	554	10,397	1,348	6,301	2,326	11,321	2,311	326	62,077	8,608	8,608	4,750	9,848	182,000
1979–0[b]	6,800	8,230	329	8,460	1,508	6,680	1,886	11,238	2,121	406	45,500	8,156	6,150	4,600	9,550	157,000
1980–1[c]	7,200	7,163	339	11,041	910	6,300	2,000	11,235	2,000	450	57,200	8,720	7,100	4,650	9,600	172,000
1981–2[c]		10,414		13,384												

Source: Foreign Agricultural Service. Department of Agriculture, U.S.
[a]Data prior to 1964–1965 are in millions of bushels.
[b]Preliminary. [c]Estimated.

TABLE 2. Salient Statistics of Barley

	United States and Canada														
	Acreage				Farm Disposition		Average[a] Price		Exports (July to June)		Canadian[a] Supply and Distribution				
Year	Planted (1,000 Acres)	Harvested	Yield Per Harvested Acre (Bushels)	Farm Value of Product (Millions of Dollars)	Feed and Seed (Millions of Bushels)	Sold	Chicago Feed (Cents per Bushel)	Winnipeg[b] 3 West.	Grain[c]	Malt	Stocks August 1st (Millions of Bushels)	Production	Total Supply[d]	Exports[e]	Domestic Disappearance
1961	15,623	12,806	30.6	376	118.5	273.9	111.4	129.0	82.1	2.3	112	113	225	43	124
1962	14,380	12,214	35.0	386	130.4	297.4	104.2	116.1	64.5	3.0	58	166	224	15	120
1963	13,452	11,236	35.0	350	110.8	282.0	98.8	107.4	68.0	2.7	89	221	310	47	145
1964	11,652	10,277	37.6	365	91.4	294.7	101.6	117.0	58.3	2.3	118	168	286	37	160
1965	10,123	9,166	42.9	400	92.9	300.2	114.3	122.1	74.3	2.4	89	218	307	38	171
1966	11,184	10,250	38.3	412	103.8	288.3	117.1	125.1	43.0	2.4	98	301	399	59	208
1967	10,077	9,230	40.5	374	104.2	269.3	100.7	113.2	29.6	1.8	132	249	381	41	209
1968	10,486	9,732	43.8	390	110.4	315.8	77.9	96.1	11.5	2.0	131	325	456	26	232
1969	10,291	9,557	44.7	378	116.6	310.4	83.1	98.0	27.6	1.7	200	378	578	88	290
1970	10,490	9,725	42.8	400	114.9	301.3	104.9	104.3	110.0	2.2	200	416	616	180	292
1971	11,115	10,151	45.7	459	125.7	337.9	96.3	125.7	50.8	2.7	144	602	746	231	321
1972[f]	10,639	9,707	43.6	507	110.3	313.2					194	518	712	156	363
1973[f]	11,335	10,527	40.3	853							193	470	663		
1974[f]	9,534														

United States (1975–1981)														
	Supply				Disappearance							Ending Stocks		
					Domestic Use									
Year and Periods Beginning June 1st	Beginning Stocks	Production	Imports	Total Supply	Food	Alcoholic Beverages	Seed	Residual Feed	Total	Exports	Total Disappearance	Government Owned[g]	Privately Owned[h]	Total Stocks
1975–1966	92.2	379.2	15.7	487.1	8.6	124.8	15.7	334.8	23.9	258.7	—	128.4	128.4	
1976–1977	128.4	383.0	10.8	522.2	8.6	131.5	18.2	171.3	329.6	66.2	395.8	—	126.4	126.4
1977–1978	126.4	427.8	9.4	563.6	8.6	133.1	16.7	174.9	333.3	57.2	390.5	—	173.1	173.1
1978–1979	172.1	449.2	10.7	632.0	8.6	147.5	14.7	206.8	377.6	25.7	403.3	2.5	225.5	228.0
June–September	172.1	449.2	2.8	624.1	2.9	52.5	1.2	77.7	134.3	18.8	153.1	0.8	471.3	472.1
October–December	471.0	—	2.8	473.8	2.1	33.0	2.2	41.5	78.8	4.7	83.5	1.4	389.8	391.2
January–March	390.3	—	3.1	393.4	2.1	35.5	3.7	55.4	96.7	0.8	97.5	2.3	294.1	296.4
April–May	295.9	—	2.0	297.9	1.5	26.5	7.6	32.2	67.8	1.4	69.2	2.5	225.5	228.0
1979–1980[f]	228.0	382.8	11.8	622.6	8.6	151.3	4.0	201.8	375.7	54.8	430.5	3.2	188.9	192.1
June–September	228.0	382.8	3.7	614.5	2.9	51.9	1.1	86.9	142.8	9.9	152.7	2.9	458.9	461.8
October–December	461.8	—	2.8	464.6	2.1	34.0	2.0	38.5	76.6	22.4	99.0	3.1	362.5	365.6
January–March	365.6	—	3.2	368.8	2.1	37.4	3.4	52.5	95.4	11.1	106.5	3.3	259.0	262.3
April–May	262.3	—	2.1	264.4	1.5	28.0	7.5	23.9	60.9	11.4	72.3	3.2	188.9	192.1
1980–1981[i]	192.1	358.5	10.0	560.6	8.6	149.0	14.0	185.0	356.6	75.0	431.6			129.0
June–September	193.1	358.5	3.5	354.1	2.9	56.6	1.0	77.9	138.4	24.9	163.3	3.5	387.3	390.8
October–December	390.8	—	2.3	393.1	2.1	35.0	2.0	30.1	69.2	21.4	90.6	3.5	299.0	302.5

Sources: Economic Research Service; Department of Agriculture, U. S. [a]Year beginning August. [b]In U.S. currency. [c]Does not include pearl barley. [d]Includes imports which are normally quite small. [e]Including barley malt. [f]Preliminary. [g]Uncommitted inventory. [h]Includes quantity under loan and farmer-owned reserve. [i]Estimate.

TABLE 3. Contract Specifications

Winnipeg Commodity Exchange—Domestic Feed Barley	
Delivery months	October, December, March, May, and July
Trading unit	100-tonne board lot, 20-tonne job lot
Quotation	Canadian dollars per tonne
Minimum fluctuation	$0.10 per tonne
Daily price movement limits	$5.00 per tonne
Deliverable grade	No. 1 feed, or No. 2 feed at $3 per tonne discount
Delivery	Thunder Bay, Ontario
Trading hours	9:30 a.m.–1:15 p.m. central time
London Grain Futures Market—Barley	
Delivery month	September, November, January, March, and May
Trading unit	100 tonnes (2,240.6226 lbs)
Minimum fluctuation	£0.05 (pounds sterling) per tonne
Daily price limits	None
Position limits	None
Grades deliveable	Conforms to European Economic Community standards: **1.** Barley is to be sound and sweet and to contain not more than 3% heat damage. **2.** Natural weight not less than 50 lb per bushel. **3.** Moisture content not to exceed 15.5%. **4.** Admixture of seeds, farinaceous grains, and dirt is not to exceed 5%; dirt not to exceed 1%. **5.** Sprouted grains not to exceed 5%.
Delivery	From storage approval by the Clearing House Committee of the GAFTA and to be located within the mainland of Great Britain.
Trading hours	11:00 a.m.–12:30 p.m. 2:45 p.m.–4:00 p.m.

PRODUCTION. Flaxseed is grown in temperate climates in well-drained sandy loam. It is sown in May and June and harvested in September and October.

World production of flaxseed from 1977–1978 to 1981–1982 averaged 2.69 million tonnes per year, 8% more than in the previous 5 years. Argentina is the world's largest producer of flaxseed, followed by Canada and India. The United States and the Soviet Union are also significant producers of flaxseed.

Canada is the largest exporter of raw flaxseed. Over the last 5 years, an average of 449,000 tonnes of flaxseed, about 75% of Canada's production, has been exported.

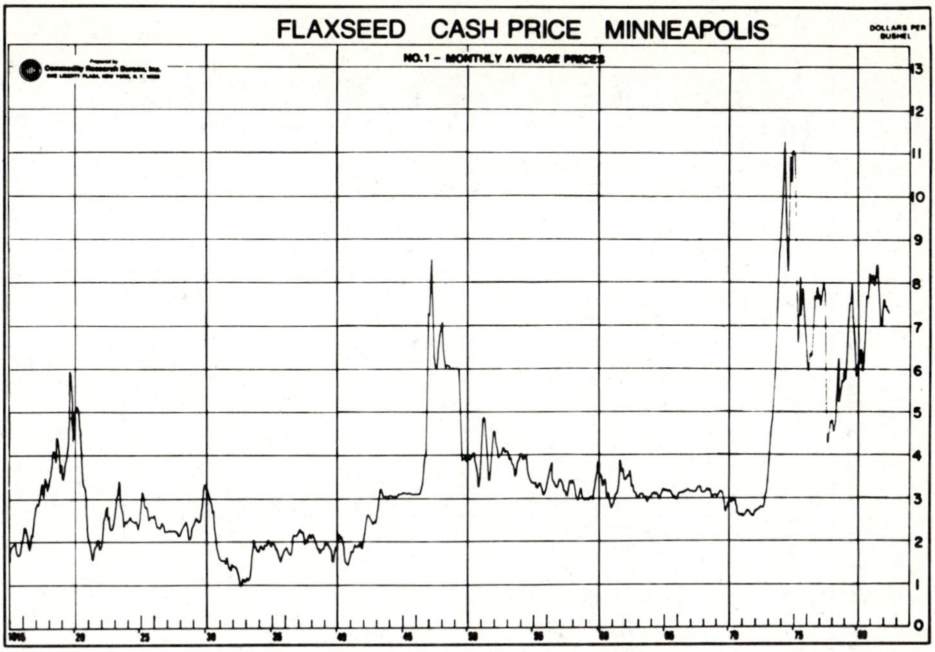

FIGURE 2. Flaxseed cash price—Minneapolis.

Argentina and India crush virtually all of their production domestically. Argentina is the largest exporter of linseed oil and linseed meal. It exports an average of 201,000 tonnes of oil annually, 93% of its production, and 431,000 tonnes of meal, 98% of its production.

CONSUMPTION AND USAGE. Flaxseed is crushed commercially to produce linseed oil and linseed meal. Commercial crushing of flaxseed yields about 42% of its weight in oil. Linseed oil is the world's major industrial oil derived from plant origin. It is used as a drying oil in paints, printing inks, and varnishes.

The crushing operation also produces linseed meal which is used for livestock feed. Linseed meal is high in protein and has a high mineral content.

The European Economic Community is the major importer of flaxseed and flaxseed products from North and South America. In the last 5 years, the EEC has imported an average of 330,000 tonnes of flaxseed, 614,000 tonnes of meal, and 98,000 tonnes of linseed oil.

Japan and the United States are also significant importers of flaxseed. Japanese imports are fairly consistent, averaging 99,000 tonnes over the last 5 years. United States imports vary significantly, depending on the level of domestic flaxseed production. Over the last 5 years, imports have ranged from a low of 18,800 tonnes in 1977–1978 to a high of 95,200 tonnes in 1980–1981.

FUTURES MARKET. Flaxseed futures are traded on *The Winnipeg Commodity Exchange*. Contract specifications appear in Table 6.

TABLE 4. World Production of Flaxseed (in Thousands of Tonnes)[a]

Crop Year	Argentina	Australia	Brazil	Canada	Ethiopia	France	India	Mexico	Poland	Romania	Turkey	Uruguay	United States	USSR	World Total
1961–1962	32,203	504	1,098	14,318			15,558	787			709	3,770	22,178	18,500	121,562
1962–1963	33,014	1,030	1,717	16,042			17,960	737			748	3,324	32,230	—	133,650
1963–1964	30,353	1,181	802	21,116	2,047	2,104	17,038	737	2,401	709	709	2,444	31,041	17,900	136,583
1964–1965	32,085	1,864	2,114	20,313	2,165	1,972	14,920	748	1,378	937	689	2,808	24,140	17,600	131,231
1965–1966	22,440	244	1,659	29,254	2,205	1,094	19,806	787	3,031	1,374	551	1,482	35,402	22,835	147,735
1966–1967[a]	597	14	36	559	57	39	335	14	72	38	11	40	594	607	3,111
1967–1968	385	11	28	238	60	33	260	15	73	39	12	27	509	519	2,319
1968–1969	510	20	28	500	60	22	438	10	65	30	12	56	685	485	3,033
1969–1970	640	37	31	700	62	20	329	10	57	38	12	105	887	451	3,499
1970–1971	680	31	22	1,243	64	19	469	30	65	42	7	64	751	404	3,995
1971–1972	316	10	12	567	70	21	474	40	75	58	7	43	462	464	2,748
1972–1973	330	11	12	448	69	18	530	10	54	51	6	29	353	413	2,446
1973–1974	297	14	12	493	72	18	428	11	51	45	6	26	409	507	2,393
1974–1975	381	33	10	351	72	6	564	20	40	39	7	39	358	388	2,416
1975–1976	377	13	8	445	75	32	598	27	36	45	8	62	395	340	2,564
1976–1977	750	12	7	277	50	16	431	8	49	50	7	46	199	337	2,347
1977–1978	855	35	5	650	50	44	527	18	38	50	6	40	409	300	2,987
1978–1979	630	16	6	571	50	44	514	16	50	50	6	31	277	250	2,472
1979–1980[b]	743	16		815		35	270	16	24		6	60	305	250	2,664
1980–1981[c]	620			465			525						206	250	2,363
1981–1982	600			477			400						198	200	2,079

Source: Department of Agriculture, Foreign Agricultural Service, U.S.
[a]Data prior to 1966–1967 are in thousands of bushels. [b]Preliminary. [c]Estimate.

TABLE 5. Supply and Distribution of Linseed Oil in the United States (in Millions of Pounds)

	Supply				Domestic Disappearance								
					Drying Oil Products								
Crop Year	Stocks June 1st	Production	Total	Exports & Shipments	Paint & Varnish	Linoleum & Oilcloth	Resins	Other	Total	Lubricants & Similar Oils	Fatty Acids	Total	Flaxseed (Oil Equivalent of Exports)[a]
1963–1964	131	394	525	14	388	14	19	10	381	2	4	388	72
1964–1965	144	418	557	20	294	14	22	8	338	3	3	344	130
1965–1966	198	463	661	84	283	14	19	8	324	5	7	336	105
1966–1967	241	405	646	121	278	14	21	11	324	6	—	329	149
1967–1968	196	331	527	53	227	10	19	11	267	4	1	273	101
1968–1969	201	300	501	77	223	20	20	10	273	1	1	275	197
1969–1970[d]	152[d]	290	442	40	220	13	19	18	239	12	2	272	131
1970–1971	130	363	495	47	209	8	19	19	239	13	1	261	64
1971–1972	187	428	615	66	221	7	21	16	258	13	3	274	18
1972–1973	275	393	668	256	224	11	25	21	270	14	—	285	200
1973–1974	127	344	471	142	205	11	21	22	248	10	—	259	13
1974–1975	71	263	334	143	112	3	11	12	134	8	—	142	7
1975–1976	49	231	279	42	154	—	10	9	173	10	4	187	19
1976–1977	49	217	266	14	126		13	8	156	9	8	164	4
1977–1978[1b]	88	232	320	25	177		23	15		7	3	225	20
1978–1979[2c]	70	260	330	54									
1979–1980[2c]	44	225											
1980–1981[c]		148											

[a]Based on 20 lbs of linseed oil per bushel of flaxseed exports. [b]Preliminary. [c]Estimate. [d]Data prior to 1969 has crop year beginning July and stocks as of July 1.

TABLE 6. Contract Specifications

Winnipeg Commodity Exchange Flaxseed	
Delivery month	October, December, March, May, and July
Trading unit	100-tonne board lot, 20-tonne job lot
Quotation	Canadian dollars per tonne
Minimum fluctuation	0.10 per tonne
Daily price movement limits	$10.00 per tonne
Deliverable grade	No.1 C, or No.2 C at $2 per tonne discount
Delivery	Thunder Bay, Ontario
Trading hours	9:30 a.m.–1:15 p.m. central time

RAPESEED

The name *rapeseed* comes from the Latin word *rapum*, which means turnip. Rapeseed is closely related to a number of familiar vegetables, including turnip, rutabaga, cabbage, brussel sprouts, and mustard.

Ancient Asian and Mediterranean civilizations used rapeseed oil in lamps and as a cooking oil, and records show that rapeseed was grown in Europe in the 13th century. Production of rapeseed did not become extensive, however, until the development of steam power, when rapeseed oil was found to have superior lubricant powers.

The use of rapeseed for the production of *edible oil* has increased significantly since the mid-1950s, at least in part as a result of plant breeders' efforts to alter the genetic makeup of rapeseed. In Canada, the world's largest producer and exporter of rapeseed, 90% of production is of varieties which produce oil extremely low in erucic acid, a fatty acid, and a meal low in glucosinolates (sulfur compounds). Other major producing countries are moving to the production of varieties with similar chemical qualities.

PRODUCTION. World *rapeseed production* rose steadily through the 1970s to reach a projected 11.8 million tonnes, 7% of the total world production of all oilseeds, by 1981–1982.

Canada is the major producer and exporter of rapeseed. Canada's 5-year average annual production is 2.6 million tonnes, about 25% of the world total. China and India are traditionally the other major producers of rapeseed, although both countries consume all of their production domestically. In recent years, France has also become a major producer and exporter of rapeseed.

Rapeseed may be seeded in the fall or in the spring, depending on the severity of the winter in the growing area. Spring rapeseed, which is the major type grown in Canada, is seeded in May and early June and harvested from August through October.

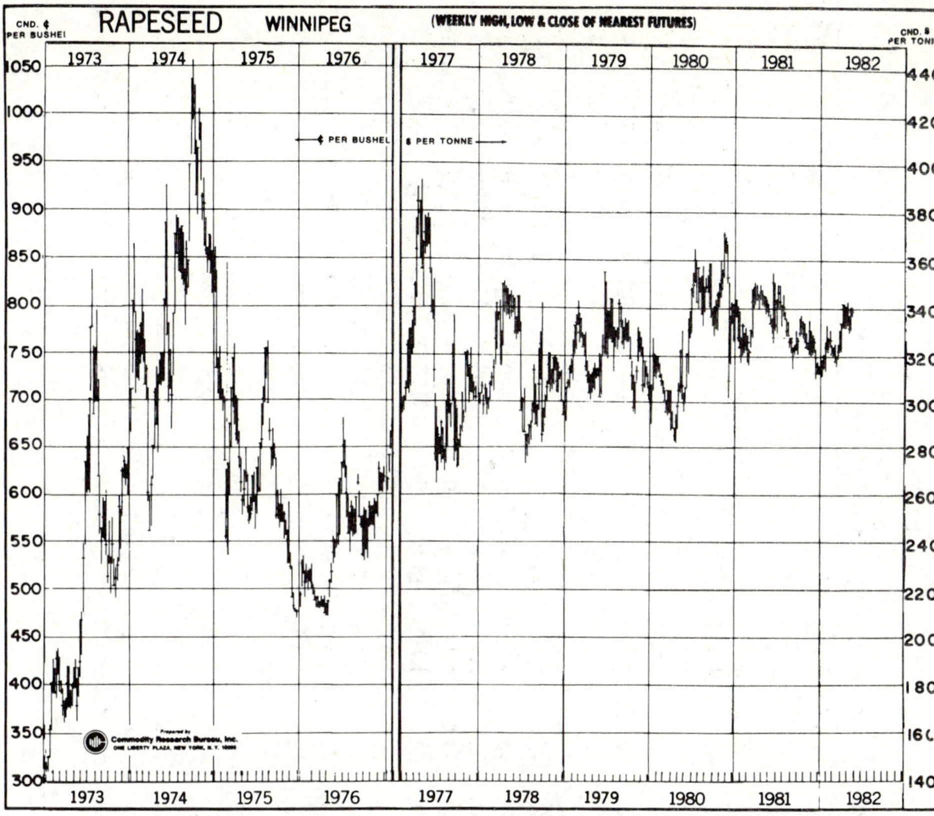

FIGURE 3. Rapeseed weekly nearest futures price—Winnipeg.

CONSUMPTION AND USAGE. Rapeseed yields about 42% of its weight as oil. The oil is used in foods, as cooking oil, and in margarine. Rapeseed meal is a high-protein livestock feed.

Canada exports more than half of its rapeseed production, but domestic crush rose steadily through the last 10 years and now accounts for about 40% of production.

France, which doubled its production of rapeseed in the last 2 years, crushes more than 60% of its production domestically. France currently exports about 35% of its crop.

Japan is the largest importer of rapeseed. Western Europe is also a major importer.

FUTURES MARKET. Rapeseed futures are traded on *The Winnipeg Commodity Exchange*. Contract Specifications appear in Table 8.

RYE

Rye is a cereal grass which is grown on every continent except Africa. Rye was probably originally cultivated in southwest Asia about 6000 B.C. Production of

TABLE 7. World Production of Rapeseed (in Thousands of Tonnes)[a]

Year[b]	Canada	China	Czecho-slovakia	Denmark	France	East Germany	West Germany	India	Japan	Bangladesh	Pakistan	Poland	Sweden	Chile	World Total
1962	280.5	645.0	92.6	29.1	117.4	191.0	82.0	1,485	301.5	—351.1—		283.3	130.0		4,189
1963	146.5	575.0	52.9	57.4	176.3	182.2	127.1	1,484	272.0	—341.6—		397.9	160.8		4,130
1964	209.0	625.0	45.2	29.1	148.8	141.3	105.6	1,426	120.0	—399.8—		250.2	113.4	55.9	3,778
1965[a]	300.1	660.0	46.0	52.3	246.6	175.7	108.7	903.0	134.6	—301.8—		267.0	181.1	50.9	3,557
1966	512.6	700.0	74.0	49.9	337.8	213.8	106.5	1,466	125.5	—306.8—		504.0	216.5	60.0	4,802
1967	585.1	735.0	78.0	33.1	317.	210.8	98.7	1,276	94.6	—278.4—		448.0	95.0	77.0	4,455
1968	560.2	800.0	85.0	39.2	432.5	272.6	124.6	1,228	79.2	120.0	270.0	651.0	245.7	60.7	5,127
1969	440	688.0	48.0	21.1	514.0	163.8	158.1	1,347	48.0	126.0	246.0	204.0	208.0	63.6	4,751
1970	758	780.0	63.0	22.2	582.0	181.0	185.0	1,564	30.1	136.0	265.0	566.0	191.0	69.9	6,461
1971	1,638	830.0	100.6	51.0	668.0	197.0	228.2	1,975	22.8	112.1	269.0	595.0	254.0	82.0	7,815
1972	2,155	1,000	107.0	51	722.0	234.0	248.7	1,433	15.9	106.0	301.0	430.0	327.0	77.9	6,624
1973	1,300	1,050	117.0	92	661.0	246.0	242	1,808	13.0	98	287.0	512.0	339	35.0	7,001
1974	1,207	1,075	85	112	690	280	301	1,692	9	107	293	523	351	33	7,022
1975[c]	1,163	1,090	115	115	532	250	194	2,300	7	110	305	726	327	55	7,989
1976[c]	1,749			90	561							980	279		
1977[d]	1,940	1,380		110	440			1,650			240	650	256		8,060
1978[d]	3,497	1,868	166	91	568	301	322	1,860	5	137	243	691	330	65	10,703
1979[d]	3,414	2,402	81	148	510	195	362	1,433	5	140	300	233	297	73	10,180
1980[d]	2,509	2,350	180	150	1,140	256	380	2,000	5	140	300	564	373	75	11,097
1981[d]	1,794	3,800			1,023			2,200				486			12,005

Source: U.S. Department of Agriculture, Foreign Agricultural Service. [a]Data prior to 1965 are in thousands of short tons. [b]Harvest generally occurs in the first half of the calendar year given in all major producing countries except Canada. [c]Preliminary. [d]Estimate.

TABLE 8. Contract Specifications

Winnipeg Commodity Exchange Rapeseed	
Delivery months	January, March, June, September, and November
Trading unit	100-tonne board lot, 20-tonne job lot
Quotation	Canadian dollars per tonne
Minimum fluctuation	0.10 per tonne
Daily price limits	$10 per tonne
Deliverable grade	No. 1 CR, or No. 2 CR at $13 per ton discount
Delivery	Vancouver, British Columbia, with alternate points: Moose Jaw Saskatchewan; Saskatoon, Saskatchewan; Edmonton, Alberta; Calgary, Alberta; Lethbridge, Alberta.
Trading hours	9:30 a.m.–1:15 p.m. central time.

rye spread west and north from there. Today, rye is grown extensively in Europe, particularly in the north, where it is staple food in some countries.

Rye is the only cereal grain other than wheat with the necessary qualities to make bread. It has approximately the same protein level as wheat and also contains small amounts of potassium and B vitamins. It does not, however, have the same elasticity as wheat and, as a result, bread made solely of rye flour is very dense and very dark. Bread made from 100% rye flour is known as black bread. To compensate for the lack of elasticity, most rye bread made today is from a blend of rye and wheat flours.

PRODUCTION. Rye is generally grown where soil and climate conditions are unfavorable for other grains or where temperatures are too cool to support production of winter wheat. No other cereal grain is as tolerant of poor soil conditions, and rye's ability to withstand cool temperatures allows it to be grown almost as far north as the Arctic Circle.

Average annual world production of rye has fallen in recent years to about 25 million tonnes. The USSR is the largest producer of rye by far, accounting for 40% of total world production. Eastern European countries are also large producers.

Rye production in the United States has fallen in recent years as a result of a decline in acreage. In Canada, on the other hand, rye acreage has increased recently. Rye is normally seeded in September and October and harvested in late July and August.

Canada is a relatively small producer of rye averaging less than 600,000 tonnes per year, but it is the world's major exporter. More than one-third of total world trade in rye originates in Canada.

CONSUMPTION. The largest part of North American rye production in recent years has moved into the export market. The Soviet Union and Poland are the major buyers.

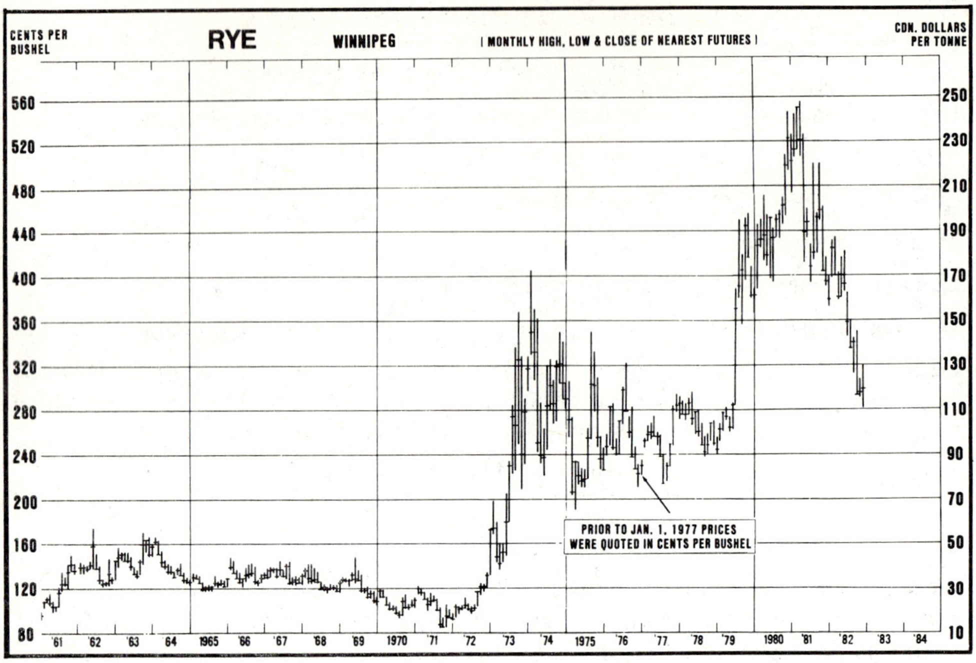

(a)

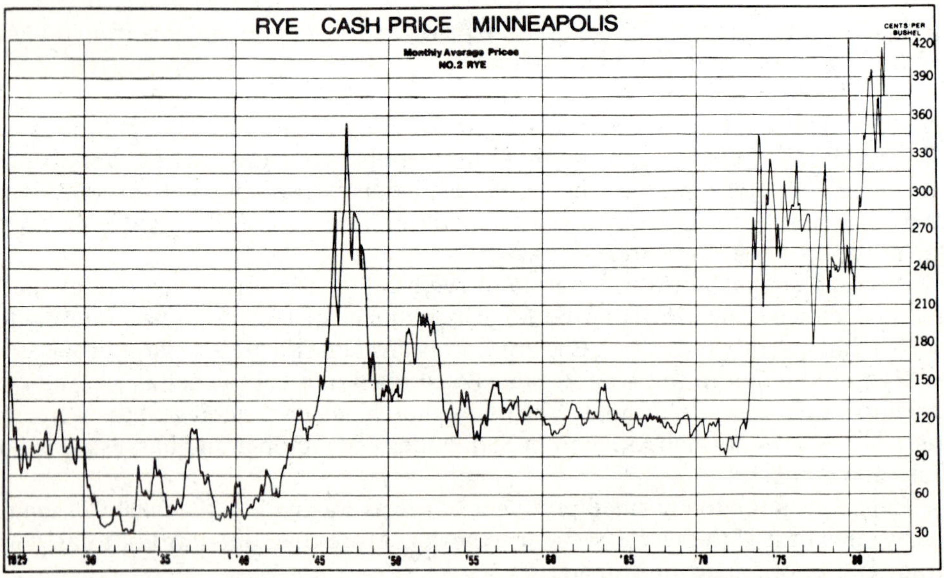

(b)

FIGURE 4. (*a*) Rye cash price—Winnipeg. (*b*) Rye cash price—Minneapolis. (*Source*: Commodity Research Bureau)

TABLE 9. World Production of Rye (in Thousands of Tonnes)[a]

Crop Year	Argentina	Austria	Canada	Czecho-slovakia	Denmark	France	West Germany	East Germany	Hungary	Nether-lands	Poland	Spain	Turkey	USSR	United States	World Total
1961	20.9	18.6	6.5	37.8	20.2	15.3	98.9	59.2	11.7	11.9	238.5	13.8	24.0	600	27	1,340
1962	6.5	18.4	12.0	36.1	20.2	14.0	116.6	63.9	9.2	13.4	263.2	17.8	24.6	540	41	1,246
1963	21.2	12.7	12.8	34.6	12.6	14.1	127.5	62.0	8.5	12.3	280.5	16.7	33.5	460	29	1,182
1964	25.6	15.3	12.2	34.3	11.5	15.3	142.1	74.4	10.4	14.0	275.0	13.8	26.6	504	32	1,256
1965–1966	9.6	12.4	16.7	32.4	10.4	15.2	111.2	75.2	11.3	9.8	326.3	13.4	27.6	571	33	1,327
1966–1967	10.6	14.3	17.2	30.9	5.5	14.0	106.1	64.6	9.5	7.5	306.7	14.1	30.7	472	28	1,170
1967–1968[a]	352	377	304	689	118	365	3,218	1,986	225	239	7,645	336	825	11,900	608	30,280
1968–1969	360	413	331	769	127	351	3,247	1,936	238	239	8,438	364	780	12,700	583	31,879
1969–1970	377	440	419	687	126	330	2,928	1,544	235	207	8,166	348	770	9,800	767	28,057
1970–1971	181	363	570	454	134	306	2,701	1,483	155	172	5,433	256	680	10,800	936	25,596
1971–1972	256	448	557	619	150	308	3,188	1,754	182	209	7,827	269	900	10,600	1,252	29,605
1972–1973	500	402	344	633	155	350	2,954	1,947	171	151	8,149	263	755	9,600	741	28,212
1973–1974	613	400	363	688	140	327	2,693	1,699	175	105	8,268	252	690	10,759	660	28,859
1974–1975	306	415	480	671	168	315	2,559	1,949	175	78	7,881	254	560	15,218	483	32,629
1975–1976	273	347	523	530	163	292	2,126	1,563	147	63	6,270	241	750	9,064	457	23,702
1976–1977	330	410	440	561	214	284	2,100	1,455	156	65	6,922	214	740	13,991	381	29,397
1977–1978	170	351	392	540	320	375	2,546	1,500	142	74	6,257	205	690	8,471	462	23,440
1978–1979[b]	210	410	605	625	326	432	2,452	1,895	136	68	7,427	259	620	13,603	665	30,583
1979–1980[c]	170	336	525	500	280	360	2,082	1,800	100	47	5,000	217	600	8,000	599	21,393
1980–1981[c]	190	383	448	585	199	407	2,189	1,700	130	40	6,600	290	600	9,800	419	24,806

Source: U.S. Department of Agriculture, Foreign Agricultural Service. [a]Data prior to 1967–1968 are in millions of bushels. [b]Preliminary. [c]Estimate.

TABLE 10. Salient Statistics of Rye

United States (1961–1967)

Year Beginning July	Acreage (1,000 Acres)		Yield per Harvested Acre (Bushels)	Farm Value of Product (Millions of Dollars)	Farm Disposition (Millions of Bushels)			National Average Support Rate		Canadian Rye (Millions of Bushels)				
										Supply			Disappearance	
	Planted[a]	Harvested[b]			Seed	Feed	Sold	Dollars Per Bushel	Percent of Parity	August 1st Stocks	Production	Total[c]	Domestic	Exports (including Flour)
1961	4,157	1,543	17.7	27.7	1,868	4,512	20,956	1.02	69	7.4	6.5	14.0	5.8	4.4
1962	4,880	1,981	20.5	39.0	1,897	4,345	34,456	1.02	70	3.8	12.0	15.9	4.4	7.3
1963	4,376	1,588	18.4	31.9	1,855	3,307	24,016	1.07	75	4.2	12.8	17.2	4.6	5.5
1964	4,552	1,696	19.1	34.0	1,856	3,341	27,279	1.07	78	7.1	12.2	19.3	6.1	4.9
1965–66	4,237	1,473	22.6	32.8	1,562	3,347	28,398	1.02	73	8.3	16.7	25.0	6.4	8.1
1966–67	3,980	1,276	21.8	29.9	1,458	3,119	23,214	1.02	73	10.5	17.2	27.7	9.4	10.0
1967–68	3,660	1,063	22.5	26.2	1,293	2,626	20,030	1.02	73	8.3	12.0	20.3	8.0	4.8

United States (1968–1981)

Year Beginning June 1st	Supply: Stocks, June 1st: Privately Owned[d]	Supply: Stocks, June 1st: Government[e]	Supply: Total Stocks	Supply: Production	Supply: Imports	Supply: Total Supply	Disappearance: Domestic Use: Food	Disappearance: Domestic Use: Alcoholic Beverages	Disappearance: Domestic Use: Seed	Disappearance: Domestic Use: Feed[f]	Disappearance: Domestic Use: Total	Disappearance: Exports	Disappearance: Total Disappearance	Acreage: Planted	Acreage: Harvested for Grain	Yield Per Harvested Acre
			(Thousands of Bushels)											(Millions of Acres)		Bushels
1968–69			19,519	22,971	1,056	43,546	5,563	4,697	5,753	9,157	25,170	1,082	26,252	3,425	996	23.1
1969–0			17,294	30,204	472	47,970	5,392	4,310	6,054	9,529	25,285	805	26,090	3,959	1,291	23.4
1970–1			21,880	36,840	1,047	59,767	5,430	3,522	6,873	11,407	27,232	3,204	30,436	4,196	1,427	25.8
1971–2			29,331	49,223	241	78,795	5,195	3,005	5,262	16,276	29,738	2,177	31,915	4,842	1,751	28.1
1972–3			46,880	28,256	154	75,290	5,122	3,038	5,321	16,458	29,939	6,535	36,474	3,458	1,050	26.9
1973–4			38,816	24,677	1	63,494	6,250	2,547	4,967	8,042	21,806	27,513	49,319	3,380	955	25.8
1974–5	14,175	—	14,175	17,506	277	31,958	5,459	1,386	4,215	7,811	18,871	6,465	25,336	2,828	784	22.3
1975–6	6,622	—	6,622	15,924	944	23,524	4,172	2,060	4,217	7,554	18,003	1,117	19,120	2,829	728	21.9
1976–7	4,404	—	4,404	14,891	248	19,500	3,696	1,930	4,217	5,304	15,147	38	15,100	2,652	719	20.7
1977–8	4,418	—	4,418	16,543	127	21,100	3,648	1,875	4,806	6,800	17,100	24	17,100	2,652	677	24.4
1978–9[g]	4,137	—	4,137	24,065	145	28,200	3,690	2,369	4,900	7,900	18,900	300	19,200	2,865	t926	26.0
1979–0[g]	8,973	—	8,973	22,389	—	31,400	3,500	2,100	4,200	7,000	16,800	2,400	19,200	2,921	869	25.8
1980–1[b]	12,000	192	12,192	16,265	—	28,500	3,500	2,200	4,200	8,500	18,400	6,500	24,900	2,527	664	24.5
1981–2[b]	4,000	145	4,145	18,621		22,800	3,500	2,100	4,200	7,000	16,800	2,000	18,800	2,594	697	26.7

Source: Economic Research Service, U.S.A. [a] Preliminary. [b]For grain. [c]Includes imports. [d]Includes total loans. [e]Uncommitted, government. [f]Residual; approximates total feed use. [g]Acreage seeded in preceding fall. All purposes. [h]Forecast.

TABLE 11. Contract Specifications

Winnipeg Commodity Exchange Rye	
Delivery months	October, December, March, May, and July
Trading unit	100-tonne board lot, 20-tonne job lot
Quotation	Canadian dollars per tonne
Minimim fluctuation	\$0.10 per tonne
Daily price movement limits	\$5 per tonne
Deliverable grade	No. 1 CW, or No. 2 CW at \$2 per tonne discount
Delivery	Thunder Bay, Ontario
Trading hours	9:30 a.m.–1:15 p.m. central time

Rye is also used domestically in both the United States and Canada as a component in livestock feed, by the milling and baking industry for making bread, and by distillers for the manufacture of whiskey.

Production of rye in the United States has averaged about 480,000 tonnes per year recently. An average of about 38% of rye use is for livestock feed. About 18% is milled for flour and another 11% is distilled. Exports vary widely from a recent high of 26% of production to almost none.

Canadian rye moves much more steadily into the export market. In recent years, more than 60% of Canadian rye production has been exported. Domestic use in Canada has been declining, with distillers consuming 12% of total use, 22% being fed to livestock and 2% distilled.

FUTURES MARKET. Rye futures contracts are traded on *The Winnipeg Commodity Exchange*. Contract specifications appear in Table 11.

CHAPTER 30

THE SOYBEAN COMPLEX CASH AND FUTURES MARKETS

CONTENTS

THE MARKETING CHAIN 4

SOYBEAN PRODUCTION 6

SOYBEAN PROCESSING 6

THE SOYBEAN CASH MARKET 7

World Markets 7
U.S. Market 10

THE SOYBEAN MEAL CASH MARKET 19

World Markets 19
U.S. Markets 19

SOYBEAN OIL CASH MARKET 26

World Markets 26
U.S. Market 30

FUTURES TRADING IN THE SOYBEAN COMPLEX 33

TRADING PRACTICES IN THE CASH AND FUTURES MARKETS 33

Gross Processing Margin and the Crushing Hedge 36

CONCLUSION 38

APPENDIX A: GLOSSARY OF SOYBEAN TERMS 38

APPENDIX B: STANDARDS FOR SOYBEANS 44

APPENDIX C: CONVERSION TABLE 47

BIBLIOGRAPHY 48

ORGANIZATIONS 49

CHAPTER 30

THE SOYBEAN COMPLEX CASH AND FUTURES MARKETS

Frank S. Rose
Randall E. Sheldon

The soybean has been an important cultivated crop of the world for many centuries. The soybean originated in northern China and, in writings dating from 2838 B.C., was described as being one of the five sacred grains essential to Chinese civilization. Commercial development of the soybean industry began in the 18th and 19th centuries and may be related to two major developments—the extraction of soybean oil and the introduction of the soybean to Europe in 1712 and to the United States in 1804.

Nearly a century and a half elapsed between the introduction of the soybean into the United States and the advent of large-scale production. But by 1937, 10,000 varieties of soybeans had been brought into the United States, forming a sound basis for the development of the types of soybeans suited to the soil and climatic conditions of the United States. Since then, American soybean production has grown spectacularly—doubling in both the 1960s and 1970s and reaching a record 2.27 billion bushels in 1979.

Today soybeans are grown on more acreage in the United States than any other crop except corn and wheat. The farm value of U.S. soybean production in 1980 and 1981 was higher than any other domestic crop except corn. However, the principal economic value of the soybean does not lie with the soybean itself, but with the oil and meal derived from it. Nearly all of the domestic soybean production is processed (either at home or abroad) into these products which have a variety of food, feed, and industrial uses.

This chapter discusses the production and marketing of the commodities in the soybean complex—soybeans, soybean oil, and soybean meal—giving special emphasis to the factors which influence the prices of the three commodities. The section "The Marketing Chain" traces the path of the soybean through the marketing chain—from the farm, through the various stages of handling and processing, to the ultimate consumer, at home or abroad. Then, following this overview of the entire marketing chain, the individual links are examined more closely. In the sections "Soybean Production" and "Soybean Processing," soybean production and processing are described. The national and international supply-and-demand picture of the three commodities is discussed in the sections "The Soybean Cash Market," "The Soybean Meal Cash Market," and "The Soybean Oil Cash Market," with particular attention given to the factors associated with supply, demand, and price changes in recent years. Following this discussion of the performance of the cash market, the futures markets for soybeans, oil, and meal are described in the section "Futures Trading in the Soybean Complex" and the specifications of available futures contracts are outlined. Then, the cash and futures markets are linked in the section "Trading Practices in the Cash and Futures Markets," in a discussion of the merchandising considerations and trading practices of those producing and marketing soybeans and their products. Supporting data and sources of further information are given in the Appendixes.

THE MARKETING CHAIN

Soybeans are grown in a large production area which includes the Midwest, the Mississippi River basin, and parts of the southeastern and mid-Atlantic states. Production centers, though, are in the Corn Belt states of Illinois, Iowa, Missouri, Indiana, Minnesota, and Ohio. These states accounted for over 60% of national output in 1982.

After the harvest in the fall, most of the crop moves from the farm to country elevators located in producing regions, though farmers may hold some of the crop in on-farm storage facilities or ship directly to processors, to larger subterminal elevators, or to large grain terminals in cities like Chicago, Minneapolis, and Kansas City. The bulk of the shipments from country elevators in soybean production areas is destined for the larger subterminal elevators and grain merchants located near soybean processors and export positions, although some soybeans move directly to the processors. From the subterminal and terminal elevators, soybeans move either to domestic processors or into export channels. In recent years, about one-half of the soybean crop has flowed to the U.S. processing industry and much of the rest has been exported as whole soybeans. Eighty percent of the soybean exports pass through gulf ports. The inland waterway system provides the principal transportation link to these ports.

Most of the soybean processing capacity in the United States is located in the main soybean production areas. In 1981 Illinois and Iowa accounted for over 40% of the nation's soybean meal production. Because it is high in crude and digestible protein and low in fiber, soybean meal is an important ingredient in animal feeds, principally those mixed for nonruminant animals such as poultry and hogs. Most soybean meal is used for this purpose, both in the United States and abroad, though it has numerous other uses (see Table 1). From the processor, the meal moves by barge, rail, or truck into three main market channels: export, feed manufacturing, and direct sales to farmers. Nearly 30% moves into export—mostly via New Orleans—and most of the remainder is used in commercially prepared feeds and rations. Farm buyers are typically large operators who mix their own feed.

TABLE 1. Uses of Soybeans, Soybean Oil, and Soybean Meal

	Foods	Feed	Industrial	Seed
Whole soybeans	Baked soybeans Dietetic foods Full-fat soy flour Roasted soybeans Soy butter Soy cereal	Puffed soybeans Roasted soybeans Steamed soybeans		Hybridization planting
Soybean oil	(Refined soybean oil) Cooking oil Margarine Mayonnaise Prepared foods Salad oil Spreads (Soybean lecithin) Coatings Emulsifiers Nutrients		(Refined soybean oil) Adhesives Disinfectants Inks Plastics (Soybean lecithin) Antifoam agents Antiknock additives Dispensing agents (Sterols) (Fatty acids) (Glycerols)	
Soybean meal	(Basic meal) Baby foods Bakery Beverages Cereals Confections Dietetics Meat analogs Meat products Soups (Isolated proteins) (Soy flour, grits)	(Basic meal) Millfeeds Livestock feeds Pet foods Poultry feeds (Soybean millfeeds)	(Basic meal) Fertilizers Fillers (Soy flour, grits) Adhesives Coatings	

Source: Commodity Trading Manual, Chicago Board of Trade, 1982.

Like meal, oil has a variety of end uses (see Table 1). Oil dominates the edible oil market in the United States just as meal dominates the high-protein feed market. After extraction at the processing plant, the crude oil moves through several intermediate stages of refining and manufacturing on the way to its final use. Some of the refining facilities are owned by processing firms and are located near their soybean processing plants. In other cases, the crude oil is shipped from the processing plant to distant refining and manufacturing firms and to export positions. About 20% of the crude soybean oil produced in this country is sold overseas.

SOYBEAN PRODUCTION

The soybean plant is a legume which usually grows to about waist height. The soybeans develop in pods which grow in clusters of three to five. Two, three, or more soybeans may develop in each pod. The plant has a root system which extends 5 to 6 ft deep, giving it good drought resistance. The soybean grows best on sandy loam soils which are also suitable for cotton and corn. Currently, over 150 varieties of soybeans are grown in the United States. Yields vary widely and are influenced by many factors including variety, growing area, and weather. In 1982, yields in the United States averaged 32 bushels per acre. The highest yields were recorded in Indiana (40 bushels per acre), Illinois (39), and Iowa (37.5).

Planting usually takes place in May and June, after corn planting is completed. Because of the large production area, the planting times can vary from north to south by as much as 2 months. The flowering and maturity of soybeans are controlled largely by photoperiodism—the length of the daily dark period. The length of this daily dark period begins to increase starting in late June, and when the critical point for a given variety of soybeans is finally reached, flowering is triggered. Because of this photoperiodic growth, a specific variety of soybeans will mature on approximately the same calendar date even if time of planting varies somewhat. The leaves begin to yellow in August and harvest takes place in September and October, when the leaves have fallen and the moisture content of the beans is about 13%.

At the various stages of its growth cycle, the soybean plant requires certain climatic conditions for optimal development. Though the seedling is hardy after emergence, a good supply of soil moisture during the germination period is critically important. The plant requires the most moisture around mid-July, when vegetative growth is most rapid and in August when the seeds are filling out. In fact, soybeans often require more moisture than is provided by rainfall during the growing season and good subsoil reserves must make up the deficit. August is a particularly critical month not only with regard to moisture, but also to temperature. Dry weather may limit growth, inhibit seed filling, and reduce the number of seeds per pod. On the other hand, proper moisture levels in August may completely overcome any damage which the plant suffered because of inadequate moisture during flowering. Abnormally high August temperature can sharply reduce yields but increase oil content. Cool temperatures have the opposite effect.

SOYBEAN PROCESSING

Soybeans usually contain between 18 and 22% oil and between 38 and 45% protein. Soybean processing involves separating this oil and meal from the soybeans. Four different methods are used to process the beans into usable oil and meal: hydraulic press, screw press (continuous expeller), solvent, and pre-press solvent. Today, most processing in the United States is done by the solvent extraction method though the mechanical processes are still used for other oilseeds and in other parts of the world. This method is much more efficient than the mechanical methods, leaving only 1% of the oil in the residue, compared to 4–15% left by the mechanical methods. In the solvent extraction process, the dehulled, cracked, and flaked soybeans are put into a solvent, usually hexane, which dissolves the oil component of the soybean. The solvent is then evaporated, leaving crude soybean oil. A 60-lb bushel of soybeans yields about 10.7 lb of crude soybean oil.

The soybean cake, which remains after the extraction of the oil, is cooked and ground into soybean meal. The hulls, which were removed earlier, may be used as feed extenders or gelatinous carriers in molasses and other syrup-type products, or may be put back into the raw meal to adjust its protein content. If the hulls are removed prior to processing, meal containing 49% protein is produced. If hulls are not removed or if hulls are returned to the meal after processing, 44%-protein meal results. About 47.5 lb of soybean meal may be obtained from a bushel of soybeans.

Crude soybean oil must be degummed and refined before it is consumed. Degumming, often done at the extraction plant, involves separating out the gums (phosphatides) using mechanical or chemical means. Refining techniques vary according to end use. A typical procedure used in the United States involves combining caustic soda with the crude oil, separating the resulting soap from the oil by centrifuge, bleaching the oil under conditions of heat and pressure with a bleaching clay, and deodorizing the oil by a steam distillation process. A large part of the soybean oil used for edible purposes is also hydrogenated to some extent.

THE SOYBEAN CASH MARKET

WORLD MARKETS. In the past 10 years, world soybean production has nearly doubled. Though U.S. production has also increased, the U.S. share of world output has dropped from about 75 to 60% as other countries, particularly Brazil and Argentina, have emerged as important producers. World trade has also increased sharply and while the United States dominates with about an 80% share, Argentina and Brazil are becoming increasingly important (see Table 2).

The growth in world soybean consumption in recent years has been due to a rapid growth in world demand for high-protein feed, particularly in North America, Europe, the USSR, and East Asia, and an expansion of demand for vegetable oils in the developing countries.

Government policies have played—and likely will continue to play—an important role in determining changes in production, consumption, trade, and price of soybeans. Brazilian government policy has provided incentives to farmers to replace other crops and pasture with soybeans and has protected the domestic processing industry with favorable tax treatment, export subsidies, and export controls on raw soybeans. In the United States, government incentives have been somewhat less direct in that efforts to restrict wheat, feed grain, and cotton output have not been applied to soybeans. In Western Europe, particularly in the European Commodity (EC) countries, government policies have encouraged greater consumption of soybeans. In the mid-1960s, the EC agreed, in international trade negotiation, not to impose any import restriction on soybeans. This agreement, combined with the EC restrictions imposed on the import of corn and other grains, has spurred European soybean consumption in recent years. This growth has been further encouraged by heavy imports of cassava from Southeast Asia for animal

TABLE 2. Soybeans: World Production, Trade, and Crush,[a] 1977/1978–1981/1982 (1,000 metric tons)

	1977/1978	1978/1979	1979/1980	1980/1981 Preliminary	1981/1982 April	1981/1982 May
Production:						
United States	48,097	50,859	61,722	48,772	55,260	55,260
Brazil	9,534	10,236	15,153	15,200	13,500	12,800
Argentina	2,700	3,700	3,650	3,500	4,300	4,300
Paraguay	333	549	575	600	625	625
China, Mainland	7,250	7,565	7,460	7,880	8,100	9,245
Other	4,204	4,454	5,067	4,665	5,067	5,114
Total	72,118	77,363	93,627	80,617	86,852	87,344
Gross exports:						
United States	19,061	20,117	23,818	19,712	23,677	24,225
Brazil	830	638	1,239	1,711	1,200	700
Argentina	1,972	2,791	2,374	2,704	2,300	2,300
Paraguay	192	347	415	525	550	550
EC 10	237	352	325	160	215	215
Other	222	434	289	291	448	436
Total	22,514	24,679	28,460	25,103	28,390	28,426
Gross imports:						
EC 10	11,232	12,148	12,217	10,603	11,561	11,386
Belgium–Luxembourg	1,061	1,004	910	1,221	1,250	1,250
Germany	3,613	3,673	3,902	3,034	3,700	3,700
Italy	1,279	1,706	1,393	1,184	1,400	1,200
Netherlands	2,665	3,267	3,495	3,050	3,300	3,300
United Kingdom	1,238	999	1,159	1,155	955	955
Eastern Europe	630	744	813	620	550	565
Poland	129	202	278	120	50	50
Romania	241	260	280	200	200	200
Yugoslavia	215	243	205	230	250	250
Portugal	181	229	260	266	750	700
Mexico	580	633	783	1,370	850	800

Brazil	11	217	367	1,067	1,100	1,000
Japan	4,260	4,132	4,401	4,197	4,100	4,200
Spain	2,178	2,237	3,214	2,970	2,900	3,100
China, Mainland	188	261	810	540	400	500
China, Taiwan	959	1,111	939	1,000	1,080	1,080
Soviet Union	906	1,765	1,085	1,200	2,000	2,000
Other	2,135	2,522	2,799	3,039	4,390	3,837
Total	23,079	25,770	27,428	26,606	28,931	28,468
Crush:						
United States	25,220	27,701	30,573	27,773	28,712	28,712
Brazil	9,862	9,621	10,591	13,827	13,300	13,200
Argentina	646	726	733	946	1,400	1,400
EC 10	10,832	11,668	11,509	9,990	11,045	10,850
Portugal	208	233	224	262	740	700
Mexico	1,000	913	1,303	1,570	1,570	1,650
Japan	3,296	3,397	3,453	3,252	3,500	3,500
Spain	2,174	2,248	3,050	3,020	3,100	3,100
China, Mainland	3,045	3,123	3,340	3,401	3,400	3,936
China, Taiwan	788	867	832	838	870	870
Soviet Union	1,304	1,486	1,285	1,200	2,150	2,150
Eastern Europe	996	1,149	1,407	1,214	1,030	1,049
Other	3,179	3,723	4,138	4,208	5,236	5,070
Total	62,342	66,622	72,214	71,239	75,313	75,487
Ending Stocks[b]:						
United States	4,386	4,738	9,770	8,655	9,117	8,573
Brazil	2,582	1,841	4,554	4,445	3,545	3,445
Argentina	508	533	898	560	960	960
Other	1,707	2,483	2,679	2,822	2,558	2,591
Total	9,183	9,595	17,901	16,482	16,180	15,569

Source: *Foreign Agriculture Circular—Oilseeds and Products,* Foreign Agricultural Service, May 1982.

[a]For northern hemisphere countries, marketing years begin in the first year shown, and southern hemisphere countries begin in the second year, Argentina and Brazil are converted to an October–September basis.

[b]Stocks data are not estimated for all countries.

feed. Cassava has no protein and thus large quantities of high-protein meals are required when cassava is used in feed rations in place of grains. Japan, too, has relaxed restrictions on soybean imports and the increased livestock production, prompted in part by international limitations imposed on offshore fishing, has increased soybean consumption in that country. Government policies aimed at raising living standards by increasing meat consumption in the USSR and Eastern Europe have also boosted demand.

U.S. MARKET. Soybeans have become the number two cash crop in the United States[1] and rank number three in terms of acreage harvested.[2] The Corn Belt, while still the premier production region, has seen its share of national production erode somewhat in the past 30 years as the South and Southeast have grown in relative importance.

In the last decade, U.S. production has increased by about 70%. Table 3 (pages 12–17) illustrates the trends of increasing planted acreage, production, domestic crushing, and exports which have characterized the soybean market in recent years.

Space limitations do not permit a full discussion of the factors influencing soybean prices, but Figure 1 presents the salient features of the interdependencies involved in determining not only soybean prices, but also prices for soybean meal and soybean oil.

As Figure 1 shows, the government plays a role in the domestic supply-and-demand picture and in the resulting price performance in the soybean complex through its price-support activities. In recent years, the government has not been a factor in soybean ownership (see Table 3), but support prices have been set in most years, giving soybean farmers the option of borrowing money from the Commodity Credit Corporation (CCC) using stored crop as collateral. Under the Agricultural and Food Act of 1981, soybean support prices are set by formula instead of being entirely at the discretion of the Secretary of Agriculture. According to the formula, the support price for the 1982–1985 crops is equal to 75% of the average price received by farmers in 3 of the previous 5 years, with the high and low years omitted. However, a minimum support price of $5.02 per bushel has been specified which the Secretary may lower as much as 10% per year, down to $4.50 per bushel, if the season average price falls below 105% of this minimum. The acreage limitation and reserve programs which are permitted for other crops are not allowed for soybeans.

[1]Behind corn.

[2]Behind corn and wheat.

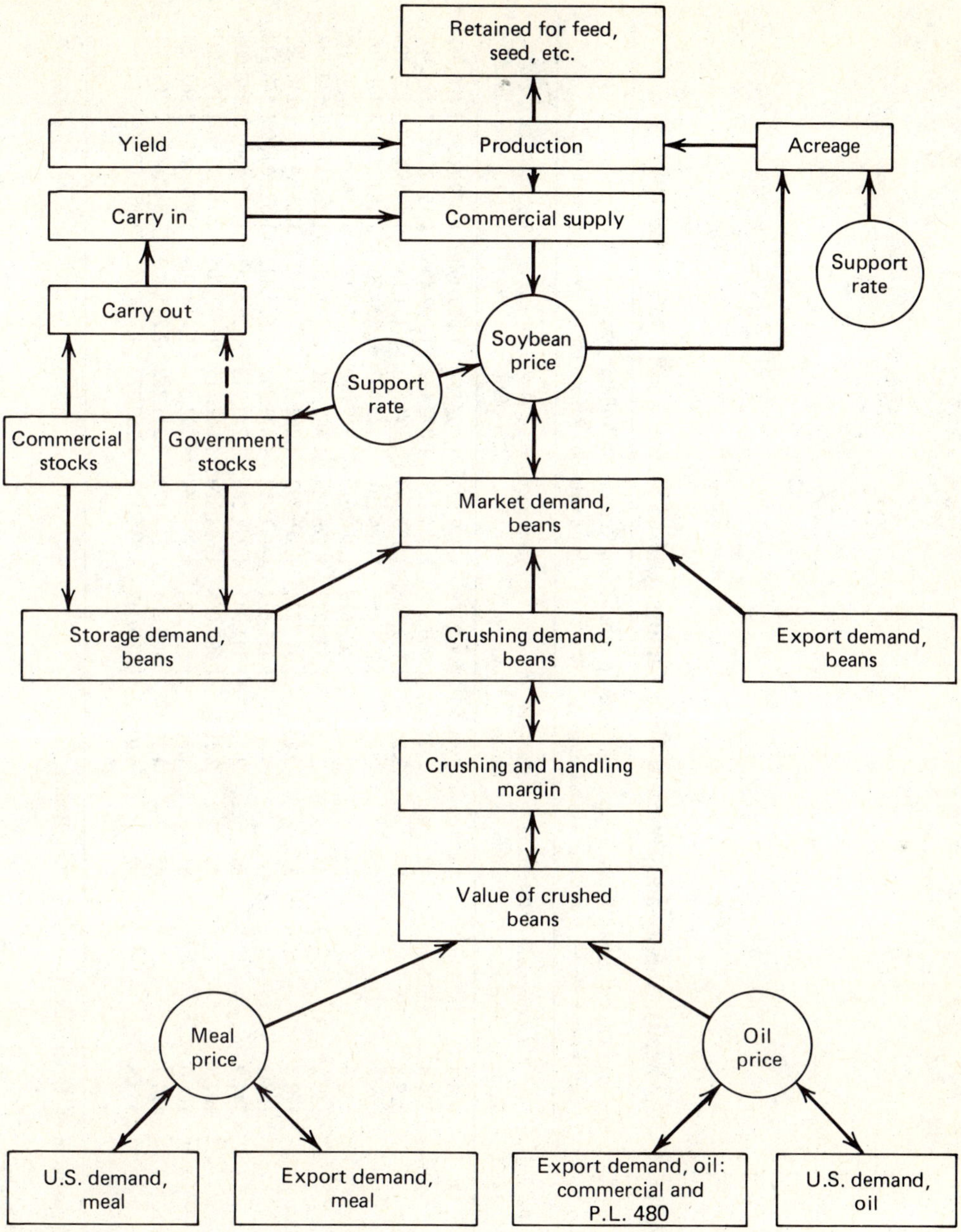

FIGURE 1. Factors influencing prices in the soybean complex. (*Source:* Houck et al., *Soybeans and Their Products—Markets, Models and Policy*.)

TABLE 3. Soybeans: Supply-and-Demand Price Factors, United States, 1968/1969–1980/1981

U.S. Soybean Price-Support Program and Official Crop Production Reports (in Millions of Bushels)

Year	Quantity Put Under Support	Deliveries to CCC	September 1 Stocks: Total	September 1 Stocks: Government Owned	National Average Support: Percent of Parity	National Average Support: Dollars Per Bushel	Crop Production Reports (in Thousands of Bushels): August 1	September 1	October 1	November 1	December 1	Final
1968	340.3	170.1	166.3	137.9	74	2.50	1,064,358	1,079,627	1,065,552	1,079,490	1,079,662	1,106,958
1969	179.5	0.2	326.8	336.8	62	2.25	1,060,859	1,054,722	1,070,182	1,094,466	1,116,876	1,133,120
1970	146.4	[b]	229.8	196.9	60	2.25	1,113,566	1,133,193	1,134,595	1,134,151	1,135,769	1,127,100
1971	168.2	[b]	98.8	11.4	56	2.25	1,235,451	1,186,301	1,175,447	1,200,201	1,169,361	1,176,101
1972	90.6	[b]	72.0	1.5	54	2.25	1,269,616	1,286,015	1,317,090	1,350,517	1,276,290	1,270,608
1973	124.2	[b]	59.6	—	45	2.25	1,539,771	1,598,746	1,588,361	1,574,586	1,566,518	1,547,543
1974	34.6	—	170.8	—	37	2.25	1,314,232	1,315,792	1,262,352	1,243,912	1,233,425	1,216,287
1975	—	—	188.2	0.4	—	—	1,457,672	1,442,422	1,473,782	1,519,882	1,521,370	1,548,344
1976	22.5	—	244.9	—	34	2.50	1,344,343	1,274,263	1,249,713	1,252,148	1,287,560	1,288,608
1977	97.5	—	102.9	—	46	3.50	1,602,065	1,644,220	1,647,315	1,682,705	1,761,755	1,767,267
1978	64.2	—	161.0	—	51	4.50	1,765,024	1,772,364	1,792,064	1,810,389	1,870,181	1,868,754
1979[a]	120.0	—	174.1	—	45	4.50	2,129,254	2,174,179	2,213,289	2,235,869	2,267,647	2,267,901
1980[a]			358.8	—	40	5.02	1,880,342	1,831,172	1,757,272	1,774,742	1,817,097	
1981						5.02						

Source: U.S. Department of Agriculture, Crop Reporting Board.

[a]Preliminary.

[b]Less than 50,000 bushels.

Soybean Stocks in the United States (in Thousands of Bushels)

Year	On Farms				Off Farms				Total Stocks			
	January 1	April 1	June 1[b]	September 1	January 1	April 1	June 1[b]	September 1	January 1	April 1	June 1[b]	September 1
1968	350,816	235,842	120,742	60,709	432,333	301,182	164,389	105,618	783,149	537,024	285,131	166,327
1969	410,168	276,930	141,360	70,551	550,329	452,343	316,815	254,992	960,497	729,300	458,175	325,543
1970	372,069	209,236	78,711	40,580	683,425	525,001	324,676	189,256	1,055,494	734,237	403,387	229,836
1971	391,960	246,491	90,595	20,554	553,012	369,063	190,832	78,225	944,972	615,554	281,427	98,779
1972	397,605	218,609	58,438	11,779	491,387	333,677	174,394	60,183	888,992	552,286	232,832	71,962
1973	429,071	145,333	33,855	9,415	437,924	358,372	145,352	50,222	866,995	503,705	179,207	59,637
1974	608,160	331,885	151,104	64,545	552,756	405,943	190,865	106,337	1,160,916	737,828	341,969	170,882
1975	483,869	331,241	165,324	75,114	505,392	323,317	191,704	109,922	989,261	654,558	357,028	185,036
1976	590,466	411,366	253,963	86,150	665,689	456,283	300,938	158,781	1,256,155	867,649	554,901	244,931
1977	473,120	227,723	92,374	32,748	559,045	390,214	243,335	70,168	1,032,165	617,937	335,709	102,916
1978	672,861	393,684	207,102	59,000	652,400	455,448	298,815	102,044	1,325,261	849,132	505,917	161,044
1979	699,556	412,570	241,255	61,509	692,534	467,646	284,850	112,579	1,392,090	880,216	526,105	174,088
1980[a]	892,934	602,779	396,650	128,888	877,896	580,322	378,152	229,880	1,770,830	1,183,101	774,802	358,768
1981[a]	738,845	539,645			790,300	493,907			1,529,541	1,033,552		
1982												

Source: U.S. Department of Agriculture, Crop Reporting Board.

[a]Preliminary.

[b]Data prior to 1976 are as of July 1.

TABLE 3 Continued

U.S. Commercial Stocks of Soybeans on the First of the Month (in Millions of Bushels)

Year	January	February	March	April	May	June	July	August	September	October	November	December
1968	23.1	21.5	21.0	20.0	14.9	11.8	12.6	9.1	5.5	6.5	41.3	48.9
1969	45.6	46.9	51.1	50.7	48.2	39.1	35.9	31.9	32.7	34.1	60.2	80.2
1970	79.4	84.8	82.5	82.3	72.4	59.0	43.8	8.7	34.3	17.8	30.1	40.7
1971	47.2	51.4	54.4	57.1	54.2	41.6	35.0	36.5	17.3	12.1	48.5	48.8
1972	41.8	37.7	41.1	49.0	48.4	36.1	27.1	18.8	13.6	7.0	25.0	32.0
1973	39.1	32.0	56.8	59.7	48.9	31.8	22.8	16.6	12.1	10.5	30.4	35.6
1974	33.6	32.0	35.3	36.2	27.3	21.2	21.2	20.3	18.0	14.3	51.6	55.4
1975	48.1	43.3	40.5	31.1	18.0	12.8	16.6	13.0	12.6	14.2	60.2	62.5
1976	52.0	55.7	57.1	51.7	42.5	37.0	32.5	30.4	21.3	27.9	54.4	52.2
1977	46.8	49.5	51.1	52.3	55.4	50.0	38.7	19.6	8.5	10.9	43.6	50.9
1978	46.2	44.3	41.8	49.1	47.9	42.7	30.6	23.0	10.7	13.0	58.3	63.2
1979	60.9	57.6	62.0	60.8	52.5	40.7	37.6	31.2	19.3	11.5	77.6	84.9
1980	76.5	71.5	73.2	72.3	56.5	52.6	53.2	51.8	44.8	51.5	80.6	79.5
1981	73.1	71.1	69.0	53.1	45.3							

Source: U.S. Department of Agriculture, Foreign Agricultural Service.

Salient Statistics of Soybeans in the United States

Crop Year	Planted Alone (1,000 Acres)	Acreage Harvested (1,000 Acres)	Yield Per Acre (Bushel)	Farm Price (Dollars per Bushel)	Farm Value (Millions of Dollars)	Pounds Per Bushel Crushed: Yield of Oil	Pounds Per Bushel Crushed: Yield of Meal	U.S. Exports of Soybeans Crop Year (September–August) (Thousands of Metric Tons[b]): Grand Total	Belgium–Luxembourg	Denmark	Canada	West Germany	Japan	Netherlands	Taiwan	USSR
1968/1969	42,265	41,391	26.7	2.43	2,689	10.61	47.43	286.8	10.2	11.8	37.9	30.5	69.9	42.7	16.6	—
1969/1970	42,534	41,337	27.4	2.35	2,664	10.66	47.36	432.6	16.1	18.4	70.0	41.8	101.4	57.4	21.2	—
1970/1971	43,802	42,249	26.7	2.85	3,215	10.83	47.39	433.8	13.2	21.4	42.2	53.0	102.8	57.9	19.6	—
1971/1972	43,472	42,705	27.5	3.03	3,560	10.98	47.43	416.8	5.7	16.2	31.3	52.0	107.4	64.1	23.9	0
1972/1973	46,885	45,683	27.8	4.37	5,551	10.59	47.04	479.4	8.2	17.4	22.1	54.7	121.0	84.3	19.6	31.5
1973/1974	56,675	55,667	27.8	5.68	8,787	10.76	47.18	539.1	13.2	12.5	37.9	72.9	98.8	101.1	20.5	0.7
1974/1975	53,507	51,341	23.7	6.64	8,070	10.51	47.48	420.7	5.6	5.9	26.9	51.0	96.9	77.7	24.4	0
1975/1976	54,550	53,617	28.9	4.92	7,618	10.94	47.27	555.1	17.7	15.1	28.0	45.6	118.1	130.5	32.8	11.4
1976/1977	50,226	49,401	26.1	6.81	8,769	11.09	47.81	15,351.0	411.0	306.0	462.0	1,520.0	3,219.0	3,007.0	697.0	825.0
1977/1978	58,760	57,830	30.6	5.88	10,352	10.89	47.34	19,061.0	475.0	423.0	264.0	1,521.0	3,636.0	4,086.0	854.0	744.0
1978/1979	64,708	63,663	29.4	6.66	12,450	11.07	47.63	20,115.0	420.0	341.0	352.0	1,486.0	3,865.0	4,012.0	1,271.0	1,178.0
1979/1980[a]	71,632	70,566	32.1	6.28	14,250	10.74	47.96	23,818.0	584.0	342.0	392.0	1,318.0	3,868.0	6,035.0	780.0	813.0
1980/1981[a]	70,087	67,856	26.8	8.39	15,253											
1981/1982[a]	69,817															

Source: U.S. Department of Agriculture, Crop Reporting Board.
[a]Preliminary.
[b]Data prior to 1976 and 1977 are in millions of bushels.

TABLE 3. Continued

Supply and Distribution of Soybeans in the United States (in Millions of Bushels)

Crop Year Beginning September 1	Supply						Distribution					
	Stocks, September 1											
	Farms	CCC	Mills, Elevators[c]	Total	Production	Total Supply	Crushings	Exports	Seed	Feed	Residual	Total Distribution
1968	60.7	—	105.6	166.3	1,107.0	1,273.3	605.9	286.8	47.3	0.9	5.4	946.4
1969	70.6	5.3	247.3	326.8	1,133.1	1,459.9	737.3	432.6	48.5	0.9	10.8	1,230.1
1970	40.6	8.7	180.5	229.8	1,127.1	1,356.9	760.1	433.8	48.1	1.1	15.1	1,258.2
1971	20.6	—	78.2	98.8	1,176.1	1,274.9	720.5	416.8	51.0	1.1	13.5	1,202.9
1972	11.8	0	60.2	72.0	1,270.6	1,342.6	721.8	479.4	60.8	1.1	19.8	1,282.9
1973	9.4	0	50.2	59.6	1,547.5	1,607.1	821.3	539.1	56.1	1.2	18.7	1,436.4
1974	64.5	0	106.3	170.9	1,216.3	1,387.2	701.3	420.7	57.2	1.0	21.7	1,201.9
1975	75.1	0	109.9	188.2	1,548.3	1,736.5	865.1	555.1	53.5	1.2	15.7	1,490.6
1976	86.2	0	158.8	244.9	1,288.6	1,533.5	790.2	564.1	61.0	1.0	13.3	1,429.6
1977	32.7	0	70.2	102.9	1,767.3	1,870.2	926.7	700.5	68.0	1.0	7.5	1,703.7
1978	59.0	0	102.0	161.0	1,868.8	2,029.8	1,018.0	753.0	75.0	1.0	11.0	1,858.0
1979[a]	61.5	0	112.6	174.1	2,267.9	2,442.0	1,123.0	875.0	67.0	1.0	17.0	2,083.0
1980[b]	128.9	0	229.9	358.8	1,817.1	2,175.9	1,075.0	800.0	69.0	1.0	21.0	1,966.0
1981												

Source: U.S. Department of Agriculture, Economic Research Service.
[a]Preliminary.
[b]Estimates.
[c]Also warehouses.

Production of Soybeans for Beans in the United States by Selected States (in Millions of Bushels)

Year	Arkansas	South Carolina	Illinois	Indiana	Iowa	Louisiana	Michigan	Minnesota	Mississippi	Missouri	North Carolina	Ohio	Tennessee	Nebraska	Kentucky
1968	91.3		209.9	103.9	178.0	38.8	12.0	71.1	56.3	102.6	17.0	70.9	24.2		
1969	92.4	22.5	228.8	106.0	177.1	33.0	11.6	75.0	50.7	80.3	23.0	73.0	29.0	24.9	12.6
1970	99.0	20.2	210.8	101.6	184.6	40.5	13.3	78.8	58.1	88.4	20.8	72.7	26.5	17.9	14.3
1971	92.5	23.0	236.0	111.4	178.8	39.5	10.3	63.9	56.6	97.3	23.8	80.3	31.7	15.2	20.8
1972	81.0	20.0	259.4	108.8	216.0	38.3	13.6	90.3	48.0	108.9	29.1	79.8	28.6	23.0	23.6
1973	116.3	23.0	281.3	135.1	263.5	34.8	16.6	127.3	60.5	126.9	34.8	89.8	36.9	36.3	26.0
1974	81.7	24.0	202.6	97.3	199.1	44.0	13.2	84.0	46.3	93.5	30.5	79.8	31.9	28.2	25.0
1975	117.5	30.4	299.5	121.6	237.0	48.0	15.9	98.6	70.2	113.6	33.4	102.3	46.3	32.4	29.7
1976	82.1	21.4	249.5	111.5	200.0	63.0	11.6	66.4	71.5	84.0	24.6	95.0	40.5	19.6	28.9
1977	105.8	26.7	336.3	144.3	251.3	63.0	21.6	133.8	78.5	148.8	29.0	120.0	52.2	40.7	40.9
1978	115.2	32.3	309.5	144.2	283.1	76.0	21.6	146.2	81.7	155.0	40.3	127.7	56.9	42.5	40.8
1979	144.2	39.8	379.1	159.1	306.4	93.8	30.3	162.6	118.9	183.6	45.8	144.8	70.7	54.7	54.0
1980[a]	69.6	22.4	309.9	157.7	322.5	70.4	30.4	152.3	61.6	138.3	35.7	135.4	48.5	53.1	36.8
1982															

Source: U.S. Department of Agriculture, Crop Reporting Board.

[a]Preliminary.

Source: *Commodity Yearbook–1981*, Commodity Research Bureau. (Note: This table draws on three tables from the *Commodity Yearbook–1981*.)

Price movements over the past 10 years have been erratic during some periods, as illustrated in Figure 2. To understand the interdependencies underlying soybean price behavior, it is instructive to look at the factors associated with the escalation of prices in 1972 and 1973. It may be noted from Table 3 that in each of the 3 years prior to the 1972 harvest, distribution had exceeded production. With demand at record levels and increasing each year, a series of events triggered the sharp price increase. First, a short sunflower seed crop and ambitious livestock production goals prompted the USSR to purchase large quantities of 1972 crop soybeans in August 1972. Second, rains delayed the U.S. harvest, reduced yields, and even destroyed some of the 1972 crop. These wet conditions further exacerbated the supply shortfall by reducing the amount of meal which could be crushed from the beans. Third, reduced production of Peruvian fish meal, another important source of protein for feed, increased the value of soybean meal. Fourth, a drought in India, a major supplier of peanuts, reduced world supplies of yet another source of protein meal. Fifth, two devaluations of the dollar, the last in February 1972, "cheapened" the value of U.S. exports—including soybeans—to foreign buyers. Sixth, rumors of a possible export embargo—subsequently imposed—and wet planting conditions in spring 1973, increased fears that the

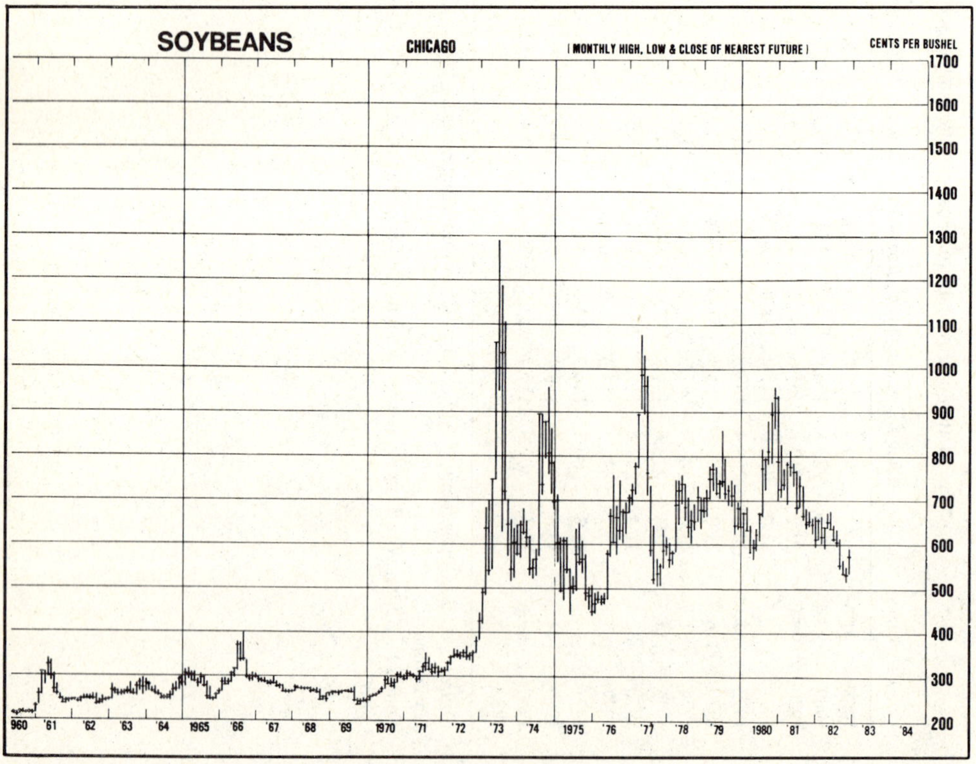

FIGURE 2. Soybean prices at the Chicago Board of Trade (monthly high, low, and close of the nearby futures). (*Source:* Commodity Research Bureau, Incorporated.)

supply shortage would grow worse and users sought to cover their needs at any price. Other factors which influenced the price behavior in 1972–1974 have been cited, for example, "inflation psychology," unresponsiveness of consumption to price, and possible overselling of the 1972 crop. Since then, many of the same general factors have continued to influence soybean prices, but supply-and-demand conditions have not combined to produce a price higher than the $12.90 per bushel which the July futures contract at the Chicago Board of Trade reached on June 5, 1973.

THE SOYBEAN MEAL CASH MARKET

WORLD MARKETS. Table 4 shows the salient features of the world soybean meal market. Of the major high-protein meals produced in the world,[3] soybean meal is the most important, comprising about two-thirds of total high-protein meal production. Its production has grown about 9% per year over the past decade. The United States accounts for over one-third of world soybean meal production; Brazil and EC each produce between 15–20% of world output. In recent years, Brazil has vied with the United States for the role of number one world exporter as Brazilian trade policies have favored exports of soybean products rather than the soybeans themselves.

The EC is the principal consumer of U.S. soybean meal and by far the major world importer. The EC consumption of soybean meal, second only to U.S. consumption, grew rapidly in the 1970s due to the expansion of its domestic pork and poultry industries. The EC crushing capacity expanded concurrently with this consumption growth. The most rapid consumption growth recently has occurred in foreign countries outside the EC—principally in developing countries—as income and population increases have stimulated meat demand and, hence, demand for high-protein rations.

U.S. MARKETS. Soybean processing plants are primarily located near the main centers of soybean and livestock production in the Midwest and along the Mississippi River system. The number of these processing plants has been steadily dropping since 1970 as Table 5 shows, though the total capacity and capacity per plant have risen. In 1978 over one-half of the plants were owned by 11 multiplant corporations, one-fifth by cooperatives, and the rest by single plant corporations. Many of the processors have become more involved in the later stages of the soybean meal marketing chain—that is, with feed manufacturing and even livestock production.

Table 6 describes the supply-and-demand situation of the U.S. soybean meal market over the past 10 years. About three-fourths of the domestic production is used for domestic animal feed with the balance entering the export market. The EC market accounts for one-half of these exports sales and Canada, Spain, Poland, and Japan, most of the rest.

[3]Soybean, cottonseed, fish, peanut, sunflower seed, rapeseed, and flaxseed.

TABLE 4. Soybean Meal: World Production, Trade, and Consumption,[a] 1977/1978–1981/1982 (1,000 metric tons)

	1977/1978	1978/1979	1979/1980	1980/1981, Preliminary	1981/1982 April	1981/1982 May
Production:						
United States	20,296	22,094	24,589	22,055	22,922	22,922
Brazil	7,652	7,451	8,134	10,584	10,200	10,120
Argentina	492	551	571	725	1,076	1,076
EC 10	8,694	9,329	9,284	8,013	8,858	8,703
Portugal	168	192	184	216	595	565
Mexico	780	712	1,016	1,225	1,225	1,270
Japan	2,542	2,645	2,693	2,536	2,735	2,735
Spain	1,728	1,787	2,425	2,386	2,449	2,449
China, Mainland	2,594	2,661	2,846	2,898	2,890	3,353
China, Taiwan	618	676	648	654	678	678
Soviet Union	999	1,152	939	925	1,656	1,656
Eastern Europe	779	904	1,114	956	818	829
Other	2,347	2,757	3,108	3,131	3,559	3,461
Total	49,689	52,911	57,551	56,304	59,661	59,817
Gross exports[b]:						
United States	5,516	5,997	7,196	6,149	6,532	6,532
Brazil	6,312	5,446	5,489	8,603	7,400	7,400
Argentina	330	382	350	365	700	700
EC 10	2,689	3,114	3,575	3,898	3,625	3,630
Other	401	538	653	597	665	666
Total	15,248	15,477	17,263	19,612	18,922	18,928

Gross imports[b]:						
EC 10	7,853	8,445	9,427	10,508	10,321	10,501
Portugal	169	171	267	267	30	30
Mexico	56	103	156	177	50	100
Japan	340	283	326	214	210	200
Spain	483	385	57	110	110	110
Soviet Union	0	52	440	1,000	1,200	1,200
Eastern Europe	3,170	3,490	3,929	4,092	3,550	3,585
Other	2,447	2,871	3,119	3,334	3,287	3,458
Total	14,518	15,800	17,721	19,702	18,758	19,184
Consumption:						
United States	14,767	16,075	17,430	15,963	16,329	16,329
Brazil	1,484	1,815	2,315	2,516	2,700	2,700
Argentina	165	158	238	310	366	366
EC 10	13,563	14,649	15,180	14,651	15,543	15,523
Belgium–Luxembourg	854	810	893	826	860	860
Denmark	983	1,035	1,076	1,232	1,288	1,288
France	2,862	3,249	3,438	3,694	3,811	3,811
West Germany	3,552	3,745	3,846	3,166	3,694	3,694
Italy	2,002	2,579	2,269	2,057	2,100	2,110
Netherlands	1,629	1,582	1,787	1,794	1,850	1,850
United Kingdom	1,369	1,285	1,523	1,526	1,540	1,540
Eastern Europe:	3,869	4,407	5,076	5,014	4,364	4,405
Czechoslovakia	502	536	669	647	619	619
East Germany	932	932	874	885	984	924
Hungary	637	652	667	587	598	598
Poland	833	1,099	1,365	1,196	780	740
Romania	457	644	840	1,025	858	858

TABLE 4. Continued

	1977/1978	1978/1979	1979/1980	1980/1981, Preliminary	1981/1982 April	1981/1982 May
Consumption: (*continued*):						
Portugal	335	334	422	426	620	550
Mexico	766	835	1,132	1,222	1,425	1,430
Japan	2,855	2,944	2,993	2,716	2,945	2,943
Spain	2,163	2,248	2,388	2,416	2,400	2,400
China, Mainland	2,575	2,649	2,831	2,883	2,875	3,338
China, Taiwan	633	676	658	654	678	678
Soviet Union	999	1,204	1,379	1,925	2,856	2,856
Other	4,375	4,984	5,607	6,031	6,357	6,408
Total	48,549	52,978	57,649	56,727	59,458	59,926
Ending stocks:						
United States	220	242	205	148	209	209
Brazil	338	529	859	324	424	344
Argentina	18	29	12	62	72	72
EC 10	351	362	318	290	305	341
Japan	115	99	124	158	160	150
Other	389	427	530	733	470	746
Total	1,431	1,688	2,048	1,715	1,640	1,862

Source: *Foreign Agriculture Circular—Oilseeds and Products*, Foreign Agricultural Service, May 1982.

[a]For northern hemisphere countries, marketing years begin in the first year shown, and southern hemisphere countries begin in the second year. Argentina and Brazil are converted to an October–September basis.

[b]Stocks data are not estimated for all countries.

TABLE 5. Number of U.S. Soybean Processing Plants, Estimated Number of Soy Oil Mills and Processing Capacity, 1951–1980.

Year Beginning September	Processing Mills[a] (Number)	Annual Processing Capacity Total[b]	Utilized[c] (Millions of Bushels)	Excess[d]	Ratio of Utilized to Total Percentage	Average Per Mill Processing Capacity (Millions of Bushels)	Capacity Utilized[c] (Millions of Bushels)
1951	193	310	244	66	79	1.6	1.3
1955	152	(355)	282	73	79	2.3	1.9
1960	125	525	406	119	77	4.2	3.2
1961	131	(535)	431	104	81	4.1	3.3
1962	130	550	473	77	86	4.2	3.6
1963	132	575	437	138	76	4.4	3.3
1964	125	585	479	106	82	4.7	3.8
1965	125	600	537	63	89	4.8	4.4
1966	129	650	559	91	86	5.0	4.3
1967	135	750	576	174	77	5.5	4.3
1968	134	750	606	144	81	5.6	4.5
1969	132	800	737	63	92	6.1	5.6
1970	130	875	760	115	87	6.7	5.8
1971	123	900	720	180	80	7.3	5.9
1972	117	925	722	203	78	7.9	6.2
1973	113	1,000	821	179	82	8.8	7.3
1974	108	1,050	701	349	67	9.7	6.5
1975	103	1,100	865	235	79	10.7	8.4
1976	103	1,200	790	410	66	11.7	7.7
1977	99	1,250	927	323	74	12.6	9.4
1978	95	1,300	1,018	282	78	13.7	10.7
1979[e]	94	1,350	1,123	227	83	14.4	11.9
1980[f]	n.a.[g]	1,425	1,040	385	73	n.a.	n.a.

Source: *1981 Soya Bluebook*, American Soybean Association.

[a]Estimates developed from census data and directories. Includes cottonseed and other oilseed mills that process significant quantities of soybeans.

[b]Estimates shown here are approximations of capacity at the beginning of the marketing year. Capacity fluctuates during any year due to new plants coming into operation and additions to existing mills, some mills becoming dormant (due to explosions, fires, strikes, etc.), and dismantling of older mills.

[c]Soybeans actually crushed. [d]Difference between total capacity and soybean utilized (crushed). [e]Preliminary.

[f]Forecast. [g]n.a. = not available.

TABLE 6. Soybean Meal: Supply-and-Demand Factors, United States, 1968/1969–1980/1981

	Supply and Distribution of Soybean Meal in the United States (in Thousands of Short Tons)									Price Per Ton Bulk, Decatur	
	Supply					Distribution					
			Production								
Year Beginning October	For Stocks October 1	Total	For Animal Feed	For Edible Protein Products	Total	(Domestic) Feed[d]	Exports	Shipments to U.S. Territories	Total	44% Protein	49 or 50% Protein
1969	157	17,596			17,753	13,514	4,035	67	17,616	78.45	86.61
1970	137	18,035			18,172	13,406	4,559	61	18,126	78.51	84.33
1971	146	17,024			17,170	13,110	3,805	63	16,978	90.20	98.20
1972	192	16,709			16,900	11,920	4,745	52	16,717	228.99	253.42
1973	183	19,674	n.a.[c]	n.a.	19,858	13,766	5,548	36	19,350	146.35	160.57
1974	507	16,701	16,437	265	17,209	12,501	4,299	50	16,850	130.86	141.26
1975	358	20,754	20,395	359	21,112	15,552	5,145	61	20,758	147.77	157.68
1976	355	18,488	18,101	388	18,843	14,001	4,559	55	18,615	199.80	218.73
1977	228	22,371	21,961	410	22,599	16,209	6,080	67	22,356	164.20	179.45
1978	243	24,354	23,986	368	24,597	17,645	6,610	75	24,330	190.10	206.30
1979[a]	267	27,105	26,808	297	27,372	18,915	7,908	85	27,146	181.90	
1980[b]	226	25,094			25,320	18,900	6,700		25,050	225.00	

Source: U.S. Department of Agriculture, Economic Research Service.

[a]Preliminary.

[b]Estimate.

[c]n.a. = not available.

[d]Includes small quantities used for industrial purposes, estimated at 30,000 tons annually.

U.S. Exports of Soybean Cake and Meal by Country of Destination (in Thousands of Metric Tons[a])

Year Beginning October 1	Belgium–Luxembourg	Japan	Canada	Denmark	France	West Germany	Spain	Ireland	Italy	Netherlands	Philippines	Poland	United Kingdom	Yugoslavia	Grand Total
1969	219.0	40.3	270.9	32.5	622.8	855.9		60.4	309.5	659.0	49.1	109.9	42.9	173.8	4,035
1970	308.8	32.8	242.1	85.6	712.1	987.4		36.5	330.8	675.4	53.8	112.3	100.1	186.8	4,559
1971	328.4	24.5	204.5	95.5	610.3	705.0		72.4	295.6	482.8	58.0	65.8	58.3	116.2	3,805
1972	179.8	287.0	199.2	114.3	678.5	987.7	140.0	76.3	445.0	248.4	14.2	337.0	48.5	152.2	4,745
1973	204.7	137.2	289.8	56.6	866.6	1,192	96.0	53.3	631.6	313.3	49.9	287.6	60.2	316.4	5,548
1974	243.8	0.1	224.5	17.6	786.7	995.4	69.0	37.3	422.2	428.7	12.6	220.6	91.4	—	4,299
1975[a]	238.2	120.1	277.8	35.1	761.9	1,008	347.3	49.1	421.4	102.5	0.1	360.8	54.5	183.5	4,667
1976	83.4	217.5	256.4	36.8	131.0	953.1	143.3	36.1	428.8	565.8	—	256.9	46.7	95.2	4,117
1977	37.0	271.3	339.5	26.1	146.6	1,004	237.3	83.6	741.6	654.7	21.0	493.3	65.0	113.1	5,515
1978	3.8	204.5	414.0	65.6	355.1	717.6	253.5	117.9	691.1	748.1	—	243.0	66.8	57.9	5,996
1979[b]															7,174
1980[b]															6,078

Source: U.S. Department of Commerce, The Bureau of the Census.
[a]Data prior to 1975 and 1976 are in thousands of short tons.
[b]Preliminary.

Figure 3 illustrates how the soybean meal futures prices have behaved over the past 10 years. Notable aspects of the figure are the sharp price rises which occurred in the period. The factors associated with soybean meal price were illustrated by the previous discussion of the 1972–1974 world market situation. In general, the main factors influencing these prices are soybean prices, demand for meat, and livestock numbers at home and abroad; the prices of other high-protein meals and grain substitutable in any way for soybean meal in feeding rations; and international currency levels. Government policies—particularly those in the EC and Brazil—also have important long- and short-run implications for the U.S. soybean meal price.

SOYBEAN OIL CASH MARKET

WORLD MARKETS. As soybean meal dominates other high-protein meals in the world markets, so soybean oil reigns as the principal edible oil, accounting for about one-third of world production.[4] The United States, Brazil, and the EC are the largest producers and exporters, as Table 7 shows. The EC is one of the

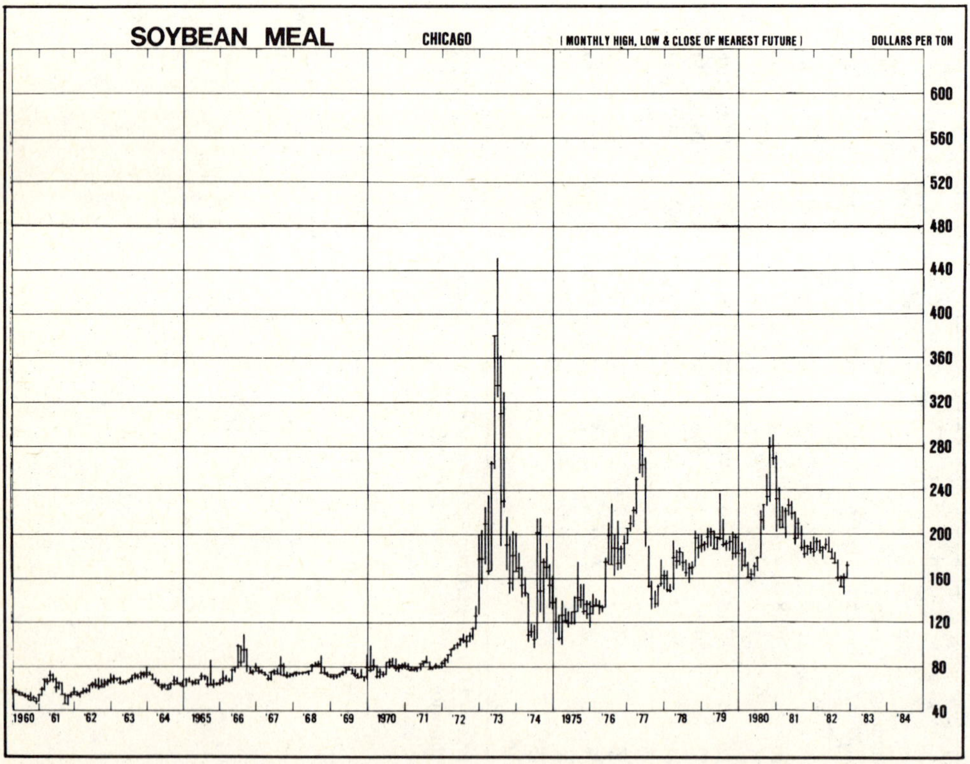

FIGURE 3. Soybean meal prices at the Chicago Board of Trade (monthly high, low, and close of the nearby futures), 1972–1981. (*Source:* Commodity Research Bureau, Incorporated.)

[4]Principal edible oils, in order of importance, are soybean, sunflower, palm, cottonseed, coconut, peanut, rapeseed, and olive.

TABLE 7. Soybean Oil: World Production, Trade, and Consumption,[a] 1977/1978–1981/1982 (1,000 metric tons)

	1977/1978	1978/1979	1979/1980	1980/1981 Preliminary	1981/1982 April	1981/1982 May
Production:						
United States	4,666	5,136	5,491	5,112	5,121	5,121
Brazil	1,828	1,767	1,996	2,589	2,475	2,455
Argentina	103	118	125	161	238	238
EC 10	1,903	2,073	2,036	1,766	1,952	1,917
Portugal	36	41	39	46	130	123
Mexico	180	164	235	270	283	295
Japan	598	621	618	591	613	613
Spain	385	398	540	528	543	543
China, Mainland	365	375	401	408	408	472
China, Taiwan	142	147	141	142	153	153
Soviet Union	221	253	219	204	366	366
Eastern Europe	177	203	246	216	184	186
Other	513	605	673	683	778	754
Total	11,117	11,901	12,760	12,716	13,244	13,236
Gross exports:						
United States	933	1,059	1,220	739	885	88
Brazil	675	557	523	1,266	900	900
Argentina	69	52	106	105	170	170
EC 10	845	932	881	854	954	957
Portugal	3	13	18	32	70	42
Spain	273	311	369	427	400	400
Other	22	47	86	84	90	93
Total	2,820	2,971	3,203	3,507	3,469	3,447

TABLE 7. Continued

	1977/1978	1978/1979	1979/1980	1980/1981 Preliminary	1981/1982 April	1981/1982 May
Gross imports:						
EC 10	438	449	457	492	497	517
Mexico	34	5	28	25	10	50
Brazil	0	0	127	0	0	0
India	510	555	662	675	650	650
Pakistan	181	260	213	260	260	260
China, Mainland	184	122	100	80	25	25
Soviet Union	3	25	50	100	150	150
Eastern Europe	88	94	197	210	205	205
Mid East/North Africa	512	558	616	654	631	631
Other						
Latin America	314	329	357	464	435	477
Other	361	318	411	493	487	495
Total	2,625	2,715	3,218	3,453	3,350	3,460
Consumption:						
United States	3,752	4,056	4,074	4,135	4,331	4,331
Brazil	1,053	1,199	1,387	1,480	1,550	1,550
Argentina	36	44	41	50	52	52
Other						
Latin America	365	409	467	511	533	554
EC 10	1,460	1,502	1,607	1,454	1,496	1,475
Portugal	31	26	21	15	60	30
Mexico	184	174	253	290	313	345
Japan	594	609	616	613	675	675
Spain	104	107	90	110	110	110
China, Mainland	545	491	500	482	427	491
China, Taiwan	140	143	139	146	152	152
Soviet Union	224	278	269	304	516	516
Eastern Europe	251	291	449	411	388	390

Consumption: (*continued*):						
India	536	588	708	745	728	728
Pakistan	181	260	213	260	260	260
Mid East/North Africa	640	656	751	792	762	767
Other	614	627	728	801	808	797
Total	10,710	11,460	12,313	12,599	13,161	13,223
Ending stocks[b]:						
United States	331	352	549	787	692	692
Brazil	275	285	498	341	366	346
Argentina	4	26	4	10	26	26
EC 10	74	162	167	117	70	119
Spain	48	44	136	131	174	174
Other	180	227	204	235	198	290
Total	912	1,096	1,558	1,621	1,526	1,647

Source: *Foreign Agriculture Circular—Oilseeds and Products*, Foreign Agricultural Service, May 1982.

[a]For northern hemisphere countries, marketing years begin in the first year shown, and southern hemisphere countries begin in the second year. Argentina and Brazil are converted to an October–September basis.

[b]Stocks data are not estimated for all countries.

principal consumers, with the United States and Brazil, and is also an important importer. However, the EC imports most of the oil it uses in the form of soybeans, crushes the beans domestically, and exports the oil it does not consume at home. The developing countries, for example, India, Pakistan, and North African countries, are also major markets for oil.

U.S. MARKET. Because soybean oil and meal are joint products, U.S. soybean oil production has increased with soybean meal output over the past 10 years (Table 8). Most of the oil is used in food products—principally shortening, margarine, and cooking and salad oils. India and Pakistan are the major foreign buyers of U.S. soybean oil.

Soybean oil prices (Figure 4) have often followed those of soybeans and soybean meal. However, the demand-side factors are different for oil and meal and, consequently, the prices can move independently. Demand for meal can have an influence on the price of oil owing to the nature of the production process. If, for example, strong meal demand triggers active crushing in the face of sluggish oil demand, the resulting buildup of oil stocks could have a depressing effect on oil prices.

An important demand-side factor to consider is the price of substitute oil on the domestic and world markets. In the past few years, increases in world palm, sunflower, and rapeseed production have put these oils in an increasingly competitive position with soybean oil. A factor of possible future importance is the

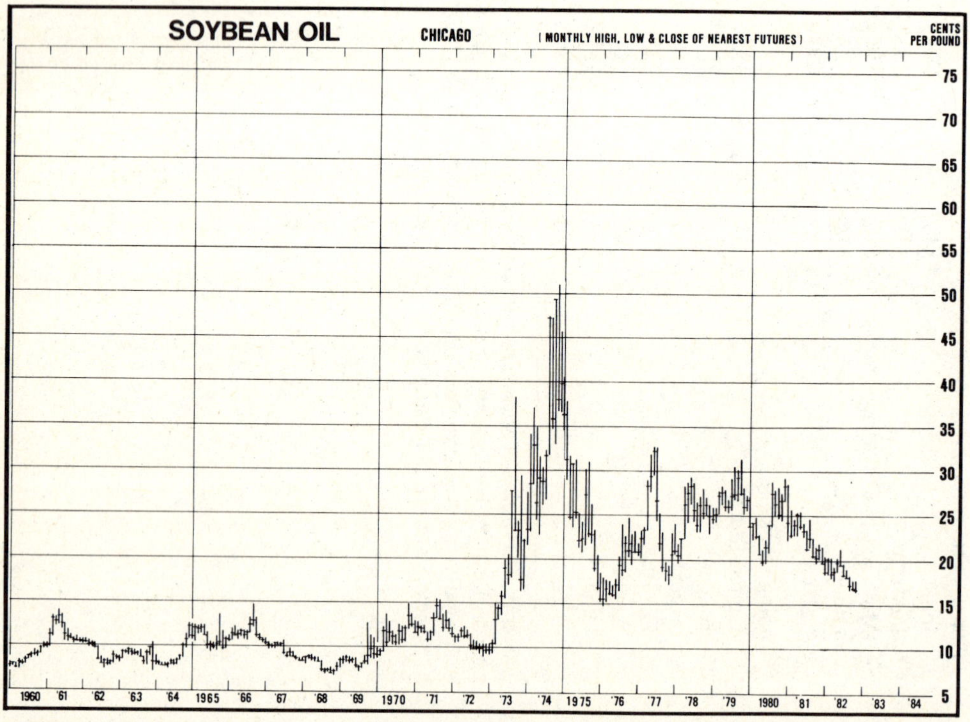

FIGURE 4. Soybean oil prices at the Chicago Board of Trade (monthly high, low, and close of the nearby futures), 1972–1981. (*Source:* Commodity Research Bureau, Incorporated.)

TABLE 8. Soybean Oil: Supply-and-Demand Factors, United States, 1968/1969–1980/1981

Production, Consumption, Stocks, and Foreign Trade of Soybean Oil in the United States. (in Millions of Pounds)

Year	Production		Consumption		Stocks December 31		Imports for Consumption	Exports	
	Crude	Refined	In Refining	In End Products	Crude	Refined		Crude	Refined
1968	6,150	5,228	5,487	5,411	305.4	283.2	—	576.8	364.0
1969	6,805	5,860	6,093	5,948	274.9	242.3	—	542.2	333.6
1970	8,086	6,276	6,523	6,322	450.7	304.9	—	1,119.4	367.6
1971	8,082	6,298	6,551	6,323	447.6	354.6	—	1,288.6	427.5
1972	8,084	6,521	7,032	6,827	581.5	315.0	—	841.6	452.1
1973	7,540	6,509	7,046	6,831	411.7	278.8	—	723.9	243.8
1974	8,705	6,812	7,000	7,039	375.6	299.4	0.1	1,607	
1975	7,861	6,423	6,686	6,830	495.3	304.6	—	758	
1976	9,640	7,185	7,476	7,577	1,141.0	347.1	—	901.7	77.3
1977	8,836	7,790	8,092	7,451	524.0	340.0	0.2	1,427.3	81.3
1978	10,625	8,618	8,955	8,175	623.1	347.5	—	1,560.8	77.8
1979[a]	11,504	9,110	9,456	8,656	656.6	373.5	—	2,371	
1980[a]	12,098	8,985	9,300	8,586	1,369.6	368.2		2,316	

Source: U.S. Department of Commerce, Bureau of Census.

[a]Preliminary.

TABLE 8 Continued

U.S. Exports of Soybean Oil,[a] by Country of Destination (in Thousands of Metric Tons[b])

Year Beginning Oct. 1	Australia	Colombia	Canada	Chile	Ecuador	Haiti	Peru	India	Israel	Mexico	Morocco	Pakistan	Panama	Egypt	Grand Total
1968		—	29.0	30.5		19.2	—	327.9	34.2	4.2	28.1	113.8			869.6
1969		—	51.0	37.8		19.2	—	247.6	37.7	18.2	52.9	355.0			1,420
1970		17.0	50.0	58.0		26.0	111.0	284.0	41.0	1.0	90.0	278.0			1,742
1971		15.0	43.0	2.0		27.0	84.0	144.0	44.0	—	122.0	142.0			1,398
1972		7.0	38.0	2.0	30.0	21.0	92.0	95.0	51.0	33.0	7.0	130.0	11.0	2.0	1,066
1973		24.0	73.0	69.0	29.0	16.0	135.0	94.0	21.0	135.0	43.0	197.0	39.0	3.0	1,435
1974		18.0	44.0	6.0	28.0	26.0	56.0	8.0	15.0	119.0	5.0	26.0	24.0	8.0	1,028
1975[b]	13.1	14.2	31.8	1.0	19.5	14.3	14.5	15.8	9.9	3.1	4.9	150.8	13.2	0.5	443
1976	20.1	27.3	26.0	12.0	16.2	17.2	57.3	252.2	3.1	15.4	3.0	119.2	12.5	1.4	702
1977	21.0	44.1	27.7	22.0	26.0	13.8	68.6	247.7	6.3	29.6	5.6	95.8	8.3	6.1	933
1978[c]	16.2	84.1	20.9	22.8	22.4	17.2	29.4	181.1	9.8	5.1	6.0	163.3	19.0	13.9	1,059
1979[c]															1,220
1980[c]															794

Source: U.S. Department of Commerce, The Bureau of the Census.

[a]Crude and refined oil combined as such.

[b]Data prior to 1975 and 1976 are in millions of pounds.

[c]Preliminary.

potential usage of vegetable oils as a fuel. The United States, Brazil, South Africa, and other countries are testing the feasibility of using vegetable oils to extend diesel fuels. Brazil, in particular, has an ambitious program of testing and has announced a goal to replace 16% of its diesel oil consumption with vegetable oils by 1985. It has been estimated that if Brazil were to meet its goals today it would need to import 2 million tons of vegetable oils. Currently, Brazil is a net exporter.

FUTURES TRADING IN THE SOYBEAN COMPLEX

Soybean futures contracts are currently traded at two domestic exchanges. Trading began in 1936 at the Chicago Board of Trade (CBT) and in 1940 at the MidAmerica Commodity Exchange (MCE). The principle difference between the contracts is the size. At the CBT, the unit of trading is 5,000 bushels; at the MCE, 1,000 bushels. Contracts in soybean oil and soybean meal have been traded at the CBT since 1950 and 1951, respectively. Salient features of these domestically traded futures contracts are shown in Table 9.

Futures trading in the soybean complex is also conducted at the following foreign exchanges:

Soybeans	Soybean Meal	Soybean Oil
Hong Kong Commodity Exchange	Bourse de Commerce de Paris	Vegetable Oil Terminal Market Association (London)
Sao Paulo Commodity Exchange (Brazil)	Grain and Feed Trade Association (London)	
Tokyo Grain Exchange (Japan)		
Osaka Grain Exchange (Japan)		
Nagoya Grain Exchange (Japan)		
Kobe Grain Exchange (Japan)		
Kanmon Commodity Exchange (Japan)		
Hokkaido Grain Exchange (Japan)		

TRADING PRACTICES IN THE CASH AND FUTURES MARKETS

The availability of futures contracts in the three commodities of the soybean complex provides a variety of hedging opportunities to participants in the cash market. In fact, hedging is an integral part of doing business for many farmers, elevator operators, exporters, processors, and others who handle soybeans and

TABLE 9. Futures Contracts in the Soybean Complex—United States

Chicago Board of Trade Soybeans	
Delivery months:	January, March, May, July, September, and November.
Trading unit:	5,000 bushels.
Price quotations and minimum fluctuation:	Quoted in cents and quarters of a cent per bushel, with a minimum fluctuation of ¼ cent per bushel ($12.50 per contract).
Daily price movement limits:	Subject to change; consult latest official notices from the exchange.
Position limits:	3 million bushels (CFTC limit) in any one future or in all futures combined; positions of 200,000 bushels or more require reports to the CFTC.
Grades deliverable:	No. 2 yellow soybeans and substitutions at differentials established by the exchange.
Delivery:	By registered warehouse receipts issued by warehouse persons against stocks in Chicago, IL and Toledo, OH warehouses that have been declared regular by the exchange.
Trading hours:	9:30 a.m. to 1:15 p.m. central time.

Chicago Board of Trade Soybean Meal	
Delivery months:	October, December, January, March, May, July, and September.
Trading unit:	100 tons or 2,000 lb each.
Price quotations and minimum fluctuation:	Quoted in dollars and cents per ton, with a minimum fluctuation of $0.10 per ton ($10 per contract), basis F.O.B. railcars bulk, Decatur, IL.
Daily price movement limits:	Subject to change; consult latest official notices from the exchange.
Position limits:	720 contracts in any one future or in all futures combined; positions of 50 or more contracts require reports to the CFTC.
Grades deliverable:	One grade of meal only with minimum protein of 44%; see regulations for further specifications.
Delivery:	Under shipping certificates from shipping plants approved by the exchange in six territories. These include the states of Arkansas, Illinois, Indiana, Iowa, Kentucky, Missouri, Ohio, and Tennessee, and parts of Mississippi.
Trading hours:	9:30 a.m. to 1:15 p.m. central time.

TABLE 9. Continued

Chicago Board of Trade Soybean Oil	
Delivery months:	October, December, January, March, May, July, and September
Trading unit:	60,000 lb (one standard tank car).
Price quotations and minimum fluctuation:	Quoted in dollars and cents per 100 lb (cents and hundredths of a cent per pound), with a minimum fluctuation of \$0.01 per 100 lb (\$6 per contract), basis Decatur, IL, with freight adjusted to Decatur–New York City.
Daily price movement limits:	Subject to change; consult latest official notices from the exchange.
Position limits:	540 contracts in any one future or in all futures combined; positions of 50 or more require reports to the CFTC.
Grades deliverable:	One grade only; see regulations for specifications.
Delivery:	By registered warehouse receipts issued by warehouse persons against stocks in Midwest warehouses that have been declared regular by the exchange.
Trading hours:	9:30 a.m. to 1:15 p.m. central time.
MidAmerica Commodity Exchange Soybeans	
Delivery months:	January, March, May, July, September, and November.
Trading unit:	1,000 bushels.
Minimum fluctuation:	⅛ cent per bushel (\$1.25 per contract).
Daily price movement limits:	Subject to change; consult latest official notices from the exchange.
Position limits:	3 million bushels (CFTC limit) in any one future or in all futures combined.
Grades deliverable:	No. 2 yellow soybeans at par, other grades deliverable at differentials.
Delivery:	From Chicago, IL and Toledo, OH, elevators approved by the exchange.
Trading hours:	9:30 a.m. to 1:30 p.m. central time.

Source: Commodity Trading Manual, Chicago Board of Trade.
(Specifications are incomplete and subject to change. Consult the exchanges for precise and current specifications.)

products. Space limitations do not permit full discussion of marketing strategies in the cash markets and the role of future trading in these strategies. Nevertheless, some examples are given.

The soybean farmer, like other farmers, seeks to combine production inputs in an efficient way and to market crops at a price which covers the costs and yields a profit. On the marketing side, the soybean farmer has several alternatives, each providing a different degree of flexibility and each having a different degree of risk. The farmer may enter into a *cash contract* before harvest to specify an exact cash price he or she will receive for crops. Another way of pricing before harvest is for the farmer to sell a *futures contract* in a month beyond harvest at a futures price which, given the farmer's local basis history, will provide an acceptable cash price at harvest. Though the farmer can sell a soybean futures contract at any time before harvest, giving the farmer considerable time in which to choose an acceptable price, the ultimate cash price is not as certain under this alternative because of the existence of basis risk. Perhaps the most common marketing alternative is for the farmer to harvest the soybeans and *deliver them to a local elevator*, accepting the prevailing price. While this provides immediate income, prices at harvest are usually at annual lows. If the farmer decides to store the soybeans instead, the farmer may then watch local cash market prices, hoping prices reach a level which will cover production and storage costs in addition to providing a profit, or the farmer may price the soybeans for future delivery using a forward cash contract or the futures market. Again the cash contract gives more price certainty, and the futures contract gives more flexibility. A final marketing option is for the farmer to deliver the soybeans to an elevator but *delay the final pricing decision*. The farmer may, for example, accept a "basis contract"—say, $0.20 under the CBT January futures contract—and then wait until the futures contract price reaches an acceptable level to specify the futures price to be used in the final calculation. Another method of delayed pricing is for the farmer to sell the soybeans on the cash market harvest but, thinking prices will rise, buy on the futures market. The farmer then can benefit from a price appreciation (or lose if prices fall) even though the farmer no longer owns the actual soybeans.

The local elevators which buy the farmer's soybeans often enter the futures market as soon as they take control of the product to hedge against some of the risks of carrying the soybeans in inventory. Further along the marketing chain, exporters of soybeans and products must often quote a selling price long before they are able to buy the commodity for export shipment. Their risk—which may be reduced by hedging—is that prices will rise before they can cover the forward sale, eliminating profits. Cattle feeders facing risks of rising feed costs may control costs of soybean meal by purchasing soybean meal futures contracts. Soybean processors employ one, two, or all three soybean complex futures markets in the course of business. The methods by which processors incorporate futures trading into their operations are illustrative of practices used by others in the soybean complex and will be discussed in somewhat more detail.

GROSS PROCESSING MARGIN AND THE CRUSHING HEDGE. Soybean processing is the focal point of the marketing chain because the soybeans must be converted to oil and meal before they take on their full economic value. The profitability of processing is thus an important factor in the supply-and-demand situation in the soybean complex. Low profitability, for example, will result in curtailed processing operations, reduced demand for soybeans, and lower soybean prices on the one hand, and lower oil and meal supplies and eventual higher oil and meal prices on the other.

The gross processing margin (GPM) is a measure of the profitability of processing. It measures the extent to which the processors' return from the sale of the products covers (or fails to cover) the cost of buying the soybeans and converting them to oil and meal.

Example 1 illustrates the computation of the GPM. In calculating the GPM, the meal price per ton and the oil price per pound are converted to the price for the amounts of these products which may be obtained from a bushel of soybeans. Oil and meal yields vary among plants and among batches of soybeans processed, but generally a 60-lb bushel of soybean yields about 47 to 48 lb of meal and 10 to 11 lb of oil. Processing losses account for the remainder:

Example 1: Computation of the GPM[5]

	Prices	Yields Per Bushel of Soybeans
Soybean meal	\$189 per ton	47.91 lb
Soybean oil	19.71 cents per lb	10.58 lb
Soybeans	\$6.45 per bushel	
Value of meal:	(\$189 ÷ 2000) × 47.91	= \$4.53 per bushel
Value of oil:	(19.71 × 10.58) ÷ 100	= \$2.09 per bushel
Value of products:		\$6.62 per bushel
Cost of soybeans:		− \$6.45 per bushel
GPM:		\$0.17 per bushel

In the past, the GPM has varied widely. In June 1975, for example, when a GPM of \$0.15–\$0.17 per bushel was needed by processors to break even, processing margins fell as low as \$0.06 per bushel. A year earlier, margins of as much as \$0.78 per bushel prevailed. Furthermore, seasonality is often observed in the GPM. Farmers sell nearly 50% of their crop in the first 3 months after harvest (October–December). During this period of heavy supply, soybean prices usually reach their lowest levels of the year and GPMs are usually the most favorable.

The soybean processor clearly faces three types of price risk. Soybeans are the processor's principal input and an increase in their price increases the cost of doing business. Decreases in oil and meal prices reduce the processor's revenue. The existence of the futures contracts in the three commodities allows the processor to hedge each risk separately or to simultaneously use all three futures contracts to hedge against an unfavorable GPM—making use of a technique called "putting on the crush" or "BOM (bean, oil, and meal) spread." Basically this involves determining the "board crushing margin"[6] from the futures prices listed

[5]*Source: Grain and Feed Market News*, U.S. Department of Agricultures, Vol. 30, No. 14, April 19, 1982.

[6]Standard yields often used in this determination are 11 lb of oil and 48 lb of meal per bushel of soybeans.

in the three contracts in an appropriate distant month and predicting whether or not it will deteriorate between now and then. If a deterioration is expected—implying that a processor's own GPM will deteriorate—a processor may put on the crush by buying soybean futures and selling oil and meal futures contracts[7] for that distant month. This establishes a processor's GPM (related to the board crushing margin via basis relationships) for the quantity of soybeans represented by this position. When the time comes to buy the soybeans, the processor liquidates the soybean futures position; when the oil and meal from those soybeans is sold (prior to expiration of the futures contract), the processor liquidates the oil and meal futures positions.

When, because of high soybean prices, low product prices, or both, the GPM drops to the point when processing is no longer profitable, processors may continue to process—albeit at a lower level—and put on the "reverse crush spread." This involves taking the opposite futures market position, that is, *selling* soybean futures contracts and *buying* oil and meal futures contracts. In the cash market, reduced processing lowers demand for soybeans and supply of products. This would tend to lower soybean prices and raise product prices. These tendencies are reinforced in the futures market by selling pressure on soybeans and buying pressure on meal and oil. Together, these actions in the cash and futures markets would serve to readjust the bean-oil–meal price relationship in favor of the processors. The reverse crush position can be closed out when processing margins become profitable and (usually) a gain on the reverse crush position can help to offset processing losses incurred.

CONCLUSION

This discussion of the soybean complex has been necessarily brief. Nevertheless, some of the principal characteristics of the marketing chain, supply and demand, price determination, futures market, and trading strategies have been highlighted by way of introduction. Further detail on these and other aspects of the soybean complex may be obtained by referring to the sources of information which follow.

APPENDIX A: GLOSSARY OF SOYBEAN TERMS[a]

Terms Used in Conjunction With the Processing of Soybeans and the Utilization of Soy Oil and Other Soy Products

ACIDULATED SOYBEAN SOAPSTOCK: The product that results from the complete acidulation of soybean soapstock. The contract grade should contain not less than 85% total fatty acid.

BREAK MATERIAL: Flocculent material (precipitate) that appears in and can be separated from crude soy oil that has been rapidly heated to temperatures between 250–300°C (482–572°F). Found to be very high in ash content rich

[7]For equivalence at the standard yields given previously, for every 10 soybean futures contract bought, 12 meal and 9 oil contracts would be sold.

[a]*Source. 1981 Soya Bluebook* (American Soybean Association).

in phosphorus, calcium, and magnesium. Presumed to be derived from phospholipids which are thermally decomposed at these high temperatures. It is sometimes referred to as "foots."

COLD PRESSED SOY OIL: Soy oil produced from domestic-grown, undamaged, mature, cleaned yellow soybeans by mechanical processing without application of heat, and then filtered. Such oil is usually sold in health food stores.

CRUDE SOY OIL: Is sometimes referred to as crude raw soybean oil. The unrefined oil is produced by any one of the procedures described for the processing of soybeans. It is customary to filter the oil and/or allow it to settle after being processed from the soybeans as required by the standard trade specifications.

A mixture of triglycerides composed of unsaturated fatty acids (oleic, linoleic, and linolenic) and saturated fatty acids, together with usually not more than 1.5% of free fatty acids and 1.8–3.2% of phospholipids, depending on the quality and kind of soybeans and the procedure used in the processing.

DEGUMMED SOY OIL: Sometimes is referred to as crude degummed soy oil. The product resulting from washing crude soy oil with water and/or steam or another degumming agent for a specified period of time and then separating the oil-and-water mixture, usually by centrifugation, to remove the phosphatides. It shall not contain more than 0.02% of phosphorus without a discount penalty.

EDIBLE CRUDE SOY OIL: Soy oil of any of the following designated types produced from domestic-grown, mature yellow soybeans (1) expeller pressed, (2) expeller pressed degummed, (3) hydraulic pressed, (4) hydraulic pressed degummed, (5) solvent extracted, (6) solvent extracted degummed, and (7) mixtures of any of the above-described types. When the oil is produced by solvent extraction, the name of the solvent used in the process must be given.

EDIBLE REFINED SOY OIL: Crude or degummed soy oil which has been subjected to special refining processes to adapt it specifically for use in food products. In addition to treatment with alkali, bleaching, partial hydrogenation, and deodorization, the oils may be also winterized. These oils are further classified as salad oils, cooking oils, or shortenings.

FULLY REFINED SOY OIL: The oil produced from crude or degummed soy oil which has been treated with dilute alkali solution (refining), decolorized by treatment with absorbent clay materials (bleaching), and subjected to steam distillation at high temperatures under vacuum (deodorizing).

HYDROGENATED SOY OIL: During the process of hydrogenation, the soy oil is exposed to hydrogen gas in the presence of heat and a catalyst (nickel, copper chromite) and the hydrogen combines with certain of the chemical components (unsaturated fatty acids) of the triglycerides with a resultant increase in the melting point of the oil. This process is sometimes referred to as "hardening."

ONCE-REFINED SOY OIL: Oil produced from crude soy oil which has been subjected only to the dilute alkali solution (refining) treatment or a comparable chemical treatment.

SLUDGE: The solid residue which settles to the bottom of the tank or car in which crude soy oil is stored or shipped. It cannot be pumped out or removed by rubber-faced scrapers from the surface to which it adheres. Steam must be applied to facilitate its removal. Is sometimes referred to as "tank bottoms" or "foots."

SOYBEAN(S): A legume whose botanical name is Glycine max (L.) Merrill. It is a summer annual varying in height from less than 1 foot to more than 6 feet and in habit of growth from stiffly erect to prostrate. The cultivated plant may reach a height of 3 feet or more. The seeds (soybeans) are borne in pods that grow in clusters of three to five with each pod usually containing two or three or more seeds. The oil content of the soybean varies from 13–26% (average 18–22%) and from 38–45% of protein (on a moisture-free basis). It was grown for centuries in the Orient and first introduced to the United States early in the 19th century. Soybeans grow best in areas having hot, damp summer weather, but they can be grown under a great variety of climatic conditions. The term "soybean" has been accepted as standard in the United States in preference to "soya bean," "soy bean," "soya-bean," or "soja bean." It is incorrect to use the term "beans" when referring to soybeans.

SOYBEAN FATTY ACIDS: The product obtained when glycerine is split off from the triglycerides in soy oil by any method of hydrolysis. In the field of industrial usage, soybean fatty acids are usually further classified according to the treatment to which they are subjected subsequent to hydrolysis.

SOYBEAN LECITHIN: The mixed phospholipids product obtained from soy oil by the degumming process, contains lecithin, cephalin, and inositol phosphatides, together with glycerides of soy oil and traces of tocopherols, glucosides, and pigments. It shall be designated and sold according to conventional descriptive grades with respect to consistency and bleaching. The dehydrated emulsion of mixed phosphatides and soy oil is further processed to produce the commercial grades which may be described as follows: plastic or firm consistency, soft consistency, fluid, unbleached, consistency, soft consistency, fluid, unbleached, bleached, and double-bleached high-quality commercial lecithin containing 60–65% phosphatides.

SOYBEAN SOAPSTOCK: The by-product that results from the alkali refining of soy oil. It averages about 6% of the volume of crude oil refined. It sometimes is referred to as "foots" since it accumulates at the bottom (foot) of the refining tank. Contract grade should contain not less than 30% total fatty acid.

SOYBEAN PROCESSING: The procedure involved in the separation of the oil and the protein meal. There are two types of processes presently used in the United States for this purpose:

1. *Solvent Extraction.* The process whereby the oil is leached or washed (extracted) from flaked soybeans by the use of hexane as the solvent. The level of oil in the extracted flakes can be reduced to 1% or less by this processing method. The products resulting from the use of this process are designated in the trade as "solvent extracted," for example, "solvent extracted soybean meal," "dehulled solvent extracted soybean meal," "solvent extracted soy grits," and "solvent extracted soy flour." Practically all soybeans processed in the United States are processed by the solvent extraction system.

2. *Mechanical Processing* A continuous pressing process, at elevated temperatures, using expellers or screw presses which utilize a worm shaft continuously rotating within a pressing cylinder or cage to express the oil from soybeans after they have been ground and properly conditioned. The oil content of the resulting press cake is reduced from 4% to 6% by this processing method. Although technically incorrect, the products resulting from this type of processing are often referred to as "expeller," for example, "expeller soybean meal." The term "expeller" applies specifically to the screw press manufactured by Anderson IBEC of Strongsville, Ohio, whereas the screw press manufactured by the French Oil Mill Machinery Company of Piqua, Ohio, is designated as a "mechanical screw press."

A third type of processing, called "hydraulic pressing" is not used at present in the United States to any appreciable extent, but is used in some parts of the world for recovering the oil from soybeans and other oil-bearing materials. It is the oldest process known to the vegetable oil processing industry. It consists of an intermittent pressing operation carried out at elevated temperatures in a hydraulic press after the soybeans have been rolled into flakes and properly conditioned by heat treatment.

SOYBEAN PROCESSOR: An individual, or a group of two or more individuals working together as a company or firm, whose primary business is the separation of the oil and meal in soybeans. The activities of a processor may also include refining and/or distribution of the oil, as well as distribution of the soybean meal or soy protein.

TECHNICAL GRADE REFINED SOY OIL: Includes a wide variety of soy oils that are specially refined and further processed to meet requirements and/or specifications for a definite industrial use.

WINTERIZED OIL: Oil which has been treated in a manner to partially remove the saturated glycerides which have relatively high melting points and are soluble only to a limited extent in the unsaturated glycerides. The process consists of chilling the oil slowly and then maintaining it at 5°C (41°F) for a specified period of time and removing the crystallized glycerides from the liquid fraction of the oil by the use of filter presses. Soy oil does not require winterizing unless it has been partially hydrogenated to increase stability.

Standard Specifications

These have been adopted for certain soy products as follows by the National Soybean Processors Association (NSPA) and made a part of their trading rules governing purchase and sale of soybean meal in the United States:

DEHULLED SOYBEAN FLAKES, 49%-PROTEIN SOLVENT EXTRACTED SOYBEAN MEAL: Produced by cracking, heating, and flaking dehulled soybeans and reducing the oil content of the conditioned flakes by the use of hexane or homologous hydrocarbon solvents to 1% or less on a commercial basis. Standard specifications are as follows:

Protein (when loaded by seller)	minimum 49.0%
Fat	minimum 0.5%

Fiber (when loaded by seller)	maximum 3.3%
Moisture (when loaded by seller)	maximum 12.0%

SOYBEAN CAKE, SOYBEAN CHIPS: The product after the extraction of part of the oil by pressure or solvents from soybeans. A name descriptive of the process of manufacture, such as expeller, hydraulic, or solvent extracted shall be used as part of the brand name. It shall be designated and sold according to its protein content.

SOYBEAN FLAKES, 44%-PROTEIN SOYBEAN MEAL: Produced by conditioning ground soybeans and reducing the oil content of the conditioned product by the use of hexane or homologous hydrocarbon solvents to 1% or less on a commercial basis. Standard specifications are as follows:

Protein (when loaded by seller)	minimum 44.0%
Fat	minimum 0.5%
Fiber (when loaded by seller)	maximum 7.0%
Moisture (when loaded by seller)	maximum 12.0%

Soy Protein

The following terms and their definitions are widely used and accepted in the trade in conjunction with the production and utilization of soy flour and other soy products.

AMINO ACIDS: Chief components and determinants of the characteristics of a protein and the building blocks of living tissues. Eighteen different amino acids commonly occur in our food supply and eight are considered essential because the body cannot produce them.

DEFATTED SOY FLOUR: Flour produced by the nearly complete removal of the oil from soybeans by the use of hexane or other homologous hydrocarbon solvents. It usually contains about 1% of fat.

FULL-FAT SOY FLOUR: Flour containing all of the oil originally present in the raw soybeans. It usually contains 18–20% of fat.

HIGH-FAT SOY FLOUR: Flour produced by adding back soy oil and/or lecithin to defatted soy flour to a specified level, usually in the range of 15%.

LOW-FAT SOY FLOUR: Flour produced either by partial removal of the oil from soybeans or by adding back soy oil and/or lecithin to defatted soy flour to specified level, usually in the range of 5–6%.

PROTEIN: A naturally occurring combination of amino acids, containing the chemical elements carbon, hydrogen, oxygen, nitrogen, and usually sulphur. Is one of the essential constituents of all living things and of the diet of the animal organism.

SOY GRITS and/or FLOUR: The ground, screened, graded product obtained after extracting most of the oil from selected, sound, clean, dehulled soybeans. They are produced from grinding the defatted soy flakes. Grits are coarser ground than soy flour. Protein range is 40–60%.

Soy Products

The following have been adopted officially by the American Feed Control Officials, Incorporated (AFCO):

DEHULLED SOLVENT EXTRACTED SOYBEAN MEAL: The product obtained by grinding flakes which are obtained by removing most of the oil from dehulled soybeans. Heat shall be applied during the process. It must be designated and sold according to its protein content and must not contain more than 3% crude fiber (proposed 1960, adopted 1961). NSPA states not less than 3.3% fiber, not more than 49% protein, and not greater than 0.5% fat.

GROUND SOYBEANS: The product obtained by grinding whole soybeans without cooking or removing any of the oil. (Is sometimes erroneously called "soybean meal," Adopted 1933).

HEAT PROCESSED SOYBEANS: The product resulting from heating whole soybeans without removing any of the component parts. It may be ground, pelleted, flaked, or powdered. It shall be sold according to its protein content (proposed 1960, adopted 1964).

ISOLATED SOY PROTEIN: Protein which has been greatly concentrated from its native location by chemical or mechanical means. It is produced by extracting white flakes or flour with water or a mild alkali. Isolate generally has a protein content of 90%.

LECITHINATED SOY FLOUR: A type of low-fat or high-fat soy flour in which lecithin is added to defatted soy flour to a specified level, usually in a range up to 15%.

MEAT ANALOGS: Material usually prepared from vegetable protein to resemble specific meats in texture, color, and flavor.

MEAT EXTENDERS: Use of soy or other vegetable proteins as partial substitutes for meat in processed items such as patties, chili, casseroles, and so forth.

SOLVENT EXTRACTED SOYBEAN FEED: The material resulting from the partial removal of protein-free and nitrogen-free extract from dehulled, solvent extracted soybean flakes. It shall be designated and sold according to its protein content (adopted 1948, amended 1960 and 1964).

SOYBEAN HULLS: The product consisting primarily of the outer covering of the soybean (adopted 1948). NSPA states that a typical analysis is 13% moisture.

SOYBEAN MEAL: The product obtained by grinding the cake, chips, or flakes which are products obtained by removal of most of the oil from soybeans by several methods, hydraulic, expeller and solvent extracted, respectively. The name must include one of the terms "hydraulic," "expeller," or "solvent extracted" to indicate the method of manufacture of the source material. Heat shall be applied during the process. It may be sold in various physical forms other than "meal," such as "cubes," "pellets," "pea size," "cake," "chips," or "flakes." It must be designated and sold according to its protein content and shall contain not more than 7% crude fiber (proposed 1960, adopted 1961).

SOYBEAN MILL FEED: The by-product resulting from the manufacture of soy flour or grits and is composed of soybean hulls and the offal from the tail of the mill. It shall contain not less than 13% crude protein and not more than 32% crude fiber (proposed 1960, adopted 1961, amended 1964). NSPA states that a typical analysis is 13% crude protein, 32% crude fiber, and 13% moisture.

SOYBEAN MILL RUN: The product resulting from the manufacture of dehulled soybean meal and is composed of soybean hulls and such bean meats that adhere to the hull in normal milling operations. It shall contain not less than 11% crude protein and not more than 35% crude fiber (proposed 1960, adopted 1961). NSPA states that a typical analysis is 11% crude protein, 35% crude fiber, and 13% moisture.

SOY PROTEIN CONCENTRATE: Produced from defatted soybean flakes or flour by a process which immobilizes the protein and removes soluble sugars, minerals, and so forth. Concentrate has a protein content of 70%.

TEXTURED VEGETABLE PROTEIN: Soy or other vegetable protein that has texture imparted by spinning a fiber and combining the fiber in layers to achieve the desired texture, or by a thermoplastic extrusion process.

TOASTING: The term commonly but erroneously applied to the processes (moist) of cooking soybean meal, flour, or grits by atmospheric or pressure methods for the purpose of increasing the protein efficiency of these soy products or improving their functional properties and/or improving physical texture.

APPENDIX B: STANDARDS FOR SOYBEANS[b]

§ 26.601 Terms Defined

For the purposes of the U.S. Standards for Soybeans:

1. *Soybeans.* Soybeans shall be any grain which consists of 50% or more of whole or broken soybeans which will not pass readily through an 8/64 sieve and not more than 10% of other grains for which standards have been established under the U.S. Grain Standards Act.

2. *Classes.* Soybeans shall be divided into the following five classes: yellow soybeans, green soybeans, brown soybeans, black soybeans, and mixed soybeans.

3. *Yellow Soybeans.* Yellow soybeans shall be any soybeans which have yellow or green seed coats, and which in cross section are yellow or have a yellow tinge, and may include not more than 10% of soybeans of other classes.

4. *Green Soybeans.* Green soybeans shall be any soybeans which have green seed coats, and which in cross section are green, and may include not more than 10% of soybeans of other classes.

5. *Brown Soybeans.* Brown soybeans shall be any soybeans with brown seed coats, and may include not more than 10% of soybeans of other classes.

[b]This Appendix is taken from the U.S. Standards for Soybeans as published in the *1981 Soya Bluebook*, American Soybean Association. The specifications of these standards shall not excuse failure to comply with the provisions of the Federal Food, Drug, and Cosmetic Act.

6. *Black Soybeans.* Black soybeans shall be any soybeans with black seed coats, and may include not more than 10% of soybeans of other classes.

7. *Mixed Soybeans.* Mixed soybeans shall be any mixture of soybeans which does not meet the requirements of the classes yellow, green, brown, or black soybeans. Bicolored soybeans shall be classified as mixed soybeans.

8. *Grades.* Grades shall be the U.S. numerical grades, U.S. sample grade, and special grades provided for in § 26.603.

9. *Bicolored Soybeans.* Bicolored soybeans shall be any soybeans with seed coats of two colors, one of which is black or brown.

10. *Splits.* Splits shall be pieces of soybeans that are not damaged.

11. *Damaged Kernels.* Damaged kernels shall be soybeans and pieces of soybeans which are heat-damaged, sprouted, frosted, badly ground-damaged, badly weather-damaged, moldy, diseased, stinkbug-stung, or otherwise materially damaged. Stinkbug-stung kernels shall be considered damaged kernels at the rate of one-fourth of the actual percentage of the stung kernels.

12. *Heat-Damaged Kernels.* Heat-damaged kernels shall be soybeans and pieces of soybeans which are materially discolored and damaged by heat.

13. *Foreign Material.* Foreign material shall be all matter, including soybeans and pieces of soybeans, which will pass readily through an 8/64 sieve and all matter other than soybeans remaining on such sieve after sieving.

14. *Stones.* Stones shall be concreted earthy or mineral matter and other substances of similar hardness that do not disintegrate readily in water.

15. *8/64 Sieve.* An 8/64 sieve shall be a metal sieve 0.032 in. thick perforated with round holes 0.125 (8/64) in. in diameter with approximately 4,736 perforations per square foot.

§ 26.602 Principles Governing Application of Standards

The following principles shall apply in the determination of the classes and grades of soybeans:

1. *Basis of Determination.* Each determination of class, splits, damaged kernels, and heat-damaged kernels, and of black, brown, and/or bicolored soybeans in yellow or green soybeans, shall be upon the basis of the grain when free from foreign material. All other determinations shall be upon the basis of the grain as a whole.

2. *Percentages.* All percentages shall be upon the basis of weight. The percentages of splits shall be expressed in terms of whole percents. All other percentages shall be expressed in terms of whole and tenths percents.

3. *Moisture.* Moisture shall be ascertained by the air-oven method prescribed by the U.S. Department of Agriculture, as described in Service and Regulatory Announcement No. 147, issued by the Agricultural Marketing Service, or ascertained by any method which gives equivalent results.

4. *Test Weight Per Bushel.* Test weight per bushel shall be the weight per Winchester bushel as determined by the method prescribed by the U.S. Depart-

ment of Agriculture, as described in Circular No. 921, issued June 1953, or as determined by any method which gives equivalent results.

§ 26.603 Grades, Grade Requirements, and Grade Designations

The following grades, grade requirements, and grade designations are applicable under these standards:

1. *Grades and Grade Requirements for Soybeans.* [*See Also (3) of this Section.*]

		Maximum Limits of—					
			Damaged Kernels				
U.S. Grade No.	Min. Test Weight Per Bushel	Moisture	Splits	Total	Heat-Damaged	Foreign Material	Brown, Black, and/or Bicolored Soybeans in Yellow or Green Soybeans
	Pounds	Percent	Percent	Percent	Percent	Percent	Percent
1	56.0	13.0	10.0	2.0	0.2	1.0	1.0
2	54.0	14.0	20.0	3.0	0.5	2.0	2.0
3[a]	52.0	16.0	30.0	5.0	1.0	3.0	5.0
4[b]	49.0	18.0	40.0	8.0	3.0	5.0	10.0
Sample grade:	U.S. sample grade shall be soybeans which do not meet the requirements for any of the grades from U.S. No. 1 to U.S. No. 4 inclusive; or which are musty, sour, or heating; or which have any commercially objectionable foreign odor; or which contain stones; or which are otherwise of distinctly low quality.						

[a]Soybeans which are purple mottled or stained shall be graded not higher than U.S. No. 3.
[b]Soybeans which are materially weathered shall be graded not higher than U.S. No. 4.

Grade Designation

2. *Grade Designations for Soybeans.* The grade designations for soybeans shall include in the order named, the letters "U.S."; the number of the grade or the words "sample grades," as the case may be; the name of the class; and the name of each applicable special grade. In the case of mixed soybeans, the grade designation shall also include, following the name of the class, the approximate percentages of yellow, green, brown, black, and bicolored soybeans in the mixture.

3. *Optional Grade Designations.* Soybeans may be certificated (under certain conditions[c]), when supported by official analysis, as "U.S. No. 2 or better soybeans," "U.S. No. 3 or better soybeans," and so forth. The optional grade designation for soybeans shall include the name of the class immediately preceding the word "soybeans" in the grade designation. The special grade designation, when applicable, also shall be included (under certain conditions)[c] in the certification.

[c]The conditions are listed in the Grain Inspection Manual, GR Instruction 918.6. Copies may be obtained from the Inspection Division, Federal Grain Inspection Service, U.S. Department of Agriculture, 1400 Independence Avenue, S.W., Washington, D.C. 20250.

Special Grades for Soybeans

4. *Special Grades, Special Grade Requirements, and Special Grade Designations for Soybeans.* (a) *Garlicky Soybeans:* (i) *Requirements*—Garlicky soybeans shall be soybeans which contain five or more garlic bulblets in 1,000 g. *(ii) Grade Designation*—Garlicky soybeans shall be graded and designated according to the grade requirements of the standards applicable to such soybeans if there were not garlicky and there shall be added to and made a part of the grade designation the word "garlicky." (b) *Weevily Soybeans:* (i) *Requirements*—Weevily soybeans shall be soybeans which are infested with live weevils or other live insects injurious to stored grain. (ii) *Grade Designation*—Weevily soybeans shall be graded and designated according to the grade requirements of the standards applicable to such soybeans if they were not weevily, and there shall be added to and made a part of the grade designation the word "weevily."

Interpretations [Added]

§ 26.901 Interpretation With Respect to the Term "Distinctly Low Quality"

The term "distinctly low quality," when used in the U.S. Standards for Grain, shall be construed to include grain which contains more than two crotalaria seeds (Crotalaria spp.) in 1,000 g of grain.

§ 26.902 Interpretation With Respect to the Term "Purple Mottled or Stained"

The term "purple mottled or stained," when used in the U.S. Standards for Soybeans [see § 26.603(1)] shall be construed to include soybeans which are discolored by the growth of a fungus; or by dirt; or by a dirtlike substance including nontoxic inoculants; or by other nontoxic substances.

§ 26.903 Interpretation With Respect to the Term "Bicolored Soybeans"

The term "bicolored soybeans," when used in the U.S. Standards for Soybeans [see item (9) § 26.601], shall be construed to include any soybeans with seedcoats of two colors, one of which is black or brown, when the black and/or brown color covers 50% or more of the seedcoat. The hilum of a soybean shall not be considered a part of the seedcoat.

APPENDIX C: CONVERSION TABLE[d]

1 bushel of soybeans = 60 lb.
1 short ton (2,000 lb) = 33.33 bushels of soybeans.
1 long ton (2,240 lb) = 37.33 bushels of soybeans.
1 metric ton (2,205 lb) = 36.74 bushels of soybean.
1 bushel of soybeans = 10.7 lb of soybean oil.
1 bushel of soybeans = 47.5 lb of soybean meal.

[d]This appendix is taken from the 1981 Soya Bluebook, American Soybean Association.

1 short ton of soybean meal = 42.08 bushels of soybeans.

1 long ton of soybean meal = 47.13 bushels of soybeans.

1 metric ton of soybean meal = 46.39 bushels of soybeans.

79.2% of a bushel of soybeans is manufactured into soybean meal.

17.8% of a bushel of soybeans is manufactured into soybean oil.

Manufacturing loss = 3%.

BIBLIOGRAPHY

Books

Caldwell, B.E. (Ed). *Soybeans: Improvement, Production and Uses*. Madison, WI: American Society of Agronomy, Incorporated, 1973.

Chicago Board of Trade. *Commodity Trading Manual*. Chicago, IL, 1980.

Chicago Board of Trade. *Grains—Production, Processing, Marketing*. Chicago, IL, 1982.

Chicago Board of Trade. *The Sunflower Phenomenon*. Chicago, IL, 1974.

Corbin, F.T. *Proceedings—World Soybean Research Conference II*. Boulder, CO: Westview Press, 1980.

Hill, L.D. (Ed.). *Proceedings—World Soybean Research Conference, Champaign, Illinois—1975*. Danville, IL: Interstate, 1976.

Houck, J.P., Ryan, M.E., and Subotnik, A. *Soybeans and Their Products—Markets, Models and Policy*. Minneapolis, MN: University of Minnesota Press, 1972.

Leath, M.N., Hill, L.D., and Fuller, S.W. *Soybean Movements in the United States—Interregional Flow Patterns and Transportation Requirements in 1977*. Illinois Bulletin 766, Agricultural Experiment Station, College of Agriculture, University of Illinois at Urbana-Champaign, January 1981.

Merrill Lynch, Pierce, Fenner and Smith. *The Soybean*. New York, NY, April 1969.

Peck, A.E. (Ed). *Views From the Trade, Book III, Readings in Futures Markets*. Chicago, IL: Chicago Board of Trade, 1978.

Soybean—Production, Marketing and Use. Bulletin Y-69, National Fertilizer Development Center, Tennessee Valley Authority, Muscle Shoals, AL, March 1974.

Periodicals

American Soybean Association. *Soya Bluebook* (annual).

American Soybean Association. *Soybean Digest* (monthly).

Commodity Research Bureau. *Commodity Yearbook* (annual).

U.S. Department of Agriculture, Agricultural Marketing Service. *Grain and Feed Market News* (weekly).

U.S. Department of Agriculture, Crop Reporting Board, Statistical Reporting Service. *Crop Production* (monthly).

U.S. Department of Agriculture, Economic Research Service. *Agricultural Outlook* (monthly).

U.S. Department of Agriculture, Economic Research Service. *Fats and Oils—Outlook and Situation* (quarterly).

U.S. Department of Agriculture, Foreign Agricultural Service. *Foreign Agricultural Circular—Oilseeds and Products* (monthly).

U.S. Department of Agriculture, Foreign Agricultural Service. *Foreign Agriculture* (monthly).

U.S. Department of Commerce, Bureau of Census. *Current Industrial Reports M20J, Fats and Oils—Oilseed Crushings* (monthly).

U.S. Department of Commerce, Bureau of Census. *Current Industrial Reports M20K, Fats and Oils—Production, Consumption and Stocks* (monthly).

ORGANIZATIONS

American Soybean Association
P.O. Box 27300
St. Louis, MO 63141
Telephone (314) 432-1600

National Soybean Processors Association
1800 M. Street, N.W.
Washington, D.C. 20036
Telephone (202) 452-8040

Food Protein Council
1800 M. Street, N.W.
Washington, D.C. 20036
Telephone (202) 467-6610

State Research Experiment Stations

Alabama	Agricultural Experiment Station, Auburn, AL 36830
	Alabama A&M University, Normal, AL 35762
Arkansas	University of Arkansas, Fayetteville, AR 72701
	University of Arkansas, Pine Bluff, AR 71601
	Arkansas State University, State University, AR 72467
Florida	University of Florida, Gainesville, FL 32640
	Agricultural Research Center, Rt. 3, P.O. Box 575, Jay, FL 32565
	Agricultural Research and Evaluation Center, P.O. Box 470, Quincy, FL 32351
Georgia	College Experiment Station, Athens, GA 30602
	Agricultural Experiment Station, Experiment, GA 30212
	Coastal Plain Experiment Station, Tifton, GA 31794
Illinois	University of Illinois, Urbana, IL 61801
Indiana	Agricultural Experiment Station, West Lafayette, IN 47907
Iowa	Agricultural Experiment Station, Ames, IA 50010
Kansas	Southeast Kansas Branch Experiment Station, Mound Valley, KS 67354
	Kansas State University, Manhattan, KS 66506
Kentucky	University of Kentucky, Lexington, KY 40506
Louisiana	Louisiana State University, Baton Rouge, LA 70803
	Northeast Louisiana Experiment Station, P.O. Box 438, St. Joseph, LA 71366

	Red River Valley Experiment Station, Box 5477, Bossier City, LA 71111
	Rice Experiment Station, P.O. Box 1429, Crowley, LA 70526
Maryland	University of Maryland, College Park, MD 20742
Minnesota	Agricultural Experiment Station, St. Paul, MN 55108
Mississippi	Mississippi Agricultural and Forestry Experiment Station, Mississippi State, MS 39762
	Delta Station, Stoneville, MS 38776
	South Mississippi Station, Poplarville, MS 39470
Missouri	University of Missouri, Columbia, MO 65211
	University of Missouri Delta Center, P.O. Box 160, Portageville, MO 63873
Nebraska	University of Nebraska, Lincoln, NE 68583
New York	Agricultural Experiment Station, Ithaca, NY 14853
North Carolina	Agricultural Research Service, Raleigh, NC 27650
North Dakota	North Dakota State University, Fargo, ND 58105
Ohio	Ohio Agricultural Research and Development Center, Wooster, OH 44691
	Ohio State University, Columbus, OH 43210
South Carolina	Clemson University, Clemson, SC 29631
	Edisto Experiment Station, Blackville, SC 29817
Tennessee	University of Tennessee, P.O. Box 1071, Knoxville, TN 37901
	West Tennessee Experiment Station, Jackson, TN 38301
Texas	Texas A&M University Agricultural Research and Extension Center, Rt. 3, Lubbock, TX 79401
	Texas A&M University Agricultural Research and Extension Center, Beaumont, TX 77706
Virginia	Agricultural Experiment Station, Blacksburg, VA 24061
	Eastern Virginia Research Station, Warsaw, VA 22572
Wisconsin	University of Wisconsin, Madison, WI 53706

Futures Exchanges

Chicago Board of Trade
LaSalle at Jackson
Chicago, IL 60604
Telephone (312) 435-3500

MidAmerica Commodity Exchange
175 West Jackson Boulevard
Chicago, IL 60604
Telephone (312) 435-0606

New Orleans Commodity Exchange
308 Board of Trade Place
New Orleans, LA 70130
Telephone (504) 524-2184

CHAPTER 31

PRIMARY FACTORS CONSTITUTING A DYNAMIC CATTLE INDUSTRY

CONTENTS

THE COW/CALF SECTOR 4

Land Valves 5

Consumer Dollar 6

CATTLE-FEEDING SECTOR 7

PRICE/DEMAND RELATIONSHIPS 12

CATTLE SEASONALITY 15

Filtering By Demand 16

HISTORICAL CATTLE PRICE MOVEMENTS 16

CATTLE FUTURES MARKETS 18

SUMMARY 22

CHAPTER 31

PRIMARY FACTORS CONSTITUTING A DYNAMIC CATTLE INDUSTRY

Bruce A. Ginn

The cattle industry is complex, consisting of many interrelationships with other sectors of the economy, as well as natural market forces. These phenomena lead to changes which can dramatically affect the cattle supply and demand balance and therefore price levels. Partially due to the lack of predictability in the course of natural events, it is often difficult to forecast, with a large degree of certainty, changes in key factors and their subsequent impact. Nevertheless, an understanding of the factors that comprise the complex interrelationships in the cattle industry leads to a better understanding of the mechanisms which constitute the industry.

Decisions of producers and cattle feeders regarding production levels for the individual feeding operation will be based first on the availability and cost of feed. Weather conditions have a dramatic impact on the availability of forage and feed grains. In addition to feed costs, the overall rate of inflation in the U.S. economy in general and agriculture in particular will influence costs for individual ranchers and cattle feeders.

Due to the structure of the cattle industry, cattlemen are price takers, not price markers. This means that the prices for cattle will be subject to a host of developments extraneous to the cattle industry, but more closely related to the overall U.S. economy. Overall profitability in the cattle industry is a direct function of the prices received for products, as well as cost of production. Over time the respective levels of profitability will lead to changes in production decisions regarding supplies. Therefore the interrelationships among prices, supplies, demand, feed, inflation, and so forth are very relevant to the cattle industry and therefore important to the consumer.

It is readily apparent that the industry is dynamic, since the factors that constitute interrelationships in the cattle industry often change. Obviously, variations in weather patterns throughout the year have a major influence over the supplies of feed and therefore the cost of production. Economic developments which influence levels of consumer income, as well as inflation rates, have a direct consequence on the prices and costs for individual cattlemen. Demographic changes also constitute a major force. Since meat is a perishable product, what is produced must be consumed within a relatively short time. There is no effective storage of beef during times of surplus for distribution at a later time. Therefore, consumption patterns of meat will change relative to other foods, as production of individual meats and meat products vary.

Technological developments provide stimuli for changes over the long term. As production technology changes, new meat products become available, which further causes processing and distribution methods to vary. Change in the industry has been prompted by various extraneous institutional and social forces. These will take many different forms, including changing taste preferences, distribution channels (i.e., the hotel, restaurant, and institutional trade), as well as government regulation. Regulation will include various degrees of meat inspection, grading, and especially tax legislation. Finally, change itself is a primary factor that leads to a dynamic industry.

There are additional sectorial considerations in the beef industry. Seldom are all sectors of the beef industry simultaneously profitable. An underlying reason is that the total dollars allocated to the beef industry by consumers are not infinitesimal. As such, the demands in the consumer dollar require that a greater outlay in one direction means that fewer dollars are left for allocation to other sectors. As the cattle feeder pays more to the rancher for feeder cattle, the profitability of the finished cattle will be reduced. Packers who pay too much for live cattle in comparison to what the consumer will pay for the end product will find their margins in the red, and their problems compounded. Finally, the two primary sectors of the cattle industry—the ranch, or the cow/calf operation, and the cattle-feeding sector, are both impacted by the overall price/supply-and-demand/cost structure that influences the entire industry.

THE COW/CALF SECTOR

The cow/calf industry is the important driving force of the cattle cycle. Decisions regarding production levels made by the rancher determine the size of the calf crop year after year, the number of cattle that will be available for slaughter, and eventually the total beef supply. Again, these decisions are a function of profitability over time, and will be reflected in the size of the cow herd.

Changes in cow numbers result from two basic factors: (1) the rate of cow slaughter and (2) the rate of heifer retention. Basically, when the rate of heifer retention is declining, cow slaughter escalates, and the total cow inventory will decline. Conversely, increases in the number of heifers, or rate of heifer retention occurring in conjunction with declining cow slaughter, will lead to a buildup in cow inventories. Historical data confirm these patterns. Limited cow slaughter in the early 1970s was associated with relatively high rates of heifer retention, and led to a buildup in the cow herd to almost 57 million cows. The herd was severely liquidated in the late 1970s to a level of under 48 million head as cow slaughter and the rate of heifer retention declined. However, indications are that these trends have reversed as cow slaughter and heifer retention have been esclating.

Profitability in the cow/calf sector will influence herd management decisions. If calf prices rise at a rate faster than cost and profitability results, producers receive a signal to reduce the culling rate of cows, retain heifers and increase cow inventories as well as the subsequent output of the calf crop. The converse is also true. From 1977 to 1979, calf prices increased 120%, which substantially outpaced the overall rate of inflation and the cost of production. However, for the period 1979–1982, calf prices declined 25%. At the same time, cost of pro-

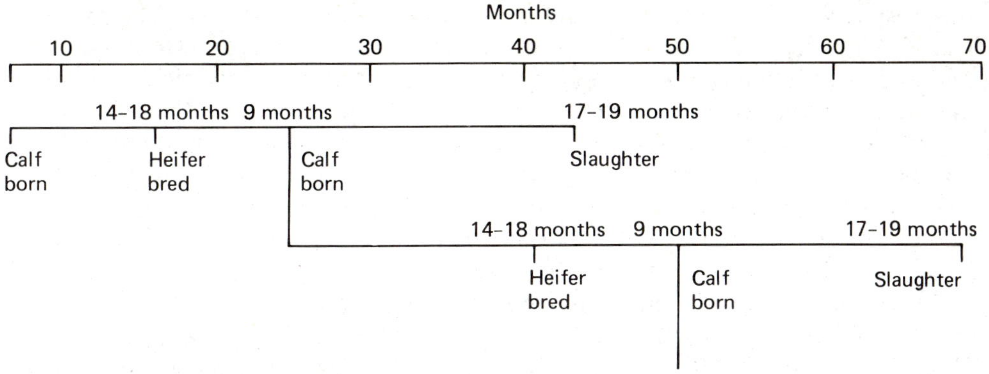

FIGURE 1. Beef production cycle. (*Source*: U.S. Department of Agriculture, Economics, Statistics, and Cooperatives Service, February 1979.)

duction from 1979 to 1982 continued to escalate by at least 25%. Analysis has also shown that in 1982, the cost of production for cow/calf producers weaning a 400-lb calf will be in the \$0.95 to \$1.20 per lb range. Since calf prices in 1982 will average near \$70 per cwt, it is obvious that the cow/calf producer in recent years has faced deteriorating financial conditions combined with a substantial price/cost squeeze.

LAND VALUES. Another significant consideration in the cow/calf business is that of land values, which, in turn, are related to other factors. The cow/calf

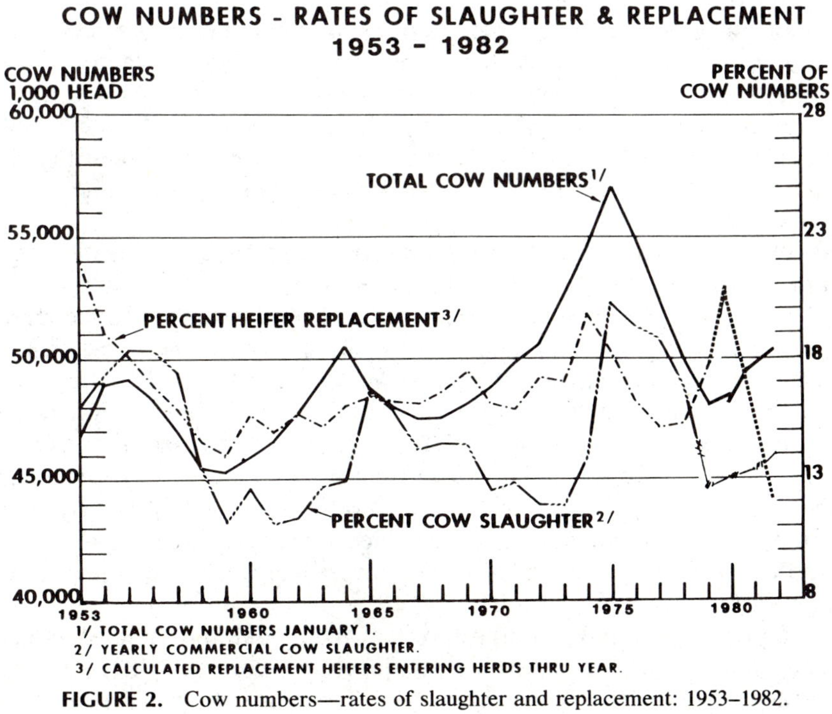

FIGURE 2. Cow numbers—rates of slaughter and replacement: 1953–1982.

business is very land-intensive, and in many operations, land costs constitute at least 25% of the total cost required to produce a calf. To a large extent, cow/calf operators are actually in the land business, as the return over time is heavily contingent upon the appreciation in land values. Analysis has shown that the returns to equity and investment based solely on income from cow/calf operations are basically modest, especially in terms of opportunity cost. Therefore the attractiveness of long-term investments in the cow business emanate from considerations more expansive than the profitability of the cow/calf business alone. The trend in land values over time is very significant to the rancher.

In agriculture, land values are impacted by several factors, including farm income and real interest rates. Net farm income for 1982 was expected to be about half of that in 1979. On a deflated basis as suggested by current inflation rates, real net farm income in 1982 was expected to be at the lowest level since the depressed state of the early 1930s. The U.S. farm economy has truly approached depression conditions, which limits cash flow and funds available for investment. At the same time, bankruptcies have increased, which has resulted in the forced sale of many farms and ranches, pushing land values lower. Many of these liquidations are the result of land purchased in the mid-1970s at high prices following 3 years of exceptionally high farm income. The poor cash flow situation in the agricultural sector caused by low crop and livestock prices has resulted in a sharply reduced demand for the additional land that has become available.

A factor that significantly impacts land values and has taken on more importance in the past 5 years is the rate of inflation and interest rates. Land is considered a good investment when inflation rates are high and money or borrowed funds to purchase land is readily available. If the rate of inflation is substantially above the cost of borrowed money, ranch land, as well as other real estate, will be a relatively attractive investment. In recent years, a number of factors forced interest rates higher and the rate of inflation lower. These factors had a negative impact on demand for land. Therefore, the combination of declining net farm income, as well as very high *real* interest rates, negatively impacted the value of land and adversely influenced the overall financial condition for ranchers.

CONSUMER DOLLAR. The primary product of a cow/calf operation is either calves or yearlings. However, demand for those calves and yearlings is actually derived from consumer demand for beef. As such, the price the producer receives for calves or yearlings is contingent upon (1) the size of the total "pie"—the total dollars consumers are willing to allocate to the beef industry, and (2) the producers' share of the consumer dollar. Experience has shown there is a significant relationship between the supply of beef and the relative amount received by the producer. For example, in the mid-1970s, calf prices were extremely low and the producer received slightly over $0.20 of the consumer's beef dollar. By 1979, calf prices improved substantially and the producer received almost $0.60. Since that time, the trend has been downward. Not surprisingly, this corresponds with an upward trend in the supply of beef.

Cow/calf operations have another product that should not be overlooked as a significant source of beef supply—cow slaughter. Cow slaughter represents a substantial portion of the domestic supply of ground and processed beef. This

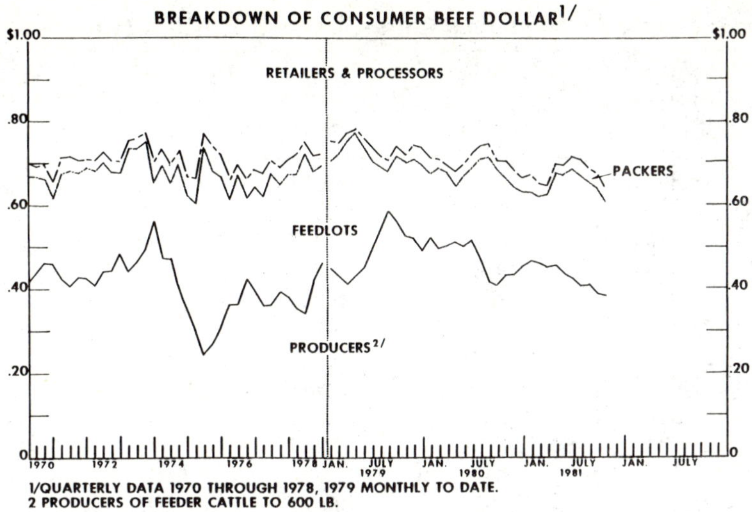

FIGURE 3. Breakdown of consumer beef dollar. Quarterly data 1970 through 1978, 1979 monthly to date.

ground and processed beef will account for 40–50% of the domestic beef supply over time, and 35–45% will be comprised of cow and bull beef. Basically, when the rancher decides to liquidate cows, the supply of ground and processed beef increases with the cow slaughter.

CATTLE-FEEDING SECTOR

One of the most substantial changes that has taken place in the cattle business in recent decades has been the evolution of *cattle feeding*. The rise of the cattle-feeding industry has corresponded with other factors that form the basis of the interrelationship that exists between the cattle feeder and other segments of the industry. Rising incomes and increased affluence helped generate a demand for the type of product which was facilitated by feeding cattle. Production technology underscored the economics of cattle feeding. The process of feeding cattle a concentrated ration in confined facilities has led to heavier marketing weights, and, consequently, much larger production on a cow-unit basis.

Cattle are most often fed where the resources exist that are necessary to accommodate this enterprise. The availability of feeder cattle and grain are essential prerequisites to a cattle-feeding program. It is much more efficient to ship the finished cattle to market and reduce the transportation of grain, since a much larger quantity of grain is necessary to production. Since these resources primarily exist in the Corn Belt and Plains states, this is where the majority of cattle-feeding operations have been established. However, in recent years the significant expansion of cattle feeding in the Southern Plains has slowed down and, in fact, the cattle-feeding industry has begun relocation in the Corn Belt, where feed is more abundant and relatively cheaper.

The location of cattle-feeding activity is relevant to the beef packers who in

TABLE 1. Annual Commercial Cattle Slaughter by Class (1,000's of Head)

Year	Fed Cattle	Nonfed Steers and Heifers	Cows	Bulls and Stags	Commercial Cattle Slaughter
1965	18,850	4,921	8,074	502	32,347
1966	20,540	5,112	7,556	519	33,727
1967	21,830	4,813	6,757	469	33,869
1968	23,670	3,970	6,843	543	35,026
1969	24,910	2,825	6,918	584	35,237
1970	25,710	2,621	6,117	577	35,025
1971	26,060	2,517	6,375	633	35,585
1972	27,670	1,472	5,992	645	35,779
1973	25,890	873	6,248	676	33,687
1974	23,880	4,598	7,514	820	36,812
1975	21,210	7,047	11,557	1,097	40,911
1976	25,040	5,997	10,619	998	42,654
1977	25,969	5,120	9,864	903	41,856
1978	27,850	2,434	8,470	798	39,552
1979	25,566	1,553	5,930	629	33,678
1980	24,004	2,745	6,334	724	33,807
1981	23,818	3,717	6,643	775	34,953

TABLE 2. Percentages of Commercial Slaughter

Year	Fed Cattle	Nonfed Steers and Heifers	Cows	Bulls and Stags	Commercial Cattle Slaughter
1965	58.3	15.2	25.0	1.5	100.0
1966	60.9	15.2	22.4	1.5	100.0
1967	64.5	14.2	19.9	1.4	100.0
1968	67.6	11.3	19.5	1.6	100.0
1969	70.7	8.0	19.6	1.7	100.0
1970	73.4	7.5	17.5	1.6	100.0
1971	73.2	7.1	17.9	1.8	100.0
1972	77.3	4.1	16.8	1.8	100.0
1973	76.9	2.6	18.5	2.0	100.0
1974	64.9	12.5	20.4	2.2	100.0
1975	51.8	17.2	28.3	2.7	100.0
1976	58.7	14.1	24.9	2.3	100.0
1977	62.0	12.2	23.6	2.2	100.0
1978	70.4	6.2	21.4	2.0	100.0
1979	75.9	4.6	17.6	1.9	100.0
1980	71.1	8.1	18.7	2.1	100.0
1981	68.2	10.6	19.0	2.2	100.0

Source: Livestock Business Advisory Services, Incorporated.

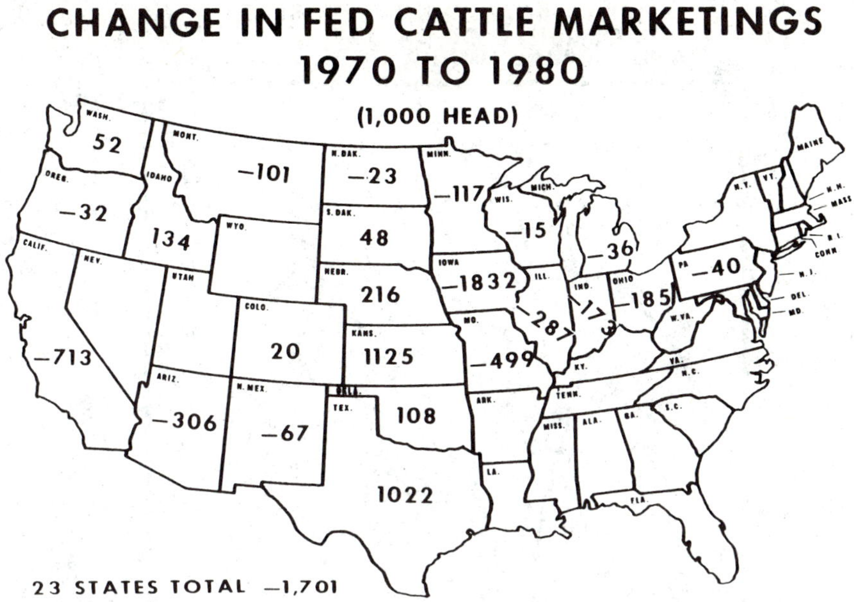

FIGURE 4. Change in federal cattle marketings: 1970–1980 (1,000 head).

recent years have found it advantageous to locate their industry near an abundant supply of slaughter cattle. In the infant stages of the beef-slaughtering industry, packers located their industry near primary market outlets, which at that time were terminal markets. This, in effect, provided packers with an adequate supply of cattle that could be procured rather efficiently. This was necessary to enhance the profitability of a plant which must be operated at a high level of capacity. However, in recent years, cattle have been marketed direct from the cattle feeder to the packer. As such, the importance of terminal or auction markets has declined.

Cattle feeders have accounted for 50–75% of the domestic cattle slaughter. The percentage of the domestic beef supply made up by the cattle-feeding industry is actually larger, since feedlot cattle are marketed at heavier weights. Consequently, production changes by the cattle feeder will have a substantial impact in the beef industry, as well as other segments of agriculture (i.e., feed grains as well as competitive products of hogs and poultry).

Decisions to place cattle on feed are usually based on profitability. If corn prices decrease, placements of cattle on feed will rise. This, in turn, will boost future beef supplies since the cattle-feeding industry accounts for a larger domestic beef production. In the short term, cheap grain is usually associated with a gain in profitability, which will eventually lead to larger numbers of cattle going on feed and larger beef production at some point in time. The converse also holds.

Another significant relationship is the price of feeder cattle relative to grain prices and the anticipated price of finished cattle. Cheap grain leads many cattlemen, as well as Midwestern farmers who also feed cattle, to believe that profitability will result or be enhanced from feeding cattle this relatively cheap grain.

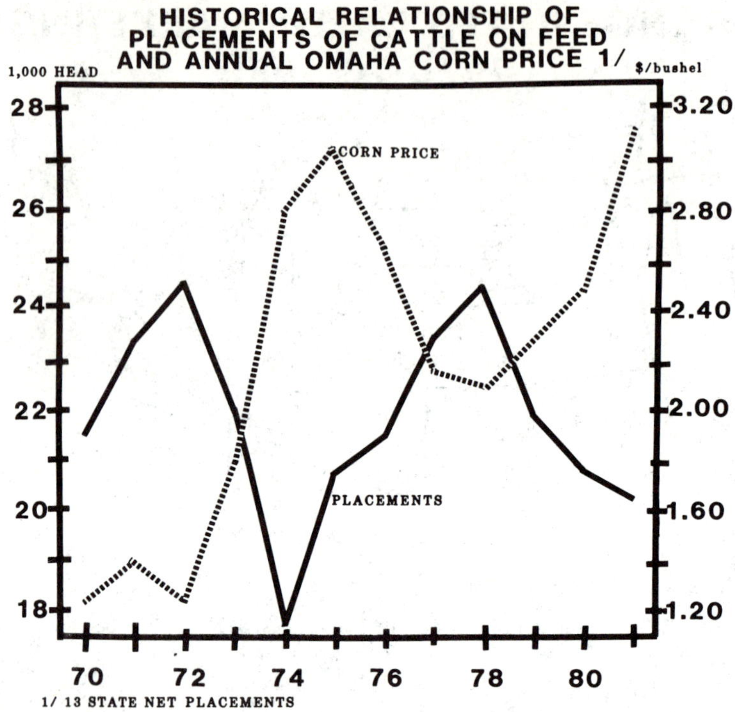

FIGURE 5. Historical relationship of placements of cattle on feed and annual Omaha corn price (13 state net placement).

As such, low grain prices can be expected to be translated into relatively expensive prices for feeder cattle. Consequently, low corn prices have generally been associated with rising prices of feeder cattle, as demand for cattle to place on feed has increased while grain supplies are large and grain prices depressed. In this type of environment, the cattle feeder is willing to bid aggressively for feeder cattle; hence, feeder-cattle prices will increase relative to slaughter-cattle prices.

Over time, most feeder cattle will be channeled into feedlots. However, some yearling cattle may be slaughtered by packers directly from pastures. This practice will occur normally when corn prices are high and feeder-cattle prices are relatively low. This is because relatively cheap corn stimulates the demand for feeder cattle, and cattle feeders bid these cattle away from packers. Due to relatively low yields on range-fed yearling cattle, packers are very limited in what they will pay. When demand for feeder cattle increases, however, cattle feeders will pay relatively more for the yearlings than will packers.

These relatively simple relationships have profound influence on the cattle industry, as well as other sectors of the economy that will be influenced by developments in the major cattle-feeding areas. Because feeder cattle and corn are primary inputs to the production process, these aspects must be monitored closely to ascertain changing developments in the industry. In so doing, a better understanding, and perhaps anticipation, of changes in the industry can be garnished.

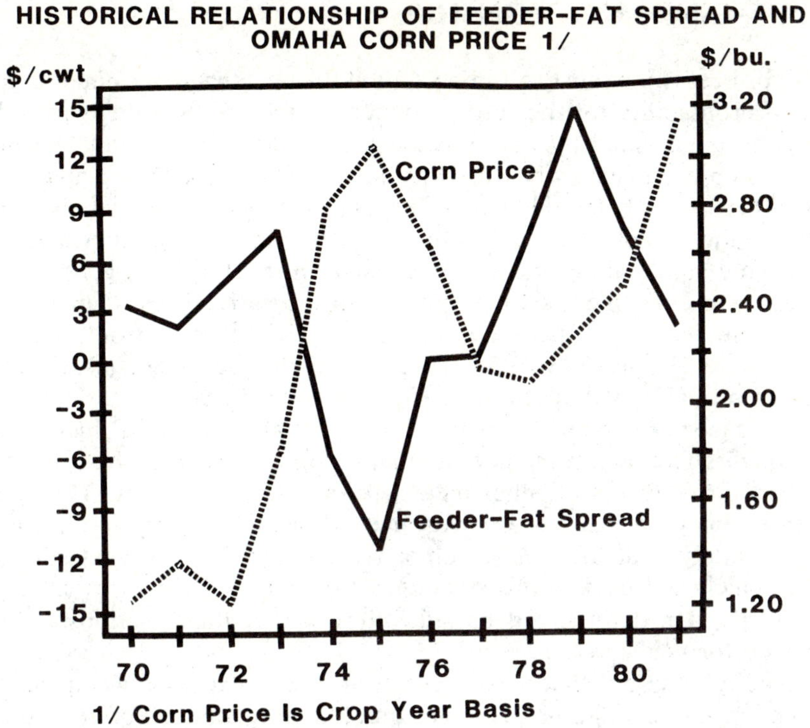

FIGURE 6. Historical relationship of feeder-fat spread and Omaha corn price (corn price is crop year basis).

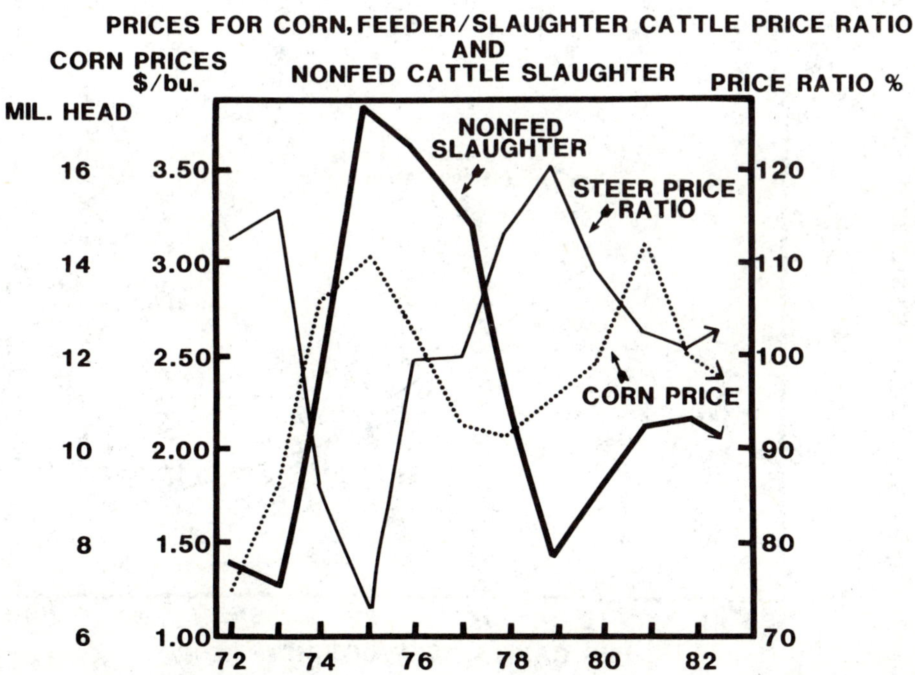

FIGURE 7. Prices for corn, feeder/slaughter cattle price ratio and nonfed–cattle slaughter.

PRICE/DEMAND RELATIONSHIPS

Demand for beef is obviously all-important in the eventual determination of cattle prices and profitability for the cattle producer or feeder. Beef demand is directly or indirectly determined by the consumer, since the result of all the interrelationships is represented by what the consumer is willing to pay for a given quantity of beef, other things held constant. It is this price/quantity relationship that represents demand, which, in inself, is dynamic. It is noteworthy that beef demand was relatively stable along the same schedule in the 1960s, as generally higher quantities were consumed at lower prices. In the early 1970s, demand for beef increased, but the slope of the demand curve also "flattened out," or became relatively more elastic. However, in the late 1970s, beef demand definitely declined, and probably will continue to slip in the early 1980s.

Several reasons can be cited for the shift in demand for beef. Principal demand factors which effect a shift include population, income (and the relative expenditures of income), prices of other meats, taste, and preferences. The latter factors—taste and preferences—are extremely difficult to quantify and, as such, cannot be totally evaluated on an objective basis without special surveys and analyses which address overall consumer psychology. However, many of the other factors can be definitely identified with respect to their relationship to prices and demand for beef.

It is readily apparent that an inverse relationship exists between the supply, or production, of beef and prices. Over time, larger quantities of beef have been consumed at lower prices, with some adjustment for beef supplies which fluctuate seasonally within the cattle cycle. In the mid-1970s, beef production escalated substantially, which, in turn, resulted in lower prices. By the late 1970s, however,

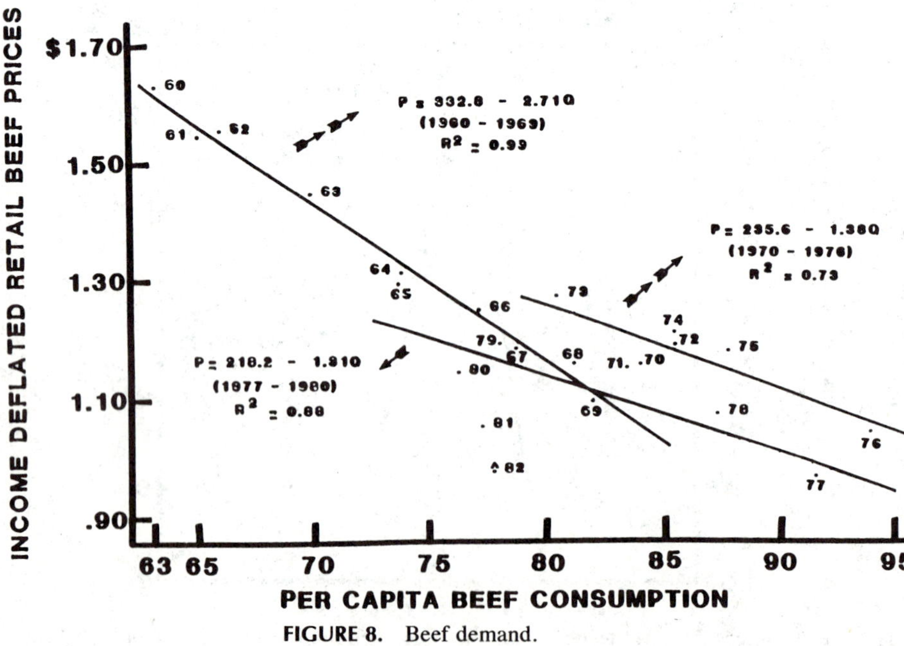

FIGURE 8. Beef demand.

the production of beef declined to lower levels and prices increased quite dramatically. Since 1979, beef production has been trending generally upward, while cattle prices have not only failed to increase, but have dropped.

Consumer income has a very direct influence on beef prices. Higher levels of consumer income have been associated with generally higher cattle prices. This is true whether or not income and prices are considered in either current or real dollars. However, beginning in the late 1970s, consumers spent less of their income for beef. Consumer expenditures are basically derived from the amount of beef consumed at alternative prices. Beginning from 1976–1977, the increases in consumer income outpaced the rise in estimated expenditures for beef. Although cattle prices did increase to record levels in the late 1970s, the increases were not commensurate with previous levels of consumer spending for beef.

Over the long term, consumers have spent an average of 2.6% of their income for beef. More recently, however, consumers have spent less than 2% of their income for beef. While the difference may seem small, a change of only 0.1% of the disposable income spent for beef equates roughly to \$3 per cwt charge in slaughter-steer prices. It is easy to observe that the deterioration in this statistic has been associated with cattle prices ranging from \$15 to \$20 per cwt less than what would have been the case had the integrity of the historical relationships been preserved.

The cattle industry is subject to the influence of the other meat sectors. About 80% of the relationship between cattle and hog prices can be explained by the changes in the respective production or supply levels between the two sectors. For example, in the mid-1970s, when beef production increased very substantially, cattle prices became relatively cheap in comparison to hog prices. When production declined cyclically into the late 1970s, cattle prices increased relative to hogs. More recently, the supply of beef relative to that of pork increased, which

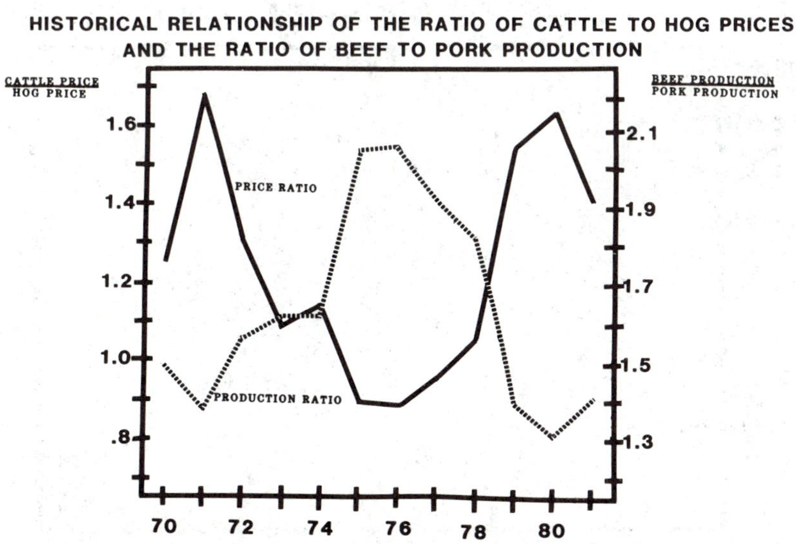

FIGURE 9. Historical relationship of the ratio of cattle to hog prices and the ratio of beef to pork production.

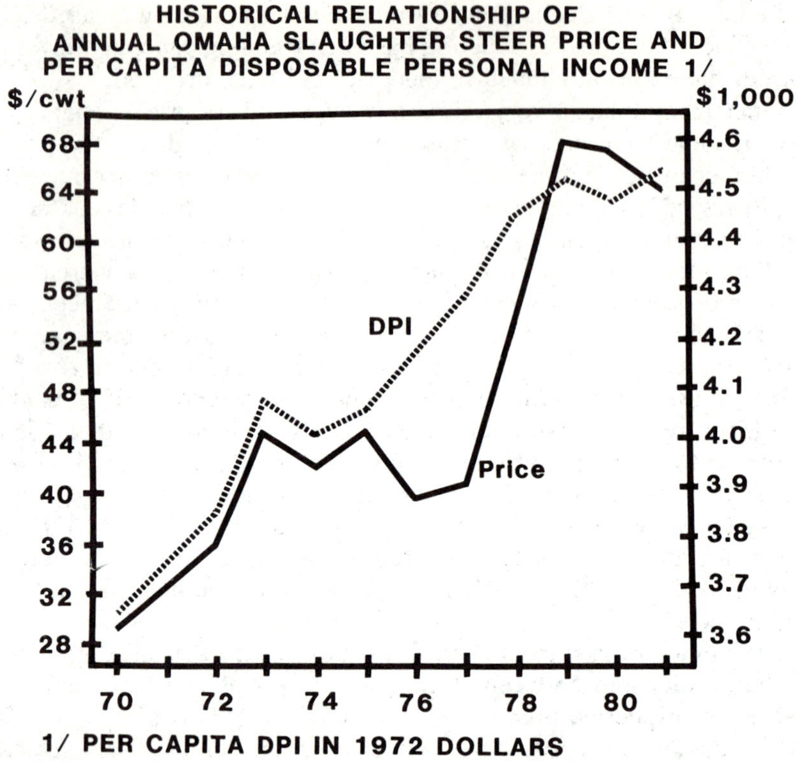

FIGURE 10. Historical relationship to annual Omaha slaughter-steer price and per capita disposable personal income (per capita DPI in 1972 dollars).

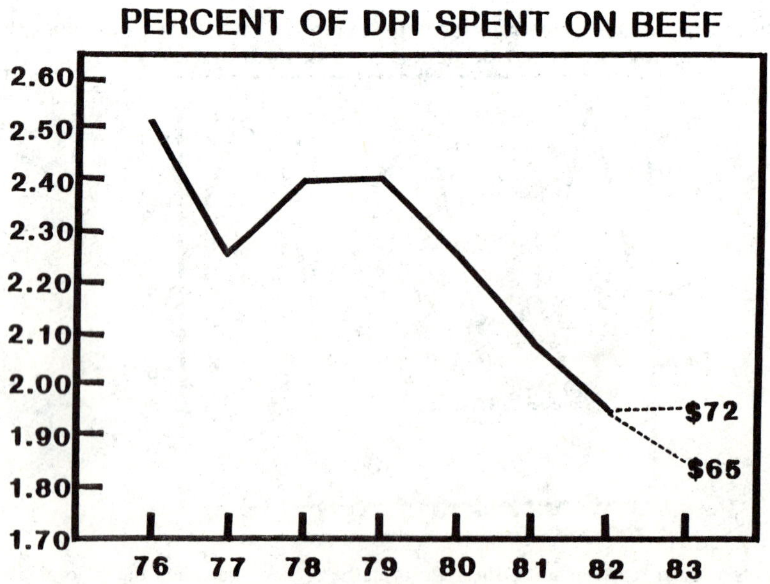

FIGURE 11. Percent of disposable personal income spent on beef.

resulted in lower cattle prices with respect to hogs. Thus the price differences between cattle and hogs narrowed. Since the production, or supply, of beef and pork is cyclical relative to changes in inventories of cattle and hogs, the price ratio between beef and pork to a large extent is also cyclical.

Finally, the aspect of derived demand for beef which entails price spreads will influence cattle prices at the producer and feeder level. Generally speaking, large supplies of beef will correspond to increased demand for services of the middleman. This is also associated with weaker bargaining power of cattlemen. Therefore larger beef supplies are normally associated with a wider price spread between the producer and the consumer. However, lower beef supplies will result in the opposite situation, where the spread between the producer and the consumer becomes less. Therefore, as supplies fluctuate cyclically, the price spread can also be expected to change.

CATTLE SEASONALITY

Although the seasonality of the cattle market is well-defined the profit potential is not attractive. What appears to be a well-defined seasonal trend for low prices during February to March and higher prices in August is actually highly variable. This is primarily a result of the longer "cattle cycle" which dominates the seasonal movement during many years.

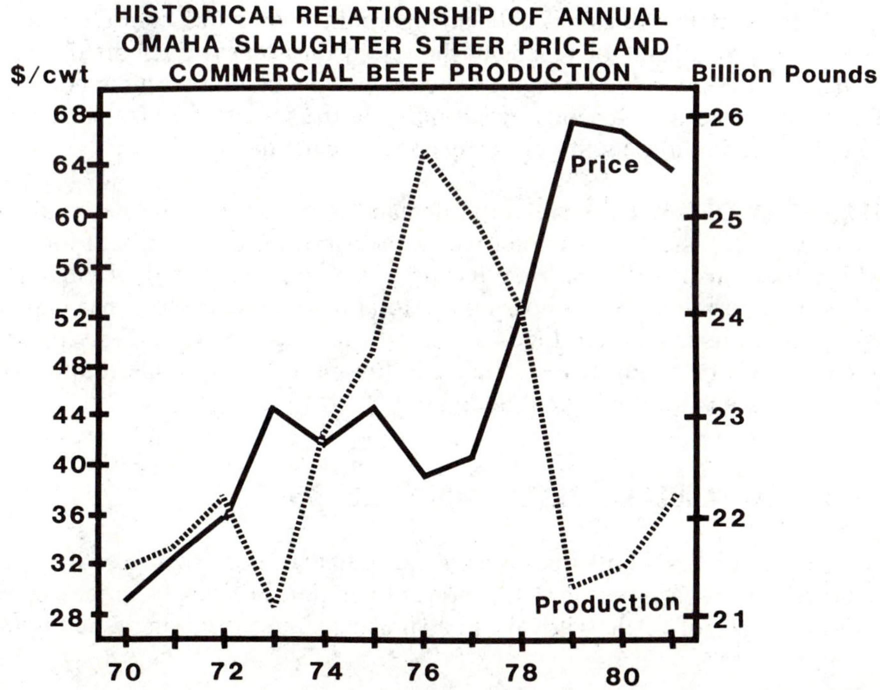

FIGURE 12. Historical relationship of annual Omaha slaughter-steer price and commercial beef production.

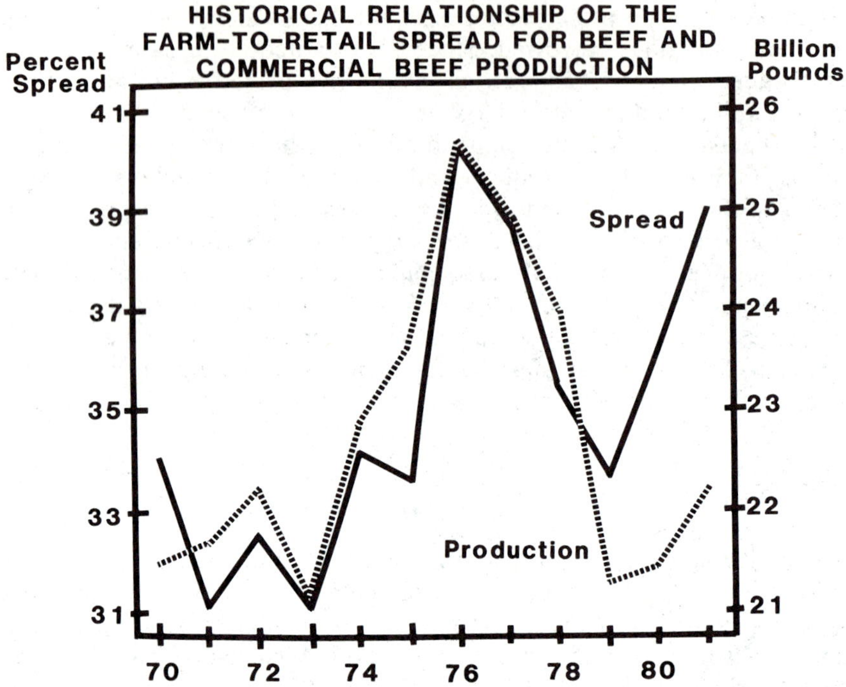

FIGURE 13. Historical relationship of the farm-to-retail spread for beef and commercial beef production.

An analysis of the seasonal data in Figure 14 shows that the average price move was very small and the reliability showed inconsistency. Even the risk/reward ratio was hardly favorable enough to encourage speculation with confidence.

The appearance of a seasonal trend must be the result of consumer demand, since cattle production could not correspond to calendar years.

FILTERING BY DEMAND.[1] Since the demand is assumed to be determined by the seasonality of the cattle market we can separate price movement into years in which the consumer's food-purchasing power was high or low. "High" or "low" was determined by comparing the total disposable income per capita divided by the Consumer Price Index against the average for 1966–1980. Figure 15 shows the more pronounced seasonality in low-ratio years, while the high-ratio years show no apparent seasonal fluctuation.

HISTORICAL CATTLE PRICE MOVEMENTS

A number of factors—both the supply and demand side—will explain a large percentage of the variation in cattle prices over time. Basically, prices of most classes and types of cattle will vary in a similar manner from one time period to

[1]David Handmaker, "Low-Frequency Filters in Seasonal Analysis," *Journal of Futures Markets*, **1** (3), 367–378 (1981). See Appendix B.

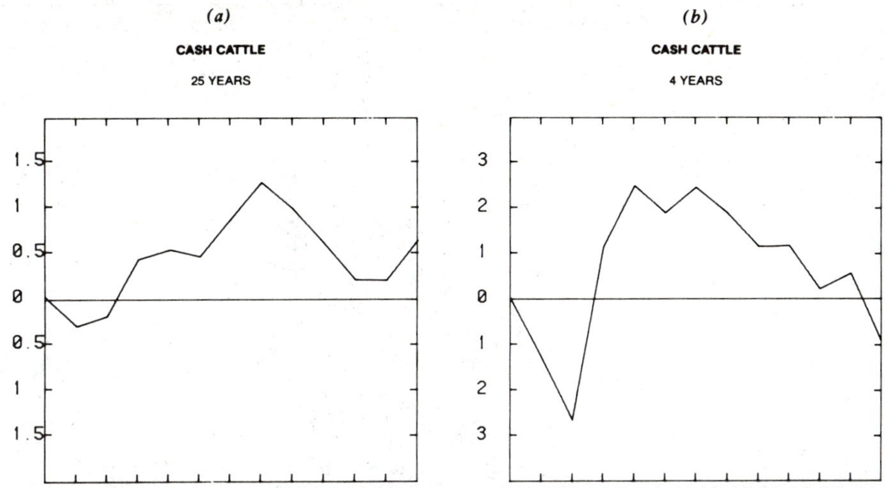

	J-F	F-M	M-A	A-M	M-J	J-J	J-A	A-S	S-O	O-N	N-D	D-J
Average Move	-0.4	0.1	0.6	0.1	-0.1	0.4	0.4	-0.3	-0.4	-0.5	-0.1	0.4
% Reliable	64	60	48	44	56	60	56	44	76	64	52	72
Avg. Up Move	1	1	1.9	1.5	0.8	1.3	1.5	0.7	0.6	0.7	0.8	1.1
Avg. Down Move	1.2	1.3	0.7	1.1	0.9	1	1.1	1.6	0.7	1.1	0.8	1.5
Greatest Up Move	2.9	2.3	6.9	7	2.1	5.7	5.2	2.1	1.9	1.2	3.2	7.7
Greatest Down Move	3.4	3.6	1.4	2.5	2.6	2.7	3.5	7.9	3.3	2.7	2.4	3.9

J-F	F-M	M-A	A-M	M-J	J-J	J-A	A-S	S-O	O-N	N-D	D-J
-1.3	-1.4	3.7	1.3	-0.6	0.5	-0.6	-0.8	0	-1	0.3	-1.5
100	75	75	50	75	50	75	50	50	75	50	75
0	1.3	5.5	4.4	2	3.2	2.9	1.1	1.4	1.2	1	0.4
1.3	2.3	1.4	1.8	1.5	2.2	1.8	2.7	1.4	1.7	0.4	2.1
0	1.3	6.9	7	2	5.7	2.9	2.1	1.9	1.2	1.2	0.4
2.4	3.6	1.4	2.5	2.6	2.7	3.5	5.3	1.8	2.7	0.6	3.9

FIGURE 14. Cattle cash price and seasonality. (*a*) 25 years. (*b*) 4 years.

the next. However, the magnitude of the price change for some types of cattle may not parallel price changes for other types of cattle. Nevertheless, the variation in prices, over time, can be explained to a large extent by fundamental economic factors.

Cattle prices generally increased in the early 1970s as supplies of beef and meat

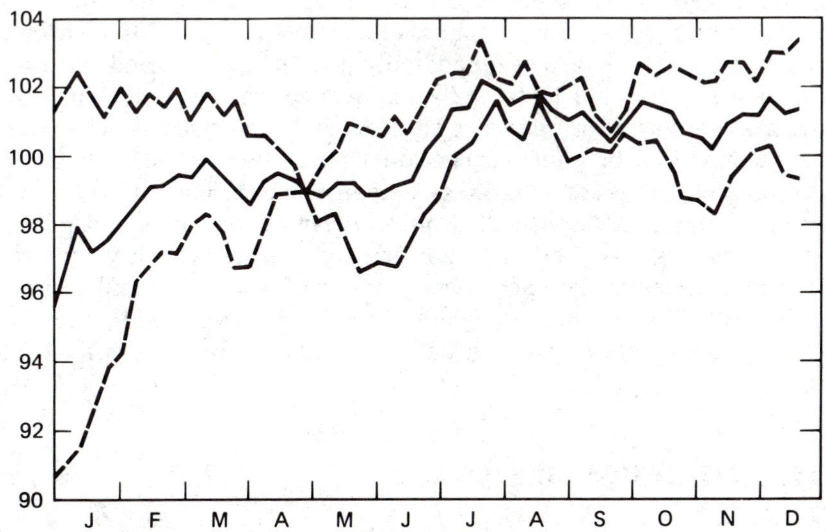

FIGURE 15. Cattle price seasonality, filtered by demand. Seasonality during all years (—); high ratio years (----); low ratio years (—–—).

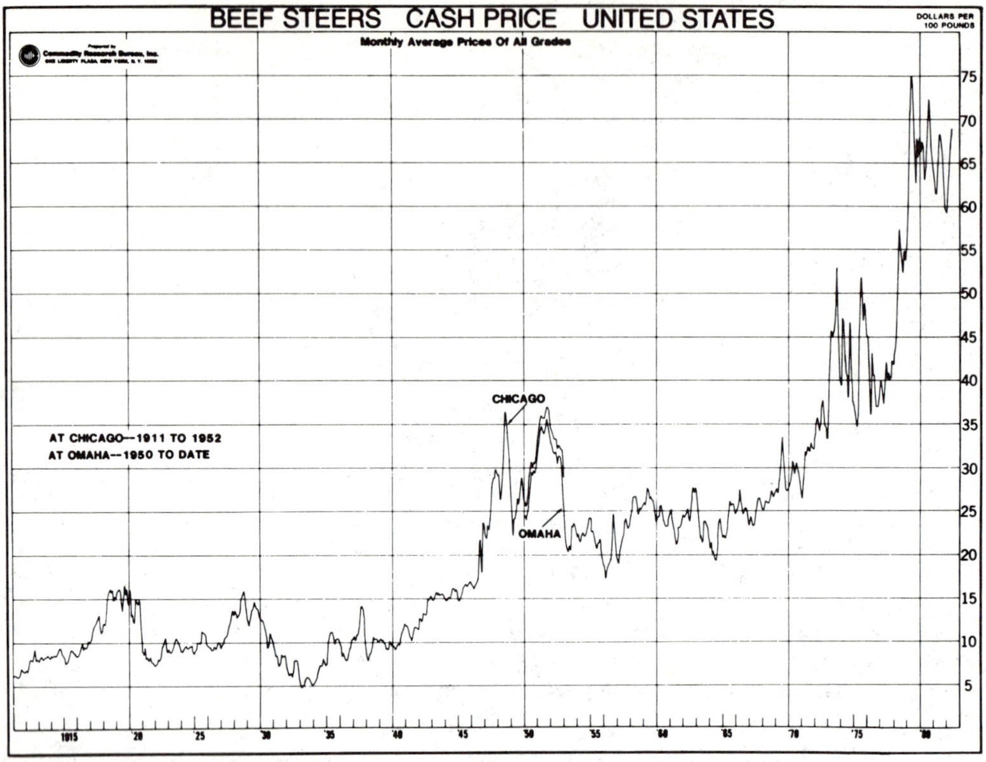

FIGURE 16. Beef steers monthly cash price—United States.

were not particularly burdensome, and demand for beef was growing with a vibrant U.S. economy. However, generally profitable operations in the early 1970s led to larger inventories of cattle and supplies of beef by the mid-1970s. Consequently, prices declined as the industry liquidated cattle inventories and increased the supply of beef. In the mid-1970s the price decline was more profound for cow and calves, as well as yearling feeder cattle, than for slaughter-steer prices. This is because demand for breeding stock and feeder cattle was relatively depressed, as was profitability in the cattle business, and provided the impetus for the industry to discontinue the liquidation and, in fact, expand inventories and production. Larger beef supplies, together with poor demand in a recessionary economy, led to lower cattle prices in the early 1980s. As prices for calves and feeder cattle increased relatively more than slaughter cattle in the late 1970s, prices of these types of cattle also suffered more dramatic price declines in the early 1980s.

CATTLE FUTURES MARKETS

Cattle is an active commodity traded on the Chicago Mercantile Exchange (CME) and the MidAmerica Commodity Exchange. The smaller MidAmerica contract, one-half of the CME contract, is readily available to smaller hedgers and spec-

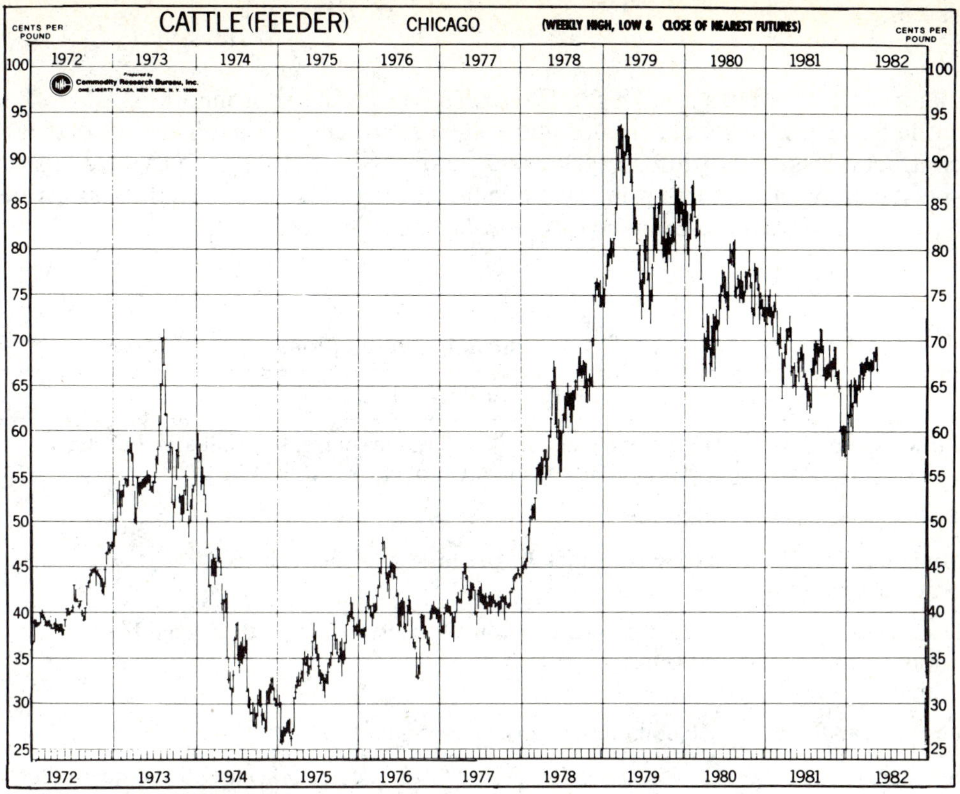

FIGURE 17. Feeder cattle weekly nearest futures—Chicago.

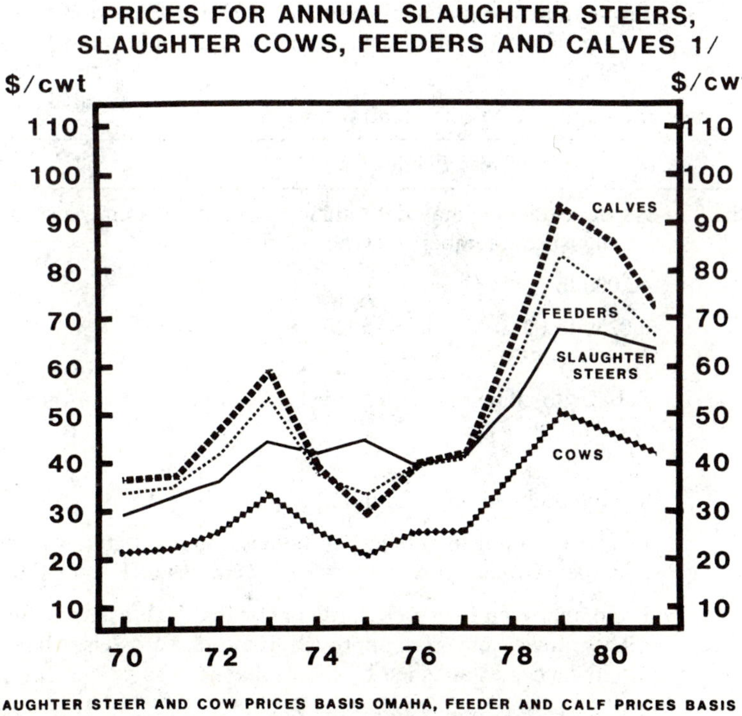

FIGURE 18. Prices for annual slaughter steers, slaughter cows, feeders, and calves (slaughter steer and cow prices basis Omaha, feeder and calf prices basis Kansas City).

ulators due to arbitrage with the CME. Volume in the spot month of CME live cattle is typically between 11,000 and 16,000 contracts per day. The feeder-cattle contract is less active, doing 1,000–2,000 contracts daily. Table 3 gives the contract specifications of the three primary cattle futures markets, as well as the less active New York Mercantile Exchange *Imported Lean Beef* contract.

TABLE 3. Contract Specifications

CME Live Beef Cattle	
Delivery months	As the exchange may determine, currently, January, February, April, June, August, October, and December.
Trading unit	40,000 lb
Minimum fluctuation	0.025¢ per lb ($0.01 per lb = $400 per contract)
Daily price movement limits	Subject to change; consult latest official notices from the exchange.
Position limits	300 contracts in any one month
Standards	Choice grade; according to the USDA official U.S. Standards for Grades of Slaughter Cattle with substitutions and allowances as established by the exchange.
Delivery	From approved livestock yards in Omaha, Nebraska, or Sioux City, Iowa, Guyman, Oklahoma, Joliet, Illinois, and Peoria, Illinois.
Trading hours	9:05 a.m.–12:45 p.m. central time
CME Feeder Cattle	
Delivery months	As the exchange may determine, currently, March, April, May, August, September, October, and November.
Trading unit	42,000 lb
Minimum fluctuation	0.025¢ lb ($0.01 per lb = $420 per contract)
Daily price movement limits	Subject to change; consult latest official notices from the exchange.
Position limits	300 contracts in any one month.
Standards	Feeder steers of the choice, or better, and good grades as defined in the "Official U.S. Standards for Grades of Feeder Cattle."
Delivery	From approved livestock yards in Omaha, Nebraska, or Sioux City, Iowa, and from approved livestock yards elsewhere with allowances established by the exchange.
Trading hours	9:05 a.m.–2:45 p.m. central time

TABLE 3. Continued

MidAmerica LiveBeef Cattle	
Delivery months	January, February, April, June, August, October, and December.
Trading unit	20,000 lb
Minumum auctuation	.025¢ per lb ($.01 per lb = $200 per contract).
Daily price movement limits	Subject to change; consult latest official notices from the exchange.
Daily trading limits	Purchase and sale of 900 contracts in any delivery month
Standards	USDA choice steers yield grade 1, 2, 3, and 4. Maximum 4 yield grade 4 steers. Cattle must average between 1,050 and 1,200 lb with no steer weighing more than 100 lb above or below the average. Steers averaging between 1,050 and 1,125.5 lb must have a hot yield of 62%. Steers averaging between 1,125.6 and 1,200 lb must average a hot yield of 63%. For steers deliverable at a discount, consult MidAmerica rules.
Delivery	Stockyards at Peoria, Illinois, Joliet, Illinois, Omaha, Nebraska, Sioux City, Iowa, and Guyman, Oklahoma.
Trading hours	9:05 a.m.–1:00 p.m. central time.
NYMEX Imported Lean Beef	
Delivery months	January, March, May, July, September, and October.
Trading unit	36,000 lb
Minimum fluctuation	.02¢ per lb ($.01 per lb = $360 per contract).
Daily price movement limits	Subject to change; consult latest official notices from the exchange.
Daily trading limits	None
Position limits	None
Standards	Hard frozen, boneless, manufacturing quality beef, full carcass less briskets and all or part of plates, but may include shanks or tenderloins, or both, with deviations and allowances as established by the exchange, imported from Australia, New Zealand, Mexico, Canada, or Ireland.
Delivery	By warehouse receipt from refrigerated warehouses in the Port of New York, the Port of Philadelphia, or other ports approved by the exchange with an ICC rate allowance.
Trading hours	10:15 a.m.–1:45 p.m. eastern time

Source: Commodity Trading Manual, Chicago Board of Trade.

SUMMARY

This chapter underscores the fact that the cattle industry is, in fact, dynamic. The primary reason is that the overall environment in which the cattle industry must operate is dynamic. Changes in such factors as weather, politics, the economy, world developments, and so forth, will impact the individual cattleman and the profitability of the cattleman's operation. This, in turn, will influence commodity price as well as costs of production. The primary key to survival and recognition of opportunity in this environment is to understand which factors will lead to changes and to anticipate those changes.

CHAPTER 32

THE PORK COMPLEX

CONTENTS

SUPPLY	4	SPREADS	11
SEASONALITY FILTERING	7	HOG/CORN RATIO	12
FROZEN PORK INVENTORY	8	SOURCES OF INFORMATION	18
DEMAND	8	SELECTED BOOKS	18
PORK BELLIES	10		

CHAPTER 32

THE PORK COMPLEX

Patrick J. Luby

Pork has always maintained an important place in the American diet. Commercial pork production in the United States reached a record peak of over 16.4 billion lb in 1980. This was derived from the slaughter of slightly more than 96 million hogs. Using retail weights, this represented an average consumption of 68.3 lb of pork per person. Using carcass weights, per capita pork consumption was 75.1 lb in 1980. Since 1950 pork consumption per person, in carcass weight equivalent, has ranged from a low of 55.4 lb per person in 1975 to a high of 78.7 lb per person in 1971.

Hog production has changed considerably in recent years. Hogs and pork are much leaner than several decades ago. For example, from 1956 to 1980, commercial production of pork increased 60%, while the number of hogs slaughtered increased only 22%. The amount of pork produced per hog rose more than 30%, from 131 to 171 lb. A small part of this increase can be explained by an increase of 4% in the average weight of hogs slaughtered, from 232 to 242 lb. The vast majority of the change resulted from the production of a much leaner and more muscular hog. Despite an increase in the average weight of hogs slaughtered, average lard production per hog declined from 32.6 lb in 1956 to 12.5 lb in 1980. The ratio of pork production to lard production in 1956 was 4.02. By 1980 it had risen to 13.66, accompanied by a corresponding increase in lard prices (see Figure 2).

Hog production remains an important part of American agriculture, contributing a gross income of more than $9.1 billion in 1980. For many years, the number of hog producers has declined while the average size has increased. The number of hog operations in the United States was 3,014,000 in 1949, fell to 1,081,000 by 1964, to 670,000 in 1980, and to a new low for this century of 581,000 in 1981. As of December 1, 1981, 4.7% of the hog operations, or a little over 27,000 production units, accounted for 26.7 million hogs, or 45.5% of all the hogs on U.S. farms. These hog operations contained more than 500 hogs at the time the survey was taken. Three years earlier, hogs in production units of this size accounted for only 37.3% of the total.

Hog production is concentrated in the Midwestern Corn Belt states, and the degree of concentration has tended to become slightly greater during recent years. As of December 1, 1981, 27.8% of the hogs in the United States were in Iowa. Almost two-thirds, or 65.9%, of the hogs were in the six states of Iowa, Illinois, Minnesota, Indiana, Nebraska, and Missouri.

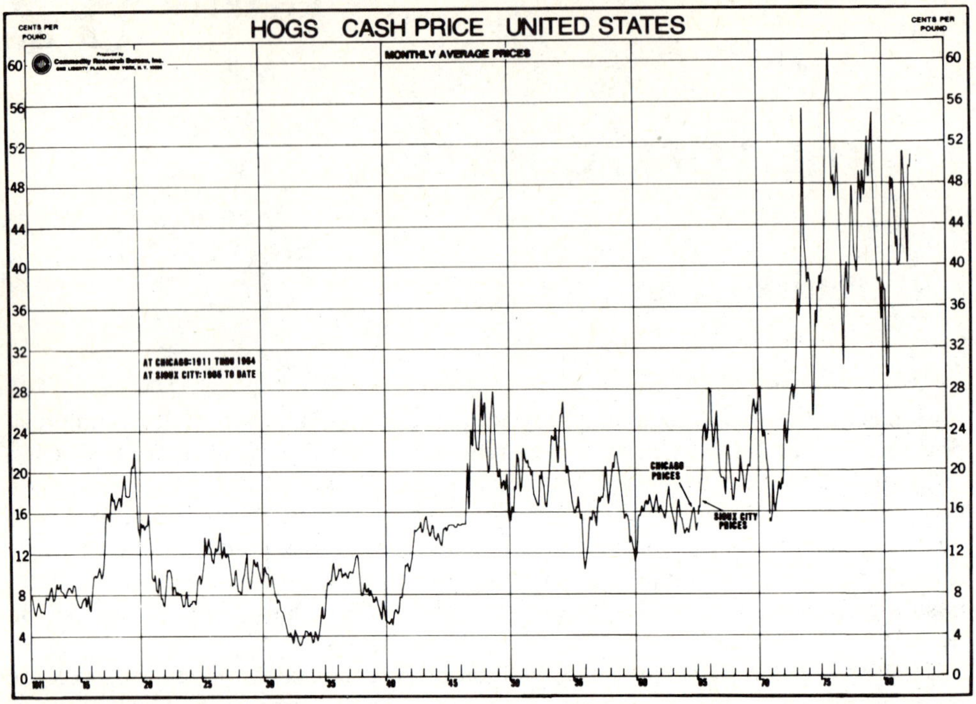

FIGURE 1. Hog cash prices. (*Source:* Commodity Research Bureau, Incorporated Yearbook.)

SUPPLY

The supply of pork is influenced by the hog producers' recent experience regarding the profitability of producing hogs and their expectations for profit within the following year. Feed costs represent about two-thirds of the cost of producing hogs. Corn and soybean meal are the most important feed inputs. Since it is nearly a year from the time the decision is made to produce and the time that hogs can be marketed, and since the majority of the costs of production (mainly feed costs) take place during the last several months of this time period, it is very difficult for producers to accurately estimate or anticipate their total costs of production at the time the production decision must be made (see Figure 3). Corn or soybean meal prices are themselves quite volatile. They are influenced by weather in the United States and other important grain-producing countries, by world demand for feed and food, by currency exchange rates, and many other factors. (Also see section "Hog-Corn Ratio.")

Thus, the hog producer is in the unenviable position of attempting to estimate the demand for pork and the costs of important feed inputs nearly a year ahead of when he or she makes the production decision. Both the demand and the costs can be quite volatile, adding to the complexity and difficulty of the decision.

Hog production has become more volatile since 1970. During the 1950s and 1960s, feed costs were quite stable as excessive grain and land reserves were available in the United States. Several severe droughts in the United States, particularly in 1974 and 1980, periodic droughts in the USSR in the 1970s, the

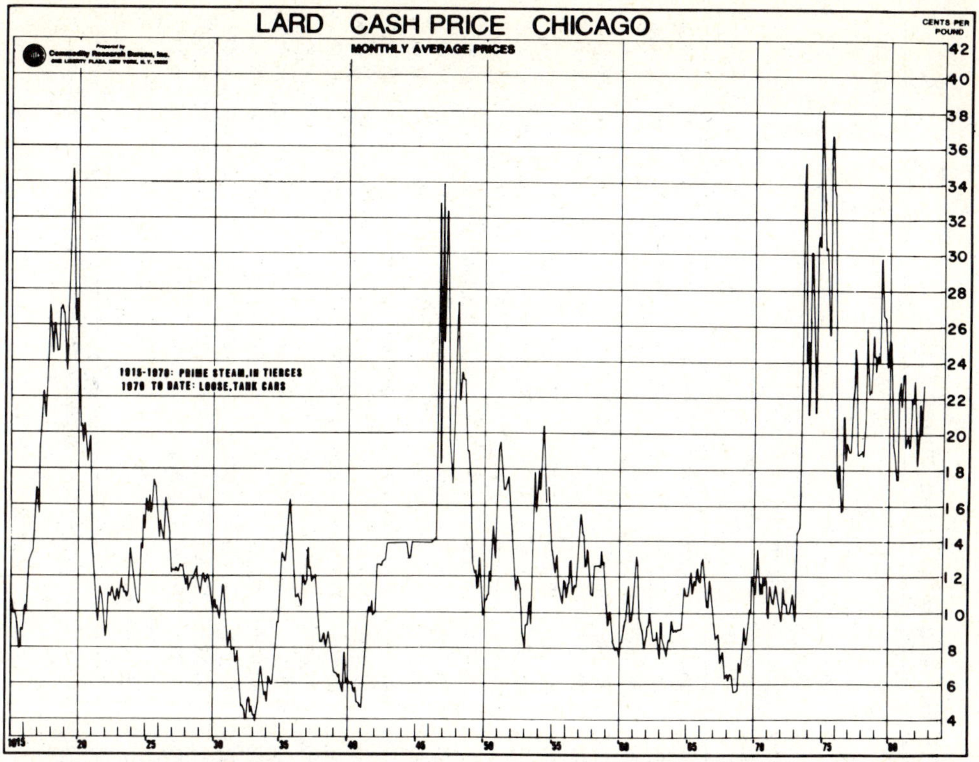

FIGURE 2. Lard cash prices. The increase in lard prices after 1972 is considered the result of production of a much leaner, more muscular hog. (*Source:* Commodity Research Bureau, Incorporated Yearbook.)

corn blight of 1970 in the United States, and the huge increase in demand for U.S. grains and protein meal from all parts of the world combined to cause grain prices to become more volatile in the 1970s. In addition, the recessions of 1974 and 1975, and 1980 and 1981, were more severe than earlier recessions. Thus hog producers were faced with greater volatility. The average annual change in pork production in the 11 years from 1970 through 1981 was 8.5%. The average annual change in the 17 years from 1953 through 1970 was 5.1%. The largest annual increases were 15.7% increases, recorded in 1959 and 1979. The largest annual decrease was 16.7% in 1975 following the severe drought of 1974.

Although the annual variation in pork production has increased, the seasonal variation of pork production is considerably less on a relative price basis than during earlier decades. Hog production has become a major enterprise on many farms and often is carried out in expensive buildings using expensive equipment. Farmers attempt to keep the facilities utilized to lower per unit costs. In addition, the modern facilities permit hog production during the harsh midwestern winters and hot, muggy summers.

The more uniform seasonality in farrowings has resulted in much less variability in the seasonality of hog marketings. Historically, hog marketings were very large during the winter months and very small during the summer. The low point in the year remains in July, but, relatively, summer marketings have increased

TABLE 1. Salient Statistics of Pigs and Hogs in the United States

	Pig Crop (in Thousands of Head)					Value of Hogs on Farms, Dec. 1[e]					Hogs Slaughtered (in Thousands of Head)				
	Spring[c]		Fall[d]								Commercial				
Year	Sows Farrowed	Pigs Saved	Sows Farrowed	Pigs Saved	Total Pig Crop	Dollars Per Head	Total Millions of Dollars	Hog Marketings (in Thousands of Head)	Quantity Produced (Live Weight) Millions of Pounds	Value of Production Millions of Dollars	Federally Inspected	Other	Total	Farm	Total
1961	7,018	50,366	5,918	42,347	92,713	27.20	1,541	80,326	20,167	3,355	65,632	11,702	77,335	4,635	81,970
1962	6,996	49,535	6,098	44,073	93,608	27.50	1,556	81,743	20,275	3,312	67,770	11,564	79,334	4,090	83,424
1963	7,099	50,749,	5,987	43,307	94,056	27.50	1,596	86,163	20,960	3,128	71,577	11,747	83,324	3,793	87,117
1964	6,596	47,682	5,525	39,862	87,544	23.40	1,328	86,086	20,217	2,989	71,667	11,352	83,018	3,266	86,284
1965	5,890	42,526	5,006	36,415	78,941	24.50	1,244	78,127	18,252	3,573	63,708	10,076	73,784	2,674	76,458
1966	6,208	45,471	5,810	42,133	87,604	45.20	2,144	75,761	19,149	4,491	63,729	10,282	74,011	1,371	75,382
1967	6,559	48,117	5,901	43,551	91,668	28.30	1,663	85,256	20,636	3,940	70,915	11,209	82,124	1,296	83,420
1968	6,659	49,077	6,130	45,078	94,156	30.50	1,857	87,726	21,034	3,897	74,789	10,371	85,160	1,257	86,417
1969	6,323	46,521	5,745	42,155	88,676	39.00	2,225	88,074	20,600	4,561	75,682	8,156	83,838	1,130	84,968
1970	7,134	52,126	6,882	49,588	101,921	23.50	1,584	86,919	21,823	4,955	78,187	7,630	85,817	1,235	87,052
1971	7,303	51,918	6,297	46,006	98,512	28.50	1,780	98,644	22,832	3,991	86,667	7,771	94,438	1,210	95,648
1972	6,512	47,523	5,967	43,053	90,828	42.00	2,477	89,555	20,919	5,245	78,759	5,948	84,707	1,158	85,865
1973	6,459	46,125	5,864	41,998	88,199	60.40	3,663	82,419	20,154	7,738	72,264	4,531	76,795	1,095	77,890
1974	6,372	44,792	5,466	38,952	83,954	44.90	2,457	85,504	19,976	6,838	77,071	4,691	81,762	1,321	83,083
1975	4,973	35,530	4,952	35,656	71,186	80.40	3,959	73,627	16,835	7,756	64,926	3,761	68,687	1,193	69,880
1976	5,777	42,177	5,850	42,218	84,395	47.00	2,583	75,747	18,160	7,856	70,454	3,330	73,784	1,175	74,959
1977	6,050	42,960	6,009	43,202	86,162	63.20	3,575	80,939	19,021	7,485	74,019	3,285	77,303	1,139	78,442
1978	6,034	42,481	6,398	46,031	88,512	83.20	5,023	81,271	19,466	9,066	74,139	3,176	77,315	1,102	78,417
1979	7,179	50,571	7,306	52,120	102,691	56.00	3,775	92,327	22,595	9,416	85,425	3,674	89,099	1,080	90,179
1980[a]	7,229	52,286	6,829	49,256	101,542	74.70	4,821	100,452	23,426	8,874	91,882	4,192	96,074	1,100	97,174
1981[a]	6,440	47,600	6,258	46,176	93,776	70.10	4,115				87,850	3,697	91,547		
1982[b]	5,760	41,500													

Source: Commodity Research Bureau, [a]Preliminary. [b]Breeding intentions. [c]December—May. [d]June–November. [e]Data prior to 1967 are for January 1 of the following year.

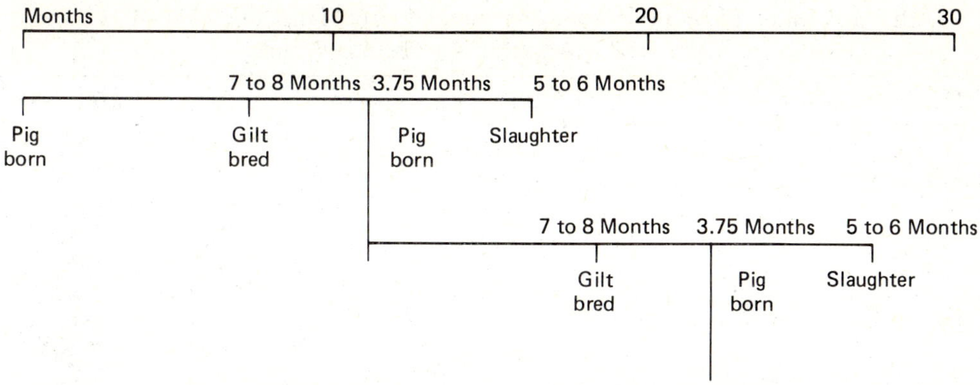

FIGURE 3. Pork-production cycle. (*Source:* U.S. Department of Agriculture, Economics, Statistics and Cooperatives Service, February 1979.)

considerably. Hog marketing peaks are reached during March and April and again in October and November (see Figure 4).

SEASONALITY FILTERING[1]

Using a *food-purchasing power* filter to analyze the seasonality of hog prices, we find that a much clearer seasonal pattern appears. The normal price increase which begins in the fall and carries into the winter months can be seen as starting sooner, and continuing with greater consistency and magnitude using "high-ratio" years. A high-ratio year is one in which the food-purchasing power qualifies as "high." The seasonal pattern becomes much clearer during these years.

During low-ratio years, the seasonal price pattern is quite different. When the consumer has less to spend on food, it is expected that the demand for pork will increase, since it represents a cheaper substitute. The result is that the seasonality, responding to consumer demand, should be more pronounced, representing a

TABLE 2. Distribution of Sow Farrowings by Quarter, 1951 and 1981

	Percent of Total	
Quarter	1951	1981
December–February	12.8%	22.9%
March–May	48.6	27.8
June–August	18.2	25.2
September–November	20.4	24.1
	100.0%	100.0%

[1]D. Handmaker, "Low Frequency Filters in Seasonal Analysis," *The Journal of Futures Markets*, Vol. 1, No. 3, Wiley, New York, NY, 1981. (See Appendix B for method of calculation.)

TABLE 3. Index of Monthly U.S. Commercial Hog Slaughter, 1950–1953 and 1978–1981 (Adjusted for Secular Trend)

Month	1950–1953	1978–1981
January	127	102
February	96	93
March	106	103
April	96	106
May	88	102
June	84	94
July	73	91
August	78	96
September	88	98
October	109	110
November	122	103
December	133	102

compounded demand for meat. This hypothesis is supported by the pattern shown in Figure 5.

FROZEN PORK INVENTORY

The amount of pork that is frozen and stored for future use is normally a small part of the total supply, but it can be a very important price-influencing factor at times. Frozen pork in storage in recent years has ranged from a low of 145.5 million lb (end of August 1977) to 403.5 million lb (end of April 1981), or approximately 1–2.5% of annual pork production. The seasonal low in frozen stocks is normally reached at the end of August or September and the normal high is at the end of April or May. About 4% of the pork consumed during June, July, and August represents a net out-movement from freezers. Most of the in-movement occurs during the two autumn months of October and November and the two spring months of March and April. On the average, between 2 and 3% of the pork produced during those four months is frozen for future use.

DEMAND

Demand for pork is influenced by the size and the age mix of the population, real income of consumers, consumers' "taste" for pork compared with its closest competitors, and the availability and price of competing protein foods, particularly beef and poultry. In the short run, the most volatile and important factors are the real income of consumers and the prices of competing products.

There are six principal pork cuts which make up most of the value of hogs. The largest and most important are hams and loins. In addition, there are picnics, Boston butts, bellies, and spareribs. These cuts account for over 40% of the weight and nearly 90% of the value of hogs. Most of the remaining value is in pork trimmings, miscellaneous edible products, lard, and other inedible products.

CASH HOGS

25 YEARS

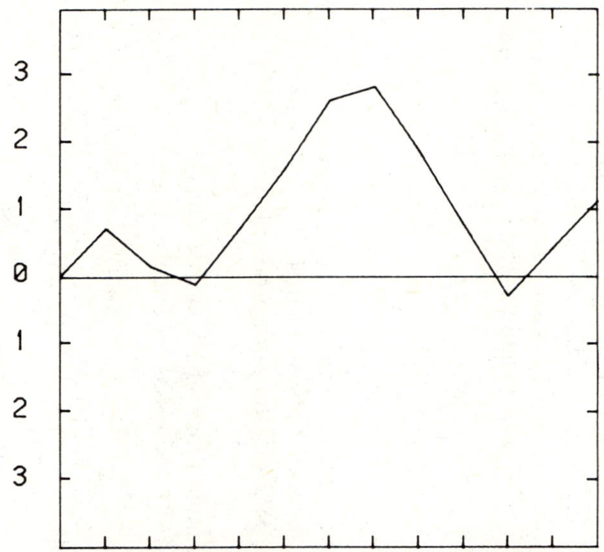

	J-F	F-M	M-A	A-M	M-J	J-J	J-A	A-S	S-O	O-N	N-D	D-J
Average Move	0.6	-0.6	-0.3	0.8	0.8	1	0.2	-1	-1.1	-1.1	0.7	0.7
% Reliable	72	60	56	60	80	72	56	68	84	88	52	80
Avg. Up Move	1.1	0.7	0.8	2	1.3	1.8	1.4	1	1.5	0.4	2.1	1
Avg. Down Move	0.6	1.5	1.2	0.9	1	1.2	1.4	1.9	1.6	1.3	0.9	0.6
Greatest Up Move	4.1	2.1	1.9	5.4	4.5	8	9.5	4.3	3.5	0.8	6.3	4
Greatest Down Move	1	4.1	4.5	4.6	3.4	2.6	4.3	12.4	6.8	9	1.7	1.2

CASH HOGS

4 YEARS

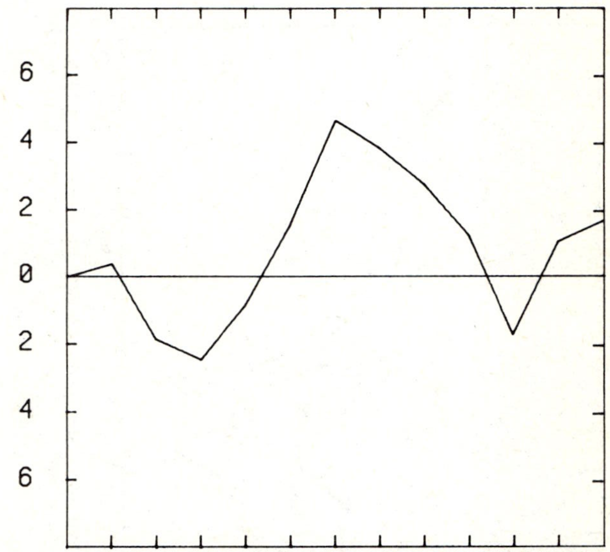

	J-F	F-M	M-A	A-M	M-J	J-J	J-A	A-S	S-O	O-N	N-D	D-J
Average Move	0.3	-2.3	-0.7	1.6	2.3	3.1	-0.9	-1.1	-1.6	-3	2.7	0.6
% Reliable	75	100	50	75	100	75	50	75	75	100	75	50
Avg. Up Move	0.8	0	1.2	3.6	2.3	5	1.2	4.3	3.5	0	4.1	1.6
Avg. Down Move	0.9	2.3	2.5	4.6	0	2.6	2.9	3	3.2	3	1.5	0.5
Greatest Up Move	1	0	1.3	5.4	4.5	7.7	1.3	4.3	3.5	0	6.3	1.9
Greatest Down Move	0.9	4.1	4.5	4.6	0	2.6	4.3	4.7	6.8	9	1.5	0.8

FIGURE 4. Seasonality of cash hog prices. The seasonal bias shown by these studies indicates that on-farm production of pork remains an important factor in annual price patterns. The relative bias of six units from peak to valley in the recent 4 years is not as volatile at current price levels as the three-unit bias over 25 years. (*Source:* J. Gruschow and C. Smith, *Profits Through Seasonal Trading*, Wiley, New York, NY, 1980.)

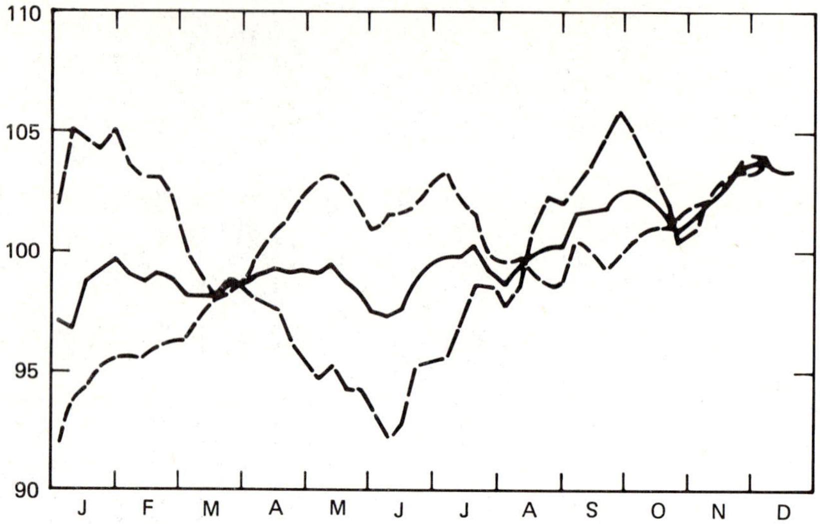

FIGURE 5. Seasonality filtering for live hogs. Seasonality during all years (——); high-ratio years (· · · ·); low-ratio years (– – –).

Each of the pork cuts has individual characteristics of demand. Most of the loins and butts are sold in fresh form. Most of the other major pork cuts are processed before sale. Demand for hams is particularly strong just before Christmas and Easter. Demand for bellies usually peaks in the late summer. Together, the various pork cuts provide a variety of products which keeps pork and hogs in demand throughout the year.

PORK BELLIES

The belly is the primal pork cut derived from the underside of the hog and is processed into bacon. Bellies represent about 12 to 13% of the total weight of hogs produced and about 17 to 18% of total pork production.

TABLE 4. Average Frozen Pork Stocks, End of Month, 1978–1981 (Adjusted for Secular Trend)

End of Month	Millions of Pounds
January	268
February	262
March	284
April	331
May	333
June	298
July	247
August	198
September	190
October	228
November	262
December	275

Frozen inventories are probably a more important factor in the belly markets than in hogs. The seasonal low is normally reached at the end of September and the seasonal high at the end of May. During recent years, frozen belly inventories have ranged from a low of 4 million lb in 1977 to a high of nearly 133 million lb in 1981. Figure 6 shows the price history of pork bellies since 1950 and its significant volatility during this period.

During recent years an average of about 7 to 10% of the bellies produced during March, April, November, and December were placed into freezers. June–September represents the months of largest out-movement of bellies from freezers. During July and August, frozen bellies represent an average of nearly 15% of the total bellies used for bacon production. Normal seasonality can be seen in Figure 7.

SPREADS

Hog and belly futures are often used by traders who specialize in placing spreads in the markets. As in other commodities, spreaders operate within the various months in hog futures markets and in the belly futures markets (*intracommodity spreads*). Since hogs are not in the strict sense a storable commodity, the various months in the hog futures market are not "held together" by a cost of storage factor. This makes them a popular commodity for spreaders. In the belly market, the February–August contracts represent bellies within the same storage season. In addition to belly spreads within the same storage season, many traders will spread bellies between the current and the following season. For example, July or August bellies of the current year are spread against February of the following year. These spreads often vary widely within the year and from year to year.

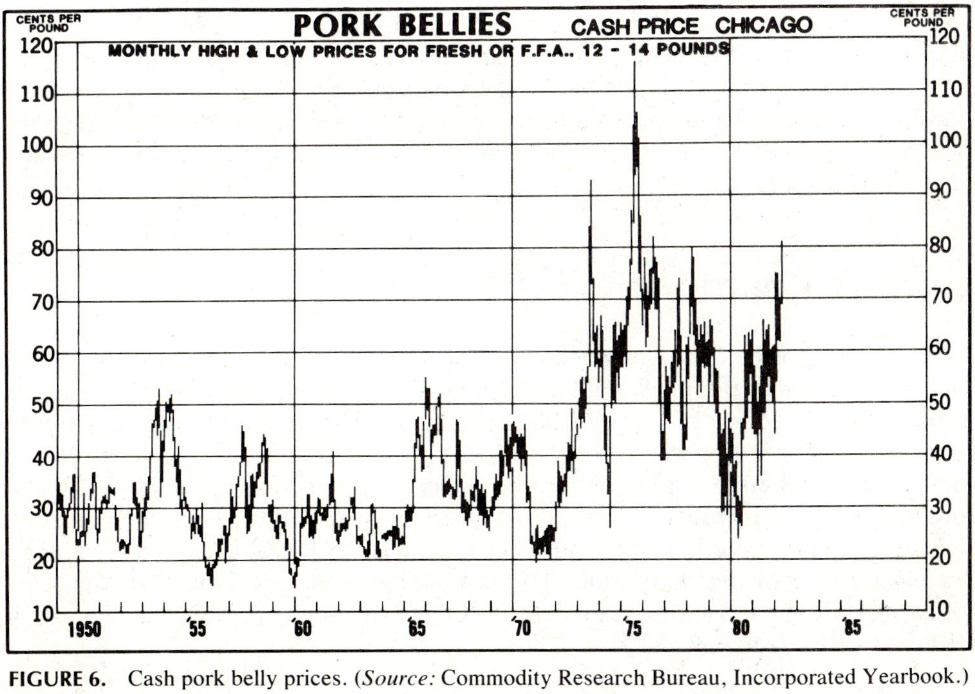

FIGURE 6. Cash pork belly prices. (*Source:* Commodity Research Bureau, Incorporated Yearbook.)

TABLE 5. Average Frozen Pork Belly Stocks, End of Month, 1978–1981 (Adjusted for Secular Trend)

End of Month	Millions of Pounds
January	58
February	57
March	74
April	93
May	103
June	93
July	60
August	27
September	13
October	22
November	45
December	66

In addition to the intracommodity spreads, many traders place *intercommodity spreads* between hogs and bellies. Variations in demand and in the elasticity of demand for hogs and bellies and the importance of frozen stocks in the belly contract create possibilities for volatile differences in values between these two closely related commodities. The following table of the open, high, low, and close of the February and July hog and belly contracts on the Chicago Mercantile Exchange for the years 1971–1980 gives some indication of the spreading possibilities between the two contracts.

Many spreaders operate in the hog and cattle markets. Even though the demand factors for pork and beef may be somewhat similar, differences in seasonal and cyclical production patterns between cattle and hogs often cause volatile differences in the values of these two commodities. These differences can span more than one production cycle. Table 7, showing the open, high, low, and close of the December hogs and cattle contracts on the Chicago Mercantile Exchange for the years 1971–1980, gives some indication of the spreading possibilities between the two contracts.

HOG/CORN RATIO

The hog/corn price ratio has been used for decades as an easy-to-calculate and useful indicator of the profitability of the hog-production enterprise. The ratio is obtained by dividing the price of hogs per hundred pounds by the price of corn per bushel. The ratio was probably a slightly better indicator of profitability in past decades when the value of corn was a larger proportion of the total costs of producing hogs. In recent years, other protein meals, other feed supplements, housing, equipment costs, interest expense, and other "fixed" costs have tended to make up a growing share of the hog-production expenses. However, the price of corn is still the most important cost factor and the hog/corn ratio is still a useful indicator. (See Table 8.)

PORK BELLIES NEAREST FUTURES

10 YEARS

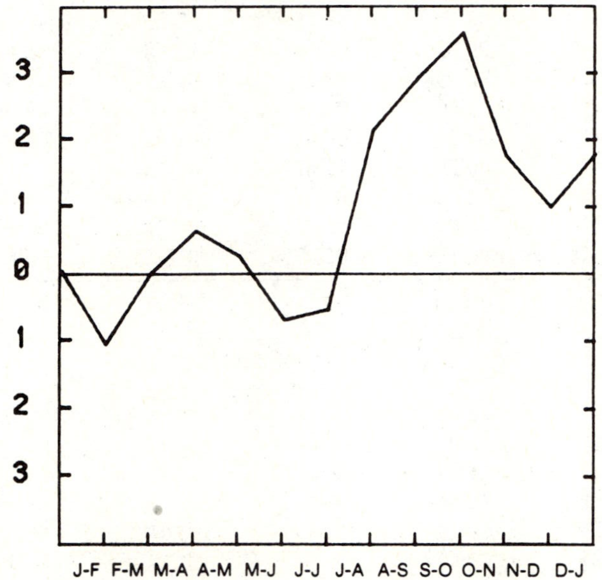

	J-F	F-M	M-A	A-M	M-J	J-J	J-A	A-S	S-O	O-N	N-D	D-J
Average Move	-1.1	1	0.6	-0.4	-1	0.1	2.6	0.7	0.6	-1.9	-0.8	0.7
% Reliable	60	90	40	50	60	40	60	70	50	70	40	70
Avg. Up Move	1.4	2	3.8	2.6	2.6	6.8	7	3.2	3	1	2	2.1
Avg. Down Move	2.8	7.6	1.6	3.5	3.4	4.3	3.9	5.1	1.7	3.1	5.1	2.5
Greatest Up Move	2.6	5	6.1	5.3	5.1	15	15	10.7	8.8	1.7	4	6.1
Greatest Down Move	5.4	7.6	3.6	9.1	5.5	11.2	8.8	12	4.6	9.7	10.9	4.6

PORK BELLIES NEAREST FUTURES

4 YEARS

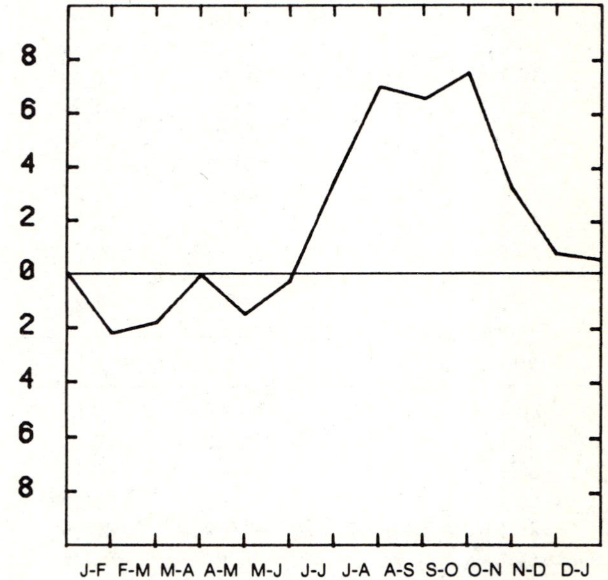

	J-F	F-M	M-A	A-M	M-J	J-J	J-A	A-S	S-O	O-N	N-D	D-J
Average Move	-2.3	0.4	1.7	-1.5	1.2	3.7	3.4	-0.5	0.9	-4.3	-2.5	-0.3
% Reliable	75	75	50	50	75	75	50	50	50	100	50	50
Avg. Up Move	2.6	3	5.8	2.5	3.2	8.7	11.5	6.2	4.8	0	3.5	1.8
Avg. Down Move	3.9	7.6	2.4	5.5	4.7	11.2	4.8	7.2	3	4.3	8.6	2.3
Greatest Up Move	2.6	5	6.1	3.5	5.1	15	15	10.7	8.8	0	4	2
Greatest Down Move	5.4	7.6	3.6	9.1	4.7	11.2	8.8	12	4.6	9.7	10.9	4.6

FIGURE 7. Seasonality of pork belly futures. The seasonality of pork belly prices is consistent with those of hogs, showing lowest levels at times of peak stocks immediately following the periods of greatest marketing of hogs.

TABLE 6. Relationship of Pork Belly to Live Hog Prices

	February Bellies				February Hogs				Ratio
Year	Open	High	Low	Close	Open	High	Low	Close	Bellies/ Hogs
1971	$35.50	$37.00	$22.57	$26.62	$20.75	$21.25	$15.80	$20.57	1.29
1972	33.00	44.17	26.77	39.72	21.50	29.35	20.00	27.07	1.47
1973	38.50	53.75	31.90	52.37	23.00	38.30	22.97	38.02	1.38
1974	55.00	83.80	45.05	53.70	28.25	58.85	28.00	41.70	1.29
1975	61.00	72.50	36.30	65.70	48.50	48.50	26.20	41.72	1.57
1976	60.00	104.10	55.25	69.22	42.95	62.35	38.30	50.30	1.38
1977	65.70	71.20	45.60	54.67	40.50	44.45	29.75	41.12	1.33
1978	48.00	73.97	43.50	69.12	33.40	51.00	32.60	49.82	1.39
1979	73.00	73.70	50.20	70.87	33.00	57.02	33.00	56.17	1.26
1980	50.00	56.50	37.20	39.25	44.00	50.65	33.50	38.35	1.02

	July Bellies				July Hogs				Ratio
Year	Open	High	Low	Close	Open	High	Low	Close	Bellies/ Hogs
1971	$33.00	$36.20	$20.70	$21.00	$23.50	$24.00	$18.25	$21.62	0.97
1972	34.00	42.40	27.75	40.15	25.20	30.50	21.27	30.25	1.33
1973	40.00	72.70	36.80	72.70	26.50	49.50	24.95	48.02	1.51
1974	64.25	81.10	28.75	55.00	35.70	57.25	24.02	39.05	1.41
1975	38.70	89.10	36.75	89.05	38.00	59.10	36.72	57.52	1.59
1976	69.50	94.95	63.70	68.47	43.80	56.15	40.90	48.37	1.42
1977	66.75	67.40	47.00	56.72	39.30	49.00	32.60	46.95	1.21
1978	54.75	85.75	44.50	50.50	35.70	57.30	32.97	48.35	1.04
1979	72.25	72.25	32.85	33.00	45.10	56.45	38.70	39.65	0.83
1980	51.50	58.85	27.30	43.10	43.90	47.70	32.67	44.87	0.96

TABLE 7. Relationship of Live Cattle to Live Hog Prices

Year	December Cattle				December Hogs				Ratio Cattle/ Hogs
	Open	High	Low	Close	Open	High	Low	Close	
1971	$28.00	$35.90	$27.90	$35.45	$20.00	$23.90	$18.60	$23.82	1.49
1972	31.20	39.65	31.00	38.25	22.65	33.95	22.65	33.75	1.13
1973	37.50	61.70	36.45	41.30	24.25	58.85	23.50	44.47	0.93
1974	49.75	53.90	34.30	37.90	44.50	50.45	24.15	42.62	0.89
1975	40.30	48.75	35.75	47.07	46.00	65.60	38.75	52.82	0.98
1976	43.50	47.80	36.90	40.90	41.50	44.95	29.70	41.62	0.98
1977	45.00	46.05	36.60	43.05	36.55	46.50	32.75	46.75	0.92
1978	40.45	59.60	40.15	58.15	31.10	55.40	30.60	53.12	1.09
1979	55.00	76.00	53.00	68.37	42.20	51.90	32.05	41.25	1.66
1980	73.00	74.95	60.60	65.65	40.60	53.45	36.50	45.97	1.43

TABLE 8. Hog/Corn Price Ratio at Omaha[a]

Year	Jan	Feb	Mar	Apr	May	June	July	Aug	Sept	Oct	Nov	Dec	Avg
1961	15.8	16.1	15.9	15.9	14.7	15.0	15.7	16.2	16.6	15.7	14.9	15.7	15.7
1962	16.0	15.5	14.7	14.4	13.6	14.9	16.4	17.0	17.1	15.5	15.6	14.6	15.4
1963	13.3	12.8	11.9	11.7	12.6	13.7	14.5	13.5	11.9	13.3	12.9	12.2	12.7
1964	12.2	12.4	12.0	11.6	11.8	12.9	14.3	13.9	13.5	13.0	12.5	12.8	12.7
1965	12.5	13.5	13.3	13.5	15.6	18.5	19.4	21.0	19.3	20.0	21.1	23.0	17.6
1966	21.7	21.9	20.6	17.7	18.6	20.1	18.6	18.6	17.1	15.9	15.0	14.5	18.4
1967[b]	14.5	14.7	14.0	13.9	16.6	17.0	17.6	17.8	16.7	15.9	15.5	14.9	15.5
1968	15.8	16.8	16.2	15.9	15.4	17.1	18.4	18.1	16.8	15.3	14.9	15.8	16.2
1969	16.3	17.1	17.0	16.2	17.8	19.8	21.1	22.0	22.1	21.7	22.0	23.0	19.5
1970	22.8	23.5	21.7	19.6	18.8	18.8	19.5	16.2	14.5	13.2	11.5	10.8	16.9
1971	11.0	13.2	11.6	11.3	11.8	12.2	13.9	15.1	16.3	17.2	16.7	16.6	13.6
1972	19.7	20.6	19.0	18.2	19.7	21.5	22.8	23.5	22.6	21.8	20.6	20.5	20.6
1973	21.5	23.3	25.4	23.4	19.5	16.9	19.9	20.8	18.4	17.8	16.9	15.7	19.3
1974	14.8	13.4	12.5	12.1	10.2	10.0	11.2	10.5	10.3	10.6	11.0	11.8	11.3
1975	12.6	14.1	14.3	14.1	16.4	17.9	19.4	18.6	20.7	21.2	19.4	18.5	16.9
1976	18.6	18.6	17.7	18.3	17.7	17.6	16.8	16.2	15.1	13.7	14.4	16.3	16.8
1977	16.4	16.8	15.9	16.0	18.8	20.7	23.8	26.4	24.6	22.6	19.2	21.0	20.1
1978	22.6	24.0	22.1	20.4	20.9	20.6	21.9	24.5	25.1	25.5	23.1	23.4	22.8
1979	24.0	25.5	22.6	19.9	18.1	16.4	14.2	15.4	16.2	14.6	15.3	16.0	18.2
1980	16.5	16.1	15.2	12.3	12.0	13.8	15.3	16.1	15.6	15.2	13.8	13.5	14.6
1981[c]	13.0	13.0	12.4	12.3	12.9	15.2	15.9	18.1	19.8	18.7	17.5	16.8	15.5

Source: Commodity Research Bureau Yearbooks.

[a]Ratio computed by dividing average price packer and shipper purchases of barrows and gilts by average price No. 2 yellow corn both at Omaha. This ratio represents the number of bushels of corn required to buy 100 lb of live hogs.

[b]Prices prior to 1967 are for "at Chicago."

[c]Preliminary.

TABLE 9. Effect of Extremes in Hog/Corn Price Ratio

Hog/Corn Price Ratio[a]			Subsequent Price of Hogs[b]		
Ratio		Month	Price Per Cwt		Month
23.5	(high)	February 1970	$15.67	(low)	December 1970
10.8	(low)	December 1970	56.68	(high)	August 1973
25.4	(high)	March 1973	26.09	(low)	May 1974
10.0	(low)	June 1974	61.23	(high)	September 1975
21.2	(high)	October 1975	32.05	(low)	November 1976
13.7	(low)	October 1976	54.42	(high)	February 1979
25.5	(high)	October 1978	28.86	(low)	April 1980
12.0	(low)	May 1980	50.92[c]	(high)	August 1981[c]

[a]Omaha basis.
[b]Average monthly price of barrows and gilts, seven leading midwest markets.
[c]High as of end of 1981.

When the hog/corn ratio is high, profitability is usually high and some hog producers expand their output. The subsequent increase in hog marketings usually causes hog prices to fall. The hog/corn ratio falls, production becomes unprofitable, and production is curtailed. Table 9 presents the highs and lows of the hog/corn ratio since 1970 and the subsequent lows and highs in hog prices.

SOURCES OF INFORMATION

There are several key reports with which a participant in the hog and pork belly markets should be familiar. Of primary importance is the quarterly *Hogs and Pigs* report, published about the 22nd of each December, March, June, and September by the Crop Reporting Board of the Statistical Reporting Service of the U.S. Department of Agriculture, Washington, D.C. 20250. This reports the results of a survey of hog producers taken about 3 weeks earlier. The December and June reports cover all 50 states. The March and September reports cover only 10 of the most important hog-producing states which account for over 75% of the total hogs. The report gives state-by-state quarterly data on the number of pigs saved, number of sows farrowing, and pigs saved per sow, as well as producers' intentions for the number of sows to farrow during the following two quarters.

The same USDA source publishes an important *Cold Storage* report about the 20th of each month reporting freezer holdings of bellies, picnics, hams, loins, spareribs, trimmings, other pork, and total pork as of the end of the preceding month. It also reports on the storage holdings of canned hams and other canned meat, as well as holdings of beef, poultry, and many other commodities.

Complete monthly data on hog slaughter can be found in the *Livestock Slaughter* report also published by the USDA on about the 20th of each month. Much more detailed historical data can be found in the annual *Livestock and Meat Statistics* compiled by the Economic Research Service, Statistical Reporting Service, and Agricultural Marketing Service and published by the USDA.

The USDA also reports daily hog and pork prices from many markets and the daily number of hogs slaughtered under federal inspection. This information is relayed to the public by many services, public and private. The Agricultural Marketing Service of the USDA also publishes many statistics on hogs and pork in the weekly *Livestock, Meat and Wool Market News*.

There are many private sources of information serving the industry. Among them are daily meat-price reporting services, the "Yellow Sheet" of the National Provisioner, Chicago, and the pink "Meat Sheet" published by Meat Sheet, Inc., Elmhurst, Illinois. There are many private consultants, brokerage firms, news services, and technical chart services with information and analysis concerning the hog and pork belly markets.

SELECTED BOOKS

Bakken, H.H. (Ed.). *Futures Trading in Livestock*. Madison, WI: Mimir Publishers, 1970.

Bundy, C.E. *Swine Production* (4th ed.). Englewood Cliffs, NJ: Prentice-Hall, 1976.

Dunn & Hargitt. *Consistent Profits in Pork Bellies*. Lafayette, IN: Dunn & Hargitt, n.d.

Dyer, I.A., and O'Mary, C.C. *The Feedlot* (2nd ed.). Philadelphia, PA: Lea & Febiger, 1977.

Ensminger, M E. *Swine Science* (4th ed.). Danville, IL: Interstate, 1970.

Leuthold, R.M., and Dixon, P. (Eds.). *Livestock Futures Research Symposium, Proceedings*. Chicago, IL: Chicago Mercantile Exchange, 1980.

McCoy, J.H. *Livestock and Meat Marketing* (2nd ed.). Westport, CT: AVI, 1979.

Purcell, W.D. *Agricultural Marketing: Systems, Coordination, Cash and Futures Prices*. Reston, VA: Reston, 1979.

Rhodes, V.J. *The Agricultural Marketing System*. Columbus, OH: Grid, 1978.

Shepherd, G.S., and Futrell, G.A. *Marketing Farm Products* (6th ed.). Ames, IA: Iowa State University Press, 1976.

Van Arsdall, R.N. *Structural Characteristics of the U.S. Hog Production Industry*. Washington, D.C.: U.S. Department of Agriculture, Economics, Statistics, and Cooperatives Service, 1978.

CHAPTER 33

BROILERS

CONTENTS

INDUSTRY BACKGROUND 3

BROILER PRODUCTION 3

SUPPLY 5

DEMAND 7

SEASONALITY STUDIES 8

FUTURES MARKETS 9

SOURCES OF INFORMATION 10

CHAPTER 33

BROILERS

Stan Ostrowski

INDUSTRY BACKGROUND

Induced by economies of scale, the structure of the broiler industry has changed dramatically over the past 25 years. The production of broilers, once dependent upon the output of numerous independent small-farm flocks is today mainly the consequence of the management decisions of large, highly integrated commercial firms. These firms own or contract with a hatchery for the supply of broiler chicks which are grown out to market weight on either company farms or under contract with individual farm units. When the broilers are of market weight (3½ to 4 lb), they are typically slaughtered in the firm's own processing plant.

This type of organizational structure in the broiler industry has been particularly well suited for the development and implementation of advances in the areas of breeding, production techniques, nutrition, and animal health. For example, broiler chicks are grown to market weight in approximately 8 to 9 weeks. Twenty-five years ago the grow-out period was about 12–14 weeks. Food required to produce 1 lb of live weight has been reduced from 4 lb in the 1940s to 2 lb or less today. Bird mortality has been reduced from 10–20% 25 years ago, to only 2–4% today.

Managerial, technological, and scientific innovations adopted by the broiler industry have enabled it to meet a significant growth in demand. Live-weight production increased from 884 million lb in 1946 to more than 15 billion lb in 1980. This increase in demand has not been solely due to population growth. Per capita consumption of broilers over the same period, has increased tremendously from only 4.1 to 47 lb.

BROILER PRODUCTION

Broiler production is concentrated in a few states, mainly Arkansas, Georgia, Alabama, North Carolina, and Mississippi. Other data also reveal industry concentration in terms of the size of broiler grow-out and processing operations. USDA data show that in 1977 the four largest firms accounted for one-fifth of broiler slaughter; the output of the 20 largest firms accounted for more than one-half of the broilers slaughtered under federal inspection in that year. Further, average output per farm increased from 33,600 birds in 1959 to 72,400 birds in 1974.

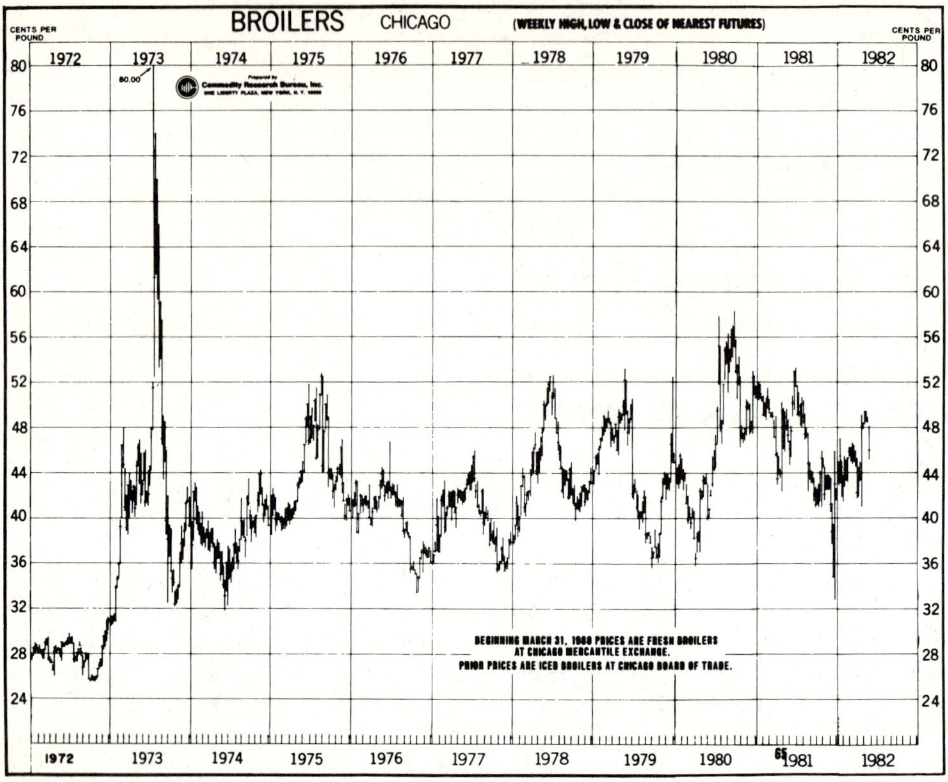

FIGURE 1. Weekly broiler prices—Chicago, nearest futures.

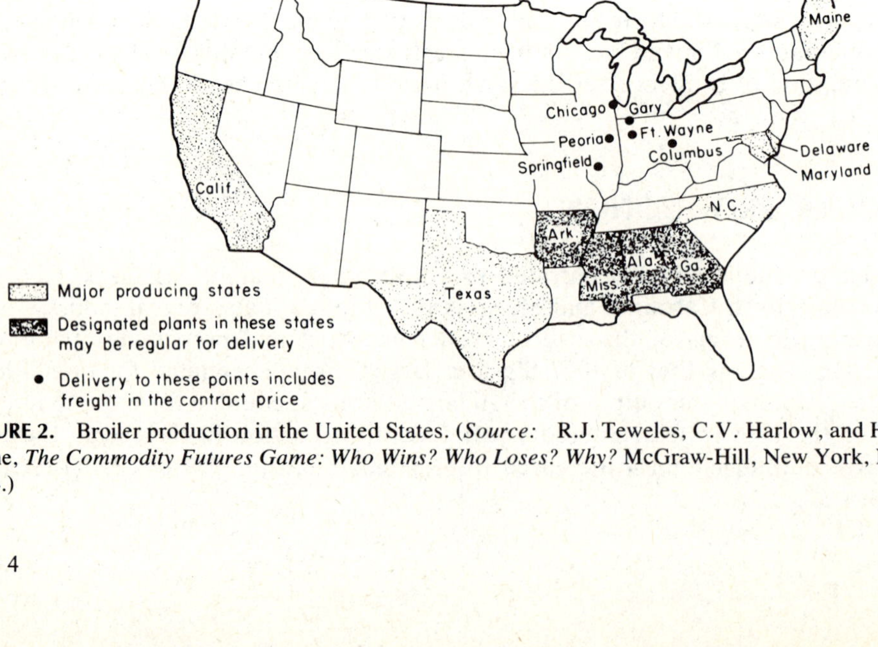

FIGURE 2. Broiler production in the United States. (*Source:* R.J. Teweles, C.V. Harlow, and H.L. Stone, *The Commodity Futures Game: Who Wins? Who Loses? Why?* McGraw-Hill, New York, NY, 1974.)

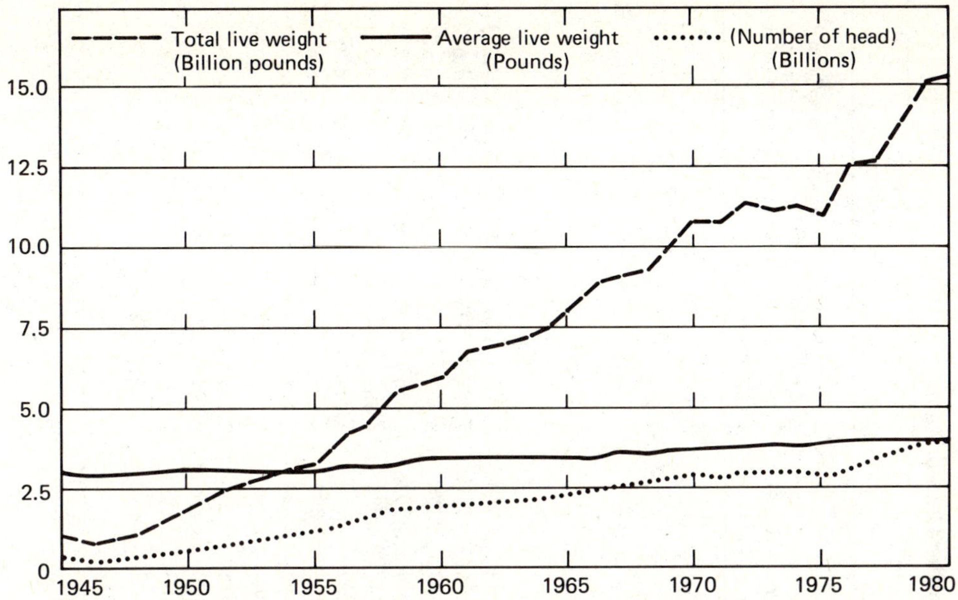

FIGURE 3. Annual broiler production, 1945–1980. (*Source:* Agricultural Economic Report, No. 381, Economic Research Services, U.S. Department of Agriculture Poultry and Egg Situation, U.S. Department of Agriculture, Economics, Statistics, and Cooperatives Service.)

At the processing plant, broilers are killed, cleaned, inspected, chilled, graded, sized, and packed in 65- or 70-lb cartons in a matter of hours. Since broilers have a shelf life after slaughter of about only 7 days, they are moved quickly through marketing channels. Broilers move to wholesalers or directly to large retail chains partially under formula pricing based on some published quotation and partially under weekly negotiated pricing. Published cash prices include a weekly nine-city, weighted-average wholesale price for iced broilers, and the processing plant's dock prices from several southern states.

Because of the short grow-out period for broilers and the degree of integration of production and processing, the broiler industry is not characterized by the lengthy underproduction and overproduction cycles which characterize cattle and hogs. However, since the production planning horizon extends well beyond the 2-month grow-out period, supply-and-demand imbalances can easily occur and can result in adjustments of large magnitude.

SUPPLY

A major component of the cost of producing live broilers is feed. The ratio of current and anticipated broiler prices to feed costs is an important and easily observable indicator of potential changes in supply. Labor is still the major component of broiler processing costs. However, energy and overhead costs have increased in relative importance.

TABLE 1. Broiler Salient Statistics in the United States

Year	Commercial[b] Production: Number (Millions)	Commercial[b] Production: Live Weight (Millions of Pounds)	Average: Live Weight Per Bird (Pounds)	Average: Farm Price (Cents per Pound)	Value of Production (Millions of Dollars)	Young Chickens Civilian Disappearance (Millions of Pounds)	Total Chickens[c] Supply and Distribution (In Millions of Pounds): Commercial Broilers	Other Chickens	Total	Storage Stocks Jan 1	Exports and Shipments	Consumption: Military	Consumption: Civilian
1961	1,991	6,832	3.43	13.9	947								
1962	2,023	6,907	3.41	15.2	1,049								
1963	2,102	7,276	3.46	14.6	1,063								
1964	2,161	7,521	3.48	14.2	1,070								
1965	2,334	8,111	3.48	15.0	1,217								
1966	2,571	8,989	3.50	15.3	1,371								
1967	2,592	9,183	3.54	13.3	1,223								
1968	2,620	9,326	3.56	14.2	1,326	1,737	6,653	769	7,422	170	162	100	7,233
1969	2,789	10,048	3.60	15.2	1,531	1,835	7,175	732	7,907	97	166	88	7,640
1970	2,987	10,819	3.62	13.6	1,475	1,958	7,687	778	8,465	110	182	69	8,161
1971	2,945	10,818	3.67	13.8	1,487	1,974	7,724	792	8,516	163	202	75	8,253
1972	3,075	11,480	3.73	14.1	1,623	2,039	8,147	740	8,887	149	206	52	8,667
1973	3,009	11,220	3.73	24.0	2,690	1,985	8,025	736	8,761	111	203	47	8,476
1974	2,993	11,320	3.79	21.5	2,436	2,044	8,126	789	8,915	146	235	34	8,617
1975	2,950	11,096	3.76	26.3	2,915	2,035	8,127	696	8,823	175	273	39	8,572
1976	3,283	12,517	3.81	23.6	2,953	2,262	9,067	684	9,751	114	451	33	9,226
1977	3,400	12,993	3.82	23.6	3,067	2,315	9,418	700	10,118	115	481	26	9,627
1978	3,516	13,656	3.88	26.4	3,682	2,400	10,129	665	10,794	139	505	32	10,294
1979[a]	3,843	15,111	3.93	26.0	4,031		11,188	732	11,920	102	597	33	11,250
1980[a]	3,881	15,277	3.94	27.8	4,304		11,348			142			
1981[a]	4,071	16,267	3.99	28.0	4,555		12,005			136			

Source: Department of Agriculture, Economic Research Service. [a]Preliminary. [b]Beginning 1970, data are for the marketing year starting December through November 30th. [c]Ready-to-cook basis.

Prices to retailers for broiler chickens generally reflect added costs of transportation and handling. Retail prices may vary between cities because of differing retailer pricing policies. This use of broilers as a price special is a common practice. Such a pricing practice may disrupt orderly producing and marketing arrangements, or serve as a means of reducing buildups in supply.

As with the production of most agricultural commodities, the average monthly ratios of broiler slaughter in federally inspected plants vary seasonally. The low production months tend to be November through April, and the high production months are May through October. This seasonal variation has, however, been moderating over time and is small compared to those of some other commodities.

Formulation of broiler-supply outlooks requires an understanding of the fundamental determinants of that supply. One fundamental determinant of broiler supply in a given period is, clearly, the size of the laying flock in a prior period. The size of the laying flock can be adjusted by changing the rate of culling old hens and by changing the rate of pullet chick replacement. In addition to the size of the laying flock, such factors as extreme weather, age distribution of the laying flock (both of which affect the rate of lay), and diversion of eggs to egg-breaking plants for processing into food products also influence the broiler chick supply.

Customarily, broiler pullets require about 6 months of rearing before they mature and join the laying flock. The useful laying life of a hen is about 8 to 9 months. A hen reaches her peak output in her second month of lay; thereafter, the rate of lay gradually declines, and eventually the quality and hatchability of her eggs also declines. Thus the typical age distribution of layers in the laying flock is between 6 and 14 months of age. Since eggs require 21 days of incubation before hatching, the current month's hatch of broiler chicks, then, is usually from hens placed as pullet chicks 7–15 months earlier.

The USDA reports the number of pullet chicks placed in rearing houses monthly. A simple moving sum of pullet chick placements of 7–15 months earlier can be used to approximate the size of the laying flock. This approximation is affected, of course, by changes in the rate of culling old hens and the age at which they are culled.

The *Crop Reporting Board* of the USDA in the 21 largest broiler-producing states publishes weekly information on the broiler eggs set in incubators. Growout of chicks to slaughter weight requires 7 to 8 weeks. Weather, food conversion efficiency, mortality rates, and management are some of the factors affecting timing, numbers, and weight of marketed broilers.

Thus, a near-term broiler-supply projection of up to about 9 weeks forward may be based on the USDA reports of chicks hatched. A supply projection for 9–12 weeks forward begins with consideration of the USDA reports on eggs set in incubators. Finally, a broiler-supply projection of from 12 weeks to 9 months forward requires, as a beginning, consideration of the USDA reports of pullet chick placements.

DEMAND

The seasonal variation of broiler slaughter was discussed in the previous section. Consumption also varies seasonally. Consumption tends to be highest during the second and third quarters of the year and lowest during the first and fourth quarters. Specifically, since warm weather tends to stimulate both cooking out and eating away from home, there tends to be a stronger demand for broilers during summer months. The reverse occurs at Thanksgiving and the winter holidays, when consumers tend to favor turkey and ham.

The level of disposable income is a determinant of consumer expenditures. Consumers apportion their expenditure among chicken, turkey, pork, beef, lamb, fish, and other protein sources on the basis of both relative prices and taste. A rise in the price of one of these items tends to stimulate spending on the other relatively less expensive items. Thus it is essential to monitor the expected supplies and prices of competing meats when attempting to forecast broiler demand and prices. Historically, pork has been the meat which is most competitive with broilers, followed by beef, turkey, and lamb. Since changes in consumer tastes tend to be gradual, so do the demand impacts of these changes. Important long-term demand factors to be considered are the growth of both fast-food franchise operations and population.

Data on broiler exports, which have represented a relatively small component of total sales in the past, are published by the USDA.

SEASONALITY STUDIES

An analytic look at seasonality confirms our previous comments on supply. Low production expected during November through April and higher production in

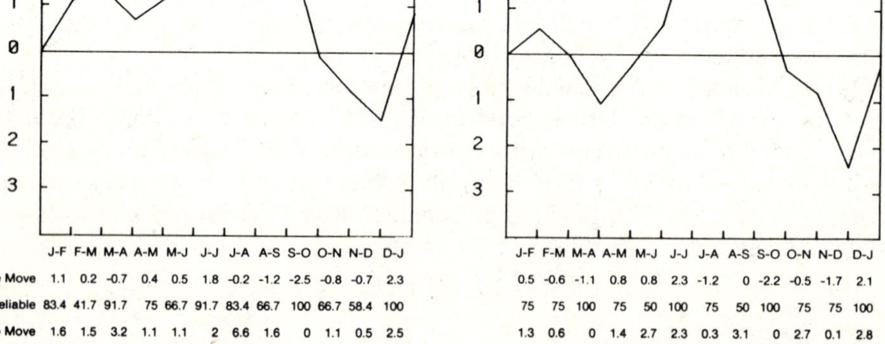

(a)

	J-F	F-M	M-A	A-M	M-J	J-J	J-A	A-S	S-O	O-N	N-D	D-J
Average Move	1.1	0.2	-0.7	0.4	0.5	1.8	-0.2	-1.2	-2.5	-0.8	-0.7	2.3
% Reliable	83.4	41.7	91.7	75	66.7	91.7	83.4	66.7	100	66.7	58.4	100
Avg. Up Move	1.6	1.5	3.2	1.1	1.1	2	6.6	1.6	0	1.1	0.5	2.5
Avg. Down Move	1.5	0.8	1.1	1.5	0.7	0.3	1.6	2.4	2.5	1.7	1.5	0
Greatest Up Move	3.5	4.8	3.2	2.5	4.5	5.7	12.9	3.1	0	2.7	1.7	4.3
Greatest Down Move	2	1.3	2.3	3.2	1.8	0.3	2.5	12	8.2	5.1	4	0

(b)

	J-F	F-M	M-A	A-M	M-J	J-J	J-A	A-S	S-O	O-N	N-D	D-J
Average Move	0.5	-0.6	-1.1	0.8	0.8	2.3	-1.2	0	-2.2	-0.5	-1.7	2.1
% Reliable	75	75	100	75	50	100	75	50	100	75	75	100
Avg. Up Move	1.3	0.6	0	1.4	2.7	2.3	0.3	3.1	0	2.7	0.1	2.8
Avg. Down Move	2	1	1.1	0.9	1.1	0	1.8	1.5	2.2	1.6	2.2	0
Greatest Up Move	2.7	0.6	0	2.5	4.5	4	0.3	3.1	0	2.7	0.1	3.6
Greatest Down Move	2	1.3	2.2	0.9	1.8	0	2	1.6	3.7	2	4	0

FIGURE 4. Broiler seasonality. (*a*) Cash broilers, 12 years. (*b*) Cash broilers, 4 years.

May through October is reflected in both the long- and short-term studies shown in Figure 4(*a*) and 4(*b*). A small response lag in the cash market may account for a 1- to 2-month offset in the pattern.

Cash broilers are considered to be one of the best seasonal markets, containing several very strong moves combined with high reliability. Although production increases in the spring, peak prices are reached in early summer followed by a decline into the Thanksgiving and Christmas holiday season—a period of low demand for broilers. After the holiday season is over, prices begin a sharp rebound.

FUTURES MARKETS

Broilers are traded on the Chicago Mercantile Exchange; however, it has become illiquid in recent years. Because of the importance of the broiler industry to the

TABLE 2. Broiler Contract Specifications

	CME Fresh Broiler Chickens
Delivery months	As determined by the Board of Governors, including February, April, June, July, August, October and December
Trading unit	30,000 lb
Minimum fluctuation	.025¢ per lb ($.01 per lb = $300 per contract)
Daily price movement limits	There shall be no trading at a price more than $0.02 per lb above or below the previous day's settlement price ($600 per contract).
Position limits	750 contracts in all futures combined; not more than 300 contracts in the spot month.
Grades deliverable	Whole, eviscerated, ready-to-cook, broiler-fryer chickens USDA Grade A with wrapped or bagged neck and giblets as harvested (which means that some giblet parts may be missing). Each delivered unit must be processed in a single plant approved by the USDA and the Chicago Mercantile Exchange. The fresher broiler chickens may be shipped ice-packed or CO_2 chilled.
Delivery	Delivery is made under a Certificate of Delivery issued by broiler plants approved by the exchange. At the buyer's option, delivery may be made in either the plant's or the buyer's truck: delivery is to be made to one of the following delivery points with corresponding allowances. Par delivery may be made at Chicago, Illinois, Columbus, Ohio, or Indianapolis, Indiana. Delivery may be made at Cleveland, Ohio, Detroit, Michigan, or Minneapolis, Minnesota at .25¢ per lb premium or at New York, NY, at .50¢ per lb premium. If the buyer supplies the truck, the buyer is entitled to a discount of 1.75¢ per lb.
Trading hours	9:10 a.m.–1:00 p.m. central time

U.S. consumer, it would not be surprising to find the contract revitalized. Specifications of the Chicago Mercantile Exchange's *Fresh Broiler Chicken* contract appear in Table 2.

SOURCES OF INFORMATION

American Poultry Historical Society. *American Poultry History 1823–1973: Anthology Overviewed of 150 Years: People, Places, Progress*, Mt. Morris, IL, 1974.

Chicago Board of Trade, *Statistical Annual*.

Chicago Mercantile Exchange, *Yearbook*.

Books

Ensminger, M.E. *Poultry Science*. Danville, IL: Interstate, 1971.

Miracle, D.J.S. "The Role of the Egg Futures Market in the Egg Economy: 1940 to 1966." Ph.D. dissertation Stanford University, 1971.

Sawyer, G. *The Agribusiness Poultry Industry: A History of Its Development*. New York, NY: Exposition, 1971.

Tobin, B. F. *Dynamics of Adjustment in the Broiler Industry*. Boston, MA: Harvard Business School, 1964.

Periodic Reports

U.S. Department of Agriculture. Economics, Statistics, and Cooperatives Service:

Cold Storage—monthly, annual.

Eggs, Chickens, and Turkeys—monthly.

Feed Situation—5 years.

Hatchery Production Report.

Livestock Slaughter and Meat Production.

Poultry and Egg Situation—5 years.

Poultry Market Statistics—annual.

Poultry Slaughter and Processing—monthly, annual.

Pullet Chicks for Broiler Hatchery Supply Flocks.

Turkeys and Chickens Tested.

U.S. Foreign Agricultural Service:

Foreign Agriculture Circular. Poultry and Eggs FPE—irregular.

National Broiler Council, Washington, D.C.:

Washington Report—biweekly.

Poultry and Egg Institute of America, Arlington, VA:

Hot Line—weekly.

Also see the Bibliography in this book for a complete list of sources of information for broilers.

CHAPTER 34

THE MARKET FOR COCOA

CONTENTS

COCOA AND CHOCOLATE PRODUCTION 3

CONSUMPTION OF COCOA AND CHOCOLATE 8

PRICE DYNAMICS IN COCOA 9

Gold as an International Standard 12
Seasonality 12
Cyclic Analysis 14

FUTURES TRADING IN COCOA 16

HEDGING APPLICATIONS IN COCOA BEANS 20

Trading Price is Fixed 20
Trading Price: Differential Basis 23
Cocoa Butter Hedging Strategy 26

CONCLUSION 28

REFERENCES 28

CHAPTER 34

THE MARKET FOR COCOA

Todd E. Petzel

Cocoa was being used as a beverage in Central America prior to the European discoveries. Spanish conquistadors reported that cocoa was so valuable in the Indian civilizations that it was the predominant drink of the ruling classes, and it frequently was used as a medium of exchange. The product quickly moved to the old world where cocoa processing centers were established throughout the Mediterranean by the mid-16th century. Consumption of cocoa, restricted to beverages, grew only gradually until the 19th century. A Dutch manufacturer, Van Houten, discovered in 1828 that some of the fat content of the bean could be extracted. He added this fat, called cocoa butter, and sugar to ground cocoa beans and produced chocolate. Later in the century a Swiss candy maker, Daniel Peter, blended milk with chocolate, increasing the desirability of the candy, and expanding the demand for cocoa beans. Since the turn of the century, world production and trade in cocoa has exploded, with supplies growing from 100 thousand metric tons to currently over 1.5 million metric tons (Watling and Morley, 1974, p. 141). Unlike sugar, which has only a small fraction of world production traded internationally, over two-thirds of cocoa supplies enter into international trade. Production is centered in West Africa and South and Central America, while over 70% of all cocoa imports go to the United States and Western Europe (see Table 1). This has the effect of creating a global market for cocoa where supply-and-demand shocks are translated into price changes affecting most consumers.

COCOA AND CHOCOLATE PRODUCTION

The cocoa tree grows best in tropical regions of the world where rainfall measures 50 in. or more per year. Prior to the later 1800s, production was concentrated in Central and South America, but since the turn of the century the dominant source of supply has become West Africa. Ghana, the Ivory Coast, and Nigeria all regularly export more than 100 thousand tonnes (Gill and Duffus Quarterly, May 1982). Brazil's exports have fluctuated around 120 thousand tonnes through the decade of the 1970s. Cameroon, Ecuador, the Dominican Republic, Malaysia, and New Guinea are other important sources of supply.

Cocoa production must be planned for the long term in that the trees do not begin to offer commercial quantities of beans until the fifth year. After remaining at low levels for a few years, yields grow rapidly until about the 15th year, when

TABLE 1. World Production of Cocoa Beans in Principal Producing Countries (in Thousands of Metric Tons)

Crop Year[a]	Brazil	Colombia	Dominican Republic	Ecuador	Equatorial Guinea[b]	Cameroon	Ghana	Ivory Coast	Nigeria	Sao Tome and Principe	Trinidad and Tobago	Venezuela	Asia and Oceania	World Total
1961–2	116.0	15.0	34.2	40.0	26.0	73.7	416.0	81.0	193.9	9.6	6.5	12.4	22.3	1,123
1962–3	111.0	13.5	39.9	42.0	31.5	76.4	428.4	103.0	178.7	10.3	6.4	14.6	25.6	1,162
1963–4	122.7	14.5	40.9	36.0	33.4	87.9	445.2	98.2	219.5	8.5	5.2	22.3	29.1	1,238
1964–5	118.6	16.0	26.1	47.0	34.7	90.0	563.3	147.5	298.3	8.6	5.4	21.9	32.6	1,490
1965–6	171.0	17.0	28.7	36.0	35.0	77.2	415.6	113.3	184.6	9.7	5.3	22.9	27.7	1,219
1966–7	173.3	17.0	28.5	53.0	38.5	84.2	381.4	149.7	267.3	10.0	4.7	21.0	31.5	1,336
1967–8	144.7	18.0	30.0	70.0	34.0	91.5	421.6	146.8	238.5	11.0	6.3	24.7	34.8	1,352
1968–9	165.0	19.0	21.0	43.0	38.0	103.8	338.9	145.0	192.0	9.0	4.7	18.0	41.0	1,242
1969–0	201.0	19.0	43.0	55.0	24.0	108.3	416.0	181.0	223.0	9.7	5.0	19.0	35.8	1,435
1970–1	182.0	21.0	25.0	61.0	30.0	111.7	392.0	180.0	308.0	10.4	4.1	18.9	44.0	1,499
1971–2	167.0	22.0	41.0	67.0	22.0	123.0	464.0	226.0	255.0	10.0	5.0	17.0	45.0	1,583
1972–3	162.0	23.0	28.0	43.0	10.0	107.0	418.0	241.0		11.0	5.0	19.0	40.0	1,398
1973–4	246.0	23.0	30.0	72.0	12.0	110.0	350.0	209.0	215.0	10.0	4.0	17.0	53.0	1,448
1974–5	273.0	25.0	27.0	78.0	13.0	118.0	377.0	242.0	214.0	7.0	5.0	19.0	57.0	1,549
1975–6	258.0	26.0	30.0	63.0	10.0	96.0	397.0	231.0	216.0	8.0	3.0	15.0	60.0	1,510
1976–7	234.0	29.0	30.0	72.0	6.0	82.0	320.0	230.0	165.0	6.0	4.0	15.0	60.0	1,339
1977–8	283.0	29.0	30.0	75.0	6.0	108.0	268.0	304.0	205.0	6.0	4.0	18.0	64.0	1,503
1978–9	314.0	31.0	33.0	90.0	6.0	106.0	250.0	312.0	137.0	5.0	3.0	17.0	69.0	1,480
1979–0[c]	294.0	30.0	27.0	98.0	6.0	122.0	290.0	373.0	169.0	5.0	2.0	17.0	77.0	1,617
1980–1[d]	350.0	35.0	27.0	75.0	8.0	115.0	255.0	352.0	165.0	5.0	3.0	18.0	79.0	1,584
1981–2[d]	345.0	42.0	30.0	35.0	10.0	110.0	265.0	400.0	170.0	5.0	2.0	15.0	90.0	1,726

Source: Gill and Duffus, Ltd. [a]Crop years are for the 12 months, October 1st to September 30th. [b]Includes Fernando Po and Rio Muni. [c]Preliminary. [d]Forecast.

TABLE 2. World Cocoa Supply and Demand (in Thousands of Metric Tons)

Crop Year[a]	Stocks October 1st	Net World Crop[b]	Total Availability	Seasonal Grindings	Closing Stocks	Stock Change
1961–2	523	1,113	1,636	1,083	553	+ 30
1962–3	553	1,152	1,705	1,133	572	+ 19
1963–4	572	1,204	1,629	1,180	449	+ 25
1964–5	606	1,467	1,916	1,320	590	+141
1965–6	788	1,193	1,783	1,370	411	−179
1966–7	627	1,320	1,731	1,366	367	− 44
1967–8	581	1,320	1,901	1,384	517	− 64
1968–9	572	1,230	1,802	1,369	433	−139
1969–0	433	1,421	1,854	1,356	498	+ 65
1979–1	498	1,484	1,982	1,417	565	+ 67
1971–2	565	1,567	2,132	1,517	615	+ 50
1972–3	615	1,384	1,999	1,607	392	−223
1969–0	433	1,421	1,854	1,354	500	+ 67
1970–1	500	1,484	1,984	1,415	569	+ 69
1971–2	569	1,567	2,136	1,515	621	+ 52
1972–3	621	1,384	2,005	1,605	400	−221
1973–4	392	1,433	1,825	1,507	318	− 82
1974–5	318	1,532	1,850	1,428	422	+104
1975–6	422	1,495	1,917	1,511	406	− 16
1976–7	412	1,326	1,738	1,423	315	− 97
1977–8	315	1,488	1,803	1,371	432	+117
1978–9	432	1,465	1,897	1,425	472	+ 40
1979–0[c]	472	1,601	2,073	1,452	621	+149
1980–1[d]	621	1,568	2,189	1,476	713	+ 92

Source: Gill and Duffus, Ltd. [a]Crop year season is October through September. [b]The net world crop is obtained by adjusting the gross world crop for 1% loss in weight. [c]Preliminary. [d]Forecast.

the peak is reached. This high level of production can be maintained for another 15 years, and then yields slowly decline until the tree is no longer productive, sometime between its 40th and 50th year of age. This characteristic of the trees leads to an inelastic supply in the short run. Farmers need to expect high prices to persist before they will undertake new plantings, and short-term low prices are not sufficient incentive to destroy trees in their prime. As long as prices are above the marginal cost of picking and handling, mature cocoa trees will be maintained. Some farmers cut back on their weeding and fertilizing when cocoa prices are low, but the impact of this on aggregate supply is quite limited.

Estimates of supply elasticities exploit the lag structure when forming the functional relationships; the price variable is frequently formed as a discounted stream of expected returns. Bateman has done an extensive analysis of the Ghanaian market and found that the supply elasticities range from 0.3 to 0.4. Ascari and Cummings report the evidence from different supply studies with elasticities falling in a broad range of 0.3 to 1. These high elasticities of supply are unusual

TABLE 3. World Exports of Cocoa Beans by Principal Producing Countries (in Thousands of Metric Tons)

Year	Brazil	Costa Rica	Dominican Republic	Ecuador	Equatorial Guinea	Cam-eroon	Ghana	Malaysia	Ivory Coast	Mexico	Papua New Guinea	Nigeria	Sao Tome and Principe	Trinidad and Tobago	Vene-zuela	Asia and Oceania	Togo	Grand Total
1961	104.2	10.2	11.7	32.5	24.6	58.3	411.9		88.5	5.5		186.9	10.3	5.7	9.7	15.7		1,015
1962	55.3	11.9	18.6	31.5	29.9	59.9	428.0		101.0	12.1		197.8	10.6	5.8	10.9	20.7		1,035
1963	68.7	9.5	23.8	35.3	31.0	71.2	411.0		99.7	18.1		177.4	9.2	6.5	12.6	22.7		1,035
1964	74.7	9.2	26.2	26.8	35.8	53.9	387.6		124.3	3.4		200.0	8.7	4.6	12.1	23.5		1,030
1965	92.0	6.8	22.4	39.3	30.5	77.5	501.9		126.4	9.3		310.2	8.9	4.9	12.1	26.8		1,306
1966	112.5	7.7	25.9	32.2	36.4	78.1	397.9		124.3	8.4		193.3	10.1	4.8	11.8	25.1		1,108
1967	114.4	7.2	23.9	45.0	31.5	69.8	334.9		105.2	6.1		248.2	11.7	4.7	12.4	28.0		1,082
1968	75.8	5.2	25.3	65.1	39.7	69.7	335.3		121.5	5.9		208.9	11.7	6.0	14.4	31.7		1,054
1969	119.6	9.1	25.1	32.4	31.0	73.8	308.6		118.9	5.3		173.6	8.3	3.9	10.6	32.5		999
1970	119.8	3.3	34.4	36.1	19.1	72.0	367.3		143.2	5.5		195.9	10.1	6.0	11.9	30.6		1,120
1971	119.1	3.6	27.8	50.9	15.0	79.9	314.2		146.9	3.9		271.7	10.4	3.6	11.5	40.8		1,175
1972	102.3	6.1	32.2	45.4	21.6	81.6	412.2		159.4	14.8		227.5	12.1	5.0	11.6	35.0		1,239
1973	82.8	4.7	23.0	30.0	6.4	84.2	373.8	6.5	142.0		22.6	213.9	11.8	3.4	9.9		17.7	1,089
1974	129.9	4.4	26.4	68.9	9.0	88.9	313.9	9.7	205.3		34.0	197.1	9.8	3.8	11.5		15.9	1,170
1975	176.6	5.4	22.3	37.8	3.0	72.5	322.2	11.8	167.5		30.5	194.7	5.2	4.8	14.4		16.2	1,125
1976	128.8	4.2	24.5	22.2	7.0	68.6	327.6	14.8	191.4		31.3	223.0	5.6	3.0	7.6		11.8	1,115
1977	107.6	5.1	25.6	20.1	5.0	56.8	249.1	13.6	158.5		29.4	167.5	6.1	3.2	7.4		19.6	919
1978	134.1	5.8	27.6	16.2	5.0	61.6	207.0	17.6	245.0		28.0	185.9	6.1	3.2	6.4		17.2	1,011
1979[a]	156.9	5.2	26.0	13.2	5.0	61.1	200.0	24.2	195.0		27.5	113.0	8.2	2.6	6.8		11.7	904

Source: U.S. Department of Agriculture, Foreign Agricultural Service. [a]Preliminary.

in agricultural supply analysis, but probably accurately reflect the *long-term* flexibility of cocoa producers.

The biggest shocks to supply come from the incidence of bad weather, affecting both yields and transportation efficiency, and viral tree diseases which, if unchecked, can destroy large productive stands. Market watchers, therefore, closely monitor the weather and crop reports from Ghana, the Ivory Coast, Nigeria, and Brazil.

The cocoa bean, once harvested, is fermented anywhere from 2 to 9 days. The fermentation generates heat, which kills the germ of the bean and activates enzymes to form the compounds that give cocoa its characteristic flavor. Considerable variation in quality can result from improper or incomplete fermentation. After fermentation, the beans are dried, either by mechanical or natural means, and then bagged for shipping. It is most unusual for cocoa beans to be stored at the point of production, since the quality of the dried beans can deteriorate rapidly in the humidity of the tropics.

The cocoa beans become ripe continuously over several months, so the harvest is not a short-term, labor-intensive activity, as it is for so many agricultural products in the developing world. For the major growing regions, the main-crop harvest goes from October through March, and there is a lower yielding midcrop harvest from May through September. This allows for a continuous supply of cocoa throughout the year and reduces somewhat the seasonality of the marketings.

Once the beans are shipped to the processor, they are cleaned, blended, and roasted. Variations in roasting and blending affect the flavor and aroma of the final product. After roasting, the thin shells of the bean are cracked and removed, leaving the meat or "nibs." The nibs, containing anywhere from 50 to 54% cocoa butter, are crushed mechanically to produce chocolate "liquor." The heat generated by the crushing is enough to liquefy the mass, which may be molded and cooled to form unsweetened or cooking chocolate, or may be left as an intermediate product to be processed further. If the liquor is pressed hydraulically, cocoa butter may be squeezed out to any degree desired. The remaining cocoa cake is ground to produce cocoa powder, on which various government labeling restrictions apply. Low-fat cocoa may contain less than 10% fat, while medium-fat, or just plain "cocoa," has a fat content of 10 to 22%. "Breakfast cocoa" is the richest classification, containing a minimum of 22% fat.

The extracted cocoa butter has a variety of end uses, ranging from cosmetics to pharmaceuticals, but its main use is in the manufacture of chocolate candy. Chocolate liquor, sugar, and cocoa butter are combined in roughly a 3:3:1 ratio to produce sweet chocolate (Wickizer, 1951, p. 311). Other combinations, including other ingredients, are prepared to produce a wide variety of chocolate products.

Historically, the demand for chocolate has driven producers to extract great quantities of cocoa butter, providing far more cocoa powder than the market will absorb. Cocoa powder from which virtually all of the fat has been extracted is of low commercial value and is frequently disposed of. It is difficult, therefore, to systematically relate the total production of cocoa butter to the output of cocoa powder. The price relationships between these two products will be discussed below.

The marketing of cocoa by producing countries varies considerably. The West African nations, almost without exception, have government marketing boards that maintain monopolies over the purchase of beans from the farmers, and the export of beans and cocoa products. Brazil, on the other hand, allows most of the cocoa market to operate in the private sector. The most dramatic marketing change in the last 10 years has been the increase in Brazilian cocoa grindings, and consequent increase in their liquor exports (Gill and Duffus, *Cocoa Statistics*, 1982). The African producing countries have not followed this pattern of trying to increase the domestic value-added of their cocoa industries.

CONSUMPTION OF COCOA AND CHOCOLATE

Six countries in the world (the United States, West Germany, the Netherlands, the USSR, the United Kingdom, and France) dominate imports of cocoa, taking, in 1980, more than two-thirds of the world trade (Gill and Duffus, *Cocoa Statistics*). Consumption data show similar patterns with North America and Europe consuming more than three-quarters of the world total. Other major consumers are Brazil and, to a lesser degree, Japan. With such concentration of consumption in high-income countries, it is a straightforward process to forecast the demand side of the world cocoa market.

The major factors affecting demand are prices, income, and population. Given the consumption patterns to date, one can infer a reasonable long-term income elasticity of demand. This bodes well for the chocolate market in the long run, as countries in South America and Africa improve their per capita incomes. The Asian countries have not proven to be a lucrative market, with consumption being virtually stagnant for the past 10 years at less than 5% of the world total. Cultural and political barriers to expanding the market in that part of the world appear significant.

Aggregate elasticities of demand with respect to cocoa bean price have been estimated to be between −0.25 and −0.5, which is high relative to other major foodstuffs traded internationally (FAO, 1961; Weymar, 1968). This sensitivity can be traced to several factors, including the "luxury" nature of the good, and the willingness of some manufacturers to use butter and powder extenders and substitutes during times of high prices. There is also the practice of holding considerable stocks (3–9 months' worth of grindings) of cocoa by manufacturers, which allows flexibility in timing purchases with respect to current prices.

The major price which can affect the cocoa market is that of sugar. As previously noted, a large fraction of finished chocolate is sugar, so one might expect a complementary relationship between the two inputs. However, sugar-based confections are the chief competitor to chocolate, so there are also strong substitution possibilities. The difficulties in measuring the impact of sugar prices on cocoa consumption stem largely from the tremendous differences in the pattern of sugar prices in the major consuming countries. Considering the EEC, the Soviet Bloc, and the United States, none has allowed complete transmission of international sugar prices to their domestic markets. Casual empiricism suggests the complementary effect may dominate somewhat. In 1980, with rapidly increasing sugar prices, and cocoa prices falling, U.S. cocoa grindings *fell* from their depressed 1979 level. Western Europe, which more effectively insulates its sugar prices, increased their grindings slightly over the same period.

The rate of growth of consumption has recently declined. In the 1950s, 1960s, and 1970s, grindings increased 19, 48, and 9%, respectively (Gill and Duffus, *Cocoa Statistics*). This is largely explained by the price environment, which showed the decade of the 1960s to have an average nominal price 20% *lower* than the 1950s. Of course, the 1970s saw commodity prices grow dramatically in both nominal and real terms, which considerably reduced the long-term trend of higher consumption. The next section discusses the price dynamics of the cocoa market which can be used to anticipate the long-term pattern of production and consumption.

PRICE DYNAMICS IN COCOA

Comparing commodities traded internationally over the decade of the 1970s, one sees cocoa standing apart. Since its end uses are limited and there are no major substitutes, cocoa depends more on its own supply-and-demand fundamentals than food and feed grains, oilseed crops, or sugar. Despite large real price increases in the 1970s, cocoa did not experience the cyclical peaks of most commodities in 1973–1974 and 1979–1980. As seen in Figure 1 (Commodities Research Bureau, Incorporated), cocoa's big rise was in 1977, but this came on the heels of a more

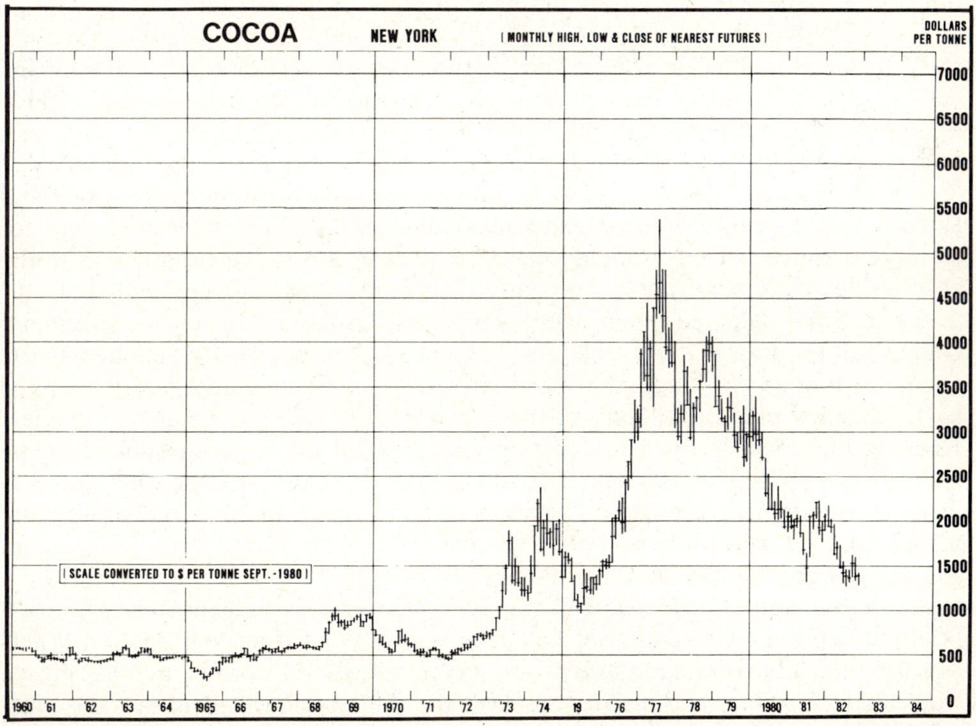

FIGURE 1. Cocoa monthly prices, New York (nearest futures). (*Source*: Commodity Research Bureau, Incorporated.)

or less steady increase in cocoa prices since 1972. The decline since 1977 has been erratic, but the trend has been clear.

Commodity analysts and chartists try to identify long- and short-term cycles, but frequently have difficulty in finding an economic rationale for the apparent periodicity. Cocoa is different for reasons mentioned above. Market commentators like Gill and Duffus and ACLI International have noted that the recent increase in output can be traced to new plantings gaining maturity in places like Brazil and Malaysia. These new growths were the logical and predictable supply response to the high real cocoa prices from 1974 to 1979. There are more young trees yet to come into production in the 1980s, so, in general, large supplies and low prices should be expected to persist for several years. Weymar talked about a 9-year cycle of cocoa prices due to the considerable lags between planting and commercial levels of production. Writing in the period of low prices in the 1960s, he noted the move from the lows of the 1930s and 1940s to the higher prices of the 1950s. Extrapolating his commentary, one would have anticipated the price advance of the early and mid-1970s, and the subsequent decline in the 1980s.

The effect of government on this cycle must be examined on a case-by-case basis. As previously noted, Brazil's cocoa output rose dramatically from 1970 to 1980. A more striking example is that of Malaysia, whose output grew from only 4 thousand tons in 1970 to over 40 thousand tons in 1981. These expansions were the product of joint efforts by the private and public sectors. The government assistance ranged from technical agronomic research to economic subsidies helping farmers finance the first unproductive years. Adding this support to a healthy price environment produced the dramatic supply response.

The West African experience was considerably different, with little growth in total output from 1970 to 1980. The Ivory Coast grew somewhat, while Ghana actually declined, reflecting the policy choices made by the two countries. Table 4 contains the real producer prices for cocoa in Ghana, the Ivory Coast, and Brazil. In each case the nominal price paid farmers was deflated by an index of local food prices to arrive at the real series. The data were taken from Gill and Duffus, *Cocoa Market Reports*, and adjusted so that 1970 was the base year for all three countries. There should be no comparison across the countries as to the absolute levels of prices, but the relative movements clearly may be discerned.

While Brazil allowed much of the world price volatility to reach its farmers, Ghana and the Ivory Coast took a more controlled approach. Relying heavily on cocoa for foreign exchange, the West African countries give their farmers a fixed local currency price and then sell the cocoa internationally for hard currencies. Keeping the cocoa price at a constant real level seems to be the policy of the Ivory Coast, while Ghana, either to encourage domestic food production or to increase the implicit tax rate on exports, or both, has chosen to reduce the real price of cocoa for its farmers. This divergence of real prices has led to a significant smuggling trade between the two countries, making it difficult to determine how much of the output expansion in the Ivory Coast was homegrown. The total production for the two countries has been virtually flat from 1970 to 1981 (1,098 to 1,046 thousand metric tons). By way of contrast, Brazil's production has grown from 182 to 324 thousand metric tons over the same period. Any efforts the West African governments have made to increase their revenue base have failed to overcome the lack of incentive that low domestic prices offer farmers.

TABLE 4. Real Producer Price Indexes, 1970 = 100

Year	Ghana	Ivory Coast	Brazil
1970	100.0	100.0	100.0
1971	94.0	106.1	71.2
1972	96.3	107.1	91.1
1973	92.6	98.6	179.0
1974	89.6	113.2	219.5
1975	77.6	142.6	173.2
1976	55.5	135.1	238.0
1977	37.1	104.7	458.8
1978	42.8	122.0	339.6
1979	50.8	106.1	291.6
1980	40.1	101.4	233.8

Source: Gill and Duffus, *Cocoa Market Report,* No. 303, September 1982, p.24.

While the policies of Brazil and Malaysia may appear to be quite positive for the farmers, and those of West Africa negative, it is important to note that if all producing countries had encouraged new plantings in the 1970s, the long-term price cycle would have been exaggerated considerably. The subsidies produce a larger supply adjustment than the private market would have generated, and consequently, lower prices in the cyclical trough. The high capital costs and long recovery period for new cocoa plantings make "countercyclical" supply policies impractical for most individuals and governments. To anyone predicting long-term supply, it is critical to examine the producers on a case-by-case basis, since it is obvious there is no such thing as a single world price to which everyone responds.

One avenue out of this dilemma, which has been tried by Brazil, is to expand processing capacity in the producing countries. Since cocoa liquor is more storable than cocoa beans, producers having processing capabilities have much more control over their inventory positions. Having both suppliers and demanders able to make storage decisions gives the market more balance and should reduce the amplitude of the price cycle. Side benefits of third-world processing include the increase in value-added, and the lower shipping costs of cocoa liquor.

Very recently, the International Cocoa Agreement (ICCA) was established to stabilize the world price between $1.10 and $1.50 per pound. If prices fall below the $1.10 level, the International Cocoa Organization is authorized to build buffer stocks totaling 250 thousand tonnes or more. On the high end of the scale, the release of these stocks may be mandated. Large supplies, a weak world economy, and a strong dollar have driven the price well below the floor level. It is not clear yet whether the provisions of the ICCA are too weak, or if the buffer-stock scheme is underfunded to achieve its goals, but so far this international stabilization plan has been ineffectual. It will always be important to watch the negotiations surrounding the ICCA, but presently, there is little evidence to suggest that this approach will break the long-term price cycle.

The short-term price behavior is largely a function of weather, pests, and politics. Since so much of production is traded, and that production is concentrated in a few countries, any shock affecting the crop in these countries will immediately affect the world price. Many trading and manufacturing firms directly monitor the situation in the key growing areas. Since this information hits the market randomly, and is factored in quickly, there is little that can be identified by way of regular-period short-run price cycles.

A factor limiting price volatility in the short run is the practice of cocoa processors to maintain large inventories of beans. Like coffee, cocoa beans vary considerably in taste. Chocolate manufacturers search across these beans, and blend various growths to produce the character they desire in their chocolate. Since there are considerable economies to continuous production, and not all growths are always available in the marketplace, there is a strong desire to maintain large stocks. As large as these stocks are, they are not price-inelastic. The stock-consumption ratio is a good indicator of the expected direction of supply and demand, and many traders correlate the histories of prices and inventories to anticipate future movements.

GOLD AS AN INTERNATIONAL STANDARD. In the case of most commodities, the representation of prices in U.S. dollars is commonly accepted. We must consider, however, that the tropical products, especially cocoa, may be also expressed in terms not tied directly to U.S. currency. The USSR, a major importer of cocoa, may make its buying decisions based on the value of cocoa relative to its own currency or some international standard. In recent years of economic problems in the USSR, it has been accepted that the Soviets will sell gold to meet many of their import commitments. It is therefore reasonable to look at the price of cocoa in terms of what can be purchased for 1 oz of gold.

In Figure 2(*b*) we see both the spot price of cocoa (solid line) and the spot price of gold (broken line). During the period from October 1980 through January 1983 the price of cocoa, in U.S. dollars, declined from $2,200 per tonne to $1,300 per tonne, then rallied back to $2,200 and declined to new lows before recovering. During this period, gold prices declined rapidly before beginning a recovery in June 1982. Since a high gold price means relatively cheap cocoa in the case of the Soviets, Figure 2(*a*) shows prices rising instead of falling during the first months. As the price of gold declines the rising price of cocoa becomes exceptionally sharp. This perspective on cocoa prices can help explain the timing of cocoa purchases that would not be evident in terms of other currencies or standards.

SEASONALITY. There is only a very weak seasonal pattern to prices, despite a large seasonal component to consumption. As previously noted, the cocoa harvest is almost continuous from October through March in the major producing areas. One might expect a seasonal low in prices to occur in the last calendar quarter, but the evidence here is weak. Gill and Duffus reports monthly New York spot prices for Ghanaian beans from 1925. Excluding the price-controlled war years and the period in which spot prices were unavailable, there are 47 crop years. The low price of the season occurred in the October–December quarter 17 times, and the low was in the second through fourth quarter, 11, 11, and 8 times, respectively. The new crop fails to offer the season's lowest price in even a majority

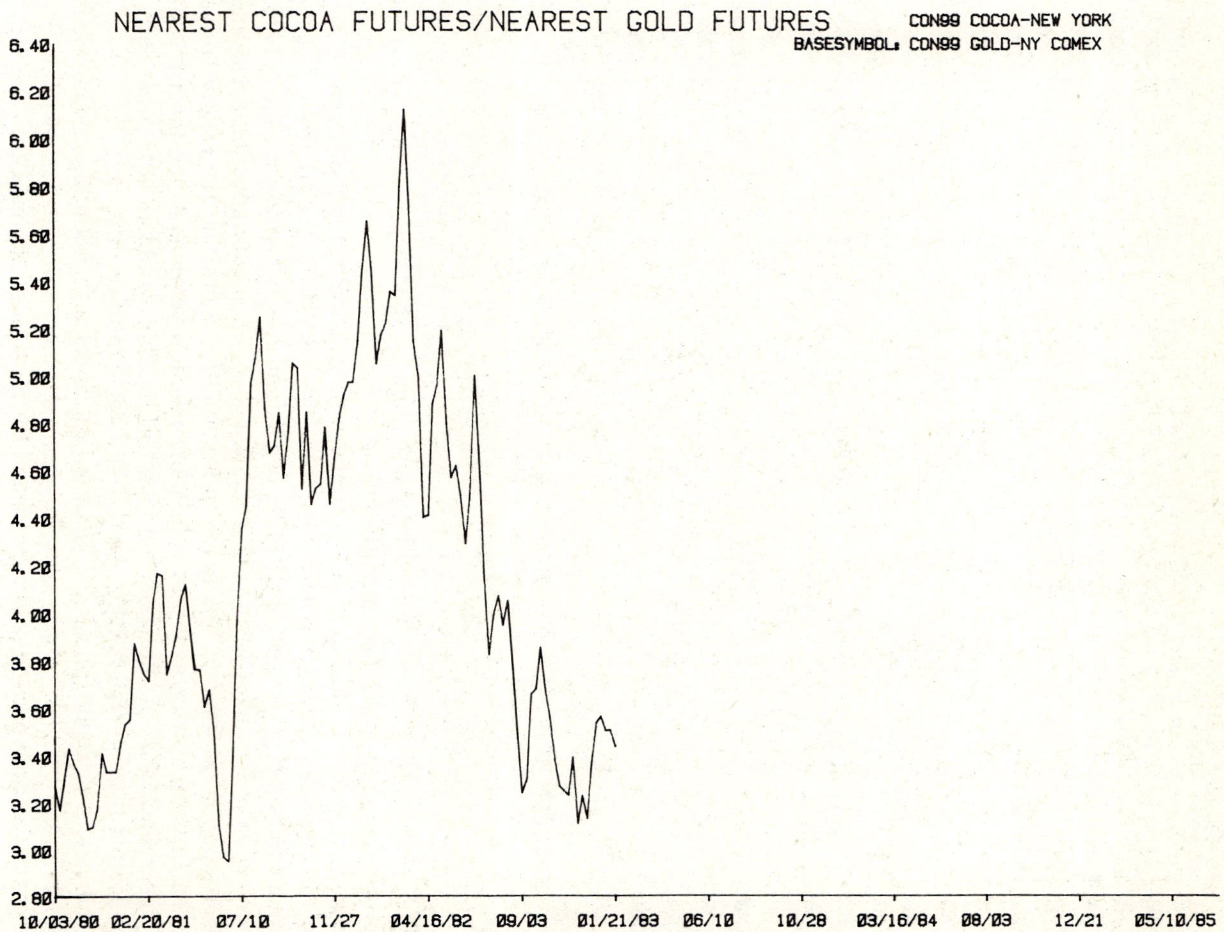

FIGURE 2. (*a*) Cocoa divided by gold (cocoa per oz of gold)

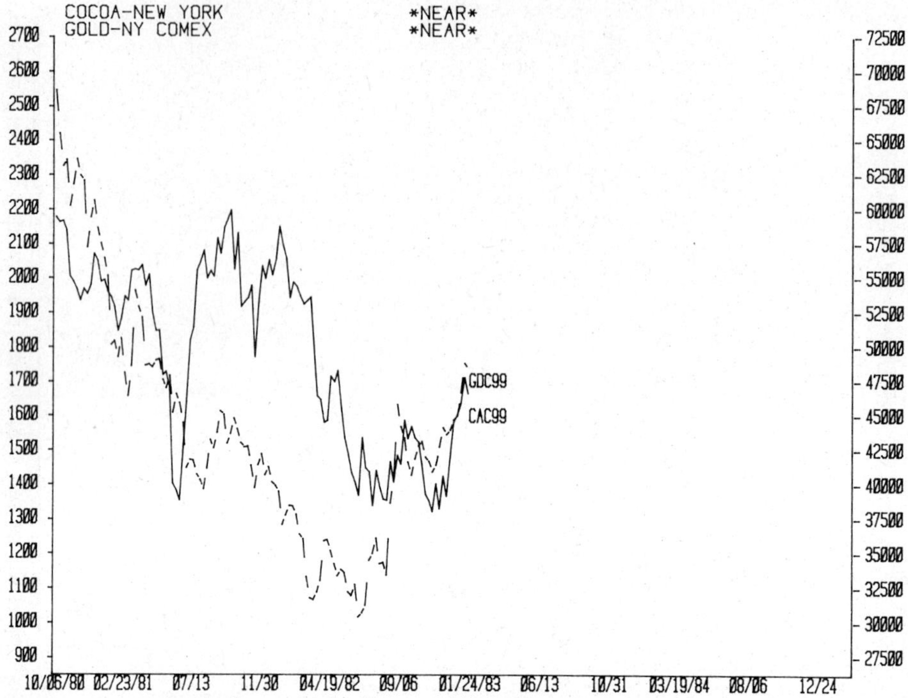

(*b*) Cocoa cash prices weekly (gold-dash; cocoa-solid).

FIGURE 2. Continued.

of the years, which shows how supply-and-demand shocks throughout the year can disguise a normal seasonal pattern.

Figure 3 shows a statistical analysis of cocoa seasonality. Although there is a decline in prices during the early harvest, the combined period from August through February shows a moderately consistent downward trend. Since 1976, when cocoa prices moved from \$0.60–\$2.00 per lb, we must expect an aseasonal distortion in these figures. The scale on Figure 3(*b*) shows that the relative price movements were twice as large in the most recent 4 years as in the most recent 11 years [inclusive of the data in Figure 3(*b*)]. This would indicate that price movements from 1976 forward would easily distort the results.

Labys and Granger (pp.66–68) analyzed the spectra for monthly cocoa prices from 1950 through 1965 (see Figure 4), representing a long stretch of relatively stable prices. In general, the spectra found for most other commodities were flat and the authors conclude that most can be accounted for by a random walk model. Cocoa, however, seemed to be an exception, exhibiting evidence of seasonal tendencies.

CYCLIC ANALYSIS. Very few commodities show nonrandom cyclic behavior, but cocoa is among those that seem to have a significant pattern. According to another study by Labys and Granger (p.77), a spectral analysis of daily prices for a 1-year interval showed the presence of a rising trend in the spectrum. This implies that the first differences in prices, which represent the trending component, are negatively autocorrelated. Given the short intervals of the data used, this

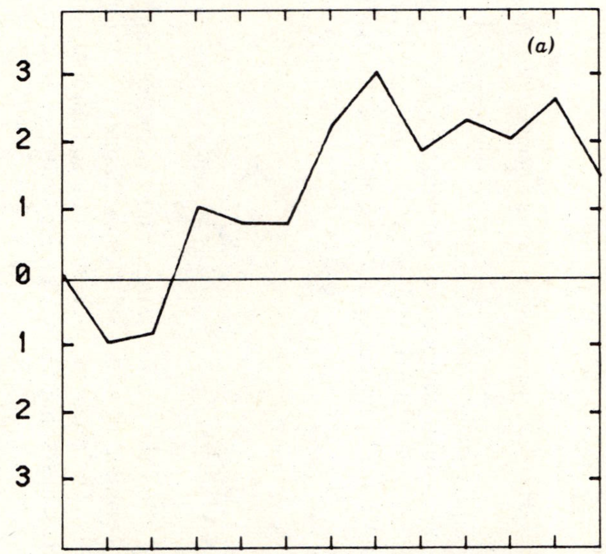

	J-F	F-M	M-A	A-M	M-J	J-J	J-A	A-S	S-O	O-N	N-D	D-J
Average Move	-1	0.1	1.8	-0.3	-0.1	1.4	0.7	-1.2	0.4	-0.3	0.5	-1.2
% Reliable	72.8	63.7	72.8	54.6	36.4	72.8	72.8	54.6	63.7	63.7	54.6	63.7
Avg. Up Move	0.8	1.2	2.9	2.1	0.8	2.8	1.9	3	1.7	2	2.1	2.1
Avg. Down Move	1.7	1.8	1	2.3	1.5	2.3	2.4	4.7	1.8	1.7	1.3	3.1
Greatest Up Move	1.3	3.6	9.1	4.8	1.6	8.5	4.9	5.5	3.6	5.1	3.1	5.1
Greatest Down Move	3.4	5	1.3	4.3	3.9	4.4	4.7	12	2.9	4.6	3.4	4.8

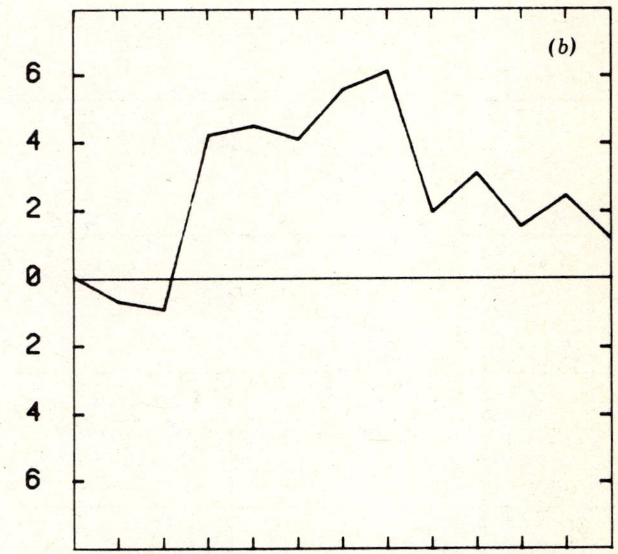

	J-F	F-M	M-A	A-M	M-J	J-J	J-A	A-S	S-O	O-N	N-D	D-J
Average Move	-0.8	-0.3	5.1	0.2	-0.5	1.4	0.5	-4.2	1.1	-1.6	0.9	-1.3
% Reliable	75	50	100	50	25	50	75	75	75	75	50	75
Avg. Up Move	1.3	2.5	5.1	4.2	0.7	5.9	2.2	5.5	2.4	0.8	2.8	5.1
Avg. Down Move	1.5	3	0	3.7	3.9	3.1	4.7	7.5	2.9	2.4	1.1	3.4
Greatest Up Move	1.3	3.6	9.1	4.8	1.2	8.5	4.7	5.5	3.6	0.8	3.1	5.1
Greatest Down Move	2.8	5	0	4.3	3.9	4.4	4.7	12	2.9	4.6	2	3.8

FIGURE 3. Cocoa seasonality, nearest futures. (*a*) 11 years. (*b*) 4 years.

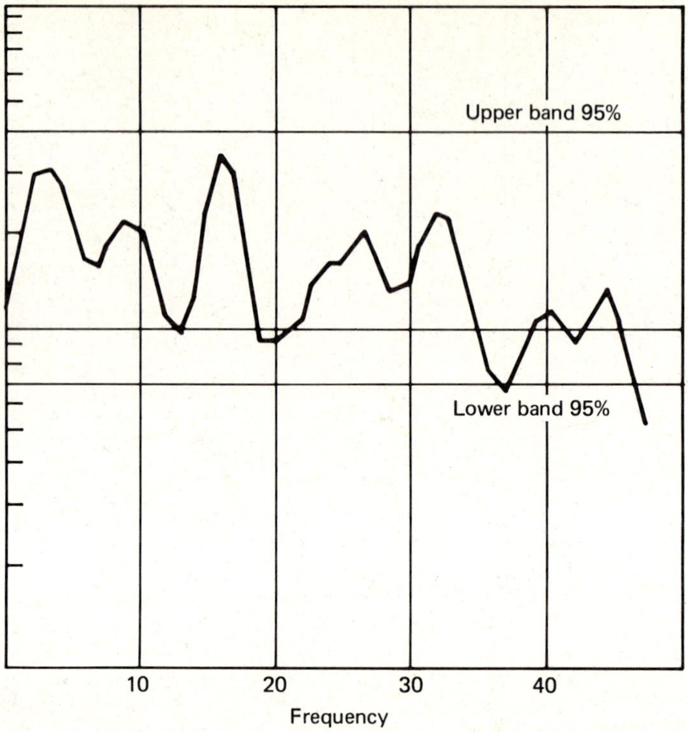

FIGURE 4. Power spectrum of first differences, cocoa futures prices monthly, 1950–1965.

result could not be caused by a seasonal component, but must be attributed to shorter-length trading cycles or other actual price behavior. In other tests of the cross spectrum (cash prices and three consecutive futures prices), cocoa again showed coherence.

FUTURES TRADING IN COCOA

Cocoa futures are actively traded on the Coffee, Sugar and Cocoa Exchange in New York and at the London Terminal Market. Smaller exchanges are found in Amsterdam, Hamburg, and Paris. The range of interests in these futures markets is wide, and this section will discuss some of the trading patterns and market participants.

The Cocoa Association of London was formed in 1926 following a sharp increase in cocoa trade after World War I. The dealers used the futures market, established 2 years later, to hedge increasing stocks resulting from new production. There was erratic volume and little speculative participation for the first 10 years. Trading was suspended during 1940–1950 when the price of cocoa, as well as its distribution, was controlled by the Ministry of Food. After trading resumed in 1951, volume slowly grew until shortages in the late 1960s caused substantially increased business. Basic trading information is shown in Table 5.

TABLE 5. Cocoa—The London Cocoa Terminal Market Association

Contract size	10 metric tons
Price quotation	Pounds sterling and decimals per metric ton
Minimum price fluctuation	£0.50 per metric ton or £5.00 per contract
Maximum price fluctuation	When, during trading hours, there is in respect of any position other than the spot month an accepted bid or trade of £40 below or above the closing price of the previous day, the market will close for 15 min and will reopen with a special call with limitless trading until the close of the day.
Trading hours	Monday–Friday, 1000–1300 hr; 1430 hr to close of 1650 hours call. Calls at 1000, 1250, 1530, and 1645 hr.
Delivery points	London, Liverpool, Avonmouth, Hull, Teesside, Amsterdam, Antwerp, Hamburg, and Rotterdam
Customary delivery months	March, May, July, September, and December beginning 15 months prior to expiration
Grades	Cocoa is acceptable from countries defined in the No. 5 Cocoa Contract Rule. Cocoa deliverable against the contract shall be 10 metric tons net weight of a gross and quality as defined in the rules exwarehouse-approved by the association in the United Kingdom or delivered in approved warehouse in Amsterdam, Antwerp, Hamburg, and Rotterdam.

The trading in New York changed in two ways in 1979. First, the New York Cocoa Exchange merged with the New York Coffee and Sugar Exchange, and moved to the modern trading facilities shared by the major New York futures exchanges. Second, the contract was respecified to deliver 10 metric tons (22,046 lb) of cocoa instead of 30,000 lb. This latter move made the New York contract conform to the London weight specification. The two changes exposed the contract to much more trading interest, expanding the liquidity in the process. The complete specifications of the New York contract are given in Table 6, showing the premia associated with different growths, and the delivery procedures.

Participants in the market include a wide range of hedgers and speculators, but not all of the parties in the cocoa industry are equally represented. It seems that the major government exporting groups in West Africa do not hedge their crops in the futures markets, preferring fixed-rate contracts with dealers. Several reasons have been suggested why these exporters do not hedge, including the financing difficulties associated with hard currency margins, and basis risk associated with London or New York deliveries. These may be disadvantages preventing these contracts from being a perfect exporter's instrument, but they have not prevented other, primarily private, exporters from hedging their cocoa. A more likely reason is that the committee structure of these government boards does not allow the flexibility necessary to trade effectively on the futures exchanges. The potential gains from a good hedging strategy are significant, and may prove a more fruitful

TABLE 6. Cocoa—New York Coffee, Sugar, and Cocoa Exchange Incorporated

Contract unit	10 metric tons
Price quotation	Dollars per metric ton
Minimum price fluctuation	\$1 per metric ton or \$10 per contract
Maximum daily price fluctuation	\$88 above or below the previous day's settlement price. Limits are expandable to \$132. Limits removed from the spot month on and after the first notice day.
Trading hours	9:30 a.m.–3:00 p.m. eastern time
Delivery	From licensed warehouses in the Port of New York District, Delaware River Port District, or Hampton Roads
Customary delivery months	March, May, July, September, and December
Deliverable growths	The growth of any country of clime, including new or yet unknown growths. Growths are divided into three classifications: Group A deliverable at a premium of \$160 per tonne (including Ghana, Nigeria, the Ivory Coast, among others). Group B deliverable at a premium of \$80 per tonne (including Bahia, Central America, Venezuela, among others). Group C deliverable at par (including Sanchez, Haiti, Malaysia, and all others). Deliveries are discounted for subnormal-size beans.
Grades	Established by exchange licensed graders in accordance with specified tolerances for defects, bean count, and other standards
Position limits	None
CFTC large trader reporting level	25 contracts or more
First notice day	10 full business days prior to the first business day of the delivery month. Beginning with the September 1982 delivery, the first notice day will be 10 full business days prior to the first business day of the delivery month
Last notice and last trading day	10 full business days prior to the last business day of the delivery month. Trading in the current month ceases at noon (eastern standard time) on the last notice and last trading day. Notices may not be issued, nor warehouse certificates delivered on exchange half-days.

avenue for the developing countries than the complex and sometimes troublesome international agreements.

Once the cocoa is out of the producing countries' hands, a host of dealers and processors become active. Those dealing in beans or liquor, the price of which moves in a parallel fashion, usually make offsetting purchases and sales of futures against specific shipments of cocoa beans or beans in the warehouse. The futures transactions may be independent decisions, or if a seller wishes to make delivery, but not in New York, the seller may find an appropriate buyer, and they would enter into an "against actuals" contract, which would involve commitments to trade futures and physical commodities.

Manufacturers and consumers of chocolate products have a slightly more complex problem. Of course, chocolate makers may hedge their purchase of beans, or their inventories of raw product, but to hedge their sales, they need a strong price relationship between cocoa beans and its component products. Since the end uses of butter and powder are related, and neither face significant competition in their end uses, one might expect a strong relationship, but, in fact, there can be a surprising degree of variation.

As previously noted, butter and powder can be produced in variable proportions, with the relative demand for butter usually being strong enough to produce an excess supply of powder. This leads to a situation where, historically, butter prices "drive" bean (and liquor) prices. A good example is seen in 1973, when butter and bean prices doubled but powder prices increased by only 28% (Gill and Duffus, *Cocoa Statistics*). By 1977 the situation was different. With surpluses being worked off, powder prices rose by 255%, while beans and butter increased 110 and 39%, respectively. Figure 5 represents the 1970–1981 price history of New York spot West African beans and the ratio of powder to butter prices. The relationship is not perfect, but it is clear that in periods of severe shortage, powder escapes from its excess supply situation and is priced according to what the traffic will bear.

This type of variation in product prices tests the abilities of the merchant, since simple hedges in the cocoa bean market will provide only imperfect protection against price risk. Here combinations of futures, forward sales, and inventory control will provide the best results. It is no accident that firms that deal in manufacturing cocoa products work in all three markets (liquor, butter, and powder) so that they may have several instruments under their control. This approach can be viewed as a portfolio which is adjusted depending on the returns of the particular market segment. The hedging possibilities in this portfolio are a major source of risk management.

This perspective on cocoa prices can help explain the timing of cocoa purchases that would not be evident in terms of other currencies of standards.

There are a number of identifiable categories of cocoa speculators. These range from day traders acting on short-term price swings, to international arbitrageurs between London and New York, and position traders who speculate on the basis of charts or fundamentals. The speculators add liquidity to the market, facilitate price discovery, and consequently, enhance the efficiency of hedging.

The following section details the mechanics of hedging in cocoa beans and products, and documents the complex ways in which the cash and futures markets interact.

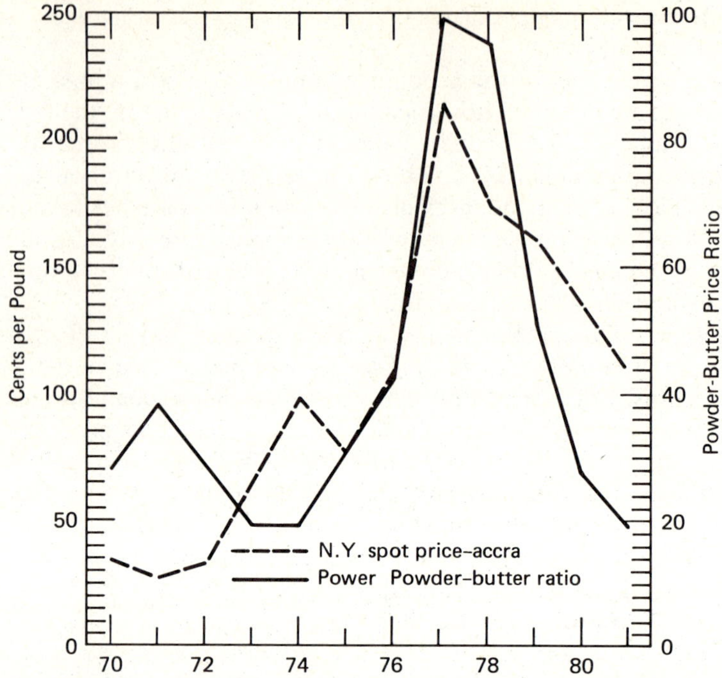

FIGURE 5. Cocoa spot prices (ACCRA, NY) vs. cocoa powder–butter price ratio.

HEDGING APPLICATIONS IN COCOA BEANS[1]

TRADING PRICE IS FIXED. Cocoa beans may be processed into cocoa liquor, cocoa butter, cocoa cake, and cocoa powder. A business which is involved in any one of these stages may use the futures market to hedge itself against unpredictable price fluctuations. The first illustration will show how hedging may be applied to transactions where the trading price of cocoa beans is fixed.

Suppose that an international trade house agrees to buy 10,000 metric tons of cocoa beans from the Ghanaian Marketing Board on September 1st. The terms of the sales contract call for delivery in December and the agreed-upon price is $2,400 per metric ton F.O.B. Once the trade house enters into the commitment, it has one of two options readily available to it. It may wait for a higher price at which to sell its cocoa beans or hedge itself by participating in the futures market. Under the first alternative, the trade house is capable of earning windfall profits if a tightening demand in Ghanaian cocoa causes prices to rise. Should prices fall, however, the trade house may suffer huge financial losses. Under the second alternative, the trade house can minimize its chances of "making or breaking" by using the futures market as a hedging mechanism. The house does this by selling 1,000 contracts of December futures at $2,300 per metric ton on September 1st(see Table 7). The trade house thereby manages to insulate itself from the fluctuation of bean prices. A month passes and December cocoa falls to $2,100

[1]D. Koutras, E. Meir, and R. Ng, *Commodity Hedging Operations and Strategies: An Introduction*, Drexel Burnham Lambert, New York, NY, 1982.

TABLE 7. Hedging in Beans When Trade Price Is Fixed

Ghanaian Cocoa Marketing Board	International Trade House X	Bean Processor Y
	September 1st	
Cash market: Sells 10,000 metric tons of Ghanaian cocoa for December delivery at $2,400 per metric ton F.O.B.	Cash market: Buys 10,000 metric tons of Ghanaian cocoa for December delivery at $2,400 per metric ton F.O.B.	Cash market: No activity.
Futures market: Nothing is done since sales transaction was price-fixed and there were no previous hedges placed in the futures market.	Futures market: Sells 1,000 December futures at $2,300 per metric ton to hedge its physical purchase.	Futures market: No activity.
	October 1st	
Cash market: No activity.	Cash market: Sells 10,000 metric tons of Ghanaian cocoa for December delivery at $2,200 per metric ton F.O.B.	Cash market: Buys 10,000 metric tons of Ghanaian cocoa at $2,200 per metric ton F.O.B.
Futures market: No activity.	Futures market: Buys 1,000 December futures at $2,100 per metric ton. Gain from futures $2 million.	Futures market: Sells 1,000 December futures to hedge against a possible decline in cocoa bean prices at $2,100 per metric ton.

TABLE 7. Continued

Ghanaian Cocoa Marketing Board	Trade House X	Bean Processor Y
	December 15th	
Cash market: Receives $24 million from trade house.	Cash market: Pays $24 million to Ghanaian Marketing Board and receives $22 million from Processor Y. Loss from cash market $2 million.	Cash market: Pays $22 million to trade house, receives 10,000 metric tons of cocoa. However, spot is currently $2,150 per metric ton. Loss from cash market and $500,000.
Futures market: No activity.	Futures market: No activity.	Futures market: Buys 1,000 December futures at $2,050 per metric ton to release hedge. Gain from futures equals $500,000.
Net gain or loss: $0	Net gain or loss: $0	Net gain or loss: $0

Therefore, hedging enables all parties involved in our example to ''price fix'' at an acceptable level by avoiding any losses or gains from any unnecessary price fluctuations.

per metric ton from $2,300 per metric ton. At the same time, Ghanaian cocoa is approximately $2,200 per metric ton (December) and the trade house finds a willing buyer at this price.

Once the trade house sells 10,000 metric tons of December delivery cocoa to bean processor Y, it lifts its hedge by buying back 1,000 December contracts. Consequently, it realizes a gain of $2 million from the futures transaction, but loses the same amount in the cash market. Altogether, its net gain and loss is zero. Meanwhile, the bean processor now assumes the risk of price fluctuations. The processor may hope for an increase in the price of cocoa beans or hedge against a possible decline by selling cocoa bean futures. The processor chooses to hedge by selling 1,000 December futures on October 1st at $2,100 per metric ton. When Processor Y receives the cocoa, say on December 18th, processor Y will pay $22 million for the shipment and buy back 1,000 December futures at $2,050 per metric ton, since futures prices have declined over the interim. Had Processor Y not hedged and prices of cocoa beans declined, Processor Y would have been hurt by the higher price paid for bean purchases at $2,200 per metric ton when spot can currently be attained at about $2,150.

Hedging is possible because cash and future prices generally move in the same direction and experience the same proportionate change. However, a perfect hedge is seldom attainable because of the difference which exists between the quantity and type of bean intended for hedging and that which is specified for futures delivery. Therefore, it is important that one analyze the situation completely in order to arrive at as perfect a hedge as possible.

TRADING PRICE: DIFFERENTIAL BASIS. The previous example illustrated how hedging would work in a theoretical case where the price of physicals was fixed at the time of the transaction. The price of physicals, however, is often pegged against the value of futures. The following illustration presents such an example.

Suppose the Ghanaian Cocoa Marketing Board sells 10,000 metric tons of December shipment to Merchant X on September 1st at $100 above December. Through trade practice, the two parties understand that whatever December closes at prior to the first day of delivery notices, that price plus $100 will serve as their binding transactions price. For purposes of illustration, we have assumed that delivery notices are not posted until December 15th and that the Ghanaian Marketing Board has formerly sold 1,000 December futures to hedge its 10,000 metric ton inventory. Table 8 shows the process of lifting the hedge conducted by the Ghanaian Marketing Board on September 1st. The Ghanaian Marketing Board appropriately buys back 1,000 December futures once it completes the cash deal with Trade House X. Trade House X in turn hedges itself by buying 1,000 December futures at $2,300, since it must pay $100 over December upon delivery. Merchant X does this for fear that bean prices will rise substantially between the present date and December. If this happens, Merchant X may no longer be in a viable business because merchants who have hedged would be capable of successfully undercutting X's prices. By hedging, Merchant X will not only be able to insulate against price swings, but also be able to project budget and expenses with a smaller margin of error because of the prices X has locked in.

On October 1st, Merchant X receives a call from Processor Y who is interested in buying 10,000 metric tons of cocoa beans for December delivery. X decides to

TABLE 8. Hedging in Beans When Trade Price Is Given on a Differential Basis

Ghanaian Cocoa Marketing Board	Trade House X	Bean Processor Y
	September 1st	
Cash market: Sells 10,000 metric tons of Ghanaian cocoa to Trade House X for December shipment at $100 above December.	Cash market: Buys 10,000 metric tons of Ghanaian cocoa for December delivery at $100 above December.	Cash market: No activity.
Futures market: Buys back the 1,000 lots of December that it sold previously on the futures market as a hedge against its 10,000 metric ton inventory.	Futures market: Buys 1,000 December contracts at $2,300 per metric ton as a hedge against X's cash purchase above.	Futures market: No activity.
	October 1st	
Cash market: No activity.	Cash market: Sells 10,000 metric tons of Ghanaian cocoa to Processor Y at 150 points above December for December delivery.	Cash market: Buys 10,000 metric tons of Ghanaian cocoa from Trade House X at 150 points above December, to be received in December.
Futures market: No activity.	Futures market: Sells 1,000 December contracts at $2,325 per metric ton upon cash sale above. Previous hedge is lifted. Gain from futures: $250,000 ($250 per contract multiplied by 1,000 contracts).	Futures market: Buys 1,000 December contracts at $2,325 per metric ton to hedge against Y's cash purchase.

Ghanaian Cocoa Marketing Board	Trade House X	Bean Processor Y
	December 14th	
Cash market: Receives \$25 million. December futures is \$2,425 and \$100 over December is \$2,525. (\$2,525 per metric ton × 10,000 metric tons)	Cash market: Receives \$25 million (\$2,425 + \$150) × 10,000 metric tons. Pays \$25 million. Cash gain is \$500,000.	Cash market: Pays \$25 million (\$2,525 + \$150) × 10,000 metric tons. Receives 10,000 metric tons. Implicit loss in cash market is \$1 million, \$25.75–\$24.75 million, the October 1st bygone purchase price.
Futures market: No activity.	Futures market: No activity.	Futures market: Sells 10,000 December contracts at \$2,425 per metric ton to release Y's hedge. Gain on futures market is \$1 million.
Net gain or loss: \$0	Net gain: \$750,000	Net gain or loss: \$0

offer 10,000 metric tons of December shipment for $150 above December. Taking into account the present market conditions, Processor Y finds the price agreeable and decides to take Merchant X up on the offer. Once both parties consent to the sale, X lifts the formerly placed hedge by selling 1,000 contracts of December futures at $2,325. Merchant X makes a $250,000 profit in the process. Similarly, Processor Y buys 1,000 December futures at $2,325 to hedge against the unpredictable price swings of cocoa beans. Regardless of the beans' trend, Processor Y expects to earn a reasonable rate of return once the acceptable bean prices are locked-in. On December 14th, Processor Y receives 10,000 metric tons of beans and pays $25.75 million for them. In turn, it releases a hedge by selling back 1,000 December futures at $2,425. Through the entire transaction, Processor Y earns $0. This is summarized in Table 7. At this point, Processor Y may elect to sell additional contracts of futures to hedge against the possible decline of beans that are now in inventory.

COCOA BUTTER HEDGING STRATEGY. Cocoa butter constitutes an important element in the manufacture of confectionaries. Instead of processing cocoa beans directly, many chocolate manufacturers find it more convenient to buy cocoa butter directly. They enter into purchase agreements where the agreed price of cocoa butter is linked to the so-called "butter ratio." The butter ratio is defined as the ratio of cocoa butter price over bean price. Under this type of arrangement, the buyer is generally empowered with the authority to fix prices. The following illustration offers such an example.

Suppose Trade House X buys 200 metric tons of cocoa butter for March delivery at $5,000 per metric ton on January 2nd because it sees that as a reasonable offering price (see Table 9). Early next morning (January 3rd) Chocolate Manufacturer Y approaches Trade House X to see whether it would sell 200 metric tons of cocoa butter for May delivery. After allowing for storage, transportation, and a small markup, Trade House X decides that it would be feasible to sell May delivery at $5,300 per metric ton. Based on the prevailing price of May beans ($2,000), X thereupon tenders an offer to Manufacturer Y at a butter-to-bean ratio of 2.65: butter price of $5,300 per May bean futures price of $2,000 (see Table 9). Since 2.65 is in line with current market conditions and delivery will be promptly made in May, Manufacturer Y accepts the offer. Upon consummation of the sale, Trade House X becomes fearful that bean prices will decline between now and May. If prices decline substantially, Trade House X's anticipated profit may turn into an unexpected loss. To avoid such an unpleasant experience, Trade House X sells an equivalent amount of May beans—530 metric tons (2.65 × 200 metric tons), or 53 contracts, in the futures market. Likewise, Chocolate Manufacturer Y is fearful that bean prices will rise between the present date and May delivery. Since Manufacturer Y has agreed to buy butter at a 2.65 butter-to-bean ratio, Manufacturer Y buys an equivalent amount of beans (530 = 2.65 × 200 metric tons), or 53 Mays at $2,000 as a hedge. This is illustrated in Table 9.

By February 3rd, May beans have fallen to $1,670 per metric ton. Manufacturer Y thinks that this is the lowest price that May beans can conceiveably fall to before delivery notices are issued. Manufacturer Y therefore instructs X's broker to buy 53 contracts of May for X's account. Once the broker buys 53 Mays at $1,670, the cash butter deal that X and Y struck on January 3rd becomes binding

TABLE 9. Hedging in Cocoa Butter When Butter Price Is Based on Butter Ratio

Trade House X	Chocolate Manufacturer Y
January 2nd	
Cash market: Buys 200 metric tons of cocoa butter for March delivery at \$5,000 per metric ton.	Cash market: No activity.
Futures market: No activity.	Futures market: No activity.
January 3rd	
Cash market: Sells 200 metric tons of cocoa butter for May delivery at a price of 2.65 butter-to-bean ratio, against May beans. X arrives at this ratio through the following calculation: $\frac{\$5,300 \text{ (May butter after storage and markup)}}{\$2,000 \text{ (May futures on January 3rd)}} = 2.65.$	Cash market: Buys 200 metric tons of cocoa butter for May delivery at a 2.65 butter-to-bean ratio.
Futures market: Sells 53 contracts of May beans at 2,000 per metric ton to hedge against an unforeseen decline in bean prices. Since Trade House X wishes to maintain a butter-to-bean ratio of 2.65, it has to sell 2.65 × 200 = 530 metric tons of beans to cover the cash transaction above. This is equivalent to 53 May contracts.	Futures market: Buys 53 contracts of May beans at \$2,000 per metric ton to hedge against an unforeseen rise in bean prices. The price Y will pay for cash butter (above) is contingent upon the price at which Y will fix May beans.
February 3rd	
Cash market: Price is fixed by the buyer (Manufacturer Y) at 2.65 × \$1,670 = \$4,425.50, with \$1,670 being the prevailing price of May beans. The cash sale that the two parties made on January 3rd becomes binding at \$4,425.50 per metric ton. Loss from each transaction: (\$5,000 − \$4,425.50) = \$574.5 per metric ton.	Cash market: Cocoa butter price for January 3rd is finalized at \$4,425.50 (2.65 × 1,670 per metric ton), once Y instructs X's broker to buy 53 Mays at \$1,670 for X's account. Implicit savings from cash market \$5,300 (January 3rd) − \$4,425.50 (February 3rd) = \$874.5 per metric ton gain.
Futures market: Price of May futures is now at \$1,670 per metric ton. Liquidated futures hedge initiated on January 3rd by buying back 53 Mays at \$1,670. Gain from future transaction: (\$2,000 − \$1,670) = \$874.5 per metric ton.	Futures market: Lifts hedge initiated on January 3rd by selling 53 Mays at \$1,670. Loss from future transaction: (\$2,000 − \$1,670) × 2.65 = \$874.5 per metric ton.
Net gain or loss: \$300 per metric ton.	Net gain or loss: \$0

In conclusion, Trade House X managed to lock in a profit of \$300 per metric ton on January 3rd when it hedged by selling 53 May futures upon the cash butter sale.

at $4,425.50 metric tons (2.65 × $1,670). Moreover, Trade House X's short futures position automatically becomes eliminated. In the process, Trade House X acknowledges losing $574.50 per metric ton in the cash market. However, it manages to earn $874.50 per metric ton in the futures market because of its hedging practice. The Trade House's net gain is $300 per metric ton. Similarly, Manufacturer Y loses $874.50 per metric ton in the futures market upon selling the 53 Mays at $1,670 per metric ton. However, Manufacturer Y has indirectly saved $874.50 per metric ton in the cash market by buying May delivery at $4,425.50, as opposed to $5,300 on January 3rd. In essence, Manufacturer Y fixed the cash butter price at $5,3000 per metric ton, when Y bought the 53 Mays on January 3rd. Y did this because he expected to earn a reasonable return on the chocolate candy once cocoa butter was available at $5,300 per metric ton.

CONCLUSION

The cocoa markets in London and New York form the basis for an active international trade. Producing countries have the opportunity to sell in any of a number of competing consuming nations, with the confidence that the price they receive is a fair reflection of world supply and demand. Consumers of cocoa have the same advantage. With active trade and speculation, the markets show considerable efficiency in price discovery, and short-run price distortions are more readily avoided.

In the long run the cocoa market seems destined to continue in decade-long swings of high and low prices. In some cases these swings may have been exaggerated by government policies artificially encouraging supply in times of high prices. Attempts to form an international agreement to mitigate these long-term swings have not worked to date. The decade of the 1980s will probably show reduced plantings of new trees, and, in extreme cases where prices are kept very low, failure to replace unproductive trees. The growth in consumption, due to low prices and increases in population and income, may then catch up with cocoa supplies and the cycle of increased prices and production could begin anew. In the short run the price of cocoa can be expected to deviate from these long-term values as sudden changes or "shocks" hit both supply and demand.

An idealistic, long-term solution to the cocoa cycle would be futures contracts with several years to maturity. Producing countries could hedge over several seasons and provide a stable return, dampening out the boom and bust cycle. The suggestion is impractical in that the current volume of trade in the existing "distant" contracts (1 year out) is quite small, reflecting a lack of interest in long-term hedging or speculating. Until parties on both sides of the transaction have planning horizons of several years, so that both suppliers and demanders can identify a hedgable risk, there will continue to be a lack of interest in far distant futures.

REFERENCES

ACLI International. *Commodity Research Bulletin*. "Cocoa—A Special Report," New York, NY, April 1980.

Akari, H., and Cummings, J. T. *Agricultural Supply Response, A Survey of the Econometric Evidence*. New York, NY: Praeger, 1976.

Bateman, M. *Cocoa in the Ghanaian Economy: An Econometric Model*. Amsterdam: North-Holland, 1968.

Chatt, E. M. *Cocoa*. New York, NY: Interscience, 1953.

Food and Agriculture Organization (of the U.N.). *The Cocoa Situation: Recent Developments and the Outlook for Production and Demand*. Rome, Italy, 1961.

Gill and Duffus. *Cocoa Statistics*. annual, London.

Gill and Duffus. *Cocoa Market Report*. quarterly, London.

Labys, W. C., and Granger, C. W. J. *Speculation, Hedging and Commodity Price Forecasts*. Lexington, MA: Heath, 1973.

Parry, J. *Guide to World Commodity Markets* (3rd ed.). New York, NY: Kogan Page, 1982.

Payer, C. (Ed.). *Commodity Trade of the Third World*. New York, NY: Wiley, 1975.

Understanding the Cocoa Market. New York, NY: Commodity Research Publications Company, 1978.

U. S. Department of Agriculture. *Foreign Agriculture Circular*. Washington, D.C.

U. S. Department of Agriculture. *Sugar and Sweetener Report*. Washington, D.C. (Reports on cocoa supply and demand appear periodically.)

Watling, T.F. and J. Morley. *Successful Commodity Futures Trading*. London, England: Business Books Limited, 1974.

Weymar, F. H. *The Dynamics of the World Cocoa Market*. Cambridge, MA: MIT Press, 1968.

Wickizer, V. D. *Coffee, Tea, and Cocoa*. Stanford, CA: The Food Research Institute of Stanford University, 1951.

CHAPTER 35

THE MARKET FOR COFFEE

CONTENTS

SUPPLIERS OF COFFEE 3

The Role of Brazil 5

Seasonality 7

COFFEE CONSUMPTION 8

Inelasticity of Demand 10

Shift in Demand 10

INTERNATIONAL AGREEMENTS AND SHORT-RUN PRICE DYNAMICS 12

FUTURES TRADING IN COFFEE 14

SUMMARY 14

REFERENCES 17

CHAPTER **35**

THE MARKET FOR COFFEE

Todd E. Petzel

Considering the world's beverages, coffee dominates the international trade picture, far outdistancing tea, cocoa, and popular, though largely locally produced, alcoholic beverages. Like tea and cocoa, production of coffee is concentrated in the tropical and subtropical regions of the world, while the bulk of consumption occurs in Europe and industrial America. This leads to a value of world trade that rivals the internationally traded grains and raw materials. In 1976 coffee was second only to petroleum among primary products in terms of dollar value of trade. Despite this extensive network of producers, traders, and consumers, the futures markets for coffee in London and New York are not large by comparison to those of the grains or precious metals. Many factors contribute to this state of affairs, including the existence of an active *International Coffee Organization (ICO)*, and the concentration of both production and consumption. This chapter will discuss the factors of supply, demand, and market organization that mesh together to form one of the more dynamic elements in the international marketplace.

SUPPLIERS OF COFFEE

Despite being a plant native to the Middle East (hence the classification *Caffea Arabica*), extensive production and trade did not occur until the Spanish and Portuguese developed the New World. In the 17th century, coffee became the dominant nonalcoholic drink of Europe and the Americas, with the exception of the British Isles and its possessions (which, on the basis of the East India company's marketing skills, switched almost entirely to tea in the mid-1700s). The demand for coffee in the western world grew steadily, and was met almost entirely by Brazil and other South and Central American producers. It was not until after World War II that African producers became a force in the market. Africa has moved from producing less than 1% of the world crop at the turn of the century to a current position exceeding 25% of the total.

The various market participants have followed different paths to reach the current situation, and it is instructive to consider the microeconomics of coffee supply, as well as the broader institutional picture, in helping to understand the history of coffee production.

First, it is useful to divide the market into two groups, *arabicas* and *robustas*. Arabicas are a mild coffee, the production of which is concentrated largely in

Brazil, Colombia, and other Latin American countries. Altitudes exceeding 2,000 ft and moderate and steady temperatures are requisites for quality arabica production. The tree itself does not come into commercial production for 3 or 4 years and then good yields may be achieved over a 15- to 18-year period. After 30 years or so, yields decline to a point where the tree is no longer commercially viable.

If the trees are left without pruning, they grow to heights exceeding 35 ft, but usually they are trimmed regularly to a height of 8–15 ft. This makes the harvest more manageable and presumably directs the tree's energies into producing fruit instead of additional wood. The mature coffee tree can have flowers and ripe and unripe berries simultaneously, making it possible to vary the method of the harvest. In most countries except Brazil, only the ripe berries are picked at any given time, leading to anywhere from two to four pickings per season. By contrast, Brazil traditionally has a single stripping of the trees when most of the berries are ripe. This saves on harvesting costs, but produces a lower quality of coffee, since not all the beans are at their peak ripeness and flavor potential.

After the harvest there are two processes which may be used to prepare the green coffee beans. The *wet method* begins with the mechanical removal of most of the outer pulp from the berries. Next, the berries are washed and fed into a tank where fermentation occurs. Careful timing of the fermentation is an essential ingredient in providing quality coffee, since acidic reactions negatively affect both color and flavor. After a second washing to halt fermentation and to remove the final traces of mucilage, the berries are dried until the inner thin skin can be removed. This wet process is used to produce the finest "washed" arabicas in the world.

An alternative available to regions that cannot meet the heavy water demands of the wet process, and that have a prolonged period of warm, dry weather is the *natural process* of drying the berries in the sun. Once very popular in Brazil, this procedure allows for the sorting of berries by degree of ripeness. The risks involved stem from the uncertainty of the weather and the consequent negative impact on the quality. This is recognized in the trade by the market premia paid to washed arabicas over their unwashed or natural counterparts.

Arabicas are frequently further divided between Brazilians, Colombians, and "other" milds. Reflecting traditional quality variations, these distinctions are useful guides in assessing the state of the arabica market.

The growth in African production has largely been the story of *C. Robusta*, which, as its name implies, is a hardier plant than its arabica cousin. Robustas are grown anywhere from 500 to 2,000 ft in elevation and, most importantly, are resistant to the diseases that destroyed early Asian and African arabica trees. Robustas are not as flavorful as arabicas, but their expanded use can be traced to the suitability for use in lower-quality blends and in soluble (instant) coffees. Up to half of soluble coffee may be robustas, so as the demand for convenience has grown, so has this market. African arabica production comprises about 25% of Africa's total and is restricted largely to the higher elevations of Ethiopia and Kenya. The Ivory Coast is the dominant producer of robustas.

Econometric studies of supply (Askari and Cummings) have centered on the long-term price response of new plantings. Usually done on a country-by-country basis, these studies show acreage to be relatively responsive to price, with elasticities in the 0.4 to 0.8 range. This price responsiveness is of concern to some developing country governments who see coffee production squeezing out subsistence crop farming. This has led, in some cases, to attempts to control coffee producing, but acting as a strong counterbalance to such controls are the large export earnings generated by coffee. Ethiopia and Nicaragua are two arabica producers who have not always handled this issue adroitly. Recent political problems in Kenya have interrupted production, but so far the major producers have been relatively free from the shocks due to political instability.

THE ROLE OF BRAZIL. Historically, the world supply of coffee has best been thought of as a Ptolemaic system with everyone rotating around a centrally positioned Brazil. In the 1930s Brazil produced over 60% of the world crop (Wickizer, p.68), and its marketing policies reflected the power of the market position. During the international depression of the 1930s, Brazil divided its crop into a fraction sold, another part stored, and a third part destroyed. The extreme of this policy occurred in 1937 when over 17 million bags were burned.

In the short run this artificial shortage of Brazilians worked off an inelastic demand curve to raise the price, but at the same time, it produced the unwanted effect of reducing the premiums paid for Colombians and other washed milds. This increase in the *relative* price of Brazilians played into the hands of Colombia and other producers who, in the long run, increased their market shares considerably at Brazil's expense. There were several attempts by Brazil to form an international production cartel to not only support Brazil's price, but also to raise the entire spectrum of arabica prices. The smaller producers obviously found more to be gained in market share at Brazil's expense than they were losing in low prices, since none of these cartel attempts ever succeeded.

This history of the 1930s is instructive since repeatedly Brazil has tried to use its market share as a lever on the entire market. In the short run there is no doubt about the impact of these policies, but it is also quite clear that the dynamic growth of African and other Central American producers since World War II has been encouraged by the price environment created by Brazil.

There is also more to the issue than just the size of Brazil's crop. Unlike most of the Latin American producers who grow coffee in climatological zones characterized by regularity of temperature and rainfall, Brazil's major producing area is subject to both frosts and droughts. Given the importance of Brazil's contribution to the world crop, these weather-induced uncertainties impact on all of the producing and consuming nations. Figure 1, taken from the USDA, contrasts the regularity of Colombia and other Latin American producers to the large swings experienced by Brazil during the 1960s and 1970s.

It is also important to note the timing of weather-induced shocks to Brazilian production. In July 1975 a major frost hit the states of Paraná and São Paulo, killing some 200 million trees out of a tree population of 2.76 billion. A far larger number of trees were badly damaged and had to be deeply pruned or stumped to induce new growth. Since the annual harvest occurs between April and August, the key impact of the frost was not so much on the ripe berries, but on the tree's ability to flower for the next season. Production for the crop year 1975–1976 was about 23 million bags, falling to under 10 million for 1976–1977 (U.S. Department of Agriculture, *Coffee Production and Trade in Latin America*). This lag between the weather shock and the disruption in supply allows the market to assess the

TABLE 1. World Green Coffee (Exportable)[a] Production (in Thousands of Bags of 60 KG Each)

Crop Year[b]	Angola	Brazil	Camer-oon	Colom-bia	Costa Rica	Ethiopia	Guate-mala	Indo-nesia	Ivory Coast	Kenya	Mexico	Salvador	Uganda	Zaire (Congo, KI)	World Total
1960–1965	2,859	18,840	780	6,800	937	1,152	1,500	1,756	3,135	605	1,521	1,702	2,416	940	51,453
1965–1966	2,740	30,200	1,170	7,000	895	1,170	1,835	1,850	4,500	855	1,800	1,690	2,585	925	66,244
1966–1967	3,240	12,000	970	6,350	1,080	1,385	1,450	1,490	2,145	915	1,350	1,825	2,435	850	44,483
1967–1968	3,340	14,745	1,070	6,700	1,210	1,380	1,625	1,650	4,445	630	1,500	2,260	2,685	950	51,726
1968–1969	3,040	8,000	1,070	6,570	1,115	1,420	1,505	1,500	3,350	780	1,400	1,755	3,320	950	43,410
1969–1970	3,200	10,250	1,170	7,080	1,250	1,375	1,510	1,500	4,535	880	1,575	2,350	3,335	1,025	48,078
1970–1971	3,200	1,500	1,125	6,390	1,095	1,450	1,590	1,450	3,950	988	1,680	2,015	2,985	1,150	40,110
1971–1972	3,300	14,850	1,220	5,750	1,190	1,490	1,845	1,320	4,400	973	1,835	2,440	2,830	1,200	53,083
1972–1973	3,400	15,000	1,533	7,430	1,160	1,410	1,990	1,650	4,985	1,240	2,100	1,935	3,280	1,265	57,285
1973–1974	3,095	6,370	1,213	6,250	1,400	1,005	1,925	1,795	3,219	1,073	1,690	2,203	3,078	1,184	43,674
1974–1975	3,352	19,500	1,766	7,400	1,237	1,051	2,255	1,700	4,432	1,082	2,156	3,130	3,302	1,017	62,862
1975–1976	1,100	15,000	1,455	7,100	1,104	1,011	1,753	2,033	5,107	1,224	2,456	2,350	2,192	922	54,307
1976–1977	267	1,800	1,281	7,900	1,147	1,049	1,915	2,219	4,782	1,644	2,080	2,788	2,634	1,270	42,777
1977–1978	1,172	10,000	1,344	9,500	1,264	1,354	2,236	2,586	3,357	1,367	2,001	2,210	1,838	954	52,016
1978–1979	533	12,000	1,599	10,970	1,533	1,342	2,517	3,735	4,551	1,181	3,034	2,991	1,585	1,120	59,288
1979–1980	290	14,000	1,530	10,550	1,297	1,130	2,332	3,823	4,056	1,376	2,320	2,530	2,070	1,210	60,644
1980–1981[c]	265	13,500	1,618	10,575	1,660	1,250	2,275	4,175	4,101	1,191	2,300	2,200	2,270	1,205	60,003
1981–1982[c]	400	32,500	1,790	14,500	1,875	3,200	2,600	5,420	4,666		3,850	2,214	1,900	1,300	95,584

Source: Department of Agriculture, Foreign Agricultural Service, U.S. [a]Exportable production represents total harvested production minus estimated domestic consumption. [b]Coffee marketing year begins in July in some countries and in others about October. [c]Preliminary.

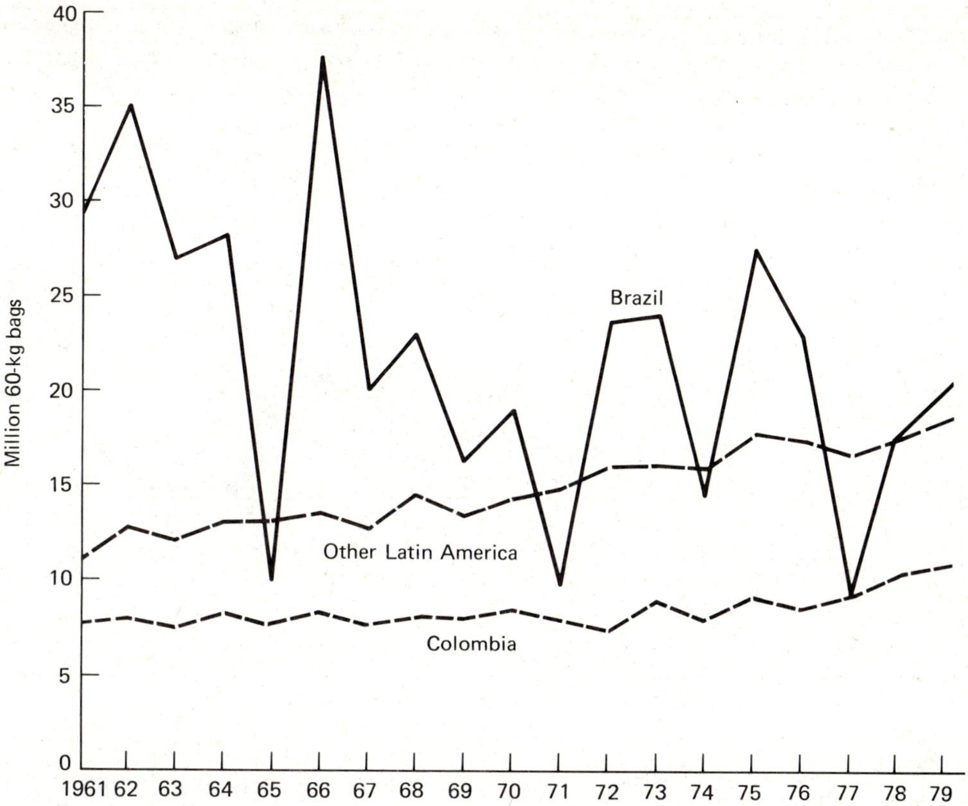

FIGURE 1. Latin America: Trends in coffee production, 1961–1979 (crop years ending September 30). (*Source*: 1978 to 1979 Forecast based on U.S. Department of Agriculture, Foreign Agricultural Service Coffee Circular FCOF, January 1979.)

extent of damage and allocate existing stocks and other countries' production over the period of irregular supply.

The final concern in the subject of supply has to do with the physiology of the tree. Frequently, large yields in a given season are followed by low yields as the tree recovers from the burdens placed on it by the heavy production. Favorable weather can mitigate this somewhat, but if a weather shock hits while the bulk of the trees are in a recovery state, the results, as they were for Brazil in 1975, can be devastating.

SEASONALITY. Coffee has a highly seasonal, although erratic, price movement. It is prone to price "shocks" due to freezes which will then affect prices for as much as 3 years afterwards. The possibilities of a freeze in coffee-producing countries have caused an anticipatory psychology among traders. There is a clear reluctance to hold short positions in the early summer. Although a freeze is uncommon, the risk of being short seems to outweigh the rewards for the speculator. Early summer is characterized by volatile, uncertain price movement for coffee much the same as the frozen orange juice market in winter or the potato market in May.

FIGURE 2. Weekly price of coffee—New York.

The two charts showing the seasonal coffee patterns in Figure 3 confirm the highly volatile patterns. The 4 years evaluated in the second chart show the effects of more than one damaging freeze which caused prices to move steadily higher with magnitude great enough to distort the previous long-term chart.

COFFEE CONSUMPTION

After green coffee leaves the countries of origin, it enters into an international marketing chain of shippers, dealers, roasters, and distributors. Unlike sugar, which has a myriad of end uses, the path traveled by coffee is well-defined. The basic problem on the demand side stems from the fact that coffee is not a homogeneous product. Green coffees need to be blended and roasted to harmonize the characteristics of the different growths. Nearly all of the regular and instant coffees sold today are blends, and while the exact composition of any given blend is a closely guarded trade secret, a typical U.S. blend would consist of Colombian or Central American milds mixed with Brazilians. High-grade coffee would consist of practically all milds and no Brazilians.

With the exception of Brazilian and Colombian beans, no single growth is produced in large enough quantities to ensure adequate supplies year after year. As weather shocks hit a particular country disrupting supply, the price differential of that growth, relative to other growths, can change. The mark of a good coffee blender is that the blender can adjust his or her blend according to the availability of given growths, maintaining a cost-effective final product with stable flavor characteristics.

CASH COFFEE

22 YEARS

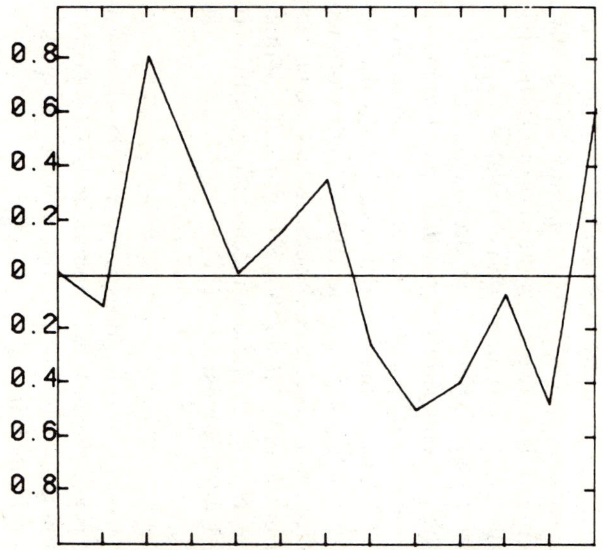

	J-F	F-M	M-A	A-M	M-J	J-J	J-A	A-S	S-O	O-N	N-D	D-J
Average Move	-0.2	0.9	-0.5	-0.4	0.1	0.1	-0.7	-0.3	0.1	0.3	-0.5	1
% Reliable	41	63.7	50	50	59.1	45.5	45.5	54.6	41	63.7	50	77.3
Avg. Up Move	1.8	3.5	0.4	0.6	1.1	2.7	1.9	2.1	2.4	1.4	0.7	3.3
Avg. Down Move	2.2	1.9	1.2	1.3	1	1.3	2.9	1.6	1.2	1.2	1.4	1.2
Greatest Up Move	5	9.7	1.2	1.7	4	6.5	7.5	6	6.7	5	2.7	11.2
Greatest Down Move	12.5	7	4.5	3.5	2.8	5	12.8	3.8	4.3	2.8	3.5	2.5

CASH COFFEE

4 YEARS

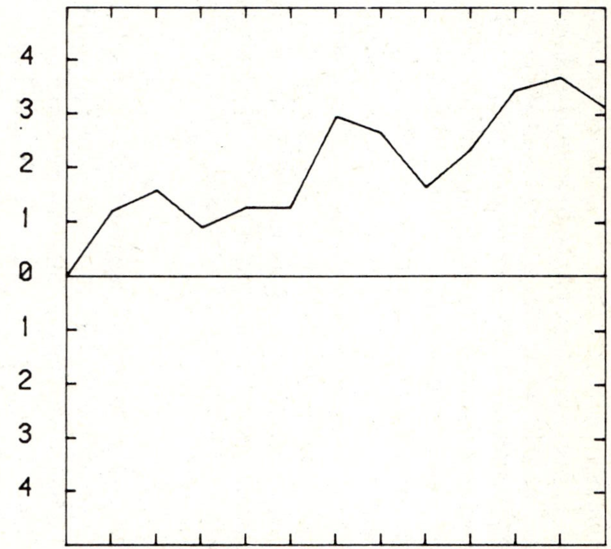

	J-F	F-M	M-A	A-M	M-J	J-J	J-A	A-S	S-O	O-N	N-D	D-J
Average Move	1.2	0.3	-0.7	0.3	0	1.6	-0.4	-1	0.6	1.1	0.2	-0.6
% Reliable	75	75	50	75	75	50	25	50	50	75	75	25
Avg. Up Move	2.9	2.8	0.3	1.3	1.2	4.7	3.8	2.5	4	2.1	1	0.1
Avg. Down Move	1	7	1.8	1.3	2.5	1.4	9	3.3	0.7	2	1	2.5
Greatest Up Move	5	4	0.5	1.7	2	6.5	7.5	2.5	4	5	1	0.1
Greatest Down Move	1	7	3	1.3	2.5	2	9	3.5	1	2	1	2.5

FIGURE 3. Coffee cash price seasonality: (left) 22 years; (right) 4 years. *Source:* J. Grushcow and C. Smith, *Profits Through Seasonal Trading,* New York, NY, Wiley, 1980

In the short run, these changes in blends should not be of great significance, but when a group of cheaper coffees are substituted into a blend without consumer resistance, the composition of the coffee trade is changed dramatically. It is difficult to sort out all of the changes that have occurred in coffee marketing over the last 30 years, but two features stand out. First of all, there has been increased use of robustas, which is seen by some as a deterioration of quality, despite the preferences of a significant fraction of consumers (*World Coffee and Tea*, September 1982). The second factor reflects both technology and the demand for convenience, and that is the rise of *soluble* (instant) coffees. The quality of instant coffee has improved dramatically over the last 20 years despite the fact that these blends contain a high fraction of robustas. This improved flavor and ease of preparation has shifted demand away from regular coffee internationally, and, consequently, has altered the market position of robustas versus milds.

INELASTICITY OF DEMAND. Examining the aggregate demand side of the coffee equation is a much easier exercise than trying to forecast supply. Almost exclusively used as a beverage, with only a small fraction being employed in flavorings, coffee is a product whose consumers are firmly attached to their consumption habits. Long-term trends have affected these consumption patterns, but in the short run, the lack of effective substitutes and coffee's limited end uses make for an inelastic demand. Estimates by the USDA (*U.S. Coffee Consumption, 1946–1976*, 1977) give a price elasticity of -0.21, and no statistically significant measure of income elasticity. It is clear that, in the short run, the price of coffee has to increase dramatically before consumption is curtailed.

A trend away from coffee consumption is apparent over the last 20 years in the United States. Both the percentage of the population consuming coffee, and the per capita consumption have declined steadily. It has been suggested that the decline in coffee demand is due to a rising popularity of soft drinks. If this is true, it is not a price-responsive relationship, as the USDA could not identify a significant cross-price elasticity. More likely, young consumers are not acquiring the coffee habit to the extent of the older generations and this demographic cultural shift explains, to a great extent, both the decline in coffee and the rise of soft-drink consumption in the United States.

SHIFT IN DEMAND. The problem this poses for coffee producers is clear. If the shift away from coffee is not price- or income-induced, but reflects the culture of the young, these consumers may be lost forever, making remote any prospect of a change in trend for the United States.

Outside the United States, the demand for both regular and instant coffee has grown enough to offset the United States decline to produce a steady upward trend. Gains since World War II have been especially strong in Eastern Europe, Japan, and the countries of the old British Commonwealth, where tea held a virtual monopoly for over 150 years. It remains to be seen if the lifestyle changes that have affected U.S. consumption will be exported to Western Europe and other parts of the world, bringing about a long-term reversal in the growth in demand for coffee.

TABLE 2. **Total Coffee Imports (for Consumption) into the United States (in Thousands of 60-Kg Bags)**

Year	Jan	Feb	Mar	April	May	June	July	Aug	Sept	Oct	Nov	Dec	Total
1967	1,979	1,618	2,092	1,717	1,722	1,647	1,748	1,818	1,599	2,103	1,845	1,424	21,312
1968	2,202	2,461	1,755	2,398	1,956	1,641	2,481	2,397	2,322	1,687	2,132	1,945	25,377
1969	363	1,111	2,015	2,195	1,664	1,747	1,714	1,476	1,778	2,327	2,167	1,675	20,232
1970	1,783	1,841	1,716	1,639	1,644	1,891	1,550	1,616	1,355	1,713	1,597	1,382	19,727
1971	2,002	1,530	1,480	2,032	1,759	1,941	2,132	2,720	2,754	621	875	1,818	21,669
1972	2,547	2,172	1,137	1,146	1,784	1,452	1,434	1,947	2,149	2,057	1,643	1,288	20,757
1973	1,996	1,844	2,101	2,050	2,494	1,710	1,573	1,731	1,399	1,624	1,624	1,652	21,799
1974	2,182	2,022	2,457	2,264	1,873	1,529	1,499	1,152	821	740	1,159	1,550	19,248
1975	1,852	1,656	1,535	1,448	1,365	1,736	1,626	1,868	2,533	1,784	1,587	1,299	20,289
1976	1,664	1,744	2,311	1,636	1,546	1,864	1,909	1,637	956	1,013	1,649	1,858	19,788
1977	1,994	1,707	1,839	1,824	1,224	1,137	756	695	678	635	972	1,347	14,808
1978	1,682	1,575	1,707	1,557	1,345	1,249	1,316	1,124	1,337	1,901	1,689	1,651	18,133
1979	1,747	1,353	1,631	2,037	1,619	1,617	1,597	1,404	1,632	1,273	1,593	1,893	19,396
1980	2,020	1,366	1,421	1,642	1,566	1,663	1,533	1,386	1,062	1,292	1,386	1,715	18,153
1981	1,858												

Source: U. S. Department of Commerce.

INTERNATIONAL AGREEMENTS AND SHORT-RUN PRICE DYNAMICS

Given the steadiness of global demand and the concentration of production in Brazil, the short- and intermediate-run price dynamics in coffee are linked directly to the previously mentioned weather shocks to supply. Each year traders anticipate the weather news and then try to assess the impact of any adverse shocks. The problem is not a simple one since the Brazilian production has to be balanced against the rest of the world supply, which includes stocks.

Green coffee can be stored under appropriate conditions for long periods of time. Since most coffee is grown in areas of moderate temperature and humidity, coffee producers, unlike their counterparts in cocoa, can store a significant fraction of their crop domestically without spending great sums on elaborate storage facilities. This distributes the storage decision across producers and consumers, balancing market power and mitigating, to a certain extent, large swings in price. However, as can be seen in Figure 4, there can still be significant price variation in the short run.

Some market commentators attribute these swings to speculative ebbs and flows, but a more likely story is that there can still be significant uncertainty about deliverable supplies in the short run. Despite the fact that ultimate demand is heavy around a winter/summer seasonal pattern, buyers of coffee will time their purchases to take advantage of perceived dips in the price. This "anticipatory" hedging adds uncertainty to the state of supply and demand and allows short-run swings in price to occur.

Attempts to mitigate swings in both the long run and short run have been tried

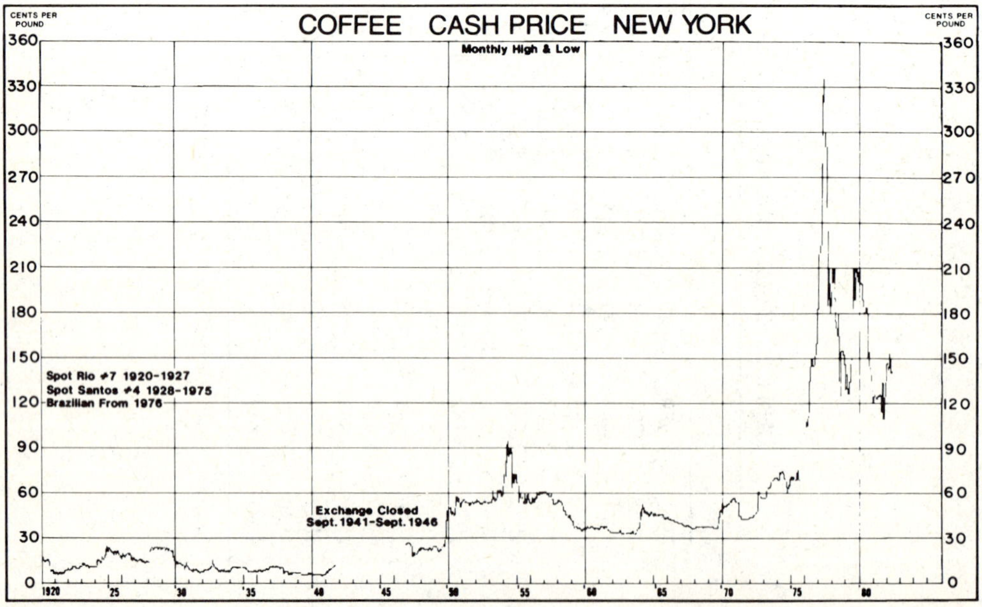

FIGURE 4. Spot price of Coffee—New York (monthly). (*Source*: Commodity Research Bureau, Incorporated.)

at the international level since the 1930s. Early efforts at forming a coffee producers' cartel, with Brazil as the focal member, failed because the smaller producers had no individual incentive to curtail output as long as Brazil supported the world price. An extreme result of this kind of one-sided producer policy occurred in the early 1960s, when Brazil held over 60 million bags in reserve stocks, and went on a multiyear program of uprooting productive trees.

The early 1970s saw prices moving into the $0.50–$0.80 per lb range as the excess supplies were slowly worked off. This environment of rising real prices provided the incentive for coffee-consuming countries to participate in an international accord, and the basic framework of the current International Coffee Agreement (ICA) was established in January 1976. Unfortunately, from a stabilization perspective, the severe Brazilian frost of July 1975 hit at a time of reduced stocks, and there was no chance for the ICA to work in preventing a dramatic price explosion. From a level around $0.90 per lb in January 1976, the price of the Coffee "C" Contract in New York peaked in April 1977 at over $3.40 per lb, only to fall below $2 by end of 1977. Since 1978 the price of coffee has moved erratically, but has generally been above the lower level of the ICA support range.

The provisions of the ICA are unique in that they internalize the costs of support to the producing countries. Instead of having a general buffer-stock agency charged with regulating supply, as the cocoa producers do, the ICA sets regular export quotas for producing members according to the price level. A country like Colombia takes its total production and divides it into domestic consumption, quota exports, and exports to non-ICA members (mostly in Eastern Europe). The remainder of production, if any, must be stored domestically, and the cost of this program is carried by either the producers or the exporting government. Since the bulk of international trade occurs between member nations, there is little opportunity to circumvent the intention of the agreement.

The pricing provisions of the current agreement attempt to regulate exports to maintain a $1.20–$1.40 composite price. This composite, a weighted average of other mild arabicas and robusta prices, is released daily by the ICO. As the price falls into the lower ranges the quotas are restricted, and the converse happens as the price goes up. Quotas are issued on an annual basis, but are divided into equal quarterly portions. It is possible to "borrow" on future quarters to a limited extent, but in general, the quarterly provisions have been restrictive in the amount of coffee they allow to move at any given point in time. If an imbalance in the stocks held by consuming and producing countries occurs, the quota provisions can prevent a rapid adjustment. This can have the peculiar effect of having the quota-controlled supply-and-demand picture move opposite to the underlying world conditions (*World Coffee and Tea*, September 1982, pp. 14–15).

To date, the provisions are working much better to support and stabilize price than the agreement for cocoa, largely due to the fact that the target-price range, in real terms, is a reasonable value for both producers and consumers. Consuming member nations are not supposed to import coffee from nonmember exporters, and as long as prices are stable at a moderate level, they have little incentive to do so. The biggest problem on the horizon is the accumulation of stocks in the producing countries. Both Brazil and Colombia are having net additions to their stock holdings, despite a mild Brazilian freeze in 1981. If this is typical of world stock holdings, countries in need of foreign exchange will be under great pressure to abrogate the terms of the ICA. At the moment, the solidarity of the consuming nations has prevented any major producers from breaking ranks, but continued excess supply at current prices offers consumers the prospect that dropping out of the cartel could provide considerable savings.

FUTURES TRADING IN COFFEE

There are two main coffee futures contracts traded internationally; the Coffee "C" Contract for arabica coffees traded on the Coffee, Sugar and Cocoa Exchange in New York, and the robusta contract traded on the London Coffee Terminal Market. These differences reflect the geographical concentration of production of the two types of coffee more than they represent a European–North American split in consumption habits. The "C" Contract, the specifications of which are in Table 3, calls for the delivery of arabica coffees from 19 different nations (*not* including Brazil) with appropriate discounts and premia prescribed to account for fundamental quality differences. Trading in the Coffee "B" Contract, calling for delivery of Brazilian arabicas, had not been active for several years and, in 1982, the contract was formally suspended. The Coffee "C" Contract provides for an adequate hedging vehicle for Brazilian coffee.

Specifications of the London robusta coffee contract are shown in Table 4.

Hedging possibilities exist on both sides of the market. Coffee roasters may sell futures against an unsold inventory of cash coffee, or they may buy futures against a forward commitment to deliver. Since futures contracts are traded for deliveries exceeding a year from the present, a wide latitude may be allowed in the timing of purchases and sales.

Coffee producers use futures by hedging their forward sales, or if they think prices are low, selling their cash crop and buying futures. This substitution of futures for actuals has the advantage of giving the grower use of money while the grower is waiting for the price to increase; and, if the price should move, either according to the grower's expectations or against the grower, futures are much more liquid than the cash commodity.

Speculators in coffee can trade on the basis of their expectations of broad price trends, or on the intertemporal price relationships between different contract months. Arbitrage between London and New York is possible if the speculator believes the arabica/robusta or pound sterling/dollar relationships are out of line. In any event, it is critical to follow the world supply-and-demand picture, and the terms of and participation in the ICA. As previously mentioned, the market prices produced in any agreement environment can diverge from the underlying supply-and-demand fundamentals.

SUMMARY

The international coffee futures markets in London and New York are active centers to a vast world trade. Buyers and sellers from all over the world can acquire accurate, up-to-the-minute, information concerning the state of the world market, and can form firm commitments several months into the future.

TABLE 3. New York Coffee "C" Contract Specifications

Contract unit	37,500 lb
Price quotation	Cents per pound
Minimum price fluctuation	1/100¢ per lb or $3.75 per contract
Maximum daily price fluctuation	$0.04 (400 points) above or below the previous day's settlement price. Limits are expandable to $0.06 (600 points). Limits do not apply to the spot month.
Trading hours	9:45 a.m.–2:28 p.m. Trading is suspended at 2:28 p.m. and the closing call begins at 2:30 p.m. eastern time.
Delivery	From exchange-licensed warehouses in the Port of New York District and the Port of New Orleans
Delivery months	Trading is permitted beginning 18 months prior to the expiration of the contract. The trading months are March, May, July, September, and December.
Deliverable growths	Washed arabica coffee of Mexico, Salvador, Guatemala, Costa Rica, Nicaragua, Honduras, Colombia, Kenya, Tanzania, Uganda, New Guinea, Peru, Venezuela, Dominican Republic, Burundi, Ecuador, India, and Rwanda. Beginning with the May 1982 delivery month, unwashed arabica coffee of Ethiopia will also be deliverable against the contract.
Standards	Coffee shall be sweet in the cup, of good roasting quality, and of bean size and color in accordance with the description established by the exchange. No delivery shall be permitted of coffee containing more than 15 full imperfections below the basis, except that in the case of Colombian (and Ethiopian, when it becomes deliverable) no delivery shall be permitted of coffee containing more than 10 full imperfections below the basis.
Differential price for delivery	Growths of Mexico, Salvador, Guatemala, Costa Rica, Nicaragua, Kenya, Tanzania and Uganda are deliverable at basis. Growths of Colombia are deliverable at a premium of 200 points. Growths of New Guinea and Honduras are deliverable at a discount of 100 points. Growths of Peru and Venezuela are deliverable at a discount of 400 points. Growths of Dominican Republic, Burundi, Ecuador, India, and Rwanda are deliverable at a discount of 550 points. Effective with the May 1982 contract, growths of Ethiopia will be deliverable at a discount of 800 points.
Position limits	None
CFTC large trader reporting level	25 contracts or more
First notice day	Seven business days prior to the first business day of the delivery month
Last notice and last trading day	Seven business days prior to the last business day of the delivery month

TABLE 4. London Robusta Coffee Contract Specifications

Contract unit		5 tons (long tons)
Price quotation		Sterling per tonne
Minimum price fluctuation		£0.50 per tonne or £2.50 per contract
Maximum daily price fluctuation		no limits
Trading Hours	London Time	New York Time
Opening call	10:30–10:40 A.M.	05:30–05:40 A.M.
Free trading	10:40–12:20	05:40–07:20
Midday call	12:20–12:30	07:20–07:30
Lunch break	12:30–14:30	07:30–09:30
P.M. call	14:30–14:40	09:30–09:40
Free trading	14:40–16:50	09:40–11:50
Closing call	16:50–17:00	11:50–12:00

Contract particulars (quality)
Coffee deliverable against the contract shall be 5 tonnes net weight (with a tolerance of up to 3% more or 3% less) of sound Robusta CIMAL Standard or other grades with allowances, or premiums in accordance with these rules in warehouses nominated by the association from time to time in London/Home Counties, Bristol, Amsterdam, Rotterdam, and Le Havre areas.

Delivery points
London/Home Counties, Bristol, Hull, Amsterdam, Rotterdam, Le Havre, Hamburg, Bremen.

On the supply side, Brazil will no doubt continue its dominant role, and the weather-induced shocks will make up a considerable portion of the market uncertainty. With ICA quotas being based on historical export positions, further deterioration of Brazilian market share will be limited. Demand will probably continue to grow moderately at the world level despite the downward trend of U.S. consumption. If the ICA succeeds in maintaining a reasonable price range, the stability of coffee prices could be translated into more dependable long-term demand.

The ICA itself has succeeded over the last several years in maintaining its targeted range of prices. This has been by limiting exports of producers, and having them build up stocks. The last weather shock, a mild frost in Brazil in 1981, provided a test of the provisions, and adequate supplies were forthcoming to keep the prices in line. The ultimate test for the agreement will occur if aggregate supply continues to grow in excess of the export quotas. Since the individual countries bear the cost of their own excess supply, either they will institute production controls to align supply to the quota, or they will be tempted to break out of the cartel. Only time will tell which outcome will come about. If the agreement does break down, extra attention will be thrust upon the futures markets as a means to allocate production and consumption over time.

REFERENCES

Abbott, S. "How International Commodity Agreements Affect Futures." *Commodities,* December 1981, pp. 42–43.

Ascari, H., and John Cummings. *Agricultural Supply Response, A Survey of the Econometric Evidence.* New York, NY: Praeger, 1976.

Complete Coffee Coverage. George Gordon Paton and Company, Incorporated. New York (Daily).

International Coffee Organization. *International Coffee Agreement.* London, England, 1976.

Payer, C. (Ed.). *Commodity Trade of the Third World.* New York, NY: Wiley, 1975.

U. S. Department of Agriculture, Foreign Agricultural Service. *Coffee Production and Trade in Latin America.* FAS Circular No. M-288, May 1979.

U. S. Department of Agriculture, Foreign Agricultural Service. *Coffee Production in Africa.* FAS Circular No. M-266, September 1975.

U. S. Department of Agriculture, Foreign Agricultural Service. *U.S. Coffee Consumption, 1946–76.* FAS Circular No. M-275, February 1977.

Watling, T.F. and J. Morley. *Successful Commodity Futures Trading.* London, England: Business Books Limited, 1974.

Wickizer, V.D. *Coffee, Tea, and Cocoa.* Stanford, CA: The Food Research Institute of Stanford University, 1951.

World Coffee and Tea. "Is America Ready for a Good Cup of Coffee?" September 1982, pp. 22–30.

World Coffee and Tea. "The Only Reality is the Agreement." September 1982, pp. 14–15.

Coffee Models

Bacha, E.L. "An Econometric Model for the World Coffee Market: The Impact of Brazilian Price Policy." Unpublished Ph.D. dissertation, Yale University, 1976.

Epps, M.L.S. "A Computer Simulation Model of the World Coffee Economy." Unpublished Ph.D. dissertation, Duke University, 1970.

Labys, W.C. *Dynamic Commodity Models: Specification, Estimation, and Simulation.* Lexington, MA: Heath, 1973.

Wickens, M., Greenfield, J., and Marshall, G. *A World Coffee Model.* CCP.71/W.P.4, Food and Agricultural Organization of the United Nations, Rome, 1971.

CHAPTER 36

ORANGE JUICE

CONTENTS

PRODUCTION 3

Effects of Weather 3
Foreign Production 9
Effects of Supply on Price 9

ORANGE JUICE DEMAND 9

SEASONALITY 10

Seasonal Studies 12
Basis 13

PRICE DYNAMICS 13

TRADING OF FCOJ 13

Speculation 19
Contract Specification 20

SOURCES OF INFORMATION 20

CHAPTER **36**

ORANGE JUICE

Charles M. Barley

The *frozen concentrated orange juice* (FCOJ) market began in 1966, the result of increased popularity of frozen juice since World War II. Frozen concentrated orange juice was conceived by the Florida Citrus Commission and developed by Dr. L. G. MacDowell. MacDowell succeeded in improving a product which had existed, but had not been as popular. The FCOJ futures market offers an opportunity for processors, middlemen or fruit procurers, growers, and end users to hedge their needs.

PRODUCTION

The orange juice market is unique. Two-thrids of all production is centered in Florida, and, combined with the possibility of damaging freezes, the market is subject to "price shocks" resulting in drastic changes in supply. In some ways the price movements of the FCOJ market are comparable to Brazilian coffee.

Orange juice production in Florida has been expanding for many years, but may be waning with the severe freezes in the past 10 years, continued urbanization, cost of land increases, production cost increases, and competition from worldwide production increases, especially from Brazil. Table 1 shows that Florida still produces such a large percentage of the total crop that its impact is enormous. Tables 2 and 3 show Florida production of citrus in more detail. The sharp rise in production in 1966 parallels the beginning of the FCOJ futures market. The steady increase that followed during the next 10 years seems to be stabilizing.

EFFECTS OF WEATHER. A *freeze* is a major event which can affect the supply of oranges. Few commodities will react as severely and as frequently as this market. Since the inception of the FCOJ futures market, four major freezes have occurred in 1971–1972, 1976–1977, 1980–1981, and 1981–1982.

Orange trees are sensitive to sudden changes in temperature. Normally, adverse weather conditions will result in lower juice yields. However, a drop in temperature to 25° may damage both fruit and trees. Lower temperatures may result in severe damage. Trees are protected by artificial heat during cold spells, since replacement trees require about 5 years to produce a good crop.

Production in Florida, after freezes, had shown a rapid recovery until the devastating freezes of 1980–1981 and 1981–1982. These record-setting back-to-

TABLE 1. Salient Statistics of Oranges in the United States

Season	Production[a] (Millions of Boxes)					Farm Price ($ Per Box)	Farm Value (Millions of Dollars)	Foreign Trade[b]		Florida Crop Processed (Millions of Boxes)					
												Chilled Pdt's			
	Arizona	California	Florida	Texas	Total			Domestic Exports	Imports	Quantities Processed	Frozen Concentrates	Juice	Sections and Salads	Other Processed	Total Processed
1961–1962	1.4	20.7	113.4	2.3	133.0	2.68	356.9	5.0	0.2	95.7	Not available				
1962–1963	1.6	28.8	74.5	0.1	102.4	3.46	354.0	4.4	0.8	71.7	47.2	5.6	0.5	9.2	62.5
1963–1964	2.2	32.0	58.3	0.2	88.5	4.67	413.6	5.1	1.7	52.3	34.2	4.9	0.6	5.7	45.5
1964–1965	2.4	31.6	86.2	0.9	116.4	3.16	367.3	5.6	1.1	74.6	54.5	7.3	0.5	7.3	69.6
1965–1966	2.6	36.9	100.4	1.3	135.5	2.48	335.9	6.7	0.7	92.1	61.8	12.3	0.8	8.0	82.9
1966–1967	3.9	36.8	139.5	2.7	182.9	1.84	337.3	7.9	0.3	134.1	96.8	16.5	0.8	10.2	124.3
1967–1968	3.1	19.2	100.5	1.8	124.6	3.08	383.8	3.6	1.7	91.7	62.0	16.0	0.8	6.8	85.5
1968–1969	5.4	44.3	129.7	4.5	183.9	2.43	447.0	7.1	1.1	138.6	92.1	17.8	0.8	9.4	120.1
1969–1970	4.6	39.0	137.7	4.2	185.8	2.09	388.0	6.8	0.9	141.0	100.7	18.6	0.8	8.2	128.4
1970–1971	3.6	37.5	142.3	6.2	189.4	2.45	465.1	6.2	1.1	145.4	103.5	19.8	0.7	8.8	132.8
1971–1972	4.9	43.4	137.0	6.2	191.5	2.87	549.4	7.7	1.1	148.0	104.4	19.5	0.5	7.7	132.2
1972–1973	5.1	42.1	169.7	7.8	224.7	2.87	549.4	7.1	1.2	182.3	132.2	20.5	0.6	8.9	162.3
1973–1974	3.4	40.4	165.8	6.6	216.2	2.69	603.3	8.2	1.1	171.3	132.5	20.4	0.6	7.5	161.0
1974–1975	5.0	55.1	173.3	4.5	237.8	2.78	600.7	12.6	0.9	183.6	135.5	22.8	0.5	7.6	166.4
1975–1976	2.7	52.8	181.2	6.1	242.8	2.75	653.8	11.6	0.5	192.5	144.5	24.0	0.6	7.6	176.7
1976–1977	4.0	45.3	186.8	6.9	243.0	2.80	678.7	10.7	1.1	195.8	148.7	27.3	0.4	8.8	185.2
1977–1978	2.6	42.6	167.8	6.1	220.1	3.34	811.2	8.9	0.6	175.5	132.2	25.3	0.4	8.1	166.0
1978–1979[c]	2.9	37.3	164.0	6.4	210.6	5.45	1,198.7	7.8	0.6	170.5	130.2	22.8	0.3	6.5	159.8
1979–1980[c]	3.5	59.6	206.7	4.0	273.8	6.15	1,296.0				174.9	24.4	0.3	7.0	206.6
1980–1981[c]	3.1	64.0	171.6	4.4	243.1	4.76	1,304.2								

Source: U.S. Department of Agriculture, Economic Research Service. [a]Fruit ripened on trees, but destroyed prior to picking is not included. [b]Year beginning November 1st. [c]Preliminary.

TABLE 2. Florida Production of Round Oranges and Grapefruit (in Thousand Boxes[a])

Crop Season	Oranges			Grapefruit			
	Early and Midseason	Valencia	Total	Seeded	White Seedless	Pink Seedless	Total
1955–1956	48,700	39,500	88,200	17,700	15,600	5,000	38,300
1956–1957	51,600	38,700	90,300	15,800	15,500	6,100	37,400
1957–1958	51,200	29,800	81,000	13,500	12,600	5,000	31,100
1958–1959	44,100	38,900	83,000	15,600	14,000	5,600	35,200
1959–1960	45,100	42,500	87,600	10,400	13,400	6,700	30,500
1960–1961	47,000	35,700	82,700	12,400	11,900	7,300	31,600
1961–1962	52,300	56,500	108,800	11,100	14,700	9,000	34,800
1962–1963	43,500	29,000	72,500	10,000	12,500	7,500	30,000
1963–1964	24,400	20,500	54,900	6,600	12,100	7,600	26,300
1964–1965	42,600	39,800	82,400	10,200	13,000	8,700	31,900
1965–1966	47,000	48,900	95,900	11,200	14,400	9,300	34,900
1966–1967	73,200	66,300	139,500	13,500	18,600	11,500	43,600
1967–1968	51,400	49,100	100,500	9,200	14,300	9,400	32,900
1968–1969	69,700	60,000	129,700	12,200	17,000	10,700	39,900
1969–1970	72,900	64,800	137,700	9,500	17,700	10,200	37,400
1970–1971	82,100	60,200	142,300	11,800	20,200	10,900	42,900
1971–1972	68,800	68,200	137,000	10,900	23,800	12,300	47,000
1972–1973	90,000	79,700	169,700	10,200	23,500	11,700	45,400
1973–1974	92,100	73,700	165,800	10,000	25,900	12,200	48,100
1974–1975	96,600	76,700	173,300	7,200	25,900	11,500	44,600
1975–1976	98,800	82,400	181,200	7,800	28,300	13,000	49,100
1976–1977	115,000	71,800	186,800	9,100	29,900	12,500	51,500
1977–1978	88,300	79,500	167,800	8,400	28,700	14,300	51,400
1978–1979	91,000	73,000	164,000	7,300	29,400	13,300	50,000
1979–1980	117,900	88,800	206,700	7,900	31,100	15,800	54,800
1980–1981	105,600	66,800	172,400	7,300	28,400	14,600	50,300

Source: Florida Crop and Livestock Reporting Service, *Citrus Summary*.
[a]Oranges, 90 lb and grapefruit, 85 lb.

TABLE 3. USDA Crop Estimate by Months: Florida Oranges and Grapefruit (in Thousand Boxes[a])

	Oranges				Grapefruit		
	Early and Midseason	Valencia	Total	Temples	Seeded	Seedless	Total
1978–1979:							
October	95,000	72,000	167,000	4,800	10,000	41,000	51,000
December	95,000	72,000	167,000	4,800	10,000	41,000	51,000
January	93,000	70,000	163,000	4,800	10,000	41,000	51,000
February	93,000	70,000	163,000	4,800	9,000	41,000	50,000
March	93,000	70,000	163,000	4,800	9,000	41,000	50,000
April	91,000	72,000	163,000	4,700	7,000	41,000	48,000
May	91,000	72,000	163,000	4,600	7,200	42,000	49,200
June	91,000	72,000	163,000	4,600	7,200	42,600	49,800
July	91,000	73,000	164,000	4,600	7,300	42,700	50,000
Final	91,000	73,000	164,000	4,600	7,300	42,700	50,000
1979–1980:							
October	115,000	85,000	200,000	5,400	7,000	44,000	51,000
December	115,000	85,000	200,000	5,400	7,000	44,000	51,000
January	115,000	85,000	200,000	5,400	7,000	44,000	51,000
February	115,000	85,000	200,000	5,400	8,000	43,000	51,000
March	115,000	85,000	200,000	5,400	8,000	43,000	51,000
April	118,000	85,000	203,000	6,000	8,000	43,000	51,000
May	118,000	85,000	203,000	6,000	8,000	45,000	53,000
June	117,900	87,000	204,900	6,000	7,900	46,500	54,400
July	117,900	89,000	206,900	6,000	7,900	46,900	54,800
Final	117,900	88,800	206,700	6,000	7,900	46,900	54,800
1980–1981:							
October	115,000	88,000	203,000	5,700	8,000	45,000	53,000
December	115,000	88,000	203,000	5,700	8,500	43,500	52,000
January	115,000	88,000	203,000	5,700	8,500	43,000	52,000
February	107,000	66,000	173,000	3,500	8,000	40,500	48,500
March	107,000	66,000	173,000	3,500	8,000	40,500	48,500
April	105,600	66,000	171,600	3,600	7,500	42,500	50,000
May	105,600	63,000	168,600	3,600	7,300	43,200	50,500
June	105,600	63,000	168,000	3,600	7,300	43,200	50,500
July	105,600	66,500	172,100	3,600	7,300	43,000	50,300
Final	105,600	66,800	172,400	3,600	7,300	43,000	50,300

Source: U.S. Department of Agriculture, ESCS, Citrus Forecast Releases. [a]Oranges, 90 lb. and grapefruit, 85 lb.

TABLE 4. Florida Production, Round Oranges and Temples: Bearing Acreage and Yield Per Acre (in Thousand Boxes[a] and Acres)

	Early and Midseason Oranges			Valencia Oranges		
Season	Production	Bearing Acreage	Box Yield Per Acre	Production	Bearing Acreage	Box Yield Per Acre
1963–1964	24,400	183.0	113	30,500	205.0	149
1964–1965	42,600	211.0	202	39,800	224.0	178
1965–1966	47,000	232.0	203	48,900	240.0	204
1966–1967	73,200	261.0	280	66,300	261.0	254
1967–1968	51,400	283.7	181	49,100	273.9	179
1968–1969	69,700	309.8	227	60,000	288.8	208
1969–1970	72,900	332.3	219	64,800	303.8	213
1970–1971	82,100	348.3	236	60,200	312.2	193
1971–1972	68,800	323.3	213	68,200	301.0	227
1972–1973	90,000	320.3	281	79,700	299.3	266
1973–1974	92,100	316.3	291	73,700	298.3	247
1974–1975	96,600	314.8	307	76,700	295.6	259
1975–1976	98,800	308.4	320	82,400	288.0	286
1976–1977	115,000	306.9	375	71,800	287.4	250
1977–1978	88,300	299.0	295	79,500	280.0	284
1978–1979	91,000	295.5	308	73,000	276.0	264
1979–1980	117,900	298.9	394	88,800	277.7	320
1980–1981	105,600	297.2	355	66,800	276.2	226

	Total Florida Oranges			Temples		
Season	Production	Bearing Acreage	Box Yield Per Acre	Production	Bearing Acreage	Box Yield Per Acre
1963–1964	54,900	388.0	141	3,400	16.0	213
1964–1965	82,400	435.0	189	3,800	16.0	238
1965–1966	95,900	472.0	203	4,500	17.0	265
1966–1967	139,500	522.0	267	5,000	18.0	278
1967–1968	100,500	557.6	180	4,500	18.3	246
1968–1969	129,700	595.6	218	4,500	19.7	228
1969–1970	137,700	636.1	216	5,200	21.8	239
1970–1971	142,300	660.5	215	5,000	23.0	217
1971–1972	137,000	624.2	219	5,300	22.4	237
1972–1973	169,700	619.6	274	5,100	22.3	229
1973–1974	165,800	614.6	270	5,300	21.9	242
1974–1975	173,300	610.4	284	5,300	21.9	242
1975–1976	181,200	596.4	304	5,500	20.5	268
1976–1977	186,800	594.3	314	3,800	20.3	187
1977–1978	167,800	579.0	290	4,900	18.9	259
1978–1979	164,000	571.5	287	4,700	18.3	257
1979–1980	206,700	576.6	358	6,000	18.2	330
1980–1981	172,400	573.4	301	3,600	17.7	203

Source: Florida Crop and Livestock Reporting Service, *Citrus Summary*.
[a]90 lb.

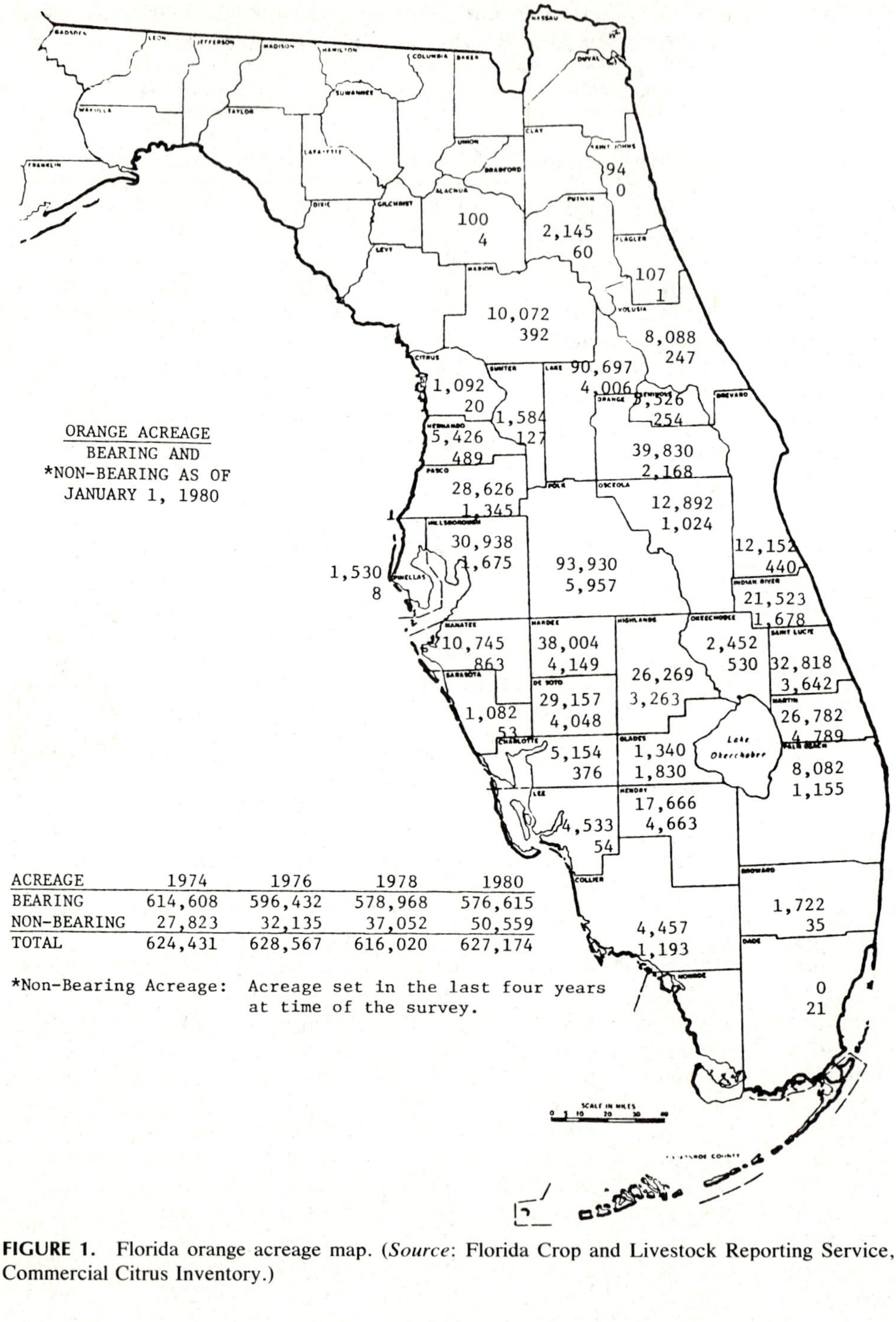

ACREAGE	1974	1976	1978	1980
BEARING	614,608	596,432	578,968	576,615
NON-BEARING	27,823	32,135	37,052	50,559
TOTAL	624,431	628,567	616,020	627,174

FIGURE 1. Florida orange acreage map. (*Source*: Florida Crop and Livestock Reporting Service, Commercial Citrus Inventory.)

back freezes (never before occurring) have taken a hard toll on both tree survival and fruit production.

The 1980–1981 freeze hit the northern and central citrus-producing areas the hardest, while the 1981–1982 freeze affected the central and southern citrus-producing areas. The shift in plantings from northcentral Florida to the Lake Okeechobee area following the 1971–1972 and 1976–1977 freezes was done because seldom have devastating weather conditions reached this far south. These freezes in recent times have caused concern among Florida citrus growers.

FOREIGN PRODUCTION. The big concern of Florida growers is the continuing expansion of production in Brazil and Central America. The Brazilian crop is challenging Florida's production for size. Brazil has ultramodern plants, good financing, and increased production knowledge. Inflation, government controls, and competition from Florida are negative factors in Brazil, but the severest Brazilian problem is their lack of marketing skill.

At present, Brazil does not have any real retail marketing program for orange juice. Its principal effort is aimed at selling bulk frozen concentrated orange juice to Europe, Canada, and the United States. While the demand from Europe is expanding, quality standards for European shipments are less than the U. S. demands. United States consumption of Brazilian juice has been dependent on severe production losses in Florida. Major imports have been restricted to those years in which a freeze has severely reduced the U.S. crop.

The freezes in the past 10 years have encouraged Brazilian production increases. It is expected that when Florida production recovers to normal levels, the lower Brazilian prices will tend to become even a bigger deterrent to higher Florida prices. FCOJ is truly influenced more by world supply and demand factors than ever before.

EFFECTS OF SUPPLY ON PRICE. Until the 1980–1981 freeze, Florida's own production was the principal factor in determining price. With the large imports both in 1981 and 1982, a price ceiling was formed. Even though the freeze of 1981–1982 caused less juice availability than anytime in the past 10 years, prices of the FCOJ futures plunged to below the previous year's low immediately after reaching new highs. The reason was simple. Florida purchased enough Brazilian FCOJ to more than make up the deficit in lost supply while raising the prices to retailers. Since this occurred at the same time as a major U.S. and world recession was progressing, the artificially high price of juice could not be sustained.

Production figures from Brazil are difficult to obtain. It is most likely to be accomplished "after the fact." This unknown is a major consideration in futures trading. In addition, some Florida processors have recently taken advantage of an obvious entrepreneurial venture by purchasing Brazilian production beyond their immediate needs and selling it for delivery to the FCOJ futures market.

ORANGE JUICE DEMAND

Demand for orange juice in the U.S. has continued its basic upwards spiral. Improved marketing procedures, advertising, and quality control have all helped to increase the demand for orange juice. Recently, a shift in consumption has

TABLE 5. Florida Frozen Concentrated Orange Juice Pack, Box Utilization, Yield, and Imports

Season	Net Pack (45° Gal)	Boxes[a] (1⅗ Bushel)	Yield (45° Gal per Box)	Foreign Imports (45° Gal)	Total Pack (45° Gal)
1964–1965	88,868,804	54,467,268	1.63160	1,473,378	90,342,182
1965–1966	70,831,316	57,317,447	1,23577	888,206	71,719,522
1966–1967	127,610,559	93,686,282	1.36210	400,498	128,011,057
1967–1968	83,697,047	61,965,460	1.35070	3,643,671	87,340,718
1968–1969	103,750,060	92,125,322	1.12618	2,459,756	108,042,918
1969–1970	124,947,460	100,738,932	1.24030	161,963	126,402,136
1970–1971	125,187,449	103,521,122	1.20909	3,980,943	133,744,515
1971–1972	134,229,151	104,339,222	1.28572	6,563,746	145,896,809
1972–1973	176,073,382	132,210,060	1,33176	1,230,034	180,174,409
1973–1974	171,845,896	132,468,892	1.29725	3,464,865	176,445,126
1974–1975	178,174,349	135,511,676	1.31482	5,777,713	184,917,159
1975–1976	186,264,679	144,526,082	1.28879	6,472,776	203,501,872
1976–1977	158,035,253	147,771,842	1.06945	9,455,888	181,833,316
1977–1978	161,203,606	130,928,816	1.23123	27,749,619	200,488,934
1978–1979	173,052,541	129,122,923	1.34021	28,734,917	216,419,164
1979–1980	231,256,856	173,229,054	1.33501	16,533,601	256,441,876
1980–1981	174,537,195	144,321,960	1.20935	56,850,587	249,617,683

Source: Florida Citrus Processors Association, *Weekly Report.*
[a]90 lb.

started to occur. The growth of *chilled juice* sales has shown greater strength than that of FCOJ. The marketing effort by large processors from Florida and their competitors in the rest of the United States has helped the growth of this convenient and attractive package. Although the increase in price which followed the freezes of 1980–1981 and 1981–1982 combined with a national recession to curtailed growth of sales in this new area, the trend has been established.

With the mergers of some Florida processors with very large national food and drink distributors, a positive change is just beginning to have its effect on the well-established upward trend of increased consumer demand. New types of packaging, marketing skills, and even new products may serve to continue this basic trend upwards.

SEASONALITY

The season for FCOJ begins with the USDA's release of its crop estimate in October of each year. This report sets the stage for futures prices. Almost immediately, the concern over a winter freeze begins and prices tend to move higher within a few days of the report, whether that report is "bullish" or "bearish" to futures prices.

Hedging by processors begins in earnest after the release of the crop-estimate report and continues through February. Since most freeze scares occur on the

TABLE 6. Florida Frozen Concentrated Orange Juice Movement, Pack, and Inventories (in Thousand Gallons)

Season	Beginning Inventory	Net Season Pack	Foreign Imports	Movement	Ending Inventory
1955–1956	9,713	69,592	n.a.	66,462	12,843
1956–1957	12,843	72,455	n.a.	74,009	11,556
1957–1958	11,566	56,764	n.a.	61,601	6,719
1958–1959	6,719	79,981	n.a.	70,096	16,605
1959–1960	16,605	77,999	n.a.	83,929	9,663
1960–1961	9,663	84,374	n.a.	80,405	13,631
1961–1962	13,631	115,866	n.a.	95,745	33,750
1962–1963	33,750	51,648	n.a.	69,979	15,399
1963–1964	15,399	56,124	1,739	61,386	10,136
1964–1965	10,136	90,342	1,473	77,933	21,814
1965–1966	21,814	77,577	888	86,568	12,828
1966–1967	12,828	132,155	400	117,758	27,225
1967–1968	27,225	87,341	3,644	101,681	12,885
1968–1969	12,885	108,043	2,460	103,686	17,400
1969–1970	17,400	126,402	162	120,844	26,566
1970–1971	26,566	133,744	3,981	140,094	22,568
1971–1972	22,568	145,897	6,564	140,251	27,750
1972–1973	27,750	180,174	1,230	159,743	47,372
1973–1974	47,371	176,445	3,465	174,956	48,861
1974–1975	48,861	183,366	5,778	187,216	50,759
1975–1976	50,759	186,265	6,473	192,185	53,709
1976–1977	53,709	158,035	9,456	198,480	25,526
1977–1978	25,526	161,204	27,750	180,205	30,909
1978–1979	30,909	173,053	28,735	200,659	37,386
1979–1980	37,386	231,257	16,534	232,829	54,802
1980–1981[a]	57,281	174,537	56,851	228,505	66,251

Source: Florida Citrus Processors Association, *Weekly Report.*
[a]43.4° Brix.
n.a. = not available.

"full moon," prices tend to be highest near this monthly phenomenon and lowest immediately afterwards with the absence of frost. In fact, prices have had a seasonal tendency to be lowest relative to the cash market between the full moon in December and January, even though they generally make their actual lows (without frost) in futures prices as well as recording the narrowest basis in April to May.

A December freeze that hits the majority of Florida producers has never occurred while there has been a futures market in FCOJ. The 1961–1962 freeze was the last one of record. In December 1980, such a freeze was predicted for Florida, but cloud cover moved in at the last moment and saved all but the southwest growing areas.

Florida citrus trees are not usually dormant in December; a freeze at that time would be considered devastating to Florida because not only would the fruit loss be the highest, since the fruit is less mature and susceptible to frost, but trees would be in danger of being killed. If a freeze occurred, then the supply problems generated would have their effect on futures prices for years to come. That is why futures prices usually decline after the December full-moon period is past, and the chances of a damaging freeze are greatly reduced.

There is no proven validity to the "full-moon" freeze phenomenon except that recent freezes have occurred during these periods. Obviously, freezes can occur at any time during the winter.

Freezes in Florida are very difficult to predict, and rarely occur because Florida is a peninsula. Usually Pacific cold patterns are not harmful to Florida. For a major freeze to develop, it requires a very strong high-pressure system to move down from the North Pole, down past the Rocky Mountains towards Texas and Oklahoma, and then due East toward Florida. The positioning, movement, and degree of pressure of the major high-pressure zone determine the extent of the freeze.

Most Florida growers along with major commodity brokerage firms contract weather information from either internal or external short- and long-term weather forecasters and climatologists. As a matter of interest, NOAA provides an excellent weather commentary daily on a Public Broadcasting System (PBS) program entitled "A.M. Weather."

The FCOJ futures have a strong but unreliable seasonal trend. Generally, futures trend lower along with a reduction in volume and open interest after the winter scare is decided. Once "harvest" is complete, usually in June, futures prices tend to move higher as speculation of drought, hurricanes, and the October estimate are the main considerations.

Even though FCOJ follows a strong seasonal tendency of being highest during preharvest and the winter season and lowest immediately afterwards, supply and demand always prevail. Watching for imports, weekly movement figures, pack, and goods on hand are major considerations on a weekly basis as to futures prices.

SEASONAL STUDIES. Seasonal studies which use the method of averaging the price movements of orange juice generate poor, weak results. As shown in Figure 2(*a*), the 11-year analysis of the cash market has a slow upwards bias, as though inflation, rather than the seasonal factors, was the only influence on the orange juice market. This, however, can be greatly misleading.

Orange juice has been subject to price "shocks" due to severe weather influences. Four freezes have occurred in the past 10 years. This situation results in both hedgers and speculators forming the opinion that the risk of a short position in the early winter is far greater than the possible rewards. Prices tend to rise as winter nears in October and November [see Figure 2(*b*)] and they experience a severe "shock" upwards if a freeze occurs or a significant decline if a freeze does not materialize. The statistics in Figure 2(*b*) however, show that the pattern is highly unreliable. Although the price movement is expected, it is formed by only a few extreme cases, reducing its reliability.

The orange juice market would be ideally suited for a "filtered" seasonal study. Developing weather patterns, identified by lower-than-average temperatures in Florida, could be used to separate annual price data. It could be easily expected that these years of lower temperatures showed stronger, more reliable price movements in late fall and early winter. The January movement would still be severe in either an upwards or downwards direction, depending on the actual occurrence of a freeze and would therefore still be expected to be unreliable.

BASIS. The *basis* for FCOJ is generally derived by using the *nearby futures less the delivered cash price* of fruit. That figure is obtained from the Florida Citrus Processors Association's weekly figures using weekly total boxes and weighted-averages of the combined price of "weekly prices" and "intermediate prices" of oranges used in FCOJ and comparing this figure to nearby futures.

The widest basis, except for a period immediately after a freeze, usually occurs around the time of the October estimate, again between the full moon of December and January, and finally settles out in the last weeks of harvest (see Figure 3).

In a general sense Florida processors, and of late Brazilian interest in cooperation with Florida processors, are sellers of a wide basis, covering shorts at a narrow or negative basis. Conversely, end users usually purchase contracts on a weak basis and become sellers on a wide basis.

Although deliveries are still very large relative to open interest there has been a great deal of effort on the part of takers and brokers to "ex-pit" rather than going to the expense of a delivery. Deliverers have attempted to be secretive about their intentions and in some cases have tried to influence the trends in futures prices by making and taking deliveries.

PRICE DYNAMICS

The price of orange juice has been greatly dependent upon the supply. It is likely, however, that competition from foreign markets will dampen the price "shocks" caused by sudden damage to U.S. crops and allow demand to be a greater factor in the price equation.

Figure 4 shows the weekly price of the nearest futures contract of FCOJ. It is clear that anticipation and real changes in supply have caused prices to be highly volatile. Figure 5 shows the FCOJ prices as a weighted seasonal average.

TRADING OF FCOJ

The spot market, traded between 2:00 p.m. and 2:30 p.m. when the futures market is open, is really determined by the prices of nearby futures, time, cost of money and storage rather than necessarily reflecting the current bulk equivalent. The volume traded in the spot market readily reflects this. Whether futures and/or spot transactions lead bulk prices or vice versa remains undetermined.

The "trade" in FCOJ is unique because most at present are Florida interests with the exception of a few northern end users and a handful of foreign concerns. The trade consists of Florida bulk processors, integrated processors, growers, cash fruit dealers ("bird dogs"), and chilled juice users. Because of the standards and delivery points (Florida only) many potential retail users and other end users do not avail themselves of the ability to hedge their needs.

TABLE 7. Temperature Record By Months Showing Average and Lowest Reading for the Month From 17 Selected Stations

Stations		1977–1978				1978–1979				1979–80				1980–1981			
		Nov.	Dec.	Jan.	Feb.	Nov.	Dec.	Jan.	Feb.	Nov.	Dec.	Jan.	Feb.	Nov.	Dec.	Jan.	Feb.
Arcadia	Average temperature	67.4	60.9	56.4	56.0	70.7	66.6	58.9	60.7	69.0	62.6	61.5	58.0	67.8	58.8	51.2	61.8
	Lowest[a]	36	28	27	26	46	44	29	29	39	35	31	27	37	34	18	28
Avon Park	Average temperature	67.9	59.7	55.2	55.1	70.8	66.5	57.1	58.8	69.1	62.3	58.5	56.5	66.9	58.2	50.1	60.5
	Lowest[a]	38	27	28	30	48	42	28	29	37	36	32	36	35	34	16	30
Bartow	Average temperature	67.7	60.3	55.1	55.9	71.3	66.3	57.9	60.3	68.1	62.7	61.6	58.0	67.4	59.4	52.6	62.6
	Lowest	37	28	25	28	43	44	27	33	36	36	32	30	38	36	19	32
Bradenton	Average temperature	67.6	60.2	55.3	54.8	70.7	66.3	58.4	60.2	68.7	62.5	60.9	57.4	67.8	59.4	50.7	61.8
	Lowest[a]	39	32	29	31	45	44	30	33	40	34	31	31	36	35	23	31
Brooksville	Average temperature	66.9	59.7	53.8	52.9	69.5	64.5	56.0	58.3	68.1	61.2	60.0	57.0	67.2	56.0	51.5	61.4
	Lowest[a]	37	30	25	26	40	38	21	28	31	33	30	25	34	32	13	26
Clermont	Average temperature	66.8	59.0	54.5	53.5	70.4	65.0	57.4	59.0	67.8	61.3	59.6	57.1	65.7	57.3	50.6	61.2
	Lowest[a]	39	29	28	30	26	30	26	24	35	34	27	23	33	31	8	25
Fort Myers	Average temperature	70.2	63.3	59.2	57.2	74.2	69.7	62.5	64.0	73.8	66.9	65.1	60.7	70.8	62.8	55.7	65.8
	Lowest[a]	43	35	33	32	49	44	34	39	45	45	40	36	43	39	28	32
Fort Pierce	Average temperature	70.6	63.5	58.5	57.2	73.1	70.0	61.8	62.3	72.6	65.9	63.2	59.1	70.2	62.0	54.6	64.4
	Lowest[a]	43	34	32	32	48	50	32	33	41	42	30	32	41	38	24	32
Kissimmee	Average temperature	68.6	61.2	57.4	56.3	71.6	67.5	59.9	60.4	68.8	62.7	61.3	58.3	67.3	59.7	52.8	62.0
	Lowest[a]	38	30	29	28	43	41	28	29	38	37	33	28	37	38	20	29
Lakeland	Average temperature	68.2	59.9	55.3	55.0	71.4	66.8	59.2	61.2	68.7	63.0	61.1	58.3	67.5	58.9	53.1	63.2
	Lowest[a]	44	34	29	32	42	42	27	32	37	35	33	29	40	36	20	31
Mt. Lake	Average temperature	68.1	61.3	57.5	56.2	71.5	67.6	60.0	61.5	69.2	64.3	62.5	59.0	67.6	59.4	52.2	63.2
	Lowest[a]	36	26	26	28	41	38	28	28	39	36	33	29	35	35	17	24

Ocala	Average temperature	65.1	56.2	51.5	50.6	68.1	62.2	54.9	56.1	64.6	59.3	57.4	55.1	63.0	55.1	48.7	58.7
	Lowest[a]	27	20	20	22	38	33	24	24	30	26	27	23	31	31	13	25
Orlando	Average temperature	69.6	61.0	56.8	55.8	72.3	66.8	58.2	58.4	68.3	62.6	60.5	57.2	67.1	59.0	51.3	61.7
	Lowest[a]	41	31	30	31	43	38	25	27	35	35	30	26	38	36	19	32
Tampa	Average temperature	67.7	58.7	55.0	53.2	71.7	66.2	57.8	59.3	68.7	63.0	62.0	56.6	66.4	57.5	50.4	61.4
	Lowest[a]	40	30	29	28	41	37	27	31	34	32	32	32	37	32	15	28
Tarpon Springs	Average temperature	68.0	59.2	55.3	53.0	70.3	65.1	57.8	59.3	68.4	61.4	59.7	55.7	66.4	58.0	49.9	61.4
	Lowest[a]	39	30	30	28	42	43	28	29	36	32	30	30	38	34	15	30
Titusville	Average temperature	66.8	58.8	54.0	53.1	n.a.	n.a.	n.a.	n.a.	69.1	62.1	58.7	55.0	66.7	58.7	49.5	n.a.
	Lowest[a]	40	30	29	28	n.a.	n.a.	n.a.	n.a.	38	38	33	32	35	36	17	32
West Palm Beach	Average temperature	72.6	67.3	62.1	60.4	73.7	71.3	62.7	63.7	73.2	67.1	64.1	60.9	72.4	65.5	58.7	67.6
	Lowest[a]	47	39	37	32	49	51	34	30	46	41	39	36	37	34	25	33

Source: Records of Federal–State Agricultural Weather Service, Ruskin, Florida.

[a]From Frost Warning Station—generally nearby low-ground locations—average from Climatological Stations.

n.a. = not available.

TABLE 8. Miscellaneous Data Relating to Citrus Showing Records of Annual Precipitation (in Inches)

Year	Brooksville	West Palm Beach	Avon Park	Bartow	Fort Myers	Clermont	Orlando	Arcadia	Lakeland
1960	77.49	66.77	65.87	73.85	54.33	66.27	68.74	62.32	65.42
1961	44.03	37.76	39.53	43.15	54.74	32.28	41.78	34.30	3583
1962	46.28	48.56	45.62	51.55	58.15	40.33	50.35	57.95	38.16
1963	48.03	53.31	63.80	63.65	42.90	50.04	45.28	53.65	46.26
1964	71.35	79.30	47.45	45.31	32.83	55.15	54.39	49.68	47.53
1965	61.45	58.26	60.10	46.68	50.83	47.81	47.40	53.95	48.35
1966	55.43	79.75	59.14	48.70	44.99	56.62	55.39	51.62	45.47
1967	48.69	51.54	44.08	44.63	49.39	53.53	40.91	60.96	37.80
1968	47.07	77.42	55.60	51.85	70.29	53.39	52.10	54.71	55.37
1969	58.87	79.75	61.29	56.38	71.94	63.71	55.18	64.53	53.00
1970	52.95	55.28	48.85	49.18	58.84	48.21	43.96	45.62	46.56
1971	56.53	51.31	42.45	52.44	47.32	49.77	40.09	41.80	42.91
1972	58.61	75.15	50.42	42.55	56.71	46.67	51.31	40.12	38.29
1973	51.83	54.74	55.51	52.39	44.33	54.94	55.37	52.65	45.41
1974	58.92	58.46	47.55	42.48	52.83	45.39	44.38	52.35	43.89
1975	46.31	44.40	45.95	45.27	51.50	49.81	47.04	45.60	41.50
1976	50.78	55.32	47.69	51.26	48.67	55.96	47.08	37.33	49.94
1977	40.70	64.26	39.31	48.45	54.06	40.41	38.12	43.89	45.18
1978	45.33	62.21	49.57	55.35	53.10	50.79	50.59	46.45	46.15
1979	55.61	61.18	56.22	60.68	66.98	67.36	50.23	67.99	69.72
1980	53.75	56.67	44.32	46.11	45.00	40.10	41.21	37.06	46.80
1981[a]	19.12	17.27	16.80	13.97	18.68	19.75	20.90	18.72	14.87

Freezing Point for Citrus Degrees of at least 2 Hours Duration	
Small green oranges	28.5
Green oranges and grapefruit	27.5
Half ripe oranges and grapefruit	27.5
Full ripe oranges and grapefruit	27.0
Tangerines	29.5
Tender growth	27.0
Dark green growth	24.0
Buttons	24.0
Open bloom	30.0

[a]Through June.

Source: The above records of annual precipitation compiled from records of the National Weather Service Office, Ruskin, Florida, Record of freezing points furnished by the above source.

Processing plants that purchase fruit rather than a cooperative unit (an integrated production processing association) will either hedge their purchases using futures or allow sellers to "fix the price" at delivery time, setting the basis "on-call" (see Rinehimer, Chapter 9 in this book).

Cooperatives tend to use the futures market less than cash purchasers of fruit. They may, however, sell their excess production or purchase shortfall rather than

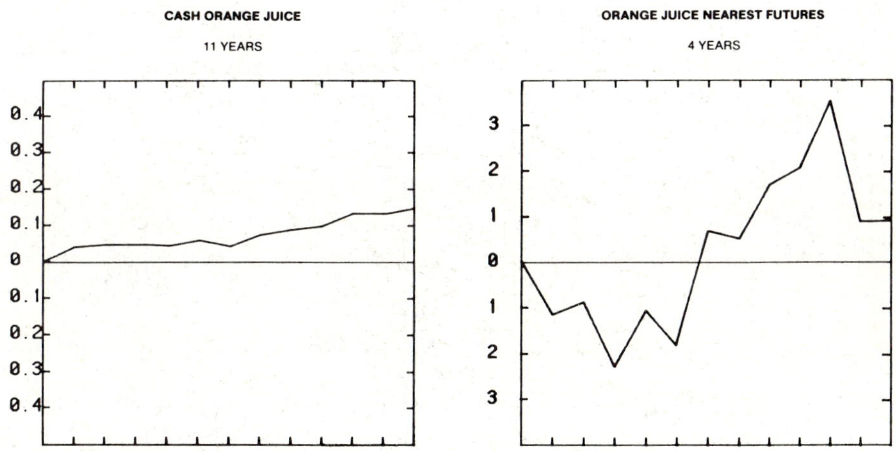

	J-F	F-M	M-A	A-M	M-J	J-J	J-A	A-S	S-O	O-N	N-D	D-J
Average Move	0	0	0	-0.1	0	-0.1	0	0	0	0	-0.1	0
% Reliable	63.7	81.9	72.8	27.3	91	45.5	100	100	91	81.9	18.2	91
Avg. Up Move	0.2	0.1	0	0.1	0	0	0	0	0	0.1	0	0
Avg. Down Move	0.2	0.2	0.1	0.1	0.1	0.1	0	0	0.2	0.1	0.1	0.1
Greatest Up Move	0.7	0.1	0	0.1	0.1	0	0.1	0.1	0.1	0.2	0	0
Greatest Down Move	0.4	0.3	0.1	0.2	0.1	0.2	0	0	0.2	0.1	0.1	0.1

(*a*)

	J-F	F-M	M-A	A-M	M-J	J-J	J-A	A-S	S-O	O-N	N-D	D-J
Average Move	-1.2	0.2	-1.5	1.2	-0.8	2.4	-0.2	1.1	0.3	1.4	-2.7	0
% Reliable	75	75	100	75	50	75	50	50	25	75	100	50
Avg. Up Move	1.2	1.4	0	2	0.3	3.8	1.2	2.5	4.3	2.3	0	2.7
Avg. Down Move	2	3.2	1.5	1.2	1.9	1.6	1.6	0.2	1	1.3	2.7	2.7
Greatest Up Move	1.2	1.7	0	3.9	0.5	4.9	1.7	3.2	4.3	3.5	0	4.8
Greatest Down Move	2.3	3.2	2.8	1.2	3.6	1.6	3	0.3	1.8	1.3	3.5	3.4

(*b*)

FIGURE 2. Seasonal analysis of orange juice. (*a*) Cash orange juice, 11 years. (*b*) Orange juice nearest futures, 4 years.

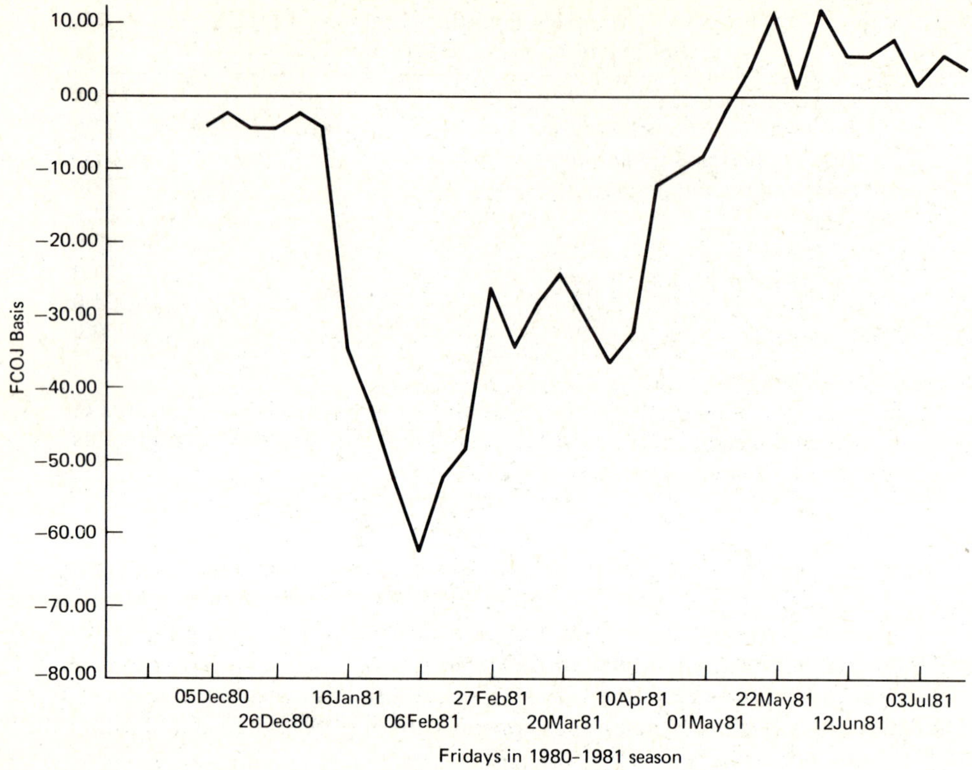

FIGURE 3. FCOJ basis study.

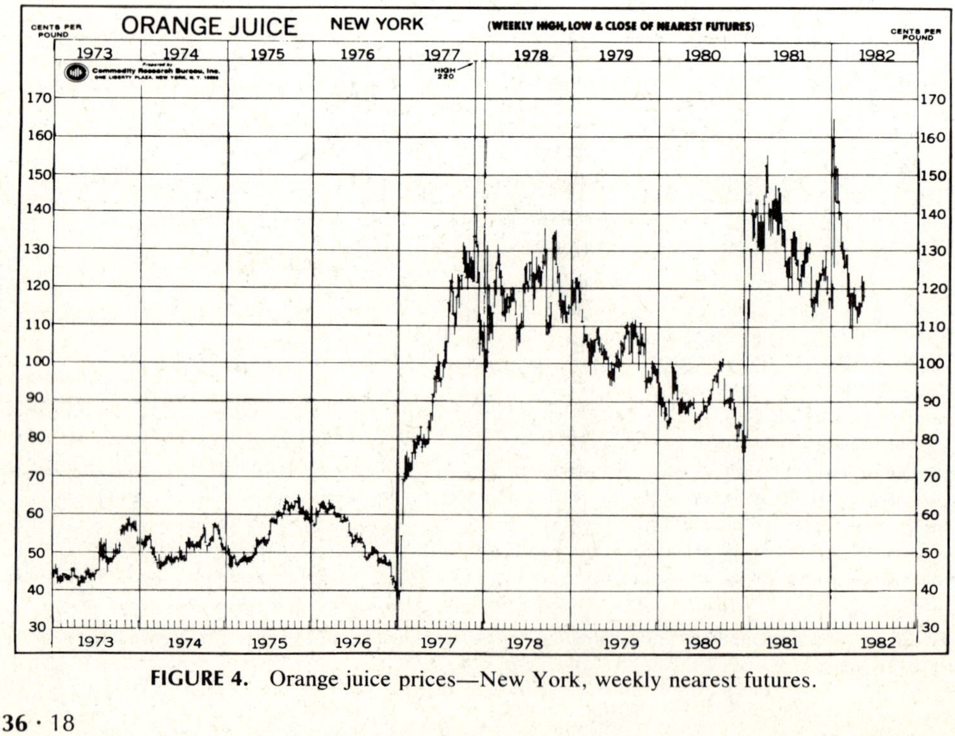

FIGURE 4. Orange juice prices—New York, weekly nearest futures.

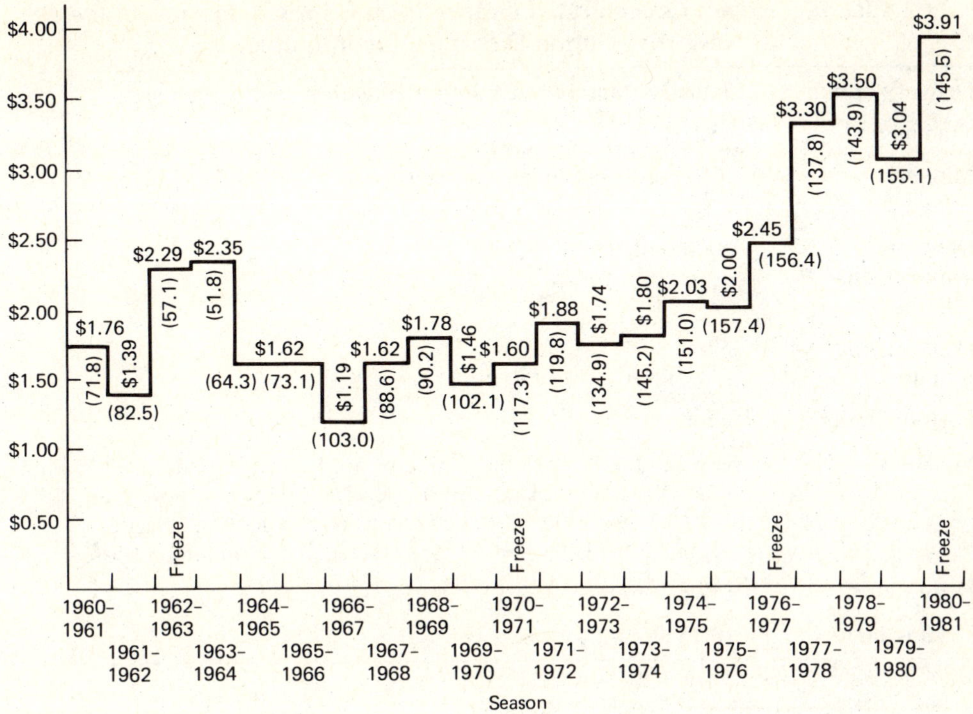

FIGURE 5. FCOJ prices, weighted seasonal average FCOB prices per dozen 6-oz cans. (Retail and institutional volume in million concentrate gallons: 42° Brix 1960–1961 through 1964–1965; 45° Brix 1965–1966 through 1979–1980; 43.4° Brix 1980–1981.)

use normal futures "basis" trading or manage their inventories through futures hedging. In fact, many large processors use the futures market *only* as a source of supply rather than as a management tool.

SPECULATION. Nearly all of the "trade" speculates in the FCOJ futures as do members of all commodities groups. After all, agriculture at its very best is always a speculation. The largest speculative portion of the trade is the grower and cash fruit dealer "bird dog." The "bird dog" is constantly "hedging" needs from day to day depending on minor changes in fundamentals rather than long-range consideration involved in hedging. These speculations are an integral and important segment of this market and to a great deal keep it liquid.

The role of the speculator, both domestic and foreign, has had a large effect on futures prices in the past several years. The fundamental information available to large speculators (either individual or managed pools) and the continued improvement in technical trading techniques have improved to a great extent giving the speculator a better edge.

The *Traders Position* released by the exchange on Tuesdays gives the position of traders for the previous week and is one source of important information for both the trade and speculators. Likewise, the release of the weekly Florida Citrus Processors Association *movement figures* on Thursdays is also a tool of importance in trading. However, an improvement in this type of information is still

TABLE 9. Frozen Concentrated Orange Juice (Citrus Associates of the New York Cotton Exchange, Incorporated)

Delivery months	January, March, May, July, September, and November
Trading unit	15,000 lb
Minimum fluctuation	.05¢ per lb ($7.50 per contract)
Daily price movement limits	500 points ($0.05 per lb)
Daily trading limits	None
Position limits	None
Standards	U.S. Grade A, with brix value of not less than 51 degrees, having a brix value acid ratio of not less than 13:1 nor more than 19.5:1, with the factors of color and flavor each scoring 37 points or higher and 19 for defects, with a minimum score of 94
Delivery	From warehouses in Florida licensed by the exchange
Trading hours	10:15 a.m.–2:45 p.m. eastern time

needed. National or even international figures of movement, pack, imports, exports, and goods on hand are needed to give all traders a better true perspective of the supply-and-demand relationship.

CONTRACT SPECIFICATIONS. At the present time FCOJ calls for 41.8 brix juice. This was a change from 42.3 brix in 1980 and down from 44.5 brix for years prior to this. The lower the brix the greater the amount of the FCOJ production for the same quality of fruit. There have been moves by some quarters in Florida to revert to a higher brix level, but because the national standard is 41.8 brix any move so far has met great competition by "northern" dealers using the national standard.

SOURCES OF INFORMATION

Citrus Summary (Florida Department of Agriculture), annual.

Florida Crop and Livestock Reporting Service (Florida Department of Agriculture).

Fruit Situation Report (USDA), quarterly February, July, September, and November.

Monthly Cold Storage Reports (USDA), midmonth.

Summary of the Citrus Fruit Industry (USDA), annual October.

Traders Position (New York Cotton Exchange).

Triangle (Florida Citrus Manual).

Weekly Statistics (Florida Canners Association).

CHAPTER 37

THE POTATO MARKET

CONTENTS

Structuring Markets 4
Perishability 6

SUPPLY OF POTATOES 8

Seasonal Distribution 8
Estimates of Supply 9
Variations in Production 10
Disappearance 15

SEASONALITY 18

FUTURES MARKETS 20

REFERENCES 21

SOURCES OF INFORMATION 21

CHAPTER 37

THE POTATO MARKET

Perry J. Kaufman

The potato market would seem an ideal choice for futures trading, but has rarely in its long history been able to satisfy the demand of its diverse industry. Prices themselves have always been the most volatile of all products; the inelastic demand and inconsistent supply causes frequent price explosions in the late winter and early spring. By comparing the price movements in Figures 1 and 2 we can readily see that the futures market serves to dampen most price movements where the cash market has continued to be highly volatile.

Selection of the best futures contract has been a problem since futures trading in potatoes began. Although Maine and the eastern region continue to be a dominant market force, its share has been decreasing as production becomes more highly concentrated in the western states. In 1970 the U.S. fall potato production was segregated as follows:

Eastern states (Maine, New Hampshire, Vermont, Massachusetts, Rhode Island, Connecticut, New York–Long Island and upstate New York, and Pennsylvania)—24.9%.

Central states (Ohio, Indiana, Michigan, Wisconsin, Minnesota, North Dakota, South Dakota, and Nebraska)—20.6%.

Western states (Montana, Idaho, Wyoming, Colorado, Utah, Nevada, Washington, Oregon, and California)—54.5%.

By 1980 this scenario had changed dramatically to:

Eastern states—15.8%
Central states—22.3%
Western states—61.9%

Futures trading in potatoes began in 1931 at the Chicago Mercantile Exchange (CME). The CME contract failed to generate sustained interest among traders for Idaho russet potatoes. In 1941 the New York Mercantile Exchange (NYME) introduced trading in *Maine potatoes*, round whites of Maine origin. The NYME

My appreciation to Karen Forstik of the New York Mercantile Exchange for her help and to Jack Schwager for his continued excellence in his own research and writing (see "References" section).

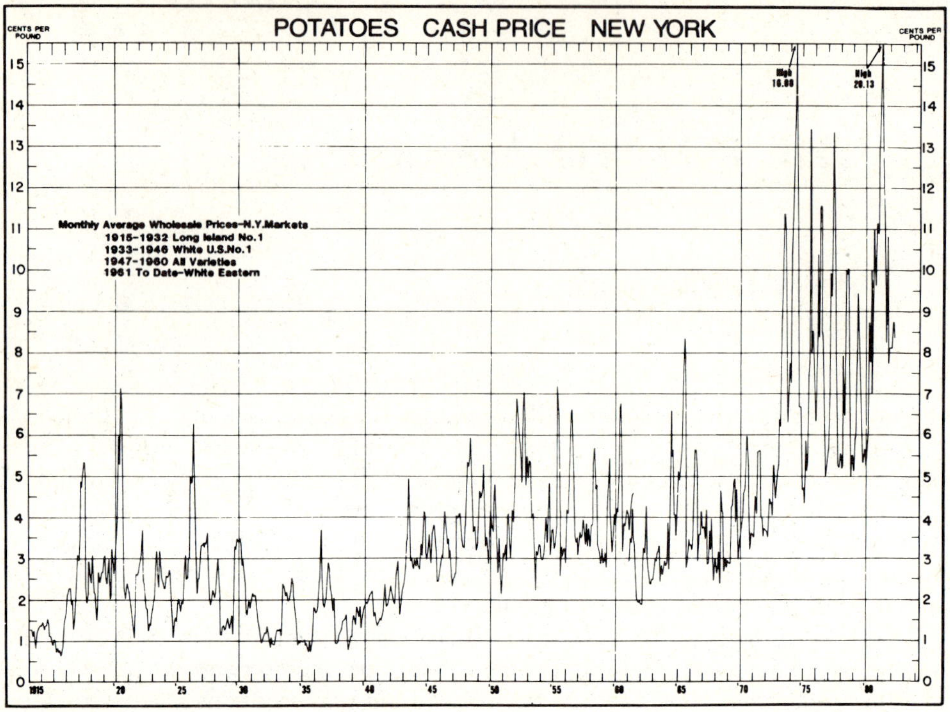

FIGURE 1. Potato prices cash—New York. *Source:* Commodity Research Bureau Inc.

has accounted for nearly all of the futures trading in potatoes despite periodic efforts by the CME to alter and revitalize the western potato contract.

STRUCTURING MARKETS. It would seem surprising that an eastern potato contract would succeed while the CME western potatoes contract would not. Russets account for approximately 70% of U.S. potato production while round whites amount to only 25%. There are several explanations for this problem[1]:

1. Russets are often contracted before planting and are primarily used for processing, while round whites are used almost exclusively for table stock.
2. Russets are more likely to be marketed by large corporations.
3. Because of the diverse markets it is difficult to choose a single, central delivery point for russets.
4. The uncertainty of delivery points combined with the contract F.O.B. provisions have put buyers at a disadvantage.
5. There is a perceived quality difference between russets grown in different states.

[1]J. D. Schwager, "A Trader's Guide to Analyzing the Potato Futures Market," *1981 Commodity Yearbook*, Commodity Research Bureau, New York, 1981.

Many of the problems associated with western potato futures are the result of the geographic expansiveness of the industry and the high cost of transporting potatoes. In the eastern potato market alone, a much smaller area, the transportation costs were once a substantially greater portion of the retail price than the farmers' receipts. In the west the magnitude of the shipping problem is far greater.

This same transportation problem prevents the eastern and western markets from competing in all but rare instances; however, the strong marketing and packaging effort introduced by the larger western organizations have made inroads into the eastern consumer markets.

Two key events hurt the potato futures market during the 1970s, forcing a change of rules and delivery specifications. The 1976 default resulted from large short positions held primarily by two western producers unable to deliver the proper grade against the contract. This was resolved by only a partial settlement of delivery.

In 1979 trading was terminated when 49 of 57 contracts delivered failed to meet the grade specifications. To avoid a recurrence of this situation the exchange eliminated trading in the May contract, the last of the season, and expanded the

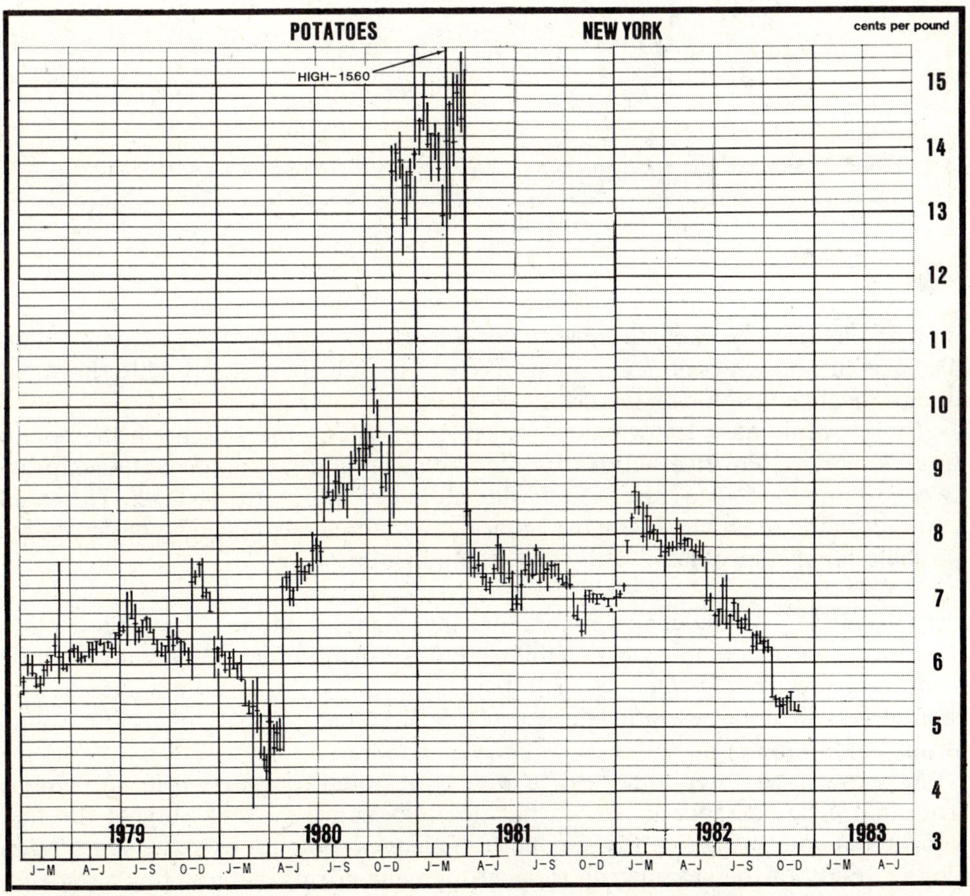

FIGURE 2. Potato prices futures—New York. *Source:* Commodity Research Bureau Inc.

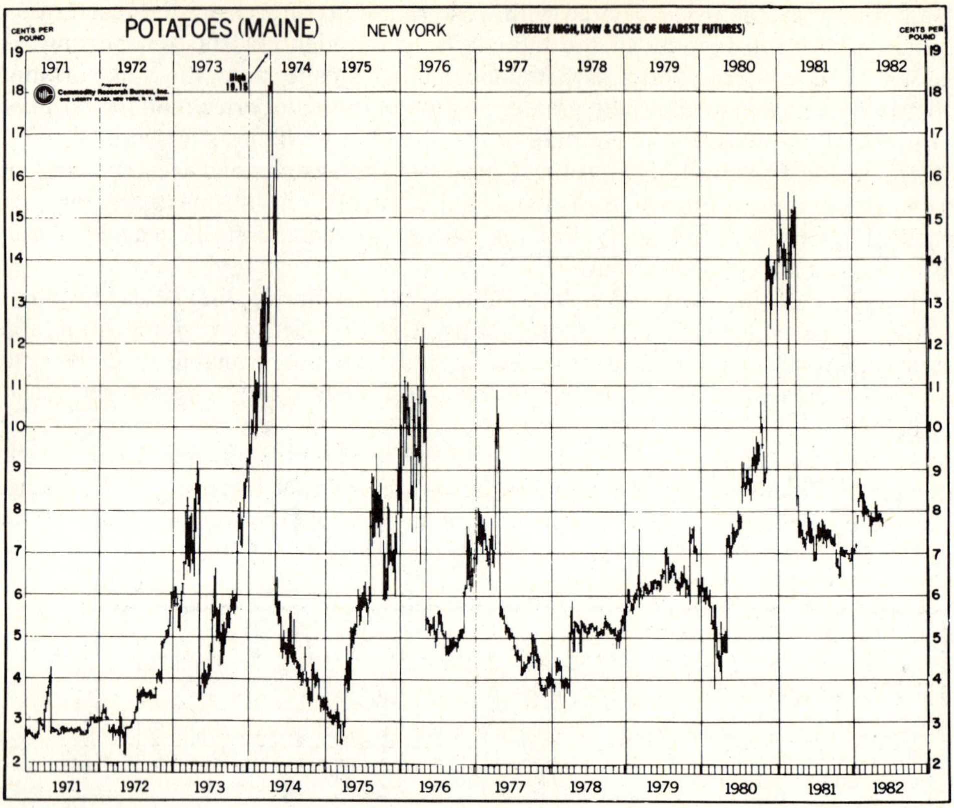

FIGURE 2. Continued.

deliverable areas to include upstate New York, Long Island, and Connecticut. The current futures contract is not as likely to be subject to deliverable shortages due to localized problems or quality.

These events have unfortunately taken their toll on the volume in the potato futures market. Positive actions by the exchange and the good relationship between futures prices and the cash market still keep the contract viable. The small contract value, compared to most other commodities, also makes potato trading possible for the speculator with small capitalization.

PERISHABILITY. One quality of potatoes that makes it different from many other agricultural products is its perishability. Unlike many other commodities, there is no "carryover"; in fact, the shrinkage and other problems associated with storage of fall potatoes into late spring cause concern among buyers and may result in extreme price shifts.

As we will see later, there is a gap in U.S. potato production in the winter. The final disappearance of stored fall potatoes and the availability of the first substantial late spring or early summer crop leaves room for extreme speculation on the ability of the stored crop to meet the demands of the next few months.

TABLE 1. Salient Statistics of Potatoes in the United States

Year	Acreage (1,000 Acres)		Yield Per Harvested Acre (cwt)	Farm Disposition: Used Where Grown (Million cwt.)			Farm Disposition	Farm Price (Dollars per cwt.)	Value of (Millions of Dollars)		Stocks on January 1st[d] (1,000 cwt.)	Foreign Trade[e] (1,000 cwt.)		Civilian Consumption Per Capita (in Pounds)
	Planted	Harvested		Seed	Feed	Household Use	Sold[b]		Production[c]	Sales		Domestic Exports	Imports	
1961	1,511	1,480	198	7.2	20.9	4.8	260.3	1.36	400	354	103,595	2,347	871	109
1962	1,378	1,347	197	6.0	17.0	4.0	237.9	1.67	441	398	122,215	3,359	912	107
1963	1,337	1,323	205	5.9	16.6	3.4	245.2	1.78	483	435	115,770	1,699	1,490	111
1964	1,311	1,272	190	7.4	12.2	2.8	218.7	3.50	846	756	115,000	1,617	3,482	111
1965	1,418	1,383	210	6.5	19.6	2.6	263.2	2.53	731	665	94,205	2,855	1,129	107.8
1966	1,498	1,463	210	8.1	31.4	2.4	265.0	2.04	623	543	124,170	2,247	2,743	113.6
1967	1,499	1,460	209	7.4	25.3	2.3	270.3	1.87	568	503	128,050	3,592	1,283	109.2
1968	1,415	1,383	214	6.9	20.9	2.1	264.2	2.23	657	589	139,170	2,569	2,636	115.8
1969	1,458	1,416	221	6.9	24.2	1.5	279.8	2.24	697	623	130,350	2,971	1,846	116.8
1970	1,450	1,421	229	10.0	23.9	1.4	291.9	2.21	714	644	138,140	2,928	1,230	117.5
1971	1,432	1,391	230	8.9	27.9	[a]	282.5	1.90	603		147,550	3,241	1,098	118.7
1972	1,301	1,256	236	7.9	20.0	[a]	268.5	3.02	896	808	148,600	4,430	759	119.4
1973	1,330	1,307	230	6.5	18.4	[a]	275.1	4.90	1,472	1,343	132,500	4,975	1,874	116.8
1974	1,422	1,392	246	6.5	32.5	[a]	303.4	4.01	1,355	1,215	131,600	4,545	1,453	114.3
1975	1,304	1,260	256	6.6	22.2	[a]	293.5	4.48	1,445	1,305	160,100	9,317	691	122.1
1976	1,407	1,371	261	6.8	26.2	[a]	324.7	3.59	1,283	1,167	156,220	11,617	806	116.1
1977	1,398	1,360	261	6.8	31.0	[a]	316.8	3.55	1,254	1,126	172,230	3,630	980	121.7
1978[f]	1,401	1,375	267	6.3	34.3	[a]	324.6	3.38	1,222	1,097	175,300	2,025	617	121.1
1979[f]	1,310	1,270	270	6.0	30.2	[a]	306.8	3.43	1,174	1,053	193,520			118.3
1980[f]	1,183	1,155	261								176,020			116.0
1981[f]	1,200										143,960			

Note: 60 lb equals one bushel. [a]Also feed. [b]For all purposes, including food, seed processing, livestock feed. [c]Farm weight basis. [d]Merchantable stocks held by growers and local dealers. [e]Year beginning July. [f]Preliminary. [g]Fresh and processed. *Source:* U.S. Department of Agriculture, Economic Research Service.

SUPPLY OF POTATOES

Potatoes are produced in almost every state in all seasons of the year. In recent years, nearly 70% of all production has originated in Aroostook County, Maine, the Small River area of Idaho, Kern County, California, and various regions of New York, Minnesota, and North Dakota. In 1981 the seven largest potato-producing states and their corresponding production levels were (in 1000's cwt):

State	Production
Idaho	80,040
Maine	26,520
Minnesota	13,300
North Dakota	20,125
Oregon	21,710
Washington	52,328
Wisconsin	18,191
	232,214

SEASONAL DISTRIBUTION. The USDA categorizes potatoes according to their harvest time. Most of the crops, with the exception of the primary ''fall'' harvest, are marketed out of harvest rather than stored. The late summer and fall crops account for 85% of the total annual production and all of the stocks which carry over until the early harvests of the next year. Table 2 indicates the terminology used to designate seasonal potato crops.

TABLE 2. Seasonal Categories of Potato Crops

Seasonal Crop	Approximate Time of Harvest
Winter	January—March
Early spring	April 1–May 15
Late spring	May 16–June 30
Early summer	July 1–September 30
Fall	October–December

Source: R.J. Teweles, C.V. Harlow, and H.L. Stone, *The Commodity Futures Game, Who Wins? Who Loses? Why?* McGraw-Hill, New York, NY, 1974.

Figure 3 shows the distribution of seasonal production. It is easy to see a natural progression from warmer to cooler climates as production moves from winter and early spring to late summer and fall. In recent years the winter harvest has accounted for only 1% of annual production, the spring and summer harvest each about 7%, and the fall harvest the remaining 85%. Since futures markets trade contracts with delivery from November through April, the fall crop becomes the sole determinant of prices.

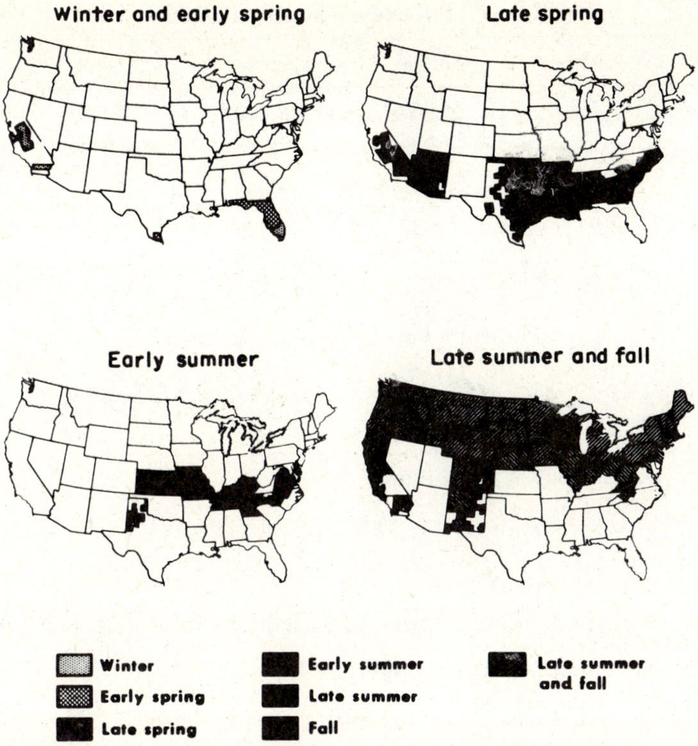

FIGURE 3. Principal potato-producing areas. (*Source:* U.S. Department of Agriculture, Economic Research Service.)

ESTIMATES OF SUPPLY. Since it is accepted that demand for potatoes is highly predictable and greatly inelastic, the key to price determination is both the anticipated and actual supply. There are three phases to this process:

1. Estimated versus actual planting.
2. Actual acreage (estimated yields) versus actual yields.
3. Estimated demand and availability versus actual disappearance (demand, shrinkage, spoilage).

Estimation of anticipated acreage to be planted late summer and fall for Maine fall harvest has been studied extensively by the USDA statistical service. For the period 1953–1970, the anticipated acreage for *Maine* was shown to be

$$A_t = 22.68 + 0.0610P_{t-1} + 0.0186P_{t-2} + 0.7534A_{t-1} \quad (R^2 = 0.7068)$$

where

A_t = Current year's planted acreage in Maine

A_{t-1} = Previous year's planted acreage in Maine

P_{t-1} = Season's average price received by Maine farmers in the previous year

TABLE 3. Potatoes—Supply (1,000 CWT)

Crop Year	Winter	Spring	Summer	Fall	Total
1970	3,582	25,907	28,400	267,827	325,716
1971	3,088	23,658	25,922	266,686	319,354
1972	2,327	21,011	23,776	248,841	295,955
1973	2,853	21,213	21,478	253,866	299,410
1974	2,933	25,032	25,421	288,674	342,060
1975	2,887	19,958	21,018	278,391	322,254
1976	2,984	24,722	22,541	307,427	357,674
1977	2,660	22,870	21,982	307,064	354,576
1978	2,621	17,896	20,941	324,856	366,314
1979	2,383	21,348	21,847	296,919	342,497
1980	2,363	17,067	16,999	266,428	302,857
1981	2,198	20,765	20,035	290,684	333,682

Source: U.S. Department of Agriculture.

and

P_{t-2} = Season's average price received by Maine farmers 2 years prior

For *all states not including Maine*, the results were

$$A_t = 13.63 + 0.4616P_{t-1} + 0.1464P_{t-2} + 0.8580A_{t-1}\ (R^2 = 0.8086)$$

For *Idaho* alone we get

$$A_t = -0.2416 + 0.2282P_{t-1} - 0.0458P_{t-2} + 0.9080A_{t-1}$$

These results show good correlations, indicating a positive response to price; planting of additional acreage would be interpreted as a direct response to higher prices. The USDA, however, expressed caution that the 1964 high prices resulting in an extreme increase in acreage during 1965 and 1966 may have distorted these results.[2]

VARIATIONS IN PRODUCTION. Although yields per acre are highly variable in different sectors of the country, the total production of potatoes has been extremely predictable. Each year the USDA has published crop estimates in October, November, and December, with the December estimates being the final; the widest variance seen in the past 18 years has been 2%.

This accuracy is surprising due to the nature of eastern and northern potato production. It seems that midyear weather conditions have little to do with the outcome of the crop; potatoes flourish in summer heat with or without what would be considered an "adequate" temperature and moisture profile. The two events which *most* critically affect production are planting and harvesting. Rain causes the primary delay in planting potatoes, as with most other crops. Long periods

[2]A previous USDA study for a shorter interval, 1952–1960, resulted in

$$A_t = 118.183 + 69.321P_{t-1} + 0.688A_{t-1} + 0.970T_{t-1},$$

where T is an index of technology.

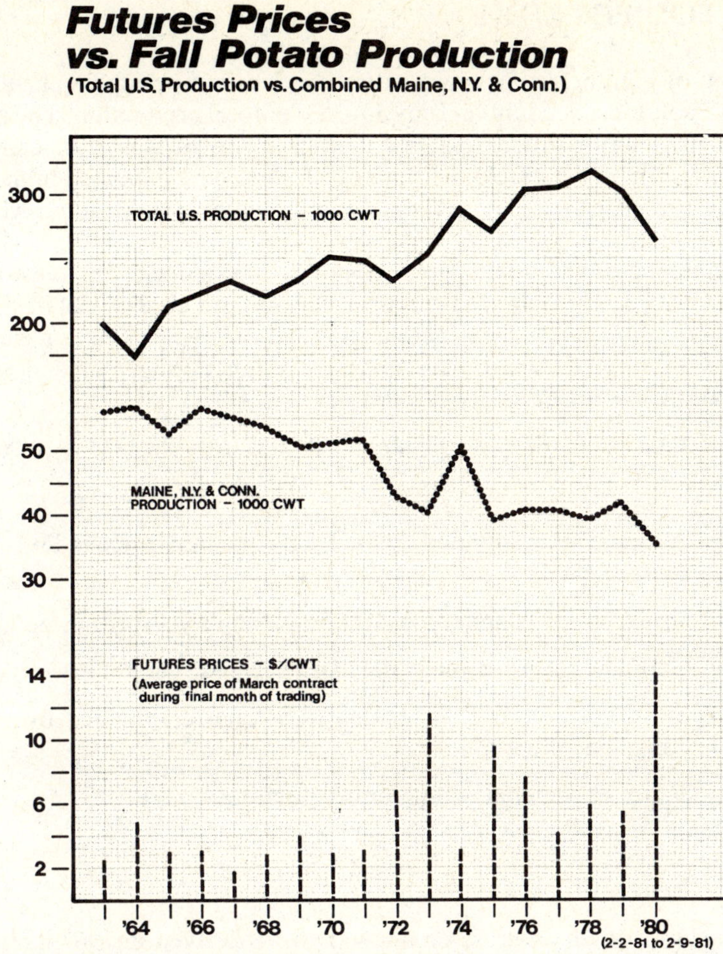

FIGURE 4. Futures prices vs fall potato production (total U.S. production vs combined Maine, N.Y., and Conn.).

of rain will prevent farmers from getting into the field and often make the planting process slower. In the northeast, there are few alternatives for the intended potato acreage and delays in planting are reflected in smaller yields.

The focus of potato production has always been the eastern harvest. Each year a fear of an early winter causes both commercials and speculators to watch harvest patterns. Farmers fight against the deadline of hardening soil as temperatures drop. As mid-October approaches, many large companies and brokerage firms estimate the number of days (and hours) necessary to complete harvest and forecast final yield based on current estimates of yield at anticipated harvest speed. Each day the harvesting equipment begins slightly later, after the topsoil thaws, and stops earlier as the ground again freezes. Days with rain become critical in the later part of harvest, therefore production is not only a function of planting and yield, but greatly dependent upon the ability to get the potatoes out of the ground.

DEMAND FOR POTATOES

The utilization of potatoes is far more extensive than most people believe. Table stock, or fresh potatoes, account for only 30–35% of total production. The majority of usage, 45–50%, is for processing, for various forms of frozen or canned potatoes, as well as for some starch and flour. This should be expected in the potato industry since the crop is highly perishable and delays in processing will result in a loss of product.

Of the remainder of the potato crop, about 7–10% is used for livestock feed and commercial seed. The balance is retained for on-farm seed or lost in shrinkage and spoilage. *Normal loss* has been estimated at 10–15% of production each year.

The USDA attempted to estimate price as a function of demand with the following relationship for *fall storage potatoes*[3]:

$$P_f = 9.351 - 0.188C_f + 0.698P_s - 0.00257D - 0.013M + 0.96_t$$

where

P_f = Average price (divided by the BLS consumer price index) received by farmers

C_f = Apparent per capita consumption (January–April) in pounds

P_s = Comparable price for winter and early spring potatoes

D = Per capita disposable income (first quarter) divided by the BLS consumer price index

M = Index of the cost of marketing potatoes

and

t = Year (1947 = 1)

Since the constants of this regression analysis were derived in 1967 it should be noted that a new estimate is appropriate before proceeding to use such a relationship.

EXPORTS. Neither imports nor exports are considered a significant factor in the potato market; however, every rule has its exceptions. In 1975 and 1976 Europe experienced two disastrous crop years. While U.S. exports of both fresh and processed potatoes had remained at about 1 to 2% of the total crop in previous years, there was a surprising jump in those 2 years. The 1974–1975 crop year resulted in total net exports of only 1.84 million hundredweight (cwt), while the 1975–1976 exports were 14–19 million cwt followed by 21.8 million cwt in 1976–1977. For a market with inelastic demand, the results were reflected in the prices as seen in Figures 1 and 2.

The surge in exports in 1975–1976 opened a new market for the U.S. potato industry. Exports remain well above normal pre-1975 levels, but have fallen off slowly. Even though exports may return to old levels, the possibilities of a radical shift in demand due to outside markets will always remain.

[3]R.J. Teweles, C.V. Harlow, and H.L. Stone, *The Commodity Futures Game, Who Wins? Who Loses? Why?* New York, NY:McGraw-Hill, 1974, p. 587.

FIGURE 5. (See facing page) Local climatological data, monthly summary, May 1977, Caribou, Maine. (*Source:* U.S. Department of Commerce.)

MAY 1977
CARIBOU, MAINE
NATIONAL WEATHER SERVICE OFC
MUNICIPAL AIRPORT

Local Climatological Data

MONTHLY SUMMARY

LATITUDE 46° 52 ′N LONGITUDE 68° 01 ′W ELEVATION (GROUND) 624 FT. STANDARD TIME USED: EASTERN WBAN #14607

MAY 1977 CARIBOU, MAINE

DATE	TEMPERATURE °F: MAXIMUM	MINIMUM	AVERAGE	DEPARTURE FROM NORMAL	AVERAGE DEW POINT	DEGREE DAYS BASE 65°: HEATING (SEASON BEGINS WITH JULY)	COOLING (SEASON BEGINS WITH JAN.)	WEATHER TYPES ON DATES OF OCCURRENCE (1 FOG, 2 HEAVY FOG, 3 THUNDERSTORM, 4 ICE PELLETS, 5 HAIL, 6 GLAZE, 7 DUSTSTORM, 8 SMOKE, HAZE, 9 BLOWING SNOW)	SNOW, ICE PELLETS OR ICE ON GROUND AT 07AM IN.	PRECIPITATION: WATER EQUIVALENT IN	SNOW, ICE PELLETS IN.	AVG. STATION PRESSURE IN. ELEV. 628 FEET M.S.L.	WIND: RESULTANT DIR.	RESULTANT SPEED M.P.H.	AVERAGE SPEED M.P.H.	FASTEST MILE: SPEED M.P.H.	DIRECTION	SUNSHINE: MINUTES	PERCENT OF POSSIBLE	SKY COVER TENTHS: SUNRISE TO SUNSET	MIDNIGHT TO MIDNIGHT	DATE
1	2	3	4	5	6	7A	7B	8	9	10	11	12	13	14	15	16	17	18	19	20	21	22
1	67	27*	47	3		18	0	RECORD OF OCCURRENCES INCOMPLETE	0	0	0	29.54								7		1
2	56	35	46	2		19	0		0	.19	0	29.21								9		2
3	45	32	39	-5		26	0		0	0	0	29.36								7		3
4	58	32	45	0		20	0		0	0	0	29.37								0		4
5	67	31	49	4		16	0		0	0	0	29.16								6		5
6	51	48	50	4		15	0		0	.17	0	29.03								10		6
7	48	30	39	-7		26	0		0	T	0	29.06								6		7
8	41	28	35*	-12		30	0		0	0	0	29.10								8		8
9	51	30	41	-6		24	0		0	0	0	29.15								8		9
10	46	37	42	-5		23	0		0	.05	T	29.08								10		10
11	59	36	48	0		17	0		0	T	0	29.07								7		11
12	68	34	51	3		14	0		0	T	0	28.98								9		12
13	50	36	43	-6		22	0		0	.09	T	28.80								9		13
14	42	35	39	-10		26	0		0	.08	T	28.92								10		14
15	56	39	48	-2		17	0		0	0	0	29.26								7		15
16	75	39	57	7		8	0		0	0	0	29.24								10		16
17	83	52	68	18		0	3		0	T	0	29.04								9		17
18	64	43	54	3		11	0		0	0	0	29.30								5		18
19	72	37	55	4		10	0		0	0	0	29.37								4		19
20	74	50	62	11		3	0		0	0	0	29.39								3		20
21	85	42	64	12		1	0		0	0	0	29.48								7		21
22	96*	60	78	26		0	13		0	T	0	29.37								3		22
23	95	69	82*	30		0	17		0	0	0	29.41								2		23
24	94	62	78	25		0	13		0	0	0	29.38								4		24
25	84	52	68	15		0	3		0	.12	0	29.11								8		25
26	64	45	55	1		10	0		0	0	0	29.08								1		26
27	56	35	46	-8		19	0		0	0	0	29.01								2		27
28	57	35	46	-8		19	0		0	.04	0	29.03								8		28
29	68	45	57	2		8	0		0	0	0	29.29								5		29
30	75	46	61	6		4	0		0	0	0	29.33								4		30
31	85	50	68	13		0	3		0	0	0	29.23								0		31
	SUM	SUM				TOTAL	TOTAL			TOTAL	TOTAL	FOR THE MONTH:						TOTAL	%	SUM	SUM	
	2032	1272				406	52	NUMBER OF DAYS		.74	T	29.20							FOR	188		
	AVG.	AVG.	AVG.	DEP.	AVG.	DEP.	DEP.	PRECIPITATION		DEP.						DATE:		POSSIBLE	MONTH	AVG.	AVG.	
	65.5	41.0	53.3	3.6		-68	52	≥ .01 INCH	7	-2.22										6.1		

NUMBER OF DAYS				SEASON TO DATE			
MAXIMUM TEMP.		MINIMUM TEMP.		TOTAL	TOTAL	SNOW, ICE PELLETS ≥ 1.0 INCH	0
≥ 90°	≤ 32°	≤ 32°	≤ 0°	9893	52	THUNDERSTORMS	
				DEP.	DEP.	HEAVY FOG	
3	0	7	0	431	52	CLEAR 7 PARTLY CLOUDY 12 CLOUDY 12	

GREATEST IN 24 HOURS AND DATES: PRECIPITATION		SNOW, ICE PELLETS		GREATEST DEPTH ON GROUND OF SNOW, ICE PELLETS OR ICE AND DATE	
.19	2	T	14+	0	

* EXTREME FOR THE MONTH - LAST OCCURRENCE IF MORE THAN ONE.
T TRACE AMOUNT
+ ALSO ON AN EARLIER DATE, OR DATES.
HEAVY FOG: - VISIBILITY 1/4 MILE OR LESS.
FIGURES FOR WIND DIRECTIONS ARE TENS OF DEGREES CLOCKWISE FROM TRUE NORTH. 00 = CALM.
DATA IN COLS. 6 AND 12-15 ARE BASED ON 7 OR MORE OBSERVATIONS PER DAY AT 3-HOUR INTERVALS.
FASTEST MILE WIND SPEEDS ARE FASTEST OBSERVED ONE-MINUTE VALUES WHEN DIRECTIONS ARE IN TENS OF DEGREES. THE / WITH THE DIRECTION INDICATES PEAK GUST SPEED.
ANY ERRORS DETECTED WILL BE CORRECTED AND CHANGES IN SUMMARY DATA WILL BE ANNOTATED IN THE ANNUAL SUMMARY

SUMMARY BY HOURS

HOUR LOCAL TIME	AVERAGES: SKY COVER TENTHS	STATION PRESSURE IN.	TEMPERATURE: AIR °F	WET BULB °F	DEW PT. °F	RELATIVE HUMIDITY %	WIND SPEED M.P.H.	RESULTANT WIND: DIRECTION	SPEED M.P.H
01		29.20	46						
04		29.21	44						
07	6	29.23	48	42	35	61	12.8	31	7.4
10	6	29.22	57	46	35	46	14.7	32	10.4
13	6	29.19	62	48	34	39	16.8	31	11.4
16	6	29.16	63	49	34	37	16.2	32	11.3
19	5	29.18	57	46	34	45	11.9	31	8.2
22	5	29.20	50	43	34	57	10.8	30	6.9

HOURLY PRECIPITATION (WATER EQUIVALENT IN INCHES)

DATE	A.M. 1	2	3	4	5	6	7	8	9	10	11	12	P.M. 1	2	3	4	5	6	7	8	9	10	11	12	DATE
1																									1
2								T	.01	.01	.08	.05	T			.04									2
3																									3
4																									4
5																									5
6										.02	.01	T								.01	.04	.08	.01		6
7								T	T																7
8																									8
9																									9
10													.01	.01	.02	.01		T	T	T					10
11					T	T																			11
12																			T	T		T	T	T	12
13				.04	T									T	T	T	T	.01	.02	.01	T	.01	T	T	13
14	T				T	T	T	T	T	T	.01	.01	.01	.01	.01	T	.01	.01	T	.01	T	T	T	T	14
15																									15
16																									16
17															T						T	T			17
18																									18
19																									19
20																									20
21																									21
22																						T			22
23																									23
24																									24
25															.02	.01		.01	.02	.01	T	.05	T	T	25
26																									26
27																									27
28																			T	T	T	.01	.02	.01	28
29																									29
30																									30
31																									31

SUBSCRIPTION PRICE: $2.55 PER YEAR. FOREIGN MAILING $1.85 EXTRA. SINGLE COPY: 20 CENTS FOR MONTHLY ISSUE. 20 CENTS FOR ANNUAL SUMMARY. OTHER DATA IN RECORDS ON FILE CAN BE FURNISHED AT COST VIA MICROFILM, MICROFICHE, OR PAPER COPIES OF ORIGINAL RECORDS. MAKE CHECKS PAYABLE TO DEPARTMENT OF COMMERCE, NOAA. SEND PAYMENTS, ORDERS, AND INQUIRIES TO NATIONAL CLIMATIC CENTER, FEDERAL BUILDING, ASHEVILLE, NORTH CAROLINA 28801.

I CERTIFY THAT THIS IS AN OFFICIAL PUBLICATION OF THE NATIONAL OCEANIC AND ATMOSPHERIC ADMINISTRATION, AND IS COMPILED FROM RECORDS ON FILE AT THE NATIONAL CLIMATIC CENTER, ASHEVILLE, NORTH CAROLINA 28801.

noaa NATIONAL OCEANIC AND ATMOSPHERIC ADMINISTRATION / ENVIRONMENTAL DATA SERVICE

Daniel B. Mitchell
DIRECTOR, NATIONAL CLIMATIC CENTER

OBSERVATIONS AT 3-HOUR INTERVALS

Columns: Hour; Sky cover (tenths); Ceiling (hnds. of ft.); Visibility: whole miles, 16ths mile; Weather; Temperature: air °F, wet bulb °F, dew pt. °F; Rel. hum. %; Wind: dir, speed (knots)

DAY 01

HOUR	SKY COVER TENTHS	CEILING HNDS. OF FT.	VISIBILITY WHOLE MILES	VISIBILITY 16THS MILE	WEATHER	AIR °F	WET BULB °F	DEW PT. °F	REL. HUM. %	WIND DIR	WIND SPEED KNOTS
01						30					
04						28					
07	3	UNL	30			37	31	21	52	19	6
10	9	180	30			53	40	20	27	15	13
13	6	UNL	30			64	47	27	25	18	16
16	10	200	30			65	48	29	26	16	18
19	9	200	30			60	46	30	32	18	16
22	3	UNL	30			53	42	27	37	22	14

DAY 02

HOUR	SKY COVER TENTHS	CEILING HNDS. OF FT.	VISIBILITY WHOLE MILES	VISIBILITY 16THS MILE	WEATHER	AIR °F	WET BULB °F	DEW PT. °F	REL. HUM. %	WIND DIR	WIND SPEED KNOTS
01						47					
04						44					
07	10	80	30			48	42	34	59	19	15
10	10	50	5		RF	48	44	40	74	31	4
13	10	20	7			51	48	46	83	22	10
16	10	10	10			55	49	44	67	32	10
19	0	UNL	10			46	42	38	74	33	5
22	1	UNL	10			40	35	26	57	32	13

DAY 03

HOUR	SKY COVER TENTHS	CEILING HNDS. OF FT.	VISIBILITY WHOLE MILES	VISIBILITY 16THS MILE	WEATHER	AIR °F	WET BULB °F	DEW PT. °F	REL. HUM. %	WIND DIR	WIND SPEED KNOTS
01						34					
04						34					
07	9	40	30			35	29	16	46	32	20
10	8	40	30			40	32	19	43	31	19
13	10	40	30			42	34	19	40	30	20
16	6	40	30			45	35	20	37	31	20
19	0	UNL	30			42	33	16	35	31	14
22	0	UNL	30			36	30	17	46	30	10

DAY 04

HOUR	SKY COVER TENTHS	CEILING HNDS. OF FT.	VISIBILITY WHOLE MILES	VISIBILITY 16THS MILE	WEATHER	AIR °F	WET BULB °F	DEW PT. °F	REL. HUM. %	WIND DIR	WIND SPEED KNOTS
01						34					
04						33					
07	0	UNL	30			39	31	16	39	32	17
10	0	UNL	30			48	37	18	30	32	16
13	0	UNL	30			55	41	20	25	29	13
16	0	UNL	30			58	41	16	19	32	12
19	0	UNL	30			52	38	17	25	33	6
22	0	UNL	30			43	34	18	37	26	4

DAY 05

HOUR	SKY COVER TENTHS	CEILING HNDS. OF FT.	VISIBILITY WHOLE MILES	VISIBILITY 16THS MILE	WEATHER	AIR °F	WET BULB °F	DEW PT. °F	REL. HUM. %	WIND DIR	WIND SPEED KNOTS
01						36					
04						32					
07	9	80	30			38	34	27	65	24	5
10	9	80	30			55	43	27	34	00	0
13	3	UNL	30			64	47	25	23	14	4
16	4	UNL	30			66	47	24	20	11	6
19	4	UNL	30			61	46	27	27	04	4
22	5	UNL	20			54	42	27	35	10	5

DAY 06

HOUR	SKY COVER TENTHS	CEILING HNDS. OF FT.	VISIBILITY WHOLE MILES	VISIBILITY 16THS MILE	WEATHER	AIR °F	WET BULB °F	DEW PT. °F	REL. HUM. %	WIND DIR	WIND SPEED KNOTS
01						48					
04						46					
07	10	4	2	8	F	46	45	44	93	16	15
10	10	7	7		R	48	46	45	89	14	12
13	10	20	10			49	46	43	80	18	10
16	10	20	10			50	47	44	80	16	9
19	10	20	10			50	46	42	74	15	12
22	10	15	7		RW	48	47	46	93	16	8

DAY 07

HOUR	SKY COVER TENTHS	CEILING HNDS. OF FT.	VISIBILITY WHOLE MILES	VISIBILITY 16THS MILE	WEATHER	AIR °F	WET BULB °F	DEW PT. °F	REL. HUM. %	WIND DIR	WIND SPEED KNOTS
01						47					
04						44					
07	10	10	10			39	37	34	82	32	18
10	8	20	20			40	36	30	68	32	18
13	7	30	30			44	37	27	51	29	20
16	1	UNL	30			46	37	23	40	32	19
19	0	UNL	30			36	30	18	48	33	18
22	0	UNL	30			31	26	17	56	31	13

DAY 08

HOUR	SKY COVER TENTHS	CEILING HNDS. OF FT.	VISIBILITY WHOLE MILES	VISIBILITY 16THS MILE	WEATHER	AIR °F	WET BULB °F	DEW PT. °F	REL. HUM. %	WIND DIR	WIND SPEED KNOTS
01						30					
04						29					
07	3	UNL	30			31	26	15	51	31	15
10	10	30	30			33	27	14	45	28	10
13	10	100	30			38	30	14	37	32	17
16	9	200	30			41	32	15	35	34	13
19	9	50	30			37	30	18	46	30	8
22	4	UNL	30			32	28	20	61	32	7

DAY 09

HOUR	SKY COVER TENTHS	CEILING HNDS. OF FT.	VISIBILITY WHOLE MILES	VISIBILITY 16THS MILE	WEATHER	AIR °F	WET BULB °F	DEW PT. °F	REL. HUM. %	WIND DIR	WIND SPEED KNOTS
01						31					
04						30					
07	9	30	30			33	31	27	79	35	7
10	8	35	30			44	38	31	60	36	12
13	10	30	30			49	40	28	44	[illegible]	10
16	4	UNL	30			51	41	29	43	01	16
19	9	50	30			47	40	31	54	01	8
22	10	60	15			44	38	29	56	02	11

DAY 10

HOUR	SKY COVER TENTHS	CEILING HNDS. OF FT.	VISIBILITY WHOLE MILES	VISIBILITY 16THS MILE	WEATHER	AIR °F	WET BULB °F	DEW PT. °F	REL. HUM. %	WIND DIR	WIND SPEED KNOTS
01						40					
04						40					
07	10	20	30			40	36	30	68	03	20
10	10	20	30			43	38	30	60	04	20
13	10	15	5		RF	39	36	31	73	03	18
16	10	12	30			39	37	34	82	02	15
19	10	14	10		R	38	35	30	73	02	18
22	10	15	10			37	35	31	79	01	17

DAY 11

HOUR	SKY COVER TENTHS	CEILING HNDS. OF FT.	VISIBILITY WHOLE MILES	VISIBILITY 16THS MILE	WEATHER	AIR °F	WET BULB °F	DEW PT. °F	REL. HUM. %	WIND DIR	WIND SPEED KNOTS
01						37					
04						37					
07	10	25	30			40	37	32	73	35	12
10	10	25	30			45	39	32	60	36	16
13	8	100	30			53	43	31	43	36	19
16	4	UNL	30			58	44	27	31	32	22
19	2	UNL	30			50	40	25	38	32	8
22	0	UNL	15			44	36	23	44	28	6

DAY 12

HOUR	SKY COVER TENTHS	CEILING HNDS. OF FT.	VISIBILITY WHOLE MILES	VISIBILITY 16THS MILE	WEATHER	AIR °F	WET BULB °F	DEW PT. °F	REL. HUM. %	WIND DIR	WIND SPEED KNOTS
01						38					
04						35					
07	10	UNL	30			43	38	32	65	20	3
10	10	UNL	30			61	46	29	30	31	10
13	10	230	30			66	48	27	23	28	13
16	10	100	30			64	48	30	28	30	10
19	10	45	30		RW	55	47	38	53	29	9
22	10	100	15		RW	52	46	40	64	27	8

DAY 13

HOUR	SKY COVER TENTHS	CEILING HNDS. OF FT.	VISIBILITY WHOLE MILES	VISIBILITY 16THS MILE	WEATHER	AIR °F	WET BULB °F	DEW PT. °F	REL. HUM. %	WIND DIR	WIND SPEED KNOTS
01						48					
04	10					44					
07	9	30	30			42	38	32	68	34	16
10	4	UNL	30			45	38	27	49	31	23
13	8	35	30			47	38	24	41	32	24
16	10	35	30		RW	42	37	29	60	32	23
19	10	20	5		RW	37	35	32	82	32	22
22	10	20	7		RW	38	36	33	82	31	19

DAY 14

HOUR	SKY COVER TENTHS	CEILING HNDS. OF FT.	VISIBILITY WHOLE MILES	VISIBILITY 16THS MILE	WEATHER	AIR °F	WET BULB °F	DEW PT. °F	REL. HUM. %	WIND DIR	WIND SPEED KNOTS
01						38					
04	10					36					
07	10	25	7		SW	37	33	27	67	32	22
10	10	30	12		RW	40	36	30	68	34	24
13	10	12	7		R	39	36	33	79	33	23
16	10	28	7		R	42	37	31	65	32	23
19	10	35	7		R	39	36	33	79	30	19
22	10	35	7		R	39	37	34	82	32	21

DAY 15

HOUR	SKY COVER TENTHS	CEILING HNDS. OF FT.	VISIBILITY WHOLE MILES	VISIBILITY 16THS MILE	WEATHER	AIR °F	WET BULB °F	DEW PT. °F	REL. HUM. %	WIND DIR	WIND SPEED KNOTS
01						39					
04	9					39					
07	8	35	30			44	40	36	74	33	13
10	10	30	30			46	40	31	56	33	17
13	5	UNL	30			54	45	34	47	32	18
16	5	UNL	30			54	43	30	40	33	13
19	3	UNL	30			51	42	30	45	31	8
22	0	UNL	30			44	38	29	56	24	5

DAY 16

HOUR	SKY COVER TENTHS	CEILING HNDS. OF FT.	VISIBILITY WHOLE MILES	VISIBILITY 16THS MILE	WEATHER	AIR °F	WET BULB °F	DEW PT. °F	REL. HUM. %	WIND DIR	WIND SPEED KNOTS
01						39					
04	10					41					
07	10	80	30			43	39	34	71	24	6
10	10	100	30			56	47	37	49	19	4
13	10	80	30			71	56	43	37	17	4
16	10	UNL	30			74	58	45	36	11	6
19	10	UNL	30			69	56	45	42	28	9
22	0	UNL	15			58	51	44	60	25	8

DAY 17

HOUR	SKY COVER TENTHS	CEILING HNDS. OF FT.	VISIBILITY WHOLE MILES	VISIBILITY 16THS MILE	WEATHER	AIR °F	WET BULB °F	DEW PT. °F	REL. HUM. %	WIND DIR	WIND SPEED KNOTS
01						57					
04	10					60					
07	7	100	30			65	55	46	50	27	12
10	8	300	30			79	63	53	41	29	16
13	8	250	30			79	63	53	41	31	15
16	8	40	30			77	64	55	47	33	16
19	8	40	30			67	57	50	55	31	11
22	10	40	15		T	57	53	49	75	29	10

DAY 18

HOUR	SKY COVER TENTHS	CEILING HNDS. OF FT.	VISIBILITY WHOLE MILES	VISIBILITY 16THS MILE	WEATHER	AIR °F	WET BULB °F	DEW PT. °F	REL. HUM. %	WIND DIR	WIND SPEED KNOTS
01						51					
04	6					46					
07	6	UNL	30			46	38	28	50	36	11
10	3	UNL	30			54	43	28	37	36	8
13	3	UNL	30			60	46	28	30	35	8
16	5	UNL	30			62	46	26	25	34	9
19	8	UNL	30			56	44	28	34	34	11
22	6	UNL	30			46	37	23	40	01	9

DAY 19

HOUR	SKY COVER TENTHS	CEILING HNDS. OF FT.	VISIBILITY WHOLE MILES	VISIBILITY 16THS MILE	WEATHER	AIR °F	WET BULB °F	DEW PT. °F	REL. HUM. %	WIND DIR	WIND SPEED KNOTS
01						42					
04	5					38					
07	3	UNL	30			45	38	29	54	10	3
10	2	UNL	30			55	45	33	43	24	5
13	4	UNL	30			63	49	35	35	21	8
16	2	UNL	30			72	53	35	26	27	7
19	8	100	30			67	52	37	33	00	0
22	10	90	15			58	48	38	48	28	6

DAY 20

HOUR	SKY COVER TENTHS	CEILING HNDS. OF FT.	VISIBILITY WHOLE MILES	VISIBILITY 16THS MILE	WEATHER	AIR °F	WET BULB °F	DEW PT. °F	REL. HUM. %	WIND DIR	WIND SPEED KNOTS
01						56					
04	0					51					
07	2	UNL	30			58	46	33	39	33	12
10	3	UNL	30			65	48	29	26	33	12
13	2	UNL	30			72	52	32	23	30	14
16	1	UNL	30			72	51	28	19	35	14
19	10	UNL	30			64	48	30	28	36	6
22	3	UNL	15			56	43	27	33	02	7

DAY 21

HOUR	SKY COVER TENTHS	CEILING HNDS. OF FT.	VISIBILITY WHOLE MILES	VISIBILITY 16THS MILE	WEATHER	AIR °F	WET BULB °F	DEW PT. °F	REL. HUM. %	WIND DIR	WIND SPEED KNOTS
01						47					
04	10					43					
07	10	UNL	30			50	42	32	50	12	7
10	10	UNL	30			66	52	39	37	21	8
13	4	UNL	30			81	59	41	24	19	15
16	2	UNL	30			83	61	45	26	20	11
19	1	UNL	30			76	60	48	37	22	8
22	0	UNL	15			66	56	47	51	21	8

DAY 22

HOUR	SKY COVER TENTHS	CEILING HNDS. OF FT.	VISIBILITY WHOLE MILES	VISIBILITY 16THS MILE	WEATHER	AIR °F	WET BULB °F	DEW PT. °F	REL. HUM. %	WIND DIR	WIND SPEED KNOTS
01						62					
04	6					60					
07	2	UNL	10			75	64	58	56	23	8
10	0	UNL	10			91	69	56	31	28	11
13	4	UNL	10			95	68	51	22	29	21
16	4	UNL	10			94	67	49	22	27	15
19	1	UNL	10			86	66	54	33	26	10
22	8	80	7			77	64	55	47	27	7

DAY 23

HOUR	SKY COVER TENTHS	CEILING HNDS. OF FT.	VISIBILITY WHOLE MILES	VISIBILITY 16THS MILE	WEATHER	AIR °F	WET BULB °F	DEW PT. °F	REL. HUM. %	WIND DIR	WIND SPEED KNOTS
01						72					
04	0					71					
07	7	UNL	4		H	75	66	60	60	22	7
10	2	UNL	5		H	87	69	59	39	28	16
13	4	UNL	15			93	68	53	26	27	14
16	2	UNL	15			93	67	50	23	26	15
19	1	UNL	15			86	63	47	26	26	7
22	1	UNL	15			74	59	48	40	28	9

DAY 24

HOUR	SKY COVER TENTHS	CEILING HNDS. OF FT.	VISIBILITY WHOLE MILES	VISIBILITY 16THS MILE	WEATHER	AIR °F	WET BULB °F	DEW PT. °F	REL. HUM. %	WIND DIR	WIND SPEED KNOTS
01						68					
04	6					63					
07	0	UNL	7			70	62	57	64	23	5
10	0	UNL	7			87	68	57	36	28	5
13	6	100	15			94	66	48	21	29	15
16	8	180	15			93	65	47	21	27	15
19	9	250	15			82	62	47	29	31	11
22	10	120	7			71	62	57	61	18	9

DAY 25

HOUR	SKY COVER TENTHS	CEILING HNDS. OF FT.	VISIBILITY WHOLE MILES	VISIBILITY 16THS MILE	WEATHER	AIR °F	WET BULB °F	DEW PT. °F	REL. HUM. %	WIND DIR	WIND SPEED KNOTS
01						67					
04	10					66					
07	2	UNL	8			71	65	61	71	27	7
10	8	30	6		H	79	68	62	56	27	10
13	10	40	8		T	77	65	57	50	32	20
16	9	40	10			67	62	59	76	32	22
19	10	20	10		RW	57	55	54	90	31	18
22	10	12	6		RW	52	50	49	90	32	20

DAY 26

HOUR	SKY COVER TENTHS	CEILING HNDS. OF FT.	VISIBILITY WHOLE MILES	VISIBILITY 16THS MILE	WEATHER	AIR °F	WET BULB °F	DEW PT. °F	REL. HUM. %	WIND DIR	WIND SPEED KNOTS
01						51					
04	3					48					
07	4	UNL	30			49	43	35	59	32	20
10	0	UNL	30			56	45	33	42	30	18
13	1	UNL	30			62	46	26	25	33	20
16	1	UNL	30			63	44	18	17	32	22
19	0	UNL	30			57	42	20	24	33	15
22	0	UNL	30			46	37	23	40	31	7

DAY 27

HOUR	SKY COVER TENTHS	CEILING HNDS. OF FT.	VISIBILITY WHOLE MILES	VISIBILITY 16THS MILE	WEATHER	AIR °F	WET BULB °F	DEW PT. °F	REL. HUM. %	WIND DIR	WIND SPEED KNOTS
01						44					
04	2					38					
07	1	UNL	30			41	33	19	41	31	20
10	2	UNL	30			48	37	20	33	33	20
13	5	UNL	30			54	41	22	29	34	17
16	1	UNL	30			56	42	22	27	34	15
19	0	UNL	30			53	40	21	29	32	16
22	0	UNL	15			43	36	25	49	30	8

DAY 28

HOUR	SKY COVER TENTHS	CEILING HNDS. OF FT.	VISIBILITY WHOLE MILES	VISIBILITY 16THS MILE	WEATHER	AIR °F	WET BULB °F	DEW PT. °F	REL. HUM. %	WIND DIR	WIND SPEED KNOTS
01						42					
04	2					35					
07	2	UNL	30			48	40	31	56	32	9
10	8	200	30			63	42	29	40	30	10
13	10	80	30			56	45	31	39	31	8
16	10	40	30			56	45	32	40	28	5
19	10	40	20		RW	53	46	38	57	03	8
22	10	50	15		RW	47	45	42	83	30	5

DAY 29

HOUR	SKY COVER TENTHS	CEILING HNDS. OF FT.	VISIBILITY WHOLE MILES	VISIBILITY 16THS MILE	WEATHER	AIR °F	WET BULB °F	DEW PT. °F	REL. HUM. %	WIND DIR	WIND SPEED KNOTS
01						46					
04						46					
07	2	UNL	30			52	45	37	57	35	9
10	7	120	30			60	49	37	43	34	19
13	7	250	30			63	50	36	37	35	13
16	8	35	30			66	51	37	34	32	15
19	4	UNL	30			60	49	38	44	32	7
22	7	90	15			54	48	41	62	27	5

DAY 30

HOUR	SKY COVER TENTHS	CEILING HNDS. OF FT.	VISIBILITY WHOLE MILES	VISIBILITY 16THS MILE	WEATHER	AIR °F	WET BULB °F	DEW PT. °F	REL. HUM. %	WIND DIR	WIND SPEED KNOTS
01						49					
04						46					
07	8	120	30			56	50	45	67	27	4
10	4	UNL	30			67	54	43	42	33	11
13	5	UNL	30			73	53	34	24	31	16
16	4	UNL	30			74	53	33	22	29	15
19	2	UNL	30			67	51	34	30	33	5
22	1	UNL	15			54	47	39	57	27	5

DAY 31

HOUR	SKY COVER TENTHS	CEILING HNDS. OF FT.	VISIBILITY WHOLE MILES	VISIBILITY 16THS MILE	WEATHER	AIR °F	WET BULB °F	DEW PT. °F	REL. HUM. %	WIND DIR	WIND SPEED KNOTS
01						50					
04						50					
07	2	UNL	30			60	53	47	62	00	0
10	0	UNL	30			75	55	36	24	32	10
13	0	UNL	30			79	58	40	25	30	9
16	0	UNL	30			84	60	42	23	34	8
19	1	UNL	30			76	58	44	32	24	5
22	0	UNL	15			64	53	43	47	25	8

STATION: CARIBOU MAINE

YEAR & MONTH: 77 05

NOTES

CEILING
UNL INDICATES UNLIMITED

WEATHER

- * TORNADO
- T THUNDERSTORM
- Q SQUALL
- R RAIN
- RW RAIN SHOWERS
- ZR FREEZING RAIN
- L DRIZZLE
- ZL FREEZING DRIZZLE
- S SNOW
- SP SNOW PELLETS
- IC ICE CRYSTALS
- SW SNOW SHOWERS
- SG SNOW GRAINS
- IP ICE PELLETS
- A HAIL
- F FOG
- IF ICE FOG
- GF GROUND FOG
- BD BLOWING DUST
- BN BLOWING SAND
- BS BLOWING SNOW
- BY BLOWING SPRAY
- K SMOKE
- H HAZE
- D DUST

WIND

DIRECTIONS ARE THOSE FROM
WHICH THE WIND BLOWS. IND
CATED IN TENS OF DEGREES
FROM TRUE NORTH: I.E.. 09
FOR EAST. 18 FOR SOUTH. 2
FOR WEST. ENTRY OF 00 IN
THE DIRECTION COLUMN INDI
CATES CALM.

SPEED IS EXPRESSED IN KNO
MULTIPLY BY 1.15 TO CONVE
TO MILES PER HOUR.

U.S. DEPARTMENT OF COMMERCE
NATIONAL CLIMATIC CENTER
FEDERAL BUILDING
ASHEVILLE. N.C. 28801

FIGURE 5. Continued.

DISAPPEARANCE. If ever a market had a focal point, the *rate of disappearance* of potato stocks may well be the most widely watched figure. Each month from December through May the Statistical Reporting Service of the USDA releases its *Potato Stocks Report*. Reports appear in the second week of the month and reflect information as of the end of the previous month. The rate of disappearance, relative to the production size, will determine the direction of price movement.

Potato prices react violently to the outcome of this report. The first report, issued in December, states the final crop production for that season and the disappearance to-date, usually about ⅓ of the total crop. After that we can expect about a 10% per month disappearance, allowing for steady consumption from December through the beginning of June and for loss due to shrinkage and spoilage. With demand declining in the spring months this pattern has resulted in a supply-and-demand balance. Tables 4 and 5 show crop production, and indicate stocks and disappearance.

It is also possible to calculate disappearance in advance of the USDA report by subscribing to the Maine Department of Agricultural Reporting Service, which provides daily accounting of all shipments of potatoes and other vegetables from each county in Maine. Daily calculations, however, are only one part of the disappearance equation. In order to complete the task, an analyst must estimate the processing demands (which may come from existing stocks), shrinkage, and spoilage. Exports and new stocks received by processors are part of shipments. The quality of potatoes held on-farm for seed or feed is a small, but sometimes important, part of the results.

The *quality* of potatoes will affect the distribution of use. Potatoes harvested during extremely wet conditions may be subject to faster spoilage and sold to processors sooner at lower prices. It is not unusual for the first potato stocks report to include the warning[4]:

> Due to the extremely wet conditions during potato harvest in the northeast region of the U.S., there is major concern about the condition of potatoes in storage in this area.
>
> In Maine, growers are reporting higher than usual shrink and grading losses with some breakdown in storage. Storage problems are due primarily to water rot and blight. . . . Grading losses are expected to be higher than normal this season.

The original estimate of fall production can be used to get the apparent domestic free supply, S (fall estimated production minus exports and diversion), combined with the *estimated deliverable supply*, D, of round whites in the northeast, and adjusted by the *producer price index*, PPI, to get a general price forecasting model of the form[5]:

$$\mathrm{P/PPI} = a + b\mathrm{S} + c\mathrm{D}$$

where a, b, and c are found by regression analysis.

[4]Crop Reporting Board, U.S. Department of Agriculture, Statistical Research Service, December 1977.

[5]J.D. Schwager, "A Trader's Guide to Analyzing the Potato Futures Market," *1981 Commodity Yearbook*, Commodity Research Bureau, New York, 1981.

TABLE 4. Potato Stocks, Disappearance, and Crop Production Estimates in the United States (In Millons of CWT)

	In Millions of CWT								Crop Production Estimates				
	Storage Stocks[a]				Disappearance of Previous Fall Crop Until				Crop Production Estimates				
Year	Jan. 1	Feb. 1	Mar. 1	Dec. 1	Dec. 1	Jan. 1	Feb. 1	Mar. 1	Sep. 1	Oct. 1	Nov. 1	Dec. 1	Final
1961	103.6	82.7	62.6	145.0	n.a.[c]	n.a.	n.a.	n.a.	278.4	279.3	284.0	290.9	293.2
1962	122.2	96.1	73.0	135.7	n.a.	n.a.	n.a.	n.a.	266.9	265.4	264.9	268.3	264.8
1963	115.8	92.0	70.3	137.0	n.a.	n.a.	n.a.	n.a.	268.0	273.4	275.1	275.5	271.2
1964	115.0	89.3	67.3	114.6	n.a.	n.a.	n.a.	n.a.	247.0	245.9	244.0	242.9	241.1
1965	94.2	73.1	54.5	147.8	n.a.	n.a.	n.a.	n.a.	286.7	290.9	290.4	288.9	291.1
1966	124.2	98.7	74.9	153.6	69.7	93.3	n.a.	n.a.	283.6	296.3	300.0	300.9	307.2
1967	128.1	103.6	79.6	161.5	75.1	100.4	n.a.	138.5	297.9	301.5	303.2	305.9	305.8
1968	139.2	112.6	86.4	152.8	69.5	91.9	118.5	144.8	283.5	289.6	293.0	293.4	295.4

Source: U.S. Department of Agriculture, Crop Reporting Board. [a]Held by growers and local dealers in the fall producing areas. [b]Preliminary. [c]n.a. = not available.

TABLE 5. Potato Crop Production Estimates, Stocks, and Disappearance in the United States (In Millions of CWT)

	Crop Production Estimates						Total Storage Stocks[a]					Disappearance of Previous Fall Crop Until				
	Total Crop			Fall Crop				Following Year					Following Year			
Year	Oct. 1	Nov. 1	Dec. 1	Oct. 1	Nov. 1	Dec. 1	Dec. 1	Jan. 1	Feb. 1	Mar. 1	Apr. 1	Dec. 1	Jan. 1	Feb. 1	Mar. 1	Apr. 1
1969	305.4	305.1	307.2				162.8	138.1	111.5	87.6		76.0	100.5	127.3	151.1	
1970	320.2	323.5	324.9				171.6	147.6	120.7	95.9		78.4	103.1	131.3	156.7	
1971	317.0	318.5	316.1				172.6	148.6	122.4	97.2		77.5	102.4	129.4	168.2	
1972	296.0	294.5	294.5				155.2	132.1	105.7	82.5	57.9	90.4	114.5	141.7	165.5	198.0
1973	297.5	298.6	297.4				154.9	131.6	105.4	80.5	55.5	96.1	120.3	147.3	172.7	209.6
1974	337.8	339.0	340.1	286.6	287.9	287.7	183.9	160.1	131.5	103.0	75.2	97.8	122.6	152.2	181.4	200.6
1975	307.6	310.3	315.6				181.7	156.2	129.7	102.9	71.0	88.6	114.9	142.9	169.4	201.4
1976	349.9	349.3	353.4	299.8	299.2	302.8	198.6	172.2	142.0	112.8	81.1	99.1	128.3	157.8	188.0	218.4
1977	350.6	350.4	352.0	303.6	303.4	304.4	202.6	175.3	147.9	119.9	88.7	93.8	122.8	149.9	177.9	210.2
1978[b]	353.6	357.7	360.5	312.0	316.0	318.7	219.9	193.5	163.0	132.6	99.3	94.6	122.0	153.0	185.0	218.0
1979[b]	347.9	348.3	347.6	300.3	300.7	301.6	200.8	176.0	147.9	121.7	92.6	87.5	114.0	143.0	170.0	200.0
1980[b]	296.9	296.9	301.0	260.7	260.7	264.6	169.8	144.0	118.5	94.2		84.1	110.0	135.0	160.0	

Source: U.S. Department of Agriculture, Crop Reporting Board. [a]Held by growers and local dealers in the fall producing areas. [b]Preliminary.

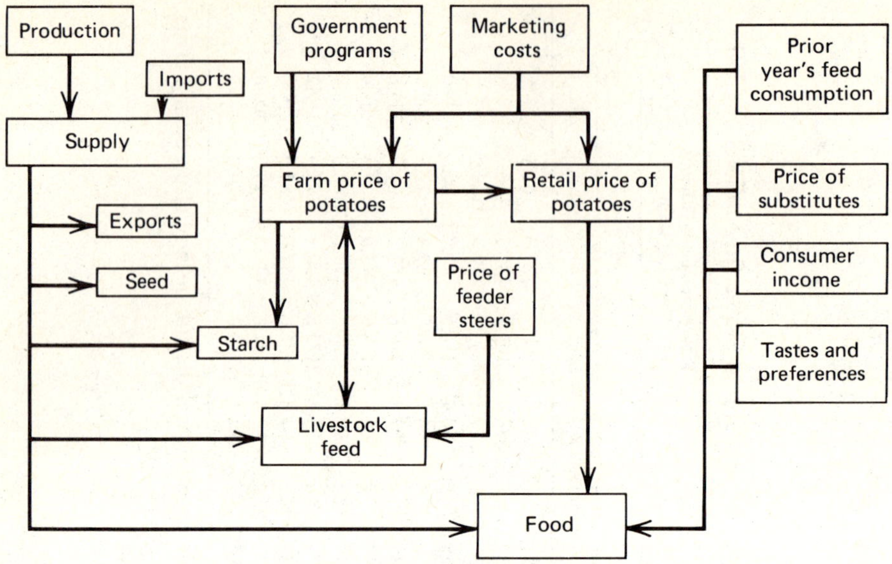

FIGURE 6. Potato marketing. (*Source:* Teweles, Harlow, and Stone. *The Commodity Futures Game, Who Wins? Who Loses? Why?* McGraw-Hill, NY, 1974).

It is easy to see that the potato market lends itself to statistical analysis and forecasting. The USDA summarized the structure of the potato market in a simple diagram which is shown in Figure 6.

SEASONALITY

The uniqueness of the potato market is reflected in the seasonal analysis shown in Figures 7 (*a*) and 7 (*b*). The cash study, Figure 7 (*a*), seems to be a normal representation of a U.S. fall crop seasonality, peaking in midsummer when weather causes production concerns, and bottoming near harvest completion in November. Although patterns are as expected, reliability is moderate with the preharvest decline in August indicated as the most consistent performer and the price rise following harvest as the next best.

The futures market study portrays a very different picture. Since the only two active contracts were November and May at the time of the analysis, there is a noticeable discontinuity after the May delivery, when prices shift to the November new crop contract, always trading at a significant discount to the old crop. Once the shift is made to November there is a steady rise. The futures market seems to fully discount the price of the new crop when it begins trading in the spring rather than in anticipation of harvest in the late summer.

As the season approaches the last traded contract in May (although April is now the final delivery), prices tend to move in extremes. In March and April, traders tend to react bullishly whenever possible. The risk of being caught short is always greater than that of being long during these months. There is a tendency to cover shorts and shift to the long side of the market in the event final disap-

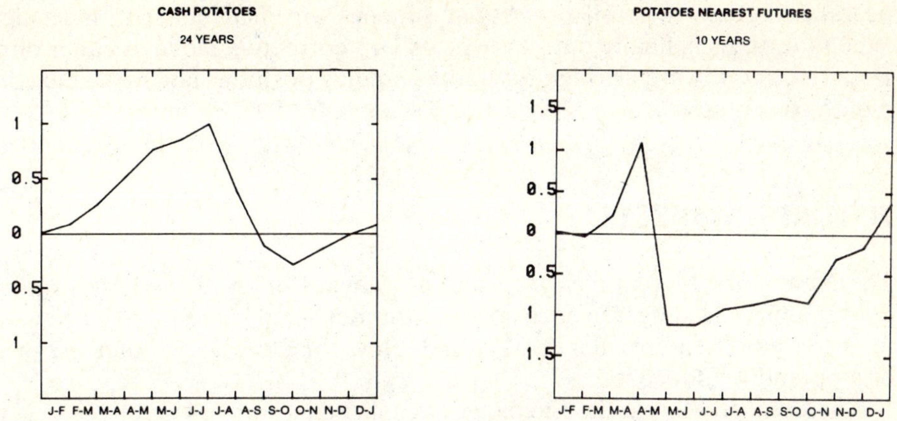

	J-F	F-M	M-A	A-M	M-J	J-J	J-A	A-S	S-O	O-N	N-D	D-J
Average Move	0	0.1	0.2	0.2	0	0.1	-0.7	-0.6	-0.2	0.1	0.1	0
% Reliable	62.5	70.9	79.2	75	50	58.4	87.5	100	91.7	75	70.9	83.4
Avg. Up Move	0.2	0.3	0.3	0.4	0.6	0.5	0.3	0	0	0.2	0.2	0.2
Avg. Down Move	0.2	0.2	0.2	0.3	0.6	0.4	0.8	0.6	0.2	0.1	0.1	0.5
Greatest Up Move	1.3	1	1.4	1.2	1.8	1.3	0.4	0	0.1	0.9	1.4	0.8
Greatest Down Move	0.5	0.3	0.3	1	1.6	1.1	2.8	1.6	0.6	0.3	0.2	1.7

(*a*)

	J-F	F-M	M-A	A-M	M-J	J-J	J-A	A-S	S-O	O-N	N-D	D-J
Average Move	-0.1	0.2	0.8	-2.3	0	0.1	0	0	-0.1	0.5	0.1	0.5
% Reliable	70	70	90	80	40	70	40	60	50	90	60	70
Avg. Up Move	0.5	0.4	1	0.6	0.2	0.3	0.4	0.2	0.1	0.5	0.3	0.8
Avg. Down Move	0.4	0.3	0.4	3	0.2	0.1	0.3	0.2	0.4	0.1	0.3	0.3
Greatest Up Move	1	1.2	4.3	1	0.5	1.3	1.3	0.8	0.5	1.6	0.7	2.3
Greatest Down Move	0.8	0.4	0.4	10.5	0.9	0.2	0.5	0.5	1.1	0.1	0.4	0.4

(*b*)

FIGURE 7. Potato market seasonality. (*a*) Cash potatoes, 24 years. (*b*) Potatoes nearest futures, 10 years. *Source:* J. Grushcow and C. Swith, *Profits through Seasonal Trading,* Wiley, New York, 1980.

TABLE 6. Contract Specifications

NYMEX Round White Potatoes	
Delivery months	November, February, March, and April
Contract unit	50,000 lb
Price quotation	Cents per lb, including freight costs to New York City
Minimum price fluctuation	.01¢ per lb ($5 per contract)
Maximum daily price fluctuation	.5¢ per lb above or below the preceding day's settling price. No limit on last trading day. Maximum daily price fluctuation is subject to variable limits formula.
Standards	Round white varieties (except cobbler and warba types) grown in the states of Maine, New York, and Connecticut, grading U.S. No. 1, Size A, 2-in. minimum, 4-in. maximum
Delivery	Buyer's choice, F.O.B. point of origin or delivered in Hunt's Point, New York City, grade guaranteed
Trading hours	10:00 a.m.–2:00 p.m. eastern time
Position limits	350 in all months combined, with no more than 150 each in February, March, and April, and 300 in November

Note: Position limits submission is awaiting CFTC approval. It would govern both speculative and hedge positions for all commodities.

pearance figures in April prove that supplies are inadequate to meet demand. When the news is finally out, there is a sharp corrective move in either direction. Both risk and reward are high for traders holding positions late in the final delivery month for potatoes.

FUTURES MARKETS

The New York Mercantile Exchange has always enjoyed the largest interest in potato futures trading. On occasion the contract specifications have been changed to accommodate a broader market and allow for delivery without the problems of a potential "squeeze."

The Chicago Mercantile Exchange revitalized its western potato contract a few years ago, but it has never attracted the interest of the eastern delivery. An additional market with reasonable activity has been the *Potato Terminal Market* in Amsterdam, The Netherlands. Established in 1960, it has maintained an active part in European economics within the framework of the EEC and despite special quotas imposed by Great Britain.

Specifications of the futures contracts are shown in Tables 6 and 7.

TABLE 7. Contract Specifications

Associate Mercantile Market Division of the CME Russet Burbank Potatoes	
Delivery months	As the exchange may determine, currently January, March, April, May, and November
Trading unit	80,000 lb
Minimum price fluctuation	.01¢ per lb ($8 per contract)
Maximum daily price fluctuation	Subject to change; consult latest official notices from the exchange
Standards	Russet Burbank potatoes grown in the states of Washington, Oregon, Idaho, Colorado, Wisconsin, Michigan (Upper Peninsula only), and California (Modoc and Siskiyou counties only) meeting USDA standards for No. 1 washed.
Delivery	If delivery is by rail, par delivery shall be F.O.B. Pocatello, ID with deliveries to be made F.O.B. from elsewhere with allowances established by the exchange. If delivery is by truck, delivery shall be F.O.B. point of origin, basis par delivery Pocatello, ID with the same allowances.
Trading hours	9:00 a.m.–1:00 p.m. central time
Position limits	No more than a total of 350 contracts, with a maximum of 300 in November, 300 in January, 150 in April, and 150 in May

REFERENCES

Books and Articles

Grushcow, J., and Smith, C. *Profits Through Seasonal Trading*. New York, NY: Wiley, 1980.

Schwager, J.D. "A Trader's Guide to Analyzing the Potato Futures Market," *1981 Commodity Yearbook*. Commodity Research Bureau, Incorporated, New York, NY, 1981.

Teweles, R.J., Harlow, C.V., and Stone, H.L., *The Commodity Futures Game, Who Wins? Who Loses? Why?* New York, NY: McGraw-Hill, 1974.

SOURCES OF INFORMATION

Government Agencies

Statistics Canada, Agriculture Division, Ottawa, Canada K1A OT6:

Fruit and Vegetable Production, Crops Section—monthly reports of (Canadian) potato storage and/or production.

U.S. Department of Agriculture (Maine), Presque Isle, ME 04769:

Federal–State Market News Service, Federal Building—daily reports on the cash market situation in various key sections of the country and the industry.

U. S. Department of Agriculture (New York), Riverhead, NY 11901:

Federal–State Market News Service, L.I. Potato Report, 127 E. Main Street—daily reports on the cash market situation in the various key sections of the country and the industry.

U. S. Department of Agriculture, Washington, DC 20250:

Cold Storage Section, Economic, Statistics, and Cooperative Service—monthly cold storage figures on frozen french fried potatoes and other frozen potato products.

Crop Reporting Board, Economic, Statistics, and Cooperative Service—monthly reports of acreage, yield per acre, and production.

"Potato Facts," Commodity Economics Division, Economic, Statistics, and Cooperative Service—quarterly figures on potatoes.

Periodicals

Ag Marketer, P.O. Box 1467, 1110 South 7th Avenue, Yakima, WA 98907.

American Potato Journal, The Potato Association of America, Orono, ME 04473.

Chipper Snacker, 26250 Euclid Avenue, Suite 915, Euclid, OH 44132.

Fraser's Potato Newsletter, Harry Fraser, RR 1, Charlottetown, Prince Edward Isle, Canada.

Potato and Onion World, 3722 North Cicero Avenue, Chicago, IL 60641.

Spudlight, Potato Division, 1019 19th Street, N.W., Washington, DC 20036.

Tabb's Market Service, Incorporated, One Gateway Center, Suite 300, Kansas City, KS 66101.

The Journal of Commerce, 99 Wall Street, New York, NY 10005.

The Maine Potato Councillor, Presque Isle, ME 04769.

The Packer, One Gateway Center, Kansas City, KS 66101.

The Produce News, 333 Sylvan Avenue, Englewood Cliffs, NJ 07632.

United Fresh Outlook, United Fresh Fruit and Vegetable Association newswire, 1019 19th Street, N.W., Washington, DC 20036.

Trade Associations

National Potato Board, Denver, CO.

National Potato Council, Denver, CO.

Potato Association of America, Orono, ME.

Potato Chip/Snack Food Association, Euclid, OH.

United Fresh Fruit and Vegetable Association, Washington, DC.

Other

Food Research Institute, Stanford University, Stanford, CA.

Smith, O. *Potatoes: Production, Storing, Processing*. Westport, CT: AVI Publishing, 1968.

University of Maine, Department of Agriculture and Resource Economics, Orono, ME.

CHAPTER **38**

THE MARKET FOR SUGAR

CONTENTS

SUGAR CONSUMPTION	4	THE FUTURES MARKET FOR SUGAR	12
SUGAR CANE PRODUCTION	5	SUGAR USER'S HEDGE	15
SUGAR BEET PRODUCTION	7	OPTIONS ON SUGAR FUTURES	16
THE INTERNATIONAL SUGAR AGREEMENT (ISA)	8	CONCLUSION	22
RECENT PRICE DYNAMICS	8	REFERENCES	22

CHAPTER 38

THE MARKET FOR SUGAR

Todd E. Petzel
Kevin P. Klarnet

The most common form of sugar (sucrose) is produced from cane and beets grown throughout the world. Though the production and processing procedures differ significantly, the final refined product is indistinguishable by source. The sugar cane plant, believed to have originated in the South Pacific, is largely cultivated by countries between the 30° north and south latitudes. Beet cultivation is a temperate zone activity, requiring 10–20 in. of rain (or irrigation equivalent) during the growing season. It is grown in climates as diverse as those in Scandinavia and the Imperial Valley of California.

Production has expanded from around 12 million metric tons in 1900 to a record estimated 98 million metric tons (about 65% of which is cane sugar) for the 1981–1982 season (*Sugar and Sweetener Outlook and Situation,* September 1982). Despite the fact that almost every country in the world produces sugar, over half of the total is concentrated in about 10 countries. Brazil, Cuba, and India are the leading cane sugar producers, while the USSR and Europe account for over 80% of the world's beet sugar. The United States, unique in producing significant quantities of both beet and cane sugars, had a 1981–1982 crop year output of about 5.5 million metric tons.

Although cane sugar is believed to have originated in the South Pacific, it is accepted that sugar was first processed in India. It did not spread through the Mediterranean region until the seventh and eighth centuries A.D. with the Moslem expansion into Northern Africa and Spain. By the 14th century, a solid industry was established in Venice, providing sugar as a luxury good to the wealthy of Europe.

The discovery of the Americas was followed closely by the expansion of sugar cultivation into the New World. The Portuguese had the first commercial production in Brazil, followed closely by Spanish, English, and French colonists. The Dutch concentrated their efforts in the East Indies, developing a large sugar industry in Java.

The Napoleonic wars and the resulting British blockade of continental shipping spurred the development of the sugar beet as a source of refined sugar. Since that time, European governments have promoted the domestic growth of beets as a secure source of supply.

SUGAR CONSUMPTION

Internationally, sugar consumption has grown dramatically since World War II. The demand for sugar is affected by four major factors: (1) per capita income, (2) price, (3) population, and (4) the price and substitutability of alternative sweeteners. Rapid population growth and economic development in much of the third world has led to dramatic increases in sugar consumption. The developed world's sugar consumption has grown more slowly due to a low income elasticity and the wide availability and acceptance of alternative sweeteners.

The demand for sugar is generally considered to be price inelastic, though in the long run artificially high prices for sugar in the European Economic Community (EEC) and the United States have produced significant shifts away from sugar toward high-fructose and glucose corn syrups. Figure 1, taken from the USDA publication *Sugar and Sweetener Outlook and Situation,* May 1981, documents the 20-year relative decline of sugar consumption in the United States.

High-fructose corn sweetener (HFCS) first appeared in 1967. The ability of HFCS to compete with sugar is somewhat limited because it is only economically available in liquid form. HFCS also has special handling requirements which pose additional limitations on potential users. The industries where there may be significant market penetration include (1) beverages, (2) bakery and cereal products, (3) dairy products and ice cream, and (4) canned foods, jams, and preserves.

A form of consumption that needs to be considered in the long run is in the production of fuel grade alcohols from sugar cane. Brazil has been a pioneer in this area, having the potential to produce sufficient ethanol to replace its petroleum

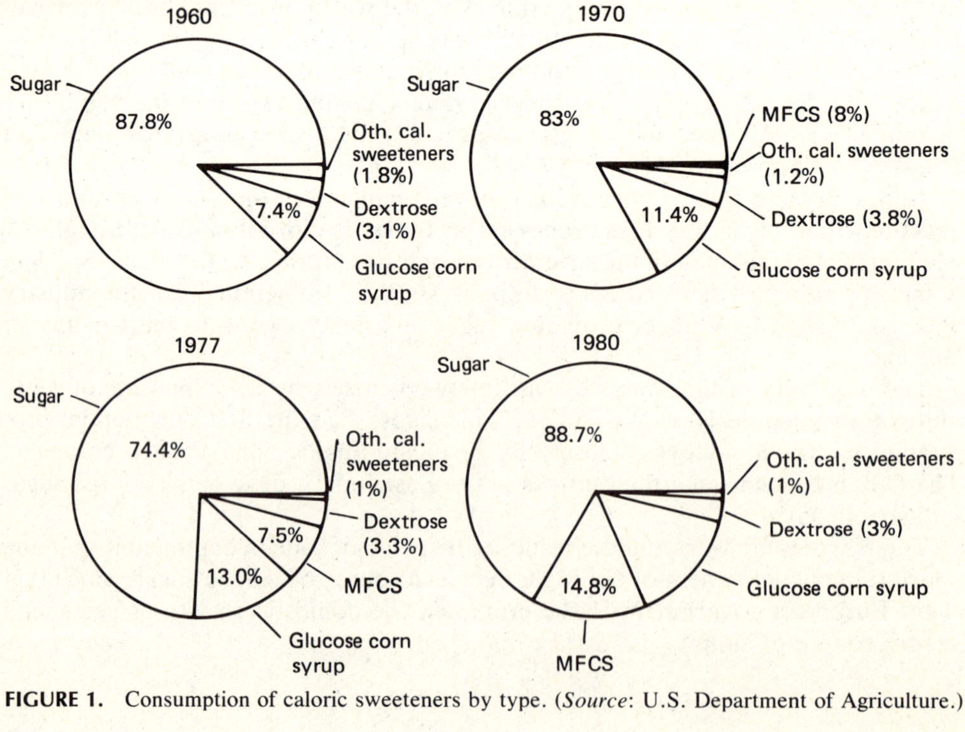

FIGURE 1. Consumption of caloric sweeteners by type. (*Source*: U.S. Department of Agriculture.)

needs by the end of the century (Yates, 1980). Current technology still produces economic yields only with low sugar and high petroleum prices, but progress to date has been significant. Whether alcohol production will grow fast enough to absorb excess stocks on the market, or whether there will be a further supply response maintaining low prices, remains to be seen. It is virtually certain, however, that if large capital intensive distilleries are constructed, they will be supplied with raw material, making the demand for sugar even less sensitive to price changes.

In the short run, the low price elasticity of demand has resulted periodically in large percentage swings in prices. Most recently, a worldwide production decline of 6.6 million metric tons (7.2%) from the 1978 to 1979 crop years produced a near trebling of the world price from October 1979 to October 1980. The existence of international marketing agreements, which will be discussed further below, can affect these price swings on the open market, but the origin of the swings lies in a low short-run price elasticity of demand. Recent production data and a graphical view of price swings are found in Table 1 and Figure 2, respectively.

SUGAR CANE PRODUCTION

Countries producing cane for export are usually underdeveloped or are in the middle stage of the development process. Cuba (6 million metric tons in 1980–1981), Brazil (2.3 million metric tons), the Philippines (1.7 million metric tons), and the Dominican Republic (1 million metric tons) all rely significantly on the export earnings of sugar cane. Australia (2.7 million metric tons) is the only developed country which is a significant cane exporter.

Price changes can have a dramatic impact on exporters' macroeconomies (Labys et al., 1980), which has led to the development of international trade agreements in an attempt to stabilize export receipts. Historically, a large percentage of the world trade has been tied up in bilateral and multilateral agreements which in many instances specify both quantity and price provisions. Different conclusions have been reached about the agreements' long-term benefits to the exporting countries, but it is clear that the open market has become a residual market where small changes in supply and demand can cause significant price volatility.

In addition to international trade controls, there are frequently domestic production and marketing controls. The acreage of sugar planted is one variable many governments specify. Some governments go so far as to set factory and field workers' wages and government export monopolies are not uncommon.

The supply of sugar cane is price inelastic in the short run. This is due in large part to the production technologies that dictate several cuttings from a given planting. Even if prices drop significantly, it could still be uneconomical to abandon a productive stand. Increases in price must be perceived to be sufficiently long term in order for acreage expansion to be justified. The government controls on production and marketing mentioned above seem only to add to the insensitivity to price changes.

This price inelasticity does not mean that the supply of exportable cane is stable. Devastating shocks can come from a variety of pests and severe weather conditions, which are monitored closely by the international market participants.

TABLE 1. World Production of Sugar (Centrifugal Sugar—Raw Value) (In Thousands of Short Tons)

Crop Year	Australia Cane	Brazil Cane	Cuba Cane	Hawaii Cane	India Cane	Indo-nesia Cane	Philip-pines Cane	Poland Beet	United States Beet	United States Cane	USSR Beet	Mexico	France	Puerto Rico Cane	China (Main-land)	West Germany	World Total All
1961–1962	1,512	3,934	5,308	1,120	3,693	709	1,618	1,808	2,404	858	7,170			1,009			56,989
1962–1963	2,000	3,576	4,211	1,101	2,979	648	1,714	1,464	2,598	853	6,600	1961–1965	1961–1965	990			54,895
1963–1964	1,883	3,620	4,400	1,179	3,470	725	1,856	1,570	3,086	1,184	6,475	Average	Average	989			59,919
1964–1965	2,132	4,152	6,600	1,218	4,285	715	1,767	1,975	3,332	1,147	11,270	(2,043)	(2,225)	897			72,567
1965–1966	2,187	5,324	4,950	1,234	4,514	671	1,590	1,620	2,820	1,104	10,700	2,320	2,585	883			69,293
1966–1967	2,564	4,807	6,200	1,191	3,039	661	1,718	1,856	2,860	1,215	10,304	2,679	1,967	818			71,112
1967–1968	2,686	4,922	5,500	1,232	3,092	716	1,759	2,109	2,694	1,457	11,531	2,575	1,905	645			73,007
1968–1969	3,052	4,804	5,200	1,180	4,640	775	1,760	1,880	3,510	1,214	10,922	2,826	2,623	483			74,537
1969–1970	2,440	5,063	9,406	1,162	5,523	835	2,124	1,683	3,471	1,071	9,570	2,974	2,648	460			79,250
1970–1971	2,702	5,642	6,530	1,286	4,963	800	2,270	1,659	3,321	1,253	9,904	2,729	2,972	321			77,739
1971–1972	3,015	5,939	4,837	1,124	4,222	750	2,062	1,887	3,531	1,206	8,813	2,778	3,530	298			77,547
1972–1973	3,162	6,909	5,787	1,155	5,151	981	2,549	2,017	3,663	1,749	9,370	3,053	3,285	300			84,085
1973–1974	2,592	6,959	5,800	944	4,949	950	2,643	1,817	2,918	1,253	9,568	2,805	3,255		2,065[c]	2,500	80,488
1974–1975	2,927	7,400	6,300	1,004	5,794	1,000	2,466	1,557	2,645	1,334	7,730	2,696	2,948		2,400	2,438	78,620
1975–1976	2,988	6,200	6,200	953	5,464	1,030	2,875	1,860	3,646	1,657	7,700	2,698	3,239		2,311	2,540	81,679
1976–1977	3,405	7,500	6,100	938	6,043	1,068	2,753	1,801	3,534	1,519	7,350	2,696	2,974		2,153	2,734	86,263
1977–1978	3,322	8,863	7,200	934	8,201	1,125	2,397	1,819	2,820	1,497	8,825	3,029	4,268		2,450	3,076	92,454
1978–1979	2,978	7,740	7,500	962	7,071	1,385	2,347	1,763	2,984	1,436	9,300	3,058	4,000		2,675	2,997	91,111
1979–1980	2,967	6,968	6,500	928	5,170	1,313	2,325	1,582	2,612	1,488	7,800	2,765	4,257		2,507	3,095	84,150
1980–1981	3,387	8,101	6,400	966	6,534	1,370	2,373	1,126	2,798	1,547	6,900	2,518	4,187		3,052	2,982	86,741
1981–1982[b]	3,550	8,500	6,800	939	8,194	1,520	2,450	1,021	3,025	1,660	7,100	2,700	5,086		3,356	3,350	95,756

Source: U.S. Department of Agriculture, Foreign Agricultural Service.

[a]Preliminary.

[b]Estimated.

[c]Average 1969/1970–1973/1974.

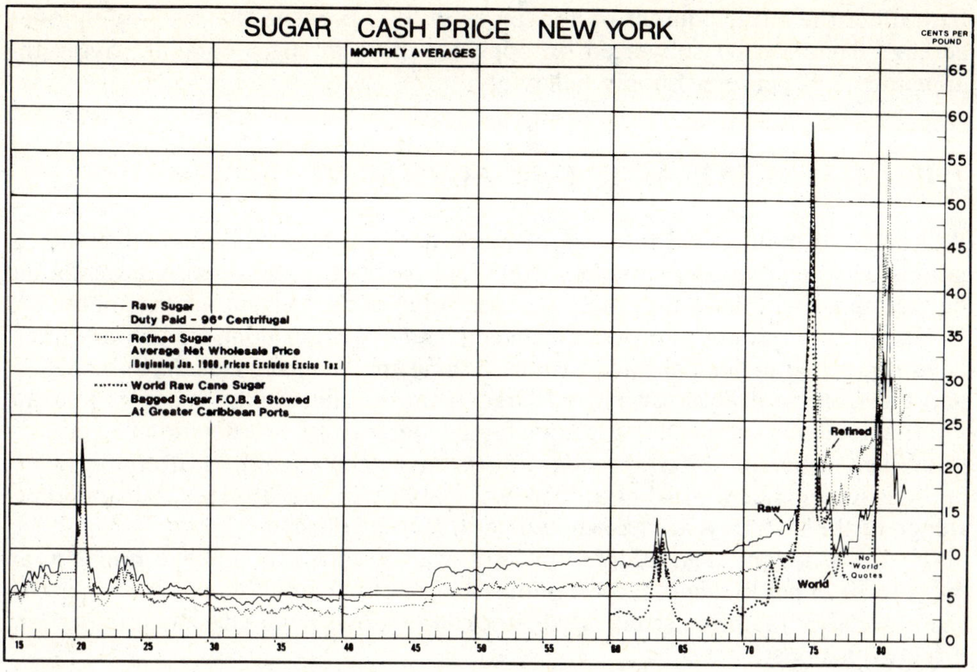

FIGURE 2. Sugar cash prices monthly, New York (*Source*: Commodity Research Bureau, Incorporated).

SUGAR BEET PRODUCTION

Western and Eastern Europe and North America are the primary sources of beet sugars. Many cost of production studies have shown that beet sugar is at a strong comparative disadvantage to cane sugar grown in the tropics. This had led to the evolution of import quotas and levies in both the European Economic Community (EEC) and the United States to protect domestic sugar. The price wedges that result between international and domestic prices can be extreme. In early October 1982, the world spot price was about $0.05 per lb, while the U.S. domestic spot price in New York was over $0.20 per lb (*CSCE Daily Market Reports*). The EEC prices have frequently been kept higher yet. The subsidies given to farmers in these two areas provide secure sources of domestic supply, but severely limit the exports and incomes of developing country producers.

The level of subsidy in Europe is so high that production has often exceeded demand. In the two crop years 1980 and 1981, the EEC had net exports of 3.3 and 2.9 million metric tons, respectively, making it the world's second leading exporter after Cuba (*World Sugar Journal*, December 1981). The sale of these large supplies can have a severe effect on international prices and tends to discourage production in the developing world.

Since beet sugar is an annual crop, there is more flexibility in altering production in response to short-run changes in price. Unfortunately, since most beet producers are not exposed to international market forces, there is little opportunity for world sugar surpluses to impact appropriately on these sources of supply. Final output can vary either because of total beet tonnage or weather conditions that affect the sugar content of a given crop. It is possible that well-intentioned acreage decisions be subverted by opposite shifts in sugar content, giving the appearance of perverse supply behavior.

THE INTERNATIONAL SUGAR AGREEMENT (ISA)

Bilateral and multilateral trade agreements have traditionally dominated the relations between exporters and importers. No analysis of the sugar market should be attempted without a thorough understanding of the current arrangements.

Historically, groups of producers and consumers, often along old colonial lines, have negotiated individual trade treaties. Prominent examples include Cuba–USSR and the Commonwealth Countries–Great Britain. These treaties segmented the international market and left any hope for a wider level of coordination and control unfulfilled. Since the 1960s, broader efforts have been attempted. Both producers and consumers seem to want a degree of stability in world prices, but the experience of the last 15 years has shown control to be elusive.

The most recent ISA, adopted in 1978, was designed to stabilize prices in an $0.11 to $0.21 per lb range. Export quotas and stock accumulations were to support the low end of the price scale, while stock draw-downs were designed to prevent price explosions.

The effectiveness of this most recent agreement was undermined at the outset by the large world stocks, and consequent low price, in 1978. Some exports were withheld by ISA members in 1978 and 1979, but they were not sufficient to bring the world price into the target range. The low worldwide production in 1979–1980 produced a big run-up in prices starting in late 1979. From October 1979 to April 1980, the world prices passed through the ISA range, eventually exceeding $0.40 per lb in October 1980. The price reversal was not quite as abrupt, but from March 1981 to April 1982, the world price fell from $0.21 to $0.10 per lb.

The failure of the current ISA is due to many factors, including the EEC being treated as a "special exporter" that is not bound by the agreement's provisions. The International Sugar Organization prevailed on the EEC in 1982 to limit its exports, but there is some question as to whether the resulting stock buildup would not have happened anyway given the severely depressed price level.

The basic problem with the ISA appears to be that, while the reserve stock and quota provisions appear restrictive, they, in fact, fall within the range of behaviors expected under normal market situations. Stocks are usually accumulated during periods of low prices in anticipation of a recovery, and are run down as prices move to higher ground (Working, 1949). Until provisions are agreed upon that effectively limit supplies during low-price episodes, or increase available supplies during large run-ups in price, little can be expected for international price stability.

RECENT PRICE DYNAMICS

Over the last 10 years world sugar prices have shown a great deal of volatility, swinging between prolonged periods of surplus and brief moments of accelerating prices. Figure 3 (Commodity Research Bureau, Incorporated) shows the behavior

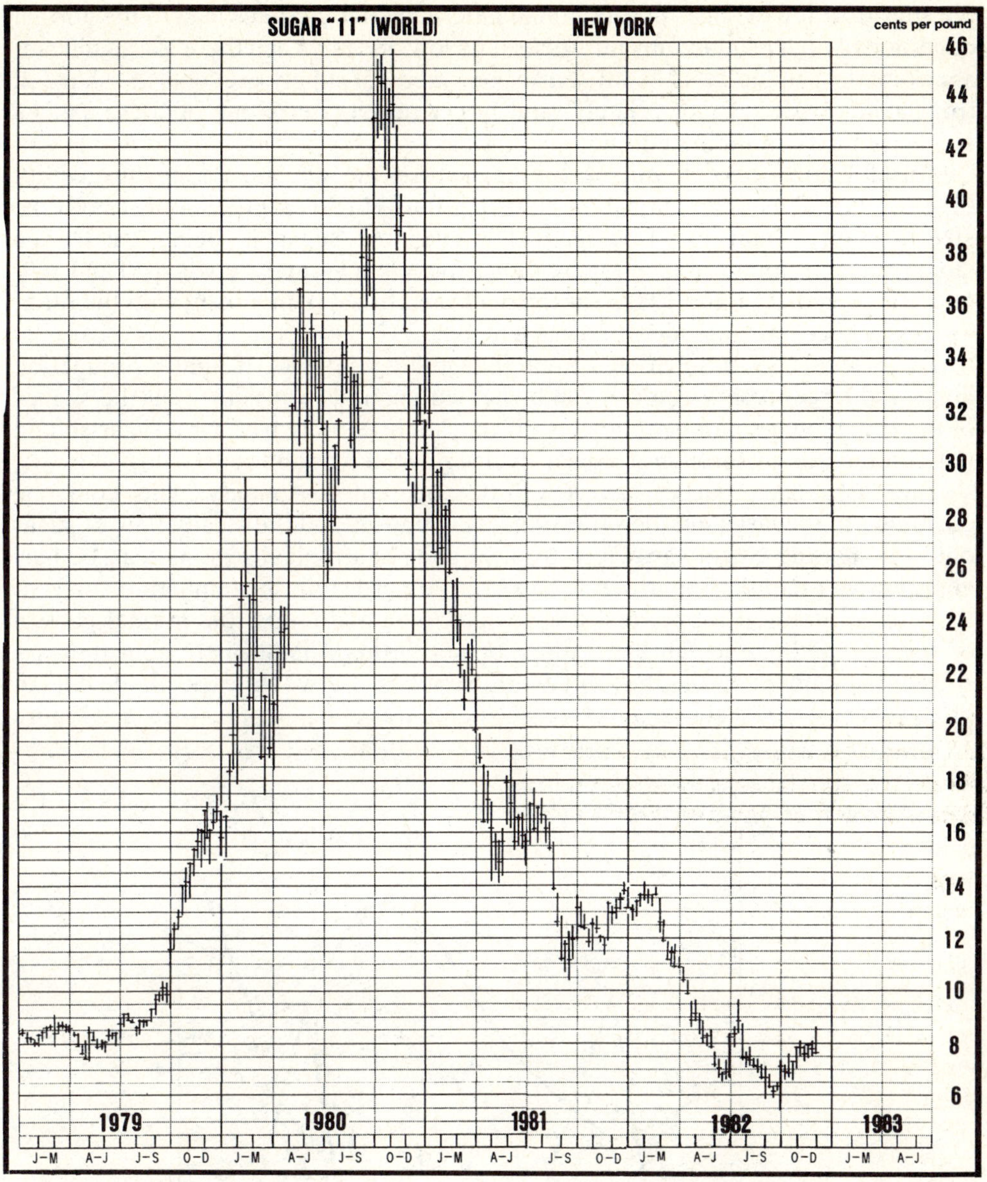

FIGURE 3. Sugar No. 11 prices weekly, New York (*Source*: Commodity Research Bureau, Incorporated).

of nearby futures contracts in New York for international sugar from 1972 through 1982. The shift from a relatively stable price regime, to one more typical of agricultural commodities traded internationally, occurred when the long-term trade agreements began to lose effectiveness in the 1960s. This breakdown is probably more political than economic in nature, as countries in the developing world have sought to become more independent in the marketing of their export crops.

The events that combine to produce these shifts between high and low prices may appear to follow a regular frequency, but in fact there is no economic evidence of a fixed periodicity. The fundamentals of short-run inelastic demand linked with the subsidization of sugar production in EEC and United States lead to the normal condition of high production and stocks, and low prices. When there is a significant shock on the production side, the basic inelasticity of supply prevents the shortfall from being made up immediately, and prices accelerate. None of these shocks can be regularly anticipated.

A useful indicator of the current market status is the ratio measuring the quantity of sugar stocks as a percentage of consumption. This measure captures both the size of supply and the rate at which available sugar is being used. The stock/consumption ratio (see Figure 4) has moved in a range between 20 and 36% over the period 1971 and 1982. Sugar prices tend to move inversely with the ratio, as can be seen dramatically for 1974 and 1980.

The current ISA is scheduled to be renegotiated in 1984. If tighter production limits and larger reserve stocks can be agreed upon, it is possible that the swings of the last 12 years can be tempered. If not, there is no reason why sugar should not continue to go through irregular cycles of price variability.

The cash sugar market has very little apparent seasonality. This could be attributed to the large number of producing countries and the steady flow of sugar onto the market. Sugar, grown in tropical and semitropical regions, can be harvested in any month. Sugar beets, however, are grown in the temperate zones of the United States, Europe, and the Soviet Union and follow the normal pattern of spring planting and fall harvesting. If the northern hemisphere contributes a substantial amount to the movable world supplies, we would expect a decline in price at harvest. The charts of both cash and futures indicate otherwise (see Figure 5).

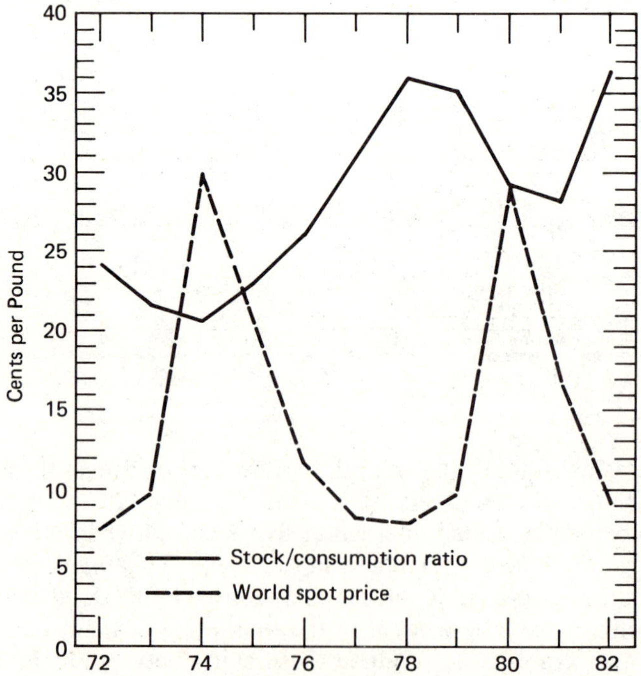

FIGURE 4. World spot price vs the stock consumption ratio.

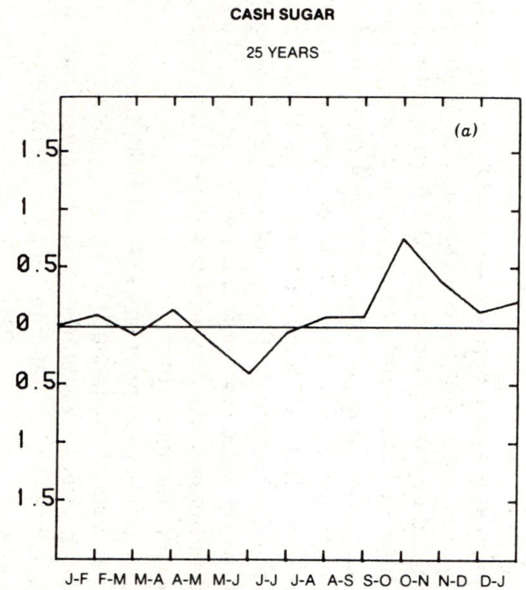

	J-F	F-M	M-A	A-M	M-J	J-J	J-A	A-S	S-O	O-N	N-D	D-J
Average Move	0	-0.2	0.2	-0.3	-0.3	0.3	0.1	0	0.6	-0.4	-0.3	0
% Reliable	52	28	76	36	48	72	64	64	44	48	32	48
Avg. Up Move	0.3	0.3	0.5	0.3	0.2	0.6	0.5	0.5	1.8	0.2	0.2	0.6
Avg. Down Move	0.2	1.4	0.6	1.5	0.9	0.4	0.5	0.9	0.4	1.1	1.4	0.3
Greatest Up Move	1.2	1.3	3.7	3.2	2	4.6	3.1	5.1	18.4	1.6	1.2	4.4
Greatest Down Move	0.7	8.8	1.9	8.7	4.8	1.4	3.2	5	2.4	10.6	9.3	1.3

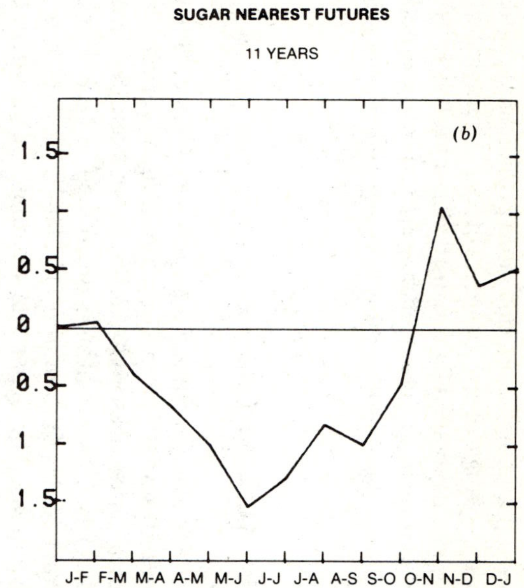

	J-F	F-M	M-A	A-M	M-J	J-J	J-A	A-S	S-O	O-N	N-D	D-J
Average Move	0	-0.5	-0.3	-0.4	-0.6	0.2	0.4	-0.2	0.5	1.5	-0.7	0.1
% Reliable	45.5	45.5	45.5	36.4	72.8	63.7	45.5	54.6	81.9	54.6	54.6	81.9
Avg. Up Move	1.2	0.3	0.2	0.5	0	0.6	1.8	0.7	0.8	3	0.9	0.8
Avg. Down Move	1.1	1.5	1	1.8	0.8	0.5	0.8	1	0.7	0.3	2.1	3.2
Greatest Up Move	5.7	1.2	0.8	1.7	0.1	2.7	6.4	2.5	4.5	16.4	1.7	3.2
Greatest Down Move	4.7	6.8	2.4	6.7	3.4	1	2.8	3.1	1.2	0.8	10.8	6.4

FIGURE 5. (*a*) Seasonality of sugar cash market, 25 years. (*b*) Seasonality of sugar nearest futures, 11 years.

Futures seasonality seems to have the same, but more pronounced, pattern as the cash market. Annual price swings of the nearest futures, averaging $0.025, could be substantial if sugar prices averaged less than $0.10 per lb. It is interesting to note that the seasonality shown in the chart of nearest futures is exactly the opposite of the normal temperate zone crop with lows occurring at planting and highs at harvest.

THE FUTURES MARKET FOR SUGAR

There are two major futures for sugar located in New York (Coffee, Sugar and Cocoa Exchange, Incorporated) and London (London United Terminal Sugar Market). Given the significant differences that can exist between the protected U.S. market and the world market, two contracts are traded in New York. The Sugar No. 11 (world) contract trades 50 long-ton (112,000 lb) lots of raw sugar from 26 different producing nations. The Sugar No. 12 (domestic) contract trades the same raw commodity, but deliverable at four different domestic points. The key difference is that for the domestic contract, the sugar has either been produced in the United States or, if imported, has had its transportation and import duties paid. The world contract trades "free" sugar that is subject to whatever import restrictions and fees are imposed by the consuming nation. Complete contract specifications are in Tables 2 and 3.

Hedgers in the futures market come from both the production and consumption side. Since the composition of the sugar industry is a combination of government and private parties, the size and economic backing of the participants can vary considerably. Still, the number of buyers and sellers is quite large, leading to highly competitive futures markets with no one party dominating the trade.

The major exporters and importers operate at two market levels. As previously mentioned, a large fraction of world trade occurs through prearranged average price contracts. After these trades are made, further supply-and-demand decisions are made at the prevailing world price levels. Increasingly, the world market trades are being performed on futures markets where suppliers and purchasers do not need to seek out specific trading partners.

With the exception of the big run-ups in price in 1974 and 1980, the world price of sugar has been reported as being lower than the cost of production in many cane exporting countries. These periods cannot be expected to persist indefinitely, and hence offer consuming nations an outstanding hedging opportunity to lock-in a low price source of supply.

On the selling side, exporting countries could have locked-in price far exceeding their costs of production during both 1974 and 1980. This was done to a certain extent, but several factors have limited the level of this activity. The cost of margin calls, given high international interest rates, can severely tax developing countries that have limited hard currency reserves. An exporter that sold September 1981 sugar short in the spring of 1980, when the price reached $0.35 per lb for the first time in 5 years, would have had to meet margin calls as the price peaked around $0.41 in the fall of that year. The ultimate choice of the short sale for the 1981 crop year would have been a very wise one, but it would have required significant reserves in the short run.

TABLE 2. World Sugar No. 11

Contract Unit	112,000 lb (50 long tons)
Price quotation	Cents per pound
Minimum price fluctuation	1/100¢ per lb or $11.20 per contract
Maximum daily price fluctuation	1/2¢ (50 points) above or below the previous day's settlement price. Limits are expandable in increments of 1/2¢ (50 points) to a maximum of $0.02 (200 points). Limits do not apply to the nearest 2 months.
Trading hours	10:00 a.m.–1:43 p.m. Trading is suspended at 1:43 p.m. and the closing call begins at 1:45 p.m. eastern time.
Basic grade	Raw centrifugal cane sugar based on 96° average polarization.
Delivery months	Trading is permitted beginning 18 months prior to the expiration of the contract. The trading months are January, March, May, July, September, and October.
Deliverable Growths	Argentina, Australia, Brazil, Honduras, Colombia, Costa Rica, Dominican Republic, El Salvador, Ecuador, Fiji Islands, French Antilles, Guatemala, India, Jamaica, Mauritius, Mexico, Nicaragua, Peru, Republic of the Philippines, South Africa, Swaziland, Taiwan, Thailand, Trinidad, United States, and Zimbabwe. Growths of Malawi shall be deliverable with respect to the January 1983 delivery month and all delivery months thereafter.
Delivery points	A port in the country of origin or, in the case of landlocked countries, at a berth or anchorage in the customary port of export, F.O.B. and stowed in bulk.
Delivery responsibility	Deliverer shall be responsible for all expenses pertaining to delivery and loading of sugar into the vessel, including freight taxes and other taxes of the country of origin of any nature. Normal pilotage, wharfage charges, customs fees, and similar charges pertaining to the entry or exit of the vessel at loading port are for the account the receiver. The receiver shall provide vessels suitable for carrying sugar. These vessels shall be ready to load at the loading port on any day from the first calendar day of the delivery month up to and including the 15th calendar day of the second succeeding calendar month.
Position limits	None
CFTC large trader reporting level	100 contracts or more
Last trading day	last full business day of the month preceding the delivery month
Notice day	Next business day following last trading day

TABLE 3. Domestic Sugar No. 12

Contract unit	112,000 lb (50 long tons)
Price quotation	Cents per pound
Minimum price fluctuation	1/100¢ per lb or $11.20 per contract
Maximum daily price fluctuation	1/2¢ (50 points) above or below the previous day's settlement price. Limits are expandable in increments of 1/2¢ (50 points) to a maximum of $0.02 (200 points). Limits do not apply to the nearest 2 months.
Trading hours	10:00 a.m. to 1:43 p.m. Trading is suspended at 1:43 p.m. and the closing call begins at 1:45 p.m. eastern time.
Basic grade	Raw centrifugal cane sugar based on 96° average polarization.
Delivery months	Trading is permitted beginning 18 months prior to expiration of the contract. The trading months are January, March, May, July, September, and November.
Deliverable growths	Cane sugars of the United States, duty free; foreign origin, duty paid and delivered in bulk.
Delivery points	New York (including Yonkers), Philadelphia, Baltimore, or New Orleans (including Grammercy, Burnside, and Reserve)
Position limits	None
CFTC large trader reporting level	100 contracts or more
Last trading day	Eighth calendar day for the month preceding the delivery month. If not an exchange business day, then the following business day.
Notice day	Next business day following last trading day

Forward average price sales are also an impediment to using world sugar futures. If an exporting country commits a large fraction of its expected sales in average price contracts, it may be reluctant to sell additional futures contracts on the world market. A significant negative shock to its production could turn the country into a futures market speculator, exposing the country's reserves to considerable risk.

The conclusion to be drawn from this is not that the futures market performs poorly for importers and exporters, but that having a larger fraction of the international trade pass through the free market would produce clearer aggregate supply-and-demand signals and a more efficient allocation. A possible defect in the current ISA is its reliance on programs dealing with physical commodities. Large stockholding schemes are expensive to implement by either consumers or producers. It may be effective to include in the next agreement a cash pool to finance legitimate hedges in the world futures markets. In that way many of the costs of futures hedging could be reduced, and the market would better perform its allocative function.

Other active participants in the futures market include refiners and consumers of refined sugar and other sweetners. Since refining costs are reasonably stable, the prices for raw sugar are highly correlated with those in the refined market, making the Nos. 11 and 12 contracts effective hedging vehicles for both raw and refined sugar users. Other sweeteners, like high-fructose corn syrup, that do not have their own futures contracts, can be cross hedged in the sugar market. Even though the correlation between the two markets is not perfect, the risk-reducing potential of these cross hedges can be significant.

The numerous uses of sugar lead to a composition of hedgers that represents all of the major food industries. Beverage manufacturers, bakers, chocolatiers, and cereal producers, all use large quantities of sugar and other sweeteners, and may use the futures markets to hedge their risks.

The form of trading on futures markets can vary with the needs of the participants. Hedging may be direct short or long positions where all that is at risk is the basis between the futures price and the relevant cash price. Frequently, trades are made "against actuals," where the long and short hedgers exchange their futures contracts, netting their positions to zero, after agreeing on the value of the basis. This practice goes by a variety of terms including "exchange for physical," and "versus cash." Other types of trades rely on the futures market as a price guide in forming forward contracts. No matter what form these trades take, the effectiveness of hedging is directly related to the liquidity and accuracy of the futures market.

SUGAR USER'S HEDGE[1]

Assume a sugar industrial user is buying 1,000 long tons (2.24 million lb) of sugar every month. During the first 8 months of 1980, without making use of the futures market, the user would have paid the following prices (in cents per lb):

January	February	March	April	May	June	July	August	Average Price
18.00¢	23.25¢	21.12¢	22.35¢	32.44¢	32.63¢	29.25¢	32.72¢	26.47¢

For the same months, the monthly purchases of 1,000 long tons (2.24 million lb) would be:

January	February	March	April	May	June	July	August	Average Price
$403,200	$520,800	$473,080	$500,640	$726,650	$730,910	$655,200	$732,928	$592,925

We can see that sugar prices over the course of the 8 months have risen considerably. If the user bought sugar each month (as needs warranted), we would see that the user would pay increasingly higher prices for sugar with each passing month. The example illustrates the considerable risk the user assumes if the user is committed to buy sugar from a volatile cash market.

[1]D. Koutras, E. Meir, and R. Ng, *Commodity Hedging Operations and Strategies: An Introduction*, Drexel Burnham Lambert, NY 1982.

As an alternative, the industrial user could hedge any needs. In this case, the user needing 1,000 tons of sugar every month, for the next 8 months, would buy 160 futures contracts equivalent to 8,000 tons. Should sugar prices rise as they did from April on, the user would be paying more for sugar purchases, but these extra outlays would be offset by a profit generated by a long futures position.

Let us now illustrate how the user could use the futures market to protect against adverse price fluctuations. The user could possibly consider the following two strategies for hedging needs during the coming 8 months:

1. The user could price *all* the sugar needed in the futures market by buying 160 September contracts (equivalent to 8,000 tons) in January 1980. Doing so, the user would lock-in a certain price for sugar for the next 8 months. The user would then liquidate 20 contracts (1,000 tons) every month as the user makes 1,000-ton purchases in the cash market.
2. The user could also decide to buy *some* coverage only up to May, and then buy additional coverage from May to August. The user may feel that he or she does not want to be locked-in to one price for the next 8 months; instead the user wants to have the opportunity to price sugar at two separate intervals.

Let us say that the second strategy is chosen. As a result the user will buy 80 futures contracts to cover 4,000 tons of sugar, which is what the user's needs will be for 4 months. Every time a monthly purchase of 1,000 tons of sugar is made, an equivalent amount of futures contracts (20 contracts) will be liquidated (sold). Table 4 goes through the hedging process in detail.

As we can see from Table 5 the sugar user managed to hold the average price for sugar to 24.9¢ (excluding commissions), whereas without the hedge the cost per pound would have been 26.5¢. The hedge in this example generated an overall profit of $279,276, lowering the total cash outlay needed to purchase the sugar.

The user would have lowered the average price for sugar even more than the 24.9¢ had the user opted for the first strategy, namely, pricing all needs in January. In this situation, the user would have locked-in a price of 18.09¢ for the entire 8 months, and the hedge would have generated greater profits. However, in real situations hedgers seldom take full coverage, preferring to take partial coverage at different intervals to ensure greater flexibility.

OPTIONS ON SUGAR FUTURES

Since October 1982, put and call options on the Sugar No. 11 Contract have been available on the Coffee, Sugar and Cocoa Exchange. Specifications of the contract are in Table 6. These American options differ from the options traded in London in that they are written at fixed strike prices and are easily traded. Viewed as a complement to futures contracts, options provide an opportunity for hedgers to segment their risk coverage depending on the degree of coverage desired. A major advantage of option hedging is the elimination of the uncertainty of margin calls arising from daily marking to the market. There is no possibility of extreme credit demands forcing the liquidation of a hedge position when the option is owned, exposing the buyer or seller of physical sugar to extreme risks in a volatile market.

TABLE 4. Chronological Hedging Process

	January	February	March	April	May	June	July	August
One contract = 112,000 lb								
1 long ton = 2,240 lb								
At the beginning of January 1980, the hedger buys 80 May contracts equivalent to 4,000 tons at 18.09¢. Another 80 September contracts would be purchased in May.	20 Contracts liquidated at 18.09¢. Profit: 0	20 Contracts liquidated at 24.68¢. Profit: $147,616	20 Contracts liquidated at 21.12¢. Profit: $67,872	20 Contracts liquidated at 22.35¢. Profit: $95,424	80 September contracts purchased at 32.61¢. 20 liquidated at 32.61¢. Profit = 0	20 Contracts liquidated at 34.47¢ Profit: $41,664	20 Contracts liquidated at 29.25¢ Loss: ($75,264)	20 Contracts liquidated at 32.72¢. Profit: $2,464
Cash prices paid for monthly 1,000-ton purchases	18.00¢	23.25¢	21.12¢	22.35¢	32.44¢	32.63¢	29.25¢	32.72¢

TABLE 5. How Profits Made on the Hedge by the Sugar User Helped Lower the User's Overall Costs

	Jan	Feb	March	April	May	June	July	Aug	Total Paid	Average Level
Cost per pound without hedging	18.09¢	23.25¢	21.12¢	22.35¢	32.44¢	32.63¢	29.25¢	32.72¢	—	26.47¢
Monthly purchase of 1,000 tons without hedging	$403,200	$520,800	$473,080	$500,640	$726,650	$730,910	$655,200	$732,928	$4,743,408	$592,925
Hedging profit or (loss)	$0	$147,616	$67,827	$95,424	$0	$41,664	($75,264)	$2,464	($279,276 total profit)	
Net cost per ton after hedge	$403,200	$373,184	$405,208	$405,216	$726,650	$689,746	$730,464	$730,464	$4,464,132	$58,017
Net cost per pound after hedge	18.00¢	16.60¢	18.08¢	18.09¢	32.43¢	30.80¢	32.61¢	—		24.90¢

TABLE 6. Contract Specifications for the Options Contract on the Sugar No. 11 (World) Contract[a]

Delivery months underlying option contracts	March, July, October and first of these months in next year for which futures trading has begun		
Normal trading hours	9:30 a.m.–1:43 p.m. New York time		
Trading unit	One Sugar No. 11 (world) futures contract		
Minimum fluctuations	1/100 or 0.01¢ per lb (equivalent to $11.20 per contract)		
Strike price increments	Futures Contract Price	2 Nearby Months	Deferred Months
	Less than $0.15	½¢—50 points	$0.01—100 points
	Between $0.15 and $0.40	$0.01—100 points	$0.02—200 points
	Above $0.40	$0.02—200 points	$0.04—400 points
Expiration date and time	12:00 noon New York time on the Saturday following the second Friday of the month *preceding* the delivery month of the underlying futures contract. Note: Customer exercise notices cannot be submitted after the last trading day.		
Last trading day	Second Friday of the month preceding the delivery month of the underlying futures contract		
Position limits	The CFTC requires the exchange to set speculative position limits. These limits are subject to change; check with your broker		
Daily price limits	None		

[a]Option contract specifications are those which were filed for approval with the CFTC on December 8, 1981. The approved specifications may be different and they are subject to change. You must verify current specifications with your broker.

A further advantage of options is that they may go unexercised. This makes it possible to manage quantity risk as well as price risk via options hedging. For example, a producer unsure of the size of a crop can hedge the maximum possible size by buying puts. If this crop is smaller, some options would expire unexercised. This level of protection is clearly costly, but may be worthwhile if there is considerable quantity uncertainty prior to harvest.

Finally, a liquid options market also serves an informational need in the market place. In the same way that futures markets serve a "price discovery" function, an options market serves in a discovery role regarding the volatility of the underlying asset. Given a level of interest rates, an underlying futures price, and the time to expiration, the market pricing of an option implies a volatility. This information can be used effectively in the planning of both producers and consumers.

In summary, the market for futures contracts and options on futures provides a menu of instruments for both the long and short hedgers. In periods of stable

TABLE 7. Comparison of Sugar Futures Contracts

	World Sugar No. 11	Domestic Sugar No. 12	Refined Sugar
Exchange	New York Coffee, Sugar, and Cocoa Exchange	New York Coffee, Sugar, and Cocoa Exchange	MidAmerican Commodity Exchange
Size	112,000 lb (50 long tons)	112,000 lb	20,000 lb
Grade	Raw centrifugal sugar, 96° average polarization	Raw centrifugal sugar, 96° average polarization	Free-flowing bulk extrafine granulated
Delivery months	January, March, May, July, September, and October beginning 18 months prior to expiration	January, March, May, July, September, and November beginning 18 months prior to expiration	Current and subsequent
Delivery points	Port in country of origin or customary port of export F.O.B. bulk	New York, Philadelphia, Baltimore, and New Orleans.	F.O.B. origin, freight off Chicago
Minimum price fluctuation	1/100¢ per point or $11.20 per contract	1/100¢ per point	1/100¢ per lb or $2.00 per contract
Maximum daily price fluctuation	½¢ (50 points) Expandable to $0.02 (200 points), no limits on two nearest months	½¢ (50 points) Expandable to $0.02 (200 points), no limits on two nearest months	½¢ (50 points)
Trading hours	local 1000–1343 (eastern time)	1000–1343 (eastern time)	900–1300 (central time) 1000–1400
Currency	U.S. dollars	U.S. dollars	U.S. dollars

	Raw Sugar and White Sugar	Domestic Sugar No. 12	White Sugar
Exchange	London Sugar Terminal Market	Tokyo Sugar Exchange	International Market of White Sugar of Paris
Size	50 long tons	Raw 10 tonnes, white 9 tonnes	50 tonnes
Grade	Raw centrifugal cane sugar, 96° minimum polarization White sugar minimum polarization, 99.8°		White beet or cane sugar, 99.7° minimum polarization
Delivery months	January, March, May, August, and October beginning 15 months prior to expiration		
Delivery points	Port in country of origin		Ports of designated countries, primarily in Europe
Minimum price fluctuation	£ 0.05 per ton £ 2.50 per lot		
Maximum daily limit	± £ 20 per ton	±3 yen	150–400 francs expandable at specified price levels
Trading hours	1030–1230, 1430–1640, kerb until 2000	930, 1030, 1330, and 1430	1000–1300 1500–1830
Eastern time	430–630, 830–1040, kerb until 1400		400–700 900–1230
Currency	Sterling	Yen	French francs

price changes, the risk of margin calls is limited, and trading futures contracts can provide strong protection against price movements. In more volatile markets, hedgers can choose to pay the options premium on an instrument that provides them with the degree of price risk they find acceptable, and completely avoid the possibility of margin calls.

CONCLUSION

The sugar market reflects the economic and political events of producing and consuming countries. Like many agricultural commodities that have a small fraction of total production traded internationally, sugar price movements can be rapid and extreme. The current layers of international trade agreements keep a significant fraction of the sugar traded out of the open market, probably adding to the volatility, and certainly reducing the allocative efficiency of the market. In such an environment, it is critical to have well-functioning futures markets to meet the hedging needs of producers and consumers. The growth of futures trading in sugar demonstrates the efficiency with which the New York and London markets meet that need with a variety of sugar instruments available. (Table 7 presents a comparison of sugar futures contracts.)

REFERENCES

Ballinger, R. A. *A History of Sugar Marketing Through 1974.* U.S. Department of Agriculture, Economics, Statistics, and Cooperatives Service, Agricultural Economic Report No. 382, 1978.

Bates, T. H., and Schmitz, A. *A Spatial Equilibrium Analysis of the World Sugar Economy.* Gianini Foundation Monograph No. 23, California Agricultural Experiment Station, Berkeley, CA, May 1969.

Bogosian, T. *Sweet Solutions.* WGBH Educational Foundation, 1979.

Bohall, R., et al. *The Sugar Industry's Structure Pricing and Performance.* Commodity Economics Division, Economic Research Service, U.S. Department of Agriculture, Agricultural Economic Report No. 363, 1977.

Commodity Research Bureau, Incorporated. *Commodity Yearbook*, New York, NY.

F.O. Licht's International Sugar Report. Ratzeburg, Germany.

F.O Licht's World Sugar Statistics 1980/1981. Ratzeburg, Germany, 1981.

Inkeles, D. M. "How to Analyze the World Sugar Futures Market." In *Forecasting Commodity Prices*, Commodity Research Bureau, New York, 1975.

Labys, W. C. Nadiri, M. I. and Nunez Del Arco, J. *Commodity Markets and Latin American Development.* Cambridge, MA: Ballinger, 1980.

Statistical Bulletin. International Sugar Organization, London, England.

Stone, M. J. C. "The Trade View of the Market." In *The Future of Sugar*, International Sweetener and Alcohol Conference, 1980.

Sugar and Other Sweeteners: An Industry Assessment. Report to the Congress of the United States by the Comptroller General, Washington, D.C., 1979.

Tewes, T. "Sugar: A Short-Term Forecasting Model for the World Market, with a Forecast of the World Market Price for Sugar in 1972–1973." *The Business Economist* **4,** Summer 1972, pp. 89–97.

U.S. Department of Agriculture, Economics and Statistics Service. *Sugar and Sweetener Outlook and Situation.* Washington, D.C. (Annual)

U.S. Department of Agriculture, Foreign Agricultural Service. *Foreign Agricultural Circular.* Washington, D.C.

Working, H. "The Theory of the Price of Storage." *American Economic Review* **39,** 1949, pp. 1254–1262.

World Sugar Journal, Berkshire, England.

Wymer, C. R. "Estimation of Continuous Time Models with an Application to the World Sugar Market." Mimeographed. London School of Economics and Political Science, 1972.

Yates, R. A. "Best Alternative Renewable Raw Material for Alcohol Production." In *The Future of Sugar*, International Sweetener and Alcohol Conference, 1980.

CHAPTER 39

REFINED SUGAR CASH AND FUTURES MARKETS

CONTENTS

HISTORY OF SUGAR PRODUCTION 3

CURRENT PRODUCTION 4

REFINERY PRODUCTION 4

MARKETING 6

Substitutes 6

GOVERNMENT PROGRAMS 7

THE INTERNATIONAL SUGAR AGREEMENT 7

FUTURES CONTRACTS 7

CHAPTER 39

REFINED SUGAR CASH AND FUTURES MARKETS

Donna Nielsen Murphy

This chapter is not intended to review all the factors of sugar supply and distribution, but to point out the more important areas of the *refined sugar* segment of that industry. There are, however, some interesting events in the growth of sugar production that have not been discussed in the previous chapter.

HISTORY OF SUGAR PRODUCTION

Mankind has enjoyed sweet substances throughout history. Honey, the original sweetener, was first collected from wild stores, but the Egyptians practiced the art of beekeeping as early as 2500 B.C. Sugar cane originated in the South Pacific islands. The art of processing sugar cane into a curious substance which looked like salt but tasted like honey was developed in the Middle East, then spread by the Crusaders throughout Europe.

Columbus brought sugar cane to the New World, yet the 13 colonies depended heavily on molasses imports. The Sugar Act, passed by the British Parliament in 1764, sparked bitter protest against stiff tariffs and helped contribute to the outbreak of the American Revolution. John Adams later wrote, "I know not why we should blush to confess that molasses was an essential ingredient in American Independence. Many great events have proceeded from much smaller causes." Sugar cane production began in the southeastern United States in 1794, but it was not until 1835 that the crop was first introduced to Hawaii. Sugar cane is currently grown in Florida, Louisiana, Texas, and Hawaii.

In 1747 a Prussian chemist proved that sugar produced from beets and cane was identical. When the continental blockade deprived France of imported sugar, Napoleon spurred commercial production of sugar beets. The first beet sugar factory in the United States was established in California in 1838 but it was not until 1890, when the government passed a protective tariff and the Sugar Bounty

Parts of this section were taken from the "Application for Designation as a Contract Market of Refined Sugar," prepared by the MidAmerica Commodity Exchange, August 31, 1981.

Act, that sugar factories began to flourish. Sugar beets are currently produced in 16 states, all west of the Mississippi except for Michigan and Ohio. Particularly important production areas include California and the Minnesota–Dakota Red River valley.

The sugar beet is a member of the goosefoot family and is distinguished by its white tapering root, which averages 1 ft in length and 2 lb in weight, slender side roots, and a cluster of crinkled leaves on top. Beets are planted in early spring and harvested before freezing weather takes hold in the fall; they grow best in temperate climates.

Sugar cane is a perennial tropical grass. Its stem ranges from 8 to 12 ft tall and from ½ to 2 in. in diameter. Cane is harvested after 1 or 2 years of growth, and requires a tropical climate of warmth and moisture.

CURRENT PRODUCTION

The domestic sugar beet production is the primary supply of U.S. refined sugar. Although the United States is one of the leading sugar producers in the world, it is also one of the largest importers, purchasing amounts nearly equal to its own production. Sugar beets are grown in 16 different temperate climate states, and with the exception of Ohio and Michigan, all are west of the Mississippi River. Minnesota and California are the two largest producers.

The *recovery rate* of refined sugar from sugar beets is consistently about 13% of the total weight. This compares to somewhat lower and more variable conversion rates for sugar cane, which range from 7.7 to 10.2%. Sugar statistics will often be quoted in terms of *raw value*, indicating that the beet or cane sugar has been processed, but not refined. To convert the raw value into refined sugar statistics, the raw figures should be divided by 1.07.

During the past 20 years, refined beet sugar, produced domestically, has supplied 20–30% of total caloric sweetener consumption in the United States. The remaining total supply has come from domestic cane sugar (15–30%), imported cane sugar (30–45%), corn sweeteners (10–20%), and such minor caloric sweeteners as honey and maple syrup.[1]

REFINERY PRODUCTION

Refiners process and refine cane and beets brought directly from the farmer, and refine imported raw cane sugar. Refining storage is highest at the beginning of the crop year, which runs from September to August, and lowest at the end of the crop year. The farmer may own a share of the refinery, work directly for the refinery, or sell to the refinery on a contractual basis. The refiner's product will

[1]U.S. Department of Agriculture, *Beet Sugar Supply Response in the United States,* Washington, D.C., 1977, Economic Research Service Report No. 371, p.2.

TABLE 1. U.S. Cane and Beet Sugar, Raw Value, 1978–1980

	Cane			Beet		
	1978	1979	1980	1978	1979	1980
Recovered sugar (%)	10.5	10.6	9.7	12.8	13.0	12.5
Yield per acre (short tons)	3.7	3.9	3.8	2.6	2.6	2.5
Production (1,000 short tons)	2,612	2,700	2,618	3,289	2,879	2,913

Source: U.S. Department of Agriculture, *Sugar and Sweetener Outlook and Situation,* Vol. 6, No. 1, February 1981.

vary according to buyer specifications, such as large granulation for decorative use on bakery products, or liquid form for soft-drink companies.

In the refining process, the refiner slices and squeezes the beets, then processes them either directly into refined white sugar, or into an intermediate product called "thick juice," which is more easily storable. Thick juice is stored in tanks on site at the refinery, then processed into refined white sugar and shipped as needed throughout the remainder of the marketing year.

Refined beet sugar is produced at all plants that process sugar beets. Plants processing sugar beets are located close to sugar beet production areas, since beets are perishable and bulky and cannot be transported economically for long distances.

Sugar cane refining is less seasonal than beet refining since cane refiners obtain their raw product from the world supplies as well as the domestic market. World raw sugar (96% sucrose) is produced from cane in a number of tropical countries and shipped out for further processing. The cane refiner is not concerned about maintaining thick-juice inventories and purchases sugar as needed to fulfill customer orders. Mills processing domestic sugar cane are highly integrated and located mainly in Louisiana. Other cane refiners are located in or near five Atlantic coast cities, two Gulf Coast cities, and one Pacific Coast city, close to ports where ships from Hawaii, Puerto Rico, and various foreign countries berth, and also near large metropolitan areas where a portion of their output is consumed.

The seasonality of refined sugar production is illustrated by the 1980 monthly refinery production statistics displayed in Table 2. The beet sugar production cycle is especially noteworthy. During October through February, months immediately following harvest, 2.205 million short tons of refined sugar were produced, as compared to 732,000 short tons total for the seven other months. Note that these figures are intended only to indicate seasonality; they do not include the production of all domestic beet refiners. Cane sugar production is less seasonal, but nevertheless exhibits a distinct pattern. Table 2 indicates that domestic production peaks in August and September, and reaches a low in December.

TABLE 2. 1980 Refined Sugar Production by Month (1,000 Short Tons, Raw Value)

	Cane Sugar Refiners	Beet Sugar Refiners[a]
January	556	367
February	587	226
March	621	88
April	600	79
May	627	181
June	670	158
July	685	70
August	725	61
September	731	95
October	686	487
November	563	538
December[b]	413	587
Total	7,464	2,937

Source: U.S. Department of Agriculture, *Sugar and Sweetener Outlook and Situation,* Vol. 6, No. 1, February 1981. [a]Incomplete coverage. [b]Preliminary.

MARKETING

The refiner sells the sugar directly to end users within the food industry, to wholesalers, to companies which liquefy or bag the sugar, to brokers, or, when price-support programs are in effect, to the U.S. government, which may in turn sell to any of the above categories of sugar market participants. Marketing intermediaries serve as a bridge between the raw sugar producer, the refiner, and the end user. Operators are important in matching up foreign raw sugar producers and refiners. Cash brokers are paid by the refineries to locate buyers for their product. Distributors actually purchase the sugar from refineries and sell it to end users, hoping to accumulate volume discounts and turn over inventory rapidly. Two types of intermediaries change the form of the sugar to meet the special needs of some buyers. Liquefiers add water to the refined sugar to transform it into liquid form, while baggers place the bulk sugar in sacks for buyers without bulk unloading facilities.

SUBSTITUTES. Per capita consumption of refined sugar has decreased over time, from 101.8 lb per person in 1970 to 84.9 lb in 1980, yet per capita consumption of all sweeteners has increased over the period, from 128.4 to 134.4 lb. Inroads have been made into the market by corn sweeteners, especially high-fructose corn syrup (HFCS), as well as noncaloric sweeteners such as saccharin. The new sweetener aspartame may eventually develop a favorable market share, since it is extremely low in caloric content, does not cause dental caries, is not believed to be carcinogenic, and resembles sugar more closely in taste than does saccharin.

GOVERNMENT PROGRAMS

The Agriculture and Food Act of 1981 established a 1981 crop year minimum loan trigger level of \$0.17 per lb raw sugar at the refinery. When the price of sugar declines to this level, the refiner may receive a loan for \$0.17 per lb, which the refiner will in turn pay to the sugar beet and sugar cane growers. The refiner stores the sugar until such time as the refiner decides to repay the loan plus interest, or default to the Commodity Credit Corporation.

There is also a duty/market stabilization program for raw sugar imported into the United States. The applicable duty during May 1982 was 2.8125¢ per lb. The market stabilization price equaled \$19.08 per lb; an adjustable fee is charged such that the market price of sugar, plus transportation costs, duties, and fees equals the market stabilization price. The fee during February 1982 was 2.14180¢, and is subject to frequent adjustment depending on market conditions.

In May 1982, President Reagan imposed import quotas to complement the government price-support programs. Quotas for each country will be based on its average exports to the United States between 1975–1981, excluding the highest and lowest years. Imports cannot rise above 6.9 million short tons for any fiscal year.

THE INTERNATIONAL SUGAR AGREEMENT

The International Sugar Agreement (ISA), first established in 1937, represents a multilateral attempt to stabilize the world price of sugar. The ISA provides for the buildup of reserve stocks and the imposition of export quotas during periods of low sugar prices, and the release of stocks and suspension of quotas when prices rise again. Such tools are highly dependent on the participation of the world's large sugar producers; lack of cooperation in the past has enabled the ISA to achieve only limited success.

FUTURES CONTRACTS

Futures contracts in refined sugar are traded on the MidAmerica Commodity Exchange. Table 3 shows contract specifications.

TABLE 3. Contract Specifications

MidAmerica Commodity Exchange Refined Sugar Contract	
Trading unit	40,000 lb of free-flowing bulk extrafine granulated sugar
Delivery months	January, March, May, July, September, November
Trading hours	9:00 a.m.–1:00 p.m. central time
Minimum fluctuation	1/100¢ per lb
Daily price limit	1/2¢ per lb above or below previous day's settlement price.

TABLE 3. (*Continued*)

MidAmerica Commodity Exchange Refined Sugar Contract	
Position limits	20,000 short tons in any one future or 100,000 in all futures combined. Limits do not apply to *bona fide* hedgers.
Standards	
Sucrose polarization	99.8% minimum
Ash	0.02% maximum
Moisture	0.05% maximum
Invert	0.05% maximum
Color	35 RBU maximum
Granulation:	
On U.S. 20 screen	5% maximum
On U.S. 40 screen	10–70%
On U.S. 70 screen	85% maximum
On U.S. 100 screen	3% maximum
Through U.S. 100 screen	5% maximum
	No objectionable odors
Delivery	F.O.B. origin, freight off Chicago, using the bill of lading as the delivery instrument. Sugar may be shipped to or from any point within the continental United States. The contract provides strong incentives for delivery by jumbo airslide railcar and grants the buyer a 400-lb crustings allowance per railcar shipped.

The specifications are written to ensure that they closely mirror cash market conditions, and the months of trading are usually selected because of their significance in the crop marketing year. When a far month trades at a premium to a nearby month which exceeds the cost of carrying (storage, interest, and insurance) the physical commodity between the 2 months, the market is bullish on long-term prices. When the difference between the nearby and far months does not cover the carrying charge, the market is bearish on long-term prices. An inverted market occurs when the nearby actually trades at a premium. New crop months (those months beginning with June of the subsequent year) generally trade at a premium to the prior months of old crop, although new crop may fall to a discount on reports of slackening demand or bountiful supply.

CHAPTER 40

THE COTTON MARKET

CONTENTS

PRODUCTION OF COTTON 4

Cotton Types 4
Cotton Classing 5
The Supply and Distribution of Cotton 6
Government Programs 10

DEMAND FOR COTTON 13

PRICE DYNAMICS 15

FUTURES MARKETS 18

CHAPTER 40

THE COTTON MARKET

Herman S. Kohlmeyer, Jr.

> "What is cotton? Cotton is the overcoat of a seed, planted and grown in the southeastern states to keep the producers broke and the buyers crazy. The fiber varies in color and weight, and the man who can guess the nearest as to the length of fiber is called a cotton man by the public, a fool by the farmer, and a poor business-person by the creditors.
>
> The price of cotton is fixed in New York and goes *up* when you have sold and goes *down* when you have bought. A buyer working for a group of mills was sent to New York to watch the cotton market, and after a few days deliberation, wired his firm to this effect: "Some think it will go up, some think it will go down. I do, too."
>
> A traditional saying goes as follows: Whatever you do will be wrong, so act at once. Cotton is planted in the spring, mortgaged in the summer, and left in the fields in the winter. There are other definitions, but none better than this.

This familiar quotation, which decorates most of the cotton offices in this country as well as abroad, shows how confounded everyone is about what the price of cotton will be. As much as we know about cotton, the greatest mystery still remains: *What will happen to the price*?

Cotton has a long, complicated, and romantic history. Evidence of its cultivation 5,000 years ago in China has been found. It was mentioned in western literature by Herodotus, and was probably first uncovered during Alexander the Great's travels in Asia Minor. Cotton from Persia and India found its way to the West over the trade routes that were established by Alexander the Great. The Moors brought the weaving industry to Europe when they introduced its techniques into Spain in the 13th century. These techniques were eventually transferred by the Spanish to the Netherlands, and then, in the 17th century, in spite of the protest of the British woolen industry, were smuggled into England. England did everything possible to preserve its manufacturing monopoly, but Samuel Slater crossed the Atlantic with the plans of the *Arkwright water frame* firmly in his mind, and helped establish the first American mill on the Blackstone River at Pawtucket, Rhode Island in 1790. However, the English inventions of Kay, Hargraves, Arkwright, and Crompton would have come to naught without Eli Whitney's *cotton gin*. With the invention of the gin in 1793, there was at last a method of producing sufficient cotton to satisfy the beginnings of a fledgling textiles industry in this country as well as in Europe. The cotton gin increased the productivity of the harvest by 50-fold, and another equally giant step was not taken until the introduction of mechanical spindle pickers in the early 1950s.

PRODUCTION OF COTTON

Cotton is grown in some 80 countries. Its general growth requirements are about 180 days of frost-free growing conditions, with the minimum summer average temperature at least 80° F. The United States, Russia, and China easily dominate the world scene, with these three countries accounting for about one-half of the total production. This was not always the case, of course. Russia and China represent modern challenges to American dominance. By contrast, in 1937, the U.S. produced one-half of the world crop. India always ran a distant second until after World War II. India now lies in fourth place, usually producing slightly less than 10% of the world crop. Pakistan's crop is about half that of India's, with Brazil, Egypt, and Turkey usually producing slightly over 2 million bales each.

COTTON TYPES. Most of the cotton which moves in the world trade is known by the general term of *upland* cotton. That label distinguishes the cotton from the earlier variety first grown in this country on the coastal plains and islands of Georgia and South Carolina, known as *Sea Island* cotton. Upland cotton, *Gossypium hirsutum,* comprises the vast majority of the American crop plus the major medium and medium-long staple cottons grown around the world. Long and extralong staple cotton can be mostly traced from *Gossypium barbadense,* a native of the West Indies. Long staple cotton production expanded prominently in Egypt at the time of the Civil War as English and French interests attempted to find a replacement for the American cotton. The Sudan became a second area of importance in the mid-1920s. Yet another strain of long staple cotton is grown in Peru, though in only moderate amounts. Production of long staple cotton in this country amounts to only 1% of the crop, half of which is grown in Arizona. The present seed is a cross of Egyptian, Peruvian, Sea Island, and Upland varieties. The cotton name *Pima* was first introduced here in 1902 by the USDA in an effort to reduce American dependence on Egyptian cultivators.

TABLE 1. Production of Cotton by Principal Countries, 1973–1983 (1,000 Bales)

Year	United States	Russia	China	World
1973	12,961	11,030	11,700	63,637
1974	11,545	12,220	11,300	64,401
1975	8,302	11,610	10,900	53,997
1976	10,581	12,050	9,400	57,235
1977	14,389	12,710	9,400	63,907
1978	10,856	12,257	9,950	59,460
1979	14,629	13,126	10,150	65,060
1980	11,122	13,500	12,400	64,505
1981	15,646	13,275	13,600	70,589
1982	11,963	11,900	16,500	67,800
1983 (est.)	7,100	12,600	16,500	

Source: USDA.

COTTON CLASSING. The complexity of cotton is best illustrated by the fact that any single bale of cotton could be described with about 300 combinations of grade, staple, and micronaire. The USDA has administered official cotton grades since 1923, when passage of the Federal Cotton Standards Act made our standards universal for world trading. The grade of cotton is determined by three factors: *color, foreign matter,* and *preparation. Color* is described in terms of the *relative brilliance* or *spotted character* of the color, the so-called spotted quality usually resulting from rainfall on open bolls. Foreign matter is a function of the amount of leaf, bract, bark, dirt, and the like, which is itself determined by both the harvesting and ginning methods. Preparation refers to the relative roughness and uniformity of the fibers. The USDA prepares official boxes containing samples of each standard grade, and these boxes are used whenever American cotton is bought and sold. There are a total of 14 such grades, plus an additional 31 descriptive grades for which official boxes are not prepared, but which nonetheless describe variations and are accepted in commerce.

Equally important in determining the value of cotton is its *staple*. Cotton is described in broad terms as being short staple if the fiber length is under $\frac{13}{16}$ in. Medium and medium-long staple cotton ranges from $\frac{13}{16}$ to $1\frac{3}{32}$ in. Long staple cotton ranges from $1\frac{1}{8}$ to $1\frac{5}{16}$ in., and extralong staple covers the length from $1\frac{3}{8}$ in. and over. Official cotton standards developed by the USDA cover each $\frac{1}{32}$ in. variation beginning from $\frac{13}{16}$ up through $1\frac{1}{4}$ in. American pima cotton is found in staples of up to $1\frac{1}{2}$ in. Certain varieties of Egyptian cotton staple are even longer.

Beginning in the 1950s, cotton began to be described and traded by the additional measurement of *micronaire*, known as "mike." This marked the initial introduction of instrument classification in the cotton, since grade and staple are generally determined by sight. Micronaire measurement is done with an airflow instrument that calculates the fiber maturity. It was introduced into trading by the USDA, which recognized that cotton which was overly mature or immature was not worth as much to the buyer as properly matured fibers. The desirably mature cotton trades at par value, while the immature or overly mature cotton brings discounts to the farmers, so no real values have been added to the cotton because of this new measurement.

The USDA is attempting to force acceptance of instrument classification of both grade and staple into the commercial handling of cotton. It is generally conceded to be a feasible, if not necessarily desirable step, and will undoubtedly bring into pricing the classification of features such as fiber uniformity, tensile strength, and others. The classification of American cotton has been provided farmers by the government since 1937 under the Smith–Doxey Act, and was free until 1981.

When cotton futures trading began in 1870, the *par value* of the contract was *middling* $\frac{7}{8}$ *in*. This has been gradually changed so that in 1967 the contract par became *strict low middling* $1\frac{1}{16}$ *in. premium mike*. The change in terms tells a lot about what has happened to cotton over the years. The reduction in grade is a consequence of machine picking, which gathers more trash than if the cotton were snapped from the plant by hand. The increase in staple is a reward for agronomists, who have steadily worked to improve fiber characteristics, and have had their success in the miniscule lengthening of the staple. Middling cotton today is found in the United States only in desert growing areas. At times, it will account for one-third of the California crop. In the Mississippi Delta area, strict low middling cotton accounts for almost half the grade in a normal year. The majority of staple cotton grown in both California and the Delta is now $1\frac{3}{32}$ in. The difference in value for $\frac{1}{32}$ in. staple for Mississippi cotton is about $3 a bale.

THE SUPPLY AND DISTRIBUTION OF COTTON. The dynamics of the cotton market naturally represent the forces of supply and demand. In fact, the key feature of the equation is supply, since demand usually manifests itself as a consequence of shortages or surpluses. Measuring supply in cotton means determining the size of crops in the United States, Russia, and China. Understanding U.S. agricultural policies is equally important. Actually, the USDA has played a heavier hand in determining the price of American cotton for the past 50 years than has the weather. A short history of the major producing areas should add some spice to the statistics that illustrate the overall picture.

United States. The American Cotton Belt is generally divided into four sections: the Southeast, the Midsouth or Central Belt, the Southwest, and the Far West. Beginning with the end of World War II, cotton has been on a westward migration and is now settling down into three major areas.

The first of these regions is about 3 million acres along both sides of the Mississippi River, from the boot-heel of Missouri down to the northeast corner of Louisiana. The second is about a $4\frac{1}{2}$-million-acre block of land around Lubbock, Texas in that part of the state known as the *Texas High Plains*. The third is $1\frac{1}{2}$ million acres in the southern half of the San Joaquin Valley of California. Other producing areas have only a peripheral effect on the market. The Rio Grande Valley in Texas is the earliest planted region. Although the area only covers around 200,000 acres, the Valley gets more than its share of attention because of its early start in mid-March, some $2\frac{1}{2}$ months ahead of the High Plains.

The Southeast has seen a general erosion of its cotton production due to normal cultural problems and to a far greater success in that area with soybeans. Therefore, in spite of the fact that almost the entire textiles industry is located there, only a minor effort is made to grow cotton for home consumption. The area is best remembered in the trade as the site of the famous *Sea Island* cotton, the first extralong staple grown for commercial consumption, which made its appearance on Hilton Head Island off the coast of South Carolina in 1790, having journeyed from the West Indies. Sea Island cotton stapled as long as $2\frac{1}{4}$ in., and set an all-

TABLE 2. Production and Percent Distribution of Cotton by Regions (1,000 Bales)

Year	Southeast	Percent	Central	Percent	Southwest	Percent	Far West	Percent	Total
1940	3,540	28	4,122	33	4,036	32	868	7	12,566
1950	1,669	17	3,518	35	3,188	32	1,639	16	10,014
1960	1,929	13	4,435	31	4,707	34	3,076	22	14,237
1970	1,175	12	3,819	37	3,402	33	1,796	18	10,192
1982	952	8	3,707	31	2,961	25	4,322	36	11,963

Source: USDA.

TABLE 3. Harvest Acreage by Region, and Each Region as a Percentage of Total Harvested Acreage (1,000 Acres)

Year	Southeast	Percent	Central	Percent	Southwest	Percent	Far West	Percent	Total
1940	6,056	25	6,835	29	10,295	43	675	3	23,861
1950	3,829	21	5,493	31	7,495	42	1,026	6	17,843
1960	2,493	16	4,284	28	6,955	45	1,577	10	15,309
1970	1,375	12	3,355	30	5,346	48	1,079	10	11,155
1982	623	6	2,381	25	4,769	49	1,954	20	9,728

Source: USDA.

time record by selling for $2 per lb in 1828. It has completely disappeared from production, but is the ancestor of the long-staple cotton grown in all other parts of the world. The richest area of remaining cotton production in the Southeast is in the northeast corner of Alabama.

The five-state area of Mississippi, Louisiana, Arkansas, Missouri, and Tennessee is regarded as the home of the cotton industry, and Memphis, Tennessee has long laid claim to being the cotton capital of the world. So-called Memphis styles of cotton, however, no longer dominate the markets, although the news from that area captures more than its share of attention. The Delta grows basic upland cotton, with staples from $1\frac{1}{32}$ to $1\frac{1}{8}$ in. About two-thirds of the cotton finds its way into the domestic trade. As many as 10 million acres were devoted to cotton in this five-state area before World War II, but present production has shrunk to a core of about 3 million acres. Although some land, of course, has fallen victim to urban sprawl, soybeans have been the main ravager of cotton acreage. Soybean acreage in the five-state area in 1982 was $19\frac{3}{4}$ million acres, compared to $7\frac{1}{2}$ million acres only 20 years before. Acreage will shift back and forth between the two crops to a minor extent each year, with a rule of thumb of 10:1 being a rough measure of which crop yields the greater potential. The cost of producing cotton runs about $2\frac{1}{2}$ to 3 times the cost of farming soybeans, but when the price of soybeans per bushel is less than 10 times the price of cotton per pound, cotton acreage will show a minor gain.

The High Plains of Texas, comprising the 25 counties around Lubbock, is the largest block of land devoted to cotton in this country. More importantly, due to the weather, it is the most volatile producing area in the world. The High Plains, which was range land in the 1920s, has been gradually converted to a highly intensive region for cotton because of the attractive government-support programs and the development of irrigation systems which can carry the cotton through the normally dry summers. The cotton, again of the upland variety, staples an average of about 1 in., and sells at a discount to all other styles of American cotton. Approximately one-half to two-thirds of this cotton finds its way into the export markets. Open-end spinning techniques have made it possible to use this shorter staple cotton in a variety of constructions, and the cotton is no longer a stepchild of the American trade. However, the production of cotton on the High Plains carries the highest risk of any major American crop. Month-long droughts during the planting and growing season are not uncommon, severe summer hailstorms can destroy blocks of as much as 200,000–300,000 acres of cotton overnight, and the northern latitudes and high altitudes of the region expose the crop to the risk of early frosts. In June 1982, a series of severe hailstorms over a 2-week period completely destroyed 2 million acres of cotton in The High Plains and adjoining Oklahoma. It was one of the most devastating localized setbacks in the history of our agriculture, amply illustrating the extreme unreliability of the region's growing conditions.

California has had spectacular success with its cotton industry. It was established in 1920 as a result of efforts by the USDA to develop an alternate supply for Egyptian-style cotton. Cotton had been tried in the state off and on since the turn of the 18th century, but with no success. After several false starts, and with no luck at all growing long-staple varieties, the USDA found that the Acala variety of upland cotton, a native of Mexico, was well-suited for the San Joaquin Valley. In a unique and successful experiment which has not been duplicated anywhere else in the world, the California state legislature in 1925 passed a single variety act requiring that all cotton in the San Joaquin Valley and adjoining counties must be planted with the same variety Acala seed. The 55,000 acres planted in 1921 were better than doubled in 3 years, remained around 300,000 acres in the late 1930s and early 1940s, and exploded after World War II, reaching 1 million acres in 1951. From that time, most of the progress in California has been as a result of better yields rather than expanded acreage.

Higher yields have frustrated American cotton producers since 1963. The remarkable growth in productivity which characterized all farming came to a halt in the cotton belt at that time. The three consecutive years producing about 520 lb per acre have not been duplicated since. Instead, and in sharp contrast to other segments of agriculture, yields actually declined for nearly a generation. Farmers were forced to shift from dependable insecticides because of environmental concerns, new chemicals were not well understood, and seed breeders were frustrated in coaxing greater productivity from their stock. The erratic yield trends since the early 1960s simply reflected the vagaries of the weather, most sharply illustrated by a record-setting drought and unrelenting high temperatures across the entire belt in 1980. The remarkable record in the 1982 season raises the hopes that farmers and seed breeders have a way to move yields to a higher plateau.

Russia. The importance of Russia in the cotton economy is best scored by the fact that Russian exports surpassed the levels of the United States in the 1975–1976 season, making Russia the most dominant factor in world trade. This was a remarkable achievement for a comparatively young industry. Although cotton has been traced as far back in Russia as the 10th century A.D., its cultivation under Czarist rule was relatively primitive, and production just before the outbreak of World War I was only about 700,000 bales, on about 1.7 million acres. After the Revolution, production began to advance as more modern techniques were developed based on American seeds. Russia emerged from World War II by producing about 2½ million bales on about 3½ million acres, doubled that production in 3 years, and finally doubled the amount again to pass the 10 million bale mark for the first time in 1970. By that time, cotton acreage had expanded to about 6.8 million acres. From 1956, all Russian cotton has been confined to irrigated soils, with the vast majority of the production being concentrated in the territory to the north of Afghanistan and to the south of the Aral Sea. The principal Russian

TABLE 4. Yield Per Harvested Acres by Regions (pounds)

Year	Southeast	Central	Southwest	Far West	Total
1940	280	289	189	616	241
1950	209	307	204	764	282
1960	371	497	331	937	454
1965	453	610	394	1,047	498
1970	403	546	306	798	467
1975	422	457	292	997	453
1978	473	493	294	709	420
1979	501	609	393	976	547
1980	355	409	229	988	404
1981	541	548	381	1,125	543
1982	707	716	297	1,017	590

Source: USDA.

producer is the republic of Uzbekistan, which of late has grown approximately 60% of the Russian crop.

Russian cotton has gradually moved into commercial channels of the western world, and by 1977, less than half of Russian exports were confined to Soviet Block nations. Since 1973, Russia has been the largest supplier to Western European markets, its cotton enjoying an obvious freight advantage over American growths. France is Russia's largest customer in the free world, accounting for about half of France's needs. Japan is Russia's major trading partner in the Far East, although Russia has supplied only about 15% of that nation's requirements.

Russian production has been characterized by an uneventful and gradual expansion, keeping in step with increases in consumption. With minor exception in 1968 and 1969, the crop rarely suffered a setback. With relatively modern production techniques and major investments in irrigation facilities, cotton had none of the problems which plagued the grain industry. Russian harvesting practices are considerably different from this country's. Russia has made the conversion to machine picking, but differs from this country in that cotton is placed in enormous stacks, most of which are uncovered, where it may await ginning for more than 6 months. These stacks are about 60 times the size of an American module, which itself yields about 11 bales of cotton. Unusual rainfall in Russia both during and after the 1982 harvest created harmful moisture levels in the seed cotton, resulting in substantial deterioration in the stacks. A significant percentage of the crop was simply unspinnable, with a profound loss of production. Even with our satellite surveillance, however, this phenomenon was not detected by any segment of the free-world cotton trade until Russia began its unprecedented purchases of cotton from the United States in late February 1983.

China. China has always been the big mystery to the cotton market, since China has been, until recently, completely closed off to American trade. As it recouperated after the war, China produced 2½ million bales of cotton in 1947, roughly doubled that amount by 1951, and finally reached the 10-million-bale mark in 1971, on some 12 million acres. China's production closely matched that of Russia's, though with substantially lower yields. Since the early 1970s, acreage has increased by less than 10%, with some land diverted to China's food needs. The foundation for a significant increase in acreage was laid in 1979, when agricultural planning was decentralized to give local communes greater autonomy over what they would plant. At the same time, the government raised its procurement price for cotton to make it a more attractive cash crop. As a result, acreage expanded 12% from 1979 to 1981, with a further, though yet undetermined, increase in 1982. As a further result of the incentives, yields surpassed the bale-per-acre mark for the first time in 1980, and have, in fact, improved every year beginning with the 1977 season. By contrast, yields in the mid-1950s were only ½ bale per acre. Production is concentrated in the central provinces, with Shandong having the largest acreage—close to 20% of the total. With the significant increase in yields, production reached 13.6 million bales in 1981, and perhaps close to 16½ million bales in 1982.

China's widespread acreage seems impervious to the ravages of weather. China uses the country's enormous population to its best advantage, with as many as six workers per acre engaged in the careful production of the cotton crop. Production did nonetheless slide some 2 million bales from 1974 to 1976, and China's entries into the world export markets have provided two of the major upward thrusts in our futures markets in the past 10 years. The western world has been almost completely unsuccessful in gaining insight into the progress of the Chinese crop, so our first indications are when China's buying interests hit the marketplace. China has gone on two major splurges in recent times, first purchasing 1.8 million bales of American cotton in the 1972–1974 seasons, and then again 6 million bales in the years 1977–1980. Needless to say, those activities were the principal market factors in those periods. The first purchases were a response to a few seasons of declining production. The later purchases coincided with profound changes in the Chinese political scene, particularly the decision to enter the modern era by a significant modernization and expansion of the country's domestic textiles industry.

GOVERNMENT PROGRAMS. Supply-and-demand analysis of the cotton market should be sufficient to deduce its ways, but quite often the biggest force on the markets has nothing to do with old-fashioned economics. In fact, the U.S. government and its programs is a bigger factor in the market most seasons than the weather or normal business considerations. All this began in 1929, when the *Agricultural Marketing Act* established the Federal Farm Board as a mechanism to promote orderly production and marketing of cotton and other farm commodities. The first loan for cotton was established in October of that year at $0.16 per lb.

Almost nothing done in 1929 would have stabilized prices in any sector of the economy, and the failure of that board led the Roosevelt Administration to pass the *Agricultural Adjustment Act of 1933*, the aim of which was to bolster the prices of most basic commodities, including, of course, cotton. Farmers could take land out of production in return for benefit payments; in addition, a loan was established, this time at $0.10 per lb. The 1930s saw a number of different efforts by Congress to provide farm relief, most prominently in 1937 an act which provided up to $130 million for price-adjustment payments to cotton and wheat farmers.

Cotton farmers could receive a direct payment of up to $0.03 a lb on cotton sold for less than $0.12. The legislation during the 1930s emphasized production controls, but the outbreak of the war shifted the emphasis to make it more attractive to expand production of all commodities. With that intent, cotton prices which were supported under the loan program at between 52 and 75% of parity were gradually raised during the war until in 1945 the *Commodity Credit Corporation* purchased cotton at 100% of parity. The loan increased from $0.089 in 1940 to $0.209 in 1945.

The concept of parity as a method to establish a fair support level for farmers continued to be the guiding philosophy in the postwar period, although the level was gradually reduced to 90% in 1949 and to 75% in 1959. A new concept, that of the soil bank, was introduced in 1956 in an effort to reduce surplus production by paying growers for taking land out of production. Programs in the 1960s added an additional feature by introducing a subsidy for cotton sold in the export trade, this being an effort by the government to permit the expansion of cotton into the world trade without undermining domestic price levels.

The biggest effect of government support programs in the postwar period was that, with the umbrella of American price supports, foreign cotton production grew rapidly. As foreign cotton consumption expanded in the healthy postwar period, foreign producers expanded their acreage in line with their consumption increases. They took all the additional business plus a part of the market that American producers already had. In the period 1947–1955, our growers reduced their acreage 21%, while foreign producers increased their acreage 79%. Consequently, our exports in the mid-1950s actually were a million bales less than in the period right after the war. The high support levels and the land diversion payments simply made it very attractive to produce cotton for the government programs. As a result, our cotton carryover grew significantly, finally reaching a record of nearly 17 million bales in the mid-1960s, with the Commodity Credit Corporation owning almost 75% of these stocks. In other words, farmers were producing for the government rather than for the marketplace. The government programs were extremely complex, consisting of parity and loan levels, production quotas, export subsidies, direct payments to growers and mills, production allotments, and special export financing benefits.

In the early 1970s, government cotton policy took a significant turn away from support toward that of a free-market orientation. In other words, the industry was encouraged to produce according to the dictates of the market, with Congress simply no longer willing to funnel monies into programs which only accumulated stocks and benefited farmers at the expense of all taxpayers. The most significant feature of the *Agricultural Act of 1970* was that the loan rate for cotton was established at 90% of the world price of cotton for the two preceding years. In other words, the government would no longer support cotton producers at some level of parity, but would rather peg the loan at world market levels. The *Agriculture and Consumer Protection Act of 1973* provided for deficiency payments to cotton as well as wheat- and feed-grain producers if prices dropped below specified so-called target-price levels. Table 5 shows the loan level and target price for 1972–1983.

Only with the 1981 crop did the target price become operative. As a consequence of the *Agricultural Act of 1980,* the target price for all commodities gained

TABLE 5. Price Support Levels, Target Price Levels, and Average Prices Received by Farmers (Year Beginning August 1st)

	Level of Support				
Year	Price Support (Strict low middling $1\frac{1}{16}$ in.)	Price Support Payment	Target Price	Target Price Payment	Season Average
1972	19.71	15.0	—	—	27.2
1973	20.65	15.0	—	—	44.4
1974	27.06	—	38.0	0	42.9
1975	36.12	—	38.0	0	51.3
1976	38.92	—	43.2	0	64.1
1977	44.63	—	47.8	0	52.3
1978	48.00	—	52.0	0	58.4
1979	50.23	—	57.7	0	62.5
1980	48.00	—	58.4	0	74.7
1981	52.46	—	70.9	7.67	54.3
1982	57.08	—	71.0	13.92	58.0
1983	55.00	—	76.0		

Source: USDA.

an automatic escalation clause, which for cotton guarantees that the target price is increased by $0.05 a year for 5 years. The likely consequence of this generosity meant that farmers, beginning in 1982, would grow cotton not only for the government loan program as they did in the 1950s, but also for the deficiency payment. This payment reached the maximum level of $0.1392 per lb in the 1982 season, and at one time threatened to reach as much as $0.20 per lb for the 1983 season. All of a sudden, government-support programs for the major crops, which had been anticipated in 1981 to cost somewhat slightly over 1 billion, were threatening to cost the government considerably in excess of $12 billion.

It was in response to government outlays of crisis proportions that the USDA, just before the end of 1982, introduced yet another program, namely, the *payments-in-kind*. Realizing the extraordinary outlay of funds which would result from a combination of both a high loan level and an even higher deficiency payment, the government developed a program which required acreage reduction upwards of 20% by cotton farmers in order to qualify for program benefits. In addition to those 20% cutbacks, growers who then cut back an additional 30% were paid by the government by a return of the commodity already owned by the government in its loan program. For the 1983 season, growers of cotton as well as growers of wheat, feed grains, and rice face the prospects of receiving 80% of their normal yields for acreage-reduction schemes that will retire up to 50% of their acreage. Because of this program, cotton farmers in 1983 will produce the *smallest acreage* in this country since 1869! All of this of course is a direct consequence of the very heavy hand of the federal government in our agricultural markets. Whether the so-called invisible hand of Adam Smith and the free market would have developed a better record of balancing supply and demand at a level equally attractive to farmers, end users, and taxpayers, remains to be seen, but the governments's role raises more questions than it answers. The first-year effect of the payments-in-kind program had a greater impact on supply than any drought or hailstorm.

DEMAND FOR COTTON

The demand side of the cotton equation is, for all practical purposes, a function of supply. In other words, with only a few exceptions, year-to-year changes in demand are relatively static except in response to crop conditions.

In general, postwar consumption patterns have paralleled population trends and general prospects. Production has kept pace with consumption, responding and adjusting to textile demand and general business conditions.

The first major interruption in the steady increase in cotton consumption came in 1974. In that year, the explosion of crude oil prices which resulted from the Israeli–Arab war sharply affected disposable consumer income in all parts of the world. Several years would go by until the global economy could recover from that shock. Inroads into cotton by synthetics are barely perceptible in worldwide statistics, although the Third World and emerging nations are beginning to witness the beginnings of that phenomenon.

The demand structure of the American textile picture is completely different from that of the world at large. Synthetics have made major inroads into our markets. Consumption has steadily declined, and by the 1974 recession, mill usage had shrunk to the lowest levels since 1932. After enjoying a brisk recovery following that recession, consumption in the 1982 recession retreated to the lowest levels since 1911.

The progress of *polyester* has been dramatic, and cotton's loss of market share is an old story. The automobile tire is just one example of cotton's use which has

TABLE 6. World Production and Consumption of Cotton (1,000 bales), 1952–1982 (Year Beginning August 1st)

Year	Production	Consumption
1952	37,229	34,894
1962	48,218	45,147
1972	63,272	60,358
1973	63,637	62,183
1974	64,401	58,219
1975	53,997	61,063
1976	57,235	60,594
1977	63,907	60,803
1978	59,460	63,000
1979	65,060	65,195
1980	64,505	65,956
1981	70,589	65,276
1982	67,800	66,713

Source: USDA.

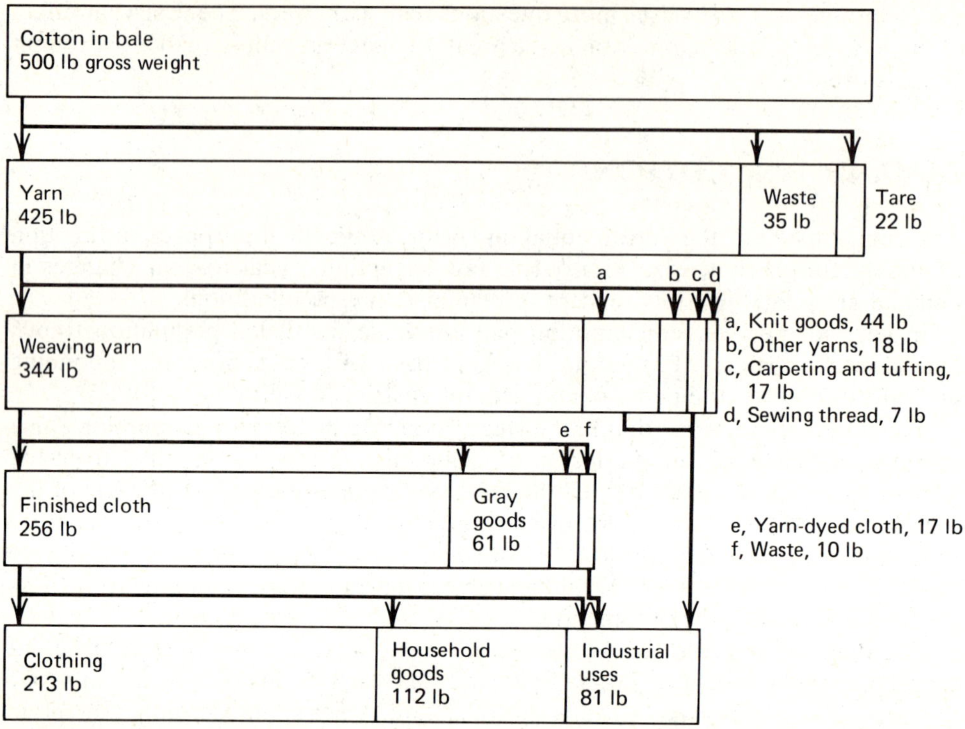

FIGURE 1. Cotton processing chain. (*Source:* U.S. Department of Agriculture, Economic Research Service.)

TABLE 7. American Cotton Consumption and Percentage of Cotton to Total Fiber Consumption, 1952–1982 (Year Beginning August 1st)

Year	Cotton Consumption	Cotton Percentage
1952	9,461	68.1
1962	8,400	59.4
1972	7,769	33.8
1973	7,472	29.8
1974	5,834	30.3
1975	7,228	29.3
1976	6,674	30.7
1977	6,463	27.3
1978	6,435	26.8
1979	6,463	25.9
1980	5,870	27.5
1981	5,264	
1982	5,397	

Source: USDA.

been relegated to the history books, but invasions of synthetics into apparel and home furnishings has been almost as successful. The first beachhead on cotton's turf was gained by rayon in the later 1930s. At the end of World War II, cotton's share of the fiber market was 71%, and it continued to slip by the mid-1950s to 65%, based entirely on rayon's price advantage. Then came a new wave of competition. The case for polyester is a simple one—its no-iron characteristic and its resilience are very appealing. Sheeting, which was 100% cotton only a generation ago, now uses only 35% cotton in the vast majority of its production. Cotton's only success story has been in denim and corduroy construction, and even with these, synthetics have made minor inroads. In the past few years, cotton has begun to hold its own in the fashion markets, thanks in large part to farmer-funded research and promotional efforts through Cotton, Incorporated of Raleigh, North Carolina.

American markets have also been invaded by growing textiles imports, mostly from the Far East, and most recently from China. A trickle of imports in the early post-war years reached flood proportions as a result of the U. S. government two-price system of high farmer loan supports and export subsidies. The cheap cotton we sent abroad came back to our shores as cheap fabrics. Imports of cotton textiles in 1955 were only 181,000-bale equivalents. By 1966, imports had swollen to 1.1 million-bale equivalents, and they continue to expand. By 1981, in spite of the recent success in the building of a modest export trade in cotton textiles, the net deficit for the cotton trade was 1.6 million-bale equivalents.

PRICE DYNAMICS

With supply-and-demand characteristics somewhat in place, what do they tell us about the market? The cotton trade has had a long and glamorous association with the futures market, and the history of the New York Cotton Exchange closely paralleled that of the Chicago Board of Trade, being organized in September 1870. A similar market started trading in New Orleans 5 months later, and organized exchanges flourished during much of the first half of this century in Liverpool, Bremen, Alexandria, and Bombay—in other words, wherever spot cotton was traded. The history of both the New York and New Orleans exchanges is replete with various corners and squeezes, but regardless of the extremes that captured

TABLE 8. Estimated Mill Consumption of Raw Cotton by Major Types, Percentage of Total, 1981

Sheeting and toweling, all cotton	18.2
Denim	16.9
Print cloth, all cotton	5.1
Corduroy	4.7
Polyester blends	22.7
Knit fabrics	23.1

Source: National Cotton Council.

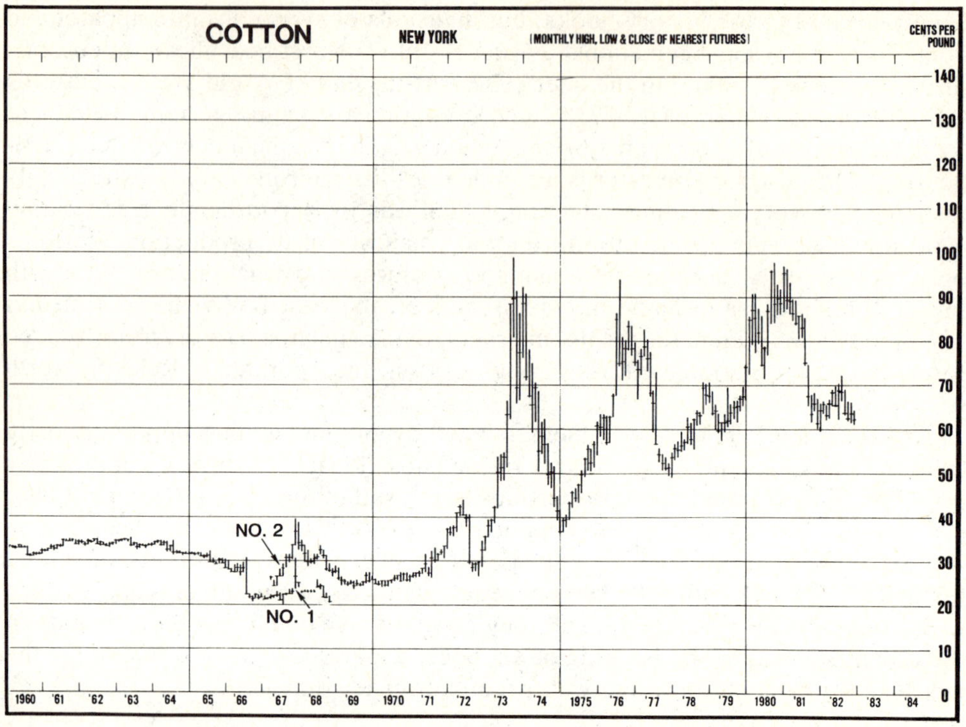

FIGURE 2. Cotton prices. *Source*: Commodity Research Bureau.

the headlines, the use of the market was vital in the marketing and the merchandising of cotton.

However, the current interest in the market is relatively new. Trading in the 1950s and 1960s had become increasingly moribund, due to the influence of government programs and the resulting buildup, in the mid-1960s, of enormous Commodity Credit Corporation stocks. The New York Cotton Exchange was forced to move to smaller quarters, and the New Orleans Cotton Exchange went into liquidation. In contrast to the relatively robust trading in the grain and soybean markets, cotton enjoyed its last hurrah with the Korean War, when futures rose from \$0.30 to \$0.45 in a year's time. From 1953 to 1964, prices barely fluctuated, and trading almost vanished. Trading was confined between \$0.31 and \$0.37 for the entire period. A break in 1967 carried prices down to \$0.20, a level last seen in 1943. A brief splurge caused by sharply reduced plantings and poor weather caused a brief rally to \$0.40, and then trading again subsided for a few years.

Cotton emerged from its cocoon in the early 1970s, following the liquidation of government stocks. Since then, we have been treated to three major bull markets, each of which was climaxed by an assault on the \$1 level.

The most dramatic of those three bull markets topped out at \$0.99 basis the October contract in September 1973. This was the highest price recorded for cotton since the summer of 1864, when spot cotton sold for \$1.90 in New Orleans as Europe panicked over the shortage of the American crop. The 1973 market got underway in the fall of 1972, with prices languishing at \$0.27. It was spurred on by the startling entry of China into our markets, so that the level of our export trade nearly doubled in that time. Cotton prices also shared in the general explosion of most all commodity prices, 1973 being the year when soybeans traded at \$12.90 a bushel. It was a vintage year for the bulls.

The next big advance developed from the trough of the 1974–1975 textiles recession. From the end of 1974 until July 1976, cotton soared from \$0.37 to \$0.94, a somewhat less exaggerated climb in a somewhat greater span of time. The 1975 crop proved to be the smallest since 1967, and the second smallest since 1921, due to poor growing conditions, and, more importantly, generally low prices and a negative outlook at planting time. The rally extended through the first 7 months of 1976, much in gear with a near doubling of soybean prices, with continued good business, and with the prospects of a small carryover.

The third market peak, at 97.78 for October in September 1980, may be cotton's last hurrah for a while. Coming almost 7 years to the day from the 1973 top, cotton climaxed an extended rally which got underway at the end of 1977. Exactly as in 1975, low prices at planting time discouraged plantings, and poor weather produced a crop that year 35% smaller than in 1975. The bull market finally peaked out after the record-breaking drought during the summer of 1980. Although the advance from \$0.52 to \$0.98 spanned three seasons, the common thread through it was the presence of the Chinese purchases. China bought a breathtaking 2.1 million bales in the 1979–1980 season, and exports soared to 9.2 million bales, the largest since 1926.

All three major moves had the usual ingredients of bull markets—reduced plantings, small crops, better business, and increased demand. However, are there seasonal trends in the cotton picture? The normal pattern would show prices advancing from harvest-time lows through the growing season. The following page shows cotton's record for the July contract since futures trading recovered.

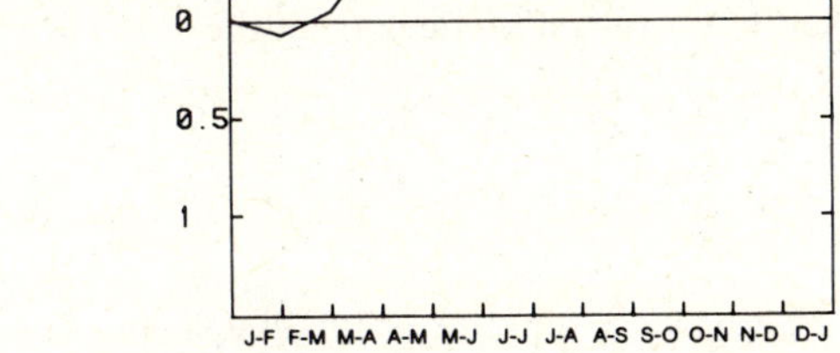

	J-F	F-M	M-A	A-M	M-J	J-J	J-A	A-S	S-O	O-N	N-D	D-J
Average Move	-0.1	0.1	0.3	0.2	0	0.1	-0.7	0.2	-0.1	-0.2	0.1	0
% Reliable	37.5	75	66.7	79.2	66.7	54.2	70.9	33.4	54.2	41.7	50	66.7
Avg. Up Move	0.6	0.5	0.7	0.6	0.7	1	1.9	2	0.5	0.7	1.7	0.7
Avg. Down Move	1.4	1.2	0.5	1.5	1.6	0.8	1.8	0.8	0.5	1.1	1.5	1.3
Greatest Up Move	4.8	3.6	4.4	3.9	8.7	4.5	8.9	12.4	3.3	1.7	9.3	2.7
Greatest Down Move	9.3	4.7	1.8	5.6	9	3.5	7.6	4.7	2.4	6.9	12.6	6.7

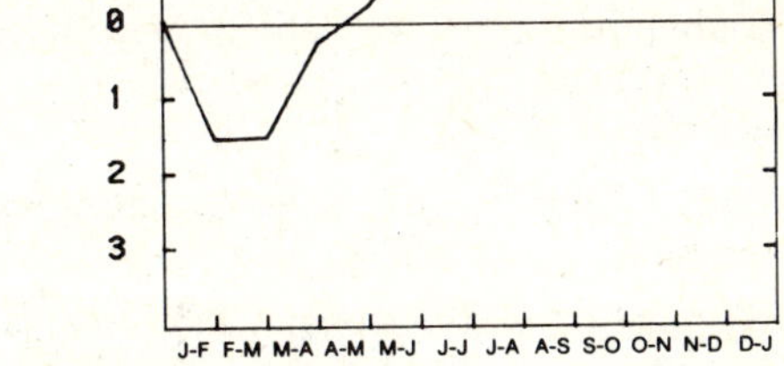

	J-F	F-M	M-A	A-M	M-J	J-J	J-A	A-S	S-O	O-N	N-D	D-J
Average Move	-1.6	0	1.2	0.4	0.8	1.4	0.6	0.8	-0.7	-1.2	1.6	0
% Reliable	66.7	66.7	66.7	88.9	55.6	77.8	44.5	44.5	44.5	88.9	77.8	55.6
Avg. Up Move	0.4	1.3	2.2	1.7	2.4	3.2	4.6	3.7	1.7	3.8	2.9	1.8
Avg. Down Move	2.6	2.6	0.8	9.5	1.3	5.1	2.6	1.5	3.6	1.8	2.7	2.2
Greatest Up Move	0.6	2.4	6	4.9	10.9	7.9	15.6	12.4	5.4	3.8	7.4	3.6
Greatest Down Move	10.3	7.1	1.4	.9.5	2.9	8.4	5.8	2.9	10.8	5.1	3	6.3

FIGURE 3. Cotton seasonality. (*a*) Cash cotton, 24 years. (*b*) Cotton nearest futures, 9 years.

Year	Harvest-Time Low		Subsequent High	
1971	December	$0.23	May	$0.31
1972	October	0.33	May	0.44
1973	October	0.28	September	0.99
1974	October	0.62	January	0.87
1975	December	0.38	September	0.56
1976	October	0.54	July	0.92
1977	January	0.68	March	0.82
1978	December	0.52	May	0.62
1979	6-month decline from October highs			
1980	October	0.68	February	0.90
1981	9-month decline from December highs			
1982	December	0.65	April	0.70
1983	November	0.67	June	0.82

Undoubtedly, with the prominent exception of two recent years, cotton prices show a dominant tendency to advance from the harvest period, and for a rather extended period of time.

FUTURES MARKETS

Both the New York Cotton Exchange and the New Orleans Commodity Exchange have contracts in cotton futures. Table 9 shows the contract specifications.

TABLE 9. Contract Specifications

	New York Cotton Exchange Cotton (No.2)
Delivery months	As determined by the exchange
Trading unit	50,000 lb (100 bales)
Minimum fluctuation	0.01¢ per lb ($0.01 per lb = $500 per contract)
Daily price movement limits	Subject to change, consult latest official notices from the exchange
Daily trading limits	Same as position limits
Position limits	300 contracts in any one future or in all futures combined
Standards	Strict low middling 1 1/16 in. U.S. grown white cotton
Delivery	From Galveston, Texas, Houston, Texas, New Orleans, Louisiana, Memphis, Tennessee, and Greenville, South Carolina
Trading hours	10:30 a.m.–3:00 p.m. eastern time

TABLE 9. *(Continued)*

	New Orleans Commodity Exchange Cotton[a]
Delivery months	March, May, July, October, and December
Trading unit	50,000 lb (100 bales)
Minimum fluctuation	0.01¢ per lb ($0.01 per lb = $500 per contract)
Daily price movement limits	$0.02 per lb ($1,000 per contract)
Standards	Strict low middling 1 in. Other grades deliverable at a premium or discount.
Delivery	Exchange declared regular warehouses in Houston, Texas, Galveston, Texas, Corpus Christi, Texas, and New Orleans, Louisiana
Trading hours	9:15 a.m.–2:00 p.m. central time
Last trading day	Business day prior to the last 16 business days
First delivery day	Fourth business day prior to the first business day of the delivery month

[a]Not active.

CHAPTER 41

AN INTRODUCTION TO THE LUMBER AND PLYWOOD MARKETS

CONTENTS

PRODUCTION OF LUMBER AND PLYWOOD 5

Timber Harvest 5
Lumber Production 5
Plywood Production 6

USES OF LUMBER AND PLYWOOD 7

FUNDMENTAL ANALYSIS OF THE LUMBER AND PLYWOOD MARKETS 9

Supply-Side Factors 9
Demand-Side Factors 11

HISTORICAL PRICE BEHAVIOR 14

Lumber Versus Plywood 15
Spreading Across Months 15
Seasonality 17

FUTURES TRADING IN LUMBER AND PLYWOOD 18

CONCLUSION 22

CHAPTER 41

AN INTRODUCTION TO THE LUMBER AND PLYWOOD MARKETS

Michael Gorham

The North American lumber and plywood markets provide the basis for the only two active forest product futures contracts in existence at this writing. This chapter will attempt to describe these markets, discuss the factors which influence lumber and plywood prices, and examine the role of lumber and plywood futures markets.

Let us first set the botanical boundaries of this chapter. All wood can be divided into *soft woods* and *hard woods*. We will discuss only softwoods, which account for roughly 85% of total lumber and plywood consumption in the United States and are the only woods deliverable on existing forest products futures contracts. The essential difference between hardwoods and softwoods is not degree of hardness as one might expect, but rather whether or not the species has exposed seeds—softwoods do and hardwoods do not. Hardwoods hide their seeds within a fruit; they have true flowers, have broad leaves, and are almost always *deciduous* (they lose their leaves in fall and grow them back in spring). The exposed seeds of softwoods are usually in cones; thus these trees are often called *conifers*. They are also called *evergreens* since they keep their needles year round.

Clearly, not all wood is consumed in the form of lumber and plywood. In fact, together they account for less than 60% of all wood consumed in the United States.[1] Pulp products account for another third of total wood consumed. About one-quarter of U.S. wood consumption is derived from trees grown elsewhere, mainly Canada.

In fact, the United States is very dependent upon Canada as a source of softwood lumber. In 1979, for example, the United States produced 30.4 billion board feet (bbf) of softwood lumber, imported another 11.2 bbf, exported 1.8 bbf, leaving an apparent consumption of 39.8 bbf. The United States thus imported 28% of its softwood lumber needs and 99.5% of these imports came from Canada. However, Canada is also quite dependent on the United States since 60% of its total production of softwood lumber (18.5 bbf) found its way into the United States in 1979. It should be noted that two-thirds of all Canadian softwood lumber is produced in British Columbia.

The two countries, however, are quite independent when it comes to plywood. Because of a protective duty imposed by the United States and very different

[1]Data in this section taken from Alice H. Ulrich, *U.S. Timber Production, Trade, Consumption and Price Statistics, 1950–1980,* Miscellaneous Publication No. 1408, U.S. Department of Agriculture, Forest Service, August 1981.

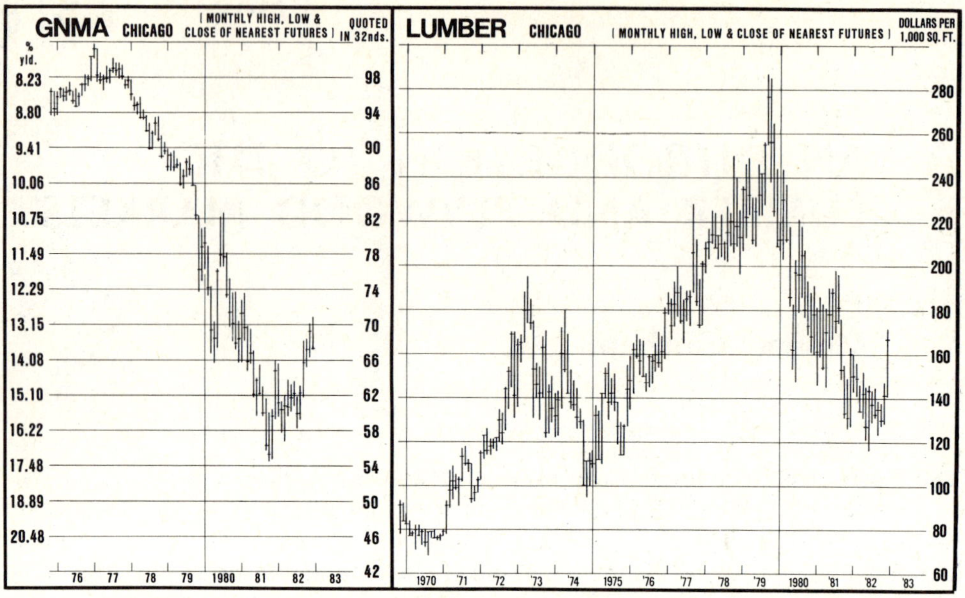

FIGURE 1. Lumber prices, monthly. (*Source:* Commodity Research Bureau)

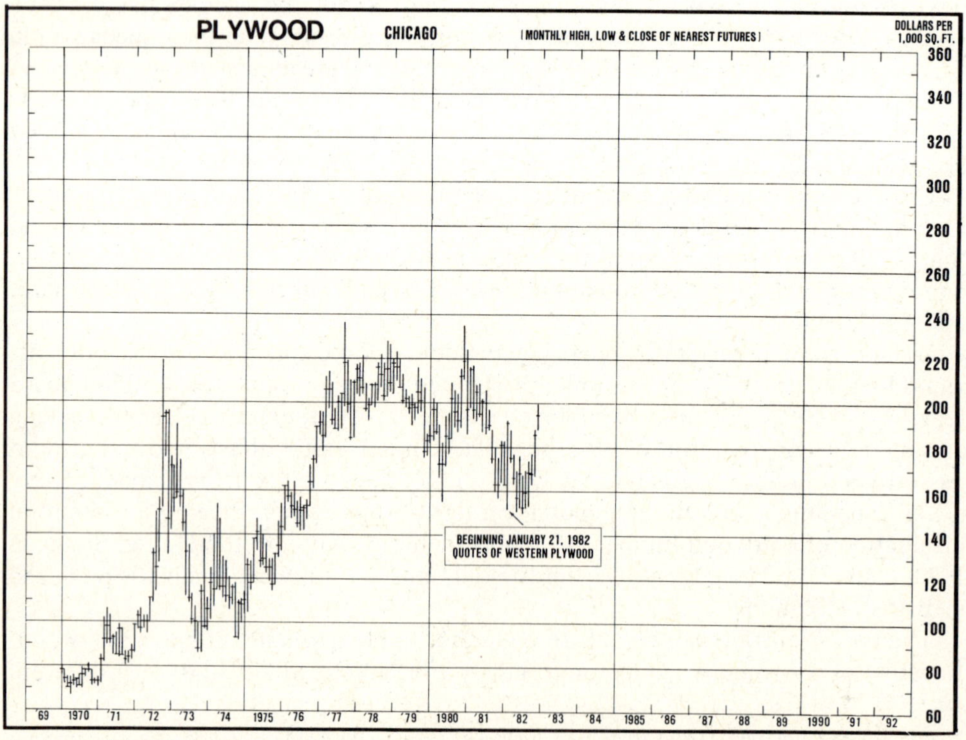

FIGURE 2. Plywood prices, monthly. (*Source:* Commodity Research Bureau)

grading systems, little plywood is exported by Canada into the United States. In 1979 the United States produced 18.6 billion square feet (bsf) of plywood (on a $\frac{3}{8}$-in. basis), exported 0.4 bsf, imported a trivial amount, leaving an apparent consumption of 18.2 bsf.

PRODUCTION OF LUMBER AND PLYWOOD

In order to understand the various factors which can affect the supply side of price determination, it is useful to briefly walk through the process through which standing forests are transformed into lumber and plywood at the construction site.

TIMBER HARVEST. Most harvesting of lumber is done by the mill on land not owned by the mill. The land is leased for timber rights either from private individuals or the federal, state, or local government. In British Columbia, 94% of all forested land is owned by the province. In the United States, one-third of commercial forest land and 58% of softwood growing stock is publicly owned.

Mills employ lumbermen who fell the trees with chainsaws or mobile machines, trim the branches and tips, saw or *buck* the trunk into desired lengths, *skid* the logs to an assembly point, and then transport them to the mill via water or truck. Once at the mill, the logs are often stored in water to prevent damage by insects, fungi, or *end checking*, small cracks which result from rapid drying of the log ends while the interior of the log remains wet. Alternatively, the logs may be piled in the open air and sprayed with insecticides and fungicides and have their ends coated to prevent rapid moisture loss.

Prior to sawing (for lumber) or peeling (for plywood), the bark is removed from the logs since it can be used for fuel, fiberboard, garden mulch, and other products and it could cause excess wear or damage to saws or plywood veneer cutting knives. The bark is removed by machines which either beat it off with hammers and chains, peel or shave it off, or force it off with high-pressure water jets. It is at this stage that the basic difference emerges between lumber and plywood production.

LUMBER PRODUCTION. After bark removal, logs destined to become lumber are conveyed to the *headsaw*, which is the focal point of the sawmill. The log is typically passed by the headsaw several times until all usable lumber and boards have been extracted. While a *circular saw* is still used in many smaller mills, most large, modern mills use a *bandsaw* (where the blade is a continuous steel band) and some use a multibladed *gang saw*, which reduces the log to lumber at one pass. The rounded edges of the log are converted to chips and then used in the production of composition board or paper.

After their creation at the headsaw, the boards and lumber pass through an *edger* which evens the edges, and a *trimmer* which trims the ends. The wood is then sorted by size and grade in preparation for *seasoning* (i.e., the removal of moisture from the wood, via either kiln or air drying). The seasoned lumber is dressed (surfaced) by a *planing* machine for the purpose of attaining smoothness of surface and uniformity of size.

While a number of regional grading systems exist, there is a national grading system which emerged in 1970 under the title American Softwood Lumber Standard, or the Voluntary Product Standard 20-70 (PS 20-70, for short) and published by the U.S. Department of Commerce. Grades are determined by both natural and manufacturing characteristics of the lumber which affect its strength, stiffness, and appearance. Grade generally declines with increases in the number or size of knots, increases in the number of splits and checks (small, limited splits), the amount of wane (presence of bark or lack of wood on an edge or corner of the lumber), and the extent of decay and honeycomb (pits in lumber caused by fungus), to name a few of the relevant factors.

The Chicago Mercantile Exchange contract specifies delivery of No. 1 and No. 2 lumber (two of the top three grades in the "Structural Light Framing" use category) or "construction and standard lumber" (the top two grades in the "Light Framing" use category). The other use classes of dimension lumber are "Studs" (2–6 in. wide) and "Structural Joists and Planks" (5 in. and wider), but neither of these are deliverable on the contract.

Once graded and sorted by size, the lumber is then seasoned or dried. There are several reasons for seasoning lumber. Dry lumber (CME contract spec lumber must be dried to 19% moisture content) is cheaper to ship; easier to nail, screw, glue, paint, or preserve; more resistant to insects, fungi, and decay; and stronger and less likely to shrink and cause structural damage. Air drying (simply stacking the lumber in the yard to expose it to sun and wind) is cheap, but takes a relatively long time (10–200 days). Drying in a kiln (an enclosure in which temperature, humidity, and air movement can be controlled) is much faster but more expensive than air drying. These are the two most commonly used methods of seasoning. Drying with chemicals, microwaves, or radio waves is not widely used at this time. Of all wood sold in the West, 55% is sold kiln dried, 5% is sold air dried, and 40% is sold green.[2]

Following the surfacing process, the lumber is typically banded with steel straps, *wrapped* (covered with a protective sheet of plastic or water-resistant paper), and loaded by forklifts onto flatcars or into boxcars for the trip to the next point of distribution.

PLYWOOD PRODUCTION. As is evident in the appearance of the final product, the steps involved in producing plywood are quite different from those involved in producing lumber. Plywood is an ingenious invention. It is simply several layers of thin wood veneer glued together. With the direction of the grain of each thin sheet of wood being placed at right angles to the adjoining sheet, the resultant piece of plywood has tremendous strength for its weight.

After the logs are debarked, they are cut into short lengths called *peeler blocks*. These 8–ft, 4-in. peeler blocks are then either steamed or soaked in hot water to make them easier to *peel*. In plywood production, peeling is not simply taking off the surface as in the peeling of potatoes or carrots, but rather using a long-knifed machine to peel off a continuous ribbon of wood which is $\frac{1}{10}$ to $\frac{1}{4}$ in. thick and 8 ft, 4 in. wide. The length of the ribbon, of course, depends upon the diameter

[2] *1981 Statistical Yearbook of the Western Lumber Industry*, Western Wood Products Association, Portland, OR.

of the log. During peeling, the knife is stationary while the wood is rotated on a lathe. After peeling each log, a peeler core of 3- to 4-in. diameter remains in the lathe and this is often used for lumber. This ribbon, which is referred to in the industry as *veneer*, is then cut into sheets of various lengths and dried in ovens to a moisture content of roughly 5%. This is lower than the 19% for lumber because of the need for the glue to be absorbed into veneers to establish a strong bond. Following drying, several veneer sheets are glued together, with the grain in each sheet placed at right angles to the grain of adjacent sheets. When enough sheets have been stacked to achieve the desired thickness, these veneer sandwiches are sent to the hot press for bonding under heat and pressure. The plywood panels are then trimmed to the desired size, sanded as required, graded, and stamped.

Veneers used in the construction of plywood panels are graded on the basis of such factors as smoothness of cut, knotholes, and other defects. The highest quality veneer is graded N, followed in order of decreasing quality by grades A, B, C, C-plugged, and D. The grades of both exposed veneers, or plys, are identified on the panel. A CDX panel, for example, has a grade C face ply, a grade D back ply, and is bonded with exterior (waterproof) glue (X for exterior glue). Plywood with this glue bond is intended for protected construction and industrial uses where protection against moisture exposure is required. The Chicago Board of Trade plywood contract calls for unsanded, $\frac{1}{2}$ in., CDX plywood.

USES OF LUMBER AND PLYWOOD

Most softwood lumber and plywood finds its way into construction. During the late 1970s and early 1980s, roughly 40% of all softwood lumber was used in residential construction, 17% in nonresidential construction, 21% for repairs and remodeling, 12% for materials handling, and 10% for other uses, including furniture, cabinets, power line poles, and railroad ties. However, as can be seen from Table 1, the share used in construction varies directly with housing starts and the shares used in repair and remodeling varies inversely with housing starts. However, construction is so important that increases in housing starts result in rising total lumber consumption and decreases in housing starts result in declining total lumber consumption.

In residential construction, dimension lumber is used mainly for *framing*, that is, for creating the framework or skeleton of the building, while plywood is used mainly for *sheathing*, that is, creating the first level of cover for a portion of the frame of the dwelling. Thus, plywood is used as subflooring in walls, especially near corners, and in roofs.

While different types of residences use different amounts of lumber and plywood, the most important distinction to make is between single family and multifamily dwellings. During the late 1970s and early 1980s, the average one-family dwelling used 10,297 board ft of lumber and 5,784 square ft of plywood per unit (see Table 2). In contrast, multifamily dwellings used only 4,050 board ft of lumber and 2,856 square ft of plywood on average. The implication, of course, is that when translating housing start figures into wood consumption, each single family dwelling should increase lumber and plywood consumption by 2.5 and 2.0 times as much, respectively, as does a unit of a multifamily dwelling.

TABLE 1. Distribution of Softwood Lumber Consumption by Use

	1976	1977	1978	1979	1980	1981
Residential construction (%)	40.8	46.4	44.8	40.3	35.8	32.5
Nonresidential construction (%)	16.0	14.2	14.8	16.4	18.2	20.1
Repair and remodeling (%)	20.7	18.7	19.2	20.2	24.4	25.3
Materials handling (%)	10.8	11.0	11.2	12.7	12.2	11.7
Other (%)	11.7	9.7	10.0	10.1	9.4	10.4
Total (in bbf)	35.6	40.1	41.4	39.3	32.5	30.1
Housing starts	1,538	1,987	2,020	1,745	1,292	1,084

Source: Adapted from *1981 Statistical Yearbook of the Western Lumber Industry*, Western Wood Products Association, Portland, OR.

TABLE 2. Amount of Lumber and Plywood Used per Unit in Single Family and Multifamily Dwellings, 1967–1981[a]

	Lumber		Rough Plywood		Sanded Plywood	
	Single Family	Multifamily	Single Family	Multifamily	Single Family	Multifamily
1967	11,066	4,909	3,945	1,922	678	293
1968	10,836	4,879	4,021	2,038	632	290
1969	10,534	4,686	4,153	2,039	580	278
1970	9,852	4,510	4,255	2,332	499	264
1971	9,960	4,573	4,614	2,613	503	268
1972	10,139	4,467	4,795	2,733	438	227
1973	10,233	4,321	5,063	2,742	428	208
1974	10,064	4,135	5,505	2,914	407	186
1975	10,435	4,131	5,499	2,806	393	174
1976	10,813	4,176	5,455	2,655	389	164
1977	10,747	4,073	5,439	2,571	371	152
1978	10,698	4,001	5,501	2,563	356	140
1979	10,336	4,058	5,458	2,692	347	144
1980	9,970	4,019	5,420	2,805	329	142
1981	9,734	4,103	5,384	2,926	317	144

Source: U.S. Forest Service Survey, 1968 and 1972; American Plywood Association, since 1970, and interpolations for nonsurvey years by Data Resources, Incorporated.
[a]Lumber in board feet, plywood in square feet, $\frac{3}{8}$ in. basis.

FUNDAMENTAL ANALYSIS OF THE LUMBER AND PLYWOOD MARKETS

In order to discuss those factors which influence the prices of lumber and plywood, it is convenient to divide them into the two traditional economic sets of supply-side factors and demand-side factors.

SUPPLY-SIDE FACTORS. The supply-side factors in any market are essentially those which in any way change the cost to the producers of bringing the product to market. Any increase in this cost, whether it be due to labor, stumpage prices, transportation, or whatever, should cause producers to require a higher price to maintain any given level of production. Buyers, of course, will begin to look around for substitutes or even go without the commodity as prices rise, so the net effect is that less will be sold at a higher market price than would have been the case without the increase in production cost.

In the forest products industry, the two major costs are raw materials and labor, so the price analyst should note any significant changes in the price of either logs or labor. Since logs used in plywood production (*veneer logs*) command prices which have averaged about 60% more than the prices of logs used in lumber production (*saw logs*), a given percent change in log prices, other things being equal, should have a greater effect on the cost of producing plywood than on the cost of producing lumber (see Table 3). If the structure of demand were the same for both lumber and plywood, then a 10% change in log prices should have a larger effect on the price of plywood than on the price of lumber. The precise effect of such an increase is dependent upon the elasticity of demand, a parameter which is not estimated in this study.

TABLE 3. Average Prices of Saw Logs and Veneer Logs in Western Washington and Northwest Oregon, 1970–1979 (dollars per million square feet, Scribner log scale)

	Saw Logs	Veneer Logs	Veneer ÷ Saw
1970	$ 89.30	$136.60	1.53
1971	90.20	132.60	1.47
1972	95.10	148.90	1.57
1973	172.30	320.40	1.86
1974	180.50	299.30	1.66
1975	168.70	274.40	1.63
1976	202.90	277.70	1.86
1977	242.80	322.20	1.33
1978	284.60	446.40	1.57
1979	382.20	571.30	1.49
Percent change 1970–1979	427.8%	418.2%	—

Source: Alice H. Ulrich, *U.S. Timber Production, Trade, Consumption and Price Statistics, 1950–1980*, U.S. Department of Agriculture, Forest Service, August 1981.

In addition to changes in the cost of major inputs to the production process are act-of-God or act-of-man interruptions in supply. There are, for example, two ways in which prices might be affected by weather. Drought or extremely dry situations can lead either to fire or such a serious threat of fire (known to some as "hoot owl conditions") that logging operations cease until conditions improve. The effect that this has on the market clearly depends upon existing log and lumber inventories.

The second supply-side weather effect is unanticipated mud. There is a period each spring during snow melt when conditions are too wet and muddy to allow machinery to move through the forest. Normally, this is anticipated and sufficient log stockpiles are created to tide the mills over during this period. However, should the period arrive much earlier or last longer than anticipated, temporary shortages and price increases would occur.

The acts-of-man which interrupt supply are essentially strikes by either lumber or transportation workers. There is, however, a difference between the two. A mill worker strike cuts production and raises the price of lumber and plywood everywhere. A transportation strike, on the other hand, would tend to raise the price of lumber in consumption areas where there is a shortage and lower it at the point of production which experiences a growing glut of unsold lumber. It must be noted that rumors of strikes are more abundant than strikes themselves. During the decade 1972–1982, there has been only one lumber worker strike (July–August 1981 by Canadian lumber workers) and one transportation strike (September 1982 by U.S. rail workers).

There is one final factor which probably could be placed on the demand-side list as easily as on the supply-side list and that is the U.S./Canadian exchange rate. The bottom line here is that a decline in the value of the Canadian dollar is bearish and an increase is bullish. The logic is fairly simple. A cheaper Canadian dollar means that when a Canadian producer receives U.S. $180 per mbf for lumber, the Canadian producer is able to convert this into more Canadian dollars with which to pay workers, log suppliers, and himself or herself. In effect, the producer is receiving the same U.S. dollar price but a higher Canadian dollar price than before. This increase in price makes Canadian producers eager to supply more wood to the U.S. market. The increased supply tends to lower the U.S. price of lumber in the U.S. market. This decline in the U.S. price begins to remove some of the romance of the U.S. market for Canadian producers, but unless the U.S. price fell by as much as the decline in the value of the Canadian dollar, Canadian producers are still receiving a higher Canadian dollar price for lumber they sell into the United States. The net effect is that a new equilibrium is reached with greater Canadian imports, a lower U.S. price and, most likely, less U.S. production. The U.S. producers would be discouraged by the lower prices and would, consequently, cut back their production levels.

Should the Canadian dollar rise in value, the opposite scenario should emerge. A new equilibrium would find Canadian sellers reducing their lumber flow into the U.S. market, a consequent rise in the U.S. dollar price of lumber and increased production by U.S. mills. Note that since there is minimal U.S./Canadian trade in plywood, exchange rate changes should have virtually no effect upon U.S. plywood prices.

DEMAND-SIDE FACTORS. Lumber and plywood have many uses. However, since the construction sector accounts for such a significant portion of all lumber and plywood use, it is this sector which must be closely monitored by the analyst. *Housing starts* is the most popular and widely recognized indicator of residential construction activity. It is published monthly and most commonly used in an annualized and seasonally adjusted form. Seasonal adjustments are essential since much of the movement in housing starts is the predictable summer increase and winter decline. To be annualized means that when you read that April starts are 1.2 million, this means that if the other 11 months of the year behaved as did April, there would have been 1.2 million units built that year. In fact, the number of units actually started in April (assuming no seasonal adjustment for a moment) would have been 100 million (i.e., 1.2 million ÷ 12 months).

As can be seen from Figures 3 and 4, during the period 1970–1982, housing starts moved dramatically. Within one 2-year period (early 1973 to early 1975), housing starts tumbled from almost 2.5 million down to less than 1.0 million. During roughly that same period of time, lumber prices fell from about \$170 to \$105 per mbf and plywood prices dropped from about \$180 to \$110 per msf (million square feet). Close examination of the charts, however, shows that prices and starts do not move in lockstep with one another and sometimes even move in opposite directions.

Another way to examine this relationship is to ask how much of the variation in monthly lumber and plywood prices is explained by movements in housing starts. Estimating a regression equation is the easiest way to do this since the R^2

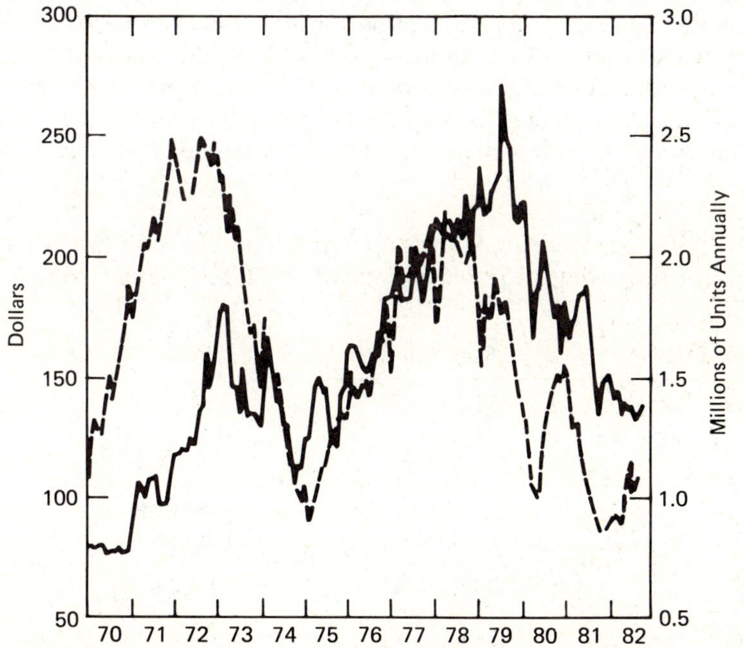

FIGURE 3. Lumber prices (solid line) vs housing starts (dotted line). (*Sources:* Chicago Mercantile Exchange, Chicago Board of Trade, and U.S. Department of Commerce Report No. C20, 1970–1982.)

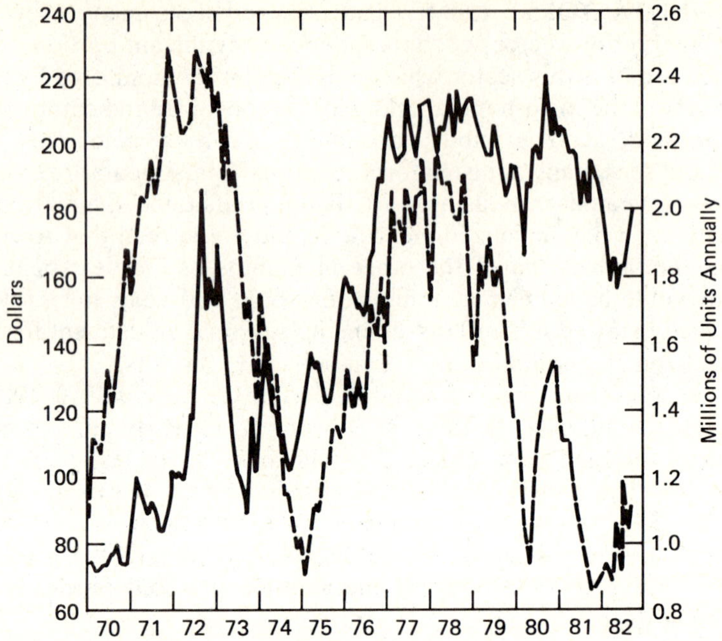

FIGURE 4. Plywood prices (solid line) vs housing starts (dotted line). (*Sources:* Chicago Mercantile Exchange, Chicago Board of Trade, and U.S. Department of Commerce Report No. C20, 1970–1982.)

statistic gives the percentage of the movement in one factor explained by movements in another factor. The results of performing this exercise (see Table 4) lead to several observations. First, housing starts alone do a generally poor job in explaining concurrent changes in lumber and plywood prices. Fourteen percent was the greatest amount of price variation explained by any of the equations and most did much more poorly. Second, total starts can be broken down into single

TABLE 4. Effect of Housing Starts on Lumber and Plywood Prices and Results of Regressions for Period January 1970 to October 1982

For Lumber Prices	Constant	Effect of Starts	R^2
Total starts	136.2 (10.3)[a]	12.0	0.009
Single family	91.7 (7.1)	61.0 (5.1)	0.142
Multifamily	176.1 (20.0)	−35.5 (−2.5)	0.034
For Plywood Prices	**Constant**	**Effect of Starts**	R^2
Total starts	158.5 (11.4)	− 3.4 (0.4)	−0.005
Single family	110.4 (7.7)	40.6 (3.1)	0.053
Multifamily	188.5 (21.1)	−61.9 (4.3)	0.104

[a] *t* statistic in parentheses. Values above 2.0 are generally considered to indicate statistical significance.

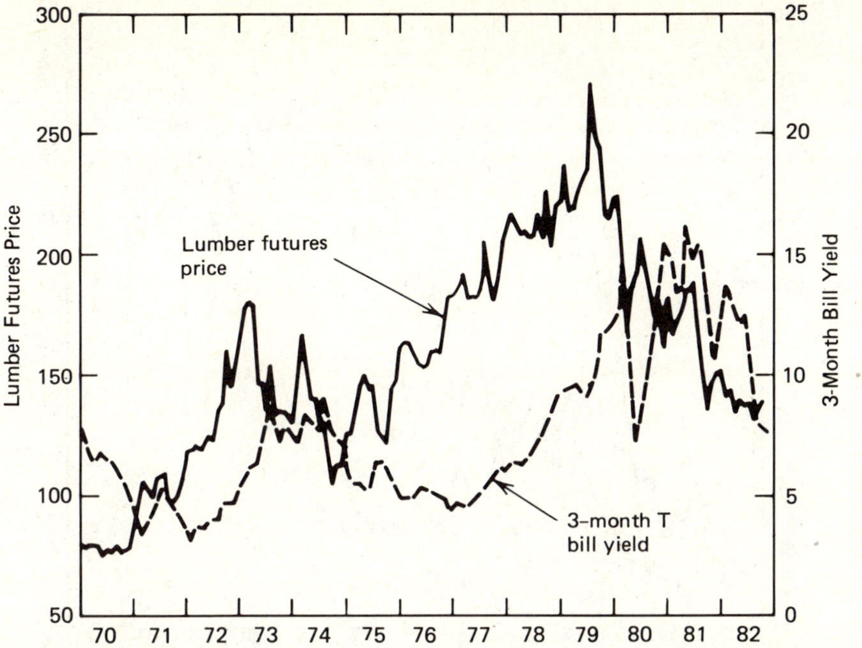

FIGURE 5. First option lumber futures vs yield on government 3-month bills. Monthly—January 1979 to October 1982.

family and multifamily starts and single family starts do a much better job of explaining lumber and plywood prices than do total starts. Third, multifamily starts have a strange negative relationship with lumber and plywood prices, the reason for which is not readily apparent.

The housing-start series is not the only indicator of the production of new housing. There are at least three others: housing authorizations (the problem is that the time lag between permit or authorization and start of construction is not constant), value of new residential construction put in place (tries to measure actual construction for the month), and housing completions (which measure what is implied and have been available only since 1968).

It is also possible to step back in the chain of causation and ask what factors affect the level of construction activity. Most housing experts appear to believe that changes in monetary conditions are the primary cause of fluctuations in residential construction.[3] Interest-rate changes actually affect both the supply and demand for housing in the same direction. Thus, a rise in rates makes it more expensive for both the contractor to build and the potential occupant to purchase housing. The net effect is less housing is built and the demand for lumber weakens, putting downward pressure on lumber prices. Therefore, one would expect to see interest rates and lumber and plywood prices move in opposite directions, with perhaps the change in interest rates leading the change in prices. Figures 5 and 6 illustrate the fact that while there is empirical content in the above statement,

[3]M. Sumichrast and M. Seldin, *Housing Markets,* Dow Jones Irwin, Incorporated, Homewood, IL, 1977, p. 160.

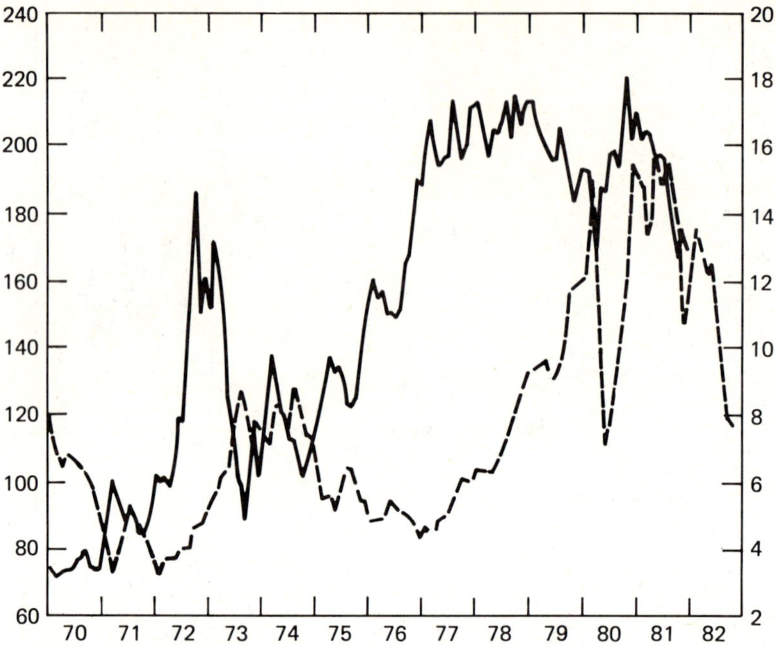

FIGURE 6. First option plywood futures vs yield on government 3-month bills. Monthly—January 1979 to October 1982.

the relationship is quite loose and unpredictable. For example, while interest rates more than doubled between 1977 and 1979, lumber prices made a dramatic upwards move from below $180 to above $250 per mbf, not a downwards move as might have been expected on the basis of interest rates alone.

One final demand-side factor should be mentioned. Normally, transportation costs are not considered important among those variables which influence price. In the case of lumber and plywood, however, transportation costs can be extremely important. It is not unusual to find that a third or more of the delivered cost of British Columbia lumber shipped to the Midwest or southern United States could be accounted for by shipping costs. Therefore, significant changes in railroad or trucking freight rates in this deregulated area could be an important determinant in the demand for northwestern lumber and plywood by contractors in the eastern portion of the United States.

HISTORICAL PRICE BEHAVIOR

There are several observations which can be made regarding historical price behavior which could be useful to anyone trading lumber or plywood. These concern (1) the relationship between lumber and plywood prices, (2) the relationship among prices for different delivery months in lumber and plywood futures, and (3) seasonal movements in lumber and plywood prices. Each is considered in turn.

LUMBER VERSUS PLYWOOD. Since the set of factors which affects lumber prices has much in common with the set of factors which affects plywood prices, one might expect to see those two prices move quite closely together. The evidence suggests that while the two prices do move together, there are times when they can move considerably far from one another. As can be seen in Figure 7, for several years (1975–1978) monthly lumber prices never drifted more than \$10 above or \$20 below plywood prices. However, during 1979 and 1980, lumber prices shot more than \$50 above and dropped to almost \$50 below plywood prices.

Using our regression approach to explain the daily movement in plywood by the daily movement in lumber prices, we find the following percentages of the former explained by the latter: 55% in 1978, 7% in 1979, 1% in 1980, 47% in 1981, 43% in 1982, and 44% over the entire 1978–1982 period. Both the figure and these results suggest that while there may be interesting spread opportunities between lumber and plywood, there is a degree of risk involved.

SPREADING ACROSS MONTHS. One of the major differences between the plywood and lumber futures contracts is that the former allows taking delivery in one month and redelivering in a subsequent month, while the latter does not. This means that should traders observe a deferred plywood month rise in price above the nearby month by more than the anticipated cost of holding the commodity for the period of time between the 2 months, then the trader would go long nearby and short the deferred contract. If the prices did not come back together while the trader held two futures positions, the trader could always take delivery of the

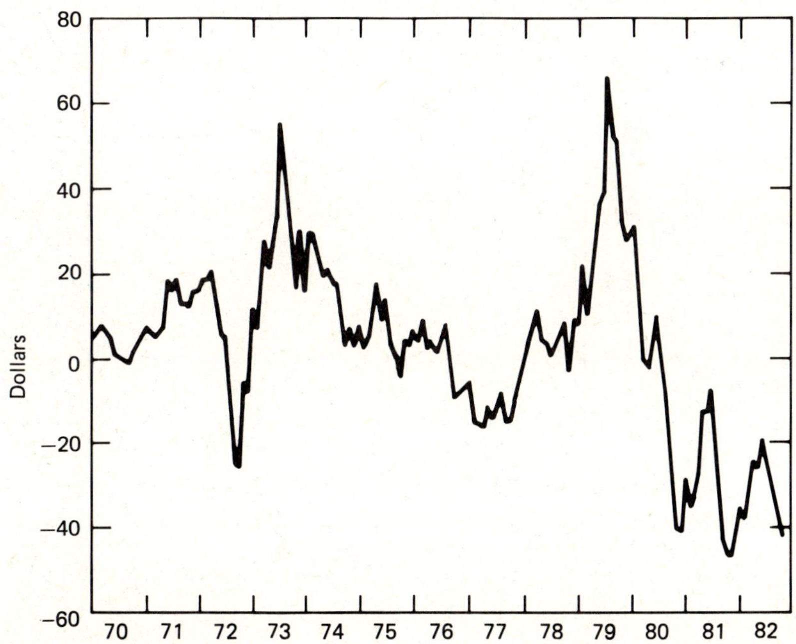

FIGURE 7. Lumber price less plywood price. (*Source:* Chicago Mercantile Exchange and Chicago Board of Trade, 1970–1982.)

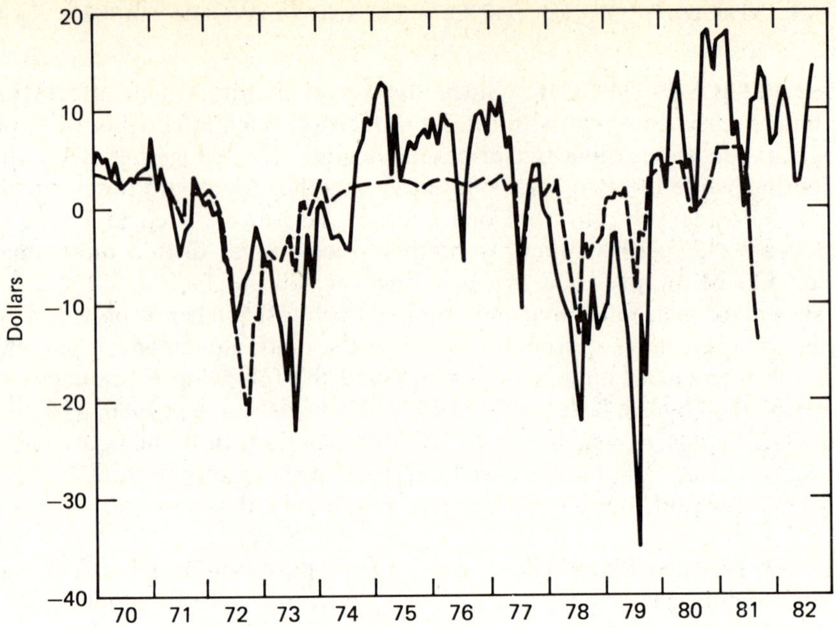

FIGURE 8. Deferred price less nearby price: lumber (solid line) and plywood (dotted line). (*Source:* Chicago Mercantile Exchange and Chicago Board of Trade, 1970–1982.)

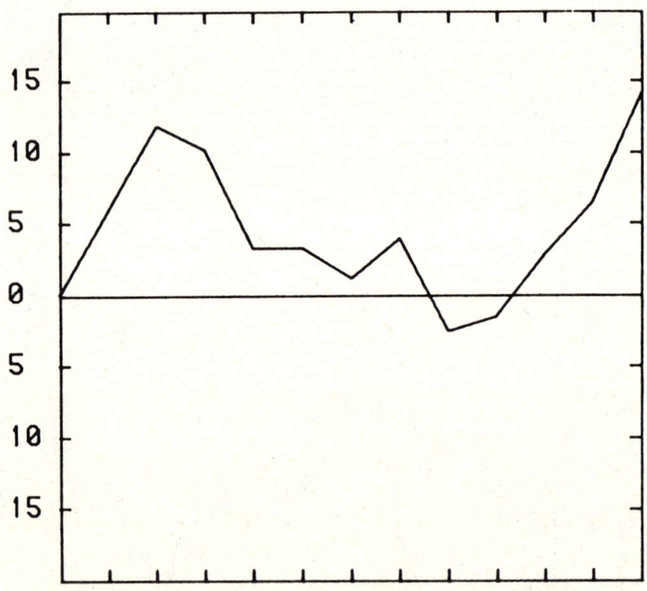

	J-F	F-M	M-A	A-M	M-J	J-J	J-A	A-S	S-O	O-N	N-D	D-J
Average Move	5.9	5.9	-1.8	-7	0	-2.2	2.8	-6.6	•1	4.4	3.6	7.5
% Reliable	57.2	100	85.8	71.5	28.6	42.9	57.2	57.2	28.6	71.5	71.5	85.8
Avg. Up Move	11.1	5.9	13	2.1	6.8	1.6	9.8	2.3	11.3	9.4	5.8	9.2
Avg. Down Move	1	0	4.2	10.6	2.7	7.3	6.6	13.2	3.1	8.3	1.9	2.5
Greatest Up Move	19.4	16.7	13	3.7	8.4	2.5	18.8	4.3	19.3	20.8	9.3	13.6
Greatest Down Move	1.5	0	11	30	6.6	10.5	18.6	21.2	8.6	15.5	2.8	2.5

FIGURE 9. Seasonality: Lumber nearest futures (7 years).

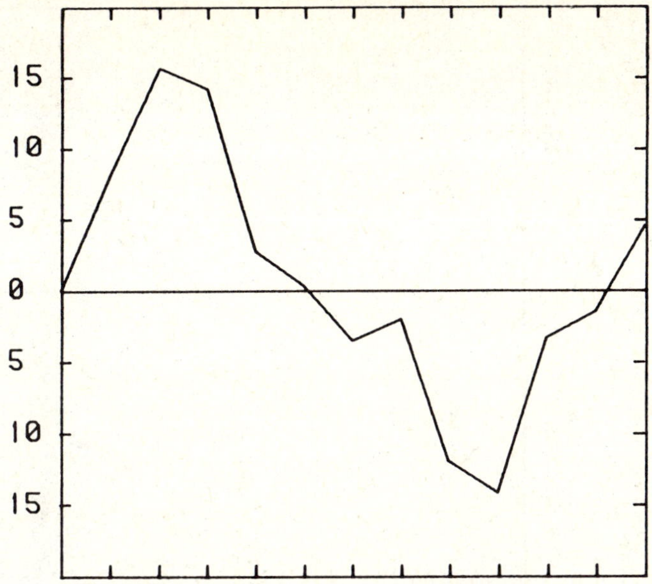

	J-F	F-M	M-A	A-M	M-J	J-J	J-A	A-S	S-O	O-N	N-D	D-J
Average Move	8	7.5	-1.5	-11.5	-2.5	-3.8	1.5	-10.1	-2.2	10.9	1.8	5.9
% Reliable	75	100	75	75	100	50	50	75	75	75	50	75
Avg. Up Move	11.2	7.5	13	3.7	0	1.8	12.6	0.3	3.3	14.8	5.5	8.8
Avg. Down Move	1.5	0	6.4	16.5	2.5	9.5	9.5	13.5	4.1	1	1.9	2.5
Greatest Up Move	19.4	16.7	13	3.7	0	2.5	18.8	0.3	3.3	20.8	6.6	13.6
Greatest Down Move	1.5	0	11	30	6.6	10.5	18.6	21.2	8.6	1	2.8	2.5

FIGURE 10. Seasonality: Lumber nearest futures (4 years).

nearby, hold it, and redeliver when the short position in the deferred contract matured. Such low-risk arbitraging leads to a greater degree of intermonth stability in plywood than exists in lumber.

As can be seen in Figure 8, this difference in stability was especially apparent in 1979 when lumber experienced more than a $40 per mbf shift in the difference between the deferred and nearby contract. Over the entire 1970–1982 period, the mean and standard deviations of the deferred less nearby spreads were lumber, 1.057 and 9.102; plywood 0.224 and 4.958.

Clearly, there is more room for both profit and loss from intermonth spreading in lumber than there is in plywood.

SEASONALITY. Given the previous discussion of significant seasonal changes in the level of construction activity—the main use of lumber and plywood—it should be no surprise that these two commodities experience fairly reliable seasonal price patterns. A recent book on seasonal price movements by Grushcow and Smith found lumber and plywood among the best commodities for reliable seasonal price

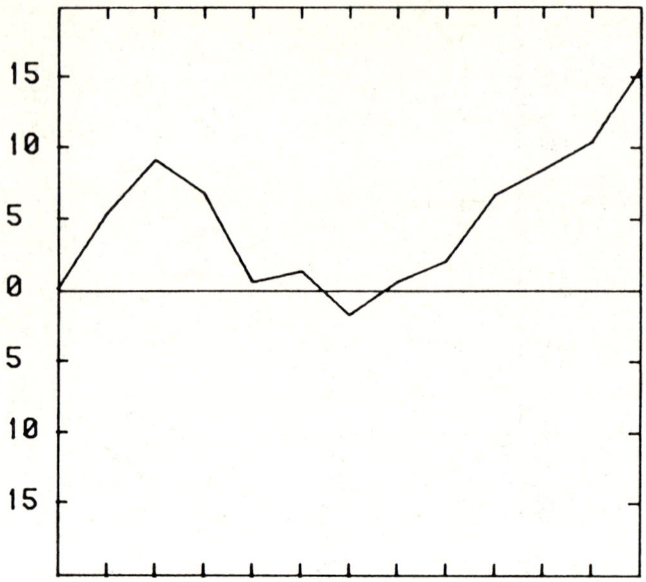

	J-F	F-M	M-A	A-M	M-J	J-J	J-A	A-S	S-O	O-N	N-D	D-J
Average Move	5.3	3.7	-2.4	-6.3	0.8	-3.1	2.3	1.4	4.6	1.8	1.9	5.1
% Reliable	71.5	57.2	57.2	71.5	57.2	71.5	42.9	42.9	57.2	71.5	85.8	71.5
Avg. Up Move	8.4	8.9	4.1	3	4.2	2.9	9.4	11.5	10.4	9.6	4.9	8.8
Avg. Down Move	2.5	3.1	7.3	10	3.8	5.5	3.1	6.1	3.1	17.9	16.4	4.3
Greatest Up Move	17.8	17.8	9.3	5.6	13.9	3.1	24.9	18.8	21.9	15.4	9	11.4
Greatest Down Move	2.6	5	15.1	23	7.4	15.7	8.1	11.1	5.5	34.8	16.4	7.6

FIGURE 11. Seasonality: Plywood nearest futures (7 years).

movements.[4] In general, both prices tend to rise from fall to spring as lumber and plywood are stored in anticipation of the spring and summer burst in construction activity. There also tends to be a price decline from spring to fall. Grushcow and Smith's lumber and plywood charts are reproduced here in Figures 9–12.

FUTURES TRADING IN LUMBER AND PLYWOOD

At this writing there are only two actively traded forest product futures contracts: a lumber contract at the Chicago Mercantile Exchange and a plywood contract at the Chicago Board of Trade. Both of these contracts were initiated in 1969. Two other attempts at plywood trading, by the New York Mercantile Exchange in 1969 and the Chicago Mercantile Exchange in 1981, were unsuccessful.

[4] J. Grushcow and C. Smith, *Profits Through Seasonal Trading*, Wiley, New York, NY, 1980.

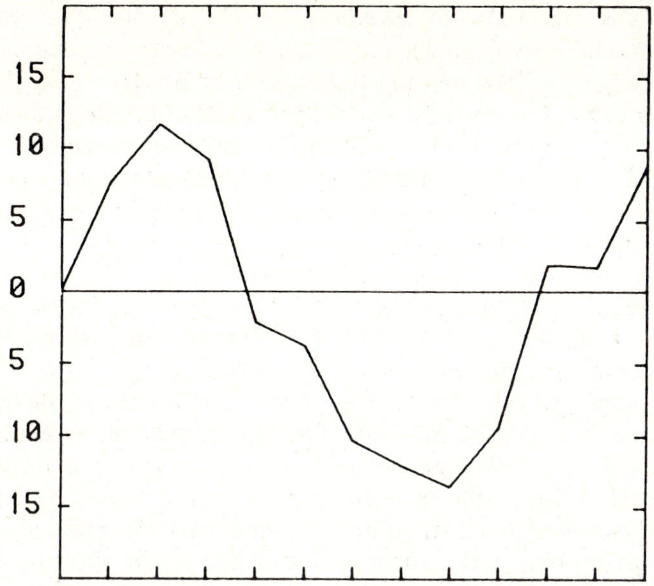

	J-F	F-M	M-A	A-M	M-J	J-J	J-A	A-S	S-O	O-N	N-D	D-J
Average Move	7.6	4	-2.6	-11.4	-1.7	-6.6	-1.8	-1.5	4.1	11.3	-0.3	7.1
% Reliable	100	50	50	100	50	100	75	75	75	100	25	75
Avg. Up Move	7.6	12.6	5.4	0	1.2	0	3	12.9	6.5	11.3	5.1	9.8
Avg. Down Move	0	4.6	10.5	11.4	4.6	6.6	3.4	6.2	3.3	0	16.4	1.1
Greatest Up Move	17.8	17.8	9.3	0	1.7	0	3	12.9	13.9	15.4	6.2	11.4
Greatest Down Move	0	5	15.1	23	7.4	15.7	8.1	11.1	3.3	0	16.4	1.1

FIGURE 12. Seasonality: Plywood nearest futures (4 years).

Currently, the Chicago Mercantile Exchange lumber contract calls for delivery of 130,000 board ft of 2 × 4's of random lengths (varying from 8 ft. to 20 ft), loaded on two railroad flat cars at a mill in any of two Canadian provinces (British Columbia or Alberta), or seven western states (Washington, Oregon, California, Montana, Idaho, Nevada, and Wyoming). Deliverable species, identified by being stamped with the appropriate species name on the wood, include: Alpine fir, Englemann spruce, Hem fir, Lodgepole pine, and spruce pine fir. Deliverable grade is "construction and standard" for "light framing" classification and No. 1 and No. 2 for the "structural light framing" classification. However, the lower grades, standard and No. 2, may not account for more than one-half of the delivery unit.

Freight billing practices in the contract attempt to mirror those in the cash market. Thus, the buyer tells the seller where to ship; the seller ships and pays the railroad for the actual weight shipped, then bills the buyer for freight on the assumption that the wood weighs 1,800 lb per board ft. In fact, deliverable lumber generally weighs less than this and the difference between the actual weight and

1,800 lb per mbf is referred to as the *underweights*. The value of these underweights to the shipper could vary from zero to as much as $6 per cwt depending upon the weight of the wood shipped and the freight rate involved.

In order to protect buyers from very large freight rates which could result from being matched with a remotely located mill, the contract puts a limit on the freight bill paid by the buyer to the seller. That cap is the rate from Vancouver to the buyer's destination for delivery from Canadian mills and the rate from Portland for delivery from U.S. mills.

The Chicago Board of Trade plywood contract is known formally as the Western Plywood futures. This is because the CBT (as well as the CME) has considered the possibility of creating a Southern Plywood futures contract at some later time. The plywood contract calls for delivery of 76,032 square ft of $\frac{1}{2}$ in., 48 by 96 in., CD, exterior glue plywood. This translates into 2,376 panels or one boxcar, though delivery into truck is also permissible. The plywood is delivered F.O.B. mill or warehouse from any *regular* (exchange-approved) mill or warehouse in Oregon, Washington, Idaho, Montana, or California north of Fresno. A major difference between the plywood and lumber contracts is that there must be a physical delivery of lumber for every long and short matched, whereas the short delivering on the plywood contract gives the long a Western Plywood shipping certificate which represents a claim on plywood. The assigned long may exercise this claim immediately, may hold onto it indefinitely before calling for delivery, may sell it in the cash market, or may establish a short position and redeliver it back into the futures market. Holders of certificates must pay a fee ($1.65 per contract per day at this writing) to certificate issuers as long as the certificates are outstanding.

Both contracts have undergone a number of modifications since their 1969 inception, and those who wish to analyze historical price patterns should be aware of those changes which might have affected the value of the contracts. The lumber contract began as a 40,000 board ft U.S. white fir contract in 1969. The size was increased to 90,000 board ft in 1971, to 100,000 board ft in 1972, and finally to 130,000 board ft in 1981. British Columbia was added in 1974, but Canadian deliveries were not economical until the species list was expanded to that mentioned above in 1981. The 1981 change also added Alberta, Canada and Wyoming to the list of permissible origins and created a separate rate ceiling for Canadian mills by having Vancouver rates serve as the cap for deliveries from Canadian origins and leaving Portland rates as the cap for deliveries from U.S. origins.

The plywood contract underwent a major change in 1981 when its pricing basis was switched from F.O.B. Portland to F.O.B. the delivering mill. In addition, the buyer was given the option to call for delivery by truck.

At this writing, activity in both lumber and plywood is below previous peaks. For the 12 months ending October 1982, volume of trading was 527,844 contracts in lumber and 116,932 contracts in plywood. Plywood has dropped considerably from the volume highs it reached in 1974 and 1977. Lumber volume has generally been building each year except for 1981 and 1982. The major reason given for depressed activity in both contracts is the depressed condition the lumber industry has been in for several years now. However, if the recent decline in interest rates translates itself into renewed vigor in construction, there is reason to believe activity and liquidity could again pick up in both contracts.

TABLE 5. Selected Contract Specifications

CBOT Western Plywood	
Delivery months	January, March, May, July, September, and November
Trading unit	Boxcars of 36 banded units of 66 pieces each (2,376 pieces, 76,032 square ft total per car)
Price quotations and minimum fluctuation	Quoted in units of 1,000 square ft, with a minimum fluctuation of \$0.10 per 1,000 square ft (\$7.603 per contract), basis F.O.B. mill or warehouse
Daily price movement limits	Subject to change; consult latest official notices from the exchange
Position limits	600 contracts in any one future or in all futures combined; positions of 25 or more contracts require reports to the CFTC
Grades deliverable	Panels of plywood 48 × 96 in., 4 or 5 ply, $\frac{1}{2}$ in. thick, CD, exterior glue, with an identification index of 32/16
Delivery	By shipping certificate issued by either plywood mills or warehouses approved by the exchange in Washington, Oregon, Montana, Idaho, or California north of Fresno
Premium charge	\$1.65 per day per contract
Trading hours	9:00 a.m.–1:05 p.m. central time

CME Random Length Lumber	
Delivery months	January, March, May, July, September, and November
Trading unit	100,000 board ft
Minimum fluctuation	\$0.10 per 1,000 board ft (\$10 per contract)
Daily price limits	\$5.00 per 1,000 board ft
Position limits	1,000 contracts, with a maximum of 300 in any one contract month.
Grades deliverable	Construction and standard on No. 1 and No. 2 grade not to exceed 50% standard grade nominal 2 × 4's of random lengths from 8 to 20 ft manufactured in California, Idaho, Montana, Nevada, Oregon, Washington, Wyoming and Alberta, British Columbia, Canada. Standard grade specifies size, quality, and moisture content
Delivery	On track and shall be unitized and each unit shall be individually paper wrapped and loaded on flatcars. Par delivery of Hem fir, Alpine fir, Englemann spruce, Lodgepole pine, or spruce pine fir.
Trading hours	9:00 a.m.–1:05 p.m. central time

CONCLUSION

Both the Chicago Board of Trade plywood contract and the Chicago Mercantile Exchange lumber contract have been trading since 1969. The prices of both commodities are influenced significantly by the level of construction activity, which in turn, is affected by the level of interest rates, though these relationships may not be as tight as some might believe. While lumber and plywood prices generally move together, the difference between the two prices is sometimes extremely unstable. This can partially be explained by the different uses of the two products, but also by the fact that while virtually all plywood consumed in the United States is domestically produced, imports (mainly from Canada) play an important role in the U.S. lumber market. Plywood futures prices exhibit more intramonth stability than do lumber futures prices because the plywood contract allows for redelivery while the lumber contract does not. During the past half-decade, lumber futures trading has exceeded plywood futures trading by a considerable amount, though activity in both contracts is currently depressed, likely by depressed conditions in the forest products industry. There is reason to believe that a general economic recovery accompanied by a decline in interest rates should stimulate construction activity, lumber and plywood prices, and lumber and plywood futures trading.

CHAPTER 42

ENERGY FUTURES

CONTENTS

REFINERY BASICS 3

CRUDE OIL 7

Grades and Specifications 7
Reserves of Crude Oil 8
Production of Crude Oil 8
Demand for Crude Oil 11
Stocks of Crude Oil 14
Cash Market Transactions 18
Cash Market Structure 18
Futures Contracts Proposed 19

HEATING OIL 19

Grades and Specifications 19
Sources of Supply 22
Demand 22
Cash Market Transactions 24
Heating Oil Futures 25

GASOLINE 29

Grades and Specifications 29
Supply 30
Demand 30
Cash Market Structure 31
Futures Contracts 33

LIQUEFIED PROPANE GAS 34

Grades and Specifications 34
Supply 38
Demand 38
Propane Futures 41
Sources of Information 41

CHAPTER 42

ENERGY FUTURES

David J. Hirschfeld

Energy represents one of the most dynamic areas of growth in the futures industry today. The New York Mercantile's heating oil contract (New York harbor delivery) experienced an eightfold increase in volume from 1979 to 1983 and promises to continue growing. During 1981 the New York Mercantile (NYMEX) introduced a leaded gasoline contract (also for New York harbor delivery) which has since achieved notable success. During 1982–1983 the Chicago Board of Trade (CBT) began trading its own contracts in heating oil, gasoline, and crude petroleum. During 1984 the Chicago Mercantile Exchange (CME) is likely to trade its own gasoline and crude oil contracts, the most successful of which has been the crude oil contract. There are also indications that new contracts are being considered in residual oil, jet fuel, and other bulk energy commodities. This flurry of exchange activity has stimulated great commercial and speculative interest and it is entirely possible we are witnessing the birth of a revolution in the petroleum industry, akin to that which has been witnessed in the financial community.

This chapter begins with an introduction to refinery operations. Being knowledgeable about any petroleum futures contract requires at least a working knowledge of how the product is produced (or refined in the case of crude). Such knowledge is important for pricing, arbitraging, and spreading the various contract markets.

Later sections of this chapter will discuss the individual market characteristics of crude oil, gasoline, heating oil, and liquid propane gas. Each section presents material on the product's supply and demand and its pricing in the cash market, as well as a comparison of various futures contracts offered.

REFINERY BASICS

The earliest refineries were little more than fancy stills: crude oil was slowly heated and the gaseous products later captured and condensed. Today, refineries are complex behemoths employing thousands of intricate operations. Yet, most modern refineries begin with distillation techniques not dissimilar to those employed more than 100 years ago.

Our story begins at a well, where crude is produced and then shipped, trucked, or piped to awaiting storage tanks at a refinery. Storage plays a crucial role in most refinery operations, allowing the refinery to operate continuously in the face of irregular deliveries. Storage also allows greater control of the quality of crude processed. During storage, some impurities (salt, metals, water, and other contaminants) separate from the crude itself. Many refineries process their crudes to further remove such impurities before they begin refining the crude.

Actual distillation begins by heating the crude in an atmospheric column. As the crude is heated, the lighter portions (called "cuts" or fractions") of the crude are given off as gases. As more and more heat is added, a larger portion of the crude is vaporized. The column itself is arrayed vertically with many trays, each of which is designed to capture (through condensation) only a selected portion of the rising gas. Lighter fractions of the crude continue to rise until they reach a tray which is capable of turning them into a liquid state.

Each fraction of the crude which is heated may be identified as a separate product. Figure 1 shows the temperature at which certain products will separate from the crude and become gaseous. This is one way of defining such products (and of classing crudes) and such a figure is called a "distillation curve." Note how progressively more of the crude is vaporized as the temperature rises until

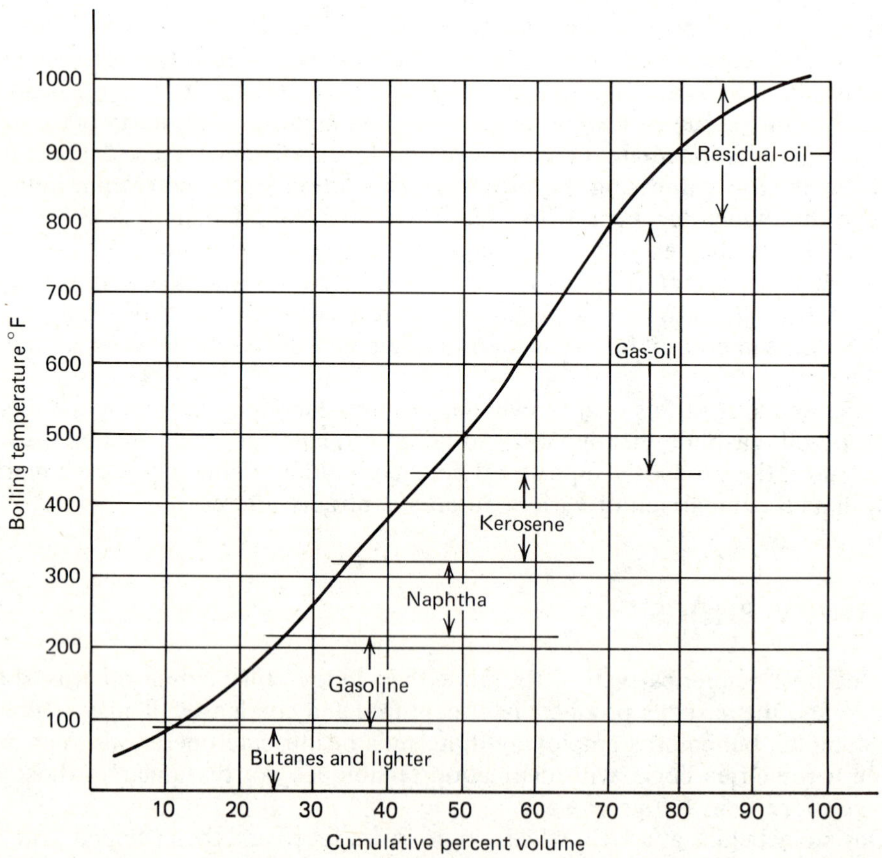

FIGURE 1. Crude oil distillation curve and its fractions. (*Source*: William L. Leffler, *Petroleum Refining for the Non-Technical Person*, p. 7.)

all that remains is a residue. Distillation curves can vary significantly among crudes, as may be seen in Figure 2 which shows curves for five common types of crude oil.

Simple distillation, as described above, is often augmented by passing the residual produced in an atmospheric column into a vacuum column. As suggested by its title, a vacuum column has zero air pressure and is often accompanied by higher temperatures than those employed in an atmospheric column. Vacuum columns are used to increase the production of certain products such as motor gasoline and jet fuel, which are generally in greatest demand.

For extremely "light" crude oils simple distillation (atmospheric and vacuum) may be all that is done to the oil. More typically, the crude is subject to additional chemical and thermal processes to fully exploit the production of the most highly valued products. Cracking and reforming are two very important and commonly used such processes. Cracking involves breaking the heavier molecules into smaller (and hence lighter) ones. There are two major types of cracking—thermal and

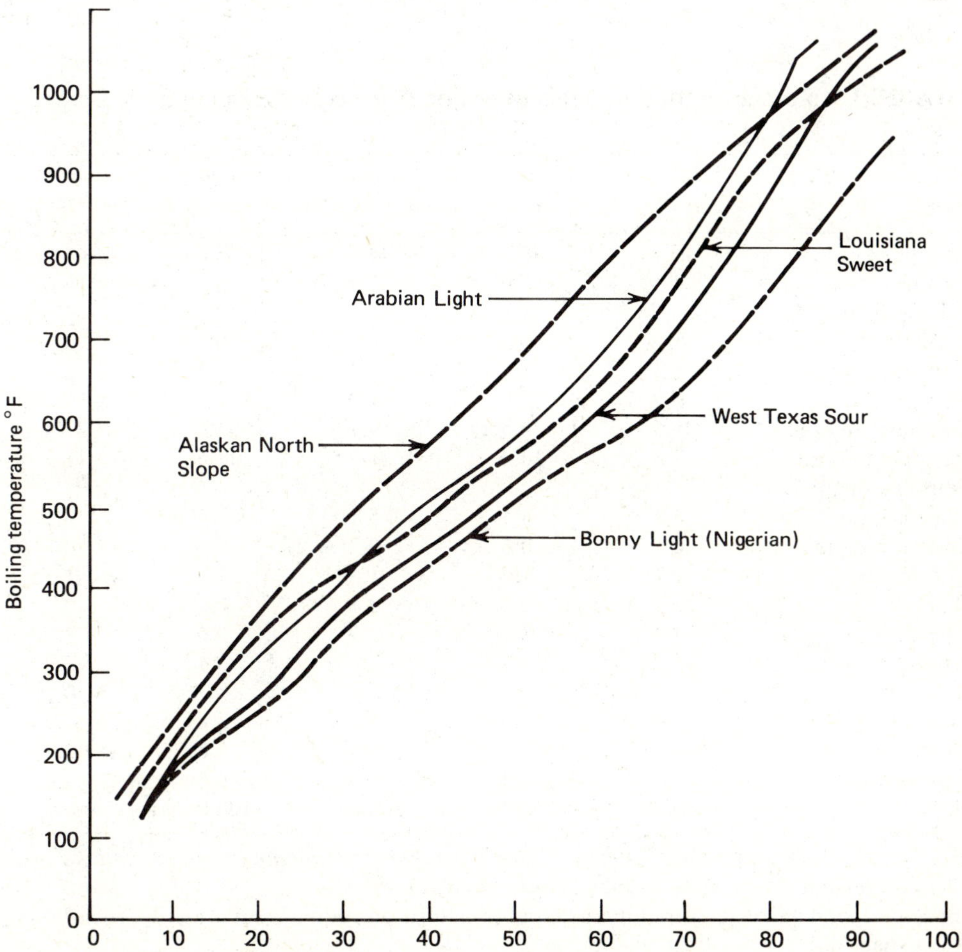

FIGURE 2. Distillation curves for some crude oils.

catalytic. Thermal cracking involves heating the residual from simple distillation, in a vacuum, to extremely high temperatures. Catalytic cracking involves using chemicals to force the residual to crack. Both processes are expensive and are most profitable when the refinery is using a lot of heavy crude oil.

There are many processes used to enhance the quality of a particular product. For example, virgin gasoline (i.e., gasoline produced from simple distillation techniques) is typically not high enough in octane to use commercially. Reforming and hydrogenization are chemical processes to raise that octane level. (They are used for other purposes too.) Desulfurization is another quality-enhancing process and involves removing sulfur from virgin products slated for immediate sale to the public and also those slated to undergo further processing. The removal of sulfur is important because sulfur has a tendency to destroy both catalysts and plant equipment and is a pollutent to the environment. The high cost of desulfurization is responsible for the discount demanded of most high sulfur crudes.

The previous description is meant as a brief introduction to refinery operations and nomenclature. Actual refinery operations are far more complex and involve many additional processes (e.g., alkyation and polymerization) than just dis-

TABLE 1. Percent Refinery Yields of Major Petroleum Products from Crude, U.S. Totals

Item	1982	1981	1980 (Percentages)	1979	1978
Gasoline[a]	46.2	44.5	44.5	43.0	44.1
Jet fuel	8.3	7.9	7.4	6.9	6.6
Ethane (including ethylene)	[b]	0.1	[b]	0.1	0.1
Liquefied gases	2.2	2.4	2.4	2.3	2.3
Kerosene	0.9	0.9	1.0	1.3	1.0
Distillate fuel oil	21.5	20.5	19.7	21.5	21.4
Residual fuel oil	8.8	10.4	11.7	11.5	11.3
Petrochemical feedstocks	3.4	4.5	5.1	4.7	4.1
Special napthas	0.4	0.6	0.7	0.6	0.7
Lubricants	1.2	1.3	1.3	1.3	1.3
Wax	0.1	0.1	0.1	0.1	0.1
Coke	3.4	3.1	2.7	2.6	2.5
Asphalt	2.7	2.7	2.9	3.1	3.2
Road oil	[b]	[b]	0.1	[b]	0.1
Still gas	4.6	4.5	4.0	3.8	3.7
Miscellaneous	0.7	0.7	0.8	0.8	0.9
Shortage	−4.4	−4.0	−4.4	−3.6	−3.4
Total[c]	100.0	100.0	100.0	100.0	100.0

Source: U.S. Department of Energy, *Crude Petroleum, Petroleum Products, and Natural Gas Liquids* and *Petroleum Supply Annual,* final summaries.

[a]Based on total gasoline output minus input of natural gas liquids and other hydrocarbons.

[b]Less than 0.05%.

[c]Totals may not sum due to rounding.

cussed. One way to appreciate this fact is to consider the range of products typically produced from a barrel of crude. Table 1 provides such a listing from 1978 and 1982. (Table 1 lists only the major products; actually, there are well over 2,000 separate petroleum-refined products.) Note how the product yields vary from year to year reflecting changing demand, technology, and crude slate.

The figures in Table 1 are aggregates and thus should not be taken to imply that each and every refinery produces these products, and in those quantities, on a regular basis. In fact, except for some of the very largest refineries (i.e., processing capacity in excess of 250,000 barrels of crude a day) most refineries are not equipped to produce all of these products. Production of the more obscure products is typically done by specialized refineries employing very specific types of crudes or product feedstock from a more conventional refinery.

CRUDE OIL[1]

Petroleum is this country's most important source of energy.[2] In addition to supplying energy products, crude petroleum is an important feedstock for a wide range of products, such as fertilizers, plastics, chemicals, and lubricants. Virtually every major industry in America today depends on petroleum in one form or another.

This section presents material on crude petroleum, including its grades and specifications, reserves, production, U.S. imports, demand, stocks, cash market transactions, and cash market structure. Much of the material on cash market transactions and structure is directly applicable to heating oil, gasoline, and propane.

GRADES AND SPECIFICATIONS. Crude oil is typically defined on the basis of three variables—field of origin, API gravity, and sulfur. While all three variables are important in characterizing a particular crude, the single most important variable is the crude oil's field of origin. The field of origin serves as a reference for many characteristics (such as pour point, viscosity, color, flash and fire points, distillation yields, and metallic contaminants), which are associated with that particular field and have been determined through previous analyses.

API gravity and specific gravity are inversely related, with "heavier" (i.e., denser) oils having a lower API gravity. Gravity is a good indication of the volume of various products that may be produced. Lighter crudes (high API gravity) produce larger amounts of the lighter products, such as gasoline. Sulfur (as a percent of weight) is important because of its contribution to pollution and destruction of catalysts and plant equipment.

For rough identification purposes, crude oil is often classed according to its sulfur content and API gravity. "Sweet" crudes are those with less than 0.5%

[1]A portion of the following section was written by the author for, and is part of, the CBT's application to the CFTC for permission to trade crude oil futures.

[2]According to the DOE, in 1981, petroleum accounted for nearly 45% of all U.S. total energy consumption, while natural gas, coal, and other sources of energy (e.g., hydroelectric, nuclear, and geothermal power) accounted for approximately 25, 20, and 10%, respectively. (See various issues of the *Monthly Energy Review*.)

sulfur (by weight), while "sour" crudes are those with more than 0.5% sulfur. "Light" crudes are generally those with an API gravity greater than 35°, while "heavy" crudes are those with an API gravity less than 24°.

Crude oils may also be grouped according to field similarities in refining properties, sulfur, and gravity. (Throughout the remainder of this chapter, "gravity" shall refer to API gravity.) The groupings are so well-defined and recognized throughout the petroleum industry that they constitute "commodities" and are traded as such. Some commodities come from a single large field, while many others represent groupings of numerous fields. Domestically, the four most widely traded commodities, which include numerous fields, are West Texas Sour (WTS), West Texas Intermediate (WTI), Light Louisiana Sweet (LLS), and Alaskan North Slope (ANS).

Figure 3 ranks a select group of domestic crude oils with some well-known foreign crudes on the basis of gravity and sulfur. Most of the major domestic fields are reported. The diagrams in Figure 3 must be interpreted very cautiously, however, since only two variables are shown and no allowance has been made for differences in distillation curves.

RESERVES OF CRUDE OIL. Petroleum reserves of the top 20 countries are given in Table 2. Middle Eastern countries account for more than 55% of the world's total reserves. Saudi Arabia surpasses all other countries with 24.7% of the world's total reserves.

PRODUCTION OF CRUDE OIL. Crude oil production is as much politically determined as it is economically determined. Much of this "politicalization" is due to OPEC which has effectively dictated total world production of petroleum since 1973. Many OPEC nations are extending this control to include the type of oil extracted. For example, Saudi Arabia allows only 65% of its total production to consist of its "marker," 34°, crude. The rest must consist of heavier crude oils. This ratio is consistent with Saudi Arabia's known reserves. The principal consequence of this policy (which is also helped by the fact that domestic fields are producing much heavier grades of crude) is that oil companies are forced to update their existing refining facilities to include more complex equipment for desulfurization and crude upgrading.

Table 3 provides 1982 production data for the top 15 producing countries. The OPEC countries supplied 35.3% of the world's total production for 1981. A little known fact is that the United States was once as great a producer of oil as all the Middle Eastern countries combined.[3] The United States is still one of three world giants (the USSR, 22.7%, and Saudi Arabia, 12.2%, are the other two) with 16.3% of the world's total oil production for 1982. Mexico is a distant fourth with only 5.2%. It is important to note that the individual production rates of countries vary enormously from year to year and the rankings and rates in Table 3 are constantly in a state of flux.

United States production of crude oil and lease condensate is given in Table 4, by state. (Lease condensate is a type of oil which has gaseous properties and is lighter than crude oil. It is drawn out of a natural gas well and generally

[3] *International Petroleum Encyclopedia,* 1980.

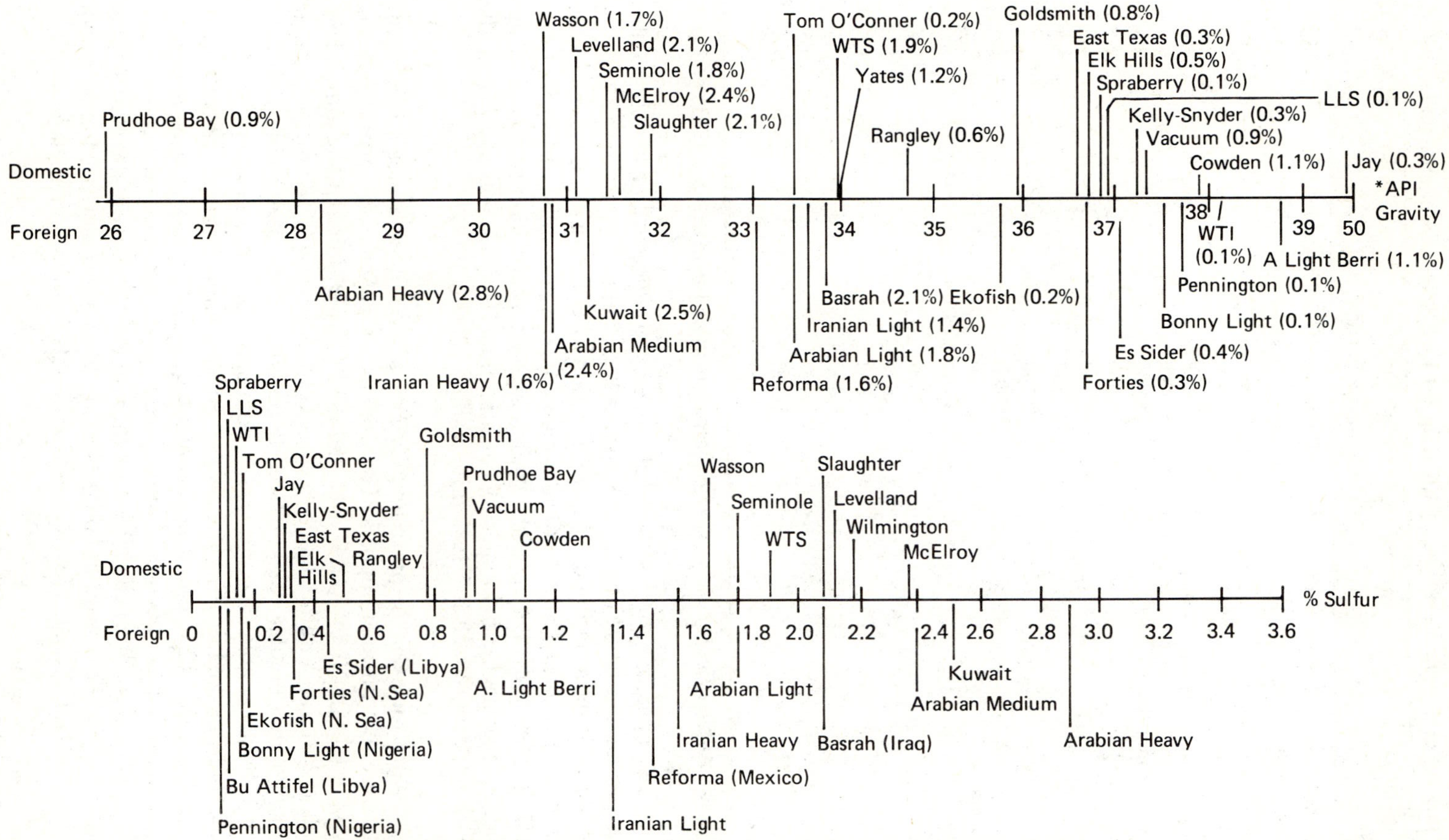

FIGURE 3. Crude oils by qualities. [*Sources:* *A Guide to World Crudes* and *Evaluations of World's Important Crudes* (both reprints of *Oil and Gas Journal* articles by the Petroleum Publishing Company); the Department of Energy's database of domestic crudes (Bartlesville, OK).]

TABLE 2. Petroleum Reserves of the Top 20 Countries, December 31, 1982

	Total (Millions of Barrels)	Percent of Total
Saudia Arabia	165,300	24.7
Kuwait	67,200	10.0
USSR	63,000	9.4
Iran	55,300	8.3
Mexico	48,300	7.2
Iraq	41,000	6.1
United Arab Emirates	32,400	4.8
USA	29,800	4.5
Venezuela	21,500	3.2
Libya	21,500	3.2
China	19,500	2.9
Nigeria	16,800	2.5
United Kingdom	13,900	2.1
Indonesia	9,600	1.4
Algeria	9,400	1.4
Canada	7,000	1.0
Norway	6,800	1.0
Qatar	3,400	0.5
India	3,400	0.5
Egypt	3,300	0.5
Total world	670,200	100.0

Source: *1982 Annual Energy Review,* U.S. Department of Energy, April 1983, p. 45.

represents a small percentage of the total crude oil produced domestically.) Table 5 reports production figures for the 25 largest U.S. fields.

Table 6 details information on the composition of U.S. crude oil supplies over the last few years. United States consumption fell approximately 7% in 1981 (after falling 8% in 1980 and 10% in 1979), while domestic production remained about the same. The decrease in domestic consumption for 1981 was mainly at the expense of imports, which fell 19% (after falling 20% in 1980).

U.S. Imports of Crude Oil. Approximately 29% of the United States's 1982 crude oil needs were met through imports. The principal suppliers were Mexico (20%), Saudi Arabia (16%), Nigeria (15%), Canada (14%), the United Kingdom (13%), Venezuela (12%), the Virgin Islands (9%), and Indonesia (7%). These percentage shares change on a regular basis, reflecting both economic and political factors. (Until 1982, Saudi Arabia was the U.S.'s dominant source of crude oil imports: its market share peaked in 1979 at 21%.) OPEC accounted for 61% of total U.S. imports, with Arab OPEC countries accounting for 24% of total U.S. imports.[4] (These percentages have been declining steadily over the past few years.)

Although some foreign crude oil enters the country throughout the states along the Atlantic and Pacific Coasts and on the Great Lakes, the majority enters through ports along the Gulf Coast. New Orleans accounts for the lion's share of these

[4]Data drawn from the latest issue of the U.S. Department of Energy's *Monthly Energy Review*.

TABLE 3. Average Crude Oil Production of Top 15 Countries, 1982 (1,000 barrels/day)

Country	Total	Cumulative Percent of Total
USSR	12,053	22.7
USA	8,671	39.0
Saudi Arabia	6,470	51.2
Mexico	2,749	56.4
Iran	2,214	60.6
United Kingdom	2,117	64.6
China	2,029	68.4
Venezuela	1,891	72.0
Indonesia	1,339	74.5
Nigeria	1,295	76.9
Canada	1,241	79.2
United Arab Emirates	1,214	81.5
Libya	1,158	83.7
Iraq	972	85.5
Kuwait	827	87.1
Total world	53,190	100.0

Source: Monthly Energy Review, U.S. Department of Energy, August 1983.

imports with 17.8% of the U.S. total for 1980. With the exception of Philadelphia (8.8%), all other major ports of entry (greater than 4% total imports) are located along the Gulf Coast: Beaumont (7.5%), Houston (7.1%), Corpus Christi (5.6%), Port Arthur (5.3%), Baton Rouge (5.1%), Freeport (4.4%), Galveston (4.2%), and Pascagoula (3.8%). The largest West Coast port of entry, Los Angeles, accounted for only 2.7% of the United States's total 1980 imports.[5]

DEMAND FOR CRUDE OIL. Various grades of crude oil are demanded on the basis of refinery specifications and consumer demand for refined products. To exploit obvious economies, most refineries are constructed to operate most efficiently with a limited range of crude oils. Shifts in the demand for certain refined products (e.g., away from gasoline and toward heating oil) will cause the refiner to use a different grade of crude, but only within the technological restrictions of the refiner's specific refinery.

In the United States, most oil refineries are located in a small number of geographic locations. This may be seen in Table 7 below which provides information on refinery runs. A small portion of foreign crude oil is refined at intermediate points and then shipped to the United States.

A major source of concern for oil companies is the recent trend of oil-producing countries (especially those belonging to OPEC) to build their own refineries. Apparently, these countries see this as a way to expand their market power in the long term with the hope that at some point in the future they may deal primarily in refined petroleum products rather than crude oil.

[5]CBT analysis using 1980 data supplied by I.P. Sharp, Incorporated.

TABLE 4. U.S. Production of Crude Oil and Lease Condensate (in Thousands of Barrels Daily)

	1982[a]	1981	1980	1979	1978	1977	1976	1975	1974	1973	Total[b] 1859–1982
District I[c]:	93	117	133	149	145	144	140	135	120	109	2,509,054
Total District I	93	117	133	149	145	144	140	135	120	109	2,509,054
District II:											
Illinois	72	66	62	60	63	71	72	71	76	84	3,195,769
Indiana	18	13	14	11	13	14	12	13	13	15	485,578
Kansas	195	180	164	156	153	158	160	162	169	181	5,044,310
Kentucky	18	18	16	15	15	18	21	21	21	24	670,912
Michigan	87	89	92	93	92	90	83	67	49	40	902,117
Nebraska	19	18	17	17	16	16	17	17	18	20	397,014
North Dakota	126	124	110	84	64	64	59	56	54	55	687,481
Ohio	37	37	35	35	34	33	32	32	26	24	896,285
Oklahoma	425	422	410	393	418	428	441	447	487	524	12,206,217
Others[d]	6	7	4	4	4	4	4	3	2	2	21,147
Total District II	1,013	974	924	863	872	396	901	889	915	969	24,506,830
District III:											
Alabama	56	57	61	52	53	50	40	37	36	33	283,440
Arkansas	51	50	50	52	56	55	49	45	45	49	1,529,079
Louisiana	1,252	1,231	1,283	1,355	1,460	1,542	1,686	1,796	2,018	2,278	17,718,146
Gulf Coast	1,155	1,135	1,194	1,267	1,363	1,441	1,581	1,693	1,911	2,168	—
Rest of state	97	96	89	88	97	101	105	103	107	110	—
Mississippi	95	94	98	105	110	118	126	127	139	154	1,779,173
New Mexico	194	196	206	217	230	239	251	259	267	276	3,693,488
Texas	2,536	2,589	2,672	2,776	2,948	3,117	3,251	3,347	3,454	3,546	46,862,903
Gulf Coast	465	482	484	488	651	686	725	765	813	793	—

West Texas	1,394	1,427	1,503	1,688	1,557	1,037	1,689	1,724	1,829	1,829	—
East Texas fld.	147	154	160	165	170	177	184	189	198	207	—
Rest of state	530	526	525	535	570	617	653	669	614	717	—
Total District III	4,184	4,217	4,370	4,557	4,857	5,121	5,403	5,611	5,959	6,336	71,866,229
District IV:											
Colorado	85	83	81	89	101	108	106	104	102	100	1,354,211
Montana	85	84	81	82	82	90	90	90	95	94	1,109,709
Utah	66	71	68	75	84	90	93	108	108	89	753,600
Wyoming	333	358	345	361	376	306	319	349	386	389	4,937,348
Total District IV	569	596	575	607	643	594	608	651	691	672	8,154,868
District V:											
Alaska	1,698	1,609	1,617	1,402	1,245	463	173	191	193	199	3,670,698
Arizona	1	1	1	1	1	1	2	2	2	2	19,086
California	1,095	1,055	975	966	935	958	892	883	884	921	19,594,012
Coast	209	185	160	169	172	186	189	200	207	216	—
Los Angeles region	222	222	227	242	259	280	308	337	344	363	—
San Joaquin	664	648	588	555	504	492	395	346	333	342	—
Nevada	2	2	2	3	3	2	—	—	—	—	8,740
Washington	—	—	—	—	—	—	—	—	—	—	12
Total District V	2,796	2,667	2,595	2,372	2,184	1,424	1,067	1,076	1,079	1,122	23,290,548
Total United States	8,655	8,572	8,597	8,553	8,701	8,179	8,119	8,362	8,764	9,208	130,327,529

Source: *Oil and Gas Journal*, January 31, 1983, p. 85.

[a]Preliminary.

[b]Thousands of barrels.

[c]Includes Florida, New York, Pennsylvania, Virginia, West Virginia.

[d]Includes Missouri, South Dakota, and Tennessee.

TABLE 5. Largest Domestic Fields

Domestic Field	Location[a]	1982 Production (1,000 Barrels)	Cumulative Percent of United States[b]
Prudhoe Bay	Alaska	560,665	17.8
Elk Hills	California	59,788	19.7
East Texas	Texas (6)	53,000	21.4
Wasson	Texas (8-A)	47,700	22.9
Yates	Texas (8)	46,512	24.4
Midway/Sunset	California	45,680	25.8
Kern River	California	44,607	27.2
Wilmington	California	38,617	28.4
Belridge South	California	35,634	29.5
Kuparuk	Alaska	32,672	30.5
Giddings	Texas (3)	31,000	31.5
Seminole	Texas (8-A)	29,196	32.4
Slaughter	Texas (8-A)	27,012	33.3
Kelly-Snyder	Texas (8-A)	23,508	34.0
Sho-Vel-Tom	Oklahoma	19,868	34.6
Levelland	Texas (8-A)	19,536	35.2
Vacuum	New Mexico	18,732	35.8
Tom O'Conner	Texas (2)	17,580	36.4
Jay	Florida	17,304	36.9
Spraberry Trend	Texas (8-A)	16,932	37.4
McArthur River	Alaska	15,946	37.9
Rangley	Colorado	15,300	38.4
Cowden (N)	Texas (8)	14,412	38.9
Hondo	California	13,452	39.3
Cowden (S)	Texas (8)	12,360	39.7

Source: *Oil and Gas Journal,* January 31, 1983, pp. 112–114.

[a]Texas is subdivided into 12 districts: Districts 8 and 8-A are in West Texas; District 10 is in the Panhandle; Districts 1, 7-B, 7-C, and 9 are in Central Texas; Districts 5 and 6 are in East Texas; and Districts 2, 3, and 4 are along the Texas Gulf Coast.

[b]Total U.S. production for 1982 is estimated at approximately 3,159 million barrels. *Source*: U.S. Department of Energy. *Monthly Energy Review*, June 1982.

STOCKS OF CRUDE OIL. There are three major systems used for storing crude oil (1) in tanks, (2) underground, and (3) in ships ("floating"). Commercial tanks vary in size from 100 to 1 million barrels, with an average being about 20,000 barrels.[6] Tanks are generally located at either the refinery, the well, the point of landing, the exporting port, or major terminaling points. Tank farms are huge tracts of land set with many tanks. These tanks are used for a wide variety of refined products, in addition to crude oil.

Underground storage may involve either the original well or an alternate well. The advantages of an alternate well are that it is often closer to the point of refining, less deep than the original well, and easier to extract oil from. Salt domes make excellent alternate wells and are currently used for storing oil for the Strategic Petroleum Reserve (SPR) program. The Louisiana Offshore Oil Port (LOOP)

[6]Information supplied by GATX Terminals Corporation.

TABLE 6. U.S. Crude Oil[a] Supply (Average, Thousand Barrels Per Day)

	1983[b]	1982	1981	1980	1979	1978	1977
Total production	8,669	8,649	8,572	8,597	8,552	8,707	8,245
Alaskan	1,713	1,696	1,609	1,617	1,401	1,229	464
Other		6,956	6,963	6,980	7,151	7,478	7,781
Stock withdrawal[c]		−157	−290	−97	−148	−79	−170
SPR[d]	−216	−174	−336	−45	−67	−163	−20
Other	−6	38	46	−52	−81	84	−150
Unaccounted-for crude		71	83	34	−11	−57	−6
Crude used directly and losses	NA	−62	−63	−28	−29	−30	−30
Total							
Total imports[e]	2,884	3,488	4,396	5,263	6,519	6,356	6,615
SPR	217	165	256	44	67	162	21
Other	2,667	3,323	4,141	5,219	6,452	6,195	6,594
Exports[f]		236	228	287	235	158	50
Total ending stocks[g]	688	644	594	466	430	376	348
SPR	332	294	230	108	91	67	7
Other primary	356	350	363	358	339	309	340
Total available for domestic use[h]			13,413	14,034	15,283	15,206	15,284

Source: U.S. Department of Energy, *Monthly Energy Review*, August 1983.
[a]Includes lease condensate.
[b]Data only up to June.
[c]A negative sign indicates a stock increase.
[d]SPR is Strategic Petroleum Reserve.
[e]Includes shipments from U.S. possessions and territories.
[f]Includes shipments to U.S. possessions and territories.
[g]Stocks as of December 31, except 1983, which is to June.
[h]Totals may not equal sum of components due to independent rounding.

TABLE 7. Refinery Runs by District

	Percent of Capacity 1982	1982[a]	Percent of Total 1981	1981	1980	1979	1978	1977	1976	1975	1974
						(Thousands of Barrels Daily)					
East Coast	70.5	1,106	9.7	1,202	1,300	1,478	1,537	1,496	1,415	1,250	1,246
Appalachian District 1	95.9	94	1.0	132	158	167	180	178	170	158	163
Total District 1	72.0	1,200	10.7	1,334	1,458	1,645	1,717	1,674	1,585	1,408	1,409
Appalachian District 2	77.3	51	0.4	54	51	65	60	65	62	57	57
Illinois, Indiana, Kentucky	71.0	1,705	14.5	1,803	2,070	2,353	2,425	2,406	2,286	2,180	2,141
Minnesota, Wisconsin, Dakota	86.0	252	1.8	229	238	294	279	267	257	238	222
Oklahoma, Kansas,				823							
Montana	88.9	763	7.0		945	1,017	1,044	1,040	995	937	912
Total District 2	76.6	2,771	23.7	2,969	3,304	3,729	3,808	3,778	3,600	3,412	3,332
Texas											
Inland	77.5	459	3.7	469	445	472	476	477	462	432	420
Gulf Coast	68.6	2,739	22.9	2,829	3,151	3,462	3,524	3,442	3,102	2,884	2,835
Louisiana Gulf	70.9	1,935	16.3	2,030	2,091	2,167	2,140	2,158	1,903	1,709	1,631
North Louisiana, Arkansas	52.2	164	1.4	163	186	200	214	196	161	155	155
New Mexico	66.7	78	0.6	81	87	89	84	87	81	80	62
Total District 3	69.4	5,375	44.9	5,572	5,960	6,390	6,438	6,360	5,717	5260	5,103
Total District 4	75.6	418	3.4	425	442	477	488	469	442	426	420
Total District 5	65.2	2,011	17.3	2,171	2,354	2,405	2,288	2,324	2,072	1,936	1,869
Total United States	70.2	11,775	100.0	12,471	13,518	14,646	14,739	14,605	13,416	12,442	12,133

Source: Oil and Gas Journal, January 31, 1983, p. 90.
[a]Preliminary; thousands of barrels daily.

also has plans to use eight such caverns, with an average 4 million barrels storage capacity each. These storage facilities will be used primarily for foreign crudes and will be available to firms using LOOP's facilities for off-loading foreign, imported crudes.

Floating storage generally involves using tank ships which may or may not be anchored. During periods of glut (as in the first half of 1982), it is not unusual to have a vessel steam at less than a normal speed. This economizes on limited storage at home, saves transportation fuel, and grants the owner greater flexibility should the owner decide to market that oil in the spot market. With a VLCC (very large crude carrier) or ULCC (ultralarge crude carrier), storage costs are currently competitive with some onshore facilities (between $\frac{1}{2}$ and $\frac{3}{4}$ cents per barrel, per day).

In October 1977 the United States began filling its Strategic Petroleum Reserve as provided for in the Energy Policy and Conservation Act of 1975. At the end of June 1983, the SPR stood at about 332 million barrels. Because of the recent oil glut, the SPR has been taking on oil at a record rate. Most of this oil is stored in PAD III, particularly, Texas and Louisiana. (There are currently five major sites, all salt domes in the Gulf Coast, at Bryan Mound, West Hackberry, Bayou Choctaw, Weeks Island, and Sulfur Mines.) The SPR is now facing serious legislative difficulties with respect to funding and provisions for allocation in the event the oil is actually needed.

Table 8 gives yearly information, by PAD district, of domestic and foreign crude oil stocks within the United States, as of January of the years 1980, 1981, and 1982. Stocks have been increasing over the last few years. PAD III surpasses all other areas with a consistent average of 36% of total U.S. domestic stocks and 13% of total U.S. foreign stocks. Unlike stocks of refined products, stocks of crude oil do not exhibit strong seasonal patterns.

In 1980, the majority of U.S. crude oil stocks (67.4%) were located at tank farms and pipelines, while most of the rest (28.4%) were at refineries. PAD Dis-

TABLE 8. Crude Stocks of Domestic and Foreign Oil in the United States as of January 1st (Thousands of Barrels)

		PAD Districts					
		I	II	III	IV	V	Total United States
1980	Domestic	4,968	63,885	114,447	16,266	50,578[a]	343,167
	Foreign	15,602	26,659	41,746	1,377	7,644	
1981	Domestic	5,555	68,816	129,884	16,712	57,442[a]	374,581
	Foreign	14,445	21,891	48,860	564	10,412	
1982	Domestic	5,516	69,056	125,182	14,091	72,321[a]	366,441
	Foreign	15,578	15,096	40,874	761	7,966	
1983	Domestic	4,917	64,288	120,783	11,725	76,493[a]	626,690
	Foreign	13,151	11,926	39,162	1,416	4,623	

Source: Oil and Gas Journal, various annual summary issues.
[a]Includes Alaskan oil in transit.

tricts I and V were notable exceptions in that a majority of oil was stored at refineries, while PAD II stocks were fairly evenly split between refineries (52%) and tank farms and pipelines (46%).[7]

CASH MARKET TRANSACTIONS. Transactions (including swaps, trades, exchanges, and the like) in crude oil are numerous and it is not unusual for a single barrel of crude to be traded many times before it is finally refined. There are many factors which encourage transactions in crude oil. First, there is typically an imbalance between what producers produce and what refiners need. Second, even if a company produced enough crude oil to meet its individual refining needs, it would probably be of the wrong quality. Refineries are built to run most efficiently with a limited range of crudes. Rather than force the refinery's equipment to operate inefficiently, the refiner/producer will normally trade undesirable crude for the specific type of crude the refinery handles best. The trade does not necessarily have to be for higher-quality oil either. For example, if the refiner had a high-gravity, low-sulfur oil and the refinery was built to handle middle- to low-gravity, high-sulfur crudes, the refiner could probably profit from trading the crude, depending on the premium the market placed on that crude.

Sometimes it is not a question of quality, but of location and timing; that is, trading may allow a refiner/producer to get the same type of oil more cheaply by avoiding storage and/or transportation costs. Trades of this nature are often called "swaps."

CASH MARKET STRUCTURE. Members of the petroleum industry are typically divided into two classes—majors and independents. Originally, the majors were seven very large, vertically integrated oil companies that dominated the U.S. and world markets for crude oil and refined products. The "seven sisters" were Standard Oil of New Jersey (Exxon), Mobil, Standard Oil of California (Socal), Gulf, Texaco, Royal Dutch Shell, and British Petroleum (BP). An eighth company, Compagnie Francaise de Petroles (CFP), was often added to this list. These companies were all active in the production, transportation, storage, refining, distribution, and marketing aspects of the petroleum industry, and continue to be today. While these companies are still the dominant members of the industry, many new names have been added to the list of majors, including Atlantic Richfield (ARCO), Getty, Continental (Conoco), Phillips, and Standard Oil of Indiana (Amoco).

"Independent" is a term which is often used to refer to an oil company involved principally with one aspect of the industry. Originally, the independents were producers, refiners, distributors, and marketers who bought (or sold) excess crude and refined products from the majors. Often they were local or regional and were not viewed as a major source of competition to the majors. This aspect of the oil industry changed radically with the increased politicalization of the industry and the emergence of OPEC. Independents which had previously been dependent on the majors for their supplies began to actively search for and develop their own supplies. (The majors also had less excess crude and refined products to sell.) Integration into other aspects of the petroleum industry followed and today the distinction between major and independent is much less important.

[7]U.S. Department of Energy, *Crude Petroleum, Petroleum Products, and Natural Gas Liquids*, 1980, p. 10.

FUTURES CONTRACTS PROPOSED. At this writing only the Chicago Board of Trade and the New York Mercantile Exchange are trading crude oil contracts. The Chicago Mercantile Exchange, the Cotton Exchange, the International Petroleum Exchange, and the New Orleans Exchange are all thought to be developing crude oil contracts. The salient features of the CBT's and NYMEX's proposed contracts are shown in Table 9.

HEATING OIL

Heating oil represents nearly 17% of the products produced from a typical barrel of crude oil. Known also as No. 2 fuel oil or as gas oil, heating oil is an important source of energy for the residential and commercial sectors of the U.S. economy.

This section presents material on various aspects of the cash market for heating oil, including supply, demand, and the structure of the cash market. A comparison of the various futures contracts, trading and proposed, is also provided.

GRADES AND SPECIFICATIONS. Heating oil is part of a broader group of petroleum products called distillates. (It represents about 85% of the "distillate family.") In terms of the temperature at which they are produced (350–800°F) distillates represent the middle range of petroleum-refined products. Refiners typically divide distillates into two groups: No. 1 oil and No. 2 oil. (A third group, No. 4 oil is sometimes added, but the amount of this oil produced is minimal.) No. 1 oil includes kerosene, while No. 2 oil includes diesel fuel oil and heating oil. It is not unusual, however, for data to identify distillate solely on the basis of No. 2 oil and to class No. 1 oil separately as kerosene. For convention, the latter definition is used here.

Heating oil and diesel fuel are very close substitutes, varying slightly in cetane (a measure of fuel performance in the engine) and sulfur. While most diesel fuel can be burned as heating oil, the converse is typically not true. Most data do not distinguish distillate production on the basis of quality, but rather on the basis of demand. Estimates by U.S. Department of Energy (DOE), however, suggest that approximately 85% of all distillates qualify as heating oil.

Heating oil, like most refined products and many crude oils, is commonly shipped via pipeline commingled with oils of all one type (i.e., in a common stream). To preserve the integrity of all the oils in a particular batch, the pipeline must set rigid standards for the quality of the product to be shipped in that stream. While the standards set by most pipelines are the same (following standards common to the industry and in accordance with standards suggested by the American Society for Testing and Materials, ASTM), there are exceptions. Exceptions are often based on regional differences in the quality of product demanded. Colonial Pipeline provides the most widely recognized standards for refined products.

It is interesting to note that standards for heating oil vary across countries too. For example, the United States has more stringent air pollution laws than most of Europe and thus, most heating oil produced in this country has a sulfur content of less than 0.2% versus 0.3% in Europe. (Heating oil is more commonly known as gas oil in Europe.)

TABLE 9. Comparison of Crude Petroleum Futures Contracts[a]

Contract Highlights	CBT	NYMEX
Unit of Trading	1,000 barrels (42,000 gal) per contract	1,000 barrels (42,000 gal) per contract
Price Basis	F.O.B. the Capline System in St. James, Louisiana or F.O.B. seller's designated port facility in either St. James, St. John the Baptist, St. Charles, Jefferson, Orleans, St. Bernard, and Plaquemines Parishes, Louisiana. Prices quoted in dollars and cents per barrel.	F.O.B. buyer's designated pipeline storage facility in Cushing, Oklahoma. Prices quoted in dollars and cents per barrel. Contract A is for a light, sweet crude, while Contract B is for a heavy, sour crude.[b]
Delivery options	Buyer shall choose a pipeline delivery (at the Capline System in St. James, Louisiana) or a nonpipeline delivery (at the seller's designated port facility). Nonpipeline deliveries shall be into buyer's barge or tanker, or by any of the following methods, if seller's designated facility allows—into shoreside tankage, by "pump-over," or by "book-transfer."	Buyer chooses the pipeline storage facility to receive oil at. Seller can deliver oil to buyer's designated pipeline facility in any manner acceptable to that pipeline. In addition to having oil delivered into a pipeline's storage facilities, a buyer may also specify one of the following methods of deliveries, if the involved facilities so permit—"book-transfer," "pump-over," or delivery into the designated pipeline.
Standard origin	Domestic crude petroleum produced in Southern Louisiana, crude petroleum from the LOOP's Segregation Number 1, or foreign crude petroleum with one of the following stream designations: Bonny Light, Brass River, Ekofish, Escravos, Qua Iboe, Saharan blend, and Zarzaitine.	Not specified
Sulfur (by weight)	50% maximum	Contract A: 0.50% maximum Contract B: 1.0–2.0%
Gravity (API at 60°)	35.0° minimum	Contract A: 35.0°–45.0° Contract B: 25.0°–35.0°

TABLE 9. *(Continued)*

Contract Highlights	CBT	NYMEX
Pour point	55°F maximum for summer and 33°F maximum for other months.	Contracts A and B: 50°F maximum
Viscosity	325 SUS maximum at 100°F	Contracts A and B: 550 SUS maximum at 60°F
Reid vapor pressure	9.5 psi maximum at 100°F	Contracts A and B: 9.5 psi maximum at 100°F
Water and sediment (by volume)	1.0% maximum	Contracts A and B: 1.0% maximum
Quality differentials	$0.02 per barrel premium per degree, or fraction thereof, above 35° and up to 40°	Par specified at bottom of quality ranges (both contracts). Payment adjusted upward by $0.15 per barrel for each full degree API above 25° and $0.02 per barrel for each full degree API above 35°. There is no adjustment for gravity above 40° API. Payment adjusted upward $0.03 per barrel for each 0.1% sulfur above par.
Price fluctuations	Minimum—$0.01 per barrel ($10 per contract) Maximum—$1 per barrel ($1,000 per contract)	Minimum—$0.01 per barrel ($10 per contract) Maximum—$1 per barrel ($1,000 per contract)
Last day of trading	Second business day prior to the 15th calendar day of the month prior to delivery	Seventh business day prior to the 25th calendar day of the month prior to delivery
Payment	By 2:00 p.m. of the second business day following seller's receipt of documents attesting to title transfer and the quality and quantity of crude oil delivered	By 12:00 noon of the 20th calendar day of month following delivery of the crude oil

[a]Consult exchanges for most recent contract terms.
[b]The NYMEX has yet to receive approval on its sour crude contract.

SOURCES OF SUPPLY. Even though the United States imports a substantial amount of foreign crude oil, most of its refined products are produced domestically. For example, during 1982 the United States imported only 33 million barrels of distillate or about 3.5% of the total distillate used domestically. This was down sharply from 7% in 1977. These and other figures concerning distillate fuel oil supply are provided below in Table 10. (As indicated earlier, distillate production data is rarely disaggregated.)

Refineries typically do not alter product yields in the short and medium run to exploit seasonal and temporary changes in demand. Instead, refineries usually alter the quantity of crude oil refined, in addition to draw-downs and buildups of their inventory. Of these two methods, inventory management is the most important, as may be seen in Figures 4 and 5. Distillate stocks typically reach a peak in October and November at the start of the home heating season and reach a trough in February and March when demand for heating oil is coming to an end. June and July mark the beginning of "summer-fill" programs, when refineries prepare for the upcoming season.

DEMAND. The market for distillates is strongly regional and seasonal in demand. This is understandable considering that the principal use for distillates is for the production of heat. Figure 6 provides a more detailed breakdown of distillate demand on the basis of use. (Remember that about 85% of distillate production may be classified as heating oil.)

As a primary source of heat, heating oil competes chiefly with electricity and natural gas; it also competes with coal and liquefied petroleum gas (LPG), but to a much lesser extent. Table 11 provides data on the proportion of U.S. homes which are heated with oil, electricity, natural gas, and various other fuels. In 1979 approximately 55% of all homes were heated with natural gas while 20 and 17% were heated with fuel oil and electricity, respectively. While the relative proportion of homes heated with natural gas has remained virtually unchanged since 1970, fuel oil has lost substantial market share (from 26 to 20%) to electricity (from 8 to 17%). It is important to note that the relative proportion held by each

TABLE 10. Distillate Fuel Oil Supply (Average, Thousands of Barrels Daily)

	1983[a]	1982	1981	1980	1979	1978	1977
Total production	2,273	2,606	2,613	2,662	3,153	3,167	3,278
Crude used directly	NA	10	10	1	1	1	1
Stock withdrawal	395	35	38	64	−34	93	−176
Total	2,668	2,651	2,585	2,599	3,188	3,075	3,455
Imports	90	93	173	142	193	173	250
Exports	87	74	5	3	3	3	1
Ending stocks[b]	112	179	192	205	229	216	186
Total available for domestic use	2,783	2,849	2,945	2,943	3,607	3,461	3,954

Source: U.S. Department of Energy, *Monthly Energy Review,* August 1983.
[a]Data only up to June.
[b]Stocks data for end of year.

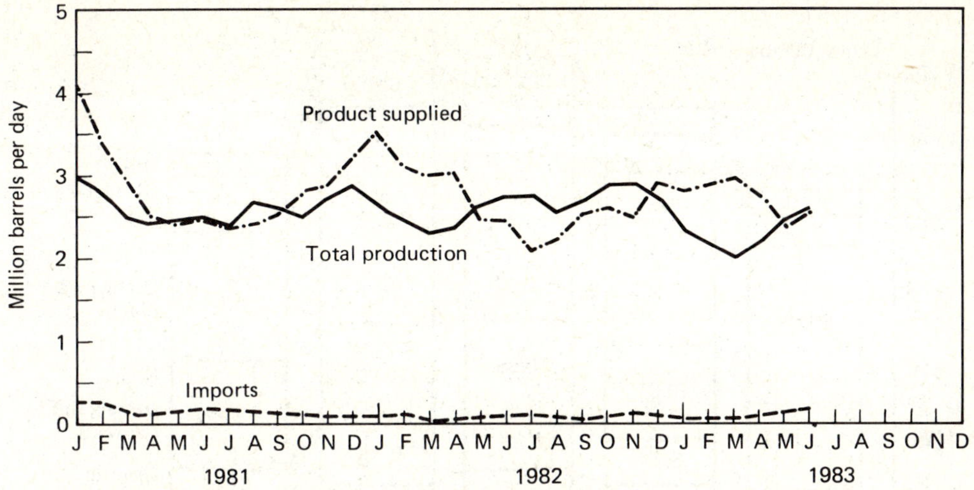

FIGURE 4. Heating oil supply. (*Source*: U.S. Department of Energy, *Monthly Energy Review*, various issues.)

fuel varies substantially from region to region depending on relative price and availability. For example, heating oil accounted for about 54% of the market in the Northeast during 1979, while it held less than 5% in the West for the same year.

Conversion costs are also an important determinant of which fuel the consumer chooses to heat the home with. Many consumers converted their furnaces to gas during the 1970s as a result of sharply rising heating oil costs and encouragement from the federal government. This trend is likely to slow or even reverse in the near future as natural gas prices are decontrolled and allowed to rise to more realistic levels. Of course, to the extent that heating oil is a refined petroleum

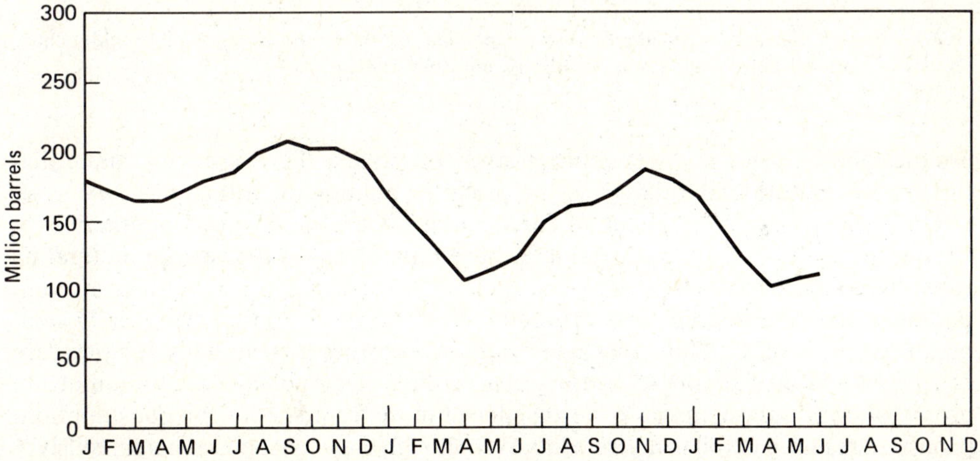

FIGURE 5. Heating oil stocks.

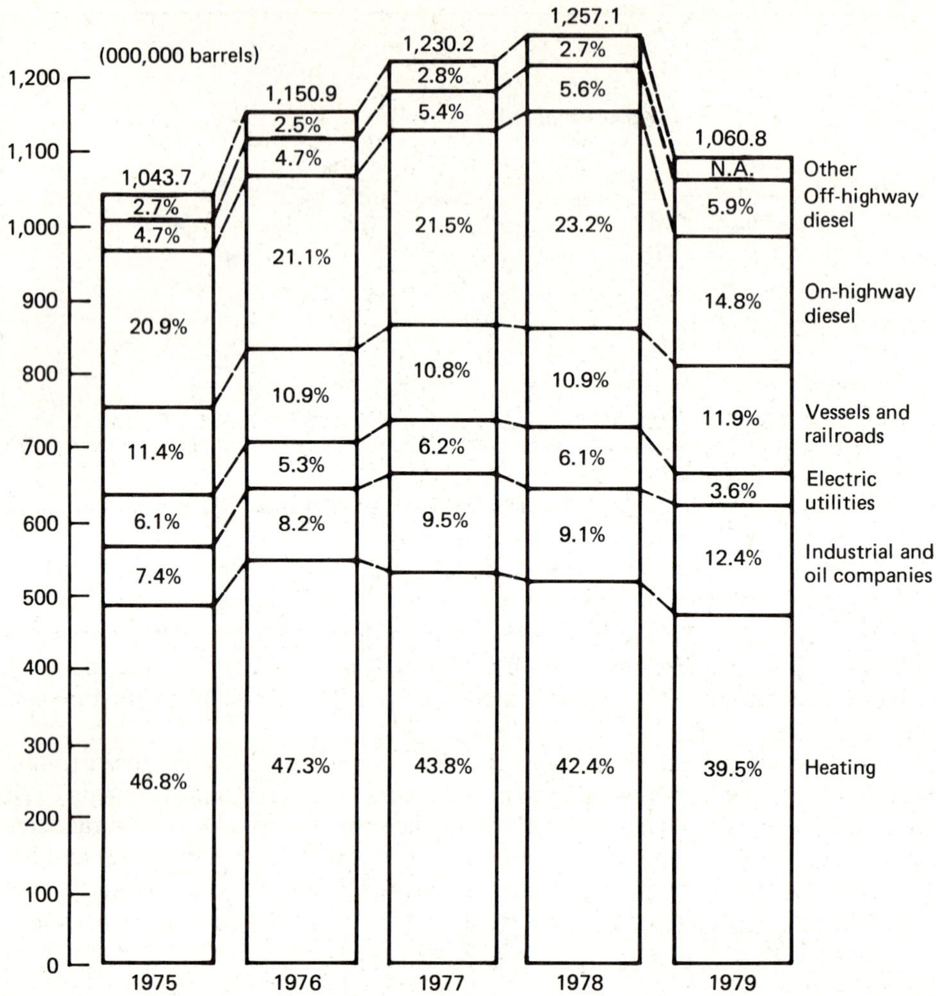

(a)

FIGURE 6. (*a*) Sales of distillate by use as percent of total. (*b*) Heating oil weekly chart. (*Source*: National Petroleum News, *Fact Book*, mid-June 1981, p. 73.)

product and its price is dependent on crude oil prices, there is no guarantee that the price of natural gas relative to the price for heating oil will rise.

On an absolute level, demand for heating oil can be seen as a function of temperature. Obviously, as the temperature falls, demand for heating oil (and its substitutes) increases. Degree days are relative measurements of outdoor air temperature. Heating degree days are defined as the deviation of mean daily temperature below 65°F. Thus a weather station reporting a mean daily temperature of 20°F would also report 45 heating degree days. Degree days are an important proxy for consumer demand in the absence of more frequent data on consumption. (Consumers purchase oil in discrete lots even though they consume oil continuously.)

CASH MARKET TRANSACTIONS. Transactions in the heating oil cash market are really no different than those in the crude oil cash market: Swaps and exchange

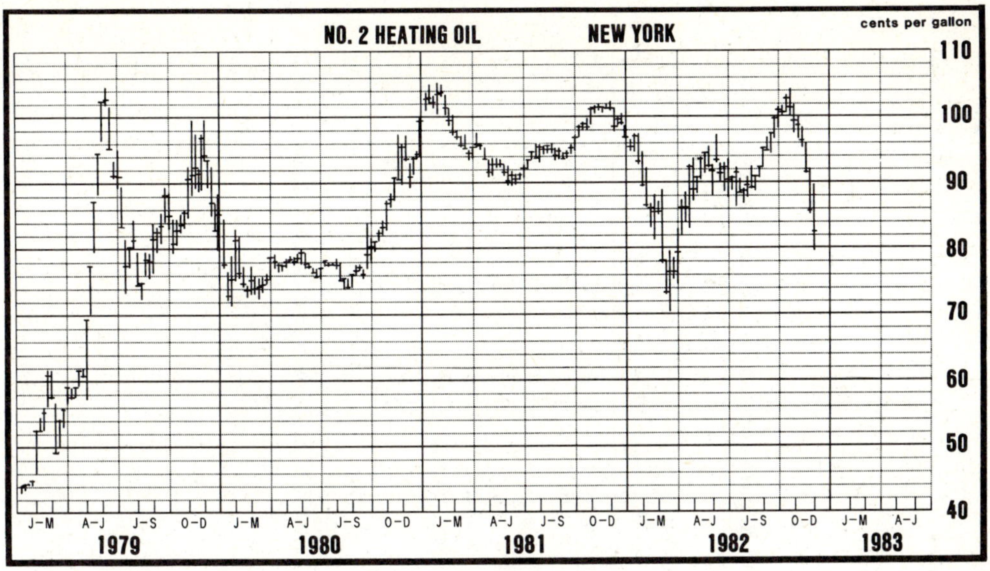

(b)

FIGURE 6. Continued.

and supply agreements are commonplace. What distinguishes the heating oil market, and the gasoline market too for that matter, is the diversity of the distribution network and the sheer number of market participants.

There are many patterns of heating oil (and gasoline) distribution, depending on the location of the market and the nature of its wholesalers and consumers. Bulk terminals, stations, and plants provide a necessary link between wholesalers (or large consumers) and refineries. A bulk terminal is generally any facility with storage capacity in excess of 50,000 barrels, while a station is a facility with less capacity. Bulk plants are normally smaller than bulk stations, although there is no widely accepted distinction. Bulk terminals and stations may be owned and operated by a refinery or by an independent firm. Refineries intending to sell a product under their own name will often own and operate the terminal and any station necessary to further distribute the product. In addition to performing an important distribution function, terminals (independent and branded) account for a substantial portion of the stocks which are maintained throughout the system.

Independently owned bulk terminals and stations generally buy directly from a refinery or importer and sell to large industrial users (or utilities), jobbers, and independent oil dealers. From the jobbers and independent oil dealers the oil may be either resold or may be distributed on a retail basis to the ultimate consumers.

HEATING OIL FUTURES. Prior to 1982, only the New York Mercantile Exchange and International Petroleum Exchange (IPE) (London, England) offered futures contracts in heating oil. Since then the Chicago Board of Trade has introduced its own futures in heating oil but with very limited success. Table 12 provides a comparison of the various contracts offered. The contracts vary substantially and individuals desiring to spread the various contracts are well-advised to study the differences carefully. The IPE and CBT contracts call for receipt delivery, while the NYMEX contracts call for physical delivery of the oil. The

TABLE 11. Residential Fuel Consumption, by Fuel Type and Region (Amounts in Percentages)

Type of Fuel	Total United States 1979	Total United States 1970	South 1979	South 1970	North Central 1979	North Central 1970	Northeast 1979	Northeast 1970	West 1979	West 1970
Utility gas	55.1	55.2	47.1	50.0	70.2	66.8	38.3	37.1	67.2	71.1
Bottled, tank or LPG	5.3	6.0	8.9	10.9	6.3	6.3	0.7	1.1	2.9	3.8
Fuel oil[a]	19.9	26.0	12.5	18.9	13.2	19.6	52.9	54.3	4.8	8.8
Electricity	16.9	7.7	27.6	13.2	9.1	3.1	6.5	3.1	20.9	11.7
Coal or coke	0.5	2.9	0.6	3.2	0.3	3.3	0.8	3.5	0.1	0.7
Wood	1.4	0.1	2.5	2.9	0.7	0.4	0.7	0.2	1.6	1.3
Other fuel	0.1	0.4	[b]	0.2	0.2	0.5	0.1	0.7	0.2	0.4
None	0.7	0.6	0.8	0.6	0.1	0.1	0.1	0.1	2.2	2.2
Survey sample	78,572	63,445	25,585	19,585	20,565	17,536	17,123	15,483	15,299	11,169

Source: Data adapted from the *1979 Annual Housing Survey*, Bureau of the Census, U.S. Department of Commerce.
[a]Includes kerosene.
[b]Less than 0.1%.

TABLE 12. Comparison of Heating Oil Futures Contracts[a]

Contract Highlights	IPE	NYMEX	CBT
Unit of trading	100 metric tons (=735.7 barrels or 30,898 gal)	1,000 barrels (=42,000 gal or 138.95 metric tons)	1,000 barrels (=42,000 gal or 138.95 metric tons)
Price basis	F.O.B. approved facilities in Amsterdam, Rotterdam, or Antwerp. Prices quoted in U.S. dollars and cents per ton.	F.O.B. seller's exshore facility in the New York Harbor area into buyer's barge or tanker. If seller's facility permits, delivery may also be completed, at buyer's option, by truck ($0.25/gal surcharge), book transfer, or interfacility or intrafacility transfers. Prices quoted in U.S. dollars and cents per gallon.	F.O.B. barge or pipeline (Colonial, Texas Eastern, or Explorer) in Harris, Galveston, or Jefferson Counties, Texas. Prices quoted in U.S. dollars and cents per gallon.
Standards[b]			
Gravity	34° minimum	30° minimum	30° minimum
Sulfur	0.3% maximum	0.2% maximum	0.2% maximum
Water, sediment	Unspecified	0.05% maximum	0.05% maximum
Viscosity	Unspecified	Kinematic, centistokes at 100°F-minimum 2.0, maximum 3.6	Kinematic, centistokes at 100°F-minimum 2.0, maximum 3.6
Pour point	−9°C	−18°C	−18°C

TABLE 12. *(Continued)*

Contract Highlights	IPE	NYMEX	CBT
Delivery tolerance	For deliveries involving up to 500 warrants: 1%; for deliveries involving more: 0.5%	5% (50 barrels) per contract	For waterborne deliveries of 1,000–5,000 barrels: 1.0%.
Trading months	Nine consecutive months including the current month	15 consecutive months including the current month	An 18-month cycle, which includes the current month, the next 4 months, plus the remaining even-numbered months
Minimum price fluctuation	$0.25 per metric ton ($25 per contract)	.01¢ per gallon ($4.20 per contract)	.025¢ per gallon ($10.50 per contract)
Maximum price fluctuation	$300 per metric ton ($3,000 per contract)	$0.02 per gallon ($840 per contract)	$0.03 per gallon ($1,260 per contract)
Delivery instrument	Warrant receipt	Wet barrels	Depository receipt
Trading hours	3:30 a.m.–6:30 a.m. and 8:45 p.m.–12:20 p.m. Chicago time	9:00 a.m.–1:45 p.m. Chicago time	9:45 a.m.–2:30 p.m. Chicago time
Last trading day	Last business day of the delivery month	Last business day of the month preceding the delivery month	Third to last business day of the delivery month

[a]Consult exchanges for most recent contract terms.
[b]IPE and NYMEX standards are exchange-specified, while CBT standards are given by Colonial Pipeline.

CBT and NYMEX contracts call for heating oil with similar characteristics, while IPE heating oil is higher in gravity and sulfur. The CBT contract calls for a fairly narrow delivery area versus a much larger delivery area for the NYMEX's Gulf Coast contract. The CBT and NYMEX contracts also call for contracts in 1,000 barrel lots versus the IPE contract which specifies a 100-metric-ton lot. These and other factors (in addition to any differences in market liquidity) have important implications for potential spreaders and arbitrageurs of these contracts.

GASOLINE

Gasoline accounts for the lion's share of refined products produced from a typical barrel of crude. In fact, the desire to maximize gasoline production is often credited with providing the incentive for many of the improvements which have been made in petroleum refining techniques.[8]

This section presents material on various aspects of the gasoline market, including grades and specifications, supply, demand, and cash market structure. This section concludes with a brief comparison of the various futures contracts offered for trading gasoline.

GRADES AND SPECIFICATIONS. As nearly every motorist knows, there are primarily four grades of gasoline: leaded regular, leaded premium, unleaded regular, and unleaded premium.[9] The two most important quality variables are vapor pressure and octane. "Vapor pressure is a measure of the surface pressure it takes to keep a liquid from vaporizing."[10] The vapor pressure must be sufficiently high to allow the car to start in cold weather but not so high that the gasoline vaporizes too easily resulting in a condition called "vapor lock." Octane is a measure of how much "engine knock" a gasoline produces. The higher the percentage of isooctane (a pure chemical compound, C_8H_{18}) the less knock. By lowering a car's compression ratio (the ratio of cylinder volume before and after ignition) it is possible to use lower octane gasolines. For much of the 1950s and 1960s, retailers used octane ratings as part of their marketing programs, much in the same way that they used prices and services. Today, with sharply escalating prices, consumers are concerned more with prices and availability. New cars also do not need high-octane-rated gasolines because of engineering advances which have made low-compression engines more common.

The development of two separate groupings of gasoline, leaded and unleaded, is a reflection of government restrictions on automobile emissions. These restrictions require the use of catalytic converters and force new automobiles to burn only unleaded gasoline. Originally, refiners added lead (usually tetraethyl, TEL, or tetramethyl, TML) to raise the octane rating of the gasoline. To produce

[8]Some petroleum economists believe that during the 1980s, there will be significant innovations in the handling and processing of sour crudes. Such innovations will be necessary if refiners are to continue current product yields.

[9]What constitutes "premium" gasoline varies from year to year. A commonly used benchmark in 1981 was an octane rating greater than 91.

[10]W. L. Leffler, *Petroleum Refining for the Non-Technical Person,* Penn Well Publishing Company, Tulsa, OK, 1979, p. 88.

TABLE 13. Finished Motor Gasoline Supply (Average, Thousand Barrels per Day)

	1983[a]	1982	1981	1980	1979	1978	1977
Total production	6,163	6,338	6,405	6,506	6,852	7,169	7,033
Stock withdrawal	94	25	28	−66	2	54	−72
Total	6,069	6,313	6,377	6,572	6,850	7,115	7,105
Imports	224	197	157	140	181	190	217
Exports	5	20	2	1	(s)[c]	1	2
Ending stocks[b]	222	235	253	261	237	238	258
Total available for domestic use	6,510	6,725	6,785	6,972	7,268	7,542	7,578

Source: U.S. Department of Energy, *Monthly Energy Review,* August 1983, p. 40.
[a]Data only up to June.
[b]Stocks data for end of year; includes motor gasoline blending components.
[c](s) = less than 500 barrels per day.

unleaded gasoline today, with a sufficiently high octane rating, refiners often employ advanced reforming techniques. These techniques (along with blending) are part of a refiner's normal operations to achieve specific standards in octane, vapor pressure, and many other quality characteristics.

The total unleaded market has grown substantially from 1975 when federal controls first came into effect. Today, this market accounts for just over 54% of the total gasoline market.[11] Projections call for this portion to continue increasing (at between 3 and 5% a year) as older cars are continually replaced by newer ones. The unleaded premium market is still in its infancy (less than 1% in 1981) but should eventually grow to capture most of the market covered by leaded premium now (about 3% in 1981, down from 4.3% in 1970).[12]

SUPPLY. Table 13 provides basic supply data on gasoline. In 1980, the United States imported only 2% worth of its gasoline needs, compared to 3% in 1979 and 1978. Total gasoline usage in 1980 was down 6% from 1979 which was down 5% from 1978. Currently, 1981 usage is about equal to that for 1980. Forecasts are highly dependent upon the existence of a recession.

DEMAND. Gasoline is used almost exclusively for transportation purposes. As many consumers will verify and as was shown clearly with the gas lines in 1973, gasoline demand is relatively inelastic (i.e., unresponsive to price) in the short run. In the longer run, gasoline demand is much more elastic, as many OPEC countries have discovered.

For cars already on the road, the only alternative to gasoline is conversion to an alternative fuel such as LPG. Such alternate fuels are imperfect substitutes, however, since their prices are often as closely tied to crude oil prices as are gasoline prices and are more likely to have availability problems. The conversion costs can also be substantial. Consumers purchasing new cars have much more

[11]See the U.S. Department of Energy's latest issue of the *Monthly Energy Review.*

[12]National Petroleum News, *Fact Book,* Annual 1982 Issue, p. 106.

flexibility in the type of fuel they burn and many are choosing cars which burn the relatively cheaper diesel fuel. Table 14 shows that the gasoline's share of the market for motor fuel has steadily declined from 96% in 1960 to 88% in 1980.

Gasoline consumption by vehicle type is dominated by passenger cars. Table 15 provides information of vehicle registrations and fuel consumption. In 1980, there were nearly four times as many passenger cars as trucks and these cars consumed about 65% of all the motor fuel oil (compared to 35% consumed by trucks). Relative fuel consumption of passenger cars has decreased relatively since 1970 (when it stood at 71%).

To a large extent, gasoline demand is the mirror image of heating oil demand. However, while both show strong seasonal patterns, gasoline demand is not nearly as variant regionally as is heating oil. Figure 7 shows the seasonal pattern for gasoline demand. Notice how demand peaks during the summer months of June, July, and August. Not unexpectedly, gasoline stocks reach a peak in May and April and a trough in September and October. The inverse seasonality between heating oil and gasoline works well with the limited storage facilities of most refineries and terminal operators.

CASH MARKET STRUCTURE. Many aspects of the structure of the gasoline cash market have already been discussed in the sections on crude oil and heating oil. One thing that was emphasized was the huge number of firms doing retail and wholesale business in refined products. This is particularly true with gasoline, where there are many retail outlets, not all of which offer the same array of products and services. Table 16 illustrates the wide diversity of retail outlets for gasoline. This wide diversity represents one of the most interesting changes to come about in recent years (largely as a result of sharply increased prices)—the acceptance of self-serve stations. Figure 8 shows how consumer attitudes towards self-serve stations, as well as other types of retail outlets, have changed, based on a survey conducted by the Amoco Oil Company. (Two states, Oregon and New Jersey, still ban self-serve stations.) Hoping to further exploit the trend towards self-service, some oil firms are even experimenting with fully automatic stations that depend strictly on bank credit cards.

TABLE 14. Motor Fuel Consumption[a] (Thousands of Barrels per Day)

	Gasoline[b]	Other Fuels[c]	Total
1960	3,953	159	4,112
1965	4,644	269	4,913
1970	5,845	439	6,284
1975	6,719	628	7,347
1980	6,820	896	7,716
1981	6,726	969	7,695
1982	6,703	998	7,701

Source: U.S. Department of Energy, *1982 Annual Energy Review*, p. 193.

[a]Includes only motor fuel taxed at the prevailing tax rates in each state. In 1979 the total motor fuel consumption quantity cited here was 99.1% of the gross reported fuel consumption.

[b]Includes motor gasoline, aviation gasoline, and gasohol.

[c]Includes distillate fuel oil (diesel oil), LPG, and kerosene when they are used to operate vehicles on highways.

TABLE 15. Vehicle Registration and Fuel Consumption

	1970	1975	1980
Passenger cars			
Registrations (millions)	89.2	106.7	121.7
Mileage (thousands of miles per vehicle)	9.98	9.63	9.14
Total fuel consumption (billions of gallons)	65.6	76.0	73.4
Motorcycles			
Registrations (millions)	2.8	5.0	5.7
Mileage (thousands of miles per vehicle)	3.61	4.50	3.14
Total fuel consumption (billions of gallons)	0.1	0.4	0.4
Buses			
Registrations (millions)	0.4	0.5	0.5
Mileage (thousands of miles per vehicle)	13.31	11.14	12.10
Total fuel consumption (billions of gallons)	1.0	1.0	1.0
Trucks			
Registrations (millions)	18.8	25.8	33.6
Mileage (thousands of miles per vehicle)	11.45	10.65	11.43
Total fuel consumption (billions of gallons)	25.7	31.7	40.1
All motor vehicles			
Registrations (millions)	111.2	137.9	161.6
Mileage (thousands of miles per vehicle)	10.08	9.64	9.41
Total fuel consumption (billions of gallons)	92.3	108.9	114.9

Source: U.S. Department of Energy, adapted from *1982 Annual Energy Review,* pp. 191 and 193.

Retail and wholesale gasoline outlets also vary in terms of ownership. There are three major types of marketers—refiner marketers, nonbranded independents, and branded independents. Refiner marketers are obviously refiners who market their own oil, under their own brand name. An independent is a marketer who buys oil from a refinery and either sells the oil under the refiner's brand or his or her own (nonbranded) label. In 1980, the branded independent's share of total gasoline sales was about 69%, while the market share for refiner marketers and for nonbranded independents was about 19 and 11%, respectively.[13] While branded independent's have the greatest market share, this is being steadily eroded by the other groups. (For example, in 1975, branded independents captured 75% of the market.)[14]

[13]*Ibid.,* p. 107.

[14]*Ibid.*

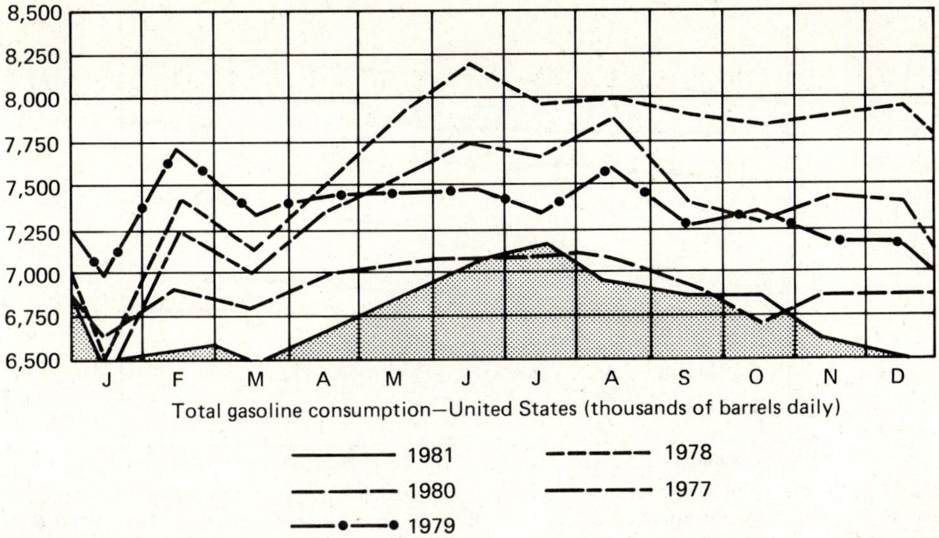

FIGURE 7. Total gasoline consumption, United States. (*Source*: National Petroleum News, *Facts Book*, Annual 1982 Issue, p. 80.)

FUTURES CONTRACTS. At this writing, only the NYMEX's New York harbor contract is actively traded. The CBT's unleaded gasoline contract, after some initial success, is currently not trading and exchange officers are looking to alter the contract to make it for physical delivery. Neither the CME or the IPE expects to list their gasoline contracts before the summer of 1984. Both the NYMEX and the CBT have the same contract specifications for their gasoline contracts as for their heating oil contracts (with the obvious exception of standards). In addition to differences associated with pricing and delivery, the CBT and NYMEX con-

TABLE 16. Where Gasoline is Sold (1980)

Type of Outlet	Weighted Number[a]	Weighted Percentage[a]
Full service	67,041	38.2%
Split island	41,594	23.7
Self-service	22,289	12.7
Convenience store	20,358	11.6
Miniservice	7,020	4.0
Car care centers	5,441	3.1
Pumpers	4,739	2.7
Truck stops	3,686	2.1
Car washes	3,335	1.9
Total	175,503[b]	100.0%

Source: National Petroleum News, *Fact Book,* mid-June 1981, p. 110.

[a]Weighted averages were obtained from National Petroleum News questionnaires and were extrapolated to reflect the industry as a whole, based on 1980 retail population totals.

[b]This total includes 158.500 service stations and 17,000 convenience stores selling gasoline in 1980. See Retail Market section for service-station and C-store population counts. (*Source:* NPN questionnaires.)

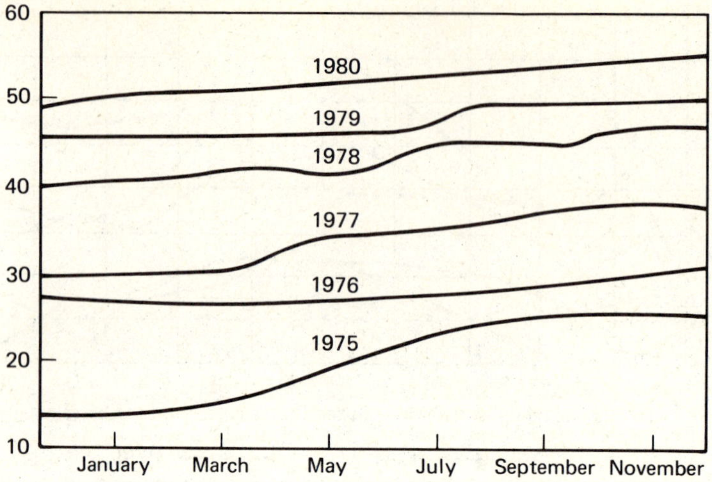

FIGURE 8. United States self-serve motorist gasoline market share (percent). (*Source*: Results of a survey by Amoco Oil Company, January 1981. Reported by National Petroleum News, *Fact Book*, mid-June 1981, p. 110.)

tracts vary in grade specifications (the NYMEX's Gulf Coast gasoline contracts never managed to trade much and the CBT never chose to list its leaded regular gasoline contracts). Differences among the various proposed and traded contracts are given in Table 17.

LIQUEFIED PROPANE GAS

William Leffler describes propane as "probably the most ubiquitous commodity of all products associated with the petroleum industry."[15] This is a strong statement and might come as something of a surprise to most consumers who are familiar with liquefied propane only as a minor source of energy to cook and heat with. Most consumers do not realize how versatile and common a product liquefied propane gas is and how important it is to the industrial and chemical sectors both as an energy source and as a chemical feedstock.

This section will discuss liquefied propane gas, which is also known as bottled or tank gas, LPG, LP-gas, and propane. (Many of these terms are misnomers as will be shown later.) Specifically, this section presents material concerning grades and specifications, supply, and demand. The terms of the Cotton Exchange's futures contract in liquefied propane gas are also presented.

GRADES AND SPECIFICATIONS. Unlike most refined products, propane is a chemically pure compound, represented by the formula C_3H_6. Propane has certain chemical characteristics which make it an attractive source of energy. For example, under normal atmospheric conditions it is a gas, but subject to high pressure and low temperatures, it becomes a liquid.

[15]W. L. Leffler, *The Technology and Economic Behavior of the U.S. Propane Industry*, Petroleum Publishing Company, Tulsa, OK, 1973, p. 1.

TABLE 17. Comparison of Gasoline Futures Contracts[a]

Contract Highlights	NYMEX	CME	CBT
Unit of trading	1,000 barrels per contract	1,000 barrels per contract	1,000 barrels per contract
Price basis	F.O.B. seller's exshore facility in the New York harbor area into buyer's barge or tanker. If seller's facility permits, delivery may also be completed, at the buyer's option, by truck ($0.25/gal surcharge), book transfers, or interfacility or intrafacility transfers. Prices quoted in dollars and cents per gallon.	F.O.B. buyer's barge or tanker at seller's facilities in Harris, Galveston, and Jefferson Counties, Texas or F.O.B. any Colonial Pipeline origin station. Prices quoted in dollars and cents per gallon.	F.O.B. barge or pipeline (Colonial, Texas Eastern, or Explorer) in Harris, Galveston, or Jefferson Counties, Texas. Prices quoted in dollars and cents per gallon. Contract A is for leaded regular gasoline, while Contract B is for unleaded regular gasoline.
Standards[a]			
Octane $\frac{(R+M)}{2}$	89 minimum	87 minimum	Contract A: 89.0 minimum Contract B: 87.0 minimum, but less than 91.0
Color	Yellow or bronze	Undyed	Contract A: Orange or bronze Contract B: Undyed or yellow
Lead	4 g/gal maximum	0.01 g/gal maximum	Contract A: 4.00 g/gal maximum Contract B: 0.01 g/gal maximum
Gravity	52° minimum	80° API maximum	Contracts A and B: 80° API maximum

TABLE 17. *(Continued)*

Contract Highlights	NYMEX	CME	CBT
Corrosion	1 maximum	1 maximum	Contracts A and B: 1 maximum
Doctor or inercaptan sulfur	Negative or 10 ppm	Negative or 0.002% (by weight)	Contracts A and B: Negative or 0.002% (by weight)
Distillation and Reid vapor pressure[c]	Northern grade[b]	Southern grade[b]	Contracts A and B: Southern grade[b]
Trading months	12 consecutive months not including the current month	Not specified yet	An 18-month cycle, which includes the current month, the next 4 months, plus the remaining even-numbered months
Minimum price fluctuation	.01¢ per gallon ($4.20 per contract)	.025¢ per gallon ($10.50 per contract)	.025¢ per gallon ($10.50 per contract)
Maximum price fluctuation	$0.02 per gallon ($840 per contract)	$0.02 per gallon ($840 per contract)	$0.03 per gallon ($1,260 per contract)
Delivery instrument	Wet barrels	Wet barrels	Depository receipt
Trading hours	8:45 a.m.–2:15 p.m. Chicago time	Not specified yet	8:30 a.m.–2:30 p.m. Chicago time
Last trading day	Last business day of the month prior to the delivery month	Last business day of the month prior to the delivery month	Third to last business day of the delivery month

Delivery tolerance	5% (50 barrels) per contract	5% (50 barrels) per contract	For waterborne deliveries of 1,000–5,000 barrels: 1.0%; for waterborne deliveries of more than 5,000 barrels: 0.3%; for pipeline deliveries: 25 barrels per shipment

[a]NYMEX standards are exchange-specified, while CBT and CME standards are given by Colonial Pipeline specifications. Only those specifications listed by the NYMEX are compared here—Colonial does list additional specifications for its tangible grades of unleaded gasoline.

[b]Southern Grade	Northern Grade
Class D: January, February, March, November, and December	Class E: December, January, and February
Class C: April, May, September, and October	Class D: March, April, October, and November
Class B: June, July, and August	Class C: May and September
	Class B: June, July, and August

[c]Distillation and Reid Vapor Pressure Classes

	B	C	D	E
10% evaporation °F maximum	149	140	131	122
50% evaporation °F maximum	170	170	170	170
50% evaporation °F maximum	245	240	235	230
90% evaporation °F maximum	374	365	365	365
End point °F maximum	430	430	430	430
Pounds °F maximum	10	11.5	13.5	14.5

Propane accounts for a major portion of all liquefied gases supplied for domestic use (67% in 1980).[16] On this basis, propane is often labeled as liquefied petroleum gas (or LP gas) even though this term actually encompasses a broader group of products. These other products include primarily butane, butane–propane mixture, and ethane–propane mixture. In 1980, these products accounted for 16, 3, and 14%, respectively, of the total amount of liquefied gases supplied for domestic use.[17]

SUPPLY. There are two major sources of propane supply: petroleum refineries and gas processing plants. Propane is a natural by-product of refining operations. Originally, the amount of propane produced was small, but with the introduction of cracking and reforming, the quantity of propane produced has increased substantially. Propane is also one of two major products produced at a gas-processing plant (the other is butane). The feedstocks for gas-processing plants may be either natural gas, casing head gas (gas which accompanies the production of crude), or other gases released during the petroleum refining process. If the propane was produced at a refinery, it is sometimes labeled LRG, for liquefied refinery gas; if the propane was produced at a gas processing plant, it is often labeled LPG, for liquefied petroleum gas. In 1980, 74% of all liquefied gases (and 62% of the propane) were produced at gas processing plants.

Table 18 presents information on the supply of propane. (The year 1980 is the most recent one for detailed data on propane supply.) In 1980 the United States imported propane to meet about 9% of its domestic needs, this was down from 10% in 1979. About 2% of the propane produced domestically is used at either the refinery or the processing plant (generally for fuel purposes).

Propane stocks (LPG stocks are shown in Figure 9) have a tendency to follow the seasonal pattern of heating oil stocks. This is because propane and other types of liquefied gases compete with heating oil as a source of heat in the residential and commercial markets.

Distribution of propane and other LP gases is different than that for most other refined products for two reasons: (1) to remain liquid, propane must be cooled and subject to low pressures; and (2) a greater portion of propane sales are at the wholesale level.

DEMAND. Propane has two principal uses—as a source for fuel and as a chemical feedstock. As a source of fuel, propane offers some significant advantages over various alternate fuel types. Specifically, it is clean burning, highly portable, and easily adapted to meet a wide variety of energy requirements. As a chemicalf feedstock, propane is used primarily to make ethylene and propylene, which Leffler describes as the "building blocks" of the chemical industry.[18] Ethylene and propylene are called olefins and are used to make many things, including polyethylene (for plastics), polyvinyl (for pipes and tiles), and polyester.

[16]U.S. Department of Energy, *Crude Petroleum, Petroleum Products, and Natural Gas Liquids*, 1980, p. 8.

[17]*Ibid.*

[18]Leffler, *op. cit.*, p. 32.

TABLE 18. Propane Statistics (Thousands of Barrels)

	1980	1979	1978
Production:			
At refineries (LRG)			
For fuel use	72,347	70,135	70,129
For chemical use	26,178	28,934	28,962
Total	98,525	99,934	98,291
At gas processing plants (LPG)	161,681	164,256	178,516
Total	260,206	263,325	276,807
Stocks:			
Refinery propane/propylene:			
For fuel use	4,624	4,037	4,914
For chemical use	217	107	237
Total	4,841	4,144	5,151
Plant propane:			
At refineries	590	140	567
At plant	59,925	59,509	81,167
Total	60,515	59,649	81,734
Total	65,356	63,793	86,885
Imports	25,387	32,368	20,639
Exports	3,621	2,873	3,379
Plant propane used at refineries	4,440	5,003	4,767
supplied for domestic use:			
Refinery propane/propylene:			
For fuel use	71,760	71,012	70,085
For chemical use	26,068	29,064	28,198
Total	97,828	100,076	98,283
Plant propane	178,141	209,782	185,576
Total	275,969	309,858	283,859

Source: U.S. Department of Energy, *Crude Petroleum, Petroleum Products, and Natural Gas Liquids,* various annual summaries.

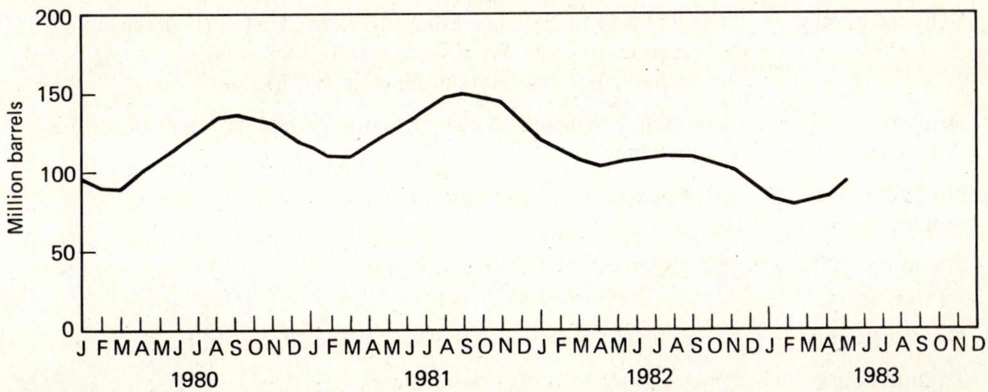

FIGURE 9. Stocks of liquefied petroleum gases. (*Source*: U.S. Department of Energy, *Monthly Energy Review*, various issues.)

TABLE 19. Demand for Propane

	1980	1979
	(Percentages)	
Residential and commercial	39.8	42.5
Chemical	27.3	23.7
Miscellaneous (including agriculture)	16.1	16.6
Industrial	8.9	9.5
Engine fuel	4.6	4.0
Utility gas	3.3	3.7
Total use (thousand gallons)	10,944,175	11,133,324

Source: U.S. Department of Energy, *Sales of LP-Gas and Ethylene in 1980.*

Table 19 provides information on propane consumption by broad industry groupings. The residential and commercial market accounted for about 40% of all propane use in 1980 (down from 42% in 1979). Most propane use in this sector is for heating purposes. As detailed earlier in the section "Heating Oil," propane and other LP gases compete heavily in this sector with natural gas, fuel oil, and electricity. In 1979, LP gas (of which propane is the most important, especially for this purpose) accounted for about 5% of the fuel market for residential heating.

The agricultural sector is an important consumer of propane, using it for such diverse things as crop drying (propane furnaces require very little maintenance), flame weeding, and poultry and pork brooding, as well as for heating and transportation purposes.

TABLE 20. Liquefied Propane Gas Contract Salient Features[a]

Unit of trading	1,000 barrels (42,000 gallons) per contract
Price basis	F.O.B. licensed facilities. Prices quoted in cents per gallon.
Standards	Liquefied propane gas meeting the specifications of NGPA-HD-5 (Natural Gas Processors Association publication No. 2140-68), or any subsequent revisions thereof
Delivery points	(A) licensed facilities in Mont Belviere, Texas. (B) licensed facilities in Conway, Kansas (with differentials from (A) based on published commercial pipeline tariff rates)
Delivery instrument	Shipping certificate issued by a storage facility licensed by the exchange
Minimum daily price move	.01¢ per gal ($4.20 per contract)
Maximum daily price move	$0.02 per gal ($840 per contract)
Months traded	The current month and the 11th succeeding months
Trading hours	9:45 a.m.–2:35 p.m. eastern time

[a]Consult exchange for most recent contract terms.

The industrial sector uses propane for transportation (it does not give off emissions, making it ideal for indoor vehicle use) and as a source of heat for such things as glass manufacturing and welding. Many plants find propane attractive because it is portable and it provides steady and clean heat.

PROPANE FUTURES. Only the Petroleum Associates of the New York Cotton Exchange offer a futures contract in propane. Originally introduced in 1971, their contract failed to attract substantial interest. Reintroduced in the fall of 1981, the Petroleum Associates hope to capitalize on the interest generated by futures in heating oil and gasoline. In reintroducing the contract, exchange officials have lowered the size of the contract from 100,000 to 42,000 gal so as to be more compatible with other energy contracts. After several months of trading, volume in the new contract is still very low. Contract specifications are given in Table 20.

SOURCES OF INFORMATION

General Energy Publications

American Petroleum Institute. *Standard Definitions for Petroleum Statistics*. Washington, D.C.

American Society for Testing and Materials. *ASTM Specifications For Petroleum Products*. Philadelphia, PA: American Society for Testing and Material, 1978.

British Petroleum. *Our Industry Petroleum*. London, England: BP Company, Limited, 1977.

International Petroleum Encyclopedia. Tulsa, OK: Penwell Publishing Company.

Wolbert, G. S. *U.S. Oil Pipelines*. Washington, D.C., American Petroleum Institute, 1979.

Refining

Leffler, W. L. *Petroleum Refining for the Non-Technical Person*. Tulsa, OK: PenWell Books, 1979.

National Petroleum Council. *Refinery Flexibility*. Washington, D.C., December 1980.

U.S. Department of Energy. *Trends in Refinery Capacity and Utilization*. September 1978.

Crude

Banks, F. E. *Political Economy of Oil*. Lexington Books, 1980.

Oil and Gas Journal. *A Guide to World Export Crudes*. Tulsa, OK: The Petroleum Publishing Company, 1976.

———. *Evaluation of World's Important Crudes*. Tulsa, OK: The Petroleum Publishing Company, 1973.

Wyant, F. R. *The United States, OPEC, and Multi-national Oil*. Lexington Books, 1977.

Heating Oil

R. Shriver Association. *Middle Distillate Market Profile Report*. Washington, D.C.: U.S. Department of Energy, July 1979.

Schmidt, F. P. *Fuel Oil Manual*. New York, NY: Industrial Press, Incorporated, 1969.

Gasoline

American Petroleum Institute. *Gasoline Marketing*. Washington, D.C., December 1976.

———. *Recent Changes in Retail Gasoline Marketing*. Washington, D.C., January 1981.

Ethyl Corporation. *The Story of Gasoline*. New York, NY, 1964.

Seiferlein, K. E., *Motor Gasoline Supply and Demand 1967–1978*. U.S. Department of Energy, Energy Information Administration, Washington, D.C., August 1978.

Propane

Butane-Propane News, Incorporated. *An Introduction to LP-Gases*. Arcadin, CA: Butane-Propane News, Incorporated, 1973.

Leffler, W. L. *The Technology and Economic Behavior of the U.S. Propane Industry*. Tulsa, OK: Petroleum Publishing Company, 1973.

Periodicals

Energy User News. Washington, D.C.: Fairchild Publishing Company.

Fuel Oil Week. Washington, D.C.: Observer Publishing Company.

National Petroleum News. New York, NY: McGraw-Hill.

Oil and Gas Journal. Tulsa, OK: PenWell Publishing Company.

Oil Buyers' Guide. Lakewood, NJ: Petroleum Publications, Incorporated.

Oil Daily. New York, NY: Oil Daily, Incorporated.

Platt's Oilgram. New York, NY: McGraw-Hill.

The Petroleum Economist. London, England: Petroleum Press Bureau Limited.

The Petroleum Intelligence Weekly. New York, NY: Petroleum and Energy Intelligence Weekly, Incorporated.

U.S. Department of Commerce, Bureau of Economic Analysis: *Survey of Current Business*.

U.S. Department of Energy: *Crude Petroleum, Petroleum Products, and Natural Gas Liquids; Energy Data Report; Monthly Energy Review; Monthly Petroleum Statement; Petroleum Market Shares; Sales of LP Gases and Ethane;* and *Weekly Petroleum Status Report*.

Associations

American Gas Association—Arlington, VA.

American Petroleum Institute—Washington, D.C.

American Petroleum Refiners Association—Washington, D.C.

American Society for Testing and Materials—Philadelphia, PA.

Gas Processors Association—Tulsa, OK.

Gas Research Institute—Chicago, IL.
Independent Petroleum Association of America—Washington, D.C.
Independent Refiners Association of America—Washington, D.C.
National LP-Gas Association—Oak Brook, IL.
National Oil Jobbers Council, Incorporated—Washington, D.C.
National Petroleum Council—Washington, D.C.
National Petroleum Refiners Association—Washington, D.C.
Petroleum Industry Research Foundation, Incorporated—New York, NY.

CHAPTER 43

THE GOLD MARKET

CONTENTS

CHRONOLOGY 3

PRODUCTION OF GOLD 5

South Africa 6
Soviet Union 6
Canada 6
United States 6

SUPPLY OF GOLD IN THE FREE WORLD 7

DEMAND FOR GOLD 7

GOLD FUTURES MARKET 10

Summary of Uses for Gold Futures 16

PUT AND CALL OPTIONS ON GOLD FUTURES 17

Price Structure in Gold Futures Market 18
The Value of an Option on Gold Futures 18
Summary of Uses for Options on Gold Futures 20

GLOSSARY 20

CHAPTER **43**

THE GOLD MARKET

Robert C. Teetsell

Gold is the best known of the precious metals. It has been used over the centuries as a medium of exchange, a store of value, and an ornament. Recently, gold has become a major industrial commodity in the manufacturing of electronic components, where its qualities of indestructibility, malleability, and electrical conductivity make it uniquely applicable for many uses. In addition, individuals have begun to hold gold as a form of insurance against the uncertainty of currency values.

The use of gold as a medium of international exchange and as a store of wealth for individuals has, at times, greatly affected its price during periods of economic and political uncertainty. Nations and individuals turn to gold because of its safety, portability, and universal acceptance.

CHRONOLOGY

During the past centuries there have been events which demonstrate the significance of gold to world economies, despite attempts to reduce its importance. The following brief chronology is appended from *Wolff's Guide to the London Metal Exchange* (Rudolf Wolff & Company, Limited, 2nd ed., Metal Bulletin Books, Surry, England 1980):

17th–18th century: London replaces Amsterdam as the center of gold trading.

1819: England adopts the gold standard.

1871–1877: Adoption of International Gold Standard by other countries (Germany in 1871, United States in 1873).

1880–1890: South Africa becomes a major gold producer.

1914: Gold standard abandoned.

1914–1918: Bank of England agrees to purchase entire South African production.

1919: Gold takes on role of inflation and currency hedge. Bank of England allows South Africa to market gold.

1919 (September): First London gold fix at £4 18s 9d set by bullion houses of Johnson Matthey, Limited, Mocatta & Goldsmid, Limited, Samuel Montagu & Company, Limited, N.M. Rothschild & Sons, Limited, Sharps Pixley, Limited. United States purchases large supplies.

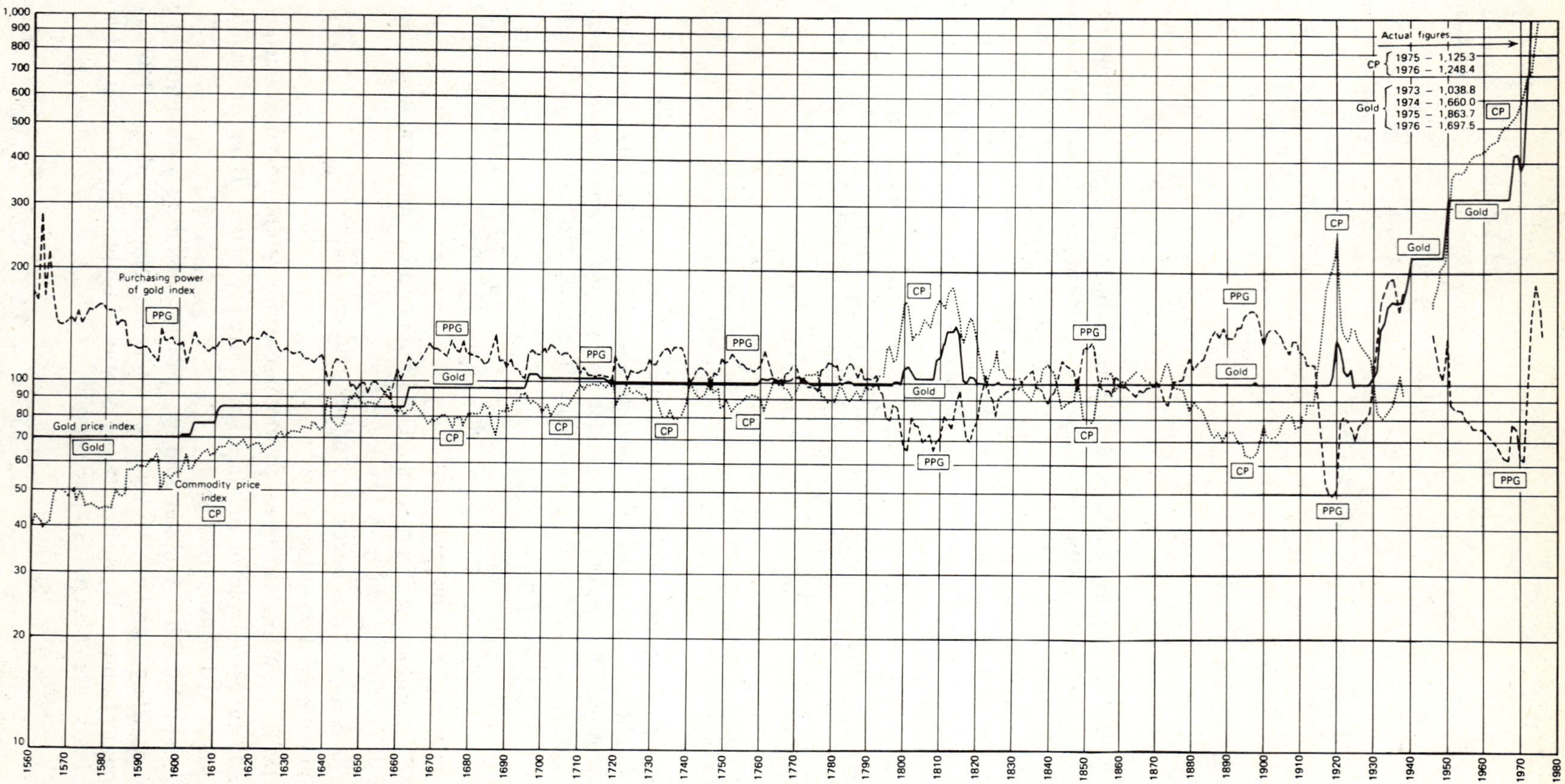

FIGURE 1. Indices of the price of gold, 1560–1976 (1930 = 100). (*Source*: *The Golden Constant: The English and American Experience 1560–1976* by Jastram, R.W. Published by John Wiley & Sons, Inc., 1977.

1922: New International Monetary Agreement allows nations to include foreign currency holdings in reserves. Sterling and U.S. dollar become reserve currencies of the world.

1925: Britain attempts to support sterling by adopting Gold Bullion Standard based on the buying and selling of bullion at fixed prices by the Bank of England.

1931: Britain abandons gold standard.

1934: United States dollar devalued; gold price raised to $35 per oz from $20.67. United States citizens relinquish gold for currency. United States dollar becomes major world reserve currency.

1940: South African production begins steady climb.

1944: Formation of the International Monetary Fund (IMF). Convertible currencies become world reserves jointly with gold. The IMF sets conversion rates between currencies and provides for conversion to U.S. dollars and gold at $35 per oz.

1945: Gold backing for U.S. Federal Reserve notes reduced to 25% from 40%.

1958: United States dollar becomes less attractive to foreign holders; gold prices rise.

1960: United States citizens prohibited from owning gold abroad.

1961: United States Treasury sells gold to hold price to $35. London Gold Pool formed to prevent conversion of U.S. dollars to gold.

1965: Reserve required of 25% for U.S. member bank deposits is removed.

1968: Reserve requirements of 25% for U.S. Federal Reserve notes is removed. Widespread dollar switching attributed to Vietnam war results in the beginning of the free market price for gold. Zurich gold market becomes prominent.

1971 (August 15th): IMF "Smithsonian" agreement canceled $35 per oz conversion rate. Currencies now float based on individual economic strengths.

1974: Increases in oil prices push gold to $200 per oz. United States announces that citizens can hold gold beginning in 1975.

1975: United States Treasury auctions begin.

1975 (August): IMF announces gold auction.

1976 (August): Gold prices fall to $100 under auction pressure.

1977: Concern over U.S. inflation causes gold prices to begin to rise.

1978 (April): United States Treasury increases frequency of auctions.

1979 (March): European Monetary System (EMS) enacted. Central banks use free market price to value gold.

1979 (October): United Kingdom citizens allowed to own gold.

1980: Russian gold sales decrease. South African gold production declines.

1980 (February): Gold rises to $850 as silver crisis reaches peak.

1980 (May): IMF auctions end.

PRODUCTION OF GOLD

Though mined worldwide, the major producers of gold during the last three decades have been South Africa and the USSR, which together produce more than 75%

of the total world production of gold. South Africa, alone, accounts for more than 50% of the world gold production and about 75% of the free-world production.

The following discussion is limited to South Africa and the USSR, as well as Canada and the United States. The production in these four countries accounts for about 80% of the total world production. The People's Republic of China is also a very large producer of gold. However, there is little public information about Chinese production of gold.

SOUTH AFRICA. There are over 40 large mines operating in South Africa. The gold-bearing ore is mined along narrow slopes and then treated and refined into 1,000 oz bricks of 88%-gold content. The average yield in South Africa is approximately 1 oz of 88% pure gold to 3 tons of ore. Of the 12% impurity, about 9% is silver and 3% is other metals, such as palladium and platinum. The 1,000-oz gold bars are refined at the Rand Refinery in Gemiston, owned and operated by the South African Chamber of Mines, an association of the South African Mining Industry. The final product has 99.6–99.9% of pure gold content.

Once the gold has been refined and cast into 400-oz bars, ownership is transferred to the South African Reserve Bank in Pretoria. The bank directs the refinery to send gold to purchasers. The majority of shipments are to London and Zurich, the two largest gold bullion markets in the world.

SOVIET UNION. Information about gold production in the USSR is not disclosed by the Soviet authorities. Therefore, the size of the Soviet production can only be estimated. Gold production is entirely under the jurisdiction of "Glavzolot," the ministry responsible for nonferrous metallurgy. The most productive mines are those of Eastern Siberia. Soviet exports of gold bullion are handled through the Vneshtorgbank and seem solely dependent on the need for foreign currencies.

CANADA. Canada is the third largest world producer of gold. Currently, there are about 30 operating mines in Canada. By-product production of gold accounts for approximately one-third of total Canadian production. This production falls when base metal prices are depressed, since mining companies curtail their production of base metals.

UNITED STATES. United States gold production is mainly a by-product of other mining activities. Only four of the 25 gold-producing mines are primarily gold producers. Therefore, as in Canada, variables other than the price of gold affect gold production. Most of the gold-mining activities in the United States occur in South Dakota, Utah, Nevada, and Arizona. The Homestake Mine in South Dakota is the world's largest mine, though gold production is only one of its many mining operations.

In the years 1970–1979, production of gold decreased steadily. Since 1979, there has been an upward trend in gold production. In 1979, production was 1.015 million troy oz; in 1980, 1.115 million troy oz were produced. The projected production for 1981 is 1.48 million troy oz. The United States is the only major producing country in which production increased from 1979 to 1980, when the price of gold reached unprecedented heights.

SUPPLY OF GOLD IN THE FREE WORLD

In addition to new mine production from the noncommunist world, marketable gold supplies include net sales by communist countries and net sales by official financial organizations. Table 1 shows the supply of gold to the free world.

As can be seen from Table 1, the supply of gold in 1981 increased an estimated 16% from the 29.5 million troy oz available in 1980. The incremental supply from the Communist bloc accounted for most of this increase in supply.

Because of its store of value and medium of exchange characteristics, gold has been held throughout the ages. Groups that currently hold significant gold stocks include central banks, international organizations such as the IMF, the Communist bloc, and private holdings. The central bank reserves account for about 50% of the total stocks. About 27% of the central bank reserves are held by the Federal Reserve System. The total world stocks is an estimate because there is incomplete information about stocks held in the communist world and in private hands. Table 2 reports the estimated distribution of world gold stocks and central bank gold reserves for the years 1980 to 1981. It is important to draw attention to the significance of gold stocks for the world gold market. A price change, a change in balance of trade, a bad crop year in the USSR, and so forth may induce holders of gold to sell part of their stocks. Thus the supply of gold available to the marketplace greatly exceeds the amount currently produced.

DEMAND FOR GOLD

There are three principal sources of demand for gold: industrial demand, investor demand, and a special subset of investor demand—the demand for official coins.

TABLE 1. Gold Supply and Distribution

	1977	1978	1979	1980[a]	1981[b]
	(Million Fine Troy Ounces)				
Supply					
Mine production in noncommunist world	31.1	31.2	30.9	30.4	31.0
Supply flow from communist countries	12.9	13.2	7.4	2.7	6.0
Net official sales	8.6	11.6	18.5	−3.5	−2.0
Total supply	52.6	56.0	56.8	29.5	35.0
Distribution of supply					
Industrial fabrication	40.7	41.6	31.9	12.0	20.0
Official coins	4.4	9.0	10.4	8.0	7.0
Net private bullion purchases	7.5	5.4	14.5	9.5	8.0

Sources: 1977–1978, Consolidated Gold Fields; 1979–1981, J. Aron Precious Metals, Research Department.

[a]Preliminary. [b]Estimated.

TABLE 2. Estimated World Gold Stocks, September 1980[a]

	Million Troy Ounces
Central bank reserves	
United States	264.5
Germany	95.2
France	81.9
Switzerland	83.3
Italy	66.7
Other	344.3
Total	935.9
International organizations	
IMF	103.4
BIS	7.3
EMCF	85.7
Total	196.4
Total of official stocks	1,132.3
Communist countries[a]	
USSR	57.0
China	13.0
Total	70.0
Private holdings[a]	
France	201.0
Other European countries	65.0
Middle East	52.0
Far East	43.0
India	120.0
United States	120.0
Other	61.0
Total	662.0

Source: J. Aron Precious Metals, Research Department.
[a]Estimated.

Industrial demand, which accounts for 57% of the total demand, comes from the jewelry sector, the electronics industry, dentistry, the decorative industry, and other users. As Table 1 shows, the industrial sector is the largest component of demand. Investor demand, which accounts for an additional 23%, comes from individuals, businesses, and other institutions who buy gold as a hedge against inflation and foreign exchange depreciation, and as a store of value.

Because of gold's physical properties, it is used for many different purposes. The beauty of gold makes it the most widely used material in jewelry production. It is not corroded by air or water and, therefore, is heavily used in dentistry. Gold is a good conductor of electricity and thus is important in the electronics industry. Because it is an excellent reflector of light and extremely malleable, it is used as a coating on windows to reduce air-conditioning costs and has been used in space programs as a reflector for space craft.

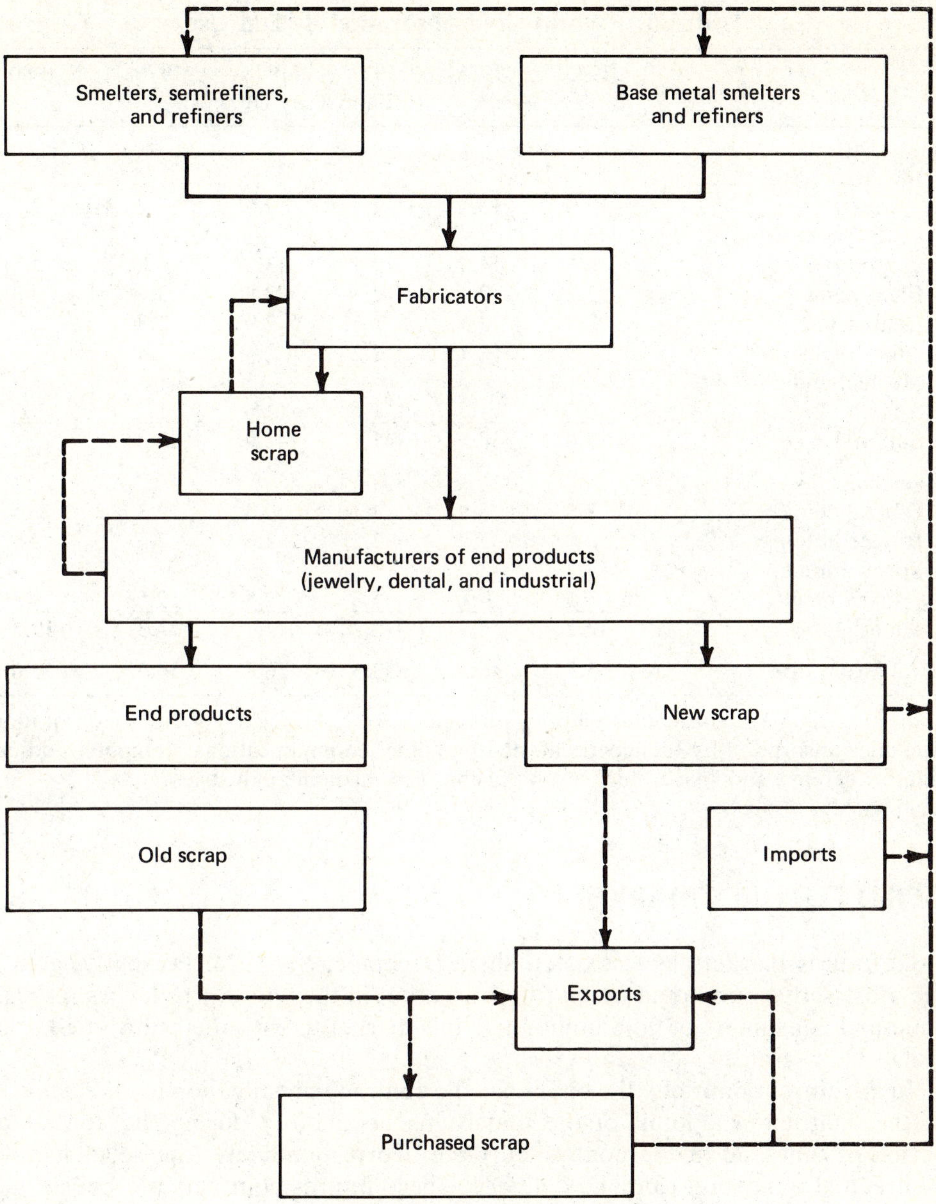

FIGURE 2. Secondary gold flow.

Table 3 depicts world gold absorption by end use over recent years. Each category of industrial use declined during 1980 as the price of gold rose to modern highs. As the price of gold increases, industry uses substitutes or lowers the amount of gold used for a task by utilizing alloys with lower gold content. Even with successful reduction of gold use per task, use of total gold could still increase as demand increases for products which utilize gold.

TABLE 3. World Gold Absorption By End Use

	1975	1976	1977	1978	1979	1980
			(Million Troy Ounces)			
Industrial						
Jewelry—advanced countries	10.0	15.1	17.4	19.0	17.7	9.5
Jewelry—developing countries	6.6	14.9	14.9	13.3	6.0	(4.5)
Electronics	2.2	2.4	2.5	2.8	3.0	2.8
Dentistry	2.0	2.5	2.6	2.9	2.8	2.3
Other industrial[a]	1.9	2.1	2.2	2.4	2.4	1.9
Medals, and so forth	0.7	1.5	1.5	1.6	1.1	0.5
Subtotal	23.4	38.5	41.1	42.0	33.0	12.5
Investment						
Official coins	7.8	5.9	4.7	9.3	9.3	7.5
Private holdings	0.0	5.7	2.2	2.6	2.5	2.5[b]
Speculation and investment	4.4	(3.9)	5.3	2.8	9.5	9.5[b]
Subtotal	12.2	7.7	12.2	14.7	21.3	19.5
Total absorption	35.7	46.2	53.3	56.7	54.3	32.0

Source: *Metal Statistics,* 1981 edition, 1979 and 1980, J. Aron Commodities Corporation.
[a]Includes absorption by the electrical, photographic, communications, computer and calculator, defense and space, nuclear and fusion, and medicine industries.
[b]Estimated.

GOLD FUTURES MARKETS

Gold futures markets have existed since December 31, 1974. Presently, gold is the most active and liquid metal futures market in the world. Producers, processors, and consumers of gold bullion use this market to shift their unwanted price risk.

In all futures contracts, the buyer has the contractual obligation to take delivery of the contracted amount of the underlying commodity during the contracted period of time and at the contracted price. Correspondingly, the seller has the contractual obligation to make delivery. These futures contracts are bought and sold on organized commodity futures exchanges around the world.

Since most commodity futures exchanges are located in the United States,[1] we shall focus on these. (Gold futures trading began on December 31, 1974.) Trading was started in Chicago on the Chicago Board of Trade, International Monetary Market division of the Chicago Mercantile Exchange, and the MidAmerica Exchange, and in New York on the Commodity Exchange, Incorporated and the

[1]The reader should be aware, though, that there are also gold futures exchanges in Tokyo, Hong Kong, London, Sydney, Australia, and Winnipeg, Canada. There is a gold futures exchange planned in Sao Paulo, Brazil. Furthermore, there are major gold bullion exchanges in London, Paris, Zurich, Hong Kong, and Singapore.

New York Mercantile Exchange. As the volume of trading grew from 7,475 total contracts on the first day to 13.37635 million total contracts for all of 1981, the Commodity Exchange, Incorporated grew to dominate the gold futures markets. The International Monetary Market is presently an important satellite market, while the smaller MidAmerica Exchange contract is significant for the small investor. Annual trading volume for all U.S. gold futures contracts is presented in Table 4. A summary of the specifications of the dominant contracts is presented in Table 5.

The difference between the price embodied in the futures contract and the spot price of gold primarily reflects the costs of carrying gold bullion until the contract matures. Thus, if the price of gold bullion is \$400 per troy oz and the cost of carrying gold until the contract matures translates into \$40 per troy oz, the price of that futures contract is about \$440 per oz. The longer the time to maturity of the futures contract, the greater is this cost of carry. The principal component in the cost of carrying gold is the cost of funds invested in the bullion. Thus, if the carry period were 1 year, the \$40 cost of carry in the above example would represent a 10% cost of funds, or interest rate.

Figure 4 depicts the typical price structure in the COMEX gold futures market. The price of gold bullion is S. F is the price for the futures contract maturing at time t. The difference between the futures price and the spot price is the cost of carry. If the price of gold bullion does not change during the life of the futures contract, the price of the futures contract maturing at time t will slide down the price curve to be approximately equal to the spot price S, as t goes to zero.

This typical price structures gives rise to the commercial "cash-and-carry" transaction. A cash-and-carry transaction is a spread transaction consisting of a long bullion position and a short futures position. This is a potentially profitable transaction whenever the cost of carry in the futures market is greater than the commercial firm's own costs of carrying the bullion position. The risk of this transaction is due to the differences in the mechanics of the cash market and the futures market.

Should the price of gold change, the final result of the transaction, net of financing costs will still be the initial differences between the purchase price of the bullion and the sale price of the futures. However, the futures position is marked-to-market daily with gains received and losses paid. Therefore any losses sustained on the futures position must be financed until the bullion is sold and the futures position is offset.

A method to recoup the financing costs incurred due to a losing futures position is with a "tail." Generally, a "tail" is an extra position or positions in the near leg of the spread. For example, in this cash-and-carry transaction the near leg might consist of 1,000 troy oz of gold, while the distant leg consists of nine short futures contracts for 100 troy oz of gold each. Thus, if the price of the gold futures rises, the gain on the extra 100 troy oz of bullion offsets the financing costs incurred on the nine short futures contracts.

Tails can also be used with futures spreads to set an interest rate for borrowing or lending at some time in the future. In this case, both legs of the spread would be futures contracts. The tail necessary to lock up this financing cost is $r + E(\Delta r)$ per spread, where r is the carry rate or financing costs, and $E(\Delta r)$ is the expected change in this carry rate. Thus, if r_0, equal to (distant − nearby)/nearby, is 0.10,

TABLE 4. Annual Gold Futures Trading Volume

	1974	1975	1976	1977	1978	1979	1980	1981
COMEX								
(100 oz)	2,550	393,517	479,363	981,551	3,742,378	6,541,893	8,001,410	10,373,706
CBOT								
(3 kg)	1,143	54,331	10,940	13,758	56,470	12,844	78	0
(100 oz)	—	—	—	—	—	97,509	71,401	14,749
IMM								
(100 oz)	2,131	406,698	340,921	908,180	2,812,870	3,558,960	2,543,419	2,518,435
NYMEX								
(1 kg)	1,230	36,733	2,351	1,017	620	171	10	0
(400 oz)	—	—	—	2,633	2,748	533	0	—
MidAmerica								
(1 kg)	421	6,872	2,573	2,650	3,214	4	0	—
(33.2 oz)	—	—	—	—	41,939	200,359	447,494	469,460
Total	7,475	898,151	836,148	1,909,789	6,660,239	10,412,273	11,063,812	13,376,350

TABLE 5. Summary of Gold Futures Contract Specifications[a]

Exchange	COMEX	IMM	MidAmerica Exchange	CBOT	London Gold Futures Market	Winnipeg	Winnipeg	Hong Kong	Sydney
Contract size	100 troy oz	100 troy oz	33.2 troy oz	100 troy oz	100 troy oz	400-oz standard	100-oz centum	100 troy oz	50 troy oz
Contract months	Current month plus the next 2 months and all subsequent months of February, April, June, August, October, and December, but not more than 23 months distant	Current month and all subsequent months of March, June, September, and December, the last of which is not to be more than 24 months distant	All calendar months with no specific limit on time to maturity	All months	Spot plus each month for the next 6 months	October, January, April, and July plus 1 year forward	August, November, February, and May plus 1 year forward		March, June, September, and December up to 24 months distant
Deliverable grade	0.995 fine	0.995 fine	0.995 fine	0.995 fine	0.995 fine	0.995 fine	0.995 fine	0.995 fine	0.995 fine
Delivery	By depository receipt	By depository receipt	By depository receipt	By depository receipt		By depository receipt	By depository receipt		
Depositories	New York	New York and Chicago	New York and Chicago			Toronto	Toronto		
Minimum price change	$0.10 per troy oz	$0.10 per troy oz	$0.025 per troy oz	$0.10 per troy oz	$0.10 per troy oz			$0.10 per troy oz	$0.10 per troy oz
Maximum daily price change	$25 per troy oz	$50 per troy oz	$50 per troy oz	$25 per troy oz	$30 per troy oz	Normal $10 per troy oz	$40 per troy oz		

[a]For a list of trading hours see M. Riess, Chapter 4.

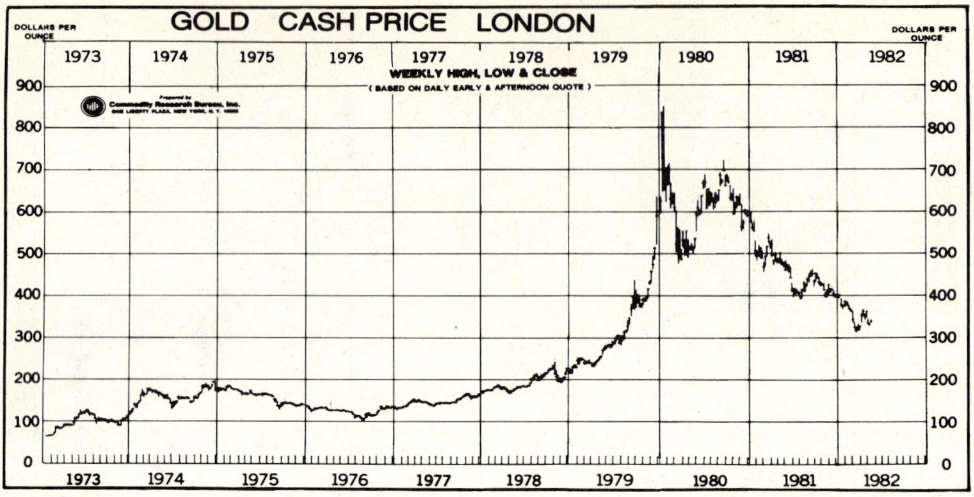

FIGURE 3. Gold cash price—London. (*Source*: Commodity Research Bureau, Incorporated.)

and the expected change in the rate is +0.01, or 100 basis points, for a maturity of length (distant − nearby), to occur *before* the tailed-spread is to be offset, there should be 1.11 nearby contracts for every distant contract. This can be shown mathematically as follows:

Proof. Let N_0 = initial price of the nearby contract;
N_1 = final price of the nearby contract;
D_0 = initial price of the distant contract;
D_1 = final price of the distant contract;
r_0 = initial interest rate of the spread;
r_1 = final interest rate of the spread.

Then $(r_1 - r_0)\,N_0$ is the desired profit or loss on the futures transaction such that a profit on the futures transaction exactly offsets the loss on the cash transaction or vice versa. If G is the gain (loss), then

$$
\begin{aligned}
G &= D_1 - D_0 + (1 + r_0 + \Delta r)(N_0 - N_1)\\
N_1 &= N_0 + \Delta N\\
D_0 &= N_0 + r_0 N_0\\
D_1 &= N_1 + r_1 N_1\\
D_1 &= N_0 + \Delta N + r_0 N_0 + r_0 \Delta N + \Delta r N_0 + \Delta r \Delta N\\
G &= N_0 + \Delta N + r_0 N_0 + r_0 \Delta N + \Delta r N_0 + \Delta r \Delta N - N_0\\
&\quad - r_0 N_0 + (1 + r_0 + \Delta r)(N_0 - N_0 - \Delta N)\\
&= \Delta N + r_0 \Delta N + \Delta r N_0 + \Delta r \Delta N - \Delta N - \Delta r_0 N - \Delta r \Delta N\\
G &= \Delta r N_0
\end{aligned}
$$

The signs are correct because the gain or loss is given by the difference between the sell price and the buy price. In this case, the initial trade was to buy the nearby and sell the distant. Thus, if rates rise, the futures transaction gives a loss,

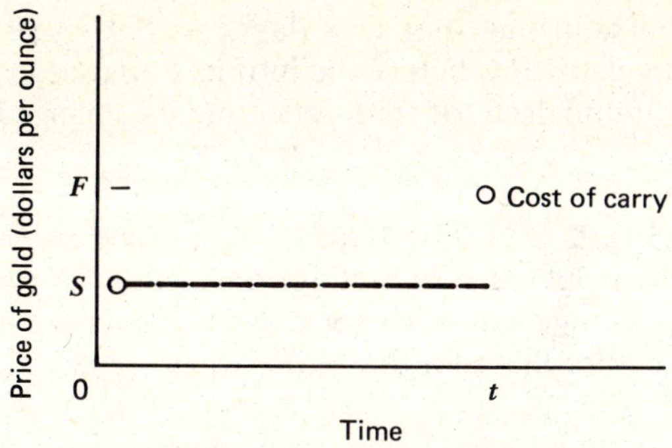

FIGURE 4. Gold price structure.

that is, r is positive for a loss. Buying the nearby and selling the distant hedges an *investment* interest rate. A rate rise when investing is a cash market gain. Multiplying the transaction equation through by -1 converts it to a borrowing rate hedge. In this case, the sign on G would obviously be negative, that is, r is positive for a gain on the futures transaction. This is the desired result because for a borrowing transaction, a rate rise is a cash market transaction loss. The following example will clarify the use of the investment rate hedge.

Example: Investment rate hedge ($40 million):

$N_0 = 400$
$D_0 = 450$
$r_0 = 0.125$
$r = 0.02$
$N_1 = 450$
$D_1 = 515.25$
$r_1 = 0.145$

Day 1: Buy 1,145 N_0 at $400 per oz; value = $45.8 million.
Sell 1,000 D_0 at $450 per oz; value = $45.0 million.

Day 2: Sell 1,145 N_1 at $450 per oz; value = $51.525 million.
Buy 1,000 D_1 at $515.25 per oz; value = $51.525 million.

Results: Total value sold:
$51,525,000
+45,000,000
$96,525,000

Total value bought:
$45,800,000
+51,525,000
$97,325,000

Loss on futures transaction is $80,000.
Gain on cash investment = (14.5% − 12.5% = 2%) ($40 million)
= $80,000

In practice, the tail is managed in accordance with revised expectations of Δr. If the initial Δr becomes too low before the futures transaction is offset, additional nearby contracts are purchased (or sold) reflecting the change in expectations and vice versa.

SUMMARY OF USES FOR GOLD FUTURES. Gold futures can be used to hedge the price risk in an anticipated gold bullion transaction. For example, suppose a bullion dealer has inventory which is expected to be sold in 6 months. If the price of gold were to fall before the sale, the dealer would receive less than its present market value.

Selling a futures contract sets a sale price, thereby hedging the price risk. If the price does fall, the futures contract will be closed out at the lower price. The net gain from the futures transaction will approximately offset the loss in market value from the gold bullion transaction. The mirror image of this general example is buying futures contracts to hedge the price risk of an anticipated purchase.

In addition to hedging price risk, a gold dealer can recoup the costs of carrying the gold bullion through the sale of the gold futures contracts. As shown before, the price structure of the gold futures market primarily reflects the cost of carrying bullion. Thus the price set through the futures sale includes the market's expectation of the cost of carrying 1 oz of gold over the remaining life of the futures contract. The following example makes this clear.

Suppose a gold dealer anticipates selling 100 troy oz of gold 1 year hence. The present market value is \$400 per oz; the cost of carrying the gold for the year totals \$40 per oz. The price of the futures contract is then \$440 per oz. Assuming that the anticipated sale, indeed, occurs in 1-year's time as the futures contract is expiring, the net gain from the bullion and futures transactions will be approximately \$40 per oz, excluding transactions costs. The following two cases illustrate this result:

Case 1. Gold prices fall to \$350 per troy oz:

	Cash Market	Futures Market
Day 1	Hold 100 troy oz of gold. Market price is \$400 per oz; market value is \$40,000.	Sell one futures contract maturing in 1 year. Futures price is \$440 per oz; total value is \$44,000.
Day 366	Sell 100 troy oz of gold. Market price is \$350 per oz; market value is \$35,000.	Buy back existing short futures position. Futures price is \$350 per oz; total value is \$35,000.
Results	There was a \$50 per oz loss in value of the gold bullion. However, there was a \$90 per oz gain on the futures transaction. The net gain is \$40 per troy oz, or the cost of carrying 1 oz of gold for 1 year in this example.	

Case 2. Gold prices rise to $450 per troy oz:

	Cash Market	Futures Market
Day 1	Hold 100 troy oz of gold. Market price is $400 per oz; market value is $40,000.	Sell one futures contract maturing in 1 year. Futures price is $440 per oz; total value is $44,000.
Day 366	Sell 100 troy oz of gold. Market price is $350 per oz; market value is $35,000.	Buy back existing short futures position. Futures price is $450 per oz; total value is $45,000.
Results	There was a $50 per oz gain in value of the gold bullion. However, there was a $10 per oz loss on the futures transaction. The net gain is $40 per troy oz, or the cost of carrying 1 oz of gold for 1 year in this example.	

Two caveats are necessary to bring this hypothetical example to reality. The first is known as *basis risk*. The futures contracts are based upon 0.995 fine gold bars. To the extent that the bullion which is being hedged is not 0.995 fine gold bars, the dollar change for the actual bullion need not be exactly the same as the dollar change in 0.995 gold bars. Therefore, actual results may not be as precise as shown in the example.

The second is known as *variation margin*. In Case 2 where the futures transaction was losing money, the daily loss is paid the following day as the futures position is marked-to-market. This represents a cash drain, since the bullion is not generating a positive cash flow. This cash drain, even though of a temporary nature, must be financed by some means. The cost of this financing could become onerous, if the futures loss is large.

The opposite side of the above example is that of a hedge against an anticipated gold purchase. The purchaser of the futures contract pays the cost of carry to the seller. However, the purchaser does not have to tie up capital in the gold bullion inventory to hedge the risk of a price increase.

In addition to these uses by a hedger, an investor can use gold futures as a highly leveraged investment in a variety of ways. If the investor has an opinion about a future change in the price of gold, the investor can buy or sell a futures contract by depositing a relatively small initial margin. Excluding the effects of variation margin and the cost of carry discussed above, the investor will reap the benefits of the price change, if the investor's expectations are correct, without having to invest directly in bullion.

PUT AND CALL OPTIONS ON GOLD FUTURES

The market for options on gold futures is a new type of complementary market which augments the gold futures market. Both parties to a gold futures contract have an obligation. The seller of the contract is obligated to deliver 100 troy oz of gold at the agreed-upon price. The purchaser is obligated to take delivery of the 100 troy oz of gold at the agreed-upon price. Of course, one or both parties to a gold futures contract can end their obligation by offsetting their contract prior to its maturity.

Only one party—the seller—to an option contract, however, has an obligation and, then, only if the option contract is exercised. The buyer of an option contract has the right to exercise the option contract whenever the buyer chooses, so long as the contract has not already expired. The buyer does not have the obligation to exercise the option. Just as with gold futures contracts, one or both parties to an option contract can end their obligation or right to exercise by offsetting their option contract prior to its expiration.

There are two types of options on gold futures contracts, call options and put options. A call option contract on a gold futures contract gives the buyer the right, but not the obligation, to purchase the underlying futures contract to buy gold at the strike price. If a call option purchaser exercises the right to purchase the underlying futures, a seller of that option is obligated to sell the underlying futures contract to deliver gold at the strike price.

A put option contract, conversely, gives the buyer the right, but not the obligation, to sell the underlying futures contract to deliver gold at the strike price. If a buyer of a put option exercises the right to sell the underlying futures contract, a seller of that put option is obligated to buy the underlying futures contract for gold at the strike price.

PRICE STRUCTURE IN A GOLD FUTURES MARKET. The gold futures markets are structured around a series of contracts for future delivery of a specific amount of gold during one of a specific set of possible months in the future at a specific price.

The option purchaser's right to exercise the option has a limited duration. After the option's expiration date, the purchaser abandons the right to exercise the option. The option seller's obligations also end at the option's expiration. After the option has been abandoned, it no longer has any value.

THE VALUE OF AN OPTION ON GOLD FUTURES. Options on gold futures contracts have value only in relationship to the specific underlying futures contract. There are two components to an option's value: the *intrinsic value* and the *time value*. The *intrinsic value* is the immediate gain the option purchaser would receive, if the purchaser were to exercise the option. The *time value* is the expected gain over and above the existing intrinsic value, if the option is not immediately exercised.

Since a call option gives the purchaser the right to purchase a gold futures contract at the strike price, a call option has intrinsic value so long as the strike price is less than the futures price of gold, providing that the call option has not expired. The purchaser of the call option gains if the purchaser exercises the right to purchase a futures contract at a lower price, that is, the strike price rather than the market price for the futures contract. The amount of the gain (per troy ounce) from exercising a call option is the difference between the strike price and the market price of the futures contract. This gain is the call option's intrinsic value and can never be less than zero.

An option's intrinsic value can never be less than zero because the option purchaser is not obligated to exercise the call option and thereby purchase a gold futures contract at the strike price. Clearly, the purchaser of a call option would not exercise the option if the market price of gold for that specific futures contract were less than the strike price of the call option.

A put option has intrinsic value so long as the strike price is greater than the market price of the underlying gold futures contract, providing the put option has not expired. The purchaser of the put option gains if the purchaser exercises the right to sell a gold futures contract at a higher price, that is, the strike price rather than the market price for the futures contract. The amount of the gain is the difference between the strike price, that is, the price at which the put option purchaser has the right to sell the futures, and the market price of the futures. This amount is the put option's intrinsic value.

The second component of an option's value is its *time value*. The time value component measures the option's likely value at expiration, or exercise, above and beyond any intrinsic value the option may already have. Thus an option has little time value if its strike price is far away from the market price of gold in the futures contract. An option also has little time value if the price of gold has been steady and is expected to remain so. Finally, an option has little time value if expiration is near at hand.

If an option's strike price is far away from the market price of gold for the underlying futures contract, the option has little time value. The market price of gold is presumed to be as likely to fall as it is to rise. Therefore, if an option has significant intrinsic value, the option is about as likely to lose its existing intrinsic value as to gain additional value. Thus, the net likely gain is small, but typically positive.

Similarly, if the option's strike price is far away from the market price of gold for the underlying futures contract, and the option has no intrinsic value, the option has little time value. The market price of gold would have to change significantly for the option to have any intrinsic value. Although this change may occur, it also may not occur or even be negative. Thus, the net likely gain from holding the option is small, but typically positive.

The net likely gain from holding an option, that is, its time value, is typically positive. Since the value of an option cannot fall below zero because the option holder is not obligated to exercise, the likely gain will generally be greater than the likely loss. Therefore an option's time value will typically be greater than zero.

If the price of gold has been steady and is expected to remain so, an option will have little time value. If the price of gold does not change much, there is little likelihood that the option will gain or lose much additional intrinsic value before it expires. Therefore, if the price of gold has been steady, the option's time value is likely to be small, but positive.

Finally, the shorter the time to the option's expiration, the smaller the time value. The less time an option has to potentially gain in value, the less value the option can gain or lose. The net likely gain from holding the option for that short period of time would be small. Again, the time value is likely to be small, but positive, in this case.

SUMMARY OF USES FOR OPTIONS ON GOLD FUTURES. Holders of gold bullion can ensure themselves against the risk of a price decrease by selling gold futures. If the price does not change or decreases, the holders will recoup their carrying cost and offset the effects of the price decrease. However, if the price of gold rises, the holders may not be able to recoup all of their carrying cost since they will have to finance any calls for variation margin on the futures position. Similarly, purchasers of gold bullion can ensure themselves against the risks of a price increase by buying gold futures.

Holders and purchasers of gold bullion can also ensure themselves against price risks by using options on gold futures. Since call options gain intrinsic value when the price of gold rises above the strike price, the purchase of call options ensures a gold bullion purchaser against a price increase above the strike price of the call option. The purchase of a gold call futures option is distinctly different, in effect, from the purchase of a gold futures contract when the price falls. The holder of a call option retains the benefits of a price decline below the strike price of the option. The call option will expire worthless; however, the purchase is then made at the lower price.

Gold futures put options, on the other hand, gain intrinsic value when the price of gold futures falls below the strike price. Therefore, the purchase of the put options ensures the bullion holder against the adverse effects of a price decline, while allowing the retention of the benefits of a price increase.

Holders and buyers of gold bullion can also use gold futures options to generate income. By granting, that is, selling, an option, the seller collects the premium as income. This usage entails similar risks to those of futures contracts in that variation margin must be paid and financed if the price moves against the position.

Private investors can, also, use gold futures options as a way of benefiting from a correctly anticipated price change, while limiting the risks of being wrong. The most an option purchaser can lose is the premium paid for the option. Thus the full extent of the risks is known at the time the option is purchased. The investor would purchase a call option if the price of gold were expected to rise. A put option would be purchased if the price were expected to fall.

The uses of gold futures options presented here are the elementary ones. By mixing purchases and sales of put options, call options, and futures, a hedger or investor can construct a complex portfolio maximizing the potential reward while minimizing the accepted risk.

GLOSSARY

CALL OPTION: This option gives the purchaser the right to buy the underlying commodity futures contract at a particular price, known as the strike price, any time between the purchase date and the expiration of the option. Thus, an option to buy a futures contract, a "call," is bought in expectation of rising prices for the underlying futures contract.

TABLE 6. **Gold Options Summary**

	COMEX	Mocatta	Winnipeg
Quantity	100 troy oz	100 troy oz	100 troy oz
Strike price intervals	\$10 per oz below \$300 per oz \$20 per oz, \$300–\$500 per oz \$30 per oz, \$500–\$800 pe oz \$40 per oz over \$800 per oz	\$10 per oz	\$10 per oz
Contract months	Group 1: February, June, and October Group 2: April, August, and December Series of contracts is determined by taking the nearest month from Group 1 and all of Group 2 for a total of four contracts.	March, June, September, and December for up to 16 months	March, June, September, and December

PUT OPTION: This option gives the purchaser the right to sell the underlying commodity futures contract at the strike price any time between the purchase date and the expiration of the option. Thus, an option to sell a futures contract, a "put," is bought in expectation of declining prices for the underlying futures market.

STRIKE PRICE: The price at which the holder of a futures option may purchase or sell the underlying futures contract upon exercise. Also known as the "striking price' or "strike."

EXERCISE: The conversion of an option into the underlying futures contract through the COMEX Clearing Association.

EXPIRATION DATE: The time and day on which a particular option may no longer be offset or exercised, that is, the time it becomes worthless. Also, the month in which options expire is known as the expiration month.

PREMIUM: The amount of money that the buyer agrees to pay for an option with a particular expiration month and strike price. Premiums will fluctuate daily and will be determined competitively through open outcry at the Gold Futures Options Ring on the exchange floor. The premium will be quoted in terms of dollars per ounce.

INTRINSIC VALUE: The amount by which the settlement price of the underlying futures contract exceeds a call option's strike price, or the put option's strike price exceeds the futures price. Options with positive intrinsic value are said to be "in the money." Options with no intrinsic value are said to be "out of the money." Intrinsic value is reflected in the premium of an option.

TIME VALUE: The part of the premium which accounts for potential changes in the price of the underlying futures contract prior to an option's expiration. Time value is influenced by the price volatility of the underlying futures contract and the time remaining until expiration of the option.

SERIES: Options of the same type (either puts or calls) which cover the same underlying futures contract, have the same strike price, and the same expiration month.

SPREAD (STRADDLE): A combination of option positions with other options positions or with futures positions such that there is offsetting risk. Thus, a long-call/short-call position would be considered a spread, while a long-call/short-put position would not, since it does not contain the element of offsetting risk.

CHAPTER 44

THE SILVER MARKET

CONTENTS

SUPPLY OF SILVER 3

Mine Production 3

Secondary Supply-Scrap Production and Hoarding 6

THE DEMAND FOR SILVER 9

Industrial Use 10

Coinage Demand 14

Commemorative Coins and Medals 14

Investment Demand 16

THE CURRENT SITUATION AND FUTURE OUTLOOK 17

SILVER FUTURES MARKETS 17

The Use of Silver Futures 19

Options on Silver 19

A Comparison Between the LME and COMEX 21

CHAPTER 44

THE SILVER MARKET

Avner S. Wolf

Silver has been known for at least 5,000 years, and is one of the most important precious metals. Over the centuries it was used as a medium of exchange, as a store of value, and for ornamentation.

Recently, silver has become the most important precious metal used in industrial production. Its unique technical properties and qualities, among which are sonority, ductility, malleability, high degree of polish, and very high thermal and electrical conductivity, make silver a very useful metal in photography, electronics, computer, and communications industries. In addition, the relatively low price of silver compared to the other precious metals (which have similar qualities) makes the use of silver very attractive.

In the past, silver was mostly used for monetary and artistic purposes because of its relative scarcity and resistance to corrosion. However, in more recent years these uses have been surpassed in importance by industrial consumption due to the discovery of its outstanding physical and chemical properties and its electrical conductivity.

Traditionally, silver has been used in decorative objects, coinage, and tableware. But, it seems that the future growth of silver as an indispensable resource lies in the industrial field. Hence, more than in the past, the industrial growth rate will be strongly related to silver prices (futures and spot) and to its production rate (see Figure 1 for the history of silver prices, and Figure 2 for the mine production of silver).

SUPPLY OF SILVER

There are three sources for the supply of silver:

1. Mine production—primary supply.
2. Scrap production—secondary supply.
3. Hoarding—secondary supply.

MINE PRODUCTION. About 70% of the mine production of silver comes not from silver mines as such, but as a by-product of lead, nickel, copper, and zinc ores. It is also derived (to a lesser extent) as a by-product from gold mining. Today most of the silver mined in the world comes from five countries: Mexico,

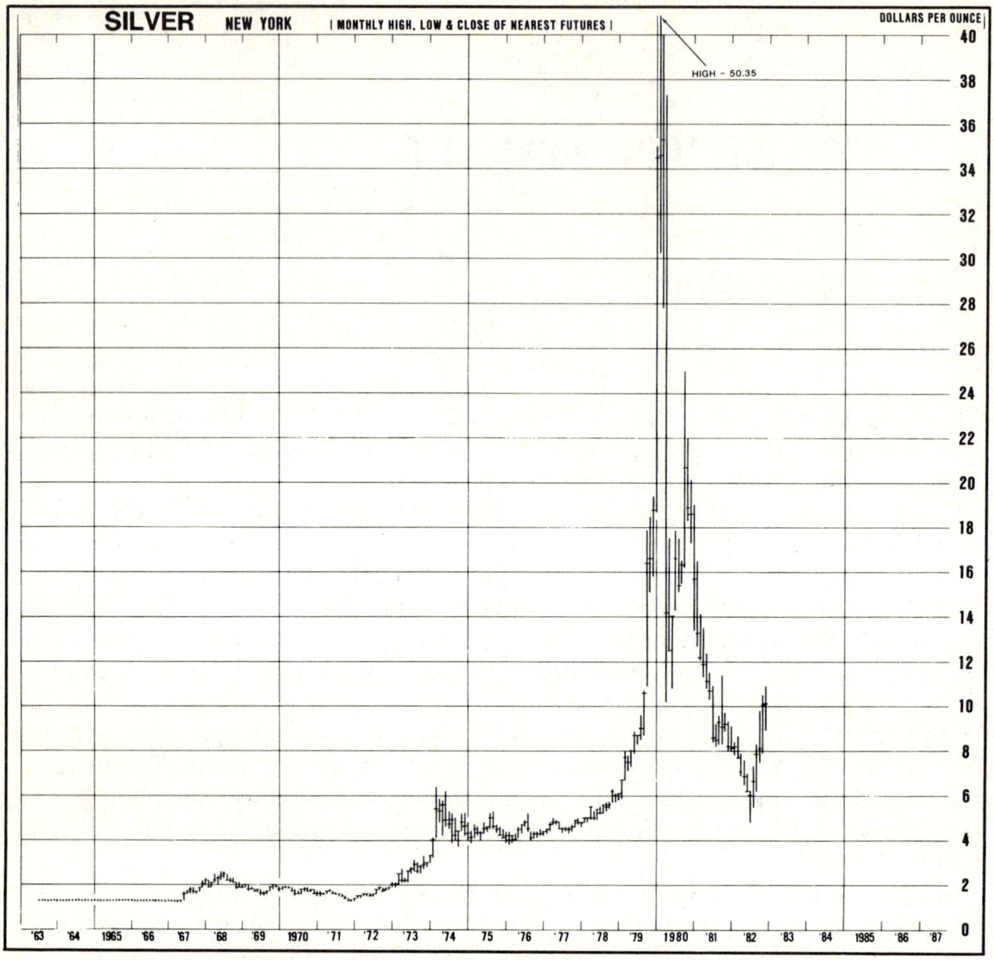

FIGURE 1. Silver prices, monthly—New York.

Peru, Canada, the United States, and Australia. Figure 2 summarizes the mine output in these producing countries from 1976.

Silver production was expanded significantly from the end of World War II (see Figure 3) until 1980. The decline in production since 1980 by roughly 65 million oz has been partly a consequence of widespread business recession.

Recently, most of the net increase in mine production occurred in two countries, Mexico and Australia. It is expected that Mexico will achieve an 11% increase to about 58 million oz, and that Australia will increase its production by 9.4% to about 28 million oz. Table 1 shows the mine production of the main producers since 1960. In Table 2 is shown the mine production by country for the years 1979 and 1980.

The production part of the supply of silver is highly inelastic to a change in prices. Since silver in most cases is a by-product of the production of other metals, its production does not respond markedly to a market price change. The silver production depends primarily on the production and the market conditions for

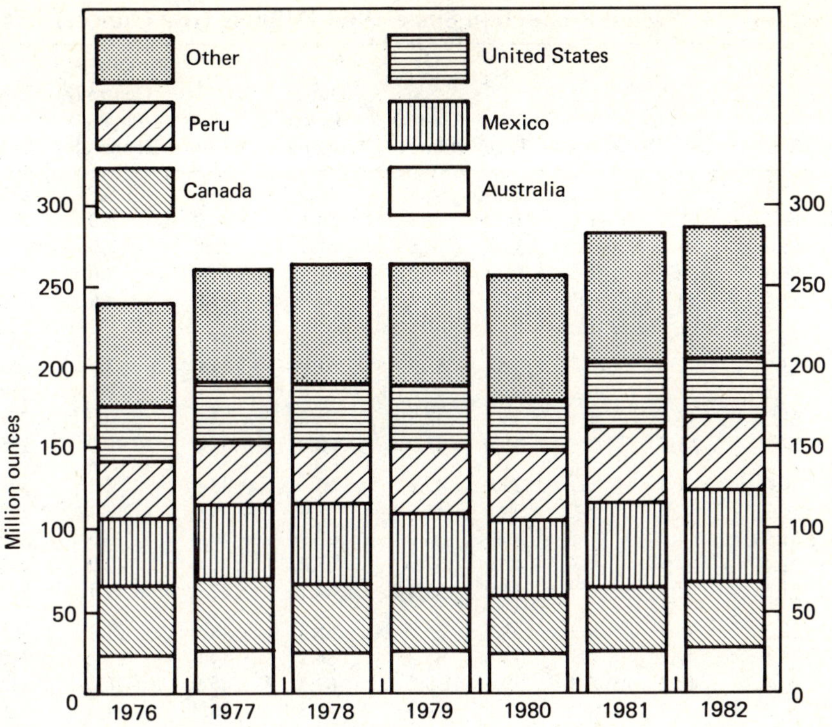

FIGURE 2. Mine output in major producing countries. (*Source: Annual Silver Review and Outlook*, July 1982, J. Aron & Company.)

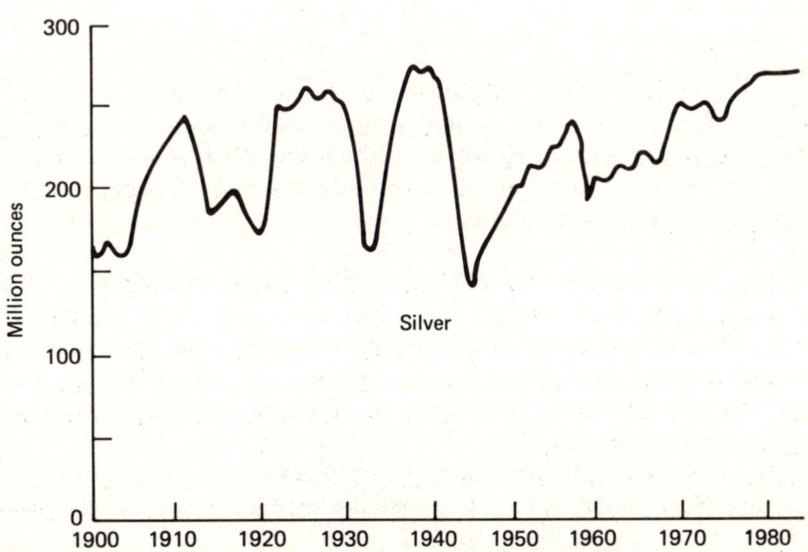

FIGURE 3. Silver production, 1900–1980.

TABLE 1. Mine Production Since 1960 (Million Troy Ounces)

	Australia	Canada	Mexico	Peru	United States	Other Market Economies	Soviet Union	Other Centrally Planned Economies	Total
1960	15.2	34.0	44.5	30.8	30.8	46.5	25.0	8.5	235.3
1961	13.1	31.4	40.3	34.2	34.8	50.1	25.0	8.0	236.9
1962	17.6	30.7	41.2	33.1	36.8	51.4	27.0	8.0	245.8
1963	19.6	29.8	42.8	35.2	35.2	51.4	28.0	8.0	250.0
1964	18.4	29.9	41.7	34.4	36.3	50.8	29.0	8.0	248.5
1965	17.3	32.3	40.3	36.5	39.8	52.2	31.0	8.0	257.4
1966	18.9	32.8	42.0	32.8	43.7	55.0	33.0	8.5	266.7
1967	19.8	37.2	38.3	32.1	32.3	55.0	35.0	8.5	258.2
1968	21.3	45.0	40.0	36.4	32.7	54.8	35.0	9.5	274.7
1969	24.5	43.5	42.9	35.9	41.9	60.0	37.0	10.0	295.7
1970	26.0	44.3	42.8	39.8	45.0	60.6	38.0	12.1	308.6
1971	21.7	46.0	36.7	38.4	41.6	62.8	39.0	13.1	299.3
1972	21.9	44.8	37.5	40.2	37.2	67.3	40.0	16.3	305.2
1973	22.4	47.5	38.8	42.0	37.8	65.2	41.0	17.2	311.9
1974	21.5	42.8	37.5	34.9	33.8	66.1	42.0	19.1	297.7
1975	23.3	39.7	38.0	37.5	34.9	65.6	43.0	21.1	303.1
1976	23.6	41.2	42.6	35.6	34.3	64.2	44.0	25.3	310.8
1977	26.4	42.2	47.0	39.1	38.2	69.3	45.0	28.0	335.2
1978	24.6	40.7	50.8	37.0	39.4	72.8	48.3	31.4	345.0
1979	25.8	36.9	49.4	41.9	38.1	74.6	47.9	30.8	345.4
1980	24.1	34.4	47.3	43.0	31.3	74.7	48.0	30.4	333.2
1981	25.6	38.7	52.5	46.9	40.7	80.0	49.0	29.4	362.8
1982[a]	28.0	39.0	58.0	44.7	36.6	81.5	50.0	30.0	367.8

Sources: U. S. Bureau of Mines; Silver Institute; Energy, Mines, and Resources Canada; *The Andean Report;* Consejo de Recursos Minerales Mexico; J. Aron Research Department; *Annual Silver Review and Outlook*, July 1982, J. Aron & Company.

[a]Projections.

copper, lead, and zinc. These base metals are highly sensitive to business cycles. As can be seen in Table 1 the estimated mine production was increased in the centrally planned economies. However, if the price of silver does not exceed the $15 level, the future increase of silver production will be dependent upon the improvement in the market conditions.

SECONDARY SUPPLY—SCRAP PRODUCTION AND HOARDING. The secondary supply accounts for about 34% of the total supply. Before 1960 only about 15% of the total supply came from secondary supply. The two most important components of the secondary supply are old scrap and hoarding, which accounts for about 85% of it. The scrap production is the single most important component of the secondary supply—60%.

The increase in the secondary supply from 1978 to 1980 was due to a substantial price increase (see Figure 1), but after 1980 the secondary supply fell sharply (see Figure 4).

TABLE 2. Mine Production by Country (Thousand Troy Ounces)

	1979	1980		1979	1980
Africa			Europe		
Algeria	100	80	Finland	1,028	1,000
Ghana	20	20	France	2,429	2,500
Morocco	2,418	2,300	Greece	1,752	1,800
Namibia	1,606	1,610	Greenland	765	547
South Africa	3,236	3,125	Ireland	897	925
Tunisia	231	236	Italy	1,065	1,233
Zaire	3,892	4,000	Portugal	31	32
Zambia	914	764	Spain	3,168	3,200
Zimbabwe	977	949	Sweden	5,649	5,000
Total	13,394	13,084	West Germany	1,042	1,000
			Yugoslavia	5,214	4,790
			Total	23,040	22,027
Asia			North and Central America		
Burma	340	425	Canada	36,874	34,402
India	370	370	Costa Rica	2	2
Indonesia	662	680	Dominican Republic	1,774	1,600
Japan	8,680	8,930	El Salvador	152	155
Malaysia	450	437	Guatemala	10	10
Philippines	1,830	1,930	Honduras	2,167	2,850
South Korea	2,278	2,292	Mexico	49,409	47,344
Taiwan	85	95	Nicaragua	318	164
Turkey	250	200	United States	38,087	31,327
Total	14,945	15,349	Total	128,793	117,854

TABLE 2. Continued

	1979	1980		1979	1980
Oceania			Centrally Planned Economies		
Australia	25,808	24,107	Bulgaria	860	865
Fiji	10	11	Czechoslovakia	1,200	1,200
New Zealand	2	2	East Germany	1,550	1,550
Papua New Guinea	1,428	1,180	Hungary	65	65
Total	27,248	25,300	Poland	22,600	22,000
			Romania	985	950
South America			Soviet Union	47,900	47,950
Argentina	2,193	2,200	China	2,000	2,200
Bolivia	5,742	6,099	North Korea	1,525	1,600
Brazil	580	640	Subtotal	78,685	78,380
Chile	8,740	9,050			
Colombia	99	150	World Total	345,416	333,158
Ecuador	57	58			
Peru	41,900	42,957			
Total	59,311	61,154			
Subtotal	266,731	254,778			

Sources: U.S. Bureau of Mines; Silver Institute; Energy, Mines, and Resources Canada; *The Andean Report;* Consejo de Recursos Minerales Mexico; J. Aron Research Department.

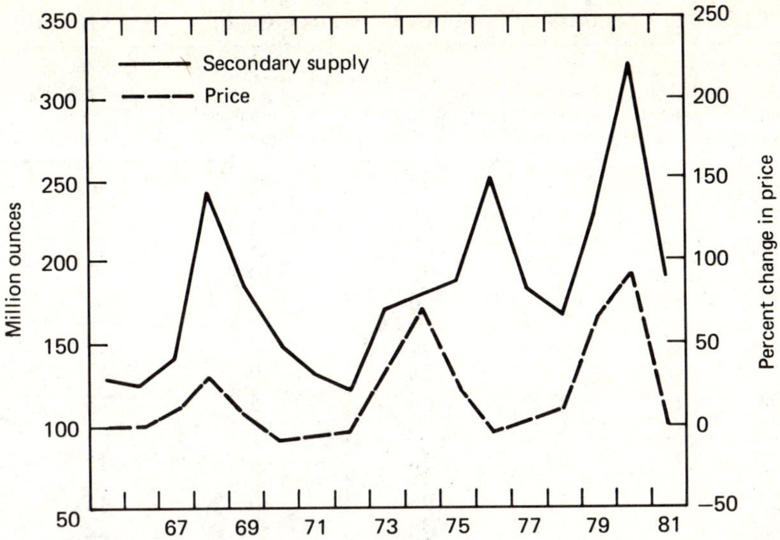

FIGURE 4. Secondary supply and the price of silver. (Note: Price series in a 2-year moving average.)

Table 3 shows the secondary supplies by source from 1960 to 1981. The importance of old scrap relative to the other secondary sources can be seen in this table.

In sharp contrast to the mine production, secondary supply is very sensitive to silver price changes. This was especially apparent in 1980 following the dramatic price rise; 1981 secondary supply reflects the rapid price decline. The sensitivity of the secondary supply to the change can be seen in Table 1 in conjunction with Figure 4.

The future secondary supply may also depend on the public belief about new price levels in the future. This has to do with the extent to which the public believes that silver may serve as a hedge against inflation. The increase in production of the scrap depends on the relative stability of silver prices when the spot reaches high levels.

To summarize the supply side, it seems that the future increase of silver production from mines mainly depends upon the improvement of the world market for the base metals. This is so because the silver is produced mainly as a by-product of these metals. The secondary supply is more sensitive to prices than to business cycles; hence price hikes will increase scrap production and will cause reduction in the hoarding of silver.

THE DEMAND FOR SILVER

The main components of the demand for silver are:

1. Industrial demand—photography, electrical products, medicine, jewelry, silverware, electronic, and coinage demand.
2. Investment demand.

TABLE 3. Secondary Supplies by Source (Million Troy Ounces)

	Old Scrap	Indian Domestic Use	South Asian Exports	Demonetized Coin	Government Stocks	Net Exports From Centrally Planned Economies	Total
1960	40	2	—	10	12	10	74
1961	43	2	—	20	7	55	127
1962	47	2	—	20	4	25	98
1963	50	3	—	15	10	—	78
1964	54	12	—	20	20	—	106
1965	57	16	—	30	17	9	129
1966	61	16	—	28	10	10	125
1967	59	15	17	35	5	8	139
1968	75	16	86	50	15	—	242
1969	80	16	28	50	—	11	185
1970	55	16	31	25	10	13	150
1971	68	16	23	20	5	—	132
1972	73	13	11	15	10	—	122
1973	72	13	22	15	45	—	167
1974	82	15	60	35	20	—	212
1975	90	13	54	20	12	3	192
1976	92	18	53	72	10	7	252
1977	93	18	25	33	5	8	182
1978	82	21	28	21	9	7	168
1979	130	23	18	45	3	14	233
1980	164	23	21	94	5	13	320
1981	113	27	20	16	4	8	188

Sources: U. S. Bureau of Mines; Handy & Harman; Samuel Montagu; Silver Institute; Japanese, European, and Indian trade sources; J. Aron Research Department; *Annual Silver Review and Outlook,* July 1982, J. Aron & Company. (Excludes U. S. Treasury sales.)

Table 4 gives the breakdown of the U.S. silver consumption by category, and Table 5 gives the United States and the world industrial consumption of silver between the years 1960–1980. As can be seen from Table 4, the industrial portion of the consumption accounts for most of the consumption demand in the United States. Hence we will devote most of this section to discussion of industrial use.

INDUSTRIAL USE. The use of silver in industry has grown rapidly since 1940. Since silver has unique properties, there are many uses of it in industry. Specifically, it has a high degree of malleability, ductility, and light sensitivity. Therefore it is widely used in photography, plating for electrical contacts, switches, medicine, coating used in mirrors, optical usage, and heat-reflecting surfaces. It is also used in aircraft engine parts, for batteries, and as parts of the amalgam used in silver dental fillings. In most of its uses, the cost of silver used in these industries represents only a small fraction of the total manufacturing cost. In 1981, 1982, and 1983, the industrial demand rose very little, despite lower prices. The reason

TABLE 4. U.S. Consumption of Silver, 1970–1980 (millions of troy ounces)

	1970	1971	1972	1973	1974	1975	1976	1977	1978	1979	1980
Photographic materials	38	36	38	52	50	46	55	54	64	66	49
Electrical and electronic products	32	34	43	44	35	32	36	37	37	38	32
Other industrial[a]	18	16	18	27	25	24	26	25	23	22	16
Jewelry, mirrors, and sterlingware[b]	37	38	46	63	45	48	45	34	34	28	18
Medallions and coins[c]	3	6	6	10	22	7	9	4	3	3	4
Total industrial consumption	128	130	151	196	177	157	171	154	161	157	120
Coinage	1	2	2	7	1	3	1	—	—	—	—
Total consumption	129	132	153	197	178	160	172	154	161	157	120

Source: U. S. Bureau of Mines, Department of the Interior.

[a]Includes bearings, brazing alloys and solders, catalysts, medical and dental, and miscellaneous uses.

[b]Includes electroplated ware.

[c]Includes commemorative objects.

TABLE 5. Industrial Demand by Country (Million Troy Ounces)

	United States	Canada	Mexico	United Kingdom	France	West Germany	Italy	Japan	India	Other	Total
1960	102.0	4.3	4.3	16.5	13.0	40.2	[a]	21.6	1.5	31.9	235.3
1961	105.5	4.5	3.4	20.0	14.0	43.5	20.0	19.1	1.5	36.2	267.7
1962	110.4	4.5	3.3	20.0	13.5	41.8	22.0	19.6	1.5	37.0	273.6
1963	110.0	4.6	3.2	20.0	13.9	40.5	25.0	20.0	2.5	37.4	277.1
1964	123.0	5.0	4.1	23.0	14.8	46.3	25.0	20.0	12.0	42.7	315.9
1965	137.0	5.7	4.7	25.0	14.0	54.6	25.0	25.8	16.0	48.0	355.8
1966	183.7	5.8	3.9	25.0	14.7	48.2	30.0	31.5	16.0	56.1	414.9
1967	171.0	5.8	5.0	24.0	14.7	48.2	28.2	33.2	15.0	53.9	399.0
1968	145.3	6.2	5.0	23.0	18.0	50.0	22.5	35.0	16.0	50.0	371.0
1969	141.5	5.7	4.4	24.5	19.3	50.0	29.0	41.5	16.0	51.9	383.8
1970	128.4	6.0	5.4	25.0	15.5	48.2	32.0	46.0	16.0	50.4	372.9
1971	129.1	6.8	5.1	25.0	15.6	59.9	30.5	46.5	16.0	52.1	386.6
1972	151.7	8.3	7.0	27.0	16.5	60.0	32.0	54.3	13.0	57.6	427.4
1973	196.4	10.4	10.5	31.5	22.5	60.0	33.5	69.0	13.0	69.7	516.5
1974	176.0	10.3	6.5	33.0	21.0	55.0	30.0	57.7	14.0	62.8	466.3
1975	157.7	10.3	5.6	28.0	21.0	38.9	28.9	46.4	13.0	54.7	404.5
1976	170.6	9.3	6.5	27.6	31.8	52.9	38.5	60.8	18.0	65.0	481.0
1977	153.6	9.1	5.5	29.4	32.6	48.1	36.3	63.2	17.6	61.8	457.2
1978	160.2	9.6	5.8	29.0	24.6	42.0	31.0	64.9	21.0	60.7	448.8
1979	157.3	7.3	5.5	27.6	24.1	39.8	33.3	68.7	22.5	60.3	446.4
1980	124.7	8.3	3.1	19.5	19.8	31.9	21.8	61.5	22.5	49.9	363.0
1981	133.0	9.0	3.4	18.4	18.9	29.3	21.8	59.8	26.5	50.8	370.9

Sources: U. S. Bureau of Mines; Handy & Harman; Japanese, Indian, and European trade sources; J. Aron Research Department.
Notes: Excludes Centrally Planned Economies. Totals may not equal sums of countries due to rounding.
[a]Included in "other" category.

for the sluggish demand is the high levels of interest rate. Table 5 shows the fabrication demand by country since 1960.

Photography. Silver is the only substance known to amplify (in reaction with light) each photon of light a billion times, therefore making it possible to produce high-quality photographs. New developments and innovations allow, for example, an instant processing of x-ray pictures. Another example of an innovation is the use of silver in improving photographic films which are processed very quickly without the need of processing chemicals. The fast growth and development of electronic photography will increase the use of silver in this industry. The U.S. photographic industry uses about 50 million troy oz of silver a year. But because silver accounts only for a very small portion of the total cost per unit production, the demand of this industry is not extremely elastic to a price change. Its demand is more elastic to the overall market conditions. Figure 5 shows the U.S. photographic use and the price of silver from 1969 to 1982.

Electrical and Electronic Use. There are three characteristics of silver which make it vital for particular applications: (1) It conducts electricity more efficiently than other metals; (2) it conducts heat more efficiently than other metals; and (3) it does not oxidize in the air as most other metals do. Similar to silver's use in photography, only a small portion of the cost is due to the use of silver in the production process. For this reason the demand of the electronic industry is not very sensitive to a change in the silver's price. Figure 6 shows the U.S. electrical industry output and silver use from 1969 to 1982.

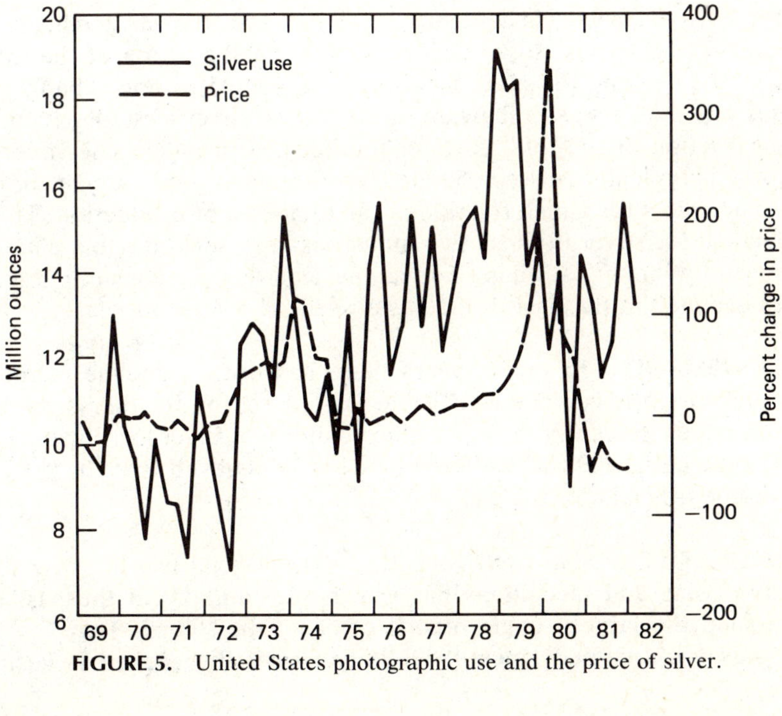

FIGURE 5. United States photographic use and the price of silver.

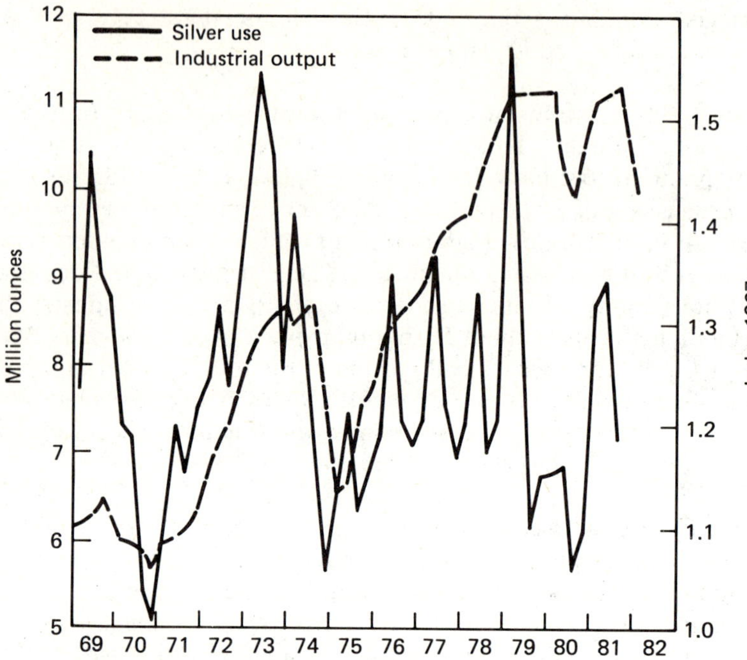

FIGURE 6. United States electrical industry output and silver use.

Other Industrial Use. An important use of silver is in batteries. When size and weight are important silver batteries are more effective because they have twice the electrical capacity of lead-acid batteries of the same size.

Silver has also been used in dentistry, medicine, and other related fields. Similar to the first two industries, silver accounts for a small fraction of the total cost. This makes the demand for silver inelastic with respect to price changes.

There is one industry, sterlingware, in which the silver content accounts for a significant fraction of the total costs of the finished product. The silver cost in this industry is typically between 50 to 60% of the final product cost. In jewelry, silver also accounts for a high fraction of the total cost of production. This factor makes demand for silver in these two industries very sensitive to a change in its price. Indeed by looking at Figure 5 it can be seen that the consumption in these industries declined in the past decade as a result of a price increase.

COINAGE DEMAND. In recent years there has been a decline in the use of silver in official silver coinage (see Table 6). The reason for this is the extreme volatility in prices. Recently, however, the volatility of silver has declined (mainly after 1981, excluding February, 1983); hence it is believed that there will be an increase in the official coinage use.

COMMEMORATIVE COINS AND MEDALS. The official use of silver for commemorative coins and medallions has grown substantially in the past decade. Mexico issued the largest single official coinage, the "Onza Troy." About 10 million coins were minted since 1949. Italy issued the second largest official

TABLE 6. Industrial Demand, Annual (Thousand Troy Ounces)

	1973	1974	1975	1976	1977	1978	1979	1980	1981[a]
Photography	51,979	49,579	46,074	55,530	53,679	64,299	65,978	49,825	53,055
Electrical contacts and conductors	40,209	31,305	27,211	32,329	31,316	30,756	33,506	27,796	31,334
Sterlingware	29,386	22,147	23,717	19,815	16,690	17,908	13,088	9,082	5,779
Brazing alloys and solders	17,736	14,514	13,582	11,198	12,362	10,987	10,912	8,508	9,699
Batteries	4,155	4,195	4,253	3,490	5,783	6,029	4,583	5,976	5,108
Jewelry	5,778	5,102	12,734	10,995	8,059	6,766	5,358	5,893	6,600
Coins, medallions, and commemorative objects	20,108	21,432	7,186	8,240	4,252	2,727	4,676	4,693	3,332
Electroplated ware	14,542	13,177	8,717	9,534	6,844	7,274	8,065	4,350	5,527
Catalysts	5,988	7,293	8,785	12,267	8,883	8,197	5,637	3,035	5,360
Dental and medical supplies	3,022	2,401	1,503	1,942	2,232	2,033	2,295	2,212	1,946
Mirrors	2,579	3,947	3,150	4,622	2,131	1,862	1,850	672	615
Bearings	375	416	458	273	523	373	332	649	250
Miscellaneous	529	519	281	324	859	954	978	2,005	4,365
Total, industrial	196,386	176,027	157,651	170,559	153,613	160,165	157,258	124,696	132,970

Source: *Annual Silver Review and Outlook*, July 1982, J. Aron & Company.

[a]Projections.

TABLE 7. Reported and Inferred Silver Holdings (Million Troy Ounces)

	Reported Stocks (Stock Levels)				Year-to-Year Changes		
	Government	Exchange	Dealer	Total	In Reported Stocks	In Inferred Stocks	Total
1970	357.7	135.0	82.2	574.9	n.a.[a]	n.a.	n.a.
1971	311.9	135.7	57.1	504.7	−70.2	36.2	−34
1972	333.6	107.9	51.9	493.4	−11.3	−80.7	−92
1973	277.2	108.0	38.4	423.6	−69.8	−54.2	−124
1974	319.2	99.5	49.3	468.0	44.4	−92.4	−48
1975	250.8	142.0	34.6	427.4	−40.6	36.6	−4
1976	257.0	144.3	30.6	431.9	4.5	−20.5	−16
1977	319.0	149.8	35.6	504.4	72.5	−119.5	−47
1978	318.8	141.1	29.0	488.9	−15.5	−41.5	−57
1979	314.6	146.2	16.1	476.9	−12.0	32.0	20
1980	326.5	147.7	18.0	492.2	15.3	185.7	201
1981	n.a.	124.8	20.6	N.A.	21.5	67.5	89

Sources: U. S. Bureau of the Mint; U. S. Bureau of Mines; COMEX; Chicago Board of Trade; J. Aron Research Department.
[a]n.a. = not available.

minting in 1980, 1.5 million 500-lire coins. The world's largest private mint is the Franklin Mint in Philadelphia, Pennsylvania. In 1980, total sales of this mint had reached $360 million and of this total, 25% or $90 million were silver items. Table 6 shows the U.S. industrial demand from 1973. It can be seen that the photography and electrical industry accounted for most of the industrial use in 1981, while coinage has continued to decline.

INVESTMENT DEMAND. Typically, the motives of investors are (1) hedge against inflation and (2) the expectation of a substantial price appreciation. During recent years, the first motive cannot be taken as a significant factor in determining the investment demand. However, despite the sharp price decline in late 1980, there is still speculative demand for silver. There are still a number of large investors who expect the silver price to increase substantially in the coming years.

The current high levels of the short-term interest rates affect the speculative demand for silver. But, if the recent trend of declining interest rates continues, it may increase substantially the demand for silver and also the silver prices.

It is not clear how much of the silver accumulated during recent years will find its way back to the market. To a large extent, it depends on the inflationary and the silver price expectations. If prices continue to remain low (below $15 per oz), not too many investors will risk selling their silver. If silver prices increase by more than the inflation rate, investors will accumulate more.

Changes in investment holdings in recent years have been more important than stock changes in other categories. Known stocks at the end of 1981 reached 462 million oz. About 316 million oz were held by governments, 125 million oz were stored in exchange warehouses, and 21 million oz were held by refiners, dealers, and importers.

It is clear that the investment demand depends on how well the whole world economy is doing, and to a large extent the shape of the world economy depends on the share of the U.S. economy. Table 7 shows the reported and inferred silver holdings from 1970 to 1981 in the United States. It can be seen that there is not a one-to-one relationship between the stock levels held by government and dealers. This indicates that a change in economic conditions has different effects on the private sector than on the central planner.

THE CURRENT SITUATION AND FUTURE OUTLOOK

Both mint output and secondary supply have been constrained by low prices. But the demand has been held back (despite the prices) by bad economic conditions and high interest rates. As interest rates decline and the business cycle causes an upturn in the demand, supply and prices will increase.

There have been three major price cycles since the late 1960s, when the U.S. government ended its active intervention in the silver market. The peaks, which were about 6 years apart, occurred in 1968, 1974, and 1980. In the current cycle prices have fallen for three consecutive years. This suggests from the experience of past cycles that prices may soon start rebounding. (For past cycles, see Figure 7.)

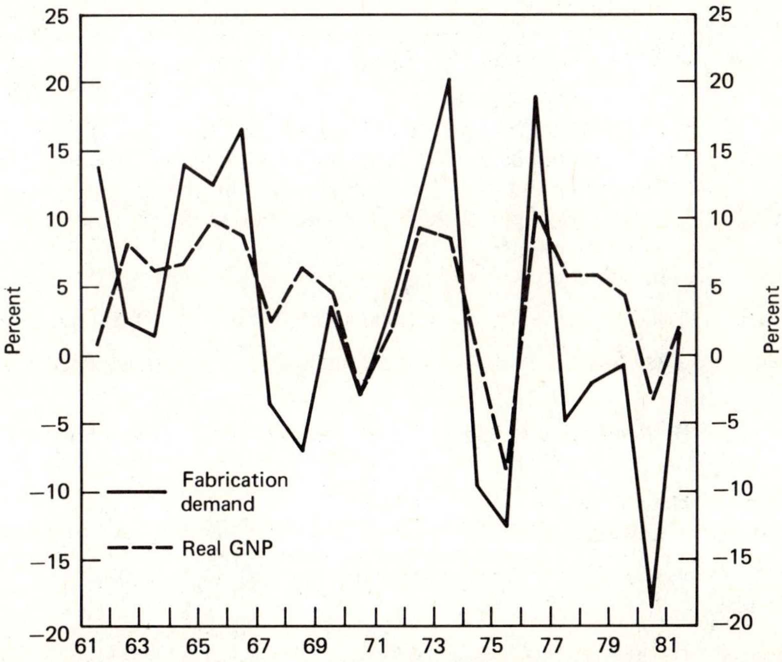

FIGURE 7. Fabrication demand and real GNP. (Note: Real GNP is the inflation-adjusted growth in output in the OECD nations. Both series are plotted as year-to-year percent changes.) (*Source: Annual Silver Review and Outlook*, July 1982, J. Aron & Company.)

It seems that the new federal monetary policy will have a positive effect on the current economic situation. Relaxing the tight monetary policy has already caused short-term interest rates to fall. Since the federal policy war against inflation was successful, the new policy will help the recovery process initially through the private sector's investment demand. This will push unemployment down and we may see a stronger upward trend in the economy, which will be reflected in higher silver prices.

SILVER FUTURES MARKETS

There are three major markets for silver futures—the London Metal Exchange (LME), the Commodity Exchange, Incorporated (COMEX), and the Chicago Board of Trade (CBT). In Table 8 there is a summary of the specifications of the contracts in these three dominant exchanges.

In all of the futures markets, the sellers (buyers) have contractual obligations to make (take) delivery, respectively. Futures contracts are traded on organized commodity exchanges in many locations around the world. COMEX is currently the most important precious metal exchange in the United States, and carries the largest volume of trading in all silver contracts. The prices of silver futures are disseminated continuously throughout the trading hours from the Chicago Board

TABLE 8. Summary of Silver Futures Contracts Specifications

Exchange	COMEX	CBT	LME
Trading hours	9:05 a.m.–2:15 p.m.	8:05 a.m.–1:25 p.m.	11:50 a.m.–11:55 a.m. 4:35 p.m.–4:40 p.m.
Contract months	January, March, May, July, September, December and current year plus 2 years by months, 23 months out	Even months and current month plus 2 nearby months, 18 months out	3, 6, 9, and 12 months
Contract size	5,000 oz	1,000 and 5,000 oz	10,000 oz
Deliverable grade	0.999 fine	0.999 fine	0.999 fine
Delivery	By depository receipt	By depository receipt	By depository receipt
Depositories	New York and Chicago	Chicago	London, Amsterdam, and Rotterdam
Minimum price change	\$0.001	\$0.001	\$0.001
Maximum price change	\$0.50	\$0.50	None

of Trade and the COMEX and twice a day from the London Metal Exchange. The silver futures prices are also reported in most of the world's financial newspapers.

The difference in the price of silver for the various contract months reflects the *cost of carry*. This includes interest, storage, and insurance charges which are determined by the price level and the time of delivery. Although there is substantial industrial use of silver, the investment value makes it a pure carry market. It is not likely that a sudden demand for physical silver will cause the spot market to rise above the deferred months, since that would imply a negative return on investment—a situation which should reduce investment demand sharply.

Prices on the world silver futures markets are kept in line by active arbitrage. The difference in price should always remain closely related to current interest rates. If the implied interest is greater than the current available bank rate for the same period, an investor need only buy the physical silver and sell the future delivery month to ensure the higher interest rate. If specific future delivery months move out of line with interest rates during the respective period those delivery months may be arbitraged by buying (selling) the near and selling (buying) the deferred if the implied rates are too high or low, respectively.

THE USES OF SILVER FUTURES. Silver futures can be used by both hedgers and investors (speculators). Hedgers (producers and bullion dealers) can hedge the risk of fluctuation in the spot price by assuming a position in the silver futures markets. For example, if a bullion dealer expects to buy a certain amount of bullion 6 months from now, but the dealer believes the silver price will increase, the dealer can immediately buy the silver futures contracts for delivery in 6 months. If a silver miner is expected to produce a certain amount of silver 12 months from now, but suspects that the price will fall, the miner can sell silver futures contracts for delivery in 12 months. In these two examples, the hedger ensures against the adverse fluctuations of the silver prices. Adverse changes in the price of physical silver will be offset by profits in the futures markets.

Some hedgers can also be considered speculators since they are still left exposed on the basis. The protection to the producer who hedges by selling futures for delivery in 12 months does not include relative price changes due to variation in interest rates. The price relationship of the deferred futures contracts will vary directly with the changing interest rates which determine the cost of carry. To be fully protected, a hedger must also take the proper position in a corresponding delivery month of financial futures.

A trader should be aware of two risks associated with futures contracts. The first is the risk that upon taking or making a silver delivery the fineness of the silver bars will not be the required 0.999. The second is that when a futures contract is liquidated prior to maturity there is a risk that the futures price at the liquidation date will be different from the spot price (the basis is usually defined as the futures price minus the spot price). Hence any unforeseen change in the basis is defined to be the *basis risk*.

OPTIONS ON SILVER. At the time of writing, the most active silver options were Mocatta options. Mocatta Metal Corporation offers three types of silver options. Table 9 summarizes the specifications of these options.

TABLE 9. Mocatta Metal Options On Silver

Commodity	Options Available	Grantor	Quantity	Equivalence	Striking Prices in Increments	Expiration Dates up to 7 Months Forward
Silver	Puts and calls	Mocatta Metal Corporation	1,000 troy oz of 0.999 fine silver	⅕ of one CBT or COMEX silver contract	$1 per oz	February, March, May, June, and August–November
U.S. silver clad coins	Calls	Mocatta Metal Corporation	One bag containing $1,000 face value of U.S. silver clad half-dollars minted between 1965–1969 inclusive.	295 troy oz silver	$200 per bag increments	January, March, April, June, July, September, October, and December
U.S. silver dollars	Calls	Mocatta Metal Corporation	One bag containing $1,000 face value of U.S. 90% silver dollars minted between 1837–1935.	760 troy oz of silver	$1,000 per bag	January, February, April, May, July, August, October, and November

It is very likely that in the near future the CFTC will approve the second phase of the 3-year pilot program of trading options. Then, it is conceivable that one or two of the major exchanges will trade options on silver futures.

A COMPARISON BETWEEN THE LME AND COMEX. Most of the trading in silver (spot and futures) is concentrated in the two U.S. exchanges, COMEX and CBT, and in the LME in England. The silver contract in the LME is more like a forward contract, while the counterparts in COMEX and CBT are futures contracts where the accounts of the traders are marked to the market daily. Hence a brief comparison between the COMEX and the LME will help potential users of the U.S. and British silver markets to understand these two distinct markets:

1. All trades on the COMEX are cleared by the COMEX Clearing Association, Incorporated which becomes the buyer to each clearing member who sells a contract and the seller to each clearing member who buys a contract. The LME has no clearinghouse, hence sellers and buyers act as principals. To become an LME ring member, a company must be well established financially.
2. On the COMEX new information about trades is continually disseminated to the public throughout the trading day. On the LME only settlement prices are officially recorded.
3. On the COMEX settlement payments may take place on any day up to, and including, expiration. On the LME payments take place only upon expiration of the contract.
4. On the COMEX the broker commissions are negotiable and based on the contract volume. On the LME the commission is a percentage of the contract value.
5. On the COMEX there are maximum position limits. On the LME there are no limits.
6. On the COMEX there are maximum daily price movements. On the LME there are no limits.
7. On the COMEX the trading hours are fixed by the exchange. On the LME there is additional trading on the "kerb," which supplements the official sessions.

CHAPTER 45

THE COPPER MARKET

CONTENTS

THE PRODUCTION PROCESS 3

PRODUCTION OF COPPER 5

Primary Copper Production 5

Scrap Recovery 6

DEMAND FOR COPPER 8

SEASONALITY 10

Filtering Housing Starts 10

COPPER FUTURES MARKETS 12

The Commodity Exchange, Incorporated (COMEX) 12

The London Metal Exchange 14

A COPPER EXPORTER'S HEDGE 15

CHAPTER 45

THE COPPER MARKET

Robert J. Anthes

Copper is a major nonferrous industrial metal which is valued around the world for its many versatile properties. It is an essential element utilized by major industries and thus has become an actively traded commodity.

The use of copper dates back several thousand years, when it was originally utilized for the purpose of ornamentation and in the making of various implements and tools. With the introduction of the Industrial Revolution, the need arose for strong, versatile, and cost-effective metals. Since that time, copper has become highly recognized, especially for its high degree of electrical conductivity and its ability to resist corrosion. These qualities, combined with its malleability, strength, and shiny appearance, have made the metal useful in multifarious applications, among which are wiring and electronics, plumbing, and jewelry. Copper is either used by itself or is combined with other metals to create a variety of consumer products and capital goods.

The electrical, housing, and automotive industries all make use of copper on a very large scale. Combined, these industries represent a significant percentage of the entire domestic consumption of the metal.

Although in recent years strong competition from aluminum and fiber optics have impacted on copper's use, the copper industry still represents a multibillion-dollar business having major economic importance. This is evident in Table 4 which shows that total world consumption of refined copper has increased considerably since 1975. Because copper is such a key element in the electrical, housing, and automotive industries, the copper market tends to be greatly affected by the state of the economy. Generally, during a recessionary economy the demand for copper tends to slack off due to the decreased demand for automobiles, housing, and capital goods. Conversely, the usage of copper typically increases during healthy economic situations. Thus, over the years, copper prices have been very volatile in reaction to the cyclical swings of the economy. This volatile price pattern is very evident in Figure 1.

THE PRODUCTION PROCESS

Copper is primarily mined in open pits, which requires the use of large and costly mechanical equipment. Enormous quantities of ore must be removed from the earth in order to obtain small amounts of copper. In fact, only 8 to 72 pounds of recoverable copper are typically obtained from one ton of overburden. The re-

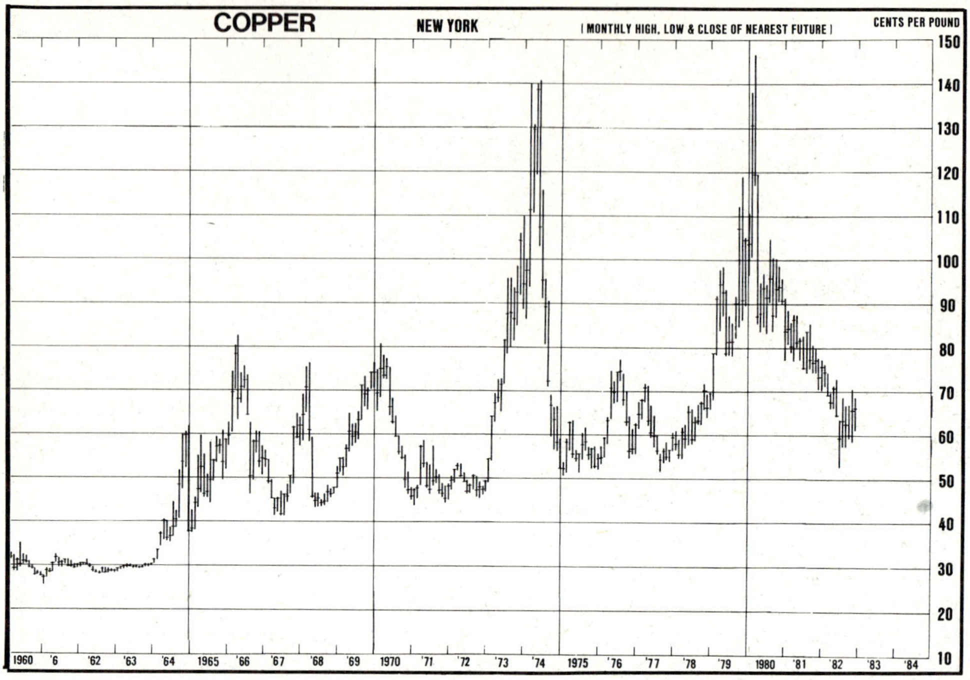

FIGURE 1. Copper, Monthly Prices—New York.

coverable amount of copper differs among various regions of the world because of their different concentrations of ore bodies. The Philippines has the lowest recoverable rate of copper ore; Zaire is estimated to have the highest. The difficult recovery process, combined with large labor forces and governmental pressures to control pollution, have made copper production a costly and complicated business requiring large capital investments.

Most of the mined copper in the United States today is obtained from copper sulfide ores, which often contain small amounts of other metals such as gold, silver, and platinum. After mining, the ore goes through three processes—basically milling, smelting, and refining—to ultimately yield pure copper. Afterwards, the copper is fabricated into many useful sizes and shapes.

During milling, the rock is crushed, ground, and sent through a flotation process which results in the formation of copper concentrates containing 30% copper or less. By intensely heating the copper concentrates, the smelting process further removes impurities. Initially, a "matte" is created (containing 30 to 45% copper) which is subsequently converted into "blister copper" consisting of about 99% pure copper. The copper is then usually fire refined or electrolytically refined. The latter process is most common and utilizes an electrolysis process to remove any remaining impurities. In this process, copper sheets are placed in a tank filled with a chemical solution. An electric current causes any impurities to separate and settle at the bottom of the tank while pure copper forms on cathode sheets. Ultimately, copper cathodes are produced which weigh about 300 lbs. They typically measure about 3½ feet square, and consist of about 99.9% pure copper.

Currently, cathodes are the most commonly used shape of copper for trading purposes.

PRODUCTION OF COPPER

Most of the world's copper production is accounted for either by mine production or through the recovery and processing of scrap copper. Scrap production has become a major supply factor in recent years and should continue its importance in the future. The noncorrosive property of copper ensures an abundance of available scrap and a relatively long lasting source of supply.

PRIMARY COPPER PRODUCTION. The primary production of copper comes from various countries throughout the world, as is indicated in Table 1.

TABLE 1. World Mine Production of Copper (in Thousand Metric Tons)

	1975	1976	1977	1978	1979[a]	1980[b]
Canada	733.8	730.9	759.4	659.4	636.4	708.4
United States	1,282.2	1,456.6	1,364.4	1,357.6	1,143.5	1,168.3
Chile	828.3	1,005.2	1,056.2	1,035.5	1,061.5	1,067.7
Mexico	78.5	89.0	89.7	87.2	107.1	175.4
Peru	165.8	218.8	326.6	366.5	397.2	365.3
Other America	12.7	10.7	8.1	7.7	11.5	6.8
Total America	3,101.3	3,511.2	3,604.4	3,513.9	3,357.2	3,491.9
Yugoslavia	114.9	120.1	116.2	123.3	111.4	116.8
Other Europe	180.8	178.1	172.4	176.9	169.1	168.1
Total Europe	295.7	298.2	298.6	300.2	280.5	284.9
South Africa	178.9	196.9	216.1	209.3	203.2	211.9
Zaire	494.8	444.6	481.6	423.8	399.8	549.7
Zambia	676.9	708.9	656.0	643.0	588.3	595.8
Other Africa	112.1	120.2	113.5	94.9	96.0	90.4
Total Africa	1,462.7	1,470.6	1,467.2	1,371.0	1,287.3	1,357.8
Japan	85.0	81.6	81.4	72.0	59.1	53.2
Philippine Republic	225.8	237.6	273.6	263.4	300.5	304.6
Other Asia	141.3	166.2	156.0	150.8	150.3	133.4
Total Asia	452.1	485.4	511.0	486.2	509.9	491.2
Australia	219.0	218.5	221.6	222.1	237.4	231.8
Papaua New Guinea	172.5	176.5	182.3	198.6	170.8	146.8
Total	391.5	395.0	403.9	420.7	408.2	378.6
Poland	230.0	267.0	289.0	318.0	340.0	343.0
USSR[c]	1,100.0	1,130.0	1,100.0	1,140.0	1,150.0	1,150.0
China and other[c]	283.4	296.7	306.5	315.6	312.5	318.8
Total	1,613.4	1,693.7	1,695.5	1,773.6	1,802.5	1,811.8
World total	7,316.7	7,854.1	7,980.6	7,865.6	7,645.5	7,816.2

Source: Metal Statistics 1982.
[a]Revised. [b]Estimated. [c]Preliminary.

The major copper-producing nations of newly mined copper are the United States, USSR, Chile, Canada, Zambia, and Zaire. Together they account for approximately 65% of world new mine production. According to 1980 statistics, world mine production totaled 7,816.2 thousand metric tons,[1] a 2.2% increase over 1979. A similar increase of 2.4% for 1981 world mine production was recorded.

The United States continues its 100 year-dominance as the world's largest mine producer, with output ranging from 15% to 19% of the world's total mine production. United States mine production in 1980 was 1,143 thousand metric tons and increased by approximately 30% in 1981 to 1,520 thousand metric tons. Total production of refined copper decreased in 1981, however, due to a decrease in scrap production. As Table 2 indicates, the major producing mines in the United States are located in Arizona, Utah, New Mexico, Montana, and Nevada which combined account for over 90% of U.S. mine production. By itself, the state of Arizona annually produces about 65% of U.S. copper mine production. Although the United States has dominated world mine production over the years, Chile, which continues to increase its mining capacity, may soon surpass the U.S. In 1981, Chile produced 13% of the total world figure; it is currently the world's second largest mine producer of the metal.

Another large mine producer of copper, the USSR, tends to have a relatively consistent rate of production varying only slightly since 1975. Estimated mine production in 1980 was 1,150 thousand metric tons, the same as in 1979.

Besides Canada, most of the other significant copper-producing nations are less-developed countries. In 1980, Peru, Zambia, Zaire, and the Phillipines together accounted for approximately 23% of new mine production. Most of these countries typically keep copper steadily flowing to the market due to their need for foreign currencies.

SCRAP RECOVERY. The secondary production of copper has become a major factor in the total supply picture. In the past years, scrap (or secondary) production has represented a significant portion of total U.S. consumption as well as consumption by other nations. Copper is similar to other metals that have a high degree of resistance to corrosion in that a significant portion of the copper produced over the years is still available for recycling. This can be a major market factor during times of short supply. Scrap metal also represents a ready available source of long-term future supply.

The significance of scrap recovery as a part of the total production picture becomes very evident by comparing Table 3 with Table 1. Table 1 specifically refers to primary or new mine production. On the other hand, Table 3 includes primary production as well as some secondary production. Due to the difficulty of obtaining information on total scrap recovery, Table 3 is used for comparative purposes. It should be noted that scrap which does not go through the refining process is not included in Table 3. Based on these statistics, world production of refined copper has steadily increased since 1975. Also, the secondary production of refined copper which is accounted for in Table 4, has apparently been increasing since 1976. This statistic is obtained by taking the total world production of refined copper (Table 3) less world mine production of copper (Table 1).

[1]One metric ton = 2,204.6 lb.

TABLE 2. Mine Production of Copper in the United States—By States[a]

	1973	1974	1975	1976	1977	1978	1979	1980[b]	1981[c]
Arizona	927,271	858,783	813,211	1,024,421	923,778	982,606	946,002	757,314	1,037,192
California	369	194	344	375	221	[d]	[d]	[d]	[d]
Colorado	3,123	3,012	3,560	2,431	1,896	1,313	362	461	[d]
Idaho	3,625	2,841	3,192	3,362	4,052	4,286	3,618	3,103	3,519
Maine	1,107	1,522	2,024	1,766	1,337	—	—	—	[d]
Michigan	72,221	67,012	73,690	43,707	42,375	38,380	[d]	[d]	[d]
Missouri	10,273	12,665	14,258	11,050	11,737	11,925	13,021	13,576	8,752
Montana	132,466	131,131	87,959	91,111	86,203	74,214	69,854	37,749	61,918
Nevada	93,702	84,101	81,210	58,160	67,061	22,546	[d]	[d]	[d]
New Mexico	204,742	196,585	146,263	162,360	164,698	140,906	164,281	149,394	154,204
Pennsylvania	1,845	—	—	—	—	—	—	—	—
Tennesee	8,500	6,304	10,041	11,131	6,187	12,444	[d]	[d]	[d]
Utah	256,589	230,593	177,155	185,458	194,130	205,394	193,082	157,755	207,821
Other states	2,107	2,259	459	254	291	2,469	53,335	48,941	55,781
Total	1,717,940	1,597,002	1,413,366	1,605,586	1,503,966	1,496,483	1,443,556	1,168,311	1,529,007

Source: Metal Statistics 1982. [a]Figures are in short tons through 1978 and metric tons thereafter. [b]Revised. [c]Preliminary. [d]Withheld; included in "other states."

TABLE 3. World Production of Refined Copper[a]

	1975	1976	1977	1978	1979[b]	1980[c]
Canada	529.2	510.5	508.8	446.3	397.3	505.2
United States	1,610.2	1,715.0	1,677.0	1,843.4	1,975.8	1,682.6
Chile	535.2	632.0	676.0	749.1	781.8	810.7
Mexico	69.8	75.4	71.9	83.0	100.8	102.4
Other America	82.6	166.7	216.7	212.1	264.2	269.5
Total America	2,827.6	3,099.6	3,150.4	3,333.9	3,519.9	3,370.4
Belgium	331.6	425.0	464.7	388.6	368.8	373.7
France	39.6	39.3	45.0	41.3	45.3	46.5
West Germany	422.2	446.6	440.2	403.4	382.5	373.8
Spain	130.2	141.9	159.0	147.0	140.4	153.7
Sweden	56.7	64.9	61.7	64.4	61.7	55.7
United Kingdom	151.5	137.2	122.2	125.6	121.7	161.3
Yugoslavia	137.9	136.5	143.5	150.8	137.5	131.3
Other Europe	107.3	116.4	122.1	109.6	116.8	126.4
Total Europe	1,377.0	1,507.8	1,558.4	1,430.7	1,374.7	1,422.4
South Africa	92.4	102.4	145.9	152.5	152.3	147.9
Zaire	225.9	65.3	98.7	102.5	103.2	144.2
Zambia	629.1	694.6	649.0	621.1	563.6	607.3
Other Africa	29.0	33.0	30.2	28.2	10.4	9.5
Total Africa	976.4	895.3	923.8	904.3	829.5	908.9
Japan	818.9	864.4	933.7	959.1	983.7	1,014.3
Other Asia	61.7	83.7	99.2	115.4	131.3	141.2
Total Asia	880.6	948.1	1,032.9	1,074.5	1,115.0	1,155.5
Australia	193.5	188.3	183.1	174.5	171.4	182.9
East Germany[d]	47.0	50.0	51.0	49.0	51.0	51.0
Poland	248.6	270.1	306.6	332.0	335.8	357.3
USSR[d]	1,400.0	1,420.0	1,440.0	1,480.0	1,480.0	1,450.0
China and other[d]	385.0	407.7	432.2	449.1	292.7	280.8
Total	2,080.6	2,144.8	2,229.8	2,310.1	2,330.9	2,322.0
World total	8,335.7	8,783.9	9.078.4	9,228.0	9,341.4	9,362.1

Source: Metal Statistics 1982. [a]Figures are in thousand metric tons. [b]Revised. [c]Preliminary. [d]Estimated.

DEMAND FOR COPPER

The demand for copper rests primarily on the industrial sector. As Table 4 indicates, most refined copper is consumed by those developed countries which have a large industrial capacity.

The United States plays the leading role in both the production and consumption of copper. A significant amount of the metal must be imported to fully meet its consumption needs. In 1980 the United States consumed 1,866 thousand metric tons, a 13.8% decrease from 1979.

TABLE 4. World Consumption of Refined Copper[a]

	1975	1976	1977	1978	1979[b]	1980[c]
Canada	185.2	206.2	219.2	250.1	243.3	208.6
United States	1,396.5	1,808.0	1,985.9	2,181.1	2,164.9	1,866.1
Brazil	155.2	179.3	210.9	180.8	228.7	246.0
Mexico	70.8	82.3	77.3	83.1	103.9	123.2
Other America	80.7	105.8	102.7	111.2	141.2	117.7
Total America	1,888.4	2,381.6	2,596.0	2,806.3	2,882.0	2,561.6
Belgium	177.4	228.1	295.4	289.5	303.1	303.9
France	364.5	367.1	326.1	319.0	358.4	433.4
West Germany	634.6	744.6	779.9	800.0	794.1	747.8
Italy	290.0	322.0	326.0	344.0	352.0	388.0
Spain	119.4	130.5	135.0	128.5	132.5	135.5
Sweden	94.4	87.5	81.1	103.5	107.6	105.3
United Kingdom	450.5	457.6	512.0	501.6	498.9	409.2
Yugoslavia	103.2	99.6	120.4	156.1	132.0	148.9
Other Europe	171.7	189.9	194.3	174.4	170.8	203.9
Total Europe	2,405.7	2,626.9	2,770.2	2,816.6	2,849.3	2,875.9
South Africa	65.3	56.7	52.2	60.3	69.3	89.9
Other Africa	22.0	19.6	23.5	26.1	27.5	26.0
Total Africa	87.3	76.3	75.7	86.4	96.8	115.9
India	34.7	57.0	55.7	57.0	63.3	71.0
Japan	827.4	1,050.3	1,127.1	1,241.4	1,330.1	1,325.5
Other Asia	91.1	115.7	143.0	166.9[e]	196.1	240.4
Total Asia	953.2	1,223.0	1,325.8	1,465.3	1,589.5	1,636.9
Total Europe	2,405.7	2,626.9	2,770.2	2,816.6	2,849.3	2,875.9
South Africa	65.3	56.7	52.2	60.3	69.3	89.9
Other Africa	22.0	19.6	23.5	26.1	27.5	26.0
Total Africa	87.3	76.3	75.7	86.4	96.8	115.9
India	34.7	57.0	55.7	57.0	63.3	71.0
Japan	827.4	1,050.3	1,127.1	1,241.4	1,330.1	1,325.5
Other Asia	91.1	115.7	143.0	166.9[e]	196.1	240.4
Total Asia	953.2	1,223.0	1,325.8	1,465.3	1,589.5	1,636.9
Australia[d]	97.7	121.4	107.9	117.4	128.8	132.4
West Germany[e]	112.0	118.0	115.0	118.0	122.0	120.0
USSR[e]	1,220.0	1,250.0	1,290.0	1,330.0	1,360.0	1,300.0
Other Eastern Europe[e]	323.5	349.3	351.1	358.3	459.7	456.2
China and other[e]	316.0	336.0	346.0	367.0	357.0	347.2
Total	2,019.5	2,108.3	2,160.6	2,237.3	2,298.7	2,223.4
World total	7,451.6	8,537.5	9,036.2	9,529.3	9,845.1	9,546.1

Source: Metal Statistics 1982. [a]Figures are in thousand metric tons. [b]Revised. [c]Preliminary. [d]Includes small amount of consumption in New Zealand. [e]Estimated.

In 1980 Japan was the second largest consumer of the red metal. Japan's consumption pattern has greatly increased over the past several years, making it one of the world's largest importers. It accounted for approximately 14% of total world consumption in 1980, using 1,326 thousand metric tons. This represented a slight decrease in tonnage from the previous year.

Estimated Russian consumption statistics have remained relatively steady since 1975. Consumption in 1980 was 1,300 thousand metric tons, a 4.5% decline from 1979.

Combined, the three largest copper consumers, the United States, the USSR, and Japan, accounted for about 47% of total world consumption in 1980.

Other major consuming nations include West Germany, France, the United Kingdom, Italy, and China. Most of the major consuming countries are somewhat dependent upon imports to satisfy their total usage requirements.

Copper's multifaceted properties make it useful in an assortment of products. Some items which utilize copper are: machines, automotive parts, switchgear, utensils, radios, televisions, and appliances. Copper is used extensively in electronic parts and wiring, for its ability to conduct electricity. A few of the largest consumers of the metal are the telecommunications, electronics, and public utility industries mainly because of copper's outstanding ability to conduct electricity.

Corrosion resistance makes copper valuable in plumbing. This property, combined with its ability to conduct heat, also makes copper useful in radiators and cooling systems. Solar panels also contain copper because of its heat transferring ability.

Coin and jewelry producers use copper for its strength and shiny appearance. For instance, copper is used in the production of gold coins to add strength to the softer metal and give the coins more durability.

The utilization of copper is also important in the production of brass and bronze, as well as many other alloys. A significant percentage of the copper consumed in the United States is combined with other metals.

SEASONALITY

Copper is considered highly seasonal, containing two periods of significantly reliable and long-lasting trends. The strong upwards movement in the early spring can be attributed to the combined demand of two of the largest users of copper—the housing and automobile industries. Both groups must purchase early to assure continuity of production in the summer.

Since commitments have been made before the heavy summer schedule, prices begin to decline prior to the summer. Prices normally continue this decline until fall, with the exception of years in which the supply has been interrupted. As can be seen in Figures 2(a) and 2(b), the seasonal movements for copper are well-defined.

FILTERING HOUSING STARTS. A closer look at the seasonality of copper may be accomplished by separating those years in which housing starts were high from years in which they were low. Figure 3 shows that years with low housing starts have the normal seasonal peak in the spring, but fail to rise in the late fall. We

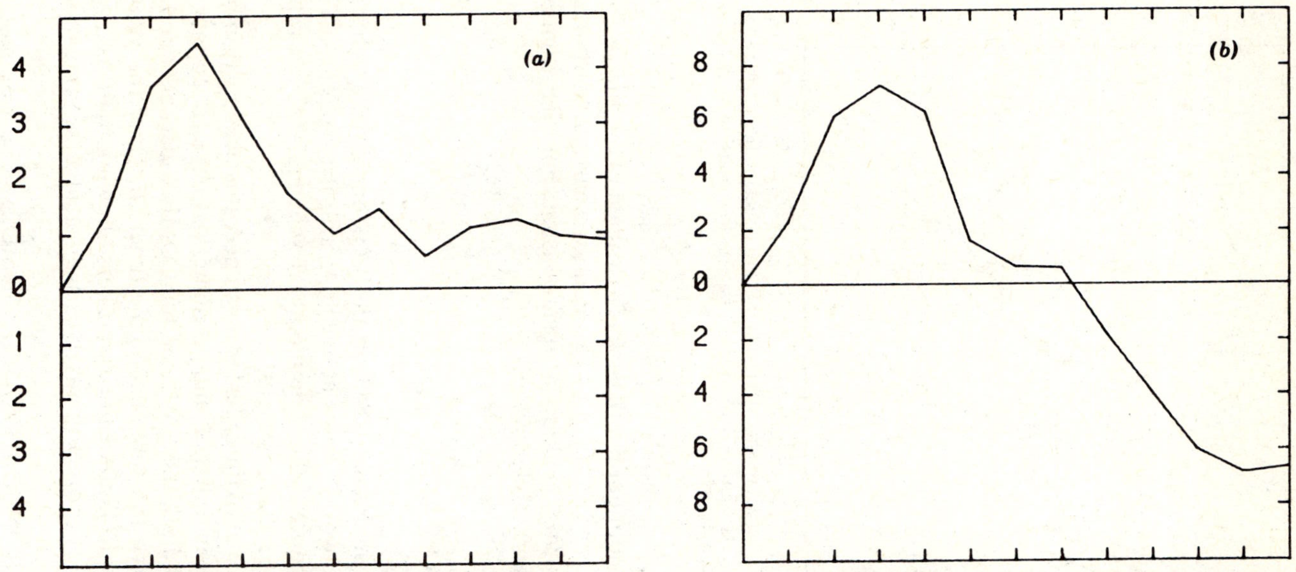

(a)

	J-F	F-M	M-A	A-M	M-J	J-J	J-A	A-S	S-O	O-N	N-D	D-J
Average Move	1.3	2.3	0.7	-1.4	-1.4	-0.8	0.4	-0.9	0.5	0.1	-0.4	-0.1
% Reliable	88.3	88.3	70.6	76.5	58.9	53	53	64.8	58.9	58.9	58.9	35.3
Avg. Up Move	1.8	3.1	2.3	1.1	1.5	1.4	3.2	1.2	2.7	1.9	2.3	1.5
Avg. Down Move	1.1	2.3	2.5	2.2	3.3	2.3	2.8	2.1	2	1.9	1.8	3.2
Greatest Up Move	5.8	7.2	4.1	2.1	2.9	3.2	15.5	2.5	7	6.4	4.9	3.8
Greatest Down Move	1.4	4.6	6.7	5	13.1	9.3	13.9	7.9	5.3	3.9	3.9	7.3

(b)

	J-F	F-M	M-A	A-M	M-J	J-J	J-A	A-S	S-O	O-N	N-D	D-J
Average Move	2.2	3.8	1	-1	-4.7	-1	-0.1	-2.4	-2.2	-2.1	-0.9	0.2
% Reliable	75	100	50	75	100	50	75	75	75	75	75	50
Avg. Up Move	3.5	3.8	2.6	2.1	0	3.1	4.1	1.3	0	0	0	1
Avg. Down Move	1.4	0	0.5	2.1	4.7	5.1	1.5	3.7	2.9	2.8	1.1	0.7
Greatest Up Move	5.8	6.4	3.1	2.1	0	3.2	4.1	1.3	0	0	0	1.1
Greatest Down Move	1.4	0	0.9	2.8	13.1	9.3	2.2	7.9	5.3	3.6	2.1	1.3

FIGURE 2. Copper price seasonality. (*a*) Cash copper, 17 years. (*b*) Cash copper, 4 years. *Source:* J. Gruschcow and C. Smith. *Profits Through Seasonal Trading,* Wiley, New York, 1980.

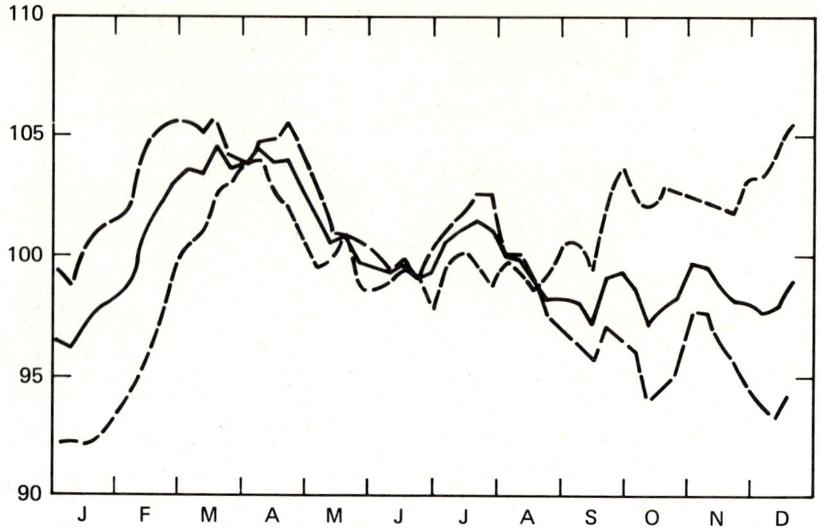

FIGURE 3. Filtering copper seasonality using housing starts. Copper price seasonality during all years (solid line), years with high housing starts (dotted line), and years with low housing starts (dashed line). *Source:* D. Handmaker (see Appendix B).

can conclude that the smaller amount of purchasing is restricted to the early spring months. In the case of high housing starts, purchasing begins early in the fall and increases sharply in the early spring, peaking in April as usual. For this situation, the summer price lull is short and moderate.

COPPER FUTURES MARKET

Copper futures trading has existed since 1883 on the London Metal Exchange (LME), which is still one of the world's most active copper futures markets. The other major copper futures market, the Commodity Exchange, Incorporated (COMEX), started trading copper futures in 1933.

The copper futures market is one of the oldest in existence. It is used by primary producers, fabricators, refiners, merchants, and consumers of physical copper to hedge their price risk. Although both the LME and the COMEX markets operate quite differently, they both serve the same economic function. Over the years, both markets have developed into liquid futures markets allowing their users to easily and relatively inexpensively protect themselves against adverse price risks.

THE COMMODITY EXCHANGE, INCORPORATED (COMEX). The Commodity Exchange, Incorporated (COMEX), located in New York City, is the world's largest metals futures exchange. COMEX accounts for two times more volume of metals futures than all futures exchanges in the United States.

Established in 1933, the COMEX copper market has developed into one of the world's most active copper futures markets. The price volatility of copper in the past, combined with the significance of the U.S. market, have spurred the growth of copper futures markets both in New York and London.

A futures contract is an obligation to buy or sell a particular amount of a commodity at a future point in time at a specified, mutually agreed-upon price. Copper futures, like all of the COMEX contracts, are traded in a "ring" or "pit" by the open outcry method. The "pit" essentially concentrates buyers and sellers into a small area for the purpose of efficiently facilitating trading in an orderly fashion. It also allows the exchange to effectively enforce its rules. Because such a market promotes a competitive environment for everyone, it attracts major participants from all over the world. Thus prices traded on COMEX represent the supply and demand for world copper.

As trades are executed, the transaction prices are immediately known by all interested parties as such prices are flashed on an electronic display board on the trading floor and are simultaneously disseminated throughout the financial world. This price discovery mechanism representing supply and demand factors of the entire world market serves as one of the primary economic functions of all futures markets. In past years, and most recently in late 1982, many North American producers have been pricing their copper production according to a formula based on COMEX prices. Similarly, many producers outside North America base their prices on the LME copper market.

Table 5 shows the contract specifications for the COMEX copper futures market.

Merchants, producers, arbitrageurs, and consumers account for a substantial amount of trading activity on the COMEX. The merchants are the largest users of COMEX from this group. COMEX has also developed into a "user" market attracting many copper consumers.

Only a small percentage of the COMEX copper futures contracts are actually settled by delivery. In 1981, 47,783 contracts were delivered on the COMEX. However, the futures market serves important economic functions, providing commercials with a means of shifting their unwanted price risk and providing a price discovery mechanism. For example, suppose a copper merchant wants to protect existing inventory from falling prices. The merchant intents to sell the

TABLE 5. Summary of Comex Copper Contract Specifications

Contract size	25,000 lb.
Contract months	Trading occurs for 23 months into the future and includes the current (spot) and next 2 calendar months plus any January, March, May, July, September, and December.
Deliverable grade	Base price deliverable grade is electrolytic cathodes. Also deliverable at various discounts or premiums are electrolytic wirebars and ingot bars, fire refined high conductivity ingot bars, and fire refined ingot bars.
Delivery	At the seller's option at any Exchange-approved warehouse by the use of a warehouse receipt.
Depositories	Various locations in the United States.
Minimum price changes	$\frac{5}{100}$¢ per lb (equal to $12.50 per contract).
Maximum daily price change	$0.05 per lb. During times of high price volatility, limits can expand according to a predetermined formula.
Trading time	9:50 a.m. to 2:00 p.m., eastern time.

inventory at some future date and must protect its value until that time. Without some protection the inventory would be held at risk, and thus the merchant stands the chance of absorbing a substantial loss. A large loss could have a serious impact on the firm's profitability. By taking an equal short position in the futures market the merchant can significantly decrease the risk of an adverse price movement. As prices declined, futures market gains would absorb the losses of the cash market position. Thus, the value of the inventory has been protected and, simultaneously, the future course of business has become more predictable. Also, the futures market may partially compensate the merchant for carrying the inventory, since futures prices typically include "carrying costs."[2]

The following example (Table 6) explains how a merchant could use the futures market to an advantage through a short hedge.

In Table 6, the merchant not only hedges a downward price risk (by selling futures), but also receives compensation for the cost of carrying inventory. Of course, not every hedging transaction has the same results as the one above.

There are other risks inherent in hedging, such as basis risk, whereby the price of physical inventory may not change exactly with the futures price. However, this risk is not nearly as significant as price risk which is greatly reduced by hedging (see Rinehimer, "Hedging").

Other hedging strategies can also be used depending on the intent of the trader. For example, consumers of copper could buy futures contracts as an anticipatory hedge against expected price increases of copper. An example of an exporter's hedge is provided in a later section of this chapter. A producer may also want to take delivery on the futures market during times when the producer is lacking physical copper and must meet a forward sale. All of these trading techniques can also be applied on the London Metal Exchange as well.

THE LONDON METAL EXCHANGE. The London Metal Exchange (LME) method and form of trading has several important differences from the COMEX. First, the LME is a principals market, in which each ring-dealing member is the guarantor of its trades. In the United States futures exchanges operate on a clearinghouse system which charges position holders an original margin fee and then each position is marked-to-market daily. Each position holder in the United States is required to pay variation margin if prices move adversely against their positions. Conversely, if prices moved favorably, funds would flow to the account from the clearinghouse. Unlike U.S. futures markets, the LME has no clearinghouse and the system is essentially based on member financial solvency. Likewise, there are no margin requirements between ring-dealing members and any changes in price are settled when the contract matures.

Copper has been traded on The London Metal Exchange since 1883. Today, the LME trades two separate copper contracts—a copper higher-grade contract which calls for the delivery of copper wirebars and high-grade copper cathodes, and a standard copper-cathode contract. Although both contracts are traded, the higher-grade copper contract is much more actively traded. Since continuous casting was introduced a few decades ago, copper cathodes have become increas-

[2]Carrying costs take into account financing charges (interest), insurance, and warehousing fees.

TABLE 6. Copper Short Hedge

	Cash	Futures
November 24th	Buys 1 million lb of copper at $0.70 per lb.	Sells 40 March futures contracts at $0.72 per lb.
February 24th	Sells 1 million lbs of copper at $0.67 per lb. Loss = $0.03 per lb $30,000	Lifts short hedge by buying 40 futures contracts at $0.67 per lb. Gain = $0.05 per lb or $50,000

ingly used in trade because they are of high grade and can be easily transformed into other usable shapes.

Each LME contract is for 25 metric tons of copper. The LME trades a spot (or cash) and 3-month forward contract. Trading is done in specific dates as opposed to trading in future months as is done on the U.S. markets. Deliveries are made by means of a warehouse receipt from warehouses located in various locations throughout Europe. Each delivery of copper must meet certain purity and weight specifications. Ring trading (by open outcry) occurs twice during the morning and twice in the afternoon for a period of about 5–10 min for each session. However, members can trade outside of ring-dealing times. Trading may take place over the phone or anywhere outside of the ring. This type of trading done outside of the ring is traditionally known as "kerb" trading.

One other important feature at the LME worthy of second mention is the high-quality grade of copper which is traded. The LME is extensively used by merchants, consumers, and fabricators. Generally speaking, the quality of copper is slightly higher than the average grade which is traded on the COMEX. Thus LME cathodes typically trade at a slight premium over COMEX quoted prices. Similar to the COMEX, however, only a small percentage of contracts traded are held to maturity and result in delivery.

A COPPER EXPORTER'S HEDGE[3]

Consider the situation of a copper exporter who in January 1979, concludes a deal to sell 600,000 lb of copper to a customer abroad at a set price of $0.88 per lb. The foreign customer wants the copper shipped by the end of the year. The exporter is now committed to sell 600,000 lb of copper to the foreign client at $0.88 per lb.

The exporter may already have the copper in stock in which case subsequent arrangements will be made to ship the copper. If, however, the exporter does not have the copper in stock, the exporter will have to buy it over the course of the

[3]D. Koutras, E. Meir, and R. Ng, *Commodity Hedging Operations and Strategies: An Introduction*, Drexel Burnham Lambert, New York, NY 1982.

year. In this situation, the exporter is assuming considerable risk. Copper prices may rise drastically over the course of the year, while the exporter is only receiving a fixed price for the copper from the client. As a result, the exporter will incur a loss if copper prices rise above the $0.88 selling price. On the other hand, should copper prices drop below the selling price, the exporter will widen the profit margin since the exporter will be buying copper at a cheaper price.

Let us assume that the copper exporter in fact has no copper in stock and as a result has to purchase copper over the course of the year (1979). Suppose the exporter makes four equal monthly purchases of 150,000 lb for subsequent delivery to the foreign client.

The purchases are made in March, June, September, and December of 1979. The merchant would therefore pay the following prices for the purchases:

March	91.6¢ per lb
June	83.2¢ per lb
September	91.9¢ per lb
December	95.3¢ per lb.

If the copper was purchased at the above prices, the exporter would have incurred the following profits and losses:

	Selling Price	Purchase Price	Net Profit or (Loss) Per Pound
March 1979	$0.88	91.6¢ per lb	(3.6¢)
June 1979	$0.88	83.2¢ per lb	4.8¢
September 1979	$0.88	91.9¢ per lb	(3.9¢)
December 1979	$0.88	95.3¢ per lb	(7.3¢)

Total dollar losses and profits for each 150,000-lb purchase are subsequently calculated as follows:

	Profit or (Loss)	Total Profit or (Loss) on 150,000-lbs Purchase
September	(3.6¢)	($ 5,400)
June	4.8¢	7,200
September	(3.9¢)	(5,850)
December	(7.3¢)	(10,950)
		($15,000)

Adding the above figures we could see that in all but one case, each of the exporter's purchases and subsequent sale, resulted in a loss. A total loss of $15,000 was registered for the whole deal. (If on the other hand, copper prices had declined instead of risen, the exporter would have made a profit, since the exporter's profit margin would have increased).

The example illustrates more than anything else the considerable risk the exporter assumes when operating in such an unprotected or unhedged environment. The exporter is obligated to deliver copper at a fixed $0.88 per lb, while the exporter has to make purchases from a volatile physicals market. As a result, the merchant's final loss or profit is contingent upon price movements more than anything else.

Let us now rework this example by introducing the concept of hedging and illustrating how the exporter's risk factor can be brought under considerably more control. By hedging, the exporter would assume a position in the futures market equivalent in quantity and quality to the physical purchase, but *opposite* in price direction. Since, in January 1979, the exporter agreed to *sell* the foreign client 600,000 lb of copper at $0.88 per lb, shipping it over the course of the year, the exporter would simultaneously, in January of 1979, *buy* 24 (January 1980) copper futures contracts at 93.4¢. These 24 contracts would be equivalent to 600,000 lb of copper.

After the exporter has purchased these copper contracts, the merchant is effectively hedged. If prices for copper subsequently rise during the year, the merchant will have to pay higher prices for the physical copper purchases. However, unlike the first case, the exporter will not incur losses since any rise in copper prices would translate into a *profit* on the exporter's long futures position. Conversely, if copper prices drop lower, the exporter would lose money on the long position, but widen the profit margin on the physicals sale, since the exporter will be buying the copper at cheaper prices. Table 7 illustrates the process in detail. We should note that throughout the hedging process, every time a purchase is made in the cash market, a simultaneous liquidation (selling) will take place in the futures market.

By hedging, the exporter managed to offset a good amount of the losses that occurred in the first case where the exporter was unprotected. On balance, the exporter lost $4,650 as opposed to the $15,000 loss sustained when unhedged.

The example displays how a hedge insulates a commodity exposure from adverse price movements. This is mainly because of the fundamental concept that a loss on one side of a transaction (cash or futures) will be offset by an approximate profit or loss on the correspondingly opposite side.

Hedging also enabled the exporter to lower the average cost of the copper purchases. Before hedging the exporter paid the following average price for the copper purchased:

	91.6¢ per lb
	83.2¢ per lb
	91.9¢ per lb
	95.3¢ per lb
Average	90.5¢ per lb

Incorporating the results of the futures transactions (profit or loss), we get the

TABLE 7. The Copper Exporter's Hedge

Cash Market	Futures Market
(1) In January 1979 the exporter agrees to sell a foreign client 600,000 lb of copper at $0.88 per lb.	(2) Simultaneously, the exporter purchases 24 January 1980 contracts at 93.4¢ per lb on the COMEX.
(3) In March 1979 the exporter buys the first quantity of copper (150,000 lb) at 91.6¢ per lb. The exporter sustains a loss of 3.6¢ per lb on the cash purchase, equivalent to $5,400 on 150,000 lb.	(4) In March 1979 the exporter liquidates (sells) six January 1980 contracts equivalent to 150,000 lb at $0.95 per lb. The exporter makes a profit of 1.6¢ per lb, equivalent to $2400 on 150,000 lb.
The combination of these two transactions resulted in a $3,000 loss: ($5,400) − $2,400 = ($3,000).	
(5) In June 1979 the exporter buys an additional 150,000 lb of copper at 83.2¢ per lb. The exporter makes a profit of 4.8¢ per lb, equivalent to $7,200 on 150,000 lb.	(6) In June 1979 the exporter sells six contracts at $0.91 per lb. The exporter loses 2.4¢ per lb on the futures transaction, equivalent to a loss of $3,600 on 150,000 lb.
The combination of these two transactions resulted in a gain of $3,600: $7,200 − ($3,600) = $3,600.	
(7) In September 1979 the exporter buys an additional 150,000 lb at 91.9¢ per lb. The exporter loses 3.9¢ per lb on this transaction, equivalent to $5,850 on 150,000 lb.	(8) In September 1979 the exporter sells another six contracts (150,000 lb) of the futures position at 97.8¢ per lb. The exporter makes 4.4¢ on the futures transaction, equivalent to $6,600 on 150,000 lb.
The combination of these two transactions result in a profit of $750: ($6,600 − $5,850) = $750.	
(9) In December 1980 the exporter buys the remaining 150,000 lb of copper at 95.3¢ per lb. The exporter sustains a loss of 7.3¢ on this transaction, equivalent to a $10,950 loss on 150,000 lb.	(10) In December 1980, the exporter sells the remaining six contracts at 96.7¢ per lb. The exporter makes a profit in this case of 3.3¢ per lb, equivalent to $4,950 on 150,000 lb.
The combination of these two transactions yields a loss of $6,000: ($10,950) − $4,950 = (6,000).	

Totaling the results of the hedge we get the following results:

March 1979 transaction	($3,000)
June 1979 transaction	$3,600
September 1979 transaction	$ 750
December 1979 transaction	($6,000)
Total loss	($4,650)

following average price (a profit on the futures transaction would lower the purchase price, while a loss would increase it):

91.6¢	−	1.6¢	=	90.0¢ per lb
83.2¢	+	2.4¢	=	85.6¢ per lb
91.9¢	−	4.4¢	=	87.5¢ per lb
95.3¢	−	3.3¢	=	92.0¢ per lb
Average			=	88.77¢ per lb

CHAPTER **46**

PLATINUM AND PALLADIUM

CONTENTS

PLATINUM 3

Platinum Supply 3
Platinum Demand 6
Market Analysis 7
Platinum Prices 8

PALLADIUM 9

Palladium Demand 9
Palladium Supply 14
Palladium Prices 15

FUTURES MARKETS 15

SOURCES OF INFORMATION 15

Platinum, Palladium, Gold, and U.S. Silver Coins 15

CHAPTER **46**

PLATINUM AND PALLADIUM

Karen Marie Forstik

Platinum and palladium are the most important metals of the "platinum group," comprised of platinum, palladium, iridium, osmium, rhodium, and ruthenium. Together they account for 95% of the total metal produced from the platinum-group ores. Although most consumers are more familiar with platinum because of its use in fine jewelry, it amounts to only one-half of the production of palladium. Since the two metals have very similar metallurgical characteristics, they are often combined in use or used interchangeably.

PLATINUM

Platinum is a white, precious metal capable of taking a beautiful, high, permanent polish. It is virtually nonoxidizable, has a high melting point, and is attacked by acids only under very special conditions. Therefore, it is used appropriately in situations calling for the maximum ability to withstand high temperature, disintegrating atmospheres, and great stress. These properties have led to significant applications in such varied fields as the manufacture of chemicals, glass, petroleum, electrical equipment, and now in antipollution devices. For the fortunate, a modest amount becomes jewelry.

Current 1982 estimates place the world reserve base of platinum-group metals at approximately 1.2–1.5 billion troy oz. These reserves are greatly concentrated, with combined South Africa and Soviet Union figures amounting to 97.9% of total reserves (see Table 1).

PLATINUM SUPPLY. Although the United States is the world's largest consumer, U.S. native deposits account for only a very small percentage of total world production. The United States therefore, depends upon imports for most of its domestic needs.

Worldwide, the bulk of new platinum production derives from three principal countries—South Africa, Canada, and the Soviet Union. Of the three major producing nations, only in South Africa is platinum produced principally as a primary product rather than as a by-product.

The three largest South African producers are Rustenburg, Impala, and Western. In 1980, mine production out of these firms amounted to over 2,000 thousand

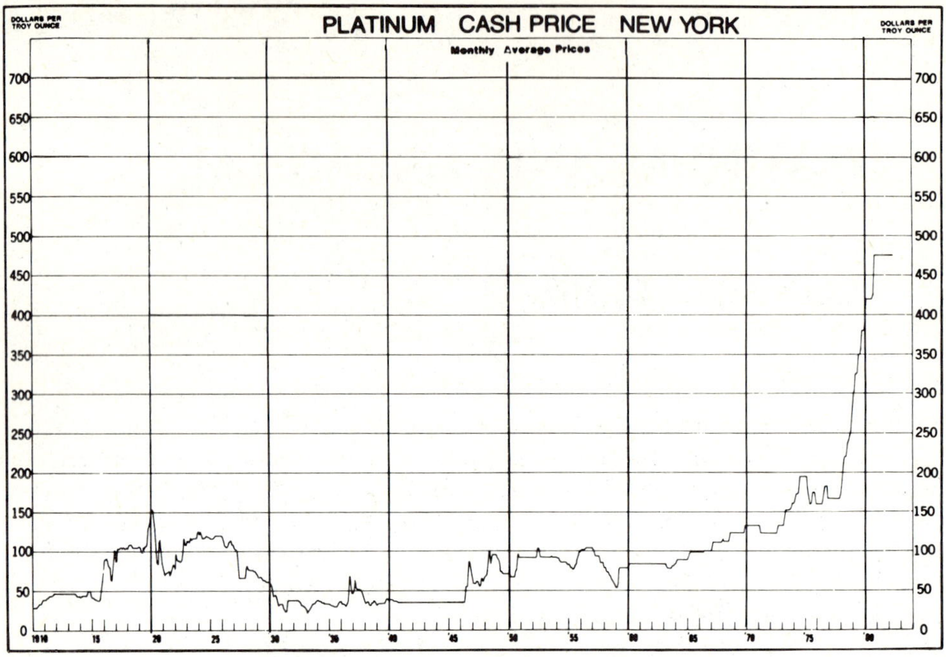

FIGURE 1. Platinum cash price—New York.

troy ozs. Production is centered in the Merensky Reef in the Bushveld Igneous Complex, which is estimated to have the world's greatest reserve of primary platinum metals. It is the only known location of significant lode deposits of platinum.

The Soviet Union is the second largest platinum-producing nation. However, platinum production is considered a consequence of palladium and nickel production. Platinum is mined as a by-product of nickel in Norilsk in northwestern Siberia. Also, the ratio of platinum to palladium contained in Russian ores is low. Soviet ores are estimated to contain approximately 70% palladium and 25% platinum. This compares to South African ores which contain approximately 60% platinum and 25% palladium.

Definitive production statistics are not available from the Soviet Union. However, Soviet sales comprise a substantial proportion of overall supply. Canadian production of platinum is largely concentrated in Ontario's Sudbury district. In Canada, platinum is produced as a by-product in the mining and refining of nickel.

TABLE 1. World Reserve Base of Platinum-Group Metals (Percent of Total)

South Africa	81.2
Soviet Union	16.7
United States	1.3
Canada	0.8
	100.0

Source: U.S. Bureau of Mines—Mineral Industry Surveys, December 1981.

TABLE 2. World Production of Platinum-Group Metals (in Troy Ounces)

Year	Australia	Philippines	Finland	Canada	Colombia[a]	Ethiopia[a]	Japan	South Africa	USSR	United States	Yugoslavia	World Total
1962		—	—	470,787	14,100	180	3,244	305,600	800,000	28,742		1,625,000
1963		—	—	357,651	22,983	180	3,040	305,185	1,300,000	49,750		2,038,805
1964		—	—	376,238	20,647	180	4,074	604,135	1,500,000	40,487		2,545,761
1965		—	—	463,127	11,141	353	5,418	753,820	1,700,000	35,026		2,968,885
1966		—	—	396,059	15,671	318	8,227	783,400	1,800,000	51,423		3,055,098
1967		—	—	401,263	19,000	282	6,399	832,000	1,900,000	16,365		3,175,300
1968		—	—	485,891	22,280	349	6,436	864,000	2,000,000	14,793		3,993,749
1969		—	—	310,404	27,805	343	7,017	964,000	2,100,000	21,586		3,431,155
1970	—	1,230	645	482,428	26,358	273	7,906	1,502,800	2,200,000	17,316		4,238,956
1971	—	2,459	600	475,169	25,610	217	8,826	1,253,200	2,300,000	18,029		4,084,110
1972	—	7,522	650	406,048	24,111	248	9,899	1,453,000	2,350,000	17,112		4,269,990
1973	975	6,656	725	354,223	26,358	235	10,197	2,362,800	2,450,000	19,980		5,232,149
1974	1,120	3,665	650	384,618	21,094	230	15,205	2,830,000	2,500,000	12,657		5,769,239
1975	1,830	1,415	600	399,218	22,114	162	19,401	2,600,000	2,650,000	18,920		5,713,660
1976	11,108	—	600	416,821	16,779	145	26,795	2,700,000	2,800,000	6,116	n.a.[d]	5,978,364
1977	13,278		640	465,371	17,300	100	32,453	2,870,000	2,900,000	5,545	5,690	6,310,377
1978	13,000		640	346,213	13,939	123	34,145	2,860,000	3,050,000	8,246	5,900	6,332,206
1979[c]	11,500		720	185,000	15,000	100	34,000	3,200,000	3,200,000	7,300	5,700	6,659,520
1980[b]				220,000				3,250,000	3,200,000	6,000		6,740,000
1981[b]				350,000				3,100,000	3,250,000	6,000		6,780,000

Source: U.S. Bureau of Mines. [a]Placer platinum. [b]Estimate. [c]Preliminary. [d]n.a. = not available.

In view of the by-product nature of Canadian production, platinum output is very dependent upon developments in the nickel industry. As a result, Canada has been limited in its ability to equate platinum production with fluctuating market needs. The International Nickel Company of Canada, Ltd. dominates the Canadian platinum picture. Flaconbridge Nickel Mines, Ltd., represents a secondary source of Canadian supply.

An additional factor influencing platinum supply is secondary production—that is, platinum obtained through recycling. Two companies, Engelhard Minerals and Chemicals Corporation and Johnson, Matthey and Company, Ltd. dominate platinum refining and fabricating in the market-oriented economies.

PLATINUM DEMAND. Platinum is known as a metal with great resistance to attack. Its many uses in industry derive from its ability to withstand high temperatures, acid damage, disintegrating atmospheres, and great stress. In 1980, U.S. platinum purchases revealed the following end-use consumption pattern:

Application	Purchases	Percent
Automotive	517,143	47.43
Electrical	142,442	13.07
Petroleum	116,609	10.69
Chemical	141,197	12.95
Glass	51,843	4.76
Jewelry and decorative	38,360	3.52
Dental and medical	26,191	2.41
Miscellaneous	56,372	5.17
	1,090,157	100.00

Source: U.S. Bureau of Mines.

The *American automotive industry* emerged in 1974 as the largest single major outlet for platinum. The use of platinum in the automotive industry is concentrated almost entirely in the emission-control area. As a consequence of concern regarding atmospheric pollution and federal and state directives, the utilization of precious metal-based *catalytic-converter* devices for most new automobiles commenced on a major scale during the 1975 model year. These catalytic units, installed in automotive exhaust systems, serve to reduce emission of unburned hydrocarbons and carbon monoxide. In 1980, purchases of platinum by the industry for stockpiling and consumption totaled 517,143 ozs.

Introduction of the catalytic converter has created a very substantial on-going market for platinum, not only with domestic manufacturers, but with European and Japanese manufacturers serving the large American market. The worldwide nature of the pollution problem has resulted in the use of platinum-containing catalytic converters in Japan and suggests possible future use in many countries of the world. It should be noted that the level of total consumption of platinum in the automobile industry is very dependent on the level of activity in that industry. Changing consumer attitudes related to the cost of automobile purchase, operation, and maintenance, if translated into less frequent new-car purchases, could have a negative impact on the total quantity of platinum used for new cars.

In both the *petroleum* and *chemical industries*, platinum is used principally as a catalyst. Platinum plays a critical catalytic role in the manufacture of gasoline and of nitric acid, a vital intermediate for fertilizers, explosives, and plastics.

Electrical and electronic uses of platinum include a wide variety of applications, ranging from temperature measuring devices to circuit elements. The glass industries consume platinum in the manufacture of fiberglass and in other uses. Gem settings constitute the single most important jewelry use. Medical applications include the *pacemaker*, a device to stimulate the heart muscle.

The use of platinum as a fuel-cell catalyst in the production of electrical energy represents what could be a promising new outlet for this versatile metal. The fuel cell is a pollution-free energy generating device consisting of the nonexplosive combination of hydrogen and oxygen with the assistance of platinum as a catalyst. Fuel-cell prototypes have been developed in New York and Japan. Table 3 lists recent demand figures for platinum.

MARKET ANALYSIS. Overall, *precious metals* (i.e., platinum, gold, and silver) prices are affected by many factors. However, the bottom-line pricing element is the *supply-and-demand balance*. Prices rise as demand outpaces supply or in response to a depleted supply. Conversely, prices fall with the trend reversal.

Aside from obvious supply-and-demand components, including mine output, secondary reflow, and automobile sales, a variety of additional factors are known to influence this balance. For example, precious metal prices are influenced by the state of the economy and the corresponding interest rates. As rates rise, other interest-bearing instruments become more attractive to the investor; subsequently, demand for precious metals decreases and prices fall.

The *global political situation* is also important when evaluating precious metal prices. As political tensions increase, metal prices usually escalate. Investors are more apt to place their capital into metals as they are viewed as safeguards against the consequences of political upheavals.

Analysts of the platinum market recognize a relationship between platinum and gold. Prices of these two metals often move in tandem. Gold, a metal associated with high speculative interest, will have a greater price response to the afore-

TABLE 3. Platinum Demand—Comparison of Purchases for 1975–1980

Industrial Application	1975	1976	1977	1978	1979	1980
Automotive	273,000	480,965	354,388	597,538	803,229	517,143
Chemical	148,813	83,560	84,414	149,696	98,600	116,609
Petroleum	107,988	59,103	74,772	108,365	170,013	141,197
Glass	33,813	41,683	59,995	98,094	88,594	51,843
Electrical	73,624	89,319	90,217	106,422	115,775	142,442
Dental and medical	17,097	26,858	27,083	44,139	27,053	26,191
Jewelry and decorative	22,900	23,371	34,650	25,751	27,712	38,360
Miscellaneous	21,318	46,246	64,350	66,336	77,949	56,372
	698,553	851,105	789,819	1,196,341	1,408,925	1,090,157

Source: U.S. Bureau of Mines.

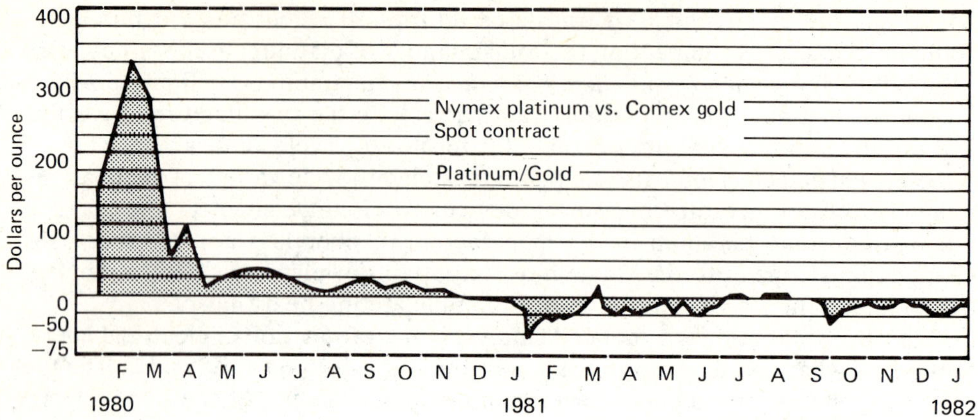

FIGURE 2. Platinum/gold spread chart. (*Source*: New York Mercantile Exchange.)

mentioned factors than will platinum. Therefore platinum often takes the price movement of gold as an overall cue for its own direction.

Historically, platinum has commanded a premium over gold. This is attributed to the relative rarity of platinum as compared to gold. In early 1980, platinum's premium exceeded $300. However, by the beginning of 1981 the spread reversed itself, with gold commanding a premium over platinum for most of 1981 and into 1982. Such a reversal is due to the fact that platinum is generally regarded as an industrial metal and therefore will respond with a greater degree of negative movement to weak economic conditions, that is, high interest rates, decreased automotive activity, and poor jewelry demand (see Figure 2).

PLATINUM PRICES. In the United States, three distinct markets exist for platinum. Each of these markets generates its own platinum price. The first price, the *producer price*, is quoted for refined platinum, F.O.B. refinery, by the two major suppliers, *Engelhard Minerals and Chemicals Corporation and Johnson, Matthey and Company, Ltd.* A second price, referred to as the *dealer price*, is quoted by metal merchants trading in platinum. Dealer platinum is derived from international primary sources, principally from the USSR, with lesser quantities from Colombia and elsewhere or from secondary supply. A third price is determined in the *futures market* in daily trading on the New York Mercantile Exchange.

Figure 3 demonstrates the following points:

1. The volatility of dealer and futures prices.
2. The relative stability of producer prices.
3. The frequent existence of substantial differences among the different prices, particularly dealer and futures prices compared with producer prices.
4. The good correlation between the movement of dealer prices and futures prices.

The stability of producer prices is not surprising. There are only two major suppliers in the producer market, and their principal interest revolves more around

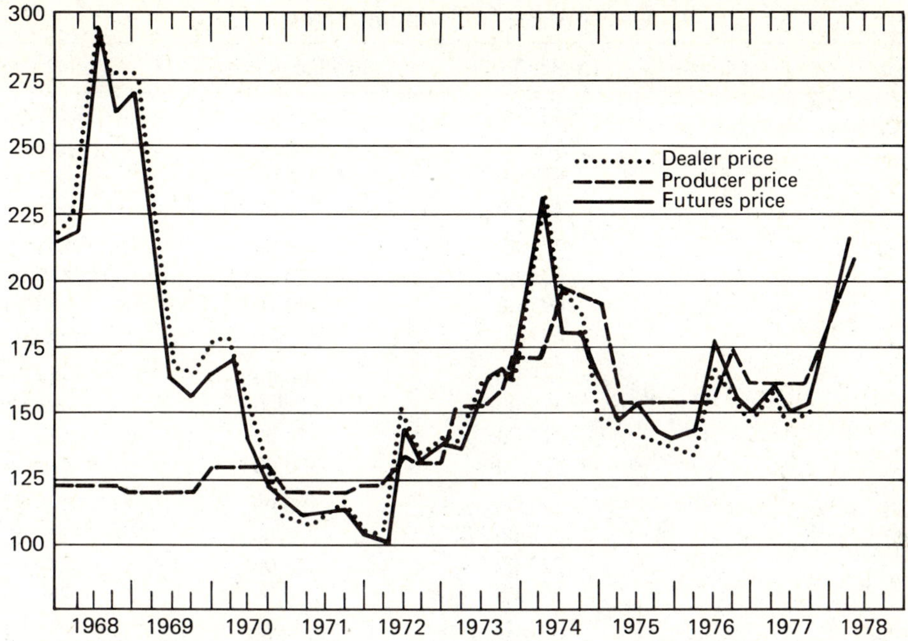

FIGURE 3. Comparison of platinum dealer, producer, and futures prices.

the sale of fabricated platinum products than platinum metal in bar form. In contrast, the dealer market consists of some 20–30 firms, while the *New York Mercantile Exchange* futures market includes a very large number of participants. During times such as the late 1960s, when platinum was in great shortage, dealer prices rose to substantial premiums over the slower-to-respond producer quotations. The reverse has been true during times when the supply has exceeded demand, such as in the late 1970s. The futures market, being highly responsive to changing economic conditions, has followed a similar course in relation to the producer price.

Both the dealer and futures markets have been in existence for a limited period of time. Accordingly, only producer prices provide a long-term picture of platinum prices. Average annual producer prices for platinum covering the entire post-World War II period, 1945–1981, are shown in Figure 4 and Table 4. Examination of the figure reveals the typical volatility of platinum prices, understated greatly by the fact that these are producer and not dealer or futures prices. Overall, platinum prices are now three times those that prevailed at the end of World War II.

PALLADIUM

PALLADIUM DEMAND. Although not as well known as platinum, palladium is a beautiful precious metal with diversified and growing end-use applications. In 1980, U. S. users purchased 911,967 oz of palladium. The following chart reveals the end-use purchase pattern for palladium in 1980.

TABLE 4. Platinum Prices

Year	Quarter	Dealer Price	Producer Price	Futures Price
1981	I	$509.00	$475.00	$495.00
	II	466.00	475.00	450.00
	III	420.00	475.00	416.50
	IV	404.00	475.00	400.00
1980	I	775.00	420.00	806.50
	II	528.00	420.00	520.00
	III	695.00	420.00	700.00
	IV	692.00	475.00	690.00
1979	I	343.00	300.00	344.00
	II	385.00	325.00	386.00
	III	413.00	350.00	419.00
	IV	575.00	380.00	632.30
1978	I	181.00	180.00	190.80
	II	208.00	205.00	217.50
	III	243.00	220.00	240.60
	IV	295.00	250.00	287.50
1977	I	149.50	162.00	150.50
	II	158.00	162.00	161.00
	III	146.50	162.00	148.80
	IV	152.00	162.00	153.10
1976	I	138.00	155.00	142.80
	II	135.00	155.00	144.30
	III	167.00	155.00	178.00
	IV	156.50	175.00	158.20
1975	I	150.63	190.00	163.60
	II	148.00	155.00	147.80
	III	145.00	155.00	155.20
	IV	140.00	155.00	146.30
1974	I	168.00	172.50	165.80
	II	226.75	172.50	231.00
	III	200.00	195.00	182.80
	IV	185.25	190.00	182.60
1973	I	140.00	132.50	140.60
	II	140.00	152.50	138.50
	III	165.00	152.50	160.10
	IV	165.75	160.50	168.30
1972	I	104.00	122.50	104.10
	II	102.00	122.50	101.20
	III	149.00	135.00	148.20
	IV	133.00	132.50	134.50
1971	I	110.00	120.00	118.00
	II	107.00	120.00	110.50
	III	111.00	120.00	111.20
	IV	115.00	120.00	112.00

TABLE 4. Continued

Year	Quarter	Dealer Price	Producer Price	Futures Price
1970	I	176.00	130.00	166.10
	II	175.00	130.00	172.80
	III	150.00	130.00	140.00
	IV	127.00	130.00	122.70
1969	I	276.00	120.00	273.00
	II	220.00	120.00	223.00
	III	171.00	120.00	164.00
	IV	165.00	120.00	156.00
1968	I	216.00	122.50	215.00
	II	227.00	122.50	218.00
	III	292.00	122.50	293.00
	IV	276.00	122.50	263.00

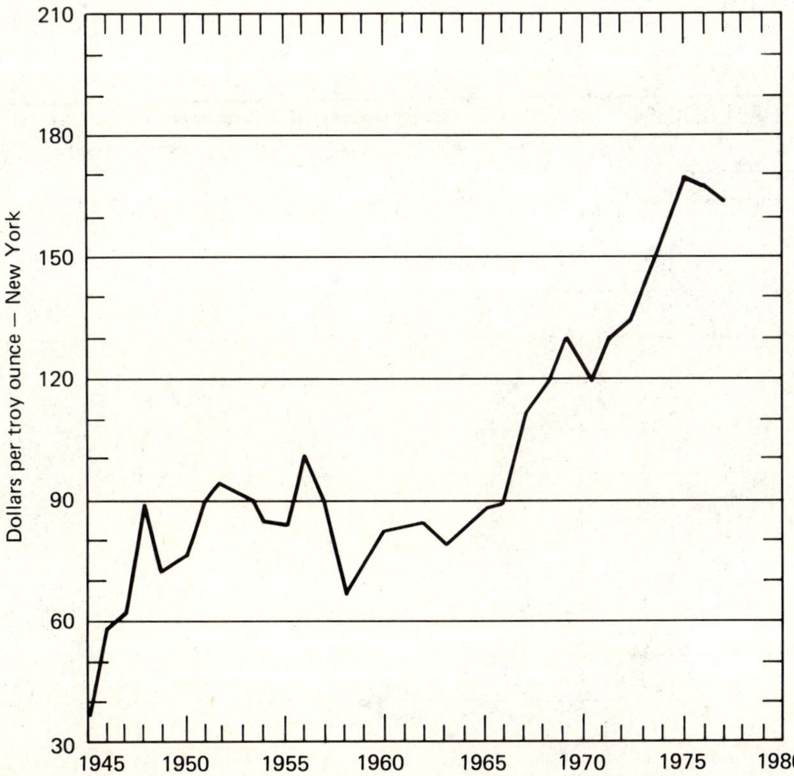

FIGURE 4. Average annual platinum producer prices, 1945–1981. 1978—$215.00; 1979—$335.00; 1980—$435.00; 1981—$475.00. [*Source: Metal Statistics* (1945–1977); *American Metal Market* (1978–1981).]

Application	Purchases	Percent
Electrical	289,797	35.58
Automotive	176,518	21.68
Dental/medical	174,832	21.47
Chemical	116,515	14.31
Petroleum	21,391	2.63
Jewelry/decorative	12,874	1.58
Glass	1,121	0.13
Miscellaneous	21,325	2.62
	814,373	100.00

Source: U.S. Bureau of Mines.

Electrical applications have accounted for the largest single segment of palladium end use. Important electrical applications include serving as the materials of construction for low-current electrical contacts and use in temperature thermocouple devices and in resistor elements. The great use of palladium in the electrical field derives from the excellent electrical properties of the metal and its comparative low cost.

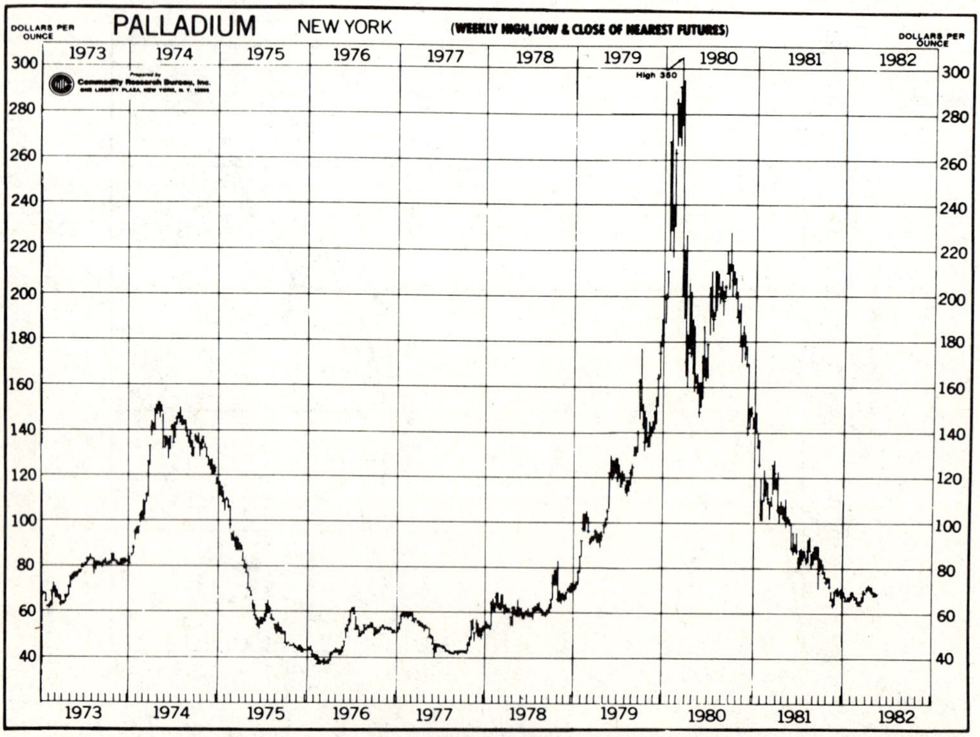

FIGURE 5. Palladium weekly nearest futures—New York.

TABLE 5. U.S. Salient Statistics of Platinum and Allied Metals (in Troy Ounces)

Year	Net Import Reliance as a Percent of Apparent Consumption	Production Crude[a]	Refinery		Stocks as of December 31st[b]				Imports for Consumption	Value of Imports (Millions of Dollars)	Exports		
			New Metal	Secondary Metal	Platinum	Palladium	Other	Total			Platinum	Other Groups[d]	Other[c]
1961		43,248	79,453	85,971	255,654	244,910	54,881	555,445	884,463	36.8	41,385	20,460	
1962		28,472	54,775	132,102	256,755	285,173	56,174	598,102	720,352	32.7	49,651	10,940	
1963		49,750	80,208	117,099	320,601	315,756	63,218	699,575	1,003,608	50.4	51,236	11,776	
1964		40,487	71,090	120,147	378,896	317,691	70,677	767,264	882,705	50.5	125,139	21,167	
1965		35,026	61,723	108,525	422,804	427,450	76,119	926,373	1,172,643	69.0	72,925	30,172	
1966		51,423	73,615	103,321	459,669	574,651	95,284	1,129,607	1,352,256	83.5	102,031	103,425	
1967		16,365	29,663	365,799	327,919	460,624	80,668	869,211	1,321,278	92.1	161,585	118,267	
1968		14,793	12,305	329,932	322,932	393,882	85,897	802,711	1,773,984	125.7	222,998	172,159	
1969		21,586	17,875	371,659	361,305	608,716	98,087	1,068,108	1,225,851	93.9	223,569	277,495	
1970		17,316	19,822	350,176	291,544	332,726	85,754	710,024	1,410,786	104.8	270,584	143,182	
1971		18,029	21,184	278,175	385,828	316,126	94,837	796,791	1,388,043	93.7	320,842	83,768	
1972		17,112	15,380	255,641	426,611	405,793	98,449	930,853	1,892,184	144.1	417,037	121,949	
1973		19,980	19,916	265,901	446,522	493,078	93,524	1,033,124	2,504,181	248.8	439,452	188,074	
1974		12,657	13,234	325216	532,675	478,210	110,921	1,121,806	3,251,311	504.6	474,494	361,260	
1975	83	18,920	16,571	270,101	420,770	335,621	92,819	849,210	1,820,284	272.8	284,796	283,435	91,654
1976	90	6,116	7,101	215,355	536,318	459,765	89,620	1,085,703	2,667,059	291.5	138,951	186,602	186,854
1977	91	5,545	5,199	195,219	438,055	475,358	99,409	1,012,812	2,510,374	273.0	149,023	137,324	140,284
1978	90	8,246	8,303	257,191	369,823	369,937	121,651	861,411	2,921,411	450.2	166,095	356,990	179,462
1979[e]	89	7,300	8,868	309,022	305,605	323,865	131,812	761,282	3,479,128	840.5	207,832	502,548	189,218
1980[f]	87	6,000	6,000	345,000	493,000	293,831	114,198	901,029	3,505,942	117.8	250,000	330,000	170,000
1981[f]	85	6,000	—407,316—		435,515	401,169	114,267	950,951	2,849,617	800.3	391,194	258,745	212,426

Source: Bureau of Mines. [a]From crude platinum placers and by-product platinum-group metals. [b]In hands of refiners, importers and dealers. [c]Ore and concentrates. Bars, ingots, sheets, wire, sponge, and other forms, including waste, scrap, and sweepings. [d]Palladium, rhodium, and iridium, osmium ruthenium, and osmium metals and alloys, including scrap. [e]Preliminary. [f]Estimate.

In 1980 the *automotive industry* purchased 176,518 oz of palladium, which accounted for 21.68% of total purchases. As in the case of platinum, palladium purchases result from the use of catalytic emission-control devices.

In the *chemical industry*, palladium is used principally as a catalyst. Palladium catalysts serve effectively in the chemical industry for combining oxygen and hydrogen, and for the processing of organic compounds.

Due to dramatic price increases in gold and platinum, palladium has become increasingly important to the dental and medical fields. Palladium's other outlets include jewelry and decorative applications and use in the petroleum and glass industries.

PALLADIUM SUPPLY. Worldwide, the bulk of newly mined palladium, similar to platinum, is produced by three countries—the Soviet Union, South Africa, and Canada. Palladium is found in the nickel–copper ores of Canada, in the pyroxinite deposits of South Africa's Merensky Reef, and in the Soviet Union in association with deposits of platinum. The Soviet Union is by far the world's largest producer of palladium. In addition to the supply of "new" palladium, considerable quantities of recycled palladium augment the overall supply.

World production of palladium in 1980 approximated 3.2 million oz. Breakdown estimates place the Soviet Union with 65–70%, South Africa with 25%, and Canada with 3% of total production. The two leading platinum companies, Engelhard and Johnson, Matthey, also dominate palladium refining and fabricating in the United States.

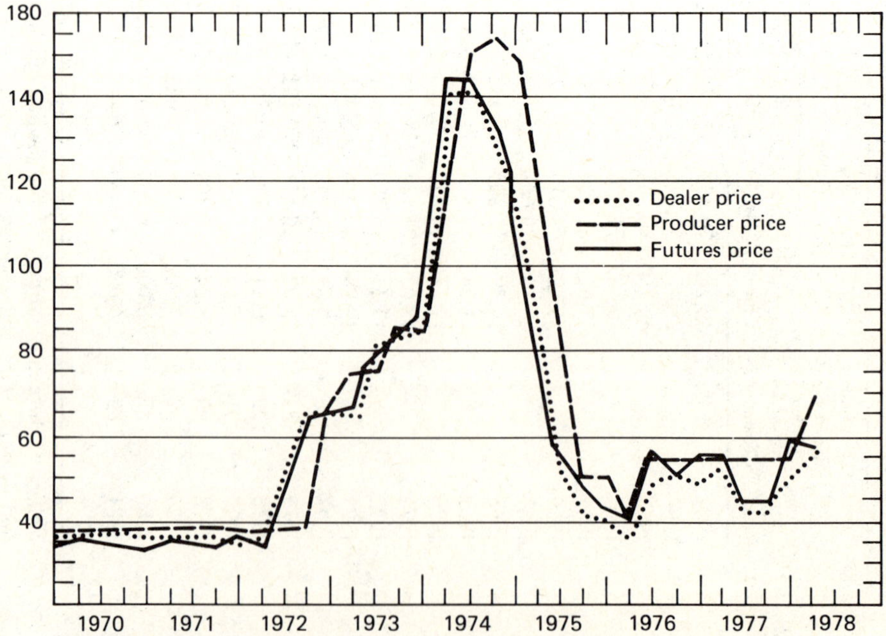

FIGURE 6. Comparison of palladium dealer, producer, and futures prices.

TABLE 6. Palladium Demand—Comparison of Purchases for 1975–1980

Industrial Application	1975	1976	1977	1978	1979	1980
Automotive	194,496	97,000	125,010	198,809	222,156	176,518
Chemical	128,229	142,975	161,234	146,352	199,743	116,515
Petroleum	7,291	2,225	8,507	18,909	24,588	21,391
Glass	2,989	17,633	907	2,757	1,729	1,121
Electrical	152,312	132,247	223,748	286,574	392,372	289,797
Dental and medical	139,279	114,970	112,473	206,312	243,627	174,832
Jewelry and decorative	5,700	23,026	15,567	12,570	11,766	12,874
Miscellaneous	26,766	11,942	53,023	45,645	36,640	21,325
	657,062	542,018	700,469	917,928	1,132,621	814,373

Source: U.S. Bureau of Mines.

PALLADIUM PRICES. Three distinct markets exist for palladium, each generating its own price.

Producer prices are established by the principal palladium producers, Rustenberg and Impala, as a basis for long-term supply agreements. The *dealer market* reflects cash prices quoted daily by metals merchants, and is closely paralleled by the New York Mercantile Exchange palladium *futures market*, which has been in existence since 1968.

Historically, dealer prices for palladium have been extremely volatile, reflecting the fluctuations in the short-term balances between supply-and-demand characteristics of the palladium field. Futures price movements have generally been closely correlated with those of dealer prices. Producer prices have been relatively much more stable.

FUTURES MARKETS

Both platinum and palladium are traded on the New York Mercantile Exchange. Volumes in both contracts have been increasing with overall market interest. Table 8 presents the contract specifications for both platinum and palladium.

SOURCES OF INFORMATION

PLATINUM, PALLADIUM, GOLD, AND U.S. SILVER COINS

Government Agencies

U. S. Department of the Interior, Bureau of Mines, Washington, DC 20241:

Mineral Industry Surveys—statistics and trade developments; published quarterly.

Minerals and Materials—a monthly survey; statistics published monthly.

Minerals Yearbook—statistics and long-range developments; published at intervals of approximately 5 years.

TABLE 7. Palladium Prices

Year	Quarter	Dealer Price	Producer Price	Futures Price
1981	I	$122.50	$176.90	$117.30
	II	102.40	134.25	98.80
	III	85.00	125.00	84.12
	IV	73.50	125.00	71.73
1980	I	247.50	186.00	239.55
	II	178.00	225.00	160.50
	III	205.50	225.00	202.40
	IV	182.00	217.85	178.10
1979	I	91.50	90.85	89.00
	II	108.00	104.00	107.35
	III	125.25	122.50	122.62
	IV	149.50	136.50	146.78
1978	I	50.00	55.00	58.95
	II	56.50	70.00	58.40
	III	60.50	70.00	60.35
	IV	71.85	77.75	69.92
1977	I	50.00	55.00	55.15
	II	53.50	55.00	54.65
	III	43.00	55.00	44.20
	IV	42.50	55.00	44.25
1976	I	40.00	50.00	42.50
	II	35.00	40.00	40.50
	III	49.00	55.00	56.85
	IV	51.75	55.00	51.30
1975	I	111.00	150.00	110.65
	II	87.00	120.00	84.50
	III	53.00	80.00	60.00
	IV	42.00	50.00	47.50
1974	I	86.00	84.00	89.25
	II	140.40	125.00	145.00
	III	141.00	151.25	144.00
	IV	134.00	155.00	134.50
1973	I	65.05	68.00	65.45
	II	65.43	75.00	66.60
	III	81.20	75.00	78.30
	IV	82.00	84.00	89.25
1972	I	34.50	36.00	35.55
	II	35.50	36.00	34.25
	III	48.90	38.00	48.20
	IV	65.21	38.00	64.25
1971	I	35.00	36.00	33.55
	II	35.00	36.00	34.95
	III	35.25	37.00	34.35
	IV	35.25	37.00	33.80
1970	I	35.50	37.00	33.75
	II	36.00	37.00	34.35
	III	36.00	36.00	34.45
	IV	36.00	36.00	34.30

TABLE 8. Contract Specifications

NYMEX Platinum	
Delivery months	January, April, July, and October, including current 3 months
Trading unit	50 troy oz
Minimum fluctuation	$0.10 per oz ($5 per contract)
Daily price movement limits	Subject to change; consult latest official notices from the exchange
Daily trading limits	None
Position limits	None
Grades deliverable	Minimum 99.9% pure platinum metals with a minimum 99.5% pure platinum, sheet or bar
Delivery	By depository receipt from a depository within the New York metropolitan area and approved by the exchange
Trading hours	9:30 a.m.–2:30 p.m. eastern time
NYMEX Palladium	
Delivery months	March, June, September, and December, including current 3 months
Trading unit	100 troy oz
Minimum fluctuation	$0.05 per oz ($5 per contract)
Daily price movement limits	Subject to change; consult latest official notices from the exchange
Daily trading limits	None
Position limits	None
Grades deliverable	Minimum 99.8% pure palladium
Delivery	By bank depository receipt from a depository within the New York metropolitan area and approved by the exchange
Trading hours	9:50 a.m.–2:20 p.m. eastern time

Periodicals

American Metal Market, 7 East 12th Street, New York, NY 10003.

Coin Age, Behn–Miller Publications, Incorporated, Sparta, IL.

Coin World, Sidney Printing and Publishing Company, Sidney, OH.

Metal Bulletin Monthly, 45/46 Lower Marsh, London, England.

Metals Week, 1221 Avenue of Americas, New York, NY 10020.
The Platinum Metals Review, Johnson, Matthey and Company, Ltd., London, England.

Trade Associations

Gold Institute, Washington, DC.
International Precious Metals Institute, Brooklyn, NY.

Other

Metal Statistics, Fairchild Publications, 7 East 12th Street, New York, NY 10003; annual statistical summary by the publishers of American Metal Market.
Yearbook of the American Bureau of Metal Statistics, American Bureau of Metal Statistics, New York, NY.

CHAPTER 47

FOREIGN EXCHANGE FUTURES

CONTENTS

THE THEORY AND HISTORY OF FOREIGN EXCHANGE 4

The Evolution of Money 4
The Mercantilist View 5
Emergence of the Gold Standard 6
The Bretton Woods System 7
From "Dollar Shortage" to "Dollar Glut" 8
"Clean" and "Dirty" Floats 12

THE MARKETS FOR FOREIGN EXCHANGE 12

The Nature of the Interbank Market 13
The Widget Example 16

FORWARD VERSUS FUTURES 17

Hedging Versus Speculation 19

PRICE DETERMINATION 19

The Role of Expectations 20
Interest Rates: The Critical Link 21
Quick Lunches 22
Class B Arbitrage—Sprinters Needed 23

CONCLUSION 24

APPENDIX 24

BIBLIOGRAPHY 28

Sources of Information—Periodicals 30

CHAPTER 47

FOREIGN EXCHANGE FUTURES

James E. Higgins
Allan M. Loosigian

Scarcely a day goes by when we do not learn of some major international development that has been affected by exchange rate fluctuations; for example, Mexico's external debt problems are aggravated by repeated devaluations of the peso. European nations reap little or no benefit from the declining price of oil, for the U.S. dollar, in which oil bills are denominated, has risen in value as the oil price has fallen. American manufacturers, already plagued by high domestic interest rates, suffer weakened demand for exports as these same interest rates keep the dollar too strong to make American products internationally competitive.

In the dealings of individual corporations, the importance of exchange rates is no less pronounced. Exxon Corporation absorbed a charge against earnings of nearly a quarter billion dollars in 1977 because of unfavorable exchange-rate movements. The collapse of the Franklin National Bank in 1974—the largest bank failure in U.S. history—resulted from unauthorized ventures in the foreign exchange market.

Why has the International Monetary Market grown? On an average trading day more than 25,000 contracts in eight currencies, with a face value of billions of dollars, change hands at the Chicago Mercantile Exchange's International Monetary Market. Yet little more than a decade ago, the foreign currency futures market did not exist. Why the dramatic growth? This chapter answers this question and unravels some of the other mysteries surrounding the futures market for foreign exchange. The chapter is addressed to readers with a speculative interest in foreign exchange, as well as to those whose primary concern is hedging foreign exchange risk.

The chapter begins with an examination of the theory and history of foreign exchange. Following this examination will be an outline of the nature of the various markets for foreign exchange—spot, forward, and futures. The section "Forward Versus Futures—What the Difference Is" will deal with the differences and the similarities among these markets. The section "Price Determination" will broach the confusing subject of price determination in the foreign exchange futures market. The more abstruse mathematical formulae are relegated to the appendix.

THE THEORY AND HISTORY OF FOREIGN EXCHANGE

Economic activity consists principally of the exchange of one good for another, or for several others. In any modern economy the good which is present in almost every such exchange is money. Workers exchange their labor for money. You exchange your money for a copy of *The Wall Street Journal* at the corner newsstand. For all the mystique surrounding it, money is really just another type of economic good. Like every other good in the economy, money has special uses which make it a desirable object to hold. The special use of an automobile, for example, is to provide relatively clean, fast, convenient transportation. There are three special uses which money traditionally has had: to serve as a store of wealth, to serve as a means of exchange, and to serve as a unit of value.

It is this third use, the unit-of-value function, that makes money so seemingly mysterious. Money is often not thought of as simply another good because virtually all other goods in the economy are priced in units of money. Economists call the good which serves this function a *numeraire*. Thinking of money as just another type of good helps to avoid the pitfall of the many newscasters who tell us "Rising prices caused inflation last month," when in fact rising prices of goods other than money *are* inflation.

Virtually all modern money has another property which distinguishes it from other goods: *It is produced by governments*. This characteristic also is responsible for the very existence of foreign exchange.

To understand the implications of this fact, consider the case of a good which is not produced mainly by governments (at least not in noncommunist countries), namely, record albums. If you travel to Europe and bring back a long-playing record, you can use it on your American-built stereo. But if you travel to Europe and bring back some European currency, you will have a rather difficult time putting it to its normal use, that is, spending it, without first exchanging it for U.S. dollars. This is so because what is money abroad is *foreign exchange* here.

Foreign exchange, then, is money held in a country different from the country where it was issued. To return to the example of the record album, to buy the LP in the first place you would have to trade in your U.S. dollars for local currency, say Deutsche marks if you were traveling in Germany. To the Germans your U.S. dollars are foreign exchange.

THE EVOLUTION OF MONEY. Money first emerged in the marketplace thousands of years ago, when traders began to recognize that bartering ("I'll give you three chickens for 2 bushels of grain") was far too cumbersome to facilitate commerce. Governments—principally the imperial government of Rome—came into the picture when rulers realized it was to their advantage to provide coinage (paper money came much later) of standardized weight and purity. By the time Christ said "Give unto Caesar . . .," the idea of government money was well-established.

But while government-produced coinage helped to solve the problems of underweight and impure money, it created another problem: what to use as a means of payment in financial dealings abroad. Through most of the history of the Roman Empire and as late as the Middle Ages, this problem mainly amounted to the question of relating the bullion content of one country's coins to those of other countries.

The acceptance of paper money more or less coincided with the later Middle Ages and the Renaissance. Bills of exchange (the forerunners of checks) and bank notes gradually superseded bullion as the standard means of international settlement. In 1694 the British government sold the Bank of England a monopoly on the issuance of bank notes. From that time, national currency was firmly entrenched in the world's financial system.

It was at about this same time that early economists began to develop theories of exchange rates, that is, the ratios at which various national currencies were exchanged for one another. There was soon general agreement that a major factor in determining the foreign exchange value of a particular country's currency was the size of the surplus (deficit) which that country ran of exports over (under) imports. In its simplest form this "balance-of-payments" theory held that a large surplus of exports over imports led to a large net foreign demand for the exporting country's currency, thereby driving up the foreign exchange price of that currency. Conversely, a trade deficit (imports exceeding exports) would lead to an excess supply of the deficit country's currency on the world market, thereby causing that currency to lose value, that is, to *depreciate*. Note that this theory suggests that foreign trade imbalances will tend to disappear. A country in trade surplus will see its currency rise in price (*appreciate*). This appreciation will raise the effective price of the surplus country's exports to any potential buyer who must exchange his or her own national currency for that of the exporter in order to buy the exports. On the other side of the coin (or bank note, as the case may be), a deficit country's currency depreciation will make its goods relatively less expensive on the international market.

At about the same time that the balance of payments theory of exchange rates was emerging, another theory of exchange rates was also being developed. This other theory evolved from the general realization that the foreign exchange value of a currency should have some relationship to the ratio of domestic currency to real goods in that country.

The resulting "purchasing power parity" theory holds that, in the absence of such administrative obstacles to trade as tariffs and exchange controls (which were in practice seldom absent, particularly in the 18th century), exchange rates should come to rest, that is, "equilibrate," in economists' jargon, in such a way that the real price of the same good in any two countries should differ only by the cost of shipping that good between the two countries.

Notice that the "balance of payments" theory and the "purchasing power parity" theory are complementary in that they both suggest that a country's currency will depreciate if its products are too expensive on the world market and appreciate if its products are relatively cheap.

THE MERCANTILIST VIEW. Today it is commonplace to say that a relatively stable international monetary system is a good thing, but at the time the first theories of foreign exchange were developed such a view was so unorthodox that it was not even expressed. The dominant international economic policy of the time was what later came to be known as "mercantilism." According to the mercantilist view, a country's prosperity depended upon the amount of bullion in its treasury. The best way to increase the size of the bullion stock was to run a surplus of exports over imports, and doing this implied keeping a country's exchange rate relatively low. It also meant erecting barriers to trade such as protective tariffs and import quotas to prevent rival nations from running trade surpluses at the home country's expense.

Such a policy has certain benefits in a narrowly nationalistic sense, but only if your country is the only one applying it. But in the 18th century all the major trading nations were using this policy. It is not difficult to see that, for example, if I am trying to prevent your citizens from exporting into my country and you are trying to prevent my citizens from exporting into yours, international trade will be virtually choked off. This is precisely what happened in the 18th century. (Regrettably, it also happened in the 1930s, when worldwide policies of high tariffs and competitive devaluations seriously aggravated the Great Depression.)

The beginning of the end for this period of international trade and finance came in 1776 with the publication of Adam Smith's *An Inquiry into the Nature and Causes of the Wealth of Nations*. Smith argued that it was the size of a country's production, not the size of its bullion surplus that determined prosperity. As this doctrine gradually found its way into economic policy, trade, even imports if necessary, came to be viewed as beneficial. Only at this time did the search begin for a monetary system which would facilitate, and not hinder, international trade. The loosely organized system which eventually came into being was the *classical international* gold standard. Under this system, governments issued gold notes each backed by a specified fixed amount of gold bullion held in the national treasury. The governments agreed to redeem the gold notes for actual gold (and vice versa) at fixed prices.

EMERGENCE OF THE GOLD STANDARD. The classical international gold standard emerged in the late 18th century, and remained in effect until the 1930's. (The costs of financing World War I forced the belligerents to suspend redemption in one way or another, and postwar restoration of the standard proved unworkable.) There had been, moreover, relatively brief periods of nonredemption during the gold standard period, as when the United States issued "greenbacks" to finance the Civil War.

International trade greatly expanded during the classical gold standard period. It is easy to see why such a regime would put merchants at ease. Suppose I am an American businessperson considering the sale of some product to a British buyer who proposes to pay in pounds sterling. If (to use purely hypothetical numbers) the U.S. Treasury will give 1 oz of gold for every \$20 turned in to it and the Bank of England will give 1 oz of gold for every £5 turned in to it, I know that I will be sure of being able to exchange each pound sterling I receive for four U.S. dollars—at least as long as both countries maintain the same prices for gold, or *gold parities*.[1]

The classical international gold standard imposed a degree of fiscal and monetary discipline on governments the likes of which we may never see again: prices in Britain in 1931 stood a scant 0.6 percentage points above where they had stood

[1] 20/5 = 4

in 1752, and prices in the United States were actually three percentage points *lower* in 1933 than they were in 1808. (The United States had moved to the gold standard somewhat later than Britain had.) Nevertheless, the gold standard has had its reputation tarnished because of several economic contractions associated with it, notably two in the United States following the Civil War and one in Britain following World War I. All of these periods of contractions were caused by attempts to reestablish prewar parities that had been rendered unfeasible by wartime inflation.

The 1930s saw nations go off the gold standard and engage, as was noted above, in *competitive devaluations* of their currencies in efforts to rescue the trading positions of their depression-wracked economies.[2] Free international trade and finance virtually came to a halt during World War II.

By 1944 it was clear to the Allied forces that they would soon win the war and would then be faced with the task of rebuilding the world's financial system.

To address this task, delegates from the Allied powers assembled in July 1944 at what has come to be known as the Bretton Woods Conference after the New Hampshire resort which hosted them. John Maynard Keynes headed the British contingent, and Harry Dexter White led the Americans.

THE BRETTON WOODS SYSTEM. The system which was devised at Bretton Woods remained intact for 27 years—remarkable durability, by contemporary standards. The two principal provisions of the agreement were: (1) that the United States would fix the value of the dollar at 1/35 of 1 oz of gold (i.e., the gold price would be $35 per oz) and would exchange dollars for gold or gold for dollars at the request of any foreign government, although not for any individuals; and (2) all other countries would have the choice of fixing, or "pegging," the value of their currencies to gold or to the dollar. (In practice, they all chose to peg to the dollar.) Countries would be allowed to change their pegs only in the event of an undefined "fundamental disequilibrium."

The agreement was to be administered by the newly created International Monetary Fund (IMF). The IMF was also given another important role in the system. Each country that agreed to participate was required to deposit a "quota" of gold and currency reserves with the fund. When a particular country was suffering from a "temporary disequilibrium"—say, a bad harvest in a particular year—that threatened to prevent the country from maintaining the value of its currency in international markets, it could borrow from the fund to tide itself over.

The objectives of the Bretton Woods system were to provide stability and flexibility in international payments, as well as to provide adequate liquidity to rebuild the world's economy. This last objective was no small matter, for by the end of the war the United States was holding three-quarters of the world's gold reserves.

The most fundamental effect of Bretton Woods (although it likely would have happened under virtually any other type of regime as well) was that the U.S.

[2]A technical distinction should be made here: *revaluation* and *devaluation* denote discrete government actions to raise and lower the foreign exchange value of the domestic currency. *Appreciation* and *depreciation* mean that a currency is bid up or down in the foreign exchange market.

dollar supplanted both gold and the pound sterling as the world's financial reserve. This effect was achieved by so overvaluing the dollar relative to other currencies that the United States would run what was virtually a permanent payments deficit. Table 1 gives the official parities that were in effect for most of the Bretton Woods period.

By 1949 the parities that were, in most cases, to prevail for the next two decades were in place. From that year on, the United States ran payments surpluses in only three of the years (1957, 1968, and 1969) that the Bretton Woods system remained in force.

Such repeated deficits did not create major difficulties as long as foreign governments and residents were eager to acquire liquidity in the form of dollars to rebuild their economies. But the devastated European (and Japanese) economies gradually began to develop enough liquidity to fuel their own growth. By 1958 the postwar European capital controls and exchange controls which had prevented the existence of an unfettered foreign exchange market were removed.

FROM "DOLLAR SHORTAGE" TO "DOLLAR GLUT." By the mid-1960s it began to be apparent that the "dollar shortage" which had followed the war had been superseded by a "dollar glut." In the mid-1950s a scant one-tenth of the surplus dollars shipped abroad returned to be exchanged for U.S. gold; by the late 1960s more than half of these surplus dollars were coming back. Other countries were having their own problems. Years of inflationary nationalization policies in England led to massive speculative selling of the British pound in November 1967. The British government virtually exhausted its dollar reserves defending its currency and was forced to devalue by 14%—from $2.80 to $2.40. In September 1969 West Germany found itself in a different sort of dilemma: unwilling to accede to an inflationary expansion of its domestic money supply (Germans well remembered the paper money hyperinflation of 1923) that would mop up the huge inflow of excess dollars, the German government revalued the mark from $0.25 to $0.27, an 8% rise. In 1971, Austria and Switzerland revalued their currencies, and Holland and Germany allowed upward floats of their units. Faced with a flight from the dollar, President Richard Nixon on August 15, 1971, "closed the gold window," unilaterally suspending America's obligation to redeem its own currency in gold.

TABLE 1. Currency Parities in U.S. Dollars (1951)

Currency	Parity
British pound	2.8000
Canadian dollar	1.0169
Deutsche mark	0.2380
Dutch guilder	0.2632
French franc	0.2857
Japanese yen	0.00277
Mexican peso	0.1156
Swiss franc	0.2286

Source: International Monetary Fund, *International Financial Statistics*, May 1976.

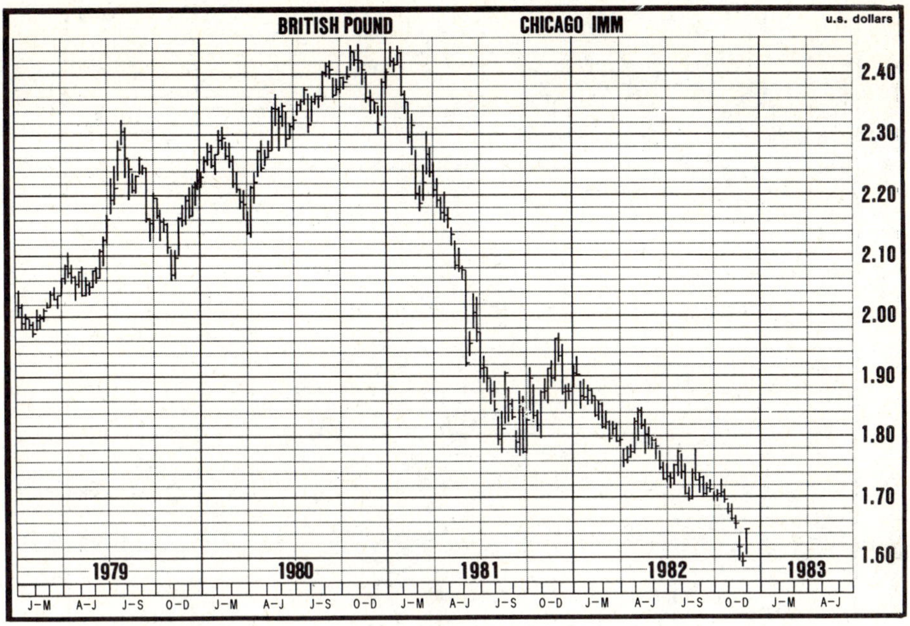

(*a*)

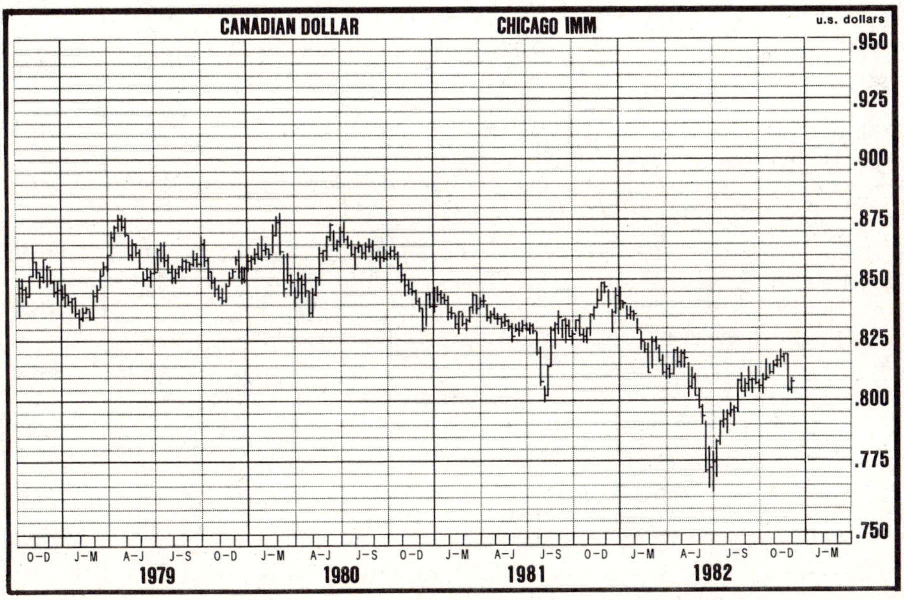

(*b*)

FIGURE 1. (*a*) British pound weekly prices. (*b*) Canadian dollar weekly prices. (*c*) Deutsche mark weekly prices. (*d*) Japanese yen weekly prices. (*e*) Mexican peso weekly prices. (*f*) Swiss franc weekly prices. *Source:* Commodity Research Bureau.

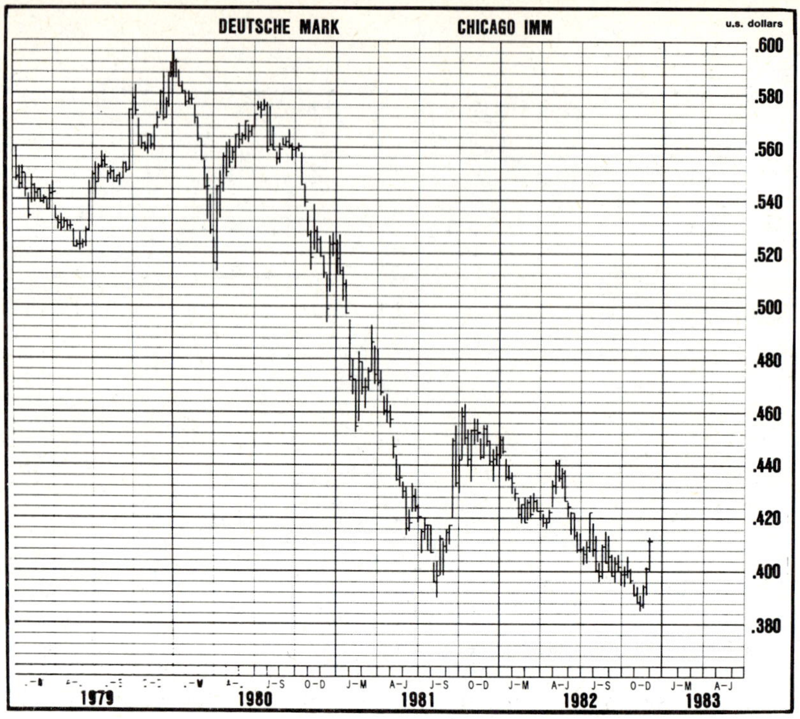
DEUTSCHE MARK
CHICAGO IMM
u.s. dollars
.600
.580
.560
.540
.520
.500
.480
.460
.440
.420
.400
.380
J-S
O-D
J-M
A-J
J-S
O-D
J-M
A-J
J-S
O-D
J-M
A-J
1979
1980
1981
1982
1983

(c)

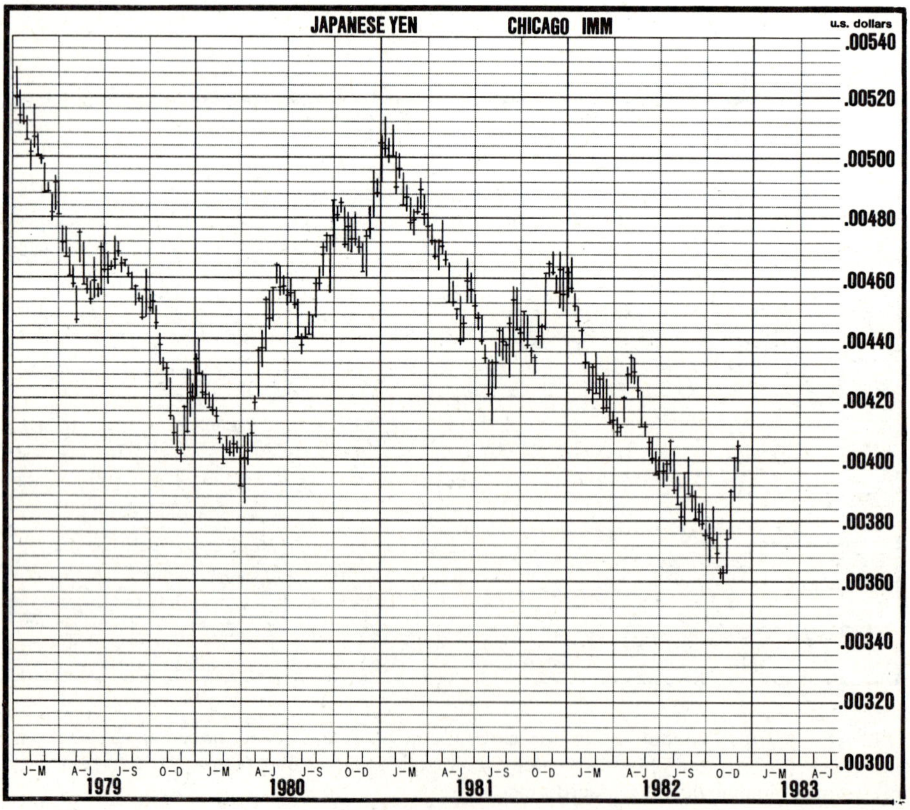
JAPANESE YEN
CHICAGO IMM
u.s. dollars
.00540
.00520
.00500
.00480
.00460
.00440
.00420
.00400
.00380
.00360
.00340
.00320
.00300
J-M
A-J
J-S
O-D
J-M
A-J
J-S
O-D
J-M
A-J
J-S
O-D
J-M
A-J
J-S
O-D
J-M
A-J
1979
1980
1981
1982
1983

(d)

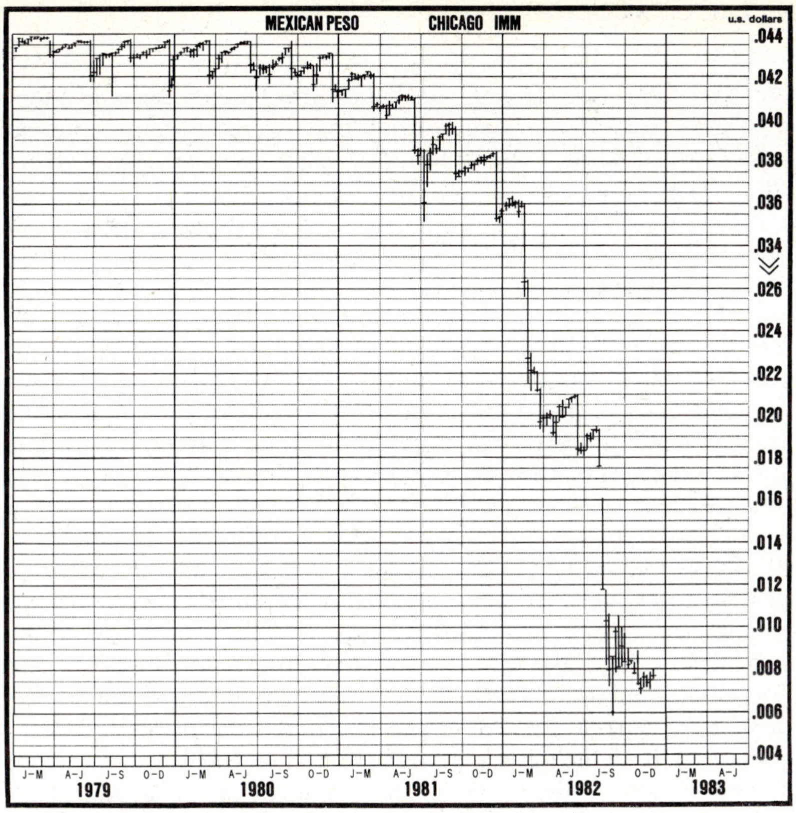
MEXICAN PESO
CHICAGO IMM
u.s. dollars
.044
.042
.040
.038
.036
.034
.026
.024
.022
.020
.018
.016
.014
.012
.010
.008
.006
.004
J–M A–J J–S O–D J–M A–J J–S O–D J–M A–J J–S O–D J–M A–J J–S O–D J–M A–J
1979
1980
1981
1982
1983

(e)

SWISS FRANC
CHICAGO IMM
u.s. dollars
.68
.66
.64
.62
.60
.58
.56
.54
.52
.50
.48
.46
.44
J–M A–J J–S O–D J–M A–J J–S O–D J–M A–J J–S O–D J–M A–J J–S O–D J–M A–J
1979
1980
1981
1982
1983

(f)

In December 1971 government financial officials from around the world attempted to put the fixed-rate regime back together again at a conference at the Smithsonian Institution in Washington, D.C. The "Smithsonian Agreement" established a system similar to the Bretton Woods regime. The major changes were that the dollar was devalued by 8.5% and that gold convertibility of the dollar was permanently ended. This system was not destined to have a long life, however. Buying pressures continued on the strong currencies—the Deutsche mark and Swiss franc—and selling pressure continued on the weak currencies—the dollar, the pound, and the Italian lira. This activity suggested that the set of Smithsonian adjustments—for that was what the Smithsonian Agreement really was—was too little and too late. In February 1973 the dollar was again devalued, but this action was still insufficient. Foreign exchange markets were ordered closed on March 1, 1973. When they were allowed to reopen several weeks later, exchange rates floated freely. The era of fixed exchange parities had come to an end.

"CLEAN" AND "DIRTY" FLOATS. However, the post-Bretton Woods world of exchange rates has not been an unregulated free market, or so-called "clean float," of every currency against every other currency. Many small countries still peg their currencies to the dollar, pound, or French franc. Most major central banks continue to intervene periodically in the foreign exchange markets to "stabilize" the value of their currency or to defend it against speculative attacks. It is this central bank activity which gives the current system the names "managed float" or, more colloquially, "dirty float." The countries in the European Economic Community have made several efforts to establish a "snake," or narrow band of parities which members are obliged to maintain among themselves. The most recent effort, which is still in effect as of this writing, is the European Monetary System (EMS), which includes Germany, France, Belgium, Luxembourg, the Netherlands, Denmark, Italy, and Ireland. The system does not include Great Britain. Each country in the snake is pledged to maintain the value of its currency vis-á-vis the other currencies in the system within a band of ±2.25% from initially agreed-upon parities. Each must obtain the consent—at least tacitly—of the others to devalue or revalue.[3]

THE MARKETS FOR FOREIGN EXCHANGE

At about the same time that the fixed-parity system of exchange rates was collapsing, the first futures market for foreign exchange was established. Trading began in seven foreign currency contracts on the Chicago Mercantile Exchange (CME) on May 15, 1972. The CME created a new submarket for the contracts: the International Monetary Market (IMM).

Trading in foreign exchange futures was the brainchild of Leo Melamed, the chairman of the CME. Melamed had the intellectual and moral support of Dr. Milton Friedman, then a professor at the University of Chicago. Moral support was certainly useful at the time, since futures markets in 1972 were very different from what they are today. Futures contracts in debt instruments such as Treasury

[3]The only exception is Italy, which has pledged to maintain the lira only within a band of ±6%.

bonds and certificates of deposit did not yet exist, and trading in stock index futures was a full decade away. In fact, it was only in the 1960s that the CME had expanded futures trading beyond its previous domain in such commodities as wheat and cotton and into contracts for livestock.

Melamed and Friedman's idea was not warmly received when they first suggested it in 1970. Not only was there no precedent for a futures contract in a financial instrument, there was considerable skepticism as to whether such contracts were needed. Melamed and Friedman presciently recognized that the days of fixed exchange rates were rapidly coming to a close; but other members of the financial community were not quick to agree. And after all, without floating exchange rates, there would be little interest in the market except from those who expected a one-time devaluation (or revaluation) of a particular currency.

Fortunately for Melamed and Friedman (not to mention all the other participants who had a stake in the IMM), their pessimism about the continued viability of fixed exchange rates proved correct. Trading on the IMM started slowly but has grown to where more than 25,000 contracts change hands on an average trading day. Several other attempts have been made since 1972 to set up alternate foreign exchange futures markets, notably by the New York Futures Exchange (NYFE), but none has been successful. These other exchanges learned the hard way a basic truism of futures markets: Unless your market is for a substantially different product than one for which there is already a functioning futures market, it is a risky undertaking to challenge an established exchange.

The specifications for each contract are listed in Table 2. The contracts are written for different quantities of each type of foreign currency in order to make their U.S. dollar values roughly equal. Of course, this equalization does not always hold over long periods of time. Since the contract on the Mexican peso was first traded, each unit of the Mexican currency has lost more than 90% of its value.

These facts about the foreign exchange futures market raise a major question. We established in the section "The Theory and History of Foreign Exchange" that there will always be a demand for foreign exchange as long as both national currencies and international transactions exist. Where, then, did foreign exchange trading take place before the advent of the IMM? The answer is that it took place where the bulk of such transactions still take place today—among the foreign exchange trading rooms of the world's major banks. Most (but by no means all) of these trading rooms are located in the "money center" cities of the world—New York, London, Zurich, Frankfurt, Tokyo, and Hong Kong.

THE NATURE OF THE INTERBANK MARKET. This trading system is known as the *interbank market*. It is not a "market" in the sense of the New York Stock Exchange or the Chicago Mercantile Exchange—that is, "interbank market" does not denote a physical location or locations. The buying and selling takes place by telephone among traders who are watching closely the price quotations on one or more cathode-ray tubes (television screens) in front of them. Trades are made only in large volume, usually multiples of 1 million units of one of the currencies being traded. Each participant bank posts two quotations of its own on this worldwide price quotation system. One quotation is the "bid" price—the price at which that bank will buy the quoted currency. The other price is the "offer" or "asking" price—what the bank is charging for purchases of that currency. The

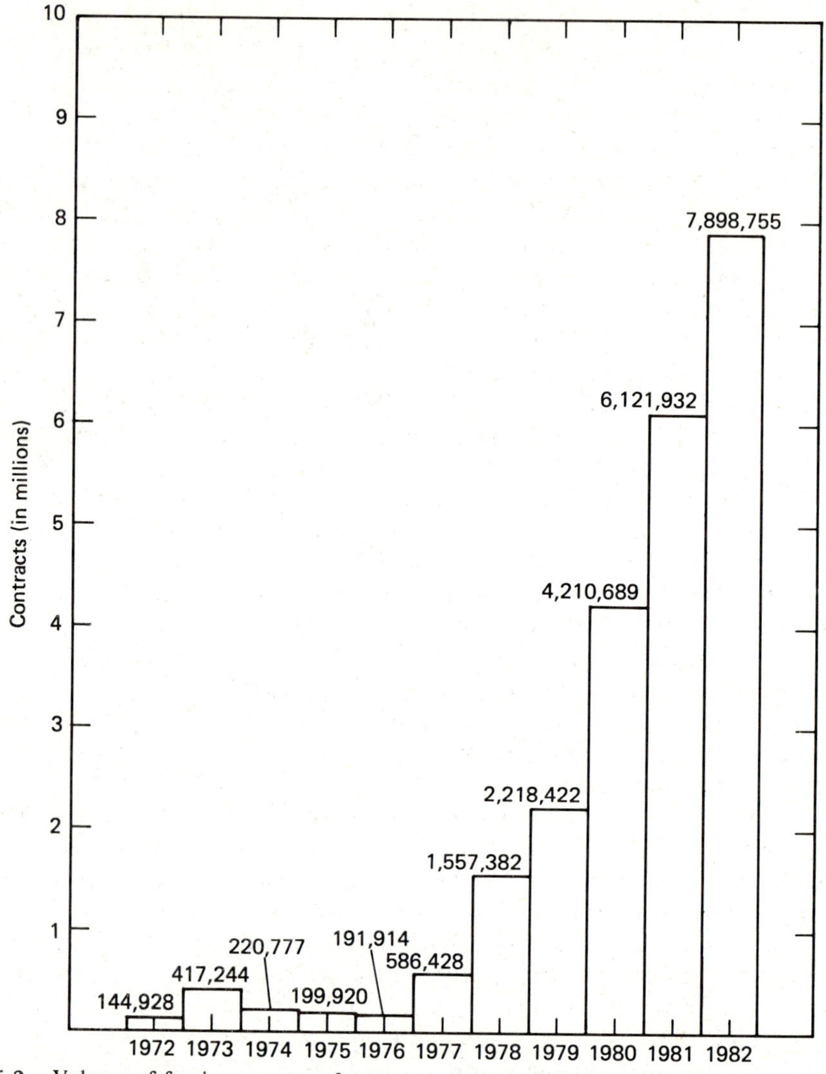

FIGURE 2. Volume of foreign currency futures contracts traded, International Monetary Market, 1972–1982 (May–December 1972 and January–November, 1982).

bid price, naturally, is always lower than the asked price. It is the existence of this difference between the two prices, or the "spread," that makes it profitable for a bank to maintain its trading operation.

At a first glance the "spread" may appear very tiny indeed. To choose purely hypothetical numbers, a bank's spread on the Swiss franc on a particular day might be 0.4999–0.5001. That is, the bank is offering to sell Swiss francs for U.S. dollars at \$0.5001 per franc and to buy francs at \$0.4999 per franc. A spread of \$0.0002 per franc may not seem like a very substantial profit, but if the bank buys 1 million Swiss francs at \$0.4999 and sells them immediately at \$0.5001, it has earned a profit before expenses of \$200.

TABLE 2. Contract Specifications on the IMM as of October 1982

	British pound	Canadian dollar	Deutsche mark	Dutch guilder	French franc	Japanese yen	Mexican peso	Swiss franc
Ticker symbol	BP	CD	DM	DG	FF	JY	MP	SF
Contract size	£25,000	C$100,000	DM125,000	125,000DG	FF250,000	Y12.5 mil	1 mil MP	125,000SF
Approximate U.S. dollar value	$45,000	$80,000	$50,000	$45,000	$37,000	$50,000	$8,000	$62,000
Minimum fluctuation	0.0005 ($12.50)	0.0001 ($10.00)	0.0001 ($12.50)	0.0001 ($12.50)	0.00005 ($12.50)	0.000001 (12.50)	0.00001 ($10.00)	0.0001 ($12.50)
Normal daily limit	0.0500	0.0075	0.0100	0.0100	0.00500	0.0100	0.00150	0.0150
Delivery months	All contracts: March, June, September, and December							
Trading hours	All contracts: approximately 7:30 a.m.–1:30 p.m. central standard time[a]							

Source: Chicago Mercantile Exchange.

[a]Foreign currency contracts do *not* all have precisely the same trading hours. They all close within several minutes of each other, at times posted in advance. These precise times are subject to change, and potential traders—particularly those who intend to day trade—should consult with their broker in advance to determine exactly what the trading hours are. It is not unknown for potential profits to disappear from under the nose of a trader who thought that a particular currency stopped trading at 1:24 p.m. when the correct closing time was 1:22 p.m.

There is, of course, a risk associated with this type of transaction. Suppose that the bank buys the 1 million Swiss francs for $0.4999, but finds that it cannot sell them immediately. Suppose that the bid/ask quotation drops to $0.4995–$0.4997, not an unusually large move in a world of floating exchange rates. When the bank sells its francs it will suffer a *loss* of $200 rather than earn a profit of that amount. In practice, sudden price swings can be much larger than this illustration suggests. Thus it is apparent why banks limit the foreign exchange positions their traders may take at any one time.

There is no necessary reason why the spread must remain at exactly $0.0002. The more active and competitive a particular market is, the smaller the spreads in it generally are. However, when a period of extreme price volatility occurs—for example, when some major and unexpected economic news item comes over the wires—banks may try to "play it safe" by expanding the spreads.

The participants in the interbank market may be speculators, the banks themselves, arbitrageurs, or nonbank firms that are trying to limit their foreign exchange exposure.

The interbank foreign exchange market is divided into two segments: the *spot* (or "cash") and *forward* markets. Spot transactions are those in which the currencies are exchanged immediately after the agreement to trade them is made.[4] Forward trades call for the exchange of funds to be made some specified number of days after the transaction is consummatted. Usually, forward contracts are executed, or "mature," 30 days, 60 days, 90 days, 6 months, or 1 year from the date they are agreed to. The story of why anyone would want to buy or sell foreign exchange now for delivery at a future date is a familiar one to anyone who has been introduced to futures markets for agricultural commodities. The usual example which is offered as an explanation of the existence of these agricultural futures markets is that of a farmer who expects to have a crop of wheat ready to bring to market in 6 months. Seeing a good market price for wheat now, the farmer wants to assure himself of favorable terms for the harvest of wheat. To do this the farmer *goes short* in the wheat futures market, selling a promise to deliver some amount of wheat 6 months hence. In exchange for this promise, the farmer establishes a predetermined price.

THE WIDGET EXAMPLE. Consider now the case of a manufacturer who exports goods. The manufacturer knows that in 6 months products will be delivered—widgets, to use as an example the favorite industrial product of economists—to a distributor in West Germany and the manufacturer will receive 1 million Deutsche marks in exchange. Like the farmer, the manufacturer wants to protect, or *hedge*, against a sudden decline in the value of the forthcoming "crop" of marks. The manufacturer might well call a bank and have it sell short the 1 million marks for delivery 6 months from now. If the value of the Deutsche mark falls during the ensuing 6 months, the implicit loss the manufacturer suffers on the payment for the widgets will be offset by an implicit profit on the forward sale. The other possibility is that, if the mark rises in value rather than falls during the intervening

[4]Strictly speaking, deliveries on most spot transactions are made 2 business days after the trade itself is made. This institutional detail is not an essential economic feature of the contracts. It is merely intended to give parties in (perhaps) different time zones enough time to gather and transfer the funds traded.

6 months, the manufacturer will forego a potential foreign exchange profit. In practice, one can seldom obtain a hedge as perfect as this stylized example would indicate.

Virtually all banks that trade spot foreign exchange in the interbank market also trade forward contracts.

FORWARD VERSUS FUTURES

The institutional relationship between the spot and forward interbank market has been discussed previously. The relationships among the prices of the various types of contracts will be analyzed at length in the sections "Price Determination." Like Earle Stanley Gardner, we set the stage early but leave the solution to the mystery for the very end. The institutional and technical differences between the forward market and the futures market are the subject of this section.

It is perfectly reasonable to ask why there is a futures market at all for foreign exchange. If the wheat farmer can hedge in the futures market and the widget manufacturer in the forward market, why should there be another market? To answer this question, let us examine just what distinguishes a futures contract from a forward contract.

First, and perhaps most important, is the matter of size. The futures contracts listed in Table 2 are far smaller than the million-unit multiples in which banks operate. Most of these futures contracts are one-tenth or one-twentieth the size of a forward contract. This relatively modest size makes the futures contracts more attractive both to potential hedgers and to potential speculators who need or wish to deal in those quantities. A firm may have foreign exchange exposure which it wishes to hedge, but that exposure may be only a fraction of the size of an interbank contract. Hedging on the interbank market in that case would actually *increase* the risks facing the firm. Speculators see similar, although not identical advantages in the futures market. Anyone you know who has speculated in futures contracts will tell you that the futures market offers plenty of volatility. Futures speculators on the whole would find it excessive to multiply their positions–and thus their risks—by a factor of 10 or 20, even if their banks would let them.

Second, futures contracts are more uniform than are forward contracts. A forward contract usually is deliverable some specified number of days from the day it is written. All foreign exchange futures contracts on the IMM expire and are deliverable the third Wednesday of March, June, September, or December. Forward contracts may be written for virtually any multiple of 1 million units of some currency. All futures contracts for a particular currency are uniform in size, having the dimensions listed in Table 2. The opposite party in any forward contract is the party with whom the agreement was made. Even though futures traders buy and sell futures contracts among themselves, the opposite party in every futures contract once the transaction is made is actually the clearinghouse which is affiliated with the IMM. The reason for this last type of uniformity is investor protection: futures exchanges do not want to have their reputations damaged if some trader with a losing position fails to live up to the contractual obligation. The clearinghouse maintains its own pool of capital to ensure that the trades are settled in any event.

Third, there is the matter of how "the house" makes its money. We have already said that banks in the interbank market do so by maintaining a bid/ask spread but futures markets are auction markets—there are no bid/ask spreads. Traders on the futures exchanges use one (or both) of two methods. Trading on the floor of the futures markets is, as on the stock exchanges, limited to those who have bought memberships. Some members are in business for themselves. Called "scalpers" or simply "locals," these traders depend on trading profits for their livelihood. Other memberships are held by brokerage houses. Like stock brokers (in fact, many of them are also stock brokers), these commodity brokers charge commissions to their nonmember customers as a fee for buying or selling a contract on the customer's behalf.

Fourth, the types of contract differ in how the principals guarantee their performance. All of the banks which participate in the interbank market are presumed to have the resources to carry out the trades to which they agree. Documentation of trades consists of an exchange of telex messages between the banks to ensure that there is no discrepancy between the parties' understandings of the terms of the agreement. Futures traders, in contrast, are required to deposit with the clearinghouse (through their brokers) some minimum amount of margin as a good-faith deposit. This margin, usually is several thousand dollars per contract for speculators. Hedgers, who will have cash gains to offset any futures losses, enjoy somewhat lower margin requirements. If the value of a trader's position declines by more than a specified amount, the trader must deposit additional margin or have his position liquidated by the broker. On the positive side, traders with profitable positions can withdraw some of their surplus margin—or use it as margin for additional positions. It is important to note that futures "margin" is not the same as stock "margin." If you buy shares of a stock "on margin," you actually own the shares, but have borrowed from your broker some of the money to pay for them. Futures margin really is no more than a good-faith deposit; you do not "own" anything by having a contract to accept or deliver foreign exchange at a future date.

Fifth, futures exchanges impose limits on how much the price of a contract may change in a single trading day. There are no such limits in the interbank market. There are several reasons why futures exchanges impose such limits. The principal one is to deter manipulation of the market. The dangers of such manipulation are far more pronounced in a futures market than in the interbank market. The interbank foreign exchange market is where the actual world prices of foreign exchange are set; manipulating the value of a major currency for more than a few minutes is probably beyond the resources of any player in the foreign exchange market. The foreign exchange futures market is less liquid and, being highly leveraged, is potentially more volatile than the interbank market. In the absence of "daily limits," a group of floor traders could engineer a 1-day plunge (or jump) in the value of a currency. Since positions are "marked to market" (i.e., valued at the current price) every day, numerous traders on the wrong side of the market would receive "margin calls" from their brokers asking for additional margin by the beginning of the next trading day. Those who could not meet these margin calls would be forced to liquidate, driving the contract's price further in the direction that it was moving the previous day. The traders who arranged the initial price movement would profit from these forced liquidations. Daily limits effectively restrict the number of traders being "called out" of the market on any given day.

HEDGING VERSUS SPECULATION. Finally, the futures and interbank market serve different economic functions. There are two principal objectives of participants in the foreign exchange futures market: hedging business risk and seeking speculative profit. While the ultimate buyers and sellers in the interbank market (who are not necessarily the traders themselves) may have one or both of these objectives in mind, their major intention is usually obtaining actual foreign exchange for use in business transactions. Statistics on the ultimate disposition of the two types of contract bear out this distinction. Over 95% of all futures contracts are liquidated before the contracts mature; the longs and shorts settle with each other in U.S. dollars.[5] Almost all forward contracts for foreign exchange are carried out as drawn. This difference between futures and forward contracts is further borne out by the very design of the contracts. The uniformity of the futures contracts makes them easily tradeable. Someone who wishes to go long in December Deutsche marks, for example, does not care which December Deutsche mark contract to buy. Indeed, there is no way for the buyer to know exactly which contract the buyer will get. Thus there is (almost) always a demand for contracts that position holders wish to dispose of. This is not the case for the forward market. If someone or some firm decides that they want to go long in an existing contract for December Deutsche marks, quite a search problem lies ahead. Suppose they locate a contract for December Deutsche marks. Does the contract come due on December 1, December 31 or some intermediate date? Where is delivery to be made or taken? *What is the size of the contract?* The difficulties involved in finding answers to every one of these problems make forward contracts unwieldy vehicles for a trader who does not actually intend to deliver or receive foreign exchange as specified in the contract.

Thus far this chapter has been singularly silent on the subject which probably most interests the reader—how foreign exchange futures prices are determined. The next section will address this question.

PRICE DETERMINATION

We have already noted that actual current exchange rates under the floating-rate system are determined in the spot interbank market. This is the case because the spot interbank market is where the bulk of actual currency exchange occurs. The earlier discussion of the theory and history of foreign exchange contained hints as to the determinants of the spot rate. Let us now list those determinants explicitly:

1. The magnitude of external demand for a country's goods and services.
2. The magnitude of such transfers as gifts, pensions, and international aid to that country.

[5]Actually, both longs and shorts settle with the clearinghouse (through their brokers, in the case of nonmembers). Since the clearinghouse maintains exactly equal long and short positions, it is easiest to think of the traders as settling with each other.

3. The extent of foreign demand for investments (stocks, bonds, real estate, etc.) in that country.
4. The desire of foreign individuals, government agencies, and private organizations (such as banks) to hold that country's currency.

The supply of a country's currency available for foreign exchange is determined by the converse of each of these items: supply of exported goods and services, magnitude of domestic transfers to foreigners, domestic demand for foreign investments, and the desire of domestic individuals and agencies to hold foreign currency. As in any market for a good, the "supply curve" for a currency as foreign exchange will be upward sloping and the "demand curve" downward sloping. Foregoing economists' jargon, this statement simply means that the amount of a currency supplied will increase as that currency's foreign exchange "price" rises; and the amount demanded will decrease as the price rises.

THE ROLE OF EXPECTATIONS. Foreign exchange theoreticians have made much of the role of the expectations of market participants concerning the future trend of a country's exchange rate. Indeed, this is an important matter. Expectations about the future spot rate play a major role—some analysts would say *the* major role—in determining a country's current spot rate. That may seem a peculiar statement at first glance, since "expectation of the future spot rate" does not even appear in the above list of exchange rate determinants. The explanation is that such expectations appear implicitly as a determinant of various participants' desires to increase (or decrease) their holdings of various foreign currencies.

This effect is somewhat subtle. While it operates under both fixed and floating exchange rates, it is easier to see in the fixed-rate case.

Suppose that the U.S. dollar-Deutsche mark spot rate today under fixed rates is $0.50. And suppose further that all the traders in the market expect that this rate will hold for some time to come. Now assume that for some reason (leak, rumor, or otherwise) all the traders suddenly believe that the U.S. government will devalue the dollar against the mark by 10%—to $0.55—and will do so *tomorrow*. Suppliers of marks at $0.50 will suddenly become very scarce. In fact, they will completely disappear. This disappearance of buyers of dollars and sellers of marks is identical with the disappearance of a demand for dollars at $0.50. The spot rate will plunge to roughly $0.55. This behavior is perfectly sensible. Why should holders of marks sell them for 2.00 marks per dollar today when they know that they will only have to pay 1.82 marks per dollar tomorrow?[6] The same principle applies to a floating-rate regime. If all the traders suddenly expect that the dollar will depreciate by a certain percentage tomorrow, they will stop demanding dollars and supplying foreign exchange at the spot rate which prevailed before the expectations changed.

There are several important points to note from the numerical example above. First, the spot rate shifted dramatically without any change whatsoever in the fundamental economic situation. That is, for neither Germany nor the United States did the trade balance, inflation rate, or other "real" factor shift suddenly, although such shifts may have precipitated the devaluation. Only the expectations

[6] 1/0.55.

changed instantly. Second, you may have found such a sudden and unanimous change in market expectations to be implausible. If you did, you were right. But even if expectations do not as a rule change so abruptly, the general thrust of the analysis still holds. If market sentiment shifts over some period from a consensus that the dollar will appreciate in the months ahead to one that the dollar will depreciate, the spot market value of the dollar will in fact decline. It will merely do so more slowly and gradually than it did in our example.

Return now to the figures cited in the above example. If the market believes that the dollar will be devalued from $0.50 to $0.55 per Deutsche mark, the spot rate for the dollar will certainly decline today to precisely $0.55, correct? Almost, but not quite. Money, be it domestic money or foreign exchange, has a price over time, namely, the interest rate. Anyone who has observed the huge gyrations in the U.S. bond market in the late 1970s and early 1980s knows that the interest rate has a powerful effect on the current value of payments to be made or received in the future. Generally, there are two important propositions to remember about the effect of interest rates on current values. They are: (1) all other things equal, the higher the interest rate, the lower the current value of some nominally fixed payment at some time in the future; and (2) the further in the future a payment is to be made, the more pronounced this effect will be. In all cases a unit of currency next week or next year is worth less than the same unit of currency today.[7]

INTEREST RATES: THE CRITICAL LINK. Interest rates play a major part in determining exchange rates, and they are the critical link between the spot market and the forward market. But in considering the role that interest rates play in determining the spot and forward exchange rates of a pair of currencies, it is necessary to examine the interest rates in *both* countries. The tradeoff which a potential trader must weigh before entering the market for foreign exchange is this: Does the combination of the "price" of the foreign exchange which I am considering buying compensate me for the interest payments on my domestic currency which I am forgoing to make the purchase *after the potential for earning interest in the foreign currency is taken into account?* This question usually appears in business decisions in a somewhat more practical form.

Suppose an importer knows that he will need 1 million Deutsche marks in 6 months. Suppose further that the importer has the funds on hand now in the form of dollars. Should the importer invest the funds in the U.S. money markets for the 6 months and obtain a forward contract to purchase the marks at the end of that period, or should the importer buy the marks now on the spot market and invest them in the German money market until the Deutsche marks are needed to pay the bills? Answering this question requires careful analysis of both exchange and interest rates.

For the moment, purely for purposes of simplification, assume that both the spot exchange rate and the 6-month forward exchange rate are $0.55 per Deutsche mark. Also assume that the market interest rate is 5% in the United States and

[7]Technically, there are some cases where this is not true, as signaled by a negative interest rate. But these cases, which involved either a prolonged deflation or stringent capital controls under fixed exchange rates, are not of immediate interest to most futures and forward market traders.

10% in Germany. The importer's choice is clear: the importer should buy spot marks and invest them in the German money market. If the U.S. interest rate were 10% and the German rate 5%, the importer should make the opposite decision. Of course, such a happy situation cannot possibly persist for any length of time in a world of nimble traders who track exchange rates and interest rates closely every day. If the first situation described above were to occur, traders and investors would rush to buy spot marks and sell forward marks, thereby raising the spot rate for marks and depressing the forward rate. The result of this process would be that marks would sell at a *forward discount* to dollars. If the second situation described above were to arise, the opposite process would occur. Marks would be sold in the spot market and bought in the forward market until there existed a *forward premium* sufficient to offset the interest-rate differential.

As a general rule, currencies will sell at a forward discount to currencies of countries which have lower domestic interest rates and at a forward premium to currencies of countries with higher domestic interest rates. That is quite a mouthful, but it is really just a corollary to the adage that "There's no such thing as a free lunch." In this case, an investor contemplating the purchase of another currency will never be certain of obtaining both a better interest rate than the domestic one for investing the foreign exchange, and a higher exchange rate than the spot rate when the investor eventually switches funds back into his or her own domestic currency.

QUICK LUNCHES. The forward and futures rates which correspond to any given world set of domestic interest rates and spot exchange rates can be computed with precision. The basic formulae for the *arbitrage* operations which keep these rates in proper alignment are given in the Appendix. There are a number of varieties of arbitrage which ensure that any free lunches the exchange markets have to offer are quickly consumed. In general, an arbitrage operation is one in which a trader earns a (virtually) certain profit by simultaneously buying and selling foreign exchange in two or more forms.

The first such type of operation is interest-rate arbitrage—the type most often thought of when the word "arbitrage" appears in the context of futures or forward markets. The trader with the sharpest pencil (or quickest draw on the hand calculator) sees that the forward or futures price of some currency for some maturity is too high given the relative levels of interest rates in the two countries. The trader goes *long* in the spot interbank market buying foreign exchange and *short* in the forward or futures market, selling it. The positions must offset each other exactly. The implicit profit is made by depositing the foreign exchange in the other country's money market until it is due for delivery and earning higher interest than would have been earned on it domestically. Conversely, if a trader spots a futures or forward contract with "too low" a price, the trader will go *short* the foreign currency in the spot market and *long* the currency in the futures or forward market, depositing the funds in the *domestic* money market for the intervening period. Before you head for the futures page of *The Wall Street Journal* to look for arbitrage opportunities, be forewarned that this game is virtually the exclusive province of the professionals. First, pricing discrepancies are typically spotted within minutes of arising, putting the player without access to interbank video screens at a severe disadvantage. Second, this is not a leveraged operation. You must have the funds available to meet your obligations in full under the spot agreement. (In the second case you must start off having these funds *in the foreign currency!*) But the professionals do play this game, and it is exactly this type of operation which maintains the term structure of foreign exchange—the constant relationships between spot and futures or forward prices discussed above—more or less in line.

The second type of operation in this category is called spatial arbitrage. "Spatial" here refers to geographic space. Traders in New York, for example, may notice that the interbank bid price for Japanese yen quoted by a London bank is higher than the asking price which another bank in New York is quoting. As long as this disparity persists, the traders assure profits by simultaneously buying yen at the New York bank and selling yen at the London bank. Clearly, this sort of relationship will not exist for long in an intensely competitive market. Spatial arbitrage can be conducted between two spot rates or two forward rates. (Theoretically, it could also be conducted between two futures markets, but there are not currently two functioning futures markets for foreign exchange.) It maintains the virtual equality of bid/ask quotations across all bank trading rooms that are open at a given hour.

The third type of arbitrage is conceptually somewhat more confusing and thus requires a numerical example. It is called triangular arbitrage and serves to keep the prices of all currencies in alignment in a world (such as ours) where more than two currencies exist. It can take place among spot quotations or among forward quotations (or futures quotations), but not among a mix of contracts for spot delivery and contracts not for spot delivery—at least not without interest-rate arbitrage finding its way into the transaction. Suppose that Deutsche marks are quoted at $0.40 and French francs are quoted at $0.20. Clearly, one Deutsche mark should exchange for two French francs. But suppose that the mark appreciates to $0.50, while the dollar/franc and mark/franc exchange rates remain unchanged. A trader could earn sure profits by exchanging $1 million for 5 million French francs, then exchanging the francs for 2.5 million Deutsche marks and completing the circle by exchanging the marks for $1.25 million, thus earning $250,000 risk free. Conceptually, such an operation is not extremely difficult to understand, but it can easily be confusing at the first application. The best way to develop a feel for the workings of triangular arbitrage is to pick any three exchange relationships among currencies, arbitrarily change only *one* of the three exchange rates, and figure on paper which sets of trades will earn risk-free profits. The moral of the story (with important analogies in physics) is that it is impossible to change, for any extended period, just one exchange rate in a world of multiple currencies. Eventually, all exchange rates must be brought into line with one another. It is triangular arbitrage that accomplishes this.

CLASS B ARBITRAGE—SPRINTERS NEEDED. There is one final type of arbitrage which the advent of foreign exchange futures markets has made possible. Known as *Class B arbitrage,* this operation involves simultaneous purchases and sales to take advantage of price discrepancies between the futures market and the interbank forward market. "Class B" is actually the name of the type of membership which the IMM has established to accommodate those firms who engage exclusively in this type of trading. Such a lower-grade membership is appropriate because firms engaging exclusively in this variety of arbitrage face much less risk than does the typical IMM "Class A" member, provided that the "Class B" member's positions are covered at all times. For this reason, the IMM has elaborate control procedures to ensure that Class B members do not assume uncovered positions. (In practice, it is only possible for the IMM to monitor what positions these members hold overnight.) What is most needed for success in Class B arbitrage is a good sprinter or a good hand-signaling team. Forward trading is, as we have noted, done over telephone lines and television screens. Futures trading is done by open outcry in pits which have neither lines nor screens connecting traders with the interbank market. Thus the successful Class B arbitrageur must have some way of knowing the futures and forward quote at virtually the same instant. Several years ago Charles O. Finley, then the iconoclastic owner of the Oakland Athletics, hired an Olympic sprinter to pinch run for more slow-footed players. To date there have been no reports of Class B arbitrage firms hiring either Olympic sprinters to run between the pit and the phone lines or third-base coaches to give hand signals to or from the pit. This is not to say that neither action will be taken in the future.

CONCLUSION

This chapter has attempted to introduce the reader to the futures market for foreign exchange—essentially a hybrid market of traditional forward foreign exchange trading and traditional commodity futures trading. Those readers who are seriously considering entering the foreign exchange futures market should follow price movements of the market in the financial news section of the newspaper. If possible, chart one or more of the markets; for charting over time gives one a good "feel" for market action. This suggestion applies equally to those who are interested in hedging business risk with foreign exchange futures and to those who are interested in trying their hands at speculation.

Potential traders should also read regularly one or more of the periodicals listed in the Bibliography and, where possible, study some of the books also listed. These volumes each treat in detail one or more of the topics which this chapter could discuss only briefly.

APPENDIX

Foreign Exchange Calculations

1. *Formula to Compute Purchasing Power Parity (PPP) Exchange Rates.*

$$\text{PPP} = \frac{I_A}{I_B} \times \text{Exchange Rate}$$

where I_A = Index number of prices in country A

I_B = Index number of prices in country B

Exchange Rate = Rate of exchange in base period between countries A and B

Example. Assume prices for the same product in countries A and B are both 20 in the base period when two units of country A's currency are equal in terms of dollars to one unit of country B's currency.

If, during a subsequent period, the product price in A increases by 50%, while the comparable price in country B remains unchanged, the new PPP rate between the two countries would then be \$3 instead of \$2, as follows:

$$\frac{30}{20} \times \$2 = \$3$$

A primary drawback of the PPP approach to exchange rate analysis lies in the difficulty of selecting the most suitable price index. Among the possible choices, there is no all-inclusive index which, through the application of the formula cited above, produces the "correct" exchange rate.

Another limitation of the PPP theory and resulting formula is that the exchange rate produced by the calculation applies only to those goods and services that move between the two countries involved. Moreover, the theory does not take into account exchange rate changes brought about by capital flows and interest-rate fluctuations, except for the effect of the latter on general price levels.

Nor does the PPP theory explain exchange rate fluctuations due to underlying economic and technological changes, apart from their effects on the particular price indices selected as the units of comparison.

2. *Formula to Compute the Effect of a Change in the Balance of Payments (BP) on an Exchange Rate.* The *balance of payments* is defined as the difference between the quantity of a country's currency demanded and supplied in international foreign exchange markets.

If the quantity of, say, Deutsche marks (DM) demanded exceeds the quantity of Deutsche marks supplied, there is a balance-of-payments surplus. If the supply of Deutsche marks is greater than the demand for them, there is a BP deficit, so that

$$BP = Q^{D}_{DM} - Q^{S}_{DM}$$

Changes in $BP^{(d)}$ can be further expressed in terms of changes in the exchange rate d\$/DM, so that

$$\frac{dBP}{d\$/DM} = \frac{dQ^{D}_{DM}}{d\$/DM} - \frac{dQ^{S}_{DM}}{d\$/DM}$$

Example. Assume that the quantity of DM demanded increases by 5%, while the quantity of DM supplied remains unchanged. In that case, the DM balance-of-payments surplus increases by 5%, causing an equivalent increase in the \$/DM exchange rate, hence

$$\frac{\text{DM 3 billion}}{0.0250} = \frac{\text{DM 63 billion}}{0.50 + 0.0250} - \frac{\text{DM 55 billion}}{0.50 + 0.0250}$$

A DM 3-billion increase in a DM balance-of-payments surplus will accordingly spur an increase in \$/DM, in the example, from 0.5000 to 0.5250.

3. *Formula to Compute Implied Interest-Rate/Forward-Rate Parity.* The future value (forward rate) of a currency is equal to its present value (spot rate) plus the interest to be earned on assets denominated in that currency over a stated period. (Conversely, by discounting that interest rate, one can convert the currency's future monetary value to its present equivalent.)

To illustrate, if the annual interest rate in Germany is labeled I_{Ger}, the value of Deutsche marks 1 year in the future ($DM_{1\ yr}$) is equal to their present value (DM_{spot}) plus the accrued interest, that is,

$$DM_{1\ yr} = DM_{spot}\,(1 + I_{Ger})$$

The future value of the dollar is likewise determined by the interest rate prevailing in the United States, that is,

$$\$_{1\ yr} = \$_{spot}\,(1 + I_{U.S.})$$

Dividing the second equation by the first produces the following equation:

$$\$/DM_{1\ yr} = \$/DM_{spot}\,\frac{1 + I_{U.S.}}{1 + I_{Ger}}$$

Example. If $I_{U.S.}$ is 12%, I_{Ger} is 8%, and $\$/DM_{spot}$ is 0.5000, the 1-year forward rate would be

$$\$/DM_{1\ yr} = 0.5000\,\frac{1.12}{1.08}$$

$$\$/DM_{1\ yr} = 0.5185$$

Under the same conditions, the 3-month forward rate is

$$\$/DM_{3\ mo} = 0.5000\,\frac{(1.12/1.08)}{4}$$

$$\$/DM_{3\ mo} = 0.5046$$

Thus the present exchange rate is equal to its future (forward) counterpart when each currency is translated into its future value by the relevant interest rate.

4. *Formula to Compute Annualized Percentage Cost, or Gain, of Hedging Foreign Exchange Exposure Through the Use of Forward Contracts.*

$$\frac{\text{Forward rate} - \text{spot rate}}{\text{Spot rate}} = \frac{360}{T} \times 100 = \text{percent per annum}$$

where T is the number of days remaining to the maturity of the forward contract employed to hedge the corporation's exchange exposure.

If the exposed position calls for the sale of a forward contract priced at a discount to the spot rate, the above calculation will produce a negative figure that should be regarded as a hedging cost, while a forward premium under the same circumstances will produce a positive figure that is an incidental benefit.

A contrary position involving the purchase of a forward contract is construed as a cost when the forward rate is quoted at a premium, and as a gain when it is quoted at a discount.

Example 1. Buying 3-month forward Deutsche marks at 0.4624 to hedge a short position when the spot rate is 0.4577:

$$\frac{0.4624 - 0.4577}{0.4577} \times \frac{360}{90} \times 100 = 4.10\% \text{ per annum}$$

Example 2. Selling 6-month forward Canadian dollars at 0.8347 to hedge a long position when the spot rate is 0.8378:

$$\frac{0.8347 - 0.8378}{0.8378} \times \frac{360}{180} \times 100 = 0.74\% \text{ per annum}$$

5. *Formula to Compute Equilibrium in the Foreign Exchange and International Money Markets (Ignoring Transaction Costs).*

$$\frac{I_d - I_a}{1 + I_a} = \frac{R_f - R_s}{R_s}$$

where I is the interest rate, R is the exchange rate, d is domestic, a is abroad, f is forward, and s is spot.

Example.

$$\frac{0.12 - 0.09}{1.09} = \frac{0.5260 - 0.5120}{0.5120}$$

$$0.027 = 0.027$$

When the equilibrium condition indicated above is reached, there will continue to be arbitrage transactions carried out to the extent necessary to maintain equality of interest-rate and forward exchange differentials. If the arbitrage were to cease completely, differentials would reappear and the markets would return to a state of disequilibrium.

In keeping with Calculation 3, when the term structure of interest rates in two countries is known, it is possible to compute the forward premium or discount from present spot rates at which equilibrium would exist and further arbitrage transactions would not be profitable.

6. *Calculating Foreign Exchange Translation and Transaction Gains or Losses.* Exposure definitions: *Currency exposure* and *translation exposure* are the exposure of an entity in any currency, including that entity's own currency. *Transaction exposure* is the exposure of an entity in any other currency than its own.

Foreign exchange gain (loss) formulas:

currency gain (loss)	=	currency exposure times the exchange rate change of the exposed currency.
transaction gain (loss)	=	transaction exposure times the exchange rate change of the exposed entity's currency.
translation gain (loss)	=	translation exposure times the exchange rate change of the exposed currency less the exchange rate change of the exposed entity's currency.

Example. The German subsidiary of a multinational corporation has a pound sterling receivable equal to $100 when the Deutsche mark is revalued by 5%, and while the British pound is devalued by 10%.

$$\text{Translation gain (loss)} = \$100 \times 0.05 = \$5$$

$$\text{Transaction gain (loss)} = \$100 \times (-0.10 - 0.05) = \$(15)$$

$$\text{Currency gain (loss)} = \$100 \times -0.10 = \$(10)$$

BIBLIOGRAPHY

Below is a list of what are, in our judgment, the most useful books currently in print on foreign exchange or on futures markets. For a more extensive discussion of the topics of this chapter, see Allan M. Loosigian, *Foreign Exchange Futures,* Homewood, IL, Dow Jones Irwin, 1981.

Aliber, R. Z. *The International Market for Foreign Exchange*. New York, NY: Praeger, 1969.

———. *The International Money Game*. New York, NY: Basic Books, 1973.

Angell, J. W. *The Theory of International Prices*. New York, NY: Augustus M. Kelley, 1965.

Baldwin, R. E., and Richardson, J. D. (Eds.). *International Trade and Finance*. Boston, MA: Little, Brown, and Company, 1974.

Black, S. W. *Floating Exchange Rates and National Economic Policy*. New Haven, CN: Yale Univ. Press, 1977.

Canterberry, E. R. *Foreign Exchange, Capital Flows, and Monetary Policy*. Princeton, NJ: Princeton Studies in International Finance No. 15, 1965.

Caves, R. E., and Jones, R. W. *World Trade and Payments*. Boston, MA: Little, Brown, and Company, 1981.

Clarke, W. M., and Pulay, G. *The World's Money: How It Works*. New York, NY: Praeger, 1971.

Coninx, R. *Foreign Exchange Today*. New York, NY: Wiley, 1978.

Crump, N. *The ABC of the Foreign Exchanges*. New York, NY: Macmillan, 1963.

Dreyer, J. S., Haberler, G., and Willett, T. D. (Eds.). *Exchange Rate Flexibility*. Washington, D.C.: American Enterprise Institute, 1978.

Dufey, G., and Giddy, I. H. *The International Money Market*. Englewood Cliffs, NJ: Prentice-Hall, 1978.

Eckes, A. E. *A Search for Solvency*. Austin, TX: Univ. of Texas Press, 1975.

Einzig, P. *A Dynamic Theory of Foreign Exchange*. London, England: Macmillan, 1961.

———. *The Euro-Bond Market*. New York, NY: St. Martin's Press, 1975.

———. *The Euro-Dollar System*. New York, NY: St. Martin's Press, 1974.

———. *The Exchange Clearing System*. London, England: Macmillan, 1935.

———. *Exchange Control*. London, England: Macmillan, 1934.

———. *Finance and Politics*. London, England: Macmillan, 1932.

———. *Foreign Balances*. London, England: Macmillan, 1938.

———. *The History of Foreign Exchange*. New York, NY: St. Martin's Press, 1967.

———. *A Textbook on Foreign Exchange*. New York, NY: St. Martin's Press, 1966.

Evans, T. G. *The Currency Carousel: A New Era in Monetary Affairs*. Princeton, NJ: Dow Jones Books, 1977.

Evitt, H. E. *A Manual of Foreign Exchange*. London, England: Sir Isaac Pitman & Sons, 1965.

Fatemi, N. S. *The Dollar Crisis*. New York, NY: Fairleigh Dickinson Univ. Press, 1964.

Federal Reserve Bank of Boston. *Managed Exchange Rate Flexibility: The Recent Experience*. Conference Series No. 20, 1978.

Glahe, F. R. *An Empirical Study of the Foreign Exchange Market: Test of a Theory*. Princeton, NJ: Princeton Studies in International Finance, No. 20, 1967.

Haberler, G. *Money in the International Economy*. Cambridge, MA: Harvard Univ. Press, 1965.

Halm, G. N. *A Guide to International Monetary Reform*. Lexington, MA: Lexington Books, 1975.

Hayek, F. A. *Denationalisation of Money*. London, England: Institute of Economic Affairs, 1978.

Heller, H. R. *International Monetary Economics*. Englewood Cliffs, NJ: Prentice-Hall, 1974.

Holbik, K. (Ed.). *Monetary Policy in Twelve Industrial Countries*. Boston, MA: Federal Reserve Bank of Boston, 1973.

Holgate, H. C. F. *Exchange Arithmetic*. London, England: Sir Isaac Pitman & Sons, 1961.

Isard, P. *Exchange Rate Determination: A Survey of Popular Views and Recent Markets*. Princeton, NJ: Princeton Univ. Press, 1978.

Jastram, R. *The Golden Constant*. New York, NY: Wiley, 1977.

Katz, S. I. (Ed.). *U.S.—European Monetary Relations*. Washington, D.C.: American Enterprise Institute, 1979.

Krause, L. B. *Recent International Monetary Crises: Causes and Cures and Fixed and Gliding Exchange Rates*. Washington, D.C.: The Brookings Institution, 1971.

Kubarych, Roger. *Foreign Exchange Markets in the United States*. New York: Federal Reserve Bank of New York, 1978.

Mayer, M. *The Fate of the Dollar*. New York, NY: New American Library, 1981.

Merns, S. *Decision-Making on Exchange Rates*. Washington, D.C.: The Brookings Institution, 1970.

Murphy, J. C. *The International Monetary System: Beyond the First Stage of Reform*. Washington, D.C.: American Enterprise Institute, 1979.

Ohlin, B. *Interregional and International Trade*. Cambridge, MA: Harvard Univ. Press, 1967.

Prindl, A. *Foreign Exchange Risk*. New York, NY: Wiley, 1976.

Quinn, B. Scott. *The New Euromarkets*. New York, NY: Wiley, 1975.

Riehl, H. *Foreign Exchange Markets: A Guide to Foreign Currency Operations*. New York, NY: McGraw-Hill, 1979.

Rolfe, S. E., and Burtle, J. *The Great Wheel: The World's Monetary System, A Reinterpretation*. New York, NY: New York Times Book Company, 1973.

Scammell, W. M. *International Monetary Policy*. New York, NY: St. Martin's Press, 1961.

Solomon, R. *The International Monetary System, 1945–1976: An Insider's View*. New York, NY: Harper & Row, 1977.

Stein, J. L. *The Nature and Efficiency of the Foreign Exchange Market*. Princeton, NJ: Princeton Univ. Press, 1962.

Teweles, R. J., Harlow, C. V., and Stone, H. L. *The Commodity Futures Game*. New York, NY: McGraw-Hill, 1977.

Wasserman, M. J., Prindl, A., and Townsend, C. C., Jr. *International Money Management*. New York, NY: American Management Association, 1972.

Yeager, L. B. *The International Monetary Mechanism*. New York, NY: Holt, Rinehart, & Winston, 1968.

———. *International Monetary Relations: Theory, History, and Policy*. New York, NY: Harper & Row, 1966.

SOURCES OF INFORMATION—PERIODICALS

Newspapers

Financial Times (London). 75 Rockefeller Plaza, New York, NY 10020. Daily, Monday–Saturday. For anyone with an interest in world economic affairs, this is the best daily in the English language—possibly in any language. Unfortunately, the *FT* does not carry price quotations for American futures markets.

Journal of Commerce. 99 Wall Street, New York, NY 10005. (Daily, Monday–Friday) Originally a shipping journal, this publication focuses on trade.

The Wall Street Journal. 200 Burnett Road, Chicopee, MA 01021. Daily, Monday–Friday. Comprehensive quotations on all currency futures, brief news and market summaries, and in-depth analyses of major economic and market news.

Weekly Publications

International Money Markets and Foreign Exchange Rates. Harris Trust and Savings Bank, 111 West Monroe Street, Chicago, IL 60690.

International News Letter. Federal Reserve Bank of Chicago, Chicago, IL.

The Economist (British). P.O. Box 2700, Woburn, MA 01888.

The Money Manager. The Bond Buyer, One State Street Plaza, New York, NY 10004.

Monthly Publications

Monetary Trends. Federal Reserve Bank of St. Louis, St. Louis, MO.

National Economic Trends. Federal Reserve Bank of St. Louis, St. Louis, MO.

World Financial Markets. Morgan Guaranty Trust Company, 23 Wall Street, New York, NY 10004.

Bimonthly Publications

Euromoney. Euromoney Publications, PLC, 14 Finsbury Circus, London, EC2, England.

International Currency Review. 11 Regency Place, London, SW1 2EA, England.

CHAPTER 48

INTEREST-RATE FUTURES

CONTENTS

OVERVIEW 3

Interest rates 4

INTEREST-RATE FUTURES MARKET 8

US Treasury bills 9

Domestic Certificates of Deposit 12

Eurodollars 17

Government National Mortgage Association (GNMA) 19

U.S. Treasury notes and Treasury bonds 23

CHAPTER **48**

INTEREST-RATE FUTURES

Steven G. Saltzgaber
Paul T. Wilkinson

The development of interest-rate futures contracts can be traced to the introduction in the 1960s of futures contracts based upon nonstorable commodities such as pork bellies, plywood, and iced broilers. The successful introduction of trading in foreign currency contracts in 1971 by the International Monetary Market (IMM) division of the Chicago Mercantile Exchange (CME) further demonstrated that the concepts of futures markets could be translated into financial instruments. The currency contracts also introduced futures to the financial community, thereby playing an important educational role in the financial marketplace.

OVERVIEW

Interest-rate futures began trading in October 1975, when the Chicago Board of Trade (CBT) introduced an intermediate-term futures contract based upon GNMA mortgage-backed securities, the GNMA–CDR contract. In January 1976 the IMM followed with the introduction of a short-term futures contract based upon 3-month U.S. Treasury bills. Long-term U.S. Treasury-bond futures were then introduced by the CBT in August 1977. To date, these contracts have been the three most successful interest-rate futures contracts. Additional interest-rate futures contracts have been offered based upon 30-day and 90-day commercial paper, 3-month domestic Certificates of Deposit and Eurodollars, 1-year Treasury bills, and 2-year, 4-year, 4- to 6-year, and 6½- to 10-year Treasury notes.

The volume of interest-rate futures contracts traded in the United States has more than doubled each year on average since the introduction of the GNMA–CDR contract (see Table 1). The GNMA–CDR contract traded 20,000 contracts during 1975. By 1981 total volume of all interest-rate futures contracts had grown to 22.865 million contracts. This total represents 23.2% of all futures contracts traded in the United States.

Of the total volume of interest-rate futures contracts traded in 1981, the CBT Treasury-bond contract comprised 61%, while the IMM Treasury bill and CBT GNMA–CDR contracts represented 25% and 10% of such volume, respectively. The success of the concept of interest-rate futures is demonstrated by the fact that the CBT Treasury-bond contract is currently the most actively traded futures contract in the world.

TABLE 1. Historical Interest-Rate Futures Volume by Year: 1975–1981 (All Values in 1000's of Contracts)

	1975	1976	1977	1978	1979	1980	1981
All futures contracts	32,200	36,876	42,847	58,462	75,966	92,096	98,522
Interest-rate futures:							
Annual volume	20	239	780	2,325	5,607	12,470	22,865
Market share	0.05%	0.74%	1.8%	4.0%	7.4%	13.5%	23.7%

This chapter will examine the most successful interest-rate futures contracts and their underlying cash markets. The salient features of the contracts will be outlined and differences between the contracts of the different exchanges will be highlighted. The interest-rate futures contracts to be discussed include:

U.S. Treasury bills
Domestic Certificates of Deposit
Eurodollar Deposits
Government National Mortgage Association (GNMA) Futures
6½- to 10-year U.S. Treasury notes
U.S. Treasury bonds

Preceding the discussion of these cash and futures markets will be an overview of interest rates in general, and the factors which influence rates on a day-to-day basis.

INTEREST RATES. This section briefly examines the concepts of yield curves and credit risk, and the principal determinants of the level of interest rates.

Interest rates are best viewed as the price of credit in the financial markets. No single interest rate, however, can encompass the differences which exist across market segments. Interest rates are generally segmented by the term to maturity, and also according to the credit risk of the borrower.

Yield Curve. The *yield curve* is a graphical device which plots interest rates versus time to maturity. Credit risk is held constant across a yield curve, thus a different curve exists for each market segment. For example, the most common yield curve reflects yields of Treasury securities. The shape of the yield curve not only provides investors with the current relationship between yields and time to maturity, but also includes the market's expectations of future interest rates.

Historically the yield curve has had a positive slope, that is, interest rates rise with the term to maturity. This is to compensate investors for the greater uncertainty and illiquidity of long-term lending. Recently, however, the yield curve has occasionally inverted, where short-term rates exceed long-term rates. A negative slope suggests market expectations of declining interest rates in the future.

Figures 1 and 2 depict actual positive and negative yield curves, using yields of Treasury securities.

Credit Risk. For a given time to maturity, securities can be segmented on the basis of credit risk. Credit risk is the market's perception of the likelihood that a borrower might default on his or her obligation for the timely payment of principal and interest.

Securities issued by the U.S. Treasury have no default risk, as they possess the unconditional guarantee of the federal government. Other borrowers, such as state and local governments and corporations, are not immune from default risk. A credit-risk premium is added to yields on Treasury securities to compensate investors for this additional risk. This risk premium will vary across financial instruments, borrowers, and time to maturity, and with the level and volatility of yields. Investors must examine the credit worthiness of each specific issue to ensure that the return is adequate compensation for the level of risk.

Interest-Rate Determinants. The ultimate determinant of interest rates is the supply and demand for funds within the various segments of the credit markets. Investors, those market participants with excessive cash reserves, are the lenders and represent the supply of funds in the economy. Borrowers represent the demand for funds and credit. The relative supply and demand for loanable funds will determine their price, that is, the interest rate.

A single "interest rate" does not exist, however. Each market segment has unique supply-and-demand factors. Segmentation occurs on the basis of term to maturity and credit risk, in addition to characteristics such as tax status and convertibility features. Although interrelated, different interest rates prevail across maturities in the Treasury, municipal, and corporate debt markets, each of which responds differently, as market expectations and supply-and-demand relationships change.

A number of factors exist which affect the overall supply and demand of loanable funds. The most important of these, Federal Reserve activity and general economic conditions, are discussed below.

Federal Reserve Activity. The Federal Reserve System, or "Fed," is charged with the task of economic stabilization via monetary policy. Through its actions, the Fed can have a dramatic impact on interest rates.

This impact is achieved by the manipulation of bank reserves through open market operations, and adjustments to the Fed discount rate and bank reserve requirements. Open market operations, the most important tool available to the Fed, entail the sale or purchase of government securities. Open market purchases of securities result in an increase in the supply of loanable funds as the securities are converted into cash. This increase in the supply of funds, combined with a decrease in the outstanding supply of securities, will result in a general reduction in interest rates.

The Fed can also increase reserves without actually purchasing securities. Reserves can be expanded by conducting repurchase agreements, or "repos." A

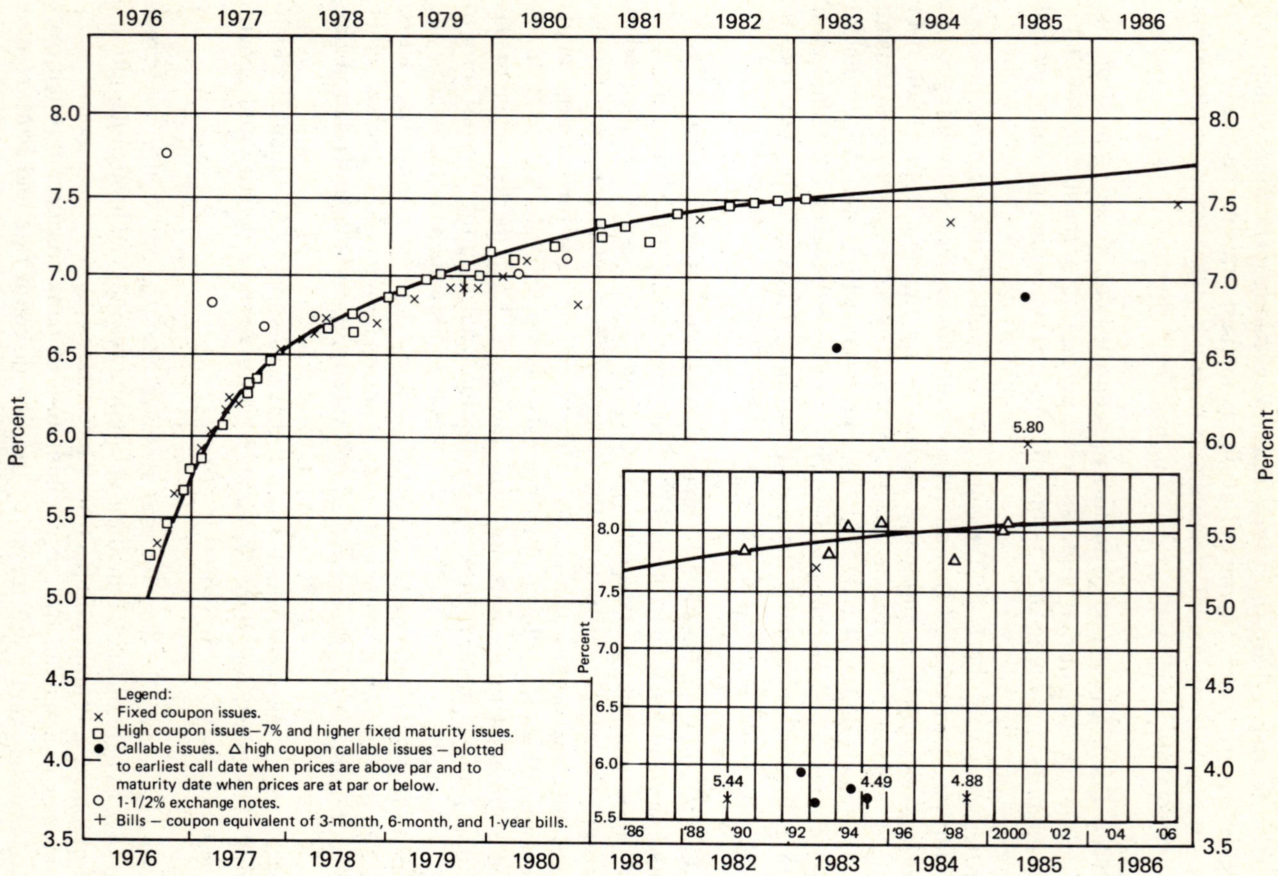

Note: The curve is fitted by eye. Market yields on coupon issues due in less than 3 months are excluded.

FIGURE 1. Yields of Treasury securities—positive yield curve, April 30, 1976. (Based on closing bid quotations.)

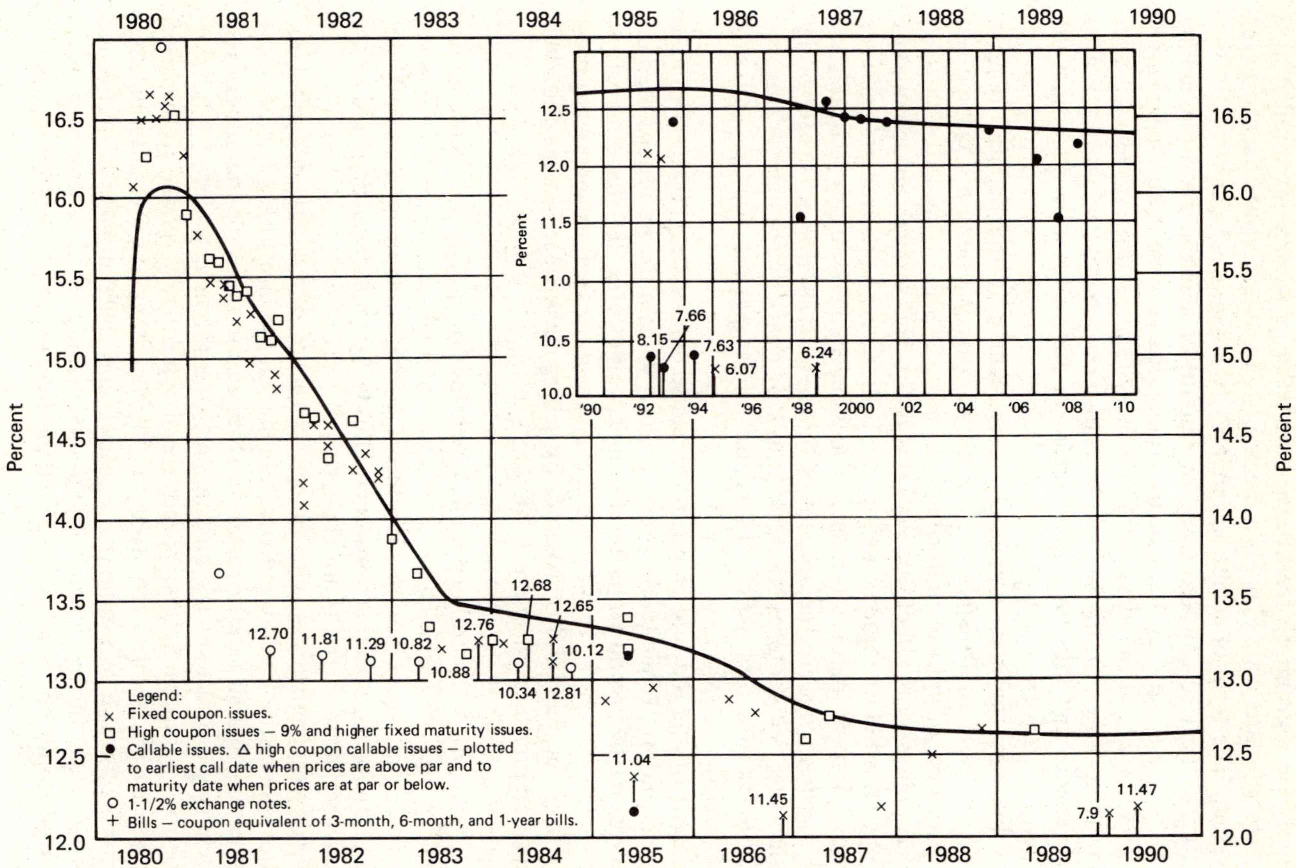

Note: The curve is fitted by eye and based only on line most activity traded issues. Market yields on coupon issues due in less than 3 months the excluded.

FIGURE 2. Yields of Treasury securities—negative yield curve, March 31, 1980. (Based on closing bid quotations.) (*Source:* Treasury Bulletin, U.S. Treasury Department, Office of the Secretary, Washington, D.C.)

repo is simply the purchase of a security with the agreement to resell it at a specified price at a later date. This is a mechanism to temporarily inject reserves into the system. The term of a repo is generally overnight to 7 days.

Alternatively, the Fed can decrease the amount of loanable funds by selling securities from the system account or by conducting reverse repurchase agreements. *Reverse repos*, or matched sales, are the sale of securities with an agreement to repurchase them in the future. As with repos, matched sales are only a temporary measure and thus have less impact on the financial markets than the outright sale of securities.

Treasury bills are the most commonly used security in the Federal Reserve open market operations. Roughly 85% of all such transactions are carried out using Treasury bills of various maturities.

Other Fed policy tools affect interest rates indirectly. Though less commonly used than open market operations, changes in bank reserve requirements and the discount rate can have important consequences on the level of interest rates.

Reserve requirements are the amount of funds, expressed as a percent of deposits, which the Fed requires member banks to hold. Increasing the reserve requirement leads to a contraction in loanable funds, and thus upward pressure on interest rates.

The *discount rate* is the rate charged to member banks who borrow from the Fed discount window. While banks prefer to borrow from the Fed funds market, some reserves are borrowed from the discount window. As the discount rate is increased, banks will tend to reduce borrowings from the Fed, by increasing their borrowings from the Fed funds market, or by selling securities. Either action will result in upward pressure on interest rates.

Economic Conditions. General economic conditions obviously affect the supply and demand for credit and therefore the level of interest rates. Variables such as the inflation rate, the Gross National Product (GNP), the unemployment rate, and the number of housing starts, are watched closely by market participants to ascertain the direction of interest-rate changes.

Interest rates vary positively with changes in the level of anticipated inflation. Interest rates rise as the level of anticipated inflation increases because investors require a greater nominal rate of return to compensate them for the anticipated loss of purchasing power over the holding period of the investment.

Indicators of a strengthening economy are also positively related to the level of interest rates. As economic activity increases, the demand for credit increases to finance an expansion of productive capacity and the purchase of consumer goods. This increase in the demand for credit not only increases interest rates directly, but also indirectly through a resulting increase in anticipated inflation.

INTEREST-RATE FUTURES MARKETS

The myriad of financial instruments available in today's credit markets, each part of a different market segment, make it necessary to have more than one interest-rate futures contract. Futures contracts have been introduced to cover many of the most important market segments. Actively traded futures in the short-term segment of the yield curve include the IMM's 3-month Treasury bill, domestic

Certificate of Deposit, and Eurodollar contracts. Intermediate-term futures contracts include the Chicago Board of Trade's 6½- to 10-year Treasury note and GNMA–CDR contracts. Finally, the long-term segment is limited to the CBT Treasury bond contract. These six contracts, and their respective cash markets, will each be discussed in detail in this section.

U.S. TREASURY BILLS

Cash Market. Treasury bills are short-term debt obligations of the U.S. Treasury. The Treasury issues debt for the purpose of refinancing existing obligations, funding the Federal debt, and the financing of off-budget items. Treasury debt may be separated into marketable and nonmarketable securities. Of the two, marketable debt is the larger, comprising about two-thirds of all government debt. Treasury bills comprise about one-third of the total marketable debt.

Treasury bills are issued through the Federal Reserve System in maturities of 13, 26, and 52 weeks. The Fed acts as agent for the Treasury in the sale of Treasury bills. Treasury bills are sold in the cash market on a discount rate basis. Discount securities do not pay coupons; instead, the return to the investor takes the form of an increase in the value of the security from its purchase price to its face value. The rate of return on a Treasury bill, the discount rate, equals the amount of the discount expressed as a percentage of face value, annualized on the basis of a 360-day year.

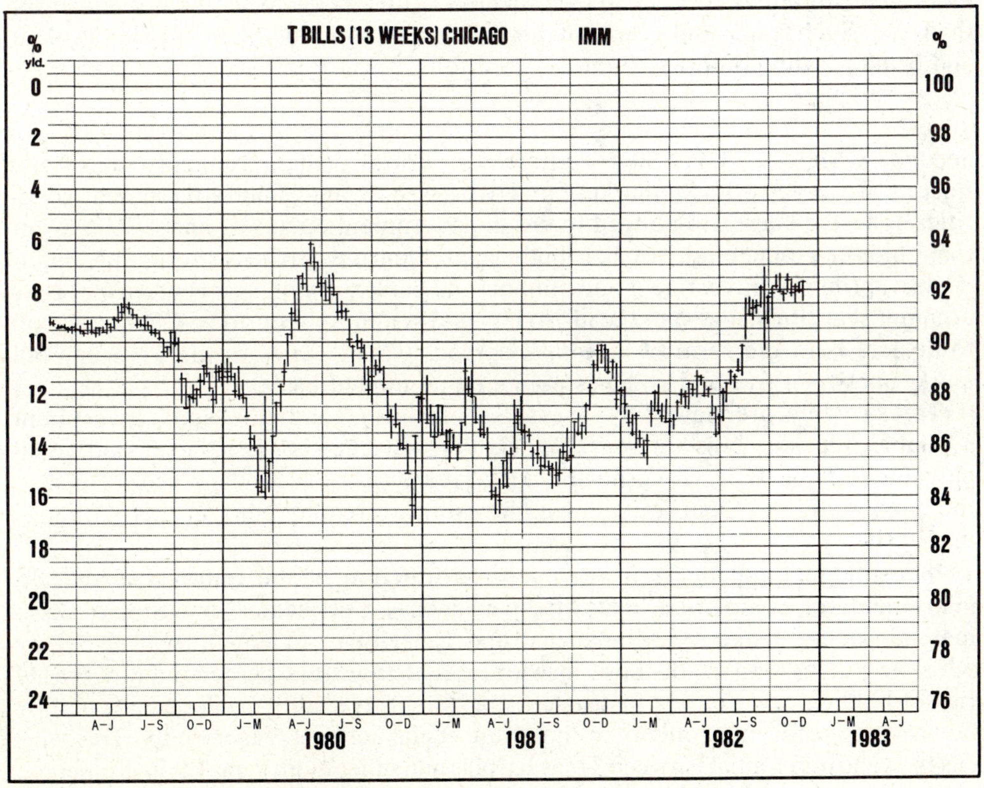

FIGURE 3. U.S. Treasury bills—price chart.

Primary Market. Treasury bills are issued by the Federal Reserve through regularly scheduled auctions. Commercial banks, government securities dealers, and the Federal Reserve itself are the most active buyers of Treasury bills in the primary market. The remaining bids are divided among states and local governments, foreign central banks, corporations, and individuals.

Both competitive and noncompetitive bids can be submitted in a Treasury auction. Large investors and money market dealers typically make the competitive bids, while small, particularly individual, investors enter noncompetitive bids. The Treasury accepts all noncompetitive bids up to $1 million per bid at a rate equal to the average of the accepted competitive bids.

The auctions for 13- and 26-week Treasury bills are conducted on a weekly basis. The auction is announced on a Tuesday, at which time the dollar amount to be issued per maturity is provided. The auction is conducted on the following Monday, and the results of the auction are announced that evening. The Treasury bills are issued to investors on the Thursday following the auction.

The 52-week Treasury bill auction takes place every 4 weeks. The auction is announced on the fourth Thursday of each month, with the auction occurring on the following Wednesday. Issuance of the Treasury bills occurs the following Tuesday.

Payment for Treasury bills is made in either maturing Treasury bills or in federal funds. Ownership is transferred by way of book entry, through the Federal Reserve wire system. Book-entry transfer protects investors from potential loss, and substantially reduces the cost to the Treasury of issuing the Treasury bills. Book entry also simplifies the transfer of such securities prior to the final maturity of the issue. Such transactions are conducted via a network of money market dealers and brokers who comprise the nucleus of the Treasury bill secondary market.

Secondary Market. Over 30 government securities dealers are approved by the Federal Reserve to make markets in Treasury bills and other government securities. These dealers are obliged to bid in government auctions, and, in the event their bids are accepted, to distribute such securities to investors. The major dealers, primarily investment and commercial banks, maintain inventories of government securities, and stand ready to buy and sell these securities. Compensation to dealers is in the form of a bid/ask spread, which varies in the Treasury bill market between five and 10 basis points on an annual basis.

Treasury bills are viewed by investors as the safest and most liquid investment available. Treasury bills are free from default risk as they possess the unconditional guarantee of the U.S. Government. The Treasury bill secondary market is also the most liquid debt market, allowing investors to readily convert their holdings into cash.

Investor demand for Treasury bills is a function of the return available on instruments of comparable maturity, particularly Certificates of Deposit, Commercial paper, bankers' acceptances, and Eurodollars. Demand will also vary with the perceived risk of these instruments. If investors perceive an increased risk of holding private-debt instruments, a "flight to quality" will occur whereby investors transfer investments from private securities to Treasury bills. This widens the yield differential between Treasury bills and other money market instruments.

Treasury Bill Futures Market. The International Monetary Market introduced futures trading in 90-day Treasury bills in January 1976. In the 6 years since its introduction, this contract has grown to be the third most active futures contract. Average monthly volume for the IMM contract in the first year of trading was just over 9,000 contracts. This has grown to almost 550,000 for the first half of 1982.

Four additional contracts calling for delivery of Treasury bills have been introduced by various exchanges since 1976. The IMM tried unsuccessfully to open futures trading in 1-year Treasury bills. This contract, introduced in September 1978, was similar to the original contract with the exception of the maturity and face value. The face value was reduced to $250,000 to maintain a constant price basis with the shorter-term Treasury bill contract.

The New York Futures Exchange introduced trading in 13-week Treasury bill futures in August 1980. This contract expanded the deliverable grade to include the delivery of an original 1-year Treasury bill with 13 weeks' remaining maturity.

The Commodity Exchange began trading a 90-day contract in October 1979. The specifications of this contract were virtually identical to those of the IMM contract.

The most recent Treasury bills futures contract was introduced by the MidAmerica Commodity Exchange. This contract began trading in April 1982 and calls for cash settlement rather than physical delivery. The final settlement price used by the exchange is the final settlement price of the IMM's 90-day Treasury bill futures contract. The advantage of this contract is a smaller face value, $500,000, which appeals to individual speculators. The smaller size reduces the dollar price risk, allowing the exchange to require lower margins.

The IMM's 1-year Treasury bill contract, and the COMEX and NYFE 90-day Treasury bill contracts, have failed to gain any market share. The original contract represents virtually 100% of the Treasury bill futures market. For this reason, the following description of the Treasury bill futures market will be limited to the IMM's 90-day Treasury bill futures contract.

IMM 90-Day Treasury Bill Futures Contract. Treasury bills in the cash market are quoted on the basis of an annualized discount rate. The IMM futures contract is priced on a similar basis, although the discount rate is subtracted from 100 to provide a futures "price." This system keeps intact the conventions of futures trading, that is, as prices rise, the long gains at the expense of the seller, and vice versa. In the fixed income markets, as interest rates rise, prices fall. Subtracting the discount rate from 100 provides this inverse relationship.

The minimum fluctuation of this index of one basis point, 1/100 of 1%, is consistent with cash market trading. The dollar value of this minimum movement is $25. The computation of this value is as follows:

$$\text{basis point value} = 0.0001 \times \$1 \text{ million} \times 90/360 = \$25$$

The IMM contract allows for delivery of Treasury bills which mature 90 days from the first delivery day. The current contract standards, which apply through the March 1983 contract, allow delivery on three successive business days, beginning with the settlement date of the 13-week auction in the third week of the delivery month. In addition to the newly issued 13-week Treasury bill, the 26-week Treasury bill issued 3 months earlier is also deliverable.

The IMM has changed their delivery specifications to include delivery of an original 1-year Treasury bill with 13 weeks to maturity. This requires the exchange to modify the delivery days, because the 1-year Treasury bill is auctioned once every 4 weeks. Therefore the first delivery day for the contract months after March 1983 will be the first day of the delivery month in which both a 13-week Treasury bill is issued, and a 1-year Treasury bill has 13 weeks' remaining maturity. This will generally be a Thursday, as is the current case, although the week of delivery will vary across delivery months.

The exchange revised the contract standards in this way to expand the deliverable supply of Treasury bills. This was in part due to the suggestion of federal regulators, who felt excessive pressure is placed on deliverable issues at delivery, particularly the deliverable 13-week auction.

The actual delivery process of the futures market further mirrors cash market practices. The Federal Reserve wire system is used to transfer both the Treasury bills themselves, as well as the cash payment. Delivery can be made to any Chicago bank approved by the exchange, as specified by the buyer. The invoice price is computed using the settlement price on the last day of trading as follows:

$$\text{invoice price} = \$1 \text{ million} - \frac{(\text{days} \times \text{settlement yield} \times \$1 \text{ million})}{360}$$

where

days = the remaining maturity of the delivery instrument

and

settlement yield = 100 minus settlement price, expressed as a decimal

A summary of salient features of the IMM 90-day Treasury bill contract is presented in Table 2.

DOMESTIC CERTIFICATES OF DEPOSIT

Cash Market. Domestic Certificates of Deposit (CDs) are negotiable receipts for deposits at U.S. banks. They are bearer instruments which at maturity entitle the holder to the par value of the CD plus accrued interest. Interest on a CD is computed on a 360-day basis. The rate of interest is fixed in most cases although some variable-rate issues have recently been offered.

Domestic CDs are offered with maturities ranging from 1 to 18 months. The most common maturity is 3 months. CDs are differentiated on the basis of when within a month they mature. Early-month CDs mature on or before the 15th day of a month, while late-month CDs mature on or after the 16th day of the month.

History. Domestic CDs were first issued by banks in the early 1960s as a new means of attracting funds. The need for new methods had arisen as corporations

TABLE 2. Salient Features of the IMM 90-Day U.S. Treasury Bill Futures Contract

Trading unit	13-week U.S. Treasury bills having a face value at maturity of \$1 million
Price basis	Prices are quoted as an index, equal to 100 minus the annualized discount rate expressed as a percent (e.g., 87.50 for a discount rate of 12.50%).
Minimum price fluctuation	One basis point, which is 1/100 of 1%. Dollar value, based on \$1 million face value, 90-day maturity, and a 360-day year, equals \$25 per contract.
Price limit	60 basis points above or below the settlement price of the previous trading day. No limit exists on the last day of trading.
Deliverable grade	U.S. Treasury bills maturing 90, 91, or 92 days from delivery day, at the option of the seller. All Treasury bills in a delivery unit must have the same maturity date.
Delivery period	Delivery can occur on any of three consecutive business days, beginning with the third business day following the 3- and 6-month Treasury bill auction of the third week of the delivery month.
Last day of trading	Trading in the current month ceases on the business day preceding the first delivery day.
Delivery method	Delivery is made by book-entry wire transfer to a Chicago bank specified by the buyer which is a member of the Federal Reserve System and registered with the exchange. Payment is made to the seller in federal funds, to a bank designated to the short.
Invoice price	The amount paid to the seller is computed as follows: $\$1{,}000{,}000 - \frac{(\text{days} \times \text{settlement yield} \times \$1{,}000{,}000)}{360}$ where days = remaining maturity of deliverable Treasury bills and settlement yield = 100 − settlement price on the last day of trading expressed as a decimal
Delivery months	Current delivery months are listed in March, June, September, and December and January, April, July, and October cycles.
Trading hours	8:00 a.m.–2.00 p.m. Chicago time.
Ticker symbol	TB

had begun to invest their excess cash in short-term investments rather than maintaining large cash balances with their banks.

Early growth of the domestic CD market was hampered from time to time by Regulation Q. Disintermediation would occur in the CD market whenever short-term interest rates exceeded the interest-rate ceilings set forth in Regulation Q. This would result in a contraction of bank lending as funds for loans would not otherwise be readily available.

These interest-rate ceilings were gradually relaxed as market interest rates steadily rose throughout the 1960s and early 1970s. Finally, in May 1973, all interest-rate ceilings on large CDs (greater than $100,000) were removed. Since that time, the domestic CD market has grown steadily to its present size of $130 billion as of April 1982. Today, CDs compete directly with Treasury bills and commercial paper for short-term loanable funds.

Primary Market. Activity in the primary market for domestic CDs is a function of the demand for bank borrowing. To make the loans to meet this demand, banks must be able to access capital quickly. Traditionally, this was accomplished by managing the asset side of a bank's balance sheet. Banks would either maintain extra cash on hand, or sell securities to meet their capital needs. The problem with asset management is its cost, either in terms of the opportunity cost of maintaining the larger-than-otherwise cash balances, or the cost of not being able to time the disposition of the bank's securities.

Recently, banks have begun practicing liability management. Liability management is the issuance of short-term liabilities as a means of raising needed capital to meet the demand for bank loans. These liabilities are comprised essentially of domestic CDs and Eurodollars. Liability management has grown increasingly popular because of its flexibility and low cost relative to asset management. Its practice is effectively restricted, however, to larger banks as they alone can issue CDs in sizes required by the primary market (greater than $1 million).

As loan demand increases, banks issue more CDs to accommodate this demand. Banks also issue more CDs if interest rates are expected to increase in the future in order to take advantage of the lower cost of obtaining funds.

Secondary Market. Secondary market activity for domestic CDs is largely a function of their yield and level of perceived risk relative to other financial instruments of comparable maturity—Treasury bills, commercial paper, and Eurodollars. Liquidity in the secondary market is aided by 25 dealer firms, who stand ready to quote bids and offers on CDs.

The risk of a domestic CD is largely a function of the credit worthiness of the bank which issued it. The credit worthiness of the nation's banks ranges from that of the highly diversified, truly national banks to small, single industry regional banks. Because of this, secondary market dealers often group different banks into tiers on the basis of their perceived credit worthiness. The top of these tiers is comprised of the 10 largest U.S. banks—Bank of America, Bankers Trust, Chase Manhattan, Chemical Bank, Citibank, Continental Illinois, First Chicago, Manufacturers Hanover, Morgan Guaranty and Security Pacific. Because of their large size, diversification, and perceived financial strength, the top 10 banks are able to offer their CDs at lower interest rates than other banks.

The top tier of bank-offered CDs is especially important because of the current secondary market practice of trading them "on the run," or on a "no-name" basis. That is, an investor is given a price quote without knowing which bank CD is being offered. Only after the offer is accepted does the investor find out which bank CD was purchased.

Domestic CD Futures Market. Trading in 3-month domestic Certificates of Deposit futures began in July 1981. The introduction of domestic CD futures was unique in that three futures exchanges—the NYFE, the CBT, and the IMM—began trading a domestic CD futures contract within a month of each other. Within a year, the IMM had won the competition for market share in the domestic CD futures market. As of June 30, 1982, the IMM was trading approximately 140,000 CD contracts per month. Because of the dominance of the IMM domestic CD futures contract, this section will only discuss the terms of that contract.

IMM 3-Month Domestic CD Futures Contract. As with the Treasury bill futures contract, the domestic CD futures contract is quoted as an index, where the value of the index equals 100 minus the CD yield. The CD yield differs from the yield on a Treasury bill as it is an add-on yield rather than a discount yield. The add-on yield can best be viewed as a coupon rate on a 360-day basis assuming no reinvestment of the accrued interest.

The minimum fluctuation of the IMM add-on index is one basis point. The dollar value of the one basis point move equals \$25, the same as a one basis point move in the Treasury bill contract.

The IMM domestic CD futures contract calls for the delivery of late month CDs, that is, domestic CDs maturing after the 15th calendar day of the third month, following the delivery month. Certificates of Deposit delivered into the contract may have between $2\frac{1}{2}$ and $3\frac{1}{2}$ months remaining maturity, although the delivery window for any given day is at most 15 days.

Certificates of Deposit deliverable into the IMM contract are restricted to those banks which are on a list approved by the exchange. This list is composed of those bank CDs which are perceived by the market to be of the lowest credit risk and which trade at identical yields in the secondary market. The list is updated on the second business day prior to the 15th calendar day of each month, on the basis of a survey of active cash market dealers of domestic Certificates of Deposit.

Delivery under the IMM domestic CD contract is accomplished via the transfer of the CD to a New York City bank specified by the long, which is both a member of the Federal Reserve System and registered with the exchange. Payment is made to the seller in Fed funds, where

$$\text{invoice price} = \frac{\text{maturity value}}{1 + (\text{settlement yield} \times \text{days}/360)}$$

where

maturity value = principal plus interest due at maturity
settlement yield = 100 minus the settlement price, in decimals
days = number of days remaining maturity

Salient features of the IMM 90-day domestic CD futures contract are presented in Table 3.

TABLE 3. Salient Features of the IMM 3-Month Domestic Certificate of Deposit Futures Contract

Trading unit	Domestic Certificates of Deposit having a face value at maturity of $1 million
Price basis	Prices are quoted as an index, equal to 100 minus the annualized discount rate expressed as a percent (e.g., 85.50 for a discount rate of 14.50%).
Minimum price fluctuation	One basis point which is 1/100 of 1%. Dollar value, based on $1 million face value, 90-day maturity, and a 360-day year, equals $25 per contract.
Price limit	80 basis points above or below the settlement price of the previous trading day. No limit exists on the last day of trading.
Deliverable grade	Domestic CDs issued by approved banks having a maturity value, principal plus accrued interest, of not less than $1 million and not more than $1.2 million. Also, deliverable CDs must not have an interest payment between delivery day and the date of maturity, and cannot have more than 185 days' accrued interest as maturity. CDs must mature on a business day between the 16th and the last calendar day of the third month following delivery.
Delivery period	Any business day in the period beginning with the 15th calendar day of the contract month, and ending on the last business day
Last day of trading	Business day prior to the last permissible delivery date
Delivery method	Delivery is made to a New York City bank which is registered with the exchange and a member of the Federal Reserve System, as specified by the long. Payment is made to the seller in federal funds.
Invoice price	The amount paid to the seller is computed as follows: $$\text{invoice price} = \frac{\text{maturity}}{1 + (\text{settlement yield} \times \text{days}/360)}$$ where maturity value = principal plus interest due at maturity; settlement yield = 100 minus settlement price, in decimal; days = remaining maturity
Delivery months	Current delivery months are listed in a March, June, September, and December cycle.
Trading hours	7:30 a.m.–2:00 p.m. central time
Ticker symbol	DC

EURODOLLARS

Cash Market. The simplest definition of Eurodollar time deposits, or Eurodollars, is *international dollars*. Eurodollars are U.S. dollar-denominated deposits in banks located outside of the United States. This would include deposits in foreign branches of U.S. banks. All principal and interest payments are made in dollars, regardless of the country in which the transaction takes place.

The currencies of other major countries can also be deposited outside of the country of origin creating other types of "Eurocurrency" deposits. Other important Eurocurrency deposits are denominated in Canadian dollars, Japanese yen, German marks, British pounds, and Swiss and French francs. Eurodollars are the largest and most important segment of the Eurocurrency market, representing three-fourths of the entire market.

Time deposits are the most common form of deposit in the Eurodollar market. Time deposits are made for a fixed period of time, and at a specified rate of interest. The deposit cannot be withdrawn prior to maturity. Consequently, there is no secondary market in Eurodollars.

Eurodollar deposits are available in a wide range of maturities, extending from overnight deposits to deposits with a maximum maturity of 5 years. Banks typically offer deposits in maturities of overnight, 7 days, 1–6 months (in monthly increments), and 1–5 years (in yearly increments).

The capital on which the Eurodollar market is based, the net liabilities, is provided by a broad spectrum of depositors. This includes domestic, foreign, and multinational corporations; central banks and other governmental entities; wealthy individuals; and international organizations such as the Bank of International Settlements (BIS). In addition, banking institutions (foreign and domestic) utilize the market as a depository of idle funds, or excess reserves in the case of U.S. banks. In this capacity, U.S. banks are using the Eurodollar market in conjunction with the federal funds market.

Trading activity in the Eurodollar market extends far beyond the original deposits, however. Eurodollars are constantly traded among banks in the Eurodollar market. Trading activity among banks is conducted within the interbank placement market.

Loans to other banks are made by depositing the Eurodollars in a time deposit account at the borrowing bank. This borrowing and lending compounds the value of the original deposit, as the deposit remains on the books of each institution.

This "pyramiding" of Eurodollar deposits overstates the value of credit extended to the financial sector. Roughly half of the gross Eurodollar deposits—which includes interbank placements—are actual claims on the financial sector, or net liabilities.

At the end of 1971 gross Eurocurrency liabilities totaled \$150 billion. This total grew to almost \$1.5 trillion by the end of 1980. There are numerous reasons for this tremendous growth in the Eurodollar market. First, the Eurodollar market allows U.S. banks to avoid Regulation Q, which governs the rate paid on domestic deposits. Second, large U.S. balance-of-payment deficits and post-1973 oil price increases have led to a huge supply of dollars overseas. Third, capital controls instituted by Congress have limited the access of foreign subsidiaries of U.S. corporations to domestic sources of funds. The fourth and final reason, is the growing use of the Eurodollar market by (foreign and domestic) commercial banks as a part of liability management and by central banks as a supplement to monetary policy operations.

Primary Market. While a Eurodollar deposit could exist in any bank, in any country outside of the United States, trading activity is concentrated in select centers throughout the world. The market began in London, and London is currently the largest and most important center. Over 200 major U.S., European, Canadian, and Japanese banks operate in London, as well as numerous smaller banks. Important trading centers in addition to London are the major European capitals, Singapore, Hong Kong, Nassau, and the Grand Cayman Islands. These last two centers are conveniently located in the same time zone as New York, and act as brokering centers for transactions originating in the United Sates.

Interbank trading activity in the Eurodollar market is facilitated through the use of Eurodollar brokers. Brokers provide a centralized location where bids and offers are made available to all market participants via a vast collection of telephones and telexes. Eurodollar brokers are centered in London, with branches in major centers around the world.

Yields on Eurodollar deposits are a function of supply-and-demand conditions in both the United States and the other countries which participate in the market. In the long run, there is a very close correlation between Eurodollar rates and rates on similar domestic securities (e.g., commercial paper and Certificates of Deposit). Any extended divergence would cause an outflow of dollars from the lower- to the higher-yielding market.

The relationship between the yields on foreign and domestic dollar investments is not so consistent on a daily or intradaily basis, however. Foreign central banks or other major market participants can offset domestic economic and Federal Reserve factors, causing short-term aberrations in the spread between domestic and Eurodollar rates.

The interest rate at which a bank is willing to lend Eurodollars is a function of the risk of the borrower. There are two components of this risk. The first is specific to the borrower; the second is sovereign risk, or the risk of the country in which the borrower legally resides.

Credit risk in the interbank market is reflected in two ways—in the price at which the loan is made, and in the amount of funds one bank is willing to lend to another. Price risk adjustments are used only for loans to smaller, less active participants in the interbank market or to banks perceived as poor credit risks. The risk premium can range from a few basis points to a full percentage point, depending on the nature of both specific and sovereign risk.

The principal method of adjusting credit-risk differentials among London interbank participants is in the form of restrictions on loan amounts, or credit lines. Each participant assigns credit lines to banks with which it trades Eurodollars. Obviously, the greater the perceived risk of the borrower—based on size, capitalization, profitability, reputation, and country of origin—the lower is the credit line.

Sovereign risk explains the Eurodollar yield differential among financial centers throughout the world. Financial centers in areas perceived as being less politically stable will generally trade at higher yields.

Eurodollar Futures Market. Trading in Eurodollar futures was introduced by the IMM in December 1981. This contract was unique in that it was the first contract where final settlement is in cash rather than physical delivery of Eurodollars. Cash settlement is necessary in this case bcause Eurodollars are nonnegotiable deposits. As such, Eurodollar deposits cannot be readily transferred across market participants, and the long taking delivery would be forced to hold the deposit to maturity.

Cash settlement is little different from daily mark-to-market margin procedure. Open positions at the close of trading in a contract month are settled at the final settlement price, which is determined by the exchange.

The IMM contract is priced off London Eurodollar rates. The exchange randomly samples 12 banks from a broader list of top-tier banks in the London market. These banks provide the rate at which Eurodollar deposits are being offered at which Eurodollar deposits are being offered to the most credit-worthy participants. These samples are taken at the close of trading, and at a time, also randomly selected, within the 90 minutes just prior to the close of trading. The final settlement price is equal to the average of these two samples, after dropping the highest and lowest quote from each sample.

Remaining specifications of the Eurodollar contract are similar to those of the IMM domestic CD contract. The price basis is an index equal to 100 minus the money market yield, with a basis point valued at $25. The daily price limit of 100 basis points is higher in the Eurodollar contract, however, reflecting the greater volatility of this market.

A summary of salient features of the IMM 3-month Eurodollar contract is presented in Table 4.

GOVERNMENT NATIONAL MORTGAGE ASSOCIATION (GNMA)

Cash Market. GNMA securities represent an ownership interest in a pool of at least $1 million principal amount of FHA–VA guaranteed mortgages. Mortgage pools are assembled by originators, often a mortgage bank or savings and loan association. The originator handles the paperwork and manages the cash flows on the underlying mortgages in exchange for a servicing fee.

Two basic types of GNMA securities exist: GNMA pass-through securities and GNMA modified pass-through securities. All GNMAs are pass-through securities; that is, the payment of principal and interest on the underlying mortgages is "passed-through" to the security holder by the pool originator. Payment of principal and interest is guaranteed because of the FHA–VA guarantee on the underlying mortgages. The modified pass-through security differs from the straight pass-through security in that the *timely* payment of principal and interest is guaranteed regardless of the financial condition of the originator. This guarantee is provided by the Government National Mortgage Association, which is backed by the full faith and credit of the U.S. Government.

The mortgages underlying a GNMA pool must bear the same coupon rate, and must mature in 29 to 30 years from the time of the formation of the pool. Principal and interest payments on the mortgages are passed through to the GNMA holders monthly. The yield of a GNMA is calculated assuming prepayment of the principal of the mortgage in its 12th year.

TABLE 4. Salient Features of the IMM 3-Month Eurodollar Time Deposit Futures Contract

Trading unit	Eurodollar time deposit having a face value of $1 million
Price basis	Prices are quoted as an index, equal to 100 minus the annualized discount rate expressed as a percent (e.g., 85.50 for a discount rate of 14.50%).
Minimum price fluctuation	One basis point which is one 1/100 of 1%. Dollar value, based on $1 million face value, 90-day maturity, and a 360-day year, equals $25 per contract.
Price limit	100 basis above or below the settlement price of the previous trading day. No limit exists on the last day of trading.
Deliverable grade	Contracts are settled by cash settlement. Final settlement price is based on the average Eurodollar rate offered by the market to prime banks in the Eurodollar market, as quoted by a random sample of 12 reference banks. Sample rates are taken at the close of trading and at a randomly selected time in the 90 minutes prior to the close of trading. The final settlement price is equal to the average of the two samples after eliminating the two highest and two lowest quotes.
Delivery period	Last day of trading
Last day of trading	Second London business day prior to the third Wednesday of the contract month
Delivery method	Cash settlement in accordance with normal variation margin procedures
Delivery months	Current month and the March, June, September, and December cycle months.
Trading hours	7:30 a.m.–2:00 p.m. central time
Ticker symbol	ED

History. GNMA securities were first offered in 1970, as a means of increasing the liquidity of the secondary U.S. housing market. Prior to that time, institutional investors were largely precluded from investing in the housing industry because of the problems of mortgage heterogeneity, mortgage servicing requirements, and the lack of a liquid secondary market for mortgages. The problem of heterogeneity arises because each individual mortgage differs in its terms—interest rate, maturity, and so forth—and in the credit worthiness of the mortgagee. This resulted in high information costs of properly evaluating a potential mortgage investment.

GNMA mortgage-backed securities have been successful in fulfilling the objective of increasing mortgage market liquidity. They are homogeneous with respect to terms and credit risk, servicing requirements are handled by the originator in exchange for a 44 basis point servicing fee, and an active secondary market for GNMA securities has developed. With the major constraints upon their participation in the housing market removed, institutional investors have become increasingly involved in the domestic housing industry. In 1981 over $14 billion

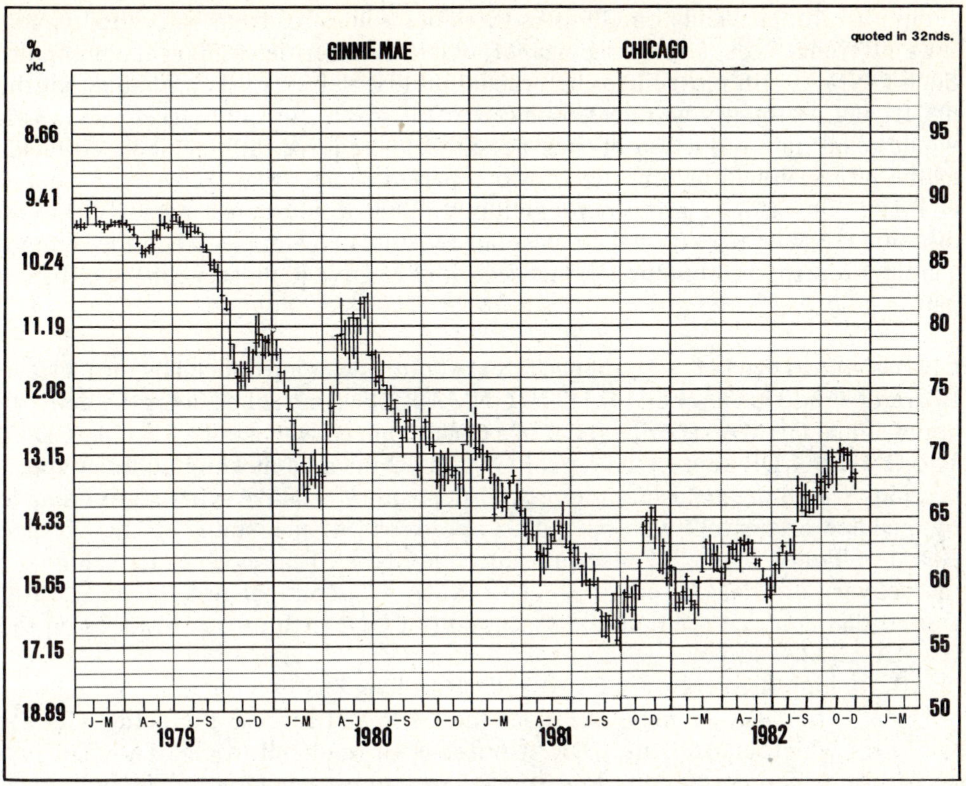

FIGURE 4. Ginnie Mae (GNMA) price chart.

of GNMA mortgage-backed securities were issued, bringing the total principal value of GNMA securities outstanding to over $105 billion.

Primary Market. GNMA securities are issued by the Government National Mortgage Association after an originator has assembled at least $1 million principal value of mortgages and transferred them to a custodian bank. Once issued, they are sold to investors in the primary market. GNMA securities are also sold in the primary market prior to their issuance through the use of forward and standby commitments. A forward commitment is a contractual agreement whereby the originator promises to deliver a pool of mortgages to the investor at a specified price at some time in the future. Standby commitments differ from straightforward commitments in that the originator has the option to walk away from the contract in exchange for a fee if the market moves against the originator.

Secondary Market. Because of their homogeneity, a secondary market has developed in GNMA securities. As in any secondary market, a group of dealers stands ready to make bids and to accept offers on GNMAs prior to maturity. Compensation to the dealers is in the form of a bid/ask spread, which currently varies between $\frac{8}{32}$ and $\frac{16}{32}$ of a point.

Although yields on GNMA securities are calculated assuming prepayment in the 12th year, actual prepayment experience often differs greatly from this assumption. Actual yields on GNMAs therefore will differ from calculated yields. This difference is especially important for GNMA securities trading at a premium. Such GNMAs will most likely be prepaid prematurely, as it is probable that the underlying mortgages will be refinanced at the lower current market rates. This would result in a reduction of their actual yields relative to the calculated yields as the premium will be amortized over a period shorter than 12 years. Discount GNMAs can also be prepaid prematurely. This would cause actual yields on discount GNMAs to exceed their calculated yields. Investors will therefore require a greater return for premium GNMA securities relative to those selling at or below par.

GNMA Futures Market. Trading in GNMA futures was introduced by the Chicago Board of Trade in October 1975. The GNMA–CDR contract calls for the delivery not of actual GNMA securities, but of a Collateralized Depository Receipt (CDR). The GNMA–CDR represents actual GNMA certificates meeting contract specifications which are held in an approved depository. GNMA–CDRs are issuable by qualified originators who have been approved for such status by the Chicago Board of Trade. The CBT also introduced a GNMA futures contract calling for the delivery of GNMA securities, the GNMA–CD contract in September 1978. Due to this contract's illiquidity, discussion of GNMA futures will focus on the GNMA–CDR contract.

After taking delivery on a GNMA–CDR, a long has two options. A long may hold onto the CDR or may surrender the CDR and receive the actual GNMA securities which backed the CDR. Until it is surrendered, a GNMA–CDR is a perpetuity which entitles the long to $635 of interest per month. The difference between the coupon income on the contract standard 8% GNMA ($667 per month) and the interest paid on the CDR accrues to the CDR originator as a servicing fee. Upon surrender, the originator has up to 15 business days in which to deliver the actual GNMA certificates to the long.

The actual amount of GNMA securities which must be delivered to the long depends upon the coupon of the GNMAs being delivered. The CBT GNMA–CDR contract calls for the delivery upon surrender of $100,000 principal amount of GNMA 8% coupons or the equivalent principal balance of another coupon. The equivalent principal balance is simply that amount of GNMAs which has a present value of $100,000, assuming that the mortgages have an original maturity of 30 years and are prepaid in 12 years, when discounted at 7.96%. As an example, the equivalent principal balance of a GNMA 15% coupon is $65,359.50. That is, $65,359.50 of GNMA 15% is equivalent in present value terms to $100,000 of GNMA 8% securities.

Upon surrender of the GNMA–CDR, the originator may deliver an amount of GNMAs equal to the equivalent principal balance plus or minus a 2.5% delivery tolerance or "tail." The difference between what is delivered and the equivalent principal balance is settled at par in cash between the CDR originator and the long.

The cash settlement value of the tail is computed as follows:

$$\text{tail} = \frac{\$100{,}000}{\text{EPB} \times (\text{PVD} - \text{EPB})}$$

where

$$EPB = \text{equivalent principal balance}$$

and $$PVD = \text{principial value delivered}$$

The equivalent principal balance and deliverable range of principal on the GNMA–CDR contract for a number of GNMA coupons are illustrated in Table 5.

U.S. TREASURY NOTES AND TREASURY BONDS

Cash Market. Treasury notes and Treasury bonds are marketable debt obligations of the U.S. Treasury. Treasury notes and Treasury bonds pay coupons semiannually, and the principal of the security at maturity. Timely payment of principal and interest is backed by the unconditional guarantee of the U.S. Government. Treasury notes are issued with maturities of 1–10 years, while Treasury bonds have maturities of greater than 10 years.

TABLE 5. Equivalent Principal Balances

Stated GNMA Interest Rate (Percent)	8% Par Equivalent Balance	Deliverable Range of Principal Balance	Maximum Overage or Underage
6½	$112,123.30	$109,320.22–$114,926.38	$2,803.08
7	107,816.70	105,121.28–110,512.12	2,695.42
7½	103,806.20	101,211.04–106,401.36	2,595.16
8	100,000.00	97,500.00–102,500.00	2,500.00
8½	96,501.80	94,089.25–98,914.35	2,412.55
9	93,167.70	90,838.51–95,496.89	2,329.19
9½	90,032.20	87,781.39–92,283.01	2,250.81
10	87,146.00	84,967.35–89,324.65	2,178.65
10½	84,328.90	82,220.68–86,427.12	2,108.22
11	81,743.90	79,700.30–83,787.50	2,043.60
11½	79,032.10	77,319.55–81,284.65	1,982.55
12	76,972.40	75,048.09–78,896.71	1,924.31
12½	74,766.40	72,897.24–76,635.56	1,869.16
13	72,674.40	70,857.54–74,491.26	1,816.86
13½	70,721.40	68,953.36–72,489.44	1,768.04
14	68,823.10	67,102.52–70,543.68	1,720.58
14½	67,057.80	65,381.35–68,734.25	1,676.45
15	65,359.50	63,725.51–66,993.49	1,633.99
15½	63,745.00	62,151.37–65,338.63	1,593.63
16	62,208.40	60,653.19–63,763.61	1,555.21
16½	60,744.10	59,225.50–62,262.70	1,518.60
17	59,347.20	57,863.52–60,830.88	1,483.68

TABLE 6. Salient Features of the CBT GNMA–CDR Futures Contract

Trading unit	$100,000 principal balance of GNMA 8% coupon or equivalent
Price basis	Prices are quoted as a percentage of par and expressed in 1/32 of a point. Par value is 100 points.
Minimum price fluctuation	1/32 of one point. The dollar value of 1/32 is equal to $31.25 (0.01 × 1/32 × $100,000).
Price limits	Two points (64/32) above or below the previous day's settlement price. There is no limit during the delivery month on or after the first notice day.
Deliverable grade	Modified pass-through mortgage-backed certificates guaranteed by the Government National Mortgage Association, with coupons of an equivalent principal balance based on an 8% coupon yielding 7.96% at par, assuming a 30-year mortgage prepaid in the 12th year.
Last day of trading	Seventh business day prior to the last business day of a delivery month
Delivery period	Any business day within the delivery month
Delivery method	Via delivery of a registered GNMA Collateralized Depository Receipt (CDR)
Invoice price	($100,000 × settlement price) plus accrued interest
Delivery months	March, June, September, and December cycle
Trading hours	8:00 a.m.–2:00 p.m. central time.
Ticker symbol	M

Primary Market. U.S. Treasury notes and bonds are offered at regularly scheduled auctions; 2-year Treasury notes are auctioned monthly. Three-year, 4-year, 5-year, 7-year, 10-year, 20-year, and 30-year security issues are auctioned quarterly at different times during the year. The regular issuance of Treasury bonds is interrupted from time to time, however, because of legislative restrictions on the amount of long-term Treasury debt outstanding.

As in a Treasury bill auction, both competitive and noncompetitive bids are permitted, where the price of the noncompetitive bid equals the average of the competitive bids accepted. The major participants in the primary market for Treasury notes and Treasury bonds include commercial banks, government securities brokers and dealers, and the Federal Reserve.

Secondary Market. Trading in the secondary market for Treasury notes and Treasury bonds is aided by a network of government securities brokers and dealers. Treasury notes and Treasury bonds are generally quoted on the basis of $1,000 face value. Three different yield measures are quoted in the note and bond markets—the coupon yield, the current yield, and the yield to maturity.

The *coupon yield* is the annual coupon payment of the security in dollars divided by its face value. The *current yield* is the annual coupon payment divided by the

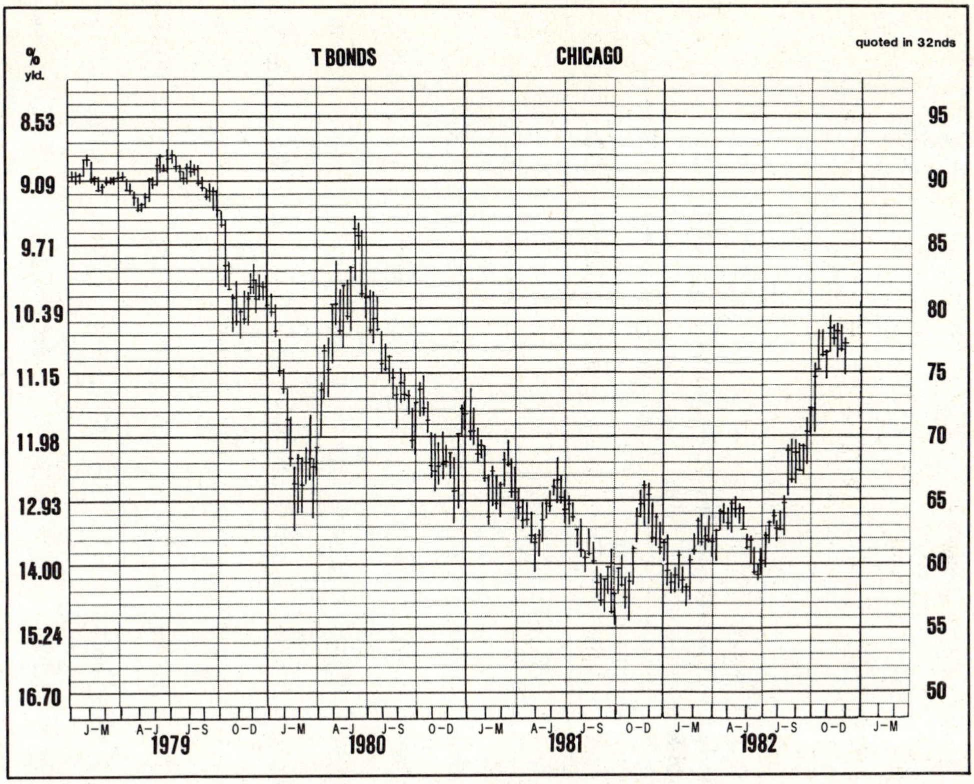

FIGURE 5. U.S. Treasury bonds price chart.

current price of the note or bond. These two measures indicate the yield provided by the income stream of the coupon payments per dollar of the security's face value and its price, respectively.

The most important yield measure in the Treasury note and Treasury bond markets is the *yield to maturity*. The *yield to maturity* is the discount rate which equates the present value of the income stream of the security with its price.

Treasury notes and Treasury bonds are investment opportunities for investors with longer time horizons. As with any security, demand for Treasury notes and Treasury bonds is a function of their yield relative to securities of comparable maturity—corporate notes and bonds, Eurobonds, and municipal securities.

U.S. Treasury Note and Treasury Bond Futures Market. Following the successful introduction of the GNMA–CDR futures contract, the Chicago Board of Trade introduced a futures contract based upon long-term U.S. Treasury bonds in August 1977. The CBT Treasury bond contract has proven to be the most successful futures contract ever introduced. As of June 30, 1982, the CBT Treasury bond contract was trading an average of 1.3 million contracts per month, representing over $130 billion face value of U.S. Treasury bonds. The NYFE also introduced a Treasury bond futures contract in August 1980. Because of its lack of commercial success, this section will only discuss the CBT Treasury bond contract.

TABLE 7. Long-Term Treasury Bond Futures Contract March Cycle Conversion Factors (Bonds Deliverable as of June 30, 1982)

Coupon	Issue Date	Maturity	Sep 1982	Dec 1982	Mar 1983	Jun 1983	Sep 1983	Dec 1983	Mar 1984	Jun 1984	Sep 1984	Dec 1984
8¼%	2/15/78	May 15th 2000–05	1.0233	1.0230	1.0230	1.0226	1.0227	1.0223	1.0223	1.0220	1.0220	1.0216
7⅝%	2/15/77	February 15th 2002–07	0.9633	0.9637	0.9637	0.9641	0.9641	0.9645	0.9646	0.9650	0.9651	0.9655
7⅞%	11/15/77	November 15th 2002–07	0.9876	0.9875	0.9878	0.9876	0.9879	0.9878	0.9880	0.9879	0.9882	0.9881
8⅜%	8/15/78	August 15th 2003–08	1.0375	1.0375	1.0371	1.0371	1.0367	1.0367	1.0363	1.0363	1.0359	1.0359
8¾%	11/15/78	November 15th 2003–08	1.0757	1.0751	1.0750	1.0744	1.0742	1.0736	1.0734	1.0728	1.0726	1.0720
9⅛%	5/15/79	May 15th 2004–09	1.1146	1.1138	1.1135	1.1128	1.1125	1.1117	1.1113	1.1105	1.1102	1.1093
10⅜%	11/15/79	November 15th 2004–09	1.2440	1.2427	1.2419	1.2406	1.2397	1.2383	1.2374	1.2360	1.2350	12336
11¾%	2/15/80	February 15th 2005–10	1.3866	1.3853	1.3833	1.3820	1.3799	1.3785	1.3764	1.3749	1.3727	1.3711
10%	5/15/80	May 15th 2005–10	1.2072	1.2061	1.2055	1.2044	1.2037	1.2025	1.2019	1.2007	1.1999	1.1987
		November 15th										

12¾%	11/17/80	2005–10	1.4960	1.4938	1.4921	1.4898	1.4880	1.4856	1.4838	1.4813	1.4794	1.4768
11¾%	1/12/81	February 15th 2001	1.3565	1.3545	1.3520	1.3500	1.3473	1.3452	1.3425	1.3403	1.3374	1.3351
13⅛%	4/ 2/81	May 15th 2001	1.4905	1.4872	1.4845	1.4811	1.4783	1.4747	1.4718	1.4681	1.4650	1.4612
13⅞%	5/15/81	May 15th 2006–11	1.6181	1.6155	1.6135	1.6108	1.6087	1.6058	1.6036	1.6007	1.5984	1.5954
13⅜%	7/ 2/81	August 15th 2001	1.5172	1.5145	1.5110	1.5082	1.5046	1.5016	1.4979	1.4948	1.4910	1.4877
15¾%	10/ 7/81	November 15th 2001	1.7505	1.7458	1.7418	1.7369	1.7327	1.7276	1.7233	1.7180	1.7134	1.7080
14%	11/16/81	November 15th 2006–11	1.6359	1.6333	1.6313	1.6286	1.6265	1.6238	1.6216	1.6187	1.6165	1.6135
14¼%	1/ 6/82	November 15th 2002	1.6083	1.6052	1.6014	1.5982	1.5942	1.5909	1.5868	1.5833	1.5790	1.5753
14⅜%		4/15/89	1.3183									
9½%		5/15/89	1.0624									
10¾%		11/15/89	1.1452	1.1410	1.1373							
10¾%		8/15/90	1.1563	1.1529	1.1488	1.1452	1.1410	1.1373				
13%		11/15/90	1.2913	1.2844	1.2780	1.2708	1.2641	1.2566	1.2496			
14½%		5/15/91	1.3954	1.3868	1.3787	1.3698	1.3613	1.3521	1.3433	1.3337	1.3245	
14⅞%		8/15/91	1.4264	1.4182	1.4091	1.4005	1.3911	1.3822	1.3724	1.3631	1.3529	1.3433
14¼%		11/15/91	1.3956	1.3876	1.3802	1.3719	1.3641	1.3555	1.3474	1.3385	1.3301	1.3208
14⅝%		2/15/92	1.4269	1.4193	1.4109	1.4030	1.3942	1.3860	1.3769	1.3683	1.3588	1.3499
13¾%		5/15/92	1.3776	1.3705	1.3640	1.3566	1.3498	1.3421	1.3350	1.3271	1.3197	1.3114

TABLE 8. Salient Features of the CBT Long-Term U.S. Treasury Note Futures Contract

Trading unit	U.S. Treasury notes having a face or par value at maturity of \$100,000.
Price basis	Prices are quoted as a percentage of par in points and expressed in 1/32 of a point. Par value is 100 points.
Minimum price fluctuation	1/32 of one point. The dollar value of 1/32 is equal to \$31.25 (0.01 × 1/32 × \$100,000).
Price limits	Two points (64/32) above or below the previous day's settlement price. There is no limit during the delivery month on or after the first notice day.
Deliverable grade	U.S. Treasury notes having a maturity, as of the first business day of a delivery month, of not less than 6½ years, and not more than 10 years. All notes delivered against a contract must be of the same issue.
Delivery period	Delivery can occur on any business day of the delivery month.
Last day of trading	Seventh business day prior to the last business day of a delivery month
Delivery method	Delivery is made by book-entry wire transfer to any bank which is both a member of the Federal Reserve System and has capital in excess of \$100 million. Payment is made in federal funds to a bank which meets the specified requirements as stated above, by the short.
Invoicing procedure	The invoice price is computed using a conversion factor system. Futures prices are quoted based on an 8% coupon. Notes bearing coupons other than 8% are deliverable at a price equal to the futures price times the conversion factor for that note specified by the exchange. The seller also invoices the buyer for accrued interest in accordance with U.S. Treasury procedures.
Delivery months	March, June, September, and December cycle.
Trading hours	8:00 a.m.–2:00 p.m. central time
Ticker symbol	TY

Three futures exchanges have offered short- to intermediate-term Treasury note futures contracts. In June 1979, the CBT introduced a 4–6 year Treasury note contract. The IMM also introduced a 4-year Treasury note contract in July 1979. Finally, the Commodities Exchange (COMEX) offered a 2-year Treasury note futures contract in December 1980. None of these contracts has achieved any substantial liquidity, and thus will not be discussed.

The Chicago Board of Trade began trading a 6½- to 10-year Treasury note contract in May 1982. The introduction of the contract was an immediate success, setting an opening day record volume of 33,502 contracts. The early success of the contract may be traced to the spread opportunities resulting from its similarity

TABLE 9. Salient Features of the CBT Long-Term U.S. Treasury Bond Futures Contract

Trading unit	U.S. Treasury bonds having a face or par value at maturity of $100,000.
Price basis	Prices are quoted as a percentage of par in points and expressed in 1/32 of a point. Par value is 100 points.
Minimum price fluctuation	1/32 of one point. The dollar value of 1/32 is equal to $31.25 (0.01 × 1/32 × $100,000).
Price limits	Two points (64/32) above or below the previous day's settlement price. There is no limit during the delivery month on or after the first notice day.
Deliverable grade	U.S. Treasury bonds having a maturity, as of the first business day of a delivery month, of at least 15 years are noncallable and which, if callable, are not callable for at least 15 years. All bonds delivered against a contract must be of the same issue.
Delivery period	Delivery can occur on any business day of the delivery month.
Last day of trading	Seventh business day prior to the last business day of a delivery month
Delivery method	Delivery is made by book-entry wire transfer to any bank which is both a member of the Federal Reserve System and has capital in excess of $100 million. Payment is made in federal funds to a bank which meets the specified requirements as stated above, by the short.
Invoicing procedure	The invoice price is computed using a conversion factor system. Futures prices are quoted based on an 8% coupon. Notes bearing coupons other than 8% are deliverable at a price equal to the futures price times the conversion factor for that note specified by the exchange. The seller also invoices the buyer for accrued interest in accordance with U.S. Treasury procedures.
Delivery months	March, June, September, and December cycle
Trading hours	8:00 a.m.–2:00 p.m. central time
Ticker symbol	US

to the CBT Treasury bond contract, and to the increasing importance of the 7–10-year segment of the Treasury debt schedule.

This section will discuss the CBT 6½- to 10-year Treasury note and long-term Treasury bond futures contracts. The terms of the contracts are essentially identical except for the term to maturity of the deliverable grade. The Chicago Board of Trade Treasury note and Treasury bond contracts allow delivery of a market basket of issues. As of June 30, 1982, there were 18 deliverable bond issues, and 11 note issues. This large number of deliverable securities, each with its own coupon rate, term to maturity, and price, poses a potential problem for the pricing of a futures contract. The Chicago Board of Trade has overcome this problem via a factor system of invoicing.

Futures prices for both contracts are stated on the basis of an 8% coupon standard. The conversion factor is multiplied by the futures price to arrive at the amount invoiced. This procedure adjusts the single futures price, which by itself reflects the current level of yields, to reflect the value differences of bonds and notes of various coupon rates and terms to maturity. Conversion factors for the CBT Treasury note and Treasury bond contracts are available from the Financial Publishing Company of Boston, Massachusetts (Publication No. 765).

Table 7 provides a listing of conversion factors for each deliverable note and bond, for each delivery month in the period September 1982–December 1984 (as of June 30, 1982).

The salient features of the CBT Treasury note and Treasury bond contracts are provided in Tables 8 and 9.

CHAPTER 49

STOCK INDEX FUTURES: THE KANSAS CITY BOARD OF TRADE VALUE LINE AVERAGE (VLA) CONTRACT

CONTENTS

SYSTEMATIC RISK 3

STOCK OWNERSHIP IN THE UNITED STATES 4

Patterns of Individual Stock Ownership 5

HISTORICAL BACKGROUND 6

Other Submissions and Litigation 7

HOW THE KCBT–VLA CONTRACT WORKS 10

Hedging with the Contract: A Numerical Example 11

Mechanics of the Market: KCBT–VLA Delivery 14

Short-Hedging Uses of the Contract 14

Long Hedging 15

Terms and Conditions of the Contracts 15

THE UNDERLYING STOCK MARKET INDICATORS 15

THEORETICAL CONSIDERATIONS 19

The "Market Factor" 21

The Econometrics: Summary 21

Quantifying the Market Factor 22

Equal Weighting 23

STOCK INDEX FUTURES STATISTICAL PRICE SUMMARY 24

Cash Indexes: 1982 24

Rationale for Stock Index Futures Contracts 30

BIBLIOGRAPHY 30

Other Sources of Information 32

CHAPTER **49**

STOCK INDEX FUTURES: THE KANSAS CITY BOARD OF TRADE VALUE LINE AVERAGE (VLA) CONTRACT

Neil S. Weiner

For more than a century, futures markets have provided a way for the holders and processors of agricultural commodities to reduce the risks of inventory price exposure. Any inventory which fluctuates in price, and hence value, subjects its owners to risk exposure during the course of storing, merchandising, and processing. By utilizing a trading technique known as "hedging" on organized futures markets, inventory holders wishing to mitigate the price risks of ownership can shift those risks to other individuals willing to assume them.

More recently futures markets have expanded to provide inventory price protection for some industrial products and precious metals. During the decade of the 1970s, the volatility of interest rates fostered a wide range of futures contracts on government and commercial debt instruments. Until 1982, a similar price-risk protection mechanism for those who hold and trade common stocks had not been available.

SYSTEMATIC RISK

The tenets of modern portfolio and capital market theory focus on the following distinction, namely, that the risks inherent in common stock price variability can be separated into two components—"systematic" and "unsystematic" risks. At a first approximation, systematic risk is the degree of correspondence of a security's price movements with the general stock market. Since the empirical evidence is overwhelming to the effect that security prices tend to move up and down together, "it might reasonably be thought that they are affected by a common market *factor*" (Aber, 1973, p. 11).

Unsystematic risk can be diversified away, however, when a given security is combined with others to form an efficient portfolio. Thus, with adequate and proper diversification, the *sole* source of uncertainty about the rate of return of

Options on market and industry indexes, which have recently appeared, are not considered in this chapter.

an efficient portfolio is its degree of "systematic," or market, risk. Stated another way, diversification is protection against a decline which impacts a particular industry or firm, but it is not protection against a general market decline. Regardless of portfolio policy or stock selection criteria, the best-reasoned equities position—no matter how well-diversified—is not safe from the hazards or risks of a general market downturn.

A stock index futures contract provides protection against such a decline. The purpose of this new futures instrument is to furnish a flexible alternative to investors for safeguarding portfolio values from fluctuations in the stock market. The data in Table 1 suggest that on the average, the "systematic" market risk accounts for about 34% of the price variability of common stocks. For a large number of individual issues, however, the market risk can account for as much as 50–70%. Similarly, as mentioned above, for well-diversified portfolios systematic risk accounts for nearly *all* of the uncertainty.

STOCK OWNERSHIP IN THE UNITED STATES

The extent of the public's holdings of common stock is shown in Table 2 for the years 1960–1980. By the end of 1980 the estimated value of the stock in the aggregate was nearly $1.4 trillion. In commodity market parlance, the outright ownership of assets without offsetting protection (i.e., a hedge position in futures contracts) equates to the risk exposure of a speculative "long" position. Without the capability to effectively manage the risks of portfolio holdings, the investing public has been compelled to hold a "speculative long" position with respect to common stocks.

TABLE 1. Value Line Index Risk Classes, Monthly Data, 1975–1979 Descriptive Statistics

VLA Risk Class[a]	Number of Stocks	R^2 Average	R^2 Range	Number of Stocks Less Than R^2 of
I	179	0.4658	0.7318–0.1479	0.30 = 16
II	178	0.4436	0.7619–0.1135	0.30 = 25
III	175	0.4078	0.7126–0.1234	0.30 = 29
IV	176	0.3777	0.6049–0.0963	0.20 = 11
V	173	0.3729	0.5853–0.1265	0.20 = 11
VI	170	0.3465	0.6026–0.0871	0.20 = 15
VII	175	0.3080	0.5339–0.0370	0.20 = 24
VIII	173	0.2860	0.5402–0.0556	0.10 = 4
IX	161	0.2462	0.4371–0.0186	0.10 = 10
X	122	0.1368	0.3945–0.0289	0.05 = 15
Total	1,682	0.3391		

[a]Ranked by estimated β values, risk class I represents those stocks with the highest values; class II, the stocks with the next highest values, and so forth.

TABLE 2. Market Value (Billions of Dollars)

Year End	NYSE Number of Issues Listed	NYSE	All Common Stocks (Estimated)
1960	1,126	307.7	345.7
1961	1,145	388.0	436.0
1962	1,168	340.0	383.5
1963	1,194	403.0	452.5
1964	1,227	466.1	523.6
1965	1,254	526.5	594.4
1966	1,267	470.9	534.7
1967	1,255	587.5	687.1
1968	1,253	664.3	789.4
1969	1,290	600.3	710.8
1970	1,330	607.8	701.5
1971	1,399	705.7	828.2
1972	1,478	838.7	994.0
1973	1,536	682.1	792.8
1974	1,543	481.1	546.9
1975	1,531	652.1	739.2
1976	1,550	815.9	915.0
1977	1,549	760.8	869.1
1978	1,552	798.8	912.9
1979	1,536	936.0	1,069.7
1980	1,540	1,215.4	1,389.0

Source: *NYSE Fact Books* et al.

PATTERNS OF INDIVIDUAL STOCK OWNERSHIP. Although somewhat dated, one of the more recent published analyses of stock-ownership patterns for individuals is that of Blume, Crockett, and Friend (1974). It was found that in tax year 1971 individuals held highly undiversified portfolios. Imputations made from a large sample of that year's income-tax returns suggested that about 34% of the individuals held only one stock, 50% held no more than two different stocks, and only about 11% held more than 10 stocks (Levy, 1980). Since there is ample evidence that investors are risk averse, this lack of effective diversification led the authors to question some of the basic assumptions typically made in capital asset pricing theory. In addition, the lack of effective diversification was also deemed to have important social implications *"since, in a major downturn in the stock market, a high proportion of investors will do very much worse than the market"* (Blume, 1974, pp. 17–18).

In a later study, Schlarbaum, Lewellen, and Lease (1978) conducted a longitudinal analysis based on a sample of actual securities transactions for individual brokerage house accounts for the period January 1964–December 1970. With regard to holding periods, trading pattern data suggested a mean investment cycle duration of approximately 8½ months and a median of 4 months, "by either standard a rather brief horizon" (pp. 305–306). The most favorable-rates-of-return results tended to be concentrated in the short duration cycle of holding periods.

Furthermore, a broad range of trading styles among investors was evident: The most active 10% accounted for 57% of all the round trips. An important comment of the authors in this respect was that "the observed round trips took place, on balance, *at times of marginally less favorable market moves than the 7 year average*. The performance of the investor sample, therefore, does not seem to be attributable to any skill in investment *timing,* but instead to skill in individual security selection" (Schlarbaum, Lewellen, and Lease, 1978, p. 315).

Stock index futures contracts provide a hedging or risk-management tool for holders and traders of corporate equities. This futures contract allows those polarized in either high market risk or no market risk situations to more effectively balance positions along the dimension of uncertainty. Thus, these new futures instruments provide expanded opportunities for more efficient risk management of financial assets.

HISTORICAL BACKGROUND

The exact origin of the stock index futures concept is difficult to pin down. Others have reported that in foreign countries stocks regularly trade on both a cash and futures settlement basis (Figlewski and Kon, 1982, p. 3). And in Amsterdam, from 1973 to 1975, Arthur Lipper operated the Forward Contract Exchange Company. At this company primarily institutional clients traded forward contracts based on the Dow Jones Industrial Average, the Financial Times Index of Ordinary Shares, and the Tokyo Dow Jones Index (Lipper, 1978, pp. 136–142).

In 1977 the Kansas City Board of Trade formed a special committee to explore potential new futures contracts. The committee retained Dr. Roger W. Gray of Stanford University as a consultant. After considerable research, the committee determined that a futures contract based on a stock index or average would offer the greatest economic utility. Due to the vast inventory of stocks which might be hedged (approximately $1.5 trillion) and the potential participation of 30 million stockholders, the expectations for success of such a contract were high.

The first submission to the Commodity Futures Trading Commission (CFTC) of a proposal to trade a futures contract based on a stock index occurred in October 1977. The Kansas City Board of Trade (KCBT) proposed a futures contract based on the Dow Jones 30 Industrial Average. Public hearings on the stock index futures submission were held by the CFTC in Washington, D.C. during October 1978. Over 400 pages of testimony were presented by interested parties, who generally affirmed the positive public interest of the innovative proposal. However, final agreement was never reached with Dow Jones and Company regarding the use of the Dow Industrial Average. On April 20, 1979, the Kansas City Board of Trade amended its proposal to the CFTC to base its futures contract on the Value Line Composite Index.

Due to regulatory disagreement concerning jurisdiction of the new contract, CFTC action on the proposal was delayed for many months. However, with the appointments in 1981 of Philip M. Johnson as Chairman of the Commodity Futures Trading Commission and John Shad as Chairman of the Securities and Exchange Commission, the bureaucratic logjam was finally broken. The new chairmen reached an accord with regard to the lines of jurisdiction for new financial products. The

Shad/Johnson agreement was instrumental in the KCBT's proposal being approved on February 16, 1982—after a total delay of nearly 4 years.

The Kansas City Board of Trade–Value Line futures contract's first day of trading occurred only 8 days later on February 24. Amid an euphoric atmosphere on the exchange's trading floor, the KCBT–VLA stock index futures contract was off to a fairly robust start. The first day's trading volume amounted to nearly 1,800 contracts.

Trading in two other stock index futures contracts followed soon thereafter. On April 20, 1982, the Chicago Mercantile Exchange (CME) received CFTC designation as a contract market for a stock index contract based on the Standard and Poor's (S&P) 500 Stock Index. The CME began trading one day after approval, on April 21. The initial volume totaled 3,963 contracts. Two weeks later, on May 4, 1982, the New York Futures Exchange (NYFE) received CFTC approval to trade its stock index future based upon the NYSE Composite Index. The first day's trading volume on May 6 amounted to 6,162 contracts. The comparative terms and conditions of the three contracts (KCBT, CME, and NYFE) and selected statistical aspects appear in the sections "How the KCBT–VLA Contract Works" and "Stock Index Futures Statistical Price Summary," respectively.

OTHER SUBMISSIONS AND LITIGATION. The extensive hedging potential and trading activity of stock index futures contracts have resulted in a virtual deluge of proposed index futures submissions to the Commodity Futures Trading Commission. Competition among the various exchanges has been keen, active, and hard fought from the very beginning. Some of the participants have sought resolution in the courts. The number of combatants involved in various forms of litigation seems reminiscent of the simultaneous gladiator duels in the Coliseum of ancient Rome. These stock index legal battles are briefly described and summarized.

1. *KCBT* v. *CFTC* (et al.). During the week before the CFTC's scheduled approval of the CME–S&P contract, the Kansas City Board of Trade sought to enjoin the CFTC from approving any other stock index futures contracts for a 1-year period. In a suit filed in the Kansas City U.S. District Court, the KCBT argued that the inordinate delay by the CFTC in approving its submission had eroded the KCBT's competitive advantage. With neither copyright nor patent protections, the KCBT as innovator of the stock index futures concept asked that an adequate period be granted for exclusive trading in order to recoup its investment in development costs. The KCBT argued further that the longer-term impacts would likely be a dilution of the incentives for the smaller futures exchanges to submit innovative proposals to the CFTC. Already rather highly concentrated in Chicago, the futures industry would not be as viable and competitive without the participation of the smaller exchanges in new product development.

The Chicago Mercantile Exchange, in the role of intervenor in the proceedings, contended that there would be no provable damages if the CME–S&P contract were to trade the following week; and even if there were damages, the KCBT could litigate an appropriate suit at a later time. On the following Monday, April 19, 1982, Judge Joseph E. Stevens, Jr. denied the Kansas City Board of Trade's petition, and the CFTC approved the CME–S&P contract for trading the next day.

2. *Standard and Poor's Corporation* v. *COMEX*. On April 28, 1982, the CFTC approved the application of the New York Commodity Exchange (COMEX) to trade a futures contract based on an index of 500 stocks, the "COMEX 500." On the same day, in New York federal district court, Judge Milton Pollack granted S&P a temporary restraining order which prevented COMEX from actually trading the approved contract. The S&P suit charged COMEX with "misappropriation of proprietary information, unfair competition, and dilution of S&P's trademark."

Judge Pollack on May 13 granted a further preliminary injunction against the New York Commodity Exchange prohibiting trading of the COMEX 500 contract. The judge said that COMEX "intended improperly to link S&P with COMEX as a commercial prop," thereby trading on S&P's name "without authorization and over S&P's objections." Judge Pollack felt that COMEX would have been "misappropriating the skill, expenditures, labor, and reputation of S&P in generating and producing the S&P 500 Index." In addition, he felt that COMEX's promotional literature was somewhat misleading and confusing as to whether S&P supported the COMEX 500 contract (*Wall Street Journal,* May 14, 1982, p. 15).

COMEX filed an immediate appeal of that decision. Two weeks later, on June 30, 1982, a federal appeals court unanimously upheld the lower court's ruling prohibiting COMEX from trading the "500" stock index futures contract (*Wall Street Journal,* July 1, 1982, p. 26).

3. *Dow Jones* v. *Chicago Board of Trade* (et al.). The most active and colorful of the stock index litigations involve the Dow Jones Averages. Originally the Kansas City Board of Trade had intended to use a 30 industrial average (DJIA, though not identified by name) as the basis for its stock index contract. As described above, when Dow Jones and Company objected to even that passive arrangement, the KCBT established a formal agreement with Arnold Bernhard and Company to use the Value Line Composite Index, and amended its CFTC application accordingly.

In its original stock index application, the Chicago Board of Trade (CBT) planned to employ "portfolio futures." The CBT proposed 10 industry indices, each composed of about five stocks, and an 11th portfolio future, the aggregate of the other 10 industry groups, a composite to represent "the market."

In March 1982, however, the CBT sought designation from the CFTC as a contract market for futures based on stock indexes remarkably similar to the Dow Jones Averages. Previously, the CBT had been refused use of the averages by Dow Jones and Company. Robert Wilmouth, then president of the CBT, described the industrial contract "as based on a stock market index, composed of 30 industrial stocks" (*Wall Street Journal,* March 1, 1982, p. 44). Three separate court actions arose from the CBT's new submission to the CFTC:

CBT v. *Dow Jones* (Cook County, Illinois): The initial legal action was filed by the Chicago Board of Trade in Cook County court in March 1982. Claiming that its stock index proposal to the CFTC would not violate Dow Jones's rights, the CBT asked for a declaratory judgment to that effect. Dow Jones responded that the Cook County court did not have jurisdiction, and asked that the suit be dismissed.

Dow Jones v. *CBT* (New York): Simultaneously with its response in Illinois, Dow Jones and Company filed a suit in New York federal court to enjoin the CBT from trading the proposed stock index futures contract. Dow Jones contended that "the proposed CBT stock indexes are in fact the Dow Jones Averages . . . and that the proposed trading by the CBT would constitute copyright and trademark infringement, false representation of goods and services, misappropriation of property, and injury to Dow Jones's business reputation." Dow Jones repeatedly objected to its name or product being associated with a "speculative trading device" (*Wall Street Journal,* April 1, 1982, p. 38).

Dow Jones v. *CFTC* (Washington, D.C.): The third legal action, in May 1982, was Dow Jones's request in federal court to enjoin the CFTC from approving the Chicago Board of Trade's application to trade the disputed stock index futures contracts (*Wall Street Journal,* May 11, 1982, p. 10), claiming that the CBT "would cause severe and irreparable injury to Dow Jones's property interests." Judge Charles Richey dismissed the Dow Jones suit since the CBT had voluntarily pledged to delay trading until the Cook County, Illinois, suit had been decided. The CBT also stated that the Dow Jones name would not be used to promote the contracts. The CFTC approved the "Chicago Board of Trade Stock Market Index Contract." However, the Illinois and New York lawsuits remained pending.

Not finished yet, the venerable Dow Jones organization "threatened to alter or suspend publication of its stock averages" because of the dispute. In a letter to the CFTC, Dow Jones reiterated its contention that "use of the Dow Jones indices as a trading vehicle poses a substantial threat 'to the company's reputation and value of its indices'" (*Wall Street Journal,* May 14, 1982, p. 15).

In New York federal court, those arguments were not persuasive. During July 1982 Judge Robert L. Carter denied Dow Jones's copyright infringement injunction request. Because Dow Jones had "shown neither the probability of success on the merits nor possible irreparable harm." Judge Carter stressed "that the decision related solely to the alleged copyright infringement" (*Wall Street Journal,* July 19, 1982, p. 8).

In Illinois the Chicago Board of Trade also initially won the lawsuit against Dow Jones. State Judge James Murray ruled that trading in the CBT's stock index futures contracts would not be harmful to Dow Jones since the latter's name would not be used. Moreover, the CBT had said it would print a disclaimer of Dow Jones sponsorship in all advertising and promotional materials (*Wall Street Journal,* June 7, 1982, p. 10). That, in the opinion of the judge, differentiated the case from the COMEX–S&P suit, partly because COMEX had used Standard and Poor's name to promote the contract. However, the CBT victory turned out to be rather hollow—Judge Murray also granted a temporary stay of ruling to permit Dow Jones to appeal the decision.

An Illinois appellate court extended that stay indefinitely, until the New York copyright infringement case had been decided. The appeals court later reversed the earlier circuit court decision, and ruled in favor of Dow Jones. The court did not issue its opinion, which was to be forthcoming at a future date. Until that opinion was issued no further legal action could have been undertaken.

The opinion of the three-judge appellate court was issued about 30 days later. In overturning the lower court's decision, in favor of Dow Jones, the opinion stated that the CBT would be misappropriating the averages, even if Dow Jones's name wasn't used in connection with the contract. The misappropriation did not relate to the name, but to "the property right of Dow Jones to its averages and the good will and public respect attendant to them" (*Wall Street Journal*, August 8, 1982, p. 25). The court further opined that "the strong correlation of the Dow Jones average to the general pattern of stock market activity is essential to the usefulness of the [Board of Trade's] index contract." There was no doubt in the court's mind that the name and reputation of Dow Jones figured heavily in the CBT's plans. The CBT immediately appealed to the Illinois Supreme Court. In December 1982, that court agreed to review the appellate court's decision. That action remained pending as of the end of 1982.

HOW THE KCBT–VLA CONTRACT WORKS

Since it was the first proposed and first approved, the Kansas City Board of Trade–Value Line Average is employed below to illustrate transactions and hedging with stock index futures contracts. The essence of an index futures contract is the use of a stock market indicator to represent the systematic risk component of stock price variability. Thus, the "underlying commodity" for the KCBT–VLA stock index futures is the Value Line Composite Average (VLA). Published and maintained by Arnold Bernhard and Company, Incorporated, it is an equally weighted geometric average of stock prices expressed in index form, with June 30, 1961 set at 100. The nearly 1,700 issues included in the VLA account for more than 96% of all dollar trading volume in U.S. equity markets. Approximately 90% of those issues are traded on the New York Stock Exchange.

The KCBT–VLA stock index futures contract is priced and traded in accordance with the VLA's index values. The contract's size is 500 times the futures price. Thus, if the futures price were $100, the corresponding contract's value would be $50,000.

The futures prices are quoted and fluctuate in increments of 0.05 (equal to a $25 change in the contract's value). However, in order to be directly comparable with the actual (or "spot") VLA index, the delivery settlement prices are determined in increments of 0.01. Trading in the contract is authorized for six forward months with the maturity of the contracts occurring at the end of each calendar quarter, the months being March, June, September, and December. Table 3 shows the contract specifications for the Kansas City Board of Trade Value Line Contract. Terms and conditions of this stock index futures contract and trading rules are subject to change by the KCBT, with CFTC approval.

The general aspects of trading stock index contracts are illustrated in the following:

Example. On June 5, 1982, the September 1982 maturity of the KCBT–VLA futures traded at a price of $118. Suppose Trader A thinks the September 1982 futures contract will rise in price from $118, while Trader B believes the price will fall.

If the traders had initiated positions in the September 1982 contract at that price ($118), the purchase cost to A would have been $59,000 ($118 × 500); similarly, the sales value to B would also have been $59,000. Consequently, Trader A is said to be "long" (since A bought first) and Trader B "short" (sold first). Until each completes a round turn, they are both said to have "open" positions.

TABLE 3. KCBT–VLA Stock Index Future: Contract Specifications

Ticker symbol	KV (Kansas City Value Line)
Exchange	Kansas City Board of Trade
Trading hours	9:00 a.m.–3:15 p.m. Kansas City time; 10:00 a.m.–4:15 p.m. New York time
Price quotations	Futures prices are based on the VLA Composite Stock Index. The value of a contract is 500 times the futures price (at a futures prices of $140 the value equals $70,000).
Minimum price change	Futures prices are quoted and fluctuate in increments of 0.05. The minimum price change would result in a $25 change in the value of a contract. However, delivery prices are settled in increments of 0.01, in order to be directly comparable to the spot VLA index.
Daily price change limit	Initially none; 5.00 point limit effective August 1982.
Delivery months	March, June, September, and December for six forward contract maturities; however, other months may be added.
Maturing contract trading termination	All contracts are marked to the market, and any remaining open contracts settled with the Clearing Company on the day after the last trading day of the expiring month. Settlement is made with U.S. funds based on the Value Line Index as of the close of the last day of trading.
Minimum customer margins	Set by the exchange.
Value Line Index	Published by Arnold Bernhard and Company. The Value Line Composite is a geometric average expressed in index form, comprised of approximately 1,700 actively traded stocks; June 30, 1961 = 100. It is computed every 3 minutes (subject to change) and is available from most quote vendors (ticker symbol: VLIC).

Six weeks later, on July 14, 1982, the September 1982 KCBT–VLA contract was trading at $123.30. If Trader A had decided to close out his position (sold), the sales value would have been $61,650 ($123.30 × 500). Trader A would have realized a profit of $2,650 ($61,650 − $59,000). On the other hand, if Trader B had closed out his position at $123.30, B would have sustained a loss of $2,650 (Trader B had been "short").

HEDGING WITH THE CONTRACT: A NUMERICAL EXAMPLE. The primary economic purpose of stock index futures is to provide a price or value protection mechanism for portfolio ("inventory") holdings. Due to the vast amounts of stock held by the "public," including institutions, the most natural type of hedge is the *short hedge*. A short hedge is accomplished through the "sell first" sequence of trading. However, there are a number of instances where a *long hedge* would be

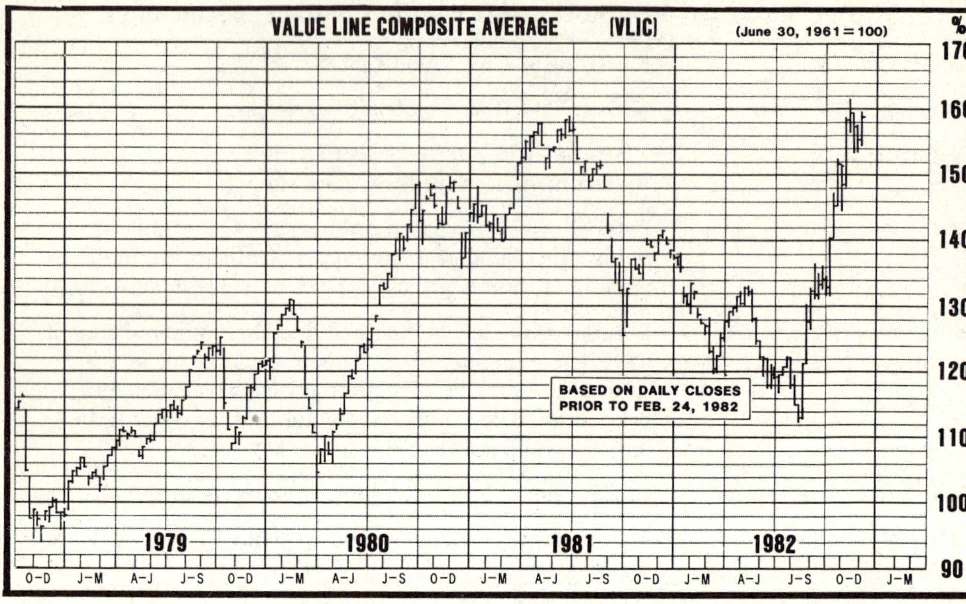

FIGURE 1. Value line composite average.

appropriately used to reduce risk, as well as various other types of "position" hedging.

The following example illustrates short hedging:

Example. Suppose an individual held a portfolio of each of the following stocks, as of April 15, 1982:

Stock	Number of Shares	Price	Market Value
Bausch and Lomb	100	44¼	$ 4,425.00
Corning Glass	100	45⅛	4,512.50
Dresser	200	23⅜	4,675.00
DuPont	100	35½	3,550.00
General Electric	100	63⅞	6,387.50
Ingersoll Rand	100	46¼	4,625.00
International Paper	100	35½	3,550.00
Martin Marietta	100	29⅞	2,987.50
Merck	100	72	7,200.00
PPG	100	32⅛	3,212.50
Squibb	100	34¼	3,425.00
Stauffer	200	20⅛	4,025.00
Tenneco	200	28⅞	5,775.00
Texas Instruments	100	86⅞	8,687.50
Total portfolio value			$67,037.50

At that time, the individual who desired to protect the value of holdings could have engaged in a "short hedge" by *selling* a forward maturity of the contract. The futures price of the June 1982 KCBT–VLA contract was \$130.40 on April 15, 1982. The contract transaction is as follows:

Closing price of June 1982 KCBT–VLA = \$130.40
Value of contract sold (\$130.40 × 500) = \$65,200

At the end of June 1982, the respective portfolio and futures contract values would have been the following:

Stock	Number of Shares	Price	Market Value
Bausch and Lomb	100	42⅛	\$ 4,212.50
Corning Glass	100	43⅜	4,337.50
Dresser	200	17⅞	3,575.00
DuPont	100	33	3,300.00
General Electric	100	63⅝	6,362.50
Ingersoll Rand	100	39½	3,950.00
International Paper	100	36⅞	3,687.50
Martin Marietta	100	25½	2,550.00
Merck	100	67½	6,750.00
PPG	100	33¼	3,325.00
Squibb	100	34⅜	3,437.50
Stauffer	200	18¼	3,650.00
Tenneco	200	24¾	4,950.00
Texas Instruments	100	86⅝	8,662.50
Total portfolio value			\$62,750.00

Other information pertinent to the hedge position is:

VLA Index on June 30, 1982 = \$120.57
Final price for the June 1982 KCBT–VLA contract = \$120.57
Value of contract (purchase cost): (\$120.57 × 500) = \$60,285

If the portfolio holder had closed out the KCBT–VLA stock index futures position on June 30, 1982, the net results of the hedging operation would have been the following:

Date	Portfolio Values	Stock Index Contract Transaction	Net Result From Hedging
4/15/82	\$67,037.50	\$65,200.00 (sale)	
6/30/82	62,750.00	60,285.00 (purchase)	
	–\$ 4,287.50 (loss)	\$ 4,915.00 (gain)	\$627.50 (gain)

During this period, the example portfolio declined $4,287.50 in value; however, that loss was more than offset by a gain of $4,915 on the stock index futures transaction. The portfolio hedge resulted in a slight overall net gain as the individual was "insulated" from a severe market decline in the value of stock holdings. That is precisely the intended price-risk-transferral function afforded by the hedging alternative. Stock index futures provide a mechanism for risk management. These futures are *not* intended as a *substitute* for securities, but as a viable *supplement* to them.

MECHANICS OF THE MARKET: KCBT–VLA DELIVERY. In futures markets, both buyer (long) and seller (short) must close out their positions by the end of the delivery (maturity) month for a contract. This is accomplished either by executing offsetting trades (round turn), or by actual delivery and receipt of the underlying commodity. Delivery and payment occur through the market's clearinghouse.

Generally, only 1 to 2% of all futures contracts created result in actual delivery. Futures transactions are principally undertaken for either speculative gain or hedging protection, and *not* for the acquisition or sale of the underlying commodity. However, delivery in settlement of futures transactions does serve a positive economic purpose in that it assures the *convergence* of the futures price and the cash price of the commodity at the contract's expiration.

The delivery mechanism for the KCBT–VLA stock index futures is a funds settlement, or more loosely, a "cash delivery." No securities or warehouse receipts are deliverable under this system. The Value Line Composite Average (VLA), an index of stock prices, acts as the "underlying commodity" for this contract. An index is merely an abstract mathematical entity, a dimensionless ratio.

In this system, convergence of the futures price with the "cash market price" is automatic in that the final *settlement* price equals the *actual (spot) VLA index value* on the last trading day of the expiring contract. The *delivery price* is *not* determined in the trading pit but by the actual cash market, by the closing prices of the 1,700 "spot" components which comprise the VLA index. With this mechanism, there is no advantage to either longs or shorts for the final "pit price" to differ from the actual VLA spot index. All open contracts are "marked to the market," the *cash* market, on the last day of trading. Finally, since U.S. funds (i.e., wire transfers) constitute the "deliverable supply," there are no concerns about manipulation, "squeezes," or "corners."

SHORT-HEDGING USES OF THE CONTRACT. In addition to the protection of equity portfolio holdings, other potential short hedgers in a stock index futures contract are listed below:

1. Someone tendering stock, but unsure whether or not the tender was accepted.
2. Buyers of call options and sellers of puts.
3. A corporation issuing rights for new stock might wish to "hedge" against a market decline during the financing period.
4. Investment bankers and underwriters of new issues.

5. Executors of estates, "locked-in" to a given portfolio during the period of probate, might opt to protect stock values with a short hedge.
6. Specialists and brokers, "market makers," who normally carry large common stock inventory positions.

LONG HEDGING. Hedging on the "long" side (i.e., buying a forward maturity) is appropriate for mitigating risk in a variety of circumstances. The most obvious long-hedge position is for someone currently or prospectively "short stock."

Similarly, specialists, dealers, or brokers who "make the market" in particular issues often find it necessary to be in a net "short" position to maintain orderly trading. Also, sellers of "naked" calls, or buyers of puts, could "hedge long" by buying a forward maturity of the stock index contract. The predominant use of the long hedge, however, would generally involve "anticipatory" transactions or positions to be established in the future. Potential users of a long hedge include:

1. Institutions which receive funds on a relatively regular basis. They could use the long hedge to improve the timing of establishing long positions in stocks (also dealers who commit to provide future delivery of securities to large institutional buyers).
2. An institution switching large positions, a process that might occur over a period of time. It could hedge long (or short) during the transition.
3. Foreign investors in U.S. stocks, who have restrictions on the rate at which capital can be liberated from their countries.
4. A firm planning to grow by acquisitions. It could use a long hedge to offset the risk of a market rise in target company stocks; on the other side, the seller of a company whose transaction is fixed in dollar terms might wish to retain future stock purchasing power by buying the stock index contract.

More theoretical treatments of hedging with stock index futures can be found in Weiner (1981) and in Figlewski and Kon (1982).

TERMS AND CONDITIONS OF THE CONTRACTS. Basically the three stock index futures contracts—KCBT, CME, and NYFE—are very similar in their specifications. All three are "sized" at 500 times the futures prices, which in effect are the respective cash index values (identical at contract maturity). The major differences among the contracts relate to the last trading day for each and daily price change limits (see comparative specifications in Table 4).

Minimum customer margins are set by each exchange. The initial speculative margin, through informal suggestion by the Federal Reserve Board, was set at about 10% of each contract's value when trading began. The comparative contract specifications are shown in Table 4.

THE UNDERLYING STOCK MARKET INDICATORS

The "underlying commodities" for the three stock index futures contracts are the Value Line Composite Average (KCBT), the S&P 500 (CME), and the New

TABLE 4. Stock Index Futures Contracts: Contract Specifications

KCBT: Kansas City Board of Trade–Value Line Index.
CME: Chicago Mercantile Exchange–Standard & Poor's 500 Index.
NYFE: New York Futures Exchange–New York Stock Exchange Composite Index.

Size of contract and price quotations	All three are 500 times the respective index value: e.g., KBCT, 130 × 500 = \$65,000; CME, 115 × 500 = \$57,500; and NYFE, 70 × 500 = \$35,000.
Trading hours	10:00 a.m.–4:15 p.m. Eastern time; 9:00 a.m.–3:15 p.m. Central time (all three contracts)
Minimum price change	0.05 × 500 = \$25 (all contracts)
Daily price change limits	KCBT, none initially, \$5 limit instituted August 1982; CME, \$5 (changed from \$3 on July 6, 1982); and NYFE, none.
Delivery months	March, June, September, and December (plus 2 additional maturities, same cycle—all contracts)
Last day of trading	KCBT, last business day of delivery month; CME, third Thursday of delivery month; and NYFE, next-to-last business day of delivery month.
Delivery	All three contracts are settled in cash, marked-to-market at the closing value of the respective underlying "spot" stock market index on the last day of trading.
Settlement	Business day following last trading day, in U.S. funds. All contracts settled to 0.01 (\$5) in terms of cash index.
Margins	Minimum customer margins are set by each exchange.

York Stock Exchange Composite Index (NYFE). The novelty of utilizing an index as the basis for a futures contract is more apparent than real. Learned students of futures markets recognize that for some years the bases of several existing futures contracts could have been interpreted as "indexes."

For example, the soybean oil contract has been characterized as an index representation for other oils hedged in that market, including cottonseed oil and palm oil. In addition, the GNMA and U.S. Treasury-bond futures contracts are more comprehensively viewed as representative of a wide range of long-term debt instruments.

Moreover, delivery terms permitting partial financial settlements and the substitution of different qualities and locations suggest the "index" characteristic of many contracts. One contract allows for complete financial settlement (delivery), if the buyer so chooses. Finally, Eurodollar futures contracts, approved by the CFTC in 1981, are explicitly based on an index.

Both the S&P 500 and the NYSE Index are *capitalization-weighted* indexes. That is, each stock's price in the index is weighted by its number of shares outstanding. Stocks of large, "heavily capitalized" companies tend to have significant influence on the movement of the indexes. The NYSE Composite Index, by definition, consists of all stocks listed on the New York Stock Exchange. The S&P 500 is composed of the prices of 400 industrials, 20 transportation companies, 40 utilities, and 40 financial institutions. The market value of the S&P 500 is nearly 80% of the NYSE Index; thus, it is apparent that the same few stocks dominate the movement of both indexes. Table 5 shows this correspondence in statistical terms; the S&P 500 and the NYSE Index have a correlation of 0.99 in almost all of the years shown: 1962–1982.

The Value Line Composite Average has a number of interesting features. First, the issues covered by the index account for over 96% of all dollar trading volume in U.S. equity markets. Second, the geometric averaging procedure provides a distortion-free measure of successive percentage changes in stock prices. This procedure gives equal weight to the percentage fluctuations in the prices of all stocks, regardless of their price levels, or total market value.

With some exceptions (e.g., 1972) Table 5 shows that for the most part, the Value Line Average is generally highly correlated with other market barometers

TABLE 5. Major Stock Market Indicators[a]

Annual correlation coefficients, weekly close, 1962–1982

Year	*R*(VL,DJ)	*R*(VL,SP)	*R*(VL,NY)	*R*(DJ,SP)	*R*(DJ,NY)	*R*(SP,NY)
1962	0.974	0.989	0.987	0.995	0.997	0.999
1963	0.908	0.938	0.935	0.983	0.986	0.999
1964	0.982	0.966	0.991	0.962	0.990	0.971
1965	0.960	0.955	0.971	0.992	0.994	0.995
1966	0.972	0.982	0.984	0.987	0.985	0.999
1967	0.910	0.968	0.980	0.909	0.893	0.996
1968	0.933	0.981	0.988	0.970	0.963	0.999
1969	0.974	0.937	0.958	0.978	0.975	0.992
1970	0.489	0.749	0.830	0.931	0.879	0.991
1971	0.946	0.866	0.849	0.950	0.938	0.997
1972	−0.134	−0.284	−0.134	0.973	0.984	0.987
1973	0.960	0.975	0.986	0.981	0.986	0.993
1974	0.955	0.983	0.989	0.982	0.973	0.999
1975	0.908	0.946	0.964	0.966	0.961	0.997
1976	0.839	0.846	0.868	0.799	0.767	0.995
1977	0.299	0.507	0.610	0.945	0.913	0.992
1978	0.962	0.966	0.977	0.989	0.986	0.999
1979	0.581	0.966	0.979	0.626	0.563	0.995
1980	0.978	0.965	0.972	0.966	0.968	0.999
1981	0.909	0.882	0.919	0.955	0.944	0.993
1982	0.952	0.977	0.984	0.958	0.986	0.999

[a]VL = Value Line Composite Average; DJ = Dow Jones Industrial Average; SP = Standard & Poor's 500 Composite Index; and NY = NYSE Composite Index.

in reflecting major market movements. This latter aspect is illustrated in the regressions shown below for the decade of the 1970s. Equations (1)–(3) relate monthly returns on the New York Stock Exchange Index (NYSE, the dependent variable) to monthly returns on the Value Line Composite Index (VLA, the explanatory variable). The specification employed is the logarithmic–linear form. Cash dividends are omitted for both market indexes. The returns are not expressed in "excess of a risk-free rate, but are total returns, in terms of the underlying stocks and index "prices."

January 1970–December 1979:

$$\log(\text{NYSE}_t/\text{NYSE}_{t-1}) = 0.1406 + \underset{(28.3747)}{0.6932} \log(\text{VLA}_t/\text{VLA}_{t-1}) \quad (1)$$

(*t* ratio) (28.3747) $R^2 = 0.8628$, $F = 805.1230$

January 1970–December 1974:

$$\log(\text{NYSE}_t/\text{NYSE}_{t-1}) = 0.5293 + \underset{(19.9166)}{0.7102} \log(\text{VLA}_t/\text{VLA}_{t-1}) \quad (2)$$

(*t* ratio) (19.9166) $R^2 = 0.8629$, $F = 396.6707$

and

January 1975–December 1979:

$$\log(\text{NYSE}_t/\text{NYSE}_{t-1}) = -0.1473 + \underset{(20.3806)}{0.7035} \log(\text{VLA}_t/\text{VLA}_{t-1}) \quad (3)$$

(*t* ratio) (20.3806) $R^2 = 0.8683$, $F = 415.3684$

As Eqs. (1)–(3) show, the monthly returns for the VLA and NYSE indexes are highly correlated, in about the same degree for the entire 1970–1979 period, and for the two 5-year subintervals as well. The "beta" regression coefficients of roughly 0.7 indicate that a given percentage change in the VLA Index, on the average, was associated with a smaller corresponding change in the NYSE Index. That is, the equal-weighted VLA Index was more volatile than the capitalization-weighted NYSE Index and the S&P 500 as well (due to the high 0.99+ intercorrelation of the NYSE and S&P and their similar construction).

With respect to the equal weighting and broad coverage of the Value Line Composite Index, it is important to recognize that the rationale for choosing any particular weighting scheme depends upon the purpose of the index. In this regard, an important clarification is that the market *portfolio* of the Capital Asset Pricing Model is a different and distinct concept from the market *factor*. It is only the latter, in the terminology of portfolio theory, which has been distinguished as the systematic influence affecting stock prices. Benjamin King (1966) stressed that a well-designed representation of the "market factor" should be insensitive to the noise resulting from news that is pertinent only to individual firms.

Lorie and Hamilton (1973) suggest that an index should be value weighted (i.e., capitalization weighted) for *indicating changes* in the *aggregate market* value of stocks. Thus "changes in general market value are more important for studies of relationships between stock prices and other things in the national economy." Value-weighted indexes are also "macroconsistent" with the total aggregate value of stock holdings. As mentioned earlier, value-weighted indexes attach great importance to a relatively few large companies.

Equal-weighted indexes according to Lorie and Hamilton, are "more appropriate for indicating movements in the prices of typical or average stocks," and "are better indicators of the *expected* change in the prices of stocks selected at random" (1973, p. 55).

They observed that "although long-run movements are similar, indexes may differ markedly over short periods of time. This is reflected both in turning points and volatility. On one occasion, there was a significant difference in the turning points of the market as a whole as measured by a comprehensive equal-weighted index and the Dow Jones Averages or Standard & Poor's Indexes. In 1929 the equal-weighted index reached its peak 6 months before the month-end peak in the other two. This suggests that the prices of stocks in relatively small companies turned down before the prices of stocks in large companies. In this instance at least, the use of the index giving greater weight to small companies could have had enormous value. The equal-weighted index also reached its trough in 1932, 1 month before either of the other two indexes. All other turning points occurred in the same month" (p. 68).

That observation appeared in the Lorie and Hamilton book, which was published in 1973, and was obviously written a year or two preceding. In more recent retrospect, the Value Line Composite (VLA) Index "peaked" in early 1972, equaling its 1971 high. Then the equal-weighted VLA turned down fully 8–10 months before the Dow, S&P, and NYSE began to reflect the bear market decline of 1973–1974.

THEORETICAL CONSIDERATIONS

There is an immense literature on capital market theory and related empirical testing. While an extensive survey is well beyond the scope of this chapter, some distinctions and clarifications are important for understanding the application of a stock index futures contract. However, only the briefest of summaries must suffice (see "Bibliography" of this chapter).

Modern portfolio theory is usually dated from the studies of Harry Markowitz (1952) which showed that an individual who maximizes "expected utility inevitably chooses a diversified portfolio which is efficient in terms of the mean and variance of returns" (Sarnat, 1974, p. 1,241). In order to implement the Markowitz technique, however, one "requires a vector of estimated expected yields for the securities under consideration and also a matrix of estimated variances and covariances" (King, 1966, p. 165).

Sharpe's contribution reduced the dimensionality problem of the portfolio variance-covariance matrix by regressing the returns of individual stocks on a single market index. Each stock's return is then decomposed into common (i.e., market factor), or "systematic," and unique, or "unsystematic," components. Off-diagonal elements of the matrix thereby take on values of zero.

This method has been extended as an explanation for the equilibrium conditions attendant to the pricing of all capital assets. The theory, dubbed the Capital Asset Pricing Model (CAPM), is formulated in *ex ante* terms, but testable only from *ex post* data. The measure of systematic risk in the CAPM is the "beta" coefficient β generally obtained from the following regression equation (or a variant thereof). The expected return for asset i (or portfolio p), $E(R_i)$, is expressed as

$$E(R_i) - R_f = \beta_i[E(R_m) - R_f] \tag{4}$$

where R_f is the risk-free borrowing and lending rate and β_i is defined as covariance (R_i,R_m)/variance R_m, where R_m is the return on the "market portfolio"—which strictly speaking includes *all wealth* whose return is uncertain.[1]

Two important clarifications relate to Eq. (4). One is that the relationship is two-dimensional. The regression estimate of beta indicates the degree of responsiveness of the security's (or portfolio's) return to that of the market. Often interpreted as an elasticity parameter, a coefficient of 1.0 implies "systematic" returns variability equal to the market's. Similarly, coefficients less than 1.0 imply less than proportional systematic returns, and those greater than 1.0 imply more.

The other dimension of Eq. (4) is the *extent* of market dependency, as measured by the R^2 statistic, the coefficient of determination. For individual securities, that proportion of return variability "explained" by the market ranged from about 76 to 2% as shown in Table 1. For portfolios, the introductory discussion suggested that almost all of the return variability would be due to the market, *if* the portfolios were efficiently diversified.

The second clarification regarding Eq. (4) is that the market *portfolio* of the CAPM is a different and distinct concept from the market *factor*. It is only the latter, in the terminology of portfolio theory, which has been distinguished as the systematic influence affecting stock prices.

The distinction in this regard is crucial between the market *portfolio m* and the market *factor* μ. The two are not *identical*. The return on the market portfolio, R_m, is then

$$R_m = \sum_j x_{jm}(a_j + b_j\mu + u_j)$$

where x_{jm} is the total market value of all outstanding shares in firm i divided by the total market value of all outstanding shares of all firms. Fama (1971, p. 46) has shown that even if a scale is chosen such that $\Sigma x_{jm}b_j = 1$, from the above equation,

$$R_m = \Sigma x_{jm}a_j + \mu + \Sigma x_{jm}u_j$$

so that the return on the market portfolio, R_m, is μ, the market factor, *plus* the additional terms involving a_j and u_j.

In any event, estimates of β in Eq. (4) necessarily involve past (*ex post*) data. The extent to which such estimates can be relied upon as predictors for the future

[1]Cf. Sharpe (1970) and especially Friend and Blume (1970) for an excellent discussion of the CAPM assumptions. The systematic risk of a portfolio, β_p, is equal to average systematic risk of its component securities, weighted by their proportionate value of the portfolio; that is, $\beta_p = \text{Cov}(R_p,R_m)/\text{Var}(R_m) = \Sigma x_i\beta_i$, where x_i is the proportion invested in security i; R_p and R_m are the returns on the particular portfolio and the market portfolio, respectively.

is always subject to uncertainty. Benjamin King, one of the earlier investigators of the Markowitz model, cautioned about the dangers of extrapolating from the past: "The main objection, however, is that changes in the characteristics of firms may prevent historical behavior from being applicable to the future" (1966, p. 165). (And also the perceptions of investors about the extent and actual significance of these changed characteristics.)

THE "MARKET FACTOR." King's model specified that the first difference in the logarithm of a stock's price change was functionally related as a linear combination of factors. The basic random variable for the security, *j*, was defined as

$$Y_{jt} = \log\left(\frac{\text{price}_{jt}}{\text{price}_{jt-1}}\right) = \log(P_{jt}) - \log(P_{jt-1})$$

that is, "the first difference in the logarithm of the prices of security *j*, observed at time *t*" (1966, pp. 143–144). Using the Guttman–Harris method of factor analysis, this methodology provided a view such that each change in log price consisted of two main parts, a *systematic* part and a *unique* part. This quantification of an estimated market factor was expressed as a column of normalized eigenvectors.

King's results suggested that the market effect accounted for about 50% of the observed security-return variance and industry effects for only about 10%. He cautioned, however, that the Sharpe "diagonalization" process may result in an oversimplification of the true relationships among residual yields (1966, p. 166). It must be kept in mind then that the "market model" is a simplifying (computational) algorithm intended to reduce the dimensionality. However, since the empirical evidence is overwhelming to the effect that security prices (and thus returns) tend to move up and down together, it might reasonably be thought that they are affected by a common market factor (Aber, 1973, p. 11).

King then compared his estimate of the "market factor" to an existing index for the period involved in the analysis: June 1927–December 1960. For this comparison, the Standard & Poor's Index of 90 stocks was chosen due to its "ready availability" (1927–1957), and the S&P 500 (1957–1960). The S&P series was transformed as follows: "The first difference in the logarithm of its values is calculated and then this variable is standardized by subtracting its mean and dividing by its standard deviation in order to make it comparable with the market factor" (1966, p. 161).

King found a high degree of correlation between his series and the transformed S&P 90/500 series, the lowest value being 0.9072 for the fourth subperiod of August 1952–December 1960. His analysis showed "how it is possible to estimate the market factor and employ this quanity as an indicator of the direction and magnitude of change in log price that affects *all securities* to some degree. . . . Although our conclusions are only tentative, it appears that a large number of stocks is unnecessary for an index of market change *if* one can weight the component stocks according to their association with the appropriate factor or factors that we choose to call the market" (1966, p. 167).

THE ECONOMETRICS: SUMMARY. There are various regression problems inherent in estimating the parameters of the linear CAPM specification. The significance of these statistical difficulties is that estimators B of β must be interpreted with some caution. The extent and implications of these problems are summarized below.

First, the true "market factor" μ is never observable, even later. The use of the "return on the market portfolio," R_m, introduces a proxy variable, with all of the accompanying errors-in-variables complications. The application of ordinary least-squares yields biased and inconsistent estimates of α and β, for individual securities (cf. Johnston, 1963, p. 149).

Second, the error components do not "average out" in calculating portfolio risk levels. It has been shown that when portfolios are formed on the basis of estimated security β coefficients, portfolio βs ("risk levels") contain a systematic bias, "even if the estimation functions for the individual securities are unbiased" (Frankfurter, 1974, p. 412). It should be added that "bias alone, of course, does not invalidate an estimator. But appropriate caveats should accompany such estimates" (Frankfurter 1974, p. 414).

Third, the econometric problems are compounded when both errors in variables and autocorrelated disturbance terms are present. Scott and Brown show that under these conditions, application of ordinary least squares produces *unstable* and *biased* estimates of β. More important, the instability can be observed in the regression coefficients "even if *true* betas are *constant* over time" (1980, p. 55).

QUANTIFYING THE MARKET FACTOR. The previous discussion indicated that the market factor and market portfolio are different theoretical concepts. Strictly speaking, the "return on the market portfolio" of the capital asset pricing model refers to an all-wealth perspective. Indeed, some investigators have found evidence of market imperfections (or perhaps institutional segmentation), which have persisted over significantly long periods of time, with respect to the risks and returns of common stocks vis-à-vis both government and corporate bonds (Sarnat, 1974).

This result also seems to account for the observed differences in the "market price of risk" among various asset types reported by Friend and Blume (1975). And again, even within the narrower context of only stocks the market factor and market portfolio remain two different and distinct concepts, as demonstrated by Fama (1971).

In this regard, King's approach to the (normative) design of an index number of security prices is enlightening: "Most of the discussion of the adequacy and appropriateness of such a measure has been in terms of a problem in *descriptive statistics,* that is, the construction of a number that will summarize the cross section of prices or price changes and enable us somehow to see at a glance what is going on within the market. . . . Few builders of index numbers have explicitly viewed these measures as functions on a set of jointly distributed random variables, making possible the *contemplation of a statistical distribution* for the index number itself. Implicit in this proposed correlation study is the isolation of a market-wide impact on price changes and the estimation of the loadings of that effect in the changes for the various securities. If one is interested in an index of price change that shows what the market as a whole is doing, then a good index would be one that is highly correlated with that part of the changes in anticipation that is felt throughout the market; and it should be relatively *insensitive* to the noise resulting from news that is pertinent only to *individual* firms" (1966, p. 143).

Further, King commented on the design of such an optimal index number: "One should aim for an index number or average that is maximally correlated with the part of each security's movement that results from a market-wide change. Furthermore, it would be undesirable to allow securities with large components of unique variance to carry much weight in the index" (1966, p. 161).

With regard to isolating this market-wide impact statistically, Pettit and Westerfield hypothesized that there may in fact be more than *one* market factor. If a security's price represents the discounted future stream of expected earnings, "two market-wide factors will determine asset returns, namely, an earnings factor and a capitalization rate factor" (1974, p. 590). The β coefficient β_i can then be seen as a weighted average of the security's earnings beta β_{ei} and the respective capitalization rate beta β_{ci} or

$$\beta_i = \chi\beta_{ei} + (1 - x)\beta_{ci}$$

(Pettit and Westerfield, 1974, p. 591).

EQUAL WEIGHTING. With regard to the use of stock market indicators as a yardstick for portfolio performance, Latané and Tuttle (1970) have suggested that a value-weighted construction is not necessarily appropriate. "Questions have been raised from time to time as to how rational it is to compare portfolio performance with value-weighted measures. It has been argued that investors do not consciously attempt to invest in an individual stock in an amount proportionate to its aggregate market value relative to that of all other stocks in the portfolio. They would be more likely to distribute their net worth in approximately equal dollar amounts in industries with highly favorable expected returns relative to expected risk. . . . But they would not concentrate their investments in IBM, AT&T, GM, and Jersey Standard simply because these stocks have large common stock capitalizations" (p. 170).

Similarly, Fisher's comments about index weighting are worth noting:

> Although holders of common stocks as a whole (including corporations whose own stocks are listed) must have their holdings distributed proportionally to the market value of all shares outstanding, there is no need for any particular investor to distribute his own holdings in this manner or any reason to believe that those shares in existing portfolios that were acquired during any particular period of time are so distributed. . . . In the indexes presented here a given relative change in the price of one stock has the same effect on the index as an equal relative change in the price of any other common stock on the New York Stock Exchange. Thus an increase of 10 per cent in the price of the stock of any company has an effect on the index that is independent of either the size of the company that issued the stock or the absolute price of the stock.
>
> This is the method of allocation in our previously published studies. Its justification may be summarized by pointing out that the individual investor may allocate his resources any way he pleases. If the resources used to own common stock listed on the New York Stock Exchange were distributed at random among the stocks by the individual investor, the number of dollars' worth of each stock held would be expected to be equal independent of the number of shares a company had outstanding or of the price of each share." (1966, p. 195)

Finally, in this regard, Bogue's approach to quantifying "the market return" is also instructive:

> Throughout this study the *equally weighted average return* of all common stocks listed on the New York Stock Exchange has been taken as the return on the market. This, of course, represents only a surrogate for the true market return. For there are many securities not listed on the New York Stock Exchange, and there are other assets available to investors not represented by any securities, certain real estate for example. Furthermore, in the true market portfolio securities are weighted in proportion to their total value outstanding. However, it has been repeatedly shown that all extremely well-diversified portfolios are very highly correlated and represent a good surrogate for the market. (1973, p. 1)

These considerations seem to imply that a value or capitalization-weighted index may not be the most efficient proxy for representing the *market factor*.

STOCK INDEX FUTURES STATISTICAL PRICE SUMMARY

Actual trading of stock index futures contracts began on February 24, 1982 at the Kansas City Board of Trade. The Chicago Mercantile Exchange followed with the S&P contract on April 21, and the New York Futures Exchange began trading on May 6, 1982. While trading has been fairly active on all three exchanges, only an abbreviated history of actual futures prices exists at the time of this writing. Sophisticated analyses will have to await longer data series. However, some statistical descriptions and estimates can be indicated.

One question which had been asked repeatedly during the 3- to 4-year approval delay can now be answered. That question concerned the profile of forward maturity prices: would the more forward prices show increasing premiums over the nearby contracts and the cash index? Or would the profile of forward maturity prices ever show discounts, that is, less than the current cash index value? The answer is both, and variants thereof.

On June 14, 1982, for example, the forward maturities for all three stock index futures contracts, KCBT, CME, and NYFE, closed at discounts to the respective cash ("spot") indexes. On the other hand, on May 20, 1982 all forward maturities closed at premiums to the cash indexes. On other days, some maturities have been at discounts, while other maturities have shown slight premiums; "V"-shaped forward price profiles are not uncommon. In general, even when at a discount from the cash index, more distant maturities tend to reflect higher premiums.

Initially some analysts thought that the futures price profile of stock index contracts would reflect a normal "cost-of-carry" relationship, possibly as a function of the "risk-free" interest rate. Rather, at least in the incipient stages of trading, the pricing of forward maturities seems to be more consistent with an "expectational" hypothesis of the future value(s) of the underlying cash index. However, the most common profile pattern of futures prices does reflect premiums to the cash indexes.

CASH INDEXES: 1982. The initial year of actual trading of stock index futures contracts, 1982, was a year of fairly dramatic market movements and volatility.

From the beginning of 1982 until mid-August, the stock market was in a rather unglamorous "free fall," with but a minor respite during the early spring, March to May. On August 17th the market suddenly turned around: the Dow Jones Industrial Average (DJIA) gained 38.81 points that day, and stock prices rallied almost without interruption throughout the remainder of the year.

The statistics shown in Table 6 for the stock market indexes underlying the futures contracts have been segmented by periods conforming to the contracts' maturities. Period I, May 6 to June 17, is dated from the time when all three contracts were "up and trading" to the date of earliest delivery for the June 1982 maturity, the CME/S&P contract. The other two contracts, KCBT and NYFE, do not expire until about the month-end; unfortunately, this aspect distorts the comparisons somewhat. The CME contract converges to the cash index about 10 to 12 days before the other contracts mature. However, this distortion is not material, as we find out in the analysis of the daily price movements of the futures.

Period II, June 18 to September 16, covers the maturity of the September 1982 contracts, again pegged to the CME maturity date. In addition, Period II is divided into two subperiods: IIa, June 18 to August 16, the "tail" of the bear market, and IIb, August 17 to September 16, the beginning of the great bull market rally of 1982. Period III, September 17 to December 16, covers the maturity period for the December 1982 contracts. The data discussed in this chapter are also generally segmented along the same lines.

As is apparent in Table 6, the volatility of these indexes decreased both absolutely (standard deviations) and relatively (coefficients of variation) until August 17, at which time the turnaround in the market resulted in substantially higher measured volatility. Generally, the order of variability among the three indexes (the coefficients of variation) remained very close in all of the periods and subperiods. The minor exception was the Value Line Composite Index (VLIC) in Periods I and III, when the coefficient of variation measure showed some small increase over the other two. Notice also in Table 6 that the variability of the S&P and New York Stock Exchange (NYSE) indexes increased over the VLIC in Period II as a whole, suggesting that the heavier capitalized, larger company stocks became relatively more volatile in the early part of the market's rise (i.e., coefficients of variation in Period II were larger). However, as noted above, the VLIC caught up and passed the other two, in terms of variation in Period III.

A similar analysis of relative variability (coefficient of variation) among the daily futures prices of the stock index contracts appear in Tables 7, 8, and 9. These tables are organized with respect to the June, September, and December 1982 maturities as before, again with subperiods IIa and IIb, shown in Table 8. In addition to the closing (settlement) futures prices, these tables include the correspondence relationships among the daily high and low futures prices, as well. This additional dimension was included to investigate whether the closing price relationships obsured some important range aspects (high–low). As the tables readily disclose, each contract's high and low variations are well reflected by the close settlement prices. The sets of coefficients of variation differ only at the third decimal point, if at all.

Similarly, for each maturity set, and subperiod segmentation, the coefficients of variation of the CME/NYFE/KCBT contracts are nearly identical. The only exception appears in Table 9 for Period III. As noted for the VLIC cash index,

TABLE 6. Spot Indexes, Stock Market Indicators Underlying Stock Index Futures Contracts, Daily Observations

Index	Mean ($\overline{X}$)	Standard Deviation (s)	Coefficient of Variation ($s/\overline{X}$)
	Period I: May 6–June 17, 1982		
VLIC	126.021	4.766	.038
S&P	113.549	3.681	.032
NYSE	65.413	2.168	.033
	Period IIa: June 18–August 16, 1982		
VLIC	118.626	2.792	.024
S&P	108.038	2.687	.025
NYSE	62.062	1.517	.024
	Period IIb: August 17–September 16, 1982		
VLIC	128.196	5.319	.041
S&P	118.304	4.798	.041
NYSE	67.818	2.757	.041
	Period II (overall): June 18–September 16, 1982		
VLIC	121.968	5.980	.049
S&P	111.623	6.066	.054
NYSE	64.072	3.422	.053
	Period III: September 17–December 16, 1982 (III)		
VLIC	149.145	9.770	.066
S&P	134.140	6.712	.050
NYSE	77.209	3.975	.051

TABLE 7. Futures Prices—June 1982 Contracts—Daily Observations, Period I: May 6–June 17, 1982

Futures Price	Mean ($\overline{X}$)	Standard Deviation (s)	Coefficient of Variation ($s/\overline{X}$)
KCBT—settlement	124.900	5.168	.041
KCBT—high	125.910	5.028	.040
KCBT—low	124.327	5.336	.043
CME—settlement	113.222	4.079	.036
CME—high	114.182	3.991	.035
CME—low	112.613	4.168	.037
NYFE—settlement	65.155	2.450	.038
NYFE—high	65.665	2.310	.035
NYFE—low	64.820	2.526	.039

TABLE 8. Futures Prices—September 1982 Contracts—Daily Observations

Futures Price	Mean ($\overline{X}$)	Standard Deviation (s)	Coefficient of Variation ($s/\overline{X}$)
	Period IIa: June 18–August 16, 1982		
KCBT—settlement	118.407	3.863	.033
KCBT—high	119.623	3.655	.031
KCBT—low	117.196	3.864	.033
CME—settlement	109.161	3.707	.034
CME—high	110.306	3.481	.032
CME—low	107.912	3.656	.034
NYFE—settlement	62.734	2.175	.035
NYFE—high	63.415	2.057	.032
NYFE—low	62.026	2.164	.035
	Period IIb: August 17–September 16, 1982		
KCBT—settlement	128.471	5.234	.041
KCBT—high	129.714	5.180	.040
KCBT—low	126.448	5.801	.046
CME—settlement	118.304	4.798	.041
CME—high	119.456	4.946	.041
CME—low	116.211	5.485	.047
NYFE—settlement	67.859	2.757	.041
NYFE—high	68.605	2.748	.040
NYFE—low	66.709	3.084	.046

TABLE 9. Futures Prices—September 1982 and December 1982 Contracts—Daily Observations

Futures Price	Mean ($\overline{X}$)	Standard Deviation (s)	Coefficient of Variation ($s/\overline{X}$)
	Period II: June 18–September 16, 1982		
KCBT—settlement	121.921	6.503	.053
KCBT—high	123.147	6.421	.052
KCBT—low	120.427	6.387	.053
CME—settlement	112.308	5.983	.053
CME—high	113.502	5.952	.052
CME—low	110.810	5.892	.053
NYFE—settlement	64.072	3.422	.053
NYFE—high	65.227	3.392	.052
NYFE—low	63.661	3.363	.053
	Period III: September 17–December 16, 1982		
KCBT—settlement	149.298	10.384	.070
KCBT—high	151.012	10.711	.071
KCBT—low	147.625	10.289	.070
CME—settlement	134.564	7.305	.054
CME—high	136.268	7.556	.055
CME—low	133.022	7.202	.054
NYFE—settlement	77.486	4.314	.056
NYFE—high	78.492	4.466	.057
NYFE—low	76.521	4.197	.055

the December 1982 KCBT contract exhibited higher relative variation (.07 versus .05 for CME and NYFE).

The regression equations fitted to the daily futures price data are summarized in Tables 10, 11, and 12. The estimates relate to the various corresponding maturities and subperiods IIa and IIb. Here again, the high and low relationships did not differ materially from the correlations and $\hat{B}$'s of the closing-settlement price equations. The higher variation in the KCBT June 1982 contract's coefficients (Period I) declined relative to the CME and NYFE September 1982 contracts in Period IIa ($\hat{B}$). That relative decrease seemed to hold throughout Period II, although in IIb, the KCBT/NYFE $\hat{B}$ regression coefficient increased slightly. As expected from the coeffficients of variation in Table 9, the KCBT December 1982 contract increased in price volatility, relative to the CME and NYFE (Period III). For the CME, $\hat{B}$ increased from around 1.08 in Period II to 1.34 in Period III for the KCBT maturity; relative to the NYFE, the KCBT $\hat{B}$ increased from 1.9 in Period II to over 2.3 in Period III.

The regression coefficients for the CME/NYFE price relationships, as in the case for the respective cash indexes, remained at about 1.7 for all 1982 maturities, and the subperiods. The R^2 values for the futures prices relationships also correspond closely, generally suggesting almost "perfect positive" correlation. Again, the only exception was the KCBT Period III change in volatility, which resulted in R^2 values for KCBT/NYFE and KCBT/CME relationships of about .90.

TABLE 10. Futures Price Regressions, Stock Index Contracts by Contract Maturity, Daily Observations

Dependent Variable (Y)	Regression Coefficient ($\hat{B}$)	Explanatory Variable (X)	R^2
Contract: June 1982; Period I: May 6–June 17, 1982			
KCBT—settlement	1.259	CME—settlement	.988
KCBT—high	1.252	CME—high	.986
KCBT—low	1.273	CME—low	.990
KCBT—settlement	2.102	NYFE—settlement	.992
KCBT—high	2.169	NYFE—high	.992
KCBT—low	2.105	NYFE—low	.994
CME—settlement	1.663	NYFE—settlement	.998
CME—high	1.724	NYFE—high	.996
CME—low	1.647	NYFE—low	.996
Contract: September 1982; Period IIa: June 18–August 16, 1982			
KCBT—settlement	1.029	CME—settlement	.993
KCBT—high	1.038	CME—high	.977
KCBT—low	1.043	CME—low	.974
KCBT—settlement	1.751	NYFE—settlement	.972
KCBT—high	1.749	NYFE—high	.968
KCBT—low	1.760	NYFE—low	.971
CME—settlement	1.702	NYFE—settlement	.997
CME—high	1.689	NYFE—high	.996
CME—low	1.687	NYFE—low	.997

TABLE 11. Futures Price Regressions, Stock Index Contracts by Contract Maturity, Daily Observations

Dependent Variable (Y)	Regression Coefficient ($\hat{B}$)	Explanatory Variable (X)	R^2
Contract: September 1982; Period IIb: August 17–September 16			
KCBT—settlement	1.062	CME—settlement	.993
KCBT—high	1.044	CME—high	.993
KCBT—low	1.055	CME—low	.996
KCBT—settlement	1.911	NYFE—settlement	.992
KCBT—high	1.874	NYFE—high	.987
KCBT—low	1.879	NYFE—low	.997
CME—settlement	1.796	NYFE—settlement	.994
CME—high	1.790	NYFE—high	.990
CME—low	1.777	NYFE—low	.998
Contract: September 1982; Period II: June 18–September 16, 1982			
KCBT—settlement	1.082	CME—settlement	.991
KCBT—high	1.075	CME—high	.993
KCBT—low	1.080	CME—low	.992
KCBT—settlement	1.897	NYFE—settlement	.990
KCBT—high	1.882	NYFE—high	.989
KCBT—low	1.890	NYFE—low	.990
CME—settlement	1.752	NYFE—settlement	.997
CME—high	1.752	NYFE—high	.996
CME—low	1.751	NYFE—low	.998

TABLE 12. Futures Price Regressions, Stock Index Contracts by Contract Maturity, Daily Observations

Dependent Variable (Y)	Regression Coefficient ($\hat{B}$)	Explanatory Variable (X)	R^2
Contract: December 1982; Period III: September 17–December 16, 1982			
KCBT—settlement	1.339	CME—settlement	.888
KCBT—high	1.342	CME—high	.896
KCBT—low	1.351	CME—low	.895
KCBT—settlement	2.297	NYFE—settlement	.911
KCBT—high	2.295	NYFE—high	.916
KCBT—low	2.353	NYFE—low	.921
CME—settlement	1.687	NYFE—settlement	.993
CME—high	1.687	NYFE—high	.993
CME—low	1.709	NYFE—low	.992

RATIONALE FOR STOCK INDEX FUTURES CONTRACTS. Systematic risk is never observable, even later. Nonetheless, stock index futures contracts provide risk-reduction potential based simply on the observation that all stock prices tend to fluctuate together. This means that every stock price has a positive systematic component. While β estimates may be useful for some purposes, the precision of such estimates (or lack thereof) is not the underpinning for stock index futures contracts. These contracts afford a flexible instrument for risk mitigation, portfolio "fine tuning," and timing adjustments to investors. In terms of their risk preferences and expectations, portfolio holders can more closely achieve risk efficiency (cf. Weiner, 1981, 1984).

BIBLIOGRAPHY

Aber, J. W. *Beta Coefficients and Models of Security Return.* Lexington, MA: Lexington Books, 1973.

Arrow, K. J. *Essays in the Theory of Risk-Bearing.* Chicago, IL: Markham, 1971.

Blume, M. E. "On the Assessment of Risk." *Journal of Finance,* March 1971, pp. 1–10.

Blume, M. E. "Betas and Their Regression Tendencies." *Journal of Finance,* June 1975, pp. 785–795.

Blume, M. E., Crockett, J., and Friend, I. "Stockownership in The United States: Characteristics and Trends." *Survey of Current Business,* November 1974, pp. 16–40.

Blume, M. E., and Friend, I. "A New Look at the Capital Asset Pricing Model." *Journal of Finance,* March 1973, pp. 19–33.

Blume, M. E., and Friend, I. "The Asset Structure of Individual Portfolios and Some Implications for Utility Functions." *Journal of Finance,* May 1975, pp. 585–603.

Bogue, M. C. III. *The Estimation and Behavior of Systematic Risk.* Unpublished Ph.D. dissertation, Stanford University, 1973.

Bowman, R. G. "The Theoretical Relationship Between Systematic Risk and Financial (Accounting) Variables." *Journal of Finance,* June 1979, pp. 617–630.

Caves, R. E. "Organization, Scale, and Performance of Grain Trade." *Food Research Institute Studies,* XVI, e, 1977–78, pp. 107–123.

Cohn, R. A., Lewellen, W. G., Lease, R. C., and Schlarbaum, G. G. "Individual Investor Risk Aversion and Investment Portfolio Composition." *Journal of Finance,* May 1975, pp. 605–620.

Cootner, P. H. (Ed.). *The Random Character of Stock Market Prices,* rev. ed. Cambridge, MA: MIT Press, 1964.

Cootner, P. H. "Speculation and Hedging." *Proceedings of a Symposium on Price Effects of Speculation in Organized Commodity Markets, Food Research Institute Studies,* Supplement to Vol. VII, 1967, pp. 65–104.

Ederington, L. H. "The Hedging Performance of the New Futures Markets." *Journal of Finance,* March 1979, pp. 157–170.

Fama, E. F. "Risk, Return, and Equilibrium." *Journal of Political Economy,* January 1971–February 1971, pp. 30–54.

Figlewski, S., and Kon, S. J. "Portfolio Management with Stock Index Futures." *Financial Analysts Journal,* January 1982–February 1982, pp. 3–11.

Fisher, L. "Some New Stock Market Indexes." *Journal of Business,* January 1966, pp. 191–218.

Fisher, L., and Lorie, J. H. "Some Studies of Variability of Returns on Investments in Common Stocks." *Journal of Business,* April 1970, pp. 99–134.

Frankfurter, G. M. "The Effect of 'Market Indexes' on the Ex-Post Performance of the Sharpe Portfolio Selection Model." *Journal of Finance,* June 1972, pp. 949–955.

Frankfurter, G. M., and Frecka, T. J. "Efficient Portfolios and Superfluous Diversification." *Journal of Financial and Quantitative Analysis,* December 1979, pp. 925–938.

Frankfurter, G. M., Phillips, H. E., and Seagle, J. P. "Bias in Estimating Portfolio Alpha and Beta Scores." *Review of Economics and Statistics,* August 1974, pp. 412–414.

Friend, I., and Blume, M. E. "Measurement of Portfolio Performance Under Uncertainty." *American Economic Review,* September 1970, pp. 561–575.

Friend, I., and Blume, M. E. "The Demand for Risky Assets." *American Economic Review,* December 1975, pp. 900–932.

Hadar, J., and Russell, W. R. "Rules For Ordering Uncertain Prospects." *American Economic Review,* March 1969, pp. 25–34.

Hanoch, G., and Levy, H. "Efficient Portfolio Selection With Quadratic and Cubic Utility." *Journal of Business,* April 1970, pp. 181–189.

Houthakker, H. S. "The Scope and Limits of Futures Trading." In *The Allocation of Economic Resources,* Essays in Honor of Bernard Francis Haley. Stanford, CA: Stanford Univ. Press, 1959.

Jensen, M. C. "Risk, The Pricing of Capital Assets, and the Evaluation of Investment Portfolios." *Journal of Business,* April 1969, pp. 167–247.

Johnston, J. *Econometric Methods.* New York, NY: McGraw-Hill, 1963.

King, B. F. "Market and Industry Factors in Stock Price Behavior." *Journal of Business,* January 1966, pp. 139–90.

Klemkosky, R. C., and Martin, J. D. "The Effect of Market Risk on Portfolio Diversification." *Journal of Finance,* March 1975, pp. 147–154.

Kon, S. J., and Jen, F. C. "The Investment Performance of Mutual Funds: An Empirical Investigation of Timing, Selectivity and Market Efficiency." *Journal of Business,* April 1979, pp. 263–289.

Latané, H. A., and Tuttle, D. L. *Security Analysis and Portfolio Management.* New York, NY: Ronald Press, 1970.

Levy, H. "The CAPM and Beta in an Imperfect Market." *The Journal of Portfolio Management,* Winter 1980, pp. 5–11.

Lipper, A. In Commodity Futures Trading Commission, In the Matter of "Application of Kansas City Board Of Trade For Designation As A Contract Market In Transactions For Futures Delivery Based Upon 30 Industrial Stocks Average Index." Hoover Reporting Company, Incorporated, Washington, D.C., October 25–October 26, 1978, pp. 136–142.

Lorie, J. H., and Hamilton, M. T. *The Stock Market: Theories and Evidence.* Homewood, IL: Irwin, 1973.

Markowitz, H. "Portfolio Selection." *Journal of Finance,* March 1952, pp. 77–91.

Niederhoffer, V., and Zeckhauser, R. "Market Index Futures Contracts." *Financial Analysts Journal,* January 1980–February 1980, pp. 49–55.

Pettit, R. R., and Westerfield, R. "Using the Capital Asset Pricing Model and the Market Model to Predict Security Returns." *Journal of Financial and Quantitative Analysis,* September 1974, pp. 579–607.

Sarnat, M. "Capital Market Imperfections and the Composition of Optimal Portfolios." *Journal of Finance,* September 1974, pp. 1241–1253.

Schlarbaum, G. G., Lewellen, W. G., and Lease, R. C. "Realized Returns on Common

Stock Investments: The Experience of Individual Investors.'' *Journal of Business,* April 1978, pp. 299–325.

Scott, E., and Brown, S. ''Biased Estimators and Unstable Betas.'' *Journal of Finance,* March 1980, pp. 49–55.

Sharpe, W. F. *Portfolio Theory and Capital Markets.* New York, NY: McGraw-Hill, 1970

Simkowitz, M. A., and Beedles, W. L. ''Diversification in a Three-Moment World.'' *Journal of Financial and Quantitative Analysis,* December 1978, pp. 927–941.

Simonson, D. G. ''The Speculative Behavior of Mutual Funds.'' *Journal of Finance,* May 1972, pp. 381–391.

Smith, K. V. ''Stock Price and Economic Indexes For Generating Efficient Portfolios.'' *Journal of Business,* April 1964, pp. 326–336.

Tosini, P. A., and Moriarty, E. J. ''Potential Hedging Use of a Futures Contract Based on a Composite Stock Index.'' *The Journal of Futures Markets,* Vol. 2, Spring 1982, pp. 83–103.

Tsiang, S. C. ''The Rationale of The Mean-Standard Deviation Analysis, Skewness Preference, and The Demand for Money.'' *American Economic Review,* June 1972, pp. 354–371.

Weiner, N. S. ''The Hedging Rationale for a Stock Index Futures Contract.'' *Journal of Futures Markets,* Vol. 1, Spring 1981, pp. 59–76.

Weiner, N. S. *Stock Index Futures: A Guide For Traders, Investors and Analysts,* New York, NY, John Wiley, 1984.

OTHER SOURCES OF INFORMATION Chicago Mercantile Exchange, Index and Option Market. *Inside S&P 500 Stock Index Futures,* 1982, Chicago, Illinois.

The Kansas City Board of Trade. *The Future is Here: Futures Trading and The Value Line Stock Index,* 1982, Kansas City, Missouri.

The New York Futures Exchange. *Introducing New York Stock Exchange Index Futures,* 1982, New York, New York.

The Wall Street Journal (various editions).

APPENDIX **A**

CHICAGO BOARD OF TRADE MEMBERSHIP TRANSACTIONS

Jeff Requarth

The following data itemize the individual transactions which determined membership rates for the Chicago Board of Trade from March 20, 1928 through October 19, 1982. Table 1 shows the range of transactions, from high to low, for each year, beginning in 1898.

OBTAINING MEMBERSHIP

Gaining membership on any of the U. S. commodity exchanges follows a similar procedure. One must apply, be approved, and subsequently purchase the membership. The following comments will briefly describe the qualifications and process.

ELIGIBILITY. The applicant must be 21 years of age, must not be an employee of the exchange, have good credit and reputation, and show financial responsibility. An application, obtained from the Exchange Member Services, must be filed with an accompanying application fee. This application must be signed by two member sponsors.

SPONSORS. Each sponsor must have known the applicant for at least 90 days (or be a partner or officer of a firm which had satisfactory business relations with the applicant) and must be fully informed as to the applicant's character, financial standing, integrity, and business background.

FINANCIAL REQUIREMENTS. The applicant must provide a financial statement, including assets, liabilities, and net worth. Persons not meeting the financial requirements may provide a second-party guarantee as prescribed by each exchange. The guarantee covers obligations due both the exchange and other members.

FINANCING OF MEMBERSHIPS. Applicants must pay for membership privileges from their own funds; however, an applicant who will be employed by

The Chicago Board of Trade is not responsible for compiling this information and does not vouch for its accuracy nor its completeness.

another member may arrange financing by his or her employer. It is also possible for membership title and value to be vested in a member firm.

INVESTIGATION OF APPLICANTS. Applicant names are posted for public viewing and Member Services investigates all information submitted on the application. Any intentional misstatement or omission will disqualify the application and render the applicant ineligible for future membership.

APPEARANCE BEFORE THE MEMBERSHIP BOARD. After the investigation, the applicant appears before the Membership Committee. Applicants satisfying the Membership Committee will be recommended for membership to the Board of Directors.

ACHIEVING MEMBERSHIP. After election for membership by the Board of Directors, the applicant is allowed 60 days to purchase or arrange membership transfer.

TRANSFERS. Memberships may be transferred from an existing member to a new member by filing a notice with the Board of Directors and paying a transfer fee.

PURCHASING A MEMBERSHIP. Buying and selling memberships are performed through the Exchange Association. The approved applicant submits a bid to buy and the present member submits an offer to sell to the Department of Financial Services. The bid and offer are listed at the exchange along with the last sale. These quotes may also be obtained at the exchange by telephone.

FINAL STEP. The final step in gaining membership is performed by the Financial Services Department. The approved applicant pays either the transfer amount or the agreed-upon price to the exchange, as well as a transfer fee for the membership. The exchange will then pay the seller the appropriate amount and both parties must sign the exchange ledger. The approved applicant is then a member.

TABLE 1. Membership's High and Low Prices

Year	High	Low	Year	High	Low
1898	800	665	1935	6,600	4,500
1899	910	650	1936	6,200	3,650
1900	2,100	800	1937	6,325	2,700
1901	3,000	1,950	1938	4,100	1,500
1902	4,350	3,200	1939	2,200	1,150
1903	3,750	2,650	1940	1,950	450
1904	3,925	2,925	1941	612.50	100
1905	3,350	2,850	1942	550	25
1906	3,800	1,875	1943	1,875	200
1907	2,600	1,900	1944	3,500	800
1908	2,650	2,100	1945	4,000	2,000
1909	2,600	2,300	1946	6,000	2,850
1910	3,125	2,800	1947	5,600	2,750
1911	2,850	2,125	1948	4,500	3,000
1912	2,350	2,250	1949	6,600	1,750
1913	2,200	2,000	1950	3,200	1,700
1914	2,600	2,000	1951	3,500	2,180
1915	3,500	2,450	1952	3,900	2,800
1916	7,600	3,350	1953	5,000	3,000
1917	7,000	4,000	1954	7,250	3,750
1918	6,350	3,075	1955	7,500	3,750
1919	11,100	6,050	1956	7,500	5,200
1920	10,450	5,750	1957	9,850	4,500
1921	8,400	5,500	1958	5,000	3,600
1922	7,400	5,300	1959	6,300	4,500
1923	5,475	4,550	1960	8,750	3,550
1924	8,600	3,500	1961	9,000	4,100
1925	9,200	7,500	1962	17,000	6,400
1926	6,700	6,700	1963	14,000	8,700
1927	10,600	6,500	1964	13,950	9,100
1928	45,000	8,300	1965	13,950	10,300
1929	62,000	19,000	1966	29,950	13,000
1930	20,500	7,500	1967	24,450	18,000
1931	12,475	6,000	1968	19,800	12,900
1932	9,500	3,500	1969	44,000	18,500
1933	16,000	3,750	1970	41,000	18,500
1934	9,500	5,000			

Year	High	Low	Average	Sales	Transfers
1971	36,000	27,000	33,676	88	60
1972	40,000	28,000	31,932	110	58
1973	65,000	30,000	34,783	88	47
1974	90,000	51,000	46,318	138	78
1975	125,000	77,000	70,364	139	63
1976	168,000	115,000	95,931	86	60
1977	167,000	100,000	141,636	86	76
1978	225,000	140,000	139,692	85	59
1979	259,500	215,000	173,263	86	62
1980	330,000	141,000	233,462	81	59
1981	320,000	210,000	226,488	75	58

1928

March:
20—9,100.00
22—9,000.00
28—9,000.00
28—8,700.00
High: 9,100.00
Low: 8,700.00
Average: 8,950.00
Transfers: 0
Sales: 4

April:
5—transfer
5— 8,700.00
9— 9,000.00
10— 8,300.00
11— 8,300.00
17— 8,750.00
18— 9,000.00
21—11,500.00
23—11,000.00
24— 9,500.00
24—12,000.00
24—12,000.00
28—12,500.00
28—transfer
30—15,000.00
High: 15,000.00
Low: 8,300.00
Average: 10,403.00
Transfers: 2
Sales: 13

May:
1—17,500.00
12—17,500.00
11—17,000.00
12—transfer
17—16,500.00
21—16,000.00
25—15,950.00
High: 17,500.00
Low: 15,950.00
Average: 16,744.00
Transfers: 1
Sales: 6

June:
5—15,000.00
6—14,750.00
7—14,500.00
9—14,750.00
26—13,000.00
26—12,250.00
26—transfer
High: 15,000.00
Low: 12,250.00
Average: 14,041.00
Transfers: 1
Sales: 6

July:
13—10,500.00
13—10,000.00
19—10,600.00
23—10,500.00
27—transfer
31—transfer
High: 10,600.00
Low: 10,000.00
Average: 10,400.00
Transfers: 2
Sales: 4

August:
2—transfer
3—10,000.00
18—10,500.00
10—10,000.00
14—10,500.00
18—10,600.00
21—transfer
29—transfer
High: 10,600.00
Low: 10,000.00
Average: 10,320.00
Transfers: 3
Sales: 5

September:
14—13,000.00
15—13,000.00
27—13,000.00
29—12,500.00
High: 13,000.00
Low: 12,500.00
Average: 12,875.00
Transfers: 0
Sales: 4

October:
6—13,000.00
8—13,000.00
12—13,000.00
18—12,500.00
18—13,000.00
18—13,000.00
18—13,600.00
18—13,000.00
19—13,000.00
19—14,000.00
19—15,000.00
19—16,000.00
20—17,300.00
27—18,000.00
27—18,000.00
27—17,000.00
29—17,000.00
29—17,200.00
30—18,000.00
31—17,800.00
31—18,000.00
High: 18,000.00
Low: 12,500.00
Average: 15,257.00
Transfers: 0
Sales: 21

November:
1—11,250.00
1—transfer
5—15,000.00
5—15,000.00
5—15,000.00
8—15,000.00
8—transfer
8—21,000.00
8—21,000.00
9—26,500.00
9—28,500.00
13—28,500.00
14—28,500.00
14—28,500.00
15—29,000.00
15—transfer
18—transfer
16—28,500.00
16—29,500.00
17—29,500.00
17—30,000.00
19—30,000.00
20—30,000.00
20—30,000.00
21—35,000.00
21—37,000.00

1928

21—39,500.00
21—40,000.00
22—40,000.00
22—45,000.00
23—45,000.00
23—45,000.00
24—45,000.00
24—45,000.00
26—transfer
28—38,000.00
30—40,000.00
30—40,000.00
High: 45,000.00
Low: 11,250.00
Average: 31,053.00
Transfers: 5
Sales: 33

December:
1—38,500.00
3—38,500.00
3—40,000.00
3—38,500.00
3—38,500.00
4—42,000.00
5—35,000.00
5—40,000.00
6—43,000.00
12—43,000.00
14—36,000.00
18—40,500.00
18—33,000.00
27—transfer
29—32,500.00
High: 43,000.00
Low: 32,500.00
Average: 38,464.00
Transfers: 1
Sales: 14

1929

January:
3—33,000.00
4—33,500.00
4—35,000.00
11—33,500.00
11—35,000.00
11—35,000.00
12—38,500.00
12—transfer
14—transfer
14—38,500.00
15—39,500.00
15—39,500.00
15—39,500.00
16—40,500.00
16—40,500.00
17—41,000.00
18—transfer
18—transfer
21—42,500.00
23—44,000.00
23—44,000.00
24—45,000.00
25—44,000.00
26—45,000.00
29—45,300.00
30—45,000.00
30—42,000.00
High: 45,300.00
Low: 33,000.00
Average: 39,969.00
Transfers: 4
Sales: 23

February:
18—39,000.00
26—37,000.00
28—37,500.00
High: 39,000.00
Low: 37,000.00
Average: 37,833.00
Transfers: 0
Sales: 3

March:
2—38,000.00
9—35,500.00
16—35,000.00
12—33,000.00
21—35,000.00
23—35,000.00
36—35,000.00
High: 38,000.00
Low: 33,000.00
Average: 35,214.00
Transfers: 0
Sales: 7

April:
3—35,000.00
6—transfer
10—30,000.00
12—30,000.00
13—29,500.00
15—29,500.00
15—29,500.00
24—34,000.00
24—34,500.00
25—37,500.00
26—39,700.00
27—40,500.00
29—40,650.00
High: 40,650.00
Low: 29,500.00
Average: 35,195.00
Transfers: 1
Sales: 12

May:
2—39,200.00
8—39,200.00
10—transfer
10—38,900,00
18—transfer
22—35,000.00
25—36,000.00
High: 39,200.00
Low: 35,000.00
Average: 37,660.00
Transfers: 2
Sales: 5

June:
5—34,700.00
7—30,000.00
7—34,000.00
13—31,000.00
13—30,000.00
15—30,000.00
18—30,500.00
20—transfer
20—33,000.00
24—36,800.00
High: 36,800.00
Low: 30,000.00
Average: 32,222.00
Transfers: 1
Sales: 9

July:
13—38,500.00
13—38,500.00
15—39,600.00
15—39,750.00
17—39,650.00
18—39,700.00
19—40,000.00
19—transfer
20—45,000.00
22—46,500.00
24—41,000.00
25—44,000.00
26—44,700.00
26—45,000.00
26—45,000.00
26—49,500.00
29—49,600.00
29—50,000.00
29—50,400.00
30—52,000.00
30—53,000.00
30—56,000.00
30—60,000.00
31—60,000.00
31—transfer
31—62,000.00
High: 62,000.00
Low: 38,500.00
Average: 46,339.00
Transfers: 2
Sales: 24

August:
5—58,000.00
10—58,000.00
16—50,000.00
17—58,000.00
28—55,000.00
High: 58,000.00
Low: 50,000.00
Average: 55,800.00
Transfers: 0
Sales: 5

September:
5—transfer

1929

7—transfer
10—45,000.00
13—50,000.00
14—transfer
18—50,000.00
18—50,000.00
24—transfer
24—transfer
High: 50,000.00
Low: 45,000.00
Average: 48,333.00
Transfers: 5
Sales: 4

October:
2—36,500.00
2—35,500.00
4—35,500.00
4—transfer
8—40,000.00
18—transfer
High: 40,00000
Low: 35,500.00
Average: 36,875.00
Transfers: 2
Sales: 4

November:
5—25,000.00
9—21,000.00
12—20,000.00
22—transfer
22—transfer
26—transfer
29—transfer
High: 25,000.00
Low: 20,000.00
Average: 22,000.00
Transfers: 4
Sales: 3

December:
2—20,000.00
2—20,000.00
10—transfer
12—21,000.00
13—24,000.00
16—22,500.00
18—22,000.00
21—transfer
28—20,000.00
28—20,500.00
27—transfer
31—21,000.00
31—19,000.00
31—19,000.00
High: 24,000.00
Low: 19,000.00
Average: 30,818.00
Transfers: 3
Sales: 11

1930

January:
3—transfer
8—18,000.00
8—18,000.00
8—18,000.00
9—transfer
13—transfer
15—17,000.00
16—17,000.00
25—transfer
28—16,500.00
29—18,000.00
30—transfer
High: 18,000.00
Low: 16,500.00
Average: 17,583.00
Transfers: 4
Sales: 8

February:
14—15,100.00
15—15,000.00
26—17,500.00
28—16,000.00
High: 17,500.00
Low: 15,000.00
Average: 15,900.00
Transfers: 0
Sales: 4

March:
5—17,500.00
8—18,000.00
12—18,500.00
14—transfer
17—transfer
17—transfer
29—16,000.00
High: 18,500.00
Low: 16,000.00
Average: 17,500.00
Transfers: 3
Sales: 4

April:
2—transfer
3—18,000.00
3—18,000.00
4—18,000.00
4—18,500.00
7—transfer
8—18,000.00
9—transfer
11—17,000.00
14—17,600.00
15—18,000.00
16—transfer
16—transfer
19—17,000.00
24—16,500.00
24—16,500.00
24—16,500.00
24—transfer
24—transfer
30—17,500.00
High: 18,500.00
Low: 16,500.00
Average: 17,469.00
Transfers: 7
Sales: 13

May:
6—transfer
9—16,500.00
10—transfer
12—16,000.00
14—16,300.00
14—17,500.00
15—18,800.00
15—18,800.00
16—transfer
17—20,000.00
17—transfer
19—29,500.00
High: 20,500.00
Low: 16,000.00
Average: 17,950.00
Transfers: 4
Sales: 8

June:
3—transfer
11—transfer
12—18,000.00
12—18,000.00
17—19,500.00
24—transfer
24—16,500.00
25—16,500.00
26—16,500.00
High: 19,500.00
Low: 16,500.00
Average: 17,500.00
Transfers: 3
Sales: 6

July:
1—17,000.00
1—17,000.00
10—transfer
17—17,000.00
19—transfer
21—transfer
23—18,500.00
High: 18,500.00
Low: 17,000.00
Average: 17,375.00
Transfers: 3
Sales: 4

August:
5—18,500.00
9—17,500.00
9—17,500.00
13—17,000.00
16—17,500.00
18—16,500.00
18—16,500.00
27—16,500.00
28—16,500.00
High: 18,500.00
Low: 16,500.00
Average: 17,111.00
Transfers: 0
Sales: 9

September:
4—16,000.00
10—16,000.00
15—15,500.00
15—15,000.00
29—14,000.00
29—13,500.00
30—13,500.00
High: 16,000.00
Low: 13,500.00
Average: 14,785.00
Transfers: 0
Sales: 7

October:
1—14,000.00
6—13,000.00
8—13,000.00
14—13,000.00
18—13,000.00
21—12,750.00
22—12,000.00
22—12,000.00

1930

29—12,000.00
29—12,000.00
29—12,000.00

High:	14,000.00
Low:	12,000.00
Average:	12,613.00
Transfers:	0
Sales:	11

November:

7—12,100.00
12—11,000.00
12—10,000.00
12—10,000.00
12—10,000.00
13—10,000.00
18—10,000.00
20—10,000.00
20—10,000.00
20—10,000.00
24—10,000.00
28— 9,500.00

High:	12,100.00
Low:	9,500.00
Average:	10,216.00
Tranfers:	0
Sales:	12

December:

1—9,400.00
4—9,000.00
5—9,000.00
5—9,000.00
5—transfer
6—transfer
7—transfer
8—9,000.00
11—transfer
13—8,500.00
13—8,000.00
15—8,000.00
16—8,000.00
16—8,000.00
16—8,000.00
17—7,500.00
19—8,000.00
19—8,000.00
23—8,000.00
22—8,000.00
22—8,000.00
23—7,500.00
29—transfer
31—7,800.00

High:	9,400.00
Low:	7,500.00
Average:	8,247.00
Transfers:	6
Sales:	19

1931

January:
6—7,700.00
6—7,800.00
15—7,600.00
High: 7,800.00
Low: 7,600.00
Average: 7,700.00
Transfers: 0
Sales: 3

February:
4—8,000.00
10—8,000.00
11—transfer
18—8,000.00
26—8,500.00
High: 8,500.00
Low: 8,000.00
Average: 8,125.00
Transfers: 1
Sales: 4

March:
2—transfer
2—transfer
2—8,800.00
11—transfer
13—10,000.00
16—10,500.00
High: 10,500.00
Low: 8,800.00
Average: 9,766.00
Transfers: 3
Sales: 3

April:
2—10,500.00
7—10,000.00
13—10,000.00
18—10,000.00
27—10,000.00
27—10,000.00
27—10,000.00
27—10,000.00
High: 10,500.00
Low: 10,000.00
Average: 10,062.00
Transfers: 0
Sales: 8

May:
4—10,000.00
6—10,000.00
13—13,000.00
14— 9,000.00
15— 9,200.00
18—transfer
18— 9,000.00
23— 8,500.00
25—transfer
25— 8,000.00
28— 7,500.00
High: 13,000.00
Low: 7,500.00
Average: 9,355.00
Transfers: 2
Sales: 9

June:
2—6,500.00
3—7,000.00
8—transfer
9—transfer
16—transfer
16—transfer
17—9,000.00
18—9,000.00
26—9,000.00
29—9,500.00
30—9.500.00
High: 9,500.00
Low: 6,500.00
Average: 8,500.00
Transfers: 4
Sales: 7

July:
6—9,000.00
8—transfer
13—transfer
14—8,500.00
22—8,500.00
24—8,000.00
24—8,000.00
27—7,600.00
28—8,000.00
28—8,000.00
High: 9,000.00
Low: 7,600.00
Average: 8,200.00
Transfers: 2
Sales: 8

August:
3—8,000.00
4—transfer
7—8,000.00
10—7,500.00
21—transfer
High: 8,500.00
Low: 7,500.00
Average: 7,833.00
Transfers: 2
Sales: 3

September:
3—7,500.00
3—7,000.00
8—transfer
14—7,050.00
High: 7,500.00
Low: 7,000.00
Average: 7,191.00
Transfers: 1
Sales: 3

October:
6—6,500.00
8—6,000.00
15—6,500.00
19—6,500.00
19—transfer
21—6,900.00
24—7,500.00
24—transfer
28—7,500.00
30—7,700.00
30—transfer
30—8,500.00
High: 8,500.00
Low: 6,000.00
Average: 7,066.00
Transfers: 3
Sales: 9

November:
3—10,000.00
3—10,000.00
3—10,000.00
3—11,000.00
3—12,000.00
4—12,000.00
5—12,000.00
5—12,475.00
5—12,000.00
6—12,200.00
9—12,000.00

1931

10—12,000.00
12—11,900.00
16—11,700.00
19—10,500.00
28— 8,500.00
30— 8,000.00

High:	12,475.00
Low:	8,000.00
Average:	11,075.00
Transfers:	0
Sales:	17

December:
11—7,250.00
15—transfer
17—7,500.00
17—7,500.00
19—8,000.00

High:	8,000.00
Low:	7,250.00
Average:	7,563.00
Transfers:	1
Sales:	4

1932

January:
7—transfer
7—7,500.00
9—transfer
12—transfer
16—7,000.00
16—7,500.00
18—7,500.00
18—7,500.00
High: 7,500.00
Low: 7,000.00
Average: 7,400.00
Transfers: 3
Sales: 5

February:
4—7,500.00
13—7,500.00
17—7,500.00
18—8,000.00
18—7,800.00
26—7,000.00
26—transfer
26—transfer
High: 8,000.00
Low: 7,000.00
Average: 7,550.00
Transfers: 2
Sales: 6

March:
4—7,000.00
9—6,750.00
16—6,750.00
21—6,600.00
21—6,700.00
21—6,750.00
23—6,700.00
31—transfer
High: 7,000.00
Low: 6,600.00
Average: 6,750.00
Transfers: 1
Sales: 7

April:
1—6,800.00
4—6,500.00
8—6,100.00
11—transfer
14—6,000.00
18—5,600.00
29—transfer
High: 6,800.00
Low: 5,600.00
Average: 6,200.00
Transfers: 2
Sales: 5

May:
1—5,500.00
5—4,500.00
7—4,800.00
21—4,500.00
24—4,500.00
25—4,900.00
25—5,000.00
31—4,200.00
31—4,100.00
High: 5,500.00
Low: 4,100.00
Average: 4,666.00
Transfers: 0
Sales: 9

June:
6—4,500.00
21—4,300.00
22—3,700.00
24—transfer
29—3,800.00
29—transfer
High: 4,500.00
Low: 3,700.00
Average: 4,075.00
Transfers: 2
Sales: 4

July:
6—3,800.00
6—4,000.00
11—transfer
18—4,000.00
19—4,100.00
19—4,075.00
20—4,000.00
27—4,000.00
27—4,000.00
28—4,200.00
High: 4,200.00
Low: 3,800.00
Average: 4,018.00
Transfers: 1
Sales: 9

August:
1—4,400.00
3—4,500.00
4—4,900.00
4—5,000.00
4—5,000.00
6—5,500.00
9—7,500.00
9—7,000.00
15—transfer
17—7,000.00
23—7,000.00
25—7,725.00
25—8,100.00
30—8,100.00
30—8,000.00
High: 8,100.00
Low: 4,400.00
Average: 6,408.00
Transfers: 1
Sales: 14

September:
3—transfer
3—9,500.00
15—transfer
22—5,000.00
High: 9,500.00
Low: 5,000.00
Average: 7,250.00
Transfers: 2
Sales: 2

October:
6—6,000.00
10—5,500.00
20—transfer
24—transfer
25—5,500.00
High: 6,000.00
Low: 5,500.00
Average: 5,666.00
Transfers: 2
Sales: 3

November:
3—5,800.00
10—5,600.00
14—5,000.00
29—4,500.00
30—4,500.00
High: 5,800.00

1932

Low: 4,500.00
Average: 5,080.00
Transfers: 0
Sales: 5

December:
2—4,500.00
8—4,500.00
9—4,250.00
10—4,250.00
10—4,250.00
15—4,900.00
20—4,000.00
20—4,100.00
29—3,500.00
High: 4,900.00
Low: 3,500.00
Average: 4,250.00
Transfers: 0
Sales: 9

1933

January:
No sales

February:
No sales

March:
No sales

April:
6—7,000.00
11—7,500.00
11—7,500.00
11—transfer
20—7,350.00
20—7,500.00
20—7,350.00
20—7,500.00
29—transfer

High:	7,500.00
Low:	7,000.00
Average:	7,385.00
Transfers:	2
Sales:	7

May:
1—7,700.00
1—7,900.00
1—transfer
4—7,900.00
5—8,000.00
6—8,000.00
6—8,000.00
6—8,000.00
8—8,000.00
10—9,000.00
11—9,400.00
12—9,500.00
12—9,500.00
15—9,800.00
20—9,800.00
26—9,000.00
29—9,500.00
31—9,500.00

High:	9,800.00
Low:	7,700.00
Average:	8,735.00
Transfers:	1
Sales:	17

June:
1— 9,000.00
5— 9,000.00
7— 9,000.00
8— 9,000.00
9— 9,000.00
10— 9,000.00
12— 9,500.00
13— 9,500.00
15— 9,600.00
19— 9,500.00
21— 9,500.00
23— 9,500.00
26— 9,650.00
26— 9,750.00
26— 9,800.00
26— 9,900.00
26—10,000.00
27—10,300.00
28—10,500.00
28—10,500.00
30—10,500.00
30—10,400.00

High:	10,500.00
Low:	9,000.00
Average:	9,654.00
Transfers:	0
Sales:	22

July:
5—10,500.00
6—10,700.00
6—11,000.00
8—11,000.00
8—11,500.00
8—11,900.00
10—11,900.00
13—14,000.00
13—14,500.00
13—14,500.00
14—12,000.00
14—15,000.00
17—15,500.00
19—15,900.00
20—15,000.00
21—13,500.00
22—10,000.00
22— 9,500.00
27—11,500.00
27—11,000.00

High:	15,900.00
Low:	9,500.00
Average:	12,520.00
Transfers:	0
Sales:	20

August:
3—11,000.00
3—10,500.00
4—10,000.00
8—10,000.00
16— 8,000.00
16— 8,000.00
24—transfer
25—10,000.00
26—10,000.00

High:	11,000.00
Low:	8,000.00
Average:	9,687.00
Transfers:	0
Sales:	8

September:
7—10,000.00
12— 9,500.00
18—10,500.00
18—10,500.00
21—10,100.00
26—10,000.00
26—transfer

High:	10,500.00
Low:	9,500.00
Average:	10,100.00
Transfers:	1
Sales:	6

October:
3—Transfer
11—9,000.00
13—8,750.00
14—8,500.00
14—transfer
14—transfer
16—transfer
17—7,500.00
19—7,000.00
25—8,000.00
25—transfer
30—transfer

High:	9,000.00
Low:	7,000.00
Average:	8,125.00
Transfers:	6
Sales:	6

November:
3—7,250.00
7—transfer

1933

8—transfer
9—7,250.00
15—6,800.00
17—6,800.00
24—7,000.00
27—transfer
29—transfer
High: 7,250.00

Low: 6,800.00
Average: 7,020.00
Transfers: 4
Sales: 5

December:
1—6,750.00
14—7,250.00
18—6,750.00
26—transfer
29—transfer
High: 7,250.00
Low: 6,750.00
Average: 6,916.00
Transfers: 2
Sales: 3

1934

January:
2—7,500.00
2—7,700.00
4—7,700.00
8—7,800.00
10—8,000.00
11—8,300.00
11—8,900.00
12—9.000.00
15—transfer
17—9,000.00
24—9,000.00
24—9,250.00
25—8,700.00
26—9,250.00
29—transfer
31—9,400.00
High: 9,400.00
Low: 7,500.00
Average: 8,535.00
Transfers: 2
Sales: 14

February:
10—7,500.00
13—9.000.00
21—transfer
High: 9,000.00
Low: 7,500.00
Average: 8,250.00
Tranfers: 1
Sales: 2

March:
7—8,900.00
21—7,200.00
28—5,000.00
29—5,500.00
29—5,500.00
29—7,000.00
High: 8,900.00
Low: 5,000.00
Average: 6,516.00
Transfers: 0
Sales: 6

April:
7—7,000.00
11—7,000.00
13—7,300.00
13—7,200.00
18—7,000.00
High: 7,300.00
Low: 7,000.00
Average: 7,100.00
Transfers: 0
Sales: 5

May:
1—6,500.00
3—6,500.00
5—transfer
8—6,500.00
9—6,500.00
19—transfer
21—6,000.00
28—6,500.00
31—6,500.00
High: 6,500.00
Low: 6,000.00
Average: 6,428.00
Transfers: 2
Sales: 7

June:
1—7,200.00
4—transfer
13—7,000.00
15—7,500.00
16—7,600.00
19—8,000.00
22—8,000.00
30—7,500.00
High: 8,000.00
Low: 7,000.00
Average: 7,542.00
Transfers: 1
Sales: 7

July:
6—7,575.00
9—transfer
12—6,750.00
13—7,100.00
14—7,100.00
18—7,200.00
18—7,500.00
24—7,400.00
26—7,250.00
28—7,250.00
31—7,500.00
High: 7,575.00
Low: 6,750.00
Average: 7,262.00
Transfers: 1
Sales: 10

August:
2—7,600.00
3—transfer
3—8,000.00
4—8,000.00
8—9,000.00
8—9,500.00
9—9,500.00
11—9,000.00
15—8,500.00
15—8,000.00
15—8,100.00
16—7,800.00
22—7,200.00
29—7,500.00
High: 9,500.00
Low: 7,200.00
Average: 8,284.00
Transfers: 1
Sales: 13

September:
4—7,000.00
4—7,000.00
7—7,000.00
11—7,500.00
12—7,400.00
13—7,500.00
15—7,500.00
19—transfer
19—7,000.00
20—7,000.00
20—transfer
29—7,400.00
High: 7,500.00
Low: 7,000.00
Average: 7,230.00
Transfers: 2
Sales: 10

October:
1—7,200.00
5—transfer
5—transfer
13—7,000.00
16—7,000.00
17—7,200.00
27—7,000.00
17—7,200.00

1934

27—7,000.00

High:	7,200.00
Low:	7,000.00
Average:	7,080.00
Transfers:	2
Sales:	5

November:

5—6,500.00

9—6,500.00

16—6,000.00

20—6,000.00

High:	6,500.00
Low:	6,000.00
Average:	6,250.00
Transfers:	0
Sales:	4

December:

3—5,800.00

4—5,500.00

6—6,000.00

High:	6,000.00
Low:	5,500.00
Average:	5,825.00
Transfers:	0
Sales:	3

1935

January:
5—6,200.00
9—transfer
11—6,000.00
24—6,500.00
28—5,500.00
30—5,500.00
High: 6,500.00
Low: 5,500.00
Average: 5,940.00
Transfers: 1
Sales 5

February:
1—5,000.00
2—4,800.00
26—4,800.00
High: 5,000.00
Low: 4,800.00
Average: 4,866.00
Transfers: 0
Sales: 3

March:
5—4,600.00
5—4,600.00
11—4,500.00
16—transfer
16—transfer
25—4,700.00
28—4,500.00
High: 4,700.00
Low: 4,500.00
Average: 4,580.00
Transfers: 2
Sales: 5

April:
5—5,000.00
10—5,000.00
12—5,000.00
19—5,500.00
27—5,300.00
High: 5,500.00
Low: 5,000.00
Average: 5,160.00
Transfers: 0
Sales: 5

May:
3—5,500.00
8—5,250.00
10—5,000.00
17—5,100.00
24—5,100.00
25—transfer
28—5,000.00
28—transfer
31—5,100.00
High: 5,500.00
Low: 5,000.00
Average: 5,150.00
Transfers: 2
Sales: 7

June:
1—5,000.00
14—5,500.00
14—5,500.00
20—transfer
24—5,200.00
28—transfer
29—5,500.00
High: 5,500.00
Low: 5,000.00
Average: 5,340.00
Transfers: 2
Sales: 5

July:
1—5,500.00
9—5,500.00
12—5,700.00
13—5,800.00
25—5,800.00
27—5,900.00
29—6,050.00
High: 6,050.00
Low: 5,500.00
Average: 5,750.00
Transfers: 0
Sales: 7

August:
1—6,250.00
6—5,850.00
6—5,950.00
13—5,800.00
17—5,500.00
23—5,300.00
28—5,300.00
29—transfer
High: 6,250.00
Low: 5,300.00
Average: 5,705.00
Transfers: 1
Sales: 7

September:
10—5,300.00
14—transfer
18—5,400.00
20—5,700.00
24—5,700.00
High: 5,700.00
Low: 5,300.00
Average: 5,525.00
Transfers: 1
Sales: 4

October:
1—5,800.00
2—6,000.00
3—6,000.00
3—6,000.00
4—6,060.00
19—transfer
21—6,000.00
23—6,000.00
23—transfer
High: 6,060.00
Low: 5,800.00
Average: 5,980.00
Transfers: 2
Sales: 7

November:
1—6,400.00
2—6,475.00
6—6,400.00
21—6,450.00
22—6,450.00
26—6,250.00
27—6,500.00
29—6,600.00

1935

High:	6,600.00	December:	28—5,750.00	
Low:	6,250.00	6—6,000.00	High:	6,000.00
Average:	6,440.00	11—6,000.00	Low:	5,750.00
Transfers:	0	13—transfer	Average:	5,880.00
Sales:	8	16—transfer	Transfers:	2
		20—5,800.00	Sales:	4

1936

January:
2—transfer
4—transfer
8—5,570.00
10—5,800.00
16—6,000.00
20—5,600.00
27—6,200.00
28—transfer
28—transfer

High:	6,200.00
Low:	5,750.00
Average:	5,870.00
Transfers:	4
Sales:	5

February:
1—6,050.00
7—5,800.00
19—5,300.00

High:	6,050.00
Low:	5,300.00
Average:	5,716.00
Transfers:	0
Sales:	3

March:
5—transfer
5—5,500.00
5—transfer
30—5,400.00
30–tranfer

High:	5,500.00
Low:	5,400.00
Average:	5,450.00
Transfers:	3
Sales:	2

April:
7—4,600.00
13—4,800.00
18—transfer
20—5,000.00
20—5,000.00
22—4,900.00
23—4,940.00

High:	5,000.00
Low:	4,600.00
Average:	4,873.00
Transfers:	1
Sales:	6

May:
1—5,000.00
6—4,750.00
7—5,000.00
8—4,600.00
18—3,650.00

High:	5,000.00
Low:	3,650.00
Average:	4,600.00
Transfers:	0
Sales:	5

June:
2—4,500.00
2—4,100.00
4—4,300.00
12—4,600.00
16—4,600.00
17—4,300.00
17—4,300.00
17—4,300.00
25—4,500.00

High:	4,600.00
Low:	4,100.00
Average:	4,388.00
Transfers:	0
Sales:	9

July:
7—3,900.00
11—4,300.00
13—4,500.00
18—4,300.00
21—transfer
24—4,400.00
25—4,400.00
29—transfer
30—4,400.00
30—4,400.00
31—4,500.00

High:	4,500.00
Low:	3,900.00
Average:	4,344.00
Transfers:	2
Sales:	9

August:
5—4,850.00
6—5,000.00
7—5,200.00
8—5,500.00
11—5,500.00
17—transfer
18—5,500.00
19—5,500.00
21—5,100.00
24—transfer

High:	5,500.00
Low:	4,850.00
Average:	5,268.00
Transfers:	2
Sales:	8

September:
3—4,700.00
8—transfer
8—5,500.00
10—5,000.00
12—5,200.00
16—5,200.00
19—transfer
25—transfer

High:	5,500.00
Low:	4,700.00
Average:	5,120.00
Transfers:	3
Sales:	5

October:
15—4,200.00
19—4,500.00
23—4,600.00
26—4,500.00
27—transfer

High:	4,600.00
Low:	4,200.00
Average:	4,450.00
Transfers:	1
Sales:	4

November:
10—4,300.00
10—4,000.00
16—4,250.00
16—4,100.00
19—4,200.00

High:	4,300.00
Low:	4,000.00
Average:	4,170.00
Transfers:	0
Sales:	5

1936

December:	14—4,800.00		Low:	4,200.00
1—4,200.00	15—4,800.00		Average:	4,614.00
2—4,400.00	16—4,800.00		Transfers:	0
3—4,500.00	High:	4,800.00	Sales:	7
9—4,800.00				

1937

January:
4—5,050.00
4—5,250.00
5—5,500.00
5—5,500.00
6—5,500.00
13—5,750.00
14—6,300.00
14—6,325.00
23—transfer
25—6,000.00

High:	6,325.00
Low:	5,050.00
Average:	5,686.00
Transfers:	1
Sales:	9

February:
5—transfer
6—5,500.00
11—5,600.00
18—5,600.00
20—5,500.00
27—5,400.00
27—5,500.00
27—5,700.00

High:	5,700.00
Low:	5,400.00
Average:	5,542.00
Transfers:	1
Sales:	7

March:
1—5,100.00
6—5,300.00
9—5,600.00
15—5,250.00
23—4,900.00
30—5,200.00
31—transfer

High:	5,600.00
Low:	4,900.00
Average:	5,225.00
Transfers:	1
Sales:	6

April:
2—5,400.00
6—5,450.00
7—5,500.00
8—5,500.00
12—5,300.00
15—transfer
16—5,400.00
19—5,400.00
20—5,500.00
20—transfer
23—5,300.00
27—5,500.00

High:	5,500.00
Low:	5,300.00
Average:	5,425.00
Transfers:	2
Sales:	10

May:
1—5,300.00
4—5,300.00
5—5,300.00
11—5,400.00
26—5,000.00
26—5,000.00
26—5,150.00

High:	5,300.00
Low:	5,000.00
Average:	5,207.00
Transfers:	0
Sales:	7

June:
1—5,150.00
9—4,895.00
9—transfer
12—transfer
17—transfer
17—transfer
19—transfer
23—4,900.00
25—transfer
25—transfer
29—4,600.00
30—4,600.00

High:	5,150.00
Low:	4,600.00
Average:	4,829.00
Transfers:	7
Sales:	5

July:
7—4,750.00
10—4,500.00
12—4,750.00
13—4,800.00
14—4,750.00
16—4,850.00
20—transfer
24—4,500.00
26—4,500.00
29—4,750.00
30—4,800.00

High:	4,850.00
Low:	4,500.00
Average:	4,695.00
Transfers:	1
Sales:	10

August:
11—4,300.00
17—4,300.00
20—transfer
24—4,500.00
25—4,300.00
26—4,500.00
30—transfer
31—transfer

High:	4,500.00
Low:	4,300.00
Average:	4,380.00
Transfers:	3
Sales:	5

September:
8—transfer
11—4,250.00
13—transfer
18—transfer
18—transfer
21—4,000.00
24—4,250.00
28—4,250.00
29—4,250.00
30—4,200.00
30—transfer

High:	4,250.00
Low:	4,000.00
Average:	4,200.00
Transfers:	5
Sales:	6

October:
8—4,000.00
11—3,750.00
13—3,500.00
16—3,500.00
22—3,250.00
23—transfer

1937

29—transfer

High:	4,000.00
Low:	3,250.00
Average:	3,600.00
Transfers:	2
Sales:	5

November:
3—3,450.00
3—3,500.00
8—3,250.00
15—3,250.00
17—transfer
18—3,050.00
18—3,000.00
20—transfer
20—transfer

High:	3,500.00
Low:	3,000.00
Average:	3,250.00
Transfers:	3
Sales:	6

December:
1—transfer
1—transfer
4—3,000.00
7—3,000.00
9—3,000.00
9—3,000.00
10—transfer
10—transfer
13—transfer
14—2,750.00
16—2,700.00
18—2,850.00
18—transfer
20—2,850.00
20—2,800.00
23—transfer
24—3,000.00
29—2,900.00

High:	3,000.00
Low:	2,750.00
Average:	2,885.00
Transfers:	7
Sales:	11

1938

January:
8—transfer
12—3,500.00
13—3,600.00
13—3,700.00
13—3,650.00
13—transfer
17—transfer
19—4,100.00
26—3,900.00
26—3,900.00
27—3,700.00
High: 4,100.00
Low: 3,500.00
Average: 3,756.00
Transfers: 3
Sales: 8

February:
17—3,500.00
17—3,500.00
19—transfer
26—3,100.00
High: 3,500.00
Low: 3,100.00
Average: 3,366.00
Transfers: 1
Sales: 3

March:
4—3,200.00
4—transfer
4—transfer
4—transfer
8—3,200.00
9—3,350.00
17—3,000.00
17—3,000.00
24—2,800.00
29—2,500.00
29—2,500.00
29—2,500.00
29—2,500.00
30—2,500.00
31—2,600.00
High: 3,350.00
Low: 2,500.00
Average: 2,804.00
Transfers: 3
Sales: 12

April:
5—2,900.00
5—3,000.00
6—3,000.00
7—3,150.00
12—3,200.00
16—3,300.00
24—transfer
26—3,300.00
27—3,500.00
28—3,500.00
High: 3,500.00
Low: 2,900.00
Average: 3,211.00
Transfers: 1
Sales: 9

May:
11—3,100.00
11—3,000.00
17—3,100.00
18—3,000.00
19—3,000.00
19—3,000.00
20—3,000.00
21—transfer
25—3,000.00
26—transfer
27—3,000.00
28—transfer
31—3,000.00
High: 3,100.00
Low: 3,000.00
Average: 3,022.00
Transfers: 3
Sales: 10

June:
2—3,000.00
4—3,000.00
7—3,100.00
8—transfer
14—transfer
14—3,000.00
14—2,900.00
15—3,000.00
15—3,100.00
16—transfer
17—transfer
17—transfer
17—transfer
21—3,000.00
28—3,000.00
28—3,000.00
30—3,050.00
High: 3,100.00
Low: 2,900.00
Average: 3,018.00
Transfers: 6
Sales: 11

July:
1—transfer
2—3,200.00
5—3,300.00
8—3,000.00
13—3,200.00
18—3,000.00
22—3,100.00
29—3,000.00
High: 3,300.00
Low: 3,100.00
Average: 3,133.00
Transfers: 1
Sales: 7

August:
10—2,900.00
23—2,750.00
High: 2,900.00
Low: 2,750.00
Average: 2,850.00
Transfers: 0
Sales: 2

September:
26—2,350.00
26—2,350.00
High: 2,350.00
Low: 2,350.00
Average: 2,400.00
Transfers: 0
Sales: 2

October:
4—2,600.00
10—2,350.00
19—2,400.00
22—2,400.00
24—2,300.00
28—2,250.00
High: 2,600.00
Low: 2,250.00
Average: 2,2358.00
Transfers: 0
Sales: 6

November:
1—2,100.00

1938

2—transfer		December:	20—1,650.00	
3—2,000.00		1—1,850.00	22—1,600.00	
7—2,000.00		8—transfer	23—1,650.00	
14—transfer		8—1,700.00	23—1,650.00	
15—1,900.00		8—1,650.00	27—transfer	
22—1,850.00		13—1,600.00	30—1,550.00	
22—1,800.00		13—transfer	High:	1,850.00
30—1,500.00		15—1,600.00	Low:	1,525.00
30—1,500.00		15—1,550.00	Average:	1,661.00
High:	2,100.00	16—1,550.00	Transfers:	3
Low:	1,500.00	17—1,525.00	Sales:	14
Average:	1,837.00	17—1,550.00		
Transfers:	2			
Sales:	8			

1939

January:
4—2,050.00
6—transfer
10—2,000.00
17—transfer
17—2,100.00
18—2,000.00
24—2,000.00
25—2,000.00
27—2,000.00
High: 2,100.00
Low: 2,000.00
Average: 2,021.00
Transfers: 2
Sales: 7

February:
6—1,750.00
7—1,750.00
7—1,700.00
8—1,700.00
9—transfer
9—1,600.00
14—1,600.00
14—1,600.00
17—1,600.00
17—1,600.00
24—1,600.00
High: 1,750.00
Low: 1,600.00
Average: 1,650.00
Transfers: 1
Sales: 10

March:
7—1,500.00
14—1,450.00
16—1,550.00
20—1,500.00
22—1,500.00
25—1,500.00
29—1,500.00
High: 1,550.00
Low: 1,450.00
Average: 1,500.00
Transfers: 0
Sales: 7

April:
1—1,350.00
11—1,500.00
12—1,400.00
High: 1,500.00
Low: 1,350.00
Average: 1,431.00
Transfers: 0
Sales: 3

May:
1—1,475.00
1—1,500.00
1—1,600.00
1—1,600.00
2—1,500.00
4—1,500.00
16—1,600.00
19—1,650.00
19—transfer
25—1,700.00
29—transfer
29—1,900.00
High: 1,900.00
Low: 1,475.00
Average: 1,616.00
Transfers: 2
Sales: 10

June:
9—1,900.00
2—1,950.00
5—2,000.00
5—2,000.00
5—1,900.00
13—transfer
15—1,700.00
16—1,700.00
16—1,700.00
23—1,700.00
24—transfer
26—1,700.00
29—1,700.00
29—1,700.00
High: 2,000.00
Low: 1,700.00
Average: 1,796.00
Transfers: 2
Sales: 12

July:
No sales

August:
3—transfer
10—1,400.00
11—transfer
19—1,350.00
24—transfer
31—transfer
High: 1,400.00
Low: 1,350.00
Average: 1,375.00
Transfers: 4
Sales: 2

September:
1—1,400.00
1—1,450.00
1—transfer
5—2,000.00
5—2,000.00
6—2,000.00
7—2,000.00
9—transfer
13—2,000.00
13—transfer
26—2,000.00
27—2,200.00
28—2,000.00
High: 2,200.00
Low: 1,400.00
Average: 1,905.00
Transfers: 3
Sales: 10

October:
14—2,000.00
18—1,750.00
27—1,800.00
High: 2,000.00
Low: 1,750.00
Average 1,850.00
Transfers: 0
Sales: 3

November:
8—1,625.00
10—1,000.00
15—1,250.00
18—transfer
18—transfer
22—1,350.00
28—1,300.00
29—1,250.00
High: 1,625.00
Low: 1,000.00
Average 1,379.00

1939

Transfers: 2
Sales: 6

December:
2—1,150.00
2—transfer
6—1,150.00
7—1,150.00
7—1,200.00
8—transfer
11—1,200.00
11—1,200.00
11—1,250.00
12—1,200.00
14—1,250.00
14—1,300.00
14—1,300.00
15—1,450.00
16—1,500.00
18—1,600.00
18—1,700.00
18—1,800.00
18—1,900.00
18—2,000.00
19—2,000.00
19—2,000.00
19—2,000.00
19—2,000.00
20—2,100.00

High:	2,100.00
Low:	1,150.00
Average:	1,539.00
Transfers:	2
Sales:	23

1940

January:
3—1,900.00
5—1,950.00
6—transfer
6—transfer
6—transfer
8—1,800.00
11—transfer
15—1,800.00
22—1,600.00
22—1,650.00

High:	1,950.00
Low:	1,600.00
Average:	1,783.00
Transfers:	4
Sales:	6

February:
14—1,600.00
17—1,650.00
20—1,600.00
20—1,650.00
20—1,700.00
21—1,750.00
24—1,850.00
28—1,850.00
28—1,850.00
28—1,850.00
28—1,850.00
28—1,850.00
29—1,850.00

High:	1,850.00
Low:	1,600.00
Average:	1,761.00
Transfers:	0
Sales:	13

March:
9—1,850.00
14—1,800.00
14—1,800.00
14—transfer
18—1,700.00
25—transfer
27—1,700.00
29—1,850.00
29—1,850.00

High:	1,850.00
Low:	1,700.00
Average:	1,792.00
Transfers:	2
Sales:	7

April:
1—1,850.00
3—transfer
9—1,800.00
11—1,800.00
12—1,750.00
12—transfer
18—1,700.00
18—1,700.00
20—1,800.00
22—1,700.00
23—1,850.00
23—1,850.00
23—1,850.00

High:	1,850.00
Low:	1,700.00
Average:	1,786.00
Transfers:	2
Sales:	11

May:
4—transfer
4—1,750.00
10—1,775.00
13—1,775.00
15—1,750.00
17—1,750.00
20—1,700.00
20—1,500.00
20—1,500.00
28—1,300.00

High:	1,775.00
Low:	1,300.00
Average:	1,644.00
Transfers:	1
Sales:	9

June:
12—1,200.00
13—1,200.00
17—1,100.00
18—1,200.00
21—1,200.00
21—transfer
28—1,000.00
29—1,200.00

High:	1,200.00
Low:	1,000.00
Average:	1,157.00
Transfers:	1
Sales:	7

July:
5—transfer
8—transfer
9—1,000.00
9—1,000.00
12—1,000.00
16—1,000.00
24—1,100.00
26—1,100.00
27—1,100.00

High:	1,100.00
Low:	1,000.00
Average:	1,042.00
Transfers:	2
Sales:	7

August:
14—1,000.00
15—1,100.00
22—transfer
24— 900.00
28— 950.00

High:	1,100.00
Low:	900.00
Average:	987.00
Transfers:	1
Sales:	4

September:
12—750.00
12—transfer
20—750.00
23—800.00
25—transfer
26—800.00
28—800.00
28—transfer

High:	800.00
Low:	750.00
Average:	780.00
Transfers:	3
Sales:	5

October:
3—900.00
9—850.00
15—750.00
15—750.00
19—700.00
21—737.00
21—transfer
23—737.00

1940

24—737.00
29—750.00
29—750.00

High:	900.00
Low:	700.00
Average:	766.00
Transfers:	1
Sales:	10

November:
2—800.00
6—750.00
8—700.00
15—675.00
16—transfer
19—transfer
22—625.00
27—600.00

High:	800.00
Low:	600.00
Average:	691.00
Transfers:	2
Sales:	6

December:
2—591.00
3—600.00
6—525.00
9—500.00
9—500.00
9—500.00
10—450.00
10—450.00
11—450.00
16—450.00
16—475.00
16—500.00
18—475.00
20—450.00
20—450.00
21—transfer
21—475.00
22—475.00
24—450.00
27—450.00
31—450.00
31—450.00

High:	600.00
Low:	450.00
Average:	481.00
Transfers:	1
Sales:	21

1941

January:
2—550.00
2—575.00
8—550.00
9—550.00
9—575.00
9—600.00
11—613.00
14—550.00
16—540.00
18—550.00
21—450.00

High	613.00
Low:	450.00
Average:	570.00
Transfers:	0
Sales:	11

February:
1—500.00
8—450.00
15—450.00
25—425.00
27—425.00
28—475.00

High:	500.00
Low:	425.00
Average:	454.00
Transfers:	0
Sales:	6

March:
3—450.00
10—425.00
11—420.00
12—425.00
19—425.00
20—425.00
26—400.00
26—400.00
26—425.00
26—450.00
31—440.00
31—450.00

High:	450.00
Low:	400.00
Average:	427.00
Transfers:	0
Sales:	12

April:
4—transfer
4—475.00
8—475.00
14—475.00
12—transfer
16—450.00
24—500.00

High:	500.00
Low:	450.00
Average:	475.00
Transfers:	2
Sales:	5

May:
2—400.00
2—400.00
3—transfer
23—375.00
28—350.00
29—390.00
29—400.00
29—400.00

High:	400.00
Low:	350.00
Average:	387.00
Transfers:	1
Sales:	7

June:
3—625.00
3—650.00
3—675.00
7—650.00
10—410.00
11—425.00
12—400.00
12—440.00
13—213.00
24—transfer

High:	675.00
Low:	213.00
Average:	498.00
Transfers:	1
Sales:	9

July:
7—625.00
8—650.00
10—600.00
14—350.00
14—700.00
17—650.00
18—transfer
25—625.00

High:	700.00
Low:	350.00
Average:	600.00
Transfers:	1
Sales:	7

August:
2—375.00
9—375.00
13—375.00
14—transfer
15—transfer
15—transfer
18—350.00
20—375.00
23—375.00
25—390.00
30—375.00

High:	390.00
Low:	350.00
Average:	374.00
Transfers:	3
Sales:	8

September:
2—400.00
2—400.00
8—400.00
10—440.00
12—450.00
13—425.00
15—440.00
15—450.00
17—transfer
18—425.00
19—400.00

High:	450.00
Low:	400.00
Average:	423.00
Transfers:	1
Sales:	10

October:
2—transfer
4—400.00
6—375.00
6—400.00
7—400.00
8—400.00
14—400.00
14—400.00

1941

22—350.00
30—375.00
30—350.00

High:	400.00
Low:	350.00
Average:	385.00
Transfers:	1
Sales:	10

November:
2—350.00
5—transfer
5—375.00
14—300.00
25—275.00
26—250.00
27—225.00
27—transfer
27—transfer
27—200.00
27—200.00
28—200.00

High:	375.00
Low:	200.00
Average:	264.00
Transfers:	3
Sales:	9

December:
1—175.00
1—175.00
2—200.00
3—225.00
3—275.00
3—300.00
3—350.00
3—350.00
3—350.00
3—350.00
3—350.00
3—325.00
5—300.00
5—300.00
8—225.00
13—150.00
15—200.00
16—200.00
20—200.00
30—200.00
30—200.00
30—200.00
30—200.00
31—200.00

High:	350.00
Low:	150.00
Average:	250.00
Transfers:	0
Sales:	24

1942

January:
7—200.00
8—300.00
12—350.00
12—350.00
13—350.00
17—300.00
19—transfer
19—450.00
19—450.00
23—400.00
23—350.00
24—400.00
24—425.00
26—425.00
28—450.00
28—450.00
28—475.00
28—475.00
28—475.00
28—500.00
31—550.00

High:	550.00
Low:	200.00
Average:	406.00
Transfers:	1
Sales:	20

February:
2—550.00
3—550.00
3—550.00
4—550.00
4—525.00
5—550.00
7—550.00
11—550.00

High:	550.00
Low:	525.00
Average:	546.00
Transfers:	0
Sales:	8

March:
7—300.00
30—200.00
30—transfer
30—200.00
30—100.00
31—150.00

High:	300.00
Low:	100.00
Average:	190.00
Transfers:	1
Sales:	5

April:
4—275.00
4—300.00
4—transfer
10—225.00
14—250.00
15—250.00
16—250.00
18—250.00
20—125.00
21—200.00
21—700.00
24—225.00
25—200.00
29—200.00

High:	700.00
Low:	125.00
Average:	275.00
Transfers:	1
Sales:	13

May:
1—175.00
1—250.00
2—transfer
2—transfer
6—200.00
12—250.00
14—175.00
14—225.00
21—200.00
25—150.00
25—transfer

High:	250.00
Low:	150.00
Average:	203.00
Transfers:	3
Sales:	8

June:
2—175.00
3—175.00
11—125.00
11—150.00
11—125.00
16—165.00
23—100.00
29—transfer

High:	175.00
Low:	100.00
Average:	139.00
Transfers:	1
Sales:	8

July:
9—150.00
13—175.00
23—175.00
28—200.00
30—200.00

High:	200.00
Low:	150.00
Average:	180.00
Transfers:	0
Sales:	5

August:
1—transfer
11—200.00
12—200.00
21—100.00
21—200.00

High:	200.00
Low:	100.00
Average:	175.00
Transfers:	1
Sales:	4

September:
1—175.00
4—transfer
24— 90.00
29—200.00

High:	200.00
Low:	90.00
Average:	130.00
Transfers:	1
Sales:	3

October:
7—175.00
(the only sale made in this month)

November:
2—transfer
12—25.00
17—25.00
17—25.00
17—75.00
17—75.00

1942

20—50.00
20—50.00
25—25.00
30—50.00

High:	75.00
Low:	25.00
Average:	50.00
Transfers:	1
Sales:	9

December:
2— 70.00
2— 75.00
2— 75.00
2— 75.00
3— 75.00
5— 50.00
7— 50.00
11— 50.00
14— 50.00
15— 50.00
15— 50.00
15— 70.00
17— 70.00
17— 70.00
18— 75.00
18— 75.00
26—transfer
29— 75.00
29— 25.00
30—100.00
31—125.00
31—150.00

High:	150.00
Low:	25.00
Average:	71.00
Transfers:	1
Sales:	21

1943

January:
5—250.00
11—250.00
13—250.00
23—250.00
26—transfer
30—250.00

High:	250.00
Low:	250.00
Average:	250.00
Transfers:	1
Sales:	5

February:
4—275.00
4—300.00
5—275.00
8—300.00
9—transfer
25—500.00

High:	500.00
Low:	275.00
Average:	330.00
Transfers:	1
Sales:	5

March:
1—450.00
5—450.00
16—transfer
22—400.00
25—transfer
29—300.00
31—300.00

High:	450.00
Low:	300.00
Average:	380.00
Transfers:	2
Sales:	5

April:
7—transfer
13—transfer
26—200.00

High:	200.00
Low:	200.00
Average:	200.00
Transfers:	2
Sales:	1

May:
7—200.00
12—250.00
14—250.00
24—250.00
25—250.00
29—250.00

High:	250.00
Low:	200.00
Average:	241.00
Transfers:	0
Sales:	6

June:
4—250.00
7—200.00
12—300.00
17—300.00
21—300.00
22—350.00
22—350.00
23—300.00
29—450.00

High:	450.00
Low:	200.00
Average:	311.00
Transfers:	0
Sales:	9

July:
2— 500.00
8— 500.00
14— 525.00
15— 675.00
19— 525.00
24— 825.00
26—1,075.00

High:	1,075.00
Low:	500.00
Average:	660.00
Transfers:	0
Sales:	7

August:
2—1,250.00
13—1,475.00
19—1,500.00
26—1,250.00
31—1,250.00

High:	1,500.00
Low:	1,250.00
Average:	1,345.00
Transfers:	0
Sales:	5

September:
3—1,300.00
18—transfer
27—1,500.00

High:	1,500.00
Low:	1,300.00
Average:	1,400.00
Transfers:	1
Sales:	2

October:
7—1,500.00
16—1,800.00
16—transfer
16—transfer
20—1,800.00
25—1,875.00
27—1,800.00

High:	1,875.00
Low:	1,500.00
Average:	1,755.00
Transfers:	2
Sales:	5

November:
1—1,700.00
4—1,500.00
19—1,000.00
19—1,000.00
24—transfer

High:	1,700.00
Low:	1,000.00
Average:	1,300.00
Transfers:	1
Sales:	4

December:
7— 800.00
8— 800.00
14— 825.00
21—transfer
27— 825.00
29—1,000.00

High:	1,000.00
Low:	800.00
Average:	850.00
Transfers:	1
Sales	5

1944

January:
3—1,400.00
14—transfer
29—1,000.00
High: 1,400.00
Low: 1,000.00
Average: 1,200.00
Transfers: 1
Sales: 2

February:
2—transfer
14—1,000.00
23— 975.00
24—1,000.00
29—1,000.00
High: 1,000.00
Low: 975.00
Average: 994.00
Transfers: 1
Sales: 4

March:
20—transfer
28—1,100.00
31— 800.00
High: 1,100.00
Low: 800.00
Average: 950.00
Transfers: 1
Sales: 2

April:
3—transfer
19—1,000.00
24—1,150.00
27—1,000.00
High: 1,150.00
Low: 1,000.00
Average: 1,050.00
Transfers: 1
Sales: 3

May:
1— 800.00
10—transfer
12— 850.00
19— 950.00
22—1,000.00
31—1,000.00
High: 1,000.00
Low: 800.00
Average: 920.00
Transfers: 1
Sales: 5

June:
5—1,000.00
6—1,000.00
14—1,150.00
16—1,300.00
16—transfer
30—1,600.00
High: 1,600.00
Low: 1,000.00
Average: 1,215.00
Transfers: 1
Sales 5

July:
10—1,600.00
11—1,800.00
14—2,000.00
24—2,250.00
High: 2,250.00
Low: 1,600.00
Average: 1,912.00
Transfers: 0
Sales: 4

August:
6—2,250.00
11—2,250.00
12—2,300.00
13—2,300.00
14—3,000.00
21—3,250.00
26—3,500.00
26—3,500.00
26—3,500.00
High: 3,500.00
Low: 2,250.00
Average: 2,872.00
Transfers: 0
Sales: 9

September:
No record of the sales for September

October:
3—transfer
23—3,500.00
(the only two sales made in this month)

November:
4—transfer
13—2,200.00
29—transfer
High: 2,200.00
Low: 2,200.00
Average: 2,200.00
Transfers: 2
Sales: 1

December:
6—2,800.00
7—2,900.00
7—3,000.00
8—3,000.00
14—transfer
20—3,100.00
21—transfer
High: 3,100.00
Low: 2,800.00
Average: 2,960.00
Transfers: 2
Sales: 5

1945

January:
10—transfer
11—2,500.00
13—transfer
17—transfer
31—2,750.00
31—transfer

High:	2,750.00
Low:	2,500.00
Average:	2,625.00
Transfers:	4
Sales:	2

February:
9—2,250.00
14—transfer
14—transfer
19—2,250.00
28—2,400.00

High:	2,400.00
Low	2,250.00
Average:	2,300.00
Transfers:	2
Sales:	3

March:
10—2,500.00
12—2,250.00
15—transfer
16—transfer
28—transfer
31—2,250.00

High:	2,500.00
Low:	2,250.00
Average:	2,333.00
Transfers:	3
Sales:	3

April:
3—2,000.00
10—2,250.00
13—transfer
27—transfer

High:	2,250.00
Low:	2,000.00
Average:	2,125.00
Transfers:	2
Sales:	2

May:
1—2,400.00
1—2,900.00
7—2,950.00
7—3,000.00
10—3,200.00
12—transfer
12—2,250.00
14—transfer
18—4,000.00
18—4,000.00

High:	4.000.00
Low:	2,250.00
Average:	3,087.00
Transfers:	2
Sales:	8

June:
5—3,200.00
15—3,950.00
20—4,000.00
27—3,500.00

High:	4,000.00
Low:	3,200.00
Average:	3,662.00
Transfers:	0
Sales:	4

July:
5—transfer
9—2,000.00
21—3,000.00
27—3,000.00

High:	3,000.00
Low:	2,000.00
Average:	2,666.00
Transfers:	1
Sales:	3

August:
2—transfer
7—2,000.00
13—3,000.00
13—3,500.00
13—3,700.00
17—transfer
17—transfer
23—transfer
24—3,750.00

High:	3,750.00
Low:	2,000.00
Average:	3,190.00
Transfers:	4
Sales:	5

September:
7—transfer
8—transfer
19—transfer
19—transfer
20—transfer
20—3,750.00
27—3,900.00

High:	3,900.00
Low:	3,750.00
Average:	3,825.00
Transfers:	5
Sales:	2

October:
19–3,500.00
30—3,650.00
30—3,700.00

High:	3,700.00
Low:	3,500.00
Average:	3,616.00
Transfers:	0
Sales:	3

November:
14—transfer
20—3,450.00
26—3,500.00
28—3,250.00

High:	3,500.00
Low:	3,250.00
Average:	3,400.00
Transfers:	1
Sales:	3

December:
7—3,500.00
11—3,500.00
12—3,300.00
17—3,650.00
22—3,600.00

High:	3,650.00
Low:	3,300.00
Average:	3,510.00
Transfers:	0
Sales:	5

1946—1948:

No records of sales

1949

January:
3—3,600.00
4—3,200.00
10—transfer
19—transfer
20—3,150.00
22—transfer
25—3,250.00
28—3,200.00
28—3,200.00
28—3,200.00

High:	3,600.00
Low:	3,150.00
Average:	3,257.00
Transfers:	3
Sales:	7

February:
4—3,400.00
8—3,000.00
18—3,000.00
21—2,850.00
21—2,900.00
25—2,900.00

High:	3,400.00
Low:	2,850.00
Average:	3,100.00
Transfers:	0
Sales:	6

March:
5—2,800.00
7—2,700.00
15—2,750.00
21—2,650.00
21—2,600.00
23—2,600.00
28—2,400.00
29—2,400.00

High:	2,800.00
Low:	2,400.00
Average:	2,612.00
Transfers:	0
Sales:	8

April:
1—transfer
4—transfer
7—transfer
7—2,250.00
19—transfer
19—2,300.00
22—2,250.00
29—2,000.00

High:	2,300.00
Low:	2,000.00
Average:	2,200.00
Transfers:	4
Sales:	4

May:
5—1,800.00
9—1,800.00
11—1,800.00
13—1,800.00
13—1,800.00
17—transfer
17—2,000.00
17—2,000.00
19—2,100.00
20—2,250.00
26—2,250.00
31—2,250.00

High:	2,250.00
Low:	1,800.00
Average:	1,986.00
Transfers:	1
Sales	11

June:
8—2,100.00
15—2,000.00
17—transfer
17—transfer
18—2,000.00
20—2,000.00
21—transfer
22—transfer
24—1,800.00
28—2,000.00
29—transfer
29—transfer
29—transfer

High:	2,100.00
Low:	1,800.00
Average:	1,983.00
Transfers:	7
Sales:	6

July:
7—2,050.00
7—2,450.00
8—transfer
8—2,250.00
14—2,250.00
15—2,500.00
20—2,500.00
21—2,500.00
21—2,500.00
22—2,500.00

High:	2,500.00
Low:	2,050.00
Average:	2,388.00
Transfers:	1
Sales:	9

August:
1—2,800.00
8—2,750.00
8—transfer
8—transfer
12—2,700.00
13—2,650.00
13—2,500.00
23—2,225.00
29—2,250.00

High:	2,800.00
Low:	2,250.00
Average:	2,557.00
Transfers:	2
Sales:	7

September:
No record of sales for this month

1949

October:
3—transfer
10—transfer
10—2,250.00
20—transfer

High:	2,250.00
Low:	0
Average:	2,250.00
Transfers:	3
Sales:	1

November:
3—2,300.00
4—transfer
15—2,250.00
16—2,100.00

High:	2,300.00
Low:	2,100.00
Average:	2,216.00
Transfers:	1
Sales:	3

December:
1—2,100.00
5—2,000.00
7—transfer
8—transfer
9—transfer
9—2,000.00
9—2,000.00
9—2,000.00
10—2,000.00
22—2,200.00
31—transfer

High:	2,200.00
Low:	2,000.00
Average:	2,042.00
Transfers:	4
Sales:	7

1950

January:
4—2,300.00
9—2,400.00
10—2,250.00
11—transfer
13—2,200.00
13—transfer
16—2,000.00
17—2,000.00
18—1,900.00
18—1,700.00
20—1,800.00
24—2,000.00
27—2,000.00

High:	2,400.00
Low:	1,700.00
Average:	2,050.00
Transfers:	2
Sales:	11

February:
2—2,000.00
7—1,900.00
8—transfer
23—2,000.00
24—2,075.00
24—2,200.00

High:	2,200.00
Low:	1,900.00
Average:	2,035.00
Transfers:	1
Sales:	5

March:
1—2,000.00
1—2,000.00
7—2,000.00
10—transfer
20—2,000.00
23—transfer
23—2,000.00
27—transfer
29—1,850.00
29—transfer

High:	2,000.00
Low:	1,850.00
Average:	1,975.00
Transfers:	4
Sales:	6

April:
12—2,000.00
15—1,950.00
20—2,150.00
21—1,900.00
24—transfer
26—2,100.00
27—1,950.00

High:	2,150.00
Low:	1,900.00
Average:	2,008.00
Transfers:	1
Sales:	6

May:
2—1,950.0
3—transfer
3—2,200.00
3—2,500.00
3—2,500.00
10—2,400.00
11—2,200.00
11—transfer
17—transfer
18—2,300.00
23—2,200.00
24—2,200.00
31—2,250.00
31—2,450.00

High:	2,500.00
Low:	1,950.00
Average:	2,286.00
Transfers:	3
Sales:	11

June:
1—2,500.00
8—3,000.00
9—3,000.00
29—2,600.00
29—transfer
29—2,500.00
29—transfer

High:	3,000.00
Low:	2,500.00
Average:	2,750.00
Transfers:	2
Sales:	5

July:
5—transfer
7—transfer
13—2,300.00
14—3,000.00
17—3,200.00
20—2,800.00
21—2,100.00
24—transfer
25—2,500.00
26—2,500.00
27—2,500.00

High:	3,200.00
Low:	2,100.00
Average:	2,612.00
Transfers:	3
Sales:	8

August:
3—2,200.00
10—transfer
16—transfer
23—2,400.00
28—2,300.00
28—transfer

High:	2,400.00
Low:	2,200.00
Average:	2,300.00
Transfers:	3
Sales	3

September:
6—2,300.00
13—2,000.00
26—2,000.00
27—2,000.00
27—2,000.00

High:	2,300.00
Low:	2,000.00
Average:	2,060.00
Transfers:	0
Sales:	5

October:
5—2,100.00
9—2,100.00
13—2,200.00
17—transfer
18—transfer
21—2,100.00
30—2,200.00

High:	2,200.00
Low:	2,100.00
Average:	2,140.00
Transfers:	2
Sales:	5

1950

November:
1—2,400.00
8—2,400.00
14—2,400.00
16—transfer
20—2,500
21—2,400.00
27—2,600.00
High: 2,600.00
Low: 2,400.00
Average: 2,450.00
Transfers: 1
Sales: 6

December:
13—2,600.00
13—2,400.00
17—2,050.00
21—2,050.00
21—2,200.00
26—2,050.00
28—2,050.00
28—2,200.00
High: 2,600.00
Low: 2,050.00
Average: 2,200.00
Transfers: 0
Sales: 8

1951

January:
2—2,200.00
5—2,200.00
11—2,000.00
15—2,200.00
18—2,500.00
18—2,600.00
23—transfer
24—2,600.00
25—2,500.00

High:	2,600.00
Low:	2,000.00
Average:	2,350.00
Transfers:	1
Sales:	8

February:
1—2,500.00
2—2,400.00
2—2,200.00
8—transfer
9—transfer
9—transfer
19—2,250.00
19—2,300.00
19—2,300.00
19—2,400.00
21—3,000.00
21—3,000.00
21—3,000.00

High:	3,000.00
Low:	2,200.00
Average:	2,535.00
Transfers:	3
Sales:	10

March:
1—2,950.00
6—2,700.00
6—2,500.00
6—2,500.00
10—transfer
15—transfer
20—2,500.00
21—2,800.00
28—3,000.00
30—2,800.00

High	3,000.00
Low:	2,500.00
Average:	2,718.00
Transfers:	2
Sales:	8

April:
6—transfer
9—2,800.00
18—2,500.00
30—2,300.00

High:	2,800.00
Low:	2,300.00
Average:	2,533.00
Transfers:	1
Sales:	3

May:
7—2,500.00
7—transfer
16—transfer
21—2,150.00
22—2,250.00
24—transfer

High:	2,500.00
Low:	2,150.00
Average:	2,300.00
Transfers:	3
Sales:	3

June:
5—transfer
6—transfer
12—transfer
15—transfer
22—3,000.00
25—transfer
26—transfer

High:	3,000.00
Low:	3,000.00
Average:	3,000.00
Transfers:	6
Sales:	1

July:
6—2,800.00
16—2,800.00
17—transfer
24—3,000.00
24—3,000.00
26—3,200.00

High:	3,200.00
Low:	2,800.00
Average:	2,960.00
Transfers:	1
Sales:	5

August:
14—2,900.00
22—3,100.00
27—3,000.00

High:	3,100.00
Low:	2,900.00
Average:	3,000.00
Transfers:	0
Sales:	3

September:
4—2,950.00
6—2,800.00
9—transfer
10—2,850.00
21—transfer
21—2,500.00
21—transfer
21—2,750.00

High:	2,950.00
Low:	2,500.00
Average:	2,770.00
Transfers:	3
Sales:	5

October:
1—2,850.00
8—2,850.00
9—2,600.00
19—2,600.00
22—2,950.00
22—2,900.00
24—3,100.00
29—3,500.00

High:	3,500.00
Low:	2,600.00
Average:	2,950.00
Transfers:	0
Sales:	8

November:
12—3,500.00
16—transfer
16—3,500.00
16—3,500.00
23—3,200.00
23—3,250.00
23—3,250.00

1951					
23—3,250.00		December:		High:	2,900.00
28—3,250.00		26—2,900.00		Low:	2,500.00
High:	3,500.00	26—2,900.00		Average:	2,700.00
Low:	3,200.00	27—2,500.00		Transfers:	0
Average:	3,314.00	29—2,500.00		Sales:	4
Transfers:	1				
Sales:	7				

1952

January:
3—3,000.00
9—transfer
14—3,000.00
19—3,100.00
20—3,000.00
23—2,850.00
High: 3,100.00
Low: 2,850.00
Average: 2,990.00
Transfers: 1
Sales: 5

February:
3—3,200.00
5—3,200.00
14—3,100.00
14—transfer
15—transfer
High: 3,200.00
Low: 3,100.00
Average: 3,166.00
Transfers: 2
Sales: 3

March:
1—transfer
7—3,350.00
7—3,500.00
10—3,500.00
14—transfer
15—3,600.00
17—transfer
25—3,300.00
High: 3,600.00
Low: 3,350.00
Average: 3,450.00
Transfers: 3
Sales: 5

April:
15—3,500.00
16—3,700.00
21—3,500.00
25—transfer
28—3,400.00
30—3,400.00
High: 3,700.00
Low: 3,400.00
Average: 3,500.00
Transfers: 1
Sales: 5

May:
2—3,500.00
13—3,400.00
13—3,400.00
13—transfer
13—transfer
14—3,400.00
14—3,400.00
15—3,300.00
15—3,300.00
20—3,300.00
20—3,300.00
23—3,300.00
27—3,450.00
27—3,300.00
28—3,400.00
31—3,500.00
High: 3,500.00
Low: 3,300.00
Average 3,400.00
Transfers: 2
Sales: 15

June:
2—transfer
4—transfer
5—3,250.00
7—transfer
9—3,000.00
22—3,300.00
30—3,000.00
30—3,000.00
High: 3,300.00
Low: 3,000.00
Average: 3,110.00
Trasfers: 3
Sales: 5

July:
9—3,300.00
18—3,300.00
21—3,300.00
22—3,150.00
22—transfer
25—transfer
29—3,200.00
30—transfer
31—3,100.00
High: 3,300.00
Low: 3,100.00
Average: 3,225.00
Transfers: 3
Sales: 6

August:
5—3,050.00
7—transfer
14—3,150.00
14—transfer
15—3,275.00
15—transfer
21—3,200.00
22—3,200.00
26—3,450.00
High: 3,450.00
Low: 3,050.00
Average: 3,300.00
Transfers: 3
Sales: 6

September:
9—3,200.00
15—3,000.00
17—transfer
17—3,100.00
24—3,000.00
High: 3,200.00
Low: 3,000.00
Average: 3,050.00
Transfers: 1
Sales: 4

October:
14—3,000.00
16—3,300.00
23—3,250.00
26—3,300.00
27—transfer
29—3,500.00
30—3,700.00
30—3,900.00
31—3,700.00
High: 3,900.00
Low: 3,000.00
Average: 3,456.00
Transfers: 1
Sales: 8

November:
5—transfer
7—transfer
10—3,600.00
13—3,700.00

1952					
17—3,300.00		December:		18—3,000.00	
20—3,300.00		1—3,300.00		23—3,300.00	
High:	3,700.00	3—transfer		31—2,800.00	
Low:	3,300.00	8—3,300.00		High:	3,400.00
Average:	3,475.00	10—3,200.00		Low:	2,800.00
Transfers:	2	11—3,400.00		Average:	3,181.00
Sale:	4	12—transfer		Transfers:	2
		16—3,150.00		Sales:	8

1953

January:
6—transfer
7—3,000.00
7—3,200.00
7—2,250.00
14—transfer
14—3,300.00
15—3,300.00
15—3,500.00
15—3,600.00
19—transfer
19—transfer
26—3,600.00
28—3,600.00
High: 3,600.00
Low: 2,250.00
Average: 3,261.00
Transfers: 4
Sales: 9

February:
2—3,500.00
3—3,800.00
3—4,000.00
19—3,900.00
19—3,900.00
20—3,900.00
27—transfer
High: 4,000.00
Low: 3,500.00
Average: 3,833.00
Transfers: 1
Sales: 6

March:
3—4,000.00
10—transfer
11—transfer
13—transfer
16—transfer
16—3,700.00
17—3,900.00
18—3,900.00
20—4,000.00
25—transfer
27—4,000.00
30—transfer
31—4,000.00
31—3,900.00
High: 4,000.00
Low: 3,700.00
Average: 3,925.00
Transfers: 6
Sales: 8

April:
1—transfer
2—4,000.00
8—4,100.00
8—4,000.00
13—4,200.00
16—4,400.00
17—4,400.00
20—4,500.00
27—4,550.00
27—4,550.00
27—4,550.00
30—transfer
High: 4,550.00
Low: 4,000.00
Average: 4,320.00
Transfers: 2
Sales: 10

May:
13—transfer
15—transfer
25—4,000.00
26—3,750.00
27—4,000.00
28—4,000.00
High: 4,000.00
Low: 3,750.00
Average: 3,937.00
Transfers: 2
Sales: 4

June:
10—4,000.00
10—transfer
10—transfer
16—3,750.00
18—4,000.00
18—3,600.00
18—3,800.00
18—3,650.00
30—transfer
30—3,600.00
30—transfer
High: 4,000.00
Low: 3,600.00
Average: 3,771.00
Transfers: 4
Sales: 7

July:
2—3,500.00
2—3,500.00
7—3,650.00
8—transfer
10—3,500.00
15—3,500.00
17—transfer
17—3,500.00
22—3,500.00
24—3,500.00
28—3,300.00
29—transfer
High: 3,650.00
Low: 3,300.00
Average: 3,494.00
Transfers: 3
Sales: 9

August:
5—3,300.00
7—transfer
10—3,000.00
11—3,300.00
15—3,300.00
18—3,300.00
20—3,600.00
25—3,900.00
25—transfer
26—4,000.00
27—4,000.00
High: 4,000.00
Low 3,000.00
Average: 3,522.00
Transfers: 2
Sales: 9

September:
2—transfer
3—3,900.00
8—3,500.00
15—3,250.00
15—3,100.00
16—transfer
22—transfer
25—transfer
28—transfer
30—3,200.00

1953

High: 3,900.00
Low: 3,100.00
Average: 3,390.00
Transfers: 5
Sales: 5

October:
1—3,300.00
1—3,300.00
2—3,300.00
7—transfer
8—transfer
16—3,500.00
16—3,500.00
23—3,600.00
24—3,600.00
27—3,500.00
30—transfer
High: 3,600.00
Low: 3,300.00
Average: 3,445.00
Transfers: 3
Sales: 9

November:
3—transfer
4—transfer
12—3,500.00
16—3,600.00
19—3,500.00
25—3,500.00
27—3,500.00
30—transfer
High: 3,600.00
Low: 3,500.00
Average: 3,520.00
Transfers: 3
Sales: 5

December:
1—3,900.00
2—4,000.00
4—4,000.00
8—4,000.00
8—4,000.00
8—4,500.00
8—4,500.00
8—4,500.00
8—4,750.00
9—5,000.00
15—transfer
23—4,000.00
24—4,000.00
24—4,000.00
29—4,500.00
31—5,000.00
High: 5,000.00
Low: 3,900.00
Average 4,296.00
Transfers: 1
Sales: 14

1954

January:
5—transfer
6—4,000.00
7—4,000.00
7—4,000.00
7—4,000.00
7—4,000.00
12—4,100.00
14—transfer
18—3,750.00
21—transfer
21—3,900.00
23—3,800.00
27—3,750.00
27—transfer
27—3,800.00
High: 4,100.00
Low: 3,750.00
Average: 3,918.00
Transfers: 4
Sales: 11

February:
1—4,000.00
8—3,900.00
10—3,900.00
10—3,900.00
11—3,700.00
16—transfer
17—3,750.00
17—3,750.00
18—3,750.00
19—transfer
23—3,800.00
25—transfer
25—3,800.00
28—transfer
High: 4,000.00
Low: 3,700.00
Average: 3,825.00
Transfers: 4
Sales: 1

March:
2—3,800.00
5—transfer
9—4,000.00
9—4,500.00
17—4,500.00
19—4,250.00
22—transfer
23—4,500.00
23—4,500.00
25—4,600.00
30—transfer
31—4,900.00
31—transfer
High: 4,900.00
Low: 3,800.00
Average: 4,394.00
Transfers: 4
Sales: 9

April:
2—5,000.00
7—transfer
9—4,600.00
9—5,000.00
14—4,600.00
22—transfer
23—4,600.00
23—transfer
26—4,300.00
28—5,000.00
28—transfer
30—transfer
High: 5,000.00
Low: 4,300.00
Average: 4,728.00
Transfers: 5
Sales: 7

May:
13—transfer
13—transfer
26—4,700.00
High: 4,700.00
Low: 4,700.00
Average: 4,700.00
Transfers: 2
Sales: 1

June:
1—4,700.00
4—4,400.00
11—4,250.00
14—transfer
15—4,600.00
16—4,600.00
23—4,800.00
23—4,800.00
28—4,600.00
29—4,500.00
High: 4,800.00
Low: 4,250.00
Average: 4,583.00
Transfers: 1
Sales: 9

July:
1—4,600.00
1—transfer
2—4,600.00
6—4,600.00
8—4,800.00
9—5,500.00
10—5,000.00
13—5,000.00
14—transfer
14—transfer
20—4,700.00
High: 5,000.00
Low: 4,600.00
Average: 4,850.00
Transfers: 3
Sales: 8

August:
6—4,900.00
9—transfer
10—4,900.00
11—4,900.00
13—5,000.00
16—4,800.00
23—4,800.00
High: 5,000.00
Low: 4,800.00
Average: 4,883.00
Transfers: 1
Sales: 6

September:
2—transfer
3—3,900.00
8—3,500.00
15—3,250.00
15—3,100.00
16—transfer
22—transfer
25—4,000.00
28—transfer
30—3,200.00
High: 4,000.00
Low: 3,000.00
Average: 3,491.00

1954

Transfers: 4
Sales: 6

October:
1—3,000.00
2—3,000.00
7—3,000.00
8—3,000.00
16—3,000.00
16—transfer
16—3,000.00
16—3,600.00
23—3,600.00
24—3,600.00
27—3,600.00
30—transfer
High: 3,600.00
Low: 3,000.00
Average: 3,240.00

Transfers: 1
Sales: 10

November:
3—transfer
11—transfer
12—3,500.00
16—3,600.00
19—3,500.00
25—3,400.00
27—3,500.00
30—transfer
High: 3,600.00
Low: 3,400.00
Average: 3,500.00
Transfers: 2
Sales: 5

December:
1—3,000.00
2—4,000.00
4—3,750.00
8—4,400.00
8—4,500.00
8—4,500.00
8—4,500.00
8—4,500.00
9—5,000.00
15—transfer
23—4,000.00
24—4,000.00
24—4,000.00
29—4,500.00
High: 5,000.00
Low: 3,000.00
Average: 4,207.00
Transfers: 1
Sales: 14

1955

January:
4—transfer
5—4,000.00
6—6,000.00
7—4,000.00
7—4,000.00
7—4,000.00
7—4,000.00
12—4,100.00
18—3,750.00
21—transfer
21—3,900.00
27—3,800.00
27—3,750.00
27—transfer
27—3,750.00

High:	6,000.00
Low:	3,750.00
Average:	4,087.00
Transfers:	3
Sales:	12

February:
1—4,000.00
8—3,900.00
10—3,900.00
10—3,900.00
11—3,700.00
16—transfer
17—3,750.00
17—3,750.00
18—3,750.00
19—transfer
23—3,800.00
25—transfer
25—3,800.00
28—transfer

High:	4,000.00
Low:	3,700.00
Average:	3,825.00
Transfers:	4
Sales:	10

March:
2—3,800.00
5—transfer
9—4,000.00
9—4,500.00
9—4,500.00
17—4,500.00
19—4,250.00
22—transfer
23—4,500.00
23—4,500.00
25—4,600.00
30—transfer
31—4,900.00
31—transfer

High:	4,900.00
Low:	3,800.00
Average:	4,405.00
Transfers:	4
Sales:	10

April:
2—5,000.00
7—transfer
9—4,600.00
9—5,000.00
14—4,600.00
22—transfer
23—4,600.00
23—transfer
26—4,300.00
28—5,000.00
28—transfer
30—transfer

High:	5,000.00
Low:	4,300.00
Average:	4,750.00
Transfers:	5
Sales:	7

May:
13—transfer
13—transfer
26—4,700.00

High:	4,700.00
Low:	4,700.00
Average:	4,700.00
Transfers:	2
Sales:	1

June:
1—4,700.00
4—4,400.00
4—transfer
11—4,250.00
15—4,600.00
16—4,600.00
23—4,800.00
23—4,800.00
29—4,500.00

High:	4,800.00
Low:	4,250.00
Average:	4,581.00
Transfers:	1
Sales:	8

July:
No record of sales for this month

August:
1—transfer
11—transfer
16—transfer
21—6,900.00
24—6,800.00
26—6,800.00
29—6,550.00

High:	6,900.00
Low:	6,550.00
Average:	6,762.00
Transfers:	3
Sales:	4

September:
1—7,000.00
2—transfer
12—transfer
19—transfer
19—7,000.00
21—7,000.00
26—6,500.00

High:	7,000.00
Low:	6,500.00
Average:	6,875.00
Transfers:	3
Sales:	4

October:
5—6,200.00
6—transfer
17—transfer
17—6,200.00
27—6,300.00
31—6,500.00

High:	6,500.00
Low:	6,200.00
Average:	6,300.00
Transfers:	2
Sales:	4

November:
1—6,300.00

1955

14—6,400.00
14—transfer
15—6,500.00
15—6,500.00
21—6,500.00
21—6,500.00

High:	6,500.00
Low:	6,300.00
Average:	6,450.00
Transfers:	1
Sales:	6

December:

15—5,600.00
15—5,600.00
21—5,600.00
21—5,500.00
27—5,850.00
27—5,800.00
30—transfer

High:	5,850.00
Low:	5,500.00
Average:	5,658.00
Transfers:	1
Sales:	6

1956

January:
3—5,500.00
4—5,500.00
5—6,000.00
12—6,000.00
13—transfer
16—transfer
18—transfer
19—5,750.00
23—5,800.00
23—5,550.00
24—5,750.00
27—5,850.00
31—5,750.00

High:	6,000.00
Low:	5,500.00
Average:	5,750.00
Transfers:	3
Sales:	10

February:
1—5,850.00
2—transfer
2—5,600.00
3—transfer
23—5,300.00
28—transfer

High:	5,850.00
Low:	5,300.00
Average:	5,600.00
Transfers:	3
Sales:	3

March:
8—5,600.00
20—transfer
21—transfer
23—5,500.00
27—5,300.00

High:	5,600.00
Low:	5,300.00
Average:	5,450.00
Transfers:	2
Sales:	3

April:
2—transfer
5—transfer
6—5,200.00
9—5,600.00
9—6,000.00
9—6,000.00
9—6,000.00
9—6,000.00
9—6,000.00
9—6,000.00
11—6,000.00
12—6,500.00
13—6,000.00
19—6,000.00
19—6,200.00
23—7,000.00
25—6,700.00
26—transfer

High:	7,000.00
Low:	5,200.00
Average:	6,000.00
Transfers:	3
Sales:	15

May:
9—7,000.00
11—7,250.00
11—7,250.00
15—7,500.00
21—7,500.00
21—7,500.00
24—7,500.00
28—7,250.00

High:	7,500.00
Low:	7,000.00
Average:	7,350.00
Transfers:	0
Sales:	8

June:
1—6,800.00
6—7,500.00
11—7,250.00
12—7,500.00
12—transfers
19—7,100.00
21—7,100.00
25—transfer
29—7,200.00

High:	7,500.00
Low:	6,800.00
Average:	7,200.00
Transfers:	2
Sales	7

July—October:
No record of sales for these months

November:
27—6,900.00
27—7,250.00
30—7,250.00

High:	7,250.00
Low:	6,900.00
Average:	7,133.00
Transfers:	0
Sales:	3

December:
11—7,500.00
11—transfer
11—transfer
11—transfer
11—transfer
12—7,500.00
13—transfer
14—7,250.00
28—7,500.00
28—7,500.00
28—7,500.00

High:	7,500.00
Low:	7,250.00
Average:	7,458.00
Transfers:	5
Sales:	6

1957

January:

- 2—transfer
- 2—7,750.00
- 7—transfer
- 9—transfer
- 22—7,800.00
- 24—transfer
- 25—8,500.00
- High: 8,500.00
- Low: 7,750.00
- Average: 8,017.00
- Transfers: 4
- Sales: 3

February:

- 5—9,300.00
- 7—9,400.00
- 8—9,400.00
- 11—9,400.00
- 19—9,500.00
- 19—9,500.00
- 19—9,500.00
- 20—9,850.00
- 20—transfer
- 27—transfer
- High: 9,850.00
- Low: 9,300.00
- Average: 9,481.00
- Transfers: 2
- Sales: 8

March—June:

No record of sales for these months

July:

- 6—8,650.00
- 23—transfer
- 23—7,900.00
- High: 8,650.00
- Low: 7,900.00
- Average: 8,275.00
- Transfers: 1
- Sales: 2

August:

- 20—7,450.00
- 20—7,100.00
- 20—7,100.00
- 21—6,700.00
- 21—6,700.00
- 21—transfer
- 21—transfer
- High: 7,450.00
- Low: 6,700.00
- Average: 7,010.00
- Transfers: 2
- Sales: 5

September:

- 4—6,300.00
- 18—6,400.00
- High: 6,400.00
- Low: 6,300.00
- Average: 6,350.00
- Transfers: 0
- Sales: 2

October:

- 1—6,600.00
- 1—6,700.00
- 1—6,700.00
- 1—6,800.00
- 1—6,825.00
- 1—6,500.00
- 1—6,825.00
- 2—6,850.00
- 2—transfer
- 3—transfer
- 15—6,800.00
- 15—6,800.00
- 17—6,700.00
- 22—6,250.00
- 29—transfer
- High: 6,850.00
- Low: 6,250.00
- Average: 6,695.00
- Transfers: 3
- Sales: 12

November:

- 12—5,800.00
- 12—5,800.00
- 13—5,500.00
- 22—4,500.00
- 26—4,500.00
- 26—4,700.00
- 26—transfer
- 27—transfer
- High: 5,800.00
- Low: 4,500.00
- Average: 5,141.00
- Transfers: 2
- Sales: 6

December:

- 10—transfer
- 10—4,700.00
- 26—4,700.00
- 26—4,700.00
- 26—4,700.00
- 26—4,750.00
- 26—4,750.00
- 26—4,800.00
- 26—transfer
- 26—transfer
- 26—4,800.00
- 31—transfer
- High: 4,800.00
- Low: 4,700.00
- Average: 4,737.00
- Transfers: 4
- Sales: 8

1958

January:
4—4,900.00
21—4,975.00
21—4,975.00
21—5,000.00
21—transfer
High: 5,000.00
Low: 4,900.00
Average: 4,962.00
Transfers: 1
Sales: 4

February:
4—4,750.00
6—transfer
13—4,900.00
18—4,900.00
18—4,900.00
18—4,950.00
19—transfer
28—4,950.00
High: 4,950.00
Low: 4,750.00
Average: 4,892.00
Transfers: 2
Sales: 6

March:
4—4,950.00
4—4,900.00
4—transfer
4—5,000.00
18—4,925.00
18—transfer
19—4,925.00
20—4,925.00
High: 5,000.00
Low: 4,900.00
Average: 4,938.00
Transfers: 2
Sales: 6

April:
1—4,925.00
1—4,925.00
18—4,800.00
21—4,900.00
High: 4,925.00
Low: 4,800.00
Average: 4,888.00
Transfers: 0
Sales: 4

May:
1—transfer
1—transfer
2—4,900.00
4—4,650.00
4—4,600.00
21—4,400.00
High: 4,900.00
Low: 4,400.00
Average: 4,638.00
Transfers: 2
Sales: 4

June:
23—3,850.00
24—3,900.00
25—3,900.00
26—4,000.00
27—4,200.00
High: 4,200.00
Low: 3,850.00
Average: 3,970.00
Transfers: 0
Sales: 5

July:
9—transfer
22—4,000.00
22—4,000.00
22—4,050.00
23—4,100.00
High: 4,100.00
Low: 4,000.00
Average: 4,038.00
Transfers: 1
Sales: 4

August:
6—4,200.00
16—4,200.00
19—4,250.00
19—4,250.00
19—4,275.00
High: 4,275.00
Low: 4,200.00
Average: 4,235.00
Transfers: 0
Sales: 5

September:
2—4,200.00
2—4,225.00
2—4,250.00
3—4,250.00
3—transfer
10—4,200.00
17—4,250.00
17—4,250.00
30—4,200.00
30—4,225.00
30—4,250.00
High: 4,250.00
Low: 4,200.00
Average: 4,230.00
Transfers: 1
Sales: 10

October:
15—4,100.00
28—4,000.00
High: 4,100.00
Low: 4,000.00
Average: 4,050.00
Transfers: 0
Sales: 2

November:
11—3,900.00
11—3,900.00
11—transfer
28—3,850.00
High: 3,900.00
Low: 3,850.00
Average: 3,884.00
Transfers: 1
Sales: 3

December:
9—3,800.00
9—3,800.00
11—3,600.00
12—3,750.00
16—3,750.00
23—3,800.00
23—transfer
High: 3,800.00
Low: 3,600.00
Average: 3,750.00
Transfers: 1
Sales: 6

1959

January:
4—4,900.00
21—4,975.00
21—4,975.00
21—5,000.00
21—transfer
High: 5,000.00
Low: 4,900.00
Average: 4,962.00
Transfers: 1
Sales: 4

February:
4—4,750.00
6—transfer
13—4,900.00
18—4,900.00
18—4,900.00
18—4,900.00
18—4,950.00
19—transfer
28—4,950.00
High: 4,950.00
Low: 4,750.00
Average: 4,891.00
Transfers: 2
Sales: 7

March:
3—3,600.00
3—3,600.00
3—3,750.00
3—transfer
3—3,800.00
18—3,750.00
31—3,750.00
31—3,750.00
High: 3,800.00
Low: 3,600.00
Average: 3,714.00
Transfers: 1
Sales: 7

April:
14—3,750.00
15—3,750.00
28—3,800.00
29—3,800.00
29—3,850.00
29—transfer
30—3,850.00
High: 3,850.00
Low: 3,750.00
Average: 3,758.00
Transfers: 1
Sales: 6

May:
12—transfer
12—3,850.00
26—3,850.00
26—3,900.00
26—4,000.00
27—4,000.00
High: 4,000.00
Low: 3,850.00
Average: 3,920.00
Transfers: 1
Sales: 5

June:
2—3,900.00
9—4,000.00
10—4,000.00
10—4,000.00
23—4,250.00
23—transfer
23—transfer
High: 4,250.00
Low: 3,900.00
Average: 4,030.00
Transfers: 2
Sales: 5

July:
8—4,250.00
8—4,250.00
8—transfer
21—4,200.00
22—4,350.00
23—4,500.00
High: 4,500.00
Low: 4,200.00
Average: 4,310.00
Transfers: 1
Sales: 5

August:
5—transfer
5—transfer
18—4,200.00
18—4,250.00
High: 4,250.00
Low: 4,200.00
Average: 4,225.00
Transfers: 2
Sales: 2

September:
1—4,400.00
15—4,900.00
17—4,950.00
25—5,000.00
25—4,500.00
29—5,000.00
30—4,900.00
30—4,900.00
30—4,900.00
High: 5,000.00
Low: 4,400.00
Average: 4,827.00
Transfers: 0
Sales: 9

October:
8—4,800.00
13—4,800.00
27—transfer
27—4,900.00
High: 4,900.00
Low: 4,800.00
Average: 4,833.00
Transfers: 1
Sales: 3

November:
10—4,900.00
10—4,950.00
11—4,000.00
11—5,000.00
11—5,000.00
11—5,000.00
24—6,000.00
24—6,000.00
24—6,000.00
24—6,000.00
25—6,000.00
High: 6,000.00
Low: 4,000.00
Average: 5,350.00
Transfers: 0
Sales: 11

December:
2—transfer
3—transfer

1959

8—6,000.00	22—6,800.00	23—6,800.00	
8—transfer	22—6,900.00	23—transfer	
16—6,000.00	22—6,900.00	High:	6,950.00
22—6,000.00	22—6,950.00	Low:	6,000.00
22—6,000.00	22—6,850.00	Average:	6,475.00
22—6,000.00	22—transfer	Transfers:	5
22—6,500.00		Sales:	12

1960

January:
7—6,300.00
21—5,500.00
21—5,250.00
22—transfer
26—5,200.00
High: 6,300.00
Low: 5,200.00
Average: 5,562.00
Transfers: 1
Sales: 4

February:
2—5,500.00
2—transfer
3—transfer
9—5,500.00
16—5,500.00
16—5,600.00
16—5,700.00
16—5,800.00
16—6,000.00
17—6,000.00
17—transfer
19—transfer
High: 6,000.00
Low: 5,500.00
Average: 5,700.00
Transfers: 4
Sales: 8

March:
1—5,950.00
1—5,950.00
2—5,500.00
15—transfer
21—5,200.00
30—transfer
30—5,550.00
30—5,500.00
High: 5,950.00
Low: 5,200.00
Average: 5,592.00
Transfers: 2
Sales: 6

April:
6—5,500.00
13—transfer
13—transfer
High: 5,500.00
Low: 5,500.00
Average: 5,500.00
Transfers: 2
Sales: 1

May:
10—transfer
11—transfer
12—transfer
24—5.050.00
24—5,050.00
24—5,050.00
24—5,050.00
31—5,050.00
31—5,000.00
High: 5,050.00
Low: 5,000.00
Average: 5,412.00
Transfers: 3
Sales: 6

June:
1—5,000.00
1—5,000.00
1—5,000.00
2—5,000.00
2—5,000.00
2—5,000.00
2—5,000.00
3—5,000.00
3—5,000.00
3—5,000.00
3—5,000.00
3—5,000.00
3—5,000.00
3—5,000.00
3—5,000.00
3—5,000.00
3—5,000.00
3—5,000.00
5—transfer
21—4,700.00
21—4,700.00
21—4,700.00
22—5,500.00
30—4,700.00
High: 5,000.00
Low: 4,700.00
Average: 4,969.00
Transfers: 1
Sales: 23

July:
12—4,625.00
12—transfer
13—4,650.00
13—transfer
High: 4,650.00
Low: 4,625.00
Average: 4,637.00
Transfers: 2
Sales: 2

August:
16—transfer
30—transfer
30—transfer
30—transfer
Transfers: 4
Sales: 0

September:
13—4,250.00
15—4,250.00
27—4,100.00
27—4,100.00
28—transfer
High: 4,250.00
Low: 4,100.00
Average: 4,175.00
Transfers: 1
Sale: 4

October:
11—3,900.00
12—3,650.00
25—3,750.00
25—3,700.00
25—3,700.00
25—3,700.00
25—transfer
26—transfer
High: 3,900.00
Low: 3,650.00
Average: 3,740.00
Transfers: 2
Sales: 6

November:
14—3,550.00
14—transfer
17—3,700.00
22—3,800.00

1960

22—transfer		December:	20—4,200.00	
23—transfer		6—3,900.00	20—4,100.00	
High:	3,800.00	6—4,600.00	22—4,000.00	
Low;	3,550.00	6—4,000.00	29—4,000.00	
Average:	3,683.00	8—4,000.00	High:	4,600.00
Transfers:	3	20—4,100.00	Low:	3,900.00
Sales:	3	20—4,100.00	Average:	4,111.00
		20—transfer	Transfers:	1
			Sales:	10

1961

January:
3—4,100.00
3—transfer
4—4,100.00
4—4,400.00
17—4,750.00
17—4,750.00
17—transfer
23—transfer
High: 4,750.00
Low: 4,100.00
Average: 4,450.00
Transfers: 3
Sales: 5

February:
14—5,500.00
14—5,500.00
14—6,000.00
14—6,000.00
14—transfer
14—6,000.00
14—6,250.00
14—6,400.00
14—6,500.00
14—6,500.00
16—6,500.00
19—6,500.00
20—transfer
28—6,400.00
28—6,500.00
28—7,000.00
28—7,000.00
28—6,500.00
28—7,800.00
28—8,000.00
28—8,000.00
28—transfer
28—transfer
High: 8,000.00
Low: 5,500.00
Average: 6,571.00
Transfers: 4
Sales: 19

March:
1—transfer
1—8,750.00
6—8,500.00
14—8,000.00
14—7,900.00
14—8,000.00
14—8,000.00
14—8,00.000
14—transfer
17—transfer
28—7,700.00
28—7,900.00
28—7,900.00
28—7,950.00
30—8,000.00
High: 8,750.00
Low: 7,700.00
Average: 8,050.00
Transfers: 3
Sales: 12

April:
5—transfer
6—7,500.00
21—7,200.00
25—7,300.00
25—7,300.00
25—7,300.00
25—7,300.00
25—7,300.00
25—7,450.00
25—7,450.00
25—transfer
25—transfer
26—7,450.00
28—7,450.00
High: 7,500.00
Low: 7,200.00
Average: 7,364.00
Transfers: 3
Sales: 11

May:
1—transfer
1—7,300.00
1—7,450.00
2—transfer
9—7,200.00
9—7,250.00
9—transfer
9—transfer
10—transfer
17—7,000.00
23—6,700.00
High: 7,450.00
Low: 6,700.00
Average: 7,150.00
Transfers: 5
Sales: 6

June:
5—6,100.00
5—6,150.00
5—6,250.00
5—6,250.00
5—6,300.00
5—6,250.00
5—transfer
5—transfer
18—6,300.00
20—transfer
20—transfer
High: 6,300.00
Low: 6,100.00
Average: 6,229.00
Transfers: 4
Sales: 7

July:
5—6,100.00
5—6,150.00
5—6,250.00
5—6,250.00
5—6,300.00
5—6,250.00
5—transfer
5—transfer
18—6,300.00
20—transfer
20—transfer
High: 6,300.00
Low: 6,100.00
Average: 6,229.00
Transfers: 4
Sales: 7

August:
1—transfer
1—transfer
1—6,350.00
15—6,350.00
15—6,400.00
25—transfer
29—6,200.00
29—6,400.00
30—6,500.00
High: 6,500.00
Low: 6,200.00
Average: 6,367.00
Transfers: 3
Sales: 6

1961

September:
8—6,500.00
12—6,750.00
12—6,750.00
25—6,750.00
26—6,750.00
26—6,750.00
26—7,000.00
26—7,000.00
27—7,000.00
27—7,200.00
28—7,000.00

High:	7,200.00
Low:	6,500.00
Average:	6,859.00
Transfers:	0
Sales:	11

October:
2—7,200.00
9—7,200.00
10—7,300.00
10—transfer
10—transfer
31—7,000.00

High:	7,300.00
Low:	7,000.00
Average:	7,175.00
Transfers:	2
Sales:	4

November:
7—7,000.00
7—7,250.00
7—7,250.00
21—transfer

High:	7,250.00
Low:	7,000.00
Average:	7,167.00
Transfers:	1
Sales:	3

December:
19—6,700.00
20—6,800.00

High:	6,800.00
Low:	6,700.00
Average:	6,750.00
Transfers:	0
Sales:	2

1962

January:
2—transfer
2—transfer
2—6,400.00
16—6,750.00
16—6,750.00
16—6,750.00
17—6,750.00
17—transfer
17—transfer
30—6,600.00
30—6,600.00
30—6,650.00
30—6,700.00
31—transfer
31—6,750.00
31—6,750.00
31—transfer
31—transfer
High: 6,750.00
Low: 6,400.00
Average: 6,677.00
Transfers: 7
Sales: 11

February:
5—transfer
13—6,750.00
13—6,750.00
13—6,800.00
13—6,850.00
13—7,000.00
13—7,000.00
13—7,000.00
13—7,250.00
14—transfer
15—transfer
23—7,300.00
27—7,500.00
27—transfer
High: 7,500.00
Low; 6,750.00
Average: 7,020.00
Transfers: 4
Sales: 10

March:
13—transfer
13—7,700.00
13—7,500.00
13—7,700.00
13—7,750.00
13—7,800.00
13—7,850.00
13—transfer
13—transfer
13—7,900.00
15—8,000.00
27—7,800.00
28—7,900.00
28—7,900.00
High: 8,000.00
Low: 7,500.00
Average: 7,500.00
Transfers: 3
Sales: 11

April:
25—transfer
Transfers: 1
Sales: 0

May:
8—7,850.00
8—7,850.00
8—7,880.00
22—7,800.00
22—7,900.00
22—7,900.00
High: 7,900.00
Low: 7,800.00
Average: 7,863.00
Transfers: 0
Sales: 6

June:
5—8,000.00
6—8,000.00
19—8,200.00
19—transfer
19—transfer
19—8,200.00
19—8,200.00
20—transfer
20—transfer
20—8,850.00
20—8,950.00
High: 8,950.00
Low: 8,000.00
Average: 8,342.00
Transfers: 4
Sales: 7

July:
3—9,000.00
5—transfer
13—8,800.00
17—8,700.00
17—transfer
31—transfer
31—8,450.00
High: 9,000.00
Low: 8,450.00
Average: 8,738.00
Transfers: 3
Sales: 4

August:
28—transfer
28—7,900.00
High: 7,900.00
Low: 7,900.00
Average: 7,900.00
Transfers: 1
Sales: 1

September:
4—8,000.00
11—7,900.00
12—8,000.00
12—8,000.00
25—8,100.00
25—transfer
25—8,100.00
High: 8,100.00
Low: 7,900.00
Average: 8,016.00
Transfers: 1
Sales: 6

October:
9—8,200.00
9—8,200.00
23—8,750.00
23—8,300.00
23—8,400.00
23—8,400.00
23—8,500.00
23—transfer
23—transfer
24—8,500.00
24—8,500.00
24—8,600.00
24—8,700.00
24—8,750.00
24—8,750.00
24—8,750.00

1962

24—8,750.00
24—8,800.00
24—transfer

High:	8,800.00
Low:	8,200.00
Average:	8,523.00
Transfers:	3
Sales:	16

November:
7—8,500.00
7—transfer
20—8,500.00
20—8,500.00

High:	8,500.00
Low:	8,500.00
Average:	8,500.00
Transfers:	1
Sales:	3

December:
4—8,650.00
4—8,650.00
4—8,700.00
4—8,700.00
4—transfer
18—8,700.00
18—8,700.00
18—8,800.00
18—8,800.00
18—8,850.00
20—transfer
20—transfer

High:	8,850.00
Low:	8,650.00
Average:	8,727.00
Transfers:	3
Sales:	9

1963

January:
15—8,700.00
15—8,750.00
15—8,700.00
15—8,750.00
15—8,800.00
16—transfer
29—8,700.00
29—8,800.00
29—transfer
30—8,850.00
High: 8,850.00
Low: 8,700.00
Average: 8,757.00
Transfers: 2
Sales: 8

February:
12—8,850.00
12—9,000.00
13—8,900.00
15—8,900.00
26—8,900.00
High: 9,000.00
Low: 8,850.00
Average: 8,910.00
Transfers: 0
Sales: 5

March:
13—transfer
13—7,700.00
13—7,500.00
13—7,700.00
13—7,750.00
13—7,800.00
13—7,850.00
13—7,900.00
13—9,000.00
13—7,800.00
13—9,350.00
13—transfer
13—transfer
High: 9,350.00
Low: 7,500.00
Average: 8,035.00
Transfers: 3
Sales: 10

April:
10—9,300.00
11—9,400.00
19—9,350.00
23—9,300.00
23—9,300.00
23—transfer
23—transfer
23—9,256.00
High: 9,400.00
Low: 9,256.00
Average: 9,318.00
Transfers: 2
Sales: 6

May:
6—9,000.00
7—8,800.00
8—transfer
21—8,800.00
21—8,900.00
High: 9,000.00
Low: 8,800.00
Average: 8,875.00
Transfers: 1
Sales: 4

June:
18—8,800.00
18—transfer
18—transfer
18—transfer
18—transfer
High: 8,800.00
Low: 8,800.00
Average: 8,800.00
Transfers: 4
Sales: 1

July:
2—8,800.00
2—transfer
2—transfer
16—8,850.00
16—8,850.00
16—8,900.00
16—9,000.00
17—8,850.00
24—8,900.00
30—9,000.00
30—9,000.00
30—9,100.00
30—9,100.00
30—9,500.00
30—transfer
30—transfer
High: 9,500.00
Low: 8,850.00
Average: 8,987.00
Transfers: 4
Sales: 12

August:
12— 9,300.00
13— 9,400.00
13— 9,500.00
13— 9,500.00
13—transfer
15— 9,550.00
19—10,000.00
27—10,000.00
27—10,000.00
27—10,000.00
High: 10,000.00
Low: 9,300.00
Average: 9,694.00
Transfers: 1
Sales: 9

September:
10—11,750.00
10—12,000.00
10—12,000.00
10—transfer
11—transfer
11—11,300.00
11—transfer
11—transfer
13—11,400.00
High: 12,000.00
Low: 11,300.00
Average: 11,690.00
Transfers: 4
Sales: 5

October:
8—13,800.00
8—13,900.00
8—transfer
15—14,000.00
22—13,500.00
22—transfer
22—transfer
22—14,300.00
22—13,900.00
22—13,800.00
22—14,000.00

1963

22—14,500.00
23—14,500.00
23—14,500.00

High:	14,500.00
Low:	13,500.00
Average:	14,064.00
Transfers:	3
Sales:	11

November:
19—14,900.00
19—15,000.00
19—15,000.00
19—transfer
19—16,000.00
19—17,000.00
19—17,000.00
26—16,500.00
27—14,900.00

High:	16,500.00
Low:	14,900.00
Average:	15,615.00
Transfers:	1
Sales:	7

December:
3—16,560.00
3—17,000.00
3—17,000.00
10—14,000.00
17—transfer

High:	17,000.00
Low:	14,000.00
Average:	16,140.00
Transfers:	1
Sales:	4

1964

January:
2—14,000.00
2—transfer
7—13,200.00
14—transfer
14—12,000.00
15—transfer
28—11,300.00
29—14,000.00
31—transfer
High: 14,000.00
Low: 11,300.00
Average: 12,900.00
Transfers: 4
Sales: 5

February:
7—10,200.00
11— 9,900.00
13—transfer
25— 9,900.00
25— 9,900.00
High: 10,200.00
Low: 9,900.00
Average: 9,975.00
Transfers: 1
Sales: 4

March:
10—9,600.00
10—9,600.00
10—9,600.00
11—9,600.00
12—9,600.00
24—transfer
24—9,500.00
24—9,500.00
24—9,500.00
High: 9,600.00
Low: 9,500.00
Average: 9,562.00
Transfers: 1
Sales: 8

April:
7—9,350.00
7—9,350.00
7—9,350.00
9—9,100.00
16—9,200.00
21—transfer
21—9,300.00
21—9,300.00
21—9,300.00
21—9,300.00
21—transfer
21—transfer
High: 9,350.00
Low: 9,100.00
Average: 9,283.00
Transfers: 3
Sales: 9

May:
5—9,300.00
5—9,300.00
5—9,300.00
5—9,400.00
5—9,400.00
7—9,400.00
19—9,700.00
20—9,750.00
20—transfer
20—9,750.00
20—9,300.00
21—9,800.00
High: 9,800.00
Low: 9,300.00
Average: 9,490.00
Transfers: 1
Sales: 11

June:
1—9,800.00
2—transfer
2—9,800.00
2—transfer
2—transfer
4—transfer
5—9,800.00
10—9,800.00
16—transfer
30—9,600.00
30—9,600.00
30—9,650.00
30—transfer
High: 9,800.00
Low: 9,600.00
Average: 9,721.00
Transfers: 6
Sales: 7

July:
8—transfer
28—transfer
28—9,400.00
28—9,400.00
High: 9,400.00
Low: 9,400.00
Average: 9,400.00
Transfers: 2
Sales: 2

August:
3—transfer
11—9,200.00
11—9,200.00
11—9,200.00
11—9,200.00
11—transfer
11—transfer
11—9,200.00
26—9,150.00
26—9,150.00
26—transfer
26—9,500.00
High: 9,500.00
Low: 9,150.00
Average: 9,225.00
Transfers: 4
Sales: 8

September:
8—transfer
10—9,200.00
10—transfer
22—9,200.00
22—9,200.00
22—9,200.00
22—9,200.00
22—9,200.00
22—transfer
22—9,200.00
High: 9,200.00
Low: 9,200.00
Average: 9,200.00
Transfers: 3
Sales: 7

October:
20—9,200.00
20—transfer
20—transfer
High: 9,200.00
Low: 9,200.00
Average: 9,200.00

1964

Transfers: 2
Sales: 1

November:
4—9,200.00
4—9,200.00
4—transfer
12—9,200.00
17—9,200.00
17—transfer
17—9,200.00
17—9,200.00
High: 9,200.00
Low: 9,200.00
Average: 9,200.00
Transfers: 2
Sales: 6

December:
1— 9,200.00
1— 9,200.00
1— 9,500.00
1— 9,600.00
1—11,100.00
1—12,000.00
1—transfer
14—12,000.00
15—13,000.00
15—13,900.00
15—13,900.00
15—transfer
29—transfer
30—13,950.00
High: 13,950.00
Low: 9,200.00
Average: 11,577.00
Transfers: 3
Sales: 11

1965

January:
8—13,950.00
13—13,750.00
20—13,800.00
26—transfer
26—transfer
27—13,700.00
27—transfer
27—transfer
27—transfer
27—transfer
27—transfer
27—transfer
28—transfer
High: 13,950.00
Low: 13,700.00
Average: 13,800.00
Transfers: 9
Sales 4

February:
1—13,800.00
9—transfer
23—13,000.00
23—13,000.00
23—transfer
23—transfer
26—12,950.00
High: 13,800.00
Low: 12,950.00
Average: 13,150.00
Transfers: 3
Sales: 5

March:
1—transfer
5—12,950.00
9—12,850.00
9—12,850.00
23—transfer
23—transfer
23—12,300.00
High: 12,950.00
Low: 12,300.00
Average: 12,738.00
Tranfers: 3
Sales: 4

April:
6—11,500.00
6—11,500.00
6—11,500.00
6—10,995.00
6—transfer
6—10,995.00
20—11,000.00
21—11,000.00
21—transfer
21—transfer
High: 11,500.00
Low: 10,995.00
Average: 11,212.00
Transfers: 3
Sales: 7

May:
3—10,500.00
6—10,300.00
6—transfer
12—10,300.00
18—10,300.00
19—transfer
20—10,400.00
High: 10,500.00
Low: 10,300.00
Average: 10,360.00
Transfers: 2
Sales: 5

June:
1—10,500.00
1—10,500.00
1—10,500.00
1—10,800.00
1—transfer
2—transfer
3—10,900.00
3—transfer
15—10,750.00
15—10,780.00
15—10,800.00
15— transfer
15—10,800.00
15—transfer
15—10,500.00
18—10,800.00
24—10,800.00
24—10,800.00
29—transfer
High: 10,900.00
Low: 10,500.00
Average: 10,710.00
Transfers: 6
Sales: 13

July:
1—transfer
13—10,700.00
13—10,700.00
13—10,800.00
22—10,700.00
26—10,900.00
28—transfer
27—10,900.00
27—transfer
27—transfer
27—10,900.00
High: 10,900.00
Low: 10,700.00
Average: 10,800.00
Transfers: 4
Sales: 7

August:
11—10,900.00
11—10,900.00
16—10,900.00
17—10,900.00
High: 10,900.00
Low: 10,900.00
Average: 10,900.00
Transfers: 0
Sales: 4

September:
2—transfer
7—10,850.00
7—10,775.00
8—transfer
8—transfer
21—10,700.00
22—transfer
23—transfer
24—transfer
24—transfer
High: 10,850.00
Low: 10,700.00
Average: 10,775.00
Transfers: 7
Sales: 3

October:
5—10,400.00
5—transfer
6—tranfer
6—transfer
13—transfer

1965

19—10,600.00
19—10,600.00
20—transfer
20—10,600.00

High:	10,600.00
Low:	10,400.00
Average:	10,550.00
Transfers:	5
Sales:	4

November:

2—11,800.00
2—12,000.00
2—12,000.00
2—transfer
16—12,000.00
16—12,000.00
16—12,000.00
17—12,300.00
17—12,500.00
30—12,500.00

High:	12,500.00
Low:	11,800.00
Average:	12,122.00
Transfers:	1
Sales:	9

December:

3—transfer
14—12,500.00
14—12,500.00
14—12,900.00
14—13,000.00
15—13,500.00
28—13,400.00
28—13,400.00
28—13,500.00
29—13,500.00
29—13,500.00

High:	13,500.00
Low:	12,500.00
Average:	13,170.00
Transfers:	1
Sales:	10

1966

January:
3—transfer
11—13,000.00
11—13,500.00
12—transfer
25—13,800.00
25—14,000.00
26—13,750.00
26—transfer
26—14,000.00
27—transfer
28—15,000.00
High: 15,000.00
Low: 13,000.00
Average: 13,864.00
Transfers: 4
Sales: 7

February:
3—transfer
8—15,000.00
8—15,500.00
8—15,800.00
8—16,000.00
8—transfer
8—transfer
18—transfer
23—17,000.00
23—16,500.00
23—16,900.00
23—16,900.00
23—17,200.00
23—transfer
23—transfer
23—17,300.00
26—transfer
High: 17,300.00
Low: 15,000.00
Average: 16,410.00
Transfers: 7
Sales: 10

March:
1—17,250.00
3—17,500.00
3—transfer
7—17,500.00
8—17,500.00
8—19,000.00
8—17,500.00
8—transfer
8—18,500.00
8—19,700.00
9—transfer
18—18,500.00
22—17,500.00
22—transfer
22—transfer
29—18,500.00
High: 19,700.00
Low: 17,250.00
Average: 18,086.00
Transfers: 5
Sales: 11

April:
1—transfer
6—17,850.00
6—17,850.00
7—transfer
19—17,450.00
20—17,450.00
High: 17,850.00
Low: 17,450.00
Average: 17,650.00
Transfers: 2
Sales: 4

May:
3—17,350.00
4—17,300.00
17—transfer
17—transfer
17—transfer
High: 17,350,00
Low: 17,300.00
Average: 17,325.00
Transfers: 3
Sales: 2

June:
1—16,900.00
14—16,800.00
14—16,800.00
14—16,800.00
14—16,800.00
14—16,800.00
14—16,800.00
14—16,800.00
15—transfer
27—16,600.00
28—16,600.00
High: 16,900.00
Low: 16,600.00
Average: 16,770.00
Transfers: 1
Sales: 10

July:
12—16,700.00
12—16,700.00
12—16,700.00
14—16,700.00
14—16,700.00
26—transfer
26—16,900.00
26—16,900.00
26—16,900.00
29—16,900.00
High: 16,900.00
Low: 16,700.00
Average: 16,788.00
Transfers: 1
Sales 9

August:
9—16,900.00
9—17,000.00
10—17,000.00
23—17,500.00
23—17,100.00
23—19,700.00
23—20,000.00
23—transfer
25—29,950.00
31—24,000.00
High: 29,950.00
Low: 16,900.00
Average: 19,905.00
Transfers: 1
Sales: 9

September:
1—23,500.00
6—25,000.00
6—transfer
7—24,500.00
7—25,000.00
7—25,000.00
7—25,000.00
12—23,500.00
13—23,000.00
20—23,500.00
20—transfer
20—transfer
20—24,000.00

1966

20—25,000.00
21—27,500.00
31—transfer

High:	27,500.00
Low:	23,000.00
Average:	24,541.00
Transfers:	4
Sales:	12

October:

6—24,000.00
6—transfer
7—24,000.00
18—25,000.00
18—26,000.00
18—transfer
18—transfer
18—transfer
31—24,000.00

High:	26,000.00
Low:	24,000.00
Average:	24,600.00
Transfers:	4
Sales:	5

November:

1—24,250.00
1—transfer
15—22,750.00
15—22,750.00
15—transfer
15—transfer
16—21,000.00
21—transfer
29—19,750.00
29—transfer
30—transfer
30—transfer

High:	24,250.00
Low:	19,750.00
Average:	22,100.00
Transfers:	7
Sales:	5

December:

1—transfer
3—transfer
7—transfer
13—18,500.00
14—18,000.00
15—transfer
27—18,400.00
27—18,400.00
27—transfer

High:	18,500.00
Low:	18,000.00
Average:	18,325.00
Transfers:	5
Sales:	4

1967

January:
- 10—transfer
- 10—transfer
- 20—18,250.00
- 24—transfer
- 24—18,000.00
- 24—18,500.00
- 26—transfer
- 30—transfer

High:	18,500.00
Low:	18,000.00
Average:	18,250.00
Transfers:	5
Sales:	3

February:
- 7—18,500.00
- 7—18,450.00
- 7—transfer
- 7—transfer
- 7—18,500.00
- 9—20,000.00
- 21—20,000.00
- 21—transfer
- 21—transfer
- 23—transfer
- 27—transfer
- 27—transfer
- 27—transfer

High:	20,000.00
Low:	18,450.00
Average:	19,090.00
Transfers:	9
Sales:	5

March:
- 6—20,000.00
- 6—transfer
- 7—20,200.00
- 7—20,800.00
- 14—transfer
- 21—transfer
- 21—21,000.00
- 21—23,500.00
- 22—transfer
- 23—23,000.00
- 23—22,000.00

High:	23,500.00
Low:	20,000.00
Average;	21,500.00
Transfers:	4
Sales:	7

April:
- 6—transfer
- 6—transfer
- 10—24,000.00
- 10—24,000.00
- 11—transfer
- 18—24,400.00

High:	24,400.00
Low:	24,000.00
Average:	24,133.00
Transfers:	3
Sales:	3

May:
- 1—24,450.00
- 3—24,450.00
- 5—transfer
- 16—23,500.00
- 17—23,000.00
- 17—23,500.00
- 31—23,800.00
- 31—transfer

High:	24,450.00
Low:	23,000.00
Average:	23,500.00
Transfers:	2
Sales:	6

June:
- 1—transfer
- 1—transfer
- 7—transfer
- 13—21,800.00
- 27—19,500.00
- 28–transfer

High:	21,800.00
Low:	19,500.00
Average:	20,650.00
Transfers:	4
Sales:	2

July:
- 5—transfer
- 12—transfer
- 12—19,450.00
- 19—19,500.00
- 25—21,000.00
- 26—21,000.00
- 26—21,000.00

High:	21,000.00
Low:	19,450.00
Average:	20,390.00
Transfers:	2
Sales:	5

August:
- 1—transfer
- 2—21,000.00
- 8—21,425.00
- 9—21,450.00
- 10—21,000.00
- 14—transfer
- 22—transfer
- 23—transfer
- 23—transfer

High:	21,450.00
Low:	21,000.00
Average:	21,235.00
Transfers:	5
Sales:	5

September:
- 7—transfer
- 19—20,950.00
- 19—21,000.00
- 20—transfer
- 27—transfer
- 27—transfer
- 28—transfer

High:	21,000.00
Low:	20,950.00
Average:	20,975.00
Transfers:	5
Sales:	2

October:
- 4—transfer
- 4—20,400.00
- 4—20,400.00
- 6—20,500.00
- 13—transfer
- 18—transfer
- 18—transfer

High:	20,500.00
Low:	20,400.00
Average:	20,433.00
Transfers:	4
Sales:	3

November:
- 1—transfer
- 1—20,000.00
- 1—transfer
- 1—19,500.00
- 2—19,750.00

1967

6—transfer
8—19,500.00
14—20,000.00
14—20,000.00
14—20,000.00
15—20,500.00
16—transfer
16—transfer
16—transfer
16—20,500.00
30—20,400.00

High:	20,500.00
Low:	19,500.00
Average:	20,015.00
Transfers:	6
Sales:	10

December:
4—19,500.00
12—transfer
13—transfer
13—transfer
13—transfer

High:	19,500.00
Low:	19,500.00
Average:	19,500.00
Transfers:	4
Sales:	1

1968

January:
9—transfer
23—transfer
24—transfer
24—19,200.00
24—transfer
24—18,500.00
25—transfer
25—transfer
26—transfer
26—transfer
31—19,200.00
High: 19,200.00
Low: 18,500.00
Average: 18,966.00
Transfers: 8
Sales: 3

February:
8—20,000.00
28—transfer
28—20,200.00
28—20,800.00
28—transfer
28—transfer
29—21,000.00
29—23,500.00
29—transfer
High: 23,500.00
Low: 20,000.00
Average: 21,100.00
Transfers: 4
Sales: 5

March:
1—transfer
1—transfer
1—transfer
1—transfer
1—18,500.00
6—18,900.00
6—18,900.00
6—18,975.00
6—19,000.00
8—18,000.00
12—18,750.00
20—transfer
20—transfer
20—transfer
20—transfer
21—transfer
22—transfer
High: 19,000.00
Low: 18,000.00
Average: 18,717.00
Transfers: 10
Sales: 7

April:
1—19,800.00
3—transfer
15—transfer
16—transfer
18—19,425.00
19—transfer
19—transfer
22—transfer
22—19,425.00
24—transfer
29—18,900.00
29—transfer
High: 19,800.00
Low: 18,900.00
Average: 19,387.00
Transfers: 8
Sales: 4

May:
28—18,000.00
28—18,250.00
28—18,450.00
28—transfer
31—18,000.00
31—18,000.00
31—transfer
High: 18,450.00
Low: 18,000.00
Average: 18,140.00
Transfers: 2
Sales: 5

June:
3—transfer
3—transfer
5—transfer
27—18,000.00
27—18,000.00
27—transfer
27—18,000.00
27—transfer
27—transfer
High: 18,000.00
Low: 18,000.00
Average: 18,000.00
Transfers: 6
Sales: 3

July:
2—17,750.00
11—17,000.00
19—16,500.00
24—transfer
24—18,900.00
25—transfer
High: 18,900.00
Low: 16,500.00
Average: 17,537.00
Transfers: 2
Sales: 4

August:
5—transfer

September:
3—14,250.00
5—transfer
17—transfer
24—13,750.00
24—13,250.00
24—transfer
25—transfer
25—transfer
High: 14,250.00
Low: 13,250.00
Average: 13,750.00
Transfers: 5
Sales: 3

October:
1—transfer
22—13,000.00
22—13,000.00
22—13,000.00
24—13,000.00
High: 13,000.00
Low: 13,000.00
Average: 13,000.00
Transfers: 1
Sales: 4

November:
21—12,900.00
25—12,950.00
25—13,000.00
25—transfer
25—transfer
26—13,250.00

1968

26—13,250.00
26—transfer

High:	13,250.00
Low:	12,900.00
Average:	13,070.00
Transfers:	3
Sales:	5

December:
3—transfer
5—13,000.00
17—13,250.00
17—13,000.00
17—16,500.00
17—17,900.00
17—18,950.00
18—18,000.00
18—transfer
18—18,000.00
18—transfer
18—17,900.00
19—17,900.00

High:	18,950.00
Low:	13,000.00
Average:	16,440.00
Transfers:	3
Sales:	10

1969

January:
8—18,500.00
16—transfer
28—19,000.00
28—19,000.00
28—19,850.00
28—19,900.00
28—19,900.00
28—20,400.00
29—transfer
29—21,000.00
30—transfer
30—20,000.00
30—21,050.00
30—transfer
31—19,500.00
High: 21,050.00
Low: 18,500.00
Average: 19,850.00
Transfers: 4
Sales: 11

February:
3—21,000.00
3—transfer
5—transfer
12—20,900.00
18—20,000.00
18—21,000.00
19—21,000.00
20—21,000.00
20—transfer
24—21,000.00
27—22,000.00
27—21,750.00
High: 22,000.00
Low: 20,000.00
Average: 21,072.00
Transfers: 3
Sales: 9

March:
18—22,000.00
18—22,000.00
18—22,000.00
18—transfer
18—22,000.00
19—transfer
19—22,000.00
19—22,400.00
22—transfer
26—23,500.00
High: 23,500.00
Low: 22,000.00
Average: 22,271.00
Transfers: 3
Sales: 7

April:
1—transfer
15—transfer
16—24,000.00
18—24,000.00
18—transfer
21—transfer
23—transfer
High: 24,000.00
Low: 24,000.00
Average: 24,000.00
Transfers: 5
Sales: 2

May:
20—24,400.00
20—24,500.00
20—transfer
21—transfer
21—transfer
21—transfer
22—transfer
26—24,500.00
27—transfer
High: 24,500.00
Low: 24,400.00
Average: 24,450.00
Transfers: 6
Sales: 3

June:
4—23,000.00
11—transfer
17—21,000.00
17—22,250.00
18—22,000.00
19—transfer
20—21,500.00
20—21,000.00
20—22,000.00
High: 23,000.00
Low: 21,000.00
Average: 21,821.00
Transfers: 2
Sales: 7

July:
3—transfer
15—21,500.00
16—transfer
17—transfer
17—transfer
17—21,500.00
22—20,800.00
23—21,400.00
24—20,250.00
29—20,000.00
30—transfer
31—21,000.00
High: 21,500.00
Low: 20,000.00
Average: 20,921.00
Transfers: 5
Sales: 7

August:
4—20,000.00
7—20,000.00
8—20,500.00
19—20,800.00
20—transfer
20—20,500.00
20—20,800.00
25—transfer
27—transfer
29—20,000.00
High: 20,800.00
Low: 20,000.00
Average: 20,371.00
Transfers: 3
Sales: 7

September:
16—21,500.00
16—21,850.00
16—22,000.00
16—22,500.00
16—transfer
16—22,000.00
16—transfer
17—transfer
17—transfer
19—22,400.00
23—transfer
24—22,900.00
30—23,000.00
High: 23,000.00

1969

Low: 21,500.00
Average: 22,268.00
Transfers: 5
Sales: 8

October:
3—23,000.00
21—25,000.00
21—27,000.00
21—27,500.00
21—24,400.00
21—34,000.00
21—40,000.00
21—40,000.00
21—transfer
21—39,500.00
21—transfer
21—40,000.00
24—transfer
24—28,500.00
28—28,000.00
29—38,000.00
29—35,000.00
31—25,000.00
31—transfer
High: 40,000.00
Low: 23,000.00
Average: 31,660.00
Transfers: 4
Sales: 15

November:
18—35,000.00
18—transfer
19—39,000.00
19—38,000.00
20—transfer
24—transfer
24—39,000.00
24—40,000.00
24—transfer
High: 40,000.00
Low: 35,000.00
Average: 38,200.00
Transfers: 4
Sales: 5

December:
5—38,500.00
8—transfer
16—39,200.00
16—40,000.00
17—transfer
17—transfer
17—transfer
17—44,000.00
17—transfer
17—transfer
17—transfer
17—42,000.00
18—transfer
18—transfer
18—transfer
18—40,000.00
18—40,000.00
18—41,000.00
18—44,000.00
18—42,000.00
19—transfer
19—39,500.00
19—39,000.00
31—42,000.00
High: 44,000.00
Low: 38,500.00
Average: 531,200.00
Transfers: 11
Sales: 13

1970

January:
5—transfer
20—41,000.00
22—transfer
22—34,000.00
23—transfer
26—41,000.00
High: 41,000.00
Low: 34,000.00
Average: 38,667.00
Transfers: 3
Sales: 3

February:
9—34,000.00
10—transfer
16—35,000.00
17—transfer
19—34,000.00
20—36,000.00
20—transfer
24—35,500.00
High: 36,000.00
Low: 34,000.00
Average: 34,900.00
Transfers: 3
Sales: 5

March:
4—33,000.00
4—35,000.00
17—38,000.00
17—39,450.00
17—39,500.00
17—transfer
18—transfer
19—transfer
19—36,000.00
19—transfer
20—39,450.00
20—transfer
20—40,000.00
24—38,000.00
24—transfer
31—transfer
High: 40,000.00
Low: 33,000.00
Average: 37,600.00
Transfers: 7
Sales: 9

April:
21—transfer
21—38,000.00
21—38,000.00
21—39,750.00
21—40,000.00
21—39,900.00
21—39,750.00
21—39,000.00
22—transfer
22—37,500.00
22—39,500.00
22—transfer
22—39,800.00
23—transfer
23—40,000.00
28—39,000.00
30—transfer
High: 40,000.00
Low: 37,500.00
Average: 39,183.00
Transfers: 5
Sales: 12

May:
19—39,500.00
19—35,800.00
19—35,750.00
20—35,800.00
20—transfer
21—transfer
21—30,000.00
High: 39,500.00
Low: 30,000.00
Average: 34,337.00
Transfers: 2
Sales: 5

June:
16—18,500.00
17—transfer
17—transfer
25—transfer
High: 18,500.00
Low: 18,500.00
Average: 18,500.00
Transfers: 3
Sales: 1

July:
21—35,000.00
21—30,000.00
21—transfer
22—34,000.00
22—34,500.00
22—transfer
22—transfer
23—transfer
23—transfer
23—34,000.00
24—transfer
24—transfer
24—27,000.00
24—34,000.00
24—transfer
29—35,000.00
High: 35,000.00
Low: 27,000.00
Average: 32,937.00
Transfers: 8
Sales: 8

August:
4—transfer
4—31,250.00
7—31,500.00
7—26,000.00
10—31,000.00
18—34,800.00
18—transfer
18—transfer
18—31,000.00
18—34,000.00
19—34,000.00
19—34,000.00
19—transfer
19—transfer
19—transfer
19—transfer
19—transfer
19—transfer
19—transfer
20—transfer
20—34,500.00
20—33,000.00
High: 34,800.00
Low: 26,000.00
Average: 32,277.00
Transfers: 11
Sales: 11

September:
11—33,500.00
15—33,000.00
15—33,500.00
15—34,500.00
15—34,500.00

1970

16—34,500.00
16—34,500.00
16—33,000.00
16—34,500.00

High:	34,500.00
Low:	33,000.00
Average:	33,944.00
Transfers:	0
Sales:	9

October:

2—transfer
2—transfer
5—transfer
8—transfer
20—32,000.00
20—32,900.00
20—33,000.00
20—33,000.00
21—32,500.00
22—transfer
22—transfer
22—transfer
22—transfer
23—33,000.00
23—33,000.00
23—33,500.00
27—transfer
30—32,000.00
30—32,000.00
30—transfer

High:	33,500.00
Low:	32,000.00
Average:	32,690.00
Transfers:	10
Sales:	10

November:

2—transfer
10—transfer
17—33,800.00
17—34,900.00
17—37,000.00
17—transfer
18—34,950.00
18—35,000.00
19—35,000.00
20—35,000.00
24—33,000.00

High:	37,000.00
Low:	33,000.00
Average:	34,631.00
Transfers:	3
Sales:	8

December:

14—33,000.00
15—35,000.00
15—transfer
15—transfer
16—35,000.00
18—34,000.00
21—34,900.00
21—transfer
21—transfer
21—35,000.00
21—transfer
30—33,000.00

High:	35,000.00
Low:	33,000.00
Average:	34,630.00
Transfers:	5
Sales:	7

1971

January:
8—34,000.00
18—33,000.00
19—35,000.00
19—35,500.00
19—35,500.00
19—tranfer
19—transfer
20—35,300.00
20—35,000.00
21—34,000.00
25—36,000.00
25—33,000.00
28—transfer
High: 36,000.00
Low: 33,000.00
Average: 34,630.00
Transfers: 3
Sales: 10

February:
1—transfer
2—32,250.00
5—32,500.00
5—32,000.00
16—35,000.00
16—35,000.00
16—35,000.00
16—35,500.00
16—35,500.00
16—transfer
16—transfer
17—35,500.00
17—34,000.00
17—32,500.00
17—transfer
17—transfer
17—transfer
18—35,000.00
18—35,000.00
19—34,000.00
23—33,900.00
24—34,250.00
26—35,500.00
26—transfer
High: 35,500.00
Low: 32,000.00
Average: 34,258.00
Transfers: 7
Sales: 17

March:
1—transfer
9—34,000.00
15—transfer
15—34,000.00
16—34,500.00
16—35,000.00
16—35,000.00
16—35,500.00
17—35,000.00
17—35,000.00
17—35,750.00
17—35,750.00
18—transfer
18—35,000.00
18—34,250.00
18—transfer
18—35,000.00
18—34,250.00
22—34,000.00
22—35,000.00
High: 35,750.00
Low: 34,000.00
Average: 34,750.00
Transfers: 4
Sales: 6

April:
7—transfer
12—32,500.00
20—33,500.00
20—transfer
20—33,900.00
20—34,000.00
20—transfer
21—transfer
21—transfer
21—transfer
21—34,000.00
21—33,800.00
21—33,400.00
22—transfer
22—transfer
22—transfer
23—transfer
23—transfer
26—34,000.00
29—transfer
30—33,500.00
High: 34,000.00
Low: 32,500.00
Average: 33,622.00
Transfers: 12
Sales: 9

May:
18—transfer
18—32,800.00
18—33,100.00
19—33,500.00
19—33,000.00
19—transfer
19—transfer
19—33,000.00
19—transfer
21—transfer
21—transfer
24—transfer
27—32,900.00
28—transfer
High: 33,100.00
Low: 32,800.00
Average: 33,050.00
Transfers: 8
Sales: 6

June:
15—32,150.00
15—32,250.00
15—32,500.00
16—transfer
16—transfer
21—transfer
29—31,000.00
High: 32,500.00
Low: 31,000.00
Average: 31,975.00
Transfers: 3
Sales: 4

July:
13—29,500.00
14—28,000.00
20—31,000.00
20—32,000.00
20—32,000.00
20—31,000.00
21—31,900.00
21—transfer
26—transfer
High: 32,000.00

1971

Low: 28,000.00
Average: 30,771.00
Transfers: 2
Sales: 7

August:
3—30,000.00
10—31,500.00
17—31,000.00
17—32,000.00
17—31,000.00
18—transfer
18—31,900.00
18—32,000.00
18—30,750.00
18—31,900.00
19—transfer
23—30,500.00
23—30,500.00
27—29,500.00
30—32,000.00
High: 32,000.00
Low: 29,500.00
Average: 31,119.00
Transfers: 2
Sales: 13

September:
15—31,500.00
19—36,000.00
19—35,000.00
20—transfer
20—35,000.00
21—32,500.00
22—35,000.00
22—33,000.00
25—32,000.00
25—36,500.00
26—transfer
26—transfer
High: 36,500.00
Low: 31,500.00
Average: 34,400.00
Transfers: 3
Sales: 9

October:
16—36,000.00
17—38,500.00
17—39,000.00
17—39,800.00
17—39,800.00
17—40,000.00
17—40,000.00
18—39,500.00
18—39,600.00
18—39,700.00
18—40,000.00
18—transfer
20—transfer
20—39,900.00
20—38,500.00
24—transfer
25—transfer
High: 40,000.00
Low: 36,000.00
Average: 39,300.00
Transfers: 4
Sales: 13

November:
3—transfer
21—transfer
22—38,900.00
22—transfer
22—transfer
22—transfer
27—35,500.00
28—35,000.00
28—38,400.00
28—transfer
29—38,900.00
High: 38,900.00
Low: 35,000.00
Average: 37,400.00
Transfers: 6
Sales: 5

December:
11—transfer
19—transfer
20—transfer
Transfers: 3
Sales: 0

1972

January:
7—transfer
12—28,500.00
13—29,500.00
18—30,000.00
18—transfer
18—30,000.00
18—30,500.00
18—transfer
19—30,000.00
19—30,000.00
19—29,950.00
19—transfer
20—29,950.00
24—30,900.00
High: 30,900.00
Low: 28,500.00
Average: 29,930.00
Transfers: 4
Sales: 10

February:
4—30,500.00
15—30,750.00
15—30,850.00
15—30,900.00
16—transfer
16—31,500.00
17—30,500.00
18—31,000.00
18—31,000.00
18—31,200.00
18—31,500.00
18—30,500.00
High: 31,500.00
Low: 30,500.00
Average: 30,927.00
Transfers: 1
Sales: 11

March:
14—33,000.00
15—32,500.00
17—32,000.00
17—32,000.00
17—32,500.00
17—32,500.00
17—32,500.00
17—33,000.00
30—transfer
High: 33,000.00
Low: 32,000.00
Average: 32,437.00
Transfers: 1
Sales: 8

April:
13—32,500.00
18—32,900.00
18—34,000.00
18—35,000.00
18—35,000.00
18—transfer
18—transfer
19—39,500.00
19—39,500.00
19—39,000.00
20—40,000.00
20—transfer
20—transfer
21—transfer
21—39,000.00
24—34,000.00
26—transfer
High: 40,000.00
Low: 32,500.00
Average: 36,400.00
Transfers: 6
Sales: 11

May:
1—36,000.00
3—transfer
16—39,000.00
16—transfer
16—39,000.00
16—38,500.00
17—39,000.00
17—transfer
17—38,500.00
17—transfer
17—38,500.00
17—transfer
18—transfer
18—transfer
30—38,500.00
High: 39,000.00
Low: 36,000.00
Transfers: 7
Sales: 8

June:
8—36,000.00
8—38,000.00
9—37,000.00
20—36,900.00
20—transfer
21—36,800.00
21—transfer
21—transfer
21—36,900.00
21—37,000.00
21—transfer
22—36,900.00
26—36,000.00
28—transfer
30—transfer
High: 38,000.00
Low: 36,000.00
Average: 36,750.00
Transfers: 6
Sales: 9

July:
17—transfer
19—35,000.00
19—transfer
19—transfer
20—31,500.00
24—29,000.00
25—34,950.00
High: 35,000.00
Low: 29,000.00
Average: 32,612.00
Transfers: 3
Sales: 4

August:
1—transfer
16—transfer
17—32,500.00
17—28,000.00
22—transfer
31—transfer
31—transfer
High: 32,500.00
Low: 28,000.00
Average: 30,250.00
Transfers: 5
Sales: 2

September:
15—31,500.00
19—36,000.00
19—35,000.00
20—transfer

1972

20—35,000.00
21—32,500.00
22—35,000.00
22—33,000.00
25—32,000.00
25—36,500.00
26—transfer
26—transfer

High:	36,500.00
Low:	32,000.00
Average:	34,055.00
Transfers:	3
Sales:	9

October:
16—36,000.00
17—38,500.00
17—39,000.00
17—39,800.00
17—39,800.00
17—40,000.00
17—40,000.00
18—39,500.00
18—39,600.00
18—38,700.00
18—40,000.00
18—transfer
20—transfer
20—39,900.00
20—38,500.00
24—transfer
25—transfer

High:	40,000.00
Low:	36,000.00
Average:	39,253.00
Transfers:	4
Sales:	13

November:
3—transfer
21—transfer
22—38,900.00
22—transfer
22—transfer
22—transfer
27—35,500.00
28—35,000.00
28—38,400.00
28—transfer
29—38,900.00

High:	38,900.00
Low:	35,000.00
Average:	37,340.00
Transfers:	6
Salew:	5

December:
11—transfer
19—transfer
20—transfer

Transfers:	3
Sales:	0

1973

January:
1—transfer
17—transfer
17—32,500.00
17—33,000.00
17—33,000.00
19—transfer
19—transfer
22—34,000.00
26—transfer
26—30,000.00
26—34,000.00
27—transfer
High: 34,000.00
Low: 30,000.00
Average: 32,750.00
Transfers: 6
Sales: 6

February:
20—35,000.00
20—35,000.00
20—34,000.00
20—39,500.00
20—38,750.00
21—35,000.00
21—40,000.00
21—35,000.00
21—40,000.00
21—38,000.00
21—35,000.00
21—34,000.00
22—40,000.00
23—transfer
24—transfer
High: 40,000.00
Low: 34,000.00
Average: 36,865.00
Transfers: 2
Sales: 13

March:
20—40,000.00
20—45,000.00
20—64,900.00
20—transfer
20—transfer
20—transfer
20—49,500.00
21—54,000.00
21—50,000.00
21—65,000.00
21—42,500.00
21—39,500.00
22—55,000.00
22—transfer
23—48,000.00
23—49,500.00
28—40,00.00
29—49,000.00
30—transfer
30—transfer
30—transfer
30—transfer
30—transfer
30—transfer
30—transfer
High: 65,000.00
Low: 39,500.00
Average: 49,421.00
Transfers: 11
Sales: 14

April:
17—59,200.00
17—54,000.00
17—59,300.00
17—transfer
17—transfer
17—53,000.00
17—55,000.00
19—50,000.00
19—transfer
24—56,000.00
High: 59,300.00
Low: 53,000.00
Average: 55,214.00
Transfers: 3
Sales: 7

May:
2—49,600.00
14—49,500.00
15—53,800.00
16—53,500.00
16—transfer
17—54,900.00
17—55,000.00
18—54,000.00
23—53,900.00
30—transfer
30—40,000.00
High: 55,000.00
Low: 40,000.00
Average: 51,577.00
Transfers: 2
Sales: 9

June:
4—42,000.00
13—transfer
18—transfer
20—48,000.00
20—transfer
21—44,000.00
21—48,000.00
21—40,250.00
21—transfer
21—transfer
21—49,000.00
21—40,000.00
21—transfer
21—transfer
21—transfer
22—transfer
25—41,000.00
26—transfer
26—transfer
27—transfer
27—transfer
High: 49,000.00
Low: 40,000.00
Average: 39,031.00
Transfers: 13
Sales: 18

July:
2—37,500.00
10—36,000.00
11—33,000.00
16—33,000.00
16—33,000.00
17—40,000.00
17—transfer
17—40,000.00
18—42,000.00
18—transfer
18—transfer
18—transfer
18—transfer
18—transfer
18—transfer
18—40,000.00
19—44,000.00
23—43,000.00
23—transfer

1973

23—transfer
24—transfer
25—transfer
25—transfer
31—43,000.00
High: 44,000.00
Low: 33,000.00
Average: 38,269.00
Transfers: 12
Sales: 13

August:
7—42,500.00
13—38,500.00
17—38,000.00
21—40,000.00
21—41,000.00
21—42,000.00
21—46,000.00
21—transfer
21—transfer
21—45,000.00
21—44,500.00
21—42,000.00
22—42,000.00
22—44,000.00
22—45,900.00
22—transfer
22—42,000.00
22—transfer
22—transfer
22—transfer
22—44,900.00
28—45,750.00
29—transfer
High: 46,000.00
Low: 38,000.00
Average: 42,753.00
Transfers: 7
Sales: 16

September:
13—45,000.00
13—44,000.00
14—44,000.00
14—44,000.00
17—46,000.00
18—46,000.00
18—50,900.00
18—55,000.00
18—55,000.00
18—51,000.00
18—50,000.00
19—46,000.00
19—52,500.00
19—50,000.00
19—46,000.00
19—47,500.00
19—55,000.00
19—55,000.00
19—transfer
20—51,500.00
20—transfer
24—55,000.00
27—transfer
27—transfer
High: 55,000.00
Low: 44,000.00
Average: 49,425.00
Transfers: 4
Sales: 20

October:
2—57,000.00
2—transfer
9—52,000.00
12—54,000.00
15—54,000.00
15—52,000.00
15—transfer
16—55,000.00
16—55,000.00
16—56,000.00
16—57,000.00
16—55,000.00
16—54,500.00
16—transfer
16—transfer
17—transfer
17—54,900.00
17—transfer
18—54,000.00
19—54,000.00
23—52,000.00
31—50,000.00
High: 57,000.00
Low: 50,000.00
Average: 54,150.00
Transfers: 6
Sales: 16

November:
1—46,000.00
1—47,500.00
1—transfer
14—46,000.00
15—48,000.00
20—50,000.00
21—49,900.00
21—transfer
21—50,000.00
21—transfer
21—49,000.00
High: 50,000.00
Low: 46,000.00
Average: 48,300.00
Transfers: 3
Sales: 8

December:
4—49,500.00
4—49,500.00
5—50,000.00
6—transfer
13—50,000.00
17—50,000.00
17—50,000.00
17—transfer
18—52,000.00
18—51,000.00
18—transfer
18—transfer
19—transfer
28—transfer
31—transfer
High: 52,000.00
Low: 49,500.00
Average: 50,250.00
Transfers: 7
Sales: 8

1974

January:
2—51,000.00
15—55,000.00
15—55,000.00
15—55,000.00
15—transfer
16—transfer
16—56,000.00
17—54,000.00
18—55,000.00
24—transfer
24—56,000.00
31—55,000.00
High: 56,000.00
Low: 51,000.00
Average: 54,555.00
Transfers: 3
Sales: 9

February:
4—54,000.00
19—56,500.00
19—58,000.00
19—57,500.00
19—52,500.00
19—57,000.00
19—56,000.00
19—transfer
20—59,000.00
20—59,000.00
20—55,000.00
20—transfer
21—59,000.00
21—54,500.00
22—59,000.00
22—55,000.00
27—transfer
28—transfer
High: 59,000.00
Low: 52,500.00
Average: 56,433.00
Transfers: 4
Sales: 4

March:
5—59,000.00
12—60,000.00
19—60,000.00
19—61,000.00
19—65,000.00
19—65,000.00
19—65,000.00
19—65,000.00
19—65,000.00
19—67,000.00
19—67,000.00
19—74,000.00
19—74,000.00
19—transfer
20—64,000.00
20—60,900.00
20—transfer
20—71,000.00
21—62,000.00
21—transfer
21—transfer
22—65,000.00
22—transfer
22—72,000.00
22—72,000.00
25—72,000.00
27—71,500.00
High: 74,000.00
Low: 60,000.00
Average: 66,268.00
Transfers: 5
Sales: 22

April:
3—71,000.00
8—73,000.00
9—73,000.00
10—74,000.00
10—transfer
11—74,500.00
16—75,000.00
16—79,000.00
16—79,600.00
16—80,000.00
16—75,000.00
16—78,000.00
17—transfer
17—transfer
17—77,500.00
18—80,000.00
18—transfer
18—75,000.00
22—79,000.00
22—73,500.00
22—79,900.00
23—transfer
29—71,500.00
High: 80,000.00
Low: 71,000.00
Average: 76,884.00
Transfers: 5
Sales: 18

May:
9—71,500.00
15—74,500.00
21—transfer
21—76,400.00
21—transfer
21—76,000.00
21—transfer
21—transfer
21—74,900.00
21—75,000.00
28—transfer
28—76,400.00
29—75,000.00
31—73,000.00
31—73,000.00
High: 76,400.00
Low: 71,500.00
Average: 74,770.00
Transfers: 5
Sales: 10

June:
4—74,500.00
6—75,000.00
10—77,500.00
10—74,500.00
11—77,500.00
12—78,900.00
14—79,000.00
18—80,000.00
18—81,000.00
18—transfer
18—79,000.00
18—89,250.00
18—90,000.00
19—90,000.00
19—transfer
19—transfer
19—transfer
20—79,750.00
21—85,000.00
24—transfer
24—transfer
26—85,000.00
High: 90,000.00
Low: 74,500.00

1974

Average: 80,962.00
Transfers: 6
Sales: 16

July:
16—81,000.00
16—81,000.00
16—81,000.00
16—transfer
16—transfer
16—transfer
16—transfer
16—transfer
16—transfer
17—transfer
17—85,000.00
17—84,500.00
18—81,000.00
18—79,000.00
19—85,000.00
High: 85,000.00
Low: 79,000.00
Average: 82,187.00
Transfers: 7
Sales: 8

August:
5—77,000.00
9—transfer
9—transfer
15—74,000.00
20—74,900.00
20—75,000.00
20—transfer
20—transfer
20—transfer
20—transfer
20—74,000.00
21—transfer
21—77,000.00
21—75,000.00
27—69,000.00
High: 77,000.00
Low: 69,000.00
Average: 74,487.00
Transfers: 7
Sales: 8

September:
11—60,000.00
17—71,500.00
18—71,000.00
18—transfer
19—72,000.00
20—72,000.00
20—72,000.00
24—72,000.00
30—transfer
High: 72,000.00
Low: 60,000.00
Average: 70,071.00
Transfers: 2
Sales: 7

October:
1—transfer
1—transfer
8—70,000.00
11—64,000.00
15—72,500.00
15—70,000.00
15—transfer
15—transfer
16—transfer
16—transfer
17—68,000.00
17—68,000.00
18—70,000.00
18—62,000.00
23—70,000.00
High: 70,000.00
Low: 62,000.00
Average: 68,278.00
Transfers: 6
Sales: 9

November:
4—transfer
15—60,000.00
18—60,000.00
19—65,000.00
19—transfer
20—transfer
20—68,000.00
21—70,000.00
21—67,000.00
21—67,000.00
21—transfer
22—71,000.00
26—transfer
26—transfer
27—66,500.00
High: 71,000.00
Low: 60,000.00
Average: 66,055.00
Transfers: 6
Sales: 9

December:
3—68,000.00
11—71,000.00
16—71,500.00
16—72,500.00
17—79,000.00
17—79,500.00
17—74,500.00
18—transfer
18—74,000.00
20—86,000.00
20—75,000.00
23—transfer
31—75,500.00
High: 86,000.00
Low: 68,000.00
Average: 75,136.00
Transfers: 2
Sales: 11

1975

January:
15—78,000.00
20—transfer
21—84,000.00
21—83,000.00
22—83,400.00
22—83,000.00
22—transfer
23—78,000.00
27—84,900.00
27—84,000.00
28—85,000.00
28—82,000.00
High: 85,000.00
Low: 78,000.00
Average: 82,530.00
Transfers: 2
Sales: 10

February:
4—transfer
5—80,000.00
7—transfer
12—84,000.00
12—84,500.00
18—87,000.00
18—transfer
19—87,500.00
19—transfer
19—92,300.00
19—87,500.00
20—89,000.00
25—transfer
25—transfer
27—transfer
27—87,500.00
High: 92,300.00
Low: 80,000.00
Average: 86,588.00
Transfers: 7
Sales: 9

March:
5—85,500.00
5—81,000.00
11—transfer
11—transfer
11—transfer
11—transfer
12—transfer
12—transfer
12—77,000.00
13—85,000.00
17—transfer
18—transfer
19—85,000.00
19—transfer
20—82,500.00
24—88,000.00
High: 88,000.00
Low: 77,000.00
Average: 83,429.00
Transfers: 9
Sales: 7

April:
1—transfer
15—85,500.00
15—86,000.00
16—86,000.00
16—86,000.00
16—transfer
16—transfer
17—transfer
21—transfer
21—86,500.00
24—transfer
30—86,500.00
High: 86,500.00
Low: 85,500.00
Average: 86,083.00
Transfers: 6
Sales: 6

May
1—transfer
8— 90,000.00
9— 88,000.00
12— 90,000.00
16— 90,000.00
19—transfer
21—transfer
21—100,000.00
21—transfer
21—transfer
21—transfer
22—transfer
22—transfer
23—transfer
27— 97,000.00
27—107,500.00
27— 97,500.00
27—100,000.00
30—105,000.00
High: 107,500.00
Low: 88,000.00
Average: 96,500.00
Transfers: 9
Sales: 10

June:
17—105,000.00
17—114,000.00
17—transfer
18—105,000.00
18—transfer
18—103,000.00
19—102,000.00
19—110,000.00
20—111,000.00
25—110,000.00
30—113,000.00
High: 114,000.00
Low: 102,000.00
Average: 108,111.00
Transfers: 2
Sales: 9

July:
2—transfer
9—transfer
16—transfer
17—113,500.00
18—113,500.00
21—110,000.00
21—110,000.00
22—transfer
23—108,000.00
25—transfer
28—transfer
28—105,000.00
28—transfer
31—transfer
High: 113,500.00
Low: 105,000.00
Average: 110,000.00
Transfers: 8
Sales: 6

August:
5—110,000.00
19—transfer
19—transfer
21—110,000.00
22—109,500.00
High: 110,000.00

1975

Low: 109,500.00
Average: 106,833.00
Transfers: 2
Sales: 3

September:
9—101,000.00
17—transfer
18—109,000.00
18—107,500.00
High: 109,000.00
Low: 107,500.00
Average: 105,833.00
Transfers: 1
Sales: 3

October:
2—107,500.00
16—transfer
22—107,500.00
22—110,500.00
22—transfer
23—109,500.00
23—107,000.00
23—109,000.00
24—110,000.00
27—107,500.00
27—transfer
27—107,500.00
28—transfer
28—105,000.00
29—110,000.00
High: 110,500.00
Low: 105,000.00
Average: 108,272.00
Transfers: 4
Sales: 11

November:
13—108,000.00
18—110,000.00
18—transfer
18—transfer
19—114,000.00
19—transfer
19—114,500.00
24—transfer
24—transfer
High: 114,500.00
Low: 108,000.00
Average: 111,625.00
Transfers: 5
Sales: 4

December:
1—transfer
1—transfer
2—transfer
12—113,000.00
16—115,000.00
16—115,500.00
16—118,000.00
16—120,000.00
17—transfer
18—119,000.00
18—114,000.00
19—125,000.00
High: 125,000.00
Low: 113,000.00
Average: 117,437.00
Transfers: 4
Sales: 8

1976

January:
6—transfer
14—125,000.00
14—125,000.00
20—transfer
20—150,000.00
20—139,500.00
20—transfer
21—130,000.00
21—transfer
21—transfer
21—135,000.00
21—125,000.00
22—transfer
22—137,500.00
23—138,000.00
24—transfer
28—transfer
29—transfer
High: 150,000.00
Low: 125,000.00
Average: 133,888.00
Transfers: 9
Sales: 9

February:
18—148,000.00
18—149,000.00
18—149,400.00
19—transfer
19—transfer
19—transfer
20—149,000.00
23—148,500.00
23—transfer
25—transfer
27—132,000.00
High: 149,400.00
Low: 132,000.00
Average: 146,133.00
Transfers: 5
Sales: 6

March:
8—148,500.00
12—146,000.00
17—135,000.00
19—transfer
22—135,000.00
24—137,000.00
29—transfer
30—128,500.00
31—135,000.00
High: 148,500.00
Low: 128,500.00
Average: 137,857.00
Transfers: 2
Sales: 7

April:
13—128,000.00
20—132,000.00
20—132,000.00
20—132,000.00
20—transfer
20—transfer
20—transfer
21—transfer
21—140,000.00
21—138,000.00
21—transfer
21—transfer
21—transfer
21—transfer
21—transfer
21—135,000.00
21—135,000.00
22—134,500.00
22—transfer
28—transfer
29—137,500.00
High: 140,000.00
Low: 128,000.00
Average: 134,400.00
Transfers: 11
Sales: 10

May:
10—transfer
13—transfer
18—transfer
19—transfer
19—transfer
19—125,000.00
19—transfer
20—transfer
24—transfer
25—transfer
26—115,000.00
High: 125,000.00
Low: 115,000.00
Average: 120,000.00
Transfers: 9
Sales: 2

June:
15—125,000.00
18—transfer
18—transfer
21—122,500.00
21—transfer
21—120,000.00
24—transfer
28—120,000.00
High: 125,000.00
Low: 120,000.00
Average: 121,875.00
Transfers: 4
Sales: 4

July:
13—122,000.00
19—125,000.00
20—127,500.00
20—134,800.00
20—135,000.00
20—transfer
21—128,500.00
21—135,000.00
21—transfer
21—transfer
21—transfer
22—transfer
22—transfer
23—125,000.00
23—transfer
26—140,000.00
27—transfer
27—130,000.00
29—transfer
30—transfer
High: 140,000.00
Low: 122,000.00
Average: 130,280.00
Transfers: 10
Sales: 10

August:
5—transfer
5—transfer
17—142,450.00
17—transfer
18—144,950.00
18—144,000.00
18—143,000.00
19—148,500.00
19—143,000.00

1976

19—148,000.00
20—142,000.00
20—150,000.00
23—transfer
23—transfer
24—transfer
25—140,000.00

High:	150,000.00
Low:	140,000.00
Average:	144,590.00
Transfers:	6
Sales:	10

September:
21—148,000.00
21—transfer
21—158,000.00
21—158,900.00
21—transfer
21—168,000.00
22—167,500.00
22—transfer
22—transfer
23—158,900.00
23—transfer
23—152,000.00
23—transfer
24—159,000.00
24—155,000.00
30—160,000.00
30—150,000.00

High:	168,000.00
Low:	148,000.00
Average:	157,754.00
Transfers:	6
Sales:	11

October:
19—160,000.00
19—transfer
19—transfer
20—160,000.00
20—transfer
21—150,000.00
29—162,500.00

High:	162,500.00
Low:	150,000.00
Average:	158,125.00
Transfers:	3
Sales:	4

November:
4—150,000.00
16—158,000.00
16—159,000.00
16—transfer
17—transfer
17—transfer
17—159,000.00
19—162,000.00
19—157,000.00
19—transfer
19—transfer
23—transfer
24—159,000.00

High:	162,000.00
Low:	150,000.00
Average:	157,714.00
Transfers:	6
Sales:	7

December:
1—transfer
8—150,000.00
9—150,000.00
21—145,000.00
22—transfer
22—transfer
22—130,000.00
23—135,000.00
27—transfer
29—135,000.00
29—120,000.00
30—transfer

High:	150,000.00
Low:	120,000.00
Average:	137,857.00
Transfers:	5
Sales	7

1977

January:
5—transfer
6—100,000.00
13—125,000.00
18—135,000.00
19—145,000.00
19—transfer
19—transfer
19—transfer
19—142,500.00
20—140,000.00
20—transfer
20—146,900.00
20—transfer
21—transfer
21—144,900.00
21—transfer
25—140,000.00
28—135,000.00
High: 146,900.00
Low: 100,000.00
Average: 135,430.00
Transfers: 8
Sales: 10

February:
15—139,000.00
15—140,000.00
15—transfer
15—transfer
16—140,000.00
16—133,000.00
17—135,000.00
17—130,000.00
22—transfer
23—transfer
28—122,000.00
28—120,000.00
High: 140,000.00
Low: 120,000.00
Average: 132,375.00
Transfers: 4
Sales: 8

March:
7—137,500.00
10—130,000.00
15—135,000.00
15—transfer
15—147,000.00
15—transfer
16—143,500.00
16—138,500.00
16—transfer
17—140,000.00
18—140,000.00
23—137,000.00
30—135,000.00
High: 147,000.00
Low: 130,000.00
Average: 138,300.00
Transfers: 3
Sales: 10

April:
6—transfer
6—135,000.00
13—140,000.00
19—147,000.00
19—148,700.00
19—149,000.00
19—150,000.00
19—transfer
20—transfer
20—transfer
20—transfer
20—transfer
20—150,000.00
20—transfer
21—144,000.00
21—153,000.00
26—150,000.00
26—145,000.00
27—transfer
27—transfer
High: 150,000.00
Low: 135,000.00
Average: 146,518.00
Transfers: 9
Sales: 11

May:
2—150,000.00
5—153,500.00
13—160,000.00
17—transfer
18—160,000.00
18—transfer
19—160,000.00
20—transfer
20—162,000.00
20—transfer
20—167,000.00
High: 167,000.00
Low: 150,000.00
Average: 158,928.00
Transfers: 4
Sales: 7

June:
21—transfer
21—transfer
22—154,600.00
22—transfer
22—154,800.00
22—150,000.00
23—154,900.00
24—154,500.00
24—transfer
29—135,000.00
High: 154,900.00
Low: 135,000.00
Average: 150,633.00
Transfers: 4
Sales: 6

July:
5—135,000.00
6—130,000.00
7—transfer
20—transfer
21—125,000.00
21—transfer
21—transfer
22—120,000.00
25—transfer
29—transfer
High: 135,000.00
Low: 120,000.00
Average: 127,500.00
Transfers: 6
Sales: 4

August:
3—120,000.00
16—transfer
16—transfer
17—transfer
17—transfer
18—108,000.00
24—120,000.00
24—transfer
29—125,000.00
High: 125,000.00
Low: 108,000.00
Average: 118,250.00

1977

Transfers: 6
Sales: 4

September:
6—117,500.00
12—120,000.00
12—transfer
19—128,000.00
21—transfer
21—transfer
21—transfer
26—128,000.00
27—130,000.00
High: 130,000.00
Low: 117,500.00
Average: 124,700.00
Transfers: 4
Sales: 5

October:
4—135,000.00
7—transfer
12—137,500.00
18—135,000.00
18—transfer
19—transfer
19—transfer
19—transfer
20—transfer
20—transfer
21—134,000.00
24—135,000.00
High: 137,500.00
Low: 134,000.00
Average: 135,300.00
Transfers: 7
Sales: 5

November:
4—135,000.00
4—135,000.00
4—134,500.00
7—135,000.00
10—138,000.00
16—transfer
16—135,000.00
18—transfer
22—138,500.00
High: 138,500.00
Low: 134,500.00
Average: 135,857.00
Transfers: 2
Sales: 7

December:
13—140,000.00
16—142,500.00
20—160,000.00
21—transfer
21—transfer
21—transfer
22—143,000.00
22—139,000.00
23—160,000.00
23—158,500.00
27—165,000.00
30—142,500.00
30—transfer
High: 165,000.00
Low: 140,000.00
Average: 150,055.00
Transfers: 4
Sales 9

1978

January:
3—150,000.00
5—144,000.00
6—transfer
13—140,000.00
20—148,000.00
20—148,000.00
23—transfer
25—150,000.00
30—transfer
31—transfer

High:	150,000.00
Low:	140,000.00
Average:	146,660.00
Transfers:	4
Sales:	6

February:
2—150,000.00
13—150,000.00
16—transfer
16—151,000.00
21—151,000.00
21—154,000.00
22—157,000.00
22—transfer
22—transfer
23—transfer
24—transfer
24—155,000.00
27—transfer
27—155,000.00
28—152,000.00

High:	155,000.00
Low:	150,000.00
Average:	152,777.00
Transfers:	6
Sales:	9

March:
2—150,000.00
8—155,000.00
9—149,000.00
13—152,500.00
17—158,900.00
21—transfer
22—170,000.00
22—174,000.00
22—160,000.00
22—transfer
22—transfer
22—167,500.00
23—transfer
27—160,000.00
29—169,000.00
31—175,000.00

High:	175,000.00
Low:	149,000.00
Average:	161,741.00
Transfers:	4
Sales:	12

April:
3—179,500.00
3—180,000.00
7—180,000.00
11—transfer
12—transfer
12—transfer
17—transfer
19—transfer
19—170,500.00
19—transfer
19—transfer
19—172,500.00
20—177,500.00
20—170,500.00
21—177,400.00
24—172,000.00
24—transfer
24—177,300.00
28—168,000.00

High:	180,000.00
Low:	168,000.00
Average:	175,018.00
Transfers:	8
Sales:	11

May:
5—165,000.00
10—transfer
15—163,000.00
17—transfer
17—transfer
18—167,000.00
19—transfer
30—transfer
31—transfer
31—160,000.00

High:	167,000.00
Low:	160,000.00
Average:	163,750.00
Transfers:	6
Sales:	4

June:
5—160,000.00
19—160,000.00
20—164,500.00
20—170,000.00
20—transfer
21—170,500.00
21—160,000.00
21—169,000.00
21—transfer
21—160,000.00
21—transfer
21—160,000.00
21—transfer
21—160,000.00
26—172,500.00
26—transfer
28—160,000.00

High:	172,500.00
Low:	160,000.00
Average:	164,227.00
Transfers:	5
Sales:	12

July:
3—transfer
6—transfer
7—transfer
18—178,500.00
18—transfer
19—transfer
19—172,500.00
20—179,000.00
20—transfer
21—176,000.00

High:	179,000.00
Low:	172,500.00
Average:	176,500.00
Transfers:	6
Sales:	4

August:
1—175,000.00
15—transfer
16—180,000.00
16—172,000.00
16—transfer
16—177,500.00
17—182,500.00
17—transfer
18—172,500.00
21—transfer

1978

21—transfer
21—184,000.00
25—185,000.00
25—185,000.00
25—transfer
High: 185,000.00
Low: 172,000.00
Average: 179,277.00
Transfers: 6
Sales: 9

September:
18—185,000.00
19—200,000.00
19—206,000.00
19—transfer
19—transfer
20—transfer
20—204,000.00
20—transfer
20—transfer
20—203,000.00
21—202,000.00
21—transfer
21—207,000.00
21—transfer
22—205,000.00
27—210,000.00
High: 210,000.00
Low: 185,000.00
Average: 202,444.00
Transfers: 7
Sales: 9

October:
2—215,000.00
18—210,000.00
19—200,000.00
19—transfer
High: 215,000.00
Low: 200,000.00
Average: 208,333.00
Transfers: 1
Sales: 3

November:
21—transfer
22—transfer
22—transfer
22—transfer
22—210,000.00
27—210,000.00
High: 210,000.00
Low: 210,000.00
Average: 210,000.00
Transfers: 4
Sales: 2

December:
4—transfer
4—transfer
13—200,000.00
19—217,000.00
19—215,000.00
19—transfer
19—transfer
20—transfer
20—transfer
22—220,000.00
22—225,000.00
26—225,000.00
27—210,000.00
High: 225,000.00
Low: 210,000.00
Average: 216,000.00
Transfers: 6
Sales: 7

1979

January:
9—transfer
12—215,000.00
19—216,000.00
19—transfer
23—215,000.00
23—transfer
30—transfer
High: 216,000.00
Low: 215,000.00
Average: 215,333.00
Transfers: 4
Sales: 3

February:
16—220,000.00
16—transfer
20—220,000.00
21—223,500.00
22—224,000.00
23—222,500.00
23—222,000.00
27—219,500.00
27—transfer
High: 224,000.00
Low: 219,500.00
Average: 221,642.00
Transfers: 2
Sales: 7

March:
8—transfer
15—transfer
15—transfer
15—transfer
20—224,400.00
21—223,000.00
21—transfer
21—transfer
21—transfer
21—transfer
22—223,500.00
26—transfer
27—223,500.00
High: 224,400.00
Low: 223,000.00
Average: 223,600.00
Transfers 9
Sales: 4

April:
2—223,500.00
17—232,500.00
17—228,500.00
18—transfer
18—233,000.00
18—233,500.00
19—234,000.00
19—235,000.00
19—234,500.00
19—234,000.00
19—222,500.00
19—234,000.00
19—235,000.00
20—227,500.00
20—223,000.00
20—230,000.00
23—233,000.00
24—230,000.00
30—transfer
High: 235,000.00
Low: 222,500.00
Average: 230,794.00
Transfers: 2
Sales: 17

May:
10—225,000.00
15—229,900.00
15—230,000.00
16—229,800.00
16—transfer
17—227,500.00
21—transfer
23—220,000.00
23—transfer
29—224,000.00
29—transfer
High: 230,000.00
Low: 220,000.00
Average: 226,600.00
Transfers: 4
Sales: 7

June:
11—225,000.00
13—220,000.00
14—227,000.00
19—transfer
19—transfer
20—225,000.00
21—229,000.00
22—223,000.00
25—239,000.00
27—238,000.00
29—transfer
29—transfer
29—224,500.00
High: 239,000.00
Low: 220,000.00
Average: 227,833.00
Transfers: 4
Sales: 9

July:
11—238,000.00
13—235,000.00
17—transfer
18—transfer
18—transfer
18—transfer
18—258,000.00
19—249,000.00
19—transfer
20—255,000.00
23—250,000.00
23—259,000.00
23—transfer
23—transfer
25—transfer
High: 259,000.00
Low: 235,000.00
Average: 249,142.00
Transfers: 8
Sales: 7

August:
7—transfer
16—transfer
21—transfer
21—250,000.00
21—259,500.00
22—258,500.00
22—transfer
24—259,000.00
30—250,000.00
31—250,000.00
High: 259,500.00
Low: 250,000.00
Average: 254,500.00
Transfers: 4
Sales: 6

September:
18—transfer
19—245,000.00
19—249,000.00

1979

19—transfer
20—245,000.00
20—245,000.00
20—245,000.00
20—249,000.00
21—248,500.00
24—transfer
27—247,000.00
High: 249,000.00
Low: 245,000.00
Average: 246,928.00
Transfers: 3
Sales: 7

October:
11—246,500.00
12—transfer
16—235,000.00
16—247,400.00
16—247,500.00
18—transfer
18—transfer
18—247,500.00
18—transfer
19—248,000.00
19—transfer
21—transfer
22—transfer
22—transfer
High: 248,000.00
Low: 235,000.00
Average: 245,316.00
Transfers: 8
Sales: 6

November:
20—224,900.00
21—transfer
27—transfer
High: 224,900.00
Low: 224,900.00
Average: 224,900.00
Transfers: 2
Sales: 1

December:
4—234,000.00
5—220,000.00
6—222,500.00
7—transfer
12—225,000.00
13—transfer
14—transfer
17—224,500.00
20—transfer
20—transfer
21—transfer
21—transfer
21—transfer
27—transfer
27—transfer
High: 234,000.00
Low: 220,000.00
Average: 225,200.00
Transfers: 10
Sales: 5

1980

January:
11—transfer
17—200,000.00
17—212,000.00
21—180,000.00
21—202,000.00
30—190,000.00
High: 212,000.00
Low: 180,000.00
Average: 196,000.00
Transfers: 1
Sales: 5

February:
15—205,000.00
19—205,000.00
19—205,000.00
22—transfer
22—transfer
26—215,000.00
High: 215,000.00
Low: 205,000.00
Average: 207,500.00
Transfers: 2
Sales: 4

March:
3—200,000.00
3—transfer
6—189,000.00
12—transfer
21—transfer
21—189,500.00
21—transfer
21—181,000.00
24—transfer
24—186,000.00
24—187,000.00
24—transfer
28—170,500.00
28—170,000.00
28—187,000.00
31—186,000.00
High: 200,000.00
Low: 170,000.00
Average: 184,600.00
Transfers: 6
Sales: 10

April:
1—165,000.00
3—165,000.00
7—141,000.00
8—transfer
15—165,000.00
15—188,000.00
15—169,500.00
16—transfer
16—transfer
17—160,000.00
22—transfer
28—transfer
High: 188,000.00
Low: 141,000.00
Average: 164,785.00
Transfers: 5
Sales: 7

May:
5—transfer
13—transfer
19—185,000.00
20—185,000.00
20—transfer
20—190,000.00
20—190,000.00
21—188,000.00
21—transfer
21—transfer
22—transfer
27—transfer
High: 190,000.00
Low: 185,000.00
Average: 187,600.00
Transfers: 7
Sales: 5

June:
4—183,000.00
6—181,000.00
12—transfer
16—182,000.00
17—185,000.00
18—transfer
18—183,000.00
18—transfer
20—195,000.00
20—transfer
23—transfer
23—transfer
26—195,000.00
High: 195,000.00
Low: 181,000.00
Average: 186,285.00
Transfers: 6
Sales: 7

July:
1—transfer
1—200,000.00
1—transfer
2—transfer
11—transfer
15—224,700.00
15—205,000.00
15—230,000.00
16—transfer
16—transfer
21—transfer
29—240,000.00
31—230,000.00
High: 240,000.00
Low: 200,000.00
Average: 221,616.00
Transfers: 7
Sales: 6

August:
15—240,000.00
15—240,000.00
15—245,000.00
15—252,000.00
19—257,500.00
19—269,000.00
20—230,000.00
20—241,000.00
21—230,000.00
25—275,000.00
28—230,000.00
28—transfer
28—230,000.00
28—transfer
High: 275,000.00
Low: 230,000.00
Average: 244,958.00
Transfers: 2
Sales: 12

September:
2—219,000.00
10—transfer
10—transfer
12—transfer
15—272,500.00
15—275,000.00

1980

15—285,000.00
15—285,000.00
16—transfer
16—transfer
17—transfer
17—300,000.00
18—transfer
23—300,000.00
23—300,000.00
25—325,000.00
29—300,000.00
30—transfer

High:	325,000.00
Low:	219,000.00
Average:	286,277.00
Transfers:	8
Sales:	1

October:
1—329,000.00
20—330,000.00
27—329,400.00
29—320,000.00
29—transfer
30—transfer
31—transfer

High:	330,000.00
Low:	320,000.00
Average:	327,100.00
Transfers:	3
Sales:	4

November:
3—310,000.00
5—transfer
6—transfer
11—transfer
18—transfer
18—transfer
19—transfer
19—transfer
19—320,000.00
19—transfer
20—transfer
24—transfer
25—320,000.00

High:	320,000.00
Low:	310,000.00
Average:	316,666.00
Transfers:	10
Sales:	3

December:
15—280,000.00
15—265,000.00
16—transfer
16—transfer
19—transfer
30—transfer
31—282,000.00
31—transfer

High:	282,000.00
Low:	265,000.00
Average:	275,666.00
Transfers:	5
Sales:	3

1981

January:
20—transfer
22—300,000.00
23—312,000.00
28—318,000.00
29—316,000.00
29—310,000.00
29—transfer
High: 318,000.00
Low: 300,000.00
Average: 311,200.00
Transfers: 2
Sales: 5

February:
10—301,000.00
11—transfer
13—301,000.00
13—312,000.00
13—312,000.00
13—300,000.00
18—transfer
18—transfer
23—transfer
25—315,000.00
25—320,000.00
26—transfer
26—316,000.00
High: 320,000.00
Low: 300,000.00
Average: 309,625.00
Transfers: 5
Sales: 8

March:
2—transfer
3—315,000.00
4—300,000.00
9—300,000.00
9—275,000.00
17—transfer
17—transfer
17—transfer
19—transfer
20—transfer
20—transfer
23—transfer
23—300,000.00
24—transfer
24—300,000.00
24—transfer
26—310,000.00
High: 315,000.00
Low: 275,000.00
Average: 300,000.00
Transfers: 10
Sales: 7

April:
1—transfer
6—transfer
14—310,000.00
14—315,000.00
16—transfer
16—transfer
22—transfer
22—transfer
22—transfer
23—310,000.00
23—transfer
23—transfer
23—transfer
24—302,000.00
27—transfer
28—transfer
High: 315,000.00
Low: 302,000.00
Average: 309,250.00
Transfers: 12
Sales: 4

May:
13—transfer
15—287,000.00
18—transfer
19—285,000.00
21—275,000.00
22—transfer
29—275,000.00
High: 287,000.00
Low: 275,000.00
Average: 280,500.00
Transfers: 3
Sales: 4

June:
4—transfer
16—transfer
16—transfer
17—transfer
22—259,000.00
22—230,000.00
22—transfer
23—235,000.00
25—255,000.00
25—242,000.00
25—258,000.00
29—235,000.00
High: 259,000.00
Low: 230,000.00
Average: 244,851.00
Transfers: 5
Sales: 7

July:
23—242,000.00
23—260,000.00
28—transfer
31—254,000.00
High: 260,000.00
Low: 242,000.00
Average: 252,160.00
Transfers: 1
Sales: 3

August:
6—225,000.00
6—236,000.00
7—transfer
7—231,000.00
7—228,000.00
12—transfer
18—transfer
18—223,000.00
24—215,000.00
24—220,000.00
25—224,000.00
26—230,000.00
27—218,000.00
31—215,000.00
31—210,000.00
31—transfer
High: 236,000.00
Low: 210,000.00
Average: 222,000.00
Transfers: 4
Sales: 12

September:
3—225,000.00
9—224,000.00
9—transfer
11—223,500.00
15—235,000.00
15—231,000.00
17—transfer

1981

17—transfer
21—235,000.00
21—transfer
21—230,000.00
24—transfer
29—transfer
30—transfer

High:	235,000.00
Low:	223,500.00
Average:	229,100.00
Transfers:	7
Sales:	7

October:
2—222,000.00
8—222,500.00
12—219,000.00
12—226,000.00
14—230,000.00
14—transfer
15—220,000.00
19—transfer
20—transfer
21—transfer
21—223,500.00
21—230,000.00
21—215,100.00
22—223,000.00
26—231,000.00
26—transfer
29—222,500.00
30—235,000.00
30—235,000.00
30—220,000.00

High:	235,000.00
Low:	215,000.00
Average:	224,257.00
Transfers:	5
Sales:	14

November:
4—234,000.00
10—transfer
17—230,000.00
19—transfer
19—transfer
20—235,000.00
23—transfer

High:	235,000.00
Low:	230,000.00
Average:	233,000.00
Transfers:	4
Sales:	3

December:
7—235,000.00
9—240,000.00
9—255,000.00
14—249,000.00
15—241,000.00
16—transfer
18—transfer
18—260,000.00
21—260,000.00
21—transfer
22—transfer
23—transfer
30—245,000.00

High:	260,000.00
Low:	235,000.00
Average:	248,125.00
Transfers:	5
Sales:	8

1982

January:
12—transfer
15—transfer
15—245,000.00
19—transfer
20—255,000.00
20—transfer
20—transfer
21—transfer
28—transfer
28—250,000.00
29—255,000.00
High: 255,000.00
Low: 245,000.00
Average: 251,250.00
Transfers: 7
Sales: 4

February:
1—250,000.00
8—250,000.00
9—transfer
10—transfer
10—transfer
12—243,000.00
16—transfer
18—transfer
22—255,000.00
High: 255,000.00
Low: 243,000.00
Average: 249,500.00
Transfers: 5
Sales: 4

March:
3—245,000.00
5—transfer
11—transfer
12—235,000.00
17—transfer
19—transfer
22—transfer
25—244,000.00
25—transfer
26—transfer
29—233,000.00
31—transfer
High: 245,000.00
Low: 233,000.00
Average: 239,250.00
Transfers: 8
Sales: 4

April:
2—245,000.00
5—transfer
7—250,000.00
12—250,000.00
20—232,000.00
20—232,000.00
21—transfer
23—245,000.00
23—250,000.00
26—transfer
28—250,000.00
29—transfer
High: 250,000.00
Low: 232,000.00
Average: 246,000.00
Transfers: 4
Sales: 7

May:
4—transfer
18—transfer
19—transfer
19—234,000.00
19—transfer
19—transfer
21—transfer
24—220,000.00
27—220,000.00
27—transfer
27—215,000.00
28—205,000.00
28—200,000.00
28—225,000.00
28—225,000.00
High: 234,000.00
Low: 200,000.00
Average: 218,000.00
Transfers: 7
Sales: 8

June:
1—transfer
2—transfer
7—transfer
7—199,000.00
11—transfer
14—185,000.00
14—180,000.00
14—180,000.00
16—transfer
17—transfer
18—161,000.00
21—177,000.00
21—175,000.00
22—184,000.00
29—170,000.00
30—184,000.00
30—185,000.00
High: 199,000.00
Low: 161,000.00
Average: 180,000.00
Transfers: 6
Sales: 11

July:
1—170,500.00
12—175,000.00
13—182,000.00
20—185,000.00
22—185,000.00
28—transfer
29—transfer
30—185,000.00
30—transfer
30—transfer
High: 185,000.00
Low: 170,500.00
Average: 180,416.00
Transfers: 4
Sales: 6

August:
6—187,000.00
12—190,000.00
12—175,000.00
16—175,000.00
18—175,000.00
19—182,500.00
19—transfer
19—transfer
23—182,000.00
24—170,000.00
25—172,500.00
26—transfer
26—172,000.00
30—transfer
30—185,000.00
30—170,500.00
31—170,000.00
31—transfer
High: 190,000.00
Low: 170,000.00
Average: 177,423.00

1982

Transfers: 5
Sales: 13

September:
2—transfer
3—190,000.00
8—181,000.00
8—189,000.00
9—189,000.00
9—190,000.00
14—193,000.00
18—176,000.00
20—180,000.00
20—transfer
21—199,000.00
22—185,000.00
23—180,000.00
24—182,000.00
28—189,900.00
29—185,000.00
29—175,100.00
30—187,000.00
30—transfer
High: 199,000.00
Low: 175,100.00
Average: 185,681.00
Transfers: 3
Sales: 16

October:
1—transfer
12—transfer
14—177,000.00
15—transfer
19—184,000.00
High: 184,000.00
Low: 177,000.00
Average: 180,500.00
Transfers: 3
Sales: 2

APPENDIX B

LOW-FREQUENCY FILTERS FOR SEASONAL ANALYSIS

David Handmaker

The use of low-frequency filters and the APP method of seasonal analysis were first introduced in David Handmaker's "Low-Frequency Filters in Seasonal Analysis" (*The Journal of Futures Markets,* Vol. 1, No. 3, Wiley, New York, NY, 1981, pp. 367–378). Through this technique, an APP for each of the 52 weeks of the year is calculated. That number (APP_i, i = 1, 2, . . . , 52) represents the average over the years of the ratio of that week's price to the year's average price. That is,

$$APP_i = 100 \left\{ \frac{1}{N} \left[52 \sum_{n=1}^{N} \left(P_{in} / \sum_{j=1}^{52} P_{jn} \right) \right] \right\}$$

where APP_i is the Average Percentage Price in week *i; i* is a week number from 1 to 52; *N* is the number of years in the analysis; and P_{jn} is the commodity price in week *j* of year *n*.

This analysis yields an ordered vector with 52 elements. The calculated number in the 27th slot tells how prices during the 27th week have compared to the years' average price levels over time. The number is expressed as a percentage. If the vector's 27th element is 60, then over the years calculated, prices have been at 60% of the year's average price level during the 27th week, or 40% below the average.

This technique automatically compensates for any inflationary bias brought on by generally increasing price levels over the years. The elements in the APP vector represent their respective weeks' average price over the years, with each year's weekly prices normalized by their yearly averages. Although a steady, long-term price increase could show up as a tendency for APP values to increase toward the end of the vector, the percentage values will depict price levels accurately relative to their time of occurrence. In this way, the APP vector provides all the seasonal information—even that part frequently dismissed as an upward trend.

The application of low-frequency filters when using the APP technique is very straightforward. Because the APP technique treats each year as an observation in a larger sample, market years can be singled out easily and then excluded from the analysis. The best filter to use is one that divides a set of all years into two different sets of similar, or analogous, years. To obtain such a filter, one must first determine the main reason for the commodity's price seasonality, then develop an indicator of the impact of that reason as it has varied over the years. This indicator will be the basis of the filtering process. If the level of the indicator is positively correlated with the degree of seasonality, then an expectation for the indicator to be at high levels translates directly to an expectation that there will be a true seasonal pattern. In some cases, the indicator can be chosen so well that completely different patterns can be estimated for the separate groups.

When using the filter to divide a set of all years into sets of analogous years, it is best to stop at two mutually exclusive sets, except when there are large amounts of data available (50–100 years). If the breakdowns become too complex and there are too many sets of analogous years, problems arise. With too many sets of years, each set will have so few years that the APP values will be meaningless. Perhaps more important, if the filtering process becomes too complicated the conclusions drawn will be difficult to apply. Various results of this technique have been incorporated into the chapters "The Soybean Complex Cash and Futures Markets," "Corn," "The Pork Complex," and "The Copper Market" in this book.

BIBLIOGRAPHY

1. BIBLIOGRAPHIES

Brealey, R. A. and C. Pyle. *A Bibliography of Finance and Investment*. MIT Press, Cambridge, 1973.

Chicago Board of Trade. *Community Futures Trading: A Bibliography*. Chicago Board of Trade, Chicago, cumulative through 1976, 1978.

Chicago Board of Trade. *Commodity Futures Trading: A Bibliography*. Chicago Board of Trade, Chicago, (A).

Woy, James B. *Commodity Futures Trading, A Bibliographic Guide*. Bowker, New York, 1976.

2. GENERAL COMMODITY MARKET LITERATURE

Books

Appleman, Mark J. *The Winning Habit; How Your Personality Makes You a Winner or Loser in the Stock Market*. McCall, New York, 1970.

Arthur, Henry B. *Commodity Futures as a Business Management Tool*. Harvard University Press, Cambridge 1971.

Baer & Saxon. *Commodity Exchanges and Futures Markets and Trading*. Harper, New York, 1948.

Bakken, Henry. *Futures Trading in Livestock—Origins and Concepts—1919–1969*. Mimir Publishers, Madison, WI, 1970.

Bakken, Henry. *Theories of Markets and Marketing*. Mimir, Madison, WI, 1952.

Baruch, Bernard. *My Own Story*. Holt, New York, 1957.

Bernstein, Jacob. *The Investor's Quotient*. Wiley, New York, 1981.

Besant, Lloyd, et al., eds. *Commodity Trading Manual*. Chicago Board of Trade, Chicago, 1980.

Besant, Lloyd, et al., eds. *Grains: Production, Processing, Marketing*. Chicago Board of Trade, Chicago, 1977.

Block, Arthur. *Murphy's Law and Other Reasons Why Things Go Wrong!*. Price/Stern/Sloan, Los Angeles, 1977.

Burns, Joseph M. *A Treatise on Markets, Spot, Futures, and Options*. American Enterprise Institute for Public Policy Research, Washington, 1979.

Chicago Board of Trade. *International Futures Trading Seminar*. Proceedings, Vol. 4, Chicago Board of Trade, Chicago, 1976.

Chicago Board of Trade. *International Futures Trading Seminar*. Proceedings, Vol. 5, Chicago Board of Trade, Chicago, 1978.

Additional bibliographical material may appear at the end of each chapter.

Chicago Board of Trade. *International Futures Trading Seminar*. Proceedings, Vol. 6, Chicago Board of Trade, Chicago, 1979.

Chicago Board of Trade. *International Futures Trading Seminar*. Proceedings, Vol. 7. Chicago Board of Trade, Chicago, 1980.

Chicago Board of Trade. *Industry Research Seminar*, Proceedings, Vol. 1, Chicago Board of Trade, Chicago, 1980.

Chicago Board of Trade. *Research on Speculation: Seminar Report*. Chicago Board of Trade, Chicago, 1980.

Chicago Board of Trade. *Commodity Trading Manual*. Chicago Board of Trade, Chicago, 1981.

Commodity Research Bureau. *Commodity Yearbook*. Jersey City, NJ (A).

Commodity Research Bureau. *Understanding the Commodity Futures Markets*. Commodity Research Bureau, New York, 1977.

DeKeyser, Ethel, ed. *Guide to World Commodity Markets*. 3rd ed., Nichols, Kogan Page, London, New York, 1982.

Dow Jones-Irwin. *The Dow Jones Commodities Handbook: A Guide to Major Futures Markets*. Dow Jones Books, Princeton, NJ (A).

Durant, Will. *Our Oriental Heritage*. Simon & Schuster, New York, 1963.

Eames, F. L. *The New York Stock Exchange*. Thomas G. Hall, New York, 1984.

Emmanuel, A. *Unequal Exchange*. New Left Books, London. 1972.

Gardner, L. *Economic Aspects of New Deal Diplomacy*. University of Wisconsin Press, Madison, WI, 1964.

Geczi, Michael L. *Futures, The Anti-Inflation Investment*. Avon, New York, 1980.

Glick, Ira O. *A Social Psychological Study of Futures Trading*. Unpublished doctoral dissertation, Department of Sociology, University of Chicago, 1957.

Gold, Gerald. *Modern Commodity Futures Trading*. 7th ed. rev., Commodity Research Bureau, New York, 1975.

Goss, B. A. and B. S. Yamey. *The Economics of Futures Trading*. Wiley, New York, 1976.

Goss, B. A. *A Theory of Futures Trading*. Routledge and Kegan Paul, Boston, 1972.

Gould, Bruce G. *Dow Jones-Irwin Guide to Commodities Trading*. Dow Jones-Irwin, Homewood, IL, 1973.

Granger, C. W. J. *Getting Started in London Commodities*. 2nd ed., Investor Publications, Waterloo, IA, 1975.

Granger, C. W. J. *Trading in Commodities*. 3rd ed., Woodhead-Faulkner, Cambridge, England, 1979.

Halliday, F. *Arabia Without Sultans*. Penguin, Harmondsworth, England, 1974.

Hammonds, Timothy M. *The Producer's and Lender's Guide to Futures Trading*. Conrad, Corvallis, OR, 1974.

Hambridge, Jay. *Dynamic Symmetry, The Greek Vase*. Yale University Press, New Haven, 1931.

Handbook of Futures Markets, Wiley, New York 1984.

Harper, Henry H. *The Psychology of Speculation*. Fraser, Burlington, VT, 1978.

Harris, Thomas A. *I'm OK—You're OK*. Harper & Row, New York, 1967.

Hayden, Jack. *What Makes You a Winner or Loser in the Stock and Commodity Markets?* Investors Intelligence, Larchmont, NY, 1967.

Hieronymus, Thomas. *Economics of Futures Trading for Commercial and Personal Profit*. Commodity Research Bureau, New York, 1977.

Horn, Frederick F. and Victor W. Farah. *Trading in Commodity Futures*. 2nd ed., New York Institute of Finance, New York, 1979.

Houthakker, H. S., and L. G. Telser. *Commodity Futures II: Gains and Losses of Hedgers and Future Speculators*. Cowles Commission Discussion Paper, Economics, No. 2090, December 1952.

Huff, Charles. *Commodity Speculation for Beginners: A Guide to the Futures Markets*. Macmillan, New York, 1980.

Irwin, Harold. *Evolution of Futures Trading*. Mimir, Madison, WI, 1954.

Jain, Arvend K. *Commodity Futures Markets and the Law of One Price*. University of Michigan, Ann Arbor, 1980.

Johnson, Philip McBride. *Commodity Regulation*. Little, Brown, Boston, MA.

Keynes, J. M. *Treatise on Money, Vol. II: The Applied Theory of Money*. Harcourt, New York, 1930.

Kindleberger, Charles P. *Mania's, Panics and Crashes: A History of Financial Crisis*. Basic Books, New York, 1978.

Klein, Frederick C. and John A. Prestbo. *News and the Market*. Henry Regnery, Chicago, 1974.

Kroll, Stanley and Irwin Shisko. *The Commodity Futures Market Guide*. Harper & Row, New York, 1973.

Laurence, Michael. *Playboy's Investment Guide*. Playboy Press, Chicago, 1971.

Le Bon, Gustare. *The Crowd*. Viking, New York, 1960.

Lefevre, Edwin. *Reminiscences of a Stock Operator*. American Research Council, New York, 1923. Also Books of Wall Street, Burlington, VT, 1980.

Leuthold, Raymond. ed. *Commodity Markets and Futures Prices*. Chicago Mercantile Exchange, Chicago, 1979.

Levin, Jonathan. *The Export Economies*. Harvard University Press, Cambridge, 1960.

Longstreet, Roy W. *Viewpoints of a Commodity Trader*. Frederick Fell, New York, 1968.

Lurie, Jonathan. *The Chicago Board of Trade 1859–1905*. University of Illinois Press, Champaign-Urbana, 1974.

MacKay, Charles. *Extraordinary Popular Delusions and the Madness of Crowds*. L. C. Page, London, 1932.

Magee, John. *Wall Street—Main Street—And You*. John Magee, Springfield, MA, 1972.

Odell, P. R. *Oil and World Power: Background to the Oil Crisis*. Rev. ed., Penguin, Harmondsworth, England, 1974.

Parris, Frank G. and Joseph J. Tedesco. *The Commodity Market—How It Works*. Rev. and enl. ed., Parris, Ft. Lauderdale, FL, 1976.

Parry, John. *Guide to World Commodity Markets*. 3rd ed., Nichols, New York, 1982.

Peck, Anne, ed. *Readings in Futures Markets, 1: Selected Writings of Holbrook Working*. Chicago Board of Trade, Chicago, 1977.

Peck, Anne, ed. *Readings in Futures Markets, 2: Selected Writings on Futures Markets*. Chicago Board of Trade, Chicago, 1977.

Peck, Anne, ed. *Readings in Futures Markets, 3: Views from the Trade* Chicago Board of Trade, Chicago, 1978.

Powers, Mark J. *Getting Started in Commodity Futures Trading*. 2nd ed., Investor Publications, Cedar Falls, IA, 1977.

Powers, Mark J. and David Vogel. *Inside the Financial Futures Markets*. Wiley, New York, 1980.

Prestbo, John. ed. *The Dow Jones Commodity Handbook: A Guide to Major Futures Markets*. Dow Jones Books, Princeton, NJ 1977.

Reinach, Anthony M. *The Fastest Game in Town: Trading Commodity Futures*. Commodity Research Bureau, New York, 1973.

Reisman, David. *The Lonely Crowd,* Yale University Press, New Haven, CT, 1950.

Schwed, Fred, Jr. *Where are the Customer's Yachts?* John Magee, Springfield, MA, 1955.

Shannon, F. A., *The Farmer's Last Frontier, Agriculture 1860–1897*. Holt, Rinehart & Winston, New York, 1945, reprinted, 1961.

Smidt, Seymour. *Amateur Speculators: A Survey of Trading Styles, Information Sources and Patterns of Entry Into and Exit from Commodity–Futures Markets by Non-Professional Speculators*. Cornell University Graduate School of Business and Public Administration, Ithaca, NY, 1965.

Smith A, *The Money Game*. Random House, New York, 1967.

Smith A, *Supermoney*. Random House, New York.

Teweles, Richard J., Charles V. Harlow, and Herbert L. Stone. *The Commodity Futures Game—Who Wins? Who Loses? Why?* 2nd ed., McGraw–Hill, New York, 1974.

Venkataramanar, L. S. *The Theory of Futures Trading*. Asia Publishing House New York, 1965.

Wyckoff, Richard D. *Wall Street Ventures and Adventures Through Forty Years*. Harper & Brothers, New York, 1930.

Yarry, Mark Robert. *The Fastest Fame in Town: Commodities*. Prentice-Hall, Englewood Cliffs, NJ, 1981.

Articles

Adelman, M. "Is the Oil Crisis Real?" *Foreign Affairs,* Winter 1972–1973.

Arrow, Kenneth. "Futures Markets—Some Theoretical Perspectives." Columbia University CSFM Working Paper Series No. 3, January 1981.

Blau, Gerda. "Some Aspects of the Theory of Futures Trading." *Rev. Econ. Stud., 1944–1945,* 1–30. Also in A. E. Peck, ed., *Readings in Futures Markets, 3, Views from the Trade,* Chicago Board of Trade, Chicago 1977, pp. 5–40.

Conhaim, Louis. "The New York Futures Exchange: The Big Board's Challenge in Financial Futures." *Rev. Bus.,* Summer 1980, 6–10.

Cootner, Paul. "Common Elements in Futures Markets for Commodities and Bonds." *Am. Econ. Rev.: Papers and Proceedings,* May 1961, 173–193.

Cootner, P. H. "Returns to Speculators: Telser versus Keynes." *J. Polit. Econ.,* **68** (4) August 1960, 396–414. "Reply," 404–415 and P. H. Cootner, "Rejoinder," 415–418.

Cootner, Paul. "Speculation and Hedging." In *Food Research Institute Studies,* Stanford University Press, Stanford, CA, 1976, supplement, 65–105.

Cox, J. C. "Futures Trading and Market Information." *J. of Polit. Econ.,* 1976, 1215–1237.

Dillon, Laura White. "The New York Futures Exchange Grapples with Its Future." *Instit. Investor,* June 1980, 183–184.

Edwards, Franklin. "The Regulation of Futures and Forward Trading by Depository Institutions: A Legal and Economic Analysis." Columbia University CSFM Working Paper Series No. 16, January 1981.

Edwards, Franklin R. "The Regulation of Futures Markets: A Conceptual Framework." Columbia University CSFM Working Paper Series No. 23, October 1981.

Emery, Henry Crosby. "Speculation on Stock and Produce Exchanges of the U.S." *Stud. Hist., Econ., Public Law,* **7** (2), Columbia University, NY, 1896.

Francis, Jack Clark. "Speculative Markets: Valuable Institutions or Dens of Iniquity?" *Federal Reserve Bank of Philadelphia Bus. Rev.*, July 1972, 3–11.

Frank, Andre Gunder. "Capitalism and Underdevelopment in Latin America." *Monthly Review Press,* New York, 1969; Penguin, London, 1971.

"Frontiers in Futures." Columbia University CSFM Working Paper Series No. 12, December 1979 Conference Proceedings.

Girvan, N. "Multinational Corporations and Dependent Underdevelopment in Mineral-Export Economies." *Soc. and Econ. Stud.*, Mona, Jamaica, December 1970.

Gray, R. W. "The Attack upon Potato Futures Trading in the United States." *Food Research Institute Studies,* Stanford University Press, Stanford, CA, 1964, pp. 97–121.

Gray, Roger. "Some Current Developments in Futures Trading." *J. Farm Econ.*, May 1958, 334–351.

Gray, Roger and D. J. S. Rutledge. "The Economics of Commodity Futures Markets: A Survey." *Rev. Mark. Agric. Econ.* **39** (4), 1971, 57–108.

Gray, R. W. (1963). "Onions Revisited." as reprinted in Peck, ed., *Readings in Futures Markets, 2: Selected Writing on Futures Markets,* Chicago Board of Trade, Chicago, 1977, pp. 325–328.

Gray, Roger. "Why Does Futures Trading Succeed or Fail: An Analysis of Selected Commodities." in A. E. Peck, ed., *Readings in Futures Markets, 2: Selected Writings on Futures Markets*. Chicago Board of Trade, Chicago, 1977, pp. 235–248.

Harlow, Charles and Richard Teweles. "Commodities and Securities Compared." *Financ. Anal. J.*, September/October 1972, 64–70.

Harris, P. S. "The Rhodesian Blockade and Internal Structural Change." *Mon. Rev.*, December 1974.

Hoogvelt, A. M. and D. Child. "Rhodesia: Economic Blockade and Development." *Mon. Rev.*, October 1973.

Kaldor, N. "Speculation and Economic Stability." *Rev. Econ. Stud.*, 1939, 1–27.

Kamara, Avraham. "Issues in Futures Markets: A Survey." Columbia University CSFM Working Paper Series No. 30.

Krasner, S. D. "Trade in Raw Materials: The Benefits of Capitalist Alliances." In J. R. Kurth and S. Rosen, eds., *Testing the Theory of Economic Imperialism,* Heath, Lexington, Washington, D.C., 1974.

Kuhn, Betsey A. *Determinants of Speculative Margin Requirements*. Chicago Mercantile Exchange, 1974.

Levish, Richard and Lawrence White. "Price Controls and Futures Contracts: An Examination of the Markets for Copper and Silver During 1971–1974." Columbia University CSFM Working Paper Series No. 8, January 1981.

Matuszewski, T. I. "Trader's Behaviour—An Alternative Explanation." *Rev. Econ. Stud.*, 126–130.

Melamed, Leo. "The Futures Market: Liquidity and the Technique of Spreading." *J. Futures Mark.*, Fall 1981, 405–412.

Payer, C. *The Debt Trap: The IMF and the Third World*. Penguin, Harmondsworth, England, 1974, Monthly Review Press, New York, 1975.

Phillips, J. "The Theory and Practice of Futures Trading." *Rev. Mark. Agric. Econ.*, June 1966, 43–63.

Powers, Mark. "Effects of Contract Provisions on the Success of a Futures Contract." *J. of Farm Econ.*, November 1967, 883–893.

Powers, Mark and Paula Tosini. "Commodity Futures Exchanges and the North–South Dialogue." *Am. J. Agric. Econ.*, December 1977, 977–985.

Puff, Harold. *Report and Teaching Guide on Commodity Futures*. Chicago Mercantile Exchange, Chicago, 1972.

Quantz, Lloyd and Murray Hawkins. "Futures Trading: A Review." *Can. J. Agric. Econ.*, July 1974, 48–54.

Riess, Michael. "Employment Opportunities in the Commodity Business." Columbia University CSFM Working Paper Series No. 4, January 1981.

Ross, Ray. *Financial Results of Trading in Commodity Futures*. Chicago Mercantile Exchange, Chicago, 1973.

Saltlin, Sheldon. "Commodity Pools—the Newest Investor Product." *J. Finan. Plann.*, April 1978, 137–142.

Seidman, A. "Old Motives, New Methods: Foreign Enterprise in Africa Today." in C. Allen and R. W. Johnson, eds., *Afr. Perspect.*, Cambridge University Press, Cambridge, England, 1970.

Silber, William. "Innovation, Competition and New Contract Design in Futures Markets." Columbia University CSFM Working Paper Series No. 14, January 1981.

Singer, H. W. "The Distribution of Gains Between Investing and Borrowing Countries." *Am. Econ. Rev.*, **40,** 1950.

Snyder, Linda. "The Weather and the Futures Markets." *Fortune,* April 1977, 59–60

Telser, Lester. "Margins and Futures Contracts." Columbia University CSFM Working Paper Series No. 17, January 1981.

Telser, Lester and Harlow Higinbotham. "Organized Futures Markets: Costs and Benefits." *J. of Polit. Econ.*, October 1977, 969–1000.

Telser, Lester. "The Supply of Speculative Services in Wheat, Corn and Soybeans." in *Food Research Institute Studies*, 1967, supplement, Stanford University Press, Stanford, CA, 131–176.

Tomek, William. "Futures Trading and Market Information: Some New Evidence." *Food Research Institute Studies, 1979–1980* Stanford University Press, Stanford, CA, pp. 351–359.

Wilmouth, R. K. "Don't Destroy Markets Economic Function." *Commodities,* August 1981, 24.

Wilmouth, Robert. "Exchange Views of Speculation." *Research on Speculation: Seminar Report,* Chicago Board of Trade, 1980, 1–7.

Working, H. (1970). "Economic Functions of Futures Markets." As reprinted in A. E. Peck, ed., *Readings in Futures Markets, 1: Selected Writings of Holbrook Working,* Chicago Board of Trade, Chicago, 1977, pp. 267–297.

Working, Holbrook. "Whose Markets? Evidence on Some Aspects of Futures Trading." *J. Marketing,* 1954, 1–11.

Periodicals

Barrons. Dow Jones & Co., Inc., 22 Cortlandt Street, New York, NY 10007 (W).

Commodities Magazine. 219 Parkade, Cedar Falls, IA 50613 (M).

Consensus. 30 W. Pershing Road, Kansas City, MO 64108 (W).

The Economist. The Economist Newspaper, Ltd., P.O. Box 190, 23 St. James Street, London SWIA 1HF England.

Futures Industry. 224 Joseph Square, Columbia, MD 21044 (B-W).

The Journal of Commerce. Twin Coast Newspapers, Inc., 90 Wall Street, New York, NY 10005 (D).

The New York Times. The New York Times Co., 229 West 43 Street, New York, NY 10036 (D).

Securities Week. McGraw-Hill, Inc., 1221 Avenue of the Americas, New York, NY 10020 (W).

The Wall Street Journal. Dow Jones & Co., Inc. 22 Cortlandt Street, New York, NY 10007 (D).

Wall Street Letter. 488 Madison Avenue, 14th Floor, New York, NY 10022 (W).

3. HEDGING—BOOKS

Chicago Board of Trade Clearing Corp. *Basis—the Economics of Where and When*. Chicago Board of Trade Clearing Corp., Chicago, 1977.

Hammonds, Timothy M. *The Commodity Futures Market from an Agricultural Producer's Point of View*. MSS Information, New York, 1972.

Leuthold, Raymond M. *An Analysis of the Basis for Live Beef Cattle*. University of Illinois Department of Agricultural Economics, Urbana, IL, 1977.

Miller, Jarrott T. *The Long and Short of Hedging*. Henry Regnery, Chicago.

Nettles, Donald M. *Hedging, the Use of Commodity Markets*. Farm Credit Administration, Washington, D.C., 1975.

Oster, Merrill J. *Commodity Futures for Profit. . . A Farmer's Guide to Hedging*. Investor Publications, Cedar Falls, IA, 1979.

Oster, Merrill J. *Professional Hedging Handbook: A Guide to Hedging Crops & Livestock*. Investor Publications, Cedar Falls, IA.

Williams, Willard F. *The TARA Handbook for Hedgers*. TARA, Lubbock, TX.

Articles

Agri-Finance and William Uhrig. "Lender's Guide to Hedging." *Agri-Finance*, July/August 1976, 21–51.

Anderson, Ronald W. and Jean–Pierre Danthine. "Cross Hedging." Columbia University CSFM Working Paper Series No. 24, March 1980.

Anderson, R. W. and J. P. Danthine. "Hedger Diversity in Futures Markets: Backwardation and the Coordination of Plans." Columbia University, Graduate School of Business, Working Paper Series No. 7A, 1980.

Anderson, R. W. and J. P. Danthine. "The Time Pattern of Hedging, Volatility of Futures, and the Resolution of Uncertainty." Columbia University CSFM Working Paper Series No. 7, 1980.

Anderson, R. W. and J. P. Danthine. "Cross Hedging." *J. of Polit. Econ.*, 1981, 1182–1196.

Arthur, Henry. "The Nature of Commodity Futures as an Economic Business Instrument." In *Food Research Institute Studies*, Stanford University Press, Stanford, CA, 1972, pp. 257–268.

Bailey, Fred. "Understanding the Mechanics of Making and Taking Delivery." *Commodities*, September 1980, 66–67.

Bobst, W. B. (1971). "The Effects of Location Basis Variability on Livestock Hedging in the South." in R. M. Leuthold, ed., *Commodity Markets and Futures Prices*, Chicago Mercantile Exchange, Chicago, 1979, 171–202.

Bobst, Barry and Joseph Davis. "Effects of Within–and Among–Contract Basis Variation on the Production Hedging of Feeder Cattle." *MidSouth J. Econ.*, **4** (1), 1980, 59–64.

Breeden, Douglas T. "Consumption Risk in Futures Markets." Columbia University CSFM Working Paper Series No. 5, 1980.

Brennen, M. J. "The Supply of Storage." *The Am. Econ. Rev.*, 1958, 50–72.

Dalton, M. E. "Benefits and Costs of a National Marketing Authority Hedging with Production Uncertainty." *International Futures Trading Seminar, Proceedings,* 1976, 32–48. Discussion, 49–59.

Danthine, Jean-Pierre and Ronald Anderson. "The Time Pattern of Hedging and the Volatility of Futures Prices." Columbia University CSFM Working Paper Series No. 7, April 1981.

Diercks, H. R. "Futures as a Corporate Tool." In A. E. Peck, ed., *Readings in Futures Markets, 3: Views from the Trade,* Chicago Board of Trade, Chicago, 1978, pp. 57–65.

Driscoll, James Lawrence. "An Analysis of Expected Returns to Oklahoma Grain Elevators from Alternative Hedged Wheat Storage Practices." Unpublished doctoral dissertation, Oklahoma State University, 1969.

Duke, R. Alton, Jr., *Hedging with Futures Contracts in the Southeast.* Chicago Mercantile Exchange, 1977.

Ederington, Louis. "Hedging Performance of the New Financial Futures Market." *J. Finance,* March 1979, 157–170.

Ehrich, Rollo. "Cash–Futures Price Relationships for Live Beef Cattle." *Am. J. Agric. Econ.,* February 1969, 26–40.

Evans, E. B. "Country Elevator Use of the Market." In A. E. Peck ed., *Readings in Futures Markets, 3: Views from the Trade,* Chicago Board of Trade, Chicago, 1978, pp. 79–84.

Fitz, James J. *Analysis of Alternative Hedging Programs for the Pork Belly Merchandiser.* Chicago Mercantile Exchange, 1972.

Goldman, Barry and Howard B. Sosin. "On the Pattern of Spot Prices for Harvestable and Storeable Commodities." Columbia University CSFM Working Paper Series No. 27, January 1982.

Gray, Roger. "The Importance of Hedging in Futures Trading and the Effectiveness of Futures Trading for Hedging." In A. E. Peck, ed., *Readings in Futures Markets 2; Selected Writings on Futures Markets,* Chicago Board of Trade, Chicago, 1977. pp. 223–234.

Gray, Roger. "Risk Management in Commodities and Financial Markets." *Am. J. Agric. Econ.,* May 1976, 280–285. Discussion by Clifford Hildreth, Konrad Biedermann, and Richard Sandor, 296–304.

Goss, Barry. "Aspects of Hedging Theory." *Aust. J. Agric. Econ.,* December 1980, 210–223.

Gum, R. and J. Wildermuth. "Hedging on the Live Cattle Futures Contract." *Agric. Econ. Res.,* October 1970, 104–106.

Gunnelson, Jerald and Paul Farris. "Use of Soybean Futures Markets by Large Processing Firms." *Agric. Econ. Res.,* April 1973, 27–40.

Hall, Kristen. "How Hedgers Use Brokerage Firms." *Commodities,* April 1981, 76.

Heifner, Richard. "Optimal Hedging Levels and Hedging Effectiveness in Cattle Feeding." *Agric. Econ. Res.,* April 1972, 25–36.

Hieronymus, T. A. "Basis Patterns." In A. E. Peck, ed., *Readings in Futures Markets, 3: Views From The Trade,* Chicago Board of Trade, Chicago, 1978, pp. 45–56.

Hieronymus, Thomas "Farmers Use of the Markets." In A. E. Peck, ed., *Readings in*

Futures Markets, 3: Views from the Trade, Chicago Board of Trade, Chicago, 1978, pp. 69–77.

Holland, David, Wayne Purcell, and Terry Hague. "Mean-Variance Analysis of Alternative Hedging Strategies." *South. J. Agric. Econ.,* July 1972, 123–128.

Holthausen, D. M. "Hedging and the Competitive Firm Under Price Uncertainty." *Am. Econ. Rev.,* 1974, 989–995.

Jackson, Barbara Bond. "Manage Risk in Industrial Pricing." *Harvard Bus. Rev.,* July/August 1980, 121–133.

Jaffray, Benjamin. "Hedging in the Corporate Financial Structure." *Industry Research Seminar, Proceedings,* Chicago Board of Trade, Chicago, 1980, 4–12. Discussion, 13–19.

Johnson, A. C. "Effects of Futures Trading on Price Performance in the Cash Onion Market, 1930–1968." As reprinted in A. E. Peck, ed., *Readings in Futures Markets, 2: Selected Writings in Futures Markets,* Chicago Board of Trade, Chicago, 1977, pp. 329–336.

Johnston, Larry Dan. *A Dynamic Approach to Integrated Hedging for Feedlots in the Texas High Plains.* Chicago Mercantile Exchange, Chicago, 1976.

Johnson, L. L. "The Theory of Hedging and Speculation in Commodity Futures." *Rev. Econ. Stud.,* 1960, 139–151.

Jones, Claude. "Theory of Hedging on the Beef Futures Market." *Am. J. Agric. Econ.,* December 1968, 1760–1766.

Johnson, Leland. "The Theory of Hedging and Speculation in Commodity Futures." *Rev. Econ. Stud.,* June 1960, 139–151. Also in A. E. Peck, ed., *Readings in Futures Markets, 2: Selected Writings on Futures Markets,* Chicago Board of Trade, Chicago, 1977, pp. 209–222.

Kahl, Kandire. "An Analysis of Intertemporal Basis Movements, 1960–1975." *International Futures Trading Seminar, Proceedings, 1976,* 1–20. Discussion, 21–31.

Kahl, Kandice and William Romek. "Effectiveness of Hedging in Potato Futures." *J. Futures Mark.,* Spring 1982, 9–18.

Kenyon, David and Steven Kingsley. "An Analysis of Anticipatory Short Hedging Using Predicted Harvest Basis." *South. J. Agric. Econ.,* July 1973, 199–203.

Kenyon, David and Neil Shapiro. "Profit Margin Hedging in the Broiler Industry." *Industry Research Seminar, Proceedings,* Chicago Board of Trade, Chicago, 1980, 58–70. Discussion, 71–83.

Larson, Arnold. "Estimation of Hedging and Speculative Positions in Futures Markets." In *Food Research Institute Studies,* Stanford University Press, Stanford, CA, 1961, pp. 203–212.

Leuthold, Raymond and Scott Mokler. "Feeding–Margin Hedging in the Cattle Industry." *International Futures Trading Seminar, Proceedings,* 1978, 56–68. Discussion, 69–77.

Longson, Ian Geoffrey. *Forecasting the Ontario Hog Basis and the Evaluation of Hedging Strategies for Ontario Hedgers.* Chicago Mercantile Exchange, Chicago, 1977.

Marcus, Alan and David Modest. "Futures Markets and Production Decision." Columbia University CSFM Working Paper Series No. 34, 1982.

Niles, James. "Forecasting FCOJ Futures Prices." *Comm. J.,* September/October 1976, 17–25.

O'Bryan, Stephen, Barry Bobst, and Joe Davis. "Factors Affecting Efficiency of Feeder Cattle Hedging in Kentucky." *South. J. Agric. Econ.,* July 1977, 185–189.

Oster, Merrill. "20 Rules for Successful Commodity Hedging." *Commodities,* October 1976, 20–23.

Patterson, Harlan Ray. *Hypothetical Case Study—Bank Lending Policy of Hedged Collateral.* Chicago Mercantile Exchange, Chicago, 1972.

Parrott, Robert. "A Professional's View of Hedging." *Business Horizons,* June 1977, 12–22. Also in A. E. Peck, ed., *Readings in Futures Markets, 3: Views from The Trade,* Chicago Board of Trade, Chicago, 1978, pp. 193–205.

Paul, A. B. "The Pricing of Binspace—A Contribution to the Theory of Storage." *Am. J. Agric. Econ.,* 1970, 1012.

Peck, Anne. "Futures Markets, Supply Response, and Price Stability." *Q. J. Econ.,* 1976, 407–423.

Peck, Anne. "Hedging and Income Stability: Concepts, Implications and an Example." *Am. J. Agric. Econ.,* August 1975, 410–419. Also in A. E. Peck, ed., *Readings in Futures Markets, 2: Selected Writings on Futures Markets,* Chicago Board of Trade, Chicago, 1977, 237–250.

Peck, Anne. "The Influence of Hedging on Futures Markets Activity." *International Futures Trading Seminar, Proceedings, 1979,* 1–23. Discussion, 24–35.

Peck, Anne. "Reflections of Hedging on Futures Market Activity." In *Food Research Institute Studies,* 1979–1980, Stanford University Press, Stanford, CA pp. 327–349.

Peeples, Furman S. *Cash-Futures Price Relationships: Effects on Egg Hedging Strategies.* Chicago Mercantile Exchange, Chicago, 1975.

Pickett, J. C. (1972). "The Supply of Storage for Frozen Pork Bellies." In R. M. Leuthold, ed., *Commodity Markets and Futures Prices,* Chicago Mercantile Exchange, Chicago, 1979, 203–230.

Pidgeon, Edward. "Factors Affecting Corn Basis in Southwestern Ontario," *Am. J. Agric. Econo.,* February 1980, 107–112.

Powers, Mark. "Hedging: The Basis." *Commodities,* May 1973, 37–40.

Rolfo, Jacques. "Optimal Hedging Under Price and Quantity Uncertainty: The Case of a Cocoa Producer." Columbia University CSFM Working Paper Series No. 21, 1981.

Rolfo, Jacques and Howard Sosin. "Alternative Strategies for Hedging and Spreading." Columbia University CSFM Working Paper Series No. 22, April 1981.

Rutledge, David. "Hedgers Demand for Futures Contracts: A Theoretical Framework with Applications to the United States Soybean Complex." In *Food Research Institute Studies,* Stanford University Press, Stanford, CA, 1972, pp. 227–256.

Schaefer, Henry Hollis. *The Determination of Basis Patterns and the results of Various Hedging Strategies for Live Cattle and Live Hogs.* Chicago Mercantile Exchange, Chicago, 1974.

Scholes, Myron. "Economics of Hedging and Spreading." Columbia University CSFM Working Paper Series No. 18, January 1981.

Schureman, Thomas R., *Hedging Strategies for Cattle Feeders.* Chicago Mercantile Exchange, Chicago, 1978.

Sexauer, B. "The Storage of Potatoes and the Maine Potatoes Futures Market." *Am. J. Agric. Econ.* 1977, 220–224.

Snape, R. H. and B. S. Yamey. "Test of the Effectiveness of Hedging." *J. Polit. Econ.,* October 1965, 540–544.

Snider, Thomas. "Using the Futures Market to Hedge: Some Basic Concepts." *Month. Rev. (Fed.) Res. Bank Richmond),* August 1973, 2–7.

Spahr, Ronald and William Sawaya. "Analysis of a Complete Hedging Strategy in the Futures Markets for Feeder Cattle as a Contradiction to Totally Efficient Markets." *MidSouth J. Econ.,* **3,** (1), 1979, 85–92.

Stein, Jerome. "The Opportunity Locus in a Hedging Decision: A Correction." *Am. Econ. Rev.*, 1964, 762–763.

Stein, Jerome. "The Simultaneous Determination of Spot and Futures Prices." *Am. Econ Rev.*, December 1961, 1012–1025. Also in A. E. Peck, ed., *Readings in Futures Markets, 2: Selected Writings on Futures Markets,* Chicago Board of Trade, Chicago, 1977, pp. 223–235.

Stevens, Neil. "The Futures Market for Farm Commodities—What It Can Mean to Farmers." *Fed. Res. Bank St. Louis Rev.*, August 1973, 10–15.

Stoll, H. R. "Commodity Futures and Spot Price Determination and Hedging in Capital Market Equilibrium." *J. Fin. Quant. Anal., Proceedings,* 1979, 873–894.

Telser, L. G. (1958). "Futures Trading and the Storage of Cotton and Wheat." as reprinted in A. E. Peck, ed., *Readings in Futures Markets, 2: Selected Writings on Futures Markets*. Chicago Board of Trade, Chicago, 1977, 105–129.

Telser, L. G. (1960), "Reply." as reprinted in A. E. Peck ed., *Readings in Futures Markets, 2: Selected Writings on Futures Markets,* Chicago Board of Trade, Chicago, 1977, pp. 52–64.

Telser, L. G. "The Supply of Speculative Services in Wheat, Corn and Soybeans." *Food Res. Inst. Stud., 1967 Supplement,* Stanford University Press, Stanford, CA, 1967, 131–176.

Telser, Lester. "Safety First and Hedging." *Rev. Econ. Stud.*, 1955, 1–16.

Tier, T. J. and P. R. Kidman. "Price Movements In and Between the Wool, Wool Tops and Worsted Yarn Spot and Futures Markets." *Q. Rev. Agric. Econ.*, April 1971, 63–81.

Urnovsky, S. J. "Futures Markets, Private Storage, and Price Stabilization." *J. Public Econ.*, 1979, 301–327.

Vollink, William and Ronald Raikes. "An Analysis of Delivery-Period Basis Determination for Live Cattle." *South. J. Agric. Econ.*, July 1977, 179–184.

Ward, Ronald and Frank Dasse. "Empirical Contributions to Basis Theory: The Case of Citrus Futures." *Am. J. Agric. Econ.*, February 1977, 71–80.

Weymar, H. F. "The Supply of Storage Revisited." *Am. Econ. Rev.*, December 1966, 1226–1234.

Wiese, Virgil. "Introduction to Hedging." In A. E. Peck, ed., *Readings in Futures Markets, 3: Views From the Trade,* Chicago Board of Trade, Chicago, 1978, pp. 3–11.

Wiese, Virgil. "Use of Commodity Exchanges by Local Grain Marketing Organizations." In A. E. Peck ed., *Readings in Futures Markets, 3: Views From the Trade,* Chicago Board of Trade, Chicago, 1978, pp. 85–90.

Wilson, Raleigh. "Merchandising and Inventory Management of Commodities: Carrying Charges and Basis." In A. E. Peck, ed., *Readings in Futures Markets, 3: Views From the Trade, Chicago Board of Trade, Chicago, 1978, pp. 27–33.*

Wood, J. E. "Analysis of Potential Hedging Criteria for Live Hogs Using Seasonal Indices." *Am. J. Agric. Econ.*, December 1972, 972.

Working, Holbrook. "Futures Trading and Hedging." *Am. Econ. Rev.*, 1953, 314–343. Also in A. E. Peck, ed., *Readings in Futures Markets 1: Selected Writings of Holbrook Working,* Chicago Board of Trade, Chicago, 1977, pp. 139–163.

Working, Holbrook. "Hedging Reconsidered." *J. Farm Econ.*, 1953, 544–561.

Working, Holbrook. (1948), "Theory of the Inverse Carrying Charge in Futures Markets." As reprinted in A. E. Peck, ed., *Readings in Futures Markets, 1: Selected Writings of Holbrook Working,* Chicago Board of Trade, Chicago, 1977, pp. 3–24.

Working, Holbrook, (1949a). "The Theory of Price of Storage." As reprinted in A. E. Peck, ed., *Readings in Futures Markets, 1: Selected Writings of Holbrook Working,* Chicago Board of Trade, Chicago, 1977, pp. 25–31.

Working, Holbrook. "The Theory of the Price of Storage." *Am. Econ. Rev.,* 1949b, 1254–1262.

Working, Holbrook. "The Investigation of Economic Expectations." *Am. Econ. Rev.,* 1949c, 158–161.

Working, Holbrook, (1953). "Hedging Reconsidered." As reprinted in A. E. Peck, ed., *Readings in Futures Markets, 1: Selected Writings of Holbrook Working,* Chicago Board of Trade, Chicago, 1977, pp. 123–138.

Working, Holbrook. "Speculation on Hedging Markets." In *Food Research Institute Studies,* Stanford University Press, Stanford, CA, 1961, pp. 185–220.

Working, Holbrook. "Theory of the Inverse Carrying Charge in Futures Markets." *J. Farm Econ.,* 1948, 1–28.

4. OPTIONS

Books

Bokron, N. *How to Use Put and Call Options.* John Magee, Springfield, MA, 1975.

Breeden, Douglas T. *Futures Markets and Commodity Options.* Columbia University CSFM Working Paper Series No. 20, 1980.

Clasing, H. *The Dow Jones—Irwin Guide to Put and Call Options.* Dow Jones—Irwin, Homewood, IL, 1978.

Cracraft, Perry J. *London Options on Commodities: A Primer for American Speculators.* Contemporary Books, Chicago, 1977.

Davis, G. and M. Jacobson. *Stock Options Strategies.* Badger, Cross Plains, WI, 1976.

Gastineau, G. *The Stock Options Manual.* McGraw-Hill, New York, 1979.

Hoag, James W. *An Introduction to the Valuation of Commodity Options.* University of California at Berkeley, May 1978, Columbia University CSFM Working Paper Series No. 19, 1980.

McMillian, L. *Options as a Strategic Investment.* Institute of Finance, New York, 1980.

Malkiel, B. and C. R. Quand. *Strategies and Rational Decisions in the Securities Options Market.* MIT Press, Cambridge, 1969.

Noddings, T. *How the Experts Beat the Market.* Dow Jones-Irwin, Homewood, IL, 1976.

Zieg, Kermit C., Jr. and William E. Nix. *The Commodity Options Market: Dynamic Trading Strategies for Speculation and Commercial Hedging.* Dow Jones-Irwin, Homewood, IL, 1978.

Zieg, Kermit C., Jr. and Susannah H. Zieg. *Commodity Options.* Investors Intelligence, Larchmont, NY 1974.

Articles

Black, F. "The Pricing of Commodity Contracts." *J. Financ. Econ.,* January/March 1976.

Black, F. and M. Scholes. "The Pricing of Options and Corporate Liabilities." *J. Poli Econ.,* May/June 1973.

Cox and S. A. Ross. "The General Structure of Contigent Claim Pricing." 1975.

Mehl, P. "Trading Privileges on the Chicago Board of Trade." U.S. Department of Agriculture USDA Circular, No. 323, Washington, D.C., 1934.

Wolf, Avner. "Fundamentals of Commodity Options on Futures." Columbia University CSFM Working Paper Series No. 35, 1982.

5. PRICE ANALYSIS, TIME SERIES, AND EFFICIENT MARKET STUDIES

Books

Cootner, Paul H., Ed. *The Random Character of Stock Market Prices*. MIT Press, Cambridge, MA, 1964.

Dahl, Dale C. and Jerome W. Hammond. *Market and Price Analysis, The Agricultural Industries*. McGraw-Hill, New York, 1977.

Dewey, Edward R. *Cycles, Selected Writings*. Foundation for the Study of Cycles, Pittsburgh, 1970.

Dewey, Edward R. *Cycles, the Mysterious Forces that Trigger Events*. Hawthorne Books, New York, 1971.

Dooley, Peter C. *Elementary Price Theory*. 2nd ed., Prentice-Hall, Englewood Cliffs, NJ 1973.

Jiler, Harry, ed. *Forecasting Commodity Prices: How the Experts Analyze the Market*. Commodity Research Bureau, New York, 1975.

Johnson, D. G. *Forward Prices for Agriculture*. University of Chicago, Chicago, 1967.

Labys, Walter and C. W. J. Granger. *Speculation, Hedging, and Commodity Price Forecasting*. Lexington Books, Lexington, MA, 1970.

Leuthold, Raymond M., ed. *Commodity Markets and Futures Prices*. Chicago Mercantile Exchange, Chicago, 1979.

Meadows, Dennis L. *Dynamics of Commodity Production Cycles*. Wiley, New York, 1970.

Shepherd, Geoffrey S. and Gene A. Futrell. *Agricultural Price Analysis*. Iowa State University, Ames, 1969.

Tomek, William G. and Kenneth L. Robinson. *Agricultural Product Prices*. Cornell University, Ithaca, NY, 1972.

Watson, Donald S. and Mary A. Holman. *Price Theory and Its Uses*. 4th ed., Houghton Mifflin, Boston, 1976.

Wilson, Louise. *Catalog of Cycles*. Foundation for the Study of Cycles, Pittsburgh, 1964.

Articles

Allingham, M. G. "Futures Price Oscillations." *Economica,* May 1976, 169–172.

Bachalier, L. (1900). "Theory of Speculation." *The Random Character of Stock Prices,* P. H. Cootner, Ed., MIT Press, Cambridge, MA, 1964.

Bear, Robert. "Martingale Movements in Commodity Futures." Unpublished doctoral dissertation, University of Iowa, 1970.

Bear, Robert. "Risk and Return Patterns on Overnight Holdings of Livestock Futures." In R. M. Leuthold, ed., *Commodity Markets and Futures Prices,* Chicago Mercantile Exchange, Chicago, 1979, pp. 13–24.

Black, Fischer. "The Pricing of Commodity Contracts." *J. Financ. Econ.*, January/March 1976, 167–179.

Blank, Steve. "Are Commodity Futures Prices 'Accurate'?" *Commodities,* September 1977, 24–26.

Bodie, Zvi and Victor Rosansky. "Risk and Return in Commodity Futures." *Financ. Anal. J.*, May/June 1980, 27–31.

Brinegar, Claude. "A Statistical Analysis of Speculative Price Behavior." In *Food Research Institute Studies,* supplement, Stanford University Press, Stanford, CA, pp. 1–58, 1967.

Brooks, William, Henry Wiebe, James Hier, and C. E. Francis. "Testing a Model for Predicting Commodity Futures Prices." *Am. Econ.*, Spring 1980, 24–31.

Cargill, Thomas and Gordon Rausser. "Temporal Price Behavior in Commodity Futures Markets." *J. Finance,* September 1975, 1043–1053.

Cargill, Thomas and Fordon Rausser. "Time and Frequency Domain Representations of Futures Prices as a Stochastic Process." *J. Am. Stat. Assoc.*, March 1972, 23–30.

Clark, Peter. "A Subordinate Stochastic Process Model with Finite Variance for Speculative Prices." *Econometrica,* January 1973, 135–155.

Clark, Peter. "A Subordinated Stochastic Process Model of Cotton Prices." Unpublished doctoral dissertation, Harvard University, Cambridge, MA, 1970.

Clough, Malcolm. "Are Futures Markets Good Forecasters?" *Commodities,* June 1973, 10–15.

Cootner, P. H. "Speculation and Hedging." In *Food Research Institute Studies,* supplement, Stanford University Press, Stanford, CA 1967, pp. 65–106.

Cox, J. C., J. E. Ingersoll, Jr., and S. A. Ross. "The Relation Between Forward Prices and Futures Prices." *J. Fin. Econ.*, **9,** 1981, 321–346. Also Columbia University CSFM Working Paper Series No. 9, May 1981.

Danthine, J. P. "Martingale, Market Efficiency and Commodity Prices." *Eur. Econ. Rev.*, October 1977, 1–17.

Danthine, M. P. (1978). "Information, Futures Prices and Stablilizing Speculation." *J. Econ. Theory,* **17,** 79–98.

Elam, Emmett. "A Strong Form Test of the Efficient Market Model Applied to the U.S. Hog Futures Market." Unpublished doctoral dissertation, University of Illinois, Urbana, 1978.

Fama, Eugene F. "Efficient Capital Markets: A Review of Theory and Empirical Work." *J. Fin.*, May 1970, 387–388.

French, K. P. "The Pricing of Futures Contracts." University of Rochester, Mimeo, 1981.

Frey, Norman and John Labuszewski. "Newspaper Articles and Their Impact on Commodity Price Formation—Case Study: Copper." *J. Fut. Mark.*, Spring 1981, 89–91.

Gardner, B. L. "Futures Prices in Supply Analysis." *Am. J. Agric. Econ.*, 1976, 81–84.

Goss, B. A. "Trading on the Sydney Wool Futures Market: A Test of a Theory of Speculation at the Level of the Individual." *Austr. Econ. Pap.*, December 1972, 187–202.

Grauer, F. L. A. "Equilibrium in Commodity Futures Markets: Theory and Tests." Unpublished doctoral dissertation, Stanford University, Stanford, CA 1977.

Grauer, F. L. A., and R. H. Litzenberger. "The Pricing of Commodity Futures Contracts, Nominal Bonds and Other Risky Assets Under Commodity Price Uncertainty." *J. Fin.*, March 1979, 69–83.

Gray, Roger. "The Characteristic Bias in Some Thin Futures Markets." *Food Res. Inst. Stud.*, Stanford University Press, Stanford, CA 1960, 296–312. Also in A. E. Peck, ed., *Readings in Futures Markets, 2: Selected Writings on Futures Markets,* Chicago Board of Trade, Chicago, 1977, pp. 83–102.

Gray, Roger. "The Emergence of Short Speculation." In *International Futures Trading Seminar Proceedings,* 1978, 78–100. Discussion, 101–115.

Gray, Roger. "Price Effects of a Lack of Speculation." In *Food Research Institute Studies,* Stanford University Press, Stanford, CA, Supplement, 1967, 177–194. Also in A. E. Peck, ed., *Readings in Futures Markets, 2: Selected Writings on Futures Markets,* Chicago Board of Trade, Chicago, 1977, pp. 191–207.

Gray, Roger. "The Relationship Among Three Futures Markets: An Example of the Importance of Speculation." In *Food Research Institute Studies,* Stanford University Press, Stanford, CA, 1961, pp. 21–32.

Grossman, S. J. "The Existence of Futures Markets, Noisy Rational Expectations and Informational Externalities." *Rev. of Econ. Stud.,* 1977, 431–449.

Grossman, S. J. and J. E. Stiglitz. "On the Impossibility of Informationally Efficient Markets." *Am. Econ. Rev.,* 1980, 393–408.

Handmaker, David. "Low-Frequency Filters in Seasonal Analysis." *J. Futures Mark.,* Fall 1981, 367–378.

Helmuth, John. "Futures Trading Under Conditions of Uncertainty." Unpublished doctoral dissertation, University of Missouri, 1970.

Helmuth, John. "A Report on the Systematic Downward Bias in Live Cattle Futures Prices." *J. Futures Mark.,* Fall 1981, 347–358.

Houthakker, H. S. "Can Speculators Forecast Prices?" *Rev. Econ. Stat.,* May 1957, 143–151. Also in A. E. Peck, ed., *Readings in Futures Markets, 2: Selected Writings on Futures Markets,* Chicago Board of Trade, Chicago, 1977, pp. 155–166.

Houthakker, H. S. "Systematic and Random Elements in Short-Term Price Movements." *Am. Econ. Rev.,* 1961, 164–172.

Hunt, B. F. "Short Run Price Cycles in the Sydney Wool Futures Market." *Aust. J. Agric. Econ.,* August 1974, 133–143.

Jarrow, R. A. and G. S. Oldfield. "Forward Contracts and Futures Contracts." *J. Financ. Econ.,* 1981, 373–382.

Jones, Donald. "The Misbehavior of Commodity Prices." *Commodities,* August 1975, 20.

Kahl, K. H. "An Analysis of Intertemporal Basis Movements, 1960–1975." *International Futures Trading Seminar,* Vol. 5, Chicago Board of Trade, Chicago, 1978, 1–31.

Kaufman, Perry and Kermit Zieg. "What Are Commodity Price Movements Really Like?" *Commodities,* December 1973, 20–26, 40.

Kendall, David and Grant Scobie. "Intertemporal Price Relationships in Noninventory Futures Markets." *International Futures Trading Seminar, Proceedings,* Chicago Board of Trade, Chicago, 1980, 106–151. Discussion, 152–161.

Kofi, Tetteh. "A Framework for Comparing the Efficiency of Futures Markets." *Am. J. Agric. Econ.,* November 1973, 534–594.

Kreiling, Tilmon, Jr. *Intemporal Price Research in Commodity Futures.* Chicago Mercantile Exchange, Chicago, 1971.

Kroch, Eugene. "Do Futures Markets Enhance Intertemporal Allocative Efficiency?" Columbia University CSFM Working Paper Series No. 28, November 1981.

Larson, A. B. "Evidence on the Temporal Dispersion of Price Effects of New Information." Unpublished doctoral dissertation, Stanford University, 1960.

Larson, A. B. "Measurement of a Random Process in Futures Prices." In *Food Research Institute Studies,* Stanford University Press, Stanford, CA, 1960, 313–324. Also in

Western Farm Economics Association Proceedings, 1960, 101–112. Also in A. E. Peck, ed., *Readings in Futures Markets, 2: Selected Writings on Futures Markets,* Chicago Board of Trade, Chicago, 1977, 295–306.

Leuthold, Raymond. "Random–Walk and Price Trends—the Live Cattle Futures Market." *J. Fin.,* September 1972, 879–889.

Leuthold Raymond and Peter Hartmann. "A Semi-Strong Form Evaluation of the Efficiency of the Hog Futures Market." *Am. J. Agric. Econ.,* August 1979, 482–489. "Comments," Donald Panton, August 1980, 584, and E. C. Pasour, 581–583, "Reply," 585–587.

Logan, Robert. "Application of Tests for Normality to a Microeconomic Theory of Futures Prices." Unpublished doctoral dissertation, Texas A&M University, 1973.

Mandelbrot, Benoit. "Forecasts of Futures Price, Unbiased Markets and Martingale Models." *J. Bus.,* January 1966, 242–255.

Mandelbrot, Benoit. "The Variation of Certain Speculative Prices." *J. Bus.,* October 1963, 394–419.

Mandelbrot, Benoit. "The Variation of Some Other Speculative Prices." *J. Bus.,* October 1967, 393–413.

Mann, Jitendar. "Intraday Commodity Price Movements." *Agric. Econ. Res.,* April 1980, 44–47.

Mann, J. S. and R. G. Heifner. "The Distribution of Shortrun Commodity Price Movements." U.S. Department of Agriculture, *USDA Technical Bulletin,* No. 1536, Washington, DC, 1976.

Marquardt, Ray. *An Evaluation of the Relative Price Forecasting Accuracy of the Futures Market for Beef, Hogs, Wheat, Corn and Soybeans.* Chicago Mercantile Exchange, Chicago, 1974.

Marquadt, Ray. "An Evaluation of the Relative Price-Forecasting Accuracy of Selected Futures Markets." In R. M. Leuthold, ed., *Commodity Markets and Futures Prices,* Chicago Mercantile Exchange, Chicago, 1979, pp. 125–142.

Martell, Terrence. "Adaptive Control Models and the Martingale Hypothesis." Unpublished doctoral dissertation, Pennsylvania State University, 1973.

Martell, Terrence and George Philippatos. "Adaption, Information, and Dependence in Commodity Markets." *J. Finance,* May 1974, 493–498.

Martell, T. F. and B. P. Helms. (1978). "A Reexamination of Price Changes in the Commodity Futures Market." In Chicago Board of Trade, ed., *International Futures Trading Seminar, Vol. 5,* Chicago Board of Trade, Chicago, 1978, pp. 136–159. Also in *International Futures Trading Seminar, Proceedings,* 1978. Discussion, 153–159.

Miller, Katherine Dusak. *Investigation of Relation Between Time Series Properties of Spot Prices and the Variability of Futures Prices.* Chicago Mercantile Exchange, Chicago, 1972.

Dusak-Miller, K. (1972). "The Relation Between Volatility and Maturity in Futures Contracts." In R. M. Leuthold, ed., *Commodity Markets and Futures Prices,* Chicago Mercantile Exchange, Chicago, 1979, pp. 25–36.

Oliviera, R. A., et. al. "Time Series Forecasting Models of Lumber: Cash, Futures, and Basis Prices." *Forest Sci.,* June 1977, 268–280.

Patterson, Harlan. "The Relative Volatility Issue: Commodity Prices Versus Stock Prices." *Univ. Mich. Bus. Rev.,* July 1978, 1–6.

Peck, Anne. "Measures and Price Effects of Changes in Speculation on the Wheat, Corn, and Soybeans Futures Markets." In Chicago Board of Trade, ed., *Research on Speculation: Seminar Report,* Chicago Board of Trade, Chicago, 1980, pp. 138–149. Discussion, 150–153.

Praetz, Peter. "On the Methodology of Testing for Independence in Futures Markets: Comment." *J. Finance,* June 1976, 977–979. "Reply" by Robert Bear and Richard Stevenson and by Raymond Leuthold, June 1976, 980–985.

Praetz, P. D. "Testing the Efficient Market Theory on the on the Sydney Wool Futures Exchange." *Aust. Econ. Pap.,* 1975, 240–249.

Protopapadakis, Aris, and Hans R. Stoll. "Spot and Futures Prices and the Law of One Price." Columbia University CSFM Working Paper Series No. 32.

Rausser, Gordon C. and Thomas Cargill. "The Existence of Broiler Cycles: An Application of Spectral Analysis." *Am. J. Agric. Econ.,* February 1970, 109–121.

Rausser, G. C. and R. E. Just (1979). "Agricultural Commodity Price Forecasting Accuracy: Futures Markets Versus Commercial Econometric Models." In Chicago Board of Trade, *International Futures Trading Seminar, Vol. 6,* Chicago Board of Trade, Chicago, 1979, pp. 116–165.

Rendleman, R. J., Jr. and C. E. Carabini. "The Efficiency of the Treasury Bill Futures Market." *J. Finance,* 1979, 895–914.

Richard, Scott, R. and M. Sundaresan. "A Continuous Time Equilibrium Model of Forward Prices in a Multigood Economy." Columbia University CSFM Working Paper Series No. 26, February 1981.

Rocca, Leroy. "Time Analysis of Commodity Futures Prices." Unpublished doctoral dissertation, University of California, Berkeley, 1969.

Rockwell, Charles. "Normal Backwardation, Forecasting, and the Returns to Commodity Futures Traders." In *Food Research Institute Studies,* supplement, Stanford University Press, Stanford, CA, 1967, pp. 107–130. Also in A. E. Peck, ed., *Readings in Futures Markets, 2: Selected Writings on Futures Markets,* Chicago Board of Trade, Chicago, 1977, pp. 167–189.

Rockwell, Charles. "Profits, Normal Backwardation, and Forecasting in Commodity Futures." Unpublished doctoral dissertation, University of California, Berkeley, 1964.

Rutledge, David. "A Note on the Variability of Futures Prices." *Rev. Econ. Stat.,* February 1976, 118–120. Also in A. E. Peck, ed., *Readings in Futures Markets, 2: Selected Writings on Futures Markets,* Chicago Board of Trade, Chicago, 1977, pp. 307–311.

Rutledge, David. "Trading Volume and Price Variability: New Evidence on the Price Effects of Speculation." In Chicago Board of Trade, ed., *International Futures Trading Seminar, Proceedings,* Chicago Board of Trade, Chicago, 1976, pp. 160–174. Discussion, 175–186.

Samuelson, P. A. (1957). "Intertemporal Price Equilibrium: A Prologue to the Theory of Speculation." In *The Collected Scientific Papers of Paul A. Samuelson,* Vol. 2, MIT Press, Cambridge, MA, 181–219.

Samuelson, Paul. "Is Real-World Price a Tale Told by the Idiot of Chance?" *Rev. Econ. Stat.,* February 1976, 120–123. Also in A. E. Peck, ed., *Readings in Futures Markets, 2: Selected Writings on Futures Markets,* Chicago Board of Trade, Chicago, 1977, 313–319.

Samuelson, Paul. "Proof That Properly Anticipated Prices Fluctuate Randomly." *Ind. Manage. Rev.,* Spring 1965, 41–50.

Samuelson, P. A. "Spatial Price Equilibrium and Linear Programming." *Am. Econ. Rev.,* 1952, 283–303.

Sanford, Donald. "Research on Non–Random Elements of the Commodity Futures Markets." Unpublished doctoral dissertation, Florida Atlantic University, Boca Raton, 1974.

Schneider, Alfred. "Short-Term Price Fluctuations: An Analysis of Shell Egg Futures Contracts." Unpublished doctoral dissertation, New York University, 1967.

Scott, Ernest. "The Risk Premium in Commodity Markets." Unpublished doctoral dissertation, University of British Columbia, Vancouver, 1976.

Simonoff, Jeffrey. "Application of Statistical Methodology to the Evaluation of Timing Devices in Commodities Trading." *J. Futures Mark.,* Winter 1981, 649–656.

Smidt, S. "A New Look at the Random Walk Hypothesis." *J. Financ. Quant. Anal.,* September 1968, 235–261.

Smidt, S. "A Test of the Serial Independence of Price Changes in Soybean Futures." In *Food Research Institute Studies,* 1965, pp. 117–136. Also in A. E. Peck, ed., *Readings in Futures Markets, 2: Selected Writings on Futures Markets,* Chicago Board of Trade, Chicago, 1977, pp. 257–277.

Stein, Jerome L. "Rational, Irrational and Over-Regulated Speculative Markets." Columbia University CSFM Working Paper Series No. 36.

Stein, J. L. (1961). "The Simultaneous Determination of Spot and Futures Prices." As reprinted in A. E. Peck, ed., *Readings in Futures Markets, 2: Selected Writings on Futures Markets,* Chicago Board of Trade, Chicago, 1977, pp. 223–235.

Stein, J. L. "Spot, Forward and Futures." *Res. Finance,* 1979, 225–310.

Stein, J. L. "Speculative Price: Economic Welfare and the Idiot of Chance." *Rev. Econ. Stat.,* 1977, 223–232.

Stevenson, Richard and Robert Bear. "Commodities Futures: Trends or Random Walks?" *J. Finance,* March 1970, 65–81. Also in A. E. Peck, ed., *Readings in Futures Markets, 2: Selected Writings on Futures Markets,* Chicago Board of Trade, Chicago, 1977, pp. 279–294.

Stewart, B. "An Analysis of Speculative Trading in Grain Futures." U.S. Department of Agriculture, *USDA Technical Bulletin,* No. 1001, Washington, D.C., 1949.

Stoll, Hans. "Commodity Futures and Spot Price Determination and Hedging in Capital Market Equilibrium." *J. Financ. Quant. Anal.,* November 1979, 873–894.

Sundaresan, M. "Empirical Investigation of the Term Structure of Futures Prices." Columbia University, Graduate School of Business, Working Paper No. 361A, 1980.

Tomek, William. "Speculation and Price Behavior in Commodity Markets: A Survey." In Chicago Board of Trade, ed., *Research on Speculation: Seminar Report,* Chicago Board of Trade, Chicago, 1980, pp. 8–23. Discussion, 24–29.

Tomek, W. G. and R. W. Gray (1970). "Temporal Relationships Among Prices on Commodity Futures Markets: Their Allocative and Stabilizing Role." As reprinted in A. E. Peck, ed., *Readings in Futures Markets, 2: Selected Writings on Futures Markets,* Chicago Board of Trade, Chicago, 1977, pp. 137–148.

Vaughn, Richard, Marvin Kelley and Frank Hochheimer. "Identifying Seasonality in Futures Prices Using X-11." *J. Fut. Mark.,* Spring 1981, 93–101.

Yeaney, Woodrow, Jr. "Investment Characteristics of Commodity Futures Contracts." Unpublished doctoral dissertation, Pennsylvania State University, 1978.

Working, Holbrook. "Frontiers in Uncertainty Theory: The Evidence of Futures Markets: New Concepts Concerning Futures Markets and Prices." *Am. Econ. Rev.: Papers and Proceedings,* May 1961, 160–163. Discussion, 184–193.

Working, Holbrook. "Measurement of Cycles in Speculative Prices." In *Food Research Institute Studies,* Stanford University Press, Stanford, CA, 1974, pp. 37–60.

Working, Holbrook. "New Concepts Concerning Futures Markets and Prices." *Am. Econ. Rev.,* June 1962, 431–459. Also in A. E. Peck, ed., *Readings in Futures Markets, 1: Selected Writings of Holbrook Working,* Chicago Board of Trade, Chicago, 1977, pp. 243–265.

Working, Holbrook. "Note on the Correlation of First Differences of Averages in a Random Chain." *Econometrica,* 1960, 916–918.

Working, Holbrook. "Price Effects of Futures Trading." *Food Res. Inst. Stud.*, February 1960, 3–31. Also in A. E. Peck, ed., *Readings in Futures Markets, 1: Selected Writings of Holbrook Working,* Chicago Board of Trade, Chicago, 1977, pp. 45–75.

Working, Holbrook. (1954). "Price Effects of Scalping and Day Trading." As reprinted in A. E. Peck, ed., *Readings in Futures Markets, 1: Selected Writings of Holbrook Working,* Chicago Board of Trade, Chicago, 1977, pp. 181–194.

Working, Holbrook. "A Random-Difference Series for Use in the Analysis of Time Series." *J. Am. Stat. Assoc.*, 1934, 11–24.

Working, Holbrook. "Speculation in Hedging Markets." In *Food Research Institute Studies,* Stanford University Press, Stanford, CA, 1960, pp. 185–220.

Working, Holbrook. "Tests of a Theory Concerning Floor Trading on Commodity Exchanges." In *Food Research Institute Studies,* Stanford University Press, Stanford, CA, 1967, supplement, pp. 5–48. Also in A. E. Peck, ed., *Readings in Futures Markets, 1: Selected Writings of Holbrook Working,* Chicago Board of Trade, Chicago, 1977, pp. 195–239.

Working, Holbrook. "A Theory of Anticipatory Prices." *Am. Econ. Rev.*, May 1958, 188–189. Also in A. E. Peck, ed., *Readings in Futures Markets, 1: Selected Writings of Holbrook Working,* Chicago Board of Trade, Chicago, 1977, pp. 33–44.

Working, Holbrook. "Price Effects of Futures Trading." As reprinted in A. E. Peck, ed., *Readings in Futures Markets, 1: Selected Writings of Holbrook Working,* Chicago Board of Trade, Chicago, 1977, pp. 45–75.

Working, Holbrook. "New Concepts Concerning Futures Markets and Prices." As reprinted in A. E. Peck, ed., *Readings in Futures Markets, 1: Selected Writings of Holbrook Working,* Chicago Board of Trade, Chicago, 1977, pp. 243–266.

Yamey, B. S. "Short Hedging and Long Hedging In Futures Markets: Symmetry and Asymmetry." *J. Law Econ.*, October 1971, 413–434.

6. PRICES AND STATISTICAL INFORMATION

Books, Articles and Periodicals

Barron's. 22 Cortlandt St., New York, NY 10007 (W).

Bashaw, W. I. *Mathematics For Statistics.* Wiley, New York, 1969.

Boyle, J. E. *Chicago Wheat Prices for Eighty-One Years.* unpublished manuscript, 1922.

Chicago Board of Trade Annual Report. (A, 1858 to date.)

Chicago Board of Trade Statistical Annual. Chicago Board of Trade, Chicago (A).

Chicago Board of Trade Year Book. Chicago Board of Trade, 141 W. Jackson St., Chicago, IL (A).

Chicago Mercantile Exchange Year Book. Chicago Mercantile Exchange, 444 West Jackson Blvd., Chicago, IL, (A, 1923 to date.)

Commodity Research Bureau. *Commodity Yearbook.* Commodity Research Bureau, New York (A).

Hoffman, G. W. and J. W. T. Duvel. *Grain Prices and the Futures Market: A 15 Year Survey.* U. S. Department of Agriculture, USDA Technical Bulletin, No. 747, Washington, DC, January 1941.

Journal of Commerce. 110 Wall St., New York, NY 10005 (D).

New York Mercantile Exchange Year Book. New York Mercantile Exchange, New York (A).

Thomsen, F. L. and R. J. Foote. *Agriculture Prices*. McGraw–Hill, New York, 1952.

USDA Commodity Exchange Authority. "Commodity Futures Statistics." U. S. Department of Agriculture Washington, DC, 1947.

USDA Commodity Exchange Authority "Grain Futures Statistics", 1921–1951. U. S. Department of Agriculture, USDA Statistical Bulletin, No. 131, Washington, DC, 1952.

USDA Consumer and Marketing Service. "Cotton Price Statistics." U. S. Department of Agriculture, Washington, DC.

USDA Consumer and Marketing Service. "Grain and Feed Statistics." U. S. Department of Agriculture, Washington, DC.

USDA Economic Research Service. "Statistics on Cotton and Related Data, 1925–62." U. S. Department of Agriculture, USDA Statistical Bulletin, No. 329, Washington, DC, 1963.

Wall Street Journal. 22 Cortlandt St., New York, NY 10007 (D).

Wasserman, Paul. *Commodity Prices: A Source Book and Index*. Gale Research, Detroit, 1974.

Working, Holbrook. "Prices of Cash Wheat and Futures at Chicago since 1883." *Food Research Institute Wheat Studies*. **10,** November 1934, 103–117.

Working, Holbrook and Sidney Hoos. "Wheat Futures Prices and Trading at Liverpool since 1886." *Food Research Institute Wheat Studies,* **15,** November 1938.

7. PROBABILITY, RISK, RISK AVERSION, PERFORMANCE MEASUREMENT, PORTFOLIOS, RETURNS

Books, Articles, and Periodicals

Anderson, Ron. "The Determinants of the Volatility of Futures Prices." Columbia University CSFM Working Paper Series No. 33, 1982.

Aronson, David and Leon Rose. "A 'Sharpe' Way to Measure Managed Accounts." *Commodities,* July 1979, 34–37.

Baumol, William J. "An Expected Gain-Confidence Limit Criterion for Portfolio Selection." *Manage. Sci.,* **10,** October 1963, 174–182.

Bear, R. M. "Risk and Return Patterns on Overnight Holdings of Livestock Futures." In R. M. Leuthold ed., *Commodity Markets and Futures Prices,* Chicago Mercantile Exchange, Chicago, 1979, pp. 13–23.

Bicksler, James and Paul Samuelson, eds. *Investment Portfolio Decision Making*. Lexington Books, Lexington, MA, 1974.

Bierman, H., "Diversification: Is there Safety in Numbers?" *J. Portfolio Manage.,* Fall 1978, **5**(1), 29–32.

Blattberg, R. C. and N. J. Gomedes. "A Comparison of the Stable and Student Distributions of Statistical Models for Stock Prices." *J. Bus.,* **47,**(2), April 1974, 244–280.

Bodie, Z., and V. I. Rosansky. "Risk and Return in Commodity Futures." *Financ. Anal. J.,* 1980, 3–14. Also Columbia University CSFM Working Paper Series No. 1, 1980.

Borch, Karl. "A Note on Uncertainty and Indifference Curves." *Rev. Econ. Stud.,* January 1969, 1–4. Also reprinted in J. Bicksler and P. Samuelson, Eds., *Investment Portfolio Decision. Making, Lexington Books, Lexington, MA, 1974, pp. 29–34.*

Cootner, P. H. "Returns to Speculators: Telser Versus Keynes." *J. Polit. Econ.,* 1960, 396–404; "Reply,", L. G. Telser, 404–415. "Rejoinder," 415–418. Also in A. E. Peck, ed., *Readings in Futures Markets, 2: Selected Writings in Futures Markets,* Chicago Board of Trade, Chicago 1977.

Cornell, Bradford. "The Relationship Between Volume and Price Variability in Futures Markets." Columbia University CSFM Working Paper Series No. 6, 1980.

Breeden, D. T. "Consumption Risk in Futures Markets." *J. Finance,* 1980, 503–520.

Cootner, P. H., "Returns to Speculators: Telser versus Keynes." As reprinted in A. E. Peck, ed., *Readings in Futures Markets, 2: Selected Writings in Futures Markets,* Chicago Board of Trade, Chicago, 1977.

Dalrymple, Brent. "Risk Analysis Applied to Commodity Speculation." *J. Finance,* June 1971, 790–791.

Danthine, Jean-Pierre and Ronald Anderson. "The Time Pattern of Hedging and the Volatility of Futures Prices." Columbia University CSFM Working Papers Series No. 7, 1981.

Dickinson, John P., ed., *Portfolio Analysis, a Book of Readings.* Lexington Books, Lexington, MA, 1974.

Dusak, Katherine. "Futures Trading and Investor Returns: An Investigation of Commodity Market Risk Premiums." *J. Polit. Econ.,* November/December 1973, 1387–1406.

Gray, Roger. "The Search for a Risk Premium." *J. Polit. Econ.,* 1961, 250–260. Also in A. E. Peck, ed., *Readings in Futures Markets, 2: Selected Writings in Futures Markets,* Chicago Board of Trade, Chicago, 1977.

Elton, Edwin J. and Martin J. Gruber. *Modern Portfolio Theory and Investment Analysis.* Wiley, New York, 1981.

Elton, E. J., M. J. Gruber and M. W. Dadberg. "Optimal Portfolios from Simple Ranking Devices." *J. Portfolio Manage.,* Spring 1978, **4**(3), 15–19.

Epstein, Richard A., *The Theory of Gambling and Statistical Logic.* Academic Press, New York, 1977.

Fama, Eugene F., "The Behavior of Stock Market Prices." *J. Bus.,* **38,** January 1965, 34–105.

Feder, G., R. E. Just and A. Schmitz. "Futures Markets and the Theory of the Firm under Price Uncertainty." *Q. J. Econ.,* 1980, 317–328.

Feller, William. *An Introduction to Probability Theory and Its Applications.* 2nd ed., 1957, 168.

Fischer, Lawrence. "Outcomes for 'Random' Investments in Common Stocks Listed on the New York Stock Exchange." *J. Bus.,* **37,** June 1964.

Francis, Jack Clark and Stephen H. Archer. *Portfolio Analysis.* 2nd ed., Prentice-Hall, Englewood Cliffs, NJ, 1979.

Gehm, F., "Avoiding Avoidable Risk Through Portfolio Theory." *Commodities,* July 1980, 46–50.

Gehm, F., *Commodity Market Money Management.* Wiley, New York, 1983.

Grauer, F. L. A., and J. Rentzler. "Are Futures Contracts Risky?" Presented at the First Annual Conference, The Center for the Study of Futures Markets, Columbia Business School, 1980.

Gray, R. W., "The Characteristic Bias in Some Thin Futures Markets." As reprinted in A. E. Peck, ed., *Readings in Futures Markets, 2: Selected Writings in Futures Markets,* Chicago Board of Trade, Chicago, 1977.

Gray, R. W. (1961). "The Search for a Risk Premium." As reprinted in A. E. Peck, ed., *Readings in Futures Markets, 2: Selected Writings in Futures Markets,* 71–82.

Griffin, P. *The Theory of Blackjack.* Gamblers Press, Las Vegas, 1981.

Holthausen, Duncan and John Hughes. "Commodity Returns and Capital Asset Pricing." *Financ. Manage.*, Summer 1978, 37–44.

Jobman, Darrell. "How Readers Rate Advisory Service Newsletters." *Commodities*, March 1980, 40–43.

Jobman, Darrell. "How Readers Rate Major Brokerage Newsletters." *Commodities*, February 1980, 36–39.

Kaufman, P. J., "Safety-Adjusted Performance Evaluation." *J. Futures Mark.*, **1**, 1981, 17–31.

Kelly, J. L., "A New Interpretation of Information Rate." *Bell System Tech. J.*, **35**, 1956, 917–926.

Lee, C. F. and R. M. Leuthold. *Impact of Investment on the Determination of Risk and Return in the Commodity Futures Markets*. Chicago Mercantile Exchange, Chicago, 1980.

Levy, Haim and Marshall Sarnat. *Investment and Portfolio Analysis*. Wiley, New York, 1972.

Lore, James H. and Mary Hamilton. *The Stock Market—Theories and Evidence*. Richard D. Irwin, Homewood, IL, 1973.

Mandelbrot, B., "The Variation of Certain Speculative Prices." *J. Bus.*, **36**(4), 1963, 394–419.

Markowitz, Harry M., "Portfolio Selection." *J. Finance*, March 1952, 77–91.

Markowitz, Harry M. *Portfolio Selection: Efficient Diversification of Investments*. Cowles Foundation Monograph No. 16, Wiley, New York, 1959.

Miller, Edward M. "Portfolio Selection in a Fluctuating Economy." *Financ. Anal. J.*, May/June 1978.

Philippatos, George C. and Charles J. Wilson. "Entropy, Market Risk, and the Selection of Efficient Portfolios." *Appl. Econ.*, **4**, 1972, 209–220. Also reprinted in J. P. Dickinson ed., *Portfolio Analysis*, A Book of Readings, Lexington Books, Lexington, MA, 1974, 59–73.

Powers, M. J. "Does Futures Trading Reduce Price Fluctuations in the Cash Markets?" *Am. Econ. Rev.*, 1970, 460–464.

Praetz, P. D. "The Distribution of Share Price Changes." *J. Bus.*, **45**, January 1972, 49–55.

Pratt, John. "Risk Aversion in the Small and in the Large." In J Bicksler and P. Samuelson, eds., *Investment Portfolio Decision Making*, Lexington Books, Lexington, MA, 1974, 49–65.

Rockwell, C. S. "Normal Backwardation, Forecasting and the Returns to Commodity Futures Traders." In *Food Research Institute Studies*, supplement, Stanford University Press, Stanford, CA, 1967, 107–130.

Ross, Ray. "Financial Consequences of Trading Commodity Futures Contracts." *Ill. Agric. Econ.*, July 1975, 27–31.

Ross, Ray. "Financial Results of Trading Commodity Futures Contracts: Speculating Public and Commercial Traders." Unpublished doctoral dissertation, University of Illinois, 1973.

Roy, A. D. "Safety First and the Holding of Assets." *Econometrica*, **20**, June 1952, 431–449.

Rutledge, D. J. S. "A Note on the Variability of Futures Prices." As reprinted in A. E. Peck, Ed., *Readings in Futures Markets 2: Selected Writings in Futures Markets*, Chicago Board of Trade, Chicago, 1977, pp. 307–311.

Rutledge, D. J. S. "Trading Volume and Price Variability: New Evidence on the Price

Effects of Speculation." *International Futures Trading Seminar, Proceedings,* Vol. 5, Chicago Board of Trade, Chicago, 1978 pp. 160–186.

Schimler. "Speculation, Profitability, and Price Stability—A Formal Approach." *Rev. Econ. Stat.,* February 1973, 110–114.

Sharpe, William F. "Capital Asset Prices: A Theory of Market Equilibrium under Conditions of Risk." *J. Finance,* September 1964, **19,** 425–444.

Sharpe, William F. *Investments.* Prentice Hall, Englewood Cliffs, NJ, 1978, 389–426.

Sharpe, William F. "Mutual Fund Performance." *J. Bus.,* **39,** January 1966, 119–138.

Simkowitz, N. A. and W. L. Beedles. "Asymmetric Stable Distributed Security Returns." *J. Am. Stat. Assoc.,* June 1980, 306–312.

Synder, William D. *Simulation of Optimal Cash Reserves for Commodity Trading.* Chicago Mercantile Exchange, Chicago, 1975.

Stiglitz, Joseph E. "Risk, Futures Markets and the Stabilization of Commodity Prices." Columbia University CSFM Working Paper Series No. 25, 1980.

Swalne, R. O. "Utility Theory—Insights into Risk Taking." *Harvard Bus. Rev.,* November/December 1966, 123–125.

Taylor, G. S. and R. M. Leuthold (1974). "The Influence of Futures Trading on Cash Price Variation." As reprinted in A. E. Peck, ed., *Readings in Futures Markets, 2: Selected Writings in Futures Markets,* Chicago Board of Trade, Chicago, 1977, pp. 367–373.

Telser, Lester. "A Theory of Speculation Relating Profitability and Stability." *Rev. Econ. Stat.,* 1959, 295–301. "Reply." W. J. Baumol, 301–302.

Thomas, Conrad W. *Risk and Opportunity.* Dow Jones–Irwin, Homewood, IL.

Thorp, E. O. "The Kelly Money Management System." *Gambling Times,* December 1979, 91–92.

Thorpe, ed. "Portfolio Choice and the Kelly Criterion." *Business and Economic Statistics Section of Proceedings of the American Statistical Association,* 1971, 215–224. Also reprinted in J. Bicksler and P. Samuelson, eds., *Investment Portfolio Decision Making,* Lexington Books, Lexington, MA, 1974, pp. 253–270.

Tobin, James. "Comment on Borch and Feldstein." *Rev. Econ. Stud.,* January 1969, 13–14. Also reprinted in Bicksler and Samuelson, 1974, 35–36.

Working H. "Tests of a Theory Concerning Floor Trading on Commodity Exchanges." As reprinted in A. E. Peck, ed., *Readings in Futures Markets, 1: Selected Writings of Holbrook Working,* Chicago Board of Trade, Chicago, 1977. pp. 195–239.

Zeeman, E. C., *Catastrophe Theory: Selected Papers, 1972–1977.* Addison-Wesley, Reading, MA, 1977.

8. SPREADS

Books

Angell, George. *Computer-Proven Commodity Spreads.* Brightwaters, Windsor, NY, 1981.

Angell, George and R. Earl Hadady. *Spread Trading for the Risk-Conscious Speculator.* Hadady, Pasadena, CA, 1979.

Breeden, Douglas T. "Variability in Gold and Silver Futures Spreads." Breeden, December 1979, Columbia University CSFM Working Paper Series No. 3, 1980.

Dobson, ed. *Commodity Spreads.* Traders Press, Greenville NC.

Esserman, Wayne, *Odds On Grain Spreading.* EWW Publishing, Delphi, IN, 1979.

Kallard, Thomas. *Make Money in Commodity Spreads*. Optosonic Press, New York, 1974.

Meyer, Richard L. *Profitability of Spread Positions in Pork Bellies Over a Ten-Year Period*. 1977.

Rolfo, Jacques and Howard Sosin. "Alternative Strategies for Hedging and Spreading." Columbia University CSFM Working Paper Series No. 22, April 1981.

Smith, Courtney. *Commodity Spread Analysis*. Wiley, New York, 1982.

9. TRADING METHODS

Books

Allen, R. C. *How to Build a Fortune in Commodities*. Best Books, Chicago, 1972.

Allen, R. C. *How to Use the 4 Day, 9 Day and 18 Day Moving Average to Earn Larger Profits from Commodities*. Best Books, Chicago, 1974.

Angas, L. L. B. *Investment For Appreciation*. Somerset, NY, 1936.

Angell, George. *Winning in the Commodities Market—A Money-Making Guide to Commodity Futures Trading*. Doubleday, Garden City, NY, 1979.

Angrist, Stanley W, *Sensible Speculating in Commodities*. Simon & Schuster, New York, 1972.

Appel, George. *Winning Market Systems, or 83 Ways to Beat the Market*. Rev 2nd ed., Signalert, Great Neck, NY, 1974.

Appel, Gerald and Martin E. Zweig. *New Directions in Technical Analysis*. Signalert, Great Neck, NY, 1976.

Armour, Lawrence A. *The Young Millionaires*. Playboy Press, Chicago, 1973.

Arms, Richard W. *Profits in Volume*. Investors Intelligence, Larchmont, NY, 1971.

Barnes, Robert M. *Taming the Pits: A Technical Approach to Commodity Trading*. Wiley, New York, 1979.

Barnes, Robert M. *1981 Technical Commodity Yearbook*. Van Nostrand Reinhold, Florence, KY, 1981.

Beckman, Robert C. *Supertiming, the Unique Elliott Wave System, Keys to Anticipating Impending Stock Market Action*. The Library of Investment Study, Los Angeles, 1980.

Belveal, L. Dee. *Charting Commodity Market Price Behavior*. Commodities Press, Wilmette, IL, 1969.

Belveal, L. Dee. *Commodity Speculation with Profits in Mind*. Commodities Press, Wilmette, IL, 1967.

Bernstein, Jacob. *The Handbook of Commodity Cycles: A Window on Time*. Wiley, New York, 1982.

Bernstein, Jacob. *The Investor's Quotient*. Wiley, New York, 1981.

Bernstein, Jacob. *Commodities Now Through 1984*. MBH Commodity, Winnetka, IL, 1978.

Bernstein, Jacob. *MBH Seasonal Futures Charts a Study of Weekly Seasonal Tendencies in the Commodity Futures Markets*. MBH Commodity, Winnetka, IL, 1979.

Bernstein, Jacob. *Seasonal Chart Study 1953–1977, An Analysis of Seasonal Cash Commodity Price Tendencies*. MBH Commodity, Winnetka, IL, 1977.

Blumenthal, Earl. *Chart for Profit Point & Figure Trading*. Investors Intelligence, Larchmont, NY, 1975.

Bolton, A. Hamilton. *The Elliott Wave Principle: A Critical Appraisal*. Monetary Research, Hamilton, Bermuda, 1960.

Charell, Ralph. *A Great Way to Make Money; 51 Consecutive Profits in 5 Months*. Stein and Day, New York, 1976.

Cleeton, Claude. *The Art of Independent Investing*. Prentice–Hall, Englewood Cliffs, NJ, 1976.

Cohen, A. W. *How to Use the Three–Point Reversal Method of Point–and–Figure Stock Market Trading*. 5th ed., Chartcraft, Larchmont, NY, 1972.

Cole, George. *Graphs & Their Application to Speculation*. Commodity Research Institute, Hendersonville, NC, 1979.

Commodity Perspective. *Encyclopedia of Historical Charts*. Investor Publishing, Chicago, 1977. (Also Supplements for 1978 and 1979).

Commodity Trades Club. *Comparative Performances*. Messena, New York, 1969. (Reprint).

Cox, Houston A. *A Common Sense Approach to Commodity Futures Trading*. Reynolds Securities, New York, 1968.

Cox, Houston A. *Concepts on Profits in Commodity Futures Trading*. Reynolds Securities, New York, 1972.

Crane, Burton. *The Sophisticated Investor: A Guide to Stock Market Profits*. Simon and Schuster, New York, 1959.

Cycles, Foundation for the Study of Cycles, Pittsburgh, PA, January, 1976.

Dahl, Curtiss. *Consistent Profits in the Commodity Futures Markets*. Tri–State Offset Co., Cincinnati, OH, 1960.

Davis, Robert Earl. *Profit and Probability*. R. E., Davis, West LaFayette, IN, 1969.

Davis, R. E. and C. C. Thiel, Jr. *A Computer Analysis of the Moving Average Applied to Commodity Futures Trading*. (Research report), Ouiatenon Management Co., West LaFayette, IN, 1970.

DeVilliers, Victor. *The Point and Figure Method of Anticipating Stock Price Movements*. Traders Press, New York, 1966 (reprint of 1933 Ed.).

Davey, Edward R. and Og Mandino. *Cycles*. Hawthorn Books, New York, 1971.

Dines, James. *How the Average Investor Can Use Technical Analysis for Stock Profits*. Dines Chart Company, New York, 1972.

Dobson, Edward D. *Commodities: A Chart Anthology*. Edward D. Dobson, Greenville, SC.

Dobson, Edward D. *Commodity Spreads: A Historical Chart Perspective*. 2 vols., Traders Press, Greenville, SC.

Dobson, Edward D. *The Trading Rule That Can Make You Rich*. Traders Press, Greenville, SC, 1979.

Doyle, Thomas L., Jr. *Live Cattle, Live Hogs and Frozen Pork Bellies*. Futures Research Co., Los Altos, CA, 1976.

Dunn, Dennis D. *Consistent Profits in June: Live Beef Cattle*. Dunn and Hargitt, West Lafayette, IN, 1972.

Dunn and Hargitt. *Consistent Profits in Pork Bellies*. Dunn and Hargitt, West Lafayette, IN.

Dunn and Hargitt. *Point and Figure Commodity Trading: A Computer Evaluation*. Dunn and Hargitt, West Lafayette, IN, 1971.

Dunn and Hargitt. *Trader's Handbook: Trading Methods Checked by Computer*. Dunn and Hargitt, West Lafayette, IN.

Dunnigan, William. *One Way Formula*. Dunnigan, Palo Alto, CA, 1955.

Dunnigan, William. *Select Studies in Speculation*. Dunnigan, San Francisco, 1954, (includes "Gain in Grains," and "The Thrust Method in Stocks").

Dunnigan, William. *117 Barometers for Forecasting Stock Price*. Dunnigan, San Francisco, 1954.

Edwards, Robert D. and John Magee. *Technical Analysis of Stock Trends*. 5th ed., John Magee, Springfield, MA, 1966.

Elliot R. N. *Nature's Law, The Secret of the Universe*. Elliot, New York, 1946.

Elliot, R. N. *The Wave Principle*. Elliot, New York, 1938.

Epstein, Eugene. *Making Money in Commodities*. Praeger, New York, 1976.

Floss, Carl William. *Market Rhythm*. Investors, New York, 1955.

Fosback, Norman G. *Stock Market Logic*. The Institute for Econometric Research, Ft. Lauderdale, FL, 1976.

Frost, Alfred J. and Robert R. Prechter. *Eliot Wave Principle, Key to Stock Market Profits*. New Classics, New York, 1978.

Gann, William D. *The Basis of My Forecasting Method For Grain*. Lambert–Gann, Pomeroy, WA, 1970 (orginally 1935).

Gann, William D. *Forecasting Grains by Time Cycles*. Lambert–Gann, Pomeroy, WA, 1976.

Gann, William D. *Forecasting Rules for Cotton*. Lambert–Gann, Pomeroy, WA, 1976.

Gann, William D. *Forecasting Rules for Gain—Geometric Angles*. Lambert-Gann, Pomeroy, WA, 1976.

Gann, William D. *How to Make Profits in Commodities*. Rev. ed., Lambert–Gann Publishing, Pomeroy, WA, 1951.

Gann, William D. *Master Calculator for Weekly Time Periods to Determine the Trend of Stocks and Commodities*. Lambert-Gann, Pomeroy, WA, 1976.

Gann, William D. *Master Charts*. Lambert-Gann, Pomeroy, WA, 1976.

Gann, William D. *Mechanical Method and Trend Indicator for Trading in Wheat, Corn, Rye or Oats*. Lambert-Gann, Pomeroy, WA, 1976.

Gann, William D. *Rules for Trading in Soybeans, Corn, Wheat, Oats and Rye*. Lambert-Gann, Pomeroy, WA, 1976.

Gann, William D. *Speculation, A Profitable Profession (A Course of Instruction in Grains)*. Lambert-Gann, Pomeroy, WA, 1976.

Gann, William D, *45 Years in Wall Street*. Lambert-Gann, Pomeroy, WA, 1949.

Gardner, R. L. *How to Make Money in the Commodity Markets*. Prentice–Hall, Englewood Cliffs, NJ, 1961.

Gehm, Fred, F. *Commodity Money Management*. Wiley, New York, 1983.

Gehm, Fred, F. *A Timing Method for Fundamentalists*. Gehm and Associates, Berkeley, CA.

Gould, Bruce G. *Bruce Gould's Commodity Trading Manual*. Bruce Gould, Seattle, 1976.

Gould, Bruce G. *Bruce Gould's My Most Successful Technique for Making Money*. Bruce Gould, Seattle, 1975.

Gould, Bruce G. *Dow Jones–Irwin Guide to Commodities Trading*. Dow Jones–Irwin, Homewood, IL, 1973.

Hardy, C. Colburn. *Investor's Guide to Technical Analysis*. McGraw-Hill, New York, 1978.

Hieronymus, Thomas A. *Economics of Futures Trading for Commercial and Personal Profit*. 2nd ed., Commodity Research Bureau, New York, 1977.

Hieronymus, Thomas A. *When to Sell Corn—Soybeans—Oats—Wheat*. University of Illinois College of Agriculture, Urbana, 1967.

Hill, John R. *Scientific Interpretation of Bar Charts*. Commodity Research Institute, Hendersonville, NC, 1979.

Hill, John R. *Stock and Commodity Market Trend Trading by Advanced Technical Analysis*. Commodity Research Institute, Hendersonville, NC, 1977.

Hurst, J. M. *The Profit Magic of Stock Transaction Timing*. Prentice–Hall, Englewood Cliffs, NJ, 1970.

Jiler, Harry, ed. *Forecasting Commodity Prices: How the Experts Analyze the Market*. Commodity Research Bureau, New York, 1975.

Jiler, William L. *How Charts Can Help You in the Stock Market*. Trendline, New York, 1962.

Jiler, William L. *Forecasting Commodity Prices With Vertical Line Charts*. Commodity Research Bureau, New York, 1966.

Jiler, William L. *Volume and Open Interest, A Key to Commodity Price Forecasting*. Commodity Research Bureau, New York, 1967.

Kaufman, Perry J. *Commodity Trading Systems and Methods*. Wiley, New York, 1978.

Kaufman, Perry J. *Handbook of Futures Markets*. Wiley, New York, 1984.

Kaufman, Perry J. *Technical Analysis in Commodities*. Wiley, New York, 1980.

Keltner, C. W. *How to Make Money in Commodities*. Keltner Statistical Service, Kansas City, MO, 1960.

Kroll, Stanley. *The Professional Commodity Trader*. Harper & Row, New York, 1974.

LaBuda, David M. *The Selection and Timing of Commodity Futures*. LaBuda & Associates, Dayton, OH.

Lange, Elmer. *The Golden Fleece*. Esposition, Hicksville, NY, 1976.

Lawrence, James C. *Your Fortune in Futures: A Guide to Commodity Futures Trading*. St. Martin's, New York, 1976.

Leslie, Conrad. *Conrad Leslie's Guide for Successful Speculating*. Dartnell Press, Chicago, 1970.

Lindsay, Charles. *Trident, A Trading Strategy*. 2nd ed., Investor Publications, Waterloo, IA, 1977.

Longstreet, Roy W. *Viewpoint of a Commodity Trader*. Frederick Fell, New York, 1968.

Lloyd, Humphrey E. D. *The Moving Balance System*. Windsor Books, Brightwaters, NY.

Massino, John P. *The Point and Figure Method of Commodity Futures Trading*. Comchart, Milwaukee, WI, 1972.

Maxwell, Joseph R., Sr. *Commodity Futures Trading with Moving Averages*. Speer, Port Angeles, WA, 1975.

Maxwell, Joseph R., Sr. *Commodity Futures Trading With Point and Figure Charts*. Speer, Cupertino, CA, 1978.

Maxwell, Joseph R., Sr. *Commodity Futures Trading Orders*. Speer, Port Angeles, WA, 1975.

Maxwell, Joseph R., Sr. *Commodity Futures Trading with Stops*. Speer, Port Angeles, WA 1977.

McMaster, R. E., Jr. *Trader's Notebook 1978*. The Reaper, Phoenix, AZ, 1978.

Merrill, Arthur A. *Behavior of Prices on Wall Street*. The Analysis Press, Chappaqua, NY, 1966.

Miller, Lowell. *The Momentum-Gap Method*. G P Putnam's Sons, New York.

Nash, R. M. H. *Commodities for Potential Gains*. C. A. Printers, Pasadena, CA, 1967.

Neill, Humphrey B. *The Art of Contrary Thinking*. 4th ed., Caxton, Caldwell, OH, 1963.

Ney, Richard. *Making It In The Market*. McGraw-Hill, New York, 1975.

Nofri, Eugene and Jeanette Nofri Steinberg. *Success in Commodities . . . the Congestion Phase System*. Rev. ed., Success, Santa Monica, CA, 1980.

Oster, Merrill J. *Commodity Futures for Profit*. Professional Farmers of America, Waterloo, IA., 1979.

Oster, Merrill J. *How the Young Millionaires Trade Commodities*. Investor Publications, Waterloo, IA.

Oster, Merrill J. *How to Multiply Your Money . . . Beginner's Guide to Commodity Speculation*. Investor Publications, Waterloo, IA, 1979.

Powers, Mark J. *Getting Started in Commodity Futures Trading*. Rev. ed., Investor Publications, Inc., Waterloo, IA, 1980.

Reinach, Anthony M. *The Fastest Game in Town*. Commodity Research Bureau, New York, 1979.

Schabacker, R. W. *Stock Market Theory and Practice*. B. C. Forbes, New York, 1930.

Schultz, John W. *The Intelligent Chartist*. WRSM Financial Service, New York, 1962.

Shaw, John E. *A Professional Guide to Commodity Speculation*. Parker, West Nyack, NY, 1972.

Sklarew, Arthur. *Techniques of a Professional Commodity Chart Analyst*. Commodity Research Bureau, New York, 1980.

Smyth, David and Laurance F. Stuntz. *The Speculator's Handbook*. Henry Regnery, Chicago, 1974.

Synder, Julian M. *Rules for Financial Survival, 1979*. International Moneyline Press, New York, 1979.

Stoken, Dick A. *Cycles, What They Are, What They Mean, How to Profit by Them*. McGraw-Hill, New York, 1978.

Taylor, George Douglass. *The Taylor Trading Technique*. Lily, Los Angeles, 1950.

Thiel, Charles and R. E. Davis. *Point and Figure Commodity Trading: A Computer Evaluation*. Dunn and Hargitt, West LaFayette, IN, 1970.

Thies, Terry. *Technical Trading of Financial Markets*. American TransEuro, Chicago, 1978.

Thorp, Edward O. *Beat the Dealer*. Vintage, New York, 1966.

Tubbs, "Tubbs' Stock Market Correspondence Lessons."

Turner, Dennis and Stephen H. Blinn. *Trading Silver—Profitably*. Arlington House, New Rochelle, NY, 1975.

Vichas, Robert P. *Getting Rich in Commodities, Currencies, or Coins—Before or During the Next Depression*. Arlington House, New Rochelle, NY, 1975.

Watling, Thomas F. and Jonathan Morley. *Successful Commodity Futures Trading: How You Can Make Money in Commodity Markets*. Business Books, London, 1974.

Wheelan, Alexander H. *Study Helps in Point and Figure Technique*. Morgan, Rogers, New York, 1966.

Wilder, J. Welles, Jr. *New Concepts in Technical Trading Systems*. Trend Research, Greensboro, NC, 1978. (Also Winsor Books, Brightwaters, NY.)

Williams, Larry R. *How I made $1,000,000 Trading Commodities Last Year*. 2nd ed., Conceptual Management, Monterey, CA, 1972.

Williams, Larry R and Michelle Noseworthy. *Sure Thing Commodity Trading, How Seasonal Factors Influence Commodity Prices*. Windsor, Brightwaters, NY, 1977.

Wyckoff, Richart D. *The Richard D. Wyckoff Method of Trading and Investing in Stocks*. Wyckoff Associates, Park Ridge, ID, 1936.

Wyckoff, Richard D. *Stock Market Technique, Number One*. Wyckoff, New York, 1933.

Zieg, Kermit C., Jr. and Perry J. Kaufman. *Point and Figure Commodity Trading Techniques*. Investors Intelligence, Larchmont, NY, 1975.

Articles

Angrist, Stanley. "Trading on the Weather." *Forbes*, March 3, 1980, 116.

Arms, Richard W., Jr. "Equivolume—A New Method of Charting." *Commodities*, April 1973.

Baumol, W. J. "Speculation, Profitability and Stability." *Rev. Econ. Stat.*, August 1957, 263–271.

Busby, William. "A Model for Speculation in Pork Belly Futures." Unpublished doctoral dissertation, University of Southern California, 1971.

Dalio, Ray. "The Hidden Profits in Commodity Arbitrage." *Commodities*, February 1976, 16–18.

Diener, William. "Managed Portfolio Approach to Commodity Trading." *Commodities*, November 1979, 38–39.

Donchian, Richard D. "Donchian's 5–and 20–Day Moving Averages." *Commodities*, December 1974.

Earp, Richard B. "Correlating Taylor and Polous." *Commodities*, September 1973.

Gallacher, Bill. "Systems and the Art of Self Deception." *Commodities*, March 1977, 30–33.

Hallberg, N. C. and V. I. West. "Patterns of Seasonal Price Variations for Illinois Farm Products." Circular 861, University of Illinois College of Agriculture, Urbana, 1967.

Hays, D. "Why Pros Like Trends . . . and Trade Contrarily." *Commodities*, February 1977, 30–31.

Hochheimer, Frank. "The Best Computer-Tested Trading Techniques for 14 Major Commodities." *Commodities*, July 1979, 44–46.

Kaufman, Perry J.. "The Mapping System of Test Strategy." *Commodities*, December 1978, 62–67.

Kaufman, Perry J. and Kermit C. Zieg, Jr. "Measuring Market Movement." *Commodities*, May 1974.

Lofton, Todd. "Different Approach To Commodity Futures." *Commodities*, September 1974, 10–13.

Logan, S. H. and J. B. Bullock. "Speculation in Commodity Futures: An Application of Statistical Decision Theory." *Agric. Econ. Res.*, October 1970, 96–103.

Manternach, Dan. "Using Butterflies to Spread Soybeans." *Commodities*, November 1980.

Perrine, Jack. "Taurus the Bullish." *Commodities*, September 1974.

Polous, E. Michael. "The Moving Average As a Trading Tool." *Commodities*, September 1973.

Reiman, Ray. "Handicapping the Grains." *Commodities*, April 1975.

Riess, Michael. "Arbitrage as a Trading Medium." *Commodities*, March 1973, 24–27.

Rome, M. "Simple Systems *vs.* the Computer." *Commodities*, August 1977, 38–41.

Shellans, S. "Building Technical Trading Models." *Commodities*, December 1980, 46–48.

Steinberg, Jeanette Nofri. "Timing Market Entry and Exit." *Commodities,* September 1975.

Taylor, Robert Joel. "The Major Price Trend Directional Indicator." *Commodities,* April 1972.

10. COMMODITIES

BROILERS

Alwood, James K., and Donald J. Wissman. *Cost-Benefit Analysis of Irradiation—Pasteurization of Selected Foods—Broilers.* Cunlap and Association, January 1969.

American Poultry Historical Society., *American Poultry History, 1823–1973.* American Poultry Historical Society, 1976.

Arnold, E. L. "Heat Recovery from Livestock and Poultry Ventilation Systems." University of Vermont, Agricultural Experimentation Station, Bul. 674, Burlington, November 1973.

Bailey, Fred and Rod Swoboda, "Understanding the Iced Broiler Futures Market." *Forecasting Commodity Prices,* Commodity Research Bureau, NY 1975.

Benjamin, E. W., *Marketing Poultry Products.* 5th ed., Wiley, New York, 1960.

Benson, Verel W. "A Guide to Energy Savings for the Poultry Producer." U.S. Department of Agriculture, Economic Research Service and Federal Energy Administration, Washington, DC, June 1977.

Benson, Verel W., Gerald R. Rector, and Theresa Y. Sun. unpublished research on broiler demand analysis. U.S. Department of Agriculture, Economic Research Service, Washington, DC,

Blase, Kenneth E., George M. Hickman, and Sandra F. Lesesne. "Prices and Price Spreads for Eggs, Frying Chickens, and Turkeys in 12 Major Cities, 1966–71." U.S. Department of Agriculture, Economic Research Service, Stat. Bul. 524, Washington, DC, August 1973.

Brandow, George E. "Interrelations Among Demands for Farm Product and Implications for Control of Market Supply." Pennsylvania State University, Agricultural Experimentation Station, Bul. 680, University Park, August 1961.

Broiler Industry. "1975 Broiler Marketing/Distribution Flow." Graden State, Sea Isle City, NJ, October 1976.

Broiler Industry. "Gas Flush Packaging Brooms Wilson's Sales." Garden State, Sea Isle City, NJ, June 1976.

Broiler Industry. "Holly's Quiet Miracle: Brands One-half Billion Pounds." Garden State, Sea Isle City, NJ, October 1975.

Broiler Industry. "How You Market Your Broilers." Garden State, Sea Isle City, NJ, April 1976.

Broiler Industry. "Institutional Market Claims 3 Out of Every 10 Chickens." Garden State, Sea Isle City, NJ, October 1969.

Brooks, R. C., and H. S. Kennett. "Labor Efficiency in Poultry Processing Plants." North Carolina Agriculture Extension Service, September 1975.

Carawan, Roy E., et al. "Water and Waste Management in Poultry Processing." U.S. Environmental Protection Agency, EPA-660/2-74-031, Washington, DC, May 1974.

Clise, James D. "Poultry Processing Wastewater Treatment and Reuse." U.S. Environmental Protection Agency, EPA-660/2-74-060, Washington, DC, March 1974.

Faber, Fred L., and William W. Gallimore. "Changes in Firm and Plant Size in Broiler and Turkey Processing." U.S. Department of Agriculture, Economic Research Service, Poultry and Egg Situation 259, Washington, DC, November 1969.

Faber, Fred L., and Ruth J. Irvin. "The Chicken Broiler Industry: Structure, Practices, and Costs." U.S. Department of Agriculture, Economic Research Service, Mktg, Res. Rpt. 930, Washington, DC, May 1971.

Forsht, R. Gar, Clark R. Burbee, and William M. Crosswhite. "Recycling Poultry Waste as Feed: Will it Pay?" U.S. Department of Agriculture, Economic Research Service, Agr. Econ. Rpt. 254, Washington, DC, March 1974.

Gaede, Harold W., and Robert L. Christensen. "Economic Interrelationships of the Poultry Industry with Other Sectors of the Economy." University of Massachusetts, Research Bul. 607, Amherst, MA, May 1974.

Hale, Kirk K. "An evaluation of Poultry Processing." University of Georgia, Athens, March 1973.

Harris, Marshall, and Dean F. Massey. "Vertical Coordination Via Contract Farming." U.S. Department of Agriculture, Economic Research Service, Misc. Pub. 1073, Washington, DC, March 1968.

Hein, Dale. "An Economic Analysis of the U.S. Poultry Sector." Am. J. of *Agric. Econ.*, **58,** (2), May 1976.

Hudson, B. L., G. L. Cole, and R. C. Smith. "An Economic Analysis of Poultry Processing Wastewater in Delaware." University of Delaware, Bul. 383, Newark, December 1970.

International Atomic Energy Agency. "Meeting on Food Irradiation." International Atomic Energy Agency, PR 76/18, Vienna, Austria.

Jones, H. B., and William L. Henson. "Broiler Production Costs in the South and Northeast." U.S. Department of Agriculture Economic Research Service, Poultry and Egg Situation 286, Washington, DC, June 1975.

Josephson, E. S. *Low Dose Food Irradiation at "Natick."* U.S. Army Natick Research and Development and Command, Natick, MA, October 1975.

Kahan, R. S., and J. J. Howker. "Retention of Fresh Chicken Quality in Refrigerated Poultry Using Radiation and Other Techniques." U.S. Army Natick Laboratories, Natick, MA, August 1970.

Kerns, Waldon R., and Harold B. Jones. "Cost of Required Water Pollution Abatement on Poultry Processing Plants." *South. J. Agric. Econ.*, July 1974.

Klose, A. A. "Perspective on Evaporative Chilling of Poultry." *Poul. Sci.*, **54,** 1889–1893, 1973.

Knott, E. M. "Homemakers" Opinions About and Preferences for Broiler-Fryers and Turkeys." U.S. Department of Agriculture, Stat. Rptg. Serv., Mktg. Res. Rpt. 760, Washington, DC July 1966.

Malone G. W., and L. M. Kilgo. "Consumer Attitudes About Broiler Meat." Mississippi Agricultural and For. Experimentation Station, July 1976.

Marion, Bruce W., and Charles R. Handy. "Market Performance: Concepts and Measures." U.S. Department of Agriculture, Economic Research Service, Agr. Econ. Rpt. 244, Washington, DC, Sept. 1973.

Mountney, G. F. *Poultry Products Technology*. AVI, 1966.

National Commission on Food Marketing. *Organization and Competition in the Poultry and Egg Industries*. National Commission on Food Marketing, Tech. St. 2, June 1966.

O'Mara, Gerald K. "An Analysis of Alternative Forecast Models for Predicting Monthly Prices and Production for the Broiler Industry." Unpublished M.S. thesis, North Carolina State University, Raleigh, 1970.

Ranken, M. D. "Chlorination in Poultry Processing." *Br. Poul. Sci.,* **6** (4), October 1965.

Rauniker, Robert, J. C. Purcell, and K. E. Ford. "Spatial and Temporal Aspects of the Demand for Food in the United States: II, Beef. University of Georgia, Research Bul. 63, Athens, GA, August 1969.

Rauniker, Robert, J. C. Purcell, and J. C. Elrod. "Spatial and Temporal Aspects of the Demand for Food in the United States: III, Pork." University of Georgia, Res. Bul. 85, Athens, September 1970.

Rauniker, Robert, J. C. Purcell, and J. C. Elrod. "Spatial and Temporal Aspects of the Demand for Food in the United States: IV, Poultry." University of Georgia, Res. Bul. 87, Athens, September 1970.

Rogers, George B. "Changes in Regional Self-Sufficiency in Egg and Poultry Supplies, 1955–1975." U.S. Department of Agriculture, Economic Research Service, Poultry and Egg Situation 291, Washington, DC, September 1976.

Rogers, George B., "Costs and Returns for Poultry and Eggs 1955–1975." U.S. Department of Agriculture, Economic Research Service, Poultry and Egg Situation 290, Washington, DC, June 1976.

Rogers, George B. "Price Spreads, Costs, and Productivity in Poultry and Egg Marketing, 1955–74." U.S. Department of Agriculture, Economic Research Service, Agr. Econ. Rpt. 326, Washington, DC, Feb. 1976.

Rogers, George, Verel W. Benson, and Donald L. Van Dyne. "Energy Use and Conservation in the Poultry and Egg Industry." U.S. Department of Agriculture, Economic Research Service, Agr. Econ. Rpt. 354, Washington, DC, October 1976.

Rogers, George, and Frank M. Conley. "Marketing Poultry Eggs." U.S. Department of Agriculture, Economic Research Service, Service, ERS 324, Washington, DC, October 1966.

Rogers, George, and Ruth J. Irvin. "Interregional Movements of Eggs and Poultry, 1955–75." U.S. Department of Agriculture, Economic Research Service, Stat. Bul. 565, Washington, DC March 1977.

Rogers, George. "Shell Egg Packing and Broiler Processing Costs in Major Regions." U.S. Department of Agriculture, Economic Research Service, Poultry and Egg Situation 291 Washington, DC, September 1976.

Spencer, J. V., and W. J. Stadelman. "Effect of Certain Holding Conditions on Shelf-Life of Fresh Poultry Meat." *Food Tech.* **19,** (7), 358–360, 1955.

Sykes, Geoffrey, *Poultry—A Modern Agribusiness.* Crosby Lockwood, London, 1963.

Thomson, James E. "Poultry: 8° Can mean 9 Days." Refrig. Transp., **8,** (9), 41–42, 1972.

Thomson, James E., W. K. Whitehead, and A. J. Mercuri. "Chilling Poultry Meat—A Literature Review." *Poul. Sci.,* **53,** (4), 1268–2281, 1974.

USDA. "Regulations Governing the Inspection of Poultry and Poultry Products." U.S. Department of Agriculture, Consumer and Marketing Service, Washington, DC, March 1968.

USDA. "Agriculture—the Third Century." U.S. Department of Agriculture, Economic Research Service, Washington, DC, July 1976.

USDA. "Cost Components of Farm-Retail Price Spreads for Selected Foods." U.S. Department of Agriculture, Economic Research Service, Agr. Econ. Rpt. 343, Washington, DC, July 1976.

USDA. "The Broiler Industry." U.S. Department of Agriculture, Packers and Stockyards Administration, Washington, DC, August 1967.

U.S. Department of Commerce. "Census of Agriculture, 1969" U.S. Department of Commerce, Bureau of the Census, Washington, DC, October 1973.

U.S. Department of Commerce. "Census of Agriculture, 1974." Preliminary reports, U.S. Department of Commerce, Bureau of the Census, Washington, DC.

Van Kooij, J. G. "Wholesomeness Testing of Irradiated Foods and Authorization Procedures in the Netherlands." Institute for Atomic Sciences in Agriculture, Wageningen, The Netherlands.

Vertrees, James G. "The Poultry Processing Industry: A Study of the Impact of Water Pollution Control Costs." U.S. Department of Agriculture, Economic Research Service, Mktg Research Rpt. 965, Washington, DC, June 1972.

Walker, H. W., and J. C. Ayres. "Incidence and Kinds of Microorganisms Associated with Commercially Dressed Poultry." *Appl. Microbiol.*, **4,** (6), November 1956.

Waugh, Frederick, V. "Demand and Price Analysis—Some Examples from Agriculture." U.S. Department of Agriculture, Tech. Bul. 1316, Washington, DC, June 1970.

Wierlicki, Eugene. "Preservation of Meats by Ionizing Radiation—An Update." U.S. Army, Natick Development Center, Natick, MA, September 1975.

Cocoa

ACLI International, Commodity Research Bulletin. "Cocoa—A Special Report." New York, April 1980.

Akari, Hossein and John Thomas Cummings. *Agricultural Supply Response, A Survey of the Econometric Evidence*. Praeger, New York, 1976.

Bateman, Merrill. *Cocoa in the Ghanain Economy: An Econometric Model*. North-Holland, Amsterdam, 1968.

Chatt, Eileen M. *Cocoa*. Interscience, New York, 1953.

FAO. *The Cocoa Situation: Recent Developments and the Outlook for Production and Demand*. Food and Agriculture Organization of the United Nations, Rome, 1961.

Feldman, Jill B. *The Price Effects of Futures Trading in Relation to International Coffee and Cocoa Markets*. Mount Holyoke College, South Hadley, MA, 1973.

Gill & Duffus. *Cocoa Statistics*. Gill & Duffus, London,

Gill & Duffus. *Cocoa Market Report*. Gill & Duffus, London, Quarterly.

Labys, Walter C. and C. W. J. Granger. *Speculation, Hedging and Commodity Price Forecasts*. D C Heath, Lexington, MA, 1973.

Payer, Cheryl. *Commodity Trade of the Third World*. Wiley, New York, 1975.

Rolfo, Jacques. *Optimal Hedging Under Price and Quantity Uncertainty: The Case of a Cocoa Producer*. World Bank, November 1979.

Stern, William. "A Method of Forecasting Cocoa Prices." *Forecasting Commodity Prices*, Commodity Research Bureau, New York, 1975.

USDA. "Foreign Agriculture Circular." U.S. Department of Agriculture, Washington, DC

USDA. "Sugar and Sweetner Report." U.S. Department of Agriculture, Washington, DC (Reports on Cocoa Supply and Demand Appear Periodically.)

Watling, T. F. and A. J. Morley. *Successful Commodity Futures Trading*. Business Books, London, 1974.

Weymar, F. Helmut. *The Dynamics of the World Cocoa Market*. MIT Press, Cambridge, MA, 1968.

Wickizer, V. D. *Coffee, Tea, and Cocoa*. The Food Research Institute of Stanford University, Stanford, CA, 1951.

Coffee

Abbott, Susan. "How International Commodity Agreements Affect Futures." *Commodities,* December 1981, 42–43.

Andres, Uribe C. *Brown Gold.* Random House, New York, 1954.

Akari, Hossein and John Cummings. *Agricultural Supply Response, A Survey of the Econometric Evidence.* Praeger, New York, 1976.

Atwood, A. C. "An Analysis of the Coffee Futures Market." Unpublished doctoral dissertation, Princeton University, 1969.

Bacha, E. L. "An Econometric Model for the World Coffee Market: The Impact of Brazilian Price Policy." Unpublished doctoral dissertation, Yale University, New Haven, 1968.

Eisenhower, D. D. "Waging Peace 1956–1961." In *The White House Years,* Vol. 2, Doubleday, Garden City, NY, 1965.

Epps, May Lee S. "A Computer Simulation Model of the World Coffee Economy." unpublished doctoral dissertation, Duke University, 1970.

Fisher, B. *The International Coffee Agreement: A Study in Coffee Diplomacy.* Praeger, New York, 1972.

FAO. *The World Coffee Economy.* Food and Agricultural Organization of the United Nations, Commodity Bulletin Series 33, Rome, 1961.

Geer, Thomas. *An Oligopoly: The World Coffee Economy and Stabilization Schemes.* Dunellen, New York, 1971.

International Coffee Organization. *Basic Information Concerning the International Coffee Organization.* International Coffee Organization, London, 1971.

International Coffee Organization. *International Coffee Agreement.* International Coffee Organization, London, 1976.

Krasner, S. D. "Business Government Relations: The Case of the International Coffee Agreement." *International Organization,* **27,** (4), Fall, 1973a.

Krasner, S. D. "Manipulating International Commodity Markets: Brazilian Coffee Policy 1906–1962." *Public Policy,* **21,** (4), Fall, 1973b.

Labys, Walter C. *Dynamic Commodity Models: Specification, Estimation, and Simulation.* DC Heath, Lexington, MA, 1973.

Pan American Coffee Bureau. *Annual Coffee Statistics.* Pan American Coffee Bureau, New York.

Payer, Cheryl, ed. *Commodity Trade of the Third World.* Wiley, New York, 1975.

Payer, C. *The Debt Trap: The IMF and the Third World.* Penguin, Harmondsworth, England, 1974.

Rowe, J. W. F. *The World's Coffee.* HMSO, London, 1963.

Sivetz, M. *Coffee: Origin and Use.* Coffee Publications, Corvallis, OR, 1973.

Struning, William C. "Understanding the Coffee Market." *Forecasting Commodity Prices,* Commodity Research Bureau, New York, 1975.

USDA. "U.S. Coffee Consumption, 1946–1976." U.S. Department of Agriculture, Foreign Agricultural Service, FAS M-275, Washington, DC, February 1977.

USDA. "Coffee Production in Africa." U.S. Department of Agriculture, Foreign Agricultural Service, FAS M-266, Washington, DC, September 1975.

USDA. "Coffee Production and Trade in Latin America." U.S. Department of Agriculture, Foreign Agricultural Service, FAS M-288, Washington, DC, May 1979.

U.S. Senate, Committee on Foreign Relations. "Hearings on the International Coffee Agreement." Washington, DC, March 12, 1963.

Walsh, Joseph M. *Coffee, Its History, Classification and Description.* Henry T. Coates, Philadelphia, 1894.

Wickens, M., J. Greenfield, and G. Marshall. *A World Coffee Model.* Food and Agricultural Organization of the United Nations, CCP.71/W.P.4, Rome, 1971.

Wickizer, V. D. *Coffee, Tea, and Cocoa.* Food Research Institute, Stanford University, Stanford, CA, 1951.

Wickizer, V. D. *The World's Coffee Economy, with Special Reference to Control Schemes.* Food Research Institute, Stanford University, Stanford, CA, 1943.

World Coffee & Tea. "Is America Ready for a Good Cup of Coffee?" *World Coffee & Tea,* September 1982, 22–30.

World Coffee & Tea. "The Only Reality is the Agreement." *World Coffee & Tea,* September 1982, 14–15.

ENERGY COMPLEX

Books

Adelman, M. A. *The World Petroleum Market.* Johns Hopkins University Press, Baltimore, MD, 1971.

API. "Gasoline Marketing." American Petroleum Institute, Washington, DC, December 1976.

API. "Recent Changes in Retail Gasoline Marketing." American Petroleum Institute, Washington, DC, January 1981.

API. "Standard Definitions for Petroleum Statistics." American Petroleum Institute, Washington DC

ASTM. "ASTM Specifications for Petroleum Products." American Society for Testing and Materials, Philadelphia, PA, 1978.

Banks, Ferdinand E. *Political Economy of Oil.* Lexington Books, Lexington, MA, 1980.

British Petroleum. *Our Industry Petroleum.* British Petroleum Co., London, England, 1977.

Butane-Propane News. *An Introduction to LP-Gases.* Butane-Propane News, Arcadin, CA, 1973.

Dasgupta, B. *The Oil Industry in India.* F. Can & Co., London, 1971.

Ethyl Corporation. *The Story of Gasoline.* New York, 1964.

Hartshom, J. E. *Oil Companies and Governments.* 2nd ed., Faber, London.

Penwell. *International Petroleum Encyclopedia 1981.* Penwell, Tulsa, 1981.

Leffler, William L. *Petroleum Refining for the NonTechnical Person.* Penwell Books, Tulsa, 1979.

Leffler, William L. *The Technology and Economic Behavior of the U.S. Propane Industry.* Petroleum Publishing Company, Tulsa, 1973.

National Petroleum Council. "Refinery Flexibility." National Petroleum Council Washington, DC, December 1980.

Odell, P. R. *Oil and World Power.* 4th ed., Penguin Books, London, 1975.

Oil and Gas Journal. *A Guide to World Export Crudes.* Petroleum, Tulsa, 1976.

Oil and Gas Journal. *Evaluation of World's Important Crudes*. Petroleum, Tulsa, 1973.

Penrase, E. T. *The Large International Firm in Developing Countries: A Case Study of the International Oil Industry*. Allen & Unwin, London, 1968.

K. E. Seiferlein. *Motor Gasoline Supply and Demand 1967–1978*. Department of Energy, Energy Information Administration, Washington, DC, August 1978.

Tanger, M. *The Political Economy of International Oil and the Underdeveloped Countries*. Temple Smith, London, 1970.

Tanger, M. *Petroleum, Raw Materials and Development*. (memorandum prepared for the UN General Assembly by the Government of Algeria), 1974.

Schmidt, F. Paul. *Fuel Oil Manual*. Industrial Press, New York, 1969.

R. Shriver Assoc. *Middle Distillate Market Profile Report*. U.S. Department of Energy, (ODE/ERA/6379-1), Washington, DC, July 1979.

USDE. "Trends in Refinery Capacity and Utilization." U.S. Department of Energy, Washington, DC, September 1978.

USDE "Survey of Current Business." U.S. Department of Commerce, Bureau of Economic Analysis, Washington, DC, January 1977, 1978, 1979, and 1981.

Wolbert, George S. U.S. Oil Pipelines. American Petroleum Institute, Washington, DC, 1979.

Wyant, Frank R. *The United States, OPEC, and Multinational Oil*. Lexington Books, Lexington, MA, 1977.

Periodicals

American Petroleum Institute. Washington, DC (M, W).

Energy User News. Fairchild Publishing, Washington, DC (W).

Fuel Oil News. Publex Corp., Whitehouse, NJ (M).

Fuel Oil Week. Observer Publishing, Washington, DC (W).

Lundberg Letter. North Hollywood, CA (W).

National Petroleum News. McGraw-Hill, New York (M).

Oil Buyer's Guide. Petroleum Publications, Lakewood, NJ. (W).

Oil Daily. Oil Daily, Inc., New York (D).

Oil and Gas Journal. PennWell, Tulsa (W).

Oil Price Information Service. Silver Spring, MD (W).

The Petroleum Economist. Petroleum Press Bureau, London, England (M).

The Petroleum Intelligence Weekly. Petroleum and Energy Intelligence Weekly, New York (W).

Platt's Oilgram News. McGraw-Hill, New York (D).

Platt's Oilgram Price Report. McGraw-Hill, New York (D).

U.S. Department of Energy. *Crude Petroleum, Petroleum Products, and Natural Gas Liquids. Energy Data Report. Monthly Energy Review. Monthly Petroleum Statement. Petroleum Market Shares. Sales of LP Gases and Ethane. Weekly Petroleum Status Report.*

U.S. Department of the Interior, "Bureau of Mineral Industry Surveys" (M). "International Petroleum Annual" (A).

U.S. Oil Week, Capital Publications, Arlington, VA (W).

FINANCIAL INSTRUMENTS

Books

Arthur Anderson & Co. *Interest Rate Futures Contracts: Accounting and Control Techniques For Banks*. Arthur Anderson & Co., Chicago, 1978.

Baxter, Nevins D. *The Commercial Paper Market*. Bankers Publishing, Boston, 1966.

Berstein, Peter L. ed. *The Theory and Practice of Bond Portfolio Management*. Institutional Investor Books, New York, 1977.

Carroll McEntee & McGinley. *Handbook of U.S. Treasury and Federal Agency Securities, Including Other Short-Term Money Market Instruments*. 2nd ed., Street, New York, 1977.

Clayton Brokerage Co. *Hedge Guide for the Interest Rate Futures Market—A Guide for the Management of Risk Associated with Fluctuations in Interest Rates*. Clayton, St. Louis, 1979.

Collins, Patrick S. *Fixed Income Futures Hedging*. First Boston Corporation, New York, 1980.

Commodity Year Book. Emery, Walter L. Ed., Commodity Research Bureau, New York (A).

Continental Illinois National Bank and Trust Company. *Financial Instruments Futures—A Better Way to Manage Interest Rate Risks*. Continental Illinois National Bank and Trust Company, Chicago, 1978.

Cook, Timothy. *Instruments of the Money Market*. Federal Reserve Bank of Richmond, Richmond, VA, 1977.

Culbertson, William Patton. *GNMA Futures Trading: Its Impact On The Residential Mortgage Market*. Culbertson, 1978.

Darst, David. *The Complete Bond Book, A Guide to All Types of Fixed-Income Securities*. McGraw-Hill, New York, 1975.

Dow Jones Irwin. *The Dow Jones Commodities Handbook, A Guide to Major Futures Markets*. Dow Jones Books, Princeton, NJ (annual).

Fabozzi, Frank J. and Frank G. Zarb, eds. *Handbook of Financial Markets*. Dow Jones-Irwin, Homewood, IL, 1981.

Federal Reserve Bank of Cleveland. *Money Market Instruments*. Federal Reserve Bank of Cleveland, Cleveland, OH, 1971.

First Boston Corp. *Handbook of Securities of the United States Government and Federal Agencies, and Related Money Market Instruments*. 28th ed., First Boston, New York, 1978.

GNMA Mortgage-Backed Securities Dealers Assn. *The Ginnie Mae Manual*. Dow Jones-Irwin, Homewood, IL, 1978.

Gold, Gerald. *Modern Commodity Futures Trading*. 4th ed., Commodity Research Bureau, New York, 1972.

Goss, B. A. *The Theory of Futures Trading*. Rutledge & Kegan Paul, Boston, 1972.

Guttentag, Jank M. and Phillip Cagan. *Essays on Interest Rates*. National Bureau of Economic Research, New York, 1969–1971.

Harris Trust and Savings. *Primer on Relative Yield Curve Values*. Harris Trust, Chicago, 1977.

Harris Trust and Savings. *The U.S. Government Securities Market*. 3rd rev., Harris Trust, Chicago, 1976.

Hawk, William A. *The U.S. Government Securities Market*. Harris Trust, Chicago, 1976.

Henning, Charles N. *Financial Markets and the Economy*. 2nd ed., Prentice-Hall, Englewood-Cliffs, NJ, 1978.

Hoel, Arline. *A Primer on the Futures Markets for Treasury Bills*. Federal Reserve Bank of New York, New York, 1977.

Homer, Sidney. *A History of Interest Rates*. 2nd ed., Rutgers, New Brunswick, NJ, 1977.

Homer, Sidney and Martin L. Leibowitz. *Inside the Yield Book: New Tools for Bond Market Strategy*. Prentice-Hall, Englewood Cliffs, NJ, 1972.

Ibbotson, Roger G. and Rex A. Sinquefield. *Stocks, Bonds, Bills, and Inflation: The Past (1926–1976) And Future (1977–2000)*. Financial Analysts Research Foundation, Chicago, 1977.

Kessel, Reuben A. *The Cyclical Behavior of the Term Structure of Interest Rates*. National Bureau of Economic Research, New York, 1965.

Lindow, Wesley. *Inside the Money Market*. Random House, New York, 1972.

Little, James M. *Financial Futures Hedging Guide*. Clayton Brown & Associates, Chicago, IL, 1979.

Loosigian, Allan M. *Interest Rate Futures—A Market Guide for Hedgers and Speculators*. Dow Jones, Princeton, NJ, 1980.

Massaro, Vincent G. *A Guide to Forecasting Interest Rates*. Conference Board, New York, 1973.

Meiselman, David. *The Term Structure of Interest Rates*. Prentice-Hall, Englewood Cliffs, NJ, 1962.

Merrill Lynch Pierce Fenner & Smith, Inc. publications: 1. *The Merrill Lynch Guide to Interest Rate Futures*. 2. *Hedge Guide for Mortgage Bankers and Institutional Investors*. 3. *Outlook for GNMA Interest Rate Futures*.

Monhollon, Jummie R. and Glenn Picou, eds. *Instruments of the Money Market*. Federal Reserve Bank of Richmond, Richmond, VA, 1974.

Mortgage Bankers Association of America, International Management Committee. *Accounting for GNMA Mortgage Interest Rate Futures Market Transactions: A Statement of Opinion Approved By The International Management Committee, Mortgage Bankers Association of America*. The Association, Washington, DC.

Nelson, Charles R. *The Term Structure of Interest Rates*. Basic Books, New York, 1972.

Pacific Bancorporation Financial Services. *A Total Financial Management System Designed to Manage Uncertainty*. Pacific Bancorporation, Bakersfield, CA, 1979.

Pease, Robert A. and Lewis O. Kenwood, eds. *Mortgage Banking*. McGraw-Hill, New York, 1965.

Powers, Mark J. and David Vogel. *Inside the Financial Futures Markets*. Wiley, New York, 1981.

Roll, Richard. *The Behavior of Interest Rates: An Application of the Efficient Market Model to U.S. Treasury Bills*. Basic Books, New York, 1970.

Rosen, Lawrence R. *Dow Jones-Irwin Guide to Interest*. Dow Jones-Irwin, Homewood, IL, 1974.

Schwartz, Edward. *How to Use the Money Market Futures Contracts*. Dow Jones-Irwin, Homewood, IL, 1979.

Stigum, Marcia, and John Mann. *Money Market Calculations: Yields, Breakevens, and Arbitrage*. Dow Jones-Irwin, Homewood, IL, 1981.

Stigum, Marcia. *The Money Market: Myth, Reality and Practice.* Dow Jones-Irwin, Homewood, IL, 1978.

Thomson McKinnon Securities, Inc. *A Traders Guide to Interest Rate Futures.* One New York Plaza, New York, 10004.

Van Home, Janes C. *Function and Analysis of Capital Market Rates.* Prentice-Hall, Englewood Cliffs, NJ, 1970.

Walmsley, Julian. *A Dictionary of International Finance.* Greenwood Press, Westport, CT 1979.

Weberman, Ben. *Interest Rate Futures—Profits and Pitfalls.* Ben Weberman, New York, 1979.

Willett, Edward R. *Interest Rate Futures: The Basics.* Willett Institute of Finance, Boston, 1979.

Winikates, James. *GNMA Mortgage Futures Market: A Financial Managers Guide.* Financial Managers' Society for Savings Institutions, Chicago, 1977.

Articles

Angell, George. "A Technical Approach to Trading Interest Rate Futures Markets." *Commodities,* **6**(6), 46–48, June 1977.

Angrist, Stanley W. "How to Hedge Interest Rate Risks." *Forbes,* December 15, 1976.

Angrist, Stanley W. "Commercial Paper Reaches the Pits." *Forbes,* May 1, 1978.

Angrist, Stanley W. "Interest Rate Inversion." *Forbes,* December 10, 1979.

Arenson, Karen W. "Use of Financial Futures Grows as a Hedge on Rates of Interest." *New York Times,* D-1, December 28, 1978.

Bacon, Peter W. and Richard E. Williams. "Interest Rate Futures—New Tool for the Financial Manager." *Financ. Mang.,* **5**(1), 32–38, Spring 1976.

Bard, Susan. "More Interest Rate Futures and How They'll Work." *Commodities,* October 1977.

Beardsley, George. "Board of Trade Writes Interest Rate Contract." *Chicago Tribune,* 3.9, August 7, 1972.

Beaver, William. *Accounting for Interest Rate Futures Contracts.* Graduate School of Business, Stanford University, March 1981; also Columbia University CSFM Working Paper Series No. 11.

Bench, Joseph. "Computerized Analysis, An Aid to Competance in Financial Futures Mart." *Money Manager,* May 1, 1978.

Black, Fischer. "The Pricing of Commodity Contracts." *J. of Finac. Econ.,* January 1976.

Blackwell, James Marvin. "The Ramifications of Hedging Interest Rates by Commercial Banks." James Marvin Blackwell, University of Texas, Austin, 1978.

Board of Governors of the Federal Rserve System. "The Federal Funds Market—A Study by a Federal Reserve System Committee, Clay J. Anderson, Chairman." Washington, DC, 1959.

Bohnsack, William H. "The Interest Rate Futures Market." *Bankers Month. Mag.,* 22–26, November 15, 1977.

Bohnsack, William H. "Interest Rate Futures: A Weapon Against Monetary Uncertainty." *Money Manager,* March 20, 1978.

Boileau, Winfield. "GNMA Pass Through: Overwhelming Success Story." *Mortgage Banker,* **37**(5), 20–28, February 1977.

Boyd, Michael A., Jr. "GNMA Futures: The Long Hedge." *Finac. World*, April 1, 1978.

Boyd, Michael A., Jr. "GNMA Futures Hedgers." *Financ. World*, **147**(10), 67, May 15, 1978.

Branch, Ben. "Testing the Unbiased Expectations Theory of Interest Rates." *Financ. Rev.*, 51–66, Fall 1978.

Brier, Charles. "A New Look at Tax Straddles." *Commodities*, 38–40, December 1977.

Brown, Jeffrey. "The Interest Rate Market." *Financ. Times*, 18, October 4, 1978.

Cagan, Philip. *Financial Futures Markets—Is More Regulation Needed?* Columbia University CSFM Working Paper Series No. 15, January 1981.

Capozza, Dennis R. and Bradford Cornell. *Treasury Bill Pricing in the Spot and Futures Markets*. Chicago Mercantile Exchange, Chicago, 1978.

Cleary, John. "Success in Futures Transactions Demands System and Caution." *Mortgage Banker*, 24–26, February 1978.

Commodities. "'Commodities' Interviews Bob Zellner: How a Big Grain Company Hedges Exchange and Interest Rates," *Commodities*, **7**(6) 28–31, June, 1989.

Commodities. Commercial Hedgers' Issue. *Commodities*. 1979.

Connelly, Julie, "The Irrepressible Growth of Commercial Paper," *Inst. Investor* 25–27, March 1978.

Connelly, James J. "Historical Analysis of the GNMA Market—Its Yield and Yield Spreads." *Mortgage Banker* **37**(8) 83–92, May 1977.

Cook, Timothy Q., ed. "Instruments of the Money Market" 4th ed., Federal Reserve Bank of Richmond, Richmond, VA, 1977.

St. Louis Globe Democrat. "Corporations to Expand Use of New Financial Instruments." *St. Louis Globe Democrat*, July 5, 1978.

Cox, Larry. "Shopping in the Futures Market: Risks and Returns on GNMA Contracts." *FHLBB J.*, 15–19, February 1978.

Cox, Meg. "Commercial Paper Futures Appear to Stimulate Little Interest So Far." *Wall Street J.*, December 30, 1977.

Cox, Meg. "Hot New Game: Interest Rate Futures Gain Popularity: Lure Hedgers, Speculators." *Wall Street J.*, **58**,(77), February 2, 1978.

Daane, Kenneth E. and Albert J. Fredman. "How Banks Can Use Interest Rate Futures." *Bankers Month. Mag.*, 26–29, April 15, 1979.

Delfino, W. J. "Futures Markets In Interest Rates: A Tool For Risk Minimization." *Bus. Econ. Rev.*, **23**(5), 10–14, April 1977.

Dew, Kurt. "CPI Futures." *Fed. Res. Bank San Francisco Weekly Letter*, 1–3, September 22, 1978.

Elias, Christopher. "Commercial Paper Trade Grows Slowly." *J. Comm.*, October 25, 1977.

Ederington, Louis H. and Wayne L. Plumly Jr. "The Now Interest Rate Futures Markets." Working Papers Department of Economics, School of Business Administration, Georgia State University, Atlanta.

Edwards, John. "Financial Contracts Fuel Expansion." *Financ. Times*, 15, October 4, 1978.

Ehrobar, A. F. "The Only Certainty About Interest Rates is Their Uncertainty." *Fortune*, **93**(1), 77, January 1976.

Erdvig, Eleanor. "Bank Participation in the Residential Mortgage Market." *Econ. Perspect.*, 8–10, May/June 1977.

Etter, Wayne E. and Donald Fraser. "Mortgage Bankers and The GNMA Futures Market." *Mortgage Banker*, August 1979.

Etter, Wayne E. "Everybody Loves Ginnie Mae," *Forbes,* **118**(9), 69, November 1, 1976.

Etter, Wayne E. "Fast Action in Interest Rate Futures." *Bus. Week,* 68, August 7, 1978.

Feduniak, Robert B. "Interest Rate Futures." *Financ. World,* **147**(15), 48, August 1, 1978.

Florez, Bob. "Money Markets Gain." *Chicago Bus. Rev.,* March 1978.

Florez, Bob. "Forward Trading That Vexes Treasury." *Bus. Week,* 60–61, August 22, 1977.

Franke, Richard J. "The Bond Market." *Commerce,* **75**(4), 21, May 1978.

Froewiss, Kenneth C. "GNMA Futures: Stabilizing or Destabilizing?" *Econ. Rev.,* Federal Reserve Bank of San Francisco, 20–29, Spring 1978.

Froewiss, Kenneth C. "Futures and Taxes, Tax Spreads: Handle with Caution." *Commodities,* 27, October 1978.

Ganis, David R. "GNMA Futures Market Has Advantages, But Not a Way to Make or Take Delivery." *Mortgage Banker,* **36**(4), 16, January 1976.

Ganis, David R. "All About the GNMA Mortgage-Backed Securities Market." *Real Estate Rev.,* **4**(2), 55–56, Summer 1974.

Ganis, David R. "Cash Market or Futures Market: Which One is Best For Mortgage Bankers?" *Mortgage Banker,* **39**(2), November 1978.

Geisst, C. R. "How Futures Trading Applies to Interest Rates." *Euromoney,* May 1970.

Gotthelf, Philip. "A Systems Approach to Financial Futures Markets." *Commodities,* **7**(8), 28–29, August 1978.

Gray, Roger W. "Risk Management in Commodities and Financial Markets." *Am. J. Agric. Econ.,* **58**(2), 280–285 and 296–304, May 1976.

Guild, Gerald A. "Financial Futures Bond Interest." *Financ. World,* December 15, 1979.

Gulf Coast Lumberman. "Commodity Exchange Proposes Trading in GNMA Futures Contract." *Gulf Coast Lumberman,* 9, June 1975.

Haggerty, William. "New Way to Cut the Risk of Running a Business." *Nations Bus.,* **65**(12), 74, December 1977.

Hall, William. "Brokerage Houses Branch Out." *Financ. Times,* 16, October 4, 1978.

Hamilton, Milo. "Growth Potential for the 'Ultimate' Commodity." *Commodities,* **7**(9), 50, September 1978.

Hammond, James H., Jr. "Accounting for GNMA Mortgage Interest Futures." *Mortgage Banker,* **37**(10), 57–59, July 1977.

Harding, John "Don't Look Past Financial Futures." *Pension World* **13**(7), 42, July 1977.

Harding, John. "GNMA Futures Options Provide New Vehicle to Transfer Risk." *Mortgage Banker,* **37**(11), 56–60, August 1977.

Harding, John. "GNMA's Not Following Script: Outlook Still Uncertain." *Commodities,* **6**(8), 18–19, August 1977.

Harding, John. "Housing in the Recovery." Federal Reserve Bulletin, **63**(6), 189–199, June 1977.

Harding, John. "How GNMA Futures Will Lessen Risks—Increase Profits." *Bankers Res.,* 1–3, October 10, 1975.

Jurley, Evelyn M. "The Commercial Paper Market." *Fed. Res. Bull.,* **63**(6), 525–536, June 1977.

Hurley, Evelyn M. "How to Protect Against Rising Interest Rates: A Technique for Bondholders." *Indic. Dig.,* May 21, 1976.

New York Times. "Interest Futures Are Widening Field." *New York Times,* June 26, 1978.

Jacobs, Steven F. and James R. Kozuch. "Is There a Future for a Mortgage Futures Market?" *Real Estate Rev.,* 109–113, Spring 1975.

Jacobs, Steven F. "The Short Hedge-Financial Boom For Mortgage Bankers." *Mortgage Banker,* **37**(5), 44–45, February 1977.

Jacobs, Steven F. "Mortgage Bankers Must Develop Knowledge and Strategy to Use GNMA Futures Market." Mortgage Banker, **37**(7), 53–57, April 1977.

Kane, Edward, J. "Arbitrage Pressure and Divergences Between Forward and Futures Interest Rates." Columbia University CSFM Working Paper Series No. 24.

Kasriel, Paul L. "Hedging Interest Rate Fluctuations." *Business Conditions—The Federal Reserve Bank of Chicago,* 3–10, April 1976.

Keene, J. "Market in Mortgage Futures Will Begin Trading This Fall." *House and Home,* **42**(20), August 1972.

Kinney, J. "Mortgage Futures Market—A Useful Tool for Reducing Risk." *Mortgage Banker,* 38–44, September 1976.

Kozuch, James R. and Michael K. Stamper. "A Study Analyzes Risks Facing Issuers of GNMA Mortgage-Backed Securities." *Mortgage Banker,* **37**(5), 8–18, February 1977.

Kozuch, James R. and Michael K. Stamper. "Ladies and Gentlemen, Hedge Your Best in the Newest Game in Town!" *Forbes,* 128, September 18, 1978.

Kozuch, James R. and Michael K. Stamper. "How Salomon Brothers Hedged The IBM Deal." *Bus. Week,* 50, October 29, 1979.

Lahey, Mark K. "Streamlined GNMA Futures Schemes Differ, But Share Promise." *Money Manager,* August 28, 1978.

Lahey, Mark K. "Why Interest Rate Futures Spreads Change." *Commodities,* 71, April 1979.

Laing, Jonathan R. "Interest Rate Futures Market Attracts Avid Interest, Diverse Trading Strategy." *Wall Street J.,* April 17, 1978.

Lang, Richard W. and Robert H. Rosche. "Yields on Futures and Forward Rates." *Comm. J.,* **14**(3), 1–4, July/August 1979.

Lang Richard W. "Las Vegas in Chicago: Speculating on Interest-Rate Futures is the Hottest New Game in Town." *Forbes,* **120**(1), 31–32, July 1, 1977.

Leibler, Max. "Your Next Opportunity: Trade the Stock Market as a Commodity." *Commodities,* **7**(12), 42–43, December 1978.

Long, Richard W. and Robert H. Rasche. "A Comparison of Yields on Futures Contracts and Implied Forward Rates." *Fed. Res. Bank St. Louis Rev.,* **60**(12), 12–30, December 1978.

Lowery, Andy. "GNMA Futures: A Selective Marketing Tool." *Mortgage Banker,* February 1978.

Lowler, Thomas. "Seasonal Movements in Short Term Yield Spreads." *Fed. Res. Bank Richmond Econ. Rev.,* **60**(4), 10–17, July/August 1978.

Lutz, F. A. "Structure of Interest Rates." *Q. J. Econ.,* 36–63, November 1940.

Martin, Preston. "A Futures Market in Your Future." *Fed. Home Loan Bank Board J.,* **5**(10), 1–4, October 1972.

Mathews, Gordon, "Major Role in Real Estate Market Predicted for Mortgage Futures Trading." *Am. Banker,* **141**(83), 1, April 29, 1976.

Mathews, Trevett. "Possible GNMA Futures Market Should Alert Mortgage Banker to Workings of Commodity Exchanges." *Mortgage Banker,* **35**(10), 11–18, July 1975.

Mayberry, J. H. "Financial Futures: Wall St. Takes Aim at Chicago." *Money Manager,* 1978.

Meyer, Janet, "Varied Reaction on New Futures Contracts." *City Star,* Kansas City, MO, December 5, 1977.

Miller, M. and D. A. Orr. "A Model for the Demand for Money by Firms." *Q. J. Econ.* **80,** 413–435, August 1966.

Miller, Thomas C. "Growth, Acceptance to Improve Liquidity of GNMA Security." *Mortgage Banker,* **37**(5), 30, February 1977.

Miller, Thomas C. "Mortgage Futures Market A Useful Tool For Reducing Risk." *Mortgage Banker,* **36**(12), 38–44, September 1976.

Miller, Thomas C. "A Mortgage Banker and a GNMA Dealer Exchange Views." *Mortgage Banker,* **38**(5), 7, February 1978.

Miller, Thomas C. "Mortgage Bankers Begin to Use the GNMA Futures Market." *Mortgage Banker,* April 1976.

Miller, Thomas C. "Mortgage Futures Market Booms." *San Diego Union,* March 25, 1978.

Miller, Thomas C. "Mortgage Future Gets Support of FHLBB Chairman." *HUD News,* 2, November 6, 1972.

Morgan Guaranty Survey. "What Markets Can Tell You About Interest Rates." Morgan Guaranty Trust Company, New York, 8–15, July 1977.

Mutter, Alan. "Financial Instruments Futures Use Up," *Chicago Sun-Times,* April 8, 1978.

Nagan, Peter S. and Kenneth A. Kaufman. "How the Interest Rate Futures Market Works—And When a Bank Can Use It Profitably." *Banking,* May 1978.

Nagan, Peter S. "A New Futures Market Reduces Some Risks." *Bus. Week,* 105, October 10, 1977.

Nagan, Peter S. "New Option Plays In Debt Investment." *Bus. Week* 76–77, November 1, 1976.

Nagan, Peter S. "Opening A Market In Mortgage Futures." *Bus. Week* 62–64, November 3, 1975.

Osteryoung, Jerome S., Daniel E. McCarty, and Gordon S. Roberts. *Riding A Hedged Yield Curve with Treasury Bill Futures.* Chicago Mercantile Exchange, Chicago, 1979.

Pepper, Andrew C. "Howdy Ginnie Mae." *Euromoney,* 93–97, January 1976.

Plant, Kenneth M. "A Futures Market In Your Future." *Fed. Home Loan Bank Board J.,* **5**(11), 1–7, November 1972.

Plant, Kenneth M. "Using the GNMA Futures Market." *Fed. Home Loan Bank Board J.,* **9**(7), 1–7, July 1976.

Plant, Kenneth M. "Playing the Futures Market Game." *Fed. Home Loan Bank Board J.* **8**(11), 16–21, November 1975.

Platt, Gordon. "Interest Rate Futures: Their Use As Hedging Device Gaining Ground." *Money Manager,* special SIA Convention issue, November 28, 1977.

Poh, Cari. "Hedging In GNMA Futures Made Simple." *Wisc. Sav. Loan League,* December 1975.

Polarus, Mark F. and David C. Fischer. "Banking on Interest Rate Futures," *Bank Admin.,* August 1979.

Powers, Mark J. "How Money Talks In The Commodity Trading World." *Commodities* **7**(5), 52–53, May 1978.

Powers, Mark J. "Yield Curve: The 'Strip'." *Commodities* **7**(12), 22, December 1978.

Powers, Mark J. "Yield Curves." *Commodities,* **7**(8), 42–43, August 1978.

Powers, Mark J. "Yield Curves—Part II." *Commodities,* **7**(9), 16, September 1978.

Powers, Mark J. "The Feds Are Coming, The Feds Are Coming." *Commodities,* 62–63, January 1979.

Powers, Mark J. "Financial Futures Help Federal Policy Makers." *Commodities,* 66–67, April 1979.

Powers, Mark J. "Yield Curves Re-Visited." *Commodities,* 20, May 1979.

Powers, Mark J. "The GNMA/T-Bond Spread." *Commodities* 23–25, October 1979.

Powers, Mark J. "Analyzing T-Bill Yield Curves." *Commodities,* 24–25, November 1979.

Powers, Mark J. "Hedging CD's in the T-Bill Futures Market." *Commodities,* 22–23, December 1979.

Quint, Michael. "50 National Banks Seek to Trade T-Bill, GNMA Futures." *Am. Banker,* **142**(154), 1, August 10, 1977.

Quint, Michael. "Rates Futures Gain As Hedgers On CD Costs." *Am. Banker,* November 25, 1977.

Robbins, William. "Hedging With Interest Futures." *New York Times,* 5–6, November 9, 1979.

Rout, Lawrence. "Exposed Position Bond Market's Plunge Caught Most Investors with Hedges Down." *Wall Street J.,* 1–30, **60**(28), November 21, 1979.

Sandor, Richard L. "Trading Mortgage Interest Rate Futures." *Fed. Home Loan Bank Board J.,* **8**(9), 2–9, September 1975.

Sandor, Richard L. "The Interest Rate Futures Market: An Introduction." *Commodities,* **5**(9), 14–17, September 1976.

Sandor, Richard L. "Commercial Paper and Treasury Bonds: More Interest Rate Futures Innovation and How They'll Work." *Commodities,* 22–25, October 1977.

Sandor, Richard L. "S&L's Give Ginnie Mae Futures a Cold Shoulder." *Commer. Financ. Chron.,* **221,** 19, June 28, 1976.

Schadrack, Frederick C., Jr. "Demand and Supply in the Commercial Paper Market." *J. Finance,* **25**(4), 837–852, September 1972.

Sciaudone, John and Thomas Coleman. "CD GNMA Futures: A Second GNMA Futures Contract at the CBOT." *Mortgage Banker,* **39**(2), November 1978.

Schwarz, Edward W. "The GNMA Futures Market—Is It For Mutual Savings Banks?" *Sav. Bank J.,* August 1976.

Shakin, Bernard. "Interest Rate Futures: They've Opened Up a Whole New Financial World." *Barron's,* **58**(46), 4–5, November 13, 1978.

Shearson Hayden Stone. "Guide To Speculating And Hedging In Mortgage Futures." Unpublished, October 10, 1975.

Smith, Brian. "GNMA Futures Market: Trading Complexities FHLBB Rules Impede Association Activity." *Sav. Loan News,* 48–53, January 1976.

Smith, Brian. Special Financial Futures Supplement. *Money Manager,* June 11, 1979.

Sternlight, Peter D., "The Federal Reserve and The Government Securities Market." remarks given to Public Securities Association, May 5, 1978.

Stevens, Neil A. "A Mortgage Futures Market: Its Development, Uses, Benefits, and Costs." *Fed. Res. Bank St. Louis Rev.,* 20–27, April 1976.

Taver, Loren. "Use of the U.S. Treasury Bond Futures Market by Rural Commercial Banks to Increase Bond Portfolio." Unpublished doctoral dissertation, Iowa State University, August 1978.

Tilton, John R. "Interest Rates." *Commerce,* **75**(4), 26, May 1978.

Tilton, John R. "Trading Interest Rate Futures." *International Curr. Rev.,* **10**(3), 30–32.

Tilton, John R. "Trading Inaugurated in Non-Agricultural Futures." *Commerce,* **67,** 139, March 1970.

Tilton, John R. "When Interest Rates Begin To Bud." *Citibank Month. Econ. Letter,* 10–12, April 1978.

Tilton, John R. "Will Interest Rates Sizzle or Fizzle?" *Commodities,* **7**(8), 21–25, August 1978.

White, Shelby. "The Siren Call of Ginnie Maes." *Instit. Investor,* 81–82, December 1976.

White, Shelby. "Everyone Into the Pool: Ginnie Mae Pass-Throughs Have Made Quite a Splash." *Barrons,* **56**(27), 11, July 5, 1976.

Wilson, S. "Futures Imperfect: Can Mortgage Pit Trading Really Help Housing?" *House & Home,* **48**(6), 16, December 1975.

Winn, James S. Jr., "GNMA Repos and the Mortgage Banker." *Mortgage Banker,* **39**(2), November 1978.

Wojnilower, Albert M. "The Distressing Outlook for Interest Rates." *Fortune,* June 1978.

Yardeni, Edward. "Managing Interest Rate Risk with Bond Futures." Columbia University CSFM Working Paper Series No. 10, June 1981.

Young, C. D. "Commodity Futures for Institutional Investors?" *Bankers Month.,* **91,** 34–38, October 1974.

Young, Clarke D. "Interest Rate Futures Win Growing Acceptance." *Bankers Month.,* **95**(9), 24, September 15, 1978.

Zachary, Phillip E. "Hedging Against Interest Rate Risk." *Bankers Month.,* 24, August 15, 1978.

Periodicals

Bank Credit Analyst. 1010 Sherbrooke St. West, Montreal, Canada H3A 2R7 (M).

Federal Reserve Bulletin. Board of Governors Federal Reserve System, Washington, DC 20551 (M).

Interest Rate Forecast. 1010 Sherbrooke St. West, Montreal, Canada, H3A 2R7 (M).

Investment Dealers' Digest. 150 Broadway, New York, NY 10038 (W).

The Money Manager. Bond Buyer, 1 State Street Plaza, New York, NY 10004 (W).

Monetary Trends. Federal Reserve Bank of St. Louis P.O. Box 442, St. Louis, MO 63166 (M).

National Economic Trends. Federal Reserve Bank of St. Louis, P.O. Box 442, St. Louis, MO 63166 (M).

Selected Interest & Exchange Rates, Weekly Series of Charts. Board of Governors, Federal Reserve System, Washington, DC 20551 (W).

U.S. Financial Data. Federal Reserve Bank of St. Louis, P.O. Box 442, St. Louis, MO 63166 (M).

FOREIGN EXCHANGE

Adler, Michael. "Bankers' Swaps, Foreign Exchange Futures and Exchange Risk." Columbia University CSFM Working Paper Series No. 29.

Aliber, Robert Z. *The International Market for Foreign Exchange.* Frederick A. Praeger, New York, 1969.

Aliber, Robert A. *The International Money Game.* 2nd ed., Basic Books, New York, 1976.

Angell, James W. *The Theory of International Prices.* Augustus M. Kelley, New York, 1965.

Baldwin, Robert E., and Richardson, J. David, eds. *International Trade and Finance.* Little, Brown, Boston, 1974.

Bernstein, Peter L. *A Primer on Money, Banking and Gold.* 2nd ed., Random House, New York, 1968.

Black, Stanley W. *Floating Exchange Rates and National Economic Policy.* Yale University Press, New Haven, 1977.

Bloomfield, A. I. *Speculative and Flight Movements of Capital in Postwar International Finance.* Princeton University, Princeton, NJ, 1954.

Brown, Brendon. *The Dollar-Mark Axis on Currency Power.* St. Martin's, New York, 1979.

Brown, Harry. *How You Can Profit from the Coming Devaluation.* Arlington House, New Rochelle, NY, 1970.

Canterbury, E. R. *Foreign Exchange, Capital Flows and Monetary Policy.* Princeton University, Princeton, NJ, 1965.

Caves, Richard E., and Jones, Ronald W. *World Trade and Payments.* Little, Brown, Boston, 1981.

Clarke, W. M. and G. Pulay, *The World's Money: How It Works.* Allen & Unwin, London, 1970.

Coninx, Raymond G. F. *Foreign Exchange Today.* Wiley, New York, 1978.

Coombs, Charles A. *The Arena of International Finance.* Wiley, New York, 1976.

Crump, Norman. *The ABC of the Foreign Exchanges.* Macmillan, New York, 1963.

Darst, David. *The Complete Bond Book, a Guide to All Types of Fixed-Income Securities.* McGraw-Hill, New York, 1975.

deRoover, R. *Gresham on Foreign Exchange.* Harvard University, Cambridge, MA, 1949.

Dominguez, John R. *Devaluation and Futures Markets.* Lexington Books, Lexington, MA, 1972.

Dreyer, Jacob S., Gottfried, Haberler, and Thomas D. Willett, eds. *Exchange Rate Flexibility.* American Enterprise Institute, Washington, DC, 1978.

Dufey, Gunter and Ian H. Giddy. *The International Money Market.* Prentice-Hall, Englewood Cliffs, NJ, 1978.

Dushek, Charles and Carol Harding. *Trading in Foreign Currencies, Speculative Practices and Techniques.* American TransEuro, Chicago, 1978.

Eckes, Alfred E. *A Search for Solvency.* University of Texas Press, Austin, 1975.

Einzig, Paul. *A Dynamic Theory of Forward Exchanges.* 2nd ed. Macmillan, London, 1967.

Einzig, Paul. *The Euro-Bond Market.* St. Martin's, New York, 1975.

Einzig, Paul. *The Euro-Dollar System.* St. Martin's, New York, 1974.

Einzig, Paul. *The Exchange Clearing System.* Macmillan, London, 1935.

Einzig, Paul. *Exchange Control.* Macmillan, London, 1934.

Einzig, Paul. *Finance and Politics.* Macmillan, London, 1932.

Einzig, Paul. *Foreign Balances.* Macmillan, London, 1938.

Einzig, Paul. *The History of Foreign Exchange.* St. Martin's, New York, 1967.

Einzig, Paul. *A Textbook on Foreign Exchange.* St. Martin's, New York, 1966.

Ensor, Richard and Boris Antl. *The Management of Foreign Exchange Risk.* Euromoney, London, 1978.

Evans, Thomas G. *The Currency Carousel: A New Era in Monetary Affairs*. Dow Jones Books, Princeton, NJ, 1977.

Evitt, H. E. *A Manual of Foreign Exchange*. 7th ed. rev. by R. F. Pither, Pitman, London, 1971.

Fatemi, Nasrollah S. *The Dollar Crisis*. Fairleigh Dickinson University Press, New York, 1964.

Federal Reserve Bank of Boston. *Managed Exchange Rate Flexibility: The Recent Experience*. Federal Reserve Bank of Boston, Conference Series No. 20, Boston, 1978.

Galbraith, John Kenneth. *Money: Whence It Came, Where It Went*. Houghton Mifflin, Boston, 1975.

Glahe, Fred R. *An Empirical Study of the Foreign Exchange Market: Test of a Theory*. Princeton Studies in International Finance, No. 20, 1967.

Grubel, Herbert G. *Forward Exchange, Speculation, and the International Flow of Capital*. University Microfilms, Ann Arbor, MI, 1977.

Haberler, Gottfried. *Money in the International Economy*. Harvard University Press, Cambridge, Ma., 1965.

Halm, George N. *A Guide to International Monetary Reform*. Lexington Books, Lexington, Ma., 1975.

Hayek, F. A. *Denationalisation of Money*. Institute of Economic Affairs, London, 1978.

Heller, H. Robert. *International Monetary Economics*. Prentice-Hall, Englewood Cliffs, NJ, 1974.

The History of Foreign Exchange. 2nd ed., St. Martin's, New York, 1970.

Holbik, Karel, ed. *Monetary Policy in Twelve Industrial Countries*. Federal Reserve Bank of Boston, Boston, 1973.

Holgate, H. C. F. *Exchange Arithmetic*. Pitman & Sons, London, 1961.

Horwitz, Paul. *Monetary Policy and the Financial System*. Prentice-Hall, Englewood Cliffs, NJ, 1969.

Hurst, James Willare. *A Legal History of Money in the U.S., 1774–1970*. University of Nebraska Press, Lincoln, NE, 1973.

International Monetary Fund. *Balance of Payments Yearbook*. International Monetary Fund, Washington. (A).

Isard, Peter. *Exchange Rate Determination: a Survey of Popular Views and Recent Markets*. Princeton University Press, Princeton, NJ, 1978.

Jacque, Laurent L. *Management of Foreign Exchange Risk*. Heath, Lexington, MA, 1978.

Jastram, Roy. *The Golden Constant*. Wiley, New York, 1977.

Katz, Samuel I., ed. *U.S.–European Monetary Relations*. American Enterprise Institute, Washington, DC, 1979.

Krause, Lawrence B. *Recent International Monetary Crises: Causes and Cures and Fixed and Gliding Exchange Rates*. The Brookings Institution, Washington, DC, 1971.

Kubarych, Roger F. *Foreign Exchange Markets in the United States*. Federal Reserve Bank, New York, 1978.

Lietaer, Bernard A. *Financial Management of Foreign Exchange: An Operational Technique to Reduce Risk*. MIT Press, Cambridge, MA, 1971.

Loosigian, Allan M. *Foreign Exchange Futures*. Dow Jones-Irwin, Homewood, IL, 1981.

Mayer, Martin. *The Fate of the Dollar*. New American Library, New York, 1981.

Meek, Paul. *Open Market Operations*. Federal Reserve Bank of New York, New York, 1973.

Merns, Stephen. *Decision-Making on Exchange Rates*. The Brookings Institution, Washington, DC, 1970.

Money Hard and Soft on the International Currency Markets. Wiley, New York, 1978.

Murphy, J. Carter. *The International Monetary System: Beyond the First Stage of Reform*. American Enterprise Institute, Washington, DC, 1979.

National Monetary Policies and the International Financial System. University of Chicago, Chicago, 1974.

New Profits from the Monetary Crisis. Morrow, New York, 1978.

Ohlin, Bertil. *Interregional and International Trade*. Harvard University Press, Cambridge, MA, 1967.

Pick, Franz, ed. *Pick's Currency Yearbook*. Pick, New York. (A).

Prindl, Andreas. *Foreign Exchange Risk*. Wiley, New York, 1976.

Quinn, Brian Scott. *The New Euromarkets*. Wiley, New York, 1975.

Riehl, Heinz and Rita M. Rodriguez. *Foreign Exchange Markets*. McGraw-Hill, New York, 1977.

Rolfe, Sidney E. and James L. Burtle. *The Great Wheel: The World Monetary System-A Reinterpretation*. McGraw-Hill, New York, 1975.

Scammell, W. M. *International Monetary Policy*, St. Martin's, New York, 1961.

Solomon, Robert. *The International Monetary System 1945–1976: An Insider's View*. Harper & Row, New York, 1977.

Stein, Jerome L. *The Nature and Efficiency of the Foreign Exchange Market*. Princeton University Press, Princeton, NJ, 1962.

Tew, Brian. *The Evolution of the International Monetary System, 1945–1976*. Wiley, New York, 1977.

Teweles, Richard J., Charles V. Harlow, and Herbert L. Stone. *The Commodity Futures Game—Who Wins? Who Loses? Why?* 2nd ed., McGraw-Hill, New York, 1974.

A Textbook on Foreign Exchange. 2nd ed., Macmillan, London, 1969.

Yeager, Leland B. *The International Monetary Mechanism*. Holt, Rinehart, and Winston, New York, 1968.

Yeager, Leland B. *International Monetary Relations: Theory, History, and Policy*. Harper & Row, New York, 1966.

You Can Profit from a Monetary Crisis. Macmillan, New York, 1974.

Wasserman, Max J., Andreas Prindl, and Charles C. Townsend, Jr. *International Money Management*. American Management Association, New York, 1972.

Periodicals

Bank Credit Analyst. 1010 Sherbrooke St. West, Montreal, Canada H3A 2R7 (M).

The Economist. P.O. Box 2700, Woburn, MA 01888 (W). U.S. Address: 527 Marisur Ave., Room 1414, N.Y., N.Y. 10022 (W).

Euromoney. Nestor House, Playhouse Yard, London EC4V 5EX England (M).

Euromoney. Euromoney Publications, PLC, 14 Finsbury Circus, London, EC2, England (B-M).

Euromoney Currency Report. Nestor House, Playhouse Yard, London EC4V 5EX England (M).

Financial Times of Canada. 1885 Leslie Street, Dun Mills, Ont., M3B 3J4 Canada (W).

International Bank Credit Analyst. 1010 Sherbrooke St. West, Montreal, Canada H3A 2R7 (M).

International Currency Review. 11 Regency Place, London, SW1 2EA, England (B-M).

International Economic Conditions. Federal Reserve Bank of St. Louis, P.O. Box 442, St. Louis, MO 63166.

International Financial Statistics. International Monetary Fund, Washington, DC 20431 (M).

International Monetary Fund Staff Papers. International Monetary Fund, Washington, DC 20431 (3/yr).

International Money Markets and Foreign Exchange Rates. Harris Trust and Savings Bank, 111 West Monroe St., Chicago, IL 60690 (W).

International News Letter. Federal Reserve Bank of Chicago, Chicago, IL (W).

Journal of Commerce. 99 Wall St., New York, NY 10005 (D/M–F).

London Financial Times. 75 Rockefeller Plaza, New York, NY 10020 (D).

Main Economic Indicators. Organization for Economic Cooperation and Development, Suite 1207E, 1750 Pennsylvania Ave., Washington, DC 20006 (M).

Monetary Trends. Federal Reserve Bank of St. Louis, P.O. Box 442, St. Louis, MO 63166 (M).

The Money Manager. The Bond Buyer, One State Street Plaza, New York, NY 10004 (W).

National Economic Trends. Federal Reserve Bank of St. Louis, St. Louis, MO (M).

The Times of London. U.S. Address: 201 E. 43rd St., New York, New York, 10017 (D).

Wall Street Journal. (midwest ed.), 200 W. Monroe St., Chicago, IL 60606 (D/M–F).

World Financial Markets. Morgan Guaranty Trust Company, 23 Wall St., New York, NY 10004 (M).

FOREST PRODUCTS

Books and Articles

Clawson, Marion. *Decision Making in Timber Production*. Harvest and Marketing, Recourses for the Future, Washington, 1977.

Irland, Lloyd C., James P. Olmedo Jr., and Robert O. McMahon, eds. *Futures Trading: Its Uses in Forest Industry*. Yale School of Forestry, New Haven, CT, 1977.

Jackson, David H. *The Micro-Economics of the Timber Industry*. Westview, Boulder, CO, 1980.

Olmedo, James P., Jr. "Understanding the Lumber & Plywood Futures Markets." *Forecasting Commodity Prices*, Commodity Research Bureau, New York, 1975.

Rich, Stuart U. *Marketing of Forest Products*. McGraw-Hill, New York, 1970.

Rosen, Kenneth T. *Seasonal Cycles in the Housing Market: Patterns, Costs and Policies*. MIT Press, Cambridge, MA, 1979.

Studdard, Charles H. *Essentials of Forestry Practice*. 3rd ed., Wiley, New York, 1978.

Story, Harry. "An Economic Analysis of the Plywood Futures Market." Unpublished doctoral dissertation. University of Oregon, 1975.

Sumichrast, Michael and Maury Seldin. *Housing Markets, the Complete Guide to Analysis and Strategy for Builders, Lenders and Other Investors*. Dow Jones-Irwin, Homewood, IL, 1973.

Youngquist, W. G. and H. O. Fleisher. *Wood in American Life 1776–2076*. Forest Products Research Society, Madison, WI, 1977.

Periodicals

American Forests. 1319 18th St., N.W., Washington, DC 20036.

British Columbia Lumberman. 200 W. 12th Avenue, Vancouver, BC V6J 4M8 Canada.

Building Supply News. 5 S. Wabach Avenue Chicago, IL 60603.

Bureau of The Census, U.S. Dept. of Commerce, Washington, DC 20250. Construction Reports, Housing Charts. Construction Review. Lumber Production & Mill Stocks.

Crow's Weekly Letter. 834 S.W. St. Clair Avenue, Portland, OR 97205.

Forest Industries. 500 Howard St., San Francisco. CA 94105.

Logging Management. 300 W. Adams, Chicago, IL 60606.

Monthly Market Report. American Plywood Assoc., P.O. Box 71700, Tacoma, WA 98411.

NAHB Builder. 15th & M. Sts., N.W., Washington, DC 20005.

Plywood Statistics. American Plywood Assoc., P.O. Box 11700, Tacoma, WA 98411.

Random Lengths. Box 867, Eugene, OR 97401.

Statistics Canada, Main Building, Tunney's Pasture, Ottawa, Ontario K1A 016 Canada. Production, Shipments & Stocks on Hand of Sawmills in British Columbia.

U. S. Department of Agriculture, Washington, DC 20250. *The Demand and Price Situation for Forest Products 1979–1980. Forest Products. Forest Products Review. Stumpage Prices for Sawtimber Sold from National Forests, by Selected Species and Region.*

Western Timber Industry. 733 S.W. Oak St., Portland, OR 97205.

Western Wood Products Assoc. 1500 Yeon Building, Portland, OR 97204.

Wood & Wood Products. 300 West Adams St., Chicago, IL 60606.

World Wood. 500 Howard Street San Francisco, CA 94105.

GRAINS—GRAINS & SOYBEAN COMPLEX

Books

Ainsworth, Ralph M. *Profitable Grain Trading*. Traders Press, Greenville, SC, 1980.

Aldrich, Samuel R., Walter O. Scott, and Earl R. Leng. *Modern Corn Production*. 2nd ed., A & L, Champaign, IL, 1975.

Brody, Julius. *Fishery By-Products Technology*. AVI, Westport, CT, 1975.

Brown, William A. *Corn Price Action*. Comtab, Libertyville, IL, 1975.

Brown, William A. *Soybean Price Action*. Comtab, Libertyville, IL, 1976.

Brown, William A. *Wheat Price Action*. Comtab, Libertyville, IL, 1975.

Caldwell, B. E., ed. *Soybeans: Improvement, Production and Uses*. American Society of Agonomy, Madison, WI, 1973.

Chicago Board of Trade. *Grains: Production, Processing, Marketing*. Chicago Board of Trade, Chicago, IL, 1972.

Chicago Board of Trade. *The Sunflower Phenomenon*. Chicago Board of Trade, Chicago, IL, 1974.

Chicago Board of Trade. *The 1978 6-Year Soybean and Oilseed Statistical Summary*. Chicago Board of Trade, Chicago, IL, 1979.

Corbin, Frederick T. *World Soybean Conference II,* Proceedings, Westview Press, Boulder, CO, 1980.

Freivalds, John. *Grain Trade*. Stein & Day, New York, 1976.

Goldberg, Ray A. *Agribusiness Coordination: a Systems Approach to the Wheat, Soybean, and Florida Orange Economics*. Ballinger, Cambridge, MA, 1965.

Grennes, Thomas. *The Economics of World Grain Trade*. Praeger, New York, 1978.

Hill, Lowell D., ed. *World Soybean Research Conference. Proceedings,* Interstate, Danville, IL, 1976.

Houck, James P., Mary E. Ryan, and Abraham Subotnick. *Soybeans and Their Products—Markets, Models, and Policy*. University of Minnesota Press, Minneapolis, MN, 1972.

Inglett, George E., ed. *Corn: Culture, Processing, Products*. AVI, Westport, CT, 1970.

Inglett, George E., ed. *Wheat: Production and Utilization*. AVI, Westport, CT, 1974.

Inglett, George E. ed. *Symposium: Seed Proteins*. AVI, Westport, CT, 1972.

Lowell, Fred R. *Profits in Soybeans*. Keltner Statistical Service, Kansas City, MO, 1966.

Lowell, Fred R. *The Wheat Market*. Keltner Statistical Service, Kansas City, MO, 1968.

Merrill Lynch Pierce Fenner & Smith. *The Soybean*. Merrill Lynch, New York, April 1969.

Milner, Arthur R. *Grain Marketing, Pricing, Transportation*. West-Camp Press, Westville, OH, 1970.

Morgan, Dan. *Merchants of Grain*. Viking, New York, 1979.

Oster, Merrill J. *Multiply Your Money Trading Soybeans*. Investor Publications, Cedar Falls, IA, 1981.

Schonberg, James. *The Grain Trade, How It Works*. Exposition, Hicksville, NY, 1956.

Scott, Walter O., and Samuel R. Aldrich. *Modern Soybean Productions*. S & A Publications, Champaign, IL, 1970.

Smith, Allan K., and Sidney J. Circle, eds. *Soybeans: Chemistry and Technology*. AVI, Westport, CT, 1965.

Stansby, M. E., ed. *Fish Oils*. AVI, Westport, CT, 1967.

Turnbull, Roderick. *Turnbull on Grain*. Interstate, Danville, IL, 1978.

Weiss, Theodore J. *Food Oils and Their Uses*. AVI, Westport, CT, 1970.

Wills, Walter J. *Introduction to Grain Marketing*. Interstate, Danville, IL, 1972.

Articles

Emery, Walter L. "How to Analyze the Soybean Futures Market" *Forecasting Commodity Prices*. Commodity Research Bureau, New York, 1975.

Emery, Walter L. "Understanding the Soybean Oil Market" *Forecasting Commodity Prices*. Commodity Research Bureau, New York, 1975.

Emery, Walter L. "Understanding the Wheat Futures Market" *Forecasting Commodity Prices*. Commodity Research Bureau, New York, 1975.

Firch, Robert. "Futures Markets as Inverse Forecasters of Postharvest Prives for Storable Agricultural Commodities." *Review of Research in Futures Markets,* 62–73. Discussion, 74–89.

Fulton, Ralph Thomas. "The New Issues: Land, Water, Energy." *The Wilson Quarterly,* Summer 1981.

Gray, Roger. "The Chicago Wheat Futures Market: Recent Problems in Historical Perspective." *Food Research Institute Studies,* Stanford University Press, Stanford, CA, 1981, pp. 89–115.

Inkeles, David. "Understanding the Oats Futures Market." *Forecasting Commodity Prices.* Commodity Research Bureau, New York, 1975.

Konjiing, Kharisri Srisawasdi. "An Analysis of the Economic Performance of the U.S. Corn Futures Market." Unpublished doctoral dissertation, University of Minnesota, 1977.

Mackel, Chris. "An Investigation of the Effect of Institutional Factors on the Level of Agricultural Commodity Futures Trading, With Particular Reference to the London Grain Futures Market." 24–44. Discussion, 45–55.

Rausser, Gordon and Richard Just. "Agricultural Commodity Price Forecasting Accuracy: Futures Markets Versus Commercial Econometric Models." 116–153. Discussion, 154–165.

Tomek, William. "A Note on Historical Wheat Prices and Futures Trading." *Food Research Institute Studies,* Stanford University Press, Stanford, CA, 1971, pp. 109–113.

Periodicals

Commodity Futures Trading Commission *Stocks of Grain in Deliverable Positions* (W).

The Farmer-Stockman. P.O. Box 25125, Oklahoma City, OK 73125 (M).

Farm Futures. 534 N. Broadway, Milwaukee, WI 53202 (M).

Feedstuffs. P.O. Box 67, Minneapolis, Minnesota 55440.

Grain Age. 5100 Edina Industrial Blvd., Minneapolis, MN 55435.

Grain & Feed Journal. 141 W. Jackson Boulevard, Chicago, IL 60604.

Milling & Baking News. 4800 Main St., Room 650, Kansas City, MO 64112.

SOYA Bluebook. American Soybean Association, (A).

Soybean Digest. American Soybean Assoc., P.O. Box 158, Hudson, IA 50643 (M).

U.S. Agricultural Marketing Service. *Feed Market News* (W). *Grain Market News* (W). *National Stocks of Grain* (W).

U.S. Bureau of the Census—*Current Industrial Reports, Fats and Oils M20J and M20K* (M/A). *Flour Milling Products* (M).

U.S. Department of Agriculture, Crop Reporting Board. *Acreage. Agricultural Prices* (M). *Agricultural Statistics* (A). *Crop Production. Grain Stocks. Prospective Plantings. Soybean Stocks.*

U.S. Department of Agriculture, Economic Research Service *Fats and Oils—Outlook and Situation* (Q2). *Agricultural Outlook* (M).

U.S. Department of Agriculture, Economics, Statistics, and Cooperatives Service *Agricultural Prices* (M/A). *Agriculture Supply and Demand Estimates* (9/Yr). *Crop Production* (M/A). *Fats & Oils Situation. Feed Situation* (Q). *Grain Stocks* (Q). *Handbook of Agricultural Charts* (A). *Statistical Abstract of the United States* (A). *Wheat Situation* (Q).

U.S. Foreign Agricultural Service—Foreign Agriculture Circulars *Foreign Agriculture* (M). *Grain FG* (Irreg.). *Oilseeds and Products* (M).

GRAINS—AGRICULTURE YIELD ESTIMATION

Arizona Crop and Livestock Reporting Service. "Arizona Agricultural Statistics." Arizona

State Statistical Office, Economics, Statistics, and Cooperatives Service, Bulletin No. S-14, April 1979.

Baker, J. R. and E. M. Mikhail. "Geometric Analysis and Restitution of Digital Multispectral Scanner Data Arrays." Laboratory for Application of Remote Sensing, Purdue University, Information Note 052875, Lafayette, IN.

Cardenas, M., M. Blanchard, and M. Craig. "On The Development of Small Area Estimators Using LANDSAT Data as Auxiliary Information." Economics, Statistics, and Cooperatives Service, U.S. Department of Agriculture, Washington, DC, August 1978.

Cochran, William G. *Sampling Techniques*. 3rd ed. Wiley, New York, 1977.

Craig, M., R. Sigman, and M. Cardenas. "Area Estimates by LANDSAT: Kansas 1976 Winter Wheat." Economics, Statistics, and Cooperatives Service, U.S. Department of Agriculture, Washington, DC, August 1978.

Fleming, M. D., J. S. Berkebile, and R. Hoffer. *Computer Aided Analysis of LANDSAT-1 MSS Data: A Comparison of Three Approaches Including a Modified Clustering Approach. Proceedings* of the 1975 Symposium on Machine Processing of Remotely Sensed Data, Purdue University, West Lafayette, IN.

Gleason, C., R. Starbuck, R. Sigman, G. Hanuschak, M. Craig, P. Cook, and R. Allen. "The Auxiliary Use of LANDSAT Data in Estimating Crop Acreages: Results of the 1975 Illinois Crop Acreage Experiment." Statistical Reporting Service, U.S. Department of Agriculture, SRS-21, Washington, DC, October 1977.

Goldfeld, Stephen M. and Richard E. Quandt. *Nonlinear Methods in Econometrics*. North-Holland, Amsterdam.

Hanuschak, G. *LANDSAT Estimation with Cloud Cover Proceedings,* 1976 Symposium on Machine Processing of Remotely Sensed Data, Purdue University, West Lafayette, IN.

Hanuschak, G., R. Sigman, M. Craig, M. Ozga, R. Luebbe, P. Cook, D. Kleweno, and C. Miller. "Obtaining Timely Crop Area Estimates Using Ground Gathered and LANDSAT Data." Economics, Statistics, and Cooperatives Service, U.S. Department of Agriculture, Washington, DC, August 1979.

House, Carol C. "A Within-Year Growth Model Approach to Forecasting Corn Yields." Yield Research Branch, Statistical Research Division, Economics, Statistics, and Cooperatives Service, U.S. Department of Agriculture, Washington, DC.

House, Carol C. "Forecasting Corn Yields: A Comparison Study Using 1977 Missouri Data." Yield Research Branch, Statistical Research Division, Economics, Statistics, and Cooperatives Service, U.S. Department of Agriculture, Washington, DC.

Huddleston, H. F., and Wilson, W. W. *Research In Yield Forecasting, Proceedings.* National Conference of the Statistical Reporting Service, U.S. Department of Agriculture, Washington, DC, 74–88, 1975.

Larsen, Greg A. "Alternative Methods of Adjusting for Heteroscedasticity in Wheat Growth Data." Yield Research Branch, Statistical Research Division, Economics, Statistics, and Cooperative Service, U.S. Department of Agriculture, Washington, DC, 1978.

Larsen, Greg A. "Forecasting 1977 Kansas Wheat Growth." Yield Research Branch, Statistical Research Division, Economics, Statistics, and Cooperatives Service, U.S. Department of Agriculture, Washington, DC, 1978.

Larsen, Greg A. "1978 Kansas Winter Wheat Yield Estimation and Modeling." Yield Research Branch, Statistical Research Division, Economic, Statistics, and Cooperatives Service, U.S. Department of Agriculture, Washington, DC, 1979.

NASA. "LANDSAT Data Users Handbook." Goddard Space Flight Center, National Aeronautics and Space Administration Document No. 76SDS4258, September 1976.

NASA. "LANDSAT Newsletter." Goddard Space Flight Center, National Aeronautics and Space Administration Bulletin No. 27, November 15, 1979.

Nealon, Jack. "The Development of Within-Year Forecasting Models for Spring Wheat (Other Than Durum)." Research and Deveiopment Branch, Research Division, Statistical Reporting Service, U.S. Department of Agriculture, Washington, DC, 1976.

Nealon, Jack. "The Development of Within-Year Forecasting Models for Winter Wheat." Research and Development Branch, Research Division, Statistical Reporting Service, U.S. Department of Agriculture, Washington, DC, 1976.

Nealon, Jack. "Within-Year Spring Wheat Growth Models." Research and Development Branch, Research Division, Statistical Reporting Service, U.S. Department of Agriculture, Washington, DC, 1976.

Ozga, M., W. Donovan, and C. Gleason. *An Interactive System for Agricultural Acreage Estimates Using LANDSAT.* Proceedings of the 1977 Symposium on Machine Processing of Remotely Sensed Data, Purdue University, West Lafayette, IN.

Rockwell, Dwight A. "Illinois and Iowa Corn Growth Study—1977." Methods Staff, Estimates Division, Economic, Statistic, and Cooperatives Service, U.S. Department of Agriculture, Washington, DC, 1978.

Rockwell, Dwight A. "Nonlinear Estimation." Research and Development Branch, Research Division, Statistical Reporting Service, U.S. Department of Agriculture, Washington, DC, 1975.

Rockwell, Dwight A. and Nealon, Jack. "An Application of Nonlinear Estimation." presented at the Ninth International Biometric Conference, Research and Development Branch, Research Division, Statistical Reporting Service, U.S. Department of Agriculture, Washington, DC, 1976.

Swain, P. H. *Pattern Recognition: A Basic for Remote Sensing Data Analysis.* LARS information note 111572.

USDA. "Oven Methods for Determining Moisture Content of Grain and Related Agricultural Commodities." Grain Division, Consumer and Marketing Service, U.S. Department of Agriculture, GR Instruction 916-16, Washington, DC.

USDA, Crop Reporting Board. "Corn, Cotton and Soybeans Enumerator's Manual." Crop Reporting Board, Statistical Reporting Service, U.S. Department of Agriculture, Washington, DC, 1976.

USDA, Research Division. "Corn Growth Research Project Enumerator's Manual." Research Division, Statistical Reporting Service, U.S. Department of Agriculture, Washington, DC, 1976.

USDA, Research Division. "Corn Growth Research Project Laboratory Manual." Research Division, Statistical Reporting Service, U.S. Department of Agriculture, Washington, DC, 1976.

Wigton, W. "The Technology of LANDSAT Imagery and Its Value in Crop Estimation for the U.S. Department of Agriculture." Statistical Reporting Service, U.S. Department of Agriculture, Washington, DC, March 1976.

Wilson, Wendell W. "Preliminary Report On the Use of Time Related Growth Models in Forecasting Components of Corn Yield." Research and Development Branch, Research Division, Statistical Reporting Service, U.S. Department of Agriculture, Washington, DC, 1974.

GRAINS—CLIMATE

Angell, J. K. and J. Korshover. "Estimate of the Global Change in Tropospheric Temperature between 1958 and 1973." *Month. Weather Rev.*, **103**, November 1975, 1007–1012.

Angell, J. K. and J. Korshover. "Estimate of the Global Change in Temperature, Surface to 100 mb, between 1958 and 1975." *Month. Weather Rev.*, **105,** April 1977, 375–385.

Arkin, G. F., S. J. Maas, and C. W. Richardson. "Forecasting Grain Sorghum Yields Using Simulated Weather Data and Updating Techniques." *Trans. of ASAE,* **23**(3), 1980, 676–680.

Barr, A. J., J. H. Goodnight, and J. P. Sall. *SAS Users Guide.* 1979 ed., SAS Institute Inc., SAS Circle, Box 8000, Cary, NC 27511.

Berman, M. B. *Generating Gamma Distributed Variates for Computer Simulation Models.* Rand Corporation Publication, R-641-PR, Santa Monica, CA, 1971.

Bond, D. C. *Generating Daily Weather Values by Computer Simulation Techniques for Crop Yield Forecasting Models.* Research Division, SRS, U.S. Department of Agriculture, Washington, DC, 1979.

Borzenkova, I. I., K. Y. Vinnikov, L. P. Spirina, and D. I. Stekhnovskiy. "Change in Air Temperature in the Northern Hemisphere during the Period 1881–1975." *Meteorology and Hydrology,* (7), July 1976, 27–35.

Broecker, W. S. "Climatic Change: Are We On the Brink of a Pronounced Global Warming?" *Science,* **189,** August 1975, 460–463.

Bruhn, J. A., W. E. Fry, and G. W. Fick. "Simulation of Daily Weather Data Probability Distributions." *J. of Appl. Meteorol.*, 1980.

Bryson, R. A. "Drought In Sahelia." *Ecologist,* **3,** October 1973, 366–371.

Bryson, Reid A. "The Lessons of Climatic History." *Environ. Conserv.*, **2**(3), Autumn 1975.

Bryson, Reid A. and Gerald J. Dittberner. "A Non-Equilibrium Model of Hemispheric Mean Surface Temperature." *J. Atmos. Sci.*, **33,** November 1976, 2094–2106.

Bryson, Reid A. and Thomas B. Starr. "Chandler Tides in the Atmosphere." *J. Atmos. Sci.*, **34,** December 1977, 1975–1986.

Budyko, M. I. and K. Y. Vinnikov. "Global Warming." *Meteorol. Hydrol.* (7), July 1976, 16–26.

Charney, J. G. "Dynamics of Deserts and Drought in the Sahel." *Q. J. R. Meteorol. Soc.*, **101,** April 1975, 193–202.

Charney, Jule and Peter H. Stone. "Drought in the Sahara: A Biogeophysical Feedback Mechanism." *Science,* **187,** February 1975, 434–435. (See also: E.A. Ripley's comments and reply by Jule Charney and Peter H. Stone in *Science,* **191,** January 1976, 100–102.)

Conover, W. J. *Practical Nonparametric Statistics.* Wiley, New York, 1971.

Damon, Paul E. and Steven M. Kunen. "Global Cooling? No. Southern Hemisphere Warming Trends May Indicate Onset of the CO_2 'Greenhouse' Effect." *Science,* **193,** August 1976, 447–453.

Eddy, J. A. "The Maunder Minimum." *Science,* **192,** 1976, 1189–1202.

Eddy, J. A. "The Sun Since the Bronze Age." in Vol. 2: *Physics of Solar Planetary Envirnoments,* A G U, 1976, pp. 958–972.

Flohn, H. "Climate and Energy: A Scenario to a 21st Century Problem." *Clim. Change,* **1**(1), March 1977, 5–20.

Gentilli, J. *Geol. Mag.*, (article relating to temperature changes after volcanic eruptions), **85** (3), 1948, 172–175.

Gentilli, J. "The Climates of Australia and New Zealand." In *World Survey of Climatology,* Vol. 13, Elsevier Press, New York, 1971, pp. 157–161, 190–193.

Greenwood, J. A. and D. Durand. "Aids for Fitting the Gamma Distribution by Maximum Likelihood." *Technometrics,* **2,** 1960, 55–65.

Hare, F. K. *Climate Change, Food Production, and Interstate Conflict, Report of a Conference, Bellagio, Italy, June 1975*. Rockefeller Foundation, New York, 1976.

Humphrey, W. J. *Physics of the Air*. McGraw-Hill, New York, 1940.

Johnson, N. L., and S. Kotz. *Distributions in Statistics: Continuous Univariate Distributions*. Vols. 1 and 2, Wiley, New York, 1970.

Jones, J. W., R. F. Colwick, and F. D. Threadgill. "A Simulated Environmental Model of Temperature, Evaporation, Rainfall and Soil Moisture." *Trans. of ASAE 15,* 1972, 366–372.

Kellog, W. W. "Mankind as a Factor in Climate Change." in E. W. Erickson and L. Waverman, Eds., *The Energy Question,* University of Toronto Press, Toronto, 1974, pp. 241–258.

Kellogg, W. W. "Climatic Non-Limits to Growth." *Proceedings of Conference on Atmospheric Quality and Climatic Change,* University of North Carolina, Chapel Hill, NC, 1975, 76–89.

Kellogg, W. W. "Climate Change and the Influence of Man's Activities on the Global Environment." in S.F. Singer and D. Reidel, Eds., *The Changing Global Environment,* Dordrecht, Holland, 1975, pp. 13–23.

Kellogg, W. W. "Global Influences of Mankind on the Climate." in J. Gribbin, Ed., *Climate Change,* Cambridge University Press, Cambridge, England, in press.

Kellogg, W. W. "Anthropogenic Influences on Climate." World Meteorological Organization Technical Note, Geneva, in press.

Kellogg, W. W., J. A. Coakley, and G. W. Grams. "Effect of Anthropogenic Aerosols on the Global Climate." in *Proceedings of WMO/IAMAP Symposium on Long-Term Climatic Fluctuations,* (Norwich, U.K.), WMO Document 421, Geneva, 1975, 323–330.

Kellogg, W. W. and Schneider, S. H. "Climate Stabilization: for Better or for Worse?" *Science,* **186,** 1974, 1163–1172.

Kellogg, W. W. and Schneider, S. H. "Desertification, Human Activities, and Climate." in M. Glantz Ed., *Desertification,* Westview Press, Boulder, CO.

Lamb, H. H. *Climate: Present, Past and Future*. Vols. 1 and 2, Methuen, London, 1972 and 1977.

Landsberg, H. E. "Sahel Drought: Change of Climate or Part of Climate?" *Arch. Met. Geoph. Biokl.,* Ser. B, **23,** 1975, 193–200.

Landsberg, H. E. and Albert, J. M. "Some Aspects of Global Climatic Fluctuations." *Arch. Met. Geoph. Biokl.,* Ser. B, **23,** 1975, 165–176.

Leith, C. E. "The Natural and Radiatively Perturbed Troposphere." CIAP Monograph 4, Chapter 3, Report No. DOT-TST 75–54, September 1975.

Machta, L., K. Hanson, and C. D. Keeling, "Atmospheric Carbon Dioxide and Some Interpretations." in *Proceedings of the Hawaiian Meeting: The Fate of Fossil Fuel Carbon Dioxide,* January 1976, in press.

Manabe, Syukuro and Richart T. Wetherald. "The Effects of Doubling the CO_2 Concentration on the Climate of a General Circulation Model." *J. Atmos. Scie.,* **32,** January 1975, 3–15.

Marshall, J. R. "The Annual Volume of United States Precipitation and the Variation for the Period 1931–1971." *J. Geophys. Res.,* **81,** 1976, 4485–4486.

Mason, B. J. "Man's Influence on Weather and Climate." *J. Roy. Soc. Arts,* February 1977.

Matalas, N. C. "Mathematical Assessment of Synthetic Hydrology." *Water Resour. Res.,* **3**(4), 1967, 937–945.

Matthews, W. H., W. W. Kellogg, and G. D. Robinson, eds. *Man's Impact on the Climate.* MIT Press, Cambridge, MA, 1971.

Mavi, H. S. and J. E. Newman. "Crop Production Potential in India—A Water Availability Based Analysis." *Agric. Meteorol.,* **17,** 1976, 387–395.

Miles, M. K. and C. K. Follard. "Changes in the Latitude of the Climatic Zones of the Northern Hemisphere." *Nature,* **252,** 1974, 616.

Mock, Steve and W. D. Hibler. "The 21 Year Oscillation in Eastern North American Temperature." *Nature,* **261,** 1976, 484–486.

National Academy of Sciences, Panel on Water and Climate. "Climatic Change, and Water Supply." National Academy of Sciences, Washington, DC, 1977.

National Science Foundation, Interdepartmental Committee for Atmospheric Sciences. "Report of the Ad Hoc Panel on the Present Interglacial." National Science Foundation, ICAS 18b-FY75, August 1974.

National Academy of Sciences, Panel on Energy and Climate. "Energy and Climate." National Academy of Sciences, Washington, DC, 1977.

Newell, Reginald E. and Bryan C. Weare. "Factors Governing Tropospheric Mean Temperature." *Science,* **194,** December 1976, 1413–1414.

Nicks, A. D. "Stochastic Generation of the Occurrence, Pattern and Location of Maximum Amount of Daily Rainfall." Proceedings of the symposium on Statistical Hydrology, U.S. Department of Agriculture, Agricultural Research Service, Misc. Pub., Washington, DC, pp. 1275: 154–176.

Nicks, A. D., and J. F. Harp. "Stochastic Generation of Temperature and Solar Radiation Data." *J. Hydrol.,* **48,** 1980, 1–17.

Richardson, C. W. "Stochastic Simulation of Daily Precipitation, Temperature, and Solar Radiation." *Water Resour. Res.,* **17**(1), 1981, 182–190.

Salinger, M. J. "New Zealand Temperatures Since 1300 AD." *Nature,* **260,** March 1976, 310–311.

Salinger, M. J. and J. M. Gunn. "Recent Climatic Warming Around New Zealand." *Nature,* **256,** July 1975, 396–398.

Smagorinsky, Joseph. "Stratospheric Ozone Research and Effects." *Hearings Before the Subcommittee on the Upper Atmosphere,* United States Senate, Committee on Aeronautical and Space Sciences, Washington, DC, 94th Congress, 2d session, February 25–March 1, 1976.

Tanaka, M., B. C. Weare, A. R. Navato, and R. E. Newell. "Recent African Rainfall Patterns." *Nature,* **255,** 1975, 201–203.

Tucker, G. B. "Climate: Is Australia's Changing?" *Search,* **6,** August 1975, 323–328.

Tyson, P. D., T. G. J. Dyer, and M. N. Mametse. "Secular Changes in South African Rainfall: 1880 to 1972." *Q. J. R. Meteorol. Soc.,* **101,** 1975, 817–833.

United Nations, World Meteorological Organization. "Drought." WMO Special Environmental Report No. 5, United Nation, WMO No. 403, Geneva, 1975.

United Nations, World Meteorological Organization. "An Evaluation of Climate and Water Resources for Development of Agriculture in the Sudan-Sahelian Zone of W. Africa." WMO Special Environmental Report No. 9, United Nations, WMO No. 459, Geneva, 1976.

United Nations, World Meteorological Organization. "A Technical Report by the WMO Executive Committee Panel of Experts on Climatic Change." WMO Bulletin 26, Geneva, January 1977, 50–55.

van Loon, Harry and Jill Williams. "The Connection Between Trends of Mean Temperature and Circulation at the Surface: Part 1., Winter." *Month. Weather Rev.*, **104,** April 1976, 365–380.

van Loon, Harry and Jill Williams. "The Connection Between Trends of Mean Temperature and Circulation at the Surface: Part II., Summer." *Month. Weather Rev.*, **104,** August 1976, 1003–1011.

van Loon, Harry and Jill Williams. "The Connection Between Trends of Mean Temperature and Circulation at the Surface: Part III. Spring and Autumn." *Month. Weather Rev.*, **104,** December 1976, 1591–1596.

van Loon, Harry and Jill Williams. "Comparisons of Surface Changes in the Northern Hemisphere With the Upper Air and With the Antarctic in Winter." *Month. Weather Rev.*, **105,** May 1977, 636–647.

Wang, W. C., Y. L. Yung, A. A. Lacis, T. Mo, and J. E. Hansen. "Greenhouse Effects Due to Man-Made Perturbations of Trace Gases." *Science,* **194,** November 1976, 685–690.

Wetherald, Richard T. and Syukuro, Manabe. "The Effects of Changing the Solar Constant on the Climate of a General Circulation Model." *J. Atmos. Sci.,* **32,** November 1975, 2044–2059.

Willett, Hurd C. "Do Recent Climatic Fluctuations Portend an Imminent Ice Age?" *Geofis. Int.,* **14,** 1974, 265–302.

Willett, Hurd C. "The Prediction of Great Salt Lake Levels on the Basis of Recent Solar-Climatic Cycles." Paper presented at International Conference on Terminal Lakes, Weber State College, Ogden, UT, May 1977.

Willett, Hurd C. and John T. Prohaska. "Patterns, Possible Causes and Predictive Significance of Recent Climatic Trends of the Northern Hemisphere." The Solar Climatic Research Institute, pre-publication paper, Cambridge, MA, March 1977.

Winstanley, Derek. "Recent Rainfall Trends in Africa, the Middle East and India." *Nature,* **243,** June 1973, 464–465.

Winstanley, Derek. "Rainfall Patterns and General Atmospheric Circulation." *Nature,* **245,** September 1973, 190–194.

Winstanley, Derek. "Climate Changes and the Future of the Sahel." in M. H. Glantz, ed., *The Politics of a Natural Disaster: The Case of the Sahel Drought,* Praeger, New York, 1976, pp. 189–213.

LIVESTOCK

Books

Bakken, Henry H., ed. *Futures Trading in Livestock.* Mimir, Madison, WI, 1970.

Boykin, Calvin C. *Structural Characteristics of Beef Cattle Raising in the United States.* U.S. Department of Agriculture, Economics, Statistics and Cooperative Services, Washington, DC, 1980.

Bundy, Clarence E. *Swine Production.* 4th ed., Prentice-Hall, Englewood Cliffs, NJ, 1976.

Dunn, Dennis D. *Consistent Profits in June Live Beef Cattle.* Dunn & Hargitt, West Lafayette, IN, 1972.

Dunn & Hargitt. *Consistent Profits in Pork Bellies.* Dunn & Hargitt, West Lafayette, IN.

Dyer, Irwin A. and Clayton C. O'Mary. *The Feedlot.* 2nd ed., Lea & Febiger, Philadelphia, PH, 1977.

Ensminger, M. E. *Beef Cattle Science.* 5th ed., Interstate, Danville, IL, 1976.

Ensminger, M. E. *Swine Science*. 4th ed., Interstate, Danville, IL, 1970.

Juergenson, Elwood M. *Approved Practices in Beef Cattle Production*. 5th ed., Interstate, Danville, IL, 1980.

Leuthold, Raymond M. *An Analysis for the Basis for Live Beef Cattle*. University of Illinois, Department of Agriculture Economics, Urbana, IL, 1977.

Leuthold, Raymond M. and Parry Dixon, eds. *Livestock Futures Research Symposium, Proceedings*. Chicago Mercantile Exchange, Chicago, 1980.

McCoy, John H. *Livestock and Meat Marketing*. 2nd ed., AVI, Westport, CT, 1979.

Neumann, Alvin L. *Beef Cattle*. 7th ed., Wiley, New York, 1977.

O'Mary, Clayton C. and Irwin A. Dyer. *Commercial Beef Cattle Production*. 2nd ed., Lea & Febiger, Philadelphia, 1978.

Oster, Merrill J. *Professional Hedging Handbook: A Guide to Hedging Crops and Livestock*. Investor Publications, Cedar Falls, IA.

Oster, Merrill J. *Commodity Futures for Profit . . . A Farmers Guide to Hedging*. Investor Publications, Cedar Falls, IA, 1979.

Purcell, Wayne D. *Agricultural Marketing: Systems, Coordination, Cash and Futures Prices*. Reston, Reston, VA, 1979.

Rhodes, V. James. *The Agricultural Marketing System*. Grid, Columbus, OH, 1978.

Shepherd, Geoffrey S. and Gene A. Futrell. *Marketing Farm Products*. 6th ed., Iowa State University Press, Ames, IA, 1976.

United States General Accounting Office. *Beef Marketing: Issues and Concerns*. U.S. General Accounting Office, Washington, DC, 1978.

Van Arsdall, Roy N. *Structural Characteristics of the U.S. Hog Production Industry*. U.S. Department of Agriculture, Economics, Statistics & Cooperatives Service, Washington, DC, 1978.

Williams, Willard F. *Economics of the Livestock-Meat Industry*. MacMillan, New York, 1964.

Articles & Reports

Anderson, Davis W. *Analysis of Forward and Futures Contracting of Live Hogs*. Chicago Mercantile Exchange, Chicago, 1973.

Bear, Robert M. *Risk and Return Patterns of Overnight Holdings of Livestock Futures*. Chicago Mercantile Exchange, Chicago, 1972.

Billings, Terry Michael. *Cattle Feeding Strategies and Financial Risk*. Chicago Mercantile Exchange, Chicago, 1978.

Bobst, Barry W. *Effects of Location Basis Variability on Hedging of Livestock in the South*. Chicago Mercantile Exchange, Chicago, 1971.

Cox, P. Thomas and M. Anthony Wright. *The Feeder Cattle Information System*. Chicago Mercantile Exchange, Chicago, 1977.

Cekander, Danny. "Evaluating the Pork-Belly Futures Market Performance with Quarterly Predictive Model." Unpublished doctoral dissertation, University of Illinois at Urbana-Champaign, 1979.

Duke, R. Alton, Jr., *Hedging with Futures Contracts in the Southeast*. 1977.

Ehrich, R. L. "Cash-Futures Price Relationship for Live Beef Cattle." *Am. J. Agric. Econ.*, **51**, 24–40.

Fitz, James J. *Analysis of Alternative Hedging Programs for the Pork Belly Merchandiser*. Chicago Mercantile Exchange, Chicago, 1972.

Hartmann, Peter. "The Forward-Pricing Efficiency of the Live-Hog Futures Market." Unpublished doctoral dissertation, University of Illinois at Urbana-Champaign, 1979.

Johnston, Larry Dan. *A Dynamic Approach to Integrated Hedging for Feedlots in the Texas High Plains*. Chicago Mercantile Exchange, Chicago, 1976.

Larson, Arnold. "Price Prediction of the Egg Futures Market." *Food Research Institute Studies,* 1967, supplement, Stanford University Press, Stanford, CA, pp. 117–194.

Leuthold, R. M. "An Analysis of the Futures-Cash Price Basis for Live Beef Cattle." *North Cent. J. Agric. Econ.,* **1,** 47–52, 1979.

Leuthold, Raymond. "Evaluating the Price Performance of the Live Beef Cattle Futures Contract." *Illinois Agric. Econ.,* January 1975, 21–25.

Leuthold, Raymond, "The Price Performance on the Futures Market of a Nonstorable Commodity: Live Beef Cattle." *Am. J. Agric. Econ.,* May 1974, 271–279,

Longson, Ian Geoffrey. *Forecasting the Ontario Hog Basis and the Evaluation of Hedging Strategies for Ontario Hedgers*. Chicago Mercantile Exchange, Chicago, 1977.

Marousek, Gerald. *Review of Live Cattle Futures Contracts and Feasibility of Carcass and Feeder Contract*. Chicago Mercantile Exchange, Chicago, 1970.

Martin, Larry and Philip Garcia. "The Price-Forecasting Performance of Futures Markets for Live Cattle and Hogs: A Disaggregated Analysis." *Am. J. Agric. Econ.,* May 1981, 209–215.

Miller, Stephen Ernest. *Live Hog Futures Prices as Expected Prices in the Empirical Modeling of the Pork Sector*. Chicago Mercantile Exchange, Chicago, 1977.

Patterson, Harlan Ray. *Hypothetical Case Study—Bank Lending Policy of Hedged Collateral*. Chicago Mercantile Exchange, Chicago, 1972.

Paul, A. G. and W. T. Wesson. "Pricing Feedlot Services Through Cattle Futures." *Agric. Econ. Res.,* U.S. Department of Agriculture, RES-351, Washington, DC, 1967.

Peebles, Furman S. *Cash—Futures Price Relationships: Effects on Egg Hedging Strategies*. Chicago Mercantile Exchange, Chicago, 1975.

Pickett, John. *The Supply of Storage for Frozen Pork Bellies*. Chicago Mercantile Exchange, Chicago, 1972.

Powers, Mark. "An Economic Analysis of the Futures Market for Pork Bellies." Unpublished doctoral dissertation, University of Wisconsin, 1966.

Schaefer, Henry Hollis. *The Determination of Basis Patterns and the Results of Various Hedging Strategies for Live Cattle and Live Hogs*. Chicago Mercantile Exchange, Chicago, 1974.

Schlenker, Thomas S. *The Implications of Economic Factors and Market Information Reports for Various Swine Marketing Strategies with Implications to the Changing Patterns of Ohio Swine Marketing Habits*. Chicago Mercantile Exchange, Chicago, 1976.

Schuneman, Thomas R. *Hedging Strategies for Cattle Feeders*. Chicago Mercantile Exchange, Chicago, 1978.

Skadberg, J. M. and G. A. Futrell. "An Economic Appraisal of Futures Trading in Livestock." *J. Farm Econ.,* December 1966, 1485–1489.

Strader, Michael. "Evaluating the Live-Cattle Futures with a Quarterly Predictive Model." Unpublished doctoral dissertation, University of Illinois at Urbana-Champaign, 1979.

Periodicals

American Meat Institute Newsletter. P.O. Box 3556, Washington, DC 20007 (W).

Beef. 1999 Shepard Rd., St. Paul, MN 55116 (M).

Beef Business Bulletin. National Cattlemen's Association, 1001 Lincoln St., Denver, CO 80203 (W).

Better Beef Business. P.O. Box 16050, Kansas City, MO 64112 (M).

Big Farmer. 131 Lincoln Hwy., Frankfort, IL 60423 (11/yr).

Calf News. Suite 409, 18345 Ventura Blvd., Tarzana, CA 91356 (M).

The Drovers Journal. One Gateway Center, Kansas City, KS 66101 (W).

The Farmer-Stockman. P.O. Box 25125, Oklahoma City, OK 73125.

Feedlot Management. P.O. Box 67, Minneapolis, MN 55440 (M).

Feedstuffs. P.O. Box 67, Minneapolis, MN 55440 (W).

High Plains Journal. P.O. Box 760, Dodge City, KS 67801 (W).

Hog Farm Management. P.O. Box 67, Minneapolis, MN 55440 (M).

Livestock. P.O. Drawer 17F, Denver, CO 80217 (M).

National Hog Farmer. 1999 Shepard Rd., St. Paul, MN 55116 (M).

National Live Stock Producer. 733 N. Van Buren, Milwaukee, WI 53202 (9/yr).

Record Stockman. 4877 Packinghouse Rd., Denver, CO 80216 (W).

Southern Beef Producer. 229 Largo Dr., Nashville, TN 37211 (M).

U.S. Department of Agriculture, Crop Reporting Board, Room 0005, Washington, DC 20250. *Agriculture Prices. Agriculture Statistics* (A). *Cattle* (Jan, Jly). *Cattle on Feed* (M). *Cold Storage* (M). *Hogs & Pigs* (Q). *Livestock Slaughter Annual Summary* (A, March). *Meat Animals-Production, Disposition, and Income* (Annual, April).

U.S. Department of Agriculture, ESCS Information Staff, Publications Unit, Room 0054 - South, Washington, DC 20250. *Agricultural Supply and Demand. Feed Situation. Handbook of Agricultural Charts. Livestock and Meat Situation* (M). *Livestock Feed Relationships - National and Geographic* (A).

Superintendent of Documents, U.S. Government Printing Office, Washington, DC 20402. *Agricultural Outlook. Statistical Abstract of the United States.*

METALS

Books

Andrews, P. W. *The American Zinc Industry Under the Import Quota Program*. Department of Energy, Mines and Resources, Mineral Resources Branch, MR 107, Ottowa, 1970.

Butts, A., ed. *Copper—The Metal, Its Alloys and Compounds*. Rheinhold, New York, 1954.

Butts, Allison, ed. *Silver; Economics, Metallurgy and Use*. Reprint of 1967 ed., *Krieger, Huntington, NY, 1975.*

Charles River Associates. *Economic Analysis of the Copper Industry*. Cambridge, MA, 1969.

Charles River Associates. *Economic Analysis of the Silver Industry*. Cambridge, MA, 1969.

Gold, Gerald. *Financial Survival in the 70's with Gold, Silver, Platinum*. RHM Press, New York, 1975.

International Lead and Zinc Study Group. *Lead and Zinc: Factors Affecting Consumption*. International Lead and Zinc Study Group, November 1966.

McMahon, A. D. *Copper, A Material Survey*. U.S. Department of the Interior, Bureau of Mines, 1965.

Persons, Robert H. *The Investor's Encyclopedia of Gold, Silver and Other Precious Metals*. Random House, New York, 1974.

Prain, Sir R. *Copper: The Anatomy of an Industry*. Mining Journal Books, London, 1975.

Robie, Edward H., ed. *Economics of the Mineral Industries*. 2nd ed., American Institute of Mining, Metallurgical, and Petroleum Engineers, New York, 1964.

Rowe, J. W. F. *Price Mechanism For Lead and Zinc*. International Lead and Zinc Study Group, 1964.

U.S. Department of the Interior. "The U.S. Zinc Industry: A Historical Perspective." U.S. Department of the Interior, Bureau of Mines Information, Circular 8629, Washington DC, 1974.

U.S. Senate. "Inquiry into the Strategic and Critical Material Stockpiles of the United States," draft report of the National Stockpile and Naval Petroleum Reserves Subcommittee of The Committee on Armed Services, United States Senate, 88th Congress, 1st session.

Periodicals

American Bureau of Metal Statistics, New York. *Non-Ferrous Metal Data* (A).

American Metal Market. 7 East 12th Street, New York NY 10003 (D).

Annual Bullion Review. Samuel Montagu & Co., U.K.

Coin Age. Behn-Miller Publications Inc., Sparta, IL.

Coin World. Sidney Printing & Publishing Co., Sidney, OH.

Engineering and Mining Journal. McGraw-Hill (M)

J. Aron and Co., New York. *Annual Review and Outlook: Metal Markets* (A). *Gold Statistics and Analysis* (A). *Monthly Review* (M). *Silver Statistics and Analysis* (A).

The Metal Bulletin. Metal Bulletin Ltd. (W).

Metal Bulletin Monthly. 45/46 Lower Marsh, London, England.

Metal Statistics. Fairchild Publications, 7 East 12th Street, New York, NY 10003 (A).

Metals Week. McGraw-Hill, 1221 Avenue of the Americas, New York, NY 10020 (W).

Mining Annual Review. The Mining Journal Ltd.

Mining Journal. The Mining Journal Ltd. (W).

The Platinum Metals Review. Johnson-Matthey & Co., Ltd., London, England.

The Silver Market. Handy and Harman. New York, NY (A).

U.S. Bureau of Mines *Mineral Facts and Problems* (5 yrs.). *Mineral Industry Surveys, Copper* (M). *Mineral Industry Surveys, Gold and Silver Monthly* (M). *Mineral Industry Surveys, Platinum-Group Metals* (Q). *Minerals and Materials/A Monthly Survey* (M). *U.S. Bureau of the Mint Annual Report of the Director* (A). *Minerals Yearbook* (A).

World Metal Statistics. World Bureau of Metal Statistics, Birmingham.

Yearbook of the American Bureau of Metal Statistics. American Bureau of Metal Statistics, New York, NY (A).

ORANGE JUICE

Books and Articles

Dominick, B. A., and F. W. Williams. *Futures Trading and the Florida Orange Industry*. University of Florida, Agricultural Experiment Station, Gainesville, 1965.

Ward, Ronald. "Measuring Market Liquidity: Case Study of FCOJ Futures." *Commod. J.*, January/February 1975, 33–40.

Ward, Ronald. "Market Liquidity in the FCOJ Futures Market." *Am. J. Agric. Econ,* February 1974, 150–154.

Periodicals

Traders Position, New York Cotton Exchange (M).

Florida Department of Agriculture, *Florida Crop and Livestock Reporting Board Citrus Summary* (A).

Florida Citrus Association, *Weekly Statistics,* Triangle.

New York Cotton Exchange, *Traders Positions* (M).

USDA. *Fruit Situation Report* (Q). *Summary of the Citrus Fruit Industry* (A-Oct.). *Monthly Cold Storage Reports* (M).

POTATOES

Periodicals

Ag Marketer. P.O. Box 1467, 1110 S. 7th Avenue, Yakima, WA 98970.

American Potato Journal. The Potato Association of America, Orono, ME.

Chipper Snacker. 26250 Euclid Avenue, Suite 915, Euclid, OH 44132.

Fraser's Potato Newsletter. Harry Fraser, R.R. 1, Charlottetown, Prince Edward Isle, Canada.

The Journal of Commerce. 99 Wall Street, New York, NY 10005.

The Maine Potato Councellor. Presque Isle, ME.

The Packer. One Gateway Center, Kansas City, KS 66101.

Potato and Onion World. 3722 N. Cicero Avenue, Chicago, IL.

The Produce News. 333 Sylvan Avenue, Englewood Cliffs, NJ.

Spudlight. Potato Div., 1019 19th Street, N.W. Washington, DC 20036.

Tabb's Market Service, Inc., One Gateway Center, Suite 300, Kansas City, KS 66101.

United Fresh Outlook. Fruits & Vegetable Association Newswire, 1019 19th Street, N.W., Washington, DC 20036.

U.S. Department of Agriculture, Washington, DC 20250. Crop Reporting Board, Economic, Statistics & Cooperative Service—monthly reports of acreage, yield per acre and production. Cold Storage Section, Economic, Statistics & Cooperative Service—monthly cold storage figures on frozen French fried potatoes and other frozen potato products. "Potato Facts," Commodity Economics Division, Economic, Statistics & Cooperative Service—quarterly figures on potatoes.

U.S. Department of Agriculture (Maine), Presque Isle, ME 04769. Federal–State Market News Service, Federal Building—daily reports on the cash market situation in various key sections of the country and the industry.

U.S. Department of Agriculture (New York), Riverhead, NY 11901. Federal–State Market News Service, *L.I. Potato Report,* 127 E. Main Street—daily reports on the cash market situation in the various key sections of the country and the industry.

Statistics Canada, Agriculture Division, Ottawa, Canada K1A OT6. Fruit and Vegetable Production, Crops Section—monthly reports of (Canadian) potato storage and/or production.

Other Sources of Information

Food Research Institute, Stanford University, Stanford, CA.

University of Maine, Department of Agriculture & Resource Economics, Orono.

Smith, Ora, Ph.D. *Potatoes: Production, Storing Processing,* AVI, Westport, CT, 1968.

STOCK INDEX

Aber, John W. *Beta Coefficients and Models of Security Return.* Lexington Books, Lexington, MA, 1973.

Ansbacher, Max G. *The New Options Market.* Walker, New York, 1979.

Arrow, Kenneth J. *Essays in the Theory of Risk-Bearing.* Markham, Chicago, 1971.

Arrow, Kenneth J. "Limited Knowledge and Economic Analysis." *Am. Econ. Rev.,* March 1974, 1–10.

Balch, William F. "Market Guides, Indexes of Stock Prices Lately Have Multiplied." *Barron's,* September, 22, 1966.

Black, Fischer. "Equilibrium in the Creation of Investment Goods Under Uncertainty." In M. Jensen, ed., *Studies in the Theory of Capital Markets,* Praeger, New York, 1972, pp. 249–265.

Black, Fischer. "Capital Market Equilibrium with Restricted Borrowing." *J. Bus.,* July 1972, 444–455.

Black, Fischer. "Fact and Fantasy in the Use of Options." *Financ. Anal. J.,* July–August 1975, pp. 36–41, 61ff.

Black, Fischer. "The Pricing of Commodity Contracts." *J. Financ. Econ.,* **3,** 1976, 167–179.

Black, Fischer and Myron Scholes. "The Pricing of Options and Corporate Liabilities." *J. Polit. Econ.,* May 1973, 637–354.

Blume, Marshall E. "On the Assessment of Risk." *J. Finance,* March 1971, 1–10.

Blume, Marshall E. "Inflation, the Pricing of Capital Assets, and Real Balance Effects." In M. Sarnat, ed., *Inflation and Capital Markets,* Ballinger, Cambridge, MA, 1978, pp. 101–112.

Blume, Marshall E. "Betas and Their Regression Tendencies." *J. Finance,* June 1975, 785–795.

Blume, Marshall E., and Irwin Friend. "A New Look at the Capital Asset Pricing Model." *J. Finance,* March 1973, 19–33.

Blume, Marshall E., and Irwin Friend. "Risk, Investment Strategy and the Long-Run Rates of Return." *Rev. Econ. Stat.,* August 1974, 259–269.

Blume, Marshall E., and Irwin Friend. "The Asset Structure of Individual Portfolios and Some Implications for Utility Functions." *J. Finance,* May 1975, 585–603.

Blume, Marshall E., Jean Crockett, and Irwin Friend. "Stockownership in The United States: Characteristics and Trends." *Surv. Curr. Bus.,* November 1974, 16–40.

Board of Governors of the Federal Reserve System. KCBT's submission of proposal to begin trading a futures contract as a Stock Index. office correspondence, J. Charles Partee, January 25, 1980.

Bogle, John C. and Jan M. Twardowski. "Institutional Investment Performance Compared: Banks, Investment Counselors, Insurance Companies, and Mutual Funds." *Financial Anal. J.,* January/February, 1980, 33–40.

Bogue, Marcus C., III. "The Estimation and Behavior of Systematic Risk." unpublished doctoral dissertation, Stanford University, Stanford, CA, 1973.

Bowman, Robert G. "The Theoretical Relationship Between Systematic Risk and Financial (Accounting) Variables." *J. Finance,* June 1979, 617–630.

The Bureau of National Affairs. Securities Regulation and Law Report. Number 558, Washington, DC June 18, 1980, pp. 2, F-1 to F-12.

Burns, Joseph M. *A Treatise on Markets: Spot, Futures, and Options.* American Enterprise Institute for Public Research, Washington, DC, 1979.

Business Week. "The Popular Indexes Don't Tell The Whole Story." *Bus. Week,* July 7, 1973, 74–76.

Business Week. "The Death of Equities." *Bus. Week,* August 13, 1979, 54–59.

Calderwood, Stanford. "The Truth About Index Funds." *Financial Anal. J.,* July/August 1977, 36–47.

Capozza, Denis R. and Cornell, Bradford. "Treasury Bill Pricing in the Spot and Futures Markets." *Rev. Econ. Stat.,* November 1979, 513–520.

Castanias, Richard P., II. "Macroinformation and the Variability of Stock Market Prices." *J. Finance,* May 1979, 439–450.

Caves, Richard E. "Organization, Scale, and Performance of Grain Trade." *Food Research Institute Studies,* Vol, 16e, Stanford University Press, Stanford, CA, 1977–1978, 107–123.

Cesta, John R. "Financial Futures and the Social Benefit Hypothesis." Paper presented at the 1980 Midwest Finance Association, March 28, 1980.

Cohn, Richard A., Wilbur G. Lewellen, Ronald C. Lease, and Gary G. Schlarbaum. "Individual Investor Risk Aversion and Investment Portfolio Composition." *J. Finance,* May 1975, 605–620.

Cohen, Kalman J. and Bruce P. Fitch. "The Average Investment Performance Index." *Manage. Sci.,* February 1966, B195–215.

Cooley, Philip L., Rooney L. Roenfeldt, and Naval K. Modani. "Interdependence of Market Risk Measures." *J. Bus.,* July 1977, 356–363.

Cootner, Paul H. "Returns to Speculators: Telser Versus Keynes." *J. Polit. Econ.,* August 1960, 396–404.

Cootner, Paul H., ed. *The Random Character of Stock Market Prices.* Rev. ed. MIT Press, Cambridge, MA, 1964.

Cootner, Paul H. "Stock Market Indexes—Fallacies and Illusions." *Commer Financ. Chron.,* September, 29, 1966, 18–19.

Cootner, Paul H. "Speculation and Hedging." proceedings of a symposium on Price Effects of Speculation in Organized Commodity Markets, *Food Research Institute Studies,* supplement to Vol. 7, Stanford University Press, Stanford CA, 1967, pp. 65–104.

Cox, Charles, C. "Futures Trading and Market Information." *J. Polit. Econ.,* **84** (6), 1976, 1215–1237.

Cox, John C., and Ross, Stephen A. "The Valuation of Options for Alternative Stochastic Processes." *J. Financ. Econ.,* **3,** 1976, 145–66.

Dusak, Katherine. "Futures Trading and Investor Returns: An Investigation of Commodity Market Risk Premiums." *J. Polit. Econ.,* December 1973, 1387–1406.

Ederington, Louis H. "The Hedging Performance of the New Futures Markets." *J. Finance,* March 1979, 157–170.

Elia, Charles J. "Swinging Stocks: Market's Volatility Has Grown in Decade." *Wall Street J.,* March 30, 1979, 1.

Elton, Edwin J., Martin J. Gruber, and Thomas J. Urich. "Are Beta's Best?" *J. Finance,* December 1978, 1375–1384.

Fama, Eugene F. "Efficient Capital Markets: A Review of Theory and Empirical Work." *J. Finance,* May 1970, 383–417.

Fama, Eugene F. "Risk, Return, and Equilibrium." *J. Polit. Econ.,* January/February 1971, 30–54.

Fama, Eugene F., and Richard Roll. "Some Properties of Symmetric Stable Distributions." *J. Am. Stat. Assoc.,* September, 1968, 817–36.

Farrell, James L., Jr. "Analyzing Covariation of Returns to Determine Homogeneous Stock Groupings." *J. Bus.,* April 1974, 186–207.

Figlewski, Stephen and Stanley J. Kon. "Portfolio Management with Stock Index Futures." *Financ. Anal. J.,* January/February 1982, 3–11.

Financial Analysts Journal. "If You Can Forecast The Market, You Don't Need Anything Else." editor's comment, *Financ. Anal. J.,* January/February, 1980.

Financial World. "Protecting His Assets." professional profile, *Financ. World.,* June 15, 1980, 70–71.

Fisher, Lawrence. "Some New Stock-Market Indexes." *J. Bus.,* January 1966, 191–218.

Fisher, Lawrence, and James H. Lorie. "Some Studies of Variability of Returns on Investments in Common Stocks." *J. Bus.,* April 1970, 99–134.

Fosback, Norman G. *Stock Market Logic.* Institute for Econometric Research, Ft. Lauderdale, FL, 1976.

Fox, Edward A. "Comparing Performance of Equity Pension Trusts." *Financ. Anal. J.,* September/October 1968, 121–129.

Frankfurter, George M. "The Effect of 'Market Indexes' on the Ex-Post Performance of the Sharpe Portfolio Selection Model." *J. Finance,* June 1976, 949–955.

Frankfurter, George M., Herbert E. Phillips, and John P. Seagle. "Bias in Estimating Portfolio Alpha and Beta Scores." *Rev. Econ. Stat.,* August 1974, 412–414.

Frankfurter, George M., and Thomas J. Frecka. "Efficient Portfolios and Superfluous Diversification." *J. Financ. Quant. Anal.,* December 1979, 925–938.

Friend, Irwin. "The Demand for Risky Assets: Some Extensions." In Levy and Sarnat, eds., *Financial Decision Making Under Uncertainty,* Academic, New York, 1977.

Friend, Irwin and Marshall Blume. "Measurement of Portfolio Performance Under Uncertainty." *Am. Econ. Rev.,* September 1979, 561–575.

Friend, Irwin and M. E. Blume. "The Demand for Risky Assets." *Am. Econ. Rev.,* December 1975, 900–932.

Friend, Irwin, Yoram Landskroner, and Losq Etienne. "The Demand for Risky Assets Under Uncertain Inflation." *J. Finance,* December 1976, 1287–1297.

Goldman, M. Barry, Howard B. Sosin, and Lawrence A. Shepp. "On Contingent Claims That Insure Ex-Post Optimal Stock Market Timing." *J. Finance,* May 1979, 401–413.

Gonedes, Nicholas J. "A Note on Accounting-Based and Market-Based Estimates of Systematic Risk." *J. Financ. Quant. Anal.,* June 1975.

Gray, Roger W. "Price Effects of a Lack of Speculation." proceedings of a symposium on Price Effects of Speculation in Organized Commodity Markets, *Food Research Institute Studies,* supplement to Vol. 7, Stanford University Press, Stanford CA, 1967, pp. 177–94.

Gray, Roger W. *The Feasibility of Organized Futures Trading in Residential Mortgages.* Federal Home Loan Mortgage Corporation, Washington, DC, 1974.

Grossman, Sanford J. "The Existence of Futures Markets, Noisy Rational Expectations and Informational Externalities." *Rev. Econ. Stud.,* October 1977, 431–449.

Hadar, Josef and William R. Russell. "Rules For Ordering Uncertain Prospects." *Am. Econ. Rev.,* March 1969, 25–34.

Hanoch, G. and H. Levy. "Efficient Portfolio Selection With Quadratic and Cubic Utility." *J. Bus.,* April 1970, 181–189.

Hamada, Robert S. "The Effect of the Firm's Capital Structure on the Systematic Risk of Common Stocks." *J. Finance,* May 1972, 435–52.

Hieronymus, Thomas A. *Economics of Futures Trading.* Commodity Research Bureau, New York, 1971.

Hopewell, Michael H. "Comment: A Model of Capital Asset Risk." *J. Financ. Quart. Anal.,* March 1972.

Houthakker, Hendrick S. "The Scope and Limits of Futures Trading." In *The Allocation of Economic Resources, Essays in Honor of Bernard Francis Haley,* Stanford University Press, Stanford, CA, 1959.

Houthakker, Hendrik S. "Systematic and Random Elements in Short Term Price Movements. Frontiers in Uncertainty Theory," *Am. Econ. Rev.,* **51,** 1961, 164–72.

Hurtado-Sanchez, Luis. "Short Interest: Its Influence As A Stabilizer Of Stock Returns." *J. Financ. Quant. Anal.,* December 1978, 965–985.

Jensen, Michael C. "Random Walks: Reality or Myth–Comment." *Financ. Anal. J.,* November/December 1967, 77–85.

Jensen, Michael C. "Risk, the Pricing of Capital Assets, and the Evaluation of Investment Portfolios." *J. Bus.,* April 1969, 167–247.

Johnston, J. *Econometric Methods.* McGraw-Hill, New York, 1963.

Joehnk, Michael D. and William J. Petty, II. "The Interest Sensitivity of Common Stock Prices." *J. Portfolio Manag.,* Winter 1980, 19–25.

King, Benjamin F. "Market and Industry Factors in Stock Price Behavior." *J. Bus.,* January 1966, 139–90.

Klemkosky, Robert C. and Terry S. Maness. "The Impact of Options on the Underlying Securities." *J. Portfolio Manage.,* Winter 1980, 12–18.

Janssor, Solveig. "The New Appeal of Specialized Managers." *Inst. Investor,* March 1980, 67–74.

Kon, Stanley J. and Frank C. Jen. "The Investment Performance of Mutual Funds: An Empirical Investigation of Timing, Selectivity and Market Efficiency." *J. Bus.,* April 1979, 263–289.

Kubarych, Roger M. *Foreign Exchange Markets in the United States.* Federal Reserve Bank of New York, New York, 1978.

Latane, Henry A. and Donald L. Tuttle. "Criteria For Portfolio Building." *J. Finance,* September 1967, 359–73.

Latane, Henry A. and Donald L. Tuttle. *Security Analysis and Portfolio Management.* Ronald Press, New York, 1970.

Latane, Henry A., Donald L. Tuttle, and William E. Young. "Market Indexes and Their Implications for Portfolio Management." *Financ. Anal. J.,* September/October 1971, 75–85.

Latane, Henry A. and William E. Young. "Test of Portfolio Building Rules." *J. Finance,* September 1969, 595–612.

Lee, Cheng F. "On the Relationship Between the Systematic Risk and the Investment Horizon." *J. Financ. Quant. Anal.,* December 1976, 803–814.

Levy, Haim. "Equilibrium in an Imperfect Market: A Constraint on the Number of Securities in the Portfolio." *Am. Econ. Rev.,* September 1978, 643–58.

Levy, Haim. "The CAPM and Beta in an Imperfect Market." *J. Portfolio Manage.,* Winter 1980, 5–11.

Levy, Robert A. "Random Walks: Reality or Myth." *Financ. Anal. J.,* November/December 1967, 69–67.

Levy, Robert A. "On The Short-Term Stationarity of Beta Coefficients." *Financ. Anal. J*, November/December 1971, 55–62.

Lintner, John. "Inflation and Security Returns." *J. Finance*, May 1975, 259–280.

Lorie, James H. and Mary T. Hamilton. *The Stock Market: Theories and Evidence*. Richard D. Irwin, Homewood, IL, 1973.

Lorie, James H. "The Second Great Crash." *Wall Street J.*, June 2, 1980.

Mains, Norman E. "Risk, The Pricing of Capital Assets, and The Evaluation of Investment Portfolios: Comment." *J. Bus.*, July 1977, 371–384.

Malkiel, Burton Gordon. *The Term Structure of Interest Rates: Expectations and Behavior Patterns*. Princeton University Press, Princeton, NJ, 1966.

Malkiel, Burton G. "The Capital Formation Problem in the United States." *J. Finance*, May 1979, 291–306.

Markowitz, H. "Portfolio Selection." *J. Finance*, March 1952, 77–91.

Murray, Roger, F. "A New Role For Options." *J. Financ. Quant. Anal.*, November 1979, 895–899.

New York Stock Exchange. *NYSE 1979 Fact Book*. New York Stock Exchange, June 1979.

New York Stock Exchange. *Stocks and Specialists*. New York Stock Exchange, October 25, 1978.

Niederhoffer, Victor and M. F. M. Osborne. "Market Making and Reversal on the Stock Exchange." *J. the Am. Stat. Assoc.*, December 1966, 897–916.

Niederhoffer, Victor and Richard Zeckhauser. "Market Index Futures Contracts." *Financ. Anal. J.*, January/February 1980, 49–55.

Officer, R. R. "The Distribution of Stock Returns." *J. Am. Stat. Assoc.*, December 1972, 807–812.

Officer, R. R. "The Variability of the Market Factor of the New York Stock Exchange." *J. Bus.*, (46), 1973, 434–53.

Pease, Robert H. and Lewis O. Kerwood. *Mortgage Banking*. 2nd ed., McGraw-Hill, New York, 1965.

Pettit, R. Richardson and Randolph Westerfield. "A Model of Capital Asset Risk." *J. Financ. Quant. Anal.*, March 1972.

Pettit, R, Richardson and Randolph Westerfield. "Using the Capital Asset Pricing Model And the Market Model to Predict Security Returns." *J. Financ. Quant. Anal.*, September 1974, 579–607.

Rendleman, Richard J. and Christopher E. Carabini. "The Efficiency of the Treasury Bill Futures Market." *J. Finance*, September 1979, 895–914.

Renshaw, Edward F. "Portfolio Balance Models in Perspective: Some Generalizations That Can Be Derived from the Two-Asset Case." *J. Financ. Quant. Anal.*, June 1967, 123–49.

Rolfo, Jacques. "Optimal Hedging Under Price and Quantity Uncertainty: The Case of A Cocoa Producer." *J. Polit. Econ.*, February 1980, 100–116.

Rothstein, Marvin. "On Geometric and Arithmetic Portfolio Performance Indexes." *J. of Financ. and Quant. Anal.*, September 1972, 1983–1992.

Rubinstein, Mark. "The Strong Case for the Generalized Logarithmic Utility Model as the Premier Model of Financial Markets." in Levy and Sarnat, eds., *Financial Decision Making Under Uncertainty*, Academic, New York, 1977.

Rudnitsky, Howard. "On the Razor's Edge of a Financial Panic." *Forbes*, March 31, 1980, 29–30.

Ryan, James C. and Mack Dritzman. "Catch 500: The Irony in Indexing." *J. Portfolio Manage.*, Winter 1980, 30–32.

Sarnat, Marshall. "Capital Market Imperfections and the Composition of Optimal Portfolios." *J. Fin.*, September 1974, 1241–53.

Schlarbaum, Gary G., Wilbur G. Lewellen, and Ronald C. Lease. "Realized Returns on Common Stock Investments: the Experience of Individual Investors." *J. Bus.*, April 1978, 299–325.

Schulz, John W. "Pale Blue Chips." *Barron's,* February 11, 1980, 11ff.

Scott, Elton, and Stewart Brown. "Biased Estimators and Unstable Betas." *J. Finance,* March 1980, 49–55.

Sharpe, William F. *Portfolio Theory and Capital Markets*. McGraw-Hill, New York, 1970.

Sharpe, William F. "The Capital Asset Pricing Model: A 'Multi Beta' Interpretation." In Levy and Sarnat, eds, *Financial Decision Making Under Uncertainty,* Academic, New York, 1979, pp. 127–135.

Sharpe, William F. and Guy M. Cooper. "Risk-Return Classes of New York Stock Exchange Common Stocks, 1931–1967." *Fin. Anal. J.*, March/April 1972, 46 ff.

Simkowitz, Michael A. and William L. Beedles. "Diversification in a Three-Moment World." *J. Financ. Quant. Anal.*, December 1978, 927–941.

Simonson, Donald G. "The Speculative Behavior of Mutual Funds." *J. Fin.*, May 1972, 381–391.

Smith, Keith V. "Stock Price and Economic Indexes for Generating Efficient Portfolios." *J. Bus.*, April 1964, 326–336.

Starr, Roger. *Housing and the Money Market*. Basic Books, New York, 1975.

Stevens, Guy V. G. "On the Impact of Uncertainty on the Value and Investment of the Neoclassical Firm." *Am. Econ. Rev.*, June 1974, 319–336.

Stigum, Marcia. *The Money Market: Myth, Reality and Practice*. Dow-Jones-Irwin, Homewood, IL, 1978.

Stoll, Hans R. "Commodity Futures and Spot Price Determination and Hedging in Capital Market Equilibrium." *J. Financ. Quant. Anal.*, November 1979, 873–894.

Stone, Bernell K. *Risk, Return and Equilibrium*. MIT Press, Cambridge, MA, 1970.

Stone, James M. *One Way for Wall Street*. Little, Brown, Boston, 1975.

Telser, Lester G. and Harlow N. Higinbotham. "Organized Futures Markets: Costs and Benefits." *J. Polit. Econ.*, October 1977, 969–1000.

Tsiang, S. C. "The Rationale of the Mean-Standard Deviation Analysis, Skewness Preference, and the Demand for Money." *Am. Econ. Rev.*, June 1972, 354–371.

Weiner, Neil S. "The Hedging Rationale for a Stock Index Futures Contract." *J. Futures Mark.*, **1,** (1), 59–76, 1981.

Willis, Parker B. *The Federal Funds Market: Its Origin and Development*. Federal Reserve Bank of Boston, Boston, 1970.

Winikates, James. *GNMA Mortgage Futures Market: a Financial Manager's Guide*. Financial Society for Savings Institutions, Chicago, 1977.

Yeaney, Woodrow Wilson, Jr. "Investment Characteristics of Commodity Futures Contracts." Unpublished doctoral dissertation, Pennsylvania State University, 1978.

Yule, G. Udny, and M. C. Kendall. *An Introduction to the Theory of Statistics*. Charles Griffin, London, 1965.

Young, William E. and Robert H. Trent. "Geometric Mean Approximations of Individual Security and Portfolio Performance." *J. Financ. Quant. Anal.*, 179–199.

SUGAR

Adamson, A. H. *Sugar without Slaves: The Politics of British Guiana 1838–1904*. Yale University Press, New Haven, 1972.

Artschwager, E. and E. W. Brandes. *Sugar Cane: Origin, Classification, Characteristics, and Descriptions of Representative Clones*. U.S. Department of Agriculture, Handbook No. 122, Washington, DC, 1958.

Ballinger, R. A. *A History of Sugar Marketing*. U.S. Department of Agriculture, Economic Research Service, Agricultural Economic Report No. 197, Washington, DC, 1971.

Ballinger, Roy A. *A History of Sugar Marketing through 1974*. U.S. Department of Agriculture, Economics, Statistics and Cooperative Service, Agricultural Economic Report No. 328, Washington, DC, 1978.

Ballinger, R. A. *The Structure of the US Sweetener Industry*. U.S. Department of Agriculture, Economic Research Service, Agricultural Economic Report No. 213, Washington, DC, 1971.

Barnes, A. C. *The Sugar Cane*. Interscience, New York, 1964.

Bates, Thomas, H., Andrew Schmitz. *A Spatial Equilibrium Analysis of the World Sugar Economy*. Gianini Foundation, California Agricultural Experiment Station, Monograph No. 23, Berkeley, CA, May 1969.

Birch, G. G., L. F. Green, and C. B. Coulson. *Glucose Syrups and Related Carbohydrates*. Elsevier, Amsterdam, 1970.

Birch, G. G., L. F. Green, and C. B. Coulson. *Sweetness and Sweeteners*. Applied Science, London 1971.

Bogosian, Theodore. *Sweet Solutions*. WGBH Educational Foundation, 1979.

Bohall, Robert, et al. *The Sugar Industry's Structure Pricing and Performance*. Commodity Economics Division, Economic Research Service, U.S. Department of Agriculture, Agriculture Economic Report No. 363, Washington, DC, 1977.

Coleman, O. H. "Syrup and Sugar from Sweet Sorghum." In J. S. Wall, and W. M. Ross, eds., *Sorghum Production and Utilization*, AVI, Westport, CT, 1970, pp. 416–440.

Commodity Research Bureau, Inc. *Commodity Year Book*. New York (Annual).

Daniels, R. *Sugar Substitutes and Enhancers*. Noyes Data Corporation, Park Ridge, NJ.

Deerr, N. *The History of Sugar*. 2 Vols., Chapman and Hall, London, 1949–1950.

Dunn, R. S. *Sugar and Slaves: The Rise of the Planter Class in the English West Indies, 1624–1713*. Jonathan Cape, London, 1973.

Edelman, J. "The Role of Sucrose in Green Plants." In J. Yudkin, J. Edelman, and L. Hough, eds., *Sugar: Chemical, Biological and Nutritional Aspects of Sucrose*, Butterworths, London, 1971, pp. 95–102.

Fisher, E. "What Is the Significance of the World Sugar Market"? *Sugar Azucar*, **62**, (1), 1967, 29–30.

FAO, *The World Sugar Economy in Figures, 1880–1959*. Food and Agriculture Organization, Commodity Reference Series No. 1, Rome, 1961.

F. O. Licht's International Sugar Report. Ratzeburg, Germany.

F. O. Licht's World Sugar Statistics 1980/1981. Ratzeburg, Germany.

Hagelberg, G. B. "Economic Comparisons: the Cautionary Case of Beet and Cane Sugar." *Economy and History*, **16**, 1973, 37–54.

Hagelberg, G. B. *The Caribbean Sugar Industries: Constraints and Opportunities*. Antilles Research Program, Yale University, New Haven, CT, 1974.

Han, Y. W., C. E. Dunlap, and C. D. Callihan. "Single Cell Protein from Cellulosic Wastes." *Food Technol.*, **56**, February, 1971, pp. 32–5.

Harris, S., and I. Smith. *World Sugar Markets in a State of Flux*. Trade Policy Research Centre, London, 1973.

Hickson, J. L. "Utilisation of Sucrose by the Chemist." in J. Yudkin, J. Edelman, and L. Hough, ed., *Sugar: Chemical, Biological and Nutritional Aspects of Sucrose*, Butterworths, London, 1971, pp. 60–8.

Honig, P. *Principles of Sugar Technology*. 3 Vols., Elsevier, Amsterdam, 1953, 1959, 1963.

Hoynak, P. X. and G. N. Bollenback. *This Is Liquid Sugar*. 2nd ed. Refined Syrups and Sugars, Inc., Yonkers, 1966.

Hugot, E. *Handbook of Cane Sugar Engineering*. 2nd ed., Elsevier, Amsterdam, 1972.

Humbert, R. P., *The Growing of Sugar Cane*. Rev. ed. Elsevier, Amsterdam, 1968.

Inkeles, David M. "How to Analyze the World Sugar Futures Market". *Forecasting Commodity Prices*, Commodity Research Bureau, New York, 1975.

International Sugar Council, *Sugar Yearbook*. ISC/O. London, 1956.

International Sugar Council, *ISC/O. The World Sugar Economy: Structure and Policies*. 2 vols., London, 1963.

International Sugar Organization, ISO. *Statistical Bulletin*. London, England.

Johnson, R. T., et al. *Advances in Sugar Beet Production: Principles and Practices*. Iowa State University Press, Ames, 1971.

Joshi, B. C. and N. Gopinathan. *Sugar Yielding Palms as a Potential Source of Sugar Supply." Proceedings, International Society of Sugar Cane Technologists*, 9th Congress, Vol. 2, 1956, pp. 287–98.

Josling, T, and S. Harris. "The Revolution in World Commodity Markets." *Round Table*, (254), 1974, pp. 187–202.

Junk, W. R. and H. M. Pancoast. *Handbook of Sugars for Processors, Chemists and Technologists*. AVI, Westport, CT, 1973.

Labys, Walter C., M. Ishaq Nadiri, and Jose Nunex Del Arco. *Commodity Markets and Latin American Development*. Ballinger, Cambridge, MA, 1980.

Lewis, W. A. "A Review of Economic Development." *Am. Econ. Rev., Papers and Proceedings*, **55**, Part 2, 1965, 1–16.

Lyle, O. *Technology for Sugar Refinery Workers*. 3rd ed. Chapman and Hall, London, 1957.

Madsen, G. B. and E. E. Norman. "New Specialty Glucose Syrups." In G. G. Birch and L. F. Green, eds., *Molecular Structure and Function of Food Carbohydrate*, Applied Science, London, 1973, pp. 50–64.

Mauch, W. "The Chemical Properties of Sucrose." *Sugar Technol. Rev.*, **1**, 1971, 239–90.

McGinnis, R. A. *Beet-Sugar Technology*. 2nd ed., Beet Sugar Development Foundation, Fort Collins, CO, 1971.

Meade, G. P. *Spencer-Meade Cane Sugar Handbook*. 9th ed., Wiley, New York, 1963.

Methot, J. R., and N. Rompre. *Maple Sugar Industry in Quebec*. Horticultural Service, Department of Agriculture, Quebec, 1953.

Nearing, H. and S. *The Maple Sugar Book*. John Day, New York, 1950.

Parker, K. J. "The Role of Sucrose Syrups in Food Manufacturing." in G. G. Birch, L. F. Green, and C. B. Coulson, eds., *Glucose Syrups and Related Carbohydrates*, Elsevier, 1970, pp. 58–85.

Paturau, J. M. *By-Products of the Cane Sugar Industry*. Elsevier, Amsterdam, 1969.

Preston, T. R. "Beef and Milk Production from Sugar Cane." *CIDA Seminar on Sugar Cane as Livestock Feed*, Barbados, January 1973, pp. 30–31.

Sheridan, R. B. *Sugar and Slavery: An Economic History of the British West Indies, 1623–1775*. Caribbean Universities Press, Barbados, 1974.

South African Sugar Association, Experiment Station. *Annual Report, 1972/73*. Mount Edgecombe, Natal.

Stevenson, G. C. *Genetics and Breeding of Sugar Cane*. Longmans, London, 1965.

Stone, M. J. C. "The Trade View of the Market." in *The Future of Sugar,* International Sweetener and Alcohol Conference, 1980.

Tewes, T. "Sugar: A Short-Term Forecasting Model for the World Market, With a Forecast of the World Market Price for Sugar in 1972–1973." *The Business Economist,* **4** Summer 1972, 89–97.

Timoshenko, V. P. and B. C. Swerling. *The World's Sugar: Progress and Policy*. Stanford University Press, Stanford, CA, 1957.

U.S. Congress. *Sugar and Other Sweetners: An Industry Assessment*. report to the Congress of the United States by the Comptroller General, 1979.

USDA. *Sugar and Sweetener Outlook and Situation*. U.S. Department of Agriculture, Economics and Statistics Service, Washington, DC (A).

USDA. "Foreign Agricultural Circular." U.S. Department of Agriculture Foreign Agricultural Service, Washington, DC.

Vinton, A. "World Sugar Outlook for the 1970s." *Sugary Azucar,* **64** (12), 1969, 13–14, 18.

Vinton, A. "Sugar prospects: Opportunities and problems." *Sugar y Azucar,* **66,** (4), 1971, 30–32.

Vinton, A. "The Prospects and Problems of Sugar." *International Symposium Devoted to the Situation of the World Sugar Economy and Its Future Development,* Confederation Internationale des Betteraviers Europeens/Comite Europeen des Fabricants de Sucre, Brussels, 1971.

Vinton, A. "Ruckgand des Zuckerpreises um 40% in zwanzig Jahrem." *Zucker,* **25,** (6), 1972 185–89.

Vinton, A. "How Cheap Is Sugar!" *Sugar y Azucar,* **67,** (9), 1972, 26–30, 40.

Vinton, A. "The Future of Sugar Consumption in Latin America." *Sugar y Azucar,* **68,** (1), 1973, 36–7.

Vinton, A. "Sugar: Leaner and Dearer Years Ahead." *Zietschrift fur die Zuckerindustrie,* **23,** (5), 1973, 267–70.

Vinton, A. "Steigerung des Zuckerangebots: Eine Herausforderung fur die Zuckerruben- und Zuckerrohrproduzenten." *Zeitschrift fur die Zuckerindustrie,* **23,** (7), 1973, 383–6.

Vinton, A. "Zucker Wird Teures." *Zucker,* **26,** (10), 1973, 548–51.

Vinton, A. "Sugar in Latin America and Africa: Needs and opportunities." *Sugar y Azucar,* **69,** (1), 1974, 23–6.

Vinton, A., and F. Pignalosa. *Trends and Forces of World Sugar Consumption*. FAO, Commodity Bulletin Series No. 32, Rome, 1961.

Willits, C. O. *Maple Sirup Producers Manual*. U.S. Department of Agriculture, Agricultural Research Service, Agriculture Handbook No. 134, Washington, DC, 1965.

Working, Holbrook. "The Theory of the Price of Storage." *American Economic Review,* **39,** 1949, 1254–1262.

World Sugar Journal. Berkshire, England

Wymer, C. R. *Estimation of Continous Time Models with an Application to World Sugar Market*. mimeographed, London School of Economics and Political Science, 1972.

Yates, R. A. "Best Alternative Renewable Raw Material for Alcohol Production." in *The Future of Sugar,* International Sweetener and Alcohol Conference, 1980.

Yedkin, J. "Sugar as a Food: An Historical Survey." in J. Yedkin, J. Edelman, and L. Hough, eds., *Sugar: Chemical, Biological and Nutritional Aspects of Sucrose,* Butterworths, London, 1971, pp. 11–17.

GLOSSARY

ACCUMULATE: To establish and to add to a position over a period of time.

ACREAGE ALLOTMENT: A voluntary limitation on the number of acres farmers plant of a given crop, established under the federal farm program to stimulate production of certain crops of limited supply and reduce production of others in ample supply; one aspect of a larger acreage diversion policy of the farm program.

ACREAGE RESERVE: An arrangement under which farmers agree to withdraw a stated acreage of cropland from production for a specified number of years. This is a conservation measure under the Soil Bank Program, which provides for annual compensation for any loss of income.

ACTUALS: Physical commodities, as distinguished from futures contracts; also cash commodities. Those commodities that are readily available. More commonly referred to as "physicals" in London.

AFLOATS: Commodities loaded in vessels that are in harbor or in transit but have not arrived at destination.

AMORTIZE: An artificial method of allocating, over the life of the instrument, income received or given up at maturity.

ANIMAL UNIT: The amount of grain or feed necessary for an animal to attain full growth.

ARBITRAGE: The simultaneous purchase of one commodity contract against the sale of another to take advantage of a price disparity. When this procedure involves actuals and futures it is known as *hedging*. If only futures are involved it is known as *spreading*. Whereas arbitrage includes the simultaneous purchase and sale of different delivery months of the same commodity, the same delivery month on two different exchanges, and the purchase of one commodity against the sale of another commodity, it also implies the existence of a well-defined relationship between the two items as well as limited risk. When commodities are arbitraged in different countries, price distortions implicitly involve currency variations.

ASSAY: The independent evaluation of the composition of a metal. Registered brands must conform to a typical assay for the brand in question.

ASSOCIATED PERSON: A person associated with any futures commission merchant (or with any agent of a futures commission merchant), commodity trading advisor, or commodity pool operator as a partner, officer, or employee. Also, any person occupying a similar status or performing similar functions, in any capacity that involves (a) the solicitation or acceptance of customers' orders (other than in a clerical capacity) or (b) the supervision of any person or persons so engaged.

AT-THE-MARKET: An order to buy or sell at the best price obtainable when the order reaches the trading floor. Speed of execution is the most important consideration. Also called a *market order*.

AUCTIONS: Periodic events dominated by the IMF and the U.S. Treasury (GSA) in which gold or silver is auctioned. The IMF auction was designed to help underdeveloped countries acquire gold to "strengthen" their currencies; the Treasury auctions have been designed to improve the U.S. balance of payments.

AUTHENTICITY: The actual gold or metal content in any lot in hand, authenticated by a reliable seller.

BACKPRICING: Fixing the price of a commodity for which the commitment to purchase has been made in advance. The consumer can fix the price relative to any monthly or periodic delivery using the futures markets.

BACKWARDATION MARKET: A futures market where the far-out months trade at a discount to (less than) the nearby months because of tight supply in nearby or cash markets. In this case demand exceeds near-term supply. See also *contango market*.

BANKER'S ACCEPTANCE: A draft or bill of exchange accepted by a bank where the accepting institution guarantees payment. Used extensively in foreign trade transactions.

BANS: Bond anticipation notes issued by state and local governments prior to the issue of bonds to even out cash flow.

BAR CHARTS: Charts of futures prices drawn with vertical lines, showing the high, low, and closing prices. Price forecasts and trading signals are derived from these diagrams using *chart analysis*.

BASIS: The difference between a cash price at a specific location and the price of a particular futures contract. To be "long" the basis or "short" the basis refers to hedging a position in the cash market by taking an equal and opposite commitment in futures. A basis that is "under" or "over" a specified futures month refers to the relationship of the cash price to that futures month. In a normal market the basis is "under" reflecting carrying charges. When the basis is over, short-term demand is indicated.

BASIS GRADE: The grade or grades specified by the exchange as deliverable against a futures contract. Other grades may be tendered for delivery at a discount or premium to the contract, or basis grade.

BASIS POINT: The measurement of a change in the yield of a security. One basis point equals 1/100 of one percent.

BASIS PRICE: The price agreed upon between the seller and buyer of an option to become the price at which the option can be exercised. The basis price is usually the current market price of the commodity, for the delivery month, at the time the option is sold. Also called the *striking price*.

BASIS QUOTE: Offer or sale of a cash commodity in terms of the difference above or below a futures price.

BEAR: One who believe prices will move lower.

BEAR COVERING: The closing of a short position. Also *covering*.

BEAR MARKET: One in which prices are declining.

BEAR SPREAD: (1) The simultaneous purchase and sale of two futures contracts in the same or related commodities with the intention of profiting from a decline in prices. In the agricultural products this is accomplished by selling a nearby delivery and buying a deferred. It can also be placed when a metals market is expected to change from a *backwardation* to a *contango* market. (2) An option strategy which involves the simultaneous purchase of a higher strike price option and selling of a lower strike price option of the same expiration. Can be applied to both Puts and Calls.

BEARER SECURITY: A security which promises to pay the holder of the security on demand.

BEST ORDERS: Buy or sell orders executed by the broker at what is considered to be the best available price. Also termed buying (or selling) "at best."

BETA (BETA COEFFICIENT): A measure of the variability of rate of return (or rarely, price) of a stock or portfolio compared to that of the overall market.

BID: An offer to buy a specific quantity of a commodity at a stated price.

BLACKSPOT: A fungus disease which attacks cocoa pods.

BOARD ORDER: See *market-if-touched* (MIT) order.

BOARD TRADING: Verbal bids in futures trading not conducted in the pit or ring but recorded on blackboards. A procedure followed in some less liquid markets.

BOND INDENTURE: Legal statement enumerating duties of the issuer and the rights of the holder.

BOOK ENTRY: A security transaction that is completed by a credit and debit to the seller's and buyer's books, correspondingly, for the security and is reversed for money transfer. The actual security may exist as a piece of paper in a centralized clearinghouse, or its existence may be limited to an entry on the computer of the Treasury.

BORROWING: Purchase of a nearby delivery date and simultaeous sale of a forward date. Derived from "borrowing metal from the market" and used mainly on the London Metal Exchange. See also *cash and carry*.

BREAK: A rapid, significant decline in price, frequently falling below a commonly recognized "support" level.

BREAKOUT: A movement of prices to outside a well-defined trading range.

BROAD TAPE: Term commonly applied to newswires carrying price and background information on securities and commodities markets, in contrast to the exchanges' own price transaction wires, which use a narrow "ticker tape."

BROKER: (1) A person paid a fee or commission for acting as an agent in making contracts, sales, or purchases. (2) When used as *floor broker,* it means a person who actually executes someone else's trading orders on the trading floor of an exchange. (3) When used to mean *account executive,* it means the person who deals with customers and their orders in commission-house offices (also called *registered commodity representative*). (4) The firm through which the transaction takes place. See also *Futures Commission Merchant* (FCM).

BROKERAGE: A fee charged by a broker for execution of a transaction; an amount per transaction or a percentage of the total value of the transaction; usually referred to as a commission fee.

BUCKET, BUCKETING: Illegal practice of accepting orders without any intention of executing them. Bucketing may also refer to the illegal use of margin deposits without disclosure to the customer. A *bucket shop* is the firm participating in such a business practice.

BULGE: A rapid, significant advance in price, usually through a commonly accepted "resistance" point. See also *break*.

BULL: One who expects prices to rise.

BULL MARKET: One in which prices are rising.

BULL SPREAD: (1) The simultaneous purchase and sale of two futures contracts in the same or related commodities with the intention of profiting from a rise in prices. In the agricultural products this is accomplished by buying the nearby delivery and selling the deferred. It can also be placed when a metals market is expected to change from a *contango* market to a *backwardation* market. (2) An option strategy that involves the simultaneous purchase of a lower strike price option and the sale of a higher strike price option of the same expiration. This can be applied to both Puts and Calls.

BULLION: Bars of metal but most commonly gold. Can range from 1 kilogram to 400 oz. and must be .995–.999 pure to be readily transferable.

BULLION COINS: Coins struck from gold which may contain less than .995 or .999 purity but sufficient "fine gold" to act as a substitute for the bullion. These coins are designed to fill needs of gold buyers who may not have the means or the inclination to collect gold bars and ingots. Popular bullion coins are the South African Krugerrand, the Austrian 100 Kroner, the British Sovereign, the Mexican 50 Peso, and the French Napoleon. While the coins are generally restruck in order to meet demand, the Krugerrand is legal tender and the French Napoleon has not been restruck as yet. Bullion coins carry a premium over the cost of gold bullion.

BUTTERFLY HEDGE: This hedge incorporates the underlying commodity and an excess number of Calls sold against the commodity, with the upside liability defined by the purchase of Calls at the higher strike price sufficient to balance the excess number of options sold. The strategy is neutral to moderately bullish depending on the relationship of the strike price of the options sold to the commodity price.

BUTTERFLY SPREAD: (1) Simultaneous purchase of one unit of a near month and a far month with concurrent sale of two units of an in-between month. This is considered an extremely low risk spread, since it reduces potential profits and losses due to changes in carry. (2) Options: applied to both Puts and Calls, it consists of buying the lower and higher strike price option, selling twice as many of the option in-between. All options must have the same expiration.

BUYER: A market participant who takes a long futures position, or buys an option. An option buyer is also called a taker, holder, or owner.

BUY IN: (1) Offsetting a previous sale by a purchase. Also known as *short covering*. See also *cover*. (2) A method of compensation for failure to deliver in the cash bond market.

BUYING BASIS: The difference between the cost of a cash commodity at a specific location and a futures contract sold as a hedge. See also *selling basis*.

BUYING HEDGE (OR LONG HEDGE): buying futures contracts to protect against possible increased cost of commodities that will be needed in the future. See also *hedging*.

BUY (OR SELL) ON CLOSE: An order to buy or sell within the closing price range.

BUY (OR SELL) ON OPENING: An order to buy or sell within the opening price range.

C. & F.: Cost and freight paid to port of destination.

CALL: (1) A period designated by an exchange in which the price for each futures contract is established, that is, an opening or closing call. (2) *Buyer's Call*: a purchase of a specified quantity of a specific grade of a commodity at a fixed number of points above or below a specific delivery month in futures, with the buyer being allowed a certain period of time in which to fix the price by either purchasing a futures contract for the account of the seller, or indicating to the seller when he wishes to fix price. (3) *Seller's Call*: same as the buyer's call except that the seller has the right to determine when the price shall be fixed.

CALL DATE: Date upon which the issuer can exercise a call feature. See also *Call feature*.

CALL FEATURE: An option on the part of the issuer to redeem a bond issue at a predetermined price prior to maturity.

CALL MONEY: Also, *call loans*. Money lent by banks to brokers, collateralized by securities, and subject to repayment upon demand.

CALL OPTION: A contract that entitles the buyer/taker to buy a fixed quantity of a commodity at a stipulated basis or striking price at any time up to the expiration of the option. The buyer pays a premium to the seller/grantor for this contract. A call option is bought, therefore, in the expectation of a rise in prices. See also *put option*.

CALL PRICE: Price at which a bond issue can be called, usually at par value or or at a slight premium.

CARGO: The load capacity of an ocean vessel.

CARLOAD: The capacity of a railroad car.

CARRY, CARRYING: The cost of financing; general term used for both *borrowing* and *lending*. *Negative carry*: the condition where the cost of financing (the short-term rate of interest) is above the current return of the financial instrument. *Positive carry*: the condition where the cost of financing (the short-term rate of interest) is less than the current return of the financial instrument.

CARRYING CHARGES: (1) Those costs incurred in owning the physical commodity, generally including interest, insurance, and storage, but may also include transportation, grading, sampling, and so forth. (2) *Full carrying charge market*: a situation in the futures market when the price difference between delivery months reflects the full costs of interest, insurance, and storage.

CARRYING CHARGE MARKET: See *contango market*.

CARRY-OVER: That portion of current supplies of a commodity comprised of excess stocks from previous production/marketing seasons.

CASH (COMMODITY): The physical commodity, as distinguished from futures contracts; the commodity as acquired through a cash market; sometimes call the *spot commodity,* although the later term refers to the nearest futures delivery. See also *actuals*.

CASH AND CARRY: An investment strategy which applies when a contango exists, and the premium of the forward position over the prompt or spot generally reflects an unusually wide carry, implying high financing rates. When a commodity is in surplus, the contango may widen to the point where banking operations are attractive. Capital may be invested by buying the cash commodity and, simultaneously, selling forward where it yields, after costs, better returns than the prevailing money markets. This strategy is generally applied to metals, or *pure carry* markets. See also *borrowing*.

CASH FORWARD SALE: The sale of a cash commodity for delivery at a later date. Price may be fixed at the time of the agreement, or there may be an agreement to determine the price at the time of delivery on the basis of prevailing local cash price or on some futures price. Also known as "deferred delivery" or "forward sale."

CASH MARKET: (1) Market for the physical commodity. (2) An organized, self-regulated central market, such as a commodity exchange. (3) A decentralized over-the-counter market. (4) A local organization, such as a grain elevator or meat processor, which provides a market for a small region.

CASH METAL: Cash metal is prompt and due for delivery on the following day.

CASH PRICE: The price of the physical commodity (on the LME, the spot price).

CASH SETTLEMENT: Transaction in which securities are delivered, versus federal funds, on the same day the transaction is made.

CD: See *Certificate of Deposit*.

CERTIFICATED STOCKS: Supplies that have been approved as deliverable grades and have been stored at warehouses or delivery points designated as regular or acceptable by the exchange on which the commodity is traded.

CERTIFICATE OF DEPOSIT (CD): A time deposit with a specific maturity evidenced by a certificate. Large-denomination CDs are typically negotiable.

CFTC: See *Commodity Futures Trading Commission*.

CHARTING: The use of graphs and charts in analysis of market behavior in order to plot trends and patterns of price movements, volume, and open interest, in the expectation that such graphs and charts will help to anticipate and profit from price movements. An aspect of technical analysis as contrasted with fundamental analysis.

CHARTIST: Technical trader who reacts to signals read from graphs of price movements.

CHEAP: Common expression implying that a commodity is underpriced.

CIF: Cost, insurance and freight paid at point of destination included in price.

CLEARANCES: Aggregate shipments of a commodity made by sea on a specified date.

CLEARINGHOUSE: The separate agency or corporation associated with a futures exchange through which futures contracts are offset or fulfilled and through which guarantees and financial settlement are made.

CLEARING PRICE: See *settlement price*.

CLERK: An assistant to floor broker, most often an LME ring dealer. The clerk may be "authorized" (empowered to deal in the absence of the dealer) or "unauthorized" (empowered only to record and check transactions).

CLOSING-OUT: Liquidating an existing long or short futures position with an equal and opposite transaction, also known as "exiting."

CLOSING PRICE: The price for a commodity futures contract generated by trading through open outcry during the closing period of a trading session.

CLOSING RANGE: A range of prices at which transactions took place at the closing of the market; buying and selling orders placed market-on-close might have been filled at any point within such a range.

COMBINATION: Puts and calls held either long or short with different strike prices and expirations that are not otherwise denominated.

COMEX: (1) The New York Commodity Exchange Incorporated. (2) Market abbreviation for the copper or silver price in New York, such as "COMEX is 11.50," meaning that COMEX silver is $11.50 per ounce.

COMMERCIAL PAPER: Unsecured promissory notes of corporations, 270 days or less in length, usually sold on a discount basis.

COMMISSION: The charge which a commodity broker must make to his or her client when the broker buys or sells contracts. Traditionally this charge is levied at the time of liquidation; however, there is a shift toward charging one-half when the position is entered. See also *round-turn*.

COMMISSION HOUSE: Also *Futures Commission Merchant* (FCM). A company which trades on behalf of clients for a commission. The term is used primarily in the United States. In London it refers to a company introducing client business to a ring dealing broker. Many companies introducing business in London as commission houses are themselves members of exchanges in the United States and vice versa. Individuals acting in this capacity are often referred to as half-commission agents because they are rewarded for introducing the business and maintaining local contact with the client by a half share of the ring dealer's commission.

COMMISSION MERCHANT: See *Futures Commission Merchant*.

COMMITMENT: An agreement to lend money at a future date to a borrower.

COMMODITY CREDIT CORPORATION (CCC): A government-owned corporation established in 1933 to assist U.S. agriculture by providing price-support programs in which the CCC purchases excess supplies of commodities and by assisting in the export of agricultural commodities.

COMMODITY FUTURES TRADING COMMISSION (CFTC): A federal regulatory agency empowered under the Commodity Futures Trading Commission Act of 1974 with regulation of all commodities trading on all domestic contract markets. The CFTC consists of five commissioners, one of whom is chairperson. All are appointed by the President subject to Senate confirmation. The CFTC replaced and assumed all powers of the Commodity Exchange Authority.

COMMODITY PRICE INDEX: Index or average, which may be weighted, of selected commodity prices, intended to be representative of the markets in general or a specific subset of commodities, for example, grains or livestock.

COMMODITY SOLICITOR: A registered commodity representative employed by, and soliciting business for, a futures commission merchant. Also called an *account executive* or *customer's man.* See also *associated person.*

CONGESTION: In technical analysis, a price range within which buying power and selling pressure are about equal, resulting in a sideways movement of prices.

CONSOLIDATION: A price pattern represented by a prolonged period of narrowing price movement.

CONSIGNMENT: An arrangement under which the seller places an unsold shipment of a commodity with an agent for sale at the best possible price. Title to the commodity rests with the seller until it is disposed of in accordance with the terms of the agreement.

CONTANGO: Also *forwardation.* The situation when the price of a commodity for forward or future delivery stands at a premium over the cash or spot price of that commodity. Contangos occur when there is a normal or surplus supply of the product. The size of the contango does not normally exceed the carrying charges of the commodity over the future delivery period. See also *cash and carry* and *backwardation.*

CONTRACT: An agreement to buy or sell a specified amount of a particular commodity. The contract details the amount and grade of the product and the date on which the contract will mature and become deliverable if it is not liquidated earlier.

CONTRACT GRADES: The standard or grade of a commodity, as specified in the exchange rules, that is deliverable on a futures contract. Basic contract grade is the one deliverable at par. There may be more than one basic grade. Other grades are deliverable at a premium or discount.

CONTRACT MARKET: An exchange designated by the CFTC to conduct futures trading.

CONTRACT MONTH: Month in which a given contract becomes deliverable, if not liquidated or offset before the date specified.

CONTRACT WEIGHTS: Deliverable weights of contract, as shown on warehouse receipts.

CONTRACT UNIT: The specific amount of the commodity represented by the futures contract. For example, 100 troy ounces is the contract unit for gold futures traded on COMEX, and 5000 bushels of grain is the contract unit on the Chicago Board of Trade.

CONTRARIAN: A trader who takes positions opposite to the market direction anticipated by the majority of traders.

CONTROLLED ACCOUNT: A commodity account controlled by someone other than the owner or customer. A controlled account requires prior written authorization (power of attorney) to be given by the customer to the manager.

CONVENTIONAL LOAN: Mortage loan without a government guarantee or insurance.

CONVERGENCE: The tendency for prices for physical and futures to approach one another, usually during the delivery month. Also called a "narrowing of the basis."

CORNER: The securing of significant control of a commodity, enabling price manipulation, often called a "squeeze"; in its extreme, the control of more contracts requiring delivery than the available supply.

CORPORATE BOND: An instrument evidencing indebtedness of a corporation.

COST OF TENDER: Total of various charges incurred to have a commodity certified and delivered.

COUNTER-TREND TRADING: In technical analysis, the method by which a trader takes a position contrary to the current market direction in anticipation of a change in that direction.

COUPON (COUPON RATE): A fixed dollar amount of interest payable per annum, stated as a percentage of principal value, usually payable in semiannual installments.

COVARIANCE: The degree of related movement between two variables, such as the price or rate of return of two commodities. It is the sum of the products of the differences of each pair of observations from their averages, divided by the number of pairs of observations.

COVER: In hedging, the amount of physical or futures commitments purchased to offset anticipated production needs.

COVERING: Offsetting a previously established futures short position by a purchase. Also "evening up" or "liquidating."

CROP YEAR: Period beginning with the harvesting of a crop to the corresponding period of the following year, as used statistically.

CURRENT DELIVERY: A futures contract that will mature and become deliverable during the current month. Also called "spot month."

CURRENT YIELD: The amount of money received (currently), divided by the instrument's purchase price.

CUSTOMER'S MAN: See *commodities solicitor*.

CUSTOM SMELTER: A smelter which relies mostly on concentrate purchased from independent mines rather than its own captive main sources, or scrap. See also *refinery*.

DATED DATE: The date from which interest begins to accure on a new bond issue.

DAY ORDER (GFD): An order that, if not executed during the day it is entered, automatically expires at the end of that trading session. On the LME a day order can specify a particular session (i.e., premarket, lunchtime, evenings) or "all markets."

DAY TRADE: A trade which is entered and liquidated on the same trading day, as different from an *overnight trade*.

DEALER: Individual or firm in the cash market who acts as principal in transactions. The dealer maintains an inventory of securities from which he or she draws on in sales and to which he or she adds in purchases. A dealer on the LME serves the same role as a broker on a U.S. exchange.

DEBENTURE: A debt instrument whose backing lies in the goodwill of the issuer rather than on any tangible assets.

DEBIT BALANCE: An accounting total that represents the total charges (i.e., money borrowed from the broker) against a customer's margin account.

DEBIT LEVERAGE: The concept of borrowing money to buy securities. Any increase or decrease in the total value of the securities accrues to the borrower alone, not the lender.

DECLARATION (OF OPTIONS): The exercising of the rights of the option purchaser made through the broker of the purchaser to the broker of the party granting the option at an agreed, specified time before the prompt date. Failure to do this is construed as abandoning the option.

DECLARATION DATE: The date on which the buyer's right to exercise the purchased option expires.

DEFAULT: (1) The failure to make or take delivery of the physical commodity as require under a futures contract. (2) Under the farm load program, the decision not to repay a government loan, instead surrending the crop that has been pledged as collateral.

DEFERRED DELIVERY: The more distant months in which futures trading is taking place, as distinguished from the nearby futures delivery months. Also see *cash forward sale*.

DELIVERY: Tender of a commodity either by (1) issuing a warehouse receipt or a bill of lading, (2) issuing a shipping certificate for some commodities, or (3) delivery of actuals against a futures contract.

DELIVERY BASIS: Difference between the spot or cash price at a primary market and the price at specified locations to which the commodity in a futures contract may be physically delivered in order to satisfy the terms of the contract.

DELIVERY DATE: Also *prompt date*, on which the commodity must be delivered to fulfill the terms of the contract.

DELIVERY MONTH: The calendar month in which the futures contract matures and within which delivery of the physical commodity can be made.

DELIVERY NOTICE: Written notice from a seller through the clearinghouse stating intention to make delivery on a short futures position on a particular date. This notice also specifies quantity, grade, and place of delivery. A notice precedes and is distinct from a warehouse receipt or shipping certificate, which are instruments representing transfer of ownership.

DELIVERY POINTS: The places specified by a commodity exchange to which delivery of a physical commodity can be made in fulfillment of the contract.

DELIVERY PRICE: Price fixed by the clearinghouse where futures deliveries are invoiced. Also, price at which a commodities futures contract is settled when deliveries are made.

DEPOSIT: The initial outlay required by a broker of a client to open a futures position, returnable on liquidation of that position.

DEPOSITORY OR WAREHOUSE RECEIPT (WARRANT): A certificate of physical deposit, issued by a bank or warehouse, which indicates ownership of the commodity or physical metal stored in an approved depository or warehouse. Ownership is transferred when the receipt is endorsed by its current owner to another party.

DIAGONAL TIME SPREAD: A variation of the conventional time spread, the diagonal consists of selling a nearby at-the-money option and using the proceeds to buy a larger number of deferred options with a higher strike price.

DIFFERENTIALS: Price differences between classes, grades, and locations of different stocks of the same commodity.

DISCOUNT: (1) The lower price allowed for delivery of stocks of a commodity of lesser than contract grade against a futures contract. (2) The price difference between futures of different delivery months, as in the phrase "July at a discount to May," indicating that the price of the July futures is lower than that of the May.

DISCOUNT BASIS: Method of quoting securities where the price is expressed as an annualized discount from maturity value.

DISCOUNT BOND: A bond selling below par.

DISCOUNT RATE: Rate of interest charged by the Federal Reserve to member banks that borrow from it.

DISCRETIONARY ACCOUNT: See *controlled account*.

DISTANT DELIVERY: Distant futures delivery months as distinguished from nearby futures delivery months. Also *deferred delivery*.

DISTRIBUTION: In technical analysis, a period in which prices move sideways at a relatively high level prior to a decline.

DOLLARING AVERAGING: A method of cummulative purchasing in which equal dollar amounts are used to determine the quantity purchased. As the price of the commodity increases, smaller quantities are purchased.

DOLLAR BONDS: A type of municipal revenue bond whose price quotes are given in dollars (e.g., 91 or 105) instead of on a yield basis.

DOUBLE OPTION: An option which gives the buyer or taker of the option the right to either buy from or sell to the seller or giver of the option at the basis price.

DUTCH AUCTION: Method of sale whereby the lowest price at which the entire issue can be sold is established as the uniform price for the entire issue.

ECONOMETRICS: The application of statistical and mathematical methods in the field of economics in testing and quantifying economic theories and the solution of economic problems.

ECONOMETRIC RESEARCH: The application of econometrics in forecasting.

EFFICIENT MARKET: A market in which new information is immediately and costlessly available to all investors and potential investors. A market in which all information is instantaneously assimilated and therefore has no distortions.

EFFICIENT PORTFOLIO: A portfolio having the highest expected return for its particular risk level; or one having the lowest risk for a given level of expected return.

EFP (EXCHANGE FOR PHYSICAL): Trade between two parties—one buys physicals and sells futures contracts, the other sells physicals and buys futures contracts. An EFP is composed of four parts: the purchase and sale of futures contracts and the simultaneous sale and purchase by the same two parties of an equal quantity of the physical commodity. This technique often follows the use of physical markets to hedge a futures position when the futures markets are not open.

ELASTICITY: A characteristic of commodities that describes the interaction of supply, demand, and price. *Elasticity of demands* exists when a price change creates an increase or decrease in consumption. If price change has little or no effect on consumption, it is known as inelasticity of demand. *Elasticity of supply* exists when a price change creates an increase or decrease in the production of a commodity. If supply is unresponsive to price change, it is known as *inelasticity of supply*.

ELEVATORS: See *public elevators; terminal elevators*.

ELLIOT WAVE PRINCIPLE: In technical analysis, a charting method based on the belief that all prices act as waves rising and falling rhythmically. Elliot's primary waves are comprised of five parts, each containing three subwaves.

END CONSUMER (END USER): A company that is the ultimate receiver or consumer of the commodity and then produces a more complex product.

EQUITY: The value of a commodity futures account.

EUROCURRENCY: CDs, bonds, deposits, or any capital market instrument issued outside of the national boundaries of the currency in which the instrument is denominated—for example, Euro-Swiss francs, Euro-Deutsche marks. See also *eurodollars, eurodollar bonds, eurodollar CDs*.

EURODOLLARS: U.S. dollars on deposit with a bank outside of the United States and, consequently, outside the jurisdiction of the United States. The bank could be either a foreign bank or a subsidiary of a U.S. bank.

EURODOLLAR BONDS: Bonds issued in Europe by corporate or government interests outside the boundary of the national capital market, denominated in dollars.

EURODOLLAR CDs: Dollar-denominated certificates of deposit issued by a bank outside of the United States, either a foreign bank or U.S. bank subsidiary.

EVENING-UP: See *covering* and *liquidating*.

EXCESS: The amount of money that can be withdrawn from a futures account without liquidating the positions; the amount by which equity exceeds margin requirements.

EXCHANGE (COMMODITY): An organized marketplace where particular commodities are bought and sold.

EXCHANGE OF SPOT (OR CASH COMMODITY) FOR FUTURES: Simultaneous exchange of a cash commodity for the equivalent in futures. This is used when the two parties carry opposite hedges in the same delivery month. Also known as "against actuals." See also *EFP*.

EXIT: See *covering* or *liquidating*.

EX-PIT TRANSACTIONS: Trades made outside the trading pit or ring. (1) A *transfer trade* involving the transfer of a customer's account between brokerage firms. (2) An exchange of cash for futures involving the purchase of cash commodities in exchange for a futures contract, at a price difference mutually agreed upon. This technique is often used by commercial accounts to close out a hedged position.

FABRICATOR: A company which makes semifabricated products from refined metal or, on occasion, from scrap.

FACE VALUE: The amount of money printed on the face of the certificate; the original dollar amount of indebtedness incurred.

FAIL: See *default*.

FEDERAL FUNDS: Member banks' deposits held by the Federal Reserve; also implies immediately available funds.

FEDERAL FUNDS RATE: The rate of interest charged for the use of federal funds.

FEDERAL HOME LOAN BANK: One of twelve federally chartered banks which regulates credit to its member institutions.

FEDERAL HOUSING ADMINISTRATION (FHA): A division of HUD that insures residential mortgage loans and sets construction standards.

FEDERAL NATIONAL MORTGAGE ASSOCIATION (FNMA): A corporation created by Congress to support the secondary mortgage market; it purchases and sells residential mortgages insured by FHA or guaranteed by the Veteran's Administration.

FEDERAL RESERVE SYSTEM: A quasigovernmental organization of twelve regional banks and a governing board of directors. The system attempts to actively manage the U.S. economy through its influence on monetary variables, such as money supply.

FEED RATIO: The relationship of the cost of feed to market-weight compared to sales price, expressed as a ratio, such as the *hog/corn ratio*. These serve as indicators of the profit margin or lack of profit in feeding animals to market weight.

FIA: See *Futures Industry Association*.

FIRST MORTGAGE BONDS: Bonds which are collateralized by a first lien on tangible assets. In the event of a default, a first mortgage bond holder can demand liquidation of those assets in satisfaction of the debt.

FIRST NOTICE DAY: (1) The first day on which notices of intention to deliver actual or physical commodities against a short futures contract can be presented by sellers through the clearinghouse. The first notice day varies with each commodity and exchange, but it usually precedes the beginning of the delivery period. (2) The first day on which notices are issued indicating delivery in a specific delivery month.

FIX, FIXING: The setting of a metals price by representatives of the London Metals Market, once in the morning and once in the afternoon. The *London fix* provides a reference point for metals dealing in world trade. See also *gold fixing*.

FLAT: Trading without accrued interest.

FLOOR BROKER: A member of the commodity exchange or representative of a member firm of the commodity market or ring who is "on the floor" (i.e., in the market, ready to do business) at all times when the market is open. See also *broker*.

FLOWER BONDS: Specific government bonds which are eligible to be used as payment at par value for federal estate taxes.

FOB: Free on board; indicates that all delivery, inspection, and elevation or loading costs involved in putting commodities on board a carrier have been paid, but not transportation costs to destination.

FORCED LIQUIDATION: The situation in which a customer's account is liquidated (all open positions are offset), by the brokerage firm holding the account, after adequate notification (margin calls), due to undercapitalization in the account.

FORCE MAJEURE: A clause in a supply contract which permits either party not to fulfill the contractual commitments due to events beyond their control. These events may range from strikes to export delays in producing countries.

FORWARDATION: See *contango.*

FORWARD CONTRACT: A cash market transaction in which two parties agree to the purchase and sale of a commodity at some future time under such conditions as the two agree—in contrast to *futures contracts.* The terms of forward contracts are not standardized; a forward contract is not transferable and usually can be cancelled only with the consent of the other party; refers to any cash market purchase or sale agreement for which delivery is not made "on the spot."

FORWARD METAL: See *forward contract.*

FORWARD SALE (OR PURCHASE): See *forward contract.*

FORWARD SHIPMENT: Contract covering actual commodity shipments at a specified date in the future. See also *forward contract.*

FREE SUPPLY: Supply of a commodity in the open market, exclusive of government owned or controlled stocks.

FULL CARRYING CHARGE, FULL CARRY: See *carrying charges.*

FUNDAMENTAL ANALYSIS: The forecasting of price movement traditionally using factors such as supply and demand, government programs, yields and techniques of econometrics, as contrasted with technical analysis or charting. Analysis which focuses on determining political policy and its anticipated effects on prices.

FUNGIBILITY: The interchangeability of futures contracts for the same commodity and delivery month because of standardization of contract specifications by the exchange where the commodity is traded.

FUTURES: Contracts for the purchase and sale of commodities for delivery some time in the future on an organized exchange and subject to all terms and conditions included in the rules of that exchange.

FUTURES COMMISSION MERCHANT (FCM): Individuals, associations, partnerships, and corporations engaging in soliciting or in accepting orders for the purchase or sale of any commodity for future delivery (on and subject to the rules of any contract market) and registered with and regulated by the CFTC.

FUTURES CONTRACT: An agreement to make or take delivery of a standardized amount of a commodity, of standardized quality grades, during a specific month, under terms and conditions established by an authorized exchange.

FUTURES EXCHANGE: Membership organization whose activity involves trading sessions between members in the specific commodities listed for trading on the exchange. Operations of the exchanges are divided broadly into floor operations (trading) and clearing (processing the trades between members through the clearinghouse).

FUTURES INDUSTRY ASSOCIATION (FIA): A membership organization preceding the National Futures Association which serves as a means of educating, disbursing information, and lobbying for members of the Futures Industry but primarily supported by the large futures commission merchants.

GENERAL OBLIGATION BONDS: Securities issued by states and municipalities which are secured by the full faith and credit, hence, taxing power, of the issuer.

GIVE-UP: A contract executed by one broker for the client of another broker that the client orders to be turned over to the second broker. The broker accepting the order from the customer collects a wire toll from the carrying broker for the use of the facilities. Often used to consolidate many small orders or to dispurse large ones.

GOLD CERTIFICATE: A certificate attesting to a person's ownership of a specific amount of bullion paid for and stored at some approved depository.

GOLD DEALER: See *dealer*.

GOLD FIXING (GOLD FIX): The setting of the gold price at 10 AM (first fixing) and 3 PM (second fixing) in London by five representatives of the London gold market. See also *fixing*.

GOLD FUNDS: Funds which pool investors' monies in either gold mining stocks or bullion.

GOLD SHARES: Shares of stock in gold mining companies in South Africa and other countries.

GOLD/SILVER RATIO: The number of ounces of silver required to buy one ounce of spot gold at current spot prices.

GOOD 'TIL CANCELLED ORDER (GTC): Order which is valid at any time during market hours until executed or cancelled by the client. Also known as an "open order."

GOVERNMENT NATIONAL MORTGAGE ASSOCIATION (GNMA): A quasigovernment organization formed when FNMA was split into two divisions in 1968. GNMA administers and guarantees mortgage-backed securities.

GOVERNMENT NATIONAL MORTGAGE ASSOCIATION SECURITIES (GINNIE MAES): Security backed by an underlying pool of insured guaranteed mortgages. These securities carry the full faith and credit of the U.S. government.

GRADES: Standards set for the quality of a commodity.

GRADING CERTIFICATES: Certificates which verify the quality of the commodity.

GRAIN FUTURES ACT: A federal statute enacted on June 22, 1923 for the purpose of regulating grain futures trading, administered by the USDA. The act was amended in 1936, creating the Commodity Exchange Authority; the act has since been referred to as the Commodity Exchange Act. See also *Commodity Futures Trading Commission*.

GRANTOR: The seller or writer of an option.

GROSS PROCESSING MARGIN (GPM): The price relationship between the raw material and the value of products derived from it. In soybeans, it is the difference between the cost of soybeans and combined sales income of soybean oil and soybean meal, which results from the processing of soybeans. The same relationship exists for crude oil and other commodities.

GTC: See *good 'til cancelled order.*

HARDENING: A market condition characterized by gradual firming of price; slowly advancing market.

HEAVY: A market condition characterized by overhanging sell orders without a corresponding number of buy orders; prices demonstrate an inability to advance, and more often they display a tendency to decline slowly.

HEDGING: The establishment of an opposite position in the futures market from that held in the physicals.

HUD: Department of Housing and Urban Development.

INITIAL DEPOSIT: The sum which the broker requires the client to deposit before market positions may first be taken in the client's account.

IN SIGHT: The amount of a particular commodity at locations near producing areas. The term implies that reasonably prompt delivery can be made.

INSTITUTIONAL CUSTOMER: One with large holdings in securities, primarily financial instruments, either long or short, who is using the futures markets for the purpose of hedging risk. Analogous to the commercial customer in other markets.

INTEGRATED PRODUCER: A producer of metal who owns mines, smelters, and refineries, and, in some instances, fabricating plants. Also called *vertical integration.*

INTERCOMMODITY SPREAD: A spread in which the long and short leg are in two different but generally related commodity markets. Also called an *intermarket spread.* See also *spreads.*

INTERDELIVERY SPREAD: A spread involving two different delivery months of the same commodity. Also called in *intracommodity spread.* See also *spread.*

INTEREST RATE PARITY: Traditional theory of foreign exchange which states that the forward premium or discount on one currency relative to another is directly related to the interest rate differential between the two countries. Because capital controls, restraints to trade, and national economic policy may affect any or all of the variables, actual realization of the theory may be difficult.

INTER-MARKET: The period between the close of the morning kerb and the opening of the afternoon ring when LME members conduct interoffice dealings by telephone. The opening of COMEX takes place during this period.

INTERMARKET SPREAD: See *spread* and *intercommodity spread.*

INTERNATIONAL COMMODITIES CLEARINGHOUSE (ICCH): An independent organization which serves as a clearinghouse for most London futures markets.

IN-THE-MONEY: A term used to describe an option that has intrinsic value. A call at 400 on gold trading at 410 is in-the-money 10 dollars.

INTRACOMMODITY SPREAD: See *spread* and *interdelivery spread.*

INTRINSIC VALUE: A measure of the value of an option or a warrant if immediately exercised.

INVERTED MARKET: Futures market in which distant-month contracts are selling below near-month contracts. Also called *backwardation*. This situation is often caused by short-term supply shortages.

INVESTMENT BANKER: A firm that engages in the origination, underwriting, and distribution of an issue.

INVISIBLE SUPPLY: Stocks in the hands of wholesalers, manufacturers, and producers (outside the commercial channels) which cannot be counted but are theoretically available for market.

JOB LOT: Unit of trading smaller than the regular contract unit. See also *round lot*.

KERB TRADING OR DEALING: That dealing which takes place after the official market has ended. Originally it took place in the street on the kerb outside the market. In modern times it also refers to trading on the telephone or by other dealing outside the ring or market.

LAST TRADING DAY: The day on which trading ceases for a particular delivery month. All contracts that have been liquidated by an offsetting purchase or sale by the end of trading on that day must thereafter be settled by delivery of the actual physical commodity.

LENDING: Sale of a nearby delivery date coupled with the simultaneous purchase of a more distant date (LME term).

LETTER OF WARNING: A written notice issued by the CFTC to an individual or firm ordering the recipient to cease and desist an improper practice or violation of law.

LEVERAGE: Buying or selling using deposits, collateral, or margin less than the face value of the item being traded. Commodity futures markets usually require about 10% of the face value of the contract, giving 90% leverage. The U.K. term for leverage is *gearing*.

LEVERAGE CONTRACTS: General term for contracts which allow for leverage, but are not as closely regulated as traded options.

LICENSED WAREHOUSE: A warehouse designated for delivery by the exchange on which a commodity is traded. Only such designated warehouses may be used to store a commodity for delivery. Also referred to as a "regular" warehouse.

LIFE OF CONTRACT (DELIVERY): The period of time from the first trading day in a futures month through the last trading day.

LIMIT (UP OR DOWN): The maximum price advance (or decline) that the rules of the exchange permit from the previous day's settlement price in one trading session. Does not apply to the LME or all contracts of a commodity or U.S. markets.

LIMIT ORDER: An order that has some restriction on execution, such as price or time.

LIMIT-ONLY (LIMIT ORDER): The definite price stated by a customer to a broker restricting the execution of an order to buy for not more than, or to sell for not less than, that stated price. Also called "or better" (OB).

LIMIT PRICE: Largest permitted price fluctuation in a futures contract during a trading session, as fixed by the contract market's rules. See also *limit (up or down)*.

LIMITED-RISK SPREAD: A carrying charge spread. See also *spread*.

LIMITS: See *price limits, variable limits, position limits*.

LIQUIDATION: The closing-out of a long position. The term is sometimes used to denote closing out a short position, but this is more often referred to as "covering."

LIQUID MARKET, LIQUIDITY: A market where selling and buying can be accomplished with ease because of the presence of a large number of interested buyers and sellers willing and able to trade substantial quantities at small price differences. Often measured by volume and open interest.

LOAN PRICES: Prices at which the U.S. government will lend producers (farmers) money for their crops.

LOAN PROGRAM: U.S. government agricultural price support operations. A program under which farmers commit their crops to the government with the assurance that they will receive a certain minimum loan price. If the price of the commodity rises above the loan price, the farmers may sell their crops in the open market. If the price of the commodity falls below the loan level, the nonrecourse character of the loan makes it possible for farmers to deliver their crops to the CCC (Commodity Credit Corporation), discharging their obligation in full.

LOCALS: Members of U.S. exchange who trade for their own account and/or fill orders for customers and whose activities provide market liquidity.

LOCKED-IN: A hedged position which cannot be lifted without offsetting both sides of the hedge (spread). See *hedging*.

LONDON GOLD MARKET: Those dealers who set (fix) the gold price; (1) Mocatta & Goldsmid (2) N. Rothschild & Sons, (3) Johnson Matthey, (4) Sharps Pixley, and (5) Samuel Montagu & Co.

LME: London Metals Exchange.

LONG: (1) One who purchases futures contracts or who owns actuals. A net long is a trader whose total purchases exceed total sales in open futures contracts. (2) Starting a transaction by the purchase of a futures contract.

LONG HEDGE: Purchase of futures against the sale of a cash commodity.

LONG LIQUIDATION: Closing of long positions.

LONG THE BASIS: A hedge consisting of ownership of actuals against short futures in a particular commodity. See also *hedge*.

LONGSIDE TRADING: Taking only long positions in the market, usually within an overall upwards trend, by buying short-term weakness and selling short-term strength.

LOT: A unit of trading (round lot, job lot). The minimum unit of trading for a commodity.

M1: Money supply as measured by the amount of demand deposits at commercial banks plus currency in circulation.

M2: M1 plus deposits and time certificates of deposit.

M3: M2 plus average deposits of mutual savings banks, savings and loan shares, and credit union shares.

M4: M2 plus large-denomination certificates of deposit.

M5: M3 plus large-denomination certificates of deposit.

MAINTENANCE MARGIN: See *margin*.

MAJOR TREND: See *price trend*.

MANAGED ACCOUNT: See *controlled account, discretionary account*.

MARGIN: Money or collateral deposited by both buyers and sellers of futures contracts that serves as a performance guarantee. It is not a downpayment, nor is it part of the purchase price. The difference between the margin deposit and the full contract value does not have to be borrowed as in the equities market. (1) ORIGINAL (INITIAL) MARGIN. The amount of money required by a brokerage house (FCM) when a futures position is established, either long or short. In general, margin requirements are highest for speculators, lower for hedgers and lowest for spreaders. (2) MINIMUM MARGIN: The smallest allowable deposit for the establishment of a futures position. Whereas the minimum is set by the individual exchanges for their traded commodities, brokerage houses may require larger original margin deposits based on their own assessment of risk. (3) MAINTENANCE MARGIN: The amount of margin or equity that must be on deposit at all times. An account whose equity falls below the maintenance level will be issued a margin call requiring additional deposits to restore the account level to original margin (also called *variation margin call*). (4) VARIATION MARGIN: The daily changes in equity as compared to the original margin.

MARGIN CALL: A written communication from a brokerage firm to a customer calling for additional money that will bring the equity to original margin level. The clearinghouse of an exchange can also issue margin calls to brokerage houses calling for additional deposits. For clearing purposes, a member of the clearinghouse generally carries two accounts, a house account and a customer's account. Current policy requires a margin call to be issued when the account equity falls below 75% of the original margin.

MARKET CORRECTION: In technical analysis, a smaller reversal in prices following a significant trending period.

MARKET-IF-TOUCHED (MIT) ORDER: An order to buy or sell when the market reaches a specified price. An order to buy becomes a market order when the commodity sells (or is offered) at or below the order price; an order to sell becomes a market order when the commodity sells (or is bid) at or above the order price. An order to buy is placed below the current market price; an order to sell is placed above the current market price. Also known as a "board order."

MARKET-ON-CLOSE (MOC): A qualifier to an order which indicates that the order is to be executed only during the closing session of the market. For example, buying gold at "450.00 limit MOC" indicates that the order is to be filled during the closing period only at a price of 450.00 or better.

MARKET-ON-OPEN: Also "on-the-open." A qualifier to an order indicating that the order is to be executed only during the opening period of the market, if possible.

MARKET ORDER: An order to buy or sell at the best price available and as soon as possible after the order reaches the trading floor of the exchange. See also *limit order.*

MARKET QUOTA: Government restriction on the amount of a commodity a producer is allowed to sell.

MARKET VALUE: The current value of all commodities and securities held in a margin account.

MATURITY: Period within which a futures contract can be settled by delivery of the actual commodity; the period between the first notice day and the last trading day of a commodity futures contract. Also, the due date of a loan, note, bond, or mortgage-backed security.

MAXIMUM PRICE FLUCTUATION: The limit of fluctuation in the price of a futures contract during any one trading session, as established by the exchange.

MEMBER RATE: Commission charged for the execution of an order for a person who is a member of the exchange.

MEMO: Metal Exchange Monitoring Operation.

MERCHANT: A metal merchant, as distinct from a producer's agent or broker, often acts as a principal, buying metal or concentrates from producers and others and selling the metal to others. Metal will often be held in the account of the merchant while waiting for a buyer.

MINIMUM PRICE FLUCTUATION: The minimum unit by which the price of a commodity can fluctuate, as established by the exchange.

MINOR TREND: See *price trend.*

MODEL: The formulated method of analysis, referring to the forecasting of prices, supply, or other commodity factors.

MODERN CAPITAL MARKET THEORY: A theory of prices which has substantial origin in Markowitz and includes capital asset pricing, efficient markets, efficient portfolios, expected rates of return, systematic and specific risk, and random walk theory as its components.

MOMENTUM: In technical analysis, the relative change in price over a specific time interval. Often equated with speed or velocity and considered in terms of *relative strength.*

MONEY SUPPLY: See *M1, M2, M3, M4, M5.*

MORTGAGE: A conveyance of interest in real property given as security for the payment of debt.

MORTGAGE BANKER: An intermediary that originates loans to permanent investors.

MORTGAGEE: A party to whom property is conveyed as collateral for a loan.

MORTGAGOR: A borrower of funds.

MOVING AVERAGE: In technical analysis, a method of averaging prices of the most recent days in an effort to determine and/or forecast the direction of movement.

NAKED CALL: A call option originated by an option writer who does not own or buy the underlying commodity on which the option is written but rather leaves cash or other unencumbered equity in his or her account as a surety that a contract will be honored.

NAKED PUT: A put option originated by an option writer who does not sell short the underlying commodity on which the option is written but rather leaves cash or other unencumbered equity in his or her account as a surety that a contract will be honored.

NEARBY DELIVERY (MONTH): The futures contract closest to maturity. Also called "spot month."

NET POSITION: (1) Difference between the number of open commodity contracts held long and short in an account. (2) The difference held by a FCM with a clearinghouse.

NFA: National Futures Association.

NOMINAL PRICE: An estimate of the price for a futures month or date in which no trading has taken place.

NONMEMBER FCM: A brokerage firm (FCM) that does not own its own seats on futures exchanges; a firm that executes its orders through another member FCM.

NORMAL MARKET: See *contango market* and *carrying charge market*.

NOTE: One of a variety of debt securities "treasury notes" refer to coupon securities with a maturity of one to 10 years; municipal notes are short-term promissory notes.

NOTICE DAY: See *first notice day*.

NOTICE OF INTENTION TO DELIVER: A notice that must be presented by the seller to the clearinghouse. The clearinghouse then assigns the notice and the subsequent delivery instrument to the longest-standing buyer on record.

OFFER: A price at which a trader is willing to sell; the asking price.

OFFSET: (1) Liquidation of a long or short position by the opposite transaction. (2) A practice of commission merchants of setting total longs against total shorts for the purpose of determining net long or net short position.

OMNIBUS ACCOUNT: An account of one commission merchant carried by another commission merchant for clearing purposes in which the transactions of customers are combined and treated as one account. The identity of the individual account is not disclosed to the clearing FCM.

ON TRACK (OR TRACK COUNTRY STATION): A type of deferred delivery in which the price is set FOB seller's location and the buyer agrees to pay freight costs to his or her destination.

OPEN CONTRACTS: Contracts bought or sold and not offset by an opposite trade. See also *open interest*.

OPENING RANGE: Range of prices at which transactions took place during the period designated as "the opening" of trading by an exchange.

OPEN INTEREST: The total number of futures contracts of a given commodity that have not yet been offset by opposite futures transactions or fulfilled by delivery of the commodity; the total number of open transactions. Each open transaction has a buyer and a seller, but for calculation of open interest, only one side of the contract is counted.

OPEN ORDER: See *good 'til cancelled*.

OPEN OUTCRY: Method of trading required in the exchange trading pits or rings by the CFTC. All futures trades must be made with verbal bids and offers with the exception of expit transactions.

OPEN POSITION: A market position which has not been closed out.

OPPORTUNITY: The expected gain due to trading as determined by the expected level of price entry and the anticipated price change. See also *risk*.

OPTION: An agreement which permits the taker (purchaser) the right to buy from or sell to the grantor (seller) of the option at any time before its expiration a specified quantity of the commodity concerned at an agreed price (the basis price). The cost to the purchaser of the option is called the "premium." Also, a term erroneously applied to a futures contract or to a specific delivery of a commodity.

OPTION BUYER (TAKER): The person who buys calls, puts, or any combination of calls and puts.

OPTION SELLER (GRANTOR): Also, *option writer*. The person who originates an option contract by promising to perform a certain obligation in return for the price of the option.

ORIGINAL MARGIN: See *margin*.

ORIGINATE A LOAN: Make or issue a loan.

OUT-OF-THE-MONEY: A term used to describe an option that has no intrinsic value. A call at 400 on gold trading at 390 is out-of-the-money 10 dollars.

OVERBOUGHT: In technical analysis, the situation or opinion that prices have risen too sharply and too quickly in relation to underlying fundamental factors.

OVERNIGHT TRADE: A trade which is not liquidated on the same trading day in which it was entered. Such a trade is subject to margin deposits, as differs from a *day trade*.

OVERPRICED: (1) In technical analysis, see *overbought*. (2) In options, a premium which is considered too high for the price and/or volatility of the underlying commodity.

OVERSOLD: In technical analysis, an opinion that the market price has declined too steeply and too fast in relation to underlying fundamental factors.

P & S STATEMENT: See *purchase and sale statement*.

PAR: A particular price, 100% of principal value; "100".

PARALLEL PRICES: The normal constant relationship between cash and futures markets, the difference between the two being the basis.

PARITY: A theoretically equal relationship between farm product prices and all other prices. In farm program legislation, parity is defined in such a manner that the purchasing power of a unit of an agricultural commodity is maintained at its level during an earlier historical base period. Parity prices are issued monthly by the USDA showing the price necessary for the farmer in order to maintain current power.

PASS THROUGH: Security in which the periodic interest and principal are passed from a mortgagor to an investor through an intemediary.

PEGGED PRICE: The price at which a commodity has been fixed by agreement.

PHYSICAL: See *actuals*.

PIT: Place where futures are traded on the floor of a commodity exchange. See also *ring*.

POINT: (1) Unit expressing minimum price change. Synonymous with "minimum price fluctuation." (2) A dollar amount equal to 1% of principal value of a note or other debt instrument. (3) See also *basis point*.

POINT-AND-FIGURE: A method of charting which uses prices to form patterns of movement without regard to time. It defines a price trend as continued movement in one direction until a reversal of a predetermined criteria is met.

POINTS: The units of price quoted, based on the minimum price unit. A $1.00 price movement may be called 100 points.

POSITION: A market commitment. A buyer of futures contracts is said to have a long position, and conversely, a seller of futures contracts is said to have a short position.

POSITION LIMIT: The maximum number of contracts, net long or net short, in any one delivery or in all deliveries of one commodity combined that may be held open by one person in certain regulated commodities according to the provisions of the CFTC. Also a limit on positions, held by one person, established by an exchange. Also called *trading limit*.

POSITION TRADER: A commodity trader who holds contracts for an extended period of time, as distinguished from a day trader, who initiates and closes out a position on the same day.

PREMARKET: Trading among brokers' offices before the rings open. See also *kerb* and *back-pricing*.

PREMIUM: (1) The amount by which a cash commodity price sells over a futures price or another cash commodity price. The excess of one futures contract price over another. (2) In options, the price, in effect, paid by the purchaser of the option to the grantor (seller). (3) That portion of an option price that is in excess of the intrinsic value, if any. In cases where the strike price and the stock price are the same, the total cost of the option is premium.

PRICE: (Verb). To fix the price of a purchase or sale based on a futures market quotation.

PRICE LIMIT: The maximum daily price fluctuation on a futures contract during any one trading session, as determined by the exchange. Also known as "limit." See also *variable price limit*.

PRICE TREND: See *trend*.

PRICING: The act of fixing the price. See *price*.

PRIMARY MARKET: Key distribution centers at which physical commodities are originally accumulated for commercial distribution.

PRINCIPALS' MARKET: A futures market where the ring dealing members act as principals for the transactions they conclude across the ring and with their clients.

PRIVATE WIRES: Electronic communications networks leased by a commission merchant for private use.

PROMPT DATE: See *delivery date*.

PROTEIN RATIOS: The relative protein value in various feedgrains for the purpose of nutritional substitution in livestock production.

PROVISIONAL PRICE: In cotton, a tentative price set on call cotton until a final price is fixed.

PUBLIC ELEVATORS: Storage facilities for grain, licensed and regulated by federal and state agencies. Grain of the same grade but owned by different persons is usually commingled, or mixed together. Some elevators are designated as regular for delivery by exchanges dealing in commodities stored at these elevators.

PURCHASE AND SALE (P & S) STATEMENT: A statement sent by an FCM to a customer when his or her futures position has changed, showing the number of contracts involved, the prices at which the contracts were bought or sold, the gross profit or loss, the commission charges, and the net profit or loss on the transactions.

PUT OPTION: A put option provides the purchaser the right to sell to the grantor of the option on the futures market a futures contract at an agreed price (the basic price) at any time during the life of the option. A put option is bought in the expectation of a decline in price.

PYRAMIDING: Adding to existing positions as the market moves favorably; allows profits on existing positions to be used as margin on new commitments.

RALLY: An upward movement of price after a decline.

RANGE: The difference between the highest and lowest prices recorded during a given trading session, week, month, life of contract, or any given period.

RATE OF RETURN: As specified by the CFTC, the monthly percentage return as determined by the monthly starting equity plus all additions, less all withdrawals, divided by the net profit or loss (after commissions and other costs) for that month.

RATIO HEDGE: The number of options compared to the number of relative futures contracts taken in a position necessary to be a hedge; that is, risk protection. A ratio less than 1 indicates that the underlying position is not fully protected. A ratio of 1 is considered a *perfect hedge*.

RATIO SPREAD: This strategy applies to both puts and calls. The put ratio spread consists of buying the higher strike price options and selling a larger number of the lower strike price options, all with the same expiration. The put ratio spread is considered moderately bearish, while the call ratio spread is correspondingly bullish.

REACTION (UP OR DOWN): A reversal of short duration to a major trend.

REFINERY: As distinct from a smelter, which produces crude metal by treating mine feed (concentrate), a refinery produces high purity metal either by electrolytic or fire refining. Refiners (and smelters) also treat scrap materials.

REGRESSION ANALYSIS: A basic tool of statistics and econometrics which determines the relationship between any two variables. This relationship is commonly termed *linear* or *nonlinear*.

REGULAR WAREHOUSE: See *licensed warehouse*.

REGULATED COMMODITIES: Commodities subject to the provisions of the Commodity Futures Trading Commission Act of 1974.

RELATIVE STRENGTH: In technical analysis, the difference between price and some measurement of "normal" price, moving average, or smoothed trend line. A price is considered stronger (or weaker) if it is further above (or below) its "normal" value.

REPORTING LIMIT: Position sizes set by the Commodity Futures Trading Commission and/or exchanges at or above which traders must file daily reports to the CFTC and/or to the exchange on position size, delivery month, and purpose of trading.

RESISTANCE: In technical trading, a price area where new selling will emerge to dampen a continued rise. See also *support*.

RESTING ORDER: Any order to buy below the current market price or sell above the current market price, such as limit, MIT, and GTC orders.

RESTRICTED STOCK: Quantities of a commodity off the market for a period of time; stockpiles resulting from defaulted loans and/or periods of government controls.

RETENDER: The act of selling an equivalent amount of futures represented in the notice of retention, to deliver during the same day, and return (retender) the same notice to the clearinghouse, along with the name of the party that bought the contract. Retendering can be accomplished only with certain commodities and only within a specified period of time.

RETRACEMENT: A reversal within a major price trend.

REVERSAL: A change of direction in prices.

REWARD: The rate of return, or expected rate of return.

RFC: Regulated futures contract as defined by the Commodity Exchange Act.

RING: (1) Space on a trading floor where futures are traded. Also known as a "pit" in the US; (2) the official trading period of five minutes on the LME, occurring four times each day for each metal traded.

RISK: The possibility of loss; the dollar difference between the current price and the point at which the liquidation of open position would occur.

RISK-AVERSION: The policy or procedure of reducing risk or choosing the least-risk course from given alternatives.

RISK PREFERENCE (UTILITY): The risk choice of an investor.

RISK/REWARD RATIO: The relationship between the probability of loss and that of profit. This ratio is often used as a basis for trade selection or comparison.

ROLL, ROLLING FORWARD: See *switching*.

ROUND LOT: Trading unit corresponding or equal in size to the futures contract in that commodity—for example, 5,000 bushels in grains, 100 bales of cotton.

ROUND-TURN (ROUND-TRIP): The entering of a long or short futures position and the subsequent exiting of that position; a complete transaction.

SCALPER: A speculator on an exchange floor who trades in and out of the market on very small price fluctuations. The scalper, trading in this manner, provides market liquidity but seldom carries a position overnight.

SECONDARY METAL DEALER: A firm which specializes in buying and selling scrap metal. The metal purchased and sold is often in alloy form (such as brass) or in a fabricated form but is always at risk from fluctuations in the value of the basic metal.

SELLER: A risk-taker who takes a short future position or grants (sells) a commodity option. An option seller is also called a maker, grantor, or granter.

SELLER'S CALL: The purchase of a commodity, the contract for which specifies quality and fixes the price in the future.

SELLER'S OPTION: The right of the seller to select commodity quality, time, and place of delivery within the limits prescribed by the exchange upon which futures contracts are traded.

SELLING BASIS: Expression which means that the buying basis is increased to include costs and profits.

SELLING HEDGE: See *hedging*.

SEMI-FABRICATOR: See *fabricator*.

SESSION: One of the two periods of LME trading, one in the morning and one in the afternoon. Each session comprises essentially two five minute "rings" for each metal and a fifteen minute "kerb" period.

SETTLEMENT DATE: See *forward contract*.

SETTLEMENT PRICE: The average price on the close of the day, or a price determined to be in line with actual closing values. Settlement prices are used to set the next trading day's price fluctuation limits and are used as the basis for adjusting margins and determining equity by the clearinghouse for contracts traded on each exchange.

SHARPE RATIO: After William P. Sharpe, a measurement of trading performance calculated as the average return divided by the variance of those returns.

SHIPPING CERTIFICATE: A document issued by an exchange-licensed storage facility calling for delivery of a specific number of contract units to the bearer within a given number of days. Commonly used for propane.

SHORT: Starting a transaction by the sale of a futures contract. An open position on a futures market which was initiated by a sale.

SHORT HEDGES: The sale of futures against holdings of the physical commodity. See *hedging*.

SHORT COVERING: See *cover*.

SHORTSIDE TRADING: Taking only short positions in a market, usually during periods in which the price trend is down.

SHORT THE BASIS: The purchase of futures as a hedge against a commitment to sell in the cash or spot market. See also *hedging*.

SILVER/GOLD RATIO: See *gold/silver ratio*.

SOFTEN: The process of a slowly declining market price.

SOIL BANK: See *acreage reserve*.

SOLICITOR: See *commodity solicitor*.

SPECULATOR: A person using the futures market for a purpose other than hedging and willing to assume varying degrees of risk in exchange for potential profit. A speculator commonly avoids physical delivery but may take spread positions.

SPLIT CLOSE: Term which refers to price discrepancies and to the range of commodity prices at the close of any market session.

SPOT: (1) The characteristic of being available for immediate (or nearly immediate) delivery; usually refers to a cash market price for the physical commodity available for immediate delivery. (2) Sometimes used in reference to the futures contract of the current month, in which delivery is possible at any time.

SPOT MONTH: The first deliverable month for which a quotation is available on the futures market.

SPOT COMMODITY: Actual or physical commodity, as opposed to a futures contract. See *actuals*.

SPOT MARKET: The market in which cash or spot transactions occur.

SPOT MONTH: See *current delivery*.

SPOT PRICE: The commodity cash sale price, as opposed to a futures price.

SPREAD (STRADDLE): (1) The purchase of one futures delivery month against the sale of another futures delivery month of the same commodity; the purchase of one delivery month of one commodity against the sale of that same delivery month of a different commodity; or the purchase of one commodity in one market against the sale of that commodity in another market. The purpose of any on these transactions is to take advantage of distortions in normal price relationships. The term "spread" is also used to refer to the difference between the price of one futures month and the price of another month of the same commodity. There are four basic types of spreads: (a) *Interdelivery spread:* The purchase and sale of the same commodity, in the same market, in different delivery months. Also called an *intramarket spread.* (b) *Intermarket spread:* The purchase and sale of the same commodity, in the same or different delivery months, in two different markets. (c) *Intercommodity spread:* The purchase and sale of different but related commodities, in the same or different markets, in the same or different delivery months. (d) *Commodity product spread:* The purchase of futures raw material and the sale of the derived processed products futures, or vice versa. (2) In the option market, a spread is a put and call combination on the same commodity with each option having a different strike price. A spread may also be a combination of buying a call and writing a call with a different strike price or expiration date option on the same commodity.

SQUEEZE: Pressure on a particular delivery month which makes the price of that date firmer in relation to other delivery months.

STANDARD DEVIATION: Also called *mean square deviation,* a common measure of variation or dispersion which is calculated by taking the square root of the variance.

STANDBY COMMITMENT: A put option in Ginnie Mae trading; holder has the right to make delivery.

STATISTICAL RESEARCH: The use of statistical techniques, including probability, multiple regression, and other computer applications, in order to forecast price movement.

STOP-CLOSE-ONLY ORDER: A stop order which can only be executed, if possible, during the closing period of the market. Also *MOC*.

STOP ORDER, STOP LOSS ORDER: An order which becomes a market order to buy only if the market advances to a specified level or to sell only if the market declines to a specified level. As soon as this specified level is traded, the order is executed for the client at the next obtainable price. There is no guarantee the order will be executed at the price specified. A stop loss order is used to prevent or minimize losses in either a short or long position.

STRADDLE: A spread in a commodity other than grains. See *spread*.

STRIKE PRICE: (1) The price at which an option can be exercised. See also *basis price*. (2) The price at which Ginnie Mae securities can be sold on a standby commitment.

STRONG CURRENCIES: Currencies that reflect better economies and balance of trade than the United States.

STRONG HANDS: In trading, the ownership of the commodity or security which has considerable financial strength.

SUPPLY/DEMAND EQUATION: The relationship which states, for a given commodity, that if supply exceeds demand the price should decline and if demand exceeds supply the price should rise. If supply and demand are equal, the price should be stable.

SUPPORT: In technical analysis, a price area where new buying is likely to come in and stem any decline. See also *resistance*.

SWAP: Exchange of one security for another; usually involves two similar (maturity coupon, security) bonds.

SWING: (1) The fluctuation of a price within a specified time interval. (2) The amount by which a consumer may vary the tonnage taken up in a given period under a period pricing contract.

SWITCHING: (1) Liquidation of a position in one delivery month of a commodity and simultaneous initiation of a similar position in another delivery month of the same commodity. When used by hedgers, this tactic is referred to as "rolling forward the hedge." (2) On the LME, switching refers to exchanging metal in one warehouse for that in another, for example, Rotterdam for London.

SYSTEMATIC RISK: Risk due to price fluctuations which cannot be eliminated by diversification.

TAKER: See *buyer*.

TECHNICAL ANALYSIS: An approach to forecasting commodity prices based on the study of price movement itself without regard to underlying fundamental market factors. Contrasted with fundamental analysis.

TECHNICAL RALLY: (1) Price variations arising from factors other than those affecting supply and demand for a commodity. (2) An unaccountable rally following a significant decline.

TECHNICAL TRADING: Systematic trading based on charts or technical analysis that indicate buy and sell signals. See also *technical analysis*.

TENDER: Delivery of the physical commodity against a futures contract by notification given through the clearinghouse. See also *retender*.

TENDERABLE GRADES AND STAPLES: Grades and staples designated as deliverable against a futures contract.

TERMINAL ELEVATOR: In the movement of grains, a storage facility located at a point of accumulation or distribution.

TERMINAL MARKET: Usually synonymous with commodity exchange or futures market, specifically in the United Kingdom. Also used to specify principals' market, as opposed to futures market.

TICKER TAPE: A continuous paper tape transmission of commodity or security prices, volume, and other trading and market information, which operates on private wires leased by the exchanges, available to their member firms and other interested parties on a subscription basis.

TIME AND SALES: The sequential record of each transaction which occurs on the exchange, specified by time of sale and transaction price.

TIME SPREAD: Applicable to both puts and calls, the selling of a nearby option and buying a more deferred option with the same strike price.

TO-ARRIVE CONTRACT: A type of deferred shipment in which the price is based on delivery at the destination point and the seller pays the freight in shipping it to that point.

TRADER: A person who takes positions in the futures market, usually without the intention of making or taking delivery.

TRANSFERABLE NOTICE: A notice of intention to deliver that may be passed on to an eligible buyer.

TRANSFER TRADE: A trade for the purpose of transferring a customer's account from one brokerage firm to another. It is executed outside the trading pit.

TREND: The general direction of price movement, within a specified time interval.

TRENDLINE: In charting, a line drawn across the bottom or top of a price chart indicating the direction or trend of price movement. If up, the trendline is called *bullish;* if down, it is called *bearish.*

TURNOVER: See *volume.*

UNCERTAINTY: Usually refers to risk, but may mean opportunity as well.

UNDERPRICED: (1) In technical analysis, see *oversold.* (2) In options, a premium which is considered too low for the price and/or volatility of the underlying commodity.

UNDERWRITER: A firm that purchases new issues and distributes them. When issues trade, the term refers to a trade during a time interval when a new issue is sold and actually distributed. Until the issue is distributed, it trades on a "when, as, and if issued" basis.

UTILITY: See *risk preference.*

VALUE: An LME term referring to a price which is traded in a volume sufficient to satisfy the current buyers and sellers at the price—there are neither buyers nor sellers "over" at that price.

VARIABILITY: The nature of the price fluctuations of a commodity as well as the risk and reward associated with such fluctuation. Statistically measured by standard deviation.

VARIANCE: A statistical measure of variation or dispersion that is calculated by determining the average of all observations (e.g., of rates of return), determining the differences between each observation and the average, summing the squares of the differences, and dividing by the number of observations.

VARIABLE PRICE LIMIT: A price limit schedule, determined by an exchange, that permits variations other than the normally allowable price movements for any one trading day.

VARIATION MARGIN: See *margin*.

VENTURE CAPITAL (RISK CAPITAL): Monies not needed for routine living expenses and basic savings that are available for purposes of investing or speculating.

VOLATILITY: A measure of price fluctuation.

VOLUME: The quantity of business or transactions done. Also *turnover*.

WAREHOUSE RECEIPT: Document guaranteeing the existence and availability of a given quantity and quality of a commodity in storage; commonly used as the instrument of transfer of ownership in both cash and futures transactions.

WARRANT OF SETTLEMENT (WAREHOUSE OR DEPOSITORY RECEIPT): Documentary evidence of title to a cited quantity of a physical commodity of a certain type and quality, signed by the warehouse in which it is stored—in effect, a "demand note" to the warehouse. (The holder of the warrant is responsible for the storage and insurance costs of the commodity in question.)

WEAK CURRENCIES: Currencies of countries with weaker economies or a less favorable balance of trade than that of the United States.

WEAK HANDS: In trading, the ownership of the commodity or security which has weak financial capability.

WET BARRELS: Oil trading term signifying delivery of product rather than the transfer of a tanker receipt.

YIELD: A measure of the annual return on an investment expressed as a percentage.

YIELD TO MATURITY: The current yield augmented or decreased by the amortized difference between the purchase price and the maturity value.

INDEX

Acceleration, **15**•17–19
  interpretation, **15**•18
Accounting and back-office operations, **18**•49–51
Acidulated soybean soapstock, **30**•38
Acreage report, **8**•5
Actual commodities, **4**•11, **13**•13–14, **13**•14–17
Adjusted gap, **11**•6, **11**•8
Advance guarantees, *see* Commodity options
African coffee production, **35**•5
Against actuals, **9**•49, **9**•50, **38**•15
Aggregate market value of stocks, **49**•18–19
Agricultural Act of 1970, **40**•11
Agricultural Act of 1980, **40**•11–12
Agricultural Adjustment Act of 1933, **40**•10
Agricultural cooperatives, **5**•13
Agricultural Marketing Act of 1929, **40**•10
Agricultural Marketing Service, **32**•18
Agricultural prices, **8**•12
Agricultural Stabilization and Conservation Service (ASCS), **8**•7–10, **8**•12
Agriculture, **25**•3–20
  crop spreads, **25**•14–18
    diverging prices, **25**•14–15
    London grain markets, **25**•18
    miscellaneous, **25**•15–18
    volume of futures trading, **25**•18–19
  exports, **25**•3
    grain market uncertainties, **25**•3–6
  forecasting and estimation, **25**•8–13
    anticipated acreage, **25**•9
    food consumption, **25**•9
    price, **25**•8–9
    satellite data, **25**•13–14
    USDA reports, **25**•9
    weather modeling, **25**•9–10
    yield estimation (corn and wheat), **25**•10–12
  grain price forecast, **25**•6–8
    demand, **25**•7
    market price, **25**•7–8
    supply, **25**•6–7
  penalties, increased output, **25**•3
Agriculture and Consumer Protection Act of 1973, **40**•11
Agriculture and Food Act of 1981, **26**•8, **27**•10, **30**•10, **39**•7
AgRISTARS (Agricultural and Resources Inventory Surveys Through Aerospace Remote Sensing), **25**•13
Alaskan North Slope (ANS), **42**•8
Alchemical symbols, **4**•11
ALGOL (ALGOrithmic Language), **18**•10
Allocation of capital, **20**•3–4
Alternative orders, **2**•16
Aluminum, **45**•3
  alchemical symbol, **4**•11
American Commodities Exchange (ACE), **1**•36, **10**•12
American Feed Control Officials, Incorporated (AFCO), **30**•43
American option, **13**•4, **13**•44
American Society for Testing and Materials (ASTM). **42**•19
American Softwood Lumber Standard, **41**•6
American Soybean Association, **30**•49
American Stock Exchange, **13**•13
Amino Acids, **30**•42
Anidata, **18**•60
Anticipated acreage forecast, **25**•9
APL (A Programming Language), **18**•10
Apple Computer, Incorporated, **18**•61
Applications packages ("canned software"), **18**•10, **18**•36
APP method of seasonal analysis, **B**•1–2
Appreciation, currency, **47**•5
Arabicas, **35**•3–4, **35**•14
Arbitrage, **4**•20, **9**•38, **12**•26, **34**•19
  financial futures markets, **10**•39–42, **10**•43–49
  foreign exchange futures, **47**•22–24
  interest-rate futures market, **10**•16–17
  U.S. and U.K. markets, **4**•26–28
  world financial futures markets, **4**•20–21
Arbitrage Class B, **47**•23–24
Arbitrage interest-rate, **47**•22–23
Arbitrage spatial, **47**•23
Arbitrage triangular, **47**•23
Arbitration committee, **1**•7, **1**•24
Arithmetic mean, **17**•4
Arithmetic method, **21**•16
Ascending triangle, **14**•19–20
Aspartame (sweetener), **39**•6
Assemblers, computer language, **18**•9–10
Associated persons, regulation of, **5**•19–20
Associate Mercantile Market, **1**•34
  futures trading opening dates, **1**•35
At the limit, **15**•33
At-the-money, **13**•44

At risk, **6**•28
Auctions, Treasury bill, **48**•24
Automatic Data Processing (ADP), **18**•28, **18**•61
Automobiles:
  use of palladium, **46**•14
  use of platinum, **46**•6–7
  vehicle registration and fuel consumption, **42**•32
Average maximum retracement (AMR), **22**•14–15
  using to construct performance measures, **22**•16–18
Averages (or measures of central location), **17**•4
Average velocity, **15**•17

Backwardations, **4**•27
Balance-of-payments, **47**•5
  exchange rate formula, **47**•25–26
Balance sheet, **25**•6
Band, used as stop-loss, **15**•14
Bank CDs, *see* Certificates of deposit
Bank of England, **4**•24–25, **43**•3, **47**•5, **47**•6
Bank of International Settlements (BIS), **48**•17
Bank risk management, *see* Risk-management techniques
Bar charting, **14**•3–22
  bar charts, **14**•6–8
    weekly and monthly continuation **14**•7–8
  basic technical concepts, **14**•8–14
    gaps, **14**•13–14
    percentage retracement, **14**•12–13
    support and resistance, **14**•9–10
    trend, **14**•8–9
    trendlines and channels, **14**•10–12
  continuation patterns, **14**•17–20
    flags and pennants, **14**•18
    triangles, **14**•19–20
  distinction between technical analyst and chartist, **14**•4–5
  Dow theory, **14**•5–6
  reversal patterns, **14**•14–17
    double tops or bottoms, **14**•15–16
    head and shoulders top or bottom, **14**•16
    rounding or saucer top or bottom, **14**•16–17
    spike or V top or bottom, **14**•16
    triple tops or bottoms, **14**•16
  what it is (and what it is not), **14**•3–5
Barley, **29**•3–4
  cash price (Minneapolis), **29**•4
  consumption and usage, **29**•3–4
  contract specifications, **29**•8
  futures markets, **29**•4
  production, **29**•3
  statistics, **29**•6–7
  world production, **29**•5
Barter, **1**•19
BASIC (Beginner's All-purpose Symbolic Introduction Code), **18**•10
Basis (application of futures to hedging price risk), **9**•11–30
  convergence, **9**•14
  cost of carry, **9**•12–14
  differences, **9**•11
  distortions in carrying charges, **9**•16–17
  hedging, **9**•19–21
  hedging applications, **9**•21–30
  inverted markets, **9**•17
  method of quoting, **9**•11
  risk and profit maximization, **9**•17–19
  seasonality, **9**•14–16, **9**•19
  supply shortages, **9**•11–12
Basis risk, **43**•17, **44**•19
Batch processing, **18**•6
Batteries, silver, **44**•14
Bear market, **19**•8
Bear spread, **12**•4–5, **12**•24–26
Beef production cycle, **31**•5
Beet sugar, *see* Sugar
Belgian franc, **10**•7
Bermuda, **1**•41
Bicolored soybeans, **30**•45
Bids, *see* Commodity options
Bill of exchange, **1**•3, **47**•5
Black soybeans, **30**•45
Blister copper, **45**•4
Blue Lakes Software, **18**•61
Board crushing margin, **30**•37
Board orders, **2**•15
BOM (bean, oil, and meal) spread, **30**•37
Bona fide hedging transaction, **9**•3
Bottoming pattern, **14**•15
Bourse, meaning of, **1**•5
Bourse de Commerce, **1**•41–43, **30**•33
Brass, **45**•10
Brazilian coffee production, **35**•5–7
Breakaway gap, **14**•13
Break material, **30**•38–39
Bretton Woods system, **47**•7–8
British Association of Grain, Seed, Feed, and Agriculture Merchants, **25**•18
British pound, **4**•21, **10**•7
  devaluation, **47**•8
  IMM contract, **47**•15
  parity in U.S. dollars (1951), **47**•8
  sterling-denominated contracts, **4**•3
  weekly prices, **47**•9
Broilers, **33**•3–10
  contract specifications, **33**•9
  demand, **33**•7–8
  futures markets, **33**•9
  industry background, **33**•3
  production, **33**•3–5
  seasonality, **33**•8–9
  sources of information, **33**•10
  statistics, **33**•6
  supply, **33**•5–7
  weekly prices (Chicago, nearest futures), **33**•4
Brokerage house, selecting, **2**•3–4
Brokerage Systems, Incorporated (BSI), **18**•51, **18**•61–62
Bronze, **45**•10
Brown soybeans, **30**•44

Bullion broker, **4**•18
Bull market, **19**•8
Bull spread, **12**•4–5, **12**•24–26
Buses, vehicle registration and fuel consumption, **42**•32
Business conduct committees, **1**•24
Business cycle, **7**•3
Business International Corporation, **18**•62
Butter and Cheese Exchange of New York, **1**•11
Butterfly spread, **12**•9
Buyer's call, **9**•49
Buyer's call price fixed later, **9**•49
Buying hedge, **9**•9–11, **9**•20

Calculated or ideal basis, **9**•19
Calendar spread, **13**•34, **13**•44
Call, **4**•25, **13**•4
Call chairman, **4**•20
Call option, **13**•4, **13**•44
  fair-value premiums, **13**•24–25
Call purchase, **13**•4
Call writer (or option seller), **13**•4
Caloric sweetener consumption, **39**•4
Canada:
  effect on U.S. grains, **25**•15
  gold production, **43**•6
  oats, **28**•7
  palladium supply, **46**•14
  platinum production, **46**•3, **46**•4
  sources of information, **25**•19–20
  wheat production, **26**•5
  Winnipeg grain markets, **29**•3–20
Canadian dollar, **10**•7
  IMM contract, **47**•15
  parity in U.S. dollars (1951), **47**•8
  weekly prices, **47**•9
Cancel former order (CFO), **2**•17
Cancellation, **2**•17
Cane sugar, *see* Sugar
Canned software, **18**•10, **18**•36
Capital:
  conservation of, **21**•7–8
  as factor for production, **7**•3–4
Capital gains conversion, **6**•7
Capital gains and losses, **6**•5
Capitalization, money management and, **20**•3–8
  allocation, **20**•3
  balancing risks, **20**•5–6
  new accounts, **20**•4
  redistribution, **20**•4–5
  risk control structure, **20**•8
  trading performance and capital contribution, **20**•6–8
Capital requirements, **6**•22, **16**•7–8
Carrying charge market, **12**•20–21, **12**•22–23
Carrying charges, **12**•16, **12**•18–20, **12**•23–24
  financing costs, **12**•20
  implied yields, **12**•24
Carry loss, **10**•15
Cash-and-carry, **6**•4, **10**•33
  tax consequences, **6**•9–10
Cash markets, **1**•20, **10**•4
  financial futures and, **10**•23–49
    alternative investments, **10**•30–33
    arbitrage strategies, **10**•39–42, **10**•43–49
    external factors, **10**•29
    integration, **10**•33–43
    overview, **10**•49
  soybean complex, **30.7–19**
    meal, **30**•19–26
    oil, **30**•26–33
Cash settlement, **1**•7, **1**•26, **10**•14
Catalytic-converter devices, **46**•6
Catalytic cracking process, **42**•6
Cattle hedge, **9**•42–43
Cattle industry, **31**•3–22
  cow/calf sector, **21**•4–7
    beef production cycle, **31**•5
    consumer dollar, **31**•6–7
    land values, **31**•5–6
    slaughter, **31**•4–5
    slaughter and replacement (1953–1982), **31**•5
    feeding sector, **31**•7–11
    and Omaha corn price, **31**•10, **31**•11
  futures markets, **21**•18–21
  historical price movements, **21**•16–18
  live hog prices and, **32**•15
  price/demand relationships, **21**•12–15
  seasonality, **21**•15–16
  weekly nearest futures (Chicago), **21**•19
Cattle on Feed reports, **8**•4, **8**•5, **12**•14
Cattle spread, **12**•14
CBOT, *see* Chicago Board of Trade
CBT, *see* Chicago Board of Trade
Central Securities Administrators Council (CSAC), **5**•41
Central states, potato production, **37**•3
Certainty equivalent, **23**•8
Certificates of deposit (CDs), **1**•30, **1**•31, **10**•13–14, **10**•20, **13**•13, **13**•14, **13**•21, **48**•3, **48**•12–16
  cash market, **48**•12–15
  futures market, **48**•15–16
  history, **48**•12–14
  IMM, **48**•15–16
  interest-rate ceilings, **48**•14
  primary market, **48**•14
  secondary market, **48**•14–15
CFATS (Commodity Fund Accounting through Time Sharing), **18**•50
CFC, *see* Controlled foreign corporations
CFM Corporation, **18**•62
CFTC, *see* Commodity Futures Trading Commission
Channel, used as stop-loss, **15**•14
Channel line, **14**•10–12
Chart analysis, *see* Bar charting
Chart formations, commodity point-and-figure chart, **15**•5–6

Chase Econometrics/Interactive Data Corporation (Chase/IDC), **18**•27–28, **18**•62
Check-sum procedure, **18**•30
Chicago Board of Trade (CBOT), **1**•17, **1**•25, **1**•29, **1**•30, **4**•19, **10**•5, **13**•13, **30**•50, **40**•15, **42**•3, **48**•3
  CD futures, **48**•15
  clearing association, **3**•11–14
  commodities traded, **1**•33–34
  corn contract, **27**•14
  crude oil contracts, **42**•19, **42**•20–21
  founded, **1**•10–11
  gasoline futures contracts, **42**•35–37
  GMNA-CDR futures contract, **48**•24
  gold contract, **43**•13
  gold trading volume, **43**•12
  heating oil, **42**•25, **42**•27–28
  long-term Treasury bond contract, **48**•29
  long-term Treasury note contract, **48**•28
  membership transactions, **A**•1–101
    qualifications and process **A**•1–2
    range of transactions, **A**•3–101
  oats contract, **28**•8–9
  plywood contract (Western plywood futures), **41**•20, **41**•21
  rules and regulations, **1**•19
  silver futures, **44**•18, **44**•21
  soybean complex, **30**•33, **30**•34
  soybean meal, **30**•34
  soybean oil, **30**•35
  trading specifications, compared to U.K., **4**•4–5
  unleaded gasoline contract, **42**•33–34
  wheat contract, **26**•12
  wheat traded, **25**•14
Chicago Board of Trade Stock Market Index, **10**•8
CBT v. *Dow Jones,* **49**•8
Chicago Board Options Exchange (CBOE), **13**•3, **13**•13, **13**•14
  straddle, **6**•30–31
Chicago Butter and Egg Board, **1**•11, **1**•17
Chicago Markets:
  of 1835–1875, **1**•10–11
  of 1898–1960, **1**•17
Chicago Mercantile Exchange (CME), **1**•11, **1**•17, **1**•29, **1**•30–31, **4**•19, **10**•5, **37**•3, **41**•6, **41**•18, **42**•3, **42**•19, **47**•3, **47**•12, **47**•13, **49**•7
  cattle futures, **31**•18, **31**•20
  clearing association, **3**•11–14
  commodities traded, **1**•34
  feeder cattle, **31**•20
  fresh broiler chickens, **33**•9
  futures trading opening dates, **1**•35
  gasoline futures contracts, **42**•35–37
  live beef cattle, **31**•20
  lumber contract, **41**•19
  random length lumber contract, **41**•21
  stock index futures contracts, **49**•16
Chicago Open Board of Trade, **1**•11, **1**•17
Chicago Produce Exchange, **1**•11, **1**•17
Chilled juice, **36**•10
China, **25**•4–5, **25**•14
  corn production, **27**•4, **27**•5
  cotton production, **40**•9–10
  crop areas, **25**•5
  wheat production, **26**•5
Chi-square test, **17**•20
Cho-ai-mai ("rice trade on book" futures market), **1**•7
Chocolate:
  consumption, **34**•8–9
  production, **34**•2–8
  see also Cocoa
Churning, **2**•9
Class B arbitrage, **47**•23–24
Class buyers, **25**•14
Class of option, **13**•45
Clean floats, **47**•12
Clearing associations, **4**•21–25
Clearinghouses, **2**•10, **2**•19, **2**•26, **3**•3–15, **47**•19
  comparative analysis of associations, **3**•11–14
  daily reporting, **3**•8
  evolution, **3**•4–5
  financial safeguards, **3**•6–8
  futures transactions, **3**•3
  handling of deliveries, **3**•9–15
  lack of, in London, **4**•12
  margin calls, **3**•8–9
  matching up, **3**•3–4
  original margin, **3**•8–9
  principle of substitution, **3**•6
  services provided, **3**•4
  theory and purpose, **3**•5–6
  variation margin, **3**•8–9
Clearing margins, **3**•8–9
Close-only stop, **12**•13
Closing purchase, **13**•45
Closing sale, **13**•45
Club or white wheat, **26**•5
CME, *see* Chicago Mercantile Exchange
Coal, **42**•22
COBOL (COmmon Business Oriented Language), **18**•10
Cocoa, **34**•3–29
  bean exports, **34**•6
  consumption, **34**•8–9
  cyclic analysis, **34**•14–16
  futures trading, **34**•16–19
  gold and, **34**•12, **34**•13–14
  hedging in cocoa beans, **34**•20–28
  impact of sugar, **34**•8–9
  long-term flexibility, **34**•7
  monthly prices (New York, nearest futures), **34**•9
  price dynamics, **34**•9–12
  production, **34**•3–8
  real producer price indexes, **34**•11
  seasonality, **34**•12–14
  speculators, **34**•19

trading price, differential basis, **34**•23–26
trading price is fixed, **34**•20–23
world production, **34**•4–5
Cocoa Association of London, **34**•16
Cocoa butter, **34**•7
hedging strategy, **34**•26–28
Coffee, **35**•3–17
aribicas and robustas, **35**•3–4
cash coffee, **35**•9
consumption, **35**•8–11
contract specifications, **35**•15, **35**•16
exports, **7**•6
futures trading, **35**•14
imports for consumption (U.S.), **35**•11
inelasticity of demand, **35**•10
international agreements, **35**•12–14
Latin American production trends, **35**•7
natural process, **35**•4
role of Brazil, **35**•4–7
seasonality, **35**•7–8
shift in demand, **35**•10
short-run price dynamics, **35**•12–14
spot price (New York), **35**•12
suppliers, **35**•3–5
weekly price (New York), **35**•8
wet method, **35**•4
world green coffee (exportable) production, **35**•6
Coffee, Sugar, and Cocoa Exchange, **1**•36, **6**•26, **34**•16
clearing association, **3**•11–14
cocoa extract, **34**•18
coffee "C" contract, **35**•14, **35**•15
domestic sugar No. 12 contract, **38**•14
sugar options, **38**•16
world sugar No. 11 contract, **38**•13
Coffee Terminal Market Association of London Ltd., **1**•45, **4**•18
robusta coffee contract, **35**•14, **35**•16
Coinage:
copper use, **45**•10
silver, **44**•14–16
Cold pressed soy oil, **30**•39
Cold Storage report, **32**•18
Collateralized Depository Receipt (CDR), **48**•22
Columbian coffee production, **35**•5
COMEX, *see* Commodity Exchange, Incorporated
Comm-Basic Associates, Incorporated, **18**•62
Commemorative coins, **44**•14–16
Commercial Exchange, **1**•10
Commercial paper contract, **10**•10–11
Commingling, **5**•18
Commission:
charges, **2**•23
LME, **4**•17
rates, **19**•14–15
transfer an account, **2**•26
Committees, **1**•23–24
Committee of subscribers, **4**•17
COMMODEX System, **18**•63
Commodities:
agriculture, **25**•3–20
barley, **29**•3–4
broilers, **33**•3–10
cattle industry, **31**•3–22
CEA definition, **5**•8
cocoa, **34**•3–29
coffee, **35**•1–17
copper, **45**•3–19
corn, **27**•3–15
cotton, **40**•3–19
energy futures, **42**•3–43
crude oil, **42**•7–19
flaxseed, **29**•4–12
gasoline, **42**•29–34
heating oil, **42**•29–34
liquefied propane gas, **42**•34–41
foreign exchange futures, **47**•3–30
gold, **43**•3–22
interest-rate futures, **48**•3–30
lumber and plywood, **41**•3–22
oats, **28**•3–9
orange juice, **36**•3–20
palladium, **46**•9–15
platinum, **46**•3–9
pork complex, **32**•3–19
potato market, **37**•3–22
rapeseed, **29**•13
refined sugar, **39**•3–8
rye, **29**•13–20
silver, **44**•3–21
soybean complex, **30**•3–50
stock-index futures, **49**•32
sugar, **38**•3–23
wheat, **26**•3–14
Winnipeg grain markets, **29**•3–20
Commodity Accounting Systems (CAS), **18**•50, **18**•63
Commodity accounts:
agreement, **2**•4, **2**•6
closing, **2**•26
establishing, **2**•4–9
see also Futures trading
Commodity Communications Corporation, **18**•29, **18**•63
Commodity concepts, **18**•63
Commodity Credit Corporation (CCC), **8**•12, **8**•18, **30**•10, **39**•7, **40**•11, **40**•16
Commodity Exchange, Incorporated (COMEX), **1**•15, **1**•36, **4**•19, **6**•26, **10**•12
clearing association, **3**•11–14
commodities traded, **1**•37
copper futures, **45**•12–14
futures contract, **10**•22
gold contract, **43**•12
gold trading volume, **43**•12
90-day Treasury bill contract, **48**•11
silver futures, **44**•18
compared to LME, **44**•21

Commodity Exchange, Incorporated (*Continued*)
trading specifications, compared to U.K., **4**•4–5
2-year Treasury note, **48**•28
Commodity Exchange, Incorporated 500 Stock Index, **10**•8
Commodity Exchange Act (CEA), **5**•6–33, **13**•11
CFTC, **5**•6, **5**•8–33
contract markets, **5**•10, **5**•12–17
current issues, **5**•33–42
duties, **5**•10–12
jurisdiction, **5**•8–10
1928 Act, **5**•3–6
regulation of trading, **5**•24–33
regulation of trading professionals, **5**•17–24
created, **5**•6–8
existing regulation and, **5**•7–8
hedgers' concerns, **5**•7
self-regulation and, **5**•7
speculators' concerns, **5**•7
Commodity Exchange Act of 1893 (Japan), **1**•8
Commodity Exchange Act of 1950 (Japan), **1**•9
Commodity fund, taxation of, **6**•27–29
domestic funds, **6**•27–28
offshore funds, **6**•28–29
Commodity Futures Trading Commission (CFTC), **1**•3, **1**•29, **2**•4, **2**•21, **3**•8, **4**•24–25, **5**•6, **5**•8–33, **9**•8, **10**•6, **10**•18–20, **13**•3, **13**•14, **19**•5, **19**•12, **19**•17, **24**•8, **49**•6, **49**•7
contract markets, **5**•10, **5**•12–17
designation, **5**•12–15
duties, **5**•15–16
rules, **5**•16–17
created, **13**•12
current issues, **5**•33–42
jurisdictional issues, **5**•37–41
pilot program, **5**•35–37, **6**•26, **13**•12
reauthorization, **5**•41–42
role of NFA, **5**•33–35
duties, **5**•10–12
informational activities, **5**•11
organization and coordination of activities, **5**•11–12
regulation, **5**•10–11
remedying violations of CEA, **5**•11
rules, **5**•16–17
equity index futures contracts, **10**•20–23
jurisdiction, **5**•8–10, **5**•37–41
commodity futures contracts, **5**•8–9
commodity options, **5**•9
in general, **5**•8
leverage transactions, **5**•9–10
new and pending contracts, **1**•32
1928 Act, **5**•3–6
pilot program, **5**•35–37, **6**•26, **13**•12
regulation of trading, **5**•24–33
antifraud rules, **5**•24–25
criminal conduct, **5**•32
general prohibitions, **5**•25
government enforcement, **5**•30–32
practices of floor brokers and FCMs, **5**•25–26
private claims, **5**•29–30
prohibition of manipulation, **5**•28
remedying violations of CEA, **5**•29
reporting requirements, **5**•28–29
speculative practices, **5**•26–28
regulation of trading professionals, **5**•17–24
associated persons, **5**•19–20
commodity pool operators, **5**•20–24
commodity trading advisors, **5**•20–24
floor brokers and FCMS, **5**•17–19
SEC jurisdictional agreement, **5**•5–6, **5**•37–41
background, **5**•37–38
boundaries, **5**•38–40
state boundaries, **5**•40–41
Commodity Futures Trading Commission Act of 1974, **3**•8, **5**•6, **13**•11–13
Commodity Information Services Company (CISCO), **18**•32, **18**•37, **18**•44, **18**•63, **22**•18
Commodity News Service, **18**•38–39, **38**•64
Commodity options, **13**•3–47
CFTC jurisdiction, **5**•9
commercial applications, **13**•38–42
as alternative to futures, **13**•38–39
delta hedging, **13**•40–42
price and quantity risk, **13**•40
fundamental concepts, **13**•4–6
glossary, **13**•44–47
margining, **13**•42–44
1982 Act, **5**•3
risk reward, **13**•6–9
diagram, **13**•8–9
"in-the-money" and "out-of-the-money," **13**•7–8
ways to profit, **13**•6
strategies, **13**•26–38
trading, **13**•4–6
history, **13**•10–13
in 1980s, **13**•13–17
pricing, **13**•17–26
see also specific commodities
Commodity pool operators, (CPO), **5**•5, **5**•20–24
antifraud rules, **5**•24
defined, **5**•21
disclosure documents, **5**•22–23
evaluating, **19**•13–14
handling of funds, **5**•23
presentation of performance, **24**•7–8
registration, **5**•21–22
reporting requirements, **5**•23–24
Commodity prices, market outlook, **7**•3–28
crude oil and commodity prices, **7**•19–22
exchange rate effects, **7**•25–27
factors of production, **7**•3–4
futures markets, **7**•6–14
inventory cycles, **7**•27–28
1979–1982 crucible, **7**•14

real interest rates, **7**•16–19
spikes and craters, **7**•14–16
world trade, **7**•4–6
Commodity QuoteGraphics, **18**•64
Commodity Research Bureau, Incorporated (CRB), **7**•15–16
Commodity Research Bureau (CRB) Index, **9**•3, **14**•21
Commodity Spreads, *see* Spread
Commodity Systems, Incorporated (CSI), **18**•29, **18**•30–32, **18**•64
Commodity Systems reports, **18**•64–65
Commodity Trading:
early evolution, **1**•3–5
in Japan, **1**•5–9
taxation, **6**•26–27
in U.S., **1**•9–17
see also Trading performance
Commodity trading advisors (CTA), **5**•5, **5**•20–24
antifraud rules, **5**•24
defined, **5**•20–21
disclosure documents, **5**•22–23
handling of funds, **5**•23
presentation of performance, **24**•7–8
registration, **5**•21–22
regulation, **5**•20–24
reporting requirements, **5**•23–24
Commodity transactions, taxation and, **6**•3–32
cash-and-carry, **6**•4, **6**•9–10
categories, **6**•4
commodity traders, **6**•26–27
domestic funds, **6**•27–28
ERTA rules, **6**•3, **6**•10–24
carry-back provisions, **6**•13–14
cash-and-carry, **6**•22
constructive ownership rules, **6**•20–21
identification requirements, **6**•23–24
identified straddles, **6**•18–19
loss deferral rule, **6**•16–18
mark-to-market concept, **6**•11–13
mixed straddles, **6**•21–22
reporting considerations, **6**•22–23
RFCs, **6**•11–13
short-sale rules, **6**•20
transitional rules, **6**•15–16
wash-sale rules, **6**•19–20
futures options, **6**•26
hedging, **6**•25–26
nonhedge transactions, **6**•4–6
offshore commodity funds, **6**•28–29
stock options, **6**•29–31
straddles, **6**•6–9
Treasury bill futures, **6**•24–25
Commodity World News, **18**•65
Common gap, **14**•13
Communications applications, **18**•37–53
accounting and back-office, **18**•49–51
analytical, **18**•43–49
choice of computer, **18**•51–53
data transmission, **18**•38
day trading and news wires, **18**•38–40
dedicated terminal services, **18**•40–41
microcomputer services, **18**•41–43
microcomputers and time-sharing, **18**•37–38
trading applications, **18**•40
Compilers, computer language, **18**•9–10
Complete hedge, **9**•48–50
Complex trigonometric curve fitting, **17**•14–15
Compound wave, **17**•11
CompuServe, **18**•65
Computer Information Service (CIS), **18**•50, **18**•65
Computerized Research International, **18**•65
Computers, **16**•5, **18**•3–81
applications, **18**•36
communications applications, **18**•37–53
accounting and back-office, **18**•49–51
analytical applications, **18**•43–49
choice of computer, **18**•51–53
data transmission, **18**•38
day trading and news wires, **18**•38–40
dedicated terminal services, **18**•40–41
microcomputer services, **18**•41–43
microcomputers and time-sharing, **18**•37–38
trading applications, **18**•40
databases, **18**•26–36
comparing vendors, **18**•30–32
fulfilling needs, **18**•35–36
fundamental analysis, **18**•27–28
management, **18**•32–35
pricing and file structure, **18**•31
technical analysis, **18**•28–30
development, **18**•5–13
costs, **18**•10–11
dependence, **18**•3
hardware, **18**•5–8
software, **18**•9–10
hardware, **18**•13–26
decision-making, **18**•22–26
microcomputers, **18**•19–22
minicomputers, **18**•16–19
time sharing, **18**•14
impact on trading, **18**•53–55
list of commercial services, **18**•56–81
using in system development, **15**•33–36
point-and-figure, **15**•34
real-time analysis, **15**•34–35
testing, **15**•33–34
Computer service bureaus, **18**•4
CompuTrac, Incorporated, **18**•66
CompuTrac Technical Analysis Group, **18**•38, **18**•41, **18**•46–47
Confirmations, **2**•12
chart pattern, **14**•21
in England, **4**•14
liquidation, **2**•23
Conifers, **41**•3

Consumer price index (CPI), **7**•17
Contango, **4**•27
Continuation patterns, **14**•17–20
  flags and pennants, **14**•18
  triangles, **14**•19–20
Continuously compounded rate, **23**•23
Contract facts, **2**•17–19, **2**•20
Contract markets, **5**•10, **5**•12–17
  designation, **5**•12–15
    agricultural cooperatives, **5**•13
    CFTC guidelines, **5**•14
    denial, suspension, or revocation, **5**•14–15
    exchange operations, **5**•13
    in general, **5**•12
    location **5**•13
    membership, **5**•12–13
    proposed CFTC rules, **5**•14
    public interest requirement, **5**•13–14
  duties, **5**•15–16
    arbitration procedures, **5**•16
    delivery terms, **5**•15
    enforcement programs, **5**•15–16
    in general, **5**•15
    warehouses, **5**•15
  rules, **5**•16–17
    altering or supplementing, **5**•16–17
    approval process, **5**•16
    CFTC emergency powers, **5**•17
    recordkeeping and reporting, **5**•17
Contracts:
  standardization of, **1**•18
  Sterling-denominated, **4**•3
  see also specific commodities; exchanges
Contract size, **2**•19, **47**•19
Contratrend systems, **15**•20–21
Controlled foreign corporations (CFC), **6**•29
Controlled or managed accounts, **2**•9
Convergence, **9**•14
Copper, **45**•3–19
  alchemical symbol, **4**•11
  consumption, **45**•9–10
  contract specifications, **45**•13, **45**•15
  demand, **45**•8–10
  exporter's hedge, **45**•15–19
  filtering housing starts, **45**•12
  futures market, **45**•12–15
  monthly prices (New York), **45**•4
  production, **45**•3–8
    primary, **45**•5–6, **45**•7
    process, **45**•3–5
    refined, world production, **45**•8
    scrap recovery, **45**•6
  seasonality, **45**•10–12
Copper spread, **12**•15
Corn, **27**•3–15
  acreage and supply (U.S.), **27**•7
  cash price (Chicago), **27**•4
  contract specifications, **27**•14
  distribution, **27**•8–9
  feeder cattle, price, and, **31**•10, **31**•11
  futures markets, **27**•12–15
  government programs, **27**•10–11
  hedge, **9**•44
  hog/corn ratio, **32**•12–18
  marketing, **27**•6
  maturing dates (Illinois), **27**•13
  prices, **27**•6–10
  production, **27**•3–6
  production growth, **25**•4
  seasonality, **27**•11–12
  world production uses, **27**•6
  yield estimation, **25**•10–12
Corn Belt region, **27**•4, **27**•6
Corn hybrid, **27**•3
Corn oil, **27**•6
Correlation, **21**•13–14
Correlation coefficient, **17**•7, **17**•8, **21**•13
Cost of carry, **9**•12–14, **44**•19, **49**•24
  inverted market structure, **9**•37
Cotton, **40**•3–19
  contract specifications, **40**•19
  demand, **40**•13–15
  first American mill, **40**•3
  futures markets, **40**•18–19
  government programs, **40**•10–13
  history, **40**•3
  payments-in-kind, **40**•12
  price dynamics, **40**•15–18
  price support levels, **40**•12
  production, **40**•4–13
    classification, **40**•5–6
    by principal countries, **40**•4
    types, **40**•4
    world (1952–1982), **40**•13
  raw, estimated mill consumption, **40**•15
  supply and distribution, **40**•6–10
    China, **40**•9–10
    Russia, **40**•8–9
    U.S., **40**•6–8
  USDA analysis, **8**•15–18
  yields, **40**•8
Cotton, Incorporated, **40**•15
Cotton gin, **40**•3
Cotton merchant's account, **9**•48
Cotton and Wool Outlook and Situation report, **8**•18
Coupon yield, **48**•24
Covered option buying, **13**•31–33
Covered option writing, **13**•31–33
Covered writer, **13**•45
Cow/calf industry, **31**•4–7
  beef production cycle, **31**•5
  consumer dollar, **31**•6–7
  land values, **31**•5–6
  slaughter, **31**•4–5
  slaughter and replacement (1953–1982), **31**•5
  see also Cattle industry
Cox, M.E., **10**•7

CPRS (Computer Price Reporting System), **18**•5, **18**•13
CPU (Central Processing Unit), **18**•23
Cracking process, crude oil, **42**•5–6
Credit risk, **48**•5
 interbank market, **48**•18
Crop Production report, **8**•5–7, **8**•18
Crop Reporting Board, **8**•5, **33**•7
Crop spreads, **25**•14–18
 diverging prices, **25**•14–15
 London grain markets, **25**•18
 miscellaneous, **25**•15–18
 volume of futures trading, **25**•18–19
Crop yields, satellite data, **25**•12–13
Cross long arbitrage, **10**•48
CRT (cathode-ray tube), **18**•28–29
Crude oil, **42**•7–19
 cash market structure, **42**•18
 cash market transactions, **42**•18
 commodity prices and, **7**•19–22
 contract specifications, **42**•20–21
 cracking and reforming process, **42**•5–6
 distillation curve, **42**•4, **42**•5
 exports, **7**•6
 futures contracts, **42**•19, **42**•20–21
 glut periods, **42**•17
 grades and specifications, **42**•7–8
 largest domestic fields, **42**•14
 majors and independents, **42**•18
 production, **42**•8–10, **42**•11
 by qualities, **42**•9
 refinery runs by district, **42**•16
 refinery yields (major products), **42**•6
 reserves, **42**•8, **42**•10
 sources of information, **42**•41
 stocks, **42**•14–18
 storáge costs, **42**•17
 U.S. imports, **42**•10–11
 U.S. production, **42**•12–13
 U.S. supply, **42**•15
Crude soy oil, **30**•39
Crushing hedge, **30**•36–38
Crushing margin, **9**•46, **12**•8
Crush spread, **9**•47–48, **12**•8–9, **12**•30–33
Currency hedge, **9**•40
Currency spread, **12**•19
Current basis, **9**•19
Current yield, **48**•24–25
Curvilinear curve, **17**•9
Cycles, as trading tool, **15**•22–29
 major regular cycles, **15**•25–27
 other growing cycles, **15**•24–25
 phasing using moving averages, **15**•27–28
 seasonality, **15**•22–24

Daily Limits, **47**•18–19
 LCE, **4**•20
Daily reporting, clearinghouse, **3**•8
Damaged kernels, **30**•45
Database access, **18**•37
Database commercial services, **18**•57
Databases, **18**•26–36
 comparing vendors, **18**•30–32
 fulfilling needs, **18**•35–36
 fundamental analysis, **18**•27–28
 management, **18**•32–35
  accuracy, **18**•33–34
  storage media, **18**•34–35
 pricing and file structure, **18**•31
 technical analysis, **18**•28–30
Data errors, **18**•33–34
Data management software, **18**•33
Data Resources, Incorporated (DRI), **18**•27–28, **18**•66–67
Data services, **18**•29
Data storage, time-sharing systems, **18**•14–15
Data transmission, **18**•38, **18**•39
Data update services, **18**•30
Day order, **2**•15
Day trading, methods of, **15**•30
Day trading techniques, **15**•29–30
Dealer options, **13**•17, **13**•20
Decline guarantees, *see* Commodity options
DEC VAX Systems, **18**•7
Defatted soy flour, **30**•42
Deferment, tax, *see* Straddles
Degrees of freedom, **22**•6
Degummed soy oil, **30**•39
Dehulled solvent extracted soybean meal, **30**•43
Dehulled soybean flakes, **30**•41
Deliver on sale contract, **1**•20
Delivery, **2**•25
 handling, **3**•9–15
 KCBT-VLA, **49**•14
 LME, **4**•13–14
Delivery of the commodity, **2**•19
Delivery dates, **2**•19
Delivery day, **3**•10
Delivery default, **2**•20
Delivery months, **2**•19
Delivery notice, **3**•10
Delta, **13**•45
Delta hedging, **13**•40–42
Demand, **17**•21
 changes in elasticity, **17**•21–22
 elasticity, **17**•21
 of grain, **25**•7
 see also specific commodities
Demand side, world trade, **7**•22–25
Dent corn, **27**•4
Department of Agriculture, *see* USDA
Depreciation, currency, **47**•5
Descending triangle, **14**•19–20
Desulfurization, **42**•6
Detrended seasonal bias, **15**•22
Deutsche mark, **4**•21, **10**•7, **47**•12, **47**•19
 IMM contract, **47**•15
 parity in U.S. dollars (1951), **47**•8

Deutsche mark (*Continued*)
triangular arbitrage, **47**•23
weekly prices, **47**•10
Diagonal spread, **13**•34, **13**•45
Dialog Information Services, Incorporated, **18**•67
Diamond exports, **7**•6
Difference or settlement account, **4**•14
Differentiation technique, **17**•12–13
Digital Equipment Corporation, **18**•67
Directors, **4**•17
Dirty floats, **47**•12
Disappearance, potato, **37**•15, **37**•16
Disclosure, performance, **19**•12–13
Disclosure information, **19**•15–17
Discount rate, **48**•8
Discretionary account, **2**•9–10
Diskettes, **18**•24
Disks, **18**•34–35
Dispersion, **17**•6–7
Distillation curves, crude oil, **42**•4, **42**•5
Distributed processing, **18**•4, **18**•17
Distribution, **17**•3–5
Diversification, commodity selection and, **16**•6
Diversification correlation, **21**•13–14
Dojima rice market, **1**•7
Dollar decline, **1**•29
Dollar shortage to dollar glut, **47**•8–12
Dollar-weighted method, **21**•16
Double exponential smoothing, **15**•13, **17**•17
Double options, **4**•26
Double tops or bottoms, **14**•15–16
Dow Jones v. *CFTC*, **49**•9–10
Dow Jones v. *Chicago Board of Trade*, **49**•8, **49**•9
Dow Jones & Company, Incorporated, **18**•67
Dow Jones Industrial Average, **10**•22, **49**•6
Dow Jones News Retrieval Service, **18**•38–39
Dow theory, **14**•5–6, **14**•8
Dual trading, **5**•18
Dunn & Hargitt, **18**•67–68
Durum wheat, **26**•5
Dutch guilder, **10**•7
IMM contract, **47**•15
parity in U.S. dollars (1951), **47**•8

Earth Satellite Corporation, **18**•68
Eastern states, potato production, **37**•3
Econometric analysis, **18**•43
Econometrics, **49**•21–22
Economic Recovery Tax Act of 1981 (ERTA), **6**•3, **6**•10–24
carry-back provisions, **6**•13–14
cash-and-carry transactions, **6**•22
constructive ownership rules, **6**•20–21
identification requirements, **6**•23–24
identified straddles, **6**•18–19
loss deferral rule, **6**•16–18
mark-to-market concept, **6**•11–13
mixed straddles, **6**•21–22
reporting considerations, **6**•22–23
RFCs, **6**•11–13
short-sale rules, **6**•20
transitional rules, **6**•15–16
wash-sale rules, **6**•19–20
Economic Research Service (ERS), **8**•7, **8**•11
Edible crude soy oil, **30**•39
Edible refined soy oil, **30**•39
Efficiency criteria, **23**•10–11
Efficient frontier, **21**•15–16, **21**•17
Ehrlich Cycle Finder, **15**•26
Elasticity of demand, **17**•21
Elasticity of supply, **17**•23
Elastic market, **17**•21
Electronic Computer Originated Mail (E-COM), **18**•5
Electronic photography, use of silver, **44**•13
Electronic worksheets, **18**•48
Elliott Wave Theory, **14**•5
Employee Retirement Income Security Act of 1974, **5**•5
End checking, **41**•5
Energy futures, **42**•3–43
crude oil, **42**•7–19
gasoline, **42**•29–34
heating oil, **42**•19–29
liquefied propane gas, **42**•34–41
refinery basics, **42**•3–7
sources of information, **42**•41–42
Energy Policy and Conservation Act of 1975, **42**•17
England, **1**•43–45
comparison of U.S. and London exchanges, **4**•3–28
London commodities, **1**•46–49
London grain markets, **25**•18
options trading, **13**•11
see also London exchanges; *names of exchanges*
Equally weighted average return, **49**•23–24
Equilibrium:
demand and supply, **17**•23–24
foreign exchange formula, **47**•27
Equity index futures contracts, **10**•20–23
Equity shares, **3**•7
ERTA, *see* Economic Recovery Tax Act of 1981
Estimated deliverable supply, potato market, **37**•15
Ethylene, **42**•38
European Commodity (EC) countries, **30**•7
definition, **48**•17
futures market, **10**•14, **48**•19
IMM 3-month contract, **48**•19, **48**•20
LIFFE, **4**•20–21
primary market, **48**•18
trading activity, **48**•17–18
Eurodollars, **1**•30–31, **7**•22, **10**•20, **13**•44, **48**•3, **48**•17–19
European Economic Community (EEC), **25**•18, **29**•9, **38**•4, **38**•7, **38**•10, **47**•12
European Monetary System (EMS), **47**•12

European option, **13**•4, **13**•45
European Options Exchange (EOE), **1**•49–53
Evergreens, **41**•3
Exchange for Physical (EFP), **4**•18, **9**•49, **9**•50, **38**•15
Exchange rate effects, **7**•25–27
Exchanges:
  arbitration, **1**•24
  committees, **1**•23–24
  commodities traded, **1**•32–40
  comparisons, U.S. and London, **4**•3–28
  domestic relationship, **1**•22–23
  evolution, **1**•4–5
  foreign, **1**•41–54
  membership, **1**•25
  organization, **1**•23
  and today's market, **1**•25–26
  see also specific exchanges
Exercise, **13**•14
Exercise price, **13**•45
Exercising an option, **13**•4
Exhaustion gap, **14**•13
Expectations, future spot rate, **47**•20–21
Expected net profit per trade (ENPPT), **22**•17
Expiration, option, **13**•4
Expiration date, **13**•45
Ex-pit transactions, **9**•49, **9**•50
Exponential curve, **17**•9
Exponential smoothing, **15**•12–13, **17**•16
  relating to standard moving averages, **15**•13–14
Exports, agricultural products, **25**•3
  grain market uncertainties, **25**•3–6
Export Sales report, **8**•11
Extrinsic value, **13**•22, **13**•45
EZ Model Builder System, **18**•44–46

Fair letter, **1**•3
Fair value, **13**•45
Fair-value premiums, call option, **13**•24–25
Fall storage potatoes, **37**•12
Faroll v. *Jarecki*, **6**•27
Fats and Oils Outlook and Situation report, **8**•15
FCMs, *see* Futures Commission Merchants
FCOJ, *see* Frozen concentrated orange juice
Federal Cotton Standards Act, **40**•5
Federal Farm Board, **40**•10
Federal Reserve System, **2**•10, **10**•18, **48**•5–8
Feeder cattle, **31**•7–11
Feeder cattle hedge, **9**•42–43
Feedlot hedge, **9**•42–45
Feed Outlook and Situation report, **8**•12
FHA-VA guaranteed mortgages, **48**•19
FIA, *see* Futures Industry Association
Fiber optics, **45**•3
FILETRAN (Data Resources, Incorporated), **18**•32
Filtered by demand, cattle price seasonality, **31**•16, **31**•17
Filtering housing starts, **45**•10–12
Finance committees, **1**•24
Financial futures markets, **10**•3–49
  arbitrage, **10**•39–42, **10**•43–49
  bank CD, **10**•13–14
  beginnings, **10**•5–7
  cash market, **10**•23–49
    potential relations, **10**•28
  chronological development, **10**•3–23
  debt and equity market, **10**•7–10
  de facto moratorium, **10**•19
  equity, **10**•9
  equity index, **10**•20–23
  Eurodollar, **10**•14
  failures, **10**•10–13
  Fed/Treasury study, **10**•19–20
  foreign currency, **10**•7
  growth, **1**•29–30, **10**•23
  hedging, **10**•12–13, **10**•15
  interactions between cash and, **10**•23–49
    alternative investments, **10**•30–33
    arbitrage strategies, **10**•39–42, **10**•43–49
    external factors, **10**•29
    integration, **10**•33–43
    overview, **10**•49
    potential relations, **10**•28
  intermediate-term debt, **10**•9
  long-term debt, **10**•9
  margins, **10**•4–5
  maturity, **10**•10
  perishable products, **10**•10
  regulation, **10**•18–20
  short-term debt, **10**•9
  stock index futures contracts, **10**•8
  storable products, **10**•9–10
  structure, **10**•17–18
  10-year Treasury note, **10**•15
  traded (Jan. 1977–Aug. 1982), **10**•24–27
  uses and users, **10**•15–17
Financial Futures Service (Monchik-Weber Corporation), **18**•43
Financial Times Index of Ordinary Shares, **49**•6
Financing costs, carrying charges, **12**•20
First notice, **2**•19
First and second differences, **15**•17
5- and 20-day moving average method, **19**•4
Fixings, London, **4**•18
Flag pattern, **14**•18
Flagpole, **14**•18, **14**•19
Flaxseed, **29**•4–12
  cash price (Minneapolis), **29**•9
  consumption and usage, **29**•9
  contract specifications, **29**•12
  futures market, **29**•9
  production, **29**•8–9
  supply and distribution (linseed oil), **29**•11
  world production, **29**•10
Flint corn, **27**•4

Floor brokers, **2**•12
  business practices regulation, **5**•18
  registration, **5**•17
  regulation, **5**•17–19
  trading practices, **5**•25–26
  use of, **2**•3–4
Floor conduct committees, **1**•24
Floppy disks, **18**•24
Florida Citrus Processors Association, **36**•13
Flour corn, **27**•4
Food consumption forecasts, **25**•9
Food Protein Council, **30**•49
Food-purchasing power filter, **32**•7
Forced liquidation, **2**•25
Forecast-driven models, interest rate, **11**•4–5
Forecasting methods and tools:
  agriculture, **25**•8–13
    anticipated acreage, **25**•9
    food consumption, **25**•9
    price forecasts, **25**•8–9
    satellite data, **25**•13–14
    USDA reports, **25**•9
    weather modeling, **25**•9–10
    yield estimation (corn and wheat), **25**•10–12
  bar charting, **14**•3–22
  computer, **18**•3–81
  mathematical aids, **17**•3–28
  quantitative trading, **15**•3–36
  selecting a trading system, **16**•3–9
Foreign Agricultural Service (FAS), **8**•7
Foreign currency futures, **10**•7, **47**•14, **47**•15
Foreign exchange futures, **47**•3–30
  calculations, **47**•24–28
  contract specifications, **47**•15
  forward *vs.* futures, **47**•17–19
  markets, **47**•12–17
    forward contracts, **47**•16, **47**•17–18
    hedging *vs.* speculation, **47**•19
    IMM, **47**•12–13
    interbank, **47**•13–16
    spot transactions, **47**•16–17
    spread, **47**•14–16
  price determination, **47**•19–24
    arbitrage, **47**•22–24
    interest rates, **47**•21–22
    role of expectations, **47**•20–21
  theory and history, **47**•4–12
    Bretton Woods system, **47**•7–8
    clean and dirty floats, **47**•12
    dollar shortage and dollar glut, **47**•8–12
    evolution of money, **47**•4–5
    gold standard, **47**•6–7
    Smithsonian Agreement, **47**•12
Foreign exchange gain (loss) formulas, **47**•27–28
Foreign exchanges, **1**•41–54
  Bermuda, **1**•41
  England, **1**•43–45
  France, **1**•41–43
  Hong Kong, **1**•53–54
  Netherlands, **1**•45
  see also specific exchanges
Forest product futures, *see* Lumber and plywood
FORTRAN (FORmula TRANslator), **18**•10
Forward (to arrive), **1**•20
Forward contracts, **1**•5, **1**•9–10, **1**•18–19, **5**•9
  annualized percentage cost or gain of hedging formula, **47**•26–27
  difference between futures and, **47**•19
  foreign exchange, **47**•16, **47**•17–18
Forward discount, **47**•22
Forward physical market, **4**•18
Forward premium, **47**•22
Framing, lumber and plywood, **41**•7
France, **1**•41–43
Franklin Mint, **44**•16
Franklin National Bank, **47**•3
French franc, **10**•7
  frequency distribution, **17**•3–5
  IMM contract, **47**•15
  parity in U.S. dollars (1951), **47**•8
  triangular arbitrage, **47**•23
Frequency of time series, **18**•26
Front loading, **15**•12
  weighted moving average, **17**•16
Frozen concentrated orange juice (FCOJ), **36**•3–20
  acreage map (Florida), **36**•8
  basis, **36**•13
  demand, **36**•9–10
  Florida production, **36**•5, **36**•7
  freezing point for citrus, **36**•17
  price dynamics, **36**•13
  production, **36**•3–9
  seasonality, **36**•10–13
  statistics, **36**•4
  temperature records by months, **36**•14–15
  trading, **36**•13–20
    contract specifications, **36**•20
    speculation, **36**•19–20
  USDA crop estimates by months, **36**•6
Frozen pork, **32**•8
Fuel consumption, residential, **42**•26
Full carrying charges, **12**•19
Full-fat soy flour, **30**•42
Fully refined soy oil, **30**•39
Fundamental analysis:
  commercial services, **18**•58, **18**•60
  databases, **18**•27–28
  lumber and plywood, **41**•9–14
Fundamental analysis packages, **18**•48–49
Fundamental approach to trading, **16**•5–6
Fungibility, option, **13**•5
Futures Commission Merchants (FCMs), **5**•17–19
  business practices regulation, **5**•18
  defined, **5**•17
  handling of customer funds, **5**•18–19
  net-capital requirements, **5**•18

registration, **5**•17
regulation, **5**•17–19
trading practices, **5**•25–26
Futures contract, **1**•9, **1**•20
CFTC jurisdiction, **5**•8–9
defined, **13**•45
new and pending, **1**•30–32
options, **13**•14, **13**•15–16
see also specific commodities; types of trading strategies
Futures exchanges:
functions (objectives) common to all, **1**•22
relations, **1**•22–23
see also specific exchanges
Futures Industry Association (FIA), **1**•3
Futures markets, **1**•20, **7**•6–14
barley, **29**•4
broiler chickens, **33**•9
cattle industry, **31**•18–21
CDs, **48**•15–16
cocoa market, **34**•16–19
coffee, **35**•14
computer applications, **18**•36
computer development, **18**•11–13
copper, **45**•12–15
corn, **27**•12–15
cotton, **40**•18–19
Eurodollars, **48**•19
flaxseed, **29**•9
gasoline, **42**•33–34, **42**•35–37
GNMA securities, **48**•22–23
gold, **43**•10–17
growth (U.S.), **7**•7–14
heating oil, **42**•25–29
linkage of commodity production and trade, **7**•6–7
liquified propane gas, **42**•34–41
lumber and plywood, **41**•18–21
oats, **28**•8–9
orange juice, **36**•13–20
palladium, **46**•15
platinum, **46**•15
pork complex, **32**•3–19
potatoes, **37**•20
rapeseed, **29**•13
refined sugar, **39**•7–8
rye, **29**•20
silver, **44**•18–21
soybean complex, **30**•33–35
sugar, **38**•12–15
Treasury bill, **48**•11
Treasury notes and bonds, **48**•25–30
wheat, **26**•11–14
Futures options, *see* Commodity options; Options trading
Futures Order Execution Systems, Incorporated, **18**•68
Futures trading:
evolution (1850s–1870s), **1**•18–19
mechanics, **2**•3–26
closing accounts, **2**•26
contract facts, **2**•17–19
establishing commodity accounts, **2**•4–9
liquidating transactions, **2**•19–20
margins, **2**•10–12
orders, **2**•12–17
prices, **2**•20–22
profit-or-loss calculation, **2**•22–25
third-party accounts, **2**•9–10
trading facilities, **2**•3–4
unusual liquidations, **2**•25
telecommunications and, **1**•21–22
Futures Trading Act of 1921, **13**•10
Futures Trading Act of 1978, **13**•12
Futures Trading Act of 1982, **5**•3–6
commodity options, **5**•3
commodity pool operators, **5**•5
commodity trading advisors, **5**•5
emergency powers, **5**•4
leverage transactions, **5**•3–4
new registration categories, **5**•4–5
NFA authority, **5**•5
private right of action, **5**•4
SEC/CFTC jurisdictional agreement, **5**•5–6
state enforcement powers, **5**•5

GAFTA, *see* Grain and Feed Trade Association
GAFTA Soy Bean Meal Futures Association Ltd., **1**•45, **4**•19
Gains and losses, tax consequences, **6**•27
Gambling, compared to speculation, **1**•21
Gap analysis, **11**•5–9
shortcomings, **11**•6–9
Gap-driven bank balance-sheet models, **11**•5–6
Gaps, **14**•13–14
Gas/oil contract, **4**•20. *See also* Heating oil
Gasoline, **42**•29–34
cash market structure, **42**•31
consumption, **42**•31
and vehicle registration, **42**•32
contract specifications, **42**•35–37
demand, **42**•30–31
futures contracts, **42**•33–34
grades and specifications, **42**•29–30
seasonality, **42**•31
sources of information, **42**•42
supply, **42**•30
where gas is sold, **42**•33
Geometric mean, **17**•4–5, **17**•16
Geometric mean rate g, **23**•21, **23**•22
Geometric method, **21**•16
Ghanaian Marketing Board, **34**•20
Ginnie Maes (Government National Mortgage Association Securities), **1**•29, **1**•30, **10**•5, **10**•18, **13**•13, **13**•14

Ginnie Maes (*Continued*)
cash markets, **48**•19–21
contract specifications, **48**•24
equivalent principal balances, **48**•23
futures contract, **10**•8–9
futures market, **48**•22–23
price chart, **48**•21
primary market, **48**•21
secondary market, **48**•21–22
types of, **48**•19
yield, **48**•19
GNMA-CDR contract, **48**•3
Gold, **43**•3–22
bull markets, **12**•25
cash price (London), **43**•14
chronology, **43**•3–5
cocoa prices and, **34**•12, **34**•13–14
contract specifications, **43**•13
currency, **47**•8
demand, **43**•7–10
futures market, **43**•10–17
summary of uses, **43**•16–17
glossary, **43**•20–22
price indices, **43**•4
production, **43**•5–6
put and call options, **43**•17–20
price structure, **43**•18
summary of uses, **43**•20
value, **43**•18–20
relationship between platinum and, **46**•7–8
secondary gold flow, **43**•9
supply, **43**•7
trading volume, **43**•12
uses, **43**•8
world absorption by end use, **43**•10
Gold coins, copper in, **45**•10
Gold fix, **4**•18, **43**•3
Gold standard, **43**•3, **47**•6–7
Good-faith deposits, **2**•10
Good-til-canceled (GTC) orders, **2**•15
Government National Mortgage Association. *See* Ginnie Maes
Government programs:
corn, **27**•10–11
cotton, **40**•10–13
refined sugar, **39**•7
wheat, **25**•15, **26**•8–10
Government relations committee, **1**•24
Grading of samples, **1**•18
Grain:
crop spreads, **25**•14–18
export market uncertainties, **25**•3–6
London market, **25**•18
mathematical forecasting, **25**•8–13
penalties for increased output, **25**•3
price forecast, **25**•6–8, **25**•8–9
sources of information **25**•18–20
volume of trading, **25**•18
Winnipeg markets, **29**•3–20
Grain and Feed Trade Association (GAFTA), **4**•3, **4**•21, **25**•18
trading specifications, compared to U.S., **4**•5
Grain embargo, **25**•4, **26**•8
Grain Futures Act of 1922, **13**•10
Grain Stocks report, **8**•5, **8**•7
Grapefruit:
Florida production, **36**•5
USDA crop estimate by months, **36**•6
Graphics packages, **18**•29
Green soybeans, **30**•44
Gross crushing margin, **9**•46
Gross National Product (GNP), **48**•8
Gross processing margin (GPM), **12**•8, **12**•31, **30**•36–38
Ground soybeans, **30**•43
Growth and organization, **1**•3–54
arbitration committees, **1**•24
committees, **1**•23–24
early evolution, **1**•3–5
evolution of futures trading (1850s–1870s), **1**•18–19
financials, **1**•29–30
foreign exchanges, **1**•41–54
Bermuda, **1**•41
England, **1**•43–45
France, **1**•41–43
Hong Kong, **1**•53–54
Netherlands, **1**•45
forms of market transactions, **1**•19–20
futures trading and telecommunications, **1**•21–22
general membership, **1**•25
Japan, **1**•5–9
early market, **1**•5–8
Meiji regime, **1**•8–9
markets today, **1**•25–26
new and pending contracts, **1**•30–40
open interest, **1**•27–29
organization of exchanges, **1**•23
relationship of domestic exchanges, **1**•22–23
self-regulation, **1**•17
speculation, **1**•20–21
standardization of contracts, **1**•18
Western world, **1**•9–17
Chicago (1835–1875), **1**•10–11
Chicago (1895–1960), **1**•17
New York (1725–1862), **1**•9–10
New York (1870–1947), **1**•11–15
GTE, Financial Services Division, **18**•68
Guarantee fund, **3**•7

Hard red winter wheat, **26**•5
Hardware, **18**•3, **18**•5–8, **18**•13–26
commercial services, **18**•56
decision-making, **18**•22–26
microcomputers, **18**•19–22

minicomputers, **18**•16–19
time sharing, **18**•14
Hard woods, **41**•3
Harmonic mean, **17**•5
Head and shoulders top or bottom, **14**•16
Heat-damaged kernels, **30**•45
Heating oil, **1**•31, **4**•20, **42**•19–29
cash market transactions, **42**•24–25
contract specifications, **42**•27
conversion costs, **42**•23–24
demand, **42**•22–24
futures, **42**•25–29
grades and specifications, **42**•19
seasonality, **42**•22
sources of supply, **42**•22
stocks, **42**•23
support and resistance levels, **14**•10
temperature and demand, **42**•24
Heat processed soybeans, **30**•43
"Heavy" crudes, **42**•8
Hedged yield curve ride, **10**•33
Hedging, **1**•21, **6**•4, **9**•3–51, **21**•14, **47**•16, **49**•4, **49**•6
basis, **9**•11–30
convergence, **9**•14
cost of carry, **9**•12–14
differences, **9**•11
distortions in carrying charges, **9**•16–17
hedging, **9**•19–21
hedging applications, **9**•21–30
inverted markets, **9**•17
method of quoting, **9**•11
risk and profit maximization, **9**•17–19
seasonality, **9**•14–16, **9**•19
supply shortages, **9**•11–12
benefits, **9**•36–39
financing, **9**•39
minimizing financial liability, **9**•36–37
price distortions, **9**•37–39
reduced costs, **9**•39
CEA and, **5**•7
complete hedge, **9**•48–50
copper exporter's **45**•15–19
defined, **9**•8–9
delta, **13**•40–42
futures contracts, **10**•12–13, **10**•15
futures and interbank market, **47**•19
integrated, **9**•42–48
establishing, **9**•43
feedlot hedge, **9**•42–45
soybean processing **9**•45–46
in inverted market, **9**•31–36
objectives, **9**•8–9
options (in London), **4**•25–26
price risk, **9**•7–8
questions to consider, **9**•39–42
cost evaluation, **9**•40–41
evaluation, **9**•40
indirect relationships, **9**•41
quantity and method, **9**•41–42
risk management, **9**•3
tax consequences, **6**•25–26
Tokugawa era (Japan), **1**•6
types of **9**•9–11
see also specific commodities
Hewlett-Packard, **18**•68
H & H Trading Company, **18**•68
High-fat soy flour, **30**•42
High-fructose (corn) content, **27**•3
High-fructose corn syrup (HFCS), **27**•6, **39**•6
High negative correlation, **21**•13
High Plains of Texas, **40**•5, **40**•6
Historical background, *see* Growth and organization
Hoarding, silver, **44**•6–9
Hog/corn ratio, **32**•12–18
Hog production, **32**•3. *See also* Pork complex
Hogs and Pigs reports, **8**•4–5, **25**•19, **32**•18
Hokkaido Grain Exchange, **30**•33
Holder, **13**•45
Hong Kong Commodity Exchange, **1**•53–54, **4**•19, **30**•33
gold contract, **43**•13
Horizontal count, **15**•8
Horizontal option spread, **13**•34, **13**•35, **13**•45–46
Housing starts, **41**•11, **41**•12–13
filtering copper seasonality, **45**•10–12
plywood prices *vs.*, **41**•12
Hybridization, **27**•3
Hydraulic pressing, soybean oil, **30**•41
Hydrogenated soy oil, **30**•39

Identification, option, **13**•5–6
Identified straddles, **6**•18–19, **6**•21
IMM, *see* International Monetary Market
Implicit forward rate, **10**•34–35
Implied Interest-rate/forward-rate parity formula, **47**•26
Implied yields, carrying charges, **12**•24
Inbread (corn) strain, **27**•3
Income deferment, **6**•8
Indemnities, *see* Commodity options
Individual accounts, **19**•11–12
Individual trades, **21**•6–7
Inelastic market, **17**•21
Information processing, **18**•3
Information sources, money management, **19**•17–19
Information transmission, **18**•3
Initial margins, **3**•8–9, **20**•3, **24**•4
Instantaneous velocity, **15**•17
Instant update, **18**•69
Insurance value, **13**•46
INSYTE (Remote Computing Corporation), **18**•32
Integrated hedges, **9**•42–48
establishing, **9**•43
feedlot, **9**•42–45
soybean processing, **9**•45–48

Integration, cash and future markets interest rates, **10**•33–43
  arbitrage, **10**•39–42
  arbitrage over HP3, **10**•43
  investment over holding period HP1, **10**•38–39
  investment over HP3, **10**•42–43
  slope of yield curve, **10**•36
Intelligent terminals, **18**•41
Interactive Data Services, Incorporated, **18**•69
Interactive Software Research, Incorporated, **18**•69
Interagency Committees (IAC), **8**•7, **8**•10, **8**•12
Interbank market, **47**•13–16
  credit risk, **48**•18
Intercommodity spreads, **12**•3, **12**•8, **12**•9, **12**•28–29, **32**•12
  commodity *vs.* product, **12**•8–9
  quotes, **12**•9–11
Intercrop spread, **12**•5–7
Interdelivery spread, **12**•3, **12**•4–5
  butterfly, **12**•9
Interest-rate arbitrage, **47**•22–23
Interest-rate futures, **48**•3–30
  interest rates, **48**•4–8
  markets, **48**•8–30
    CDs, **48**•12–16
    Eurodollars, **48**•17–19
    GNMA securities, **48**•19–23
    Treasury bills, **48**•9–12
    Treasury notes and bonds, **48**•23–30
  success of, **48**•3–4
  volume by year (1975–1981), **48**•4
Interest-rate futures markets, *see* Financial futures markets
Interest-rate risk, **11**•3–11
  benchmark to use **11**•9–10
  forecast-driven model, **11**•4–5
  gap analysis, **11**•5–9
    shortcomings, **11**•6–9
  qualitative analysis, **11**•11
Interest rates, **7**•16–19, **48**•4–8
  credit risk, **48**•5
  determinants, **48**•5–8
  exchange rates, **47**•21–22
  yield curve, **48**•4–5, **48**•6
Intermarket spreads, **12**•3, **12**•26–28
  orders, **12**•12–13
Internal Revenue Code, **6**•3
Internal Revenue Manual (IRM), **6**•31
Internal Revenue Service (IRS), **6**•3, **6**•31–32. *See also* Taxation of transactions
International Business Machines Corporation, **18**•69
International Cocoa Agreement (ICCA), **34**•11
International Cocoa Organization, **34**•11
International Coffee Organization (ICO), **35**•3, **35**•13, **35**•14, **35**•16
International Commodity Clearing House (ICCH), **3**•11–14, **4**•18, **4**•22
  margining, **4**•23–24
International Future Exchange Ltd. (INTEX), **1**•41
International gold exchanges, **4**•19
International gold standard, **47**•6
International Monetary Fund (IMF), **7**•22–23, **43**•5, **43**•7, **47**•7
International Monetary Market (IMM), **1**•29, **1**•30, **1**•34, **10**•5, **10**•22, **47**•3, **47**•17, **48**•3, **48**•15
  certificates of deposit (CDs), **10**•13–14, **48**•15–16
  Class A members, **47**•24
  Class B members, **47**•23–24
  created, **47**•12–13
  Eurodollar contract, **10**•14, **48**•19, **48**•20
  foreign currency contracts, **47**•15
  4-year Treasury note contracts, **48**•28
  futures trading opening dates, **1**•35
  gold contract, **43**•13
  gold trading volume, **43**•12
  90-day Treasury bill futures contract, **48**•11–12, **48**•13
  1-year Treasury bill contract, **48**•11
  3-month Treasury bill, **48**•8–9
  trading specifications, compared to U.K., **4**•4–5
International Petroleum Exchange (IPE), **1**•45, **4**•19, **4**•20, **42**•19, **42**•25, **42**•27–28
International Sugar Agreement (ISA), **38**•8, **38**•10, **38**•14, **39**•7
International Sugar Organization, **38**•8
Interval of a time series, **18**•26
INTEX exchange **18**•13, **18**•55
In-the-money option, **13**•7–8, **13**•46
Intracommodity spread, **12**•3, **32**•11
Intrinsic value, option's, **13**•22, **13**•46
Inventory cycles, commodity price behavior, **7**•27–28
Inverted markets, **9**•17, **12**•21–22
  hedging, **9**•31–36
  meaning of, **12**•22–23
Investment vehicles, tax consequences, **6**•28
Investors, system diversification for, **21**•5–7
Investor's Macro Software, **18**•69
Island reversal, **14**•13–14
Isolated soy protein, **30**•43
Isooctane, **42**•29
Italian lira, **10**•7, **47**•12

Japan:
  Meiji regime, **1**•8–9
  Tokugawa era (1603–1868), **1**•5–8
  see also specific exchanges
Japanese yen, **4**•21, **10**•7
  hedging, **9**•40
  IMM contract, **47**•15
  parity in U.S. dollars **47**•8
  weekly prices, **47**•10
Jet fuel, **42**•3, **42**•5
Jewelry, **43**•8, **44**•14, **45**•10, **46**•6
Jobbing, **4**•3
Johnson-Shad Agreement, **10**•21, **13**•13, **13**•14

Kanmon Commodity Exchange, **30**•33
Kansas City Board of Trade (KCBOT), **1**•31, **1**•38, **10**•22
  Value Line Average (VLA), **49**•3–32
    contract, **49**•16
    historical background, **49**•6–10
    how it works, **49**•10–15
    rationale, **49**•30
    statistical price summary, **49**•24–30
    stock ownership in U.S., **49**•4–6
    systematic risk, **49**•3–4
    theoretical considerations, **49**•19–24
    underlying commodities, **49**•15–19
  wheat contract, **26**•13
  wheat traded, **25**•14
Karob software, **18**•70
Kate's Komputers Distributing Corporation, **18**•70
KCBT v. *CFTC*, **49**•7–8
Kelly measure, **23**•21–23
Kerb trading, **4**•14, **4**•20, **45**•15
Kerosene, **42**•19
Kidder Reports, Incorporated, **18**•70
Kobe Grain Exchange, **30**•33
Kondratieff wave, **15**•25

Labor, as factor of production, **7**•3–4
Lag of a trend, **15**•20
Land, as factor of production, **7**•3–4
LANDSAT program, **25**•12–13
Lard cash prices, **32**•5
Largest loss string (LLS), **16**•7–8, **16**•9
Law of motion, **16**•5
LCE, *see* London Commodity Exchange Group
Lead, alchemical symbol for, **4**•11
Leaded gasoline, **42**•29–30
Least-squares, **17**•9, **17**•14–15, **25**•11
Least-squares sinusoidal, **17**•10
Lecithinated soy flour, **30**•43
Leg of a cycle, **15**•26
Legging-in or legging-out process, **12**•14
Legging mistakes, **12**•15
Legs, **6**•6, **12**•3
Leverage, **10**•4, **14**•10, **20**•5, **20**•6
  CFTC jurisdiction, **5**•9–10
  defined, **13**•46
  1982 Act, **5**•3–4
  option contract, **13**•17–21
  trading system risk, **16**•4
LGFM, *see* London Gold Futures Market
LIFFE, *see* London International Financial Futures Exchange
"Light" crudes, **42**•8
Light Louisiana Sweet (LLS), **42**•8
Limited partnerships, **19**•12
Limited power of attorney, **2**•9
Limit moves, **2**•21, **15**•33
Limit order, **2**•12–15, **12**•12
  "or better," **2**•15
"Limit up" or "limit down," **2**•21
Linear regression, **17**•8
Linseed meal, **29**•4
Linseed oil, **29**•4, **29**•9
  supply and distribution (U.S.), **29**•11
Liquified petroleum gas (LPG), **42**•22
  demand, **42**•38–41
  futures, **42**•41
  grades and specifications, **42**•34–38
  sources of information, **42**•42
  statistics, **42**•39
  stocks, **42**•38
  supply, **42**•38
Liquidation, **19**•11–12, **20**•3
  confirmation, **2**•23
  transactions, **2**•19–20
  unusual, **2**•25
Liquidation by delivery, **2**•25
Liquidity, **10**•4, **10**•12, **16**•4
  futures market, **7**•12
  market orders, **12**•11–12
LISP (LIS Processing Language), **18**•10
Livestock, Meat and Wool Market News, **32**•18
Livestock cycles, **15**•24–25
Livestock and Meat Situation and Outlook, **8**•5
Livestock and Meat Statistics, **32**•18
Livestock Slaughter report, **32**•18
LME, *see* London Metal Exchange
Locals, **47**•18
Locked-limit days, **12**•17, **15**•33
Logica, **18**•70
London Cocoa Terminal Market Association Ltd., **1**•45, **4**•18, **34**•16, **34**•17
London Commodity Exchange Group (LCE), **1**•45, **4**•3, **4**•18–20, **4**•21
  categories of membership, **4**•19–20
  trading specifications, compared to U.S., **4**•6
London exchanges, compared to U.S., **4**•3–28
  local traders, **4**•3
  options, **4**•25–26
  sterling denominated contracts, **4**•3
  trading specifications, **4**•4–9
  see also specific exchanges
London Gold Futures Market (LGFM), **4**•3, **4**•18, **4**•19, **4**•21
  gold contract, **43**•13
  trading specifications, compared to U.S., **4**•4
London Grain and Feed Trade Association, **30**•33
London Grain Futures Market, **4**•3, **4**•21
  barley contract, **29**•8
  wheat contract, **26**•14
London International Financial Futures Exchange (LIFFE), **4**•3, **4**•20–21
  trading specifications, compared to U.S., **4**•5
London Metal Exchange (LME), **1**•43, **4**•3, **4**•11–17
  copper futures, **45**•14–15
  delivery by value date, **4**•13–14
  extent of delivery, **4**•11–12
  margining, **4**•14, **4**•21–25

London Metal Exchange (*Continued*)
membership and management, **4**•17
principals' market, **4**•12
ring, **4**•10
rings and kerb, **4**•14
settlement, **4**•13
silver futures, **44**•18
compared to COMEX, **44**•21
trading limits, **4**•17
trading specifications, compared to U.S., **4**•4
transfer of contracts, **4**•14–17
London Metal Exchange Monitoring Operation (MEMO), **4**•21
London Potato Futures Association Ltd., **4**•21
London Rubber Terminal Market Association Ltd., **1**•45, **4**•19
London United Terminal Sugar Market, **38**•12
London Vegetable Oil Terminal Market Association Ltd., **4**•19, **30**•33
London Wool Terminal Market Association Ltd., **1**•45, **4**•19
Long the basis, **9**•20
Long the currency, **47**•19, **47**•22
Long futures arbitrage, **10**•45–49
Long hedges, **9**•9–11, **10**•4
KCBT-VLA stock index futures, **49**•15
Long the local basis, **9**•49
Long side of the crush spread, **9**•47
Loss deferral rule, **6**•16–18
Louisiana Offshore Oil Port (LOOP), **42**•14–17
Lower confidence limit, as a preference measure, **23**•16–17
Lower level languages, **18**•10
Low-fat soy flour, **30**•42
Low-frequency filters, APP technique, **B**•1–2
Lumber and plywood, **41**•3–22
amount used (single and multifamily dwelling), **41**•8
contract specifications, **41**•21
distribution by use, **41**•8
fundamental analysis, **41**•9–14
demand-side, **41**•11–14
supply-side, **41**•9–10
futures trading, **41**•18–21
grades and grading, **41**•6
historical price behavior, **41**•14–18
lumber *vs*• plywood, **41**•15
seasonality, **41**•17–18, **41**•19
spreading across months, **41**•15–17
housing starts, **41**•11, **41**•12–13
lumber prices, monthly, **41**•4
plywood prices, monthly, **41**•4
processing, **41**•5
production, **41**•5–7
lumber, **41**•5–6
plywood, **41**•6–7
timber harvest, **41**•5
uses, **41**•7–8
Macroeconomic factors, **7**•3–28
crude oil and commodity prices, **7**•19–22
exchange rate effects, **7**•25–27
factors of production, **7**•3–4
futures markets, **7**•6–14
growth (U.S.), **7**•7–14
linkage of commodity production and trade, **7**•6–7
inventory cycles, **7**•27–28
1979–1982 crucible, **7**•14
real interest rates, **7**•16–19
spikes and craters, **7**•14–16
world trade, **7**•4–6
demand side, **7**•22–25
Maine Department of Agricultural Reporting Service, **37**•15
Maine potatoes, **37**•3–4
anticipated acreage (1953–1970), **37**•9
Maintenance margin amount, **24**•4
Maintenance margins, **2**•10–11
Major move, **24**•6
Managed Account reports, **19**•5, **19**•8, **19**•17–18, **21**•9
Managed accounts, **2**•9–10, **19**•3–5
evaluation, **24**•3–9
availability of information, **24**•7
benchmarks, **24**•6
major move, **24**•6
performance content, **24**•8–9
presentation of performance, **24**•7–8
publication of performance, **24**•5
simulated performance, **24**•9
selecting a program, **19**•11–12
Management committees, **1**•24
Management Services, **18**•70–71
Margin adjusted AMR (MAAMR), **22**•15–16
using to construct performance measures, **22**•16–18
Margin calls, **2**•25, **3**•8–9, **4**•17, **47**•18
Margin futures, compared to stock, **47**•18
Margining, London exchanges, **4**•14, **4**•21–25
ICCH, **4**•23–24
legal and regulatory safeguards, **4**•24–25
LME, **4**•22–23
Margins, **2**•10–12
defined, **13**•46
options, **13**•42–44
on spread positions, **2**•11
Market Data Systems, **18**•29, **18**•71
Market-if-touched (MIT) order, **2**•15
Market Information, Incorporated, **18**•71
Market maker, **6**•29
tax effect, **6**•31
Market order, **2**•12, **2**•21, **2**•22, **12**•11–12
Market patterns, short-term trading, **15**•32
Market penetration, **7**•12–14
Markets:
development (in U•S•), **1**•9–17

forms of transactions, **1**•19–20
influence:
macroeconomic factors, **7**•3–28
USDA information system, **8**•3–21
operation:
clearinghouse, **3**•3–15
growth and organization, **1**•1–54
mechanics, **2**•3–26
regulation of the industry, **5**•3–52
taxation on transactions, **6**•3–32
U.S. and U.K. compared, **4**•3–28
use:
commodity options, **13**•3–47
commodity spreads, **12**•3–34
financial futures market, **10**•3–49
hedging, **9**•3–51
interest-rate risk, **11**•3–11
Marketview Microsystems, **18**•71
Marketvision, **18**•72
Mark-to-market concept, **3**•8–9, **6**•11–13, **10**•4, **13**•21, **13**•46, **45**•14, **47**•18
Matched sales, **48**•8
Matching up, **3**•3–4, **3**•9
Mathematical aids, **17**•3–28
actual *vs.* expected, **17**•20
complex trigonometric curve fitting, **17**•14–15
dispersion and skewness, **17**•6–7
distribution, **17**•3–5
double exponential smoothing, **17**•17
least-squares sinusoidal, **17**•10
moving average, **17**•15–16
multivariate analysis, **17**•9–10
nonlinear regression, **17**•9
probability of success and ruin, **17**•18–20
regression analysis, **17**•7–8
risk preference, **17**•17–18
supply and demand, **17**•21–28
trigonometric curve fitting, **17**•10–14
Maximum loss (ML) as a risk measure, **22**•16–18
Mean, **17**•7
Mean deviation, **17**•6
Mean variance, **23**•12
Mean-variance model, preference space, **23**•12–23
cautionary warnings, **23**•19–21
lower confidence limit, **23**•16–17
restrictive efficient criterion, **23**•13–16
Sharpe ratio, **23**•17–19
Measures of central location (or averages), **17**•4
Measuring gap, **14**•13
Meat analogs, soy, **30**•43
Meat extenders, use of soy, **30**•43
Median, **17**•4
Meiji regime (Japan), **1**•8–9
Membership, exchanges, **1**•25, **A**•1–2
Memory Systems, Incorporated, **18**•72
Mercantilism, **47**•5–6
MERLIN, **18**•44
Metal Market Exchange Company Ltd., **4**•17
Metal symbols, **4**•11
Mexican peso, **10**•7, **47**•13
IMM contract, **47**•15
parity in U.S. dollars (1951), **47**•8
weekly prices, **47**•11
Microcomputers, **18**•19–22
buying, **18**•20
commercial services, **18**•56–57
communications applications, **18**•41–43
decision to use, **18**•23–25
limitations, **18**•21–22
personal quality, **18**•20–21
security, **18**•20
time-sharing, **18**•37–38
Microcomputing Research, **18**•72
Micro Futures, **18**•72
Micronaire ("mike"), **40**•5
MidAmerica Commodity Exchange, **1**•11, **1**•17, **4**•19, **30**•50
clearing association, **3**•11–14
commodities traded, **1**•32–33
corn contract, **27**•14
gold contract, **43**•13
gold trading volume, **43**•12
live beef cattle, **31**•21
oats contract, **28**•9
refined sugar, **39**•7–8
soybean complex, **30**•33, **30**•35
trading specifications, compared to U.K., **4**•4–5
wheat contract, **26**•12
wheat traded, **25**•14
Midwest Stock Exchange, **13**•13
Mine production of silver, **44**•3–6
Minicomputers, **18**•6–7, **18**•16–19
burdens, **18**•18–19
commercial services, **18**•56
decision to use, **18**•22–23
leasing or buying, **18**•17
power and independence, **18**•18
security, **18**•17–18
Minicontracts, **1**•17, **2**•19
Minimum fluctuation, **2**•20–21
Minneapolis Grain Exchange, **1**•38, **25**•15
wheat contract **26**•13
wheat traded, **25**•14
Mixed soybeans, **30**•45
Mixed straddles, **6**•21–22
MJK Associates, **18**•72–73
Mocatta Metal Corporation, **44**•19–21
Mode, **17**•4, **17**•7
MODEM (MOdulator/DEModulator), **18**•24, **18**•26
Modernization policy (China), **25**•5
Modern portfolio theory, **21**•3
Momentum, **15**•15–16
Monchik-Weber Corporation, **18**•73
Money:
evolution of, **47**•4–5
uses of, **47**•4

Money management, **16**•3
capitalization and, **20**•3–8
allocation, **20**•3
balancing risks, **20**•5–6
new accounts, **20**•4
redistribution, **20**•4–5
risk control structure, **20**•8
trading performance and capital contribution, **20**•8
commission costs, **19**•14–15
disclosure information, **19**•15–17
growth of, **19**•5–7
managed accounts, **19**•3–5
evaluating, **24**•3–9
selecting a program, **19**•11–12
performance disclosure, **19**•12–13
portfolio selection, **21**•8–16
diversification correlation, **21**•13–14
efficient frontier, **21**•15–16
elements, **21**•8
returns, evaluating, **21**•16
risk control, **21**•3–8
conservation of capital, **21**•7–8
diversification of systems and portfolios, **21**•7–8
effects of varying reserve, **21**•4–5
success and failure, **19**•8–11
trading performance:
measuring, **22**•3–26
preference space evaluation, **23**•3–26
Money manager, evaluating performance, **22**•21–25
inadequacy of return/risk ratio, **22**•22–25
return/risk measures, **22**•21–22
MoniResearch Corporation (MRC), **18**•44–46, **18**•73
Monitor (Cathode-Ray Tube), **18**•24
Monitoring Committee, **4**•22
Monthly continuation charts, **14**•7–8
Monthly statement, **2**•23
Motor vehicles, motorcycles, registration and fuel consumption, **42**•32
Moving average technique, **15**•11, **15**•22, **17**•15–16
phasing using, **15**•27–28
Multimarket system, evaluating performance, **22**•18–20
Multivariate analysis, **17**•9–10

Nagoya Grain Exchange, **30**•33
Naked option, **13**•30–31, **13**•46
Naked position, **13**•27
National Association of Futures Trading Advisors (NAFTA), **19**•17
National Futures Association (NFA), **5**•4, **5**•.33–35
admission, **5**•34–35
approval, **5**•33
arbitration, **5**•35
authority of, **5**•5
Board of Directors, **5**•33–34
discipline, **5**•35
ethical standards, **5**•34
FCM financial requirements, **5**•34
funding, **5**•35
mandatory membership, **5**•34
objective, **5**•33
National Hide Exchange, **1**•15
National Metal Exchange, **1**.15
National Potato Board, **37**•22
National Potato Council, **37**•22
National Silk Exchange, **1**•15
National Soybean Processors' Association, **8**•14, **30**•41, **30**•49
Natural coffee process, **35**•4
Natural exponential rate, **23**•23
Negative carrying charges, **12**•23
Negative interest rate, **47**•21
Netherlands, **1**•45–53
Neutral hedge ratio, **13**•46
New accounts, treatment of, **20**•4
New Orleans Board of Trade (NOBT), **1**•40
New Orleans Commodity Exchange, **1**•38–40, **30**•50, **42**•19
cotton contract, **40**•19
New Orleans Cotton Exchange, **40**•16
New York Cocoa Exchange, **1**•12
New York Coffee Exchange, **1**•11–12
New York Coffee and Sugar Exchange, **1**•12
New York Cotton Exchange, **1**•11, **1**•19, **1**•36, **40**•15, **40**•16, **42**•19
contract specifications, **40**•18
propane futures, **42**•41
New York Futures Exchange (NYFE), **1**•31, **10**•12, **47**•13, **49**•7
certificates of deposit (CDs), **10**•13–14, **48**•15
Eurodollar CD futures, **10**•14
90-day Treasury bill contract, **48**•11
stock index futures contracts, **49**•16
Treasury bond futures, **48**•25
New York markets:
of 1725–1862, **1**•9–10
of 1870–1947, **1**•11–15
New York Mercantile Exchange, **1**•11, **1**•36, **37**•3, **41**•18, **42**•3
clearing association, **3**•11–14
crude oil contracts, **42**•19, **42**•20–21
gasoline contract, **42**•33–34, **42**•35–37
gold trading volume, **43**•12
heating oil, **42**•25, **42**•27–28
imported lean beef, **31**•21
palladium contract, **46**•17
platinum contract, **46**•17
potato contract, **37**•20
round white potatoes, **37**•19
New York Produce Exchange, **1**•10, **1**•19
New York Stock Exchange (NYSE), **1**•26, **1**•31, **10**•12, **10**•22

New York Stock Exchange Composite Index, **10•**8, **10•**22
New York Stock Exchange Financial Sector Stock Index, **10•**8
New York Stock Exchange Industrial Sector Stock Index, **10•**8
New York Stock Exchange Utility Sector Stock Index, **10•**8
New York Times Information Service, Incorporated, **18•**73
NFA, *see* National Futures Association
Nibs, cocoa bean, **34•**7
Nickel, alchemical symbol for, **4•**11
90-day commercial paper, **48•**3
90-day domestic CD futures contract, **48•**15–16
90-day Treasury bill futures contract, **48•**11–12, **48•**13
No correlation, **21•**13
Nominations committees, **1•**24
Nonhedge transactions, **6•**4
  tax consequences, **6•**4–6
Nonlinear regression, **17•**9
Nonring dealing, **4•**17
Nonstorable commodities, **9•**17
Nontransferable notice, **3•**10
Normal or carrying charge market, **9•**12
Normal equations, **17•**8, **17•**14
Normalized preference space, **23•**10
Normalizing gain, **22•**3–5
North American Securities Administrators Association (NASAA), **5•**41
No. 1 oil, **42•**19
No. 2 oil, **42•**19
No. 4 oil, **42•**19
Numeraire, **47•**4
NYMEX, *see* New York Mercantile Exchange

Oats, **28•**3–9
  cash price, **28•**3, **28•**4
  consumption and usage, **28•**4–5
  contract specifications, **28•**8–9
  futures markets, **28•**8–9
  production, **28•**4
  seasonal bias, **28•**5, **28•**8
  statistics (U.S.), **28•**7
  world production, **28•**6
OCO Commodities, Incorporated, **18•**73–74
Octane, **42•**29–30
Offers, *see* Commodity options
Offset, *see* Liquidation
Offshore commodity funds, taxation of, **6•**28–29
Oil embargo of 1973, **7•**4
Olamic Systems Corporation, **18•**74
Old-new crop spread, **25•**15
Omega Microware, Incorporated, **18•**74
On-call transactions, **9•**49, **9•**50
Once-refined soy oil, **30•**39
One cancels the other (OCO), **2•**16
1 month delivery, **4•**13
Onza Troy, **44•**14
Opening price, **15•**33
Opening purchase, **13•**46
Opening sale, **13•**46
Open interest, **1•**27–29, **1•**31, **3•**8, **7•**12, **7•**13, **14•**6–7
  heating oil volume, **1•**31
Operating systems, computer, **18•**10
Options Market, London, **4•**25–26
Options trading, **13•**4–6, **13•**10–38
  fundamental concepts, **13•**4–6
  history, **13•**10–13
    banned, **13•**11–12
    London markets, **13•**11
    pilot program of 1981, **13•**12
    precommodity exchange act, **13•**10–11
    security exchanges, **13•**12–13
  in 1980s, **13•**13–17
    actual securities, **13•**14–17
    dealer options, **13•**17
    futures contract, **13•**14, **13•**15–16
  pricing, **13•**17–26
    leverage and insurance value, **13•**17–21
    model, **13•**25–26
    relationship between market and strike price, **13•**21–23
    short-term interest rates, **13•**24–25
    term until expiration, **13•**25
    and underlying market volatility, **13•**23–24
  strategies, **13•**26–28
    buying, **13•**29–30
    covered writing, **13•**31–33
    naked option selling, **13•**30–31
    spreads, **13•**34–36
    straddles, **13•**36–38
  tax consequences, **6•**26
  see also Commodity options
Orange juice, **36•**3–20
  acreage map (Florida), **36•**8
  contract specifications, **36•**20
  demand, **36•**9–10
  Florida production, **36•**5, **36•**7
  freezing point for citrus, **36•**17
  price dynamics, **36•**13
  production, **36•**3–9
    effects of weather, **36•**3–9
    foreign, **36•**9
    supply and price, **36•**9
  seasonality, **36•**10–13
  statistics, **36•**4
  temperature records by months, **36•**14–15
  trading of FCOJ, **36•**13–20
  USDA crop estimates by months, **36•**6
"Or better," **2•**15
Order cancels order (OCO), **2•**16

Orders:
  confirmation, **2**•12
  delays, **2**•21
  pool, **2**•21
  types of, **2**•12–17
Order tickets, **2**•13
Ordinary income conversion, **6**•8
Organization, commodity exchanges, **1**•23
Organization of Petroleum Exporting Countries (OPEC), **7**•3, **7**•4, **7**•14, **42**•10, **42**•18
  pricing formula, **7**•22
Organizer Systems, Incorporated, **18**•74
Original equipment manufacturers (OEMs), **18**•17, **18**•22
Original margin, **3**•7, **3**•8–9
Orion Management, Incorporated, **18**•74
Osaka Chemical Fibre Exchange, **1**•9
Osaka Grain Exchange, **30**•33
Oscillator, **15**•15–16, **15**•17
OTC, *see* Over-the-counter
Out-of-the-money option, **13**•7–8
Overnight positions, **15**•30–32
Over-the-counter (OTC), **13**•3

Pacific Stock Exchange, **13**•13
Palladium, **46**•9–15
  contract specifications, **46**•17
  demand, **46**•9–14
  end use, **46**•12
  futures markets, **46**•15
  prices, **46**•14, **46**•15, **46**•16
  sources of information, **46**•15–18
  supply, **46**•14
  weekly nearest futures (New York), **46**•12
Par deliverable quality, **9**•14
Paris International Futures Market, **1**•41
Payments-in-kind, **40**•12
Peachtree Software, Incorporated, **18**•74
Pear Technical Analysis, **18**•44
Peeler blocks, **41**•6
Pennant pattern, **14**•18
Percentage retracement, **14**•12–13
Percent risk, **22**•23
Perfect correlation, **21**•13
Performance:
  actual *vs.* expected, **17**•20
  disclosure, **19**•12–13
  evaluating managed account, **24**•3–9
  publicly offered commodity funds, **19**•6–7
  risk and money management:
    disclosure, **19**•12–13
    measuring, **22**•3–26
    preference space evaluation, **23**•3–26
  time weighted or dollar weighted, **21**•16
Periodic waves, **17**•11
Period movement, least-squares sinusoidal, **17**•10
Perishability, potatoes, **37**•6
Perishable products, **10**•10
Personal computer, **18**•6, **18**•19. *See also* Microcomputers
Personal property, **6**•16–17
Petroleum, *see* Crude oil
Phase of the wave, **17**•11
Phasing using moving averages, **15**•27–28
Philadelphia Stock Exchange, **13**•13
Photography, use of silver, **44**•13
Physical commodities, **13**•13
Physical position, **6**•19
Pima cotton, **40**•4, **40**•5
Planting Intentions, **25**•19
Platinum, **46**•3–9
  bull markets, **12**•25
  cash price (New York), **46**•4
  contract specifications, **46**•17
  demand, **46**•6–7
  futures market, **46**•15
  market analysis, **46**•7–8
  prices, **46**•8–9, **46**•10–11
  production, **46**•5
  relationship between gold and, **46**•7–8
  sources of information, **46**•15–18
  statistics, **46**•13
  supply, **46**•3–6
  world reserve base, **46**•4
Platinum/gold spread chart, **46**•8
PL/1 (Programming Language 1), **18**•10
Plywood, *See* Lumber and plywood
Pod corn, **27**•4
Point-and-figure charting, **15**•3–11
  chart formations, **15**•5–6
  computer use, **15**•34
  concepts, **15**•11
  daily rules, **15**•6
  plotting prices, **15**•4–5
  price objectives, **15**•8
  short-term trading, **15**•32
  trading techniques, **15**•7–8
  trendlines, **15**•6–7, **15**•8
Polyester, **40**•13, **40**•15
Pool, **2**•21
Popcorn kernels, **27**•4
Pork bellies, **32**•10–11
  cash price (Chicago), **32**•11
  frozen stocks, **32**•12
  nearest futures, **32**•13
  relationship to live hog prices, **32**•14
Pork complex, **32**•3–19
  demand, **32**•8–10
  distribution of sow farrowings by quarter, **32**•7
  hog cash prices, **32**•4
  hog/corn ratio, **32**•12–18
    effect of extremes, **32**•17
    at Omaha, **32**•16
  hog production, **32**•3
  lard cash prices, **32**•5
  principal cuts, **32**•8

relationship of live cattle to live hog prices, **32**•15
seasonality, **32**•7–8, **32**•9
slaughter, **32**•8
sources of information, **32**•18
spreads, **32**•11–12
statistics, pigs and hogs, **32**•6
supply, **32**•4–7
Pork Terminal Market, **1**•45
Portfolio selection, **21**•8–16
diversification correlation, **21**•13–14
efficient frontier, **21**•15–16
elements, **21**•8
Position limits, **24**•3
Potato Association of America, **37**•22
Potato Chip/Snack Food Association, **37**•22
Potatoes, **37**•3–22
anticipated acreage, **25**•9
carrying charges, **12**•26
climatological data, **37**•13–14
contract problems, **37**•3
contract specifications, **37**•19, **37**•20
crop production estimates, **37**•17
delivery, **37**•4
delivery default, **37**•5–6
demand, **37**•12–18
disappearance, **37**•15, **37**•16
exports, **37**•12
futures markets, **37**•20
futures prices *vs*. fall production, **37**•11
marketing, **37**•18
normal loss, **37**•12
perishability, **37**•6
production, **37**•3–4
seasonality, **37**•18–20
sources of information, **37**•21
statistics, **37**•7
structuring markets, **37**•4–6
supply, **37**•8–11
estimates, **37**•9
seasonal distribution, **37**•8
variations in production, **37**•10–11
Potato Stocks report, **37**•15
Potato Terminal Market (Amsterdam), **1**•45, **37**•20
Power curve, **17**•9
Precious metals, **46**•7
Predicasts, Incorporated, **18**•75
Preference space, trading system performance, **23**•3–26
choosing the best, **23**•3–4
connotations, **23**•3
Kelly measure, **23**•21–23
mean-variance model, **23**•12–23
cautionary warnings, **23**•19–21
criteria for, **23**•4–5
finding suitable reward and risk measures, **23**•10–11
lower confidence limit, **23**•16–17
ordering, **23**•4–12
quantitative ordering, **23**•7–10
restrictive efficient criterion, **23**•13–16
risk-aversion characteristics, **23**•5–7
Sharpe ratio, **23**•17–19
Premium, **13**•5, **13**•6
defined, **13**•46
effects of market conditions, **13**•27
fair-value, how to calculate, **13**•28
Premium gasoline, **42**•29
Presentation of performance, **24**•7–8
Price buyer, **25**•14
Price forecasts, **25**•8–9
Price objectives, **15**•8
Price risk, hedging program, **9**•6–7. *See also* Basis
Prices, **2**•20–22
factors of supply and demand, **17**•21–28
option trading, **13**•17–26
leverage and insurance value, **13**•17–21
model, **13**•25–26
relationship between market and strike price, **13**•21–23
short-term interest rates, **13**•24–25
term until expiration, **13**•25
underlying market volatility, **13**•23–24
plotting, using point-and-figure method, **15**•4–5
see also Commodity prices
Principal's market, **4**•12
Printer, computer, **18**•24
Private commodity pools, **19**•11–12
Privileges, *see* Commodity options
Producer hedge, **28**•5
Producer price index, potato market, **37**•15
Professional Farm Software, **18**•75
Profit-or-loss calculation, **2**•22–25
Profit maximization, basis risk, **9**•17–19
"Prompt," definition of, **2**•25
Propane, *see* Liquefied propane gas
Propylene, **42**•38
Prospective Plantings reports, **8**•5, **25**•19
Protein, soy, **30**•42
Publication of performance, **24**•5
Publicly offered commodity funds, **19**•11–12
Public relations committees, **1**•24
Pudd's Exchange, **1**•11
Pullbacks, trading on, **15**•7
Purchase-and-sales report (P&S), **2**•23 in England, **4**•14
Purchasing power parity (PPP) exchange rates, **47**•24–25
Purchasing power parity theory, **47**•5
Pure long arbitrage **10**•48
Put, **4**•26, **13**•4
Put and Call Dealers Association, **13**•12
Put option, **13**•4, **13**•46
intrinsic value, **13**•22
risk/reward structure, **13**•9

Putting on the crush, **9•**46, **30•**37
Put writer, **13•**4
PWA Commodity Research, **18•**75

Quadratic mean, **17•**5
Qualitative analysis, risk-return management, **11•**11
Quantitative ordering, **23•**7–10
  normalized *vs.* unnormalized, **23•**10
  reward/risk ratios, **23•**8–9
  riskless equivalent reward, **23•**7–9
Quantitative trading methods, **15•**3–36
  cycles, **15•**22–29
    major regular cycles, **15•**25–27
    other growing cycles, **15•**24–25
    phasing using moving averages, **15•**27–28
    seasonality, **15•**22–24
  point-and-figure charting, **15•**3–11
    chart formations, **15•**5–6
    concepts, **15•**11
    daily rules, **15•**6
    plotting prices, **15•**4–5
    price objectives, **15•**8
    trading techniques, **15•**7–8
    trendlines, **15•**6–7, **15•**8
  short-term trading, **15•**29–32
    day-trade, **15•**29–30
    market patterns, **15•**32
    overnight positions, **15•**30–32
    point-and-figure use, **15•**32
    time of day, **15•**30
  smoothing, **15•**11–19
    defined, **15•**11
    exponential, relating to standard moving averages, **15•**3–4
    objective, **15•**11
    trading methods, **15•**14–17
    velocity and acceleration, **15•**17–19
  system tradeoffs, **15•**19–21
    contratrend, **15•**20–21
    trend-following, **15•**19–20
  use of the computer, **15•**33–36
    point-and-figure, **15•**34
    real-time analysis, **15•**34–35
    testing, **15•**33–34
Quotas, refined sugar, **39•**7
Quotations and market reports committees, **1•**24
Quotrader Corporation, **18•**38, **18•**41, **18•**75
Quotron Systems, Incorporated, **18•**75

Radin Research Group, Incorporated, **18•**75
Radio Data Systems, **18•**29, **18•**76
RAM (Random Access Memory), **18•**23
Rapeseed, **29•**12–13
  consumption and usage, **29•**13
  contract specifications, **29•**15
  futures market, **29•**13
  production, **29•**12
  weekly nearest futures price (Winnipeg), **29•**13
  world production, **29•**14
Rate of change, momentum value, **15•**16
Rate of disappearance, potato stocks, **37•**15
Rate of return, trading system (noncompounded), **16•**8
Ratio rate, **19•**14
Raw value, U.S. cane and beet sugar, **39•**4, **39•**5
R&B Futures Software, **18•**76
Real interest rates, **7•**16–19
Real-time analysis, **15•**34–35
Real-time data transmission, **18•**40
Reauthorization process, **5•**41–42
Recovery rate of refined sugar, **39•**4
Rectangle, **14•**18
Redistribution of capital, **20•**4–5
Refined sugar, **39•**3–8
  contract specfications, **39•**7–8
  current production, **39•**4, **39•**6
  futures contracts, **39•**7–8
  government programs, **39•**7
  history of sugar production, **39•**3–4
  International Sugar Agreement, **39•**7
  marketing, **39•**6
  raw value, **39•**4, **39•**5
  recovery rate, **39•**4
  refinery production, **39•**4–6
  seasonality, **39•**5
  substitutes, **39•**6
  see also Sugar
Refinery basics, energy futures, **42•**3–7
Reforming process, crude oil, **42•**5–6
Regression analysis, **17•**7–8
Regression analysis, autoregressive integrated moving average (ARIMA), **18•**48
Regulated futures contract (RFC), **6•**6, **6•**11–13, **6•**26
  defined, **6•**11–12
  gains and losses, **6•**27
Regulation, **5•**3–52
  arbitration, **1•**24
  CFTC and Bank of England, **4•**24–25
  Commodity Exchange Act, **5•**6–33
  current issues, **5•**33–42
    CFTC jurisdiction, **5•**37–41
    CFTC options pilot program, **5•**35–37
    reauthorization process, **5•**41–42
    role of NFA, **5•**33–35
  interest-rate futures contracts, **10•**18–20
  recent developments (1928 Act), **5•**3–6
Regulation Q., **48•**14, **48•**17
Regulations committees, **1•**24
Remote Computing Corporation (RCC), **18•**29, **18•**44, **18•**76–77
Replacement order, **2•**17
Repo rate, **10•**15
Report on Traders' Commitments, **3•**8
Repos, **48•**5–8

Reserve, **20**•3
Reserve requirements, **48**•8
Residual oil, **42**•3
Resistance level, **14**•9–10
Returns, **21**•9
  evaluating, **21**•16
Reuters, **18**•38–39, **18**•77
Reversal chart patterns, **14**•14–17
  double tops or bottoms, **14**•15–16
  head and shoulders top or bottom, **14**•16
  rounding or saucer top or bottom, **14**•16–17
  spike or V top or bottom, **14**•16
  triple tops or bottoms, **14**•16
Reverse crush spread, **9**•48, **12**•9, **12**•31–32
Reverse repos, **48**•8
Reversing method, **16**•3
Reward/risk ratio:
  preference measure, **23**•8–9
  spreads, **12**•17–18
RFC, *see* Regulated futures contract
Riding the yield curve, **10**•30, **10**•32–33
Ring dealing, **4**•17
Ring method, **3**•5
Rings, **4**•14
Ring trading, **45**•15
Risk, **21**•10, **23**•5, **44**•19, **48**•5
  capitalization and money management, **20**•5–6
    control structure, **20**•8
  commodity options, **13**•40
  trading system, **16**•4
  trend-following, **15**•19–20
  as variability in percent return, **23**•12
Risk-aversion characteristics, **23**•5–7
Risk control, **21**•3–8
  conservation of capital, **21**•7–8
  diversification of systems and portfolios, **21**•5–7
  effects of varying reserve, **21**•4–5
Risk-free return, **22**•5
Risk of income, **10**•30
Riskless equivalent reward, **23**•7–8
Risk letters, **2**•4, **2**•8
Risk-management, **49**•6
Risk-management hedging, **9**•3
Risk-management techniques, **11**•3–11
  benchmark to use, **11**•9–10
  forecast-driven model, **11**•4–5
  gap analysis, **11**•5–9
    shortcomings, **11**•6–9
  qualitative analysis, **11**•11
Risk and money management:
  commission costs, **19**•14–15
  concepts, **21**•3–17
  disclosure information, **19**•15–16
  effects of capitalization, **20**•3–8
  evaluating a trading advisor, **19**•13–14
  information sources, **19**•17–18
  managed accounts, **19**•3–5
    evaluating, **24**•3–24
  performance:
    disclosure, **19**•12–13
    measuring, **22**•3–26
    preference space evaluation, **23**•3–26
  selecting a program, **19**•11–12
  success and failure, **19**•8–11
Risk preference, **17**•17–18
Risk premium, **48**•5
Risk of principal, **10**•30
Risk/reward, option contract, **13**•6–9
  diagram, **13**•8–9
  "in-the-money" and "out-of-the-money," **13**•7–8
  ways to profit, **13**•6
Risk of ruin, **17**•18–19
Robustas, **35**•3, **35**•4, **35**•14
Robust measure of risk, **21**•10
ROM (Read-Only Memory), **18**•23
Rounding or saucer top or bottom, **14**•16–17
Round oranges, Florida production, **36**•7
Round-turn commission, **2**•22
Round whites, *see* Maine potatoes
Rubber, kerb trading, **4**•20
Rubber Exchange of New York, **1**•15
Rules of trade, **1**•4
Runaway gap, **14**•13
Russet potatoes, **37**•4
Rye, **29**•13–20
  cash prices (Minneapolis and Winnipeg), **29**•16
  consumption, **29**•15
  contract specifications, **29**•20
  futures market, **29**•20
  production, **29**•15
  statistics, **29**•18–19
  world production, **29**•17

Saccharin, **39**•6
Sao Paulo Commodity Exchange, **30**•33
Satellite data, **25**•12–13
Saw logs, **41**•9
Scalpers, **47**•18
Scatter diagram, **17**•7
Scrap recovery of copper, **45**•6
Scrap silver production, **44**•6–9
Sea Island cotton, **40**•4, **40**•6–7
Seasonality, **25**•15
  broiler, **33**•8–9
  cash sugar market, **38**•10
  cattle, **31**•15–16
  cocoa, **34**•12–14
  coffee, **35**•7–8
  copper, **45**•10–12
  corn, **27**•11–12
  cycles, **15**•22–24
  gasoline demand, **42**•31
  heating oil, **42**•22
  lumber and plywood, **41**•17–18, **41**•19
  oats, **28**•5, **28**•8

Seasonality (*Continued*)
pork complex, **32**•7–8, **32**•9
potatoes, **37**•8, **37**•18–20
sugar cane refining, **39**•5
wheat, **26**•10–11
Seasonality of basis, **9**•13–15, **9**•18
SEC, *see* Securities Exchange Commission
Second derivative, **15**•17
Securities Exchange Commission (SEC), **1**•29, **2**•10 **10**•18, **10**•19, **13**•13, **19**•12
CFTC jurisdictional agreement, **5**•5–6, **5**•37–41
background, **5**•37–38
boundaries, **5**•38–40
state boundaries, **5**•40–41
Security exchange options, **13**•18–19
SEC v. *Goldstein, Samuelson, Incorporated,* **13**•11
Self-regulation, **1**•17
Sell hedge, **9**•20
Selling hedge, **9**•9–11
Semivariance, **23**•20
Sequences of trades, **21**•6–7
Series of options, **13**•46
Settlement price, **3**•8
Sharp Associates Limited (I.P.), **18**•77–78
Sharpe ratio (SR), **21**•16, **21**•17, **22**•5–14, **23**•17–19
dependency on time interval, **22**•9–10
drawbacks, **22**•8–14
intermittent and consecutive losses, **22**•8–9
reward/risk ratio in (E, σ), **23**•17–19
trade entry data equity, **22**•12–14
upside and downside fluctuations, **22**•11–12
Sheathing, lumber and plywood, **41**•7
Short the basis, **9**•20
Short the currency, **47**•19, **47**•22
Short futures arbitrage, **10**•43–45
Short hedge, **9**•9–11, **10**•4
copper, **45**•15
KCBT-VLA stock index futures, **49**•14–15
Short sales, **2**•10, **6**•20
Short sale tax rule, **6**•7
Short side of the crush spread, **9**•47–48
Short-term interest rates, option premium, **13**•24–25
Short-term trading, **15**•29–32
day-trade, **15**•29–30
market patterns, **15**•32
overnight positions, **15**•30–32
point-and-figure use, **15**•32
time of day, **15**•30
Silver, **44**•3–21
alchemical symbol, **4**•11
bull markets, **12**•25
consumption (U.S.), **44**•11
contract specifications, **44**•18, **44**•20
current situation and future outlook, **44**•17–18
demand, **44**•9–17
coinage, **44**•14–16
dentistry and medicine, **44**•14
electronic use, **44**•13
fabrication and GNP, **44**•17
industrial use, **44**•10–13, **44**•15
investment, **44**•16–17
photographic, **44**•13
futures market, **44**•18–21
hedging, **44**•19
options, **44**•19–21
risks, **44**•19
uses, **44**•19
holdings (troy ounces), **44**•16
price cycles, **44**•17
prices, **44**•4
secondary supply, **44**•9
production, **44**•5
supply, **44**•3–9
mine production, **44**•3–6, **44**•7–8
scrap and hoarding, **44**•6–9
secondary, **44**•10
uses, **44**•3
Silver fix, **4**•18
Silver straddles, **6**•7–8
Simple moving average, **16**•15
Simulated performance, **24**•9
Singapore Gold Exchange, **4**•19
Skewed distribution, **17**•3
Skewness, **17**•6–7
Skewness in distributions, **23**•20
Slightly overbought market, **15**•20–21
Slightly oversold market, **15**•20–21
Sludge, **30**•39–40
Small Grains report, **8**•18
SMART (Securities Market Analysis, Reporting, and Transaction), **18**•47, **18**•49, **18**•51
Smith-Jacobson decision, **6**•8–9, **6**•31
Smithsonian Agreement, **47**•12
Smoothing, **15**•11–19
defined, **15**•11
exponential, relating to standard moving averages, **15**•3–4
moving average, **17**•15–16
objective, **15**•11
trading methods, **15**•14–17
velocity and acceleration, **15**•17–19
Smoothing constant, **15**•13
Snake, **47**•12
Soft red winter wheat, **26**•5
Software, **18**•3, **18**•5, **18**•9–10
commercial services, **18**•58–60
Software Options, Incorporated, **18**•78
Software Resources, Incorporated (SRI), **18**•29, **18**•38, **18**•47, **18**•78
Soft woods, **41**•3
Soil erosion, **25**•3
Solvent extracted soybean feed, **30**•43
Source Telecomputing Corporations, **18**•78
"Sour" crudes, **42**•8, **42**•29
South Africa, gold production, **43**•6
Sovereign risk, **48**•18

Soviet Union, **25**•4, **25**•5, **25**•14
cocoa imports, **34**•12
corn production, **27**•5
cotton production, **40**•8–9
flaxseed production, **29**•8
gold production, **43**•6
oats production, **28**•4
palladium supply, **46**•14
platinum reserves, **46**•3, **46**•4
wheat production, **26**•5
Soya Bean Meal Futures Association Ltd•, **4**•21
Soybean cake, **30**•42
Soybean chips, **30**•42
Soybean complex, **30**•3–50
cash market, **30**•7–19
U.S., **30**•10
world markets, **30**•7–10
world production, **30**•8–9
conversion table, **30**•47–48
factors influencing prices, **30**•11
futures trading, **30**•33
glossary of terms, **30**•38–44
marketing chain, **30**•4–5
meal cash market, **30**•19–26
meaning of, **30**•40, **30**•44–45
oil cash market, **30**•26–33
organizations, **30**•49
prices (Chicago Board of Trade), **30**•18
processing, **30**•6–7, **30**•40–41
production, **30**•6, **30**•17
standards, **30**•41–44, **30**•44–47
grades, grade requirements and designations, **30**•46–47
principles governing application, **30**•45–46
products, **30**•43–44
protein, **30**•42
specifications, **30**•41–42
terms defined, **30**•44–45
state research experiment stations, **30**•49–50
statistics, **30**•15
stocks, **30**•13–14
supply-and-demand price factors, **30**•12
supply and distribution, **30**•16
trading practices (cash and futures markets), **30**•33–38
crushing hedge, **30**• 36–38
gross processing margin, **30**•36–38
hedging, **30**•33–36
USDA analysis, **8**•12–15
uses, **30**•5
Soybean fatty acids, **30**•40
Soybean flakes, **30**•42
Soybean hulls, **30**•43
Soybean lecithin, **30**•40
Soybean meal, **30**•43
cash market, **30**•19–26
number of U.S. processing plants, **30**•23
production, trade, and consumption, **30**•20–29
supply and demand factors, **30**•24
U.S. markets, **30**•19–26
world markets, **30**•19
uses of, **30**•5
Soybean mill feed, **30**•44
Soybean mill run, **30**•44
Soybean oil:
cash market, **30**•26–33
exports (U.S.), **30**•32
prices (Chicago Board of Trade), **30**•26
production, trade, and consumption, **30**•27–29
supply-and-demand factors, **30**•31–32
U.S. market, **30**•30–33
world markets, **30**•26–30
uses of, **30**•5
Soybean processing hedge, **9**•45–48
Soybean processor, **30**•41
Soybean protein concentrate, **30**•44
Soybean soapstock, **30**•40
Soybean Stocks, 25•19
Soy grits, **30**•42
Spatial arbitrage, **47**•23
Specialized Industries Audit Guidelines and Examination of Tax Shelters Handbook, **6**•31
Speculation, **1**•20–21, **16**•4
CEA and, **5**•7
cocoa, **34**•19
compared to gambling, **1**•21
FCOJ futures, **36**•19–20
futures and interbank market, **47**•19
hedgers, **1**•21
interest-rate futures markets, **10**•16, **10**•17–18
role of the speculator, **1**•20–21
Speculative long position, **49**•4
Spike or V top or bottom, **14**•16
Splits soybean, **30**•45
Spot, **6**•9, **10**•4
foreign exchange, **47**•16–17
Spot delivery, **4**•13
Spot markets, **1**•20
Spread, **1**•20, **10**•4, **10**•15, **12**•3–34, **21**•14
bull and bear, **12**•4–5, **12**•24–26
butterfly, **12**•9
carrying charge market, **12**•20–21, **12**•23
carrying charges, **12**•16, **12**•18–20, **12**•23–24
crop, **25**•14–18
crush, **12**•8–9, **12**•30–33
defined, **13**•46
entering the order, **12**•13–14
feed and protein relationships, **25**•15
financing costs, **12**•20
foreign currency, **47**•14–16
hog and belly futures, **32**•11–12
implied yields, **12**•24
intercommodity, **12**•3, **12**•8, **12**•9, **12**•28–29
quotes, **12**•9–10
wheat *vs.* corn, **12**•29–30
intercrop, **12**•5–7

Spread (*Continued*)
- interdelivery, **12**•3, **12**•4–5
- intermarket, **12**•3, **12**•26–28
  - wheat, **12**•27–28
- intermarket orders, **12**•12–13
- inverted markets, **12**•21–22, **12**•23
- knowledge of, **12**•18
- legging-in or legging out, **12**•14
- less margin, **12**•16–17
- limited risk, **12**•16
- locked-limit days, **12**•17
- lower risk, **12**•16
- market, limit, and time orders, **12**•11–12
- option, **13**•34–36
- orders, **2**•17
- reason for, **12**•15–16
- reward/risk ratio, **12**•17–18
- stop orders, **12**•13
- storage and insurance, **12**•20
- terminology, **12**•3–4
- trading, **12**•11
- unprofitable into profitable, **12**•15

Spread position margin, **2**•11
Standard deviation, **17**•6, **17**•8, **22**•6
Standard error, linear regression, **17**•8
Standardization of contracts, **1**•18
Standard and Poor's Corporation v• *COMEX,* **49**•8
Standard & Poor's 500 Index, **1**•31, **10**•8, **10**•22
Staple, cotton, **40**•5
Stationary moving average, **15**•16
Statistical Research Service (SRS), **25**•9
Step-weighted moving average, **17**•16
Step-weighting, **15**•12
Sterling, *see* British pound
Sterling-denominated contracts, **4**•3
Sterlingware, **44**•14
Stock index futures, **10**•8, **49**•3–32
- contract specifications, **49**•11, **49**•16
- as hedging or risk-management tool, **49**•6
- historical background, **49**•6–10
  - origins, **49**•6–7
  - submissions and litigations, **49**•7–9
- KCBT-VLA, **49**•10–15
  - contract specifications, **49**•11
  - delivery, **49**•14
  - example, **49**•10–11
  - hedging, **49**•11–14
  - long-hedging, **49**•15
  - short-hedging, **49**•14–15
  - terms and conditions, **49**•15
- rationale, **49**•30
- statistical price summary, **49**•24–30
- stock ownership in U.S., **49**•4–6
  - market value, **49**•5
- systematic risk, **49**•3–4
- theoretical considerations, **49**•19–24
  - econometrics, **49**•21–22
  - equal weighting, **49**•23–24
  - "market factor," 49•21
  - quantifying market factor, **49**•22–23
- underlying commodities, **49**•15–19
  - major market indicators, **49**•17

Stock options:
- tax consequences, **6**•29–31
- trading, **13**•4–6

Stocks of Grains in All Positions report, **25**•19
Stop limit, **2**•16
Stop-loss order, **13**•34, **21**•6
- channel or band used as, **15**•14

Stop orders, **2**•15–16, **12**•13
Storable products, **10**•9–10
Storage and insurance charges, **12**•20
Straddles, **6**•4
- carrying charges, **6**•10
- defined, **13**•47
- option, **13**•36–38
- silver, **6**•7–8
- tax consequences, **6**•6–9
- Treasury bill futures, **6**•24
- *see also* Spread

Strategic Petroleum Reserve (SPR), **42**•14
Strict low middling cotton, **40**•5–6
Strike price, **13**•4–5, **13**•47
- relationship between market and, **13**•21–23

Strip of futures, **10**•31
Substitution, **3**•6, **3**•9
Success and ruin, probability of, **17**•18–20
Sugar, **4**•20, **38**•3–23
- beet production, **38**•7–8
- cane production, **38**•5–6
- cash sugar, **38**•11
- consumption, **38**•4–5
- contract specifications, **38**•13, **38**•14
- futures market, **38**•12–15
- hedgers, **38**•12, **38**•15–16
  - chronological process, **38**•17
  - profits and lower user's overall costs, **38**•18
- impact on cocoa prices, **34**•8–9
- International Sugar Agreement, **38**•8
- No• 11 prices (New York), **38**•9
- options, **38**•16–22
  - comparison of contracts, **38**•20–21
  - No• 11 contract, **38**•19
- price dynamics, **38**•8–12
- production, **38**•3
- user's hedge, **28**•15–16
- world production, **38**•6
- world spot price *vs.* stock consumption ratio, **38**•10
- *see also* Refined sugar

Sugar Act of 1764, **39**•3
Sugar arbitrage, **4**•20
Sugar beet, **39**•4
Sugar Bounty Act of 1890, **39**•3–4
Sugar cane, **39**•4
Sugar industrial user's hedge, **38**•15–16

Sugar No. 11 (world) contract trades, **38**•12, **38**•13
  specifications for options contract, **38**•19
Sugar No. 12 (domestic) contract trades, **38**•12, **38**•14
Sugar and Sweetener Outlook and Situation, **38**•3, **38**•4
Suitability, determining, **2**•4–9
"Summer-fill" programs, **42**•22
Supply and demand, **17**•21–28
  changes in short-run demand elasticity, **17**•21–22
  demand, **17**•21
  elasticity of demand, **17**•21
  elasticity of supply, **17**•23
  equilibrium, **17**•23–24
  models, **17**•24–28
  supply side, **17**•22–23
  see also specific commodities
Support and resistance, **14**•9–10
Surplus fund, **3**•7
Swaps, **42**•18, **42**•24–25
Sweet corn, **27**•4
"Sweet" crudes, **42**•7–8
Swiss franc, **4**•21, **10**•7, **15**•27, **47**•12, **47**•14
  IMM contract, **47**•15
  parity in U.S. dollars (1951), **47**•8
  weekly prices, **47**•11
Switch, *see* Spread
Sydney Futures Exchange, **4**•19
  gold contract, **43**•13
Symmetrical triangle, **14**•19–20
Systematic risk, **49**•3–4
System tradeoffs, quantitative methods, **15**•19–21
  contratrend, **15**•20–21
  trend-following, **15**•19–20

Tails, **43**•11–12
Take your time (TYT) orders, **12**•13
Tandem Computers, Incorporated, **18**•79
Tandem Non-Stop Systems, **18**•7
Tandy Corporation/Radio Shack, **18**•79
Taxation of transactions, **6**•3–32
  cash-and-carry, **6**•4, **6**•9–10, **6**•22
  categories, **6**•4
  commodity traders, **6**•26–27
  domestic commodity funds, **6**•27–28
  ERTA rules, **6**•3•, **6**•10–24
    carry-back provisions, **6**•13–14
    constructive ownership, **6**•20–21
    identification requirements, **6**•23–24
    identified straddles, **6**•18–19
    loss deferral, **6**•16–18
    mark-to-market concept, **6**•11–13
    mixed straddles, **6**•21–22
    reporting considerations, **6**•22–23
    RFCs, **6**•11–13
    short-sale, **6**•20
    transitional rules, **6**•15–16
    wash-sale, **6**•19–20
  futures options, **6**•26
  hedging, **6**•25–26
  nonhedge transactions, **6**•4–6
  offshore commodity funds, **6**•28–29
  stock options, **6**•29–31
  straddles, **6**•6–9
  Treasury bill futures, **6**•24–25
Tax-deductible or tax-deferred retirement plan, **6**•27
Tax Reform Act of 1981, **4**•14
Tax-shelter, **6**•5
Taylor Trading Technique, **15**•32
Technical analysis:
  commercial services, **18**•58, **18**•59–60
  type of data useful, **18**•28–30
Technical analysis packages, **18**•44–48
Technical approach to trading, **16**•5–6
Technical Corrections Act, **6**•12
Technical Data Company, **18**•79
Technical grade refined soy oil, **30**•41
Telecommunications, futures trading and, **1**•21–22
Telerate Systems, Incorporated, **18**•79
Temple oranges, Florida production, **36**•7
10-day moving average, **15**•11
10-Year Treasury note, **10**•5
Textured vegetable protein, **30**•44
Thick juice, **39**•5
Third-party accounts, **2**•9–10
Third-party clearing, **1**•11
30-day commercial paper, **48**•3
3-month delivery period, **4**•13–14
Timber harvest, **41**•5
Time of day, **15**•30
Time orders, **2**•17, **12**•12
Time and sales, **2**•21–22
Time series, **18**•26
  correlation using, **17**•8
Time-sharing, **16**•5, **18**•4, **18**•6, **18**•14–16, **18**•51–52
  benefits, **18**•15–16
  costs, **18**•14
  data storage, **18**•14–15
  decision to use, **18**•22
  microcomputers and, **18**•37–38
  negative aspects, **18**•16
Time stamps, **2**•21
Time value, **13**•47
Time-weighted method, **21**•16
Timing, investment, **49**•6
Tin, alchemical symbol for, **4**•11
Toasting, soybean meal, **30**•44
Tokugawa era (Japan), **1**•5–8
Tokyo Dow Jones Index, **49**•6
Tokyo Grain Exchange, **30**•33
Total exports or total imports, **7**•22
Trade-based profit and loss ratio (TBPLR), **22**•17
Tradecenter Incorporated, **18**•79
Trade entry date, **22**•12–14, **22**•18
Trade executions, U.S. compared to London, **4**•14

Trading, regulation of, **5**•24–33
  antifraud rules, **5**•24–25
  criminal conduct, **5**•32
  general prohibitions, **5**•25
  government enforcement actions, **5**•30–32
    administrative actions, **5**•30–31
    cease-and-desist orders, **5**•31
    denial of registration, **5**•31
    injunctions and compliance, **5**•31
    investigative powers, **5**•31
    power over exchanges, **5**•30
    state enforcement, **5**•32
  practices of floor brokers and FCMs, **5**•25–26
  private claims, **5**•29–30
    arbitration, **5**•29–30
    lawsuits, **5**•30
    reparations proceeding, **5**•29
  prohibition of manipulation, **5**•28
  remedying violations of CEA, **5**•29
  reporting requirements, **5**•28–29
  speculative practices, **5**•26–28
    aggregation of positions, **5**•28
    general, **5**•26–27
    hedging exemption, **5**•27
    miscellaneous exemptions, **5**•27–28
    position limits, **5**•27
Trading advisor, evaluating, **19**•13–14
Trading authority, **2**•9
Trading facilities, **2**•3–4
Trading hours, **2**•19
Trading limits, **4**•17
Trading methods, **16**•3, **16**•4
  distinction between trading system and, **16**•3
  quantitative, **15**•3–36
  see also Mathematical aids
Trading performance:
  capital contribution, **20**•6–8
  measuring, **22**•3–26
    AMR as risk measure, **22**•14–15
    margin adjusted AMR, **22**•15–16
    ML as a risk measure, **22**•16
    money managers, **22**•21–25
    multimarket system, **22**•18–20
    need to normalize gain, **22**•3–5
    practical considerations, **22**•21
    Sharpe ratio, **22**•5–14
  preference space evaluation, **23**•3–26
    mean-variance model, **23**•12–23
    ordering of trading systems, **23**•4–12
Trading professionals, regulation of, **5**•17–24
  associated persons, **5**•19–20
  commodity pool operators, **5**•20–24
  commodity trading advisors, **5**•20–24
  floor brokers, **5**•17–19
  Futures Commission Merchants, **5**•17–19
Trading range, **14**•8, **14**•18
Trading system, **16**•3–9
  approaches, **16**•5–6
  capital contribution, **20**•6–8
  capital requirements, **16**•7–8
  characteristics, **21**•9
  commodity selection and diversification, **16**•6
  distinction between trading method and, **16**•3
  evaluating returns, **16**•8–9
  leverage risk, **16**•4
  rate of return, **16**•8
  volatility, **16**•7
  see also Mathematical aids
Trading techniques, point-and-figure formations, **15**•7–8
Trading volume, **1**•25–26
Transferable notice, **3**•10
Transfer accounts, **2**•26
Transfer of contracts, on the LME, **4**•14–17
Transfers of funds, **2**•4
Transformations, skewness of a data series, **17**•7
Trans-Lux Corporation, **18**•79–80
Treasury bills, **1**•29, **1**•30, **3**•7, **6**•24–25, **13**•14, **48**•3, **48**•9–12
  cash market, **48**•9–10
  futures contract, **10**•9, **10**•10–12, **10**•13
  futures market, **48**•11
  IMM 90-day contract, **48**•11–12, **48**•13
  primary market, **48**•10
  secondary market, **48**•10
  use, as margins, **2**•10
Treasury bonds, **1**•29, **3**•7, **10**•5, **13**•14, **48**•23–30
  contract specifications, **48**•29
  futures contract, **10**•10, **10**•12
  futures market, **48**•25–30
  long-term, **48**•26–27
  price chart, **48**•25
  primary market, **48**•24
  secondary market, **48**•24–25
Treasury notes, **1**•30, **3**•7, **48**•23–30
  futures market, **48**•25–30
  primary market, **48**•24
  secondary market, **48**•24–25
Trend, **14**•8–9
Trend-following methods, **16**•7
Trend-following risks, **15**•19–20
Trend-following systems, **20**•7–8
Trendlines, **14**•10–12, **15**•3
  point-and-figure, **15**•6–7, **15**•8
Triangles, **14**•19–20
Triangular arbitrage, **47**•23
Trident Systems Publications, **18**•80
Trigonometric curve fitting, **15**•26, **17**•10–24
  complex, **17**•14–15
Triple tops or bottoms, **14**•16
Troy-Folan Productions, Incorporated, **18**•80
Trucks, vehicle registration and fuel consumption, **42**•32
Trusler v. *Crooks,* **13**•11

Two-dimensional preference space (efficiency criterion), **23**•10–11
Two moving averages, **15**•14–15

ULCC (ultralarge crude carrier), **42**•17
Underlying commodity, **13**•47
stock index futures contracts, **49**•15–19
Underweights, **41**•20
United Fresh Fruit and Vegetable Association, **37**•22
USDA (U.S. Department of Agriculture), **8**•3–21, **25**•9
analysis and estimate procedures, **8**•12–20
cotton, **8**•15–18
soybean complex, **8**•12–15
wheat, **8**•18–20
decision-making factors, **8**•10–12
information and data, **8**•3–10
monthly schedule of reports, **8**•21
U.S. Department of Energy (DOE), **42**•19
U.S. Futures Corporation, **18**•80
United Terminal Sugar Market Association Ltd., **1**•45, **4**•19, **4**•25
Units, **2**•20, **19**•12
UNIVAC I computer, **18**•6, **18**•9
Unleaded gasoline, **42**•29–30
Unnormalized space, **23**•10
Unsystematic risk, **49**•3–4
Upland cotton, **40**•4, **40**•7
Urban Aggregates, Incorporated, **18**•80
Utility, concept of, **21**•10
Utility theory of preference, **23**•3, **23**•13, **23**•18

Value dates, **4**•13–14
Value Line Average (VLA) contract, **49**•3–32
historical background, **49**•6–10
origins, **49**•6–7
submissions and litigations, **49**•7–9
how it works, **49**•10–15
contract specifications, **49**•11, **49**•16
delivery, **49**•14
example, **49**•10–11
hedging, **49**•11–14
long-hedging, **49**•15
short-hedging, **49**•14–15
terms and conditions, **49**•15
rationale for, **49**•30
risk classes, monthly data, 1975–1979, **49**•4
statistical price summary, **49**•24–30
stock ownership in U.S., **49**•4–6
market value, **49**•5
patterns, **49**•5–6
systematic risk, **49**•3–4
theoretical considerations, **49**•19–24
econometrics, **49**•21–22
equal weighting, **49**•23–24
"market factor," **49**•21
quantifying market factor, **49**•22–23
underlying commodities, **49**•15–19
major market indicators, **49**•17
Value Line Average Stock Index, **10**•8
Value Line Composite Index, **10**•22
Value Line Index, **1**•26, **1**•31
Variation margin or pay, **3**•8–9, **43**•17
Varying reserves, **21**•4–5
Vegetable Oil Terminal Market Association Ltd•, **1**•45
Velocity, **15**•17–19
interpretation, **15**•18
Veneer, **41**•7
Veneer logs, **41**•9
Vertical count, **15**•8
Vertical spread, **13**•34, **13**•47
Videocom, **18**•40–41
Videocom Quotation Service, **18**•28–29
Virgin gasoline, **42**•6
VisiCorp, **18**•38, **18**•48, **18**•80–81
VisiTerm, **18**•38
VLCC (very large crude carrier), **42**•17
Volatility pattern, **16**•7
Volume, bar charting, **14**•6
Voluntary Product Standard, **20–70**, **41**•6

Wall Street Software Company, **18**•81
Warehouse and license committees, **1**•24
Warehouse receipt, **2**•19
Warrant, **1**•3, **1**•9, **1**•17
Wash-sale, **6**•6–7, **6**•19–20
Weather modeling, **25**•9–10
Weather Services International Corporation, **18**•81
Wedge, **14**•18
Weekly continuation charts, **14**•7–8
Weekly Grain Market News, **25**•19
Weighing, **1**•17, **1**•23
Weighted geometric moving average, **17**•16
Weighted moving average, **17**•15
Western states, potato production, **37**•3
West Texas Intermediate (WTI), **42**•8
West Texas Sour (WTS), **42**•8
Wet method, coffee process, **35**•4
Wheat, **26**•3–14
cash price (Chicago), **26**•4
cultivation, **26**•3–5
demand, **26**•5–8
futures contracts, **26**•11–14
government programs, **26**•8–10
hedging, **25**•15–18
marketing, **26**•8
prices, **26**•8
production growth, **25**•4
seasonality, **26**•10–11
stocks, production, and exports (by classes), **26**•7
supply and distribution, **26**•9
USDA analysis, **8**•18–20
U.S. production, **26**•5

Wheat (*Continued*)
  world production, **26**•4, **26**•5, **26**•6
  yield estimation, **25**•10–12
  see also Agriculture; Grain
Wheat *vs*. corn spreads, **12**•29–30
Wheat Situation report, **25**•19
Wheat spreads, **12**•27–28
Wholesale price index (producer price index), **7**•17
Winchendon Group, **18**•81
Winnipeg, gold futures contract, **43**•13
Winnipeg grain markets, **29**•3–20
  barley, **29**•3–4
  domestic feed barley, **29**•8
  flaxseed, **29**•4–12
  oats contract, **28**•9
  rapeseed, **29**•12–13, **29**•15
  rye, **29**•13–20
  wheat contract, **26**•13–14
  wheat traded, **25**•14
Winterized oil, **30**•41
Winter Wheat Seeding, **25**•19
World Agricultural Outlook Board (WAOB), **8**•7
World Agricultural Supply and Demand Analysis, **8**•5, **8**•7
World Crop Production report, **8**•7
World trade, **7**•3
  demand side, **7**•22–25
  role commodities, **7**•4–6

Yardley Group, Incorporated, **18**•81
Yellow soybeans, **30**•44
Yield curve, **48**•4–5, **48**•6
Yield curve ride, **10**•33
Yield forecasting, **25**•10–12
  use of satellite data, **25**•12–13
Yield to maturity, **48**•25
Yields:
  carrying charges, **12**•24
  Eurodollar deposits, **48**•18

Zinc, alchemical symbol for, **4**•11